10 EVENTFUL YEARS

Eisenhower's Welcome

10 Eventful Years

VOLUME FOUR
SCULPTURE to
ZOOLOGY
& INDEX

A RECORD OF EVENTS
OF THE YEARS PRECEDING
INCLUDING AND FOLLOWING
WORLD WAR II

1937 THROUGH 1946

Prepared Under the Editorial Direction of

WALTER YUST

Editor of Encyclopaedia Britannica

The University of Chicago

ENCYCLOPÆDIA BRITANNICA, INC.

CHICAGO · LONDON · TORONTO

PRINTED IN U.S.A.

10 Eventful Years

Sculpture

At the outset of the decade 1937–46, sculpture was still suffering from lack of appreciation; the struggles of sculptors for recognition, especially the younger artists who were experimenting with new ideas, were great. Art critics gave very little notice to sculpture, and art magazines contained few reproductions. For some unexplained reason, critics often completely ignored sculpture when exhibited in conjunction with painting. No wonder, therefore, that the public responded slowly.

The situation, however, changed greatly during the ensuing ten years, and great forward strides in sculpture were made. In the United States, many new sculptors, with opportunities formerly nonexistent, came to the fore. The public generally became more conscious of this art form and gradually introduced it into the home as an intrinsic element of the decorative scheme. Architects co-operated more widely with sculptors; museums gave more importance to exhibitions of sculpture; and, with the advent of the federal art projects and government sponsorship, sculpture received a new impetus which would have continued had World War II not intervened. The United States seemed to lead in this development; little news concerning sculpture came from Europe. After Aristide Maillol, Charles Despiau, Constantin Brancusi, Jacques Lipschitz, Ossip Zadkine, Jacob Epstein and Henry Moore, there had not been many new men whose work was known, and these sculptors retained their position of eminence. Their influence was world-wide and was felt in the works of most of the new sculptors. Wilhelm Lehmbruck's influence also lived, although this great German artist died shortly after World War I.

The increasing number of sculptors who cut directly into the material, sometimes without any preconceived ideas, brought about great changes during the decade. This approach led to more solidity and a more sculpturesque quality, together with more individuality and greater depth. Experiments were made with new plastic materials. Sculptors returned more and more to cutting directly in marble, stone and wood, "cherchant dans la matière." They also built and modelled in plaster. These trends to a great extent initiated a style directed more toward the simplification of forms and abstraction, thus departing from too close a reproduction of nature, which in turn gave their work a more personal quality. Thus, the sculptors' approach separated them more and more from the surface manipulation and the splashy style of Auguste Rodin and Antoine Bourdelle, whose influence almost disappeared during the decade.

Work of Individual Sculptors.—A great loss was the death in 1944 of Maillol, one of the greatest sculptors of his time. Maillol's forms were concise, sensuous, smooth and well-rounded. He understood simplification, and his style showed his great admiration for the ancients. His drawings were wonderful expressions of a sculptor's approach in that medium. Maillol's memorial to Paul Cézanne, his titanic "Action in Chains," "Ile de France," "Venus," "Pomona," "The Mediterranean" and his war memorials were his great works.

Despiau, another great French sculptor, differed from Maillol in that he was much more interested in portraiture. In this accomplishment he was unique and was perhaps one of the greatest portrait sculptors of his period. Although portraiture comprised the bulk of his work, he also did full figures. "Eve" stands out as one of his finest—a very beautiful, simple, sensitive figure of a girl standing erect with legs apart. Among his later portraits, that of Antoinette Schulte has power and is a good likeness. Despiau had a knack for getting likenesses. Although

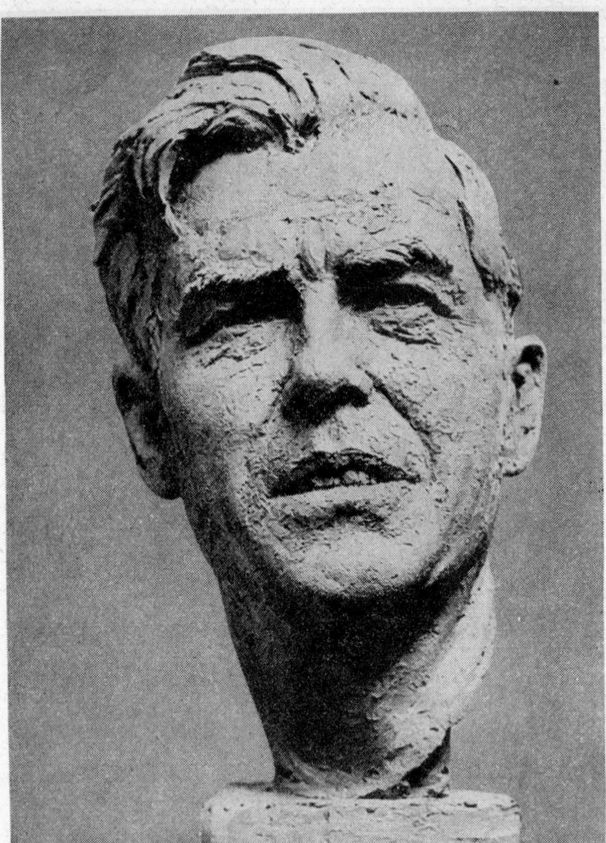

Bust of Henry A. Wallace modelled from life by Jo Davidson in 1942

his work has the appearance of spontaneity, it was the result of long and arduous work. Earlier portraits, such as "Portrait de Mme. S.," "Maria Lani," "Madame André Derain," are among his finest. They are austere, laboriously modelled, but always surprisingly fresh.

Henri Laurens worked mostly in the abstract, and Naum Gabo introduced new ideas and materials in his abstractions.

Lipschitz and Zadkine, connected with L'École de Paris, were both in the United States during World War II. Their visit was a great stimulus to the sculptors of that country, both young and old. Lipschitz's interesting interpretations of "Europa" and his drawings remained a cachet of his visit. Zadkine's "Prometheus" struggling with the eagle, leaned toward abstraction. One of his later works, "La Prisonnière," was an outstanding achievement; an imprisoned torso, inspired by World War II, represented all the occupied countries. This sculptor's style was uniquely his own.

Georg Kolbe remained the outstanding German sculptor after the death of Lehmbruck. His work was done mostly in clay and cast in bronze; he was brilliant in handling this material. Many of his figures, caught in action, are very alive with a free technique recalling Rodin's style. Kolbe, in that sense, remained closer to nature. His "Grosser Wächter" (1937), of a kneeling man with a bow, was considered among his best works.

Ernst Barlach was influenced strongly by the early German wood sculpture. His figures generally have a pleasing rhythm with solid forms. Renée Sintenis did interesting animal sculptures. Gerhardt Marck's work was in the primitive trend. William Ehrich, who moved to the United States in 1929, worked interestingly in wood.

Chana Orloff, the Russian sculptor, exhibited in New York. Her style shows individuality; "Girl With Basket" is interestingly simple, but her "Maria Lani" is less profound than Despiau's interpretation of the same.

Moore, at his best, was reminiscent of Pablo Picasso's "Dinard Period of 1928" and also his "Bone Period." Moore's drawings were entertaining and showed more originality than his sculpture. Eric Gill was another accomplished British artist of the decade.

In the United States, several sculptors of merit appeared. John B. Flanagan worked largely in hard natural stones, cutting not very deeply into the material but profiting by allowing the shape of the stone to suggest his subjects. Thus he obtained a primitive effect, and his elongated forms often resemble the manner of Lehmbruck. His animal sculptures were considered among his best. One of his last works was a figure in limestone made for the Ellen Phillips Samuel memorial in Philadelphia.

José de Creeft was also an important and prolific artist in this period, exhibiting almost every season. He made use of the odd shapes of materials such as marble and stone, and also worked successfully in hammered lead. Among his later pieces in *taille directe,* "The Kiss," is an excellent example, as are also the earlier works, "Head," in black Belgian granite, and "Maternity," which won the first prize in the Artists-For-Victory exhibition at the Metropolitan Museum of Art in 1942.

William Zorach worked mostly in marble, stone and wood, occasionally using clay. He was at his best when cutting directly, and his "Mother and Child" remained one of his best-known pieces. Also memorable works were: "The Dance," cast in aluminum and placed in Radio City music hall, and his later "Head of Christ" in black granite, in the collection of the Museum of Modern Art.

Chaim Gross, a younger man, worked in lignum vitae and other woods usually, although he also used marble and stone. The figures are arbitrarily short and bulky, constituting a style of his own. His acrobats, generally two or three figures standing or riding on each others' shoulders, were subjects that brought him renown. Gross received the second prize in the Artists-For-Victory exhibition in 1942.

Oronzio Malderelli cut directly into the material and also worked in plaster. He was among the leaders doing strong, monumental work. A simplified head of a girl in stone received a prize at the Chicago Art institute.

David Smith, at one time an iron founder, worked interestingly in steel, zinc and copper. His former trade influenced him and made him very adept at forging his own creations and achieving unique patina.

Alexander Calder made a special place for himself in the art world. His "mobiles" are abstract, moving forms in wire, steel, wood and other materials, frequently introducing colour. Some of them were used successfully in scenic designs for the theatre. Calder was an exhibitor at the Museum of Modern Art, in which collection he was well represented.

Epstein, an American who lived mostly in Great Britain, gave the art world some exciting moments. Two of his later works were "Adam," an over-life-size figure in pink alabaster, and "Jacob and the Angel," also in alabaster. An earlier work, "Mother and Child," in marble and owned by the Museum of Modern Art, suggests the sculpture of Amedeo Modigliani.

Heinz Warnecke did interesting animal sculpture and also greatly simplified figures such as the "Prodigal Son."

Turku Trajan received full recognition of his work only during the decade, and was somewhat different from most

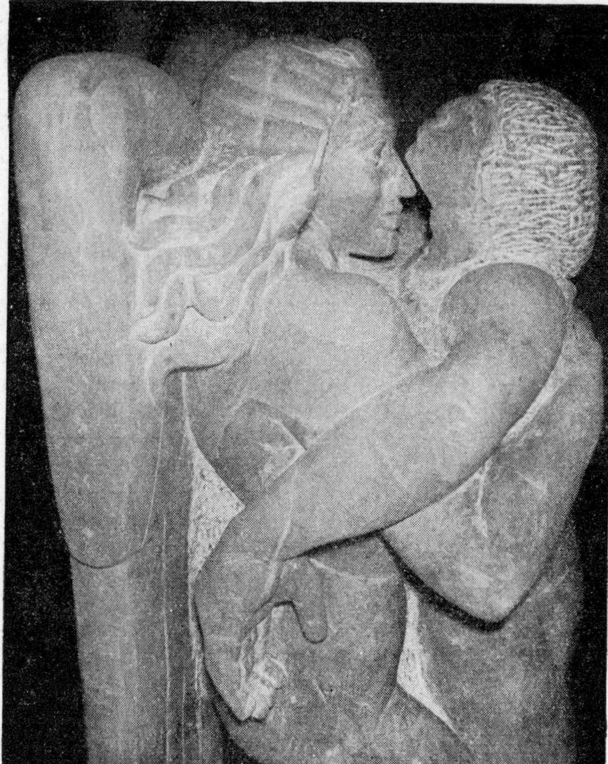

Detail from "Jacob and the Angel," a work in alabaster by Jacob Epstein, based on the Old Testament story, which was exhibited in London in 1942

sculptors in that he refused to be limited by what he claimed to be the almost universal tendency: considering the material of prime importance. Trajan had a strong inner conviction in regard to sculpture and strove for deep spiritual expression. He worked in keen cement and plaster, and has frequently colour. His "Fallen Angel" was considered one of his best pieces.

Alfeo Faggi worked in clay. Of his earlier works, "Eve" and "Pieta" remained among the best, as did his portraits of Rabindranath Tagore and Noguchi.

Concetta Scaravaglione was outstanding among the women sculptors. Her "Girl with Gazelle" is marked by an individual style. Lu Duble was another talented woman sculptor whose "Calling the Loa Haiti" shows movement and is distinctly personal. Minna Harkavy also accomplished work of note.

Cornelia Chapin, an animal sculptor with a good sense of design, reminded one at times of the French animal sculptor, François Pompon. Saul Baizerman hammered coppers and beaten metals.

Raoul Hague, among the late discoveries, did splendid work in stone, winning the Audubon first prize for sculpture in 1945. John Rood, who worked in wood, showed great technical ability and was very productive. Ronald Kraus, whose "Justice," completed under the treasury art project for the Newark federal court house, won him success, received the sculpture prize at the Golden Gate International Exposition in 1939. Kraus modelled chiefly in clay.

Alexander Archipenko worked in many materials and was one of the first abstractionists. His "Moses," a symbolic figure, became well known. Mahonri Young's sporting subjects made him familiar to many. Richmond Barthé was accepted as the foremost Negro sculptor, and held a prominent place in this field of art.

Hugo Robus worked in smooth, simplified forms. "Woman Combing Her Hair" was considered one of his best. Louis Slobodkin also remained in the front rank; his fine "Lincoln" was a source of considerable controversy. Henry Kreis achieved recognition for his work in stone, of which one of the best was "Woman With Violin." He worked under the federal art project in Washington, D.C.

Lee Laurie's large figure of "Atlas" on Fifth avenue in front of Radio City shows Assyrian influence. Carl Milles's fountains and colossal figures kept his name before the public. He acquired a wide reputation as a teacher.

Isamo Noguchi, another outstanding sculptor, worked for Radio City music hall in an interesting style. Other sculptors who gained prominence during this period were Carl Schmitz, Charles Rudy, Bertha Margoulies, John Hovannes, Anita Weschler, Anthony de Francisci, Simon Moselsio, Ben-Schmuel, Harold Cash, Albino Cavallito, Vincent Glinsky, Mitzi Solomon, Paul Fiene, Jean de Marco, Maurice Glickman, Ruben Nakian and Warren Wheelock.

Competitions and Exhibitions.—The New York World's Fair in 1939 proved a great incentive to sculptors. Many were given a chance for the first time to work on a large scale; the results were surprisingly good. Through the federal art projects, some of the younger men achieved their first success. Many well-known sculptors were represented at the fair: Paul Manship's "Time and the Fates of Man" held a central position; Gaetaro Cecere had two very successful over-life-size groups; James Earle Fraser's colossal "Washington," and works by Zorach, Leo Friedlander, Edmond Amateis and others, were exhibited. The French building had a fine collection of sculpture containing work

Alexander Calder's "Stabile," an abstraction in Plexiglas which won first prize in a national competition and was exhibited at the New York World's Fair in 1939

by Maillol and Despiau. Latin-America's exhibit was interesting in some instances, and Cuba was represented by Fernando Boada's excellent "Head."

The plexiglas competition for the Hall of Industrial Science at the fair created an interesting experience for sculptors in that it introduced a new material. More than 200 artists entered the competition. The jury consisted of Katherine S. Dreier, James Johnson Sweeney and Robert Laurent. First prize went to Calder for an interesting piece in this transparent plastic. Other winners were Herman Matter and Werner Drewes.

Still another great opportunity for sculptors was the Golden Gate International Exposition in San Francisco.

In 1939 attempts were made to popularize sculpture by reproduction. Limited editions of small pieces in cast stone, plaster and terra cotta were introduced. The prices ranged from $15 to $100. These enterprises worked fairly well, and probably would have continued had it not been for the small return to the artists. The list of names included such men as: Warren Wheelock, Oronzio Malderelli, Zorach, De Creeft, Laurent, Gross, Flanagan, Polygnoto Vagis, Scaravaglione, Dorothy Greenbaum and Maurice Glickman.

Glass was tried also as a material and was used by some factories as an experiment in reproducing sculpture within the range of the ordinary citizen's pocketbook.

One of the outstanding events during the decade was the second Out-Door exhibition held in 1940 at the Philadelphia Museum of Art under the sponsorship of the Ellen Phillips Samuel memorial. This very ambitious sculptural project along the Schuylkill river in Fairmount park extended over a period of many years. It was of great importance to the advancement of modern sculpture and was representative of works from all schools and from all parts of the world. Commissions were awarded for monuments commemorating events in the history of the U.S. Those for the first two principal groups were given to Gaston Lachaise and Laurent respectively.

Lachaise, one of the foremost sculptors of his day, had been given the subject "Welcoming the Peoples." He died while still working on the sketch, a model of which was cast in bronze for the Philadelphia museum. "Standing Woman" by Lachaise, a cast of which was placed in the collection of the Whitney Museum of American Art, was acknowledged as an important contribution to sculpture by critics and connoisseurs alike. He was given a one-man exhibition at the Museum of Modern Art and was one of the three sculptors included in the "Pioneer Exhibition," held in the spring of 1946 at the Whitney museum, the other two being Zorach and Laurent.

After the untimely death of Lachaise, the commission went to Maurice Sterne, who was known as a painter but worked in sculpture as well. His "Awakening," a figure in bronze, was an outstanding example of his work. This commission, together with Laurent's "Spanning the Continent," comprise two over-life-size groups cast in bronze, and were placed on an exedra along the Schuylkill. Other sculptors who later received commissions for this memorial were: Warnecke, J. Wallace Kelly, Helene Sardeau, Flanagan and Wheeler Williams. Among the exhibitors from Europe in this Out-Door exhibition were such important sculptors as: Barlach, Brancusi, Ernesto de Fiori, Despiau, Epstein, Kolbe, Lipschitz, Maillol, Zadkine, Pablo Gargallo, Sintenis and Henri Matisse, the famous French painter who did interesting quick sketches in sculpture, as other painters had done in the past—notably Pierre Auguste Renoir, Hilaire Degas, and, later, Modigliani and Picasso.

In 1941 the International Business Machines corporation made a selection of sculptures typifying that art in the western hemisphere. The Latin-American countries, Canada, the United States and its possessions were all represented. This selection was added to the permanent collection of I.B.M. Each country in Latin America was represented generally by two sculptors, and many of the pieces were in wood. Among the interesting artists were Agustín Riganelli, Marina Nuñez Del Prado, Maria Martins and Francisco Narvaez. Canada was represented by ten sculptors, including Don Stewart, whose "The Dancer" in terra cotta was noteworthy, as was Sheila Wherry's "Mother and Child" in plaster. The United States's exhibitors included such artists as Arnold Ronnebeck, Paul Hyun, Robert Davidson, Reuben Kramer, Laurent, Charles Cutler, Waylande Gregory, Ben Schmuel, Simon Moselsio, Dan Olney and Marie Louise Felden.

In 1944 an exhibition was shipped to Britain to illustrate "The Art of Today" in the United States. This was a major undertaking during wartime, and because of the difficulties of transportation, only small pieces were accepted. Approximately 50 sculptors were included, covering all schools and directions, from Fraser to Robus. The jury of selection consisted of Archipenko, Manship and George Lober. Before being shipped, the group was exhibited in New York city.

Many other competitions in sculpture took place during this period, including that of the Metropolitan Life Insurance company and those of the "Artists-For-Victory."

The Sculptors' guild, a society numbering among its members most of the younger group, attracted much attention by holding outdoor exhibitions in New York City. Its members employed *taille directe*. Their exhibitions kept abreast of the latest trends in sculpture during the decade.

Museums, as well as universities, became more interested in exhibitions of sculpture. The Whitney Museum of American Art had always welcomed new talent, and many young sculptors experienced their first success there. The museum's permanent collection was very representative of the new movement in sculpture. The Museum of Modern Art was interested chiefly in the ultramodern sculptors, and its superb collection embraced works done in Europe as well as the western hemisphere. The Philadelphia Museum of Art, the Corcoran Gallery in Washington, D.C., the Albright Art Gallery in Rochester, N.Y., the Brookgreen Gardens, S.C., the Carnegie institute in Pittsburgh, together with others, aided the development of sculpture during the period.

Among the colleges and universities which contributed to the general interest was Indiana university where, in the fall of 1944, an exhibition of sculpture was held showing the work of Maillol, Despiau, Gross, Lipschitz, Zorach, Laurent, Lehmbruck, Flanagan, Kolbe, Lachaise and Barlach. In the spring of 1946, Yale university exhibited contemporary sculpture showing the variety of activities in this field. Many of the pieces shown were early works by well-known artists; also, later works by Zadkine, Lipschitz, Smith, and some excellent abstractions by Anton Pevsner done in celluloid, copper and zinc. Pevsner's "Torso" was entertaining with its curved transparent planes. He also showed a portrait of Marcel Duchamp. Many of the items had been presented to the university by Miss Dreier and

→

The last of the giant stone faces of four American presidents—that of Theodore Roosevelt—was unveiled on Mount Rushmore, South Dakota, July 2, 1939. Gutzon Borglum, the sculptor, died in 1941

THE SHRINE OF
MT. RUSHMORE NATIONAL

Duchamp, the latter having done interesting wire sculpture besides making a name for himself at the time of the armory show with his famous painting, "Nude Descending The Staircase."

Another experiment which made the U.S. public more sculpture-conscious was the yearly (except for the war years) open competitions in soap sculpture sponsored by Procter and Gamble. Every exhibition had several thousand entries and started many young artists trying their talent at cutting directly into some material.

Thus, the decade 1937–46 witnessed an increasing appreciation of sculpture on the part of the general public, and the great productivity of the established artists, coupled with the emergence of so many new talents, helped to keep pace with the growing interest. (*See* also ART EXHIBITIONS.) (R. LT.)

BIBLIOGRAPHY.—B. Adriani, *Problems of the Sculptor* (1943); A. T. Broadbent, *Sculpture Today in Great Britain* (1945); H. Buchtal, *Western Aspects of Gandhara Sculpture* (Oxford, 1946); S. Casson, *Sculpture of Today* (1939); J. Epstein, *Let There Be Sculpture* (1940); A. T. Gardner, *Yankee Stonecutters* (1945); R. G. Harris, *Techniques of Sculpture* (1942); M. Hoffman, *Sculpture Inside and Out* (1939); H. S. Moore, *Sculpture and Drawings* (1944); B. Putnam, *Sculptor's Way* (1939); L. Rothschild, *Sculpture Through the Ages* (1942); Sculptor's Guild, *Outdoor Sculpture Exhibition* (1938 *et seq.*); *Sculpture of the Western Hemisphere* (1942); United American Sculptors, *Annual Exhibition* (1939 *et seq.*); W. R. Valentiner, *Origins of Modern Sculpture* (1946). Consult also *Art Index* for specific person's references.

Seabees

First authorized on Dec. 28, 1941, the U.S. naval construction battalions, popularly known as the "Seabees," participated in every major amphibious operation of World War II, including the occupation of Japan and Japanese-controlled areas in China.

Operating in basic units (1,082 men and 34 officers) sufficiently diversified to be completely self-contained and capable of performing any type of advance base construction work, the Seabees, trained construction men commanded by experienced officers of the Civil Engineer corps U.S. navy and U.S. naval reserve, built, operated and maintained more than 400 naval bases in outlying areas.

In 1942 the construction efficiency of the Seabees was estimated to be in the ratio of five to one as compared with that of Japanese construction troops. By the end of the war, when 83% of the more than 240,000 Seabees on active duty were serving overseas, the construction potential of the average Seabee battalion had been increased by 300% over that of original battalions.

In addition to these construction battalions, special battalions were trained in stevedoring operations. Other battalions and detachments were organized to handle the navy's pontoons as causeways, barges and a variety of other uses. Still others specialized in truck operation, camouflage, automotive repair, demolition work, fog generation

Seabees climbing down a rope cargo net. Such nets were used for getting soldiers overside on landing craft during invasion operations in World War II

and petroleum supply. When construction work had been completed, quarter-battalion-size maintenance units took charge, freeing construction battalions for other assignments.

In Europe the Seabees assisted in the construction of and manned the artificial harbour units, and operated pontoon "Rhino" ferries and causeways during the Allied invasion of France, as well as all invasions in the Mediterranean. They assisted in handling stores for the Allied armies over the open beaches of Normandy and southern France and participated in the restoration of damaged ports.

Starting westward from Guadalcanal on the south and the Aleutians in the north, Seabee construction projects mounted into the hundreds. Warehouses, hospitals, personnel structures, airfields, roads, harbours and fleet facilities were provided. Among the largest were those in the Marianas, Guam, Tinian and Saipan, taken in 1944 and completed by mid-1945. The field at Tinian, for example, could accommodate eight B-29s per minute for the bombing of Japan.

On all three islands vast networks of airfields were placed in operation, and supply and staging area facilities expanded.

On the small land area of Iwo Jima such construction was not possible. However, three airfields were built there. The largest of these, called Central airfield, had one of the longest runways in the Pacific—9,800 ft. Serving as an emergency landing point for bombers unable to return to the Marianas after sweeps over Japan, Central airfield during the closing months of the war was used by more than 5,000 B-29s.

The last major Seabee project of the war was the base at Okinawa. This was planned as the greatest single wartime construction undertaking in military history. Installations scheduled included 22 airfields and 1,100 miles of road.

Planned as a wartime organization, the Seabees were scheduled in 1946 to become a permanent branch of the peacetime navy. Plans called for the training of Seabees at Port Hueneme, Calif., for continued overseas advanced base assignments, and for the continued development of advance base type of materials and specialized construction techniques. (J. J. Mg.)

BIBLIOGRAPHY.—W. B. Huie, *From Omaha to Okinawa, the Story of the Seabees* (1945); "Seabees," *American Mercury* 58:19–26 (Jan. 1944). *See* also U.S. Dept. of Navy, *Annual Report* (1942 *et seq.*).

Sea Blockade

See BLOCKADE; SUBMARINE WARFARE.

Seaquake

See SEISMOLOGY.

SEC

See SECURITIES AND EXCHANGE COMMISSION.

Secondary Education

See EDUCATION.

Secondary Metals

The salient features of the secondary metals industry in the U.S. during 1937–45 are shown in the accompanying table. In presenting these data, however, it should be emphasized that only recoveries from old scrap, discarded from the pool of metal in use, represent an increase in the available supply; the reworking of new scrap merely

reconditions for use such portions of new metal not yet in use as may have been discarded in the process of manufacture, and so makes no addition to the current supply.

Recoveries of Secondary Metals in the United States

	1937	1939	1941	1943	1945
NONFERROUS METALS					
Copper (Thousands of short tons)					
As metal	285.6	151.4	135.9	137.9	112.9
In alloys	246.5	345.1	580.7	935.1	875.0
In chemical compounds	?	3.2	9.8	13.0	18.7
Total	532.1	499.7	726.4	1,086.0	1,006.5
From old scrap	408.9	286.9	412.7	427.5	559.8
From new scrap	123.2	212.8	313.7	658.5	446.7
Mine output, new copper	842.0	728.3	958.1	1,090.8	772.9
Lead (Thousands of short tons)					
As metal	154.5	86.9	75.3	58.3	61.1
In alloys	120.6	148.8	322.1	283.8	301.9
Total	275.1	241.5	397.4	342.1	363.0
From old scrap	?	210.8	380.3	310.7	310.8
From new scrap	?	30.7	17.1	31.4	52.2
Mine output, new lead	464.9	414.0	461.4	453.3	390.8
Zinc (Thousands of short tons)					
As metal	64.5	36.0	89.7	78.9	83.9
In alloys	62.8	98.9	143.8	257.9	234.6
In chemical compounds	?	54.8	48.5	31.6	41.9
Total	127.3	189.6	284.0	368.5	360.4
From old scrap	?	45.1	81.5	84.2	121.6
From new scrap	?	144.5	202.8	284.3	238.8
Mine output, new zinc	626.4	583.8	749.1	744.2	614.4
Aluminum (Thousands of short tons)					
As metal	29.4	2.9	8.3	5.9	2.1
In alloys	33.2	51.0	97.6	306.8	295.4
In chemical compounds	?	?	0.9	1.2	0.8
Total	62.6	53.9	106.9	314.0	298.4
From old scrap	?	37.8	43.1	33.1	27.3
From new scrap	?	16.2	63.7	280.9	271.1
Smelter output, new aluminum	146.3	163.5	309.1	920.2	496.5
Tin (Thousands of short tons)					
As metal	8.3	4.4	5.9	5.2	3.7
In alloys	20.3	23.0	35.0	32.3	31.0
In chemical compounds	1.7	0.7	1.1	0.3	0.5
Total	30.3	29.2	42.0	37.8	35.1
From old scrap	?	16.9	29.6	25.2	24.0
From new scrap	?	12.3	14.4	12.6	11.2
Consumption, new tin	72.9	66.6	103.1	46.3	55.6
Antimony (Thousands of short tons)					
Total (mostly alloys)	12.3	9.8	21.6	15.5	17.1
From new scrap		9.7	21.6	15.4	15.1
From old scrap		0.1	0.1	0.1	2.1
Consumption, new antimony	18.1	11.6	30.0	19.5	25.8
Magnesium (Thousands of short tons)					
Total (mostly alloys)	?	?	1.7	11.4	9.2
From old scrap	?	?	—	0.1	0.8
From new scrap	?	?	1.7	11.3	8.4
Smelter output, new magnesium	2.3	3.4	16.3	183.6	32.8
Nickel (Thousands of short tons)					
Total (mostly alloys)	2.4	2.9	5.3	6.9	6.5
From old scrap	?	1.0	2.1	1.9	2.2
From new scrap	?	1.9	3.2	5.0	4.3
Available supply, new nickel	50.2	55.0	117.7	132.4	119.8
PRECIOUS METALS					
Platinum (Thousands of troy ounces)	55.9	45.4	37.5	68.6	58.9
Consumption, total platinum	96.0	100.3	190.1	344.7	336.9
Palladium (Thousands of troy ounces)	12.7	13.0	12.6	23.6	33.0
Consumption, total palladium	69.6	51.4	78.9	137.7	185.2
O. P. M.* (Thousands of troy ounces)	3.6	5.0	1.4	9.4	4.2
Consumption, total O. P. M.	6.6	6.7	19.4	26.8	28.0
Gold† (Millions of troy ounces)	10.4	8.9	8.6	3.0	8.9
Consumption†	11.3	11.1	19.1	27.7	40.0
Silver† (Millions of troy ounces)	23.6	25.0	20.4	44.1	58.4
Consumption†	51.3	69.6	92.8	162.1	184.7
IRON AND STEEL					
Consumption of scrap (Millions of short tons)					
Total used	38.0	36.3	59.2	61.7	56.2
Steel furnaces	28.4	27.5	44.5	47.5	43.2
Old scrap	13.4	12.1	18.1	18.4	17.9
New scrap	15.0	15.3	26.4	29.1	25.2
Steel made	56.6	52.8	82.8	88.8	79.7
Iron furnaces‡	9.6	8.9	14.7	12.8	12.4
Old scrap	4.8	4.6	7.3	7.0	6.5
New scrap	4.9	4.3	7.5	5.9	5.9

*Other Platinum Metals. †Industrial uses only, with no reference to monetary uses. ‡Furnaces using scrap in making pig iron or iron castings; total includes uses other than steel and iron furnaces.

World War II brought marked increases in the recovery of secondary metals. On the one hand, shortages in the supply of practically all important metals led to greater activity in the collection and utilization of old scrap, and at the same time the greatly increased fabrication activity required by the war program inflated the amounts of plant scrap that had to be reworked to put it in shape for use.

Of these two factors, the latter was the greater with most metals, so that the ratio of plant scrap to old scrap was increased.

The table includes data on all of the metals for which secondary recoveries were reported. In addition to total recoveries, broken down according to whether the recovered metal is in the form of pure metal, alloys, or compounds, the total is also divided according to the amounts recovered from old or purchased scrap, and new or plant scrap.

And finally, in order to give the reader an idea of the relative importance of secondary recoveries in comparison with the production of the primary metal, there are added data on the magnitude of the primary industry.

The ideal figure for this comparison would be the consumption of the primary metal in question, but since consumption data were not available in all cases, the next best substitute was used; the first choice is mine production, but for some items smelter production must be used. Nickel was a special case, in which none of these data were at hand, nor was any other figure directly indicative of the demand for nickel; the best that could be done was to use the available supply, that is, domestic production, plus imports, less exports.

This figure is at fault in that it does not take into account changes in stocks, which were considerable during the years of World War II; furthermore, the published data on imports and exports were only approximate, in that they included the gross weights of any ore, matte or alloys, and not the nickel content, giving figures appreciably higher than the actual supply, but still the best approximation that could be made.

The major item in secondary metals is iron and steel scrap, three-quarters of which is used in the production of steel. The increased steel output demanded by the war program soon brought on a shortage of scrap, necessitating the use of more pig iron and less scrap in the steel furnaces.

While increased production activity expanded the supply of plant scrap, purchased scrap was short in supply and more than offset the increase in plant scrap. Purchased scrap decreased from 529 lb. per ton of steel made in 1937 to 406 lb. in 1944, while plant scrap increased from 594 lb. to 657 lb., giving a drop in total scrap used from 1,122 lb. to 1,062 lb., and necessitating an increase in pig iron used from 1,141 lb. to 1,207 lb.

The scrap content of the charge rose to 1,083 lb. in 1945, of which 450 lb. was purchased scrap—the highest ratio of purchased scrap used since 1939. In the first half of 1946 the scrap used rose to 1,138 lb., including 598 lb. of plant scrap and 540 lb. of purchased scrap, a ratio slightly better than that of 1937; this improvement, however, did not indicate a return to normal, but was the result of the disorganization of plant operations during the steel and coal strikes, and especially the shortage of pig iron caused by the latter strike.

By mid-1946 stocks of scrap had declined to a point even lower than in the critical year of 1941, and increased steel output to recoup strike losses was seriously handicapped.

Among the leading nonferrous metals it is significant to note the shift in form of recovery. While recoveries in the form of alloys doubled and redoubled, those as pure metal declined sharply in most cases.

Fabrication for war production created so much plant scrap that recoveries grew rapidly. Only in the cases of lead and tin did recoveries from old scrap keep ahead of those from new scrap.

After 1943 secondary recoveries turned back toward normal, as was evidenced by decreasing totals, and even more so by a trend toward an increase in the ratio of old scrap to new scrap; however, it was possible that some of this latter shift was due to increasing recoveries from used war materials.

There were also significant changes in the secondary recovery of the precious metals during World War II, responding to increased consumption. Because of their relatively high values, the recoveries of these metals were more complete and more prompt than with the cheaper nonferrous metals.

Especially striking were the increasing industrial uses of platinum, gold and silver, and their corresponding increases in secondary recovery.

And finally, the comparison of secondary and primary outputs as shown in the table, emphasize the great importance of the secondary recoveries as a factor in metal supply, and the magnitude of the conservation of mineral resources made possible through the commercialization of the junkpile. (G. A. Ro.)

Second World War

See World War II.

Secret Service, U.S.

The United States secret service, treasury department, was established during the Civil War. Its major duties include the protection of the person of the president of the United States, the members of his immediate family and the president-elect; the protection of the White House and its grounds; the suppression of the counterfeiting and alteration of all government obligations; the protection (by the secret service uniformed force) of treasury buildings, money and securities; and the enforcement of other laws relating to the treasury department.

The ten years from 1937 to 1946 marked a new secret service trend in law enforcement, a trend toward the prevention of crime. In the early 1930s, counterfeit bills were circulating to the extent of nearly $1,000,000 a year. Because the centre of big-time counterfeiting activity was in New York city, the secret service organized a special squad of carefully-selected agents to crack down on certain underworld "syndicates" known to be dealing extensively in counterfeit money. By shadowing, "roping" and tireless investigating, the agents traced and captured hundreds of makers, distributors and passers of fake notes and coins, and seized thousands of counterfeits before they could reach circulation. By 1937 losses to victims of counterfeits were considerably on the downward trend. To help protect potential victims, and to wage a more effective war on counterfeiting, the secret service devised new methods—not to supplant, but to reinforce the enforcement techniques.

Thus the secret service crime prevention program was conceived and integrated with enforcement methods already in use.

Before 1937 it had been the policy of the secret service to give very limited publicity to new types of counterfeit money, lest the public become suspicious of all currency. As a result, few persons except bankers and police had any definite knowledge of what counterfeit money looked like, how to detect it, or what action to take if counterfeit money was passed to them. The situation in 1937 convinced the secret service that by making the crime of counterfeiting difficult and dangerous to commit, the counterfeiter could be driven out of business.

In the four-year period 1933–36, inclusive, losses suffered by victims of counterfeit bills had averaged about $771,000 a year. In 1937 the first attempts were made to put merchants on the alert against the counterfeiter. Thousands of illustrated warning notices were distributed to show essential differences between counterfeit and genuine paper money, so that potential victims would know counterfeits when they saw them and could thus guard against bad-money losses. In April 1938 a special corps of secret service agents centred prevention activities in New York city, long the hotbed of counterfeiting. They lectured to 93,000 business people assembled at 2,160 public meetings. They went from store to store, giving oral instruction to more than 100,000 retailers, and distributed about 900,000 warning notices. For the year ended June 30, 1938, losses to counterfeiters' victims dropped to $519,000.

In the next fiscal year, 1939, the crime prevention work was broadened in an intensified nation-wide "Know Your Money" campaign. More warnings were distributed, and counterfeit-detection material was used effectively in radio broadcasts, newspapers, magazines, leaflets, posters and placards. At the close of that year, losses to victims of bogus bills had dropped to $294,057—almost $225,000 less than the 1938 losses. It was also during 1939 that efforts of the secret service resulted in a conference among representatives of the post office department, the Works Projects Administration and the treasury department, to improve methods of preparing and distributing government cheques and to prevent thefts and forgeries of such cheques.

In Jan. 1940 secret service personnel completed a sound motion picture called "Know Your Money," destined to be shown extensively in the nation's high schools, and to groups of bankers, storekeepers and other money handlers. The actions which had started as crime prevention skirmishes against the counterfeiter now became integrated in a purposeful secret service crime prevention program, which included the "Know Your Money" and "Know Your Endorser" campaigns, the latter directed against cheque thieves and forgers.

A 32-page booklet entitled "Know Your Money" was first published by the secret service in Sept. 1940. Filled with enlarged photographs of genuine and counterfeit bills and coins, the booklet's text told in simple language the story of money, how to detect counterfeits, and how to avoid losses from forged cheques. By 1946 about 100,000 copies had been sold by the government printing office, and several hundred thousand were in use in more than 15,000 high schools, to which they were presented by the secret service for use as standard study courses.

Part of the tools and equipment of a counterfeiter's shop seized by U.S. secret service agents in New York city in Jan. 1942

Use of the booklet in high schools was in keeping with the long-range objectives of the secret service crime prevention program. The boys and girls graduating from secondary schools to enter the commercial world gained much practical knowledge about money from this study. They were preparing themselves to face the realities of business more confidently, and to become better citizens by helping to prevent crime and delinquency.

The "Know Your Money" campaign was endorsed by the U.S. office of education and the National Education association. Many publishers included counterfeit-detection material in standard school textbooks on civics, economics, history, problems of democracy and general business. Schools in various states held "Know Your Money" essay contests in which local banks or merchants furnished war bond prizes to high school students writing the best essays on the subject. In New York city the Chase National bank and *Life* magazine sponsored an impressive secret service exhibit at Rockefeller Center in 1942. Entitled "The Silent Saboteur," the display stressed the potential dangers of counterfeit money as a weapon of war. National advertisers produced merchandising displays on the backs of which they printed counterfeit-detection material and warnings against specific issues of counterfeit bills. With the displays placed on store counters near cash registers, the warnings were thus readily available to merchants and cashiers. Transit companies in many towns and cities printed millions of street car and bus transfers bearing "Know Your Money" warnings, and thousands of instructive car cards were posted in subway trains, trolley cars and busses in big cities.

By 1943 the campaign was progressing favourably of its own momentum, and counterfeiting losses were less than $29,000 for that fiscal year. However, cheque forgery became a growing problem, with the government sending more than 300,000,000 cheques a year to dependents of soldiers and sailors, to social security beneficiaries, to farmers, veterans and others. Forgery was another underworld business conducted for illicit profit, and the secret service attacked it by seeking to make it unprofitable and dangerous. Profiting by experience gained in the offensive against the counterfeiter, the "Know Your Endorser" campaign was intensified to defeat the forger.

Through secret service efforts, all government cheques were imprinted with the pertinent warning: "Know Your Endorser—Require Identification." Also, convinced that merchants and other money handlers should be on the alert against forgers of commercial cheques as well as government cheques, the secret service sought the co-operation of private business in having the "Know Your Endorser—Require Identification" inscription printed on commercial and personal cheques. The response was overwhelming. Life insurance companies, auto manufacturers and other industrialists, state, county and municipal governments, chain stores and independent business men, makers of safety paper for cheques, and other organizations printed the warning on millions of cheques. As in the "Know Your Money" campaign, newspaper and magazine articles, hundreds of radio broadcasts, pamphlets, posters, placards and educational exhibits played an important part in putting potential victims of the cheque forger on guard against him. Printed warnings were sent with cheques to persons who received government cheques by mail, cautioning them to foil mail thieves by getting cheques upon delivery and by keeping mail boxes locked. A large insurance company co-operated by producing a motion picture in colour, called "Check and Double Check," and another on counterfeiting, entitled "Doubtful Dollars," and presented several prints to the secret service for use in both campaigns. Public utility companies, department stores and banks promoted and exhibited educational displays designed to make money-handlers cheque-conscious and counterfeit-conscious.

Secret service crime prevention techniques were not confined to the combatting of counterfeiting and forgery. They were effectively applied in security work involving protection of the president, members of his family, and protection of numerous foreign dignitaries and other personages. Secret service agents protected President Roosevelt during his historic journeys to foreign countries and his wartime inspection tours in the United States. They were with President Truman at the United Nations conference in San Francisco, and the United Nations Charter was transported from San Francisco to Washington, D.C., in secret service custody. Careful preparations were made for Truman's conference at Potsdam with Stalin, Churchill and Attlee, and agents provided security for the president enroute and abroad at all times.

Among notables protected by the secret service, especially during World War II, were Crown Princess Martha of Norway and her family; Queen Wilhelmina and Princess Juliana of the Netherlands; Churchill; Attlee; Lord Beaverbrook; members of the British imperial staff; Sergio Osmeña, president of the Philippine commonwealth; Madame Chiang Kai-shek; the Earl of Athlone, governor-general of Canada; Mackenzie King, prime minister of Canada, and others.

One important security mission accomplished by the secret service shortly after war was declared was not revealed until after V-E day. On Dec. 26, 1941, secret service agents provided security during transportation of several priceless historic documents which were moved from the Library of Congress in Washington, D.C., to the government's gold depository at Fort Knox, Ky. The treasures included the originals of the Constitution of the United States, the Declaration of Independence, the Articles of Confederation, the Lincoln Cathedral copy of the Magna Carta, Abraham Lincoln's Gettysburg Address and Second Inaugural Address, and the Gutenberg Bible.

Despite the fact that more than 41% of secret service personnel joined the armed forces, its enforcement and crime prevention work progressed. Convictions of counterfeiters and forgers averaged more than 97% in cases which went to trial, the security work was performed efficiently and the crime prevention program rolled forward, thanks largely to the hearty co-operation of police departments, school authorities, banks and private business. (*See* also FEDERAL BUREAU OF INVESTIGATION.)

BIBLIOGRAPHY.—Frederic Majer, *Our Country's Money* (1939); Joseph Leeming, *From Barter to Banking* (1940); *Know Your Money*, U.S. Secret Service booklet, Wash. D.C. (1940); Robert Disraeli, *Uncle Sam's Treasury* (1941); Irving Crump, *Our United States Secret Service* (1942); John J. Floherty, *Money-Go-Round* (1944); Laurence Dwight Smith, *Counterfeiting—Crime Against the People* (1944). (F. J. W.)

Securities

See BUSINESS REVIEW; LAW; STOCKS AND BONDS.

Securities and Exchange Commission

At the beginning of the ten-year period 1937–46, the Securities and Exchange Commission (SEC), a quasi-judicial agency of the United States government, was administering three statutes designed for the protection of investors and enacted by the congress as a part of the early reform program of the New Deal. With these and four subsequent enactments a well-rounded pattern of securities regulation was established.

The SEC continued to be composed of five members, appointed by the president by and with the advice and consent of the senate. A bipartisan agency, not more than three of its members might be of the same political party. Its decisions were reviewable by the U.S. circuit courts of appeal at the instance of any person aggrieved by a decision of the commission affecting his rights and interests.

Administration of the 1933 Act.—The two basic objectives of the Securities Act of 1933 were: (1) to prevent fraud in the sale of securities, of whatever nature under penalty of fine or imprisonment, or both; and (2) to provide for disclosure to public investors of the facts they needed to know in order to determine whether to purchase securities offered for public distribution.

Disclosure of the facts was obtained through a requirement that registration statements be filed with the commission. The statements so filed were made publicly available for anyone's inspection. Specified items of information had to be reported, describing the terms and provisions of the security being registered as well as pertinent information concerning the issuer. A prospectus or selling circular was required to be made available to investors and to contain an accurate summarization of the facts thus disclosed. The commission did not guarantee accuracy of the representations, but persons responsible for the filing of false information subjected themselves to the risk of fine or imprisonment, or both; and investors had a right of recovery against the company, the underwriters and others for losses suffered in reliance upon false information.

The act of 1933 did not give the commission any power to disapprove the issuance of securities for lack of investment merit. However, the commission could deny or suspend the effectiveness of the registration statement if after hearing it found that the factual disclosures were materially inaccurate or inadequate. Such "stop orders" operated to prohibit the sale of the securities until the statement was amended to correct the deficiencies. If such corrections were made, the stop order had to be lifted. Thus, registration served only to make information available for investors. In no sense was registration to be considered by investors as a guarantee or assurance against investment risk in the purchase of registered securities. The investors themselves had to appraise the securities in light of the facts thus disclosed; otherwise the benefits of registration and disclosure were dissipated.

Securities in the aggregate amount of $28,649,609,000 became effectively registered for sale to the public during the ten-year period, 1937–46, bringing the total of securities so registered under the act to $35,643,000,000. Securities registered during the year ended June 30, 1946, aggregated $7,073,280,000, the highest annual volume of registrations to that date.

On that date, effective registration statements numbered 5,511.

As of the same date, 6,572 registration statements had been filed with the commission, proposing security offerings aggregating $39,754,000,000. Of these, 913 were withdrawn, some because of changes in financing plans and many others because of unwillingness to make the required disclosure of facts about the security or the issuer. A total of 326 stop orders were issued, based upon material misstatements and omissions in the registration statements. Of these, 144 were lifted when the statements were corrected.

The registration requirements of the act did not apply to nonpublic offerings and intrastate distributions of securities, if properly circumscribed. Another provision exempted relatively small security offerings, the amount thereof having been increased from $100,000 to $300,000 under a May 1945 amendment to the act. In respect of such latter offerings, a simple letter of notification had to be filed with the commission, together with copies of the selling circulars.

Regulation of Trading Practices.—The beginning of the decade 1937–46 found the commission well advanced in its administration of the statute of 1934, designed by congress to regulate securities trading practices on exchanges and in the over-the-counter market. Passage of this legislation to eliminate abuses from interstate traffic in securities traded upon the nation's securities markets was a necessary adjunct to the 1933 law providing protection to investors in connection with new offerings or secondary distributions of securities.

Administration of the Securities Exchange act had contributed much to the advancement of the interests of investors and the public. Under the act, annual and other corporate reports of companies with securities listed upon exchanges were accumulated. These reports contained detailed information concerning such securities and the issuing companies. Filed, subject to legal penalties for misstatements, this information served as a valuable guide to the proper market appraisal of the investment merit of the securities. The importance of such disclosure requirements of the act and the extent of the public interest involved was emphasized by the annual dollar volume of securities traded on exchanges, which in 1945 approximated $18,000,000,000.

The misuse by management officials of "inside" information was curbed through operation of provisions of this act (1) requiring such officials to report monthly to the commission their holdings and transactions in their companies' listed equity securities; and (2) making their short-term trading profits in such securities recoverable by the company.

Management officials also were forbidden to engage in short sales.

So, too, did the operation of the act during the decade 1937–46 result in greater participation by investors in the determination of the affairs of their companies than ever before. The exercise by investors of their important voting rights was greatly facilitated by commission rules governing the solicitation of proxies from holders of listed securities. These rules required disclosure of all facts pertinent to the particular matter upon which the votes of security holders were being solicited. Also, stockholder proposals might be included in management solicitations and thus submitted to a vote of the entire body of security holders.

Approximately 1,700 proxy solicitations were reviewed annually by the commission for compliance with the disclosure requirements of its rules.

It is important to observe, however, that the foregoing discussion of the protective provisions of this act applied only to securities listed upon exchanges. Only 3,585 security issues of 2,188 issuing companies were listed in 1946. However, there were several thousand other securities traded exclusively in the over-the-counter market; and with respect to all of these (except securities of companies subject to the Public Utility Holding Company and Investment Company acts) there were no comparable provisions requiring disclosure of information, curbing misuse of "inside" information, or regulating proxy solicitations. Recognizing the added benefits to investors which would flow from a more universal application of these protective provisions of the law, the commission, in June 1946, presented a report to congress recommending their extension to securities of the larger U.S. corporations not then listed.

Securities trading practices, both on exchanges and in the over-the-counter market as well as among brokers and dealers generally, were the subject of other provisions of the act designed for the protection of investors and the public. These provisions divided themselves into: (1) outright prohibitions against misstatements, deceit, market manipulation, and other fraudulent acts and practices; and (2) provisions for the regulation of trading practices upon exchanges and in the over-the-counter market and of the activities of brokers and dealers, to eliminate malpractices and establish new and improved standards of business conduct and fair dealing. Regulation by the board of governors of the federal reserve system of the extension of credit or "margin" on transactions in listed securities contributed a stabilizing influence over exchange trading.

The first step in the process of improving the standards of conduct in the financial community involved registration with the commission of the nation's securities exchanges. As a prerequisite to such registration, a showing was required that the exchanges' constitutions, bylaws, rules and procedures were such as to meet the prescribed standards of the act. Among these were fair trade practice rules applicable to the membership; powers of discipline over members for conduct inconsistent with just and equitable principles of trade; and undertakings to comply with the act and regulations thereunder, and to enforce compliance by exchange members. Nineteen exchanges maintained registrations with the commission as meeting these standards; and during the course of the intervening years, numerous revisions of the rules of the exchanges were made to meet new and changed situations (many being recommended by the commission to afford additional protection to investors and the public). Foremost among these was a basic reorganization of the administrative machinery of the New York Stock exchange in 1938, providing among other things for direct representation of the public on its board of governors. The commission was empowered to modify exchange rules whenever necessary for the protection of investors.

Similar regulatory provisions applied to the over-the-counter market. Brokers and dealers were required to register with the commission and to conform their business practices with standards prescribed in the act and in commission regulations as necessary for the protection of investors. On June 30, 1946, 4,132 brokers and dealers were registered with the commission. Pursuant to the Maloney act amendment passed by congress in 1938, a national organization of over-the-counter brokers and dealers was organized, under the name of National Association of Securities Dealers, incorporated (N.A.S.D.). Its membership approximated 2,500 in 1946. This association prescribed fair trade practice rules governing its membership, and had powers of discipline for rule violations; its rules and disciplinary actions were subject to review by the commission.

Both the exchange and the over-the-counter markets were under constant surveillance by the commission in the interest of curbing misrepresentation, market manipulations, and other fraudulent acts and practices. The penalty for such offenses might be suspension or expulsion from exchange membership, the commission having invoked such remedies in a number of cases; or the commission might deny or revoke the registrations of brokers or dealers, or suspend or expel them from membership in the N.A.S.D. Registrations denied or revoked numbered 290 as of June 30, 1946, the number of suspensions and expulsions from the N.A.S.D. being 28. Other sanctions included civil actions to enjoin continued violations, and criminal prosecutions.

In many of its "disciplinary" actions, the commission found that unscrupulous dealers had defrauded investors by selling securities to them or buying securities from them at prices far above or below the current market, while misrepresenting or withholding facts which the investor was entitled to know concerning the market—the dealer exacting exorbitant profits in the process. As an aid to the elimination of this abuse, the N.A.S.D. set up a procedure under which sales or purchases at more or less (respectively) than 5% above or below the current market would set in motion an inquiry as to whether, under all the circumstances, fair treatment had been accorded the customer; if not, disciplinary action was taken.

Another significant development involved the public offering of securities registered under the Securities act. An SEC study showed that in a number of cases the securities sold substantially above the specified public offering price almost immediately after the commencement of the offering. It further appeared that one of the primary causes was the withholding by underwriters and distributors of substantial blocks of the securities with the result of artificially restricting the available supply of stock; this created a correspondingly excessive demand for the available stock, carrying the price to higher levels and permitting the later sale of the withheld stock at a higher margin of profit to the underwriters and distributors. Arising during a period of heavy demands for new stock offerings, this abuse was a good illustration of the new and varying problems with which the commission had to cope in its efforts to protect investors.

Administration of the Public Utility Holding Company Act.—Enacted as a result of public investigations into the evils and abuses which marked the growth of huge utility empires during the 1920s, the Public Utility Holding Company act of 1935 directed the commission to regulate the financial and related practices of holding company systems of electric and gas companies in the interest of curbing such practices. It further directed the commission to take such action as might be necessary to delimit the systems, so that their operations would be confined to economically integrated units and related businesses, and to simplify the corporate and capital structures of system companies and provide an equitable redistribution of voting power among security holders.

Opposition to such regulation precipitated a bitter congressional battle; and this opposition was carried over into the courts following enactment of the measure. Accordingly, when the major holding companies refused to register upon passage of the law (because of alleged unconstitutionality), the commission prosecuted a test case (against Electric Bond and Share company) which resulted in a U.S. supreme court ruling in March 1938, upholding the constitutionality of the act's registration requirements.

Thus, the industry was subjected to regulation in the interest of protecting investors, consumers and the public against corporate practices which previously had resulted in huge losses to U.S. investors and the bankruptcy of many holding and operating companies. Vast concentrations of control over far-flung and unrelated properties had been accomplished by methods which led to the creation of unsound and top-heavy financial structures, many of which could not weather slight declines in earnings. This control was to be broken up, permitting the return of local control and management and of effective state regulation and limiting system operations to integrated, economic units.

Administration of these requirements for readjustment, characterized by the commission as the "key provisions of the act" and the real target of the opposition before congress, occupied a considerable portion of the commission's time and efforts. Much progress was made in the integration of the physical properties of the nation's utility systems and in the simplification and rehabilitation of their corporate structures, these accomplishments being attributable both to voluntary action by holding companies and to action ordered by the commission to effectuate its objectives. Despite the protests of the opposition that the legislation would lead to the destruction of security values, actual experience demonstrated that the reverse was true. In no instance was there a dumping of securities upon a market unable to pay a fair price for them; on the contrary, there were numerous instances of sharp increases in the market prices of securities attributable in substantial part to steps taken to comply with the act. Many holding company stocks had more than doubled in price upon announcement of company plans for integration or simplification.

Other beneficial effects of compliance with the act's objectives included the substitution of sound structures providing fair voting rights in place of top-heavy structures under which public security holders, who had supplied almost all the capital, were disfranchised; the release of operating utility companies from absentee control, permitting local management and regulation; the distribution of underlying portfolio securities to the stockholders of holding companies who were far removed from the ultimate source of earnings and dividends; and the simplification of capital structures, often permitting the resumption of dividends after years of default.

While, as indicated, much of this progress resulted from voluntary company action, there were several court contests of commission orders directing compliance. Among these were SEC orders (1) directing two major holding companies to divest themselves of scattered properties found not to be retainable with their respective principal, integrated systems; and (2) directing the liquidation of two large subholding companies in one major system because they served no useful or economic function and constituted undue and unnecessary complexities in the system. By mid-1946, only one of these cases had been decided by the supreme court, to which they ultimately were appealed; and in that case the court upheld the constitutionality of the integration clause of the act (that being the only issue which the case posed for court determination). In the other undecided integration case, questions of administrative interpretation were involved; and both the constitutionality of the corporate simplification clause and questions of administrative interpretation were involved in the two liquidation cases remaining undecided. In these and related cases appealed to and decided by the courts, the commission's rulings in all cases had been sustained, except for a reversal on a minor issue in one case. In all other cases involving court review of commission decisions under this act, only one important but incidental ruling failed of court affirmation.

One measure of the progress toward accomplishment of these objectives of the act was reflected in the $6,100,000,000 of utility and nonutility properties whose proscribed control by particular holding companies had been eliminated as of June 30, 1946. An additional $3,250,000,000 of properties were then under orders requiring similar divestment. Plans numbering 68 for corporate simplification and redistribution of voting power among security holders had been approved by the commission; and numerous other cases had been carried to advanced stages. In all such cases, the commission had to find that fair and equitable treatment was accorded each class of security holders affected and that the objectives of the act otherwise were effectuated.

As of June 30, 1946, the issuance and sale of securities of holding and operating companies in the aggregate amount of $9,700,000,000 had been passed upon by the commission as meeting applicable standards of the act. Conformance to these standards brought about more conservative accounting, depreciation, dividend and financing policies by companies affected, thus strengthening their financial condition and safeguarding the interests of investors and consumers. Maintenance of competition for the underwriting of securities was required. Other protective provisions of the law applied to the purchase and sale of securities and other assets; mergers and consolidations; solicitations of proxies and other authorizations; dividend and accounting policies; servicing contracts and other similar arrangements; and other related matters. The law also forbade political contributions.

Trust Indenture Act of 1939.—This act required that indentures under which the larger public offerings of bonds, debentures, notes and similar debt securities were to be made, should contain specified provisions designed to safeguard the interests of the purchaser. Provisions relating to the indenture trustee, as representative of the security holders, included a requirement for a corporate trustee with minimum combined capital and surplus, prohibited certain conflicts of interest, imposed high standards of conduct and responsibility, precluded the preferential collection of certain claims owing to the trustee and provided for reports and notices by the trustee to the investor. Other provisions related to the maintenance of bondholders' lists and the supplying of evidence to the trustee of compliance with indenture provisions. As of June 30, 1946, trust indentures qualified as meeting the applicable standards of the act covered an aggregate of $9,085,000,000 securities proposed for public sale.

Investment Company Act of 1940.—While the sale of investment company securities was subject to the registration provisions and fraud prohibitions of the Securities act, special legislation was found necessary to curb abuses prevalent in the conduct of investment company affairs. Accordingly, such companies were subject to regulation under the act and were required to conform their business practices to various standards prescribed therein in the interest of protecting investors. Among these were special prohibitions against transactions between companies and affiliated persons unless found by the commission to be fair and to involve no overreaching. Management abuse of trust obligations to security holders became a statutory ground for their removal by courts upon application of the commission. Mergers and consolidations were subjected to special SEC scrutiny.

Investment companies numbering 361 and having aggregate assets perhaps exceeding $3,500,000,000 were registered with the commission at the close of the period.

Investment Advisers Act of 1940.—There were registered with the commission on June 30, 1946, 853 individuals and firms engaged in the business of advising others with respect to their securities investments. Under the act, they were required to conform their activities to the prescribed standards, including disclosure of any adverse interest they might have in transactions for their clients. Acts or practices constituting fraud were prohibited.

Bankruptcy Act.—In reorganization proceedings for debtor corporations in which there was a substantial public interest, the commission, pursuant to the provisions of chapter X of the Bankruptcy act, was to participate as an independent, expert adviser to the courts. The commission's special concern in these proceedings was the fairness of the terms of reorganization plans as they applied to the several classes of security holders whose interests were at stake, and the feasibility of the plans, particularly in terms of the ability of the reorganized company to continue as a going concern. The commission's views on these and related problems normally were presented orally or by memorandum to the courts; in the larger and more complicated cases, however, the commission prepared advisory reports for the information of the courts and interested security holders.

Enforcement Activities.—In addition to the commission's administrative powers previously discussed, the commission had the duty of investigating complaints and other indications of securities violations. Where evidence developed of a violation of law, the commission might seek a court order enjoining the acts and practices complained of; or, if fraudulent misconduct was apparent, it might refer the facts to the department of justice for prosecution.

By 1946 the commission had obtained court orders enjoining 1,054 companies, firms and individuals from continuing acts or practices alleged to violate the securities laws. Persons convicted of fraudulent securities transactions numbered more than 1,200. (*See* also LAW; STOCKS AND BONDS.) (R. K. M.; O. L. DS.)

BIBLIOGRAPHY.—C. C. Bosland, "Investment Company Act of 1940 and Its Background," *Journal of Political Economy*, 49:477–529, 687–721 (Aug., Oct. 1941); H. V. Cherrington, *Investor and the Securities Act* (1942); Prentice Hall, *Federal Securities Regulations Service* (1933 *et seq.*, looseleaf). *See* also publications of the Comm.: *Annual Report, Bulletin, Decisions and Reports, Rules of Practice, Work of the Sec. and Exc. Comm.*

Security Council, United Nations

See UNITED NATIONS.

Sedition

See FEDERAL BUREAU OF INVESTIGATION.

Seismic Wave

See SEISMOLOGY.

Seismology

Turkey suffered more than any other country in earthquake casualties during the decade 1937–46. The Erzingan earthquake of Dec. 27, 1939, killed 23,000 persons. Twenty-seven hundred were killed in the Samsun area on Nov. 26, 1943, more than 1,300 in Anatolia on May 31, 1946, and nearly 1,000 in the Gerede area on Feb. 1, 1944. Several hundred were lost in each of six other shocks. Casualties were caused largely by the tendency of native mud-wall and tile-roof structures to collapse under relatively moderate earthquake forces.

In South America casualties ran high in five earthquakes. Ten thousand were killed in the destruction of Chillan, Chile, on Jan. 24, 1939. At San Juan, Argentina, on Jan. 15, 1944, 3,500 were killed and damage was estimated at $100,000,000. On May 24, 1940, 249 were killed at Callao, Peru, and there was great damage. Guayaquil, Ecuador, on May 13, 1942, suffered $2,500,000 damage and the loss of 200 lives. Two hundred were killed in Cuzco province, Peru, on Jan. 30, 1943.

Japan remained relatively quiescent. The most notable shock occurred on May 1, 1939, when hundreds were lost as the village of Aikawa was destroyed. A seaquake greater than the Tokyo earthquake of 1923 centred 100 mi. off Honshu Island on Dec. 7, 1944, but only slight damage occurred along the coast.

A strong shock killed 17 at Accra, Gold Coast, Africa on June 22, 1939; 276 were reported killed at Constantine, Algeria, on Feb. 14, 1946. On Nov. 10, 1940, 400 were killed, great damage done and oil fires started at Focsani, Rumania. A shock near Colima, Mexico, on April 15, 1941, killed 90 and caused $1,000,000 damage in Mexico City.

In the U.S., the Imperial valley earthquake of May 18, 1940 killed 9 persons and caused $6,000,000 damage. In the Torrance-Gardena area of Los Angeles an earthquake on Nov. 14, 1941, caused $1,000,000 damage. On Sept. 5, 1944, earthquake damage at Cornwall, Canada, and Massena, New York, reached $2,000,000. Strong shocks also occurred in Ohio, New Hampshire, Washington and California.

Seismographers at the Fordham university seismic station in New York city, source of most public information in the U.S. concerning earthquakes and tremors

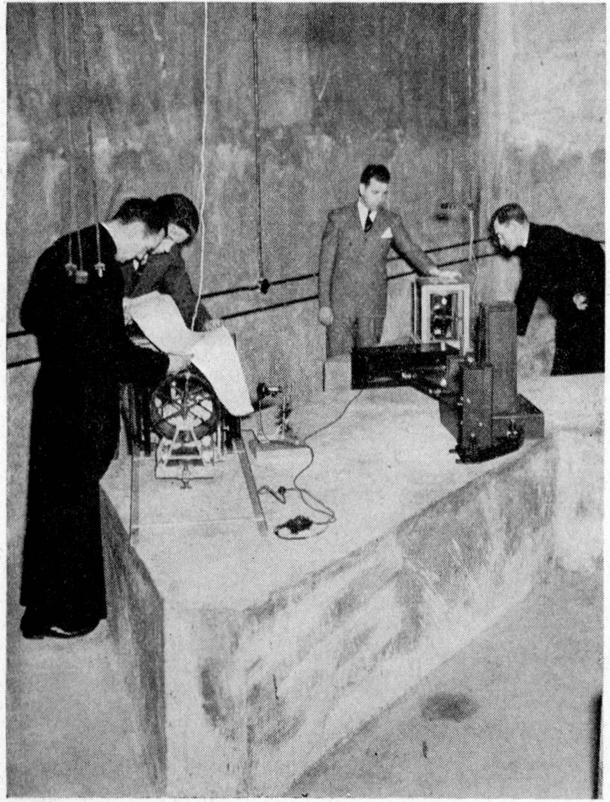

On Nov. 27, 1945, a violent seaquake in the Arabian sea generated a sea wave which was reported to have killed 4,000 on the coast near Karachi, India. On April 1, 1946, the greatest seismic sea wave in the Pacific in many years swept down from the Aleutian Islands, killing nearly 200 at Hilo, Hawaii, and causing $10,000,000 damage. The wave there was 20 ft. high. It spread out over the entire Pacific basin.

Paricutin volcano in Mexico, breaking through a cultivated field on the afternoon of Feb. 20, 1943, caused prolonged but localized seismic activity. The atom bomb test explosion in New Mexico on July 16, 1945, was recorded as a light earthquake on seismographs in the U.S.

In California, plans were made by public officials and public utilities groups for joint action in case of disastrous earthquakes. A new building code covering earthquake forces was published in the U.S. under federal auspices, and similar codes were under consideration in many other countries, especially South and Central America. Earthquake insurance was discussed in papers by A. C. Chick (U.S.) and O. Seiler (Switzerland).

Engineering-Seismological Research.—Basic instrumental data on destructive ground motions, obtained by the U.S. coast and geodetic survey, were used in research on the design of earthquake-resistant structures. Strong-motion seismographs were installed in several South and Central American countries. The mathematically laborious problem of computing earthquake stresses in structures was solved by a torsion pendulum device. Results obtained with it emphasized the important influence of foundation conditions on earthquake damage.

At Boulder dam sensitive seismographs were successfully used to investigate local shocks caused by changing water loads. The shocks were generally associated with local fault patterns.

Data Used to Detect and Track Hurricanes.—Minute ground waves called microseisms are continually recorded on seismographs all over the world and are known to be of meteorological origin. By utilizing a newly discovered method of measuring the direction of propagation of these complex waves at an observing station, the U.S. navy was successful in detecting and tracking hurricanes in the West Indies and adjacent areas. The method was originally demonstrated at St. Louis university, Missouri, by Rev. J. Emilio Ramirez and Rev. James B. Macelwane. In some cases low pressure areas were detected thousands of miles away. Important microseismic investigations based primarily on amplitude fluctuations were made in India, China, England, the U.S. and some other countries in attempts to learn more of the mechanics of their origin.

Earthquake Investigations.—Publication of epicentres of the earthquakes of the world, based on instrumental data, continued at Oxford university, England, under the auspices of the International Seismological association. Work on descriptive catalogues was advanced in Spain, Switzerland, Jamaica, Germany, New Zealand and especially in South and Central American countries. A comprehensive study of the seismicity of the earth was made by Beno Gutenberg and Charles F. Richter (Pasadena), and periodicity studies based on 131 catalogues were published by Charles Davison (Cambridge).

Use of the Pasadena earthquake magnitude scale, utilizing instrumental data, greatly advanced knowledge of the frequency and energy distribution of earthquakes. It revealed that about 80% of the total earthquake energy released in one year (by possibly 100,000 shocks) may be expended in one great earthquake. A definite relation was developed between the instrumental magnitude scale and an intensity scale based on observed surface effects. Deep focus earthquakes which occasionally originate as much as 500 mi. below the surface were given further study especially by U.S. and British seismologists, and there was wide discussion on their geological implication.

Instrumental Investigations.—Harry O. Wood (Pasadena) published a new list of the seismographic stations of the world as they existed at the start of World War II. The war caused many disruptions. New stations were established in the Americas, Africa and on islands of the Pacific. Perry Byerly (Berkeley) used seismographic data to verify the existence of mountain "roots." Maurice Ewing (Woods Hole Oceanographic institute) determined the structure of a section of the continental shelf on the east coast of the U.S. Seismographic data were also used to investigate the structure of the continents, the extent of continental layering in the oceanic basins, density variations in the earth's interior, the mechanism of faulting, changes in the physical state of the earth's interior with depth and kindred subjects. Studies of seismic wave propagation and earth structure were supplemented in other fields by high pressure laboratory experiments on rocks. Further investigation of regional variations in the speeds of seismic waves and the development of seismological tables for deep focus earthquakes materially improved the accuracy obtained in locating earthquakes. A comprehensive work on seismic wave analysis was published in Finland. During the war seismographs were used to locate earthquakes in axis occupied territory. (*See* also DISASTERS; GEOLOGY.)

BIBLIOGRAPHY.—Perry Byerly, *Seismology* (1942); Joseph Lynch, *Our Trembling Earth* (1940); L. Don Leet, *Practical Seismology and Seismic Prospecting* (1938); A. W. Lee, *Earthquakes and Other Earth Movements* (London, 1939); B. Gutenberg and eight collaborators, *Internal Constitution of the Earth* (1939); A. Imamura, *Theoretical and Applied Seismology* (Tokyo, 1937); S. Irwin Crookes, *Earthquake Resistant Buildings* (New Zealand, 1939). (F. NN.)

Selective Service, U. S.

Selective Service in the U.S. during World War II was predicated upon at least one proposition as old as society itself, that every citizen is under obligation to join in the common defense of his country, his community, his hearthstone. Another proposition was that in a national emergency, the national government has absolute authority over its armed forces. And the all important proposition that local self-government is the fundamental basis of U.S. democracy was often called the heart and soul of Selective Service.

The Selective Training and Service act of 1940 embraced these propositions closely. Liability for military service was placed equally upon all male persons between the specified ages of 21 and 36. There were very few exceptions. Men were to serve in the national forces instead of in state or local militia, as they served during the early days of the country. And selection was to be made by neighbours and fellow civilians under a system of supervised decentralization. In principle, though with many modifications, 1917 Selective Service legislation was used as a "lesson book."

The 1940 act was the first peacetime military training law in the nation's history, and there were several limitations in the original legislation which took into account the peacetime situation. Not more than 900,000 men were to be in training at one time; the inducted men were to serve and be trained for a period of 12 months or less, unless sooner relieved, or unless congress declared the national interest imperilled, and they were not to be employed beyond the limits of the western hemisphere, except in U.S. territories and possessions. These limitations were removed by congress a few days after the Japanese struck the U.S. at Pearl Harbor in Dec. 1941.

The president was authorized to defer men from training and service by reason of age, occupation or dependency, but deferments were to be made on the status of the individual, and no deferments could be made by occupational groups or by groups of individuals in any plant or institution. Bounties and the hiring of substitutes were prohibited. The statute exempted ministers of religion and certain high public officials from the liability for training and service during the time they held office, and permitted men opposed to participation in war by reason of "religious training and belief" to undergo either noncombatant or nonmilitary service, depending on the degree of their objection. A significant new feature was the re-employment provision, which sought to guarantee the citizen-soldier reinstatement in the position he left to enter service, upon the completion of that service. This provision, as well as the other main provisions of the act, will be discussed in detail under appropriate sections following.

Termination date of the act was May 15, 1945, except for the provisions relating to reserves, re-employment and pay of enlisted men. The termination date later was changed successively by congressional action to May 15, 1946; June 30, 1946; and finally March 31, 1947.

Actual planning for the mobilization of U.S. manpower in case of an emergency had begun in 1926, with the appointment of a Joint Army and Navy Selective Service committee, to carry out the will of congress expressed in the National Defense act of 1920, providing that it was to be the duty of the war department general staff "to prepare plans . . . in conjunction with the naval forces . . . for the mobilization of the manhood of the nation."

The first effort of this committee was to analyze and study the experience of Selective Service during World War I. The group was made up of four officers, one from the navy, one from the marine corps and two from the war department. They foresaw the need for more personnel to undertake a long-range program of study, research and planning, and as a result of their recommendations there was assigned to the committee an allotment of 95 civilian reserve officers, drawn from all parts of the U.S., representing a cross section of national life and varied civilian endeavours. These reserve officers met and conferred once a year, learning from officials who had been associated with Selective Service the principles and problems, and studying plans and regulations for the organization and operation of a nation-wide manpower procurement agency—in the event that it might be needed.

By 1935, complete details of the organization had been worked out on a national level, and the adjutant general of the national guard in each state had been asked to co-operate in the organization and administration of Selective Service within his state. Reserve officers, reinforced by national guard officers, assigned to the Joint Army and Navy Selective Service committee, were attending one of the 4 annual regional conferences of 14 days' duration. Nearly 7,000 extension course lessons were being completed every year by these officers.

In June 1940, after the flames of war abroad threatened to spread to the United States, the congress of the U.S. began to study plans for the training and service of men "to augment the armed forces." The Joint Army and Navy Selective Service committee was ready with results of its own studies and planning. The committee's allotment of 95 reserve officers was prepared to function as a national headquarters and as liaison officers with the various states. The adjutants general of the states were ready with their staffs to function as a state headquarters. Altogether there were about 350 officers of the army, navy and marine corps in reserves and in the national guard who were trained specialists in Selective Service.

Organization.—Before proceeding to a detailed discussion of the operations of Selective Service, it would be well to examine the organization which carried out these operations. Selective Service was administered by a civilian agency under the direction of the president. This agency, the Selective Service system, consisted basically of units known as local boards, a headquarters in each state and territory and a national headquarters in Washington, D.C., under a director of Selective Service. The 6,443 local boards, at least 1 in every county or similar area in the nation, were composed of 3 or more civilian members who were citizens of the U.S., residents of the area over which their board had jurisdiction and at least 35 years of age. They were appointed by the president upon recommendation of the governors of the states and served without compensation. Upon these local board members was placed the responsibility of selecting men for training and service. Though these men were unpaid, and usually had other full-time occupations, they met frequently to carry out the duties assigned them.

Also attached to each local board were one or more re-employment committeemen to advise and protect veterans in their rights to obtain their old jobs back as provided in the Selective Service act; medical and dental examiners to assist local boards in classifying registrants whose mental or physical conditions would disqualify them for military service; and a government appeal agent to carry appeals in behalf of the registrant or the government. There were also one or more boards of appeal for each state. Each of these Selective Service officials was uncompensated. At the peak of Selective Service operations, there were some 180,000 citizens contributing their services to the program.

The work of the local boards was directed and co-ordinated, within the states, by a state headquarters under a state director appointed by the president upon the recommendation of the governor, and the entire system was operated by the national director, appointed by the president and directly responsible to him. Dr. Clarence A. Dykstra, president of the University of Wisconsin, was the first national director, serving from Oct. 15, 1940, until his resignation March 21, 1941. He was succeeded by Maj. Gen. Lewis B. Hershey, then a brigadier general, a regular army officer and veteran of World War I, who had served as executive officer of the Joint Army and Navy Selective Service committee from 1936 until 1940, and then as deputy director under Dykstra.

The Job.—Selective Service consisted of three fundamental processes: registration, classification and delivery for induction. By registration was meant the listing by name of all men within prescribed age groups in order to obtain an inventory of manpower for military service. Classification was the determination of the relative availability for military service of the individuals registered, and the selection of those most available. Delivery for induction was the final step, in which the men selected were sent to army and navy induction stations, where those acceptable to the armed services were inducted and became members of the land or naval forces. Although there were changes in details, each of these functions remained substantially the same after Selective Service was put into operation in 1940.

Added to these basic tasks, Selective Service was charged, under the act of 1940, with administering re-employment provisions of the Selective Service act, guaranteeing the citizen-soldier restoration to the position he left to enter service; and, further, with the management of a program of "work of national importance" for men whose religious training and belief forbade their participation in any form of war.

Some idea of the magnitude of the Selective Service task can be obtained when it is considered that between the years 1940 and 1946, more than 45,000,000 men were registered; some 32,000,000 were classified, many of these more than once; and 11,000,000 men were forwarded and accepted for induction by the armed forces. Each of these millions of men was treated as an individual case. Every man had a record to be made and kept. Changing circumstances—the status of the individual, the needs of the armed forces and the requirements of industry—demanded constant scrutiny of each classification and necessitated changing many classifications many times, as indicated by the fact that although 32,000,000 men were classified, classification actions totalled more than 250,000,000.

After passage of the act, and while the organization in the state and local communities was still being perfected, the task of registration was accomplished. The legislation prescribed that, with certain exceptions, every male citizen and alien between the ages of 21 and 36 residing in the U.S. on the registration day would be required to register. The act provided that the president should proclaim when, where and how the registration would be held. Excepted from liability for registration were those already in the military or public health service, and certain aliens of recognized status.

On the same day as passage of the act, the president issued a proclamation calling for the first national registration to be held Oct. 16, 1940. Seven days later regulations were published, outlining the manner in which the registration was to be carried out. The president called upon governors of the states and all public officials to cooperate. Local election machinery formed the basis for the registration system, but this was augmented by many volunteer workers. It was estimated that 1,000,000 persons conducted the registration throughout the nation, in school houses, polling places and other centres. The final total of the first registration was 16,565,037.

During Oct. and Nov. 1940 separate registrations were held, by special proclamation, for the territories of Alaska, Hawaii and Puerto Rico.

The second national registration, for those men who had become 21 years of age after Oct. 16, 1940, was set by presidential proclamation for July 1, 1941. The statutory basis of this registration was the provision of the original act which made male persons between the ages of 21 and 36 liable for registration. In view of the fact that fewer than 1,000,000 men were involved, the registration was carried on through the local boards. The second registration likewise proceeded smoothly and without untoward incident. A total of 850,451 men was enrolled in the U.S. and its territories.

The third registration was held a year and a half later,

on Feb. 16, 1942, and was an immediate aftermath of the declaration of war by the U.S. The congress passed public law 360 on Dec. 20, 1941, extending the liability for registration and military service to men between the ages of 20 and 45. Under the first and second registrations men aged 21 to 36 had already been enrolled, so the third registration included those aged 20, those who had become 21 after the second registration and men between the ages of 38 and 45. In the three registrations, more than 26,000,000 men had been registered, all of them liable for military service. The third registration totalled 8,635,236 in the U.S. and its territories.

Three months later, on April 27, 1942, a fourth registration was held, to include men between the ages of 45 and 65 years. These men were not liable under the existing legislation for military service, but their registration was provided for under public law 360, passed Dec. 20, 1941. Again, as in the first registration, there was comprehensive use of the election machinery in carrying out this registration, because of the great numbers involved; 14,369,325 men were registered in the U.S. and territories. No order numbers were assigned these men, and they were never considered for classification, but they were required to fill out and return a special occupational questionnaire, inquiring into their industrial, agricultural and professional skills. A copy of this form was given to the U.S. employment service.

Although men aged 18 and 19 years were not made liable for military service until near the end of 1942 their liability for registration had been established in the Dec. 1941 legislation, dependent upon presidential proclamation setting a time and a place. Registration date for these men was June 30, 1942, and at that time 2,871,121 men were registered in the U.S. and territories.

Thus, 5 registrations were held during the period Oct. 1940 to June 1942, including a total of approximately 42,000,000 men between the ages of 18 and 65 years, of whom approximately 26,000,000 were at that time liable for military service. Five months later, with the passage of public law 772, men aged 18 and 19 were made liable for military service, increasing the militarily liable manpower pool to approximately 28,700,000.

The sixth registration was, in fact, two registrations. The first part of it included those men who had become 18 years of age after June 30, 1942, and was held between Dec. 11 and 31, 1942. A total of 521,738 was registered in the U.S. and territories.

The second part of the sixth registration was a continuing process which began Jan. 1, 1943, the next day after the close of the first part of the registration. In it every man was required to register as he became 18 years of age, excepting those already in the services by that time. In addition, men who were in the service at the time that men of their age group were required to register, were expected to perform that duty within ten days after their discharge from service. Hence, the sixth registration was a cumulative but only partial inventory of men who became 18 years old each month, since there were excluded those who enlisted in the army or navy before reaching 18. In addition to the 18-year-olds, then, were those from other age groups who had not previously registered, including men discharged from the land or naval forces, and men returning from foreign countries or leaving institutions of various kinds.

A seventh registration, for U.S. citizens abroad, was called for in a presidential proclamation of Oct. 26, 1943, to be held between the dates of Nov. 16 and Dec. 31, 1943. In a sense, this was not a distinct registration from those previously held, but a new opportunity for U.S. citizens residing abroad who were required to register under the six previous proclamations. These persons did not have to register while they remained abroad, but were required to do so the first time they entered the continental limits of the U.S., or Alaska, Hawaii or Puerto Rico. The Oct. 1943 proclamation, however, extended the liability to register to these men wherever they might be. The registration was made before any diplomatic or consular officer of the U.S., who was a U.S. citizen, or before any duly appointed registration official, or any member or clerical assistant of a Selective Service local board. The age limits were placed at 18 through 44, thus excluding those men more than 45, though men 45 to 65 years of age had been required to register in the U.S., but for occupational reasons only. As of Oct. 1, 1945, there had been registered 31,944 men under the seventh registration.

Classification.—As used in Selective Service, classification referred to the determination of the relative availability for military service of the men who had registered. Their selection for service obviously followed when they were needed. Registrants were classified by the local boards, under provisions of the Selective Training and Service act of 1940, as amended, and under regulations prescribed by the president.

The act provided (section 4a) that "the selection of men

Table I.—*Total Registrants, Excluding Fourth Registration, by State of Registration* Oct. 1, 1946

	Total Registrants except Fourth Registration		
	Total	White	Negro
Total	35,717,264	31,913,720	3,803,544
Continental U.S.	35,074,950	31,360,876	3,714,074
Alabama	759,427	504,328	255,099
Arizona	143,585	138,542	5,043
Arkansas	497,595	373,686	123,909
California	2,068,034	2,017,385	50,649
Colorado	280,981	277,653	3,328
Connecticut	475,016	463,221	11,795
Delaware	73,358	61,329	12,029
District of Columbia	244,515	167,605	76,910
Florida	534,551	368,390	166,161
Georgia	827,155	544,288	282,867
Idaho	138,470	138,262	208
Illinois	2,094,289	1,957,649	136,640
Indiana	890,113	852,359	37,754
Iowa	601,655	597,367	4,288
Kansas	426,804	411,077	15,727
Kentucky	724,417	666,315	58,102
Louisiana	655,154	422,843	232,311
Maine	205,083	204,812	271
Maryland	529,863	431,459	98,404
Massachusetts	1,072,489	1,058,518	13,971
Michigan	1,465,260	1,387,368	77,892
Minnesota	686,787	684,272	2,515
Mississippi	559,763	288,669	271,094
Missouri	940,483	867,140	73,343
Montana	144,765	144,491	274
Nebraska	306,678	302,813	3,865
Nevada	35,462	35,093	369
New Hampshire	119,233	119,085	148
New Jersey	1,152,132	1,078,020	74,112
New Mexico	139,941	138,388	1,553
New York city	2,119,688	1,959,388	160,300
New York (excl. N.Y.C.)	1,520,137	1,485,361	34,776
North Carolina	969,938	700,168	269,770
North Dakota	157,832	157,795	37
Ohio	1,804,223	1,699,506	104,717
Oklahoma	576,829	534,108	42,721
Oregon	290,858	289,953	905
Pennsylvania	2,633,427	2,485,514	147,913
Rhode Island	183,623	181,015	2,608
South Carolina	509,408	300,741	208,667
South Dakota	152,578	152,478	100
Tennessee	781,705	632,536	149,169
Texas	1,756,761	1,491,991	264,770
Utah	142,507	142,045	462
Vermont	84,944	84,856	88
Virginia	756,058	560,314	195,744
Washington	476,107	473,447	2,660
West Virginia	513,347	479,399	33,948
Wisconsin	786,437	782,587	3,850
Wyoming	65,485	65,247	238
Territories	642,314	552,844	89,470
Alaska	22,289	22,280	9
Hawaii	133,372	133,315	57
Puerto Rico	481,169	396,612	84,557
Virgin Islands	5,484	637	4,847

Secretary of War Stimson being blindfolded before selecting the first capsule in the U.S. draft lottery Oct. 29, 1940, at Washington, D.C. President Roosevelt (left) watched the drawing made from the same "goldfish bowl" used in the 1917 draft. The first number drawn was 158

for training and service . . . shall be made in an impartial manner . . . from the men who are registered and classified but not deferred or exempted, provided . . . that there shall be no discrimination against any person on account of race or color." The local boards, the act stated, "shall have power within their respective jurisdictions to hear and determine, subject to the right of appeal . . . all questions and claims with respect to inclusion for, or exemption or deferment from, training and service under this Act of all individuals within the jurisdiction of such local boards." (Section 10a[2].)

The regulations pointed out that classification was "the key to selection, and it must be accomplished in the spirit of the Selective Training and Service Act, in the preamble of which Congress has declared 'That in a free society the obligations and privileges of military training and service should be shared generally in accordance with a fair and just system.' "

Four main classes were established, generally defined as follows: class I, men available for military service; class II, men necessary in their civilian capacity (deferred because of occupational status); class III, men with dependents (deferred because of dependents); class IV, men deferred specifically by law; those unfit for military service; and conscientious objectors available for civilian work of national importance.

Each of these main classes was subdivided. The subdivisions were changed somewhat during the course of Selective Service operations to meet changing conditions, but the nature of the four main classes remained unchanged. These subdivisions will be discussed later in more detail.

The task of Selective Service was to provide manpower for the land and naval forces of the U.S., but, as the regulations pointed out, "with the least possible disruption of the social and economic life of the Nation." The task was relatively simple during the period from Oct. 1940 to Dec. 1941 because there were 17,000,000 registrants to select from, and the act provided that not more than 900,000 men could be in training at any one time. In one sense, however, it was more difficult to induct a man in peacetime than during wartime. For there are no drums beating in peacetime, no flags waving for the "hero going forth to do or die for his country." Induction during peacetime is apt to be a mundane affair in the eyes of the inductee and his friends, even though peacetime service is as honourable and patriotic as wartime service. At any rate, when war came to the U.S., the needs of the armed forces grew at the same time that the need for more men for war production increased. And the decision had to be made individually, in every case, as to where a man would be most useful to the national interest in a uniform or at the civilian job he was doing. Classification, in short, was not a mechanical process by which the local board merely took men as their order numbers came in sequence and forwarded them for induction. The case of each man had to be considered as to his rights under the law and the regulations; if he had dependents, the hardship which might be suffered because of his induction had to be determined. Finally, consideration was given as to whether he would serve the national interest better in the armed forces or as a civilian.

One of the major problems in connection with Selective Service was that of determining which of several hundred or thousand registrants a local board should consider for military service first. It was patently unfair to go through the list alphabetically, or in the order in which they happened to register, or in any other manner subject to individual variations among local boards. The order in which registrants were considered meant a considerable difference in the time at which an individual registrant might be called up for military service. The problem was solved in 1940, as it had been in 1917, by means of a national lottery.

First, the individual registration cards in each local

board were shuffled indiscriminately. Then each was assigned a number, which became known as the serial number, but which at this point had no particular significance. Then at Washington, D.C., there was held a national lottery, in which numbers 1 to 9,000 were drawn—numbers which corresponded to the highest number of serial numbers which had been assigned by any local board. The order in which these numbers were drawn was officially and carefully recorded on what was known as the national master list, and this list became the basis on which local boards considered registrants. Thus, serial number 158 was the first number drawn in the first lottery, which meant that every registrant who had been assigned serial number 158 was placed in the position of order Number 1, or the first man to be considered by his local board for military service. The order number was again used by the local board in calling up men for military service after they had been classified.

This method was used in the first, second and third registrations. Separate national lotteries were held for each registration. In the fifth and sixth registrations no lotteries were held, but the order numbers were determined by the date of birth of each registrant, and men born on the same day were assigned numbers alphabetically by name. For the fourth registration serial numbers were assigned, but no order numbers, because the men included in this registration were not liable for military service.

As soon as registration cards had been assigned order numbers, the local board was ready to commence classifying the registrants, in the sequence of the order numbers. In order to facilitate the classification process there was needed more detailed information than that contained on the registration card, which merely told the man's name, address, age, place of employment and similar details. Consequently, registrants were required to fill out comprehensive questionnaire forms, on which they listed information concerning their physical condition, education, occupation, family status, citizenship, military service and any other factors which they desired to have considered by the local board in determining the classification. Registrants who by religious training and belief were conscientiously opposed to war in any form, were given an opportunity of stating their case in this questionnaire. Local boards were empowered to summon any person to appear and testify under oath as a witness, in order to obtain additional information concerning a registrant.

Selective Service headquarters in New York city as workers checked names and numbers during the lottery of March 17, 1942

To assist the registrants in filling out questionnaires, registrants' advisory boards consisting officially of three attorneys, with associate members in many instances, were established.

After receiving the registrant's questionnaire, the local board proceeded to determine in which class the registrant should be placed. The classification was made on the basis of the questionnaire and all other information in the registrant's file, and was made in accordance with an established sequence by placing the registrant in the first class for which grounds had been established. This sequence varied from time to time, but fundamentally the board considered first whether the registrant might be deferred by reason of having been honourably separated from the land or naval forces of the U.S. or of cobelligerent nations. If this classification did not apply, the board then decided whether he might be deferred or exempted by specific provision of the act, as a minister or public official, or by reason of age, as a registrant over or under the age groups currently liable for military service. If the registrant did not fall into any of these categories, it was then determined whether he should be deferred by reason of dependency or hardship, on occupational grounds or moral unfitness.

If no grounds were established for placing the registrant in any of the deferred or exempted classes, he was then classified "I-A," available for military service, provided that if he claimed to be a conscientious objector, the claim should be determined. If the board found that he was conscientiously opposed to combatant service only, he was classified "I-A-O," and if he was found to be a conscientious objector to both combatant and noncombatant military service, he was classified "IV-E."

Registrants classified in these three groups were, after Feb. 1, 1942, physically examined by medical representatives of the land or naval forces before they were ordered to report for induction. This step was known as the "preinduction physical examination." Men were selected for this examination by sending first volunteers for induction in the sequence in which they had volunteered, followed by other registrants in the sequence of their order numbers. When the local board was of the opinion that a registrant had a manifestly disqualifying defect, the local board examining physician might conduct the examination, and the local board might classify the registrant accordingly.

After the registrant had been given the preinduction physical examination, if he had been found acceptable for service, his classification remained as it was "I-A, available for service." If for any reason he had been found disqualified for military service, the registrant was reclassified "IV-F."

It should be pointed out that whenever any registrant was found to be physically or mentally unfit for any military service, he was classified in the first one in sequence of the deferred or exempted classifications for which grounds had been established.

The preceding paragraphs present a bare outline of the classification procedure, to which some of the more important ramifications and problems, including occupational deferments, dependency deferments, physical examination procedures and others will be discussed later. At this point there should be discussed the right of appeal from the local board classification, which was provided in the basic legislation, and which also provided that the president should establish such appeal boards and agencies of appeal as might be necessary to carry out the provisions of the act, and that these boards and agencies should be composed of civilians, citizens of the U.S. Regulations outlining the method of appeal stated that the registrant, any of his dependents, his employer, the government appeal agent or the state director or national director of Selective Service might appeal a local board classification.

The appeal procedure did not follow the pattern of judicial review. Liberal provision was made for the registrant to be heard. He could appeal by making a written request, for which no particular form was prescribed. He could be accompanied by an interpreter, but not by an attorney. He had ten days after the notice of his classification was mailed by the local board to appeal to the appeal board.

The governor of each state divided the state into appeal board areas, each containing about 70,000 registrants of the first registration, or about 300,000 population. Throughout the Selective Service system there were 332 boards of appeal. Members, normally five in number, were appointed by the president—male citizens of the United States, residents of the area over which their board had jurisdiction, and not members of the land and naval forces. Usually the membership was composed of a lawyer, a physician, and representatives from labour, industry and agriculture where applicable. Appeal boards maintained offices and had paid clerical assistance, but members were not compensated for their services.

The decision of the appeal board was made on the basis of the record of the registrant which had been received from the local board, although the appeal board might ask the local board for more information. The appeal board's decision was final, except that another appeal, this time to the president, might be taken under certain circumstances. During the period in which an appeal was being taken, the induction of the registrant was automatically stayed.

The registrant, or any dependent of his, or any person who had filed written information relative to the registrant's occupational status within ten days after the mailing of the classification notice, might appeal to the president, provided that the registrant had been classified in Class I-A, I-A-O, or IV-E, and provided that one or more members of the board of appeal dissented from that classification. The ten-day period could be extended by the local board if it felt that the registrant failed to appeal because he did not understand his rights.

The registrant could not be inducted while an appeal to the president was pending, and when the appeal had been decided the registrant was notified of a continuance of classification or new classification, according to whether the appeal had been affirmed or denied. By the end of 1946, there had been approximately 68,000 appeals to the president, of which approximately 60% sustained the classification of the appeal board.

Generally speaking, age, occupation and dependency were the three chief factors bearing upon the classification procedure. Added to these considerations were, of course, statutory exemptions and deferments, as in the case of certain public officials, ministers of religion and conscientious objectors. Again, broadly speaking, the tendency was for younger men to be more desirable to the armed forces, and hence it was more difficult for them to obtain deferment. All three of the major considerations were interwoven in the classification process.

The Age Factor.—At the outset of Selective Service in Oct. 1940 men between the ages of 21 and 36 were, under the act, liable for military service; as a consequence, men in this age group who were not otherwise eligible for deferment were forwarded for induction in the armed forces. On Aug. 16, 1941, congress limited induction to ages 21 through 27, and provided that men more than 28 could be released from active duty upon their request and with the approval of the secretary of war. At that time, there were 183,966 men more than 28 who could be released from the armed forces under this provision.

Liability for military service was extended to ages 20 through 44 on Dec. 20, 1941, when congress again amended the Selective Service act. This amendment also provided that the president could defer from training and service, by age group, men whose age was such that their deferment was advisable in the national interest. Less than a year later, Nov. 13, 1942, 18- and 19-year-olds were made liable for military service. Shortly thereafter, on Dec. 5, 1942, the age group acceptable for induction was reduced to ages 18 through 37. This age group continued to be the basis for classification until after the end of the war. On Aug. 15, 1945, the induction of men aged 26 and over was discontinued by executive order of the president.

During the postwar period, the age group for military liability was twice changed by the congress. On May 14, 1946, in extending the Selective Service act 45 days, congress limited inductions to men between the ages of 20 through 29. Public law 473, approved June 29, 1946, which extended the basic legislation to March 31, 1947, permitted inductions of men aged 19 to 44, inclusive, but by administrative action the upper age limit was retained at 29.

The age groups from which inductions were actually made at various times were as follows:

Period	Ages (inclusive
Sept. 16, 1940–Aug. 15, 1941	21–35*
Aug. 16, 1941–Dec. 19, 1941	21–27*
Dec. 20, 1941–Nov. 12, 1942	20–44*
Nov. 13, 1942–Dec. 4, 1942	18–44*
Dec. 5, 1942–Aug. 14, 1945	18–37†
Aug. 15, 1945–May 15, 1946	18–25†
May 16, 1946–June 30, 1946	20–29*
After July 1, 1946	19–29†

*Congressional action.
†Administrative action (further limiting age groups previously set by congress).

Age had a bearing on occupational deferments, in that deferments for younger men for occupational reasons were much more stringent, beginning with the spring of 1944. In April of that year, three age groups were established within the ages then liable for induction: 18–25, 26–29 and 30–37. Men under age 26 faced rigid requirements in order to obtain occupational deferments; requirements were more liberal for each of the older groups in turn.

Age, as a factor in classification, was relatively simple, once the age limits had been established by law or policy. The great variables in classification, subject both to legislative action and administrative interpretation, and on top of that in the final analysis to local board interpretation, were dependency and occupation. No matter how carefully definitions were drawn it was up to the local board to decide in each individual case whether to grant deferment for occupation or dependency.

Occupational Deferment.—Occupational deferment was one of the most difficult problems which faced local boards in their classification meetings. If all physically fit men were forwarded for induction as their order numbers came up, industry would be forced to release workers it could not replace without a reduction of productivity. Since the production of war materials was important to the prosecution of the war, the total industrial productivity had to

→

Send-off by a Chicago, Ill., high school band for local draftees bound for induction centre in June 1942

be taken into account. Some men, because of their training and experience, were more essential than others to the continuing production of war goods. Not only in industry, but in other aspects the national health, safety and interest would be imperilled if men were inducted without regard to their civilian work. The order in which men were to be forwarded for induction was dictated by chance, by the instrument of the national lottery. But where chance interfered with essential production of war materials and food, and with the national health, safety and interest, the laws of chance had to be repealed by deferment policies, a factor recognized in the original legislation.

The Selective Service act authorized the president to "provide for the deferment of . . . those men whose employment in industry, agriculture, or occupations or employment, or whose activity in other endeavors, is found . . . to be necessary to the maintenance of the national health, safety and interest." Thus there was left to the president to define the meaning of a "necessary" man, which was done in the initial regulations published a week after the act was approved. However, the act specifically placed occupational deferment on an individual basis, forbidding deferments by groups or occupations as a whole. It further provided that the deferment should cease when the cause for deferment no longer existed. No extensive changes in the act were made relative to occupational deferments immediately following the U.S. declaration of war in Dec. 1941. The first major change in the act occurred with the passage on Nov. 13, 1942, of the Tydings amendment, which provided that registrants found to be "necessary to and regularly engaged in an agricultural occupation or endeavor essential to the war effort . . . shall be deferred until a satisfactory replacement can be obtained."

In April 1943 a law was passed to establish procedures for deferment of federal government employees, by setting up a review committee to pass upon all requests for deferment by reason of federal government employment. Later that year, an amendment was enacted which in effect postponed the induction of 18 and 19-year-old high-school students for the remainder of a school year, if they were ordered to report for induction during the last half of an academic year.

One more wartime change was made in the original legislation, by an amendment approved Dec. 5, 1943, which specified that all occupational deferment cases should be submitted for review and classification to the appeal board having jurisdiction over the area in which the registrant was employed.

In addition to the changes made by legislation, administrative policies pertaining to occupational deferment underwent numerous changes during the course of Selective Service operations. At the outset, in 1940, only 900,000 men had to be selected during a year, and there were 17,000,000 from whom to choose. Even after deferments were granted those men specifically deferred by law, and nearly 10,000,000 men on dependency grounds, the occupational deferment regulation did not need to be drawn very tightly to yield the required numbers for training and service. Hence, the original regulation stated that a man was "necessary" in his civilian activity, when he was "engaged in such activity . . . could not be replaced satisfactorily because of a shortage of persons with his qualifications or skill . . . and his removal would cause a material loss of effectiveness in such activity."

In June 1941 a new class, II-B, was created, in which any registrant found to be a "necessary" man in the "national defense program" was placed. Class II-B deferments were given precedence over Class II-A deferments, in that those in II-B were not limited to a maximum duration, while those in II-A were to be for no more than six months, though the deferments might be renewed. In Feb. 1942 the designation of Class II-B was changed, since the United States had entered the war, to read "man necessary to the war production program," and a maximum limit of six months, subject to renewal, was placed on deferments in II-B, similar to the limit on II-A. Furthermore, renewal of deferment in either class was dependent upon the employer or the registrant convincing the local board that a replacement could not be found.

Provision for individual deferment by reason of both dependency and occupation was established April 23, 1942, with the creation of Class III-B, "in which . . . shall be placed any registrant with one or more dependents, and who is engaged in a civilian activity which is necessary to war production or which is supporting the war effort."

Two new classes were added Nov. 18, 1942, in order to carry out the provisions of the Tydings amendment providing for the deferment of agricultural workers. Local boards were informed that "In Class II-C shall be placed any registrant who has no grounds for deferment other than his occupation or endeavor and who is found to be necessary to and regularly engaged in an agricultural endeavor necessary to the war effort." Class III-C was established for agricultural workers who were also deferred by reason of dependency.

From the beginning, Selective Service operated on the principle that deferments were to be made by the local board on the basis of information available to board, but the War Manpower commission was created by executive order of the president in the spring of 1942 to co-ordinate all civilian manpower functions of the federal government with special reference to war production. At the same time, it became apparent that more detailed information was needed on each job and each worker in the most important manufacturing plants and industrial operations. In April 1942 Selective Service headquarters began helping local boards with their problem of granting industrial deferments by sending out lists of essential occupations which had been prepared with the advice of the war and navy departments and other federal agencies. The War Manpower commission continued this function, issuing directives and regulations concerning "the use and classification of manpower needed for critical industrial, agricultural and governmental requirements." Thus there was a general tightening up of occupational deferments. In March 1942 Selective Service headquarters sent local boards a comprehensive statement which started out "War has necessitated a revised determination of policy with regard to occupational classifications." The statement, in ten parts, dealt with the necessity of getting men for the armed forces and at the same time maintaining an adequate labour force for war production. Civilian activities in support of the "national health, safety and interest" were defined to include only those activities which directly supported the war effort, and "mere convenience and comfort" was excluded. Critical occupations and necessary men were discussed and defined, and a list of essential activities was included.

The number of men without dependents, who were deferred in Class II-A because their civilian occupation was essential to the national health, safety and interest, was 457,218 on Nov. 30, 1942. At the same time, 609,229 men without dependents were deferred in Class II-B because they were essential in war production. It should be noted that these did not comprise the total number of men who had been deferred during 1942 for occupational reasons. Actually, the total would be much greater, since Classes II-A and II-B were actually a revolving pool, with men being moved in and out daily all over the country, by every local board. Totals of men deferred show only the men who happened to be in a deferred status on the day that the total was taken. Furthermore, the bulk of the nation's civilian manpower was still, in 1942, in Class III, deferred because of dependency.

The entire classification picture at the end of 1942 is shown in Table II.

Table II.—*Numbers in Each Classification, Dec. 31, 1942*

Classification	Number*
Total Living Registrants	28,864,091
Unclassified	2,819,613
Classes I-A and I-A-O	1,285,972
Class I-C	5,777,660
Classes II-A and II-B	1,051,776
Classes II-C and III-C	192,364
Classes III-A and III-B (men with dependents deferred in occupations other than agriculture)	14,436,217
Classes IV-B, IV-C, IV-D and IV-E†	209,586
Class IV-F	2,417,875
Class IV-H (men deferred by reason of age)	387,211
All other classes	285,817

*Includes registrants 18 through 44 years of age.
†Includes registrants in Classes IV-ELS, IV-E, IV-E Disc. and IV-E Dec.

Further controls over the manpower program were enacted in Nov. 1942 with the development of the Manning tables and replacement schedules for all major war production industries. The Manning table was, in effect, a report on the number and kinds of jobs and workers required in a given plant. The replacement schedule was developed following the introduction of the Manning table, to require employers to show what plans they had for training replacements for deferred workers, and to promote an orderly release of those workers who could be replaced so that they might take their places in the armed forces. By Sept. 1, 1943, there were more than 14,000 replacement schedules in operation. An estimated 10,000,000 employees were involved, listing some 1,600,000 employees as liable for induction under policies then in effect.

The Selective Service system was placed under the War Manpower commission by executive order of the president on Dec. 5, 1942. Volunteer enlistment of men between the ages of 18 and 38, requiring all male enlisted personnel between those ages for both army and navy to be inducted through Selective Service, was also stopped by this order. In the winter of 1943, Selective Service headquarters warned workers in occupations nonessential to the war effort to get into war production or lose their deferment for dependency.

In Dec. 1943 the Selective Service system was taken out from under the War Manpower commission. The total classification situation at the end of that year is shown in Table III.

Table III.—*Numbers in Each Classification, Dec. 31, 1943*

Classification	Number*
Total Living Registrants	22,158,001
Unclassified	101,940
Classes I-A and I-A-O	1,159,000
Class I-C	9,159,858
Classes II-A and II-B	2,759,170
Classes II-C and III-C	1,667,506
Classes III-A and III-B (men with dependents deferred in occupations other than agriculture)	3,573,167
Class III-D	97,053
Classes IV-B, IV-C, IV-D and IV-E†	152,709
Class IV-F	3,428,189
All other classes	59,409

*Includes registrants 18 through 37 years of age.
†Includes registrants in Classes IV-ELS, IV-E, IV-E Disc. and IV-E Dec.

Early in 1944, the president wrote the director of Selective Service:

> The Nation's manpower pool has been dangerously depleted by liberal deferments and I am convinced that in this respect we have been overly lenient, particularly with regard to the younger men. . . . Deferments for industry include over a million non-fathers, of whom three hundred eighty thousand are under 26 years of age. Of almost a million non-fathers deferred in agriculture, over five hundred fifty thousand are under 26. Agriculture and industry should release the younger men who are physically qualified for military service. The present situation is so grave that I feel the time has come to review all occupational deferments with a view to making available the personnel required by the armed forces.

Local boards were asked to review the cases of all occupationally deferred registrants, with particular attention to those under 26 years of age. Deferment for those between the ages of 18 and 21 was virtually eliminated, with the exception of men in agriculture. To be deferred, these men had to be regularly engaged as necessary men in essential war production, and recommended by the state director of the state in which they were employed. In March this policy was extended to include men aged 18 through 25. There was continued pressure from all sides to meet calls from the armed forces for men.

In April 1944 the war and navy departments announced that they had reached their planned strength, but the war department announcement added:

> Inductions through Selective Service must continue, however, with the emphasis on young men who are needed to replace losses due to combat and to normal attrition. . . . It is essential that from seventy-five thousand to one hundred thousand men be inducted each month to maintain the strength of seven million seven hundred thousand. This means that the army will need from seven hundred thousand to a million men during the remainder of 1944.

As a result of this expressed need for younger men, Selective Service postponed induction of men 26 years and older who were making a contribution to essential agriculture, war production or war supporting activities, until the induction of those under 26 had been substantially completed. Hence, the rigid requirements for occupational deferments for registrants in the 18 through 25 year old group remained in effect. Men aged 26 through 29, who were found to be necessary to and regularly engaged in war production or a war supporting activity "had the prospect," local boards were told, "of remaining in civilian life for the time being, subject to adjustment as the needs of the armed forces change." The prospect for men 30 through 37, the announcement continued,

> regardless of their physical condition . . . who are regularly engaged in and who remain in activities in war production or in support of the national health, safety and interest, is that they will remain in civilian life for an indefinite period, subject to adjustment as the needs of the armed forces change.

The manpower situation as of Dec. 31, 1944, is shown in Table IV.

Table IV.—*Numbers in Each Classification, Dec. 31, 1944*

Classification	Number*
Total Living Registrants	22,084,858
Unclassified	58,782
Classes I-A and I-A-O	796,641
Class I-C	10,753,323
Classes II-A and II-B	4,198,884
Classes II-A(L), II-B(L), II-A(F) and II-B(F)	864,427
Classes II-C and III-C	1,472,340
Classes II-C(L) and II-C(F)	132,026
Classes III-A and III-B (men with dependents deferred in occupations other than agriculture)	19,744
Class III-D	50,472
Classes IV-B, IV-C, IV-D and IV-E†	140,143
Class IV-F	3,582,823
All other classes	15,253

*Includes registrants 18 through 37 years of age.
†Includes registrants in Classes IV-ELS, IV-E, IV-E Disc. and IV-E Dec.

While at the beginning of 1945 ultimate victory was considered likely, the immediate military situation was not favourable to the Allies. The Germans had broken through in the Ardennes during Dec. and had inflicted serious losses. President Roosevelt told congress, Selective Service and the public that all physically fit men under 30 who could be spared from war production must be inducted to meet the urgent needs of the fighting forces, and that their places in the production lines must be taken by older men, those unacceptable for military service and women.

Local boards were advised that there should be the "least possible" number of deferred men in the age group 18 through 29, and that men who left the position for which they were deferred without convincing the local board that the change would benefit the war effort were to be forwarded for immediate induction. The boards were informed that the army physical standards applied to these men would be drastically lower than the standards for general military service.

By March 1, 1945, about one-half of the 22,000,000 registrants 18 through 37 years old had been inducted or had enlisted. About 25% were unavailable for military service because of physical disability, extreme hardship to dependents or statutory exemption. Of the remaining 25%, comprising about 6,314,000 men, more than four-fifths (5,251,000) were deferred in essential occupations; 62,000, mostly 18-year-olds who had just registered, were unclassified, and about one-sixth (1,001,000) were in the I-A classes, available for military service. Only 106,000 of those occupationally deferred were under 26 years of age.

After the end of the war in Europe, in May 1945 the need for young men continued, but local boards were asked to liberalize occupational deferments for men more than 30 years of age, particularly fathers, and to review the cases of previously rejected registrants under 26, to see whether some of these men might be acceptable for general or limited service.

With the surrender of Japan in Aug. 1945 manpower needs of the army and navy were reduced to replacements for war veterans of long service and those with dependents. The services had, following the end of the European war, instituted a point system of demobilization, based on total length of service, overseas service and campaigns, and number of children. President Truman lowered monthly calls on Selective Service and reduced the top age of acceptability for induction from 38 to 26 years. Class II-B, for registrants deferred because they were necessary to and regularly engaged in war production, was eliminated on Sept. 4, and men classified II-B were transferred to class II-A, which contained registrants deferred because they were necessary to and regularly engaged in an activity in support of the national health, safety and interest. Also in September, provisions were announced that students who entered high school before they reached the age of 18, might have their inductions postponed until they graduated, or reached the age of 20, whichever was the earlier, provided their course of instruction was pursued continuously and satisfactorily.

The manpower situation at the approximate end of the war, as of July 31, 1945, is shown in Table V.

Occupational deferment policies in effect after the end of the war remained virtually the same until July 1946 except for minor changes granting consideration to scientific and technical personnel and students. In July Selective Service headquarters informed local boards that in order to meet war department calls for men it would be necessary to "limit occupational deferment to those few

Table V.—*Numbers in Each Classification, July 31, 1945*

Classification	Number*
Total Living Registrants	22,028,732
Unclassified (18 year old men and other men who had registered but had not yet been classified)	87,448
Classes I-A and I-A-O (including men who had passed their physical examinations and were awaiting induction, men who were being processed for preinduction physical examination, men whose inductions had been postponed and men whose cases were on appeal, etc.)	613,302
Class I-C (registrants who had become members of the armed forces; not including registrants 38 years of age or over, women, or nonregistered enlisted men, *i.e.*, enlisted at age 17, etc. This classification included approximately 2,300,000 who had been discharged or transferred to the reserves and retained in this classification to identify them as having been members of the armed forces)	11,429,722
Classes II-A and II-B (including men deferred by reason of occupation in war production and work in support of national health, safety or interest. Most of these men had not had a physical examination; when, as and if they were physically examined, a large per cent would be rejected)	3,444,229
Classes II-A(L), II-B(L), II-A(F) and II-B(F) (same as II-A and II-B, except these men had been physically examined and rejected for military service)	1,409,689
Classes II-C and III-C (deferred by reason of agricultural work. Most of these men had not had a physical examination; when, as and if they were physically examined a large per cent would be rejected)	1,265,097
Classes II-C(L) and II-C(F) (same as II-C, except they had been physically examined and rejected for military service)	271,326
Class III-D (men deferred by reason of extreme hardship and privation to wife, child or parent)	44,648
Classes IV-B, IV-C, IV-D and IV-E† (IV-B, public officials; IV-C, aliens; IV-D, ministers and divinity students; IV-E, conscientious objectors)	138,746
Class IV-F (registrants rejected for military service)	3,256,082
All other classes	68,443

*Includes registrants 18 through 37 years of age.
†Includes registrants in Classes IV-ELS, IV-E-, IV-E Disc. and IV-E Dec.

registrants who are determined by the local boards to be indispensable and irreplaceable to the national existence except that registrants in agriculture will continue to be considered for deferment under the provisions of the Tydings Amendment." College students could no longer obtain a stay of induction to complete a semester or quarter, it was announced.

Dependency Deferments.—The third chief factor in classification, in addition to age and occupation, was dependency. It was paramount in U.S. thinking about Selective Service that single men without dependents should be

Joint session of the U.S. senate and house military affairs committees at which Senator Burton K. Wheeler (centre) opposed the drafting of U.S. fathers in 1943

the first to be called, and that those with children should be the last. The Selective Service act provided (Section 5[e]) that "The President is authorized to provide for the deferment . . . of those men in a status with respect to persons dependent on them for support which renders their deferment advisable."

The original regulations prescribed in 1940 defined and elucidated this provision for the guidance of local boards, advising them to classify in Class III (deferred for dependency) "any registrant upon whom one or more dependents . . . depend for support in a reasonable manner: Provided, however, that it is not advisable to defer any such registrant if he acquired such status for the purpose of avoiding training and service, and therefore no registrant should be placed in Class III if he acquired such a status after the day when he was required to be registered," except for special cases which proved to be within the "course of human affairs," and not to provide the registrant with a basis for deferment. To be considered as a dependent, the regulations stated, a person had to be either (1) the registrant's wife, child, parent, grandparent, brother or sister, or (2) a person under 18 years of age, or a person of any age who was physically or mentally handicapped and whose support the registrant has assumed in good faith. The dependent, at the time the registrant was classified, had to depend "in fact" for support in a reasonable manner on income earned by the registrant by his work.

The term "child" was defined to include an unborn child, one legally adopted or born out of wedlock. The terms "child," "brother" and "sister" were defined to include only persons under 18 years of age unless physically or mentally handicapped.

As a consequence of these provisions, only unmarried registrants were forwarded for induction during the first two years of Selective Service operations. While dependency, as defined and limited in the act, was the basis for deferment rather than marriage, it was recognized that most "dependencies" grow out of marriage, and it was further recognized that there were other than financial problems involved, even though that was the only aspect of dependency recognized by the law. On the other hand, Selective Service local boards were aware that marriage could be used as a means of avoiding training and service, and took this factor into consideration.

As early as April 1942 Selective Service headquarters began looking at Class III with an idea of the imminent need for taking men from this group. Local boards were running out of single men, and needs of the armed forces were increasing. Accordingly, the first step was taken April 23, 1942, when Class III was divided into two classes, and registrants who were deferred for dependency alone were placed in Class III-A; in Class III-B were placed those registrants who had dependents and were also "engaged in a civilian activity which is necessary to war production or which is supporting the war effort." Thus, for the first time, dependency and occupation were combined as bases for deferment, although, unlike those registrants in Class II-B, deferred for occupation alone, Class III-B registrants did not have to qualify as "necessary to" the civilian activity in which they were engaged, only that they be engaged in an occupation which was itself necessary to the war effort.

On June 23, 1942, the whole concept of dependency deferment was changed, with the enactment of the Servicemen's Dependency Allowance act of 1942. It provided for the payment of monthly family allowances to the dependents of enlisted men in the lower four grades, consisting of contributions by the government and the enlisted man from his pay. The total allowance amounted to $50 a month for a wife, plus added amounts for children. There were corresponding provisions for other dependents, including parents, brothers and sisters or grandchildren, who had been dependent upon the enlisted man for a substantial portion of their support.

Thus, there was eliminated at least some of the basis for deferment on the grounds of financial need of dependents and that section of the Selective Service act dealing with the definition of dependency was amended accordingly. However, the new amendment pointed out that payments of allowances "shall not be deemed conclusively to remove the grounds for deferment when the dependency is based upon financial considerations." Furthermore, the amendment went on to state there might be grounds for dependency deferment which were other than financial. Finally, the president was authorized to provide for the deferment of "any or all categories of those men who have wives or children, or wives and children, and with whom they maintain a bona fide relationship in their homes." Under the new Selective Service regulations it was provided that a registrant's claim for a dependency status "must have been acquired prior to December 8, 1941 or at a time when the registrant's selection was not imminent."

Registrants with wives but no children, and those with collateral dependents only, began to be forwarded for induction during the middle part of 1942.

During 1943, the entire problem of dependency as a basis for deferment from training and service was debated in the halls of congress, in the press and among the general public. Ultimately, on Dec. 11, dependency as a factor in deferment was practically discontinued, except for cases of extreme hardship. Early in 1943 it became apparent that fathers would have to be made available for induction, if calls were to be met. Bills were introduced in both house and senate during the spring of 1943 on the question of inducting fathers. Inductions began to be short of calls in April, and by July Selective Service was lagging one-third in meeting demands of the armed forces. On July 31, 1943, the director of Selective Service asked local boards to begin reclassifying fathers for induction, though none was actually to be forwarded before Oct. 1. In the meantime, the term "father" had been defined by Selective Service as a registrant who maintained a bona fide family relationship with his child or children in their home, provided such status was acquired prior to Dec. 8, 1941. A child was defined to exist from the date of conception, and a child born before Sept. 12, 1942, was regarded as qualifying the registrant for claim to dependency status.

In Sept. 1943 a local board inventory determined that there were not enough men in other available categories to postpone inducting fathers after Oct. 1. Accordingly, local boards were directed to commence forwarding fathers for induction, and the process began very slowly in October. On Dec. 5, 1943, congress amended the Selective Service act to stipulate that

> registrants shall, on a Nation-wide basis within the Nation and on a State-wide basis within each State, be ordered to report for induction in such manner that registrants, regardless of their occupations or the activities in which they may be engaged, who were married prior to December 8, 1941, who have maintained a bona fide relationship with their families since that date and who have a child or children under 18 years of age, will be inducted after the induction of other registrants not deferred, exempted, relieved from liability, or postponed from induction under this Act or the rules and regulations prescribed thereunder who are available for induction and are acceptable to the land and naval forces.

Applied to practice, this meant that local boards were to fill the calls with nonfathers insofar as they were available and to fill the remainder of the calls with fathers. Local boards still remained reluctant to forward fathers for induction, and it was not until June 1944, nine months after the induction of fathers was directed, that the monthly call was filled completely. The percentage of fathers inducted ranged from a low of about 7% of the total inductions in Oct. 1943 to more than 52% in April 1944, after which the proportion gradually decreased. This decrease was due in part to a reduction in the size of the calls and to the demand of the armed forces for younger men, a demand which was the cause of more stringent occupational deferment policies.

From Nov. 1944 to May 1945 the numbers and proportions of fathers inducted increased somewhat, to a high of nearly 45% of the total monthly inductions in April 1945 —the result of a virtual depletion of available registrants in the 18 through 25 year age group, and the increase in the calls resulting from events on the European front, during the battle of the Bulge late in 1944.

After May 1945 inductions of fathers tapered off, and on Nov. 5, 1945, fathers of three or more children were relieved from eligibility for induction. At this time the so-called "pre-Pearl Harbor father" definition became obsolete, and fatherhood, in Selective Service usage, did not depend upon any date. A month and a half later, on Dec. 19, all fathers were relieved of liability for induction. During the entire period in which fathers were being inducted, Oct. 1, 1943, to Dec. 19, 1945, the total number inducted was 944,000 or slightly more than one-tenth of the registrants listed as fathers on the local board inventory in Sept. 1943. The number of fathers inducted was also about one-tenth of the total number of men inducted throughout the entire period of the war.

The induction of fathers was specifically prohibited by congress in both extension acts of 1946.

Physical Examinations and Rejections.—Men inducted, the Selective Service act specified, had to be acceptable to the land and naval forces. This was a departure from the 1917–18 practice, when Selective Service inducted the men who had been selected. In 1940–46, Selective Service selected the men and sent them to the land and naval forces, where they might be accepted or rejected.

At the outset, Selective Service undertook a complete examination of every registrant, under war department standards. This work was accomplished by volunteer examining physicians, and later dentists, attached to each local board. As a result of the examination, registrants were classified as fit or unfit for service, and those found acceptable were ordered to report for induction as their order numbers came in sequence. However, all registrants

With his back to the wall, Gen. Dwight Eisenhower listened, in Jan. 1946, as G.I. wives demanded that their husbands be demobilized and returned home to their families

"Green Light," a cartoon by Shoemaker in the *Chicago Daily News* echoing Gen. Eisenhower's opinion that extension of the draft was necessary to secure the peace. In June 1946, the Selective Service act was extended to March 31, 1947

were again examined at the induction station, and it developed that from 10% to 30% of those who had been previously pronounced acceptable for service were turned down by induction station doctors. Part of this discrepancy was due to the time lapse between the two examinations, often several months, and the rest to differing interpretations of the standards. The hardship and inconvenience to registrants who had been found fit for service and had made plans accordingly and were later rejected, required drastic revisions in the examination procedure.

By early 1943 the physical examination at the local board level consisted only of a screening type examination, by which it was sought to eliminate from further consideration those registrants with obviously and manifestly disqualifying defects. Only one complete physical examination was given, at the induction station. This plan eliminated duplication and conflicting decisions, but not the period of waiting and uncertainty after the registrant was classified "I-A" by his local board and before he was finally accepted or rejected for service at the induction station. This period might be several months, and during that time these men were not only unable to make their plans, but they were a liability in the whole manpower picture since employers were unable to count on their services. Problems of the local boards were increased as well by this plan because in order to be certain of sending enough men to fill the call, the boards had to send sometimes as many as 50% more men than the call to allow for probable rejections. Hence, the plan for preinduction physical examination was developed.

Under this arrangement, all "I-A" registrants were examined at the induction station as soon as possible after their classification, and without relation to the possible date of their being forwarded for induction. Then if they were rejected at the induction station, they were reclassified accordingly; and if they were accepted, they were retained in "I-A" and could look forward to probable future induction.

This plan was in use during the balance of the period, though it still did not eliminate the element of uncertainty entirely, since a registrant accepted and found fit for military service at the preinduction physical induction examination might still be rejected in the final examination at induction, and sometimes as many as 10% of those previously found acceptable were so rejected.

During the period from Oct. 1940 to Nov. 30, 1946, an estimated 20,000,000 men forwarded by Selective Service were examined for military service; some 16,000,000 were found acceptable.

Table VI.—*Physical Rejections by Occupational Group*

Occupational Group	Total	White*	Negro
All occupations	42.6	40.3	56.1
Professional and semiprofessional	42.2	41.9	49.1
Farmers and farm managers	56.4	54.4	64.5
Proprietors, managers and officials, except farm	46.4	46.1	57.9
Clerical, sales and kindred workers	37.5	37.4	39.2
Craftsmen, foremen and kindred workers	40.7	39.8	54.9
Operatives and kindred workers	37.2	35.7	52.8
Domestic service workers	59.6	62.1	58.8
Protective service workers	42.7	42.2	56.9
Service workers, except domestic and protective	49.1	48.5	50.0
Farm labourers and foremen	52.8	49.1	63.5
Labourers, except farm and mine	46.6	41.5	58.2
Emergency workers and unemployed	56.5	55.6	60.4
Students	25.7	25.6	28.6
Nonclassifiable returns and no entry	44.5	43.1	54.3

*Includes all races other than Negro.

Selective Service made a comprehensive study based on a 20% sample of the results of the physical examinations of more than 9,000,000 men examined between April 1942 and Dec. 1943. During the period covered by the study, rejections ranged from 31.4% in Jan. 1943 to 46.9% for Dec. 1943 with an over-all average for the period of 36.4%. The rejection rate increased directly in relation to age of the registrants, reaching a rate of slightly more than 50% at age 34 and more than 67% at age 46.

Table VII.—*Principal Causes for Physical Rejection*

Causes	Number	Percent
Total	4,828,000	100.0
Manifestly disqualifying defects	510,500	10.6
Mental disease	856,200	17.7
Mental deficiency*	676,300	14.0
Physical defects	2,708,700	56.1
Musculoskeletal	367,600	7.6
Cardiovascular	317,500	6.6
Hernia	260,600	5.4
Syphilis	254,800	5.3
Neurological	235,400	4.9
Eyes	234,300	4.9
Ears	189,700	3.9
Tuberculosis	129,900	2.7
Lungs	86,900	1.8
Underweight and overweight	69,600	1.4
Feet	69,200	1.4
Abdominal viscera	64,700	1.3
Kidney and urinary	53,300	1.1
Varicose veins	48,200	1.0
Genitalia	48,000	1.0
Endocrine	45,300	0.9
Teeth	36,200	0.7
Neoplasms	32,200	0.7
Skin	31,900	0.7
Nose	29,400	0.6
Haemorrhoids	19,300	0.4
Gonorrhoea and other venereal	18,400	0.4
Mouth and gums	12,500	0.3
Infectious and parasitic	6,000	0.1
Throat	4,400	0.1
Blood and blood-forming	4,400	0.1
Other medical	39,000	0.8
Nonmedical	76,300	1.6

*Includes (1) registrants with more than one disqualifying defect who were rejected for educational deficiency prior to June 1, 1943; (2) registrants rejected for failure to meet minimum intelligence standards beginning June 1, 1943; (3) morons, imbeciles and idiots rejected Nov. 1940–July 1945.

(*See* also EDUCATION; FEDERAL BUREAU OF INVESTIGATION; HEART AND HEART DISEASES; INDIANS, AMERICAN; LAW; MEDICINE; REHABILITATION OF THE DISABLED. For conscription in Great Britain, *see* COMPULSORY SERVICE, BRITISH.)

(L. B. H.)

BIBLIOGRAPHY.—Selective Service System, *Handbook, Veterans*

Assistance Program of the Selective Service System (1945 *et seq.*); *ibid., Local Board Memoranda* (1945); *ibid., Medical Statistics Bulletin* (1941 *et seq.*); *Report of the Director* (1941 *et seq.*); *ibid., Selective Service Regulations* (1941 *et seq.*); *ibid., Special Monographs* (1945 *et seq.*).

Selenium

Salient statistics of selenium in the United States and Canada during 1937–45 were as follows, in thousands of pounds:

	United States				Canada
	Production	Sales	Stocks	Imports	Production
1937	436	283	306	93	397
1938	226	166	365	101	359
1939	227	346	247	125	368
1940	329	369	207	134	180
1941	620	682	146	198	407
1942	506	317	342	84	495
1943	636	522	456	82	374
1944	485	424	517	98	299
1945	542	666	393	219	419

Since selenium is recovered as a byproduct in copper refining, output was determined more by the demand for copper than for selenium itself. During most of the years of World War II output was ahead of demand, and stocks increased. In 1945 production and sales increased sharply in spite of record imports, giving an available supply ahead of anything previously recorded. All of the U.S. imports continued to come from Canada.

Several other countries with electrolytic copper refineries recovered small amounts of selenium, but no production data were available. The most important uses for selenium were in rubber compounding and glass making. Selenium produces a heat-resistant rubber; in glass small quantities are used as a decolorizer, to remove the greenish tint caused by iron; larger amounts give a pink tint, and still more, along with cadmium, gives a ruby colour. Small amounts in stainless steel and copper alloys improve machineability. Selenium is used in pigments and is a constituent of certain types of alternating current rectifiers and photoelectric cells. (G. A. Ro.)

BIBLIOGRAPHY.—H. G. Byers, *Selenium Occurrence in Certain Soils* (Dept. Agric. Tech. Bull., 1935 *et seq.*); G. R. Waitkins, "Industrial Utilization of Selenium and Tellurium," *Industrial and Engineering Chemistry*, 34:899–910 (Aug. 1942).

Semantics

Semantics may be defined as (1) In modern logic, the study of the laws and conditions under which signs and symbols, including words, may be said to have meaning, and the study of the kinds of meanings possible to be conveyed; semiotic; (2) The study of human responses of signs and symbols; the study of the relationship between words and things, between language and behaviour; significs.

The decade 1937–46 saw a continuation and intensification of the intellectual confusion and the conflict of values characteristic of the years following World War I. Philosophic and moral scepticism was, in the years of the depression, aggravated by political and economic doubts. A marked tendency of thought from the middle '30s on was a progression beyond the simpler scepticism of the '20s (the decade of the "debunkers") to a higher scepticism. One form which this higher scepticism took was the tendency to go beyond the critical examination of accepted facts and beliefs to the examination of the mechanisms by means of which facts and beliefs are given form, namely, language and symbolism.

Furthermore, the rise of Adolf Hitler had shown, among other things, the amazing power of radio and a controlled press as instruments for organizing and directing public opinion. The knowledge that the powerful modern instruments of communication, instead of being used for enlightenment, could be and were being used to arouse dangerous mass hysterias, brought many U.S. educators to an alarmed sense of their responsibility to try to prevent the occurrence of any such phenomena in the United States. Such factors as the success of Father Charles E. Coughlin on the radio and the knowledge of the increasing concentration of ownership and control of the means of mass communication contributed to their sense of urgency. Among the results of this concern were a marked development of scientific research into public opinion and the introduction into many colleges, universities and high schools of courses of study variously labelled public opinion, propaganda analysis, communications study, etc. In 1937, the journal *Public Opinion Quarterly* was founded at Princeton university, and the Institute for Propaganda Analysis (which suspended operations in 1940) was founded at Teachers college, Columbia university, by Professor Clyde R. Miller. Propaganda analysis, when pursued at anything beyond the most superficial level, also became a concern with the mechanisms by means of which facts and opinions are given form—language and symbols.

Both the temper and the needs of the decade therefore led to enquiry into language and symbolism. But such enquiry had hitherto been a highly theoretical and little-known branch of learning, cultivated principally by philosophers, by mathematicians with a philosophical turn of mind or by linguistic theorists. When the popular writer on economic topics, Stuart Chase, published his entertaining *Tyranny of Words* in 1938, he performed the exceedingly useful service of bringing to the attention of a public bewildered by controversy and propaganda the existence of the abstruse theoretical literature of semantics, which, he said, was just what was needed to introduce some sanity and order into public discussion.

It is possible to trace semantics back to the Greeks if one wishes to, but modern semantics can be said to originate in Lady Viola Welby's "significs" ("the science of meaning or the study of significance, provided sufficient recognition is given to its practical aspect as a method of mind,") and in Bertrand Russell's and A. N. Whitehead's *Principia Mathematica* (1910). Lady Welby found that the study of the complete interpretive act, including insight into motivation and ethical evaluation was necessary, as opposed to the study of meanings as a purely verbal discipline. She perceived, as Alfred Korzybski was later to emphasize, that civilizations had been content to retain modes of speech which had become totally inadequate. She also perceived grave shortcomings in the habits of interpretation inculcated by the educational methods ("senseless formalism" and "barren controversy") of her times.

Russell's and Whitehead's concern was with the foundations of mathematics. In trying to solve certain apparently inescapable logical contradictions, they proposed the theory of types, the principal point of which was that ambiguities of language conceal certain "illegitimate totalities," which, when undetected, lead to "vicious circle fallacies." For example, need a statement about *all* statements apply to itself? The statement in the following parentheses illustrates this type of proposition: (All statements in these parentheses are false). If we suppose the statement true, then we must conclude that it is false; if we suppose it false, we must conclude that it is true. The "all" in such propositions is the "illegitimate totality." The "all" must be limited so that a statement about that totality must itself fall outside the totality.

Russell and Whitehead were exceedingly influential. No small part of the achievement of the logical positivist or physicalist school of philosophy (the "Vienna circle") was due to the stimulus which they gave to the analysis of language. Ludwig Wittgenstein, a leader of this school, showed through logical analysis that practically all the traditional problems of philosophy were, from this point of view, "senseless," and that most philosophic propositions arose from the lack of understanding of the "logic of our language." This school contributed much to semantics by distinguishing sharply the various functions of language, by pointing out the kinds of statements which are of necessity impossible to verify and therefore fruitless to discuss and by showing that another large class of utterances turn out on analysis to be statements not at all about reality, but about language. The "logical syntax" of Rudolf Carnap attempted to show that, properly speaking, the only philosophic method was the analysis of the form and rules of language. In 1938 a group of logical empiricists, as philosophers of this general persuasion also called themselves (Otto Neurath, Niels Bohr, Bertrand Russell, John Dewey, Rudolf Carnap, Charles W. Morris), started the publication of the *International Encyclopedia of Unified Science,* a series of studies based on the conviction that an adequate theory of signs would provide the basis for the ultimate unification of knowledge by the study of the relationships of the languages of the special sciences to each other, and of the relationships of scientific language to the languages of other areas of human activity. An ambitious later attempt to state the foundations of a theory of signs was Charles W. Morris' *Signs, Language, and Behavior* (1946).

Another semantic development was the increasing influence of the operationalism of P. W. Bridgman—a theory which held that the meaning of scientific statements lay solely in the operations involved in verifying them, and that if no operations, actual or theoretical, could be employed in the testing of a statement, such a statement was to be regarded as meaningless. It was not coincidence, but a revealing symptom of the needs of the times, that almost identical ideas were being expounded in such an apparently unrelated field as the law. "Our legal system is filled with supernatural concepts, that is to say, concepts which cannot be defined in terms of experience and from which all sorts of empirical decisions are supposed to flow," wrote Felix S. Cohen in 1935. "Against these unverifiable concepts modern jurisprudence presents an ultimatum. Any word that cannot pay up in the currency of fact, upon demand, is to be declared bankrupt, and we are to have no further dealings with it." Owing much inspiration to Oliver Wendell Holmes (who made a profound contribution to semantics in his famous remark, "The prophecies of what the courts will do in fact, and nothing more pretentious, are what I mean by the law"), modern students of law of the "functionalist" and "legal realist" schools (Morris R. Cohen, Jerome Frank, Thurman Arnold, Karl Llewellyn, Glanville Williams and others) steadily increased their strength, although, in a field more permeated with transcendental concepts and fictions than any other learned profession, their influence was of necessity slow.

In literary circles the examination of meaning was deeply influenced by I. A. Richards, whose *Principles of Literary Criticism* (1924), *Practical Criticism* (1929), *Interpretation in Teaching* (1938) and *How to Read a Page* (1942) stimulated a revival of interest in the accurate explication of texts. Hugh R. Walpole's *Semantics* (1941) and F. A. Philbrick's *Understanding English: An Introduction to Semantics* (1942) also contributed to this interest, the former being especially concerned with translating texts into basic English as Richards had suggested, in order to understand them better and to lay bare problems of meaning. In one sense, however, Richards and his school, because of their relatively limited literary and pedagogical concerns, disappointed the expectations aroused by Richards' earlier book (written with C. K. Ogden), *The Meaning of Meaning* (1921), which was a brilliant continuation of the study of significs initiated by Lady Welby. This earlier work, however, continued to be influential in legal, scientific, sociological and philosophical thought.

Anthropological researches into language initiated earlier by such men as Leonard Bloomfield, Edward Sapir and Bronislaw Malinowski continued to provide material for semantic thought in the findings of such scholars as Benjamin Lee Whorf (1897–1941) and Clyde Kluckhohn. Increasingly, examination of the language and behaviour of speakers of non-Indo-European languages confirmed the observation made by earlier semanticists that language, far from simply expressing thoughts, actually determines the character of the reality one apprehends. Furthermore, anthropologists gave added evidence supporting the semantic principle that linguistic events are not to be studied in isolation, but in relation to the whole of the behaviour, the social forms and the antecedent and subsequent nonlinguistic events which constitute their total context.

The assault against meaninglessness; the determination to build new syntheses on simpler, less metaphysical and more functional principles than had been inherited from past systems; the searching enquiry into the legitimacy of traditional systems of language and symbolism—these were the tendencies the decade 1937–46 called semantics. The fact that these tendencies were strong in the decade even outside the semantics movement was revealed in other fields, *e.g.,* in architecture and art, where Frank Lloyd Wright's long war against meaningless symbols and forms (pillars supporting nothing, false fronts, sham mediaevalism) came perceptibly closer to final victory, and in the theories of such abstractionists as Gyorgy Kepes (*Language of Vision,* 1945) and L. Moholy-Nagy (*The New Vision,* 1946) who, explicitly rejecting the traditional symbolisms of artistic representation, sought a new "language" of vision by means of an analysis of the fundamental psychophysiological events that constitute visual experience.

The most ambitious and more controversial, however, of all the systems of semantics being evaluated, discussed and applied during the decade was that known as general semantics.

General Semantics.—General semantics is the name which Alfred Korzybski, Polish-U.S. scientist and engineer, gave to a new educational discipline, the purpose of which was to make the methods of modern science the basis for everyday living. Like other modern students of language, Korzybski regarded the language of everyday life as permeated with prescientific and primitive beliefs and assumptions. He went further than others, however, in studying the consequences of this fact. Error and confusion in intellectual life were, to him, serious but relatively superficial consequences of prescientific language. He found even graver consequences in the fact that moment-to-moment behaviour and reactions are determined to a large degree by the prescientific assumptions embedded in language.

Korzybski introduced his system in 1933 in his *Science and Sanity: An Introduction to Non-Aristotelian Systems and General Semantics.* In calling his discipline general semantics (the term semantics was coined by M. Bréal in

1897 and is derived from the Greek, *semaneien,* "to signify"), he stated its goal as the achievement, in science and thought, of "non-Aristotelian orientations," and in everyday life, of a "non-Aristotelian orientation." In calling his goals non-Aristotelian, he was at once paying tribute to Aristotle as the individual who had had more influence than anyone else in the systematization of thought in western culture, and stating the limitations of Aristotelian traditions for modern times—just as mathematicians, in speaking of non-Euclidean geometries, at once paid tribute to Euclid and stated their claim to have gone beyond him.

The aim of general semantics was not, therefore, simply to point out errors of fact, opinion or logic, *i.e.,* to correct verbalizations. The metaphysics which men hold, their theories of knowledge, their philosophies, Korzybski believed, necessarily end up in their nervous systems as involuntary, or almost involuntary, patterns of reaction. The Indo-European languages categorize events in parts of speech such as nouns, verbs and adjectives, and form propositions by means of them. This language structure, based on the unconscious philosophical assumptions of primitive people, still shapes everyday speech and thought. Within the area of special sciences, each with its own language, men had succeeded to some degree in escaping the primitive structure of their language. In everyday life, however, patterns of reaction were still largely governed by the metaphysics of our linguistic ancestors. The problem then, as Korzybski regarded it, was to enable an escape from that tyranny by making mistaken assumptions conscious, and by substituting as a basis for daily living the assumptions of modern science.

Like the anthropological linguists, Korzybski was not willing to regard Aristotle's laws of thought as in any sense final. He deplored the followers of Aristotle who, regarding the Aristotelian laws as universally valid, had made them the basis of education in western culture. He felt that western philosophical tradition, predominantly Aristotelian, had reinforced the influence of language in making prescientific philosophies the basis of reaction patterns. Consequently, he named those age-old reaction patterns the Aristotelian orientation, and set out to uproot them in favour of his non-Aristotelian orientation, by which he meant patterns of reaction more general in character, not limited by the accidents of particular language structures.

Science is a social and linguistic product, the result of co-operative endeavour made possible by observations accurately made and by communications accurately given and understood. Korzybski had remarked earlier, in his *Manhood of Humanity* (1921), on the vast difference existing between those areas of human thought, such as science and technology, in which progress had been rapid and grew even more rapid with each new success, and those areas, such as philosophy, ethics and politics, in which confusion remained general and progress often appeared impossible. To him this contrast between progress and stalemate was crucial. In *Science and Sanity,* he attributed this difference to the non-Aristotelian orientations general in the sciences and the Aristotelian orientations general in other fields. With the attainment of non-Aristotelian orientations in economic, social, political, moral and personal life, Korzybski believed western culture would overcome its most serious cultural lag, namely, the much-deplored failure of social wisdom to keep pace with the progress of technology. His proposal of general semantics as a discipline for the attainment of this end constituted, therefore, the manifesto of a cultural revolution of the most ambitious kind—a proposal that practically the whole of western culture be born again.

General semantics was based on an extraordinarily broad survey of diverse fields of knowledge, among them mathematics, mathematical logic, mathematical physics (quantum mechanics, relativity theory), biology, neurology, colloidal chemistry, the various schools of psychology (Freud, Jung, Adler, Adolf Meyer, behaviourism, the Gestalt school) and psychiatry. In each of these he examined tendencies of thought, the evaluative habits, the methods of approaching problems. It should be explained here for the benefit of the nonscientific reader that each of these fields was either new, or had made revolutionary progress, in the twentieth century. In each of them dogmas and assumptions which had been held unquestioned for centuries had been overthrown—in physics, such basic concepts as those of space, time, and matter; in psychology, the traditional notions of mind; in social thought, the traditional beliefs about the differences between savage and civilized men; in logic, the belief that propositions had to be either true or false, etc.

General semantics, then, was a summary, in a few simple and general formulations, of the basic habits of evaluation which Korzybski believed to be common to the most advanced contemporary thinkers—just as Aristotle's laws of thought were in his time a descriptive summary of the habits of thought of his contemporaries. The modern habits of evaluation appear to rest, Korzybski said, on three fundamental non-Aristotelian premises. Comparing the relationship of language (as well as of thought, memory, mental images) to reality with the relationship of maps to the territories they represent, he laid down the following premises: (1) a map *is not* the territory (words *are not* the things they represent); (2) a map *does not* represent *all* of a territory (words *cannot* say *all* about anything); (3) a map is *self-reflexive,* in the sense that an ideal map would have to include a map of the map, which in turn would have to include a map of the map of the map, etc. (it is possible to speak words about words, words about words about words, etc.; in terms of behaviour this means that it is possible to react to our reactions, react to our reactions to our reactions, etc.).

These three premises, Korzybski said, arose directly out of Russell's and Whitehead's theory of types. He stated further that they had to be understood in neurological terms, instead of being left simply in the realms of mathematical theory. Understood neurologically, they could, he argued, be translated into behavioural reactions. In order to accomplish this translation, he offered a set of rules to govern language, thinking, behaviour and attitudes. Appropriating from formal logic the term "extension," which means the aggregate of things denoted by a term (as opposed to "intension," the qualities or properties implied by a term), he called his rules extensional devices. They were as follows:

1. *Indexes.* Words lump together unique individuals under a common name. In nature no two things are identical. Names give a false impression of identity to non-identical objects and events, and this impression when translated into behaviour results in uniform, identical reactions to all individuals to which the same name can be given. For example, some persons have fixed reactions to "Republicans," "unions," "subsidies," etc. Hence, the practice of adding index-numbers to all our terms serves as a reminder of the uniqueness of all individuals: $Republican_1$, $Republican_2$ . . . $subsidy_1$, $subsidy_2$ . . . etc. Indexes remind us that there are differences as well as similarities among individuals of the same name.

2. *Dates.* Heraclitus said that you cannot step into the same river twice. The world and everything in it is in process of change. But many behaviour patterns, opinions, beliefs, tend to remain fixed and static in spite of changes in circumstances. "Maps" of yesterday are used as guides to the "territories" of today. All terms, statements, opinions and beliefs should therefore be dated: Supreme Court_{1946}, Supreme Court_{1947}. . . John $\text{Smith}_{\text{Monday}}$, John $\text{Smith}_{\text{Tuesday}}$ . . . This principle also takes into account the fact that the same object or individual is different in different environments: *e.g.*, $\text{violin}_{1\ (\text{rainy day})}$ is not identical with $\text{violin}_{1\ (\text{dry day})}$. The habit of dating all terms and statements, when translated into patterns of reaction and behaviour, makes rigidity of attitudes impossible and a dynamic time-minded orientation habitual.

3. *Et cetera.* All statements should be accompanied by an implicit "et cetera," to remind one of the second premise, namely, that "maps" do not represent all the "territory." The habitual et cetera prevents dogmatism, since it is a constant reminder that, language being the product of an abstractive (selective) process, no statement about events or objects in the real world can ever be final. This rule induces what Korzybski called "permanent consciousness of abstracting."

4. *Quotation marks.* Many terms in everyday language have pre-scientific metaphysical or structural implications. However, ordinary vocabulary often contains no better terms. Hence such terms ("mind," "substance," "objective," "subjective," "same," etc.) should be used in quotation marks to remind us that they are not to be trusted.

5. *Hyphens.* Traditional language separated verbally many things that cannot actually be separated. A revolution in physics was accomplished by Einstein's demonstration that space and time cannot be separately considered and that one should think in terms of space-time. Similar revolutions were going on in other fields, as in psychosomatic medicine, which does not separate physical and mental disorders; and in bio-physics, which offers general methods for dealing at once with the living and the nonliving. Terms such as psycho-biological, socio-cultural, psycho-social, geo-political and socio-economic in the sciences of human behaviour also show the new orientation. The use of such hyphens sharpens the awareness of the inter-relatedness of events which traditional language treated as unrelated. Indeed, hyphens often reveal that what seemed to be two or more separate events can more fruitfully be regarded as different aspects of the same event.

Korzybski did not intend these extensional devices simply as things to say by rote or to sprinkle through one's writing. Each of them was intended to point beyond itself to subverbal levels—to observing and feeling and absorbing as directly perceived data the nonlinguistic actualities distorted by language. Nevertheless, a common error among the general public regarding general semantics was the tendency to regard it as some kind of purely intellectual discipline (like defining one's terms) incapable of touching one's emotional life. This misunderstanding was due in part to earlier definitions of semantics as the science of meanings, but it was due even more, as Korzybski often pointed out, to one of the very errors his extensional devices were intended to correct, namely, the habit of separating the intellectual and the emotional into discrete categories. The use of the devices was intended as a discipline of (to use the prescientific terms) the senses, the emotions, and the mind—or to use modern terms—a discipline of the "organism-as-a-whole." Continued practice in the use of the devices would, Korzybski claimed, gradually liberate the individual from his Aristotelian orientations and make a modern man of him—a non-Aristotelian.

A unique feature of general semantics was that it offered, for what its originator believed to be the first time in scientific history, a positive, functional theory of sanity. The extensional devices were purported to describe not only how the best scientific minds do work, but how all human minds ought to work. Here Korzybski made use of his study of the mentally ill, as well as of his studies of political controversy, philosophical disputation and other areas of stalemate. In these areas he found lack of indexing (*e.g.*, confusion of words with things, prejudices), lack of dating (inflexibility, adherence to outworn notions), lack of consciousness of abstracting (treating verbal worlds as realities in themselves; dogmatism), reliance upon word-magic and incantation, and other violations of his rules to be extremely common. To thinkers on political and ethical problems he therefore proposed systematic application of his extensional devices as a way of helping to make their fields scientific. To psychiatrists, he proposed them as a basis for the re-education of patients.

If sound, a positive theory of sanity could not but be regarded as a tremendous contribution to science. Both psychiatrists and cultural anthropologists, finding certain patterns of behaviour normal in one culture and abnormal in others, had difficulty in offering grounds for preferring, in any general sense, some behaviour patterns over others. In the light of general semantics, however, any widespread "lack of consciousness of abstracting," any systematic failure in indexing (*e.g.*, race prejudice), any over-valuation of symbols at the expense of the realities symbolized (*e.g.*, preoccupation with money rather than with the economic actualities of goods and services), in individuals or in cultures, could be described as blocking the full development and utilization of human evaluative resources, and therefore from an engineering point of view as undesirable—in short, unsane.

During the decade 1937–46, the number of individuals willing to concede that general semantics was all that Korzybski claimed it to be increased steadily. Whatever the shortcomings of the system, there was no question that it was one of the most impressive intellectual syntheses yet produced in the 20th century, purporting as it did to be at once a science of sciences, a value theory (theory of sanity), a new system of education capable of being introduced even to the very young (*e.g.*, indexes and dates could be taught to kindergarten children), and the blueprint of a cultural revolution. The very ambitiousness of the system, however, antagonized as many as it excited to admiration. Academic and scientific officialdom was slow in accepting it, so that by the beginning of 1947 only a few colleges and universities in the United States (University of Iowa, Iowa City, Ia., Northwestern university, Evanston, Ill., Illinois Institute of Technology, Chicago, Ill., University of Denver, Colo., University of Michigan, Ann Arbor, Mich.) were offering courses of instruction in the subject.

The spread of general semantics was in considerable measure due to Korzybski's own efforts. In 1935, the first Congress of General Semantics was held in Ellensburg, Washington, at the Central Washington College of Education. In 1938, Korzybski founded in Chicago the Institute of General Semantics, where he began to give annually three or four seminars—intensive courses of instruction often lasting two or three weeks—which were attended by scientists, physicians, educators, business men and many others. In 1941, the second Congress of General Semantics was held at the University of Denver and attracted considerable attention. Some 150 to 200 persons were trained at the institute each year, and in 1947 the seminars were being continued in the institute's new location at Lakeville, Conn.

Especially after the foundation of the institute, students of Korzybski's seminars began to make his influence felt in many fields of activity. In education the small number of courses offered in general semantics gave little indication of the extent of its influence, since courses in many branches of instruction were modified or radically changed in the light of Korzybski's doctrines. Some journalists, publicists and radio commentators showed considerable semantic influence in their utterances, while a number of business executives introduced changes into such areas as accounting, personnel policies and intercompany communication systems as a result of the study of general semantics. Korzybski also attracted the attention of writers with a bent for popular presentation who spread the news of the doctrine far beyond the extent to which new theoretical systems are usually publicized. Besides Stuart Chase's *The Tyranny of Words* (1938), S. I. Hayakawa's *Language in Action* (1941; a Book-of-the-Month club selection), Irving Lee's *Language Habits in Human Affairs* (1941) and Wendell Johnson's *People in Quandaries* (1946) had a wide popular sale, stimulating much general interest in the subject.

In 1942, interested individuals organized the Society for General Semantics and in the following year began the publication of a quarterly, *ETC.: A Review of General Semantics,* edited by S. I. Hayakawa. At the end of 1946, chapters of the society had been formed in New York, Chicago, Boston, Pasadena, Los Angeles, Iowa City, St. Paul, Milwaukee, Winnipeg (Canada), and Sydney (Australia), each of them devoted either to general discussion and instruction or to the study of special applications of the theories.

At the close of the decade the cultural revolution outlined by general semantics still remained far off. Nevertheless, the depth of conviction exhibited by proponents of the system appeared to indicate that the movement would continue to grow, challenging outworn practices and creeds.

The translation of the theories of general semantics into actual daily practice remained to be accomplished in many fields. Under Professor Wendell Johnson the activities of the Psychological and Speech clinic of the University of Iowa were profoundly reshaped by general semantics theory. Instruction in English, speech and education was influenced by changes introduced into existing practices by such teachers as Professors Irving Lee (Northwestern), Thomas C. Pollock (New York university, N.Y.), Elwood Murray (Denver), Hayakawa (Illinois Institute of Technology), and O. R. Bontrager (State college, California, Pa.). In psychotherapy and the prevention of mental illnesses, new applications of general semantics were devised by Drs. Douglas G. Campbell, C. B. Congdon, Douglas M. Kelley, Alfred Bay and others, but accounts of these had not appeared widely as yet in the scientific press. The usefulness and validity of Korzybski's general theories remained to be demonstrated so far as most fields of special endeavour were concerned. Also, institutional changes in education or in industry needed to be devised which would enable the observation of the effects of non-Aristotelian training applied on a wide scale. (*See* also PHILOSOPHY.)

BIBLIOGRAPHY.—Thurman W. Arnold, *The Symbol of Government* (1935); *The Folklore of Capitalism* (1937); A. J. Ayer, *Language, Truth, and Logic* (1936); Eric T. Bell, *The Search for Truth* (1934); P. W. Bridgman, *The Logic of Modern Physics* (1927); Rudolf Carnap, *Philosophy and Logical Syntax* (1935); *Logical Syntax of Language* (1937); Stuart Chase, *Tyranny of Words* (1938); *ETC.: A Review of General Semantics,* Quarterly (1943 *et seq.*); Jerome Frank, *Law and the Modern Mind* (1930); S. I. Hayakawa, *Language in Action* (1941); H. R. Huse, *The Illiteracy of the Literate* (1933); Wendell Johnson, *People in Quandaries* (1946); M. Kendig, editor, *Papers from the Second American Congress on General Semantics* (1943); C. J. Keyser, *Mathematical Philosophy* (1922); Alfred Korzybski, *Science and Sanity* (1933; 2nd edition, 1941); *Manhood of Humanity* (1921; 2nd edition, 1947); Irving J. Lee, *Language Habits in Human Affairs* (1941); C. W. Morris, *Signs, Language, and Behavior* (1946); Elwood Murray, *The Speech Personality* (1944); C. K. Ogden and I. A. Richards, *The Meaning of Meaning* (1923); F. A. Philbrick, *Understanding English: An Introduction to Semantics* (1942); Jean Piaget, *The Language and Thought of the Child* (1926); Thomas C. Pollock, *The Nature of Literature* (1942); I. A. Richards, *Practical Criticism* (1929); *Interpretation in Teaching* (1938); *How to Read a Page* (1942); Bertrand Russell and A. N. Whitehead, *Principia Mathematica* (1910); Edward Sapir, *Language* (1921); Hugh R. Walpole, *Semantics* (1941); Viola Welby, *What is Meaning?* (1903); Ludwig Wittgenstein, *Tractatus Logico-Philosophicus* (1922); George K. Zipf, *The Psycho-Biology of Language* (1935).

(S. I. H.)

Senate

See CONGRESS, UNITED STATES; ELECTIONS.

Serbia

See YUGOSLAVIA.

Serrano y Suñer, Ramón

Serrano y Suñer (1901–), Spanish statesman, was born in Zaragoza (Saragossa), Spain. He studied law at the University of Bologna in Italy and on his return to Spain took up practice in his native city. In 1923, he became a member of the cortes as deputy of the Catholic party and during the Spanish Civil War (1936–39), he was minister for press and propaganda in the insurgent cabinet headed by his brother-in-law, Gen. Francisco Franco. On good terms with Hitler, Ribbentrop, Mussolini and Ciano, Serrano y Suñer exploited these contacts to obtain more war materials for Franco's armies. He became interior minister and was named foreign minister on Oct. 18, 1940. At the start of World War II, he linked his country closely with axis policies in Europe. However, dependence on Britain for food prevented Spain from effecting a complete rupture with the Allies.

Although Serrano was vocally sympathetic with the aims of Hitler and Mussolini, politically he seemed to doubt the advisability of permitting Germany to extend its influence to Gibraltar and North Africa.

On Sept. 3, 1942, Franco reshuffled his cabinet, ousting his brother-in-law as foreign minister and forcing him to relinquish his post as head of the Falange's political council. However, Serrano continued to exert considerable influence within the Spanish fascist party and as late as 1944, he was said to be one of Franco's inner circle of confidantes and advisers.

Serum Therapy

See MEDICINE.

Service Organizations, United

See UNITED SERVICE ORGANIZATIONS.

Seventh-day Adventists

On Sept. 30, 1936, Seventh-Day Adventist membership in the United States and Canada was 162,735; in 1946, it was 218,160. World membership in 1936, 429,833; in 1946, 583,923. Total receipts in United States and Canada for the year ending Sept. 30, 1936, were $6,878,031, or $42.27 per capita; for 1946, receipts were $27,036,001, or $123.92 per capita. Parochial school enrolment, grades 1 to 16, in the United States and Canada during 1936 was 26,362; in 1946, it was 39,999. During the decade a Spanish seminary was opened in New Mexico, and permanent quarters for an English Theological seminary were erected in Washington, D.C. Sales of denominational literature in the United States and Canada for 1936 were in excess of $1,900,000; for 1946, $6,600,000. World sales for 1936 were $3,600,000; for 1946, $8,400,000. The denomination's total investment in 1936 was in excess of $57,000,000; in 1946, $118,000,000. In the decade ending Dec. 31, 1945, 1,174 missionaries were sent out.

On Jan. 4, 1942, a radio program, "The Voice of Prophecy," was put on a nationwide hook-up in the United States through 85 stations. By 1946, a total of 400 stations carried the program; in addition, an overseas program was carried on 139 stations.

About 12,000 of the denomination's youth in the United States were trained in medical noncombatant service in parochial schools, ready to enter the army at the outbreak of war. One noncombatant Adventist youth, Cpl. Desmond T. Doss, was decorated with the Congressional medal of honour.

A $5,000,000 fund was created for rehabilitation of overseas work. About 750 tons of clothing were sent to war-stricken countries.

In 1944 a plan was approved for separate conferences in the United States for the Negro constituency. A hospital for Negro patients and for nurses' training was established in Nashville, Tenn.

At the annual Autumn council, held in Grand Rapids, Mich., in Oct. 1946, a budget in excess of $13,000,000, was voted for 1947. This was largely for overseas work and was the largest annual budget ever set up. (F. D. N.)

Sewage Disposal

See Public Health Engineering.

"Sextant" (Cairo) Conference

See International Conferences, Allied (World War II.)

Seychelles

See British East Africa.

Seyss-Inquart, Arthur

Seyss-Inquart (1892–1946), Austrian politician, was born July 22, 1892, in Stannern, in the Sudeten district of Czechoslovakia. While studying law in Vienna in 1908, he established his permanent residence in the Austrian capital. He was graduated from the University of Vienna and practised law in that city. During World War I he served in the Austro-Hungarian army for three years and in 1928 he joined the Austrian nazi party, becoming one of its leaders.

When Chancellor Kurt von Schuschnigg reorganized the Austrian cabinet Feb. 15, 1938, at Adolf Hitler's command, he appointed Seyss-Inquart minister of the interior and security. After Schuschnigg's resignation on March 12, 1938, Seyss-Inquart became chancellor and urged the earliest possible dispatch of German troops to Austria to "restore order." Two days after the formal proclamation of anschluss, Seyss-Inquart was appointed statthalter (governor) of Austria. The following month, he relinquished real authority (although he remained statthalter) to Joseph Buerckel, who became commissioner of Ostmark (as Austria was known under the nazi regime).

In May 1940 Seyss-Inquart was made German high commissioner for the conquered Netherlands. In this capacity he employed ruthless measures to stamp out all opposition to the German occupation. He fled from the Netherlands after its liberation and was taken prisoner in Germany on May 8, 1945. Seyss-Inquart, along with other top nazi leaders, was indicted Aug. 29, 1945, on charges of war crimes before the International War Crimes tribunal at Nuernberg. Found guilty of crimes against the peace, war crimes and crimes against humanity, he was sentenced to death on the gallows Oct. 1, 1946, and was executed Oct. 16, 1946.

Sforza, Carlo

Count Sforza (1873—), Italian statesman, was born at Montignoso di Lunigiana. After entering the diplomatic service, he was minister at Peiping (1911) and at Belgrade (1916). Two years later, he became Italian high commissioner in Turkey. Created senator in 1919, he served as foreign minister (June 1920–July 1921). Appointed ambassador in Paris in Feb. 1922, he resigned after Benito Mussolini's accession to power, becoming a leader of the anti-Fascist opposition in the senate. After the murder of Giacomo Matteoti in 1924, Count Sforza left Italy and went into self-imposed exile. He returned in Oct. 1943 after Mussolini's downfall; on his arrival he refused to support the Pietro Badoglio regime and charged that the house of Savoy had become an "obnoxious" symbol of fascism through its close association with Mussolini.

The fall of the first Ivanoe Bonomi cabinet, Nov. 26, 1944, put Sforza in the forefront as a possible candidate for premier. Anthony Eden, then Britain's foreign secretary, ruled against Sforza, however, and charged that he had worked against the Bonomi government. Winston Churchill offered the further explanation that Sforza was "untrustworthy" and had conspired to overthrow the Badoglio regime in violation of a pledge made to the Allies. Sforza denied these charges of intriguing, but British pressure prevailed in the dispute. Sforza subsequently declined Bonomi's offer of an ambassadorship to the United States. In 1945 Sforza was appointed president of the Italian consultative assembly.

Shallots

See Vegetables.

Shaposhnikov, Boris Mikhailovich

Shaposhnikov (1882–1945), Russian army officer, was born Oct. 4, 1882, in Zlatoust, Russia. At 19 he entered the Moscow Military school and after completing his studies went into active service. He was graduated from the Academy of the General Staff in 1910, was commissioned an officer in the tsarist army, and was aide to Grand Duke Nicholas on the general staff during World War I. In May 1918, his offer to serve the Red army was accepted; he was appointed an assistant commissar by Nicolai Lenin and Leon Trotsky, and in 1930 he joined the Communist party. He was chief of the general staff, 1929–31, and was again appointed to that position in 1937 when he also became a member of the central executive committee of the U.S.S.R. For his achievements in the Finnish campaign, 1939–40, he was promoted to the rank of marshal in May 1940. In the summer of that year, he resigned from the general staff because of ill health, but was recalled Oct. 31, 1941, when the Germans were nearing Moscow. Under his direction, the Red army traded space for time, and curtailed the power of the blitzkrieg technique with a defense-in-depth strategy. His planning enabled the soviets to repulse the German army at Stalingrad in 1942. Recognition of his achievements was evidenced by a nation-wide observance of his 60th birthday. As chief of the Frunze Red Banner Military academy, 1932–35, Shaposhnikov trained many of the outstanding Red army commanders and helped lay the groundwork for the creation of a modern army. He was vice-commissar for national defense, 1941, Stalin's personal military adviser and deputy of the supreme soviet of the U.S.S.R. In April 1943, it was announced that owing to protracted illness, Shaposhnikov had been replaced as chief of staff by Marshal A. M. Vasilevsky. His publications included *The Cavalry* (1923), *On the Vistula* (1924) and *The Brain of the Army,* 3 vols. (1927–29). He died March 26, 1945.

Sharpening Stones

See ABRASIVES.

Sheep

The number of sheep and lambs on United States farms had declined in 1937 to 51,019,000 head; thereafter an increase started which continued until a record peak of 56,735,000 was reached in 1942. Another decline then set in, and by 1946 the Jan. 1 estimate was down to 44,241,000 head. The 1945 lamb crop was estimated at 28,500,000 head, compared with a ten-year (1934–43) average of 30,589,000. The number of lambs on feed remained fairly constant—5,597,000 head in 1937 and 6,630,000 in 1945. By 1942 the demand for U.S. meat was reflected in the increasing number of sheep and lambs; the total of these animals on farms and produced during the year rose to about 88,000,000 head. This brought the sheep industry to a high level that could not be continued with the strong competition for feed. By 1943 the number of stock sheep had declined; the lamb crop was estimated at 31,100,000, or 1,500,000 fewer head than in 1942 and the lowest after 1939. Again in 1944 the Jan. 1 estimates showed a decline, about 7%, and the lamb crop was only 29,600,000 head, a loss of 5%. The principal cause of the decline was the acute labour shortage in the range and livestock feeding regions; prices had not declined. In 1945 another drop was recorded and by Jan. 1, 1946, sheep numbers were down to a new low point for two decades.

Number of Sheep in United States, 1937–46
(On Jan. 1)

Year	Number	Year	Number
1937	51,019,000	1942	56,735,000
1938	51,210,000	1943	55,775,000
1939	51,595,000	1944	51,769,000
1940	52,399,000	1945	47,780,000
1941	54,283,000	1946	44,241,000

Prices of sheep and lambs began a sharp increase in 1941 which continued through 1946. The average May price of sheep at Chicago was $4.10 per 100 lb. in 1937 and advanced to $6.93 in 1943; lambs were selling at $10.69 per 100 lb. in 1937 and advanced to a top of $14.46 in 1942. These prices in 1942–43 were not sufficient to maintain production in the face of the labour shortage and higher wages. Subsidies were paid to slaughterers from 1943 to 1945, when a direct payment to producers was begun and continued into 1946. These payments varied from $1.50 to $3.15 per 100 lb. on different weights

A newborn black lamb being tagged at a stock farm near Los Angeles, Calif., in 1945. The farm sold breeding ewes and raised sheep for Persian lamb, Karakul and broadtail skins

of lambs at different seasons. The announced purpose was to prevent increases in the price of the meat to consumers. The plan did not operate to increase production, which continued to decline.

The fall in sheep values began in 1943, when the price of pelts was no longer fixed by the government. Large stocks of wool had a depressing effect on the sheep market. The great war need had begun to pass, and mill consumption declined because of labour shortage. Since wool prices were particularly subject to the effects of government action, sheep raisers were not inclined to expand nor even to maintain production in the face of uncertainties. Wool production increased from about 423,000,000 lb. in 1937, when the average price was 32 cents per pound, to 459,000,000 lb. in 1942 and then declined to about 400,000,000 lb. in 1946, although the price was 42.4 cents per pound. Large amounts of wool were imported duty free in 1942–44 and stored for other governments. This wool was not to be used by U.S. mills, and much of it had been exported by Jan. 1946. The United States had been on a wool-importing basis for many years for domestic use.

The U.S. sheep industry suffered in comparison with other farm enterprises because of the shortage of skilled labour. This need could be replaced only slowly, as competent herdsmen could not be trained quickly. Sheep numbers were low in the range states, and the unsettled wool market was not encouraging to ranchmen. The per capita consumption of lamb and mutton averaged 6.7 lb. in 1935–39 and rose to a high point of 7.2 lb. in 1945, when the shortage of meats for civilian use was most acute. (*See* also LIVESTOCK; MEAT; WOOL.) (J. C. Ms.)

BIBLIOGRAPHY.—For statistics of various countries, *see* U.S.

Dept. Agric., *Agricultural Statistics;* J. F. Walker, *Breeds of Sheep* (1942).

Shenyang

See MUKDEN.

Shidehara, Kijuro

Baron Shidehara (1872–), Japanese statesman and diplomat, graduated from the Imperial university, Tokyo, in 1895 and entered the diplomatic service the following year. He was appointed Japanese minister to the Netherlands in 1914 and vice-minister of foreign affairs in 1915. As Japanese ambassador to Washington he attended the Washington conference (1921–22). Created a baron in 1920, he was foreign minister from 1924 to 1927 and from 1929 to 1931. On his resignation in 1931, in protest against Japanese seizure of Manchuria, he earned a reputation as a "liberal."

Shidehara lived in relative seclusion until the fall of the first postwar cabinet of Prince Naruhiko Higashi-Kuni, after which he formed the new government, on Oct. 6, 1945. The baron-premier promised establishment of a "liberal" regime, but did not state whether his government would include all the leftist parties. He advocated caution in abolition of Shinto as the state religion, defended the authority of the emperor and reluctantly complied with directives from Gen. Douglas MacArthur to allow Japanese women to vote, encourage labour unions, liberalize education methods and democratize Japanese economic institutions. He reorganized his cabinet, Jan. 12, 1946, for the fourth time since its inception in order to eliminate five ministers mentioned in Gen. MacArthur's "purge" directive. The Shidehara cabinet resigned (April 22, 1946) after the first postwar elections. He was named vice-premier in the cabinet formed by his successor, Shigeru Yoshida, May 22.

Called on to testify at the Tokyo trial of high Japanese charged with war crimes, he admitted June 26, 1946, advance knowledge of Japanese plans to invade Manchuria.

Shigemitsu, Mamoru

Shigemitsu (1887–), Japanese statesman and diplomat, was born July 29, 1887, in Oita-ken. Educated at the Tokyo Imperial university, where he received his law degree, he entered the foreign service in 1911 and held minor diplomatic posts in Europe and the U.S., 1911–18. Struck by fragments of a bomb hurled at him by a Korean patriot at Shanghai in 1932, he lost a leg. He was made vice-minister of foreign affairs, 1933, ambassador to the soviet union, 1936, and ambassador to England, 1938.

Tokyo ordered Shigemitsu in 1941 to leave his British post and return home; while en route to Japan, he paid a courtesy visit to Washington. On Dec. 9, 1941, two days after Japan's attack on Pearl Harbor, Shigemitsu was appointed ambassador to the Chinese puppet regime at Nanking. In April 1943 Premier Hideki Tojo reshuffled his cabinet and named Shigemitsu foreign minister. Before the Pearl Harbor attack Shigemitsu was reported to favour Japanese co-operation with Great Britain and the United States; he was said to be highly critical of the ruling Japanese military clique. He was retained as foreign minister in the Koiso cabinet but was not in the succeeding Suzuki regime.

After Prince Higashi-Kuni formed the first postwar cabinet of defeated Japan (Aug. 16, 1945) Shigemitsu was returned to his old post as foreign minister. In his first statement, Aug. 18, he advised his countrymen to admit their defeat and said Japan must win the world's sympathy and understanding. He signed the Japanese surrender document aboard the U.S. battleship "Missouri," Sept. 2. Two weeks later (Sept. 17), he was dismissed as foreign minister. Shigemitsu was one of the 28 Japanese defendants who appeared before the Allied tribunal in Tokyo (the sessions started Apr. 29, 1946). He was indicted on 55 counts, including crimes against the peace, war crimes and crimes against humanity.

Shimada, Shigetaro

Shimada (1883–), Japanese naval officer, was born in Tokyo. In World War I, he was Tokyo's military attaché to Italy and later held many administrative and command posts. He was vice-admiral and commander in chief of Japan's 2d fleet, 1937. In 1941 he was successively commander in chief of the Japanese fleet in China waters, commandant of the Yokosuka naval station and navy minister in the Tojo cabinet formed in Oct. 1941. After the U.S. landings in the Marshall Islands and the blistering air attack against Truk Island in Feb. 1944 he relieved Fleet Admiral Osami Nagano as navy chief of staff and assumed this additional post himself. As Japan was defeated in successive naval engagements through 1944, Shimada was ousted as navy minister, July 17, 1944, and as naval chief of staff, Aug. 2, 1944. His retirement "at his own request" was announced Jan. 20, 1945.

Shimada was one of the 28 Japanese leaders brought to trial (Apr. 29, 1946), before an Allied tribunal in Tokyo, and was indicted on 55 counts which included crimes against the peace, "conventional war crimes" and crimes against humanity.

Shinwell, Emanuel

Shinwell (1884–), British cabinet member and politician, was born Oct. 18, 1884, in London. A high-ranking member of the Labour party, he was a member of the house of commons from 1922 to 1927 and from 1928 to 1931, and was re-elected in 1935. He was financial secretary in the war office (1929) and secretary for mines (1924 and 1930–31).

A caustic-tongued debater, Shinwell's exchanges with the Churchill government leaders enlivened discussions in commons. During World War II he criticized the Churchill government for the failure of British arms in the Malaya, Hong Kong and Libya campaigns. As he did not spare members of his own party, the Labour party executive board in late 1942 was pondering disciplinary measures to curb his acidulous attacks. An avowed left-winger, Shinwell surprised his supporters in Dec. 1942 with a spirited defense of the criticized Darlan agreements; he stated that if the Allies could conquer North Africa with Darlan's aid the agreements were justified.

After the Labour party took over the government in the summer of 1945 Prime Minister Attlee appointed Shinwell to the post of minister of fuel and power. An advocate of nationalization of the coal mines, he introduced in commons (Dec. 19,1945) a bill to "establish public ownership and control of the coal mining industry and certain allied activities." The Coal Nationalization bill, passed by the house of commons, Jan. 30, 1946, established a nine-man board for control of the coal industry and made the board responsible to Shinwell.

Shipbuilding

The decade 1937–46 was epochal in the history of the shipbuilding and ship repairing industry, not only in the United States but in the world. Never before had the industry achieved a performance record even approaching that attained in the building of both merchant and naval vessels in the United States during World War II. Employment in the industry in 1943, at its peak in that year, was some 18 times as great as at the beginning of the ten-year period.

Employment of personnel in the U.S. industry in 1937 was approximately 100,000, of which two-thirds was in the privately operated yards and one-third in government-operated naval shipyards. Taking into account the employment in the allied industries, therefore, the total employment provided by the industry was approximately 200,000 at the beginning of the decade.

In 1938, employment was slightly less than that of 1937. At about the time of the outbreak of war in Europe in 1939, however, employment had begun to increase, and continued upward until it reached a maximum of 1,722,500 at the end of 1943. Of this peak number, 1,396,400 were employed in the privately operated shipyards and 326,100 in government naval shipyards. Of those engaged in the private industry at that time, about 10% were engaged on ship repairing. As between naval and merchant work, the privately operated yard forces were about equally divided in the war period.

From the beginning of 1944 to the end of 1946, employment gradually decreased, although it remained more than 1,000,000 until the surrender of Japan in 1945. After that time the liquidation of employment was heavy, and at the end of 1946 was about 110,000, a figure which nevertheless was substantially more than the figure which prevailed in the immediate prewar years.

Geographical Shifts in the U.S. Industry.—During the peacetime years immediately preceding the beginning of the European war in Sept. 1939, there were only 22 privately owned U.S. shipyards engaged in the building of large naval and seagoing commercial vessels. The larger part of this work was performed on the east coast of the United States. There were, however, many smaller yards engaged in the building of barges, towboats, carfloats, ferries and miscellaneous small craft for both commercial and government use, and some 15 or more inoperative shipyards with facilities that would have enabled them to build seagoing commercial vessels, if the volume of work had been sufficient to necessitate their use. These smaller yards were well distributed over all the coastal areas, on the Great Lakes and along the great rivers.

During the first part of the war period, all of the coastal areas, at first, and later all areas, which included the Great Lakes and the rivers, contributed considerably to the building of both merchant and naval craft, although seagoing naval and commercial vessels of the larger sizes were built in the coastal yards.

Prior to the war, construction on the Great Lakes had been confined largely to vessels for lake service, as the canal locks and depth of water channels limited the size of vessels built there capable of navigating to the seas. During the war, however, after changes had been made in bridges in the Chicago area, commercial vessels up to 321 ft. in length and submarines of 307 ft. in length, assembled in large part on the Great Lakes, reached the sea via the Chicago Drainage canal and the Illinois and the Mississippi rivers.

Prewar U.S. Construction.—Naval contracts in private yards had brought about substantial activity in shipbuilding at the beginning of the decade 1937–46. Work for the yards was further increased by a $50,000,000 appropriation for auxiliary naval vessels in 1937. Another act of congress, in 1938, authorized an increase in naval building beyond the strength permitted by the Washington and London naval treaties, and permitted the number of and tonnage restrictions on combatant vessels to be expanded approximately 23%.

All of these naval increases antedated the outbreak of the war in Europe in 1939.

In 1940, two acts of congress greatly increased the then authorized strength of the U.S. navy. The first act, sometimes referred to as the "Eleven Per Cent Increase," was passed on June 14, 1940. The second, passed on July 19, 1940, increased the existing authorized strength of the U.S. navy by approximately 70% in the combatant categories. It was commonly referred to as the "Two-Ocean Navy Program." This act also authorized the building of 100,000 tons of auxiliary vessels and an expenditure of $50,000,000 to construct patrol, escort and miscellaneous craft. In May 1941 congress authorized the construction of 550,000 tons of auxiliary vessels in addition to those heretofore authorized and in Nov. 1941 authorized the construction of 400 smaller vessels for local defense.

All of these authorizations or appropriations were made before the United States declared war in Dec. 1941.

Wartime Naval Construction.—Acts later in 1941, shortly after Pearl Harbor, provided for a still further increase of 150,000 tons in combatant vessels to make good the losses of battleship strength which at that time were thought to have been permanently incurred in the Pearl Harbor attack, plus the construction or acquisition of 800,000 tons of auxiliary vessels and an additional 400 smaller vessels for harbour defense purposes. This was followed in rapid succession by the enactment of the so-called "Emergency Construction Program" for 1,799 minor combatant, auxiliary and patrol vessels of various types, the Submarine act, authorizing the construction of 200,000 tons of combatant ships and finally the act of July 9, 1942, providing for the construction of an additional 1,900,000 tons of combatant ships. This last authorization, which was greater than the total tonnage provided by the preceding authorizations, resulted in expanding the original "Two Ocean Navy Program" into a "Five Ocean Navy Program."

Private shipbuilding yards delivered 1,027 combatant vessels of 2,538,065 displacement tons of the following types: battleships, aircraft carriers, cruisers, destroyers, destroyer escorts, high speed transports (destroyer escort type), frigates, minelayers (destroyer type), gunboats and submarines in the years 1941–45. The government-owned and -operated naval shipbuilding yards delivered 325 combatant vessels of similar types of 962,975 displacement tons or a grand total of 1,352 combatant vessels of 3,501,040 displacement tons. Private yards also delivered 166 auxiliary naval vessels of 1,061,959 displacement tons of the following types: seaplane tenders, destroyer tenders, motor torpedo boat tenders, repair ships, aircraft carrier escorts, submarine tenders, submarine rescue vessels, mine layers, ammunition ships, oilers, fuel oil ships, store ships, transports and landing ship vehicle (formerly large net layers), in the years 1941–45. Government-owned and -operated naval shipbuilding yards produced 13 auxiliary vessels of similar types of 69,310 displacement tons or a grand total of 179 auxiliary vessels of 1,131,269 displacement tons.

Other naval vessels of miscellaneous types were constructed during the years 1943, 1944 and 1945 as follows:

Shipways at Baltimore, Maryland, during a night shift in 1943 →

Many boys under draft age worked full-time schedules at standard wages in U.S. shipyards during the peak periods of war production

patrol and mine craft, 1,984 units of 538,772 displacement tons; landing craft, 73,787 units of 2,815,577 tons, and district craft, 1,895 units of 589,527 tons. The privately owned shipyards of the United States constructed more than 90% of the vessels of these smaller types.

Tables I and II show the major categories of naval vessels built in private shipyards and government naval building yards during the ten-year period 1937–46.

In addition to the building of naval vessels the private ship repair yards participated extensively in the repair and reconversion of various types of naval vessels throughout World War II.

Merchant Shipbuilding.—The program of U.S. merchant vessel construction under way in the early years of the decade was prompted by the merchant marine act of 1936. The Maritime commission, an agency created by this act, was directed to make a survey of U.S. shipping to determine what additions and replacements were required to carry forward a national policy, declared in the act, of providing and maintaining an adequate U.S. merchant marine. It further was directed to study, perfect and adopt a long-range program for replacements and additions that would insure a well-balanced merchant fleet, including vessels of all types, and to provide shipping service on all routes essential for maintaining the free flow of the foreign commerce of the United States.

Under the mandate of this act, the Maritime commission studied and later developed a ten-year plan for the building of 50 seagoing vessels a year. Contracts for the first group of 50 ships were placed in 1938.

When war broke out in Europe in 1939, the schedule of 50 merchant ships a year was doubled. In 1940 it again was doubled, thus providing for the building of 200 high-grade vessels available for either war or peacetime service. Late in 1940, two contracts were placed by the British for the construction of 60 standard cargo vessels, half to be built on the Atlantic coast and half on the Pacific coast.

Early in 1941, these British contracts were followed with the first emergency Liberty fleet program for 200 cargo ships for the Maritime commission account, followed a little later by a lend-lease program of 227 vessels, some of the emergency Liberty and some of standard C types. Then came the first national defense program of 541 ships of both emergency Liberties and standard C types. All of this commercial work had been awarded, and much of it was actually under construction, when the United States entered the war in Dec. 1941.

Great activity in the industry developed from the various actions taken by congress and formalized by the navy and by the Maritime commission. A large staff of technicians was built up in the shipbuilding industry, and at the outbreak of war in the Pacific they were engaged actively in the design of both naval and merchant vessels. The working forces in the shipyards and in the allied marine industries likewise were built up to a degree that placed the industry in a particularly advantageous position to perform the constantly increasing task placed upon it throughout the subsequent war years.

After the U.S. declaration of war, the volume of work for the Maritime commission, the navy and other government departments progressively increased to meet losses and the needs of the armed forces.

In 1937, the facilities in the shipbuilding and ship repairing industry were adequate to handle any probable normal peacetime demands for the building and repairing of either commercial or government vessels. Prior to the war, substantially all building of seagoing vessels was confined to coastal areas.

In 1938, two yards that had been engaged only in repair work since World War I entered the shipbuilding field, one on the west coast and one on the Gulf. In 1939, six additional yards entered the building field, two of which

Table I.—*Number and Displacement Tonnage of Steel Combatant* Naval Vessels Built in U.S. Shipyards and Delivered in 1937–46 (by Geographical Regions)*

Year delivered	Built in private shipyards								Built in navy yards						Combined total	
	East coast		West coast		Gulf and inland		Total		East coast		West coast		Total			
	No.	Tons	No.	Tons	No.	Tons	No.	Tons	No.	Tons	No.	Tons	No.	Tons	No.	Tons
1937	10	42,360					10	42,360	12	26,610	5	7,330	17	33,940	27	76,300
1938	11	69,900	2	3,000			13	72,900	6	25,800	1	1,450	7	27,250	20	100,150
1939	16	32,600					16	32,600	9	30,060	2	2,950	11	33,010	27	65,610
1940	12	31,705					12	31,705	14	21,060	1	1,630	15	22,690	27	54,395
1941	15	45,915					15	45,915	13	87,360	3	4,555	16	91,915	31	137,830
1942	75	310,015	14	22,820	5	9,925	94	342,760	29	80,685	6	9,150	35	89,835	129	432,595
1943	206	622,425	60	112,095	121	148,950	387	883,470	119	253,790	39	48,050	158	301,840	545	1,185,310
1944	175	527,050	65	106,645	147	175,610	387	809,305	66	258,750	16	25,805	82	284,555	469	1,093,860
1945	87	345,835	17	41,200	40	69,580	144	456,615	31	189,105	3	5,725	34	194,830	178	651,445
1946	42	238,459	8	17,600	9	19,800	59	275,859	6	60,304			6	60,304	65	336,163
Total	649	2,266,264	166	303,360	322	423,865	1,137	2,993,489	305	1,033,524	76	106,645	381	1,140,169	1,518	4,133,658

*These tonnages comprise the following categories of vessels: battleships, aircraft carriers, cruisers, destroyers, destroyer escorts, high speed transports (destroyer escort type), frigates, minelayers (destroyer type), gunboats and submarines, and is exclusive of all other types of naval craft.
Source: Shipbuilders Council of America, 21 West St., New York 6, N.Y.

Table II.—*Number and Displacement Tonnage of Steel Auxiliary* Naval Vessels Built in U.S. Shipyards and Delivered in 1937–46 (by Geographical Regions)*

Year delivered	Built in private shipyards								Built in navy yards						Combined total	
	East coast		Gulf and inland		West coast		Total		East coast		West coast		Total			
	No.	Tons	No.	Tons	No.	Tons	No.	Tons	No.	Tons	No.	Tons	No.	Tons	No.	Tons
1937																
1938																
1939																
1940	4	36,500					4	36,500							4	36,500
1941	1	9,180					1	9,180			3	12,640	3	12,640	4	21,820
1942					10	93,765	10	93,765	3	9,300	3	12,390	6	21,690	16	115,455
1943			1	5,220	61	386,545	62	391,765			1	9,000	1	9,000	63	400,765
1944			10	63,696	59	329,431	69	393,127	1	8,300	1	9,000	2	17,300	71	410,427
1945			2	11,220	22	162,902	24	174,122			1	8,680	1	8,680	25	182,802
1946	5	7,086	2	16,000	11	84,958	18	108,044	1	8,000			1	8,000	19	116,044
Total	10	52,766	15	96,136	163	1,057,601	188	1,206,503	5	25,600	9	51,710	14	77,310	202	1,283,813

*These tonnages comprise the following categories of vessels: seaplane tenders, destroyer tenders, motor torpedo boat tenders, repair ships, aircraft carrier escorts, submarine tenders, submarine rescue vessels, mine layers, ammunition ships, oilers, fuel oil ships, store ships, transports, landing ship vehicles (formerly large net layers) and miscellaneous auxiliary ships (ice breakers), and is exclusive of all other types of naval craft.
Source: Shipbuilders Council of America, 21 West St., New York 6, N.Y.

had been previously engaged in repair work only. Three of these yards were located on the Pacific coast, two on the Gulf and one on the east coast. All of these shipyards began building merchant vessels under contracts placed by the Maritime commission in those two years. These added facilities went into operation before Sept. 1939.

As the European war progressed and the demand for ships increased greatly, additions were made in both structures and equipment in existing U.S. building and repair yards. The first two newly built shipyards for building merchant vessels on a quantity basis were those for the construction of vessels for the British account, previously mentioned; they were started in 1940.

The first new government-owned shipyards for the building of Liberty vessels were started early in 1941 and were in full operation at the time the United States entered the war the following December. Two Liberty vessels, the "Patrick Henry" on the east coast and the "Star of Oregon" on the west coast, were delivered from these yards at the close of the year.

More and more facilities, both for naval and commercial types of vessels, were added through 1942 and 1943 to meet the ever-increasing demand for ships and more ships. To the extent practicable, the new shipyards were developed under the control and management of existing shipbuilding organizations. In planning shipyard lay-outs, the experience gained in the construction programs of World War I, as well as that of the few years preceding World War II, were utilized. Advantage was taken of the latest advancements in manufacturing and construction methods in other fields. As experience in the operation of the first new yards was gained, still other lessons were learned that were utilized in later shipyard layouts, making possible more production and shorter times for ship deliveries.

New shipyards were laid out on quantity production principles with a view to turning out the maximum number of ships of identical design. Not more than one or two types at a time were built in any new yard. These new plants first were distributed over the particular coastal areas where the greatest reservoir of labour was believed to be available. Later on, as demands became more pressing, the Great Lakes and the great rivers were brought extensively into the building project.

The original schedule of these newer yards for the building program of Liberty ships was formulated on a basis of 180 days from keel-laying to delivery. This plan governed the number of building ways within each yard. Later on, this plan was stepped up to 105 days from keel-laying to delivery. Eventually, at the peak of production, Liberty ships were delivered in less than 40 days average time by the several yards engaged in the building of vessels of that type.

The aggregate tonnage of seagoing merchant vessels of 2,000 gross tons and over produced in the United States in the war years 1941 to 1945, inclusive, was about 37,710,000 gross tons. Of this total, 12,499,873 gross tonnage was constructed in the single year of 1943. The production of combatant naval vessels and large size naval auxiliaries for the same years was approximately 4,632,309 displacement tons, of which 3,501,040 displacement tons were represented by vessels in the combatant category.

Table III.—*Gross Tonnage and Numbers of Steel Self-Propelled Merchant Vessels (by Types of Ships)*
Built in U.S. Private Shipyards and Delivered in 1937–46
(Includes only vessels of 2,000 gross tons and over)

Year	Cargo		Tanker		Passenger and cargo		Total	
	No.	Gross tons	No.	Gross tons	No.	Gross tons	No.	Gross tons
1937 . .			15	121,852			15	121,852
1938 . .	8	43,476	16	137,930	2	4,252	26	185,658
1939 . .	14	91,560	11	119,429	3	30,063	28	241,052
1940 . .	31	227,275	16	148,509	6	68,943	53	444,727
1941 . .	61	423,019	28	267,979	6	58,107	95	749,105
1942 . .	652	4,678,988	61	612,121	11	101,844	724	5,392,953
1943 . .	1,410	10,116,973	231	2,163,147	20	219,753	1,661	12,499,873
1944 . .	1,175	8,457,190	240	2,485,923	48	461,291	1,463	11,404,404
1945 . .	833	5,384,610	188	1,769,583	46	509,169	1,067	7,663,362
1946 . .	68	500,254	7	78,533	9	76,666	84	655,453
Total . .	4,252	29,923,345	813	7,905,006	151	1,530,088	5,216	39,358,439

Source: Shipbuilders Council of America, 21 West St., New York 6, N.Y.

Table III shows by types and number of vessels the total gross tonnage of commercial vessels constructed in the United States during the ten-year period 1937–46.

40

New Production Methods.—Much experience had been gained prior to World War II in the use of welding on both naval and commercial work, in the lay-out of the new shipyards and expansion of older yards and in the design of ships to be built in them. Welding became an important factor; it was particularly suitable where a large number of ships was produced from one design.

Provision was made in new shipyard lay-outs for the subassembly of large sections of the hull structure. This necessitated plenty of space for pre-assembly platens and for the convenient storage of assembly units as needed; but with ample land available at the new sites, this did not present a serious problem. The subassemblies required a supply of cranes of large lifting capacity for transporting heavy assembly units from the ground to the building slip or to storage spaces.

The advantages of subassembly had been well recognized for many years in the old-time shipyards, but its extent had been limited by crane lifting capacity. In at least one of the older yards, subassemblies up to 100 tons had been handled for years. The advantages of subassembly were so great that the new shipyards were fitted with cranes of large lifting capacity—the earlier ones with cranes of 25 to 30 tons capacity and the later ones with 40 to 50 tons capacity and some with cranes of 100 tons capacity or greater. These cranes handled completely assembled and equipped "deck houses" and "pilot houses." Ground space in most shipyards was hard-surfaced, in order to provide for rapid transportation of small parts to assembly and storage spaces by means of trucks, electric cranes and other units. Rails likewise were used for this purpose.

Work was farmed out wherever practicable to large numbers of small enterprises, many of which previously had not been associated in any way with the marine industry. No less than 5,000 plants, large and small, situated throughout the entire country and employing hundreds of thousands of workers, were called upon to produce materials and equipment and to deliver them to the shipyards on time schedules and in the order and the quantities necessary to make possible a continuous, orderly program of building. Shipbuilding hence became an inland as well as a waterfront industry, and the shipyards for the construction of vessels of duplicate types were for the most part assembly plants.

Standardization was exemplified in the Liberty ship as well as in the naval destroyer escorts and some other types. Not only was the basic design standardized but component parts manufactured in different plants were interchangeable. The Liberty ships were built in 17 different private shipyards and the destroyer escorts in 11 private yards and 6 government navy yards.

Within the shipyards, the greatest factor in meeting delivery schedules was repetitive work. It was the first time in the history of shipbuilding that the real effects of multiple production had been achieved. This was demonstrated in the reduced time of construction as the number of ships of a duplicate type increased, and in the lesser number of man-hours required as the number of ships laid down increased. As previously stated, the average time in the construction of a Liberty ship at the peak of production was as low as 40 days from keel-laying to delivery. The average number of man-hours per ship required after 60 ships of the same type had been built was less than half the working hours required for the building of each ship in the first group of ten. Similar notable reductions were shown with oil tankers, destroyer escorts and other vessels that were duplicated in considerable numbers.

The average number of man-hours required for the construction of each navy destroyer escort after 69 of these vessels had been built in a private shipyard was less than one-half of the man-hours required for the construction on each of the first 3 vessels.

Subassembling was a very important factor, too, not only in the easier assembly and welding of the structural material itself on the platens away from the building ways, but in the ability to outfit each subsection and complete within the subassembly the work on foundations, piping, electrical and other fixtures. Men carried on their work with less exertion and less interference than if performed on the building ways.

Duplicate construction permitted the use of "mock-ups" and jigs and fixtures for the production of component parts on a simplified quantity basis. Large sections of hull plating were built up on the ground on "mock-up" forms and were completely welded before being hoisted into place on a ship's side.

Overcoming the Labour Shortage.—The recruitment of shipbuilding and ship repair workers was a major problem and necessitated speedy accessions from all walks of life. Extensive courses were instituted for training of craftsmen and supervisory employees, and the ability rapidly to expand the working forces and put them on the job was due to the great volume of duplicate work, which made it possible to utilize employees with limited training on repetitive work.

The basic working schedule in the industry during the war continued to be a 40-hour week, with overtime beyond 8 hours a day or 40 hours in 5 days. Much of the work was carried on during the greater part of the program on an around-the-clock basis; that is, with continuous operation of equipment, but with few employees working more than six days a week continuously except in emergencies. Average hourly earnings in the industry increased from 84.6 cents at the beginning of 1940 to $1.306 at the end of 1945, and weekly earnings from $32.00 a week at the beginning of 1940 to a maximum of $68.00 a week near the end of the program.

Shipbuilding and ship repair employed few women—less than ½%, mostly in office jobs—prior to Pearl Harbor. All tradition was against hiring women to do such heavy work, but with a dearth of manpower large numbers of women were employed. On new construction work at the wartime peak, approximately 120,000 women were employed in the following trades: blacksmith and forge; electrical (including manufacturing); foundry and pattern; joiner, carpenter and shipwright; machine (including boiler); paint (including manufacturing); pipe and copper; blueprinting; rigger (including labourers and erectors); sail and flag; service and maintenance; sheet metal; shipfitting (including welders, burners, riveters, mould loft, fabricating and drafting); and toolroom.

The greatest number of women was employed in the shipfitting and machine trades groups. Their employment was also greatest where the greatest volume of repetitive work was carried on. About 10% of the working forces were women but the percentage varied widely in the individual yards. Their employment in repair yards was not large.

Problems of Naval Shipbuilding.—The problems in connection with facilities and employment for naval building were similar to those for merchant building. The construction of the largest and most highly specialized types of

Shipyard cranes formed giant "Vs" at the California Shipbuilding Corp. yards in Los Angeles, Calif., as workers dropped their tools after the announcement of Japan's surrender in Aug. 1945

combatant vessels was restricted to the older shipyards that previously had been engaged in this type of work. The old-time private shipyards built battleships, cruisers and the larger aircraft carriers and destroyers, as well as the larger auxiliaries and great numbers of smaller craft.

Submarines were built in three private shipyards and in three government naval shipyards. Two private shipyards that had not engaged in the building of submarines prior to World War II participated in the submarine program, one of these yards under direct contact with and under the guidance of a shipyard that had been engaged in the building of submarines for many years prior to the war.

Some new shipyards were built which, because of their size, were restricted to the building of smaller types of naval vessels, while in the construction of the very smallest types, such as tugs, barges, landing craft and other miscellaneous boats, every facility in the country that could be used to advantage was brought into service.

In 1939, there were available in the United States approximately 156 building ways of 200 ft. and more in length suitable for the building of seagoing merchant vessels and the larger size combatant naval vessels and auxiliaries. At the end of the program, there were in existence 84 shipyards of such capacity, with 578 building ways. While building ways in themselves were not necessarily a measure of the capacity of the industry unless other facilities were balanced with them, these figures indicated the large increase in plant capacity necessary to carry on the war program.

More than $1,000,000,000 was invested in new shipyards and in additional shipbuilding and ship repairing facilities, and approximately another $500,000,000 in the expansion of facilities in various allied marine industries for the construction of naval and merchant vessels.

Naval vessels are of a much more complicated design than commercial vessels, requiring many more man-hours per ton in their construction. This fact was responsible for the much smaller reported tonnage of naval vessels than of merchant vessels built during the war. If converted to the equivalent of merchant tonnage, the total program of U.S. merchant and naval vessels combined built in the years 1941 to 1945, inclusive, would be equivalent to about 75,000,000 gross tons of the merchant type.

In addition to the merchant and naval program, 13,105 vessels of various types, mostly small, were built for the army. Also a considerable number of vessels of various types were produced for the coast guard.

Ship Repair.—It is difficult to measure the important part played by the ship repairing industry during World War II, as no two repair or conversion jobs were ever exactly alike. This segment of the industry, however, was called upon to repair commercial ships in the shortest possible time and to convert certain types of naval vessels to other types best suited for war purposes. Some record, although inadequate to measure the real service rendered by these repair yards, was shown in the statement that not less than 67,902 vessels were repaired or converted in the shipyards of the United States in the four years, 1942 to 1945, inclusive.

The ship repair yards which were active throughout the war in the conversion of merchant vessels to wartime use were engaged at the end of the decade in the reconversion of these vessels back to peacetime requirements. While the ship repair yards were extensively engaged in the repair and conversion of various types of naval vessels during the war, their participation in such work in peacetime was not expected to be of large proportions.

Postwar Shipbuilding.—In the merchant field, the U.S. Maritime commission and ship owners in 1946 were contemplating the construction of a few large vessels for several services. There were numerous disturbing elements, however, in this building program. Shipbuilding wages had been increased substantially, as well as the pay of seagoing personnel, the latter being more than double what it was before the war. The higher cost of operation would be a controlling factor in a consideration of new tonnage orders.

Another factor was the unsettled tax problem. Ship operators holding operating-differential contracts with the commission were required by the act of 1936 to deposit in statutory reserve funds their profits above a certain level, to be applied against their subsidy accounts.

Although payment of operating differential subsidies was suspended for the period that the war caused abandonment of regularly scheduled operations on essential routes, operators holding subsidy contracts with the commission continued to deposit into the statutory funds proceeds from the loss or sale of vessels, depreciation funds and profits from operations, in accordance with the act of 1936, or as the Maritime commission specified under its granted powers. Considerable sums had been set aside for this purpose. It was the evident intent of congress that operators should set aside such sums for the building of new vessels. However, certain legal problems had arisen in connection with the status of funds reserved during wartime operation, and a demand was made on the operators by the treasury department to subject some of the earnings set aside in these funds to taxation. This matter was having a serious effect on new construction. (H. G. S.)

Bibliography.—A. W. Carmichael, *Practical Ship Production* (1941); J. P. Comstock, *Introduction to Naval Architecture* (1944); W. B. Ferguson, *Shipbuilding Cost and Production Methods* (1944); H. F. Garyantes, *Handbook for Shipwrights* (1944); W. Hovgaard, *Structural Design of Warships* (1940); A. Kari, *Design and Cost Estimating of all Types of Merchant and Marine Passenger Ships* (1938); W. P. Leidy, *Shipbuilding and Marine Engines* (1941); G. C. Manning, *Basic Design of Ships* (1945); H. L. Sheed, *Ship Structure and Blueprint Reading* (1942); U.S. Bureau of Ships, *Technical Bulletin* (1940); U.S. Federal Trade Commission, *Shipbuilding Corporations* (1941); *See* also various issues of U.S. Dept. of Labour, *Monthly Labor Review*.

Great Britain.—The revival in freights in 1937 brought a rush of business to the shipyards, where prices were already beginning to rise; many orders were placed prematurely in anticipation of further advances. Britain led the world for 1937 with Japan second and Germany third, but only about two-thirds of the available slipways were occupied in December, with approximately 250,000 gross tons more commercial shipping under construction than at the end of 1936. Of that tonnage, 60% was steam-driven, against about 33% of tonnage built in continental yards.

Unemployment figures dropped from 11.6% to 8% during 1937, but many men, although registered as shipbuilders, had really left the industry. In some sections this caused a serious shortage, assisted by the dearth of apprentices. Various claims for improved pay and conditions were presented.

During the depression many firms had kept their experimental and designing staffs busy and they, as well as the national physical laboratory, had carried out a large number of experiments which had striking results on the design of ships ordered when business revived. Most were to increase economy by reducing resistance and weight. The diesel engine slowly gained favour, particularly in the opposed-piston type, which was successfully adopted in more tramps.

In 1937, also, the royal navy started its rearmament program, claiming priority in the facilities suitable for building cruisers, destroyers and other specialist types. The business was valuable but was not an unmixed blessing, for it increased prices in all directions and by almost monopolizing the yards which normally built liners forced a number of companies to send their orders abroad. The new types of smaller warship which could be built in the nonspecialist yards were not ordered until later.

By that time the flow of orders for tramp tonnage had slowed down, for costs were rising rapidly. In Jan. 1938 the price of a cargo ship of simple specification was 50% higher than in the middle of 1936. Many factors contributed but particularly raw materials, labour and subcontracts, over which the shipbuilders had no control. Price combined with a shortage of shipbuilding steel to send more contracts abroad. As regards passenger ships, 1939 was noteworthy for the launching of the Cunard White Star liner, "Queen Elizabeth" (85,000 tons).

Among the foreign contracts were numerous small motor coasters from Holland, although some of the British yards were gaining a high reputation in that branch. Many coasting and short sea trading companies were not only acquiring motor ships of lighter draught than the old type of steamer but were also replacing their larger steamers by a greater number of small motor vessels in order to maintain more frequent sailings, on some routes daily.

Immediately before the outbreak of World War II there was a spate of orders for cargo tonnage because shipbuilding stood to benefit under the government's scheme for state aid, which provided for building loans. These orders fitted in with the government plans for shipbuilding in the event of war. Control had been proved necessary by World War I to secure the maximum carrying capacity of new ships and to arrange the rival claims of the navy and commercial shipping. The former had priority, so that all shipbuilding resources were placed under a new section of the admiralty, the merchant shipbuilding department, under experienced builders. The admiralty controlled repairs as well as new construction, and its local officers decided whether suggested work was necessary; after the war it gave up absolute control but it retained practical control by a system of permits, without which no contract could be placed. Repeated suggestions were made that a ministry of merchant ship construction should be established, but were turned down because it was felt that interdepartmental rivalry would inevitably ensue. Even when the ministry of production was established in Feb. 1942, the admiralty was left with the sole responsibility for shipbuilding, repairs and equipment, but acting in co-operation. Generally speaking, this arrangement worked very well, particularly when the great U.S. shipbuilding effort altered the situation.

To avoid another mistake of World War I when production was held up to permit the new system of standardized construction to be started and to keep in mind the primary necessity for new ships of the tramp type, the admiralty examined the standardized designs to which a number of yards were already building and, when they were suitable (as they were in most cases), arranged for them to be continued on government account. Such yards already possessed all the necessary data, patterns, etc., and frequently stocks of material which permitted much quicker delivery. Minor alterations were made, measures for defensive armament were provided and the designs were simplified in matters of detail, but that was quickly done. Each ship of special design already under construction was considered on its merits; those nearly completed were finished, and a large proportion of the remainder were taken over by the admiralty and converted to auxiliaries.

All the yards which specialized in naval work, or in the construction of high-class types which made their plant and labour well suited to the building of warships, were largely occupied on men-of-war. Several capital ships already under construction were suspended to make way for more urgently needed types (cruisers, destroyers, submarines, etc.), while the royal dockyards concentrated principally on repairs and reconstruction. New designs were soon necessary, and improved constructional methods were adopted where it was possible to do so without slowing down production; in many yards the repair of air raid damage gave the opportunity of improving the plant for welding and other methods, and in all cases every opportunity was taken to have component parts made in other plants and assembled in the shipyards.

Under the prewar rearmament program, orders for the smaller types of warship (escort vessels, corvettes, minesweepers, trawlers, etc.) were already placed with ordinary commercial yards and, as the war on commerce increased the demand for vessels of those classes, this policy was increased. The necessity for counteracting the magnetic mine led to large numbers of wooden minesweepers being built in old and small yards all round the United Kingdom, as well as in the dominions' yards, which had formerly been used for yachts and fishing craft. The first preparations in 1942 for the invasion of France led to the building of many landing craft; the sections of others were built in various engineering works and assembled in special establishments.

As losses mounted, many designs were submitted to the admiralty to combine the functions of warships and carriers. The merchant aircraft carriers, popularly known as M.A.C. ships, were started in 1942 to carry aircraft for the defense of convoys and at the same time to transport oil or grain themselves. The first was laid down in Aug. 1942, a 13½-knot motorship of about 8,000 tons, well armed with a flight deck over the hull, hangars and other fittings of the aircraft carrier but still able to carry more than 8,000 tons. Such ships provided protection for convoys without reducing their carrying capacity.

As the war progressed, standardization increased also; more yards were employed on fewer slow tramp types while more ships of higher speed were built for operational purposes. The standardized tramps were mostly about 7,050 tons gross, 10,000 deadweight with simple steam, later frequently diesel, machinery, for 11 knots. Smaller types were of 4,700 tons deadweight. The use of prefabricated sections, but not complete ships, increased steadily. All the tankers in the early part of the war were conservative in design with a maximum speed of 12 knots; 5,000, 12,000 or 14,500 tons, deadweight. For the Normandy invasion, and later for the anticipated Pacific operations in numerous islands, a number of standardized coasters, tugs, small colliers, etc., were built and, because of the steaming distance in the east, various special types ranging from crane ships to 15-knot cargo liners of about 10,000 tons gross were built with remarkable speed. Frequently the machinery and fittings differed widely, but the hulls were as uniform as possible. Several 15½-knot refrigerated cargo liners, 8,560 tons gross with diesel engines, were also built for the food supply service. Special 15-knot geared turbine tankers of about 8,200 tons gross, 11,900 deadweight, were also built and proved invaluable.

British shipyard workers lowering the plate for a new ship into place before a completed freighter cleared the runways after its launching in 1941

On the question of speed the admiralty was bitterly criticized in press and parliament, even while it was building a number of fast ships for the invasion under cover of censorship. The cost in material and labour of increasing the speed of the tramp-type ships would have been prohibitive and they would have had no opportunity of using it in convoy owing to the standards of most of the escort vessels.

In finish, fittings and accommodation, all these were of "austerity" design to economize in material and labour. It was often acknowledged to have been taken too far, and the regulations were relaxed after experience with the first ships; in some the saving in weight led to serious disadvantages which had to be rectified. Most were delivered by the British yards as soon as they were sufficiently completed to make an outward voyage in reasonable safety; the missing fittings were installed in dominion or Allied ports, particularly those of the United States.

Every attention was paid to the design and, with due care for production difficulties, the greatest pains were taken by tank tests and other means to procure the most satisfactory hull forms for capacity, speed and economy. Some measures taken to simplify construction proved exceedingly efficient at sea. The accommodation, for passengers where it was fitted, and for the crew in all cases, was of the simplest possible description; for the crew it was often far inferior to the standards set by the private shipowners well before the war in size and furnishing. Owners who later bought the ships had to incur considerable expense before officers and men would serve in them.

Bottlenecks and supply difficulties had been considered in the prewar plans and the calculations proved to be remarkably correct. Tankers were such a tempting target and so vulnerable to attack that a serious oil shortage had been anticipated; all the earlier tramp-type ships were therefore built to burn coal. Triple expansion engines were fitted in many types which would normally have been given geared turbines and, in the early days, the supplies of diesel engines were strictly reserved, although later the opposed-piston type was permitted for many ships of low speed. Single screws were ordered wherever possible, even for fast ships. As the situation eased, and improved measures reduced the losses, it was possible to relax the restrictions considerably, and as the navy put the results of all its experiments at the disposal of merchant shipping the later ships were, generally speaking, up-to-date in every respect and with a little adaptation could be made excellent for postwar trading. The earlier types, however, were unattractive to shipowners.

Shipowners always had the right to submit requests for licences to build ships to their own design, subject to admiralty approval. Very few were granted before 1942, but thereafter the number increased steadily, although the designs were frequently greatly modified and the necessity for many of the modifications, nominally to save materials, was questioned.

As in World War I, attempts were made to conserve steel by concrete construction, but on a much smaller scale. Few seagoing ships were constructed, although a very large number of lighters for port work were built to replace steel barges requisitioned by the services. The technique was considerably improved and the proportion of steel was reduced, but not nearly to the extent necessary to make concrete a real rival of steel in peacetime. On the other hand, the use of aluminum and other light metal alloys was successfully adopted and saved a great deal of steel, although supplies were very severely rationed because of the priority of the aircraft industry. In the later stages, plastics were also used for nonstrength parts, after they had been greatly improved. The shortage of timber when the northern European sources were cut off led to the development of numerous substitutes after experiments in the national physical laboratory and elsewhere.

Welding also made immense progress although not to the same extent as in the United States, because of the impossibility of holding up production while the new shipyards necessary for its successful employment on a large scale were built. Nevertheless, its employment where suitable, and for repair work, led to a great saving of weight and man-hours, and unskilled labour could be very much more rapidly trained for it than for riveting. A large number of women were successfully employed. Welding also overcame the serious bottleneck of very large castings for stern frames, etc.

The same necessity for uninterrupted delivery prevented adoption of prefabrication in large ships, as it was in the U.S.A. and Canada, but partial prefabrication for large ships was usefully employed in the fully standardized designs. For the small craft built for the Normandy and Pacific campaigns, complete prefabrication was adopted, most of the assembling being done in special establishments, including reopened yards that had been closed down and cleared of their equipment during the depression. Fabrication within the shipyards, and the assembly of large sections in convenient places away from the slipway made great strides.

As the admiralty always worked on the principle that a ship which was not too badly damaged could be repaired and sent to sea again very much more quickly than a new ship could be built, the repair sections were very busily employed, demanding a fluidity and mobility of labour which was not easily contrived. The repair yards were constantly under air attack and were severely handicapped by the blackout regulations; yet the work done was far beyond expectations. Welding was largely employed, but when the demand for repairs became so great, as much as possible was done in overseas yards, the government paying owners the difference between their prices and the British level. All repairs, both damage and maintenance, were subject to a special licence, and the rules for regular survey were relaxed. Under lend-lease, the U.S. yards carried out a large proportion of this repair work; in the early days their price was much higher, but by 1945 there was little difference in most jobs. The facilities of the royal dockyards were quite insufficient to cover the repairs demanded by the navy, and many warships were serviced in private establishments.

Labour was one of the greatest problems of the industry at the beginning of the war and remained so until the end. In 1939 about 90,000 workers were employed, about 26,000 on merchant ships; owing to the constant demand for warships, the latter figure never averaged more than 35,000,

H.M.S. "Eagle," largest aircraft carrier in the Royal navy at the time of its launching at Belfast by Princess Elizabeth on March 19, 1946

excluding those on repair work. The unions made every reasonable concession with regard to demarcation and the dilution of labour to increase output, with the understanding that their privileges would be restored after the war. Yard committees were set up to settle doubtful points, and although they were occasionally accused of exceeding their functions they worked well and avoided many disputes. Skilled shipbuilders were withdrawn from the territorial army and returned to the trade; genuine craftsmen were exempted from conscription, but its intensification in 1942 increased the shortage of the unskilled labour which was doing excellent work. The Essential Work orders applied to shipyards and directed a number of former shipbuilders, and technicians who were ordinarily employed on housebuilding and similar work, to them. Many of these who had been out of the industry for a long time were found to have lost their skill and nerve when working at a height. Highly skilled and supervising labour remained a great difficulty, particularly on isolated jobs, like repairing ships afloat, which demanded an unusual proportion.

As the shortage increased women were admitted into the yards. On the new construction side they proved themselves able to cover an unexpectedly large range of work and had a smaller percentage of accidents than the men; on the repair side they naturally had less scope, although they undertook the lighter jobs with conspicuous success.

All branches of shipyard labour earned good money during the war; at the end the average for men more than 21 years of age was 145*s.* 6*d.* a week, the highest wage in the country except (by a very small margin) the motor vehicle and aircraft industries. With overtime, many earned much more than that. Most of the labour troubles which occurred were after 1942, when it was found that excessive hours cut down the output and official attempts were made to reduce overtime, including Sunday work. There were comparatively few strikes, practically all unofficial and against the advice of the unions.

As was only to be expected, shipyard prices rose steadily in all branches from the beginning of the war to the end. The admiralty contracts were kept down to a very low level compared with those of owners who ordered ships under licence; when contracts were again placed freely it proved that the price for a simple cargo ship had increased by at least 100%, and in the case of fast, passenger or special-purpose ships by very much more. Repair costs advanced still more; by the beginning of 1944 they were already about 140% more than the prewar level, after which no official figures were published, but the increase was accelerated.

The total mercantile output of the British yards between the outbreak of war and Dec. 1944 was approximately 5,750,000 gross tons in ships of more than 100 tons each. Owing to the more elaborate fittings it was impossible to make an exact comparison with the effort during World War I, but the output per man was estimated as between 50% and 75% greater, a result largely obtained by improved machinery and modernized layout of the yards.

The change-over from war to peace started in 1945, but it had to be achieved gradually. Owing to the important posts in the wartime administration given to men who were connected with shipyard labour, the difficulties were fully understood; shipbuilding was excluded from the government's scheme of nationalization in 1945.

The industry was immediately faced with an immense amount of new construction and overdue repairs, quite apart from the reconditioning of a large number of ships which had been radically changed for their war service. For instance, the final stage of the reconditioning of the "Queen Elizabeth" at Southampton (June–Sept. 1946) was the greatest piece of reassembly ever undertaken and was possible only because the original furniture and fittings, stored in various parts of the world, were intact. Her sister ship the "Queen Mary," holder of the Atlantic blue ribbon since Aug. 1938, was in process of reconditioning at the end of 1946.

Facilities being still limited, all new orders remained subject to admiralty licence, granted according to the national importance of each particular type and the losses which the owners had sustained. This gave precedence to cargo liners, whaling depot ships, fishing vessels and certain other types, while the needs of tramp shipowners, unless they could prove a good case, had to be satisfied by the purchase of government-built ships; passenger liners of normal design had to be reconditioned for further service even if they were over age. The cost of all types was very high, particularly those of which the furnishing, etc., demanded a number of subcontracts; the great majority of outstanding warship contracts were cancelled at the first opportunity, and the firms concerned turned to other branches of shipbuilding whenever possible, otherwise to entirely different industries in which their machinery could be adapted.

British Commonwealth.—The dominions started shipbuilding in 1940 from practically nothing, yet Canada and Australia made a very important contribution to the Allied effort, and others according to their ability and conditions. Canada's output was by far the most important, with yards operating on the Atlantic and Pacific coasts and the Great Lakes. The output of the Pacific yards was the greatest, unhampered as they were by climatic conditions which impeded winter work in the other areas. The majority of the ships turned out were of the North Sands type, similar to the British Empire and U.S. Liberty ships, but later the yards turned to an adaptation of the faster U.S. Victory design and numerous naval auxiliaries. Establishments which could not construct such big ships built vessels of 4,700 tons deadweight, while those from the Great Lakes were of smaller tonnage to pass through the canals.

Starting with only nine big slipways, Canadian yards built 456 merchant ships of a little less than 4,000,000 tons deadweight by April 1945; in 1944 their output equalled that of Britain and 70% came from British Columbia. During the peak period, 75,000 men and women were employed. In addition Canada repaired and refitted a large number of ships and built destroyers, minesweepers, corvettes and other small warships for the royal and Canadian navies.

Australian shipbuilding had to face even greater difficulties, depending for its steel almost entirely on the Broken Hill company. It began by concentrating on naval small craft but turned to cargo ships of somewhat similar types to the Canadian. In the latter stages of the war, most of the labour had to be diverted to repairing Allied ships damaged in the Pacific. Its great handicap was high costs; similar ships cost £68 (Australian) per deadweight ton, £45 in the U.S.A., £37 in Canada and £26 in Britain. After the conclusion of the war, great efforts were made both in Australia and Canada to keep the shipbuilding industry alive.

Compared with Australia and Canada, the new construction in South Africa, New Zealand and India was small, largely because of difficulties with material and labour. A certain number of useful small warships and auxiliary craft were built, but the main effort in these countries was in repair work, with which their facilities were fully occupied. (*See* also SHIPPING, MERCHANT MARINE.) (F. C. Bo.)

Shipping, Merchant Marine

The United States merchant marine during the decade 1937–46, became the largest merchant fleet ever to sail under one flag. A ten-year plan by which the United States Maritime commission—established by the Merchant Marine act of 1936—hoped to place 500 new oceangoing merchant vessels in service under the U.S. flag was multiplied more than ten times. The stimulus of World War II brought forth a shipbuilding effort in which every known record for speed and quantity of construction was shattered, and at the end of hostilities the U.S. merchant fleet contained three-fifths of all the tonnage afloat in the world.

The story of this accomplishment properly begins with the shipbuilding for the war of 1917–18, for the vessels in the U.S. merchant marine in 1937 were principally those built in the five-year shipbuilding period that began with U.S. entrance into World War I and ended in 1922. Consequently, the U.S. merchant fleet, lacking the addition of a single cargo ship from 1922 to 1936, was in exceeding need of replacements.

On June 29, 1936, President Roosevelt signed the Merchant Marine act. He had recommended to congress that more realistic legislation be enacted than the laws which had failed to give soundness to the merchant fleet. There was considerable apathy and opposition to the bill in congress, and it passed the house of representatives by only eight votes. As it emerged on the statute books, however, it was a sincere attempt to right a number of ills that had beset the shipping industry for many years. It attempted to be comprehensive in all phases of maritime activities which the government was called on to assist or regulate.

The United States Maritime commission created by the act was to consist of five members, one to be designated as chairman. Broad authority was granted the commission to operate in matters of a commercial nature. A survey of the existing fleet was ordered as the basis for a long-range construction program. The Maritime service was established to provide training for United States citizens as licensed or unlicensed merchant seamen. Finally, the act provided for subsidization, both for construction and operation of ships, by the fairest and most practical plan yet devised.

Joseph P. Kennedy was confirmed by the senate as the commission's first chairman on April 15, 1937. On that same day, Edward C. Moran, Jr., Rear Admiral H. A. Wiley, USN (retired), Thomas M. Woodward and Rear Admiral Emory S. Land, USN (retired) were confirmed as members. The commission immediately began fulfilment of the act's stipulation that an inventory should be taken of U.S. maritime resources. An economic survey of the merchant marine was submitted to the congress on Nov. 10, 1937.

Its revelations were startling and its recommendations frank.

The report made clear many of the weaknesses in U.S. maritime structure. It stated many of the problems that had to be resolved before the U.S. merchant marine would be in a position to accomplish the aims outlined in the declaration of policy. It discussed the various theories of the causes of U.S. maritime degeneration with considerable thoroughness, but the underscoring of shipping in its national defense aspects was significant. It pointed out that in time of war the United States invariably had turned to offense as the best means of defense, and that a corollary of this action was adequate supply for a war at a distance from U.S. shores; that there were 60 or more harbours and 7,000 mi. of coastline to be guarded by the navy; that to transport an army and its equipment overseas would take an amazing number of ships.

Though the report stressed the military value of a strong merchant fleet, the nation was not at war, nor was Europe, in 1937. Consequently, in point of design, the fleet ostensibly would be rejuvenated according to peacetime requirements; but there would be incorporated whatever modifications were possible to render ships more suitable as fleet auxiliaries, or more readily adaptable to the purposes of war.

The report disclosed that on May 31, 1937, the U.S. merchant marine consisted of 1,422 ocean-going vessels (of 3,000 deadweight tons or more) having a carrying capacity of 12,600,000 deadweight tons and that by 1942–5 years was taken arbitrarily as the time required to replace any considerable part of the fleet—92% of the ships embracing 88% of the tonnage would be obsolescent. The fleet had been built almost as a unit and it was growing obsolete in the same way.

On the basis of the findings and recommendations in the economic survey and the basic needs of auxiliary ships expressed by the navy, the commission expressed its determination to build 500 ships within the ensuing decade, at the rate of 50 per year. The commission's technicians went to work on a basic design for a cargo vessel. Leading naval architects were consulted, the opinions of qualified individuals and organizations were studied, and there emerged the design that became the famed C-2.

The C-2 proved eminently satisfactory in every respect. It embraced every point of modernness that could be devised. Its designed speed was 15½ knots, though it could make more. Its characteristics were such that it could be adapted to almost any general purpose. It could be a general cargo vessel, a cargo-passenger ship within a wide ratio, or a pleasure vessel. It met universal favour, and with the larger and smaller versions of its design, remained the standard product of the commission at the end of the decade 1937–46.

From a military point of view, tankers were also of prime consideration. One of the first acts of the commission was to enter into negotiations with the Standard Oil company of New Jersey, which was then preparing to construct 12 tankers, for an increase in their speed to make them suitable for conversion to naval auxiliaries. The tankers normally would make 11½ knots. The commission agreed to bear the cost of installing equipment which would raise their speed 50% or more, of gun emplacements, oiling-at-sea gear and other features that would make them highly desirable in case of emergency. The cost was close to $900,000 for each vessel, but the cost was repaid when the emergency did arise, and they went immediately into naval service.

The first cargo vessel delivered in the long range program went into service in June 1939. By that time there were shipyards in California, Florida, Pennsylvania, New Jersey, Massachusetts and Mississippi. Six months later, there were 16 yards in 12 states and 21 new C-type vessels had been put into service.

In September 1939 the outbreak of World War II in Europe caused a sharp revision of commission schedules. Even before that time, the commission had realized that with unrest in Europe reaching a critical stage, there would be an inevitable shortage of vessels to conduct what would remain of world trade. With the sanction of the administration and of congressional leaders, the commission increased its construction schedules to 100 ships a year, and went into 1940 with the assumption that it would be called on to bear the heaviest load of construction and operation in its history.

The events of 1940 were as critical for the Maritime commission as for any branch of the government. The army and navy frankly were preparing for any eventuality by increasing their personnel and their armament. The commission could do no less. It doubled its schedules again, for it had to consider not only the possibilities of the future, but also immediate, imperative needs.

In Jan. 1941 the president issued a plea for "More Ships —More Speed." The administration and the congress had conceived the lend-lease legislation by which there would be a legal basis for extending unlimited supplies to the anti-axis nations. It was clear by this time that even though cargo ships and tankers were being built much faster in the U.S. than by any previous methods, the nation was running a terrifying risk of being caught in a shipping squeeze. By unspoken agreement, the U.S. had become shipbuilder to the world, and the United States had to find a faster means of producing tonnage, else Europe would fall and the rest of the world become the prey of the axis.

It still required 9 to 12 months to build a ship in 1940. That was faster than the old methods, but not fast enough.

The British were experiencing large shipping losses in

Basic training for deck hands at a U.S. maritime training station →

1940. The United States, still a legally neutral nation, could not substitute in Britain's shipping tasks without violating whatever remained of neutral obligations. England placed an order in U.S. shipyards for 60 cargo vessels and sent over the plans on which a British tramp steamer, the Sunderland type, had been built.

It was a simple vessel, not particularly graceful, but sturdy. It was selected deliberately because it was believed its construction would be less complicated than most, therefore speedier. The commission's technicians reported that, with a few changes in design, a high degree of standardization both in design and methods, and a centralized system for getting ship components into yards, there would be excellent possibilities of instituting a shipbuilding procedure to build vessels of 10,000 deadweight tons in four-and-one-half to six months.

The commission drew up a design that standardized every 1 of the 15,000 or more parts that went into the vessel. It substituted welding for riveting wherever possible. The plans were drawn so that whole sections of the superstructure and other unified sections of the ship could be fabricated at the yard or miles away, whichever was convenient. The shipyards were to be laid out on an assembly-line basis, for a new technique was to be applied. The old orthodox method of shipbuilding was to build almost every component inside the yard. The new conception was for a shipyard to be the focal point for sources of supply that would reach into every state of the union. Shipyard workers were not to build ships, but to assemble them. The emphasis was entirely on speed.

Obviously, to build such a system there had to be a co-ordination of shipyards with sources of manufacture and supply. Hundreds of plants making components ranging in size from the smallest bolt to steam engines had to be supplied with drawings detailing the rigidly standardized specifications. Then, once these parts were manufactured, a most intricate system of scheduling had to be perfected, requiring closest relations not only between the commission and the manufacturer, but among transportation systems as well.

A major difficulty arose when propulsion for the new ship was considered. The navy's huge building program had pre-empted most of the capacity for building turbines. With extreme reluctance the commission was forced to adopt the steam reciprocating engine for the Liberty ship. The 10,000 ton vessel would do little better than 11 knots with the 2,500 horsepower, but there was no choice.

International developments in 1941 underscored the commission's hurried efforts. Sinkings of British and other Allied vessels rose from 453,000 deadweight tons in February to 774,000 in April. Occasions of German ruthlessness on the high seas were galling to America. The famous seizure of the "City of Flint" was one case in point. The culmination of these actions was the order given the navy on Sept. 11, to "shoot on sight" any axis molesters of U.S. vessels and the passage by congress of a bill permitting the arming of U.S. ships and their entry into all combat zones. The merchant marine was virtually at war.

By Jan. 1941 the number of commission shipyards had grown to 18, with 71 ways. Before the year was out there were 40 yards with 275 ways capable of constructing vessels 400 feet long with a 60-foot beam. In addition, there were yards building smaller vessels on the Great Lakes.

The distinction of launching the first Liberty ship went to the Bethlehem-Fairfield shipyard of Baltimore. Eight months after its keel had been laid, the "Patrick Henry," first of more than 2,600 identical Liberty ships, sailed from Baltimore in the service of the United States and the United Nations as well, for the Japanese had struck at Pearl Harbor three weeks before.

The outbreak of war between the United States and the axis powers unleashed the real shipbuilding power of the nation. For three years or more the shipbuilders had been developing their talents for design and for organization. It was to be a race against time; ships had to be built within weeks and days instead of months.

Sixty days after Pearl Harbor, the War Shipping administration (WSA) was created by executive order of the president. The commission was left free to build ships, and WSA was given control over all vessels in ocean commerce, power to seize alien vessels, the right to requisition U.S. flag vessels. Its authority was broad in all respects, for it not only controlled U.S. shipping, but represented the United States, as a leading maritime power, in the control of all Allied shipping. Within two months WSA had requisitioned the ships of the American merchant fleet, and was preparing for the increase expected from the emergency construction program.

The request for shipping made by President Roosevelt after Pearl Harbor took the breath of U.S. shipbuilders. Production in 1941 had been 105 vessels aggregating 1,142,500 deadweight tons. The president's directive was for 8,000,000 tons to be delivered in 1942, and twice that much in 1943.

American shipbuilders were expected to build, within 24 months, more than twice the tonnage of the U.S. merchant fleet at the time of Pearl Harbor. There was no solution but a concentration on the Liberty program. Six new yards were added. Eight million tons of shipping meant almost 800 ships of 10,000 or more tons each, more than 2 each day of the year. The president's order did not contemplate launchings, but deliveries of vessels with steam up, ready to sail.

Liberty ships were welded instead of riveted in 90% of their construction. Women proved especially adaptable to welding, for the improvements in welding technique had made it less heavy and arduous, and women in shipyards, dressed in protective clothes against the welding arc, be-

Apprentice seamen of the U.S. maritime service drilling in the use of life suits

A new record for building a merchant ship was set at the Kaiser shipyards in Portland, Ore., on Sept. 23, 1942. Present at the launching of the "Joseph N. Teal," a Liberty ship completed in ten days, were President Roosevelt (left), and Henry J. Kaiser, owner of the yards. The shipyard later lowered this record to three days

came a commonplace part of the shipbuilding scene.

Delivery time fell rapidly. The Liberty ships delivered in Jan. 1942, required, on a national average, 241 days to build. In June, when 51 Libertys went into service, this national average fell to 122 days. By September the yards were delivering an average of 3 ships every day of the month and at the end of the year there had been delivered 746 ships of all types, having an aggregate total of 8,089,732 deadweight tons. Five hundred and forty-two of them were Liberty ships.

By 1942 the commission had solved the turbine production problem. With the aid of the Defense Plants corporation and the expenditure of $50,000,000 the small number of plants in the nation with the knowledge and skill to build this complicated machinery had been greatly expanded and new facilities created. By Sept. 1942 deliveries of C-types were doubled over previous months. As 1943 approached, production of C-types and tankers was being redoubled.

The banner year was 1943. In February of that year, production exceeded 1,250,000 tons, more than had been built in all of 1941. Before the end of March, five vessels were being delivered every day from American yards. By the end of June, the tonnage exceeded 1942 production, and long before, the commission had promised that if there was no lessening in supply of labour and materials, the year's tonnage total would not be 16,000,000, but in excess of 19,000,000 deadweight tons.

In Dec. 1943 close to 80 shipyards were building vessels under direction of the commission. They had passed the president's mark in November. During the last month of the year, 208 ships were delivered. The month's tonnage passed the 2,000,000 mark and brought the year's total to 19,238,626 tons deadweight.

In two years American shipbuilders had built almost two and a half times the total of the nation's prewar tonnage. They had replaced all the shipping losses of the Allies. The navy and the merchant marine had won the battle of the Atlantic, for monthly tonnage losses had declined from a high point of slightly more than 1,000,000 deadweight tons in March—the peak of the "wolf pack" tactics—to 257,000 tons in December.

The commission's program now entered a new phase. With Allied tonnage at the 1939 level, axis raiding halted to a great degree, and adequate capacity for building turbine propulsion machinery, the commission stopped the emergency Liberty construction program, and turned to increased production of C-types, tankers, military vessels and the new Victory ship.

The Victory ship grew out of the Liberty program and was built by the same rapid methods. Making 18 knots or better when propelled by the larger of 2 turbine installations of 6,000 or 8,500 horsepower, it had the same deadweight capacity as the Liberty, but its speed made it a far more valuable ship.

The WSA was principally concerned, in the spring of 1944, with supplying General Eisenhower's command for the invasion of Normandy that came in June. The tempo of Atlantic shipping rose sharply. Materials moved into eastern ports with clocklike regularity, to disappear immediately down the hatches of vessels that came in a steady flow. WSA estimated that 3,700 ship days a month were added to the Atlantic run—the equivalent of adding 123 vessels to the fleet.

The surrender of Germany in May 1945 presented new problems. The army planned to withdraw more than 3,000,000 men from the European theatre. Many of them were destined for the Pacific—across the Atlantic, the United States and 4,000 to 7,000 mi. into the Pacific. Most of their equipment, routed through the Panama canal, traveled 14,000 mi. The commission immediately began preparation for the huge troop movement by conversion of 400 cargo ships to troop carriers.

The surrender of Japan, however, brought the mer-

Merchant Fleets of Ten Selected Countries in Order of Their Importance, Number and Gross Tonnage of Sea-going Iron and Steel Steam and Motor Vessels of 1,000 Gross Tons and Over as of Dec. 31, 1945

(Excluding vessels operating on the Great Lakes and inland waterways and special types such as cable ships, ice breakers, etc.)

Country	Total		Type of vessel: Combination Pass. and Cargo		Freighters		Tankers	
	No.	Gross tons	No.	Gross tons	No.	Gross tons	No.	Gross tons
Total	10,796	66,490,862	756	5,994,324	8,151	45,779,503	1,889	14,717,035
United States	5,745	41,084,290	154	1,554,125	4,533	30,510,225	1,058	9,019,940
British empire	2,666	15,403,958	345	2,890,204	1,905	9,786,774	416	2,726,980
Norway	588	2,768,993	20	68,093	399	1,292,797	169	1,408,103
Netherlands	300	1,614,094	70	488,067	153	742,856	77	383,171
Sweden	436	1,384,348	30	157,411	368	901,143	38	325,794
France	246	1,295,402	51	534,599	169	587,040	26	173,763
U.S.S.R.	305	937,175	43	170,261	240	683,367	22	83,547
Denmark	236	715,017	36	100,531	189	525,975	11	88,511
Panamá	131	703,634	3	8,033	60	206,464	68	489,137
Greece	143	583,951	4	23,000	135	542,862	4	18,089

Source: United States Maritime Commission Division of Economics and Statistics.

Vessels acquired through capture, seizure, transfer, etc., and operating under a country's temporary control were excluded from such country's Dec. 1945 merchant fleet and added to that of the country from which acquired.

Included in the United States merchant fleet were (1) vessels which may or may not have undergone some degree of conversion when acquired by the United States army or navy, and (2) military type vessels originally designed as merchant ships and constructed under the United States Maritime commission construction program. Vessels strictly of military type such as LST's, frigates, aircraft carriers, etc., constructed by the commission were excluded.

chant marine to the end of the shooting war, as it did for the armed services. For the merchant fleet, however, the work was not over. Seven million fighting men were abroad. Nine out of every ten servicemen sailed home on ships under WSA control. By April 1946 most American soldiers had been repatriated. In addition to this transportation of troops, there was an insistent demand for cargo space for relief shipments to devastated areas.

As the tenth anniversary of the establishment of the Maritime commission passed in Sept. 1946, there were still major problems before the commission and the shipping industry. The wealth of tonnage that cost U.S. taxpayers more than $15,000,000 was for sale under provisions of a Ship Sales act passed in March 1946. The Maritime commission was deep in its task of aiding conversion of the war-built fleet to private operation. It was selling war-built vessels to whomever would buy them, giving U.S. citizens first choice as to sale or charter, then permitting foreigners to purchase on specified terms. (W. W. SH.)

Great Britain

The year 1937 was aptly described as the "false dawn of British shipping" after the long depression; the rise in freights, satisfactory as it was for the moment, was not so much due to improved trade as to the political results of Italy's Ethiopian war of 1935 and subsequent international events. The influence of the years following World War I was shown by the fact that the gross tonnage of British merchant ships, excluding tankers, was 17,400,000 compared with 45,500,000 under other flags, whereas in 1913 the figures had been 18,300,000 and 22,500,000 respectively. Britain's share of the world's carrying trade, particularly on the short sea routes to the continent, had declined steadily since 1920, and even the coasting trade had been invaded by foreign tonnage. Nevertheless, the earnings of shipping from foreign clients during 1937 supplied an invisible export which wiped out 30% of the visible adverse trade balance. The average age of the ships was satisfactory and in fast ships, refrigerated tonnage and ocean-going tankers Britain's share of the world's total was large.

In both the tramping and the liner sections, however, particularly the former, the situation was serious. The Shipping (Continuation of Subsidy) act remained in force for 1937, but as the average level of freights was above the 1929 datum line, no money was actually paid in spite of the decline at the end of the year. Until Aug. 1937, the tramp rates were satisfactory, permitting several owners to make up arrears of depreciation and declare a dividend, but in September they broke, partly through a reduction in business and partly through the delivery of a number of ships ordered when the revival started in 1935. By the end of the year they were down to the level which had been agreed as the minimum and continued to decline in 1938; by the end of Aug. 1939 they were nearly 40% below the level of Sept. 1937.

Later comparisons were impossible owing to lack of statistics during the war period.

The industry realized that a scheme of voluntary co-operation would be necessary after the end of the subsidy, and discussions were started to continue and increase the system which had operated effectively to maintain minimum freights for three years. The tramp administrative committee was established, with co-operation from the liner companies, and by the end of 1937 included 90% of tramp and a considerable majority of liner tonnage. The minimum rates were based principally on the main grain trades, but markets not covered by them fell rapidly.

Foreign competition continued to be serious; in some cases it was assisted by lower running costs, in some by subsidies and in some by parties to trade treaties successfully insisting on buying f.o.b. and carrying all the British goods so bought in their own ships. In some cases the competition was largely political, as in the far east, where the Japanese carried out a vigorous campaign to exclude foreign, and particularly British, shipping. Liner business, being very largely controlled by international conferences, did not suffer to the same extent but frequently operated under a considerable handicap.

In the passenger section the sale or demolition of numerous ships during the slump had its effect, but those in commission did reasonably well and, to the surprise of many people, the Cunard White Star record-breaker "Queen Mary" of 1936 proved to be not only an excellent figurehead but also a very profitable ship. New tonnage, on improved standards, was built for the long distance services, although prices were high and few of the companies could order what they needed. Cruising continued to employ liners during the slack season on the various passenger routes.

The decline from the end of 1937 was shown by the fact that in the summer of 1938, 438,000 gross tons of British shipping were laid up, against 97,000, 12 months previously; in 1932 the figures had been 3,556,000, but many of those ships had been sold to foreign interests or broken up.

In view of the rapid increase of all running costs it was feared that a further reduction in freights or volume of trade would mean further large-scale laying up.

The very short period of revival, coupled with the obvious threats of Germany, caused the authorities to take action. In July 1938 the president of the board of trade stated that the government was willing to assist shipping, even to a considerable sum, but felt that the first move should come from the industry itself.

Fact-finding committees were appointed to carry out exhaustive inquiry into conditions and the influences which had depressed them.

Early in 1939 the shipowners presented their report on conditions and their suggestions for state assistance. They included a renewal of the tramp subsidy for 5 years, with the sliding scale previously used, so that the assistance would be reduced when freight rates approached the 1929 average and be abolished altogether when they exceeded it by 5%.

Allowance was made for the increased working expenses in allocating the total sum. On the liner side it was suggested that a defense fund should be set up, to be called upon only in certain circumstances, including state aid to rival flags.

In May 1939 the house of commons provided £2,000,000 for the purchase of merchant ships to form a reserve and £100,000 for their maintenance. The price of old tonnage to the shipbreakers was low, and a number of ships were purchased and registered in the name of the board of trade.

The outbreak of World War II in Sept. 1939 immediately put an end to the subsidy suggestions and the government reserve of ships showed its value. Many were added to it which had already gone to the shipbreakers but the demolition of which had not begun. The total tonnage under the British flag when World War II broke out was 17,891,134 tons gross, of which 15,508,000 tons was in ships of 2,500 tons or more. These included 360 passenger and mixed liners, 778 cargo liners, 808 tramps and 395 ocean-going tankers.

Government Control.—A large measure of government control was recognized as being necessary in wartime and before World War II began, preparations were made under the board of trade and admiralty. The nucleus of a ministry of shipping was established within the former, having the advantage of existing legal, financial and establishment services while it was being developed. That arrangement was continued in the earliest days of the war, although there was an agitation for a separate ministry from the beginning. The ministry of transport was concerned with war plans to facilitate the rapid turn-round of ships in the ports and to avoid congestion.

The ministry of shipping was established on Oct. 20, 1939, taking over the duties and staff of the marine department of the board of trade. The clerical staff was immediately greatly augmented; numerous volunteers entered from the shipping business and various bodies connected with the industry.

The new organization was soon bitterly criticized. It had inherited the duty of licensing every overseas voyage, and the tramping section of the industry complained that the absence of experienced tramp men in the executive caused constant misdirection and waste of tonnage. There was also considerable overlapping and lack of co-operation with other departments and it was complained that the ministry lacked authority when the ministry of transport or the admiralty demanded tonnage. Later the demands of the ministry of food and ministry of supply, and the control of dock labour by the ministry of labour added to the confusion.

The suggestion was constantly put forward that all merchant shipbuilding should be the sole responsibility of the ministry, but after much discussion it was successfully maintained that as priority was bound to be a matter of conflicting claims it should be kept in the hands of the admiralty, with proper liaison, as naval needs had to be considered first.

Growing criticism, and constant confusion through lack of co-operation between shipping, the ports and land transport caused the ministry of war transport to be formed in May 1941, combining the ministry of shipping and the ministry of transport. On the shipping side numerous departments and divisions operated, some of them inherited from the old organizations and some new.

Requisitioning and Management.—One of the first duties of the government was to arrange for the requisition of the ships which it needed for military and supply services and for the management of vessels taken from the axis, acquired before the outbreak of World War II as a reserve, or purchased later. In the first class there was no difficulty, for charter parties had long been agreed with the owners for the complete temporary acquisition of merchant ships, required as auxiliary cruisers or for other naval purposes. The unprecedented range of official demands complicated the matter, and the requisitioning of individual ships introduced many problems; in Dec. 1939 it was necessary to demand tonnage for badly needed Atlantic cargoes without any previous agreement having been made for rates of hire, and a comprehensive scheme was essential.

The general requisition of all ships except certain coasters was gradually applied during the first part of 1940, the ships being taken up as they reached a convenient port and then being managed by the owners on account of the government. Terms were finally agreed after long negotiation; the basis was that payments should cover average operating expenses, calculated by practical experience with each class of ship, plus 5% per annum for depreciation of liners and dry cargo ships and 6% for tankers, with an additional 5% to cover the interest on capital. That was calculated on the actual first cost in the case of liners and on agreed average value for each class of tramp and tanker. The shipowners protested that the narrow limits laid down by the government for discussion were unfair, but the agreement was made subject to revision at any time. Such revision was repeatedly necessary as the running expenses increased.

The basic rate was by the month; for cargo liners it was 8*s.* per gross ton and for passenger liners from 10*s.*5*d.* to 13*s.*7*d.* per gross ton according to speed. For deep-sea tramps it varied from 6*s.* to 8*s.* per deadweight ton according to size, which governed the running costs to a great extent. There were many variations for special ships; an extra payment was made for motorships.

From time to time there were popular suggestions that large profits were being made by the owners under these agreements, but official investigation by the select committee on national expenditure and constant examination by the ministry showed that such charges were unfounded and that, owing to the inevitable time-lag between increased running costs and new agreements, the rates very frequently failed to cover the intended depreciation and interest on capital.

All ships under requisition, as well as those owned by the government, and prize vessels, were managed by the practical shipowners. They were under constant direction and were allocated to various routes, often far different from those for which they were designed, according to the needs of the moment. They were then loaded by the companies on whose berth they ran in rotation, involving an immense amount of accountancy and administrative work with reduced staffs. After 1940 when London and the east coast ports were constantly raided by German aircraft, all possible overseas ships were diverted to west coast ports, where their owners frequently had no organization, and special wartime ports were opened on the Clyde and elsewhere. A large part of their cargoes was transshipped to coasters and carried to ports which were regarded as dangerous for the big ships.

New ships built during World War II and those acquired by the government before the war, or captured from the axis or while blockade-running, or later acquired by the government either by purchase abroad or after war damage which caused them to be regarded as constructive total losses, were rechristened with names beginning with the word Empire and placed under the management of established firms at agreed rates. As the war progressed a number of the U.S. Liberty ships were transferred to the British flag for operation under bare-boat charter terms. They were all given names having the prefix Sam (Samadang, Samcalia, Samtucky, etc.) to signify Uncle Sam, and were allocated to the companies for management. Many ships which escaped from occupied Allied territory, or were chartered from neutrals, were managed in the same way without rechristening.

Non-Commercial Service.—During World War II the work of merchant ships was divided into commercial (although principally on behalf of the state) and non-commercial service, the latter being entirely for the fighting forces. Merchant ships had been the reserve of the navy from the earliest days; their functions had changed but they were still essential.

Charter parties for these non-commercial services were adapted from previous ones in force long before the war, varying according to whether the owners managed the ships, supplying and feeding the crews, or the government took them over "bare boat" and did everything necessary. When the admiralty supplied the crew, the majority temporarily joined the royal naval reserve. These charters could be terminated at any time in any port, but naturally that was done only when the ship could be immediately employed on cargo work; an auxiliary warship took months to reconvert at the responsibility of the admiralty.

Their principal naval duties were as auxiliary cruisers and aircraft carriers. Medium-sized ships of big fuel capacity were the most valuable in the former role as they could overcome bunkering difficulties. Nevertheless, they were recognized as being very vulnerable, for it was impossible to give them more than the most primitive protection, and several were lost with heavy casualties. Among these were the Peninsular and Oriental "Rawalpindi" and the Aberdeen-Commonwealth "Jervis Bay," sunk fighting against impossible odds. In the acute shortage of regular cruisers, and with the long distances to be patrolled, their use was unavoidable, but they were paid off as soon as possible. They mounted six to eight 6-in. guns with anti-aircraft backing; some carried aircraft and catapults. The great majority of the auxiliary (escort) aircraft carriers were American ships under lend-lease, but certain fast British cargo ships were converted.

An enormous number of small craft were commissioned in combatant roles. Minesweepers included fishing vessels, shallow-draught paddle excursion steamers and a few miscellaneous small vessels. Other excursion steamers, having broad decks for their passengers, made excellent anti-aircraft ships. In non-combatant roles ships were used for carrying naval stores and defense boom material; fitted with racks and safety devices, they were used as ammunition issuing ships to replenish warships' magazines. Numerous coasters did naval work, while privately owned tugs were commissioned for dockyard and other work and were the mainstay of the salvage section. Coastal liners and short sea traders were specially fitted as rescue ships to follow the convoys and pick up survivors without endangering the other ships.

Other merchantmen, including passenger liners, were converted into depot ships for various types of small warships. They were generally fitted to carry out repairs as well as to house the crews in port and to dispense the necessary stores and ammunition. Some were converted into "amenities ships" for the Pacific, elaborately fitted to afford men rest and relaxation and even to carry a brewery. Others became floating dockyards able to effect a remarkable range of repair work. Many ships were so altered by conversion that it was impractical to reconvert them to commercial use. The coastal command of the royal air force also used tonnage for depot and repair purposes.

In the case of the army, most of the ships were required for trooping and store carrying, the normal functions of the merchantman in war. In the former the authorities were handicapped by the reduction in the number of passenger ships, particularly those of handy size, between World Wars I and II. In 1939 and 1940 troopships, although largely gutted for their conversion, carried the same number of troops as passengers on commercial work, but later the number was increased by stages and comfort diminished. The capacity of the Cunard White Star liners "Queen Mary" and "Queen Elizabeth" was approximately 5,000 when they were first commissioned; in the latter stages they were carrying 15,000 officers and men. Cargo vessels and, for the shorter distances, cross-channel packets and excursion steamers, were also used for trooping, many being lent to Allied governments. Considering the circumstances the losses of transports, especially when loaded, were remarkably small.

In the case of hospital ships, the structural alterations were not usually so great; a wide range of types were employed, principally handy-sized liners and packets, and the losses were heavy owing to the fact that under the Geneva convention they were not escorted like transports.

In the case of ordinary store and supply ships, little or no conversion was necessary and it was usual for them to pick up a commercial cargo as soon as their military stores were discharged. With operations ranging from Normandy to the Pacific, every type was employed. One important duty was the carrying of gasoline for the army and R.A.F., for which certain preparations were necessary. It was originally packed in "flimseys" at great risk to the ship, but later the familiar "jerry cans" were used, the holds being protected to prevent incendiary bullets penetrating the sides and starting fires.

Commercial Service.—Commercial voyages, after the general requisition in 1940, were all on behalf of the government; an increasing proportion of the cargoes were on government account and when they were for private interests the profit went to the treasury.

In Sept. 1939 freight rates of British ships were rigidly restricted and voyages were made subject to licence; wheat and other necessities already being imported by the government were at fixed rates. In November British ships received 32*s*.6*d*. a ton for grain from the River Plate, but the supply was not nearly sufficient and the government was paying neutral ships 60*s*. On Dec. 4 increases were announced, 43*s*.6*d*. for British ships and 65*s*. for neutrals, with the latter becoming more difficult to arrange as they found greater profit on safer voyages elsewhere. On the export side efforts were made to maintain the slogan "Business as Usual," and to encourage exports for the sake of foreign currency; but as mobilization proceeded and the munitions industry demanded more labour the policy had to be abandoned. Exports were strictly controlled, while British dominions and Allied countries were forced to restrict their imports for economic reasons. All shipments of commercial cargo gradually came under a permit system of some sort.

The progress of World War II constantly changed the character of the commercial service. Until the German invasion of Norway, a large traffic still remained with northern Europe in spite of losses. When the Scandinavian timber trade was interrupted by the blockade, supplies had to be obtained from Canada, both east and west, and a certain amount from South America. Mediterranean services were maintained by their normal type of short sea trader carrying foodstuffs, etc., until Italy entered the war. Then the closing of the central Mediterranean forced ships to use the Cape route, demanding a vessel with bigger bunkers. The small ships caught in the eastern Mediterranean maintained a feeder service to Egypt, where the cargo was transshipped. When the United States passed the "cash-and-carry" legislation, all the available fast cargo ships were transferred to the north Atlantic service, but after Pearl Harbor the rapidly growing U.S. merchant service took a large part.

To increase essential imports, troopships and army supply ships collected as much commercial cargo as possible

Huge fleet of 114 merchant vessels in New York harbour in Sept. 1941, including British, Norwegian, Dutch and Icelandic ships

on their return voyages, providing it did not interfere with their military work; but the diversion had to be as small as possible although fast meat ships would return from the middle east campaign via South America.

Measures were taken to increase the carrying capacity of the available tonnage. The greatest difficulty was waste of time, unavoidable when convoys had to be protected by insufficient escorts but frequently unnecessary and exasperating. Great improvements in that direction were effected by the establishment of the ministry of war transport in 1941. Ships were allocated to the shortest haul possible; imports from the north Pacific, for instance, were finally covered almost entirely by the delivery voyages of new ships built in western Canada and the U.S.A. The freeing of the Mediterranean saved thousands of tons. Many ships were made to carry more by raising the load line under careful precautions and much time was saved by reducing the number of loading ports to one or two; sometimes small vessels were used for feeder services from the remainder.

Careful peacetime precautions were impossible with tonnage in short supply, and cargoes had to be loaded with small regard to possible contamination, but surprisingly little food was spoiled. Block purchases permitted "block loading" of cargo, with a saving of space and time at the ports.

There was a struggle for priority between the different importing departments, which caused great waste in the early days; later the demands were examined by the director of commercial services in the ministry of war transport and approved requirements were then reported to the allocation of shipping tonnage division which, in conjunction with the ship operating division, arranged details.

In spite of the need for raw materials and munitions, foodstuffs had first priority. Every care was taken to make the greatest use of the available space; on the day World War II started wireless orders were sent out to all ships carrying chilled meat to freeze it down at once. Dairy produce was given high priority, particularly cheese on account of its food value and the small space that it occupied. Eggs in the shell were soon prohibited, and fruit after the end of 1940. With some adaptation many fruiters carried ordinary meat cargoes successfully. Refrigerated meat ships made a special target for the Germans and casualties were high.

The passenger side had equal difficulties, especially as so many of the biggest and fastest ships were taken up by the navy and army as auxiliary cruisers or transports. As many ships as possible, however, were left to the service, and some relief was afforded by the U.S. government prohibiting its nationals from travelling in belligerent ships, but later only the minimum number of ships were left to maintain necessary skeleton services. The mails were carried by any convenient ship, naval or mercantile.

When all ships came under general requisition, the whole of the profits of the passenger business went to the ministry. The owners did all the necessary business and management for set fees; the ministry received the fares and fixed the rates and conditions. All passages were subject to strict priority, and the accommodation of each ship was distributed as the ministry considered necessary; naval and military passengers came first; officials with wives and families and civil servants followed them. The rest was allocated to the dominion and colonial authorities on the route to distribute to their people according to the necessity of their voyage; if any passage remained it went to civilians travelling in the national interest or, in exceptional circumstances, to those who could show strong compassionate grounds. The ships were packed to their utmost capacity, extra berths being fitted wherever possible, and the normal limit of 12 passengers without a special licence was relaxed, although lifeboat and other safety regulations continued. Each passenger was bound to strict secrecy concerning the name of his ship, voyage, port of departure and any information that could be dangerous. Booking was "blind," without the passenger knowing what accommodation or what ship he would get, and very short notice was given to assemble at a named place, often an open roadstead in which the convoy was assembling.

Manning.—Manning proved one of the greatest problems during World War II, not from lack of spirit but from difficulties of training and organization. A general invitation to seamen and engineers who had left the sea to register for return in war met with a ready response; the registration of all former seamen between the ages of 18 and 60 was made compulsory in 1941, but it was found unnecessary to call upon any who had been ashore for a long period.

The number of men choosing sea service under the National Service act was more than the royal navy could absorb, and the rest were trained as merchant seamen in special establishments.

The ordinary voyage articles were changed to suit war conditions in 1940, and before the invasion of Normandy special articles ("V-articles") were prepared which covered the increased danger and met with a very fine response. Discipline varied; a great deal of trouble was admittedly experienced, and it was often necessary to prosecute under the defense regulations with severe penalties, but the conduct in action was almost invariably excellent.

Opportunity was taken to try the longed-for experiment of continuous service for seamen instead of the majority being paid off after every voyage. In May 1941 the Essential Work order was extended to the merchant navy, and the M.V. reserve pool was established. All officers and men became members at the end of current articles and remained on pay until appointed to another ship. Arrangements were made for companies to retain their regular employees, and they were allowed to maintain domestic pools provided they did not withdraw too many men from active service. Officers and men enjoyed their regular leave on pay and could be employed on relieving work, guard duties in port, etc., until they were required to return to sea. There were a number of cases of men defrauding the pool, but the great majority appreciated its facilities.

During World War II the basic rates of pay remained almost stable, but they were greatly supplemented by allowances. The first scale of war risk bonus was published in Sept. 1939, varying with rank, and was later greatly increased. It was paid while the officer or man was on articles, and a special war risk bonus was paid for dangerous service. Differential monthly payment was adopted in Dec. 1940, and qualifications in gunnery, etc., received allowances.

Compensation for injuries and pensions for dependents were arranged on naval scales for comparative ranks; many details were left uncovered and had to be arranged by

Deck drill aboard the "Queen Mary" for U.S. troops en route to England in Nov. 1944. Britain's two giant luxury liners, the "Queen Mary" and the "Queen Elizabeth," carried 1,243,538 troops across the Atlantic while serving as transports during World War II

agreement, but the owners voluntarily increased their obligations in cases not covered by the regulations.

The Postwar Period.—Immediately after the surrender of Germany some relaxation was possible in the wartime regulations, but there was no general cancellation until the defeat of Japan. Even then it had to be gradual, with the large fighting forces still in the field to be supplied and relief work urgently needed in liberated countries. The Allies and certain neutrals pooled their tonnage for a certain period, while each country maintained its own measures of control. When the general requisition scheme came to an end, British shipowners regained a measure of control over their own ships but they were still regulated as to the voyages that could be undertaken and the freights charged.

In addition, a number of ships remained under particular requisition, especially transports and army storeships. The former were employed repatriating British, dominion and Allied troops in units and, when demobilization was started, a large number of time-expired men in details. The system left a number of berths vacant for civilian passengers under the same conditions as in the later stages of the war, and until the latter part of 1946 the ministry still retained control of the passenger bookings of the ships which were in their owners' hands and reserved a large part of their accommodation for official travellers. Meanwhile the waiting lists on all the principal routes ran into many thousands and numbers of travellers on important business had to go by air.

Bottlenecks in the passenger business were caused by the delayed release of ships on transport duty, and the fact that many liners requisitioned by the navy had been so drastically altered that reconversion was slow or impossible. A minimum of 6 months was usual, and the cost frequently ran to £1,000,000. The Cunard White star "Queen Elizabeth," with a gross tonnage of 83,673, was reconverted as a passenger ship, in Oct. 1946.

During World War II the ministry had inaugurated a scheme for replacing war losses by permitting owners who had suffered to register for the purchase of government-built ships after the end of hostilities, managing them in the meantime. This still left a large number for disposal, in addition to tonnage surrendered by the axis. In Jan. 1946 the first invitation to tender was issued, cataloguing 528 vessels of various types with the minimum price that would be accepted for their purchase or bare-boat time charter. In the case of practically all the ships of satisfactory design and condition the former was largely exceeded but many tramp owners, in particular, preferred to charter for a period of years.

Demobilization of the seamen who had gone to sea under the Military Service act was based on the age-and-service system of the fighting services, but owing to different conditions it was impossible to carry it out so methodically. All were given the opportunity of remaining in the merchant navy; a number of the young men, as well as many temporary ratings demobilized from the navy, embraced it eagerly but the great majority of the older men preferred to take their discharge.

British Dominions.—The large coasting fleets under the Canadian, Australian and New Zealand flags were greatly depleted by requisitioning for war service, but the numerous ocean-going ships built in the two former dominions were kept under state ownership, although a large proportion was chartered to the British government, until after World War II. Then many of the Canadian ships were sold to private owners, but the process proved more difficult in Australia. The South African government fleet was augmented by prize tonnage and was used principally for national supplies; at the end of World War II there was great enthusiasm for shipping and a number of new companies were launched, mostly with purchased ships. In India there was equal enthusiasm, and numerous native ownerships were started for Asiatic international traffic as well as coastal, with the hope of very generous help from the new government. (F. C. Bo.)

Bibliography.—R. G. Albion, *Sea Lanes in Wartime* (1942); *Annual Review of Shipping, Shipbuilding and Marine Engineering* (London, 1945); *Shipping World Yearbook* (London); E. A. Turpin, *Merchant Marine Officers Handbook* (1943); U.S. Bureau of Census, *Statistical Abstract* (ann.); U.S. Bureau of Foreign and Domestic Commerce, *Foreign Commerce Yearbook;* P. M. Zeis, *American Shipping Policy* (1938). Periodical: *World Ports.*

Shipping Administration, War

See War and Defense Agencies.

Shock Treatment

See Medicine; Nervous System; Psychiatry.

Shoe Industry

The ten years 1937 through 1946 were the most eventful years in shoe history. During that period the industry was confronted with problems that had no precedent, for, in addition to the peaks and valleys, recessions and booms that had become the accepted pattern, there was the terrific influence of World War II. Ten eventful years in the shoe industry did not record the same astounding advances and progress that the sciences or the fields of invention made, but they indicated that shoes are universal—the one article of wearing apparel that is a common necessity and as such influences all civilized people.

United States.—In 1937 the country was beginning to emerge from almost ten years of depression, and industry was again thinking in terms of manufacturing, merchandising and distributing its shoes. In 1946 the first full postwar year with its problems of economic readjustment, there were shortages of materials and greater demand than ever for shoes because of the high rate of employment and earnings. The intervening years had their full complement of difficulties, hazards and rewards.

The United States, as the largest consumer of leather and the greatest shoe-producing country, maintained a steady per capita production and consumption in the years prior to the war. Far-reaching international and domestic events catapulted the industry out of its normal channels and, beginning with 1941, demand for shoes caught up and almost outdistanced supply. With the entrance of the United States into World War II production was stimulated and organized to the limit of the nation's resources. Every available man and machine was employed. The greatest problem of the industry was to bridge the gap between supply and demand—a gap created by the diversion of supplies to the armed forces and by extraordinary purchasing power. Consumption of shoes increased sharply and would have continued to increase but for the limiting factors of wartime supply.

All branches of the industry—tanners, manufacturers and retailers—co-operated wholeheartedly in the transition from peacetime operation to all-out war effort. The government became the biggest and most important customer for boots and shoes. For the first time in history, heavy government buying was accomplished without an immediate spiral of prices on consumer goods; but it was inevitable that priorities, allocations, restrictions upon consumption, price control and rationing would follow. Various government agencies were established, and key men were recruited from industry to draft the orders and administer the laws. The War Production board was set up to regulate production, and the Office of Price Administration was established to keep prices from getting out of line. The shift from abundance to the economic realities of war and slowly growing scarcities had to be clearly and plainly translated to the public.

Demand and potential supply were brought into closer balance by Footwear Conservation order M-217, eliminating wasteful shoe practices, banning new designs and constructions, limiting colours to black, white and three shades of brown; and directing available supplies of critical sole leather into the manufacture of the most essential types of shoes. Amendments to order M-217 were issued from time to time, and in Aug. 1944 colour restrictions were eliminated. New designs, lasts and patterns were allowed, providing manufacturers could adopt them without employing additional workers, for the manpower shortage was becoming increasingly acute.

Industry withstood the impact of greater production for the armed forces, lend-lease and civilians until the growing concern over shortages in sole leather and materials necessitated that the country go on a shoe rationing basis in order to ensure an equitable distribution of available shoes. On Feb. 7, 1943, Shoe Ration order 17 was issued, limiting consumption to three pairs per person per year. This per capita consumption was reduced to two pairs per year during the later course of the war and ebbed to almost one pair before shoe rationing was lifted Oct. 30, 1945.

Despite shoe rationing, however, the civilian population of the United States was well shod during the war period. Non-rationed shoes, which did not utilize leather or other essential materials in short supply, and which could be manufactured with the available manpower, supplemented shoe wardrobes and helped fill consumer demand for extra shoes.

The shoe industry stripped down to the bare essentials and became a part of a restricted, restrained and regulated war machine. The end of hostilities, first in Europe and then in Japan, eased the situation to some extent. Large army cutbacks released some leather which could be routed through for civilian production.

As soon as it was feasible, many of the controls were lifted and the industry was back to the job of reconverting for peace. Enormous shortages, accumulated during the war years, however, still remained.

Table I.—*Production of Boots and Shoes in U.S.**

1937	411,968,780 pairs
1939	424,136,411 "
1941	483,096,625 " †
1943	418,512,387 " †
1945	443,893,317 " †

*Statistics from U.S. Dept. of Commerce.
†Excludes shoes for military production.

When the United States entered World War II, the demand for leather (*q.v.*) was almost trebled. Military requirements were the first consideration and took up more than 30% of the sole leather. A substantial supply of leather was allocated for repair and rebuilding, and these operations by the army conserved some 22,000,000 sq.ft. of military quality upper leather. Of the U.S. army's total footwear procurement in 1944, 17% was provided through rebuilt shoes, which totalled 6,000,000 pairs—issued to troops stationed in the United States only. About 4,000,000 pairs that could not be put into condition for army use were repaired and sent to the liberated countries.

United States tanners did a magnificent job—supplying not only the huge military requirements and civilian needs but taking care of lend-lease and United Nations Relief and Rehabilitation administration obligations as well. The United States filled a good part of soviet Russia's military shoe requirements in addition to furnishing leather and shoes to the British, French, Polish, Yugoslav, Philippine and Chinese armies. Sole leather produced in the United States was worn by the fighting men of the United Nations all over the world.

Since the major part of the available sole leather supply was marked for the military, shoe men were hard put to get enough soling material for their civilian requirements. New materials and substitutes evolved. Plastic soles and composition rubber soles came into production and helped solve the situation to some degree. Because these soles were durable and long-wearing, they were used effectively on men's and boys' and children's shoes.

Table II.—*Production of Boots and Shoes in the U.S. for Military Purposes**

1941	15,284,574 pairs
1942	40,875,494 "
1943	46,884,617 "
1944	45,122,197 "
1945	42,333,254 "

*Statistics from U.S. Dept. of Commerce, bureau of the census.

In view of the fact that 80% of the world's hides ordinarily had gone into boots and shoes, it was imperative to set up some board that would equitably allocate hides and skins, and the Combined Raw Materials board was put into effect. The United States, Great Britain and Canada co-operated in this initial action and invited other nations to participate—in order to prevent unrestrained price inflation and ensure a fair channelling and distribution of exportable surpluses. Careful studies were made by the C.R.M.B., and joint commissions were sent to Argentina, Brazil and Uruguay, the largest hide producers in South America. Exchange visits also took place between the United States and the United Kingdom, in order to determine the world's supply and a proper distribution of those materials.

The Combined Raw Materials board was replaced by the International Hides, Skin and Leather committee, an international body on which the United States, Great Britain, Canada, Belgium, Denmark, France, the Netherlands, Norway, Spain, Sweden and Switzerland—the major leather-consuming nations of the world—were represented. Its duties were to determine the types of raw, semitanned and tanned hides which were in global short supply and to recommend appropriate agencies, national and international, for fair distribution of supplies. This international committee functioned effectively in maintaining controls until it was dissolved June 26, 1946.

With the war over and international controls dropped a leather-hungry world frantically tried to obtain hides and skins and tanning materials from all parts of the globe. It might seem strange that bankrupt nations would fight to buy world raw stock and leather at higher prices; but the answer was that they would do without almost everything else to get foot coverings.

Peak producing and selling of shoes in the United States could be credited to the progress achieved by U.S. designers. At the decade's end fashion was originating in the various centres of the United States and then gravitating to the European countries.

Stretchable shoes were introduced in the United States in 1938. Elasticized yarn was used as a backing for leather, and the shoes yielded to every movement of the foot—but always returned to the original contour. Buckles for fastening and gores for snugness could be discarded, and there was an immediate acceptance in the women's field. From a meagre 800,000 pairs in 1939, production increased to 80,000,000 pairs in 1942 before elasticized yarn became an essential war product.

One of the outstanding developments in the shoe field in the United States was the introduction of the slip-lasted or California process of shoemaking. This process was used in the production of most of the platform type, casual shoes which were, in the main, unrationed and therefore had a wide appeal.

In its simplest form the California process was nothing more than the assembly, as a unit, of upper, sock lining and platform cover to form a pocket into which the last was inserted before the platform material and outer sole were attached. Lasting could be done by hand, in which case it was generally said to be slip lasted.

Great Britain.—Despite limited resources of raw materials, shoe production in England had always ranked high in national importance. In 1935 England produced about 132,468,000 pairs of shoes, and although no statistics were available for the years 1936 through 1941, production undoubtedly remained steady and consistent. During World War II boot and shoe retailers, along with other merchants, carried on courageously, but shortages of leather and other materials, as well as restrictions in trade, produced a great many changes in the established economic and social structure. A considerable number of stores were forced out of business since civilian footwear for the domestic market was radically curtailed. Some of the better stores had to close their doors several days of the week, having no stock to offer their customers.

A clothes-rationing system went into effect June 1941 with the object of providing a fair distribution of available supplies. The government gave as its basic reason for rationing the maldistribution of clothing and footwear.

In England shoes were not rationed specifically as such but rather fitted into the wider field of clothing. Each civilian had an issue of coupons which were expendable for clothing, including footwear. Men's shoes were scaled to 17 coupons, women's 5, children's 2 and infants' 1. Originally 66 coupons were issued, but these were cut down later to 48 per year.

Clothing coupons in England put a different value on things. No one considered the cost in money but rather in cost of coupons. High-priced articles were in greatest demand for it was felt that they would last longer. Consumer rationing in Great Britain limited consumption for leather footwear and other apparel to about 50% of the prewar figure.

In order to ease the shoe situation wooden-soled shoes were introduced, and Britain's board of trade ruled that a percentage of civilian footwear had to consist of wooden-soled shoes. Utility shoes—plain, practical, extremely limited in design—were standard in England for a full 50% of production; the other 50% were free of all restrictions of colour or price.

The British shoe industry didn't let the war stop its investigation in connection with the improvement of the product; techniques, shoemaking, lasts and general efficiency. Studies were continued throughout the war by the British Boot, Shoe and Allied Trades Research association and, although making of new machinery for the footwear industry was greatly restricted, small improvements were affected in existing machines.

With the war over England again looked to her export markets, and several groups of British shoe men made trips to the United States and other countries to re-establish their contacts, for British shoes, especially in the men's lines, had a good acceptance abroad.

Table III.—*Production of Shoes in England**

1935	132,468,000 pairs
1942	105,623,208 "
1943	101,421,924 "
1944	99,729,480 "
1945	99,813,852 "

*Statistics from the British Information service.

Canada.—In Canada, too, shoes proved to be a common denominator. All the problems and difficulties that confronted the shoe industry in the United States and England were part and parcel of the problems and difficulties that Canadian shoe manufacturers faced. Materials shortages and lack of skilled manpower were acute, and the armed forces took a large percentage of the output of men's shoe factories and factories making women's welt shoes.

An Imperial Hide pool was created for the underlying purpose of ensuring adequate supplies of hides and skins to the tanners, and the Canadian Wartime Price and Trade board was given the power to fix maximum prices and mark-ups and to control exports of hides and skins—in order to maintain price stability. During the course of the war this same board issued orders further restricting styles, colours and finishes of leather.

The Canadian method of controlled raw materials at the source permitted better distribution of shoes, and Canada never had rationing as the United States had it. The retail stores imposed their own rationing on customers to maintain a control of shoe sales. Some of the large establishments did rather extensive shoe repairing to help consumers straddle the gap and extend the life of the shoes they had in their wardrobes.

Price controls operated successfully in Canada and in spite of restrictions, Canadian trade, in the aggregate, fared well.

Table IV.—*Shoe Production in Canada**

1942	33,199,912 pairs
1943	34,139,945 "
1944	35,285,807 "
1945	38,955,725 "
1946†	22,553,508 "

*Statistics from the Division of the Dominion Bureau of Statistics, Ottawa, Canada.
†January to June only.

Europe.—European countries, generally, found it impossible to maintain production. War activity, heavy military requirements (for despite mechanization and modernization, armies still travelled on their feet), materials shortages, regulated production, controlled consumption, price-fixing and lack of manpower all contributed to their difficulties. Stoppages of leather and other raw material imports drastically curtailed shoemaking, and almost every European country resorted to substitutes of one kind or another. It was amazing what necessity and ingenuity could produce.

In Sweden, where the living standard was above the level of the rest of Europe, it was necessary to institute drastic rationing when the supply of leather from the Argentine stopped. Overnight a ration of one pair of shoes for each adult for 18 months was applied, and only one repair for the same period was permitted. Most of the other European countries followed suit—to stretch available supplies.

In prewar Czechoslovakia the Bată shoe organization at Zlin shipped to the United States more pairs of shoes than all the combined manufacturers in the United States exported to all the countries of the world. These were low-priced shoes and caused manufacturers in the U.S. great concern. When Hitler came into power and captured the plant, its equipment, goods and capital, the United States immediately terminated all concessions granted to Czechoslovakia in which shoes from that country were given favourable tariff consideration. After the war the Czechoslovakian government took over the factory in Zlin and its facilities shifted to state ownership; but the Batå interests in the Netherlands, France, Switzerland, England, Canada and South America continued to be very active.

Frogskins were introduced in France and made into elegant shoes; the French could always be relied upon for that spark of genius that made Paris the fashion centre of the world. During World War II that centre of fashion shifted to the United States, but the French later made a determined effort to get it back.

Wooden-soled shoes were accepted, grudgingly at first but matter-of-factly thereafter, in all the European countries. Pigskin, used in Germany for years in the manufacture of gloves and bookbindings, was substituted for calf and kidskin leather in the manufacture of shoes. Ersatz products included glass shoes of nonsplintering plexiglass.

Latin America.—A study of the shoe industry during the eventful decade would be incomplete without mention of the South and Latin American countries, which became increasingly important as factors in the production of shoes and leather. The decade was marked by a steady expansion of shoe-manufacturing facilities. Many plants were built in areas where none existed before, and shoe machinery was imported from the United States, Germany, Great Britain and France. Growth of domestic leather production in these countries after 1939 was chiefly caused by a greater dependence of manufacturers upon domestic materials; during the war it was not always possible to obtain needed products from foreign sources, and the industry had to turn more and more to local manufacture for fabrics, rubber and other products as well as labour. Hides were available for shoe production in sufficient quantities in most of the countries for shoes to be produced both on mass scale in factories and by hand.

South American styling in patterns and colours was remarkable, for shoemakers had available manpower and the people of the countries had money and a desire for new and unusual footwear.

Argentina was one of the outstanding South American countries in the shoe and leather industry. Hides available for export, after taking care of domestic needs, were in quantities to give Argentina a favoured place in the international market. After the International Hides, Skin and Leather committee was dissolved and international allocations were dropped, the competitive market for Argentina's hides was wide open.

Shoe production was a natural development in the South American countries inasmuch as both raw hides and quebracho extract were readily available. Large tanneries were built in Brazil, Chile, Colombia, Ecuador and Peru.

In Mexico there was a decided increase in the production of leather shoes during the war years. Mainly responsible for this trade were the increased purchasing power of much of the population and the dwindling supplies of domestic footwear with canvas uppers and rubber soles. Wartime conditions and demands had a favourable effect on the footwear industries in Mexico after 1939. Production improved in quality and quantity. Huarachos—the sandal type with uppers of woven or plaited leather and soles of leather—made the most important gain as far as pairage was concerned. A considerable quantity was exported to the United States. Alpargatas, with fabric uppers and cord or rope soles, were more generally purchased by the native population, for they were available at a low price.

Japan.—The Japanese found that they could get a 750-ft. hide off a whale, and its 3-inch thickness split into three sheets for a possible production of 2,250 ft. of leather; and the Japanese fishermen caught about 800,000 sharks annually. These could be converted into the manufacture of about 2,000,000 pairs of shoes or about one-third of Japan's annual requirements before the war. Philippine mountain snakes were tanned for shoes but because the supply was so limited, they could be used only in high-priced footwear. (*See* also FASHIONS, WOMEN'S; LEATHER.)

BIBLIOGRAPHY.—*Boot and Shoe Recorder* from which the basic material of this study was obtained. (E. G. AN.)

Short, Walter Campbell

Short (1880–), U.S. army officer, was born March 30, 1880, in Fillmore, Ill. A graduate of the University of Illinois (1901), he entered the army in 1902 as an infantry lieutenant and saw service in the Philippines, 1908, and in the Mexican expedition, 1916. During World War I he was attached to the 1st division general staff in France and was assistant chief of staff of the 3d army. He was promoted to a lieutenant general and was assigned to command the Hawaiian department, Feb. 8, 1941, but was relieved of this post, Dec. 17, 1941, in the army shake-up that followed the Japanese blitz on Pearl Harbor. His request for retirement from the army was approved Feb. 28, 1943.

The army, in a report of Aug. 29, 1945, ascribed part of the blame for the Pearl Harbor disaster to Gen. Short, declaring he had failed to take adequate measures "to alert his command for war." On the same day, Gen. Short replied that he had acted in accordance with information "available" to him at the time, adding: "My conscience is clear."

Shows (Animal)

Livestock, Agricultural.—Livestock and agricultural shows reached a maximum of size and influence during the five years preceding the outbreak of World War II. World-wide restrictions of travel, transportation and trade during the four years from 1942 through 1945 had a marked curtailing effect on such events. With the cessation of the active phases of war, these fairs and expositions returned to some measure of their prewar status in the United States, Canada and South America. Great Britain, however, first to suffer cancellation of its long established shows of this nature, was not able to resume them immediately.

The oldest established major livestock show of the United States was still the Southwestern Exposition and Fat Stock show at Fort Worth, Tex., a huge and colourful exposition reflecting in spirit and substance the vast cattle country of the southwest U.S. The Fort Worth show suffered less from wartime restrictions than did most events of its class. Formerly held in the Fort Worth stock yards, its exhibits were cut to include market animals only—steers, wethers and barrows—in 1943; but in 1944 it was reopened on a much more extensive basis in the Will Rogers Memorial amphitheatre. The full exposition went on that year and was repeated in March of 1945 and 1946. A rodeo—one of the country's finest—continued to be the chief entertainment feature of this exposition.

The National Western Stock show in Denver, Colo., was the only large sectional exposition in the United States that continued uninterruptedly during the decade 1937–46. The Denver show was held adjacent to—and in some of its phases—directly in the Denver union stock yards. Its coliseum was one of the few show buildings in the United States not requisitioned for war and military purposes for the duration of hostilities. At the end of the decade, the show was planning a new coliseum.

Always in the fore-rank among the country's livestock shows from the time of its inception in 1907, the Denver show was the setting of impressive displays of Hereford and Aberdeen-Angus cattle. During the war, competition for quarter horses was introduced. These classes developed into one of the principal features of the show. Quarter horses vied for top interest with the perennially popular Hereford; huge ringside crowds followed both of these events.

Denver is also famed for its huge exhibitions of commercial feeder cattle, shown, judged and sold in carload units, as well as for its purebred beef bulls, also exhibited in carlots. These continued to be featured in the stock yards proper; this phase of the show was established as a source of supply of top quality cattle in feeder flesh for cornbelt fattening and for quality bulls for range use. It also remained the setting of one of the largest purebred Hereford cattle sales of the year, an event highlighted in 1945 by the sale of two bulls at $50,000 each. Following the sale, the bulls were brought to the Brown Palace hotel and led into the lobby on the occasion of a banquet.

A Texas show which grew to national note during the decade 1937–46 was the Houston Live Stock show—a January event featuring both beef and dairy exhibits.

Prior to 1941, the Pacific International Livestock exposition at Portland, Ore., the American Royal Livestock show in Kansas City, Mo., and the Aksarben Livestock and Horse show in Omaha, Neb., were all of major national rank. During the war, however, competitions were restricted to fat stock only, and on a far smaller scale.

The American Royal—after an interval of four years—returned to its former prewar status as a full exposition in 1946. Staged in a spacious amphitheatre at the Kansas City stock yards, it drew the largest attendance of its history in that year. Its horse shows drew capacity crowds at each performance and its exhibits of purebred Hereford, Aberdeen-Angus and Shorthorn cattle came close to matching the best turnouts of these breeds in prewar times.

The American Royal in 1946 was the focus of national attention and publicity in the sale of its grand champion steer—a white-faced specimen, shown by an Iowa 4-H boy, which far outdistanced in price any other ever sold at any show in the world. In an auction the steer brought $35.50 a pound or a total price of $42,600.

An important west coast sectional show was the Great Western Live Stock show in Los Angeles, Calif., scheduled annually during the first week of December. Added to the list of postwar events in that area was the Grand National Live Stock exposition in the famous Cow Palace in San Francisco, Calif. This show was held Nov. 15–24, 1946—becoming one of the major sectional western events of postwar times.

State fairs occasionally matched some of the winter ex-

Four-year old Aberdeen Angus bull, valued at $100,000, which was named champion for its class at the International Livestock exposition held at Chicago, Ill., in Dec. 1946

positions in the size of their livestock exhibits and exceeded them in displays of farm produce. Shows of this class were forced to shut down completely during the war period, for the most part, after having arrived at a pinnacle of influence in the five years that preceded the war. Almost all fair grounds of importance were taken over by the military.

Despite problems incident to reconditioning of these grounds, most of the major state fairs were again held in 1946 after an average lapse of four years. By comparison with the quality and number of livestock displays that distinguished these shows in the five years prior to war, the exhibits in 1946—particularly of livestock—were under par. This was attributed to high prices of feed, scarcity of farm labour, and the long time required to prepare animals for show. Most of these shows revived on short notice.

The New York state fair, one of the east's largest, and the Kentucky state fair, outstanding for its prewar saddle horse shows, were among the few state fairs that did not reopen in 1946. The Minnesota state fair, noted in prewar times as the largest farm machinery show in the country, was scheduled to reopen in 1946 during the last week of August; but it was cancelled at the last minute because of an unusually severe epidemic of infantile paralysis.

The U.S. leading livestock show for four decades prior to World War II was the International Live Stock Exposition and Horse show in Chicago, Ill. Founded in 1900, it progressed and grew in size and significance each year until 1914 and 1915, when a national epidemic of hoof and mouth disease forced its cancellation. Returning in 1917 on a larger scale than before, the International went on each year through 1941, when it closed at midnight on Dec. 6, a few hours before the attack on Pearl Harbor. Not even the Chicago stock yard fire of May 19, 1934, which destroyed all the show buildings that had housed the International, caused its interruption. The new International amphitheatre was built in less than five months and was ready for the 1934 exposition to go on as scheduled.

Meeting in the spring of 1942, the International's board of directors voted to cancel the exposition for the duration of the war in compliance with the request—just issued—of the Office of Defense Transportation that all such shows be curtailed. The signal corps of the army took over the International amphitheatre soon after, and it was occupied by them until Aug. 1, 1946.

Four substitute shows, known as the Chicago Market Fat Stock shows, were held during the first week of December under sponsorship of the Union Stock Yard and Transit company, operators of the Chicago market. Consisting only of the classes for fat cattle—steers, lambs and hogs, shown individually and in carlots—which had formerly made up a major part of the full International Live Stock exposition, there was no added burden to transportation. Exhibits consisted only of animals that would have moved to market anyway, and they served the purpose of sustaining much of the spirit and purpose of the International during the war period. The shows were held in the pens, buildings and sheds of the market place.

The average entry of livestock at the International show for the five year period from 1937 through 1941 was 12,304 animals; the peak year was 1939, with an entry of 13,332. During the wartime market shows, from 1942 through 1945, an average of 5,500 animals were shown each year—the largest series of straight fat stock shows put on in the United States during the war period.

Immediately prior to the 1945 show, the International secured permission from the Office of Price Administration to sell all the animals that had qualified for show purposes above the ceiling prices on all slaughter animals. The action resulted in several record prices. The grand champion steer brought $10 a pound, the grand champion carload of 15 fat steers $2 a pound, or $30,660 for the load, the grand champion wether $3 a pound, and the grand champion barrow $7 a pound.

The "Victory" International Live Stock Exposition and Horse show reopened in the International amphitheatre Nov. 30 through Dec. 7, 1946. Attendance for the week exceeded all past records. The gate was close to 500,000. Visitors came from every state in the union and Canada. Exhibits totalling 10,490 animals, were sent to the show by breeders, feeders, horsemen and farm youths from 35 states and Canada. The value of livestock exhibited was approximately $15,000,000.

The International Junior Live Stock Feeding contest survived the war and the participation of farm boys and girls from 13 states at the 1946 International was 113% greater in terms of the number of animals shown than it was at the last prewar exposition in 1941.

National contests featured at the "Victory" exposition in 1946 were a collegiate livestock judging contest; a junior livestock judging contest, in which state-champion teams of boys of high school age matched their skill in livestock judging in competition for the national title; a collegiate meats judging contest; and the International Grain and Hay show—world's largest competitive farm crops show.

One of the great specialty shows of the United States in prewar years, the National Dairy show, did not survive World War II. Founded at Chicago in 1906, it was held annually in the same setting occupied by the International Live Stock exposition until 1920, when it became an itinerant show. It was last held in Oct. 1941 at Memphis, Tenn. The closest approach to a national show for the dairy interests thereafter was the Dairy Cattle Congress and National Belgian Horse show at Waterloo, Iowa. Forced into suspension for three years of the war, from 1943 through 1945, the congress was reopened in 1946. Despite the inroads of tractors into the draught horse business as a means of farm power, the exhibit of Belgians at Waterloo in 1946 was larger than it was in 1942. Another breed of draught horse staging a strong postwar come back in 1946 was the Percheron. The national show of this breed was held that year in connection with the Indiana state fair at Indianapolis and drew more entries than at the last prewar national show in 1942 at the Minnesota state fair, St. Paul.

The Eastern States exposition—one of the strongest shows of the east from 1937 through 1941, with particular emphasis on dairy breeds, remained a war casualty in 1946.

In Canada, the only show to survive the war years was the Calgary Exhibition and Stampede—a July event that attracted a huge attendance not only from the dominion but from the western United States as well. In 1946, three other Canadian summer shows were restored. These were the Edmonton exhibition, the Saskatoon exhibition, and the Regina Provincial exhibition—all held in July of that year. Another Canadian show returned to the September calendar in the Exposition Provinciale at Quebec; and the Royal Winter fair at Toronto—after a wartime interval of seven years—returned in Nov. 1946, the 25th anniversary year of this event. It was Canada's leading livestock show in 1946. The Canadian National exposition, founded in 1879 at Toronto, was not held after 1940.

Seven years had elapsed since the last of Great Britain's

oldest and longest established livestock shows—the Highland Show of Scotland, and the Royal Agricultural show of England. The Highland celebrated its 108th anniversary in 1939 and the Royal was 98 years old the same year. Neither was revived in 1946. The only show of importance in Great Britain to survive the war period was the annual Perth Show and Sale in Scotland. It featured Shorthorn and Aberdeen-Angus cattle. A world record price for a Shorthorn bull was established at the 1946 Perth show when the champion Shorthorn bull was purchased by a U.S. buyer for 14,500 guineas, or $68,000 by the time of delivery in the United States.

South America's largest show, the Palermo, held annually in August at Buenos Aires, continued without cessation during World War II. It became noted as the world's largest show of Shorthorn cattle. An international exhibition every fifth year, it normally had drawn exhibits from other South American countries and from Great Britain; but because of war conditions and the difficulty of shipping, exhibits at the 1943 international of the Palermo were confined to those from the Argentine and Uruguay. This show also featured Hereford and Angus cattle as well as Holsteins and Guernseys, the two principal dairy breeds of the Argentine. (W. E. O.)

Dogs.—The U.S. canine population increased from around 12,000,000 to 13,000,000 (by estimated figure, in the absence of official statistics, state or federal) during the decade 1937–46.

In 1937 the three largest dog shows, based on number of dogs actually competing, were: Morris and Essex (outdoors at Madison, N.J., discontinued 1942 through 1945, re-

Champion for the second successive year, "My Own Brucie," a black cocker spaniel, was selected from among 2,547 entries of all breeds in the Westminster Kennel club show in New York city Feb. 12, 1941

sumed 1946), 3,500; Westminster (or Garden show), New York city, 2,753; Cleveland, Ohio, 1,300.

Morris and Essex held this lead through 1941, reaching a top in 1939 with 3,862 dogs, the United States' largest all-time show (and edging ahead of Crift's of London, which had held that distinction). Westminster held second through 1941 and then took top place 1942 through 1946 with Morris and Essex second in 1946; Long Beach, Calif., third.

Katonah, N.Y. (discontinued after 1946) was third in 1939 through 1941 with its highest in 1940—1,792 dogs; it was second in 1942 and 1943. Chicago, Ill., discontinued in wartime after 1942 (1,334 dogs), was resumed in 1946, placing fourth.

In 1946 the American Kennel club registered approximately 196,000 dogs, an all-time high, comparing with 84,525 in 1937 (to that date the highest total); 1941 saw a new high, 88,000. The coming of World War II, contrary to fears at the time, did not retard activity in the dog field, since 1942 had 89,100 registrations. This fell to 77,400 in 1944.

An outstanding aspect was that the merry little cocker spaniel led the 112 breeds every year from 1937 through 1946, more than doubling in the latter year its 1937 total of 15,110.

The Boston terrier kept second place for three years, a high of 9,400 in 1937 and in 1940 yielded to the little beagle, which maintained it steadily with an average of 8,000. The Scottish terrier held third in 1937 with 7,700 but went down to sixth as the decade closed in 1946. The fox terrier held between fourth and fifth place, while a wartime surprise was the dachshund, creeping up to fifth place in 1943 with 2,779. The Pekingese held the top billing among the toy dogs, capturing fourth place in 1944 with 2,726, when the collie took fifth.

The world's largest dog, the Saint Bernard Yocub, weighing 247 lb., died in 1938. New breeds admitted to the registry—the barkless African dog, the basenji (as hound); the gray German pointer Weimaraner; and two U.S.-developed breeds, the American water spaniel and the black-and-tan coon hound. The last applicant of the decade was the Irish wheaten terrier, partially recognized.

The smallest dog exhibited was an eight weeks old chihuahua (smallest of all breeds, one lb. up matured, a native Mexican breed), at a match of the Kennel Club of New Jersey, Feb. 23, 1940. (W. Ju.)

Horses.—Public interest in the horse as a show animal was growing steadily at the beginning of the decade 1937–46. While the number of work horses was declining steadily, the popularity of the light horse for riding and racing was demonstrated by the holding of horse shows in connection with county fairs; local riding and hunt clubs; and with all types of livestock exhibitions. Attendance at these shows was positive evidence of the favour of the general public. Estimates placed the total of all types of shows at about 1,000. The American Horse Shows association reported 174 shows in 1938 recognized under its supervision; 187 in 1939; 162 in 1940; and 171 in 1941.

World War II checked the expansion of horse exhibitions, and by 1942 most of the larger annual exhibitions had been cancelled entirely or reduced to very local competitions. Most of the state fairs were closed, and hundreds of small community shows were omitted. Many of the state fairs and other large exhibitions gave up their buildings for military uses as camps or storehouses. Restrictions were put on shipments of horses for show purposes by rail or truck. With general travel restricted, the attendance was comparatively small at such shows as were held.

Important developments under way before the war recess were the growing international competitions of jumping teams. The United States and South American countries were taking a more active place in such competitions; a United States team also competed in London in 1937. A team from Chile won first place at the National Horse show at New York city in Nov. 1938.

Light-gaited horses were popular, and the new walking horse, developed in Tennessee, appeared at several shows. Heavy draught horses, although declining in numbers, were shown at most of the larger horse shows as well as at the general livestock shows.

By 1944 the revival of the shows began, and some new ones were projected. The National Horse show, New York city, was a small exhibition chiefly for juniors. The new Chicago Horse show was held in Dec. 1944 with more than 1,500 entries in 125 classes and was such a success that plans were expanded. At the second Chicago show in 1945, the 1,705 entries in 125 classes attracted 588 animals. In 1945 the American Horse Shows association reported 108 shows held under its auspices, as compared with 62 in 1944. While the former leading shows in the east continued to be restricted, several important exhibitions were held in the west and south, notably at the Kentucky state fair at Churchill Downs; Spokane, Wash.; Los Angeles, Calif.; and Memphis, Tenn.

The state fairs listed more entries for heavy horses as they resumed their normal exhibitions.

In 1946 the National Horse show, New York city, staged a successful revival with a record for entries and attendance. The third Chicago show exceeded the two preceding exhibitions. Kansas City, Mo., St. Louis, Mo., San Francisco, Calif., Portland, Ore., Houston, Tex., and the state fairs all expanded their exhibitions. The revival of the community show of saddle horses and children's ponies was also evident. (J. C. Ms.)

Shvernik, Nikolai Mikhailovich

Shvernik (1888–), soviet statesman, was the son of a St. Petersburg worker. At the age of 14, he became a turner's apprentice in an electrical machine plant. Three years later he joined a revolutionary party and was active in agitating among factory workers. He joined the Bolsheviks and at the outbreak of the Russian Revolution in 1917 was elected chairman of the All-Russian Union of Ordnance Workers. During the civil war, he enlisted in a guerrilla detachment and later held command posts in the new Red army. Returning to trade union work in 1921, he was elected chairman of the metal workers' regional committee in the Donbas; two years later, he was appointed people's commissar of Workers and Peasants Inspection. In 1930 he was elected to head the entire trade union movement in the U.S.S.R. as first secretary of the Central Council of Soviet Trade Unions. He was also chairman of the Council of Nationalities of the supreme soviet, and during World War II was named chairman of the Extraordinary commission investigating axis crimes in the soviet union. Shvernik also became a member of the central committee of the Communist party in the U.S.S.R.

Upon the retirement of President Mikhail Kalinin, who died shortly thereafter, Shvernik's appointment as his successor to the post of chairman of the praesidium of the supreme soviet was announced March 19, 1946.

Siam (Thailand)

A constitutional monarchy, Siam is situated in southeast Asia, bordered by Burma on the north and west, French Indo-China on the north and east and the Malay peninsula on the south. Area: 198,247 sq.mi.; pop. (1937 census): 14,464,489 including *c.* 500,000 Chinese, *c.* 500,000 Indian and Malayan, 60,000 Cambodian and Annamese and 2,000 Europeans; (est. March 1940) 15,717,000. Chief towns (1937 census): Bangkok (cap., 681,214); Chiengmai (544,001); Khonkaen (473,475); Chiengrai (443,476). Language: Siamese. Religion (1937): Buddhists 13,752,091; Mohammedans 626,907; Christians 69,227; others 15,880. Rulers: King Ananda Mahidol, succeeded to the throne on March 2, 1935; reputedly assassinated on June 9, 1946, he was succeeded by his brother Prince Phumiphon Aduldet. Prime ministers: Colonel Phya Phahol Pholphayuha Sena (1935–Dec. 15, 1938); Field Marshal Luang Pibul Songgram (Dec. 15, 1938–July 29, 1944); Major Kuang Kovit Aphaiwong (Aug. 2, 1944–Aug. 17, 1945); Seni Pramoj (Sept. 19, 1945–Jan. 31, 1946); Kuang Kovit Aphaiwong (Jan. 31, 1946–Aug. 21, 1946); Thawan Thamrong Nawasawat (after Aug. 23, 1946).

"Land of the Free."—In June 1939 the Siamese government announced that henceforth its country would be known as Thailand ("Land of the Free"), and this became the keynote to Siamese policy in the years 1937–41, when Siam was emerging as an independent and nationalistic state. In the words of its foreign minister, it had suddenly grown up and become a modern nation, and in the context in which it was used this was no overstatement. In 1936 Siam denounced all its existing treaties and in 1937 signed revised ones with Great Britain, the United States, Japan, Switzerland, France, Belgium, Sweden, Denmark, Norway, Italy, Germany and the Netherlands. These new treaties brought to an end the system of extraterritoriality and gave Siam unrestricted jurisdiction over its own territory, at the same time placing its trade relations with the outside world on a basis of complete equality. The government's economic policy was to foster rice production and existing industries for the greater benefit of the Siamese producer and to develop the country's land, water and air communications to facilitate the exploitation of its natural wealth. In the social field the government laid stress on vocational training and the inculcation of the savings habit among the people. Considerable progress was made in the establishment of a co-operative credit movement.

The government's policy was challenged in Sept. 1938 when an elected member of the Siamese parliament demanded a detailed account of expenditure. Although co-opted members supported the demand, the prime minister refused to supply the information; parliament was dissolved and a general election was held on Nov. 12–15. The cabinet was reconstructed, and Field Marshal Luang Pibul Songgram, leader of the militarist-nationalist movement, was appointed prime minister, combining that office with the ministries of defense and the interior. Shortly before he took office an attempt was made on his life, and in Jan. 1939 a plot was revealed to dethrone the king and restore his uncle, ex-king Prajadhipok.

During the years 1937–39 Siam had embarked on a rearmament program; this, backed by the fact that Japan was spending large sums in Siam, was interpreted by many foreign observers as the development of a sinister friendship between the two countries. At the same time those who knew Siam well were convinced that the strongly nationalistic sentiment and independent nature of the Siamese made this unlikely; there was certainly no evidence of anti-European feeling among Siamese in responsible positions. On his appointment Pibul announced a policy of strongly defended neutrality.

War with Vichy.—On the outbreak of war in Europe in Sept. 1939 Siam proclaimed its neutrality and in June 1940 signed nonaggression pacts with Great Britain, France and Japan. The pact with France, however, remained unratified, and on Sept. 6 Siam opened diplomatic negotiations with the Vichy government for rectification of the frontier with French Indo-China in the Savannakhet region, cession of parts of western Laos, retrocession of Battamberg and Siem-Reap provinces and an assurance that if Japan seemed likely to force French withdrawal from Indo-China the entire states of Laos and Cambodia should be ceded. These demands, historically justifiable, if opportunist, were rejected by Vichy; they were repeated and again rejected. On Oct. 18 popular demonstrations for the use of force were made in Siam and French and Siamese troops began massing at the frontier. On Nov. 23 Siamese troops were reported to have crossed the border and fighting began. Border warfare continued throughout December but on Jan. 23, 1941, a Japanese offer of mediation was accepted by the French, and hostilities ceased five days later. At the peace conference which opened in Tokyo on Feb. 7, Japan proposed a much larger cession of French territory than Siam had originally demanded and, by the terms of the treaty signed on May 9, France ceded the districts of Paklay and Bassac and the larger part of Cambodia; Siam agreed to pay France 6,000,000 piastres in six annual instalments. In two protocols to the agreement, France and Siam agreed that any future dispute should be mediated by Japan.

Japanese Occupation.—Japan's declaration of war on Great Britain and the United States emphasized Siam's position as a buffer state between two great powers and made its oft-repeated policy of independent neutrality untenable. In Nov. 1941 the premier was given absolute authority for a period of 12 months and defense preparations were made. The official radio meanwhile tried to calm the fears of the Siamese that their country would become a battleground for the British and Japanese. By Dec. 5 the Japanese had long-range bombers and 60,000 troops in Indo-China. On Dec. 9 Japanese troops entered Siam and met with practically no resistance; on Dec. 21, 1941, a ten-year treaty of alliance was signed at Bangkok. Siam declared war on Great Britain and the United States on Jan. 25, 1942, and soon afterward recognized the puppet Wang Ching-wei regime in China. Riots followed the declaration of war and were again reported in August, but the only effect of any effort to assert independence was an increase of Japanese control. In Oct. 1942 the powers of the national assembly were transferred to Pibul's puppet government for the duration.

Economically Siam was now thrown on its own resources, which were in any case being steadily milked by the Japanese. The currency was drastically devalued in terms of yen, which made the worth of the Japanese loan of 200,000,000 yen, negotiated in June 1942, more apparent than real. The strategic value of Siam to the Japanese in the Burma campaign was increased by the building of the Siam "railway of death" as it came to be known, connecting southern Siam with Burma. This railway was begun by the Japanese in Nov. 1942 and completed in Sept. 1943, and is said to have cost the lives of some 16,000 Allied prisoners and more than 150,000 Asiatics. (It was announced in Oct. 1946 that the Siamese government was to buy for £1,250,000 that part of the Burma-Siam railway built with prisoner-of-war labour.)

Siamese troops proclaimed a victory in the Shan states area of Burma in Jan. 1943, and the two Shan states and the four northern Malay states of Perlis, Kedah, Kelantan and Trengganu were formally transferred by the Japanese to Siam on July 5, 1943. These transfers were not recognized by the British government or regarded by it as permanent. Territorial gains were accompanied by a tightening of the Japanese grip and an increasingly totalitarian regime. For instance, betel-chewing, a universal habit among the Siamese, was banned; innumerable irksome governmental orders were made. Prime Minister Pibul was now openly called a quisling, and in July 1944 he and his government resigned, to be succeeded on Aug. 2 by Major Kuang Aphaiwong, one of the original supporters of the democratic revolution. Under the leadership of Aphaiwong and the Regent Pridi Panomyong, better known to the world as Luang Pradit, Siam now pursued a policy of non-co-operation with the Japanese, while the resistance movement sponsored by the Allied Southeast Asia Command, though never given the chance to prove itself openly, gave considerable help to the Allies.[1]

King Phumiphon Aduldet of Siam (wearing glasses), who succeeded to the throne under a regency council in 1946. He is shown approaching the throne room at the palace in Bangkok to attend funeral services for his brother, King Ananda Mahidol, who died of a bullet wound on June 9

[1]*The Times* of London in an account published on Dec. 22, 1945, was the first to tell the true story of the part played during the war by Pridi Panomyong. Lord Mountbatten of Burma, former supreme Allied commander, Southeast Asia Command, speaking in London on Dec. 17, 1946, elaborated in detail the account of *The Times*. He disclosed many details about the "unique relationship" of an Allied supreme commander exchanging vital military plans with the head of a state technically at war with the United Nations.

Peace with Britain.—On Aug. 16, 1945, Siam repudiated its declaration of war on Great Britain and the United States, but the repudiation was rejected by Britain as unconstitutional. After prolonged discussion and consultation with the United States a peace treaty was signed between Great Britain and India and Siam (after Sept. 7, 1945, officially known as Siam once more) on Jan. 1, 1946. Under its terms Siam agreed to return all acquisitions of British territory, to provide 1,500,000 tons of rice for Asia, to take part in regional security arrangements in southeast Asia under the provisions of the United Nations charter and to undertake that no canal linking the Gulf of Siam with the Indian ocean would be cut across Siamese territory without the prior concurrence of the British government. Agreement was also reached on future economic collaboration, Siam undertaking to observe the treaty of commerce of 1937 pending the signature of a new commercial treaty, and agreeing not to exclude British commercial or industrial interests from participation in Siam's economy and trade "on grounds of nationality." It also agreed to participate in any general international arrangement regarding tin or rubber, to prohibit exports except under the direction of the Combined Boards and to regulate trade and stimulate production of rice, tin, rubber and tea. Siam was slow in producing the agreed quota of rice in 1946, partly because of the difficulties of transporting it from the interior, partly because it now represented the country's only asset. Inducements made by the Siamese government to merchants did, however, speed up deliveries.

Siam: *Statistical Data*

Item	1938 Value (000's omitted)	1938 Amount or Number	1940 Value (000's omitted)	1940 Amount or Number
Exchange rate				
United States		1 baht or tical =44.44 cents		1 baht or tical =34.81 cents
Great Britain		11 ticals=£1		11 ticals=£1
Finance				
Government revenues	$44,904 (£9,185)		$45,890 (£11,982)	
Government expenditures	$44,900 (£9,184)		$45,899 (£11,984)	
Gold reserves	...		$32,049 (£8,368)	
National debt	$34,502 (£7,057)		$25,510 (£6,661)	
Transportation				
Railroads		1,925 mi.		
Highways		1,815 "		
Airways		444 "		
Communication				
Telegraph lines		5,784 "		
Radio sets		29,834		
Minerals				
Tin		16,468 tons		
Tungsten		553,355 lb.		
Gold		13,804 oz.		
Crops				
Rice		5,021,754 tons		
Peas		16,075 "		
Tobacco		8,854 "		
Cotton		7,808 "		
Livestock				
Bullocks		5,711,720		
Buffaloes		5,551,232		
Horses		385,565		
Forest products				
Teak wood*	$4,050 (£828)	73,458 tons	$3,083 (£805)	...
Yang wood*	$106 (£22)	...	...	...
Exports—total	$75,338 (£15,410)	...		
Rice and rice products	$33,489 (£6,850)	1,215,000 tons		
Tin and tin ore	$16,681 (£3,412)	24,000 "		
Rubber, waste and substitutes	$10,076 (£2,061)	37,000 "		
Teak	$4,050 (£828)	73,000 "		
Imports—total	$49,705 (£10,167)	...		
Cotton textile manufactures	$8,327 (£1,703)	...		
Provisions and foodstuffs	$5,661 (£1,158)	...		
Mineral oil	$4,924 (£1,007)	...		
Iron and steel manufactures	$4,044 (£827)	...		
Defense				
Standing army personnel		30,000		...
Standing navy personnel		...		5,078
Standing air force personnel		...		30,000
Military expenditures	$12,001 (£2,455)			
Education				
Government schools		429†		
Students		61,297†		
Local public and municipal schools		11,072†		
Students		1,484,483†		
Universities		2†		
Students		11,525‡		

*Exports only. †1939. ‡1937.

French Dispute.—Disturbances on the Indo-Chinese border added to Siam's postwar difficulties. The French government did not recognize the cession of territory by Vichy, and in the early months of 1946, efforts were made to arrange a conference which would formally end the state of war between France and Siam and restore the disputed territory. The situation was complicated by the presence of armed bands of refugee Annamites hostile to France on the Siam side of the border, and the fact that French frontier police were constantly crossing the frontier in pursuit of guerrilla troops. On May 24 the Siamese government reported that about 800 French troops had crossed the Mekong, and on June 1 made a formal protest to the United Nations against French activities, appealed for sympathy and assistance and at the same time asked for admission to membership of the United Nations. On the same day the French government requested the United States and Great Britain to draw the attention of the Siamese government to the fact that Siam had not yet returned the territories of Laos and Cambodia acquired in 1941. On July 16 Siam asked that the situation be brought before the Security council as one threatening the maintenance of peace. So diverse were French and Siamese reports of the situation that it was generally felt that even if the threat to world peace was an exaggeration it would be well if the whole matter were ventilated in the Security council. Siam, however, requested a postponement of the discussion, and negotiations instituted by France on Aug. 1 for bringing the case before the International Court of Justice were also broken off. On Oct. 15 the Siamese parliament, after heated debate, endorsed the government's decision to return disputed territory (nearly 44,000 sq.-mi. in extent) to Indo-China. A Franco-Siamese agreement providing for the return was signed at Washington on Nov. 17, 1946; diplomatic relations were restored; Siam withdrew its complaint to the Security council and France its opposition to the admission of Siam to the United Nations.

King's Death.—On June 9, 1946, the young king Ananda Mahidol was found dead in his bedroom from a gunshot wound. An official statement issued by the Siamese legation in London said that his death could be presumed to be an accident "as a result of his Majesty having handled a gun according to the royal inclination and habit." A commission aided by a committee of 19 medical members was appointed to inquire into his death, and on July 2 an official police statement declared that 12 out of the 19 members reported that murder was the most likely explanation. Prince Phumiphon Aduldet, 18-year-old brother of the late king, was unanimously selected by the legislature to succeed to the throne, and a council of regency was appointed.

BIBLIOGRAPHY.—K. P. Landon, *Siam in Transition* (1939) and *The Chinese in Thailand* (1941); V. M. Thompson, *Thailand: the New Siam* (1941); R. Emerson, L. A. Mills and V. M. Thompson, *Government and Nationalism in South-East Asia* (1942); H. G. Deignan, *Siam: Land of Free Men* (1943); B. Lasker, *Peoples of South East Asia* (1944); Sir Josiah Crosby, *Siam: Past and Future* (London, 1945). (J. RA.)

Siberia

See UNION OF SOVIET SOCIALIST REPUBLICS.

Sierra Leone

See BRITISH WEST AFRICA.

Sikorski, Wladyslaw

Sikorski (1881–1943), Polish politician and army officer, was born May 20, 1881, in Tyszowce Narodovy, Austrian Galicia, and studied engineering at the Lwów University Technical college, graduating in 1908. One of the leaders of the nationalist movement in Poland, he was trained in the Austrian army, 1905–06, commanded a regiment of the Polish legions in World War I and fought in the Polish-Russian conflict, 1920. After the assassination of Polish Pres. H. Narutowicz in Dec. 1922, Gen. Sikorski, then chief of the general staff, was made premier and interior minister, remaining in office until Dec. 1923. He served as war minister, 1924–25, then returned to army service as commander of the Lwów military area. His dismissal from the army in 1928 was only one of the many personal changes effected by Marshal Joseph Pilsudski in the civil and army administrations after he took power. Sikorski subsequently went to France, where he wrote extensively on political and military matters. At the outbreak of the war with Germany in Sept. 1939, his request for an assignment to active service was refused. After the collapse of Poland, however, he became premier of the Polish government-in-exile; in addition, he was made commander in chief of the Polish legions that fought on battlegrounds in France, Britain and the middle east. Politically, he mended his fences with the Czechoslovak government-in-exile, but ran into a snag on the issue of relations with the U.S.S.R. On June 23, 1941, Gen. Sikorski secured an agreement with Moscow which invalidated the Soviet-German pact partitioning Poland in 1939. But dissatisfied with the conduct of anti-soviet elements within the Sikorski cabinet, the U.S.S.R. ruptured diplomatic relations in April 1943. Sikorski's continued efforts to mend relations with the soviet union were interrupted by his death in a plane crash, July 4, 1943, while he was en route from Gibraltar to London.

Silesia

Of this former Prussian province, the eastern part of Upper Silesia was ceded to Poland as a result of the plebiscite of June 15, 1922. It was organized as a province, Slask, with an area of 1,633 sq.mi. and a population of 1,124,967 with the capital Katowice (Kattowitz), pop. 134,000 (1939 est.). After the defeat of Germany in World War II, all the remaining parts of Prussian Silesia passed under Polish administration. This Polish acquisition consisted of the Upper Silesian district of Oppeln with an area of 3,750 sq.mi. and a population of 1,379,408; the Lower Silesian district of Liegnitz with an area of 5,257 sq.mi. and a population of 1,235,093; and the Lower Silesian district of Breslau with an area of 5,019 sq.mi. and a population of 1,897,172.

The province of Silesia included, in addition to great industrial wealth and natural resources, some of Germany's principal towns, like Breslau (1939 pop. 615,006), Hindenburg (126,402) and Beuthen (100,644). In 1946 the German population was everywhere being replaced by Polish settlers. Under Polish administration Silesia was divided into three provinces: Lower Silesia with the capital at Wroclaw (Breslau), Middle Silesia with the capital at Opole (Oppeln) and Upper Silesia with the capital at Katowice (Kattowitz). The German University of Breslau, (established 1702 and united in 1811 with the ancient University of Frankfurt-on-Oder, founded 1506) was reopened as a Polish university in Breslau. A small part of the province of Silesia, especially the territory around Kladsko (Glatz) and Ratibor (Raciborz), was claimed by Czechoslovakia. (H. Ko.)

BIBLIOGRAPHY.—G. Kaeckenbeeck, *International Experiment of U. Silesia* (1942); S. Kudlicki, *U. Silesia* (1944); *Oberschlesischer Heimatkalender* (Breslau, ann.).

Silk

The last of the golden days of the silk industry coincided almost exactly with the decade 1937–46. In those ten years the use of silk declined to the point of complete obliteration in 1941, when the Japanese embarked on a world war that meant severance of the last remaining ties between the world's largest silk producer and the world's largest silk consumer, the United States, and the cutting off of supplies to other silk-consuming countries. At first the decline was not apparent to many students of silk consumption, because the U.S. hosiery industry was using an increasing amount and there was still a substantial use in French, Italian, British and U.S. fine fabrics for women's underwear, men's neckwear and the high-style dress fabrics of both France and the United States. But the turn had come earlier. In 1933, U.S. fabric manufacturers had indicated to their Japanese suppliers that silk was no longer of substantial importance to them. The peak of silk consumption in the United States came in 1931. By 1937, the imports were the lowest since 1924. When the last normal trading year, 1940, arrived, imports were down to 1919 levels. Except for silk used for war materials, and already stocked in the respective countries, imports of raw silk were nominal until 1946, when U.S. military authorities opened the sale of Japanese raw silk to the world through public sale by the United States Commercial company, a government selling agency operating under the Reconstruction Finance corporation in Washington, D.C.

Table I.—*Imports of Raw Silk into the United States*

	Quantity (millions of pounds)	Value (millions of dollars)
1937	57.8	106.6
1938	55.2	88.8
1939	51.6	120.9
1940	44.8	124.9
1941	23.1	61.8
1942	25.6	72.5
1943	.2	.4
1944	nominal	nominal
1945	1.7	1.2
1946	11.9*	113.9

*Estimated.

Brazilian Silk Bubble.—A slight flurry was caused in 1945 by imports from Brazil, which saw in the elimination of Japan as well as China during World War II, an opportunity to enter the supposedly lucrative U.S. silk market. Japanese workers on farms in southern Brazil, primarily around São Paulo, had long held ambitions to become a new source of supply, but the price of the reeled silk and

Table II.—*Consumption of Raw Silk in U.S. 1936–39 compared with 1929*
(Millions of Pounds and Percent of total)

	1929		1936		1937		1938		1939	
Hosiery	22.2	27.3%	27.0	46.7%	35.0	65.3%	37.4	72.2%	38.4	81.2%
Broad goods, etc. . . .	59.1	72.7%	30.8	53.3%	18.6	34.7%	14.4	27.8%	8.9	18.8%
	81.3	100%	57.8	100%	53.6	100%	51.8	100%	47.3	100%

the uncertainty of available supplies as well as quality of workmanship had prevented any buyer interest. As suppliers of a fibre unobtainable elsewhere in the world, however, Brazil found buyers for raw silk at $15 a pound in 1943–45, but the quality was not equal to prewar standards and hosiery manufacturers found it impracticable. Its only use was in dress fabrics that were four times the price of prewar fabrics and of a quality that found much to be desired. The result was elimination of the Brazilian market, as far as United States imports were concerned, once the Japanese and Chinese silk reappeared in 1946. Brazil, however, was reported to be planning domestic manufacture of the fibre for export to other South American countries who found it difficult to buy sufficient textiles in a clothes-hungry world.

Consumers.—The sharp decrease in silk imports between 1940 and 1941 was due primarily to the introduction of nylon as a yarn for hosiery manufacture. The hosiery makers had been the best customers of the silk-producing countries since 1936, as shown in Table II.

In 1940, when the first nylon hosiery was accepted with much enthusiasm by U.S. women, hosiery manufacturers were using substantially all of the silk imported. By 1941 (during the last six months), 28% of the full-fashioned hosiery for women was nylon, and the writers for radio comedians throughout World War II found nylon hosiery a popular theme for indicating something more precious than gold to feminine listeners. The hosiery market, for this reason, was watched closely by potential suppliers of raw silk, when the Japanese and Chinese markets were again open in 1946. The response was not encouraging, and it was conceded that the silk hosiery field was lost to the synthetic fibres. During 1946, the prices of silk hosiery steadily declined on the retail market. The manufacturers observed this trend, and their purchases of raw silk fell to a minimum by the end of that year.

In reverse, it was the fabric manufacturer who showed the only interest in silk of the postwar era and that, too, was limited. But most merchandising analyses made during 1945 and 1946 as to the future possibilities of silk consumption agreed that the best opportunities lay in the manufacture of luxury type dress and underwear fabrics, as well as the specialty neckwear fabrics. Despite these indications, the dearth of buyers among fabric manufacturers resulted in estimates by Dec. 1946, that silk consumption in the United States would not exceed 10% of prewar imports; and that even the 10% would not be achieved immediately for reasons that were not based primarily on consumer demand.

Consumers were reported by retailers as interested in silk, but it was recommended that prices be decreased to reach any quantity market. Silk dresses in 1946 were selling at $75 and more, compared with 1939–40 prices of $25. Newspaper advertising gave prominence to silk garments but still the manufacturers using raw silk did not respond. The reasons were twofold. First, silk yarn could not be handled as easily as synthetic; it was not as uniform in size of thread as synthetics and did not run through the loom as easily. It required much more preparatory treatment before weaving, could not be used on the high-speed modern automatic looms and required much more manual labour than synthetics. In a time of labour shortages, a fibre with such handicaps was shoved aside in a weaving mill. Second, instability of price plus an artificially high price level reminded manufacturers of past losses caused by rapidly changing market values and were in glaring contrast to the stability in price of rayon, the fibre which had become the chief source of supply to former silk manufacturers.

The Price Problem.—A comparison of price movements in the chief textile fibres during 1937–46 demonstrates the difference between synthetics and natural fibres, including silk (Table III).

Table III.—*Prices of Textile Fibres and Yarns 1937–46*
(Dollars per pound average monthly)

	Raw Silk	Rayon Yarn	Raw Cotton	Wool—Scoured Basis
1937	1.86	.57	.118	1.02
1938	1.69	.62	.089	.70
1939	2.71	.59	.093	.83
1940	2.77	.53	.102	.96
1941	2.94	.54	.139	1.09
1942	nominal	.55	.193	1.19
1943	"	.55	.203	1.18
1944	"	.55	.212	1.19
1945	"	.55	.226	1.18
1946	6.79*	.56	.306	1.03

*July–December only.

From 1936–41, the price of raw silk was largely determined by Japanese dealers who were believed to be closely controlled by their government. When representatives of the Japanese industry first approached their former major customers in 1933, the U.S. fabric manufacturers, regarding support of a program for publicizing silk, one of the chief complaints from the buyers had been the instability of price, which had become highlighted because of the relatively stable rayon prices even at that time. On the other hand, other advisers said that silk must be reinstated as a luxury fibre and therefore the price should not be as close to the rayon prices as current trends indicated. The result was that the price of silk rose slightly for three or four years, then dropped once more for a year, only to rise sharply just before World War II removed it from the scene. At the same time, rayon continued its even way. When silk reappeared, its price was far above the prewar levels. At the first sale on July 1, 1946, the weighted average of prices paid was $9.72 per pound. At the second sale, the average was $7.96 per pound. On Sept. 30, 1946, minimum prices for each grade were established ranging from $6 to $10.50 per pound. At these and subsequent sales, buyers represented the United States, Great Britain, Switzerland, Sweden, Mexico and South America.

Effect of Silk Decline on World Politics.—The fact that the silk market of the world fell apart during the same era in which war was again rampant in its most virulent form offered some interesting comparisons. The close interest of the Japanese government in raw silk prices was claimed to be tied up with policy concerning world diplomatic relationships. When silk prices declined rapidly during the early 30s, it was stated freely in the U.S. market that the Japanese government was subsidizing the Japanese silk merchants in order to build up cash returns and thus enable the government to buy the supplies it needed for gaining world prowess. Silk, constituting the largest single item exported, represented approximately 13% of the total value of exports during the period 1937–40. Observers pointed out that 1941, the year when Japan launched its ambitious plan for world power, was the year when it must have been finally convinced that its hold on world trade through raw silk was gone. This was the end of a ten-year period in which the United States had indicated its growing lack of interest in silk.

When the U.S. military government took stock of Japan's assets for world trade in the fall of 1945, first consideration was given to silk. In October, General Douglas MacArthur issued a directive ordering the Japanese government to furnish figures on stocks and estimated production in which he made clear that the silk industry would have to assume a considerable share of the responsibility for furnishing export commodities acceptable as payment for vital imports. Japanese stocks were estimated to be 46,000 bales, approximately four to six weeks' supply to the United States before 1941. At that time, it was estimated that the value was $18,500,000, or approximately $3 a pound. The first offering of Japanese silk under this plan was in July 1946, when 5,130 bales were offered for sale under sealed bids. During 1946, five more sales were conducted but with decreasing interest from users. At all sales, most of the silk went to dealers who hoped to supply the domestic trade as the yarn was needed. The minimum or "upset" prices also steadily declined, not without anxiety on the part of those responsible for carrying out General MacArthur's plan for Japan's financing.

By the end of 1946, there was serious discussion as to whether Japan could depend upon its silk trade for any substantial part of its support; whether it would be better to discard silk for other agricultural products. At the end of the decade, and the beginning of a new era for the Japanese people, the history of silk was one of a lost cause.

U.S. Silk Raising.—The appearance of new attempts to raise silk in the United States attained substantial publicity during 1942–46. Such attempts were fostered by promised high returns and the absence of customary imports. Congressional committees visited Japan, looking for a supposed superior type of mulberry tree that the Japanese used in order to attain their high production but the committees reported that the Japanese used the ordinary type of mulberry found throughout the United States. Local chambers of commerce vaunted the performance of their particular citizens who had achieved new ways of reducing the cost of breeding the silkworms, reeling the silk, etc. Farmers were invited to share in the potential profits by buying mulberry cuttings and silkworm eggs to rear the cocoons from which raw silk is obtained. For an additional sum, some of the promoters offered to sell wonder-working machines which would reduce the cost of reeling the silk, almost entirely a manual process. Estimates of profits were based on published figures of consumption and imports for the period 1931–41 and at prices that were being currently quoted for Brazilian silk, $12 a pound. But by the end of 1946, no reports had been published as to any commercial production of silk from those sources, and domestic users stated that they had no expectation of receiving any. (*See also* RAYON AND OTHER SYNTHETIC FIBRES; TEXTILE INDUSTRY.)

BIBLIOGRAPHY.—*Textile Organon* (New York); Department of Commerce publications; *New York Times; Daily News Record* (New York); *Raw Silk on the American Market*, The Chase National Bank (New York); U.S. Commercial Company, Washington, D.C., announcements of raw silk sales; *Silk Journal & Rayon World* (Manchester, England).

(I. L. BL.)

Silver

In general, gold and silver continued to be closely associated in nature during the decade 1937–46. and few countries produced appreciable quantities of one unaccompanied by the other; silver usually took precedence in amount, but in a few cases gold predominated, as with several of the African producers. The production of silver was so widely scattered, with so many producers of small amounts, that complete world production could not be determined. Producers of more than 1,000,000 oz. a year, as listed in Table I, accounted for about 95% of the world total, while much of the remainder was covered by the unknown soviet output.

World silver production, unlike that of gold, suffered a severe decline during the depression years of the early 1930s, caused mostly by the relatively larger amounts of silver recovered as a by-product from the base metals, and partly by declines in countries like Mexico, where silver output greatly outranked that of gold. By 1937, world production had recovered to better than the predepression level, only to meet another heavy cut in the recession of 1938, which extended into 1939. The 1940 total came back to the 1937 high, but subsequently war conditions began to show their effects, with successive reductions of output each year.

When gold production was officially restricted in the United States and Canada, silver was likewise affected. In addition, producers everywhere were hampered by shortages of labour, equipment and supplies, and by increasing costs. Total output had shrunk by one-third in 1944, with further declines in 1945.

United States.—After the recession of 1938, silver production in the United States recovered slowly and in 1941 had not yet reached the 1937 level. In 1942 shortages of labour and equipment, coupled with governmental restriction of gold production, began to take a heavy toll on output, and by 1945 the accumulated losses from year to year had reduced the year's total 59% below that of 1941. Even

Table I.—*World Production of Silver*
(Thousands of fine ounces)

	1937	1938	1939	1940	1941	1942	1943	1944	1945
United States	71,299	61,689	63,872	68,287	71,076	55,860	40,874	35,651	29,332
Canada	22,978	22,219	23,164	23,834	21,754	20,695	17,345	13,627	12,867
Newfoundland	1,448	1,664	1,421	1,494	1,657	1,106	1,259	1,163	1,076
Mexico	84,681	81,019	75,871	82,640	78,364	84,865	76,633	65,460	61,098
Honduras	3,210	3,335	4,214	3,902	3,528	3,484	3,164	3,115	3,003
Argentina	2,122	2,636	4,772	3,713	2,918	2,844	?	?	?
Bolivia (Exp.)	9,454	6,374	7,241	5,626	7,349	8,121	7,300	6,798	6,684
Chile	1,855	1,376	1,181	1,516	1,242	1,317	1,094	1,095	?
Peru	17,453	20,553	18,802	19,366	15,119	16,035	14,660	15,832	16,082
Czechoslovakia	1,103	1,190	805	870	805	740	740	675	?
Germany	6,774	7,010	6,393	6,208	5,691	5,642	?	?	?
Sweden	946	1,124	1,123	762	761	986	862	1,048	923
Yugoslavia	2,243	2,524	2,294	?	?	?	?	?	?
Belgian Congo	3,962	3,122	2,800	3,537	3,472	3,955	3,113	2,609	2,500
South Africa	1,101	1,135	1,183	1,292	1,483	1,478	1,334	1,213	?
Burma	6,180	5,920	6,807	6,057	5,937	1,225	?	?	?
Japan	9,902	10,100	10,100	13,225	13,523	13,012	6,377	5,029	?
Philippines	720	1,168	1,350	1,299	1,260	231	26	?	?
Australia	14,293	14,589	15,320	15,872	15,413	14,242	10,330	9,367	9,400
Total	277,718	267,676	266,902	275,387	261,566	247,749	217,041	186,200	?

Table II.—*Data of the Silver Industry in the United States*
(Thousands of fine ounces or dollars)

	1937	1938	1939	1940	1941	1942	1943	1944	1945
Production (mine)	64,363	61,706	64,373	70,549	67,259	54,091	41,461	34,474	29,024
Imports	$91,877	$230,531	$85,307	$58,434	$47,053	$41,103	$27,903	$23,373	$27,278
Exports	$12,042	$7,082	$14,630	$3,674	$5,673	$1,999	$30,689	$126,915	90,937
Industrial use	51,292	38,620	69,585	67,063	92,794	131,419	162,113	176,289	184,661
Secondary recovery	23,565	18,439	24,972	22,564	20,361	30,021	44,113	56,189	58,361
Net consumption	27,727	20,182	44,613	44,499	72,432	101,399	118,000	120,100	126,300
Treasury stocks*					2,872	2,838	2,687	2,345	2,005

*Millions of ounces.

after the gold limitation order was rescinded on July 1, 1945, production continued to decline, not reaching a minimum until Feb. 1946, when the month's mine output was 1,637,091 oz., a third lower than the average rate for 1945. By Oct. 1946, the monthly total had increased to 2,073,079 oz., and the total for the 10 months was 17,178,176 oz.; this figure was equivalent to an annual rate of 20,414,000 oz., well below that of 1945.

The war era of decreasing output was paralleled by decreased imports of foreign silver, while at the same time industrial uses of silver expanded at such a rate as to create a definite shortage of supply. Much of this shortage was met by the sale of metal from U.S. treasury stocks which had not yet been incorporated into the monetary system. In addition to these sales of free silver, the treasury loaned thousands of tons of its silver reserve to government-owned aluminum and magnesium plants for use in making bus bars to carry the heavy currents required, thus saving large amounts of copper, the supply of which was critically short at the time these plants were built. A considerable proportion of the loaned silver was returned to the treasury, and eventually all of it would be.

Canada.—Although there was a pronounced decline in silver production in Canada, output was maintained much better than in the United States. After reaching a peak in 1940, production declined only 9% in 1941 and 5% in 1942; war restrictions then became more pronounced, with declines of 16% in 1943 and 21% in 1944, tapering off to 9% in 1945. Altogether, the drop was 46% from the high of 1940. Postwar recovery brought an output of 12,778,218 oz. in 1946, 1% less than in 1945.

Mexico.—Except for occasional off years, Mexico had been the world's largest producer of silver for the preceding 50 years, though during much of the time the margin above the United States was not great. As in the United States, the recession of 1938 cut production heavily, with recovery so slow that the war peak of 1942 barely surpassed the 1937 level. Subsequent output declined but in 1945 was only 28% below the 1942 peak.

Other Countries.—Data were still incomplete from several countries where the producing areas had been involved in the fighting zones or had been subject to axis occupation, chiefly Germany, Yugoslavia, Burma and the Philippines. Other producers in this category were so small that their output did not greatly affect the world totals. (*See* also MINERAL AND METAL PRODUCTION AND PRICES.) (G. A. RO.)

BIBLIOGRAPHY.—L. Addicks, *Silver in Industry* (1940); R. H. Leach, "Uses of Silver in Wartime," *Mining and Metallurgy* 23:456-8, (Sept. 1942); "Silver in Peace and War," *Scientific American* 169:151-3 (Oct. 1943); U.S. Bureau of Mines, *Minerals Yearbook*.

Simeon II

King Simeon of Bulgaria (1937–) was born June 16, 1937. On Aug. 28, 1943, Simeon's father, King Boris, died under mysterious circumstances—it was variously reported that his death was due to a heart attack, poisoning or shooting—and six-year-old Simeon ascended the throne. In Sept. 1943, Prince Cyril, Boris' brother; Lt. Gen. Nikola Michov, former war minister; and Bogdan Philoff, former premier, formed a regency to rule Bulgaria in the king's name until Simeon reached his majority. All three of the regents were executed Feb. 1, 1945, as enemies of the regime and as collaborators with the Germans, and on Sept. 8, 1946, the Bulgarians voted the monarchy out of existence. Simeon and his mother, Queen Ioanna, left Bulgaria on Sept. 17, 1946, and went into exile in Alexandria, Egypt.

Simovitch, Dushan

Simovitch (1882–), Yugoslav statesman and army officer, was born in Kragujevac, Serbia. A graduate of the military academy in Belgrade (1900), he entered the army with the rank of a lieutenant of artillery and was a major on the general staff during World War I. After the war, he was chief of staff (1919–27) of the 3rd and 4th Yugoslav armies and later took charge of the army's mechanized instruction schools in Sarajevo. In 1938 he was appointed commanding general of the Yugoslav air force. Gen. Simovitch engineered the coup in March 1941 which led to the overthrow of Premier Dragicha Cvetkovitch's pro-axis government which had signed a pact with Germany and Italy.

Simovitch became premier of the new pro-Allied government, which repudiated the pact, proclaimed the end of the regency and installed young Peter II as active monarch of Yugoslavia. Following Germany's crushing defeat of Yugoslav arms in April 1941, Simovitch fled with Peter to Jerusalem and then to London, where the Yugoslav government-in-exile was set up. In early 1942, Simovitch was replaced as prime minister of the government-in-exile by Slobodan Yovanovitch.

At the height of the rivalry between the exiled regime and the Tito movement, Simovitch came out with a judicious appeal (May 19, 1944) recommending that King Peter form a government composed of all parties, including representatives of the partisans. In the same speech, he swung away from the monarchy by praising Marshal Tito's fight against the axis. After the war, Simovitch returned to Yugoslavia. Testifying at the trial of Gen. Draja Mikhailovitch in Belgrade, he declared June 28, 1946, that the defendant, far from being pro-German, was pro-British.

Simpson, Mrs. Wallis

See WINDSOR, DUCHESS OF.

Simpson, William Hood

Simpson (1888–), U.S. army officer, was born May 19, 1888, at Weatherford, Tex. A graduate of the U.S. Military academy at West Point (1909), he served in the Philippines (1910–12), in the Mexican campaign (1916) and as a divisional chief of staff with the U.S. forces in France (1918–19). After studying at various army institutions, he became an instructor in military science and tactics, teaching at the Army War college, 1936–40. Following the outbreak of World War II, Simpson held several command posts. He was made commanding general of the 4th army on Sept. 28, 1943, and a lieutenant general the same month.

In the early phase of the fighting in France in 1944, Gen. Simpson led the attack on German-held Brest. On Sept. 13, 1944, it was disclosed that he was in command of the 9th U.S. army on the western front. The following November the 9th army went into action as Gen. Dwight D. Eisenhower launched a general offensive on the western front. Simpson's 9th army was in the thick of the Ardennes battle, and participated in the cleanup of the Ruhr and the Rhineland in 1945.

Announcement of Simpson's presence in China in July 1945 lent weight to reports that the U.S. 9th army, the only force definitely scheduled for redeployment to the Pacific, might be shipped to that theatre, but the war ended before the 9th could get into action.

Sinclair, Sir Archibald

Sir Archibald Sinclair (1890–), British politician, was born Oct. 22, 1890, in London. He was educated at Eton and Sandhurst and joined the army in 1910, but later resigned to enter politics. Elected to commons in 1922 as Liberal member for Caithness and Sutherland, he was chief Liberal whip, 1930–31, and served as secretary of state for Scotland, 1931–32. After the party split over the issue of joining the Stanley Baldwin government, Sinclair became leader of the Independent Liberals. When Winston Churchill formed his wartime coalition cabinet in May 1940, he made Sir Archibald secretary of state for air. A year later, when the R.A.F. intensified its raids over Germany, the air minister warned the reich that it would be bombed "night after night until the German people, shattered and disillusioned, decide for the second time that war is not worth while." The R.A.F. more than kept the promise. After dissolution of the coalition wartime cabinet on May 23, 1945, Sir Archibald was not reappointed to his post as secretary of state for air, which passed on to the hands of Harold Macmillan.

Singapore

See Malayan Union.

Sinkiang (Chinese Turkestan)

Largest and most remote of the provinces of China, Sinkiang has an area of 705,769 sq.mi. and a population of 3,700,000.

From the days of legend, beyond the recall of written chronicles, the history of Sinkiang has swung in cycles of terrifying violence and seductive peace. In 1937 an evanescent quiet was settling over the oases of the desert land. The remnant bands of the Moslem uprising of the early 1930s were being finally liquidated, while in the capital, Tihwa, a Chinese governor, Sheng Shih-tsai, made firm his grip on power with the aid of the soviet union.

The alliance between Sheng Shih-tsai and the soviet union had been born of necessity four years before. Sheng, leader of the Chinese minority—5% of the province's population—had been isolated by a rebellion of the overwhelmingly Moslem majority. The central government of China, nominal suzerain of the province of Sinkiang, had been unable to succour him from disaster. The soviet union, immediately across the border in central Asia, had been alarmed itself by the Moslem uprising, which seemed to the soviets a menacing form of Japanese intrigue. When invited by Sheng to assist in crushing the uprising, the soviets moved to his rescue with troops, airpower and materials.

Having thoroughly crushed the uprising by 1937, Sheng proceeded to reorganize the social structure of the province under soviet tutelage. A broad policy of racial tolerance was made part of governmental principle. Improved seed strains and livestock were imported from the soviet union, while village schools were fostered till their number multiplied by 20 during the course of the decade. Taxes were slashed to a fraction of those that prevailed in China proper. Highways were laid down, hospitals established, the Moslem clergy sharply restricted in its activity.

The program of social reconstruction was paralleled by a political program of harshest regimentation. Government censors rigidly suppressed all independent expression of opinion, concentration camps of the cruelest sort were established for dissidents and the secret police of the provincial government won a reputation for spectacular ferocity that coursed from end to end of Asia.

The provincial government was bound by closest ties to the soviet union. A loan of 5,000,000 gold roubles stabilized the chaotic provincial currency, soviet troops garrisoned the town of Hami against attack from China proper while soviet advisers infiltrated key government bureaus. The oil resources of the province were opened in 1939 as a joint soviet-provincial enterprise. So close had relations become that by the summer of 1939, Gov. Sheng himself applied for permission to join the Communist party and was refused.

Soon after 1939 the emotional and political ties that had bound Sheng to the soviet union began to wither. By 1941 relations between Sheng and the U.S.S.R. were under great strain, and the compulsions that had brought them together no longer obtained. Sheng, on the one hand, no longer feared the Moslems who had been crushed, and the benefits he enjoyed from trade with the soviet ceased when the German invasion concentrated all soviet production on war. The soviet union, on the other hand, no longer needed Sheng as an ally on its flank, for it was now allied with the central government of China itself.

In the spring of 1942 the younger brother of Sheng Shih-tsai was assassinated in the provincial capital. The Chinese communists charged that he was murdered by Sheng. Sheng claimed that the murder was committed by the communists. Whatever the truth of the matter, Sheng made the incident pretext for a complete breach with the soviet union. He invited the Chinese central government to reenter the province, which it did, and by the fall of 1943 soviet influence had apparently vanished.

In the summer of 1944 native discontent again made itself manifest, breaking out in a revolt against the Chinese authorities in the Ili valley. The central government of China deposed Sheng, brought him to Chungking and attempted to placate the rebels by political concessions. In 1946 the Chinese government was still engaged in the political pacification of the turbulent Moslems, but dispatches from the interior of Asia gave little indication of what success was being achieved. (T. H. We.)

Bibliography.—*China Handbook 1937–43,* (1943); A. Kamel, *Land Without Laughter* (1940); E. Lattimore, "Report on Sinkiang," *Far Eastern Survey,* 14:77–79 (April 11, 1945); M. R. Norins, *Gateway to Asia* (1944).

Sino-Japanese War

See World War II.

Sinuses

See Ear, Nose and Throat, Diseases of.

Sister Kenny Treatment

See Infantile Paralysis.

Six-Day Bicycle Racing

See Cycling.

Sjahrir, Sutan

Sjahrir (1910?), Indonesian statesman and politician, joined the Indonesian Socialist party and refused to collaborate with the Japanese during their occupation of the Netherlands Indies, 1942–45. His anti-Japanese stand made him more acceptable than Soekarno (*q.v.*) to the British and Dutch when the latter returned to the East Indies after Japan's surrender in 1945. Thus, in Nov. 1945, at the height of the Indonesian revolt, Sjahrir became premier. He overhauled the cabinet, assuming the portfolios of foreign minister and home minister for himself and ousted from office all but one of Soekarno's cabinet appointees.

Sjahrir resigned in late Feb. 1946 over a dispute with opposition members who wanted him to form a more representative cabinet, but winning a vote of confidence in the national committee, he was renamed premier on March 2, and formed a new government, March 12. On June 29, it was disclosed that Sjahrir and five members of his cabinet had been kidnapped by an armed band. Sjahrir was released July 1 and he later disclosed that he had been kidnapped by troops of his army who thought he was a Dutch spy. When they finally realized that they had abducted their own premier, they were "dismayed" and released him promptly. The explanations were not taken at face value by some foreign observers in Batavia, who asserted that the kidnapping was staged by Soekarno, who wanted to assume dictatorial power for himself.

After nearly a year of fighting between Indonesian and Dutch forces, Sjahrir and Netherlands officials signed a truce Oct. 14, and the following month (Nov. 15, 1946) Sjahrir initialed a draft plan under which the Netherlands agreed to recognize the Indonesian republic and the latter's claims for equality and freedom.

Skating

See Ice Skating.

Skiing

Of all sports, skiing was perhaps hardest hit by World War II, but it quickly regained its growing popularity in 1946 and promised to reach major status, both among spectators and participants. The ski-train industry, which transported thousands of city folk to snow resorts each winter week end, was eliminated by the transportation problems created by World War II, but started anew in 1946. Proof of the war's effect on skiing came in the 1942 and 1943 Bear mountain jumping classics. In 1942 the event attracted 19,500 fans; in 1943 the war held the crowd to a mere 1,500.

Competitive skiing in the United States was largely dominated by Richard Durrance of Dartmouth college, Alf Engen of Salt Lake City, Utah and Sun Valley, Ida., Arthur Devlin of Syracuse university, the Ruud brothers, Sigmund and Birger, and Torger Tokle, the latter three of Norway. Women's competition was dominated by the Sun Valley duo of Shirley McDonald and Mrs. Gretchen Fraser.

The world jumping record was established in 1938 by Joseph Brandl of Austria, who leaped 350.96 ft. at Planica, Yugoslavia. The U.S. record was extended on seven different occasions during the ten-year period, starting with Engen's jump of 242 ft. in 1937 and climaxed by Tokle's leap of 289 ft. at Iron Mountain, Mich., in 1942.

In 1937 the Ruuds dominated ski jumping, Sigmund winning the National title and Birger capturing the world championship. Sigmund Ruud's victory in the national was not declared until July 31, the committee having previously announced Alf Engen of Sun Valley as the victor. Richard Durrance, the Dartmouth university star, won both the national amateur and national open slalom titles, as well as the national downhill event. Emile Allais of France won the world's downhill championship.

In 1938 Birger Ruud topped United States skiers with a jump of 216 ft. to win the national championship at Brattleboro, Vt. Ulrich Beutter of Germany won both the national downhill and combined championships, while Dick Durrance of Dartmouth university won the National Intercollegiate. The world jumping title went to Asbjorn Ruud of Norway with 226.4 points.

Sgt. Torger Tokle won the first half of a novel tournament staged at Wrigley field, Chicago, Ill., in Jan. 1944

Durrance led U.S. ski competition in 1939 by winning the open and amateur championships in the downhill, slalom and combined. Both Engen and Bob Roecker, of Duluth, Minn., broke the national ski-jumping records, Engen soaring 251 ft. at Big Pines, Calif., and Roecker going 257 ft. at Ironwood, Mich. Helmut Lantschner of Germany won the world's downhill title, while Stanislaw Narusarz of Poland won the world jumping crown with distances of 241 ft. $1^{41}/_{46}$ in. and 234 ft. $6^{57}/_{64}$ in.

Engen won the American Ski trophy as the nation's outstanding skier of 1940 on the strength of his victory in the National ski championship. He won the title with leaps of 219 and 217 ft.

Durrance repeated as champion in the slalom and downhill combined.

During 1941, Tokle took charge of U.S. ski jumping with the record leaps which brought him the national, central and eastern titles. He twice broke the national jumping record, once with a leap of 273 ft. at Leavenworth, Wash., and again with a distance of 288 ft. at Olympian Hill, near Seattle, Wash. Toni Matt won the national open downhill and combined titles. Bill Redlin of the University of Washington won the amateur downhill, slalom and combined.

Ola Aangesen, a member of the royal Norwegian air force stationed in Canada, won the national ski-jumping championship in 1942 with jumps of 191 and 180 ft. Aangesen dethroned Tokle, who in turn set a U.S. distance record of 289 ft. at Iron Mountain, Mich. Engen won the U.S. open downhill-slalom combined title, while Barney McLean of Denver, Colo., swept the amateur events.

All U.S. ski championships were called off in 1943 because of the war. Arthur Devlin featured the limited competitive jumping. The University of New Hampshire topped collegiate skiing by winning the 34th Dartmouth Outing club carnival and the Senior Intercollegiate Ski union championship.

Featuring the war-restricted season, the Norge Ski club staged a novel ski jumping tournament in 1944 at Wrigley field, home of the Chicago National League baseball club. Sgt. Tokle of Camp Hale, Colo., and Lieut. Walter Bietila of the U.S. navy divided honours. In 1945 Merrill Barber of Brattleboro, Vt., won the only jumping test of importance, defeating Arthur Devlin in a Bear Mountain tournament.

In 1946 Alf Engen won the national open jumping title with a leap of 259 ft. Steve Knowlton of Aspen, Colo., won both the open and amateur downhill titles. Dick Movitz of Salt Lake City, Utah, won the national slalom, while Barney McLean of Denver, Colo., captured the combined championship. (M. P. W.)

BIBLIOGRAPHY.—*Annual Report of the National Ski Patrol System;* V. A. Firsoff, *Ski Track on the Battlefield* (1943); F. Elkins, *Complete Ski Guide* (1940); Federal Writers' Project, *Skiing in the East* (1939); F. Harper, *Military Ski Manual* (1943); J. Langdon-Davies, *Invasion in the Snow* (1941). Periodical: *Ski Bulletin.*

Skin Diseases

See DERMATOLOGY.

Slate

Sales of slate in various forms in the United States were as follows during the period 1937–45, in short tons:

	1937	1939	1941	1943	1945
Roofing	137,400	149,410	140,830	35,370	38,240
Mill stock	21,480	21,710	18,680	15,950	11,520
Flagstones	8,620	8,480	21,480	21,990	19,900
Granules	193,950	265,830	323,740	292,330	374,800
Flour	83,060	85,950	113,930	103,220	107,430
Total	444,510	531,380	618,660	468,860	551,890

Total sales of all types of slate reached a high of 670,070 tons in 1929, but declined heavily during the depression years and had not yet regained its former high level in 1946. The construction program of World War II increased consumption heavily, to within 8% of the former high, but production declined to about the prewar level in 1943. There were marked improvements in 1944 and 1945, and the postwar building program was expected to bring further increases. (G. A. Ro.)

Slim, Sir William Joseph

Sir William Slim (1891–), British army officer, was born Aug. 6, 1891. He received a grammar school education in Birmingham and during World War I shipped as an officer of the Royal Warwickshires to France. Later he fought at Gallipoli, where he was severely wounded, and in Mesopotamia. Slim continued in the services after World War I, and in 1939 he was commandant of a senior officers' school in Bombay province. In World War II, he participated in fighting in Italy, east Africa and the middle east. Transferred to the Burma theatre, after Japan's entry into the war, he was made head of the 1st Burma corps in March 1942. In Oct. 1943 Slim was given command of the 14th British army which halted the Japanese drive into Manipur state, India, in June 1944. He then opened the arduous campaign to regain all of Burma and recaptured Mandalay in March 1945 and Rangoon in May. He relinquished command of the 14th army in Aug. 1945 to Gen. Miles C. Dempsey. Slim was made a knight of the Order of the British Empire on Jan. 1, 1946.

Slovakia

The eastern part of Czechoslovakia, as constituted in 1918, had an area of 18,895 sq.mi. and a pop. of 3,329,-793 (1930), of whom the great majority were Slovaks, a Slav people closely akin to the Czechs. Of the minorities there were 529,337 Magyars, 154,821 Germans, 95,359 Ruthenians and 72,678 Jews. Of the population, 78% were Catholic (of whom 72% were Roman Catholic), 17% Protestants and 4% Jews. Before 1918 Slovakia had been for almost 1,000 years a part of Hungary. In 1938 some Slovak territory was ceded to Hungary. The rest (an area of 14,848 sq.mi. with a pop. of 2,800,000) became an independent republic in March 1939. Capital, Bratislava; chief cities: Bratislava (123,852); Trnava (23,948); Nitra (21,283). The president was Msgr. Josef Tiso; premier, Dr. Bela Tuka. In 1945 Slovakia became an autonomous part of the reconstituted Czechoslovak republic.

Slovakia as an independent state came into existence in March 1939 through German help. On March 18, 1939, it signed a treaty with Germany for 25 years according to which German armed forces received the right to occupy Slovakia at any time and to erect military plants there. Slovakia pledged itself to conduct its foreign policy and to organize its army in agreement with Germany. All its economic life was co-ordinated with national socialist economy. On Nov. 24, 1940, Slovakia adhered officially to the Rome-Berlin-Tokyo military alliance. As a result of that pact, Slovakia participated in Germany's war against the soviet union after June 22, 1941, and declared itself to be in a state of war with the United States after Germany's similar declaration of war Dec. 11, 1941. But many Slovaks, dissatisfied with the German vassalage, with the fascist trend and with the anti-Slav stand taken by the Slovak government, worked for the re-establishment of the Czechoslovak republic. A number of Slovaks participated in the Czechoslovak government which resided in England under Dr. Eduard Beneš as president.

During 1942 the nazification of Slovakia made rapid progress. On Oct. 22 the totalitarian character of the state was officially proclaimed. The Slovak People's party, a Catholic nationalist party founded by Father Andreus Hlinka (1864–1938), was recognized as the only party and its leader received the title *vodca,* the Slovak word for fuehrer. It comprised an armed militia, the Hlinka guards, and a youth organization, the Hlinka youth. Slovaks living abroad were to be organized as members in the same way as the German national socialists had built up their foreign organizations. The German anti-Semitic legislation was vigorously enforced in Slovakia.

In the summer of 1944 Slovak antifascist forces rose against the clerical fascist regime and succeeded quickly in seizing most of Slovakia's territory and in establishing a well-ordered administration with Baňská Bystrica as its centre. Most of the regular army and police forces of the government went over to the newly established regime. In this crisis President Tiso accepted the resignation of the cabinet of Dr. Bela Tuka and appointed his relative, Stephen Tiso, prime minister and also minister of foreign affairs and justice. The war minister and commander in chief, Gen. Ferdinand Čatloš, resigned from the Tiso government. On the other hand, the Slovak national council in Baňská Bystrica proclaimed the restoration of the Czechoslovak republic. Delegates of this council arrived on Oct. 13, by air, in London to establish direct relations with the Czechoslovak government there, while the London government sent Gen. Rudolf Viest to assume command of the forces in Slovakia. In the liberated territory all totalitarian organizations were dissolved. Jews were liberated from concentration camps and their rights restored; state and church were separated. U.S., British and Russian liaison officers co-operated with Gen. Viest. Strong German armed forces were sent against the Slovaks, however, and after two months of bitter fighting the Germans succeeded in defeating the Czechoslovak army. The new German occupation was short-lived. By the end of the year Russian armies had penetrated into Slovakia from the east and from the north.

With the victorious advance of the Russian armies, the Tiso regime in Slovakia came to an end in 1945. By the end of the year, the country was under the Slovak national council, composed equally of communists and democrats. The council enjoyed a large autonomy in the domestic affairs of Slovakia. In the Czechoslovak government in Prague the Slovaks were represented by six members in the cabinet and by two of the five vice-premiers. In the Czechoslovak provisional national assembly the Slovaks had one-third of the deputies. These 100 Slovak delegates, half communists and half democrats, were elected in the city of Baňská Bystrica, on Aug. 29. The party which formerly ruled Slovakia, the Catholic People's party, was outlawed and its leaders were placed under arrest. The elections of May 1946 assured the victory of the Slovak Democrats with the Communist party taking the second place. (*See* also CARPATHO-UKRAINE; CZECHOSLOVAKIA.)

(H. Ko.)

BIBLIOGRAPHY.—E. Benes, *Democracy Today and Tomorrow* (1940); V. Krajcovic, *La Estructura de la Economia Eslovaca* (Madrid, 1945); *Die Slovakische Industrie* (Bratislava, ann.); *The Slovak Question,* Slovak Council (Geneva, 1940); *Statesman's Yearbook.*

Smaller War Plants Corporation

See WAR AND DEFENSE AGENCIES.

Smigly-Rydz, Edward

Smigly-Rydz (1886–), Polish army officer and statesman, studied philosophy and painting in Cracow, where he met Josef Pilsudski. He fought against Russia on the Eastern Front in 1914–17, and again during the Polish campaign of 1919–20. He was inspector of the Polish army, 1922–35, and became one of Pilsudski's closest associates during this period. After Pilsudski's death in 1935, Smigly-Rydz became virtual dictator of Poland, assuming the post of inspector-general of the army. Prior to the German invasion in 1939, Marshal Smigly-Rydz was designated commander in chief of the army and successor to Pres. Ignacy Moscicki. Less than three weeks after the Germans invaded his homeland, he fled to Rumania, where he was interned. In Oct. 1940, he was arrested in Bucharest, following charges that the entire Polish embassy staff and many Polish refugees in Rumania were employed by the British to blow up the Ploesti oil wells. A Bucharest report (Dec. 20, 1940), said Smigly-Rydz, who had been held in the Dragoslav prison camp in Rumania, escaped from the camp to an unknown destination.

Smith, Alfred Emanuel

Smith (1873–1944), U.S. politician, was born Dec. 30, 1873, in New York city. Four times governor of New York state, Smith was Democratic candidate for president in 1928. In the 1936 and 1940 presidential elections he abandoned the party line and stumped for the Republican candidates. Although violently opposed to Pres. Roosevelt's policies during the peace years, Smith rallied behind the administration after the Pearl Harbor attack and called for national unity. An outstanding Catholic layman, Smith was appointed Knight of St. Gregory and papal chamberlain in 1938. He died in New York city, Oct. 4, 1944.

Smith, Holland McTyeire

Smith (1882–), U.S. marine corps officer, was born April 20, 1882, in Russell county, Ala. A graduate of the University of Alabama (1903) he practised law for a brief period and then joined the marine corps. Commissioned a second lieutenant in 1905, he was promoted through the grades to major general in 1941, and became commanding general of the Atlantic fleet's amphibious force the same year. Smith commanded U.S. amphibious forces during the battle for the Aleutians and in the invasion of Tarawa and Makin in 1943. He was also assault commander of operations in the Marshall Islands, Feb. 1944, and of landings on Saipan, June 1944. On Sept. 9, 1944, he disclosed that he had been "forced" to remove Maj. Gen. Ralph Smith, commander of an army division, during the Saipan battle. Although the marine general refused to discuss details, there were reports that the two Smiths disagreed on strategy, with the army commander refusing to accept the marine thesis of achieving quick victory without regard to immediate cost in casualties. Gen. Holland Smith, who was succeeded by Lt. Gen. Roy S. Geiger as commanding field officer of the marine corps on June 22, 1945, was made head of the marine training and replacement command at San Diego, Calif. On his retirement from the marine corps, Aug. 7, 1946, Smith was promoted to a full general.

Smith, Walter Bedell

Smith (1895–), U.S. army officer, was born Oct. 5, 1895, in Indianapolis, Ind. Shortly after the U.S. entry into World War I he entered the army direct from civilian life. After receiving his commission as a second lieutenant, he went overseas in April 1918, serving until Sept. and then returning to Washington, D.C., for duty in military intelligence. With the war department general staff after 1939, Smith was promoted to brigadier general in 1942 and was made U.S. secretary of the combined chiefs of staff. For his services in this post, he was awarded the distinguished service medal in 1943.

In Sept. 1942, as a major general, Smith became chief of staff in the European theatre, with headquarters in England, and subsequently chief of staff to Gen. Dwight D. Eisenhower in North Africa. He remained with Eisenhower throughout World War II and handled many details involved in preparation for the invasions of Sicily, Italy and Normandy. Promoted to the rank of temporary lieutenant general in Jan. 1943, he was made major general (permanent) in Oct. 1945. On Feb. 14, 1946, President Truman named Smith ambassador to the soviet union, succeeding W. Averell Harriman.

Smithsonian Institution

The year 1946 marked the 100th anniversary of the founding of the Smithsonian institution.[1] The centennial was observed by suitable ceremonies. A three-cent commemorative postage stamp was issued by the post office de-

[1]The following bureaus of the government were administered by the Smithsonian during the decade 1937–46: *U.S. National museum, Bureau of American Ethnology,* National Collection of Fine Arts, *Freer Gallery of Art,* International Exchange Service, National Zoological Park and the Astrophysical observatory. The *National Gallery of Art* also became a Smithsonian bureau under a separate board of trustees.

partment, special publications were issued by the institution to mark the event and special exhibits were shown to illustrate the work of the institution during its first century.

Research and Exploration.—In 1941 Dr. Frank H. H. Roberts, Jr., concluded several years of work on the Folsom man problem, centering mainly on the Lindenmeier site in northern Colorado. There he unearthed numerous artifacts, including the distinctive Folsom projectile points, which indicated that the area had been a hunting ground for Folsom men at a time when animals now extinct roamed over Colorado. Geological studies at the site indicated an age for the artifact-bearing deposits of 10,000 to 25,000 years, with the geologists' preference leaning toward the higher figure.

In 1938 the Smithsonian participated in the presidential cruise to the Galápagos Islands, Dr. Waldo L. Schmitt accompanying the expedition as biologist. In 1939, in co-operation with the National Geographic society, there began a series of joint archaeological expeditions to Mexico, under the leadership of Dr. Matthew W. Stirling, chief of the Bureau of American Ethnology. These added measurably to knowledge of Mexican archaeology, establishing what became known as the La Venta culture. The same year marked the end of Dr. Aleš Hrdlička's anthropological field investigations in Alaska begun in 1926, in which he gathered many important specimens and much data relating to the origin of early man in America. Two expeditions were notable in bringing back live animals for the National Zoological park. The first, in 1937, to the East Indies, was conducted in co-operation with the National Geographic society, while the second, in 1940, to Liberia, was made possible by the Firestone Tire & Rubber Co., of Akron, O. Both were under the direction of Dr. W. M. Mann, director of the zoo, and both were eminently successful in the number and variety of animals obtained.

The staff of the Astrophysical observatory devoted several years to the revision of the daily solar radiation values recorded at the Smithsonian solar observing stations on Mt. Montezuma, Chile, Table mountain, Calif., and Mt. St. Katherine, Egypt, from 1923 to 1939. The final values were published in 1942 as vol. 6 of the *Annals of the Astrophysical Observatory*. They clearly indicated the variation of the sun ranging up to about 3%, with the variation shown to be composed of 14 periodicities ranging from 8 to 273 months. In 1938 the solar observation station at Mt. St. Katherine in Egypt was abandoned and a new one was established at a more accessible location on Burro mountain, near Tyrone, N.M.

The Division of Radiation and Organisms continued its work on photosynthesis. The importance of carbon-dioxide assimilation as a function of wave length of light was shown, and the spectrographic method of determining small amounts of carbon dioxide was further improved and utilized in the measurement of photosynthesis and respiration in plants. Emphasis was placed on the wave-length effects of light on plant growth and on growth substances found in plants. Development of instrumentation accompanied this specialized research.

Biological research and field work conducted under the Walter Rathbone Bacon travelling scholarship of the Smithsonian institution saw notable results. During the decade this scholarship was awarded to three recipients: Dr. Richard E. Blackwelder for studies of the staphylinid beetles of the West Indies; Dr. Hobart M. Smith for investigations relating to the herpetology of Mexico and Philip Hershkovitz for a study of the distribution of mammals in Colombia.

The coming of World War II suspended most of the research and exploration activities of the institution except those directly pertaining to the war effort.

In 1943 the Institute of Social Anthropology was added to the Smithsonian institution, operating as an autonomous unit of the Bureau of American Ethnology and receiving its funds through the department of state. The institute's stated purpose was to carry out co-operative training in anthropological teaching and research, with two objectives in mind: (1) to introduce modern social science theories and techniques to other countries so that they might train their scholars for such work and (2) to accumulate basic social science data about the rural populations in those countries. During the first three years of its organization, with Dr. Julian H. Steward, anthropologist, in charge, the institute operated chiefly in Mexico, Peru and Brazil.

War Work.—World War II was literally a war of science and during the war years the services of the Smithsonian were utilized to an unprecedented extent. Shortly after Pearl Harbor the secretary appointed a war committee to canvass the institution's possibilities and to recommend specific lines of action. As a result a large part of the effort of the staff was devoted to war work, and the Smithsonian became an essential cog in the great war machine in Washington, D.C.

Probably the Smithsonian's most effective contribution to the war was its ability to answer urgent calls from the U.S. army and navy for information in a variety of fields—mainly anthropology, biology, geology, geography, physics and astrophysics, engineering, textiles and fibres and woods. Many of the requests were for information that had only an indirect war connection, but others led straight to the fighting fronts and had a direct bearing on the progress of the war. Among the latter were calls for means of identification of various kinds of disease-bearers such as mosquitoes, rats and molluscs; for reports on geography, peoples and other features of areas ahead of the actual fighting; for transliteration of Chinese, Japanese and Siamese names on maps of war areas; for preparation of a survival manual for aviators and other personnel stranded in unfamiliar areas and for many other items of equal importance.

As a means of bringing together in one place all the known resources of specialized and regional knowledge urgently needed by the army and navy, particularly in the early days of the war, the institution joined with the National Research council, the American Council of Learned Societies, and the Social Science Research council in setting up the Ethnogeographic board with offices in the Smithsonian building. The board proved almost immediately to fill a place among the Washington, D.C., war agencies. Besides making available to the army and navy a great regional file of specialists able to assist in the solution of problems relating to all parts of the world, the board produced on request numerous special reports on particular regions for use in planning military operations, and served as a clearinghouse for spot information in many different fields.

The facilities and staff of the Astrophysical observatory, including the Division of Radiation and Organisms, were occupied for a considerable time with research on the heat-radiation properties of various textiles, pigments and other materials used for war purposes, and on the deterioration of impregnated cloth, cardboard and other materials used by the navy. A number of special instruments were developed and constructed for the navy. At the request of the Office of Scientific Research and Development, an extended study was made to find a filter that would exclude undesired types of radiation and transmit certain desired wave lengths.

In geology one museum staff member was in the field continuously throughout the war directing an investigation for the U.S. Geological survey of Mexico's resources of strategic minerals. Another member was engaged in a study of the geological structure in an economic survey of the ore and mineral deposits of northern Mexico, and later investigated Devonian stratigraphy in Illinois in connection with oil-resource studies. Much of the work in the field of biology was in the nature of continuous assistance to war-agency personnel through identification of specimens, instruction in various fields of medical biology, training of military personnel in identification work, conferences on recognition and control of harmful organisms, reports on the occurrence and identification of strategic plant material and other similar activities. In anthropology staff members prepared a number of reports and articles involving research on the native peoples of various war areas at the request of army and navy intelligence officers. Studies of arctic clothing were made for the army quartermaster corps, based on the extensive collections of Eskimo garments in the National museum. For use in the design of oxygen and gas masks, data were worked out and supplied to the army on the variations in size and form of the human head and features.

Another war project was the publication of a series of 21 papers on the peoples, history, geography and other features of war areas. These were issued under the title *Smithsonian War Background Studies* and covered practically every country and island group involved in the war in the Pacific, in addition to several on other war areas of special interest and on general war background topics. The series became popular at once and large numbers of copies were used for orientation work in the armed services.

In all, more than 600,000 copies were printed.

Soon after the beginning of the war thousands of the priceless and irreplaceable specimens in the collections of the National museum were evacuated to a place of safety outside of Washington.

By the end of 1945 all this material was returned to the museum.

Art.—Smithsonian activities in the realm of art received unprecedented impetus in 1937 when Andrew W. Mellon gave to the people of the United States through the Smithsonian institution his unexcelled art collection and a $15,000,000 gallery building, the whole to be known as the National Gallery of Art. The building, a monumental structure in Washington's Mall section, was completed and opened to the public on March 17, 1941. Starting with Mellon's own collection of 111 choice old masters and 21 pieces of sculpture, the National gallery collection soon grew greatly in size and importance through the gifts of several valuable assemblages of art works, including those of Samuel H. Kress, Joseph E. Widener, Lessing J. Rosenwald, Chester Dale and others. With these priceless acquisitions the National gallery became from the start a centre for the study of art in the United States and one of the great galleries of the world.

Prior to the Mellon gift, the national art collections in the custody of the Smithsonian had been known as the "National Gallery of Art." In 1937 this name was changed to "National Collection of Fine Arts" in order to make the former name available for the new "Mellon" gallery. Although congress approved a building site the steadily growing National Collection of Fine Arts was still housed in temporary quarters in the natural history building of the National museum.

Publications.—In 1941, under the direction of Dr. Julian H. Steward, work was begun on the preparation and editing of the *Handbook of South American Indians,* a project of encyclopaedic proportions undertaken in co-operation with the state department's interdepartmental committee on cultural and scientific co-operation and with the National Research council. By the end of 1946 two of the five projected volumes (*The Marginal Tribes* and *The Andean Civilizations*) had been published and vols. 3 and 4 were in galley proof. These finely illustrated books, written by leading South American as well as North American anthropologists, provided for the first time a comprehensive summary of existing knowledge of the Indians of South America.

For many years, as a service to scientists and students throughout the world, the Smithsonian had maintained a group of publications in the nature of handbooks of information on geographical, physical and mathematical subjects. Three volumes of these publications were revised and reprinted during the period—*Smithsonian Meteorological Tables,* in 1939; *Smithsonian Mathematical Formulae and Tables of Elliptic Functions,* in 1939; and *Smithsonian Mathematical Tables* (*Hyperbolic Functions*), in 1942; in addition, *World Weather Records,* a monumental 2-vol. reference work in meteorology, was reprinted in 1944 under a grant from John A. Roebling.

The *Annual Reports* of the Smithsonian had been published for 100 years without a break. Throughout this time, hundreds of distinguished articles by leading scientists had been given wide distribution in the appendices of these reports, and altogether they formed a unique record of scientific progress during the century.

Other Activities.—Beginning in 1937 radio was used by the Smithsonian institution for the first time on an extensive scale in the diffusion of knowledge. "The World Is Yours," a half-hour dramatized program, sponsored jointly by the Smithsonian institution, the U.S. office of education and the National Broadcasting Co., first went on the air on June 7, 1936, and nearly every week for more than 300 weeks the program presented some phase of science, invention, history and art to a nation-wide radio audience. The series from the beginning struck a responsive chord in radio listeners throughout the country, and twice from an official rating service the program received top rating among all non-commercial programs on all networks. Because of the urgent demand of war agencies for radio time the series was terminated on May 10, 1942.

World War II temporarily disrupted the activities of the International Exchange service. This agency, with the function of facilitating the distribution of scientific publications to and from foreign countries, had been a part of the Smithsonian from 1849. In 1939, approximately 715,000 packages of scientific publications passed through the service.

At the end of 1946 the Smithsonian library, including all its several branches plus the Smithsonian deposit at the Library of Congress, aggregated nearly 1,000,000 volumes.

The ten years saw important personnel changes in the Smithsonian organization.

On January 16, 1942, Chief Justice Harlan F. Stone was elected chancellor of the institution to succeed former

Chief Justice Charles E. Hughes. Justice Stone served until his death on April 22, 1946. Dr. Charles G. Abbot, astrophysicist, who had been secretary of the institution from 1928, resigned on July 1, 1944, and on the following Jan. 12, Dr. Alexander Wetmore, biologist, was named by the board of regents to succeed Dr. Abbot. Dr. Wetmore had been assistant secretary of the institution from 1925. John E. Graf was advanced from associate director of the National museum to assistant secretary of the institution on April 1, 1945.

The Freer Gallery of Art lost its director in the death of John Ellerton Lodge on Dec. 29, 1942. Lodge, a gifted linguist and orientalist, served 22 years as director of the gallery, and during that period he added to the original Freer collection many works of major importance in the fields of Chinese bronzes, paintings, jades, sculpture and ceramics; Indian paintings and sculptures; Arabic, Persian and Armenian manuscripts and paintings; and Syrian and Persian glass, pottery and metal work. Archibald G. Wenley became the new director of the Freer gallery on Jan. 16, 1943.

At the end of the fiscal year 1936 the capital funds of the institution totalled $6,462,121. By the end of 1945 this figure had risen to $8,621,189 by reason of various gifts and investments. One of the largest gifts in this period was an addition of $400,000 to the Charles D. and Mary Vaux Walcott research fund for development of geological and palaeontological studies and publishing results thereof, from Mrs. Walcott's estate. Another was $300,000 received from Miss Annie May Hegeman to establish the Henry Kirke Porter fund in honour of her stepfather.

In 1937, under an allotment from Public Works administration funds, five new buildings were added to the National Zoological park. Located in Rock Creek park in Washington, the zoo had grown to be one of the chief attractions of the city, and the new buildings added greatly to the attractiveness of the park as well as providing more adequate facilities for the animals.

The number of visitors to Smithsonian buildings reached an all-time high in 1940, when more than 2,500,000 were recorded. (A. Wt.)

Smuggling

See Immigration and Emigration, U.S.

Smuts, Jan Christiaan

Smuts (1870–), South African statesman, soldier and philosopher, was born May 24, 1870, near Riebeek West in Cape Colony. He was educated at Cambridge university, England, and was admitted to the Capetown bar in 1895. During the Boer War, Smuts joined the Boer army in 1900, eventually becoming chief of a commando detachment.

After the restoration of peace, he actively campaigned to smooth over political and racial differences. Upon the outbreak of World War I in 1914, Smuts became commander of South African armies preparing for battle with the Germans in Southwest Africa. That same year, Louis Botha, with Smuts's co-operation, helped put down the Dutch rebellion. Smuts was a member of the peace conference in Versailles and in 1919 wrote his celebrated memorandum on the League of Nations, which was endorsed by Lloyd George and Woodrow Wilson; in substance, it became the League covenant.

Smuts was prime minister of South Africa from 1919 to 1924. Inactive in South African politics after 1924, he re-entered the political arena as war with the axis threatened. Britain's declaration of war against Germany on Sept. 3, 1939, brought him back as prime minister. On Sept. 6 Smuts formed a war cabinet, and the Union proclaimed a state of war with Germany. He was made a field marshal in the British army in 1941.

In a speech at London on Nov. 25, 1943, Smuts predicted that Britain would emerge from the war as the weakest member of a trinity of states that would include the United States and the soviet union. To offset this weakness, he suggested that Britain take the smaller states of postwar Europe into its orbit. The marshal attended the sessions of the United Nations conference in San Francisco, Calif. (April–June 1945), as a delegate of the Union of South Africa. He also attended the 21-nation peace conference in Paris in the late summer and early fall of 1946. At the U.N. general assembly sessions in Lake Success, N.Y., he warned the U.N. in Nov. 1946 that if it did not approve South Africa's proposal to annex the former Southwest Africa mandate, South Africa would continue ruling the area with or without U.N. approval.

Snyder, John Wesley

Snyder (1896–), U.S. government official, was born June 21, 1896, at Jonesboro, Ark. A student at Vanderbilt university, Nashville, Tenn., 1914–15, he joined the army in 1917 and was promoted to artillery captain. While in France, he met Capt. Harry S. Truman and the two continued their friendship after the war. Entering the banking profession, Snyder became national bank receiver in the office of the comptroller of currency in Washington, D.C., 1930. He held important posts with the Reconstruction Finance corporation and its subsidiary from 1937 to 1943. In the latter year, Snyder resigned from his various governmental posts to return to private banking. On April 17, 1945, President Truman appointed Snyder federal loan administrator; three months later (July 16), he was made director of the Office of War Mobilization and Reconversion. On June 6, 1946, the president named Snyder as secretary of the treasury, succeeding Fred Vinson, who had been appointed chief justice of the U.S. supreme court. Snyder also served as board chairman of both the world bank and the international fund until Oct. 3, 1946, when he was succeeded by Hugh Dalton, British chancellor of the exchequer.

Soap, Perfumery and Cosmetics

The beginning of the decade, 1937–46, found the soap, perfumery and cosmetics industries struggling in the toils of a federal excise tax law, so-called. Actually, the tax was originally one on gross sales. The burden of it was sufficiently heavy—10% on cosmetics and perfumes, 5% on soaps—to impel resort to a variety of expedients that would legitimately minimize the load. The most notable of these was the creation of the "independent" subsidiary sales company which bought goods from the parent "at arm's length," at prices which covered only manufacturing costs. Even so, prime producers had to pay tax on containers, often the most expensive part of their products. A confused situation arose, in which companies existed by a method that could best be described as "taking in each other's washing." While no supporting data existed, it finally became clear that for the government the cost of collecting (and policing) the law grew out of all proportion to the income received from it. Of its cost to the industries there was no doubt. And while the intent was to collect a tax from manufacturers that could not be passed on to the ordinary man or, in this instance, the ordinary woman, nevertheless, however indirectly, the law probably added greatly to the ultimate public cost of the goods in question.

In the fall of 1941 the burden of this tax was at last shifted to where, from every point of view save that of the acutely vote-conscious politician, it had always properly belonged: directly on the ultimate consumer. Thus the cost of collection to the federal government was minimized; the gross revenue increased with almost no extra cost to the consumer; the industries were relieved of a wasteful and irritating situation and were able to set their several corporate houses in order. This transfer of a luxury tax from producer to consumer constituted no more than reversion to a system that had already served the people and the government satisfactorily in 1861, 1898 and 1914.

Another and far more important development during the decade arose out of the enactment of a new federal Food, Drug and Cosmetics act. This act became operative on Jan. 1, 1940, when it superseded the wholly ineffective Pure Food law of 1906. The most obvious effect of the new law to the public was probably the extent to which it compelled irresponsible advertisers to tone down their extravagant claims, with (it was hoped) some benefit to the consumer as well as to those manufacturers who always were restrained with respect to their claims in advertising by some sense of social responsibility.

The law, in this connection, had the somewhat curious effect of turning the imaginative attentions of these industries to perfume, as the touchstone for happiness-ever-after. It was significant that in one periodical—a magazine by no means limited to feminine editorial appeal—fully 40% of all the advertising in the issue immediately preceding Mother's day, 1946, was devoted to perfume. This was, however, precisely where such advertising appeal—if it had any justification at all—belonged; since at even the highest levels of intelligence human beings actually are, to a large extent, emotionally governed and guided, impelled or restrained, by their sense of smell.

The law also proved to be of great practical benefit not only to the socially minded producer but also to the consuming public. For among the manufacturers, irresponsibility did not confine itself to windy words and specious phrases. Under the 1906 law, so long as he shunned downright deadly poison, a maker could put almost anything he wanted into his compounds. There was no doubt that many were using materials, and selling finished goods, that were definitely if not invariably harmful. If any direct evidence of this should be needed it could be found in the steady increase during, say, the 20 years 1920–40, of the use of protective insurance by manufacturers against the liability of damage awards to injured customers by the courts. It was further a fact that during that period certain types of commodities were continuously offered to the public on which no insuring company would assume a risk. The new law effectively protected the people against the worst of those risks to which they were previously unwittingly exposed.

The history of World War II's influence on these three industries was by and large the history of its influence on all industries catering to the ultimate consumer: an ever-increasing demand created almost entirely by full employment and the monetary inflation, versus a steadily decreasing supply. From Sept. 1939 until well into 1946 these industries enjoyed a sellers' market.

Annual sales at retail for the decade of perfumes, cosmetics and toilet preparations, as estimated by the Toilet Goods association, were as follows: 1937, \$352,000,000; 1938, \$366,100,000; 1939, \$387,600,000; 1940, \$400,000,000; 1941, \$419,600,000; 1942, \$439,600,000; 1943, \$461,000,000; 1944, \$546,300,000; 1945, \$655,000,000; 1946, \$699,600,000.

The biggest single factor in this rise undoubtedly was the very large increase in trademarked lines, generally consisting of such items as shaving soaps, shaving lotions, talcum powders, toilet waters, pomades, sun-tan preparations, etc.—lines designed exclusively for male consumption. To be sure, men had always bought and used such products but certainly never before to the extent that they did during the decade. The market for men's toiletries was variously estimated at from \$50,000,000 to \$80,000,000 a year in 1946.

By early 1941 exports from the United States to the British dominions and colonies, the largest part of the export market, had been brought to a standstill. Those U.S. firms with British subsidiaries—and almost all of any size or consequence had them after 1931—could divert this business to their British houses. For although Great Britain had already severely limited production for home use, it was still anxious to retain all possible export luxury trade for the sake of foreign exchange balances. However, as early as 1942, it was obliged to restrict even this business, partly because of increasing scarcity of such essential materials as paper and boxboard, but largely for politico-military considerations. Thus, the whole lend-lease position might have been jeopardized if while obtaining under it the pulp vitally needed to manufacture paper and explosives Britain had continued to export luxury goods packed in paper and cardboard.

As late as the third quarter of 1946, these industries were still operating "under wraps" in Great Britain. As a part of the "austerities program," domestic limitations on production were in full wartime force. Additional quota for export was readily obtainable. However, this quota was expressed in money (sterling) and it still did not solve the primary problem of obtaining the materials for which it was permissive. Many of these materials normally came from France where, in the case of the best perfume materials, the situation arising from the stringency of fuel power and transportation afflicting all industries was still further aggravated by the continuing shortage of fats.

BIBLIOGRAPHY.—Charles Lazar, *Manual of Cosmetics* (London, 1937); Marcelle Auclair, *Toute La Beauté* (Paris, 1937); E. G. Thomssen and C. R. Kemp, *Soap Making* (1937); Herman Goodman, *Principles of Professional Beauty Culture* (1938); A Mueller, *Schöne Frau: Ein Kosmetisches Brevier* (Leipzig, 1938); S. L. Mayham, *Marketing Cosmetics* (1938); Mme. Albert Lechapt, *Manicure, Massage Facial Soins De Beauté* (Paris, 1939); Sven Holm, *Kosmetik* (Copenhagen, 1939); R. Rockwood and I. Ruddock, *Modern Cosmetology* (1940); S. B. Jeffries, *Profitable Beauty Shop Management* (1940); American Medical Association, *Review of Some Actions of Government Agencies and other Information on Cosmetics, 1930–40* (1941); H. A. Toulmin, Jr., *A Treatise on the Law of Food, Drugs and Cosmetics* (1942). (H. T.)

Soapstone

See TALC.

Soccer

The east dominated soccer during 1937–46, sweeping all 10 national amateur challenge cups and capturing 7 national open challenge cups, emblematic of the United States championship. Chicago teams upheld the west in the annual playoffs, the Spartas winning in 1938 and the Vikings in 1946. The Spartas and Baltimore, Md., Soccer club were tied for the championship in 1940.

Prompted by the tours of several outstanding British

U.S. National Soccer Champions, 1937–46

Year	National Challenge Cup	National Amateur Challenge Cup
1937	New York Americans	Highlanders, Trenton, N.J.
1938	Sparta A. B. A., Chicago, Ill.	Ponta Delgada S. C., Fall River, Mass.
1939	St Mary's Celtics S. C., Brooklyn, N.Y.	St. Michael's A. C., Fall River, Mass.
1940	Sparta and Baltimore, Md., tied	Morgan, Pa., Football Club
1941	Pawtucket, R.I., Football Club	Fall River, Mass., S. C.
1942	Gallatin Football Club, Donora, Pa.	Fall River, Mass., S. C.
1943	Brooklyn Hispano Soccer Club	Morgan Strasser S. C., Morgan, Pa.
1944	Brooklyn Hispano Soccer Club	Eintracht Sports Club, Brooklyn, N.Y.
1945	Brookhattans, Bronx, N.Y.	Eintracht Sports Club, Brooklyn, N.Y.
1946	Vikings, Chicago	Ponta Delgada S. C., Fall River, Mass.

teams before and after World War II, soccer gained considerable popularity in the United States during the 1937–46 decade. The Charlton athletics of England attracted much attention during a U.S. tour in 1938, as did the Scottish All-Stars in 1939. The Liverpool Football club of Liverpool, England, brought the United States its first international soccer of the postwar period and was victorious in both its U.S. appearances. (M. P. W.)

BIBLIOGRAPHY.—S. Fralick, *Soccer* (1945); *Official Soccer Guide Including the Official Laws* (A. S. Barnes, ann.); *Official Soccer, Speedball and Field Ball Guide for Women and Girls* (ann.); U.S. Office of Naval Operations, *Soccer* (Aviation Training Division) (1943).

Social Credit

See ALBERTA.

Socialism

The decade 1937–46 began in Europe with democratic socialist parties as the strongest parties in the Scandinavian countries and in control of their respective governments; as the principal opposition party in Great Britain, and as the largest party in the popular front which in 1936 had come to power in France. Nevertheless, socialism was already on the defensive as against fascist and communist totalitarianism. It had been driven completely underground in Germany and Austria and, with the coming of World War II, it fell before Hitler's advancing armies, while, during the decade, the Labour and Socialist International disappeared. By the end of 1946, the international had not yet been reconstituted, but conferences of European Socialists had been held in England to lay the foundation for a new international.

In every country Socialist parties or the dominant factions in them strove in the '30s to keep out of war. This desire for peace at home and abroad led Léon Blum, the Socialist prime minister of the popular front in France, to support a so-called nonintervention policy. Until late in 1937 the British Labour party backed the Conservative government of Britain in a similar policy, though it later opposed the policy which led to the Munich pact.

With the ending of World War II socialist parties emerged from their grim underground existence with surprising strength in all countries in Europe which were not under dictatorship or in the soviet sphere of influence. In most European countries, socialism presented itself as the principal alternative to communism. Labour and Socialist parties constituted the largest single parties in Great Britain, Sweden, Norway, Denmark, Belgium, Switzerland and Finland, constituted the governments in the three first-named countries and were members of coalition cabinets in Austria, Belgium, Czechoslovakia, France, the Netherlands, Hungary, Italy and other countries. The most significant victory of democratic socialism immediately after the war was that of the British Labour party in June 1945.

In the western hemisphere, in both Americas, the labour movement made substantial gains during the decade. Organized socialism, however, made no such progress except in Canada, where the Co-operative Commonwealth federation showed growing strength.

In Asia Japanese socialism showed increasing strength under the occupation after World War II. Socialists were a factor of some consequence in the India Congress party during this period, Jawaharlal Nehru, head of the interim government, being a socialist in philosophy. The Indonesians likewise selected Sutan Sjahrir, a socialist leader, as head of the struggling Indonesian republic.

In Australia and New Zealand socialist and labour forces maintained control of the governments throughout the decade. A brief recapitulation of events in various countries follows.

Great Britain.—The British Labour party at the beginning of the decade was his majesty's chief opposition, with 154 members of the house of commons against 387 Conservatives. It swung to bold opposition to nazi aggression slowly but more rapidly and vigorously than did the Conservatives. It supported the war but criticized the Chamberlain government for failing to mobilize Britain's full resources. On the resignation of the Chamberlain cabinet May 10, 1940, the Labour party joined the war coalition government under Winston Churchill, and its leaders (among them C. R. Attlee, Ernest Bevin, Herbert Morrison, Hugh Dalton and A. V. Alexander) served in important posts throughout the war. The small, leftist Independent Labour party remained outside the coalition. So did the newly formed Common Wealth party, a socialist but definitely non-Marxist organization.

Shortly after the defeat of Germany in 1945 the Labourites resigned their seats in the cabinet and asked for a general election. In the ensuing campaign the party issued a manifesto, "Let Us Face the Future," in which it pledged itself, if elected, to legislate for the public ownership of some of the key industries, a comprehensive national health service and an extensive housing program, while working for the gradual establishment "of the socialist

"The Painless Way," a 1945 cartoon by Shoemaker of the *Chicago Daily News* comparing the methods chosen in Great Britain and Russia for adopting socialism

commonwealth of Great Britain free, democratic, efficient, progressive, public spirited."

In the elections of July 1945, 393 Labourites were elected out of a total of 640, as compared with 197 Conservatives. The Labour party thus obtained, for the first time in its history, a majority of parliamentary seats. Attlee became prime minister; Bevin, foreign minister; Morrison, lord president of the council and leader of the house of commons; Dalton, chancellor of the exchequer and Sir Stafford Cripps, president of the board of trade, in an all-Labour cabinet.

During its first year of office the Labour government nationalized the Bank of England and the coal-mining industry, enacted the National Insurance bill which provided cradle to grave social security for the entire nation and rescinded the Trade Disputes and Trade Unions act passed by the Conservative government in 1927 after the general strike of 1926. It introduced bills for the nationalization of civil aviation, of telecommunications and of atomic energy and for complete medical, dental and specialist services under the national health service. The government likewise announced its intention of bringing electricity, gas and power and inland transportation under public ownership.

In international affairs the government gave to India the choice of self-government within the British commonwealth of nations or of becoming an independent nation. At the end of the year it was still negotiating with the Jews and Arabs regarding the solution of the Palestinian problem. (*See* also LABOUR PARTY, GREAT BRITAIN.)

In the neighbouring country of Northern Ireland Labour in the July 1945 election won two parliamentary seats, while in Eire, June 1944, Labour sent to the first chamber eight representatives.

Sweden.—The one European country in which socialists remained at the head of the government throughout the decade 1937–46 was Sweden. In the 1936 parliamentary elections the Social Democratic party, a moderate socialist party, won 112 seats in the lower chamber, 45.9% of the total.

Following the election Per Albin Hansson, leader of the Social Democrats, again assumed the premiership and appointed to his cabinet eight Socialists and four Agrarians. After the outbreak of World War II the Social Democrats, as a means of preserving national unity, organized a new four-party coalition government. In 1940 a new parliamentary election was held which resulted in the Social Democrats' obtaining 134 seats out of 230. One of the chief aims of the government during the following years was the preserving of the nation's neutrality and its independence against the pressures from the third reich. The Social Democrats during World War II gave great aid to the Norwegian and Danish underground and to the cause of the Allies.

In the 1944 elections the Social Democratic party returned 115 members to the lower house. In July 1945 the four-party coalition government was dissolved and on July 31 an all-Social Democratic cabinet was formed.

On Oct. 5, 1946, Prime Minister Hansson died, after serving as prime minister for 14 years. Tage Erlander, minister of education, was chosen as Hansson's successor.

Norway.—In the neighbouring Scandinavian countries of Norway and Denmark the socialist parties, which were in charge of their respective governments during most of the '30s, were forced underground when the Germans occupied those countries during World War II. Following the liberation these parties again became powerful political forces in their respective countries.

In the 1936 elections in Norway the Norwegian Labour party was returned to power, Labour winning 70 seats in a unicameral legislature of 150 representatives. Johan Nygaardsvold, Labour premier from 1932, was again called upon to form the cabinet.

When the Germans invaded the country, many of the leaders of the Labour government escaped from Norway and established in London on June 10, 1940, the official Norwegian government—a coalition government of Labour, Conservatives, Liberals and Agrarians. This government assumed control of the powerful Norwegian merchant marine and directed much of the underground movement which conducted a continuous sabotage against the Germans and the Quisling government set up by the Germans.

Following the defeat of Germany the Norwegian government-in-exile resigned and was reconstituted with Einar Gerhardsen, chairman of the Labour party and formerly mayor of Oslo, as prime minister. In the ensuing elections of Oct. 8, 1945, the first elections held on the European continent after the end of the war, the Norwegian Labourites won a majority of the seats in parliament—76 out of 150. The communists elected 11 members. Gerhardsen again became Norway's prime minister. Trygve Lie, minister of foreign affairs in the Norwegian cabinet from 1940, left this post in 1946 to become secretary general of the United Nations.

Denmark.—In Denmark, where Thorvald Stauning, Social Democrat, had served as prime minister from 1929, the year 1935 found the left-wing parties for the first time in the history of Denmark represented by a majority of members in both the lower and the upper chambers of parliament. This revolution to a Socialist-Radical-controlled legislature made possible the passage of progressive legislation on a scale hitherto unheard of in Danish history. Four years later, on the eve of World War II, the Social Democrats won 64 seats in a house of 149, a decrease of 4, and the Radical party, 14.

On April 9, 1940 when Hitler ordered the invasion of Denmark, King Christian appealed to the people to refrain from resistance on the ground that such resistance would lead to Denmark's annihilation. The Germans occupied the country and deprived the government of most of its power. On July 3, 1940, leaders of the five principal parties decided to "abandon all points of disagreement and unite to make secure the independence and integrity promised our country."

In the following years of World War II, the German government brought great pressure on the Danish government to become a mere puppet of the reich. Many of Hitler's demands, however, were refused. Stauning remained in office and kept the free trade unions intact. Shortly before Stauning's death in May 1942, the reich forced the cabinet to accept Eric Scavenius, collaborationist, as foreign minister, and on Nov. 8, 1942, the Germans compelled the reorganization of the cabinet with Scavenius as premier. On March 23, 1943, in one of the few elections held in Europe during the war, the Social Democrats obtained 45.5% of the total, while the pro-nazi Farmers' and nazi parties received less than 3.5% of the total and the distinctly German nazi party, a little more than 1%.

On May 9, 1945, following the defeat of Germany, a provisional government was formed under Vilhelm Buhl, Social Democrat, an underground leader. In the general elections of Oct. 30, 1945, the Socialist representation in parliament, however, fell to 48. The Communists increased their parliamentary membership to 18, while the Agrarians won 38 seats out of a total of 149. Though the Social Democrats were still the largest party, Buhl refused to form a minority or coalition government, and the Agrarians undertook to organize the first non-socialist government in Denmark since 1929.

France.—At the beginning of the decade 1937–46, the French Socialist party was one of the most prominent of the socialist political organizations on the European continent. In the May 1936 elections Socialists had joined with Radicals, and with Communists, two trade union federations and several other left-wing groups in a popular front movement with a view of effectively fighting fascist forces in France. In the spring elections the Socialist party increased its representation from 101 to 148, and the Communist party, from 10 to 73.

The popular front parties, controlling a majority of seats in the house of deputies, proceeded to form the government. On June 4, 1936, Léon Blum, leader of the Socialist party, was selected as premier. The Socialists were represented in the cabinet by 19 members; the Radicals with 16. The Communists, refusing to join, declared that they would support the government, "while continuing to administer to the masses." The house of deputies, under the leadership of Premier Blum, passed liberal educational, social insurance, taxation and agrarian legislation and authorized the government to take over armament manufacturing plants.

In the spring of 1937 Premier Blum asked for emergency financial powers to protect the franc and public credit against speculative attack. On being denied these powers, he resigned on June 21, 1937. Blum again assumed the premiership March 10, 1938. The senate, however, refused to go along with his financial plan for a graduated capital levy, and he handed in his resignation on April 8, 1938. Socialists refused to accept posts in the ensuing Daladier cabinet, an action which spelled the virtual death of the popular front.

In Sept. 1939, at the outbreak of World War II, the French Socialist party voted its support of the war. It opposed attempts to suppress parliamentary activity and urged a progressive policy in the French control of the country's North African colonies. Party members later became prominent in the war ministry.

With the defeat of France in 1940 and the creation of the Pétain government, the Socialist party was outlawed and Léon Blum and other Socialists were put on trial at Riom, accused of responsibility for France's defeat. As a result of Blum's forceful defense of his role in France as prime minister, the trial was discontinued and Blum and other Socialists were removed from France to prevent their taking part in a revolt against Hitler.

Through the period of the Pétain government Socialists and Communists—the latter after Hitler's invasion of the U.S.S.R.—took an active part in the underground movement. The Socialist party affiliated itself with the National Council of Resistance, which drew up a charter on March 15, 1944, calling, among other things, for the nationalization of mines, electric power, big banks and insurance companies and the abolition of trusts in fields left to private enterprise.

In early 1945 Socialists took an active part in the De Gaulle government, and following the defeat of Germany participated vigorously in the French elections. In the elections of Oct. 21 for the national assembly, the Socialist party came third in the number of parliamentary seats, electing 139 deputies, as compared with 151 for the Communists and 150 for the Popular Republican (Catholic) party. These three parties obtained nearly nine-tenths of the popular vote.

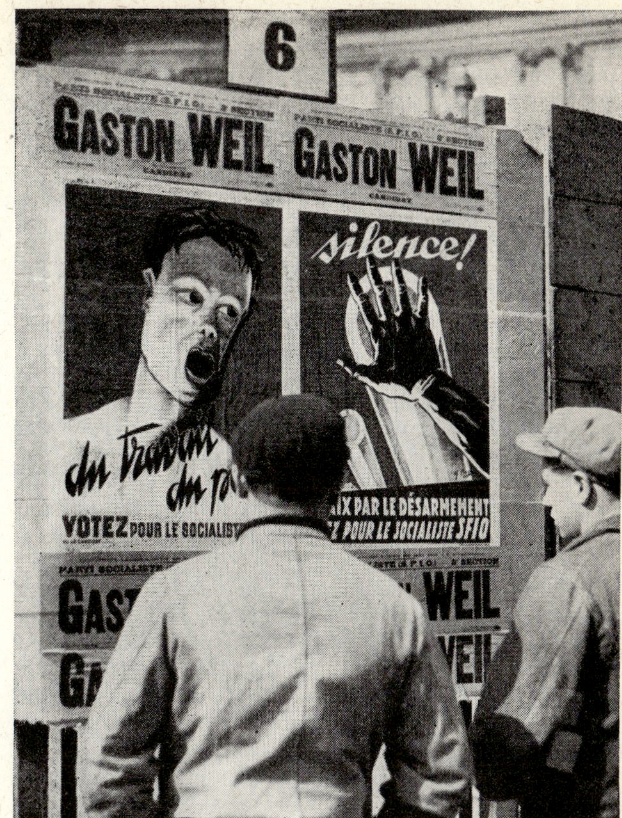

Campaign poster for a French Socialist candidate prior to the general elections of Oct. 1945, in which workers were promised peace through disarmament

In the coalition cabinet formed following the elections under Gen. de Gaulle, Socialists received six important posts and Felix Gouin, Socialist, was elected president of the assembly. On Jan. 20, 1946, Gen. de Gaulle resigned from the presidency; the Socialists, among others, had opposed his demand for increasing military appropriations and an independent executive—and three days later Gouin, Socialist leader, was elected president.

On Jan. 26, 1946, Gouin organized a three-party cabinet containing seven Socialists, six Communists, six Popular Republicans and one nonparty man. Under Gouin's presidency the constituent assembly in March voted for the nationalization of France's electrical and gas industries, these industries to be directed by an 18-member commission composed equally of representatives of the state, the consumers and the industry. In April the constituent assembly decreed the nationalization of many of France's largest insurance companies, following the nationalization of the Bank of France, the four principal deposit banks and many of the mines.

The Socialist party joined with the Communists in supporting a constitution which proposed giving to a unicameral national assembly power to elect a premier from among its members and to select a president of the republic, who would exercise little but honorary functions. The French people, however, rejected the proposed constitution. On June 2, 1946, in the new elections for the assembly, Socialists elected 122 deputies, Communists 149, Popular Republicans 162, Edouard Herriot's Radical party 40 and the Right parties 54. Gouin immediately resigned his presidency and Georges Bidault, of the Popular Republicans, was chosen to lead the nation. On Oct. 13, a new and revised draft of the constitution, supported by the three principal parties, was adopted by a small majority against the opposition of Gen. de Gaulle. The preamble of the constitution, among other things, declared that "all property and all businesses whose exploitation has acquired the characteristics of a national public service or a monopoly in fact should become the property of the community."

Belgium.—In the elections of 1936, the Belgian Labour party had elected 70 deputies, and again became the country's largest single party, with the Catholics' representation dropping from 79 members in the lower chamber to 63. In the new four-party cabinet formed by Paul van Zeeland, Catholic leader, Paul-Henri Spaak, Socialist, was appointed minister of foreign affairs. In the electoral fight of 1937, the Labourites supported Prime Minister van Zeeland in his successful fight against Léon Degrelle, Rexist (fascist) leader.

Early in 1938 Spaak became prime minister, heading a coalition government. On Christmas day 1938 the Belgian socialist movement lost by death its most distinguished leader, Emile Vandervelde. In the elections of 1939 the Labour party again gave place to the Catholics as the country's leading party, and during the next year Hubert Pierlot, Catholic, and Spaak, Socialist, alternated as premiers. Following the German invasion of May 1940 many leading Socialists left Belgium and Spaak and other Socialist leaders became affiliated with the Belgian government-in-exile.

On Feb. 11, 1945, following the return of the government, Achille van Acker, a leading member of the Belgian underground, was asked to form a four-party cabinet with Spaak again as foreign minister. The following year, in the parliamentary elections of Feb. 17, 1946, the Catholic party won first place, electing 92 deputies out of 202; the Labourites 69 and the Communists 23.

During the next month or so temporary coalition cabinets were formed under Van Acker and Spaak. On March 31, 1946, Van Acker formed a government of Socialists, Communists and Liberals, with the Catholics as the government's chief opposition. In the following days the question as to whether Belgium should invite King Leopold to return continued to provide a subject for much bitter discussion within and without parliament, the Socialists and other left-wing groups urging the abdication of the king. On July 26 the chamber of deputies, in voting its confidence in the Van Acker government, indirectly voiced its support of the abdication proposal.

Another political crisis, however, soon took place, resulting in the organization on Aug. 2 of another coalition government, this time headed by Camille Huysmans, veteran Socialist, long burgomaster of Antwerp.

Netherlands.—In the Netherlands the mid-'30s found the Social Democratic Labour party the second largest in the field with the Catholic party occupying first place. In the elections of May 1937 the S.D.L.P. secured 23 seats out of a total of 100, the Catholics 31 and the Communists 3. Two years later, in Aug. 1939, on the eve of World War II, the Social Democrats entered the cabinet for the first time in the country's history.

When the Germans invaded the Netherlands in May 1940, the queen and all members of the cabinet left the country and set up a government-in-exile in London. Queen Wilhelmina entrusted Willem Drees, leader of the Social Democratic party, and Willem Schermerhorn, leader of the Peoples movement, with the formation of the cabinet. A provisional coalition cabinet was set up containing Social Democratic, Catholic, Christian Historical and Peoples movement representatives. Schermerhorn, a former professor of geodesy and a resistance leader during the occupation, was elected premier.

Following the formation of the cabinet, members of the Peoples movement merged with the Socialists, with the Liberal Democratic party and with advanced Catholic and Protestant groups, to form a Dutch Labour party. The party, in its inaugural program, expressed itself in favour of the nationalization of mines, the Bank of the Netherlands, the nation's railroads, blast furnaces and business monopolies.

The first postwar elections in May 1946, resulted in giving the Catholic People's party 32 seats, the Labour party 29, the four Protestant parties 23, the Communists 10 and the Liberals 6. As Labour came out second in these elections, Schermerhorn resigned as premier and was succeeded by Louis J. M. Beel, liberal Catholic.

The Catholics, following the elections, asked Labour to form a coalition cabinet with them. Labour replied that it would join only if its conciliatory Indonesian policy were accepted and applied by persons acceptable to it. Following several weeks of negotiation a coalition cabinet of five Catholics, five Labourites and three nonpolitical specialists was formed. Prof. Schermerhorn was appointed commissioner general of the Netherlands Indies. In the July 1946 municipal elections, Labour led the field in Rotterdam and the Hague, and the Communists in Amsterdam.

Spain.—In the Spanish elections of 1936 Socialist, Communist and other groups had banded together under the name "popular front" and in the elections of that year won 256 seats, against 165 captured by the right and 52 by the centre party. The ensuing government, under Pres. Manuel Azaña and Premier Casares Quiroga, threw down a challenge to fascist forces which soon began to mobilize under Gen. Francisco Franco, who declared his goal to be a "broadly totalitarian" government.

Gen. Franco received much aid from the governments of Hitler and Mussolini and soon became the ruler over much of Spain. A serious dissension occurred within the anti-Franco movement when anarcho-syndicalists staged an uprising in Barcelona in May 1937. After this outbreak anarcho-syndicalists were eliminated from the new cabinet headed by Dr. Juan Negrín, who succeeded Largo Caballero. Negrín and his cabinet were in turn ousted by a council of defense, formed on March 5, 1939, of all parties except the Communist. On March 28, 1939, following a week of revolt on the part of the Communists and the former premier's supporters, the loyalist government surrendered. All Socialist and Radical groups were suppressed, and all political groups were merged in one government party under the control of Gen. Franco. Thousands of antifascists were arrested, imprisoned and executed.

On Nov. 22, 1943, many of the republican leaders set up a Spanish Committee of Liberation to prepare a provisional regime to succeed Franco. On Aug. 29, 1945, a Spanish Republican government-in-exile, headed by former Premier José Giral, was formed. During the succeeding months this group conducted a widespread campaign against Franco.

Switzerland.—The middle of the 1930s found the Swiss Social Democratic party the largest in the country, with a total of 50 seats in the lower house's 194. In 1943, for the first time, a Socialist was admitted to the Swiss federal council of seven, chosen by parliament. In the election of that year the Social Democratic party increased its representation in the national council to 54—28% of the total membership—7 seats more than its nearest rival, the Radical Democratic party. During and following the parliamentary campaign the Social Democrats advocated as a part of their postwar program the nationalization of heavy industries and of private enterprises of a monopolistic nature.

Austria.—In central Europe the end of the decade saw the formerly powerful socialist movements in Austria, Hungary and Germany on the road to revival, following years of suppression. In Austria, from 1934 until the defeat of Germany in 1945, the Socialists existed only as an underground movement. On April 29, 1945, when it was clear that the defeat of Germany was imminent, an Austrian provisional government was set up in Vienna under the leadership of Dr. Karl Renner, Socialist and former chancellor of the Austrian republic.

Elections for the national and provincial assemblies were held on Nov. 25, 1945, resulting in the election of 84 members of the Catholic People's party to the national legislature, 76 Social Democrats and only 5 Communists, in a body of 165 members. In Vienna the Social Democrats elected the largest number of councilmen and the city's mayor. Following the establishment in December of the second Austrian republic, Dr. Renner was elected president, and Leopold Figl of the Catholic party took over the chancellorship. Karl Gruber, Social Democrat, was chosen vice-chancellor.

On the initiative of the Social Democrats the Austrian parliament during 1946 passed a law for the nationalization of a number of branches of industry, including oil, shipping, electric power, metallurgy and banking. The soviet military commander demanded that this law be annulled on the ground that these industries, many of which had been forcibly Germanized under the nazi regime, belonged to the soviet government. The U.S. commander, with the support of the British, rejected this demand, with the result that the law went into effect on Sept. 9, 1946. Soviet authorities, however, arrested a number of Austrians who attempted to carry out the parliamentary decrees.

Germany.—In 1933 the socialists and all parties except the nazi party were outlawed in Germany. Many socialists, communists and other anti-nazis were active in the underground movement, and many were sent to concentration camps and executed.

On the defeat of Germany, the territory remaining in the former reich was temporarily partitioned into soviet, British, French and U.S. zones. On Sept. 13, 1945, the U.S.S.R. announced the establishment of a German government for its entire occupation zone, composed of Communists, left-wing Socialists, Christian Democrats, Liberal Democrats and Independents. The U.S.S.R. occupying forces threw their weight on the side of the Communists. As a result of strong pressure exerted by the soviet occupying authorities, Social Democrats in the zone in April 1946, joined with Communists in a Socialist Unity party. Social Democrats in other zones overwhelmingly defeated the proposal of organic unity with the Communists.

During the year, state elections took place in the British, U.S. and French zones. In the U.S. and French zones, the Christian Social Union (Catholic party) obtained the largest number of votes; the Social Democrats came second and the Communists a poor third. In the soviet zone the Socialist Unity party won first place. In the municipal elections in the four zones of Berlin on that date, however, the Social Democrats, who refused to join the Communists, received 49% of the nearly 2,000,000 votes; the Christian Democratic party 22%, the Socialist Unity party 20%, and the Liberal Democrats (conservative) 9%.

Hungary.—In Hungary, Socialists under the dictatorship of Adm. Nicholas Horthy had been a negligible political force during the 1930s. However, when the soviets entered Hungary in Dec. 1944, a provisional national assembly was set up, which formed on Dec. 23, 1944, a provisional government.

In the cabinet thus organized a number of Socialists were appointed to ministerial posts, together with Small Landowners and Communists.

A year later, in the parliamentary elections of Nov. 4, 1945, the Communists urged that a single all-party election list be drawn up. This proposal was rejected by the other parties. In the elections the conservative Small Landowners party scored a decisive victory over the Socialist and Communist opponents, the Small Landowners winning 245 seats, 60% of the total, as compared with 69 seats for the Social Democrats, 70 for the Communists and 23 for the Peasant party. In the four-party cabinet formed following the election, under the Small Landowners' leader, Premier Zoltan Tildy, Socialists were appointed to head the ministries of justice, commerce and industry.

The soviets who were occupying the country, however, through the Communist control of the important ministries of communications, interior, public welfare and other positions, and their domination of many industries formerly under nazi control secured a dominating control over the economic and political life of that country.

Italy.—After World War II the Italian Socialists (who had functioned underground during Mussolini's regime) were represented in the six-party government formed in June 1945, under Ferrucio Parri and later under Alcide de Gasperi, by Pietro Nenni, vice-premier, and others. In the general elections of June 2, 1946—the first elections for a democratic parliament in more than 20 years—the socialist party obtained second place, receiving more than one-fifth of the total votes and electing 115 deputies. The Christian Democrats came first with 207 deputies and the Communists third with 104 successful candidates out of a total of 556.

Following the election, Socialists and Communists received four seats in the De Gasperi cabinet, with the Christian Democrats taking eight seats, the Republicans two and the independents one. Pietro Nenni, leader of the Socialist party, became a minister without portfolio and later minister of foreign affairs.

On Oct. 24, 1946, the Italian Socialist party signed an agreement with the Communists in which both parties pledged themselves, while retaining their autonomy and individuality, to co-ordinate their respective activities in liquidating fascist remnants, defending the republic and public freedoms, providing among other things for the nationalization of monopolistic industries, large banks and public services, improvement of living conditions, abolition of large estates and strengthening of co-operatives.

Eastern Europe.—In eastern Europe, not including the soviet union, the strongest socialist movements during the decade 1937–46 were those in Finland and Czechoslovakia. In the Finnish elections of 1939 the Social Democrats won 80 out of the 200 seats in the country's unicameral parliament, the Agrarians trailing with 56 representatives. In 1939 the Social Democrats joined with other parties in resisting the soviet invasion. In the elections of March 1945 the Social Democrats won 52 seats; the Popular Democrats, composed of Communists and their sympathizers, 51. On March 24, 1946, M. Pekkala, Socialist, became premier in a coalition cabinet. As a result of pressure from the U.S.S.R., a number of Finnish leaders were tried on charges of leading Finland into the war with the soviet union and Väinö Tanner, leader of the prewar Socialists and co-operators, was declared guilty of failing to take advantage of offers to mediate for a settlement of the war with the soviet union.

In Czechoslovakia prewar Socialists were divided into Czech and German Social Democrats. In a coalition government under Pres. Eduard Beneš, Socialists held a number of key positions.

On the return of the government-in-exile to Czechoslovakia early in April 1946, a four-party coalition government was formed with Zdeněk Fierlinger, Social Democrat, as premier. In Oct. 1946, Socialists supported the government in nationalizing all enterprises with more than 400 to 500 employees.

On May 27, 1946, Czech Communists won 93 seats; Slovak Communists 21; Czech Social Democrats 37; other parties 94. On July 3 Klement Gottwald, Communist, was elected premier, and a coalition government was formed with Communists in the majority. The government parties pledged themselves to a foreign policy favourable to the U.S.S.R.

In Poland Socialists exercised but little influence in the semidictatorship prevailing in that country following the 1935 dissolution of parliament. Socialists were active in the government-in-exile in London during World War II and in the Polish underground movement. After World War II the party leadership was split over the question of co-operation with the Lublin government set up by the U.S.S.R. and later recognized, following some changes, by the United States and Great Britain. Edward Osubka-Morawski, left-wing Socialist, became premier of this coalition government.

At the meeting of the deputies to the Polish Provisional National council in Feb. 1946 a motion was passed to nationalize all essential industries employing more than 50 workers, industries which contained 40% of all employees in trade and industry and 10% of all wage earners, agriculture included.

This decision was ratified in a referendum passed by the electorate on June 30, 1946.

Throughout the decade 1937–46 Socialists in Bulgaria, Rumania, Yugoslavia and Greece were in a weak position. In 1946, in all those countries except Greece, the Communist party, backed by military force, was the directing force in the governments. In the Bulgarian elections of Oct. 27, 1946, Communists secured 277 seats out of 465; Social Democrats, 9. In Yugoslavia the opposition parties refused to take part in the Nov. 11, 1945, elections for the constituent assembly, and Premier Marshal Josip Brozovich (Tito) announced that his opponents had cast only 10% of the vote. In Greece Socialists participated in the National Unity government under George Papandreou in late 1944, but were not represented in the cabinet formed after the return of the monarchy in 1946.

Australia.—In the countries of the Pacific during the decade 1937–46, the most stable labour and socialist movements were those in Australia and New Zealand. In the 1930s the Australian Labour party constituted the chief opposition in the country, and it was not until Oct. 1941, after occupying the opposition benches for a decade, that the party, under the leadership of John Curtin, formed the government.

In constituting the cabinet, Labour invited the opposition to take part in the Advisory War council on a 50–50 basis.

In the elections of Aug. 1943 Labour won another sweeping victory, electing 49 out of 75 members of the lower house and all of the 19 seats in the senate for which elections were held. This was the first time that the party had had a majority of seats in both the senate and the lower house of the Australian parliament.

On July 5, 1945, Prime Minister Curtin died and was succeeded by Joseph B. Chifley, treasurer and minister of postwar reconstruction in the Curtin cabinet. During the ensuing year the government nationalized all interstate civil air-line operations and extended the sphere of public banking. In the elections of Sept. 29, 1946, the first since the conclusion of the war, Labour was again victorious, winning 44 seats, with the Liberals trailing with 17, the Country party with 11 and the Independent Labourites with 2.

New Zealand.—The beginning of the decade found the New Zealand Labour party the majority party in parliament as a result of the 1935 elections. Under Labour Prime Minister Michael Joseph Savage, the government during the succeeding years enacted much advanced social and economic legislation, including a comprehensive Social Security law.

On the death of Premier Savage, Peter Fraser became prime minister on April 30, 1940, with Walter Nash as deputy premier. In the Sept. 24, 1943, elections, the Labour party won 45 seats as compared with 34 for the National party. Following the elections the premier continued an all-Labour party cabinet.

Japan.—The Social Democratic party was revived after the defeat of Japan. In Dec. 1945 it demanded that the government of Kijuro Shidehara resign en masse because this government had "demonstrated that it lacks power to meet the current situation." In the April 1946 elections Socialists elected 94 members to the diet out of a total of 466, Liberals 142, Co-operatives 17 and Communists 5.

India.—There was little organized Socialist activity in India during the decade, but great socialistic sentiment, as witnessed by the fact that Pandit Jawaharlal Nehru, prominent Socialist, became India's most important political leader with the possible exception of Gandhi, being chosen to head the Indian Congress party and in 1946 the Indian interim government.

Latin America.—The decade saw a considerable growth of socialist influence in Latin America. The party, however, actually lost ground in Argentina where by 1940 it achieved considerable strength both in popular vote and in representation in congress. It was the victim of the quasi-fascist movement which in 1946, in a legitimate election, confirmed the power of Juan D. Perón, who had won considerable working-class support. The Socialists, part of the coalition against him, won no seats in congress.

In Peru, the socialistic Aprista party—later called the People's party—long suppressed by the Peruvian semidictatorship—was the strongest element in a popular front movement which, on June 10, 1945, in the first free election for decades, put José Bustamento Rivero in the president's chair.

In Venezuela, socialists were active in the Democratic Action party which won a substantial victory in the election of Oct. 27, 1946. The party was committed to a considerable degree of nationalization of industry and the breaking up of large estates.

In Chile, 1946 found the Communists more powerful than the Socialists. During the existence of the nazi-soviet pact, the Socialists had demanded that the Communists be excluded from the popular front which then controlled the government. The Radicals refused, and the Socialists formally withdrew from the popular front, although the Socialist ministers continued in the cabinet. Some sort of co-operation continued in the 1941 elections and in 1942 the Socialists supported Juan Antonio Rios, the successful Radical candidate for the presidency and received three cabinet posts. But in 1946 the Socialist party ran its own candidate, Bernado Ibanez, who obtained but 12,000 votes as against 190,000 for the winning Radical-Communist candidate, Gabriel Gonzalez Videla. The latter also received the support of some of the Socialists.

In general, through all Latin-American countries, including Mexico, Cuba and Brazil, Communist influence at the end of the decade was stronger than Socialist influence in the growing labour movement, and Communist propaganda was better organized and far better financed than Socialist.

Canada.—The principal progress of organized socialism on the North American continent was in Canada. In 1932 the Co-operative Commonwealth federation (C.C.F.) was formed in Calgary, Alta., and in 1933 in Regina, Sask., adopted a Socialist program of action. Originally it was a coalition of various groups, including avowed Socialists. In a comparatively short time it grew into a unified party, which, by June 1944, won an overwhelming victory in the Saskatchewan elections and set up a government headed by Thomas C. Douglas. This government made remarkable progress in such social legislation as lay within the field of a Canadian province.

In the federal elections of 1945 the C.C.F. parliamentary representation increased from 10 to 28 and its vote doubled to 806,000 (⅙ of the total). As a result of provincial elections that year, the party secured 38% of the vote in British Columbia; 34% in Manitoba; 22% in Ontario. M. J. Coldwell, leader of the C.C.F. in parliament, became the party's president following the death of J. S. Woodsworth, one of the chief founders of the party.

United States.—In the United States, by far the richest and most powerful country in the world after World War II, private capitalism retained a degree of vigour and power which everywhere else it had lost. Nevertheless, state intervention in economic life, begun by the first Roosevelt administration under depression conditions, continued. Many welfare measures once regarded as socialist were adopted, and organized labour, especially in the C.I.O. took a more vigorous and better-organized interest in political action than at the beginning of the decade. The agency of such action was principally the Political Action committee, which followed the line of endorsing progressive candidates. At the end of the decade, however, there was considerable discussion of the formation of a new party. In New York state, under favourable election laws, two new statewide parties had been formed; first the American Labor party in 1936, and later the Liberal party, which had split off from the A.L.P. on the ground that the latter was communist-dominated. Both parties had socialistic platforms, but for major offices usually endorsed the Democratic candidates.

In 1946 a National Education committee for a New Party was organized to stimulate the formation of a party analagous to the C.C.F. in Canada. Its program could be described as socialistic, and the Socialist party at its 1946 convention made more definite and emphatic its long-standing endorsement of the emergence of a new mass party. The Socialist party, the Social Democratic federation, the Michigan Commonwealth federation and various progressive groups sent official or unofficial representatives to the conferences, out of which the new committee was formed. John Dewey was made its honorary president and J. Philip Randolph, president of the Brotherhood of Sleeping Car Porters, its acting president.

The Socialist party itself continued its own electoral activities but, on the whole, lost ground, a process which was first noted in the 1936 election. Part of the reason was the steady tendency in important states to monopolize the ballot by new and more stringent election laws or by more stringent interpretation of old laws. The principal reason, however, for the decline in Socialist votes was the general swing of labour and progressive elements to support of Roosevelt in his various campaigns. In 1936 the Social Democratic federation split off from the party over various issues of policy and in particular because of fear that the party was becoming too friendly and co-operative with Communists.

The S.D.F. supported Roosevelt from the 1936 campaign on. In New York state, where their principal strength lay, they participated in the formation of the American Labor party and later of the Liberal party. Connecticut Socialists under Jasper MacLevy, mayor of Bridgeport, withdrew in 1936 from the Socialist party on the issue of state autonomy but supported the party ticket in national elections. By the end of the decade cordial relations were re-established between the Socialist party and the S.D.F., and there was talk of organic unity.

In 1936, 1940 and 1944 Norman Thomas was Socialist presidential candidate. His running mates for vice-president were George Nelson of Wisconsin in 1936, Maynard Krueger of Illinois in 1940 and Darlington Hoopes of Pennsylvania in 1944. The recorded vote fell to 80,419 in 1944. In the same year the Socialist Labor party, rigid Marxists according to the semisyndicalist interpretation of Daniel DeLeon, received 45,335 votes.

Until the Japanese attack on Pearl Harbor the Socialist party opposed U.S. entry into World War II. Its 1944 platform called for: (1) a political offensive to help win the earliest peace that would last, followed by the forma-

Norman Thomas (left) with Maynard C. Krueger, who was elected national chairman of the U.S. Socialist party at the party's convention in Milwaukee, Wis., June 1, 1942, after Thomas declined to run again

tion of an inclusive international federation and by co-operative action to remove the causes of war; (2) social ownership and democratic control of "the commanding heights of" the economic order—natural resources, money, banking and credit and monopolies, semimonopolies and other exploited industries; (3) the establishment of equality of rights and obligations among all races; and (4) "a democratic socialist party with mass support" similar to the Canadian C.C.F. (*See* also COMMUNISM; LABOUR PARTY, GREAT BRITAIN; LIBERALISM.)

BIBLIOGRAPHY.—British Labour Party, *Proceedings of Annual Conferences;* M. J. Coldwell, *Left Turn Canada* (1945); Margaret Cole and Charles Smith, editors, *Democratic Sweden* (1938); A. Gray, *Socialist Tradition* (1946); Harry W. Laidler, *Social-Economic Movements* (1945); Walter Nash, *New Zealand —A Working Democracy* (1943); Joseph A. Schumpeter, *Capitalism, Socialism and Democracy* (1946); Adolph Sturmthal, *The Tragedy of European Labor* (1943); Norman Thomas, *We Have a Future* (1941); Barbara Wooton, *Freedom under Planning* (1945); Periodicals: *The Call; Modern Review; New Leader; Fabian Quarterly* (London); *Tribune* (London). *See* also publications of Socialist Vanguard and Socialist Clarity Groups (London). (H. W. L.; N. T.)

Socialist Soviet Republics

See UNION OF SOVIET SOCIALIST REPUBLICS.

Socialized Medicine

See MEDICINE.

Social Legislation

See LAW.

Social Security

The U.S. Social Security act of 1935 and its subsequent amendments, provided measures to improve the general welfare through eight programs for which the Social Security administration carried federal responsibilities. Under organizational changes effective in July 1946, federal responsibilities for social security were vested in the Social Security administration, one of four main units of the Federal Security agency (*q.v.*). The Social Security administration included all bureaus of the Social Security board, which was abolished in the reorganization, and in addition included the children's bureau, which was transferred with all but its child labour functions from the department of labour.

Federal old-age and survivors insurance, financed by employer and employee contributions, afforded insured industrial and commercial workers continuing retirement income in old age and monthly income for their dependents and survivors, as well as lump-sum death payments.

Under federal-state unemployment insurance, a federal tax of 3% was levied on industrial and commercial employers of eight or more workers, and these employers credited, against as much as 90% of the federal tax, the amounts they paid—or would have paid but for experience-rating reductions in state contribution rates—to state unemployment funds. Benefits were financed largely from employer contributions under state laws, which provided weekly payments to persons in approximately the same employments when they were out of work through no fault of their own. Administrative costs of these state programs were paid from federal grants to states.

Federal-state public assistance provided, under three separate programs (old-age assistance, aid to dependent children and aid to the blind), for federal grants-in-aid to states to meet part of the costs of monthly payments to needy aged persons, the needy blind and children deprived of parental support or care, and part of the costs of administering these programs.

Under three federal-state programs for maternal and child welfare, federal grants-in-aid to the states met part of the costs of state programs for maternal and child health services, services for crippled children and child welfare services.

Provisions for similar federal grants-in-aid to states for development and expansion of their programs for vocational rehabilitation and for public health services, first incorporated in the Social Security act, were embodied in separate federal laws enacted in 1943 and 1944, respectively. Other provisions for regular insurance payments or related income to persons who had acquired rights—through employment or earnings—to retirement, disability or unemployment benefits, and sometimes benefits to their dependent survivors, were established under separate programs for railroad workers, war veterans, federal employees and employees of some state and local governments, and under workmen's compensation programs. General assistance, financed without federal co-operation, was made available as a form of public assistance in all states, but was often meagre in rural areas.

Table I indicates the changes in the amounts paid under public programs to provide continuing income to persons who acquired rights to social insurance and related benefits and to those who qualified for public aid. The table also includes figures on the number of insurance beneficiaries and recipients of public aid on the rolls of each program in June of the years 1937–45. Table II (p. 86) shows the aggregate wages and salaries in employments that carried social insurance or related protection under contributory retirement and unemployment insurance programs; it also indicates the amounts contributed to those programs and the assets of the trust funds through which such programs were financed.

In 1937, at the opening of the decade, the Social Security act of 1935 still represented a new and virtually untried experiment in the United States. The Social Security board had begun to set up the machinery for a nation-wide system of old-age insurance for industrial and commercial workers, and millions of persons had applied for and received their "social security account numbers." States similarly had made preparations for administering their unemployment insurance programs. The three federal-state programs for old-age assistance, aid to dependent children and aid to the blind were in operation in about two-thirds of the 51 jurisdictions of the United States. Acceptance of federal sharing in financial responsibility for continuing income to needy persons was only slowly gaining ground. The public health and maternal and child health provisions of the act, in contrast, were in operation in all jurisdictions, those for vocational rehabilitation in all but 2, while 45 jurisdictions received federal aid toward services for crippled children and for child welfare services.

Early in 1937, decisions of the supreme court of the United States, by affirming the constitutionality of the insurance programs of the Social Security act, allayed fears that these new ventures in social insurance might be declared inconsistent with the principles on which the nation was founded. The Social Security board—established under that act—had already foreseen that the scope of the act would need expansion. Working with an advisory council, appointed with the co-operation of the senate committee on finance, the board had begun to study ways to strengthen the social security program.

President Franklin D. Roosevelt, the Social Security board and many other persons and organizations were

Table I.—*Selected Data on Social Security and Related Programs in the United States, 1937–45*
(In thousands)

Program	1937	1938	1939	1940	1941	1942	1943	1944	1945
	Beneficiaries under social insurance and related programs, June								
Retirement, disability and survivor programs*:									
Old-age and survivors insurance	...	...	...	95.5	336.2	529.9	676.3	846.3	1,106.0
Railroad retirement	7.3	108.3	132.3	144.3	153.0	156.9	160.0	164.1	171.5
Federal employee systems:									
Civil service	53.8	56.7	59.0	62.7	66.9	70.0	74.8	79.2	88.0
Other contributory†	.5	.5	.6	.6	.7	.8	.8	.9	1.0
Noncontributory†	26.5	28.0	29.8	32.2	36.7	33.5	30.6	32.2	35.8
Rhode Island sickness compensation‡	...	...	...	...	...	...	6.0	8.3	7.1
State and local employee systems†	§	§	§	152.3	158.2	171.0	182.6	195.5	208.0
Veterans' pensions and compensation	911.2	907.8	919.4	928.7	935.4	939.8	937.8	1,150.9	1,681.5
Workmen's compensation	§	§	§	§	§	§	§	§	§
Unemployment insurance programs:									
State unemployment insurance‡	§	870.0	802.2	1,268.6	683.9	552.7	100.3	77.9	129.4
Railroad unemployment insurance‖	...	...	...	31.4	11.4	4.7	.7	.4	.8
Veterans' unemployment allowances¶	...	...	...	...	...	...	...	...	31.8
Public assistance programs♀:	Recipients of public assistance, June								
Old-age assistance	1,290	1,657	1,842	1,967	2,167	2,250	2,167	2,087	2,038
Aid to dependent children:									
Children	473	638	748	831	942	949	747	653	647
Families	192	258	311	346	391	395	304	261	256
Aid to the blind	50	62	68	72	74	79	78	74	71
General assistance	1,277	1,648	1,568	1,355	934	607	354	258	234
Subsistence payments to farmers	191	93	69	60	40	12	...	...	...
Federal work programs♀:	Persons employed on federal work programs, June								
Civilian Conservation corps	277	245	266	240	195	53	...	...	...
National Youth administration:									
Students	249	219	280	313	357	133	§	...	...
Out-of-school	173	209	214	269	384	184	...	...	...
Work Projects administration	1,874	2,741	2,569	1,734	1,370	671	2	...	...
	Payments under social security and related programs, calendar year								
Total	$3,269,045	$4,458,660	$4,428,743	$4,296,268	$3,824,683	$3,259,470	$2,534,678	$2,774,341	$3,834,331
Retirement, disability and survivor programs*	938,101	1,014,779	1,055,587	1,130,803	1,251,202	1,363,607	1,473,353	1,764,804	2,281,554
Old-age and survivors insurance	1,278	10,478	13,896	40,594	93,923	137,045	172,850	218,097	287,757
Railroad retirement	40,445	98,440	110,659	118,111	124,892	128,523	133,060	138,062	147,050
Federal employee systems	108,664	113,687	118,862	125,491	129,502	132,570	145,636	190,691	248,478
Civil service	61,574	64,048	66,129	71,106	75,718	80,580	91,114	128,100	176,978
Other contributory†	911	1,044	1,147	1,212	1,560	2,093	2,523	2,955	3,500
Noncontributory†	46,179	48,595	51,586	53,173	52,224	49,897	51,999	59,636	68,000
Rhode Island sickness compensation	...	...	...	...	...	...	2,857	5,035	4,669
State and local employee systems†	144,000	151,000	157,000	163,000	175,000	194,000	210,000	218,000	228,000
Veterans' pensions and compensation	399,714	406,174	420,257	427,507	436,712	440,578	451,833	605,365	957,117
Workmen's compensationδ	244,000	235,000	234,913	256,100	291,173	330,891	357,117	389,554	408,483
Unemployment insurance programs	2,132	393,786	434,994	534,661	358,858	350,352	80,560	67,080	563,180
State unemployment insurance	2,132	393,786	429,298	518,700	344,321	344,084	79,643	62,385	445,866
Railroad unemployment insurance‖	...	...	5,696	15,961	14,537	6,268	917	582	2,359
Veteran's unemployment allowances¶	...	...	...	...	...	...	...	4,113	114,955
Public assistance programs♀	839,839	1,007,566	1,067,889	1,053,266	1,002,503	965,089	930,234	942,457	989,597
Old-age assistance	310,442	392,384	430,480	474,952	541,519	595,152	653,171	693,338	726,422
Aid to dependent children	70,451	97,442	114,949	133,243	153,153	158,435	140,942	135,015	149,667
Aid to the blind	16,171	18,958	20,752	21,826	22,901	24,660	25,143	25,342	26,593
General assistance	406,881	476,203	482,653	404,963	272,649	180,571	110,978	88,762	86,915
Subsistence payments to farmers	35,894	22,579	19,055	18,282	12,281	6,271	...	...	...
Federal work programs♀	1,488,973	2,042,529	1,870,273	1,577,538	1,212,120	580,422	50,531	...	...
Civilian Conservation corps	245,756	230,318	230,513	215,846	155,604	34,030	...	...	...
National Youth administration:									
Student work	24,287	19,598	22,707	26,864	25,118	11,328	3,794	...	...
Out-of-school	32,664	41,560	51,538	65,211	94,032	32,009	...	...	...
Work Projects administration	1,186,266	1,751,053	1,565,515	1,269,617	937,366	503,055	46,737	...	...

*Beneficiaries represent persons receiving monthly benefits; exclude persons receiving lump-sum payments only. Payments include lump-sum death payments and, for the federal civil service and state and local employee systems, refunds.
†Data estimated; for 1945, preliminary.
‡Average weekly number.
§Not available.
‖Average number of persons receiving benefits for unemployment in a 14-day registration period. Benefit payments began in July 1939.
¶Average weekly number, under Servicemen's Readjustment act of 1944, effective Sept. 1944. In addition, readjustment allowances were paid to 10,600 self-employed veterans during June 1945. Self-employment allowances totalled $102,000 in 1944 and $11,675,000 in 1945.
♀Data through 1942 for continental United States only.
δCash and medical benefits. Data estimated; for 1945, preliminary.

concerned about the limited coverage of the insurance programs, which excluded agricultural labour, domestic service, employment by private nonprofit and governmental agencies, maritime service and self-employment, types of service for which little or no insurance protection was afforded under other public measures. They were concerned also with the low levels of benefits and the lack of adequate protection against the risks of disability and death of the family wage earner, the wide variations among states in adequacy of unemployment insurance provisions, and the meagre provisions which some of the states and localities could afford to make for public assistance to needy persons and for health and welfare services.

Old-age, Survivor, and Disability Insurance.—Significant changes were made in the old-age insurance program by the Social Security act amendments of 1939. Following closely the recommendations of the Advisory council, whose report was issued at the close of 1938, the program was revised to begin monthly benefit payments in 1940, rather than in 1942, to provide supplementary benefits to dependents of retired workers and monthly survivor benefits to survivors of deceased workers, to increase the amount of benefits payable in the early years of the system and to permit workers to acquire wage credits after the age of 65. The amendments also repealed provisions for lump-sum payments to workers at the age of 65, established the old-age and survivors insurance trust fund to take over the assets of the old-age reserve account and provided for automatic appropriation to that fund of all employer and employee contributions toward financing the program.

Recommendations for wide extension of the coverage of the program were not adopted, however, and the employer and employee contribution rates were kept at 1% each until 1943, when rates were to double. This scheduled increase was later postponed, however, each year that it became imminent. In 1944, congress authorized the appropriation of federal funds to the old-age and survivors insurance trust fund of any additional amounts which might be needed to finance future benefits, and the house com-

Table II.—*Pay Rolls in Employments Covered by Selected Contributory Social Insurance and Related Programs, Contributions Collected and Trust Fund Assets, 1937–45*
(In millions)

Year	Total	Retirement programs: Old-age and survivors insurance	Retirement programs: Railroad retirement	Federal civil-service retirement	State and local government retirement	Unemployment insurance programs: Total	Unemployment insurance programs: State unemployment insurance	Unemployment insurance programs: Railroad unemployment insurance
Total pay rolls in employments covered by specified program								
1937	$37,968	$32,770	$2,290	$1,050	$1,858	*	*	...
1938	34,164	29,026	2,028	1,139	1,971	$28,228	$26,200	$2,028
1939	37,638	32,222	2,161	1,221	2,034	31,230	29,069	2,161
1940	41,721	35,668	2,273	1,430	2,350	34,723	32,450	2,273
1941	52,606	45,417	2,687	1,912	2,590	44,833	42,146	2,687
1942	67,919	58,147	3,382	3,600	2,790	58,178	54,796	3,382
1943	81,972	69,747	4,085	5,100	3,040	70,191	66,106	4,085
1944	86,637	73,310	4,507	5,600	3,220	73,628	69,121	4,507
1945†	85,156	71,311	4,514	5,840	3,491	70,444	65,930	4,514
Contributions collected								
1937	725	493	93	37	102	567	567	...
1938	734	474	111	39	110	778	778	...
1939	831	568	113	42	108	841	825	16‡
1940	929	637	130	50	112	921	854	67
1941	1,123	789	148	71	115	1,080	1,006	74
1942	1,482	1,012	193	157	120	1,235	1,139	96
1943	1,855	1,239	232	256	128	1,434	1,325	109
1944	2,021	1,316	286	280	139	1,450	1,317	133
1945	2,007	1,285	279	293	150†	1,292	1,162	130
Trust fund assets at end of year§								
1937	1,273	766	111	396	*	638	638	...
1938	1,730	1,132	135	463	*	1,072	1,072	...
1939	2,416	1,724	148	544	*	1,525	1,500	25
1940	2,811	2,031	146	634	*	1,958	1,805	153
1941	3,678	2,762	166	750	*	2,744	2,516	228
1942	4,907	3,688	256	963	*	3,698	3,379	319
1943	6,553	4,820	391	1,342	*	5,147	4,711	436
1944	8,326	6,005	573	1,748	*	6,583	6,015	568
1945	10,041	7,121	737	2,183	*	7,537	6,833	704

*Not available.
†Preliminary.
‡Tax effective July 1, 1939.
§Excludes state and local government retirement.

mittee on ways and means was authorized to make a thorough study of financial and other provisions of the program.

Relatively little additional change was made in the old-age and survivors insurance program until 1946. Early in that year, the technical staff appointed by the house committee on ways and means published its report, "Issues in Social Security," covering a study of insurance and assistance programs under the Social Security act. Subsequently, the committee held prolonged hearings on these and other proposals for improving the social security system. The Social Security act amendments of 1946, which resulted from these hearings, were, however, relatively limited in scope. The contribution rates for old-age and survivors insurance were held at 1% each for workers and their employers through 1947. Provisions were enacted to give temporary protection under federal old-age and survivors insurance for survivors of certain veterans of World War II dying within three years after discharge from active service. The permanent changes effected by these amendments removed some of the anomalies and administrative complexities of the old-age and survivors insurance program.

During the decade, substantial changes were made in the Railroad Retirement act. Credits for military service were allowed under this program, as under the federal civil-service system, and the railroad act was amended in 1946 to provide higher contribution rates and more effective provisions for benefits to survivors of covered workers. The Federal Civil Service Retirement act was also amended, in 1942, to require higher contribution rates, provide higher and also deferred annuities and prohibit refunds of contributions to workers leaving with five or more contribution years to their credit.

Relatively little legislative action was taken in the decade to furnish protection against the risk of wage loss from disability. Rhode Island and California, in 1942 and 1946 respectively, enacted laws to provide cash sickness benefits to workers covered by their unemployment insurance programs, and in 1946 the Railroad Unemployment Insurance act was amended to include benefits during maternity and sickness. The Social Security Act amendments of 1946 authorized the nine states that had deposited employee contributions in the unemployment trust fund to use that money to finance disability insurance benefits. More effective provisions for permanent disability were incorporated in the Railroad Retirement act amendments of 1946, and provisions for veterans were liberalized.

At the end of the decade, as at its beginning, public systems for retirement, survivor and disability insurance were lacking for agricultural, domestic, nonprofit and many governmental employees. Under the federal old-age and survivors insurance system, moreover, there was no provision for disability among industrial and commercial workers. Federal and state workmen's compensation laws provided temporary and permanent disability benefits, as well as survivor benefits, for workers suffering from industrial injury, but Mississippi had no such law, and the laws of most states covered industrial accident but not industrial disease.

Unemployment Insurance.—Before the end of 1937, the Social Security act had performed its initial function in unemployment insurance by stimulating all states and territories to enact laws which met the conditions for federal approval, but only one state, Wisconsin, had been collecting contributions long enough to pay benefits. By July 1939, all states were paying benefits, and the Railroad Unemployment Insurance act of 1938 was in full operation. In 1944, similar benefits were also available to unemployed veterans of World War II as federal unemployment allowances administered by states under the provisions of the Servicemen's Readjustment act of 1944. These three programs were an important aid to reconversion after fighting ceased in Europe and the far east; they provided millions of dollars in benefits to workers who were unemployed while the economy was readjusting to peacetime activities —a resource that was wholly lacking in the reconversion process that followed World War I.

A system of unemployment insurance, co-ordinated with employment services, offered the best available method of giving an unemployed worker a chance of re-employment and—if no suitable job was available—a weekly income based on his former wages. Funds were systematically collected through employer (and sometimes employee) contributions to finance these payments.

During the last months of 1937, employment had begun to decline; in Jan. 1938, when 22 states began to pay benefits, they were faced with the difficulties of inaugurating a new program and processing a heavy load of claims. Except for this initial period of recession in late 1937 and early 1938, the trend in employment was upward for several years, and more and more workers acquired wage credits in employments covered by state laws. It was not until Sept. 1945, after the capitulation of Japan, that large numbers of insured workers began to claim their rights to benefits under state laws, and demobilized servicemen availed themselves of their unemployment allowances while they were readjusting to civilian life.

The system of public employment offices, which was under state control through 1941, with federal grants-in-aid under the Wagner-Peyser act of 1933, was turned over to the federal government on Jan. 1, 1942, at the president's request, made to state governors almost immediately after the United States entered World War II.

In July 1939, under a reorganization plan which placed the Social Security board in the newly established Federal Security agency, responsibilities for the U.S. Employment service and for federal grants toward state employment services had been transferred from the department of labour to the Social Security board for integration with its functions in federal-state unemployment insurance. Shortly after the War Manpower commission was established, that office became responsible for all public employment offices, a responsibility carried until the commission was abolished in the autumn of 1945. The employment services were then administered by the labour department, which on Nov. 15, 1946, turned over to the states the facilities and functions they had relinquished during the war emergency. The labour department retained responsibility for the United States Employment service and for federal grants to states.

Additional federal aid to states for their employment services was made available under the Social Security act through federal grants covering costs of the unemployment insurance functions of public employment offices in taking claims for unemployment benefits, finding jobs for insured unemployed workers and certifying their availability for work.

Changes in federal provisions for unemployment insurance under the Social Security act were minor during the decade; in the Social Security act amendments of 1939, higher amounts were authorized for federal grants to states for administering their programs, and establishment and maintenance of merit systems for state employment security personnel were made conditions for receipt of these grants.

In 1939, and with increasing urgency in subsequent years, the Social Security board recommended wider coverage of state unemployment insurance programs, minimum benefit standards as a condition of federal approval, repeal or modification of experience-rating provisions and establishment of special provisions for maritime workers and federal employees. Although many of these proposals were presented in congressional hearings that preceded the Social Security act amendments of 1939 and 1946, relatively little was done to change the federal provisions first effective in 1935.

The decade produced important federal legislation for servicemen and railroad and maritime workers, but there was no federal legislation to enhance the unemployment benefit rights of workers covered by state laws or to lessen the variations among states in adequacy of provisions and interpretation of these provisions. The War Mobilization and Reconversion act of 1944 authorized, until July 1, 1947, advances to state unemployment funds when these funds approached insolvency, but because each state account in the unemployment trust fund had large surpluses of deposits over withdrawals for benefit payments, this provision was inoperative.

States, however, made significant changes in their laws during the decade. At the end of 1937, 29 states, with about half the covered workers in the United States, restricted their coverage to employers with eight or more workers—the coverage of the federal tax against which employer contributions to state unemployment funds were credited—and only 10, with less than one-eighth of the covered population, had no size-of-firm restriction. By the middle of 1945, 16 states, with nearly a third of the covered population, had no size-of-firm restriction, and only 22, with about a third of the covered workers, limited their coverage to firms with eight or more workers. No major changes were made, however, in extending coverage to agriculture, domestic service, nonprofit organizations or other types of employment excluded from the federal tax. The Social Security act amendments of 1946 authorized states to cover maritime workers in intercoastal shipping. The supreme court had declared in May 1943 that there were no constitutional barriers against such state coverage. These amendments also authorized a temporary federal program of reconversion benefits for seamen employed by agents of the War Shipping administration, somewhat like that for veterans, but no funds were appropriated to start operations in 1946.

During the decade, many states also greatly liberalized their benefit provisions. At the end of 1945, one state (Maryland) had abolished its waiting period and 35 required only one week; at the end of 1937, all states required a waiting period of two or more weeks before a worker could receive benefits. In 1937, the maximum weekly benefit amount was $15 in 49 jurisdictions which accounted for all but 5% of the covered workers; by the end of 1945, the maximum was $15 in only 10 states, 6 states with about one-tenth of the covered population had maximums of $24–$28 and 4 states made provisions for allowances to an unemployed worker's dependents. In view of the high wages and steady employment of the war years, however, these maximums represented less than half of customary weekly wages for the majority of beneficiaries under state laws.

The maximum duration of benefits was also liberalized. In 1937, no matter how long an insured worker was unemployed, his benefits ceased in all but 6 states after he had received benefits for as much as 16 weeks; by the end of 1945, half the covered workers were in the 11 states which paid benefits for as much as 21–26 weeks. In 1937 only one state provided for uniform duration of benefits for all workers; by 1945 the number was 14.

The trend toward increasing severity of disqualifications from benefits ran counter to these liberal tendencies, however. These severe disqualifications meant that more than half the states cancelled a worker's wage credits or reduced his benefit rights if he was disqualified because of quitting his job voluntarily without good cause, discharge for misconduct or refusal of suitable work. Other states postponed his benefits for several weeks, but considered his unemployment involuntary after the specified period had elapsed.

Experience-rating provisions were effective in all but 6

states by the end of 1946. During the war years, 12 states, fearful of postwar drains on their unemployment funds, required special war-risk contributions, which came principally from employers with large-scale war production.

Public Assistance and Other Aid.—The major proposals of the decade for strengthening the provisions for federal aid to states for assistance to needy persons stressed the need for federal sharing in general assistance, for special federal aid to low-income states, for raising or removing the limits set in the Social Security act on federal matching maximums for individual payments and for federal participation in medical assistance. Federal legislative changes in the ten years were relatively slight, however, and in some instances temporary.

The 1939 amendments to the Social Security act made establishment and maintenance of merit systems for state public assistance personnel a condition for receipt of federal grants for each of three assistance programs and provided that, in determining recipients' need, account should be taken of their resources. The federal contribution was increased for all three programs. The 1946 amendments, for a 15-month period beginning Oct. 1946, increased the federal participation in assistance still further.

Significant changes were made in state programs, however. The number of states receiving federal funds increased in the decade to nation-wide dimensions for old-age assistance, to all but one (Nevada) for aid to dependent children, and all but four (Alaska, Missouri, Nevada and Pennsylvania) for aid to the blind. Many states progressively liberalized their eligibility requirements and raised or eliminated their maximums on individual payments. They gave fuller recognition to the requirements of assistance recipients, including medical needs, and to increases in the cost of living, and, within the limitations of available funds, made assistance more nearly commensurate with need and more nearly uniform throughout the state. During the decade, assistance became increasingly a matter of right, and the concept of the unrestricted money payment, to be spent as the recipient deemed best, acquired widespread acceptance.

By July 1943 the federal work programs established in the depression years had all been liquidated, leaving old-age assistance, aid to dependent children, aid to the blind and general assistance as the only forms of public aid. The assistance rolls of each of these programs declined during the war years of full employment and high wages. In the war period, economic security was greatly enhanced by increased resources of relatives, federal allowances to dependents of servicemen and even by earnings of old and disabled persons, housewives and young children.

Upturns in the assistance rolls started in the autumn of 1945 and were accelerated in the reconversion period, with increases in the number of unemployed workers and demobilized servicemen. Social insurance rights, however, were an important resource of many persons who might otherwise have had to apply for assistance.

Health, Welfare and Medical Services.—As compared with the development of nation-wide measures for old-age insurance and assistance, progress in the application of insurance principles and pooling national resources for health was slow. As early as 1938, a National Health conference technical subcommittee on medical care issued a report on a national health program, recommending a system of public medical care for the medically needy and consideration of a program of medical care for the entire population, to be supported by general taxation or insurance payments or a combination of both. In Jan. 1939, President Roosevelt sent congress the report of the Interdepartmental Committee to Co-ordinate Health and Welfare Activities, which urged use of federal grants to expand and strengthen general state services for public health and maternal and child health and to develop needed hospital facilities and state programs for medical care. In the Social Security act amendments of 1939, larger amounts were authorized for federal grants for child health and welfare, and the provisions for these programs were extended to Puerto Rico.

The Social Security act amendments of 1946 authorized increases in federal grants for maternal and child health, services for crippled children and child welfare services, and included the Virgin Islands among the jurisdictions eligible for funds under these programs. Other federal legislation in 1946 made permanent earlier provisions for a school program and authorized federal aid in a nation-wide program for construction of hospitals and medical centres. Insurance against medical costs, however, remained available on a voluntary and limited basis only.

War Emergency Programs.—In Feb. 1942, the Federal Security agency was authorized to establish emergency benefit and assistance programs financed from emergency funds for certain civilians. Under this and subsequent authorizations, the Social Security board initiated a program of civilian war benefits providing disability and survivor benefits and a program of civilian war assistance to provide assistance of short duration to meet emergency need resulting from enemy attack or action to meet such attack or the danger thereof, and the U.S. public health service provided medical service benefits. In addition, the Social Security board established a program of aid to enemy aliens and other persons in need because of the restrictive action of the federal government. The two assistance programs, although financed entirely from federal funds, were administered by state public assistance agencies.

On March 18, 1943, federal funds were authorized for a wartime program of maternity and infant care for wives

"G.I. Joe Wants More Than a Rowboat." The need for planned reconversion to insure postwar employment after demobilization, as seen by Bishop of the *St. Louis Star-Times*

and children of the enlisted personnel of the armed forces, to be administered by states under the supervision of the U.S. children's bureau.

By July 1946, the program for enemy aliens had been terminated. Acceptance of new claims for civilian war benefits was discontinued in July 1945. This program and civilian war assistance were of special significance for U.S. citizens repatriated from Europe and the far east and for civilians who had been interned in enemy prison camps.

Program Developments.—At the start of the decade 1937–46 relatively few persons had any rights to immediate benefits under social insurance, and many had never recovered their earning capacity after the devastating years of the depression. States were struggling to raise the funds which would bring in matching federal dollars for the public assistance programs under the Social Security act and, in the meantime, were carrying heavy loads for general assistance to persons who could not be shifted to the rolls of old-age assistance, aid to dependent children or aid to the blind.

As the old-age and survivors insurance program developed, more and more workers reached the age of 65 with rights to continuing monthly benefits as retirement income for themselves, their aged wives and their young children. In June 1946, for example, some 193,240 retired workers whose wives received supplementary benefits had an average family benefit of $38.80 a month under this program; so similar income protection was available to these industrial and commercial workers before 1940. At the beginning of 1946, about 41,500,000 living workers had acquired insured status under old-age and survivors insurance. The survivorship rights acquired under this program over the decade had built up to the equivalent of more than $50,000,000,000 in term life insurance. In June 1946, the average monthly amount paid to widows of deceased insured workers with young children in their care was $51.00 for a family with three or more child beneficiaries. Table III indicates the number of workers with wage credits under the program in successive years, the number of living workers with insured status under the program at the beginning of the year and the amount paid as retirement and survivor benefits, including lump-sum death payments.

Table III.—*U.S. Workers with Social Security Wage Credits*

Year	Workers with wage credits in year	Insured living workers at beginning of year	Payments certified in year to: Living workers and their dependents	Survivors of estates of deceased workers
1937	32,904,000	...	$651,000	$627,000
1938	31,822,000	...	4,706,000	5,772,000
1939	33,751,000	...	4,575,000	9,321,000
1940	35,393,000	22,900,000	21,074,000	19,520,000
1941	40,976,000	24,900,000	55,141,000	38,783,000
1942	46,363,000	27,500,000	80,305,000	56,740,000
1943	47,656,000	31,200,000	97,257,000	75,593,000
1944	46,296,000	34,900,000	119,009,000	99,088,000
1945	45,696,000	38,400,000	157,391,000	130,366,000

In June 1946, the total number of beneficiaries of old-age and survivors insurance—retired workers, their aged wives and aged widows and aged parents of deceased workers—comprised nearly one-tenth of the estimated 10,400,000 persons in the population aged 65 and over. Perhaps an additional 6% received old-age benefits under related public programs, while one-fifth received old-age assistance. In June 1940, there were 25 recipients of old-age assistance for every aged beneficiary of old-age and survivors insurance, while 6 years later there were only 2.

For aged persons, public assistance by 1946 constituted a more important source of support than social insurance and related programs. For surviving dependents under age 65, social insurance was probably more important than public assistance.

Among fatherless children, about two were receiving social insurance and related benefits at the end of 1945 for every one receiving public assistance.

Somewhat similar relations appeared between unemployment insurance and public aid. Unemployment benefits paid under state laws, the railroad program and the Servicemen's Readjustment act greatly diminished the need for assistance and federal work programs. Table IV shows the number of workers who acquired wage credits under state unemployment insurance programs, the number of beneficiaries and of weeks compensated and the number of initial claims filed (the number of different workers claiming benefits) for each year for which comparable data were available:

Table IV.—*Statistics of State Unemployment Insurance*

Year	Workers with wage credits in year	Beneficiaries in year	Weeks of unemployment compensated in year	Initial claims for benefits in year
1938	*	*	38,076,000	9,565,000
1939	30,086,000	*	41,554,000	9,765,000
1940	31,947,000	5,220,000	51,084,000	11,140,000
1941	37,600,000	3,439,000	32,295,000	8,527,000
1942	43,400,000	2,815,000	28,158,000	6,324,000
1943	44,000,000	664,000	6,004,000	1,884,000
1944	43,000,000	533,000	4,124,000	1,503,000
1945	42,500,000	2,830,000	24,038,000	6,030,000

*Not available.

After V-J day, unemployment rose steadily with the stoppage of war production and demobilization of the armed forces. The peak level of unemployment (2,700,000) reached in March 1946, was about three times the extremely low level in Aug. 1945. In the 12-month period, Sept. 1945–Aug. 1946, a total of nearly $2,455,000,000 was paid as unemployment benefits under state laws and the programs for railroad workers and veterans brought the total paid under social insurance and related programs to $5,618,000,000, or more than five times the total ($1,020,000,000) for the calendar year 1937. Mainly because employment and earnings remained relatively high after the war, and because federal allowances to dependents of servicemen and subsistence allowances to veterans under the Servicemen's Readjustment act represented a substantial federal contribution ($2,046,000,000) to income maintenance, the total spent as public aid in the 12 months following V-J day aggregated only $1,095,000,000, or less than half the total for federal work program earnings and public assistance payments in 1937. Payments under social insurance and related programs, moreover, played a significant and increasingly important part in reducing the need for public assistance and employment on federal work programs.

The progress of public assistance under the Social Security act is indicated in Table V.

Table V.—*Number of States and Territories Participating in Federal Funds Under the Social Security Act*

Year	All three assistance programs	Old-age assistance	Aid to dependent children	Aid to the blind
1937	36	50	39	37
1938	38	51	42	42
1939	39	51	42	43
1940	40	51	43	43
1941	43	51	47	44
1942	43	51	47	45
1943	45	51	48	46
1944	46	51	49	46
1945	47	51	50	47

General assistance, the residual program which provided for needy persons failing to meet qualifications for the special types of assistance, was still financed by states and localities without federal aid. (A. J. A.)

Great Britain

During 1937, large-scale unemployment continued to be the most formidable problem of its kind ever experienced in Great Britain. As many of the 1,700,000 unemployed had been without work for periods of years, the problem of their welfare and adequate maintenance was one of progressively increasing difficulty. Responsibility for this rested largely on the unemployment assistance board, which provided allowances from state funds to those who had either exhausted their title to unemployment insurance benefit or who had not acquired a title to such benefit. During the year the number of applications for allowances to the unemployment assistance board was about 1,250,-000, and in Dec. 1937 there were nearly 600,000 applicants for assistance, representing the needs of about 2,000,000 persons. The annual expenditure on unemployment assistance allowances was £36,740,000 and on unemployment insurance benefits £33,160,000, a combined total of £69,800,-000 devoted entirely to the maintenance of those out of work.

National Administration.—In the more restricted sphere of improved security measures for the long-term unemployed, the most important development was the assumption in 1937 of full powers by the unemployment assistance board. This board had been created by the Unemployment act of 1934 to take over, in one department of the central government, a responsibility which had previously been placed on local government. This transfer from local to central administration had been arranged in two stages; the first stage, which was carried out early in 1935, was confined to those who were insurable under the unemployment insurance scheme, and had involved the newly created board in the considerable first task of taking over from about 200 local authorities responsibility for the needs of about 800,000 unemployed, who with their dependents represented about 2,500,000 persons. The second stage was delayed until April 1937, when the unemployment assistance board assumed responsibility for the remaining unemployed whose occupations were not embraced by the unemployment insurance scheme, but who had normal occupations insurable under the wider scope of the Contributory Pensions acts, such as domestic service and similar private employment. This second stage involved the transfer of approximately 90,000 persons, and so completed the change-over to direct national responsibility. With this began a great and significant change in the history of British social administration, and a further stage in the break up of the old locally-administered Poor law which had survived in much the same form since Elizabethan times. The general structure of the Poor law remained, but the responsibilities of the local authorities were now restricted to the care of the needy aged, the sick and destitute and those normally self-employed.

The year 1938 was marked by many difficulties and uncertainties arising from the threat of war; the upward trend in employment was not maintained and the number of unemployed increased until at the end of December the total was more than 1,830,000. Applications to the unemployment assistance board were again in the region of 1,250,000, of which about 445,000 were from persons who had not previously applied for such assistance. The total expenditure on unemployment allowances was £39,-297,000, an increase of £2,557,000 more than the previous year, and on unemployment insurance benefit £51,622,000, an increase of £18,462,000. The increased expenditure on unemployment insurance benefit was largely the result of the Unemployment Insurance act of 1938, which extended the range of insurance to those in domestic service and similar employment, and also made certain increases in the rates of benefit for dependents and for the younger claimants under the agricultural part of the insurance scheme.

The unemployment assistance board became increasingly concerned with the problem of prolonged unemployment among the younger applicants for assistance, which showed evidence of being more a problem of the individual than a problem of industry. Exceptional methods were devised to ensure that as many as possible in the younger age groups were specially interviewed and individually advised on their prospects of employment or suitable training.

Rearmament and War.—The expanding rearmament program which was soon to be followed by the outbreak of World War II had early and appreciable effects on the unemployment problem. The general change-over from a peace to a war economy was necessarily slow and caused dislocations of industry and employment which at first offset gains in other directions. Under the pressure of wartime demands for labour of every kind, however, the long-standing problem of mass unemployment rapidly diminished, and by the end of 1940 had ceased to be a social problem of any consequence. Some new social complications emerged in the changed conditions of war, such as the influx of refugees from abroad, the large-scale evacuation of sections of the civil population from vulnerable areas, the loss of employment or incomes caused by the cessation of certain industries and the flow of private funds from other countries. This situation had been anticipated to a large extent and was met by the provisions of the Unemployment Assistance (Emergency Powers) act of 1939, which was administered by the unemployment assistance board and came into operation soon after war was declared.

By this act the unemployment assistance scheme was extended to provide for the needs of certain classes of persons, including refugees from abroad, who were in distress as a result of the war. Fortunately the extent of such distress never assumed the proportions which had been anticipated; the largest number of such allowances in payment at any one time was 48,000. The scheme continued in operation and in 1946 seemed likely to do so as long as distress attributable to the war remained, or until a comprehensive scheme of state assistance should be evolved.

The more general and most pressing social consequence of the war was a rapid increase in the cost of living, the government index figure of which rose from 55 in Sept. 1939 to 87 in Sept. 1940. This increase was largely offset by a general rise in wage levels, but soon began to cause hardship among a large number of old-age pensioners who were in the main dependent on the small fixed pensions paid under the state insurance schemes. Those who found such pensions insufficient for their needs had normally no alternative but recourse to the locally administered Poor law, funded mainly from local taxation, and the steadily increasing numbers who were forced to seek such relief greatly increased the financial burdens of many local authorities at a time when they were least able to sustain them.

The government consequently decided to relieve the local authorities of such additional charges and also at the same time to improve the condition of the aged by transferring the whole responsibility for the additional needs of old age-pensioners to the exchequer. This decision was implemented by the Old-Age and Widows' Pensions act of 1940, which, in addition to lowering from 65 to 60 the age at which contributory old-age pensions were payable to

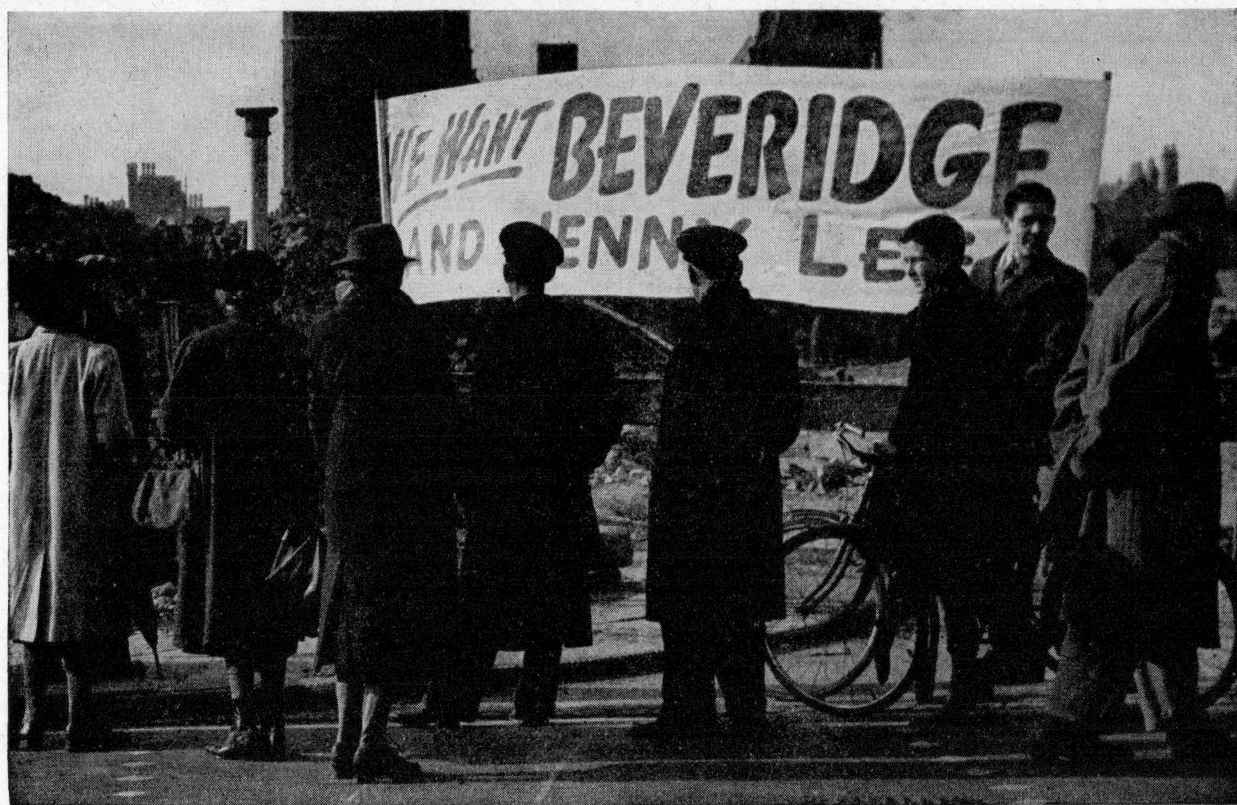

Poster in the bombed centre of Bristol, Eng., before the parliamentary by-election of Feb. 1943, in which Jenny Lee was a candidate. The Beveridge plan for social security was a key issue throughout the campaign

women, made the unemployment assistance board, under the changed name of the assistance board, responsible for the new scheme of supplementary pensions introduced by the act. The scheme provided that, subject to a test of need, the income of the pensioner and his or her dependents should be brought up to standards approved by parliament.

Prior to the operation of this act, some 275,000 old-age pensioners had been receiving assistance under the Poor law, at a total annual cost to the local authorities of about £5,000,000. Within three months of the introduction of the state scheme the number of supplementary pensioners had reached nearly 1,000,000, at a total annual cost to the exchequer in 1941—the first full year of operation—of more than £25,000,000. By the end of 1945 the number of supplementary pensioners had risen to more than 1,600,000, at a total annual cost of about £59,000,000.

The assistance board had thus become responsible for the needs and welfare of a much larger section of the community than it had been brought into being to deal with under the unemployment assistance scheme and had become the largest single welfare service in British history. In 1943 the board's responsibilities were further extended by the Determination of Needs act, by which the scheme of supplementary pensions was widened to include widow pensioners of less than 60 years of age who had an allowance for dependent children included in their pension.

Beveridge Report.—The Unemployment act of 1940 provided for certain increases in the rates of contributions and benefit for those more than 15 years of age and extended unemployment insurance to nonmanual workers earning up to £420 a year, but there still remained many inequalities both in the methods of payment and in the amounts which were provided either directly or indirectly from state funds to provide against economic insecurity. Despite the preoccupations and perplexities of war, the government had under consideration the necessity for a comprehensive survey of all of the state insurance and allied services, which had long been felt to be overdue. In June 1941 an interdepartmental committee was formed under the chairmanship of Sir William Beveridge (later Lord Beveridge) to undertake this task, but for reasons of policy the findings of this committee were published in 1942 as a personal report by Sir William Beveridge and were universally referred to as the Beveridge report. This recommended the amalgamation of all the state insurance schemes into a single unified system under the control of a minister of social insurance.

The main features of the plan were universal social insurance against the interruption or destruction of earning power, and for special expenditure arising at birth, marriage or death, embodying six fundamental principles: flat rate of subsistence benefit, flat rate of contribution, unification of administrative responsibility, adequacy of benefit, comprehensiveness, and classification. These, in combination with national assistance and voluntary insurance as subsidiary methods, would ensure freedom from want in any circumstances and remove for all time one of the fundamental defects of the social system. As a corollary of the insurance arrangements the report recommended the organization of a complete national health service which would be free and available to all.

The government accepted the general principles of the plan and in 1944 presented legislative proposals to parliament in three White Papers, one on a national health service, one on the general provisions for social insurance and one on the special provisions for workmen's compensation. The health proposals envisaged a complete state system of health and medical services controlled by the minister of health, assisted by a central medical board, and health centres established throughout the country by the local government authorities according to population requirements, the centres to be based on a system of grouped medical practice closely linked with improved and extended specialist, nursing, hospital, sanatoria and rehabilitation services. With some slight modifications, the social insurance proposals closely followed those of the Beveridge report, including sickness and unemployment benefit, retirement pensions, maternity benefit, widow's benefit and pensions, family allowances and national assistance, but proposed to deal with workmen's compensation as a separate fund with a separate range of benefits apart from the general scheme of social insurance.

National Insurance Legislation.—The first step towards giving effect to these proposals was the Ministry of National Insurance act of Nov. 1944, which established a minister of national insurance (parliament preferred this title to that of minister of social insurance which had been suggested in the Beveridge report) and transferred to the new minister responsibility for all matters relating to national health insurance, old-age pensions, widows', orphans' and old-age contributory pensions, supplementary pensions, unemployment insurance and unemployment assistance, and workmen's compensation. The first instalment of the comprehensive social security scheme was contained in the Family Allowance act of 1945, which became operative in Aug. 1946. This provided for payment to every family which included two or more children, and for the benefit of the family as a whole, an allowance of five shillings a week for each child after the first, to continue generally until the eligible children were 16 years of age. The allowances were inalienable and of universal application; there were no exceptions.

It was estimated that in the first full year of operation some 2,000,000 families would receive allowances at a cost to the exchequer of about £57,000,000. The National Insurance bill and the National Insurance (Industrial Injuries) bill were introduced in 1945 and passed by parliament in Aug. 1946, but their main provisions were not to become operative until dates to be fixed by the minister of national insurance. Both acts embodied the main principles set out in the White Papers which preceded them. The main clauses of the National Insurance bill provided for the division of the population into three insurance classes: persons employed under contract, self-employed persons and nonemployed persons, with separate contribution rates for each class, contributions by employers and additions by the exchequer.

The main points were: title to benefits to be dependent on a prescribed number of contributions; employed persons to qualify for sickness and unemployed benefit, self-employed for sickness benefit only; indefinite sickness benefit, unemployment benefit normally to be limited to 180 days, but the period might in individual cases be extended; maternity grant to be made for each child born, maternity allowances for employed women to be paid for 13 weeks before and after confinement, attendance allowances for four weeks to other women; widows' allowances with additions for children of school age to be made for 13 weeks, followed by widowed mother's allowance and subsequent widow's pension, conditional on age and ten years of marriage or physical infirmity, with retirement pension if husband was so entitled; guardians' allowances for orphan children to be made; retirement pensions for life at age of 65 (women 60), increased pensions for postponed retirement at more than 70 (women 65) to be paid without retirement condition; death grants to be made in respect of an insured person, his wife, child or dependent.

Although the scheme would probably not come into operation until 1948, the government decided as an exceptional measure that the section of the act which related to retirement and old-age pensions should come into effect from Oct. 1946. The general effect of this decision was that such pensioners received payment at the higher rates provided for in the act; for example, the joint pension of a man and wife insured in the husband's right was increased from 20*s.* to 42*s.*, single persons' pensions were increased from 10*s.* to 26*s.* and such increased pensions could, if necessary, be supplemented under the existing scheme of supplementary pensions administered by the assistance board. The main provisions of the National Insurance (Industrial Injuries) act established this as a separate insurance fund with separate rates of contributions and separate benefits. Broadly the scheme would apply to all persons working under a contract of service without income limit or provisions for contracting out. Contributions were to be paid jointly by the insured persons and their employers, with an additional contribution from the exchequer equal to one fifth of the joint contributions. The principal benefits would be as follows: injury allowances for first 26 weeks of incapacity, followed by disablement pensions if incapable of work or if permanent disability was suffered, amount of pension being assessed according to degree of disability; dependent's allowance for wife, child or adult dependent; rates of benefit the same for men or women; pensions in fatal cases for widows or adult dependents with allowances for children; the scheme was to be extended to certain industrial diseases to be prescribed by the minister.

The National Health Services act, passed in Oct. 1946, did not differ in any important particular in its general principles from the proposals in the government's White Paper of 1944, except that it was proposed that all hospitals should be brought under national ownership. There was, however, general recognition that effective planning and co-ordination of the hospital services was inseparable from ownership, with the exception of the teaching hospitals attached to the universities. A similar service was to be provided in Scotland under the terms of the National Health Services (Scotland) bill.

When these measures were in operation all of the various state social services would be transformed into one universal and comprehensive system of social security without precedent elsewhere, firmly establishing the social policy envisaged by Beveridge of a national minimum income adequate to the subsistence needs of every family and designed with the twofold purpose of providing social security for everybody and an equivalent increase in national productive efficiency. (*See* also LAW; RELIEF.)

BIBLIOGRAPHY.—*Reports of the Ministry of Labour* (Cmd. 5,717, 1937), (Cmd. 6,016, 1938); *Reports of the Unemployment Assistance Board* (Cmd. 5,752, 1937), (Cmd. 6,021, 1938), and *Reports of the Assistance Board* (Cmd. 6,700, 1944), (Cmd. 6,883, 1945); Sir William Beveridge, *Report on Social Insurance and Allied Services* (Cmd. 6,404, 1942), and *Memoranda from Organizations* (Cmd. 6,405, 1942); Government White Papers on *A National Health Service* (Cmd. 6,502, 1944); *Social Insurance,* Part 1 (Cmd. 6,550, 1944), Part 2 *Workmen's Compensation* (Cmd. 6,551, 1944); *Summary of Main Provisions of the National Insurance Scheme* (Cmd. 6,729, 1946); *National Insurance Bill* (Cmd. 6,730, 1946); *National Insurance (Industrial Injuries) Bill, Explanatory Memorandum* (Cmd. 6,651 1945); *National Insurance Act,* 1946; *National Insurance (Industrial Injuries) Act,* 1946. (J. McAT.)

Social Service

See CHILD WELFARE; RELIEF; SOCIAL SECURITY.

Societies and Associations

Following is a listing of prominent societies, associations, foundations and other organizations in the United States, Great Britain and Canada.

American Academy of Arts and Letters.—The American Academy of Arts and Letters was founded in 1904 by the National Institute of Arts and Letters for the furtherance of literature and fine arts. Membership of the academy was limited to 50, chosen only from members of the institute. The following persons were elected to the academy during the 1937–46 decade: 1937, Charles McLean Andrews, Van Wyck Brooks, Bernard Berenson, Frederick Converse, William Adams Delano, Sinclair Lewis, Jonas Lie, Herbert Putnam, Albert Spalding, Chauncey Brewster Tinker, Charles Warren; 1938, Stephen Vincent Benét, Willa Cather, Ellen Glasgow, Thornton Wilder; 1939, no elections; 1940, Ralph Adams Cram, Edna St. Vincent Millay, Carl Sandburg, Henry O. Taylor; 1941, Paul P. Cret, Charles Hopkinson, Agnes Repplier; 1942, John Alden Carpenter, Barry Faulkner, Henry R. Shepley, John Sloan, Eugene Speicher; 1943, Gifford Beal, Ernest Bloch, John Marin, Frederick L. Olmsted, Edward W. Redfield; 1944, Edward McCartan; 1945, Douglas Southall Freeman, Robinson Jeffers, Lee Lawrie; 1946, Charles Austin Beard, Gilmore D. Clarke, Archibald MacLeish.

The academy made the following awards during the 1937–46 decade: *Gold Medal of the Academy*, conferred in recognition of special distinction in literature, art or music was awarded to Ernest Bloch in 1942; *Howells Medal of the Academy*, given every fifth year in recognition of the most distinguished work of U.S. fiction published during that period, was awarded to Ellen Glasgow in 1940 and to Booth Tarkington in 1945; *Diction Medal of the Academy*, to be conferred at any time to any man or woman for good diction on the U.S. stage, was given to Paul Robeson in 1944 and to Eva La Gallienne in 1945; *Award of Merit Medal*, accompanied by a cash prize and given to a highly outstanding person in the U.S. representing painting, sculpture, novel, poetry and drama, was conferred upon Charles Burchfield (1942); Carl Milles (1943); Theodore Dreiser (1944) and Wystan Hugh Auden (1945). Between 1942 and 1946, the American Academy of Arts and Letters and the National Institute of Arts and Letters gave a number of $1,000 grants to persons for work in art, literature and music.

Officers of the academy (1946) were Walter Damrosch, president; James Truslow Adams, chancellor and treasurer; Van Wyck Brooks, secretary. Offices of the academy: 633 W. 155th St., New York 32, N.Y.

American Academy of Arts and Sciences.—Founded in Massachusetts in 1780, the American Academy of Arts and Sciences devoted itself primarly to "the cultivation and diffusion of the arts and sciences for the wealth, peace, independence and happiness of the people."

The academy, whose membership of 800 fellows and 130 foreign honourary members in 1946 represented the various sciences, the arts and humanities, continued to meet 8 times annually and on special occasions to receive and discuss communications from members or guests.

For the encouragement of research, particularly in the sciences, the academy continued to award grants-in-aid in various fields. From the Rumford fund it awarded, from time to time, the gold and silver Rumford medals and the Rumford premium for high achievement in the fields of heat and light. In the decade 1937–46 these awards were conferred on William W. Coblentz, George R. Harrison, Vladimir K. Zworykin and Charles E. K. Mees.

In recognition of high achievement in certain fields of medicine, it continued to award septennially the Frances Amory prize. In 1941 this award of $17,000 was conferred jointly upon Dr. Hugh H. Young, Dr. Joseph F. McCarthy, Dr. Carl R. Moore and Dr. Ernest Laqueur.

Publications: the *Proceedings*, scholarly and scientific papers, memoirs and special volumes. Noteworthy among these were the *Monumenta Paleographica Vetera: Series I*, dated Greek minuscule manuscripts to the year 1200, edited by Kirsopp Lake and Silva Lake in 10 fasciculi.

The officers (1946–47) were: president, Howard Mumford Jones; vice-presidents, R. G. D. Richardson, J. W. M. Bunker, E. N. Griswold and Donald Scott; corresponding secretary, J. W. M. Bunker; recording secretary, I. Amdur; treasurer, H. S. Ford; librarian, F. H. Pratt, and editor, Taylor Starck. Headquarters: 28 Newbury St., Boston, Mass.

American Academy of Political and Social Science.—Founded in 1889 to provide a forum for discussion of political, social and economic problems, the academy had a membership of slightly more than 12,000 in 1946. Publications included the *Annals*, a bimonthly magazine, and occasional monographs and pamphlets. Among some of its better-known pamphlets were *Democracy Versus the Totalitarian State in Latin America* by Samuel Guy Inman (1938); *European Plans for a World Order* by William P. Maddox (1940) and *The Core of a Continent: Problems of Central and Eastern Europe* by Henryk Strasburger (1943). Officers (1946): president, Ernest Minor Patterson; vice-presidents, Herbert Hoover, C. A. Dykstra and Carl Kelsey; secretary, J. P. Lichtenberger, and treasurer, Charles J. Rhoads. Headquarters: 3457 Walnut St., Philadelphia 4, Pa.

American Association for the Advancement of Science.—A scientific organization whose membership increased from 11,547 in 1920 to more than 30,000 in 1946, the American Association for the Advancement of Science was organized in 1848 and had 200 affiliated and associated societies in 1946. The association continued to publish three journals, the *A.A.A.S. Bulletin* (monthly), *Science* (weekly journal) and the *Scientific Monthly*, in addition to technical and nontechnical symposia. The association's technical symposium began in 1938 with a volume entitled *Tuberculosis and Leprosy* and by 1946 contained 20 vol. Two other volumes, *Human Malaria* and *Relapsing Fever*, were widely used during World War II by the U.S. army and navy medical corps in the tropics. Officers (1946): James B. Conant, president; Forest Ray Moulton, administrative secretary, and William E. Wrather, treasurer. Headquarters: 1515 Massachusetts Ave., Washington 5, D.C.

American Association of Law Libraries.—The association was founded in 1906 and incorporated in 1935 under the laws of the District of Columbia as a nonprofit organization designed to promote librarianship, develop and increase the usefulness of law libraries, and foster a spirit of co-operation among law libraries. Publications: *Law Library Journal*, a quarterly, and *Index to Legal Periodicals*, published monthly (except August). Officers for the 1946–47 period: Laurie H. Riggs, president; Arie Poldervaart, president-elect for 1947–48. Executive secretary and treasurer: Mrs. Helen M. S. Helmle, Equitable Life Assurance Society of the U.S., 393 Seventh Ave., New York 1, N.Y.

American Bankers Association.—A national organization to promote the general welfare of U.S. banks, the A.B.A. was founded in 1875; its 1946 membership embraced 96% of all U.S. banks.

In 1938 the A.B.A. carried on a campaign against government-subsidized credit where the latter allegedly was in unfair competition with chartered banks. Educational activities continued to rank high among the A.B.A.'s activities; its projects along this line included the American Institute of Banking, offering study courses to banking employees, and graduate school of banking, offering annually two weeks of graduate studies at Rutgers university, New Brunswick, N.J., for bank officers. During World War II, the A.B.A. actively encouraged its membership to promote war bond drives. The association also engaged in protecting the interests of member banks with regard to federal legislation and continued to maintain a Washington office to represent the entire membership in matters pertaining to national legislation, rulings and regulations affecting banking operations.

Officers (1946–47): president, C. W. Bailey; vice-president, Joseph M. Dodge; treasurer, S. Albert Phillips; secretary, Merle E. Selecman. Headquarters: 12 E. 36th St., New York 16, N.Y.

American Bar Association.—Organized in 1878 as a voluntary association of lawyers and jurists, the A.B.A. defined its objectives to include the advancement of the science of jurisprudence and promotion of the administration of justice. Its membership as of Sept. 1, 1946, was 37,303. During the 1937–46 decade, the association voiced vigorous opposition to President Roosevelt's plan to reorganize the supreme court (1937) and voted for support of the Vandenberg amendment to the Child Labor act. The following year, the association devoted its attention to safeguarding civil liberties.

After the start of World War II, the A.B.A. sponsored free legal aid to men in service and their families. The A.B.A. continued to grant an annual association medal for conspicuous service to U.S. jurisprudence, the Ross prize of $3,000 for an essay and the award of merit given to U.S. bar associations. Publications: the *American Bar Association Journal,* a monthly, and an annual volume of reports and proceedings and various papers. Officers (1946): Carl B. Rix, president; Joseph D. Stecher, secretary; Walter M. Bastian, treasurer. Headquarters: 1140 N. Dearborn St., Chicago, Ill.

American Bible Society.—Founded in 1816 for the purpose of encouraging wider distribution of the Holy Scriptures, the American Bible society aided in translation, publication, distribution and use of the Bible, free of notes and comments. The American Bible society continued to distribute annually about 7,000,000 volumes of the Holy Scriptures in the United States and about 3,000,000 in other lands. In co-operation with bible societies in other lands and missionary organizations, the American Bible society aided in translation of the Scriptures into more than 1,000 languages. After World War II, the society through its postwar emergency fund, devoted its efforts to furnishing free of cost about 2,500,000 new testaments and 100,000 bibles (all in the Japanese language) to Japan, and to supplying about 2,000,000 German bibles and new testaments to Germany. It also continued to publish the *Bible Society Record,* an illustrated magazine issued 10 times yearly. President of the society (1946): Daniel Burke. Headquarters: 450 Park Ave., New York 22, N.Y.

American Chemical Society.—The American Chemical society was founded in 1876 to encourage the advancement of chemistry, improve the qualifications and usefulness of chemists, increase the diffusion of chemical knowledge and promote scientific interests and inquiry. In the 1937–46 decade, membership more than doubled. In 1946 members totalled 48,000, while in 1938 its membership was slightly more than 22,000.

The organization continued to award predoctoral and postdoctoral fellowships as well as specific annual awards to individual chemists for outstanding work in their fields. Among the more prominent recipients during the 1937–46 decade were G. N. Lewis, who received the Richards medal in 1938, and James B. Conant, who was awarded the Priestley medal in 1944.

Publications: *Chemical Abstracts, Journal of the American Chemical Society, Chemical and Engineering News, Industrial and Engineering Chemistry* (industrial edition) and *Analytical Chemistry.* During World War II many of the pages of these journals were devoted largely to presenting information needed by chemists.

Officers (1946): Bradley Dewey, president; W. Albert Noyes, Jr., president-elect; Roger Adams, chairman of the board of directors; Alden H. Emery, secretary, and Robert Baldwin, treasurer. Headquarters: 1155 16th St. N.W., Washington 6, D.C.

American College of Life Underwriters.—This college grew out of the needs for efficient life underwriting and was incorporated in 1927 with the object of training students and establishing standards for the profession. It also co-operated with universities and colleges, promoted research and preparation of textbooks. The college became associated with the American Society of Chartered Life Underwriters, with chapters in 58 cities and associations with 19 insurance firms in 1946. At the end of 1946 there were 2,599 persons who had received the Chartered Life Underwriter designation. To receive the C.L.U. award, candidates had to pass 5 written examinations, which in 1946 were held at 115 universities and colleges, and then complete 3 years of satisfactory business experience. The college continued to publish an annual report containing information on its activities and trends of life underwriting. Officers (1946): chairman of the board, Julian S. Myrick; vice-chairman, William M. Duff; president, Dr. S. S. Huebner; dean, Dr. David McCahan; secretary, John A. Stevenson, and treasurer, Sewell W. Hodge. Headquarters: N.E. corner of 36th and Walnut streets, Philadelphia 4, Pa.

American College of Surgeons.—Founded in 1913 by 500 surgeons of the U.S. and Canada, the American College of Surgeons was dedicated to elevating the standards of surgery and to promoting high professional and ethical ideals. Membership in the association increased from 12,620 in 1939 to about 15,000 in 1946. Its endowment in 1946 totalled $1,000,000. In 1918, 89 hospitals met the criteria of its hospital standardization rules. This figure increased to 3,118 in 1946.

During World War II the college held war sessions in a number of U.S. cities; attendance at the 1942 sessions included nearly 40,000 physicians and medical students. Travel restrictions imposed for the duration reduced the number of sessions and attendance in the succeeding years. In 1946 the college resumed its annual clinical congress, which was suspended during the war years.

Publications: *Surgery, Gynecology and Obstetrics,* the official monthly journal; *Bulletin of the American College of Surgeons,* a quarterly; *Manual of Hospital Standardization* (revised edition 1946); *Medical Service in Industry and Workman's Compensation Laws* (new edition published in 1946).

Officers for 1946: Dr. Irvin Abell, president and chairman of the board of regents; Dr. Paul B. Magnuson, secretary, and Dr. Dallas B. Phemister, treasurer. Headquarters: 40 E. Erie St., Chicago, Ill.

American Dental Association.—Founded in 1859, the American Dental association in 1946 was composed of 58 state and territorial societies and about 440 component or local societies. The association's objectives were set forth as the improvement of dental health services to the public by promoting the art and science of dentistry; the direction and encouragement of dental research; improvement of dental education; the dissemination of knowledge of dentistry; enlightenment of public opinion on prevention of oral diseases and the maintenance of high professional standards.

The association's membership grew from 37,919 in 1937 to 63,786 in 1946, the latter figure representing seven-eighths of the total number of practising dentists in the United States.

During the 1937–46 decade, the association devoted much time and attention to dental socio-economic problems. It established the Council on Dental Health, whose principal duties were to develop programs for the provision of more adequate dental care for the public. The association also developed a set of principles deemed essential in the establishment of programs to improve dental health.

In 1938 the A.D.A. established the Council on Dental Education, which, among other things, organized and administered criteria for accreditation of institutions for the study of dentistry in the United States. As a result of the council's activities, all but 3 of the 40 dental schools in the country were approved or provisionally approved.

Through its Council on Dental Therapeutics and its research commission, the association greatly improved the quality and standards of dental medicines and dental materials. It also sponsored two bills in congress: one to provide federal funds for dental research and one to provide grants-in-aid to states for dental education of the public and dental services, particularly for children.

During World War II the association and its members actively engaged in the war effort. Approximately 22,000 dentists served in the army and navy. After the war, the association co-operated with the Veterans' administration in caring for the dental needs of veterans.

Publications: the *Journal of the American Dental Association* (issued 24 times yearly) and the *Journal of Oral Surgery*, issued quarterly. Officers (1947) were: Dr. Sterling V. Mead, president; Dr. E. B. Penn, first vice-president; Dr. B. B. McCollum, second vice-president; Dr. M. D. Huff, third vice-president; Dr. Harold Hillenbrand, secretary, and Dr. Roscoe Volland, treasurer. Headquarters: 222 E. Superior St., Chicago 11, Ill.

American Economic Association.—A professional association of economists, the A.E.A. was founded in 1885 to encourage economic research and to stimulate discussion of economic problems. During the 1937–46 decade the organization nearly doubled its membership and subscribers. In 1937 members totalled 2,713 and subscribers 1,219. In 1946 membership was 4,662 and subscribers were 2,161. The 58th annual meeting held at Cleveland, O. (Jan. 24–27, 1946), was the first of national scope since 1941. Publications: *American Economic Review* (quarterly) and *Papers and Proceedings* of the annual meetings. Officers (1946): president, E. A. Goldenweiser; vice-presidents, Carter Goodrich and Simon S. Kuznets; secretary-treasurer, James Washington Bell. Headquarters: Northwestern university, Evanston, Ill.

American Federation of Labor.—Founded in 1881 as an association of labour unions, the American Federation of Labor adopted three objectives—to organize unorganized workers, to promote the interests of its members through legislative activity and publicity and to settle disputes among its members. Final authority was vested in the federation's autumn convention. Between conventions, the federation was to be governed by an executive council made up of the president, vice-presidents and the secretary-treasurer.

Total membership of the A.F. of L. in 1936 was reported to be 3,422,398; but the defection that year of the 10 unions that later formed the Congress of Industrial Organizations sharply reduced the federation's membership, which in 1937 was reported at 2,860,933. However, a vigorous organizing campaign during the 1937–46 decade brought the federation's rolls up to 7,151,808 as of Aug. 31, 1946. Claimed membership at the end of 1946 was put at 7,500,000.

In 1938 the A.F. of L. intensified its organizing activities, particularly among white-collar workers and unorganized employees in many industries. The following year the A.F. of L.-C.I.O. schism widened after the federation's leadership made frequent complaints that the National Labor Relations board was showing favouritism toward the C.I.O. in its rulings. The Roosevelt administration made an attempt that year to patch up the quarrel between the two organizations but achieved no tangible results.

The federation pledged its full and unqualified support of the government in its war program and subscribed to a no-strike policy on all defense projects. All unions were urged to forego strikes during the war emergency, although A.F. of L. officials insisted that workers be free from legislative restrictions on their economic rights. The A.F. of L. was critical of government activities on the home front during the conflict and in 1943 it assailed the Office of Price Administration's failure to check rising living costs and demanded repeal of the Smith-Connally act.

After the close of the war, the A.F. of L. announced a postwar program that included provision for return of prewar rights and privileges voluntarily relinquished during the conflict, such as free collective bargaining, abolition of wartime controls over labour and industry, increased wages, etc. In the legislative field, the federation called for enactment of the Kilgore bill providing for broader unemployment compensation, enactment of the Murray-Wagner Full Employment bill, a postwar housing bill, a law lifting minimum wage levels and the Wagner-Murray-Dingell Social Security bill.

Internationally, the federation gave its full support to the International Labour organization and refused participation in the newly created World Federation of Trade Unions on grounds that the participating soviet trade unions were not "representative" of wage earners.

One of the key labour events of early 1946 was the return of the United Mine Workers, with its 600,000 members, to the A.F. of L., after an absence of 10 years. In that year the A.F. of L. chartered three new unions, the Maritime Trades department, the National Association of Postal Supervisors and the National Farm Labor union. The latter organization sought to organize farm workers on large plantations and commercial farms in the southern states.

Officers of the A.F. of L. elected at its convention in Oct. 1946 in Chicago were: William Green, president; George Meany, secretary-treasurer. Headquarters: the American Federation of Labor building, Washington, D.C.

American Geographical Society.—Founded in 1852 primarily as a research institution to advance geographical knowledge, the American Geographical Society of New York carried on original investigations, issued publications, sponsored exploration and gave awards, honours and medals for outstanding achievement in exploration and geographical research. The society continued to publish the *Geographical Review* (a quarterly journal) and *Current Geographical Publications,* a monthly list (initiated in 1938) of selected books, pamphlets, articles, maps and photographs, which was added to the society's special research catalog. An outstanding event in the record of the society was the completion in 1945 of the 107-sheet *Map of Hispanic America* on the scale of 1:1,000,000, on which an average of 7 compilers, draftsmen and editors had been engaged for the preceding 25 years. Work on other long-range undertakings was largely suspended during World War II in order to carry out research and cartographic projects for government agencies.

Membership in the society increased from 3,500 at the end of 1935 to 4,648 at the end of 1946. During the 10-year period, the library collection was increased from 100,400 books and volumes of periodicals, 17,100 pamphlets and 9,100 photographs to 117,756 books and periodicals, 23,523 pamphlets and 26,563 photographs. The map collection of 89,300 maps and 1,710 atlases at the end of 1935 reached a total of 144,194 maps and 2,365 atlases at the end of 1946. Fourteen volumes covering a wide range of geographical subjects were added to the society's monograph series, which totalled 70 vol. at the close of 1946.

Officers of the society (1946): Roland L. Redmond, president; Dr. John K. Wright, director. Headquarters: Broadway at 156th St., New York 32, N.Y.

American Historical Association.—Founded in 1884, the American Historical association was incorporated by an act of congress five years later "for the promotion of historical studies . . and for kindred purposes in the interests of American history." Its members, recruited chiefly from teachers and writers of history in United States and Canadian schools and colleges, numbered about 3,300 in 1937 and 3,812 in 1946.

Activities of the association during the 1937–46 decade were many, and their scope was wide. It published an important series of U.S. legal records, another important series of material relating to the history of the U.S. and a third series of historical monographs covering the whole field of history. The association co-operated with the National Council for the Social Studies in the publication of *Social Education,* dealing with the problem of teaching history in the schools. During World War II the association was engaged in preparation of discussion pamphlets for use in the armed forces.

Publications: the *American Historical Review,* a quarterly, and an annual report in three volumes. Officers (1946) were: Prof. Sidney Bradshaw Fay, president, and Dr. Guy Stanton Ford, executive secretary. Headquarters: Study Room 274, Library of Congress annex, Washington 25, D.C.

American Institute for Property and Liability Underwriters.—The institute was created in 1942 under sponsorship of seven national insurance organizations, maintaining, however, its independence in management. Its objectives were defined as the establishment of an educational standard for property and casualty insurance underwriters.

To obtain the award of Chartered Property Casualty Underwriter (C.P.C.U.), candidates were required to pass examinations in insurance principles and practices, general education, general commercial and insurance law and accounting and finance. In 1946, 89 persons held the C.P.C.U. designation.

Officers (1946) were: Dr. S. S. Huebner, chairman of the board of trustees; H. P. Stellwagen, president; Harry J. Loman, dean; Arthur C. Goerlich, secretary, and Otho E. Lane, treasurer. Headquarters: Hamilton Court, 39th and Chestnut streets, Philadelphia 4, Pa.

American Institute of Accountants.—Founded in 1887, the American Institute of Accountants adopted as its objectives the maintenance of high standards of education and practice for the profession and development of the technique of accounting to serve the public interest. Governed by a council consisting of 48 elected members, 4 elected officers and past presidents, the institute continued to prepare the official C.P.A. examinations for 44 states, the District of Columbia and 4 territories. The 40 committees of the institute continued to work toward improvement of the federal income tax system, conduct special studies in accounting and auditing problems and strive to promote better accounting and auditing for government agencies.

Membership of the organization as of Sept. 30, 1946, was 10,149. Publications: the *Journal of Accountancy,* national professional monthly magazine, and the *Certified Public Accountant,* a monthly news bulletin. Officers (1946) were: Edward B. Wilcox, president; Parry Barnes and Percival F. Brundage, vice-presidents; Maurice E. Peloubet, treasurer, and John L. Carey, secretary. Headquarters: 13 E. 41st St., New York, N.Y.

American Institute of Architects.—Founded in 1857 as the national organization of the architectural profession in the United States, the American Institute of Architects included 76 local chapters and 20 state associations in 1946. The institute continued to publish its monthly magazine, *Journal of the American Institute of Architects.* Officers (1946): president of the board of directors, James R. Edmunds, Jr.; vice-president, Samuel E. Lunden; secretary, Alexander C. Robinson, III; treasurer, Charles F. Cellarius. Headquarters: 1741 New York Ave., N.W., Washington 6, D.C.

American Institute of Chemical Engineers.—This organization was founded in 1908 for the advancement of chemical engineering in theory and practice. During World War II many of its regular activities were curtailed because of wartime restrictions. The institute's official publication: *Transactions of the American Institute of Chemical Engineers,* a bimonthly. Membership in 1946 was 6,403. Officers (1946): president, James G. Vail; vice-president, Charles M. A. Stine; secretary and executive secretary, Stephen L. Tyler; treasurer, C. R. DeLong. Headquarters: 50 E. 41st St., New York, N.Y.

American Institute of Electrical Engineers.—The institute was established in 1884 as a membership society of individual electrical engineers, devoting its efforts primarily to advancing the theory and practice of electrical engineering and allied fields and maintaining a high professional level among its members. During the 1937–46 decade its membership increased from approximately 15,000 to 27,000. Sections activities were greatly expanded as were the activities of all other divisions of the institute. Publications: *Electrical Engineering,* a monthly; *Transactions* and *Yearbook,* both annuals, and other publications appearing irregularly. Officers (1946): J. Elmer Housley, president; H. H. Henline, secretary. Headquarters: 33

W. 39th St., New York 18, N.Y.

American Institute of Mining and Metallurgical Engineers.—The American Institute of Mining and Metallurgical Engineers was founded in 1871 to promote the arts and sciences connected with the economic and scientific research for production and use of metallic and nonmetallic minerals.

Membership of the institute in 1946 was 15,000. Publications: *Mining and Metallurgy,* a monthly magazine, as well as periodicals dealing with various phases of mining and metallurgical technology. The institute's funds had a principal value of about $650,000 in 1946.

Officers (1946): Louis S. Cates, president; A. B. Parsons, secretary. Headquarters: 29 W. 39th St., New York 18, N.Y.

American Iron and Steel Institute.—The American Iron and Steel institute's predecessor organization, the American Iron association, was formed in 1855. The institute defined its purposes as the promotion of the interest of the iron and steel industry, the encouragement of the use of iron and steel and the collection of statistics and other information concerning the industry.

Within the institute 43 committees were set up, dealing with technical aspects of operations in the industry alone. Its publications included *Steel Facts* and *Steelways,* as well as occasional technical bulletins, books and pamphlets. In the critical years prior to the outbreak of World War II, defense activities were the institute's major preoccupation. After U.S. entry into World War II, the major part of the institute's activities were devoted to furthering the war effort.

Through its committees, it served as liaison between war agencies and steel producers. Officers (1946) were: Walter S. Tower, president; B. F. Fairless and Frank Purnell, vice-presidents; Harold L. Hughes, treasurer; George S. Rose, secretary. Headquarters: 350 Fifth Ave., New York 1, N.Y.

American Judicature Society.—An organization designed to promote the efficient administration of justice, the American Judicature society was founded in 1913 by Herbert Harley. It was reorganized in 1928 with a membership of 600. The organization had a period of slow but steady growth during the 1937–46 decade; its membership in 1937 was 1,272 and by Oct. 1946 it had increased to 6,912.

The A.J.C. made many notable contributions to judicial reforms and reorganization and continued to publish the *Journal,* a bimonthly magazine with a claimed circulation of 43,000 readers. Officers (1946): president, George E. Brand; chairman of the board, Albert J. Harno; secretary-treasurer, Glenn R. Winters. Headquarters: Hutchins Hall, Ann Arbor, Mich.

American Law Institute.—Founded in 1923, the American Law institute defined as its objectives the pursuit of constructive scientific work for improvement of the law. Its chief task was work on *Restatement of the Law,* a work covering a large part of the common or judge-made law of the United States.

During the 10 years beginning Jan. 1, 1936, the first *Restatement of the Law,* as planned, was completed: *Property,* vol. I (Introduction and Freehold Interests) and vol. II (Future Interests, parts 1 and 2) (1936); *Restitutions* (1936); *Torts,* vol. III (Absolute Liability, Deceit, Libel, Wrongful Litigation, Domestic Relations, Business, part 1) (1938); *Torts,* vol. IV (Miscellaneous Torts, Defenses and Remedies) (1939); *Property,* vol. III (Future Interests, parts 3 and 4) (1940); *Security* (1941); *Judgments* (1942); *Property,* vol. IV (Perpetuities and Other Social Restrictions) (1944) and vol. V (Servitudes) (1944).

Besides the *Restatement,* the most notable task completed in the 1937–46 decade was the institute's *Model Code of Evidence* published in 1942. Toward the close of the decade, the institute and the National Conference of Commissioners on Uniform State Laws were co-operating on development of the code of commercial law.

Aside from the official members there were 860 life members in 1945. Officers (1946): George Wharton Pepper, president; Learned Hand, vice-president; William Dean Embree, treasurer, and William Draper Lewis, director. Headquarters: 3400 Chestnut St., Philadelphia 4, Pa.

American Legion.—The American Legion was chartered by congress in 1919 as an organization of U.S. veterans of World War I. On Oct. 29, 1942, Pres. Roosevelt signed an act making honourably discharged veterans of World War II eligible for membership. Since its inception, the Legion's basic program had been to strengthen national defense and to safeguard the rights of veterans.

Legion membership in 1937 stood at 973,841 in 11,393 posts. The influx of returning veterans of World War II increased membership in Dec. 1946 to more than 3,322,000 in nearly 16,000 posts. Legion statistics then disclosed that more than 68% of the membership was composed of World War II veterans.

At the beginning of the 1937–46 decade, the Legion endorsed policies stressing world peace and neutrality and urged further strengthening of U.S. national defenses. In 1941 the Legion embraced an all-out war program and registered the larger part of its membership for national defense service. It also sent a mission to Britain to study civilian defense and participated in the training of many citizens in the U.S. in civil defense duties.

Between 1937 and 1941, the Legion also conducted campaigns for government protection of World War I widows and orphans and veterans' preference in civil service employment, and urged an intensive Americanism campaign. It also advocated further restrictions on immigration and opposed communism.

During the first phase of U.S. participation in World War II, the Legion was active in selling war bonds, manning aircraft warning systems, aiding the nationwide scrap metal and rubber collections and conducting a variegated number of similar services of assistance to the war effort.

On the national political front, the Legion campaigned for expediting claims of World War II veterans, for government compensation and enactment of the G.I. Bill of Rights and the measure providing financial assistance for needy dependents of deceased veterans of World War II. It also distributed Christmas gifts to wounded and sick servicemen in domestic hospitals.

In 1945 the Legion recommended a program for national security buttressed on universal training; the program included scientific research, a world-wide military intelligence system and a strong navy and urged retention of atomic bomb secrets and merger of the armed services.

Credit for five major legislative actions of benefit to war veterans in 1945–46 was claimed by the Legion. These were: (1) the bill providing for terminal leave pay for enlisted men and women: (2) amendments liberalizing the G.I. Bill of Rights; (3) a 20% cost-of-living increase in compensation and pension rates for disabled veterans; (4) amendments liberalizing the surplus property act and (5) amendments liberalizing the National Service Life Insurance act.

The Legion's national publications: the *American Legion Magazine,* a monthly, and the *National Legion-*

American Legion Conventions, 1937–46

Year	Place	National Commander Elected
1937	New York, N.Y.	Daniel J. Doherty, Woburn, Mass.
1938	Los Angeles, Calif.	Stephen F. Chadwick, Seattle, Wash.
1939	Chicago, Ill.	Raymond J. Kelly, Detroit, Mich.
1940	Boston, Mass.	Milo J. Warner, Toledo, Ohio
1941	Milwaukee, Wis.	Lynn U. Stambaugh, Fargo, N.D.
1942	Kansas City, Mo.	Roane Waring, Memphis, Tenn.
1943	Omaha, Neb.	Warren H. Atherton, Stockton, Calif.
1944	Chicago, Ill.	Edward N. Scheiberling, Albany, N.Y.
1945	Chicago, Ill.	John Stelle, McLeansboro, Ill.
1946	San Francisco, Calif.	Paul H. Griffith, Indianapolis, Ind.

naire, a semimonthly newspaper. National headquarters of the American Legion: Indianapolis, Ind.

American Library Association.—Founded in 1876, the A.L.A. became the official organization of librarians in the United States and Canada. Consisting of librarians, library trustees and others interested in libraries, the A.L.A. in 1946 was the oldest association of its kind, affiliated with more than 60 other library associations in the United States and other countries.

During the decade, the A.L.A. continued to promote one of its principal objectives: complete and adequate library coverage for the United States and Canada, particularly in the rural areas which were without access to a public library. Its activities and services continued to be carried by a large headquarters staff, about 80 committees and boards of volunteer workers. Its program included informational and advisory services, personnel service, field work and nonprofit publication of numerous professional books and pamphlets. Among its publications are the following periodicals: *A.L.A. Bulletin, Booklist, College and Research Libraries, Hospital Book Guide* and *Subscription Books Bulletin.*

The A.L.A.'s activities during the 1937–46 period were broad and varied. In 1938 the A.L.A. worked for inclusion of grants for rural library service as well as other projects in the public interest. During the decade, the A.L.A. handled funds, chiefly from the Rockefeller foundation and the department of state, totalling more than $1,500,000 in making gifts of books to libraries in war countries and in arranging exchange of personnel between foreign and U.S. libraries.

After U.S. entry into World War II, the A.L.A. encouraged the U.S. public libraries to act as war information centres, sources of research material and as disseminators of authentic ideas and facts about war and postwar problems to civilians. The association also engaged in international activities which were co-ordinated under the Board on International Relations. Acting on A.L.A. recommendations, the Office of War Information and the Co-ordinator of Inter-American Affairs established U.S. information libraries in the major cities throughout the world, these were later taken over by the department of state. A.L.A. also co-sponsored with the American Red Cross and United Service organizations the Victory Book campaign. In 1944 it published its "Bill of Rights," which recommended that books believed to be factually correct should not be banned or censored because of disapproval by some persons.

After the close of World War II, the A.L.A. opened a Library National Relations office in Washington, D.C.

Membership in the A.L.A. increased from 14,000 in 1936 to more than 16,000 in 1946. Executive secretary: Carl H. Milam. Executive offices: 50 E. Huron St., Chicago, Ill.

American Medical Association.—Founded in 1847, the American Medical association established its aim as the promotion of the art and science of medicine and the betterment of public health. Strictly a nonprofit organization, it devoted all of its income toward realization of these objectives. The association's capital in 1946, valued at about $7,100,000, consisted of securities in the amount of $5,600,000 and assets and property totalling $1,500,000. Its net income in 1945 was more than $1,000,000.

The administrative structure of the association became pyramidal in form. At the base were the numerous county medical societies; these bodies elected members to the state associations, each governed by a house of delegates. At the apex was the national house of delegates, with members elected by the state bodies. Authority to establish policies was vested in the national house of delegates, convening in official session once annually, although it could be convoked for special emergency sessions. The affairs of the association continued to be run by a board of nine trustees representing various sections of the United States—two elected each year to serve five-year terms.

The great majority of the physicians in the United States belonged to the American Medical association at the end of 1946. At the beginning of the 1937–46 decade, 105,400 physicians were listed as members of the A.M.A.; this figure increased to 128,000 by the end of the decade.

The association's list of publications continued to be headed by the *Journal of the American Medical Association,* a weekly journal with a circulation of more than 130,000. Other publications: *Hygeia,* a monthly; nine medical journals for various medical specialties; a directory of the medical profession, schools, libraries and hospitals, the *Quarterly Cumulative Index Medicus; The Standard Nomenclature of Diseases and Operations.*

During the 1937–46 decade, the association was especially active in prompt testing of some medicinal products which proved subsequently to be merely nostrums. In 1937 its laboratory was able to prove that the solvent in the so-called "elixir of sulfanilamide" was the toxic agent that caused the deaths of 73 persons.

Activities of the council on industry (which set standards and promoted improvement in care of industrial workers) and the council on medical service (which encouraged the growth of voluntary sickness insurance plans) gained importance during the decade because of the A.M.A.'s consistent opposition to administration plans for instituting a government-sponsored health insurance program. The association's objections stemmed from its concern lest "socialized medicine" result in lowered fees for physicians and the introduction of "politics" in the profession.

In World War II the American Medical association was actively engaged in helping the government war effort, and many of its operations were handled through its committee on war participation. A suboffice of the War Manpower commission, set up in its headquarters, engaged in procuring and assigning physicians for the armed forces and for civilian areas in need of medical personnel.

Officers (1946) were: Harrison H. Shoulders, president; Olin West, president-elect; George F. Lull, secretary and general manager; J. J. Moore, treasurer; Morris Fishbein, editor of publications, and Thomas R. Gardiner, business manager. Headquarters: 535 N. Dearborn St., Chicago.

American Society of Civil Engineers.—Founded in 1852, the American Society of Civil Engineers adopted as its objectives the advancement of the sciences of engineering and architecture, and the fostering of professional improvement of its members. General funds of the society totalled about $850,000 in 1946; its interest in the Engineering and Societies building accounted for another

$625,000 and its trust funds totalled about $120,000.

The society continued to conduct its activities through its professional committees on employment conditions, engineering education, registration of engineers, salaries, professional conduct, etc. Its technical divisions covered the practice of engineering in 13 categories, and its work in various communities of the country was carried on under its 65 local sections. Its student chapters worked in 123 engineering colleges.

Membership in Aug. 1946 was about 21,500. Publications: *Proceedings*, a monthly technical journal; *Transactions*, an annual, and *Civil Engineering*, an illustrated magazine. Officers: Wesley W. Horner, president; Col. William Carey, executive secretary; Charles E. Trout, treasurer. Headquarters: 33 W. 39th St., New York 18, N.Y.

American Society of Mechanical Engineers.—Organized in 1880, the American Society of Mechanical Engineers set forth as its objectives the fostering of mechanical engineering and related arts and sciences, the advancement of engineering standards and the broadening of usefulness of the engineering profession. The society grew from a membership of 189 at the time of its first annual meeting in 1880 to more than 19,000 members in 1946, grouped into 18 divisions and 70 local sections, including one in Canada. Student branches were also maintained in 120 schools. The society continued to award its A.S.M.E. medal, the Holley medal, the Worcester Reed Warner medal, the Melville medal, the Spirit of St. Louis medal and others. Publications: *Mechanical Engineering*, a monthly journal, and *Journal of Applied Mechanics*, a quarterly. Other books and material relevant to mechanical engineering continued to be published on occasion. Officers (1947); president, Eugene W. O'Brien; treasurer, K. W. Jappe, and secretary, C. E. Davies. Headquarters: 29 W. 39th St., New York 18, N.Y.

American Veterans Committee.—An organization of veterans of World War II, A.V.C. was founded on Jan. 31, 1943, and assumed its name in Oct. 1944. A.V.C.'s goal was defined as the achievement of "a more prosperous and democratic America and a more stable world." In late 1946 A.V.C. had between 80,000 and 85,000 members. It was active in support of terminal leave pay, the G.I. Bill of Rights, housing for veterans and continuation of price control. A.V.C. denounced the sentence accorded to Col. James A. Kilian at the Lichfield trials in 1946 and demanded investigation of the army's court-martial system. Official publication: the *A.V.C. Bulletin*, a semimonthly newspaper. Officers (1946): Charles G. Bolté, chairman; Gilbert A. Harrison, vice-chairman. Headquarters: 1860 Broadway, New York 23, N.Y.

American Veterans of World War II (Amvets).—Founded at Kansas City, Mo., on Dec. 10, 1944, Amvets is a veterans' organization composed exclusively of former soldiers, sailors and marines of World War II.

Eligible for Amvet membership are any honourably discharged persons who served in the U.S. armed forces, or U.S. citizens who fought in the armed forces of any U.S. ally, between Sept. 16, 1940, and the date of the close of hostilities. Membership lists are also open to any soldiers, sailors or marines on active duty who meet other specified qualifications.

By the close of 1946 there were more than 1,050 Amvet posts in all the 48 states and in Hawaii. Membership was put at about 100,000.

At its second national convention, held in St. Louis, Mo., Nov. 21–24, 1946. Amvets adopted a broad national program that stressed special privileges for veterans in the domestic field.

Ray Sawyer was elected national commander of Amvets at the Nov. 1946 convention. National headquarters are at 724 Ninth St. N.W., Washington, D.C.

Anti-Saloon League of America.—Founded in 1895, the Anti-Saloon League of America stated its objective as "extermination of the traffic in alcoholic beverages and the prevention of alcoholism and attendant evils." The league was active in securing local option, state prohibition and ratification of the 18th amendment. After the latter law was repealed by the 21st amendment in 1933, the Anti-Saloon league shifted the emphasis of its activities toward creation of greater temperance sentiment in the states and local communities.

Official organ of the league: the *American Issue*. A nonmembership organization, the Anti-Saloon league continued to be supported by voluntary contributions. Officers elected at the 1946 convention were Bishop Ralph S. Cushman, president; Bishop G. D. Batdorf, vice-president; Samuel Reid, treasurer, and Frederick W. Smith, recording secretary. National headquarters: 131 B St. S.E., Washington 3, D.C.

Authors' League of America.—A national organization of U.S. authors, dramatists, radio writers and screen writers, the Authors' League of America was founded in 1912 to procure adequate national and international copyright laws. In 1920 the organization was divided into guilds, such as the Authors' guild, Dramatists' guild and Screen Writers' guild. Most of the established writers in the United States are members of the organization.

The executive secretary of the organization is Louise M. Silcox. Headquarters are at 6 E. 39th St., New York 16, N.Y.

Boys' Clubs of America.—A federation of local groups, nonsectarian, Boys' Clubs of America was founded in May 1906, in Boston, Mass., to provide leisure-time activities under trained leadership for boys of 7 to 18, chiefly in congested urban districts. As of 1946, the organization represented 260 Boys' clubs with more than 250,000 members. Among the many services provided by the national organization were a field service to inform, advise and assist Boys' clubs, as well as services for personnel and training, building, supply and publicity. Publications: the *Boys' Club Bulletin*, the *Boys' Club Courier* and the *Boys' Club Service*. Officers (1946): chairman of the board, Herbert Hoover; president, William Edwin Hall; treasurer, Albert H. Wiggin; secretary, William Ziegler, Jr.; executive director, David W. Armstrong. Headquarters: 381 Fourth Ave., New York 16, N.Y.

Boy Scouts.—The Boy Scout movement was founded in the British Isles in 1908 and later spread to every civilized country in the world. The movement was free to boys of all races, creed or colour, and the organization's leaders continued to emphasize its nonmilitary, nonpolitical, nonclass and nonsectarian nature.

Boy Scouts of America.—Between 1937 and 1941, Boy Scouts of America (the U.S. section of the movement) engaged in its usual peacetime activities. In 1940 the scouts adopted an extensive program to be of assistance in the national emergency and after the U.S. entry into World War II placed their entire resources at the service of the government. During the conflict scouts rendered outstanding service in the salvage campaigns, in encouraging sales of war bonds, in victory gardening, etc.

At the request of the government, scouts in 1946 helped put over many postwar projects, including collection of clothing and materials to be sent abroad and cultivation of victory gardens to alleviate critical food shortages.

The total number of boys in the organization in 1946 was 1,499,184, while scout leaders numbered 493,186. The number of scout units was 64,080. Officers (1946) were: Amory Houghton, president; Elbert K. Fretwell, chief scout executive. Headquarters: 2 Park Ave., New York 16, N.Y.

Great Britain.—During the battle of Britain, scouts served as wardens, foot, cycle and motorcycle messengers and telephone operators. They formed decontamination squads, helped police air-raid shelters, trenches and sandbag emplacements, gave first-aid assistance to people injured during the bombings and formed stretcher units to speed the seriously injured to hospitals. The number of emergency war jobs performed by the scouts totalled nearly 200; and scores of individual scouts and scout units were decorated by a grateful government for their yeoman service.

Lord Baden-Powell, founder of the Boy Scout movement, died in early 1941 and Lord Rowallen was elected chief scout of the British Boy Scout association in 1945. John Skinner Wilson was appointed director of the International Scout bureau located in London.

Brookings Institution.—A nonprofit corporation, the Brookings institution was founded in 1916 for scientific and educational work in the U.S. public interest. Its principal efforts were made in research and training in the fields of economics and government. The institution's grants of research fellowships to a limited number of advanced graduate students were temporarily discontinued during World War II.

During the decade 1937–46 the Brookings institution published 46 books and 41 pamphlets in the field of economics and government. Among some of its publications were: *The Recovery Problem in the United States* (1937); *The Income Structure of the United States* by Maurice Leven (1938); *Reorganization of the National Government* by Lewis Meriam and L. F. Schmeckebier (1939); *Labor Relations in the Automobile Industry* by William H. McPherson (1940): *The Presidents and Civil Disorder,* by Bennett Milton Rich (1941); *Peace Plans and American Choices,* by Arthur C. Millspaugh (1942); *World Minerals and World Peace,* by C. K. Leith, J. W. Furness and Cleona Lewis (1943); *The Control of Germany and Japan* by Harold G. Moulton and Louis Marlio (1944); *International Tribunals: Past and Future* by Manley O. Hudson (1945) and *Relief and Social Security* by Lewis Meriam (1946).

Officers: Harold G. Moulton, president; Lewis Meriam, vice-president, and Elizabeth H. Wilson, secretary. Headquarters: 722 Jackson place, N.W., Washington 6, D.C.

Camp Fire Girls.—Camp Fire Girls, Inc., an organization in the United States serving girls between the ages of 7 and 18, was founded in 1910 and incorporated 2 years later with the objective of supplementing the training of girls in home, school and church by directing their recreational activities into the proper channels. Membership in the organization increased from 234,664 in 1936 to more than 360,000 (in more than 1,300 communities) in 1946.

Camp Fire Girl units were divided into 3 age groups: (1) the Bluebirds, ranging from 7 through 9 years of age; (2) Camp Fire Girls, from 10 through 14 and (3) Horizon Clubbers, ranging from 15 through 18.

During World War II the Camp Fire Girls carried out a "Service for Victory" program which included such activities as selling war bonds, salvaging needed materials, aiding the Red Cross, child-tending, victory gardening and helping to offset delinquency by organizing parties, outings and games for younger children.

Official magazine: the *Camp Fire Girl,* a monthly. Officers in 1946: Martha F. Allen, national director; Mrs. James C. Parker, president; Dr. Bernice Baxter, vice-president; Earle W. Brailey, chairman of the board; Glenn O. Hoffhines, treasurer; Mrs. Frank C. Love, secretary. Headquarters: 88 Lexington Ave., New York 16, N.Y.

Carnegie Trusts.—The Carnegie Trusts in 1946 comprised the second largest group of charitable foundations in the world. A brief résumé of the activities of the principal U.S. trusts during the 1937–46 decade follows:

Carnegie Corporation of New York.—Largest of all the foundations, this corporation was founded in 1911 by Andrew Carnegie for the express purpose of "the advancement and diffusion of knowledge and understanding among the peoples of the United States." Its scope was extended in 1917 to include the British dominions and colonies.

The corporation had a basic endowment of more than \$135,000,000. Book value of the total assets of the main endowment fund as of Sept. 30, 1946, was \$152,937,620. Book value of the assets of the British Dominions and Colonies fund as of the same date was \$14,305,061.

The program of this foundation included advancement of education through complete or partial support of specific undertakings in institutions of higher learning, in organizations and agencies devoted to general education in national and international affairs. It also included projects giving promise of new knowledge.

Between 1937 and 1946, the Carnegie Corporation of New York appropriated about \$38,000,000 for achievement of the above-mentioned goals. The total amount appropriated since the corporation's inception in 1911 was about \$200,000,000.

President of Carnegie Corporation of New York (1946): Devereux C. Josephs. Secretary: Robert M. Lester; and treasurer and investment officer: C. Herbert Lee.

Carnegie also founded and endowed separately five other agencies in the United States, as follows:

Carnegie Institute of Pittsburgh.—Founded in 1896, the Carnegie Institute of Pittsburgh in 1946 consisted of a museum of fine arts, a music hall, a museum of natural history, a public library and an associated institute of technology with a library school. It had a capital of \$36,000,000 in 1946.

Carnegie Institution of Washington.—Founded in 1902 to encourage scientific research, this institution had spent about \$50,000,000 by the end of 1946 in investigation, research and discovery and application of knowledge for improvement of the lot of mankind. The institution, with a capital of \$35,000,000, consisted of a combination of research departments, which conducted important research and work in astronomy, terrestrial magnetism, geophysics, animal and plant biology and in historical research. During World War II most of its staff and research facilities were largely devoted to the war effort. After the war, the regular staff members returned to their posts and the institution's normal functions in basic research were resumed.

Carnegie Hero Fund Commission.—Founded in 1904 to give merited recognition to heroic acts performed in the United States, Canada and Newfoundland and the waters of these areas by persons who normally would not perform such acts in their regular vocations, the commission made 477 awards of medals or funds totalling more than \$1,837,000 during 1937–46. From its inception, the total awards made by the commission were 3,442 and pecuniary awards totalled $6,837,051.

Carnegie Foundation for Advancement of Teaching.—This foundation was established in 1905 to provide free pensions for college professors and to advance higher education. Through its Division of Educational Inquiry (endowed by Carnegie corporation), the foundation subsidized many sweeping inquiries in the field of education. The foundation also was concerned with such activities as a teacher-testing program, graduate examination study and a comparative examination study. During the 1937–46 decade, it paid more than $17,000,000 in allowances to retired college professors or their widows, making a total of $50,077,418 paid for such purposes since its establishment.

Carnegie Endowment for International Peace.—This organization, founded in 1910 for promoting "the speedy abolition of international war between the so-called civilized nations" was divided into three sections: (1) Intercourse and Education; (2) Economics and History and (3) International Law. The endowment, with a capital of $10,000,000, was free to work in any way to encourage peace and good will between nations. The Economics and History section was responsible for a 152-vol. work on the economic and social history of World War I, prepared under the direction of Dr. James T. Shotwell and divisional editors in 16 countries, through funds made available by the endowment. This monumental task was completed in 1937. A 44-vol. study of the history of Canadian-U.S. relations was completed in 1941.

During and after World War II, the endowment continued its efforts to further international understanding through research, publication, conferences, student centres in colleges and universities, distribution of books and pamphlets to strategic centres, study of international law and studies of causes of misunderstanding and means of promoting the general cause of peace.

Catholic Community Service, National.—Founded in Nov. 1940, the National Catholic Community service was the agency designated by the Roman Catholic Church in the United States to serve men and women in the armed forces and war workers in overburdened industrial communities. A member of the United Service organizations, it was financed by public donations. The N.C.C.S. was organized to serve men and women of every creed, but differed from other war agencies in that it held special services for Catholics. During World War II, N.C.C.S. participated in several hundred operations and also sponsored independent operations in the U.S. and in areas abroad where U.S. armed forces were stationed. Its publications included *NCCS,* a monthly, as well as numerous books and pamphlets. Officers (1946) were: James S. Mitchell, executive director, and Anne Sarachon Hooley, assistant executive director. N.C.C.S. headquarters: 1312 Massachusetts Ave. N.W., Washington, D.C.

Catholic Library Association.—The Catholic Library association was founded in 1921 as the library division of the National Catholic Education association; in 1931 the library association became independent of the parent organization.

Activities were defined to include dissemination of data on library service to member organizations, compilation of bibliographical research to promote Catholic scholarship and encouragement of formations of new units to the association. The association also was organized to function as the standardizing agent of Catholic library schools and to collaborate with other organizations.

Publications: *Catholic Library World,* the official organ; *Catholic Periodical Index; Catholic Booklist,* a weekly, and the *Catholic Supplement to Standard Catalog for High School Libraries.* Officers (1946): Richard James Hurley, president; Brother Thomas, F.S.C., vice-president; Laurence A. Leavey, executive secretary. Headquarters: the Cardinal Hayes library, Manhattan college, New York, N.Y.

Commonwealth Fund.—The Commonwealth fund was established by Mrs. Stephen V. Harkness in 1918 "to do something for the welfare of mankind." Increased by gifts from the founder and from Edward S. Harkness, former president of the fund (1918–40), the fund's endowment by 1946 totalled $50,237,489. A large portion of its annual appropriations was devoted to the promotion or maintenance of physical and mental health and medical research. In addition, fellowships were provided for British graduate students at U.S. universities and aid was given to public health activities aimed at raising standards of rural hospitals and medical centres.

Early in the 1937–46 decade, the fund aided child guidance enterprises in England, maintained an advisory service for community mental hygiene clinics in the U.S. and made grants for the study of administrative law and legal history.

After the start of World War II, the fund set aside more than $1,250,000 for war relief and related services, including the rehabilitation of men rejected under Selective Service or discharged from the armed forces for psychiatric disabilities. The fund continued to publish annually a number of books and pamphlets of educational significance in its fields of operation.

Officers (1946): Malcolm P. Aldrich, president; Barry C. Smith, general director. Headquarters: 41 E. 57th St., New York 22, N.Y.

Congress of Industrial Organizations.—An organization of labour unions in the U.S. and Canada, the C.I.O. was founded on Nov. 9, 1935, as the Committee for Industrial Organization. At its first constitutional convention in Pittsburgh, Pa., Nov. 14–18, 1936, the committee changed its name, adopted a constitution and named John L. Lewis (chief of the United Mine Workers of America) as president. Vice-presidents were Philip Murray and Sidney Hillman, and James B. Carey was elected secretary. Additional vice-presidents were named at subsequent conventions.

The new labour organization was formed by representatives of eight international unions who broke off their affiliations with the American Federation of Labor in 1935 after the latter organization voted down demands of the eight groups for industrial unionization. The seceding unions then had a membership of about 912,000. In 1946 its membership was reported to be between 6,000,000 and 6,500,000, and the organization comprised about 40 international unions affiliated with it. The C.I.O. had state councils in 36 states and almost 300 city councils throughout the nation.

The C.I.O.'s first objective was to organize the employees in the mass production industries, such as steel, automobiles and textiles, into industrial unions. Its early membership drives were spectacular and were marked by tremendous gains. Its first major success occurred in 1936 when it compelled the Goodyear firm in Akron, O., to agree to union recognition. It lost subsequent strikes against four of the "Little Steel" companies, but made new gains the following year (1937) in signing up U.S. Steel and General Motors. In 1940 the C.I.O. extended its efforts to organization of craft as well as industrial unions.

John L. Lewis, who had given vigorous backing to President Roosevelt in the early phase of the New Deal, fell out with the president in 1940 and switched his support to Wendell Willkie, the Republican nominee. Lewis announced that he would resign if Roosevelt were re-elected and made good his promise; the U.M.W. later seceded from the C.I.O. Philip Murray was elected as president after Lewis' resignation.

In 1941 the C.I.O.'s most noteworthy gains were the organization of employees of the Ford Motor company, the "Little Steel" companies and other large corporations which previously had refused to sign C.I.O. contracts. It also made rapid strides in organizing U.S. defense industries. During World War II the C.I.O.'s most noteworthy record was the activity of its then 5,000,000 members in the war effort and the success of its leaders in keeping strikes at a minimum. In 1943 C.I.O. established the Political Action Committee (*q.v.*), which helped get out the vote for prolabour candidates and for President Roosevelt during the 1944 elections.

After the war the C.I.O. backed the Full Employment bill and other pending federal legislation designed to improve living standards among workers. Two major strikes marked the C.I.O.'s postwar program for higher wages to combat increasing living costs. The United Automobile Workers staged a walkout at General Motors plants for a 30% wage increase but settled the dispute in March 1946 for a smaller increase and other benefits after a 113-day strike. The month-long strike called by the United Steelworkers in the "Big" and "Little" steel corporations was settled in Feb. 1946 on conditions deemed favourable to the C.I.O.

In 1946 the C.I.O. spurred its organizing drive in the south, opposed abolition of price controls and actively campaigned against what it termed the efforts of antilabour elements to emasculate the Wagner act and other labour measures.

Principal C.I.O. publications: *C.I.O. News,* a weekly, and *Economic Outlook,* monthly. Officers (1946–47): Philip Murray, president (re-elected at 1946 convention in Atlantic City, N.J.); James B. Carey, secretary-treasurer. Headquarters: 718 Jackson place N.W., Washington 6, D.C.

Daughters of the American Revolution.—Founded in 1890 to perpetuate the memory and spirit of the men and women who achieved U.S. independence, the society devoted itself over the years to the acquisition and protection of historical spots and erection of monuments and to the preservation of relics, documents and records of the revolutionary era.

During the 1937–46 decade membership increased from 140,000 to 153,000, and about 100 new chapters were added during that period. The society continued to publish foreign language manuals for citizenship for distribution to aliens through government agencies; it also maintained and operated two schools at Grant, Ala., and Tamassee, S.C., and contributed to 18 other approved schools. The D.A.R. was active in civil defense, relief and charitable activities during World War II. Principal publications: *Daughters of the American Revolution Magazine* and *National Defense News.* Officers (1946): Mrs. Julius Y. Talmadge, president general; Mrs. Stanley Thorpe Manlove, recording secretary general, and Mrs. Charles Carroll Haig, treasurer general. National headquarters: 1720 D St. N.W., Washington 6, D.C.

DeMolay, The Order of.—Founded in 1919, the Order of DeMolay became a fraternal organization for youth between the ages of 14 and 21. DeMolay's purpose was to further the seven cardinal virtues of the Masonic order: love of parents, reverence, courtesy, comradeship, fidelity, cleanliness and patriotism. Admission to the order had two requirements: a belief in God and a good character record. No Masonic relationship was required or implied.

During World War II the order lost virtually all physically fit boys of 17 and over to the armed forces, and several hundred chapters necessarily suspended their activities for the duration. In early 1945 many of the dormant chapters asked for reinstatement.

Officers (1946) included: Frank S. Land, founder of the order, who is secretary general and chief administration officer; Stratton D. Brooks, director, and Charles A. Boyce, comptroller. Headquarters: 201 E. Armour Blvd., Kansas City 2, Mo.

Elks, Benevolent and Protective Order of.—A fraternal order, the B.P.O.E. was organized in New York city in 1868 for the purposes of practising "charity, justice, brotherly love and fidelity; to promote the welfare and enhance the happiness of its members; to quicken the spirit of American patriotism; to cultivate good fellowship." Membership in the Elks was limited to white male citizens 21 years of age and over. In 1946 there were lodges in 1,450 towns and cities in the U.S. and territorial possessions. Membership during 1937–46 doubled, increasing from 450,000 to 850,000. During that period, expenditures for charitable and welfare purposes amounted to more than $2,500,000 annually. During World War II the order's work was directed by the Elks National War commission, which urged local lodges to give full support to the war effort.

Official organ of the order: the *Elks Magazine.* Officers of the Grand Lodge, B.P.O.E.: Charles E. Broughton, grand exalted ruler; J. E. Masters, grand secretary, and John F. Burke, grand treasurer. Headquarters: Elks National Memorial Headquarters Bldg., 2750 Lake View Ave., Chicago 14, Ill.

Falk Foundation, The Maurice and Laura.—The Falk foundation was established Dec. 14, 1929, by a capital fund gift from Maurice Falk, who specified that the fund was to be used within a period of 35 years for the "betterment of mankind." Specific uses to be made of the money were left to the foundation's board of managers. Mainly the Falk fund concentrated on supporting economic research (by grants to outside organizations). From 1937 to 1946 inclusive, the foundation made research grants to such organizations as the Brookings institution, Washington, D.C.; the National Bureau of Economic Research, New York; the American Law institute; the National Conference of Commissioners on Uniform State Laws, Philadelphia and Chicago; the Committee on Postwar Tax Policy, New York, and the Committee on Public Debt Policy, New York. Many publications were issued under the foundation's grants. Throughout World War II, the foundation's principal interest was in studies designed to promote orderly economic postwar demobilization. Following the war, the foundation resumed its interests in encouraging peacetime economic stability and progress.

Grants during the 1937–46 decade totalled more than $2,500,000. Capital assets of the foundation on Dec. 31, 1946, were $6,967,025.87. Officers of the board of managers: Leon Falk, Jr., chairman; J. Steele Gow, executive director. Headquarters: Farmers Bank building, Pittsburgh, Pa.

Four-H Clubs.—Four-H clubs, organizations of rural boys and girls with activities guided by local and volunteer leaders, continued to operate under the direction of county extension agents co-operatively employed by the U.S. department of agriculture, state colleges of agriculture and county extension organizations. The name Four-H derived from the four phases of training emphasized in the work of the members—"head, heart, hands and health."

Generally the clubs were organized on the community basis, although in some states they were restricted to specific agricultural interests as dairying, canning, etc. Members usually were between the ages of 10 and 20. Each club elected its own officers and mapped out its own program for the year. No national organization of Four-H clubs was established.

The skills and experience acquired by the Four-H members enabled them to make considerable contributions to the nation's war effort, and it was estimated that during World War II, Four-H members produced and conserved enough food to feed 3,000,000 soldiers for an entire year. In addition to their work in gardening, raising crops and livestock and in conserving surplus, they also assisted in collection of scrap and in the sale of war bonds.

Membership in Four-H clubs in 1938 totalled more than 1,192,000 boys and girls, and the number of local volunteer leaders in that year was more than 125,000. By 1945 enrolments of youth in the clubs was about 1,700,000 while the local volunteer leaders totalled 175,000.

Girl Guides.—The object of the World Association of Girl Guides, formed in 1928, was stated as the promotion of unity of purpose and common understanding in the fundamental principles of Guiding and Girl Scouting throughout the world, and to encourage friendship between the girls of all nations. In 1936 there were 27 full members and 4 tenderfoot members (countries where the organization was not yet fully developed). In 1946 the membership was as follows: full members—Australia, Belgium, Brazil, Canada, Czechoslovakia, Denmark, Egypt, Finland, France, Great Britain, Hungary, India, Ireland, Luxembourg, the Netherlands, New Zealand, Norway, Poland, South Africa, Sweden, Switzerland and the United States of America; tenderfoot members—Costa Rica, Greece, Guatemala, Haiti, Italy and the Philippines.

The first postwar biennial conference—the 11th—was held in France in Sept. 1946.

Girl Scouts.—The Girl Scouts were formed in 1912 for the purpose of promoting good citizenship. During the 1937–46 decade membership in the organization increased from 435,142 to 1,213,913. Each year the Girl Scouts program has emphasized different projects for practical application of its better citizenship objective. During World War II the Girl Scouts launched the Senior Service Scouts to aid in the U.S. civilian defense program, a campaign for promoting the sale of war bonds and stamps and the Wing Scouts, a preflight aviation program for Senior Girls. Senior Scouts volunteered as farm aides, engaged in home gardening and canning, helped at blood donor centres and inaugurated an international friendship program to provide milk, clothing and school equipment to children of war-torn countries. A "share-the-food plan" was originated whereby profits from "starvation" luncheons were turned over to relief organizations.

The Girl Scouts of the United States and members of similar groups in 32 other countries became members of the World Association of Girl Guides and Girl Scouts, which before the war had a membership of more than 5,000,000.

A number of books were published by the Girl Scouts, including *Girl Scout Handbook* (*Intermediate*). Periodicals included the *American Girl* (monthly) and the *Girl Scout Leader* (10 times annually), a variety of pamphlets and an *Annual Report*.

Officers (1946): Mrs. Harry S. Truman, honorary president; Mrs. C. Vaughn Ferguson, national president; Mrs. Paul T. Kammerer, Jr., chairman, national executive committee, and Mrs. Paul Rittenhouse, national director. Headquarters: 155 E. 44th St., New York 17, N.Y.

Grand Army of the Republic.—On April 6, 1866, a handful of Civil War veterans meeting at Decatur, Ill., founded the first post of the Grand Army of the Republic, an organization of Union soldiers, sailors and marines. The idea grew in popularity among Union veterans and by 1890 the Grand Army of the Republic had a peak membership of 409,489. Thereafter old age took an increasing toll of the veterans and by 1937 the G.A.R. enrolment had shrunk to 2,443. At the close of the 1937–46 decade, the surviving members totalled about 75, many of whom were centenarians. The rules and regulations provided that the organization could carry on until the death of the last surviving member.

Affiliates of the G.A.R. included the Woman's Relief corps, Ladies of the G.A.R., Daughters of Union Veterans of the Civil War, Sons of Union Veterans of the Civil War and the Auxiliary to the Sons of Union Veterans of the Civil War.

Officers for the 1946–47 period were: commander in chief, John H. Grate; senior vice-commander in chief, Theodore A. Penland; junior vice-commander in chief, Orlando Le Valley; chaplain in chief, Robert M. Rownd, and secretary, Cora E. Gillis. Correspondence with the organization could be addressed to G.A.R., in care of Daughters of Union Veterans of the Civil War, 1326 18th St. N.W., Washington, D.C.

Guggenheim Memorial Foundation.—The John Simon Guggenheim Memorial foundation was created in 1925 with the basic objectives of improving the quality of education and the practice of arts and professions in the United States, of fostering research and of promoting better understanding between nations. In order to achieve these aims, the foundation offered a limited number of fellowships to scholars and artists for research in any field of knowledge and for creative work in any field of fine arts, including music.

During World War II, the foundation's trustees exclusively earmarked an additional $400,000 for postservice fellowships. The funds were put aside for use by young scholars, artists and writers serving in the nation's armed forces and other government services to be made available to them upon their discharge from service. In all, 157 postservice fellowships were awarded.

Funds of the foundation as of Jan. 1, 1946, totalled $20,268,324.22. Officers (1946): Mrs. Simon Guggenheim, president; Francis H. Brownell, vice-president; Otto L. Myers, treasurer, and Henry Allen Moe, secretary. Headquarters: 551 Fifth Ave., New York, N.Y.

Hayden Foundation, Charles.—The Hayden foundation was incorporated in New York in 1937 and had funds totalling more than $50,000,000 in 1946. Its purposes and objectives, as specified in Hayden's will, were to improve the training and education of the youth of the United States in order to "rear a nobler race of men who will make better and more enlightened citizens, to the ultimate benefit of mankind." To carry out these objectives, preference was given to youth living in Boston, Mass., and New York, N.Y., although the foundation's charter included provisions for extension of benefits to other localities. J. Willard Hayden became the organization's first president.

Institute of Pacific Relations.—An international research and educational organization, the Institute of Pacific Relations was founded in 1925 for the study of the peoples of the Pacific area and their mutual relations.

Member councils included: the American council, the U.S.S.R. council, Australian Institute of International Affairs, Canadian Institute of International Affairs, China Institute of Pacific Relations, Comité d'Études des Problèmes du Pacifique (France), Netherlands-Netherlands Indies council, New Zealand Institute of International Affairs, Philippine Institute of Pacific Relations and Royal Institute of International Affairs (Great Britain). Publications included the *Far Eastern Survey,* a semimonthly journal, and *Pacific Affairs,* a quarterly magazine. In addition the institute by 1946 had published more than 700 books and pamphlets prepared by scholars from various countries. Chairman (1946) of the Pacific council: Percy E. Corbett. Chairman of the American council (1946): Robert G. Sproul. Headquarters of the American council: 1 E. 54th St., New York 22, N.Y.

Kiwanis International.—An organization founded at Detroit, Mich., in 1915, the Kiwanis International was devoted principally to development of closer relationships between business, industrial, professional and agricultural leaders and to fostering of civic, social and welfare service in its respective communities. Membership was limited to two men from each of the above categories in any one community. Each local club was given autonomy, but a district and international organization was established to further co-operation for achievement of Kiwanis objectives.

After U.S. entry in World War II, Kiwanis gave full support to all activities which contributed to the conduct of the war and war-work was added to its program. Membership of Kiwanis in 1937 was about 97,000, distributed in 1,936 clubs. Membership in 1946 was about 170,000, distributed in 2,550 clubs in the U.S., Canada and Alaska. Publications: the *Kiwanis Magazine,* the *Monthly Club Bulletin* and the *Weekly Bulletin.* Officers in 1946 were: J. N. Emerson, president; O. E. Peterson, secretary. Headquarters: 520 N. Michigan Ave., Chicago 11, Ill.

Knights of Columbus.—The Knights of Columbus, a fraternal benefit society of Catholic men chartered at New Haven, Conn., on March 29, 1882, had a membership of 638,435 on Dec. 31, 1946. There were 2,561 councils of the society located in the United States, Canada, Newfoundland, Cuba, Mexico, Puerto Rico and the Philippine Islands. The society continued to operate its own insurance system for its members and, at the end of 1946, had total insurance in force amounting to $294,673,237.

At the annual meeting of the supreme council in 1944, an educational trust fund of $1,000,000 was established for the purpose of providing a complete Catholic college education for sons and daughters of veterans killed or totally disabled in military service in World War II. The Knights of Columbus blood donors program, inaugurated in 1938, was effectively carried on in more than 1,000 of the society's councils in 1946. Members co-operating in the plan had contributed almost 40,000 pints of blood for emergency cases in which "live" transfusions were required.

Publication: *Columbia* (monthly), official organ of the society. Officers (1946) were: supreme knight, Judge John E. Swift; deputy supreme knight, Timothy P. Galvin; supreme secretary, Joseph F. Lamb, and supreme treasurer, Francis J. Heazel. National headquarters: P.O. Drawer 1670, New Haven 7, Conn.

Lions Clubs, International Association of.—Founded in Chicago on June 7, 1917, the International Association of Lions Clubs became a union of businessmen's clubs with a primary objective "to create and foster a spirit of 'generous consideration' among the peoples of the world through a study of the problems of international relationships."

The idea of Lionism soon spread to other countries and in 1920, Lions clubs were established in Canada. Clubs were also formed in many Latin American countries and in China.

During the decade 1937–46 the growth of Lions International was substantial. As of June 30, 1936 (the close of the fiscal year), there were 2,725 Lions clubs in 8 countries with 85,539 members. As of Feb. 28, 1947, there were 5,828 Lions clubs in 18 nations and 314,308 members.

Lions clubs remained nonpolitical, nonsectarian civic units whose members had demonstrated leadership in business or the professions and interest in the welfare and development of their communities. During World War II Lions clubs in the U.S. and Canada co-operated with the Red Cross, civilian defense organizations and the United Service organizations. They also participated actively in war bond campaigns.

Publications: the *Lion; El León* (Spanish-language edition) and *Lions International Monthly Letter.* International president: Clifford D. Pierce; secretary general: Melvin Jones. Headquarters: 332 S. Michigan Ave., Chicago 4, Ill.

Masonic Fraternity.—Freemasonry was exported from England to the colonies in the early 18th century. Among the fundamental principles adhered to by U.S. masonic lodges were presence of the Holy Bible on the altar, belief in God, forbidding of political activity or discussion and nonsectarianism in religion. In 1936 the Masonic order was represented by 50 grand lodges (one in each of the 48 states and one each for the District of Columbia and Puerto Rico). The total number of masonic lodges was 15,981 and the membership in that year was 2,709,105. On Jan. 1, 1946, while the number of lodges had been reduced to 15,210, membership had increased to 2,874,588.

The early part of the decade 1937–46 found the grand and local bodies of the Masonic order giving vigorous support to educational work. In 1938 the attacks on freemasonry by the German and Italian governments prompted leaders of English-speaking freemasonry to reiterate that one of the cardinal principles of freemasonry was abstention from political and religious controversies.

During World War II the U.S. Masons established close ties with members in the services through the agency of the Masonic Service association of the United States, with headquarters in Washington, D.C. The close of the war and the fact that many prospective members would be veterans who were crippled or maimed in action aroused intense debate in many grand and local lodges over the bars on physical qualifications for initiation. Although the controversy heightened in 1946, the trend seemed to be toward lowering the physical qualifications.

Music Library Association.—The principal aim of the Music Library association, organized in 1931, was to promote the establishment, growth and use of music libraries and collections of music throughout the country.

M.L.A.'s activities continued to be carried on by its executive board (consisting of its officers and two members-at-large), regional chapter chairmen and various committees; the latter conducted their work in the fields of relations between libraries in the U.S. and the Americas, photoduplication, personnel and employment and periodical indexing. The Music Library association became affiliated with the American Library association and was also a member of the National Music council and the Council of National Library associations. Membership in 1946 included about 400 individual and 150 institutional members.

Publications: *Notes,* a quarterly journal; *Music and Libraries,* a volume of selected papers presented at the 1942 meetings; *Code for Cataloging Music* and a supplementary chapter on cataloguing photograph records. Officers in 1946: H. Dorothy Tilly, president; Lowell P. Beveridge, vice-president; Mary R. Rogers, secretary-treasurer. Headquarters: the Library of Congress, Washington 25, D.C.

National Academy of Sciences.—The National Academy of Sciences was incorporated in 1863 by an act of congress approved by President Lincoln. The act of incorporation provided that "it shall, whenever called upon by any department of the government, investigate, examine, experiment and report upon any subject of science or art." The charter specified that the academy should not receive compensation for its services to the government, but it could be paid for expenses involved in making such investigations and reports.

Originally membership was limited to 50, although amendments in the succeeding years eventually extended it to a total of 450 and 50 foreign associates. On July 1, 1946, the Academy had 390 members, 6 members emeriti and 44 foreign associates.

The academy was divided into 11 sections: astronomy, physics, chemistry, engineering, mathematics, geology and palaeontology, botany, zoology and anatomy, physiology and pathology, anthropology and psychology. It continued to meet twice yearly, award medals for meritorious research and discoveries and issue grants for scientific service. The academy's endowment totalled $3,550,000 in 1946.

During World War II the academy was engaged largely in government problems concerned with scientific matters related to the war. Its reports were confidential and its doors were closed to the public for the duration.

The academy continued to publish an annual report, scientific memoirs, biographical memoirs of deceased members and monthly proceedings devoted to condensed reports of scientific discoveries. Officers (1946) were: Frank B. Jewett, president; L. P. Eisenhart, vice-president; F. E. Wright, home secretary; Detlev W. Bronk, foreign secretary, and J. C. Hunsaker, treasurer. Headquarters: 2101 Constitution Ave. N.W., Washington 25, D.C.

National Association of Manufacturers.—Founded in 1895, the N.A.M. was organized for the promotion of industrial interests of the U.S., the fostering of domestic and foreign trade and dissemination of information to the public respecting furtherance of legislation supporting the principles of private enterprise. In 1932 N.A.M.'s membership was about 2,000; it increased to 16,000 in 1946. The association established six departments—taxation, industrial relations, economic security, public relations, research and law—and various committees. It issued a number of publications, including an annual report, *NAM News,* a weekly bulletin, and a weekly digest of labour rulings and decisions as well as books and pamphlets on economic, social, industrial and labour subjects.

During the 1937–46 decade the N.A.M. expanded its informational activities and urged, among other things, amendments of the Wagner act and the Wage Hour act. During World War II it was committed to a policy of stimulating management to maximum efforts in production for victory. After the close of the conflict, it waged an active campaign against continuance of the government program for price controls. At its convention in New York city (Dec. 5, 1946), N.A.M. recommended legislation to minimize labour "abuses" without taking away the legitimate rights of labour to organize and bargain collectively. It also urged a 20% reduction in personal income taxes as of Jan. 1, 1947, and called on the federal government to reduce government expenditures with the eventual goal's being a budget of not more than $20,000,000,000 annually.

N.A.M.'s president for 1947: Earl Bunting, head of the O'Sullivan Rubber company; Noel Sargent was secretary. Headquarters: 14 W. 49th St., New York, N.Y.

National Association of State Libraries.—One of the oldest organizations of its kind in the United States, the National Association of State Libraries was founded in 1889 to provide the information, data and recommendations required for improved organization and functioning of state libraries. In 1946 it had 43 institutional, 4 associate and 7 individual members as well as 1 honorary life member.

To assist in the cataloguing of state publications, the association continued to publish a series of check lists of session laws, statutes and state journals. A member of the Council of National Libraries, the association participated during World War II in the collection of large numbers of scientific and research publications scheduled for postwar distribution in devastated libraries in Europe and Africa.

Officers (1946): Dennis A. Dooley, president; Harold F. Brigham, first vice-president; Mrs. Mildred P. McKay, second vice-president. Secretary-treasurer: Alfred D. Keator, Pennsylvania State Library and Museum, Harrisburg, Pa.

National Education Association.—The N.E.A., founded in 1857, was "dedicated to the upbuilding of democratic civilization and supported by the loyal co-operation of the teachers of the United States to advance the interests of the teaching profession, promote the welfare of children and foster the education of all the people." The representative assembly of the association was composed of delegates from 52 affiliated state and territorial associations with 759,980 members and more than 1,550 local associations (1946 figures). Direct membership in the 1937–46 decade grew from about 200,000 in 1937 to 340,973 in 1946. Special branches of education were served by 29 departments, such as school administrators, classroom teachers and social studies.

During World War II N.E.A. co-operated with the U.S. Office of Education and other agencies in the war effort. It also played an important part in securing a place for education in the United Nations charter and later discussed measures for improving education and co-operation with the United Nations Educational, Scientific and Cultural organization. N.E.A., in addition, continued its active campaigning on behalf of increased salaries and improved working conditions for teachers and for correction of abuses in school systems.

Its official organ, the *Journal of the National Education Association,* continued to be issued to all members monthly except in June, July and August. Other publications included the annual volume of *Proceedings,* the *Research Bulletin, The Public and Education* (for laymen), *NEA Handbook* and *NEA Handbook for Locals,* a number of bulletins and yearbooks of departments and numerous special bulletins and reports.

President for 1946–47: Mrs. Pearl A. Wanamaker; Willard E. Givens, executive secretary. Headquarters: 1201 16th St. N.W., Washington 6, D.C.

National Geographic Society.—The National Geographic society, with headquarters in Washington, D.C., was founded in 1888 "for the increase and diffusion of geographic knowledge," with only a few hundred members. The society's official publication, the illustrated monthly *National Geographic Magazine,* was sent to every member. By 1937 the membership had grown to approximately 1,000,000.

In the decade 1937–46 the membership expanded to 1,500,000. During that period the society continued its notable series of scientific expeditions. In 1937, co-operating with the U.S. navy, it sent an expedition to the mid-Pacific Canton Island to photograph and study a total solar eclipse. The same year, joined by the Smithsonian institution, the society collected more than 1,000 wild animals and birds in the Netherlands Indies and southeast Asia, presenting them to the National Zoological park in Washington. The society also sent an expedition into Kwangsi province, south China, to study aboriginal tribes and to obtain specimens of flora and fauna.

In 1938 the society, in co-operation with Cornell university, Ithaca, N.Y., began a comprehensive investigation of auroras. In 1939 the society and the Smithsonian institution sent to the isthmus of Tehuantepec the first of eight annual expeditions to study the archaeology of the region.

In 1940 the society and the National Bureau of Standards sent a party of scientists to Patos in northeastern Brazil to observe a total eclipse of the sun. A series of expeditions to study and photograph North American birds was begun in 1944 in nesting areas on the shores of Hudson bay. The researches were continued in 1945 along the north shore of the Gulf of St. Lawrence, and in 1946 in bird refuges along the coast of North and South Carolina and in Georgia, Florida, Texas, northern Mexico and the Rocky mountains of the United States.

The National Geographic society, the U.S. army air forces and the Bartol Research foundation co-operated in the summer of 1946 in investigations of cosmic rays made from an instrument-equipped B-29 bomber flying between the Canadian border and the equator at altitudes up to 35,000 ft.

During the 1937–46 decade the society published the following technical papers on the scientific results of expeditions: *The Stratosphere Flight of 1935 in the Balloon Explorer II* (a joint expedition of the National Geographic society and the U.S. army air forces); *An Initial Series from Tres Zapotes, Veracruz, Mexico; The Solar Eclipse Expedition of 1940 to Brazil.* In this period there was a significant expansion of the society's production of maps. More than 56,500,000 wall maps in colour of continents, oceans and other major regions of the earth were issued as supplements to the *National Geographic Magazine* and were distributed to the society's membership.

During the war years the society made its fund of information and its facilities available to the armed forces to aid in solving military problems in various parts of the world. Intelligence officers from the U.S. army, navy and air forces and Allied armies were given access to more than 300,000 unpublished photographs of shore lines and of mountain, desert and jungle terrain. In addition, several million copies of the society's maps were requisitioned by the armed forces for use on land, sea and in the air.

During the 10-year period, awards for achievement in the fields of geography and exploration included a special gold medal to Thomas C. Poulter, second in command of the second Byrd Antarctic expedition, the Hubbard medal to Gen. Henry H. Arnold, U.S.A.A.F., and Franklin L. Burr prizes to Dr. and Mrs. William M. Mann, Bradford Washburn, Dr. and Mrs. Matthew W. Stirling, Dr. Alexander Wetmore, Dr. Lyman J. Briggs and Dr. Thomas A. Jaggar.

Officers: Dr. Gilbert Grosvenor, president since 1920 and editor of the *National Geographic Magazine* since 1903; John Oliver La Gorce, vice-president and associate editor; Thomas W. McKnew, secretary, and Robert V. Fleming, treasurer. Headquarters: 1146 16th St. N.W., Washington 6, D.C.

National Lawyers Guild.—The National Lawyers guild was founded in 1936 to unite the U.S. lawyers into an organization which would function as an effective social force to the end "that human rights shall be regarded as more sacred than property rights" and to protect "our civil rights and liberties and our democratic institutions."

During World War II the guild gave free and voluntary legal assistance to members of the armed forces and their dependents; its plan for utilizing voluntary services of U.S. attorneys in enforcement of rent and price ceilings was accepted by the Office of Price Administration. The guild urged abolition of the poll tax, opposed the activities of the Dies committee and advocated punishment of war criminals. In 1945 the guild supported the veto power of the U.N. Security council and advocated establishment of a new world court. In 1946 it sought to unite democratic lawyers of the world to further development of international law as an instrumentality for maintaining world peace. Officers in 1946: Robert W. Kenny, president; Robert J. Silberstein, treasurer, and Martin Popper, executive secretary. Headquarters: 902 20th St. N.W., Washington, D.C.

National League of Women Voters.—Founded in 1920, the National League of Women Voters strove to inform and educate the citizenry on major political issues, promote the general welfare and urge the citizen to broaden participation in government.

The league's program, nonpartisan, refrained from supporting or opposing any political candidate or party *per se.* It continued to support only those measures or policies which it deemed in the public interest, irrespective of party labels.

The organization in 1946 was composed of 525 affiliated leagues throughout the country. The local leagues conducted thousands of discussion groups on program items, ran campaigns to encourage a large and informed vote, did work in local government and engaged in numerous other activities. Toward the close of World War II the league advocated U.S. participation in the United Nations. On the domestic scene, it supported measures for curbing inflation, establishing a sound tax structure and developing a sickness insurance program.

Its membership in 1946 was put at 62,000 and its publications were *Trends in Government,* a biweekly news sheet, and *Action,* a bimonthly magazine.

Officers in 1946: Anna Lord Strauss, president; Mrs. Harold A. Stone, first vice-president; Mrs. Marc A. Law, second vice-president; Mrs. James G. Scarborough, secretary, and Mrs. Leonard Haas, treasurer. Headquarters: 726 Jackson place, Washington 6, D.C.

Parents and Teachers, National Congress of.—The National Congress of Parents and Teachers, often known as the P.T.A., was founded on Feb. 17, 1897, as the National Congress of Mothers.

Later broadened to include both parents and teachers,

the organization by 1936 had attracted to its ranks about 2,000,000 adults. By 1946 that membership was nearly doubled, and on April 15 of that year there were 3,910,106 members in 27,000 parent-teacher associations in the 48 states, the District of Columbia and Hawaii. Of this number, 1,130,800 were men and 402,000 were teachers.

The program of the congress was dedicated to the protection of children and youth. Its activities continued to be developed through 30 national standing committees and their counterparts at state and local levels. Parent education, health, juvenile protection, music, art, safety, mental hygiene and recreation were but a few of the many fields of endeavour carried on by the congress. As one means of improving the public schools, P.T.A. members worked consistently toward enactment of a measure providing federal aid for education. During the 1937–46 decade they made a united effort to alleviate the growing shortage of teachers and succeeded in awakening the nation to the critical situation.

A major P.T.A. project in many communities was the sponsoring of school lunches. The federal school lunch bill was passed in 1946 largely because parent-teacher members worked so diligently for its enactment.

Parent education, long a part of the parent-teacher work, was greatly broadened in the 1937–46 period; and thousands of local associations, both urban and rural, fostered the development of an enlightened U.S. parenthood.

Publications: *National Parent-Teacher,* official P.T.A. magazine; the *National Congress Bulletin,* a monthly newssheet, and numerous books, pamphlets and other informational material.

In 1945 the P.T.A. was one of four educational organizations invited by the state department to send a consultant to the San Francisco conference. In 1946 parent-teacher units made every effort to acquaint their members with the structure and purpose of the United Nations Educational, Scientific and Cultural organization, the Commission on Human Rights and other groups operating within the framework of the United Nations.

Officers (1946): Mrs. L. W. Hughes, president; Mrs. John E. Hayes, first vice-president; Charles W. Phillips, second vice-president; Mrs. Gertrude E. Flyte, secretary; G. L. Maxwell, treasurer, and Mrs. A. H. Reeve, honorary president. National headquarters: 600 S. Michigan blvd., Chicago 5, Ill.

Performing Right Societies.—Performing Right Societies throughout the world became affiliated with a central body, the International Confederation of Performing Right Societies, which in turn consisted of four international federations having to do with: (1) dramatic performing rights; (2) musical performing rights; (3) recording rights and (4) rights in general of literary persons *(gens des lettres).* The Second federation, which united with the parent body in 1927, comprised in 1946 about 25 national societies administering music-performing rights of their members. The American Society of Composers, Authors and Publishers (A.S.C.A.P.) was the only U.S. affiliate of the Second federation and also the sole U.S. unit within the framework of the confederation.

Annual congresses of the confederation were held in 1937 at Paris and in 1938 at Stockholm, Sweden. World War II interrupted these congresses, and no further meeting was held until March 1946, when a session took place in Paris, at which steps were taken for postwar reorganization and resumption of formal annual congresses. An interim meeting took place at Washington, D.C., Oct. 21–26, 1946, the first meeting of the confederation in the U.S., at which an agenda for the formal congress scheduled for London in 1947 was prepared.

While the war disrupted the international co-operation of the performing right societies, they continued to function within their respective countries. In the western hemisphere, such organizations progressed steadily and during the 10-year period the American Society of Composers, Authors and Publishers expanded to become the chief such society, with a membership of more than 2,000 and with more than 30,000 licencees. There was a drop of 10% in licences during the war, but with the resumption of normal activities, the number of licences quickly returned to the former figures. The income from commercial performance of music in radio surpassed that from any other source.

Gene Buck served as president of A.S.C.A.P. from 1924 to 1941, when he was made president emeritus, to be succeeded by Deems Taylor. After 1943, A.S.C.A.P. was increasingly active in the standard music field. Prior to that time it had administered performing rights chiefly in the popular and production fields. General offices of A.S.C.A.P.: 30 Rockefeller plaza, New York 20, N.Y.

Research Libraries, Association of.—The Association of Research Libraries was founded in Jan. 1933 by delegates of 43 research libraries of the United States and Canada. Membership was eventually expanded to 47, but in 1946 the existing members voted to reduce the participating libraries to the 45 most important research institutions.

The association continued to hold two meetings annually for discussion of topics of interest to research librarians. In 1946 publication was completed on the *Catalog of Library of Congress Cards,* in 164 vol., compiled under the association's auspices; and plans were made for publishing a photo-offset reprint of the British Museum catalog in 40 vol. Also published under the association's auspices was the annual volume of *Doctoral Dissertations Accepted by American Universities.* Executive secretary: Paul North Rice. Headquarters: New York Public library, New York 18, N.Y.

Rockefeller Foundation.—Founded in 1913 as a permanent institution, the Rockefeller foundation was consecrated to "promoting the well-being of mankind throughout the world." Specifically, it gave active assistance to the extension and application of knowledge in certain fields of the medical, natural and social sciences, the humanities and public health. Save for its limited activities in public health, the Rockefeller foundation was not an operational agency and its work was generally limited to support of other agencies and to training, through postdoctoral fellowships, of skilled personnel in the various fields of knowledge.

Funds and assets of the foundation as of Dec. 31, 1945, totalled $147,064,222 and appropriations for its work during the period between 1937 and 1945 inclusive totalled $90,947,600.

Publications: the *President's Review,* a brief illustrated account of the year's work, and the *Annual Report.* The officers in 1946 were: Walter W. Stewart, chairman of the board of trustees; Raymond B. Fosdick, president, and Norma S. Thompson, secretary.

General Education Board.—The second largest of the benevolent organizations set up by John D. Rockefeller, the General Education board had an original endowment of $129,000,000. The board, which was incorporated by an act of congress in 1903, aimed at promotion of education within the United States without distinction of race, sex or creed.

Its resources were being concentrated mostly in connection with three types of activities: the continuance of the existing program in the southern states, support of research and experimentation with regard to problems in general education and a program of child growth and development.

Between 1937 and 1945, the General Education board appropriated about $33,821,000 for work in its various fields.

Officers (1946) were: Walter W. Stewart, chairman of the board of trustees; Raymond B. Fosdick, president, and Norma S. Thompson, secretary. Headquarters: 49 W. 49th St., New York 20, N.Y.

Rosenwald Fund.—The Julius Rosenwald fund was established in 1917; under its provisions trustees were permitted to spend capital as well as income and were required to expend all the funds within 25 years of the death of its founder, that is, before Jan. 6, 1957. In 1946 total payment of funds on its several programs since inception of the organization totalled $20,120,382. Funds spent in the years 1936–46 totalled $6,883,786. At the close of the fiscal year, June 30, 1946, the value of capital assets was about $2,500,000.

During its early years, the chief function of the fund was aid in building rural public schools for Negroes. Later, its programs were extended to include improvement of the content of education for both whites and Negroes in the south; aid in building up four important centres of higher education for Negroes: Howard university, Washington, D.C.; Atlanta university, Atlanta, Ga.; Fisk university, Nashville, Tenn., and Dillard university, New Orleans, La.

Other projects undertaken by the fund were efforts in behalf of Negro health and establishment of a series of fellowships for Negroes and white southerners and efforts to improve race relations, especially relations between U.S. white and Negro citizens. Officers at the end of 1946 were: Lessing J. Rosenwald, chairman of the board of trustees; Edwin R. Embree, president, and Dorothy A. Elvidge, secretary and comptroller. Headquarters: 4901 Ellis Ave., Chicago 15, Ill.

Rotary International.—A world-wide organization of Rotary clubs, founded in 1905, was made up of groups of representative men for the purpose of furthering co-operation and goodwill in business and community life. On July 29, 1946, there were 5,842 Rotary clubs with about 280,000 members in about 70 different countries.

During World War II Rotary clubs emphasized development of plans for the economic and social readjustment of returning servicemen and clubs in the U.S. and Canada. Rotary International continued its welfare activities on a national level, and its programs included community improvement undertakings, work for crippled and underprivileged children and promotion of high ethical standards in business and professional life.

Rotary clubs also actively co-operated with their governments in rationing, salvaging and fund-raising campaigns and engaged in activities to alleviate war suffering. The organization's activities in 1945 included a program to promote an understanding of the United Nations charter. Publications: the *Rotarian* and its Spanish-language edition *Revista Rotaria*. Officers (1946–47): president, Richard C. Hedke, U.S.A.; first vice-president, Charles Jourdan-Gassin, France; second vice-president, B. T. Thakur, India; third vice-president, Carl E. Bolte, U.S.A.; secretary, Philip Lovejoy, U.S.A.; treasurer, Richard E. Vernor, U.S.A. Rotary International headquarters: 35 E. Wacker drive, Chicago 1, Ill.; with additional offices in Zurich, Switzerland, London, England, and Bombay, India.

Russell Sage Foundation.—Established in 1907, the Russell Sage foundation had an endowment of $15,000,000 at the end of 1946. General objectives of the foundation were to study causes of adverse social and living conditions in the United States and to make public information to correct or prevent these maladjustments. Divided into various departments to carry on its work, the foundation employed about 70% of its income to this purpose; and the remaining 30% was generally given as grants to organizations with similar aims.

In the years 1937–46, the Russell Sage foundation gave increasing aid to such activities as adult education, city or regional planning, housing improvement, family welfare, education and training for social work, child welfare and prevention of delinquency, social welfare publications, improvement of race relations, control of consumer credit, methods of relief, work relations in industry, social statistics and increasing public understanding of social work.

It continued to issue the *Social Work Year Book,* an annual edited by Russell Harold Kurtz. Officers (1946): president, Morris Hadley; vice-president, Joseph P. Chamberlain; secretary, John M. Glenn; treasurer, Arthur H. Ham. Headquarters: 130 E. 22d St., New York 10, N.Y.

Society of the Cincinnati.—Founded in 1783 by officers of the Continental army, with George Washington as first president general, the Society of the Cincinnati became the oldest military association of the United States. Its objectives were to care for the needy and to encourage patriotism. Membership was made hereditary, with the eldest son succeeding to membership upon the death of his father. Total membership in 1946 was about 1,500.

General officers (1946): Col. Bryce Metcalf, president general; Col. Edgar Erskine Hume, vice-president general; Francis A. Foster, secretary general; William Marbury Beall, assistant secretary general; Horace Morrison, treasurer general, and Lawrence Monck Pinckney, assistant treasurer general. Headquarters: Anderson House, 2118 Massachusetts Ave. N.W., Washington, D.C.

Sodality of Our Lady.—Founded in Rome in 1563, the Sodality of Our Lady's purposes, embodied in the first rule of the sodality, were stated as the "fostering in its members an ardent devotion, reverence and filial love towards the Blessed Virgin Mary. . . . It seeks to make the faithful . . . good Catholics, sincerely bent on sanctifying themselves." The Sodality of Our Lady was first established in the United States in 1810 at Georgetown college, Washington, D.C.

During the 1937–46 decade, the affiliated sodalities in the U.S. grew in number from 10,351 to 13,956. The U.S. active membership in 1946 was estimated at between 1,000,000 and 1,500,000. The sodality continued to disseminate its teachings through its Queen's Work press and the Institute of Social Order, the latter operated through 6,000 Jesuits in the U.S. Courses in more than 50 Summer Schools of Catholic Action (started in 1931) were conducted by staff members in all parts of North America to teach "the what, how and why of Catholic living."

Among the Sodality publications: the *Queen's Work* (monthly); *Directors' Bulletin; Sodality Union News; Faculty Adviser;* the *Semester Outline* and during the war the *Chaplain's Service.* The central secretariat was manned by 8 Jesuits and about 75 of the laity.

Special Libraries Association.—The Special Libraries association was founded in 1909 as an international body of librarians and information experts in libraries of specialized knowledge pertaining to business, industrial and related organizations. Membership totalled about 4,500 at the end of 1946. The association had 21 chapters in the United States and 2 in Canada. Publications: *Special Libraries*, published monthly from September to April and bimonthly from May to August, and the *Technical Book Review Index*, published 10 times annually. Vol. I of *Special Library Resources* was published in 1941 and vol. II in 1946.

After the close of World War II, the association's International Relations committee established contact with libraries and librarians overseas to exchange information and materials of mutual benefit. Officers (1946) were: president, Betty Joy Cole; treasurer, Paul Gay; directors, Dr. Mary Duncan Carter, Melvin J. Voigt and Elma Evans. Executive office: 31 E. 10th St., New York 3, N.Y.

Spelman Fund of New York.—Incorporated in 1928, the Spelman fund was formed for "exclusively charitable, scientific and educational purposes." These included the advancement and diffusion of knowledge concerning child life, the improvement of inter-racial relations and co-operation with public agencies.

The fund's program during the 1937–46 decade was directed toward co-operation with public agencies for advancing public administration. Its interest in this field was expressed through its support of activities of public and quasipublic agencies engaged in making public significant results of administrative experience, in developing improved methods and putting them to practical use and in experimenting with new devices and procedures under actual operating conditions.

Theatre Library Association.—An organization of persons in libraries and museums as well as private collectors and members of the theatrical profession, the Theatre Library association was founded in New York city in 1937 to preserve and make accessible to the public the records of the drama and kindred fields of entertainment. Membership, which was 47 at the time of its founding, grew by 1946 to 163. In 1940 the association published *Broadside*, a news sheet appearing at irregular intervals; in 1942 *Theatre Annual*, a yearly publication, was first issued. Officers: president, George Freedley, Theatre Collection, New York Public Library, 476 Fifth Ave., New York 18, N.Y.; treasurer, Elizabeth P. Barrett, and secretary, Sarah Chokla Gross.

Twentieth Century Fund.—Founded in 1919 by Edward A. Filene, the foundation served as a disbursing agency during its early years. After 1929 the fund experimented with surveys on important economic problems. During the 1937–38 fiscal year the organization's trustees voted to end grants to outside agencies and to devote the fund's entire income to its own work on economic research and publication. Up to the start of World War II studies of U.S. domestic economic problems of a controversial nature were stressed. Internal defense problems dominated the publications issued between 1939 and 1941. Outstanding among publications issued during World War II were the Stuart Chase reports which stressed the difficulties and opportunities that would crop up in the U.S. in the postwar era. In addition, the Twentieth Century fund published a number of public affairs pamphlets and collaborated with Encyclopædia Britannica Films Inc., in distributing adult educational films.

The fund also carried on, during the war, intensive research and an educational program on basic problems of postwar reconstruction in the U.S. In progress during 1945 and 1946 were surveys of foreign economic relations of the U.S., cartel arrangements in world trade and monopoly problems in domestic business. Officers (1946): president, John H. Fahey; chairman of executive committee, Henry S. Dennison; treasurer, Morris E. Leeds; executive director, Evans Clark. Headquarters: 300 W. 42d St., New York 18, N.Y.

Veterans of Foreign Wars.—The Veterans of Foreign Wars was founded in 1899 by a group of 13 Spanish-American War veterans at Columbus, O. In succeeding years, veterans who fought in the Boxer rebellion, the Philippine insurrection, World War I, the Nicaraguan and other armed expeditions and World War II joined the organization. Membership in 1936 was 250,000; its claimed membership 10 years later was more than 2,000,000.

Objectives of the V.F.W. were defined as follows: to strengthen comradeship between war veterans, to assist worthy comrades and their widows, to maintain allegiance to the United States and to its constitution and laws, to extend institutions of U.S. freedom and to preserve and defend the United States in case of attack.

The association was organized into three principal divisions with the central administrative authority lodged in the national headquarters in Washington, D.C. Next in the administrative hierarchy were the departments—one for each state as well as departments for the District of Columbia, the Canal Zone and Hawaii. The smallest administrative unit was the local post.

The V.F.W. consistently urged the federal government to accept the responsibility for all disabled veterans and their dependents as well as the dependents of deceased veterans. It actively sought congressional and public recognition of its contention that service in the armed forces overseas merited special legislative treatment and consideration.

In 1945–46 membership in the V.F.W. increased substantially, with the majority of members being veterans of World War II. After the war the V.F.W. endorsed peacetime compulsory military training, government control of atomic research and U.S. participation in the United Nations. On domestic affairs, the organization urged congress to seek a high level of full employment through use of free enterprise. On veterans' affairs, V.F.W. recommended adjusted service pay for all World War II veterans and liberalizing the G.I. Bill of Rights. Publications: *Foreign Service*, a monthly magazine, and the *V.F.W. National News*, a monthly newspaper. Officers (1946–47): Louis E. Starr, commander in chief; Ray H. Brannaman, senior vice-commander in chief, and Lyall T. Beggs, junior vice-commander in chief. National headquarters: 406 W. 34th St., Kansas City 2, Mo.

Woman's Christian Temperance Union.—Organized in 1874, the National Woman's Christian Temperance union actively campaigned to advance education on the evils of addiction to alcoholic beverages and raised for this purpose a national temperance education fund totalling nearly $1,000,000. Membership in the organization in 1946 was put at about 400,000 in 8,000 local unions in the United States, Alaska, Puerto Rico, Hawaii and the Virgin Islands. W.C.T.U. continued to hold annual organization workshops in Evanston, Ill., for training of officers, department heads and organizers. Summer seminars on narcotic education were given at Evanston and at Chautauqua, N.Y. Publications: the *Union Signal*, weekly; the *Young Crusader*, a monthly magazine for children; an annual report; a yearly handbook, and numerous educational pamphlets.

It added more than 131,300 new members to its rolls between 1938 and 1941. After the outbreak of World War II, W.C.T.U. augmented its department of work for soldiers and sailors.

Officers of the National W.C.T.U. (1946) were: Mrs. D. Leigh Colvin, president; Mary B. Ervin, vice-president; Violet T. Black, treasurer, and Lily Grace Matheson, corresponding secretary. Headquarters: 1730 Chicago Ave., Evanston, Ill.

Women's Clubs, General Federation of.—Founded in 1890, the General Federation of Women's Clubs in 1946 comprised a membership of about 3,000,000 women in 16,500 clubs located throughout the United States and its territories and in 31 foreign countries. There were 50 state federations (including the District of Columbia and Alaska) and 20 affiliated organizations. Objectives of the federation were defined as follows: to unite women's clubs and similar organizations throughout the world for promotion of education, philanthropy, public welfare, moral values, civics and fine arts.

After U.S. entry into World War II, member clubs of the general federation participated in innumerable activities of assistance to the war effort.

Publication: the *General Federation Clubwoman,* published monthly (except in June, July and August). Officers (1946): Mrs. LaFell Dickinson, president; Mrs. J. L. Blair Buck, first vice-president; Mrs. Hiram C. Houghton, second vice-president; Mrs. Oscar A. Ahlgren, recording secretary, and Mrs. Volney W. Taylor, treasurer. National headquarters: 1734 N. St. N.W., Washington, D.C.

World League Against Alcoholism.—The World League Against Alcoholism was founded in Washington, D.C., in June 1919. Its objective was set forth in its constitution as follows: "to attain, by the means of education, the total suppression throughout the world of alcoholism, which is the poisoning of body, germ-plasm, mind, conduct and society produced by the consumption of alcoholic beverages." The league carried on its work by distribution of periodicals, books, pamphlets, tracts and other material dealing with the problem of alcoholism and by lectures and leadership in young people's camps and institutes. To aid its program, the league established a reference library and information bureau. During World War II more than 500,000 copies of the special army series of leaflets were distributed among servicemen. Publications: the *American Issue, Scientific Temperance Journal* and the *International Student.*

Officers (1946): Ernest H. Cherrington, general secretary, and Harry B. Sowers, treasurer. Headquarters: Westerville, O.

Zonta International.—An organization of executive business and professional women selected on a classified basis, Zonta International was founded in 1919. In 1946 it comprised about 160 clubs in the United States, Canada, Hawaii, Denmark, Iceland and Sweden with about 5,500 members.

Principal objectives were defined as: community service; fostering of high ethical standards in business and the professions; improvement of the status of women and advancement of international understanding.

In 1939 Zonta established the Amelia Earhart scholarship, an award given exclusively to a qualified young woman in any country where Zonta clubs had been established, for graduate work in aeronautics. Official publication: the *Zontian,* a monthly. Officers (1946): Louise C. Grace, president; Ruth H. Gates, treasurer; Harriet C. Richards, executive secretary. International headquarters: 59 E. Van Buren St., Chicago, Ill.

Great Britain

Associated Learned Societies of Liverpool and District. —The triennial exhibition was held in Oct. 1938 at the City of Liverpool Technical college. During World War II activities were restricted, but in 1943 a small exhibition was held in the botanical laboratory of the university. By 1946 there were 15 associated societies.

British Association for the Advancement of Science.— In 1937 the annual meeting was held at Nottingham, and a delegation of 100 members left for Calcutta, India, to attend the silver jubilee of the Indian Science Congress association. The 1938 annual meeting was held at Cambridge, England, and the 1939 meeting, cut short by the imminence of war, at Dundee, Scotland. During the following years the annual meetings were discontinued, but the division for the social and international relations of science (founded in Aug. 1938) continued to carry out much of the association's work. A conference was held in London and at the Rothamsted experimental station in Sept. 1941, and further conferences took place in London in 1942 and 1943. One result of the 1941 conference was the establishment of a committee on postwar university education, which presented its report in 1944. In Dec. 1944 the division, in conjunction with the Indian group of the Royal Institute of International Affairs, held a conference for the Indian Scientific delegation. A conference on the place of science in industry was held in Jan. 1945, another on the dissemination of scientific information to the public in July 1946, in collaboration with the Royal society. On July 20, 1946, the first postwar annual meeting was held, presided over by Sir Richard Gregory, who had remained in office throughout the war.

British Medical Association.—In 1938 the association reissued its 1931 publication, *General Medical Service for the Nation,* and in 1941 appointed a medical planning commission to consider postwar reconstruction of medical services, the draft interim report of which was issued in 1943. A representative committee was appointed in 1944 to consider the government's White Paper on a national health service, and in 1945 a negotiating committee was established which discussed with the coalition government the form of a National Health Service bill. With regard to international medical relations, the association held an exploratory conference of individual medical practitioners in June 1945 to arrange a closer liaison for the medical profession in different countries; in Sept. 1946 an international medical conference was organized in London composed of delegates and observers sent by medical associations throughout the world. Thirty-one nations were represented, and the conference established a World Medical association to meet in Paris in 1947. The British Medical association set aside the sum of £10,000 for the provision of B.M.A. lectures in other countries, to be given by distinguished British practitioners. Among the association's publications during the years 1937–46 were: *Industrial Health in Factories* (1941), *Report of Committee on Mental Health* (1941), *The Returning Doctor* (1945), *Report on Rehabilitation* (1946) and *A Charter for Health* (1946). At the request of the government, the association undertook the recruitment of all medical practitioners to the forces, appointing a central medical war committee and establishing an emergency register of all practitioners in the country.

Chemical Society.—At the outbreak of World War II the society assisted the government in compiling the list of chemists on the central register for national service and later gave advice on chemical problems through the Advisory Research council. The centenary of the society fell in 1941, and postponed celebrations were to take place in 1947.

Faraday Society.—Bombed out of its old premises in 1941, the society moved to Grays Inn Square, London. During World War II its publications continued and its membership increased. Two meetings a year were held for general discussion. The meeting in Sept. 1946 took place in London under the presidency of Prof. W. E. Garner, the subject being "Shrinking and Swelling." A legacy left to the society by Lieut. Col. E. A. Bourke made possible the establishment of a fund for the entertainment of foreign visitors.

Institute of Physics.—Conferences on industrial physics were held at Birmingham in 1937 and at Leeds in 1939. In 1938 a summer school took place at Reading university informing members and others on advances in pure and applied physics. On the outbreak of World War II the institute moved to Reading university, returning in July 1946 to new premises in London. In Nov. 1941 the board appointed a planning committee, which gave immediate attention to the training of wartime physicists and their conditions of employment; and in Oct. 1942 a conference was held in London to consider problems of postwar training and education. Among activities of the institute during 1946 were the summer meeting of the London and Home Counties branch at the Dunstable station of the meteorological office and a summer school on "Applications of Theoretical Physics in Industry," held in co-operation with the University of Bristol.

Library Association.—The 60th annual meeting of the association was held at Scarborough in 1937 under the presidency of the archbishop of York (Dr. William Temple). The meeting for 1938 took place at Portsmouth and Southsea and for 1939 at Liverpool. Additional responsibilities were assumed in World War II. Steps were taken to link up the information services of public libraries with the ministry of information. The council set up a sub-committee to examine the possibilities of providing libraries for the armed forces, and in collaboration with the Lord Mayor of London's committee distributed millions of books and periodicals to the troops. The association was also represented on the Central Council (and some regional committees) for Adult Education in H. M. Forces. Sound foundations for postwar librarianship were planned. Many libraries were severely damaged in air raids, but efforts made through the National Book Recovery campaign resulted in the salvaging of nearly 2,000,000 books. An important postwar project was the establishment of schools of librarianship at technical institutions. The annual meeting for 1946 was held at Blackpool under the presidency of Dr. Arundell Esdaile, who later retired after holding office for seven years.

Linnean Society.—The 150th anniversary of the society was celebrated in May 1938, the meeting being held under the presidency of J. Ramsbottom. Queen Mary graciously consented to accept honorary membership. During World War II part of the society's library was removed to Oxford, and the collections were housed for safety at Woburn Abbey, home of the duke of Bedford. There they were photographed, and complete sets of the *Collections of Linnaeus* were sent to Sweden.

London Scientific Film Society.—The society was founded in 1937 to provide programs of general scientific and technical films for its members and to encourage the wider use of the film in science and education. Membership was restricted during World War II but was later reopened; scientific films were exhibited by the society at the Scala theatre, London.

National Farmers' Union.—In 1938 a delegation from the union attended the first empire producers' conference at Sydney, Australia. At home the union was closely concerned with the government's marketing schemes for milk, bacon pigs, potatoes and hops. During World War II the union collaborated with the war agricultural emergency committees in the effort to produce more food and later had to face the problems of world shortage. A farm accounts scheme was developed under which qualified accountants collected facts for use when farm prices were discussed with the government. Close relations were maintained with foreign agricultural bodies, and in May 1946 the union organized an international conference of primary producers, which resulted in the formation of the International Federation of Agricultural Producers.

National Institute of Economic and Social Research.—The institute was founded in 1938, and special committees were set up to deal with special research for two-year periods. Publication of the first completed studies was planned for 1939 and 1940, but the course of events made this impossible; after a temporary suspension it was decided in Dec. 1939 that the institute should continue its activities. The research staff was increased and the scope of work expanded, arrangements being made with the Cambridge University press for publication of the institute's findings. The acting secretary of the institute became secretary of the National Service Committee for Social, Economic and Statistical Research set up by the ministry of labour.

National Institute of Industrial Psychology.—With the outbreak of World War II, the institute's work was considerably changed. The majority of the firms for whom investigations had been carried out were engaged in war production, and the introduction of training schemes for new workers took first place. The institute co-operated with the air ministry in the training of gunners in the royal air force. Nevertheless, consultations continued to be given annually by the Vocational Guidance department, and as far as possible industrial investigations were also carried out.

Royal Academy of Arts.—Attendances at the summer exhibitions fell off during the early years of World War II but in 1945, when the exhibition contained the state portraits of the king and queen by Sir Gerald Kelly, rose to 200,287, as against 96,276 in 1939. The attendance for 1946 was 197,457. Subjects of the winter exhibitions were: British architecture 1937; 17th-century art in Europe 1938; Scottish art 1939. In 1940, 25 art societies collaborated in an exhibition in aid of the Red Cross society and the Artists' General Benevolent institution, repeated in 1942 and 1943. No winter exhibition was held in 1941 because of bomb damage to the galleries. Other exhibitions included those of paintings by firemen artists, (1942–43–44), of war photographs (1942), Yugoslav art (1944), soviet graphic art (1945); and in Oct. and Nov. 1945 the galleries were given over to an exhibition of national war pictures. Selections from the summer exhibitions were sent on tour annually from 1942 to 1945 by the Council for the Encouragement of Music and the Arts; and organizations which held their own exhibitions in the galleries included the Royal Institute of Oil Painters, the Royal Society of Painters in Water Colours, the Royal Society of Portrait Painters, the London group and the New English

Art club. The painting and drawing schools and the sculpture school were re-opened in 1946. In 1938 Sir Edwin Lutyens was elected president and on his death on Jan. 1, 1944, was succeeded by A. J. Munnings.

Royal Empire Society.—Weekly meetings were held throughout World War II. Although badly damaged by air attack in 1941, the library, containing more than 500,000 books and pamphlets, remained open to all accredited students and was used by several government departments. More than 100 daily papers from various parts of the empire were available; and political, industrial and economic study groups were organized, their conclusions being published in pamphlet form. In 1942 the society celebrated its 75th anniversary.

Royal Geographical Society.—In 1937 the British Graham Land expedition returned after two-and-a-half years in the antarctic, and the following year its work was recognized by the award of the Founder's medal to the leader, John Rymill. Ronald Kaulback, accompanied by N. J. F. Hanbury-Tracy, completed explorations of the Salween valley and surrounding areas in southeast Tibet. In 1938 the Mount Everest expedition, led by H. W. Tilman, was sent out by the society and the Alpine club, but was forced by adverse weather to abandon its efforts. A delegation attended the International Geographical congress at Amsterdam, the Netherlands, in the same year. Successive presidents of the society were: Field-Marshal Sir Philip Chetwode, elected on the death of Prof. Henry Balfour in 1939; the Rt. Hon. Sir George Clerk, elected 1941, and the Rt. Hon. Lord Rennell of Rodd, elected 1945. World War II put an end to expeditions, but the expedition fund was maintained. Much of the experience gained by fellows was turned to good use, as in work done by desert travellers in the Libyan campaign. On behalf of the British council the society undertook the making of a map of the middle east, with English and Arabic editions.

Royal Institute of Chemistry.—In March 1944 the name of the institute was changed by royal charter from "Institute of Chemistry" to Royal Institute of Chemistry, and all fellows and associates were authorized to use the initials F.R.I.C. and A.R.I.C. respectively. Assistance was given to the government in World War II. Later, the institute collaborated with the Institute of Physics and the Joint Council of Professional Scientists in preparing a statement on "Principles of a Suggested Code of Practice in Respect of Consulting Work Carried Out by Academic Scientists."

Royal Institution.—During World War II the institution continued its Friday evening discourses and public afternoon lectures. The juvenile Christmas lectures were discontinued from 1939 to the winter of 1943–44. In 1941 Sir William Bragg gave three lectures to cadets of the Air Training corps on "The Story of Electro-Magnetism," and on his death the following year was succeeded as Fullerton professor of chemistry and director of the Faraday research laboratory by Sir Henry Dale. In 1944 Lord Eustace Percy was succeeded as president by Lord Rayleigh; and in 1945 Sir Henry Spencer Jones, the astronomer royal, was appointed professor of astronomy in succession to Sir James Jeans.

The Royal Society.—In 1938 it was decided to admit 20 new fellows annually instead of 17. The Pilgrim trust offered 250 guineas annually for 6 years to allow lectures to be given alternately in London and Washington in conjunction with the National Academy of Science. The council, through the development committee, granted capital expenditure of £5,100 and £3,500 *per annum* to cover intensive study of the Gulf stream and Atlantic drift and their effect upon fisheries in British waters. In 1940 Sir Henry Dale became president on the retirement of Sir William Bragg; a scientific advisory committee to the war cabinet was set up under Lord Hankey. In Oct. 1941 the society held a conference with United States and empire representatives, resulting in the establishment of the British Commonwealth Science committee; and in 1942 the secretary of state for air invited the society to co-operate in the newly established Meteorological Research committee. The advisory committees on air-borne research facilities and naval research facilities gave their assistance to the government. At the instigation of Sir R. Fowler and Professor Patrick M. Blackett, the Committee on the Needs of Research in Fundamental Sciences was established. In 1945 women were admitted to the fellowship of the society for the first time.

Royal Society of Arts.—In 1936 the council of the society, feeling that industrial art had not received due recognition, instituted the distinction of Designer for Industry of the Royal Society of Arts, designated by the letters R.D.I. This honour could not be held by more than 40 designers at the same time. In Sept. 1944 the War Memorials Advisory council was set up. In Aug. 1944 Viscount Bennett, former prime minister of Canada, who was later elected president of the society, instituted the R. B. Bennett Empire prize of £1,500 for the promotion of arts, industry and commerce. The Albert medal was awarded annually; among the distinguished persons honoured were Queen Mary (1938), President Roosevelt (1941) and Winston Churchill (1945).

Royal Society of Edinburgh.—Full sessions of meetings were held throughout World War II. The library was extensively used by fellows, research workers and a number of government departments; the admiralty in particular received assistance from it.

Canada

Canadian Historical Association.—A resolution passed at the annual meeting for 1940 concerning the preservation of wartime material of historical value was sent to the secretary of state and the prime ministers of the dominion and its provinces. It was also embodied in a statement on "Historical Records and the Canadian War Effort," published in the *Canadian Historical Review*. A series of broadcasts on historical subjects was arranged by the association's radio committee and the Canadian Broadcasting corporation.

National Research Council.—In 1938 the division of biology and agriculture undertook research in the curing of bacon for the British market and in refrigeration of meat. Other subjects of research were tests of water skis for aircraft, methods of fighting forest fires and experiments in cathode ray direction finding. A fund to further the council's war efforts was opened in commemoration of Sir Frederick Banting, and a sum of more than $1,000,000 was raised by public subscription. In 1941 the council was officially designated a station of the royal Canadian navy, army and air force, and shown as a civil establishment in the records of the department of national defense. Three service committees were set up in 1942 to deal with aviation medical research, navy medical research and army medical research. In 1943–44 an extension of the scholarship system under war appropriations enabled the council to carry out work in many fields.

Royal Canadian Institute.—Lectures were given by members of government departments, the navy, army and air force and other organizations. In 1943 a committee was formed to draw up plans for the institute's centenary celebrations, scheduled to be held in 1949.

Royal Society of Canada.—Although the cultural and scientific activities of the society continued during World War II, additional work was undertaken along lines similar to that of the National Research council, with which close collaboration was maintained.

The society's research fellowships were suspended for the duration of the war, with effect from Oct. 1942.

Sociology

The course of sociology during the decade 1937–46 was one of consolidation and expansion rather than of innovation. No strikingly new variants in sociological theory, methodology or technique appeared, but extremes were either eliminated or crystallized into forms of lessening adaptability and influence, and modes of analysis and interpretation not marked by single-factor fallacies slowly gained the upper hand. It was in part because of this drift toward what in political analogy might be termed the "centre" that one of the most striking manifestations was due; namely, the fusing of selected aspects of sociology, social psychology, social and cultural anthropology and social psychiatry into a reasonably well-integrated whole which could with warrant bear the name of the science of social relations.

Value-System Approach.—One of the most interesting developments was the full realization of the significance of values in social life. Indeed, the analysis of value-systems became a favourite approach. Implied in the far earlier work of Ferdinand Tönnies, Emile Durkheim, Vilfred Pareto, C. H. Cooley, Florian Znaniecki, G. H. Mead, Sigmund Freud and literally dozens of other students of social life, it was made explicit by Robert Redfield, Talcott Parsons, Pitirim Sorokin, R. C. Angell, Howard Becker, Morris Opler, Ralph Linton, Ruth Benedict, Karen Horney, Erich Fromm and many other contemporary researchers. This was the more surprising in view of the extreme behaviourism which threatened to dominate the sociological scene in the '20s and the larger part of the '30s, and according to which the more complex value-systems were mere "speech-reactions" of utterly insignificant or even epiphenomenal character. The impact of those value-systems popularly called ideologies and "isms" during the decade 1937–46 doubtless did much to show the utter insufficiency of the sociological brand of white-rat behaviourism, but the actual scientific demonstration of its shortcomings was at least equally important. George Lundberg, S. C. Dodd and their followers no longer commanded the respectful attention once accorded them. In fact, sociology had perhaps arrived at the point where it was necessary to insist that studies of total value-systems, particularly those delivered by social anthropologists of psychoanalytic bent, be carried on with more stringency of method and technique; there was definite danger of reliance on casual impressions and the mistaking of the merely plausible for the demonstrably probable. The kind of analysis offered by Znaniecki, Opler, and George Homans, with its careful dissection of value-systems into "themes," "life-policies," "sentiments" and the like, could do much to counteract the suggestive but untrustworthy essays of Sorokin, Margaret Mead, Gregory Bateson and Benedict.

Closely related to the increased attention given to value-system analysis was the changed emphasis in the study of sociation. Where once it was thought sufficient merely to classify and rank in order of intensity the various associative and dissociative relations, it became increasingly evident that social interaction of every variety had so large a value-component that very little predictive utility could be attached to researches that ignored it or treated it as secondary. Studies of sociation could no longer run exclusively in the channels cut by Georg Simmel and his avowed or unavowed followers such as J. L. Moreno, W. L. Warner, E. D. Chapple and others focusing chiefly on the obvious externals of conduct. Pairs, "sets" and like groupings, for example, could not be adequately analyzed without direct heed to the value-systems in which they were incorporated. This was particularly obvious in the published work of the sociometrists clustering about Moreno, but fortunately practice seemed to be better than publication. If one were to take the articles appearing in *Sociometry* as they stood, instead of continually reading between the lines, one would have to conclude that the gyrations of so-called social atoms had as little reference to value-systems or fragments thereof as do the attractions or repulsions of uranium or lead. The elaborate pretense involved in using the terminology of physics and chemistry, while actually dealing with conduct not susceptible of reduction to physical and chemical interactions alone, robbed the researches of many students of sociation of their full effectiveness. Further, the perpetual intermingling of two differing analytic standpoints, viz., the situation as defined by the participant and the situation as defined by the observer, vitiated the great potential usefulness of many such studies of sociation. Among the most fruitful work in this field during the decade was that on the sociation of workers carried on at Harvard, but the criticisms just noted applied to these as well. When in F. A. Roethlisberger and W. J. Dickson's most elaborate study of pairs, triads and similar sociative groupings among employees there was no single word of reference to union or non-union ideologies, the disregard of value-system orientation was glaring indeed. If one were attempting to predict typical group responses in strike situations, of what utility would these studies of "workers' morale" actually be? Nevertheless, there could be no doubt that sociative analyses greatly advanced in relevance and precision during the ten years, and that Leopold von Wiese's conception of a sociology of economics was well on its way toward realization through the work of investigators who knew little if anything of Wiese and had only a few general ideas about Simmel. (This was not true, of course, of the sociometrists, for Moreno owed as heavy a debt to Simmel and Wiese as he did to Freud; the "psychodrama" as a process of "group therapy" is genuinely sociative in theory and practice.)

As a matter of fact, it seemed probable that the most definite theoretical influences on the Harvard analysts of workers' sociation derived from Durkheim and Pareto, particularly the latter. In general, it could be said that the stress on the non-rational aspects of conduct smacked of Pareto's "residues," and the ignoring of ideologies had more than a little flavour of "mere derivations." Pareto's vogue declined enormously during the decade, but some of its most doubtful benefits remained. Incidentally, it should be noted that Homans' magnificent treatise on the English villager likewise leaned heavily on Pareto, but that the use made of his ideas was soundly discriminating and genuinely advantageous. "Derivations" need not be treated as epiphenomenal unless the researcher is as fanatical a "positivist" as the inconsistent Pareto sometimes was.

A worthwhile phase of Pareto's analysis—by implication, at least—was the inseparability of social psychology and sociology. The development of social structures was closely bound up, all through Pareto's work, with on-going changes in social processes and the concomitant shifts in dominant personality configurations. Talcott Parsons was perhaps too charitable an interpreter of the great Italian, but there could be little doubt that Parsons' zeal for the merging of sociology and social psychology stemmed as largely from Pareto as it did from Max Weber and Durkheim. A clearer case for the merger, however, was afforded by the writings of G. H. Mead and the neo-Freudians such as Horney, for here it was made abundantly clear that man becomes human, in the social-psychological sense, only in society. Only in and through interaction with his fellows who themselves as personalities have been woven from threads forming part of societal patterns does *Homo sapiens* take on the attributes of man defined as man in any society of which there is knowledge. Differently put: physiological psychology is a branch of biology; social psychology is inextricably linked with sociology; and so-called individual psychology incessantly fluctuates between these equally necessary poles. Still otherwise: man's experience as man is essentially dramatic; he learns to play roles in a cast of societal characters, takes parts in a *dramatis personae,* responds to his own actions as others respond to them and develops an array of mirrored selves which are eventually integrated in some socially acceptable way.

The contribution of the neo-Freudians to this essentially Meadian analysis was the reinterpretation of Freud's conceptions of id, ego and super-ego. The id became the more crudely biological phase of G. H. Mead's "I"-actions; the ego represented those social roles of the "me" with which the person could feel himself identified (plus those "I"-actions of necessarily unique and less directly biological character consonant with such social roles) and the super-ego was taken to signify "me"-actions and assigned roles with which no genuine identification took place and which therefore remained somewhat external—even though this externality might become manifest only in schizoid states or extreme demoralization. Unfortunately, many neo-Freudians sometimes failed to analyze their vague referents, "society" and "culture," in terms of specific roles and their accompanying rights and duties; the result was the belligerent championing of the "environment" pole of the false "heredity *versus* environment" dilemma. Further, where Mead and his followers were wisely reluctant to catalogue "basic needs," the neo-Freudians ordinarily substituted an instinct for security for the orthodox Freudian instinct of sexuality; the derived arguments were just as circular in the one case as in the other. A sounder use of the neo-Freudian approach was evidenced by Abram Kardiner, who made a very sophisticated use of the conception of basic personality structure. If Kardiner's followers, notably Linton and Benedict, had been as circumspect as Kardiner himself, high hopes might have been entertained for the neo-Freudians. As it was, it seemed evident that they would have to become more thoroughly acquainted with the vast amount of work done on the socialization of the child and the adolescent by the ordinary "academic" psychologist, social psychologist and sociologist. At the same time, it must be granted that they rendered signal service by destroying orthodox Freudian dogmas; it was now possible to unite psychiatry of "functional" emphasis with other analytic social studies.

The importance of the value-system approach was also evident in the renewed attention to social stratification. Fifteen or 20 years prior to the decade 1937–46, sociological interest in class struggles was well-marked; Albion W. Small's most famous course dealt with precisely this topic. The waning of ideological analysis during the '20s and the early '30s, perhaps because of behaviouristic prepossessions or intimidations, was counteracted from the later '30s onward by several factors. Among these was the assimilation of numerous emigré sociologists whose experiences with naziism and fascism had rendered them keenly aware of the crucial role of class mentalities. Moreover, the depression and its aftermath made even the most obtuse and optimistic of U.S. social scientists realize how sharply class lines had come to be defined in even so relatively open-class a country as the United States. The result was a flood of articles and books on stratification topics—a flood which showed little sign of abating even during World War II and which in the immediate postwar period had not noticeably receded. Along with careful analytic distinctions such as those made by Émile Benoît-Smullyan, for example, there were of course loose but popular presentations such as W. Lloyd Warner's nine-class scheme and the bandying about of the category of caste—a category, by the way, used in its limited and proper Hindu meaning by Oliver C. Cox. Further, the "Spissies" (members of the Society for the Psychological Study of Social Issues) generated a good deal more heat than light about U.S. class discrimination, but here and there valuable insights were achieved. As matters stood at the end of the decade, sociologists insufficiently aware of social stratification and its ideological accompaniments were hard to find.

Another trend of the decade, the inaptly christened "sociology of knowledge," was closely bound up, as ordinarily presented, with stratification ideologies and their analysis. Although he had many forerunners of much greater intrinsic importance than himself, Karl Mannheim was largely responsible for the burst of interest in the field because of the strong appeal his books made to those of left-wing political allegiance or imbued with the ideology of social planning. His severest critic, Alexander von Schelting, pointed out the untenability of any theory in which all knowledge is class-bound except the variety possessed by the promulgator of the theory—Mannheim made the "free-floating intelligentsia" the court of last resort. It must not be imagined, however, that "sociology of knowledge" was necessarily embroiled in epistemological quarrels, for it was quite possible to show the functional relations of idea-systems, on the one hand, and social processes and structures, on the other, without assuming one-way "causal" flow in either direction. Some of Mannheim's own substantive work was consequently above the epistemological battle, as was likewise that of Logan Wilson, R. H. Merton, Oscar Cargill, Margaret Smith Stahl and several other writers. Znaniecki, in his *Social Role of the Man of Knowledge,* pointed the way to effective research and showed how to avoid the many pitfalls awaiting the unwary.

Even greater "skill at running cannily among the spears" was needed in another field which greatly expanded during the ten years 1937–46—sociology of religion. Nevertheless, such skill was frequently in evidence; Joachim Wach, Paul Honigsheim, Milton Yinger and J. M. Mecklin, among others, provided excellent treatises and monographs. The basic reason for the success of these studies was close adherence to the practice of taking the religious belief in question as given and proceeding to the analysis of its functional interdependences with the social world *per se.* Questions of the validity or invalidity of the belief itself were not raised. Incidentally, it may be noted that one of the most penetrating discussions of naziism to be offered in this period, Stuart P. Herman, Jr.'s *It's Your Souls We Want,* dealt with the economic and political realms involved from a standpoint akin to that of sociology of religion. A value-system for which men sacrificially live and gladly die is essentially religious even though no explicit supernaturalism is involved, and Herman made the most of this fact. Becker's *German Youth: Bond or Free,* a study of the perverting of the youth movement, was oriented in much the same direction.

War Work.—During World War II, and especially after the entry of the United States, much of the earlier work in social psychology and sociology having to do with minority groups, leadership, public opinion, population and related matters found a new focus in the "area" courses sponsored by the U.S. armed forces. Along with human geography, descriptive economics and a host of other social studies, the various aspects of the science of social relations were brought to bear on the problems of defeating the axis and on the eventual task of occupation. Here the emigré social scientists mentioned above performed yeoman service. They knew not only the component parts of the great social structures against which the Allies were contending, but in addition were able to chart the more subtle currents of axis mentality in ways which persons who had never participated in the value-systems concerned could never have envisaged. Working with them, naturally enough, were many social scientists from the Allied nations who possessed special competence in the "area" endeavour. As later events demonstrated, all too few of the men trained in the Foreign Area and Language Study Curriculum and Civil Affairs Training Program were actually placed in the military government niches for which they had been moulded, and those who were assigned to appropriate tasks were sometimes demobilized with undue haste in order to make room for ex-combat officers who did not relish the prospect of return to former peacetime rank. Military government posts looked attractive, and competitors were speedily ousted whenever possible. Yet it could be said that the effort that went into "area" training was not wasted, for the social scientists who carried out the job were brought to a vivid realization of the artificiality of most of the traditional boundary lines between many of their respective disciplines and of the consequent necessity for a regrouping of the social studies. True, there had been much effort long before the war to stimulate "interdepartmental projects" on the part of the foundations aiding research, but the projects were usually quite poorly conceived and the results frequently superficial. There was no merit in the crossing of departmental boundaries as such, but when there was a genuinely common problem or a close grouping of definitely related social sciences, the usual lines of academic jurisdiction could and should be ignored.

"Area" studies were not the only zone of operation for social scientists during the war, for they were on the staffs of a great number of the government bureaus and branches of the armed services. The information and education division of the war department used many, as did likewise the War Labor board, Board of Economic Warfare, the state department, United States Strategic Bombing survey, Office of Strategic Services, Office of War Information and scores of other agencies. After the V-days most of them returned to their peacetime posts, but U.N.R.R.A. and the United Nations absorbed a number, and the restaffing of the occupation groups with civilian personnel at the "expert" levels accounted for a few more.

A substantial part of the social-psychological and sociological work done for the armed forces was of "poll" character. There were studies of food preferences among the troops, ratings of uniforms, conceptions of fairness in redeployment and demobilization, attitudes of civilians in liberated areas toward Allied forces and so on almost *ad infinitum.* By far the greater part of the work done along these lines was essentially trivial by any scientific standard, but it was often essential to the war effort and was conscientiously performed. Other studies of less need-of-the-moment character were made, true enough, but except for the documentary value they had for peacetime research, their usefulness was exhausted when their immediate purpose was fulfilled. Documentary value, however, should not be underestimated, for although the ideal method for gathering data is to collect them with a highly specific research problem in view, the great mounds of material still held under security restrictions contained thousands upon thousands of recorded observations utilizable by all but the most hypercritical. World War II could be of some benefit to social scientists in general and to sociologists in particular if there was sufficient effort to extract that benefit.

American Sociological Society.—The American Sociological society underwent many changes, most important of which were: (1) the displacement of the *American Journal of Sociology* as the official journal in favour of the newly-founded *American Sociological Review;* (2) the splitting off of the rural sociologists from the parent body; (3) the establishment of mail voting for officers of the society and the adoption of a new constitution of considerably more flexible character than the old regional sociological societies, some of them in almost open competition with the national body, continued to spring up and grow. The tendency toward a science of social relations co-ordinating social psychology, social psychiatry, social and cultural anthropology and sociology was made most clearly manifest by the establishment in 1946 of a department of social relations at Harvard, but Chicago had the substance of such co-ordination without the name, as did Wisconsin and several other universities. The breakdown of the last stronghold of resistance to sociology on the west coast occurred in 1946; Berkeley finally installed a department of sociology and social institutions.

Latin America.—The former supremacy of Argentina in Latin American sociology gave place to a triangular situation in which Brazil and Mexico figured as the other peers. Numerous books and periodicals were published during the decade, and university instruction grew. The activities of the Pan American Union and of the state department of the United States, as well as of the Carnegie and Rockefeller foundations, facilitated exchange of personnel, and prospects for further development were bright.

Great Britain.—In Britain the movement known as "Mass Observation" gave much promise of developing into a base outside the universities for a science of social relations, but in the later war years enthusiasm seemed to wane. Only the provincial universities and London had any persons on their staffs calling themselves sociologists; Oxford and Cambridge were still recalcitrant. Herbert Spencer rejected honorary degrees from both institutions. Morris Ginsberg continued to be the only professor holding an exclusively sociological chair, for Karl Mannheim's, likewise at the University of London, was in education. Nevertheless, Mannheim became editor of the International Library of Sociology and Social Reconstruction, established early in the war. Much of the interest in sociology in Great Britain probably stemmed from two sources: (1) the influx of refugee scholars who brought with them the continental familiarity with sociology; and (2) the drastic alterations in social structure resulting, among other things, in the new Labour government and making most persons acutely aware of social relations they had formerly taken for granted.

Continental Europe.—France underwent an almost complete elimination of sociology during the war, for it had come to be identified, in the popular mind, with the ideology of the Third Republic. Its representatives either quietly submerged as did Marcel Mauss, fled as did George Gurvitch or were killed as was Maurice Halbwachs. After liberation, however, there was a genuine rebirth; a Centre of Sociological Studies was established in the buildings formerly occupied by the Institute of Intellectual Co-operation of the League of Nations, and a new journal, *Cahiers Sociologiques,* began publication under the editorship of Gurvitch.

The nazis hated no intellectual enterprise more deeply than the sociological; consequently the German Sociological society was among the first of the learned societies to be liquidated. Most sociologists lapsed into silence, fled or were imprisoned and exterminated; a few, however, seized the opportunity to rise to power and one of them, Willy Gierlichs, eventually became Himmler's aide, committing suicide with him at Flensburg. As noted above, some of the sociologists fled, reached the United States and Britain, and in many instances gave valuable assistance to governments and armed forces; others who remained in Germany and survived took over important functions in the new regime—*e. g.,* Hanna Meuter became chief councillor for public welfare in the Aachen district, and Leopold von Wiese, although advanced in years, became professor of sociology at Cologne and Bonn and president of the reconstituted German Sociological society. Unfortunately, the assassination of E. Y. Hartshorne, the military government officer most conversant with sociology and eager to aid in its re-establishment, temporarily checked further advances.

Another central European country, Czechoslovakia, actively resumed sociological teaching, research, publication and organization. President Eduard Benes was a sociologist of repute, as was his predecessor Thomas Masaryk. The Masaryk Sociological society, official organization of Czechoslovakian sociologists, renewed contact with the other sociological societies throughout the world, and there seemed every reason to believe that the high level of productivity and quality of research formerly shown by its members would once more be achieved.

Unfortunately very little was known about the state of sociology in Italy, the Balkans and the U.S.S.R. The same was true of India, China and Japan; the accounts and bibliographies published in Barnes and Becker, *Social Thought from Lore to Science,* 2 vols., (1938) badly needed supplementing, but apparently more time had to elapse before accurate and up-to-date information would make that possible. (*See* also PSYCHOLOGY.)

BIBLIOGRAPHY.—Talcott Parsons, *The Structure of Social Action* (1937); Pitirim Sorokin, *Social and Cultural Dynamics,* 1st 3 vols. (1937); *idem,* vol. 4 (summary and conclusions) (1941); Milla Aissa Alihan, *Social Ecology* (1938); George Herbert Mead, *The Philosophy of the Act* (1938); Karen Horney, *New Ways in Psychoanalysis* (1939); George Andrew Lundberg, *Foundations of Sociology* (1939); Gaetano Mosca, *The Ruling Class* (1939); Arnold Joseph Toynbee, *A Study of History,* 6 vols. (1934–1939); Harry Elmer Barnes, Howard Becker and Frances Bennett Becker, eds., *Contemporary Social Theory* (1940); Karl Mannheim, *Man and Society in an Age of Reconstruction* (1940); George C. Homans, *English Villagers of the Thirteenth Century* (1941); Robert Redfield, *The Folk Culture of Yucatan* (1941); F. J. C. Teggart, *Theory and Processes of History* (1941); W. Lloyd Warner and Paul S. Lunt, *The Social Life of a Modern Community* (1941) and succeeding volumes; Oscar Cargill, *Intellectual America* (1942); R. M. MacIver, *Social Causation* (1942); Morris Opler, *An Apache Life-Way* (1942); F. A. Roethlisberger, *Management and Morale* (1942); Logan Wilson, *The Academic Man* (1942); Henry Pratt Fairchild, *Dictionary of Sociology* (1943); Charles S. Johnson, *Patterns of Negro Segregation* (1943); Henrik Infield, *Co-operative Communities in Palestine* (1944); Karl Mannheim, *Diagnosis of Our Time* (1944); Lewis Mumford, *The Condition of Man* (1944); Gunnar Myrdal, *An American Dilemma* (1944); Joachim Wach, *Sociology of Religion* (1944); Georges Gurvitch and W. E. Moore, eds., *Twentieth Century Sociology* (1945); Abram Kardiner, *Psychological Frontiers of Society* (1945); A. H. Leighton, *The Government of Men* (1945); T. C. T. McCormick, ed., *Problems of the Postwar World* (1945); James West, *Plainville, U.S.A.* (1945); Howard Becker, *German Youth: Bond or Free* (1946); Gilberto Freyre, *The Masters and the Slaves* (1946); Hans Gerth and C. Wright Mills, eds. and trans., *From Max Weber: Essays in Sociology* (1946); Wilbert E. Moore, *Industrial Relations and the Social Order* (1946). (H. BEC.)

Sodality of Our Lady, The

See SOCIETIES AND ASSOCIATIONS.

Sodium Carbonate

The bulk of the sodium carbonate marketed continued to be made from salt, with consumption ranging from 3,037,000 short tons in 1937 to 4,693,000 tons in 1944, and declining to 4,513,000 tons in 1945. As compared with these totals, the output from natural sources was relatively small, increasing from 104,711 short tons in 1937 to 194,045 tons in 1945.

There was a small but constant output in Canada, varying from 286 tons in 1937 to a high of 9,486 tons in 1943 and a low of 44 tons in 1944, swinging back to 239 tons in 1945. (G. A. RO.)

Sodium Sulphate

Although the greater part of the sodium sulphate consumed continued to be manufactured from common salt, a considerable tonnage was produced direct from natural sources. In the United States output of natural sulphate increased from 80,053 short tons in 1937 to 178,196 tons in 1945.

In Canada, production increased from 79,804 short tons in 1937 to a peak of 131,258 tons in 1943, declining to 102,421 tons in 1944 and 86,643 tons in 1945. (G. A. RO.)

Soekarno

Soekarno (1901?–), Indonesian statesman, studied at the Bandoeng Technical institute where he received a degree in civil engineering. Following a brief career in architecture, he went into politics after World War I. He became one of the leading spirits in the leftist Perserikatan Naisonal Indonesia (National Indonesian party). Under the guidance of this party, many Indonesian nationalist groups were welded together and urged to accept the principles of nonco-operation with the Dutch, following the pattern laid down by Gandhi in India. Soekarno was arrested in 1934 and exiled to Flores island. After the Japanese conquest of Indonesia in 1942, Soekarno allegedly collaborated with the Japanese occupation authorities. Two days after Emperor Hirohito's surrender broadcast, Japanese forces appointed Soekarno president of the newly-created Indonesian republic. He formed a cabinet and attempted negotiations with the Dutch, who refused to recognize his "native" regime.

As British and Dutch troops were preparing to land in Java, Soekarno told foreign correspondents in Batavia that the Indonesians would fight any attempt to restore Netherlands sovereignty. The battles started with the landing of Dutch troops and on Oct. 12, 1945, Soekarno appealed to Pres. Truman to stop the Netherlands from using U.S. equipment to put down his independence movement.

On Nov. 13, Soekarno relinquished his ministerial duties to Sutan Sjahrir, who was named premier, but retained his duties and title as president. Soekarno, however, was believed to be the dominant figure in the government. He attended the signing, Nov. 15, 1946, of the Dutch-Indonesian draft plan under which the Dutch agreed to recognize the republic set up by him.

Softball

Its popularity enhanced by World War II and the need for employee recreation, softball made huge advances from 1937 to 1946. World championship amateur tournaments were held each year, starting at Soldier field, Chicago, and moving on to Detroit and then to Cleveland.

All sectors of the nation shared in the men's amateur championship, with Hammer field at Fresno, Calif., a wartime team, and the Fort Wayne, Ind., Zollners, scoring the only doubles. The women's tournament from 1937 to 1946 was chiefly the championship legacy of the far west and far south. Jax Maids of New Orleans, La., dominated play after 1942 with four out of five championships.

Softball reached its zenith in 1944, when two professional women's leagues were conducted in and around Chicago, centre of the sport. Salaries of from $50 to $150 a week were established, and leagues were conducted and promoted not unlike those of major league baseball.

In 1937, after a series of country-wide elimination tournaments, 84 teams gathered at Chicago for the world amateur final. The Briggs Manufacturing Co. of Detroit, Mich., won the men's title with a 1–0 victory over the B. & B. Clothes team of Sapulpa, Okla. The National Screw and Manufacturing Co. of Cleveland, O., won the women's title.

Pohler's Cafe of Cincinnati, O., won the men's amateur title in 1938 over a field of 56 teams, while J. J. Krieg's of Alameda, Calif., won the first of two successive women's tournaments.

In 1939, Carr's of Covington, Ky., outlasted Columbus, O., in the men's final, while the Alameda entry repeated as champion of the women's division.

Featuring a three-hit pitching performance by Harold Gears in the final of 1940, Kodak park of Rochester, N.Y., won the men's world tournament. The Arizona Ramblers, Phoenix, Ariz., won the women's championship.

An estimated 2,750,000 players took part in softball during 1941. Bendix Brakes of South Bend, Ind., won the men's world title in the annual tournament at Detroit, while the Higgins Midgets of Tulsa, Okla., dethroned the Phoenix Ramblers in the women's final.

In 1942, the Deep Rock Oilers of Tulsa, Okla., defeated the Briggs Bombers of Detroit, 2 to 0, in the men's world championship final. The Jax Maids of New Orleans, La., opened their reign of the women's tournament with a 4–1 final victory over Chicago.

While the Jax Maids were repeating as women's champion in 1943, Hammer field, an army air base near Fresno, Calif., won the first of its two successive championships in the men's division.

The west coast won both world titles in 1944, Hammer field repeating in the men's division and Lind-Pomeroy of Portland, Ore., capturing the women's title. Milwaukee, Wis., won the All-America Girls' professional crown, while the Kandy Kids of Chicago topped the National Girls' league.

Winner of the world's pro basketball title, the Fort Wayne Zollners added the men's amateur softball title to their accomplishments in 1945. The Jax Maids won the women's title for the third time in four years, while Rockford, Ill., captured the All-America title and the Chicago Rock-Ola Music Maids topped the National league.

The year 1946 was a repeat year in both amateur divisions, Fort Wayne, Ind., winning the men's title and the Jax Maids of New Orleans winning their fourth women's title in five years. Both champions defeated teams from the Match Corp. of America, Chicago, in the final. Racine, Wis., won the All-America Girls' Professional Ball league title, while the Chicago Blue Birds won the National Girls' Baseball league crown. (M. P. W.)

Bibliography.—L. H. Fischer, *How to Play Winning Softball* (1940); H. G. Johnson, *Baseball and Softball Rules, A Comparative Interpretation* (1941); V. Mitchell, *Softball for Girls* (1943); A. T. Noren, *Softball* (1940); *Official Rules of Softball* (1940); H. D. Wilson, *Play Softball* (1942).

Soil Chemistry

See Tennessee Valley Authority.

Soil Conservation Service

See Geology.

Soil Erosion and Soil Conservation

Many large regions of the world have been permanently lost to agriculture through soil erosion. In old lands such as the near east, and in China, wherever cultivation was extended up slopes in farming through the centuries, soils have been washed off to bedrock, making it impossible to restore the productive capacities of the land. Some of the old world's natural grasslands have been turned into deserts, useless to mankind. In North Africa, central Australia, parts of North America and central Asia, deserts expanded as semi-arid grasslands were overgrazed year after year or plowed for cultivation. Even in Central and South America, large areas of both hill lands and valleys became so eroded that they would be worthless for generations. Only in certain specially favoured climates, such as that of Great Britain and western Europe, are cultivated and grazing lands relatively free from serious erosion.

According to the best estimates, only about 4,000,000,000 ac. of the world's total land area was immediately available for production of food and fibre crops during the decade 1937–46. From the standpoint of the needs of the more than 2,000,000,000 people inhabiting the earth, the most serious soil erosion was that evident on this 4,000,000,000 ac. on all continents. This included millions of fields and farms depended upon for food, livestock feed and fibre, which no longer were capable of producing good yields because they were eroded in varying degrees. Much of this land was rapidly deteriorating either because it had been farmed intensively without protective conservation farming measures or because it had been used to grow crops for which it was unsuited.

Lands vary widely from place to place and even on parts of the same field. Every variation in the combinations of soil, slope, climate and susceptibility to erosion means a variation in the use and treatment necessary to keep land permanently productive. Thus, to prevent erosion and depletion of soils, engineering measures must be used to supplement agronomic and fertility measures, according to the needs of land, its adaptability for cropping and the economic limitations of land users. This was the basic principle underlying the new land technology developed in the United States and spread to many parts of the world by 1946.

U.S. Program.—Soil erosion had first been formally recognized as a menace to agriculture when in 1929 the United States congress passed legislation appropriating funds for the specific purpose of making investigations as to its causes and developing methods to control it. Research carried out at erosion experiment stations established under authority of this legislation (the Buchanan amendment to the Agricultural Appropriation bill for the fiscal year 1930) had formed the foundation for the national soil and water conservation program which grew and spread, in the following 15 years, to all states of the United States and to many other countries of the world.

Later historic steps in building for soil conservation in the United States had been: (1) Establishment of a technical agency (the soil erosion service) in 1933, with authority to work directly with farmers in demonstration areas in applying conservation practices to farmland, and to survey the total land of the country to determine the extent and severity of the erosion problem; and (2) adoption by congress of the Soil Conservation act, on April 27, 1935, as a law of the nation. The act set up the soil conservation service as a permanent bureau of the department of agriculture. Also in April 1935, the parliament of Canada passed the Prairie Rehabilitation act which, with subsequent amendments, authorized the dominion minister of agriculture to introduce soil and water conserving practices in those regions of the prairie provinces where soil drifting and other types of erosion were prevalent.

By the beginning of the decade 1937–46, soil and water conservation had been developed in the United States as the science and practice of using and conserving agricultural land and the water available for agricultural production. Thousands of experiments had been carried out to determine the causes and processes of accelerated erosion and to evolve measures that could be used to heal eroded soils and prevent further serious erosion on farm, range and forest lands. Between 1933 and 1937, complete soil and water conservation farming systems, based on scientific findings, had been applied to about 4,240,000 ac. in more than 500 demonstration and work areas in 42 states. Conservation methods were spreading to some farms outside the demonstration areas where they had proved effective both in controlling erosion and raising per-acre yields. Approximately 50,000 farmers and rangemen were co-operating with the demonstration program. At the same time, there was a growing consciousness of vast acreages of eroded lands far removed from the projects and of the urgent need for a new and more rapid approach to the problem of applying soil and water conservation on a national scale.

Events in 1937 supplied this need. In that year, farmers and rangers began organizing soil conservation districts under state laws. Legislative action in 18 states authorized formation of this new type of district on a community basis, with legal status, to ensure continuance and progress of soil conservation throughout the nation. The first district of this kind was chartered in Aug. 1937. It was the Brown Creek Soil Conservation district in North Carolina —the first unit of its kind in history.

Soil conservation districts were brought into existence by the initiative and vote of farmers and ranchers themselves and operated by farmers through their elected officers. Districts were served, upon request, by planning technicians and other conservation specialists of the soil conservation service, living and working within the boundaries of the districts. Other federal, state or local sources of assistance also might be drawn upon by these districts. Every landowner acquired a voice in shaping the policies of the district. The aims of the district, its co-operating policies, the land-use changes and the soil and water conservation measures it decided to apply to the land, were set forth in a district program and work plan drawn up by the district supervisors with the help of landowners and technicians. The overall objective of such a district was to put all the land of all the farms under conservation land use and practices by working together on common problems and adopting conservation techniques on a community scale.

By Jan. 1, 1942, as the United States entered upon the full-scale warfare of World War II, 38 states had passed soil conservation districts laws, and farmers and ranchers had organized 642 districts including 377,000,000 ac. of land. Conservation farming on thousands of farms producing all kinds of crops had resulted in an average per-acre yield increase of 20%, with additional savings in labour, fuel, time, money or machinery. These districts, and some 800 others formed during the war, proved an extremely important channel through which the national conservation program essential to protecting land and water resources under wartime pressure for maximum food and fibre production was carried out.

By the end of 1946, about 1,750 soil conservation districts and 21 grass conservation districts had been organized, including approximately 950,000,000 ac. and 4,160,000 farms. Several states were completely covered by soil conservation districts. All of the 48 states and Puerto Rico had enacted legislation authorizing local land owners and operators to organize for carrying out soil conservation work on the land and to obtain technical and other aid in doing it. Their common purpose was to restore eroded lands and to avoid additional devastation of still productive lands. It was to halt overcropping, plowing of grasslands, reckless timber cutting or other wasteful land use such as had caused heavy soil losses, dune formation and dust storms, gullying of large areas and serious depletion of grazing and crop lands. Such damage had been especially severe in some areas during and immediately after World War I.

Individual Planning.—The actual work of putting soil and water conservation on the land progressed with greatly increased momentum after the advent of soil conservation districts. During the ten years following establishment of the first such district in 1937, complete soil and water conservation plans were applied to some 90,000,000 ac. of farm and range land in soil conservation districts; plans were partially applied on another 10,000,000 ac.; and complete plans had been written by the soil conservation service, co-operating with farmers, for approximately 160,000,000 ac. At the same time, 130,000 more farmers and ranchers had made formal application for such plans for their land.

A complete soil conservation farm plan included specifications for use of each piece of land according to its natural properties, its capabilities for sustained production and its needs for erosion control. Such plans were based on land-capability surveys, made before farm planning began. The farmer and the farm-planning technician made the plans together directly on the land. The farmer designated the kind of farming he wished to do, the machinery available, the livestock he intended to carry and his economic outlook as related to conservation farming. The technician pointed out the practices needed to stop or prevent ero-

Formation of severely eroded nonarable soil in Mississippi

sion and make the land more productive. Land for growing row crops was selected, and rotations were worked out for all these fields. Permanent meadow or hay land, pasture and woodlots were selected from land not suitable for annual cultivation.

Erosion control practices required for each field were listed on the plan. Field boundaries might be changed so that crops could be fitted to land classes, or to permit contour cultivation, strip cropping or terracing. Green manure crops, cover crops or mulching with crop residues might suit parts of the land. If the farm was in a region of heavy rainfall, grassed waterways had to be planned; but in dry regions, a water-spreading system might be necessary for crop and pasture production. Still other practices might be considered before the plan was completed.

Once the details were agreed upon, they were recorded in a written plan, which included a farm map for the farmer to use as he installed the conservation practices with the assistance of the technicians. The chief advantage of this kind of farm planning was that each acre of land received careful consideration as to its needs for protective farming methods, developed and adapted to the land itself by scientific survey and experiment.

U.S. Soil Conservation Service.—The work of the soil conservation service, the scientific and technical federal agency responsible for soil and water conservation throughout the United States, was greatly broadened during the ten-year period 1937–46. Yearly, as public demand for farm and range conservation increased, the service's research, survey and operational activities were shaped to provide all needed information and assistance to the working units, the soil conservation districts. Experimentation was directed toward developing planting materials, equipment modifications and uses and facts about soil and water which would enable farmers to apply conservation while carrying out seasonal crop and livestock production, without extra cost or loss of crop production.

A survey charting the conservation needs of the total land of the United States was made in 1942–43, and the results were made available to farmers, farm planners, industry, municipal and civic associations and other public groups and individuals. Based on classification of land according to physical characteristics and best productive use, the conservation needs survey provided the most complete analysis of agricultural land resources ever undertaken by any country. Basic information acquired by research and surveys was moved promptly to farm planning technicians working directly with farmers. The seven regional offices of the service and the field offices throughout the country provided the system for prompt, convenient channelling of improved methods directly to the land.

By 1943, nearly 60 different soil and water conservation practices had been tested and approved, redesigned or developed by the service for use on the land. Twenty-three of them were found to be effective in increasing crop production in from one to three years. Some of the principal practices incorporated in complete conservation farm plans in soil conservation districts during the ten-year period were as follows:

Contour cultivation	15,900,000 ac.
Cover crops	5,900,000 ac.
Crop residue management	13,500,000 ac.
Strip cropping	5,000,000 ac.
Range properly stocked	40,800,000 ac.
Seeding range and pasture	9,800,000 ac.
Woodland improvement	7,500,000 ac.
Tree planting	503,000 ac.
Farm and ranch ponds	75,500
Terracing	871,000 mi.
Water diversions	100,600,000 linear ft.
Farm drainage	2,089,000 ac.
Land preparation for irrigation	607,000 ac.
Application of irrigation water	1,300,000 ac.

A survey of 9,348 farms under complete soil and water conservation farming plans, made in 1943, revealed that yields of all major crops had increased 35.7%.

Aside from assistance to soil conservation districts, the service participated in many large-scale conservation projects during the decade. These included studies of the silt-ing of reservoirs as related to erosion on agricultural lands; development of emergency erosion-control methods applicable to the Everglades region of Florida; appraisal of water resources of the United States for use in determining the feasibility of proposed water projects; snow surveys; and flood control projects on small and large watersheds. During World War II, technicians of the service assisted the war and navy departments with flood control and erosion problems at harbours, cantonments, forts, arsenals and other locations.

During 1945, technicians of the soil conservation service spent 11,810,306 man-hours on soil and water conservation activities throughout the United States. Complete conservation farming systems were applied to 13,000,000 ac., and plans were drawn up for an additional 20,500,000 ac.

No small part of the service's essential functions during the ten-year period was training of personnel. Soil conservation explored the wide ramifications of land and water problems into many fields—physics, engineering, agronomy, ecology and biology, economics and sociology, climate, soils, forestry and others. It was early recognized that permanent conservation on land could be achieved only by co-ordinating the knowledge of many sciences and techniques toward a common objective. The training program of the service was especially designed to co-ordinate all knowledge relating to land, water and farming into a practical science aimed specifically at conserving soil while using it for production. Training schools for soil conservation technical personnel were held in six regions of the country; 1,263 employees went through these training centres in 1945. Several leading colleges and universities added soil conservation courses to their curricula during the war years.

Between 1937 and the start of World War II, ten countries other than the United States and Canada took steps to improve their agriculture through soil and water conservation. Experimental work was authorized and undertaken to adapt conservation practices to land types in four Australian provinces—Victoria, New South Wales, South Australia and the Bardekin river basin of Queensland; in New Zealand; the Punjab of India; Rhodesia, Kenya and the Union of South Africa on the African continent; and in Brazil, Argentina, Colombia and Venezuela in South America.

Africa.—In 1938, a soil conservation service was established as a branch of the department of agriculture of Kenya and was given wide powers for long-term planning as well as an immediate program to apply conservation practices to lands farmed largely by East African natives. At the same time, the British ministry of state for the colonies recommended that land conservation programs be incorporated in colonial governments and arranged for free grants of money to help in defraying the cost to natives of putting anti-erosion measures on the land. Uganda, Tanganyika, Nyasaland, Northern Rhodesia, Basutoland, Bechuanaland, Swaziland and Sierra Leone in Africa, with Palestine on the Asian continent and Jamaica in the West Indies, all had soil and water conservation programs in various stages of development by 1942. Although developments were impeded during the next five years by wartime shortages of conservation staffs, labour and equipment, remarkable progress was made in various African colonies, where erosion was so serious that yields of food crops had dwindled to almost nothing. Furthest advanced was the work in Kenya, where about 300,000 ac. had been treated by terracing, grassing of drainageways, contouring, gully control dams and plantings by 1943.

In Swaziland and Basutoland, farmed mostly by Negroes, some highly successful conservation work was done with contour embankments in 1939–41. Corn yields were advanced from about 3 bu. to 12–15 bu. an acre by this practice.

During 1941, the legislative assembly of Rhodesia enacted the Natural Resources law empowering the Natural Resources board to direct use of land for pastures, cultivation methods, control of water and retirement of land from cultivation. Large-scale land use changes were made immediately, and soil conservation projects were begun on a watershed basis for protection of stream sources and valley lands subject to flooding or drying up because of upland erosion. In Uganda, also, considerable progress was made in the early 1940s. There, first attention was given to protection of grazing grounds by instituting rotational grazing on a wide scale and providing watering ponds for stock.

An area of 380 sq.mi. was reserved for permanent forest, and in cultivated areas the practice of contour strip cropping, whereby narrow grass strips were interposed between plowed strips, was enthusiastically adopted by native farmers.

As was the case everywhere, successful soil and water conservation throughout Africa presupposed active co-operation of the people in solving land problems. In some of Britain's African colonies, this co-operation had been obtained by 1945. In the territory of Tanganyika, for example, one of the features of the work was tribal organization to provide labour for putting conservation structures and methods on the land. In the Central province of Tanganyika, a 10-yr. program was organized in 1942 to control erosion completely on 5,000,000 ac. of pasture and 1,000,000 ac. of cultivated land, the work to be done through such tribal organization. With the consent of native tribes, large grazing areas were reserved for use in the dry season.

Likewise, hundreds of hilltops were closed to cultivation, gullying was controlled, and many acres of communal fuel plantations were planted.

During 1941, the senate and the house of assembly of the Union of South Africa adopted an act designed to amend the Union's laws on land use to make provision for soil and water conservation. Erosion experiments were car-

Gullies splitting grazed pasture lands in the mountain region of Bernalillo county, New Mexico

ried out, and very successful soil conservation demonstrations were established in a few localities. Difficulty was encountered in spreading conservation methods to farm and grazing land, owing largely to disinterest on the part of land holders. In 1946, a national Soil Conservation act was passed, making soil conservation a national policy. In the meantime, the land of the country was surveyed in considerable detail, and vast areas were found to be eroding with great rapidity. Large wheat-growing tracts in Cape province already were ruined and abandoned; in northern Transvaal, between Pietersburg and the Drakensburg mountains, more than 100,000 ac. had lost practically all of the original topsoil. Where lands were still in cultivation, yields had dropped from 15 bu. of maize an acre to 3 bu. or nothing. Causes of this serious erosion were pointed out as burning of veld, manures and maize stalks; indiscriminate grazing of uplands and dry lands by goats, sheep, cattle, horses and donkeys; up-and-down slope plowing; and widespread cultivation, without rotations, of soil-depleting crops. Most of South Africa's reservoirs were filling with sediment, while gullies and sheet erosion were reducing underground water supplies and permanency of streams and springs, especially throughout the Orange river basin. Average yields of tilled crops were estimated as having been reduced to 25% of the land's original capacity. In the Karroo, whole districts of originally good veld were so eroded that carrying capacity was but one-tenth of what it was before abusive land-use practices became common. It was noted that erosion had greatly altered the vegetation on hundreds of thousands of acres, while bankruptcy, abandonment of farms and even hunger were common in seriously eroded regions.

South and Central America.—During the first years of World War II, Mexico, Venezuela and Argentina had established special soil conservation agencies, while surveys to determine the condition of land, and educational programs to inform the people of the needs and advantages of conservation were in progress in most of the other Latin American countries, including Haiti and the Dominican Republic. Lack of trained soil conservation scientists and technicians was proving a handicap to these nations. The difficulty was overcome, however, when in 1942–43 arrangements were made to admit Latin American agricultural scientists to the United States for one year of training with the soil conservation service of that country. Twenty-five men, carefully chosen and sponsored by 13 Latin American governments, were trained the first year and returned to their home countries to act as leaders in various phases of land conservation.

The training program for foreign conservationists proved valuable both to the United States and to other countries involved, and it was therefore expanded and opened to countries outside the western hemisphere in 1944. By the close of 1946, the governments of 23 countries had sent nearly 100 agricultural scientists to the United States for the year of study and training in all phases of developing, establishing and carrying out soil conservation as a permanent national program. In addition, an equal number of scientists and agricultural executives from more than 30 countries spent from three to eight months touring the United States to observe soil conservation districts and to study the voluntary co-operation through which conservation practices had been developed and applied to farm and range land. Some of the countries represented, aside from Latin American countries, were China, South Africa, Belgian Congo, Tanganyika, Australia, Palestine, Greece, India, Korea, France, Holland, Turkey, U.S.S.R., England and Scotland, New Zealand and the Netherlands Indies.

A World-wide Movement.—By the end of 1946, actual work of applying soil and water conservation to land had started in more than 30 countries of the world. Even before the end of World War II, a vigorous co-operative movement toward conservation agriculture in all its complexities was in evidence, between governments, educational and experimental institutions, industrial and business groups and land users in groups and as individuals. After the war ended, this movement quickly assumed world-wide proportions, as food shortages in many parts of all continents were traced to crop losses, extremely low yields from immense acreages of eroded or seriously depleted land or to loss of water through wasteful farming methods.

Five important food-producing countries—Mexico, Venezuela, New Zealand, Australia and the Union of South Africa—passed national soil conservation laws in 1945 and 1946. Twelve countries had established and organized federal soil conservation agencies similar to the soil conservation service of the United States, to lead, plan and apply soil conservation programs by co-operating with land users. They were Mexico, Guatemala, Venezuela, Peru, Chile, Argentina, Canada, Kenya, South Africa, Rhodesia, Australia and New Zealand. Conservation personnel, working through departments of agriculture of their respective countries, were applying conservation methods to land in Costa Rica, El Salvador, Colombia, Ecuador, Uruguay, four Brazilian states, Haiti, the Dominican Republic, six East and South African native states, Kansu province in China, the Punjab, Bombay province and the state of Hyderabad of India, in many parts of the U.S.S.R. and in Great Britain in some places where pressure of wartime production had caused erosion of hill lands or depletion of lowland crop lands.

Mexico's soil conservation program was well advanced by the end of 1946. Much of the groundwork for widespread conservation had been done, even before adoption of the federal law decreeing that soil and water conservation should be applied to all of the nation's lands early in 1946. Ten soil conservation districts, covering most of central Mexico, had been established by the government, and demonstrations established in 1942 and 1943 already were becoming effective in spreading conservation practices to farm lands. The practices used included contouring, modern terracing, gully control by structures and plantings, reforestation, range and pasture improvement, and grass planting in waterways where sloping lands had to be farmed to grow food crops. In the state of Tlaxcala, where erosion had been most serious, ravines were being controlled by means of dams, alignment structures, pilot canals and other engineering devices. Extensive crop rotation experiments were in progress, so that once the hazard from flooding through the ravines was reduced, farmers could use some of the valley lands to grow crops while they gradually restored soil fertility.

Paracutín, the world's newest volcano, became a part of one of Mexico's soil conservation districts. Scientists from many countries were participating in studies undertaken in an effort to find ways of reclaiming large forests and two irrigation districts invaded by lava or choked by ash from the volcano. Old volcanic soils are common in Mexico, but never before had students of erosion had the opportunity to start with a vast area of entirely new volcanic land in studying the erosion process. Experiments were underway, in 1945, to test various kinds of plants which might be used to restore a cover of vegetation to ash-encrusted areas in the vicinity of Paracutín.

Device for gauging the amount of soil erosion from a cultivated slope

Common Problems.—Through world-wide co-operation, many soil and water conservation practices already had been improved or adapted to areas with special problems. Of particular interest was the wide distribution and study of planting materials—grasses, trees, shrubs, leguminous and fodder crops—showing promise for erosion control and having economic values. Grasses native to China were being tested in the northwestern United States to determine their potentialities for range seeding. Kudzu, originally from China and Japan, which had been planted on more than 1,000,000 ac. of eroded land in the southeastern United States, was being tried out in Australia, Chile, Mexico, Venezuela and other Latin American countries, while at the same time a tropical variety of this remarkable erosion-control forage plant had been discovered and adapted in Puerto Rico on a wide scale. In Mexico, on eroded hill lands, extensive plantings of mixed fruit-bearing trees and shrubs from many countries were being made to control erosion on steep slopes devastated by cultivation, and to provide edible fruits for local consumption. Extremely important experiments were undertaken in Bombay province, India, to adapt leguminous crops to dry lands, for use in rotation with maize, grains and other badly needed food crops. Also noteworthy were the lovegrasses from South Africa which had been planted extensively in the southwestern part of the United States. These and other exotic drought-resistant grasses were hailed by ranchers and farmers as a solution to wind erosion problems in seriously dry areas.

As the decade ended, conservation scientists of many nations were pooling their knowledge and experience in the effort to improve and co-ordinate water conservation practices for use in agricultural regions subject to periodic droughts or general semi-arid conditions. An excellent system of terracing combined with water diversion channels had been designed in Bombay province, India, and applied to about 600,000 ac. of non-irrigable land by 1946. Yields of food crops were reported to have increased from 100 to 400% on some of this land by the water-saving methods and other soil conservation practices. Mulching with crop residues, in use on large areas in the United States, had been adopted by many Australian farmers as a means of storing moisture in the soil. Both small and large water storage projects, including ponds for livestock watering and other uses as well as water impounding for community irrigation, were an important feature of the soil and water conservation program of Canada's prairie provinces and the western United States. Approximately 19,000 small stock ponds, 4,200 dams for impounding water and 1,000 irrigation projects had been constructed in the Canadian provinces as of March 1945. In addition, tree plantings on a large scale, reseeding and regulation of grazing to preserve the range and contour strip cropping where lands were plowed were becoming common land-use practices in the Great Plains regions of both Canada and the United States. In Australia, Argentina, South Africa and parts of India, these methods were under study or already used as effective in helping to solve the problems of moisture deficiencies in regions subject to soil blowing and drifting when land had been denuded of its natural cover.

Steep slope erosion, often with gigantic gullies cutting into lowland, presented a stupendous conservation problem in some parts of the world. Surveys made by the soil conservation department of Mexico revealed that 30% of the steep lands and large acreages of valley lands of that country had been made totally unproductive by such erosion. In addition, about half the country remained semi-arid. Other parts were subject to floods which destroyed entire crops and caused rapid and destructive erosion. An extremely mountainous topography further complicated planning by conservationists. Steep ranges make up 68% of the land area of Mexico, and much of the level land suitable for cultivation is in small strips between high, eroding mountains. Conservation specialists concluded that only complete revegetation of mountain regions would stop the spread of this vicious type of land destruction.

* * *

THE TEN-YEAR period 1937–46 thus marked a definite trend among the people of the world toward agricultural development based on conservation of land and water resources. Hundreds of groups—nations, states or provinces, countries, associations both rural and urban and action groups even among so-called primitive peoples—were formulating long-term land conservation plans based on the premise that peace and prosperity would be impossible without adequate sustained yields of food and fibre crops from agricultural lands. At the United Nations Food and Agriculture conference, held May 18–June 3, 1943, in the United States, representatives of 44 nations agreed that if the food needs of all peoples were to be met in future times, the agricultural land of the planet should be adequately protected from erosion and from other damage by effective methods for conserving and rebuilding the fertility of the soil.

(*See* also AGRICULTURE; AQUEDUCTS; DAMS; IRRIGATION; METEOROLOGY.)

BIBLIOGRAPHY.—Axel F. Gustafson, *Conservation of the Soil* (1937); Russell Lord, *Behold Our Land* (1938); Joseph F. Cox and Lyman E. Jackson, *Crop Management and Soil Conservation* (1937); Hugh Hammond Bennett, *Soil Conservation* (1939); R. O. Whyte and G. V. Jacks, *Vanishing Lands* (1939); H. H. Bennett and William C. Pryor, *This Land We Defend* (1942); Kenneth B. Cumberland, *Soil Erosion in New Zealand*, Soil Conservation and Rivers Control council (Wellington, 1944); Sir Harold Glover, *Erosion in the Punjab, Its Causes and Cure*, Civil and Military Gazette Press, (Lahore, 1944); Ward Shepard, *Food or Famine: The Challenge of Erosion* (1945); C. J. J. Van Rensburg and E. M. Palmer, *New World to Win*, A. C. White P. and P. Co., Ltd. (Bloemfontein, 1946); Casiano V. Quevedo, *Conservacion del Suelo*, Volúmenes 33–34, Coleccion el Campo, Editorial Suelo (Buenos Aires, 1946); H. H. Bennett, *Elements of Soil Conservation* (1946).

(H. H. BE.)

Solar System

See ASTRONOMY.

Soldiers' Bonus

See VETERANS' ADMINISTRATION.

Solid Fuels Administration

See WAR AND DEFENSE AGENCIES.

Solomon Islands

The Solomon Islands figured prominently in Japan's drive to sever communications between the United States and Australia during the early part of World War II. Japanese task forces in March and April 1942, put several thousand troops ashore in the archipelago first on Bougainville, then on Guadalcanal and smaller intervening islands. Landings met with little resistance, as the Solomons had been lightly garrisoned, and the British withdrew all troops except a few officers and enlisted men who were left to live secretly among the natives and report by radio on Japanese troop and ship movements.

A series of air attacks against a large Japanese task force in the waters of the Solomons and the Coral sea in May 1942, turned back the task force into safer waters farther north, with heavy losses to the Japanese. This was the first serious reversal of the Japanese advance toward their apparent objective, Australia, and the "Battle of the Coral sea," as it was called, marked their farthest southward reach. This victory for the Allies, who had retreated from every stand, beginning with the Philippines and Malaya, in Dec. 1941, raised Allied morale and was one of the decisive battles of the war.

Japanese forces strengthened their grip on the Solomons, however, by moving in additional thousands of soldiers, especially concentrating them on Guadalcanal, where, at Henderson Field, they had an air strip in operation by August.

On Aug. 7, 1942, a strong force of U.S. marines accompanied by a naval task force which included Australian warships, struck the small islands of Tulagi and Gavutu in a surprise attack, carrier based planes bombed Henderson Field and marines of the 2nd division went ashore under protection of naval gunfire on Guadalcanal near the field.

This marked the beginning of one of the most remarkable campaigns of the war. In dense jungle, in swamps and mountains, often in torrential rains, modern weapons other than the trench mortar and automatic small arms were useless most of the time. Marines had to learn a type

of warfare utterly foreign to them, but for which Japanese troops had been well trained. Man stalked his enemy as a panther stalks its prey. Knife, bayonet and even fist fighting were not uncommon. Survival often depended on the animal-like art of concealment.

The malaria-carrying mosquito was a deadly enemy, taking a heavy toll of both Japanese and U.S. forces. The quinine substitute, atabrin, mosquito nets and the new miracle insecticide DDT were made available to U.S. soldiers in increasing quantities as the campaign progressed, reducing casualties and providing a standing operating procedure for future invasions of tropical areas. One of

Rendova Island in the New Georgia group, Solomon Islands, as it looked to U.S. soldiers landing in invasion barges early in the morning of June 30, 1943. The Japanese garrison was routed after a short but bitter struggle

the earliest experiments in use of blood plasma for wounded soldiers was conducted among U.S. casualties on Guadalcanal.

U.S. army units in November replaced battle-weary marines and supplies began to reach the island in increasing quantities. The seesaw, often bloody, battle, however, continued to be indecisive for some time, and the island was not secured till Feb. 9, 1943.

Several daring naval engagements took place in the waters of the Solomons as Japan and the Allies struggled to reinforce their troops. Japanese naval losses were estimated at 2 battleships, 12 cruisers, 26 destroyers and numerous smaller ships; U.S. naval losses, 2 carriers, 7 cruisers, 13 destroyers and several smaller ships.

In an island-hopping campaign, U.S. forces established beachheads at Munda in Feb. 1943, at Rendova and the Trobriand and Woodlark groups in July. In November they went ashore at Empress Augusta Bay and seized an airfield, establishing a firm and highly useful beachhead on Bougainville. Mopping up operations were not pressed, however, and some fighting broke out from time to time between the Allies and 22,000 Japanese troops who were completely cut off from supplies for the rest of the war.

The war interrupted a program of education and agricultural development for the Solomon Islanders which the British colonial administration had begun in the early part of the 1930s. The experiment was to give wider governmental powers to native authorities and to provide some elementary education and some education in health and sanitation. This work was resumed as rapidly as was practicable behind advancing Allied troops. Guadalcanal was officially turned back by military forces to the British colonial administration Nov. 13, 1942, though only a small part of the island had then been cleared of Japanese. Councils of elders were formed later in the villages, each with a headman to act as spokesmen for natives with the British resident commissioner. The council organized communal activities, such as precautions against epidemics, and was given the power of courts in cases of minor offenses.

Under the British Colonial Development and Welfare act, the resident commissioner and a staff of specialists helped the natives restore vegetable gardens and plantations ransacked by the military or destroyed by military operations.

The administration also experimented with new crops to supplement copra as a source of income for the natives.

Interruption of the colonial medical program by the war permitted fresh outbreaks of yaws, which disease had been brought partially under control. But doctors again were touring the islands before the end of hostilities, giving injections and distributing drugs supplied by the United States.

Natives remained loyal to the Allies throughout the war, and not a single instance of betrayal of British scouts was recorded. The Japanese paid little attention to natives till Allied forces began to cut off Japanese supplies, after which time they pillaged native gardens and villages. Natives ambushed and annihilated the raiders on a number of occasions. (*See* also WORLD WAR II.)

The population of the Solomons in 1944 was estimated at 500 Europeans, 200 Chinese and 94,700 natives. Plans were made in 1946 to rebuild the protectorate capital at Tulagi, but this project, like others of the rehabilitation program, was hampered by shortage of shipping.

Solomon Islands: *Statistical Data, 1938*

Item	Value (000's omitted)	Amount or number
Exchange rate		
Great Britain		£A1.25 = £1
United States		£A1 = $3.895
Finance		
Government revenues	£66 ($323)*	
Government expenditures	£55 ($269)*	
Forest products		
Timber†		1,431,945 bd. ft.
Ivory nuts†		598 tons
Sea products		
Trochus shell†		239 tons
Green-snail shell†		61 tons
Exports		
Total	£233 ($1,139)	...
Copra	£207 ($1,010)	25,689 tons
Trochus shell	£12 ($58)	239 tons
Timber	£6 ($31)	1,431,945 bd. ft.
Imports		
Total	£186 ($907)	...
Rice	£16 ($78)	2,000 tons
Machinery	£15 ($73)	...
Bags and sacks	£8 ($39)	32,000 doz.
ducation		
Elementary schools		6
Students		4,697

*In 1942: Revenues: £33 ($134); Expenditures: £51 ($206)
†Exports only

BIBLIOGRAPHY.—Edgar McInnis, *The War;* "A Future for New Guinea," *Asia* (June, 1946); Richard Tregaskis, *Guadalcanal Diary.*
(U. CE.; R. H. WS.)

Somaliland, British

See BRITISH EAST AFRICA.

Somaliland, French

See FRENCH COLONIAL EMPIRE.

Somaliland, Italian

See ITALIAN COLONIAL EMPIRE.

Somervell, Brehon Burke

Somervell (1892–), U.S. army officer, was born May 9, 1892, in Little Rock, Ark., and was graduated from the U.S. military academy at West Point in 1914. He served overseas during World War I, principally as personnel and supplies officer. During the peace years, he supervised civilian engineering and construction projects in the U.S. and Europe. Appointed assistant chief of staff in charge of the army supply division on Nov. 25, 1941, he became commander of the army supply services in March 1942. He thereupon became involved in a controversy with WPB officials, who charged that the army had sought control over all war production. Somervell's denial of these charges was qualified with his statement, Dec. 7, 1942, that "we do insist on running our part of it."

In late 1942, Somervell was appointed head of the Production Executive committee, created for the purpose of avoiding rows between the army and the WPB. Nominated for promotion to a full general, Mar. 13, 1945, Somervell made his final report as commanding general of the army service forces (A.S.F.) Oct. 27; in it, he declared that the A.S.F. achieved the "impossible" in handling its tasks. He retired Jan. 1, 1946, and on the following March 25, he was elected president of the Koppers co., in Pittsburgh.

Songs, Popular

See MUSIC.

Soong, T. V.

Soong (1894–), Chinese statesman, was born at Shanghai, the eldest son of Charles Jones Soong, wealthy Bible publisher, and a brother of Mme. Chiang Kai-shek. Educated in the United States, he attended Vanderbilt, Harvard and Columbia universities, where he specialized in economics, and later worked in New York banking houses. He returned to China in 1917 and became general manager of the Canton Central bank in 1924. As finance minister, 1928–33, he introduced a budget system, central banking and unified currency. He founded and was first chairman of the Bank of China, 1936, later becoming president. On Dec. 23, 1941, Chiang appointed Soong foreign minister.

Soong was named acting premier (president) on Dec. 4, 1944, of the executive yuan, which gave him a position second in importance only to that of Chiang Kai-shek; on May 31, 1945, he succeeded Chiang, who resigned to devote his energies to other duties. Soong attended the San Francisco conference of the United Nations in April 1945 and later went to Moscow to confer with Joseph Stalin on proposals for the Russo-Chinese treaty and the soviet plans for attacking Japanese forces in Manchuria. Soong quit his post as foreign minister on July 30, 1945, because of the burden of his many concurrently-held government posts.

Discussing the civil war which followed World War II, Soong revealed on June 19, 1946, that the government was expending 80% of its revenue on a huge army totalling between 250 and 300 divisions, adding that the only way to avert disastrous inflation would be to achieve internal peace. On Aug. 31, 1946, Soong signed an agreement with the United States for purchase of U.S. wartime properties in China and the western Pacific valued at $800,000,000.

Soong Mei-ling

See Chiang Kai-shek, Madame.

Sorghum

See Syrup, Sorgo and Cane.

South Africa, British

See British South African Protectorates.

South Africa, The Union of

A self-governing dominion of the British commonwealth of nations, South Africa consists of four provinces: Cape of Good Hope, Natal, the Transvaal and the Orange Free State. The former German colony of South-West Africa (area: 317,725 sq.mi.; pop., est. 1941: European 33,600; Bantu and coloured 287,700) was administered under mandate as an integral part of the union, but the territory had not been incorporated as a province. Area 472,494 sq.mi. (incl. Walvis bay, 374 sq.mi.); pop.: (est. June 30, 1941) 10,521,700 (Europeans, 2,188,200; Bantu, 7,250,700; coloured, 844,400; Asiatic 238,400): (est. Aug. 1946) 11,258,858 (Europeans, 2,335,460). Languages: English, Afrikaans. Religion: 95.5% of the European population is Christian (Dutch Reformed church, 55%, Anglican, 19%, Methodists 6%, Presbyterians 5%, Roman Catholics 5%, others 5.5%) and 4.5% Jews; 51.5% of the non-Europeans are Christian (one-fourth of them belong to the native separatist churches, one-eighth are Methodists, one-tenth Anglicans, etc.), *c.* 44% pagan (mainly Hottentots and Bushmen) and the remainder is divided between Hinduism, Mohammedanism and Buddhism. Chief towns (pop. 1936 census): Capetown (seat of legislature, 344,223); Pretoria (seat of government, 128,621); Johannesburg (519,384); Durban (259,606); Port Elizabeth (109,841). Governors general: Sir Patrick Duncan (Nov. 16, 1936–died July 17, 1943); Nicholaas Jacobus De Wet (July 1943–Dec. 31, 1945); Major Gideon Brand van Zyl (after Jan. 1, 1946). Prime minister: Gen. James Barry Munnik Hertzog (1924–Sept. 5, 1939); Gen. (after 1941 Field Marshal) Jan Christiaan Smuts (after Sept. 6, 1939).

Preludes to War.—The close of the Empire exhibition in Johannesburg in the middle of Jan. 1937 was like the end of a chapter. The various dominions and colonies, which had sent their displays to be admired by the people of South Africa, packed up their pavilions, and the buildings erected with such care in the gardens of Milner park were demolished.

The influx of refugees from overseas had considerably diminished and was now only a trickle, but the activities of the nazis in South Africa grew steadily. Collections for winter help and other German causes, as well as visits of warships, all furnished pretexts for the German legation at Pretoria to indulge in fresh bursts of propaganda; and the utmost nazi efforts were made to obtain support from all anti-British elements. During this period an organization known as the Greyshirts made fresh efforts to win support in the backveld, but with very little success.

As though to stimulate discontent and to mark the mounting uncertainty in Europe the share market in South Africa collapsed. On April 8, 1937, the boom which had prevailed in South Africa since the relinquishment of the gold standard in 1933 was abruptly suspended. Already there had been signs of uncertainty on the stock exchanges both in Johannesburg and in London, yet the full meaning of the danger was understood by only a few. On "Black Friday" thousands of people (not only of the Witwatersrand gold fields but of all parts of South Africa) woke up to find themselves ruined. However, the gold industry remained unaffected so far as production was concerned. The gigantic workings underground, which now extended for 60 mi. with Johannesburg in the centre, continued operations at full pressure. There was no falling off in output and the stream of golden wealth continued to flow. The gold output in 1937 was 11,734,000 oz.; and it rose to 12,161,000 oz. in 1938; to 12,821,000 oz. in 1939; and to the record figure of 14,046,000 oz. in 1940. Under the stress of the later wartime labour shortages and the lack of new mining equipment there was a recession for a while; but the industry continued to function with impressive efficiency and even helped to supply the state with munitions.

Nor did "Black Friday" influence South Africa's remaining heavy industries. The new steel works at Pretoria, known as Iscor, were steadily developing. Since their opening in 1934, production had risen from 198,000 short tons yearly to more than 385,000 short tons, and before the end of the war it was more than 660,000 short tons. New blast furnaces and coke ovens were ordered, and extensions were under way at the iron mines of Thabazimbi, a mountain of ore.

Revelations of nazi activities in South Africa, published early in 1938, caused a disturbance and had echoes in parliament. At the same time, the then prime minister, Gen. J. B. M. Hertzog, remained firm in his belief that South Africa could remain at peace even though Europe should be plunged into war. Germany remained an excellent buyer of South African wool, wattle bark and other farm produce, while there seemed no limit to its appetite for manganese and other minerals used for armaments. The union's mines received big orders, and a barter agreement with Berlin was due for renewal, under which wool and other produce were supplied in return for German railway material and other finished articles.

Behind the scenes some objections were made to the closeness of relations with Germany, but on the surface it was a fairly united government (formed by a fusion of the former parties led by generals Hertzog and Smuts) which prepared for the general election of May 18, 1938. On the other hand the Nationalists, led by Dr. D. F. Malan, complained about the excessive attachment of the government to the British commonwealth, while, at the other extreme the Dominion party, led by Col. C. F. Stallard, protested at what it regarded as the placating of anti-British feeling. Much was made of the action taken by Gen. Hertzog in objecting to the anti-German sentiments expressed by certain South African newspapers. There was a stinging exchange of views between him and several outspoken editors.

The election itself was fought with vigour by both sides. The Nationalists considerably damaged their case by publishing a poster purporting to show the results of the government's alleged "colour policy." Partly as a result of this and partly because of the country's economic progress, the government won a resounding victory and returned to power with a strong working majority, the figures being: United party (government) 111; Nationalists 27; Dominion party 8; Labour party 3; others 1.

Despite this there were certain indications that there might be political trouble before long. Events in Europe in 1938 caused deep anxiety in the union. The nightmare of war loomed near. In Pretoria preparations began at defense headquarters and elsewhere to meet the possibility.

Meanwhile an event of the greatest interest to all South Africans, irrespective of their politics, had fallen due. This was the celebration of the 100th anniversary of the Great Trek, on Dec. 16, 1938. The leaders of all political parties participated in the commemoration. The Voortrekker (pioneer) memorial was designed to crown a hill and thus to be visible for miles around. The commemorative ceremony, in conformity with Afrikaans tradition, was chiefly of a religious character. One of its accompaniments was the foundation of a movement of self-help known as Reddingsdaad (act of rescue) fathered by a highly respected Afrikaans pastor, the Rev. J. D. Kestell. Another movement originating at the same time claimed to be a nonpolitical attempt to unite all sections of the white populace as true South Africans. It called itself the Ossewabrandwag (ox-wagon sentries) or, briefly, the O.B.

As Europe staggered from crisis to crisis, the local nazis paraded and demonstrated not only in Windhoek, capital of the former German colony of South-West Africa, but also in the union, particularly in various German settlements diligently visited by various German consuls. The course of South African politics received the closest attention in Berlin. On Sept. 2, 1939, South Africa received notification from London that the British would fight. It was left to the South Africans, with their free dominion status, to decide for themselves what they would do. The British government awaited the union's answer.

Constitutional Struggle.—After Great Britain had declared war on Germany there followed one of the greatest and most important constitutional struggles on record in South Africa. Gen. Hertzog, as prime minister, decided that it was in the best interests of South Africa to remain neutral. He cited the discussions which had taken place at the time of Munich, interpreting them to mean that South Africa would in no circumstances agree to fight the Germans unless it were invaded. Gen. Smuts, as deputy prime minister, opposed this view. He pleaded that the union's name would be besmirched if it stood aside. The cabinet passed through an internal struggle. Then the matter came before parliament, and Gen. Hertzog's neutrality motion was rejected by 80 votes to 67. On Sept. 5, Gen. Hertzog tendered his resignation and the governor general (Sir Patrick Duncan) called on Gen. Smuts to form a new cabinet. On Sept. 6, the union was at war with Germany.

The government's war policy was announced by Gen. Smuts a few weeks later. He said that the question indirectly raised by the neutrality issue was whether South Africa was to stand with its trusted friends in the British commonwealth or go the other way and make friends with Germany.

Recruiting started, and the small active citizen force grew rapidly. The most mobile section of the union's defenses, the air force, started the patrol of coastal waters and before long had intercepted a number of axis vessels. Within a short time other mobilization signs became noticeable. The censorship of foreign correspondence began and grew steadily more effective as the war proceeded. Simultaneously a South African navy was formed. Simonstown, famous Africa station of the royal navy, became a most important base. South Africa realized how near the war was when at the end of 1939 the tanker "Africa Shell" was sunk off the coast of Mozambique by the "Graf von Spee."

The year 1940 began quietly. Members of the parliamentary opposition made jokes about the Allies' lack of initiative. After the fall of Holland (May 1940), a stream of propaganda was loosened on the union, through the German short-wave station at Zeesen. It was systematically fed with information gathered with extraordinary speed in South Africa, transmitted to neutral Lourenço Marques, distorted by the German propaganda offices and returned through the ether. Realizing the effectiveness of reaching the people on the farms and in the backveld generally, Berlin's ministry of propaganda engaged several Afrikaans-speaking men and women to address the Afrikanders in their own language. The broadcasts had a sufficient element of truth to make fantastic stories credible. The union government, having established a bureau of information, started energetic countermeasures; and a careful record was kept of everything transmitted by the axis. Gen. Smuts showed a patience with the disloyal element in the union which sometimes distressed certain of his supporters. He allowed speeches to be delivered which in other countries would have brought the speakers into prison for sedition or even high treason. Nor did he in any way interfere with freedom of speech among members of the parliamentary opposition. Soon, however, the wisdom of this policy became manifest. Violent differences developed between the antiwar factions. Gen. Hertzog fell out with his own former supporters and retired to his farm, where he died in Nov. 1942. To the end he protested against the increasing bitterness of their racialism.

The remaining opposition leaders likewise fell out. Oswald Pirow, minister of defense in the Hertzog cabinet, proclaimed himself a supporter of the totalitarian principle being applied to South Africa. He founded an organization called the "New Order," which aimed at abolishing party government as then known and the building up of a corporate state. His aims were not dissimilar to those proclaimed by the Ossewabrandwag, which abandoned any moderation it had shown at the outset and which ranged itself behind the former administrator of the Orange Free State, Dr. J. F. van Rensburg. The O.B. became organized on a military pattern. Van Rensburg was its commandant-general and there was a hierarchy of lesser officers all working for the overthrow of the administration. Parallel with these were the Greyshirts, whose uniform was copied from the nazis, but they were less numerous than the O.B. Malan's own followers dissociated themselves from these groups and from a number of smaller

Prime Minister Jan Christiaan Smuts of South Africa delivering an address to the British parliament during his visit to England in Oct. 1942. At his immediate left is Winston Churchill

movements such as the *Boerenasie* under the former Boer War leader and rebel, Gen. Manie Maritz. Gen. Smuts who, in addition to being premier, was also minister of defense, listened patiently to the clamour. All he did at the start was to cause all rifles to be bought up by the government for adequate compensation, to forbid the wearing of uniforms and the holding of parades without authority, and to intern a limited number of the worst hotheads. More drastic measures were taken with Germans. Internment camps were opened at Baviaanspoort and elsewhere for local nazis and others in South-West Africa. Several thousands spent the war behind barbed wire at Andalusia and elsewhere, while Italians were concentrated near the former Orange Free State diamond mines.

South Africa's War Effort.—Not far from Pretoria on the property of the Premier diamond mine, which had produced the famous Cullinan stone, another kind of camp came into being. It was known as Zonderwater and here, during 1940, South Africa's expeditionary force assembled. In cantonments which spread across the veld, thousands of men were trained. Gen. Smuts decided that the union would not have conscription. Recruiting posters and propaganda were substituted for compulsion. The call went out for women as well as for men, and the response was splendid. Although the European population was barely 2,250,000, some 200,000 joined the forces. In addition, 102,000 non-Europeans—natives, Cape Coloured, Indians and Malays—joined up. For reasons of policy, it was decided not to arm the non-European troops but, instead, they were trained in non-combatant duties, particularly as drivers and medical orderlies. One out of every three white men in the union between 20 and 60 years of age came forward voluntarily for full time duty—190,000 out of 570,000. Simultaneously, the union government decided to expand the country's industry to meet war needs. Iscor works at Pretoria were turned over to the manufacture of steel for munitions. Work began on the design and manufacture of light artillery shells, parts for tanks and for thousands of other items necessary for war. Dr. H. J. van Der Bijl, chairman of Iscor, took over the post of first director-general of war supplies and then director of supplies.

New war factories grew up in lonely places and near busy cities. Not only was the union to a large degree meeting its own needs for civilian and military goods, but it was exporting on a large scale to most parts of southern Africa and even overseas. It was doing ship repairs on a large scale. As the normal sources of imports from overseas were cut off, South Africa turned to its own plants or sought new suppliers. South America, particularly the Argentine and Brazil, became vitally important as furnishers of textiles.

South Africa's first armies reached East Africa in 1940 and went into training at Gilgil and elsewhere in the hills. Before 1940 ended the first important action had been fought at Elwak on the borders of Kenya and Italian territory. It was a small affair, yet it would always be remembered in South African history, for it marked the start of the downfall of fascism on the African continent. Into Kismayu, through the sands of Somaliland, into the hills of Ethiopia and on to its capital Addis Ababa, troops of the union fought their way—particularly the steel commandos as they were called. The skill of the Afrikanders in their armoured cars recalled that of the horse commandos of the Boer war.

Yet another role came to South Africa during the war. With Rhodesia it now provided training grounds and training centres for thousands of British airmen. Schools under the Empire scheme were established, and soon they became known wherever royal air force men flew—Lyttelton, Oudtshoorn, Queenstown, Vereeniging, Potchefstrom and many more. From there fliers returned to participate in Britain's defense against the luftwaffe and later in bombing Italy and Germany into submission. With their R.A.F. comrades, the South African air force trained and fought—first in Ethiopia, then in North Africa and beyond.

By the middle of 1941 the Ethiopian campaign (save for the last stronghold at Gondar) was over. Tragic moments followed in the western desert—the bloody field of Sidi Rezegh in November and December 1941 and then, after half a year of seesaw warfare, to and fro along the north African shore, the calamity of the second siege of

Happy to be home, troops of South Africa's first division paraded through Capetown in 1943. These troops helped break German defenses at El Alamein in Oct. 1942

Tobruk. After the valorous earlier stand, it came to pass that nearly 10,000 of the best troops from the union were captured by the Germans. Yet under the inspiration of Gen. Dan Pienaar, the finest soldier South Africa produced in World War II (destined to lose his life in an air crash in the very hour of victory), the South Africans continued to fight from El Alamein to Tripoli and Algiers.

As 1942 advanced the number of ships sunk around the union became appalling. Blackouts on the coast were enforced rigidly and even inland centres such as Johannesburg organized civilian protective services to handle air raid precautions. Japan's men-of-war and secret agents were coming ever nearer in the Indian ocean. Vichy was now almost entirely pro-German. Madagascar, that huge French island colony, was only a few hours flying distance from Durban on the mainland of the union. Already the union's naval and air forces had prevented a convoy of French ships loaded with rubber and other products from reaching German-held Europe. That was in Nov. 1941. Now more drastic measures were demanded. Secretly the union helped in preparing for the occupation of Madagascar. Not only did South Africa furnish war matériel, but men, ships and aircraft were all there in May 1942, when the Allied forces (themselves under South African-born Rear-Admiral Neville Syfret) descended upon Diégo Suarez and other Madagascar ports, thereby ending the threat of a Japanese landing. In the middle east, meanwhile, teams of South African engineers and miners from the gold fields built railways and drove tunnels designed to link up the Allies more effectively with Turkey and Russia. South Africans were in Syria and in Persia where they did brilliant work.

In 1943 the life of the pre-war parliament ended. Without the slightest hesitation Gen. Smuts decided to let a general election take place as usual. Despite the bitterness shown by the opposition (one of their posters showed the prime minister as a devil with horns and a tail) the result was another resounding victory. The government side, which since the beginning of the war had included the Labour and the Dominion parties, obtained 107 seats against 43 for Dr. Malan's Nationalists.

There arose the question of whether the original "anywhere in Africa" oath taken by all men willing to serve "up north," and symbolized by the orange flash on their shoulder straps, should be extended to cover service in the new theatre of war—Europe. Legislation was introduced and, after a full debate, passed by parliament. The troops were given the choice of serving in Africa or overseas. With negligible exceptions, the mass of the army, navy and air force agreed to carry on overseas. The South African air force and the 6th South African armoured division moved forward with the Allied forces in Italy. When Mussolini's Italy collapsed in the middle of 1943. thousands of South Africans were set free from prison camps only to be recaptured by the Germans. Hundreds escaped into Switzerland and hundreds more received shelter from their former Italian enemies. In the union itself, near Pretoria, sat 80,000 Italian prisoners wondering about their fate.

Now the union government saw peace ahead and new problems approaching. It set up a directorate of demobilization to prepare for the return of the men. Elaborate facilities for technical training, hitherto earmarked for war, were to serve the needs of the homecoming troops. Gen. George Brink was placed in charge. The war machine, however, ran on at high pressure. Munition and war factories, many of them located in places like Kimberley, which had little previous experience of manufacturing industry, employed more than 60,000 men and women. They turned out hundreds of millions of rounds of ammunition, thousands of pieces of light ordnance, vast tonnages of armour plate, tens of thousands of vehicles and millions of pairs of boots. As far afield as Burma, products of the union's war industry were used. Lend-lease material from the United States came in a steady stream to supplement local production.

After V-J day, South African war prisoners came back from Europe, soldiers were demobilized and thousands of girls returned from the army and navy to the offices and kitchens. Various home defense units, such as the national volunteer brigade and the mines engineering brigade, were allowed to stand down. (Civilian guards for the time being continued to supplement the efforts of the police.) Gen. Smuts travelled backward and forward between South Africa and Europe, now meeting parliament, now in conference with statesmen in Downing street and elsewhere, to help in planning peace.

Postwar Problems.—Endless problems awaited solution—in many of which South Africa was vitally concerned. There was the future of Italian East Africa, the re-employment of soldiers, the shortage of housing, the repatriation of local nazis, and the weeding out of undesirables in South-West Africa. There was a mass of racial problems—particularly those concerning natives and Indians. The position of the Indians in Natal, especially, demanded urgent attention. Tens of millions of pounds had to be repaid to the U.S. under lend-lease, while the country itself had a war debt of around £400,000,000.

The government did not hesitate to tackle these problems. It set up organizations to deal with housing which had fallen far into arrear. It started a huge program of soil reclamation and irrigation, followed in Aug. 1946 by Gen. Smuts's announcement that immigration would be welcomed. World War II had not proved solely a matter of losses. Despite thousands of casualties and a legacy of hate, the world had learned to regard South Africa as a nation. Its prime minister had played a vital part in writing the charter of the United Nations at San Francisco in 1945. The opposition had agreed to support that body as it also accepted participation in the international bank planned at Bretton Woods. (E. Ros.)

BIBLIOGRAPHY.—H. C. Armstrong, *Grey Steel: J. C. Smuts* (1937); O. W. A. Hoops, *Der Status der Südafrikanischen Union* (1937); P. Nielsen, *The Colour Bar* (1937); H. R. Abercrombie, *Africa's Peril: The Colour Problem* (1938); W. A. Webster, *Real Union in South Africa: A Record and a Plea* (Cape Town, 1938); R. F. A. Hoernle, *South African Native Policy and the Liberal Spirit* (1939); G. H. Calpin, *There Are No South Africans* (1941); C. W. De Kiewiet, *A History of South Africa* (1941); J. C. Smuts, *Plans for a Better World* (1942); J. Mockford, *South Africa Today* (1944); L. Sowden, *South African Union* (1944).

Union of South Africa: *Statistical Data*

Item	1938 Value (000's omitted)	1938 Amount or Number	1944 Value (000's omitted)	1944 Amount or Number
Exchange rate				
Great Britain		£SA 1.011 = £1		
United States		£SA 1 = $4.841		£SA 1 = $3.98
Finance				
Government revenues	£43,188 ($211,146)		£60,233 ($243,039)*	
Government expenditures	£38,903 ($190,196)		£73,001 ($294,561)*	
Gold reserves	£44,999 ($220,000)		...	
National debt	£260,072 ($1,271,491)		£375,927 ($1,516,867)*	
Transportation				
Railroads		12,083 mi.		
Highways		85,428 "		
Airways		6,311 "		
Communication				
Telephones		175,711		232,950
Telegraph lines		...		17,189 mi.
Radio sets		189,321		...
Minerals				
Gold		12,161,392 oz.		14,046,502 oz.†
Coal		17,536,230 tons		18,934,005 tons†
Diamonds		1,238,608 carats		543,463 carats†
Crops				
Sugar cane		4,080,935 tons		
Corn		1,924,731 "		
Wheat		321,693 "		
Forest products				
Bark (extract)		32,488 tons		
Bark (wattle)		72,417 "		
Livestock				
Sheep		39,117,797		
Cattle		11,613,980		
Goats		6,213,084		
Sea products				
Fish		35,876 tons		
Crawfish		9,994 "		
Whale oil (export only)		1,337,281 gal.		
Manufactures—total	£75,234 ($367,819)	...	£126,237 ($509,368)*	...
Metal	£15,834 ($77,412)	...	£32,335 ($130,473)*	...
Food, beverage, tobacco	£14,312 ($69,973)	...	£22,910 ($92,443)*	...
Building and construction	£7,424 ($36,298)	...	£8,804 ($35,525)*	...
Exports—total	$29,268 ($143,090)	...	£23,158 ($93,442)	...
Textile materials and manufactures	£9,613 ($46,996)	...	£5,512 ($22,240)	...
Fruits and nuts	£3,262 ($15,948)	...	£1,660 ($6,699)	...
Food, beverage and tobacco	£2,807 ($13,724)	...	£8,143 ($32,858)	...
Jewellery, diamonds and precious metals	£2,750 ($13,520)	...	£7,644 ($30,845)	...
Imports—total	£94,685 ($462,917)	...	£83,669 ($337,604)	...
Vehicles	$14,580 ($71,281)	...	£1,018 ($4,109)	...
Textiles	£10,691 ($52,269)	...	£24,273 ($97,940)	...
Machinery (except electrical)	£9,916 ($48,477)	...	£2,325 ($9,382)	...
Defense				
Standing army personnel		17,422		...
Reserves		31,157		...
Military expenditures	£2,120 ($10,366)		£3,161 ($12,108)†	
Education				
State and state-aided primary and secondary schools				
European schools		4,278		3,622‡
Students		386,880		388,925‡
Non-European schools		5,001		5,229‡
Students		589,308		678,161‡
University students		9,492		11,801‡

*1942. †1940. ‡1941.

South America

See ARGENTINA; BOLIVIA; BRAZIL; BRITISH GUIANA; CHILE; COLOMBIA; ECUADOR; PARAGUAY; PERU; URUGUAY; VENEZUELA.

South Australia

South Australia was proclaimed a state of the commonwealth of Australia on Dec. 28, 1836. Area: 380,071 sq.mi.; pop.: (1937 est.) 591,201; (1946 census) 635,400. Chief towns (pop. 1945 est.): Adelaide (cap., 370,000), Port Pirie (12,000), Whyalla (8,000). Governors: Major Gen. Sir Winston Dugan (March 26, 1934–39); Sir Malcolm Buclay-Harvey (March 2, 1939–44); Lt. Gen. Sir Charles Willougby Moke Norris (after Dec. 19, 1944). Prime ministers: Sir Richard Butler (April 18, 1933–Nov. 5, 1938); Thomas Playford (after Nov. 5, 1938).

In ten years, the economic structure of South Australia changed so drastically that the state no longer could be regarded solely as agricultural and pastoral, depending on primary industries. The introduction of vast new undertakings (hastened during World War II) and the expansion of existing secondary industries, some centred in country areas, made it semi-industrial and created a more balanced economy. Wheat farmers abandoned doubtful holdings in areas where regular rainfall was not assured (more than 80% of the state has an annual rainfall of less than 10 in.).

More than 80 new industries, including a number from Great Britain, started in the first eight months of 1946 alone.

Foremost in the industrial expansion was the further exploitation of the great iron ore deposits at Iron Knob, 33 mi. inland from the port of Whyalla on the western side of Spencer's gulf. Iron Knob's expansion automatically led to the growth of Whyalla, where heavy industries were established, including a blast furnace and shipbuilding yards.

Jan. 4, 1937, marked the beginning by a liberal government of an experiment in socialist planning that attracted worldwide interest. A state housing trust was created primarily to build modern, permanent homes for renting to workers of the lower income group. It was a success. More than 3,000 of these homes were erected, and more were being built. The trust extended its activities later to build large modern homes for sale on easy terms, principally to returned servicemen. Also in 1937 a reservoir at Mt. Bold, with a capacity of 6,662,400,000 gal. (practically doubling the water storage for the metropolitan area) was completed. It was officially opened in 1938. The size of the state parliament was reduced from 46 members, representing 19 districts to 39 members from single electorates.

State elections were held in 1938, and a Liberal and Country league administration was returned under the leadership of Thomas Playford, who proved a leader of outstanding driving force and administrative ability and a man with marked foresight. Returned again in 1941 and 1944, with a reduced majority, Playford established a record for continuous office.

With the beginning of World War II, the state was mobilized promptly on a war footing. In the years 1940 and 1941, army and air force training camps were established, thousands of men and women entered the services, and civil defense sections were organized. There was great industrial expansion, the extensive motor-body-building plants were turned over to war production, railway workshops produced armaments and aeroplane components, and other industries changed to war output. Three large munition factories were built. One became the largest in the southern hemisphere, covering an area of more than 16 sq.mi. As part of the war effort at home, the government prohibited horse racing and betting within the state. Linked with the establishment of heavy industries, the most dramatic development in the industrial history of the state came with the reawakening of interest in the old Leigh Creek coalfield, 380 mi. north of Adelaide. After a detailed survey in 1940, revealing deposits of more than 400,000,000 short tons, drillings were made in 1941 and later, production was started by open cut methods.

South Australia: *Statistical Data*

Item	1938		1941		1945	
	Value (000's omitted)	Amount or Number	Value (000's omitted)	Amount or Number	Value (000's omitted)	Amount or Number
Exchange Rate						
Great Britain		£A 1.25=£1		£A 1.25=£1		£A 1.25=£1
U.S.		£A 1=$3.895		£A 1=$3.198		£A 1=$3.198
Finance						
State revenues	£9,928 ($48,536)*		£9,752 ($39,319)*		£12,348 ($49,761)*	
State expenditures	£9,826 ($48,041)*		£10,317 ($41,600)*		£12,786 ($51,529)*	
State debt	£85,604 ($418,518)*		£87,072 ($351,076)*		£86,323 ($347,882)*	
Transportation						
Railroads		2,555 mi.		2,557 mi.		2,547 mi.
Highways		23,259 "		25,008 " †		...
Communication						
Telephones		57,630		64,821		71,710
Telegraph lines		14,961 mi.*		14,740 mi.*†		14,496 mi.*
Radio sets		117,091*‡		130,895*		146,392*
Minerals						
Ironstone and ore		2,245,366 tons		...		2,182,831 tons§
Salt		74,812 "		...		184,312 " §
Gypsum		146,590 "		...		39,523 " §
Crops						
Wheat		1,302,852 tons		535,680 tons		620,714 tons‖
Hay		687,312 "		394,274 "		407,078 " ‖
Barley		207,529 "		114,624 "		121,382 " ‖
Raisins		16,609 "		15,517 "		20,739 " ‖
Oranges		802,255 bu.		754,070 bu.†		670,273 bu. ‖
Livestock						
Sheep		9,936,586		10,245,894		8,473,939¶
Cattle		318,897		399,143		391,323¶
Horses		195,834		171,092		133,003¶
Swine		71,292		190,068†		160,875¶
Sea products						
Fish		4,480		...		2,293 tons§
Crayfish		22,000 doz.		...		17,200 doz.§
Manufactures						
Total	£9,704 ($43,038)‡	...	£18,610 ($75,092)♀	...	£21,714 ($87,616)‖	...
Industrial metals, machines, implements, etc.	£4,397 ($19,500)‡	...	£9,157 ($36,950)♀	...	£9,884 ($39,882)‖	...
Food, drink and tobacco	£2,013 ($8,926)‡	...	£2,493 ($10,061)♀	...	£3,226 ($13,016)‖	...
Paper, printing and binding	£591 ($2,619)‡	...	£587 ($2,370)♀	...	£743 ($3,000)‖	...
Clothing	£535 ($2,371)‡	...	£927 ($3,742)♀	...	£994 ($4,010)‖	...
Education						
State schools		1,061		989		880§
Enrolment		78,845		72,156		69,257§
Teachers		3,050		3,078		2,734§
Private schools		162		157		151§
Enrolment		13,218		13,502		14,910§
Teachers		872		831		818§
Universities		1		1♀		1‖
Enrolment		2,307		2,003♀		2,756‖
Teachers		174		227♀		245‖
Technical schools		17		17		...
Enrolment		9,610		10,518		...
Teachers		296		307		...

*Year ending June 30. †1940. ‡1939. §1943. ‖1944. ¶Year ending March 31. ♀1942.

Installation of grading and steam drying plants was undertaken to raise the calorific value of the coal. Production from the field rose rapidly. But in 1945–46, when supplies of high-grade coal from New South Wales coalfields broke down, production from Leigh Creek was not sufficient (and in many industries boilers had not been converted for the lower grade state-produced coal) to avoid serious stoppages in industry and transport.

Late 1943 and early 1944 saw the completion and opening of the Morgan-Whyalla pipeline, an ambitious project taking water from the River Murray 223 mi. overland to Whyalla. Previously, Whyalla had relied on water carried by ship from New South Wales and on surface supplies. The new project cost nearly £A3,450,000 and was officially opened on March 31, 1944.

On April 29, 1944, the state elections were made compulsory for the first time. Playford's government was returned with a majority of one. The standing of the parties was: Liberal and Country league, 20; Labour, 16; Independents, 3.

Projects were started in 1945 for the settlement of returned servicemen on agricultural and pastoral lands and on blocks in irrigation settlements along the River Murray. The government scheme envisaged the preparation of holdings to a state of productivity before settling the soldier. Development of state timber forests in the southeast was pushed ahead, and in 1946 preliminary arrangements were completed for the building of a new deep sea port at Robe to serve the rapidly expanding district.

An important step in 1946 was the acquisition by the state government of the Adelaide Electric Supply company, which for many years supplied the power for the metropolitan area and part of the country. A state board was appointed to administer electricity supplies in the future and to arrange for extension of supplies to more country districts.

Late in 1946, South Australia jumped into world prominence when it was announced that the British and Australian governments had combined to establish an experimental range for guided projectiles at Mt. Elba. Initial development was to be up to 300 mi. missiles but it was planned to have a 3,000 mi. range later directed northwest toward the Christmas Islands in the Indian ocean. Projectiles were to be controlled by radar from point of fire to destination. The total cost of the project was estimated at $18,000,000 and there would be an annual expenditure for maintenance and equipment of about $19,000,000. South Australia was considered to have the only suitable area in the British empire for this type of experimental work. (M. W. Js.)

Bibliography.—*Annual Pocket Year Book* and *Annual Statistical Register* (Adelaide).

South Carolina

A south Atlantic state of the United States, South Carolina was eighth of the original 13 to ratify the constitution, in 1788; popularly known as the "Palmetto state." Area, 31,055 sq.mi., including 461 sq.mi. of inland water. Population (1940) 1,899,804, including 1,084,308 white; 814,164 Negro; 1,332 others; 75% rural; 24.5% urban; 0.3% foreign-born. Capital, Columbia (62,396). Other cities: Charleston (71,275); Greenville (34,734); Spartanburg (32,249). The bureau of census estimated the population of the state, July 1, 1944, at 1,923,354.

Extensive strikes in 1935-36 caused a conservative reaction. Support of Franklin Delano Roosevelt's policies continued to be overwhelming, although many senators and the state bar association condemned the proposed change in the supreme court. Gov. Olin D. Johnston's hostility to the highway department continued in 1937, characterized by his charges of political domination by the department. The governor's demand for removal of Chief Highway Commissioner Ben M. Sawyer was answered by the new commission's electing Sawyer for his fourth consecutive four-year term. While Gov. Johnston roused much feeling against the commission (having in 1935 seized their offices by military force, until restrained by the supreme court), conservatives highly valued the commission's services.

Labour troubles diminished during 1938. President Roosevelt's attempt to defeat Senator E. D. Smith with Governor O. D. Johnston resulted in Smith's overwhelming re-election for a sixth term in 1938. As a result, fewer than 500 Republicans voted in the 1938 general election. The senatorial race was not inspiring, Smith strongly playing up the race issue, and Governor Johnston the friendship of the President. John L. Lewis's opposition doubtless helped more than it hurt Smith. The governor's race in 1938 presented several unusually good candidates, of whom Mayor Burnet R. Maybank of Charleston was chosen over Wyndham M. Manning (son of Governor R. I. Manning of 1915-19) by a majority less than his large vote in Charleston. A house vote of 50 to 44 for repealing the constitutional prohibition of divorce fell below the required two-thirds for submitting amendments to the people. A senate vote for refusing marriage licences to "socially diseased" persons, and requiring a five-day interval between licence and marriage was not concurred in by the house. The general property tax for state purposes was eliminated by veto. A teachers' pension bill failed, and a popular referendum overwhelmingly defeated a constitutional amendment pensioning judges at 70.

Late in 1939, bands labelled K.K.K. in several upcountry counties occasionally committed violence against racial or political opponents or supposedly immoral persons. Vigorous investigation and early arrests resulted. The 1939 legislative session (Jan. 9 to July 1) was the longest on record for the state, because of squabbles over revenue measures, and the continued growth of local legislation of no more general concern than a town ordinance.

Governor Maybank continued, in 1940, to urge state police to supplement antiquated local law enforcement, diversion of part of an abundant road support from gasoline tax to general purposes in order to avoid increasing general taxes and a constitutional convention to modernize the constitution especially as to taxation. A few K.K.K. parades and whippings brought several prosecutions. The state voted 95% Democratic in the 1940 national election, giving Roosevelt 95,470 votes and Wendell Willkie 4,360. The people voted for biennial (instead of annual) legislative sessions and for prohibition. Large army training camps were located at Columbia and Spartanburg. A coastal hurricane of Aug. 11 killed 35 or 40 persons and wrecked about $3,000,000 worth of property.

Governor Maybank, though twice defeated by the courts, continued in 1941 to seek a means of diverting part of the gasoline tax from roads to general purposes. A probation and parole board was created, but could not be given control of pardons, as the governor desired, without constitutional change. Horse-race betting was legalized in several low-country "resort counties." Biennial sessions, twice popularly voted, again stranded on details. Prohibition, heavily voted, was enacted and provided that new revenues be found to replace the $3,000,000 from state liquor taxes by July 1, 1942. Legislation for regulating loan sharks again failed. Several Ku Klux Klansmen were sentenced to prison for masked parades or whippings. Governor Maybank was elected U.S. senator to succeed James F. Byrnes, who was appointed to the U.S. supreme court. Maybank was succeeded by J. E. Harley, lieutenant governor, Nov. 4, 1941.

Governor Harley died Feb. 27, 1942; he was succeeded for the rest of 1942 by senate president R. M. Jefferies. The 1941 law enacting prohibition if the 1942 legislature provided taxes fully replacing liquor revenues lapsed because of no action. Other defiances of heavy referendums for prohibition were manifested by the legislature and by the state Democratic convention's refusal to endorse them, though Governor-elect Olin D. Johnston (elected Nov. 3, 1942) strongly supported prohibition. Extension of the parole system, slum clearance, low-cost housing (especially for war workers) and, in two counties, old-age teacher pensions were enacted. Farmers of the state voted 91% for continued cotton acreage control. The $57,000,000 federally financed Santee-Cooper navigation and power plant began operation Jan. 31, 1942, and by December was producing 2,000,000 kw.hr. a day, exceeding its planned annual 700,000,000 kw.hr.

The legislature in 1943 extended state support for schools from eight months to nine; raised teachers' salaries (which any district might supplement) 15%; assumed practically the entire expense for bus transportation of pupils; appropriated $186,000 for school lunches; raised state employees' pay 10%; voted $50,000 for postwar planning; appropriated $6,800,000 to reduce state debt; eliminated primary election laws for fear of federal action on the rule excluding Negroes from the Democratic party, thus leaving primary regulations to private party action; passed a law requiring physically fit males between the ages of 16 and 60 to work or fight; discontinued the low state tax on general property. In addition, the governor vetoed a marriage protection act and the legislature defeated an effort to permit the $57,000,000 Santee-Cooper hydro-electric authority to buy two large companies for $40,000,000, fearing politico-economic monopoly power. A suit to compel equal pay for white and Negro teachers brought no results.

The total state appropriations in 1943 were $18,161,555, largest in the state's history. Highway gasoline revenues, however, fell to about half. Farm wages were the highest in 20 years. The only one of the penal officials charged with corruption so far tried was acquitted, though bad conditions were undoubted. A sheriff was sent to jail for 60 days for depriving a prisoner of federal constitutional rights. The 250 Catawba Indians were by agreement with the U.S. provided at joint expense with more lands, schools and direct support, admitted to citizenship and transferred to federal supervision. The state supreme court ruled that Methodists refusing membership in the reunited church might use the name Methodist Church South, but not any of its property.

Olin D. Johnston, serving his second, though not consecutive, term as governor, was elected in Nov. 1944, to the U.S. senate over the incumbent Ellison D. Smith, who died at the age of 80 on Nov. 17, 1944. Following the legislature's repeal of all primary election laws, a resolution was passed asserting devotion to white supremacy. The rejection of Negro applicants for membership in the Democratic party led to the formation of the Progressive Democrats by pro-Roosevelt Negroes. The regular Democratic electors for president received 90,601 votes (perhaps 3,500 of which were from the Negro Progressive Democrats); Southern Democratic electors (white anti-New Dealers favouring Harry F. Byrd for president) 7,799; Republican electors 4,610 (perhaps 1,300 being from bolting white Democrats); Prohibitionist electors 365. A proposal by the council for Columbia to buy for $39,500,000 gas and electric utilities serving that and some other localities was dropped because of public opposition.

Ransome J. Williams became governor on Olin D. Johnston's resignation Jan. 2, 1945, to become senator. Gov. Williams urged that criminal laws be better enforced. The sheriff's association agreed and severely criticized liberal pardons. Legislative efforts were ineffectively made for constitutional revision of the pardoning power. A resolution for referring to popular vote the removal of the constitutional prohibition of divorce failed, lacking the necessary two-thirds. An extensive alumina plant began operations in July; large hydro-electric expansion occurred; and a $12,000,000 box factory and a $10,000,000 Celanese plant were announced. A few protracted strikes in textile occurred. The National Council of Negro Democrats, meeting in Columbia and sponsored by Carolina Negro Democrats with representatives from several states, urged a systematic campaign for making Negroes politically conscious as being necessary for securing recognition in the south. From Nov. 1, 1940, through June 30, 1945, accession to U.S. army personnel from the state totalled 119,000 men and 1,886 women. Total accessions to the navy were not available; but those in service at the close of World War II totalled 45,827 men and 1,065

South Carolina: *Statistical Data*

Table I.—*Education (Public)*

	1938	1941	1942	1943	1944	1945
Elementary school pupils	412,587	397,950	379,853	372,466	364,639	358,777
High school pupils	76,162	86,800	95,357	92,986	89,345	91,451
Elementary teachers	11,240		8,187	11,498	11,492	11,411
High school teachers	3,069		4,653	3,678	3,589	3,678

Table II.—*Public Welfare*
(Money figures in thousands of dollars)

	1937	1938	1939	1940	1941
Cases on general relief	1,043	2,811	2,832	2,185	2,261
Cost of general relief	$12	$27	$28	$20	$19
Recipients of old-age pensions		23,160		19,796	17,683
Dependent children receiving aid		12,036		8,943	10,992
Blind receiving aid		862		794	801
Workers under unemployment compensation		192,258	201,705	206,200	

Table III.—*Communications*
(Money figures in thousands of dollars)

	1937	1938	1939	1940	1943	1944
Highway mileage		7,516	8,538			
Expenditures on highways	$19,630	$22,557	$17,691	$22,804		
Railroad mileage	3,543	3,502	3,486		3,563	3,563

Table IV.—*Banking and Finance*
(Money figures in thousands of dollars)

	1937	1938	1940	1942	1944	1945
State revenue	$36,341	$39,396	$66,198	$40,273	$43,987	$45,280
State expenditure	32,857	43,552				
Number of banks	151	150	152			
Total deposits	$141,900	$127,000	$154,500	$227,398		
Number of national banks	20	20	21	22	22	22
Deposits of national banks	$76,803	$76,860	$126,108	$155,688	$268,108	$339,170

Table V.—*Manufacturing*
(Money figures in thousands of dollars)

	1937	1939	1942	1943	1944	1945
Wage earners	129,748	126,983	167,331	167,718	161,122	154,384
Wages paid	$91,792	$86,616	$166,307	$208,195		
Value of products	$409,912	$397,513	$855,676	1,062,403	$1,093,101	$1,106,913

South Carolina: *Statistical Data (continued)*

Table VI.—*Agriculture*
(All figures in thousands)

	1937	1939	1940	1942	1944	1945
Acreage, principal crops.	5,223	5,088	5,124	4,897		4,416
Leading crops (bu.):						
Corn.	24,945	25,433	24,304	21,330	24,160	23,414
Cotton (bales)	1,023	871	970	699	864	675
Hay (tons)	501	541	539	550	410	508
Oats.	8,658	11,515	10,890	13,461	15,064	16,023
Peaches	1,080	1,636	2,158	3,500	2,460	5,760
Potatoes, sweet . . .	5,130	6,834	5,040	5,890	7,056	5,890
Potatoes, white . . .	3,120	3,108	3,192	3,108	1,464	2,480
Tobacco (lb.)	108,080	133,200	82,215	96,750	132,250	139,520
Wheat.	1,416	2,415	2,688	3,377	3,653	2,912

Table VII.—*Mineral Production*
(All figures in thousands of dollars)

	1937	1938	1939	1942	1944	1945
Value of mineral production	$4,022	$4,364	$5,423	$4,574	$3,359	$3,563
Leading products (value):						
Stone.	1,463	1,316	1,733			
Clay	2,242	2,159	2,877			
Gold.	87	409	484			

women. J. Strom Thurmond was elected governor in Nov. 1946. Voting by Negroes in the Democratic primary (the effective election) was not attempted. A bill abolishing the one dollar poll tax voting qualification failed.
(D. D. W.; X.)

BIBLIOGRAPHY.—J. K. Coleman, *State Administration in South Carolina* (1935); Council of State Govts., *Book of the States* (bienn.); Clerk of the House of Representatives, *Legislative Manual and Reference Book* (ann.); Federal Writers' Program, *Our South Carolina: Today From Yesterday* (1942), *South Carolina: Guide to the Palmetto State* (1940); Secretary of State, *Report to the General Assembly* (ann.); Periodical: *Monthly Checklist of State Publications.*

South Dakota

A north central state of the United States, South Dakota was admitted as the 40th state on Nov. 2, 1889, popularly known as the "Coyote state." Area, 77,047 sq.mi., including 511 sq.mi. of water. Population (1940) 642,961, with 158,087 listed as urban and 484,874 as rural; Indian population 23,347. Capital, Pierre (4,322). Principal cities: Sioux Falls (40,832); Aberdeen (17,015); Rapid City (13,844); Huron (10,843); and Mitchell (10,633). The federal census bureau estimated the population at 558,629 on July 1, 1944.

South Dakota, normally Republican, had become wholly Democratic in 1934. At the elections of 1936, Republicans placed in office the governor, lieutenant governor, one congressman and captured both houses of the state legislature. The leading state officials at the beginning of the decade 1937-46 were: Leslie Jensen, governor; Goldie Wells, secretary of state; Donald McMurchie, lieutenant governor; Raymond A. Kelly, auditor; W. H. Hinselman, treasurer; Clair Roddewig, attorney general. The chief legislative act of 1937 was a system of old-age pensions.

In 1938 the state re-established its normal politics with a complete Republican roster of state officers: Harlan John Bushfield, governor; Donald McMurchie, lieutenant governor; Olive Ringsrud, secretary of state; W. W. Warner, auditor; Will G. Douglas, treasurer; Leo Temmey, attorney general. A constitutional amendment, enlarging the legislature, was defeated. (D. Ro.; X.)

The state legislature met in 26th regular session in 1939; measures enacted included a capital punishment law and a blood test-before-marriage bill. Three amendments to the state constitution were proposed, to be voted on at the Nov. 1940 election. In all, 300 laws were passed. Governor Bushfield, 16th governor, was inaugurated on Jan. 3, 1939.

In the general election of Nov. 5, 1940, the Republicans retained complete control of the state government and the state's two congressional seats. In the presidential vote, Wendell Willkie carried the state 177,065 to 131,362 for his largest percentage in the nation. The state officials elected in Nov. 1940, in addition to Governor Bushfield were: lieutenant governor, A. C. Miller; secretary of state, Olive A. Ringsrud; auditor, W. W. Warner; treasurer, W. G. Douglas; commissioner of schools and public lands, Earl A. Hammerquist; attorney general, Leo A. Temmey; superintendent of public instruction, John F. Hines; public utilities commissioner, C. L. Doherty; judges of supreme court, H. B. Rudolph and St. Clair Smith. All except the lieutenant governor were re-elected.

Bushfield began his second term as governor Jan. 7, 1941. The state legislature met in its 27th regular session for 60 days, passing amendatory, regulatory and routine laws necessary to the conduct of state business. Reduction of the general sales tax from 3% to 2% and modification of the state income tax met with popular approval. Of 766 bills introduced, 375 became laws. The great Rushmore memorial in the Black hills was completed by Lincoln Borglum, who carried out the design of his sculptor father, Gutzon Borglum. The number of tourists passed the 1,000,000 mark, many drawn to the state by the Rushmore project.

In addition to retaining complete control of the state administration in the election of Nov. 3, 1942, Republicans won the sole congressional seat held by Democrats. In a listless campaign, Governor Bushfield was elected to the U.S. senate over former Democratic Governor Tom Berry, who had defeated Senator W. J. Bulow in the primary election. Congressmen Francis Case and Karl Mundt won re-election handily. Nominated in convention after a four-man contest in the primary had failed to produce a Republican gubernatorial nominee, M. Q. Sharpe, former attorney general, carried the whole state ticket to victory in the November election. Republicans won 100 of 110 seats in the 1943 state legislature.

Sharpe took office Jan. 5, 1943. The legislature was in session from Jan. 5 to March 5. In addition to routine legislation, administration-backed laws were passed providing for tithes from specified departments; establishing a department of audits and accounts under a comptroller; reducing the unemployment commission to one member; and authorizing a study of compulsory education through high school. The tithing law met vigorous opposition from sportsmen and from gasoline taxpayers. An action in the state supreme court nullified the law as it applied to the highway department and permitted it to be referred. Although opponents of the law circulated petitions to refer it, the referendum was denied on the grounds of insufficient legal signers.

The legislature met in special session on July 10, 1944, to enact four measures dealing with soldier voting, education for veterans, the creation of a veterans' department of five members and the establishment of a $50,000 war veterans' fund available for loans to dependents or veterans during the period when applications for federal benefits were being adjudicated. The Republicans carried the state on Nov. 7, 1944, re-electing by a wide margin Governor Sharpe, Senator Chan Gurney and Congressmen Case and Mundt. They also won 107 out of 110 seats in the legislature. Thomas E. Dewey received 135,365 votes to 96,711 for Franklin D. Roosevelt, in the presidential election. Other state officials elected included: Sioux K. Grigsby, lieutenant governor; George T. Michelson, attorney general; Mrs. L. M. Larson, secretary of state;

E. V. Youngquist, treasurer. J. F. Hines was re-elected superintendent of public instruction without opposition on a nonpartisan ballot.

Legislative enactments during the 60-day session ending March 2, 1945, included the creation of a state conservation commission; activation of a state teachers' pension and annuity system; reduction of the ore tax from 6% to 4%; increased old-age assistance benefits; and an increase in state aid to education from $1,165,000 to $2,625,000. Hazel Dean succeeded E. V. Youngquist as state treasurer.

The Republican party won all state offices in Nov. 1946, polling 108,998 against 53,294 votes in the contest for governor. State officials elected included: George T. Mickelson, governor; Sioux K. Grigsby, lieutenant governor; Sigurd Anderson, attorney-general; Miss Annamae Riff, secretary of state; Clarence Buehler, treasurer.

(L. K. F.; H. S. S.; X.)

South Dakota: *Statistical Data*

Table I.—*Education (Public)*

	1936	1938	1941	1944	1945
Elementary school pupils	115,114	104,785	95,994	86,903	84,100
High school pupils	38,049	37,729	37,384	29,415	28,724
Elementary teachers	6,948	6,488	7,952		
High school teachers	1,622	1,779			

Table II.—*Public Welfare*
(Money figures in thousands of dollars)

	1938	1939	1940	1941	1944	1945
Cases on general relief	5,155	4,072	4,849	3,126		
Cost of general relief	$79	$54	$63	$44		
Recipients of old-age pensions	16,201		14,752	14,968	13,561	14,520
Dependent children receiving aid	4,662		4,243	3,548	3,799	4,763
Blind receiving aid	219		238	281	231	254
Workers under unemployment compensation	35,092	33,825	34,000			

Table III.—*Communications*
(Money figures in thousands of dollars)

	1937	1938	1939	1940	1942	1944
Highway mileage		6,056	6,047		6,003	5,905
Expenditures on highways	$8,121	$7,558	$6,685	$9,236	$1,740	$2,433
Railroad mileage	4,151	4,127	4,127			3,990

Table IV.—*Banking and Finance*
(Money figures in thousands of dollars)

	1937	1938	1939	1940	1944	1945
State revenue	$22,625	$24,138	$25,303	29,705	36,057	32,959
State expenditure	20,419	22,060	$15,587	26,846	33,817	27,486
Number of banks	181	175	166	165		
Total bank deposits	$86,700	$82,200	89,200	97,400		

Table V.—*Manufacturing*
(Money figures in thousands of dollars)

	1937	1939
Wage earners	4,970	5,538
Wages paid	$5,485	$6,217
Value of products	$67,276	$81,172
Leading manufactured products (value):		
Meat packing	$39,025	$48,802
Creamery butter	11,198	10,369
Poultry	1,663	4,106

Table VI.—*Agriculture*
(All figures in thousands)

	1937	1939	1940	1943	1944	1945 (est.)
Leading agricultural crops:						
Barley, bu.	20,068	24,633	30,821	35,343	28,448	33,615
Corn bu.	43,820	46,848	50,112	79,718	140,292	119,250
Hay (tons)	948	707	765	2,657	3,705	3,255
Oats, bu.	30,702	43,929	53,240	70,500	92,430	146,759
Potatoes, bu.	1,534	2,400	2,016		2,550	2,904
Sorghum, grain, bu.	582	4,072	3,544	933	2,091	962
Wheat, bu.	15,381	18,990	26,221	32,057	38,847	53,098

Table VII.—*Mineral Production*
(All figures in thousands of dollars)

	1937	1938	1939	1940	1941
Value of mineral production	$23,473	$23,583	$24,811		
Leading products (value):					
Gold	20,354	20,820	21,649	$20,533	$21,358
Stone	983	899	998		
Sand and gravel	613	627	722		

Bibliography.—Council of State Governments, *Book of the States* (bienn.); Federal Writers' program, *South Dakota Guide;* Department of Finance, *Legislative Manual* (bienn.); Planning Board, *Report, Monthly Checklist of State Publications.*

Southern Rhodesia

See Rhodesia, Southern.

South Tyrol

As a result of World War I Austria ceded to Italy the South Tyrol, which was constituted as the Italian province of Venezia Tridentina with an area of 5,250 sq.mi. and a population (1936) of 669,029. It was divided into two departments, Trento or Trient in the south (area: 2,515 sq.mi. and pop. 391,309) and Bolzano or Bozen, sometimes also called Alto-Adige or Ober-Etsch according to the chief river, in the north (area: 2,735 sq.mi. and pop. 277,720). While Trento had a predominantly Italian population—according to the census of 1910 there were 360,847 Italians and Ladins and only 13,450 Germans,—the department of Bolzano was predominantly German—in 1910 there were 215,796 Germans and only 22,500 Italians and Ladins. In spite of solemn pledges given in 1919 by the Italian government assuring a fair treatment for the compact German minority, the Austro-German population was subjected to severe persecution, perhaps the worst any minority suffered before Adolf Hitler's rise to power. The Italian government tried to Italianize completely the territory of Bolzano and north to the Brenner pass. In spite of all these efforts the Germans in South Tyrol survived and retained their language and national character and their desire to be re-united with Austria.

After World War II the Austrian government presented in Nov. 1945 a formal note to the Allies demanding the return of the German-speaking parts of South Tyrol to Austria. It pointed out the unanimous will of the population for such a return, and stressed the economic necessity and the vital importance of the territory for Austria's communications. Italy pleaded the retention of Austrian South Tyrol purely for strategic reasons, regarding the Brenner pass as a military asset of great importance. In 1946 the foreign secretaries of the great four Allied Powers decided in favour of Italy. (H. Ko.)

Bibliography.—K. Baedeker, *Tirol* (1938); I. A. Morrow, *Austrian Tyrol* (1931); N. Murdoch, *Tyrolean June* (1936); F. S. Smythe, *Over Tyrolese Hills* (London, 1936); J. Wenter, *Das Land in den Bergen* (Innsbruck, 1942).

South-West Africa

See Mandates; South Africa, The Union of.

Sovereigns

For the names of all heads of state during the decade 1937–46, *see* articles on the individual nations concerned.

Soviet Arctic Scientific Station

See Exploration, Polar.

Soviet-German Pact

See Germany; Union of Soviet Socialist Republics.

Soviet Union

See Union of Soviet Socialist Republics.

Soybeans

World production of soybeans was long confined to China and Manchuria. Since the crop grows best in the same climatic conditions as corn, it was later introduced into the Danube basin of southeastern Europe. The prewar world crop, 1935–39, was estimated at 458,300,000 bu., of which 204,444,000 bu. were grown in China, 151,204,000 bu. in Manchuria, 56,167,000 bu. in the United States, 19,303,000 bu. in Korea, 12,499,000 bu. in Japan, 9,731,000 bu. in the Dutch East Indies and about 2,400,000 bu. in Europe. Canada produced only about 207,000 bu. World production was estimated to have increased to 567,000,000 bu. by 1944, the greatest gains being in the United States and Canada, where the crop was about three times the prewar output.

The soybean was slow to find its place in United States agriculture, although it had been an important food in China for 5,000 years. Before World War I it was little known and grew in favour slowly until 1930, when it began to expand rapidly. By 1946 it was one of the ten leading U.S. crops. Soybean production had increased fortyfold within 20 years and had doubled in the decade 1937–46. When World War II began in 1939, soybeans at once became a critical war crop to supply domestic needs for vegetable oil because far eastern sources were cut off. The acreage in the United States grown for beans was increased from less than 4,000,000 ac. in 1937 to more than 10,000,000 ac. in 1943, after which there was a decline. Production in 1944–46 continued high but not quite equal to the 1943 record.

Soybeans are grown for three purposes, viz: for the beans, for the hay and to be grazed or hogged off as pasture. Until 1940, the U.S. acreage grown for hay was larger than that for beans, but the war demand stimulated greater production for the oil-bearing bean; the acreage grown for hay declined to the level of 1933. The area grown for grazing also declined but not in such a large proportion. With the development of markets for soybeans crushed for oil, the proportion grown for beans expanded. In 1939, only 40% of the acreage was harvested for beans, but by 1944 more than 72% was grown for oil. At first, the crop was grown primarily in the southeastern states for hay and grazing, and beans were gathered only for seed. It was not considered a reliable crop in the northern states, but plant breeders developed quicker-maturing varieties for the shorter northern season. By 1946 the crop was produced primarily in the corn belt states. About 80% of the total acreage was grown in five states—Ohio, Indiana, Illinois, Iowa and Missouri—during the period 1941–46. Production was still large in the lower Mississippi valley and on the Atlantic seaboard from Pennsylvania to South Carolina. The improvement of varieties of soybeans was advanced rapidly by the plant breeders until there were more than 100 varieties adapted to a wide variety of soil and climatic conditions.

The use of soybeans before 1928 was principally for seed and feed in the United States. The processing for oil and feeds began to increase rapidly in the early 1930s until the amount used by mills increased suddenly from 9,105,000 bu. in 1935 to 25,181,000 bu. in 1936, or about half the harvested crop. This change continued until, in 1943, about 74% was processed. Imports of soybeans had been small, except during World War I, when large quantities were imported from Manchuria and crushed in cottonseed oil mills in the southern states. Exports were also small, except in a few years when 2,000,000 to 4,000,000 bu. were exported, and the one year 1939, when exports amounted to 10,949,000 bu. Processing for oil and meal began in 1910, when a small quantity of Manchurian beans was imported for crushing. The number of soybean-crushing plants was small before 1930, but by 1940 they numbered about 100. Stimulated by the demand for oil and feed during World War II, the number of plants was rapidly increased in 1944 to about 140 with a capacity of about 172,000,000 bu. Mills designed to use other oilseeds were also used to crush soybeans. The domestic production of oil meal and cake increased from 724,000 tons in 1937 to 3,444,000 tons in 1944. About 90% of these products was used as livestock feed. Domestic oil production rose from 194,411,000 lb. in 1937 to 1,235,806,000 lb. in 1944.

U.S. imports of soybean oil were large in the period 1920–40. This oil was first used in soapmaking, then its adaptability led to increased consumption in cooking oils, margarine, other edible products, and as a drying oil. After domestic production increased, imports shrank to very small quantities.

Prices of soybeans to U.S. growers were steady at about 80 cents per bu. in 1937 but advanced in 1941 to $1.55 per bu. and to an annual average of $2.08 per bu. in 1944. The government stimulated production in 1942 by offering $1.55 per bu. to growers. This support price was increased to $2.04 for the 1944 and 1945 crops. The value to processors was $1.70 to $1.75 per bu., the difference being paid as a subsidy by the Commodity Credit corporation. (*See* also CHEMURGY; VEGETABLE OILS AND ANIMAL FATS.)

U.S. Soybean Production by Leading States, 1937–46
(In millions of bushels)

	1937	1939	1941	1942	1943	1944	1945	1946
Total	45.2	91.2	105.5	187.1	193.1	190.4	191.7	186.1
Illinois	27.0	46.8	49.0	66.4	70.6	71.4	74.1	72.5
Iowa	4.2	11.5	16.0	35.4	39.3	42.5	34.8	32.0
Indiana	5.7	14.4	13.8	26.3	27.0	23.1	27.9	25.8
Ohio	3.2	10.1	13.1	24.3	27.9	22.4	20.0	18.2
Missouri	.5	.9	2.1	7.0	8.6	10.6	9.4	10.3
Minnesota	—	.5	1.2	3.5	3.3	4.3	6.8	9.5
Arkansas	.5	.4	1.7	3.2	2.5	3.6	3.3	3.5
North Carolina . .	1.5	2.0	1.7	3.4	2.3	2.0	2.7	2.3
Kansas	.03	.05	.5	2.5	2.3	3.3	2.7	1.8
Michigan	.08	.9	1.4	2.1	1.5	1.5	1.9	1.5
Tennessee	.2	.2	.1	.9	.9	1.0	.9	1.3
Virginia	.3	.3	.6	1.7	1.0	.9	1.3	1.2
Kentucky	.09	.1	.5	1.0	.8	—	.8	.8
Mississippi	.4	.6	.7	2.8	1.7	1.1	.9	.8
Wisconsin	.03	.3	.5	.7	1.0	.7	.6	.4
Other States . . .	—	—	—	—	—	–	2.9	2.9

(J. C. Ms.)

BIBLIOGRAPHY.—For statistics of acreage and trade, U.S. Department of Agriculture, *Agricultural Statistics;* Handbook *Official Grain Standards* (1941); *Soybean Digest* (monthly).

Spaak, Paul-Henri

Spaak (1899–), Belgian statesman, was born Jan. 25, 1899, in Brussels. At the age of 17, he attempted to cross from German-occupied Belgium into neutral Holland, but was captured and interned until after the armistice of 1918. He studied law at the Université Libre de Bruxelles, where he received his law degree. Admitted to the bar, he practiced law in Brussels. Spaak, who acquired his socialism from his mother (the first woman senator of Belgium) was elected as Socialist member from Brussels to the chamber of deputies. In 1935, he was named minister of transport, post and telegraph in the Van Zeeland cabinet, and the following year he was named foreign minister. At the time, the Belgian government rejected British and French promises of military support, hoping to remain strictly neutral. As a result, Spaak, who supported this view, conducted negotiations releasing Belgium from its commitments under the Locarno pact and the Anglo-

French-Belgian agreements. He formed a government in May 1938, but was compelled to resign in Feb. 1939, and was succeeded by Hubert Pierlot. Spaak again became foreign minister at the outbreak of World War II on Sept. 3, 1939. He fled Belgium after the collapse of Allied resistance in the summer of 1940 and went to England, where he became foreign minister and minister of labour in the Belgian government-in-exile. In Feb. 1945, he was retained as foreign minister and deputy prime minister in the Van Acker government established on Belgian soil, and the following April he headed his country's delegation to the U.N. conference at San Francisco. At the opening session of the U.N. general assembly meeting in London, Spaak was elected president of the general assembly by a 28 to 23 vote on Jan. 10, 1946, defeating Trygve Lie, who later was elected to the post of secretary general of the security council.

Spaatz, Carl

Spaatz (1891–), U.S. army air officer, was born June 28, 1891, in Boyertown, Pa. A graduate of the U.S. Military academy, West Point, N.Y., 1914, he participated in the Mexican campaign in 1916. During World War I, he commanded a pursuit squadron in the St. Mihiel offensive, 1918, and was awarded the distinguished service cross. After the war, he advanced rapidly in the air corps, becoming chief of staff to Gen. Henry H. Arnold, 1941, and U.S. air commander in Europe, July 1942. Early the following year, he was shifted to the Mediterranean theatre as commander of the 12th air force in Africa. His appointment as commander of the U.S. strategic bombing forces operating against Germany was announced by Pres. F. D. Roosevelt on Dec. 24, 1943.

During 1944 and 1945, bombers under Spaatz's command subjected Germany and German-occupied areas in Europe to intense aerial attacks. Spaatz represented the U.S. at the German surrender ceremonies in Berlin May 8, 1945. After the end of the war in Europe, he was made commander of the newly-created U.S. strategic air force in the Pacific in July 1945. Promoted to the permanent rank of major general, Jan. 22, 1946, he was named two days later (Jan. 24) to succeed Gen. Arnold as commander of all U.S. army air forces. On April 21, 1946, Spaatz urged that the army air forces be put in charge of guided-missile research.

SPAB (Supply Priorities and Allocations Board)

See War and Defense Agencies.

Spain

A southwestern European state, Spain occupies about 84% of the Iberian peninsula. After the Spanish civil war (1936–39), the chief of state (Caudillo) governed through a council of ministers not responsible to the parliament (Cortes). All political parties except the Falange were proscribed. The official religion was Roman Catholicism.

Manuel Azaña was president of the Spanish republic from May 1936 to Feb. 1939. Gen. Francisco Franco was head of the Spanish nationalist state after Oct. 1936.

The area of Spain (including the Balearic and Canary islands) is 194,945 sq.mi. The population was estimated at 25,220,000 in 1937 and 26,761,907 in 1944. By the census of Dec. 31, 1940, it was 25,877,971. Madrid is the capital. Chief cities (1944 est. pop.): Madrid (1,141,000); Barcelona (1,109,000); Valencia (508,000); Seville (348,000); Zaragoza (266,000); Málaga (259,000); Bilbao (208,000).

Political Facets of Civil War.—In July, 1936, a military uprising in Morocco plunged Spain into a civil war which ended with the final victory of the insurgents in March 1939. Although many factors underlying the revolutionary movement were misunderstood during the war period, in later years it became clear that the revolt against the second Spanish republic was inspired and materially aided by the totalitarian regimes of Italy and Germany. Ideologically and militarily Spain's civil war, as both sides proclaimed, was a tryout for World War II (*see* Spanish Civil War).

With Madrid under siege, the Republican capital was moved to Valencia in Nov. 1936. Here the Cortes met on Feb. 1, 1937, and granted the cabinet full powers over civil and military affairs. But the Republican, or Popular Front government, failed to hold in line the motley political groups pledged to defend the republic, and in May the Anarcho-Syndicalists staged a revolt which subjected Barcelona to the horrors of a civil war within a civil war. The defeat of the Syndicalists strengthened the hand of the Communists, two of whom entered the cabinet formed by Dr. Juan Negrín. On Oct. 1, 1937, the Cortes reconvened in Valencia, but at the end of the month political and military reverses dictated the removal of the government to Barcelona.

In Nationalist Spain an outstanding political development was the decree of April 19, 1937, which announced the 26-point Falangist program and merged the Falange and the Requetés into a single party, thereafter known as the Falange Española Tradicionalista y de las J.O.N.S. (generally shortened to F.E.T.). The same decree instituted a national council to study "the great national problems" of "the new totalitarian state."

Nonintervention was the keynote of international conferences on the Spanish question. In Jan. 1937 the U.S. applied the Neutrality act to Spain, thus blocking the flow of war materials which the Republicans planned to acquire in the U.S.; but European sources continued to furnish munitions and "volunteers" to both sides in defiance of the Nonintervention agreement of Sept. 1936. The control scheme adopted by the Nonintervention committee went into effect in April, with non-Spanish observers policing the land frontiers while British, French, German and Italian ships patrolled the coasts. Germany and Italy soon withdrew from the naval patrol, forcing the committee to search for a new formula for blocking foreign aid and withdrawing volunteers.

The committee tried repeatedly during 1938 to implement the plan for the repatriation of volunteers. After the Republican government had promised unilateral action, withdrawing volunteers under the supervision of the league council, the Nationalist regime responded favourably, and the first contingent of Italian troops sailed from Cádiz in Oct. 1938.

The Republican offensive, started in Dec. 1937, led to short-lived victories on the Aragonese front. After recapturing Teruel, Gen. Franco launched the drive which pushed through to the Mediterranean and cut Republican Spain in two. The breaking of communications between Barcelona and Madrid led to the appointment of Gen. José Miaja as military commander and civil governor of Republican Central Spain. After a crisis in April, 1938, Negrín's government was reconstituted to include representatives of seven groups supporting the republic: Socialists, Republican Lefts, Anarcho-Syndicalists, Communists, Republican Union, Basque Nationalists and the Catalan Esquerra. In May Negrín announced 13 Republican war aims, including a plebiscite to determine the form of government after the war. But neither this pronouncement nor the declaration (in the Cortes' October meeting) of the government's desire to explore the possibilities for a negotiated peace moved Franco from his insistence upon unconditional surrender.

Spain's appeal to the League of Nations for the right to buy war materials abroad fell on barren ground, while in the U.S. a movement to lift the arms embargo failed to win sufficient support. Severe air raids were frequent in Republican Spain. A British commission to visit bombed cities reported in Sept. 1938 that most of the attacks were made on military objectives, but more than one raid (such as that on Torrevieja) was described as a premeditated attack on civilians.

Food shortages were acute. A League of Nations commission visiting the Republican territory found widespread malnutrition among the civilian population, swelled as it was by more than 2,000,000 refugees from Nationalist Spain. In Dec. 1938, after a two years' ban on religious services, the Republican government reaffirmed the constitutional guarantees of religious freedom and appointed a commissariat-general of worship.

In Nationalist Spain the technical council of state, created three months after the outbreak of war, became a ministerial government under the decree of Jan. 30, 1938, with Gen. Franco as president of the cabinet and head of all the armed forces. The Labour charter, promulgated in March, revealed in broad outline the projected national-syndicalist structure of the totalitarian economy. In April 1938, the Jesuits recovered the privileges and property rights they enjoyed upon their expulsion in the early days of the republic; and in December the government restored to ex-King Alphonso the civil rights taken away from him in 1931.

Gen. Franco's final drive commenced in Dec. 1938, and, although a counteroffensive was launched by Gen. Miaja, the Nationalist forces advanced with no important setback. With the fall of Barcelona (Jan. 26, 1939) the Republican government moved to Gerona, and from there to Figueras, where the last meeting of the Cortes took place on Feb. 1. Determined "to continue the struggle until conditions assuring the independence of the country . . . are achieved," Negrín's cabinet returned to Madrid; but Pres. Azaña, believing that continued resistance was hopeless, fled to Paris and on Feb. 27, 1939, resigned his office.

The return of the cabinet to Madrid occasioned another civil war within the civil war. On March 6, Gen. Miaja and Col. Casado organized a *putsch* which overthrew the Negrín government. Negrín fled, but his supporters took up arms against Miaja's National Council of Defense. The revolt suppressed, the council began negotiating with Franco (as, apparently, the Negrín government had intended to do). Nationalist forces entered Madrid on March 28, and within a few days all open resistance ended. England and France had recognized the Franco government on Feb. 27; the U.S. followed suit on April 1.

Franco's Shifting Foreign Relations.—Shortly before the end of hostilities the Nationalist government adhered to the anti-Comintern pact, and in May announced its withdrawal from the League of Nations. But at the outbreak of World War II, Franco immediately reaffirmed Spain's neutrality. The Russo-German alliance and the invasion of Catholic Poland came as a great shock to the axis' former partner-in-arms against communism. With Portugal, the third country to which the Nationalists were indebted for aid in the civil war, Spain concluded a treaty of nonaggression and friendship (March), followed by a trade agreement in December.

In Spanish relations with France, gold and refugees were the main issues. By the end of March, 500,000 refugees had left Spain and taken up a precarious existence in French internment camps. The Spanish government was unprepared to arrange for their immediate repatriation, though agreeing to contribute to the maintenance of those left in France; and at the end of 1938 France was still the involuntary host to more than 100,000 Spaniards. In July, pursuant to a ruling of French courts, more than $30,000,000 of the gold which the Republican government had shipped to France was delivered to the Bank of Spain.

The German victories of 1940 and Italy's entry into World War II encouraged Spain to abandon strict neutrality and to proclaim (June 12) a policy of "nonbelligerency." Public demonstrations demanded Gibraltar and occupation of the International Zone of Morocco, despite British protests. Ramón Serrano Suñer, a rabid partisan of the axis, was appointed foreign minister. Franco's declaration of his intention "to forge an empire" supported Winston Churchill's statement that Spain "seemed to hang in the balance between peace and war." Later, it became known that Spain demanded territorial concessions, including Gibraltar and French Morocco, and military and economic assistance sufficient to make up for her dearth of munitions and foodstuffs as conditions for entering World War II. On Aug. 15, 1940, Franco told Benito Mussolini, Spain would go to war "at a favourable opportunity in proportion to the means at our disposal." The duce replied that although Spain needed a long period of recuperation, "events will not permit it, and your domestic economic condition will not get worse when you change from nonbelligerency to intervention." Franco hesitated. Adolf Hitler, in conversations with Count Galeazzo Ciano, noted caustically that the exorbitant demands for grain and armaments in exchange for Spanish "friendship" showed that Spain lacked "the same intensity of will for giving as for taking." Finally accepting Franco's invitation, Hitler journeyed to Hendaye in Oct. 1940 for talks with the Caudillo. No agreements were reached, but in December Hitler informed Franco of a plan to send troops through Spain for an attack upon Gibraltar. Franco demurred, protesting "absolutely inadequate" food supplies and insufficient preparation to enter the war as early as Jan. 1941. At the end of 1940 one concrete move toward belligerency was made: Spain agreed to permit German tankers to use sheltered bays along the Cantabrian coast for refuelling submarines.

While carrying on this flirtation with the axis, Spain improved her economic position *vis-à-vis* the non-axis countries, especially England. The Anglo-Spanish trade agreement signed in March 1940 provided a loan of £2,000,000 for purchases within the sterling area, while Spain undertook to resume payment on the outstanding commercial debts of about £7,000,000. A tripartite payments and trade agreement (England-Portugal-Spain) was concluded in July, and in September arrangements were made for oil imports under British navicerts, with guarantees against re-export.

In the Italian debt agreement of May 8, 1940, Spain undertook to pay in 25 instalments the sum of 5,000,000,000 lire for Italian assistance in the civil war. Hitler stated privately that the Spanish debt to Germany amounted to 400,000,000 marks but that Spain had been unwilling to discuss repayment.

Spain continued to give aid and comfort to the axis nations throughout 1941. In March the German consulate in Tangier was reopened, less for the sake of commercial contacts than for facilitating espionage in the Mediterranean area. Germany's attack upon the U.S.S.R. inspired the recruiting of the Spanish "Blue Division" to fight on the eastern front, enthusiasm for which was echoed by Serrano Suñer. "The extermination of Russia," he said, "is an exigency of history and of the future of Spain." But the government was not persuaded to abandon its nonbelligerent status. Hitler, still chiding Franco for spurning the proposal for entering the war, belittled Spain's economic difficulties, promised 100,000 tons of grain upon the declaration of war, and offered an equitable division of African colonial possessions. Franco replied that the Spanish people were "suffering the greatest starvation and enduring all sorts of privations and sacrifices" and that he could not demand greater sacrifices unless confident of a quick ending to the war.

Spain of necessity continued to maintain close economic ties with non-axis countries, however. New agreements with England enabled Spain to increase its imports of food and raw materials from sterling areas and to exchange oranges and mercury for British wheat and rubber. A trade agreement with Argentina further augmented Spain's supply of wheat, cotton and meat. Yet during most of the year there were shortages and hunger on every hand, and in April the American Red Cross donated to the Spanish people considerable quantities of milk, flour and medicine.

Eulogizing the German defense of Europe from the menace of Communism, Franco promised that if Berlin were endangered, not a division but 1,000,000 Spaniards would volunteer to defend the German capital. In another speech (July 1942) the Caudillo asserted that totalitarianism had "amply demonstrated its superiority" over democratic institutions. "For the countries of Europe," he said, "there exists a single danger . . . Communism." He later told Hitler he was praying for German victory "in the glorious undertaking of liberating Europe from bolshevik terror."

Other developments revealed Spain's reluctance to join the axis in a "shooting" war. Ramón Serrano Suñer was dismissed without explanation in Sept. 1942 and was replaced in the foreign office by Count Francisco Gómez Jordana y Souza, a monarchist friendly to the U.S. and Great Britain. Roosevelt personally advised Franco that the landing of U.S. troops in North Africa was "in no shape, manner, or form directed against the government and people of Spain . . . Spain has nothing to fear from the United Nations." Spain replied by partially mobilizing its armed forces, with the announced purpose of guaranteeing its isolation from the struggle. U.S. Ambassador Carlton Hayes reported that at the end of 1942 Spain was ready to enter the war on the Allied side in the event that Germany undertook military operations on Spanish territory.

In a secret agreement of Feb. 10, 1943, Germany promised "to deliver to the Spanish army in the shortest time possible . . . war material of modern quality"; in return, Spain covenanted "to resist every entry by Anglo-American forces upon the Iberian peninsula or upon Spanish territory outside of the peninsula." The hour for Spain's voluntary entry into the war had definitely passed. In April and May 1943, the government put out peace feelers, motivated by the belief that the war had reached a stalemate. Not until the last half of the year, however, were doubts of axis victory made public. In July the censorship of German news agencies was reimposed; in August Spanish newspapers were permitted to say that Allied military aims might be realized; and in October the Caudillo defined the Spanish position as one of "vigilant neutrality," ostensibly retracting the nonbelligerency adopted in 1940.

The slight improvement in relations with the United Nations was offset by the congratulations which the foreign office sent to the Japanese puppet government in the Philippines. U.S. protests brought a prompt denial of Spain's friendship for Japan and of any intention to recognize the Laurel government. The announcement of Nov. 1943 that the Blue division had been withdrawn only partially satisfied Allied demands, since Spaniards were permitted to remain on the eastern front as "legionnaires." In conversations with Franco the following month, the German ambassador disclosed Hitler's displeasure over the change in Spanish policy, citing the "unjustified internment" of U-boat crews and the passage of French fugitives through Spain to Africa as examples of pro-Allied collaboration. Franco denied (with what sincerity, it was impossible to say) any change in his policy, since "he knew for certain . . . that only the victory of Germany would make possible the continued existence of the regime . . . [while] a victory of the Anglo-Saxons . . . would mean his own annihilation."

Still "economically very dependent" (as Franco pointed out to the German ambassador), Spain was forced to yield to Allied pressure in exchange for promises of food and oil. Great Britain and the U.S. agreed to supply 100,000 tons of cotton in 1943, or enough to restore consumption to normal levels. Under the plan worked out by the British and U.S. Boards of Economic Warfare, Spain was allowed to import 541,000 tons of petroleum, or not more than 60% of normal requirements. Allied preclusive buying furnished a market (at constantly rising prices) for such varied products as sheepskins, woollens, fluor spar and wolfram. Spanish statistical sources revealed that the Allies acquired 77% of the 3,003 tons of wolfram for which export licences were granted in 1943.

Spain's abandonment of nonbelligerency did not immediately yield the advantages anticipated by the Allied governments. The continued exportation of strategic minerals to Germany, the persistence of German espionage

"What Now, Little Man?" inquired Lewis in the *Milwaukee Journal* after U.S. oil shipments to Spain were discontinued in Jan. 1944

on Spanish soil and attacks upon British and U.S. consulates cast some doubts upon Spain's strictly neutral position. In Jan. 1944 the government's refusal to embargo wolfram shipments to Germany led to a crisis in relations with the U.S. and the halting of petroleum imports, which virtually paralyzed the motor transport system. The ban was lifted in May, but not until Spain agreed to release certain Italian ships detained in Spanish ports, withdraw all military personnel from the eastern front, expel designated axis agents from Spain and Morocco, close the German consulate in Tangier, and cut to a trickle exports of wolfram to Germany.

The military reverses of Germany and, following the liberation of France, the removal of nazi troops from the Spanish border were decided stimulants to the reorientation of the country's foreign policy. But official Spain continued to insist that the Allied war aims were meaningless, and in July 1944 Franco repeated his offer of Spain's good offices in negotiating a peace. The press disparaged the Atlantic charter and predicted that a United Nations victory would only lead to Russian domination of Europe. In a letter to Churchill the Caudillo suggested that, "since we cannot believe in the good faith of Communist Russia and since we know the insidious power of Bolshevism," it would be wise to form an anti-communist bloc. In response to suggestions that Spain might furnish a haven for war criminals, the government stated that "no one has ever contemplated providing a hiding place in Spain for the enemies of the Allied countries" and added that "the Spanish regime has nothing in common with National Socialism, which is condemned by the church, while Spain's own regime is essentially based on Christian principles." Although in Nov. 1944 Franco described the Spanish state as one of "organic democracy," his bid for an invitation to the peace conferences was accorded a frigid reception. Relaxation of press and censorship regulations enabled the British and U.S. information agencies to present the case for the United Nations more effectively.

The Franco government in 1945 weathered a rising storm of foreign criticism but only at the expense of isolation from the current of international affairs. In March the country was thoroughly aroused by Japanese atrocities in the Philippines; and within a month the break in diplomatic relations ensued. As Allied armies were delivering the blows which led to Germany's unconditional surrender, the government blocked all axis-controlled assets in Spain; but only at the very end (May 7) did Spain sever relations with Germany. Pierre Laval, who fled to Spain in May, was expelled at the request of the Allies.

Domestic Problems, 1939–45.—Although reconstruction following the civil war was the major problem of 1939 a number of political changes were affected. In the face of internal bickering, Franco reorganized the F.E.T., giving the Falangist elements a predominant place in the new state. The Caudillo, by virtue of a decree of July 31, 1939, assumed "in its entire plenitude the most absolute authority. The Chief is responsible only to God and to History."

Rationing and drastic measures against hoarding and profiteering were adopted immediately after the fall of Madrid. In April 1939 the women's social service was distributing 1,500,000 rations daily in Madrid alone. To speed the work of reconstruction, Franco "adopted" the most severely damaged towns and granted extraordinary credits for the building of houses, the repair of public buildings, and the rehabilitation of the transport system. Long-range industrial development was anticipated by the decree of Oct., 24, 1939, which authorized the National Industrial institute to intervene in the management of industries of "national interest" in exchange for preferential tax treatment and a guarantee of earnings. Official unemployment statistics, beginning with Sept. 1939, showed a decrease in the number of idle from 600,000 in September to less than 450,000 in December.

The significant *Law of Syndical Unification* was published in Jan. 1940. So-called vertical syndicates, after the fashion of the Italian corporations, supplanted all trade unions and employers' associations. Syndicalist Centrals co-ordinated the national syndicates on a regional basis; at the top the organization was controlled by the National Syndicalist delegation of the Falange. In the words of the more detailed measures published in Dec. 1940, "the law insures the subordination of the syndicalist organization to the Party, since only the Party can infuse in it the discipline, unity and viewpoint necessary to make the national economy subserve the national policy." Following repeal of the Agrarian Reform law of 1932, a new National Institute of Colonization was established to carry out a program of rural electrification, irrigation and reforestation in place of the land-tenure reforms projected under the republic.

Social legislation included a law for the suppression of freemasonry and communism (March 1940) and the decree for the establishment of the Consejo de la Hispanidad, an organization avowedly designed for cultural rapprochement with the Hispanic nations.

There were further indications during the following year of the socializing effects of National Syndicalism: in Feb. 1941 the decree nationalizing the railroads became effective, and in September all tin, copper, aluminum, zinc, manganese, nickel, chromium and tungsten mines, declared to be "of national interest," were brought under the program of state aid and control. New legislation expanded the coverage and benefits of social security, including marriage loans and family subsidies. "Only nations of prolific families," explained the decree of Aug. 1, 1941, "can expand the race throughout the world and create and maintain empires." Government statisticians talked of increasing Spain's population to 40,000,000 by 1984.

The tribunal appointed to judge masons and communists handed down a number of sentences, including long prison terms for Negrín, Jiménez Asua, Victoria Kent and other outstanding Republicans. On Columbus day (Oct. 12), "Hispanidad" was again proclaimed as a purely spiritual and cultural program, but within the month Cuba requested the removal of the press attaché in the Spanish embassy on the grounds of political activity inimical to Cuban foreign policy.

Under the terms of an agreement with the Holy See, signed on June 7, the Spanish government secured the right to fill episcopal vacancies after submitting a panel of nominees to the pope.

By a law of July 17, 1942, a new type of cortes described as "the superior organism of the participation of the Spanish people in the work of the state" was created. "The principal mission of the Cortes is the planning and formulation of laws, without prejudice to the veto power which belongs to the head of the state." Party officials, presidents of learned societies, and certain public officials became members ex-officio; other members were appointed by the *caudillo,* and a third of the membership was subject to election by the national syndicates.

On the economic front, shortages of food and raw materials still hampered plans for development and reconstruction. Limited supplies were made available by the

Allied nations, while trade agreements with Argentina made it possible to exchange Spanish ores and manufactures for Argentine grain and tobacco. Allied economic warfare led to large-scale preemptive buying in an effort to keep wolfram, mercury and other strategic commodities out of axis hands. As a result, Spain acquired large reserves of foreign exchange, and in 1942 the balance of trade was favourable for the first time since 1930.

In March 1942 the government repudiated the note issues and a large part of the deposit liabilities of the Republican Bank of Spain. Deficit financing, the enormous cost of reconstruction, and the European war contributed to the persistent inflationary tendencies of the post-civil war period. By the end of 1942, prices and the cost of living were about two-thirds greater than in 1939, but unemployment was less than half the figure reported in Dec. 1939.

In 1943 except for the disbanding of the Falangist militia in December, the political and social program of the totalitarian state suffered no radical transformation. At the opening of the cortes in March 1943, Pres. Esteban Bilbao scoffed at "liberal regimes," "stupid parliaments," and "pharasaical democrats." In July the cortes approved a law for the administration of the universities, prescribing courses of study for the "political" indoctrination of students. Professors were required to submit syllabi of their courses prior to the opening of classes, and the student body was linked to the Falange by one of the ubiquitous syndicates. The national budget, with expenditures set at almost 10,000,000,000 pesetas (4,700,000,000 in 1935; 7,200,000,000 in 1940), revealed the increasing role of the state in social and economic undertakings, although allowance must be made for the rising price level.

In March 1944 four university professors were arrested for signing a memorandum in favour of Don Juan, claimant to the Spanish throne after the death of his father, ex-king Alphonso, on Feb. 28, 1941. From exile the pretender announced his complete lack of sympathy with the Franco regime. Meanwhile, restoration of the monarchy continued to be a forbidden topic.

Other expatriates kept up their propaganda for the restoration of parliamentary government, demanding the withdrawal of Franco in favour of the "third" Spanish republic. Late in 1944 guerrilla bands operating out of the French Pyrenees harassed northern Catalonia, but their marauding was more annoying than menacing.

In the sixth year after the civil war Spain was still struggling with a gigantic task of reconstruction, a task whose burden in some sectors of the economy was increased by the European war. Adverse weather, coupled with acute shortages of fertilizer, kept the production of most major crops below prewar levels, and drought severely curtailed the output of hydroelectric power. Scarcity of articles of necessity persisted; prices and the cost of living continued to rise; but unemployment dropped to the relatively low figure of 166,000 (May).

Postwar Difficulties.—At the Potsdam conference in 1945, England, Russia and the U.S. declared they "would not favour any application for membership" in the United Nations "put forward by the present Spanish government, which . . . does not, in view of its origins, its nature, its record and its close association with the aggressor states, possess the qualifications necessary to justify such membership." Replying to a message from the *caudillo,* Churchill cited the unilateral change in the status of Tangier as one reason for distrust of Spain's attempted rapprochement with the Allies. In Aug. 1945 the Morocco question was studied by experts representing Great Britain, France, Russia and the U.S., and, pursuant to the four-power agreement, in October Spain withdrew from the administration of the International Zone in favour of a committee of control.

Susceptible to foreign antipathy, the government made every effort to disassociate foreign policy from its domestic program. The official attitude was expressed by Foreign Minister José Felix Lequerica, who asserted that "the internal regime, purely Spanish, created by Spaniards and defended by them, has nothing to do with its foreign policy."

Several Latin American countries broke diplomatic relations with the Franco government; but England and the U.S., despite strong demands from certain segments of public opinion, hesitated to take this drastic step. In Mexico, where the Franco regime had never been recognized, the Spanish Committee of Liberation made some progress in harmonizing the divergent ambitions of the exiled groups working for Franco's overthrow and in Aug. 1945 formed a government-in-exile headed by Martínez Barrio (president) and José Giral (premier). Eschewing violence, the anti-Franco forces advocated a plebiscite which they hoped economic sanctions and diplomatic pressure would force Franco to accept.

Denouncing the Franco government as dictatorial, the pretender asserted that a constitutional monarchy "alone [could] provide an effective guarantee for religion, order and liberty." The Duke of Alba, considering the regime "harmful to the best interests of Spain," strengthened the hand of the monarchists by resigning his post as ambassador to England. Franco himself declared his hope that the cortes would prepare legislation to bring about the restoration.

Internally, the regime made a few polite bows to liberalism. Franco described the nation as a "Catholic state, eminently socialized . . . in which all Spaniards are equal before the law"; and in May 1945 he declared that "Spain is not a dictatorship." A cabinet shakeup in July, giving monarchists and non-Falangists a majority, was called a "further stage in Spain's spiritual and material reconstruction." An electoral census was conducted and lists of electors posted in Madrid, though no occasion was offered for the exercise of suffrage. The tribunal of political responsibilities was abolished in June, 1945 and in October full pardon was extended to prisoners convicted of political offenses committed before the end of the civil war. A bill of rights, based on the constitution of 1876, was approved by the cortes in July; but amendments to the penal code made blasphemy, contravention of the labour laws and disparagement of the regime criminal offenses.

Weather, war and politics combined to induce unfavourable economic conditions. With grain harvests abnormally low, because of the lack of fertilizer and a drought said to be the worst in half a century, the country faced the necessity of importing almost half the normal requirements of cereals. The end of Allied preclusive buying and the loss of other markets not only reacted adversely upon mining and industrial activity but drained the supply of foreign exchange needed for making purchases abroad.

Spain's exclusion from the United Nations on Feb. 8, 1946, touched off a series of diplomatic duels. The three-power talks initiated by France in Dec. 1945 led to the joint announcement of March 4, 1946, that England, France and the U.S. hoped "leading patriotic and liberal-minded Spaniards may soon find means to bring about

Carnival figure representing Spain's housing problem, on display in Valencia during April 1946

a peaceful withdrawal of Franco, the abolition of the Falange and the establishment of an interim or caretaker government" pending the free choice of their form of government by the Spanish people. In April, Poland, after recognizing the government-in-exile, brought before the United Nations Security council a proposal for breaking relations with Spain "in view of the fact that the present regime . . . is endangering international peace." By unanimous action the council set up a subcommittee to investigate the Polish charges, and on June 1 the committee made its report. After pointing out that Franco had failed, and sometimes refused, to co-operate in ridding Europe of naziism and fascism (*e.g.*, by continuing to harbour the Belgian quisling Léon Degrelle), the committee concluded that unjustifiable military strength and the existence of a rival government-in-exile constituted a potential threat to peace.

Although the subcommittee pointed out that the council could take no action in the absence of an immediate threat to peace, Russia supported Poland in insisting upon a decision. Motions to accept the subcommittee's report and to refer the question to the assembly were defeated, as was the Polish resolution for the immediate severance of relations with Spain. The motion offered by Australia and England to keep the Spanish question on the agenda was upheld, and in the fall meeting of the council Russia and Poland were intent upon making it the order of day.

Meanwhile, the Spanish government accepted the challenge and in the case of France retaliated by closing the frontiers (Feb. 28, 1946). Representatives of friendly nations were invited to Spain to observe that, contrary to the Polish allegations, no German scientists were engaged in atomic-bomb experimentation. At the opening of the cortes in May 1946, Franco declared that the law-making processes of the parliament disproved charges that his government was dictatorial and undemocratic; but Spain would rather live in "sacrificial isolation" than to acknowledge the competence of the United Nations to stand in judgment. By June, only 19 of the 51 members of the United Nations had diplomatic relations with Spain, while 7 recognized the government-in-exile. In September, Spain was explicitly debarred from the United Nations Food and Agriculture organization conference in Copenhagen, Denmark; and in October vigorous efforts were made to exclude her from the world court.

On other questions the position of the Spanish government was far from adamant. The Allied Control commission secured a satisfactory agreement for blocking business assets controlled by Germans in Spain; and by May, British sources acknowledged, the majority of German officials and military personnel had been sent back to Germany. A report on prison conditions, in response to British representations, indicated that political prisoners numbered less than 40,000 in May.

Don Juan journeyed to Portugal to talk with representatives of Gen. Franco, but no more tangible evidence emerged of the government's intentions toward the restoration. The concordat signed in July provided for the joint participation of the state and the Spanish church in the appointment of priests and dignitaries of the cathedrals.

In the economic sphere, Spain continued to suffer from low production, food shortages, rising prices and black markets. On the tenth anniversary of his rise to power (Oct. 1946) Franco admitted that the government's economic program had fallen short of its goals: industrial development, agricultural expansion and housing were

Spain: *Statistical Data*

Item	1938 Value (000's omitted)	1938 Amount or number	1940 Amount or number	1942 Value (000's omitted)	1942 Amount or number
Exchange rate					
United States		1 Peseta = 5.6 cents	1 Peseta = 9.32 cents		1 Peseta = 9 cents
Great Britain		40-42 Pesetas = £1*	40-60 Pesetas = £1 (1941)		40-50 Pesetas = £1 (1943)
Finance					
Government revenues	$253,700 (£57,204)*				
Government expenditures	$517,548 (£116,696)*				
Transportation					
Railroads		...	10,497 mi.		
Highways		71,369 mi.*	...		
Communication					
Telephones		281,418	344,780†		
Radio sets		800,000	...		
Minerals					
Copper ore (copper content)		33,069 tons ‡			
Lead		39,683 tons			
Copper		12,125 tons			
Crops					
Potatoes		4,456,048 tons*	4,303,159 tons†		
Grapes		3,520,526 tons*	2,961,990 tons†		
Wheat		3,163,491 tons*	3,100,990 tons†		
Livestock					
Sheep		14,045,100*	24,236,992		23,800,000§
Goats		4,076,900*	6,249,009		6,100,000§
Swine		2,945,600*	5,612,854		5,150,000§
Forest products					
Cork			67,198 tons		
Resin			11,567 tons		
Turpentine			3,310 tons		
Sea products					
Total			484,637 tons		
Fish			432,806 tons		
Molluscs			37,617 tons		
Crustaceans			14,214 tons		
Exports					
Total				$57,588 (£14,272)	2,543,000 tons
Oranges				$8,272 (£2,050)	254,000 "
Wines				$2,419 (£600)	7,441,000 gal.
Almonds				$159 (£39)	651 tons
Imports					
Total				$55,657 (£13,794)	2,204,000 tons
Cotton (raw)				$5,254 (£1,302)	73,000 "
Automobiles				$1,262 (£313)	5,000 "
Machinery				$1,516 (£376)	4,000 "
Defense					
Standing army personnel		350,000*	320,000		
Reserves		600,000*	300,000		
Standing navy personnel		22,300*	...		
Standing air force personnel		110,000*	100,000		
Reserves		40,000*	50,000		

*1939 †1941 ‡Exports only §1944

still lagging. Trade agreements with the Netherlands and Argentina in part relieved the domestic economy, furnishing grains and vegetables in exchange for Spanish fruits and manufactures. A treaty of commerce with Italy provided for an annual trade of 200,000,000 pesetas, but Spanish exports worth 150,000,000 were to be applied to the civil war debt. The 1946 budget (ordinary and extraordinary) called for expenditures of 13,200,000,000 pesetas, of which 5,400,000,000 represented appropriations for the military, naval and police forces. Inflationary tendencies were reflected by the rise in the note issue of the Bank of Spain to 18,900,000,000 pesetas in May (despite the ceiling of 18,000,000,000 imposed by law in March 1945). Unemployment, which reached a low of 123,000 in May 1945, rose to 177,000 in March 1946. The peseta was officially pegged at 10.95 to the U.S. dollar, although in August a "tourist" rate of 16.40 per U.S. dollar was introduced. (*See* also Fascism.)

Bibliography.—John Langdon-Davies, *Behind the Spanish Barricades* (1936); Franz Borkenau, *The Spanish Cockpit* (1937); Elliot Paul, *The Life and Death of a Spanish Town* (1937); Robert Sencourt, *Spain's Ordeal* (1938); S. Casado, *The Last Days of Madrid* (1939); E. Allison Peers, *Spain, the Church and the Orders* (1939); Henry Buckley, *Life and Death of the Spanish Republic* (1940); J. Alvárez del Vayo, *Freedom's Battle* (1940); E. Allison Peers, *Spain in Eclipse* (1943); Higinio Paris Eguilaz, *La expansión de la economía española* (1944); José Antonio de Aguirre, *Escape via Berlin* (1945); Carlton J. H. Hayes, *Wartime Mission in Spain* (1945).

(R. S. S.)

Spangler, Harrison Earl

Spangler (1879–), U.S. lawyer and politician, was born June 10, 1879, in Guthrie county, Iowa. A graduate of Iowa university law college, Iowa City, he was admitted to the bar in 1905. Active in the Republican party, he became a member of the Republican national committee in 1931, and directed Alfred Landon's presidential campaign for the midwest area in 1936. After retirement of Joseph W. Martin as chairman of the Republican national committee in 1942, Spangler was elected to this post at the G.O.P. convention in St. Louis, Mo., in Dec. 1942. He proposed on April 11, 1943, to the Democrats that the Republican party would consider favourably suggestions for a short presidential campaign in 1944 provided "satisfactory assurances" were given that Franklin D. Roosevelt would refuse a fourth term. Spangler retired as chairman on June 29, 1944.

Spanish-American Literature

World War II was only one among three historical events which had an important bearing upon Spanish-American literature in the decade 1937–46, the other two being the Spanish Civil War and the Pan-American policy of the U.S. government under the guidance of Franklin D. Roosevelt. The Spanish question divided Latin America into two irreconcilable parties, just as it did in the *Madre Patria*. Friends of the Spanish republic spared no efforts in order to contribute to the defeat of Francisco Franco. They collected money, sent medical supplies, participated in active propaganda and, when they had the talent and the capacity, composed poetry in praise of the Republican armies. Some of the finest poetry produced by Spanish Americans dealt with the Spanish Civil War, such as Pablo Neruda's *España en el Corazón* (1937); Nicolás Guillén's *España: Poema en cuatro angustias y una esperanza* (1937); César Vallejo's *España, aparta de mi este cáliz;* A. Torres-Ríoseco's *Canto a España Viva* (1941).

World War II, on the other hand, had no direct impact on Spanish-American letters during the decade; and it was doubtful whether it ever would. Spanish America played an important but secondary role in the conflict, and only Brazil and Mexico sent armies to the battle fronts. Indirectly, however, the war brought about considerable changes in the literary world of the southern continent. It caused the largest Spanish publishing houses to move out of Europe and into Latin America. Espasa-Calpe established its headquarters in Buenos Aires, Argentina. Distinguished Spanish writers went into the publishing business and managed such enterprises as Losada and the already mentioned Espasa. Argentina, Mexico and, to a lesser extent, Chile took over the book markets of their sister republics and attained a rate and a quality of production never paralleled in the history of these countries. More and better books were published. Foreign authors—North American, French, Russian, British—were still favoured over the native writers, but this tendency was counteracted by the work of such institutions as the Fondo de Cultura Económica de Mexico, which began to organize a true encyclopaedia of Spanish America through the publication of outstanding works by native essayists, novelists, historians, etc. The war also accounted for the arrival in Latin America of refugees from Spain, Poland, Austria, Italy and other countries, who effectively contributed to the cultural progress of their countries of adoption. One of the best examples perhaps was that of Dr. A. Lipschutz, the eminent physiologist who, working in Chile, turned his attention to Spanish-American problems and produced a book of exceptional significance in *El indoamericano y el problema racial en las Américas* (1945).

In regard to Pan-Americanism, it was necessary to thank the good neighbour policy for making possible the publication of an increasing number of Spanish-American books in excellent English translations. Works by writers such as G. Freyre, G. Arciniegas, E. Mallea, E. Verissimo, among others, as well as classics such as E. d'Acunha's *Os Sertões*, R. Rojas' *El Santo de la Espada*, R. Palma's *Tradiciones Peruanas* reached the English-speaking public with various degrees of success. Poets like Neruda, J. Carrera Andrade, G. Mistral and many others were made known to the American Hispanists through the efforts of anthologists like H. R. Hays, Dudley Fitts, Dudley Poore and translators of such calibre as Muna Lee, A. Flores, H. de Onís, D. Craig, L. Mallan, S. G. Morley, etc. Scholars of great prestige continued the work begun by A. Coester and published general treatises on Spanish-American letters: A. Torres-Ríoseco's *The Epic of Latin American Literature*, Rex Crawford's *A Century of Latin American Thought*, R. Spell's *Contemporary Spanish American Fiction*; the language was studied by C. E. Kany in his pioneer volume *American-Spanish Syntax*. Spanish-American writers and professors travelled through the United States and wrote articles and books giving their impressions: Erico Verissimo, Germán Arciniegas, Luis A. Sánchez, Manuel Seoane imitated John Gunther's *"Inside"* series in quick, subjective books about North America. P. Henríquez Ureña's *Literary Currents in Hispanic America* and G. Freyre's *Brazil: an interpretation* were a result of invitations to lecture in the United States; as likewise *De la Conquista a la Independencia* by M. Picón Salas, a charming display of erudition without pedantry. The "Good Neighbour" policy was also responsible for the two literary contests which the Pan American Union and the Farrar and Rinehart publishing house sponsored in 1942 and 1943, which resulted in hundreds of books being written and submitted to the national judges for a right to compete in New York. Winners of the awards—C. Alegría, G. Gilbert, M. L. Menéndez, P. and Ph. Thoby-Marcelin, A. Díaz Lozano and F. Alegría—saw their works published in English translations.

* * *

In a more detailed analysis of Spanish-American literature of the decade, one should emphasize, in the first place, the consistency with which old and new novelists subscribed to the ideas of *criollismo* or regionalism. The old masters continued to produce those long and minute descriptions of rural, provincial or city life with emphasis on the picturesque. In Mexico, M. Azuelas published *Regina Landa* (1939), *Avanzada* (1940) and *La Merchanta* (1945); J. R. Romero added to his list of poignantly realistic portrayals with *Una vez fuí rico* (1942) and *Rosenda* (1946). In Chile M. Latorre was awarded the National Literature prize (1945) for his volumes of short stories *Hombres y zorros, Mapu* and *Viento de Mallines*, all dealing with country life among the colorful *huasos;* J. Edwards Belloalso received the same prize (1943) for his lively descriptions of Valparaíso in *En el viejo Almendral.* Other *costumbrista* novels were published by E. Barrios, L. Durand, J. M. Castro and L. Yankas. The Venezuelan R. Gallegos produced one of his most important novels in 1937: *Pobre Negro*, a book of social and psychological significance; in 1945 he published another story, *Sobre la misma tierra*, which, unfortunately, did not live up to his merits and had to be considered rather as a movie script than as a novel. The Argentinean M. Gálvez wrote a book of historical interest about a famous Ecuadorean character *Vida de don Gabriel García Moreno* (1943). A. Gerchunoff, Max Dickman and others struggled to give the Argentinean novel a more modern form and a broader scope.

Younger novelists, in general, followed the realistic tradition, but became more conscious of social and economic problems. They denounced the persecution of Indian peoples in Peru—C. Alegría's *El mundo es Ancho y Ajeno*—in Ecuador—J. Icaza's *En las Calles.* They assailed the imperialistic ambitions of foreign powers—C. Uribe's *Mancha de aceite*, D. Aguilera Malta's *Canal Zone.* They described the incredible conditions in which workers laboured in coal mines: Juan Marín's *Viento Negro*; in copper mines: G. Drago's *Cobre;* in nitrate fields: A. Sabella's *Norte Grande.* Those interpreting the traditional *gaucho* or *huaso* theme managed to bring some novelty by analyzing psychological conflicts: E. Amorim's *El caballo y su sombra* (1941), or by giving an artistic treatment to an historical event: R. Lomboy's *Ranquil* (1943). Central-American rural life was described by the Guatemalan Flavio Herrera in *El tigre* (1942). The philosophical novel had two worthy representatives in E. Mallea of Argentina—*Historia de una pasión argentina* (1937), *Fiesta en Noviembre* (1938), etc., and in the more artistic and subtly pessimistic E. González of Chile (*Noche*, 1942).

The fact must be pointed out that Ecuador led Spanish America—with the possible exception of Brazil—in the novelistic production of the decade. Outstanding examples included J. Icaza's *Cholos* (1938); A. Pareja Diez-Canseco's *Baldomera* (1938); H. Salvador's *Noviembre* (1939); *Trabajadores* (1940) and *Prometeo* (1945); H. Matta's *Sumag Allpa* (1940) and *Sanagüín* (1942); E. Gil Gilbert's *Nuestro Pan* (1942); D. Aguilera Malta's *La isla virgen* (1943).

Imagination and psychological insight were displayed by such novelists as the Argentinean A. Gerchunoff in *La clínica del Dr. Mefistófeles* (1937), the Guatemalan R. Arévalo Martínez in *El mundo de los Maharachías* (1938), the Chileans M. L. Bombal in *La Amortajada* (1938) and B. Subercaseaux in *Daniel* (1941).

A number of historical characters came to literary life through the biographical novels written by the Peruvians L. A. Sánchez (*Garcilaso Inca de la Vega,* 1939) and María Wiesse (*José Carlos Mariátegui,* 1945); by the Argentinean M. Gálvez (*Vida de Hipólito Irigoyen,* 1939); the Colombian G. Arciniegas (*Jiménez de Quezada,* 1939); the Cuban Feliz Lisasso (*Pasión de Martí,* 1938); the Honduran R. H. Valle (*Iturbide, varón de Dios,* 1944); the Chilean M. Petit (*Diego Portales,* 1937).

This powerful development of Spanish-American fiction was accompanied, and perhaps conditioned, by the exhausting criticism of A. Torres-Ríoseco, *La novela en la América Hispana* (1939–43) and L. A. Sánchez, *América novela sin novelistas* (1940, 2nd ed.). Critics were beginning to undertake the task of interpreting the works of the great old masters and so, for example, R. Silva Castro and H. Díaz Arieta wrote abundantly on the life and works of A. Blest Gana.

The importance of the Spanish Civil War in Latin-American poetry has already been mentioned. World War II inspired almost no one, P. Neruda being the exception because of his memorable *Canto a Stalingrado.* Neruda, moreover, became the greatest single influence in Spanish letters. He was either admired or attacked but left no one indifferent. His book *Residencia en la Tierra* offered a strange mixture of romantic, surrealistic, patriotic and revolutionary elements. Neruda created a style of his own, about which a book was written by the distinguished philologist Amado Alonso (*Poesía y Estilo de Pablo Neruda,* 1940). Chile could also be proud of Gabriela Mistral, winner of the Nobel prize in 1945 and author of *Tala* (1938), a serious attempt in the field of vernacular poetry. Other Chilean poets joined the already famous group of Neruda, Vicente Huidobro (*Ver y Palpar,* 1941) and Pablo de Rokha (*Morfología del Espanto,* 1943) to amaze, delight or disgust the reader with their adventures in experimental technics. Juvencio Valle and H. Díaz Casanueva were newcomers of indisputable talent; L. Merino, A. de Undurraga and other younger poets struggled wholeheartedly to come out of lifeless abstractions and into a poetry which was more humane and had a greater universal appeal. Mexico followed a more conservative pattern and its poetry shone especially in the refined spiritualism of Xavier Villaurrutia (*Décima Muerte y otros poemas,* 1941); *La Nostalgia de la Muerte,* 1938); in the virtuosity of Alfonso Reyes (*Algunos Poemas,* 1941) and the philosophical seriousness of Octavio Paz (*A la Orilla del Mundo,* 1943). E. González Martínez gave in 1940 and 1942 two examples of his mild lyricism: *Poesía* and *Bajo el signo Mortal.*

In 1945 he published the first volume of an interesting autobiography: *El Hombre del Buho.*

The Negro poetry of the Antilles was in full splendour, and Nicolás Guillén was a leader with numerous disciples. Another great poet, the Ecuadorean J. Carrera Andrade, kept his fame alive by publishing both in English and in Spanish; two of his books, *Microgramas* and *País Secreto* showed him endeavouring to discover the inner poetry of a typical American reality. His *Canto al Puente de Oakland* (1941) is a sincere homage to the greatness of the United States.

One of the high marks of 1945 Latin-American poetry was the publication of *Poemas Intemporales* by the Colombian P. Barba Jacob.

Argentina's outstanding poetical accomplishments were those of L. Franco (*Suma,* 1938); S. Ocampo (*Viaje Olvidado,* 1940, *Enumeración de la Patria,* 1943); F. L. Bernárdez (*Poemas de Carne y Hueso,* 1943); V. Barbieri (*La Columna y el Viento,* 1943); González Carbalho (*Orilla Nocturna,* 1943). Uruguay had one more poetess of remarkable value in Sara Ibáñez (*Canto,* 1941). Since Spanish-American poetry had become so abundant and varied it became impossible to name all of its worthy representatives. It would also be unwise to generalize on its tendencies. It could be said, however, that abstract poetry had declined, that an eagerness to discover a new form of realism was felt in most of the younger poets. It might be true that Chile had the richest poetical production in the southern continent, but it was also true that Chilean poetry had come to a dead end and was showing alarming signs of exhaustion.

The reaction which was evidently necessary had not yet appeared.

A few words should be said about essays and plays. Spanish-American essayists were busy trying to define their world in terms of universal appeal. Few of them indulged in pure speculative work. Philosophy was studied by men like Enrique Molina (*De lo Espiritual en la Vida Humana,* 1938); Leopoldo Zea (*El Positivismo en México,* 1943); Samuel Ramos (*Historia de la Filosofía en México,* 1943). The field of aesthetics was studied by A. Menéndez y Samara (*La Estética y su Método,* 1938); C. Vaz Ferreira (*Fermentario*); A. Reyes (*Deslinde,* 1945). The majority of Spanish-American essayists dealt with historical, economic and social problems; for example, G. Arciniegas (*América, Tierra Firme,* 1938; *Los Alemanes en la Con-*

Gabriela Mistral (right), Chilean poet who was awarded the Nobel prize for literature in 1945, is shown arriving at a Paris airport for a visit at the invitation of the French government

quista de América, 1941); A. Capdevila (*Las Invasiones Inglesas,* 1939); A. Zum Felde (*El Ocaso de la Democracia,* 1939); M. Picón Salas (*Cinco discursos,* etc., 1940); S. Zavala (*Ensayos sobre la Colonización Española en América,* 1945).

The essays on literary questions were numerous, and some of them attained real success, as A. Arias' *Jorge Isaacs y su "María,"* 1937; A. J. Bucich's *Esteban Echeverría y su tiempo,* 1938; A. Reyes's *Mallarmé entre Nosotros.* 1938; M. Vitier's *Las Ideas en Cuba;* P. Henríquez Ureña's *La Cultura y las Letras Coloniales en Santo Domingo,* 1938; *Plenitud de España,* 1940; J. Jimenez Rueda's *Juan Ruiz de Alarcón y su tiempo,* 1939; N. Pinilla's *La Generación Chilena de 1842,* 1943; D. Melfi's *El Viaje Literario,* 1945. Three histories of literature deserved mention: C. González Peña's *Historia de la Literatura Mexicana* (2nd ed.), 1940; Juan J. Remos' *Historia de la Literatura Cubana,* 1945; and A. Jiménez Pastor's *Historia de la Literatura Argentina,* 1945. Brief surveys were published by Mariano Latorre (*La Literatura de Chile,* 1943) and L. A. Sánchez (*La Literatura del Perú,* 1944).

Spanish-American dramatic literature had not attained great importance. Translations and Spanish plays continued to make up the repertoire of the troupes performing in Buenos Aires, Mexico or Santiago. Two organizations, however, did an excellent job in trying to create a theatre original to Latin America: the Teatro del Pueblo, organized and directed by Leonidas Barletta in Buenos Aires and the later Teatro Experimental of the University of Chile under the direction of Pedro de la Barra. The latter believed it necessary to educate the public, the actors and the authors before a worthwhile dramatic output could begin. Accordingly, he worked mostly with classical pieces of the Spanish Golden Age and occasionally produced a play by a contemporary Chilean author. Argentina had at least one original playwright in Samuel Eichelbaum (*Un guapo del 900, Pájaro de Barro*) and a critic in J. E. Assaf (*El Teatro Argentino como Problema Nacional,* 1938); Mexico had, among others, Xavier Villaurrutia (*La Mujer Legítima,* 1942) and Miguel N. Lira (*Linda,* 1942).

BIBLIOGRAPHY.—Ciro Alegría, *El Mundo es Ancho y Ajeno* (1941); Germán Arciniegas, *América, Tierra Firme* (1938); R. Blanco Fombona, *El Espíritu de Bolívar* (1944); J. Edwards Bello, *En el viejo Almendral* (1943); J. Carrera Andrade, *País Secreto* (1940); Rómulo Gallegos, *Pobre Negro* (1937); P. Henríquez Ureña, *Literary Currents in Hispanic America* (1945); Eduardo Mallea, *Historia de una pasión argentina* (1937); Gabriela Mistral, *Tala* (1938); Pablo Neruda, *Residencia en la Tierra* (1938); J. Rubén Romero, *Una vez fui rico* (1942); A. Torres-Rioseco, *La novela en la América Hispana* (1939–43), *The Epic of Latin American Literature* (2nd ed. 1946); Leopoldo Zea, *El Positivismo en México* (1943). (F. AA.)

Spanish Civil War

The Spanish Civil War, which began on July 17–18, 1936, was an explosion brought on by deep-rooted internal conflicts. It almost immediately took on the pattern of the popular front struggle against fascism which, in turn, made it the rehearsal for World War II.

Spain, after the end of the Napoleonic period, had seen a series of military *pronunciamientos* ending in the dictatorship of generals who were called *caudillos.* There had been two civil wars in the 19th century, and the Second Republic of 1931 was brought on by a definitive revolution whose bloodshed was merely postponed. The failure of the republic to bring peace or internal stability, the reactionary period of the so-called "Black Biennium" from the end of Nov. 1931, the sanguinary, working-class uprising in the Asturias in Oct. 1934, so brutally crushed, and the constant violence all over the country reached a preliminary climax in the elections of Feb. 16, 1936, when the popular front won.

The violence was the result and expression of many long-standing conditions—a peasantry made desperately poor by an antiquated and unequal agrarian structure, a church that was enormously rich and largely monopolized the educational system, an army that was inefficient, costly and privileged, an aristocracy and monarchy that fostered reaction. The political forces of anarcho-syndicalism, socialism, communism, republicanism, falangism and regionalism were disruptive and a constant source of conflict. From outside Spain the pressure of power politics, represented by the anti-democratic forces of Italian and German fascism, the international opposition of Russian communism to fascism and the appeasement of Great Britain and France, all contributed to encouraging disruption and violence. Spain's natural riches, in which the British and French had heavy investments, and which Adolf Hitler coveted, were sources of greed.

In the elections of Feb. 1936, the popular front won a majority of seats, but the voting was close and the government formed under President Manuel Azaña was not really representative of the left and the proletarian revolutionary forces. A period of violence began, characterized by strikes, riots, mob scenes and shooting affrays, that was to merge into the Civil War. The army and Guardia Civil were undermined by subversive forces that were actively plotting rebellion. General Francisco Franco, in fact, had been demoted to the Canary Islands for disloyalty.

On July 12, 1936, Lieut. José del Castillo of the assault guards was shot down by falangists. Early the following morning, Calvo Sotelo was taken out by republicans and killed. He had supplanted José Gil Robles as head of the C.E.D.A. (Confederación Española de Derechas Autónomas) which combined most of the right political parties, and his assassination was the spark which lighted the Civil War.

The uprising was military and it aimed at a military dictatorship, but the generals soon found need for popular support and called upon falangism to provide the political framework. On the republican side, the government had failed to prepare for the shock and when it came refused to arm the people; but they rose spontaneously. The first move took place on July 17, 1936, in Spanish Morocco when a number of regiments mutinied, or rather responded to General Francisco Franco's call to arms. He had flown there the day before, finding the foreign legion, or Tercios, and the Moors ripe for trouble. The following day, garrisons rose in city after city on the peninsula at the call of rebellious generals and within 24 hours, Franco, covered by Italian and German planes, had landed and taken Algeciras and Cádiz. General Queipo de Llano, commander of the carabineros, seized strategic points in Seville and held the city until reinforcements came from Morocco in German planes.

Lineup of Power.—Although falangism was strong in Andalusia, the government held Jaén and the southeastern part of the peninsula. Galicia went to the rebels and stayed with them. In the Asturias, workers held Santander and Gijón, while Bilbao and the Basque country up to the French frontier remained loyal. Navarre, the fiercely Catholic and monarchical centre, where Carlism was still strong, became Franco's fortress and the reservoir of his best troops. It rose under General Emilio Mola. Saragossa, although overwhelmingly left, was cowed by the military garrison under General Miguel Cabanellas. The anarchists fought in the street, and some 1,500 were killed. Valencia and Murcia were seized by the workers and held for the government.

Everything hung upon the fate of Madrid and Barcelona. In Madrid the trade unions forced Azaña's hand. A militia rose spontaneously; barricades were thrown up, churches burned. General Joaquín Fanjúl, commander of the Montaña barracks, reacted too slowly. Militiamen surrounded the barracks and stormed them with heroism and desperation on the night and morning of July 19-20. Thus Madrid was saved for the republic and for its great siege.

Barcelona meanwhile was having its one period of high deeds, for it, too, was held for the republic by a popular, three-day uprising which called for sacrifice and courage. The anarcho-syndicalists were in their element and performed their greatest service of the war for the republic, although their activities were accompanied by a vicious reign of terror, wholesale assassinations, church burnings and the shooting of priests and nuns. The C.N.T. (Confederación Nacional de Trabajo) took power.

While Franco's army was advancing north, Mola's column coming down from Navarre was stopped at the Somosierra pass on the highway from Burgos to Madrid, and that line was held until the end of the war. The loyalists were developing the nucleus of an army in the "5th regiment," which had leaders who were later to become important—Enrique Lister, a Galician worker trained in the soviet union after the Asturias uprising, Juan Modesto, a former carpenter, Valentín Gonzalez, known as "El Campesino" and an Italian communist, Vittorio Vidali, who called himself "Carlos Contreras" and who acted as political commissar.

Initial Franco Successes; Deadlock at Madrid.—As a military insurrection, the rebellion had largely failed in the first week, but German and Italian arms kept it going. Four columns converged on Madrid, while a "fifth column" was supposed to be in the capital, ready to rise. The fall of Badajoz on Aug. 15 started a long series of government reverses. The slaughter by Franco's forces of 1,200 to 1,500 workers in the bull ring of Badajoz after it was taken was symbolic of the desperate and bitter character of the fighting.

Franco, who was campaigning with a small force of Moors and Tercios, aided by German and Italian tanks and planes, made a junction with his northern forces at Mérida on Aug. 16. The general soon became the acknowledged head of the insurgents, who had set up a junta at Burgos on July 22. On the government side, the conflict was accompanied by a social revolution, but unevenly and on the whole timidly. The first cabinet, under José Giral, gave way to a more radical government headed by Largo Caballero after Mola captured Irun on Sept. 4 and San Sebastian on Sept. 12, thus cutting off northern Spain from Madrid. The Italians were largely instrumental in seizing the Balearic Islands for Franco, and they made Palma de Majorca their main air base for the whole war. A front had quickly become established in Aragon and it remained unchanged for a year and a half, with Teruel and Huesca in rebel hands.

Franco diverted his troops to relieve Toledo on Sept. 27, 1936, lifting the siege of the Alcázar, he then moved on to Madrid, reaching its outskirts on Nov. 6. The government fled to Valencia on that day, leaving Gen. José Miaja at the head of a *junta de defensa.* For 36 hours the militia and the Madrileños, unaided, held back Franco and his troops. The "fifth column" proved a fiction. On Nov. 8 the first Internationals entered the lines on the edge of the city at the Casa de Campo. Three days of nip-and-tuck struggle decided the issue, and there the battle lines remained until the end of the war, two and a half years later.

Laboratory for World War II.—The most decisive factor in the war, aside from intervention by Germany and Italy, was the "non-intervention" policy of the democracies, formulated and made effective by Great Britain, initiated by the France of Léon Blum's popular front and supported by the United States. Russian help for the government did not begin until late Oct. 1936, and at no time compensated for the German and Italian aid which Franco received. The League of Nations consistently followed England's lead.

The international brigades in Spain were at first composed of scattered handfuls of foreign volunteers, mostly German and Italian exiles and a few hundred French workmen. Communists soon began gathering from various countries and became the organizers and backbone of the brigades, but there was always a minority of non-party men fighting against fascism. A nucleus of high officers and technicians, partly Russian, was sent from Moscow, remaining discreetly in the background. Before the end of 1937 nearly all of them had been withdrawn. The air force at first was mainly Russian and so were the small tank units of the early months and some artillery. There was never any Russian infantry. The International commission sent by the League of Nations in the fall of 1938 gave the over-all totals as 12,673 foreigners plus 488 prisoners in all services when the internationals were withdrawn. At the beginning of the siege of Madrid, they numbered about 1,500 and at their height totalled between 17,000 and 18,000. The heterogeneous matériel they and the Spaniards used came to a considerable degree from the soviet union and was paid for in gold. The republican army was gradually conscripted, formed and trained to supplant the volunteer "columns" and party groups of the early weeks. The internationals were then incorporated into "mixed brigades," with a majority of Spanish troops.

Franco began a determined drive for Madrid on Feb. 6, 1937, by striking up the Jarama river valley, but after three weeks of desperate fighting the line was held near Arganda and remained unchanged until the end of the war. Meanwhile the Italian expeditionary force, which had won an easy victory at Málaga on Feb. 8, launched a new drive on March 8 with five purely Italian divisions. It was an attempt to smash through Guadalajara and down the plain to Madrid and it proved a turning point in the Civil War and the history of fascism, for the Italians were first held and then routed at Brihuega on March 18.

Galeazzo Ciano, Italian minister of foreign affairs, wrote after the war that his government had sent 100,000 men to Spain between mid-Dec. 1936, and mid-April 1937, without counting naval, air, tank, artillery and technical help. Numerically, the Italian contribution was always the greatest on both sides. The Germans helped Franco more than the Italians, but by means of matériel and technicians rather than men. Their Condor legion, which was formed on Nov. 6, 1936, used up between 16,000 and 18,000 men. For both Italians and Germans, the Spanish venture was considered as training.

Guadalajara changed the course of the war, as it forced Franco to give up hope of taking Madrid. On the suggestion of the Germans, the insurgents turned on the weak and isolated Basque and Asturian sectors and eliminated them. Only the Basques fought, defending their autonomy.

Above, left: Patrol duty on a Republican front during the Spanish Civil War. This guard was armed with a modified 1901 model Russian gun and wore a helmet apparently camouflaged with smeared clay

Above, right: Young militiamen learning to construct barbed wire defenses at a school for military instruction in Madrid

Left: Spanish government troops defending Madrid. In the foreground is a stretcher for the removal of dead and wounded

Below: Teruel was taken by Republican forces in Jan. 1938, but it soon fell to Franco's army for want of defense supplies. Republicans are shown mopping up a machine gun nest overlooking the city's main street, during their brief occupation

The campaign began on April 2, 1937. Guérnica was bombed on April 26; Bilbao fell June 19, Santander Aug. 26 and Gijón Oct. 21, when the long siege of Oviedo was raised.

The Caballero government, weakened by military reverses and by internal friction, fell on May 17, 1937. Dr. Juan Negrín became prime minister and Indalecio Prieto minister of war. In order to relieve the pressure on Bilbao, a drive was launched outside Madrid that lasted from July 5 to 24 and merely resulted in the taking, and the eventual loss, of Brunete. Another drive, toward Saragossa, which commenced on Aug. 23, resulted in the capture of Belchite by the Loyalists on Sept. 1, but otherwise was a failure. At the end of Oct. 1937, the Republican government moved from Valencia to Barcelona.

Teruel and After.—A drive by Franco on Madrid had been expected all through the autumn, but the government sprang a surprise by attacking the rebel stronghold of Teruel on Dec. 15, 1937. Surrender came, in bitter weather, in Jan. 1938. This forced the insurgents to divert their troops, but they had to make four counter-offensives—the last Feb. 19–22, 1938. The loyalists were exhausted by the effort of hanging on, while Franco had mainly expended replaceable German and Italian matériel. He was therefore ready to strike again immediately, while the republicans were now in no condition to hold him. The generalissimo began on March 9, breaking through quickly, and commencing a drive that was to carry the insurgents through Aragon to the sea. The attack was on a 60-mile front with the major axis at Híjar. The loyalists were short of matériel and officers, and there was treachery. As the line melted, four Italian divisions, Moorish cavalry and the Spanish infantry poured through.

Barcelona was subjected to the first blitz of a great city—the prototype for those in World War II—when 18 raids were made in 44 hours during March 16, 17 and 18, 1938.

The line was first consolidated on the Segre river at Lérida, but further south the loyalists went steadily back until the Navarrese Requetés reached the sea at Viñaroz on April 15, 1938. Loyalist Spain was cut in two, but the line of the Ebro and Segre rivers still protected the north. The confident expectations of a quick victory in the insurgent camp and abroad were disappointed when Franco's most determined efforts to drive down from Teruel to Valencia were frustrated. It proved one of the fiercest battles of the war, and just as the lines were stabilized at Viver and Caudiel on July 24, the republicans again surprised the enemy by striking across the Ebro river between Flix and Miravet. The bridgehead then set up was to take Franco four months and seven counter-offensives to reduce.

This was the last battle in which the international brigades figured, for Negrín, in a quixotic gesture, announced to the League of Nations on Sept. 21 that the Spanish government was withdrawing them. At his request the League appointed an international commission to verify the withdrawal. Benito Mussolini thereupon agreed to pull out 10,000 of the "legionnaires" who were fighting in Spain. According to Italian official figures at the time, the total number of men was 40,000, but in any event, the Germans made no withdrawals, and what counted most was the fact that German and Italian matériel continued to flow into Spain in ever greater measure. On the loyalist side, Russian help had long ceased to be of any importance. The army was wholly Spanish. The matériel bought from the soviet union or "bootlegged" from various countries, could not get into Spain because the French held it at their ports until too late, and the German and Italian naval units at Franco's disposal made direct shipments risky. Thus the republicans had to fight their hopeless struggle alone.

Loyalist Collapse.—The consequences of the Ebro attack proved the same as at Teruel. The battle also ended with the loyalist army exhausted and without matériel, while the insurgents had received the heaviest reinforcements of matériel in the whole war. The Italian "Corpo Truppe Voluntarie" was reorganized and re-equipped under General Gastone Gambara and from then on fought hard and effectively. After five weeks of sporadic bombing raids on rearguard towns, Franco struck on Dec. 23, 1938, across the Segre river on three sectors. The Italians found an opening near a small insurgent bridgehead at Seros and poured through. Moorish cavalry followed and began a sweep around their right wing against feeble opposition by the loyalist 43rd division, but at other points the defense was heroic. Lister, who had become the greatest of the loyalist commanders, held the Italians for ten days, while Lieut. Col. Francisco ("Paco") Galán fought a stubborn retreat in the Tremp sector for as many days. But on Jan. 4, 1939, Borjas Blancas and Artesa de Segre were lost, and with them the Civil War. Franco by then had 28 divisions in the line and overwhelming matériel superiority of every kind. The loyalists did not even have nearly enough rifles to go around. The diversion that should have come from the southern zone never materialized, for its people were tired and its higher officers weak or treacherous.

Tarragona fell on Jan. 15 and after a brief pause the insurgents drove steadily toward Barcelona. The Catalan capital was not defended and was lost on Jan. 26 after having been subjected to five days of almost uninterrupted bombing. A few days before, the government moved to Figueras where the last dramatic cortes of the Second Spanish Republic gathered on Feb. 1, in the cellars of the castle overlooking the town. It was an effort to maintain constitutional legality, and the cortes had, indeed, met regularly every six months during the war, wherever possible.

The retreat, which was accompanied by more than 250,000 civilians, began to push up and then over the French frontier. Men, women, children and soldiers were packed into hastily improvised camps where most of them remained for months and years. Figueras was overrun on Feb. 8 and the government came across to the Spanish portion of Le Perthus the next day. The republican army went on fighting rearguard actions as best it could to the very end, and it succeeded at least in delaying the insurgents long enough to protect the civilian refugees and to save what matériel it had. By the afternoon of Feb. 10, 1939, Generalissimo Franco's forces were all along the whole French frontier.

All that remained was to liquidate the southern zone, where Madrid still continued its heroic defense. Dr. Negrín and a few faithful adherents, including Lister and Modesto, flew into the zone in an effort to rally the 60 divisions which were there. A much greater war was approaching and they saw that if the zone could hold out for six months or more, the democracies would have to come to the rescue. However, the forces in Madrid, nominally headed by Gen. Miaja, but really controlled by a former regular army officer, Col. Sigismundo Casado, were placed at the mercy of Franco. Parleys were held in which the generalissimo insisted on unconditional surrender. To accomplish this it was necessary to liquidate the loyal elements and this was done by inducing the anarchists and some other troops to turn on the communists and those men who wanted to fight to the end. The navy mutinied and sailed to Oran; Negrín and his followers had to fly to France, and there was nothing to stop the insurgents from entering the capital. The epic siege of Madrid ended on March 29, 1939. That same evening the Navarrese corps, followed by the Italians who had driven down to the coast without opposition, entered Valencia unopposed. Resistance had ended everywhere. Minorca, the only territory outside of the peninsula which the government had held on to, had already been turned over to Franco by the British. The Civil War was over. (*See* also INTERNATIONAL LAW.)

BIBLIOGRAPHY.—J. Alvarez del Vayo, *Freedom's Battle* (1940); Louis Fischer, *Men and Politics* (1941); J. Martin Blazquez, *I Helped to Build an Army: Civil War Memoirs of a Spanish Staff Officer* (London, 1939); Francisco Franco, *The Times and the Man* (1938); G. L. Steer, *The Tree of Gernika* (London, 1937); Franz Borkenau, *The Spanish Cockpit* (London, 1937); E. Allison Peers, *The Spanish Tragedy* (London, 1937); Frank Jellinek, *The Civil War in Spain* (London, 1938); Gerald Brenan, *The Spanish Labyrinth*, Cambridge University Press (1943); Herbert L. Matthews, *The Education of a Correspondent* (1946). (HE. L. M.)

Spanish Colonial Empire

The Spanish empire at the end of the decade 1937–46 comprised territory in Morocco, the western Sahara and Spanish Guinea. In Morocco, Ceuta Melilla, Alhucemas, Chafarines and Peñon Veliz; area 82 sq.mi.; pop. (est. 1944) 145,000; capital: Madrid (administered as part of Spain). Spanish Morocco; area 8,080 sq.mi.; pop. (1944 est.) 992,000; capital: Tetuan (protectorate). Spanish Guinea, including Fernando Poo, Rio Muni and 4 small islands; area 10,900 sq.mi.; pop. (1944 est.) 168,000; capital: Santa Isabel (colony). Western Sahara, including Ifni and Spanish Sahara; area 116,200 sq.mi.; pop. (1944 est.) 72,000; capital: Villa Cisneros (colonies).

Total area: *c.* 135,200 sq.mi.; total pop. (1944 est.) 1,377,000.

Tangier (*q.v.*) was temporarily incorporated into the empire.

During the greater part of the Spanish Civil War (1936–39), the colonies were held by Gen. Francisco Franco.

In Jan. 1937 the French government protested against the alleged infiltration into Spanish Morocco of German troops and the development of German military and commercial interests, including the building of barracks for a German armed force. Hitler replied, however, that Germany had no designs there. From Morocco Gen. Franco poured large numbers of Moorish troops into Spain, describing them (March 13, 1938) as "the flower of the army" and used them freely, notably in the capture of Santander (Aug. 26, 1937), Lérida (April 3, 1938) and Castellón (June 14, 1938).

The Republicans repeatedly bombed Ceuta.

In his first cabinet (Jan. 30, 1938) Gen. Franco assigned the government of the colonies to his vice-president, whence it passed to the foreign ministry, but on Jan. 23, 1942, it was made over to a directorate-general, responsible to the head of the state.

The first director-general was Don Juan Fontán, previously governor-general of the Spanish possessions in the Gulf of Guinea.

The principal high commissioners for Spanish Morocco were Col. Juan Beigbeder (later Spanish foreign minister), Gen. Carlos Asensio, Gen. Luis Orgaz and Gen. José Varela.

From the beginning of the Civil War, Tangier was a centre of discord, owing to its important position on the Straits of Gibraltar. Italy, *e.g.*, accused French magistrates of partiality in an inquiry into a dispute between Italian soldiers and Spanish communists, while Franco accused Italy and Germany of making unscrupulous use of propaganda in order to detach the people of Tangier from allegiance to their ruler and thus threatening the unity of Morocco.

But only during World War II was the international status of Tangier temporarily changed. During 1943–45 it became a part of the Spanish colonial empire. (*See* TANGIER.)

Spanish Morocco: *Statistical Data*

Item	1938 Value (000's omitted)	1938 Amount or Number	1941 Value (000's omitted)	1941 Amount or Number
Exchange rate				
U.S.		1 Peseta = 5.6 cents		1 Peseta = 9.13 cents
Great Britain		40–42 Pesetas =£1*		40–60 Pesetas =£1
Finance				
Government revenues	$6,260 (£1,280)†			
Government expenditures	$6,260 (£1,280)†			
Transportation				
Railroads		140 mi.		176 mi.
Highways		1,383 "		1,398 "
Minerals				
Iron ore		1,478,910 tons		566,865 tons
Antimony		103 "		204 "
Manganese		168 "		...
Graphite		...		456 "
Crops				
Barley		62,067 tons		79,340 tons
Sorghum		24,684 "		27,714 "
Wheat		22,880 "		21,356 "
Livestock				
Goats		918,100		792,300
Sheep		487,300		438,600
Cattle		226,900		308,700
Products				
Firewood		36,198 tons		49,997 tons
Esparto		3,807 "		2,178 "
Cork		1,764 "		1,843 "
Sea products—total		4,330 tons		8,046 tons
Tuna		91 "		1,517 "
Melvas		13 "		153 "
Molluscs		...		331 "
Exports—total	$7,144 (£1,611)*	...	$5,031 (£1,248)	...
Cattle, eggs, iron ore, principal commodities; no details available				
Imports—total	$1,710 (£386)*	...	$27,303 (£6,772)	...
Cereals and flour	$1,225 (£276)*	...	$1,099 (£273)	...
Textiles and yarns	$926 (£209)*	...	$1,743 (£432)	...
Sugar	$563 (£127)*	...	$1,330 (£330)	...
Education				
Primary grades				
Spanish schools				49‡
Students				6,876‡
Teachers				144‡
Moroccan schools				39
Students				3,544
Teachers				172
Private Spanish schools				17
Students				2,539
Teachers				61
Schools teaching the Koran				3,295
Students				34,766

*1939. †Budget estimate. ‡Including Tangier.

 On the British-American invasion of North Africa (Nov. 8, 1942), the two governments sent Spain a written assurance that "Spanish territory will be fully respected and Spanish interests in North Africa will not be compromised," which Spain "gratefully accepted." Gen. Miguel Yagüe, an old and tried soldier, was appointed to the command of Spanish Morocco, but no other steps were taken.

BIBLIOGRAPHY.—T. García Figueras, *Marruecos: La Acción de España en el Norte de Africa* (Barcelona, 1939); F. H. Mellor: *Morocco Awakes* (1939); J. M. Cordero Torres, *Organización del Protectorado Españo en Marruecos* (2 vols. Madrid, 1942–43); E. Allison Peers, *Spain in Eclipse* (London, 1943).

(E. A. P.)

Spanish Literature

Spain's Civil War, a sort of preview of World War II, broke out on July 18, 1936, leaving in its wake devastation, death, starvation, concentration camps, mass emigration and complete disruption of normal life. With the cessation of open warfare (1939) and the establishment of Francisco Franco's government, there was instituted a strict censorship which stifled effectively all liberal tendencies.

The gloomy war years claimed in death several notable writers. In 1938 the idealist Armando Palacio Valdés, esteemed as a gentle grandfather by the younger generation of novelists, slipped away from this life, his passing being hardly noticed during the siege of Madrid. Antonio Machado died in 1939 at Collioure in the south of France; his death resulted directly from privations suffered while escaping from Barcelona. The same year also saw the passing of Serafín Alvarez Quintero, elder of the two brothers who collaborated in writing more than 200 plays, many quite remarkable for their sprightly humour and springlike freshness, particularly conspicuous in those having their setting in Andalusia.

The Civil War furnished the topic for many books of the decade 1937–46, a number characterized by inadequate assimilation of the material to the literary form. The drama and the novel deteriorated noticeably in quality; of true novels there were few. Several émigrés won distinction through writing frank, critical, philosophical prose. The nationalists controlling Spain's destiny insisted upon preserving peninsular tradition and indigenous culture, importing nothing from the other European countries or the Americas. The most important propagandist of this doctrine was the essayist Ernesto Giménez Caballero.

The indefatigable Pío Baroja, creator of some 70-odd volumes, continued producing books, few of which, if any, served to enhance the author's reputation. He persisted in his pessimistic views and grumbled about practically everything and everybody, retaining his stubborn genuineness. In his supposed novels the action developed in an endless swift succession of incidents and characters, both equally deficient in imagination and dramatization. His style still possessed a journalistic flavour, characterized by pellucid directness. In *Rapsodias,* a collection of essays on divers literary and social themes, special interest attached to Baroja's speech delivered upon his reception in the Spanish academy. Intentionally, the author plays the part of a writer of the streets, the autobiographical information being recounted with the utmost candour. *El cura de Monleón,* the second volume of the trilogy *La juventud perdida,* is the story of a truly Barojan hero, who discovers in the end his incompatibility with his spiritual vows. *Historias lejanas* contains three fairly long stories and ten miscellaneous articles previously published in newspapers. *El caballero de Erláiz* awakens interest with its adventures in the French and Spanish Basque countries during the French Revolution. Three volumes of memoirs (*El escritor según él y según los críticos; Familia, infancia y juventud; El Final del siglo XIX y principios del XX*) relate his autobiography in fragments, boring in spots because of too many details. He sometimes gives expression to petty dislikes, speaking in a harping way of his contemporaries, both the living and the dead. His description of the dissecting room leaves a thoroughly disagreeable impression, yet his concrete realism gives way in a few places to lyricism.

José Martínez Ruiz (Azorín), awarded the Gran Cruz de Alfonso el Sabio, rivalled Baroja in his productivity. He published in 1941 two volumes of autobiographical memoirs, *Valencia* and *Madrid.* The 40 chapters of *El escritor* may be looked upon as interesting chats expressed in a language personal and simple, yet very beautiful. *Tiempos y cosas,* composed of 32 articles not previously assembled in book form, is concerned primarily with topics of artistic and literary criticism. The novel *María Fontán* analyzes the reactions of an opulent heiress, curious and restless. *Salvadora de Olbena,* another novel, likewise presents an exceptional woman character against the background of a small provincial city. *El paisaje de España visto por los españoles* is a study of Spanish landscapes through the works of authors who had best described them. *Veraneo sentimental* gives travel impressions of well-known summer resorts. *París* is made up of essays about the French capital. Still another book of essays, previously published in Spanish and Spanish-American newspapers, was *Palabras al viento.*

Salvador de Madariaga, professor, literary critic, essayist, high functionary of the defunct League of Nations, former ambassador and minister of the republic, continued to cultivate several literary genres. His *Campos eliseos* is a purported dialogue in which Goethe, Mary Stuart, Voltaire, Napoleon, Karl Marx, and President Washington discourse on 20th-century conditions: fascism and communism, the evil effects of moving pictures, the U.S. reluctance to join the League of Nations, etc. The novel *El enemigo de Dios* has for its protagonist a hunchback through whose eyes life takes on a different point of view. Later Madariaga devoted his attention almost exclusively to biography. His comprehensive life of Christopher Columbus, although replete with documental notes, bibliography and two indices, is never dull in spite of its erudition; one of the most interesting chapters takes up the oft-debated question of the great navigator's origin. Similarities between Columbus and Don Quixote are developed as the hero's life unfolds. Madariaga's biography of Hernán Cortés, equally well documented and packed with details, is a fascinating story of a real life, not just a record of historical events.

El Gran Hotel and *Los muertos, las muertas y otras fantasmagorías* possess the good humour and optimism for which Ramón Gómez de la Serna's works had become so well-known. *El circo,* in addition to its many ingenious digressions inspired by the circus, contains some biographical data by the author's brother, Julio Gómez de la Serna. *Lo cursi y otros ensayos* are full of epigrams and paradoxes. While manifesting sympathy for modern poetry and surrealism, the essayist makes use of the opportunity to condemn the submersion of literature in politics.

Ramón J. Sender, an active combatant, suffered much in the Civil War, several members of his family being executed by the fascists. Sacrifice and marked idealism endowed him with a deep humanitarian spirit. All of his works are arresting narratives. *Proverbio de la muerte,* of an autobiographical nature, is the author's account of his crossing to Mexico. The novel presents a disillusioned idealist who wins his battle in the determination to live. *El lugar del hombre* turns back the pages of time to prewar Spain, the Spanish countryside becoming a symbol of this modern world; this novel studies man's injustice and inhumanity toward his fellow. *Hernán Cortés,* written in dialogue form, draws excellent sketches of Mexico's conqueror, a complex character generally misunderstood; Marina, his *querida* and interpreter; and Xhinotecatl, the untamable young Indian leader. Novelettes, legends and animal stories form *Mexicayotl,* a panorama of ancient Mexico. The plots are closely linked with that country's salient natural features, birds and animals. *Epitalamio del Prieto Trinidad* is a sombre picture of the tortured world and its monstrous inhabitants. The tender love story of Darío and La Niña—Truth and Beauty—flowers in the unhealthy atmosphere of an island penal colony. The author termed this psychological novel "a poem of the subconscious." In *Crónica del alba,* Sender returned to the Aragón of his childhood; it is a beautiful tale of family life, youthful love, adventures in an abandoned castle, studies and boyish pranks.

Jacinto Benavente, Spain's most distinguished dramatist and Nobel prize winner in 1922, continued writing plays. His later works were: *La culpa es tuya; La enlutada; El demonio del teatro; La honradez de la cerradura; Al fin, mujer;* and *Nieve en mayo.* In 1945, while in Argentina to see to the publication of his memoirs, he was lionized at numerous literary gatherings and made corresponding member of the Argentine academy of letters. He had, moreover, the satisfaction of seeing staged in Buenos Aires his famous masterpiece, *Los intereses creados.* In Jan. 1941 Don Joaquín Alvarez Quintero, the surviving member of the distinguished pair of brother-dramatists, received appointment as *bibliotecario perpetuo* of the Spanish academy. The facile playwright Carlos Arniches Barrera produced comedies, farces and tragedies right up to the end of his life: *La venganza de la Petra, o donde las dan, las toman; ¡La condesa está triste!; La fiera dormida; Ya conoces a Paquita; Don Verdades. El galeón y et milagro,* Eduardo Marquina's drama in verse, was lavishly produced in 1945. Another of his later works, *María la viuda,* glorifies religion and mother love. Ignacio Luca de Tena, one of the most popular playwrights of the latter part of the decade, dramatized Juan Alarcón's humorous novel *El sombrero de tres picos.* The talented poet Rafael Alberti, a refugee residing in Argentina, wrote an eccentric play *El adefesio,* with the subtitle *Fábula del amor y las viejas,* in which three old spinsters oppose a young girl's love, thereby causing her suicide. The famous actress Margarita Xirgu took the leading role at its premiere in Buenos Aires. The modernist poet Manuel Machado revealed traditional Spanish faith in *El Pilar de la Victoria,* a lyric religious poem, with music by Pablo Luna and Julio Gómez, which had its initial performance in Zaragoza during the Pilar festival of 1944.

Among the older poets who remained in Spain, two wrote deeply religious works, strikingly different from what came before from their pens. Vicente Aleixandre, stricken by illness and living in retirement, ceased to be essentially a love poet. The poems of *Sombra del paraiso* presented a new perspective, expressed in elaborate symbolism tending to the baroque. Passion for the sea is evident in this poetry, often cast in a form of exquisite plastic grace. Dámaso Alonso's *Hijos de la ira,* free from the spirit of aloofness prevailing in his earlier poems, is as the subtitle indicates a "diario íntimo." The verses evoke the problem of man's relation to God and disclose concern over ultimate values. Several excellent studies added lustre to Dámaso Alonso's fame as an erudite critic and scholar, properly recognized in his appointment to membership of the Academia de la Lengua in May 1945. *La poesía de San Juan de la Cruz* shows the great mystic's indebtedness to Garcilaso and *Garcilaso a lo divino* (an adaption by Sebastián de Córdoba, who gave to Garcilaso's works a spiritual significance), the elements stemming from popular tradition and the biblical roots. Dámaso Alonso's *Ensayos sobre poesía española* consists of some thought-provoking chapters relative to both the old and new in Spanish poetry. Such dissimilar topics as *The Poem of the Cid,* sonnets attributed to Francisco Gómez de Quevedo, Gustavo Bécquer's originality, García Lorca as an expression of the Spanish spirit and Aleixandre's poetry are discussed in a stimulating manner. *Versos plurimembres y poemas correlativos* studies in detail the multipartite and correlative verses written during the "Golden Age"; the critic is not a biased partisan of Gongorism.

The poet Pedro Salinas, who became a professor at Johns Hopkins university, Baltimore, Md., published two books of a critical nature. *Reality and the Poet in Spanish Poetry* is made up of six lectures which attempt to bring together around a common thematic centre—reality and poetry—a series of spiritual reactions experienced in reading *The Poem of the Cid,* Jorge Manrique, Calderón de la Barca, Garcilaso de la Vega, Fray Luis de León, San Juan de la Cruz, Luis de Góngora and Jose de Espronceda. His volume *Literatura española, siglo XX,* divided into three sections, opens with a discussion of modernism, the generation of '98 and 20th-century literature before taking up Miguel de Unamuno, Ramón del Valle-Inclán, Antonio Machado, Jorge Guillén, García Lorca, Luis Cernuda, etc. He finds the period characterized by a lyricism, evident not only in poets but in prose writers like Unamuno, Pérez de Ayala, Azorín and even Baroja. Juan Ramón Jiménez, still Spain's greatest poet at the end of the decade, also assembled in *Españoles de tres mundos* a number of brief impressionistic sketches—by no means traditional—about Bécquer, Rosalía de Castro, Asunción Silva, Salinas, Dámaso Alonso, Guillén, Pablo Neruda, etc.

Spain could well be proud of the accomplishments of the young literary historian and critic Angel Valbuena Prat. His *Historia de la literatura española,* in two volumes, was the best book of its sort to be published in a number of years. It was the product of deep study and an incredible amount of reading. The last chapters, concerned with contemporary letters, are extremely important because of an acute discriminating taste between what is good and bad. In *La novela picaresca española,* the most complete collection of Spanish picaresque novels in one volume, Valbuena Prat discussed the genre in its satirical and social phases along with the derivation of the word *pícaro.* Brief introductions precede each of the novels. His *Teatro moderno español* is a critical examination of the theatre from the beginning of the 18th century. Three volumes of the all-comprehensive *Historia de España,* directed by the famous philologist Ramón Menéndez Pidal, and numbering among its contributors historians of authority, were published. Rodríguez Marín brought out another volume of proverbs, *Todavía 10.700 refranes más.*

The cultural life in Hispanic America was greatly quickened by the many Spanish refugees who fled there from Europe after the fall of the republic. Mexico absorbed as many of these intellectuals as all of the other Latin-American countries combined. Enrique Diez-Canedo, author, lecturer, editor and dramatic critic wrote several works of literary criticism while teaching in the Mexican capital before his death. *El teatro y sus enemigos* studies the three enemies which had brought about the decline of the theatre: the "movies," the actor and the author. *Juan Ramón Jiménez en su obra* is an examination of this poet's development, his indebtedness to others and influence on the younger generation. *Letras de América* treats literary figures belonging to practically every age and nation of Latin America. Diez-Canedo's little book of epigrams contains fleeting impressions experienced while journeying through South America, the orient and Mexico.

José Moreno Villa, archivist, poet, essayist and painter also worked in Mexico City. In *Locos, enanos, negros y niños palaciegos* he brought to light a lot of curious information relative to the entertainers in the Spanish court from 1563–1700. *Cornucopia de México* gives sensitive impressions of the habits, language and folklore of his new homeland. His unconventional autobiography *Vida en claro* holds the reader's attention with its modernist verses, the reproduction of the author's paintings and the account of life in the Residencia de Estudiantes in Madrid with glimpses of García Lorca and others.

The Valencian journalist, playwright, poet and lecturer, Max Aub, wrote prolifically in the favourable surroundings of the Mexican republic. *Morir por cerrar los ojos* is a tragedy dealing with the collapse of France, the materialism and selfishness of its citizens, their barbarous treatment of foreigners and the officials' propensity for bribery. His *Diario de Djelfa,* poems composed in Africa in a French concentration camp for interned Republicans, expresses the prisoners' feelings of despair and hope, together with an account of their physical sufferings caused by cold, hunger and ever-present death. *No son cuentos,* eight sketches written in different countries and over a period covering some six years, are records of actual experiences in the Spanish Civil War, related in short story form. The first story makes a deep impression with its portrait of the enslaved sharecropper converted into a patriot through receiving some land to cultivate as his own. Too, there are spiritual tragedies like the one of the turncoat priest.

José Bergamín, a great essayist, established in Mexico City a thriving publishing house, the Editorial Séneca. In spite of his many duties connected with this company, Bergamín found time to write articles, essays, plays, novels and ballets. His incisive style, one of the most individual in modern Spanish literature, is characterized by the use of metaphors, epigrams and aphorisms. This author is first of all a psychologist and social philosopher. His *Detrás de la cruz,* with the subtitle *Terrorismo y persecución religiosa en España,* treats of collusion between the Spanish church and fascist Italy and nazi Germany during the Civil War.

Only the future could show whether peninsular Spanish letters would again attain the world importance enjoyed by the generation of 1898. Barriers along the way to impede the realization of such a goal were strict censorship, internal dissension, chronic lethargy and the loss of numerous writers—some of high calibre—who would most likely pass the remainder of their lives in the Americas.

BIBLIOGRAPHY.—Pío Baroja, *El final del siglo XIX y principios del XX* (Madrid, 1945); José Martínez Ruiz (Azorín), *El escritor* (Buenos Aires, 1942); Salvador de Madariaga, *Christopher Columbus* (London, 1939); Ramón J. Sender, *El lugar del hombre* (México, 1939); Ramón Gómez de la Serna, *Lo cursi y otros ensayos* (Buenos Aires, 1943); Jacinto Benavente, *La honradez de la cerradura; Al fin, mujer* (Buenos Aires, 1943?); Vicente Aleixandre, *Sombra del paraíso* (Madrid, 1944); Dámaso Alonso, *Ensayos sobre poesía española* (Madrid, 1944); Pedro Salinas, *Reality and the Poet in Spanish Poetry* (1940); Angel Valbuena Prat, *Historia de la literatura, española,* 2 vols. (Barcelona, 1937); Enrique Diez-Canedo, *Juan Ramón Jiménez en su obra* (México, 1944); José Moreno Villa, *Vida en claro* (México, 1944); Max Aub, *Morir por cerrar los ojos* (México, 1944); José Bergamín, *Detrás de la cruz* (México, 1941).

(H. L. JN.)

Spanish Possessions in Africa

See SPANISH COLONIAL EMPIRE.

Spars (Women's Reserve of the U.S. Coast Guard Reserve)

See COAST GUARD, U.S.

Spearmint

See VEGETABLES.

Special Areas, British

The term "special areas" was first used in Britain in the Special Areas (Development and Improvement) act, 1934, which provided for the establishment of two commissioners, one for England and Wales and one for Scotland, whose functions were "the initiation, organization, prosecution and assistance of measures designed to facilitate the economic development and social improvement" of the special areas. These areas depended on coal mining and heavy engineering industries. Their special problem was prolonged and intensive unemployment. In 1937 the powers of the commissioners were extended by the Special Areas (Amendment) act, which enabled them to make a financial contribution not only in relief of income tax and rates but also towards rent payable in respect of new industrial undertakings and for certain street works and field drainage works.

During World War II prosperity came to the special areas, and unemployment dwindled to a vanishing point. Schemes not under construction, which the commissioners had undertaken to assist, were postponed. Those begun were, wherever possible, completed. Towards the end of the war the government began to look ahead to the postwar problems of the special areas. The 1934 and 1937 acts were repealed, and the Distribution of Industry act, 1945, was substituted. This later act set out new procedures for stimulating the industrial and social development of areas in which there was a special danger of a recurrence of unemployment. The special areas now became known as "development areas," and the board of trade took over the functions of the commissioners. Provision was made for adding to the list of development areas by order of the board of trade.

To the four areas determined before World War II (South Wales and Monmouthshire, North-Eastern area, Scottish development area and West Cumberland development area) the South Lancashire and Wrexham areas were added in 1945, by order of the board of trade.

BIBLIOGRAPHY.—"Special Areas (Amendment) Act, 1937," *Public Acts,* chap. 31, session 1936–37 (H.M.S.O., London, 1937); *Report of the Commissioner for Special Areas* (Cmd. 5896, H.M.S.O., London, 1938); "Distribution of Industry Act, 1945," *Public Acts,* chap. 36, session 1944–45 (H.M.S.O., London, 1945).

(JE. L.)

Special Libraries Association

See SOCIETIES AND ASSOCIATIONS.

Speedway Racing

See Automobile Racing.

Spellman, Francis Joseph

Cardinal Spellman (1889–), U.S. Catholic prelate, was born May 4, 1889, in Whitman, Mass. Ordained in Rome in 1916, he served as assistant chancellor of the archdiocese of Boston, Mass., 1922–25, and in the latter year became the first U.S. priest to enter active service in the papal diplomatic corps, serving in the papal secretariat of state in the Vatican. In 1932 he was appointed titular bishop of Sila, to serve as auxiliary bishop of Boston, and on May 23, 1939, he was installed as the sixth ordinary of the New York archdiocese.

Three months after the outbreak of World War II, he was appointed by the holy see to be U.S. military vicar. In this capacity he journeyed over the world for inspections of military installations and conferences with churchmen; he also met U.S. fighting men in the field.

The archbishop frequently pleaded for tolerance as "the basic American credo of religious, industrial education and social freedom." In 1945 the cardinal served as secretary of the administrative board of the National Catholic Welfare conference in Washington, D.C. Announcement of his appointment to the Sacred College of Cardinals was made Dec. 23, 1945, and he was created cardinal on Feb. 18, 1946.

Spelman Fund of New York

See Societies and Associations.

Spices

As 1937 opened, the U.S. Food and Drug act was 30 years old. On June 25, 1936, the original law of 1906 had been repealed and replaced by the U.S. Food, Drug and Cosmetic act with added police power over imports and interstate shipments of spices. Consumers became more conscious of flavour and strength and the eupeptic qualities of spices. The staple spices were 24 in number, the same as centuries before.

Mustard.—In the western hemisphere and Europe, more mustard was eaten during the decade 1937–46 than any other spice. In large measure this was due to the activity of U.S. and Canadian farmers. They were ready when World War II began, and their crops maintained adequate supplies of mustard seed from Montana, Washington, California in the United States and Alberta in Canada. The U.S. harvest of 1946 was estimated by the department of agriculture at 49,490,000 lbs. Until 1936, nearly all mustards had originated in Europe and Asia. Imports into the United States were impossible during the war, as governments refused to issue export permits. U.S. growers were protected by the 1939 reciprocal import duty of one and three-quarters cents per pound (about 16% ad valorem). The ascending popularity of salad dressings and mayonnaise explained the heavier demand. New homogenizing methods for combining oils with mustard and the other ingredients and better retail distributing methods, plus the vogue of raw, leafy vegetables, indicated still more expansion. The finest seeds continued to come from England. The three varieties cultivated during the decade in North America were yellow (*Brassica alba*), brown (*B. nigra*) and oriental (*B. juncea*). England, Denmark and Sweden resumed shipments in March 1946. The Netherlands again appeared as a seller to offer its new crop mustard for shipment in Oct. 1946.

Black and White Peppers.—Trading in peppers was turbulent throughout the decade. About 1934, the suggestion that pepper was a good hedge against inflation had been widely accepted. Pepper trading began on the New York produce exchange, which began to displace London as the world market, and margin and cash business became active. In 1939, several bumper crops depressed spot and future quotations from the six cent low of 1936 to a new low of two and three-quarters cents per lb. ex store New York (50 year average 13.6 cents). Accumulation was brisk, hastened by the diminishing gold content of the dollar. Warehoused tonnage rapidly increased. The produce exchange reported stored stocks in bags (140 lbs. each) every month. When the Office of Price Administration established price controls in 1941, it imposed a ceiling of six and three-quarters cents per lb. at which some "fright selling" occurred. A few months later the OPA reduced the ceiling to six and one-half cents, which just about ended pepper selling. As Japan invaded the Netherlands Indies and French Indo-China, where most of the world's pepper originated, imports ceased. Southwestern India became the sole source of supply; there the price was much higher than the U.S. ceiling, hence the later U.S. scarcity. Because of the need of the U.S. armed forces, the U.S. government moved to seize stored stocks at six and one-half cents (world price 18 cents), but desisted when court action seemed inevitable. OPA countered later by raising the ceiling to ten cents (world price 20 cents), when a few tons came on the market. A real pepper famine impended. From July 1, 1945, to Sept. 1, 1946, New York stocks had dropped from 58,832 bags to 7,901 bags. The impasse continued because of the impossibility of importing at the U.S. ten cent ceiling. The OPA feebly tried again by raising the ceiling to 15 cents per lb., and some sellers appeared. But replenishment from Alleppey and Tellicherry (Indian pepper ports) could not be landed in New York for less than 25½ cents.

Pepper had been plentiful and the price much below normal in 1934. There was no U.S. import duty on it; kept dry, pepper does not deteriorate and there had always been a market for it, either domestic or export, usually both. Demand had been universal. Pepper, therefore, was an excellent hedge against losses from currency depreciation, and investors switched wealth into it from securities, thus increasing the stock pile to 673,527 bags (42,100 tons) in New York warehouses by April 1939. That amount was sufficient for the United States for 3½ years; the normal consumption of 1,000 tons per month was later reduced to 250 tons by a regulation limiting distribution to 25% of the prewar normal. The plowing-under of crops and slaying of little pigs in exchange for largess were recalled as the proponents of those policies, still in power, found profits on warehoused pepper abhorrent, whether from domestic or export sales. The U.S. per capita pepper expenditure was less than 15 cents per year.

When OPA ceased temporarily to exist on June 30, 1946, active trading in pepper was resumed, and much spot tonnage changed hands at from 25 cents to 60 cents. The volume faded to nothing flat when OPA was revived July 25 and reimposed the ceiling price of 15 cents. The pepper ceiling was removed at last on Aug. 26, 1946 (world market 55 cents).

Cinnamon and Cassia.—These two spices are one and the same to consumers north of the Rio Grande. Elsewhere they are marketed under their distinctive names. The world's supply of cinnamon comes from Ceylon. Its soft, smooth, mild flavour and light colour pleases Latin

Americans. About 90% of the production ordinarily had been bought by them at prices usually much above the cost of cassia. During World War II, cinnamon was eagerly accepted as a substitute in the United States, but cassia remained the favourite. The supply from Sumatra and other East Indian islands was cut off during the war. China remained the largest producer of cassia; its best variety, Saigon cassia, remained expensive as it carried the largest percentage of the essential oil conveying flavour and strength. During 1936–37 the results of many years of effort to improve quality were noted. Certain almost tasteless varieties of cassia were excluded from U.S. markets under the National Food law as trash. During the period 1941–46 the distribution of cassia and cinnamon in the United States was limited to 25% of the prewar volume, and price was controlled by ceilings. Early in 1946, exports of fine varieties from Hong Kong were resumed, including the strongest and best flavoured Saigon variety.

Ginger.—Ginger, next in popularity, was shipped in usual volume throughout the decade 1937–46. While World War II continued, imports from Sierre Leone, West Africa—supplier of the staple variety for cakes and gingersnaps—were several times delayed; but the cochin from southern India, with its lemony flavour (for ginger wafers) was plentiful. The top U.S. favourite for lightness of colour and rich fruity flavour, produced in Jamaica, was always in good supply for ginger ale, fancy baking and the tonic purposes set forth in the U.S. *Pharmacopoeia,* 12th revision.

Cloves.—Cloves remained continually available despite the war and reduced shipping service. The two islands, Zanzibar and Pemba, sent all that was needed. Quickly following the fall of Japan, Madagascar again contributed to the clove supply. The production of vanillin from oil of cloves was expanded; this synthetic vanilla was needed in unprecedented volume by Allied armed forces. As flavouring in powder form, it required neither alcohol nor heavy bottles, both scarce during World War II.

Pimento.—The prime mincemeat spice remained known throughout the United States as allspice, because in flavour it resembles a mixture of cinnamon, cloves and nutmegs. Botanically it is *Pimenta officinalis,* a tree, native to the island of Jamaica, British West Indies, which continued to be the only successful producer. During the decade, a rival appeared on the market, listed by botanists as *Eugenia Tabasca* from Mexico, whose fruit also is baccate, same size and shade of brown as the true allspice. Because of a strong fragrance resembling bay rum, it remained unpopular in foods and hence became marketable only when its price was cheaper than the Jamaican product. Authorities administering the U.S. food law required it to be labelled Mexican allspice to prevent deception of buyers seeking Jamaica allspice or pimento.

Nutmeg and Mace.—During the decade 1937–46 production in Grenada, a British West Indian Island, increased. This was fortunate, as World War II had eliminated Banda, Siau and other nutmeg islands of the Netherlands Indies as suppliers, leaving Grenada as the only source of nutmegs and mace after 1941. From a peacetime price of ten cents, nutmeg value increased to 70 cents per lb. The Indonesian rebellion continued the Grenada monopoly. Fried cakes or crullers were unusually popular during 1937–46; to maintain consumer acceptance, these had to be flavoured with nutmegs.

Red Pepper and Paprika.—Korea, Japan and Manchuria, which had shipped most of the U.S. tonnage of these spices, dropped from the market when fighting began in the Pacific; by late 1946 they had not yet resumed exports. India, a one-time source, cultivated more staple foods. A few were obtained from Mexico, but shipments often were excluded from the U.S. market by food law restrictions against a mould growth within the pods. Arizona and California began to ship larger quantities. The sweet paprika was in continuous good supply. When Hungary was invaded, competition for the world's paprika orders diminished. Spain and Portugal were quick to raise prices about 50%. Supply was well maintained as high prices abetted production, and quality was excellent. On the U.S. family table paprika became more prominent; as late as 1937 it had been found almost exclusively in public eating places.

Cayenne.—The most pungent of all spices (also as capsicum—a useful drug) was insufficiently available during World War II. Produced in both East and West Africa near the equator, it became difficult to ship as naval operations increased. Simultaneously with the extreme scarcity, the U.S. food law administration found new reasons for excluding importations.

Herbs.—For many years the United States used the thyme, marjoram, savoury and basil grown in France. They were missed during World War II, and, as usual, substitutes appeared. Unsuspected quantities of thyme—not the same as the French product—were found in Spain. Marjoram also grew in Chile, which shipped many tons. Portugal had savoury and bay leaves (*Laurus nobilis*); the latter in prewar times was almost a Greek monopoly, so excellent

A cutting of dried sweet basil being stacked on a farm in Los Angeles, Calif., in 1942

was the flavour and colour of the latter nation's product. Shippers in Athens wrote happily of the 1946 laurel crop, explaining that no leaves had been gathered for five years, hence trees were "strong" and leaves brighter and more flavourful.

The important herb for pork sausages is true sage (*Salvia officinalis*), whose wartime substitutes in the United States were disappointing. Because of the popularity of pork products, U.S. per capita use of sage became the world's highest. It was needed too in most dressings for poultry. Some was grown in the northwestern United States, but production costs (mostly hand labour) made the price six times higher than that shipped from the Adriatic port of Dubrovnik. Various makeshifts from Mediterranean islands and Spain were tolerated, but none were genuine sage. Their common defect was a camphor-like flavour.

Chili.—When General John J. Pershing crossed the Rio Grande, his troops learned to eat chili con carne (chili with meat). This national dish of Mexico depended upon the chiles anchos, a variety of red peppers distinctive in character and not too "hot." Its carminative quality, rugged flavour and deep red colour were advantageous in breaking the monotony of roasts and fried dishes. The spice industry quickly responded with chili powder, 85% of which, under the food law of 1938, had to be chili. The popular brands after 1936 contained the genuine ancho. Some highly pungent cayennes, popular south of Texas, were omitted in U.S. formulae. The popularity of Mexican chili touched a new high during the decade 1937–46. Work on flavour combinations of spices continued during the decade. Two prominent and long-standing accomplishments in this line were curry powder and the pickling mixtures of whole spices. (C. A. T.)

For statistics of trade see U.S. Bur. Census, *Statistical Abstract;* J. W. Parry, *Spice Handbook* (Chemical 1945); *Coffee, Tea and Spices* (monthly); *Spice Mill* (monthly).

Spinach

See VEGETABLES.

Spirits

See LIQUORS, ALCOHOLIC.

Spodumene

See LITHIUM MINERALS.

Sports

The decade of 1937–46 showed with definite clarity how a world war could affect the wide field of sports, amateur and professional. On the sports field the previous decade came to a close with the holding of the Olympic games of 1936 in Berlin in a setting of unprecedented sporting splendour—with a baleful background. Under the personal attention of Adolf Hitler and for the general purposes of nazi propaganda, the Germans in control of the international sports program provided stadiums, playing surfaces, indoor courts and outdoor courses and all equipment for the comfort and convenience of athletes and spectators to an extent never before approached in the 40-year span of modern Olympic competition. There were 5,000 athletes representing 55 different nations in the Berlin games. The main stadium was filled to its capacity of 110,000 spectators every day and sometimes twice a day while the Olympic festivities were afoot. Estimates of the cost of production and operation of the Berlin games ran as high as $80,000,000, but even a quarter of that sum would have been a new Olympic record.

But for all the magnificent setting, the great gathering of athletes from all over the world, the astonishing hordes of spectators at the various events and the record-breaking competition on the fields of action, many visitors from other nations viewed the Berlin games in a brooding spirit. It was 1936. By that time Japan had walked into Manchuria and out of the League of Nations. Italy already had swallowed Ethiopia and Benito Mussolini was bellowing for more from assorted balconies in Rome. Austria was seething with internal dissension. France was torn by political strife and Paris had seen rioting in the streets and deaths by shooting on the Rue Royale. Worst of all, Hitler's war machine was in the making and there were signs of it on all sides of the Olympic games at Berlin in 1936. So the Olympic spectacle was watched by visitors with mental reservations; there was more in it than met the eye, and more behind it than the "Strength through Joy" that the nazis had been chanting. At the end of the games the visiting athletes and their camp followers scattered with a vague feeling of dread. Something was in the wind and behind the glittering trappings at Berlin. What was in the wind and behind the glittering trappings, of course, was World War II and misery and mourning for millions all over the globe.

But sports ran their merry way along the edge of the abyss for a few more years. France had its annual quota of hysteria over horse racing, bicycle riding and soccer football in 1937. In Great Britain there was the usual round of cricket, football, golf, tennis, horse racing and all the rest of it. John Bull trotted out a thin little chap named Sydney Wooderson, who ran a mile outdoors in 4:06.4, a new record for the event. T. O. M. Sopwith, for the honour of British yachting, made his second challenge for the America's cup with his "Endeavour II" and according to the custom, was beaten back by the U.S. defender, "Ranger," off Newport, R.I. In 1937 the New York Yankees were pounding ahead toward an overpowering record in baseball, and it was in this same year that Joe Louis, the outstanding pugilistic star of a war-torn decade, climbed to the heavyweight boxing throne over the fallen body of James J. Braddock, whom he knocked flat and senseless in the eighth round of their championship bout in Chicago.

War clouds were gathering on the horizon in 1938, but the horizon seemed comfortably distant to most of the players and spectators on and around the fields of sport. There was a successful racing season in France and the British, for the first time, defeated the United States team in Walker cup golf. Seabiscuit won the triple crown of the U.S. turf and Don Budge, at the peak of his redheaded career on the tennis courts of the world, won the British, French, Australian and United States singles championships, a quadrilateral triumph to rival the "grand slam" of Bobby Jones on the golf links in 1930. It was quite a year for sports in the United States. The Yankees again were unbeatable in baseball. Football was played before record crowds. Basketball was gaining ground rapidly as a public spectacle in the indoor season and, outdoors, winter sports were winning converts with each successive cold spell. There were ski tracks on a thousand snow-covered hills of the northern sector of the United States and Canada, and Sonja Henie drew 102,000 spectators to six performances of her ice show at Madison Square Garden. There was one ominous happening, however, in the field of sports. The Olympic games of 1940 had been assigned to Tokyo. Embroiled with many nations and pushing relentlessly deeper into Chinese territory week by week, it was in 1938 that Japan formally abandoned plans to hold the Olympic games of 1940 at Tokyo. Finland, a small country with a great record of Olympic competition, eagerly applied for the privilege of holding the games that the Japs had abandoned, and the Olympic games of 1940 were transferred to Helsinki.

In the forepart of 1939 the rumbling of the approaching international storm could be heard distinctly and the athletes of many European nations were afraid to venture far from such shelter as their own countries afforded. But John R. Cobb, a London fur merchant with a hankering for fast riding in a powerful car, raised the auto speed record to 368.85 m.p.h. in a series of meteoric dashes across the Bonneville Salt Flats in Utah, and Sir Malcolm Campbell pushed the speedboat record up to 141.74 m.p.h. on Lake Coniston, England. The New York Yankees set a baseball record by winning their fourth successive world series when they beat the Cincinnati Reds in straight games in Oct., but by that time it didn't seem important, because Hitler had marched into Poland, the tocsin was ringing all over Europe and Europe was aflame. On Nov. 30, 1939, Russia invaded Finland and a Russian bombing raid spattered with high explosives the main stadium, the adjacent buildings and all the playing fields that the forlorn Finns had so enthusiastically prepared for the holding of the Olympic games of 1940 at Helsinki. Thus the Olympic games, designed to promote international peace, were the first notable sports casualty of World War II.

Anno Domini 1940 saw more than half the world at war. Asia had been in a turmoil for years. The great nations of Europe were locked in a death struggle. African colonies were involved in the European war. Only North and South America were at a distance from the heavy firing, and even these continents were not untouched by war. For one thing, Canada naturally was in it on the British side. For another thing, German U-boats began to lurk along the Atlantic shipping lanes and the American coasts to sink ships carrying supplies to Great Britain and its allies. Under such circumstances the United States, the nations of Central America and the nations of South America were left to play among themselves, and even there the pressure of war was felt. The United States began to build up its military and naval forces. The Selective Service act went into force in the autumn of 1940. Track and field competition was mediocre because of the lack of international rivalry. Polo lost its tang for the same reason, and most of the U.S. polo stars went into the army or navy in a hurry. There was a proposal to hold a set of inter-American games to replace the vanished Olympic games of 1940, but the proposal was dropped for two reasons. Athletes travelling to and from such games would have to go by ship, and few ships were available for such coastwise traffic. And with so much misery and slaughter elsewhere in the world, it didn't seem quite the time to stage a big sports spectacle for all the Americas.

But what might be called the "intramural" sports program in the United States went steadily ahead. Baseball, football, racing, boxing and basketball drew huge crowds. With Canada in the war, ice hockey was hard hit for play-

Baseball enjoyed an undiminished popularity throughout the years of World War II, and night games became an established institution. This picture shows an audience of some 60,000 watching the New York Yankees play the Cleveland Indians under a battery of floodlights at Yankee stadium

ers, but the cripples and the veterans who filled out the big league rosters were good enough to hold the franchise. U.S. industry, when France surrendered on June 17, 1940, practically went on a war basis and the overtime workers in mills, factories, foundries, shipyards and aeroplane plants had plenty of money to spend on the movies and sports spectacles and other amusements in their free hours.

It was, in fact, the beginning of a fantastic period in U.S. sports history. All through 1941 the Selective Service act was drawing athletes from the playing fields of the United States. Big league ball players, college gridiron stars, varsity track stars, basketball experts, famous jockeys and boxing champions were being called up to don soldier or sailor suits. With so many good players taken away, there was a drop in the quality of the competition in all sports, but as the quality of play went down, the number of spectators rose. There were great crowds out to see Joe DiMaggio of the Yankees set a baseball record by hitting safely in 56 consecutive games. The stands and the bleachers were filled as the Brooklyn Dodgers drove to their first pennant in 21 years. Whirlaway was the star of a turf season during which mutuel betting reached a new peak, and Minnesota remained unbeaten in a football season that set new records of attendance and gate receipts. Then came Dec. 7, 1941, and the attack on Pearl Harbor.

In the months when Great Britain was standing alone against the axis, when the luftwaffe was "blitzing" an England that was short of arms, ammunition, food, housing, transportation and medical supplies, some serious folk were astounded—and perhaps shocked—to discover that the English insisted on going ahead with their customary sports program wherever possible. They had dog racing regularly, and horse racing intermittently. They played cricket and football and tennis and golf when they could find time for these games. They attended boxing matches. There was no "petrol" for their cars and no new tires for their bicycles but, where there were sports events, they gathered in such numbers that air raid wardens had to set attendance limits at any contest lest some nazi bomber set a new record not wanted in the history of British sport.

There was the same phenomenon in the United States after the attack on Pearl Harbor and the entry of the United States into World War II. The impact of war and the conditions that went with it served as a spur to the popular interest in all sports. Where the crowds gathered around sports spectacles, there were war relief collections and drives to sell war bonds.

Horse racing raised $3,000,000 for war relief in 1942 and professional baseball contributed $1,314,825 to the United Service organizations.

Through 1943, 1944 and 1945, the colleges, amateur athletic clubs and professional teams in the United States were stripped of practically all players who were sound in wind and limb. Only the hundreds of service teams—including those of the U.S. military academy and U.S. naval academy in intercollegiate competition—had players full of youth and health. Fordham, Alabama, Tennessee, Stanford, Santa Clara and other colleges noted for their fine football teams abandoned the gridiron (and in some cases all varsity sports) for the duration of the war. Some of the minor leagues in football and baseball had to close down for lack of players. But some colleges and the professional field in general went ahead in sports with young fellows whose physical handicaps kept them out of the armed forces and doddering athletic veterans called back to fill out the teams and the sports programs. Yet the crowds that turned out to watch the competition of the subnormal players and makeshift teams grew larger month by month. War workers were making high wages. There was a shortage of civilian goods on which to spend this money. Watching games provided relaxation and amusement for men and women who put in long hours on war work. So the turnstiles clicked at an ever-increasing rate, and new attendance records were set in all directions.

Gasoline rationing caused the shifting of some games, boxing bouts and race meetings in many cases, and horse racing was banned in the United States for one period of four months but, despite all handicaps, the spectators managed to reach the scenes of sporting action in record numbers. These conditions persisted long after the firing ceased in Europe and the Pacific area. Belmont Park had its first $5,000,000 betting day on Sept. 22, 1945, and in that same year more than $1,500,000,000 was poured through the mutuel machines at race tracks in the United States. Teams, leagues and sporting events of all kinds set attendance records through 1946. There was some improvement in the level of competition because of the return of many athletes from the wars, but certainly the playing was not yet up to the prewar standard, yet record crowds rushed through the turnstiles wherever there was a sports contest with a fence around it. A restless population, a supply of "loose money" and the lingering shortage of civilian goods on which to spend it accounted for these astonishing attendance records in sports.

There were some great champions and some outstanding performances in the field of sports during the decade that was dominated by World War II. Those who blandly believe that the British are a bit on the slow side should take note that, in this dramatic decade, new world speed records on the ground, on the water and in the air were set by three Englishmen—John R. Cobb, Sir Malcolm Campbell and Capt. E. M. Donaldson (*see* above).

Three U.S. athletes were outstanding in their own fields. Don Budge was the tennis star of the decade. Joe Louis became one of the great heavyweight champions of pugilistic history. Cornelius Warmerdam far outclassed all other pole vaulters in the world and hoisted the record to 15 ft. 7¾ in.

But all this—except the fast ride in the jet plane—took place before Hitler's armies poured into Poland and started the global conflagration.

It is significant that the only notable sports feature through the years of war was the joint contribution of two athletes of a neutral nation. Arne Andersson and Gunder Haegg (Hägg) of Sweden took turns lowering the mile record until Haegg finally put it at 4:01.2, only to have the whole series of record-breaking marks left under a shadow when the two great Swedish runners were suspended from amateur competition on the charge of accepting money for running. In the countries that engaged in the struggle, the war produced a novel contrast in the field of sports; a great decrease in the quality of play because so many athletes were in the armed forces, and a vast increase in the number of spectators who turned out to witness such sports events as the grim years had to offer.

(*See* also Air Races; Angling; Archery; Automobile Racing; Badminton; Baseball; Basketball; Billiards; Bowling; Boxing; Chess; Cricket; Curling; Cycling; Fencing; Football; Gliding; Golf; Gymnastics; Handball; Horse Racing; Ice Hockey; Ice Skating; Lacrosse; Motor-Boat Racing; Polo; Rowing; Shows (Animal); Skiing; Soccer; Softball; Squash Racquets; Swimming; Table Tennis; Track and Field Sports; Trap-shooting; Wrestling; Yachting.) (J. Ki.)

Spruance, Raymond Amos

Spruance (1886–), U.S. naval officer, was born July 3, 1886. He entered the navy in 1903 and was promoted through the ranks to rear admiral in Dec. 1939. He served as commandant of the 10th naval district, San Juan, Puerto Rico, 1940–41 and was sent to the Pacific theatre of operations at the outbreak of war with Japan. Adm. Spruance was in complete charge of operations during the landings of the U.S. marines on the Gilbert Islands of Makin and Tarawa, Nov. 20–23, 1943. He also directed naval operations in the Okinawa landings. After Hirohito's surrender broadcast, Spruance frankly aired his views on the war and politics in the Pacific (Aug. 25, 1945). He voiced the belief that the U.S. navy should be drastically cut and that the U.S. be satisfied with the Marshalls and Carolines and not take bases off the Asiatic coast at the risk of offending other powers. He also praised the Japanese for putting up a "hell of a fight," declaring they "fought an excellent war considering what they had to start with."

On Nov. 20, 1945, Spruance succeeded Adm. Chester W. Nimitz as commander in chief of the Pacific fleet. In turn, he was replaced (Jan. 13, 1946) by Adm. John H. Towers. Spruance left active duty to become president of the navy war college.

Squash Racquets

National dominance in squash racquets from 1937 to 1946 became principally a two-man proposition. It started with the second and third national titles for Germain G. Glidden of the Harvard club, New York city, in 1937 and 1938 and ended with the prewar and postwar dominance of Charles W. Brinton of Philadelphia. As a Princeton university undergraduate, Brinton won the national squash racquets title in 1941 and 1942 and came back for his third championship in 1946 after the tournament had recessed three years because of World War II.

Philadelphia cornered most of the squash racquets titles during the decade. After Glidden failed to defend his title in 1939, Donald Strachan, A. Willing Patterson and Brinton made the men's title the legacy of Philadelphia. Anne Page and Cecile Bowes, both of Philadelphia, dominated the women's division until the tournament was abandoned at the start of World War II. Miss Page won it in 1937 and 1939, while Miss Bowes triumphed in 1938, 1940 and 1941.

International competition for the Lapham trophy between the United States and Canada resulted in a five-to-five split during the ten-year period. In winning the 1946 test, the United States captured its 16th match in 25 with Canada.

Racquets, also hard hit during World War II, brought forth Robert Grant III of New York as its dominant figure. Except for a one-year reign of Warren Ingersoll III of Philadelphia as 1940 champion, Grant held the crown all the remaining years after 1937. He also won the amateur court tennis title in 1946 and thus became the first player in 46 years to hold both titles simultaneously. Harry F. Wolf of New York won his 11th straight squash tennis crown in 1940, after which Joseph Lordi of New York was champion in 1941 and Frank R. Hanson of Columbia university in 1946. (M. P. W.)

Bibliography.—A. Barker, *Squash Rackets* (London, 1936); H. L. Cowles, *Art of Squash Racquets* (1935); J. Skillman, *Squash Racquets* (1937).

Stabilization Administrator, Office of

See War and Defense Agencies.

Stader Splints

See Medicine.

Stainless Steel

See Metallurgy.

Stalin, Joseph Vissarionovich

Joseph Stalin (1879–), soviet statesman, was born Dec. 21, 1879, in the Georgian town of Gori, the son of a poor shoemaker named Djugashvilli. Complying with his mother's wish that he study for the priesthood, he entered the Tiflis Theological seminary in 1893. However, he developed a greater interest in socialism than theology and was expelled from the seminary five years later. During that time he had become active in the revolutionary underground and adopted various pseudonyms, including Stalin, to evade the police.

First arrested in March 1902, Stalin was exiled to Eastern Siberia. He later escaped, resumed his political activities and became associated with Lenin and other Bolshevik leaders. Between 1908 and 1917, he was exiled four times, escaping on three occasions. He was freed after the revolution of Feb. 1917; returning to St. Petersburg, he was named to the central committee of the Communist party. Recognized as an able administrator, he was appointed commissar of nationalities in Oct. 1917; he was also made People's Commissar of the Workers' and Peasants' Inspection in 1922. During the civil and interventionist wars, Stalin fought with the Red army against white Russian and Polish forces. He became a central figure in soviet politics after his appointment in 1922 to the all-powerful position of general secretary of the central committee of the Russian Communist party.

After Lenin's death, the struggle between Stalin and Leon Trotsky (*q.v.*) became critical, with Stalin leading the faction that urged establishment of "socialism in one country"; Trotsky, on the other hand, insisted on continuation of the original Marxist concept of world revolution. But the mercurial Trotsky was no match for Stalin in political manoeuvring and lost out; he was deported in 1929, and Stalin became the undisputed leader of the party.

In the succeeding years, Stalin eliminated opponents of his measures, chiefly the "Old Bolsheviks"; during the great treason purges of 1936–38, many anti-Stalinists were executed and by 1939 his position as leader of the U.S.S.R. was unquestioned. He did not hold state office until a month before the German invasion, when he assumed the post of premier, May 6, 1941. After the nazi attack, he also became commander-in-chief of the armed forces, chair-

U.S. National Racquets and Squash Champions, 1937–46

Year	Squash Racquets	Court Tennis	Racquets	Squash Tennis
1937	Germain G. Glidden	Ogden Phipps	Robert Grant III	Harry F. Wolf
1938	Germain G. Glidden	James H. Van Alen	Robert Grant III	Harry F. Wolf
1939	Donald Strachan	Ogden Phipps	Robert Grant III	Harry F. Wolf
1940	A. Willing Patterson	James H. Van Alen	Warren Ingersoll III	Harry F. Wolf
1941	Charles W. Brinton	Alastair Martin	Robert Grant III	Joseph Lordi
1942	Charles W. Brinton	No contest	No contest	No contest
1943	No contest	No contest	No contest	No contest
1944	No contest	No contest	No contest	No contest
1945	No contest	No contest	No contest	No contest
1946	Charles W. Brinton	Robert Grant III	Robert Grant III	Frank R. Hanson

Foreign Minister V. Molotov and Marshal Joseph Stalin during an intermission at the Yalta conference of 1945

man of the state committee of defense and commissar of defense. In March 1943 he was invested with the rank of marshal of the soviet union and in June 1945, he was named generalissimo of the U.S.S.R.

During World War II, Stalin proved a stern leader. In 1941, he directed the retreating Red army to pursue a "scorched earth" policy without regard to cost. In Nov. 1943 Stalin met with his wartime allies—President Roosevelt and Prime Minister Churchill—at Tehran in the first of the Big Three conferences for discussion of grand strategy and postwar policy. This parley was followed by their second meeting at Yalta (Feb. 4–11, 1945); the final parley of soviet, U.S. and British government leaders was held at Potsdam (July–Aug. 1945).

The end of World War II witnessed a rapid deterioration in relations between the soviet union on one side and the U.S. and Britain on the other. The rift was heightened by Churchill's speech at Fulton, Mo., Mar. 5, 1946, in which he called for an Anglo-U.S. "fraternal" alliance to block soviet "expansionism." Stalin subsequently retorted that the Fulton speech was a "dangerous act" intended to sow discord among the Allies. In later statements, he branded Churchill as one of the foremost "incendiaries" trying to provoke a third World War.

BIBLIOGRAPHY.—D. M. Cole, *Josef Stalin, Man of Steel* (1942); W. Kolarz, *Stalin and Eternal Russia* (1944); J. Stalin, *Great Patriotic War: War Speeches* (1946); *Stalin's Kampf: J. Stalin's Credo* (1940).

Stalingrad

At the time of the Russian Revolution, Stalingrad (then called Tsaritsyn) was a dilapidated provincial town of slightly more than 100,000 inhabitants. It contained two small metallurgical works, some handicraft industries, and many sawmills concerned with the disposal of timber floated down the Volga from the forest zone. With the development of the Caspian oil fields, the importance of Stalingrad as a transit port increased, and by 1937 it was carrying more than 30,000,000 tons of cargo annually, mainly oil going north and timber going south. But its real transformation into the third industrial city of the U.S.S.R. with a population in 1939 of nearly 500,000 was due to its key position in the first two five-year plans, involving the expansion of the Red October metallurgical works and the inauguration of the largest tractor plant in the U.S.S.R. By 1937, Stalingrad was turning out 4,000 tons of high-grade steel and rolled steel every year and supplying tractors to all the farms of the lower Volga steppe. The city owed its record expansion to its situation on the arterial Volga with a railway junction connecting it with the Caucasus on the one hand and the Donetz coal field on the other. Its history from 1937 to 1941 was intimately bound up with that of the Red army, since the famous tractor works was able to switch almost overnight to the production of tanks. Tanks were being turned out in large numbers right up to Aug. 1942, when Adolf Hitler opened his Stalingrad offensive; and for many weeks afterwards, at the height of the battle for the city, the great Stalingrad factories acted as front-line maintenance and repair shops.

The all-out attempt to seize the city was started on Aug. 23, 1942, with a 1,000-bomber raid, followed by a demand for surrender two days later. Almost at once Stalingrad had become the real and symbolic pivot of the Russian defense. Its capture, to which Hitler had publicly committed himself, and which seemed inevitable to the most optimistic, would have led to a double turning movement. involving Moscow and the whole line of the Volga on the one hand, and the Caucasus on the other. The Russian defense took its place among the epic stories of war. In its final stages the Russian headquarters, driven back to the very edge of the Volga and completely encircled by land, lived in dugouts in the steep river banks, while their men fought from room to room in ruined factories and houses. During this battle, which lasted until the final surrender of the German 6th army on Jan. 31, 1943, and which marked a turning point of the war, the new city, with its proud buildings, tree-lined avenues and parks, was totally destroyed.

But even before the war was over reconstruction was under way, and its complete restoration and enlargement was a priority under the new plan. (E. CRA.)

BIBLIOGRAPHY.—B. Agapov, *After the Battle* (London, 1944); *Stalingrad, an Eye-witness Account by Soviet Correspondents,* (London, 1943); E. Weinert, *Stalingrad Diary* (London, 1944).

Stamp, 1st Baron

Baron Stamp of Shortlands (Josiah Charles Stamp) (1880–1941), British economist and banker, was born June 21, 1880, in London. In 1896 he started work as a clerk in the inland revenue department; 40 years later he was one of the most powerful figures in British finance. During his lifetime he served as economic adviser on various government committees, was a director of the Bank of England and chairman of the board of the London Midland and Scottish railway. Lord Stamp exerted a powerful influence on British foreign policy during the critical years preceding the outbreak of World War II and he actively supported Neville Chamberlain's efforts to appease Hitler. He was appointed chief economic adviser to Chamberlain's war cabinet in Oct. 1939. Lord and Lady Stamp and their eldest son, the Hon. Wilfred Carlyle Stamp, were killed in a German air raid on London April 16, 1941.

Stamp Collecting

See PHILATELY.

Standards, National Bureau of

The national bureau of standards was established as the laboratory of the federal government, having primary responsibility for basic research in physics, chemistry and engineering, except in certain special fields which, by legislation, were assigned to other agencies. One of its primary duties is to maintain the uniformity of standards throughout the nation. It has the custody of all the national standards and it calibrates in terms of these standards the measuring equipment used by the federal government and by tax-supported agencies of the various states. This is done free of charge. Similar comparisons are made for any citizen on the payment of a fee, as required by law.

The mass production of interchangeable parts for which U.S. industry became famed was made possible by this unremitting attention to standards. When the measuring equipment used in industry conforms with the national standards, the axles of an automobile may be made in one factory, the ball bearings in another, the wheels in a third and yet the parts will assemble perfectly, without looseness or without strain.

The parts are made so nearly identical that they are entirely interchangeable.

Another activity of the national bureau of standards is the testing of apparatus, equipment and supplies purchased by government agencies, to find whether these supplies measure up fully to the requirements of the federal specification under which they were purchased. Much time is given to the work of the federal specifications board in preparing the specifications under which federal purchases are made. These specifications are widely used also by state purchasing agencies. Assistance is also given trade groups in simplifying the sizes and varieties of manufactured products to reduce costs and in developing commercial standards for certain types of goods.

High-Voltage Laboratory.—In 1938, $500,000 was appropriated for the construction of a high-voltage laboratory, a project which had been urged by electrical manufacturers for years. This enabled the bureau to extend into the field of high voltages the standardization work it had long carried on in connection with low-voltage measurements. X-ray equipment, working up to 1,400,000 volts, was also installed in the new laboratory which made it possible to undertake much-needed research and to calibrate dosage-meters for the powerful high-voltage X-ray tubes being installed in hospitals, and thus help safeguard the lives of patients receiving X-ray treatment. The high-voltage surge generator in the new laboratory was extensively used during World War II in developing ways to protect wooden gliders and their occupants from lightning. The X-ray group developed radiographic methods for detecting cavities in the T.N.T. charges of high-explosive shells, which might lead to a disastrous premature explosion in the gun itself. Similar studies were made to detect fissures in the powder charges in large rockets resulting in non-uniform burning of the powder so that the rocket did not follow its predicted path. After these methods were developed, large X-ray plants were installed by the U.S. army in suitable places for the routine inspection of explosives. The X-ray section also carried out extensive tests of X-ray equipment for the surgeon general of the army, and made surveys of X-ray equipment in navy yards, hospitals and factories in order to see that the operating personnel was fully protected from stray radiation.

Enlargement of Bureau Grounds.—In 1940 the bureau was authorized to purchase an undivided tract of 12.5 ac. immediately adjoining the bureau grounds. The land was utilized almost immediately as a site for a materials testing laboratory costing $600,000, and for three laboratories built by the war department for the use of the bureau staff in the development of proximity fuses.

Broadcasting Standard Frequencies.—In 1941, a new bureau station (WWV) for broadcasting standard radio frequencies, costing $230,000, was authorized for construction at Beltsville, Md. A limited service of this kind had been provided by the bureau for some years, but the new transmitters were sufficiently powerful to cover not only the United States and the North Atlantic, but a large part of the Pacific as well, the signals being received with ease in New Zealand. This service was utilized extensively by the navy and army throughout the war in maintaining the correct frequency of their countless transmitters. It was also widely used by firms making radio equipment, by the Federal Communications commission and by broadcasting stations generally. These standard frequencies are generated by means of a group of quartz crystal oscillators, working under conditions which are rigidly controlled as regards temperature and pressure. The signals broadcast do not vary as much as 1 part in 10,000,000 from the announced standard frequency. This is comparable with the precision with which the mass of standard kilogram or the length of the standard metre is known. But unlike the metre and the kilogram, standards of frequency cannot be stored in a vault until needed. They must be continuously generated and broadcast to serve their intended purpose.

Optical Glass.—Up to the time of World War I, the United States had been dependent entirely upon Germany, Belgium and France for the glass used in making the optical parts of periscopes, range finders, cameras and binoculars. In 1914 this supply was suddenly completely shut off, and U.S. manufacturers undertook the new and difficult job of making optical glass under the technical guidance of the geophysical laboratory of the Carnegie institution, with the co-operation of the national bureau of standards. The bureau at that time built an optical glass plant which was kept in operation after World War I through the farsighted support of the navy, and produced all the optical glass needed for the navy's peacetime requirements. During this period much was learned about the large-scale production of optical glass of high quality that would meet exacting specifications as to dispersion and refractive index and thus facilitate the mass production of optical equipment if this should prove necessary.

At the beginning of the U.S. defense program prior to World War II, the bureau foresaw the probability of a greatly expanded need for optical glass, and an appropriation of $125,000 for the enlargement of the glass plant was authorized by congress. With these new facilities the bureau and the Bausch and Lomb Optical company, the only commercial firm that had continued optical glass production after World War I, were able to supply all the optical glass needed until other firms could be brought into production. At the request of the armed services the bureau opened its glass plant for the training of the technical personnel of four U.S. firms which were about to undertake the production of optical glass, as well as to representatives of the Australian and Canadian governments for similar purposes. At this time the navy department also constructed a large annex to the bureau's glass plant, in order that production there might be further expanded.

During the war years, the bureau manufactured nearly a million pounds of optical glass of high quality, conforming strictly to the specifications of the armed services. Practically all of this was delivered in the form of moulded prisms and lens blanks with curved surfaces, these pieces being so shaped as to require the minimum amount of grinding in the subsequent finishing operations. At one period about 400 persons were engaged in this work. The whole operation was directed by the small group of experienced bureau personnel headed by P. H. Bates.

Staff.—The staff of the bureau increased from about 900 in 1939 to approximately 2,250 during the last three war years. The securing of new trained personnel became more and more difficult as the war progressed and the majority of the new appointees came with little or no laboratory experience. Deferment of technical men from induction into the armed services was at first granted, but later trained men were inducted without recognition of the fact that the early solution of the technical military problems upon which they were engaged was vastly more important to the all-out war effort than any contribution these men could make in the enlisted ranks. In all, 499 members of the bureau staff joined the armed forces.

Atomic Bomb.—The work of the federal government on this project was initiated in Oct. 1939, when President Roosevelt appointed Lyman J. Briggs, director of the national bureau of standards, as chairman of a committee to investigate the possibilities of utilizing the atomic fission of uranium in warfare. In the light of the final achievement, it is difficult to realize how little was known about uranium in those early days. The committee recognized at once the possibility of using uranium fission as a source of power but decided to concentrate its efforts on the development of a bomb. Both applications were dependent upon the possibility of establishing a chain reaction. This vitally important problem was entrusted to Prof. Enrico Fermi at Columbia university, who three years later finally saw the great pile of graphite embedded with uranium begin to heat up spontaneously. The chain reaction had been established. But this was not accomplished without painstaking and brilliant work on methods to remove impurities from the graphite and uranium and on methods to reduce the uranium ore to pure metal. In both of these lines of research the bureau of standards played an important part.

In June 1940 the uranium committee was placed by the president under the newly-organized National Defense Research committee. By this time it was known that fission occurred only in the uranium isotope 235, which constituted only .7% of the total parent mass of uranium. To secure the violent explosive chain reaction required in a bomb, it was necessary to separate and concentrate the isotope 235 in almost pure form. Isotopes cannot be separated by chemical processes and accordingly an intensive and exhaustive investigation of various physical methods for separating the uranium isotopes was undertaken. By the end of 1941, the research had advanced to the point where it was believed that an "all-out" effort, involving the expenditure of enormous sums, was justified. The project was transferred to the Office of Scientific Research and Development under the general direction of Vannevar Bush, who, in June 1942, appointed a new executive committee, consisting of J. B. Conant, chairman, L. J. Briggs, A. H. Compton, E. O. Lawrence, E. V. Murphree and H. C. Urey to supervise the vast undertaking. Procurement and engineering functions were taken over by the U.S. army engineers (Manhattan district) under Maj. Gen. L. R. Groves. By May 1, 1943, the project had reached such an advanced stage of development that it was transferred to the army for the all-out production effort.

During the war about 60 members of the bureau staff were engaged on the atomic bomb project. Some of them were assigned to the Oak Ridge and Los Alamos laboratories. The bureau served as a central control laboratory for determining the purity of the uranium and other products that were used in the project. Thousands of chemical and spectrographic analyses were made during the course of this work. Measurements were made of the radium recovered from the uranium ores. Methods for separating the uranium isotopes were studied. Yet the work was so closely guarded that the disclosure of the bureau's participation in the atomic bomb project came as a complete surprise to most of the bureau staff. (*See* also ATOMIC BOMB.)

Proximity Fuses.—One of the most important of the new weapons developed during World War II was the radio proximity fuse. This fuse causes a projectile to explode if it passes within 50 to 75 ft. of an aeroplane or at a height of 30 to 50 ft. as it approaches the ground, if the attack is against ground objectives. In other words, the proximity fuse does not need to hit the target in order to function, and this increases enormously the effectiveness of the projectiles on which the fuse is used.

The bureau served as the central laboratory of the National Defense Research committee in the development of radio proximity fuses for bombs, rockets and other nonrotating projectiles. At one period of the war about 350 bureau people were engaged in this undertaking, under the leadership of Harry Diamond. The fuse took various forms in adapting it to different types of projectiles, but in each instance it incorporated a complete miniature radio transmitting and receiving set, so small that some models could be covered by a man's hand. When the radio waves generated in the fuse struck the target, a small part of the radiation was reflected back to the approaching projectile and received by the fuse. The fuse exploded the projectile when this reflected radiation reached the required intensity. Proving ground tests showed that when a fragmentation bomb is exploded 30 ft. above the ground by means of a proximity fuse it becomes from 10 to 20 times as effective against troops in foxholes as the same bomb equipped to explode on contact with the ground. Proximity fuses were used effectively by the army air forces in the Mediterranean theatre, and such fuses on bombs and rockets were widely used by U.S. forces against Iwo Jima and other Japanese strongholds during the latter months of the war.

When the proximity fuse project reached the stage of large-scale production, and the importance of electronics in ordnance development had been convincingly demonstrated, the bureau of ordnance of the army took over the financial support of the work, and a large laboratory was constructed on the bureau grounds for the use of the proximity fuse group. Their duties at the close of the war were expanded to include other applications of electronics to ordnance development. The laboratory also was to be supported by funds from the bureau of standards for electronic research in nonmilitary fields. (*See* also RADAR.)

Guided Missiles.—Members of the bureau staff under the leadership of Dr. H. L. Dryden worked closely with the NDRC and the navy in the development of radar homing missiles, *i.e.,* missiles which automatically seek out their target and guide themselves to hit the target. This was one of the largest of the bureau's war projects, and the great hydraulic laboratory building was given over entirely to this undertaking. In one form of this weapon a bomb is housed in a glider which carries in its nose the necessary radar and control mechanism. The glider "illuminates" the target ship with short bursts of radio waves and "homes" in the direction from which come the waves that are reflected back from the target. In making an attack the glider is carried underneath a mother aeroplane to a point beyond the range of gunfire and released after being "told" what target it is to attack. According to the official navy release this guided missile destroyed many tons of Japanese combatant and merchant shipping during the last year of the war.

Forecasting "Radio Weather."—Large military operations involving the participation of ground, sea and air forces had to be definitely scheduled well in advance of the day of attack. Failure of the all-important radio communication system of the mission on the day selected, owing to magnetic storms or similar disturbances, would jeopardize the success of the whole undertaking. Accordingly the combined chiefs of staff asked the bureau's radio section to undertake the forecasting of conditions which might interfere with radio communication. This work was carried out under the leadership of Dr. J. H. Dellinger, who had shown earlier that the appearance of sun spots is often accompanied by marked disturbances in radio communication. The service inaugurated provided for both daily and long-range forecasts. So successful was the undertaking that at the end of the war the military sponsors strongly urged that a direct appropriation be made to the bureau to continue and expand the service as a peacetime aid to air and sea navigation. This recommendation was approved by congress, and a wartime development, born of necessity, found a peacetime application in safeguarding lives and shipping and in aiding transportation by air and sea.

Grading Quartz Crystals.—The "heart" of a radio transmitter is the oscillating quartz plate, for it fixes the frequency of the signal sent out. Literally millions of these crystal oscillators were made during World War II. The quartz crystals from which they were cut were imported by the government from Brazil and were classified and graded as to quality by the bureau's optics division under the supervision of F. J. Bates. Each individual crystal was examined for imperfections in an oil bath with the aid of an arc lamp. To determine the types of imperfections which would prevent the proper performance of the finished oscillators, plates were cut from crystals with various imperfections and tested as oscillators. During the years 1942 to 1945 inclusive, more than 10,000,000 lb. of quartz crystals were graded for the government in the bureau's laboratory.

* * *

Many other projects were carried out by the bureau staff for the U.S. armed services. The flag of the bureau of ordnance of the navy was awarded to the bureau of standards early in the war. The bureau was also one of the first agencies to receive the joint army-navy "E" award. On V-J day this pennant was flying at the bureau's masthead carrying five stars, symbolizing continued "excellence in production" throughout the war period.

At the close of the war Dr. Briggs retired as director of the national bureau of standards after a service of 12 years in this post. He was succeeded by Dr. Edward U. Condon, a former member of the uranium committee, who was promptly selected by the senate committee on atomic energy as its scientific adviser, and later was appointed a member of the president's committee to observe the atomic bomb experiments at Bikini. Plans were under way in 1946 at the bureau for a greatly enlarged research program in the field of nuclear physics, including the installation of a large betatron, and for an extension of its peacetime research activities in many other fields.

(L. J. Br.)

Standley, William Harrison

Standley (1872–), U.S. naval officer and diplomat, was born Dec. 18, 1872, at Ukiah, Calif. A graduate of the U.S. naval academy (1895), he was commissioned an ensign. He served in the Spanish-American War, and was a naval captain during World War I. Raised to the rank of rear admiral in 1927, he was assistant chief of naval operations, 1928–30, and was chief of naval operations, 1933–37, with the rank of admiral. Although he retired in 1937, he was recalled to active duty in March 1941 and in the fall of that year he served as a member of a mission to the U.S.S.R. to confer with British and Russian officials on means of speeding aid to Russia.

Adm. Standley was appointed ambassador to the soviet union Feb. 9, 1942. Although favourably impressed with the Russians, he nevertheless criticized their failure to publicize the amount of aid they were receiving from the United States; as a result, soviet newspapers devoted more space to this topic. His resignation as ambassador was announced Oct. 1, 1943.

Stanley, Oliver Frederick George

Stanley (1896–), British politician, son of the 17th early of Derby, was born May 4, 1946. Educated at Eton and Oxford, he was an artillery major in World War I and was awarded the military cross and the croix de guerre. On returning to civilian life after the war, he was admitted to the bar in 1919. Stanley held cabinet posts in the Ramsay MacDonald, Stanley Baldwin and Neville Chamberlain governments, and in 1940 was named secretary of state for war by Chamberlain, but was dropped by Winston Churchill when the latter became prime minister in May 1940. In Nov. 1942 Churchill reshuffled his government and Stanley returned to the cabinet as colonial secretary. In March 1943, his statement rejecting any kind of scheme for international administration of British colonies after the war—a view identical with that of Churchill—was strongly criticized by some factions in England and the United States.

He was renamed colonial secretary in the Conservative cabinet formed by Churchill after Germany's defeat in 1945, holding this post until the Labourite victory (July 1945) in the national elections swept the Conservatives out of office.

Stark, Harold Raynsford

Stark (1880–), U.S. naval officer, was born Nov. 12, 1880, at Wilkes-Barre, Pa. A graduate of the U.S. naval academy, he was commissioned an ensign in 1905. During World War I, he was on the staff of Adm. William S. Sims, commander of U.S. naval forces in European waters. He was appointed chief of naval operations, March 15, 1939, with the rank of admiral. Succeeded in this office on March 9, 1942, by Adm. Ernest J. King, he was assigned to command U.S. naval forces in European waters. In this capacity, he also acted as liaison officer between the British admiralty and Washington. In the summer of 1943, Stark, with Gen. Charles de Gaulle's assistance, was able to obtain co-operation of both civil and military French officials with U.S. armed forces in New Caledonia and New Hebrides. Stark also lent a diplomatic hand in the agreement achieved in 1943 between De Gaulle and Gen. Henri Giraud. Later he was head of the U.S. 12th fleet operating in the European theatre. Stark's retirement from the navy was announced July 14, 1945.

In the navy reports published Aug. 29, 1945, on responsibility for the Pearl Harbor disaster, Stark was blamed for failure to transmit "important information" in his possession "during this critical period." In his testimony before the Pearl Harbor congressional investigating committee, Dec. 31, 1945, Stark said that "specific warnings" of possible Japanese hostile actions were sent to Pacific commanders between Oct. 16 and Dec. 6, 1941.

Stars

See ASTRONOMY.

Starvation

See FAMINES.

Starzynski, Stefan

Starzynski (1893–1940?), Polish politician and mayor of Warsaw from 1937 to 1939, was educated in a Warsaw high school. He joined the Polish army, fought in World War I and in the Russo-Polish campaign. After the latter campaign, Starzynski was a member of the Polish delegation to the Polish-Soviet commission for repatriation, 1921–24. A close student of municipal government, he was elected mayor of Warsaw in 1937. He organized civilian resistance when German forces approached the city in Sept. 1939 and worked vigorously to maintain the morale of the capital's inhabitants. He stubbornly refused to yield the city, and his radio broadcasts appealing for British and French help were heard over the world. After the fall of Warsaw, Starzynski was taken prisoner by the Germans. London press dispatches subsequently declared that he was executed by the nazis in Dachau concentration camp, Sept. 1, 1940. This was denied by the German D.N.B. (official German news agency before the close of the war), which said Starzynski was released before Christmas 1939 but broke his word of honour and fled to a foreign country.

After the war an official of the Warsaw municipal government, who fought beside Starzynski, reported that the mayor had been killed in a German concentration camp a few months after his capture.

Stassen, Harold Edward

Stassen (1907–), U.S. politician, was born April 13, 1907, in West St. Paul, Minn. After studying at the University of Minnesota Law school, Minneapolis, Minn., 1923–29, he was admitted to the Minnesota bar in 1929. Elected governor of Minnesota on the Republican party ticket in 1938, he was inaugurated in Jan. 1939. Reelected governor for the 1941–43 term, he served as temporary chairman and keynoter of the Republican National convention in 1940 and as national chairman of the Governors' conference and of the Council of State governments, 1940–41. He resigned his governorship in 1943 to join the U.S. navy, becoming commander and flag officer to Adm. William Halsey and participating in four naval engagements. In Feb. 1945 Stassen accepted President Roosevelt's appointment as delegate to the San Francisco conference of the United Nations. He subsequently declared that U.S. acceptance of the United Nations security charter and adoption of a flexible foreign policy could give the world a minimum of 50 years of peace. Stassen was released from the navy on Nov. 15, 1945.

He was regarded as one of the "dark horse" G.O.P. candidates for the 1948 presidential nomination, although his chances had been reduced considerably by the victory of "regular" Republicans in the Nov. 1946 national elections.

State, U.S. Department of

See GOVERNMENT DEPARTMENTS AND BUREAUS.

State Guard

See NATIONAL GUARD, U.S.

State Legislation

See LAW.

Steamships

See SHIPBUILDING.

Steel

See IRON AND STEEL.

Steelman, John Roy

Steelman (1900–), U.S. economist and government official, was born June 23, 1900, in Thornton, Ark. Graduated in 1922 with an A.B. degree from Henderson Brown college (Arkadelphia, Ark.), he took his master's degree from Vanderbilt university, Nashville, Tenn., in 1924. Four years later (1928), he won his Ph.D. degree from the University of North Carolina, Chapel Hill, N.C., and became an economics professor at Alabama State College for Women, Montevallo, Ala. (1928–34). He accepted in 1934 an offer made by Frances Perkins, secretary of labour, to become a member of the U.S. conciliation service. He served as her special assistant from 1936 to 1937, becoming director of the conciliation service in the latter year. He resigned this post in 1944 to set up an industrial relations bureau in New York city, but returned to Washington in 1945 as special assistant to Secretary of Labour Lewis B. Schwellenbach.

Acting as President Truman's aide, Steelman was a central figure in settlement of the railway strike May 25, 1946, and the following June 14, the president named Steelman as director of the Office of War Mobilization and Reconversion. On July 25 Truman gave Steelman the added post of temporary stabilization chief.

Steelman, who had on several occasions interceded for John L. Lewis in labour disputes, was one of the counsels called in by President Truman for a conference on the U.M.W. coal strike staged in Nov. 1946. It was then reported that the president rejected the advice of both Steelman and Secretary Schwellenbach, who favoured negotiating with Lewis.

Stellar System

See ASTRONOMY.

Sterility

See GYNAECOLOGY AND OBSTETRICS.

Stettinius, Edward R., Jr.

Stettinius (1900–), U.S. industrialist and statesman, was born Oct. 22, 1900, at Chicago, Ill. He was educated at the University of Virginia (1919–24), Charlottesville, Va. In 1938 he was made chairman of the board of the U.S. Steel corporation. Stettinius, who had been given a number of important posts in war production agencies by President Roosevelt, was made lend-lease administrator, Aug. 28, 1941, and special assistant to the president the following month. When aid to the Allies was consolidated in the Office of Lend-Lease administration, Stettinius was named head of the new organization, Oct. 28, 1941, with blanket powers to approve disbursements. He remained in this post until Sept. 25, 1943, when Roosevelt named him successor to Sumner Welles, undersecretary of state.

Upon Cordell Hull's resignation as secretary of state because of ill health, Stettinius was appointed to the post, Nov. 27, 1944, becoming the second youngest secretary of state in U.S. history. In Dec. 1944 he told Britain that the European peoples should be permitted to work out their own governments without interference; this statement was regarded as criticism of Winston Churchill's opposition to Count Carlo Sforza's appointment as Italian foreign minister. In 1945 Stettinius attended the Yalta conference (Feb. 4–11) and welcomed delegates to the Inter-American Conference on War and Peace at Mexico City (Feb. 21–March 8). His subsequent espousal of Argentina's candidacy for United Nations membership was widely criticized because of that country's totalitarian form of government. His resignation as secretary of state was accepted June 27, 1945, by President Truman, who thereupon appointed him U.S. member of the United Nations security council and chairman of the U.S. delegation on the U.N. general assembly.

Stettinius attended the U.N. sessions in London, Jan.–Feb. 1946, and in New York city the following spring. His resignation as U.S. delegate to the U.N. security council was accepted by President Truman June 3, 1946. Ill health was the apparent reason behind his resignation, although it was believed that he was dissatisfied with his role of understudy to Secretary of State James Byrnes, who dominated U.S. activities in the security council.

Stilwell, Joseph W.

Stilwell (1883–1946), U.S. army officer, was born March 19, 1883, at Palatka, Fla. Graduated from West Point in 1904, he served with the A.E.F. in World War I. After Pearl Harbor, he was promoted to lieutenant general (Feb. 1942) and later served as chief of staff to Chiang Kai-shek. In March 1942, Chiang gave Stilwell command of the 5th and 6th Chinese armies in the Burma theatre. Retreating before the Japanese advance, Stilwell reached India. After the fall of Burma in May 1942, he candidly confessed: "I claim we got a hell of a beating. We got run out of Burma and . . . I think we ought to find out what caused it, go back and retake it." During 1943, as U.S. commander in southeastern Asia under Lord Louis Mountbatten, he was busy preparing to do so.

Stilwell's efforts were abruptly interrupted Oct. 28, 1944, when he was relieved of his command in the China-Burma-India theatre and recalled to Washington. His removal was attributed to growing friction between himself and Chiang Kai-shek over disposition of Chinese troops as well as over strategic and political problems. Prior to his recall, Stilwell had been named (Aug. 1944) a full general. It was announced Jan. 25, 1945, that Stilwell had been appointed commander of army ground forces in the U.S. On June 22, he was named commander of the U.S. 10th army in Okinawa. He took over command on June 28 and on Sept. 7, accepted the surrender of some 105,000 Japanese troops scattered throughout the Ryukyus. On Feb. 23, 1946, he was appointed commander of the reactivated 6th army on the Pacific coast. He died at Letterman General hospital in San Francisco, Oct. 12, 1946.

Stimson, Henry Lewis

Stimson (1867–), U.S. statesman and lawyer, was born Sept. 21, 1867, in New York city. He was graduated from Yale university with an A.B. degree in 1888 and from Harvard with an A.M. degree the following year; he was admitted to the New York bar in 1891. After serving as secretary of war in President William Howard Taft's cabinet, 1911–13, he went to France during World War I as a colonel in the field artillery. In 1927, he was appointed by President Calvin Coolidge as governor general of the Philippines and was secretary of state in Herbert Hoover's cabinet, 1929–33. He led the U.S. delegations to the London naval conference in 1930 and the disarmament conference in 1932. Stimson, who had advocated that the United States take a strong stand against Japanese aggressions in Manchuria in the early 1930s, was appointed secretary of war by President Roosevelt on June 20, 1940. In the cabinet, he became a militant supporter of the lend-lease bill, revision of the neutrality act to permit U.S. convoys, extension of selective service and removal of the prohibition on use of U.S. armed forces outside of the western hemisphere. After the Pearl Harbor attack, he carried out a program for building a 2,000,000-man air force and an army of at least 7,500,000 men by 1943. In Jan. 1944 he urged enactment of labour draft legislation "to extend the principles of democracy and justice more evenly" between soldier and civilian. In 1945 he endorsed a proposal for unified army-navy command under a single secretary and advocated peacetime military training.

He resigned as secretary of war Sept. 18, 1945. In a report to the Pearl Harbor investigating committee (March 21, 1946), he disclosed that Roosevelt and his war cabinet had agreed on Nov. 28, 1941, that the United States would be forced to fight if Japan attacked British Malaya because of the threat to the Philippines.

Stock Exchanges

See Stocks and Bonds.

Stockholm

The end of the 1930s saw a period of rapid development in the history of the capital of Sweden. The great increase in population (to 654,864 in 1944) gave rise to brisk building activities, with a peak in 1939. New areas were covered with up-to-date blocks of apartment houses on the outskirts of the town and in the suburbs. The volume of traffic in the central part of the town continued to increase; a project of driving an underground traffic tunnel through the town was discussed, and a thorough regulation of the district of Lower Norrmalm, called "the city," which would create new thoroughfares and lead to clearances of the built-up areas, was proposed. A clearance of the historical nucleus of the town around the castle, the old town, had begun. When World War II broke out, all these plans had to be shelved. All energies then had to be devoted to the construction of air-raid shelters and organization of air-raid precautions. As a result of the blockade, all motor vehicles had to be equipped for producer gas, and coke was replaced by wood. The fuel problem was difficult to contend with during the winters, which were the bitterest for 125 years. Help to refugees and children, first from Finland during the "winter war," and later from the other neighbouring countries, became an ever greater problem of organization. The increase of population and stagnation of building activities led to a shortage of houses in 1940, which continued up to the end of 1946.

Work was begun on the great underground line, and the reconstruction of Lower Norrmalm was decided on during the war. Parks, playgrounds and recreation areas were planned; several schools and hospitals were erected. Three museums were entirely rearranged during the war years: the State Historical museum, the Army museum and the new municipal city museum.

It was necessary to build provisional traffic lines in the centre of the town, first at the traffic junction at Tegelbacken and then over Strömmen (the stream), near the castle, a solution which was violently criticized on architectonic and aesthetic grounds. In the meantime the authorities were working on new traffic routes in the form of bridges and tunnels and on a general plan for both Stockholm and the neighbouring municipalities.

(G. SEL.)

Stock Prize

See LITERARY PRIZES.

Stocks and Bonds

Three distinct major movements took place in the U.S. stock market during 1937–46. The first of these occurred during 1937 and 1938, when stock price averages reached their highest level since 1932, namely, in March 1937. Then followed an extraordinary collapse during the last half of the year. This drastic decline continued during the first half of 1938, but that year's price range ended at about the same level as prevailed at the close of 1937.

The second major stock market movement extended from 1939 to 1942, inclusive. The four years were characterized by comparative dullness and a continuing low level of prices for all groups of stocks, the average price remaining at approximately the low level reached at the close of 1937 and 1938.

The third outstanding period of the decade commenced in 1943 and extended to the middle of 1946. It was a more or less consistent bull market for nearly four years, with the average price level of all groups of stocks, at the middle of 1946, well above the high level reached in March 1937.

Decline of 1937–38.—The outstanding development in the U.S. stock market during 1937 was a generally drastic decline in the price level for all groups of stocks. For all the major classes of stocks the record for March 1937, represented the highest monthly price level since the bottom depression figures of June 1932. Near the close of March the security market commenced to waver. By August the decline had assumed large and rapid proportions. From September to November, inclusive, the decline took on the proportions of a collapse. Railroad stocks, from March to December, were cut in half, the average price level (Standard Statistics company figures) declining from 64.8 to 32.6. Industrial stocks declined during the same period from 174.6 to 106.4, public utility stocks from 91.8 to 60.9 and copper and brass stocks from 254.0 to 129.2. The combined average for the first 3 groups of stocks—railroads, industrials and public utilities, comprising a total of 90 stocks—declined from 143.7 in March to 87.5 at the end of the year. In fact, there were few instances on record where a larger percentage decline had been experienced within so short a time.

Following the close of 1937 the decline continued further until the middle of 1938, although with a much smaller momentum. Railroad stocks reached a June level in 1938 of 22.7, industrial stocks of 97.5 in May, public utility stocks of 55.9 in June and copper and brass stocks of 103.6. Thereafter the market steadied and rose moderately until the Dec. 1938, price levels were approximately those of Dec. 1937. The railroad December stock level of 1937 was 32.6, compared with 30.7 for Dec. 1938. The industrial stock level for Dec. 1937, was 106.4, compared with 125.8 for 1938, the public utility stock level 60.9 compared with 62.7 and the copper and brass stock level 129.2 as compared with 155.5.

Table I.—*U. S. Security Market Prices, 1937-38*

	Railroads 20 stocks		Industrials 50 stocks		Public Utilities 20 stocks		Copper and Brass 7 stocks	
	1937	1938	1937	1938	1937	1938	1937	1938
Jan.	58.8	31.5	168.0	110.5	100.9	59.3	227.4	131.2
Feb.	60.8	30.2	174.5	108.5	97.2	55.8	239.1	129.8
March	64.8	25.9	174.6	101.8	91.8	52.6	254.0	124.6
April	62.1	23.0	163.9	97.7	85.5	51.6	230.6	108.5
May	60.6	23.1	156.8	97.5	79.4	56.0	204.8	112.3
June	56.0	22.7	152.1	100.3	74.4	55.9	207.5	103.6
July	55.4	29.6	161.2	120.7	81.7	63.2	218.9	143.3
Aug.	53.3	29.4	163.9	122.4	80.7	59.9	232.8	147.5
Sept.	44.1	26.4	140.7	117.6	70.8	55.9	196.1	143.7
Oct.	36.7	31.4	119.9	129.3	62.6	65.1	139.2	162.4
Nov.	33.1	31.7	107.8	129.1	63.3	66.4	115.4	165.8
Dec.	32.6	30.7	106.4	125.8	60.9	62.7	129.2	155.5

The above figures are an average for the month based on daily closing prices, except for copper and brass, which are weekly closing prices.

(Source of data—*Standard Trade and Securities, Statistical Bulletin*—Standard Statistics company, Inc.).

During the first quarter of 1937 market sentiment was extremely optimistic, and market actions seemed to indicate that the nation was emerging definitely from the 1930–36 depression. The bull market was stimulated by (1) the prospect of greatly increased production to fill the large backlog accumulated during depression years, (2) exceedingly low money rates and the large volume of lendable funds, (3) the great demand of foreign buyers for U.S. securities, (4) the increasing development of foreign markets, (5) the better balance obtained between agriculture and industry and (6) the more hopeful outlook relative to the balancing of the federal budget. By the close of March, however, and continuing all through the remainder of the year, as well as during 1938, news and happenings of a very disturbing nature seemed to overwhelm market sentiment. War in Europe, and the prospects of U.S. involvement, filled the newspapers from day to day. All through the year 1937, basic industries were also blocked with labour upheavals, causing widespread disorganization as well as severe financial loss. Corporations felt more and more the burden of taxes levied on their undivided profits and capital gains. Increasingly it also became apparent that the national budget could not be balanced, with a resulting spectre of a further increase in tax burdens. Government credit policies also tended to tighten credit. Moreover, many political measures were either launched or threatened which involved an unsettling influence upon business until the measures could be finally disposed of.

Price Levels.—Averages published by the Standard Statistics company showed that a representative list of 20 railroad stocks rose from 58.8 for Jan. 1937, to a high for the year of 64.8 in March. Thereafter a decline occurred, almost uninterruptedly month after month, until a low of 32.6 was reached for December. This average compared with 47.0 for Jan. 1936, and with a yearly average of 26.8 for 1932, the bottom depression year. For Jan. 1938 the average stood at 31.5, for June a low for the year of 22.7 was reached, while by December a recovery was made to 30.7.

A representative list of 50 industrial stocks experienced an increase from Jan. 1937 to March 1937, of from 168.0 to 174.6. Thereafter a decline occurred, again almost uninterruptedly month by month, until a low for the year—106.4—was reached in December. This low average may be compared with 129.1 for Jan. 1936, and with 53.5, the yearly average for 1932. By May 1938, the average had declined further to 97.5. Thereafter the monthly average moved back and forth, although with an improving tendency, until the closing December average stood at 125.8.

Twenty representative utility stocks slumped from 100.9 for Jan. 1937, to 60.9 for December. The decline was almost uninterrupted throughout the year. The low of 60.9 may be compared with 88.4 for Jan. 1936, and with a yearly average of 85.7 for 1932.

A representative list of 7 copper and brass stocks underwent a decline during the period March–Dec. 1937 from 254.0 to 129.2, or nearly 50%.

The combined average for the first 3 groups of stocks—railroads, industrials and public utilities, comprising a total of 90 stocks—showed a decline, during March–Dec. 1937, from 143.8 to 87.5, or nearly 40%. During 1938 this combined average declined further to an extreme low of 78.5 for April. Thereafter a gradual improvement occurred until a December average of 100.7 was reached.

Doldrums, 1939–42.—For a four-year period, following 1938, the stock market remained comparatively dull and steady. Major price trends showed many fluctuations, both bull and bear, but all were comparatively small in scope as compared with the major movement of 1937, and nothing of a sensational nature occurred marketwise in any one of the four years covered by this period. From an overall standpoint during the four-year period, it may be said that the market assumed a creepingly lower tendency. In other words, the main force of the bear market had spent itself during 1937 and 1938, but a somewhat further downward drift was experienced during the following four years of 1939–1942. Most of the leading groups of stocks ended with an average December level in 1942 of from 8.1% (railroads) to 44.3% (public utilities) under the December average of 1938.

Price Movements of Important Groups.—Averages published by the Standard Statistics company showed that a representative list of 20 railroad stocks began 1939 with a January average of 31.3, then declined to 26.8 for May, and subsequently rose to 31.7 for December. In 1940 the monthly average declined from 31.2 for January to 22.1 for June, and subsequently rose to 28.4 for December. During 1941 the monthly average rose from 29.8 for January to 30.3 for August, and subsequently declined to 24.9 for December. In 1942 the monthly average declined from 28.1 for January to 24.0 for June, and subsequently closed at 28.2 for December. This December average of 28.2 for 1942 compared with a December average of 30.7 for 1938, a decline of 8.1%.

A representative list of 50 industrial stocks began 1939 with a January average of 122.5, then declined to 105.2 for April, and subsequently rose to 120.2 for December. During 1940 the monthly average declined from 119.0 for January to 93.0 for June, and thereafter closed at 103.0 for December. The next year, the monthly average declined from 102.6 for January to 92.4 for May, and subsequently declined further, closing at 88.2 for December. In 1942 the monthly average declined further from 89.2 for January to 79.0 for April. Subsequently the average closed at 96.5 for December. This December average of 96.5 for 1942 compared with a December average of 125.8 for 1938, a decline of 23.2%.

Twenty representative public utility stocks started 1939 with a January average of 66.6, then declined to 62.1 for April, and subsequently rose to 68.5 for December. In 1940 the monthly average started with 70.4 for January, then declined to 56.8 for June, and later declined somewhat more to 53.8 for December. In the following year, the monthly average declined from 55.0 for January to 44.4 for May, and subsequently rose and declined at intervals until the December average stood at 34.3. During 1942 the monthly average declined from 35.4 for January to 28.8 for April, and thereafter rose slightly to close at 34.9 for December. The December average of 34.9 for 1942 compared with a December average of 62.7 for Dec. 1938, a decline of 44.3%.

A representative list of 7 copper and brass stocks started with a monthly average of 145.6 for January, then declined to 114.0 for May, and subsequently closed at 141.3 for December. In 1940 the January average was 134.3; thereafter a decline occurred to 92.3 for July, while the close for December showed a rise to 125.7. During 1941 the January average was 86.9 (a new base, using 1935–39 as a base period, having been adopted by the Standard Statistics service). Thereafter a decline occurred to 78.5 for April, while the December close stood at 71.6.

The combined average for the first 3 groups of stocks—railroads, industrials and public utilities, comprising a total of 90 stocks—stood at 99.3 for Jan. 1939, then declined to 89.2 for May, and subsequently rose to 98.2 for December. For 1940 the January average was 97.7; thereafter a decline reached bottom in June at 76.8, while the December close stood at 83.7. The year 1941 began with a January average of 83.8, followed by a May low of 74.9, and a December close of 69.5. During 1942 the January average stood at 70.9, followed by a decline to 62.2 for April, and a subsequent rise to 75.6 for December. The December average of 75.6 for 1942 compares with a December average of 100.7 for Dec. 1938, a decline of 24.9%.

Economic Factors.—The gradually declining seesaw market of 1939–42 was largely the outgrowth of conditions

Table II.—*U. S. Security Market Prices, 1939-42*

	Railroad Stocks 20 stocks				Industrial Stocks 50 stocks				Public Utility Stocks 20 stocks				Copper and Brass Stocks 7 stocks				Combined Groups 90 stocks			
	1939	1940	1941	1942	1939	1940	1941	1942	1939	1940	1941	1942	1939	1940	1941	1942	1939	1940	1941	1942
Jan. . .	31.3	31.2	29.8	28.1	122.5	119.0	102.6	89.2	66.6	70.4	55.0	35.4	145.6	134.3	86.9	88.3	99.3	97.7	83.8	70.9
Feb. . .	30.3	30.9	28.4	28.0	120.7	118.3	96.1	86.4	69.7	69.9	51.4	33.9	134.5	131.7	80.1	85.1	98.5	97.0	78.5	68.7
Mar. . .	31.1	30.8	28.7	26.2	120.4	117.9	96.9	82.1	69.6	67.8	50.6	30.8	136.9	133.6	81.1	81.4	98.3	96.5	79.0	64.9
April . .	25.6	31.2	29.0	24.8	105.2	119.0	93.9	79.0	62.1	68.7	47.6	28.8	115.6	137.2	78.5	76.9	86.0	97.4	76.5	62.2
May . .	26.8	26.4	28.7	24.6	108.7	102.4	92.4	79.8	65.5	60.4	44.4	29.8	114.0	117.6	83.4	70.8	89.2	84.0	74.9	62.9
June . .	27.2	22.1	28.7	24.0	110.7	93.0	96.2	84.4	66.6	56.8	44.9	31.1	117.9	99.3	88.3	71.4	90.8	76.8	77.5	66.1
July . .	27.9	26.3	30.0	25.8	113.2	95.1	101.5	87.9	68.6	61.7	45.9	30.6	123.1	92.3	94.1	76.1	93.0	79.4	81.5	68.6
Aug. . .	27.0	26.9	30.3	26.7	111.1	97.5	101.0	87.3	70.2	61.1	45.2	30.0	125.1	97.8	93.2	75.6	91.6	81.0	81.1	68.2
Sept. . .	32.6	28.8	29.4	27.2	125.1	102.2	101.7	88.1	67.1	60.9	44.6	30.4	152.3	107.5	90.8	75.3	101.4	84.4	81.3	68.9
Oct. . .	35.0	29.4	28.6	29.7	125.5	103.5	97.7	94.1	69.0	59.8	42.1	33.7	154.2	113.2	83.4	80.9	102.4	85.2	78.0	74.0
Nov. . .	33.5	30.1	27.8	29.6	123.0	106.9	93.8	95.2	69.5	59.8	37.9	35.7	146 9	124.5	82.7	76.4	100.6	85.2	74.4	75.2
Dec. . .	31.7	28.4	24.9	28.2	120.2	103.0	88.2	96.5	68.5	53.8	34.3	34.9	141.3	125.7	82.4	71.6	98.2	83.7	69.5	75.6

Copper and brass figures from 1941 on use 1935–39 as a base period. All other figures use 1926 as a base period.
The above figures are an average for the month based on daily closing prices, except for copper and brass, which are weekly closing prices.
(Source of data—*Standard Trade and Securities, Current Statistics*, Standard Statistics company, Inc.)

resulting from World War II. The first of these years showed an overall improvement in business of about 18% as compared with the close of 1938, thus causing many to believe that the stock market had failed to keep pace with business conditions. However, the actual outbreak of war in Europe was a new factor of importance. War scares were frequent during the early months of the year and were possibly responsible for the marked decline from January to April, inclusive. When World War II finally became a reality, the market seemed to have discounted the momentous event, and exhibited a remarkably steady tendency. In this respect, the stock market's actions were very different from those at the outbreak of World War I, when chaos resulted with news of the commencement of war and all stock exchanges had to be closed for a four-month period.

During 1940 despite the war news from both a national and an international point of view, stock movements, as in 1939, were in no sense extraordinary. The whole year's showing was rather surprising in view of the substantial enlargement of business activity caused by large war orders and the initiation of a huge national defense program. Probably the continued absence of substantial market movements was attributable to the fact that fundamental conditions affecting business had not changed materially. The burden of taxation upon corporations, an unbalanced national budget and a rapidly growing national indebtedness seemed to indicate in 1940 every prospect for further extensions. Increased volume of business, in other words, was counterbalanced by the fear of possible price restrictions and general governmental regimentation of business.

As was the case during 1940 market movements in 1941 were again distinctly and gradually downward, despite the tremendous enlargement of business activity occasioned by war orders and the exceptional earnings of larger corporations. All through the year the market seemed to be influenced by fear and indecision. Apparently the market was discounting future prospects and, therefore, remained uninfluenced by current improved volume of business and earnings. As in 1939 and 1940 the market lethargy and general price decline was largely attributable to a huge increase in the tax burden and the fear of governmental regimentation. But a new factor was increasingly entering the economic picture, namely, the prospect of inflationary tendencies with their increased cost of raw materials as well as increased labour costs. Despite war psychology and war controls, the year was marked by constant labour troubles. Moreover, there was a marked trend toward the adoption of priorities in business and of price restrictions. A considerable amount of selling in the stock market also had for its motive the establishment of losses for income tax deductions.

Rarely had annual stock market price fluctuations, as well as the annual volume of transactions, been smaller than in 1942. Strange as it may seem, this unusual record occurred despite momentous developments of a domestic and international character. Neither war events, favourable and unfavourable, nor extraordinary domestic news with respect to the dislocation of industry, the imposition of greatly increased taxes and the introduction of rationing and other control systems, seemed to have any real effect, except momentarily, upon either the price level of stocks or bonds or the volume of transactions. Nor did the market respond to the splendid earnings of corporations and the payment of large dividends. Instead it continued low and dull, despite the fact that for many of the listed issues of common shares, the dividend distribution to stockholders during the year equalled an 8% to 10% return on the prevailing market price.

Bull Market of 1943–46.—Although stock market price movements for the year 1943 were somewhat more extensive than was the case during 1942, the fluctuations were comparatively small considering the extraordinary economic events occasioned by World War II. As was the case during 1939–42, the market as a whole seemed largely unaffected by war events or economic happenings. However, the year was quite consistently a moderate bull year, in marked contrast to the creeping seesaw downward trend of prices during 1939–42. During 1944 stock market fluctuations were again exceptionally small, as was also the volume of trading. But the year was again marked by an upward trend, the various groups of stocks showing an appreciation for the year, as compared with 1943, of about 7.3% for railroads, 8.2% for industrials, 11.3% for public utilities and 8.2% for all three groups combined.

Compared especially with 1944 and 1943 the 1945 U.S. stock market was decidedly different with respect to (1) much greater activity, (2) a much higher price level, (3) a much greater continuity of trend and (4) a more vigorous extension of the bull market to all leading classes of stocks. In fact, the 1945 market may be described as an active bull market throughout the year (following the milder bull market of the preceding two years), with only one brief period of moderate decline in the middle of the year. At the end of December, railroad stocks showed an appreciation of 17.4% more than 1943, industrial stocks an appreciation of 38.2%, public utility stocks 28.1% and copper and brass stocks 41.5%. For all of the first 3 leading groups, the appreciation amounted to 33.6% as compared with a rise during the same period of 1944 of only 8.2%.

The vigorous bull market of 1945 was continued during the first six months of 1946. By June of that year the monthly average stood at 66.1 for the railroads, 177.8 for the industrial group, 94.5 for the public utilities group and 139.7 for the copper and brass group. This rise represented another appreciation for these groups respectively of 3.1%, 6.8%, 12.4% and 10.6% more than the averages of Dec. 1945.

Table III.—*U. S. Security Market Prices, 1943-46*

	Railroad Stocks 20 stocks				Industrial Stocks 50 stocks				Public Utility Stocks 20 stocks				Copper and Brass Stocks 7 stocks				Combined Groups 90 stocks			
	1943	1944	1945	1946	1943	1944	1945	1946	1943	1944	1945	1946	1943	1944	1945	1946	1943	1944	1945	1946
Jan.	30.2	32.3	49.3	66.7	101.8	117.4	131.8	172.8	38.2	50.2	57.7	88.5	75.2	75.2	91.2	132.2	80.2	94.1	107.1	143.1
Feb.	31.6	39.2	50.4	66.3	107.7	115.8	135.8	173.1	41.3	50.5	61.3	89.5	80.0	74.1	94.9	136.3	84.9	93.5	110.7	143.5
March	35.1	40.4	50.5	62.7	110.9	119.0	135.8	167.8	42.9	51.8	61.2	88.8	84.1	76.3	92.7	131.4	87.9	96.1	110.6	139.2
April	37.7	39.8	52.5	63.7	114.0	117.1	138.8	179.5	45.4	50.8	63.5	93.7	85.8	74.6	95.0	139.1	90.9	94.4	113.4	148.2
May	39.4	40.2	54.7	63.6	118.3	119.4	143.9	179.8	47.1	51.0	66.5	94.3	84.8	75.2	95.9	142.8	94.4	96.1	117.7	148.5
June	38.3	41.2	58.6	66.1	121.0	125.3	145.2	177.8	47.8	52.9	69.9	94.5	80.2	76.3	97.2	139.7	96.1	100.6	119.8	147.6
July	39.4	42.7	56.6	62.8	122.5	128.5	141.7	173.5	51.4	54.3	71.2	90.2	82.3	80.2	94.3	138.8	98.1	103.2	117.4	143.4
Aug.	36.7	41.7	53.4	59.9	116.2	126.2	143.3	170.5	49.9	55.4	69.8	88.4	77.4	77.7	91.3	133.9	93.2	101.8	117.7	140.6
Sept.	37.3	40.3	56.2	48.3	118.6	124.2	153.7	145.9	51.3	54.6	72.9	75.5	76.2	77.5	99.6	109.2	95.2	100.0	125.8	119.9
Oct.	37.5	42.1	59.0	45.1	117.3	127.1	159.7	142.9	51.0	55.9	77.3	74.3	77.4	82.8	110.6	109.7	94.3	102.5	131.0	117.2
Nov.	34.9	42.7	62.7	46.6	112.1	126.2	163.5	141.5	48.8	54.9	83.4	76.0	74.3	82.0	120.7	115.1	90.0	101.8	135.3	116.7
Dec.	35.0	46.6	64.0	48.4	113.8	128.5	166.7	145.3	48.9	55.1	83.2	79.5	72.7	84.8	126.3	123.8	91.2	104.0	137.6	120.2

Copper and brass figures use 1935-39 as a base period. All other figures use 1926 as a base period.
The above figures are an average for the month based on daily closing prices, except for copper and brass, which are weekly closing prices.
(Source of data—*Standard Trade and Securities, Current Statistics*, Standard Statistics company, Inc.)

168 *Price Movements of Important Groups.*—Averages published by the Standard Statistics company showed that 20 representative railroad stocks began 1943 with a January average of 30.2, then rose to 39.4 for July, and subsequently declined to close at 35.0 for December. During 1944 the monthly average rose from 32.3 for January to 42.7 for July, and subsequently closed at 46.6 for December. In 1945 the monthly average rose further from 49.3 for January to 58.6 for June, and closed with a December average of 64.0. The vigorous bull market of 1945 was maintained during the first 6 months of 1946, the monthly average standing at 66.7 for January and 66.1 for June. The January average of 66.7, the highest level for the 3½ year bull market, compared with the December average for 1942 of 28.2, an increase of 136.5%.

The representative list of 50 industrial stocks began 1943 with a January average of 101.8, then increased to 122.5 for July, and subsequently declined slightly to close at 113.8 for December. During 1944 the monthly average increased from 117.4 for January to 128.5 for July. Thereafter the monthly average held without substantial change until the December average stood at 128.5. In 1945 the monthly average rose further from 131.8 for January to 145.2 for June. Subsequently the monthly average fluctuated somewhat, but the December average reached the high figure of 166.7. This average continued to rise during the first 5 months of 1946, the figure rising from 172.8 for January to 179.8 for May. The latter average, again the highest level for the 3½ year bull market, compared with the December average for 1942 of 96.5, an increase of 83.5%.

Twenty representative public utility stocks started 1943 with a January average of 38.2, then rose to 51.4 for July, and subsequently declined slightly to 48.9 for December. During the year 1944 the monthly average started with 50.2 for January, then increased to 55.4 for August, and thereafter held to the end of the year, when the December average stood at 55.1. In the following year, the monthly average rose from 57.7 for January almost uninterruptedly to a December close for the year of 83.2. This average increased further during the first 6 months of 1946, the price level rising from 88.5 for January to 94.5 for June. This figure of 94.5 compared with the December average for 1942 of 34.9, an increase of 170.8%.

The list of 7 representative copper and brass stocks started 1943 with a January average of 75.2, then increased to 85.8 for April, and thereafter declined to 72.7 for December. In 1944 the January average was 75.2, thereafter increased to 80.2 for July, and subsequently fluctuated up and down until the December average stood at 84.8. During 1945 the January average was 91.2, an increase subsequently occurred to 97.2 for June, and subsequently a further increase took place to 126.3 for the closing month of December. During the first 5 months of 1946, the average rose from 132.2 for January to 142.8 for May—again the highest level for the 3½ year bull market, comparing with the December average of 71.6 for 1942, an increase of 99.4%.

The combined average for the first 3 groups of stocks—railroads, industrials and public utilities, comprising a total of 90 stocks—stood at 80.2 for Jan. 1943, then increased to 98.1 for July, and subsequently declined to 91.2 for December. For 1944 the January average was 94.1. Thereafter an increase occurred to 103.2 for July, and this level was substantially maintained until December, when the monthly average stood at 104.2. The year 1945 began with a January average of 107.1. Thereafter an increase occurred to 119.8 for June, and subsequently a further increase to 137.6 for December. The December average of 137.6 for 1945 was further increased during the first 5 months of 1946, rising from 143.1 for January to 148.5 for May, as compared with the December average for 1942 of 75.6, an increase of 96.4%.

The bull market of 1943–46 apparently had ended by June 1946. Following that month a very drastic decline occurred, especially after August. The decline was so large as to raise the question of whether the stock market had not discounted a serious letup in business. Railroad stocks, using the Standard Statistics company figures, declined from a June average of 66.1 to a September average of 48.3, or 26.9%. Industrial stocks during the same period declined from 177.8 to 145.9, or 18%; public utilities from 94.5 to 75.5, or 20.1%; copper stocks from 139.7 to 109.2, or 21.8%; and the first 3 groups combined from 147.6 to 119.9, or 18.8%.

Market Factors.—The year 1943 could be regarded as the first conservatively bull stock market year since the break of 1937. New economic factors began to assert themselves, as compared with the preceding four-year period, namely, heavy emphasis concerning the prospects of inflation, as well as the expected high postwar activity to meet depleted backlogs of needed goods, repairs and new construction.

During 1944 the market at all times seemed to visualize an early termination of hostilities and the gigantic problems that would ensue. Price movements, therefore, were hesitating in character, and indicated an extremely cautious financial sentiment and unusually selective buying. On the bull side of the market, emphasis was given to large earnings and the resiliency of industry to withstand high taxes, the prospect of at least a temporary high postwar activity to meet the greatly depleted backlog of consumer goods and deferred repairs and construction, and the likelihood of the elimination of governmental price and other economic restrictions. On the bear side, emphasis was given to the rapidly mounting federal debt, the likelihood of continued high taxation, the costly problems of reconversion of industry to a peacetime basis, the loss involved in the renegotiation and termination of war contracts, the drift toward inflation and increasing production costs and the prospect of greatly increased labour troubles when strikes no longer would seem inconsistent with the war effort. The attempt to balance these two groups of opposite factors very likely led to the cautiousness of market speculators and their inclination to remain conservative as speculators on the bull side of the market.

Market factors of 1945 influencing the stock price levels were again exceedingly numerous. On the bull side, ten considerations seem to have been stressed by the speculative community, namely: (1) a strong undercurrent of inflation thinking, (2) an enormous pressure of idle funds seeking investment, with outright purchases the general rule, (3) a diminution of investment bond issues owing to large refunding operations, (4) continued low interest yields on choice bonds with a much larger yield obtainable from stocks, (5) favourable corporate earnings and increased dividend declarations, (6) federal tax legislation reducing corporate taxes materially, (7) better prospects for utility shares, resulting partly from tax redemptions and partly from a likelihood of more liberal recapitalization plans for common stockholders, (8) a belief by many in a huge postwar boom to meet the needs of foreign nations as well as domestic depleted backlogs of goods, repairs and badly needed new construction, (9) the hope of abolition of price and other economic restrictions with the close of hostilities and (10) a feeling that stocks were not too high, despite their substantial rise, in view of the devalued dollar (devalued by nearly 40% in 1933). Unfavourable market factors were also plentiful, such as (1) continued heavy government deficit spending, (2) a substantial business reaction from excessive war activity, (3) a faltering reconversion of business to peacetime conditions, (4) a substantial increase in production costs, as well as a distinct trend toward higher living costs and (5) an enormous increase in strikes throughout the nation, with the automotive and steel industries paralyzed, and with a threatened stoppage of numerous other basic industries. For the time being, however, all these ominous factors seemed to be ignored by the stock market. Bad news, especially strike news, seemed to be geared to a further appreciation in stock values. Increasingly the inflation and boom psychologies seemed to brush all unfavourable factors aside and more and more to hold the market within their grip.

Toward the middle of 1946, however, bear considerations clearly gained the upper hand. Continual strikes throughout the country in nearly all leading industries made it more and more apparent that the anticipated postwar boom would not materialize immediately. Moreover, the numerous wage increase victories of labour were not accompanied by a compensating increase in prices for producers. Disappointment over the inability of leading corporations, especially the automotive industry, to get back to profitable production became increasingly keen to the thinking public. Moreover, the apprehension caused by stymied foreign policy indications, and the prospects of serious trouble with U.S.S.R. also shared in the undermining of confidence and the bringing about of the sharp market break following June 1946. Economic enterprise was also impeded by numerous serious shortages in steel scrap, freight cars, etc., and by great uncertainties concerning cost price relations and corporation taxes.

Traders on the floor of the New York Stock exchange shortly before the outbreak of war in Europe during 1939

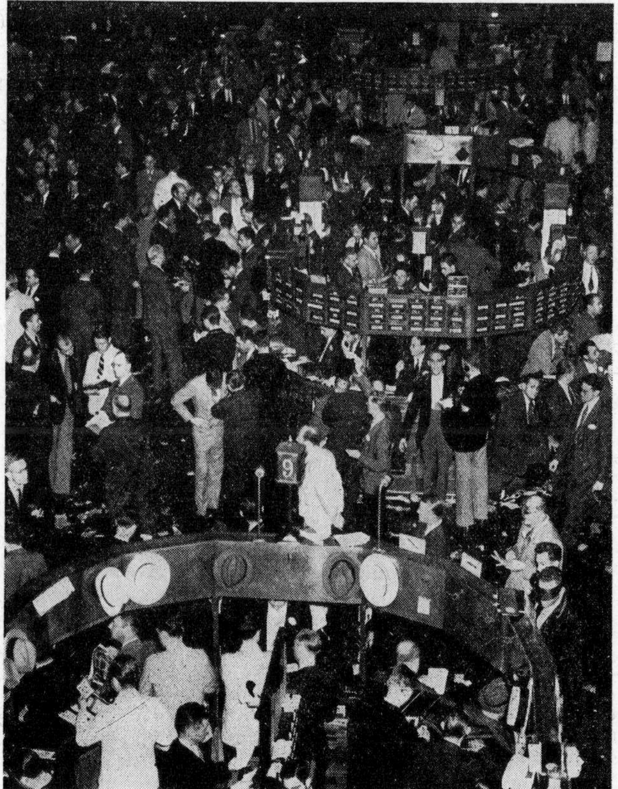

Market Values.—Using the figures of the New York Stock exchange, the total value of listed shares on the New York exchange stood at $66,864,000,000 on Oct. 1, 1946, and $69,561,000,000 on Nov. 1, 1945. This value compared with $53,087,000,000 on Nov. 1, 1944, and for the corresponding period, with $45,101,000,000 for 1943, $37,374,000,000 for 1942, $37,882,000,000 for 1941, $41,848,000,000 for 1940, $45,500,000,000 for 1939, $46,081,000,000 for 1938, $40,716,000,000 for 1937 and $62,618,000,000 for March 1937, the high mark before the bear market of 1937–42 began its course. During 1946 the total value was increased to $74,350,000,000 on Sept. 1, highest during the ten-year period under consideration.

Volume of Transactions.—Stock transactions on the New York Stock exchange during the decade 1937–46 showed a condition of unusual dullness. This was particularly true of all years except 1937, 1945 and 1946. For 1937 total sales on the New York exchange amounted to 409,468,885 shares, and for 1945 to 377,563,575 shares. For all of the intervening years the total fell below the 300,000,000 share mark, and for the 3 years 1940–42, the total stood respectively at only 208,000,000, 171,000,000 and 126,000,000. These totals seemed extremely small when compared with former totals of 1,125,000,000 shares for 1929, the highest on record, with 920,000,000 and 810,000,000 for 1928 and 1930, and with 655,000,000 and 496,000,000 for 1933 and 1936. For 1946 the total was 363,709,312.

On the New York Curb market, the second largest stock market in the western hemisphere, the showing was similar to that explained for the New York Stock exchange. Here again the largest volume of sales occurred in 1937 (with 104,000,000 shares) and 1945 (with 143,000,000 shares). For all other years the market was comparatively dull, with 1944 and 1943 alone showing sales of 71,000,000 shares, and with 1942 and 1941 dropping to the low totals of 22,000,000 and 34,000,000 shares, respectively. Even the 1945 total of 143,000,000 shares seems small when compared with the 1930 volume of sales of 220,000,000 shares, and the 474,000,000 shares of 1929, the largest on record.

Table IV.—*Yearly Totals of Share Sales on the New York Stock Exchange*

Year	Shares	Year	Shares
1929	1,124,991,490	1942	125,677,963
1937	409,468,885	1943	278,741,765
1938	297,446,059	1944	263,074,018
1939	262,015,799	1945	377,563,575
1940	207,605,359	1946	363,709,312
1941	170,534,363		

The Bond Market.—Unlike the stock market, the U.S. bond market of 1937–46 may be discussed as a single entity. Throughout the decade, bonds sold at an extremely high price level. Variations were comparatively small, with the exception of 1937, and the price trend was a gradually rising one.

Using the Standard Statistics company barometer figure for composite bonds (average for each month based on daily closing prices), the average high price for Jan. 1937, stood at 100.7, and thereafter declined to 83.6 in December. This December high level held substantially for the following 3 years, namely, 82.2 for 1938, 82.6 for 1939 and 84.4 for 1940. Thereafter the index was changed to a new basis. For 1941 the monthly high index for January was 99.87. Each succeeding year recorded an increase, namely, to 100.3 (January high) for 1942, and for the corresponding month, to 106.4 for 1943, 113.4 for 1944, 117.6 for 1945 and 120.2 for 1946. For Dec. 1946 the high average stood at 116.5.

Table V.—*U. S. Composite Bond Prices*

	January		February		March		April		May		June	
	High	Low	High	Low	High	Low	High	Low	High	Low	High	Low
1937 . . .	100.7	100.0	100.4	99.6	99.8	97.1	97.2	95.9	96.9	95.7	95.8	93.4
1938 . . .	82.5	77.7	80.2	78.1	79.9	70.7	75.3	70.9	78.2	74.8	78.1	73.5
1939 . . .	82.7	80.6	82.9	81.5	84.6	80.8	80.7	78.3	81.2	79.3	81.9	80.2
1940 . . .	83.2	82.0	82.6	81.9	82.4	81.8	83.3	82.0	82.3	76.5	80.3	77.0
1941 . .	99.87	98.39	98.65	96.45	100.0	96.75	100.4	99.05	100.0	98.67	99.55	98.74
1942 . . .	100.3	97.5	100.6	98.89	99.50	98.01	99.51	98.78	99.28	98.21	98.63	97.64
1943 . . .	106.4	104.5	107.4	105.8	109.0	107.4	109.5	109.0	110.5	109.5	110.6	109.1
1944 . . .	113.4	112.6	113.9	113.1	114.0	113.5	114.7	114.0	115.0	114.3	115.1	114.2
1945 . . .	117.6	117.0	117.9	117.0	118.2	117.8	118.3	118.1	118.0	117.7	118.4	117.8
1946 . . .	120.2	119.1	120.2	119.9	120.3	120.0	120.3	119.4	119.8	119.4	119.8	119.2

	July		August		September		October		November		December	
	High	Low	High	Low	High	Low	High	Low	High	Low	High	Low
1937 . . .	95.6	94.2	95.3	94.0	93.7	88.8	89.9	82.3	85.4	81.1	83.6	81.3
1938 . . .	82.8	78.4	82.3	80.3	80.2	77.0	82.4	79.6	83.0	81.3	82.2	80.6
1939 . . .	82.3	80.3	82.5	79.5	82.6	78.0	83.5	82.2	83.4	82.3	82.6	81.7
1940 . . .	81.7	80.3	82.1	81.0	83.5	82.1	83.8	83.3	84.3	83.6	84.4	83.6
1941 . . .	100.2	99.26	100.1	99.33	99.43	98.38	99.55	98.62	99.66	99.07	99.66	95.79
1942 . . .	99.22	98.47	99.72	98.82	101.4	99.76	102.9	101.4	103.6	102.7	104.5	102.9
1943 . . .	111.3	110.4	110.6	110.2	110.6	110.2	111.3	110.1	111.8	110.7	112.6	111.4
1944 . . .	115.0	114.3	115.0	114.6	114.8	114.3	115.9	114.8	116.2	115.5	117.3	116.4
1945 . . .	118.2	117.5	117.6	116.9	117.4	116.8	118.1	117.3	118.6	118.1	119.4	118.5
1946 . . .	119.5	118.6	119.3	118.6	119.1	115.8	116.2	114.8	116.5	115.1	116.5	115.4

1937–40 Daily Bond Price Indexes-60 Bonds Composite
1941–46 Daily Index of Medium and Lower Grade Bonds—Composite
(Source of data—*Standard Trade and Securities, Current Statistics,* Standard Statistics company, Inc.)

Using Moody's Bond Price index, the rise for "Aaa bonds" extended from a high average figure of 118.16 for 1937 to 126.61 for 1940. Thereafter a decline took place to a high average of 117.20 for 1942. Subsequently the price rise was resumed, extending from 119.41 for 1943 to 124.20 for 1946. United States government bonds showed an almost steady rise throughout the decade, from 112.78 (January high) for 1937 to 126.28 for 1946. During the decade, bond yields also showed a substantial decline. According to Moody's Bond Yield averages, the yield on the "Aaa group" of bonds declined from 3.47% for 1937 to 2.58% for 1946, whereas the yield on the "Aa group" declined during the same 10 year period from 3.60% for 1937 to 2.66% for 1946. On government bonds the yield, according to this index, declined from 2.13% for 1941 to 1.54% for 1946.

Table VI.—*Moody's Bond Prices*

	Aaa Group		Aa Group		U.S. Government	
	High	Low	High	Low	High	Low
1937	118.16	109.84	113.89	107.30	112.78	107.01
1938	118.60	112.45	111.43	102.66	112.81	105.89
1939	122.40	112.45	118.60	108.27	117.72	108.77
1940	126.61	118.60	121.94	115.57	119.61	113.02
1941	118.60	116.22	116.02	112.00	120.05	115.89
1942	117.20	115.43	114.27	112.75	118.41	115.90
1943	119.41	116.80	117.00	113.89	120.87	116.85
1944	119.20	118.20	118.00	116.22	120.58	119.20
1945	121.25	118.80	119.82	117.80	124.84	120.55
1946 (to Aug. 29) .	124.20	121.46	122.50	119.82	126.28	123.14

Moody's Bond Yield Averages

	Aaa Group[1]		Aa Group	
	High	Low	High	Low
1937	3.47	3.07	3.60	3.27
1938	3.34	3.05	3.85	3.39
1939	3.34	2.88	3.55	3.05
1940	3.05	2.70	3.19	2.90
1941	2.86	2.72	3.06	2.85
1942	2.88	2.79	3.02	2.94
1943	2.81	2.68	2.96	2.80
1944	2.74	2.69	2.84	2.75
1945	2.71	2.59	2.76	2.66
1946 (to Aug. 29)	2.58	2.45	2.66	2.53

Source: *Commercial and Financial Chronicle,* first issue of each year.

Factors Influencing Bond Prices.—Reasons for the huge rise in bond values during the decade 1937–46 were essentially three: (1) enhanced safety of bonds because of the improved solvency status of the issuing corporations, (2) the relative scarcity of available bonds, occasioned partly by rapidly growing investment funds on the part of depository institutions as well as individual investors, and partly by vast bond retirement and refunding operations by corporations and (3) an extraordinary decline in interest rates. The last two factors were the most important. Sound bond investments, when measured by the huge funds seeking investment, became acutely scarce. Moreover, interest rates sank to an extremely low level. Throughout the decade, time money rates for prime commercial paper (using New York as a basis) ranged between 0.75% and 1.00%, and call loans remained consistently at 1.00%. Owing largely to governmental policies, funds for business purposes seemed to be a drug on the market; hence the unusual demand for high grade bonds on the part of nonspeculative investors, despite the declining yield.

Number and Value of Bond Issues.—According to the N.Y. Stock exchange's compilation, the total market value of bonds listed on that exchange stood at $41,612,000,000 on Jan. 1, 1937. By Dec. 1, 1937, this market value had declined to $39,000,000,000. Subsequently the market value figure (Dec. 1) rose gradually to $50,000,000,000 for 1938, $48,000,000,000 for 1939, $51,000,000,000 for 1940, $55,000,000,000 for 1941, $63,000,000,000 for 1942, $91,000,000,000 for 1943, $102,000,000,000 for 1944, $139,000,000,000 for 1945 and $141,000,000,000 for Aug. 1, 1946. The enormous increase in the aforementioned figures was largely attributable to the issue of huge amounts of United States government securities. The New York Stock exchange's average bond price for Jan. 1, 1937, was given as 100.76 and for Dec. 1 of that year as 92.36. Thereafter a slight decline occurred to 91.24 for Dec. 1, 1939. Following 1939 a consistent rise took place, namely, to 93.58 (Dec. 1) for 1940, and for the corresponding date to 94.80 for 1941, 96.11 for 1942, 99.02 for 1943, 100.71 for 1944, 103.16 for 1945 and 103.52 (Aug. 1) 1946.

There was also a noticeable decline in the number of outstanding bond issues listed on the New York Stock exchange. Whereas the number of issues during 1938–40 was consistently near 1,400, that figure declined to 1,273 in 1941, 1,142 in 1942, 1,098 in 1943, 1,058 in 1944 and 946 in July, 1946. As already explained, bond issues became relatively scarce, owing to the large bond retirement and refunding operations of corporations.

Table VII.—*All Listed Bond Issues on the New York Stock Exchange*

	Number of Issues	Total Value (in $000,000's)	Average Price
1937 (Jan. 1)		41,612	$100.76
1937 (Dec. 1)	1,092	39,088	92.36
1938 (Dec. 1)	1,389	50,301	92.36
1939 (Dec. 1)	1,396	47,839	91.24
1940 (Dec. 1)	1,396	50,756	93.58
1941 (Dec. 1)	1,273	54,813	94.80
1942 (Dec. 1)	1,142	62,544	96.11
1943 (Dec. 1)	1,098	90,970	99.02
1944 (Dec. 1)	1,058	101,801	100.71
1945 (Dec. 1)	1,174	128,741	103.16
1946 (Oct. 1)	930	139,784	102.15

Volume of Transactions.—Throughout the decade the volume of bond transactions was comparatively meagre. Only 1943 showed bond sales on the New York Stock exchange exceeding $3,000,000,000. During 1938 and 1940 sales fell to the extreme low level of $1,859,000,000 and $1,671,000,000 respectively. For all other years the annual

Table VIII.—*Bonds Traded on the New York Stock Exchange*

1937	$2,790,323,300	1942	$2,182,625,800
1938	1,859,525,825	1943	3,254,716,525
1939	2,048,237,875	1944	2,694,703,700
1940	1,671,598,875	1945	2,261,985,110
1941	2,114,098,550	1946	1,364,177,150

total of sales ranged from a minimum of $2,048,000,000 in 1939 to a maximum of $2,790,000,000 in 1937.

U.S. Stock Exchanges.—The 1937–46 chronology of the New York Stock exchange's alterations in its rules and practices embraces an exceedingly large variety of subjects.

Governmental Reorganization.—In 1942 the governmental setup of the exchange was materially altered. The board of governors was reduced from 32 to 25; all standing committees were abolished; the rule-making powers of the committees were transferred to the board of governors and the election of the nominating committee was set to be held at the same time as the election of governors. The objectives of the change were "to establish the board of governors as the exchange's sole policy making body; to centralize administrative authority in the president and to provide the constitutional framework for a competent, responsible and representative government of the exchange."

In passing judgment upon the appropriateness of advertising, the committee on public relations of the exchange announced in 1939 that it was "pursuing a liberal, realistic policy and that its philosophy permitted all reasonable latitude."

Announcement was also made in 1939 of the establishment of panels of 504 business and professional men in Baltimore, Boston, Chicago, Los Angeles, Philadelphia, Pittsburgh, Richmond and San Francisco from which arbitrators might be drawn in cases involving members of the public.

Requirements Designed to Protect Public.—In 1939 new rules were adopted whereby the capital requirements of member firms doing a general business with the public were increased by 25%. Aggregate indebtedness of a member firm could not exceed 1500% of its net capital, whereas previously such indebtedness was limited to 2000% of net capital. In the same year all firms were required to make available to customers "on request a statement of financial condition as of a date within four months prior to such request," and notice of such availability must be sent to customers. Following this requirement, the exchange also installed a complete revision of its audit requirements in 1940. Later in 1942 the Securities and Exchange commission (SEC) adopted a rule "requiring all registered brokers or dealers dealing with the public, to file, on a standard type financial questionnaire, annual audit and financial reports with the commission." Mention should also be made of the ruling of the SEC restricting the use of customers' securities as collateral (effective Feb. 17, 1941). According to this ruling, "brokers and dealers are prohibited from commingling securities of different customers as collateral for loans without the customer's consent; from commingling customers' securities with their own securities under the same pledge; from pledging customers' securities for more than the amount the customers owe them." These new rules were designed to give customers added protection against loss in the event of brokerage failures.

Trading Procedures.—Five important actions affected trading procedures, as follows:

(1) The order of the SEC (Oct. 4, 1941) to the exchange "to amend its constitution, effective Oct. 6, to make clear that members of the exchange would not be prevented from acting as odd lot dealers or specialists upon regional exchanges in securities listed on the New York Stock exchange."

(2) Adoption of a "special offerings" plan, effective Feb. 16, 1942, providing for "the marketing on the floor of the exchange, by announcement on the ticker tape and by payment of a special commission, of blocks of listed securities which could not readily be absorbed in the auction market within a reasonable time and at a reasonable price."

(3) Adoption of an experimental trial (in 1942) to "determine if dealings in a selected list of stocks in units of trading smaller than 100 shares at active posts would improve the market for such issues." Later in the year 28 stocks were selected to be traded in units of 10 shares at active posts 1 to 15 inclusive. The purpose of the move was to see whether specialists might be able to make better markets and thus attract business away from the over-the-counter market.

(4) Issuance in 1937 of a detailed set of instructions to specialists with reference to dealings on the floor of the exchange in stocks in which they were acting as specialists.

(5) Adoption of rules (July 15, 1939) prohibiting general partners of member firms, doing a margin business with the public, from trading on margin.

Margin Requirements.—On long accounts the margin requirement was reduced to 45% in 1937 and on short sales to 50%. Effective March 1, 1943, purchases of securities selling at less than 5 could be on a cash basis only. In 1944 margins on "when issued" and "when distributed" securities were made equivalent to margins on issued securities. In 1945 the federal reserve board announced that the margin for the purchase of registered securities would be increased to 50%. In the same year the board of governors of the exchange amended its margin requirements "to provide for 100% margin on securities selling at or less than 10; a minimum of $10 a share on stocks selling at more than 10; 10% of the principal amount of any bond selling at more than 10% of its principal amount and a minimum margin account equity of $1,000." On July 5, 1945, the federal reserve board again increased margin requirements for the purchase of registered securities from 50% to 75%, and also applied this same margin to short sales. Later the margin requirement for both purchases and short sales was increased to 100%.

Commission Rates.—Effective Jan. 3, 1938, 3 important changes in commission rates were approved: (1) a new schedule for commissions, increasing non-member commissions by an estimated 11% and member rates by 5%; (2) permission to members also holding membership on another exchange to charge whatever rates of commission might be prescribed by the other market and (3) the establishment of a service charge on inactive accounts. In 1941 commissions and clearing charges for United States government bonds and New York city corporate stock were reduced by 50%. Later in the same year "the odd lot differential on stocks selling at less than $1 and more than ⅛th would be increased from 1⁄16th to ⅛th." For stocks selling at ⅛th or less, the differential, in order to cover expenses, was placed at half of the selling price. On Feb. 26, 1941, the exchange adopted an amendment "raising minimum non-member and member commission rates approximately 25% and 10% respectively."

Listing Requirements.—In 1939 listing fees were revised, involving a reduction in the initial fee on stock from $120 to $50 per 10,000 shares, a 15 year annual continuing fee of $75 per 100,000 shares for the first 2,000,000 shares, and $50 per 100,000 shares in excess of 2,000,000 shares; and a reduction from $120 to $60 per $1,000,000 principal amount in the listing fee for short term bonds.

In the same year, announcement was made of a policy (1) to place "emphasis upon national interests and quality rather than upon size as a test of listing eligibility," and (2) to delist any stock issue whose outstanding shares available for trading had become reduced to approximately 2,000 shares, or in the case of bonds to $200,000 par amount.

The exchange announced in 1940 that new preferred stock should not be listed unless the stock provided at least the following minimum voting rights; (1) the right of the stock, "voting as a class, to elect not less than two directors after default of the equivalent of six quarterly dividends," and (2) "affirmative approval of at least two-thirds of the preferred stock, voting as a class, as a prerequisite to any charter or by-law amendment altering materially any existing provision of such preferred stock."

In 1942 the exchange suggested to the presidents of listed corporations "that their inventory policy be disclosed in annual reports to stockholders." The exchange transmitted a bulletin prepared by the Committee on Accounting Procedure of the American Institute of Accounts which "discussed special reserves made necessary by wartime conditions." During the following year, the exchange requested that presidents of listed corporations report to stockholders any effect that renegotiation settlements might have on the operating figures. The exchange likewise suggested to listed corporations "that stock dividends received not be recorded as income and that stockholders be notified of the amount of earnings or earned surplus capitalized by stock dividends when issued by a corporation."

Supervision of Short Sales.—On Jan. 24, 1938, the SEC ruled that, effective Feb. 8, no person could make a short sale, other than in odd-lot transactions, "at or below the price at which the last sale thereof, regular way, was effected." The previous rule, effective since 1931, provided that "short sales could be made below the last sale." On May 25 the above-mentioned change was enlarged by a ruling of the board of governors to the effect that "a short sale in an odd-lot must be based upon a round-lot sale at a higher price than the last round-lot sale." In 1939 effective March 20, the SEC further amended its short selling rules "to permit a short sale at the price of the last sale, provided the previous different sale was lower than the last sale." Bona fide international arbitrage transactions, however, were exempted from price restrictions upon short selling.

Stock Transfer Taxes.—During the decade, frequent appeals were made for relief from the high state stock transfer tax, with respect to both the amount and the inconvenience of collection. On April 24, 1942, New York passed the Coudert-Mitchell bill, eliminating the double taxation on odd-lot transactions, a distinct benefit to investors. In the following year (April 20, 1943) New York adopted legislation eliminating the requirement that brokers affix tax stamps to transferred securities. Instead, registered stock exchanges or affiliated clearing corporations were authorized to collect the tax, thus relieving brokers of the necessity of maintaining large stocks of stamps, paid in advance. Similarly, on Oct. 15, the federal bureau of internal revenue arranged to have the payment of federal transfer taxes made by the stock clearing corporation, instead of by the use of stamps by each member firm. Effective July 1, 1945, New York state revised its stock transfer tax rates "to eliminate the emergency rate and to provide a graduated scale of charges of from one cent to four cents a share, depending on the selling price. Previous rates provided for a charge of three cents a share for stocks less than $20 and four cents for stocks $20 and more. These rates included a one and one-half cent and 2 cent per share emergency rate, respectively."

It will be noted that many of the changes effected during the decade were ordered by the SEC, and numerous complaints emanated from the exchange indicating that the burden and detailed character of government supervision was becoming increasingly apparent. Moreover, the president of the New York Stock exchange reported in 1937 that "evidence accumulates that the quality of the market has been affected. With much concern I note the continuance of narrow illiquid markets in which wide spreads between bid and asked quotations prevail and in which comparatively small volumes of buying or selling create undue fluctuations in prices." That statement was interesting in the light of the report of the Trading and Exchange division of the SEC in Jan. 1945, proposing to prohibit floor trading by members of the New York Stock exchange and the New York Curb exchange. To that proposal the president of the New York Stock exchange replied that "adoption of the rule might amount to a major surgical operation upon one of the most delicately adjusted segments of our national economy."

Bibliography.—W. E. Atkins, G. W. Edwards and H. G. Moulton, *The Regulation of the Security Markets* (1946); Roger Babson, *Babson's Business Service* (Issued weekly); R. E. Badger and H. G. Guthmann, *Investment Principles and Practices* (1941); A. F. Burns and W. C. Mitchell, *Measuring Business Cycles,* National Bureau of Economic Research (1946); *The Commercial and Financial Chronicle* (Issued weekly); C. A. Dice and W. J. Eiteman, *The Stock Market,* Second Edition (1941); S. S. Huebner, *The Stock Market;* S. S. Huebner, "Economic and Business Conditions" and "The Security and Money Markets," *American Year Book* (Published annually); D. F. Jordan, *Investments* (1941); *Moody's Bond Price Index; Moody's Bond Yield Averages; New York Stock Exchange Chronology*

New York stock exchange members and employees during a weekly drill instituted in the fall of 1942 to prepare men for military service or home defense

(Issued annually by the exchange); *New York Stock Exchange Monthly Statistics* (Issued monthly by the exchange); Standard Statistics company, Inc., *Standard Trade and Securities, Current Statistics* (Issued monthly); Standard Statistics company, Inc., *Standard Trade and Securities, Statistical Bulletin* (Issued monthly); Raymond Vernon, *The Regulation of Stock Exchange Members* (1941). (S. S. H.)

Great Britain and Europe

The history of stocks and bonds in Great Britain and Europe in the period 1937–46 was a reflection of the political strife that culminated in war. World War II was already beginning to cast its shadow over the financial scene as early as 1937, and so far as Great Britain was concerned the needs of financing of rearmament and, later, of the war itself at the lowest possible cost completely dominated the British market.

British Cheap Money Policy.—Up to 1936 a stock exchange boom had been in existence which had been touched off psychologically in 1932 by an event which was to have a major influence on stock and bond values throughout the years 1937–46. In June 1932 Neville Chamberlain, chancellor of the exchequer, announced the conversion of 5% war loan, 1929–47, into 3½% war loan, 1952, or after. More than £1,910,670,000 was converted into the new loan, representing more than ⅓ of the total amount of British government securities then quoted on the London Stock exchange. The general effect on all government and kindred securities was dramatic. At the end of 1931 interest yields on quoted irredeemable British government securities ranged from 4½% to nearly 5%; gross redemption yields from 4¾% to more than 6%; and the 3 months' treasury bill rate averaged over 3½% discount. At the end of 1932 after the great war loan conversion, interest yields on quoted irredeemable British government stocks had fallen to 3⅜% to 3½%; gross redemption yields to 1¼% to 3⅝%; and the treasury bill rate for the year to just more than 1.65% discount. The era of dear money which began with World War I had ended, and the era of cheap money had been ushered in. The latter proved to be independent of politics and probably owed its continuing impulse throughout 1937–46 to a fixed treasury policy, acceptable to different governments. Because of it, a later chancellor of the exchequer, Sir Kingsley Wood, was able to boast, in 1943, that the colossal war borrowing was being carried out at an average rate of interest of 2% *per annum*, with a net cost of only 1% after allowing for income tax.

The political events of 1937–39, leading up to World War II, greatly strained the treasury's ability to maintain the cheap money policy. Unlike the period from 1939, when a closed economy existed because of the treasury ban on purchase of securities abroad by United Kingdom residents and on new capital issues, external influences operated to affect government credit. In 1937 Europe seemed on the brink of war on more than one occasion. There was a heavy fall in all security values on the London Stock exchange, including those of the government and industrial companies, reflecting not only the approaching world disaster but also a recession in industrial activity. The rearmaments race was gathering momentum, and the government announced it would spend £1,488,834,000.

The position worsened in 1938; the business recession was not arrested until the spring. Sterling weakened in the international markets, and stability was not reached until Sept. 1939 when the sterling–dollar rate was pegged on the basis of $4.02–$4.06 to the £ sterling.

Between 1937 and 1938 the total of government loans issued to the public was only about £179,901,000, with a somewhat smaller increase in the amount of three-months' treasury bills issued. The deterioration in the effectiveness of the cheap money policy may be appreciated from the fact that between 1937 and 1939 the treasury bill rate had more than doubled and in 1939 averaged, over 1.2% discount, and that to attract subscriptions the terms of the only government stock issued in 1938—£81,000,000 of 3% National Defense loan, 1954–58, issued at 98%—had to be fixed to show a gross redemption yield of nearly 3.15% *per annum*. This was a retrograde step; at the end of 1936, a loan of similar currency had been floated with a gross redemption yield of 2.85%. Municipal loans, originally issued in many cases at an interest rate of 6%, were converted into 3% loans.

With the declaration of war on Sept. 3, 1939, the cheap money policy of the British treasury, operating within a closed economy, entered into its own again. On Aug. 24 the bank rate had been raised from 2% to 4% as a precautionary measure, and minimum prices, below which dealings on the London Stock exchange could not take place, were fixed for British government and kindred securities. The government's announcement on Sept. 1 of a £496,278,000 credit for war purposes gave an inkling of the volume of borrowing to come. Temporarily, the market in British government securities became frozen, but following the restoration of the bank rate to 2%, and a plentiful supply of funds as government war spending got under way (note circulation and bank deposits reached successively higher records), the market became unfrozen and showed a sharply rising trend which persisted, with interruptions, until the end of 1946.

The British treasury found its keenest advocate for its cheap money policy when the Labour government came to power in 1945 and Hugh Dalton was appointed chancellor of the exchequer. Dalton was responsible for the outstanding event of 1946 in the market for government securities, with an issue of a "tap" loan of 2½% savings bonds, 1964–67, at par. Holders of maturing National war bonds, 1946–48, accepted conversion into the new loan to the extent of £327,543,400, and £418,362,200 of new subscriptions were received. This loan may be said to have consolidated the ground gained throughout the previous ten years, and to have formally established British government credit over a period of 18–21 years on a 2½% basis. The advantages were extended to municipalities and public boards, which under the sponsorship of the treasury were able to place loans on similar terms.

Indeed, the effects of the cheap money policy were felt throughout the whole range of securities in Great Britain. The continuous fall in prior charges and ordinary shares (and rising yields) of British industrial companies from 1937 until June 1940, when the trough of the slump was reached, was due initially to fears of war, then to the outbreak of war and finally to fears of a stalemate result at best following the British army's evacuation from Dunkirk and the air onslaught on Great Britain. The steady recovery in share quotations to a level which approximated to the peak of the 1936 loan owed its origin to the favourable turn in the war fortunes of the United Nations, to the satisfactory earnings of industrial companies because of war spending, and, later, to prospects of a return to peacetime trading and of a reduction of heavy war taxation. It was, however, greatly assisted by the low yields on British government securities which aided the presentation of industrial ordinary shares in a relatively attractive light for income purposes.

Table IX.—*London Stock Exchange Record, 1937–46.*

(Indexes of prices compiled by the *Financial Times;* bases of indexes: Oct. 1926=100)

	Govt. securities	Home Rails	Industrials	Gold Mines	Bargains Recorded*
1937: Jan. 4	119.1	73.6	142.9	242.9	13,327
July 1	111.7	69.4	128.1	188.3	6,095
1938: Jan. 3	113.7	66.2	117.7	208.4	5,881
July 1	113.3	52.6	108.0	206.2	7,450
1939: Jan. 3	108.1	41.8	99.0	210.5	7,290
July 3	104.2	44.3	95.8	188.2	5,538
1940: Jan. 2	104.8	47.4	97.1	190.2	5,650
July 1	107.1	33.8	69.4	137.0	3,369
1941: Jan. 2	112.3	41.4	87.8	179.4	2,235
July 1	113.9	47.8	88.4	171.1	2.469
1942: Jan. 2	113.8	55.0	102.0	173.1	3,305
July 1	113.6	55.0	98.1	146.2	2,513
1943: Jan. 4	113.8	66.5	118.2	152.7	7,205
July 1	112.6	68.2	123.3	161.5	4,979
1944: Jan. 3	112.6	68.7	128.9	159.6	5,290
July 3	112.7	68.8	138.7	157.9	3,196
1945: Jan. 2	114.9	68.2	140.8	153.1	6,529
July 2	115.01	64.17	142.86	158.95	7,174
1946: Jan. 2	115.32	63.84	145.34	173.90	10,021
July 1	118.61	64.42	158.20	153.80	12,073

*Approximate figures only: there is no obligation on members of the London Stock exchange to make an official record of transactions.

The industrial share index reached a low wartime level of 61.1 on June 26, 1940.

Public Issues.—The British government's borrowing program, which resulted in public issues, including those to government departments, of more than £8,436,725,000 during World War II, did not really get under way until 1940. It was then evident from the terms of the new issues that the treasury intended to finance the war at low rates of interest. The war's first "tap" issue—a stock which remained open for subscription at the issue price at the Bank of England, usually for a considerable period—was made. This was a loan of short currency, a 2½% National war bond, 1945–47, issued at par. Lists were opened on June 24, 1940, and were not closed until Dec. 31. Subscriptions of more than £440,695,000 were attracted. Altogether, the device of the "tap" at the Bank of England as a means of mopping up surplus funds in the hands of the public, was used on 10 occasions during World War II, resulting in the subscription of some £6,352,109,000. This was, in fact, the chief means employed to obtain public subscriptions for new loans of various kinds.

The 3% war loan, 1955–59, a stock which was to become one of the leaders of the market for British funds, was also issued in that year; £302,233,250 was subscribed. Although public loans totalling only £741,439,200 were issued by the government during 1940 (excluding £243,176,000 of conversion loan, 2%, 1943–45), this was by no means the extent of government borrowing. It is significant that at the end of the financial year 1936–37 the proportion of the national debt in 3-months' treasury bills was less than 9%; by the end of 1939–40, the proportion of a rising debt had increased to about 15%, and was later to exceed this ratio.

Short-Dated Securities.—Throughout World War II the short-dated security, bearing a low rate of interest, was the principal weapon in the British government's armoury, not only for absorbing surplus funds in the banking system and thus limiting inflationary trends, but also for financing the war cheaply so far as interest was concerned. Between 1937 and 1946 the total of treasury bills in issue increased more than fivefold. For the greater part of the war the 3-months' treasury bill rate was about 1% discount. In Oct. 1945 when the cheap money policy drive was intensified, the rate was reduced to ½%. Two other important short-term bonds were issued by the government during the war at low interest rates. In July 1940 the treasury asked for 6-months' deposits from the banks at an interest rate of 1.125% *per annum.* Receipts, known as treasury deposit receipts, were issued, and the banks were assured of their liquidity by the undertaking of the Bank of England to discount them at bank rate (2%.) Another short-term instrument used for war finance and which had a value as an anti-inflationary device was the tax reserve certificate. This was created in the latter part of 1941, and was in reality a means of anticipating tax payments, which were becoming heavy following big government spending and the rise in the level of taxation. Taxpayers were invited to buy certificates at par, bearing an interest rate of 1% *per annum,* free of any kind of tax. These could be surrendered against liability for income-tax (Schedule E) and other taxes, as well as War Damage act contributions.

European Stocks and Bonds.—With Europe the centre of the political maelstrom, it was inevitable that the market for foreign bonds should have been distressed, a condition which lasted in varying degree, dependent on the country concerned, until the end of 1946. In 1937 Germany's internal economic difficulties were growing, so much so that free dealings in foreign stocks and bonds in Germany were forbidden by decree. Germany maintained the service of the Dawes and Young loans, however, although holders of state and municipal issues continued to receive interest payments in funding bonds. Both Poland and Hungary reduced rates on high-interest-bearing bonds to 4½%. Following the nazi *coup* in Austria in 1938, Germany recognized the Austrian debt, but reduced interest rates generally, including those on the German Dawes and Young loans. The credit of Hungary, Bulgaria and Rumania as foreign borrowers was temporarily raised by improved debt offers, but the beginning of World War II and invasion by Germany in 1940 destroyed the security behind most European bonds, which slumped to nominal prices on the London market.

Postwar Europe as a Debtor.—The external debt service of most European countries remained in abeyance throughout World

Table X.—*British Government Issues, 1937 46.*

		Approximate Amounts Issued (in millions of pounds)	How Issued
1937	2½% National defense bonds 1944–48	100	For cash at 99.5%
1938	3% National defense loan 1954–58	81	For cash at 98%
1939	3% Defense bonds	320	On "tap" at post offices from Nov. 22, 1939, to Aug. 31, 1946, at par
1940	2% Conversion loan, 1943–45	245	Conversion issue at par to holders of 4½% Conversion loan, 1940–44
	3% War loan, 1955–59	302	Issued at par for cash
	2½% National war bonds, 1945–47	444	On "tap" at par from June 24 to Dec. 31
1941	2½% National war bonds, 1946–48	493	On "tap" at par from Jan. 2 to Aug. 14
	3% Savings bonds, 1955–65	712	On "tap" at par from Jan. 2, 1941, to April 30, 1942
	3% National defense loan, 1954–58	120	Issued to National debt commissioners
	3% Defense bonds	789	Second issue, "on tap" at post offices from Sept. 1, 1941, at par
	2½% National war bonds, 1949–51	714	On "tap" at par from Oct. 8, 1941, to Nov. 30, 1942
	3% Funding loan, 1959–69	120	Issued to National debt commissioners
1942	3% Savings bonds, 1960–70	978	On "tap" at par from May 1, 1941, to Aug. 5, 1944
	3% Funding loan, 1959–69	120	Issued to National debt commissioners
	2½% National war bonds, 1951–53	522	On "tap" from Dec. 1, 1942, to Aug. 31, 1943
	3% National defense loan, 1954–58	120	Issued to National debt commissioners
1943	2½% National war bonds, 1952–54	807	On "tap" from Sept. 1, 1943, to Nov. 6, 1944
1944	3% Savings bonds, 1965–75	1,039	On "tap" from Aug. 7, 1944, to Dec. 15, 1945
	1¾% Exchequer bonds, 1950	327	On "tap" from Nov. 7, 1944, to June 12, 1945
1945	2½% National war bonds, 1954–56	425	On "tap" from June 13 to Dec. 15, 1945
1946	2½% Savings bonds, 1964–67	418	On "tap" at par from May 17 to July 9, 1946
	2½% Defense bonds	21	On "tap" at post offices from May 1, 1946, at par.
	Total	9,317	

War II, except for payments by exile governments in London, owing, of course, to the German occupation. After the liberation of Europe, however, France, Belgium, Czechoslovakia, Denmark, Norway and Finland again honoured their debt obligations, but Austrian, Bulgarian, German, Greek, Italian, Yugoslavian, Polish and Rumanian issues continued in default. (*See* also BUSINESS REVIEW; LAW; SECURITIES AND EXCHANGE COMMISSION.) (H. PN.)

BIBLIOGRAPHY.—"Stock Exchange Reconversion," *Economist* (London, Aug. 24, 1946); *Financial Times* (London).

Stomach Disorders

See ALIMENTARY SYSTEM, DISORDERS OF.

Stone, Harlan Fiske

Stone (1872–1946), U.S. jurist, was born Oct. 11, 1872, in Chesterfield, N.H. He received a B.S. degree from Amherst college, Amherst, Mass., in 1894, then turned to the study of law, taking his LL.B. from Columbia university school of law in 1898. He entered private practice, then returned to Columbia as professor of law in 1902. In 1910, he was made dean of the law school, but resigned in 1923 to return to private practice. The next year, President Calvin Coolidge appointed him attorney general of the United States. On March 2, 1925, Coolidge named him associate justice of the U.S. supreme court. On the court bench he frequently sided with the minority reports of Oliver Wendell Holmes, Louis D. Brandeis and Benjamin Cardozo and was known with these other eminent jurists as one of the "great dissenters." Upon the retirement of Charles Evans Hughes as chief justice, Stone was appointed in June 1941 to that post. He died at Washington, D.C., on April 22, 1946.

Stone

The production and uses of stone in the United States are shown in the accompanying table. To make the record complete, there is added to the data on the stone industry proper, the outputs of limestone used in making cement and lime, of asphaltic stone and of slate.

The World War II construction program increased the consumption of stone for building and paving, which reached a peak in 1941, declining in later years to 1945. While the postwar building revival doubled the demand for dimension stone in 1945, crushed stone continued to decline; there must have been an increased use of crushed stone in concrete aggregate for building in 1945, but presumably the rise was more than offset by a continued decline in paving.

In comparison, other uses of crushed stone showed continuing increases beyond the break in demand for construction stone.

Industrial uses reached a peak in 1943, the year in which production in general caught up with war demands; food requirements remained high, and in agricultural uses the peak was postponed until 1944, with only a small decline in 1945.

That the load on the railroads did not end with the close of the war was evidenced by the annual increases in the demand for railroad ballast, with a 16% rise in 1945 over 1944.

It should also be noted that stone was an important factor in munitions production; this was especially true of limestone, used as flux in metallurgical furnaces and in the production of calcium carbide, the source of acetylene for welding.

Dolomitic limestone and sandstone were used as a refractory in furnaces and the former as a source of magnesite and magnesium. (G. A. Ro.)

Stones, Sharpening

See ABRASIVES.

Production and Uses of Stone in the United States (Short Tons)

	1937	1939	1941	1943	1945
Dimension stone*	1,881,230	2,298,360	1,946,980	831,720	1,058,690
Basalt†	25,100	101,320	10,300	125,330	203,520
Granite	666,850	733,610	782,120	283,880	361,650
Building	294,520	471,920	506,220	93,500	136,610
Monumental	203,610	176,400	211,470	178,130	213,640
Paving‡	168,720	85,290	64,430	12,250	11,400
Limestone	713,580	1,060,670	813,620	237,080	334,480
Building	699,890	1,043,730	796,590	230,850	329,200
Flagging	13,690	16,940	17,030	6,230	5,280
Marble	95,460	123,740	69,300	43,390	59,690
Building	63,950	88,840	43,380	11,700	22,520
Monumental	31,510	34,900	25,920	31,690	37,170
Sandstone	231,630	195,560	183,040	101,380	64,240
Building	170,620	115,350	69,460	40,590	32,770
Curbing§	61,010	80,210	79,590	30,770	18,320
Other stone	64,130	83,460	88,600	40,660	35,110
Building	62,770	81,190	85,610	39,570	34,320
Flagging	1,360	2,270	2,990	1,090	790
Total tonnages					
Building	1,409,560	1,902,250	1,545,500	571,390	772,050
Monumental	249,050	211,400	237,440	209,840	250,850
Paving‡§	222,620	184,710	164,040	50,490	35,790
Total values	$24,332,537	$25,553,026	$21,395,834	$13,367,355	$17,848,638
Building	$13,476,435	$16,533,458	$10,688,010	$ 3,209,546	$ 6,033,656
Monumental	$ 8,426,623	$ 7,265,575	$ 9,110,846	$ 9,731,521	$11,360,627
Paving	$ 2,429,479	$ 1,753,993	$ 1,596,978	$ 426,288	$ 454,355
Crushed and broken*	131,262,010	145,148,770	181,160,980	170,511,530	152,346,520
Basalt	13,556,360	15,989,930	17,926,650	14,259,930	14,707,020
Riprap	507,760	1,500,630	619,570	886,750	444,970
Crushed	13,033,200	14,477,920	17,104,300	13,115,520	13,528,110
Granite	14,775,300	11,307,750	13,516,630	8,956,400	7,378,380
Riprap	6,785,270	1,084,110	1,459,340	314,740	585,310
Crushed	7,945,540	10,017,870	11,598,410	8,213,440	6,589,640
Limestone	93,863,690	99,785,420	132,349,980	128,743,190	112,239,940
Riprap	2,769,640	2,237,990	2,177,470	2,786,780	1,777,940
Fluxing	21,311,250	17,271,560	27,432,520	31,570,650	27,639,520
Crushed	56,141,800	65,693,790	78,526,520	64,318,660	51,762,570
Agricultural	5,004,930	5,459,260	11,909,640	14,521,670	17,395,570
Marble	112,300	104,340	107,160	125,400	111,540
Sandstone	4,841,030	8,658,120	7,409,780	7,306,850	4,322,750
Refractory	923,210	646,580	1,236,370	1,581,160	1,480,740
Riprap	363,890	328,050	745,910	483,460	346,610
Crushed	2,947,480	5,866,020	4,901,190	3,811,240	2,087,580
Other stone	10,374,130	9,303,210	9,850,780	11,119,760	13,586,890
Riprap	1,164,150	660,960	150,350	478,740	1,642,230
Crushed	8,493,920	7,835,420	8,833,490	10,189,220	11,405,360
Total value	$121,880,591	$132,908,489	$173,941,591	$170,952,679	$161,459,264
Grand total value	$146,213,128	$158,461,515	$195,337,425	$184,320,034	$179,307,902
Summary totals					
Basalt	13,581,460	16,091,250	17,936,950	14,385,260	14,910,540
Granite	9,265,830	12,041,360	14,298,750	9,240,280	7,740,030
Limestone	94,577,270	100,846,090	133,163,600	128,980,270	112,574,420
Marble	207,760	228,080	176,460	168,790	171,230
Sandstone	5,072,660	8,853,680	7,592,820	7,408,230	4,386,990
Other stone	10,438,260	9,386,670	9,939,380	11,160,420	13,622,000
Total	133,143,240	147,447,130	183,107,960	171,343,250	153,405,210
Slate, dimension	167,550	179,600	180,990	73,310	69,660
Crushed	277,010	351,780	437,670	395,550	482,230
Cement rock	29,547,000	30,463,000	42,735,000	35,867,000	27,332,000
Lime rock	8,250,000	8,509,000	12,159,000	13,193,000	11,841,000
Asphaltic stone	447,213	422,484	654,692	835,648	642,600
Grand total	171,832,000	187,373,000	239,275,300	221,614,500	193,772,700

*Many of the subtotals include uses too small to be itemized.
†All for building. ‡Includes curbing. §Includes flagging.

Strategic Bombing

The theory and practice of strategic bombing began in World War I, but did not advance beyond the rudimentary stage. The aeroplane had not then developed sufficient load capacity to serve as a decisive offensive weapon. It was used mostly for reconnaissance and for tactical support of armies, with only experimental air effort applied to strategic objectives.

The weapons then available for surface war favoured defense, as against offense. As a result, the western front remained comparatively stationary for the greater part of four years, "the blood-bath of positional war." Superiority of defense was a concomitant of the relative immobility of firepower entrenched behind barbed wire. Land offensives were restricted by the lack of a mobile armoured weapon. This deficiency was characteristic of surface war of the period, in which the opponents were relatively equal and similar in manpower, distribution, weapons and mobility. The objectives, of necessity, were limited to the defeat of the immediate military forces in the field and the progressive seizure of space. The tank, a mobile and offensive weapon, was not effectively employed until the final phase. ("The Black Day For The German Army," according to German authorities, was Aug. 8, 1918, when the British launched their co-ordinated tank offensive.) The only other means to force the enemy's collapse in two-dimensional war was the *external* blockade, to deprive him of outside sustenance.

The consequence of the superiority of defense resulting from immobility of firepower was that World War I, despite the many attacks and counter-attacks, remained a stalemate "in the mud" until the closing months, when U.S. reinforcements upset the balance between the opposing forces. The inescapable high cost of successful land offensives predetermined the outcome of a war of attrition; the side with the greatest resources in manpower and matériel, including food, would emerge victorious. Germany was conquered, but not invaded, during the period of combat. Under pressure of external blockade, Germany's "home front" collapsed, leaving its armies without support and therefore with no recourse but surrender. The "home front" was the Achilles heel.

The conclusion seemed plausible that constant increase of firepower, mounted in defensive works, would insure the continued superiority of defense over offense, given equality of forces engaged, and provided the "home fronts" remained unbroken. In the following years some authorities enunciated this dictum as an incontestable military doctrine. Its physical expression was the Maginot line, the classical pattern for a stalemate war.

The offensive character of the tank was a challenge to the idea of impregnable defense in that it increased the mobility of firepower, but within the limits imposed by its two-dimensional movement in surface warfare. Some new capacity was necessary.

Airmen believed that the aeroplane, operating in three dimensions, could not only give greater mobility to the offense, but also could break the deadlock of positional war by its capacity to maintain an *internal* blockade on the enemy's "home front."

The clue to this undeveloped capacity lay in the relatively insignificant experience with strategic bombing in World War I. Bombing operations were carried out with slight success by both sides in 1916. The German attacks on London in the summer of 1917, however, pointed to the strategic offensive potentials of the air weapon. These attacks led to the creation of the royal air force as a separate service and to the establishment (within the R.A.F.) of a special bombing force, the independent air force, for direct action against the heart of the German industrial system. General Jan C. Smuts, in recommending air operations independent of the army and navy to the war cabinet, Aug. 1917, declared: "aerial operations . . . may become the principal operations of war, to which the older forms of military and naval operations may become secondary and subordinate." The independent air force dropped 543 tons of bombs on Germany in 1918, causing 2,589 casualties and damage amounting to $6,000,000. These operations by light aeroplanes were small compared with those of World War II, but they did demonstrate the efficacy of the strategic air offensive.

Prophets of the offensive use of air power included Marshal of the Royal Air Force Lord H. M. Trenchard; Winston Churchill, British minister of munitions, 1917; Brig. Gen. William Mitchell, U.S. army air corps; and Gen. Giulio Douhet, Italian air force, author of *The Command of the Air* (1921). The R.A.F. staff college and the U.S. army air corps tactical school focused attention on the necessity for a new means of offense to reach the vital centres of an enemy's war production. From these studies there was gradually evolved a new concept, based on the capacities of the aeroplane.

The aeroplane was not limited by geography, except for its requirement of surface bases. Its one serious limitation, weather, could be mastered by man's ingenuity in making and using electronic instruments. The aeroplane came from anywhere; it went everywhere.

The basic problem in designing a decisive service weapon is the necessary compromise between the contradictory imperatives of firepower, mobility and protection (armour). In general experience, one of these is achieved in a weapon only at the sacrifice, to some degree, of the others. The aeroplane is peculiar in that it not only harmonizes the three imperatives, but combines them to a high degree. Its firepower is measured by the allotment in its load capacity to armament and bombs, allowance being made for fuel and crews. It has unprecedented mobility in three dimensions. Speed and altitude are its principal armour. Its offensive character is determined by the extent of its radius of action, and by power of penetration equal to its reach. These qualities made the aeroplane a decisive weapon of a high order.

The mobility of the aeroplane vastly extended the reach of firepower, and created a new large-scale capacity for offense. It brought the enemy's "home front" within immediate range during hostilities, thus altering the meaning of time and space in war operations. This capacity was the basis for changing the concept of war from limited conflict between armed forces in the field (nations in arms) to all-inclusive combat between the total human and material resources of the opposing nation-structures.

The ultimate national aim of all military action is to break the enemy's power and will to resist. Before proceeding to this ultimate objective, surfaces forces are obliged to attain a limited, intermediate objective—the defeat of the corresponding type of hostile force, the enemy's body muscles on the periphery of his strength.

Air power, on the other hand, acts not only against the corresponding hostile air force, but against all the hostile forces, land, sea and air. In addition, by reason of its power for offensive penetration, it proceeds to direct assault on the ultimate unlimited objective of all forces—the enemy's national will, his "home front," his heart,

Heligoland fortress shown before and after a single attack by R.A.F. bombers on April 18, 1945

brain and vitals, at the very core of his existence.

Concept of Strategic Air Offensive.—The nine fundamental principles of war (U.S. war department, 1921) were evolved during centuries of surface warfare, and were considered immutable. But air power was without the guidance of precedents for application of its peculiar capacities. The concept of the strategic air offensive could be stated in terms of the nine immutable principles, regrouped under the three headings: *objective, means, application.*

Objective.—In executing the national war aim of breaking the enemy's will to resist, air power may be employed to attack the hostile air, land and sea forces, or to attack the enemy's national structure, depending on the enemy's most vulnerable sources of strength. Against a heavily industrialized enemy, its maximum contribution to the national war aim is through strategic effort. It thus has both a mission which is sometimes co-ordinate, and sometimes subordinate, to the land and sea forces, and an independent mission of its own.

Its tactical mission is the destruction of military forces. Maintenance of air cover over the surface forces by bombers and fighters includes preparation for surface advance by assault on enemy ships, troops and supply lines; local control of the air; isolation of the battlefield; and airborne operations.

The independent strategic mission is destruction of war-making capacity. The main targets of an air offensive are not the enemy's military forces in the field, but his arsenals, essential war industries, transport systems, communications, fuel supplies and other elements sustaining the national will on the "home front," including civilian morale. A primary purpose is to destroy the enemy's capacity to create war power and to maintain the battle. These vital objectives had formerly been accessible on a decisive scale only at the end of successful surface campaigns. They could be reached by air power regardless of the tide of surface battle, or even when surface forces were not engaged.

Systematic destruction of the enemy's sources of war power on the "home front" breaks his will to resist through paralysis of his means. To the indirect, *external* blockade is added a direct, *internal* blockade which disrupts his means of sustenance inside the area occupied by his military forces and population. In a condition of progressive strangulation of his war effort, he loses capacity to maintain the battle and is forced to collapse from within. This assault on the whole national structure is the peculiar capacity of air power and its dominant mission in war.

Means.—The means for fulfilment of the strategic concept of air power are organized air forces, adequately equipped with aeroplanes of various types with the speed, range and firepower necessary to execute their particular missions. Auxiliary instruments include bomb sights, navigational aids, radio, aerial cameras, etc. The national sources of supply must be adequate to build and maintain the air forces and to replace battle wastage of manpower and matériel.

Application.—The application of air power includes those principles of war not listed under the objective. A special requirement is advance knowledge of the targets most vital to the enemy's war effort. These are selected from available intelligence sources, and confirmed by aerial photography.

The principle of offensive is inherent in the aeroplane; it cannot remain still. The methods of the offensive are attrition, destruction, external and internal blockade and capture. Security, in combat and at the base, is achieved by control of the air, gained by progressive destruction of the enemy's air force in the air and on the ground and stoppage in factories of his replacement capacity. The offensive for control of the air in its early stages parallels the strategic mission, as an air force on the defensive can be forced up to engage in combat by bombing "sensitive" targets. Control of the air is essential to freedom of action of all forces, land, sea and air. When the enemy's air resistance has been neutralized to the point where he can not effectively intercept strategic missions, the degree of air control advances to air supremacy which, if maintained, is tantamount to victory.

Air power achieves the principle of mass more effectively than any other armed power. By its extreme mobility, it attains an unprecedented concentration of force over single targets from bases separated by hundreds, and eventually thousands, of miles.

Economy of force is the efficiency which results from accurate bombing of the primary objective with the least expenditure of manpower and equipment and by avoidance of dissipation of strength on secondary operations. Air power is not committed to position in battle; its units retire to base to prepare for renewal of the assault. The rapid turnaround schedules permit a high degree of sustained effort on targets marked for destruction.

Movement is characterized by high flexibility in the tactical manoeuvres of combat and in employment. Strategic air forces may be used tactically; tactical air forces may be used strategically. Any component, within the limits of its capabilities, may be shifted from one target to another, from one type of operation to another or from one theatre of war to another in shuttle operations. High flexibility is a dominant characteristic of air power.

Surprise is elemental in air warfare. The enemy can never be certain of the target selected for attack. Feint attacks, camouflaged efforts and changes in direction are possible while missions are in flight. Diversionary missions cannot be evaluated in time to take successful countermeasures.

Simplicity, through unity of command, is a prerequisite of the air offensive to insure integration of effort under the principle of mass. Co-operation is attained between strategical and tactical air forces, between bombers and fighters and between the air and surface forces by careful observance of timing. Co-ordination among the air, land and sea forces is achieved through a supreme commander and the over-all offensive plan.

The combination of new medium, new capacity for offense and new concept of total war, enabled airmen to raise their sights over the traditional line-of-war to the enemy's war capacity in the rear. By its ability to utilize increased firepower to enlarge rather than reduce the mobility of armed forces, air power abolished the stalemate of positional war. By its independent strategic mission to force collapse of the national structure, it could shorten the term of hostilities. As the new and supreme instrument of national will, air power altered the dynamics by which nations at war survive.

Strategic Employment of Air Power.—The concept of strategic air offensive was not given an adequate tryout until the final year and a half of World War II. Air operations between the two world wars (against the native tribes of the middle east, against China and Ethiopia and in the Spanish Civil War) were necessarily tactical because of the lack of strategic targets in such areas. The Germans, in preparing for World War II, designed a large air force for tactical support of fast-moving ground troops, without an independent strategic mission of its own. They had not developed the strategic concept. Their bombers (Ju-88, H-111, Do-17) were inadequately armed. They used their fighters defensively in close support of the bombers instead of offensively in general support. Because of faulty concept, the luftwaffe failed to concentrate primarily on the R.A.F. and subsequently on industry and ports. They were unable to establish control of the air against the eight-gunned British fighters (Spitfire and Hurricane), aided by the warnings of secret radar. Consequently, despite the Germans' numerical superiority, their air offensive in the battle of Britain, 1940, was doomed to failure.

The royal air force did have the strategic concept, but its available bombers were inadequate for the mission. Its daylight raids on German targets in 1940 resulted in prohibitive losses. The R.A.F. bomber command was forced into night bombing from 1940 onwards. It was not until 1942 that the development of radio navigational aids and the improvement of four-engined bombers (particularly the Lancaster) made the night operations of R.A.F. bomber command demonstrably effective in destroying German war capacity. The British heavy night bomber, which sacrificed defensive armament to bomb load, was successful to a limited degree while operating unsupported in its strategic tasks by U.S. heavy day bombers; it remained the greatest load carrier of the war in Europe. With its new equipment and more effective technique for concentration, the R.A.F. bomber command, commanded by Air Chief Marshal Sir Arthur T. Harris, was able to begin mass attacks on the concentrated German industries (the first mission was over Cologne on May 20, 1942, when 1,043 bombers dropped 2,000 tons in 90 minutes). Subsequently, R.A.F. area bombing became the night shift in the round-the-clock strategic Allied air offensive; in smashing Germany's national structure, it had the effectiveness of a titanic sledge hammer. Later, because of improved techniques in aiming, night bombing from medium altitude by the R.A.F. achieved degrees of accuracy and economy of force unsurpassed by other forms of air attack on specific and individual targets.

Shortly after World War I, U.S. air leaders began to

formulate ideas for the correct methods of using air power as the new decisive instrument in war. These ideas, expressed in lecture form at the tactical school, gradually assumed the status of air doctrine—the basis of the U.S. version of the strategic concept.

The strategic plans of the U.S. army air force envisaged precision bombing from high altitudes in daylight, aided by an improved bomb sight. The prohibitive losses incurred by the German and British daylight missions were to be prevented by more and heavier guns on the bombers and the use of tactical formations in combat to gain an intense concentration of protective firepower.

At the moment of Pearl Harbor, the U.S.A.A.F. confronted war in Europe and the Pacific without the means of putting its concept into operation. It did have the advantage of time to prepare while the Allies maintained the battle; of an enormous national industrial establishment for forging the weapon; and of a vast reservoir of U.S. youth capable of being trained in air techniques.

During the ensuing two years the U.S.A.A.F. under the command of General H. H. Arnold, built the striking force necessary to execute the concept. Its strength, which was 43,118 personnel and 2,546 aeroplanes in 1940, was expanded to 2,300,000 total personnel and 80,000 aeroplanes in early 1944. Technical training was necessary in the organization of air and ground crews, as well as in intelligence and target analysis, radio, tactical air doctrine, etc. Mastery of the new technique kept pace with production of the weapons—the B-17 and B-24 heavy bombers and the P-38, P-47 and P-51 fighters for escort. The first heavy bombing unit of the 8th air force arrived in Great Britain on June 10, 1942. The first mission of the 8th bomber command was an attack by 12 B-17s on the Rouen marshalling yards, Aug. 17, 1942. On the following day, U.S. fighters, P-38s, made their first sorties.

Day bombing was tentative and experimental until the Casablanca directive, issued by the combined chiefs of staff, Jan. 21, 1943, sanctioned the "destruction and dislocation of German military, industrial, and economic system, and the undermining of the morale of the German people to the point where their capacity for armed resistance is fatally weakened." To implement this directive there was drawn up "the combined bomber offensive plan" based on an operations analysis report. This plan, also called "pointblank," was approved by the combined chiefs of staff on June 10, 1943, and issued to the air commanders of the R.A.F. and the U.S.A.A.F. The order of target priorities established were: (1) submarine construction yards and bases; (2) aircraft industry; (3) ball-bearing industry; (4) oil industry; (5) synthetic rubber plants; (6) military transport vehicle industry. This order of priorities changed as the air offensive progressed.

During 1943 the 8th air force carried out strategic missions with insufficient force to insure control of the air over the targets. Losses threatened to become prohibitive. The development of long-range escort, by installing additional fuel tanks in fighters, solved this problem and permitted deeper penetrations. By the end of 1943, the 8th air force attained the necessary build-up of strength for effective execution of its strategic mission. The advance of the Allied forces across North Africa to Italy led to activation of the 15th air force on Nov. 1, 1943, with bases in the Foggia area. This made possible the co-ordination of bombing attacks from two theatres on the same German targets, implementing the principle of mass.

The co-ordination of the strategic bombing effort by the 8th air force, commanded by Lt. Gen. James H. Doolittle, and the 15th air force, commanded by Maj. Gen. Nathan

Vapour trails behind a fleet of B-17 Flying Fortresses on their way to bomb railroad yards at Linz, Austria, Jan. 8, 1945

F. Twining, was the function of the headquarters of the U.S. strategic air forces, established in Great Britain Jan. 6, 1944, under the command of Lt. Gen. Carl Spaatz. These air forces were in two theatres of operations, the European under General Dwight D. Eisenhower and the Mediterranean under General Sir Henry Maitland Wilson. The reach and power of the strategic air arm had not made sufficient impact on the thinking of military strategists to cause organization of theatres of war in conformity with the capability of the most elastic, far-reaching powerful weapon. Under this condition, the difficulties of operating the U.S. strategic air forces in Europe were greatly augmented. However, by frequent conferences between General Spaatz and Lt. Gen. Ira C. Eaker, commanding general of the Allied air forces in the Mediterranean who had administrative control of the 15th air force, wholehearted co-operation and effective co-ordination of effort was obtained. Co-ordination within U.S. Strategic-Tactical Air Forces was attained by appointment of two deputy commanding generals, Maj. Gen. F. L. Anderson, operations, and Maj. Gen. Hugh J. Knerr, administration (supply).

The absolute necessity for furtherance of the Anglo-U.S. strategic mission and of preparations for surface invasion of the continent was control of the air over Germany. This could be won only by cutting off the replacements of the German air force and by fighting its existing force out of the sky. The rising scale of R.A.F. night bombing of industrial concentrations, augmented by U.S. daylight attacks, led to German countermeasures. In 1942 the Germans began dispersal of aircraft factories to the deep interior. They planned to quadruple their monthly output of single-engined fighters by April 1944. The 8th air force began its offensive for control of the air by an attack on the Focke-Wulf plant at Bremen, April 17, 1943. On six successive days of late July, it attacked the German aircraft industry so successfully that the production curve, which had attained double the output of 1942, was turned downward. The climax came in late Feb. 1944 (the "big week"), when during six days of perfect weather the R.A.F.-U.S.A.A.F. team dropped 16,506 tons of bombs in a series of attacks on the German aircraft industry. These fatally reduced its replacement capacity.

German aircraft production subsequently recovered; but the Allies retained control of the air during the remainder of the war.

The combined chiefs of staff retained final control of strategic bombing in Europe throughout the period of hostilities after the United States's entry into the war. Until April 14, 1944, their designated agent in exercise of control was Air Chief Marshal Sir Charles Portal, who as chief of air staff was *ipso facto* a member of the combined chiefs of staff. From that date until Sept. 15, 1944, the strategic air forces were placed at the disposal of the supreme commander, Gen. Eisenhower. During this period (operation "Overlord") they were used to prepare for and support the surface invasion of the continent. Co-ordination between the tactical and strategic air forces was effected by the deputy supreme commander, Air Chief Marshal Sir Arthur Tedder, as representative of Gen. Eisenhower. On Sept. 15, 1944, the strategic air forces reverted to the direct control of the combined chiefs of staff. Air Chief Marshal Portal and Gen. Arnold were designated joint agents, with Air Marshal Sir Norman Bottomley and Gen. Spaatz charged with co-ordination in the field.

From April 1944 onward the immediate objectives were transportation systems, with increasing effort assigned to synthetic oil production and other strategic targets of a vital nature. Total German production and imports of oil dropped from 918,000 tons per month in the first quarter of 1944 to 319,000 tons in the last quarter, a decline of two-thirds caused preponderantly by the attacks of the strategic air forces. The effect of the oil shortage was catastrophic for all the German armed forces. The German ground troops literally ran out of oil in the battle of the Bulge, beginning Dec. 16, 1944. Destruction of the German oil supply was the climactic fulfilment of the strategic air offensive in Europe. By Feb. 1945 most of the remaining aeroplanes of the German air force, including the newly developed jet-propelled, were pinned to the ground by lack of fuel. Consequently, the Allied strategic air forces could attack at will, with negligible loss, any part of Germany's armed forces or national structure selected for destruction.

Total air supremacy was achieved over the whole area of the European war.

On April 16, 1945, orders were issued to the strategic air forces as follows: "The advances of our ground forces have brought to a close the Strategic Air War waged by the United States Strategic Air Forces and the Royal Air Force Bomber Command. It has been won with a decisiveness becoming increasingly evident as our armies overrun Germany. From now onward our Strategic Air Forces must operate with our Tactical Air Forces in close cooperation with our armies."

Until the arrival in sufficient numbers of very heavy, long-range bombers, the B-29s, the air mission in the Pacific was tactical support of the navy and the amphibious forces. The objectives were Japanese land, sea and air forces, and islands which were utilized as bases as the offensive of all arms closed on Japan proper. The strategic mission began in the summer of 1944 with small attacks on the industries of Japan by B-29s based in China. Attacks

Site of a former machine tool plant in the Osaka-Kobe area left virtually stripped by the pounding of B-29s aiming at Japanese targets of strategic importance in 1945

of similar weight were begun in Nov. from the newly acquired bases on the Marianas. The necessary control of the air had already been won. On March 9, 1945, Maj. Gen. Curtis LeMay, commanding general of the 21st bomber command (the striking force of the 20th air force, then commanded by Gen. Arnold from Washington, D.C.) initiated the all-out mass offensive by low-level incendiary attack. The U.S. army strategic air forces, under the command of Gen. Spaatz, was activated July 11, 1945, with headquarters at Guam. The attacks on Japan continued at accelerated frequency and unbearable intensity. The dropping of the two atomic bombs, one on Hiroshima Aug. 6 and the second on Nagasaki Aug. 9, merely served as justification for the capitulation, Aug. 14, by the government of a nation long sinee defeated. A surface invasion proved unnecessary. For this reason the air offensive against Japan was the classic prototype of fulfilment of the strategic concept in World War II.

In its strategic effort (1942–45) the U.S.A.A.F. expended 1,050,710 U.S. tons of bombs against Germany and 179,967 tons against Japan. In similar operations the R.A.F. bomber command expended 989,320 U.S. tons against Germany (1941–45) and 13,730 tons against Japan (1943–45). Both air forces expended considerable additional tonnage in tactical operations of the air war. The combination of bombing by day and by night round-the-clock fulfilled the Casablanca directive of the combined chiefs of staff, Jan. 1943 (*see* above).

The two following extracts serve as over-all assessment of the strategic air war (from the Over-all Report [European War], of the United States Strategic Bombing Survey, Sept. 30, 1945):

"Allied air power was decisive in the war in Western Europe. . . . In the air, its victory was complete; at sea, its contribution, combined with naval power, brought an end to the enemy's greatest naval threat—the U-boat; on land, it helped turn the tide overwhelmingly in favor of Allied ground forces. Its power and superiority made possible the success of the invasion. It brought the economy which sustained the enemy's armed forces to virtual collapse, although the full effects of this collapse had not reached the enemy's front lines when they were overrun by Allied forces. It brought home to the German people the full impact of modern war with all its horror and suffering. Its imprint on the German nation will be lasting."

From the Summary Report (Pacific War) of the United States Strategic Bombing survey, July 1, 1946:

"The physical destruction resulting from the air attack on Japan approximates that suffered by Germany, even though the tonnage of bombs dropped was far smaller. The attack was more concentrated in time, and the target areas were smaller and more vulnerable. Not only were the Japanese defenses overwhelmed, but Japan's will and capacity for reconstruction, dispersal, and passive defense were less than Germany's. . . .

"The time lapse between military impotence and political acceptance of the inevitable might have been shorter had the political structure of Japan permitted a more rapid and decisive determination of national policies. Nevertheless, it seems clear that, even without the atomic bombing attacks, air supremacy over Japan could have exerted sufficient pressure to bring about unconditional surrender and obviate the need for invasion.

"Based on a detailed investigation of all the facts, and supported by the testimony of the surviving Japanese leaders involved, it is the Survey's opinion that certainly prior to 31 December 1945, and in all probability prior to 1 November 1945, Japan would have surrendered even if the atomic bomb had not been dropped, even if Russia had not entered the war, and even if no invasion had been planned or contemplated."

* * *

World War II was won through co-ordinated effort of all forces, land, sea and air, organized in over-all offensive plans. Air power did not attain its necessary striking potential until the closing 18 months. It was the new instrument of war and became the spark to success of all forces engaged. The national structures of Germany and Japan were disrupted; their defenses saturated; their home fronts dissolved in rubble. This appalling penalty was visited upon nations unable to control the air over their own territories.

Except for the two atomic bombs on Hiroshima and Nagasaki, the bombs carried the conventional type of explosives. A very small percentage of the total tonnage expended, if put in the form of atomic bombs, would have achieved the same results. Carrying a nation's power through the air and applying it to strategic objectives on the enemy's home front, had become the most powerful means to wage war.

Development of the heavy bomber was decisive in the first total war of history. Further evolution of the strategic air concept would include development of guided missiles. The military necessity of the strategic air concept thus epitomized the future issue between possible totality of destruction and the survival capacities of technical civilization. (*See* also Aviation, Military; Incendiary Warfare; Strategy of World War II; Tactics of World War II; World War II.)

Bibliography.—H. A. Jones, *The War in the Air*, vol. VI and appendices volume (1937); (for creation of the Independent Air Force, R.A.F., under Trenchard); Winston Churchill, *Extracts* of 1917 papers, in V.E.R. Blunt, *The Use of Air Power* (1942); Giulio Douhet, *The Command of the Air* (1921, translated 1943); Gen. William Mitchell, *Winged Defense, The Development and Possibilities of Modern Air Power—Economic and Military* (1925); J. M. Spaight, *Bombing Vindicated* (1944); Maj. Oliver Stewart, *Air Power and the Expanding Community* (1944); Marshal of the Royal Air Force the Viscount H. M. Trenchard, "The Effect of the Rise of Air Power on War" (1943); "The Principles of Air Power on War" (1945), "Air Power and National Security" (1946) and other pamphlets; *Reports of the Commanding General, USAAF, to the Secretary of War* (*General H. H. Arnold*) (Jan. 4, 1944; Feb. 27, 1945; Nov. 12, 1945); *Reports of the United States Strategic Bombing Survey, European War* (1945); *Pacific War* (1946); *Air Affairs* (an international quarterly journal, first issue Sept. 1946); Air Chief Marshal Sir John Slessor, *Air Power and Armies* (1933); Marshal of the Royal Air Force Sir Arthur Harris, *Bomber Offensive* (1947); H. von Rohden, *Vom Luft Kriege* (Berlin, 1938); C. Rougeron, *L'Aviation de Bombardment*, 2 vols. (Paris, 1936); General Lieutenant H. Rieckhoff, *Trumpf oder Bluff* (Geneva, 1945). (B. C. H.; C. Sz.)

Strategic Mineral Supplies

In 1937 ten commodities of mineral origin were included in the official U.S. Army and Navy Munitions board list of strategic materials—aluminum, antimony, chromium, iodine, manganese, mercury, mica, nickel, tin and tungsten. A number of other materials were considered "critical," that is, probably subject to more or less shortage in supply during an emergency, but it was for only the ten named that real concern was felt. In 1939 there were still ten items in the strategic list, but iodine had been transferred to the critical list, and radio quartz had been added. Also, two-thirds of the former critical list had been dropped to a lower category, under the designation "essential," leaving nine members of the critical list—asbestos, cadmium, cryolite, fluorspar, graphite, iodine, platinum, titanium and vanadium.

Long-continued agitation for the stock-piling of strategic materials finally culminated in the passage of the Strategic Materials act of June 1939. However, action had been delayed too long, and by the time specifications could be formulated and purchase arrangements made, war had started in Europe, and with the resulting disorganization of world markets and the channels of international trade, little could be accomplished.

A year later the purchase of emergency stocks was turned over to the Metals Reserve company, a subsidiary of the Reconstruction Finance corporation. Less hampered by red tape, Metals Reserve made much better progress, and in the ensuing years secured a large portion of the metal and mineral requirements for the war program. However, as World War II spread over wider areas and increased in intensity and momentum, it was found that supply requirements which had been considered ample were becoming hopelessly inadequate, and before long the point was reached where the supplies of only gold and lead were adequate to meet demands, and later lead also became short in supply.

Stock-piling.—During the early stages of World War II, in what was still called the defense program, and before the United States became an active belligerent, it was becoming evident that previous conceptions of strategic mineral supplies were inadequate, and long before the war was over it had been effectively demonstrated that the United States could maintain self-sufficiency in few of the many minerals and metals required in such enormous quantities by modern mechanized warfare. This being the case, the only safeguard against critical shortage of supply in any future emergency lay in the advance accumulation of stock piles, to supplement the domestic output and such imports as could be maintained.

When World War II was drawing to a close, it became necessary to look to the future, and make plans for the disposal of the surplus stocks on hand at the end of the war. In order to prevent these stocks from disorganizing postwar markets, and at the same time to start a nucleus of stock-piling for future needs, the Surplus Property act of 1944 provided that all surplus property designated by the Army and Navy Munitions board as suitable for stock-piling purposes should be added to the stock piles authorized by the legislation of 1939, unless needed by industry for current requirements.

Since the stock-piling provisions of the Surplus Property act were scheduled to expire at a specific date, it was necessary that additional legislation be provided if stock-piling were to go beyond this preliminary step. In March 1945 and again in October bills were introduced in congress to provide permanent stock-piling procedure. In the hearings on these bills the chief objections centred on the question as to whether stock pile purchases should be made from domestic or foreign producers, and the methods proposed for the protection of industry against release of stock-piled material, with consequent bad effect on the current market. After much delay the bill was reformulated and passed and approved on July 23, 1946.

The new legislation provided that "the Secretary of War, the Secretary of the Navy, and the Secretary of the Interior, acting jointly through the agency of the Army and Navy Munitions Board, are hereby authorized and directed to determine, from time to time, which materials are strategic and critical under the provisions of this Act and to determine, from time to time, the quality and quantities of such materials which shall be stock piled under the provisions of this Act." The procurement division of the treasury department was designated as the agency to make the purchases, provide for storage on approved military and naval reservations, provide for any needed refining or processing to put materials in the best form for stock-piling, provide for rotation of the stocks if necessary to prevent deterioration and to dispose of stocks as required by rotation, obsolescence or by revised determinations of requirements. The act also made permanent the temporary provision for transferring surplus war material to the stock pile, and the procurement division handled the materials received by transfer in much the same manner as new purchases. Later, the sum of $100,000,000 was appropriated by congress for current purchases.

The chief objection to the act was that under pressure from industry the "Buy American" clause was included, giving the output of domestic producers certain priorities over imported materials. This inclusion definitely weakened the protective features of the legislation. The stock-piling of domestic output depleted the already weakened domestic reserves, and contributed nothing to future security except immediate accessibility; hence it should be used only to the extent necessary to keep a marginal industry on a going basis. Only through the stock-piling of imported materials could the available supply be increased.

Army and Navy Munitions Board Report.—In the light of the experience gained in World War II, and under the conditions existing at the end of that war, it was necessary to recast the entire basis of strategic mineral supplies. The Surplus Property act provided that the Army and Navy Munitions board should report to congress its recommendations as to the maximum and minimum amounts of each strategic or critical material that should be included in the stock pile. Similar provisions were incorporated in the Strategic and Critical Materials Stock Piling act of 1946. In accordance with this directive the board made a report in which the necessity for stock-piling was the sole criterion in the determination of strategic materials, and the only differentiation between strategic and critical materials lay in the amounts recommended for the stock pile. All materials which war experience showed to be short in supply were divided into three subclasses, depending on the relative desirability and feasibility for stock-piling, as follows:

A. Those commodities for which stock-piling was considered the only satisfactory way of assuring an adequate supply for future emergency.

B. Materials the stock-piling of which was practicable and acquisition of which was recommended only so far as they might be turned into the stock pile as surplus property, on the score that future supply might be secured by stimulating output from North American sources, or by the use of substitutes.

C. Materials not recommended for stock-piling because difficulties in storage outweighed the advantages of stock-piling.

In its report to congress the board listed 43 items in Group A, 20 items in Group B and 5 items in Group C, a total of 68 items, of which 24 items were different forms or grades of the same 9 basic materials. The last prewar official list (1940) included 9 strategics and 6 criticals in the mineral and metal group; the comparison of this total of 15, against the numbers given above, was a rough measure of the extent to which the status of U.S. strategic minerals had been modified by World War II. (*See* MINERALOGY.)

Strategic Minerals in Other Countries.—Adequate discussion of the problems of strategic mineral supplies in other countries than the United States was hampered by lack of information. The United States was in a better supply position than any other country and also paid more attention than any other to the means of meeting its inherent shortages in time of emergency demand. At the same time it must be admitted that when the World War II emergency arrived it developed demands so far beyond any that had been anticipated that the supply position proved hopelessly inadequate, and supplementary provisions had to be improvised to meet the needs as they developed. At the end of the decade 1937–46 there was insufficient information available on supply and demand during World War II in other countries to make it possible to say much about the subject except in a general way. However, bearing in mind the experiences of the United States with its superior advantages, one was inevitably led to the inference that supply problems in other countries must have been even less satisfactory. This conclusion was also substantiated by the extent to which others of the United Nations received help from the United States in the way of lend-lease material. In fact, it was the necessity for extending such aid to the Allied nations that caused much of the exaggeration in the war demands in the United States, more than those that had been anticipated.

Prewar Status.—It was difficult likewise to arrive at any effective method of evaluating the comparative status of the various countries with respect to strategic mineral supplies since there was no common factor on which a direct comparison could be made. About the best that could be done was to make a rough appraisal of the self-sufficiency of the various countries with respect to the chief commodities involved in a war program. Table I, adapted from

Self-Sufficiency Ratings for Strategic Minerals in the Leading Countries

	Metallic Ores							Smelting Capacity						
	United States	Great Britain	Germany	France	U.S.S.R.	Italy	Japan	United States	Great Britain	Germany	France	U.S.S.R.	Italy	Japan
Iron	4	3	1	5	5	3	1	4	4	4	5	1	2	1
Aluminum	2	0	0	5	4	5	0	4	2	4	4	4	1	2
Zinc	4	1	2	0	1	5	2	4	1	2	1	2	4	2
Copper	4	0	1	1	2	1	2	4	1	1	2	1	1	2
Lead	4	1	1	1	2	1	1	4	1	1	2	2	1	1
Mercury	2	0	0	0	3	5	0	2	0	0	3	0	5	0
Manganese	1	0	0	0	5	1	1	3	5	4	4	5	3	4
Chromium	1	0	0	0	4	0	3	3	0	4	4	4	4	?
Platinum	1	0	0	0	5	0	0	4	5	?	5	5	0?	0?
Tungsten	2	0	0	0	2	0	0	3	5	0	2	5	0?	0?
Antimony	1	0	0	0	0	2	0	3	3	3	0	1	2	1
Tin	0	1	0	0	0	0	1	0	5	0	0	1	0	1
Nickel	0	0	0	0	1	0	0	0	5	3	1	1	0	0?
Total	26	6	5	12	34	23	11							
Nonmetallic Ores														
Fluorspar	3	5	5	3	4	4	3							
Coal	5	5	5	2	4	1	3							
Sulphur	5	0	2	1	3	5	5							
Graphite	1	0	5	0	4	3	5							
Pyrite	2	0	1	1	4	5	4							
Potash	2	0	5	4	5	0	0							
Magnesite	2	0	5	0	4	1	0							
Phosphates	5	0	0	1	5	0	1							
Petroleum	5	0	1	0	5	0	1							
Asbestos	1	0	0	1	5	2	1							
Mica	1	0	0	0	4	0	?							
Iodine	1	0	0	0	0	1	?							
Total	33	10	29	13	47	22	23							
Grand Total	59	16	34	25	81	45	34							

Legend
- ? Conditions uncertain
- 5 Surplus supply
- 4 Adequate supply
- 3 Self-sufficiency ratio more than ⅔
- 2 Self-sufficiency ratio more than ⅓
- 1 Self-sufficiency ratio less than ⅓
- 0 Supply completely or almost completely lacking

Ratings cover the home country only and do not include colonial territory.

data of this type compiled in 1939,[1] lists the approximate self-sufficiency of the United States and the 6 other most important industrial nations, with respect to 25 mineral commodities important in the development and maintenance of a war program. This list included 12 nonmetallic minerals and 13 metals for which the relative smelting capacity was also rated. In some cases, a country was rated as having a smelting capacity greater than the corresponding ore-producing capacity, indicating that the smelting capacity was dependent on imported ores to the amount of the difference. In other cases the ore capacity showed a surplus, leaving material available for export. These points were particularly important in time of war, when the country deficient in ore supply might be cut off from imports necessary to make its full smelting capacity effective, while on the other hand the country with surplus ore might not be able to export it. Of these two conditions, the former was of course the more important.

Tungsten concentrate in the form in which it is added to steel used in tool making. The only Canadian tungsten refinery, at Ottawa, contributed to the supply of the strategic metal when it became scarce after the fall of Burma in 1942

The ratings in the table show the approximate self-sufficiency, or ratio of production to consumption, for the various countries and minerals during the years preceding World War II. While in most cases data of this kind were fairly definite for a particular year, they might vary considerably from year to year; so no attempt was made to classify the ratings more closely than the rough grouping into surplus, adequate and deficient, scaling partial deficiency in thirds. In arranging the table, the minerals in the metallic and nonmetallic groups were listed approximately in the order of increasing deficiency for all countries combined, rather than for any particular country. While this order could not be determined accurately, it still served as a rough relative measure of the over-all strategic importance of the various minerals. While in general the major metals headed the list, and the less common ones followed, the order of importance varied in each country.

Interesting as the comparative status of the various minerals might be, a far more important factor was the comparison of the different countries with each other, since it gave some insight into the question as to the amount of effort required for any country to develop and maintain a munitions program. The attention of the reader is therefore directed to a study of the vertical columns of the table, rather than of the horizontal ones. At a glance it is seen that none of these countries had an adequate supply

[1] G. A. Roush, *Strategic Mineral Supplies* (1939).

of all the minerals listed, and on the other hand, none was deficient in all of them; but the over-all degree of deficiency varied widely. In general, it is also to be noted that self-sufficiency ran higher in the nonmetallic group than in the metallic.

It would not only be interesting, but also extremely valuable, if there were some way in which the various deficiencies could be given a relative weighting and so combined to show a total deficiency factor, but this could not be done. At first glance it might appear that the totals of the different country columns would give a first approximation of a relative factor of this kind, but the ratings on which these values are based are, in the first place, measures of self-sufficiency for ordinary everyday industrial operation, and not for an emergency demand. The countries are listed in the table roughly in the decreasing order of industrial activity; while the totals shown are a rough measure of self-sufficiency for the particular degree of industrial activity of the individual country, a second factor would have to be incorporated to make these figures comparable, taking into account the differences in the magnitude of the industrial activity in the different countries. The totals show that the U.S.S.R. had the best self-sufficiency ratio of the group, so far as its scale of industrial activity went, but that scale of activity was far less than in any of the countries listed in the preceding columns. Then too, the increased activity incident to a munitions program would likely revise many of these factors downward, to an indeterminate but appreciable degree. And finally, to arrive at a factor that would be comparative, it would be necessary to weight each separate commodity according to its value in the program as a whole. From a strategic standpoint the lack of a ton of manganese ore had about the same importance as the lack of 80 tons of steel, since the manganese was required in the production of the steel; or, having both and having the steel made up into finished projectiles, the whole procedure could be made ineffective by the lack of the few ounces of mercury to supply the primers required to make the projectiles function.

It being obviously impossible to develop a directly comparable self-sufficiency factor, investigators were limited to such incomplete data as shown in Table I as a basis for comparison. Furthermore, keeping in mind that these data were all of prewar origin, and the extent to which the United States fell short of expectations under war demands, the situation in the other countries, all of which had greater deficiency lists, must have been considerably worse.

Stock-piling.—Although stock-piling was not officially inaugurated in the U.S. until 1939 (*see* above), some stocking of strategic materials had been done by industry in the immediately preceding years, but only with a few commodities. On the other hand, there was abundant evidence that stock-piling of some strategic materials, especially manganese ore, was started in Europe almost immediately after the close of World War I. How much, and what materials were stocked, was not known; neither was it known to what extent the stocking was done voluntarily by industry and what part, if any, was fostered by government action. The chief evidence of stock-piling was the importation of commodities in quantities appreciably greater than were currently required by industry. For example, over a long period of years, and beginning as early as 1922, for each ton of steel produced, France imported about four times as much manganese ore as did the United States. There was similar evidence of stock-piling in other countries, especially Japan, Italy and Germany, during the immediate prewar years. Again using manganese ore as an illustration, world production per ton of steel made was more than a third greater during 1924–37 than it had been during 1911–23, the surplus presumably having gone into stocks in various countries. There were no definite records on the extent of stock-piling during the interwar years, but indications such as those cited above pointed to its rather extensive use. Though limited to a few countries and a few of the more important strategic minerals in the early years, the practice came into more extensive use in the latter 1930s when, in turn, Japan, Italy and Germany were preparing for war. (G. A. Ro.)

Bibliography.—H. Barger, *The Mining Industries,* (1944); E. Brooks, *Strategy of Raw Materials* (1937); W. O. Hotchkiss, *Minerals of Might* (1945); C. K. Leith, *World Minerals and World Peace* (1943); T. S. Lovering, *Minerals in World Affairs* (1943); H. Ries, *Economic Geology* (1937); G. A. Roush, *The Mineral Industry: Its Statistics, Technology and Trade* (1941), *Strategic Mineral Supplies* (1939); E. Sampson, *Mineral Resources and International Strife* (1938), *Stock Piles of Strategic Minerals* (Hearings before subcommittee of senate committee on mines and mining) (1943 *et seq.);* U.S. Bureau of Mines, *Minerals Yearbook;* U.S. Geological Survey, *Strategic Minerals Investigations* (1940 *et seq.*); U.S. Military Academy, Dept. of Economics, Government and History, *Strategic and Critical Raw Materials* (1944); *Mineral Industry; Mining and Metallurgy; Mining Congress Journal. See* also publications of U.S. Bureau of Mines, U.S. Geological Survey.

Strategic Services, Office of

See Psychological Warfare; Psychology; War and Defense Agencies.

Strategy of World War II

Victory in war is achieved through the tactical application of superior military power in proper directions and at the right times and places. The art of developing and applying this power to accomplish national objectives is military strategy. This is a definition dangerously subject to oversimplification. Strategy is ever complicated by obscurity of the enemy situation, by national and international politics, geography, the elements, by technical developments and most important, by unpredictable moral factors, by human strengths, genius and limitations. Once all the complications and difficulties have been resolved by the courage and wisdom of victorious leaders, their strategy will appear simple. However, as Karl von Clausewitz put it, everything in strategy is simple, but not therefore very easy.

Comparison of the opposing forces in World War II and analysis of their employment vividly illustrate all the elements of the preceding definition. Furthermore, the global features of the conflict added greatly to the complexities of evolving and implementing strategy. These difficulties were never fully surmounted by the axis powers, who never achieved a co-ordinated strategy. On the other hand the Allies, particularly the United States and the British commonwealth, did ultimately achieve relatively effective and continuous co-ordination.

In varying degrees the Allies had conflicting political, economic, social and military interests and doctrines and, to some extent, divergent interests regarding the enemy. It should be appreciated therefore that each major decision was not necessarily satisfactory to all the participants, and that complete agreements did not always exist among the war leaders of each nation. Each decision, however, was one which all accepted as effectively leading toward the final goal of decisive victory. That divergent interests were reconciled and an agreed over-all strategy evolved was due to the realization of the overriding importance of inflicting complete defeat upon Germany, Italy and Japan.

In the early stages, an effective tenet of axis strategy was to divide and conquer. The machinery and procedure for Allied co-ordination evolved slowly and did not become reasonably effective until after Pearl Harbor. Eventually the United States and Great Britain developed an effective basis for production and allocation of resources—both human and material. Only very general co-ordination was achieved with the soviet union, and not until late in World War II.

First Phases—Axis Triumphs.—As disciples of Clausewitz, the axis leaders espoused military power as an essential instrument of their expansionist policy. Adolf Hitler, in his early career, defined a specific application of this doctrine when he said, "It is not by flaming protests that oppressed lands are brought back into the embrace of the common reich, but by a sword ever ready to strike" (*Mein Kampf,* translated by Ralph Manheim, Houghton Mifflin, 1943). Even with Hitler's warning, his intended victims rationalized their estimates in accordance with their desires. The western democracies blindly formed their policies on the unwarranted assumption of continuous peace.

The bloodless occupation by the nazis of the Rhineland, Austria and Czechoslovakia evidenced their early strategy of gaining objectives by the threat of force. The axis success at Munich flowed from axis military power. By Sept. 1939 Germany had "peacefully" enlarged its territory to a relatively broad, productive base for additional expansion and increased its flexibility and potential for surprise action. However, the exasperation and growing fear of other nations had exhausted possibilities of further coups d'état by the mere threat of force.

In Aug. 1939 a trade agreement with the soviet union, followed the same month by a nonaggression pact, effectively divided the nations of Europe and seemed to ensure Germany against a two-front war—the strategic dilemma which Hitler dreaded. Attempts to obtain the Polish corridor by "diplomacy" ended on Sept. 1 when German troops invaded Poland without a declaration of war.

In less than a month, the Polish state was destroyed. Modern equipment and weapons supplied the German commander, Walter von Brauchitsch, the mobility and power to carry out a campaign that overran an entire nation in a few weeks. Manoeuvres which moved rapidly across a nation and would have been strategic in Napoleon's era had become merely battlefield tactics. The principles of war were skilfully and effectively applied to the employment of new weapons and equipment. As many claimed, there was indeed a new face to war—a mechanical face. However, the quality and type of individual genius required behind that face remain unchanged.

Success in Poland greatly improved Germany's strategic position. Elimination of the Polish corridor, acquisition of a frontier further to the east and control of a large portion of the Polish population added to its prestige, resources, depth, flexibility and security. With Poland so quickly eliminated and soviet neutrality virtually ensured, there was little chance that the forthcoming western campaign would suffer, as did Helmuth Moltke's Marne campaign in 1914, by diversions to secure an eastern front.

On Sept. 3, 1939, Great Britain and France, in a belated demonstration of vigorous policy, declared war. However, defensive thinking, feeble Allied preparations and the strength of the German west wall precluded a correspondingly vigorous strategy. As a positive measure, naval blockade produced a limited effect; however, passive measures featured the "sitzkrieg" Allied strategy by which, in 1939 and early 1940, they futilely sought to halt a strong and clever aggressor.

Much of the iron ore of Sweden, so important to German industry, came through the port of Narvik and the territorial waters of Norway. British sea power was moving to cut off the flow when Germany, uninhibited by any threat on the western front, struck (April 9, 1940) Denmark and Norway. Success not only secured the flow of ore to Germany but also acquired coastal bases which precluded an effective Allied defense against submarine and air activities in the North sea. Denial of the area to the Allies secured Germany's northern flank. Later operations from Norwegian bases against Allied convoys into Murmansk bore eloquent testimony to the farsighted strategy of this manoeuvre.

By May 1940 the bloodless preliminaries of the Rhineland, Austria and Czechoslovakia had been followed by the brutal engulfment of Poland and Norway. Germany was now well prepared to undertake the destruction of France. Great Britain and France were not yet ready to fight. Militarily, Germany was superior in equipment, had more than double the number of Allied divisions, and in addition, had an overwhelming air force. France was further weakened by lack of offensive spirit and internal class strife.

The goal of German battle strategy was annihilation of the Allied forces. The 1914 plan of an enveloping attack through Belgium was replaced by a new plan to penetrate the weakest point of the French fortifications, at the end of the Maginot line in the Ardennes forest. The pattern was a gigantic manoeuvre in which a German feint on the right (north) occupied the northern channel ports, drew Allied armies northward into Belgium, following which the main attack swept through the Ardennes and to the coast, first destroying the Allied forces in northern France and Belgium, then completing the destruction in southern and eastern France.

In a few weeks the Wehrmacht defeated the European armies of the Netherlands, Belgium, France and England. The coast of western Europe was now secure to the axis from Spain to Narvik. Destructive air and submarine operations could be launched from numerous bases located throughout its entire length. In addition, bases could be developed for direct attack on the British Isles.

After the collapse of France, the strategic initiative everywhere rested with Germany. There were at least three possible lines of action, of which it might adopt one or more. First, Germany could undertake an assault on the British Isles to obtain full control of that territory; second, it could strike through the Balkans and North Africa to gain control of the middle east; third, it could invade the U.S.S.R. In a sense Germany undertook all three. The main weight of the nazi machine was shifted to crush its major objective—the U.S.S.R.—out of which, in accordance with Hitler's concept, could be carved a greater Germany. There was good evidence that Hitler expected to achieve victory over Russia within a few months, after which he could concentrate further effort wherever the situation required.

However, contrary to the early concept of Hitler, Great Britain, as well as the whole British empire, was now Germany's enemy. The situation required that the British Isles either be conquered or neutralized. Also, British hostility increased the strategic importance of the Balkans and the middle east to the axis military position. The axis strategy, as brought out by events to follow, indicated that the British Isles were to be neutralized by air and submarine attacks, the Balkans were to be overrun and the middle east penetrated by campaigns against Egypt and perhaps through Asia Minor.

The German air assault was defeated in the battle of Britain, and the submarine menace was gradually overcome by dint of extraordinary Allied measures. As a result, the British Isles survived to become the base for launching the offensive which ultimately destroyed German power in western Europe.

Furthermore, the middle east was not conquered by the axis, and a vital gap in German planned territorial expansion was never closed. Most important, the Red army was not destroyed but eventually joined in the crushing defeat of Germany. The nazis thus failed in each of their strategic objectives. Success in any of the three undertakings of this period might have had a disastrous effect on the world's history.

In Sept. 1940, during the battle of Britain, the Italians struck eastward from Libya at the British in Egypt. Destruction of the British forces would have brought the strategic middle east under full axis control. The European axis and Japan could then have made a junction, a vital supply route to the U.S.S.R. would have been eliminated, important oil resources would have passed to the axis, India's position would have been compromised, severe repercussions might have been felt throughout the Moslem world, and North Africa, a potential base for attack against the southern flank of the axis, would have been difficult for the Allies to secure.

However, the British succeeded in their fight for time. The resistance, the delays, the losses inflicted in spite of tactical defeats and only a few victories, enabled them to hold on in the middle east. The issue was not finally determined until Gen. Erwin Rommel was turned back at El Alamein by Sir Bernard L. Montgomery's 8th army in 1942. This victory determined that the British would retain control of the middle east, an area vital to Allied strategy throughout World War II. While possession of Crete gave the axis added security in the Balkans, strategic domination of the Aegean sea and a base for offensive air operations, British determination had ensured that nothing essential to the strategic control of the middle east was lost.

Russia, by the spring of 1941, was practically isolated. It was small wonder it made a neutrality pact with Japan on April 13 of that year. Allies or potential allies could assist it only a little. The soviet for many months would have to fight its own battles and survive its own defeats.

The entire Balkan area had been secured to the axis in the spring months of 1941, and fighting in Crete was barely finished when, on June 22, 1941, Germany invaded soviet Russia. In 1941 the Wehrmacht was seeking primarily the destruction of the Russian army. Annihilation, taught by Alfred von Schlieffen, was to be accomplished through penetration and envelopment. The geographic pattern showed three terrain objectives and corresponding lines of operations—Leningrad, Moscow (initially Smolensk) and Kiev. The Red army could logically be expected to defend these vital objectives and in their defense might be destroyed. It was not clear that any specific battles were foreseen, but the tactics employed were such as to trap and devour masses of Russian troops.

On the other side, Stalin's early strategy was born of desperation and necessity. It was designed to sustain the war-making power of the nation until its strength and the attacks of its allies would permit the offensive. While initial soviet strategy was defensive, it was not passive and by no means called for defensive tactics.

The U.S.S.R. was not weak militarily. It had been rapidly preparing for war, and had absorbed the buffer Baltic states. It had almost inexhaustible manpower. In bloody engagements it could stubbornly trade space and manpower for time. Its industry, like its army, could not be destroyed in one mighty blow. Most important, the hardy Russian people possessed great determination and courage, both moral and physical, which could not be shaken by disaster.

All these factors were probably underevaluated by German strategists and statesmen as they were by the rest of the world. Only a few outside the U.S.S.R. doubted that superior German tactics and technique would quickly overcome the elements of Russian strength and accomplish the destruction of the soviet army. After the end of World War II, statements of responsible German leaders indicated that Germany expected a quick victory and prepared itself accordingly, both materially and psychologically.

By Dec. 7, 1941, Germany had advanced deep into Russia. Although it had failed to crush the Red army it had, in the eyes of the world, crowded Russia close to the brink of destruction. The situation in the U.S.S.R. on that date was of profound importance to the global strategic picture.

It is in a sense fallacious to mark Dec. 7, 1941, as a turning point in World War II. Certainly it did not mark any change in the axis procession of victories, unless to initiate for a period, more and greater ones for Japan. However, that date marked a fateful decision by Japan to make war on the United States—a development which was perhaps inevitable in view of its direct and irreconcilable conflict of interests with those of the United States.

Pearl Harbor temporarily paralyzed U.S. naval strength in the Pacific. On the other hand and of greater eventual significance, the U.S. people were immediately unified in a determination to defeat the axis. Although belated, the entrance of an angry and unified U.S. into the struggle, coupled with axis strategic mistakes and Russo-British success in preserving vital strategic areas and their armed forces, forecast eventual victory for the Allies.

In the spring of 1941 the United States had passed the lend-lease act, which was to contribute to Allied strength on every battlefield. The United States' entry into World War II stimulated this contribution and brought about combined (U.S.-British commonwealth) productive effort on a scale far greater than the axis believed possible. This industrial power, through the functioning of lend-lease and reciprocal aid, was employed to benefit all the Allies in accordance with planned priorities. It exercised a determining and overwhelming influence in the eventual Allied victory.

Allied Global Strategy.—As of Dec. 7, 1941, the strategy of World War II clearly became global; the relation between the Asiatic and European conflicts became well marked and had both a day-to-day and a long range effect. In order to allocate resources and guide preliminary operations, an over-all strategic decision was required as to the priority in which the Allies would take decisive action against their enemies. The U.S. and British leaders, Pres. Franklin D. Roosevelt and Prime Minister Winston Churchill, agreed that defeat of Hitler was to have priority over an offensive against Japan. British-U.S. preparations soon began to reflect this over-all decision.

It was an application of the best known principle of war which required the concentration of the mass of Allied resources against the major objective, in this instance, Hitler. As a corollary, the principle of economy of force had to be exercised elsewhere, especially in the Pacific and in India-Burma, where the concept required active opposition to the Japanese but with a minimum of resources.

It was a decision for the United States and the British military chiefs, who later as the combined chiefs of staff guided Allied strategy, including allocation of major resources in western Europe, the Pacific, the middle east and Asia. Especially for the United States, it was a difficult choice to make or implement. Stung by the attack on Pearl Harbor, with its countrymen on Bataan dying without hope of aid, and with its traditional friend, China, in danger of falling completely under Japanese control, the U.S. leaders could make and follow it only by exercise of the greatest courage. It was a lethal blow to the once successful "divide and conquer" strategy of the axis.

The most serious threat rested with Germany; Germany had more resources than Japan, and these resources were more efficiently mobilized for war. Furthermore, Germany was nearer than Japan, both to the centres of Allied power and to the bases from which the final blows would be launched. Fortunately, unprecedented and unexpected Allied production later provided means to overcome the relative disadvantages and even permit assumption of a Pacific offensive before the final defeat of Germany.

The important advantage of unified effort by the entire Allied coalition was largely dependent on the Hitler-first strategy. While eventual victory might also have been achieved under a Japan-first strategy on the part of the U.S., the inhibiting effect on Allied working relationships, serious doubts as to the staying power of Russia, and the time required to mount long-range operations in the Pacific were overpowering factors militating against such a course.

There were at least six factors essential to the main effort and basic in the implementation of early strategy of the combined chiefs of staff, although in themselves they could not bring about a decision. Strategic and operational decisions gave the factors full consideration. These factors were:

1. The necessity of supporting the Russians, whose forces were essential to complete defeat of the German land armies.
2. Maintenance of the security and war-making capacity of the British Isles and the western hemisphere.
3. Maintenance of the stability of the middle east and prevention of an axis drive to join Japan and Germany.
4. Control of the sea lanes in the Atlantic, Pacific and Indian oceans.
5. The necessity of stopping the Japanese before they advanced so far or became so securely entrenched as to prolong World War II unduly.
6. The need for keeping China in the war to contain Japanese forces and possibly provide bases for operations against Japan, as well as Chinese forces to mop up the Japanese spread through China.

Success in these six factors alone would not assure victory; they were nevertheless vital to the implementation of decisive offensive strategy. The factors did not change materially until very late in the conflict, when the axis power began to crumble. Although relative priorities between them could not be rigidly established, the minimum essential means were required for each, as failure in any one could not be countenanced. A single failure would have had global implications. For instance, a failure to halt the Japanese advance would have forced the United States to shift major resources to the Pacific, thereby seriously handicapping any major effort in Europe.

The basic factors in Allied strategy against Japan will be discussed later. The above factors as they relate to the defeat of the European axis are worthy of individual consideration.

Support of Russia, of paramount importance to winning the European war, was provided in two ways—by actual combat and by supply. Direct combat support, except by air, was slight until the Allied offensive in France was under way. Probably the most important early effects through combat were from the British and U.S. bomber offensives in 1943 and 1944 which reduced the capacity of German industry to support its forces in Russia and compelled withdrawal of luftwaffe fighter squadrons from the soviet front. Also, indirectly, Allied strength in the Pacific and Asia must have exercised a strong restraining influence on any Japanese desire to attack Asiatic Russia, thereby saving the Russians from the problem of a two-front war.

Long before combat support produced any direct results, U.S. and British lend-lease was reaching the U.S.S.R. in substantial amounts and made a major contribution to the soviet military effort. A single item of more than 300,000 U.S.-made vehicles was in itself important enough to improve substantially the capabilities of the Russian army. In 1941 and 1942 supply convoys to Murmansk and Archangel were attacked by German U-boat packs and aircraft from Norwegian bases, which sank about one-fourth of the ships. Before the end of World War II substantial supplies flowed through Iran, Alaska-Siberia and Vladivostok. Since the items delivered and shipping used were in great demand by all the Allies, it was only a determined unity of purpose that permitted the deliveries.

Maintaining the security and war-making capacity of the British Isles was of vast importance in the strategic pattern for the axis defeat. As an individual base, the United Kingdom was second only to the United States. The islands were a springboard for decisive sea, ground and air attacks on the axis. Of major importance also was the maintenance of the will to win in a population which furnished a large share of resources in men and matériel to bring about Allied victory. Success in this factor required success in the battle of the Atlantic and in measures to defeat the German air and V-weapon attacks. However, security was not complete until Allied infantry occupied the west coast of Europe.

Britain had long been at grips with the axis in the middle east when the U.S. entered World War II. From the Allied point of view, retention of the middle east was largely a British responsibility supported by U.S. supplies and only a limited number of troops, principally air. The British employed substantial forces and resources of all types in its accomplishment.

Control of the Atlantic sea lanes was vital to the accomplishment of any of the other undertakings. It was sustained in a continuous and widespread maritime struggle known as the battle of the Atlantic. This battle became critical within a month after the U.S. entered World War II, when effective U-boat attacks commenced against shipping in the western Atlantic. In 1942 total losses in ships exceeded ships built.

However, the U-boat was gradually subdued by a variety of measures, both defensive and offensive in character. In addition to naval surface craft, United States and British aircraft, military and civilian, were used extensively on patrols. Use of Iceland, Greenland, Newfoundland and later the Azores, as bases, greatly facilitated operations. As an offensive measure, the strategic air forces bombed German submarine bases and production facilities with limited effect. The menace of the U-boats was drastically reduced by the combined effectiveness of the various measures adopted and, after seizure of their western Europe bases in 1944, this weapon was no longer a threat.

It must be continually borne in mind that the minimum

EUROPEAN WAR
GREENLAND
ICELAND
ATLANTIC
Murmansk
Archangel
Narvik
NORWAY
SWEDEN
U S S R
Moscow
Smolensk
Stalingrad
POLAND
Kharkov
Kiev
Odessa
DENMARK
Berlin
GREAT BRITAIN
London
6 JUNE 1944
Cotentin Peninsula
Havre
GERMANY
Munich
Vienna
AUSTRIA
FRANCE
SWITZERLAND
ITALY
BALKANS
TURKEY
SPAIN
MEDITERRANEAN
SICILY
MALTA
CRETE
15 AUGUST 1944
8 NOV 1942
El Alamein
CAIRO
EGYPT
TUNISIA
LYBIA
NORTH AFRICA

demands of these vital undertakings were ever present and at times so urgent as to assume a priority higher than the main effort. In this situation, only the clearest of judgment and the greatest determination on the part of Allied leadership kept plans and their implementation directed with maximum efficiency toward the vital objective of destroying the axis military power.

Europe and the Mediterranean.—It was generally accepted in principle from early 1942 that the axis could be destroyed in Europe only by Allied victory on the continent, probably in Germany itself. Russia would play a vital role, but the western Allies would have to open a second front to make victory possible. The obvious solution was invasion of the continent at a suitable time and place to close with the axis forces and destroy them.

This was the final answer, but as stated earlier, it could be so oversimplified as to be almost meaningless in a serious analysis of the problem. There was no precedent on which to pattern the solution. There were political considerations such as the necessity for early victory and for encouraging resistance movements in occupied areas. The early liberation of France and British interests in the Mediterranean were some of the many conflicting factors to be resolved.

There was no textbook, no manual, no doctrine which could be clearly and definitely applied. The great prestige of German arms did not tempt responsible Allied leaders to reckless or audacious schemes. Massive amphibious operations on an hitherto untried scale would be required. Discounting a few late lessons from Japan against relatively weak resistance, all the wars in history provided poor precedents and no encouragement for an amphibious assault against a strong and vigorous enemy. In short, it was easy to prove that the task could not be done.

In early 1942 a cross-channel operation for the summer of 1943, known as "Roundup," was discussed by the combined chiefs of staff. If an early desperate situation on the Russian front required a diversionary attack, a lighter and earlier assault known as "Sledgehammer" would be substituted for "Roundup."

By July 1942 the situation in Russia looked unfavourable, while Rommel was threatening Egypt on the El Alamein line. Hitler's strategy was strongly offensive—aerial bombardment of Britain, break-throughs at Stalingrad and in Egypt, and later a junction in the middle east. The British and U.S. decided to undertake "Torch," an offensive against North Africa, as the only possible move having a fair prospect of success with the limited resources available. As the Allies were still on the defensive, operation "Torch" was strategically defensive. Generally speaking, the expected returns included savings in shipping, extension of the blockade, increased security of the middle east and possible reconstitution of a French army in North Africa. Also, control of the North African area was a necessary preliminary to any strategic offensive which might later be made through the Mediterranean.

The soviet counteroffensive of the winter of 1941 and 1942 inflicted heavy casualties on the Germans but suffered reverses in the Crimea and at Kharkov. Just when the soviet war was beginning to look less like a blitzkrieg and more like a war of attrition, a serious nazi threat came in the summer of 1942 with the German drive toward the Caucasus and Stalingrad. This drive, if successful, would have cut off the oil of the Caucasus from the Russian armies and opened the way for axis control of the middle east. The attack was savage, but fell short of cutting off the oil or the flow of American lend-lease supplies. When the Russians, commanded by Vassily I. Chuikoff and Georgi K. Zhukov, saved Stalingrad, the danger of disaster was past, and it was only a question of time until the Red army could commence offensive operations.

Meanwhile, Rommel's forces rolled dangerously near to Alexandria and Cairo. Further advance, however, was delayed by strong blows from the air and difficulties inherent in a long and inadequate supply line. British reinforcements at El Alamein halted Rommel and finally, by Oct. 1942, launched the attack which drove the Germans back to destruction in Tunisia. The German strategic pincers failed to close in the middle east, having met sharp tactical reverses in both Russia and Africa.

While in early 1942 cross-channel operations had been envisaged as essential to the defeat of Germany, the beginning of 1943 saw the Allied Mediterranean campaign being pressed forward with a vigour absorbing more and more resources. In Jan. 1943 the combined chiefs of staff decided to invade Sicily by midsummer in order to obtain further advantages to shipping and continue the momentum of recent successes in the area. In May 1943 the combined chiefs of staff decided that Allied pressure would extend to forcing Italy's withdrawal from World War II. The strategic advantages of success included denial of Italian manpower to Germany and the securing of a land base for launching possible invasions into the Balkans or southern France. In a sense, a second front in Europe would be created which would absorb limited German resources, although it was doubtful that the U.S.S.R. ever considered Italy sufficient diversion to be termed a second front. An important consideration was the advantage of maintaining the momentum of the successful attack on Sicily rather than to shift forces to another theatre.

Invasion of Fortress Europe.—While operations in the Mediterranean were proceeding with energy, it was accepted that defeat of the German armies in west Europe could occur only on the ancient battlefields of France and the Low Countries. Some strategists continued to press for the Allied main effort to be made through Italy and even the Balkans; however, the general determination to undertake a cross-channel invasion prevailed.

Preparations for the attack had been initiated in June 1942, but as a result of diversion of resources to the Mediterranean, consummation had to await successful conclusion of the North African campaign.

At Casablanca in Jan. 1943 the combined chiefs of staff directed definite preparations for cross-channel operations to take advantage of any sudden German weakness or for an assault in the spring of 1944 if no previous opportunity occurred. This decision gave definite impetus to the build-up of resources in the United Kingdom, to a combined bomber offensive and to formation of a combined plan for the continental assault. Although the air offensive was placed in first priority, the over-all plan evolved by mid-1943 provided for an Anglo-U.S. ground and air assault ("Overlord") in the spring of 1944.

It should be noted that definite combined (British-U.S.) planning and large-scale preparations for "Overlord" began about one and a half years before the assault was undertaken, and at a time when Allied defense around the globe was just beginning to achieve success. Preparations to carry out the simplest strategic decision often present problems of great magnitude and require substantial time prior to execution. Such was the case here.

A major element in the strategic pattern for the defeat of Germany was the combined British-U.S. air attack. This attack absorbed a substantial proportion of the total available resources and considerable effort had been expended in analyzing its effect. According to the United States Strategic Bombing survey, the number of planes involved reached a peak of some 28,000 and men in combat commands a peak of 1,300,000. The total loss in air action was about 158,000 men and 40,000 aircraft. This was a tremendous expenditure of men and treasure to implement a hitherto untried employment of a new weapon. It demonstrated the determination of the leaders to exploit fully the vast technical and industrial power of the United States and Britain as well as the possibilities of new developments in winning a war.

In addition, attacks both before and after D-day on the German transportation system, combined with devastating strikes on oil resources, severely reduced both the strategic and tactical mobility of the German forces and logistically had a paralyzing effect. The extent of these successes was extolled in the United States Strategic Bombing survey as follows:

> Allied air power was decisive in the war in Western Europe. Hindsight inevitably suggests that it might have been employed differently or better in some respects. Nevertheless, it was decisive. In the air, its victory was complete. At sea, its contribution, combined with naval power, brought an end to the enemy's greatest naval threat—the U-boat; on land, it helped turn the tide overwhelmingly in favor of Allied ground forces. Its power and superiority made possible the success of the invasion. It brought the economy which sustained the enemy's armed forces to virtual collapse. . . .

Some had hoped that Germany could be defeated in the west by air power alone, but plans had never envisioned such success. Air power was a decisive contributing factor, but the tenacious will of Germany to fight even after Allied armies crossed the Rhine demonstrated that the Allied leaders were correct in their judgment that a "second front" on the ground ("Overlord") was required to ensure early German defeat.

By D-day, June 6, 1944, the U.S.S.R. had not yet started its big summer offensives but was preparing all along the front. A co-ordinated offensive by combined forces under Field Marshal Sir Henry Maitland Wilson in Italy pinned down German forces there, and an attack by French and American troops under General Jacob L. Devers against southern France was to be launched in mid-August. The German leaders were probably aware of the forthcoming attacks on the west and east, but it is doubtful if they anticipated the strength and skill with which their coastal fortifications in France would be assailed or the paralyzing effect of the accompanying air attack. The destruction of their industry by strategic bombing and of their communications by tactical air preparations, together with loss of control of the air, was only a foretaste of the deadly blows about to be struck.

Battle strategy of the supreme allied commander in Europe, Gen. Dwight D. Eisenhower, involved a landing, amphibious and airborne, between Le Havre and the Cotentin peninsula of Normandy. In mid-August the supporting attack was landed in the south of France. The Allied advance pushed rapidly across France and Germany to a junction with the Russians along the general line of the Elbe river. There were inevitable delays caused by German resistance and the necessity for seizing and operating ports and lines of communications in support of the advance. However, as the attack progressed, large masses of German forces were progressively destroyed. At the time of the final German surrender on May 7, 1945, German military power had virtually ceased to exist.

The Russians, having held the general Leningrad-Odessa line on D-day, advanced across eastern Poland into the Baltic states in July and August. By Sept. 1944 the drives by Fedor Tolbukhin's and Rodion Y. Malinovsky's armies into the Balkans were under way and became the principal soviet effort for the remainder of the year. The Balkans were soon largely under soviet domination. In early 1945 Zhukov's forces smashed across Poland and East Prussia to stand along the Oder river, from which they subsequently advanced to the Elbe. By April their push up the Danube reopened, to reach Vienna by the end of World War II.

In north Italy, meanwhile, the Allied armies had crossed the Po river in late April and were sweeping toward the Alpine passes.

In general, therefore, the final destruction of Germany involved two great attacks, one on the east and one on the west. The western attack involved initial amphibious and airborne landings in Normandy followed by destruction of German forces in France, the Low Countries and western Germany. The eastern attack of the U.S.S.R. swept westward from the Leningrad-Odessa line, crushing German forces in its path and eventually meeting the western democracies in Germany and Austria. Contributions of the Italian front were an initial holding attack and provision of a base for supporting operations into south Europe.

The general pattern of Allied conquests found the western democracies, at the end of World War II, in control of Italy and western Germany. Eastern Europe and the Balkans were under Russian domination. This was a direct result of the military strategy employed and of great significance to the political, economic and military future of Europe.

The conclusive element in the German surrender was the Allied ground strength. Until the infantry of the western Allies and Russia joined at the Elbe, Germany's will was unbroken. However, it was useless to attempt an assessment of credit to each of the various arms, services or nationalities. The pattern for victory was dependent upon the early refusal of soviet Russia and England to accept defeat and on their retention of vital areas. The naval roles of securing the sea lanes and participating in the amphibious attack were also vital and essential. The importance of air operations has already been described. Nothing could have been accomplished without the logistic support of the military services. Civilian industry provided the sinews for all. Not least in importance was the accomplishment of the leaders in guiding the production and organization of all the vast resources required and in the strategic determination of where and how they should be used. These leaders, having defeated the European axis, had yet to complete the same task against Japan.

Japanese Objectives and Strategy.—General of the Army George C. Marshall's analysis of Japan's objectives and plans was in part as follows:

> Strategically, Japan was well poised in 1941 to carry out her aims in Asia. All the major world powers who normally maintained the status quo in Asia were absorbed in the war in Europe. France had been overrun and eliminated. England was threatened by German invasion. The U.S.S.R. was attempting to repel a German invasion on her Western front reaching to the gates of the capital. The United States had become the Arsenal of Democracy, with major efforts directed toward the support and preservation of our European Allies.
>
> The Tripartite Pact had been signed, giving Japan a free hand in Asia. She had a large and relatively well-equipped army and a moderately good air force well trained by actual combat in China. She had obtained by forced agreement a

staging area in French Indo-China. She had a fairly large navy especially strong in the transport craft available. She had accumulated by great national economy a good stockpile of strategic materiels at home for the initial effort and with each successive conquest she obtained new and important areas from which other supplies of materials could be drawn, such as oil, rubber, and metal. The Japanese mistakenly believed in the hearty cooperation of "liberated" peoples of the so-called Greater East Asia Co-Prosperity Sphere with their huge labor pools. Japan considered herself ready to strike.

Japan's objective was the conquest, consolidation, and eventual domination of the whole Far East. She intended to make her conquest in a rapid surprise drive which would overpower all resistance, to form an iron ring of outer defenses against which the spiritually inferior, pacifistic combination of opponents could beat themselves into weariness, while she consolidated her gains at leisure.

Japan's plan for accomplishment of its objectives as later known or deduced from its actions and from interrogation of leaders involved:

1. Neutralization or destruction of the United States Pacific fleet by an attack on Pearl Harbor.
2. Conquest of the Philippines, the South Pacific Islands and the Burma-Malaya-Netherlands Indies barrier in order to secure a strong southwestern flank against attack and to gain control of the sea lanes in the west and southwest Pacific, South China seas, and the eastern part of the Bay of Bengal. Control of these areas would cut China's supply line across Burma and isolate Australia.
3. Later, capture of Midway and raids on Hawaii and the west coast of the United States.
4. Invasion of the Aleutians to form a northern flank if initial success in that area warranted it.
5. Stimulation of unrest and possible revolution in India.
6. Probably eventual conquest of Siberia and the maritime provinces of U.S.S.R.

Therefore, while the German war concept had visualized the relatively unlimited objectives of the destruction of its principal enemies, the Japanese visualized a limited objective of securing a large area to its control, but without the destruction of its principal enemy, the United States. Furthermore, in contrast to Germany's doctrine of making a single main decisive effort, the Japanese strategic scheme was unorthodox. It involved simultaneous attacks in several different directions, each with a limited objective. Even with efficient internal lines of communication, such a plan is ordinarily unsound because it requires a prolonged dispersion of forces to widely scattered points.

Nevertheless, in the situation as it existed, the Japanese strategy did not appear unsound. Japan did not have means to destroy the power of the United States, but a quick victory leading to a favourable negotiated peace seemed a possibility. Special preparations permitted Japan to concentrate superior power at nearly all the points of attack. However, when the productive power of the Allies exceeded even their own expectations, Japan's underestimate of Allied determination, strength and capabilities became a logical but fatal error.

There was no indication that Japan and Germany succeeded in co-ordinating their strategy in the sense that agreements were reached on specific military operations or any combined allocation made of resources, such as submarines. The only possible co-ordination appears to have been through the timing of Japan in forcing the U.S. into a two-front war and increasing the burdens on the British empire. However, the Japanese timing had the effect of forcing Germany into a war with the United States. There was evidence that Germany actually attempted to persuade Japan to attack Russia rather than south or east in the Pacific. Thus, Germany may have foreseen the possible implications on itself of a Japanese attack on the U.S. Continued failure to co-ordinate was one of the principal blunders in axis planning and conduct of the war.

Implementation of Allied Strategy against Japan.—Considering the elements of the Japanese plan, it was apparent that success therein would have indeed accomplished the objective perhaps beyond any Allied power to penetrate the iron ring and destroy Japan without an unacceptable cost. It is, therefore, appropriate to examine each of the elements to see wherein and why Japan failed.

Neutralization or destruction of the U.S. fleet at Pearl Harbor was accomplished only temporarily and incompletely. U.S. naval power was not destroyed. The leadership, the men, the traditions, the know-how of operation and production and the repair and manufacturing facilities were unimpaired. Even the principal U.S. naval bases, except in the far Pacific, were never lost.

The objective of overcoming the Philippines, the South Pacific islands and southeast Asia including the seizure of Malaya and Burma was accomplished in 1942. However, the resources of this area were never effectively exploited by the Japanese. China's overland supply line was cut in the Burma campaign in 1942, but China was never completely isolated and soon began to receive supplies by air from India. The important thing was that China never gave up but remained in World War II in accordance with one of the basic factors of Allied strategy. The Allied navies, in continuous and widespread operations, assisted by the air and land campaign to secure Port Moresby, successfully maintained communications with Australia, thus preventing its isolation. Allied strategy required that these sea communications be maintained.

The attempt to invade Midway Island was foiled in the battle of Midway in June 1942. This and the Coral sea battle were the first decisive defeats inflicted on the modern Japanese navy. Not only was the threat to Hawaii removed, but the reduction in Japanese carrier based air strength swung naval power in the Pacific back into balance. Thereafter, until its air strength was rebuilt, the Japanese navy could operate safely only under cover of darkness or land based air protection.

The Aleutians were partially invaded and occupied in June 1942 (Kiska and Attu). However, failure in the battle of Midway and failure to push further eastward along the Aleutian chain made this occupation of no strategic importance to Japan.

India remained loyal to the Allied cause and furnished substantial resources in men and matériel contributing to the axis defeat.

Japanese strategy failed when it missed the early opportunity to capture Hawaiian bases and to isolate Australia. From these two areas were launched the advances which eventually converged on Japan and destroyed her. The grave perils of strategy with a limited objective thus bore the fruit of final defeat.

Allied Strategy for Defeat of Japan.—By mid-1944 the Allied strategic concept for complete defeat of Japan was determined. Unconditional surrender was to be achieved by preliminary wearing down of Japan's ability to resist through air and sea blockade, intense air bombardment, destruction of its air and naval strength, seizure of the necessary bases to serve as springboards and the ultimate invasion of the industrial heart of the empire. Blockade was of much greater significance against Japan, a maritime nation, than it had been against Germany. There was a possibility that destruction of the Japanese forces in Manchuria, China and elsewhere would have to be accomplished also. This latter possibility existed even at the formal surrender.

USA
ALASKA
ALEUTIANS
Attu
Kiska
Pearl Harbor
HAWAIIAN ISLANDS
Midway
SIBERIA
U S S R
P A C I F I C
P A C I F I C
MANCHURIA
Vladivostok
J A P A N
Tokyo
Hiroshima
Nagasaki
Coronet
Olympic
Okinawa
Iwo Jima
Marianas
HIMALAYAN HUMP
C H I N A
Kunming
INDIA
BURMA
BAY OF BENGAL
FR. INDO CHINA
CHINA SEA
PHILIPPINES
Truk
Carolines
Rabaul
NEW GUINEA
Port Moresby
MALAYA
Singapore
INDIAN OCEAN
AUSTRALIA

This concept required intense submarine, surface and air operations against Japanese sea communications, air bombardment of vital resources and simultaneously a continued amphibious advance across the Pacific to seize major bases from which could be launched the final overwhelming land, sea and air assault. In the advance, it was inevitable that Japanese sea power would be met in force and that its air power would have to be overcome. Japanese ground armies could be by-passed except in those areas essential to the advance. Control of the sea and air was the key factor. As long as such control was maintained, ground forces could be pushed in to seize the required islands or areas. However, sustained loss of control in any area would mean local disaster. Of course, the air and sea operations were tied to land bases which the ground forces must seize and secure. Hence, the importance of a unified land, sea and air team was magnified.

It must not be supposed that each of the various amphibious steps could be foreseen at the outset. In a geographic sense, it could not be determined at once whether or not bases on the China mainland would be required. Nor did it seem unlikely at the outset that an Allied attack would have to break through the Malaya-Netherland Indies barrier from the Indian ocean area to join eventually in the final assault. Furthermore, it required the experience of vigorous operations to demonstrate the feasibility of neutralizing and by-passing strong Japanese bases.

Japanese strategy, after the Allied assumption of the initiative, was one of passive defense. Having lost the initiative, Japan seemed largely paralyzed except for desperate naval actions and development of such extreme measures as Kamikaze or suicide attacks.

In a sense, Japan lost the strategic initiative at the battle of Midway on June 3–6, 1942. There followed a period in which the Allies gradually assumed the tactical offense but were not yet prepared to seize any of the areas vital to the Japanese position. This is sometimes called an offensive defense, and its early assumption was a necessity in the Allied concept of Pacific strategy.

Although that concept originally envisaged that the strategic offensive must await the defeat of Germany, it also required that Japan be kept off balance in the interim by tactics which would prevent consolidation of its position and further advances. This offensive defense was one of the strategic fundamentals of the combined chiefs of staff and included in its tactical objectives the acquisition and development of bases from which to launch major offensive action when means became available.

During the early phases, tactical thrusts known as island hopping were employed. It gradually became apparent that Allied naval and air superiority would permit by-passing of Japanese land forces on isolated islands, and as Allied strength and skill increased it was evident that even strong bases such as Truk could be by-passed and neutralized by air and sea operations. On the larger land masses such as New Guinea, by-passed Japanese forces required ground as well as air and naval forces for their neutralization. The first major Jap base so by-passed was Rabaul, after which it was apparent that only selected base areas need be seized. From these the Allied forces could step rapidly across the Pacific to the springboard from which the final assaults on Japan itself would be launched.

The land, sea and air arms found teamwork of primary importance. Two such teams, one commanded by Gen. Douglas MacArthur, the other by Adm. Chester Nimitz, operated under the control of the U.S. joint chiefs of staff, as independent but mutually supporting commands which co-operated not only as to the timing and the objectives of their operations but also as to transfer of resources between them. These commands advanced on converging axes, one through the Southwest Pacific from New Guinea to the Philippines; the other across the central Pacific to the Marianas, Iwo Jima and Okinawa.

The advances were in successive strides, each step securing areas which could be developed to provide supporting facilities for subsequent campaigns. It was found that carriers could provide air cover until land-based air forces were established on shore in the areas assaulted. This capability was an operational factor which increased the length of the strides. Eventually the most advanced Allied bases projected Allied power within striking range of Japan itself, and cut the empire's supply lines to the south and the China coast. Allied military and economic strength and carefully scheduled interchange of amphibious resources permitted effective support to both arms of the pincers.

Strategy in Southeast Asia and China.—In the preliminaries for the final phase, southeast Asia, India and China played an unspectacular and indirect, but nevertheless important, role. From the beginning it was basic to maintain China in World War II. Not only were there substantial Japanese forces in China, unavailable for use elsewhere, but also their logistic support was a continual drain on Japanese resources. In addition, the possible future requirement for China bases to support the final assault on Japan demanded that Chinese forces be kept in being to help secure such bases at the appropriate time. As a direct contribution, air forces operating from China attacked industry and shipping.

The support to China all channelled through India and thence over the Himalayan "hump." Therefore, in the early stages of World War II, the strategy in India was directed toward the security of India and support of China. In the fall of 1943 the combined chiefs of staff created the Southeast Asia command (Adm. Louis Mountbatten) which assumed the responsibility in that area for operations against the Japanese, initially those necessary for protecting India and securing and improving the supply line to China. As a direct contribution to the defeat of Japan, Southeast Asia command prepared to capture Singapore and advance into the South China seas. Such preparations could not be implemented prior to V-J day because of lack of resources, although the Japanese army in Burma was destroyed by the end of hostilities. The security and quantity of supplies to China were continuously increased.

Air operations from China bases contributed materially to the attrition of the Japanese air force and to Japanese shipping in coastal waters of China. In addition, China-based B-29s struck the first blows at Japanese industry.

The Allied strategy in China, India and southeast Asia thus succeeded in its basic objectives of maintaining China in World War II and projecting operations to absorb and dissipate the enormous Japanese resources in the area.

Japan's Defeat—Final Phase.—Direct preparations for final amphibious assault on the Japanese Islands were underway in early 1945 and proceeded rapidly. New advanced base areas in the Marianas, Philippines and Okinawa were secured and developed. Resources were increased through redeployment of troops and supplies from the European theatre and other areas.

Japan's shipping had already been severely reduced by attacks from U.S. submarines. Losses became more critical as Allied air and naval raids struck deep into home waters. Plans and preparations were progressing rapidly toward the full consummation of forcing Japanese surrender by seizure of vital objectives in the home islands. It appeared that the U.S.S.R. would attack the Japanese forces in Manchuria, while in China there were good possibilities of a successful Chinese offensive to seize a coastal port.

The final amphibious blow was never struck. The threat of immediate land attack from all sides, the destruction of Jap shipping, loss or isolation of many outlying areas and forces and the strategic air attack, all combined with the effects of blockade, broke the will of the Japanese people. Desperate intentions and preparations by the Japanese army and the Kamikaze air force to die in the defense of the homeland could not be sustained in the face of mounting disaster.

By late 1943 it was visualized that strategic air attacks would play a major role in wearing down Japan's ability to resist. Starting in Nov. 1944 attacks from the Marianas bases centred on the Japanese aircraft industry. In March 1945 Gen. Curtis Le May's B-29s shifted from high altitude attacks to night incendiary strikes on urban industrial areas from altitudes of 7,000 ft., aimed at the destruction of the basic economic and social fabric of Japan. This method proved so highly successful that by the end of World War II, 66 of Japan's largest cities had been heavily damaged.

Thirty per cent of the urban population had lost their homes and one-quarter had evacuated the cities as a by-product of the devastation of industrial areas. The holocaust wrought by the atomic bomb in Hiroshima and Nagasaki was the final blow. It crystallized growing intentions in the minds of Japanese leaders to surrender and brought about speedy capitulation.

As atom bombs levelled Hiroshima and Nagasaki, and the Japanese government finally made its decision to surrender, soviet armies struck into Manchuria. It does not appear that this attack materially hastened the final capitulation of Japan. However, the virtual certainty that a Russian attack would be launched eventually was undoubtedly a factor influencing an early decision to capitulate. Also, it must be realized that, throughout World War II, powerful Japanese forces were deployed in Manchuria prepared to meet a potential soviet threat. These forces could not be employed to meet Allied moves elsewhere. Therefore, it may be said that Russian forces in Manchuria did play a substantial role in Allied success in the Pacific.

Japan's surrender was brought about by developments for which each Allied service was in a measure responsible, although the final spectacular and conclusive role was played by the strategic air forces and, to a lesser extent, by raiding carrier task forces. As in Europe, it was useless to attempt to list these developments in order of importance or to allocate the credit for victory. In every campaign the various arms and services were interdependent for success. The final result could not have been achieved without the phenomenal industrial capacity of the United Kingdom and the U.S.

The important military developments which shattered the fighting will of Japan were:

1. Destruction, damage or paralysis of virtually all Japanese shipping by submarine, air attack and mining.
2. Destruction of the Japanese navy and the overpowering of its air force.
3. Actual loss or ineffectiveness of Japan's resources caused by loss of control of the sea, air and outlying key base areas.
4. Devastation of the strategic air attacks on the homeland.
5. Strategic position of Allied bases, where land, air and sea forces were poised to invade the homeland in overwhelming force.
6. Probability that the U.S.S.R. would attack the Japanese forces in Manchuria.

Aftermath of the War's Strategy.—The effects of Allied war strategy on world affairs were by no means terminated on V-J day. The wartime strategy largely determined the deployment of Allied forces at the end of hostilities and therefore in general the subsequent zones to be occupied by, or to come under the direct influence of each of the Allied nations. In Europe, the western democracies had decided to avoid major Balkan operations, which resulted in Balkan and eastern European occupation by Russia. On the other hand, the Allied strategy placed Italy, France, the Low Countries and western Germany in the areas controlled on V-E day by the armies of the west. In the Pacific, rapid thrusts took U.S. forces into Japan before the other Allies could arrive. Thus the United States played the dominant role in Japan.

The important effect of occupational control on postwar political, economic and military developments was apparent. Each of the great powers found the strength and location of its armed forces an essential factor in its influence on world affairs. In each case the occupying power was able to confront theoretical or moral persuasion by other powers with the realities of *de facto* control. (*See* also BLOCKADE; INCENDIARY WARFARE; INTERNATIONAL CONFERENCES, ALLIED [WORLD WAR II]; LOGISTICS OF WORLD WAR II; PSYCHOLOGICAL WARFARE; STRATEGIC BOMBING; SUBMARINE WARFARE; TACTICS OF WORLD WAR II; WORLD WAR II.)

BIBLIOGRAPHY.—Bernard Brodie, ed., *The Absolute Weapon* (New York, 1946); John R. Deane, *The Strange Alliance* (New York, 1947); Edward Mead Earle, ed., *Makers of Modern Strategy* (Princeton, 1943); Dwight David Eisenhower, *Report by the Supreme Commander to the Combined Chiefs of Staff on the Operations in Europe of the Allied Expeditionary Force, 6 June 1944 to 8 May 1945* (Washington, 1946); Edgar McInnis, *The War, First Year* (New York, 1941); *idem, The War, Second Year* (Toronto, 1941); Sir Halford J. Mackinder, *Democratic Ideals and Realities* (New York, 1942); Homer Lea, *The Valor of Ignorance* (New York, 1942); George C. Marshall, *Biennial Report of the Chief of Staff of the United States Army, July 1, 1941 to June 30, 1943, to the Secretary of War* (Washington, 1943); *idem, Biennial Report of the Chief of Staff of the United States Army, July 1, 1943 to June 30, 1945, to the Secretary of War* (Washington, 1945); Nicholas John Spykman, *America's Strategy in World Politics* (New York, 1942); Derwent S. Whittlesey, *et al., German Strategy of World Conquest* (New York, 1942); Report of the United States Strategic Bombing Survey, *Japan's struggle to end the war* (Washington, 1946); *The War Reports of George C. Marshall, H. H. Arnold* [*and*] *Ernest J. King* (Philadelphia, 1947). (J. E. HU.; L. J. L.)

Stratigraphy

See GEOLOGY.

Stratton, Dorothy Constance

Miss Stratton (1899–), U.S. coast guard officer, was born March 24, 1899, in Brookfield, Mo. She taught history in her native town and later, moving to California, became (1924) vice-principal and dean of girls at the senior high school in San Bernardino. She joined the faculty of Purdue university, Lafayette, Ind., in 1933 as associate professor of psychology and dean of women and was made full professor of psychology in 1940. In the summer of 1942 she joined the women's naval reserves (WAVES) as a lieutenant and in September of that year, she was appointed assistant to the commanding officer at the training centre for radio operators at Madison, Wis. When the women's reserves of the coast guard was created, she was selected to head the new unit.

Promoted to the rank of a lieutenant commander, she was sworn in Nov. 24, 1942, and was raised to a captaincy in Feb. 1944. She retired from the SPARS in early Jan. 1946.

Strawberries

See Fruit.

Streeter, Ruth Cheney

Mrs. Streeter (1895–), officer of the U.S. marine corps women's reserve, was born Oct. 2, 1895, in Brookline, Mass. She was educated in Boston and Paris schools and Bryn Mawr college. After marrying Thomas Winthrop Streeter, an attorney, in 1917, she settled in Morristown, N.J.

After the women's reserve of the marine corps was formed early in 1943, Mrs. Streeter was appointed director and was inducted with the rank of major.

Mrs. Streeter was later raised to the rank of lieutenant colonel, and on Feb. 1, 1944, was promoted to the rank of colonel. She returned from the marine corps in the summer of 1946.

Streicher, Julius

Streicher (1885–1946), German politician, was born Feb. 22, 1885, at Fleinshausen. He served in the army during World War I, and became a school teacher in Nuernberg in 1919. In the early 1920s, he joined the nazi party and participated with Hitler in the Munich putsch of Nov. 1923. In that year he also founded a weekly magazine, *Der Stuermer,* in which pornography and anti-Semitism were combined to obtain mass circulation. Encouraged by Hitler, Streicher became the most extreme anti-Semite of the Third reich. After the nazis gained power in 1933, Hitler appointed Streicher to the Academy for German Law.

He was also made gauleiter for Franconia. Streicher thereupon intensified his anti-Semitic activities, which he maintained throughout the succeeding years.

After Germany's defeat Streicher was captured May 23, 1945, by U.S. troops near Waldring, Bavaria, disguised as a painter. Indicted with a score of other top nazi leaders on charges of war crimes before the International Military tribunal at Nuernberg, in 1945, Streicher was found guilty of crimes against humanity on Oct. 1, 1946, and was sentenced to death. He was hanged on Oct. 16, 1946, in Nuernberg.

Streptomycin

See Bacteriology; Chemistry; Chemotherapy; Pneumonia; Urology.

Strikes and Lock-outs

The number of strikes in the United States from 1937 to December 1946, is shown in Table I. The years 1937, 1941, 1944–46 were characterized by marked strike activity, 1946 being the worst year for strikes in U.S. history. During Jan.–Aug. 1946, three times as much working time was lost through strikes as in any previous full year in U.S. history.

Table I.—*Number of Strikes, Workers Involved and Man-Days Lost, 1937–46*

Year	No. of strikes beginning in year indicated	Workers involved in strikes beginning in year	Man-days idle	Average days lost per employee
1937.	4,740	1,860,621	28,424,857	15.5
1938.	2,772	688,376	9,148,273	13.3
1939.	2,613	1,170,962	17,812,219	15.3
1940.	2,508	576,988	6,700,872	11.7
1941.	4,288	2,362,620	23,047,556	9.9
1942.	2,968	839,961	4,182,557	5.0
1943.	3,752	1,981,279	13,500,529	6.8
1944.	4,956	2,115,637	8,721,079	4.1
1945.	4,616	3,069,300	24,360,000	7.9
1946 (11 months).	4,335	4,545,000	107,475,000	23.4

Table II (p. 197) summarizes the major types of issues, 1937–45. The classification indicates only roughly their relative importance because few strikes, except those solely for wage increases, involved but a single issue or type of issues. Demands for a closed shop, for instance, or even union recognition, were almost always only one of many issues involved in a particular bargaining. There were no statistics to show in how many bargainings each separate issue appeared. If there were, the list would be so long as to be difficult to appraise.

Table II shows that the predominant issue of the decade 1937–46 was wages. Breakdowns in *Monthly Labor Review* showed that it appeared in bargainings concurrently with almost every other type of issue. Next in importance were the issues centring around union security—recognition, closed shop, maintenance of membership, check-off, grievance procedure, discrimination and rights of union representatives.

Strikes, Year by Year.—The 4,740 strikes of 1937 exceeded any other year up to 1944. The upsurge of union activity which started in 1934, encouraged, at least, by section 7A of the National Industrial Recovery act and the 1935 National Labor Relations act, developed into a definitely militant labour movement. The split in the labour movement in 1936, which established the C.I.O. as a rival to the A.F. of L., intensified rather than retarded labour's drive to spread unionism into hitherto unorganized areas of industry.

Sit-down strikes, a tactic still being used in 1937, tended to increase the number of strikes, since the sit-down enabled workers who were dissatisfied to call strikes without waiting for authority from their union, or without organization. The year was essentially one of offensive strikes—strikes to compel union recognition, wage increases, shorter hours and other positive gains. Few of the strikes were defensive.

The automobile industry was the worst strike area of 1937. Industrial conflict had become serious in the industry as early as 1934 and reached a peak during the spring of 1937 in the General Motors, Hudson and Chrysler strikes, all of which ended in union recognition and agreements. Of automobile workers 48,000 went out in the General Motors strike, tying up operations in 50 plants in 25 cities and directly affecting the employment of 126,000 other workers. Following the major automobile strikes there were numerous "illegal" strikes; *i.e.,* stoppages which violated the agreements with the auto manufacturers. Some of these were sit-down strikes. In November major strikes again broke out at General Motors and the Hudson Motor company, chiefly over impatience and suspicion concerning the renewal of the agreement. During the latter part of the year the United Automobile Workers (C.I.O.) staged several strikes at St. Louis and Kansas City against the Ford Motor company but during 1937 did not attempt a major strike against that company.

The Pacific coast maritime strike, which lasted 98 days and ended on Feb. 4, 1937, involved 37,000 workers directly and many thousands indirectly. Large strikes also occurred in the leading "independent" steel mills (Bethlehem Steel, Inland Steel, Republic Steel and Youngstown Sheet and Tube). More than 10,000 coal miners struck in support of the steel strike, which failed after lasting from May to July. A strike of 31,000 employees of the silk and rayon industry of New York, New Jersey and Pennsylvania

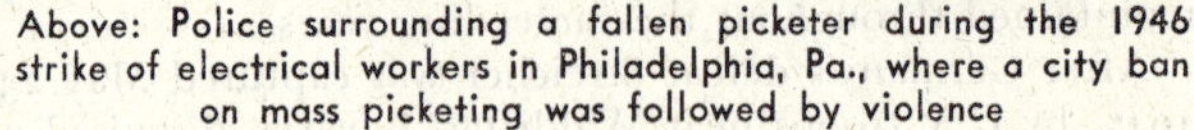

Above: Police surrounding a fallen picketer during the 1946 strike of electrical workers in Philadelphia, Pa., where a city ban on mass picketing was followed by violence

Left: Sewell L. Avery, chairman of the board of directors of Montgomery Ward & Co. being carried from his office by military police after the government took possession of Ward's Chicago, Ill., plant following a labour dispute in April 1944

Below: John L. Lewis, United Mine Workers union leader, photographed at his hotel in Washington, D.C., on Nov. 29, 1946, as he read news accounts of the soft coal strike then in progress

during the summer resulted in union agreements similar to those of the men's and women's clothing industries. Several strikes occurred in the rubber industry at Akron, O.; and a severe strike in the plants of the Remington-Rand company in New York, Ohio and Connecticut. In New York 15,000 shipyard workers were out two months in a strike for union recognition. The many strikes in retail trade, hotels, restaurants and other service industries attracted widespread attention in 1937. They involved relatively small numbers of people compared with the large manufacturing industries, but affected the convenience of the public directly and were new areas of industrial conflict.

During 1938 strikes decreased sharply in number, size and drama. The number was only 58% of 1937; man-days lost only 32%; and people involved 37%.

Only two strikes involved more than 10,000 people—the hosiery strike in Pennsylvania, New Jersey and New York and the truckers' strike in New York and New Jersey.

A quieting-down period was to be expected after the strike wave of 1936–37, and it occurred in 1938. Business recession made the situation unfavourable to labour militancy, while the success of the National Labor Relations act in forcing employers to accept collective bargaining, together with the problems which labour leaders had to face, arising out of the struggles between the A.F. of L. and C.I.O. tended toward a diminution in strikes.

Sit-down strikes were rare in 1938. The "slowdown,"—a tactic not measurable with statistics—continued to be used, but actual seizures of employers' plants had been dropped as a labour tactic. More than half of the strike activity of the year was concentrated in five industries outside the mass production industries—textile and clothing factories, trade, construction, local transportation and food manufactures.

The number of strikes decreased again in 1939. There were 159 fewer than in 1938. But nearly twice as many workers were involved and almost twice as many man-days were lost. The large loss of time was the result of the coal strike in April and May. Except for the coal strike, the disputes of 1939 were widely distributed, both industrially and geographically, and not of major importance. The principal strikes, outside of coal, were in the maritime and automobile industries.

In 1940 the number of workers on strike and of man-days lost dropped to the lowest figures of the decade 1937–46, with the exception of the year 1942. The month-long strike of painters in New York city and the strike of 12,000 Pacific coast lumbermen, which started in December and continued into January, were outstanding in a year of moderate strike activity. There was no marked concentration of strikes in particular industries or areas. Nearly one-half the man-days lost during the year resulted from strikes involving relatively small numbers of employees. In retail trade there were 482,000 man-days lost; in machinery manufacturing 816,237; in lumbering 806,773 and in transportation occupations 593,283.

A.F. of L. unions carried on 62% of the 1940 strikes, and their members constituted 53.5% of the employees on strike. C.I.O. unions called 28% of the strikes and their members were 40% of the people who struck. More of the C.I.O. strikes than of the A.F. of L. were in mass production industries, particularly automobiles, steel, rayon, aluminum, shipbuilding and aircraft. Only 3% of the strikes resulted from the controversies between the A.F. of L. and C.I.O.

In 1941 the number of strikes increased sharply. There were 70% more than in 1940. The new development in 1941 was that government representatives or boards (largely composed of people drawn into public life for the purpose) assisted in settling more than half the strikes ending that year. These disputes involved nearly three-quarters of all the workers and 85% of the strike idleness of 1941. Three plants were seized temporarily by the government on account of labour disputes which interfered too seriously with war production—the North American Aviation company (Englewood, Calif.), Federal Shipbuilding and Dry Dock company (Kearney, N.J.) and Air Associates, Inc. (Bendix, N.J.). The North American Aviation dispute was the first after 1921 to result in intervention by federal armed forces. The strikers resumed work soon after the seizure on June 9. The National Mediation board effected a settlement of the dispute. On July 2, 1941, the plant was returned to private control.

The 3-month International Harvester strike which involved 15,700, the Allis-Chalmers 76-day strike involving 7,800, the strikes of 318,000 coal miners throughout April, the "captive mines" strikes of 58,000 intermittingly in September–October and the dramatic Ford Motor "organization" strike in April illustrate the large-scale strikes which caused more than 23,000,000 man-days to be lost in 1941. The west coast welders' strike involved 12,500 welders from shipyards and metal-working plants. In 1941 the coal miners lost 4.5% of their possible working time by strikes. There was no other industry in which the employees lost so much as 1% of the possible working time. The miners constituted 17% of all the workers who struck during the year and lost 31% of the total man-days lost by all strikes in the nation. Steel had 10% of the strikers and construction 8%. The number of strikes had been exceeded previously only in 1937 and 1917, and the number of strikers exceeded only in 1919. One-twelfth of the nation's industrial workers were involved at some time during the year.

War and Decline.—Pearl Harbor quickly arrested the epidemic of strikes, and several important ones were called off. In other cases where affirmative votes had been taken the strike was cancelled. Labour organizations pledged their full support to the war effort.

New York city was the "strike-capital" of the nation as far as urban industries were concerned. It had more strikes and more strike idleness than any other city. The other urban areas most affected were Philadelphia, Detroit, Dearborn, Los Angeles, Cleveland and Chicago. The largest was at Ford's River Rouge plant, with 85,000 men out. The A.F. of L. called 54% of the strikes, but the C.I.O., with but 37% of the strikes, called out 70% of the strikers.

Table II.—*United States: Principal Issues Involved in All Strikes and Lock-outs for Years 1937–45**

	1937	1938	1939	1940	1941	1942	1943	1944	1945
All Issues (*Totals*)	4,720	2,772	2,639	2,493	4,314	3,036	3,734	4,958	4,616
Wages and hours	1,410	776	699	753	1,535	1,423	1,906	2,146	1,956
Union organization and security (*recognition, closed shop, discrimination, etc.*)	2,728	1,385	1,411	1,243	2,138	943	585	808	946
Working conditions (*job security, shop policies, etc.*)	**	**	**	**	**	497	1,094	1,800	1,510
Interunion and intraunion matters (*rival unions and factions, jurisdiction, sympathy*)	210	175	204	187	316	173	148	203	188
Other	372	436	325	310	325	—	1	1	16

*Compiled from information supplied by *Monthly Labor Review*, U.S. Bureau of Labor Statistics.
**Not tabulated as separate item for this year.

The year 1942 saw another sharp drop in strikes. Labour and industry concentrated on getting out war materials. Overtime made earnings high, and the cost of living had not yet gone up sharply. Labour leadership and industrial leadership both indicated that every effort would be made to maintain industrial peace. The government's wage and price stabilization program promised to prevent strikes caused by rising costs of living. Hope ran high throughout the country that the government agencies set up to adjust labour disputes and protect the interests of wage earners during the war would prove adequate to prevent strikes detrimental to the war program.

Strikes dropped from 4,288 in 1941 to 2,968 in 1942, the number of strikers from 2,362,620 to 839,961 and man-days lost from 23,047,556 to 4,182,557—the lowest figure for the decade 1937–46. With industrial production 16% greater than in 1941, the cost of living up 1% and employment up 7%, strikes were fewer, smaller and of shorter duration. And, of the strikes which occurred, a considerable number were not authorized by unions but originated among the local rank and file. But 46% of all the strikes which did occur and 68% of the employees involved were in industries directly related to the war effort. In mining 515,000 man-days were lost; in textile products 463,700 days; in iron and steel 270,000 days; and in leather manufacture 241,000 days. Of the strikes 72% were concentrated in such leading industrial states as New York, Pennsylvania, Massachusetts, New Jersey, Ohio, Indiana, Illinois and California. Government agencies assisted in settling 1,880 of the strikes; 1,408 through conciliation; 121 by arbitration and 349 through formal hearing by the War Labor board. In two cases, the Toledo, Peoria and Western railroad and the General Cable company of Bayonne, N.J., government seizure occurred. In the railroad case the company refused to obey an award of the War Labor board and in the cable company case there was an unauthorized strike against the decision of the War Labor board.

In 1943, with the war at peak intensity, the number of strikes increased substantially. There were 784 more strikes than in 1942, nearly twice as many strikers and more than 3 times as much loss of working time.

"Ladies and Gentlemen—the Winnah." Ross Lewis' cartoon appeared in the *Milwaukee Journal* shortly after John L. Lewis called a strike of the United Mine Workers on April 30, 1943

Coal was again the major area of conflict. The 2-year agreement negotiated in 1941 expired, and the coal miners demanded a $2-a-day increase in wages, 6 days' work per week, portal-to-portal pay, double-time for Sunday work and other substantial gains. On April 29 the president ordered all strikers back to work on pain of government seizure of the mines. Instead of complying, 325,000 bituminous and 75,000 anthracite miners quit work on May 1.

The government seized the mines the same day. On May 4, 1943, full production was resumed, with management operating the mines for the government. On May 25 the War Labor board denied most of the miners' demands but increased their vacation pay and required the operators to pay for tools and other miners' equipment.

The miners rejected the board's decision and struck again on June 1, and the president again ordered them back to work. On June 7 the union officers ordered them back until June 30. The War Labor board reaffirmed its May 25 decision, and the miners struck a third time. On June 23 the union's officers again ordered the men back to work but the miners were slow to return. About 6,000,000 man-days were lost in the series of stoppages. The miners lost an average of 19.75 days; strikers in other industries lost an average of 5 days. Their strikes decreased the year's coal output by 21,750,000 tons of bituminous and 3,500,000 tons of anthracite.

The average duration of strikes dropped steadily from 1939 through 1943. In 1939 it was 23 days; 1940, 21 days; 1941, 18 days; 1942, 12 days; and 1943, 5 days.

Many of the 1943 strikes were spontaneous stoppages, and more than one-half were for wage increases, registering the widespread dissatisfaction of labour with the government's wartime wage stabilization policy.

Passage of the War Labor Disputes act by congress in June, largely as a result of the coal strike, made illegal strikes which interfered with war production until after a 30-day notice had been filed with the government and a formal strike vote had been taken under government supervision. In 117 strike ballots under government supervision during the latter part of 1943, 102 strikes were voted but only 34 actually occurred.

The relative importance of strikes in different industrial areas during 1943 is revealed by the figures on man-days lost as follows:

Mining (mostly coal)	9,370,000 days lost
Iron and steel	726,000
Automobile factories	441,000
Other transportation equipment	382,000
Textiles	306,000
Construction	140,827
Trade	90,711

The strike pattern of 1944 was different from that of 1943. Two-thirds of the strikes occurred in manufacturing, with mining second in importance. In manufactures 6,148,117 man-days were lost in 3,257 strikes; in mining 1,412,634 days in 893 strikes. The strike area was again concentrated geographically. In Michigan 39% of the industrial workers struck at some time during the year; in Pennsylvania 13%; West Virginia 12% and Illinois 7%.

There were 16 strikes involving 10,000 people or more, as compared with 10 in 1943. The Detroit strike of 54,800 foremen attracted particular attention. It was the first large strike of foremen in U.S. history. Discontent over wages, lack of formal grievance procedures and discipline were the principal causes. The strike evidenced that foremen were not nearly so "management-minded" as management had believed. There were at least 30 foremen's strikes in 1944, involving 130,000 supervisors and 650,000 man-days lost.

Wages were the most important issue in the strikes of rank and file employees but involved much more than demands for "over-the-board" wages increases. Disputes over incentive systems, overtime, vacation pay and shift premiums were especially common. Working conditions and shop labour relations policies were next in importance. These included disputes over discipline, job assignments, job security, work loads, work schedules, shift arrangements and safety conditions. Union security, including union recognition, efforts to get a closed shop, expansion of the rights of union representatives and reforms in grievance procedure were a part of the causes of many major disputes.

Cut-backs in war production contributed to the causes of 35 strikes in 1944—forerunners of what was to come in 1945 and 1946. Loss of overtime pay, transfers to lower-rated jobs and the application of seniority provisions were typical factors in "cut-back strikes."

In 1944 more than one-third of the strikes were terminated by straight collective bargaining. These 1,653 strikes involved 488,827 workers. Government agencies assisted in the settlements of 2,942. In 2,373 some or all of the issues had to be negotiated further after the strikers returned to work. In 822 of these cases the issues were referred back to the parties for negotiation; in 147 they were submitted by the parties to private arbitrators; and in 1,404 they were discussed further with government conciliators or boards. In 347 no settlement was reached during the year.

In 1945 there were 4,750 strikes and more strikers than in any other year after 1919; 10,000,000 more man-days were lost than in any other year after such figures had begun to be compiled in 1927. The previous peak was 1937.

Coal was again the most important strike area, with 670 strikes, 678,000 strikers and 6,234,000 man-days lost. The automobile industry had the worst experience of any manufacturing group—185 strikes, 473,700 strikers and 7,308,000 man-days lost. The rubber industry had 123 strikes, 248,000 strikers and 1,521,000 man-days lost. Iron and steel had 817 strikes, 425,000 strikers and 3,731,000 man-days lost; while textiles had 187 strikes, 107,400 strikers and 1,456,000 man-days lost. This group of 4 closely related industries lost more than 14,000,000 man-days, an unprecedented occurrence in U.S. manufacturing. There were 342 transportation strikes, 157,000 strikers and 1,551,000 man-days lost.

Pennsylvania's and Michigan's industries each lost more than 6,000,000 man-days; Ohio's more than 3,000,000; and California's and Illinois's above 2,500,000 man-days. Whether examined industrially or geographically, the strike picture in 1945 was one of concentration of a major part of the strike activity in basic industries and major industrial states.

Half the strikes involved basic wages and hours but were generally complicated by union efforts to obtain actual or virtual closed shop situations. "Fringe issues," such as holiday and vacation pay, changes in the administration of incentive wage systems and payment for travel time, were of increased importance—a trend which began in 1943. The fringe issues were responsible in 1945 for a larger percentage of workers being idle and man-days lost than were demands for straight wage increases. In 1942, 6% of total man-days lost were on account of fringe issues; in 1945, 22.8%.

Efforts to obtain collective bargaining rights for supervisory workers also increased in importance. They were a major feature of the organization drive in 1945.

The number of strike ballots conducted by the National Labor Relations board increased to 1,445; and in 1,249 such ballotings the employees voted to call strikes—an enormous increase over that of the previous year. But only 213 strikes followed such ballots. They accounted for 15,015,000 man-days lost—39.7% of all strike idleness in 1945. Wages were an issue in three-quarters of these strikes. The postwar wage conflict was getting under way.

In the automobile and tire industries 17 strikes each involved more than 10,000 strikers. The largest, which included employees of Chrysler, Ford, Packard and Budd Wheel company, involved a jurisdictional dispute between U.A.W. (C.I.O.) and A.F. of L. building trades over reconversion of buildings. In this strike 47,000 were out. Chrysler had 16,000 men out in February in a dispute over production standards.

Briggs, A.C. Spark Plug, Hudson, Goodyear Tire and Rubber company, General Motors and Wright Aeronautical company all had important disputes over discipline and/or alleged discriminatory suspensions or discharges. The mine workers had 164,000 men out in portal-to-portal pay disputes. Libbey-Owens and Pittsburgh Plate Glass had 16,000 men out in 5 states over incentive pay; and Goodrich Tire and Rubber company had 21,000 employees on strike in an effort to force union participation in setting up wage rates, awarding wage increases and revision of the merit system. Chrysler corporation had 19,000 out on a demand for clean-up time. Eleven major strikes were for "over-the-board" wage increases. Textile mills in 5 eastern states had 16,000 out in November for a closed shop, increased wages and vacations after a strike in September for wage increases. The foremen's union at B. F. Goodrich called out 14,000 foremen in September because of some lay-offs. The diversity of issues, and particularly the increased variety of issues as compared with the period before 1937, was apparent in these important strikes.

First Postwar Year.—During the first 11 months of 1946 there were 4,335 strikes, involving 4,545,000 workers and loss of 107,475,000 man-days, more than 9 times the loss of time in the corresponding 11 months of 1945 and nearly 13 times the corresponding man-day loss of 1944. The strike epidemic continued into December with the coal strike and other major strikes in full swing when December began. The maritime strike of September, the stubborn Allis-Chalmers strike (which had continued, by Dec. 31, for more than 8 months), the coal strike and the New York trucking strike were the outstanding disputes in the latter part of the year. Overshadowing all others was the coal strike in which the federal government hailed John L. Lewis, president of the United Mine Workers, into court in contempt proceedings on Nov. 27 and obtained a judgment of $10,000 fine against Lewis and $3,500,000 fine against the union.

The miners were ordered back to work by Lewis shortly after the fines were imposed, and the U.S. supreme court took immediate jurisdiction over the case to decide the legality of the action of the lower court. The supreme court on March 6, 1947, upheld judgment against Lewis and the union, but reduced the latter's fine to $700,000.

The wave of important strikes in the early part of 1946 had subsided by August. In February 21,500,000 man-days were lost; in August only 1,712,000. Then came the maritime strike in September, the Trans World Airline (T.W.A.) pilot strike, bus strikes, the Pittsburgh public utility strike and the coal strike.

Armed guard watching U.S. soldiers board a Philadelphia streetcar as the army took over the Philadelphia Transportation company in Aug. 1944. The strike, involving 6,000 workers, paralyzed transportation in the city from Aug. 1–6

Measured in terms of workers involved and resulting idleness, work stoppages in Jan. 1946 exceeded any previous month in the nation's history. About 500 strikes were in progress, the largest being the strike at General Motors which started on Nov. 21, 1945, and the strikes involving the electrical manufacturing and meat-packing industries. These three accounted for about three-fourths of the strikers and of total strike idleness in January.

Wages, and their relationship to prices and profits, were the most important issues in these and many other labour disputes.

On Jan. 21, 1946, another major strike broke out, the largest on record. The steel industry was shut down by a walk-out of 750,000 members of the United Steel Workers of America (C.I.O.). They demanded a wage increase of $2 per day. More than 1,200 iron, steel and aluminum plants were directly involved. An agreement between the union and U.S. Steel was reached on Feb. 15, with an 18.5 cents per hour wage increase, with a price increase of $5 per ton allowed by the government. By Feb. 19, 450,000 steel workers had returned to work; the remainder awaited clarification of the government's wage-price policy. Approximately 200,000 electrical workers struck at 75 plants on Jan. 17—also for a $2-a-day increase. General Electric, Westinghouse and the electrical division of General Motors were involved. General Motors settled for 18½ cents an hour on February 9. The General Electric strike was settled on March 18 for the same wage increase plus some inter-occupational adjustments of inequalities, an improved vacation plan and a more satisfactory overtime pay plan. The Westinghouse strike (75,000) continued through March.

The Allis-Chalmers strike, which began on April 28 at the Milwaukee plant, and at dates close to April 28 in six other of the company's plants, was still going at Milwaukee at the end of the year, though it had terminated at other of the works. It involved wages only as a secondary issue. The company refused demands for a closed shop, freedom of union representatives to move about in the shops without control by foremen, submission of wage issues to a referee and modifications in grievance procedure and discipline desired by the union.

A series of strikes in the maritime industry virtually paralyzed all shipping in the east, west and gulf states during most of September. The disputes started in protest against a refusal by the National Wage Stabilization board to approve negotiated wage increases for two A.F. of L. maritime unions which exceeded the $17.50 per month the board had approved on June 14 for the National Maritime union (C.I.O.) and several other unions. The decision applied only to government-owned vessels. Between Sept. 5 and 7 all major ports on three coasts became strikebound. As one union after another became involved, these issues became more complicated. The A.F. of L. and C.I.O. were both alert to secure any benefits obtained by the other federation, and the employers were caught in a situation where they had to bargain separately with powerful unions from both federations and then, perhaps, to yield to each set of unions all the gains each had obtained itself plus all that its rivals had obtained. On Sept. 30, after settlement had finally been reached in the disputes involving the seamen, firemen, oilers, water-tenders, cooks and stewards, the masters, mates and pilots (A.F. of L.), and National Marine Engineers (C.I.O.) went out.

A maritime strike on the Great Lakes in August made 5,000 seamen idle for a week. It followed several months of negotiations and it caused a serious disruption of the commerce of the Great Lakes region.

On May 23, 1946, the first widespread strike of the operating brotherhoods on the railroads after 1888 occurred and for two days the nation's railroad system was tied up. The strike was the final chapter in a series of three threatened strikes over wages in 1941, 1943 and 1945. Under pressure of a strike threat the railroad-operating brotherhoods had obtained a 9½ cents per hour increase, and nonoperating occupations 10 cents in 1941. Early in 1943 the operating brotherhoods demanded a 30% increase, and after months of controversy a strike was set for Dec. 30. The railroads were seized by the government on Dec. 27, and on Jan. 17, 1944, both nonoperating and operating occupations got another increase. In 1945, 20 unions (nonoperating and operating) served notice of further demands, and a 16-cent increase on April 3, 1946, brought them up to the full 33% increase allowable under the cost-of-living formula in an executive order of Feb. 14, 1946. On May 23, 1946, the brotherhoods struck for further wage increases. The roads had again been taken over by the government on May 17 as a precaution against the impending strike. But the strike occurred anyway. After two days it was called off, and the issues were submitted to further negotiation between the government, the railroads and the brotherhoods.

The ten-day strike at the R. H. Macy & Co. stores in July of 1946 had unusual causes. It was precipitated by transfer of their delivery service, together with their drivers and helpers, to the United Parcel Service, Inc. The Macy employees were members of a C.I.O. union of wholesale and department store employees, while United Parcel had a closed-shop contract with the A.F. of L. teamsters. The C.I.O. union claimed that the transfer was a violation of its agreement with Macy's. The dispute was settled when Macy's agreed to extend to the transferred deliverymen benefits which accrued to the store employees under the C.I.O. agreement, as well as any general wage increases given to the store employees during the life of the existing agreement. These included such matters as vacations, pension rights, severance pay and overtime and other wage benefits which might exceed the terms of the A.F. of L. agreement. The transferred deliverymen were also given a separate seniority roster. With these securities guaranteed, the C.I.O. deliverymen then joined the A.F. of L. teamsters en masse and a ten-man joint A.F. of L.-C.I.O. council was set up to consider the common problems of the two groups of deliverymen.

The complexity of the patterns of strike issues from 1943 to 1946 indicated that a new era had arrived in collective bargaining; one in which unions sought to negotiate on everything touching the interests of employees and were willing to resort to strikes on matters formerly left to management to decide.

Strikes in Great Britain.—It is apparent from Table III that Great Britain did not experience a strike epidemic comparable with that of the United States. From 1938 through 1942 British labour unions kept strikes at a minimum and concentrated on war production. From 1943 onward the number of strikes and strikers increased, but only in 1944 was there strike activity approximating that of 1937.

The loss of man-days, 1938–43, was at the average annual rate of 1,341,000 days—only 38.2% of the 1937 man-day loss and 36.2% of the 1944 loss. The first eight months of 1946 indicated that the strike record for the year would approximate the 1945 record.

Table III.—*Great Britain: Number of Strikes, Number of Strikers and Man-Days Lost, 1937–46 (8 months)*

Year	Number of strikes, beginning in year or month	Number of workers made idle by the strikes beginning during year	Number of man-days lost in all stoppages in progress during year
1937	1,129	597,000	3,410,000
1938	875	274,000	1,330,000
1939	940	337,000	1,360,000
1940	922	299,000	940,000
1941	1,251	360,000	1,080,000
1942	1,303	457,000	1,530,000
1943	1,785	557,000	1,810,000
1944	2,194	821,000	3,710,000
1945	2,293	531,000	2,840,000
1946 (8 mo.)	1,498	369,800	1,496,000

The industrial distribution of strikes followed a fairly consistent pattern. Coal mining, engineering, the iron and steel industry, transportation and shipbuilding were the major areas of industrial conflict.

The long-established procedures for government mediation and arbitration of labour disputes caused the stoppages to be terminated more quickly than in the United States, even when final decision of the issues was not achieved at once.

The industrial distribution of the labour disputes of 1943, 1944, 1945, is shown in Table IV. The industrial distribution of strikes in earlier years was closely similar, the principal difference between years being in the degree of strike activity in coal, engineering, dock work and shipbuilding.

The only large strikes in 1937 were in the Yorkshire coal industry, where 400,000 man-days were lost by 95,000 miners; and 2 strikes of engineering and shipbuilding apprentices involving 10,000 and 14,000 apprentices and causing a loss of 370,000 man-days. Thirty thousand engineers and shipbuilders struck for one day in moral support of the apprentices.

In 1938–43 the only major disputes were 2 coal strikes in 1940, involving 20,000 and 26,000 miners; and in 1943, extensive strikes in coal and engineering. In 1944, 170,000 miners in 7 areas went out because an arbitration tribunal rejected their demand for increased piece rates. They lost 850,000 man-days.

The engineering, metal and shipbuilding trades lost a quarter of the total number of days lost in 1944. Their disputes started with demands for wage increases, and then spread "in protest against the prosecution and imprisonment of certain shop stewards for their participation in the strike of aircraft workers," a total of 400,000 man-days lost.

The strike tempo picked up sharply in 1945. Disputes in the transport industries caused more than one-half of the total man-days lost during the year. In March 55,000 days were lost by dock workers in a dispute over a new method of checking in when they came to work and over other disciplinary matters. The dock workers lost another 1,100,000 man-days in disputes over increases in wages, shorter hours and working conditions demands. In late September and much of October longshore work was stopped in many of the important ports.

Table IV.—*Great Britain: Industrial Distribution of Labour Disputes, 1943–45*

Industry	1943 Number Stoppages	1943 Number Workers Involved*	1943 Man-Days Lost	1944 Number Stoppages	1944 Number Workers Involved*	1944 Man-Days Lost	1945 Number Stoppages	1945 Number Workers Involved*	1945 Man-Days Lost
Fishing and agriculture . . .	—	—	—	8	700	2,000	4	2,600	12,000
Coal mining. . . .	843	294,000	89,000	1,253	568,000	2,480,000	1,306	243,000	641,000
Other mining, quarrying. . . .	19	1,700	3,000	22	3,400	13,000	13	900	3,000
Brick, pottery, glass, chemical	30	1,600	4,000	22	1,600	4,000	27	4,400	26,000
Engineering . . .	288	121,000	437,000	261	130,000	600,000	235	76,100	317,000
Shipbuilding . . .	196	32,000	137,000	199	44,000	370,000	186	28,400	143,000
Iron, steel, other metals	128	18,200	61,000	150	23,000	78,000	170	19,400	68,000
Textiles	52	6,100	17,000	48	6,600	46,000	41	4,000	10,000
Clothing	23	3,100	7,000	30	2,800	5,000	29	9,000	68,000
Food, drink, tobacco	17	8,800	27,000	8	900	3,000	9	1,800	9,000
Woodworking, furniture	4	600	1,000	10	1,200	2,000	17	1,600	4,000
Building, public works . .	71	13,200	25,000	48	5,100	7,000	36	3,200	5,000
Transport.	68	53,500	180,000	82	32,000	85,000	156	127,900	1,491,000
Gas, water and elec. supply. . .	—	—	—	5	700	2,000	5	1,600	4,000
Public administration	—	—	—	5	200	1,000	8	1,500	5,000
Commerce, distribution and finance.	8	500	1,000	10	600	1,000	9	600	3,000
Other	38	4,700	20,000	33	5,200	11,000	42	6,200	26,000
TOTALS . . .	1,785	559,000	1,810,000	2,194	826,000	3,710,000	2,293	532,200	2,835,000

*Some workers, chiefly in the coal mining industry, were involved in more than one stoppage, and therefore have been counted more than once in the year's total.

Compiled from tabulations appearing in *Ministry of Labour Gazette:* London.

In May more than 6,000 London street railway and bus operatives struck against new time schedules, and in July 6,500 more were idle in other areas for the same reason. In aircraft manufacturing there were strikes over piece rates and output bonuses.

In coal there was only one large dispute, in which 16,000 miners lost 180,000 man-days over wage demands.

Canada.—Strike activity was moderate in Canada except in the years 1937, 1943, 1945 and 1946 (Table V). The strike pattern of Canada in 1945–46 was similar to that of the United States and was undoubtedly influenced by the U.S. situation. Many of the important industries of Canada continued to be related through ownership to U.S. industries, and many important unions were also integral parts of U.S. international unions. The sharp increase in the number of man-days lost, in spite of a smaller number of strikes in 1945–46, was a noticeable feature of the Canadian strike history of those years. From the middle of 1945 through 1946 there were widespread, large and often prolonged strikes in the automobile, rubber, electrical, metals manufacturing, chemical, metal and coal mining and textile industries.

Table V.—*Canada: Number of Labour Disputes, Workers Made Idle and Man-Days Lost, 1937–46*

Year	Number of disputes	Number workers made idle	Number of man-days lost
1937	278	71,905	886,393
1938	147	20,395	148,678
1939	122	41,038	224,588
1940	168	60,619	266,318
1941	231	87,091	433,914
1942	354	113,916	450,202
1943	402	218,404	1,041,198
1944	199	75,290	490,139
1945	197	96,068	1,457,420
1946 (9 months)	178	126,436	4,069,434

The Ford strike, Sept. 12–Dec. 20, 1945, was finally arbitrated by a judge of the supreme court who denied the union an all-union shop but granted a compulsory check-off from the pay of all employes, whether members of the union or not.

The issues were identical with those being pressed in the larger strikes in the United States—increased wages, shorter hours, closed shop, seniority rules, check-off, liberal vacation plans, payment for legal holidays, resistance to discipline and protests against government wage policies. (*See also* Business Review; Labour Unions; Law; National Labor Relations Board.) (D. D. L.)

Stritch, Samuel Alphonsus

Cardinal Stritch (1887–), U.S. Catholic prelate, was born Aug. 17, 1887, in Nashville, Tenn. Ordained to the priesthood in Rome in 1910, he became chancellor of the Nashville diocese in 1913. Upon his appointment in 1921 as bishop of Toledo, he became the youngest member of the Catholic hierarchy in the U.S. Nine years later, he was appointed archbishop of Milwaukee and in 1939, he headed the archdiocese in Chicago, succeeding to this office after the death of George Cardinal Mundelein. During World War II, Stritch was active in organizing relief for war victims and directed a national campaign for shipment of canned foods to Europe and Asia. He was also chairman of the Bishops' War Emergency and Relief committee and supervised distribution of the large sums raised for relief purposes by U.S. Catholics. One of the archbishop's tenets was to distribute the food to all the needy "regardless of creed or political belief."

In his views on foreign affairs, he was a confirmed internationalist and he signed an inter-faith statement calling for international organization with economic and social controls. Under his direction, the archdiocese charity program expanded. He was elected chairman of the administrative board of the National Catholic Welfare conference in Nov. 1945. Msgr. Stritch, whose nomination to the Sacred College of Cardinals was announced Dec. 23, 1945, was created cardinal at the consistory of Feb. 18, 1946.

Strontium

The demand for strontium during the decade 1937–46 continued to be satisfied mainly by celestite, the sulphate. While pyrotechnics, tracer bullets and flares accounted for some of the increase in demand during World War II, a good share of the expansion was caused not by the need for strontium, but for a substitute for barite in oil well drilling mud. Beginning with 1940, the first year of production since 1918, the United States supply was as follows in short tons:

	Shipments	Imports
1940	350	2,751
1941	4,724	4,294
1942	4,041	10,387
1943	7,566	16,881
1944	3,005	5,793
1945	2,784	3,691

Previous to 1940, the imports of celestite were supplemented by the importation of 200–350 tons of strontium chemicals from Germany. Demand for war uses reached a peak in 1943, with the consumption of 13,387 tons in the production of strontium chemicals. (G. A. Ro.)

Subasitch, Ivan

Subasitch (1890–), Yugoslav politician, was born at Velika Gorica, near Zagreb. A graduate of the University of Zagreb, he received a doctor of law degree. Drafted into the Austro-Hungarian army during World War I, he was taken prisoner on the Russian front and later joined Serb forces fighting the Russians. After the collapse of the tsarist armies in 1917, he was sent to the Salonika front.

Subasitch joined the Croat Peasant party after the war; when Croatia was granted autonomy Subasitch became *ban* (governor) of Croatia in 1939, a post he held until the German invasion in 1941. After the collapse of the Yugoslav armies he fled to the United States and maintained residence in New York city, N.Y. Subasitch returned to Europe in May 1944 and the following month was asked by King Peter II to form a government. After conferring with Marshal Tito and reaching agreement on points of dispute, Subasitch formed a government July 7, 1944. In Nov. 1944 he conferred with Joseph Stalin in Moscow on the problems involved in establishing a policy that would prove satisfactory to both Great Britain and the soviet union.

On March 7, 1945, Tito completed his new cabinet and appointed Subasitch as foreign minister. But Subasitch quit the Tito government on Oct. 8, 1945, for "reasons of health." Unofficially, he was said to have resigned after a dispute with Tito over "undemocratic" electoral laws.

Submarine Warfare

The submarine played a paradoxical role during World War II—it was either saint or sinner, depending not on its deeds or misdeeds but on the flag it flew. In the Atlantic, the German submarines were stigmatized as the rattlesnakes of the deep—the one great menace that must be wiped out if the Allied cause were to succeed. Concurrently, the United States submarines in the Pacific and the British submarines in the Mediterranean, conducting a similar type of warfare, were hailed as the defenders of democracy. The German analyst could undoubtedly interchange the above designations with commensurate logic. The fact is that the submarines constituted a powerful offensive weapon, exploited by both the axis and the Allies with equal disregard for the prewar rules for submarine employment under international law. The Allies might rightfully argue that the Germans started the game and established the rules, and to justify this argument it is necessary to review briefly the status of undersea warfare at the outbreak of World War II.

The Battle of the Atlantic

It was the original intent of the Germans to limit the war to Poland by not inflaming the British or French people. Adolf Hitler hoped that, in spite of their declaration of war, Great Britain and France would accept the conquest of Poland as a *fait accompli* and that a major conflict could be avoided. Accordingly, to the U-boats at sea on Sept. 3, 1939, the German naval staff passed detailed orders for the conduct of the war. Merchant ships were to be attacked only in accordance with the rules of international law. Over and above this, Hitler expressly forbade attacking or stopping any passenger ship, or any ships of French nationality. Despite these orders an over-eager U-boat captain sank the "Athenia" less than nine hours after declaration of war. The reaction to the sinking was immediate—it was only a matter of days before Great Britain began to arm its merchant vessels, and hasty preparations were made for the resumption of all U-boat defenses which the Allies had used during World War I. When these steps became evident, Germany, during the latter part of September, declared its intention of sinking all British ships without warning.

Germany had neither desired nor prepared to wage unrestricted submarine warfare. When Hitler came into power in 1933, he did not consider any of the great naval powers to be among the future opponents of Germany and

U-Boat construction yards, including those at Hamburg, Emden, Kiel and Bremen, were major objectives of the R.A.F. and U.S.A.A.F. during World War II. This picture, bearing the stamp of an official German photographer (lower right), shows a submarine destroyed while under construction at Bremen

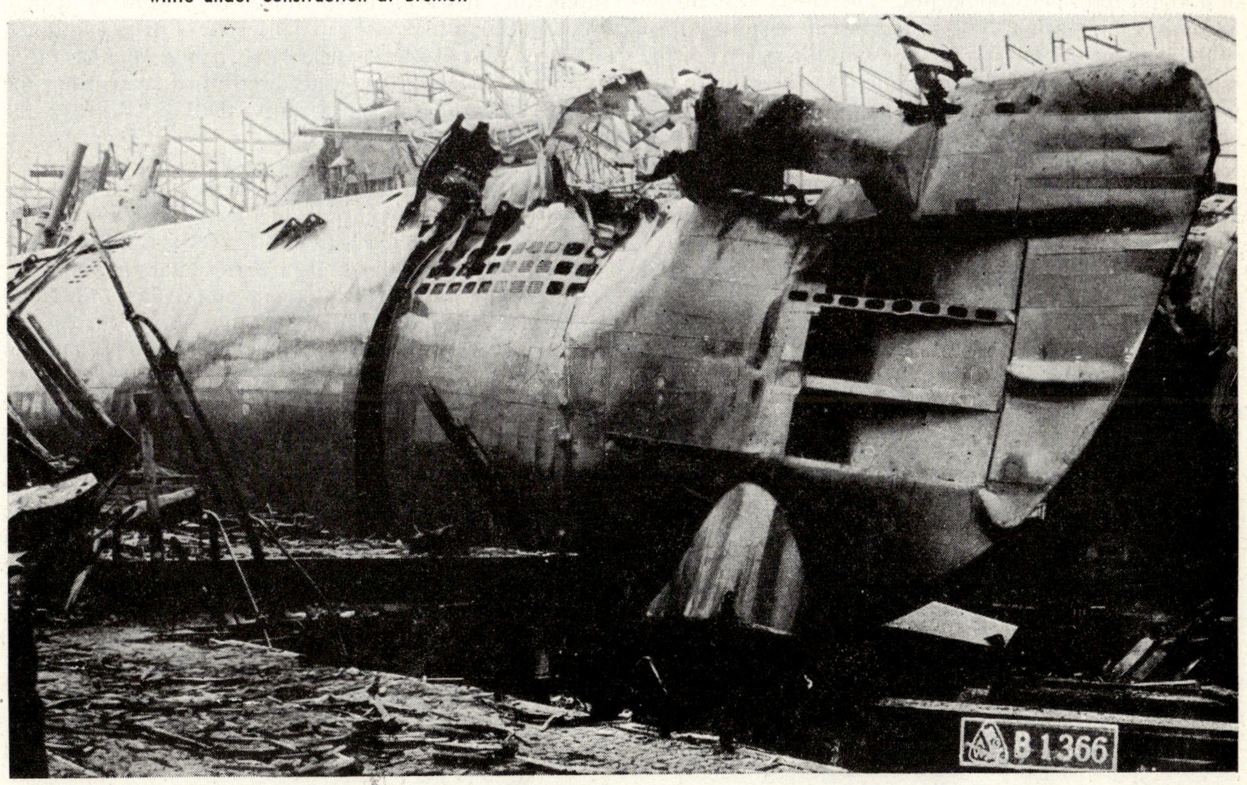

consequently he emphasized the building up of the wehrmacht and the air force. The naval service was not considered to be on a par with these other branches and had little or no influence in matters of high policy. It was Hitler's intention to create a small homogeneous fleet capable of matching the naval power of the U.S.S.R. or France, and no real effort was made to build up a large U-boat arm. Admiral Karl Doenitz, the German submarine expert, did strive for technical developments and added emphasis on submarines but was largely overruled, he then being of only captain's rank. As a result of this policy, the German navy at the outbreak of World War II consisted of the following units, in commission or nearing completion in the building yards: 4 battleships—"Scharnhorst," "Gneisenau," "Bismarck" and "Tirpitz"; 2 pocket battleships—"Scheer" and "Graf Spee"; 2 aircraft carriers—"Graf Zeppelin" and "B"; 5 heavy cruisers—"Hipper," "Bleucher," "Prinz Eugen," "Luetzaw" and "Seydlitz"; 30 destroyers; 76 submarines.

The submarines were of three general types:

	Type IX C	*Type VII C*	*Type II*
Surface displacement .	740 tons	500 tons	250 tons
Cruising radius (at 10 knots)	7,000 miles	6,000 miles	5,000 miles
Maximum submerged speed	8 knots	8 knots	7 knots
Maximum surface speed	18 knots	16 knots	13 knots
Armament	6 torpedo tubes 1 4 in. gun 2 AA machine guns	5 torpedo tubes 1 3.5 in. gun. 1 AA machine gun	3 torpedo tubes 1 AA machine gun

With the decision to conduct unrestricted submarine warfare the Germans hastened to apply the techniques and operating methods they had developed in World War I. The plan for building a homogeneous fleet was drastically changed, and an increased U-boat construction program was ordered, concentrating on the 740-ton and 500-ton types. Whereas previously the monthly output had been 2 or 3 U-boats, the new construction was expected to bring production to 25 monthly within two years.

Initially the Germans concentrated their submarines in the vicinity of the British Isles, making attacks submerged in daylight from periscope depth. The tactics were highly aggressive, and each U-boat scored heavily against Allied shipping. One of the early successes was the sinking of the aircraft carrier, H.M.S. "Courageous," in the western approaches of the Atlantic on Sept. 17, 1939. The "Courageous" had been operating with British antisubmarine forces. Following this success the U-boat command determined on a bold plan of attack against ships in harbours and close in to the coast line. The plan included submarine operations in Scapa Flow, Moray Firth, the Firth of Forth, the Shetland passages, Loch Eue, Liverpool and the Bristol channel.

For the operation against Scapa Flow, an air reconnaissance was conducted, and detailed plans for the penetration of the harbour were prepared. The mission was entrusted to one of the most able submarine commanders, Kapitan-Lieutenant Gunther Prien of U-47. In mid-October U-47 successfully penetrated the anchorage and sank the British battleship "Royal Oak." Torpedo failures denied Prien further successes against the anchored British fleet in this bold and brilliantly executed performance. In the operations against the Firth of Forth, the cruiser "Belfast" was torpedoed and damaged; at Loch Eue, the battleship "Nelson" was similarly damaged. The other planned operations were abandoned after several fruitless attempts.

During the first ten months of World War II, the average number of U-boats at sea in the Atlantic was 6; the average number of ships sunk monthly by them was 26, totalling about 106,000 tons. The principal factor in keeping Allied shipping losses low was the prompt institution of the convoy system and the rapid organization of all available antisubmarine forces into an antisubmarine warfare command.

By the conquest of the Netherlands, Belgium and France in May and June 1940, Germany gained a strategical naval position of great importance, and conditions became particularly favourable for the employment of submarines. The possession of the Bay of Biscay ports eliminated the long journeys to and from the hunting areas which had taken up much of the cruising radius of the U-boats. The sea routes were at the front door of the U-boat command, resulting in almost doubling the number of submarines that could be maintained on patrol stations.

By the fall of 1940, the danger of invasion of England had passed, and the British navy intensified its antisubmarine measures, while the royal air force was used on an increasing scale for guarding shipping routes. It became increasingly difficult for the U-boats to operate close into shore, and convoys were located less frequently. To counter these Allied defenses, the U-boat command instituted a method of group control of U-boats which permitted wide dispersion of the submarines for search, and heavy concentration for attacks. These so-called "wolf-pack" tactics were developed in the certain knowledge that location of the Allied convoys would be the greatest problem. Once a convoy was located, headquarters would direct the assembly and mass attacks of the submarines. Coupled with the wolf-pack tactics the Germans began their night surface attacks against Allied shipping. At night, trimmed down to decks awash, the submarine offered a very small silhouette to the human eye and was very difficult to detect by either radar or sonar. Having made its attack, the submarine would use its high surface speed to escape the convoy escorts, and diving was resorted to only in an extremity.

As a result of the new building program, coupled with the capture of the Biscay ports, the number of German submarines at sea increased from 6 in 1939 to 36 in mid-1941, and to as high as 93 in Jan. 1942, with 40 additional submarines available for operations in the Mediterranean and in the Barents sea, which were used for cutting the Allied supply lines to Libya and to the U.S.S.R. After the entry of the United States into the war in Dec. 1941, it was natural for the U-boats to head westward to search for weak spots in the Allied defenses. In their initial raids, the U-boats inflicted heavy losses in the areas off the eastern seaboard of the United States.

The first ten months of 1942 were by far the most successful of the war for the German submarines. The total world-wide losses suffered by the Allies during that period amounted to 878 ships of 4,587,000 gross tons. The main U-boat battle was fought in the Atlantic, where about 90% of the losses occurred. However, in this same period the Germans lost 78 submarines to the ever-increasing efficiency of the Allied antisubmarine forces. While the Germans could replace their submarine losses, they could not replace their experienced crews, and the effectiveness of the individual submarine decreased. The Germans then changed the locale of their concentrated attacks to the gap in the northwest Atlantic, where the U-boats could operate against the vital transatlantic convoys in a region beyond the range of Allied air cover. It was in these areas that the crucial war of the Atlantic was fought, and eventually won by the Allies through the employment of hunter-killer groups of escort carriers accompanied by a number of destroyer escorts. The carriers' planes would hunt and seek out the U-boats and vector the destroyer escorts into position to administer the *coup de grace.*

Between Oct. 1942 and June 1943, 112 U-boats were sunk in the Atlantic and 37 in the Mediterranean, with aircraft accounting for 76 of the total. Coupled with the severe losses, the expansion program for the U-boat fleet began to slow down as the Allied air forces' bombing began to take effect. The bombings of the construction yards and the U-boat pens seriously restricted new construction. But even so, the U-boat menace to the Allies continued as a major threat, for the Germans still had about 400 submarines in commission in mid-1943.

By late 1943, the Germans were forced to admit that the rate of submarine losses had become so great as to stop their operations effectively; reorienting their thinking, they sought to develop a submarine design that would permit operating beneath the surface most of the time, be highly manoeuvrable, and able to operate at great depths. As an interim measure the Schnorkel was developed for installation on U-boats in service. The Schnorkel was an extensible engine-breather pipe which permitted the submarine to operate her Diesels submerged at slow to moderate speeds, to charge her batteries submerged, and to replenish the air supply inside the boat. To allow the installation of the Schnorkel, as well as other devices designed to counter antisubmarine measures, the Germans withdrew many of the U-boats from the North Atlantic.

From late 1943 until May 1944, the U-boats were employed in a widely dispersed campaign in the Caribbean, off Brazil in the South Atlantic, and off Freetown, South Africa. Until all U-boats could be Schnorkel-equipped, the U-boat command hoped to gain time and minimize losses by operating in these widely dispersed areas which they considered relatively weak in antisubmarine measures. The plan met with little success. The Allied antisubmarine forces continued to increase in number and efficiency and there were few, if any, ocean areas that they did not patrol. Consequently, the losses continued to mount—from July 1943 to May 1944, a total of 199 submarines were destroyed at sea by the antisubmarine forces.

The U-boat reverses at sea were only part of the perilous war situation which confronted the nazis on all fronts by the fall of 1944. The loss of France through the Normandy landings was a setback of utmost gravity to the U-boat warfare. The submarines had to fall back on the Norwegian and home bases and, as in the beginning, the long passage from these bases to the Atlantic shipping lanes absorbed a major portion of the submarine's cruising radius. In addition, the U-boats could no longer attempt surface running—the long journey to the hunting areas had to be made for the most part submerged.

In the final phase, U-boat operations resembled those of the early months of the war. Operating from bases in Norway and the Baltic, the submarines hunted in the waters around the British Isles. In these waters the Schnorchel-equipped U-boats were able to operate in inshore waters with relative safety from aircraft detection. At first they achieved some successes, but eventually the weight of the Allied antisubmarine forces became overwhelming and finally forced the U-boats from the coastal areas. The submarine then was no longer practicable as an offensive weapon against Allied antisubmarine measures.

The battle of the Atlantic, in which the Allies won a final victory over the U-boats, came to an end with the German capitulation on V-E day. A total of 781 German submarines had been sunk, with a loss of approximately 30,000 men from a total personnel of 38,000. But, from the German viewpoint, these men did not die in vain—their successes were outstanding and represented a large portion of the price of the Allied victory. They had sunk more than 2,500 Allied ships of about 14,500,000 gross tons, including two battleships, two aircraft carriers and numerous destroyers and escort vessels.

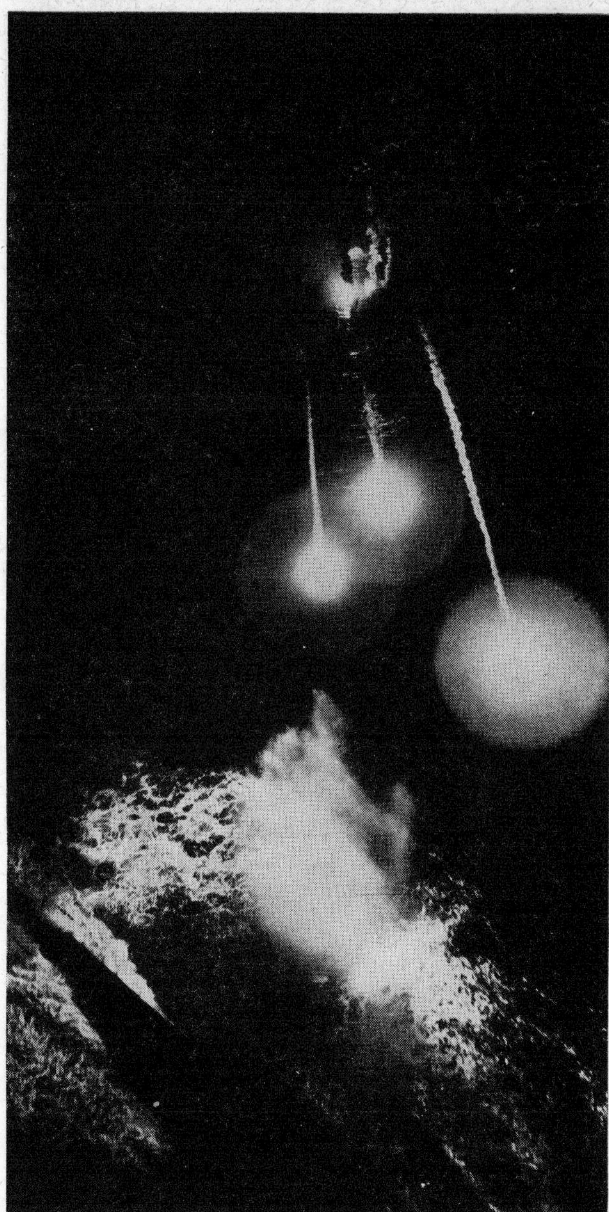

Night flares dropped above a German submarine by an R.A.F. coastal command plane flying at 75 ft. The flame-burst in the foreground was from an exploding depth charge

Admiral Karl Doenitz, the commander of the U-boats for almost the entire war, stated that the battle of the Atlantic was lost before it began. Germany, he said, was in no way prepared to fight a naval war against Great Britain. Had Germany adopted a realistic policy it would have had 1,000 U-boats available at the beginning of the war. Considering the depredations which his submarines committed on the Allies and how near to victory they were in the Atlantic, one is bound to recognize the fearful consequences which undoubtedly would have resulted had the Germans carried out such a realistic policy.

The U.S. Submarine War

In the halcyon days of 1930, Baron Kijuro Shidehara,

Shipways at Bremen harbour, where about 40 German submarines in all stages of construction and repair were captured by the Allies in 1945

foreign minister of Japan, had stated: "the number of submarines possessed by the United States is of no concern to the Japanese inasmuch as Japan can never be attacked by American submarines . . ." Eleven years later the baron's beliefs were still shared by the Japanese militarists, as was evidenced by the pattern of the attack on Pearl Harbor. The bombs and torpedoes were for the battleships and for the carriers which they hoped would be present. They could not be expended on such inconsequential targets as submarines and submarine repair facilities. The submarine base at Pearl Harbor and the few submarines based therein were ignored by the attacking planes. It was a fatal mistake.

The reasoning of the Japanese strategists was difficult to comprehend. They well knew of the effectiveness of the German submarines against the British, both in World War II and in the previous one, and Japan's position in the western Pacific was analogous to that of the United Kingdom in the eastern Atlantic—an island empire dependent upon ship-borne cargoes for the prosecution of a war as well as for the maintenance of the domestic economy. The ships bringing raw materials to the home islands and those providing logistic support for the outlying bases were the bloodstream of the Japanese war potential. The submarines, which the Japanese high command overlooked or underestimated, applied the tourniquet to that stream; the outlying bases became gangrenous and fell prey to amphibious assault. Long-range bomber forces moved into these captured bases and they, together with carrier air forces, which were free to roam the seas after the decimation of the Japanese navy by submarine, air and surface attacks, forced the empire of the mikado into acceptance of unconditional surrender. Had the submarines with their base at Pearl Harbor and their tenders in Manila bay been destroyed in the initial attacks on those places, as easily they might have been, the submarine war against Japan would have been retarded many months. Had the Japanese devoted more of their prewar effort to the development of antisubmarine weapons and to training in antisubmarine methods, the submarine results would have been greatly curtailed. While the defeat of Japan was inevitable in any event, the war would have lasted much longer without the submarine achievements and have been far more costly in both men and material.

The United States government had strongly condemned the unrestricted warfare conducted during World War I and being conducted during World War II by the German submarines. It was opposed by U.S. public opinion, as well as by government policy. Yet, within six hours after the first bomb fell on Pearl Harbor, despatch orders from the chief of naval operations directed the submarines to conduct "unrestricted warfare against Japan." The United States had cut its pattern to fit its cloth. With the bulk of the fleet incapacitated at Pearl Harbor, the submarines were the one effective weapon available, and Japan had aligned itself with the powers that sanctioned unrestricted warfare. And, though the orders permitted attacks without warning on merchant ships, actually there were no merchant ships as such in the Pacific after the war began. All Japanese shipping was engaged in the prosecution of the war—either carrying men and munitions and equipment to the areas under attack or occupation, or carrying the raw materials to manufacture more munitions and more equipment. "Transports," "freighters," "tankers," were just other names for unarmed, or poorly armed combatant ships. Considered in that light, the directive to attack this shipping did not involve such an about-face as it appears at first glance. However, it did come as a surprise to the submariners who had been taught to believe that in the event of war they would be required to abide by the provisions of the London Naval treaty, 1930, which stated:

> . . . a warship, whether surface vessel or submarine, may not sink or render incapable of navigation a merchant vessel without having first placed passengers, crew, and ship's papers in a place of safety. . . .

But, though surprised, they were not caught napping. The submarines were well trained and well organized, and they were ready for war, or as ready as the peacetime ships of a peace-loving nation could be. With their all-embracing directive, they stood out to carry the war to the Japanese. On Dec. 15, 1941, the first confirmed submarine sinking of a Japanese ship occurred—that of the 8,663-ton "Atsutusan Maru," which fell victim to "Swordfish" off Hainan island in the South China sea. Three years and eight months later "Torsk," operating in the Sea of Japan, accounted for the last two victims of the war just a few hours before the cessation of hostilities. Between these sinkings, about 1,750 steel merchant vessels (not counting ships of less than 500 tons) and 94 major men-of-war were sunk by submarines.

Submarines vs. Japanese Merchantmen.—To inaugurate the submarine campaign, the United States had a total of 51 submarines available in the Pacific at the time of Pearl Harbor. They were of two general classes—the fleet submarines, each carrying the name of a fish, and the older and smaller S-class, with numerical designations rather than names. Twenty-three of the former and 6 of the latter class were based in the Philippines, while 16 fleet type and 6 S-class were based at Pearl Harbor. The fleet submarines were not of a homogeneous type. They represented the results of 20 years of experiment to determine the most suitable type of submarine for operations in the Pacific. However, they all had one thing in common. They were all capable of long periods of sustained cruising, being able to remain at sea for periods up to 75 days and to cover about 10,000 miles at normal cruising speeds without refuelling or revictualling. On the other hand, the S-class submarines, built primarily for defense purposes in the years following World War I, were comparatively short-legged and incapable of covering the vast expanses of ocean required for Pacific patrols, while their lack of air-conditioning made them unbearably hot for submerged patrolling in tropical waters. The submarines of this class based at Pearl Harbor were transferred to the Aleutians to patrol those subarctic regions where distances were short and the waters cold. Those based in the Philippines made a number of patrols in that area and later, with their base moved to eastern Australia, they operated in the Solomons and New Guinea area but finally they also were transferred to the Aleutians.

These 51 submarines had a Herculean task assigned them. Their patrol areas extended from the Aleutians southward to the Solomons, New Guinea and the Dutch East Indies, and from Midway westward to the coast of China and French Indo-China. It was their task to drive Japanese shipping from these 8,000,000 or more square miles of ocean. Experience soon proved that not more than one-third of the 51 could be maintained on patrol station simultaneously (the other two-thirds being either en route to or from station or undergoing refit or overhaul); the submarine effort was spread exceedingly thin. However, the 20 years of experiment in submarine design had culminated the year before Pearl Harbor in the evolution of the "Gato" class submarine which, with minor refinements dictated by war experience but no basic changes, remained the standard class for all wartime construction, thus simplifying and speeding up submarine production. As fast as new submarines of this class could be turned out of the building yards they were sent to augment the submarine fleet in the Pacific. Thirty-six (plus 11 S-class transferred from the Atlantic) were added in 1942, 52 in 1943 and 76 in 1944. With each addition, the intensity of the Pacific submarine war increased.

The campaign against Jap shipping introduced many new elements foreign to the prewar training curriculum. To the submarine captain, thoroughly trained in attacks on high-speed, well-screened, zigzagging men-of-war, attacks on eight-knot, poorly-protected Jap convoys offered no serious difficulties. But there were other phases of this type of warfare not so readily assimilated. It took many months to learn that having missed his target, or sunk only a part of the convoy, the submarine could wait until the enemy was out of sight, surface in broad daylight, make a high speed "end around" and attack again. It took longer still to learn that a submarine could steal silently into a convoy on the surface at night, sink two or three ships, and escape at high speed without even diving, and perhaps repeat the performance a few hours later on the convoy remnants. But the technique was finally mastered and the success of the submarine warfare was attested by the record of Japanese ships sunk. Up until the end of 1943, the submarines accounted for 73% of Japanese ship losses from all causes. Subsequent to 1943, this percentage dropped, not because of any lessening of the submarine effort, but rather because of an increase in sinkings by other agencies, mainly carrier aircraft and, during the closing months of the war, mines laid by B-29s in the Inland sea. The previously mentioned sinking of "Atsutusan Maru" marked the initial point on an ever-rising curve of submarine sinkings. This curve reached its peak in Oct. 1944, during which month 110 ships (exclusive of ships less than 500 tons) were sent to the bottom by U.S. submarine attack. The curve then tapered off because of a paucity of Japanese shipping.

The original plan for the employment of submarines was to place them at the focal points of Jap shipping—the entrances to Tokyo bay and the Inland sea, and off Truk, Palau, the Marianas, the Bonins and Ryukyus and the important harbours of Formosa, the Philippines and Dutch East Indies. With so many focal points and so few submarines initially available, not all productive areas could be covered, but none of them was totally neglected. A submarine would work one spot until it had made its presence known by sinking a number of Jap ships and would then move to another area to confuse the Japs and cause them to diffuse their antisubmarine forces. As the number of submarines increased, more and more of the vital areas were patrolled simultaneously until, by the fall of 1943, the saturation point was reached. Submarines then started operating in co-ordinated attack groups, or "wolf packs," as they were called. Three or four submarines under a wolf-pack commander embarked in one of them would co-ordinate their patrols, maintaining radio contact with one another. The first submarine of a group to make contact with Jap ships would trail and vector its packmates into contact positions before making its attack. Rarely were the attacks co-ordinated—after all submarines of the group were in contact with the Japs, each would attack independently. Wolf packing served a triple purpose—it permitted greater density of submarines in an area without interference with one another; it multiplied the effectiveness of each submarine by permitting it to act on contacts of its packmates as well as its own; and it reduced the severity of Japanese countermeasures. The escort commander could not concentrate his escorts on the first submarine to attack when his charges might be attacked a short time later by another submarine of the pack.

The ultimate in intersubmarine co-ordination was attained by a hastily organized pack of two boats. The story merits the telling. Early in Jan. 1944, "Seawolf," commanded by Commander R. L. Gross, on patrol in the East China sea, reported that it had sunk three ships and that it had but three torpedoes remaining from its original 20. The force commander directed it to return to Pearl Harbor, patrolling en route until its remaining torpedoes were expended. Two days later "Seawolf" contacted a southbound convoy of four ships protected by three escorts. With its three torpedoes, it sank one ship of this convoy and as soon as the usual depth-charging subsided it surfaced and commenced trailing the three remaining ships, sending an urgent dispatch for another submarine to join it and destroy the covey it had flushed. The closest submarine at the time was "Whale," Commander A. C. Burroughs commanding, patrolling off the Bonin Islands about 400 miles to the eastward. It was ordered to proceed at maximum speed to intercept "Seawolf's" convoy. Two days later "Whale," acting on information from "Seawolf," made contact, and with the latter watching through its high periscope from its position beyond the horizon, sank two of the three remaining Japanese ships. The escorts promptly started depth-charging "Whale" while the last Jap ship attempted to flee unescorted to the southwest. Gross, determined that no ships of this convoy would escape, made a high speed end-around to a position ahead of the fleeing ship where he opened fire on it with his three-inch gun. The gunfire had the desired effect; the ship reversed course to rejoin its escorts, who in the meantime had broken off their attacks on "Whale," permitting it to surface. It re-established radio contact with "Seawolf" who vectored it into position to destroy with torpedoes this last ship of the convoy.

The Japanese used relatively small convoys—usually four or five ships escorted by from one to four destroyers or destroyer escorts—and there were many instances where a single submarine destroyed an entire convoy unassisted. The first of such instances was that of "Wahoo" who, on Jan. 26, 1943, contacted an unescorted four-ship convoy in the area north of New Guinea. That night, "Wahoo's" commanding officer, Lieutenant Commander Dudley W. Morton, reported ". . . IN TEN-HOUR RUNNING GUN AND TORPEDO BATTLE DESTROYED ENTIRE CONVOY OF TWO FREIGHTERS ONE TRANSPORT ONE TANKER X ALL TORPEDOES EXPENDED X RETURNING HOME . . ." Two days previously, "Wahoo" had penetrated the Japanese-held port of Wewak on the New Guinea coast to sink a destroyer therein, and this may have accounted for his finding an unescorted convoy—possibly the destroyer had been the one designated as escort. The day following the convoy battle, "Wahoo" encountered another convoy. With all torpedoes expended, Morton trailed in the hope of picking off a straggler with gunfire. The attempt was thwarted by one of the escorting destroyers who detected "Wahoo" and chased it off. Morton then sent his classic dispatch ". . . ANOTHER RUNNING GUN FIGHT X DESTROYER GUNNING X WAHOO RUNNING . . ."

There were several cases in which submarine commanding officers, using the Mohammed-and-the-mountain principle, entered Japanese harbours to seek their prey. The "Wahoo's" penetration of Wewak mentioned above was one of them, but it was not the first. As early as Nov. 1942, "Seawolf," then commanded by Commander F. B. Warder, penetrated Davao gulf in the southeastern Philippines to sink "Sagami Maru" at anchor off Taloma wharf, about 50 miles from open water. The outstanding attack of this nature was that of "Barb," which in the dark of the night of Jan. 22–23, 1945, penetrated 20 miles of water too shallow for diving to attack a group of 30 Japanese ships at anchor in Namkwan harbour on the coast of China. "Barb" fired eight torpedoes in this attack and escaped undamaged through a rain of shells from exploding ammunition ships. The following day, a press despatch from Chungking, China, reported a naval engagement off the China coast, and so it was—30 Japanese ships versus U.S.S. "Barb." Its commanding officer, Commander E. B. Fluckey, was awarded the congressional medal of honour for this outstanding performance.

By the spring of 1945, submarine and air attacks had well-nigh cleared the seas of Japanese shipping, but there still remained one important area where Japanese shipping travelled virtually unmolested—the Sea of Japan with its many ships plying the waters between Korea and the Japanese home islands. During the summer of 1943, several submarines had entered that sea to patrol therein but the patrols were discontinued because of the risks involved. All the entrances to the Sea of Japan were known to be mined and with equally as productive areas elsewhere the risks of transversing these mine fields were not warranted. However, by the spring of 1945, the other productive areas no longer existed, and the Sea of Japan remained the one great challenge to the submarines. Foreseeing this trend of circumstances, the submarine force commander inaugurated a series of exercises to train submarines to underrun anchored mine fields. Early in June, nine submarines, formed into three wolf packs, simultaneously passed through the mine fields of Tsushima strait to enter the Sea of Japan. They remained for nine days to sink 32 Japanese ships, including one submarine, for a total of more than 100,000 tons. It was the last great submarine offensive. While the submarine patrols continued until the end of hostilities two months later, and there were a number of desultory sinkings, the submarines had successfully completed their assigned task of driving Japanese shipping from the sea.

Whenever the opportunity offered, submarines attempted to rescue survivors from the ships they had sunk. Their efforts were usually resisted by the Japanese themselves who, with their suicidal complex and their inherent desire to die for the emperor, preferred death to rescue by the enemy. On several occasions submarines had to employ force to bring survivors on board; on three occasions survivors committed suicide after having been voluntarily rescued. The Japanese psychology was impossible to fathom.

While the over-all effect of the submarine war against shipping was known, the value of any individual attack was impossible to appraise. For man-of-war sinkings, the value could be judged by the size and type of the victim, but the same did not hold true in the case of the merchantmen. The lowliest tramp steamer might be carrying the most vital cargo. Two examples will suffice to illustrate this point. (1) When carrier aircraft made their first attack on presumably impregnable Truk, the air crews were pleasantly surprised by the weakness of Truk's anti-aircraft defenses. Questioned about this point after the cessation of hostilities, Captain Tamura, air staff officer at Truk, stated that the weakness was caused by lack of radar control for the guns, and when asked the reason for this lack, he stated that the ship bringing in the radar control equipment was sunk by submarine off Guam. (2) Japanese authorities generally agreed that the loss of Saipan was the turning point of the war. On June 6, 1944, "Shark II" and "Pintado" decimated a Saipan-bound convoy in the waters northwest of the Marianas. The U.S. forces landed on Saipan nine days later. The campaign was touch-and-go with the issue in doubt for several weeks. Postwar information revealed that the ships sunk by "Shark II" and "Pintado" were carrying a division of troops to reinforce Saipan and that less than half that division, completely devoid of equipment, succeeded in reaching the island. This division of troops, fully equipped, might well have been sufficient to weigh the balance in favour of the Japanese.

Submarines vs. the Japanese Navy.—From the point of view of the individual submarine, the campaign against the merchantmen and that against the Japanese navy were one and the same thing. The two went hand in hand. The submarine on patrol station in Japanese waters attacked whatever came its way, be it freighter or man-of-war, with the latter always the target of preference. The war of attrition against Japanese merchantmen throttled Japan's economy and weakened the island outposts. The attacks on the Japanese navy had the more immediate effect of reducing the offensive and defensive strength of the fleet. With but a few notable exceptions, the majority of sinkings of important Japanese combatant ships took place during 1944. Unknown at the time, this late start was not because of any failure of the submarines, but rather because of faulty torpedo exploders which, activated magnetically by the induction of a ship's hull, while effective against merchantmen, had a tendency to explode from 30 to 50 yards away from the side of large combatant ships, causing only superficial damage.

The first notable success was that of "Nautilus," which

during the battle of Midway in June 1942, sank the aircraft carrier "Soryu." "Soryu" had been severely damaged by carrier planes and was dead in the water when finished off by "Nautilus," commanded by Lieutenant Commander W. H. Brockman. Brockman was credited with an "assist" only on this sinking. Two months later "S-44," patrolling off Kavieng under the command of Lieutenant J. R. Moore, sent the heavy cruiser "Kako" to the bottom with all hits from a salvo of four torpedoes. Three days previously "Kako" had been a member of the force that had administered the greatest setback to Allied naval forces during the war. On the night of Aug. 7, the United States heavy cruisers "Vincennes," "Quincy" and "Astoria," and the Australian heavy cruiser "Canberra" were sunk off Tulagi in the Solomon Islands. "Kako" was returning from that engagement when it fell prey to "S-44."

Following the sinking of "Kako," 16 months elapsed before the next large Jap man-of-war was sent to the bottom by submarine attack. In the meantime, the torpedo exploder faults had been detected and by late summer of 1943 had been corrected. (It should be noted that "Nautilus" had sunk a previously wounded carrier, while "S-44" was using contact exploders not subject to the faults of the magnetic exploders used by the fleet-type submarines.) On the night of Dec. 3, 1943, "Sailfish," passing several hundred miles south of Tokyo bay en route to its patrol station, detected a northbound Jap task force on its radar screen. Despite typhoon winds and mountainous seas "Sailfish" trailed, and using radar bearings alone, being unable to see its target, fired four torpedoes which registered two hits on a large Japanese ship. Subsequent radar tracking indicated that the target was stopped. "Sailfish" closed again and obtained two more hits, but still the target remained afloat. "Sailfish" stayed in the vicinity and the following morning closed the target submerged to discover an aircraft carrier badly listed to starboard, with the crew abandoning ship. Two more hits sent it to the bottom. Judged by persistence, this was probably the most outstanding sinking of the war—the series of three attacks had covered a period of ten hours, and Lieutenant Commander R. E. M. Ward, making his first patrol as a submarine commanding officer, had proved his mettle. The ship was the escort carrier "Chuyo," and there was tragedy as well as triumph connected with its sinking. "Sailfish" was the name given to "Squalus" after that ill-fated submarine, which sank during its trial runs off Portsmouth, N.H., had been raised and rebuilt. When it sank, during May 1939, the submarine which located it and stood by during its salvage was "Sculpin." Postwar information disclosed that "Chuyo" at the time of its sinking by "Sailfish" was carrying 21 of the total of 41 survivors of "Sculpin," which had been sunk about two weeks previously by Japanese action off Truk. Of these 21 on "Chuyo," only 1 survived the "Sailfish" attacks.

The banner year for submarines in their campaign

Sinking from shellfire by the U.S. coast guard cutter "Spencer," this German submarine was photographed in the North Atlantic in 1943. All but one crewman left on deck had jumped overboard or been killed against the Japanese fleet was 1944. With the exception of May, not a month of that year passed without at least one important Japanese man-of-war being destroyed by submarine action. The first four months of the year each saw a light cruiser go down. In January, it was "Kuma," sunk by H.M.S. "Tallyho" off Penang, British Malaya. In February, the new light cruiser "Agano" fell victim to "Skate" north of Truk on the eve of the first carrier air attack on that island stronghold. The following day, carrier dive bombers sank the destroyer "Maikaze," which was bringing in survivors from the "Agano" sinking. In March, "Tatsuta" was sunk by "Sandlance" south of Tokyo bay, while the following month "Yubari" went down from torpedoes fired by "Bluegill."

Important as were these sinkings, they were but apéritifs for those which were to take place during the last seven months of the year. With the start of the amphibious offensive in the Pacific, the submarines were no longer free to conduct their free-lance war of attrition in Japanese waters. While these offensive patrols were continued on a reduced scale, a considerable portion of the submarine effort was devoted to the support of the amphibious landings. For each operation, submarines were placed in positions to intercept Japanese fleet units that might attempt to oppose the landings. The mission of the submarines was twofold—to report Japanese fleet movements, and to attack, with report the primary mission. The submarines' orders required that "in the event of contact with a previously unreported major enemy force moving toward the area of operations your first duty is to send a contact report." These orders were universally unpopular with the submarine captains. For the first submarine to make contact, the order to send a contact report before attacking precluded the possibility of a successful attack. The burning ambition of every submarine captain was to torpedo and sink a capital ship, and these orders were depriving him of his rightful heritage. Before a message could be drafted and enciphered, and the submarine could surface and transmit it, the ship would be far over the horizon. However, the fleet commanders insisted upon these orders. From their vantage point the damage that could be inflicted by a single submarine, important as it might be, could not possibly outweigh the value of a contact report which might prevent a surprise attack upon the hundreds of ships involved in an amphibious operation.

For both the Gilberts and the Marshalls campaigns, the submarines were stationed to guard all the entrances to Truk, and in positions between Truk and the Gilbert and Marshall islands, as it was reasoned that if the enemy fleet attempted to oppose the landings it would either come from, or stage through, Truk. The Japanese fleet did not attempt to oppose the landings in either of these campaigns and the submarine efforts, involving about ten submarines in each case, appeared to be wasted. However, for the next operation, the Marianas campaign, the plan paid big dividends.

At the time of the landings in the Marianas, in June 1944, the bulk of the Japanese fleet was known to be anchored in Tawi Tawi bay in the southwestern Philippines. To reach the Marianas from there, the Japanese would have to pass to the north or to the south of the Philippines, or through either San Bernardino or Surigao straits. To watch the Japanese fleet and to guard all the avenues of approach to the Marianas, three submarines were stationed in the vicinity of Tawi Tawi, three north of Luzon and three south of Mindanao (the northernmost and southernmost Philippines), while one was stationed at the eastern entrance to San Bernardino strait and another at the eastern entrance to Surigao strait. In addition, five submarines were stationed to the northwest of the Marianas to guard the approaches from the Japanese empire while others, as available during the operation, patrolled in the vicinity of the Palau islands and in the waters between the Philippines and the Marianas.

First information on Japanese movements came from "Harder," who on the evening of June 10, reported that three battleships, four or more cruisers and six or eight destroyers had departed Tawi Tawi on a southerly course. Subsequent information indicated that this force proceeded to an anchorage off the island of Halmahera. "Redfin," also at Tawi Tawi, made the next contact report—this time on the striking force which contained the carriers. On the evening of June 13, it reported that a force consisting of six carriers, four battleships, eight cruisers and six destroyers had left Tawi Tawi that morning and had headed north. The Japanese fleet was underway, but was it coming out to fight? The question was answered two days later by "Flying Fish."

"Flying Fish" had been maintaining a lonesome vigil at San Bernardino strait for weeks and was nearing the end of its patrol endurance. Its fuel was running low, but it held out waiting for relief to arrive. Perseverance was rewarded. On the evening of June 15, it reported that shortly before sunset the force previously reported by "Redfin" had passed through San Bernardino strait and had proceeded slightly north of due east at a speed of 20 knots. The die was cast! The long-hoped-for fleet engagement was in the offing. But what of the southbound force reported by "Harder" on June 10? "Seahorse" sent in the answer within a few hours.

While "Flying Fish" had waited weeks to make its all-important contact, "Seahorse" made its quite by accident. It wasn't included in the submarine disposition for this operation but was passing east of the Philippines en route to its station in Luzon strait after fuelling in the Admiralty Islands. Shortly after the "Flying Fish" message arrived at fleet headquarters in Pearl Harbor, an urgent message from "Seahorse" stated ". . . TASK FORCE IN POSITION 10°-11′ NORTH, 129°-35′ EAST, COURSE NORTHEAST SPEED SIXTEEN POINT FIVE KNOTS . . . SEAHORSE TRAILING. . . ." Soon thereafter, it reported that its speed had been reduced by main motor trouble and that it had lost contact and had given up the chase.

The two forces were located but they were still a long way from the Marianas. They would undoubtedly fuel before striking. Where would they rendezvous with each other and with their tankers, and from what direction would they strike? These questions also were answered by the submarines, this time by "Cavalla."

"Cavalla," a new submarine making its first patrol, was en route to San Bernardino strait to relieve "Flying Fish." Upon receipt of the latter's contact report, "Cavalla" was ordered to patrol temporarily across the estimated track of the striking force. An hour before midnight on the 16th, it made radar contact with a convoy which later was determined to consist of one large and one medium tanker with three destroyers for escort, on an easterly course making 16 knots. "Cavalla" gained position ahead for an attack but had to abandon the approach when detected and forced to go deep by one of the escorting destroyers. An hour and a half later it was on the surface to transmit its contact report. It then proceeded on the way to San Bernardino strait. "Cavalla" had failed to grasp the importance of the convoy it had contacted. Normally, a Japanese convoy in these waters would have little implication, but at this time, the only islands to the eastward being the Marianas, and they under attack by the U.S. fleet, these tankers could have but one possible mission—to fuel the Japanese fleet, and the position of that fuelling was the one bit of information vitally needed by the U.S. forces. And, if the tankers could be destroyed, the Japanese fleet would be slowed by lack of fuel and become easy prey for the carrier planes. As fast as the message could be drafted, orders were sent to "Cavalla" ". . . DESTRUCTION THOSE TANKERS OF GREAT IMPORTANCE X TRAIL X ATTACK X REPORT." "Cavalla" reversed course and started the chase at maximum speed, holding out little hope for success. It would take two days to overtake the tankers even if it knew where they were heading. The following morning, subsequent orders directed it to discontinue the high speed chase but to continue along the track at normal cruising speed.

"Cavalla's" adventures were only beginning. At 8:00 in the evening of June 18, it found itself directly on the track of the battleship force previously reported by "Harder" and "Seahorse." Knowing the need for definite information concerning the Japs, "Cavalla" rightfully elected to report rather than attack. The battleships passed directly over it without suspecting its presence. Two hours later, "Cavalla" was sending out its vital message. With its receipt, the fleet commander had sufficient information concerning the Japanese, and submarines were relieved of the restriction to "report before attacking." The following morning, "Cavalla" received its just reward for forbearance. Shortly before 11:00 o'clock on the morning of the 19th, "Cavalla" contacted the Jap carrier force. Now it was free to attack. The results are best decribed in its terse radio report of the ensuing action ". . . HIT SHOKAKU CLASS CARRIER WITH THREE OUT OF SIX TORPEDOES AT ZERO TWO ONE FIVE (11:15 A.M.) X ACCOMPANIED BY TWO ATAGO CLASS CRUISERS THREE DESTROYERS POSSIBLY MORE X RECEIVED ONE HUNDRED FIVE DEPTH CHARGES DURING THREE HOUR PERIOD X SUPERSONIC GEAR OUT OF COMMISSION X HULL INDUCTION FLOODED X NO OTHER SERIOUS TROUBLE X SURE WE CAN HANDLE IT X HEARD FOUR TERRIFIC EXPLOSIONS IN DIRECTION OF TARGET TWO AND ONE HALF HOURS AFTER ATTACK X BELIEVE THAT BABY SANK . . ." The carrier proved to be "Shokaku," one of Japan's three largest carriers in commission, and it did sink. In a brand new submarine, and making his first attack as a submarine commanding officer, Commander Herman J. Kossler had attained the submarine hall of fame.

Unknown to either "Cavalla" or to the submarine force commander, another event of equal import had taken place just three hours earlier and about 60 miles distant from "Cavalla's" attack. On this same eventful morning of June 19, "Albacore," with Commander J. W. Blanchard commanding, was patrolling on the surface in the vicinity of 12°-20′ north 137°00′ east. Shortly after 7:00 o'clock it was forced to dive to avoid detection by a Jap plane. At 7:50 it sighted through the periscope an aircraft carrier, a cruiser and the tops of several unidentified ships. The range was 13,000 yards, and "Albacore" was 70° on the carrier's port bow. From such a position an attack was impossible—the carrier would pass well outside torpedo range. However, Blanchard manoeuvred for position, hoping that a favourable zigzag would bring the targets toward him. While attempting to close the range a periscope sweep of the horizon disclosed a second carrier group of similar composition. "Albacore" was 10° on the bow of the second carrier, an ideal attack position. This was a horse of another colour, and Blanchard forgot about the first group to concentrate on the second. At 8:08 he was 1,500 yards on the target's beam and ready to fire when he noted that his fire control equipment was not indicating a correct solution to the problem. No sadder fate ever befell a submarine captain—one of the prize targets of the war crossing his bow at 27 knots and something was wrong. In a situation such as this, there was little time for thought; within two minutes the target would be beyond reach. It was now or never. Blanchard quickly estimated a solution, angled his torpedoes, and using a wide torpedo spread to compensate for the probable errors in his estimate, fired six torpedoes. He then ordered deep submergence to avoid the counterattack which he knew was coming. Two minutes after firing, "Albacore" heard what was believed to be a torpedo hit. However, at this stage of the war, hits that were heard but not seen were given slight credence. Disappointed in his results, Blanchard neglected to report this attack by radio. It was not until a month later when the patrol report was received that it came to the attention of the force commander, who credited "Albacore" with probable damage to a "Shokaku" class carrier. But the gremlins that had deprived Blanchard of his rightful quota of hits regretted their caprices and paid off in full. When "Cavalla" made its attack three hours later on what was obviously a combination of the two groups sighted by "Albacore," there was only one carrier in the formation—the other carrier must be in difficulty somewhere. Months later, information received from a Japanese prisoner of war disclosed that "Taiho" had been sunk on the morning of June 19. Information gathered after the end of hostilities proved beyond all doubt that the one chance hit from "Albacore" had, after six hours, resulted in a gasoline explosion which sent this newest of carriers to the bottom on the very day that it launched its planes for its initial attack on the U.S. forces.

There were two submarine commands operating against Japan—the Submarine Force Pacific fleet, based at Pearl Harbor, and Commander Submarines Southwest Pacific, based on the east and on the west coast of Australia, with headquarters at Perth. June 19, 1944, was the high point of the war for the former command. At that time, Japan had only three first-line carriers in commission, "Taiho," "Shokaku" and "Zuikaku," and within the space of three hours "Albacore" and "Cavalla" of the Pearl Harbor command had sent two of these three to the bottom in the initial and crucial phase of a fleet engagement. But the submarines of the Southwest Pacific were not to be outdone. They too had their day of glory, equal in importance to June 19. Some four months later, on Oct. 23, the day preceding the start of the battle for Leyte gulf, submarines of that command put four heavy cruisers out of commission, sinking two of them and sending the other two limping back to port, never again to see action during the war. But before describing these actions it should be mentioned that in these intervening four months, four light cruisers and two escort carriers were destroyed by submarine action. On July 19, "Flasher," patrolling the South China sea, sank the light cruiser "Oi." Aug. 7 marked the end of "Nagara" through action of "Croaker" in the waters north of the Ryukyus. As evidence of this sinking, "Croaker's" commanding officer, Commander J. E. Lee, brought back a reel of motion pictures taken through the periscope of this light cruiser's last moments. Eleven days later another light cruiser, this time "Natori," was sunk by "Hardhead" in the area east of the Philippines. On this same date "Rasher," operating to the north of these same islands, sank the escort carrier "Taiyo." Less than a month later another escort carrier, "Unyo," fell victim to "Barb" off the island of Hainan. On Sept. 19, "Shad," stationed south of the main Japanese island of Honshu, sank "Ihojima," the ex-Chinese cruiser "Ning-hai" which the Japanese had captured and converted to their own use. By this time the supply of light cruisers as targets for submarines was running low—the next successes were against the heavy cruisers previously mentioned.

The initial landings for the recapture of the Philippines were made on the island of Leyte on Oct. 20, 1944. At this time the Japanese fleet was based at Singapore and submarines of the Southwest Pacific command were disposed in intercepting positions between Singapore and Leyte gulf. The Japanese had their fleet plans for defense of the Philippines and were quick to react. At midnight on the night of Oct. 22–23, "Darter" and "Dace," on station in Palawan passage, that long narrow strip of water between the banana-shaped Palawan island and the unexplored Dangerous Ground to the westward, were within hailing distance of each other, and their respective commanding officers, Commanders D. H. McClintock and B. D. Claggett, were discussing plans for the next day's operations when "Darter" made radar contact with a large Japanese force at a range of 30,000 yards. McClintock, the senior of the two, gave deployment instructions to Claggett, and "Darter" and "Dace" proceeded at full speed to their positions. "Darter" drew first blood. At 5:32 A.M., from the starboard side of the Jap formation, and from a range of 980 yards, it fired six torpedoes from its bow tubes at the heavy cruiser "Atago." Torpedoes could hardly miss from that range. Not waiting to see his results, McClintock swung hard left and one minute later fired his four stern tubes, this time at the heavy cruiser "Takao." With all tubes empty, "Darter" could take no more offensive action until they could be reloaded. McClintock ordered deep submergence to reload and to evade the depth charging which was as certain to follow as night the day, but before doing so he took a quick look at his first target. It had been hit with five torpedoes and, billowing smoke from forward turret to stern, was already well on the way to its final resting place. While going deep, McClintock heard three hits in his second target, with a fourth explosion, about 25 seconds later than scheduled, which might possibly have been a hit in a third ship. "Atago" sank. "Takao" was severely damaged but succeeded in reaching Singapore. The last explosion was not explained—it was possibly the sixth torpedo of the first salvo exploding at the end of its run.

Meanwhile "Dace" was closing the Japs from the port flank. Twenty minutes after "Darter" fired her first salvo, "Dace" got off six torpedoes at "Maya." The resulting four hits sank this heavy cruiser within a few minutes.

Now it was the Japs' turn. The depth charging of "Dace" lasted for four hours; that of "Darter" for one. Neither sustained material damage, but it was early afternoon before their hecklers departed and they could return to periscope depth to take stock of the situation. They found the horizon clear with the exception of the damaged "Takao," which was heading slowly southward escorted by three destroyers. An attempted submerged attack by "Darter" was thwarted by these escorts. Both submarines surfaced after sunset and immediately embarked on a high speed chase to catch and destroy the crippled cruiser. At five minutes after midnight, on the morning of the 24th, "Darter," not having had opportunity to fix her navigational position within the past 24 hours, and making full speed in pursuit of "Takao," ran hard aground on Bombay shoal, a submerged reef to the westward of Palawan passage. A hurried despatch brought "Dace" to her assistance. "Dace," seeing there was no possibility of refloating "Darter," who was so high out of the water that its propellers were exposed, removed all "Darter's" crew and then expended all its remaining torpedoes in an attempt to destroy its helpless sister. The attempt failed—the torpedoes exploding on the rocks before they could reach their target. "Dace" then sprayed "Darter" with 21 hits from its three-inch gun to damage it beyond salvage by the Japanese. After being brought home by "Dace," the entire crew of "Darter" was ordered to the new submarine "Menhaden," then building at Manitowoc, Wis., in order to maintain intact this fighting organization which had inflicted such severe damage on the Japanese. The damage was actually greater than was known or suspected at the time. Postwar information revealed that "Atago," sunk by "Darter," had been the flagship of the Japanese fleet, and Admiral Kurita had been forced to shift his flag to "Yamato" on the eve of the greatest naval engagement in history.

On this same morning that "Darter" and "Dace" were carving their niches in history, another submarine, "Bream," commanded by Commander W. G. Chapple, on patrol off the entrance to Manila bay, was further reducing the force which was to challenge the U.S. landings on Leyte. At 1:10 A.M. Chapple sighted two heavy cruisers, with destroyer escorts heading south from Manila bay, evidently to join the forces contacted by "Darter" and "Dace." Six torpedoes fired by "Bream" at 3:24 A.M. sent the heavy cruiser "Aoba," wounded with two hits, limping back into the bay. In this case, as in the case of "Atago," the damage was tantamount to sinking. While the Japanese expended great effort to repair "Aoba" and "Atago," they were still disabled when the war ended.

Four Jap cruisers put out of action was a good day's work for any organization. Submarines of the Southwest Pacific command had had their day of triumph and had proved their parity with the Pacific fleet submarines. But the story of the submarine part in the battle for Leyte gulf was still not complete. Submarines of the Pacific fleet were to get in their blows, unimportant as they might be as compared with the work of "Darter," "Dace" and "Bream." The main fleet engagements took place on Oct. 25. The Japanese ships had approached through waters patrolled by Submarines Southwest Pacific, but if they attempted to reach Japan they would have to pass through the areas patrolled by the Pearl Harbor submarines. On the morning of Oct. 25, two submarine wolf packs of three submarines each were en route from Saipan to Luzon strait. The submarine force commander, seeing the battle shaping up, ordered these two groups to proceed at maximum speed into positions to intercept any Jap ships attempting to escape the fleet engagement. The positions chosen for these two groups were purely guesswork, yet strangely enough both groups made contact and both inflicted damage upon the Japanese. At 6:44 P.M., "Halibut" fired six torpedoes at what was believed to be a battleship of the "Ise" class and counted five hits. When "Halibut" surfaced a few minutes later nothing was in sight but a large upturned hulk. The Japanese records of this battle were very sketchy, and this sinking by "Halibut" was not confirmed. It was believed that it may have sunk a destroyer. At 11:00 o'clock the same evening "Jallao," of the other group, put three hits into a Japanese cruiser attempting to escape to the northward. It sank within a few minutes, witnessed by the group commander in "Pintado." It was the light cruiser "Tama."

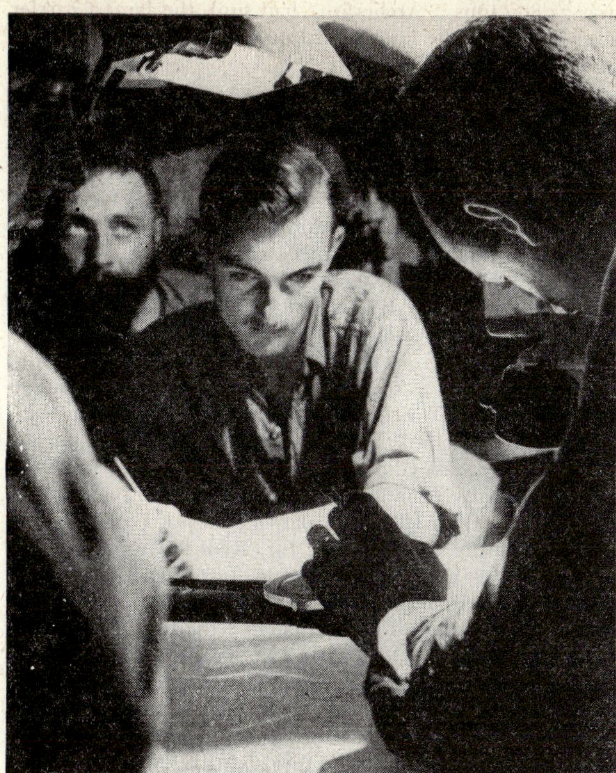

Control room of a U.S. submarine in 1945 as crew members worked tensely on a problem while a Japanese ship dropped depth charges near by. Their only recourse was to shut off their motors and hope their position would not be detected

Following the battle, a number of the Japanese ships took refuge in Manila bay. On the morning of Nov. 6, a group of these ships, attempting to reach the Japanese homeland, ran afoul of the Southwest Pacific submarines—"Guitarro," "Bream," "Raton" and "Ray," all four of whom, in the order named, attacked the largest ship of the formation, the heavy cruiser "Kumano." Best available evidence indicated that it was "Ray" who inflicted the major damage. "Kumano" had its bow blown off and was immediately beached to prevent sinking. Its position, on the west coast of northern Luzon, was reported and on the 25th of the month, its destruction was completed by carrier planes of Admiral W. F. Halsey's 3rd fleet.

Two escort carriers were the next victims on the submarine agenda. On Nov. 15, "Akitsu Maru," designed as an escort carrier but unsuccessful in that role and subsequently converted to an aircraft transport, was sunk by "Queenfish" in the Yellow sea. Two days later "Spadefish," operating in the same area and in the same wolf pack with "Queenfish," sank "Jinyo," the fifth and last escort carrier to fall victim to submarine attack. These sinkings were followed within a few days by the most important sinkings of the war, that of a battleship with a destroyer as a soupçon, and that of the largest aircraft carrier ever built.

Commander Eli T. Reich had an account to square with the Japanese. The first U.S. submarine lost to enemy action in the war was "Sealion," destroyed by aircraft bombing Dec. 10, 1941, while under overhaul at Cavite navy yard in the Philippines. Reich, a junior grade lieutenant at the time, was the engineer officer of "Sealion," and one of the two bomb hits, exploding in the engine room, killed four of his engineer ratings. "Sealion" was beyond salvage and had to be abandoned. Reich, a submarine officer without a ship, served for awhile on the island of Corregidor but before the fall of that isolated stronghold he was evacuated by, and later assigned to duty in "Stingray." Subsequently, he was ordered to "Lapon" as executive officer. By the fall of 1943, he had worked up to command rank and was given "Sealion II," which was then being completed at New London, Conn. Now with his own command he was ready to exact retribution for the loss of his four engineers. Each torpedo that he fired carried one of the four names—Foster, Ogilvie, O'Connell and Paul, and like the Four Horsemen of the Apocalypse, each took a heavy toll. On its first patrol, "Sealion II" sank four Jap ships. On its second patrol it sank six. This patrol was noteworthy in that, in addition to the ships sunk, it rescued 54 British and Australian survivors from a Japanese prison ship which it had sunk three days previously. These survivors had spent more than two years in Japanese prison camps in Malaya and all were hospital cases, suffering from malnutrition, scurvy and pellagra, as well as from the effects of three days' exposure to sun and water. Four of them died before "Sealion II," rushing at maximum speed, could reach port. (In addition to "Sealion II," three other submarines were involved in these rescues—"Pampanito," "Barb" and "Queenfish." Altogether, a total of 157 survivors were picked up, "Pampanito" alone rescuing 71.)

But Reich's greatest triumph was still to come. On the night of Nov. 20–21, 1944, "Sealion II" was patrolling north of Formosa, guarding the northern approach to Formosa straits. Twenty minutes after midnight its radar detected a group of three ships at a range of 44,000 yards—a phenomenal range for a submarine's radar—the ships must be big. Reich started tracking and as the range closed other ships showed up on the radar screen. Soon the situation clarified—contact had been made with a Jap task force consisting of a cruiser, two battleships and a second cruiser in column in the order named, with three destroyers as escorts (postwar information revealed that one of the ships identified as a cruiser was actually a third battleship, "Yamato," which explains the three ships originally detected by radar). By 2:45 A.M., Reich had determined the ships to be on course 060°, speed 16 knots, not zigzagging. He decided upon a surface attack—a hazardous method against an enemy task force. Detection would bring swift and severe retaliatory measures but, if undetected, surface action offered the greatest chances for repeated attacks on this important force. At 2:56, from a range of 3,000 yards on the Japs' port beam, six torpedoes from the bow tubes were fired at the first battleship. A quick reversal of course and three torpedoes from the stern tubes (the fourth stern tube being out of commission) were loosed at the second battleship. At 3:00 A.M. three hits were seen in the first target, and four minutes later a large and violent explosion was seen on what was believed to be the second battleship. The escorting destroyers dashed wildly to the eastward to depth charge some innocent whale, while "Sealion II," still on the surface, withdrew to westward to reload torpedo tubes and to prepare for another attack. Strangely, instead of slowing down, the Japanese formation increased speed. Whereas before it had been making 16 knots it was now making 18 and Reich, overloading his engines in an attempt to keep up, was slowly losing ground. While normally capable of 20 knots, a choppy head sea was slowing "Sealion II" to a maximum of 17. At 4:50 A.M. the break came. The Japanese formation split into two parts, three ships maintaining speed while the wounded battleship, with two destroyers for escort, dropped astern. Radar tracking first showed the rear group to be making 12 knots, but shortly thereafter indicated that the battleship was dead in the water. Reich, using the "bird in the hand" theory, abandoned his high speed chase to finish off the cripple. "Sealion II" closed to administer the *coup de grace*. The treatment was unnecessary. At 5:24, while still 12,000 yards from the crippled target, there was a tremendous explosion. The sky was brilliantly illuminated like a sunset at midnight. The target disappeared from the radar screen. It was "Kongo," the only Japanese battleship sunk by submarine attack during the entire war. Postwar information revealed that the fourth hit, rather than damaging the second battleship, had hit and sunk an intervening destroyer—"Urakaze." A battleship and a destroyer on one attack! Reich had collected his debt a hundredfold.

A newspaper hoax in the early stages of the war was the story of the U.S. submarine which lay in wait in Tokyo bay to torpedo a Jap carrier as it slid down the launching ways. Although vigorously and repeatedly denied, the story circulated rapidly and soon became a legend. But even were it true the deed of this legendary submarine could not compare with the less colourful but more important work of "Archerfish" in the early morning of Nov. 29. A carrier sliding down the launching ways is but partially completed, whereas the carrier sunk by "Archerfish" was on its trial run and nearing the stage when it would enter combatant service. On the evening of the 28th, "Archerfish," with Commander J. F. Enright commanding, was patrolling off Inamba Shima, south of Tokyo bay, when it made radar contact at 24,700 yards with a Jap force, later determined to consist of an aircraft carrier escorted by four destroyers. The base course was southwesterly, speed 20 knots, zigzagging radically. It was soon apparent that the force would pass outside of torpedo range—"Archerfish's" maximum speed of 19 knots was insufficient to permit closing. Enright parallelled the target's base course and sent out a contact report hoping to guide some other submarine into this juicy prize. His 19 knots, though insufficient to close, permitted him to keep up, the radical zigs and zags reducing the Jap speed made good. At 11:40 P.M., three hours after initial contact, the Japanese changed base course to the right. "Archerfish" on the port flank was left farther behind than ever. Enright sent out another contact report to give the new base course. The situation looked hopeless, but still "Archerfish" hung on. At 3:00 A.M., after more than six hours of maximum speed chasing, the Japanese made a radical change of course to the left and Enright found himself on the track of the formation. At 3:05, "Archerfish" submerged and started the approach. Twelve minutes later six torpedoes were fired from a position 1,400 yards on the starboard bow of the target. The four hits that resulted were all that were necessary. The Japs attempted to tow the cripple to port but it sank several hours later. Enright identified his target as a "Hayataka" class carrier of 29,000 tons. In the years immediately preceding the war, Japan had laid the keels of three superbattleships. Mounting 18-inch guns, they were to be the largest and most powerful combatant ships ever built. The first two were commissioned as "Yamato" and "Musashi." The third remained a mystery until the facts were learned at the end of the war. It had been converted to a carrier, named "Shinano," commissioned Nov. 18, and sunk by submarine attack on Nov. 29, while on its maiden voyage. Its full load displacement was 71,890 tons. "Archerfish" had sunk the largest carrier ever built and the largest ship in history to go down from submarine attack.

The practice of sinking Jap carriers before they could see action was becoming established—first "Taiho" and now "Shinano." But there was to be a third, only 20 days after Enright's outstanding performance. On Dec. 15, 1944, as a prelude to the invasion of Luzon, U.S. forces landed on the island of Mindoro in the west-central Philippines. A Japanese task force, consisting of the heavy cruiser "Ashigara" and several destroyers, attempted to destroy the Mindoro beachhead. This force, lacking air cover, was easily beaten off and two of the destroyers were sunk. Survivors from these destroyers were captured and when questioned as to the absence of air cover they stated that the carrier which was scheduled to rendezvous with them had been sunk a few days previously by submarine attack in the East China sea. This time it was "Redfish," commanded by Commander L. D. McGregor, which had replaced "Sealion II" in the patrol area north of Formosa.

Shortly after noon of Dec. 19, "Redfish" was forced to submerge by the approach of a Jap plane. McGregor stayed down to await developments. Because of earlier attacks he had only four torpedoes remaining for his forward tubes, but still had his full quota of four in the tubes and four in the racks aft. At 4:24 P.M. the masts of two destroyers were sighted and three minutes later the top hamper of an aircraft carrier came into view. At 4:35, just eight minutes after the first sighting, McGregor fired his four remaining bow torpedoes at the carrier, and a moment later let go with four stern tubes at one of the escorting destroyers. These last four missed, but one torpedo of the first salvo caught the carrier in its engineering spaces. It stopped and listed to starboard. "Redfish" remained at periscope depth while a reload was started aft. McGregor's mental strain during the next few minutes probably was beyond description—a helpless carrier less than 1,000 yards away and all tubes empty. By 4:49, one tube was ready and judgment gave way to impatience. McGregor fired his single torpedo. It struck at the point of aim—just abaft the island superstructure. The torpedo explosion was followed immediately by an unearthly series of blasts. The torpedo had set off the aircraft bombs and the thousands of gallons of aviation gasoline. McGregor kept his periscope exposed to assure himself that the ship was doomed and to take photographs of his victim. One destroyer spotted him and rushed in for the kill. Deep submergence was ordered. While passing 150 feet, the blow struck. Seven well-placed depth charges exploded all around "Redfish." The bow planes jammed in the hard rise position, the steering gear jammed with rudder hard left; the hydraulic system, the gyrocompass and all listening gear were knocked out of commission. The pressure hull was cracked in the forward torpedo room. One of the torpedoes just loaded aft made a hot run in the tube to give off gases and noise as a continuous marker of "Redfish's" position. Several battery jars were cracked; there were numerous air leaks. "Redfish" settled to the bottom in 232 feet of water to await the final blows which all hands felt were sure to come. But they never did. The depth charging became progressively farther away. "Redfish" licked its wounds and after dark blew itself to the surface to work its way home for a well-earned and much-needed overhaul. Its companion on the bottom, the new carrier "Unryu," en route to its first combat action, remained. The air cover for the Mindoro bombardment force never arrived.

The campaign for the capture of Okinawa which started on April 1, 1945, was the last major operation of the war.

For this, as for all other major amphibious operations, submarines were again used to guard against surprise attack by Jap surface forces. But by this time, Japan had only few capital ships. Not a first-line carrier remained in operating condition; the few that hadn't been sunk were under repair for damages inflicted by submarine or plane. A few cruisers were in Singapore, isolated from Okinawa and from the Japanese home islands by the U.S. occupation of the Philippines. All other remnants of the once proud Japanese fleet were based in the Inland sea, and submarines were stationed to watch the three entrances thereto—Bungo Suido, Kii Suido and Shimonoseki strait. Once again they had orders to "report before attacking." With all their losses the Japanese had one ace-in-the-hole remaining—the battleship "Yamato," the most powerful ship afloat. On the night of April 6–7, a task force consisting of "Yamato," the light cruiser "Yahagi" and seven destroyers, embarked on a suicidal attempt to break up the Okinawa landings. And suicidal it proved to be. Sortieing through Bungo Suido, the southwestern entrance to the Inland sea, they were immediately contacted by the submarines "Threadfin" and "Hackleback" who, in accordance with their orders, sacrificed their chances for attacking to trail at high speed and to send out a series of contact reports. Based on this information, planes of Admiral Raymond Spruance's 5th fleet caught the Japanese flatfooted the next morning. "Yamato," "Yahagi" and the destroyers, "Hamakaze," "Isokaze," Asashino" and "Kasumi" were sunk Only three destroyers escaped. For all practical purposes, it was the end of the Japanese navy.

But there still remained the cruisers at Singapore—"Takao," still out of commission from "Darter's" attack, the heavy cruiser "Myoko," with its stern blown off by the submarine "Bergall" on Dec. 13, 1944, the heavy cruiser "Ashigara" and the light cruiser "Isuzu." These last two were not to escape the submarines. The sun of April 7 that witnessed the destruction of the "Yamato" task force also saw, 2,000 miles to the southward along the Malay barrier, the end of "Isuzu," victim of three hits from six torpedoes fired by "Charr." "Ashigara" was the next and the last on the list of major combatant sinkings, victim of a British submarine, H.M.S. "Trenchant," commanded by Commander A. R. Hezlett, who destroyed it with five torpedo hits in a brilliantly executed attack in the shallow waters close into the coast of Sumatra on June 8, 1945.

* * *

IMPORTANCE of results was the criterion in selecting the actions described in the foregoing accounts. Space has not permitted the recounting of the many actions in which submarines sank 42 destroyers, 26 Japanese and 3 German submarines (exclusive of those sunk in European and Atlantic waters) and the countless minor combatant vessels—destroyer escorts, coast defense vessels, destroyer minelayers, picket boats, etc. The stories of these many engagements lay buried in the mass of sixteen hundred odd submarine patrol reports, awaiting the future historian to bring them to light. That future historian would uncover many deeds of skill and daring—factors which could not be gauged merely by the size or importance of the victim. The fast weaving destroyer was more difficult to hit than the lumbering battleship; the enemy submarine and the small destroyer escort were hardest of all. And for intrepidity, who could excel the submarine captain (there were more than a few of them) who deliberately exposed his periscope to an enemy destroyer, to sink it as it charged down on him with bone in its teeth and depth charges set? Those stories were still untold. Soon after the war started, submarines became known as the "silent service." Their activities and their successes were hidden behind a veil of secrecy. Anonymity rather than publicity was the watchword. They fought their battles in the Pacific, not in the daily press. An occasional communiqué announced that submarines had sunk several freighters or tankers, but rarely was the sinking of a combatant ship disclosed. Modesty had never been a national trait of the U.S. people, and the public, not understanding the submarine attitude, resented it. But it was self-preservation rather than modesty that dictated the policy. While naval vessels normally operated in groups, the submarine acted alone. Even when operating in a wolf pack, it seldom was in visual contact with its pack mates. The enemy was the only witness to the submarine's action. Rare indeed was the submarine attack which was not followed by vigorous countermeasures, and any announcement of the submarine's success would be *prima facie* evidence that it survived to tell the tale. The submarines could operate with relative impunity only as long as the Japanese maintained their blind faith in the lethality of their antisubmarine weapons. Any doubt would bring improvements and greater submarine losses. The silence policy paid huge dividends in lives of submarine personnel. Japan claimed 468 definite submarine kills. Actually, 52 U.S. submarines were lost during the war, only 42 of which could have been caused by enemy action. While these 52 submarines took a great toll of lives —approximately 16% of the total submarine operating personnel—the number was small as compared with the 781 submarines lost by the Germans, the 130 by the Japanese and the 85 lost by the Italians.

The final score sheet, as verified by Japanese records, disclosed that the submarines accounted for 54.7% of the Japanese merchantmen and 29% of the men-of-war sunk by all agencies, and this by a force which comprised but 1.6% of the total personnel of the United States navy! Impressive as these figures were they did not tell the complete story. The sinking of enemy ships, while the most important, was but one of the many phases of the submarine war. The war in the Pacific offered many unusual opportunities for the employment of submarines and, for the first time in history, they were exploited to the full extent of their capabilities. Many were the tasks assigned which had never been envisioned in prewar planning and training. The ability of the submarine to enter and remain undetected in enemy waters gave it a flexibility of movement denied to other types, and the fleet and force commanders were quick to capitalize on that ability. Evacuation of personnel from enemy-held territory, running ammunition and food into Corregidor and gasoline into Guadalcanal, supplying of guerrillas in the Philippines, landing of marine and army raiders on enemy islands, photographic reconnaissance of enemy beaches prior to amphibious landings, rescue of aviation personnel shot down over enemy waters, gun and rocket bombardments of enemy shore installations, supplying weather information for carrier strikes—these and a host of other tasks were successfully undertaken by the undersea craft. One of these extra-curricular tasks, that of air-sea rescue of aviators, assumed such major proportions that at war's end, with Japanese ships scarce and hard to find, it was absorbing almost 50% of the entire submarine effort. The story of its modest birth and rapid growth are worthy of this record.

Lifeguarding.—During the summer of 1943, ships, personnel and equipment were being assembled in the Pacific for the offensive which was to start with the Gilberts campaign in November. In August a number of new carriers, with their supporting cruisers and destroyers, were formed into task force 15, under Rear Admiral Charles A. Pownall, to conduct a series of hit-and-run raids on various Japanese islands, with the dual purpose of harassing the Japs and training the air crews. For each of these raids, Admiral Pownall requested that a submarine be stationed near the island target for the purpose of rescuing downed aviators. The first two of these air strikes on which submarines were employed, at Marcus island and at Tarawa on Sept. 1 and 20, respectively, offered no opportunities for rescues but they did prove the feasibility of the plan. The highly successful submarine air-sea rescue work, or "lifeguarding" as it came to be called, was the outcome.

The first successful lifeguard mission was that performed by "Skate," who succeeded in rescuing six aviators during and following the carrier strike on Wake island on Oct. 6 and 7, 1943. These rescues, made under most trying conditions in the face of Jap gunfire, met with general acclaim from the carriers and carrier pilots. The submarines were definitely in the lifeguard business for the remainder of the war. Thereafter, no important air strike was ever made without its submarine lifeguards. During the seven and one-half months of hostilities in 1945, submarines spent 2,739 patrol days on lifeguard station, with as many as 20 submarines on such stations simultaneously around the Japanese empire during the closing months of the war.

Altogether, a total of 504 rescues were accomplished by 86 individual submarines. "Tigrone" led with 31, followed by "Tang" with 22, while 17 submarines rescued 10 or more aviators each. In making these rescues, the submarines were catholic in their tastes—army bomber and fighter crews, marine corps fighter pilots, British and U.S. carrier pilots, with a few Japanese airmen, not included in the totals, salvaged for good measure.

Some rescues were purely by accident. A submarine heading for its station, or patrolling its area would occasionally encounter an aviator who had been adrift for days and who had long been given up for lost. On June 7, 1945, "Trutta," en route to its area, rescued an army pilot who had been drifting for six days and who had ridden out a typhoon in his one-man rubber lifeboat. More remarkable still, "Sealion II," on April 2, 1945, while passing through the South China sea, picked up an army bomber crewman who had been adrift in his rubber boat for 23 days, and who, aside from the loss of 40 pounds, was none the worse for his experiences. A few of the rescues were the result of long and thorough searches of a general area where planes were known to be down. But most rescues were the direct result of extensive planning and training which brought about effective co-operation between submarines and planes. For carrier strikes, one or two submarines would be stationed in the vicinity of the island target whereas for the B-29 attacks on the Japanese mainland, three or four would be stationed along the approach and retirement routes. The plane crews would be briefed on the location of these lifeguards, and planes in trouble would head for the submarine and ditch in its vicinity or would send a ditching message which the submarine would intercept and head for the position to start its search.

Many of the rescues were routine in nature; others were accomplished with the exercise of outstanding resourcefulness and daring. Perhaps leading the field in both of these attributes was the rescue on April 1, 1944, of a carrier pilot who had landed on the reefs of the Japanese air base at Woleai in the Caroline Islands. The story is best told in the words of the official report of the commanding officer:

0825 [8:25 A.M.] Planes sighted, headed for Woleai. Contacted aircraft by voice and learned of 'Downed Pilot' drifting toward the reefs.

0840 Made full speed on four engines. From here on, the picture in the skies looked like a gigantic "Cleveland Air Show." With dozens of fighters forming a comfortable umbrella above us, we watched a show that made the Hollywood "colossals" seem tame. We rounded the southeast coast of Woleai one to two miles off the beach and had the perfect "ringside seat." The plastering that the airmen gave this Jap base was terrific! Bombs of all sizes rained on every structure on the island. Several buildings seemed to be lifted and thrown high in the air. Causeways between the various islands were bombed. Oil or gasoline storage tanks blew up covering the islands with heavy clouds of black smoke. The runway on the island was hit time and again with large and small bombs. It was hard to believe that anything could be left on the islands after the first waves of planes had gone over, and yet some bursts of AA. fire continued to meet the planes on each attack. The bombers hit Woleai from the south, waited for the smoke to clear, reformed, and then gave it the works from east-west courses! Fighters seemed to hit the place from all directions, peeling off from high above and diving straight into the AA. fire that still persisted. Many looked as if they would go right on through the blanket of smoke and crash on the islands, but all managed to pull out just above the trees. Fires blazed intermittently on Woleai and most of its adjacent islands and gradually the AA. defense was reduced to a few sporadic bursts.

Fighters now zoomed the "Harder" one mile off the northeast corner of Woleai and guided us toward the downed pilot.

1145 He was finally sighted on the northwest tip of the second island to the west of Woleai. Battle surface stations were manned, the ship flooded down, and maneuvered into a spot about 1,500 yards off the beach. White water was breaking over the shoals only 20 yards in front of the ship and the fathometer had ceased to record. Planes now advised us that if rescue looked too difficult from here (and it did) that a better approach might be made from another direction. Backed off to make approach from another angle. The aviator had been standing on the beach and was now observed to fall and lie there outstretched on the sand. His collapse was undoubtedly due to physical exhaustion, but also to the disappointment in seeing his chances of rescue fade away. We were then advised by the plane that further air reconnaissance showed the first approach best after all. Reversed course and headed back at full speed. Made ready the rubber boat (no paddles were aboard), selected Lieutenant Sam Logan, "J" "W" Thomason, SC1c, and Francis X. Ryan, MoMM1c, from a large group of volunteers and maneuvered the ship in for a second attempt at rescue. Moved in again until the forward torpedo room reported, "Bottom scraping forward" (soundings at zero fathom) and worked both screws to keep the bow against the reef while preventing the ship from getting broadside to the waves.

1200 The three volunteers dove over the side and commenced pushing and towing their rubber boat toward the beach about 1200 yards away. A line was played out from the sub to the rubber raft in order to pull it back from the beach. Meanwhile, one of the planes had dropped another rubber boat to the stranded aviator who got in and commenced feebly paddling it to sea against the tide. When the rescue party reached a spot where they could stand up, Thomason was directed to remain with the rubber boat while Lieut. Logan and Ryan waded on through the surf toward the aviator. Both were in the breakers now most of the time and their feet and legs were badly cut by the coral reefs. After about half an hour, Logan and Ryan, alternately swimming and wading, reached the aviator whose raft had meanwhile drifted farther away. By this time he was thoroughly exhausted. They put him in the raft and by alternately pushing and swimming headed back toward their rubber boat from which a line led to the submarine about 500 yards. Meanwhile a float plane, (also attempting the rescue) taxied over the line to the raft and it parted! —The entire rescue party was now stranded. Thomason was then recalled and managed to swim back to the sub after a hard battle against the tide. Another volunteer swimmer, Freeman Paquet, Jr., GM1c, then dove over the side and finally managed to swim a line to the three men standing just inshore of the heavy breakers. This line was made fast to the raft and, little by little, the four men were pulled through the breakers and brought back to the ship.

Throughout the entire rescue, the cooperation of the aviators was superb. They kept up a continuous pounding of the islands by bombs and flew in low to strafe the Japs and divert their attention from the rescue. In spite of this, Jap snipers concealed in the trees along the beach commenced shooting at the ship and rescue party and bullets whined over the bridge, uncomfortably close. The rescue could never have been attempted without the protection afforded by the planes. Too much praise cannot be given to the officers and three men who effected this rescue. Its daring execution, under the noses of the Japs and subject to sniper fire from the beach, can be classified as a truly courageous accomplishment, and the rescued aviator—(Ensign John R. Galvin)—though physically exhausted, showed a character that refused to admit defeat. It is a privilege to serve with men such as these.

This account has been written in considerable detail partly to portray the spectacular air smashing of a Jap base, and partly in sheer pride of the volunteers who carried out the rescue . . .

Commander S. D. Dealey, who commanded "Harder" and who wrote the above report, was outstanding in everything he undertook. On the same patrol in which this rescue was made, he sank one Japanese destroyer and damaged another. On his next patrol he earned the congressional medal of honour for the unbelievable performance of sinking five Jap destroyers within the space of a few days. Commander Dealey did not live to receive this highest of all awards. "Harder" was lost with all hands on the following patrol while attempting to add another destroyer to its long list of victims.

Vying with "Harder's" rescue in resourcefulness was the rescue on June 13, 1944, of a carrier pilot just two miles off the coast of Guam when that island was still in Jap hands. While approaching this aviator, "Stingray," commanded by Commander S. C. Loomis, Jr., was forced to dive by fire from shore batteries. With shells dropping all around the periscope, "Stingray" continued in and after three unsuccessful attempts lasting almost four hours, succeeded in having the downed pilot grab hold of the periscope, to be towed out of range of the shore batteries and then taken aboard.

In addition to the lives saved, submarine lifeguarding exerted an influence on air force morale which had far-reaching effects on the progress of the war. Pilots flying their fighters or bombers hundreds of miles from their bases or carriers became more aggressive in their attacks when they realized that even were their planes shot down in Jap waters they had an excellent chance for rescue. As the curve of successful rescues rose, the confidence of the fliers in the ability of the submarines to bring them home rose with it. This confidence reached its climax during the closing days of the war, when a carrier pilot remained off the coast of Japan guarding his downed wingman until he himself ran out of gas and had to ditch. Rescued by "Whale" and asked to explain why he hadn't tried to get back to his ship, he stated that he wasn't worried; he knew there would be a submarine along to pick him up.

"Submarine fortress" constructed by the Germans on the Atlantic coast of France to shelter U-boats in port from aerial attack. This photograph was smuggled out of German-occupied France in 1942

Lifeguarding profited the rescuers as well as the rescued. Submarines had been the lone wolves of the U.S. navy. Their movements were cloaked in silence; they patrolled enemy waters denied to the surface forces. They stalked and struck and hid—a sinister arm fighting a sinister type of warfare. But with each successful rescue the submarine force and its methods became less and less a mystery to other units. By the time the war ended, submarines had attained their rightful status among the honoured branches of the armed services.

British Submarine Operations

The importance of the submarine as an offensive weapon in naval warfare was brought home to the British just seven weeks after the outbreak of World War I. On Sept. 22, 1914, the first of the German U-boat aces, Weddigen, in his U-9, sank the British cruisers "Hogue," "Aboukir," and "Cressy," with a loss of more than 1,100 lives. The action took place in the English channel, with all three ships sinking in little more than an hour after the first attack. The royal navy had had a sizable submarine fleet in commission at the time—78 as compared with

30 for the Germans—but up until this action occurred the submarine had been looked upon as a defensive weapon for coastal patrol work and little had been done to develop its offensive capabilities, or to counter the submarine when employed offensively by the enemy. Even prior to these sinkings the potential strength of the submarine had been indicated when on Sept. 5, the light cruiser "Pathfinder" went down from U-boat attack, to be avenged a week later by the sinking of the German cruiser "Hela" off Heligoland by E-9, commanded by Lieutenant Commander Max Horton. These victories of the submarine over surface vessels augured ill for the traditional supremacy of the British fleet, and the attitude of the admiralty concerning submarines changed from complacency to grave concern. Every effort was expended toward the development of antisubmarine weapons and methods.

The activities of the German submarines during World War I and how close they took Germany to final victory, are too well known to be recorded herein. The lesson learned was not to be forgotten, and in the years between the wars the British, through diplomatic means, endeavoured to outlaw the submarine as a weapon of war. In addition, in the early 1930s, the British perfected the Asdic —an echo-ranging, underwater sounding equipment for the location of submerged objects—for use on destroyers and on other antisubmarine craft. Following this development, the admiralty's attitude toward the seriousness of the submarine threat again changed; the royal navy then felt that it could successfully put down any submarine menace that might threaten, and with this confidence came a more conservative attitude toward their own submarine branch.

In the peace years, the royal navy maintained a modest submarine fleet. Small groups were stationed with the far eastern fleet, in the Mediterranean and in home waters. In Sept. 1939, there were 60 submarines ready for service. Most of these were of the "H" and "L" classes, launched during 1918–19, of limited capabilities. However, 11 were under construction and a 12th, "Thetis," which had foundered during its trials off Liverpool in June, was being salvaged, to be renamed "Thunderbolt."

Upon the outbreak of war in Europe, the British recalled their submarines from the far east for duty in home waters. Since France, her ally, possessed a very large submarine fleet, an agreement was made that French submarines would conduct the patrols in the Mediterranean. The British submarines would patrol the North sea and the Bay of Biscay.

The operating theatres of action for the British submarines in World War II shifted with the progress of the war. In the beginning, the channel and the home waters were patrolled. Then, in 1940, came the Norwegian campaign with the invasion of Norway—this opened up the Norwegian coast, the fjords of the Kattegat and the Skagerrak. After the fall of France, the patrols of the Mediterranean and the French coastal position became the royal navy's responsibility. And, finally, during the summer of 1944, British submarines joined in force the U.S. submarines operating in far eastern waters against the Japanese.

The day Germany invaded Norway, "Truant" torpedoed and sank the German cruiser "Karlsruhe" off the Norwegian coast. Following this initial success, British submarines maintained a close-in offensive in the Norwegian waters against the German transport and supply ships supporting the invasion forces and succeeded in sinking 90,000 tons of German invasion shipping during the month of April 1940. A notable event of this campaign was the sinking of the "Rio de Janeiro," a 5,000-ton German troop transport by the Polish submarine "Orzel." "Orzel" had escaped from axis custody in the Baltic and after a very dangerous voyage without compass or charts had made its way to the English coast and joined up as an operating unit of the royal navy.

With the fall of France in June 1940, Germany became an Atlantic power and made haste to use the many strategical advantages which possession of the French coast brought her. At Lorient, St. Nazaire and other French coastal ports, U-boat pens were built. The U-boats commenced to operate in force from these bases against the Allies' Atlantic life line.

The British shifted their submarine offensive at this time to the Bay of Biscay, the channel coast of France and the Mediterranean. Patrols in the channel were very hazardous because of the danger of mines, the shallow water, and the ever-present danger of attack from nearby land-based axis aircraft. In these areas, the submarines sought as their main targets the U-boats entering and leaving their coastal bases, the German blockade runners, and the small coastal convoys which the Germans attempted to operate along the French and Dutch coasts.

A keen disappointment to the royal submarines occurred when the German battleships "Scharnhorst" and "Gneisenau" successfully eluded a large group of submarines patrolling off Brest, France, in late March of 1941. Although aircraft reconnaissance had furnished good intelligence and the submarine deployment seemed sure to make contact should the "Scharnhorst" and "Gneisenau" sortie, the operation came to naught. The German ships escaped from Brest at night and, aided by rough seas and foggy weather, avoided the deployed submarines, passing through the English channel and into the North sea without damage.

Italy entered the war on June 10, 1940, on the side of the axis powers, and the Mediterranean with its contiguous waters—the Tyrrhenian, Ionian, Adriatic and Aegean seas—became the principal theatre of naval war. British submarines operated in this area for three years while the opposing armies waged the land war along the coast and over the deserts of North Africa.

In the initial stages of the campaign in the Mediterranean, the British had only a very meagre force of submarines available. Operations in the Mediterranean were difficult because of the transparent water, the coastal shallows and the frequent calms that prevailed. In such waters, the large type submarine was unsuitable for offensive work. Three of the first four large submarines that went out from Malta after Italy's entry into the war were lost.

As the war in the Mediterranean progressed, the British submarine strength increased despite losses suffered in offensive operations. New submarines of the U-class arrived and operated from Malta. These small submarines, although lacking both speed and endurance, were particularly suited for patrolling narrow waters. They concentrated on the Italian shipping routes between Tripoli and the Sicilian ports; the larger submarines operated in the eastern Mediterranean and in the Adriatic.

The advance of British land forces beyond Bengasi in Feb. 1941, marked the beginning of the first Allied major campaign in North Africa. In support of the campaign, British submarines set out to interrupt the axis convoy traffic to Libya. By the end of February, when the rout of the Italian army ended at El Agheila in the Gulf of Sirte, British submarines in the Mediterranean had sunk 100,000 tons of axis shipping.

As the land war in the Mediterranean theatre shifted back and forth from 1941 to 1943, the missions of submarines continued with additional tasks being imposed to meet the ever-changing situations. In the evacuation of Crete, H.M.S. "Thrasher" embarked 68 Allied personnel and transported them safely to Alexandria, Egypt. The larger type submarines, especially minelayers, were used in the vital service of supply to the beleaguered island of Malta. The axis powers had won control of the air over the island and had almost choked off all means of bringing in supplies by surface ships. To the submarines fell this mission of supply, and submarines operating as underwater freighters and passenger ships sailed from Gibraltar and Alexandria.

Throughout the long siege of Malta, British submarines continued to operate from the little battle-scarred island. Underground workshops and storage vaults were constructed, and safe living quarters were provided for the submarine crews resting between patrols. When the bombing became too intense, submarines in port for repairs were taken a short distance to sea, submerged, and work was continued while lying on the bottom. The spirit displayed by the British submarine personnel and their supporting forces at Malta in the face of such hardships was noteworthy and contributed much to the eventual success of the Allied naval forces in the Mediterranean theatre. As the Germans made greater efforts to supply and reinforce Gen. Erwin Rommel's troops in North Africa, the tonnage score of the British submarines rose. From February to mid-November 1941, the axis lost 300,000 tons of supply shipping to submarine attacks. Among this tonnage were five of the largest Italian liners which the axis powers were using in a desperate effort to reinforce their armies in North Africa. The importance of these sinkings was heightened by the fact that they were southbound and full of troops and war material when sunk. Such sinkings put a great strain on the German air force, which was then compelled to use large numbers of aircraft for transport and supply missions.

The policy of the Italians throughout the war in the Mediterranean was to take no undue risks with their fleet. When they did put to sea, they were generally very closely and heavily screened. For these reasons, there were few real opportunities for the British submarines to make attacks against heavy combatant ships. However, those occasions which were afforded were fully exploited. In a night surface attack, "Utmost" sank an Italian cruiser in Nov. 1941, and in 1942, the cruisers "Giovanni delle Bande Nere" and "Armando Diaz" were sunk by "Urge" and "Upright" respectively. By such sinkings, the "Unity" class submarine proved its deadly offensive power in shallow water operations.

As the land war in Africa gradually turned in favour of the Allied armies in late 1942 and early 1943, the axis powers, in an endeavour to stave off defeat, used every means to reinforce the Afrika korps and to maintain a foothold in North Africa. Although the Germans made wide use of air transport for supplies and troops, they still had to rely on ships to carry bulk supplies across the Mediterranean. The axis convoys were almost always under the protection of German land-based aircraft—either from Sicily or Tunisia. To the royal navy's submarines fell the greater share of the burden of disrupting this reinforcement traffic. An example of the effectiveness of the British submarines against this convoy traffic was the record of H.M.S. 'Splendid." In the closing months of the African war, "Splendid" sank three tankers, six supply ships, two destroyers and three antisubmarine vessels.

When the Italian fleet surrendered on Sept. 11, 1943, the Mediterranean campaign ended. Between the entry of Italy into the war and the surrender of its fleet, British submarines sank 1,335,000 tons of axis shipping in the Mediterranean. The submarines' contribution to victory was not without its cost; 41 British submarines were lost in that theatre of action during the campaign.

Although the Mediterranean theatre occupied the major share of the British submarine effort during the campaign in North Africa, some submarines did operate in the Arctic during the same period, maintaining patrols between the North Cape and Varanger fjord. The mission of the patrols was to attack German shipping bound for Kirkenes, Norway, or Petsamo, Finland, with supplies and reinforcements for the German and Finnish troops on the north Russian front. A secondary mission was to help divert attention from the passage of British convoys to Murmansk and Archangel, U.S.S.R. In these Arctic patrols, the British submarines operated in co-ordination with Russian submarines and were based at Polyarni, near the mouth of Kola inlet, at the head of which lies Murmansk. Never before had submarines of the royal navy operated under such arduous conditions. Material difficulties and personnel hardships were numerous and ever-present. However, despite great handicaps, the patrols were maintained; several heavily-laden German supply ships were sunk.

The damaging of the German battleship "Tirpitz" by British X-craft in Oct. 1943, announced to the world the British use of midget submarines. Built in 1942–43, the X-class of submarine was about 50 feet in length and had a crew of four. The cruising range of the X-craft was very limited, less than 100 miles. It was designed to be towed to the vicinity of the scene of action.

Near the end of the war in the Pacific, X-craft entered Singapore to attack the damaged Japanese heavy cruisers "Myoko" and "Takao."

The royal navy also developed a human torpedo for use during World War II. This torpedo, operated by a crew of two, was designed to permit attacks on anchored targets. On an attack it manoeuvred at slow speed toward its target and then submerged. The nose charge was fixed to the enemy hull and the crew escaped on the torpedo body, the charge being detonated some time later by the action of a time fuse. These torpedoes were used successfully in attacks against the strongly defended base at Palermo, Sicily. There on Jan. 3, 1943, they sank the Italian cruiser "Ulpio Traino" and damaged a transport. Later, in June 1944, they sank the German-manned Italian cruiser "Bolzano" in the harbour of Spezia, Italy.

During the last year of the war, British submarines operated with their U.S. colleagues in the war against Japan from bases in southwest Australia. They were formed, with the U.S. submarines, into one force under the operational control of Commander Submarines Southwest Pacific.

The story of the U.S. submarines during this period was also the story of the British.

During World War II, British submarines sank 2,000,000 tons and damaged approximately an additional 1,000,000 tons of axis naval ships and merchant shipping. Seventy-two British submarines were lost. The royal navy could well be proud of its tough, hard-hitting submarine service.

Japanese Submarine Operations

At the time of Pearl Harbor, the Japanese navy possessed a modern submarine fleet. Numerically, Japan had the largest force of cruiser-type submarines in commission. It began building up its submarine fleet after World War I, using as prototypes the surrendered German submarines that had been allotted to it by the terms of the peace treaty. The Japanese considered themselves naturally adapted as a race to submarine warfare and devoted much interest and effort to development of submarine designs in the pre-World War II years.

Between 1920 and 1940, various submarine types were designed and built for experimental and operational purposes. Of these, the long-range reconnaissance type and the midget submarines were perhaps the most noteworthy. The long-range reconnaissance type was a large submarine of about 2,000 tons surface displacement, equipped with a float plane and having a fairly high surface speed, about 22 knots. The midget submarine had been fairly well developed prior to the outbreak of hostilities, while during World War II the Japanese developed and built the very large I-400 class reconnaissance and cargo submarine. This type was designed primarily for the transportation of supplies, fuel and planes to the beleaguered outlying Japanese island garrisons. An appreciation of the unusual size of this type can be had from the following tabular comparison of the I-400 class with a standard U.S. fleet submarine, which was considered a large type:

	I-400	U.S. fleet Submarine
Length over-all	400 feet	310 feet
Displacement, surfaced	5,700 tons	1,600 tons
Complement	21 officers	8 officers
	171 men	72 men

The I-400 class was fitted with eight-bow torpedo tubes and could carry four planes. To launch and recover the aircraft, a catapult and a portable aeroplane crane were installed.

Japanese submarines, except for the midget class, were not designed for mass production. As the war progressed, Japanese building facilities could not keep up with submarine losses and, consequently, the number of submarines available gradually diminished. However, the midget class was readily mass-produced and the war's end found hundreds of midget submarines in production and ready for operational use to defend the Japanese home islands against invasion.

The Japanese conception of the strategic use of the submarine arm was principally as an adjunct to their surface fleets. The submarine was used extensively for scouting and reconnaissance in advance of their surface units. Submarine reconnaissance of an objective area was always made preliminary to an amphibious assault or invasion. Offensively, the Japanese expected to employ their submarines in strength in ambush lines—that is, they were to be deployed across an enemy major fleet's track to attack and re-attack the enemy's large combatant surface units. It was for this reason and not because of any humanitarian motives that Japanese naval policy placed little stress on the submarine's role in commerce destruction. The submarine arm was integrated into the various fleets of the navy, and there was no central operational command for the submarine effort nor any over-all plan for the efficient employment of submarines.

The navy was hampered in its submarine combat operations by serious interference from the Japanese army, which was able to force the navy to use a large portion of its available submarines for transport and supply duties. Coupled with this interference, the Japanese navy, after the first year of war, began to feel the serious shortage of scientific and technological knowledge. As compared with the Allied nations, little real progress was made in the development, production, and installation of radar, sonar, radio and fire control equipment. The Japanese were cognizant of these deficiencies very early and, as a result, planned their submarine operations with marked caution in an effort to minimize losses. The navy plan was to "save" the submarines for use against the U.S. fleet by restricting targets to the more valuable combatant ships. This encouraged in the submarine commanding officers an extreme sense of caution that amounted almost to timidity.

Three submarines accompanied the Japanese carrier task force which attacked Pearl Harbor on Dec. 7, 1941. Other submarines had left Japan earlier and conducted patrol and reconnaissance in the vicinity of the principal Hawaiian Islands to keep a close observation of the movements of the large number of U.S. fleet units present in the islands. Of the submarines directly participating in the Pearl Harbor attack, some were loaded with midget submarines. Two of the midgets made a successful penetration of the Pearl Harbor estuary and claimed the sinking of one battleship of the "Oklahoma" class. Shortly after Pearl Harbor, in the southern Pacific areas, Japanese submarines were assigned reconnaissance and mining missions in the Philippine and Singapore areas. It was a Japanese submarine that initially located the British capital ships "Prince of Wales" and "Repulse" and supplied the intelligence which enabled the Japanese to attack with torpedo planes and sink these two valuable ships in the waters north of Singapore.

Prior to the battle of Midway, the Japanese submarines were assigned reconnaissance missions in the vicinity of Midway and Pearl Harbor. To co-operate in the Midway offensive, the Japanese deployed three submarines on a scouting line to the north of their main body. In the Midway action, on June 7, 1942, the I-168 sank the crippled U.S. aircraft carrier "Yorktown."

In the Indian ocean, the Japanese waged unrestricted submarine warfare on Allied convoys in a limited fashion. At no time did they have more than a squadron (about ten submarines) available for such duty. The Germans assigned a small group of their long-range, large 1,200-ton U-boats to operate in loose co-ordination with the Japanese in this theatre. The Germans established a liaison group with the Japanese for their submarines at Penang, Batavia and Singapore. The Japanese high naval command in the Southwest Pacific area had orders from Tokyo to co-operate with the German submarines in the matter of supply and maintenance, but had nothing to do with the operational control of the U-boats. Japanese submarines sank about 70 merchant vessels in the Indian ocean areas during the period of their employment in offensive patrols against Allied commerce.

Thirteen Japanese submarines co-operated in the invasion of the Aleutians in June 1942. In May 1943, when the United States forces attacked at Attu and later at Kiska, the Japanese position became untenable. Not desiring to risk surface transports, the Japanese employed 15 submarines to evacuate the Kiska garrison of 700 men to Paramoshiri.

During 1944 and 1945, more than one-third of the available submarines were employed in transport and supply to the various isolated island bases, while German U-boats co-operated with the Japanese in blockade-running between Germany and the far east. Rubber and tin were carried to Germany and, in return, the Germans shipped plans of new weapons, optical supplies, and a variety of precision machine tools. This mission was a hazardous one; about half the U-boats engaged in the traffic failed to return.

The United States fleet suffered a serious loss on Sept. 15, 1942, when the aircraft carrier "Wasp" was sunk southeast of the Solomons Islands by I-19. Other notable successes of Japanese submarines were the sinking of the escort carrier "Liscombe Bay" during the Gilberts campaign, and that of the heavy cruiser "Indianapolis" by the I-58 on July 29, 1945, northeast of Leyte, P.I.

In comparison with their modest successes, the Japanese lost 130 submarines during the war. The reasons for their over-all ineffectiveness were several—lack of building materials, backwardness of scientific research and efficiency of Allied antisubmarine measures all contributed. But perhaps the most important cause of the failure lay in the mistaken strategy of their employment by the Japanese high command. There was lacking a unity of purpose, an over-all war plan for the integrated employment of a large submarine force. When the navy became embroiled in the war, it shunted its submarine forces here and there —subordinating them to the service of the Japanese army and avoiding too-close contact with the enemy for fear of losses.

The intrinsic military value of the submarine as a powerful weapon of opportunity, of surprise in offensive warfare, was never fully appreciated by the Japanese.

The Submarine and the Future

Of what use would the submarine be in future wars? Did the Allies develop their antisubmarine measures to a point where the submarine ceased to be a menace? Had the atomic age made the submarine, as well as all the other conventional naval types, obsolete? To these questions, only qualified answers could be made at the end of the eventful decade 1937–46.

However, it could be said positively that research and development would greatly influence the employment of submarines.

The Allies defeated the U-boat campaign in the Atlantic. However, had World War II continued and the Germans been able to place their new type high-speed, long-submerged endurance submarines into combat service, the issue might have been different. In addition to this interim type, the Germans sought to build a true submarine—one capable of remaining submerged indefinitely, possessing high submerged speed, and able to operate at great depths. It became known later that the Germans had working prototype models of a true submarine and apparently would have been able to develop the type in a short time. Whether Allied antisubmarine measures would have been able to cope with these new type U-boats remained problematical.

The atom bombs of Hiroshima and Nagasaki ushered in the atomic age of warfare. Press reports of the first and second Bikini atom bomb tests against modern naval ships left little doubt that revolutionary changes were in the offing in the design of warships to suit the requirements of atomic warfare.

It was significant that the naval type which best withstood these tests was the submarine.

It was probable that the atomic age of warfare would bring about the dispersal of great cities and industrial centres. It might force radical changes in naval tactics—the elimination of the concepts of large, surface task forces made up of battleships, carriers, cruisers and the many light and supporting forces. It might well be that the submarine would emerge as the only practical naval type able to navigate and hold the command of the seas of the world against an enemy power possessing atomic weapons.

It had been said that the future would belong to those weapons capable of operating in a medium of three dimensions—the submarine and the aeroplane. Who could say that huge atomic-powered submarines built as aircraft carriers, as battleships, or as amphibious assault ships might not rise from the ocean depths to decide the issue should a World War III engulf the world?

(*See* also Navies of the World; Shipbuilding; World War II.)

(R. G. V.; C. A. Ld.; C. W. Sr.; E. T. R.)

Bibliography.—B. Acworth, *Life in a Submarine* (London, 1941); R. H. Barnes, *United States Submarine* (1945); R. Baxter, *Stand by to Surface* (London, 1944); R. Briggs, *The Super Submarine* (1942); R. J. Casey, *Battle Below* (1945); H. F. Cope, *Serpent of the Seas* (1942); K. Donitz, *Die U-bootswaffe* (Berlin, 1943); Great Britain Admiralty, *His Majesty's Submarines* (London, 1945); A. M. Low, *Submarine at War* (1942); D. Masters, *Up Periscope* (1943); C. Mayers, *Submarines, Admirals and Navies* (1940); J. Schepke, *U-boot-fahrer von Heute* (Berlin, 1940); U.S. Bureau of Ships, *Marine Material Guide* (1944); *Submarine Safety, Respiration and Rescue Devices* (1945); H. S. Zim, *Submarines* (1945).

Subsidies

See Agriculture; Business Review; Prices.

Sucrose

See Chemistry.

Sudan

See Anglo-Egyptian Sudan.

Sudetenland

See Czechoslovakia; Germany; World War II.

Suez Canal

The prominence of the Suez canal during the years 1937–46 was the immediate outcome of the events of 1935 and 1936. Italy, having conquered Ethiopia, effected a junction between its Red sea colonies of Eritrea and Italian Somaliland. The possession of Libya had already given Italy a frontier with Egypt on the east, and by the further enlargement of its African empire, as well as by the requirements of the Ethiopian expedition, the Suez canal had assumed a new significance for Italy. The campaign had necessitated the employment of the canal for the transit of war material and when the League of Nations had imposed sanctions under Article 16 of the covenant the closing of the canal to Italian shipping had been considered. The view had prevailed, however, that such action would be contrary to the stipulations of the Suez Canal convention of 1888. Nevertheless, Italy regarded the possibility of such a closure as a potential threat to its communications, and as making it a virtual prisoner in the Mediterranean, dependent on the goodwill of Britain, although by an agreement of April 16, 1938, both Britain and Italy reaffirmed their intention to respect the terms of the convention.

From 1937 to 1939 Italy sought to secure a more favourable position in regard to the canal by activities designed to weaken Britain's relations with Egypt, and by pressing claims to representation on the board of the Suez Canal company on the ground that it was now the second largest user of the canal. These claims were resisted by the company and were resented by Egypt. The canal was in Egypt's territory and would revert to its control at the expiration in 1968 of the concession granted to the company. The defense of the canal had been a joint Anglo-

Egyptian concern since Britain had taken the place of Turkey under the Suez Canal convention by the terms of the peace treaties after World War I and any changes required the consent of both powers. By the Anglo-Egyptian treaty of 1936, full recognition had been given to Egypt's right of self-defense as an independent sovereign state, and Britain had agreed to withdraw its forces to the canal zone when preparations for their reception were completed. Unable to attain its objectives, Italy proceeded to augment its fleet and military installations in Libya, and in April 1939 it became necessary for Pres. Franklin D. Roosevelt to invite an assurance from Germany and Italy that no aggressive intentions were designed against certain countries, including Egypt.

Suez Canal Traffic Statistics

Year	Number of Transits	Net Tonnage	Receipts (in £)
1937	6,635	36,491,332	10,806,840
1938	6,171	34,418,187	9,658,670
1939	5,277	29,573,394	7,959,000*
1940	2,589	13,535,712	3,667,000
1941	1,804	8,262,841	3,092,000
1942	1,646	7,027,763	3,002,000
1943	2,262	11,273,802	4,431,000
1944	3,320	18,124,952	7,029,000
1945	4,206	25,064,966	9,922,000

*Sterling figures for 1939–45 to the nearest £1,000.

With the outbreak of World War II, and especially the collapse of France in 1940, Italy seized its opportunity. Not only was Britain fully engaged at home, but also the wings of the defensive system covering the Suez canal had folded up through the impotence of France in Tunisia and Syria and the neutralization of the French Mediterranean fleet. Late in 1940, Egypt was invaded from Libya, but the Italian forces halted immediately east of Sidi Barrani, and the British counterstroke in December forced their withdrawal to the back of Cyrenaica. Germany intervened in North Africa in 1941 and by June 1942 the axis troops were again on Egyptian soil and pressing forward to the Nile delta and the Suez canal. This time they were stopped at El Alamein, two days' march west of Alexandria. There a decisive battle was fought at the end of October and with the British victory the land threat to the Suez canal was ended. The danger to the canal from air attack and mine-laying continued, however, until the Allied victory in Tunisia (April–May 1943) and Italy's subsequent surrender. From then on, the full use of the canal became possible again, thus affording help to Burma and facilitating preparations for the campaign against Japan.

In 1945–46, the defense of the canal was under review in negotiations between Britain and Egypt. The withdrawal of British forces to southern Palestine would still permit common defense of the canal even if British garrisons were not to remain in the canal zone. Developments in international affairs in any case required a fresh instrument to replace the Suez Canal convention of 1888.

During 1937–46, the board of the Suez Canal company consisted of 32 directors (19 French, 10 British, 2 Egyptian, and 1 Dutch). Because of wartime conditions, however, there were in 1946, 4 vacancies (3 French and 1 British). After conversations between the canal company and the Egyptian government (1936–37) it was agreed that two of the directors should be Egyptian. The Egyptian government would also appoint a commissioner with right of inquiry into all the company's dealings. The company undertook to pay the government an annual rental of £E300,000 and to contribute the single payment of a like sum toward the cost of the strategic roads beside the canal provided for by the Anglo-Egyptian treaty. Other stipulations covered the employment of Egyptian staff and the basis of valuation for the maximum chargeable for dues. In 1946 the tasks immediately ahead consisted mainly in making up arrears of maintenance and in carrying out local improvements held up by the war. New works were to include improvements in Port Said harbour. (H. J. Sd.)

Bibliography.—R. Guibal, *Peut-on fermer le canal de Suez?* (Paris, 1937); B. Aglietti, *Il canale di Suez ed i rapporti anglo-egiziani* (Florence, 1939); R. Aglion, *La société du canal de Suez* (Paris, 1939); H. J. Schonfield, *The Suez Canal* (London, 1939); A. Siegfried, *Suez and Panama* (1940).

Sugar

World sugar production had increased slowly up to 1923, when the total passed 23,000,000 tons. From then until 1930 there was a relatively rapid increase to 31,800,000 tons, followed by a slight decline and then another increase to over 35,000,000 tons in 1936. After 1937 a new high record of 35,942,000 tons was set in 1940, followed by a steady decline to about 27,200,000 tons in the 1945–46 season—about 7,300,000 tons less than the prewar (1935–39) average. The losses were due to the reduction in cane sugar production in Java and the Philippines, and in beet sugar production in central Europe. In 1940, German-controlled areas reported production of over 3,000,000 tons of raw beet sugar, which had to be deducted from the world total in later years. Production fell off in other European countries; France, for instance, with a prewar (1935–39) average of over 1,000,000 tons, reported only 660,000 tons in 1943. The greater loss was in exportable surplus, which in 1945 was estimated to be almost 35% below the prewar average. Gross exports were estimated by the U.S. department of agriculture at 7,971,000 tons in 1945–46 compared with 12,603,000 tons prewar average 1935–39.

International control of sugar distribution was begun in 1937 under an agreement concluded between 21 countries, and ratified by the U.S. senate Dec. 20, 1937, to allot quotas for five years. The United States Sugar act of 1937 was passed to remedy the situation caused by the supreme court decision invalidating the processing-tax under the Jones-Costigan act of 1934 and the Agriculture Adjustment act. This act continued in force until it was suspended by executive order in 1942. The 1940 U.S. sugar production was maintained at a record level with a depressed market. South American exporting countries were cut off from European markets, and their stocks became available to the United States, resulting in the largest supply on record.

World sugar markets were divided by World War II into three major areas—Japanese-controlled Asia, German-con-

Gathering seed sugar cane in Louisiana for transport to new planting fields during the fall of 1945. Large crops were planted as sugar continued scarce in the United States

"Sugar Shortage," a reflection on the ironies of U.S. sugar rationing during World War II, by Goldberg of the *New York Sun*

trolled Europe and the United Nations areas. There was no trade among these areas; the United Nations remained dependent on the western hemisphere. Prior to the war, the hemisphere was a surplus area to the extent of about 1,300,000 tons, mostly shipped to Europe. At the beginning of 1945, sugar production accessible to the United Nations was estimated at about 20,400,000 tons of raw sugar, or 5% less than had been produced in the same area in the previous season. The year 1945 was expected to be the low point of both production and consumption. Early 1946 reports from all over the world indicated that recovery was taking place slowly. The rebuilding of sugar mills and transportation facilities in Europe had hardly begun in 1946.

The sugar situation was summarized by a committee investigation by the United States house of representatives in 1945 which said the causes of the sugar shortage were as follows: use of sugar, chiefly Cuban, for the making of alcohol to be used in synthetic rubber production; the drought in the Caribbean area; European relief needs; and heavy sugar consumption in the United States in 1944. The committee recommended continued rationing; purchase of the Cuban and Puerto Rican crops; a general review of allotments. The 1946 world production appeared to be increasing by the middle of the year, but stocks were very low so that the supplies for consumption were believed to be about the same as in 1945.

The production of sugar, cane and beet, in continental United States increased steadily up to 1937, when it reached a total of 1,720,000 tons. A decline then began, and the output dropped to 1,399,000 tons of raw sugar by 1943; but it increased to 1,760,000 tons in 1946. The U.S. supply, including that produced in the possessions, was estimated at 4,977,000 tons in 1937; it declined to 3,149,000 tons in 1943 and 3,618,000 tons in 1945. After 1941 the Philippine crop was not included. The United States supply was usually considered to include the surplus of

the Cuban crop. The total, including the Cuban supply, was 8,357,000 tons in 1937, 7,849,000 tons in 1943, and 8,068,000 tons by 1945. The shortage of sugar in the United States was the result of the several changes; reduced domestic production, loss of the Philippine supply, smaller shipments from Puerto Rico and smaller output of Cuba in some years.

Sugar beet acreage in the United States was 816,000 ac. in 1937, slightly below the average of the previous 10 years. The area increased to 1,048,000 ac. in 1942, then declined to 716,000 ac. in 1945 and increased to 865,000 ac. in 1946. The yield during the war years was near the average of 12 tons per ac. which returned a crop of 10,900,000 tons in 1946, compared with an average of 9,568,000 tons during 1935–44. The planted acreage in 1946 was estimated at 930,000 ac., an increase of 20% over 1945, as the result of a vigorous campaign to increase the crop. Abandonment was low, but the scarcity of labour caused harvesting troubles. The competition of other food crops which could be grown with machine work was a factor in holding beet acreage down during the war period.

Sugar beet production increased in the United States from 8,784,000 tons in 1937 to 12,292,000 tons in 1940, declined to 6,753,000 tons in 1944 and then increased again, to 10,916,000 tons in 1946. From these crops of beets the sugar output was 1,288,000 tons in 1937, 1,773,000 tons in 1940 and about 1,228,000 tons in 1945. Prices to beet growers advanced from $5.27 per ton in 1937 to $10.70 in 1944 and $10.20 in 1946; these included price supports of $2.02 per ton in government payments.

U.S. sugar cane production for sugar and seed continued at a stable level after 1937, the acreage for sugar ranging from 307,200 ac. in 1917 to a low of 269,700 ac. in 1940, then up to 298,800 ac. in 1946, as compared with an average of 291,210 ac. 1935–44. The later increases were almost wholly in Florida, under water control. The crop of cane for grinding ranged from 4,218,000 tons in 1940 to a top of 6,658,000 tons in 1946. Prices for the crop to farmers increased from $2.90 per ton in 1937 to over $5.00 per ton in 1946.

U.S. Sugar Production by Leading States, 1937-46
(In thousands of tons)

Beet:	1937	1939	1941	1942	1943	1944	1945	1946
U.S. Total . . .	1,288	1,643	1,484	1,613	933	987	1,228	1,901
Colorado . . .	303	262	299	321	243	230	273	
California . .	288	453	313	347	329	178	216	
Montana . . .	122	140	118	141	122	109	130	
Idaho.	99	127	107	145	111	80	108	
Michigan . . .	79	162	158	172	50	73	97	
Nebraska . . .	113	106	121	104	74	68	88	
Utah	81	100	82	82	65	55	59	
Wyoming . . .	94	92	79	92	28	40	51	
Ohio	14	42	46	54	11	17	32	
Cane:								
U.S. Total . . .	432	471	392	430	466	437	521	
Louisiana . . .	379	406	302	374	406	369	429	
Florida	53	65	90	56	60	68	92	

Under the U.S. Sugar act of 1937, the government made payments to beet and cane producers. From 1938 to 1941 the basic rate was 60 cents per 100 lb. of commercial raw sugar. Payments in 1942 and later years were at 80 cents per 100 lb., with reductions for growers producing 500 tons or more. Other payments were made for losses by abandonment, floods, drought, freeze or disease or insect damage. The total of these subsidies varied from $46,000,000 to $58,000,000 in different years. Other subsidies were paid to producers and processors for "excess" costs or as "incentive" payments to encourage the production of more sugar.

Sugar production in the United States possessions de-

Sugar beet refinery at Picture Butte, Alberta, Canada

clined as in the continental area. The Philippines produced about 1,150,000 tons from 1937 to 1940 inclusive, and thereafter none was available to the United States. In Puerto Rico over 1,000,000 tons was harvested in 1937 and the crop maintained nearly that average up to 1942. Hawaiian production, around 1,000,000 tons, dropped to 880,000 by 1944. The Virgin Islands crop amounted to an average of about only 4,000 tons after 1940. The Cuban crop, mostly bought by the United States during the war years, was 3,379,000 tons in 1937 and dropped to 2,734,000 tons in 1940 but recovered to 4,700,000 tons in 1943 and 4,450,000 tons in 1945.

Consumption of refined sugar in the United States was at a prewar average of 96.5 lb. per capita during the period 1935–39. The national supply included 1,948,000 tons from domestic production, 1,849,000 tons from the possessions, and 3,018,000 from foreign sources, mostly Cuban. Exports amounted to about 109,000 tons. By 1941, the supply had increased, because of larger crops and imports, to 11,166,000 tons; per capita domestic consumption was up to 103.6 lb. In 1942, military supplies and government purchases for export by lend-lease began by taking 608,000 tons. By 1944 these two requirements had increased to 1,330,000 tons, and the supply had shrunk to 9,209,000 tons, leaving only 89.0 lb. per capita for civilian consumption. By 1945, the per capita portion was down to 73.2 lb. and was estimated at 73 lb. for 1946. The United States had access to supplies adequate to increase production to normal levels, but the international controls held out supplies for countries dependent upon Java as a source since the Far Eastern stocks were not available. The United States government purchased the entire Cuban sugar and molasses crop, except that needed for Cuban consumption, from 1942 to 1946. The price in 1942 and 1943 was 2.65 cents per lb. for raw sugar, f.o.b. Cuba.

U.S. sugar rationing began in May 1942, and was modified at frequent intervals as the war progressed. Special allowances were made for canning and preserving under the stamp system.

The use of sugar by institutions was controlled after April 1942, beginning with 50% of the amount used in the base period in 1941.

Allotments for industrial users of sugar were held to 70% of the amount used in 1941 for most of the war period.

The Combined Food board allocated the crop among the Allied Nations, including the Cuban crop. Molasses was also allotted to alcohol-making plants and other users. The Defense Supplies corporation purchased alcohol made in Cuba from molasses. The government also purchased the entire sugar crop of Puerto Rico during 1942–46. The crops of the Dominican Republic and Haiti likewise were bought in 1942 and 1943, but in 1944 and 1945 these crops were bought by the United Kingdom. Hawaiian sugar was not bought by the U.S. government but was handled by the sugar trade as in prewar years. Price ceilings for wholesale and retail sales were maintained without change from 1943 to 1945.

Raw imported sugar was 3.74 cents per lb. at New York city.

While U.S. domestic consumption of sugar was increased somewhat in 1945 and allotments to institutions and industrial users were relaxed, the short crop of beets in Europe made it necessary to increase allotments to liberated countries in 1945 over previous years. Supplies from the Philippines were expected to be small for several years, since the Japanese had changed the sugar areas into rice and cotton production and neglected the sugar plantations. Military needs for sugar declined in 1945 and the need for alcohol also decreased.

The United States sugar supplies changed little from 1937 to 1940, and ranged at about 6,700,000 tons. In 1941 the total supply jumped to 8,140,000 tons following a big crop of beets in the United States and a large Cuban crop. Then, in 1942, supplies dropped sharply to 5,675,000 tons, because of the smaller Cuban crop and the loss of the Philippine supply. To restore an abundant supply, the U.S. government encouraged the planting of beets and cane and planned to aid in the rehabilitation of the Philippine crop.

As European agriculture became stabilized, the need of sugar for that region would shrink; Europe produced most of its sugar supply in prewar years. Recovery would be slow, however, because of the destruction of sugar refining machinery in Central Europe.

(*See* also BEEKEEPING; CHEMISTRY; MAPLE PRODUCTS; PRICE ADMINISTRATION, OFFICE OF; SYRUP, SORGO AND CANE.) (J. C. Ms.)

BIBLIOGRAPHY.—U.S. Dept. Agric., *Agricultural Statistics;* M. Lynsky, *Sugar Economics* (1938); Dept. Agric., *Sugar Division Repts.* (1939); *Sugar Intelligence* (s-mo).

Sugiyama, Gen

Sugiyama (1880–1945), Japanese army officer, was educated at the Imperial Military college. He was vice-chief of the military general staff and chief of the military affairs department of the war office, 1923–25, and attended the Disarmament conference in Geneva, 1926–28.

He became vice-minister of the army in 1930 and director of the army's aviation headquarters in 1933. He was made a member of the Japanese Supreme War council in 1935, inspector general of the army the following year and was minister of war, 1937–38.

Appointed commander in chief of the Japanese forces in North China in 1938, he held this post through the year 1939. In 1940 he was made chief of the general staff. Gen. Hideki Tojo ousted Sugiyama from this post on Feb. 21, 1944, assuming it himself. On July 18, 1944, it was disclosed that Sugiyama had been made inspector general of army education. Also a member of the board of field marshals and admirals, Sugiyama returned to the government as war minister in the cabinet of Kuniaki Koiso but was not recalled after the resignation of the Koiso government in April 1945. He then became commander of the 1st Imperial army. Unnerved by the Japanese surrender, Sugiyama and his wife committed suicide Sept. 12, 1945, in their Tokyo home.

Suicide Statistics

Comparisons of mortality from suicide are commonly based upon the number of deaths from this cause per 100,000 of population. Thus, there were 13,231 deaths from suicide in the United States during 1944; the estimated midyear population, exclusive of the armed forces overseas, was 132,552,000, so that the suicide rate was 10.0 per 100,000. These suicides accounted for 0.9% of the deaths from all causes during 1944.

International Comparisons.—Before World War II, Austria had a higher death rate from suicide (38.1 per 100,000 in 1937) than any other country for which data are shown in Table I. Mortality from suicide was generally high among the countries of central Europe. For example, rates of more than 20 per 100,000 were found in Germany (28.6 per 100,000 in 1936), Czechoslovakia (27.5 in 1937), Hungary (32.0 in 1937) and Switzerland (23.9 in 1937). Outside this area, the rates were ordinarily high in Denmark and Japan. On the other hand, they were very low in Eire, Northern Ireland, Spain (according to data for 1935) and Greece. Of the English-speaking countries, suicide rates in prewar years were generally lowest in Scotland and highest in the United States, while Australia, New Zealand and England and Wales were on about the same level.

Table I.—*Annual Deaths from Suicide per 100,000 Total Population in Certain Countries for Each Year from 1937 to 1944*

Country	1937	1938	1939	1940	1941	1942	1943	1944
North America								
United States	15.0	15.3	14.1	14.3	12.9	12.0	10.2	10.0
Canada	8.8	8.5	8.6	8.3	7.8	7.2	6.4	6.1
South America								
Chile	6.1	*	*	*	*	*	*	*
Uruguay	13.3	*	*	*	*	*		*
Europe								
Austria	38.1	*	*	*	*	*	*	*
Belgium	17.8	18.0	17.0	18.2	14.1	13.0	10.4	12.3
Czechoslovakia	27.5	*	*	*	*	*	*	*
Denmark	20.9	20.8	17.9	17.8	17.4	17.2	21.3	22.2
Eire	2.9	3.3	2.7	3.3	3.0	2.8	*	*
England and Wales	12.5	12.8	12.1	11.3	9.4	9.1	9.1	8.9
Finland	18.6	18.8	*	*	*	*	*	*
Greece	5.6	5.4	*	*	*	*	*	*
Hungary	32.0	29.6	25.7	24.7	23.8	*	*	*
Ireland, Northern	5.2	4.2	5.2	4.6	4.3	3.4	*	*
Italy	7.6	7.2	*	*	*	*	*	*
Netherlands	7.9	8.5	*	*	*	*	*	*
Norway	6.9	7.0	6.8	6.9	4.3	*	*	*
Portugal	10.7	*	*	*	*	*	*	*
Rumania	10.3	*	*	*	*	*	*	*
Scotland	9.1	9.2	9.2	8.3	8.4	7.9	8.1	*
Sweden	15.6	15.8	16.2	17.1	15.8	14.3	*	*
Switzerland	23.9	24.6	23.8	23.6	24.4	23.2	23.8	25.6
Other countries								
Australia	10.5	10.8	11.2	10.6	8.8	8.3	*	*
New Zealand	11.1	12.4	11.7	10.9	9.3	10.9	8.6	*
Union of South Africa (white)	9.6	10.3	11.3	*	*	*	*	*
Japan	20.1	17.0	*	*	*	*	*	*

*Not available.

Effect of War.—The previous experience of a decline in the death rate from suicide during wartime was duplicated in World War II. For example, the rate in the United States fell from 15.3 per 100,000 in 1938 to a little more than 14 in 1939 and 1940, and then to 12.9 in 1941, before U.S. participation in World War II. The subsequent years saw the rate drop rapidly to 10 per 100,000 in 1944. According to indications provided by the Metropolitan Life Insurance company, the death rate from suicide continued low during 1945 until the close of European hostilities in May. Beginning with that month, the monthly rates for the rest of 1945 continued at a higher level than for the year before. For the first quarter of 1946 the death rate from suicide was more than ⅓ higher than for the corresponding period of 1945.

The decline in the suicide death rate in the United States from the prewar period 1939–41 to the war years 1942–43 was studied in regard to sex and age, again using the experience of lives with industrial insurance (*Statistical Bulletin of the Metropolitan Life Insurance Company*, July 1944). It was found that among white males, the declines were greatest at the oldest ages, where the death rates from suicide are highest. Thus, at ages 55 to 74, the suicide death rate for white males was reduced by about one-third within the brief period of study; at ages 25 to 34 and 45 to 54 the reduction was by one-quarter, while at ages 35 to 44 it was by only one-eighth. The decline at ages 15 to 24 was by less than one-fifth. Among white females, on the other hand, the greatest improvement was at the youngest ages, amounting to about one-third at ages 15 to 24 and one-fifth at ages 25 to 34, the older ages showing minor gains. The marked declines among older men and young women were attributed, in large measure, to the more favourable economic conditions these groups were experiencing through their increased opportunities for work at satisfactory wages. The psychological effect of World War II upon the population, subordinating personal concerns to the general welfare of the country, was also considered to be a beneficial factor in the suicide situation. The postwar increase in suicide mortality was found to be more rapid among men than among women. Factors that may have contributed toward this rise were temporary unemployment while converting from war to peace production and, perhaps, the problems of readjusting to civilian life by men leaving the armed services.

The situation in the United States was undoubtedly duplicated, in substantial part, in other countries during World War II. For example, the death rate from suicide in Canada fell from 8.6 per 100,000 in 1939 to 6.1 in 1944. England and Wales, likewise, showed a marked improvement, from 12.1 in 1939 to 8.9 in 1944. In Scotland, the decline was less rapid, from 9.2 in 1939 to 8.1 in 1943.

Of the German-occupied countries with available data, Belgium, Denmark and Norway showed wartime reductions in suicide mortality, but the first two also showed an upward tendency in the later years. Thus, the rate for Denmark declined from 20.9 per 100,000 in 1937 to a low point of 17.2 in 1942, only to rise rapidly to a maximum of

22.2 in 1944. In Belgium, the suicide death rate rose from 10.4 per 100,000 in 1943 to 12.3 in 1944. It is likely that these late wartime rises in suicide mortality were also experienced by other overrun countries for which data were not available; this adverse situation was undoubtedly a reflection of the deteriorating economic and social conditions in the occupied countries as the war continued.

The only indication regarding the course of mortality from suicide in the axis countries during World War II was a report for large towns in Germany showing an increase of almost 20% in the deaths from this cause from 1939 to 1942.

In contrast to the wide fluctuations in the death rates from suicide in the countries engaged in World War II, the records for three neutrals with available data remained fairly stable. Thus, Eire had a low rate of 2.8 per 100,000 in 1942, practically identical with those for 1937 and 1939. The suicide rates for Switzerland hovered about a level of 24 per 100,000 from 1937 to 1943, and then moved still higher to a rate of 25.6 in 1944. In Sweden, the rate rose from 15.6 per 100,000 in 1937 to 17.1 in 1940, but fell to 14.3 in 1942.

Race, Sex, Age.—Death rates from suicide in the United States were much higher among males than among females, and also higher for white persons than for Negroes. In 1943, for example, white males had a suicide death rate of 16.4 per 100,000; white females, 5.9; Negro males, 4.8; Negro females, 1.3 (see Table II). When the wartime rates of 1943 are compared with the prewar rates of 1940, the Negro female population showed a more rapid improvement than the white female population, while males of both races showed the same improvement; the decreases amounted to 31% for Negro males, 38% for Negro females, 30% for white males, and 19% for white females.

Table II.—*Death Rates from Suicide per 100,000 Population of Specified Ages and of Specified Race and Sex, United States, 1937 to 1944**

Age; Race; Sex	1937	1938	1939	1940	1941	1942	1943	1944
Total persons								
10–14	.6	.3	.5	.4	.4	.5	.5	.4
15–24	7.0	6.7	5.9	6.1	5.7	5.0	4.5	4.3
25–34	14.3	14.4	12.9	13.5	12.5	11.5	9.2	9.2
35–44	21.1	21.3	19.0	19.3	17.2	16.3	13.2	13.5
45–54	30.0	30.5	28.0	27.6	23.1	21.1	17.5	17.3
55–64	34.6	36.7	33.9	34.0	29.5	28.1	23.5	21.4
65–74	34.9	34.8	34.2	33.4	31.2	28.3	26.4	23.9
75 and over	35.6	33.7	33.5	32.9	33.3	32.5	31.3	30.2
All ages								
White males	24.5	25.4	23.4	23.4	20.7	19.6	16.4	†
White females	7.6	7.4	7.1	7.3	6.8	6.3	5.9	†
Negro males	7.4	7.4	6.5	7.0	6.5	5.9	4.8	†
Negro females . . .	2.5	2.5	2.0	2.1	1.7	1.9	1.3	†

*Death rates for 1942 to 1944 based upon population excluding members in the armed forces overseas.

†Not available.

Death rates from suicide according to age for the United States are shown in the upper tier of Table II. The rates rose rapidly with advance in age up to 65 years. Thus, in 1944, the rate at ages 15 to 24 was 4.3 per 100,000; this rose to 21.4 at ages 55 to 64, and then to 30.2 at ages 75 and over.

Means of Suicide.—In the United States, the most frequent means of suicide was by firearms or explosives. The proportion of suicides in which this means was used varied little from year to year after 1940; in 1944, it was 36.3% (see Table III). Next in frequency as a means of self-destruction was hanging or strangulation, used in 23.1% of the cases in 1944; the percentage using this medium increased rapidly during World War II. Third in rank was suicide by poison; the proportion using this means declined gradually after 1940, and, in 1944, accounted for 11.2% of the suicides. There was a sharp drop in the percentage using motor vehicle exhaust gas as a means of suicide, from 5.6% of the total in 1940 to 2.8% in 1944; the decreases were most rapid in the last three years of this period, while gas rationing was in effect. On the other hand, the proportion of suicides using illuminating gas rose gradually to 9.4% in 1944.

There were no significant changes from 1940 to 1944 in the percentages of suicides by drowning, by crushing, or by jumping from high places.

Table III.—*Per Cent Distribution of Deaths from Suicide in the United States According to the Means Employed, 1940 to 1944*

Means	1940	1941	1942	1943	1944
Total	100.0	100.0	100.0	100.0	100.0
Solid or liquid poisons	13.6	13.3	11.9	11.4	11.2
Illuminating gas	8.0	8.5	8.6	9.5	9.4
Motor vehicle exhaust gas . .	5.6	5.3	4.0	3.0	2.8
Other gas	2.5	1.5	1.1	1.1	.9
Hanging or strangulation . . .	18.8	19.5	21.3	22.2	23.1
Drowning	4.5	4.8	4.4	4.6	4.8
Firearms and explosives . . .	37.4	37.3	38.0	37.0	36.3
Cutting or piercing instruments .	3.8	4.3	4.4	4.8	4.7
Jumping from high places . . .	4.0	3.9	4.0	4.3	4.5
Crushing	.8	.9	1.0	.9	1.2
Other means	1.0	.7	1.3	1.2	1.1

Marital Status.—The incidence of suicide was much higher among the unmarried than among the married. In the United States in 1940 the death rate from suicide among single males was 66% in excess of that among married males; among widowers the excess was 198% and among divorced males 292%.

Among unmarried women the relative excess was less. Spinsters had a death rate 38% above that for married women, widows 63% and divorced women 261%. (U.S. bureau of the census, Vital Statistics—Special Reports, Vol. 23, No. 7, Nov. 1945).

Reasons for Attempted Suicide.—Detroit records for 1942 and 1943 provided data for a study of the reasons for attempted suicide (*Statistical Bulletin* of the Metropolitan Life Insurance company, Feb. 1945). It was found that, among men, almost 40% of the attempts (whether successful or not) were caused by ill-health, about 30% by domestic difficulties, and 4% by love affairs. Among women, domestic difficulties led in importance as a cause of attempted suicide, accounting for 50% of the total; ill-health was the motive behind 20% of the cases, and love affairs in somewhat more than 10%. The proportion of successes in the attempts at suicide varied strikingly with the motive. Among men, about one-half were successful where ill-health led to the attempt, about one-seventh where there were domestic difficulties and about one-tenth in love affairs. For women, one-quarter of the attempts were successful in cases of ill-health, one-fiftieth in cases of domestic difficulties but only 1 in 114 where there was a love affair. In connection with these findings, it is interesting to observe that, in the United States in 1940, mental diseases and deficiency were reported in about two-fifths of the total suicide deaths in which a contributory cause of death was mentioned.

Place of Residence.—In the United States, suicide was most frequent in large cities and least frequent in rural areas. In 1940 the death rate from suicide per 100,000 population (adjusted to allow for differences in age distribution) in cities of 100,000 and over was 15.6; for cities of 10,000 to 100,000, the rate was 14.9; cities of 2,500 to 10,000 had a rate of 14.8 and rural areas, 12.9. Considered geographically within the United States, the death rate from suicides is generally highest in the Pacific coast states and lowest in the southern states.

BIBLIOGRAPHY.—U.S. department of commerce, bureau of the census, *Vital Statistics—Special Reports* (issued irregularly) and *Annual Reports of Vital Statistics;* Metropolitan Life Insurance company, *Statistical Bulletin* (issued monthly).

(A. J. Lo.; M. Sp.)

Sulfonamide Drugs

See Arthritis; Bacteriology; Chemistry; Chemotherapy; Dermatology; Drug Administration, U.S.; Ear, Nose and Throat, Diseases of; Gynaecology and Obstetrics; Industrial Research; Medicine; Military Medicine; Nervous System; Pneumonia; Surgery; Tuberculosis; Urology; Venereal Diseases; Veterinary Medicine.

Sulphur

In the years prior to World War II, the United States produced about 80% of the world's output of sulphur, and Sicily most of the remainder. Aside from those two, only Chile produced amounts greater than 1% of the total. By 1942 the Sicilian industry had been badly disorganized, and after the invasion of Sicily, operations almost ceased.

Sulphur production in the United States increased 26% between 1937 and 1943, and then, in the peak year of war demand for most materials, declined to below the 1937 level. The reduction was not caused by any production difficulties, but followed several years in which stocks had been accumulated to such an extent as to permit a temporary relaxation in production activity. Even with the reduction in 1942, production exceeded consumption. In 1945 production shipments and consumption rose to a new record high, and approximately the same high level was maintained through the first eight months of 1946. The increased activity of 1945 and 1946 were more because of the improved export position than because of higher domestic consumption.

From 1939 to 1944 exports averaged as much as in 1937, and in 1945 rose more than one-third above this level.

Close to 90% of the sulphur consumption went into chemicals, fertilizers and insecticides, pulp and paper and explosives. Regardless of the end use, most of it was converted first into sulphuric acid. (G. A. Ro.)

Table I.—*World Production of Native Sulphur*
(short tons)

	1937	1938	1939	1940	1941	1942	1943	1944	1945
Chile	19,600	23,474	30,239	36,333	32,194	33,118	36,243	34,026	...
Italy	378,673	419,260	392,233	364,530	329,603	250,208	102,800	41,400	89,600
United States	3,071,006	2,680,617	2,341,896	3,059,939	3,515,963	3,875,968	2,843,440	3,604,337	4,203,571
Total (est.).	3,700,000	3,360,000	3,000,000	3,700,000	4,150,000	4,500,000	3,360,000	3,900,000	4,600,000

Table II.—*Data of the Sulphur Industry in the United States*
(short tons)

	1937	1938	1939	1940	1941	1942	1943	1944	1945
Production .	3,071,006	2,680,617	2,341,896	3,059,939	3,515,963	3,875,968	2,843,440	3,604,337	4,203,571
Shipments . .	2,762,493	1,824,309	2,501,875	2,865,791	3,809,579	3,503,986	3,308,306	3,941,373	4,293,289
Imports . . .	703	2,915	15,653	31,186	32,067	28,708	18,657	36	37
Exports . . .	771,490	662,832	731,163	858,159	852,069	655,512	764,369	756,260	1,055,781
Available supply . .	1,991,707	1,164,392	1,786,365	2,038,819	2,989,577	2,877,182	2,562,594	3,185,149	3,237,545
Consumption .	2,000,000	1,232,000	1,786,400	2,069,700	2,500,000	2,767,500	2,835,800	3,270,400	3,316,300
Stocks, at mines	3,808,000	4,704,000	4,480,000	4,704,000	4,368,000	4,816,000	4,302,000	3,964,481	3,874,762
Total . . .	...	...	...	...	...	5,727,700	4,997,400	4,592,358	4,484,387

Sultan, Daniel Isom

Sultan (1885–), U.S. army officer, was born Dec. 9, 1885, in Oxford, Miss. A graduate of the U.S. Military academy (1907), he served in the Philippines, 1916–17. He was transferred to Washington, D.C., after United States' entry into World War I and was attached to the war department's general staff from 1918 to 1919. In the latter year he was assigned briefly to the A.E.F. general staff in France. On his return to the United States he attended the Command and General Staff school, being graduated in 1923 and served in Nicaragua. Gen. Sultan was commander of the 38th division at Camp Shelby, Miss., when Japan attacked Pearl Harbor. Later, he was made chief of the 8th army corps, and in Jan. 1944 he became deputy commander under Gen. Joseph W. Stilwell in the China-Burma-India theatre of war. Promoted to the temporary rank of lieutenant general in Sept. 1944, Sultan was made commander in chief of the Burma-India theatre a month later (after the split of the C.B.I. theatre into two commands). He headed the Chinese armies in Burma, Nov. 12, 1944, but came under the authority of Chiang Kai-shek. On July 9, 1945, Pres. Harry S. Truman announced Sultan's appointment as inspector general of the U.S. army.

Sumatra

See Netherlands Colonial Empire; Netherlands Indies.

Sun

See Astronomy.

Sunday Schools

Fifty-one national and international bodies interested in Christian religious education through the Sunday school and allied agencies were federated with the World's Sunday School association at the end of the decade 1937–46. The association began as a movement for the extension of Sunday schools, and the Sunday schools of the world retained a primary place in the program of all its constituent bodies. But increasingly the concern of all these bodies broadened to take account of the entire range of factors and agencies involved in Christian religious education. At a meeting of the board of managers held in London, July 1–4, 1946, steps were initiated looking toward a change of name to World Council of Christian Education.

The programs of the constituent units of the association varied greatly during the decade, as was proper to a movement everywhere indigenous. But the movement as a whole, or through some of its units, was concerned not only with the promotion and improvement of Sunday schools, but with Christian religious education through such means and agencies as the following: the family, schools and colleges, youth organizations, daily vacation Bible schools, weekday schools of religion, Christian literature, visual aids, the radio and whatever other means might be employed for the teaching and learning of Christian truth and living.

The last world's Sunday school convention prior to World War II was held at Oslo, Norway, July 6–12, 1936. It reported 369,510 Sunday schools in 129 countries, with 3,145,895 teachers and 34,139,624 scholars. There were no Sunday schools in the U.S.S.R. and Turkey.

War conditions caused the cancellation of plans to hold a world's Sunday school convention in Durban, South Africa, in 1940. In its place the quadrennial meeting of the council of the World's Sunday School association was held at Lake Mohonk, N.Y., May 8–11, with representatives of 20 countries present. Sir Harold Mackintosh, Halifax, England, was re-elected president, and Dean Luther Allan Weigle, Yale university, chairman of the council and board of managers. Dr. James Kelly, Glasgow, and Dr. Forrest Knapp, New York, were elected general secretaries.

An International Congress on Christian Education, held in Mexico City, July 16–20, 1941, under the auspices of the World's Sunday School association and the National Council of Evangelical Churches in Mexico, was attended by 962 delegates from all of the countries of the western hemisphere, with a few from mission lands. The proceedings of the congress were published in English and in Spanish. It was preceded by a smaller Conference for Sunday School Workers held at Cuernavaca, Mexico, July 13–15, and followed by a Conference on Christian Literature for Latin America, July 21–25.

The congress noted the following as reasons for encouragement: increased Sunday school attendance in many countries, increased recognition that religious education had become an integral part of the work of the church, increased interest in the reading and study of the Bible, a mutual approach of evangelism and Christian education, the greater extent to which preparation for service in Christian education was being included in the training of ministers in theological schools, the development of education for lay service of various types and increased interest of youth, where free, in religion. It recognized the need for better curriculum materials, better prepared teachers and more effective provision for the underprivileged, including the great number of illiterates.

Sunday school enrolment decreased during World War II, partly because of the dislocations of population in all countries, and partly because movements appealing to Christian youth were increasingly suspect and for the most part banned in countries controlled by the axis powers. In Spain Protestant schools were "provisionally suspended" with no likelihood of the suspension being ended. Yet encouraging word concerning the maintenance of Sunday school work came from Czechoslovakia, Finland, Sweden and Norway. "The Christian front in Norway is the hardest to control," the Quisling newspaper stated; and active in that front were the teachers of the Norwegian Sunday schools. The printing and circulation of Sunday school literature continued in spite of the nazi ban, and at the end of the war Norway reported 3,497 schools, with 12,967 teachers and 211,163 pupils.

The National Committee for Christian Religious Education in China continued effective service, publishing Sunday school literature, guiding the training of lay workers in the free areas of China, administering relief and conducting Sunday schools for refugees in territory controlled by the Japanese. When the war closed, the Sunday school board of the Churches of Christ in Japan wrote to the headquarters of the World's Sunday School association asking for information, literature and religious films, "anything that will show the Japanese children that America is a good friend and neighbor to them, who have been taught in these years by the militarists and nationalists that the Americans were demonic enemies."

A sponsoring committee for the association's postwar program of reconstruction was headed by Edward V. Rickenbacker. On Dec. 14, 1945, the association issued an appeal endorsed by Pres. Harry S. Truman, King George VI, Generalissimo Chiang Kai-shek, Queen Wilhelmina, King Christian X, King Gustav V and King Haakon VII, which declared that a just and enduring peace "must rest upon the solid foundations of strong moral and spiritual character . . . Only if the Church fulfills its teaching mission will future generations be blessed by the peace for which this generation is planning and praying."

The largest of the bodies federated in the World's Sunday School association in 1946 was the International Council of Religious Education, in which were associated the educational boards of 44 of the major Protestant denominations of the United States and Canada, enrolling almost half the Sunday school scholars of the world. At its annual meeting in 1940 this body adopted a comprehensive report on basic philosophy and policy, which was published under the title *Christian Education Today.*

Under the auspices of the International Council of Religious Education an authorized revision of the English Bible was begun in 1937 by a committee of scholars appointed by the council. The revision was in the interest of accuracy, simplicity and clarity. It sought to retain the beauty and power of the King James version, but to correct its errors and obscurities, and to eliminate obsolete and archaic forms of expression. The Revised Standard Version of the New Testament was published in Feb. 1946, and became at once a best-seller. The revision of the Old Testament was scheduled for completion in 1949.

(L. A. WE.)

Suñer, Ramón Serrano y

See SERRANO Y SUÑER, RAMÓN.

Superphosphates

Salient statistics of the superphosphate industry in the United States during 1937–45 were as follows, in thousands of short tons:

	1937	1939	1941	1943	1945
Production.	552.4	3,953.7	5,003.8	6,293.0	7,372.1
Exports	88.4	106.7	115.1	268.6	207.2
Phosphate rock used.	2,678.2	2,455.9	3,164.5	4,067.6	4,418.4

The effects of the demand for an increased food supply during World War II were clearly shown in these figures, and the general food shortage after the end of the war continued production at a high level. (G. A. RO.)

Supply, Military

See LOGISTICS OF WORLD WAR II.

Supply Priorities and Allocations Board

See WAR AND DEFENSE AGENCIES.

Supreme Court of the United States

No single decade in the history of the United States supreme court saw as many changes in personnel and shifts of doctrine as did the years 1937–46. The court was remodelled not by adding to the personnel as originally contemplated by Pres. Franklin Delano Roosevelt in his projected court program, but by resignations and deaths.

During the beginning of the ten-year period, the division in court decisions followed a very definite pattern. The four so-called conservatives, Justices James C. McReynolds, Willis Van Devanter, George Sutherland and Pierce Butler, were generally agreed. Likewise, the three so-called liberals, Justices Louis D. Brandeis, Harlan F. Stone and Benjamin N. Cardozo, were agreed. Chief Justice Charles E. Hughes and Justice Owen J. Roberts held the balance, and the decisions primarily depended upon them. If one of them joined with the conservatives, that group had a majority. It was necessary for both of them to join with the liberals in order for the liberal group to be in the majority. This pattern underwent rapid changes with the overwhelming Roosevelt victory in 1936.

Evidence of a break in the conservative group was becoming manifest. Van Devanter retired from the court on June 2, 1937. Hugo J. Black succeeded him, having been appointed on Aug. 17, 1937. Sutherland, retired from the court on Jan. 18, 1938, was succeeded by Stanley Reed, who was appointed Jan. 25, 1938. The October term of 1937 started with one new justice and another was added in the middle of the term.

Cardozo died July 9, 1938, after a relatively brief period on the bench, and was succeeded by Felix Frankfurter, appointed Jan. 17, 1939, former dean of the Harvard Law school. The vacancy created by the resignation of Brandeis, who retired on Feb. 13, 1939, was filled by William Orville Douglas on April 4, 1939. The death of Butler on Nov. 16, 1939, occasioned the appointment of the fifth of Pres. Roosevelt's nominees to the bench, in the person of Frank Murphy, former governor of Michigan and U.S. attorney-general.

The last of the old guard, McReynolds, retired Feb. 1, 1941, to be succeeded by James F. Byrnes, appointed June 25, 1941. Robert H. Jackson was appointed July 11, 1941, to fill the vacancy created by the elevation of Harlan Fiske Stone to the chief justiceship, succeeding Chief Justice Charles Evans Hughes, who retired July 1, 1941. Wiley Blount Rutledge was appointed on Feb. 11, 1943, to succeed Byrnes, who resigned Oct. 3, 1942. With the resignation of Roberts July 31, 1945, Pres. Harry S. Truman had occasion to name his first appointee on Sept. 19, 1945, Sen. Harold H. Burton of Ohio. The death of Chief Justice Harlan Fiske Stone on April 22, 1946, occasioned the choice of Fred Moore Vinson, secretary of the treasury, as the thirteenth chief justice of the United States.

Among the outstanding incidents of the period was the celebration of the 150th anniversary of the court in 1940 (October term 1939), and the leave of absence of Justice Jackson during the 1945 term to serve as chief prosecutor in the trial of the nazi war criminals.

"What a Spectacle!" a cartoon by Fitzpatrick of the *St. Louis Post-Dispatch* expressing disapproval of the controversy between Justices Hugo L. Black and Robert H. Jackson in June 1946

The New Dissent.—Personnel changes were also reflected in notable changes of doctrine. The retirement of McReynolds and Chief Justice Hughes ushered in a new era for the court. The old dissent disappeared—because the old issues had passed; in its place came a new dissent with a different basis. The new court which emerged was not reluctant to overthrow principles established by precedent, and set out to strike a new balance in the old problem of the guarantees of the individual on the one hand and adequate federal power for the protection of social welfare on the other. Among the principles announced were: (1) federal controls over business should be sustained whenever these could be justified; (2) labour organizations were to be favoured whenever possible; (3) the government should generally prevail over the taxpayer and (4) precedents need not be too rigidly binding.

The constitution did not mean the same thing to all members of the court. Conflicting interpretation of the commerce clause marked a clear break from traditional legal formulae and decisions were in the main said to be dictated by the economic and political philosophy of the justices rather than by strict adherence to constitution interpretation. (B. WE.)

Decisions of the Decade.—The most serious judicial blow to early New Deal legislation had been that of May 27, 1935, and this blow was struck by a unanimous court. Upon that date two opinions were handed down. The opinion in *Schecter* v. *U.S.*, with the opinion of the court by Chief Justice Hughes and a concurring opinion by Justice Cardozo, substantially destroyed the National Industrial Recovery act. Upon the same day a unanimous court joined in an opinion by Justice Brandeis which held invalid the original Frazier-Lemke act with respect to farm mortgages (*Louisville Joint Stock Land Bank* v. *Radford*). These two cases probably had more influence than any others in bringing about Pres. Franklin D. Roosevelt's recommendation of Feb. 5, 1937, for the reorganization of the supreme court, although his recommendations would have had little effect upon the decisions of a unanimous court.

The president's recommendations led to much discussion and hearings by the Committee on the Judiciary of the U.S. senate running from March 10 to April 23, 1937, with an adverse report by that committee on June 14, 1937. It was frequently argued that the president's recommendation constituted a threat which forced a change in the attitude of the court. No changes in the personnel of the court occurred from Jan. to June 1, 1937.

In addition to the adverse decisions referred to above, the president's program was faced with two earlier decisions: *Hammer* v. *Dagenhart* (June 31, 1918), in which federal power was held not to apply to the shipment of child-made goods in interstate commerce, and *Adkins* v. *Children's Hospital* (April 9, 1923) in which it was held that a statutory regulation of minimum wages for women was violative of due process of law. Although *Hammer* v. *Dagenhart* was not specifically reversed until the Fair Labor Standards act was sustained in *U.S.* v. *Darby Lumber Co.* (1941), Justice Stone was correct in saying in that opinion that the principle of the *Dagenhart* case was abandoned in *Kentucky Whip & Collar Co.* v. *Illinois Central R. R. Co.* (Jan. 4, 1937). The Adkins case was specifically overruled in *West Coast Hotel Co.* v. *Parrish* (March 29, 1937).

With reference to interstate commerce, the spring of 1937 produced two cases of importance in addition to that of the Kentucky Whip & Collar Co. In *Virginian Ry. Co.*

v. *System Federation* (March 29, 1937), the court held that the Railroad Labor act applied to railway shop employees. And in *National Labor Relations Board* v. *Jones & Laughlin Steel Corporation* (April 12, 1937), the court with four dissents sustained the National Labor Relations act. The opinion of Chief Justice Hughes constituted the basis for a widened scope of national power over interstate commerce, although there were four dissents. On March 29, the court unanimously sustained a revised Frazier-Lemke act as to farm mortgages, this act having previously been held invalid by a unanimous court because of constitutional defects which were now removed (*Wright* v. *Mountain Trust Bank*, March 29, 1937).

On May 24, 1937, the court sustained the Social Security act with respect to unemployment compensation and old age benefits (*Stewart Machine Co.* v. *Davis; Helvering* v. *Davis*, May 24, 1937).

There was no basis for the assertion that favourable opinions by the court from Jan. to June 1937 were occasioned by the president's action and there seemed to be a fair degree of certainty that they were independent of such influence during the period when the membership of the court remained unchanged. Such favourable decisions before June 1937 laid the basis for subsequent developments in the extension of governmental power over industry and in the expansion of federal authority through unlimited spending and interstate commerce powers. The foundation was fully established for the recognition of federal power to prescribe quotas of farm production for the farmer's use on his own farm (*Wickard* v. *Filburn*, 1942), and for federal control of insurance (*U.S.* v. *South Eastern Underwriters Association*, 1944).

The tendencies toward greater governmental regulation and toward greater federal regulatory power found a basis in changed economic and social conditions which made greater regulation necessary, and made once local problems national. The trend toward unrestricted national power found basis primarily in the commerce clause and in the taxing and spending powers.

Federal dominance was also strengthened by the court's emphasis upon the power of congress to exempt from state and local taxation the business of a federal agency common to private capital (*Pittman* v. *Home Owners' Loan Corporation*, 1939; *Maricopa County* v. *Valley National Bank*, 1943), and the power of congress to tax the business of a state agency engaged in enterprises generally pursued (*State of New York* v. *U.S.*, Jan. 14, 1946). The position of the supreme court laid the foundation for the much-urged federal taxation of state and local bonds while continuing the exemption of federal bonds from state and local taxation. It was argued that the states were protected from abuse by virtue of their representation in the two houses of congress, but this ignored the fact that the U.S. political system was organized on a federal basis.

With reference to state taxation of intangibles, the supreme court made a vital change which purported to be for the advantage of the states. Beginning in 1929 the supreme court took the view that for two or more states to tax intangibles was violative of due process of law (*Safe Deposit & Trust Co.* v. *Va.*). Although he did not dissent in this case, Justice Stone opposed the principle and, with changed personnel of the court he was able in 1939 to obtain the adoption of the principle that every state could tax the same intangibles if "within the reach of the tax gatherer there" (*Curry* v. *McCanless*, 1939). This principle was strengthened in *State Tax Commission of Utah* v.

Fred M. Vinson, formerly secretary of the treasury, taking the oath of office as chief justice of the U.S. supreme court. Ceremonies took place at the White House in Washington, D.C., on June 24, 1946

Aldrich (1942), and was in 1944 substantially adopted as to movable tangibles, with strong dissent by Chief Justice Stone (*Northwest Airlines* v. *State of Minnesota*). Multiple taxation gave more than one state an opportunity to tax the same property, but created a confusion which the national government had to meet, or which the states had to adjust by reciprocal legislation. With respect to intangibles, such legislation was in force in a number of states.

The full faith and credit clause was put into the constitution for the benefit of the states and this was properly so stated in *Magnolia Petroleum Co.* v. *Hunt* (1943), but the statement was accompanied by an opinion prejudicial to the administration of state workmen's compensation laws. Such results encouraged a movement to have workmen's compensation transferred to the federal government. However, with respect to divorces, an opinion favourable to the states was rendered in *Williams* v. *State of North Carolina* (1945).

With reference to federal and state relations, expansion of federal authority during the decade was also found in *Screws* v. *U.S.* (1945), which took the view that federal control applied to state officers acting in their capacities as state officers, and in *U.S.* v. *Classic* (1941) and *Smith* v. *Allwright* (1944) with respect to the conduct of elections.

World War II constituted an essential element in the work of the supreme court. The court exercised its authority efficiently, being less restrictive than during World War I in its construction of the Espionage act and in its view as to freedom of speech. Although the court sustained all necessary actions in support of the war, including price control, the use of court martial and the use of Japanese concentration camps, it took a liberal view in the first definition of treason and in protecting civil rights, although there might be some doubt as to its view with respect to the punishment of Japanese military officers.

Freedom of the press, of speech and of religion occupied a large part of the court's time during the ten-year period, the freedom of speech and religion centring on "Jehovah's Witnesses" and the most striking element being the sustaining of salute to the flag in *Minersville School District* v. *Gobitis* (1940), and the reversal of the *Gobitis* case in *W. Va. State Board of Education* v. *Barnette* (1943). Aside from this the most striking development was that which permitted the exercise of these freedoms upon private property (*Murdock* v. *Commonwealth of Pennsylvania,* 1943; *Marsh* v. *State of Alabama,* 1946). With respect to freedom of the press, the court adopted a wide view in regard to criticisms of the courts (*Pennekamp* v. *State of Florida,* 1946). The freedom of labour was also broadly recognized, although at least one member of the court doubted that equal freedom had been given employers.

The court at the end of the decade 1937–46 was liberal with respect to civil rights and federal powers, although the foundation for its position was largely laid before the change in the court's personnel which began with the October term of 1937. Unfortunately, there appeared to be something of a quarrelsome attitude among its members which at times reflected itself in their opinions—a situation which had presented itself only once before with respect to *Hepburn* v. *Griswold* (1870), and which did not then appear in a printed report. Moreover, the numerous concurring and dissenting opinions exceeded those of other days, often added nothing to the case and implied ignorance of a possible paper shortage upon the part of members of the court. (*See* also LAW.) (W. F. D.)

BIBLIOGRAPHY.—W. R. Barnes, *The Supreme Court Issue and the Constitution* (1937); I. Brant, *Storm over the Constitution* (1937); R. K. Carr, *Supreme Court and Judicial Review* (1942); E. S. Corwin, *Constitutional Revolution* (1941); R. J. Harris, *Judicial Power of the U.S.* (1940); R. H. Jackson, *Struggle for Judicial Supremacy* (1941); S. J. Konefsky, *Chief Justice Stone and the Supreme Court* (1945); B. F. Wright, *Contract Clause of the Constitution* (1939), *Growth of American Constitutional Law* (1943). *See* also *Reports of the Supreme Court,* and various compilations of decisions.

Surgery

The years 1937–46 were indeed ten eventful years in the progress of surgery. In spite of World War II, or probably because of it and its resultant stimulation to investigation of surgical problems, advances were rapid. The understanding of wound healing was on a sounder basis than ever before. Whereas for many years it had been known that wound healing was poor in patients with scurvy, only within the decade was it shown that a vitamin C deficiency interferes with the deposition of scar tissue, and that an optimum vitamin C content of the body is necessary for wounds to heal. Also, for some time it had been known that in patients with malnutrition wounds heal poorly. It was shown that a deficiency of the body proteins retards wound healing because of the swelling of the tissues surrounding the wound and the deficient deposition of fibrin which is essential for wound healing. Later, Champ Lyons showed that not only is it necessary to determine the percentage content of the plasma proteins, but also the total circulating plasma protein, because even though the plasma protein per cent value may be within the normal limits because of a decrease in the blood volume there may be a decrease in the total circulating protein and a consequent interference with wound healing. Also, the ordinary blood count and haemoglobin determination in the chronically ill patient is of little significance because of alteration in the blood volume, and unless the latter is determined, the presence of a severe anaemia is likely to be missed. Because of the decreased blood volume in these patients this condition was designated as chronic shock by Lyons.

Wound healing is greatly influenced by the type of suture material used. Whereas previously catgut had been the suture of choice, nonabsorbable sutures became much more popular during the decade. Steel wire was used by many surgeons. As a result of the investigations of W. H. Meade and Alton Ochsner, cotton was found to be superior to most sutures and was employed extensively in the place of other suture materials.

With the introduction of chemotherapy, better control of infections became possible. Sulfonamides were efficacious in many infections, particularly streptococci, but it was shown that in the presence of necrotic and purulent material, they were relatively ineffectual because of the presence of sulfonamide inhibitors, especially aminobenzoic acid. As originally shown by Evarts Graham, sulfonamides interfere with wound healing and, although sulfonamides were used extensively prophylactically before World War II, as a result of investigations done under the auspices of the National Research council, they were found to be of value in the prevention of wound infection and they were harmful when used locally. Sulfonamides are also toxic and should not be used indiscriminately. Other antibiotics which proved to be of great value were penicillin and streptomycin. Penicillin is effective against most streptococci, most staphylococci, gonorrhoea and syphilis. It is almost without toxicity and is very effectual in the prevention, control and treatment of many infections. With the introduction of these chemotherapeutic agents, the mortality rate from invasive infections of the soft parts, osseous tissue and the serous cavities was greatly diminished. Streptomycin, a newer antibiotic, was found particularly efficacious in the control of Gram-negative bacillary infection and particularly valuable in the control of many proteus urinary infections. It was valuable also in the treatment of tularaemia and influenzal meningitis. Its use in tuberculosis appeared promising.

Actinomycosis of the thorax and abdomen which previously had been difficult to control was treated successfully by Champ Lyons by the combination of several methods of therapy: (1) adequate surgical drainage; (2) chemotherapy, with the use of penicillin during the acute phase of the infection to be followed by prolonged administration of sulfonamides; (3) the administration of large amounts of whole blood during the acute infection in order to restore the total circulating haemoglobin and red cell mass.

The prevention and treatment of venous thrombosis continued to be of great importance because this condition was responsible for many unnecessary fatalities and many more instances of disability caused by persistent sequelae following inflammation of the veins with associated thrombus ("milk leg"). It is necessary to differentiate between two types of venous thrombosis, as emphasized by Ochsner and Michael DeBakey, one in which there is a typical "milk leg" with fever, swelling of the leg and pain and the other in which there are few or no symptoms. In the former (thrombophlebitis) the clot is firmly attached to the vein and except in rare instances does not become detached to be carried to the heart and lungs, but the patient's symptoms persist for weeks and years. In the latter (phlebothrombosis), the clot is not attached to the vein and although it produces few symptoms, a fatality is likely because the clot is early detached and can be carried to the

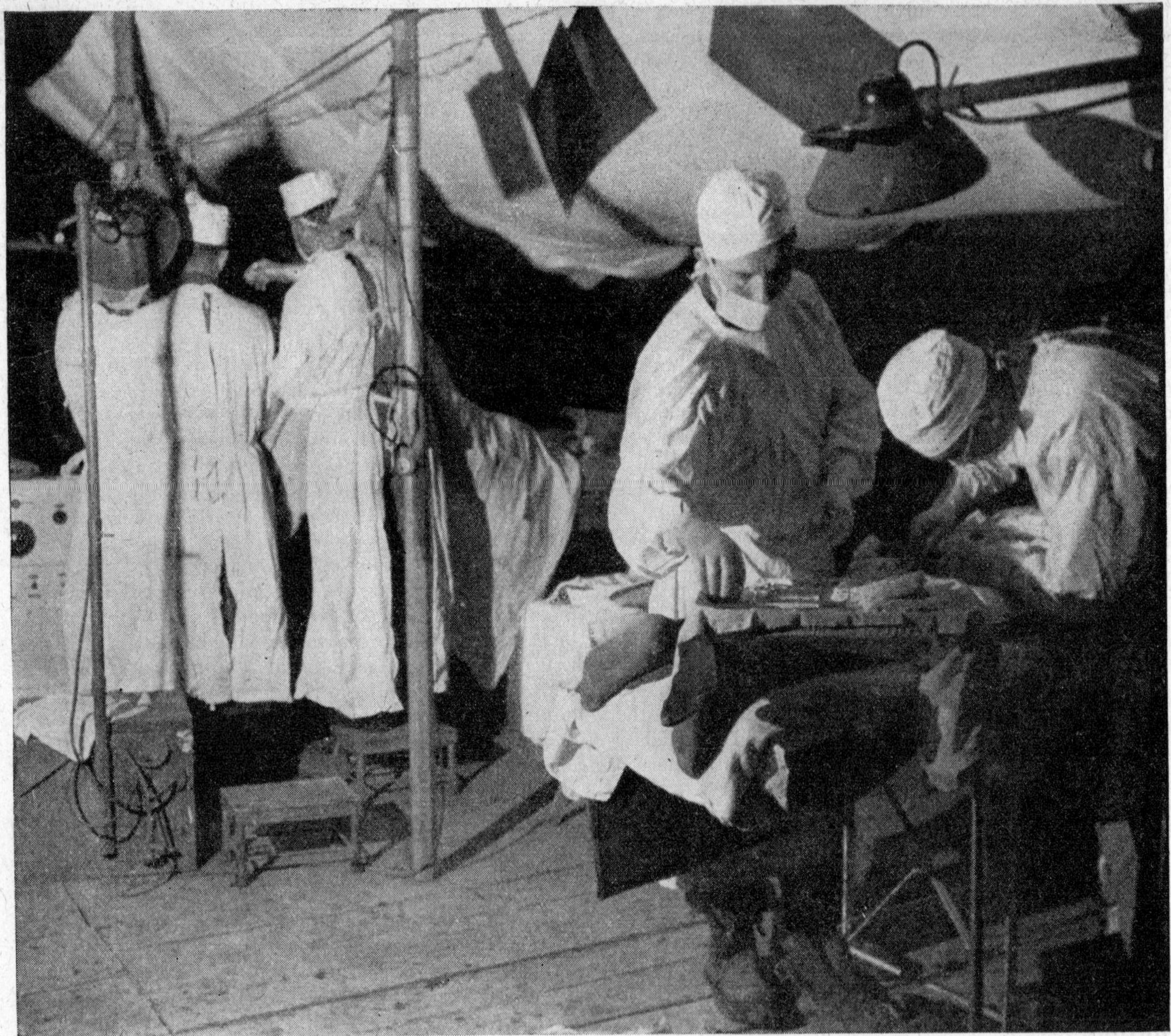

Front line evacuation hospital in Italy during 1944, showing U.S. army surgeons with two patients in the surgical tent. The team at the right was treating shell fragment wounds and that at the left was performing a brain operation

heart and lungs, resulting in a sudden fatality. The treatment of venous thrombosis consists first of prophylaxis and can be accomplished by speeding up the blood flow through the veins in lower extremities where these thrombi predominately occur. This is facilitated by deep breathing, bed exercises and by getting the patient out of bed early after an operative procedure. Anticoagulants, such as heparin and dicoumarol are occasionally useful prophylactically. A patient with true "milk leg" in which there is swelling and pain of the extremity is best treated by anaesthetizing, with procaine, the sympathetic ganglia supplying that extremity which increases the blood flow. On the other hand, the treatment of a patient with phlebothrombosis consists of ligation of the vein before the clot has had a chance to become detached.

There were few conditions in which the treatment was so changed within the decade as in the treatment of burns. The crystallization of ideas concerning treatment of burns was undoubtedly the result of the investigations made during World War II. Whereas previously tannic acid was a favourite method of treatment, it was repeatedly shown that tannic acid is dangerous not only because it destroys tissue locally, but also because of absorption of the drug into the body, producing liver damage. Burns should be treated as any other wound. They should be carefully cleansed under sterile precautions and following this, compression bandages should be applied. Because the burned patient loses considerable fluid and protein, it is necessary to replace it. Whereas previously it had been felt that the administration of salt solution or plasma was particularly advantageous in these cases, it was shown by F. A. Coller and his colleagues that the administration of whole blood is essential to the severely burned individual. G. J. Connor and S. C. Harvey showed that the application of pyruvic acid to the burned area in which there is considerable destruction of skin would bring about a more rapid separation of the dead tissue, permitting the application of skin grafts early enough.

Considerable work was done in vascular surgery. A number of congenital anomalies affecting children were treated successfully by operation. Persistence of a communication between the aorta and pulmonary artery which is necessary in the foetus, but which normally closes after the birth of the child, is responsible for heart disease. This communication was divided and the normal mechanism re-established. Blue babies with congenital defects in their heart and blood vessels were treated by making a new opening between two of the large arteries in the chest. Alfred Blalock performed this operation in many instances and, although an abnormal condition results from the operation, the condition is very much better than the original congenital defect. Another congenital abnormality of the blood vessels is a narrowing of the aorta known as coarctation. This anomaly, which causes marked elevation of blood pressure in the upper extremities, was corrected by removing the narrowed portion of the aorta and reuniting the two ends. This pioneer work was successfully done by C. Crafoord and Robert Gross.

The use of internal secretions in surgical conditions gained considerable interest. It was shown by C. Huggins that cancer of prostate, which previously was extremely difficult to treat, could be treated quite satisfactorily, although cures did not result, by removal of the testicles or by the administration of the female sex hormone, stilbestrol. In women with cancer of the breast with extension to the bones, relief of pain and recalcification of the bone was obtained by the administration of the male sex hormone.

Banti's disease, which had been unsatisfactorily treated previously, had been shown to be the result of an increase in blood pressure within the portal venous system. In order to prevent the symptoms produced by the condition, two procedures were used: (1) the making of a new opening between the portal vein and inferior vena cava or (2) a communication between the portal and systemic circulations by anastomosing the left renal vein to the splenic vein. This could be done either by direct suturing of the vessels or by the use of a vein-lined vitallium tube, as suggested by Arthur H. Blakemore.

Vitallium, an alloy, became very popular for use in surgery. It contains no iron but is composed of chromium, cobalt and molybdenum. It had been used for a long time in dentistry and can be implanted in body tissues because it produces practically no electrolytic reaction. It was used for plates to hold fractures and to reconstruct ducts within the body. Later a newer metal, tantalum, was introduced because it has the advantage over vitallium that it can be more readily handled; it can be cut, bent and hammered, whereas vitallium has to be cast to fit the part.

Heart disease, particularly coronary thrombosis, which continued to be responsible for so many deaths, was attacked surgically. The severe pain associated with angina pectoris was relieved either by injecting the sympathetic nerves with alcohol or by removing them. Claude S. Beck was able to increase the blood supply to the heart muscle by exposing the heart and either applying a flap of muscle from the chest wall to the heart or by introducing irritating substances, such as asbestos, into the pericardial cavity to produce new adhesions between the heart muscle and the surrounding tissues. These operations resulted in marked relief of symptoms and prolongation of life.

Operations on the digestive tract became much safer and more frequently performed. Whereas previously a cancer or obstruction of the oesophagus was not amenable to surgical treatment, it became possible during the decade to remove large portions, even the entire thoracic oesophagus, and to re-establish the normal continuity. These operations were done through the chest, making an opening in the diaphragm so that the oesophagus and adjacent stomach could be resected. It was possible in this way not only to remove cancer of the oesophagus and the upper part of the stomach, but also to remove strictures of the oesophagus as well. Complete removal of the stomach through the chest was made possible. Whereas the treatment of spasmodic contraction of the opening of the stomach had consisted primarily of dilatation, much was done to secure a more permanent result in these cases. In these instances, a new opening between the stomach and the oesophagus completely relieved the patients of their symptoms. Although ulcers of the duodenum were treated medically and probably should continue to be, it was quite generally agreed among surgeons that in ulcer of the stomach, because of its great tendency to become cancerous, partial removal of the stomach should be done. In the intractable ulcer of the duodenum, resection of a considerable portion of the stomach was the method of choice.

A conservative procedure for the treatment of duodenal ulcer was suggested by L. R. Dragstedt. This consisted of removing portions of the two vagus nerves supplying the stomach, following which the acid content of the stomach was diminished. Following this relatively simple procedure, the patients were relieved of their symptoms; although this operation was not without disadvantages, the results up to the end of the decade were quite satisfactory. A longer period of time was required for a true evaluation of this conservative procedure.

Operations on the liver and bile ducts in the presence of jaundice previously had been attended with a high mortality rate, because of the danger of haemorrhage. It was shown that this haemorrhagic tendency is the result of a deficiency of vitamin K, which is normally absorbed from the intestine during the digestion of fat. Whenever there is an obstruction to the flow of bile into the intestine, an interference with fat digestion occurs, preventing the absorption of vitamin K. As a result of the deficiency, the formation of thrombin, which is essential for blood clotting, is interfered with; this condition is responsible for the haemorrhagic tendency. Vitamin K was made available synthetically and can be supplied to these patients preoperatively, thus preventing the bleeding tendency in jaundice.

Although benign tumours of the pancreas had been operated upon successfully, malignant tumours of the pancreas were not amenable to surgical treatment. As the result of the investigations of Allen Whipple, it became possible to remove large portions of, or even the entire pancreas for cancer. Stones in the pancreas, producing severe pain, were successfully treated by removal of the involved portion of the gland.

The preparation of a patient with a toxic goitre for operation was greatly facilitated by the use of a thiouracil, a drug closely allied to the sulfonamides. A temporary chemical thyroidectomy is produced, resulting in a marked diminution of the toxic manifestations. Although the drug is toxic and must be used cautiously, it proved of great value in the treatment of many patients with toxic goitre. Another substance, propylthiouracil, much less toxic, was used and was found to be equally efficacious in the preoperative preparation of these extremely ill patients. Acute inflammation of the thyroid gland (acute thyroiditis), which previously required prolonged therapy, also was successfully treated with thiouracil.

Great advances were made in surgery of the lung. Cancer of the lung, the incidence of which was increasing, was treated successfully and with surprisingly low mortality rates by removal of the lung. Although the treatment of tuberculosis continued to be largely conservative, consisting principally of rest and good food, many were benefited by collapse of the lung. A few cases were treated by surgical resection of the involved lung. This method of therapy had to be limited to relatively few cases, and the indications for its use were very strict.

Even high blood pressure became a surgical condition in many instances. Although most cases had to be treated medically, there were some individuals, particularly the younger ones, who were benefited by the removal of sympathetic nerves. Although the results obtained by this procedure were not so gratifying as originally anticipated, all patients were relieved of their symptoms by the operation, and in many instances a normal blood pressure was obtained.

Great advances were made in plastic surgery. The perfection of the dermatome by Earl C. Padgett, an instrument which permits the cutting of a calibrated thickness of skin, was of great value. It became possible to cut skin of any desired thickness and of relatively large size. The use of preserved isocartilage taken from another patient or from an individual at necropsy was of importance. It was no longer necessary for the patient to donate his own cartilage when a transplant of cartilage was necessary. The isocartilage was not quite so satisfactory as the cartilage obtained from the patient himself, because there was always a certain amount of absorption. On the other hand, it proved to be as resistant to infection as (or even more so than) the patient's own cartilage obtained from another part of his body.

Whereas, previously it had been necessary to rely upon ligation of vessels and compression to control haemorrhage, great advances were made in the use of haemostatic substances during the decade. With the stimulus given to the study during World War II, it was found that fibrin, a normal product of the blood, could be made into a sponge and when left on a bleeding surface would tend to stop the haemorrhage. This was particularly true when combined with thrombin, which is normally responsible for clotting. In addition to fibrin foam, obtained from human and other blood, two other substances were made available as haemostatic agents. Gelatine foam has more body than fibrin foam and therefore is easier to use. When left in a wound, absorption occurs without reaction. Another substance, oxidized cellulose, was used as an effective haemostatic agent. All of these substances were of great value to the neurosurgeon in controlling oozing from the brain and to the general surgeon in controlling oozing from such organs as the kidney or the liver, from which haemorrhage can be stopped only with difficulty.

Myasthenia gravis, a condition in which there is severe muscular weakness, resisted most forms of therapy. It was treated successfully in many instances, however, by removal of the thymus gland, a small gland in the chest. Alfred Blalock showed that many of these patients can be operated upon safely and have their normal strength re-established.

As the result of wartime experiences many patients with severe injury to the lung or infection of the pleural cavity were rehabilitated relatively quickly by removal of blood clot or fibrin which forms on the surface of the lung. Unless this procedure is used the lung may not re-expand, because it is kept in a contracted position by the clot which may be changed into scar. By the removal of the fibrinous mass two to three weeks after injury or after infection, the lung is allowed to re-expand and re-establish its normal function. (*See* also ANAESTHESIOLOGY; DIABETES; EYE, DISEASES OF; MEDICINE; MILITARY MEDICINE.)

BIBLIOGRAPHY.—Champ Lyons and others, "Chronic Shock," presented before Clinical Congress of the American College of Surgeons (Dec. 1946); W. H. Meade and Alton Ochsner, "Spool Cotton as a Suture Material," *J.A.M.A.*, 113:2230-31 (Dec. 16, 1939); Evarts Graham, personal communication, Champ Lyons C. R. Owen and W. B. Ayers, "Sulfonamide Therapy in Actinomycotic Infections," *Surgery*, 14:99-104 (July 1943); Alton Ochsner and Michael DeBakey, "Venous Thrombosis," *J.A.M.A.*, 132:827-833 (Dec. 7, 1946); C. A. Moyer, F. A. Coller, V. Iob, H. H. Vaughan and D. Marty, "A Study of the Interrelationship of Salt Solutions, Serum and Defibrinated Blood in the Treatment of Severely Scalded Anesthetized Dogs," *Ann. Surg.*, 120:367-376 (Sept. 1944); G. J. Connor and S. C. Harvey, "The Healing of Deep Thermal Burns: A Preliminary Report," *Ann. Surg.* 120:362-366 (Sept. 1944); Alfred Blalock and H. B. Taussig, "The Surgical Treatment of Malformations of the Heart in which There Is Pulmonary Stenosis or Pulmonary Atresia," *J.A.M.A.*, 128:189-202 (May 19, 1945); C. Crafoord and G. Nylin, "Congenital Coarctation of the Aorta and Its Surgical Treatment," *J. Thoracic Surg.*, 14:347-361 (Oct. 1945); Robert E. Gross, "Surgical Correction for Coarctation of the Aorta," *Surgery*, 18:673-678 (Dec. 1945); C. Huggins, "Effect of Orchiectomy and Irradiation on Cancer of the Prostate," *Ann. Surg.*, 115:1192-1200 (June 1942); Arthur H. Blakemore, Jere W. Lord and Paul L. Stefko, "Restoration of Blood Flow in Damaged Arteries: Further Studies on a Nonsuture Method of Blood Vessel Anastomosis," *Ann. Surg.*, 117: 481-497 (April 1943); Claude S. Beck, "Principles Underlying the Operative Approach to the Treatment of Myocardial Ischemia," *Ann. Surg.*, 118:788–806 (Nov. 1943); L. R. Dragstedt and P. W. Schafer, "Removal of the Vagus Innervation of the Stomach in Gastroduodenal Ulcer," *Surgery*, 17:742–749 (May 1945); A. O. Whipple, "The Problem of Portal Hypertension in Relation to the Hepatosplenopathies," *Ann. Surg.*, 122:449–475 (Oct. 1945); Earl C. Padgett, "Calibrated Intermediate Skin Grafts," *Surg., Gynec. & Obst.*, 69:779–793 (Dec. 1939); Alfred Blalock, "Thymectomy in Treatment of Myasthenia Gravis; Report of Twenty Cases," *J. Thoracic Surg.*, 13:316–339 (Aug. 1944).

(A. O.)

Surinam (Dutch Guiana)

A Netherlands colony in northeastern South America, Surinam is bounded on the east by French Guiana, on the south by Brazil, on the west by British Guiana, and on the north by the Atlantic ocean. Area, 54,291 sq.mi. The population by 1944 estimate was 191,628; earlier official estimates were as follows: 1938, 173,089; 1940, 177,980; 1941, 183,730; 1943, 189,484. The population included approximately 1,000 Dutch, 1,000 other Europeans and Americans, 50,000 British Indians, 35,000 Javanese, 2,400 Chinese, 19,000 bush Negroes (or Djukas) and 2,600 aboriginal Indians. The capital is Paramaribo (pop., 60,723), where some two-fifths of the white population lives; other inhabited places include Nieuw Nickerie (5,000), Coronie (4,500) and Moengo (1,400). The colony is ruled by a governor, who serves as president of an executive council of four, all nominated by the queen of the Netherlands. A legislative body, the states of Surinam, includes 15 members, 10 elected and 5 appointed by the governor, all for a term of four years. The colony is divided for administrative purposes into 16 districts. The judiciary, appointed by the crown, is headed by a supreme court at Paramaribo. Governors in the decade 1937–46 included Dr. J. C. Kielstra, 1933–Jan. 3, 1944; Dr. J. C. Brons, after that date.

* * *

LITTLE of consequence occurred in the colony until about a year and a half after the invasion of the Low Countries by Germany. As a result of an earlier agreement between the United States and the Netherlands government-in-exile at London, United States troops arrived in the colony Nov. 24, 1941, with the object of providing necessary protection to the colony's valuable bauxite mines. The United States simultaneously assumed responsibility for protection of a refining plant at Paranam, on the Surinam river about 20 mi. above Paramaribo. The government of Brazil, in a corollary action, pledged itself to maintain military vigilance along the Brazil-Surinam frontier. The troops, whose numbers were not disclosed,

Native women of Surinam, parading in 1943 as auxiliary members of the Dutch colonial army

were located in some 20 or more camps and acted solely in a military capacity. The United States emphasized that its presence in Surinam in no way constituted an occupation and that Netherlands sovereignty was not in any degree infringed.

The effects of World War II continued to be mixed. Normal trade channels were even more disturbed in 1942 than previously, because of axis submarine activity in Atlantic and Caribbean waters and the lack of shipping for the customary products; but the booming bauxite exports, which in 1941 had almost equalled the combined total for 1939 and 1940, and the presence of United States troops in the colony provided an economic counterpoise. An important political event was the pledge made by Queen Wilhelmina on Dec. 6, 1942, that a postwar "equal partnership" of the Netherlands overseas territories with the mother country would be established; this was interpreted in Surinam to mean a subsequent grant of practically complete local autonomy. The arrival in late Dec. 1942 of 122 Netherlands refugees intending to settle in the colony aroused considerable interest as a possible portent of the future.

Trade conditions eased in 1943, and shortages became less acute, chiefly because of the decline of the axis submarine menace in western Atlantic and Caribbean waters. Bauxite mining continued at practically double the prewar rate of production. The colony was visited in Nov. 1943 by Crown Princess Juliana of the Netherlands, the first member of the royal house of Orange ever to go to Surinam. Earlier in the year a Surinam economic mission visited Brazil; the first Brazilian consul ever accredited to the colony arrived at Paramaribo on May 13. Surinam's first daily newspaper, *Het Nieuws,* began publication Aug. 3, 1943. The colony was faced in 1943 with an acute shortage of subsidiary coins, which was relieved in part by assistance from the United States mint. Agricultural production was abnormally low in 1943 except for pineapples, which more than doubled the volume of the preceding year.

Relative economic prosperity continued to prevail in Surinam in 1944, with agricultural production generally above the low of 1943. The colony continued to feel considerable concern, however, because of the likelihood that bauxite, which in recent years had formed more than nine-tenths of Surinam's exports, would be in sharply reduced demand with the tapering off of war needs. Plans were consequently made for financial retrenchment, although the first Netherlands government loan ever launched in Surinam was successfully floated; it totalled 4,000,000 guilders at 2½%. Plans were presented to the legislative assembly in June looking toward provision of funds for better housing and for improving educational and agricultural facilities. Representatives of Surinam took part in the first West Indian conference, held at Bridgetown, Barbados, Mar. 21–30, 1944, under the auspices of the Anglo-U.S. Caribbean commission. That agency, formed two years earlier to serve the joint research and advisory needs of the British and United States possessions in the Caribbean area, had begun to seek the co-operation of Dutch and French representatives and to broaden the basis of participation and the scope of interest. The conference in Barbados discussed plans for increasing local food production and raising standards of living, quarantine and health protection and other matters of common interest to the area. It urged that secondary industries be developed where practicable, as a means of broadening the economic base of the various colonies.

The colonies' chief problems in 1945 were those of reconversion from the World War II period. It was announced late in the year that a committee headed by a former governor would be sent subsequently to study financial and economic conditions for the Netherlands government; one of the chief problems to be discussed was that of a possible adjustment in value between the Surinam and Curaçao guilders. The position of the guilder tended to be weakened in mid-1945 because of devaluation in the Netherlands with respect to the pound sterling. A serious shortage of dollar exchange existed early in the year. Trade in 1945 continued to be largely with the United States, a shift which had taken place during the war because of the disruption of the previously normal trade with the Netherlands. Large stock piles of bauxite built up at Paramaribo during the year. Steamship sailings continued to be irregular throughout most of the year, and Pan American Airways curtailed certain of its services to Surinam in 1945, although K.L.M. (Royal Dutch Air Lines) was understood to be planning a considerable postwar expansion of its network, partly based on Surinam. Service on a portion of the short rail lines existing in the colony was abandoned in 1945 because it was not self-sustaining. The colonial government late in the year studied plans for the expenditure of 15,000,000 guilders for public works over a period of five years; dredging projects in the lower reaches of certain rivers, especially the Surinam, were a feature of this program.

The colonial government organized a department of social affairs and immigration early in 1946. Officials representing Surinam participated in a joint conference on Caribbean problems with British, French, and United States representatives, meeting at St. Thomas, Virgin Islands, beginning Feb. 21, 1946. As a partial offset to the questionable future of the bauxite industry in Surinam, interest revived somewhat early in 1946 in the possibility of gold mining, although the outlook was not especially bright in view of the lack of new fields to exploit. The anticipated financial mission arrived at Paramaribo early

Surinam: *Statistical Data*

Item	1938 Value (000's omitted)	1938 Amount or number	1940 Amount or number	1944 Value (000's omitted)	1944 Amount or number
Exchange rate					
United States		1 florin = 55 cents	1 florin = 53.13 cents		1 florin = 53.19 cents
Great Britain		8.56–8.59 florins = £1	6.66 florins = £1		
Finance					
Government revenues	$2,047 (£419)			$4,930 (£1,222)	
Government expenditures	$3,580 (£732)			$4,972 (£1,232)	
Minerals					
Bauxite		415,802 tons	676,706 tons		708,985 tons
Gold		14,154 oz.	15,921 oz.		5,723 oz.
Crops					
Rice		39,793 tons			19,841 tons
Sugar cane (sugar content)		13,448 "			1,764 "
Corn		2,425 "			...
Coffee		1,984 "			331 tons
Livestock					
Cattle		21,200*	21,396†		
Swine		7,100*	5,727†		
Goats		4,900*	7,161†		
Forest products					
Balata		302 tons			215 tons
Timber		...			1,050,000cu.ft.
Exports					
Total	$3,636 (£744)	...		$2,610 (£647)	...
Bauxite	...	433,000 tons		$236 (£58)	710,000 tons
Gold	...	17,000 "		...	...
Sugar, rum, molasses	...	12,000 "		$1 (§)	33 tons
Coffee	...	3,000 "		$16 (£4)	131 tons
Rice	...	8,000 "		$11 (£3)	161 tons
Imports					
Total	$3,775 (£772)	...		$5,935 (£1,471)	67,000 tons
Manufactures	...	...		$3,086 (£765)	7,000 tons
Foods and beverages	...	...		$1,747 (£433)	14,000 tons
Raw and semimanufactured goods	...	...		$938 (£232)	45,000 tons
Education					
Schools		132‡			...
Enrolment		21,851‡			...
Elementary schools		...			114‖
Enrolment		...			22,000‖
Secondary Schools		...			4‖
Indian and bush negro schools		33*			33‖

*1937 †1941 ‡1939 §(£247) ‖1943

in 1946 and began consideration of the adjustment of the Surinam monetary system to the Netherlands guilder. The colonial government was anxious to keep the money at its existing level with United States currency but by March it appeared likely that the Surinam guilder would subsequently be devalued.

BIBLIOGRAPHY.—Netherlands Information Bureau, *Netherlands News* (bi-weekly); *The West Indies Year Book* (annual); *The South American Handbook* (annual); J. K. Wright and William van Royen, *The Netherlands West Indies; Curaçao and Surinam* (1941); Raye R. Platt (ed.), *The European Possessions in the Caribbean Area* (1941); J. W. Nystrom, *Surinam: A Geographic Study* (1942); Philip H. Hiss, *Netherlands America; the Dutch Territories in the West* (1943); *Foreign Commerce Weekly*. (R. H. FN.)

Surplus Property Administration

See SURPLUS PROPERTY DISPOSAL, U.S.; WAR AND DEFENSE AGENCIES.

Surplus Property Disposal, U.S.

Surplus property disposal was first recognized as a special function in 1933 when the procurement division of the U.S. treasury department was assigned responsibility for disposing of surplus of World War I and even some property dating from previous wars.

World War II increased the importance and, in an enormous degree, the magnitude of the task. At a breath-taking pace, war production rushed to meet the demands of modern war. An endless assortment of property of almost every description began to accumulate as surplus as the war developed and war requirements changed. Implements became outmoded almost before they had left the production line. For example, 800 modifications were made in the original specifications of the B-17 bomber, each involving thousands of "change orders" and throwing into the surplus heap millions of parts.

At the request of President Roosevelt, Bernard Baruch and John Hancock made a report which, among other things, recommended a central authority. The Surplus War Property administration (SWPA) was accordingly created under executive order No. 9425, Feb. 19, 1944, and charged by the president with general supervision and direction of the surplus disposal program.

On Oct. 3, 1944, the Surplus Board act was approved. Its major aims, while conflicting in some respects, were to make maximum use of surplus property, establish a system of priorities for the disposal of surplus and to use existing facilities for such disposal. The act created a three-member board to carry out its provisions.

On Sept. 18, 1945, congress amended the act to replace the board by a Surplus Property administration headed by a single surplus property administrator. This centralization of authority in one individual was the only effect of the amendments; the SPA carried on the same functions as the predecessor board.

The two final redistributions of the functions originally assigned the Surplus Property board were brought about by executive order No. 9689, effective Feb. 1, 1945. By this time the SPA had largely completed an initial task of policy formulation.

World War II was over. Surplus was accumulating at an increasing pace. The time for more active disposal had arrived.

Accordingly, the Executive Order provided for the abolition of SPA and for the transfer of its function to the War Assets corporation. Excluded from this transfer was authority over surplus property abroad, which became the responsibility of the state department. Finally, and as a result of the same order, the War Assets administration came into being on March 25, 1946, taking over the functions of WAC.

Previously, the various disposal agencies had operated under and as subsidiaries of other and more permanent agencies using the facilities of such agencies for actual disposal operations. The WAA, however, was created as a separate unity. It co-operated with other agencies but functioned primarily on its own, handling the entire disposal program for over 90% of all surplus.

By late 1946, in round numbers, $13,200,000,000 worth of surplus war property had been sold by domestic disposal agencies, mainly the War Assets administration. Preliminary estimates set this figure at 31% of total World War II domestic surplus eventually to be disposed of in the United States, its territories and possessions. An overall total of $34,000,000,000 of eventual surplus was anticipated. Inventory was $9,500,000,000 which left approxi-

Reconditioned jeeps lined up at a U.S. depot in England in 1945. They were part of the huge store of U.S. surplus property throughout the world which was then awaiting disposition

mately $24,500,000,000 still to be declared by the owning agencies. (*See* also INVESTMENTS ABROAD, U.S. AND BRITISH; LEND-LEASE.) (H. E. BY.)

Suzuki, Kantaro

Baron Suzuki (1867–), Japanese statesman, was born Dec. 24, 1867, in Osaka. A graduate of the Japanese naval academy in 1887, he held many important posts in the Japanese navy, including that of commander in chief of the combined fleet and chief of the navy general staff. In 1929, he was named grand chamberlain and privy councillor concurrently. Following his resignation as grand chamberlain in 1936, he was made a baron. That same year, Suzuki was wounded in a revolt staged by young Japanese army officers, because he allegedly opposed the army extremists who dominated the government. In Aug. 1944, he became president of the privy council.

After the fall of Premier Kuniaki Koiso's cabinet (April 5, 1945,) Suzuki formed a new government. On July 29, 1945, he rejected the U.S.-British-Chinese surrender terms formulated at the Potsdam conference, but the emperor's acceptance broadcast of the decision to accept the surrender terms (Aug. 15) forced the resignation of Suzuki's cabinet. In an interview later, he was reported to have declared that he had sounded out the soviet union in June 1945 on the possibility of peace, but that this "feeler" was ignored.

According to a U.S. broadcast from Tokyo, Sept. 15, 1945, Suzuki went into hiding after the end of the war to escape possible assassination at the hands of vengeful Japanese militarists.

Swains Island

See PACIFIC ISLANDS, U.S.; SAMOA, AMERICAN.

Swanson, Claude Augustus

Swanson (1862–1939), U.S. secretary of the navy, was born at Swansonville, Va., on March 31, 1862. He graduated from Randolph-Macon college at Ashland, Va., in 1885; the next year he received his degree in law at the University of Virginia, was admitted to the bar, and began practice at Chatham, Va. His first venture into national politics was successful when, in 1893, he was elected to the U.S. house of representatives. From 1906 to 1910 he was governor of Virginia and from 1910 to 1933 U.S. senator from that state. He was appointed chairman of the senate's naval affairs committee in 1918 and secretary of the navy by President Roosevelt in 1933. When he took office in the cabinet, the United States had only 17 warships under construction. When he died at Rapidan camp, Va., on July 7, 1939, the naval forces had been increased by 197 ships either built or under construction.

Swaziland

See BRITISH SOUTH AFRICAN PROTECTORATES.

Sweden

A democratic monarchy of northern Europe, Sweden has an area of 173,341 sq.mi.; pop. (Dec. 31, 1944) 6,597,-348. Capital, Stockholm (671,525). Other principal cities: Göteborg (Gothenburg) (296,289), Malmö (167,885), Norrköping (75,792), Hälsingborg (65,357), Örebro (58,590) Religion Lutheran Evangelical. King Gustavus V reigned throughout the decade 1937–46 (since 1907). Prime minister from 1932 until his death on Oct. 6, 1946, was Per Albin Hansson; he was succeeded by Tage Erlander.

Fortified Camp.—Although Sweden was not involved in World War II, its national life was dominated by this catastrophe most of the decade 1937–46. In the prewar years the Swedish people were increasingly disturbed by the bellicose trend in international affairs. During the war itself they became isolated by German military power and preserved their independence only by a united, determined moral resistance, backed by feverish rearmament, and to a certain extent, at first, by certain concessions to Germany which seemed necessary to the responsible Swedish authorities at the time. By 1940, Sweden had become in effect a small fortified camp inside a big one. Both during the war and after it was over, unprecedented aid was given to countries less fortunate. In proportion to population the number of refugees in Sweden would have corresponded to about 4,000,000 for the U.S. Gifts to other countries added up to more than 1,000,000,000 kronor (about $280,000,000, or an average of $54 per person); 1 kronor was equal to 26 U.S. cents at par, 23.86 cents on Nov. 28, 1945.

During the war itself all elections, both national and local, were held as usual. "One way to defend democracy is to practise it" said prime minister, Per Albin Hansson. When war came close to Sweden in the fall of 1939 through Russia's attack on Finland, the Social Democrats invited the leaders of all other parties, except the Communists, to join them in a cabinet of national union, which held power throughout the war. In 1945, however, when the war was over in Europe, the Social Democrats, who had made large gains in 1940 and still held a working majority in both houses after the election in 1944, resumed sole executive authority.

In foreign affairs, Sweden retained its membership in

the League of Nations to the end, but when the war broke out announced its resumption of its traditional neutral attitude of more than 130 years, as did all the other northern states. Swedish military power of resistance grew during the war and German strength simultaneously declined; transit permits were cancelled in the fall of 1943 and a year later all commercial exchange of goods between the two countries ceased. Toward the end of the war more and more facilities and services were granted to the Allies.

The Prewar Years.—In order to understand the internal political situation in Sweden at the beginning of 1937 it is necessary to review briefly the preceding years. Although by 1935 the Swedish riksdag had been in existence for 500 years and the kings themselves had originally been elective officers, there had been no thoroughly democratic system of government based on universal suffrage, regardless of property qualifications, until the end of World War I. Universal suffrage, regardless of both wealth and sex, was then introduced, giving greatly increased power to the organized industrial workers, enrolled in the Social Democratic party, which was led by Sweden's great statesman, Hjalmar Branting. Earlier in the century, parliamentary control over the government, best exemplified by the British and the French systems, had been introduced, making the prime minister, usually the leader of the largest party, the real executive instead of the king.

In 1917, leaders of the Social Democratic party headed by Branting had entered the government for the first time, then sharing executive power with the Liberals. After World War I was over, they formed several cabinets of their own, though in the minority. In the 1928 election, when hope of a permanent, capitalistic prosperity was still over the land, they had lost several seats and were replaced by the Conservatives. In 1932, when the depression had at last struck Sweden, they were restored to power and given the task of finding a cure for unemployment. This they did by increasing social welfare payments to stimulate the domestic demand for goods and by borrowing money for public works. Taxes on large estates and incomes were increased. As foreign trade revived, however, the country recovered more quickly than had been expected, and the emergency loans were repaid much sooner than planned. The partly subsidized building boom that began in 1934 helped materially in breaking the depression.

In the 1932 election the Social Democrats had polled for the first time more than 1,000,000 votes giving them 104 seats in the dominant second chamber. Year by year, they had also made gains in the indirectly elected first chamber, renewed at the rate of one-eighth of its membership annually, but they still lacked working majorities in each of the two houses. To put through their projected unemployment program they then made an alliance for the first time with the Farmers' Union, a World War I offshoot of the Conservative party and still one of the small minority groups. In return the farmers, mostly small land owners, were promised not only their share of the improved social welfare measures, but also guarantees of stable prices on their products. Previously the practice had been to help the farmers by increasing import duties on grain, but as that also boosted the price of bread for the industrial workers as well as for all other inhabitants, the method of using government subsidies to guarantee minimum prices was used. This put the burden, of course, on the general taxpayers, and chiefly on the large income receivers and large property owners.

Incidentally, the system of government purchase of surplus grain to sustain falling prices led to the accumulation of a large grain reserve which turned out to great advantage when the two successive crops of 1940 and 1941 failed and Sweden was prevented by the German blockade from resorting to imports. By improved methods, better seed and increased use of commercial fertilizers between the wars, the Swedish farmers increased productivity so as to make the country for the first time normally independent of imports for bread stuffs. The crop failures caused by unfavourable weather, however, could not be prevented, and only the stored surplus saved the country from having to ask Adolf Hitler for bread. In 1917, Sweden had had to cede part of its merchant marine to the Allies in return for the right to buy foreign grain. But whereas the ports were then open, in 1940–45 they were blockaded by both sides in the war. Thanks to the experience of 1917, Sweden also began in 1936 to store up imported raw materials which helped to tide it over the actual war.

In the 1936 election, the Social Democrats had advanced to 112 seats in the second chamber out of a total of 230, or still a few seats short of an absolute majority. They then made a further advance toward a worker-farmer alliance by inviting the leaders of the Farmers' Union to join them in the new cabinet. (During the election campaign the farm group had formed for the first time an interim, holdover government, giving the labour leaders more time for electioneering.) The election outcome was a distinct endorsement of the Labour program; having achieved a coalition between the organized workers and the capitalistic small farmers, the returning prime minister, Per Albin Hansson, was naturally in a triumphant mood as the 1937 riksdag was about to open early in January.

On Jan. 2, 1937, Hansson published in the chief party organ, *Social-Demokraten*, of Stockholm, a signed article in which he advocated a strong government, checked always by an alert opposition. In writing this he may have had the dictators in both Berlin and Rome in mind, but the lesson was not lost on the Swedish opposition leaders either. In 1933 they had greatly deplored the alliance between the organized industrial workers and the farmers; in previous years the Social-Democrats had formed temporary coalitions, or working agreements, with the Liberals, but this was something new and unexpected.

As far as further improvements in the social welfare situation were concerned, several Liberal party organs declared that they would go a long way to support the Labour-Farmer government. But if it was to be a question of nationalizing more private enterprises, they would offer the most determined opposition.

In his address from the throne to the 1937 riksdag, in effect the government's own program, King Gustavus had said that the decrease in unemployment and the improvement in the country's economic situation warranted increased appropriations for social welfare, particularly adjustments in the old age pensions in accordance with the higher costs of living in some localities. This was the proposal on which the Social-Democrats had been defeated in the spring of 1936 and on which they had formally decided to resign and appeal to the electorate. In the spring of 1937, such a law was passed. Other measures of a similar type were adopted later.

By 1937, all government loans for public works to aid the unemployed had been paid off. The gain in 1936–37 revenue had been 59,000,000 kronor over that for 1935–36. The income estimated in the proposed budget for 1937–38 showed an advance of 96,000,000 kronor or close to 9%. This increase came partly from the higher earnings of government-owned utilities and partly from the increased

Refugees arriving on skis at the border of neutral Sweden in 1944. As the last haven among the Scandinavian nations, Sweden was generous in extending aid to those most urgently in need of medical attention or food both during and after World War II

yields of previously imposed taxes, chiefly those on income, both categories indicating a rising state of prosperity. A year later, in Jan. 1938, the 1937–38 budget was overbalanced; it showed a surplus of 19,000,000 kronor, a modest enough sum, but which, by the end of the 1938–39 budget year, was expected to be between 175,000,000 and 195,000,000. But before June 30, 1937, the government proposed to use 123,000,000 kronor to pay off old debts and write off bad investments, which would make the government's financial position sounder than it had been at the end of the previous boom in 1930.

In the four years between 1934 and 1938, government revenue from the income and estate taxes went up by 55%. A cut in income tax rates of close to 12% had been made in 1936, and since both the size and the number of taxable incomes had gone up by 1937, further cuts seemed unnecessary. In 1932, a new type of budget had been adopted, one that would be underbalanced in lean years and overbalanced in the fat ones.

Surpluses were to be put into a special equalization account, the use of which was defined in the king's address from the throne on Jan. 11, 1938.

"Our country can continue to rejoice over a favorable economic situation," said his majesty. "Neither is there any reason for expecting any change due to purely domestic causes." (On the eve of the Munich crisis he wisely hedged on foreign ones.) "But because of the decrease in economic activity in other countries with which we are closely connected in business," he went on, "the future is uncertain. Caution based on earlier experiences bids us not to meet it unprepared. Evidence of increased strength in our own private industrial enterprises is not lacking. It is my hope that this will be utilized in keeping up employment, even during an eventual future crisis. The government, too, must be prepared to act more quickly than it has done heretofore. At the first signs of depression, it must take measures to maintain employment and support the people's purchasing power. For this reason I intend to submit to you an economic preparedness budget which will take effect if and when an unfavorable development demands it."

This idea of an economic preparedness budget to fight depressions had to be abandoned, however, as the international situation grew worse. What Sweden had to achieve when Hitler had annexed both Austria and Czechoslovakia was a military preparedness budget rather than measures to combat unemployment, the chief obstacle of the 1930s. Prior to 1936, the annual national defense budget had been but 125,000,000 kronor, but by 1936–37 it had reached 154,000,000; in 1937–38, 179,000,000; in 1938–39, 262,000,000; in 1939–40, 320,000,000, later increased to 1,350,000,000; figures that clearly reflected the growing Swedish apprehensiveness over the international situation. During the war years, the military appropriations averaged 2,000,000,000 kronor, or 16 times the 1936 figure. No other small country in Europe spent that much money for its national defense.

Traditionally, the Swedish Social Democrats, like their fellow partisans in other countries, had been internationalists and strongly antimilitaristic. In 1925, they had supported the Liberals in reducing the Swedish army by about one-third, and in 1932 they naturally put social welfare and economic recovery before national defense. Hitler had just then come to power in Germany. As late as 1936 they resigned on a social welfare measure and thereby avoided the issue of voting for a proposed increase of less than 25,000,000 kronor in the military appropriations, as proposed by a mixed partisan commission.

By Jan. 1938, the original appropriations asked for national defense by the Hansson government had gone up to 180,560,000 kronor, but by March that year, when Hitler had annexed Austria, Hansson asked for 50,000,000 extra. He had seen the significance of the Hitler move. "The extra measures contemplated," he told the riksdag, "are of such a nature that they will have immediate effect." Without debate and without a dissenting vote, the money was granted. This was the first real Swedish emergency measure to prepare for World War II.

The spirit of national unity with which the Swedish people were later to face the war itself had by then taken firm root. The Social Democrats had faced the necessity of giving increased support to the national defense, just as the bourgeois parties had previously accepted the labour program of improved social welfare. Throughout the 1930s there were virtually no party differences of opinion in regard to foreign policy. All groups had supported the League of Nations, whereas there had been bitter disputes as to foreign relations before, during and after World War I.

As the 1938 riksdag opened, there was even less opposition to the Social Democratic government's proposals than there had been in 1937. If there was no tax reduction promised, there were also no new and expensive social welfare measures proposed either. This reform pause was intended to give the taxpayers a breathing spell. Even after the increased military expenditures had been voted, the expected government income was large enough to balance the 1938–39 budget without new imposts. As the foreign situation grew worse, domestic political strife died down.

The Shock of Munich.—Into this Swedish social welfare idyll of 1938 the Munich crisis broke as an unpleasant surprise.

What had Sweden done to prepare for it? In World War I, the nation had been neutral, though less united mentally than in the 1930s and 1940s. It had joined the League of Nations only after a sharp debate, but throughout its life had loyally fulfilled all obligations. Sweden had been the first neutral country elected to a seat on the League council, and it continued to be a sort of informal leader of the neutral bloc. In order to sustain the new international system, Hjalmar Branting had induced his country to accept gracefully, in 1921, the unfavourable decision of the League in regard to the Aland Islands, which were awarded to Finland. In 1925, after the Locarno agreements, Sweden had partly disarmed unilaterally, believing as it did in the new collective security. In 1935 it had taken part in economic sanctions against Italy, but had lived to regret that too; the great powers had not been sincere in their participation; the oil embargo which might have been effective was never imposed, and both France and Britain were suspected of having given Mussolini permission to proceed with his Ethiopian conquest. In 1937, the Swedish foreign minister, Richard I. Sandler, made a round of the European capitals, except Berlin and Rome, to get advance consent for a move at the next League meeting to be absolved of future obligation to take part in economic sanctions. (Sweden had made a reservation against participating in military sanctions before entering the League.) At the 1938 session, as a matter of fact, several states gave formal notice that they would never again take part in economic sanctions. To the very end Sweden kept up its membership in the League, hoping for the miracle that never was performed, but at the same time prepared for a resumption of its old neutrality policy.

During the final peace year, Sweden's main concern was to avoid affiliation with one group or the other of the great powers. It liked neither the Fascist nor the Communist camps, and the democratic powers were geographically too far away. After the Russo-German nonaggression treaty in Aug. 1939, which set off the war, there was less choice than ever.

As early as 1930, Sweden had become a member of the so-called Oslo group of small powers which had met in the Norwegian capital to discuss economic disarmament. The member nations had been able only to promise not to raise their import duties without first giving each other due notice—a modest enough commitment. This was the European small power answer, feeble as it was, to the British empire agreement about preferential duties, which in turn was a result of the U.S. tariff increases during the Herbert Hoover administration. To this vicious circle there was no end. Beside Sweden, the members of the Oslo group were Belgium, Denmark, Finland, the Netherlands, Norway, and Luxembourg (the members of the neutral bloc in the League of Nations, with Belgium taking the place of Switzerland).

Besides resumption of neutrality, Foreign Minister Sandler discussed on his travels in 1937 the idea of enlarging the Oslo convention. In July, when he visited Moscow, he was dined by Foreign Commissar Maxim Litvinov and was received cordially by Soviet President Mikhail I. Kalinin, but he did not meet Joseph Stalin and there were no visible results. The Oslo powers could not have formed a military alliance. They could not even plan a customs union. While their total foreign trade was comparable in volume to that of several of the great powers, their total trade with each other was less than that with almost any one of the big nations. As long as the latter were divided, they were helpless.

Equally futile were the attempts before the war to create some sort of Scandinavian unity. In foreign trade, even population, these states if united might have seemed impressive; but they had no geographic unity and therefore no common military front. While united mentally and in ideals of civilization, they could apply no common strategy. It would have been as hard, for instance, to get Finland to help hold the southern Danish frontier against Germany as to make either Norway or Denmark mobilize to defend Finland against Russia. Only Sweden, situated as it was, in the centre, was a common denominator. The Danes felt that it would be both foolish and futile for them to provoke Germany by rearming. They did not want, they said in effect, to make the Germans fear that their country might be used as a jumping off place by a would-be enemy of the reich. Norway seemed safe as long as it had Sweden as a buffer to the east and the British navy controlling the seas to the west. Neither of these countries therefore followed Sweden's example of at least beginning to rearm in 1936.

Only in Finland did Sweden get a favourable response. Early in 1938 a Stockholm pact was drawn up, providing for a joint defense of the Aland Islands, but it was never ratified by the Swedish riksdag, or even submitted to the other interested powers, signers of the 1921 Aland convention, by which the islands were to be demilitarized. Finland had stayed better armed than Sweden and in spirit it had not broken training, either mentally or physically, since World War I. Sooner or later it expected to be attacked by Russia, as happened at the end of Nov. 1939.

Sweden and the Finnish War.—Feeling itself menaced

too, Sweden at once sent both food and munitions, especially planes and anti-aircraft guns, medical aid and supplies, and later fully armed volunteers. Under the League of Nations' ruling that Finland had been unjustly attacked, this was not only legal but a neighbourly duty. In this war Sweden did not declare itself a neutral, but a nonbelligerent, or informally a noninterventionist. Many other countries, including Norway and Denmark as well as France and Britain, sent volunteers via Sweden, and some sent machine guns and artillery pieces, antiquated as some of them were. Almost all over the world Sweden was then berated for not taking an official and more active part. Inside Sweden, too, feeling ran high. "Finland's cause is our own," was the watchword, launched by Christian E. Guenther, the new nonpolitical foreign minister himself. Russia seemed to have no friends anywhere except the Communists in various countries.

On Feb. 13, 1940, Finland made a formal request for official aid from Sweden, but this was refused, causing Swedish public opinion to become even more aroused. The explanation given by the prime minister, Per Albin Hansson, on Feb. 15, was rather curt, and to allay the widespread excitement and disappointment, the king himself dictated a personal statement to the cabinet minutes (Feb. 19) which was at once published—a form of expression of opinion left open to him even after the adoption of the parliamentary system. In this he said, "From the very beginning Sweden has tried to aid Finland by means of volunteers and in numerous other ways, but at the very start I informed the Finnish authorities that, unfortunately, no military intervention could be expected from Sweden. With sorrow in my heart I have come to the conclusion, after serious reconsideration, that to this decision we must hold fast. For I am definitely of the opinion that if Sweden were now to intervene in Finland, we would run the greatest risk of not only becoming involved in a war with Russia, but also in the war between the great powers, and such a responsibility I am not able to assume. In such a situation, moreover, it would most probably be impossible to continue to render the not inconsiderable aid which Finland now receives from us and which it so well needs and which we are prepared to continue to give with the warmest of hearts. Sweden's vital interests, its honor, and its peace are the aims I have ever in mind. With the help of God, I hope that by following the route we have chosen we shall be able to escape all the misfortunes of war." With this conclusion the Swedish people as a whole agreed, and the demand for official aid died down.

On March 2, 1940, the Allied powers, France and Britain, made a formal request for the right to send troops across Scandinavia to aid Finland, if Finland should make such a request, which, as a matter of fact it never did; it was then too late. Both Norway and Sweden, however, replied in the negative. At least the Swedish government knew that as early as January Finland had requested, via Sweden, peace terms from Russia; and on March 12, or before any military help could have reached the north from either France or Britain, a peace treaty was signed in Moscow.

For the time being, the danger of being involved in the general European war was averted. Had the Allied request been granted, the risk of both France and Britain getting into a war with Russia would, of course, have been great. Had that happened, and had Hitler and Stalin thus been forced to become permanent partners, the outcome of World War II could very well have run a different course. The negative Norwegian and Swedish decision in March 1940 could therefore be termed a crucial turning point. During the "sitzkrieg" period on the eastern front in France in 1939–40, the opening of the northern front in Scandinavia against Germany had been openly discussed in the Paris press. On such a front Britain would have been, of course, expected to bear the major burden, a repetition of similar French agitation in World War I, when the French wanted the British to take over more of the line in northern France.

That the real objective of the Allies was less to aid Finland than to get control of the Swedish iron mines in arctic Lapland was suspected by both Norway and Sweden. The secret minutes of the Allied Supreme council on this point were later published in England and Sweden as well as in Germany.

The German Thrust North.—What would have happened had the Allied troops invaded or been admitted to the north was shown on April 9, 1940, when Germany carried out its own long-planned scheme to occupy both Denmark and Norway, the immediate excuse being that the British navy had mined certain Norwegian coastal waters in order to stop the transport of the Swedish iron ore to Germany. Germany already had charged that the Allies themselves had planned to invade Scandinavia. At the Nuernberg trials it was shown that they had planned the coup as early as the preceding fall and that they actually hoped for an Allied move in the north to give them an excuse to act. As a matter of fact, the Allies made no such move; they only talked about one, and the Germans took them by surprise. Thanks to its contacts inside Germany, Sweden had at least two weeks' advance warning, which it passed on to both Denmark and Norway. When asked about this, German diplomats deceived the Scandinavian governments by replying that their "operation Weser" was intended for the Low Countries.

Having learned that the Allies had made preparations themselves for action in the north, Sweden naturally assumed, in April 1940, that they were prepared to counter the German stroke. The ultimate German objective was after all not Norway, but Great Britain. By its help to Finland, Sweden, moreover, had badly depleted its inadequate supply of munitions, and Germany made the direct threat that under all circumstances it expected Sweden to maintain its declared policy of neutrality. Without relying on Germany's promise to leave Sweden alone as long as the latter did not interfere with German plans elsewhere, Sweden at once mobilized as never before in its whole history. Several German military scouting planes were shot down, and a complete blackout was ordered. Even the seacoast beacons were put out. Requests for the purchase of arms from Norway were turned down, as were the German demands for the right to send troops through Sweden to relieve their hard pressed units at Narvik. Later in the spring several German medical shipments and nursing staffs were allowed to pass through Sweden, and both German and British crew members of the civilian ships sunk at Narvik were evacuated through Sweden. Otherwise, while mounting guard over its own frontiers, Sweden kept inactive. Repeated German requests for troop transit privileges through Sweden were refused; each time Sweden expected to be invaded the next night or early the next morning. Finally in June the tension was eased by the Allied withdrawal from Norway and the escape of the Norwegian king and government to England. For the time being, open Norwegian resistance seemed broken.

Why did Sweden escape? At that time its military establishment was so weak that it could not have offered serious or long-drawn-out opposition to the immense German strength. Nor could the Allies have given Sweden the help they could not render even to the more accessible Norway. In the international political situation of the time Russia's attitude was obviously most important to Germany. The feeling in Finland being what it was after the bitter defeat earlier in the year, Russia must have known that if Germany had occupied the whole of Scandinavia, including Sweden, the balance of power between the two great Baltic states, Germany and Russia, would have been upset. As long as Sweden stayed neutral, there was no plausible reason Germany could give Russia for an occupation. From Moscow came reports that the German ambassador had spent five hours in the Kremlin, presumably to explain his country's intentions. Denmark was but a stepping stone to Norway, he probably pointed out, and the Norwegian coast was to be used for submarine action or even as a starting point for an invasion of England. That such was the German policy was confirmed at Nuernberg. Conversely, the occupation by Germany was intended to forestall one by the Allies, he probably told the Russians. Mountainous Norway was to be only a temporary German rampart to the north—an easily defended bastion. No such excuse could have been offered for invading a neutral Sweden. Sweden, to be sure, was an important Baltic state, the continuation of whose neutrality was a Russian concern. By occupying it, Germany would have outflanked Russia to the north, especially as Finland had not been occupied. Whatever the Russian rulers replied to the German ambassador, Sweden understood what had happened and at once sent a note of appreciation to Moscow, an act that was not officially revealed until after Germany had been defeated, when it attracted little notice, except in Sweden. Internationally, Russia's attitude was indirectly revealed at the time in a Tass news agency dispatch from Moscow which first denied certain not otherwise identified foreign press reports that Russia had put pressure on Germany in favour of Swedish neutrality, and then emphasized the desirability from the Russian point of view of a continuation of that very policy. Germany at that time knew that it must avoid a break with Russia at all costs. The western front was still intact.

How worried Germany had been that Sweden might join the Allies was revealed at the Nürnberg trial, explaining at last the announcement in Berlin on May 7, 1940, that Hitler and King Gustavus of Sweden had been in correspondence, and that the king had given Hitler his personal word that his country would remain neutral—a correspondence that was soon confirmed by the Stockholm foreign office. Against this background, the apparently uncalled for statement by the German foreign minister, Joachim von Ribbentrop, on April 26, 1940, that Sweden's neutrality had been perfect and was expected to remain so, took on a clear meaning. By indirection, Russia was thereby assured that Germany intended to leave Sweden alone. Diplomats often talk around curves.

Aside from this fear of provoking Russia, Germany had other, more direct reasons for its restraint. By leaving Sweden unoccupied, it felt, it could count on a continued exchange of goods, and since all transoceanic trade routes had been blocked by Britain every source of supply, no matter how small, was valuable. Of particular interest was Sweden's iron ore; to keep that source open, Germany was willing to ship coal to Sweden in return. And since Sweden had lost its coal supplies in both Poland and Britain, there was only Germany left. Swedish pulp and paper were less important, though worth buying at a certain price. Sweden also needed German chemicals, especially those used in medicines and commercial fertilizers. In return, Germany could demand ball bearings and other types of steel. And once Sweden was surrounded by German military power there was every reason to believe that ultimately it could be induced to join the German "lebensraum" without the expenditure of a single shell or air bomb. Finally, when the planned big drive against Russia was started, Sweden, like Finland, could be expected to join in the "crusade against bolshevism." That Sweden instead continued to rearm, resisting as many German demands as possible, and finally refusing point blank to march against Russia, was, of course, a disappointment. The German press then began to call the Swedes names such as "Communists," "a people on vacation," "a nation out of step with the times," and finally "swine in tuxedos"—a typical German nerve war.

Log piles along the streets of a Stockholm suburb where wood was used as home fuel during the wartime coal shortage in Sweden. Available supplies of coal were reserved for industrial uses

When World War II began, Sweden had attempted to carry on normal trade with both England and Germany and in Dec. 1939 concluded special treaties to that effect with each of those powers. When Sweden was surrounded in 1940 and lost about 70% of its foreign trade, chiefly from overseas, it had no choice but to increase its trade with Germany and the countries the latter had invaded and conquered. For several years before the war Swedish trade with Germany had been conducted on the barter or forced clearing basis; this system was continued throughout the war.

German coal was traded for Swedish iron ore; chemicals and rubber for ball bearings. At no time during the war did Sweden send Germany either foodstuffs or ready-made arms or munitions. In the fall of 1944, all trade stopped. Throughout the war and despite German blockade, Sweden managed to send Britain ball bearings too, but that could not be revealed until later. With Russia, Sweden concluded a wartime trade treaty in Sept. 1940, granting credits up to 100,000,000 kronor, but the trade that started then was cut off in June 1941 when Germany invaded its associate of 1939.

Under heavy German pressure, a major concession was made by Sweden early in July 1940, after the Low Countries had been overrun and France had capitulated. Sweden consented to allow German soldiers on leave to travel on Swedish trains from Norway to the German border and vice versa, and a certain number of armed men were permitted to use the Swedish railroads between points in northern and central Norway, between which there was no train service within Norway itself. German munitions were also routed through Sweden, both to Norway and Finland, a concession balanced by the charter in 1940 of one-third of the Swedish merchant marine to England for service in the convoyed transportation of both food and munitions to England. Many of these ships were torpedoed and lost. A year later, after the German war against Russia had started, Sweden agreed to transport a single German division from Norway to Finland, a favour requested by Finland as well as Germany.

Neutrality?—While the second concession was clearly a violation of neutrality, the first was a border case, partly mitigated by the fact that when it was granted, open resistance had ceased in Norway (the underground movement had not yet been formed) and that it was not in direct violation of any distinct provision in the 1907 Hague rules of neutrality—a technicality, to be sure, but still arguable. To the worried Swedish people, who had heard rumours and read newspaper reports of German soldiers on Swedish trains, the foreign office, on July 5, 1940, issued the following statement: "Since the military operations in Norway have been discontinued, the war restrictions on transit to and from Norway have become superfluous. All goods in such traffic may therefore now be transported on the Swedish railroads. Travel permission will also be given to members of the German military forces, especially soldiers on leave. For this purpose special cars will be provided." To say that the Swedish public was both bewildered and shocked would be an understatement. The Norwegian reaction was naturally even more profound. To both countries it was a painful situation.

In a public address delivered at Ludvika in central Sweden two days later, July 7, 1940, Prime Minister Hansson explained as follows: "During the war in Norway, the transit traffic was restricted and shipments through Sweden of both men and munitions was refused to both sides in the conflict. The situation has now changed. From our point of view the dominating fact is that fighting between Germany and Norway has now ceased and that the whole European situation has thoroughly changed during the past two weeks. Obviously, Sweden cannot ignore the fact that seven European countries have been occupied by Germany, either wholly or in part, and that France has accepted an armistice. Our government's main duty is to keep Sweden out of the war and safeguard our freedom and independence. Neutrality and national emergency measures are the instruments used in our efforts to save our country from war."

While there was much grumbling and criticism, this policy was ultimately supported by all parties in the national coalition cabinet. In September of that year the Social Democratic representatives were given a clear majority, 134 out of 230 seats. As attendance at the polls was about the same as in 1936, this verdict was a distinct personal triumph for Hansson and his policy.

The concession permitting a German division to cross Sweden from Norway to Finland a year later was explained by Hansson in an address at Uppsala on June 29, 1941, in which he said, "There is no occasion to conceal that this accommodation caused much hesitation, particularly in view, among other things, that it involves a deviation from the traditional concept of neutrality and that it has put a strain on the national unity. The consent was given only after careful consideration. . . . Let what has happened be what it is—an accommodation, a single concession which to be sure is of great importance, but at the same time clearly limited in scope."

The German division, which after crossing Sweden was expected to reach Murmansk and otherwise hold the extreme left wing of the German-Finnish lines, never gained its objective. Repeatedly Germany made requests for further transit concessions over the Swedish railroads, but was consistently turned down. What Germany had expected to be the beginning of Swedish accommodations, turned out to be, as announced, the last one. On that Sweden was united. In the fall of 1943, even the special permits for traffic to Norway were cancelled, ostensibly by mutual consent. Germany was then too weak to bluster in the 1940 fashion, while conversely, Sweden had made much progress in rearming.

Toward the end of the war, Swedish officers were allowed to train in Sweden young refugees from both Denmark and Norway, supposedly for police duty in their own respective countries when the Germans should withdraw, and many young Norwegians were allowed to leave by air for training in England or overseas. American air pilots who had made emergency landings in Sweden after missions over Germany were allowed to leave the country on a credit basis, the Germans being told that whenever a corresponding number of their pilots had made similar landings in Sweden they too would be repatriated. By then, however, the power of the German luftwaffe was exhausted. In the very last stages of German resistance, Sweden sent a caravan of motor buses to Germany under the command of Count Folke Bernadotte, a nephew of the king, to evacuate first the Scandinavian inmates and then as many as possible of other nationalities from the German concentration camps. Nearly 20,000 civilian prisoners of the nazis were thus brought to Sweden and helped to recuperate. The total number of war refugees in Sweden at various times and from various countries was almost 200,000, Finnish war orphans being the most numerous.

Postwar.—When the hostilities ceased, Sweden was naturally in a position to start production at once, its machinery and factories being largely intact. Prefabricated houses were delivered to England, the Netherlands and other war-torn areas, including the Danish island of Bornholm. The demand for goods of all kinds became very strong and to many countries Sweden sold goods on credit, particularly its neighbours, Denmark, Finland and Norway. The credit limit to Britain itself was set as high as 600,000,000 kronor. On a cash basis, trade with the U.S. was resumed

Sweden: *Statistical Data*

Item	1938 Value (000's omitted)	1938 Amount or Number	1944 Value (000's omitted)	1944 Amount or Number
Exchange Rate				
United States		1 Krona = 25.19 cents		1 Krona = 23.86 cents
Great Britain		19.41 Kronor = £1		16.9 Kronor = £1
Finance				
Government revenues	$365,201 (£74,699)		$663,399 (£164,411)	
Government expenditures	$342,329 (£70,020)		$941,246 (£233,270)	
Gold reserves	$149,018 (£30,480)		$249,251 (£61,772)	
National debt	$612,348 (£125,250)		$2,329,046 (£577,211)	
Transportation				
Railroads		10,300 mi.		10,197 mi.*
Highways		52,791 "		54,403 " *
Communication				
Telephones		803,228		1,075,000†
Telegraph lines		13,038 mi.		12,485 mi.*
Radio sets		1,156,781		1,710,000†
Minerals				
Gold		2,172,170 oz.		
Silver		7,059,377 "		
Iron ore		13,352,860 tons		
Copper		11,759 "		
Crops				
Hay		5,884,959 tons		4,709,734 tons†
Root crops (fodder)		2,830,817 "		2,499,307 " †
Potatoes		2,064,057 "		2,393,223 " †
Livestock				
Cattle		3,036,000		2,789,780†
Swine		1,371,000		988,642†
Horses		617,000		595,444†
Poultry		...		8,255,513†
Forest products				
Total		194,898,296 cu. ft.		
Box boards		52,682 standards‡		
Lumber (sawn and planed)		676,200 " ‡		
Manufactures				
Machinery and metal	$451,042 (£92,256)	...		
Wood and paper	$307,235 (£62,842)	...		
Exports				
Total	$464,453 (£95,000)	22,463,000 tons		
Paper and manufactures	$119,243 (£24,390)	3,069,000 "		
Iron and steel and manufactures	$67,943 (£13,897)	435,000 "		
Iron ore	$60,301 (£12,334)	13,983,000 "		
Imports				
Total	$524,543 (£107,290)	15,068,000 tons		
Coal and coke	$48,357 (£9,891)	8,502,000 "		
Iron and steel and manufactures	$34,563 (£7,070)	578,000 "		
Vehicles and parts	$33,837 (£6,921)	84,000 "		
Defense				
Standing army personnel		48,000		350,000§
Reserves		575,000		275,000§
Standing navy personnel		5,500		...
Reserves		700		...
Standing air force personnel		1,000		3,000§
Military expenditures	$46,620 (£9,536)		$84,156§ (£21,973)	
Education				
Elementary school students		567,579		529,750*
Secondary school students		90,087		53,868*
Universities		5§		5
Students		7,606§		8,937

*1942. †1943. ‡Exports only. §1940.

as soon as the seas could be swept of mines; Swedish pulp and paper were in special demand. In return Sweden was able to get some coal and crude rubber from the U.S. Business travel between Sweden and the U.S. soon became heavy, but no tourist traffic was allowed. Commercial air traffic was begun in 1946 both by the American Overseas division and all the Scandinavian air lines.

In Nov. 1946, Sweden was one of the first formerly neutral countries to be admitted to the United Nations, the others being Afghanistan and Iceland. The admission was by unanimous consent and without debate. (N. Hn.)

Bibliography.—M. W. Childs, *This is Democracy* (1938); *Cook's Traveller's Handbook*, rev. by T. G. Garman (London, 1939); N. Herlitz, *Sweden: A Modern Democracy* (1939); A. Montgomery, *Rise of Modern Industry in Sweden* (London, 1939); A. Myrdal, *Nation and Family* (1941); P. H. Norgren, *The Swedish Collective Bargaining System* (1941); A. F. Rickman, *Swedish Iron Ore* (London, 1939); *Sweden: A Wartime Survey* (Royal Ministry for Foreign Affairs, 1942).

Swedish Literature

See Scandinavian Literature.

Sweepstakes

See Horse Racing.

Sweet Potatoes

See Potatoes.

Swimming

The major developments in swimming during the decade 1937–46 were the vigorous impetus imparted to educational activities by the exigencies of World War II, the unprecedented role played by expert swimmers in actual combat, and the notable strides made in lifesaving methods, speed swimming and fancy diving.

In the early stages of the war, lack of watermanship among service men was responsible for loss of life so appalling in ship sinkings and landing operations that all belligerents came to realize the imperative need of taking immediate steps to remedy the shortcoming. Teaching centres were organized rapidly, in ever increasing numbers, and eventually millions of men and women were taught to swim, thus materially reducing the world's quota of non-swimmers and bringing about almost universal recognition of the value of swimming in lifesaving and physical development.

At these centres, too, far more efficient methods of self-protection in accidents at sea were evolved, as well as new and greatly improved techniques for the use of swimming in the rehabilitation of injured veterans and the treatment of infantile paralysis.

Here also, various service groups were trained for particular combat duties, including the famous Allied underwater demolition teams, whose task it was to blast the way for invasion and who acquitted themselves valiantly and conspicuously on the Normandy beaches, in the Mediterranean and throughout the Pacific. Never before had swimming been utilized so widely and effectively in warfare.

Water sports, meanwhile, were fostered for recreation and conditioning at the training centres and at the front, proving immensely popular and of great benefit. Allied championships were conducted in the various theatres of operations and results were successful everywhere.

Records.—The great slashes administered to world's records during the decade bore witness to the progress of speed swimming. Only eight of those established prior to 1937 remained unbroken, five of them marks for events never used in international competition.

A highlight was the downfall of the most enduring record on the official table, that of 51 sec. for the 100 yd. free style, created in 1927 by John Weissmuller, of the United States.

Sixteen years had elapsed when his young countryman, Alan Ford, clipped the record to 50.6 sec., then to 49.7 sec. in 1944.

The greatest star of the decade, however, unquestionably was Ragnhild Hveger, of Denmark, who rose to fame in 1936 and dominated the field until her retirement in 1944. She shattered all but one of the 16 free style records listed for women, several repeatedly, some by large total margins, cutting the time for 220 yd. from 2 min. 27.6 sec. to 2 min. 22.6 sec., 400 m. from 5 min. 12.4 sec. to 5 min. .1 sec. and 1,500 m. from 22 min. 36.7 sec. to 20 min. 57 sec. Thirteen of her free style records remained unbeaten, as did that of 5 min. 38.2 sec. for the 400 m. back stroke.

The only other swimmer to monopolize records throughout the period was Adolph Kiefer, United States back stroke ace, who also retired. True, one of his marks was shaded, but he disposed of the claimed record before it could be bracketed. In all, he sliced the figures for 100 yd. from 58.8 sec. to 56.6 sec., 200 m. from 2 min. 24 sec. to 2 min. 19.3 sec. and 400 m. from 5 min. 13 sec. to 5 min. 10.9 sec.

The decade opened rather dully, a natural reaction to the feverish activity caused by the Olympic games of 1936 in Berlin. Aside from the exploits of Miss Hveger and Kiefer, the only record broken was that of 20 min. 57 sec. for one mile free style, dropped to 20 min. 42.6 sec. by Ralph Flanagan, of the United States.

Things again were in full swing by 1938 and the British Empire games in Sydney provided the highlight. Australia and England fought so keen a battle for aquatic laurels that third places had to be figured before Australia could be declared the winner. Tomikatsu Amano of Japan earned glory by ripping the 11-year-old record for 1,500 m. free style from 19 min. 7.2 sec. to 18 min. 58.8 sec.; a Dutch lass, I. Van Feggelen, leaped into the spotlight, erasing all four of the back stroke standards tabled for women and doing her best at 100 m. in 1 min. 12.9 sec. and 400 m. in 5 min. 41.6 sec.; Flanagan added to his holdings a mark of 4 min. 46.2 sec. for 400 m. free style.

The European championships brought a startling upset, the favoured Dutch naiads suffering a crushing 100-to-60 defeat at the hands of their Danish rivals.

Two topnotch breast stroke swimmers stepped to the fore in 1939, Richard Hough, of the United States, lowering the records for 100 yd. to 1 min. .6 sec. and 100 m. to 1 min. 7.2 sec., Inge Sorensen, of Denmark, the women's for 400 m. to 6 min. 16.2 sec. and 500 m. to 7 min. 58 sec. Of especial interest were the first victory ever gained by a Hawaiian team in the men's championships of the U.S.A. and the success of the German men and Danish women in the European title tests, the last of the decade, held almost on the eve of the war. The start of hostilities made it necessary for the Fédération Internationale de Natation Amateur, controlling body in Olympic and international water sports, to suspend operations. It did not resume its functions until 1946.

Of chief import in 1940 was the noticeable decline of Japan's men swimmers, claimants to world leadership from 1932. In their national championships they fell short of the winning performances of 1939 in every event, except the 100 m. back stroke. All sports were curtailed in war-torn Europe, and most of the title events were abandoned for the duration, but one record fell, Miss J. Waalberg of Holland clipping the time for 500 m. breast stroke to 7 min. 49.9 sec. In the United States the standards for the 400 yd. and 400 m. relays were lowered to 3 min. 30.7 sec. and 3 min. 54.4 sec.

The discovery of a 16-year-old Hawaiian then rated the greatest middle distance swimmer of all time was paramount in 1941. William Smith, Jr., the lad in question, displayed sensational speed in slashing free style records from 220 yd. to 800 m. In particular, he swam the 800 m. in 9 min. 50.8 sec. in a 100 m. pool, time which, allowing for the gain at the turns, was equal to about 9 min. 43 sec. in a 50 m. pool, the length of course over which the former record of 9 min. 55.8 sec. was set. The standard for the 400 yd. relay was bettered thrice in the U.S.A., finally dropping to 3 min. 27.7 sec.; and Alfred Nakache of France shaved the time for 200 m. breast stroke to 2 min. 36.8 sec.

Smith continued to write swimming history in 1942; his

William Smith, 16-year-old Hawaiian swimmer, after he had set a new world's record of 2:07.7 for the 220-yd. free style at Honolulu, May 16, 1941. In one week he established five new world's records

outstanding feat was to cover 440 yd. in 4 min. 39.6 sec. in a 55 yd. pool, an approximate pace of 4 min. 29 sec. in a 25 yd. pool, the course used in creating the then tabled mark of 4 min. 40.8 sec. Hiroshi Nakama, another Hawaiian, cut the figures for one mile to 20 min. 29 sec. and a U.S.A. four cut those for the 400 m. relay to 3 min. 50.8 sec.

Of especial interest in 1943 was the mentioned threat to the back stroke supremacy of Kiefer. Harry Holiday, his fellow citizen, not only lowered the record for 100 yd. to 57 sec., but nosed out the noted ace in the national 150 yd. championship. But Kiefer soon regained standard and title. Danish girls hung up a new record of 4 min. 5.7 sec. for the 400 yd. relay; Alfred Nakache further reduced the time for the 200 m. breast stroke to 2 min. 36.4 sec. and Leonid Meshkov of Russia was credited with a mark of 5 min. 43.8 sec. for the 400 m. breast stroke, but feats by Russians could not be recognized, because the soviet union was not affiliated with the F.I.N.A.

Ann Curtis (left), 100-yd. titleholder in 1945, with Brenda Helser, whom she defeated during the A.A.U. indoor swimming meet at Chicago, Ill., on April 13

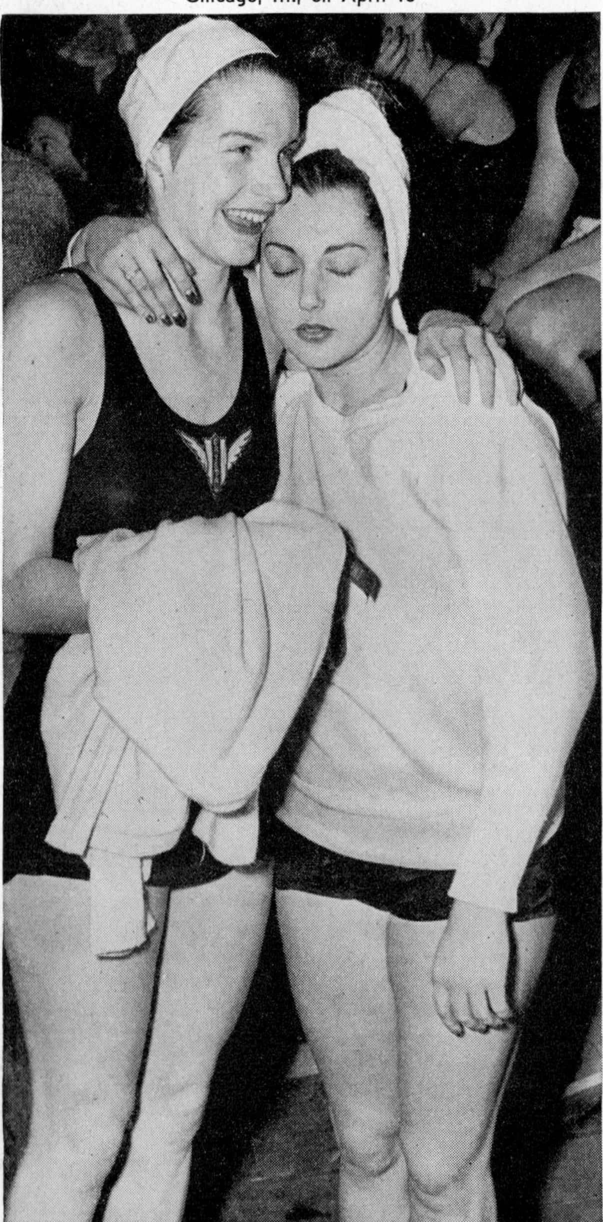

Ann Curtis of the United States made a strong bid in 1944 for the post vacated by the retiring Miss Hveger. Besides shading the latter's record for 880 yd. to 2 min. 8.6 sec., she came close to other marks and won the U.S. titles from 100 m. to one mile free style. Alan Ford clipped the standard for 100 m. free style from 56.4 sec. to 55.9 sec., and William Smith those for 200 m. and 220 yd. to 2 min. 6.2 sec. and 2 min. 7.1 sec., while a U.S.A. four cut the time for the 400 yd. relay to 3 min. 24.5 sec.

Joseph Verdeur of the United States was the only record breaker in 1945, with 2 min. 21 sec. for the 200 yd. breast stroke, but Miss Brenda Helser, same country, swam 100 yd. in 60 sec. and the 100 m. free style in 1 min. 5.8 sec. over a 50 m. course, better performances, figuring the gain at the turns, than the records of 59.4 sec. and 1 min. 4.6 sec., set in 25 m. pools. Two boys of striking ability drew attention as world prospects, James McLane of the United States, 14 years old, and Alex Jany, of France, 16. McLane won the national one and three mile titles over Nakama, one-mile record holder, and Jany achieved 57.5 sec. for 100 m. and 2 min. 9.8 sec. for 200 m., not far from standard time.

Outstanding in 1946 were a great revival of water sports in Europe and the return to activity of the F.I.N.A. A number of abandoned title meets were resumed in Europe, intercountry matches were frequent and brilliant performances marked the competition. The F.I.N.A. executive bureau held its first postwar session in London in June, revised its rules, drafted plans for the Olympic games of 1948 and approved 45 of the records set while it was inoperative. H. E. Fern, of England, was elected president, and R. M. Ritter, of the United States, secretary-treasurer.

Jany fulfilled predictions made for him, clipping the record for the 200 m. free style to 2 min. 5.4 sec., besides helping lower the time for the 300 m. medley relay to 3 min. 12.3 sec. McLane showed great improvement, winning national titles from 400 to 1,500 m. and defeating at 400 m. Smith, the record holder. Miss Nel van Vliet, of Holland, assumed front rank as a breast stroke star, breaking six records and slashing these for 200 m. from 2 min. 56 sec. to 2 min. 52.6 sec., and 500 m. from 7 min. 49.9 sec. to 7 min. 41 sec. while Joseph Verdeur dropped the men's for 200 yd. and 200 m. to 2 min. 19.5 sec. and 2 min. 35.6 sec. Russia's Leonid Meshkov was credited with an unofficial record of 1 min. 5.2 sec. for 100 m. breast stroke.

In glancing over the picture of the decade as a whole, there was evidence aplenty that the Japanese had lost in 1940 any claim they may have had to international leadership in swimming for men and that the United States was in front after that. Among women, the Danish succeeded the Dutch in 1938, retaining the lead until Miss Hveger retired.

Supremacy in fancy diving was maintained throughout by the men and women of the U.S.A., and it was a gauge of the men's margin of superiority that they introduced quite a few new and more difficult dives. Some added to the official table at the highest valuations ever listed. The ablest performers were, chronologically, Al Patnik, Earl Clark, Sam Lee, Frank Dempsey, Norman Sper, Jr., Miller Anderson, Bruce Harlan and the Misses Arlite Smith, Marjorie Gestring, Helen Crlenkovich, Ann Ross and Zoe Ann Olsen.

Water polo grew steadily in popularity, and although the war broke up standardized competition, it did not greatly reduce activity, as the game was played extensively at training centres and in the war theatres. Hungary was

Alan Ford, of Yale university, New Haven, Conn., who broke a 16-year swimming record when he swam the 100-yard free style in 50.6 seconds. He is shown using a mirror to detect flaws in his stroke during a practice swim

foremost in 1937 and 1938, lost to Germany in 1939 and regained the top in 1940, when the last determining matches took place. Results in 1946, with Hungary, Germany and England not participating, placed Sweden at the head of the list. (L. de B. H.)

Bibliography.—T. K. Cureton, *Warfare Aquatics* (1943); F. A. Greenwood, *Bibliography of Swimming* (1940); M. Mann, *Swimming Fundamentals* (1940); U.S. Off. of Naval Operations, Aviation Training Div., *Swimming* (1944).

Swing Music

See Dance; Music.

Swiss Literature

See Central European and Balkan Literature.

Switzerland

A republican confederation of 22 cantons in west-central Europe, Switzerland is bounded N. and E. by Germany, S. by Italy and W. by France. Area, 15,944 sq.mi.; pop. (census of Dec. 1, 1941,) 4,260,179. Chief towns: Berne (cap. 129,331); Zürich (333,829); Basle (161,380); Geneva (124,442); Lausanne (91,738). Languages (census of 1930): German 2,924,314; French 831,100; Italian 242,-034; Romansch 44,204 and others 24,797. Religion: Protestant 57%, mainly in the more populous cantons of Zürich, Berne, Vaud, Neuchâtel and Basle; Roman Catholic 41%, mainly in Lucerne, Fribourg, Ticino, Valais and the Forest cantons; Jews and others 2%.

The Swiss federal constitution, adopted in 1874, provided for a parliament and federal council. The parliament is the supreme legislative authority and consists of two houses: a Ständerat, or council of states of 44 members, 2 chosen by each canton by varying methods; and a nationalrat, or national council, chosen by the Swiss people in direct election for 4 years, at the rate of one deputy for every 22,000 persons; in 1937, there were 187 deputies and in 1946, 194. Laws passed by the two houses can be vetoed by the people, which means in effect that 30,000 citizens, or eight cantons, may demand that the law in question should be submitted to the direct vote of the nation, which can say only "yes" or "no." This referendum procedure is frequently used.

The chief executive authority is deputed to the bundesrat or federal council, consisting of seven members, elected for four years by the two houses of parliament sitting together as a federal assembly. The president of the Swiss confederation and the vice-president of the federal council are also both elected by the federal assembly for the term of one year from Jan. 1 to Dec. 31 and are not re-eligible to the same offices until after the expiration of another year. The vice-president may be, and usually is, elected to succeed the outgoing president. The presidents for 1937–46 were: Giuseppe Motta (1937), Johannes Baumann (1938), Philippe Etter (1939), Marcel Pilet-Golaz (1940), Ernest Wetter (1941), Philippe Etter (1942), Enrico Celio (1943), Walter Stampfli (1944), Eduard von Steiger (1945) and Karl Kobelt (1946). (S. B. F.)

Traditional Neutrality.—In joining the League of Nations in 1920, Switzerland had accepted the obligations of membership with one reservation, which safeguarded its military neutrality. Such prudence was amply motivated by the political uncertainty left by the treaty of Versailles. As the impotence of the League became increasingly evident, Switzerland was permitted in 1938 to resume its traditional, unconditional neutrality. It remained a member of the League but was freed from all obligations to participate in any kind of sanctions.

World War II did not impair the political neutrality of Switzerland. This was chiefly because of the firm attitude of the Swiss people who, under the leadership of the federal council and of Gen. Henri Guisan, were determined to defend themselves to the utmost, and also to the fact that vital military decisions were reached away from the Swiss borders. As long as Switzerland had two belligerents along its frontiers, its troops remained ready for action on all sides. Later, when the country was surrounded by axis forces only, the Swiss organized their national redoubt in the heart of their mountains, ready to abandon the lowlands and towns in order to make the decisive stand in their natural fortress.

It is true that in order to survive materially and, especially, to receive the coal supply so indispensable to its industries, Switzerland was forced into commercial agreements that operated in favour of the axis. It is true also that the liberty of the press had to be restricted through censorship. But at no time did it compromise on the fundamentals of its neutrality. On the other hand, the influx of an increasing number of refugees and escapees raised many grave problems. Although improvisation was often necessary, the helping spirit of the Swiss remained true to itself. The doors were opened to children suffering from hunger and privation. Thanks to the activity of the International committee of the Red Cross, Switzerland became the centre, during the war, for the assembly and forwarding of prisoner-of-war parcels and messages, and following the end of hostilities in Europe for the dispatch of relief supplies to distressed populations. The postwar welfare agency created by the Swiss themselves was called the Don Suisse. Its activities were first directed toward countries to the west of Switzerland, then south, north and east. The Don Suisse collaborated on many occasions with the United Nations Relief and

Through neutral Switzerland, daily mail passed between nations at war during 1939–45. In the photograph, delayed Christmas packages for British prisoners of war in Germany await delivery in a railroad station at Geneva in the spring of 1941

Rehabilitation administration and was the best illustration of the way the Swiss people intended to contribute, within their limited means, to the reconstruction of Europe.

The creation of the United Nations again brought the problem of neutrality to the fore again. No final decision had yet been taken at the end of the decade 1937–46 regarding the position of Switzerland in the new world organization, but it should be stressed that if Switzerland wished to preserve its neutrality it was precisely in order to go on rendering services so urgently needed in times of conflict. Indeed, one of the most valuable contributions which Switzerland was able to make during the war was the part it played as a protective power.

Internal Policy.—Independent development in Swiss internal policy could occur only under the protective shield of neutrality. This does not mean that Switzerland had not been influenced by the various European political currents. There, as in almost every other country, socialism had made steady progress. Aware of the economic implications of the new program, the conservatives joined hands. And while the socialists looked to soviet Russia as the one state having come closest to the realization of their ideals, the bourgeois parties at first regarded without displeasure the façade of order that the first fascist government was building in Europe. The arrival of the nazis on the political scene, however, was the danger signal to all Swiss patriots.

After World War I, party politics gradually yielded to the growing influence of economic interests. By the end of the decade 1937–46, it was mostly the trade unions, the employers associations, the industrial groups which were determining the fate of the country. In 1943, a Socialist, Ernest Nobs, was elected to the federal council. This gesture of political conciliation helped the Swiss to preserve a state of great stability.

The tendency toward political centralization grew steadily. The codes, or sets of laws, were unified, the proportion of federal taxes increased. Political and economic bodies began to rely more and more on state subsidies. Centralization brought an increase of bureaucracy, an evergrowing dependence on the federal authority.

Social Progress.—A vast project of old age insurance made progress during the decade and it was expected to be given a trial in 1948. In the organization of labour, mention should be made of an extension of collective bargaining. In the watchmaking and metallurgical industries, employers and workmen came together in 1938 and decided on a labour truce which obliged both parties to submit conflicts to arbitration. In certain fields, on the other hand, Switzerland displayed excessive conservatism. It remained one of the few countries in the world where women were still refused the right to vote.

At the beginning of World War II, a compensation fund was established to help soldiers to cope with the difficulties of prolonged mobilization. This measure went a long way toward preventing social troubles and proved of capital importance for the morale of the country. The wartime rationing system functioned almost to perfection. The black market was negligible. The country adopted an elaborate plan to intensify crops and general food production. Thus, thanks to the talent of a few men

Swiss fire fighters directing hose at a blazing structure after U.S. planes accidentally bombed Schaffhausen near the Swiss-German border on April 1, 1944. Several industrial plants were razed, and many persons were killed or injured

and the discipline of the population, Switzerland reached the end of the war with its labour and plant intact, a great social stability and sufficient reserve not to suffer from the dearth in Europe. Once the immediate danger had passed, the conflicts of interest between the bourgeois and socialist groups gained new strength.

(R. Bd.)

Bibliography.—Edgar Bonjour, *Swiss Neutrality: Its Meaning and History*, trans. by Mary Hottinger (London, 1946).

Switzerland: *Statistical Data*

Item	1938 Value (000's omitted)	1938 Amount or Number	1944 Value (000's omitted)	1944 Amount or Number
Exchange rate				
United States		1 franc=22.87 cents		1 franc=23.35 cents
Great Britain		20.40 francs=£1		17.35 francs=£1
Finance				
Government revenues	$123,275 (£25,215)			
Government expenditures	$132,194 (£27,039)			
Gold reserves	$660,972 (£135,196)			
National debt	$629,707 (£128,801)			
Transportation				
Railroads		3,218 mi.		
Highways		10,200 mi.		
Communication				
Telephones		450,380		567,517*
Radio sets		458,074		675,819*
Minerals				
Aluminum		58,422,000 lb.		
Iron ore		147,706 tons†		
Gold		1,125 oz.		
Crops				
Potatoes		893,965 tons		
Straw (grain)		619,823 tons		
Fruits (orchard)		498,460 tons		
Livestock				
Cattle		1,700,585		1,497,436
Swine		922,807		599,521
Goats		...		218,485
Forest products				
Conifers		59,666,564 cu. ft.		
Firewood		42,704,668 cu. ft.		
Timber		38,748,919 cu. ft.		
Exports‡				
Total	$301,113 (£61,590)	...		
Watches	$55,188 (£11,288)	17,000,000		
Machines	$47,320 (£9,679)	63,000 tons		
Aniline dyes	$19,189 (£3,925)	8,000 tons		
Imports‡				
Total	$367,515 (£75,172)	...		
Coal	$29,115 (£5,955)	3,678,000 tons		
Industrial chemicals	$25,433 (£5,202)	256,000 tons		
Iron and steel	$20,012 (£4,093)	406,000 tons		
Defense				
Standing army personnel		318		180,000§
Reserves		450,000		370,000§
Standing air force personnel		5,000		7,840§
Reserves		...		15,000§
Military expenditures	$28,358 (£5,800)		...	
Education				
Elementary school students		464,714		455,561§
Secondary school students		86,190		73,422§‖
Universities		...		7¶
Students		11,472		9,649¶

*1943. †Exports only. ‡Includes Liechtenstein. §1940. ‖Includes middle school students. ¶1941.

Sydney

Capital city of the state of New South Wales, Sydney is the site of the first British settlement founded in Australia, the 150th anniversary of which was celebrated in 1938. Within statistical boundaries (157,000 ac.) the population of Sydney metropolis was 1,398,000 (est. Dec. 1943). After London it had the largest European population of any city in the British commonwealth, and contained half the population of New South Wales. Its growth was late and rapid, the population being 383,000 in 1891; 630,000 in 1911; 1,235,000 in 1933; 1,279,000 in 1937. This growth was due to natural increase, overseas immigration and internal migration from other parts of Australia. Toward the end of the decade 1937–46, growth of Sydney was retarded by a lowered birth rate and temporary suspension of immigration. Plans were, however, going forward for development of the metropolis on modern extensive lines. There was no standard boundary of the metropolis and contiguous to the statistical boundaries there was a population of more than 100,000, largely suburban in character. Local government within the statistical boundaries was administered by 50 separate municipalities, while in the contiguous suburban areas there were seven local municipal and shire councils. Water and sewerage, electricity, road transport and main roads were each administered by separate authorities.

In 1945 a Cumberland county council was established to draw up an interim plan and a master plan for urban, suburban and rural development covering the entire area of county Cumberland in which urban settlement extended radially some 20 or 30 mi. from the city centre. This embraced an area of 1,630 sq.mi. and a population of (approx.) 1,550,000 in which there were 66 local government areas. In 1946 the government decided to abolish these existing local government areas and to redivide the entire county area into eight local government units.

Although Sydney was extensively prepared against air raids during World War II, no bombing occurred. On one occasion a few shells from the sea did minor damage. Midget Japanese submarines in 1942 penetrated Sydney harbour and were destroyed. During the war Sydney became a supply base of the U.S. Pacific forces and in 1944 temporary headquarters of the British Pacific fleet. For the first time in its history the commodious natural harbour was utilized by the largest naval and merchant ships afloat. The Captain Cook dock, constructed during the war at a cost of £A9,000,000, was capable of accommodating the largest ships yet built or projected.

(A. W. S.)

Bibliography.—National Fitness Council of New South Wales, *Problem of Recreation Space in the Metropolitan Area* (1941).

Symington, William Stuart

Symington (1901–), U.S. government official, was born June 26, 1901, in Amherst, Mass. He joined the army during World War I. Following the armistice, he attended Yale university, 1919–23. After completing his studies, he worked at the Symington company, a railroad equipment plant owned by his family. Later he entered the radio manufacturing field, becoming president of Colonial Radio (1930–35) and of Emerson Electric Manufacturing company in St. Louis (1938). On June 7, 1945, President Truman named Symington as chairman of the Surplus Property board with the task of disposing of billions of dollars worth of surplus war property. Later, Truman's proposal that surplus property disposal be placed under the supervision of a single man was approved by the senate and on Sept. 18 he named Symington surplus property administrator. Symington resigned in Jan. 1946, and was named assistant secretary of war for air.

Symphony Orchestras

See Music.

Synthetic Products

See Chemistry; Industrial Research; Petroleum; Plastics Industry; Rayon and Other Synthetic Fibres; Rubber; Textile Industry.

Syphilis

See Marriage and Divorce; Medicine; Military Medicine; Venereal Diseases.

Syria

Syria, an independent republic, is bounded on the north by Turkey, on the east by Iraq, on the south by Trans-Jordan and Palestine and on the west by Lebanon and the Mediterranean sea. Its area is 73,587 sq.mi. Pop. (1935 census) 2,487,000; (1942) 2,800,000. The capital is Damascus (1942 pop. 275,651). Chief cities are Aleppo (299,218); Homs (96,600); Hama (66,463); Latakia (33,223); Deir ez Zor (10,000). Arabic is the dominant and official language. Turkish is spoken in the north and Kurdish, Armenian and Syriac are used by minority communities. The latter are mostly bilingual and also speak Arabic.

Islam is the dominant religious faith, consisting of several sects. Figures for 1943 were as follows: Sunnite 1,971,053; Alawite 325,311; Druze 87,184; Ismailian 28,527; Shiite 12,742. Christian groups were as follows: Greek Orthodox 136,957; Armenian Gregorian 101,747; Greek Catholic 46,733; Syrian Orthodox 40,135; Syrian Catholic 16,247; Maronite 13,349; Protestant 11,187; Nestorian 9,176; others 10,715. Jews numbered 29,770; Yazidis 2,788.

The total population in 1945 was 3,250,000 (including about 400,000 Bedouin). Estimates in 1938 were 2,740,000 (including about 250,000 Bedouin).

Shukri el Quwatli was elected president of Syria Aug. 17, 1943. Prime ministers during the decade 1937–46 were as follows: Jamil Mardam (Dec. 28, 1936–Feb. 18, 1939); Lutfi Al Haffar (Feb. 23, 1939–March 16, 1939); Nassuh Al Bukhari (April 6, 1939–July 8, 1939); military government by the French established until April 2, 1941; Khalid Al Azm (April 2, 1941–Sept. 20, 1941); Hasan Al Hakim (Sept. 17, 1941–April 14, 1942); Husni Al Barazi (April 15, 1942–Jan. 29, 1943); Jamil Al Ulshi (Jan. 30, 1943–April 17, 1943); Ata Bey Al Ayyubi (April 17, 1943–Aug. 17, 1943); Saadullah Al Jabri (Aug. 18, 1943–Oct. 11, 1944); Faris Al Khuri (Oct. 14, 1944–Oct. 2, 1945); Saadullah Al Jabri (after Oct. 1, 1945).

"Divide et Impera."—On Dec. 26, 1936, the Syrian chamber unanimously approved the Franco-Syrian treaty signed in Paris on Sept. 9. It was to become effective Jan. 1, 1937, and promised independence in 3 years—a goal for which Syrian nationalists had struggled for 17 years. Their high hopes for self-government, unification, withdrawal of French armed forces from all but two bases and recognition as an independent state witnessed a series of frustrations and failures as the year wore on. Reactionary French officialdom persuaded the French chamber in Paris not to ratify the treaty. The prospect of eventual independence galvanized into action separatist moves which broke out in the four peripheral provinces. Enemies of Syrian independence found fertile ground in the suspicions, true or malicious, of the heterogeneous population, which were intensified by persistent propaganda. The pattern of intrigue was much the same, although its sources were different and the course of events varied in each case. From abroad, pressures were brought to bear on the sense of insecurity of cultural or religious minorities; efforts were made to intensify the fear of vested interests, such as the traditional tribal leaders; obstacles were placed in the way to impede and nullify the efforts of inexperienced national leaders. Therefore, every effort on the part of the Syrian government to consolidate its unity and independence was countered by a foreign power which played upon regional, clan, religious or linguistic susceptibilities to weaken Syrian independence and thereby maintain or enlarge a field of privileges.

There were four main areas affected by this conflict of nationalism against separatism. First was the Alexandretta (Hatay) sanjak. This province was 38.5% Turkish and under the Franklin-Bouillon agreement of 1921 it enjoyed certain linguistic, cultural and administrative privileges. Turkey claimed in 1936 that Syria would be incapable of protecting this region alone or of defending those privileges. It demanded a separate status, to which Syria protested. On May 27, 1937, France and Turkey agreed to the internal independence of what was then commonly called the republic of Hatay. It was to have a customs union with Syria but its government was to be elected by a fundamental law. This gave to the non-Turks a majority, whereupon in Dec. 1937, Turkey protested the law and demanded 22 of the 40 seats in the legislative assembly for Turkish-speaking members. In May 1938, assisted by Turkish pressure from outside, the Turkish minority began a determined drive to gain control of the assembly, causing riots, bloodshed and violence. On June 3 the French declared martial law. Meanwhile, France, needing allies, was negotiating an alliance with Turkey, which was announced on July 4, 1938. The next day the French invited Turkish troops to participate in restoring order. Once they were well entrenched, the Turks announced elections. Amid charges of intimidation and irregularities, the Turkish minority gained 63% of the members of the assembly. The latter immediately elected a solidly Turkish cabinet, thereby gaining complete domination of the government. In June 1939, the Turkish state announced annexation of the sanjak, called it Hatay, the 63rd province of Turkey, and formalized it in a treaty with France on July 23. Many Arabs and most of the Armenians preferred to abandon their homes and sought refuge in the Arab states to the south.

A second scene of discord was the Jazireh, the large semi-desert tribal northeast quarter of Syria. Mostly populated by nomads prior to 1914, it had become a place of refuge for increased numbers of Kurds, Assyrians and Armenians who disliked Arab domination. These newcomers constituted a majority in 1937 who resented inexperienced officials representing the city populations. On June 7, 1937, the Kurds revolted. Extremist nationalists represented the conflict as a question between Moslems and Christians with the Kurds assisting the Christians. The arrival of French planes and the presence of a Kurdish chief stopped the plundering indulged in by the Arab Bedouin. Ignatius Gabriel Cardinal Tappouni of the Syrian Catholic church, who had at one time openly declared that Catholicism, Christianity and French influence in the Levant were inseparable, appealed to Paris for French protection of minorities. In Dec. 1937 the newly arrived governor was kidnapped and bloodshed followed, whereupon the French established direct control. Nationalists claimed the trouble had been inspired by French *agents provocateurs.*

The third area of disaffection was the Jebel Druze. The hardy mountaineer Druze tribes were perennially restless and in early 1937 refused to co-operate with the Damascus-appointed governor. To calm their suspicions, a Druze governor was appointed in June 1937, and the hero of 1925–26, Sultan Atrash, was granted an amnesty. During 1938 the situation was relatively quiet but in July 1939, when the French were about to suspend the constitution, a few of the pro-French Druze chieftains declared the Jebel Druze independent and appealed for French protection. Other more prominent chiefs declared their loyalty to Syria. Again the nationalists blamed this on French officers stationed among the Druze.

A fourth troublesome region was the northwest Alawite (Noseiri) mountainous country. The fanatic Shia'h sectarians had always been an easy target for separatist intrigue. The French had not lost sight of this when they desired to put pressure on Damascus. There were incipient revolts in 1938 when the Alawites expelled the governor, and in 1939 when an erstwhile brigand, Suleiman Murshid, assumed religious hegemony, identifying himself as a manifestation of the divine, and seized the lands of many of his neighbours.

Mardam's Compromise.—These storms sorely beset the government of Prime Minister Jamil Mardam; but most damaging to the prestige of the National Bloc party, which dominated the cabinet, was the failure to gain ratification of the treaty. In June 1937, Dr. Abdur-rahman Shahbandar returned from exile in Egypt and used his fiery oratory to press the government for action. Mardam, feeling the disintegration of his position, decided to visit Paris to lobby his friends into ratification of the treaty. Forced into an impasse, he accepted six main modifications of the 1936 treaty which became known as the Mardam compromise. It would have granted: (1) a special internal regime for the Jazireh; (2) renewal on the original basis of the Banque de Syrie accord; (3) French concessions for the exploitation of petroleum; (4) renewal of the contracts of French employees; (5) appointment of additional French advisers; (6) recognition of the French right to intervene in defense of the minorities, which should have a special status. This compromise, announced on Nov. 15, 1938, spelled the doom of Mardam as a national leader. The French attitude had hardened. War seemed too near, and Syria was a strategic base. Oil had recently been discovered in Iraq and might be discovered in the Jazireh. The Blum government had fallen and George Bonnet announced on Dec. 14, 1938, that he had abandoned the idea of presenting the 1936 treaty to parliament. This galvanized the Syrian parliament, which announced on Dec. 31 that it would stand by the 1936 treaty and none other, and that Syria would assume full independence on schedule. These events split the National Bloc party wide open. Shurki el Quwatli resigned from the cabinet with two other members, and Dr. Shahbandar uncovered a vigorous party of opposition, denouncing the Mardam compromise as treason, bedevilling the impotence of the government in the existing business stagnation and criticizing its weakness in assisting the Arab struggle in Palestine. The result was that leadership of the bloc passed from Mardam to the trio Quwatli, Saadullah Jabri and Faris Al Khuri.

On Jan. 2, 1939, the new French high commissioner, Gabriel Puaux, arrived and issued a series of decrees for the regulation of religious communities. Mardam was caught between the surging nationalist opposition and the French. Violence flared up, and on Feb. 18, 1939, Mardam resigned. Puaux tried to fill the vacuum by two short-lived and unpopular ministries and finally on July 7 he dissolved parliament, suspended the constitution and instituted a government by decree. Syria was dismembered again by setting up four separate administrations.

Vichy Dominance.—The outbreak of World War II put an end to political bickering, and most Syrian leaders pledged loyalty to Gen. Maxime Weygand when he arrived on Sept. 3, 1939. In June 1940, he was replaced by Gen. Eugène Mittelhauser who, after the fall of Paris, announced he would remain loyal to the Pétain government. Allied troops left Syria July 5, while Vichy began to replace officials with those considered trustworthy. The whole country was stirred in July 1940, by the assassination of Dr. Shahbandar in his office. Opponents of the government accused the bloc leaders, whereupon Mardam, with three other prominent officers, fled to Iraq. The group of assassins were caught and tried in December and at that time insisted that their sole motivation had been religious zeal. The fugitive leaders returned early in 1941. Their prolonged absence had left the field clear for the rise of the renovated National Bloc under the leadership of Quwatli, who consistently gained the allegiance of not only the National Bloc factions but others as well. When Gen. Henri Dentz arrived in Dec. 1940, Quwatli was in a position to demand formation of a national government instead of the rule by decree and in March 1941 his insistence led to strikes, demonstrations and then riots when the French arbitrarily tried to enforce certain antihoarding laws.

That the axis powers had plans involving Syria became apparent on Aug. 28, 1940, when, with Vichy approval, an Italian armistice commission arrived and began touring the country. In October a group of proaxis students returning from Germany opened the Arab club. Certain politicians appeared with strong anti-British propaganda and abundant funds. In Jan. 1941, the chief of oriental affairs in the German foreign office, Georg Werner-Otto von Hentig, arrived with credentials as a minister. Then in May, in spite of earlier British warnings, several squadrons of German combat planes refuelled by permission of Vichy authorities at Syrian airfields and went on to fight the British in Iraq. Other supplies went by rail to Iraq, and strenuous efforts were made to whip up pro-Arab anti-British fervour. This proved that as long as Syria was under Vichy control, it could be used as a base for an attack upon Allied positions in the middle east.

The Allies Strike.—Early on the morning of June 8, 1941, tens of thousands of leaflets were scattered over Syrian towns bearing the proclamation of Gen. Georges Catroux which included this phrase, "I come to terminate the regime of the mandate and to proclaim you free and independent—your state of independence and sovereignty will be guaranteed by a treaty." At the same time two columns of mixed British, Australian and Free French troops crossed the borders into Syria. Contrary to Allied expectations, the French troops fought a battle of honour for their Vichy officers and even carried out two notable counterattacks. With the arrival of British reinforcements, the French fell back and after yielding Damascus, an armistice was concluded on July 10, 1941. The defeated Vichy army was given the choice of joining the Free French and remaining in the middle east or being repatriated to France. The combat troops, almost to a man, chose the latter, though most of the colonial officers who held positions in the Syrian government elected to stay.

The political situation was peculiarly delicate and difficult. In 1918 a British army allied to Arab forces had driven out the Turks and then, against the expressed will of the Syrian people, had given the mandate to France as a share in the spoils of war. Again in 1941, predominantly by British effort, Syria had been reconquered but only after definite promises had been made by the French to recognize the independence of Syria. In 1941 the Syrians were as adamant against further French control as they had been in 1919. Yet the Free French were anxious to rebuild French prestige, and the corps of French officials therefore resumed its authority as though nothing had happened since 1919, insisting that promises of independence were dependent on a treaty which would be negotiated when France was once more a nation with a recognized government. To clarify the British position, Capt. Oliver Lyttelton, British minister of state in the middle east, wrote to Gen. Charles de Gaulle on Aug. 15, "France should have the predominant position (in Syria) . . . over any other European power."

To this De Gaulle replied, ". . . the pre-eminent and privileged position." On Sept. 9, Winston Churchill stated in the house of commons, ". . . our policy, to which our Free French allies have subscribed, is that Syria shall be handed back to the Syrians, who will assume at the earliest possible moment their independent and sovereign rights. . . . But we recognise . . . the position of France in Syria is one of special privileges and that (the influence) . . . of France will be pre-eminent." The Syrian leaders consistently refused to recognize any modification of their independence. To them sovereignty and special privileges were inconsistent. Under some pressure, General Catroux proclaimed Syria as independent on Sept. 28, designating Taj-ed-Din Al Hasani as president. He was known to consider Syrians as politically immature and to favour French hegemony. The whole procedure struck a sour note among the nationalists. The new president had recently come from France and had been appointed by the French—not elected. He chose a government in which no prominent bloc leaders were included. To them it looked like a ruse to perpetuate French domination. The bloc refused to co-operate, bringing on a virtual paralysis of government. The French seemed to want to delay elections indefinitely while the British favoured them and the bloc demanded them. Finally in March 1943, a provisional government was appointed with instructions to organize elections. These were held in July, and the bloc candidates won out by large majorities even in Aleppo where there was a split between two bloc candidates. But those suspected of being pro-French were conspicuously defeated. On Aug. 17 the new chamber met and enthusiastically elected Quwatli president.

Nominal Independence.—At long last, Syria had the title and machinery of an independent state, but the exigencies of war made foreign troops essential to security. The same French officers, who for two decades had ruled Syria, remained at their posts, obviously reluctant to surrender their positions of authority and privilege. Each attempt of the new state to act as a free agent met with an open or hidden rebuff producing an increasing number of irritating incidents. On Nov. 11, news was flashed from Beirut that the French had arrested the Lebanese government and set up a pro-French regime because the Lebanese had proceeded to eliminate all references to the French mandate rights in their constitution. There was a surge of national animosity against the French in Syria, but the government acted cautiously and no untoward incidents occurred. Syria threw in its influence through the embryo Arab league then under formation and breathed a sigh of relief when the Lebanese government was released and restored to authority. But the government lost no time in pressing for a transfer of authority in relation to the 20 or more so-called common interests of both Syria and Lebanon administered by French officers. The French relinquished a few in the spring of 1944, such as antiquities, posts and telegraphs. But disagreement rose over such important questions as education, military control and security. In June 1944, the French pressed a university convention which would have riveted French cultural hegemony upon Syria and discriminated against other educational systems. But the question of jurisdiction over the maintenance of security involving the transfer of the 20,000 *troupes spéciales* paid for by the local governments but officered by the French, brought negotiations to a full stop.

Syrian parliament at Damascus after French troops took over the building on May 30, 1945, in an armed attempt to halt protest demonstrations by Syrians against the continued presence of foreign troops

The government was showing definite signs of attaining maturity. During July–Sept. 1944, it had been recognized by the soviet union, the United Kingdom and the U.S. as well as by several Arab states. In May 1944 a small riot developed when women appeared unveiled in theatres, but the government acted firmly and quickly, refusing to be intimidated by fanatical groups. In Sept. 1944, the Druze voluntarily surrendered their age-old autonomy and entered Syria as a province. On Oct. 7, Syria signed the Alexandria pact establishing the Arab league. Without incident, the chamber had revised the constitution, dropping out the last article which had made the whole conditional upon approval by the mandatory power. All these gains were encouraging, but the crucial matter of troops and security remained deadlocked. As though to punctuate their importance, a revolt broke out in the Alawite stronghold in Feb. 1945, shortly after persistent rumours indicated that a French captain had distributed arms to the partisans of Suleiman Murshid. Syrian gendarmerie started to move in but were anticipated by French troops, and the Syrians withdrew. Many incidents took place which charged the atmosphere with rancour, hurt pride and veiled threats.

Revolt.—Victory in Europe added to the tensions when on May 16, 1945, a French cruiser arrived unannounced at Beirut, carrying about 900 French troops. More were on the way. The French explanation was that some were replacements and others were to be redeployed to the far east. But the Syrians were convinced that the arrival of large numbers of French troops violated their sovereignty and doomed their independence. The French blamed the rising tide of resistance to "the intrigue of a third power," but so widespread was the popular anti-French feeling that large numbers of the Syrians in the *troupes spéciales* began to desert lest they might be forced to fire upon their own people. By May 23 sporadic incidents of violence were spreading and Gen. Fernand Oliva-Roget issued an order to his officers to be cautious inasmuch as the "paid ruffians" of a third power "would be summarily disciplined soon." On May 27, a fusillade of shots was fired at a deserter escaping the French barracks in the centre of Damascus, killing and wounding several civilians. Toward evening, French artillery began a bombardment of the city that lasted sporadically for three days. The chamber was about to convene at 7:00 P.M. but had been dismissed by the president when he noted French armoured cars moving toward the parliament buildings. Claiming that snipers were using the building, the French moved in artillery and fired point blank into the building, killing all 14 guards who had remained. About 350 were killed in the indiscriminate bombardment of the city. At Homs and Hama, Syrian tribesmen rallied to isolate and surround the French garrisons while in the Jebel Druze, French officers were disarmed and held prisoners. Thoroughly exasperated, the British sent in an armoured mobile column on the 30th, separating the fighting forces.

Repercussions were world-wide. In San Francisco the United Nations was being born to the accompaniment of shouts by the Arabs of "French war criminals," while acrid public debates took place between London and Paris. Gen. de Gaulle directly accused British agents of fomenting trouble, stated that the French had restored complete order and that therefore British intervention was unnecessary. On June 5 Churchill reviewed the situation, denying both allegations. Meanwhile, under British escort, French troops and civilians were evacuated from Syria to Lebanon and those remaining were restricted to a few bases. Even then, the Syrians were not satisfied. They recalled the intimate association between French officers and separatist "revolts" and the memory of 1920 when French troops had used Lebanon as a base for an attack upon Damascus. Wherefore in Jan. 1946, at the first meeting of the United Nations Security council in London, Syria and Lebanon registered a complaint against foreign troops on their soil in contradiction to the will of the nations. Although on Dec. 13, 1945, the United Kingdom and France began negotiating the matter of withdrawal, the conferences had broken down over details. With world attention focused on the situation, the United States delegate proposed on Feb. 16, 1946, that a definite time be set for withdrawal of troops inasmuch as it was considered a principle of policy that no small nation should have troops quartered upon its soil against the national will. The soviet representative vetoed the proposal as too weak, but both the British and French announced their intention to abide by the majority result despite the veto. By April 20 the last foreign troops left Syria. Celebrations lasting almost a week marked the occasion. A new government was formed. Its task was clear. Instead of the sterile struggle to ward off foreign domination, its reputation would stand on its ability to transform the dreams of the past into the realities of the future.

"Greater Syria."—A word should be said about the political conception of a greater Syria. Under Turkish rule —and even earlier—Syria had included Lebanon, Palestine and Trans-Jordan. Splitting it into four entities had been an accident of European designs. Greater Syria had a natural cultural, geographic and economic unity. Its political problems lay in the late creation of new political divisions and loyalties engendered by the policy of man-

Syria and Lebanon: *Statistical Data*

Item	1938 Value (000's omitted)	1938 Amount or Number	1942 Value (000's omitted)	1942 Amount or Number
Exchange rate				
United States . . .		1 French franc =2.8 cents		Syrian £=44 cents*
Great Britain . . .		179 francs=£1		8.83 Syrian £=£1*
Finance				
Government revenues . . .	$9,919 (£2,029)		$15,948 (£3,952)	
Government expenditures . .	$9,496 (£1,942)		$15,948 (£3,952)	
Transportation				
Railroads		872 mi.		
Highways		7,072 mi.		
Minerals				
Cement		88,184 tons		
Salt		11,023 tons		
Crops				
Wheat		691,544 tons		559,968 tons
Barley		421,211 tons		274,473 tons
Melons		283,528 tons		248,789 tons
Grapes		221,434 tons		654,766 tons
Livestock				
Poultry		9,257,000		2,000,000
Goats		2,291,000		1,919,000
Sheep		2,129,000		2,342,000
Exports—Total . . .	$16,853 (£3,447)	414,000 tons		
Olive oil	$1,522 (£311)	10,000 tons		
Beans, peas, lentils, etc. . . .	$1,317 (£269)	41,000 tons		
Citrus fruits . . .	$1,025 (£210)	31,000 tons		
Silk and artificial silk	$1,006 (£206)	1,000 tons		
Imports—Total . . .	$40,760 (£8,337)	. . .		
Cotton cloth and thread	$5,637 (£1,153)	12,000 tons		
Mineral oils and fuels	$3,194 (£653)	541,000 tons		
Iron and steel and manufactures . .	$3,089 (£632)	45,000 tons		
Woolen cloth and yarns	$1,755 (£359)	2,000 tons		
Defense				
Standing army personnel . . .		10,476		
Education				
Primary schools		2,654		
Pupils		279,598		
Technical schools .		188		
Pupils		19,478		
Universities and colleges		6		
Pupils		1,441		

*New unit of currency with the new status of Syria and Lebanon as independent republics.

datory powers. In addition, they were complicated by the existence of the old Christian population of Lebanon and the new Jewish community in Palestine. Some Arabs continued to favour Iraq's entering a greater Syria federation. A few Jews supported such a scheme, with modifications favouring Jewish immigration. King Abdullah of Trans-Jordan favoured the idea, if he were to be king of greater Syria. In 1945 Quwatli expressed the official Syrian attitude toward it. He favoured a greater Syria if it were to be a republic with its capital at Damascus, but his ultimate hope was Arab unity. The French, utilizing the principle of division, disliked the inclusion of Arabs under British influence. To the British, the plan had more advantages than were at first apparent, for it would serve as an instrument to fill in the security gap that would arise in case of the threat of a new war. Although greater Syria was not a concept likely to grow rapidly, its roots were fed by elements that went far back in Arab history and, in one form or another, would probably survive modern nationalism and dynasties. Pan Arabs favoured such a regional development as a step toward ultimate Arab federation. (*See* also MANDATES.)

BIBLIOGRAPHY.—Henry H. Cuming, *Franco-British Rivalry in the Post War Near East* (1938); George Antonius, *The Arab Awakening* (1939); Philip W. Ireland, *The Near East—Problems and Prospects* (1942); Majid Khadduri, "The Alexandretta Dispute," *Am. Jour. of International Law*, vol. 39, No. 3 (July 1945); Albert Hourani, *Syria and Lebanon* (1946); Charles A. Julien, "French Difficulties in the Middle East," *Foreign Affairs* (Jan. 1946); Jean Godard, *L'oeuvre politique, economique et sociale de la France combattante en Syrie et au Liban* (Beyrouth, 1943); Michael Clark, *The Nation* (March 17, 1945, June (Jan. 1946); Jean Godard, *L'oeuvre politique, économique et* 1941); "Next Step in Syria," *ibid.* (Aug. 9, 1941); Freya Stark, *The Arab Island* (1945); Pierre Vienot and G. Henry-Haye, *Les relations de la France et de la Syrie* (Paris, 1939).

Syrovy, Jan

Syrovy (1885–), Czechoslovak general and politician, was born in Bohemia. He practised architecture in Warsaw, Poland, and in 1914 joined the Czech brigade in the Russian army. Promoted to a lieutenant, he lost his right eye in the fighting on the Russian front. After the Russian Revolution, he commanded two divisions of Czech legionnaires that fought against the Bolsheviks and cooperated with the Allies. Repatriated to his homeland, he became inspector general of the Czechoslovak army in 1935. In 1938, he succeeded Dr. Milan Hodza as premier. Although he was prepared to resist a German attack, he was obliged to yield to German demands "legitimatized" by the Munich pact. After Eduard Beneš' resignation on Oct. 5, 1938, Syrovy became acting president of the republic. He promptly came to terms with the reich and began to model the government along National-Socialist lines. After Emil Hacha's election to the presidency, Syrovy resigned and on Dec. 1, 1938, he was appointed minister of national defense.

Syrup, Sorgo and Cane

The area of sugar cane harvested for syrup in the United States declined from 143,000 ac. in 1937 to a low of 102,000 ac. in 1940 and then increased again to 152,000 ac. in 1945. Total production was 23,844,000 gal. in 1937 and dropped to 13,415,000 gal. in 1940 but recovered to 24,450,000 gal. in 1946. The 10-year average 1934–43 was 20,890,000 gal. The increase in the latter year was due to favourable weather for the cane crop as well as to the advance in price. The average price to farmers was 44.5 cents per gal. in 1937 and advanced to more than $1.00 in 1945. Louisiana produced about one-third of the crop, but the price was lower than for the crop of any other cane state, being only 66 cents per gal. in 1944 compared with $1.50 in Arkansas and $1.45 in Texas, both small producers.

U.S. Syrup Production by Leading States 1937–46
(In millions of gallons)

	1937	1939	1941	1942	1943	1944	1945	1946
Sugar Cane Syrup:								
U.S. Total	25.1	24.	18.7	18.6	21.5	21.0	25.8	24.5
Louisiana	8.2	9.3	6.2	5.7	7.9	6.6	11.0	11.8
Georgia	5.4	4.7	3.5	3.9	4.2	4.3	4.6	4.0
Mississippi . . .	4.4	3.7	3.1	3.3	2.9	3.6	3.9	3.5
Alabama	3.7	3.3	2.7	2.6	2.8	2.7	3.1	2.4
Florida	1.8	1.9	1.6	1.7	2.0	2.2	2.0	2.0
Texas	.7	.7	.8	.6	.7	.7	.5	.3
South Carolina .	.4	.4	.5	.4	.6	.5	.4	.4
Arkansas	.1	.1	.1	.1	.1	.1	.1	.1
Sorgo Syrup:								
U.S. Total	12.5	10.2	10.5	13.7	11.8	12.1	10.5	12.1
Alabama	1.9	2.7	2.0	1.7	2.0	2.0	2.1	1.8
Mississippi . . .	1.3	1.6	1.8	1.8	1.4	1.9	1.6	1.4
Arkansas	1.2	.8	.8	1.1	.7	.9	.9	1.2
Georgia	.9	1.0	.7	1.3	1.3	1.2	.9	.6
Tennessee . . .	.9	1.0	.9	1.2	1.2	.9	.8	1.5
Kentucky	.7	.7	.6	.7	.7	.7	.7	1.3
North Carolina .	1.1	.8	.5	1.0	.7	.8	.6	1.2
South Carolina . .	.2	.3	.4	.7	.5	.5	.6	.6

Sorgo syrup during the decade 1937–46 was produced in 17 states, mostly in small quantities, with 6 states producing about half the U.S. crop on the average. The total acreage averaged 240,000 ac. in 1933–42 but later declined to about 200,000 ac. The average price for the whole crop advanced from 56.8 cents per gal. in 1937 to $1.37 in 1944 without apparent stimulation of the output. Total produced was 12,481,000 gal. in 1937 and reached a high of 13,772,000 gal. in 1942, only to drop to 12,074,000 gal. in 1946. (*See* also BEEKEEPING; MAPLE PRODUCTS.) (J. C. Ms.)

For statistics of consumption *see* U.S. Dept. Agric., *Agricultural Statistics;* Bur. Agric. Econ., *Farm Production* (1944).

Table Tennis

At the start of the 1937–46 decade, the International Table Tennis federation had advanced the game from a parlour pastime to an athletic sport which required a playing arena of 25 by 60 ft. for the hard-driving and deep defense of championship matches and attracted galleries of 10,000 spectators. Thirteen nations contended in the 11th annual world championships in 1937 at Baden, near Vienna, where the United States, a comparative newcomer in international competition, became the first to win both team cups simultaneously. Previous men's Swaythling cup winners were Hungary (eight times), Austria and Czechoslovakia (once each); previous women's Corbillon cup winners were Czechoslovakia (twice) and Germany (once).

To improve the game's spectator value, the I.T.T.F. congress banned hand-spin services, lowered the net from 6¾ in. to 6 in., and ruled against excessive defensive play (known as "stonewalling," "chiseling" and "pushing"). Finals of the 12th world championships in 1938 in London were played at the Empire Sports arena, Wembley, with 16 nations represented. The 13th world championships, involving 12 nations, were played in 1939 in Cairo under the patronage of King Farouk and Queen Farida. Outbreak of war in Europe caused the I.T.T.F. to suspend activities. Until then, these world titles had been won:

Men's teams (Swaythling cup)—1937, U.S.A.; 1938, Hungary; 1939, Czechoslovakia.

Women's teams (Corbillon cup)—1937, U.S.A.; 1938, Czechoslovakia; 1939, Germany.

Men's singles—1937, Richard Bergmann (Austria); 1938, Bohumil Vana (Czechoslovakia); 1939, Richard Bergmann (Austrian exile in England).

Men's doubles—1937, Robert Blattner and Jimmy McClure (U.S.A.); 1938, Jimmy McClure and Sol Schiff (U.S.A.); 1939, Viki Barna (Hungary) and Richard Bergmann (England).

Women's singles—1937, declared vacant after a draw between Trude Pritzi (Austria) and Ruth Hughes Aarons (U.S.A.), defending champion; 1938, Trude Pritzi (Austria); 1939, Vlasha Depetrisova (Czechoslovakia).

Women's doubles—1937 and 1938, Vlasha Depetrisova and Vera Votrubcova (Czechoslovakia); 1939, Hilde Bussmann and Trude Pritzi (Germany).

Mixed doubles—1937, Bohumil Vana and Vera Votrubcova (Czechoslovakia); 1938, Laszlo Bellak (Hungary) and Wendy Woodhead (England); 1939, Bohumil Vana and Vera Votrubcova (Czechoslovakia).

Istvan Kelen and Miklos Szabados, Hungarian stars, met defeat in Japan on a 60,000-mi. world exhibition tour ending in 1939. In 1940 the Japan Table Tennis association, inaugurating what were intended to be annual Pan-Pacific matches, invited Australian and U.S. teams and defeated both; the possibility of return matches was cancelled by Pearl Harbor.

The war crippled civilian play, which concentrated on benefit tournaments and exhibitions for the Red Cross and other service organizations. Most players of the warring nations being in the armed forces scattered around the world, table tennis was conducted as a recreation for troops, who played in military championship tournaments and watched exhibition matches by stars, whose schedules often required long aeroplane flights over seas, jungles and mountains.

The I.T.T.F. was revived in June 1946, and the 14th world championships were designated for Paris in Feb. 1947. As against 28 associations in full membership or good standing in 1939, in 1946 there were 18 full members (Australia, Belgium, Czechoslovakia, Egypt, England, France, India, Ireland, Luxembourg, Netherlands, New Zealand, Palestine, Poland, Sweden, Switzerland, U.S.A., Wales, Yugoslavia); 3 in good standing (Jersey, Ontario, Scotland); 3 eligible for restoration of membership (Canada, Latvia, Lithuania); 5 former axis member associations of undetermined status (Austria, Germany, Hungary, Japan, Rumania); and 10 in prospective membership, including the U.S.S.R.—a total of 39.

BIBLIOGRAPHY.—Coleman Clark, *Table Tennis* (1938); Sol Schiff, *Table Tennis Comes of Age* (1939); Emily M. Fuller, *Top-Notch Table Tennis* (1942); Jay Purves, *Table Tennis* (1942). The annual *Handbook of the International Table Tennis Federation* (W. J. Pope, London), which is published in English, French and German, was suspended during the war, as was the English monthly *Table Tennis*. The U.S.A. monthly *Table Tennis Topics* has been published continuously since 1933. (C. Z.)

Tacoma Narrows Bridge

See BRIDGES.

Tactics of World War II

In all previous wars the aim was to defeat the enemy armies and destroy his will to fight; in World War II it became possible to enlarge this aim to include total destruction of his ability to fight. This was the first total war.

In World War II, as in all wars, tactics and techniques of employment were controlled by the weapons and equipment available. World War II saw the development of mechanization to an extremely high degree. This resulted in combinations of mobility, speed, power and range previously unknown. Scientific developments in various fields, the development of subsistence and clothing, enabled full-scale campaigns to be carried out in inaccessible areas previously considered unsuitable for large military operations with weapons and equipment of modern warfare. Full exploitation of the capabilities of mechanized warfare produced dramatic and startling results whether the fighting was on the frozen wastes of the arctic tundra, the mountainous jungles of the South Pacific, the deserts of Africa, the marvelously engineered fortifications of Europe, the great amphibious operations in both hemispheres, or a vertical envelopment by airborne troops. This great variety of tactical operations caused many different adaptations and changes in standard organization and uses of equipment. Tactical success depended on the most skilful combination of the means available into a task force to accomplish the objective.

The successful application of tactics in World War II, as in earlier wars, depended upon a clear understanding by commanders of the capabilities and limitations of the forces at their disposal, and upon a vigorous application of tactical methods used on a thorough and rapid evaluation of all available information about the enemy's forces. This was equally true of the tactics of whole theatre forces down to those of the smallest combat units.

In all the main theatres of war the infantry division (and its equivalent in the U.S. marine corps) was the basis of organization of the field forces. This unit, numbering some 15,000, was the smallest unit which had within it all essential ground combat arms and services, and which could carry out operations of some importance acting alone. However, "task forces" were frequently organized to carry out special operations. These forces generally consisted of a regiment of infantry, a battalion of field artillery and attached service units as well as a headquarters similar to a division headquarters. The chief combat elements of each infantry division were three regiments of infantry, four battalions of field artillery and a battalion of combat engineers.

The U.S. army contained 67 infantry divisions (including 1 special mountain division) of which 42 fought in Europe and 25 in the Pacific. In the Pacific also were six marine divisions.

There were, in addition, five U.S. airborne divisions, four in Europe and one in the Pacific. These were smaller with generally lighter supporting weapons. Their troops moved by aeroplane and landed either by parachute or glider drop to fight. These were used against objectives within axis-held territory, but in co-operation with other forces of which infantry divisions were the principal combat elements.

The 16 U.S. armoured divisions each had as chief combat units 3 battalions, consisting of 3 companies of medium tanks and 1 company of light tanks, 3 battalions of armoured infantry transported in armoured half-tracks and 3 battalions of field artillery. All of these divisions were used in Africa and Europe. The one U.S. cavalry division, using motor and armoured vehicles rather than horses, was used in the Pacific theatre.

All types of divisions were, when necessary, augmented in strength by the support or attachment of additional field artillery, armoured (separate tank battalions), engineer, chemical, anti-aircraft and (sometimes) infantry units.

The next higher tactical unit was the corps, made up of two to as many as ten infantry, armoured and airborne divisions, and corps headquarters and supporting troops such as field artillery and tank units. The next larger unit was the army, formed of a variable number of corps plus army headquarters and supporting troops. The army group consisted of two or more armies and headquarters and additional troops. The largest field force, that in Europe, contained at its maximum two U.S. army groups (one containing certain large French units) and one British army group, together with U.S. and British tactical air units, and headquarters, supporting and service forces.

All U.S. operations and those of Allied armies were conducted on the principle that no one arm, such as infantry, armoured or air forces, could win battles, because it took the combined action of all to assure victory. It was true that the infantry units sustained nearly three-fourths of all air and ground combat casualties and 90% of those in the ground combat forces. This simply shows that infantry was the basic, central arm of close combat, not that it could have done without the tremendous supporting power of artillery, air and other types of assisting units. Infantry was the strong cutting edge of the armies, the one part capable of taking and holding ground and of keeping up a sustained direct pressure on the enemy's forces which had to be defeated and destroyed in order to win. It was also the only element of U.S. forces capable of manoeuvring on ground too difficult for armoured forces and too covered for air units to find rewarding targets. Much of the ground fought over in every theatre of war was of this type; for example, the jungle-covered islands of the Southwest Pacific area and the many forests of France and Germany. But, generally speaking, the tactics used by all the principal armies were basically infantry tactics, since what all other combat arms did depended upon how the infantry was used, in both offensive and defensive action.

The offensive tactics of the different Allied and axis armies were not radically different. Lack of supporting weapons made the organization of the Chinese combat forces somewhat simpler and the tactics were correspondingly simpler and for the most part defensive. For all armies the tactical problem was the same—how best to gain or hold a given area and reduce the strength of the enemy's defense or attack. All armies had to use large numbers of infantry, and the control and application of such combat forces could be accomplished only through organization into units of ascending size and the issuance of combat orders from the top down. Hence tactics could vary only in relatively minor respects, chiefly according to the general nature of the terrain and the means of warfare available.

Offensive Tactics

As in all preceding wars, the tactics were offensive and defensive, those used in attacking and those used in defending against an attack; and in most battles the force of one side used generally offensive tactics and the other defensive. But at any stage of the battle up to that of complete victory for one side and defeat for the other, parts of the attacking forces were often temporarily on the defensive, and parts of the defending forces on the offensive, as in making a counterattack. The offensive tactics used were in general as described below.

The purpose of offensive action was to destroy the opposing force. The commander of the attacking force, however, selected a specific physical objective, such as an area of high ground, a city or group of cities, or some other vital area well in rear of the enemy's forward position. The objective had to be one that could be reached by the attacking force or unit within the time required by the higher commander and by manoeuvre over the available ground, usually limited by the fact that other units of the same attacking force required the adjacent space for their own part of the battle. The objective had also to be one, the taking of which would either insure the capture or complete breaking up of the enemy force, or so threaten the enemy force that it was forced to retreat. Objectives had also to be good places from which to begin the next attack. Once the objective had been selected, the commander concentrated the main effort of his available troops in the direction best calculated to gain the objective.

Thus, in the well-conducted battles of World War II, the main driving power was concentrated into a small fraction of the whole front. On other parts of the front there were also attacking troops, but in much less strength than at the point of main attack. "Secondary attack groupings" had as a purpose to keep the enemy from shifting his forces, force him to commit his reserves in the wrong place and keep him from reinforcing the front of the main attack.

Once the commander began an attack he could not readily use any sizable part of his force or unit for another purpose. For once his units were spread out and fighting, they could be shifted to some other front only at risk of heavy losses. The commander could, however, influence the course of an attack already begun through the way in which he used his reserves which were the part of his force (up to one-third of it) which he held back at the beginning of an attack for later use. He could also influence the course of battle by shifting the fire of his artillery and other supporting weapons, and obtaining available additional fire or air support from a higher commander.

Attack Manoeuvres.—There were but two main kinds of attack manoeuvres—envelopments and penetrations. In an envelopment the main attack was directed around the principal forces of the enemy against their flank or rear, toward an objective in the enemy's rear. The aim was to surround the enemy's force before he could withdraw it. An enveloping action was usually supported by a secondary attack, made simultaneously or nearly so, against the enemy's front. The commander would strike fast and unexpectedly with the enveloping part of his force and avoid attacking on ground chosen by the enemy for battle. One of the major envelopments of World War II was the Allied envelopment of the German defending forces in Normandy after the U.S. forces had driven south through St. Lô into France as far as St. Nazaire and Angers and the British had reached the vicinity of Caen. This placed the Allied forces generally on the north and east of the German forces endeavouring to hold and break up the Allied invasion.

The next stage of the attack was an envelopment in which the British 2nd army and Canadian 1st army attacked from the north and the U.S. 1st army from the east, and the U.S. 3rd army drove far to the east and then turned north to cut off the German forces entirely. In this battle of the Falaise-Argentan pocket, the long U.S. envelopment manoeuvre and the shorter British gains against heavy opposition did not close completely the gap behind the German forces. Much of the armour got away, but seven infantry divisions and many other troops were surrounded and captured. This was a "double envelopment" with attacks directed to close around both flanks of the German force, and a third against its front. In the Pacific operations, envelopments in a sense were carried out by completely by-passing certain islands occupied by the Japanese and attacking others beyond them, thus cutting off the by-passed islands from shipping and therefore from supplies of food, equipment and ammunition.

Envelopments were usually less costly and more decisive than penetrations. But an envelopment was not always possible, usually because of the fact that the enemy had defenses organized from sea to sea. In World War I, the German armies stretched from Switzerland to the North sea, and it was not possible to send a force around them except by the wide route through the Mediterranean and the Balkans. In World War II the Germans held all of France, and Italy was an axis partner. But by first clearing the axis out of North Africa, it became possible gradually to attack by a great double envelopment from north and south, using sea routes. But for the two Allied forces attacking Normandy and southern France, the German defenses did not permit an envelopment initially. Each had to make penetration first. In the Pacific island-to-island campaigns, envelopments by sea could readily be made. But in most of the attacks upon the smaller and heavily fortified islands, there was little room for envelopment since the defending Japanese forces were distributed across the full width of the islands in strong fortifications, and once ashore, it was impossible for a force to manoeuvre around them.

In general, a penetration attack had to be used when envelopments were impracticable. Such attacks could be delivered faster than envelopments because there was less distance to go, and when a rapid attack had to be made for any reason, as when the enemy was known to be unready, the penetration manoeuvre was often best. A penetration might also be better when a strong attacking force could be used against a relatively weak or thinly spread defensive force.

In a penetration, as in an envelopment, a main attack and a secondary attack or attacks were made. The commander directed the main or heavy part of his whole attack toward an objective in the rear of the enemy's front but *through* that front. The aim was to strike hard and break through, thus splitting the opposing force. Upon capture of the objective the further aim was to "roll up" one or both of the parts into which the enemy's force had been divided. The main attack was made on a wider front than the width of the expected break-through. This gave the main attack force strength from which to protect the flanks of the penetration as the operation continued; but if it went far, additional units had usually to be directed to follow the main attack force for this purpose.

In 1940, the strong German attack to the channel ports was a penetration which split the British forces in Belgium and the Netherlands from the French and from their own reserves. The forces in this attack prevented the British from retreating south with the French; other German forces enveloped them from farther north through the Netherlands. Still other units were poured into the break-through and turned south to attack and defeat the French and north to attack and defeat the British. Most of the blitzkrieg attacks were rapid penetrations by strong forces against forces weak in weapons or spirit, attack which became double envelopments as the penetration forces turned to right and left from their first objectives to roll up and surround the forces caught between them. The German army used this same method successfully in 1941 and 1942 against the Russian forces. And in 1945, the Allied forces used similar tactics most successfully against the Germans, as in the operations to reach the Rhine and in the final phases of the war in Europe, including the envelopment of the Ruhr by the U.S. 9th and 1st armies, and in the operations of the U.S. 3rd and 7th armies which made the juncture with the Russian forces in Austria and southern Germany. In the Pacific warfare the penetration was often used to cut an island, and the Japanese forces on it, in two. This was done by the marine forces on Iwo Jima and by the combined army and marine forces on Okinawa. Most of the landings made from the sea and most attacks across sizable river lines made in World War II were penetrations of necessity. The attempt was made, however, to deceive the enemy to the last moment as to the actual point of the main attack, thus preventing him from strengthening his defensive forces at that point. Even so, there was usually heavy fighting to gain a good foothold, a beachhead from which to deliver further attacks. Indeed, for the bulk of the subordinate units in all the large campaigns, the offensive tactics were more generally those of penetrating the immediately opposing forces rather than enveloping them, although it was often possible to apply enveloping manoeuvre on a small scale.

Small-unit Offensive Tactics.—The tactics of the smaller combat units, the regiments, battalions, companies and platoons, followed the same general principles of surprise and concentrated application of power and, above all, teamwork that applied in the employment of larger forces. The U.S. infantrymen were trained to take full advantage of the ground and keep on advancing under fire by manoeuvre in which some men or units advanced while others covered their movement by fire. The commander on each level could manoeuvre his own subordinate units within the framework of the higher unit's mission.

Frontages of Attack.—Orders for an attack given by a high commander, for example, an army group commander, would designate the width of front for each attacking army by stating the boundaries between the armies within which each army would largely confine its own attack manoeuvre. The order would also indicate what proportion of the whole force would constitute the reserve. Each army commander's order stated which of his corps would lead the attack and which would be in reserve and gave the boundaries between the leading corps. In like manner, corps commanders designated assault and reserve divisions; and division, regimental, battalion and company commanders issued similar orders to their subordinate units. Thus on an army group front of, say, 200 mi., with 3 armies attacking, an army might be responsible for 50 to 100 mi. of front or more, a corps for 10 to 30 mi., a division for 1 to 5 mi., and so on down to companies with a few hundred yd. and platoons with a few score yd. of front. The front for any unit varied considerably, depending on whether it was a part of the main attack force or of a secondary attack force or a force that would temporarily be operating on the defensive. The main attack was, as we have seen, delivered on but a fraction of each unit's front.

Offensive Tactics of Armoured Units.—Large armoured combat units were used extensively by all the armies except the Chinese, which had but limited numbers of tanks, and the Japanese, whose limited numbers of armoured vehicles were never used in large concentrations. The experience with armour disproved the theories which arose between the two world wars that "mass armies" with infantry were no longer needed and that highly mobile armoured forces working closely with air forces had taken their place. There were too many areas where the tank could not operate freely, and the tank was vulnerable to improved antitank ground weapons and often to attack from the air. But World War II also proved that, properly employed within their limitations and used with other combat arms, armoured units were of high value.

Tanks were used in two principal ways: (1) in armoured divisions containing approximately 300 tanks organized into battalions and companies, and units of armoured infantry, artillery, engineers and other branches of a large armoured combat team; (2) in "separate tank battalions" to fight with infantry units of infantry division. Armoured divisions were used extensively in the German campaigns against France and Russia, in the campaigns in North Africa and in the final campaigns against Germany through France and from Russia. It was impossible to use large armoured units in the Pacific. In Africa, Europe, China-Burma-India and the Pacific, tanks were much used in close co-operation with infantry.

The primary role of the armoured divisions of all armies was the same as for the U.S. units—offensive operations against hostile rear areas. Throughout the war, however, even in the early stages of the blitzkrieg against France and Russia, armoured forces could not break through strong defenses with the help of air units alone. Infantry, heavily supported by all arms, had to make the opportunities for the faster-moving armoured forces to exploit. Infantry divisions first had to overcome heavy resistance, break defenses, weaken the enemy and secure ground so that armoured divisons could pass through the gap thus created and launch their attack. The battle of El Alamein (1942) which, in its second phase, was a decisive battle of tanks against tanks, opened with an attack by four British infantry divisions working with artillery, engineer and air units for four days to clear a path for the armoured units through the German defenses. And often, in other campaigns, it took long hard fighting to make the gap.

The armoured infantry battalions which formed part of the armoured divisions consisted of infantry transported in armoured half-tracks that gave protection against enemy small arms fire. Armoured infantry left its half-tracks to fight; it was especially important to armoured divisions after antitank rocket launchers had been perfected for use by the individual infantryman. Without infantry to fight opposing infantry thus equipped, tanks could become an easy prey. A mission of armoured infantry was to attack to seize terrain favourable for launching a tank attack but it was usually insufficient in numbers to make an original break-through against strong defenses, and there had to be a full-scale attack by available infantry divisions and supporting units before armoured divisions could pass through the enemy's main defenses and into his rear areas with speed. Attempts to use large armoured units against strong defenses always resulted in crippling losses, as in the British drive for the Caen area in June 1944. Thus the most important tactics of armoured divisions were those used in spearheading attacks against an enemy incompletely prepared for defense, breaking through on a wide front against a demoralized enemy, exploiting a success and pursuing a defeated enemy and completing his destruction by deep penetration and encirclement. At times, large armoured units were also used to attack enemy armoured units.

Infantry-Tank Tactics.—The U.S. tactics of close tank co-operation with the smaller infantry units were similar to those of other armies. Early in the war several separate tank battalions, not part of a larger armoured unit, were assigned to each U.S. army. But in the European campaign the need to attach one such battalion to each infantry division became apparent. These battalions fought closely with each division, usually with one of the three medium tank companies of the battalion fighting with each of the three infantry regiments. The infantry-tank combination used offensive tactics of close co-operation and mutual assistance. The infantry assisted the tanks by fire against the antitank weapons of the opposing infantry, and the tanks assisted infantry by close fire on the enemy's machine guns and other automatic weapons. On bad terrain, such as the rocky ground heavily covered with undergrowth on many Pacific islands, one or two tanks were often used to assist infantry against strong defenses. Artillery was usually a third member of the combat team, and engineer units, using explosive charges, often made a fourth. When the hostile resistance was sufficiently light, the tank units working with infantry could use mobile tactics. Possible missions of these units included leading an attack, feeling out the Japanese and developing weak spots, exploiting a success, breaking up hostile counter-attacks and assisting the infantry in mopping up. The four separate tank battalions with the U.S. 6th army in the Luzon campaign of 1944 were frequently able to operate as battalion units to good advantage.

The other armies all made similar use of close support tank units. Early in the war the Russian army frequently used single tanks as a part of small infantry combat teams. The Chinese tank units in Burma operated closely with infantry.

Defensive Tactics

The clear statement of the object of defensive warfare found in the U.S. *Field Service Regulations* could be applied to most defensive operations of all armies in World War II:

> The general object of defensive combat is to gain time pending the development of more favorable conditions for undertaking the offensive, or to economize forces on one front for the purpose of concentrating superior forces for a decision elsewhere. Under the first of these objects, a commander may assume the defensive pending the arrival of reinforcements, or he may be thrown on the defensive by inferiority in numbers, disposition, or training. He may take up a defensive position and invite attack as part of a deliberate plan to win the battle by a counteroffensive. Under the second object, the defensive is usually expressed in the mission received from higher authority. This mission may be to hold a vital area pending completion of the maneuver of other forces to protect a flank, or to contain an enemy force while an offensive is being conducted on another part of the front or in another theater.

Defensive tactics included the idea of organizing a fortified battle position to be held at all costs (Bataan and Corregidor were examples), but the Chinese forces made extensive use of defensive tactics, gradually giving way without fighting extensive battles. The following were, in general, the defensive tactics used in World War II.

Defensive Positions.—In setting up a defensive position, the commander selected the best ground for the purpose within the limits of his orders from the next higher commander. The position was selected to facilitate future manoeuvre, and make the enemy attack the position directly or conduct a time-consuming manoeuvre. The position was divided into sectors assigned to subordinate units, part of which, however, were not put into position but held as a mobile reserve. Positions might be hastily occupied when a force was surprised by an enemy ground attack; or when there was more time, positions might be deliberately selected after thorough study by the commander and his staff. Reconnaissance as thorough as the available time permitted was made to pick the best ground. Sometimes an attack was made to seize better ground for a defense.

All positions involved setting up protection against

attack from any direction—from front, flanks or rear and from the air—even when the terrain or other circumstance made attack from a particular direction highly improbable. Ridges, valleys, rivers, woods, swamps, lakes and other natural obstacles might all be important to a defensive position.

A defensive position was "organized" by placing infantry and supporting units so as to permit the most accurate and continuous fire on the attacking enemy, and permit one defending unit to direct its fire to assist other defending units nearby. Since from a given defensive position all infantry and supporting weapons could cover a considerable area with fire, a defending force was not evenly distributed over its area. The gaps of some width between small-unit positions usually consisted of ground exposed to potential enemy fire, and were covered by obstacles and fire from two or more positions. Such unoccupied ground was usually occupied at night or during foggy weather.

Within each of the subordinate defense positions making up the whole defense area, riflemen and others equipped with light automatic weapons were placed so that their fire would be most effective, not only to the front but to the flanks across the front of the positions of adjacent units. The fire of heavy types of machine guns was especially deadly for such use.

Defensive positions were organized in considerable depth. The U.S. term for the principal defense line was "the main line of resistance," an imaginary line touching the forward edges of the forward defense positions all across the front, the defenses for which extended back at least several hundred yd. Other "lines" were organized farther back more or less parallel to the main line of resistance, so that to be successful a hostile attack had to penetrate through a series of defenses that might be miles in depth.

Artillery units occupied areas in the rear of the main line of resistance and placed concentrations of fire in front of the defending infantry. Infantry supporting weapons used positions farther forward. The fire of all weapons was co-ordinated in a defense plan. Supporting tactical aviation bombed and otherwise attacked approaching enemy forces, artillery and reserves, supply and railroad establishments, airfields, bridges and any other suitable targets. Organization of a defensive position included fortification, which might begin with hastily dug foxholes and weapons emplacements but which was constantly improved as long as the defensive position was occupied.

In World War II, there were many long highly fortified places involved, such as the Maginot, Siegfried and Hitler lines in Europe, Corregidor in the Philippines and Pantelleria in the Mediterranean sea, all the work of years. Other substantial defenses, such as those of the Japanese on Iwo Jima, Saipan and Okinawa, had been developed into an intricate defensive network through many months. Engineer troops were used to plan and develop extensive fortifications.

Flexibility in shifting defensive reserves rapidly to meet new attacks was also essential in defensive tactics. The fact that the German defense of Normandy was made static by bombing of communication lines contributed much to Allied victory. The French army of 1940 was unable to move reserves rapidly or counterattack swiftly.

When the enemy's attack against a position was first discovered, artillery and air units might begin the defense by opening on all possible hostile targets. If the enemy succeeded in launching his attack, artillery fires were continued on his forces as close to the defending troops as was safe. A defensive battle position was protected from surprise by outposts to the front of the main line of resistance, which delayed the hostile attack by forcing the enemy to deploy his units, and which deceived the enemy as to the real position of the main defenses. Outposts withdrew when forced by the pressure of the enemy's attack. When the attack came within its reach, the defending infantry opened on the enemy with all its many weapons. U.S. defensive doctrine envisaged the stiffest possible defense of battle positions. *Field Service Regulations* stated: "A unit entrusted with the defense of a tactical locality under no circumstances abandons it unless authorized to do so by higher authority. Important localities on the main line of resistance must be defended to the last man." On Saipan in 1944 a force of some 5,000 Japanese infantry attacked a line held by a few hundred men of the 27th infantry division. The defenders on the main line of resistance killed more than 2,000 Japanese before being overwhelmed by sheer fanatical numbers. Russian forces defended Sevastopol and Stalingrad with similar last-man tactics.

When the enemy broke through a defensive position, the defender turned his effort to limiting the penetration and then ejecting the enemy from the main battle position. The battle of the Bulge in Europe, Dec. 1944, was perhaps the best-known large-scale example of World War II, and illustrated equally how the smaller defending units fought to limit and break up penetrations. The sudden, powerful German attack broke extensively through the hastily organized defenses of the opposing forces. Allied reserves were brought up rapidly to meet the attack. Other units were rearranged for counterattacks from north and south against the sides of the German attack, which was a threat of encirclement to the successful break-through forces. The desperate fighting of surrounded units, notably at Bastogne, cost the Germans time and effort and slowed them down. The Allied pressure from all directions soon became so intense that the attack was halted halfway to its objective—the splitting of the Allied forces and the recapture of Antwerp. And soon further Allied offensives recaptured the lost ground and more.

Retrograde Movements.—Defensive tactics included the efficient carrying out of withdrawals when they became necessary. Disengagement of a force or unit from combat was called "withdrawal from action" and might be followed by a "retirement." Planned resistance up to a certain point, followed by successive retirements to new lines of temporary resistance up to a certain point, followed by successive retirements to new lines of temporary resistance was called "delaying action." Throughout World War II there were many such operations both on a large and small scale. Their proper conduct had great importance, for it could usually save a defeated force from destruction. The two greatest retrograde movements of World War II in point of numbers involved were those of the Russian armies in the face of the German attacks of 1941 and 1942, and those of the German armies before the Russian attacks of 1943–45. Both were on a front of nearly 2,000 mi. and involved several million men. The Chinese retrograde actions from 1937 on also covered a great area and involved large numbers. Smaller but of importance were such operations as the British, and later the German, retirements across parts of North Africa, the U.S. delaying action on Luzon in 1941–42, and the U.S. and Chinese retreat from Burma in 1942. The Japanese often based their defensive tactics largely on defending in one place till overpowered, with the final result of great disorganization and heavy losses. Often, of course, it would have been impossible for them to retire from an occupied island after shipping had been destroyed by air and naval action.

Withdrawals from action by daylight, always considered difficult and costly operations, were found even more so in World War II because of detection and attack from the air. Hence, when possible, withdrawals were conducted by night or by daylight in fog or heavy weather. All retrograde operations of any size were usually carried out according to plan. Even when the enemy succeeded in making a surprise attack, commanders and their staffs speedily determined the best tactical moves to minimize losses and offset the hostile pressure. The delaying actions and retirement to Bataan of the U.S.-Philippine forces in 1942 were carried out in accordance with a plan of long standing. The retirement of U.S. units in the battle of the Bulge was under guidance of the higher commanders who planned at once how to meet the situation. When such plans were not used, or were too slowly developed, as in the French army of 1940, the retirement generally became an unmanageable rout.

Antimechanized Defense.—In World War II, antitank guns, rocket launchers, tank destroyer guns, medium and heavy calibre artillery fire and mines were the chief defense weapons of ground troops against armoured attack. An attacking as well as a defending force or unit often had to use defensive measures against tanks. Tank units themselves were considered offensive units rather than defensive but often used hit-and-run tactics to avoid continued exposure to heavy antitank fire. U.S. tanks were sometimes used in a purely defensive manner as small mobile forts; this was the usual method of tank employment by the Japanese, especially on Luzon and Okinawa.

Tank destroyers were armoured vehicles carrying powerful guns for use against tanks. Tank destroyer units used tactics of lying in wait to surprise hostile armoured forces, and fast hit-and-run battle tactics. Supporting field and anti-aircraft artillery were also important means of combat with tanks, augmenting when necessary the purely antitank means. Mines were used in vast quantities, first by the German forces and later by all World War II armies which could obtain them. Large areas and long stretches of roads were covered with mines buried close enough together to cause heavy losses to tanks attempting to traverse the areas. The removal of mines was a major task for engineer and other troops.

Combat aviation was a powerful weapon against armoured forces in open country. The Russian armies made extensive use of aviation for this purpose as did the British and U.S. armies.

Chemicals.—Nontoxic chemicals, chiefly smoke, were used extensively to add the protection of reduced visibility for the enemy. The smoke was placed on the enemy troops making them unable to fire with any accuracy until the smoke cleared away. It could be kept dense by continuing to place it on the enemy. Smoke was a "deceptive device" generally used in offensive rather than defensive operations. Smoke was also used within friendly lines to cover troop movements, and to protect areas and sites from observation.

Anti-aircraft Defenses.—Defense of ground troops and ground installations and cities from air attack was carried out by defending air units, which attacked the hostile planes; and by large numbers of mobile and stationary anti-aircraft gun units formed in battalions and similar units in the different armies. Ground combat troops also used such weapons of their own as were suitable against low-flying aeroplanes. Improved anti-aircraft gun techniques accounted for a large fraction of the aeroplanes brought down in every theatre of the war.

Special Operations and Aspects

Tactics for operations under special conditions were largely the application of the general attack and defense principles to those conditions.

Attack of Fortified Localities.—Whenever possible, fortified localities or positions were attacked by tactical air units in co-ordination with artillery preparations just prior to attack of the enemy position by ground or airborne troops. The Japanese captured the defenses of Singapore in 1942 from the rear. The German armies attempted to take Stalingrad by siege since they were unable to come at it from the rear. U.S. forces retook Corregidor early in 1945 by a combination of airborne and amphibious operations. Direct attack on fortified localities usually involved four phases: reducing the hostile outpost system to gain close contact; breaking through the fortifications at one or more favourable points; extending the gap by isolating and reducing the hostile positions on the flanks of the gap; and moving mobile reserves through the gap to complete the encirclement and isolation of the remaining fortifications while continuing the attack against them from the front. Air bombardment or action by airborne troops might precede these phases or might be a part of any one. Secrecy of preparation, thorough study of the special task to be accomplished based on detailed reconnaissance of the attack area, practice with special equipment for the purpose and careful planning were all important to success. The forces leading the attack were often specially selected and trained and usually included infantry, engineers, chemical troops and guns of high penetrating power.

Many operations began as amphibious operations against fortified localities, notably the 1944 landings in Normandy and those on Tarawa, Iwo Jima, Guam, Saipan and other fortified islands in the Pacific. Each such landing was carefully rehearsed, and many types of special equipment were involved, both in getting the troops to shore and in clearing the shore line of mines and obstacles, and in the attack on the fortifications. Preliminary naval and air bombardment was usual. During the assault heavy supporting fire or bombardment was concentrated on the hostile targets that were the greatest danger to the success of the attack, and especially on the enemy's armoured and other reserves to prevent them from reinforcing the positions being attacked. Operations were continued until the entire front selected for the major break-through was reduced and then the next phases of the attack followed at utmost speed.

Attacks Across Rivers.—Attacks across river lines also required special equipment and detailed reconnaissance and study to determine the most favourable weak points in the hostile dispositions and the best spots for the construction of bridges. In both river attacks and landing from the sea, the first objective of the attacking forces was to capture an area (beachhead) of sufficient size to permit the safe landing of further troops and the organizing of further attacks on a progressively larger scale. In river crossings, if an existing bridge could be captured before the enemy destroyed it, the operation was greatly helped. The taking of the Remagen bridge on March 7, 1945, by the U.S. 9th armoured division enabled several divisions to make a rapid crossing, secure a bridgehead, and by securing the bridgehead greatly aid the corps of engineers in the construction of ponton bridges across the Rhine river before the Remagen bridge collapsed.

Night Combat.—There was much night fighting in World War II. Japanese forces made a specialty of infiltrating into U.S. lines at night, and in the early phases of the Pacific war the U.S. units tended to cease offensive action at nightfall and set up a "perimeter defense" against expected attacks. Later, well-planned U.S. night attacks against the Japanese were usually successful. An important phase of the British victory at El Alamein in North Africa in 1943 was carried out at night. The principles of night tactics were the selection of special men and units for specific tasks, simplicity of plan and thorough rehearsal. Complicated plans usually failed. Night attacks were used particularly to complete or exploit successes of the previous day, gain ground important for further operations, attract hostile reserves away from other uses and avoid the heavy losses of attacking over open ground by day. In all armies, river crossing operations were usually begun at night. Raids of small groups into enemy lines to get information and prisoners were common night operations. Many operations of large size were begun at night but required one or more days and nights to complete. Defense against night operations included the use of fire from machine guns and other weapons fixed to cover probable approaches, open ground and other areas of probable enemy use, and the use of obstacles and mines and illumination by flares and fires of the ground the enemy had to cross to attack. The use of outguards with night sentries was a normal means of night defense.

Fighting in Towns and Villages.—Fighting in towns and villages required special tactics applied by all armies. Attacks involved the use of small combat teams to enter the outer houses and then clean out the houses and buildings one by one and room by room with a technique making much use of hand grenades, explosives and short range automatic weapons. Tanks could be used for certain co-operating purposes but were at a disadvantage in towns well protected by antitank means. Air attack by bombing, except for the atomic bombs used late in the war, could not destroy a well-built city sufficiently to weaken the defensive forces within it seriously. Stalingrad and Cassino were examples. The heavy bombing created such rubble that towns were easier to defend and harder to take. Small towns and villages were sometimes by-passed and cleaned up later by troops following the leading elements of an attack. The defensive tactics used in towns were in general those used in other fortified localities.

Combat in Woods and Jungles.—Combat in woods is similar to combat in towns. Observation is difficult, as is control of troops. A large heavy woods with irregular ground is naturally a strong defensive area, and there were many such areas in most of the war theatres. The German defenses in the Hurtgen forest and other heavily wooded and hilly areas of France and Germany were most bitterly contested in 1944, and there were many jungle battles in the Pacific and China-Burma areas. Woods lend themselves to tactical traps and ambush. It was sometimes possible in the European operations to by-pass the smaller areas of woods, completely surround them and take the enemy forces within them later. In attacking a wooded area the edge of the woods was often the first objective, with a further attack organized and launched from that area. In defending a woods, the main defenses were not often placed in the edges, for these were clear-cut targets for artillery and air bombing. Woods were usually organized with a network of defensive positions closer together than on open ground, with observers and outposts in and near the edge of the woods and of clearings in the woods.

Jungle operations were made particularly difficult by lack of roads and trails, and by the heavy, tangled growth and the usual hot, wet climates. Observation was often limited to a few feet, and units had to take great care not to become isolated. Water routes were sometimes more useful than routes on land. Jungle manoeuvre consisted chiefly in painstaking movement to outflank encountered resistance. Such tactics required special training to produce resourceful fighting men who could use the jungles as an ally. Keeping to narrow roads and trails was often dangerous; hence troops had to be able to make progress through the heavy underbrush where routes often had to be cut. All-around defense against surprise attack, by day or night, was especially important in jungle warfare. In general, the lighter infantry and supporting weapons had greater use than the heavier because it was easier to move them. However, there was a considerable use of tanks in small groups fighting in close co-operation with infantry; and it was often necessary, against substantial jungle defenses which lightly equipped troops had been unable to reduce, to bring up the heavier weapons and equipment.

Mountain Operations.—The main effect of mountainous regions on tactics in World War II, as in previous wars, was simply to make operations slower because of the greater effort required. Many mountain areas required little or no special mountain-climbing equipment. Mountainous regions were fought over extensively in Burma-China, New Guinea, Okinawa, North Africa, Greece, Italy, France, Germany and soviet Russia. Mountains lent themselves to defensive warfare, as witness the long hard campaigns of the Allied armies in Italy during 1944–45.

In mountain combat the terrain limited the means commanders could use, and success depended more upon adaptation of available means to the terrain than upon their power. Surprise manoeuvres of the smaller combat units and initiative and leadership were of the highest importance. The seizing of heights from which fire could be concentrated on routes was an important general tactical problem, and offensive operations often resolved themselves into a number of well-defined attacks by subordinate units to seize a series or line of separate mountains.

Most of the armies of World War II had specially trained mountain troops with special light equipment and transportation, including pack animals. In the U.S. army there was one mountain division used in Italy. Lack of pack animals hampered the Allied forces operating in New Guinea in 1943, and in Burma and China, in the Chinese, British and U.S. forces, it proved necessary to build up pack-animal units to carry artillery, ammunition and supplies. Supporting air units were hampered in mountains by fog, clouds and wind currents, but bombing of routes was often very effective.

Combat in Snow and Extreme Cold.—Tactical operations in snow and cold demanded special equipment such as snow vehicles, white camouflage materials and extra warm clothing. The German-Russian winter operations were conducted in the most severe weather met by any of the armies. U.S. forces did no actual campaigning under true arctic conditions. Lack of proper cold-weather equipment caused many casualties among the German forces in Russia in the winter of 1941–42, in U.S. forces on Attu in 1943 and in Italy and France in 1944–45. Snow and cold often affected the mobility of motor equipment when full preparations for winter had not been made. The organization of defensive positions required special digging equipment and use of explosives.

Desert Warfare.—In World War II, the principal desert operations were those in North Africa between the British and first Italian and later German forces from 1941 to 1944. Water supply was always a chief concern in desert operations. The terrain was generally open, and either sandy or rocky. A number of desert movements made by both the British and Germans involved careful preparation for a surprise outflanking movement sweeping around at a distance from the hostile lines. Lack of roads and landmarks made it easy for troops to lose direction, and special attention to training in compass use was required. A high degree of mobility was always desirable in applying desert tactics, particularly because movements could be so readily detected from the air that speed was often vital to success.

Partisan Warfare.—Partisan-type warfare proved of considerable importance and usually took the form of surprise attacks by small forces, even groups of a few men, against isolated detachments and against the outer flank and rear units of main forces. In some phases of World War II, such operations were conducted by a great many small forces over a wide area. Partisan methods were especially effective against supply lines. Night was the usual time for partisan actions and much use was made of noiseless methods of combat such as strangulation and assault with knives. Defense against widespread partisan action was costly in use of troops for security detachments over large areas. Air action was sometimes effective against partisan-defended areas. A complete defense required a thorough combing over of large areas to find and clean out all partisan strongholds. Large as they were, none of the armies was large enough to accomplish this thoroughly except within areas of limited size. The Japanese forces in China, numbering many divisions, could not occupy completely even the areas their armies overran. The Japanese held the cities and towns, railways and roads, but could not move within other areas except in strength. Chinese partisan warfare was an important means of capturing weapons, ammunition and supplies; but this and other sources of the means of warfare were often insufficient to permit continuous partisan combat on a large scale.

Partisan methods were extensively used by the soviet forces in the great area overrun by the German armies in 1941–42. Their tactics for completely surrounded army units included use of partisan methods. In Yugoslavia the Germans were never able to blot out the partisan Chetnik and other forces, which eventually expanded to a considerable size and activity. In the Philippines and other Pacific regions, guerrilla action continued throughout the period of Japanese occupation. In France, the underground Maquis workers took up active partisan warfare in co-operation with the Allied landing forces.

After the remnant of the British expeditionary force to France was evacuated at Dunkirk in 1940, training in partisan tactics became widespread in Britain. Invasion was expected before there would be time to build up the British army, and preparations were begun to make the invasion as costly as possible through home-guard partisan tactics. (*See* also GUERRILLA WARFARE.)

Commando, Ranger and Raider Tactics.—The tactics used by picked and highly organized forces such as the British commandos (*q.v.*) in the raids on Norway and Dieppe, the U.S. army rangers in North Africa, Sicily, Italy and Normandy, and the U.S. marine corps raiders in early Pacific operations, were essentially night infantry tactics. The units received more intensive training than it was pos-

A tactical air command headquarters where targets were singled out for attacks in support of ground operations during World War II

sible to give the rest of the combat forces. Operations were planned in great detail and rehearsed many times. Nearly all such units were disbanded by early 1944 because of their adverse effect on combat units in general which had equally difficult fighting to do. The colourful commando units received much special acclaim not received by the others and took too many of the best men from other combat units.

Airborne Tactics.—The airborne developments of World War II were highly important. With airborne forces operating in conjunction with ground forces, a commander could attack the enemy's rear by "vertical envelopment." Perhaps the most important general principle, however, of airborne operation was that such forces must not be thrown into battle too far from other forces attacking the same hostile force by ground routes. Isolated airborne units had to be supplied by air with food and ammunition for continuous operations. Three to five days was considered the maximum time airborne units could operate without a linking up and relief by ground forces.

In an airborne operation, the first troops dropped were parachute infantry with artillery and other supporting units. These were necessarily spread over an area of some size, and were required therefore to assemble speedily into organized fighting units. The first attack objective normally included an airfield or other suitable spot for glider and aeroplane landings where supporting glider infantry could land, and, later, aeroplanes with reinforcing supplies and troops.

Tactical Air Units

Combat air units were divided into strategic and tactical. The strategic air forces carried out long-distance bombing operations. Tactical air forces worked closely with the ground forces on close support missions. (*See* AVIATION, MILITARY; STRATEGIC BOMBING.)

In their early campaigns of 1939 to 1942, the German ground forces were heavily supported by dive bombers and other planes which attacked ground forces effectively from low altitudes. But against determined and experienced troops, well equipped with anti-aircraft weapons, these tactics proved to be so costly that they were generally avoided except when the hoped-for accomplishment was believed to be worth the probable cost. Hence much tactical bombing in support of ground troops was done from medium rather than extremely low altitudes. Strategic air forces were sometimes given tactical missions, for example, in augmenting the air support of the D-day landings.

Tactical air operations in offensive warfare consisted in part of close and immediate co-operation in support of front-line troops. There was by no means an "air umbrella" over every part of an attacking ground force as it was often popularly believed. An important use of tactical air units was for pin-point bombing and strafing of enemy positions prior to ground attack, and after the attack began, against hostile targets some distance from the ground forces. The destruction in the air and on the ground of hostile air units which attempted to interfere with an offensive operation was a primary mission of all tactical air forces. Air success in this regard was usually so important that when such air action was delayed by weather or other cause, large ground actions were often postponed. Air attacks to slow up the movement of hostile reserves and destroy lines of communications were also missions of great assistance to ground forces. The air superiority gained and held by the Allies over Germany from 1944 on, through the action of both strategic and tactical air forces, contributed much to the successful invasion of France and defeat of the German forces, especially through hindering the movement of German reserves. Similarly, in the Pacific, destruction of Japanese air forces by U.S. air units of the army and navy, and of Japanese shipping by air and naval forces, not only prevented reinforcement of island garrisons but enabled U.S. ships and planes to assist the landing forces freely through preliminary bombardment and later tactical co-operation. And from D-day on in Europe, the large tactical air forces which were available greatly augmented the artillery fire power in preparing break-throughs of ground forces, and were of immeasurable assistance to the rapidly moving ground forces exploiting a successful break-through. Such action was particularly effective during the German retreat after the break-through at St. Lô and the crossing of the Rhine.

In the Allied forces, a tactical "air command" composed of medium bombardment, fighter-bomber, reconnaissance and other air groups, operated in close conjunction with each of the armies. Co-operation missions were jointly planned by the commander of the army and the commander of the tactical air command working with that army. (*See* also CHEMICAL WARFARE; GUERRILLA WARFARE; INCENDIARY WARFARE; LOGISTICS OF WORLD WAR II; MUNITIONS OF WAR; PSYCHOLOGICAL WARFARE; STRATEGY OF WORLD WAR II; WORLD WAR II.)

BIBLIOGRAPHY.—Allied Forces Supreme Headquarters, *Report by the Supreme Commander to the Combined Chiefs of Staff* (H.M. Stat. Off., London, 1946); *Brassey's Naval Annual* (Clowes, London, 1940–46); L. H. Brereton, *Diaries* (1946); H. A. DeWeerd, *Great Soldiers of World War II* (1944); F. Eldridge, *Wrath in Burma* (1946); D. Garnett, *War in the Air, Sept. 1939–May 1941* (1941); R. Henri, *U.S. Marines on Iwo Jima* (1945); J. Hersey, *Hiroshima* (1946); "Capture of Attu," *Infantry Journal* (1946), "Okinawa," *ibid.* (1947); E. Kahn, H. McLemore, "Fighting Divisions," *Infantry Journal* (1945); W. Karig, *Battle Report* (1944); W. B. Kerr, *Russian Army* (1944); M. Johnson, *Automatic Weapons of the World* (1945); A. Lee, *German Air Force* (1946); E. McInnis, *The War*, 5 vol. (1940–45); G. McMillan, "Uncommon Valor," *Infantry Journal* (1946); S. Marshall, "Bastogne," *Infantry Journal* (1946), "Island Victory," *Infantry Journal* (1944); F. Miksche, *Attack* (1942); A. Moorehead, *Don't Blame the Generals* (1943); *End in Africa* (1943); F. Pratt, *The Navy's War* (1944); R. Sherrod, *Tarawa* (1944); R. Shugg and H. DeWeerd, "World War II," *Infantry Journal* (1946); R. Tregaskis, *Guadalcanal Diary* (1943); U.S. Army Air Forces, *Report of the Commanding General* (First report 1944–); U.S. Office of Naval Operations, *U.S. Navy at War, Official Reports* (1941–45); U.S. War Dept. Chief of Staff, *Reports* (1939–45); U.S. War Dept. Historical Division: *The Admiralties* (1946); *Capture of Makin* (1946); *Fifth Army at the Winter Line* (1945); *From the Volturno to the Winter Line* (1945); *Guam* (1946); *Merrill's Marauders* (1946); *Omaha Beachhead* (1946); *Papuan Campaign* (1944); *St. Lo* (1947); *Salerno* (1944); *Small Units* (1947); *With the II Corps to Bizerte* (1944); also *History of Military Units* in files of the Historical Division; O. White, *Green Armor* (1945). (J. L. D.; C. R. HU.)

Tadzhik S.S.R.

See UNION OF SOVIET SOCIALIST REPUBLICS.

Taft, Robert Alphonso

Taft (1889–), U.S. senator, was born Sept. 8, 1889, in Cincinnati, O. Son of William Howard Taft, 27th president of the U.S. he received his B.A. degree from Yale in 1910 and his LL.B. from Harvard in 1913. After completing his studies, he began the practice of law and also entered politics in Cincinnati as a precinct worker. He served during World War I as assistant counsel on the U.S. food administration. Elected to the Ohio house of representatives in 1921, he served three terms and was a member of the Ohio senate, 1931–32.

In 1938 he was elected to the U.S. senate and two years later (1940) Ohio Republicans boosted him for the presidential nomination, but he lost to Wendell Willkie. In 1944 Taft again loomed as a possibility for the presidential nomination, but the convention chose Gov. Thomas Dewey. Meanwhile, Taft gradually took a dominant position among G.O.P. members in the senate.

Committed to a stand of nonintervention before Pearl Harbor, Taft voted against Dumbarton Oaks, the Bretton Woods agreement and the Reciprocal Trade Acts agreement and on Dec. 4, 1945, he was one of the seven senators who voted against U.S. participation in the United Nations. He also assailed the proposed $3,750,000,000 loan to Britain and suggested (April 24, 1946) that Britain be given an outright gift of $1,250,000,000 instead. With regard to the soviet union, he felt that Pres. Harry S. Truman's administration was "appeasing" that country and thereby building it into "the greatest totalitarian state the world has ever known."

In domestic policy, he based most of his attacks against New Deal legislation on what he called the government's tendency to take more and more control over the nation's economy, thereby threatening the structure of private enterprise.

After the Republican victory in the elections of Nov. 1946, Taft was once more considered as a potential presidential candidate.

Tahiti

See Pacific Islands, French.

Taiwan

See Formosa.

Talc

The United States remained the world's largest producer of talc minerals—talc, pyrophyllite and soapstone. Next in importance came Manchuria, Italy, Norway, India, Canada and Spain, with outputs of the order of 100,000 tons down to 20,000 tons, which combined to make a total somewhat less than that of the United States. A number of other countries had smaller outputs, with production data so incomplete that no estimate could be made of the world total.

The salient features of the industry in the United States are indicated by the following data in thousands of short tons:

	1937	1939	1941	1943	1945
Mine production	?	?	414.5	436.2	401.2
Sales	230.0	254.0	416.4	412.9	401.1
Crude	11.1	15.7	43.8	30.2	39.3
Sawed	1.1	1.9	4.2	1.7	2.6
Ground	217.8	236.4	368.4	381.0	359.2
Imports	26.9	26.2	18.6	6.6	8.5
Used in					
Paint	59.7	67.9	120.3	129.2	96.5
Paper	32.1	30.2	37.9	34.4	27.1
Ceramics	29.8	38.4	79.0	47.9	34.3
Rubber	26.9	31.1	58.1	49.0	62.0
Roofing	23.6	30.5	40.6	47.5	46.2
Toilet preparations	4.3	9.7	21.1	17.7	19.0
Insecticides	?	?	10.3	24.5	35.7

In addition to the increased uses shown in the table, unspecified uses expanded greatly, since this group included various important war uses in the chemical warfare service and as an insulator in electrical equipment, especially for radio communication.

Full data were available from Canada only after 1941, when the total was 34,632 tons; succeeding years showed 29,868 tons in 1942, 26,163 tons in 1943, 32,597 tons in 1944 and 26,889 tons in 1945. In general, the total output was divided about evenly between talc and soapstone.

The Italian output increased from 51,200 short tons in 1937 to 90,117 tons in 1942, and the Indian from 14,839 tons in 1937 to 36,133 tons in 1942, declining to 18,731 tons in 1943. (G. A. Ro.)

Tanganyika

See British East Africa; Mandates.

Tangerines

See Fruit.

Tangier

An international territory, Tangier is one of the zones of Morocco, its legislative power being vested in an international assembly following the convention of Paris of Dec. 18, 1923. The regime is autonomous, under the nominal sovereignty of the sultan of Morocco. The sultan's representative (the mendoub) during the decade was Hadj Mohammed el Tazi. Area: 232 sq.mi.; pop. (1940 census, 102,306) (1941 est.) 100,000 (36,500 Moslems, 16,509 Europeans). Languages: French, Spanish, Arabic.

* * *

In May 1936 it had been agreed that the office of administrator in the international zone should be held for three years alternatively by a Frenchman and a Spaniard, and that a Spaniard should hold it first. The Spanish Civil War, however, supervening, the French administrator's term was extended. With France's collapse and Italy's entry into World War II, Tangier became front-page news. On June 14, 1940, Spain assumed sole control there. Since three of the four guaranteeing powers (Britain, France, Italy and Spain) were at war with each other, this proceeding was in itself perfectly normal. But newspaper headlines, demonstrations and rejoicings throughout Spain proclaimed that Tangier, "now Spanish," was to be "the gateway to the Spanish empire," and on Nov. 3, 1940, Colonel José Yuste, who had entered the zone with Moorish soldiers in June, proclaimed himself governor, announced that the charter of internationalization (1923) was annulled and dissolved the legislative assembly. This step having violated an international agreement, Britain, which with France, had concurred in the action of June, made a formal protest and reserved its position with regard to an ultimate settlement. Compensation described in the house of commons as "generous" was offered by Spain to British officials displaced by the annexation, and the rights of British nationals, together with the continuance of British institutions, were guaranteed; Spain also undertook that the zone would not be fortified.

During the five years' occupation, plans were made by Spain for the amelioration of the zone, but next to nothing was accomplished, the price paid by it for the advantage of neutrality being Spanish forms of government, the substitution of Spanish for international police and the introduction of the black market. In Jan. 1943 Tangier was formally incorporated in Spanish Morocco and the khalifa of Spanish Morocco, Sidi Muley Hassen Ben el Mehedi, made a ceremonial entry into the city. In Aug. 1945, after the defeat of Germany, a conference was held in Paris, between representatives of Britain, France, the U.S.S.R. and the United States. On Sept. 4, 1945, Spain was called upon to evacuate Tangier; the sovereign rights of the sultan of Morocco were re-established; the international administration of 1923, as modified in 1928, was restored; and the U.S.S.R. and the U.S. were invited to collaborate in this administration. These decisions were to remain in force until the conclusion of a fresh convention between the powers signatory to the act of Algeciras, among which was Spain.

The Spanish government complied with the demands of the powers, an official statement from its foreign ministry (Sept. 18) alleging that the zone had been occupied only to forestall a possible axis attack upon it. The diplomatic and consular representatives of the powers in Tangier met there and agreed to reinstate a Frenchman, Joseph le Fur, as temporary administrator for the Allied control commission, to be succeeded by a Portuguese. The Spanish undersecretary of foreign affairs, Don Cristóbal Castillo, was appointed Spanish consul-general. On Oct. 11, 1945, the 80-year old mendoub, representative of the sultan of Morocco, returned to Tangier in a French cruiser, which also brought a new garrison, and, in the sultan's name, thanked the United Nations for restoring his rights. Among the earliest reforms instituted under the new regime was the creation of an assistant administratorship of native affairs, so that problems of government might more adequately be studied before the meeting of the signatory powers to discuss the forthcoming charter. (E. A. P.)

Tangier: *Statistical Data, 1938*

Item	Value (000's omitted)	Amount or Number
Exchange rate		
United States		1 French franc=2.87c
Great Britain		178.75 francs=£1
Finance		
Government revenues	\$756 (£155)	
Government expenditures	\$798 (£163)	
Transportation		
Railroads		11 mi.
Communication		
Telephones		1,481*
Sea products—total		936 tons*
Fish		893 " *
Crustaceans		42 " *
Exports—total	\$334† (£68)	...
Goatskins (raw)	\$58† (£12)	180 " †
Preserved fish	\$43† (£9)	230 " †
Moroccan leather goods	\$30† (£6)	15 " †
Imports—total	\$3,240† (£655)	...
Wheat flour	\$478† (£97)	9,984 " †
Vegetable oils (edible)	\$107† (£22)	704 " †
Refined sugar	\$98† (£20)	2,124 " †

*1941. †1937.

Bibliography.—A. Ménard, *Étude Critique du régime spécial de la zone de Tanger* (2 vols., 1933); H. W. Petzet, *Tanger und die Britische reichsbildung* (1938).

Tanks, Military

See Munitions of War; Tactics of World War II; World War II.

Tantalum

The production of tantalum ores in the United States continued small, reaching a high of only 9,411 lb. in 1943, and declining to 5,500 lb. in 1945. The relatively large amounts used in the United States came mostly from imports, which were as follows, in thousands of pounds:

1937	20.9	1940	490.5	1943	643.1
1938	41.7	1941	403.5	1944	837.1
1939	56.6	1942	467.5	1945	630.1

In earlier years, the bulk of the supply went into electronic tubes. The other most important use of the metal was in chemical equipment resistant to acid corrosion, especially by hydrochloric and acetic acids. Tantalum received a considerable amount of publicity during World War II as a bone repair material in surgery, and in surgical and dental instruments, though the amounts thus consumed were relatively small. In compound form, the fluoride was used as a catalyst in the manufacture of the butadiene type of synthetic rubber, and the oxide and some other compounds were used as phosphors in the coating of fluorescent lights. The carbide, exceedingly hard, was used in cutting tools, wire-drawing dies and parts requiring high hardness and resistance to abrasion. (G. A. Ro.)

Bibliography.—J. S. Baker, *World Survey of Tantalum Ore* (Bureau of Mines Inform. Circ. 7319) (1945); Fansteel Metallurgical Corp., *Tantalum* (1935); C. G. Goetzel, "Refractory Metals," *Mining and Metallurgy* 25:373–5 (Aug. 1944); C. T. Olson, "Place of Tantalum in Surgery," *Industrial Medicine* 13:917–20 (Nov. 1944).

Tarawa

See Gilbert Islands; World War II.

Tariffs

The world emerged from the decade 1937–46 with substantially the same tariff systems as those employed at the beginning of that period. Although numerous duties had been changed for individual items in the import classifications of various countries, these changes were of minor importance insofar as they affected the general character of the tariff systems of the major trading nations. The foregoing statement applies with almost equal validity to both the revenue positions and the protective role of these systems. It may be somewhat misleading, however, to make the above generalization without setting it in its proper perspective. However correct it may be that tariffs in 1946 differed little from those in 1937, it should be borne in mind that the economic and political environment was altered materially during the decade. Customs duties were to function against a new and different background of international trade, world finance, political organization and programs for world collaboration; this altered environment in turn could be expected to affect both the importance and the status of tariffs in the commercial policies and revenue systems of the world.

For several decades, the importance of import duties in the fiscal systems of many countries had declined. Similarly, even their importance as an instrument of commercial policy (that is, their employment for the protection of domestic industries and for the benefit of special interest groups) had waned with the increased use of other devices such as nontariff controls over imports, state trading, bilateral agreements, export controls and the like. The global character of World War II, involving extensive preparations by the aggressor nations and, later, by the Allied Powers, the vast operations of the war itself and the comprehensive measures undertaken to prevent postwar disorganization, induced many countries to resort to nontariff import and export controls on a scale incomparable to anything imagined in the nontotalitarian countries during the prewar decade. As a consequence, therefore, tariffs were eclipsed by the wartime trading policies of most countries.

The generalization that the world emerged from the war with substantially the same tariff systems as before must also be interpreted in the light of aspirations and programs (discussed later in this article) of the United Nations to remove the many barriers which had served as continuing restrictions on the volume of world trade. These plans for liberalizing trade constituted the basis for a wider degree of multilateral trading and served to replace the autarchic and bilateral practices of the prewar decade.

Tariff Systems at the Beginning of the Decade.—The national tariff systems in force at the beginning of the decade 1937–46 were in large part the products of events which occurred during the interwar period. So far as tariffs were concerned, these events could be grouped around three rather distinct trends: (1) the general intensification of protectionism during the late '20s and the '30s; (2) the rise of autarchic-bilateralism as practised principally by the later aggressor nations and (3) the development of the reciprocal trade agreements program by the United States.

Sharply contrasting with the objectives of various programs instituted by the League of Nations to achieve greater freedom in the international exchange of merchandise was the rise of economic nationalism after the close of World War I. Even before the depression of the '30s, many countries had begun to vie with one another in raising tariff barriers and granting protective duties. Economic nationalism was given additional impetus by the newly created European states which desired to integrate their economies behind new boundaries. Other countries, beset by inflation, shortages of exchange or unemployment, sought to fortify their economies by the erection of tariff walls. Only the more stable of the European countries, particularly those which were neutral during World War I, found it expedient to pursue moderate tariff policies. In 1922 the United States, by then the world's chief creditor nation, sharply increased the level of its tariff. Heinrich Liepmann estimated that by 1927 the chief European countries had increased the height of their tariffs to about double that prevailing in 1913.[1]

The depression following 1929 gave further impetus to the erection of tariff barriers. In 1930 the United States intensified its policy of protection by increasing substantially the rates of duty on hundreds of import items. This action was followed almost immediately by sharp increases in the tariffs of many other countries. In a short while Great Britain found it necessary to abandon the gold standard and to reverse its traditional position as the leading exponent of free trade. Later, a system of empire preferences was worked out at Ottawa, Canada.

It had become increasingly difficult to consider tariffs without referring to a wide variety of complementary instruments of commercial policy. These instruments had been colourfully characterized as follows by Pres. Herbert Hoover: "Mainly out of currency instability and currency manipulations and planned economy there have grown unreasonable tariff walls, embargoes, quotas, subsidies on exports, discriminations between nations. They are all devilish devices which create scarcity and restrict world prosperity." To the list might well have been added compensation, clearing and payment agreements, exchange control and the "invisible tariff," by means of which governments extended indirect administrative protection through application of cumbersome customs formalities and regulations. During the interwar period nontariff controls over imports had become an important aspect of the international system of regulation and had contributed materially to the breakdown of the world trading system. Despite the importance of these auxiliary devices for restricting imports at the beginning of the decade 1937–46, however, the tariff continued to be the most prominent instrument of commercial policy in countries other than the totalitarian states.

By 1937 two rather carefully articulated programs of world trading were competing with one another. These systems were designated as the autarchic-bilateralism practised by such countries as Germany and Italy, and the reciprocal trade program of the United States. The first method, employed chiefly by the totalitarian states for the thoroughgoing regulation of trade, constituted leadership in the direction of more aggressive economic nationalism. It utilized quotas and other nontariff import controls, tariff discriminations and exchange control, and made extensive use of the many instruments of bilateralism, including compensation, clearing and payment agreements. Because of the vulnerability of their economies, many smaller countries were drawn into the orbit of the German trading system.

In 1934 while the new and discriminatory trade restrictions were being employed by the aggressor nations in preparation for war, the United States launched its reciprocal trade program. It was directed to the restoration of multilateral trade, and its cornerstone was "the principle of equality of treatment." The United States congress authorized the president to negotiate trade agreements with foreign countries and, in return for concessions by such countries, to grant reductions in duties on imports into the United States. All reductions thus granted were extended on an unrestricted unlimited most-favoured-nation basis to all countries not discriminating against United States products. The objective of the reciprocal trade program was that of contribution to a general liberalization and revival of world trade. By the close of 1937 the United States had negotiated most-favoured-nation agreements with 16 countries and had, thereby, exchanged reciprocal concessions providing for lower tariffs and modifying other restrictions on imports.

The Prewar Years.—During the three-year period 1937–39, the dictator nations of Europe were preoccupied with the program which eventuated in war and conquest. Meanwhile, other countries became increasingly concerned over problems of defense and consequently the commercial policies of all nations reflected the new war atmosphere. Efforts were generally directed to the achievement of a greater degree of self-sufficiency, the acquisition of essential materials and the elimination of nonessential imports. Tariffs did not readily adapt themselves to the new objectives. Thus, although import duties continued in many countries to be the most important method of trade control until the outbreak of the war, they lost ground relative to other types of restriction. More extensive use was made of quotas, licensing systems, bilateral balancing arrangements, export embargoes and state trading.

The multilateral system of international trading continued to be under attack by the German program of bilateralism, while at the same time the United States continued the attempt to revitalize multilateralism through the media of its reciprocal trade program. The German system, preliminary to its ultimate collapse, approached its zenith during this period, but, as before, the chief instruments of policy were nontariff controls over trade, including an intricately articulated system of exchange control, blocked accounts, barter transactions and highly elaborated clearing and payments agreements.

Probably the outstanding development in the field of tariffs during the years immediately before World War II was expansion by the United States of its reciprocal trade program. In addition to those already in force, new agreements were negotiated with Czechoslovakia, Ecuador, the United Kingdom, Turkey and Venezuela, and supplementary agreements were concluded with Canada and Cuba. In all of these negotiations, the agreement countries granted, on a most-favoured-nation basis, numerous concessions on United States exports in return for tariff concessions on imports of their products into the U.S.A.

[1] *Tariff Levels and the Economic Unity of Europe* (London, 1938).

During the period 1937–39 no country undertook a major revision of its import tariff. Moreover, an analysis of the more important changes which did occur reveals no discernible trend; possibly the tendency, if it may be called one, was in the direction of higher tariffs. Many changes were piece-meal and made no significant alteration in the tariff policy of the various individual countries; others were somewhat more substantial. In 1937 the United Kingdom, in a trade agreement with Canada, granted reductions to the latter country on a variety of products. In the same year duties were lowered on various iron and steel items. In 1939 the United Kingdom negotiated an agreement with Eire by which the two countries exchanged various reciprocal reductions in duties on each other's products. The earlier duties on iron and steel products were restored in that year, however, when the protective system was further elaborated by increasing the tariff on various imports including mineral oils.

In the trade agreement mentioned above, Canada in 1937 reduced its preferential duties on about 150 items from the United Kingdom. During the same year the system of imperial preference was strengthened by new agreements in which Canada granted additional preferential reductions to Australia and New Zealand. France increased all customs duties by about 13% in 1937 and also raised the levy on a variety of individual import items. Additional increases by Eire in 1938 served to make that country's tariff structure one of the highest in the world. During these three years Belgium, the Netherlands and Sweden were about the only other countries of Europe which may be said to have increased their customs duties on any substantial list of items. Outside of Europe, perhaps the most extensive change was that by Australia, which in 1937 reduced duties on a wide variety of imports, including iron pipes, sanitary ware and tiles. Although Australia reduced its tariff on a few items in 1938, duties on many others were increased during the following year. Few changes were made in the tariffs of Latin American countries. In 1938 Bolivia, in order to compensate for currency depreciation, imposed an additional surcharge on all imports. In the same year Brazil levied a much smaller surtax on imports into that country. In 1937 Ecuador increased the basic rates of duty on more than 300 commodities, as did Mexico on most of the items in its tariff schedule. In 1938 further increases, subsequently modified, were imposed on more than 200 additional import items in the Mexican schedule.

The War Period.—Because of the exigencies of World War II, customs tariffs were employed less as instruments of commercial policy during the period 1940–44 than perhaps during any comparable period in the preceding quarter century. Although prewar schedules of import duties were generally maintained, at least in form, they had less effective application during the war than before. There were scattered instances where governments increased or imposed new protective duties to foster selected industries, but these increases were scarcely representative of the war period. From time to time, also, a few nations increased their tariffs on a substantial variety of items solely for revenue purposes. Still others, such as Peru in 1940, had recourse to higher duties as a wartime measure of indirect exchange control by means of restricting the importation of nonessential items. More representative of the war period, however, was the fact that many nonbelligerent countries, impelled by the need for industrial equipment, raw materials and prime essentials, frequently sought to protect their economies by granting at least temporary exemptions or reductions in duties. Because of wartime scarcities of essential materials, the closing of important sources of supply and the blockade of others, the shortage of shipping and the greatly increased demand for strategic materials, some countries suspended temporarily the application of duties on commodities essential to the prosecution of the war.

By and large, however, the war constituted a standstill period as far as tariffs and related instruments of commercial policy were concerned. There were virtually no complete revisions or extensive modifications of tariff schedules throughout the world. Perhaps the closest to such revisions were the changes made in Bolivia and Uruguay. In 1940 Bolivia adopted a new customs classification based on the Brussels International nomenclature, and, during the three years which followed, Uruguay revised its tariff schedule more or less in accordance with the recommendations of the League of Nations committee on tariff nomenclature. It is interesting to note, however, that the new schedules in each of these countries left the prevailing rates of duty relatively unaltered.

Although import duties continued to be the mainstay of the revenue systems of many nonindustrialized nations during World War II, nontariff controls overshadowed the various national tariff systems as instruments of control over world trade. The war served to substitute a struggle for imports for the former neomercantilistic struggle for exports; it resulted also in the coinage of new slogans such as that in Turkey, where the proverbial "We buy from those who buy from us" was replaced by "We sell to those who sell to us." Almost immediately after the outbreak of the war in 1939 there was a rapid extension of control over trade in most neutral countries. There followed a widespread introduction of embargoes and licensing systems for the restriction of exports, particularly of foodstuffs, essential raw materials and industrial supplies. The belligerent powers, of course, administered increasingly tight systems of control over all aspects of foreign trade. Thus, the eclipse of tariffs became quite complete as production priorities, export licensing, shipping allocations, import permits, blocked exchange balances and state trading were employed on a wholesale scale as instruments of global warfare. The wartime subordination of the tariff was succinctly portrayed in the following remarks by the Canadian minister of finance in his budget speech of 1943:

> The customs tariff has fallen from the high position it has previously held as an instrument of fiscal and economic policy. Under the circumstances of war, the tariff has little effect except as a producer of revenue. The scope and direction of trade are now governed by the consideration of supply, transportation and enemy action. . . . Under these circumstances, changes in the customs tariff . . . are of no effect in expanding or curtailing trade.

Each of the major belligerent powers, of course, elaborated its own system of control to conserve essential supplies, promote the importation of strategic materials and prevent supplies from reaching the enemy. Nonbelligerent countries found themselves obliged to adopt similar programs in the interests of their own national economies. As one of the belligerent powers, for example, the United Kingdom instituted a system of selective control over exports through the requirement of licences. The British government negotiated many bulk purchasing agreements for foodstuffs and other vital materials. To allocate shipping space, to eliminate nonessential imports and to conserve exchange balances, an import licensing system was also applied soon after the outbreak of World

War II. Gradually the British wartime system of exchange control, designed to conserve the available free exchange balances, resulted in the blocking of millions of pounds sterling and entailed a large degree of bilateralism within the sterling area. This bilateralism resulted chiefly from the fact that the owners of the blocked balances could use their funds only to buy imports from the sterling area, principally the United Kingdom, whose import transactions had created the balance in the first place.

Although there were no over-all revisions of tariff schedules in any major country during the war, there were many piecemeal modifications, usually relatively unimportant, either raising or lowering the rates of duty for specified import items. For the most part these scattered changes displayed no decided pattern or trend; modifications providing for lower rates of duty, however, were apparently more numerous and of somewhat greater importance than those providing for increased import charges. Only the more salient of these changes will be mentioned. As the war progressed, Canada tended more and more, because of its exchange position, to favour imports from the United Kingdom. This was achieved, in part, by lowering the preferential duties on products imported from the United Kingdom. In 1941 Canada cut in half most of the duties on British products; further reductions were made in 1944. A different trend was apparent in Egypt, however, where duties levied on a specific basis were doubled in 1941. In Latin America, wartime shortages of supply induced several countries to reduce or suspend, at least temporarily, the duties on many prime necessities; such action was most apparent in Argentina, Brazil, Chile and Venezuela. Rather extensive increases in duty were imposed, on the other hand, in Cuba, Ecuador, Mexico, Paraguay, Peru and Uruguay.

Despite the onset of the war, the United States pressed its efforts to promote a more liberal basis for world trade. Not only were new trade agreements negotiated but the legal basis of the program itself was also broadened. In 1945 the congress of the United States authorized the president to continue the program of negotiating reciprocal, unconditional most-favoured-nation commercial agreements with other countries and to grant mutual concessions therein; moreover, it liberalized the terms under which such concessions could be granted. During the period 1940–46, inclusive, additional most-favoured-nation agreements involving reciprocal tariff concessions were negotiated between the United States and Argentina, Peru, Uruguay, Mexico, Iran, Iceland and Paraguay; supplemental agreements were concluded with Canada and Cuba.

Postwar Plans and Projects.—Perhaps the decade ending in 1946 would ultimately be characterized not as an interval during which tariffs were eclipsed, momentarily at least, by other devices for controlling world trade, but as a memorable transition period between the neomercantilistic bilateralism of the '20s and '30s and a new epoch of multilateral trading among nations. Although it would be premature in this summary to render such a judgment, it is highly pertinent to an appraisal of trends during the decade to record the fact that a great deal of thinking and planning was devoted to the problem of liberalizing commercial policies throughout the world. By 1946 these aspirations had progressed beyond the early stages of discussion and debate and had become the subject of international negotiation and formal commitment. Although the superstructure had not been elaborated, the foundation perhaps had been laid for a broader and freer exchange of goods and services among nations.

For many years there had developed among statesmen, a growing consciousness that autarchic and bilateral trade devices strangled commerce, impoverished peoples and created international ill will. The instrumentalities of economic warfare to which nations had had recourse included heightened tariffs, embargoes, quotas, exchange controls, multiple currencies, export subsidies and bilateral agreements. These in turn frequently set in motion spirals of retaliation and counterretaliation. During the decade ending in 1946, therefore, various proposals were advanced to reduce or eliminate trade barriers and to lay the basis of a wider multilateralism which in turn was expected to promote world prosperity and facilitate the maintenance of peace. The more important steps designed to reconstruct world trade included the signing of the Atlantic charter, the Lend-Lease agreements, the Bretton Woods program and the proposal for an international conference on trade and employment.

The Atlantic Charter.—In Aug. 1941, even before the entrance of the United States into the war, the prime minister of the United Kingdom and the president of the United States issued a joint declaration setting forth "certain common principles in the national policies of their respective countries on which they base their hopes for a better future for the world." Two of the pledges made in this renowned document, the Atlantic charter (*q.v.*), committed the two countries to liberal trading policies:

> Fourth, they will endeavor, with due respect for their existing obligations to further the enjoyment by all States, great or small, victor or vanquished, of access, on equal terms, to the trade and to the raw materials of the world which are needed for their economic prosperity;
>
> Fifth, they desire to bring about the fullest collaboration between all nations in the economic field with the object of securing, for all, improved labor standards, economic advancement and social security.

Article VII of The Master Lend-Lease Agreement.—The next important declaration of intention to work for a broader program of economic collaboration and for the elimination of world trade barriers was embodied in the master Lend-Lease agreement, signed between the United States and other members of the United Nations. Article VII of the Lend-Lease agreement between the United States and the United Kingdom, signed in Feb. 1942, read as follows:

> In the final determination of the benefits to be provided . . . the terms and conditions thereof shall be such as not to burden commerce between the two countries, but to promote mutually advantageous economic relations between them and the betterment of world-wide economic relations. To that end, they shall include provision for agreed action . . . directed to the expansion, by appropriate international and domestic measures, of production, employment, and the exchange and consumption of goods, which are the material foundations of the liberty and welfare of all peoples; to the elimination of all forms of discriminatory treatment in international commerce, and to the reduction of tariffs and other trade barriers; and, in general, to the attainment of all the economic objectives set forth in the Joint Declaration (Atlantic Charter) made on August 12, 1941, by the President of the United States of America and the Prime Minister of the United Kingdom.
>
> At an early convenient date, conversations shall be begun between the two Governments with a view to determining, in the light of governing economic conditions, the best means of attaining the above-stated objectives by their own agreed action and of seeking the agreed action of other like-minded Governments.

International Monetary Fund; World Bank.—The first

important measures to implement the objectives of the Atlantic charter and Article VII of the mutual-aid agreements were products of the United Nations Monetary and Financial conference which met at Bretton Woods, N.H., in July 1944. As a result of the Bretton Woods proposals, two agencies for international economic collaboration began initial operations in Dec. 1945; these were the International Monetary fund and the International Bank for Reconstruction and Development (*qq.v.*).

The International Monetary fund was designed to eliminate the various currency and foreign-exchange difficulties which obstructed world trade during the interwar period. Previously, widely fluctuating exchange rates, competitive depreciation of currencies, exchange allocations and preferential exchange treatment had all served as barriers to the free flow of commerce and mutual prosperity among nations. Some countries had instituted exchange control reluctantly during the depression to stabilize their currencies or to prevent further disruption of their national economies; others had used exchange regulation as an instrument of a carefully articulated program of economic aggression and still others had recourse to such controls more or less helplessly as they were caught in a world tide of economic bilateralism.

The Monetary fund constituted an agreement among nations to assist one another in reducing or avoiding monetary disturbances and provided the machinery, so far as possible, to make the currencies of its members freely convertible. Member countries undertook through the fund to keep their exchange rates as stable as possible and to alter rates only in accordance with carefully designed rules of procedure. A common pool of monetary resources was established to meet temporary shortages of exchange and to assist member countries to weather an emergency.

The resources of the Monetary fund were not available, of course, to finance capital investment and long-term transactions. Hence, a companion institution came into being after Bretton Woods to render such assistance to nations. The International Bank for Reconstruction and Development had an authorized capital of $10,000,000,000, subscribed by the member countries. Subject to the provisions of its carefully drawn article of agreement, the bank was in a position to promote the postwar rehabilitation of nations and to further their orderly economic development thereafter.

The Anglo-American Trade and Financial Agreement.—In 1946 a financial agreement was negotiated by which the United States extended a line of credit ($3,750,000,000) to assist the United Kingdom in the rehabilitation of its economy. At this time both countries agreed to support a broad program for the relaxation of trade barriers. Indeed, one announced purpose of the loan to Britain was that it would permit that country to make a more rapid transition to multilateral trading; the loan would thus enable the United Kingdom to remove exchange controls on current accounts, open up the so-called sterling area by permitting nations within the system to trade freely with other countries and eliminate quantitative import restrictions. Commitments covering all of these matters were embodied in the Anglo-U.S. agreement, which thereby served to facilitate the restoration of world trade on a multilateral, nonrestrictive and nondiscriminatory basis.

International Trade Organization.—Despite the measures of international economic collaboration outlined above, much remained to be done at the close of 1946 to achieve full implementation of the objectives of the charter insofar as international commercial policies were concerned. The Bretton Woods program was designed chiefly to promote world monetary stability and to assist in postwar economic reconstruction and development. There was still need for more direct action to eliminate trade barriers and to establish "rules of the game" to achieve international collaboration on a multilateral trading basis.

In Feb. 1946, the Economic and Social council of the United Nations adopted a resolution calling for an international conference to consider the creation of an International Trade organization (I.T.O.). It also created a preparatory committee of 19 nations to arrange for the conference, to draft the agenda for its deliberations and to prepare a draft charter for the proposed organization. When the preparatory committee met in London in Oct. 1946, the United States delegates brought with them a proposal for co-operative action (*Proposals for Expansion of World Trade and Employment*) to break down trade barriers and expand world trade. This draft, suggesting the possible character of the I.T.O. charter, embodied a code of international trading principles and suggested that the organization should constitute an agreement among the signatory powers:

(1.) To reduce trade restrictions and discriminations imposed by governments;

(2.) To eliminate restrictions on trade imposed by private business groups;

(3.) To prevent, by intergovernmental action, disorder in the markets for certain primary commodities;

(4.) To seek full employment by co-operative rather than conflicting nationalistic measures which in the past failed to accomplish their employment objectives and further restricted international commerce;

(5.) To establish an international organization—the International Trade organization—to administer the world trade charter and to provide an effective forum for later negotiation of problems of international commerce.

The various postwar projects and plans outlined above had far-reaching potentialities for the trade of the world. The basis for co-operative action among states had been laid so that restrictive trade practices might be eliminated. In anticipation of the actual signing of the charter of the new International Trade organization, the United States, in Nov. 1946, announced its intention to pursue still further its reciprocal trade agreements program by negotiating on a scale much more comprehensive than previously. The United States indicated that early in 1947 it would negotiate simultaneously with 18 leading trading nations and that it would seek most-favoured-nation agreements providing reciprocal reductions in tariff duties and modifications of other barriers. It was also suggested that should these negotiations prove successful, multilateral concessions among the other negotiating countries might be agreed upon to facilitate a general reduction of trade barriers throughout the world.

The various efforts toward international collaboration to establish more liberal trading practices were impeded, of course, by the same social forces which during the interwar period contributed to the break-down of the world trading system. In many countries, those economic interest groups, which were, or believed themselves to be, the beneficiaries of trade restrictions, indicated their staunch opposition to the projects outlined above for eliminating trade barriers. Moreover, by the close of the war a substantial number of countries, including a few in Latin America, indicated that they intended to employ protective duties or related controls (especially import and exchange controls) to preserve or expand a variety of war-born industries. Perhaps the major contradictory trend was the manifestation of an increasing expectation by citizens in the principal industrial countries that governments would intervene in economic affairs to prevent social disorganization, to stabilize the national economies and to assure some measure of full employment. This, of course, was the motive for exchange and import controls in many countries during the '30s; it served also as a rationale of the autarkic practices by the aggressive totalitarian states and it was the purpose of commodity control schemes (*e.g.,* those for sugar, wool and wheat) adopted by other countries. The victory of the British Labour party in the election of 1946 was in part a dynamic illustration of this point of view. International trade restrictions, state trading and commodity control programs thus came to be regarded in various quarters as means by which nations might insulate or protect themselves from the hazards and shocks generated in other countries. Thus, at the close of 1946 there were substantial forces resisting the program for multilateralism in world trade. (*See* also INTERNATIONAL TRADE.)

BIBLIOGRAPHY.—Percy W. Bidwell, *The Invisible Tariff* (1939), *A Commercial Policy for the United Nations* (1945); Stuart Chase, *Tomorrow's Trade* (1945); J. B. Condliffe, *The Reconstruction of World Trade* (1940); P. T. Ellsworth, *International Economics* (1938); Paul V. Horn, *International Trade Principles and Practices* (1945); League of Nations, *Commercial Policy in the Interwar Period,* Economic and Financial Series, 1942 II. A.G., Geneva, (1942); Eugene Staley, *World Economic Development* (Montreal, 1944); August Maffrey and Hal B. Larry, *Foreign Trade after the War,* U.S. Department of Commerce Economic Series No. 28 (1943); U.S. Department of State, *Proposals for Expansion of World Trade and Employment* (1945); U.S. Tariff Commission, *Economic Controls and Commercial Policy in Brazil* (1945). (One of a series of 20 monographs on economic controls and commercial policy in the Latin American republics). (D. LH.)

Tasmania

One of the six states of the commonwealth of Australia, Tasmania is an island situated 140 mi. south of the east corner of the continent of Australia. Area: including sundry small islands, 26,215 sq.mi.; pop. (1937 est.) 232,693; (1946 census) 251,260 (99% of British origin). Chief towns: Hobart (cap.) in south (pop. 10,838, 1943) and Launceston in north (35,785). Language: English. Religion: Church of England 54%, Roman Catholic 17%, Methodist 14%, Presbyterian 7%, Baptist 2%, Congregational 2%, others 4%. Governors: Sir Ernest Clark (Aug. 4, 1933–Aug. 4, 1945); Admiral Sir Hugh Binney, (after Aug. 4, 1945). Prime ministers: Albert G. Ogilvie (June 22, 1934–June 10, 1939); Edmund Dwyer-Gray (June 11, 1939–Dec. 18, 1939); Robert Cosgrave (after Dec. 18, 1939).

In 1937 Tasmania was beginning to recover from the world depression. Foremost among industrial undertakings was the state hydroelectric system, which showed an in-

Tasmania: *Statistical Data*

Item	1938 Value (000's omitted)	1938 Amount or Number	1941 Value (000's omitted)	1941 Amount or Number	1945 Value (000's omitted)	1945 Amount or Number
Exchange rate						
Great Britain		£A 1.25=£1		£A 1.25=£1		£A 1.25=£1
United States		£A 1=$3.895		£A 1=$3.198		£A 1=$3.198
Finance						
State revenues	£2,900* ($14,178)		£2,317* ($9,341)		£2,902* ($11,695)	
State expenditures	£2,894* ($14,151)		£2,461* ($9,923)		£2,917* ($11,756)	
State debt	£20,587* ($100,651)		£22,337* ($90,062)		£24,063* ($96,973)	
Transportation						
Railroads		651 mi.		642 mi.		642 mi.
Highways		7,919 "		8,039 mi.†		...
Communication						
Telephones		17,055		19,565		22,135
Telegraph lines		3,495 mi.*		3,516 mi.*‡		3,545 mi.*
Radio sets		39,392*§		44,716*		47,930*
Minerals						
Copper ore, ingot and matte		12,729 tons		...		11,148 tons‖
Zinc and concentrates		25,366 "		...		21,078 tons‖
Tin and tin ore		1,279 "		...		949 tons‖
Gold		22,200 oz.		19,908 oz.		17,245 oz.‖
Lead		10,652 tons		11,753 tons		8,633 tons‖
Crops						
Apples		115,008 "		123,552 "		192,547 " ¶
Hay		112,995 "		95,180 "		153,834 " ¶
Potatoes		99,969 "		114,041 "		217,800 " ¶
Livestock						
Sheep		2,625,690		2,682,375‡		2,156,071♀
Cattle		262,407		259,108‡		224,668♀
Swine		45,317		46,713‡		46,915♀
Horses		30,458		29,406‡		25,885♀
Sea products						
Fish		1,197 tons		...		2,803 tons¶
Crayfish		65,652 doz.		...		63,668 doz.¶
Manufactures—Total	£3,738§ ($16,577)	...	£5,601†($22,600)	...	£7,023¶ ($28,337)	...
Industrial metals machines, implements, etc.	£1,338§ ($5,933)	...	£1,757† ($7,090)	...	£2,770¶ $11,177)	...
Food, drink and tobacco	£798§ ($3,541)	...	£976† ($3,937)	...	£1,266¶ ($5,107)	...
Woodworking and basketware	£379§ ($1,682)	...	£519† ($2,095)	...	£520¶ ($2,098)	...
Paper, printing and binding	£359§ ($1,590)	...	£935† ($3,774)	...	£996¶ ($4,020)	...
Education						
State schools		459		424		369‖
Enrolment		34,553		33,354		30,916‖
Teachers		1,274		1,273		1,239‖
Private schools		64		63		62‖
Enrolment		6,523		6,886		7,403‖
Teachers		328		329		309‖
Universities		1		1†		1¶
Enrolment		288		353†		407¶
Teachers		37		42†		39¶
Technical schools		5		6		...
Enrolment		1,851		3,163		...
Teachers		133		233		...

*Year ending June 30. †1942. ‡1940. §1939. ‖1943. ¶1944. ♀Year ending March 31.

crease of plant capacity from 81,000 h.p. (1937) to 197,900 h.p. (1946). Work in hand in 1946 was estimated to provide additional 37,500 h.p., making a total of 235,000 h.p., and more additions were contemplated. Within the ensuing two or three years £A1,000,000 was to be spent on this work. The cost of the hydroelectric scheme including transmission and distributing mains equipment was, up to 1946, approximately £A9,000,000. The undertaking showed a profit after meeting all working expenses and interest and making adequate provision for redemption of loans and depreciation of assets.

Before World War II the power committee of the standards association of Australia estimated that on a basis of a 50% load factor and 80% turbine and generator efficiency, the potential water power of the whole of Australia was about 4,750,000 h.p. Of this total 3,500,000 h.p. was available in Tasmania. At 100% load factor, therefore, Tasmania's potential hydroelectric power was about 1,750,000 h.p. To realize as much as possible of this reserve of industrial power extensive developmental works were being planned, and much had already been accomplished. After the outbreak of World War II, the hydroelectric commission had installed five more power stations, with machines producing 92,000 h.p. Orders had been placed in Britain for plants that would provide an additional 34,000 h.p. Toward the end of 1946, big water diversion works were in progress so that the new plant could be put into operation in order that Tasmania, one of the least industrialized of the Australian states, could be transformed into a centre of great industrial activity.

The successful establishment during the interwar period of works for the pulping of the wood of a Tasmanian tree (*eucalyptus regnans*) and the manufacture of paper from it was the triumph, after many years of experiment, of invention and technical skill over difficulties caused by the nature of this hardwood. The first mill, situated on the northwest coast, made fine printing and writing paper. Production began in 1936. In 1939, eight Australian newspaper companies formed a company for the production of newsprint. The original plant was being extended in 1946 to make it capable of producing 100,000 tons of newsprint annually. It was estimated that this industry would ultimately save Australia some £A2,750,000 yearly, the cost of imported supplies of paper pulp for newsprint.

(C. W. Js.)

BIBLIOGRAPHY.—*Statistics of Tasmania* (1937 *et seq.*) and *Pocket Year Book of Tasmania* (1937 *et seq.*), both published by the government printer, Hobart; Walch's *Tasmanian Almanac* (1937 *et seq.*).

Tassigny, Jean de Lattre de

De Lattre de Tassigny (1889–), French army officer, was born Feb. 2, 1889, at Mouilleron-en-Paretz (Vendée department). A graduate of St. Cyr, he served in World War I and was severely wounded in the Rif campaign in 1925.

In World War II, De Tassigny commanded the "Iron Division"—so-called because of its stout resistance against the Germans in the battle of Rethel in 1940. After Pétain signed the armistice in June 1940, De Tassigny was assigned to southern Tunisia but returned to France and in Jan. 1942 assumed command of the 16th division at Montpellier.

At the time of the Allied landings in North Africa in Nov. 1942, De Tassigny prepared to organize resistance against the Germans in southern France. Vichy troops promptly countermanded his orders. Arrested, De Tassigny was tried by a Vichy tribunal Jan. 9, 1943, and was sentenced to ten years imprisonment. He escaped from prison nine months later and made his way to London, where he joined De Gaulle's movement. De Gaulle promoted him to the rank of major general and Eisenhower made him commander of French forces operating with the U.S. 7th army which took part in the Allied landings in southern France in Aug. 1944. During the final months of 1944, De Tassigny was in command of the French 1st army that was part of the Gen. Dever's 6th army group operating on the southern flank of the French-German border.

On June 5, 1945, he assumed his post as French member of the four-power Allied Control council for Germany.

Taxation

The successive impact of the great depression of the '30s and World War II left in their wake levels of taxation, debt and expenditure that dwarfed those to which the 1920s had been accustomed. The ten eventful years which ended in 1946 included what was for most countries either the closing years of an era of depression financing, or alternately a period of armaments boom. There followed in all cases the financial upheaval accompanying the outbreak of World War II. Attention will be concentrated here upon the changes which took place during these ten years in the finances of the central governments of the United States, Great Britain and Canada. Primary emphasis will be placed upon budget and tax policy, although some reference also will be made to borrowing operations.

Tables I, II and III show the movement of total revenue, total expenditure and war expenditure as well as the deficits or surpluses experienced by the central governments in the United States, Great Britain and Canada.

Table I.—*United Kingdom*

Year ending March 31	Revenue Excluding Loans	Total Expenditures	War Expenditures	Deficit or Surplus
	(In millions of pounds)			
1935–36	845	842	136	+3
1936–37	897	902	191	−5
1937–38	947	920	262	+27
1938–39	1,009	1,019	382	−10
1939–40	1,132	1,408	1,141	−276
1940–41	1,495	3,971	3,220	−2,476
1941–42	2,175	4,876	4,085	−2,701
1942–43	2,922	5,740	4,840	−2,818
1943–44	3,149	5,909	4,950	−2,760
1944–45	3,355	6,180	5,125	−2,825

Source: Great Britain. Financial Accounts of the United Kingdom (various years).

Table II.—*United States*

Year ending June 30	Revenue Excluding Loans	Total Expenditures	War Expenditures	Deficit or Surplus
	(In millions of dollars)			
1935–36	4,116	8,666	900	−4,550
1936–37	5,029	8,177	929	−3,148
1937–38	5,855	7,239	1,029	−1,384
1938–39	5,165	8,707	1,206	−3,542
1939–40	5,387	8,998	1,657	−3,611
1940–41	7,607	12,711	6,301	−5,104
1941–42	12,799	32,397	26,011	−19,598
1942–43	22,282	78,179	72,109	−55,897
1943–44	44,149	93,744	87,039	−49,595
1944–45	46,457	100,405	90,029	−53,948

Source: Annual Report of the secretary of the treasury, 1945, pp. 440–441.

Table III.—*Canada*

Year ending March 31	Revenue Excluding Loans	Total Expenditures	War Expenditures	Deficit or Surplus
	(In millions of Canadian dollars)			
1935–36	373	533	17	−160
1936–37	454	532	23	−78
1937–38	517	534	33	−17
1938–39	502	553	34	−51
1939–40	562	681	118	−119
1940–41	864	1,242	752	−378
1941–42	1,483	1,880	1,340	−397
1942–43	2,310	4,380	3,724	−2,070
1943–44	2,920	5,322	4,587	−2,402
1944–45	2,906	5,246	4,418	−2,340

Source: Various budget speeches and appendices.

A very striking difference appears at the outset of the period between the position of the British budget and those of the other two countries. In the fiscal year 1936 the United Kingdom showed an excess of revenues over expenditures, while both Canada and the United States were experiencing substantial deficits. Canadian revenues for the fiscal year 1936 covered only 70% of total expenditures; in the United States revenues were equal to only 48% of total expenditures.

As will be pointed out in some detail below, this difference reflected a variation in the budgetary policies pursued. However, it was also based to some extent upon the relative speed with which the British economy rebounded from the impact of the great depression and upon the effects of an armament boom which was just getting under way in that country.

The subsequent movement of expenditures in these countries can be followed more readily by means of Table IV, which expresses the expenditures of each year as a percentage of the amounts paid out in the fiscal year 1936. If attention is directed to the first four years of the decade, it can be seen that the British pattern again differed from that of the other two countries. British expenditures rose by roughly one-fifth, while the expenditures of Canada and the United States were both only slightly higher in 1939 than they had been in 1936.

This difference in the movement of total expenditures reflected the fact that in the United Kingdom outlays for armaments were increasing far more rapidly than in either the United States or Canada. Between 1936 and 1939 British expenditures for war purposes rose 181%. In 1936 they accounted for 16.2% of total expenditures; in 1939 they made up 37.5% of the total. During those same four years the war expenditures of the United States increased by roughly one-third; those of Canada doubled. In 1939 war expenditures were 13.8% of the total in the United States; 6.1% in Canada.

In spite of the relatively rapid increase in the total expenditures of the United Kingdom between 1936 and 1939, its budget showed a net surplus for the four year period. The accounts of both Canada and the United States showed substantial deficits. In both these countries, the size of the deficit declined with reviving business to a low point in fiscal 1938, only to rise again in the following year.

Reference to Table V, which shows the percentage of total expenditures covered by revenues other than loans,

Table IV.—Total Expenditures Expressed as a Per Cent of Total Expenditures in 1935–36

Year	Canada	Great Britain	United States
1935–36	100	100	100
1936–37	100	107	94
1937–38	100	109	84
1938–39	104	121	100
1939–40	128	167	104
1940–41	233	472	147
1941–42	353	579	374
1942–43	820	682	902
1943–44	998	702	1,082
1944–45	984	734	1,159

Table V.—Per Cent of Total Expenditures Covered By Revenues Exclusive of Loans

Year	Canada	Great Britain	United States
1935–36	70	100	48
1936–37	85	99	61
1937–38	97	103	81
1938–39	91	99	59
1939–40	83	80	60
1940–41	70	38	60
1941–42	79	45	39
1942–43	51	51	28
1943–44	52	53	47
1944–45	51	54	46

reveals the fact that the deficits in the United States were relatively much larger than those of Canada. The deficits of the dominion government ranged from 30% of total expenditures in 1936 to 3% in 1938. Those of the federal government in the United States ranged from 52% of total expenditures in 1936 to 19% in 1938. In the year prior to the outbreak of war in Europe, Great Britain financed all but 1% of its expenditures without the use of loans; Canada covered all but 9%; the United States showed a deficit equal to 41% of its total expenditures.

The outbreak of World War II in Sept. 1939 brought a sharp acceleration in the increase of public spending in both the United Kingdom and Canada. The expenditures of the United States advanced more slowly until it too entered the war in the fiscal year 1942. The so-called "defense" period which intervened was in fact a period of armaments boom similar in many respects to the British rearmament between 1935 and 1939.

The advance in public spending in these three countries during the war itself carried to levels that would have been considered stupendous a few years earlier. When British expenditures reached their peak in 1945, they were no less than 735% of the level in 1936. The expenditures of the federal government in the United States reached a peak of $100,000,000,000 in 1945, over 11 times the amount spent 10 years earlier. The peak Canadian expenditures of 1944 were ten times as large as those of 1936.

These staggering increases were of course based upon the rapid advance in war expenditures. In the peak years noted above, the latter made up 83% of the total in Great Britain, 86% in Canada and 90% in the United States.

All three countries made a valiant effort to increase their tax revenue, to compensate at least in part for this spectacular increase in war expenditures. During the decade ending in 1945, the last year of the war, Great Britain's revenues other than those derived from loans rose by about 300%, those of Canada by 600%. The revenues of the federal government in the United States in 1945 were about 11 times as large in 1945 as they had been 10 years before.

Yet even these large increases in revenue fell far short of matching the current advance in expenditures. Table V indicates that in Canada the percentage of total expenditures covered by revenues other than loans declined from 79% in 1942 to 51% in 1945; in Great Britain this percentage dropped from 80% in 1940 to 51% in 1943, in the United States from 60% in 1941 to 28% in 1943. At the close of World War II, each country was financing in the neighbourhood of half its total expenditures by methods other than borrowing.

The full impact of these wartime deficits is revealed in the statistics of public debt which are summarized in Table VI. By the end of 1945 the Canadian debt was roughly four times as large as it had been ten years earlier. The British debt was nearly three times as large; and the debt of the United States had reached a level roughly seven and one-half times that at the beginning of the decade.

To summarize, the ten eventful years brought to Great Britain, Canada and the United States a tremendous increase in the expenditures, revenues and indebtedness of their central governments. In Great Britain, war and the preparation for war had been the dominant themes of the decade. In Canada and the United States the period began with several years in which the central problem before the economy was not war but business revival. In

Table VI.—*Public Debt, 1936–45*
(as of end of fiscal year)

Fiscal Year	Canada* March 31 $ Canadian	U.K.† March 31 £	U.S.‡ June 30 $
	(In millions of national currency)		
1936	3,265	7,796	33,779
1937	3,337	7,797	36,425
1938	3,315	8,026	37,165
1939	3,386	8,163	40,440
1940	3,696	8,932	42,968
1941	4,372	11,399	48,961
1942	5,866	14,073	72,422
1943	7,861	16,855	136,696
1944	10,689	19,595	201,003
1945	13,539	22,505	258,682

*Canada. Includes internal and external debt (unmatured funded debt and treasury bills.) Data from *Annual Financial Statements* (Budget) of the Minister of Finance.
†United Kingdom. Includes internal and external debt. Data from *The Statist* (London), Oct. 13, 1945, p. 878.
‡United States. Data from *Annual Report* of the Secretary of the Treasury, 1945, p. 531.

Canada this era ended abruptly with the outbreak of World War II. In the United States there was an interval of "defense" financing between the depression finance of the first four years and the period of active participation in World War II.

Budgetary Policies.—The budget policies of the central governments in the United States and Canada during the period 1936–39 reflected the fact that the chief economic problem confronting these governments was the revival of business. In both countries the first reaction to the crisis of 1931–33 had been an attempt to restore balance in the budget of the central government as quickly as possible. This objective had not actually been attained. Instead, each country had experienced an unbroken sequence of deficits, and each had evolved a policy tending to justify the temporary maintenance of an unbalanced budget in the face of the depression emergency. The policy in question was the same in each case; it was the so-called "double budget." Under the latter, expenditures were divided into ordinary or current expenditures on the one hand, and extraordinary or emergency outlays on the other. Only the former were to be covered by current revenues. The latter, being of an emergency character, should be financed by borrowing.

In spite of the fact that President Roosevelt's budget message of Jan. 1935 forecast an over-all deficit of $3,892,000,000 exclusive of debt retirement, this double budget philosophy made it possible for him to avoid recommending additional taxation.[1] The president reported that anticipated revenues available for general purposes were $3,422,000,000, which was well in excess of the regular or ordinary expenditures of $3,302,000,000. The balance of a $7,314,000,000 total expenditure was made up of recovery and relief items, the greater part of which was to be financed by borrowing. The program which these extraordinary expenditures financed was, of course, intended to assist in the revival of business which in turn would bring with it a budget that was balanced on an over-all basis.

The Canadians had reached the same solution somewhat earlier, and in his budget speech of April 18, 1934, Finance Minister Edgar Rhodes, had explained the amount of additional taxation which was needed by comparing total revenues with *ordinary* expenditures. No estimate of *total* expenditures was mentioned in this connection. It was merely stated that the revenues would suffice to cover *ordinary* expenditures and "leave a surplus of $8,800,000 to apply on capital and extraordinary expenditures." Similar tactics were used in the budget speech of March 22, 1935. As a matter of fact, the well-established double budget policy of the dominion government provided a clear precedent for the use of this policy by President Roosevelt in his budget message of Jan. 3, 1935.

The budget policy used by the United Kingdom in 1935 was quite different. Here too the first reaction to the impact of the great crisis had been a determination to restore balance in the national budget. But, unlike Canada and the United States, Great Britain was willing and able to put into effect the economy measures and new taxes which the restoration of a balanced budget required. These results were facilitated by a somewhat more speedy recovery from the crisis of 1931–33 than had taken place in either Canada or the United States. Nevertheless, the fact remains that in 1935 Chancellor of the Exchequer Neville Chamberlain was able to set out with a budget that was in balance and a well-established policy of keeping it that way.

Depression Budgets in the U.S. and Canada, 1936–39.—President Roosevelt again used the double budget device in his message of Jan. 3, 1936. Again it was possible to forecast that revenues other than loans were adequate to cover regular expenditures. Again no additional taxes were recommended. The volume of expenditures for recovery and relief was estimated to be substantially lower than in previous years with a corresponding reduction in the amount of necessary borrowing. The tone of his message was optimistic and the president concluded with these words:

> Our policy is succeeding. The figures prove it. Secure in the knowledge that steadily decreasing deficits will turn in time into steadily increasing surpluses, and that it is the deficit of today which is making possible the surplus of tomorrow, let us pursue the course that we have mapped.

The president's budget message of Jan. 5, 1937, reflected the continued revival of business in the United States. For the first time since the great crisis, a budget message was presented which predicted a balance not merely on a partial but on an over-all basis. As a matter of fact, a surplus of $1,136,000,000 was forecast for the fiscal year 1938. Naturally, there were no recommendations for the levy of new taxes. The device of the double budget, which had been at the centre of the policy set out in the two previous messages, was not used in the message of Jan. 5, 1937.

Unfortunately, the downturn of business during the autumn of 1937 belied the optimism of this budget message. By January of the following year it was obvious that, instead of a surplus, the fiscal year 1938 would produce another deficit, albeit a much smaller one than that experienced in preceding years. The president's message of Jan. 3, 1938, emphasized the relationship between the downturn in business in 1937 and this failure to attain the predicted over-all balance in the budget. A somewhat smaller deficit was predicted for 1939, but no attempt was made to justify it by the double budget device. It was merely pointed out that the anticipated deficit was lower than that expected in the current fiscal year, and that 1939 would be the third year in succession in which the deficit would have declined. The continued recession in business conditions also belied this prediction. The actual deficit incurred in 1939 was $3,542,000,000 as compared with $1,384,000,000 in 1938.

The president's budget message of Jan. 3, 1939, was the last of the predefense period. In it a deficit of $3,972,000,000 was predicted for the current fiscal year, and one of $3,326,000,000 for fiscal 1940. In spite of his disap-

[1]The only tax action recommended was the renewal of certain excises which were due to expire at the end of the current fiscal year.

pointment over this situation, the president reaffirmed the idea that depressed business conditions were not appropriate to a formal balancing of the budget. Ordinary expenditures were again distinguished from extraordinary, and in addition it was emphasized that many of the latter were being made for projects of a self-liquidating character. The suggestion was advanced that such expenditures should not really be included among the items set out against current revenues in order to determine whether a budget was in balance, but "should occupy a separate category in budgetary reporting." This was the idea basic to the so-called "capital budget" which had been developed in Sweden. A table was presented in which the president compared the deficits of the period 1931–40 with the capital outlays of the same period. He pointed out that this table "clearly shows that the greater part of the deficits and the larger part of the increase in the public debt have gone for permanent additions to our national wealth." It was argued that "the balance has been an investment in the conservation of our human resources."

This justification of a continued deficit policy accompanied the recommendation that congress "consider moderate tax increases which would approximately meet the increased expenditures on the account of the proposed national defense program and the program for agricultural parity payments, for which no revenue provision has as yet been made."

Thus it appears that in 1939 the federal government of the United States was still operating with a substantial deficit. The president's justification for the deficit now included the idea of the capital budget as well as the distinction between ordinary and extraordinary expenditures which he had used in 1935. However, the basis for this policy was the idea that the deficits incurred would make a substantial contribution to the revival of private business.

The problem of recovery was also reflected in the Canadian budgets between 1936 and the outbreak of World War II in Sept. 1939. However, the policy of the double budget, which had been reaffirmed in Finance Minister Edgar Rhodes' message of 1935, went by the board one year later. A general election had taken place in the interval and the budget message of May 1, 1936, was presented by a new finance minister, Charles Dunning. While Dunning was not unmindful of the extent of industrial recovery achieved in Canada, he took a decidedly less optimistic position than his predecessor had done. He was not inclined to avoid unpleasant facts and disposed of the double budget with the following pithy remarks:

> It is also proposed to depart from what I have sometimes called the "bridge score" method of accounting—so much above the line and so much below the line—and to present clearly the over-all deficit in the government's accounts. In the past we have too frequently misled ourselves by the form in which our government accounts were presented. We have pointed with pride to a small surplus on ordinary account and we have tended somewhat to minimize the importance of large deficits resulting from capital and special expenditures. It is time to look the facts squarely in the face. If the people of Canada are fully aware of all the facts, I am confident they will support us in taking the steps necessary to achieve that balance of government revenues and expenditures which in my opinion cannot safely be postponed much longer.

Dunning went on to emphasize the amount of the existing deficit and to announce the policy of obtaining a balance in the budget as a whole as follows:

> I am not an alarmist. On the contrary, I am confident that common sense and sound economic policies can solve our immediate problems. Moreover I am convinced that this country can bear all the burdens which the war and the depression and past mistakes have saddled upon it, great as they have been. Nevertheless I believe that no country can go on indefinitely with heavily unbalanced budgets and continue to maintain either the confidence of investors or the basis upon which her economy can function healthily and vigorously. We have now reached the stage where delay should no longer be tolerated. We must make an immediate approach to a balanced budget and we must be able to show that complete equilibrium can be reached within a reasonable time.

Dunning's policy led him to recommend an increase in the sales tax which, together with certain other tax increases, was expected to reduce the deficit in the forthcoming fiscal year from $125,000,000 to $100,000,000.

He was not unmindful of the need for business recovery. When he turned his back on the idea that a governmental deficit should be used as a positive instrument in a recovery program, he did so in the expectation that an approach to a balanced budget would be a more effective weapon. Moreover, he proposed to supplement his budget balancing program with an excursion into the field of incentive taxation, which will be described later in some detail.

In 1937 Dunning's objective of a balanced budget seemed well within reach. Continued recovery plus the new taxes of 1936 had reduced the current deficit to $78,000,000, as compared with $160,000,000 in the previous year. Further increases in revenues were forecast, and the deficit for the coming year was estimated to be only $35,000,000. This was approximately the amount of the current deficit on the account of the Canadian National railways. Consequently, Dunning advanced no proposals for additional taxation.

"Quoth the Raven, 'Why Not Me?' " Congress continued to ignore the sales tax in 1942, as pointed out in this cartoon by Duffy of the *Baltimore Sun*

The actual experience of the dominion in the fiscal year 1938 exceeded expectations, the over-all deficit incurred being only $18,000,000. However, the downturn in business in late 1937 and the failure of the Canadian wheat crop made it quite evident that the forthcoming year would not be as satisfactory.

The budget message of June 16, 1938, again specifically rejected deficit financing as an instrument of recovery policy, both in the crude form of financing by the issue of paper money and by borrowing in order to finance deliberately incurred deficits. The finance minister's attitude towards the "pump priming" argument then receiving so much attention in the United States was summarized in the following statement:

> . . . We have had several conclusive demonstrations of the principle that government expenditure to create or stimulate employment will not have beneficial results if it is carried on in such a way or on such a scale as to create an atmosphere of fear and uncertainty. It is of little use to prime the pump of business enterprise with government expenditure if at the same time we dry up the springs of private initiative which feed the well. . . .

On the other hand, Dunning did not insist upon an absolute balance in the budget for the forthcoming year. He forecast a deficit of $23,000,000 and stated that, "in view of the current business situation, we have not thought it wise to attempt this year to wipe out a possible deficit of the moderate proportions I have indicated by imposing further burdens upon industry and upon the people."

The actual deficit of $51,000,000 experienced in 1939 was substantially larger than anticipated. Although the budget message of April 25, 1939, reported that the dominion had recovered substantially from the effects of the downturn of 1937, the minister's remarks indicated that he was under pressure both from the people who wanted him to "prime the pump" and those who wished the budget to be balanced immediately.

Before the end of the calendar year 1939 Canada was at war, and a new budget had taken the place of the one submitted by Dunning on April 25.

It is quite evident that although the deficits incurred in Canada between 1935 and 1939 followed the same general pattern as those in the United States, the policies behind them were radically different. In the United States, the continuance of the deficits was justified by the president in terms of an economic philosophy based upon the idea that such deficits were a useful instrument of recovery policy, to which he added the further thought that many of the expenditures which the deficits financed had been made on "self-liquidating" projects for the financing of which loans were an appropriate instrument. The Canadian policy turned its back on this philosophy, and aimed instead at a restoration of business confidence through the attainment of a balance in the government's budget; it attempted to stimulate the expenditures of private business further through a program of incentive taxation. However, at the close of the period in Canada, it was admitted that a balanced budget could not be obtained quickly, and it was pointed out that private enterprise had a definite role to play in the restoration of business prosperity.

Great Britain, 1935–39.—Great Britain had a balanced budget in 1935 and attempted to maintain that balance during the period of rearmament which preceded the outbreak of World War II. As Table I indicates, revenue other than loans exceeded total expenditures for the period 1936–39 taken as a whole. This was the result of a policy of levying additional taxes each year to match in full the anticipated increase in armament expenditures. The budget message of April 1936 estimated that such expenditures would produce a deficit of £21,000,000. The entire amount was to be financed by additional taxation. The message of April 1937 reported a further increase in armaments spending, anticipated a deficit of £15,000,000, and provided for additional taxes of a like amount. Again in the budget message of April 1938 a deficit of about £30,000,000 was anticipated on the basis of the increase in armaments expenditures. This deficit also was to be covered by additional taxation.

The break with this policy came in Sir John Simon's budget message of April 1939. This time the anticipated increase in armament expenditures was of far greater size, and it no longer seemed expedient to provide all of the additional revenue by taxation. On the contrary, only £24,500,000 was to come from new taxes, and £280,000,000 was to be raised by borrowing. With this budget Great Britain really entered the realm of war finance.

U.S. "Defense Period."—As has already been pointed out, there were no transitional or rearmament budgets in Canada, but there was a clearly marked transition or "defense" period in the United States which covered the interval between 1939 and the entrance of the United States into World War II. The first budget message of the so-called "defense" period was presented on Jan. 3, 1940. It was prefaced by a review of the budgetary policies of the '30s. The speed of the revival from the business recession of 1937–38 was compared with the much slower recovery from the depression following 1929, and much of the credit for this difference was assigned to the deficit policy of 1937 and 1938.

As for the immediate future, the president pointed out that although there had been substantial business recovery, there were still large numbers of unemployed. He believed that it would be dangerous to curtail too suddenly or too drastically the support which the federal deficit was giving to business activity and enunciated the following policy:

> We should count upon a natural increase in receipts from current taxes and a decrease in emergency expenditures, and we should try to offset the unavoidable increase in expenditures for national defense by special tax receipts, and thus hope to secure for the over-all picture, a gradual tapering off, rather than an abrupt cessation of the deficit.
>
> In the proposed budget I have tried to interpret the wishes of our people. They want to strengthen our national defenses and are prepared to pay additional taxes for this purpose. They wish to attain, if possible, an over-all decrease in expenditures. They would like to see a reduction in the deficit but not of a magnitude that would imperil the progress of recovery.

The deficit forecast for fiscal 1941 was $2,176,000,000. It was indicated that a tax program would be introduced providing $450,000,000 in additional revenue and reducing the anticipated deficit to $1,716,000,000.

These estimates were revised upwards very drastically later in the year as the German army began to overrun country after country in Western Europe. The defense expenditures as estimated in the budget message of Jan. 3 were about $1,940,000,000. In June this total was raised to $3,250,000,000, in August to $5,000,000,000. These figures did not include appropriations which could not be expended in the current fiscal year. If the latter were also taken into account, it appeared that by Aug. 5, 1940, congress had appropriated more than $14,000,000,000 for defense purposes exclusive of the cost of enforcing the acts for compulsory military training and putting the National Guard into active military service.

In spite of the enactment of two revenue bills by congress during 1940, one of which was calculated to produce about $1,000,000,000 additional revenue in a full year's operation while the other set up an excess profits tax that was estimated to produce a similar amount when in full operation, the federal deficit for fiscal 1941 was $5,104,000,000. This was far in excess of the $1,716,000,000 estimated in January on the basis of additional taxes of $450,000,000.

The budget message of Jan. 3, 1941, differed markedly from its predecessors. Defense had now taken the centre of the stage. Expenditures for this purpose were reported to constitute 62% of the total. The total defense program had risen to $28,480,000,000. A deficit was forecast for 1942 of $9,200,000,000 in spite of the fact that revenues were estimated to be 50% higher than in fiscal 1940, the last year prior to the defense period. This deficit was due entirely to the defense spending; anticipated revenues for 1942 exceeded the total of nondefense expenditures in that year.

In April 1941 Secretary Henry Morgenthau, Jr. appeared before the committee on ways and means to request an increase in taxes of $3,500,000,000 which would bring total revenues up to about two-thirds of anticipated total expenditures in the fiscal year 1942.

The continued acceleration of the defense program produced a drastic revision of the budget estimates in Aug. 1941. Total expenditures were estimated between $22,000,000,000 and $25,000,000,000 instead of $19,000,000,000 and the deficit was estimated between $13,000,000,000 and $16,000,000,000. In October new budget estimates were issued setting the deficit for 1942 at $12,500,000,000. Actually the deficit incurred in that fiscal year was $19,598,000,000, but before the year was out the country had moved from the defense period into a state of war.

Great Britain and Canada, 1939–45.—Reference to Tables I, II and III reveals that during the period of active participation in World War II the United Kingdom financed 50% of its total expenditures with revenues other than loans; Canada covered 57% without borrowing, the United States 41%. However, in appraising the relative vigour of the budgetary policies pursued by these countries, it must be borne in mind that the period of active participation was smaller for the United States, and that both Canada and Great Britain were covering substantially larger percentages of their total expenditures with revenues other than loans immediately prior to their entrance into the war.[2] Moreover, it must not be overlooked that although revenues equalled only 28% of total expenditures in 1943, they had risen to 46% of a much larger total in 1945.

There was a sharp contrast between the British and Canadian budget policies as expressed in the war budget messages which followed immediately upon the outbreak of World War II in Sept. 1939. In presenting his budget of Sept. 27, 1939, Sir John A. Simon estimated that in the year total outlays would be about £2,000,000,000 instead of £1,300,000,000 as he had estimated in April, and that the deficit would run to £1,110,000,000 instead of £380,000,000.

Simon stressed the inflationary impact of a spending program of this size and recommended a policy of financing the additional expenditures out of the proceeds of new taxation and loans purchased out of "genuine savings."

[2]In 1939 Canada covered 91% of its total expenditures with revenues other than loans; Great Britain 99%. In 1941 the United States covered only 60% of its total expenditures with current revenues.

The Canadian budget of Sept. 12, 1939, presented by J. L. Ilsley, also disclosed a substantial increase in the deficit. Ilsley emphasized the idea that the real cost of the war could not be postponed and could be avoided only by an increase in national productivity. However, the policy used in the British budget speech, that the current deficit should be financed without credit expansion, was rejected. Instead it was pointed out that the Canadian economic system had a good many idle resources which could be put to work through credit expansion. So long as this was true, a policy involving a certain amount of credit expansion was appropriate. When full employment was reached, deficits would become highly inflationary, and the objective of policy should be the one set out by Sir John Simon, namely, the financing of total expenditures out of taxes and loans purchased with current savings. Because Canada had not yet reached full employment, Ilsley was content with a tax program which would raise $21,000,000 during the current fiscal year, $62,000,000 when in full operation. These taxes would reduce the anticipated deficit for 1940 from $156,000,000 to $135,000,000.

In the budget speech of July 23, 1940, Sir Kingsley Wood reaffirmed the objective laid down by Sir John Simon in the preceding September. Inflation control continued to be the objective of British budget policy throughout the remainder of the war period. However, the inflationary pressure was of such magnitude that taxes and savings were only a part of a much broader program including import licensing, the allocation of raw materials and foodstuffs, price control, subsidies, rationing, full control of a segment of British industry and a limitation of the dividends which could be distributed by public companies during World War II.

The Canadian budget of June 24, 1940, repeated the general logic set out in the message of the previous September and reported that while the country had not yet reached full employment, it was approaching that level. It was reported further that although the first borrowing of the war had been from the chartered banks and hence was of an inflationary character, borrowing from the public had begun in Jan. 1940 and a war savings campaign had been inaugurated in May. A much larger deficit was in the offing, $700,000,000 as compared with $118,000,000 actually incurred in the preceding year. While new taxes were imposed, they were expected to leave a deficit of between $550,000,000 and $600,000,000.

The same general policies were reflected in the budget message of April 29, 1941. The dominion was still borrowing substantial amounts from the banks and the additional taxes proposed were calculated to yield only $250,000,000 in the current year as compared with a budgetary deficit of $618,000,000. The latter did not include the borrowing which the dominion undertook in order to finance Great Britain's exchange deficit in Canada. If this was also taken into account, the total amount of borrowing in 1942 was expected to be $1,250,000,000 in spite of the increase in taxes. There was a heavy emphasis on the need for additional savings.

By the time the next budget was reported in June 1942, it was apparent that Canada had reached the second of the two stages which Ilsley had described in 1939. Direct controls had been installed over wages, salaries and prices and existing controls over production had been extended. The deficit of the forthcoming year was estimated to be $2,228,000,000, and a tax program was recommended which would produce $378,000,000 in the current year.

The logic used in the budget of 1943 was quite similar.

"Whistling as He Works," was Bishop's idea of the average taxpayer's attitude concerning the pay-as-you-go tax bill passed by the U.S. congress in June 1943. The cartoon appeared in the *St. Louis Star-Times*

It was acknowledged that the Canadian economy had reached full employment; it was admitted that some of the current borrowing had been inflationary, and heavy emphasis was placed upon the need for stimulating voluntary savings in order to prevent inflation. This same emphasis on voluntary savings was the dominant theme of the budget message of June 26, 1944, which was really the last of the wartime series in Canada.

United States, 1941–45.—The policy of using a deficit as a device to facilitate the transition to full employment, which was the most notable feature of budgetary policy in Canada, was identical with that which President Roosevelt had enunciated in his "defense" financing budget message of Jan. 1941.

His budget message of Jan. 5, 1942, had a different emphasis. The president said:

> I stated last year in the Budget Message that extraordinary tax measures may be needed to "aid in avoiding inflationary price rises which may occur when full capacity is approached." The time for such measures has come. A well-balanced tax program must include measures which combat inflation. Such measures should absorb some of the additional purchasing power of consumers and some of the additional funds which accrue to business from increased consumer spending.
>
> A number of tax measures have been suggested for that purpose, such as income taxes collected at the source, pay-roll taxes, and excise taxes. I urge the Congress to give all these proposals careful consideration. Any tax is better than an uncontrolled price rise.

Congress was requested to impose a program of taxes which would yield $7,000,000,000 in new revenue. While this was a very large tax program, it left a deficit which was estimated at $35,400,000,000. Thus there was the same emphasis in the United States on the curtailment of private expenditures by rationing, price and credit controls as in Canada and the United Kingdom. There was also the same emphasis on the need for voluntary savings and the importance of the sale of savings bonds.

In the budget message of Jan. 6, 1943, these ideas found an even clearer expression. The president was now offering a $100,000,000,000 budget presenting "the maximum program for waging war." His message contained a full flowering of the anti-inflation philosophy which had been put forward by Sir John Simon in Great Britain in 1939 and which was to receive a strong statement in Ilsley's Canadian budget of March 1943. The president said:

> We must assure each citizen the necessities of life at prices which he can pay. . . . By a concerted effort to stabilize prices, rents, and wages we have succeeded in keeping the rise in the cost of living within narrow bounds. We shall continue those efforts, and we shall succeed.
>
> The stabilization of incomes and the absorption of excess purchasing power by fiscal measures are essential to the success of the stabilization program. I am confident that the Congress will implement that program by adequate legislation increasing taxation, savings, or both. Thus we help to "pay as we go" and make the coming peace easier for ourselves and our children. . . .
>
> We cannot hope to increase tax collections as fast as we step up war expenditures or to absorb by fiscal measures alone all excess purchasing power created by these expenditures. . . . Nevertheless the more nearly increases in tax receipts follow increases in expenditures, the better we safeguard our financial integrity and the easier the administration of price control and rationing.
>
> I believe that we should strive to collect not less than 16 billion dollars of additional funds by taxation, savings, or both, during the fiscal year 1944.
>
> On the basis of present legislation, we expect to meet 35 percent of total estimated Federal expenditures by current receipts during the fiscal year 1944. If the objective proposed in this message is adopted we shall meet approximately 50 percent of expenditures during the fiscal year 1944.

This objective of current revenues equal to 50% of total expenditures was a downward revision of a goal of two-thirds laid down by Secretary Morgenthau in April of the preceding year, when the emphasis on the inflation problem had been not nearly so great. Meanwhile, however, the level of expenditures had risen from $12,700,000,000 to an estimated $100,000,000,000, and a broad program of price and credit controls had been installed to assist in checking the rise in prices. The revenue which Morgenthau's two-thirds goal required was estimated at $9,200,000,000; that which Roosevelt's 50% objective necessitated was in the neighbourhood of $50,000,000.

There was a substantial difference of opinion between congress and the treasury with reference to the amount of additional tax revenue which should be raised in 1943. Congress was mindful of the extent of the tax burden which had already been imposed, and believed that so far as individual income taxation was concerned the country had reached the point of diminishing returns. Congress was aware that revenues had risen from $7,600,000,000 in the year prior to the outbreak of World War II to $22,000,000,000 in 1943, and Table II shows that the actual yield in the fiscal year 1944 would be no less than $44,000,000,000. Congress had good reason to be fearful of the repressive effect of additional taxation.

Congress was also left in considerable doubt as to the precise amount of money which would have to be raised if taxation was to be the primary bulwark against inflation. When Secretary Morgenthau appeared before the committee on ways and means in Oct. 1943, he did not ask for $16,000,000,000 in added taxes as the president had done in January, but for $10,500,000,000. Moreover, there were some among the president's advisers who felt that not even the $16,000,000,000 program originally proposed by the president would have served as the primary bulwark of an anti-inflation program. Hence it appeared likely that even if the treasury's program of $10,500,000,000 were adopted, primary emphasis would still have to be placed upon rationing and the control of individual prices. Consequently, the committee on ways and means stated its conviction that "the proper psychology (and freedom from fear of inflation) can be maintained only by strict economy in government expenditures through effective price control, rationing and wage control." This committee reported out a tax bill providing $2,300,000,000 in additional revenue. The bill agreed to in the conference committee was of similar size.

Before congress actually passed the Revenue act of 1943, the president had presented his budget message of Jan. 13, 1944, repeating the secretary of the treasury's request for $10,500,000,000 of additional taxation made in the preceding October. The president indicated that another $100,000,000,000 budget was in the offing and forecast a deficit of $59,000,000,000 in fiscal 1945. He stated that the $10,500,000,000 tax program was a necessary minimum.

When the much smaller tax bill passed by congress reached the president, it was vetoed, only to be passed over his veto in Feb. 1944.

The president's budget message of Jan. 3, 1945, did not repeat this request for additional tax revenue. Instead, it reported that the period of construction for war purposes had been completed and the supply lines filled. The forecast was made that war expenditures could be expected to taper off. Instead of a request for additional taxes there was a caution against premature tax reduction. The president stated:

> Wartime taxes must be maintained as long as large scale war expenditures are necessary. There is no justification for tax reductions as long as we are engaged in a major war.

In the last analysis, tax and budget policies were only a part of the anti-inflationary program in each of the three countries. Like the United States, Canada and Great Britain placed heavy reliance on controls of production, wages, prices and credit and upon rationing. Each of these countries found it inexpedient to finance the war by taxation alone. Each found it necessary to borrow on a large scale. Each tried to curb the inflationary effects of the borrowing by stimulating the purchase of government securities out of the current savings of their citizens. The net result of their anti-inflationary policies is shown in the cost of living statistics which are contained in Table VII.

Table VII.—*Cost of Living (1939=100)*

	United Kingdom*	Canada*	United States†
1939	100	100	100
1940	119	105	101
1941	129	110	106
1942	128	116	117
1943	128	118	124
1944	129	118	126
1945	132	119	129

**Monthly Labor Review*, May 1946, pp. 782–83. The 1939 and 1940 figures are for the month of August, those for later years are for June.

†Index of consumer's prices for moderate income families in large cities. *Monthly Labor Review*, May 1946, p. 793. The base was shifted from the 1935–1939 average to 1939.

The relatively small changes in the cost of living which took place during these years testified to the efficacy of the measures taken for the control of inflation. The extent of the achievement can be appreciated if it is borne in mind that during the relatively short period of 19 months during which the United States was an active participant in World War I, the cost of living in that country had risen about 38%. Between July 1914 and Nov. 1918 the cost of living in the United Kingdom had risen 120%; in Canada, 57%.

Tax Policy

The tax revenues of the central governments of Great Britain, Canada and the United States during the decade ending in 1935 are shown in Tables VIII, IX and X. Certain major differences in these three tax systems should be pointed out before attention is directed to the tax policies which these countries pursued during the succeeding decade.

In the fiscal year 1936 the federal government of the United States obtained roughly 36% of its tax revenues from levies on income. Something less than half of this amount came from the individual income tax, something more than half from that on corporate net income. An additional 10% was produced by the estate and gift taxes, and 10% more came from the customs duties. The bulk of the remaining 44% came from various types of excises, chiefly those on tobacco and liquor, and a system of excises on manufacturers' sales which had been imposed earlier in the depression period.

In the national tax system of Great Britain the income tax was somewhat more important than in the United States. It should also be borne in mind that in Great Britain the income tax continued to be essentially a levy on individuals, not broken down into a levy on individuals and one on corporations as in the United States. In 1936 the British death duties produced 12% of total tax revenues as compared with 10% in the United States. British customs duties were substantially more important than those of the United States; excises were somewhat less important. The former accounted for approximately 27% of total tax revenues in 1936, the latter for 22%. The relatively large yield of the British customs was explained in part by the in-

Table VIII.—*Revenues of the Central Government of the United Kingdom*
(Years ending March 31)
(In millions of dollars)

	1936	1937	1938	1939	1940	1941	1942	1943	1944	1945
Income and surtax	289.1	310.8	355.0	398.4	459.9	600.0	844.6	1,082.2	1,259.6	1,390.3
National defense contribution	...	...	1.4	21.9	26.9	24.1	21.9	30.6	33.4	33.3
Excess profits tax	...	...	...	...	...	72.1	247.2	346.9	466.7	477.1
Esrate duties, etc.	87.9	88.0	89.0	77.4	77.7	80.8	90.9	93.3	99.5	110.9
Customs	196.9	211.3	221.6	226.3	262.1	304.9	378.4	459.5	560.8	579.4
Excises	106.7	109.5	113.7	114.2	137.9	224.1	325.6	425.3	482.2	496.9
Stamp taxes	25.8	29.1	24.2	21.0	17.1	13.7	14.1	15.3	17.7	17.0
Motor vehicle duties	30.8	32.7	34.6	35.6	34.1	38.0	38.4	28.5	27.3	29.0
Misc. inland revenue	2.1	1.7	1.7	1.6	1.3	1.0	0.9	0.9	1.0	0.8
Total tax revenue	739.0	783.1	841.2	896.4	1,017.0	1,358.7	1,962.0	2,482.6	2,948.1	3,134.8
Non-tax revenue	39.7	41.6	31.3	30.8	32.2	50.2	112.1	337.3	90.4	103.3
Total ordinary revenue	778.7	824.7	872.5	927.2	1,049.2	1,408.9	2,074.1	2,819.9	3,038.5	3,238.1
Post office and broadcasting	66.1	71.9	76.1	79.0	83.1	86.4	100.6	102.5	110.6	116.6
Total revenues	884.8	896.6	948.6	1,006.2	1,132.3	1,495.3	2,174.7	2,922.4	3,149.1	3,354.7

Sources: *Economist* (London), April 15, 1939, p. 139; April 13, 1946, p. 595.

Table IX.—*Revenues of the Dominion Government in Canada*
(Years Ending March 31)
(In millions of dollars)

	1936	1937	1938	1939	1940	1941	1942	1943	1944	1945
Individual income tax*	82.7	44.3	50.6	56.8	56.5	116.6	324.3	561.2	840.4	796.4
Corporation income tax		58.0	69.8	85.2	77.9	131.6	185.8	348.0	311.4	276.4
Excess profits tax	...	...	...	...	...	24.0	135.2	454.6	468.7	465.8
Succession duties	...	...	...	...	...	...	7.0	13.3	15.0	17.3
Customs	74.0	83.8	93.5	78.8	104.3	130.8	142.4	119.0	167.9	115.1
Excise duties and taxes	157.1	198.5	232.8	213.0	227.0	372.8	563.5	627.4	780.7	695.0
Other taxes	3.4	2.4	2.5	2.5	2.5	2.5	2.6	12.3	7.7	8.2
Total tax revenue	317.3	387.1	449.2	436.3	468.3	778.2	1,360.9	2,136.7	2,591.8	2,374.1
Non-tax revenue	54.9	58.0	61.1	61.7	73.3	81.6	102.9	116.1	133.3	145.5
Special receipts and credits	0.4	9.1	6.4	4.2	20.5	4.8	69.6	57.5	194.9	387.2
Grand total revenue†	372.6	454.2	516.7	502.2	562.1	864.5	1,483.5	2,310.3	2,920.0	2,906.8

*Includes National Defense tax, tax on interest and dividends, and tax on rents and royalties.

†Before adjustment for amounts of income and excess profits taxes refundable after the war.

Source: *Appendix to the Budget, 1941–42*, p. 4; *ibid*, 1942–43, p. 4; budget speech, Oct. 12, 1945, p. 30.

Table X.—*Revenues of the Federal Government in the United States*

(Years ending June 30)
(In millions of dollars)

	1936	1937	1938	1939	1940	1941	1942	1943	1944	1945
Individual income tax	674	1,092	1,286	1,029	982	1,418	3,263	6,630	18,261	19,034
Corporation income tax	739	1,057	1,300	1,123	1,121	1,852	3,069	4,521	5,284	4,880
Excess profits tax*	15	25	37	27	18	192	1,670	5,146†	9,482†	11,147†
Capital stock tax	95	137	139	127	133	167	282	329	381	372
Estate and gift tax	379	306	417	361	360	407	433	447	511	643
Social security tax	‡	265	593	631	711	788	1,015	1,288	1,473	1,494
Manufacturers' excise	383	450	417	397	447	617	772	505	503	783
Liquor	505	594	567	587	624	820	1,048	1,423	1,619	2,310
Tobacco	501	552	568	580	608	698	781	923	988	932
Stamp taxes	69	70	46	41	39	39	42	45	50	66
Other excises	72	78	86	78	80	131	412	844	1,231	1,781
Subtotal—total excises	1,530	1,745	1,684	1,683	1,798	2,305	3,055	3,740	4,391	5,872
Other internal revenue	62	8	188	181	199	222	243	268	337	358
Total internal revenue	3,494	4,635	5,644	5,162	5,323	7,352	13,030	22,369	40,120	43,800
Adjustment from collections to daily treasury statement basis	+19	−302	−356	−504	−557	−651	−906	−1,328	+306	−1,181
Total internal revenue—adjusted	3,513	4,333	5,288	4,658	4,766	6,701	12,124	21,041	40,426	42,619
Customs	387	486	359	319	349	392	389	324	431	355
Total tax collections	3,900	4,819	5,647	4,977	5,115	7,093	12,513	21,365	40,857	42,974
Other receipts	216	210	208	187	273	515	286	916§	3,292§	3,483§
Total receipts‖	4,116	5,029	5,854	5,165	5,387	7,607	12,799	22,282	44,149	46,457

*Includes the declared value excess profits tax. †Before deduction for postwar refund.
‡Less than $500,000. §Includes refunds under the renegotiation of war contracts.
‖Before refunds.
Source: Annual report of the secretary of the treasury, 1945.

stallation of new and higher duties early in the depression, largely for protectionist purposes.

The dominion tax system in 1936 was quite different from those of the United States and Great Britain. Here income taxes were much less important. In 1936 they produced only 26% of total tax revenues. There were no dominion death duties, and the yield of the customs duties made up 23% of the total tax revenue. On the other hand, Canada had a general sales tax which produced 24% of its total tax revenues in 1936. In that year this sales tax plus the excises accounted for roughly one-half the dominion's total tax revenue. The importance of the sales tax in the Canadian system had been accentuated by its central position in the tax programs of the early years of the depression, and by the decline in the productivity of the customs duties. The latter had accounted for 44% of total tax revenue in 1931.

The United States, 1935–39.—As pointed out above, the first tendency to produce a fully balanced budget in the face of an acute depression situation had given way in both Canada and the United States to the "double budget" policy. This policy emphasized a balance between current revenues and ordinary expenditures. Since a balance of this limited sort was forecast in the budget presented in the United States on Jan. 3, 1935, it was not surprising that the accompanying message did not contain a request for additional taxation. The president merely suggested the extension of certain excises which were due to expire and the continuance of the three cent postage rate.

When, therefore, the president submitted a special message to congress in June 1935 requesting immediate tax revision, his action came as something of a surprise. However, it was evident from the content of this message that the primary objective was the revision of methods of taxation rather than the provision of additional revenue.

Specifically the president recommended that:

> . . . In addition to the present estate taxes, there should be levied an inheritance, succession, and legacy tax in respect to all very large amounts received by any one legatee or beneficiary; and to prevent, so far as possible, evasions of this tax, I recommend further the imposition of gift taxes suited to this end.
>
> Because of the basis on which this proposed tax is to be levied and also because of the very sound public policy of encouraging a wider distribution of wealth, I strongly urge that the proceeds of this tax should be specifically segregated and applied, as they accrue, to the reduction of the national debt. By so doing we shall progressively lighten the tax burden of the average taxpayer, and, incidentally, assist in our approach to a balanced budget.

To further reduce the "disturbing effects upon our national life that came from great inheritances of wealth and power" the president recommended "a definite increase in the taxes now levied upon very great individual net incomes." Specifically, Roosevelt took exception to the fact that progression under the existing surtax schedule stopped at incomes of $1,000,000.

The committee on ways and means began deliberations on this message on July 8, 1935. A bill was prepared by the committee on ways and means and with certain changes by the finance committee, became law on Aug. 30, 1935. As passed by the congress the bill included the following:

(1) The surtax rates on individual incomes were increased starting at $50,000, with a top rate of 75% on net incomes of more than $5,000,000. Under the act of 1934 the top rate was 59% on an income of $1,000,000.

(2) A slightly graduated tax on corporations was imposed. The rates were 12½% on corporation incomes not in excess of $2,000, 13% on incomes between $2,000 and $15,000, 14% between $15,000 and $40,000 and 15% above $40,000. Under the act of 1934 corporations had been subject to a flat rate of 13¾%. This new rate schedule did not really become effective since it was superseded by the rates set up under the revenue act of 1936.

(3) The capital stock tax was increased from $1 per 1,000 to $1.40 per 1,000, and the rates used under its companion, the declared value excess profits tax, were also increased.

(4) An intercorporate dividend tax of 1½% was in effect, imposed by allowing corporations to deduct from gross income only 90% of the dividends received from other corporations.

(5) In lieu of the inheritance tax and the gift tax on donees suggested by the president, the estate tax was increased in two respects. First, by lowering the exemption from $50,000 to $40,000 and second, by increasing the rates. The latter now began with a 2% rate on the first $10,000 of taxable estate and graduated up to 70% on taxable estates over $50,000,000.

(6) Similarly, the gift tax on donors was increased, so that the rates would be approximately three-fourths of those then used under the estate tax.

This bill was estimated to yield approximately $250,000,000, which was a small amount when compared with the deficit of $4,500,000,000 incurred in fiscal 1936.

In 1935 congress had also taken an important step in the development of social welfare legislation when it adopted the Social Security act. Systems of old age annuities and unemployment insurance were established to be financed with the proceeds of a set of new taxes on payrolls. In addition a program was set up under which the federal government and the states joined in the provision of relief for certain categories of needy persons.

While the president's budget message of Jan. 3, 1936, also stressed the balance between current revenues and ordinary expenditures and included no request for additional taxation, another special tax message asking for immediate tax legislation was sent to congress on March 3. This message was based upon the invalidation of the processing taxes used to finance the agricultural adjustment program and upon the enactment of the soldiers' bonus. The president called for a permanent additional taxation amounting to $620,000,000 annually.

To raise this amount the president suggested (1) the imposition of an undistributed profits tax on corporations, (2) a windfall tax on taxpayers who had already shifted to others the burden of the processing taxes which were to be returned to them under the supreme court decision and (3) a temporary tax on the processing of certain agricultural products. The committee on ways and means passed a bill carrying out the first two suggestions of the president but did not follow his suggestion for the imposition of a temporary processing tax on agricultural commodities.

The main controversy over this bill in congress centred around the imposition of an undistributed profits tax in lieu of the existing taxes on corporate income, capital stock and declared value excess profits. The house bill provided for a single graduated tax on corporation incomes, the graduation being based first on the size of the corporation, and second, upon the proportion of a corporation's net earnings retained in the business. The purpose of this method was (1) to prevent avoidance of surtax by individuals through the accumulation of income by corporations, (2) to remove serious inequities and inequalities between corporation, partnership and individual forms of business organizations and (3) to remove the inequity as between large and small shareholders resulting from the existing rates on corporations. There was considerable opposition to this tax, particularly on the part of business groups, who feared that the tax might force an unwise distribution of earnings needed for business expansion or as reserves to meet future contingencies.

The senate finance committee did not agree with the house bill, particularly as to repealing the existing corporate income, capital stock and declared value excess profits taxes, and offered the following as a substitute:

> (1) a corporate normal tax with rates from 15½% on the first $2,000 of income to 18% on incomes in excess of $40,000, (2) an undistributed profits tax of 7%, (3) retention of the capital stock tax and declared value excess profits tax at existing rates and (4) an increase in surtax on net incomes of individuals between $6,000 and $50,000.

As finally agreed to by the two houses, the bill contained the following: (1) a normal tax on corporate income with rates ranging from 8% on the first $2,000 of income to 15% on incomes of more than $40,000, (2) a tax on the undistributed portion of corporate net income ranging from 7% to 27% and (3) a capital stock tax of $1 per 1,000, and a declared value excess profits tax with the rates used under existing law.

The increase in surtax rates on individual incomes between $6,000 and $50,000 was eliminated, and dividends were made subject to the normal tax on individuals.

Instead of supplanting the existing array of corporation taxes with a single levy on undistributed profits, a new tax using the latter as a base had been added to the system. In view of the subsequent withdrawal of this modified version of the president's reform proposal, probably the most important action taken in 1936, from the long run point of view, was the subjection of dividends received to the normal tax on individuals.[3] This action was basic to much of the later controversy over the "double taxation" of income.

The pattern of the two preceding years was reproduced in 1937. The budget message of the president anticipated an over-all balance in the federal budget. Naturally under these conditions there was no need to request the enactment of additional tax legislation. Congress was merely asked to renew the excises which were due to expire and to continue the three cent postal rate. While a supplementary budget message of April 21 painted a more pessimistic picture, there was still no mention of the need for immediate tax revision. Then on June 1 the president submitted another special message urging immediate legislation to prevent evasion of the income tax law.

Technically, the basis for the revenue act of 1937 was the report of a joint committee on tax evasion and avoidance, set up as the result of a senate resolution. The thesis of the measure was loophole plugging. Like the act of 1936, this legislation was basically designed to make the rates used under the tax on personal incomes effective.

The legislation of 1937 included: (1) a redefinition of the personal holding company and its income, together with an increase in the rates applied thereon, (2) a new method of taxing foreign personal holding companies, (3) action disallowing losses on sales or exchanges between members of the same family, etc., (4) a new tax on income received by nonresident aliens and (5) a restriction of the exemption allowed to trusts. The anticipated yield from the measure was small.

The three tax bills enacted in 1935, 1936 and 1937 had much in common. In all of them, additional revenue was a secondary consideration. The legislation of 1935 was preceded by a tax message stressing the need for the redistribution of wealth and income; the undistributed profits tax of 1936 and the loophole plugging measure of the following year were designed to make the now highly progressive surtax rates more effective. The legislation of 1938 and 1939 reflected a different motive. There was now a strong tendency to amend the tax structure in such a way as to promote business confidence and hence facilitate business recovery.

The crux of the legislation of those two years was the revision of the undistributed profits tax. Representatives of business who had opposed the enactment of that legislation in 1936 were now loud in their complaints concerning the effects of the measure. It was argued that the surtax on undistributed profits (1) discouraged in many cases legitimate business expansion, and, therefore, had an adverse effect on employment, (2) put a penalty on corporations which found it necessary to use current earnings in payment of debt, (3) burdened the small and weak corporations more than the large and financially strong corporations and (4) was unfair to corporations with impaired capital which under state law could not legally declare dividends. It was pointed out that the relief provisions applying to corporations having contracts not to pay dividends or requiring use of current earnings for the payment of debts were so restrictive as to afford no relief in meritorious cases.

To meet these complaints the committee on ways and means completely revised the income tax on corporations. The new system contained in the committee's bill included the following provisions:

> (1) Corporations with net incomes of $25,000 or less were subject to graduated rates from 12½% to 16%,

[3]A precedent for this action could be found in the excise on dividends enacted under the NRA legislation of 1933.

with no undistributed profits tax added. This relieved 88% of the corporations from the undistributed profits tax.

(2) Corporations with net incomes in excess of $25,000 were taxed at a flat rate of 20% with a credit against the tax of 4%, or 4 cents of each dollar of dividends paid out.

(3) A special undistributed profits tax was levied on corporations whose stock was held by 10 or fewer individuals, and which had a net income of $40,000 or more. This was the famous "third basket" tax eliminated on the floor of the house.

The committee on ways and means also revised the system of taxing capital gains and losses, and rewrote the estate tax, so as to produce a single rate schedule with a credit of 16½% for state taxes paid. Under the committee bill, only one exemption of $40,000 was allowed for both estate and gift taxes.

The bill, as finally enacted after agreement with the senate conferees, retained the undistributed profits principle with respect to corporations having net incomes of $25,000 or more. The maximum rate applied to the income of such corporations which distributed no earnings was 19%. For corporations making full distribution of earnings the rate was 16½%. The spread between no distribution and a full distribution was 2½% and took the form of a dividend paid credit. This system was to be temporary and was to expire in 1939. Corporations with incomes of $25,000 or less were to be exempt from the undistributed profits tax.

In the final bill the capital gain and loss provisions were completely rewritten. Gains held for 18 months or less were taxable as ordinary income at the regular normal and surtax rates; gains realized on assets held more than 18 months but less than 2 years were taxable at a maximum rate of 20%, and gains on assets held for over 2 years were taxable at a maximum rate of 15%.[4] This supplanted a system set up in 1934 under which the percentage of gains and losses taxed as ordinary income ranged through 5 classes, from 100% on assets held 1 year or less, to 30% on assets held 10 years or more.

No changes were made in the estate tax exemption, but the annual gift tax exemption was reduced from $5,000 to $4,000.

This bill became law without the signature of the president, who expressed disapproval of the provisions relating to capital gains and the undistributed profits tax. Senator Byron Patton Harrison, in a speech in the senate on May 28, 1938, defending the tax bill stated: "I have heard no voice lifted in Congress or elsewhere to defend the undistributed profits tax as it was in the law until yesterday. Thank God, it is not in the law today." And in defending the capital gain provision, Senator Harrison stated that "the new law will release much of the frozen credit of this country and ought to be most helpful in getting some industries started and in relieving the distress caused by the unemployment situation in this country."

The policy of continuing to aid business recovery by removing deterrents from the tax laws was continued in the revenue act of 1939. Here again much controversy centred around the undistributed profits tax. As finally enacted, the revenue act of 1939 contained the following provisions:

(1) The undistributed profits tax, which was applicable to corporations with incomes of $25,000 or more, was allowed to expire with respect to taxable years beginning after Dec. 31, 1939. In lieu of this tax, corporations with incomes above $25,000 were subject to a flat rate of 18% on net income.

(2) The lower rates imposed by the 1938 act with respect to corporations with incomes of less than $25,000, were continued. These rates were 12½% upon the first $5,000 of income, 14% on the next $15,000 of income and on the next $5,000, 16%.

(3) Corporations, partnerships and individuals were permitted to carry over their net operating business losses for a period of two years.

(4) The $2,000 limitation on capital losses was repealed. If the capital asset which was sold had been held less than 18 months, the loss might only be applied against a gain from the sale of an asset held for less than 18 months. If there was not sufficient short term gain (on assets held less than 18 months) to absorb such loss, the loss might be carried over into the next year, and applied against a short term gain in that year. If the capital asset had been held over 18 months, the loss resulting therefrom was treated as a long term loss and might be applied against ordinary income.

(5) Corporations were permitted to increase their valuations for the purpose of the capital stock tax for the fiscal years ended June 30, 1939, and June 30, 1940. Under the revenue act of 1938, corporations were entitled to a new declaration (either lowering or raising their capital stock value) for capital stock tax purposes for the fiscal year ending June 30, 1941.

Another important change in the federal system of taxation adopted in 1939 was the Public Salary Tax act of 1939, which subjected to taxation for taxable years beginning after Dec. 31, 1938, the compensation of all state and local officers and employees. The states were also given the power to tax the salaries of federal officers and employees. In this same year congress also enacted into law an Internal Revenue code, which was the first statutory codification of the internal revenue laws into absolute law since 1873.

This act brought to a close the period of depression financing in the United States. By the following year the defense problem had taken the centre of the stage.

Canada, 1935–39.—In its first reaction to the impact of the great depression, the dominion government had made a vigorous attempt to raise substantial amounts of new revenue in order to bring its budget back into balance. The basis for that program had been a drastic increase in the general sales tax. By 1935, however, Canada had a well entrenched double budget policy, and hence the pressure for additional taxation was much less insistent than it had been at the beginning of the depression period. The tax program set out in the budget speech of March 22, 1935, was intended to produce additional revenues of $12,000,000. It was not intended to produce a fully balanced budget, but merely to offset certain anticipated increases in expenditures. This program included the following changes in the dominion's income tax:

(1) The installation of a surtax in investment income. This surtax applied a progressive rate schedule ranging from 2% to 10% on "investment income" in excess of $5,000. It is important to note that all income in excess of $14,000 was defined as "investment income." This measure was based upon the same philosophy as the earned income credit then used in both the United States and Great Britain.

(2) The reduction in the allowable rate of depletion

[4]A special relief provision was inserted in order to cover the small taxpayer whose income tax rate was less than these maximum rates.

for precious metal mines from 50% to 33⅓%.

(3) An increase in the rate applied on corporate net income from 12½% to 13½%. For those corporations using consolidated returns, the rate was raised from 13½% to 15%.

(4) The installation of a levy on gifts in excess of $1,000 per annum with rates ranging from 2% to 10%. The most important change in the dominion's excise system was a reduction in the levy on distilled spirits from $7.00 to $4.00 per gal.

As already pointed out, a general election brought a change of administration, and in 1936 a much more vigorous budget policy was enunciated. The double budget idea was dropped and as a first step toward a truly balanced budget a tax program was submitted intended to produce between $28,000,000 and $30,000,000 of additional revenue. The bulk of this revenue ($23,000,000) was to be raised by increasing the rates under the dominion sales tax from 6% to 8%. Most of the remainder was to come from an increase in the rate applied to corporate net income from 13½% to 15%. The rate on corporations using consolidated returns was raised from 15% to 17%.

This portion of the tax program of 1936 was in fact a reversion to the policy which Canada had used at the outset of the depression. Now, however, something new was being added. In addition to raising more revenue, Dunning proposed to enter the field of incentive taxation. His plan for the stimulation of investment in metal mining was offered in the following terms:

> The government . . . proposes to grant exemption from corporate income tax to any metalliferous mine coming into production between May 1, 1936, and January 1, 1940, such exemption to apply to its income for the first three years following the commencement of production. This definite step to encourage the development of the mining industry . . . should do much to accelerate new exploration and development work during the present year and the following two or three years.

The budget message of Feb. 25, 1937, contained no major proposals for adding to the total tax revenues, and with one exception the tax proposal of the following year were also of minor importance.[5] The exception was another experiment in incentive taxation, this time in the form of sales tax exemption to building materials, in order to stimulate the housing program.

This idea of incentive taxation was developed further in the concluding budget message of the prewar period, that of April 25, 1939. There it was proposed not only to extend the exemption to new metalliferous mines for three additional years, but also to introduce a tax credit for new investment generally.

This attempt to use tax concessions as a means of stimulating business activity was far and away the most interesting feature of the Canadian tax policy during the years immediately preceding the outbreak of World War II. In a sense, it was the counterpart of the policy of removing irritants to business which characterized the legislation of 1938 and 1939 in the United States.

Great Britain, 1935–39.—The tax measures enacted in Great Britain during these years were methods of financing an armaments boom. Hence they did not emphasize social reform as the legislation of 1935 and 1936 in the United States had done, nor did they represent an attempt to promote business revival.

In 1936 Neville Chamberlain faced a deficit of £21,000,000. He proposed to raise £12,000,000 by increasing the standard rate under the income tax (comparable to the normal tax in the United States), and the remainder by increasing the duty on tea, by instituting a series of measures intended to reduce avoidance under the income and estate taxes, and by certain transfers from the so-called Road fund. The severity of the increase in the standard rate was tempered somewhat by raising the allowances under the income tax to the levels which had prevailed before 1931.

Almost all of a deficit of £13,000,000 anticipated in the following year was to be financed with an increase in the standard rate. There was also enacted at this time a new tax called the National Defense contribution, which was an attempt to recoup trading profits arising out of the defense effort. This tax was applied to the growth of profits received by all persons engaged in industry or trade of any kind whose profits in any accounting year ended after April 5, 1937, exceeded $2,000. The base period against which the growth of profits was measured was 1933–35, but it should be borne in mind that this tax also contained an optional invested capital base. Taxable profits could also be defined as the excess of 6% over invested capital in the case of a corporation and the excess over 8% for other forms of business enterprise. In all cases, the rates applied depended upon the rate of return on invested capital. In the case of a corporation, they were 20% on a return between 6% and 10%; 25% when the return was between 10% and 15%, and 33⅓% when the return was in excess of 15%. While the National Defense contribution would not reduce the current deficit, it was calculated to yield between £20,000,000 and £25,000,000 in a year of full operation.

Again in 1938 the entire amount of the anticipated deficit was to be financed by additional taxation, and again the bulk of the money was to come from an increase in the standard rate. The balance was to be provided by increases in the excises on gasoline and tea and by the imposition of a new tax on power alcohol. By now the standard rate had reached the level where some relief for small incomes was necessary, and an adjustment was made in the rates applied in the lowest brackets. The depreciation allowance used in calculating business incomes was also increased. Like the two preceding budget messages, that of April 1938 contained a considerable discussion of the problem of tax avoidance.

"Going Up," a critical version of tax policies under the Attlee administration, as presented by Butterworth in the *Daily Dispatch* of Manchester, England

[5]Most important of these was an increase in the gift tax rates. The new rate schedule was graduated from 5% to 15%.

The final budget of the prewar period, that of April 1939, contained a much larger anticipated deficit (£400,000,000) and only a small part of it (£24,000,000) was to be financed by added taxation. For the first time in this series of rearmament budgets, there was to be no increase in the standard rate. Most of the new money was to come from additional excises on tobacco and sugar, and from additional motor vehicle duties. A special set of surcharges was to be added to the levy on estates.

The Three Tax Systems in 1939.—Between 1936 and 1939 the combination of the tax measures just summarized and a rise in business activity brought substantial increases in the tax revenues of Great Britain, the United States and Canada. The increase in the total was 38% in Canada, 28% in the United States, and 21% in Great Britain.

There was also a tendency for the revenues produced by the income tax to make up a larger percentage of the total. While corporate and personal income taxes produced 36% of the total in the United States in 1936, their yield was 44% of the total in 1939. The yield of the British income tax rose from 39% of total tax revenue to 44%; that of the Canadian income tax from 26% to 33% over this same interval.

In the United States, revenue from excises, which had made up 39% of the total in 1936, dropped to 34% in 1939. Similarly, the British excises dropped from 22% of the total in 1936 to 19% in 1939. In Canada, on the other hand, excises (including the general sales tax) provided roughly half of the total revenue in each of these years. Customs duties declined in importance in all three countries.

Defense Taxation in the United States, 1940–41.—The first revenue act of 1940 was based upon a presidential message dated May 16, 1940. That message requested $3,250,000,000 additional income for the fiscal year 1941 to finance certain defense expenditures, among them the procurement of new and additional equipment for the army and navy, an increase of production facilities and the stock pile of materials for use in the defense program, plus the cost of putting armaments production on a 24 hour basis.

The financial plan used at that time called for the issuance of $4,000,000,000 in defense obligations to be outstanding not more than five years. These obligations were in turn to be retired from the proceeds of increased taxation. The individual income, estate and gift taxes, payable under existing law were increased by 10% of the tax payable. The personal exemption for single persons was reduced from $1,000 to $800 and for married persons from $2,500 to $2,000. This added 2,290,000 new taxpayers to the tax rolls. The corporation income tax rate was increased by 1%. The tax on cigarettes was increased from $3 per 1,000 to $3.25 per 1,000. The tax on liquor was increased from $2.25 per gal. to $3.00 per gal., an increase of 33⅓%; the tax on beer from $5 per bbl. to $6 per bbl., an increase of 20%, and the tax on gasoline from 1 to 1½ cents, an increase of 50%.

This program was expected to produce about $1,000,000,000 in additional revenue. Of this amount, over half was to be placed in a special fund for the retirement of defense obligations. The remaining half was the part obtained by broadening the income tax base through lowering the exemptions, by increasing the surtax in the middle brackets, and by raising the rate on corporate income. In these cases it was difficult to segregate the increased revenue from the ordinary revenue, and it was deemed advisable to allow the former to remain in the general fund.

Another message from the president dated July 1, 1940, recommended the enactment of a steeply graduated excess profits tax to be applied to all individuals and all corporate organizations without discrimination. There had been a demand for this form of taxation when the first revenue act of 1940 was being discussed, and in its report on that measure the committee on ways and means had expressed the desire that the rearmament program should furnish no opportunity for the creation of new war millionaires or for the further enrichment of already wealthy persons.

While the committee was convinced of the need for an excess profits tax, it found it impracticable to apply such a tax to individuals and partnerships, particularly since individuals and partnerships were subject to heavy surtaxes on their income, whether or not it was left in the business, while corporate stockholders were not taxed on their undistributed earnings. Furthermore, since all of the assets of an individual, whether he was a sole proprietor or a member of a partnership, were at the risk of the business, it was extremely difficult, if not impossible, to determine the amount of capital actually invested.

In drafting the excess profits tax, the committee on ways and means also refused to follow the treasury recommendation as to the base to be used in measuring excess profits. The treasury proposal was that the tax should apply to profits in excess of a certain return on invested capital. The committee on ways and means, the finance committee and the congress believed that the invested capital base was an inadequate standard for measuring excess profits in many cases. Such a method would have favoured the corporation which had retained its earnings over a long period of time, as against the corporation which distributed its earnings and thereby permitted the government to secure the individual normal and surtax on such earnings. It would have favoured the company which by chance was incorporated in a year of high values, as compared with a company organized in a year of low values, or would have deemed the present shareholders to have realized excess profits on what the original shareholders paid for their stock.

Accordingly, in lieu of the treasury proposal, the congress adopted an alternate plan, which defined excess profits as the excess of the profits for the year over either (1) a stated return on their invested capital or (2) more than 95% of the average profits earned in the 1936–39 period. The excess profits tax rates were progressive, ranging from 25% on the first $2,000 of excess profits to 50% on excess profits above $500,000. A specific exemption of $5,000 was adopted which had the effect of limiting the excess profits tax to 70,000 to the 500,000 active corporations in the United States. In order to stimulate the corporations and private enterprises which were participating in the defense program, a special amortization deduction was allowed with respect to facilities necessary to the national defense, and profits limitations applicable to the construction of naval vessels and army and navy aircraft were suspended. This bill was enacted on Oct. 8, 1940.

In April 1941 Secretary of the Treasury Morgenthau appeared before the committee on ways and means to request the enactment of legislation designed to provide $3,500,000,000 in additional revenue. This was intended to bring revenues other than loans up to two-thirds of total expenditures. The tax bill, which was enacted by congress on Sept. 20, was expected to produce an additional $3,553,400,000 in a full year of operation.

The tax bill of 1941 lowered the single persons' exemption for income tax purposes from $800 to $750, that of married persons from $2,000 to $1,500. This action brought the total number of persons liable to the income tax to 13,181,000, and the total number of income tax returns to 22,108,000. It resulted in 2,275,000 new taxpayers.

The house committee on ways and means had inserted in the revenue act of 1941 a requirement for a mandatory joint return of husband and wife, but this was defeated by the house. In this bill, taxpayers with incomes under $3,000 were given an optional method of computing their tax, if their entire income was derived from salary, wages, compensation for personal services, dividends, rents, annuities, or royalties. The taxpayer electing this optional method had his tax already computed on a table set out in the law and on his return. The rates of the excess profits tax were increased by 10 percentage points, so that they ranged from 35% on excess profits incomes not more than $20,000 to 60% on excess profit incomes in excess of $50,000. Another very important change was made in the excess profits tax. Under the revenue act of 1940 the corporate income tax had been allowed as a deduction in arriving at excess profits net income. Under the revenue act of 1941, this deduction was not allowed, but, in order to avoid double taxation, the excess profits tax was allowed as a deduction in computing the corporation income tax.

The corporation normal tax was not changed in the revenue act of 1941, except that the 10% defense tax, which had been imposed for a period of 5 years under the revenue act of 1940, was integrated with the regular income tax. The total normal corporate rate remained at 24%. However, a special surtax on corporations was imposed at the rate of 6% on corporate surtax net income not in excess of $25,000, and 7% on corporate surtax net income in excess of $25,000. This special surtax was designed to reach partially tax exempt federal securities, which were exempt from the corporation normal tax. In 1941 the congress passed a law making the income from all federal obligations issued on or after March 1, 1941, subject to both the normal tax and the surtax.

The tax bill of 1941 also included substantial changes in the excise system. A number of new taxes were levied, and the rates used under certain existing excises were increased in order to discourage the production or use of articles needed for the defense effort.

In a letter dated July 31, 1941, to the chairman of the committee on ways and means the president took exception to certain features of the revenue act of 1941, particularly the mandatory joint return provision of the house bill, the method of permitting corporations to compute excess profits on an average earnings base, and the provisions relating to excises. However, the committee refused to modify its position, and the chairman advised the president to that effect in a letter dated Aug. 2, 1941.

Another piece of tax legislation enacted in 1941 is worth mention here. This was the set of relief amendments added to the excess profits tax enacted on March 7, 1941, which applied retroactively to Jan. 1, 1940. It had been evident at the time of enactment of the second revenue act of 1940 that the excess profits tax did not make sufficient provision for hardship cases. Hence a general relief clause had been inserted into the law giving the commissioner of internal revenue authority to make adjustments where abnormalities existed in income and capital, and giving the board of tax appeals the right to review the decision of the commissioner. The staff of the joint committee on internal revenue taxation and the treasury was instructed by the house and senate conferees under the 1940 bill to study the problem of relief and report to the appropriate committees as soon as possible. The act of March 7 was based on this report. It set up a series of specific relief provisions to take the place of the general relief clause enacted in the previous year.

U.S. War Taxation.—In 1942 the United States became an active participant in World War II. Projected expenditures rose to extremely high levels. Those for the fiscal year 1943 were estimated to exceed $73,000,000,000. Since the existing federal tax structure was expected to yield only $17,000,000,000, a deficit of $56,000,000,000 was in the offing. The gross public debt was expected to reach $133,000,000,000 by June 30, 1943.

In recognition of this situation, the congress enacted the revenue act of 1942, which was expected to provide an additional revenue of approximately $7,000,000,000. Of this total, no less than $4,966,000,000 was to come from the tax on individual incomes. The personal exemptions under the regular income tax were cut from $1,500 to $1,200 for a married person, from $750 to $500 for a single person. The credit for dependents was reduced from $400 to $350. The normal rate was raised from 4% to 6%. Surtax rates were increased drastically, the rate on the lowest bracket being increased from 6% to 13%, thus raising the basic rate applied to personal incomes from 10% to 19%.

In addition there was enacted the so-called Victory tax, which imposed a flat 5% on that part of the taxpayer's net annual income (except capital gains and interest on federal obligations) which was in excess of $624. Net income for the purpose of this tax was computed without deductions for expenses or allowances not connected with a trade or business or incurred in the production of income. Thus, charitable contributions, taxes on a residence and losses from fire or other casualty were not deductible. On the other hand, credits were allowed currently for debt reduction, insurance premium payments and bond purchases, but such credits were not to exceed the limits set for the "postwar credits" allowed under this tax. The latter were 25% of the Victory tax, or $500, whichever was less, for a single person; and 40% of the tax, or $1,000 for a married person or the head of a family, plus 2%, or $100 for each dependent. These postwar credits were allowable only to the extent that they had not been exhausted by the current credits listed above. Also it was stipulated that the Victory tax and the ordinary taxes on individual income combined were not to exceed 90% of net income. The Victory tax was imposed for the war period only and had the effect of putting nearly 50,000,000 taxpayers on the rolls.

One of the most important features of the Victory tax was the fact that it instituted a system of collection at the source which was the forerunner of the more extensive system set up under later legislation.

The act of 1942 also altered the treatment of capital gains and losses. The number of categories was reduced to two. Profits on capital assets held less than six months were now treated as taxable income. Those on assets held longer than six months were included in taxable income to the extent of 50%. The amount of deductible capital loss was limited to the extent of the capital gains plus net income, or $1,000, whichever was less; but taxpayers could carry over for five succeeding years any excess of losses over gains.

The severity of these measures necessitated certain relief provisions. Service personnel on active duty were given preferential treatment in the form of an exclusion from gross income of $250 for a single person, and $300 in the case of a married person. Pensions received for personal injuries or sickness resulting from active service in the armed forces of the Allied nations were exempt from the income tax. For taxpayers generally there was introduced a new deduction for extraordinary medical expenses, and relief was instituted for Americans who had incurred war losses abroad. In addition, taxpayers with incomes less than $3,000 from wages, salaries, dividends, interest, rent, etc., had their returns simplified, and income tax returns in general were no longer required to be made under oath.

The act of 1942 also called for $1,300,000,000 from additional taxes on corporations. The rate in corporate net income was raised from 31% to 40%, the increase coming in the surtax rather than the normal tax. The excess profits rate was raised to 90% with a postwar credit equal to 10% of the excess profits tax. This credit could be used currently up to 40% of the amount paid for retirement of debt within the year. Otherwise, it could not be used until after World War II.

As a relief for new and expanding corporations, the act limited the effective rate to be applied to normal, surtax and excess profits taxes to 80% of the corporation's net income. The general relief provisions under the excess profits tax were greatly expanded. Mutual insurance companies other than life or marine were taxed either at the regular corporate rates on their net income, or at a rate of 1% on the gross amount of their income from interest, dividends, rents and net premiums, less dividends paid to policy holders. An exemption was installed for the corporate surtax of western hemisphere corporations in cases where 80% of the income was derived from business activities in the western hemisphere.

While the act of 1942 did not alter the rates under the estate tax, the $40,000 exemption plus the $40,000 life insurance credit used under the previous law was supplanted by a single exemption of $60,000 for either or both combined.

The act of 1942 also included changes in the excise system calculated to yield about $650,000,000 of additional revenue.

While this legislation was before the finance committee, the treasury had appeared before that committee to advocate a so-called spendings tax which was to be added to the tax on incomes. This proposal was not agreed to by the committee. Proposals to adopt a federal sales tax were also rejected by congress. As a matter of fact, the Victory tax was adopted in preference to a sales tax.

In presenting his $100,000,000,000 budget in Jan. 1943, President Roosevelt made three tax recommendations: (1) that $16,000,000,000 be raised in new tax revenue, or savings, or both, (2) that the income tax be simplified and (3) that collections under the income tax be put on a pay-as-you-go basis.

The first action taken by congress in 1943, the Current Tax Payment act, was aimed at the last of these objectives. This legislation extended the withholding system which had been applied under the Victory tax of 1942, to the regular tax on individual incomes. Provision was made for withholding at the source 20% of income after allowing exemptions of $1,248 for a family and $624 for a single person. This system became effective Jan. 1, 1943, and applied to all income except that paid to members of the armed forces, that received for agricultural, casual or domestic service, for services performed by a minister of the gospel, by a non-resident alien, or by United States citizens outside the United States.

The proposal to go over to a "pay-as-you-go" system generated a considerable controversy in congress, and further difficulties were raised by the problem of the treatment of the 1942 tax which also came due in 1943. Some advocated complete forgiveness, others partial forgiveness, still others wanted full payment of the 1942 tax with actual collection spread over a period of years. Out of this controversy came the following compromise:

(1) If the tax for the lower of the two years, 1942 and 1943, was $50 or less, the tax for the lower year was cancelled.

(2) If the tax for the lower year was between $50 and $66.67, a flat $50 of the tax for the lower year was cancelled.

(3) If the tax for the lower year was more than $66.67, 75% of the tax was cancelled.

This act also provided additional relief for servicemen. It excluded from income tax $1,500 of servicemens' pay, and provided special relief from the 1942 tax after the serviceman had entered the service.

The Current Tax Payment act was signed June 9, 1943.

In October of the same year congress took up the problem of raising more revenue. By this time the treasury had reduced the goal of the proposed legislation from the $16,000,000,000 requested in January to $10,500,000,000. Congress did not choose to follow the treasury program, believing that individual income taxes were nearing the point of diminishing returns. As a result, it enacted a tax bill which was estimated to yield only slightly more than $2,300,000,000 in a full year's operation.

No changes were made in the normal or surtax rates, but the Victory tax was reduced from 5% to 3% and the refund or credit provisions of the previous laws were eliminated. The earned income credit was removed. On the other hand, a new exemption was introduced for blind persons, and the mustering out pay of service personnel was exempt from the individual income tax.

While there were no changes in the rates applied to corporate net income, the rate on excess profits was raised from 90% to 95%. The specific exemption under the excess profits tax was increased from $5,000 to $10,000, and certain important changes were made in the invested capital credit. Tax exempt organizations were required for the first time to file informational returns showing their receipts and disbursements.

Payroll tax rates were frozen at 1%, a considerable number of excises were increased, and postal rates were advanced.

This bill was unacceptable to the president, who vetoed it, but the congress passed it over his veto and it became law in Feb. 1944.

By its action with reference to the tax bill of 1943, the congress evidenced its belief that the taxes which had already been imposed were reaching the limit of the nation's taxable capacity. It was not surprising therefore that the legislation of 1944 was concerned with the simplification of the existing law rather than the production of additional revenue.

In enacting this legislation, congress had before it the following objectives: (1) to relieve the great majority of taxpayers from the necessity of computing their income tax, (2) to reduce the number of tax computations, (3) to simplify the return form, (4) to decrease the number of persons required to file declarations of estimated tax and (5) to eliminate some of the difficulties inherent in the filing of declarations of estimated tax used in the pay-as-you-go system.

The act of 1944 relieved 30,000,000 taxpayers of the necessity of computing their income taxes, permitting them to use a simple income statement in place of a detailed income tax return. Of the remaining 20,000,000 who filed such returns, 10,000,000 could use a simple tax table which showed their entire tax. The other 10,000,000 filled out returns which were more detailed but which were still much simpler than those previously required.

To achieve this simplification, certain important changes were made in the basic provisions of the individual income tax. The personal exemption for surtax purposes was changed to a uniform $500 each for the taxpayer, for his spouse and for each of his dependents. An optional $500 standard allowance for deductions was set up for persons whose gross incomes were $5,000 or more. The Victory tax was repealed and there was set up in its place a new 3% normal tax on the net income of each person in excess of a flat exemption of $500. Finally, the levies previously known as the normal tax and the surtax were combined into a new surtax with rates ranging from 20% on the first $2,000 of surtax net income to 91% on the portion of surtax net income in excess of $200,000.

The legislation of 1944 was really the last of the series of war measures in the United States, the legislation of the following year being directed at the problems of the postwar transition. Realizing the importance of taxation in the postwar economy, the joint committee on internal revenue taxation planned and conducted a study of postwar taxation early in 1945. For this purpose, the membership of the committee was increased by one minority member from the senate finance committee and one minority member from the committee on ways and means. The staff of the joint committee on internal revenue taxation, the staffs of the treasury and the bureau of internal revenue were instructed to collect and analyze data, information, and plans with regard to the problems in the transition and postwar periods. The material contained in these studies for the joint committee were used in formulating the Tax Adjustment act of 1945.

The main purpose of this act was to make available more promptly benefits already granted under existing law. The only provision which was designed to reduce tax liabilities was that which increased the specific exemption for excess profits tax purposes from $10,000 to $25,000. This provision never became effective because of the repeal of this tax as of Dec. 31, 1945. The benefits which the taxpayer actually received under the Tax Adjustment act were (1) the advance in the maturity date of the 10% postwar credit funds to Jan. 1, 1946, (2) the provision of the quick refunds of overpayments of taxes resulting from carrybacks of unused excess profits credits or net losses and (3) the recomputation of amortization deductions for emergency facilities.

On Nov. 8, 1945, congress enacted the revenue act of 1945. This was the first general reduction act since 1929. The excess profits tax was repealed as of Dec. 31, 1945; individual income taxes were reduced, corporation surtaxes were reduced by 4 percentage points for taxpayers with net incomes of less than $25,000 and by 2 percentage points in the case of taxpayers with net incomes in excess of $50,000. The capital stock tax was repealed, as was also its companion measure, the declared value excess profits tax, and about 12,000,000 individuals who had been liable for the normal income tax but not the surtax were removed from the tax rolls. Special benefits were granted to members of the armed forces and to veterans. All service pay of servicemen below the rank of commissioned officers was excluded from income if received after Dec. 31, 1940, and before the termination of World War II. The tax attributable to service pay of commissioned officers was deferred through an extension of time without interest. The wartime tax on the use of automobiles was repealed as of July 1, 1946.

War Taxation in Canada, 1939–45.—Ilsley's emergency budget of Sept. 2, 1939, called for a tax program which was expected to produce $21,000,000 in the current year, reducing the anticipated deficit from $156,000,000 to $135,000,000. The expected yield in a full year's operation was estimated to be $62,000,000. The core of this program was an excess profits tax. As in the subsequent legislation of the United States, the taxpayer was given the option of computing excess profits with reference to base period income or as a percentage return on invested capital. When the base period income was used, the rate applied was 50%. When the invested capital base was used, the rates progressed by brackets from 10% on profits between 5% and 10% of invested capital to 60% on profits in excess of 25% of invested capital. However, this system was never put into effect. It was superseded in 1940 by a tax which was applied to the increase over base period net income, and in which the invested capital base was used only for relief purposes. Like the excess profits tax used in the United States, the Canadian tax was levied in addition to the tax on corporate net income. Unlike the United States, Canada extended the tax to all forms of business organizations.

In addition to the excess profits tax, Ilsley proposed to increase the rate on corporate net income from 15% to 18% (for consolidated returns from 17% to 20%), to install a war surtax of 20% of the amount of the ordinary individual income tax and to increase the excises, particularly those on liquor, beer, wines and tobacco. The rates on tea and coffee were increased as a substitute for the reduction of the exemptions used under the individual income tax.

The deficit anticipated in the budget message of June 24, 1940, was substantially larger, and the tax-program offered at that time was calculated to yield $110,500,000 in the current year—$280,000,000 when in full operation.

From the point of view of immediate productivity, the most important items in this program were those designed to protect the international position of the Canadian dollar. A tax of 10% was levied on the value of all imports from outside the British empire. This was expected to produce $50,000,000 in the current fiscal year. A steeply graded excise on the sale of automobiles, which rose to 80% on amounts in excess of $1,200, was intended to prohibit the purchase of the better grade vehicles, which were of course primarily imported from the United States.

More significant from a longer run point of view was the aforementioned revision of the excess profits tax which turned the latter into purely and simply a levy on the wartime increase in profits. The rate was raised from 50% to 75%, and in addition it was stipulated that in no case was a corporation to pay a total income and excess profits tax which was less than 30% of its total net profit. The corresponding minimum for individuals and partnerships was 12% (30% minus the 18% rate on corporate net income). Under these arrangements, corporations which paid the 75% rate under the excess profits tax also paid a tax of 18% on corporate net income. Those which did not pay the 75% rate were in effect taxed at a flat 30%

of corporate net income. A general relief clause was inserted in the excess profits tax, and a board of referees was set up to administer it. Special relief was granted to the gold mining and oil producing industries.

The individual income tax was also revised. The existing surtaxes on the amount of the tax due were removed and the regular rate schedule was revised upward. Exemptions were cut from $1,000 to $750 for a single person and from $2,000 to $1,500 for married persons. There was no change in the dependency exemption. Failure to use the individual income tax more aggressively in 1939 was attributed to the problem of adjustment with the existing provincial taxes, some of which applied high rates in the upper brackets.

There was also enacted in 1940 a new levy on individuals called the National Defense tax. This applied a flat rate to all incomes above $600 in the case of a single person, and $1,200 in the case of a married person. The rates used were 2% for married persons and single persons whose incomes were not more than $1,200, 3% for single persons with incomes above $1,200.[6] This tax was to be collected at the source. It bore considerable resemblance to the Victory tax subsequently enacted in the United States.

Ilsley's message of April 29, 1941, forecast an even larger deficit and contained a tax program intended to produce an additional $250,000,000 in the current year, $300,000,000 when in full operation.

The basis for the tax legislation of 1941 was an agreement with the provinces which would overcome the obstacles to the development of the dominion tax system pointed out in the budget speech of the previous year. Under the terms of this agreement, the dominion undertook to make certain payments to the provinces and their municipalities compensating them for a temporary withdrawal of their taxes on personal and corporate income. In addition, in order to reconcile the provinces to the installation of a dominion tax of three cents a gallon on gasoline, the dominion agreed to guarantee to the provinces the equivalent of the current yield of their taxes on gasoline. Ilsley emphasized that these arrangements were temporary, pointed out that the provinces were not required to accept the plan, and if they did, that they could withdraw from it at the end of any fiscal year. The budget speech of 1942 indicated that all of the provinces had accepted this agreement.

Having made these arrangements with the provinces, it was possible to move more aggressively in the development of the individual income tax. The rates used under the National Defense tax were increased from 2% to 5% in the case of married persons, and from 3% to 7% in the case of individuals. However, the exemption for single persons under this tax was raised from $600 to $660, and the credit for dependents was increased from $8 to $20. The latter was the equivalent of a 5% rate on $400. The rates used under the individual income tax were also increased. They now began at 15% instead of 6%, and reached a top rate of 85% at an income of $500,000. If these rates were added to those used under the National Defense tax, the effective rate on individual income ranged from 20% at the bottom to between 90% and 92% at the top.

The tax on investment income was also revised. It now became a flat 4% on all such incomes over $1,500. The provision which had interpreted all income over $14,000 as investment income was dropped.

[6]It was stipulated that in no case was the tax to reduce the income below $600 or $1,200, as the case might be.

The charitable deduction under the income tax was sharply curtailed; the maximum deduction was cut from 50% of net income to 10%.

Finally, a plan was introduced for the payment of the individual income tax in 12 monthly installments. While the amount of the tax due was based on the previous year's income, this was a definite step in the direction of the pay-as-you-go principle.

In addition to the foregoing action relating to the income tax, the minimum rate used under the excess profits tax was increased from 12% to 22% of corporate net income. As a result, corporations not paying the 75% rate on excess profits were in effect subject to a flat rate of 40% on corporate net income. Those paying the 75% rate on excess profits were still subject to an 18% rate in corporate net income.

The arrangement with the provinces also facilitated the adoption of the first dominion death duty. This was a tax on successions. The budget message introducing it emphasized that this tax was to be temporary, and pointed out that it, in combination with the existing provincial death duties, was intended to impose a total burden "of about the same general magnitude as the British death duties."

The legislation of 1941 also included increases in the existing excise rates, particularly those on sugar, beer and automobiles. Some additional excises were introduced, including the aforementioned tax of three cents a gallon on gasoline, and the exemption of building materials under the sales tax was deleted.

This was a major tax program. In his budget speech, Ilsley concluded, "I think it will be agreed that the Dominion is attempting to carry the pay-as-you-go policy as far as is reasonably practical."

Another large deficit predicted in the budget message of June 23, 1942, was accompanied by recommendations for taxation intended to yield $378,000,000 of additional revenue in the current year.

As in the previous year, the focal point of this program was the tax on individual incomes. In 1942 the so-called National Defense tax was consolidated with the graduated tax on personal incomes, and provision was made to collect both at the source in-so-far as this was possible. However, this change was made in such fashion as to perpetuate what were really two separate taxes.

One of these imposed a flat rate of 7% on married persons and on single persons with incomes of less than $1,800. Single persons with incomes between $1,800 and $3,000 were to pay 8%, those whose incomes exceeded $3,000 were to pay 9%. As in the National Defense tax the exemptions allowed under this new levy were $660 for a single individual; $1,200 for a married person. The dependency adjustment was a tax credit of $28. This compared with $20 allowed under the National Defense contribution.

The second tax imposed in 1942 was a graduated levy on personal net income. The minimum rate was 30% as compared with the 15% rate previously in use. The new rate schedule rose to a maximum of 85% at an income of $100,000, whereas under previous law the maximum rate of 85% had been reached at an income of $500,000. Under the new levy, each taxpayer was allowed a flat exemption of $660, instead of $750 for a single person and $1,500 for a married person, plus a set of tax credits. The latter were $150 for a married person plus $80 for each child. These credits were intended to be the equivalent of the value of the exemptions previously in use under a 20% tax.

When these two new taxes were considered together, it appeared that the maximum levy ranged from 96% to 98% of net income. To reduce the severity of these rates, a new medical deduction was allowed, and it was stipulated that a substantial portion of the new tax was to represent forced saving. Against the latter portion, a credit was allowed for certain forms of voluntary savings such as the payment of premiums on life insurance, the repayment of mortgages on a home and contributions to pension funds.

These changes in the levy on individual incomes were accompanied by an increase from 75% to 100% in the rate applied to excess profits. In addition, the rate on corporate net income was raised from 18% to 30%, and a minimum excess profits tax of 10% on corporate net income was imposed. The net effect was to levy a flat rate of 40% on the net income of corporations not subject to the 100% rate on excess profits. Corporations subject to the latter also paid a rate of 30% on corporate net income.

When the latter combination was used, it was stipulated that a portion of the payment was to be offset by a postwar refund. The new rates on corporations were expected to limit profits to 70% of the prewar standard. A one year carry forward of losses was also introduced.

The legislation of 1942 also included substantial increases in selected excises, particularly those on alcoholic beverages, soft drinks, cigarettes and passenger transportation. Substantial new excises were imposed on candy, chewing gum, cabarets, jewellery, luggage and other luxury items.

The tax program advanced in the budget speech of March 2, 1943, was of smaller size. Out of a total of $152,000,000 in additional revenue, $115,000,000 was accounted for by the installation of a pay-as-you-go system under the individual income tax. This action paralleled that taken in the Current Tax Payment act in the United States in the same year. In addition to installing pay-as-you-go, certain excises were increased, particularly those on tobacco, liquor and cabarets, and the Canadian postal rates were advanced for the first time during World War II. A purchase tax of the type adopted by Great Britain was considered at length, but was rejected on the ground that if nonessential items were excluded, the productivity of such a tax would be too small to make its enactment worth while.

The program adopted in 1944 was of even smaller importance from the point of view of the expected increases in yield. The most important action taken in that year was probably the abandonment of the system of forced saving which was a part of the individual income tax. Collections on this account were to terminate at the end of June 1944 with a resulting revenue loss of $110,000,000 in a full year's operation.

There were a good many minor changes in the income taxes. A $480 deduction for the blind was installed, special relief was set up applying to the earnings of married women and the alimony deduction was revised.

The changes in the tax on corporations included the installation of a one-year carry back and a three-year carry forward. Additional relief was provided by a special postwar deduction for deferred maintenance and repairs. One-half the expenditure for such purposes "incurred in a period to be fixed by the governor in council, may be charged against the income of a previous fiscal period but not farther back than the fiscal periods ending in 1943."

To facilitate the postwar transition, the treatment of expenditures for research and technical development were amended. All such expenditures as were of a current nature were to be allowed in the year of expenditure. Those of a capital nature were to be written off over a three-year period.

It was also provided that "in respect of bona fide new investment in depreciable assets carried out after a date to be designated by the governor in council, the taxpayer should be allowed rates of depreciation which may vary at the option of the taxpayer between maximum rates and minimum rates which will be one-half the ordinary rates."

To make available more quickly the postwar refunds under the excess profits tax, the taxpayers were allowed to assign the refundable portion of tax as security "in cases in which the governor in council is satisfied that the funds so obtained will be used in capital expenditures in preparation for postwar business giving desired employment."

Like the legislation in the United States of 1945, the Canadian program of 1944 seemed to be aimed primarily at the problem of postwar adjustment.

War Taxation in Great Britain.—The budget message which Sir John Simon presented immediately following the outbreak of World War II in Europe included tax proposals intended to produce £107,000,000 of additional revenue in the current fiscal year, and £226,000,000 in a year of full operation. As in most of the tax programs of the rearmament period, an increase in the standard rate under the income tax was the heart of the first wartime program. The increase in the standard rate, together with the accompanying reduction in the amounts of the so-called allowances, accounted for £70,000,000 of the £107,000,000 immediate increase in total tax revenues. The balance was to be made up by increasing the rates under the estate tax by 10%, by advances in the surtax schedule and by additions to the excises on alcoholic beverages, tobacco and sugar. The substantial difference between the immediate and ultimate productivity of the program was accounted for by the inclusion of an excess profits tax which would not, of course, produce immediate revenues. An armaments duty had already been enacted in 1939 in connection with the compulsory military training program. Sir John Simon now proposed to generalize this tax. The rate applied was to be 60%. Unlike the excess profits tax used in the United States, no regular invested capital option was provided under the British legislation of 1939.[7] The National Defense contribution was continued, and it was stipulated that the new excess profits tax was to be due only when it exceeded in amount this earlier profits tax.

Another tax program of somewhat smaller size was presented in April 1940. An increase in the standard rate was to produce £62,700,000 out of a total of £128,000,000 in a full year of operation. The balance was to come from the excises on beer, spirits, tobacco and matches, and from increases in the rates used by the post-office, and the telephone and telegraph systems.

At this time a general relief clause was inserted into the new excess profits tax, to be administered by a board of referees.

More significant than the measures actually put forward in the budget of April 1940, was the announcement of the government's intention to install a purchase tax on

[7]The invested capital option was allowed to new companies; *i.e.*, those commencing business after July 1, 1936. In the budget message of April 1940 it was pointed out that the invested capital alternate could only be used as a relief measure.

wholesale sales. No revenue estimates were made, and no rates were announced. It was merely indicated that the tax was to be levied at the wholesale level and was to exclude exports, food, tobacco, gasoline and services.

Sir John Simon reported the government's rejection of a proposal to levy a tax on increases on personal wealth attributable to the war, as well as his doubts concerning the feasibility of the forced saving proposal advocated by Sir John M. Keynes. On the other hand, it was proposed to place a limit on the amount of dividends which could be paid out during World War II.

By July 1940 it had become clear that the deficit would be much larger than originally anticipated. Sir Kingsley Wood reported a tax program intended to produce £239,000,000 additional revenue when in full operation. As in earlier programs, the major role was to be played by the standard rate. An increase in the latter was expected to produce £84,000,000. The balance was to come from increases in the surtaxes, from the duties on beer, tobacco, wines and entertainments, from the installation of differential rates under the new purchase tax and from another increase of 10% in the rates applied to estates.

Between the budget messages of April and July 1940 the rates used under the excess profits tax had been advanced from 60% to 100%. This action alone was expected to produce £40,000,000 of additional revenue yearly.

The tax legislation introduced by Sir Kingsley Wood in 1941 was intended to obtain another £250,000,000 a year from the income tax. This was to be done by reducing the allowances and the earned income credit. The result of this action was to extend the tax to approximately 2,000,000 persons not previously taxable.

The budget message of April 1941 was notable primarily for the relief measures which it contained. This message introduced the 20% postwar credit under the excess profits tax and led to the installation of a similar credit under the tax on personal incomes. The latter was intended to be the equivalent of the taxes collected by reason of the reduction in the allowances and the earned income credit. In a sense this credit was a concession to Sir John Keynes' forced saving proposal, which had been rejected in the budget message of April 1940.

Unlike its predecessors, the program introduced in April 1942 was concerned exclusively with commodity taxation. Increases were made in the duties on alcoholic beverages, tobacco and entertainment. The luxury rates used under the purchase tax were raised from 33⅓% to 66⅔%. This action was intended to produce £186,000,000 in additional revenue in a full year's operation, and was based on the idea that by this time the bulk of the untaxed purchasing power was to be found in the lower income brackets.[8]

Under the legislation of 1942 the National Defense contribution was extended for a period of five additional years.

The philosophy basic to the budget message of April 1943 was similar. Here again a statement appeared that the bulk of the remaining purchasing power lay in the lower brackets, and a tax program was set out to produce £110,000,000 additional revenue by increasing excises.

Before the budget message of April 1944 was presented, Great Britain, like Canada and the United States, had found it necessary to bring collections under its income tax to a current basis.

While Sir John Anderson forecast a large deficit in his budget message of April 1944, he made no proposals for increasing taxes. Much of his message was devoted to a defense of the 100% rate on excess profits, and to certain proposals intended to facilitate the postwar adjustment. Chief among these was a special initial allowance of 20% on the cost of new plant and machinery, which was to be in addition to the regular depreciation allowance. To go into effect after the war, this measure was designed to assist in the re-equipment of industry. A similar allowance of 10% was to be made on new buildings, and depreciation allowances were introduced for the extractive industries. More generous treatment was also to be accorded research expenditures in the postwar period. If such expenditures were of a capital nature they were to be written off in five years, or over the life of the asset if this was shorter. If they were not capital outlays, they were to be treated as a business expense.

It is evident that by 1944 Great Britain, like the United States and Canada, had passed the peak of its wartime tax program, and was looking toward the postwar period. This statement applies equally to the budget of April 1945, in which the bulk of the discussion concerned the success of the pay-as-you-go plan during its first year of operation, the extension of relief to small business under the excess profits tax and the double taxation treaty with the United States.

Summary of Wartime Tax Experience.—The tax revenues of the federal government of the United States reached a total of $43,000,000,000 in 1945. This represented a net increase of 245% over the level of 1942, and 750% over 1939, when the defense period was just beginning. Great Britain's tax revenues reached a level in 1945 which was 250% higher than in 1939. In that country the defense period began in 1935. The net increase in tax revenues during the subsequent decade was 333%. In Canada, which had no clearly defined "defense" period, tax revenues increased 385% between 1939 and 1945.

In all these countries the tax programs of World War II, and the rise in business activity which accompanied the war, produced substantial increases in the relative share of the tax burden borne by income taxes. This tendency was most marked in the United States. In 1945 the individual income tax alone produced approximately 45% of total tax revenue. When the corporate income tax was added, the percentage rose to 56. When the excess profits tax was included as well, no less than 81% of the total tax revenues of the federal government were accounted for. In 1939 the corporate and individual income taxes had accounted for 44% of total tax revenue.

The increase in the importance of the income taxes was also very marked in Canada. In 1945 the yield of taxes on corporate and individual incomes equalled 45% of the total. If the excess profits tax was included as well, 65% of total tax revenues were accounted for. In 1939 personal and corporate income taxes made up 33% of total tax revenue.

In 1945 the British levies on income, including the excess profits tax, made up 60% of total tax revenue. In 1939 the corresponding taxes accounted for 44% of the total. However, if the excess profits tax was left out of account, the percentage of the total obtained from income taxes was no higher in 1945 than it was in 1939.

In all these countries excess profits taxes played major roles in the wartime tax program. While different approaches were made to the definition of excess profits the tax used in each of these countries was primarily a levy on

[8]The chancellor of the exchequer reported, "today personal incomes below £500 represent nearly 85 percent of all personal incomes after payment of the income tax and surtax."

the increase in earnings over the prewar period. In the United States the statute provided an invested capital option. A similar option was used in Great Britain and Canada as an administrative relief measure.[9] It is interesting to note that in the United States the treasury department urged repeatedly that invested capital be made the exclusive basis for calculating excess. However, congress did not adopt this proposal, and in effect the base period earnings method was the principal basis for calculation in the United States as it was in Great Britain and Canada. Postwar credits were used in connection with this tax in all of these countries.

World War II brought drastic changes in the individual income taxes. In all cases, rates were advanced to extremely high levels and the base of the tax was broadened substantially. Thousands of persons who had never before been subject to the individual income tax found their names on the tax rolls. In all cases this broadening of the base led to the adoption of a general system of collection at the source, and the bulk of the collections was put on a current basis.

In all three countries, provisions were attached to the levies on personal incomes which partook of the nature of forced savings. Those used in Great Britain were the most thoroughgoing. The Canadian arrangements were withdrawn before the end of World War II. Those used in the United States were of an embryonic character. They were attached to the so-called Victory tax and were withdrawn even before that tax was absorbed in the general income tax. In all cases, the forced savings arrangements were enacted in order to reduce the shock of a drastic broadening in the base of the personal income tax.

One corollary of the increase in the relative importance of the income taxes was a decline in the position of commodity taxation. In the United States, excises produced only slightly more than 13% of total tax revenues in 1945 as compared with 34% in 1939. In Great Britain, commodity taxes accounted for 17% of the total in 1945; 19% in 1939. In Canada, these taxes produced 29% of total tax revenues in 1945 as compared with 49% in 1939.

This decline in relative importance did not mean that commodity taxation was neglected. On the contrary, the yield of the excise system of the United States increased by 249% over the period 1939–45; that of the United Kingdom rose nearly 218%; that of Canada increased nearly 226%. During this period, the United Kingdom introduced a variety of wholesale sales tax known as the purchases tax. Canada, which had relied heavily upon a general sales tax during the 1930s, obtained substantial additional revenues from this source during the war period. There was constant pressure to adopt a federal sales tax in the United States, but no legislation of this sort was enacted. A spendings tax was proposed by the treasury in the United States in 1943, but met with little favour in congress.

Customs duties continued to decline in importance during World War II. They were most important in Great Britain, but even there the yield of the customs dropped from 25% to 18% of total tax revenues between 1939 and 1945. In Canada the yield of the customs duties made up only 5% of total tax revenue in 1945 as compared with 18% in 1939. In the United States, they accounted for less than 1% of the total in 1945 as compared with 6% in 1939.

Death duties also declined in relative importance. In 1945 their yield made up only 1.4% of the total in the United States and 3.6% in the United Kingdom. This also came about in spite of substantial increases in the rates applied during the war period. The new Canadian succession tax which was introduced during the war period produced a minor portion of the dominion's tax revenues in 1945.

By the end of the ten eventful years there had appeared in each of these countries a healthy trend away from deficit spending and towards a balanced budget. Between the end of the war with Germany and the end of the war with Japan, the federal government in the United States found it possible to reduce its expenditures by more than 50%.

This reflected a sound policy of retrenchment necessary to keep the credit of the country secure.

The task of the reconversion period is to determine what taxes retard production and employment and to devise ways and means for their elimination. The work of the congress of the United States for the accomplishment of these objectives was started in 1945, and gave promise of resulting in the establishment of a sound tax system for the postwar period.

(*See* also BUDGETS, NATIONAL; BUSINESS REVIEW; DEBTS, NATIONAL; LAW; MUNICIPAL GOVERNMENT.)

BIBLIOGRAPHY.—Basic to an understanding of the tax history of the period 1937–46 are the budget messages in the United States, Great Britain and Canada. An understanding of the tax legislation of the United States also requires a study of the reports on the several tax bills prepared by the finance committee and the committee on ways and means, as well as the statements which the chairmen of these committees made when submitting the final bill to their respective chambers for ratification. These statements appear in the *Congressional Record.* See also R. G. Blakey and G. C. Blakey, *Federal Income Tax* (1940); A. G. Buehler, *The Undistributed Profits Tax* (1937); L. Crum, J. F. Fennelly, L. H. Seltzer, *Fiscal Planning for Total War,* National Bureau of Economic Research (1942); H. M. Groves, *Postwar Taxation and Economic Progress* (1946); J. R. Hicks, U. K. Hicks and L. Rostas, *Taxation of War Wealth* (1941); M. S. Kendrick, *The Undistributed Profits Tax* (1937); L. H. Kimmel, *Postwar Tax Policy and Business Expansion* (1943); Roswell Magill, *The Impact of Federal Taxes* (1943); Roswell Magill, *Taxable Income* (rev. ed. 1945); J. Mertens, *The Law of Federal Income Taxation* (1942–43); H. F. Morgenthau, *Summary Report to the Congress, July 21, 1945*—reprinted as Exhibit 51 in the *Annual Report of the Secretary of the Treasury on the State of the Finances for Fiscal Year Ended June 30, 1945* (pp. 397–431); C. A. Newport, *Income Tax Law and Practice* (1945); Randolph E. Paul, *Federal Estate and Gift Taxation* (1942); A. C. Pigou, *The Political Economy of War* (2d. ed., 1940); Carl Shoup, *et al, Facing the Tax Problem* (1937); Carl Shoup, "Taxation of Excess Profits," *Political Science Quarterly,* Vols. 55 and 56 (Dec. 1940, Jan. 1941); "Consumption Taxes" *Law and Contemporary Problems,* Vol. 8, No. 3 (1941); "Excess Profits Taxation," *Law and Contemporary Problems,* Vol. 10, No. 1 (1943); *Excise Taxes: United States, Canada and the United Kingdom,* Treasury Dept., Division of Tax Research (1944); "Final Report of the Committee of the National Tax Association on Federal Taxation of Corporations," *Proceedings of the National Tax Association* (1939); *Foreign Tax Data,* Joint Committee on Internal Revenue Taxation U.S. Government Printing Office (1943); *National Income and Expenditures of the United Kingdom, 1938–1945* (1946); "Sales Tax Proposals," U.S. Treasury (78th Cong. 1st Sess., 1943) (Reprint of pp. 1095–1272 of Hearings before Committee on Ways and Means on Revenue Revision 1943). (R. L. D.)

Tea

The International Tea committee was formed in 1933 to improve the tea industry, which had experienced alternate periods of prosperity and depression. The committee regulated exports and production and inaugurated a campaign to increase consumption. The U.S. was considered the most promising field for propaganda, and The Tea Bu-

[9]Except that in Great Britain statutory relief was granted to new companies through the invested capital method.

reau, Inc., was formed in New York to direct the publicity. On the outbreak of World War II these publicity activities were reduced. Under the Tea Control order of Sept. 1939 the British government took over all stocks of tea and later the ministry of food appointed a director of tea. The ministry of food made contracts with producers in India, Ceylon and East Africa covering quantities, prices, etc. In 1942 the ministry of food began to work under the Combined Food board at Washington and became the sole purchaser of tea for the Allies. Supplies were allotted to the armies, the trade and for shipments to neutrals. The threat of shortage in 1940 forced the British to ration tea to 2 oz. per week. Prices were also fixed, wholesale and retail. The U.S. tea supply came from India, Ceylon and East Africa; no Ethopian tea was imported, since there was no market for it. While coffee was rationed in the U.S., the consumption of tea increased slightly, but with the end of rationing the swing back to coffee occurred quickly.

World trade in tea in 1937 amounted to about 870,000,000 lb., divided as follows: India 354,000,000 lb.; Ceylon 234,900,000 lb.; Netherlands Indies 142,300,000 lb.; China 91,800,000 lb.; Japan 27,300,000 lb.; Formosa 16,800,000 lb. and Indo China 1,600,000 lb. The largest consumer nations were: Britain 449,000,000 lb.; United States 87,800,000 lb.; soviet union 46,700,000 lb.; Australia 46,500,000 lb.; Canada 40,400,000 lb.; Netherlands 29,700,000 lb.; Eire 23,600,000 lb. The tea industry of China is ancient and universal, each province formerly growing small quantities for local use. The nation's total production was unknown but was estimated to be about 900,000,000 lb., or more than the trade in tea of the rest of the world. In contrast, tea culture was relatively new in other countries. In India the industry was begun by the East India company in 1600.

Most of the crop was grown by tea companies. In Ceylon tea culture was introduced when the coffee industry was wiped out in 1869 by a blight. Tea growing is an old industry in the Netherlands Indies but was of much later development in East Africa. Most of the plantations there were started after 1925. Only small areas had been grown in Brazil and Peru, although experiments on new varieties were under way in South America.

The United States imported a total of about 85,000,000 lb. of tea per annum during the decade ending in 1937. Following World War I, the imports had exceeded 100,000,000 lb. from 1915 to 1918 inclusive, but this increase was not all for consumption. The total for 1939 was 100,000,000 lb. In 1943, the tea committee of the Combined Food board reduced the U.S. allotment to 65,000,000 lb., of which 50,000,000 lb. was for civilians. In 1944 imports were up again to the average of prewar years—90,645,000 lb.—which dropped off to 89,542,000 lb. in 1945. United States per capita tea consumption changed little, but the U.S. armies in Britain came to consume more tea than usual. (J. C. Ms.)

U.S. Tea Imports, 1937–46
(In pounds)

Year	Pounds	Year	Pounds
1937–38	85,838,000	1942–43	51,840,000
1938–39	89,600,000	1943–44	90,645,000
1939–40	100,119,000	1944–45	89,542,000
1940–41	101,687,000	1945–46	86,586,000
1941–42	94,429,000		

BIBLIOGRAPHY.—U.S. Bureau of the Census, *Statistical Abstract;* R. D. Morrison, *Tea* (Intl. Tea Comm., 1943); *Tea and Coffee Trade Jl.* (mo.).

Technical Training

See EDUCATION.

Technicolor

See MOTION PICTURES; PHOTOGRAPHY.

U.S. government appraisers setting standards of quality for tea imports at an annual meeting of the board in New York city. Meetings were suspended during World War II because of the reduction of varieties in teas imported

Tedder of Glenguin, 1st Baron

Baron Tedder of Glenguin (Arthur William Tedder) (1890–), British air officer, was born July 11, 1890, at Glenguin, Sterlingshire, Scotland. He was graduated in 1912 from Magdalene college, Cambridge, where he took a degree in history, and in 1914 he was with the colonial service in the Fiji Islands. After the outbreak of World War I he joined the army, served in France and was later transferred to the royal flying corps. He was commander of the royal air force in the far east (1936-38) and was promoted to deputy commander in chief of the R.A.F. in the middle east in 1940. The following year he was made commander in chief of the R.A.F. over the vast middle east area.

Tedder was credited with having effectively co-ordinated the British air and ground forces during the preparations for the El Alamein offensive. In July 1942 he was promoted air chief marshal and the same year he was knighted. On Nov. 27, 1942, Tedder was promoted to vice chief of air staff of the R.A.F. and he was named air chief of the Mediterranean theatre Feb. 11, 1943. On Dec. 28 of that year he was appointed deputy supreme commander of Allied invasion forces under Gen. Eisenhower, and on Oct. 15, 1944, he assumed the additional post of chief of Allied air operations in western Europe.

He replaced Lord Portal as chief of the air staff and first senior member of the air council, Jan. 1, 1946 and was raised to the peerage the same day, as Baron Tedder of Glenguin.

Tehran Conference (1943)

See International Conferences, Allied (World War II).

Telegraphy

The first half of the decade 1937–46 was marked by continued development and more extensive practical application of many technical improvements already known to the industry but not fully exploited. In the latter half of the decade, orderly progress was arrested by the sudden demands of World War II. In the civilian field, wartime telegraph services were sharply curtailed and plant expansion was limited by shortages of materials, equipment and personnel. Military needs, on the other hand, required the establishment of thousands of special installations and accelerated technical developments along certain lines. Telegraph laboratories were devoted almost exclusively to the development, testing and manufacture of special equipment for war purposes.

In the years prior to the war, most of the technical advances aimed at increasing the speed, capacity and accuracy of telegraph service through the improvement and better utilization of printing telegraph equipment. Progress in this direction was accelerated during the war years by the tremendous strains imposed by the war on the U.S. telegraph system.

Technical Progress.—Maximum usage of trunk lines was achieved by the invention of "Varioplex" (*see* below) and by the expansion of the carrier system. Telegraph carrier equipment superimposed a number of different frequencies on a single pair of wires and made it possible to obtain from a pair of wires as many as 36 independent telegraph circuits, capable of carrying 288 messages simultaneously.

Improved types of repeaters, including electron repeaters, were developed for installation at intermediate points in long circuits to strengthen electrical impulses and correct for signal distortion.

The facsimile method of transmitting telegrams, known as "Telefax," was highly developed, but wartime shortages of materials prevented large-scale manufacture and distribution of the special equipment required, except for military use. In this process, the original copy, carried on a revolving drum, was scanned by an electric eye, which transmitted for each minute area of the copy an electrical impulse that varied according to the relative darkness of the area. At the receiving end, these electrical impulses passed through a stylus, which traversed an electrosensitive recording paper moving at synchronized speed on the drum of a receiving machine.

The received copy required no processing and was ready for immediate use.

Automatic sending and receiving Telefax devices were developed for use in customers' offices to expedite the transmission of messages to and from telegraph offices. Other machines for public places permitted patrons to drop handwritten or typed telegrams into a slot. The machines would then transmit the telegrams in facsimile to the central telegraph office.

The use of Telefax was extended to the transmission of train orders by railroads and the rapid handling of reservations by air lines.

The facsimile system also was applied to submarine cable operation, and photographs, drawings and typewritten matter were transmitted between Europe and the U.S. until the extraordinary demands of the Allied governments and military forces for communication by cable made it necessary to discontinue cablephoto service.

A wartime development of Telefax was its application to languages using other than the Roman alphabet. The hitherto difficult problem of sending telegrams in Chinese, with its thousands of characters, was solved by use of Telefax. Machines were shipped to China for modernization of important elements of its communications system.

A by-product of Telefax was the "Multifax," a business machine for the preparation of stencils and copies by facsimile methods. The machine, which could operate either within a single office or between two distant offices, prepared stencils of both text and drawings with absolute accuracy.

Facsimile transmission of messages was advantageously applied to radio in 1946 when Western Union inaugurated a marine news reporting service between pilot boats in the outer New York harbour and the main office building in that city. Officers on the pilot boat wrote on slips of paper data regarding the arrival of vessels and placed the slips in the transmitting cylinder of the Telefax machine installed in the wheelhouse. The messages were sent by radio beam to Western Union's marine news room, to be reproduced in facsimile. The news would then be flashed over the marine news tickers.

Another application of Telefax to radio telegraphy was the "Telecar," a mobile delivery unit developed to speed the delivery of telegrams in the outlying areas of large cities. The Telefax unit, mounted in a vehicle cruising about a prescribed area, received telegrams over the radio beam from the local main office for delivery directly to addressees within that area. As soon as the address appeared on the message, the "roving telegraph office" was on the way to make immediate delivery.

Sub-centre switching was perfected. Through this system a number of small branch telegraph offices or patrons' offices in a remote area, each having a private line to a local central point, could be automatically connected, over a limited number of trunks, with a main telegraph office in a large city for the transmission of messages in either direction.

Some of the entirely new developments during the decade were of great importance to the future of the telegraph industry. Notable among these were reperforator switching, Varioplex and radio beam telegraphy.

Reperforator switching systems were installed in 5 key cities, and 25 were scheduled to be in use by 1950. Each would serve as a central point through which telegrams would pass to and from all places in the states or areas in which they were located. These systems eliminated manual resending of telegrams and ensured greater speed, accuracy and economy of operation. With this equipment, incoming messages, arriving in the form of perforations on a tape, were automatically switched to the desired outgoing circuit, simply by pressing a button, and were automatically sent on to their destinations without manual typing. This cut transmission time for relayed messages approximately in half and reduced the possibility of error.

The Telemeter service was developed to provide direct telegraph connections between pairs of teleprinter users in distant cities. This service was made possible by the invention of the Varioplex, a multi-channel telegraph system in which the total capacity of a circuit was divided among users actively transmitting over the line at a given instant instead of being divided equally among all users, idle or busy. By means of the Varioplex system, a number of pairs of users could be connected to a telegraph wire. It was possible to set up a large number of long, lightly loaded, private-communication circuits, which formerly had been impracticable. The service became known as Telemeter service because the charge was based on the volume of words sent as shown by an automatic word-count meter on each customer's line.

During World War II several departments of the U.S. and British governments were in instantaneous and continuous contact with each other between Washington and London over Varioplex facilities. The direct Varioplex channels between the U.S. navy and the British admiralty were especially useful in the war against submarines.

Frequency modulation was successfully applied to the operation of telegraph carrier systems. Signals were transmitted by varying the tone according to the telegraph code instead of interrupting the tone, as in amplitude modulation. This added to the reliability of carrier operation, since FM signals are less susceptible to atmospheric interference.

Radio-beam transmission was perhaps the most significant advance of the decade in telegraphy. Plans were made to establish radio-beam telegraph systems with high towers 30–50 mi. apart to interconnect the major cities in the U.S. Utilizing super-high-frequency radio waves transmitted by directional beam, this system would eventually eliminate the need for the familiar trunk pole lines and hundreds of thousands of miles of wire between main telegraph centres, although wires would still be used to link tributary towns with the main centres. The radio-beam telegraph would furnish a larger number of channels for the handling of telegraph traffic. By application of the carrier system to the radio beam, it became possible to send more than 2,000 telegrams in both directions simultaneously over the radio-beam system. Since atmospheric static does not exist in the microwave region, radio-beam transmission is unaffected by electrical disturbances. It practically eliminated interruptions caused by ice and wind storms and falling trees. It also cost less to install and maintain the beam system.

Antennas equipped with parabolic reflectors transmitted the signals in a narrow beam, using a power of less than 1 watt and frequencies of more than 4,000 megacycles. Since super-high-frequency waves travel in a straight line, they must be redirected at intervals to compensate for the curvature of the earth. Unattended repeater stations located in towers on hills or any available elevations in the ground automatically relayed signals without delay or interference.

Carbonyl powdered iron was developed as the principal ingredient of magnetic cores for high-frequency coils and transformers used in carrier systems.

Wartime Developments.—Many technical discoveries by telegraph engineers during World War II were the result of specialized research for the armed forces. In addition to their purely military value, some of these developments had important peacetime applications.

Telekrypton, a cryptographic machine, automatically and simultaneously encoded messages as they were typed on the sending teleprinter, in Washington for example, and automatically decoded them as they were received in London.

Packaged telegraph units were provided by the telegraph company to the U.S. signal corps and were used with great success overseas. These were miniature semi-automatic telegraph stations designed to meet the army's need for a simple, compact and portable relay system for use in the field. Each unit combined sending and receiving sets and required only one operator. The unit could be placed in operation in 10 minutes without the use of tools, and as many as 20 units could be transported in a single truck. They were packed to withstand rough handling, vibration and immersion in salt water. Teleprinters were redesigned to increase the operating speed from the usual 65 words per minute to 100 words per minute for special applications.

An improved synchronizing method was developed for multiplex distributors, making it practicable to use four-channel multiplex printing telegraph equipment on long overseas radio circuits. This equipment, which allowed a circuit to be used for a number of high-speed channels, had previously been confined to land-line operation.

A by-product of telegraph laboratory research in wartime which was expected to find important uses in industry, apart from the field of communications, was the Western Union concentrated-arc lamp. This lamp contained permanent electrodes sealed into a glass tube filled with inert gas at atmospheric pressure. It provided an intense white light from a luminescent source as small as 0.003 in. in diameter, the nearest approach to a point source of light thus far obtained by science. It could be modulated, or dimmed and brightened, for signalling purposes, at frequencies of much more than 10,000 times a second. The concentrated-arc lamp had 5–10 times the brilliance and up to 100 times the life of a normal tungsten projection lamp of similar wattage. In addition to its use for telegraph purposes, the lamp was expected to find wide applications in such fields as photography, microscopy, optics and lensless projection.

Industrial Organization.—In 1942 the telegraph business of the United States was divided among the Western Union Telegraph company, which accounted for more than 70% of the national business; Postal Telegraph, Inc., which handled less than 20%, and the American Telephone and Telegraph company, which offered a national teletypewriter exchange service. In 1943, congress enacted legislation permitting the merger of domestic telegraph companies. The Federal Communications commission approved an agreement for the consolidation of Western Union and Postal Telegraph on Sept. 27, 1943. The merger was consummated on Oct. 7, 1943. It eliminated the duplication of public telegraph facilities throughout the U.S. and established a single national system with uniform standards of efficiency.

Cable telegraphy was made more efficient during the decade by the application of printing telegraph equipment to the cables of U.S. companies, by the use of Varioplex, and by the introduction of improved vacuum tube amplifiers, measuring and balancing devices and repeaters.

Multiplex printing telegraph equipment was applied during the war to the submarine cables to Alaska, increasing their capacity 400%. A supplementary chain of cables, known as the Alaskan Communications system, was laid by army engineers to connect strategic islands in the Aleutian group.

World War II did not interfere with U.S.-operated cables in the Atlantic except to the extent that the U-boat menace may have impeded their usual speedy repair. To assist the Allied invasion of Normandy, the former German cable from Horta, an island in the Azores, to Emden, Germany, was picked up and swung over to Cherbourg, France, by the army communications service. It was then operated for military use, by direct connection with a Western Union cable from Horta to New York, to carry printing telegraph circuits extending from Washington to Paris.

As the result of several years of experimentation early in the decade, many miles of submarine cable were buried in the ocean bed to protect it from frequent and costly damage caused by trawlers dragging fishing nets along the bottom. The burying of cables was accomplished by means of a specially constructed plow attached by chain to the cable ship. The cable was fed through the plow into a trench which filled rapidly because of the washing action of the water. An instrument known as a depthometer was devised to determine magnetically the depth to which the cable was buried in the ocean bed. (*See* also FEDERAL COMMUNICATIONS COMMISSION.) (J. L. E.)

BIBLIOGRAPHY.—J. M. Herring, "Public vs. Private Ownership," *Annals American Academy of Pol. and Soc. Sci.*, 201:96–104 (Jan. 1939). Consult *Readers' Guide to Periodical Literature* and *Industrial Arts Index.*

Teleki, Pál

Count Teleki (1879–1941), Hungarian statesman, was born Nov. 1, 1879, in Budapest. His political career started in 1905, when he was elected to parliament. He was appointed prime minister and minister of foreign affairs in 1926, and in 1939 he was again named prime minister, retaining that post until his death. While Teleki was not averse to using Germany's might in winning back the lost province of Transylvania from Rumania, he nevertheless feared that a too great dependence on Hitler would jeopardize Hungary's independence. This misgiving was seen in the disclosure after his death that Count Teleki was one of the Hungarians who backed the book *Why Germany Cannot Win the War,* which broke all sales records in the country. But the German stranglehold on Rumania and Bulgaria in early 1941 placed Hungary in a precarious position.

Worried by the grave turn of events and by the impending invasion of Yugoslavia, the 61-year-old statesman committed suicide on April 3, 1941, in Budapest.

Telephone

During the ten years from 1937 through 1946, the telephone was called upon to meet unprecedented service demands, and telephone usage mounted steadily to higher and higher levels. The communications requirements of the nations of the world increased tremendously as they recovered from the depression of the early 1930s and climbed to dizzy heights as World War II spread out from Europe to global proportions. With the end of hostilities in the summer of 1945, the demand for telephone service, instead of diminishing, continued to increase.

As the decade began, the people of the world were being served by an estimated 35,028,682 telephones, or 1.63 telephones per 100 population. More than half, or 18,862,127 telephones, were in service in the United States and Canada. In the United States alone there were almost 14 telephones for each 100 people. Great Britain at that time was served by more than 2,500,000 telephones, or 5.4 telephones per 100 population. Europe had 36% of the world's telephones and Asia less than 5%.

People in the U.S. not only had more telephones than any other people in the world, but they used the telephone much more. In 1937 the average person in the U.S. made 197 telephone calls, as compared with 40 in Great Britain, 70 in Australia, 174 in Denmark and 152 in Sweden.

By 1946, the number of telephones in the world had increased to approximately 51,500,000, or 2.24 telephones per 100 population. More than 58% of this total, or 30,-100,000 telephones, served the United States and Canada, and the number of telephones per 100 population in the United States had increased to 21. During 1946, the 4,000,000th telephone was installed in Great Britain, bringing its number of telephones per 100 population up to 8. Europe had 33% of the world's telephones, and Asia about 3%.

Great as were these increases, the gain in telephone usage was even greater. In the United States the average person carried on 284.4 conversations a year. Denmark and Sweden ran a close second with an estimated 243 calls per person. Elsewhere in the world the average was considerably less, although exact figures were not available.

Years of Recovery.—In the United States the period from 1937 to Sept. 1, 1939, when Germany invaded Poland, was one of moderate growth and of extensive improvement of telephone plant.

First of these improvements was the introduction into regular service of the combined handset telephone in 1937. This type of instrument combined the ringing apparatus and telephone into one compact set.

The conversion of central office equipment from the manually-operated type to the dial-operated type proceeded steadily both in the United States and Europe. In 1938 a new type of dial switching equipment designated as "crossbar" was introduced into the regular plant and thereafter was extensively installed in larger central offices. The name "crossbar" derived from the fact that strips of metal were placed at right angles to each other in such a way that they were caused to rock slightly by electric relays and thus establish contacts in obedience to the dial.

Although the important field of application for dial service was in switching local traffic, it was being employed for the completion of toll calls to an increasing degree both in Europe and the United States. Operator toll dialing had been in use in Switzerland and Belgium and in certain areas of the United States; and in 1938 two areas in the state of Ohio were converted from manual to dial toll. In this method of operation the outward toll operator could complete the call without the help of other operators at the terminal of the toll line or intermediate switching points, by sending impulses over the toll line to the dial switching equipment at the other end.

By 1938, U.S. telephone engineers had demonstrated that the coaxial cable was an important instrumentality for providing more abundant long distance telephone circuits. In their hands, it had provided as many as 500 telephone channels over a distance of 2,000 miles. In some of the European countries—notably England, France and Germany—the coaxial cable had been more largely stressed as a conductor for the point-to-point transmission of television programs than as an adjunct to the telephone.

The coaxial cable operated on the "carrier" principle, enabling two pairs of conductors (each pair consisting of a wire surrounded by a concentric metal pipe and used to transmit in one direction only) to provide a large group of telephone channels or, alternatively, a single television channel, depending upon the range of the filters and the amplifying devices or repeaters with which the cable was equipped. In 1939 the first commercial installations of a coaxial cable got under way between Minneapolis, Minn., and Stevens Point, Wis., a distance of 200 miles.

By 1938, broad band systems of transmission by which 12 telephone conversations could be carried simultaneously on a single pair of open wires, or on two pairs of wires in cables, had been proved satisfactory in the United States and were going into extensive commercial use. Further research later increased the number of telephone channels provided simultaneously to 16 on one pair of open wires.

Most countries in Europe added to their long distance telephone cable networks prior to World War II, principally by the use of 12-channel carrier systems on existing cables.

In the United States, exchange telephone cables also were notably improved in 1939. As many as 4,200 wires of No. 26 gauge were placed within a lead sheath of 2⅝ in. over-all diameter, an increase of 600 wires over the previous maximum.

During these years, overseas telephone service operating on an international basis experienced phenomenal growth. Inaugurated in 1927 with an overseas radio channel between the United States and England, the number of overseas radio telephone circuits for the handling of public message business had increased by 1937 to more than 175. At the time war broke out in Europe, 93% of the world's telephones, located in more than 70 countries or territories could be interconnected.

In Sept. 1938 the great hurricane which struck New England and parts of New Jersey and New York put about 600,000 telephones out of service, isolated about 500 communities completely from communication with the rest of the world, damaged or destroyed thousands of miles of toll wire, flooded central office buildings and brought transportation to a standstill.

Telephone forces in the affected areas went into action at full speed, but the damage was too great for them to repair it quickly. Within 48 hours, crews from other areas along the Atlantic seaboard, the middle west, and as far as Omaha, Nebr., had started to their assistance. Trainloads of men, fully equipped with trucks, tools and emergency supplies were en route to the affected areas; crews from nearby areas were rolling over the highways with their own trucks and equipment. More than 2,300 men with 600 vehicles moved into the stricken areas of New England to help the more than 7,000 telephone men there. They stayed there for weeks, working from dawn to dusk, and longer, until the job was done.

Defense Efforts.—Just one year later, man-made disaster struck in Europe. With it, a sudden great increase in telephone use took place in the United States. Practically overnight, the number of long distance calls increased 30% and passed all previous records. Nearly twice the normal number of calls were made to and from Europe.

First France, then England clamped rigid censorship on overseas circuits, only government calls being permitted. The volume of calls over the remaining circuits to Europe and to the rest of the world jumped instantly to new high levels.

Military establishments, government ordnance and munitions plants sprang up, many of them in remote rural areas where the existing telephone plant was inadequate to serve the new purpose. As this production effort expanded throughout the country, the demand for long distance service increased enormously.

Late in 1939 the Bell system authorized the construction of a new transcontinental cable, running 1,600 miles underground from Omaha, Neb., to Sacramento, Calif., and connecting at those points with the eastern and Pacific coast cable networks. This augmented the four existing open-wire lines west of Chicago, Ill., which then provided 170 circuits.

Network of Spiral-4 and other field cable at the 1st U.S. army headquarters on the Normandy beachhead in 1944. Each of the Spiral-4 cables could handle three telephone and four telegraph circuits

Other long distance facilities were extended in 1940 by about 500,000 circuit miles to help meet the unprecedented demands for long distance service. Approximately one-third of these circuits were provided by means of broad band transmission systems. At the end of the year, about two-thirds of all long distance telephone circuits were in cable.

At the same time, prudent measures were taken to safeguard telephone facilities. Reserve power equipment was installed or ordered at all important telephone central offices which did not already have it. The establishment of alternate toll routes between important points was speeded.

The telephone companies co-operated with the military in army manoeuvres and aeroplane warning tests and provided promptly the facilities needed at camps, air fields, arsenals and munitions plants.

The number of Bell system telephones in service increased 950,000 in 1940, at that time the largest gain ever recorded in one year, to 17,484,000. The total number of telephones in the United States at the end of that year was 21,860,000.

The average number of telephone conversations per day was 79,303,000.

By the end of 1940, overseas service to Belgium, France, Gibraltar, Greece, Luxembourg and the Netherlands was suspended because of World War II. Although transatlantic traffic fell off, calls to South America, Hawaii and Australia gradually increased, so that the total volume of overseas traffic was nearly as great as it was before the war. Facilities for additional circuits to South America were built, and facilities to the Caribbean countries were improved.

Coastal and harbour radio telephone service increased, with more than 2,500 vessels equipped by the end of 1940 for communication with any land telephone.

While these defense activities were going forward in the United States, the telephone personnel of England were grimly battling the blitz. The Germans started bombing Great Britain in April 1940. In the 11 months from Sept. 1940 to the end of July 1941, between 45,000 and 50,000 high explosive bombs fell on the London region; incendiaries were numbered in the millions.

At the same time, practically every other English city and town of any importance was visited by the bombers.

Telephone communication was seriously interrupted. In the London area alone between Sept. 1940 and Sept. 1941, bombs fractured 1,695 cables. Repairing this damage required the splicing of nearly 3,000 joints and connecting more than 500,000 wires. Damage to telephone exchanges ranged from broken windows to complete destruction in a few cases.

The demand for telephone service in the United States in 1941 was greater than in any preceding year. By the end of the year it was estimated that there were about 23,500,000 telephones in service in the United States, an estimated gain for the year of about 1,500,000, (more than 40% over the 1940 gain). The estimated average number of daily telephone conversations grew to 85,000,000, about 5,700,000 above the corresponding 1940 figure. The increase in toll calls was greatest in those parts of the country where defense activity was most intense.

To meet this unprecedented demand for telephone service, expenditures for new plant construction mounted to approximately $420,000,000. This vast expansion, carried out in the face of growing shortages of a number of materials, called for the use of substitute materials wherever they could be used effectively and for the conservation of existing facilities and materials to the fullest extent.

The War Years.—Starting in 1939 and continuing throughout World War II, conservation of vital materials and manpower was practised scrupulously in the United States by the telephone companies. By the end of 1943, the rate of use of strategic war materials showed the following savings over the high point of 1941: iron and steel 83%; nickel and zinc 91%; copper 93%; tin 95%; aluminum 98%; and crude rubber 100%. In one year alone, 20,000 tons of paper were saved in the printing of directories, one-third the amount normally used for this purpose. Foreseeing the shortage of telephone instruments, the telephone companies accumulated a stock pile of 750,000 telephone sets of all types.

In 1942, the manufacture of telephones for civilian use was stopped, not to be resumed until 1944, when a limited number of instruments were authorized by the War Production board.

To conserve manpower and offset the eventual loss of about 68,700 employees to the armed forces, the work week was lengthened in many areas, and streamlined maintenance schedules and practices were put into effect.

Camps, cantonments, airports and flying schools as well as ordnance and industrial plants, some as big as good-sized cities, were being built with remarkable speed. To provide telephone service for them frequently meant the building of cable routes miles in length and sometimes a complete new central office building and equipment. Many such projects were rushed to completion within one-third to one-half normal engineering and construction time. Altogether more than 7,000 switchboard positions and more than 600,000 telephones were installed in such establishments at a cost of nearly $100,000,000.

From the beginning, the U.S. army and navy recognized the morale-building importance of telephone service for members of the armed forces. Public telephone service was provided in and near all military and naval establishments, and at nearly all larger camps attended telephone centres were built, providing pleasant, comfortable surroundings. Telephone centres also were maintained at army and navy hospitals, with additional conveniences such as bedside service and oversize booths for wheel chairs.

In further assistance to the army and navy, the telephone companies conducted plant schools where more than 7,000 army and navy technicians received training in switchboard installation and repair, teletypewriter service and line work; operated army switchboards, 3,000 operators being engaged in this assignment at one time; provided private line services which included 400,000 miles of intercity leased telephone and teletypewriter channels and 2,600 teletypewriter stations; helped the signal corps install communications facilities along the Alaska highway; and devised a radio teletypewriter system reaching to all theatres of action.

Work which was started late in 1939 on the buried transcontinental cable was completed in 1942, more than doubling the coast-to-coast circuits. Simultaneously, through use of open wire and carrier systems, 60 additional transcontinental circuits were provided prior to Pearl Harbor. More than 8,500,000 circuit miles of toll and long distance circuits were added during the war. Most of these miles of circuits were provided by the installation of carrier systems, which used a minimum of material.

A significant step in the development of automatic long

Telephone lines on Okinawa where U.S. army linemen helped to keep communication wires in order during the campaign in the Pacific

distance switching was taken in 1943, when a new toll office housing an automatic switching system particularly suited to handling toll and long distance calls in metropolitan areas was cut into service in Philadelphia, Pa. That year, too, an automatic ticketer was placed in service in the Los Angeles, Calif., area. With this device, the customer could dial direct over a toll circuit, and a ticket was automatically printed giving the full information necessary for charging the call.

Long distance traffic volume rose sharply during the war, total toll messages for the system averaging 80% higher in 1945 than in 1939, while longer haul calls tripled over the same period. In the face of critical shortages of facilities and operating personnel, such increases presented tremendous problems.

More switchboard positions and circuits were needed than could be provided. Many additional operators had to be recruited and trained. Changes had to be devised in engineering and operating practices to make more effective use of available circuits, switchboard positions and force.

On Nov. 1, 1942, by an order of the Board of War Communications, a toll priority plan was set up under which calls essential to the conduct of the war or to public health, welfare and safety were given precedence on the wires.

A second hurricane of great intensity caused widespread destruction from Cape Hatteras to Maine in Sept. 1944. It put out of service more than 400,000 telephones and cut off nearly 50 communities from long-distance lines. With the help of nearly 1,000 men and 350 trucks and work cars from other Bell operating areas as far away as Ohio, construction and maintenance forces completed the general restoration of service in 12 days despite wartime shortages.

Return of Peace.—Following the end of World War II, it was possible to disclose some of the wartime research and production achievements of the industry. Telephone laboratories were revealed as major contributors to electronic developments such as radar, gun directors, rockets, torpedoes, guided aerial missiles, detection of submarines and magnetic mines. In all, more than 1,200 military projects were carried through to completion. In four years—1942 through 1945—telephone factories supplied to the government more than $2,000,000,000 worth of communication, electronic and other specialized equipment.

At the end of the war, more than 2,000,000 applications for telephone service were waiting because of lack of facilities. Furthermore, the new demand for additional service continued at a very high level. By a rapid reconversion of the telephone manufacturing establishments and by rapid building up of the depleted forces of the telephone companies, it was possible within a year of the war's end to increase the number of telephones in service by about 3,500,000. However, as the old applications were cleared up their place was largely taken by new ones, so that by the end of 1946 the decrease in the total number of waiting applicants was slight.

The Bell system's postwar construction program to restore adequate telephone facilities and to resume and extend the continuing programs, interrupted by the war, for the development and improvement of the telephone system was well under way by the end of 1945. Among other objectives, the program aimed to make telephone service available to 1,000,000 additional farm homes within a few years. As part of over-all plans to strengthen the long distance networks, about 1,500 miles of coaxial cable had been placed in the ground by the year's end, with several thousand more miles scheduled for completion in the next few years. Suitably equipped, this type of cable could transmit television or carry several hundred telephone conversations simultaneously. Such a system, therefore, not only provided needed additional telephone circuits in large quantity, but could also serve as the basis for a nation-wide television network.

Construction also advanced during 1946 on an experimental microwave radio relay system that was expected to be suitable for transmission of telephone conversations or television. Mobile radio-telephone service to vehicles, permitting two-way communication between mobile units and any regular telephone, was being provided as rapidly as equipment became available in major U.S. cities and on certain principal intercity highways. Progress also was made in the automatic long-distance switching program, the goal of which was to enable any operator to dial direct, without assistance of another operator, any telephone in the United States.

At the end of 1946, almost 120,000,000 calls a day were being made over the more than 30,000,000 telephones in the United States. Although a large number of applications for main telephone service still were being held awaiting the provision of facilities, many of these were filled within the year. Telephone factories were producing needed

Above: Televising the V-J day celebrations at Times square in New York city, 1945

Upper left: Engineers at the controls in the New York studios of television station WCBW of the Columbia Broadcasting system during 1945

Left: Installation work on a high frequency antenna atop the Empire State building in New York city

Below: United Nations Security council session being picked up by television cameras and relayed to overflow crowds outside the building at Hunter college, N.Y., in 1946

equipment at the highest rate in their history, and heavily augmented installation forces were placing the new facilities in service in record time.

Without question, more telephone service was being furnished to more people than ever before in history, and every effort was being exerted to make the service better than it had ever been. (*See* also FEDERAL COMMUNICATIONS COMMISSION.)

BIBLIOGRAPHY.—*Bell Telephone Magazine,* Annual Reports of the American Telephone and Telegraph Company, 1937–45; World Telephone Statistics. (W. S. G.)

Telescope

See ASTRONOMY.

Television

The scientific advances in television insofar as they had become noticeable to the general public by the end of 1946 lay principally in the field of vacuum tubes. The orthicon and the image orthicon tubes announced in 1939 and 1945, respectively, were very sensitive pickup devices, the latter making possible the showing of scenes illuminated by twilight or candlelight. This greatly extended the scope of news and sports broadcasts. The development of more efficient "picture tubes" made possible in 1946 the building of commercial receivers adapted for use in well lighted rooms.

The use of mobile television vans for the relaying of special events programs was initiated in 1937. Scenes were televised and relayed by radio to the station for rebroadcasting. On April 30, 1939, mobile units were used to televise the opening of the New York World's fair, at which time Pres. Franklin D. Roosevelt became the first chief executive of the United States to appear on television. The V-J day ceremonies in Central park, New York city, christening of the aircraft carrier "Franklin D. Roosevelt" by Pres. Harry S. Truman, the Republican National convention in Philadelphia in 1940, the Louis-Conn championship boxing match in 1946, important football games, and other events were brought to the public by this and similar equipment. The Hooper survey reported that 141,375 persons saw the Louis-Conn fight by television. In 1945, largely as the result of wartime developments, this mobile equipment was supplemented by suitcase type units, which were used for many remote pickups.

Following an experience with air-borne television in 1937–39, the Radio Corporation of America and the National Broadcasting company, during World War II developed for the U.S. government two noteworthy applications of television. The "ring" system of air-borne reconnaissance television supplied to ground stations more than 100 mi. away detailed pictures televised from heights of 10,000 ft. and more. The "block" system utilized lightweight equipment for unattended operation in aircraft and guided missiles. In these and other ways, television participated in the Allied victory.

In another useful though less spectacular service, television was used to train air raid wardens and instruct them in methods of resuscitation and fire fighting. Receivers were placed in the New York police stations, and classes there were instructed by experienced personnel in the studios. In no other way could instruction have been given so rapidly and completely to so many.

As in war, so in peace, a number of school systems in 1946 ordered television receivers for classroom use and made arrangements with broadcasting stations for programs at times when they could be utilized by the schools. To this service was added the showing of special news events, and of dramatic presentations, making these features part of the actual experience of the students.

Utilizing special types of kinescopes capable of pioneering brilliant pictures, theatre projection equipment was developed and demonstrated in 1941. A 15 ft. x 20 ft. picture was shown in the New Yorker theatre in New York on Jan. 24, utilizing scenes from Madison Square garden, Ebbets field and Camp Upton. The light from the face of the kinescope was reflected by a large spherical mirror, passed through a correction plate and thus projected on the viewing screen with a picture brilliance comparable to that of a home television receiver.

After extensive study by the Radio Technical Planning board and after public hearings lasting several months, the Federal Communications commission, in 1945, changed the frequency band for television from the assignments which had been in use for some years. The new allocation provided for 13 standard 6 megacycles (mc.) channels for commercial television in the band of 44 to 216 mc., and permitted the assignment of 16–20 mc. channels between 480 and 920 mc. for experimental transmission. The wider, higher frequency channels were provided in answer to the request for facilities suitable for the development of higher definition and for colour television.

During 1945 and 1946, manufacturers developed transmitters, receivers, special tubes and other equipment for the utilization of these frequencies. Studies were made of the propagation of signals in this little known region, and a beginning was made in determining how best to take advantage of this previously neglected part of the spectrum. These channels permitted pictures of increased clarity and gave room for the broadcasting of colour television, which required at least twice the frequency space of black and white television. Several manufacturers and broadcasters were experimenting with colour before 1940, and resumed this work after the end of the war.

The Columbia Broadcasting system, during the latter part of the period, was an active proponent of the early introduction of colour television, carried on extensive development and gave many demonstrations of its colour system. Late in 1946, the Columbia Broadcasting system applied to the FCC for a commercial licence for broadcasting colour television. This resulted in extensive hearings, discussion of standards and of the question whether or not colour television was ready for commercialization. These hearings were scheduled to be continued in 1947.

The system of colour television as demonstrated by CBS was like that of most other investigators in that it uses rotating colour filters at the transmitter and receiver. In Oct., 1946 the Radio Corporation of America demonstrated an all-electronic colour system wherein the signals representative of each of the three primary colours were simultaneously generated and transmitted. With this system one of the colour transmission channels (green) could be used to provide black and white pictures on a conventional black and white picture receiver. This system had the advantage that standardizing such a colour system would not render black and white receivers obsolete, as they could be adapted to receive in black and white the same picture transmitted in colour.

Many improvements in the received picture were made after 1941. On July 1, 1941, station WNBT became the first commercially licensed transmitter to go on the air. The number of lines in the picture were increased in 1941 from 441 to 525. This was followed by improved picture synchronization, flatter surface picture tubes, and brighter pictures of better colour and contrast to give an over-all better result in the user's receiver. Many of these developments were commercially introduced in 1946 as the post-war receivers became available.

The use and value of television, so far as broadcasters and sponsors were concerned, was a function of the number of receivers in use. In 1940 the number was only a few thousand, all in the vicinity of the few stations operating in New York, Philadelphia, Chicago and Los Angeles. Later surveys indicated a large potential market, and production in the latter part of 1946 was on a scale not known before.

In 1937, the RCA and NBC experimental stationW2XBS was active, and several other organizations were making occasional broadcasts and conducting other experimental work. In Dec., 1946, in spite of the handicaps which had been imposed by war, and the long uncertainties with respect to standards, there were 7 licensed stations giving regular service, 2 experimental stations giving limited service, 47 stations for which construction permits had been issued by the FCC, and 21 applications for stations still pending.

Programs and methods for meeting program and operating costs were in the forefront of discussion in 1945–46. The various broadcasters were experimenting with many types of programs, and brought items of fine quality and high entertainment value to the public. Boxing, wrestling, football and other sports remained in favour, and a number of dramatic presentations set an excellent mark for the future. At the end of Sept. 1946, 22 large advertisers were sponsoring television presentations of interest to the public. With this kind of participation it apeared that commercial television with high quality of home entertainment was on a practicable basis.

Television shows, unlike those of the legitimate theatre, could generally be given once only, and thus involved high expense. Networks helped to spread the cost, and consequently they were part of television planning from the earliest days. Network programming also made available to people at great distances those news events, sports and high quality dramatic presentations which otherwise would be enjoyed only by those near a particular station. The frequencies used in television were such that they could not be relayed directly or by wire for long distances. Two solutions were possible—radio relays and coaxial cables, each with intermediate repeater or booster stations. The American Telephone and Telegraph company and others were actively at work along these lines. Radio relays were in use in 1946 at a number of points, and the coaxial line from New York to Washington was in use for connecting stations along the Atlantic seaboard.

The Westinghouse Electric and Manufacturing company, with the assistance of the Glenn L. Martin Co. and broadcasters, in 1946 began tests on "stratovision," in which the television signal was rebroadcast from a plane flying at high altitude, in order that a large area, including numerous cities, could be served by one transmitter for a given program.

One of the most spectacular applications of television in 1946 was its use in connection with the Bikini atom bomb tests. Television cameras installed about three miles from the explosions, as well as others on planes, picked up and broadcast the pictures to observers, and made possible the photographing of close-up views of the results.

(B. E. Sd.; G. L. Bs.)

British Television.—Television as a public service began in Great Britain in 1936. Its first 10 years did not show the same rate of progress as sound broadcasting (which started in 1922), but six years of this period were war years.

Training instructions for New York city's air raid wardens were televised and viewed by trainees on receiving sets installed at local police precincts

The BBC television service that began in 1936 was the first regular service of entertainment value, but it was by no means the first essay in television. Experiments went back to 1929, when the BBC first lent its transmitter to the British inventor John L. Baird, who used a low definition system (30-line definition, medium-wave transmission, with a tall, narrow screen). High-definition, ultra-shortwave television came in 1936. By that time two rival systems were in the field, one promoted by Baird Television and one by Marconi-Electrical and Musical industries. When high-definition television began in 1936, both systems were used side by side. The first BBC television station was equipped with two complete systems, from studio to transmitter, one installed by Baird Television and the other by Marconi-E.M.I., the only common element being the sound transmitter. Programs were to be produced and transmitted by the two systems alternately.

The opening of the service was forestalled by a sudden demand for television entertainment at the Radio exhibition of Aug. 1936. With new equipment and untried techniques, programs were produced and relayed to the stands. Then in November came the formal opening of the station and the beginning of regular programs, and in Feb. 1937, the alternation of systems came to an end. The British postmaster general's permanent advisory committee on television recommended that the standards of the Marconi-E.M.I. system should be adopted. From then onward this remained the only television system used by the BBC.

From 1937, the BBC television station remained housed in one wing of a vast old entertainment palace on the heights of north London, 300 ft. above sea level. It had two studios, each 70 ft. by 30 ft. by 25 ft. high, one of them having four Emitron cameras and one three. Standards were 405 lines, 50 frames interlaced, giving 25 complete pictures per sec. Transmission was on 45 mc. per sec. for vision, 41.5 mc. per sec. for sound, with a peak white power of 17 kilowatts (kw.) for vision and 3 kw. for sound. The transmitting aerials were mounted on a steel mast on top of one of the towers of Alexandra palace, which reached a height of 600 ft. above sea level. The effective range of the station had been estimated at a radius of 25 mi., but experience showed that reliable results were usually obtained up to about 35 mi. and in many cases much farther, the amount of local interference being the limiting factor.

From 1936 to 1939 this station provided regular programs afternoons and evenings, with an additional morning transmission of a demonstration film on weekdays for the use of manufacturers testing sets and dealers installing them. This film was transmitted on a "telecine" apparatus designed for the purpose and consisting of two continuous-motion projectors, coupled up to two emitron cameras. Film newsreels and cartoon films were shown regularly, and film was used to provide special effects in live productions of plays, but generally the television service consisted of live programs, broadcast as they happened, either from the studio or from outside.

These prewar programs were extraordinary varied and ambitious. From the studios came plays, variety shows, cabaret, ballet, boxing and wrestling, discussions and illustrated talks. From outside, brought by special mobile units which constituted miniature television stations and sent their programs back to Alexandra palace for retransmission, came plays from London theatres, big sporting events such as the Derby, the association football cup final and the university boat race, public events like the coronation procession in 1937; this was the first television outside broadcast and one of the most memorable.

The number of homes equipped with television sets had risen by that time to some 23,000, according to a BBC estimate. Demand was growing fast; at the Radio exhibition of 1939, some 60,000 people placed orders for television sets. But before the exhibition was over, Germany had invaded Poland and Britain had issued her ultimatum. The television service ceased at the end of the morning transmission on Sept. 1, 1939.

During the six years of war, the transmitters were used by the royal air force, and one of their jobs was a fascinating form of air defense known as "bending the beam," by which German bombers were diverted from their targets. Even television research stopped as the whole resources of science and industry were turned to the immediate needs of war.

Long before the war was over, however, there were signs that television had not gone for good. In the autumn of 1943, the government set up a committee to advise on its resumption. The committee made its report at the end of 1944, and in Oct. 1945 the government indicated its acceptance of the main recommendations. These were that the service should be resumed from the prewar station, on the prewar standards, as soon as possible, with extension to the provinces and raising of standards to follow, and that it should again be run by the BBC.

The decision to resume on prewar standards meant that 1,000-line definition and colour would have to wait, but it also meant that there could be television in 1946. The service reopened on June 7, 1946, and on the following day the Victory parade was televised from the Mall.

From then on the home screens were kept alive with varied programs regularly every afternoon and evening (plus a morning demonstration film as before), transmission hours varying between 26 and 42 weekly, according to the number of outside events that fell outside the regular program hours. Thanks to the thorough overhaul before the service was resumed, the pictures from Alexandra palace were clearer than before the war. Programs were more elaborate, more ambitious, rather longer in duration. The range of the station was still reckoned conservatively at about 35 mi. but there were more reports of good regular reception well outside that distance.

On the program side, difficulties arose with entertainment interests which regarded television as a competitor and therefore wanted to delay its progress, and there were big problems such as the conditions of big-screen rediffusion in theatres, which, at the end of 1946, had not yet been solved. There was also the question of extension to the provinces; the post office announced that a double link between London and Birmingham, by line and by radio relay, was well under way. There was the even bigger question of adopting higher standards of definition, in black and white or colour; when and what to change.

The first ten years of British television, even with the wartime gap accounting for most of them, showed at least in outline what radio could do when it appealed not merely to the ear but also to the eye. (*See* also FEDERAL COMMUNICATIONS COMMISSION; RADIO.) (M. A. C. G.)

BIBLIOGRAPHY.—D. Allen, *How to Write for Television* (1946); American Television Society, *American Television Directory* (1945); F. J. Camm, *Television Manual* (1943); L. DeForest, *Television Today and Tomorrow* (1942); J. DuPuy, *Television Showmanship* (1945); W. C. Eddy, *Television: The Eyes of Tomorrow* (1945); Federal Communications Commission, *Television Report* (1941); D. G. Fink, *Principles of Television Engineering* (1940); R. W. Hubbell, *Television: Programming and Production* (1945); L. R. Lohr, *Television Broadcasting* (1940); Mass. Inst. of Tech., *Applied Electronics* (1943); National Television System Committee, *Television Standards and Practice* (1943); K. S. Tyler, *Telecasting and Color* (1946). Pers.: *Communications* (New York); *Electronics* (New York); *FM: Electronic Equipment Engineering and Design Practice* (New York).

Tellurium

The salient statistics of tellurium in the United States and Canada during 1937–45 were as follows, in thousands of pounds.

	United States			Canada
	Production	Sales	Stocks	Production
1937	51.4	23.4	93.2	41.5
1938	11.1	26.9	77.3	48.2
1939	25.2	63.4	39.1	23.0
1940	85.6	89.0	35.7	3.5
1941	224.6	240.0	20.4	11.5
1942	224.1	98.8	145.7	11.1
1943	56.2	62.3	139.4	8.6
1944	69.0	45.3	163.1	10.7
1945	80.8	60.3	183.5	42.0

Tellurium is a by-product in the refining of copper and lead. Production capacity with total recovery remained greater than demand. In 1941 and 1942, producers operated well up to the limit of capacity, apparently in the hope that war demands would absorb the extra output. However, while the uses of tellurium expanded appreciably, they still did not require anything like a full recovery.

Tellurium imparts better machineability and corrosion resistance to copper alloys; in lead it adds corrosion resistance, fineness of grain and greater strength; minute amounts in cast iron increase hardness and depth of chill. The leading use, however, continued to be in compounding rubber, to give greater toughness and resistance to abrasion. (G. A. Ro.)

BIBLIOGRAPHY.— U.S. Bureau of Mines, *Minerals Yearbook;* G. R. Waitkins, "Industrial Utilization of Selenium and Tellurium," *Industrial and Engineering Chemistry* 34:899-910 (Aug. 1942).

Temple, William

Temple (1881–1944), British divine, was born Oct. 15, 1881, at Exeter, the son of the Right Hon. Frederick Temple, 93rd lord archbishop of Canterbury. Educated at Rugby and Balliol College, Oxford, he was fellow and lecturer at Queen's College, Oxford, from 1904 to 1910, and headmaster of Repton school from 1910 to 1914, when he resigned to take charge of St. James's, Piccadilly. He was named bishop of Manchester in 1921 and archbishop of York in 1929. In 1942 he was enthroned as 96th archbishop of Canterbury. While still archbishop of York, Dr. Temple publicly criticized King Edward VIII for his determination to marry Mrs. Wallis Simpson. In international affairs, he advocated stringent but just measures for policing the axis countries after their defeat. He died at Westgate-on-the-Sea, near Margate, Kent, England, Oct. 26, 1944.

Tennessee

A south central state, Tennessee was 16th to enter the union, and is called the "Volunteer state." Land area, 41,961 sq.mi.; water area, 285 sq.mi. Population (1940) 2,915,841; rural 1,888,635; urban 1,027,206; rural farm 1,271,944; native white 2,395,586; Negro 508,736; foreign born 11,320; other races, 199. The bureau of census estimated the population on July 1, 1944, at 2,870,158. Capital, Nashville (167,402). Other cities include Memphis (292,942); Chattanooga (128,163); Knoxville (111,580).

Gordon Browning was governor at the beginning of the decade 1937–46. The legislature in 1937 adopted the county unit plan of voting.

Governor Prentice Cooper took office in 1939. Other state officers included the following: secretary of state, A. B. Broadbent; attorney general, Roy Beeler; commissioners as follows: agriculture, C. C. Flanery; conservation, J. Charles Poe; education, B. O. Duggan; finance and taxation, George McCanless; highways and public works, C. W. Phillips; institutions, A. T. Taylor; welfare, Paul Savage; insurance and banking, J. M. McCormack; labour, S. E. Bryant; public health, W. C. Williams; railways and public utilities, W. D. Hudson, Porter Dunlap and Leon Jourolman. The office of commissioner of administration was discontinued in 1939, and institutions and public welfare were separated. The legislature passed a marriage law requiring premarital examinations. It also repealed the 30-year-old prohibition law, thus leaving package sale of liquor to local determination.

The Nov. 1940 election returns were as follows: president: Franklin D. Roosevelt (Dem.) 351,601; Wendell Willkie (Rep.) 169,153; Roger Babson (Prohibition) 1,606; Norman Thomas (Socialist), 463. U.S. senator: McKellar (Dem.) 295,440; Baker (Rep.) 121,790; Neal (Ind.) 35. Governor: Cooper (Dem., re-elected) 323,466; Bruce (Rep.) 125,254. Railway and public utilities commissioner: Porter Dunlap (Dem.) 278,793; Maddox (Rep.) 103,935.

Prentice Cooper, Democrat, was re-elected governor Nov. 3, 1942. Other state officials were as follows: secretary of state, Joe C. Carr; treasurer, John W. Harton; comptroller, Robert W. Lowe; adjutant general, Thomas A. Frazier; attorney general, Roy Beeler. Commissioners were as follows: agriculture, C. C. Flanery; conservation, J. Charles Poe; education, B. O. Duggan; finance and taxation, George McCanless; highways and public works, C. W. Phillips; institutions, A. T. Taylor; welfare, Paul Savage; insurance and banking, J. M. McCormack; labour,

Tennessee: *Statistical Data*

Table I.—*Education (Public)*

	1938	1940	1941	1942	1943	1944
Elementary school pupils	540,274	524,459	521,129	511,312	503,659	496,844
High school pupils	97,646	123,672	126,285	124,514	120,838	109,576
Elementary teachers	15,652	...	...	...	...	...
High school teachers	4,619	4,935	5,227	5,428	5,570	5,074

Table II.—*Public Welfare*
(Money figures in thousands of dollars)

	1938	1939	1940	1941	1943	1944
Cases on general relief	5,200	4,000	3,800	2,600	...	...
Cost of general relief	$30	$22	$22	$15	...	...
Recipients of old-age pensions	22,324	...	40,303	40,154	39,050	38,085
Cost of pensions	$295	...	$406	$408	$556	$628
Dependent children receiving aid	26,762	...	36,041	35,921	32,510	28,394
Blind receiving aid	1,434	...	1,607	1,645	1,593	1,541

Table III.—*Communications*
(Money figures in thousands of dollars)

	1938	1939	1940	1942	1944	1945
Highway mileage	7,817	7,564	7,520	7,510	7,491	7,491
Expenditures on highways	$20,657	$37,823	$34,031	$14,193	$7,022	$10,260
Railroad mileage	3,669	3,594	3,573	3,503	3,503	3,507

Table IV.—*Banking and Finance*
(Money figures in thousands of dollars)

	1937	1938	1940	1942	1944	1945
State revenue	$48,961	$61,926	$72,752	$55,488	$55,563	$55,638
State expenditure	$46,205	$55,522	$70,955	...	...	...
State net debt	$91,007	$92,366	...	$97,026	$78,985	$75,890
State gross debt	$104,042	...	$93,054	$109,059	$88,756	$83,416
Number of banks	312	303	297	297	292	292
Total bank deposits	$480,600	$478,600	$571,900	$836,181	$1,328,123	$1,677,092

Table V.—*Agriculture*
(All figures in thousands)

	1937	1939	1940	1941	1943	1944
Acreage, principal crops	6,507	5,889	6,113	6,159	...	...
Income from crops and livestock	$138,200	$117,861	$125,049	$191,456	$300,936	$315,003
Farm value of crops	$135,250	$110,310	$132,768	$133,722	$172,605	$192,185
Leading crops (bu.):						
Corn	66,058	57,700	69,175	69,615	65,964	59,950
Cotton (bales)	661	449	509	600	491	562
Hay (tons)	1,597	1,629	1,579	2,148	2,217	1,601
Potatoes, sweet	5,610	3,713	4,335	4,664	4,752	4,128
Potatoes, white	3,081	3,024	3,388	2,604	4,380	2,464
Tobacco (lb.)	122,757	110,267	109,690	91,523	96,830	125,645
Wheat	6,750	4,117	5,116	5,415	4,116	6,714

Table VI.—*Mineral Production*
(All figures in thousands of dollars)

	1938	1939	1941	1942	1943	1944
Value of mineral production	$32,429	$40,120	$56,302	$67,224	$65,053	$63,382
Leading products (value):						
Coal	$9,007	$10,402	$16,455	$20,691	$20,907	$23,088
Stone	$4,237	$8,313	$9,158	$9,018	$10,048	$7,777
Cement	$5,064	$5,613	$8,520	$9,928	$7,343	$6,081
Clay	$347	$425	...	...	...	$764
Sand and gravel	$1,605	$1,967	$2,830	$3,086	$2,285	$2,314
Lime	$901	$893	$1,355	$1,621	$1,504	$1,247
Coke	$509	$527	$1,119	...	...	...
Zinc	...	...	$5,426	$8,179	$9,021	$9,309
Clay products	...	...	$2,041	$1,621	$1,800	$1,500
Barite	$209	$372	...	$625	$383	$280

Tennessee: *Statistical Data (Continued)*

Table VII.—*Manufacturing*
(Money figures in thousands of dollars)

	1935	1937	1939
Wage earners	112,434	135,073	131,874
Wages paid	$81,246	$109,248	$109,662
Value of products	$520,969	$707,987	$728,088
Leading manufactured products (value):			
Rayon and allied products		$59,133	$59,725
Hosiery		$29,219	$33,799
Meat packing		$29,491	$28,266
Chemicals		$38,049	$25,640
Edible fats		$36,457	$19,788
Footwear (except rubber)		$20,898	$17,741

S. E. Bryant; public health, W. C. Williams; railways and public utilities, W. D. Hudson, Porter Dunlap and Leon Jourolman. In the November election for the house of representatives, the Democrats polled 102,143 votes; the Republicans 52,368.

Mrs. Joe C. Carr became state treasurer in 1944. New commissioners included: Paul S. Mathes, education; W. O. Baird, institutions; William A. Shoaf, welfare; Dr. R. H. Hutcheson, public health; and John C. Hammer, railroad and public utilities. In the presidential election Roosevelt received 308,707 votes in Tennessee, Thomas Dewey 200,-311, Norman Thomas 892 and Claude A. Watson 882 votes. James Nance McCord, Democrat, was elected governor.

Principal state officers in 1945, in addition to Governor McCord, Joe C. Carr, secretary of state; C. C. Wallace, treasurer; Sam K. Carson, comptroller; Rufus E. Fort, Jr., adjutant general; Roy H. Beeler, attorney general. Commissioners were as follows: agriculture, O. E. Van Cleave; conservation, Paul S. Mathes; education, Burgin Dossett (superintendent of schools, appointed by governor); finance and taxation, George F. McCanless; highways and public works, C. W. Phillips; institutions, Dr. W. O. Baird; welfare, William A. Shoaf; insurance and banking, James M. McCormack; labour, W. E. Jacobs, Sr.; public health, Dr. R. H. Hutcheson; railroad and public utilities, Sam Pharr, Leon Jourolman, John Hammer; safety, Lynn Bomar; employment security, W. O. Hake.

Governor McCord was re-elected to office in the elections of Nov. 1946. (C. E. A.)

Bibliography.—Council of State Governments, *Book of the States* (biennial); Federal Writers' Project, *Tennessee: Guide to the State* (1939); M. U. Rothrock, *Discovering Tennessee* (1936); Secy. of State, *Blue Book and Official Directory* (biennial); Tennessee Taxpayers Association, *Report* (annual). Periodical: *Monthly Checklist of State Publications.*

Tennessee Valley Authority

The period 1937–46 saw the Tennessee Valley authority's greatest physical expansion. Construction of dams and reservoirs brought the Tennessee river under more complete control, for diverse purposes, than any comparable stream in the world. The rapid expansion dictated by World War II provided power for the production of atomic energy, aluminum, phosphorus, munitions and other war materials. TVA produced war chemicals and expedited the production of food, minerals and wood. The flexibility and initiative written into the TVA act by congress enabled it to shift emphasis from peace to war aims and back again, and to expand and contract its operations with a minimum of confusion and disruption. During the decade, TVA became the subject of national and world-wide study as a method of dealing with resources development on a unified and scientific basis and by democratic methods.

River Control.—In 1937 TVA had completed two dams, Norris and Wheeler. In the ensuing 10 years, TVA built and placed in operation 14 additional dams and reservoirs, 7 of them constructed as emergency projects to provide war power—Cherokee, Apalachia, Ocoee No. 3, Chatuge, Nottely, Douglas and Fontana. In 1942 TVA had under construction 12 dams and a large steam-electric generating station. Construction by force account made for speed and efficiency. Cherokee dam, built in 16 months, was closed 2 days before Pearl Harbor; by adapting Cherokee designs and using the same personnel and equipment, Douglas dam was built in 12 months. Fontana dam, fourth highest concrete dam in the world, was closed after less than three years and produced power in Jan. 1945. Kentucky dam, creating a 184-mi. reservoir in the lower Tennessee, was closed in Sept. 1944 and produced power the next month. Land and land rights were obtained on 1,759 sq.mi., in fee or by easement. Under an appraisal and nonprice trading policy, contested condemnation suits represented only 6% of the total acreage. Extensive aid in relocating satisfactorily was given the 13,000 families required to move. Housing research in connection with construction resulted in designs for factory prefabricated and fully equipped sectional houses, of which more than 5,000 were installed at the Fontana project and at atomic energy plants in Tennessee and Washington. Planning assistance to communities affected by reservoirs led to extension of state and community planning to nonreservoir towns and cities.

TVA acquired four dams in the Tennessee valley by purchase in 1939 (plus a dam in the Cumberland valley). In Jan. 1945 it assumed, by agreement, direction of the operation of five major dams of the Aluminum Company of America. The integrated system of 26 dams provided a 640-mi. navigation channel from the Ohio river to Knoxville, Tenn.; provided 11,000,000 ac.ft. of storage for flood control on the Tennessee and lower Ohio and Mississippi rivers and, with associated steam-electric stations, had a generating capacity of more than 2,500,000 kw. installed.

Power.—TVA in 1945 and 1946 became the largest integrated power-producing system in the U.S., generating nearly 12,000,000,000 kw.hr. annually. TVA power was a major reason for locating the largest of U.S. atomic energy plants at Oak Ridge, Tenn. About 75% of TVA power annually went to war production, and an estimated 10% of the total war power of the U.S. was produced in the Tennessee valley. In July 1946 a peak demand of 2,038,000 kw. was established, as compared with the wartime peak of 1,982,000 kw.

In 1946, 138 municipal and co-operative distributing systems served 675,000 ultimate consumers with TVA power, as compared with 34 distributors and 30,200 consumers in 1937. Rapid expansion of the power market followed the decision of the U.S. supreme court in *Tennessee Electric Power Co., et al.* v. *TVA,* 306 U.S. 118 (the "18 company suit") that privately owned utilities had no legal right to be free of competition. This decision followed that in *Ashwander, et al.* v. *TVA,* 297 U.S. 288, in 1936, upholding sale of power from Wilson dam. Private utility properties serving about 345,000 customers were purchased by TVA and associated municipalities and co-operatives for approximately $125,000,000.

TVA pioneered in rural electrification, with the result that farm service increased from 4% of total farms in 1932 to more than 25% in 1946. Farm customers in 1946 numbered 125,000. Postwar plans of distributors called for 30,000 mi. of rural line to serve 150,000 farm customers.

Resale rate schedules established in TVA wholesale power contracts in 1933 were in 1946 still about one-third lower than U.S. electric rates generally. By mid-1946, 20 distributors had adopted still lower rate schedules. A comparison of typical residential bills follows:

Kw.Hr. per month	25	100	250
U.S. Average 1945*	$1.37	$3.89	$7.09
TVA Rate B-1	0.75	2.50	5.00
TVA Rate R	0.75	2.25	4.13
TVA Rate R-1	0.75	2.00	3.50

*Federal Power Commission report, *Typical Residential Bills: Cities of 2,500 Population and More: 1945.*

Stimulated by low rates and promotional activities, average domestic use of electricity by TVA power consumers grew from about 600 kw.hr. in 1933 (pre-TVA) to more than 1,850 kw.hr. in 1946, the average cost per kw.hr. declining from 6 cents to 1.8 cents. Average use in the U.S. over the same period increased from 600 to about 1,280 kw.hr., average cost dropping from 5.5 cents to 3.3 cents per kw.hr. In 1939, with sales of 1,618,287,000 kw.hr., TVA power operations commenced to earn an annual net income. Up to June 30, 1945, accumulated earnings after all power expenses amounted to $55,105,000. In the fiscal year 1945, with operating revenues of $39,383,000 from sale of 10,315,000,000 kw.hr., net income was $17,982,000. Return on the net average power investment was 4.8%. For the five years ending June 30, 1945, the rate of return was 4.1%. In the fiscal year 1945, municipal and co-operative distributors, with operating revenues of $38,293,000 from sale of 3,023,000,000 kw.hr., earned a combined net income of $7,265,000.

Flood Control.—Well-defined seasons of high and low rainfall and streamflow in the Tennessee valley enabled TVA to use much of the same reservoir space for reduction of floods and for maintaining flow in dry periods for navigation and power. Minimum dry season flow was increased at the mouth of the Tennessee sixfold, from 5,000 to 30,000 cu.ft. per second. Flood storage provided by 1946 was sufficient to reduce crests at Cairo, Ill., on the Ohio and Mississippi rivers, by 2 to 4 ft. A TVA report in 1939 set the value of a 2-ft. reduction in the alluvial valley of the Mississippi at $100,000,000–$200,000,000. Reduction in flood crests added to the safety of cities, protected 9,375 sq.mi. from flooding and reduced frequency of floods on an additional 6,250 sq.mi. In the Tennessee valley, besides protection to agricultural lands and smaller cities, the TVA system substantially protected Chattanooga against a repetition of the flood of record (1867) which, if uncontrolled, would do nearly $40,000,000 in direct damage. TVA reservoirs made possible complete protection of the city against a flood 50% greater than that of record by a future levee system.

Damage averted at Chattanooga up to 1946 totalled nearly $11,000,000 in five floods, some of which would have hampered war production. This included a flood in Jan. 1946 which, uncontrolled, would have been the fifth largest in the city's history and the most destructive. Potential damage of $6,600,000 was reduced to $33,000 by lowering the flood crest 10 ft.

Navigation.—In 1939, the TVA had provided a commercially usable channel upstream to Chattanooga, and traffic volume trended sharply upward thereafter. By 1946 the channel was completed to Knoxville, except for a small amount of dredging and raising of Hales Bar dam to provide full nine-foot draft. Traffic increased from 44,000,000 ton-mi. in 1937 to 256,000,000 in 1945. Traffic included coal, wheat, corn, aluminum, fertilizer, automobiles, gasoline and oil, pig iron and steel products. In 1943–44 TVA placed in operation four public use general freight terminals and a coal terminal. Privately owned grain and oil terminals had been constructed. More than 125 new vessels, many of them ocean-going, were constructed on the Tennessee during World War II.

Soil Development.—Control of water on the land

Facts About Major TVA Dams

Main River Projects	River	State	Maximum Height (Ft.)	Length (Ft.)	Total Storage (Ac.-Ft.)	Useful Controlled Storage (Ac.-Ft.)†	Length of Lake (Mi.)	Area of Lake (Sq.Mi.)§	Shore Line of Lake (Mi.)§	Constr. Started	Closure	Constr. Completed (1st Unit on Line)	Installed Capacity Kw.	Estimated Cost‖
Kentucky	Tennessee	Ky.	206	8,422	6,002,600	4,010,800	184.3	250.1	2,380	7- 1-38	8-30-44	9-14-44	128,000	117,200,000
Pickwick Landing	Tennessee	Tenn.	113	7,715	1,091,400	418,400	52.7	66.9	496	3- 8-35	2- 8-38	6-29-38	144,000	39,600,000
Wilson	Tennessee	Ala.	137	4,862	562,500	52,500‡	15.5	24.7	154	4-14-18	4-14-24	9-12-25	335,200	41,200,000
Wheeler	Tennessee	Ala.	72	6,342	1,150,400	347,500	74.1	104.8	1,063	11-21-33	10- 3-36	11- 9-36	129,600	42,200,000
Guntersville	Tennessee	Ala.	94	3,979	1,018,700	162,900	82.1	108.0	962	12- 4-35	1-16-39	8- 1-39	72,900	34,900,000
Hales Bar*	Tennessee	Tenn.	83	2,315	135,100	11,800‡	39.9	9.5	100	10-18-05	—	4-17-14	51,100	*
Chickamauga	Tennessee	Tenn.	129	5,800	705,300	329,400	58.9	53.9	810	1-13-36	1-15-40	3- 4-40	81,000	38,100,000
Watts Bar	Tennessee	Tenn.	112	2,960	1,132,000	377,600	72.4	60.3	783	7- 1-39	1- 1-42	2-11-42	150,000	34,800,000
Fort Loudoun	Tennessee	Tenn.	122	4,190	386,500	109,300	55.0	22.7	368	7- 8-40	8- 2-43	11- 9-43	64,000	41,400,000
Tributary Projects														
Norris	Clinch	Tenn.	265	1,860	2,567,000	2,281,000	72-56¶	53.1	800	10- 1-33	3- 4-36	7-28-36	100,800	30,900,000
Hiwassee	Hiwassee	N.C.	307	1,287	438,000	364,700	22	9.8	180	7-15-36	2- 8-40	5-21-40	57,600	18,700,000
Cherokee	Holston	Tenn.	175	6,760	1,565,400	1,473,100	59	47.2	463	8- 1-40	12- 5-41	4-16-42	60,000	31,900,000
Apalachia	Hiwassee	N.C.	150	1,308	58,570	35,730	9.8	1.8	31	7-17-41	2-14-43	9-22-43	75,000	22,900,000
Nottely	Nottely	Ga.	184	2,300	184,400	184,000	20	6.7	106	7-17-41	1-24-42	—	—	5,500,000
Ocoee No. 3	Ocoee	Tenn.	110	612	14,440	9,370‡	7	0.9	24	7-17-41	8-15-42	4-30-43	27,000	8,200,000
Chatuge	Hiwassee	N.C.	144	2,850	247,800	229,300	13	11.2	132	7-17-41	2-12-42	—	—	7,200,000
Fontana	Little Tenn.	N.C.	480	2,385	1,444,300	1,157,300	29	16.7	274	1- 1-42	11- 7-44	1-20-45	135,000	73,000,000
Watauga♀	Watauga	Tenn.	318	900	677,000	627,000	17	11.1	117	2-16-42	—	—	—	28,900,000
South Holston♀	S. Fork Holston	Tenn.	290	1,550	783,000	660,000	25	14.2	241	2- 1-42	—	—	—	30,650,000
Douglas	French Broad	Tenn.	202	1,705	1,514,100	1,419,700	43.1	47.8	556	2- 2-42	2-19-43	3-21-43	60,000	42,100,000
Ocoee No. 1*	Ocoee	Tenn.	135	840	91,300	33,100	7	3.0	18	8- ?-10	12-15-11	1-10-12	18,000	*
Ocoee No. 2*	Ocoee	Tenn.	30	450	—	—	—	—	—	5- ?-12	—	10- ?-13	19,900	*
Blue Ridge*	Toccoa	Ga.	167	1,000	197,500	183,000	10	5.1	60	11- ?-25ð	12- 6-30	7- ?-31	20,000	*
Great Falls*	Caney Fork	Tenn.	92	800	54,500	49,400	22	3.5	120	?- ?-15	12- 8-16	?- ?-16	31,860	*
Totals					22,021,810	14,526,900		933.0□	10,238				1,760,960	

Notes: Power-generating facilities were provided at all but two projects, Nottely and Chatuge. The total TVA system installed capacity, including fuel plants and minor hydro plants not listed above, was 2,227,982 kw. at June 30, 1946; completion of new generating units under construction would increase the system installed capacity to 2,414,782 kw. The 1946 capacity of Alcoa plants was 311,120 kw., or a total of 2,539,102 kw. for the integrated system.

The lakes or reservoirs of the main-river projects on the Tennessee were designed to provide a channel for boats of 9-ft. draft from the mouth of the river to Knoxville, a distance of 650 mi.

*Purchased with other electric properties from the Tennessee Electric Power company.

†Useful controlled storage is the volume between the lowest operating level of the reservoirs and the top of the spillway or spillway gates.

‡Reservoir volume available for pondage, but not for seasonal storage operations.

§Maximum normal operating level.

‖Estimated cost included 1946 authorized units but was exclusive of switchyards, the total cost of which was estimated to be approximately $32,500,000.

¶72 mi. on the Clinch river; 56 mi. on the Powell river.

♀Construction deferred during World War II; resumed in 1946 under congressional appropriation.

ðConstruction discontinued early in 1926; resumed in March 1929.

□Includes 178.8 sq.mi. representing original riverbeds.

complemented its control in the river. Rainfall in the Tennessee valley averages 52 in. a year, or 6 tons per ac., and, falling on land traditionally devoted to intertilled crops, had done tremendous damage. In 1933 TVA, upon the advice of the U.S. department of agriculture and the land-grant colleges, embarked upon the development, experimental manufacture and large-scale testing of new and improved phosphate fertilizers, since phosphorus is a key mineral in which many soils are deficient.

Chemical Operations.—In the chemical plant at Muscle Shoals and a plant built in middle Tennessee, TVA developed and manufactured three different types of phosphate fertilizers—calcium metaphosphate (65% plant food), concentrated superphosphate (48%) and fused tricalcium phosphate (28%). Potassium metaphosphate, containing 90% plant food, was developed through the pilot plant stage. All but concentrated superphosphate, previously manufactured by a wet process using sulphuric rather than phosphoric acid, were new products. Shipments during the ten-year period ending June 30, 1946, were as follows:

	For TVA Test-Demonstrations and AAA (Tons)	For Lend-Lease (Tons)	Other
Concentrated superphosphate	451,631	94,394	22,048
Calcium metaphosphate	53,989	3,801	126
Fused tricalcium phosphate	10,352	0	21

War Production.—TVA research in electric-furnace production of phosphorus encouraged expansion of private capacity, so that great quantities of military-grade phosphorus were available in World War II as compared with World War I. TVA produced 58,700 tons, including 4,600 tons for lend-lease, which was a large proportion of total U.S. output. Using rehabilitated graining facilities plus a new ammonia plant, TVA produced up to June 30, 1946, 464,000 tons of ammonium nitrate, 75,000 tons for munitions use and the remainder for fertilizer. A TVA-developed process for conditioning ammonium nitrate for fertilizer use was adopted by other government munitions plants. About 43,000 tons of synthetic ammonia were sent to other munitions producers. TVA made more than 250,000

Ammonia for explosives being produced at Nitrate Plant No. 2, Muscle Shoals, Ala. During World War II, women workers were trained to do much of the work formerly done by men

tons of calcium carbide for use in synthetic rubber manufacture. A plant was built, largely of scrap materials, to produce dicalcium phosphate for cattle feed supplement. Manufacture of ammonium nitrate and dicalcium phosphate continued in 1946 to help meet critical shortages.

"Whole Farm" Test-Demonstrations. — Tests and demonstrations of TVA fertilizers went beyond testing of fertilizers *per se* and included the use of minerals in conservation and soil building. The test-demonstrations were carried out by practical farmers, selected by their neighbours or participating in area demonstrations, under the general supervision of the agricultural extension services of the states and with the assistance of their county agricultural agents. TVA provided the phosphate fertilizers free except for freight charges, in return for which farmers developed soil-conserving farm plans, kept records and measured results. Farm test-demonstrators increased from about 12,000 in 1937 to 38,900 in 29 states in 1946.

Marked changes through use of soil minerals and improved farm management included reduction of row crops and shifting such crops to less erosive land, use of winter cover crops, reduction of soil and water losses, increased pasture and hay crops leading to more and better livestock and increased production of more nutritious food for animal and human consumption.

Forestry Development.—Woodlands in 1946 covered 21,875 sq.mi., or more than half the valley, 43% on nonfarm holdings, 40% on farms and 17% publicly owned. Co-operating with federal, state and county agencies, TVA encouraged modern forestry practices in a region in which few examples existed prior to 1941. More than 400 demonstrations of sustained-yield forest management were established in co-operation with commercial timber operators and farmers, who obtained both immediate and long-term benefits in better forest operation. Organized fire control was extended to 18 counties, and TVA co-operated with state conservation commissions in extending control to 5,469 sq.mi. Two TVA forest nurseries provided 154,000,000 seedlings for planting upon both public and private lands needing reforestation and erosion control. Erosion control demonstrations were established in every valley county.

Other Benefits.—To meet malaria hazards resulting from reservoir construction, TVA developed a large-scale mosquito control program, teaming medical, biological and engineering sciences. Methods included water-level fluctuation, diking, filling and dewatering projects and spreading insecticides from planes, boats and shore. Blood samples taken in reservoir areas showed reduction in the incidence of malaria from 10% in 1939 to less than 1% in 1944. Methods developed by TVA were adapted by the U.S. army during World War II. TVA equipped 12 planes and trained pilots for the United Nations Relief and Rehabilitation administration's malaria control program in Greece.

By 1945 5 state, 8 county and 10 city parks had been established on land leased from TVA. More than 50 boat docks were in operation. Surveys indicated that fishing had increased 50-fold on storage reservoirs and 15-fold on mainstream reservoirs. Biological research by TVA, showing that only a small proportion of fish were being caught, led to discontinuance of hatcheries for stocking reservoirs and to elimination by state conservation commissions of closed fishing seasons on all TVA waters. Approximately 180 sq.mi. of TVA land were incorporated in federal and state game refuges, migratory waterfowl refuges predominating.

Research.—To implement development of resources, TVA carried on research directly and, more extensively, co-operated with existing agencies in research directed at specific regional problems in the fields of agricultural engineering, minerals development, food processing, forest products and so on. Developments included, for example, a small portable thresher adapted to the hills and small farms characteristic of much of the valley, giving impetus to growing of small grain and legume crops, and providing a machine for manufacture by private industry. A barge-borne food-processing laboratory provided new processes and guidance in handling perishable products for market, thus helping develop a new foods processing industry in the valley. Minerals research increased use of pottery clays and vermiculite, among other minerals. Three TVA studies in 1937, 1939 and 1943 gave impetus to the movement for abolition of freight rate discrimination between regions. These were typical of activities by which TVA assisted other agencies, public and private, in the field of resources development.

Personnel.—Peak employment was nearly 42,000 in 1942, declining with reduced construction activities to 11,000 in 1946. Employees, under the act, were selected on the basis of merit and efficiency and without political qualification. Collective bargaining procedures were formalized in 1940 in a general agreement with 14 A.F. of L. unions forming the Tennessee Valley Trades and Labor council. By 1946 seven unions were negotiating for TVA "white-collar" workers.

Finances.—Congressional appropriations to June 30, 1946, were $677,617,270; bonds had provided $65,000,000 and assets transferred by the war department were about $39,000,000. About $100,000,000 in receipts had been reinvested in power facilities, particularly during the wartime expansion. In Dec. 1945 TVA paid into the U.S. treasury general fund $12,600,000 representing excess of receipts over requirements of programs financed out of revenues. Congressional control over TVA was exercised through the annual budget procedure, in which TVA presented plans for programs financed both by revenues and appropriated funds, through annual audits by the comptroller general and through submission of an annual report. TVA accounting followed business rather than governmental patterns, and power accounts were kept in conformity with the uniform system prescribed by the Federal Power commission for all utilities.

The TVA board in 1946 consisted of David E. Lilienthal, chairman (resigned Oct. 28, 1946), Dr. H. A. Morgan, vice chairman, and James P. Pope. The TVA act provided for administration by a board of three directors appointed by the president and confirmed by the senate for staggered nine-year terms. (*See* also Dams.)

Bibliography.—Robert L. Duffus, *The Valley and Its People; A Portrait of TVA* (1944); Herman Finer, *The TVA: Lessons for International Application* (Montreal, 1944); Alvin H. Hansen and Harvey S. Perloff, *Regional Resource Development* (1942); Julian S. Huxley, *TVA, Adventure in Planning* (Surrey, England, 1943); David E. Lilienthal, *TVA—Democracy on the March* (1944); C. Herman Pritchett, *Tennessee Valley Authority; A Study in Public Administration* (1943); Joseph S. Ransmeier, *The Tennessee Valley Authority; A Case Study in the Economics of Multiple Purpose Stream Planning* (1942). The following indexes prepared by the TVA Technical Library and available in many libraries will give the reader additional references to the TVA program: *Indexed Bibliography of the Tennessee Valley Authority; Selected List of Books, Theses, and Pamphlets on TVA; Congressional Hearings, Reports and Documents Relating to TVA.* (K. R. K.)

Tennis

Three facts had become clear in the world of lawn tennis by the beginning of the decade 1937–46. First, the hold which France and then England had kept upon the Davis cup for ten years was seriously threatened by the rising strength of younger players in the United States and Australia. Second, the men who had dominated the game during that period, Henri Cochet, Jean Lacoste and Jean Borotra of France, William T. Tilden and Ellsworth Vines of the United States, J. H. Crawford of Australia, and Fred J. Perry and H. W. Austin of England, had either reached and passed their peak, or else turned professional. A new lot was surging forward, youngsters like J. Donald Budge, a dynamo in the best Californian tradition, Gottfried von Cramm, a classicist from Germany of the Froitzheim school, Adrian Quist, a brilliant Australian, and his compatriot, John Bromwich, who hit the ball with two hands on his racket. From them were coming the champions of the following decade.

Perhaps even more significant, however, was the fact that at last the dictators had discovered sport. By then it had become apparent to the overlords of Europe that winning a heavyweight boxing title, an international soccer championship, a Wimbledon trophy, or better still, the Davis cup, was a matter not merely of sporting but of national prestige. Stars of the game were aided by subsidies and governmental assistance of every kind. Champions—when victorious—became national heroes and heroines. Curiously, defeat did not enter into the scheme of totalitarian sport. One was not sent upon the field of sport to lose.

This was shown by the summer of 1937, and more obviously still in 1938. In that year the German Davis Cup team, after winning the European zone, was unexpectedly and badly defeated in the Interzone final of the series in the United States. Hitler probably ordered the team to return. At any rate they left immediately, without competing in the American championships several weeks later in New York, as had been planned.

On the sporting side, perhaps the rise of redheaded Donald Budge, the Californian with the McLoughlin service and the all-court game, was the most important single item of these ten eventful years. Here at last was a real successor to the mighty Tilden, and a worthy one too. By 1937 he had come into his own, capturing the Wimbledon and United States titles, and losing only three sets in all in so doing, two of them to Cramm in the finals at Forest Hills, Long Island, N.Y. Winning all his singles matches and carrying along an indifferent partner in doubles most of the time, he was the principal artisan of American victory in the Davis cup, thus returning the trophy to the land of its birth for the first time in a decade.

During the next season, 1938, he dominated the field of tennis as perhaps no one had done before. Starting in January, Budge won the Australian title in Adelaide, South Australia, the French championships at Paris in June, the All-England title at Wimbledon in July, and the U.S. at Forest Hills in September. He also helped materially by his two victories in singles to defeat Australia in the Challenge round of the Davis cup at Philadelphia, Pa., that same month. It was a remarkable athletic feat, one that had perhaps never before been equalled by any tennis champion.

Meanwhile, in women's as in the men's field, new faces

were appearing on the courts. The players who had ruled the game in the United States and abroad were passing. Alice Marble in the United States, Amita Lizana of Chile, and younger stars of both England and North America were coming to the front. However, in 1938, Mrs. Helen Wills Moody, after an absence from action for three years because of an injury, decided to return to active competition again, and entered the All-England championships at Wimbledon. From the strongest field in many seasons, including Miss Marble and Helen Jacobs of the United States, Dorothy Round and K. E. Stammers of England, Simone Mathieu of France, Hilda Sperling, the German star, and Mrs. Bobbie Heine Miller, the South African champion, Mrs. Moody came through to victory without the loss of a single set.

This was surely the most amazing feminine sporting achievement of the year.

In the summer of 1939, on the eve of battle, a hollow and ominous tone echoed over the tennis courts of the world. The quality of play fell off almost as if in sympathy with the times. Budge had turned professional and there was no outstanding star to replace him, no one like the Tilden of 1930, the Vines of 1932, the Crawford of 1933, the Perry of 1934 and 1936, and the Budge of 1938. There were only a number of mediocre players in different lands.

Thanks to Herr Hitler's timetable, all the major tennis championships were completed and the Davis cup, as on the eve of World War I, finished just as the guns began. History repeated itself. In 1914, Norman Brookes and Tony Wilding took the cup from the United States. In 1939, the Australian team of Bromwich and Quist beat an American side without the cannonball delivery of Donald Budge. Thus after 25 years the trophy returned to the antipodes.

From 1940 to 1946, tennis, like other sports, was a matter of small importance. As in World War I, the Davis cup contests were abandoned. All championships, save those in the United States, were given up. Not until 1946, the year after hostilities ended, was a general resumption of play possible.

The United States was the only major tennis-playing nation to continue tournaments, both before and even while the nation was at war. Although golf, polo and most amateur sports gave up their title events, tennis continued as usual. After 1942, the national championships consisted largely of servicemen on leave or fortunate enough to obtain permission from a commanding officer to compete.

Perhaps the most interesting feature of the period was the rise of Alice Marble of California. She won the Wimbledon and United States titles in 1939, and in 1940 repeated her triumph at Forest Hills, smothering Helen Jacobs, a former champion, with the loss of only a couple of games in the two sets. No woman had ever played such a starkly masculine game as Miss Marble; her service, court-covering, volleying and driving were as forceful as that of most men.

In 1946, the French, English and U.S. championships were held, the latter title being won by John A. Kramer, a young Californian who had been victorious in the same event in 1943 before going into the navy. For the first time since 1939, matches for the Davis cup were also resumed, with Sweden winning the European zone by defeating Yugoslavia, and the United States, the American zone.

In the Interzone final, played at Forest Hills in September, the United States beat Sweden five matches to none, thus earning the right to face Australia, holder of the cup, in the Challenge round.

The U.S. captain was faced with a difficult decision in choosing a team to represent his country in the Challenge round. He had a squad of five fine players, three of whom, Frederick R. Schroeder, John A. Kramer, and Frank Parker, had all held the singles title of the United States. He finally decided to depend on two men only—the first two-man team to play for the United States in the Challenge round since William T. Tilden and William Johnston took the trophy from Australia in 1920.

His decision was a wise one, and history repeated itself. Notwithstanding the handicap of playing in a strange land under the torrid Australian sun, the U.S. team of Schroeder and Kramer, teammates and doubles champions of the United States in 1941, dominated play completely. They won four of the five matches with the loss of but two sets, and were never, save in one contest, seriously threatened.

The Challenge round was played on Dec. 26, 27 and 30, 1946, at the Kooyong stadium, near Melbourne, before ca-

Sarah Palfrey Cooke won her first U.S. women's singles championship, defeating Pauline Betz in straight sets Sept. 7, 1941, at Forest Hills, L.I.

Frederick Schroeder (left) and John Kramer, the two-man Davis cup team which defeated Australia in the Challenge round held in Dec. 1946, near Melbourne

pacity crowds. The issue was practically settled the first afternoon, when Schroeder beat John Bromwich of Australia in five sets, and Kramer defeated Dinny Pails. The two sets lost by Schroeder were the only ones taken by the Australian side in the three days.

Most remarkable was the straight set victory of the U.S. team in doubles. For the preceding 40 years Australians had had a higher average standard in doubles than any other nation, and Bromwich and Adrian Quist were a veteran pair who had been victorious in two previous Challenge round contests played in the United States before World War II. However, they were no match for Kramer and Schroeder, and were beaten in three quick sets in a little more than an hour's play. It was the first defeat in doubles for an Australian team in a Challenge round since 1926.

This third victory gave the United States possession of the Davis cup, and the two remaining contests could not affect the decision. Kramer defeated Pails in three sets, and Gardnar Mulloy, substituting for Schroeder, was victorious by the same margin over Bromwich. This was the 13th time the United States had been victorious in the 34 years of play since the matches started in 1900.

(J. R. Tu.)

Bibliography.—C. Bowers, *Advanced Tennis* (1940); J. D. Budge, *Budge on Tennis* (1939); S. H. Cooke, *Winning Tennis and How to Play It* (1946); W. P. Jacobs, *Tennis, Builder of Citizenship* (1941); *Official Tennis Guide* (1941 *et seq.*)

Terauchi, Juichi

Count Terauchi (1879–1946), Japanese army officer, was born in Yamaguchi province. His father was an army field marshal, premier of the Japanese cabinet and governor-general of Korea. The son, after serving in various high army posts, became a member of the Supreme War council in 1935. He was named war minister in the cabinet of Premier Koki Hirota in March 1936, but his refusal to permit the diet to criticize the army resulted in the downfall of the Hirota government, although he retained his post in the succeeding cabinet. Terauchi left the cabinet in Feb. 1937 to return to the army as inspector-general of military training. Later that year, he became commander of Japanese forces in North China and directed the victorious Japanese offensive along the Peiping-Hankow front. Shortly after Japan's attack on Pearl Harbor, in Dec. 1941, Emperor Hirohito named Terauchi commander of all Japanese forces in the Southwestern Pacific.

After Hirohito's surrender broadcast (Aug. 15, 1945), Terauchi failed to comply promptly with Lord Louis Mountbatten's order to send surrender envoys to Rangoon. On Nov. 30, 1945, he formally surrendered at Saigon and was moved to Malaya where he died at his quarters in Johore Bahru, of a cerebral haemorrhage, on June 12, 1946.

Termites

See Entomology.

Ter Poorten, Hein

See Poorten, Hein ter.

Territorial Army, British

At the beginning of 1937, the British territorial army was composed of 14 divisions and army troops with an establishment of 196,075, and although the actual strength was only 141,153, this marked a modest revival as compared with previous years. The improvement was partly because of small concessions on the part of the treasury, but far more because of a growing appreciation in the country that Adolf Hitler and naziism were a menace to the peace of the world. The Munich agreement of Sept. 1938, when the anti-aircraft defenses were first mobilized, encouraged recruiting for all branches of the T.A., and thenceforward manpower ceased to be a difficulty. Unfortunately, however, there still remained the problem of equipment.

Although horses had for the most part given way to machines, the actual armament of the T.A., apart from anti-aircraft equipment, had remained practically unchanged since World War I and the manufacturing potential for which the army council importuned had not been provided by the government. Consequently, when in 1938 a scheme for a complete reorganization on modern lines was at last accepted, the means to put it into effect did not exist. Early in 1939, it was decided to raise the T.A. from peace to war establishment, and then to double it. This meant increasing the establishment to 437,349, and the men required came forward readily enough, thereby making the equipment position even more difficult. Indeed this measure, like the introduction of conscription a few months later, was more of a political gesture than an immediate addition to Britain's armed strength. Both were in the nature of a warning to Hitler that the British intended to make a stand, and although these gestures failed to check him, they were of great importance since they formed the basis for the expansion of the land forces on mobilization.

Another useful step was the creation in 1938 of the women's organization, the auxiliary territorial service (A.T.S.) which as the WAAC had been disbanded after World War I. The emergency service and the field army nursing yeomanry (F.A.N.Y.) had continued to train at their own expense, eventually providing many officers for the 307,000 women who passed through the ranks of the A.T.S. and who proved invaluable in releasing men for front line duties, or in performing those duties themselves. (*See* British Women's Services, World War II.)

On the declaration of war in 1939, the T.A. assumed complete responsibility for the coast and anti-aircraft defenses of Great Britain; its efficiency in this work reached its zenith in 1944, when over 90% of flying bombs were brought down by fire from the ground defenses. By the spring of 1940, 11 territorial divisions were with the field armies overseas. In Norway, in Belgium and in France they fought in retreats to the coast and in subsequent evacuations; a territorial battalion took part in the heroic defense of Calais. All suffered from a lack of armour and anti-tank weapons and their casualties were consequently very heavy. Later on, territorial divisions and units served on every front. As the war proceeded the necessity for replacing casualties by the wartime intake tended to affect the purely local character of many units, but despite this they retained their territorial connection. Thus the tradition and the spirit of the original volunteers survived.

By the end of 1946, all territorial divisions overseas were broken up; the government announced its intention to reform the T.A. and to include in it as many as possible of the original units which existed from 1908 to 1937.

(W. M. S. G. K.)

Bibliography.—R. G. Codrington, *The Territorial Army* (1938); J. K. Dunlop, *The Territorial Army Today* (1939); W. E. Green, *The Territorial Army in the Next War* (1939); *The Citizen Soldier* (1939).

Teschen

Before 1918 this European city and district had been part of the Austro-Hungarian monarchy; it was subsequently disputed between Czechoslovakia and Poland. The duchy of Teschen (Těšin) was originally ruled by Polish princes but became a part of the lands of the Bohemian crown in 1335. It is of great strategic and economic importance. It is the watershed between the Vistula (Baltic sea) and the Danube (Black sea) and the crossroads of the railroads from Berlin to Budapest and from Vienna to Warsaw. In its territory are important coal mines on which Czechoslovak industry largely depended.

Czechoslovakia and Poland first disputed Teschen in 1919. Its area was then 881 sq.mi., its pop. (1910) 426,000, of whom nearly 55% were Polish-speaking, 27% Czech-speaking and 18% German-speaking. The council of ambassadors decided on July 28, 1920, to partition the territory, and the solution was accepted, though against Polish wishes. Czechoslovakia received 491.5 sq.mi., with a pop. (1921) of 310,183. The city of Teschen was divided, the larger part, east of the Olsa river, going to Poland.

The weakness of Czechoslovakia at the time of the Munich crisis in 1938 was used by Poland to present an ultimatum to Czechoslovakia for the Czechoslovak part of the Teschen district. The territory annexed by Poland in Sept. 1938 amounted to 419.3 sq.mi. with a pop. of about 230,000, of whom 120,000 were Czechs and 76,000 Poles. In 1945 in spite of all protestations of Slavic brotherhood and in spite of the fact that both governments were Russian controlled, the struggle for Teschen flared up with undiminished violence between the two governments. The Polish army occupied the territory on June 19. The Czechoslovak government immediately protested. It declared that any cession of the territory to the Poles would affect the most vital interests of Czechoslovakia. (H. Ko.)

Bibliography.—B. Kozusznik, *Problem of Czeszyn, Silesia* (London, 1943); *Statesman's Yearbook;* V. L. Tapie, *Le Pays de Teschen* (Paris, 1936).

Texas

A south central state of the United States, Texas was admitted to the union as the 28th state on Dec. 29, 1845; popularly known as the "Lone Star state." Area, 263,644 sq.mi. of land and 3,695 sq.mi. of inland water surface. Population (1940) 6,414,824 including 3,503,435 or 54.6% rural and 14.5% Negroes and other nonwhites; 6,179,296 native and 235,528 foreign-born, principally from Mexico. The population was estimated at 6,876,248 on July 1, 1944. Capital, Austin (87,930). The four largest cities were Houston (384,514); Dallas (294,734); San Antonio (253,854); Fort Worth (177,662).

The principal state officers at the beginning of the decade 1937–46 were: James V. Allred, governor; William McCraw, attorney general; George H. Sheppard, comptroller; Charley Lockhart, treasurer; Edward Clark, secretary of state; Claude D. Teer, chairman board of control; L. A. Woods, superintendent of public instruction. The state legislature was in regular session Jan. 12–May 22, 1937, with called sessions convening in May and September. In politics, Texas remained strongly Democratic, with the Democrats divided into liberal and conservative wings. During the legislative sessions there was a sharp contest between the liberals, controlling the house and led by the governor, who demanded higher taxes upon the corporations exploiting the state's mineral resources, and the conservative senate, which preferred a general sales tax. Enlarged appropriations without new taxes increased the deficit in the general fund to approximately $17,000,000; but other funds had surpluses which aggregated about the same amount. Important laws enacted included those giving cities power to regulate public utilities therein and reducing the rate of return on utility investments from 10% to 8%; permitting the commitment of insane without a court trial; setting up a teachers' retirement system, but failing to provide the state's share in financing it, and repeal of the law permitting betting at race tracks. Constitutional amendments increasing the salaries of state officials and providing pensions for indigent persons above 65 years of age went into effect in 1937.

The biennial state elections of 1938 introduced a new political figure, W. Lee O'Daniel, a Fort Worth flour merchant, who was elected governor on a platform for liberalizing the old-age pension system and for promoting industries in the state. Under the pension system about 114,000 of the neediest persons more than 65 years of age received an average of $13.90 monthly (half paid by the U.S. government), while O'Daniel advocated paying all persons more than 65, $30 per month (half by the U.S.). Among other newly elected state officials were: Coke R. Stevenson, lieutenant governor; Gerald C. Mann, attorney general; Richard Critz, justice of the supreme court; G. A. Sadler, railroad commissioner, and Bascom Giles, commissioner of the general land office. All elected officials were Democrats. The 45th legislature did not meet in 1938.

Controversy over the governor's social security program made the session of the 46th legislature, which opened in Jan. 1939, one of the most turbulent. A bill known as Senate Joint Resolution 12, sponsored by the governor, would have submitted to popular vote a constitutional amendment embodying a sales tax and a tax on natural resources, but with a permanent ceiling on the latter that could not be raised. The measure was opposed by 56 members of the lower house, sufficient to prevent passage. Another bill, passed by the legislature and signed by the governor, added 50,000 old-age pensioners to the 118,000 already on the rolls, but no money was appropriated, and the sums received by the pensioners decreased within the year from an average of $14 to about $8 per month. For the first time in many years there was no special session of the legislature since the governor refused to call one.

In the presidential election of Nov. 1940, the Democratic candidates carried Texas by an overwhelming majority. The vote for presidential electors was as follows: Democrat 840,151; Republican 199,152; Socialist 728; Communist 212; Prohibition 925. W. Lee O'Daniel was re-elected governor in 1940. The opposition to him in the political campaign was bitter but ineffectual. The legislature did not meet during the year because the governor refused to call a special session. During the year the state turned its attention to the problem of national defense. Work was begun on a great army encampment at Brownwood. At Corpus Christi, construction started on a huge air-naval base. The shipyards at Orange received orders to build 12 destroyers.

The legislature met in Jan. 1941 to begin the longest session (170 days, until July 4) and to pass the heaviest tax bill in the history of the state. Little other legislation of importance was enacted, except to repress strikes in defense industries; hostility between the governor and legislature caused frequent impasses. After the death of U.S. Sen. Morris Sheppard in April 1941, the governor called a special election for June 28. Meanwhile, he appointed Andrew Jackson Houston, 87, to the vacant seat. O'Daniel himself announced his candidacy for the office; Senator Houston died in June, and O'Daniel barely defeated Congressman Lyndon Johnson, who had the strong support of the national administration. The three leading candidates were O'Daniel (175,590), Johnson (174,279), Gerald Mann (140,807). Coke R. Stevenson, lieutenant governor, was inaugurated as governor Aug. 8, 1941. Other state officers were Gerald Mann, attorney general; Charley Lockhart, treasurer; Bascom Giles, commissioner of general land office; J. E. McDonald, commissioner of agriculture; L. A. Woods, superintendent of public instruction; George H. Sheppard, comptroller; railroad commissioners, Ernest O. Thompson, G. A. Sadler and Olin Culberson. On Gov. Stevenson's inauguration, H. L. Winfield became acting lieutenant governor.

During 1942 the life and economy of the people of Texas were disrupted by World War II. The rate of enlistments in the armed services was higher than in any other state of the union. War workers crowded cities and towns and there was a scarcity of farm labour. As a result of these disruptions there was a lack of interest in local politics. In the second Democratic primary (in August) U.S. Sen. W. Lee O'Daniel defeated James V. Allred, who had the strong support of the national administration, by a narrow margin (451,359–433,203). Only a minority of qualified voters went to the polls. O'Daniel, after re-election to the senate, led the fight against the drafting of 18- and 19-year-olds. The antiadministration trend in Texas politics was echoed by Coke R. Stevenson (re-elected governor), who protested against rationing, and John Lee Smith (elected lieutenant governor), who criticized federal labour policy. Jesse James was state treasurer in 1942, and James P. Alexander, chief justice of the supreme court.

No general election was held in Texas during 1943, and there was little political activity or interest. Cities and towns with army camps or defense plants continued to bulge with newcomers. While the people remained apathetic, a strenuous campaign against the national administration and its major policies was carried on by the junior U.S. senator, W. Lee O'Daniel, the governor of the state, Coke R. Stevenson, and the lieutenant governor, John Lee Smith. The only state official of any importance who defended the administration was the attorney general, Gerald Mann. He resigned in December and was succeeded by his assistant, Grover Sellers. (C. W. Ra.; X.)

The elections of 1944 resulted in removal of only one incumbent of state office. Judge Richard Critz (Dem.) of the state supreme court was defeated by Lt. Col. Gordon Simpson (Dem.), who served in Italy during the campaign. The chief political development was the split of the dominant Democratic party over the fourth-term nomination of President Roosevelt. The election poll was 821,605 for Roosevelt; 135,439 for the Democratic "regulars" or anti-Roosevelt ticket, with uninstructed electors, and 191,425 for Thomas Dewey (Rep.). A bitter controversy developed during 1944 over differences between the board of regents of the University of Texas and its president, Dr. Homer P. Rainey, who was removed from office Nov. 1, after which three board members resigned. Principal state officers for the official biennium beginning Jan. 1, 1945, in addition to Governor Stevenson, were: lieutenant governor, John Lee Smith; secretary of state, Claude Isbell; comptroller, George H. Sheppard; attorney general, Grover Sellers; treasurer, Jesse James; superintendent of public instruction, L. A. Woods; state land commissioner, Bascom Giles; chief justice, James P. Alexander; railroad commission, Olin Culberson (chairman), Beauford Jester and Ernest O. Thompson.

The closing of large ordnance, aircraft and shipbuilding plants, built for war production, was the outstanding event of 1945, causing some redistribution of population and lessening of drastic labour shortage. The only state election in 1945 was on Aug. 25, when three constitutional amendments were adopted, increasing the supreme court from three to nine members; providing for soldier voting without poll tax for a limited time after the war and giving state agencies wider discretion in distribution of social welfare benefits; one amendment, increasing legislative pay, was defeated. Submission of these amendments was the principal permanent result of the 49th legislature in biennial session Jan. 2–June 5. The controversy over control of the university continued during 1945 with the institution placed on probation by the Southern Association of Colleges and Secondary Schools.

The year 1946 was characterized in Texas by continued postwar readjustment of industry, with a consequent reshifting of population to the rural areas, although the 500,000 who migrated to the cities during the World War II period still remained largely concentrated there. There was no session in 1946 of the biennial legislature.

Political interest centred in the gubernatorial race in the 1946 Democratic primaries; Beauford H. Jester was nominated in the runoff primary, defeating Homer P. Rainey by a vote of 700,178 to 361,178. Nomination as usual was equivalent to election. There was intense public interest in the campaign because it was the culmination of a controversy between Rainey, who was deposed as president of the University of Texas in 1944, and the university board of regents. At the general election on Nov. 5 and at a special election on Nov. 7, four constitutional amendments were adopted providing for (1) issuance of $25,000,000 in state bonds to assist war veterans to buy farms; (2) a pension system for state employees; (3) restriction of revenue from the gasoline tax to use in highway construction; (4) payment to a construction contractor for a state building whose contract had been voided by court decision.

In addition to Gov. Jester, principal state officers for the biennium beginning Jan. 1, 1947, were as follows: Allan Shivers, lieutenant governor; Price Daniel, attorney general; George H. Sheppard, comptroller of public accounts; Jesse James, treasurer, and L. A. Woods, superintendent of public instruction. (S. McG.; X.)

BIBLIOGRAPHY.—Council of State Govts., *Book of the States* (bienn.); Federal Writers' Program, *Texas: Guide to the Lone Star State* (1940); E. H. Johnson, *Basis of the Commercial and Industrial Development*, Univ. of Tex. Bur. of Bus. Res. Monograph 9 (1933); C. P. Patterson, *State and Local Govt.* (1940); R. N. Richardson, *Texas* (1943); *Texas Almanac and State Industrial Guide* (bienn.); Periodical, *Monthly Checklist of State Publications.*

Texas: *Statistical Data*

Table I.—*Education (Public)*

	1936	1938	1941	1943	1944	1945
Elementary school pupils	1,071,230	1,032,468	1,016,143	970,507	967,422	1,043,438
High school pupils	293,397	322,933	350,240	313,644	345,889	
Elementary teachers	31,245	30,791	49,210	47,334		36,602
High school teachers	12,498	13,732				

Table II.—*Public Welfare*

	1938	1940	1941	1943	1944	1945
Cases on general relief	14,250	12,523	9,503			
Recipients of old-age pensions	113,230	118,380	138,677	182,765	171,991	175,000
Dependent children receiving aid	265	230	230			
Blind receiving aid				4,427	4,617	4,600

Table III.—*Communications*
(Money figures in thousands of dollars)

	1938	1939	1941	1943	1944	1945
Highway mileage	22,296	23,161	23,997	24,565		24,664
Expenditures on highways	$42,262	$60,249	$33,066		$42,440	$46,616
Railroad mileage	16,473	16,425	22,000	22,000	15,859	15,752

Table IV.—*Banking and Finance*
(Money figures in thousands of dollars)

	1937	1938	1939	1941	1943	1944
State revenue	$177,220	$185,501	$188,187	$202,132		$254,725
State expenditure	$153,784	$164,363	$130,133	$166,073	$290,371	$182,234
State net debt	$26,649	$23,503		$37,151		
State gross debt	$29,737			$21,825		
Number of banks	874	856	844		830	832
Total bank deposits	$1,300,700	$1,341,800	$1,471,900		$3,650,129	
Number of national banks	453	499	445	446	438	439
Deposits of national banks	$1,194,463	$1,261,143	$1,409,821	$1,695,662	$3,113,803	

Table V.—*Agriculture*
(All figures in thousands)

	1937	1939	1940	1942	1944	1945
Acreage, principal crops	28,510	25,034	25,826	26,414	29,179	
Leading crops (bu.):						
Barley	1,766	2,955	3,825	4,818		
Corn	72,048	73,376	90,324		69,622	66,832
Cotton (bales)	5,154	2,846	3,234	3,038	2,640	1,820
Grain sorghums	52,336	38,115	46,397	59,675	96,724	60,921
Oats	30,432	28,750	37,125	11,210	38,600	42,441
Peaches	1,392	1,972	2,036	1,610		
Peanuts (lb.)	100,760	129,480	166,675	430,080		
Pecans (lb.)	27,000	19,000	41,000	10,300		
Potatoes	3,456	2,666	3,200			
Rice				15,498	19,208	18,000
Wheat	41,690	29,032	29,355	47,438	74,746	41,778

Table VI.—*Manufacturing*
(Money figures in thousands of dollars)

	1937	1939	1944 (est.)	1945 (est.)
Wage earners	129,501	126,992		
Wages paid	$132,505	$128,139		
Value of products	$1,581,422	$1,530,221	$4,500,000	$3,000,000
Leading manufactured products (value):				
Petroleum refining	$689,625	$698,850		
Meat packing	$97,981	$85,461		
Cottonseed oil, etc.	$52,322	$44,407		
Grain mill products	$62,874	$41,251		

Table VII.—*Mineral Production*
(All figures in thousands of dollars)

	1937	1938	1939	1941	1943	1944
Value of mineral production	813,291	740,147	701,940	836,260	1,116,056	1,160,000
Leading products (value):						
Petroleum	594,500	539,150	478,330		721,400	906,226
Natural gas	132,166	133,486	141,535		208,560	199,900
Sulphur	36,546		28,498		38,175	38,175
Natural gasoline	24,329	19,781	25,807		51,930	57,030

Textile Industry

The decade 1937–46, which left no part of the world economy unchanged, had a more profound relative effect upon the textile industry than upon industry in general. The full significance of those ten eventful years in textiles was not immediately apparent to the general public, or even to textile manufacturers themselves.

U.S. Activity.—The sharp extremes of fortune were accurately portrayed in the statistical picture for the decade. Textile-mill activity in the United States started the period in 1937 at a level well above that of the depression years, dropped sharply in 1938 to depression levels as the 1936–37 boom came to its abortive end, and then started climbing to an unprecedented volume of activity which was still in effect at the end of the decade. The result was that the bulge starting with the U.S. defense program became a boom in the years of World War II and continued so in the immediate postwar years. The activity index from 1941 to 1946 inclusive was more than 75% above the assumed prewar normal.

The decade brought sharp changes in the alignment of the major raw materials. Silk passed out of the picture well before Pearl Harbor. Completely new types of synthetic fibres, best exemplified to the general public by nylon, posed new threats not only to the natural fibres but to the old-line synthetics. However, here too World War II arrested the full manifestation of these changes. Military needs and devastated countries combined to make every pound of raw material valuable and the "Battle of the Fibres" was postponed by events on the world's battlefronts. Natural fibres, which might have receded sharply in a world percentage scale, rose instead as war took its toll of man-made fibre production in the countries in the war zones. The following figures from the *Rayon Organon*, published by Textile Economics Bureau Inc., show this shift: In 1937 the first year of the decade, cotton accounted for 81% of world production of the 4 major textile fibres; wool 10%, rayon 8% and silk 1%. In 1941 synthetics had made inroads on cotton, with the resulting alignment as follows: cotton 69%, wool 14%, rayon 16%, silk 1%. In 1945 the trend had been partly reversed with this result: cotton 75%, wool, 15%, rayon 10%, silk none.

The global nature of World War II created new textile needs for which entirely new types of research were necessary. Fabrics were required for use in the stratosphere, on the ground and under the sea; in the arctic regions and in the tropics; in the desert and in swamps; against possible use of gas and other weapons. To meet these needs, research was conducted under government auspices, by textile institutes and associations, and by corporations.

Prior to World War II, there were undercurrents of reform which were gradually removing textile manufacture from its relatively low place in public esteem to the status of a higher-wage industry. The most important single force in that direction was the inauguration of minimum-wage and maximum-hour legislation, which became effective in the United States in the fall of 1938. Also, the

Textile worker winding nylon yarn around bobbins. Nylon hosiery first went on general sale in the United States May 15, 1940, but production was severely curtailed during World War II and the immediate postwar period

acute manpower shortage throughout the years of World War II and in the immediate postwar years pushed wage levels still higher and brought new gains for labour. Although to many the pendulum may have seemed to swing too far in the other direction, the net result of the long-term trend should be of help to the ethical and progressive manufacturer.

The most important question at the end of the decade, not only from the standpoint of the textile industry itself but from that of the general public, was the effect of competition from other industries and other countries for markets hitherto supplied by the United States textile industry. Inroads by other products—particularly paper—were made before World War II. Textile manufacturers recognized that the only real defense was research. Similarly, competition from newly industrialized countries posed another threat to the textile industry of the United States. It was quite possible that the latter would have to retreat gradually from the manufacture of cheap, staple fabrics, leaving that field eventually to countries with lower wage levels and standards of living, and resorting more and more to the production of specialized fabrics with higher margins of profit. This possibility was not a threat to the alert sections of the industry. For the general public, it promised more and more intrinsic value for the dollar spent on fabrics, no matter what country or what type of enterprise produced them. It could be concluded, therefore, that the ten eventful years were most important because of the groundwork which had been laid.

(D. G. Wo.)

Bibliography.—Z. Bendure, *America's Fabrics* (1946); *Textile World* (mo.); *Quarterly Rev. of Textile Industry* (1938 *et seq.*).

Great Britain and Europe.—Before 1937 viscose, cuprammonium and cellulose acetate, the three main types of rayon, had found extended use. They were, however, defective in possessing a rather low strength (from 2.0 to 1.3 grams per denier) and in showing too great a loss in strength on immersion in water. In the case of viscose rayon, improved methods of spinning raised the strength to 3.5 grams per denier and reduced the loss in strength in water to 35% compared with 50%. Such material was marketed in Great Britain under the name of "Tenasco." Even greater strength, though accompanied by a small extensibility, was obtained by development of the Lilienfeld process. The yarn, known as "Durafil," had a strength of 5.5 grams per denier, but the extension at break was only 7%. In the case of cellulose acetate rayon, strong yarn, marketed under the name of "Fortisan," was obtained by stretching the filaments in an atmosphere of steam to induce molecular orientation, and then hydrolyzing the product to regenerate cellulose and increase molecular cohesion.

In ways such as these, the elastic properties of ordinary rayons were modified, particularly in the direction of increasing their strength, to meet a number of industrial requirements. During World War II both "Tenasco" and "Fortisan" found important military uses; *e.g.*, in the manufacture of tire cord for the reinforcement of aeroplane and motor car tires. At the same time as these developments were taking place, further attempts were made to modify the properties of viscose rayon so as to give it an affinity for acid wool dyes. For this purpose, synthetic resins were either incorporated in the spinning solution or applied to the rayon after spinning. A German product of this type was "Vistralan," while the British product was "Rayolanda."

A different approach to the problem of making rayons to imitate the properties of animal fibres like wool was made by Antonio Ferretti in Italy. He chose casein, which had long been used in the manufacture of plastics, as the raw material, and by the discovery of correct methods of isolating, dissolving and spinning the casein he was able to produce usable textile fibres. Their strength was only 0.8 grams per denier, and the loss in strength in water was as much as 60%, but satisfactory fabrics were obtained by blending the cut fibre with an equal or greater amount of wool. The low wet strength of the material was also turned to advantage in the manufacture of felts, particularly felt hats, because mixtures of casein staple fibre and wool or fur were found to felt more rapidly than wool alone. Fibres of a similar type, known as "Ardil," were made from the proteins of ground nuts in Great Britain.

The closest imitation of silk, both in appearance, strength and dyeing properties, came with the production of nylon in the United States (*see* above). Its manufacture in Great Britain during World War II was restricted to war purposes, such as parachute fabric and tow ropes for gliders. There were repercussions in Germany, where a synthesis of nylon-like fibres was worked out. Marketed under the name of "Perlon L," the rayon had the same high strength as nylon and possessed affinity for the same types of dye. Among other fibres developed in Germany were "Perlon U" (polyurethane) and PE-CE (chlorinated polyvinyl chloride). Processes were developed in Germany for the continuous production of viscose rayon. These, with Courtauld's process for making "top" directly from continuous filament rayon by means of an ingenious cutting device, did much to cheapen and increase the utilization of viscose staple fibre.

An interesting development in Great Britain during World War II was the attempt to produce satisfactory rayon from seaweed. Sodium alginate, obtained from seaweed by extraction with a solution of sodium carbonate, was dissolved in water and extruded into an acid solution of calcium chloride. The resulting calcium alginate rayon was lustrous, slightly stronger than ordinary viscose rayon and could be readily knitted or woven. It was, however, soluble in alkali. The defect was overcome by replacing all or part of the calcium by chromium or beryllium, or by treatment with an acid solution of formaldehyde. Actually, the alkali-soluble type of rayon was found to be more important than the alkali-resistant types, because it was the only one of its kind. Its uses were multitudinous. Calcium alginate fabric was, for example, used as a foundation fabric on which other yarns were embroidered; when the embroidered fabric was washed in a solution of soap and soda the alginate rayon dissolved and left the embroidery isolated.

Although the most striking advances were in the field of rayon production, considerable progress was made in the modification of natural fibres. The discovery of the main features of the constitution of wool in 1933 had given rise to constructive attack on many problems, notably that of preventing the felting and shrinking of wool textile materials during laundering. Most of the work in this field was carried out in Great Britain, and the processes included treatment of wool with a solution of sulphuryl chloride in white spirit, a dispersion in white spirit of a solution of sodium hydroxide in butyl alcohol and an acid solution of potassium permanganate. All these processes were used commercially, and a number of others, based on the formation of polymers inside and outside the fibres, were carried to the point of commercial development. Similarly, in the case of cotton, the war in the Pacific gave an impetus to research on the proofing of cotton uniforms and equipment against attack by bacteria and fungi. Several successful processes were evolved. Of special importance, too, was the "ventile" fabric from which portable and collapsible containers for water were made. (*See* also CHEMURGY; COTTON; INTERIOR DECORATION; RAYON AND OTHER SYNTHETIC FIBRES; WOOL.)

Mohair warehouse at Kerrville, Texas. Large stocks of this material, formerly used in U.S. motor car upholstery, were used to help ease the wartime wool shortage

BIBLIOGRAPHY.—Combined Intelligence Objectives sub-committee, *File No. XXVI-53* (London); British Intelligence Objectives sub-committee, *Report No. 37* (London); J. R. Whinfield, "Chemistry of 'Terylene,'" *Nature* (weekly, vol. 158, No. 4026, Dec. 28, 1946); E. Race and P. Alexander, "Fibrous Proteins," *Journal of the Society of Dyers and Colourists*, pp. 67, 199 (monthly, Dec. 1946). (J. B. SN.)

Thailand

See SIAM.

Theatre

No Sophocles, no Shakespeare emerged to make the native American drama momentous during the decade surveyed in these volumes. True, Eugene O'Neill broke his 12-year silence in 1946 with a lengthy, eloquent and often exciting examination of the dreams and illusions of bar-room riff-raff which was strangely entitled *The Iceman Cometh;* there was poetry by stealth in the often lyrical realism of Tennessee Williams' *The Glass Menagerie* (1945) and in 1943 *Oklahoma!,* the folk comedy with music by Richard Rodgers and a libretto adapted from Lynn Riggs' *Green Grow the Lilacs* by Oscar Hammerstein II, set new pace and pattern for the music show with antiphonal ballets. Yet had William Gillette lived another ten years, that distinguished playwright and actor could have uttered again the humorously truthful words he wrote shortly before his death in 1937: "I have the honor to report that the American theater is still declining."

The financial depression was still felt when this period began. Hundreds of unemployed actors were given at least a subsistence wage in the Federal Theatre project controlled by the Work Projects administration. There may have been more heart than art in this worthy governmental experiment, greater relief for the player than for the playgoer, but when in 1939 the Federal theatre expired in its fourth year, there remained encouragement for a noncommercial enterprise entitled The American National Theatre and Academy, with a federal charter.

The theatres of the United States experienced an abrupt boom directly World War II had started, even before Americans had been called to arms. This boom grew despite not only a shortage of theatres (they had been snapped up for motion picture houses during the depression), but a shortage of playwrights and players who had transferred their talents to Hollywood, many later engaging in war work at home and abroad. Countless inferior plays were produced but without retarding the public's reawakening to the pleasures of beholding living actors rather than their animated photographs. Some of the nightly plays were almost as contemporary and short-lived as the daily newspapers. Money was spent on production and at the box office as never before. The more successful New York productions lasted so many seasons that duplicate casts were engaged for Chicago and the road. But failures still numbered four against one success, and in the absence of tempting scripts many revivals were staged, not only of yesterday's popular pieces, but of day-before-yesterday's: Shakespeare was again the first playwright.

Many an unstageworthy comedy or drama died obscurely in what *Variety,* the nation's leading amusement weekly, termed "straw-hat" production at the summer theatres that mushroomed throughout the countryside and the suburbs of the eastern states, the audiences preferring revivals of Broadway and national hits. In the metropolitan theatres were staged a few plays with no scenery and few props. Orson Welles made a sceneryless presentation of *Julius Caesar* without togas; Thornton Wilder's principal properties for the bare-staging of his *Our Town* (an amiable reflex from the bitter elegy of Edgar Lee Masters' *Spoon River Anthology*), were an array of umbrellas opened against the rainless rain of the burial scene which would have brought down the final curtain had a curtain been in use.

"Movie money" moved in and out of the living theatre. It had moved in again in 1946. Hollywood writers tackled the stiffer obstacles lying behind the footlighted proscenium, and a mournful statistician counted in 1 year 39 failures in 40 attempts. The "colour question" was presented with heated partisanship by some of the playwrights, and these checkerboard dramas increased the attendance of Negro playgoers, as did Shakespearean revivals which included Paul Robeson's appearance as Othello and Canada Lee's as Caliban, not to overlook Ethel Waters' emergence as a dramatic actress in *Mamba's Daughters.* There were a number of Negro casts ranging from Orson Welles' Haitian version of *Macbeth* to *Anna Lucasta,* Philip Yordan's workmanlike play originally written with Polish-American characters before the script fell into the capable hands of New York's American Negro theatre and was profitably snapped up by commercial management. Plays in protest against anti-Semitism appeared near the end of the decade, but none was written with the avowed impartiality of Galsworthy's remembered *Loyalties;* they were more justly indignant than dramatically significant.

With the appearance of the amazingly popular *Junior Miss,* there came at least a dozen comedies of adolescence that prematurely aged those veteran critics who had not found relief in war work or foreign correspondence, but which greatly pleased not only youngsters temporarily weaned from the movies but a vast number of adults who seemed happy to find their second childhood in what several of the more morose reviewers dubbed "diaper drama."

Politics took to the stage in jest and in earnest, and the cream of political persiflage was George M. Cohan's (he died in 1942) song-and-dance impersonation of the living Pres. Franklin D. Roosevelt in *I'd Rather Be Right,* in 1937. A more serious and yet richly amusing consideration of the political scene was 1945's *State of the Union,* in which Howard Lindsay and Russel Crouse, authors of the durably laughable *Life With Father,* satirized not only the conflict between political idealism and bossism but admonitory preachments written along that line. One of the more serious admonitory dramas was novelist Sinclair Lewis' warning against fascism in America, bearing the ironic title *It Can't Happen Here* and produced in 1936 throughout the country by 18 units of the Federal Theatre project.

Most of the war plays were precipitously propagandic, and it was recalled that America's *What Price Glory?* came six years after World War I, and England's *Journey's End* ten years. Black was very black and white very white and there was hardly any gray in these abrupt and one-sided dramatic editorials. Robert E. Sherwood's fluent *There Shall Be No Night* lost nothing of its popular appeal even when a disturbance in contemporary history made tactful the change of scene from Finland to Greece. But the war plays of any quality were the lightheartedly messageless rather than the heavily-loaded propagandist, and among these were Paul Osborn's dramatization of the John Hersey novel, *A Bell for Adano,* John Patrick's *The Hasty Heart,* S. N. Behrman's adaptation of Franz Werfel's *Jacobowsky and the Colonel* and a sprightly revue written by young war veterans on the matter of reconversion and tellingly called *Call Me Mister.*

Shakespeare Redivivus.—While many of the better American playwrights served their country or Hollywood, there was always Shakespeare. As in previous periods, productions of his plays outnumbered those of any other author dead or alive. There were Shakespearean revivals lavish and sparse. The night following Orson Welles' presentation of *Julius Caesar* in mufti, Tallulah Bankhead appeared at a nearby New York theatre in the costliest *Antony and Cleopatra* ever staged. It lasted five nights.

But a brief run did not always mean a bad performance. One of the best was Welles' telescoping of the Henry histories under the title of *Five Kings,* in which his wine-stained and greasily gutteral wencher was reckoned the ripest and most richly humorous Falstaff of the 20th century by critics fortunate enough to witness the too few performances played only in Washington, D.C. The Falstaff of Ralph Richardson was widely acclaimed when Richard Aldrich, husband of Gertrude Lawrence, brought from London to New York, under guarantee, the Old Vic company for a repertory season of six weeks. Here Laurence Olivier—whose Romeo, like Vivien Leigh's Juliet, had met emphatic failure first in Chicago and then in New York several seasons earlier—was welcomed as the right man for Hotspur in the opening half of *Henry IV* and declared by many reviewers to have attained to little short of greatness when he assumed the name-part in the rarely seen translation of Sophocles' *Oedipus,* originally made by W. B. Yeats for Dublin's Abbey Theatre.

Domestic and imported actors measured their skills in *Hamlet.* Maurice Evans well-played the first unabridged Hamlet since, following the turn of the century, Ben Greet had survived a *Hamlet* without cuts in the University of California's vast open-air Greek theatre at Berkeley. Near the close of the decade, Evans staged for the armed forces at home and abroad a severely shortened *Hamlet* in costumes of the 19th century (including swords), which was somewhat expanded later when Michael Todd took it over as a commercial enterprise. Leslie Howard's Hamlet was more reflective than urgent; John Gielgud's was declaimed in the old tradition that had been followed by Edwin Booth's contemporaries, but not by Booth.

Evans was the most tireless of the Shakespeareans. In and as *Richard II* he gave his most rounded and magnetic performance. In *Macbeth* his thane was dimmed by the luminous power of Judith Anderson's Lady Macbeth. His deliberately cockneyed Malvolio to Helen Hayes' ardent Viola in the guild's *Twelfth Night* was good fun, good theatre, good acting. But his Falstaff in *Henry IV, Part One,* was mediocre. The versatile Miss Hayes had her first experience in Shakespeare in Chicago when she relieved the hard routine of *Victoria Regina* with special performances of *The Merchant of Venice.* Notwithstanding uncouth criticism that called her characterization "a half-Portia," the true comic spirit gleamed throughout the diminutive actress' portrayal. Walter Huston, a stalwart among American character actors but unschooled in verse drama, gave up Othello after 21 Broadway performances. Paul Robeson's attack on this role, which he had first acted in London a decade earlier, was more popular in New York and other large cities, although his characterization was singularly lacking in passion; here the critical posies were bestowed on the Iago of Jose Ferrer.

The road witnessed its liveliest Shakespeare when Alfred Lunt and Lynn Fontanne, with an excellent company and a most artistic yet inexpensive production left New York and toured from coast to coast in a riotously comical performance of *The Taming of the Shrew.* Another "grand tour" was made in the earliest of these days by Katharine Cornell when she duplicated throughout the country the New York success of her *Romeo and Juliet,* the poetic spell of her Juliet intensified by the highly emotional Romeo of Maurice Evans and the dazzlingly brilliant Mercutio of Ralph Richardson. Two comparatively unfamiliar revivals were *The Tempest* and *The Winter's Tale.* In the former, the versatile Negro actor Canada Lee put forth a Caliban whose speeches were more believable than his makeup, and in which the comely dancer Zorina, as Ariel, was more poetic to the eye than to the ear. The Theatre Guild's *Tale* was magnificent scenically, but, even with such veterans as Jessie Royce Landis and Florence Reed the acting did not overcome the play's traditional lethargy. And late in 1946 the newly organized American Repertory company started in Princeton, N.J., a well-received *Henry VIII* with interpolations credited by Director Margaret Webster to the Holinshed chronicles.

Other Revivals.—Early in this decade a few plays of the Elizabethan and Restoration periods were revived. Welles acted the titular character in Christopher Marlowe's *Doctor Faustus* for New York's Federal theatre, seats selling for as little as 25¢ and no higher than 50¢. His and John Houseman's short-lived Mercury theatre made a rollicking production of Thomas Dekker's *The Shoemaker's Holiday.* Ruth Gordon, who had prepared for the job by working with the Old Vic actors in London, was, as Mrs. Pinchwife, the high condiment in Gilbert Miller's staging of Wycherly's *The Country Wife.* The scarcity and mediocrity of new scripts encouraged the revival of successful plays of previous periods. Ibsen's *Hedda Gabler, Ghosts* and *An Enemy of the People* swiftly appeared and disappeared. But where Alla Nazimova, Walter Hampden and others failed to repopularize Ibsen, the saline Ruth Gordon's 1937 reconsideration of his new woman gave new life to the great Norwegian's *A Doll's House.* Anton Chekhov's work was enthusiastically revived with compelling casts. The Lunts, following a Russian pilgrimage to the Moscow Art theatre, valiantly forsook comedy for a solemn and successful disinterment of *The Sea Gull.* Miss Cornell, sharing honours with Miss Anderson and Miss Gordon in the title parts and supported by a company of unchallengeable calibre directed by Guthrie McClintic, gave *The Three Sisters* the most satisfying examination it had received since Morris Gest imported the original Moscow cast. Eva LeGallienne and Joseph Schildkraut had a lopsided revival of *The Cherry Orchard,* owing to uneven acting by their support and bits of avowedly comical stage business that provoked in the audience more embarrassment than mirth.

Miss Cornell, whose Candida in Bernard Shaw's comedy of that name was first essayed in 1924, and repeated in 1937, became its classic interpreter when, in 1942, she revived the play in New York for the Army Emergency fund and Navy Relief society with a notable cast. Miss Cornell offered still another *Candida* revival in 1946 (her gallant experiment with Lewis Galantiere's adaptation of *Antigone* failing to attract large audiences) in which Sir Cedric Hardwicke acted an elaborately low-comical Burgess. In 1941 she presented *The Doctor's Dilemma* for 121 performances in New York, a duration record for a Shaw revival that was broken only when Gertrude Lawrence restored *Pygmalion* to the American theatre in 1946.

Oscar Wilde's *The Importance of Being Earnest* was seen again in 1939, with Clifton Webb and Estelle Winwood, and in 1946 his *Lady Windermere's Fan* was sumptuously staged (there was even an original score of incidental music) for national consumption in San Francisco.

In 1937 Dublin's still intact Abbey theatre company toured the United States in a familiar repertory. W. S. Maugham's *The Circle* was revived the following year with Tallulah Bankhead and Grace George. Sean O'Casey's *Juno and the Paycock* ran to much acclaim. In 1942 Paul Muni returned to the role he had originated in Elmer Rice's *Counsellor at Law.* After playing Rudolph Besier's *The Barretts of Wimpole Street* for the U.S. armed forces in Europe in 1945, Miss Cornell gave the play back to the civilians of New York. The following year was marked by successful revivals on Broadway of Ben Hecht and Charles MacArthur's hilariously cynical *The Front Page,*

Circle: *Abe Lincoln in Illinois* by Robert E. Sherwood was hailed as a "classic" by drama critics immediately after its Broadway opening on Oct. 15, 1938. Raymond Massey (right) is shown in the title role

Above: James Thurber's *The Male Animal*, written with Elliott Nugent, became the first of Broadway's hits of 1940

Below, left: Katharine Hepburn, Joseph Cotten (left) and Van Heflin in Philip Barry's 1939 comedy success *Philadelphia Story*. It was Miss Hepburn's first stage success

Below: Principals in the dramatization of Clarence Day's *Life with Father*

Below: Monty Woolley (seated in wheelchair) in a scene from *The Man Who Came to Dinner*, a successful comedy of the 1939 Broadway season, based on apocryphal adventures of Alexander Woollcott and the Brian Hooker translation of *Cyrano de Bergerac,* acted and produced by José Ferrer.

Musical Revivals.—The ever welcome works of Gilbert and Sullivan were wittily revived in three lengthy tours of London's authoritative D'Oyly Carte company, and there were American revivals of them by the Boston Comic Opera company and the Gilbert and Sullivan Opera company. *The Mikado* survived consternating changes when the score was tricked with jazz rhythms and Negro singers voiced it as a federal enterprise first in Chicago, where it was named *The Swing Mikado.* Failing in his ambition to take over this production, manager Todd staged his own *The Hot Mikado,* with the veteran tap-dancer Bill Robinson heading the Negro cast.

The untimely death of George Gershwin in 1937 may have hastened general recognition of the enduring worth of the many compositions he had written in the idiom of jazz. His *Porgy and Bess,* the libretto based on Du Bose and Dorothy Heyward's Negro folk play, began to gain acceptance even from musicologists as the master work of its genre. During this period it was several times revived in the capital cities and on tour. Jerome Kern's *Show Boat* was happily revived for a long New York run in 1946. The composer died shortly after the first night of this reproduction, survived by at least a dozen songs that had become a melodious part of the musical consciousness of the American people. Two enormously successful operettas, *Blossom Time* and *The Student Prince,* profitably continued their annual tours despite shoddy settings, imperfect casts and resentful reviews. Victor Herbert's ancient *The Red Mill,* verging on 40 years of age, was the surprise success of the Broadway revivals of 1946. One of its producers was Paula, daughter of Fred Stone, who had starred in the original with Dave Montgomery. Among the imports revived were Oscar Straus' *The Chocolate Soldier* and Franz Lehar's *The Merry Widow,* the latter withstanding the tenoric blasts of grand opera's Jan Kiepura.

New Words and Music.—*Oklahoma!,* based on the Riggs folk-play which the Theatre guild had produced 15 years earlier, was the most undebatably popular of the decade's theatrical offerings. *Oklahoma!* sounded a new high for the play with music. Its dialogue and lyrics were painless stage literature and its score the most unpretentiously musicianly since George Gershwin's enduring music for *Porgy and Bess.* Two Theatre guild "no-star" companies voiced it on the eastern and western coasts, and no one challenged the boast that neither of these organizations had ever been confronted with an empty seat. Compared with the costly song-and-ballet plays that followed, *Oklahoma!* was an inexpensive production. It had to be, for when it was timorously tried out the guild's financial stock pile was as depleted as its dramatic stock pile. But the guild's competitors followed the formula rather than the frugality of *Oklahoma!*

The abruptly munificent Todd expended a fortune on a spacious cantata re-exposing the scandal of old New York's crooked Tweed Ring and entitled *Up in Central Park.* The guild itself became open-handed in producing the enchanting *Carousel* when it commissioned *Oklahoma's* Rodgers and Hammerstein to Americanize Ferenc Molnar's Hungarian *Liliom,* with Agnes de Mille again devising the stirring associational ballets. The upcoming Billy Rose employed the agile wit of Hammerstein in *Carmen Jones,* his gorgeous and popular all-Negro variation of the opera *Carmen,* thriftily and triumphantly refitting the royalty-less Sevillian music of Bizet to New York's Harlem, where the Spanish bullfighter became a Negro prize fighter.

As early as 1938 Maxwell Anderson provided in *Knickerbocker Holiday* a salty libretto for the satirical score of Kurt Weill and the wryly humorous acting of Walter Huston. The psychoanalytic was explored by Weill and librettist Ira Gershwin in an enormous and enormously successful music show by Moss Hart, named *Lady in the Dark.* But for Gertrude Lawrence's unsparing impersonation of the inhibited lady and Danny Kaye's uninhibited photographer it might not have been so successful. Not unlike the more ribald restoration comedies was George Abbott's fearless staging of John O'Hara's book, *Pal Joey,* as it had been made vocal by Rodgers and Hart, and was interpreted by Gene Kelly and Vivienne Segal with unflinching candour.

Lorenz Hart died in 1943 just as his and Richard Rodgers' *A Connecticut Yankee,* after—a long way after—Mark Twain's historical satire, had been revived. This industrious and gifted team had turned out during this period more than half a dozen characteristic hits, including *Babes in Arms, I'd Rather Be Right, I Married an Angel, The Boys from Syracuse* (an impudently amusing distortion of *A Comedy of Errors*) and *By Jupiter,* based on Julian F. Thompson's *The Warrior's Husband* and justifying the belated but brilliant starship of Ray Bolger, the dancer who was to score again in the Nancy Hamilton-Morgan Lewis revue *Three to Make Ready.*

Cole Porter, who like Cohan wrote his own lyrics, composed the scores of an even greater number of nationally welcomed music shows. In many of these the leading roles were sung and acted with trumpet power by Ethel Merman, notably *Red Hot and Blue, DuBarry Was a Lady* (in which she shared the robust comicalities with Bert Lahr), *Panama Hattie* and *Something for the Boys.* Other applauded Porter musicals were *Leave It to Me, Let's Face It, Mexican Hayride* and *Seven Lively Arts.*

The labour stage, expressing cultural criticism by the International Ladies' Garment Workers, turned out one of the most durable hits of this or any other theatrical period in *Pins and Needles,* with a cast composed of amateurs and semi-professionals.

Irving Berlin, undebatably the nation's most popular song writer, composed and wrote the outstanding soldier show of the World War II period. His *This Is the Army,* cast with enlisted men still under military discipline and played for the benefit of the Army Emergency Relief fund, was even more enthusiastically received than had been his *Yip, Yip, Yaphank* of World War I. Berlin's return to the commercial theatre in 1946 resulted in his phenomenally successful *Annie Get Your Gun,* in which Ethel Merman, as the riflewoman of a Buffalo Bill "Wild West" show, rang yet another bull's-eye. The freak hit among musicals of the period was achieved by Ole Olsen and Chic Johnson when in 1938 they put together the mossy remains of their vaudeville past, called it *Hellzapoppin,* and ran it for years on Broadway and throughout the country.

Biographical Plays.—There were biographical plays in the flesh as well as in the celluloid. During 1936–38 Helen Hayes was still playing extended engagements in the capitals and mighty tours on the road, impersonating England's best-loved queen in Laurence Housman's *Victoria Regina,* which marked the summit of her hard-won starship. Five years later she masqueraded as Harriet Beecher Stowe in Florence Ryerson and Colin Clements' *Harriet,* which ran 377 performances in New York alone and from which ensued several catastrophic revivals of Mrs. Stowe's *Uncle Tom's Cabin.*

London's Robert Morley caught the fancy of the more sophisticated playgoers of Manhattan in his reasonable and witty lifelikeness of the poet-playwright in Leslie and Sewell Stokes' *Oscar Wilde.* That was in 1938, the year in which the Canadian-born American actor Raymond Massey first presented his finely felt and realized portrait of the martyred president in Robert E. Sherwood's brilliant and authoritative *Abe Lincoln in Illinois.* Hopes that this was the biographical play to end all biographical plays were pleasingly discouraged in the following year when George S. Kaufman and Moss Hart wrote—without objection from the waspish and witty guest lampooned, author Alexander Woollcott—*The Man Who Came to Dinner.* No actor failed as The Man, not even Woollcott, when after several false starts he nervously certified the caricature in Chicago.

But the most durable of the biographies was dramatized from the autobiographical humoresques of Clarence Day by Howard Lindsay and Russel Crouse in 1939 and entitled *Life With Father.* The millions collected from the public in the first seven years of this thoroughly delightful comedy, concurrently acted by three companies, would encounter unbelief even if totalized in a trustworthy work of reference. Sidney Kingsley's *The Patriots,* dealing with the animosities of Jefferson and Hamilton and the godlike patience of Washington in building a young democracy, was a tired piece about tired men and more elegy than drama. Emmett Lavery's *The Magnificent Yankee* celebrated the domestic rather than the judicial life of the great minority leader of the supreme court, Justice Oliver Wendell Holmes. The mellow dignity of Louis Calhern added to the stature of that actor and balanced an uneven play into a hit.

Modern Plays.—This period proved again that it is not always possible to measure the true worth of a play by the length of its run, nor by the Pulitzer prizes and the awards made by the New York Drama Critics' circle, an organization which was formed in 1935 to protest some of the Pulitzer selections and which eventually uttered many savage unilateral protests against its own findings. Harry Brown's realistic drama of soldiers in action, *A Sound of Hunting,* produced in 1946, died in two weeks on Broadway, yet continued to live in the admiring references of the more fastidious lay and professional playgoers. Philip Barry's mystical correction of a misguided world, *Here Come the Clowns,* endured less than three months on Broadway despite good acting and sympathetic direction; and William Saroyan's likeable collection of San Francisco crackpots, *The Beautiful People,* lasted only two months in New York although a third of the critics voted it the best play of the 1941 season. But in the long run the long runs were in most cases fair appraisals of diversionary, if not dramaturgic value. The "Broadwise" had not forgotten their ivied cliché to the effect that nothing is so dead as a dead play.

Season-by-Season Review.—The over-all popular hit of 1937 was George S. Kaufman and Moss Hart's joyous lunacy, *You Can't Take It With You.* Other lighthearted successes of the year were Clare Boothe's laughable betrayal of the female nation, *The Women; Amphitryon 38,* in which Alfred Lunt and Lynn Fontanne sparkled in S. N. Behrman's sportively free translation of Jean Giraudoux's droll notion of Plautus' *Amphitryon, or Jupiter in Disguise;* Rachel Crothers' *Susan and God,* an amusing travesty on Buchmanism that owed its run to the energetic acting of Gertrude Lawrence and *Room Service,* a George Abbott-directed farce about a war between impecunious stage folk and their unpaid landlord.

Of higher and more serious aim were Maxwell Anderson's *High Tor,* not quite so successful an adventure in metrical prose as had been his *Winterset,* and *The Star-Wagon,* a prose comedy in which time alternately ran clockwise and counter-clockwise. This same season saw John Steinbeck's sometimes cruelly, sometimes compassionately realistic *Of Mice and Men,* and Clifford Odets' *Golden Boy,* whose violinist protagonist maimed his gifted hands while debasing them for money in the prize ring.

In 1938 Robert E. Sherwood, Maxwell Anderson, S. N. Behrman, Elmer Rice and Sidney Howard, who died a year later, formed the Playwrights' company, which produced and financed plays written by its members. Their three productions of that season were Sherwood's nationally welcomed *Abe Lincoln in Illinois,* Anderson's Washington Irvingesque *Knickerbocker Holiday* (with the musical score by Kurt Weill, who joined the playwrights in 1946, the year in which Behrman retired from the organization), and Rice's swiftly discarded *American Landscape.*

This was the year in which Thornton Wilder's sceneryless *Our Town* won critical as well as popular approval, and in which Sir Cedric Hardwicke built up a strong American following through his suave, ironical depiction of the proud and polysyllabic priest in Paul Vincent Carroll's uneven but absorbing *Shadow and Substance.*

The season saw another Odets play, *Rocket to the Moon,* which was more mellow but less exciting than his previous social criticisms. Death, the old reliable, was the lighthearted theme of Paul Osborn's *On Borrowed Time,* in which Dudley Digges was the expiring old gentleman who outwitted the grim reaper while he found a home for his grandson. Clare Boothe, pretending in the published preface that she had written "a political allegory on fascism in America," was represented by *Kiss the Boys Good-bye,* a laughable pasquinade on Hollywood's highly publicized search for an actress worthy of being photographed as the heroine of *Gone With the Wind.* And this was the time when adolescence began to be a best-seller in the show shops with Ian Hay's *Bachelor Born* and Clifford Goldsmith's even more profitable high school comedy, *What a Life.*

The discriminating Eddie Dowling produced another Carroll comedy-drama in 1939, *The White Steed,* in which bigotry battled tolerance without a chance and won only laughter. But Dowling's remembered offering of this season was William Saroyan's *The Time of Your Life,* which immediately established that young short-story writer's reputation as a playwright with a fresh and happy outlook on the native scene and in which the producer, not long graduated from vaudeville, gave a distinguished performance of the leading role. Another outstanding success was Lillian Hellman's *The Little Foxes,* an astringent comedy of interfamily chicaneries in which Tallulah Bankhead, as the victorious arch-schemer, scored her first definite hit in her own country, and Patricia Collinge sympathetically portrayed the bullied wife who overdrank by stealth.

Ethel Waters, heretofore known only as the foremost Negro songstress of character ballads, was the season's surprising discovery when she made Dorothy and Du Bose Heyward's *Mamba's Daughters* much more than melodrama by her tragic portrayal of a self-sacrificing mother. The Playwrights brought forth Anderson's *Key Largo,* which dealt with the conscience of an American soldier who had survived the civil war in Spain, and was the first significant token of the numerous war plays that were to follow. A forthright token of the many plays of warning against American naziism was Clare Boothe's well-received *Margin for Error.*

The native comedy of manners was represented by S. N. Behrman's not-too-smooth levity that bore the bodeful title of *No Time for Comedy,* in which Katharine Cornell made her debut as a comedienne, ably aided by Laurence Olivier; and Philip Barry's *Philadelphia Story,* a somewhat emotional farce in which Katharine Hepburn found her first stage popularity impersonating a heroine with a stubborn case of arrested spinsterhood; 1939 was the year that saw the birth of *Life With Father* and *The Man Who Came to Dinner.*

Ethel Barrymore again came into her very own in 1940 by acting with unblandished straightforwardness the genius-mothering schoolmarm who determinedly fostered a boy poet she had the wit to discover among the grimy coal miners of Wales, in Emlyn Williams' sentimental but strong *The Corn Is Green.* In a chivalrous effort to pay his debts, her brother John Barrymore, the first Hamlet of the previous generation (he was to die in 1942 and live again in the glowing pages of Gene Fowler's *Good Night, Sweet Prince*), returned to the stage after too many years in Hollywood as a caricature of himself in a drooling comedy named *My Dear Children,* wherein the actor interpolated gusty asides that were as sad and pitiful to some members of the audience as they were sidesplitting to others.

Alfred Lunt and Lynn Fontanne, the most accomplished and admired stage couple since England's Mr. and Mrs. Kendal and U.S. E. H. Sothern and Julia Marlowe, triumphed on both shores of the Atlantic in Sherwood's admonitory *There Shall Be No Night.* James Thurber and Elliott Nugent wrote (the latter appearing in) *The Male Animal,* a pewter comedy plated with silver acting. Reginald Denham and Edward Percy's deftly written mystery melodrama, *Ladies in Retirement,* suffered none of the disabilities of sea change when Gilbert Miller imported it from London for the good acting of Flora Robson and others. The farcical fortunes and misfortunes of maiden innocency exposed to the dangers of a great city were entertainingly set forth in *My Sister Eileen,* a work workmanly dramatized from Ruth McKenney's magazine sketches by John A. Fields and Jerome Chodorov.

Lillian Hellman's *Watch on the Rhine,* which might have been called *It Can Happen Here,* was not only 1941's but the decade's most dramatic propaganda against the infiltration of naziism. Here Paul Lukas made a memorable figure of the briefly visiting German anti-fascist whose American wife, the mother of three polylingual children, was forcefully played by Mady Christians. Exciting theatre (the hunted Negro, who had accidentally killed his white employer's daughter, exchanging shots and oaths with his captors when they charged down the aisles to the stage) was the very human melodrama written by Paul Green from the Negro Richard Wright's urgent social novel *Native Son,* in which the Negro actor Canada Lee took firm foothold on the American stage.

Life With Father-in-Law might have been a second title for Isabel Leighton and Bertram Block's *Spring Again,* wherein C. Aubrey Smith's seasoned acting was harmoniously matched by that of Grace George. Playscripts from England that duplicated their success throughout the United States were Noel Coward's fantastical *Blithe Spirit,* in which a husband was amusingly haunted by the wraiths of his deceased wives, and Patrick Hamilton's adult and tightly-built melodrama, *Angel Street.* Another long-lasting melodrama was Joseph Kesselring's *Arsenic and Old Lace.* Twenty-one lay henchmen of its abruptly wealthy producers, Lindsay and Crouse, profitably hazarded $1,000 apiece against the failure of a murder comedy that wound up with thirteen visible corpses taking their bows at the final curtain.

This was the year that started "diaper" comedies. Rose Franken's *Claudia* was a kindergarten of sex, whose beaming girl-bride questioned not only her own biological processes, but those of the cow, the cat, the hen, even the rooster. Jerome Chodorov and Joseph Fields' *Junior Miss* was a blurred proscenium view of Sally Benson's piercing magazine studies of preadolescence. Its popularity was more easily recorded than justified.

The only "juvenile" in 1942 was the comparatively esculent *Janie,* whose sixteen-year-old prodigy suffered comically in getting rid of scores of soldiers giving themselves a party in her home during the brief absence of her parents.

Thornton Wilder's spell-casting fantasy, *The Skin of Our Teeth,* which celebrated man's antlike perseverance in rebuilding a destroyed world from the primitive age of stone to the polished present of Excelsior, New Jersey, was rebuked by a few of the critics for not acknowledging the author's debt to James Joyce's widely unread *Finnegans Wake,* but with Miss Bankhead in the cast, unJoyceian New Yorkers vouchsafed it a long run. The still incomparable Lunts found and imparted joy in *The Pirate,* an imperfect but delightfully humorous Behrman adaptation in which Lunt, masquerading as the deadly buccaneer of Miss Fontanne's dreams, altitudinously crossed the stage to her chamber window on a clothesline.

If the war plays did not boom, at least they bombed; detonations were heard beyond the walls of their theaters. The Playwrights' Maxwell Anderson wrote *The Eve of St. Mark,* the transient heroic of an American farm boy who might have lived but for helpfully holding out on Bataan a day longer than honour compelled. It was an improvement on his *Candle in the Wind* of the previous year, whose short season would have been shorter but for the popularity of Helen Hayes. Steinbeck's *The Moon Is Down,* in which German officers as well as those they scourged were presented as victims of naziism, fared no better.

Playgoers seemed to be equally indifferent to war plays "hard" or "soft," and more friendly to the lighter adventures of the war-discomforted at home. Joseph Fields' critic-scolded *The Doughgirls* rejoiced in the turpitude of lodgingless women to whom any bed was home in crowded Washington. The long-to-be-remembered melodrama of the year was Thomas Job's *Uncle Harry,* whose melancholy villain poisoned one sister, fastened the guilt on the other and was regarded as merely a harmless liar by those to whom he confessed.

The year 1943 started the concurrent runs of *Oklahoma!,* thereby re-establishing the artistic as well as the financial credit of the Theatre guild, which for several seasons had been serving its subscribers in the capitals with the productions of other managements rather than with quickly proven guild failures.

On the more serious side was James Gow and Arnaud d'Usseau's *Tomorrow the World,* a wartime warning in which a precociously evil nazi aged 12 was miraculously reformed in an American home. It was the success of the season's dozen war plays. Moss Hart wrote for the army air forces *Winged Victory,* which was patriotically applauded.

The energetic acting of Elisabeth Bergner was the reasonable excuse for the long run of Martin Vale's *The Two Mrs. Carrolls,* a poison melodrama that was cyanide to the critical. New York was hospitable for almost two years to Phoebe and Henry Ephron's *Three's a Family,* a wartime farce about three pregnant women in crowded quarters which was less tolerantly received in other cities. The farce of this year and several following was F. Hugh Herbert's *Kiss and Tell,* a juvenile which exploited the imagination of an innocent adolescent who sought to save the reputation of her secretly married sister-in-law by declaring herself to be an expectant mother.

But the one hit comparable with the songful *Oklahoma!* was John van Druten's enduring *The Voice of the Turtle,* in which this adroit author made relishably touching as well as amusing the prenuptials of a pair of young sinners who had elsewhere previously loved and erred in vain.

There were originality and flavour in the 1944 season. Mary Chase's *Harvey,* with its happily boozing hero, with his invisible but felt and almost seen rabbit, was a novelty indeed. It brought legitimate actorhood not only to Frank Fay of vaudeville and the night-club, but to Bert Wheeler and to Joe E. Brown following his long tour of the army camps overseas.

I Remember Mama was van Druten's skillful compaction of Kathryn Forbes' *Mama's Bank Account,* which warmly chronicled the lives of a Norwegian family and their dependable matriarch in old San Francisco. This was not only the year of the mentioned *Anna Lucasta* and the warborn *Jacobowsky and the Colonel* and *A Bell for Adano,* but of Lillian Hellman's loose and cluttered anti-appeasement preachment *The Searching Wind.* A poised and polite satire on the higher inhabitants of what had once been called the nation's "Hub" was John P. Marquand and George S. Kaufman's *The Late George Apley,* which might have been as perfectly entitled There'll Always Be a Boston.

The season's one popular juvenile was Norman Krasna's *Dear Ruth,* in which the *enfant terrible* signed her big sister's name to love letters. From Ruth Gordon's twinkling typewriter and for her own enactment came *Over 21,* a smart little success which encouraged its author to declare herself ready to put by the rabbit's foot for the pen and write an autobiographical comedy.

Height was attained by American playwriting and play-acting in 1945 when Tennessee Williams' *The Glass Menagerie,* following the sensational success of its initial production in Chicago, went to New York. For at least the third time in her career the Laurette Taylor of the youthful *Peg o' My Heart,* the mature Mrs. Midget of *Outward Bound* (revived in 1938) and now the burbling mother of a poverty stricken family with her boastful and exaggerated memories of suitors among the southern aristocracy, was acclaimed a great actress. The magic of the theatre was not only in Miss Taylor's performance but in the coordination of setting, lighting and complemental music. Eddie Dowling, who not only directed the four-character play with sympathetic feeling for its poetic overtones, but who had erased the crudeness of the original script, himself acted the role of narrator-son whose memories were the story.

Howard Richardson and William Berney's *Dark of the Moon* was a "hillbilly" witch's brew fantastically based on the folk ballad of Barbara Allen. It combined tenderness, passion, racy humour and gross comedy, and was justly reckoned a worthwhile contribution to the dramatic literature of the decade. *The Hasty Heart,* mentioned earlier, was a wryly likeable Scotch soldier's adventure in dying, and deservedly popular. Sherwood's *The Rugged Path* was that author's first effort following extended service to the White House and World War II, and despite the reappearance in it of the cinema's Spencer Tracy, this study of a conscience-stricken anti-"isolationist" country editor was more homily than drama. Arnaud d'Usseau and James Gow wrote with less sincerity than had marked their *Tomorrow the World* a one-sided postwar examination of the Negro problem called *Deep Are the Roots,* which prospered beyond its dramatic merits. Yet theirs was the best of many arguments on a vital subject.

Lindsay and Crouse's durably successful *State of the Union* played politics without playing favourites. Any party, any politician, was a struck target for its breezy mirth, for at almost every performance the tireless authors telegraphed interpolations to the three companies serving the comedy.

Elmer Rice's *Dream Girl,* whose heroine, one of the longest roles ever written, beguiles her idle hours in a book-rental shop with trances gay and grave, profitably presented that playwrights' playwright as neither preacher nor propagandist and won lasting favour on Broadway and on tour.

The 1946 season, which reached its climax in Eugene O'Neill's *The Iceman Cometh,* was otherwise interesting for the six-weeks visit to New York of London's revitalized Old Vic players in a repertory that included both parts of Shakespeare's *Henry IV,* Chekhov's *Uncle Vanya* and a double bill that contrasted Sheridan's *The Critic* with Sophocles' *Oedipus.*

The Lunts returned from their long stay overseas with Terence Rattigan's *Love in Idleness,* newly named *O Mistress Mine,* a comedy more notable for the wit of its acting than its writing. The loudest laughter of the year was for Garson Kanin's *Born Yesterday,* wherein an illiterate chorus girl is so amazingly educated by a radical newspaper man hired for that purpose that she ultimately ruins the countless rackets of her nefarious protector. *Lute Song,* Sidney Howard and Will Irwin's picturesque paraphrase of China's ancient *Pi-Pa-Ki,* whose heroine is the classic oriental model of wifely fidelity, was a dramatic love song of exquisite tenderness and beauty.

The highly dramatic and debatable *The Iceman Cometh* proved to be a parabling realism densely populated by derelict spongers on a waterfront New York saloon of 1912. In the first of the four long acts one of the besotten boozily philosophized, "The lie of a pipe dream is what gives life to the whole misbegotten mad lot of us, drunk or sober." The final act attested the futility of taking pipe dreams away from the disinherited. While this work was criticized for lacking the diversification of scene and action of O'Neill's earlier "dinner-dramas" whose playing time exceeded four hours—*Strange Interlude* and *Mourning Becomes Electra*—its poignant characters and the steadily upclimbing strength of the fable which revealed them as vividly as were the misbegotten of Maxim Gorki's *The Lower Depths,* caused The Iceman to be regarded as the most distinguished American drama acted in the period considered. Dowling, who directed Williams as Kneisel had led string quartettes, directed O'Neill as Toscanini had conducted symphonies. (A. Ss.)

Tendencies in the U.S. Drama

During the period 1937–46 the only noticeable tendencies in the drama were as follows:

(1) An increasing concern of dramatists with the behaviour and the problems of the lower classes and the

underprivileged.

(2) A tendency to use the theatre as a lecture platform on which the playwright became more important than the characters he created or than the story he was attempting to tell. He had a social or political conviction which he desired to make the audience accept. The proper medium for his views was the pamphlet, the public hall, the soapbox, the periodical essay, the argumentative book or the radio time reserved for commentators with individual and personal views to state.

(3) The decline of the poetic idiom in stage presentations. Not merely had playwrights veered very far away from the poetic forms of the Greek and Elizabethan dramatists, of Jean de Racine and Pierre Corneille and of Edmond Rostand and Carl Hauptmann; they had striven for colloquialisms to such an extent, in their flight from romanticism to naturalism, that going to the theatre was often no more of an aesthetic experience than that of listening to the conversation of one's most boresome neighbours.

(4) The introduction of the ballet-pantomime into musical comedy and the musical play, as a substitute for the chorus routines of old burlesque shows which had developed into what was a distinct American contribution to the theatre—the musical comedy. It was a metamorphosis, deriving from some of the worst features of Slavic and Latin grand opera formulas, seen at its best in *Oklahoma!* and *Carousel* and one or two other Broadway productions during the decade; but it became so repetitious in musical play choreography by 1946 that the public, as well as the critics, revolted against it, and even when a musical had several ballet-pantomime numbers in it, they were not so designated but described as "dance numbers."

(5) The decline of the number of plays of an experimental nature in the treatment of theme and in originality of concept in favour of the time-tested plays designed for the broad base of popular appeal.

(6) The increasing reliance of the commercial producers upon Hollywood "box-office" names for the success of their productions, often without any consideration of the acting ability of the motion picture stars or of their suitability for the parts to which they were assigned.

(7) The rise, during the years of World War II especially, of amateur and semi-professional groups in small towns, universities and large-city cultural centres, more or less subsidized both privately and publicly. The plays put on by such groups were ordinarily those that had been successes on Broadway and they rarely were the work of new or untried writers; but these groups provided an apprenticeship in all aspects of theatrical production, from scenic designing and lighting to acting and from box-office account-management to direction; and so they were a constant source of abundant supply of talent and experience to Broadway and Hollywood. Moreover, in aggregate they paid to authors royalties amounting to close to $6,000,000 a year on productions for which, in most cases, the prescribed fee to the author was only $25 a performance, sometimes more than the gross receipts for such a performance.

(8) The decline of "drawing-room" or "smart" comedy in favour of more serious drama and in favour of comedy-drama of middle-class and lower middle-class life. This meant the elimination of wit and subtlety in favour of broad farce or melodrama, but it also meant the elimination of the wise-crack and the cynical epigram upon which so many sophisticated comedies of the '20s and of previous decades, going back to the Yellow '90s and Oscar Wilde, were based, based so much, indeed, that often such comedies were, or seemed to be, built entirely around a few clever lines. And when one uses the words clever here, one means the paradoxical or the surprising or simply an observation contrary to one's experience or to one's normal sentiments or emotions.

The British and U.S. theatres had become practically identical. That is, the plays produced with success in New York sooner or later reached the London stage and vice versa. The reception, in either case, was not always the same; a smash hit in New York might be a failure in London, and a play that had great success in London might be a complete failure in the United States. A British author might find his countrymen indifferent to his playwriting efforts and be a great success in America. On the other hand, a new American playwright such as Elsa Shelley could find a *Pick-Up Girl* (1944), pulled off the boards after a short and unprofitable run in New York, the season's (1946) hit in London, doing a larger gross business than any musical and playing the provinces with six road companies, all successful, with enthusiastic acclaim not only from the critics but from Queen Mary herself (who rarely volunteered a commendation for a play). Incidentally, the recommendation of the wife of a president of the United States, or even of the president himself, had never enhanced the commercial value of a play or a book, with one notable exception, Theodore Roosevelt's recommendation of *Penrod* by Booth Tarkington and of Edwin Arlington Robinson's merits as a poet, the latter recommendation serving to lift a fine poet out of obscurity; but Mrs. Franklin D. Roosevelt, for instance, often praised books and plays in her widely syndicated column with no appreciable demand therefrom at the bookstores or the box offices.

From 1937 to 1946 the drama was, in effect, dead in Germany, Italy, Spain, France, the Scandinavian countries, China, Japan and elsewhere in the world, except the United States, Great Britain and U.S.S.R. During World War II the drama flourished, commercially at least, in the United States in a way that it had never flourished before. Money was easy to get for productions in the United States, even with the enormous increase of production costs, because of war prosperity for workers, business men and gamblers alike. Because of income taxes, a person in the higher brackets of income could lose $10,000 in an investment in a Broadway flop and still—because it was a legitimate deduction in his income tax report—sustain an actual loss of only $1,000 or less; and if he hit the jackpot by investing in a highly successful play or musical, his income from a $10,000 investment might pay (with his cut in movie rights) from 3,000% to 6,000%.

U.S. play costs, before the actual opening, rose during World War II to an average of $70,000 for a legitimate play and to an average of $200,000 for a musical. The same productions 25 years before might have cost less than $5,000 for a straight play and less than $25,000 for a musical. The gains were labour gains, mostly, and for that reason to be applauded, because the actors' and stage-hand unions, the musicians' unions and other combinations of workers, had been effective in equalizing the profits from a gamble among all who contributed to it: it did not let the profits go mainly to the real-estate men who controlled the theatres and to other middle-men in a theatrical production.

Pity the Author.—The only ones who suffered from this situation were the authors of plays which were not successful. These authors included many whose work was highly praised by the majority of drama critics and published in Burns Mantle's *Best Plays of the Year* (including British

Above: Scene from *Oklahoma!*, a musical comedy with scores by Richard Rodgers and choreography by Agnes de Mille. The production opened in 1943 and in 1946 it broke existing long-run records for U.S. musicals with more than 1,400 performances

Right: *The Iceman Cometh* marked the first new offering by Eugene O'Neill within the decade 1937-46. Concerned with man's need for illusions, it was greeted with controversial reviews but drew full houses after its premiere in 1946

Below: Margaret Sullavan and Elliott Nugent, stars of the *Voice of the Turtle*, an appealing comedy by John Van Druten which opened in 1943 and had a successful run

Laurette Taylor and Eddie Dowling in a scene from Tennessee Williams' prize-winning play *The Glass Menagerie*, judged by the New York Drama Critics Circle in April 1945 as the best play of the season

Left: Paul Robeson was the first Negro to play Shakespeare's Othello in the U.S. He is shown (left) with Uta Hagen as Desdemona, in the production which opened in 1942 and later went on tour and translated plays as well as U.S. plays). Actors got salaries for rehearsals, tryouts and for a full week after a Broadway opening, even if the play was closed after one performance. Theatre owners got rent for 3 weeks, amounting to from $9,000 to $16,000, even if the theatre was occupied for only 1 night. All of those engaged in the sheer mechanics of a production were amply protected. The author of the play was the "patsy"—unless his play was a tremendous success.

A producer, for instance, without putting a cent of his own money into the production, might charge against production costs $2,000 a week or more as his salary. He might add another $1,000 a week as director, beginning with the first week of rehearsals. A play could last only 1 night in New York and yet pay the producer $18,000 or more, the theatre owner from $9,000 to $16,000, the actors, mechanics, costume designers and everybody (except the author) a fair return upon their investment of time, money, experience and talent.

The author, however, received $500 as an advance against royalties from the producer who was considering his play. This play might have taken the author three years to write. The producer might get into a jam trying to get persons to put up money to produce the show. Persons with money to invest in shows, "angels," sometimes wished to see the script before they invested. They might take the script with them to Maine or Bermuda, along with many other scripts, and lose their copies of it. The producer (who charged this to the author's agent, who, in turn, charged it to the author—as was right) provided the "angel" with another script. The "angel" might not read it but get his wife or secretary to read it. Or the office boy. The wife, secretary, office boy and the "angel" all were incipient playwrights. They had never tried to write a play but they knew just how a play should be written. They had suggestions. Usually these suggestions represented a dozen different plays, none of which the original author had in mind, and all of them stark plagiarisms of scenes and incidents and gags which these amateur drama critics had found pleasing to themselves in the shows for which they had been given free tickets.

The author's headaches would then begin. He would like to see his play produced, without having his orchid turned into a ragweed. He would sweat and compromise; his play would be produced. But the producer had imported a high-priced director from Hollywood with his own ideas about plays—and, under Equity rules, all actors must take the director's direction, no matter how they might differ with the director about how a scene should be played—and the leading lady (salary $3,000 a week and a percentage of the gross) might decide that all the good lines given to a comedienne (salary only $1,500 a week) must be killed. The producer would decide he couldn't lose his star, who had cost him so many telegrams and telephone calls and dinners at the Stork club with the star's adamant agent. So the show would go on. It would be bad; critics would squelch it; the audience would walk out on it in great numbers. It would be a flop. And the author's net income for his three year's work would be $500, less 10% agency fees, $225 in telephone and telegram charges and $145 in dinner, railroad and hotel charges, plus taxes. He was lucky if he emerged with 47 cents, net. But, if he hit the jackpot with his play, he would find himself the object of solicitude by the treasury department, which would need all the details about the $750,000 he made last year, out of which, when all taxes and agency legal fees were paid, he might (if lucky) emerge with $45,000 (or $15,000 a year for three years)—pretty good pay for a writer, even if not for a criminal or corporation lawyer, a political boss, a war contractor, a labour czar, a night club comedian, a stage-hand, a jazz musician, a movie pin-up girl, the head of an advertising agency or a theatrical producer.

Plays and Dictatorships.—In U.S.S.R. they ordered these things differently. The system there was payment according to one's worth to the state as a whole. This was nice for authors, composers and other artists, for a while. The Politburo at first decided that playwrights, novelists, composers, painters were very important to the state—as propagandists—so such persons enjoyed for a while the highest incomes and the highest consideration that it was possible for anyone to receive in the U.S.S.R. except members in the highest councils of the Politburo. During World War II playwrights, novelists and composers—who were supposed to entertain the people—fared very luxuriously. War-torn Russia was a hotbed of feverish theatrical activity, more plays, new and old, being produced there than in all the rest of the world combined.

But in 1946 the Politburo of the U.S.S.R. decided that all the plays by western writers (that is, plays by U.S. and British writers, such as Wilde, Maugham, Behrman, Kaufman, Hart, etc.) which had been enjoying popularity in Russia were guilty of portraying "bourgeois ideology" and that popular plays by Russian writers were guilty of the same offense. The Politburo thereupon banned all plays except those which the Politburo should find acceptable to the Politburo, that is, all plays which did not idealize the aims and achievements of the current political leaders of the U.S.S.R. It would seem that soviet writers were not yet able to produce plays by fiat and that the drama was as dead in Russia as it was in Germany, Italy and Spain under the fascist-nazi regimes.

An examination of *Annuraio del Teatro Italiano* (Annual of the Italian Theatre) April 30, 1937—June 1, 1939, showed what a totalitarian dictatorship of culture could do to that culture. In that period there were 108 original plays produced in Italy, under the reign of Mussolini, and under the reign of Hitler, who dominated Mussolini and Italy from 1938 until the defeat of the axis.

It was the theory of Hitler and Mussolini that France was a decadent country, easily to be destroyed because its birthrate had been declining for more than a century, and that Germany and Italy would become more powerful if the subjects of these countries would produce more chil-

Statistics of the Theatre in New York City (1937–46)

	1937	1938	1939	1940	1941	1942	1943	1944	1945	1946
Productions	132	117	113	116	94	110	109	126	107	110
Musical comedies	17	20	32	29	20	26	30	39	29	28
Plays	115	97	81	87	74	84	79	87	78	82
Premieres	84	84	74	75	69	73	71	82	71	68
Successful productions	21	19	29	22	21	17	20	27	18	19
Performers employed	1,724	1,833	1,829	1,659	1,414	1,679	1,856	2,449	2,047	2,026
Tickets sold	6,750,000	6,900,000	7,200,000	6,948,000	7,360,000	7,210,000	7,920,000	8,970,000	8,840,000	8,600,000
Approximate cost of production	$2,300,000	$3,000,000	$3,200,000	$2,000,000	$2,000,000+	$2,250,000	$2,500,000	$3,500,000	$4,000,000	$5,000,000
Number of shows booked for other cities	52	55	59	103	106	94	87	91	74	87

dren, *i.e.*, more "cannon fodder." Therefore both Germany and Italy offered bonuses to women who would produce children, in or out of wedlock. And their propaganda agents and official censors saw to it that no plays could be produced which did not glorify the German and Italian ideals in this as well as in all other respects. The results were 108 plays in Italy which were not only pornographic but sentimentally so—plays so repulsive to adult civilized minds that it was difficult to conceive of human beings in 20th century culture seeing them without ridicule or overt resentment.

In the United States there were many movies and radio "soap-operas" and even quite a few plays on a low intellectual level, and they were not ordered to be so written by the state; but, in this republic of (more or less) free enterprise, the highest level of theatrical productions were not represented—as it was in Italy and Germany—by claptrap. Rubbish was about all a country could expect when the politicians of a totalitarian state prescribed the sort of plays to be produced. (B. Ras.)

Great Britain

The most positive achievement of the English theatre during the years 1937–46 was a new standard of acting. So high was this standard at the period's close that it became almost a duty to believe in the dawn of a new golden age of English acting, comic as well as tragic. Contributions to serious drama were rare, and after World War II no new work of any significance appeared. The U.S.A., it would seem, had the dramatists; England the actors. However that may be, undoubtedly the most important thing that happened to the English theatre was that it was discovered by a great new public. Never at any time in its history had it meant so much to so many people; its appeal extended from London to the big cities, the towns and even the villages. It was the war which brought this new public into being.

Outside London before World War II there was constantly rumoured to be a widespread unsatisfied demand for drama. The evidence for it, unless collected with the eye of faith, was scanty and unconvincing. Amateur acting societies and playgoers' clubs might be numerous and active, but, to offset the hopes they inspired, famous provincial theatres continued to be turned into cinemas by a process that seemed automatic and irresistible; the half dozen well-known repertory theatres obviously depended on the efforts of a few brave spirits possessed of exceptional driving power and private means. Yet when London companies were driven into the country they found a surprising welcome; and for some years all things, good and bad, apparently conspired to advance the cause of the theatre from end to end of the country.

Government Help.—Even the government, with an air of doing good by inadvertence, took a hand. The Council for the Encouragement of Music and the Arts (later rechristened the Arts council), a body directly under the authority of the Board of Education, was originally formed by a few individuals in the autumn of 1939 to assist artists during the period of the nation's adjustment to war conditions by finding for them a useful part in the war effort. At the outset, drama and music were particularly hard hit, although their subsequent recovery was spectacular, and it was through the council's initiative that the government was prevailed upon to provide a grant in order that the practice of these and other arts might continue. Thus armed, the council enabled the Old Vic to form two touring companies of high quality which continuously played their way through the industrial areas, bringing Shakespeare and the classics before audiences to many of whom such things had hitherto been a sealed book. The council's support was later extended to many other theatrical ventures of genuine merit, and one frequent effect of its anomalous independence was that its acquisition of the 18th century Theatre Royal at Bristol provided the first recorded case of state purchase in the history of the English theatre. Thus by accident, as it were, the English drama was accorded official rank with the fine arts.

It is difficult to over-estimate the benefits which accrued to the theatre as a result of the assistance that it received during World War II from this curiously British organization which, under the astute and imaginative chairmanship of Lord John Keynes, continued to be a government hand doing things which the government's other hand knew nothing about. It was due to the Arts council that the Old Vic ramified into many permanent companies covering the country. It was with the support of the Arts council that the Old Vic's main company, led by Laurence Olivier and Ralph (later Sir Ralph) Richardson, was established at the end of the war in classical repertory in the heart of London. In the next few years it was to make acting history there, and there was general satisfaction when it was learned that the Old Vic company, already the strongest dramatic force in the country, was to become the nucleus of the National theatre whenever that almost fabulous project might become a reality of bricks and mortar. The skill and judgment of the Arts council in playing kindly providence was recognized when its original purposes had all been served. It was given a permanent place in the peacetime life of the country.

Discriminating Audience.—The new audience that had discovered this new theatre differed much in size and in requirements from the audience of tradition. Partly it was a listeners' audience, called into existence by the radio and the talking film, star-conscious no doubt but with a catholic taste born of its freedom from tradition and from the circumstance that only a very small proportion of it was within reach of the London theatre. Ivan Turgenev, William Congreve, G. B. Shaw, Henrik Ibsen, Michael Chekhov, all came alike to it, provided that the play was finely presented and finely acted by well-known actors. Outside London, in towns up and down the country, many and various plays of quality filled the theatres as they had not been filled since the actor-management times of Henry Irving, Herbert Tree or John Alexander. It became, during World War II, the rule rather than the exception that a London success of the better sort should be the culmination of weeks or even months of country touring. In London itself the audience of tradition remained fairly stable, and it was for this audience that the commercial syndicates continued to ply an honourable trade, supplying the musicals, the light comedies and the whimseys running for years on end. It was only after the war that this audience tended to monopolize the stage. Until a few years previous managers had been casting a shrewdly adventurous net over the centuries for plays likely to revive well, and they succeeded in revealing the singular richness of the English dramatic heritage. The wartime theatre had in truth little chance to be more than an heir, but in that role it must be allowed to have administered its noble estate with wisdom and imagination. The revival habit con-

Maurice Evans in the title role of *Richard II*. Evans' popular and critical success as a Shakespearean actor became widespread during World War II when his production of *Hamlet*, staged in relatively modern dress, played to enthusiastic audiences of U.S. servicemen and women overseas

tinued into peacetime, but, except where the Old Vic was concerned, neo-classics rather than classics were chosen and even the general public began to grow tired of the Edwardian scene.

Barren Dramatists.—The habit grew up in wartime, and there was no escaping it. If excuses could be made for the drying up of dramatic inspiration, plenty were at hand. Young British writers were born into a period highly discouraging to creative effort. In 1937 their plans may well have been unsettled by the growing sense that they were drifting between one catastrophe and another. Came the catastrophe, and the young were swept into the fighting lines. The survivors found themselves in a society which was harassed by drab uncertainties. Genius would doubtless have made light of such an atmosphere, but genius failed to appear. It seemed to be absent in 1937. Then J. B. Priestley had three new plays running simultaneously —*Time and the Conways, I Have Been Here Before* and *People at Sea.* The first two, based on the time theories of Ouspensky and Dunne, were plays of quality. And James Bridie's *Susannah and the Elders* revealed a writer of considerable ability. But neither of these dramatists was wholly to realize the hopes they then raised. Both wrote a number of entertaining and successful plays during World War II, but Priestley seemed too intent on enheartening his fellow countrymen as often as possible to concentrate his great gifts; and Bridie's brilliant first acts invariably put to shame those that followed. *They Came to a City* was Priestley's most solid work, and *Mr. Bolfry* Bridie's most sustained. Most of the dramatic honours of war fell to Noel Coward with three plays—*Blithe Spirit,* an almost purely nonsensical intellectual farce, *Present Laughter,* a slightly sophisticated comedy, and *This Happy Breed,* a somewhat self-conscious excursion into the lesser suburbs. Bernard Shaw's *Geneva* and *In Good King Charles's Golden Days* were written just before the war, but so many of his plays were revived that he never ceased to be a major figure of the period. And after the war Somerset Maugham enjoyed an outstanding vogue. Peter Ustinov had few rivals among the talented young, and his comedy *The Banbury Nose* showed a more mature psychological insight than either of his previous pieces.

Inspired Actors.—It was natural under the circumstances that critics, whether of amateur or professional status, should have concerned themselves less with the play than with the manner of its presentation. The merits and shortcomings of John Gielgud's Lear, Hamlet and Macbeth and of Donald Wolfit's playing of the same parts were eagerly disputed and with the end of World War II Laurence Olivier's Lear and Sir Ralph Richardson's Falstaff were generally felt to have challenged comparison with the great Lears and Falstaffs of stage history. Indeed, by introducing Lear as a choleric humourist, made by the habit of tyranny the slave of his own abounding whims, Laurence Olivier may be said to have made a contribution to Shakespearian interpretation; at any rate, his version made the hitherto improbable act of the division of Lear's kingdom plausible and entertainingly playable. Alongside this Lear, Laurence Olivier placed a magnificent Richard III, an unforgettable Oedipus, a brilliant Hotspur, to say nothing of his Justice Shallow and his Mr. Puff. John Gielgud showed once more that as Hamlet he had no rival. Donald Wolfit's great feats of acting did not enjoy the same measure of acclaim, perhaps because he acted in a company which seldom satisfied the exacting standards of London production. The Old Vic had magnificent leaders, but it also had a splendid team. Donald Wolfit was too often the sole attraction of his own stage. Yet it must be remembered that he and his chosen actors carried Shakespeare, Ben Jonson, John Ford and Ibsen all over the country, that they seized a London stage when theatrical life seemed near to extinction in 1940 and that they reappeared in easier times with an extensive repertory of high endeavour. Lear during these years proved to be his greatest part.

Besides these distinguished actors were many more who showed great promise, from whom should be singled out Alec Guinness and William Devlin. (A. V. Cm.)

Bibliography.—J. Anderson, *American Theatre and the Motion Picture in America* (1938); E. Capon, *Actors and Audiences in the Soviet Union* (1943); W. Bridges-Adams, *British Theatre* (1944); B. W. Brown, *Theatre at the Left* (Russia) (1938); H. W. Dana, *Handbook on Soviet Drama* (1938); H. C. Heffner, *Modern Theatre Practice* (1946); N. Houghton, *Advance from Broadway* (1941), *Moscow Rehearsals* (1936); J. T. Macleod, *Actors Across the Volga* (1946), *New Soviet Theatre* (1943); B. Mantle, *Best Plays* (1937 *et seq.*); J. W. Marriott, *Theatre* (Gt. Brit.) (1946); G. J. Nathan, *Entertainment of a Nation* (1942), *Theatre Book of the Year;* P. Noble, *British Theatre* (1946); N. De Pirro, *Theatre for the People* (Italy) (1938); E. H. Short, *Theatrical Cavalcade* (Great Brit.) (1942); M. D. Skinner, *One Man in His Time* (1938); *Theatre Annual* (U.S.); *Theatre in a Changing Europe* (1937); A. Van Gyseghem, *Theatre in Soviet Russia* (1943); G. A. Whitworth, *Theatre and the Nation* (London, 1939); Per.: *Theatre Arts Monthly; Stage.* Consult also *Dramatic Index* (1937–); John Gielgud, *Early Stages* (London, 1938); James Agate, *The Amazing Theatre* (London, 1939); P. W. Manchester, *Vic-Wells* (London, 1942).

Theatre Library Association

See Societies and Associations.

Theology

See Religion.

Theosophical Society, The

See Societies and Associations; Theosophy.

Theosophy

The Theosophical society, proclaiming as its main tenets the spiritual reality of the one life and the fact that humanity is a universal brotherhood, had naturally to suffer considerable material reverses during the decade 1937 to 1946. The national society in Germany had already been disbanded in 1933; its numerical strength was somewhat small after secession of Dr. Rudolf Steiner in 1912. The last general secretary in Germany was Baron Egenolf Roeder von Diersburg, and in 1946 it was not known whether he was alive or dead. As the German invasion of Europe gradually proceeded, the national societies were forcibly disbanded by the nazis, and their buildings and libraries confiscated. The movement in the invaded countries went underground and members continued to meet in private almost everywhere. Elsewhere the society continued its activities without losing ground.

Dr. G. S. Arundale, president from 1934 onward, died in Aug. 1945 and was succeeded by C. Jinarajadasa, a Sinhalese and Buddhist, author and traveller.

With the ending of World War II came a great resurgence of life throughout the society. Many inquiries regarding its philosophy were being made, and new members joined in countries where there was political freedom. The largest individual groups were to be found in the United States, India and Great Britain. The national president of the society in the U.S. in 1946 was James S. Perkins, and the headquarters were at Wheaton, Ill. The designation of national president corresponds to that of general secretary in Great Britain. The total membership of the society in England was 3,752 in 1946. The number of members was slightly higher in the U.S. and possibly about twice the number in India. (D. Gs.)

BIBLIOGRAPHY.—B. B. Gattell, *Light of the Mind* (1938); F. Morrish, *Outline of Metaphysics* (1945); G. Purucker, *Man in Evolution* (1941). Periodical: *Theosophical Forum* (Point Loma).

Therapy

See CHEMOTHERAPY; MEDICINE; MILITARY MEDICINE; REHABILITATION OF THE DISABLED.

Thiamin

See VITAMINS.

Thiophene

See CHEMISTRY.

Third Term

See DEMOCRATIC PARTY; ELECTIONS; UNITED STATES.

Thomas, Rolland Jay

Thomas (1900–), U.S. labour leader, was born June 9 in East Palestine, O. He completed high school and attended Wooster college (Wooster, O.) for two years. In 1923 he entered the automobile industry as a metal finisher and six years later emerged as a labour union leader at the Chrysler plant in Detroit. In 1934 he was chosen by his fellow workers on the first shop committee under the National Recovery act (N.R.A.); he was president of Chrysler Local No. 7, when it amalgamated with the United Automobile Workers (U.A.W.) in 1936. One of the militant leaders in the General Motors and Chrysler strikes of 1937, he was named one of the vice-presidents of the international union in that year.

In 1938 Thomas was elected president of the U.A.W. international union and vice-president of the Congress of Industrial Organizations (C.I.O.) in 1939. During World War II Thomas denounced wildcat strikes no matter what the provocation and adhered rigidly to the no-strike pledge.

Thomas and Walter Reuther were the leading union figures in the General Motors strike that started Nov. 21, 1945, and ended March 13, 1946. While the strike was still in progress, Thomas and Reuther disagreed. Reuther became a candidate for Thomas' post as president of the U.A.W. In the voting March 27, 1946, at the party convention in Atlantic City, N.J., Reuther was elected by a very narrow margin, but Thomas was elected first vice-president.

Thorez, Maurice

Thorez (1900–), French politician, was born April 28 in Noyelles-Godault, a village in the department of Pas-de-Calais. The son of a coal miner, he started work in the pits when he was 12 years old. After World War I he joined the Socialist party but left in 1920 to join the newly-formed French Communist party. A talented dialectician and a forceful leader, he rose high in the party ranks and in 1930 became secretary general of the Communist party in France. Two years later he was elected to the chamber of deputies from Ivry-sur-Seine, a suburb in Paris' "Red Belt." In 1936 Thorez rallied the Communist deputies to support Léon Blum's first popular front government. At the outbreak of World War II, Thorez was conscripted into the French army, but soon disappeared. Court-martialled *in absentia,* he was convicted of desertion and sentenced to serve six years' imprisonment. In 1943 it was disclosed that he was living in Moscow. That year, Thorez's appeal to be permitted to return to liberated French territory was denied by Gen. Charles de Gaulle, but in Nov. 1944 after his election, also *in absentia,* to the consultative assembly in Paris, he was amnestied under a general order pardoning French deserters who had engaged in resistance movements.

He returned to Paris on Nov. 28, 1944.

On resuming the leadership of the Communist party, Thorez followed a restrained policy. While he continued to attack the postwar remnants of the "200 families" which leftists said were the real rulers of prewar France, he agreed to three-party rule of France with the middle-of-the-road Socialists and the conservatively-inclined Popular Republican movement (M.R.P.).

Thorez made three bids for the presidency and premiership of France in 1945 and 1946, all of which failed because the Communist party, although the strongest single party in France, could not muster enough votes in the assembly to support a government of its choosing.

Throat

See EAR, NOSE AND THROAT, DISEASES OF.

Thyroid

See ENDOCRINOLOGY.

Tibet

A country of central Asia, Tibet lies north of the Himalayas and south of the Kun-lun mountains; mainly a high tableland. Nominally a Chinese dependency, it is in practice independent. Area: *c.* 463,200 sq.mi.; pop.: 1936 est. 3,722,000. Capital: Lhasa (pop. *c.* 50,000). Religion: Lamaism.

Ruler: 14th dalai lama, Lingerh Lamutanchu (born 1933, enthroned Feb. 22, 1940).

On the death of the 13th dalai lama on Dec. 7, 1933, the administration of Tibet was taken over by Reting Hutukhtu until, according to Tibetan tradition, the spirit of the deceased lama should be found reincarnated in one of its people. In 1938 Reting Hutukhtu reported the rebirth of the spirit of the dalai lama in the person of a

Portrait of Lingerh Lamutanchu, a Chinese boy, who was enthroned 14th dalai lama of Tibet in 1940. He was born in Dec. 1933

child found in Chinghai, whereupon the Chinese government appointed Wu Chung-hsin, chairman of the commission on Mongolian and Tibetan affairs, to assist Reting Hutukhtu in taking charge of the affairs concerning the rebirth of the dalai lama. A special envoy escorted the child from Sining to Lhasa, and on Feb. 22, 1940, the solemn ceremony of enthronement took place. Reting Hutukhtu was instructed by the Chinese government to continue the administration of Tibet until the dalai lama came of age.

The panchan lama, the religious head of the Tibetan state, who since 1924 had been travelling in the interior provinces of China, died on Nov. 30, 1937, on his way home to his country. The Chinese government, in recognition of his services to Tibetan-Chinese relations, conferred on him the posthumous title of "Hui Kuo Hsuan Hua Kwang Hui Yuan Chuch Ta Shih" and his remains were given an official escort back to Tibet. Panchan Chasa-ro-sang-chien-tsan was appointed to seek for the reincarnation of the panchan lama. His mission was successful, and on Feb. 8, 1944, the 10th panchan lama was enthroned. The ceremony was presided over by members of the Kuomintang's central executive committee.

The standard of living of Tibet was very low at the best of times, and during the decade 1937–46 was reduced by famine, and in the autumn of 1942 by plague in the Huangyuan region in Chinghai. The Chinese government sent relief on many occasions. Tibet for its part gave aid to China during the war, sending clothes, furs and wool, and in 1940 a comfort mission went to Chungking where it presented a banner to Generalissimo Chiang Kai-shek and a money gift for Chinese troops.

Tibetans held office in the central government of China and more frequent exchanges of visits between Tibet and China contributed to a closer feeling of unity than existed before. A delegation of 20 lamaists visiting Chiang Kai-shek on his assumption of the presidency of China asked that he help Tibet to develop politically, economically and culturally. China's policy, as stated by Chiang in 1945, was to allow Tibet a higher degree of autonomy.

BIBLIOGRAPHY.—F. S. Chapman, *Lhasa: The Holy City* (London, 1938); O. Lattimore, *Inner Asian Frontiers of China* (1940); Sir Charles Bell, *Portrait of the Dalai Lama* (London, 1946).

(J. RA.)

Tien, Thomas

Cardinal Tien (1890–), Chinese Catholic prelate, was born Sept. 27 at Changtsiu, China. Orphaned in his childhood, he was taken into the Society of the Divine Word orphanage of Puoli, run by Catholic missionaries, in Shantung. He completed his studies in both the minor and major seminaries operated by the society in Yenchowfu. After his ordination in 1918, he taught at mission schools until 1921 and was then assigned to various missions in Shantung.

Entering the Divine Word novitiate in 1929, he took his final vows in 1934. Consecrated vicar apostolic of Yangkü by Pope Pius XII, Msgr. Tien was named titular bishop of Ruspe and vicar apostolic of Tsingtao in 1942. His appointment to the Sacred College of Cardinals was announced, Dec. 23, 1945, and he was proclaimed a cardinal at ceremonies in Vatican City, Feb. 18, 1946.

Timber

See LUMBER.

Timor

See PORTUGAL; PORTUGUESE COLONIAL EMPIRE; WORLD WAR II.

Timoshenko, Semyon Konstantinovich

Timoshenko (1895–), soviet army officer, was born Feb. 18 in Furmanka, Bessarabia. The son of impoverished peasants, he had virtually no formal education and was working as a farm labourer when he was inducted in the tsarist army in 1915. He fought in the Don region against the Whites and became commander of the 6th Red cavalry division.

After the civil war, Timoshenko joined a Red army military academy to acquire the formal schooling that he had missed in his youth. On completing his studies he was made joint commander and commissar of the 3rd cavalry corps in 1925. He was assistant commander of the Kiev military district at the outbreak of World War II in Sept. 1939.

During the Russo-Finnish war, Stalin assigned Timoshenko to command the Karelian front in Dec. 1939. Timoshenko spent the entire month of Jan. 1940 preparing for a break-through of the Mannerheim line; he opened his offensive Feb. 1, 1940, and within a month his forces had broken through the fortress chain to reach the outskirts of Viipuri (Viborg).

Timoshenko was appointed people's defense commissar and was raised to the rank of a marshal May 8, 1940. When the Germans launched their invasion of the soviet union, June 22, 1941, he was in command of the central group of Red armies blocking the route to Moscow. On Oct. 23, 1941, Timoshenko was shifted to the southern front, where he launched a surprise attack against extended German lines and recaptured Rostov, Nov. 29, 1941.

The following summer, when German armies had broken through soviet lines in the Ukraine and were racing toward Stalingrad, Timoshenko conducted a rapid but orderly retreat from Rostov and Novocherkassk. Later he was transferred to the Ilmen-Leningrad front, where he launched offensive operations around Lake Ilmen.

In the summer of the year 1943 he was returned to the southern front and led the concentrated Russian drive that resulted in the final recapture of the Taman peninsula in October.

Tin

Data on world production of tin were still lacking for many countries, mostly those occupied by axis troops, after World War II.

Mine production, as compiled and estimated by the U.S. bureau of mines, is shown in Table I.

Since two-thirds of the prewar tin output originated in countries that were occupied by Japanese troops, the tin industry of the world was recast during World War II, especially the supplies of the United Nations, which had been only partially offset by increased production in countries still accessible. After the loss of the oriental smelting capacity, a tin smelter was built in the United States, making that country the largest smelter of tin in the world during the war years. Smelters of the United States, Great Britain and the Belgian Congo handled about two-thirds of the known ore supply in the latter years of World War II, while minor outputs from Australia, Canada, China, Mexico and South Africa increased the United Nations supply to nearly three-quarters of the world total. However, the total had shrunk so much below its normal level that the available supply was far less than normal, and stringent controls were necessary to restrict consumption to essential uses. To compensate as much as possible for the loss of the major oriental sources, output was expanded elsewhere, especially in Belgian Congo, Bolivia and Nigeria; in 1939 these 3 countries supplied only 26% of the world total, rising to 54% in 1942 and 82% in 1945.

Table I.—*World Mine Production of Tin*
(Short tons)

	1937	1938	1939	1940	1941	1942	1943	1944	1945
Argentina	1,594	2,112	1,854	1,659	1,032	1,118	784	887	610
Australia	3,647	3,728	3,435	3,921	3,913	3,283	2,951	2,845	2,800
Belgian Congo . . .	9,054	9,878	10,040	13,980	18,133	18,134	19,578	19,405	19,126
Bolivia	28,143	28,542	30,476	42,493	47,263	42,888	45,149	43,366	47,585
Burma	8,369	7,952	9,560	6,160	?	?	1,100	560	220
China.	14,416	12,998	11,673	6,999	9,000	7,800	5,600	3,400	1,700
Great Britain. . . .	2,225	2,239	1,829	1,814	1,690	1,527	1,522	1,444	1,112
Indo-China.	1,766	1,791	1,646	1,649	1,600	1,570	1,100	560	220
Malaya.	86,536	48,564	57,932	95,630	87,400	16,800	16,800	11,200	2,200
Netherlands Indies. .	43,829	30,575	31,086	43,376	57,000	11,200	16,949	6,797	944
Nigeria	12,076	10,054	10,588	13,453	16,800	14,000	14,172	14 000	12,900
Portugal.	1,226	1,161	1,664	1,928	2,610	2,990	3,875	2,000	700
Siam	17,680	16,468	19,404	19,541	18,300	13,500	7,800	5,600	3,300
Total	236,300	182,600	197,100	264,300	268,800	140,000	142,200	117,600	97,400

Table II.—*Data of the Tin Industry in the United States*
(Short tons)

	1937	1938	1939	1940	1941	1942	1943	1944	1945
Imports, total.	98,858	55,663	79,074	143,147	189,888	62,368	40,954	54,753	47,003
In concentrates . . .	169	—	560	3,360	32,110	32,405	27,480	39,814	37,550
Metal.	98,689	55,663	78,514	139,787	157,778	29,963	13,474	14,939	9,453
Smelter output	—	—	—	1,558	2,060	18,108	24,068	34,590	45,332
Secondary recovery . .	30,350	23,500	29,000	33,300	42,000	37,970	37,850	32,600	35,200
Consumption	100,945	66,947	92,319	108,812	150,858	95,970	89,969	100,765	93,613
Primary	81,679	53,890	74,573	81,003	115,456	63,043	51,803	66,255	62,319
Secondary.	19,266	13,057	17,746	27,809	35,402	32,927	38,166	34,510	31,294
Stocks.	?	?	?	133,291	147,564	149,584	130,910	111,751	95,410
In ore.	—	—	—	—	26,034	41,132	45,139	46,029	36,443
Metal.	?	?	?	133,291	121,530	108,452	85,771	65,622	58,967

After the fall of Japan and the reoccupation of the major producing centres in Malaya, Netherlands Indies and Burma, and the expulsion of the Japanese from Siam and Indo-China, small tonnages of Japanese-produced tin were seized and exported to replenish dwindling stocks. The conditions reported in the producing areas, however, were such as to indicate a lapse of at least two years before production could be much improved. Production during the first half of 1946 showed only a very slight improvement over that of 1945.

Widespread readjustments were required. As the occupied areas came back into production their output could be absorbed for a time in expanding consumption above the restricted wartime level, but eventually the time would come when supply would outrun demand, and production would have to be adjusted between these countries and those in which production had been pushed above normal levels by the demands of World War II. Then, too, there was the question as to whether the postwar consumption rate would be as high as the prewar rate; during the years of forced economy many uses, in which tin was formerly thought to be essential, were drastically rationed, or even eliminated entirely. It was quite possible that users in some lines of consumption had discovered that they could get by with less tin than they had formerly thought necessary. Finally, there was the problem of the disposal of the Texas smelter; this plant would continue as essential until smelting capacity in the orient and the Netherlands was sufficiently rehabilitated to handle the normal ore supply. However, the question would then have to be settled as to whether the Texas plant was to be dismantled, held in a stand-by condition or kept in operation in competition with other world smelting capacity. This problem had so many features which seriously impinged on the return to normal living in other smelting centres that it would probably become the subject of international negotiations.

The United States had long been the world's largest consumer of tin, though domestic production remained practically nil. Demand and a price up to double the normal during World War I brought a domestic output of only 157 short tons in 1916 and a total of 588 tons in 1914–18. Although agitation for the production of strategic metals led to a peak output of 189 tons in 1937, domestic production was abandoned as hopeless, and the combined total for 1942–44 was only 19 tons, with none reported in 1945. Practically the entire domestic demand had been supplied in normal years by imports of metal, but with the loss of the oriental smelters through Japanese occupation, and with the shortage of shipping to carry Bolivian ores to English smelters and then back to the United States, it became necessary to establish a domestic smelting industry. There was a small metal output from private smelters, beginning in 1940, but it was not until the government-owned plant near Galveston, Tex., went into operation in April 1942 that domestic smelting was able to carry any appreciable load. Later, 64% of the available metal supply was furnished by domestic smelters, against 36% by imports, and in 1945 the proportion rose to 83%.

Domestic smelting was established in the United States by private plants on a small scale during World War I, but after the close of that war they were not able to secure ore supplies and were forced to close down. All of the British empire ore output was produced under export restrictions, and the bulk of the Bolivian output was under contract to English smelters, and it was only as a necessary war measure that readjustments were made to provide an ore supply for the Texas smelter. As conditions were brought back to normal there would doubtless be a resumption of restrictions on the export of ore, and it was questionable whether domestic smelting could be continued except after international negotiation and agreement as to the extent that smelting in the United States might be permitted to encroach on the old established smelting interests. Commercially, these interests had the upper hand, but for security reasons it was desirable to have the smelting industry continued in the United States.

With the discontinuance of price control, in Nov. 1946, the price of tin in the United States advanced to 70 cents per pound, as compared with the controlled price of 52 cents. (*See* also Metallurgy; Mineral and Metal Production and Prices.) (G. A. Ro.)

Tinian

See Pacific Islands, Mandated; World War II.

Tires

See Rubber.

Tiso, Josef

Tiso (1887–1947), Slovakian politician and ecclesiast, was ordained a Roman Catholic priest in 1909; he joined the Slovak autonomy movement after the end of World War I and associated himself with Father Andreus Hlinka's movement.

Following the Munich pact in Oct. 1938, Czechoslovakia

granted the Slovaks their long-desired autonomy and Tiso became prime minister of the Slovak state. Suddenly ousted from his post by the Czechoslovak government on March 10, 1939, Tiso appealed to Adolf Hitler for assistance. Four days later, Slovakia, with German backing, proclaimed its independence. Reinstated as prime minister, Tiso signed a pact with Hitler on March 23, 1939, under which Germany guaranteed Slovakia's political integrity for 25 years. At that time, Hungarian forces were invading eastern Slovakia. On Aug. 18, 1939, Germany assumed military control over Slovakia and Tiso was elected first president of the Slovak republic Oct. 26, 1939.

Hostility to Tiso's rule by Czechs and left-wing Slovak elements was heightened by the Slovak premier's anti-Semitic measures and his dispatch of the Slovak army to help the Germans crush the partisan uprising in 1944 in which thousands of patriots were killed. After the collapse of Germany, he was captured by U.S. 3rd army troops.

At the opening session (Dec. 2, 1946), of his trial in Bratislava, Tiso challenged the authority of the court and the impartiality of the presiding judge, Dr. Igor Daxner. Both protests were overruled. Tiso was condemned to death and hanged April 18, 1947.

Titanium

Of the two commercial ores of titanium, ilmenite and rutile, the former continued to supply the bulk of demand, but the latter had some uses for which ilmenite was not suitable. World production of rutile prior to World War II was only of the order of 5,000 tons a year, and even the top war demand brought out not more than 20,000–25,000 tons. Australia remained the chief producer, followed by the United States, Brazil and French Cameroun. Ilmenite output, on the other hand, totalled about 320,000 tons in 1937, after a more than 10-fold increase in 20 years resulting from the expanding demand for titanium pigments—two-thirds from India and most of the remainder from Norway; the United States was the third largest producer. The output of the leading producers was as follows in short tons:

Table I.—*Production of Ilmenite*

	1937	1939	1941	1943	1945
Canada	4,229	3,694	12,651	69,437	13,307
India	200,777	?	144,525	41,933	?
Norway	92,825	60,657	67,336	72,963	?
United States	?	14,602	23,297	203,551	308,516
Total (est.)	320,000	380,000	260,000	390,000	?

When transportation conditions made it impossible to move the Indian output to the United States, production in India declined and that of the United States was developed to cover the shortage. No reports were received on Indian output after 1943, when it had dropped to under 42,000 tons, but improvement was evidenced by U.S. imports of 62,066 tons of Indian origin in 1944 and 179,693 tons in 1945. The Norwegian output declined about a third from the prewar level, while Canada developed a temporary production almost equal to the Norwegian. War demand led to increased outputs by a number of minor producers, chiefly Australia and Brazil, while shipping difficulties reduced output in Senegal.

The United States was slow in supplying increased demand for titanium pigments from domestic sources and made no great advances in domestic ilmenite production until war transportation difficulties cut off imports, most of which had come from India. Output was expanded beginning in 1942, and by 1945 was well above the prewar level of consumption. In the meantime, however, demand had continued to increase, and as soon as shipping conditions permitted, imports came back almost to the prewar level. All told, the supply in 1945 was more than double that of 1940. The salient statistics of the industry in the United States are shown in Table II.

Table II.—*Statistics of Titanium Industry*

	1937	1939	1941	1943	1945
Ilmenite					
Production	?	14,602	23,297	203,551	308,516
Shipments	?	16,872	21,526	211,715	308,518
Imports	172,472	287,191	170,689	78,093	210,066
India	?	?	156,079	8,960	179,693
Consumption	?	?	275,106	302,822	381,178
Pigments	?	?	266,244	284,573	369,433
Alloys and carbide	?	?	7,104	10,583	8,611
Welding rod coating	?	?	1,756	5,894	2,373
Stocks	?	?	352,060	129,824	272,598
Rutile					
Production	?	?	3,130	3,987	7,179
Shipments	?	?	3,431	3,941	6,837
Imports	665	787	6,291	14,338	10,602
Consumption	?	?	6,361	17,634	9,971
Welding rod coating	?	?	5,461	12,358	7,813
Alloys and carbide	?	?	709	5,221	1,923
Stocks	?	?	5,678	6,173	10,130

In the first half of 1946, the production of ilmenite dropped to 139,179 tons, but imports soared to 209,690 tons, or almost as much as in the full year 1945. Consumption rose slightly to 199,430 tons, leaving a considerable balance for stocks, which increased to 397,430 tons. Rutile production dropped to 2,840 tons and imports to 2,759 tons; consumption declined 2,994 tons, with stocks increasing to 12,643 tons.

Although much of the titanium pigment went into war uses, the most important contribution of titanium to direct war uses was in welding rod coatings and in titanium alloys and carbides. (G. A. Ro.)

Tito

Tito (Josip Brozovich or Broz) (1892–), Yugoslav army officer and statesman, was born near Zagreb in Croatia. He served in the Austro-Hungarian armies during World War I and in 1915 went over to the Russians. Returning to Croatia after the war, he became a labour leader and Communist, assuming the pseudonym Tito. After the Germans overran Yugoslavia in 1941, Tito organized a leftist guerrilla group, which effectively harried axis occupation forces. Subsequently, Tito engaged in a struggle for power with Gen. Draja Mikhailovitch, who had organized a similar guerrilla organization but with rightist leanings. Tito, whose armies were numerically larger and had more mass support, emerged from this internecine battle victorious and won Allied recognition.

On March 7, 1945, Tito formed a new Yugoslav government with himself as premier. On May 2, after the surrender of German armies in northern Italy, his partisans occupied Trieste, slightly ahead of British imperial forces also trying to seize the port. Tito's unilateral seizure was denounced by the Allies and on June 9 he reluctantly agreed to turn over command of the military government of Trieste to the Allies and to withdraw his troops to Gorizia. Tito's government held national elections on Nov. 11, 1945, although the political opposition stayed away from the polls. However, the Yugoslav electorate endorsed his policies and on Nov. 29 he proclaimed the dissolution of the monarchy and establishment of a republic. His government was recognized by the United States and Great Britain on Dec. 22, 1945.

In 1946 Tito renewed his claims to Trieste and charged that the Allied military government was encouraging infiltration of Italian "Fascist bandits" into Trieste. In the early part of the year, he made visits to Prague, Czechoslovakia, Warsaw, Poland, and Tirana, Albania, and in the summer of 1946 he visited Moscow, securing a pact

Нове мере против бандитизма
награда од 100.000 рајхсмарака у злату!
100.000 РАЈХСМАРАКА У ЗЛАТУ ДОБИЋЕ ОНАЈ КОЈИ ДОВЕДЕ ЖИВА ИЛИ МРТВА КОМУНИСТИЧКОГ ВОЂУ ТИТА.
СТОГА ЈЕ ОВАЈ ОПАСНИ БАНДИТ У ЗЕМЉИ УЦЕЊЕН СА 100 000 РАЈХСМАРАКА У ЗЛАТУ
Врховни заповедник немачких трупа у Србији

Tito's portrait on a German notice offering 100,000 marks for the capture of the Yugoslav partisan leader, dead or alive, which appeared in the Belgrade *Novo Vreme* July 21, 1943

(June 8) whereby the soviet union agreed to help rebuild Yugoslavia's industries and equip its army. In Aug. he became embroiled in a serious controversy with the United States over the shooting down of U.S. planes over Yugoslavia. On Aug. 21 the United States delivered a warning to Yugoslavia to free the occupants of one of the craft shot down, failing which the state department would take the case before the United Nations Security council. Although he complied with the U.S. ultimatum for "satisfaction" and subsequently paid a $150,000 indemnity for the deaths of five fliers, Tito maintained that infringement of Yugoslav frontiers by the U.S. planes was "deliberate."

Titulescu, Nicolae

Titulescu (1883–1941), Rumanian diplomat and statesman, was born in Craiova, the son of a prominent Rumanian jurist. Educated in Craiova and Paris, he became professor of law at the universities of Jassy and Bucharest. Titulescu entered Rumanian politics in 1912 and 5 years later, at the age of 34, he was appointed minister of finance. In 1927 Titulescu became foreign minister in the Vintila Bratianu government. Under his tutelage Rumania championed collective security, entered both the Balkan and Little Ententes and embarked on a policy of friendship with France and the U.S.S.R. His support of a pro-French policy was so militant that his political enemies called him "foreign minister-at-large of France." Titulescu's power waned with the rise of Adolf Hitler's Germany. His countrymen had lost all faith in collective security, and Titulescu was dropped from the cabinet in Sept. 1936 while he was in France. As Rumanian Fascists had openly threatened to kill him, the former foreign minister was forced to remain abroad. In 1937 he returned to Rumania, but fled again to France in 1940. He died at Cannes on March 17, 1941.

Tobacco

The place of tobacco in U.S. farm economy underwent a remarkable change during the decade 1937–46. Before World War II, tobacco was not considered an essential crop; even in the first years of the war in Europe it was not highly regarded in comparison with food crops. But by 1944 it began to hold high rank as a wartime commodity and an essential to the maintenance of morale. Consumption increased rapidly and production rose to new record heights in 1944, 1945 and 1946. When the war began, no other group of U.S. farmers was in more serious jeopardy than the growers of flue-cured and dark tobacco. More than half of these types had been exported, and the war put a sudden end to this market. Supplies of tobacco had been large for six years. Production reached a high level in 1930, and stocks reached a peak in 1932. By 1937 exports had not reached the predepression level of 1928 and 1929. Prices had declined to the lowest point in 20 years in 1931 but had recovered somewhat by 1934. The growers' income was slowly recovering and favoured some expansion of planting.

Tobacco acreage in 1937 was 1,752,800 ac., the highest for 6 years; in 1939, acreage increased to 1,999,900 ac., a record until that year except for the year 1931. The acreage then dropped to 1,305,900 ac. in 1941, followed by expansion to more than 1,900,000 ac. in 1946, almost as high as in 1939. The total acreage was less significant than that of particular types of tobacco. The remarkable increase in yield was more a factor in attaining the high production. In five of the seven years beginning with 1940 the yield per ac. was more than 1,000 lb., compared with a 10-year (1935–44) average of 952 lb. The record was made in 1944 at 1,117 lb. per ac.

Total tobacco production was high in 1937 and still higher in 1939 at 1,880,793,000 lb.—the record up to that time. Four smaller crops followed, but in 1944 a new high mark, 1,950,000,000 lb., was made which was exceeded in 1945 with 1,997,000,000 lb. and 1946 with 2,162,900,000 lb. (Aug. estimate).

Upon the outbreak of war in 1939 the British buyers, who usually took about one-third of the flue-cured crop, ceased buying. Markets were closed to prevent a collapse of prices, which were down to about 15 cents compared to 22 cents for the 1938 crop.

The U.S. government held a referendum of growers on marketing quotas and agreed to finance the grades usually taken by the British trade. A purchase and loan program supported prices for the rest of the year. The large crop of 1939 increased stocks, and exports declined. Flue-cured stocks were particularly large, and Burley supplies were high. Marketing quotas were again voted in 1940, and

U.S. Tobacco Production by Leading States, 1937–46
(In millions of pounds)

	1937	1939	1941	1942	1943	1944	1945	1946*
U.S. Total	1,562.	1,874.	1,262.	1,408.	1,402.	1,835.	1,997.	2,220.
North Carolina	604.5	821.2	459.4	574.4	552.6	748.0	814.8	891.4
Kentucky	364.9	346.1	294.1	289.4	321.7	398.1	437.6	458.8
South Carolina	108.0	133.2	69.6	96.7	86.4	128.8	139.5	162.4
Virginia	111.0	143.8	88.5	104.7	109.4	136.9	153.3	158.0
Tennessee	122.7	110.2	86.3	89.3	96.8	115.4	141.9	141.8
Georgia	75.0	95.9	55.4	59.7	63.6	95.5	105.9	110.1
Pennsylvania	28.9	30.2	58.1	42.1	40.0	50.8	46.3	53.6
Wisconsin	25.1	32.2	31.6	29.2	27.1	29.7	36.0	41.9
Maryland	22.7	32.8	30.2	28.1	20.8	32.1	21.6	39.1
Connecticut	22.2	25.1	22.8	19.6	20.0	22.8	22.8	25.0
Florida	16.7	23.7	11.7	14.7	14.9	20.0	20.0	21.5
Ohio	28.5	30.2	25.3	24.0	20.3	22.5	22.6	21.5
Indiana	11.6	11.8	8.4	8.8	10.1	12.2	13.5	12.8
Massachusetts	8.2	9.8	9.7	9.0	8.2	9.6	8.1	10.3
Missouri	5.5	6.2	5.4	5.1	5.8	7.3	6.8	7.5
West Virginia	3.5	2.7	2.6	2.2	2.7	2.5	3.7	3.5
New York	1.1	1.6	1.7	1.4	.7	.9	1.0	1.2
Minnesota	.4	.7	.7	.7	.6	.7	.9	1.0
Alabama	.2	.4	.3	.2	.2	.3	.3	.3
Kansas	.1	.5	.3	.1	.1	.3	.3	.3
Louisiana	...	...	.05	.07	.1	.2	.1	.1

*Preliminary estimate.

the loan and purchase program was continued. The foreign market for fire-cured types, 60% of which had been exported, began to decline. The outlook was so gloomy that acreage for 1941 was reduced by 600,000 ac. from the high of 1939. Prices in 1940 averaged only 16 cents per lb. national average. The law was amended to provide for marketing quotas for three years, and 86% of growers voted in favour of such quotas for 1941–43. In 1941 the law was broadened to apply to more types of tobacco, and the parity base was changed from 1919–29 to 1934–38. In May loans at 85% of parity were offered to producers of all types of tobacco who co-operated with the Agricultural Adjustment administration. Free inspection service was provided in one-third of all auction markets in 1941. The average growers' price was 26.4 cents per lb. in 1941 compared to 16 cents a year earlier. In 1942 the price advanced to 36.9 cents per lb. average.

By 1943, tobacco had come to be regarded as essential to the war effort. Cigarette manufacture increased more than 50% over that of 1940, to new high record levels. Both military and war-worker demand contributed to this expansion. The foreign demand also increased. Lend-lease took large quantities for export, about 87% to Great Britain. The use of tobacco by-products to replace the shortages of insecticides and fungicides increased. Large quantities of nicotine sulphate were made and sold under a price ceiling with subsidies for by-product manufacturers to cover the difference between the price paid for the leaf and the price at which the product had to be sold.

Changes in the consumer demand for tobacco developed rapidly during the war period. Cigarette consumption increased rapidly to about three-fourths of the total of tobacco consumed. Chewing tobacco and snuff consumption increased because of the restrictions on smoking in the military forces and in war plants. On the contrary, the use of cigars and smoking tobacco declined. The demand for most types of tobacco exceeded the supply in 1943 and price ceilings were placed on most types of tobacco.

The War Food administration allocated supplies of the 1943 crop to buyers to divide stocks equitably. The Combined Food board made international allotments. The large British requirements were supplied by the Commodity Credit corporation; two-thirds was sold for cash and one-third was shipped under lend-lease for military forces. By 1945 tobacco had become a war crop of which a very large proportion went to the military forces. Civilian cigarettes became scarce, even with the record production, which was more than 50% above the 1935–39 average. During 1944–45 cigarettes accounted for about 80% of the total volume of tobacco products, an increase of 7%; production of smoking tobacco increased 17%, and production of cigars also increased. About 30% of the cigarettes made were exported. The per capita consumption of cigarettes was estimated at 1,262 in 1937 and 1,889 in 1943.

The cigarette shortage became so acute in the United States that investigations were conducted which found that the situation was due to: (1) limitations of manufacture caused by labour shortage; (2) large military demands which were met before supplying civilians and (3) the increase of smoking by civilians with higher incomes. The lack of leaf was not a limiting factor. With the end of hostilities the military demand declined and civilian supplies became ample. The large crops of tobacco assured plenty. The termination of lend-lease put exports on a sale basis. During the war years the CCC handled about 1,700,000,000 lb. of tobacco, mostly for the military forces, and about half shipped under lend-lease. Foreign demand was expected to continue at a high level until stocks abroad were restored and foreign production recovered.

The world tobacco crop was estimated at an average of 6,560,000,000 lb. during 1935–39 and at 5,306,000,000 lb. 1940–44. The principal decline was in Europe and Asia. By 1945 the total was up to 6,027,000,000 lb. because of increases in the United States and South America and a small recovery in Asia. The early estimates for 1946 put the world crop at 6,654,000,000 lb., larger than the prewar average, mostly in the western hemisphere. The world's big tobacco producers in 1945 were the United States, 1,997,000,000 lb.; India, 1,050,000,000 lb.; China, 902,000,000 lb.; Brazil, 240,000,000 lb.; Turkey, 145,500,000 lb., all other countries producing less than 100,000,000 lb. Burma, Japan and Java produced about 100,000,000 lb. each before World War II but lost production steadily during the war. Great Britain, Europe and the soviet union greatly increased consumption during the war but produced relatively little tobacco leaf. Canada produced 72,093,000 lb. of tobacco in 1937 and increased the crop to an average of 84,484,000 lb. during 1940–44. In 1945 more than 92,000,000 lb. were raised, and a new high record of 115,000,000 lb. was estimated for 1946. The Cuban crop was much less than that of Canada—55,000,000 lb. in 1937 and an average of 53,154,000 lb. during 1940–44, with a top of 60,000,000 lb. in 1946. Mexico grew a crop slightly larger than that of Cuba, reaching 70,000,000 lb. in 1946.

Production by Types.—Flue-cured tobacco amounted to more than half the total U.S. crop in 1937 and was about twice the quantity of air-cured Burley. Production jumped from about 866,300,000 lb. in 1937 to 1,275,000,000 lb. in 1939, then declined for 4 years, after which came the 3 big crops of 1944–46. The price dropped from about 22 cents per lb. in 1937 to 15 cents in 1939 and 16 cents in 1940. It then jumped to 38 cents in 1942 and made slight gains to more than 40 cents, where it held through 1946. The total supply of this type of tobacco was more than 2,000,000,000 lb. from 1939 on, stocks being only about one-fourth larger than production.

The average price for the 1945 crop was 43.3 cents per

lb., the highest since 1919, when the average was 44.4 cents per lb. Growers voted to continue acreage controls and marketing allotments through 1949–50. The British loan was expected to be a factor in sustaining the export trade. With continuing high consumption of cigarettes, the domestic disappearance of cigarette types of tobacco seemed likely to continue high. U.S. exports of flue-cured tobacco were at the low point in 1940, then recovered in 1941 and 1942. By 1944 exports were above the level of 1937 and 1938 and then made a new high in 1945.

The U.S. Burley tobacco crop was high in 1937, 402,-200,000 lb., and did not exceed this amount until 1944, when the output jumped to 591,800,000 lb. and then held close to that amount through 1945 and 1946. The large crops of 1944 built up the supply from 974,000,000 lb. in 1937 to 1,334,300,000 lb. in 1945. Consumption was high, however, and promised to reduce the stocks. The average price of Burley rose from 16.2 cents per lb. in 1940 to 45.6 cents in 1943 and then declined a little through the next two years. The tobacco goals for 1946 did not call for any increase in Burley acreage. The large domestic consumption would probably reduce the stock to normal if the 1946 crop could be moved. The 1946 yield of Burley was highest in Virginia, 1,450 lb. per ac., and North Carolina, 1,350 lb., compared with an average of 937 lb. in 1935–44 for the whole Burley belt.

Fire-cured tobacco had begun to decline in importance before 1937, when the crop was 119,000,000 lb. The decline continued irregularly until 1945, when the crop was only 57,095,000 lb., the smallest on record in 30 years. In 1946 the crop increased to 87,700,000 lb. Prices advanced after 1941, when it was 9.5 cents per lb., to more than 24 cents in 1945. Stocks were low through the decade after 1937. The smallness of the supplies held down exports.

All of the fire-cured tobacco came from Kentucky, Tennessee and Virginia.

Dark air-cured had changed little in supply from 1926 to 1937. The crop was 48,000,000 lb. in 1937 and dropped to a low of 30,000,000 lb. in 1943, then rose again to 47,275,000 lb. in 1946. This type of tobacco was largely used in chewing tobacco and declined with the decreasing use of this form of tobacco. Exports continued small. The price rose from an annual average of 7.3 cents per lb. in 1939 to 27.3 cents in 1943. Stocks were stable within a range of 56,000,000 to 74,000,000 lb. during the whole decade. This type was still mostly grown in Kentucky, except about one-fifth from Tennessee, Indiana and Virginia.

Cigar types of tobacco amounted to 105,000,000 lb. in 1937, increased to 139,000,000 lb. in 1939, then declined slightly until 1946, when the total reached a new high of 143,378,000 lb. The cigar filler types of Pennsylvania and Ohio ranged from around 55,720,000 lb. in 1937 down to 50,000,000 lb. and then up to 59,540,000 lb. in 1946. Cigar binder types followed a similar swing—a decline after 1939 and a great increase to 72,000,000 lb. in 1946. Cigar wrapper, shade-grown types, continued with less fluctuation throughout the decade, from an average of 8,800,000 lb. during 1933–42 to 11,800,000 lb. in 1946. All of the foregoing types reflected the decline in demand for cigars during World War II.

As shipping became available, the normal U.S. export demand caused an increase in exports toward the prewar level. In 1939 the United States exported a record amount of 473,757,000 lb. of all tobacco types; it imported 76,085,-000 lb., giving net exports of 397,672,000 lb. Imports changed little until 1945, while exports increased from a low level of 179,626,000 lb. in 1940, leaving a net export of about 300,000,000 lb.

The principal destinations of exports in 1946 were Great Britain, China, Australia, New Zealand, France, the Netherlands, Norway, Sweden and India. These exports represented chiefly the movement of stocks owned by foreign buyers to storage abroad to replenish stocks. The high price of U.S. tobacco was expected to stimulate the expansion of foreign production wherever possible.

(J. C. Ms.)

Bibliography.—U.S. Dept. Agric., *Agricultural Statistics;* Agric. Marketing Serv., *Annual Report on Statistics;* Tobacco Industry (Dept. Labor 1941); *U.S. Tobacco Jl.* (wkly.).

Tobago

See West Indies, British.

Togo, Shigenori

Togo (1882–), Japanese statesman, was born in Kagoshima, Japan. He was graduated in 1908 from the Tokyo Imperial university, where he specialized in law; he entered the foreign service four years later. After holding a number of minor diplomatic posts in Europe and Asia, 1912–20, he became chief of the first section of the European and U.S. bureau of the foreign office in 1921. Later Togo headed the European and Asiatic affairs bureaus of the foreign office. He was ambassador to Berlin, 1937, and to the U.S.S.R., 1938. During his tenure as envoy to the soviet union, he helped negotiate agreements for settling the Soviet-Japanese fighting along the Manchurian border. Togo, who became foreign minister in Gen. Hideki Tojo's cabinet on Oct. 17, 1941, rejected as "fantastic" a U.S. proposal for settling the far eastern crisis, and reaffirmed Japan's determination to proceed with its expansionist program for establishing a "new order" in Asia. A week later, Japan attacked Pearl Harbor, bringing the United States into World War II.

Togo went out with the Tojo cabinet on July 18, 1944, but in the following year he returned as foreign minister in Baron Kantaro Suzuki's cabinet (April 1945). The Suzuki cabinet retired in turn after the emperor's surrender broadcast of Aug. 15, 1945. Togo was subsequently arrested by Allied authorities and was among the 28 Japanese leaders indicted April 29, 1946, in Tokyo by the Allied War Crimes tribunal.

Togoland

See British West Africa; French Colonial Empire; Mandates.

Tojo, Hideki

Tojo (1884–), Japanese army officer and politician, was born in Tokyo of a samurai family. He attended the Imperial Military academy in Tokyo and upon graduation became a sublieutenant in the army. Later he was graduated from the Military Staff college (1915). After the close of World War I, he served for a while as military attaché in Japan's embassy in Berlin; returning to Japan he became an instructor in the Military Staff college and subsequently filled a number of important war office posts.

In 1928 Tojo was made commander of the 1st infantry regiment, which, eight years later, participated in the mutiny of the Tokyo garrison. In 1937 Tojo was appointed commander of gendarmerie headquarters, and shortly thereafter he became chief of staff of the Kwantung army in Feb. 1937. He returned to Tokyo in 1938 to become vice-minister for war. Two years later (July 1940) he was appointed minister of war in the Konoye cabinet. Tojo succeeded Konoye as premier in Oct. 1941 and also assumed the war ministry and home production portfolios. On taking office, he pledged his government's firm adherence to its pro-axis and "greater east Asia" policy. Six days after the Pearl Harbor attack, Tojo declared that Japan was "fighting in self-defense and in the cause of righteousness."

Allied military successes in the Pacific in late 1942 and early 1943 caused consternation in Tokyo, and in Feb. 1943 Tojo assumed dictatorial powers over the nation's economy and political life in an effort to bolster home front morale.

He reshuffled his cabinet frequently in 1943, adding the portfolios of education, commerce and industry to those already under his control.

Further U.S. military successes in the Marshalls and in New Guinea, and the U.S. naval bombardment of Truk in early 1944 generated dissatisfaction with the rule of Tojo, who nevertheless assumed additional posts in February, becoming chief of the army general staff, minister of munitions and governor of the Imperial Rule association.

However, the successful Allied invasion of the Marianas Islands in June 1944 destroyed what remnants of confidence existed in his leadership and on July 16, 1944, he was removed as chief of staff and two days later (July 18) his entire cabinet resigned.

On Sept. 11, 1945, after Japan's formal surrender to the Allies, Tojo shot himself in a dramatic attempt at suicide. He was nursed back to health, however, and on April 29, 1946, along with 27 other Japanese leaders, was indicted by the Allied Military tribunal on 55 counts as a war criminal.

Books being returned to the shelves of the Ueno Imperial library in Tokyo. They were brought back in 1946 from small towns where they had been stored for safekeeping during World War II

Tokyo

The heart of Tokyo, capital of Japan and the world's third largest city (pop. 1940, 6,778,804) is situated in the sprawling, wood, paper and glass buildings that are the abode of the nation's spiritual and temporal leader, the emperor.

Facing the massive stone walls, gates and moat surrounding the imperial palace, many of Tokyo's citizens gathered in mid-1937 to bow in awe toward the palace and to pray for victory in the undeclared war which the emperor's forces had begun to wage in north China.

Exultant thousands paraded the streets and saluted Emperor Hirohito once again in Dec. 1941 when the government, now securely in the hands of Japan's fanatical militarists, announced that the nation was at war with England and the U.S. and revealed the startling success of the surprise attack on U.S. naval forces at Pearl Harbor. Prayers arose from Buddhist and Shinto shrines, and thousands upon thousands of young men made their way to the Yasukuni shrine, on a hillside near the palace, to pray that they might die as warriors and bring victory to their homeland.

Four years later, at the end of the eventful decade 1937–46, two-thirds of Tokyo lay in charred ruins, and the burned skeletons of perhaps 300,000 people were scattered among the ashes. All buildings in great areas of the city had disappeared completely. There were less than 5,000,000 residents of Tokyo now, poorly clad, on scant rations; many of them living in shanties of corrugated tin.

Outwardly, one thing had not changed. Tokyo's people still made pilgrimages to the imperial palace. But behind its concealing stone wall, the palace was partially burned out, too. And in addition to bowing toward the emperor, the Japanese also saluted the foreign sentries guarding his gates—U.S. soldiers of the army that occupied the country after Japan's defeat and surrender in 1945. For the first time in the 2,000-year reign of its imperial household, the flag of a foreign conqueror flew over the Japanese capital. By sufferance of the conquerors and under their orders, Hirohito still ruled, but his empire had dwindled until now it consisted of only the four main islands of Japan proper.

Few cities in history had undergone such dramatic changes as did Tokyo in the ten years from 1937 to 1946. Two dates stand out in that period: the first months of 1945, and September of that year. It was in the span from January through April that U.S. bomber planes first brought the facts of war home to the heart of Japan.

Tokyo offered an ideal target. Except for its business district, modernized after the 1923 earthquake, it consisted mostly of highly inflammable, tightly-packed buildings of wood and paper. Its industrial district stretched in a narrow belt along the railway to Yokohama, and extended into that neighbouring port city. Outside of its few modern areas, the city was composed of small villages which it had encompassed and cemented together in its centuries of growth.

Despite its size, it had never been a cosmopolitan city, nor a place of festivity. The few foreigners living there before the war had been swallowed up by the millions of Japanese. The native inhabitants of Tokyo took their pleasures in a handful of cinemas, baseball stadia or behind the closed doors of geisha houses and in the streets of the Yoshiwara. The city had no splendid vistas, no outstanding boulevards.

It was on this target that the B-29's loosed their bombs. Incendiaries spread fire and death through the capital.

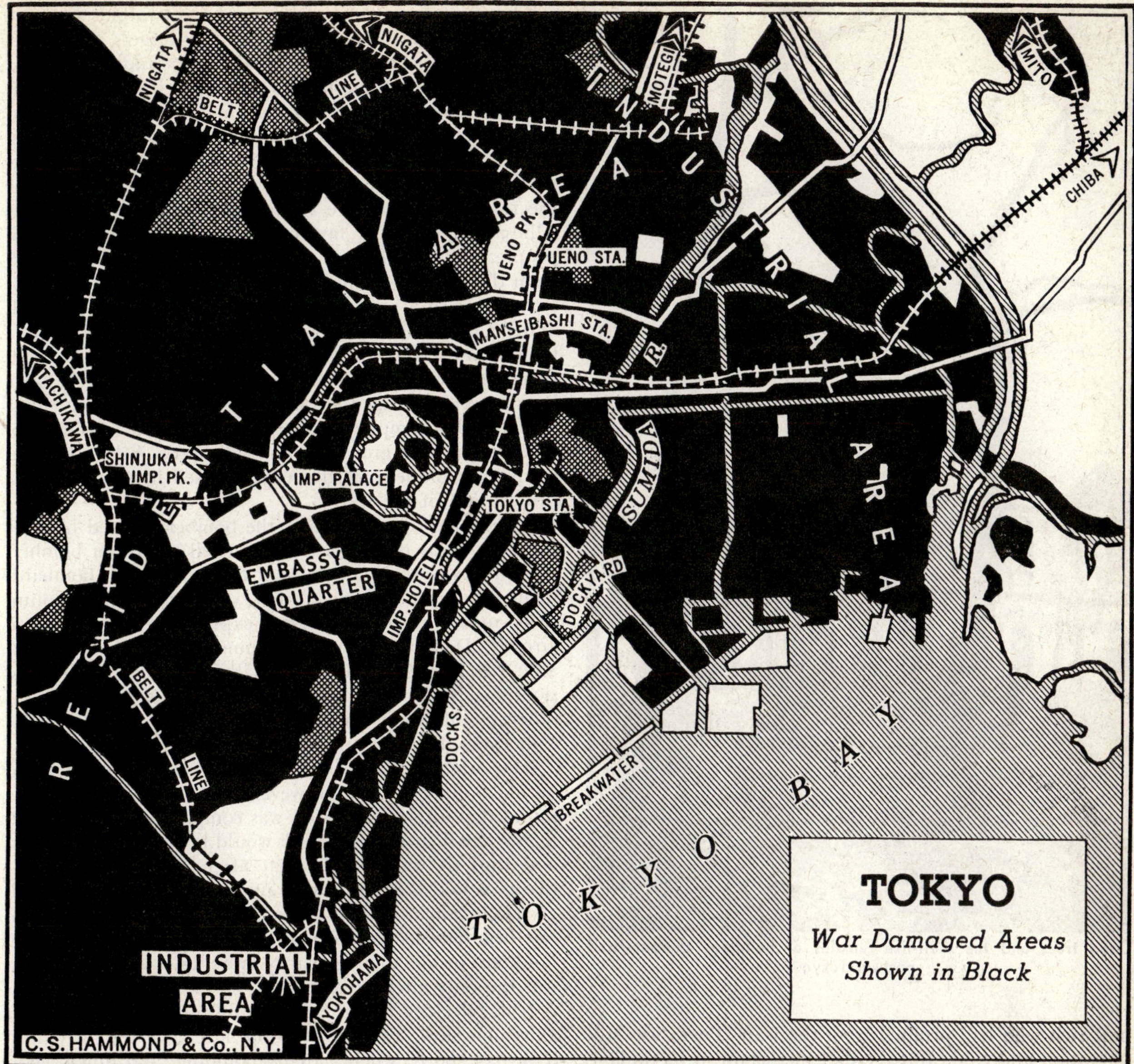

Most of the industrial section, with its war plants, was wiped out. During one raid, a 40-mile-an-hour wind swept flames through the city; paper and wood buildings burned like tinder as the antiquated fire fighting system was overwhelmed. Helplessly, Tokyo's residents battled the flames with small buckets of sand.

By government order, a mass exodus started. On foot and by crippled train facilities, millions made their way into the country and to ancestral villages. The survivors worked as best they could to get war industries reorganized. But no materials were coming in through the blockade by U.S. submarines; no rice from Korea and French Indo-China.

Truck gardens were planted in the middle of the wide Nishi Ginza and amid the ruins of the Ginza which had been Tokyo's main shopping street.

Up until the surrender on Sept. 2, 1945, government officials worked in the charred shells of their ministries. A week later, General Douglas MacArthur occupied Tokyo. A few Japanese leaders took their own lives in their Tokyo homes rather than submit. A half-hundred ordinary citizens performed hara-kiri at the gates of the palace. But Tokyo's millions, ever obedient to the emperor's orders, submitted in sullen silence to the occupation of their sacred city.

MacArthur found that the modern section of Tokyo, the buildings that housed the great firms controlling Japan's finance and industry, was nearly intact. Here he set up headquarters for the vast job of remodelling Japan from a feudal, militaristic state bent on world conquest, to a democratic nation. After the shock of the first contact between the populace and the U.S. troops, the people of Tokyo proved unexpectedly co-operative.

Hundreds of Japanese stood in the streets daily to watch MacArthur enter his offices, to take his picture or to bow reverentially.

Tokyo's jail doors were opened to free political prisoners who had starved in dark cells for years; and to admit new occupants, generals and admirals who were shortly placed on trial as war criminals, and the lesser men who had inflicted practised brutality on Allied prisoners of war. The dreaded Kempetai (military gendarmerie) was broken up; the police force reorganized as an instrument to serve the people and not to terrorize them.

After a year of occupation, black markets dealing in U.S. army goods still flourished, their customers mainly the

Dead trees and the shell-like remains of buildings characterized postwar Tokyo

new rich who had profited from the war. There was still starvation and cold. But the diet met again in its undamaged building after the first free elections in Japanese history. Rice was coming in from the U.S. Contact with the U.S. occupation troops had freed the Japanese from some of their fear and distrust of foreigners and foreign ways. Tokyo, still bleeding and ruined, was starting to rebuild for a more enlightened future. (CL. L.)

Doolittle's Raid on Tokyo.[1]—It was a month after Pearl Harbor. The United States war machine had not yet been geared to full fighting effectiveness, and the axis was riding the crest of an offensive wave from the burning sands of north Africa to the steaming jungles of the southwest Pacific. Berlin and Tokyo were making blatant and ominous threats in accompaniment to nazi and Jap victories over desperately battling, but out-manned Allied armies. This was before Midway and Guadalcanal, before El Alamein and Stalingrad.

These were crucial days—days of holding actions, defensive strategems and retreat. But in Jan. 1942, plans for a bold and daring offensive thrust against the heart of the Japanese empire were conceived in Washington, D.C. and executed successfully three months later. The plan was to bomb Tokyo itself.

[1]This section was checked by James H. Doolittle for technical and factual accuracy.

The primary purpose of this raid was twofold: to cause material damage by destroying military targets and consequently to retard Jap war production; and to effect a psychological reaction by developing a fear complex in Japan, making it necessary for their military leaders to recall combat equipment from other theatres for home defense, and thereby ease the pressure on Allied units elsewhere in the Pacific area. Secondarily, it was hoped that the raid would improve relationships of the U.S. and its Allies, and obtain a favourable response from the U.S. people who had been reading nothing but "bad news" from the fighting fronts.

It was with a great deal of satisfaction that Lieut. Col. (later Lieut. Gen.) James H. Doolittle was able to report the successful completion of the raid to Gen. H. H. Arnold, then commanding general of the army air forces. It later became evident that the raid exceeded expectations; aims were fulfilled completely, and in addition, the mission provided a proving ground upon which the A.A.F. learned many valuable lessons subsequently used in the victorious prosecution of the war.

In working out raid plans, the bomber deemed best for the attack was the B-25, the "Mitchell" medium bomber. Aeroplanes were obtained from the famed 17th bombardment group along with a small, selected group of volunteers—men who had had some experience with this type aircraft. Doolittle was put in command of the raiders, and after the planes had been specially outfitted for the mission, *i.e.*, stripped down, extra gas tanks installed and other modifications made, training began at Eglin field, Valparaiso, Fla., in early March 1942.

The original plan called for both take-off and landing on an aircraft carrier. However, in actual practice it was found that although take-off was comparatively easy, landing on the floating flight deck would be extremely difficult, and thus, it was decided that after "bombs away," the planes would head for either unoccupied China or Vladivostok in Siberia. The latter was much closer to Japan, but negotiations with Russia in connection with possible landings inside their territory were unsuccessful. China was the only alternative.

It was decided that the entire mission would be flown at extremely low altitude—tree-top level all the way into Tokyo, 1,500 ft. when actually bombing, and down again to low level the rest of the way into China. Each plane was to carry 2,000 lb. of bombs made up of both demolition and incendiary, depending on the targets each was to hit. And since the Norden bombsight was not very effective at low altitude, and was still secret, a simplified sight was installed in the aeroplanes. Called the "20-cent" sight, it was designed by Capt. (later Colonel) C. Ross Greening, one of the pilots on the raid, and was used with excellent results.

At Eglin, the entire group entered upon a three-week period of intensive and exhaustive training. Concentrated courses of instruction simulating carrier take-offs were instituted under the supervision of Lieut. Henry Miller, a naval officer. White lines were drawn on two runways of an auxiliary field near Eglin outlining a carrier's flight deck, and the pilots practised hour after hour getting the fully-loaded "Mitchells" into the air within the required distance.

There were long periods of special training in cross-country flying, night flying and navigation. Flights over the Gulf of Mexico were scheduled regularly to permit pilots and navigators to become accustomed to flying without visual or radio references or landmarks. Low altitude approaches to bombing targets, rapid bombing and evasive action were practised with diligence. Emphasis was placed on ground and air-to-ground firing for the gunners, but time did not permit drills in air-to-air tow target firing.

All the volunteers were highly capable—the cream of the nation's youth, but the transition from civilian to soldier had come swiftly; practically all of them needed more training. The pilots were the most experienced, and they were all excellent; the co-pilots were good, but required more "polish"; the bombardiers needed practice; the navigators had good training, but little practical experience; and the gunners had never before fired from an aeroplane at either moving or stationary targets. They were far from the crews trained to razor-edged sharpness which the U.S. sent into combat in later years. After three weeks, the Tokyo raiders were deemed ready, and despite the fact that additional training undoubtedly would have improved everyone's efficiency, they took off from Eglin for the last time and headed for California.

On April 2, 16 B-25s were loaded on the flight deck of the aircraft carrier "Hornet" at Alameda naval base, and a day later, the flat-top steamed out toward the take-off point deep in Jap-controlled waters—about 400 mi. off the coast of Japan. That point was never reached.

In the meantime, training continued on the carrier without respite. Lieut. Stephen Jurika, Jr., of the navy gave the raiders a series of lectures on Japan itself; Lieut. Thomas R. White, who was to play a heroic role on the mission as flight surgeon, addressed the men on first aid and sanitation; and lectures on gunnery, navigation and meteorology were given by members of the Doolittle unit and by men of the "Hornet." Gunners engaged in actual gunnery and turret practice using kites flown from the ship as targets.

The crews were briefed thoroughly on procedure to be followed on the mission. Each crew was assigned its specific targets, with alternates if conditions made it impossible to bomb the primaries. Each flight of three planes was assigned a course and coverage all its own. The entire mission was spread over a 50-mi. front in order to provide the greatest possible coverage, to create the impression that a larger number of aeroplanes took part in the raid than were actually used, and to dilute Japanese air and ground fire. This also prohibited the possibility that more than one plane would pass over any given point on the ground and assured the element of surprise.

Five flights were assigned: the first, led by Lieut. Travis Hoover, was to cover the northern part of Tokyo; the second, led by Capt. David M. Jones, was to cover the central part of Tokyo; the third, led by Capt. Edwin J. York, was to cover southern Tokyo and the north-central part of the Tokyo Bay area; the fourth, led by Capt. Greening, was to cover the southern part of Kenegawa, the city of Yokahama, and the Yokasuka navy yard; and the fifth was to go south of Tokyo, proceed to the vicinity of Nagoya and break up—one plane bombing Nagoya, one Osaka and one Kobe.

Col. Doolittle was not too encouraging in these briefings, and made it a point to emphasize that once the mission took off, the fliers were on their own. There was to be no radio communication of any kind, of course, for success and personal safety depended almost wholly on complete surprise. On shipboard, Doolittle wanted only to make sure the men knew *what* to do; he realized that they could and would do the job if it were humanly possible.

In addition to the "Hornet," the naval force consisted of another carrier, the "Enterprise," and several escort vessels. All aerial scouting and patrolling during the voyage was done by planes from the "Enterprise" since it was impracticable for the "Hornet" to release any of its own planes because of the B-25s parked on the flight deck. In command of this force was Rear Adm. William F. Halsey, who was destined in the months to come to lead powerful naval task forces which helped break the back of Japan's sea power. Commanding the "Hornet" itself was Capt. (later Admiral) Marc Mitscher.

(This mission saw the army and the navy co-operate with each other in a manner that had never been accomplished before. It was a forerunner of the eventual complete co-operation between the services attained later in all theatres of war.)

A great deal of thought, both before and during the voyage, was given to the best method of attack. It was originally decided to take off three hours before daylight, in order to provide security and ideal bombing conditions, assure surprise and permit the raiders to arrive at their destination before dark. This plan was abandoned, however, because those in charge were not too sure of the advisability of a night take-off; also, the navy was unwilling to light up the deck of the carrier in such dangerous waters.

A second plan was for a dawn take-off, early morning bombing, and arrival in China before nightfall. This was rejected because it was felt that the surprise element would be eliminated, increasing the hazards of the mission unnecessarily.

A third and final plan was agreed upon. This was to take off just before dark, bomb at night, and arrive in the morning at the destination—the town of Chuchow in unoccupied China. Doolittle's plane was to take off ahead of the others, arrive over Tokyo at dusk and fire an inflammable military target with incendiaries. This would minimize the over-all hazards and assure a well-lighted target for the following planes.

As it turned out, the fliers were not able to carry through this final plan of action either. The task force made contact with a Japanese patrol much sooner than expected.

At 3:10 A.M. on April 18, the first Jap patrol vessel was picked up on the radar. The course of the task force was changed as each new Japanese vessel appeared on the radar screen. Finally, in avoiding one ship, the U.S. force found itself closely confronted with another. This vessel was sunk, but it was believed that it had sent at least one message to the mainland before going to the bottom. Consequently, if this was to be a surprise raid, the fliers had to get started. Time was running out and, although the raiders wanted to get within 400 mi. of Japan, take-off was made at 35° 43′ N. lat., 153° 25′ E. long.—a point 824 statute miles from the heart of Tokyo.

Final instructions were given: avoid at all costs nonmilitary targets, particularly the temple of heaven. If impossible to reach the China coast, don't go to Siberia, but proceed as far west as possible, land on the water, launch the rubber boat and sail in. (This proved unnecessary for most of the planes, as they had a 25-mile-an-hour tailwind throughout the last 1,200 mi. of the flight which enabled all but one of the bombers to reach China before running out of fuel.) This plane, in direct violation of orders, went to Siberia.

After the final quick briefing, the crews climbed aboard their respective ships, and at 8:20 A.M., Doolittle's plane was the first to leave the carrier. Take-off was easy despite the heavy seas which prevailed that morning. The remaining 15 followed without mishap. In less than an hour, the

"Hornet's" flight deck was clear.

After take-off, each plane circled to the right and flew over the "Hornet," lining up the axis of the carrier with the plane's drift sight. The course of the vessel was displayed in large figures from a gun turret. This, through the use of the aircraft compass and directional gyro, enabled each pilot to check his compass and set the proper course for Tokyo. This manoeuvre was considered necessary because of the possibility of change in compass calibration, particularly on those planes which were parked close to the island of the carrier.

With Doolittle in the first ship were Lieut. Richard E. Cole, co-pilot; Lieut. Henry A. Potter, navigator; Sgt. Fred A. Braemer, bombardier and Sgt. Paul J. Leonard, gunner. Fifteen aeroplanes carrying 75 others followed Doolittle, anxious to strike the first aerial blow at Japan.

The run into the city was uneventful. The fliers were about an hour on course when they passed a camouflaged vessel which they took to be a light cruiser, and after two hours the airmen passed a multi-engined land plane headed directly for the air task force, and flying approximately 2,000 ft. From then on they passed, and tried to avoid, various civil and naval craft which dotted the water from time to time. Landfall was made north of Inubo Shuma, slightly to the right of the briefed course.

With the other flights proceeding according to instruction, Doolittle's group began to approach Tokyo from the north to drop incendiaries on selected targets. They were flying as low as terrain would permit, and noticed several small biplanes, evidently trainers, in the air above them. Ten miles from the target, the raiders encountered nine Japanese fighters, but there was no attack. Nearing the target, they climbed to 1,200 ft., dropped their bombs, lowered away to the housetops again and slid over the western outskirts of the city into some low haze and smoke. While in the target area, Japanese anti-aircraft fire became very active but inaccurate. Only one burst came close.

After leaving Tokyo, the airmen turned south again and headed out to sea, bound for the China coast. And although the skies had been clear over Japan, it was not long before the group ran into extremely bad weather. The ceiling dropped to almost zero, and when landfall was made in China, the planes climbed to 6,000 and then 8,000 ft., flying entirely on instruments.

Doolittle attempted to contact Chuchow on the command radio, but received no response. With fuel almost gone, it was time to bail out. The crew jumped, and after putting the ship on automatic pilot, Doolittle followed. He glanced at the clock on the instrument panel just before leaving the plane—it was 9:20 P.M., exactly 13 hours after he had said good-bye to the "Hornet."

Everyone in Doolittle's plane landed safely in friendly territory. They were taken to Chuchow, and in a few days reached Chungking. Before arriving there, however, Doolittle contacted Gen. Ho Yang Ling, director of the branch government in Western Chekiang province, and requested him to have a lookout kept along the seacoast, and also have all sampans and junks in the coastal area watch for planes that might have gone down at sea or had just reached shore.

By early morning of April 20, four planes and crews, in addition to Doolittle's had been located, and he wired Gen. Arnold, through the embassy at Chungking, as follows: "Tokyo successfully bombed. Due to bad weather on China coast, believe all airplanes wrecked. Five crews found safe in China so far."

As it turned out, only three of the 16 crews failed to turn up at Chungking. Capt. York's crew, being desperately short of fuel after bombing their target, headed north and landed in Siberia where they were interned by the Russians. Two crews were captured by Japanese forces in China after bailing out, one on the coast and the other inland near Lake Poyang.

Every effort was made to recover the prisoners through purchase or force. The Chinese were reluctant to use force because of the large concentration of Jap troops, but agreed to try purchasing them. They were unsuccessful, however, and it was not until the end of the war that four of the men were released from prison and returned to the U.S.: Lieutenants Chase J. Nielsen, George Barr, Robert Hite and Corp. Jacob Deshazer. Four others would never return; Lieut. Robert G. Meder died in prison of starvation, and three other airmen were executed—Lieut. Dean Hallmark, Lieut. William G. Farrow and Sgt. Harold Spatz.

Of the crewmen who landed in China (all via parachute), three were killed in accidents. Corp. Leland Faktor, an engineer-gunner, was killed after bailing out. His chute opened, but since he landed in mountainous territory, it is believed that he was the victim of a secondary fall. The other airmen, Sgt. William J. Dieter, and Corp. Donald E. Fitzmaurice, were found dead on the shore of a river.

Lieut. Ted Lawson, a pilot, was seriously injured in a crash landing, and his left leg had to be amputated. There were other injuries, but they were comparatively slight, and all recovered.

Final figures showed: of the original 80 crewmen (16 five-man planes), 64 managed to get back to safety in China, 8 were captured by the Japs (of whom 4 later returned to the U.S., 1 died in prison and 3 were executed), 3 were killed in parachute-landing accidents, and 5 were interned by the Russians.

Fourteen tons of bombs rained down on the Japanese mainland that memorable day, and hits were scored on practically all assigned primary targets. Large fires were seen by several crews as incendiaries did their deadly work on the more inflammable sections of Japan's war industries, while the demolition bombs hit factories, communication arteries, ammunition dumps, military barracks, and oil and storage warehouses.

It was actually a "hit and run" mission, with the U.S. planes gone almost before the defenders knew what was happening. One crew reported a baseball game in progress on a field directly in its line of flight, but the B-25 was over and gone before either players or spectators had a chance to dive for cover. They probably didn't realize that the city was being attacked until they heard the explosions.

Mission reports of the crews agreed that Jap anti-aircraft fire was intense, but inaccurate. The Japanese judged altitude very well, but the bursts were all to the right and left, and the raiders did not lose a ship or a man to flak. One crew saw some flak burst among some barrage balloons that were in the sky and saw two or three of the balloons go down.

The fliers learned a great deal on that mission. For one thing, that in home defense, nothing could be taken for granted. "Doolittle's Daredevils" achieved complete surprise; however, adequate defense would have made this surprise an impossibility. Japanese patrol craft which spotted the Americans must have sent radio messages to shore. They were not acted upon, and the AAF could only presume that there was poor dissemination of information on the part of the Japanese, or a complete failure of their communication system.

They had failed to provide enough fighters for interception purposes. A few fighters did make passes at the medium bombers, but with little or no effect. Several gunners reported that some of the bullets fired at them from Japanese planes actually "bounced off" the B-25s without penetrating. This was definite evidence of the inferior type of equipment committed to home defense. The fact that the interceptors made so few and ineffective attacks also demonstrated the inexperience and lack of training of the Japanese pilots. Japanese airmen in the combat areas were far superior to those at home.

The raiders had expected to be hindered by camouflage in locating the targets, but little or none was seen. Also, the targets were not dispersed enough to prevent widespread destruction from a single raid. These were costly mistakes, and they contributed materially to the success of the mission.

In Doolittle's report to Gen. Arnold after the attack, at a time when the U.S. was still in danger of a bombing raid, he recommended the following defensive measures for the country: (1) sufficient utilization of small surface craft, such as shipping boats with simple radio and simplified code, for detection purposes; (2) provision for widespread camouflage and dispersion of industry; (3) provision of the greatest number of fighters possible, to intercept bombing raids; (4) provision of an infallible detection and communication system; and (5) retention of sufficient modern aeroplanes and combat pilots within the territorial limits of the U.S. to assure adequate defense.

Japan had failed on all counts. It paid for its failure. On the other hand, the AAF learned a lot about its capabilities, its weakness and strength, and about some of the things that had to be done to achieve victory. The need for certain modifications and improvements on the aeroplanes themselves, on air equipment, including guns, gunsights, turrets, fuel pumps and other instruments and apparatus, was clearly seen.

Perhaps most important of all, the AAF saw the need for more thorough training of flight crews, especially gunners. This inadequacy was everywhere apparent. However, it was not long after this raid that a comprehensive training program was instituted in the U.S. which was to send U.S. flight personnel into combat better trained and far better equipped than any in the world. (R. D. T.)

Tokyo-Berlin-Rome Axis

See Fascism; Germany; Hungary; Italy; Japan; Union of Soviet Socialist Republics; World War II.

Tolbukhin, Fedor Ivanovich

Tolbukhin (1894–), soviet army officer, was born of peasant parentage June 16, 1894, in the Russian village of Davydovo. After completing his elementary school work, he went to St. Petersburg (now Leningrad) to continue his education. Upon the outbreak of World War I in 1914, he joined the army and was wounded in the battle of Grodno. Sent to an officer's school he was graduated in 1915 with the rank of second lieutenant. Tolbukhin, who was decorated four times for valour in action, was a captain at the outbreak of the Russian Revolution in 1917. He joined the red army, fought in the civil war and remained with the army after peace was restored. He was chief of staff of a military district when the Germans attacked the soviet union in June 1941. Later he became chief of staff on the Crimean front, and in Nov. 1942 he was in command of one of the several soviet armies that launched the counterattack on German forces besieged in Stalingrad.

After Stalingrad he was promoted to colonel general and was given command of the 4th Ukrainian army in the spring of 1943. He defeated German forces in the battles at Taganrog and Melitopol, was raised to the rank of an army general and participated in the reconquest of Sevastopol. Thereafter Tolbukhin was put in command of the 3rd Ukrainian army which swept through Rumania into Bulgaria. In Sept. 1944 he was made a marshal of the soviet union.

Tolbukhin's 3rd Ukrainian army participated in the battles of Budapest and Vienna in early 1945. In May 1945 he was made a cavalier of the soviet Order of Victory.

Toluene

See Chemistry.

Tomatoes

See Vegetables.

Tongan Island Protectorate

See Pacific Islands, British.

Topology

See Mathematics.

Tornadoes

See Disasters.

Toronto

During the decade 1937–46, Toronto made substantial progress in spite of, and perhaps partly by reason of, the conditions imposed by World War II. There was a great increase in business done; bank clearings went up from $6,465,263,740 in 1936 to $10,985,142,402 in 1945; postal revenue from $7,085,301 in 1936 to $12,290,055 in 1945; customs and excise from $54,408,397 in 1936 to $178,791,340 in 1945. There were great changes in the industrial, commercial and social life of the city. Huge quantities of material for war purposes—for the use of every branch of the services—were produced and, while the area of the city did not change appreciably, the population grew from 645,492 persons in 1936 to 681,802 in 1945 although large numbers of its finest young citizens joined the navy, the army and the air force.

Toronto continued to be an important commercial and industrial centre; its goods were distributed in quantity throughout the dominion and the empire; it enjoyed a good foreign trade. United States manufacturing and commercial enterprises in increasing numbers continued to establish subsidiaries and agencies in Toronto to manufacture and sell their products. It was found that for such purposes the situation of Toronto midway between the Atlantic and Pacific seaboards was good, that transportation and communication by land, water and air were available in every direction. Much progress was made in the provision of facilities for traffic by air.

During World War II, two important annual activities were suspended. The Canadian National exhibition, an annual affair for 63 consecutive years, was held for the last time in 1941, after which its grounds and its many buildings were turned over to the department of national defense. It was planned to reopen the exhibition in 1947. Similarly, the Royal Agricultural Winter fair, held annually since 1922, was discontinued in 1941, to be resumed

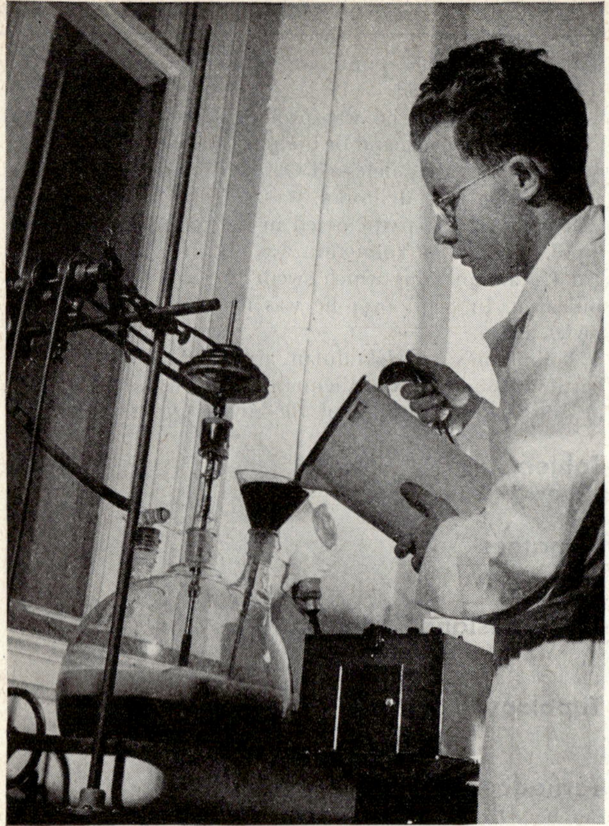

Chemist at the Connaught laboratory in Toronto, Ontario, preparing a penicillin extract for bottling

during the winter of 1946–47. The facilities of these two institutions, including 350 ac. of land, were used to great advantage by the services.

During the early part of the decade, construction was begun on a duplicate water supply system. It was completed at a cost of less than $12,000,000 and placed in operation in 1942. Thus, except in the unlikely event of two systems with widely separated intakes from Lake Ontario breaking down at the same time, Toronto was assured of an abundant supply of pure water, filtered and treated. The former method of sewage disposal had not been satisfactory, nor was the plant used for that purpose adequate. A modern and effective system was designed, and construction of the first unit, to cost $6,000,000, was under way in 1946.

The Toronto transportation system, operating the city-owned street railway and bus system, completed its 25th year of control and management in 1946. The original debenture debt of $42,000,000 (which included the cost of taking over the railway from its private owners) had been reduced to $12,000,000, and improvements to the system representing an outlay of $25,000,000 had been financed out of reserves established for that purpose. The commission had paid its way completely, and the city had not been called on for any payment whatever in connection with the reduction or servicing of the debenture debt. There were reserves adequate for all needs. At the annual municipal elections on Jan. 1, 1945, the citizens of Toronto voted by a majority of 10 to 1 in favour of a rapid transit plan submitted by the commission. This plan provided for private rights of way, partly in subway and partly in open cut, for two main transit routes leading to and through the downtown area. It is to be noted also that the city-owned hydro-electric system had always paid its way without cost to the city.

Improvements and additions were made at the Provincial museum and the Toronto Art gallery. The high standard set in music by the Toronto Symphony orchestra, the promenade concerts, the Mendelssohn choir, the Hart House quartet and various other excellent organizations was fully maintained.

The business of the immense mining industry of Canada was to a great extent carried on in Toronto, and the mining stock exchange there grew to be one of the largest, if not the largest, in the world. (G. R. G.)

Bibliography.—N. A. Deacon, "Geographical Factors and Land Use in Toronto," *Canadian Geographic Journal,* 29:80–99 (Montreal, Aug. 1944); E. C. Guillet, "Toronto's 150 Years," *Canadian Geographic Journal,* 28:204–11 (May 1944); G. Spencer, "Toronto Investigation," *Canadian Forum,* 20:315 *et seq.;* 21:19 *et seq.* (Toronto, Jan.–April 1941).

Torpedoes

See Munitions of War; Navies of the World; Submarine Warfare.

Torts

See Law.

Totalitarian State

See Fascism; Germany; Italy; Japan; Minorities; Philosophy; Rumania; Spain; Union of Soviet Socialist Republics; World War II.

Towers, John Henry

Towers (1885–), U.S. naval officer, was born in Rome, Ga., Jan. 30, 1885. Graduated from the U.S. Naval academy at Annapolis in 1906, he was one of the first naval officers to qualify for naval aviation in 1911. The following year he established a world's record endurance flight in a seaplane. During World War I, Towers was assistant director of naval aviation. Six months after the war he led a squadron of flying boats that made the first trans-Atlantic flight in history (May 1919). Towers was assistant chief of the navy department's bureau of aeronautics, 1929–31, and commanding officer of the aircraft carrier "Saratoga," 1937–38. He was named chief of the bureau of aeronautics and promoted to the rank of rear admiral in June 1939.

In Sept. 1942 he was promoted to rank of vice-admiral and given command of the Pacific fleet air force. He was appointed (Feb. 11, 1944) deputy commander of the Pacific ocean areas, becoming second in command to Adm. Chester W. Nimitz. In July 1945 he replaced Vice-Adm. John McCain as head of a naval carrier task force, and on Dec. 28, 1945, he was named commander in chief of the Pacific fleet and the Pacific ocean areas, with command of the 3rd, 5th and 7th fleets.

Under the naval reorganization plan announced on Nov. 12, 1946, Towers retained his post as commander in chief, with administrative control over U.S. naval forces in the western Pacific and in Japanese waters.

Town and Regional Planning

The eventful years of the decade 1937–46, which covered the most disastrous war in history, developed new tendencies in town and regional planning throughout the world and strengthened other trends which had appeared during the years of the so-called world depression.

Continental Europe.—Most of the devastated European cities were working on rehabilitation plans in 1946, and many of them were subsidized by their national governments. Some hoped for reparations money from their destroyers. Even during destructive hostilities, patriotic planners and architects worked on plans for their home cities, to be ready for the peacetime reconstruction.

France was committed to a plan to reshape the nation as a physical and economic unit after the Oct. 1945 elections. French leaders recognized the evils of haphazard industrial expansion and attempted to put into effect a plan for the decentralization of industry which would control the size of cities. They hoped to stem the tide of migration from farm to city by providing better cultural and recreational facilities for farm dwellers. When the German troops withdrew, there were 6,000,000 homeless persons in France. About 400,000 houses were totally destroyed. By 1946 nearly all of the injured towns had been replanned, thanks to the many architects and planners who worked throughout the war. Little actual reconstruction had been undertaken in spite of the efforts of the General Commissariat of Modernization and Equipment to supply manpower and materials. There were two schools of planners—those who would rebuild French cities as they were, and those classified as modernists, some of whom follow Charles E. J. le Corbusier for out-and-out revolution in design, and some of whom believed that a regional pattern could be superimposed on traditional plans and classic architecture.

In Germany, despite the difficulties of running the gauntlet of approval from the four nations governing the four zones, the problem of replanning Berlin was attacked. There was established an 800-man building and housing council, which had first to clear the ruins and find use for the rubble. A plan for Berlin seemed to be definitely emerging; but it was predicted that it would take at least 20 years to provide acceptable living conditions. The new plan aimed to establish livable communities with decent working and living conditions, open spaces and adequate circulation facilities and provision for housing, industry, commerce and recreation. The schedule for issuing the plan in the spring of 1946 was postponed, it was said, because of political reasons and the required approval of the four ministries.

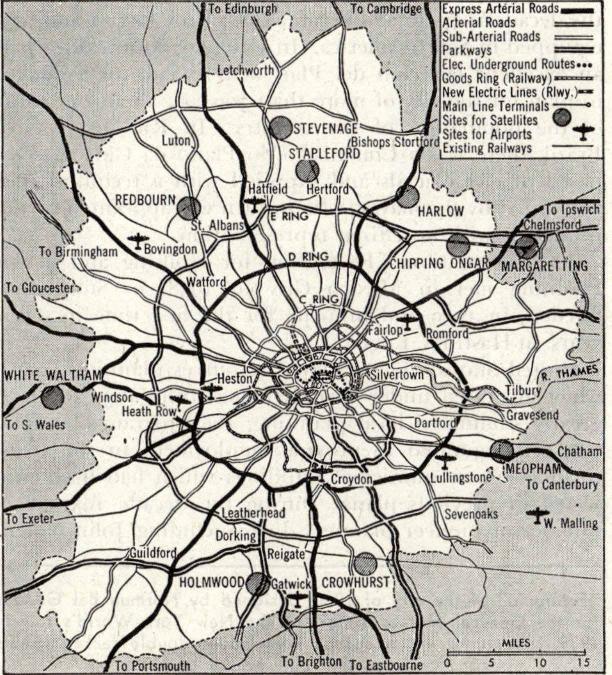

The Greater London plan, emphasizing decentralization, was prepared for official consideration while World War II was still in progress

It was proposed to reduce the average population density from 350 to 100 persons per gross acre.

In Italy there was evidence that the new planning might preserve the beauty of the old and provide the functional convenience of modern design. Before World War II, Italian cities, once famous for their charm, had already suffered from the fascists' over-elaborate architecture and grandiose planning, which totally overlooked the living conditions of the people. Even before the war there were only 33,000,000 rooms for 45,000,000 people. A movement was started in 1946 to place planning under the guidance of a single joint commission which would revise national planning laws to apply to emergency peacetime needs.

Warsaw, swept by four distinct waves of devastation from Sept. 1939 to Jan. 1945, was developing an ambitious reconstruction plan dominated by the two-dimensional pattern of the old city, applied with new standards of density. The new Warsaw was to be designed as the cultural, political and economic centre of Poland and as part of a national and regional plan. The population was to be decentralized into residential boroughs all within 30 min. of high-speed travel from the central district. The prewar economy basis of Warsaw was not expected to change. Even before World War II, the city owned much of the land within its confines. The new Warsaw was said to be committed to municipal ownership of all land; large areas left ownerless after the war were to be claimed by the city. Existing owners of single lots would be compensated; but those owning more than one lot would relinquish claims to all but the one for which they would be compensated. Rapid transit was expected to equalize land values. All industries employing more than 50 persons were nationalized. The planned locations for industry, it was said, were developed in consultation with the industries concerned; transportation facilities were planned to serve industries and workers. The basic unit was the residential colony. In 1946, 1,400 persons were employed in the Warsaw Reconstruction office; city planners and architects worked in teams of 3. The Warsaw Reconstruction office contained the Historic Buildings service, whose powers (like that of the office) permitted it to overrule any government or municipal authority. During the first year following the war, the national budget for reconstruction supplied 60% of the total cost. The city realized an income from leased lands and various municipal enterprises and public services.

Switzerland, itself untouched by the ravages of war, became a clearing house for information and work on all European reconstruction. The modern movement for planning and design in Switzerland was influenced by the ideas of Le Corbusier. There was a reported absence of slums in Swiss cities.

In Sweden, likewise immune from war damage, Le Corbusier also exerted an influence, as noted in the Stockholm exhibit of 1930.

Swedish cities before the war had developed a modern architecture of pleasing appearance which promised to keynote future planning.

Great Britain.—The opening of the decade 1937–46 found the people in England engaged in peacetime pursuits. After World War I great strides were made in local planning and in the provision of houses. From 1920 to the beginning of the depression more than 4,000,000 houses had been built—about 2,500,000 by private enterprise unsubsidized by government, and nearly 2,000,000 by local authorities and private enterprise subsidized by the state.

Then came the blitz and the incredible devastation of World War II. Through all the long years of the war, planning was a lively topic of conversation. The magazines were full of planning references. The *Rebuilding Britain* series made comprehensive and detailed proposals. A series of books called *Targets for Britain* appeared on the newsstands and had wide circulation. Of these, *A Plan for Town and Country Planning,* with a foreword by Julian Huxley, carried the gospel of planning to the general public. In 1945 *Rebuilding Britain—A Twenty Year Plan* by E. D. Simon appeared. Official reports were made to the government during the years of devastation. The Barlow, Scott and Uthwatt reports recommended plans and legislation to decentralize urban populations through density controls and the provision of open spaces and green belts. Recommendations were made that public funds be used to acquire title or restrictive rights in private property to prevent uncontrolled use of land. Two important items of legislation followed these reports—the Education bill and the Town and Country Planning bill of 1944, which provided for the acquisition and development of land for planning purposes, made amendments to the laws relating to town and country planning and provided for compensation payable in connection with land acquisition for public purposes by reference to 1939 prices. Two additional acts were also passed providing for the extension of the scope of housing subsidies and for the erection of 250,000 temporary houses.

During all the war years, planning reports for cities were listed. Perhaps the most discussed was *The County of London Plan* and *The Greater London Plan* prepared in part by Sir Patrick Abercrombie. In 1944 appeared the *Report* of the Improvements and Town Planning Committee on Postwar Reconstruction of the City of London. Some of the plans for public buildings and open spaces were very impressive; but the keynote of all these plans and proposals was decentralization, reduced densities of population and control of location of industries. Planners were thinking in terms of neighbourhood communities to be provided with schools, libraries, parks, playgrounds and shopping centres.

Plymouth, of all English cities, suffered most perhaps from war devastation, except London itself. By the spring of 1941 the citizens of Plymouth and Devonport, after 40 raids, realized their opportunity and had prepared *The Plan for Plymouth.* Of the business and industrial belt of 900 ac., 300 suffered from the blitz. The plan would reduce the densities in part in this area from 256 to 100 persons per acre. This decentralization involved overspill, and plans were made to push out into the country. Restored Plymouth would preserve historic landmarks but would profit by the principles of modern planning.

Manchester published a plan in 1945. The city suffered relatively slight damage but put forth a 50-year plan, providing for a series of ring roads and radial highways, for the relocation of passenger and goods terminals around an inner ring, the development of new industrial sites and the unscrambling of mixed areas of homes and industry, the development of large open areas connecting the heart with the country and insulating residence areas from industry. There was to be a progressive redevelopment of the school system and a well-studied housing program. The housing program was proposed upon a neighbourhood basis of 10,000 persons per neighbourhood and 50,000 for districts of 5 neighbourhoods.

Other cities issuing reports during 1940–46 included Bath, Canterbury, Durham, Glasgow, Hastings, Newmarket, Northampton, Norwich, Richmond, Sheffield, Edinburgh, Belfast, Cork and Dublin.

Latin America.—Planning in Mexico centred chiefly in Mexico City, a federal district and cultural centre; Monterrey, capital of the state of Nuevo León, also had a planning commission, as did Nuevo Laredo, on the Texas border, with necessary planning laws for a master plan. Acupulco, resort town on the Pacific coast, adopted organized planning in order to preserve the natural scenic features of its beautiful city. Tasco, the old silver town, was protected with a plan and legislation setting aside the town as a national monument. Veracruz on the Gulf of Mexico laid out a new plan and program under the guidance of Carlos Contreras.

While Mexico reserved to the local governments the initiative to form plans, the reverse was true in Peru and Chile. Central planning offices were set up by the respective governments to do all town planning throughout the countries with the aid of local offices in the larger cities. In Peru the planning was placed in charge of an office called the Section of Urban Studies, said to be one of the best-directed planning offices in South America. An effort was made to co-ordinate into a regional plan the growth and development of the 40 separate municipalities making up the Lima region. In 1929 Chilean planners were successful in having enacted the first comprehensive planning law—one which required all cities of more than 20,000 to make city plans. In 1936 there was formed a central department of urbanism in the ministry of development, with authority to make plans for all cities of more than 8,000. This office carried on planning studies for about 55 Chilean towns and cities. Legislation for each city was scheduled to become a law when the plan was approved jointly by the city authorities and the federal government, but such legislation operated without a city planning commission. Several other large cities, including Santiago, Valparaiso and Concepción, employed trained planning staffs to co-operate with the department of urbanism.

In Bolivia, La Paz, after several attempts at planning, organized a department of urbanism in 1940. In Argentina, Buenos Aires had established in the early '30s a Plan de Urbanización which operated continuously throughout the decade 1937–46 and became one of the largest and best equipped in South America. In Uruguay, Montevideo had an excellent Direción del Plan with an adequate budget to plan for the city of more than 700,000, about one-third of the population of the country. In Rio de Janeiro, Brazil, there was a Commissão do Plano da Cidade, composed of city officials and supplied with a technical staff appointed by the mayor, who in turn was appointed by the president, with no citizen representation.

The International Federation for Housing and Town Planning met in Mexico City in 1938, in Stockholm, Sweden, in 1939 and in 1946, for the first time in seven years, in Hastings, England.

United States.—The national resources planning board, which operated under various names from 1933 to 1943, greatly stimulated local planning; the program of public works inaugurated to provide employment in the 1930s included many municipal buildings which had been projected in previous plans. During the decade 1937–46, a number of pioneer planners died, including John Nolen,

"Futurama" of the city of 1960, designed by Norman Bel Geddes for the General Motors exhibit at the New York World's fair in 1939. It featured widely spaced skyscrapers, double-decked streets and parks on the roofs of low buildings

Model of a proposed civic centre to occupy the water front area in Portland, Ore., as outlined by the City Planning commission in 1944

Robert Whitten, Alfred Bettman and Warren H. Manning. During the depression years, business was not very brisk for planning consultants except as they were employed by or through the federal government. Nevertheless, under the influence of the national resources planning board, state planning boards were set up in most of the states, and some of these boards stimulated local planning. Beginning in 1941, it became the custom for states and cities to set up special postwar planning agencies or to designate existing agencies for the work. In 1944, congress authorized a program of federal planning advances or loans without interest to state and local governments to be administered by the Federal Works agency through a bureau of community facilities. For 1946 a total appropriation of $30,000,000 was made available. The Public Roads act of 1944, for the first time, appropriated federal aid funds for through highways in urban territory. By 1946 all practising planning consultants were pushed to the limit to meet the demand. New city planning commissions were set up, and those which had been inactive began to function and seek planning directors.

In recognition of the prevalence of blighted areas and slums in all of the larger cities, a movement grew up in the 1940s to bring about urban redevelopment on a comprehensive scale. The Federal Housing administration issued a *Handbook on Urban Redevelopment for Cities* in Nov. 1941 as a result, perhaps, of the city planning service which the agency had started in 1937. In 1942 the National Planning association issued a pamphlet on "Urban Redevelopment and Housing." This was supplemented by a "Proposal for Rebuilding Blighted Areas," issued by the Urban Land institute. All of these publications were much discussed. Of the states 28 had passed some sort of legislation by 1946, 12 to authorize redevelopment corporation laws permitting corporations to engage in redevelopment; 6 had passed housing redevelopment acts which would make the public housing authority the administrative as well as the constructing agency and 10 had redevelopment land agency enabling acts which would establish a redevelopment or land agency as an arm of the local government to administer the redevelopment program.

A good many planning reports were issued, most of them in serial form as parts of the master plan, including the following cities: New York, Chicago, Cincinnati (O.), Cleveland (O.), San Francisco (Calif.), Los Angeles (Calif.), Santa Barbara (Calif.), Saint Paul (Minn.), Denver (Colo.), Des Moines (Ia.), Omaha (Nebr.), Dallas (Tex.), Baltimore (Md.), Buffalo (N.Y.), Harrisburg (Pa.), Spokane (Wash.), Portland (Ore.), Portland (Me.), Louisville (Ky.), Toledo (O.), Detroit (Mich.), Kansas City (Mo.), Milwaukee (Wis.), New Haven (Conn.), Schenectady (N.Y.), Syracuse (N.Y.), Waterbury (Conn.) and many smaller cities. The National Resources Planning board experimented with a new technique in Tacoma, Wash., Salt Lake City, Utah, and Corpus Christi, Tex. In most of these reports attention was paid to densities of population, and often a degree of decentralization was recommended. In 1946 wartime congestions of population continued in most cities. In 1945 the *Toledo Blade* promoted the construction of a $250,000-scale model of the Toledo plan which caused nationwide comment. In Boston a metropolitan study contest was won by a team from Harvard university in 1944. In Chicago the *Herald-American* and the *Tribune* promoted planning and housing contests.

After the organization of the American Society of Planning Officials and the merger of the American Civic association with the National Conference on City Planning in 1935, joint planning conferences with the American Institute of Planners, and later with the National Planning association, were held in Richmond, Va., in 1936, in Detroit in 1937, in Minneapolis, Minn., in 1938, in Boston in 1939, in San Francisco in 1940, in Philadelphia, Pa., in 1941 and in Indianapolis, Ind., in 1942. After that the

American Planning and Civic association held a separate citizens' conference in Omaha in 1943, in St. Louis in 1944 and in Dallas in 1946; none was held in 1945. The American Society of Planning Officials met in New York and Chicago. The American Institute of Planners held regional meetings with each.

Canada.—The appointment of a minister of planning and development for the province of Ontario was announced in 1945. Of cities and towns in Canada 20 had city planning committees or commissions in 1946, among them Halifax (N.S.), Montreal (Que.), Saint John (N.B.), Hamilton (Ont.), Toronto (Ont.), Windsor (Ont.), Vancouver (B.C.) and Winnipeg (Man.). (*See* also HOUSING; PUBLIC HEALTH ENGINEERING.)

BIBLIOGRAPHY.—*United States:* American Planning and Civic Association, *American Planning and Civic Annual* (1937–45); American Institute of Planners, *Urban Redevelopment Bills and Statutes* (1945); American Society of Planning Officials, *Proceedings* (1937–44); *Proceedings of a Discussion Conference on Problems of Large Cities* (1945); *Planning Legislation* (1945); Chas. S. Ascher, for the National Resources Planning Board, *Better Cities* (1942); Edward M. Bassett, *The Laws, Administration, and Court Decisions during the First Twenty Years* (1940); Harland Bartholomew, *The Present and Ultimate Effect of Decentralization upon American Cities* (1940); Russell Van Nest Black, *Planning for the Smaller American City*, Public Administration Service (1944); S. R. DeBoer, *Shopping Districts*, American Planning and Civic Association (1937); Henry S. Churchill, *The City is the People* (1945); Miles Colean and Arthur P. Davis, *Cost Measurement in Urban Redevelopment* (1945); Federal Housing Administration, *Urban Redevelopment of Cities in the United States* (1941); Charles E. Merriam, *Spirit and Purpose of Planning* (Planning and Civic Comment, Jan.–March 1937); Lewis Mumford, *City Development* (1945); Eliel Saaranen, *The City, Its Growth, Its Decay, Its Future* (1943); Jose Louis Sert, *Can Our Cities Survive?* (1942); Mel Scott, *Cities Are for People* (1942); Oscar Stonorov and Louis O. Kahn, *You and Your Neighborhood* (1944); Twentieth Century Fund, *Postwar Planning in the United States* (1943–44) and numerous planning reports on cities. Journals: *American City* (monthly); American Institute of Planners, *Journal* (quarterly); American Society of Planning Officials, *News Letter* (monthly); American Planning and Civic Association, *Planning and Civic Comment* (quarterly); *Architectural Forum*—Planning With You series (monthly); Urban Land Institute, *Urban Land* (monthly). *Great Britain:* Sir Patrick Abercrombie and J. Paton, *A Plan for Plymouth* (1944); *ibid.* and J. L. Forshaw, *County of London Plan* (1944); Cadbury Bros. Lt., *Our Birmingham* (1943); L. B. Escrit, *Regional Planning* (1943); Sir Gwelyn Gibbon, *Reconstruction and Town and Country Planning* (1943); Kate K. Liepmann, *The Journey to Work and its Significance in Industrial and Community Life* (1944); Lewis Mumford, *Social Foundations of Physical Planning*, Rebuilding Britain Series, No. 9 (1943); F. J. Osborn, ed., Series on *Rebuilding Britain;* C. B. Purdom, *How Shall We Rebuild London?* (1945); British Information Service, *Postwar Planning in Britain* (1944); Royal Commission on the Distribution of the Industrial Population, *Report* (1940); Royal Institute of British Architects, *Towards a New Britain* (1943); E. D. Simon, *Rebuilding London, a 20-year Plan* (1945). Journals: *The Housing and Planning News Letter* (National Housing and Town Planning Council, bimonthly); *Journal of the Planning Institute* (bimonthly); *Town and Country Planning* (quarterly); *South America:* Francis Voilich, *Cities of Latin America: Housing and Planning to the South* (1944). (H. Js.)

Townsend, Francis Everett

Townsend (1867–) was born Jan. 13, 1867, in Fairbury, Ill. He was graduated from the Omaha Medical college in 1903, practised in the far west and was an assistant health officer at Long Beach, Calif.

During the height of the economic depression in the early 1930s, Townsend originated a scheme, later known as the Townsend plan, to provide an old age pension of $200 monthly for all persons at the age of 60 who retired from active employment. According to its terms the money had to be spent within the month. As the number of pensioners would be about 10,500,000, the annual cost of

the plan would total about $25,200,000,000; this figure represented about 37% of the national income ($68,000,000,000) in 1937. According to Townsend, the pension fund would be financed by a pyramidal tax of 2% on commercial transactions. Critics charged that the Townsend plan was an impractical scheme which if put into practice would bankrupt the nation. Townsendites answered that the plan would stimulate consumption of commodities.

Sentiment for the Townsend plan increased enormously during the national hysteria that followed the closing of the banks in early 1933. In some areas the plan was the chief political issue, and its supporters were elected to congress. Pressure from its advocates was intense, and just before the elections of Nov. 1938 as many as 16 schemes dealing with old age pensions were brought forward. President Franklin D. Roosevelt was strongly opposed to the plan, considering it a quixotic measure; but in the first term of his presidency, he was of the opinion that congress could not withstand the pressure built up by the Townsendites unless it enacted what he termed a "real" old age insurance system. The clamour for the Townsend plan was muted somewhat by the passage of the Social Security act in 1935, although it was revived temporarily by the recession of 1937. But after the elections of Nov. 1938, its popularity slumped to the point where it was no longer a force to reckon with in politics. Despite the loss of support, Dr. Townsend continued to publicize his scheme through the *Townsend National Weekly*, of which he was president, and through the Townsend foundation, of which he was both president and trustee.

Toyoda, Teijiro

Toyoda (1885–), Japanese naval officer, industrialist and statesman, was born in Aug. 1885. Graduated from the Japanese naval academy, 1905, and later from the naval staff college, he was at one time Japanese naval attaché in London and was one of the signatories to the London Naval treaty of 1930. Toyoda became chief of the general section of the naval technical department in 1934 and commander-in-chief of the Sasebo naval station in 1937.

He was minister of commerce in the cabinet of Prince Fumimaro Konoye and in July 1941 succeeded Yosuke Matsuoka as foreign minister. It was generally believed that Konoye, alarmed by Matsuoka's excessive sabre-rattling, decided to replace him with a "moderate." Toyoda's alleged moderation probably stemmed from the fact that he was pre-eminently a businessman. He had been president of Japan's Iron and Steel Control association and was associated with the giant Mitsui family combine by marriage. After the resignation of Konoye's third cabinet on Oct. 16, 1941, Toyoda was succeeded in the foreign ministry by Shigenori Togo. He virtually retired from the public eye until April 1945, when he reappeared in the government again, this time as minister of munitions in the cabinet of Baron Kantaro Suzuki.

Trachoma

See EYE, DISEASES OF; INDIANS, AMERICAN.

Track and Field Sports

It took only a glance at the world-record feats of 1937–46, minimized as they were by the long intervention of World War II, to realize that few track and field marks could survive a ten-year assault by the world's leading athletes. No fewer than 36 world marks were toppled, some several times, during the decade, while numerous others were tied.

As a result, several "ceilings" were lifted on events which, some believed, had received the maximum of human endurance. For instance the pole vault, which had a ceiling of 15 ft. for most track fans in 1937, was now looking toward a 16-ft. mark as a result of the record vaults of Cornelius Warmerdam. Warmerdam, a member of the Olympic club of San Francisco, went 15 ft. 7¾ in. in 1942 in one of the outstanding track and field developments of the decade.

Even more significant, however, was the slow approach to the four-minute mile, once regarded as an obscure dream. The speed of two Swedish contemporaries, Gunder Haegg (Hägg) and Arne Andersson, sliced a full four seconds from the mile time throughout the ten-year period. Sydney Wooderson, the great British miler, started the movement with a world-record mile of 4 min. 6.4 sec. in 1937. By the time Haegg and Andersson had finished their duels of 1943, 1944 and 1945, the mark stood at 4:01.4, held by Haegg. The record was accepted by the International Amateur Athletic federation, although both Haegg and Andersson were ruled from amateur competition for life because of professionalism.

Although he lost the mile record, Wooderson at the end of the decade still held the 880-yd. mark of 1 min. 49.2 sec., made in England in 1938. Another European middle-distance star, Rudolf Harbig of Germany, established world records in the 800-m. run in 1939 and the 1,000-m. run in 1941.

The greatest onslaught on world records, however, was made by Haegg in 1942. Within a space of 74 days, the 25-yr.-old Swedish sensation set 7 world marks and unofficially held all records ranging from 1,500 to 5,000 m. Not only did Haegg run a mile in 4:04.6 in 1942, but he accomplished such world-record performances as: 1,500 m., 3:48.8; 2,000 m., 5:11.8; 3,000 m., 8:01.2; 2 mi., 8:47.8; 3 mi., 13:32.4; 5,000 m., 13:58.2.

Taisto Maki of Finland promoted a similar landslide of world records in 1939, setting marks in 5 events, 2 mi., 3 mi., 6 mi., 5,000 m. and 10,000 m. Most of his records, however, were wiped out by Haegg three years later.

United States athletes stood out in the shorter distances and field events. Two sprint records were tied when Clyde Jeffrey of the Olympic club was timed in 9.4 sec. for the 100-yd. dash in 1940 and Grover Klemmer, also of the Olympic club, matched Ben Eastman's 46.4 for the 440-yd. dash in 1941.

Fred Wolcott of Rice Institute, Houston, Tex., rewrote the record books for the hurdle events while winning six national Amateur Athletic union (A.A.U.) titles from 1938 to 1941. Wolcott set a world record of 22.3 sec. for the 200-m. low hurdles in 1941 and a mark of 22.5 for the 220-yd. lows in 1940. He also shared the high hurdle records with Forrest Towns, both the 120-yd. and the 110-m. at 13.7 sec.

Warmerdam was not alone in creating world records on the field. Les Steers, also of the Olympic club, set a world high jump record of 6 ft. 11 in. in 1941. Bob Fitch of the University of Minnesota added more than 5 ft. to the world discus mark with a toss of 180 ft. 2¾ in. in 1946. The world javelin record was raised to 258 ft. 2⅜ in. in 1938 by Yrjo Nikkanen of Finland.

Indoor track gained considerable popularity during the 1937–46 era, with crowds of 15,000 not unusual at New York and Chicago. J. Gregory Rice, the Notre Dame distance star, featured the indoor season with regular assaults on the two-mile indoor record. The era also marked the exit of Glenn Cunningham, one of the world's greatest milers, and the blossoming of two other fine U.S. milers, Leslie MacMitchell of New York university and Gilbert Dodds, divinity student from Boston.

Team dominance was largely in the hands of the University of Southern California, whose great track dynasty was broken up only by World War II. Southern California won the National Collegiate A.A. tournament successively from 1937 to 1944, when Illinois came to the fore. The Trojans also won the A.A.U. team title in 1943. The New York Athletic club won nine out of ten national A.A.U. indoor titles, while Tuskegee institute of Alabama had the same record in the A.A.U. women's championships.

Another phenomenon of the decade was Stella Walsh, who in 1946 finished her 14th year of championship track competition and annually won two or more firsts in the national women's A.A.U. championships.

As a sideshow to the National Collegiate, the Pacific Coast and Western conferences inaugurated an annual dual meet in 1937.

Until the meet was interrupted by World War II in 1942, the Pacific Coast, led by U.S.C. and Stanford, had won four out of five. The Big Ten scored a surprise 70⅔–56⅓ victory in 1942.

Track and Field Chronology, 1934–46.—The track and field year of 1937, coming as a slight anticlimax to the 1936 Olympic games, nonetheless produced many standout performances, particularly among newcomers. Of the 21 titles decided in the A.A.U. outdoor championships, only John Woodruff, University of Pittsburgh, won his event among the 33 Olympic games athletes who competed. Woodruff won the 800-m. run in 1 min. 50 sec. Otherwise the 1937 season was a proving ground for such champions-to-be as Cornelius Warmerdam, Greg Rice, Charles Fenske, Taisto Maki and others.

The indoor season was marked by U.S. records in two distance events during the A.A.U. championships and the presence of athletes from Japan, Italy, Hungary and Canada in the numerous U.S. tournaments. Tommy Deckard of the University of Indiana set a new indoor mark of 8 min. 48.6 sec. for the 3,000-m. steeplechase, while Norman Bright of the Olympic club, San Francisco, established another U.S. record in winning the 5,000-m. run in 14 min. 45.8 sec.

Sydney Wooderson, the British middle-distance star, shattered the 3-year-old world record of Glenn Cunningham by travelling the mile in 4 min. 6.4 sec. Wooderson's record run featured the European track and field program in which Sweden stood out with a team victory over Germany, winner of the World Student championships.

Other outstanding accomplishments of the 1937 track season were: Ray Malott's time of 47.1 sec. in the 400-m. dash of the A.A.U. outdoor championships; Bill Reitz's toss of 224 ft. 9⅜ in. for the javelin, fourth longest in U.S. history; Woodruff's time of 1 min. 60.3 sec. in the 880-yd. run for a new intercollegiate record and William Sefton's 14-ft. 8⅞ in. in the pole vault, also a new intercollegiate record.

Southern California dominated the collegiate track picture in 1937, though vigorously challenged by Stanford. U.S.C. outlasted Stanford in the National Collegiate tour-

→

Cornelius Warmerdam clearing the bar during a meet in Chicago, Ill. Warmerdam set a record of 15 ft. 7¾ in. in 1942

nament, 62–50 points, and won the Pacific Coast title by a mere point, 55–54. Pittsburgh won the I.C. 4-A outdoor title by a half point over Columbia, while Michigan easily won the Big Ten indoor and outdoor championships. Indiana university's relay team of Mel Trutt, Jim Smith, Tom Deckard and Don Lash set a new 4-mi. mark of 17 min. 16.1 sec.

Women's competition in 1937 was marked by an A.A.U. indoor record of 44 ft. 11½ in. for the 8-lb. shotput by Helen Stephens of Fulton, Mo. Tuskegee institute won the A.A.U. women's indoor title. The men's A.A.U. championships went to the Olympic club of San Francisco, outdoors, and New York Athletic club, indoors.

In 1938 57 records of varying importance were toppled by U.S. track athletes, highlighted by the 4-min.-4.4-sec. mile for Glenn Cunningham on the indoor track at Dartmouth college, Hanover, N.H. The fact that the National A.A.U. outdoor championships were staged on a slow, muddy track hindered the 1938 performers' opportunities of cracking even more records.

As a result of the soggy track, only Henry Cieman, completing the 3,000-m. walk in 13 min. 39.9 sec., established a record. The National Collegiate championships, however, produced such outstanding marks as a 4:08.3 mi. by Lou Zamperini of Southern California; a 9:11.1 for the 2 mi. by Walter Mehl of Wisconsin; a 120-yd. high hurdle time of 14 sec. by Fred Wolcott of Rice institute and a high jump deadlock between David Albritton of Ohio State and Gil Cruter of Colorado at 6 ft. 8¾ in. The mile duels of Zamperini and Charles Fenske of Wisconsin featured the track season, with Zamperini downing Fenske in the National Collegiate championships and Fenske winning the Big Ten-Pacific Coast mile in the slow time of 4:20.9.

On the European front, two world records were established. In England, Sydney Wooderson set a world mark of 1 min. 49.2 sec. for the 880-yd. dash. In Finland, Yrjo Nikkanen tossed the javelin to a new record of 258 ft. 2⅜ in.

The New York Athletic club made a sweep of the A.A.U. outdoor and indoor championships in 1938, while the University of Southern California did the same in the National Collegiate and I.C. 4-A tournaments. Tuskegee institute repeated as A.A.U. women's titlist. Michigan again won the Big Ten outdoor crown with 60½ points to Wisconsin's 37, while Southern California outlasted Stanford, 63⅗–40⁷⁄₁₀, on the Pacific coast. Columbia won the indoor I.C. 4-A championship.

The A.A.U. permitted the use of starting blocks for running events for the first time in 1938.

Although the Olympic games, scheduled for Helsinki, Finland, in 1940, were called off because of gathering war clouds, track and field was not without its record-shattering performances during 1939. Taisto Maki of Finland alone broke five world records, while other standout times were offered by England's Sydney Wooderson, Germany's Rudolf Harbig and the U.S.'s Charles Fenske.

Maki started cracking world records at 2 mi. and didn't stop short of 10,000 m. He recorded a world 2-mi. mark of 8 min. 53.2 sec., a 3-mi. record of 13:42.3, a 6-mi. record of 28:55.6, a 5,000 m. record of 14:16.2 and a 10,000 m. mark of 29:52.3. His times principally surpassed those of his Finnish distance predecessor, Paavo Nurmi.

Harbig established two world records during 1939. His time of 46 sec. lowered the 400-m. mark, and he added an 800-m. world record with an excellent 1 min. 46.6 sec. Wooderson again had the year's lowest mile, going the distance in 4:07.4 to establish a new British record. He also set a world ¾-mi. record, as did Fenske in the 1,000-yd. run. Both distances, however, were not recognized as standard events.

Of 18 champions 11 were dethroned at the National A.A.U. outdoor tournament of 1939, won by the Olympic club of San Francisco. Outstanding performers included: Clyde Jeffrey of the Olympic club, who ran the 100 m. in 10.2 sec., and J. Gregory Rice, who won the 5,000-m. run in 14 min. 50.9 sec. The New York Athletic club retained its A.A.U. indoor crown, while the University of Southern California scored another double in winning the National

Gunder Haegg of Sweden, phenomenal track star of the decade 1937–46 and holder of world records in the one-mile and two-mile events. He is shown at the two-mile finish in a race at Los Angeles, Calif., in 1943, during which year he broke three U.S. speed records

Gilbert Dodds, Boston divinity student, winning the 1,500-metre run at the National A.A.U. meet in Triborough stadium, New York city, June 20, 1942. His time was 3:50.2

Collegiate and I.C. 4-A championships. Tuskegee institute repeated as women's A.A.U. champion. The I.C. 4-A indoor crown went to Manhattan, and Michigan continued its dominance of the Big Ten. Outstanding college feat of the season was a 55-ft.-10⅜-in. toss of the shot by Elmer Hackney of Kansas State. It was a new intercollegiate record.

In 1940 United States athletes staged their own "American olympics" during the National A.A.U. outdoor championships and celebrated the occasion with one world and four U.S. records, as well as a tie for a world mark. Cornelius Warmerdam featured the tournament with his pole vault of 15 ft. 1⅛ in., a world record.

Fred Wolcott, the Rice institute flier, outdid even Warmerdam in his onslaught on world records. He set a world 220-yd. low hurdle mark of 22.5 sec. and added a 200-m. record of 22.3. In the A.A.U. championships, Wolcott tied the 200-m. hurdle record of 22.6, set by Jesse Owens in 1935. Carl McBain of Los Angeles set a U.S. record in the 400-m. hurdle event at 51.6 sec. Other U.S. marks set in the A.A.U. championships were: 200 m. in 20.4 sec. by Harold Davis of the Olympic club, San Francisco, and 1,500 m. in 3 min. 47.9 sec. by Walter Mehl of Madison, Wis., only ⅒ sec. slower than the world record held by Jack Lovelock of New Zealand. In all, eight national A.A.U. records were surpassed and two were equalled during the 1940 championship meet.

Warmerdam and Wolcott, however, were not alone in the realm of world-record accomplishments. Clyde Jeffrey of the Olympic club, San Francisco, moved in with Frank Wykoff and Jesse Owens as holders of the 100-yd. record of 9.4 sec. He also tied the 100-m. mark of 10.2 sec., but the record was disallowed because of favouring conditions.

The indoor season of 1940 was also eventful. Charles Fenske emerged as the mile-king successor to Glenn Cunningham, winning 8 out of the 9 indoor mile events and recording times of 4 min. 7.4 sec. in the Millrose and New York A.C. games. J. Gregory Rice, the Notre Dame graduate, highlighted the indoor season with two world indoor records. He established new marks of 8 min. 56.2 sec. for the 2 mi. and 13 min. 55.9 sec. in the 3 mi. His 3-mi. record was one of 8 which fell in the 17 events of the national A.A.U. indoor championships.

Two intercollegiate records were broken during the 1940 nationals, Ed Dugger of Tuft going over the 120-yd. high hurdles in 13.9 sec. and Alfred Blozis of Georgetown tossing the shot 52 ft. ½ in. Blozis' mark was also a U.S. record. Southern California again won the National Collegiate championship with 47 points to 28⅔ for Stanford. Pittsburgh won the 64th annual I.C. 4-A, while Michigan again repeated as Big Ten champion, both indoor and out. Southern California narrowly won the Pacific Coast tournament, 55–53 over Stanford.

In 1941, three world records were shattered and three were tied during the U.S. outdoor season. The indoor season brought a quartet of broken records, making 1941 one of the most noteworthy in the history of track.

Cornelius Warmerdam reached 15 ft. 5¾ in. in the pole vault for a new world mark. His fellow Olympic clubman, Les Steers, established a world record with a leap of 6 ft. 11 in. in the high jump. The other world outdoor mark to topple before U.S. onslaught was the 2-mi. relay record, re-established at 7 min. 35.5 sec. by the University of California.

Leslie MacMitchell and J. Gregory Rice moved up with the world-record breakers in the 1941 track spotlight. MacMitchell dominated the feature mile, both indoors and out. He won 5 indoor classics and equalled Glenn Cunningham's and Charles Fenske's competitive indoor mile marks of 4:07.4 in winning the Baxter mile. MacMitchell also dominated the outdoor season, winning the A.A.U., National Collegiate A.A. and I.C. 4-A crowns.

Rice was voted the outstanding athlete of 1941 by New York track writers by virtue of his winning nine straight indoor races. He reduced his world indoor 2-mi. record to 8 min. 51.1 sec. in winning the *Chicago Daily News* 2-mi. test.

Grover Klemmer of the University of California tied the world 440-yd. record of 46.4, held solely by Ben Eastman of Stanford from 1932. Fred Wolcott of Rice institute tied 2 other world records, going over the 120-yd. high hurdles and the 110-m. high hurdles in 13.7 sec. each. Other outstanding performances of the outdoor season included a U.S. record of 174 ft. 8¾ in. in the discus by Archie Harris of New Jersey, and a U.S. native record of 234 ft. 3½ in. in the javelin by Bob Peoples of Southern California.

Rice had company in his record-breaking accomplishments indoors. John Borican set a world 600-yd. indoor record of 1:10.2, while Al Blozis hoisted the indoor shotput standard to 56 ft. 2⅞ in. Joe McCluskey, the New York

Contestants for the national A.A.U. 5,000 metre championship at New York city in June 1943. Gunder Haegg (extreme right) won the title, outrunning U.S. track star Greg Rice (second left) by 35 yards

A.C. veteran, registered a new indoor record of 9:35.4 for the 2-mi. steeplechase.

The Olympic club of San Francisco won its third straight A.A.U. outdoor title in 1941, while New York A.C. repeated as the indoor champion. Southern California continued to dominate the N.C.A.A., while New York university, led by MacMitchell, won the I.C. 4-A. Tuskegee institute repeated as women's A.A.U. champion. Stella Walsh of the Cleveland Polish Olympic team won individual scoring honours with 28 points.

The United States and Sweden dominated track in 1942, the U.S. with the record feats of Warmerdam, Rice and Harold Davis and Sweden with the middle-distance duo of Gunder Haegg and Arne Andersson. Their accomplishments made 1942 one of the most eventful years of the sport.

Warmerdam raised his pole vault ceiling to 15 ft. 7¾ in. outdoors and 15:7¼ indoors and cleared 15 ft. on 16 different occasions during the winter season. Rice easily stood out among the nation's distance runners and wound up with a world record of 13 min. 45.7 sec. in the 3-mi. run. The record-breaking performance marked the 48th straight victory for the former Notre Dame athlete. Harold Davis of the University of California was the other member of U.S.'s Big Three, completely dominating the sprint championships. Davis won the 100- and 220-yd. dashes in the National Collegiate championships and repeated his double with victories in the 100- and 200-m. events in the A.A.U. outdoor meet. He also produced a record-equalling 9.4 sec. in the 100-yd. dash, but the mark was disallowed because of questionable starting blocks. Roy Cochran of Indiana university set a world 440-yd. hurdle record of 52.2 sec.

Just as prodigious were the feats of Haegg and Andersson. Haegg established 7 world records within 74 days and unofficially held all marks ranging from 1,500 m. to 5,000 m. He ran the mile in 4:04.6, which was 1.8 sec. below the recognized world outdoor record of Sydney Wooderson of Great Britain, set in 1937. His other records, some of which lowered the previous world records by as much as 10 sec., included: 1,500 m., 3:48.8; 2,000 m., 5:11.8; 3,000 m. 8:01.2; 2 mi., 8:47.8; 3 mi., 13:32.4; 5,000 m., 13:58.2. Andersson's performances generally were obscured by those of Haegg, although he equalled Wooderson's accepted world record of 4:06.4 for the mile. World War II prevented a move to bring Haegg and Andersson to the United States for the U.S. outdoor season and also forced cancellation of the Pan-American games.

The National A.A.U. outdoor championships of 1942, stripped by World War II of its younger competitors, became largely a meet for repeats. Not only did Davis, Rice and Warmerdam retain titles in their specialties, but Al Blozis won his third straight shotput title, Billy Brown his fourth straight in the broad jump and Boyd Brown his fourth straight in the javelin.

The University of Southern California won its eighth straight N.C.A.A. title and captured its seventh consecutive Pacific coast crown. Ohio State won the western conference outdoor meet, Penn State dominated the east and won both the I.C. 4-A indoor and outdoor championships. New York A.C. won both the indoor and outdoor A.A.U. team titles.

Rice featured the indoor season with his record 3-mi. and also established indoor marks in the 2-, 2¼-, 2½-, 2¾-, mi. events. Gilbert Dodds, a divinity student from Boston, administered the first defeat in 20 races to Leslie MacMitchell in winning the A.A.U. indoor mile. Joe McCluskey won the 10,000- and 15,000-m. runs in the A.A.U. outdoor meet, bringing his senior championships to 23, a new record. After years of trying, John Borican won the A.A.U. outdoor 800-m. championship. Six months later he died of pernicious anaemia.

Stella Walsh wound up a decade of women's track supremacy by winning three events—the 200-m. dash, discus and broad jump, in the annual A.A.U. championship. Tuskegee institute won its sixth straight team title.

In 1943 Warmerdam, Haegg and Andersson were the Big Three of world-wide track. Warmerdam reached a new high of 15 ft. 8½ in. in the last meet of the indoor season at Chicago. Haegg toured the United States and finished with three U.S. records. Andersson remained at home in his native Sweden to lower two of Haegg's world records. He established a mile mark of 4 min. 2.6 sec. and a 1,500 m. record of 3 min. 45 sec.

Haegg did not lose a race during his summer tour of the United States, despite a long sea voyage from Sweden in a tanker. He started his eight-race tour in the two-mile event of the National A.A.U. championships, besting Greg Rice. Twenty days later he set a U.S. 2-mi. mark of 8:53.8 and later he lowered it to 8:51.3. Haegg concentrated on the mile in the last stages of his tour, setting a U.S. record of 4 min. 5.3 sec.

Harold Davis again proved king of the sprinters, once more scoring a double in the 100- and 200-m. events of the A.A.U. outdoor championships. Davis' time of 20.2 sec. in the 200-m. final was 1⁄10 sec. less than the world record of Jesse Owen. However, because of a strong following wind, the mark was not allowed. Bill Cummins of Rice joined with Davis as the two-event winners of the A.A.U. meet, taking both hurdle races. Lieut. Joe McCluskey of the U.S. naval reserve won his 24th A.A.U. senior title in the 3,000-m. steeplechase.

A four-man squad brought the University of Southern California its ninth straight National Intercollegiate track and field title. Michigan won both the outdoor and indoor championships of the Big Ten, while New York university topped the east with team victories in the A.A.U. indoor and I.C. 4-A outdoor tournaments. The mile, classic event of the indoor season, brought an ever-changing stream of victors during the winter season. The final summation found honours almost evenly divided among Frank Dixon of New York university, Gilbert Dodds of the Boston A.A., Earl Mitchell of the University of Indiana and Don Burnham of Dartmouth. Dixon won the National A.A.U. title, but Dodds turned in the season's fastest time of 4:08.5.

Otherwise the indoor season of 1943 was devoted to the consistency of Rice, Warmerdam and Hugh Short of Georgetown. Short tied the world record of 1:10.2 in the 600-m. run and was unbeaten in the middle-distance events before going into the army during mid-season. Herbert Thompson of Jersey City topped the indoor sprinting with a world-record-equalling 6.1 in the 60-yd. dash of the National A.A.U. meet.

Stella Walsh led her Polish Olympic Women's A.C. of Cleveland to the A.A.U. team championship with triumphs in 3 events, 10-m., 200-m. and broad jump. The Cleveland team's victory ended a six-year reign of Tuskegee institute.

The distance duel of Andersson and Haegg continued to hold the interest of track during the war-torn year of 1944. Andersson had the better of the conflicts by registering a new mile record of 4 min. 1.6 sec., cutting a full second from his previous record set the year before. In following his countryman across the line, Haegg also broke the old mark with a time of 4:02. Andersson added a ¾-mi. world mark to his accomplishments, his time of 2:56.6 lowering the previous record of 2:58.7 set in 1940 by Paul Moore of Stanford.

Haegg wasn't without glory during 1944. He twice shattered his world record for the 2-mi. He first lowered it from 8:47.8 to 8:46.4 and again plunged it to 8:42.8. He also out-raced Andersson over the 1,500-m. route, lowering Andersson's old record of 3:45 to 3:43.

Outside Sweden, the years' record-breaking feats were confined to the United States and Finland. Gilbert Dodds established a world indoor record of 4 min. 6.4 sec., while Stella Walsh broke the women's world record for the 220-yd. dash at 24.3 sec. Viljo Heino established the world mark in Finland, knocking more than 17 sec. off the 10,000-m. mark previously held by Taisto Maki. Heino's time was 29:35.2.

The United States track and field schedule, despite the dearth of top-flight performers, was carried on. The New York Athletic club won both the indoor and outdoor A.A.U. championships. Navy humbled favoured Army, 81 points to 35½, in the I.C. 4-A outdoor meet, but the cadets captured the indoor phase of the fixture. Illinois ended Southern California's long reign as champion of the N.C.A.A. but trailed Michigan in both the Big Ten indoor and outdoor tournaments.

Dodds highlighted the indoor season in 1944 with 7 straight mile victories, topped by a record 4:06.4 for the *Chicago Daily News* mile feature. Stella Walsh again took charge of women's track, tying her old 220-yd. record of 24.3 sec. The 33-yr.-old veteran won 3 events in the A.A.U women's championship, but Tuskegee institute still managed to dethrone her Cleveland Polish Olympic team as champion. Alice Coachman of Tuskegee equalled the world record of 6.4 sec. for the 50-yd. dash.

In 1945 dreams of a 4-min. mi. came closer to reality when Haegg traversed the distance in the world-record time of 4 min. 1.4 sec. The new mark developed from his prolonged duel with Andersson and was marred by the professional charges levelled late in the season against the pair.

Aside from the duel of the Swedish stars, there was little to distinguish the track season of 1945. Navy dominated collegiate track, winning both the National Collegiate A.A. and Intercollegiate A.A.A.A. outdoor titles. Navy became the first eastern school to win the N.C.A.A. Army captured the I.C. 4-A indoor title, while Illinois won the western conference outdoor and Michigan the indoor championships. Roland Sink, 19-yr.-old midshipman from Harvard, proved the toast of the outdoor A.A.U. meet with his victory in the 1,500 m. over such veterans as Jim Rafferty and Rudy Simms.

Norwood (Barney) Ewell, winner of the 100-m. dash in 1941, returned to recapture the sprint title in the fine time of 10.3 sec.

The New York Athletic club won both the outdoor and indoor A.A.U. championships in 1945, while Tuskegee repeated as the women's team winner. Rafferty featured the indoor season with a sweep of all nine mile races he entered. Haegg and Hurdler Haakon Lidman arrived belatedly from Sweden to compete in the indoor season, but the Swedish miler failed to reach peak condition and was unable to defeat Rafferty.

In 1946 the continued reign of foreign milers and a world record for the discus throw highlighted the exodus of track athletes from war to tournaments. Although Haegg and Andersson were barred from amateur competition, Lennart Strand carried on the Swedish tradition to dominate U.S. competition.

Bob Fitch of the University of Minnesota registered the outstanding performance of 1946 with a toss of 180 ft. 2¾ in. in the discus, a new world record. He set the new mark in the Northwest A.A.U. meet at Minneapolis, Minn., and later added a toss of 179 ft. ⅛ in. in the national A.A.U. meet at San Antonio, Tex. The former record, set in 1941, was held at 174 ft. 10¾ in. by Adolfo Consolini of Italy.

Strand's invasion of the United States started with his 30-yd. victory over Leslie MacMitchell in the national A.A.U. 1,500-m. run and wound up with a mile in 4 min. 9 sec., fastest of the season.

Collegians generally dominated the U.S. track picture. Not only did Fitch set a world discus record, but Harrison Dillard of Baldwin-Wallace tied the world 220-yd. low

National Track and Field Team Champions, 1937–46

Year	A.A.U. Outdoor	A.A.U. Indoor	National Collegiate	I.C. 4-A Outdoor	A.A.U. Women's
1937	Olympic club	New York A.C.	U.S.C.	Pittsburgh	Tuskegee Inst.
1938	New York A.C.	New York A.C.	U.S.C.	U.S.C.	Tuskegee Inst.
1939	Olympic club	New York A.C.	U.S.C.	U.S.C.	Tuskegee Inst.
1940	Olympic club	New York A.C.	U.S.C.	Pittsburgh	Tuskegee Inst.
1941	Olympic club	New York A.C.	U.S.C.	New York univ.	Tuskegee Inst.
1942	New York A.C.	New York A.C.	U.S.C.	Pa. State coll.	Tuskegee Inst.
1943	U.S.C.	New York univ.	U.S.C.	New York univ.	Cleveland, O., Polish-Olympic A.C.
1944	New York A.C.	New York A.C.	Illinois	Navy	Tuskegee Inst.
1945	New York A.C.	New York A.C.	Navy	Navy	Tuskegee Inst.
1946	New York A.C.	New York A.C.	Illinois	Navy	Tuskegee Inst.

hurdle mark of 22.5 sec. and scored the only double of the national A.A.U. championships. Herbert McKenley of the University of Illinois, a native of Jamaica, was timed in 46.2 sec. in the 440-yd. dash, but his possible world record was disallowed because of a favouring wind. McKenley did set a 300-yd. record of 29.8 sec. in a special meet at Randall Island, N.Y.

Other outstanding performers during 1946 included: Bernie Mayer, New York university, who tossed the 8-lb. shot 71 ft. 7¼ in., a U.S. record; Bill Martineson, Baylor university, who ran the 150-yd. dash in 14.1 sec., equalling the world record and Kenneth Wiesner, Marquette university, who high jumped 6 ft. 6¾ in., setting an intercollegiate record.

The University of Illinois dominated collegiate track, winning the N.C.A.A. and Big Nine championships and capturing three events in the Penn relays. The New York Athletic club won both the A.A.U. outdoor and indoor titles, while army won the I.C. 4-A indoor and navy the I.C. 4-A outdoor titles.

Sydney Wooderson continued to burn up European tracks with a 3-mi. time of 13 min. 53.2 sec., a new British record. Sweden won Europe's first track meet since 1938 Most important international development, however, was the barring for life of Haegg and Andersson by the Swedish Athletic association after Haegg's world mark of 4:01.4 for the mile had been officially accepted.

MacMitchell featured the indoor season with seven straight victories in the mile, including the coveted A.A.U. event. Fred Sickinger, back at Manhattan college after two years in the army, also won 7 races during the 1946 season, 4 1,000-yd. events, 2 ½-mi. and the I.C. 4-A 600-yd. test.

Once again Alice Coachman and her Tuskegee institute team dominated the women's A.A.U. championships. Miss Coachman repeated her triple titles in the 50 m., 100-m. and high jump. Stella Walsh, completing her 20th year of competition, scored two firsts and a second. (M. P. W.)

BIBLIOGRAPHY.—H. M. Abrahams, *Training for Health and Athletics* (1936); G. T. Breshanah, *Track and Field Athletics* (1937); G. M. Butler, *Athletics and Training* (1938); R. M. Conger, *Track and Field* (1939); D. B. Cromwell, *Championship Technique in Track and Field* (1941); *Official Track and Field Guide with the Official Rules* (Barnes, ann.); J. T. Smith, *Track and Field Athletics* (1941); U.S. Office of Naval Operations, *Military Track* (Aviation Training Div.) (1940).

National A.A.U. Senior Men's Outdoor Track Champions

Year	Champion	Affiliation	Time
		100-Metre Run	
1937	Perrin Walker	Unattached, College Park, Ga.	10.7 sec.
1938	Ben Johnson	N.Y. Curb Exchange A.A.	10.7
1939	Clyde Jeffrey	Olympic club, San Francisco	10.2
1940	Harold Davis	Olympic club, San Francisco	10.3
1941	Barney Ewell	Pa. State coll.	10.3
1942	Harold Davis	Olympic club, San Francisco	10.5
1943	Harold Davis	Olympic club, San Francisco	10.3
1944	Claude Young	Univ. of Illinois	10.5
1945	Pvt. Barney Ewell	U.S. army, Camp Kilmer, N.J.	10.3
1946	Bill Mathis	Univ. of Illinois	10.7
		200-Metre Run	
1937	Jack Weiershauser	Olympic club, San Francisco	20.9 sec.
1938	Mack Robinson	Univ. of Oregon	21.3
1939	Barney Ewell	Pa. State coll.	21.0
1940	Harold Davis	Olympic club, San Francisco	20.4
1941	Harold Davis	Olympic club, San Francisco	20.4
1942	Harold Davis	Olympic club, San Francisco	20.9
1943	Harold Davis	Olympic club, San Francisco	20.2
1944	Charles Parker	San Antonio, Tex.	21.3
1945	Elmore Harris	Shore A.C., Asbury Park, N.J.	21.9
1946	Barney Ewell	Shanahan C.C., N.Y.	21.2
		400-Metre Run	
1937	Ray Malott	Olympic club, San Francisco	47.1 sec.
1938	Ray Malott	Olympic club, San Francisco	47.6
1939	Erwin Miller	So. Cal. A.A.	48.3
1940	Grover Klemmer	Olympic club, San Francisco	47.0
1941	Grover Klemmer	Olympic club, San Francisco	46.0
1942	Cliff Bourland	So. Cal. A.A.	46.7
1943	Cliff Bourland	So. Cal. A.A.	47.7
1944	Elmore Harris	Shore A.C., Long Branch, N.J.	48.0
1945	Herbert McKenley	Boston	48.4
1946	Elmore Harris	Shore A.C., Long Branch, N.J.	46.3
		800-Metre Run	
1937	John Woodruff	Univ. of Pittsburgh	1 min. 50 sec.
1938	Howard Borck	69th Regt. A.A., N.Y.	1:51.5
1939	Charles Beetham	69th Regt. A.A., N.Y.	1:51.7
1940	Charles Beetham	Unattached, Columbus, O.	1:51.1
1941	Charles Beetham	Unattached, Columbus, O.	1:50.2
1942	John Borican	Asbury Park A.C., N.Y.	1:51.2
1943	William Hulse	New York A.C.	1:53.4
1944	Robert Kelley	Univ. of Illinois	1:51.8
1945	Robert Kelley	Univ. of Illinois	1:54.1
1946	John Fulton	Olympic club, San Francisco	1:52.7
		1,500-Metre Run	
1937	Glenn Cunningham	N.Y. Curb Exchange A.A.	3 min. 51.8 sec.
1938	Glenn Cunningham	N.Y. Curb Exchange A.A.	3:52.5
1939	Blaine Rideout	Shore A.C., Elberon, N.J.	3:51.5
1940	Walter Mehl	Unattached, Madison, Wis.	3:47.9
1941	Leslie MacMitchell	Ohrbach A.A., N.Y.	3:53.1
1942	Gilbert Dodds	Boston A.A.	3:50.2
1943	Gilbert Dodds	Boston A.A.	3:50.0
1944	William Hulse	New York A.C.	3:54.3
1945	Roland Sink	U.S.N.R., Harvard	3:58.4
1946	Lennart Strand	Sweden	3:54.5
		110-Metre High Hurdles	
1937	Allan Tolmich	Wayne univ., Detroit, Mich.	14.4 sec.
1938	Fred Wolcott	Rice institute, Houston, Tex.	14.3
1939	Joe Batiste	Unattached, Tucson, Ariz.	14.1
1940	Fred Wolcott	Rice institute	13.9
1941	Fred Wolcott	Unattached, Houston, Tex.	13.7
1942	Bill Cummins	Rice institute	14.1
1943	Bill Cummins	Rice institute	14.3
1944	Owen Cassidy	New York A.C.	14.9
1945	Charles Morgan	New Orleans A.C.	14.8
1946	Harrison Dillard	Baldwin-Wallace coll.	14.2
		200-Metre Low Hurdles	
1937	Allan Tolmich	Wayne univ., Detroit, Mich.	23.3 sec.
1938	Fred Wolcott	Rice institute, Houston, Tex.	23.6
1939	Fred Wolcott	Rice institute	22.9
1940	Fred Wolcott	Rice institute	22.6
1941	Fred Wolcott	Unattached, Houston, Tex.	22.8
1942	Bob Wright	Ohio State univ.	23.5
1943	Bill Cummins	Rice institute	22.8
1944	Elmore Harris	Shore A.C., Long Branch, N.J.	24.1
1945	Ronald Frazier	Los Angeles	24.0
1946	Harrison Dillard	Baldwin-Wallace coll.	23.3
		400-Metre Hurdles	
1937	Jack Patterson	Rice institute, Houston, Tex.	52.3 sec.
1938	Jack Patterson	Rice Institute	52.8
1939	Roy V. Cochran	Indiana univ.	51.9
1940	Carl McBain	Unattached, Los Angeles	51.6
1941	Arky Erwin	Louisiana State univ.	54.5
1942	J. Walter Smith	So. Cal. A.A.	52.0
1943	Arky Erwin	New Orleans A.C.	53.1
1944	Arky Erwin	U.S. army, New Orleans	54.0
1945	Arky Erwin	New Orleans A.C.	53.7
1946	Arky Erwin	Hot Springs, Ark.	55.5
		5,000-Metre Run	
1937	Joseph McCluskey	New York A.C.	15 min. 4.1 sec.
1938	J. Gregory Rice	Univ of Notre Dame	15:15
1939	J. Gregory Rice	Univ. of Notre Dame	14:50.9
1940	J. Gregory Rice	South Bend (Ind.) A.A.	14:33.4
1941	J. Gregory Rice	South Bend (Ind.) A.A.	14:45.2
1942	J. Gregory Rice	New York A. C.	14:39.7
1943	Gunder Haegg	Stockholm, Sweden	14:48.5
1944	James Rafferty	New York A.C.	15:22.3
1945	John Kandl	New York A.C.	16:14.4
1946	Francis Martin	New York A.C.	15:50.7
		3,000-Metre Walk	
1937	Max Beutel	92nd St. Y.M.H.A., N.Y.	14:15
1938	Henry Cieman	Achilles club, Toronto, Can.	13:39.9
1939	Otto Kotraba	New York A.C.	14:04.7
1940	Otto Kotraba	New York A.C.	13:53
1941	Joseph Medgyesi	New York A.C.	14:37.9
1942	John Connolly	New York A.C.	14:16.3
1943	James Wilson	Maccabi A.C., N.Y.	14:16.9
1944	Fred Sharaga	92nd St. Y.M.H.A., N.Y.	14:08.5
1945	Sam Bleifer	New York City	14:27.5
1946	Ernest Weber	New York City	15:50.7
		3,000-Metre Steeplechase	
1937	Floyd Lochner	Unattached, St. Louis	9 min. 26.6 sec.
1938	Joseph McCluskey	New York A.C.	9:23.3.
1939	Joseph McCluskey	Unattached, Manchester, Conn.	9:23.1
1940	Joseph McCluskey	New York A.C.	9:16.6
1941	Forest Efaw	Oklahoma A. & M.	9:13.7
1942	George DeGeorge	New York A.C.	9:16.5
1943	Lt. Joseph McCluskey	U.S.N.R., Loudonville, N.Y.	9:39.7
1944	Forest Efaw	U.S.N.T.C., San Diego, Calif.	9:39.6
1945	James Wisner	Baltimore, Md.	10:00.6
1946	James Rafferty	New York A.C.	10:01.0
		10,000-Metre Run	
1937	Eino Pentti	Millrose A.A., N.Y.	32 min. 2 sec.
1938	Eino Pentti	Millrose A.A., N.Y.	32:15.6
1939	Louis Gregory	Millrose A.A., N.Y.	33:11.5
1940	Donald Lash	Indiana state police	32:29.2
1941	Louis Gregory	Millrose A.A., N.Y.	33:11.0
1942	Joseph McCluskey	New York A.C.	32:28.3
1943	Lt. Louis Gregory	U.S. navy Pre-flight school, Iowa	33:22.0
1944	Norman Bright	U.S. army, Presque Isle, Me.	33:53.0
1945	Ted Vogel	Boston A.A.	35:30.7
1946	Edward O'Toole	New York A.C.	32:17.5

National A.A.U. Senior Men's Outdoor Track Champions—Continued

Broad Jump

Year	Champion	Affiliation	Time
1937	Kermit King	Pittsburg (Kan.) Teachers coll.	25 ft. 1½ in.
1938	William Lacefield	U.C.L.A.	25:03/10
1939	William Lacefield	Unattached, Los Angeles	25:5½
1940	William Brown	Louisiana State univ.	25:1⅛
1941	William Brown	Louisiana State univ.	25:4½
1942	William Brown	Norfolk (va.) Naval Training	24:3½
1943	Bil Christopher	Rice institute, Houston, Tex.	24:4⅝
1944	William Lund	Case institute, Cleveland, O.	23:3½
1945	Herbert Douglas	Pittsburgh	24:0⅛
1946	Willie Steele	San Diego State coll.	24:2

High Jump

Year	Champion	Affiliation	Time
1937	David Albritton	Ohio State univ.	6 ft. 8⅝ in.
1938	*Melvin Walker	Unattached, Toledo, O.	6:7
	David Albritton	Ohio State univ.	6:7
1939	Les Steers	Olympic club, San Francisco	6:8⅛
1940	Les Steers	Olympic club, San Francisco	6:8¾
1941	*William Stewart	So. Cal. A.A.	6:9¾
	Les Steers	Olympic club, San Francisco	6:9¾
1942	Adam Berry	Southern univ.	6:7
1943	Pvt. Peter Watkins	U.S. army, Fort Sam Houston, Tex.	6:7¾
1944	*Fred Sheffield	Univ. of Utah	6:7
	Willard Smith	Unattached, San Francisco	6:7
1945	David Albritton	Dayton, O.	6:5¾
	*Joshua Williamson	U.S. army	6:5¾
	Richard Schnacke	Massena, N.Y.	6:5¾
	Leslie Howe	U.S. navy	6:5¾
1946	David Albritton	Dayton, O.	6:6⅞

*Won on either jump-off or fewer misses.

Pole Vault

Year	Champion	Affiliation	Time
1937	William H. Sefton	So. Cal. Sportsmen's Assn.	14 ft. 7⅝ in.
	Cornelius Warmerdam	Olympic club, San Francisco	14:7⅝
	Earle Meadows	So. Cal. Sportsmen's Assn.	14:7⅝
	George Varoff	Olympic club, San Francisco	14:7⅝
1938	Cornelius Warmerdam	Olympic club, San Francisco	14:5½
1939	George Varoff	Olympic club, San Francisco	14:4
1940	Cornelius Warmerdam	Olympic club, San Francisco	15:1⅛
1941	Cornelius Warmerdam	Olympic club, San Francisco	15:0
1942	Cornelius Warmerdam	Olympic club, San Francisco	15:2½
1943	Ens. Cornelius Warmerdam	U.S.N.R., Del Monte, Calif.	15:0
1944	Lt. Cornelius Warmerdam	U.S.N.R., Monmouth, Ill.	15:0
1945	*Albert Morcom	U.S. army	13:6
	Robert Phelps	Univ. of Illinois	13:6
1946	Irving Moore	Olympic club, San Francisco	14:4¾

Discus Throw

Year	Champion	Affiliation	Time
1937	Phil Levy	Olympic club, San Francisco	163 ft. 7⅞ in.
1938	Peter Zagar	Olympic club, San Francisco	167:3¾
1939	Phil Fox	Olympic club, San Francisco	172:4½
1940	Phil Fox	Olympic club, San Francisco	170:4½
1941	Archie Harris	Unattached, New Jersey	167:9½
1942	Bob Fitch	Univ. of Minnesota	166:10
1943	Ens. Hugh S. Cannon	U.S.N.R., Thompkinsville, N.Y.	161:2
1944	Lt. Hugh S. Cannon	U.S.N.R., N.Y.	162:1
1945	Jack Donaldson	Rice institute	151:2
1946	Bob Fitch	Univ. of Minnesota	179:0⅛

Shot Put

Year	Champion	Affiliation	Time
1937	James Reynolds	Olympic club, San Francisco	51 ft. 7⅛ in.
1938	Francis Ryan	New York A.C.	52:1½
1939	Lilburn Williams	Xavier univ., New Orleans, La.	53:7
1940	Alfred Blozis	New York A.C.	55:0⅜
1941	Alfred Blozis	New York A.C.	54:0⅝
1942	Alfred Blozis	New York A.C.	53:8⅜
1943	Earl Audet	Unattached, Los Angeles	52:11⅜
1944	Earl Audet	Pasadena A.C., Calif.	52:8
1945	Wilfred Bangert	Normandy, Mo.	52:10
1946	Wilfred Bangert	Normandy, Mo.	52:2½

16-Pound Hammer Throw

Year	Champion	Affiliation	Time
1937	Irving Folwartshny	Rhode Is. State coll.	173 ft. 7⅝ in.
1938	Irving Folwartshny	Rhode Is. State coll.	179:3
1939	Chester Cruikshank	Unattached, Delta, Colo.	174:1½
1940	Stanley Johnson	Unattached, Brunswick, Me.	182:6 7/16
1941	Irving Folwartshny	New York A.C.	175·6⅛
1942	Chester Cruikshank	U.S. army, Fort Devens, Mass.	173:8½
1943	Henry Dreyer	New York A.C.	164:6¾
1944	Henry Dreyer	New York A.C.	166:6½
1945	Henry Dreyer	New York A.C.	166:11½
1946	Irving Folsworth	New York A.C.	169:8

56-Pound Weight Throw

Year	Champion	Affiliation	Time
1937	Louis Lepis	New York A.C.	33 ft. 7¼ in.
1938	Louis Lepis	New York A.C.	35:1½
1939	Stanley Johnson	Univ. of Maine	34:6⅞
1940	Henry Dreyer	New York A.C.	35:6
1941	Frank J. Berst	New York A.C.	35:4⅞
1942	Frank J. Berst	New York A.C.	39:3½
1943	Frank J. Berst	New York A.C.	35:2
1944	Frank J. Berst	New York A.C.	38:4¼
1945	Henry Dreyer	New York A.C.	35:2
1946	Frank J. Berst	New York A.C.	35:3⅛

Javelin Throw

Year	Champion	Affiliation	Time
1937	William Reitz	So. Cal. Sportsmen's Assn.	224 ft. 9⅜ in.
1938	Nick Vukmanic	Pa. State coll.	218:7¾
1939	Boyd Brown	Olympic club, San Francisco	215:10¾
1940	Boyd Brown	Olympic club, San Francisco	223:1⅜
1941	Boyd Brown	Olympic club, San Francisco	218:3
1942	Boyd Brown	Olympic club, San Francisco	216:7½
1943	Martin Biles	Olympic club, San Francisco	202:5
1944	Capt. Martin Biles	U.S. army, Ark.	211:0
1945	Earl Marshall	Carlsbad, N.M.	215:4
1946	Garland Adair	Austin (Tex.) A.C.	213:7

Hop, Step and Jump

Year	Champion	Affiliation	Time
1937	William Brown	Baker, La., H.S.	49 ft. 7¼ in.
1938	Herschel Neil	Maryville, Mo., Chamber of Commerce	48:5.9
1939	Herschel Neil	Maryville, Mo., Chamber of Commerce	47.9⅞
1940	William Brown	Louisiana St. univ.	50:2⅝
1941	William Brown	Louisiana St. univ.	50·11½
1942	William Brown	Norfolk (Va.) Naval Training	48·11½
1943	Ens. William Brown	U.S.N.R., Bainbridge, Md.	45·8
1944	Don Barksdale	U S. army	47:2⅞
1945	Burton Cox	Villanova coll., Villanova, Pa.	45·10⅛
1946	Ralph Tate	Oklahoma A. & M.	47:11¼

National Decathlon, Pentathlon Champions, 1937–46

Year	Decathlon	Pentathlon
1937 . . .	Not Held	Eulace Peacock
1938 . . .	Joseph Scott	John Borican
1939 . . .	Joseph Scott	John Borican
1940 . . .	William Watson	Harry March
1941 . . .	John Borican	John Borican
1942 . . .	William Terwilliger	Not Held
1943 . . .	William Watson	Eulace Peacock
1944 . . .	Irving Mondschein	Irving Mondschein
1945 . . .	Charles Beaudry	Eulace Peacock
1946 . . .	Irving Mondschein	Charles Beaudry

Trackless Trolleys

See Electric Transportation.

Tractors

See Agriculture.

Trade Agreements

See International Trade.

Trade Commission, Federal

See Federal Trade Commission.

Trade Marks

See Law.

Trade Unions

See Labour Unions.

Traffic Accidents

See Accidents.

Transbay Bridge

See Bridges.

Trans-Jordan

Trans-Jordan, an Arab nation to the east of Palestine, was formerly part of the Turkish empire. After World War I it was a British mandated territory until 1946. During that period it was under the supervision of the British high commissioner for Palestine and Trans-Jordan. It became an independent state in 1946. King: Abdullah Ibn Hussein, emir of Trans-Jordan since 1922. Area: 34,740 sq.mi.; pop. *c.* 350,000, all Arab-speaking and, with the exception of about 30,000 native Christians, Mohammedans. Capital: Amman (25,000); other cities: Es-Salt, Maan.

The relations between Great Britain and Trans-Jordan were governed by the treaty of Feb. 20, 1928. Internally Trans-Jordan was ruled according to the constitution promulgated in Amman on April 16, 1928. The development of the country with its seminomadic population had been slow, but steady progress was made after 1925 in the fields of education, public health and agriculture.

In May 1939 the British government agreed to expand the autonomy of Trans-Jordan. The constitution of the country was liberalized. In the first years of World War II, when German and Italian forces threatened to overrun the middle east, Trans-Jordan gained in importance for the

King Abdullah Ibn Hussein of Trans-Jordan who received his royal title on May 25, 1946. He is shown at the palace entrance in Amman

maintenance of the military security and stability of the middle east. When in 1941 a pro-German government rose to power through a military coup in the neighbouring Arab kingdom of Iraq, the emir of Trans-Jordan not only kept the Arab tribes loyal to their alliance with Great Britain, but also made Trans-Jordan the base for the advance of a small British force into Iraq which succeeded in re-installing the legal regent of Iraq who had taken refuge in Trans-Jordan. In reward for this important help to the cause of Britain and its allies, the country was promised independence after the conclusion of the war. The people of Trans-Jordan took a lively interest in the cause of "Arab Palestine." Emir Abdullah cabled on March 3, 1944, a sharp protest to President Franklin D. Roosevelt against the pending senate resolution of support for a Jewish Palestine. Trans-Jordan participated in the conference of Arab states in Cairo, Egypt, in the fall of 1944 to protect "Arab Palestine" and to discuss closer collaboration among the Arab states. When the Arab league began to function in 1945, as the international representation of the Arab states, Trans-Jordan was one of its seven members. The prime minister of Trans-Jordan took an active part in the affairs of the league and in the defense of Arab rights in Palestine.

On March 22, 1946, Great Britain and Trans-Jordan signed a treaty of mutual assistance and alliance. The treaty put an end to the British mandate and recognized Trans-Jordan as an independent sovereign state. In order to make the alliance effective, Trans-Jordan was to provide lines of communication through the country for Britain, which could station armed forces there. Should either party become involved in hostilities as the result of attack by a third party, the other party would immediately come to its aid. Costs incurred by Trans-Jordan in fulfilment of this treaty provision were to be borne by Britain. On May 25, 1946, Emir Abdullah assumed the title of king of Trans-Jordan and in a brief ceremony of enthronement called upon the Arab world to unite into a federation.

Bibliography.—Kenneth Williams, "Trans-Jordan's Future," *Spectator* (London, March 29, 1946). (H. Ko.)

Trans-Jordan: *Statistical Data*

Item	1938		1941		1944	
	Value (000's omitted)	Amount or Number	Value (000's omitted)	Amount or Number	Value (000's omitted)	Amount or Number
Exchange Rate		£Palestine 1 =£1 ($4,889)		£P1 =£1($4.032)		£P1 =£1($4.035)
Finance						
Government revenues	£459 ($2,245)		£514 ($1,969)*		£2,858 ($11,518)†	
Government expenditures	£463 ($2,262)		£510 ($1,954)*		£2,581 ($10,401)†	
National debt	£220 ($1,078)		...		£310 ($1,251)†	
Transportation						
Railroads		197 mi.				202 mi.†
Highways		1,220 mi.				1,220 mi.†
Communication						
Telephones						1,354‡
Telegraph lines						305 mi.‡
Radio Sets						900‡
Minerals§						
Kaolin				489 tons		2,428 tons
Ochre				470 "		63 "
Manganese				28 "		33 "
Crops						
Wheat		92,593 tons				121,253 tons
Barley		49,604 "				44,092 "
Grapes and raisins		22,046 "				23,148 "
Livestock						
Poultry		552,000				560,000
Sheep		240,673				304,107
Goats		234,138				349,323
Forest Products						
Charcoal						2,631 tons†
Firewood						3,232 " †
Plow Pieces						10 " †
Exports—Total	£472 ($2,310)	...			£774 ($3,124)‖	...
Wheat	£324 ($1,585)	35,956 tons			£231 ($931)‖	6,976 tons‖
Sheep	£25 ($122)	28,602			£53 ($212)‖	26,677‖
Fruit	£23 ($114)	6,199 tons			£118 ($476)‖	4,980 tons‖
Barley	£20 ($100)	4,426 "			£56 ($224)‖	2,980 ‖
Imports—Total	£1,306 ($6,386)	...			£2,199 ($8,874)‖	...
Cotton cloth	£130 ($637)	...			£165 ($666)‖	...
Artificial silk cloth	£50 ($244)	...			£119 ($481)‖	...
Sugar	£47 ($230)	...			£207 ($835)‖	...
Education						
Government elementary schools		70				
Students		7,408				

*1940. †1945. ‡1946. §Exclusive of products of the Dead Sea. ‖1942.

Transportation

See Aviation, Civil; Business Review; Electric Transportation; Interstate Commerce Commission, Logistics of World War II; Motor Transportation; Railroads; Shipping, Merchant Marine; War and Defense Agencies.

Transvaal

See South Africa, The Union of.

Transylvania

See Hungary; Rumania.

Trap-shooting

The Grand American handicap, world series of the trap-shooting sport, extended to 47 yr. its tradition of never crowning a champion more than once. Ten different shooters wore the crown from 1937 to 1946 during the annual August shoot at Vandalia, O.

World War II made its inroads on the Grand American championships, cutting it from 950 to 500 targets starting in 1943, but the classic was back to peacetime status in 1946. A field of 1,487 competed in the 1946 championships, firing 1,317,500 shells. Prior to World War II it was estimated that there were approximately 1,000,000 shooters in the United States who spent an average of $50 annually for shells and accessories, not including guns.

Joe Hiestand of Hillsboro, O., proved the standout individual of the decade with two noteworthy feats. In 1938 he broke 966 consecutive targets from 16 yd. for a world record. In 1944 Hiestand became the first shooter in tournament history to win a major event four times when he annexed the North American clay target championship.

In 1937 Franklin G. Carroll of Brecksville, O., outshot a field of more than 1,200 shooters to win the Grand American handicap. Shooting at 19 yd., Carroll broke all 100 targets, leaving 11 shooters tied for second with 99 out of 100. He was the third winner to break a possible 100 targets in the 38-yr. history of the Grand American. Phil Miller of French Lick, Ind., captured the North American Clay Target title with 275 out of 275, while Hal Jones of Wood River, Ill., continued the high-grade shooting by winning the champion of champions with 125 out of 125. Lela Hall of Strasburg, Mo., was crowned women's titlist, 194 out of 200. Walter Beaver of Conshohocken, Pa., won the national amateur with 198 out of 200.

O. W. "Ted" West, Coshocton, O., highway engineer, won the Grand American in 1938 with a 99 out of 100 and a 23 out of 25 in the shoot-off. The North American handicap went to Joe Hiestand of Hillsboro, O., 200 out of 200, who broke 966 consecutive targets from 16 yd. to set a world record. M. Hootman of Hicksville, O., was crowned champion of champions, 221 out of 225, while Mrs. Ryba Peters of Springfield, O., won the Grand American women's handicap with 93 out of 100. Walter Beaver of Conshohocken, Pa., repeated as national amateur champion, 99 out of 100.

In 1939 Dwight L. Ritchie, a left-handed marksman from Goshen, O., won the Grand American handicap with 99 out of 100 and 22 out of 25 in a shoot-off with G. A. Wagner of Dayton, O. P. O. Harbage of West Jefferson, O., scored a perfect 200 out of 200 to win the North American handicap, while W. A. Peterson of Lynn, Mass., won the champion of champions, 100 out of 100. Mrs. Roy Meadows of Des Moines, Ia., won the women's Grand American with 94 out of 100.

E. H. Wolfe of Charleston, W.Va., breaking 98 out of 100 birds from the 23-yd. mark, won the Grand American handicap title in 1940. Forest W. McNeir of Houston, Tex., topped the North American Clay Target field with 200 out of 200 and Sam H. Sharman of Salt Lake City, Utah, won the champion of champions crown with 99 out of 100. Mrs. Lela Hall of Strasburg, Mo., won the women's grand handicap, 95 out of 100.

In 1941 Walter L. Tulbert of Detroit, Mich., won the Grand American handicap in a shoot-off after breaking 99 out of 100 birds in the regular test. Miss W. M. Hill of Kansas City, Mo., won the women's Grand American with 96 out of 100. Walter S. Beaver of Conshohocken, Pa., was the year's leading over-all shooter, winning the class AA crown in the national amateur singles and the Class A title in the doubles, as well as the eastern states singles and doubles.

Illinois marksmen dominated 1942, topped by the victory of James F. Holderman, 32-yr. old farmer from Morris, Ill., in the Grand American handicap. Tied at 193 out of 200 with Arthur Finney of Mankato, Minn., Holderman won in a shoot-off with a possible 25 to Finney's 23. William Drennan of Utica, Ill., won the North American title, while Joe Moore of Kewanee, Ill., was crowned champion of champions. Carolyn Elliott, 19-yr. old Vanderbilt university coed, won the women's Grand American handicap at 183 out of 200.

In 1943 the state of Ohio won its 13th Grand American handicap in the 44-yr. history of the event when Jasper Rogers, 35-yr. old Dayton toolmaker, survived a six-way shoot-off after scoring 97 out of 100 in the regular test. L. E. Smith of Peru, Ind., won the champion of champions title, 99 out of 100, while Orla Booher of Farmland, Ind., won the North American with 200 out of 200. Skipper Winski, 17-yr. old girl from Wellsburg, W.Va., won both the women's Grand American and preliminary handicaps.

Leslie C. Jepsen of Dwight, Ill., won the 1944 Grand American with 97 out of 100 while firing with a borrowed gun. Joe Hiestand of Hillsboro, O., scored 200 straight to win the North American title, and Mrs. Van Marker of Evanston, Ill., won the women's Grand American, 90 out of 100. John Peterson of Racine, Wis., 98 out of 100, captured the champion of champions.

Don Englebry, a Vermilion, O., restaurant owner, broke 99 out of 100 targets to win the Grand American in 1945. Otherwise, principal honours went to Rudy Etchen, 22-yr. old gunnery specialist from the U.S. navy and Memphis, Tenn., who won three titles, the over-all with 474 out of a possible 500, the all-around with 381 out of 400 and the doubles, 96 out of 100. Mrs. Van Marker, repeated as Grand American women's titlist, 94 out of 100, while E. T. Pugh of Morris, Ill., won the North American, 199 out of 200, and Lt. Vic Reinder of Waukesha, Wis., captured the champion of champions title.

In 1946 Capt. Frank Bennett, an aeroplane pilot with 9,400 hr. of flying time, won the Grand American handicap in a three-way shoot-off after finishing with 98 out of 100. Walter Beaver of Conshohocken, Pa., won the North American event with 199 out of 200 and 25 out of 25 in the shoot-off. Mrs. Roy Meadows of Grimes, Ia., won the women's Grand American, 94 out of 100. Reinder, now a University of Wisconsin biology professor, won the men's champion of champions title, 100 out of 100, and the open title, 99 out of 100. (M. P. W.)

Bibliography.—B. Nichols, *Skeet and How to Shoot It* (1939); J. M. Robinson, *Hits and Misses of the Trapshooting and Skeet World* (1942); Sporting Arms and Ammunition Manufacturers' Institute, *Handbook on Shotgun Shooting* (1940); U.S. Bureau

Above: U.S. tankmen patrolling the troubled city of Trieste during the summer of 1946

Left: Newsstand in a workers' district of Trieste where pro-soviet sentiment could be seen in the prominent displays of poster-portraits of Stalin and Lenin

Below: Tear gas released by U.S. military police to break up a street demonstration in Trieste, where months of sporadic rioting followed the Big Four's decision to internationalize the city, as announced at Paris on July 2, 1946

of Aeronautics, *Syllabus and Instruction for Primary Gunnery Training* (Training Division) (1942). Periodical: *American Rifleman.*

Treason

See Federal Bureau of Investigation.

Treasury, U. S. Department of

See Government Departments and Bureaus.

Treaties

See International Law.

"Trident" Conference (Washington, 1943)

See International Conferences, Allied (World War II).

Trieste

Trieste is a city and port on the northeastern Adriatic (pop. 248,379 in 1936) and the chief city of the Italian province of Venezia Giulia e Zara (area 3,456 sq.mi.; pop. 977,257). This territory had formed part of Austria (Trieste from 1382) before World War I. It was then called Küstenland. It had an area of 3,084 sq.mi. with a pop. (1900) of 755,183. It consisted of three divisions, the margraviate of Istria (pop. 344,173, of whom one-third were Italian), the county of Gorizia and Gradiska (pop. 232,338, of whom one-third were Italian) and the city of Trieste. After World War I the territory was claimed by Yugoslavia and by Italy. The Italian population was preponderant in the cities; the Yugoslav population, Slovene and Croat, in the rural districts. According to the census of 1910 there were 387,000 Italians and 435,000 Slavs, almost all Roman Catholics.

The disposition of the territory played a major role at the peace conference of 1919. It was closely connected with the question of Fiume and Dalmatia. The control of the territory was settled by the treaty of Rapallo of Nov. 12, 1920, between Italy and Yugoslavia, which gave the territory to Italy. The Italian government subjected the Slav majority to rigorous measures of Italianization. Thus the racial animosities in the territory became even more bitter.

The collapse of the German armies in April 1945 brought Marshal Tito's Yugoslav forces into the occupation of the territory; Tito declared his determination to incorporate it into Yugoslavia. Italy was united in an equally determined protest against the annexation of Venezia Giulia and especially of Trieste by the Yugoslavs. The Allied armies wished to have the question settled by the peace conference and to avoid any one-sided settlement by force. The acting U.S. secretary of state, Joseph C. Grew, declared on May 12, 1945, that "it is the firm policy of the United States that territorial changes should be made only after thorough study and after full consultation and deliberation between the various governments concerned." As northeastern Italy was an Anglo-U.S. theatre of operations, an Allied military administration was established and the Yugoslav forces were prevailed upon to relinquish at least the smaller and predominantly Italian part of the territory to Allied administration until final settlement of the dispute. In an agreement concluded on June 9, 1945, the cities of Trieste, Gorizia and Pola and the territory connecting them were placed under Allied administration while the much larger part of the province east of that line was put under Yugoslavia without prejudice of the ultimate disposal of that area.

Zara in Dalmatia and Fiume came under Yugoslav administration.

In 1946 the Paris peace conference decided that the largest part of Venezia Giulia should be given to Yugoslavia, including the purely Italian cities of western Istria and the famous naval base of Pola. On the other hand, the city of Trieste and its immediate neighbourhood was to become a free state under United Nations supervision. Trieste was to establish a free port for the use of all the hinterland.

Bibliography.—A. J. P. Taylor, *Trieste* (Yugoslav Information Office, London, 1945); René Albrecht-Carrié, "The Northeastern Frontier of Italy," *Journal of Central European Affairs* (Oct. 1945); Gaetano Salvemini, "The Frontiers of Italy," *Foreign Affairs* (Oct. 1944); Isabella Massey, "Venezia Giulia," *Free Italy* (Nov. 1945). (H. Ko.)

Trinidad

See West Indies, British.

Tripartite Conference, Berlin

See International Conferences, Allied (World War II).

Tripoli

See Abrasives.

Trolley Coaches

See Electric Transportation.

Trotsky, Leon

Trotsky (1879–1940) also bore the first and middle names Lev Davidovitch; his real name was Bronstein. One of the great revolutionary leaders of his era, he was born near Elizavetgrad, Russia, the son of a middle class Jewish family, and was educated at the University of Odessa. Entering revolutionary politics at a youthful age, he was arrested in 1898 and deported to Siberia; he escaped four years later and went to England, where he became associated with Nicolai Lenin. In 1905 he returned to Russia but was soon arrested again, along with the entire St. Petersburg soviet, of which he had become a member. Once more he was successful in escaping from his Siberian exile, however, and he spent the next few years in Vienna, Constantinople, Zurich and Paris. He was expelled from France in 1916 and proceeded to the United States, where for a short while he edited a revolutionary paper, *Novy Mir* (New World). Meanwhile, the Russian revolution had broken out (March 1917), and he left for his native country. After a brief internment by the British at Halifax, he arrived at Petrograd shortly after Lenin.

For the next six years Trotsky's name was linked inseparably with that of Lenin as communist revolution leader. He organized the Red army and rebuilt the shattered Russian transportation system; he was equally brilliant as a writer and orator. After Lenin's death in 1924, it seemed natural that Trotsky would inherit the mantle of power. Actually, however, considerable opposition to him had developed within the Communist party. He was attacked by Joseph Stalin and Grigory Zinoviev in particular, and soon lost his post as commissar of war. Stalin gradually assumed power, and in Nov. 1927 Trotsky was expelled from the party; in 1928 he was banished from the country and later went to Constantinople. In 1936 he moved to Norway and the following year to Mexico, where he continued to denounce Stalin's regime as a "betrayal of the Revolution," as "undemocratic" and "nationalist-Bonapartist."

On Aug. 20, 1940, he was fatally attacked in his suburban home near Mexico City by a man whom he described, before his death the following day, as an agent of the Russian O.G.P.U. The assassin gave his name as Frank Jackson but was later identified as Jacques M. van den Dreschd.

Trotting Races

See Horse Racing.

Trucial Sheikdoms

See Arabia.

Truck Crops

See Vegetables.

Trucks

See Automobile Industry; Motor Transportation.

Truman, Harry S.

Truman (1884–), 33rd president of the United States, succeeded Franklin Delano Roosevelt upon the latter's death April 12, 1945; he had been vice-president for only three months.

He was born in Lamar, Mo., and educated in public schools. After service overseas in World War I as a lieutenant and captain of field artillery, and a brief business career, he rose rapidly in politics. Under the sponsorship of the Pendergast political organization in Kansas City, Truman became judge of the Jackson county court in 1922. In 1926 he was made presiding judge, a position he held until 1934, when he was elected to the United States senate as a Democrat. His first term was unspectacular, but he won the confidence and respect of his colleagues and revealed talent as an investigator when the Interstate Commerce committee, of which he was a member, conducted a special railroad inquiry.

After re-election to the senate in 1940, Truman offered a resolution calling for a special senate committee to investigate the national defense program. The resolution was approved in Feb. 1941 and Truman became chairman of the committee. It quickly achieved fame as it made careful investigations of the conduct of the defense and war programs. Under Truman's chairmanship no minority reports were ever written. Republicans and Democrats worked well together under his leadership. There was never any charge of partisanship made against the committee, nor any serious criticism of its methods. The committee itself was sharply critical at times of many in industry, the armed services and the civilian war agencies. The White House did not escape criticism; but the committee held the respect of the senate and the country.

As a senator, Truman's main efforts were devoted to the committee which bore his name. He seldom took a major part in floor debates or in legislative fights. He was quiet and retiring except in the work of his investigating committee. He voted for all the major foreign and domestic legislation requested by the administration, but was regarded as more middle-of-the-road than some of the more ardent Roosevelt supporters.

Early in 1944, when Democratic politicians were seeking a running mate for President Roosevelt in his fourth campaign for the presidency, Truman's name was occasionally mentioned. It was not prominently mentioned until a short time before the Democratic national convention met in July in Chicago, Ill. Conservative members of the party had persuaded the president that Henry A. Wallace, then vice-president, should not be renominated. When the convention met, Roosevelt expressed first choice for Wallace but said he would be happy to run with Truman or Justice William O. Douglas of the supreme court. The campaign for Truman had been conducted by Robert E. Hannegan of Missouri, chairman of the Democratic national committee.

President Truman delivering an Army day address at Soldier field, Chicago, on April 6, 1946. Broadcast throughout the world, his speech emphasized the need for U.S. preparedness as a safeguard for world peace

After a bitter convention fight, Truman was nominated for the vice-presidency on the second ballot. He was elected vice-president on Nov. 7, 1944, and took office Jan. 20, 1945, as the third vice-president to serve with Roosevelt.

Upon being sworn in as president in the cabinet room at the White House shortly after notification of Roosevelt's death, Truman pledged himself to carry out the policies of the late president. His first few weeks in the White House were crowded with history. He promptly announced that the San Francisco conference to draft the charter of the United Nations would open as scheduled on April 25. He urged the conference delegates to establish an organization that would "maintain peace and redeem the terrible sacrifice of the war."

The war in Europe was rapidly drawing to a close when Truman became president. On May 8, Truman announced the unconditional surrender of Germany. There was satisfaction throughout the country with the manner in which the new president handled the surrender. He continued to enjoy great popularity throughout the summer.

In July 1945 he sailed for Europe to hold his first meeting with Joseph Stalin and Winston Churchill. At Potsdam, Germany, the three leaders agreed on the control of Germany and final decisions were reached on the prosecution of the Japanese war. On Aug. 6, while on his way home, the president announced that the first atomic bomb had been dropped on Hiroshima, Japan.

On Aug. 11, he announced that the U.S.S.R. had declared war on Japan.

At 7 P.M. on Aug. 14, Truman announced that Japan, too, had surrendered unconditionally and that World War II had been won.

Shortly thereafter, Truman turned his attention to domestic problems, and his troubles began. In a long message to congress in Sept. 1945 he set forth a detailed legislative program. It was hailed as a liberal program, and brought forth cries of protest from anti-New Dealers. The fight with congress, dominated by Republicans and conservative Democrats, was just beginning. When congress recessed in December with none of the president's major demands acted upon, he took the fight to the people in a caustic radio report on congressional inactivity. But he began losing support also of progressive and labour groups, which complained that he did not fight hard enough for his legislative program. His reorganized cabinet, decidedly more conservative than the Roosevelt cabinet, was the target of criticism.

While battling his first round with congress, the Council of Foreign Ministers, which was created at the Potsdam conference, met in London and ended in failure. Relations with the soviet union had deteriorated. In Dec. 1945, therefore, Secretary of State James Byrnes flew to Moscow for extended conferences with Foreign Minister Vyacheslav Molotov and Generalissimo Stalin. A decision was reached to sponsor the establishment in the United Nations of an atomic energy commission. The problem had been carefully discussed in a White House meeting between the president, Prime Minister Clement Attlee of Great Britain and Prime Minister Mackenzie King of Canada.

Labour troubles gave the president his biggest headache early in 1946. Strikes in several basic industries, including steel and coal, brought White House intervention. Neither labour nor capital was pleased, and politicians were critical of the president. He replied that he had asked congress for long-range labour legislation, but had got nothing. At the height of the industrial conflict, the bitter fight against the nomination of Edwin W. Pauley to be undersecretary of the navy was waged in the Senate Naval Affairs committee. Amid criticisms of his chief advisers, the president withdrew the nomination on March 13, 1946.

The railroad strike in May 1946 angered the harassed president, who asked congress in a special message on May 25 for power to draft strikers against the government into the army. After 40 minutes' debate, the house passed the emergency bill.

The senate amended it substantially, but when Truman vetoed the Case strike-control bill the emergency bill was allowed to die.

A bitter fight then developed over extension of price controls. When congress passed a bill which the White House called inflationary, Truman vetoed it and demanded a stronger one. For three weeks in July 1946 the country was without price controls, and prices began to rise. Before the end of the month a new bill, which the president termed better than the one he vetoed, was passed and signed. With the spectre of inflation hanging over the country, price control became the basic issue of the 1946 congressional campaigns and the Democrats lost heavily. (*See* ELECTIONS; UNITED STATES.)

BIBLIOGRAPHY.—Frank McNaughton and Walter Hehmeyer, *This Man Truman* (1945); "Addresses and Statements of Harry S. Truman, 1935–45," *United States News* (1945). (C. KK.)

Truscott, Lucian King, Jr.

Truscott (1895–), U.S. army officer, was born Jan. 9, 1895, in Chatfield, Tex., the son of a country doctor. After finishing high school, he taught in rural Oklahoma schools. He joined the U.S. army in 1917, and retained his commission after the armistice. He studied at the Command and General Staff school, instructed at Fort Riley and was a lieutenant colonel at the time of the Pearl Harbor attack in Dec. 1941. In May 1942 he was sent to England and was attached to Adm. Mountbatten's combined operations staff. In the North African campaign Truscott led a special task force that captured Port Lyautey in the initial phases of the invasion, Nov. 1942. During the final operations in Tunisia, Truscott, then a major general, became commander of the 3rd U.S. division. The 3rd took part in the Sicilian invasion, July 1943, and fought in the Italian campaign. In March 1944 he was appointed commander of the 6th U.S. army corps and in August of the same year, he led the 6th corps in the landings in southern France.

Truscott, who was made a lieutenant general (temporary rank) in Sept. 1944 returned to Italy the following December to assume command of the Allied 5th army.

After the war, Truscott replaced Gen. Patton in Oct. 1945 as commander of the 3rd U.S. army and of the eastern military district of the U.S. occupation zone of Germany. On May 16, 1946, Truscott, in ill health, gave over command of the 3rd army to Lt. Gen. Geoffrey Keyes.

Trusteeship, Territorial

See MANDATES; UNITED NATIONS.

Tsaldaris, Constantin

Tsaldaris (1884–), Greek politician, was born in Alexandria, Egypt, in 1884. He was graduated from the University of Athens law school and later studied law and political science in France, England and Germany. On returning to Greece, he practised law for a brief period and then entered the government as minister in Crete (1920–22). A royalist by conviction, he was imprisoned in 1926 for plotting against the republic, but served only seven months of a three-year sentence. Elected to the Greek parliament in 1932, he was re-elected in 1933 and 1935. He held two undersecretaryships in the cabinet between 1934 and 1936.

Tsaldaris remained in Greece for a short time during the German occupation, but later fled to Egypt. Toward the end of World War II, he became one of the leaders of the Populist party and took a strong pro-royalist stand. He held five ministries in the short-lived Poulitsas cabinet and himself formed a cabinet (April 18, 1946), after Poulitsas resigned.

In foreign policy, Tsaldaris was committed to co-operation with the western Allies. While the Council of Foreign Ministers agreed in 1946 to return the Dodecanese to Greece, Tsaldaris' claims to Northern Epirus, corrections of the Bulgar frontier and reparations from Italy were rejected.

At home, Tsaldaris faced revolt and on Nov. 4, 1946, he broadened his government to include opposition members; in the new cabinet Populists held only 6 of the 30 portfolios.

Tsaritsyn

See STALINGRAD.

Tuberculosis

Since the beginning of the 20th century, no significant new instrument or test had been devised to diagnose tuberculosis. The period 1937–46, however, witnessed the culmination of exceedingly important demonstrations in tuberculosis control. During this ten-year period, tuberculosis was driven to its lowest level of incidence in some areas, while in other parts of the world it reached heights that had rarely been exceeded. In the world as a whole, tuberculosis continued to be the first cause of disability and death with one exceptional year, when it was superseded by malaria.

Organizations.—The National Tuberculosis association, with its some 2,900 component societies, conducted excellent educational work through numerous pamphlets, books, movie films, medical and lay journals. The Christmas Seal sale reached its peak in 1945, with a gross income of $15,638,755.37, in contrast to income of $135,000 in 1908, and $4,985,696 in 1937. The American Sanatorium association, organized in 1905, was reorganized and named the American Trudeau society in 1939; this became the medical section of the National Tuberculosis association. In 1946, 33 other nations had tuberculosis associations.

The American College of Chest Physicians, a strictly medical organization, was organized in 1934 and by 1946 was international in its scope, with members in 34 nations. Other national organizations had active committees on tuberculosis, such as the American Academy of Pediatrics, the American Student Health association, the American School Health association, the American Public Health association and the American Nurse association.

The 78th U.S. congress in July 1944 authorized the sum of $10,000,000 for the fiscal year ending June 30, 1945, and for each fiscal year thereafter a sum sufficient to carry out the tuberculosis control program of the U.S. public health service. Approximately $125,000,000 was spent on tuberculosis annually in the U.S. including funds derived from the seal sale, the public health service appropriation, the cost of operating sanatoriums, etc.

Diagnosis.—The tuberculin test continued to be extensively used as a delicate and accurate means of detecting the presence of living tubercle bacilli in the animal or human body. Its value was greatly enhanced during the decade because of the rapidly decreasing number of reactors. Tubercle bacilli may all die in the human body, after which reactors to tuberculin become nonreactors. No one knew the frequency of occurrence. However, in 1940 A. W. Dahlstrom reported that among 2,490 reactors 11.1% were later found to be nonreactors.

Old tuberculin properly prepared and PPD (purified protein derivative) were found of equal value as testing substances.

In 1937 H. Vollmer revived and modified the method of administration introduced by R. Lautier in 1908 and designated it the tuberculin patch test. Although this method of administration was extensively used after 1937, the following objections were offered: it is time-consuming to apply and requires more visits than other methods; some persons are sensitive to adhesive tape; with excessive perspiration the adhesive falls off; children often remove the tape soon after it is applied.

The intracutaneous method of administration devised by C. Mantoux continued to be universally used in testing animals and remained the standard method for testing humans. The time of reading tuberculin tests was extended from 48 to 72 hours by many physicians because "false reactions" have then disappeared and true reactions always persist even longer.

The tuberculin test found its greatest usefulness, first, in screening from any group all persons or animals with living germs of tuberculosis in their bodies and, second, as an indication for seeking the source of the infection of the reactor among his adult associates.

The use of the X-ray increased greatly during the decade because inspection of the chest by this method often detects location of areas of disease before they can be found by the conventional examination. However, during the last five years of the decade the previous overenthusiasm for the X-ray was considerably dampened by failures which resulted from its limitations. For example, not more than 25% of the persons rejected for military service in World War II largely because tuberculosis was said to be evident on X-ray film actually had this disease in significant form. Moreover, approximately two-thirds of the persons who were discharged from military service early in the war because of tuberculosis, had shadows on their induction films which were overlooked or were not considered significant. Similar errors occurred in many other places under different circumstances, largely because of the following limitations of X-ray: the shadows cast by areas of tuberculosis did not differ from those produced by other diseases of the lungs; only 75% of the lungs was visualized by the usual X-ray inspection; areas of disease had to be large enough to be seen by the unaided eye before they cast visible shadows.

Despite these limitations, X-ray inspection usually continued to supersede all other phases of the examination in determining location and extent of disease in the lungs. Once areas of disease are located, other phases of the examination are available to determine whether they are tuberculous. Thus, during the decade, X-ray was relegated to its proper place in the diagnostic armamentarium.

X-ray techniques were modified considerably. In 1937 there was available the usual 14x17 inch celluloid and paper film. The latter was also used in a new rapid method, by which 1,000 chest exposures were made with one machine in a working day with an excellent quality finished product and at a marked reduction in cost. Microfilms were introduced into the U.S. from Brazil in 1938. They were 35x35 millimetres in diameter. Later 4x5 inch films were used, and still later 70x70 millimetre films were introduced. These microfilms were known as photofluorograms, since they were photographs of images taken from the fluoroscopic screen.

There was a great deal of controversy concerning the efficacy of the various techniques used in making X-ray inspection of the chest. In 1945, however, a comparative study of the various X-ray methods of inspecting the chests of a large number of persons was made. Each of the individuals included in the study had a 35-millimetre photofluorogram, a 4x10-inch photofluorogram, a 14x17 inch paper film and a 14x17 inch celluloid film taken within a few minutes of one another. Independently, three chest specialists and two radiologists inspected the films. A preliminary report of this study revealed that in the actual experience of the five experts, the efficiency for case-finding purposes was of approximately the same magnitude for each of the four methods. It was found that such advantage as might be inherent in any one technique was very much smaller in magnitude than the human error involved in X-ray inspection.

Previously, the bane of the physician had been technical differences in X-ray films made at various times of the same chest for comparison. It was with extreme rarity that one saw two or more films made at different times in the same laboratory that were not technically different. In 1943 R. H. Morgan developed a photo-timer which accomplished uniformity of exposure of photofluorograms so that those made on one date were technically the same as those made subsequently, despite marked changes in body weight, etc. If this could be adapted to usual X-ray equipment it would be one of the true contributions to the X-ray field.

In a number of disease processes of different kinds, calcium is carried in and deposited by the blood stream in such amounts as to cast dense, usually irregular shadows on the X-ray film. Tuberculosis is only one of the diseases in which this occurs. However, as tuberculosis was thought to be the most prevalent disease of the lungs, there developed the unfortunate practice of diagnosing tuberculosis in everyone whose X-ray films presented evidence of depositions of calcium. During the decade, heated controversies, almost bitter at times, were waged between those who maintained that calcium deposits always represent tuberculous lesions and those who demanded more specific evidence. The tuberculin test was occasionally condemned by those who saw evidence of calcium deposits on X-ray films of the chests of nonreactors to tuberculin. Thus, X-ray shadows, which are never pathognomonic, were allowed to supersede the accurate and highly specific tuberculin test.

In 1942 J. D. Aronson and his associates reported a close correlation between the presence of calcium deposits in the lungs and sensitivity of the tissues to coccidioidin, suggesting that calcified nodules in the lungs might be caused by infection with a fungus known as *C. immitis*. Further observation proved that in certain areas, such as California and Arizona, a mild form of this fungus disease (coccidioidomycosis) develops in man which usually causes no significant symptoms. The primary lesions in the lungs and regional lymph nodes throughout their development, including deposition of calcium, appear identical with those of the primary tuberculosis complex. There was no way to differentiate between the lesions of these diseases except with the coccidioidin and tuberculin tests and by recovering the organisms.

While examining a large number of student nurses for tuberculosis in 1945, Carroll E. Palmer found that evidence of calcium deposits in the chest occurred with considerable frequency in the central eastern half of the U.S. The majority of these students were nonreactors to tuberculin. The histoplasmin test was administered to 3,105 such students; the incidence of reactors corresponded with that of calcifications in the chest, reaching its height in Kansas City, Mo., with 65.8%.

Although a fungus disease known as histoplasmosis, caused by Histoplasma capsulatum, was thought to be universally fatal, Palmer's work indicated that infection with this or an immunologically related organism also results in a prevalent, mild disease which can be diagnosed only by the histoplasmin test or recovery of the organism. Palmer was cognizant of the possibility that histoplasmin may not be entirely specific for histoplasma infection but may elicit the presence of some other closely related fungus infections, inasmuch as cross-reactions are frequent with such testing material as blastomycin, as shown by C. W. Emmons and his associates. Moreover, co-existence of two or more kinds of fungus infections might be possible.

Later in 1945 A. Christie and J. C. Peterson reported on histoplasmin and tuberculin tests administered to 181 children from middle Tennessee, of whom 24.9% reacted to tuberculin and 73.5% to histoplasmin. Nearly twice as many (43.6%) histoplasmin reactors showed evidence of pulmonary calcification as tuberculin reactors (24.9%).

Not all persons who develop primary tuberculosis, coccidioidomycosis or histoplasmosis present demonstrable deposits of calcium by X-ray inspection. In tuberculosis it is rare to find as many as 20% who actually have primary complexes with any evidence whatsoever by X-ray. The fact that shadows are not seen on X-ray films does not constitute proof of the absence of tuberculosis, coccidioidomycosis or histoplasmosis. Doubtless there are cases which do not calcify. In others, the deposits are so small or so located that they are not seen on the X-ray film.

These discoveries were of extreme practical value, as they emphasized that the diagnosis of any calcified or noncalcified pulmonary or pleural lesion, regardless of its location, size, or the appearance of the shadow it casts on the X-ray film, is dependent upon specific evidence, which consists of a reaction to a specific testing substance such as tuberculin or histoplasmin, or finding the causative organism by bacteriological methods. Therefore, no physician can afford to assume the tremendous responsibility which obtains when he labels any lesion or condition of the lungs or pleura as tuberculous in the absence of the tuberculin reaction or the recovery of tubercle bacilli. Thus, in the vast majority of cases, the diagnosis of chest diseases was removed from the realm of speculation during the decade 1937–46.

Case Finding Among Special Groups.—The general hospitals of the U.S. admitted approximately 15,000,000 persons and examined about the same number in their outpatient departments annually during the decade. In many of these institutions arrangements were made for persons being examined for any cause to have an adequate examination for tuberculosis.

The problem of tuberculosis among institutions for the mentally ill had long been recognized as serious. Surveys in many places showed that as many as 10% of the inmates and the personnel had this disease, many of whom were transmitting it to others. However, it was not until about 1937 that feeble attempts were made in a few places to solve the problem. By 1946, some of the states had directors of tuberculosis control work in these institutions; with a limited number of helpers, they devoted their entire time to this activity. In these states provision was being made for the isolation, in one or a few places throughout the state, of all found to have tuberculosis. There they could be treated as soon as possible, under strict contagious disease technique, thus sparing members of personnel and other patients from the contagion. The same kind of work was also instituted in prisons where, prior to 1940, tuberculosis often was a serious problem.

A campaign was instituted to make every physician's office a centre for the diagnosis of tuberculosis, so that everyone who presents himself for any cause has the tuberculin test administered, and the reactors are completely examined. This would provide for an enormous number of annual examinations.

Surveys during the decade revealed that 1 to 1.5% of pregnant women had tuberculosis to such a degree as to require treatment. Doubtless this percentage was much higher in countries where nearly all adults were infected with tubercle bacilli. In many places all women presenting themselves for obstetrical care were completely examined for tuberculosis. When significant disease was found, it was treated promptly and if it remained contagious at the time of delivery, the infant was protected against infection by having no contact with the mother after birth as long as her disease remained contagious.

In the U.S. tuberculosis was spoken of as a disease of elderly people. Indeed, the tuberculosis mortality rate was reaching its height after the age of 50 years. There were two main reasons for this situation. First, the span of life had increased; thus, the number of elderly persons had increased, and in their bodies the disease had more time to mature. Second, children and young adults had been so protected against tubercle bacilli that relatively few of them were now infected with this germ.

With the decrease in tuberculosis among children and young adults, the high incidence of the disease among elderly persons stood out in bold relief. With continued protection of children and young adults against infection, the destructive forms of tuberculosis would continue to decrease. Among the persons who had passed the 50th year there was a high incidence of tuberculous infection, inasmuch as they were not protected against tubercle bacilli when they were infants, children and young adults. Therefore, this residue of tuberculosis among elderly persons would continue to cause a great deal of contagion, illness and death. In 1946, there were more than 19,000,000 persons in the U.S. 55 years or older. Tuberculosis among elderly persons was a serious problem in nearly all parts of the world; therefore it was being given due consideration in many tuberculosis control programs.

After 1937, tuberculosis workers of the U.S., England and a few other countries put forth a great deal of effort to find the disease among industrial workers. These persons were gathered together in groups in their places of work, thus facilitating large numbers of examinations in a short time. Industrial surveys on a voluntary basis were not entirely satisfactory unless an agreement was reached in advance that every person should participate. Otherwise those who knew they had tuberculosis or even suspected it, usually shunned the examination. Moreover, industrial workers constituted a small percentage of the population in most places, and thus a tuberculosis control program was incomplete when limited only to this group.

As tuberculosis is contagious, a good deal of emphasis was placed on the examination of the contacts of persons who had recently died from tuberculosis or were known to have contagious disease. This was a good procedure, but it was inadequate because a considerable percentage of persons with contagious tuberculosis did not have the disease diagnosed. Often they died from other conditions without the tuberculosis being detected unless a postmortem examination was performed. From 10 to 40% of the persons with tuberculosis were first reported to health departments by death certificate. Thus they had been permitted to transmit tubercle bacilli to their associates over long periods of time. Furthermore, in many communities the majority of persons with tuberculosis were contagious when first diagnosed. Obviously, by examining only contacts, one never would know how many contagious cases existed at any given time, and therefore work on many contacts would begin late, if at all.

The most efficacious method continued to be the periodical examination of all adult tuberculin reactors. The type of tuberculosis which causes illness and death develops only among the reactors. This new and most effective approach in communities where the incidence of tuberculosis had reached a low level, was instituted in the entire population of whole counties after 1940. All citizens were first tested with tuberculin. The chests of the adult tuberculin reactors were inspected with X-ray films, and those who presented shadows were completely examined to determine the cause of the disease. In this manner the tuberculosis status of every citizen was determined. Those with lesions not yet contagious might be treated. Those who had no finding except the tuberculin reaction could be kept under observation, as they might have significant disease at any time. Those not reacting to tuberculin could be retested periodically, and if infection occurred they could be placed on the list for observation.

During the decade 1937–46, the Committee on Tuberculosis of the American School Health association made several reports of its activities on tuberculosis in the schools. The objective of this committee was the creation of an environment free from contagious tuberculosis in all the schools of the country; this applied to personnel as well as to students.

The committee strongly recommended that the tuberculin test be administered to all preschool children, as well as those in kindergarten and in the pre-high school grades. X-ray inspection of the chest was rarely necessary because the reinfection chronic form of tuberculosis of the lungs which becomes contagious is a rarity this early in life. Nevertheless, every child who reacts to tuberculin has been in direct or indirect contact with a contagious case of tuberculosis. Thus the tuberculin reaction in the child is a clue to such a case which is often found by adequately examining the adult associates of the child.

It was also strongly recommended that all high school students be tested with tuberculin and each reactor have X-ray inspection of the chest annually. In the event shadows appear, the examination is completed. This is the age period when the chronic reinfection type of tuberculosis begins to appear in the lungs of humans, and it may become contagious at this time. Numerous cases were reported of high school students infecting nearly all of their classmates.

One of the innovations which the committee introduced in 1943 consisted of officially certifying schools on the basis of tuberculosis work in progress.

Members of the personnel also were required to have the tuberculin test, repeated for the nonreactors at least every two years. Reactors on first or subsequent testing had X-ray film inspection of the chest. All reactors, regardless of the presence or absence of X-ray findings in the chest, had to be examined with reference to tuberculous lesions in other parts of their bodies. Students and members of personnel found to have progressive tuberculosis in any part of the body were removed from school until adequately treated and the danger of contagion was remote. An educational program was provided to make sure that the teaching staff understood thoroughly the underlying principles of tuberculosis control.

The Committee on Tuberculosis of the American Student Health association reported a gradual decrease in the incidence of tuberculin reactors among college and university students throughout the country. For the school year 1932–33, 35% of the students tested reacted; in the school year 1942–43, only 18.6%. In that year 13 colleges reported that less than 10% of their students reacted.

Miniature X-ray films such as these (35 mm.) proved an accurate medium for revealing chest lesions, according to a test of comparative X-ray methods conducted in 1945, and were recommended for mass radiography of the chest in tuberculosis prevention

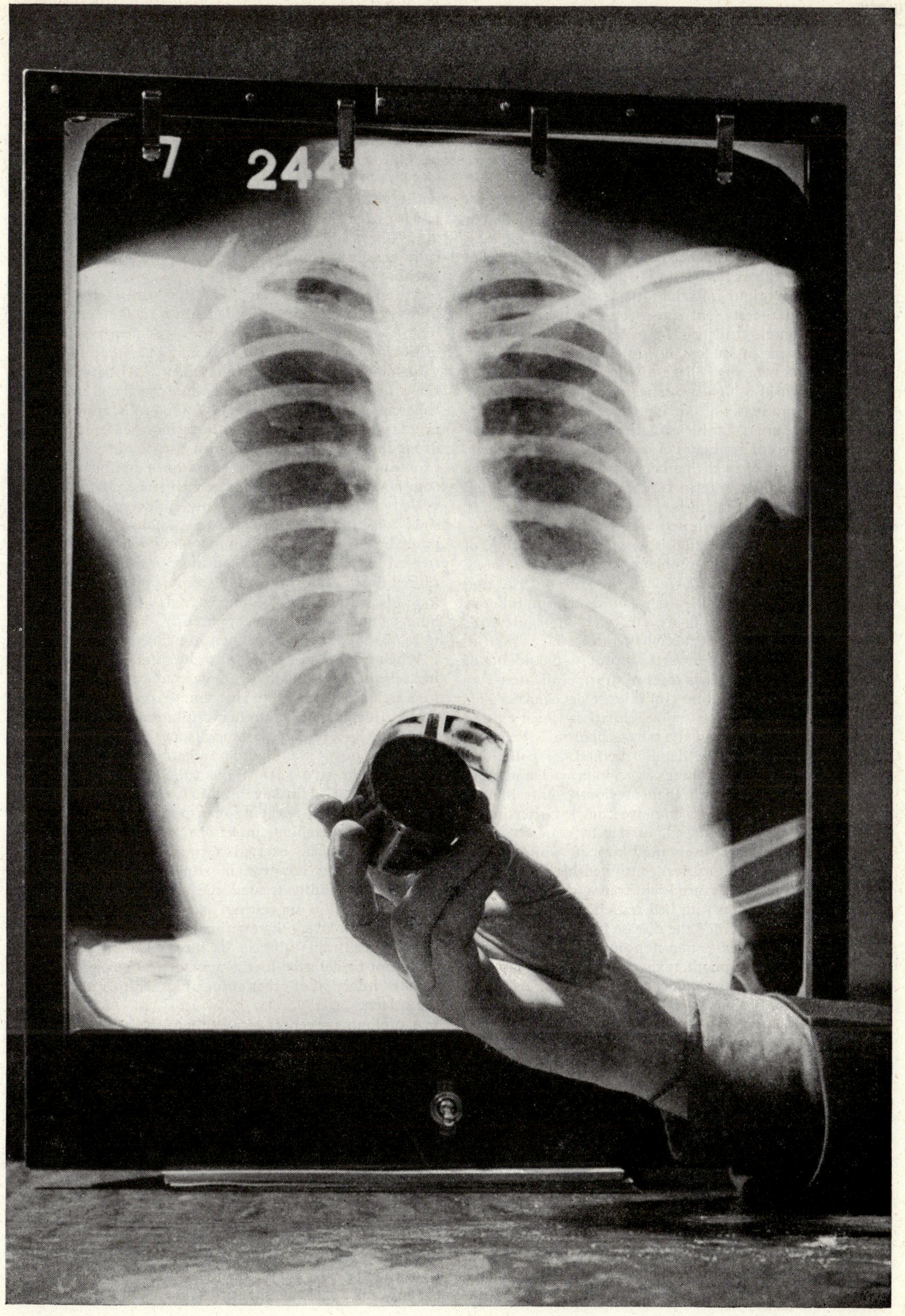
7 244

The program recommended by the committee consisted of administering the tuberculin test to all entering students, making X-ray inspection of the chests of the reactors, and a complete examination of those with areas of disease which cast shadows that might be tuberculous. This committee extended its program to faculty members and other personnel in the hope of creating an environment free from contagious tuberculosis on U.S. college and university campuses.

The most serious problem in the institutions of higher learning occurred in those with schools of nursing and medicine where the students had become infected from patients with tuberculosis. In 1939 Ruth E. Boynton found the tuberculous infection attack rate was 100 times greater among the student nurses on a general hospital service than among students in a college of education, and 500 times greater in student nurses on a special tuberculosis service than in the college of education. From many parts of the world a high incidence of tuberculosis among students and graduates of nursing were reported.

An equally unfavourable situation was found among students and recent graduates of medicine. In some places, as many students of medicine became infected during the brief time that they were in school as had been infected from birth until the time they entered professional schools. F. E. Harrington demonstrated that strict contagious disease technique on tuberculosis services was capable of solving, in large part, the problem of tuberculosis among students. Aerosols and ultra-violet light were on trial and already offered considerable promise in destroying tubercle bacilli in the air, on the floors, etc., of rooms and wards where tuberculous patients were being treated.

H. S. Diehl and his co-workers so protected students of medicine against contagious cases of tuberculosis that very few became infected, and no clinical case developed. This was in sharp contrast to a serious situation which existed among medical students in the same school in 1937.

Treatment.—During the decade methods of collapsing the diseased areas of the lungs were improved and were used much more extensively than previously. Intrapleural artificial pneumothorax was employed much earlier in the course of the disease. Indeed, in selected cases of early tuberculosis it was extensively used by 1946, while the patient remained ambulatory and continued his usual activities of life. In more advanced and contagious cases it was utilized in combination with bed rest. This form of treatment frequently prevented the disease from becoming contagious or converted cases to a noncontagious state. Extrapleural artificial pneumothorax was a development consisting of separating the outer layer of pleura from the chest wall, after which air is introduced into the space outside the pleura. The value of this procedure was limited.

Crushing the phrenic nerve, phreniphraxis, as it courses near the surface of the neck paralyzes the same side of the diaphragm and thus decreases the size of the chest space, as well as the movements of the lung during respiration. This treatment decreased in popularity during the decade, although it continued to serve a useful purpose in some cases.

Removal of the ribs over areas of disease, extrapleural thoracoplasty, continued to be a standard procedure when less drastic methods of treatment failed.

The removal of a lobe of a lung, lobectomy, or the entire lung, pneumonectomy, in the treatment of tuberculosis of the lung was developed largely during the decade. Surgical technique improved to such a degree that these operations were now performed with considerable success.

With the various procedures, including strict bed rest in a hospital, sanatorium or home, artificial pneumothorax and extrapleural thoracoplasty, the disease is not cured. Nature is only assisted in walling off the disease, but the germs of tuberculosis remain alive. Although some individuals so treated recover and have complete restoration of working capacity, their disease can never be said to be cured. With the total removal of a diseased lobe or an entire lung, likewise, the tuberculosis is not cured, inasmuch as persons who undergo such treatment practically always have elsewhere in their bodies the germs of tuberculosis, which remain a constant threat to their future health.

At the end of the decade, there was still no drug capable of destroying all germs of tuberculosis in the human body. The hope of finding such a drug was nearly abandoned until about 1937, when the sulfonamides were found to be valuable in controlling other infections. Although none of these preparations proved of value in the treatment of tuberculosis, another group of compounds known as sulfones was employed. The three most extensively used drugs in this group were known as promin, diasone and promizole. The immediate effect on experimental tuberculosis was remarkable. However, further observations revealed that they apparently only suppressed the disease, since sensitivity to tuberculin was not lost in any treated animal. Moreover, in animals apparently successfully treated for a prolonged period the disease reactivated and caused death after medication was stopped. The same sulfone derivatives were administered for tuberculosis in humans but while some apparently encouraging results were observed, none proved entirely adequate.

When penicillin was found to be so effective in destroying certain infections it was immediately used in tuberculosis in animals and humans, but it proved to be of no avail. In Jan. 1944 another antibiotic substance, streptomycin, was announced. Made from the organism *Actinomyces griseus,* it was found to exert impressive effects in vitro and in vivo against the tubercle bacillus. W. H. Feldman, H. C. Hinshaw and F. C. Mann found streptomycin effective in resolving or suppressing established experimental tuberculous infection in guinea pigs. In most instances the drug exerted a suppressive rather than a sterilizing effect; however, in approximately 39% of the animals successfully treated the sensitivity to tuberculin disappeared, thus suggesting that a germicidal effect was exerted. Moreover, these animals were found to be sufficiently free from tubercle bacilli so that the organisms could not be detected by the most delicate means of study; namely, infection of other guinea pigs with emulsions from the spleen.

A preliminary report of a study to the effects of streptomycin on tuberculosis in humans by Hinshaw and Feldman was encouraging. Thirty-four patients who had tuberculosis were treated over varying periods of time, with subsequent observation for periods up to nine months. It appeared probable that the drug exerted a limited suppressive effect, especially upon some of the more unusual types of pulmonary and extrapulmonary tuberculosis. No convincing evidence of rapidly effective bactericidal action was obtained. However, apparently significant improvement was seen in cases of early and extensive haematogenous forms of pulmonary tuberculosis, early miliary disease, tuberculosis of the genitourinary tract and suppurative tuberculous lymphadenitis. Streptomycin was not available in sufficient quantities during the latter part of the decade to make a thoroughgoing study of its efficaciousness in tuberculosis in humans. Although early reports were somewhat encouraging, final deductions awaited further observations.

Any drug capable of destroying tubercle bacilli in the human body would be most effective if administered soon after the initial invasion. Periodic tuberculin testing of uninfected individuals, constituting the majority in the U.S., would detect primary tuberculosis with almost 100% accuracy within eight weeks after tubercle bacilli were focalized. Then for some time thereafter one might expect to destroy all tubercle bacilli with a satisfactory drug. Thus the disease could be cured in the strict sense of the word before it had caused significant destruction of tissues. The only criterion of such cure would be the complete loss of allergy to tuberculoprotein, as indicated by subsequent tuberculin tests.

Re-education and Rehabilitation.—During 1944–46 great strides were made in providing for re-education and rehabilitation of persons recovering from tuberculosis. Many young adults were now able to complete high school courses or undertake other educational activities while being treated for tuberculosis. The federal government made provision for vocational training of handicapped persons, including the tuberculous, and in co-operation with state departments of health special training was offered and positions found for qualified persons. Special institutions, such as the Tomahawk Lake camp in Wisconsin, the Altro Work Shop in New York city and the Ida Potts Memorial hospital at Livingston, N.Y., began bridging the chasm between the sick bed and a gainful occupation for many persons.

During World War II the Committee on Tuberculosis in Wartime of the Medical Research Council of Great Britain recommended the provision of a special tuberculosis fund designed to ensure an adequate allowance for tuberculous patients for a period of up to one year after detection of the disease. The case of any person unable to work at the end of this period would be reviewed by a suitable authority. The needs of the patient and his family would determine the amount of the allowance. This scheme might also be linked with a fund to provide payments for supplementing to their full amount the wages of those returning to their employment on part-time basis or modified work. A similar scheme was being considered by the division of tuberculosis of the U.S. public health service. Such an arrangement would induce many persons to undergo treatment promptly upon diagnosis of their disease; otherwise these persons would be reluctant to give up their income necessary for the support of their families. The tuberculous wage earner, moreover, would be more likely to remain under treatment as long as his physician advised if an adequate income were provided to support his family.

Prevention.—The only satisfactory method of preventing tuberculosis continued to be avoidance of initial infection. The method consisted of preventing persons or animals with contagious tuberculosis from disseminating tubercle bacilli to others. This was being accomplished with a remarkable degree of success. Between 1939 and 1941, of the deaths from all causes in the U.S. 3.8% resulted from tuberculosis among the white, and 5.9% among the nonwhite population. This was in contrast to 6.9% among the white and 9.1% among the nonwhite population between 1919 and 1921.

The incidence of primary tuberculosis among U.S. university students decreased from 35% in 1932 to 18.6% in 1943. Reports from many rural communities indicated an incidence of tuberculin reactors of 5 to 10% among high school students. From the available data throughout the country it appeared that only about 12 to 15% of persons of high school age were infected with tubercle bacilli.

The incidence of tuberculosis among children was rapidly decreasing. In one state, Ruth E. Boynton called attention to a mortality rate of 130 per 100,000 among infants under 1 year of age from 1915–19. But it was only 9 per 100,000 from 1940–44, a decrease of 93%. In the largest city of this state, with approximately 500,000 population, not one child died from tuberculosis from birth to 5 years of age in 1945. In the same city the infection attack rate was now only one third of 1% per year. Thus only 2% of the children were infected at the age of 6 years. In 1946, there were sizable areas in the U.S. where no preschool child had been infected with tubercle bacilli.

F. E. Harrington found that 18.9% of children in grade schools reacted to tuberculin in 1936, but among the children in the same schools in 1944, only 7.7% reacted. At the end of 15 years of effort in protecting children against tubercle bacilli, L. S. Jordan reported 153 schools in which no child reacted to tuberculin in 1946. The same year he tested 12,000 students and personnel of schools, and only 2.7% reacted. From available data it appeared that 90% of the children of grade school age in the U.S. had been protected against tubercle bacilli.

Transients and itinerant workers had long been known to disseminate tubercle bacilli. However, little was done to solve this problem in the U.S. until 1938, when the attention of the Michigan health department was called to an undue percentage of imported Mexican labourers being admitted to some of Michigan's sanatoriums. An arrangement was promptly made whereby sugar beet labourers proposing to migrate to Michigan were examined at their

Mobile X-ray clinic at Seattle, Wash. A group of college students is shown waiting for chest examinations as part of a preventive campaign in the area during 1946

concentration headquarters in San Antonio, Tex., by the Michigan department of health. Among 4,271 such persons examined in 1939 and 5,753 examined in 1940, 202 were found to have tuberculosis. Thus the rejection of these persons for employment prevented an influx into Michigan of a considerable number of persons with contagious tuberculosis.

The U.S. bureau of animal industry had long prohibited the importation of tuberculous animals, particularly cattle, but it was not until 1943 that the U.S. public health service made an attempt to control tuberculosis imported into the country by immigrants. An examination centre was established at Mexico City, where labourers were examined prior to entrance into the U.S. to work under the program of the War Food administration. During 1943 and 1944 a total of 169,421 were examined, of whom 1,499 were rejected. Eight hundred and seventy-nine had the reinfection type of tuberculosis. This probably was the beginning of a program which would ultimately include adequate examination for tuberculosis of all persons entering the U.S. It should also be extended so that no person could leave the U.S. for a foreign country unless his passport showed freedom from contagious tuberculosis. If all nations would adopt a similar procedure the spread of tuberculosis from country to country would be promptly checked.

In Nov. 1940 the entire U.S. was designated a modified accredited area with reference to tuberculosis control among cattle. This action marked the attainment of a goal set by the veterinarians and their associates in 1917. At that time the U.S. bureau of animal industry outlined a nation-wide campaign to control tuberculosis among cattle because of the tremendous losses sustained by the owners of cattle and because the cattle type of tuberculosis is transmissible to man. The county was chosen as the unit of activity, and the work consisted of testing with tuberculin all the cattle in a county and slaughtering the reactors, regardless of apparent good health. Areas of disease were found in an overwhelming percentage of the slaughtered animals. When the disease was extensive the carcass was confined to the rendering tank. If a small amount of disease was located, it was removed and the remainder of the carcass was salvaged for food. However, the meat from such carcasses was always sterilized before being placed on the market.

Whenever the county had tuberculosis so controlled that not more than 0.5% of the cattle reacted to turberculin, it was officially designated as a modified accredited area. This recognition stimulated a tremendous amount of interest and local pride which greatly accelerated the national program. The first 17 counties were accredited in 1923. By the end of 1928 all the counties in one state, North Carolina, had been accredited, and thus the entire state was designated as a modified accredited area. By 1937 44 states had qualified, and in Nov. 1940 the last state was accredited. Between July 1, 1917, and June 30, 1946, 287,689,953 tuberculin tests were administered to cattle and the 3,911,414 reactors were slaughtered. The entire cost of accomplishing the modified accredited rating for the nation was approximately $260,000,000, but before the work was undertaken tuberculosis was costing the cattle owners $300,000,000 every ten years. This represented the greatest victory man had ever won over tuberculosis.

Inasmuch as the term "modified accredited" did not imply complete eradication, there was still a problem in many counties after accreditation was achieved. Therefore the veterinarians and their associates worked toward eradication, and they were successful in large areas where there was no longer to be found a single animal reacting to tuberculin. In fact, the testing of 8,454,463 cattle throughout the nation during the fiscal year ending June 1946 revealed only 0.23% reactors. The success of the veterinarians' program was also indicated at the postmortem examination made at the points of federal inspection. For example, in 1917 a total of 9,276,049 cattle were slaughtered under federal inspection, and 40,746 (0.3%) were condemned as inedible because of tuberculosis. During 1944, 12,900,544 cattle were slaughtered, of which 1,435 (0.011%) were condemned. Actually in proportion to the number slaughtered, 98% fewer were condemned in 1944 than in 1917.

Tuberculosis in other domestic animals, particularly fowls and swine, continued to be a serious problem in some sections of the U.S. However, much was done to control the disease in these animals in the same manner as among the cattle. In 1917, 76,807 hogs (0.19% of the total kill) were condemned for tuberculosis, whereas, in 1944, only 15,910 (0.021%) were condemned for this purpose. The decrease in the disease among hogs was considerably less than among cattle because hogs are susceptible not only to the bovine type, but also the human and the avian types of tubercle bacilli. Much of the tuberculosis among hogs was caused by bacilli transmitted from flocks of poultry with the disease. During the decade 1937–46, successful methods were developed to curb tuberculosis in poultry. The control of tuberculosis among domestic animals in the U.S. placed that nation in the most favourable position of all the countries involved in World War II to produce dairy products and meat without molestation from this disease.

Tuberculosis in cattle is readily transmissible to humans. Therefore, as the disease was controlled among the cattle county by county and state by state, the decrease in the mortality, morbidity and incidence of infection among humans was experienced. In fact, this was probably the most responsible factor for the sharp decline in the incidence of tuberculin reactors among children and young adults observed in the U.S. during the decade 1937–46. In countries where the disease had not been controlled among the cattle there still existed a great deal of tuberculosis of the bovine type among humans. In 1937 A. Stanley Griffith of England found that more than 50% of the persons with serious tuberculosis of the lymph nodes (scrofula) and nearly 50% of those with tuberculosis of the skin resulted from the cattle type of tubercle bacillus. Moreover, 25% of the cases of fatal tuberculous meningitis and 20% of those involving the bones and joints and genitourinary tract were the result of bovine infection. Griffith reported 163 cases of tuberculosis of the lungs caused by the bovine type of tubercle bacillus. In England alone during the decade, about 2,000 deaths occurred annually and 4,000 new cases of bovine type of tuberculosis developed each year in humans.

In 1942 Eric Hedvall of Lund, Sweden, published a monograph on the bovine type of tuberculosis in man in which he reported 94 cases that he had seen in the province of Skane. These 94 persons had tuberculosis in various parts of their bodies and ranged in age from 3 to 68 years. Fifty-three had pulmonary tuberculosis, 28 of which were serious; in fact, so serious that 16 of them had died by the time the report was made.

The disease caused by the cattle type of tubercle bacillus in man is just as serious as that produced by the human type. Indeed, Griffith and Hedvall stated that the course of the disease originated by these two types of organisms was identical and that the only possible way to differentiate the one from the other was through laboratory typing of the tubercle bacilli. Hedvall demonstrated that the cattle type of tubercle bacillus could be transmitted from cattle to man, from man to man, and from man back to cattle. He said that in Sweden it was imperative that the campaign against tuberculosis in cattle be carried on with the greatest energy and that the goal must be the extermination of tuberculosis among these animals. Griffith made the same plea for England but, unfortunately, when World War II began only about 3% of England's cattle herds had been attested. The Committee on Tuberculosis in Wartime of the Medical Research Council of Great Britain reported in 1942 that approximately 40% of all of England's cattle reacted to tuberculin, and lesions were found in 40% of all of those slaughtered in the abattoirs.

Tuberculosis and War.—In many parts of the world significant progress was being made in tuberculosis control just prior to the beginning of World War II. However, with the prosecution of the war in both Asia and Europe much that had been accomplished was soon dissipated. Most of the countries that entered the war attempted to prevent tuberculous individuals from engaging in military service. The X-ray was at its height of popularity, and military authorities in several nations believed that little or nothing need be done except to inspect the chests of inductees with X-ray. Unquestionably this practice screened out most persons with advanced pulmonary tuberculosis, but it missed large numbers with disease of lesser proportions. Some nations, particularly Canada, used the regular 14x17 inch films. Others used photofluorograms of various sizes. In the U.S. when the Selective Service system for induction into the army was established in Sept. 1940, only the conventional physical examination of the chest was used. However, in Oct. 1940 X-ray inspection was advised and funds were made available for contract work, but this phase of the examination was made universal only in the first three corps areas. It was not until the spring of 1942, after approximately 1,000,000 persons had been admitted to military service without X-ray inspection, that this phase of the examination was included at all induction centres. The army then adopted the 4x5 inch, and the navy the 35x35 millimetre photofluorogram, for routinely inspecting the chests of inductees. If shadows were seen on these microfilms, 14x17 inch celluloid or paper films were made. Those whose photofluorograms did not reveal shadows that appeared significant were regarded as having no tuberculosis and therefore were acceptable for military service.

Among approximately 18,000,000 persons seen at induction centres, 180,000 were rejected for tuberculosis, largely on the basis of X-ray shadows. Although it had long been known that various diseases of the lungs cast shadows with the same appearance as those produced by tuberculosis, nearly all of those seen at induction centres were regarded as representing tuberculous lesions, and a provision was made whereby persons with these findings were reported to the boards of health of their respective states. Thus, persons reported as tuberculous on the basis of X-ray findings included some with such nontuberculous conditions as pneumonia, abscess, fungus infection, etc., as well as some with tuberculosis. The only excuse for this limited procedure was that under the emergency of war there was not time at the induction centres to examine completely and determine the actual cause of the diseases which cast the shadows. It was assumed that if all were reported as tuberculous to state boards of health they would be contacted, and complete examinations would be made so that the actual diagnoses could be ascertained. In some places this was actually done, and it was found that from 10 to 14% of the rejectees had no evidence of significant lung disease. They apparently had acute infections, such as pneumonia, at the time of the induction examination and the lesions had promptly disappeared.

Follow-up studies of this kind in Detroit revealed that only about 10% of a group of more than 1,000 rejected for military service actually had tuberculosis which was in need of treatment. Of all persons rejected in three counties in Illinois this was true of only 4.4%, and among more than 4,000 rejectees from the entire state of Illinois, only 9.3%. In New York city about 37% of the rejectees were later found to have tuberculosis which was thought to require treatment. Information available in 1946 indicated that probably less than 25% of all persons rejected because of tuberculosis actually had active disease. This was a striking demonstration of the inability of physicians to determine either the cause of disease or its activity from a single X-ray shadow.

By the end of 1946, approximately 20,000 persons had been discharged from U.S. military service because of tuberculosis. These could not all be attributed to the war because many of them, probably the majority, were infected before they entered military service and would have fallen ill had they remained in their former communities. The disheartening fact was that, at least early in the war, approximately 60% of those discharged from service because of tuberculosis had shadows on their induction films which were entirely overlooked or regarded as insignificant. This again emphasized the inability of physicians to diagnose conditions within the lungs accurately from X-ray.

The most serious flaw in the examination for military service was the omission of the tuberculin test, which is much more delicate and accurate than X-ray, and all other phases of examination for tuberculosis. One reason for not including the test was that many persons still believed that nearly 100% of adults are infected with tubercle bacilli and therefore would react to the test. Another reason was that the war emergency did not permit time for administration of this test. This was somewhat paradoxical, however, since a serological test for syphilis was provided for every inductee. Probably less than 25% of inductees would have reacted to the test had it been administered, and the films of their chests could have been scrutinized more carefully, and thus the roentgenologist would not have missed so many who had unmistakable shadows at the time of induction. Moreover, the reactors to tuberculin should have been kept under close observation throughout the period of their military service, since it was from their group that most of the clinical tuberculosis developed, and often to advanced proportions before it was recognized.

The percentage of persons discharged from U.S. military service because of tuberculosis during World War II was about one tenth of that in World War I. Probably two factors were largely responsible for the difference: there was much more tuberculosis in the general population immediately before and during the first war; most of the advanced cases were rejected for military service in World War II because of the X-ray inspection of the chest; whereas in World War I much advanced disease was not detected at the induction stations.

Of those discharged from the army because of tuberculosis, about 90% had disease of the lungs and only 10% in other parts of the body. The tuberculosis rate for men more than 40 years was 8 times as high as that for those under 20 years of age. The number of persons who fell ill in the army was approximately the same among those who were leading sedentary lives as among those engaged in strenuous activities of warfare. In the navy there was no apparent difference between the incidence of tuberculosis among forces afloat and those ashore. Apparently life at sea with its ofttimes arduous duties, naval engagements, etc., did not conduce to the development of tuberculosis any more than did life at a shore station. The army and navy established hospitals where those who fell ill from tuberculosis could be immediately treated, after which, if more treatment was advisable, they were discharged to veterans' hospitals.

There was no doubt that many engaged in the military services of the U.S. were infected and reinfected while in countries where large numbers of contagious cases of tuberculosis were in the general population. Since the tuberculin test was not employed, there was no way to determine when or where they were infected. Except for acute reinfection forms of the disease, such as pleurisy with fluid, there had not been time for clinical tuberculosis to develop among them. Undoubtedly this type of disease would appear among U.S. veterans for several decades as a result of the infections sustained while in service.

Tuberculosis Among War Veterans.—Tuberculosis had always been a serious problem among veterans of wars. In Canada following World War I, for each 100 veterans pensioned for wounds, 25 were pensioned for tuberculosis. Following World War I up to 1941, 1 U.S. veteran alive or deceased, of every 42 persons who served in that war was known to suffer from tuberculosis of a pensionable or compensable degree. In fact, claims were paid to the widows and dependents of 48,330 deceased World War I veterans. From July 1918 through June 1944, tuberculosis among such veterans cost the U.S. government $1,422,545,000.

The total number of admissions of World War II veterans to hospital treatment for pulmonary tuberculosis from Dec. 7, 1941, to Feb. 28, 1946, was 23,600, of whom 16,100 were service connected. In 1946 there were 8,650 beds for tuberculous beneficiaries in operation by the Veterans administration in 14 hospitals for the tuberculous and in tuberculosis departments of 15 general hospitals. There were 775 additional beds for tuberculous patients in 22 neuropsychiatric hospitals. Plans were in progress for more beds, making a total of 14,600 by Jan. 1, 1948. The Veterans administration arranged for care of tuberculous veterans equal to that in any civilian sanatorium. Wherever veterans' hospitals were located near medical schools, affiliations were being established so that the appropriate members of the faculty were participating in the care of the veterans.

Tuberculosis Among Civilians During War.—It was still too early in 1946 to determine with exactness the extent of increase of tuberculosis among the civilians in most of the nations involved in World War II. However, enough information was available to justify the statement that it was large. There was an approximate 100% increase in the Netherlands from 1939–42, and in Greece the disease increased four and one half times. In Germany there was an increase of 24% during the same years. The mortality rate doubled in Yugoslavia, and a threefold increase occurred in Italy. According to estimates, there were about 36,000,000 active cases of tuberculosis in China in 1946. Tuberculin tests administered to children indicated that 40% to 80% were infected in Poland and Czechoslovakia. In England between 1938 and 1941 there was an increase of 12.1%. Children up to 10 years of age showed a relative increase of 50% in mortality from tuberculous meningitis. Many tuberculosis hospitals and sanatoriums were evacuated in Sept. 1939. The institution of blackout conditions interfered with ventilation and increased cross-infection. Evacuation of town populations to the country resulted in overcrowding as well as dissemination of large numbers of bovine type of tubercle bacilli through the dairy products, and contributed greatly to infection and reinfection with tubercle bacilli throughout England.

When World War II began, the examination of milk from individual herds in England showed that an average of more than 6% of all farms were sending out milk containing tubercle bacilli. Practically all bulk milk represented the mixed milk of 20 or more herds and, therefore, nearly all milk consumed was contaminated. Prior to the war, as much as 93% of the milk consumed in London was pasteurized. This was true of about 40 to 50% distributed in the aggregate of county boroughs, and about 15% was heat-treated in some other way. In the smaller towns very much less was pasteurized and practically none in rural areas. The Committee on Tuberculosis in Wartime of the Medical Research Council strongly recommended that, throughout the war, milk for human consumption be heated to a degree sufficient to destroy tubercle bacilli, which simply meant bringing it to the boiling point.

Such factors as dietary deficiency, physical and mental strain were long thought to cause increase in tuberculosis among civilians in time of war. In England during World War I there was considerable increase in tuberculosis among patients in hospitals for the mentally ill. This was thought to be caused by deficient diet. During World War II, however, special attention was paid to the diet of patients in such institutions, but tuberculosis definitely increased among them. The Committee on Tuberculosis in Wartime ascribed the increase in World War II not to diet, but to overcrowding in these institutions. The blackout was conducive to the dissemination of tubercle bacilli. Moreover, these patients did not suffer mental or physical strain more than during peacetime. The old idea that a run-down condition causes tuberculosis during peace or war was now open to question. In all probability, man had been deceived by the disease in this regard. Usually it is the tuberculosis which causes the run-down condition and which is not detected until it is in an advanced stage.

A. L. Barach observed two physicians who developed active pulmonary tuberculosis following repeated exposure to altitudes of approximately 42,000 ft. He believed that previous lesions were reactivated by local trauma to the lungs, caused when air or other gases expanded in the vicinity of the areas of disease. No evidence was produced to show that the usual altitudes attained in commercial air travel has any effect on tuberculous lesions.

Contrary to a general belief, it was shown that irritants such as chemicals and dusts, and bacterial infections like pneumonia do not influence the development of pulmonary tuberculosis or effect lesions already present. The only known exception was fine silica dust. It was formerly believed that persons with silicosis were almost certain to develop tuberculosis. Sander observed a sizable group of silicotics for periods as long as ten years and found that no more tuberculosis developed among them than in persons of the general population. However, when tuberculosis does develop in silicotics it often progresses more rapidly than among nonsilicotic individuals.

Only one factor had been established to account for an increase in tuberculosis among humans—contagion. Even though a nation might be conducting excellent tuberculosis control work in peacetime, it could be forced to relax its efforts during war. Isolation of contagious patients was practically discontinued in wartime; sanatoriums were closed or used for other purposes; patients were sent back to their home communities where they disseminated tubercle bacilli to children and adults alike; stronger ones entered industry, while the weaker might be assigned to the care of children or other light work. In April 1942 Elizabeth Dechoff, a chest specialist in Dresden, Germany, found that approximately 60% of some 400,000 persons with open pulmonary tuberculosis, and 80 to 90% of those with stationary tuberculosis, were employed partly in unsuitable occupations. Doubtless the problem became even more serious in Germany and other nations during the last months of the war.

Unfortunately, the reports regarding increase in tuberculosis during World War II were based largely upon mortality and morbidity rates. These were not satisfactory criteria, as they provided no accurate information as to the number who became infected during the war or those who had the disease in the presymptom stage. Thus the increase in tuberculosis in such nations as Germany was much greater than it yet appeared. By the end of the decade 1937–46, there had not been time for infections sustained during the war to mature into chronic, ill-producing or life-taking disease. However, many of these would mature, so that illness and death in many persons during the following quarter of a century would result from infections incurred during World War II.

In the U.S. the mortality rate from tuberculosis did not increase during the war. Neither was there any evidence of increase in the number of persons ill from the disease. In fact, the mortality rate reached an all-time low of 39.7 per 100,000 population in 1945. Most of the sanatorium beds were kept in operation, and considerable searching was done in industry and elsewhere for contagious and precontagious cases in order that they might be prevented from disseminating tubercle bacilli. In spite of all this work, tuberculosis undoubtedly did increase in the U.S. as a result of the war. There was no doubt that large numbers of service women and men who went overseas became infected or reinfected with tubercle bacilli, and among them a significant percentage would later have clinical tuberculosis as the result of those infections. (*See* also X-RAY.)

BIBLIOGRAPHY.—H. Vollmer and E. W. Goldberger, "A New Tuberculin Patch Test," *Am. J. Dis. Child.*, 54:1019–1024 (Nov. 1937); R. H. Morgan, "The Automatic Control of Exposure in Photofluorography," *Pub. Health Rep.*, 58:1533–1541 (Oct. 15, 1943); J. D. Aronson, R. M. Saylor and E. I. Parr, "Relationship of Coccidioidomycosis to Calcified Pulmonary Nodules," *Arch. Path.*, 34:31–48 (July 1942); Carroll E. Palmer, "Nontuberculous Pulmonary Calcification and Sensitivity to Histoplasmin," *Pub. Health Rep.*, 60:513–520 (May 11, 1945); H. E. Hilleboe, R. B. Haas, C. E. Palmer and W. P. Gardner, "Tuberculosis Case Finding in Institutional Populations," *Am. J. Pub. Health*, 32:516–522 (May 1942); J. A. Myers, "Tuberculosis Among Persons Over Fifty Years of Age," *Geriatrics*, 1:27–39 (Jan.–Feb. 1946); H. E. Hilleboe and R. H. Morgan, *Mass Radiography of the Chest* (1945); J. A. Myers, H. S. Diehl R. E. Boynton and T. L. Streukens, "Tuberculosis Among Students and Graduates of Schools of Law and Medicine," *Yale J. Biol. & Med.*, 15:439–451 (Jan. 1943); W. H. Feldman, H. C. Hinshaw and F. C. Mann, "Streptomycin in Experimental Tuberculosis," *Am. Rev. Tuberc.*, 52:269–298 (Oct. 1945); H. C. Hinshaw and W. H. Feldman, "Streptomycin in Treatment of Clinical Tuberculosis," *Proc. Staff Meet., Mayo Clin.*, 20:313–318 (Sept. 5, 1945); L. E. Siltzbach, *Clinical Evaluation of the Rehabilitation of the Tuberculous: Experience at Altro Work Shops 1915–1939* (1944); Ruth E. Boynton, "Tuberculosis Deaths Among Children," *Journal-Lancet*, 65:148–151 (April 1945); Herman E. Hilleboe, "Federal Tuberculosis Control Gets Under Way," *Bull. Nat. Tuberc. A.*, 31:35–36 (March 1945); J. A. Myers, *Man's Greatest Victory Over Tuberculosis* (1940); H. R. Smith, "Bovine Tuberculosis in the United States," *Am. Rev. Tuberc.*, 50:520–533 (Dec. 1944); E. R. Long, "The Problem of Tuberculosis in Military Service," *J.A.M.A.*, 117:264–266 (July 26, 1941); D. F. Smiley and H. A. Raskin, "Tuberculosis as a Navy Problem," *Dis. of Chest*, 10:210–233 (May–June 1944).

(J. A. MY.)

Tung Oil

See VEGETABLE OILS AND ANIMAL FATS.

Tungsten

World production of tungsten concentrates, so far as data were available at the end of the decade 1937–46 from the important producers, is shown in Table I.

In order to cover a longer period, data are shown for alternate years previous to 1941. The extent to which production was built up in so many countries was one of the marvels of the World War II production program. The results in the U.S. were especially noteworthy since, so far as was known, the U.S. became the leading producer in 1944. In the earlier years of World War II, Portugal and Spain furnished most of the German supply, but later the buyers of the United Nations adopted the policy of outbidding the German buyers to reduce the German supply, thus accounting for the marked rise and abrupt fall of output in these countries. When the Burma road was closed

Table I.—*World Production of Tungsten Concentrates*
(Short tons, 60% tungstic acid [WO_3])

	1937	1939	1941	1942	1943	1944	1945
U.S.	3,500	4,287	6,567	9,333	11,945	10,283	5,715
Canada	—	4	35	269	681	517	—
Mexico	36	253	201	203	569	371	148
Argentina	955	1,443	1,896	2,331	2,668	2,743	577
Bolivia	1,986	3,678	4,798	6,180	7,608	8,747	4,245
Brazil	7	8	39	10	1,393	2,448	2,471
Peru	86	187	371	562	796	700	349
Portugal	2,281	4,245	6,431	5,754	8,242	4,506	—
Spain	276	406	457	1,612	4,301	2,638	237
Sweden	140	196	334	418	426	525	?
Burma	7,599	9,081	?	?	?	?	?
China	19,726	12,765	?	9,506	13,272	9,906	?
Indo-China	714	562	?	?	?	?	?
Korea	1,753	?	?	?	?	?	11,194
Malaya	1,495	670	?	?	?	?	?
Siam	244	417	?	?	?	?	?
Belgian Congo	—	—	136	347	515	477	355
So. Rhodesia	303	298	291	556	888	835	316
Australia	955	1,134	1,259	995	1,000	743	?
Total	42,600	44,000	?	?	?	?	?

Table II.—*Data of the Tungsten Industry in the U.S.*
(Short tons of metal content)

	1937	1938	1939	1940	1941	1942	1943	1944	1945
Production	1,666	1,903	1,715	2,436	3,210	4,489	5,736	4,882	2,696
Shipments	1,666	1,449	2,040	2,531	3,125	4,441	5,684	4,893	2,720
Imports									
General	?	?	1,556	4,833	6,576	7,705	9,339	9,119	4,320
For consumption	2,781	81	743	2,805	5,761	7,163	9,723	9,198	2,387
For re-export	251	414	295	674	14	3	—	—	166
Stocks	405[1]	336[1]	1,548	4,167	5,393	6,652	11,988	14,920	12,388
Producers	?	?	142	47	132	178	229	218	195
Consumers	?	?	1,334	1,402	1,202	1,708	1,230	755	1,892
Government	—	—	72	2,709	4,059	4,766	10,529	13,947	10,302
Consumption	?	?	?	4,978	8,350	8,695	9,657	9,583	7,073

[1]Stocks in bonded warehouses; others not known.

and it was necessary to fly war supplies to China, considerable amounts of tungsten were taken out on the return trips.

United States.—As a result of war demand and the discovery and development of new deposits, tungsten production in the U.S. rose to heights that a few years previously would have been considered fantastic. The peak of production was reached in 1943, with 11,945 tons of concentrate having a tungsten content of 5,736,000 lb., almost double the maximum attained during World War I.

In spite of heavy increases in consumption, production and imports not only maintained a satisfactory supply, but built up large stocks for possible emergency demand. Consumption almost doubled over prewar levels, and would have gone much higher except for extensive substitution of molybdenum for tungsten in tool steels. That this was an emergency substitution, and not a permanent trend in use, was made clear when restrictions on the use of tungsten were removed at the end of 1943. There was an immediate swing back to tungsten with a sharp decrease in the demand for molybdenum.

The new discoveries that supplied a large share of the increased output were largely marked out by the close of the war. This condition, combined with a tapering off of war demand, led to an abrupt decline in output in 1945. Imports declined even more sharply, the two barely meeting the consumption requirements.

With little left of the additional ore reserves discovered during the war, the postwar output was expected to be of the same order as that of the prewar years. The decrease of output in 1945 continued into 1946. Production of concentrates declined from 1,693 tons in the first quarter; the total for the three quarters was 3,297 tons, as compared with 4,371 tons in the same period of 1945. Imports declined from the 1945 level, with 5,429 tons in the first three quarters of 1946, against 7,122 tons in the same period of 1945. Consumption sagged even more, dropping from 12,961 tons to 4,354 tons in the first three quarters of 1945 and 1946, respectively.

China.—Chinese production of tungsten was greatly hampered by war activities, and even more so by shipping difficulties. However, even under these handicaps, exports of ore to the U.S. were maintained on a considerable scale up to 1945.

South America.—Outside China, South American countries were the chief sources of war supplies of tungsten. For over-all output during the war period, Bolivia headed the list, followed by Argentina, Brazil and Peru. Although Brazilian production did not get under way in any appreciable scale until 1943, it built up rapidly, and the total for 1943–45 was second to that of Bolivia. It is also to be noted that Brazil was the only producer in the list which did not show a decrease in output in 1945.

Axis Supplies.—German supplies of tungsten during the war years were chiefly from Portugal and Spain, with possibly small amounts from Sweden. These sources could hardly have supplied the amounts necessary for a war program of the size that was developed, especially since in the later years of the war much of the Portuguese and Spanish output was lost through preclusive buying by U.S. agents. It was reported that investigators going into Germany at the close of the war found considerable amounts of tungsten in reserve stocks, leading to the inference that emergency stocks of considerable size had been built up during the war.

Compared with Germany, Japan apparently was in a better position as to supply, with eventual control of the outputs of Burma, Malaya, Indo-China, Siam and Korea. Indo-China and Siam were occupied without any great upheaval and it is probable that their relatively small outputs were not greatly disturbed. Burma had been a heavy producer and Malaya an intermediate one, but in the conquest of these countries most of their production capacity was presumably destroyed, and it was not known to what extent, if any, the production facilities were restored. However, the single available figure on Korean output after 1938 (11,194 short tons in 1945) leads to the inference that if supplies of any magnitude had been available from Burma and Malaya, it would not have been necessary to push the Korean output so high. (*See* also MINERAL AND METAL PRODUCTION AND PRICES.) (G. A. Ro.)

BIBLIOGRAPHY.—"Allies' Tungsten Supplies," *Economist*, 138: 116–18 (London, Jan. 20, 1940); F. H. Ellinger, "Nickel-Tungsten System," *American Society of Metals Transactions*, 28:619–45 (Sept. 1940); C. G. Goetzel, "Refractory Metals," *Mining and Metallurgy*, 25:373–5 (Aug. 1944); K. C. Li, *Tungsten* (1943); C. H. Segerstrom, "War's Effect on Tungsten," *Mining Congress Journal*, 27:38–40 (Feb. 1941).

Tunisia

See FRENCH COLONIAL EMPIRE.

Tunnels

Despite the years of World War II, when nonmilitary construction operations were greatly curtailed, the decade 1937–46 was one of the most important in tunneling history. During this decade the longest tunnel, by far, in the world was completed—the 85-mi. Delaware aqueduct for the New York city water suppply. In southern California another remarkable municipal water supply project was put into service, the Colorado river aqueduct to service Los Angeles and vicinity extending for 392 mi. across California from the Colorado river to the Pacific. Included in the aqueduct were 33 tunnels aggregating 18 mi. in length, the longest being 13.5 mi.

The longest ever driven from two portals only, without intervening shafts or adits was the Alva B. Adams water diversion tunnel under the continental divide in Colorado, a 9-ft. bore 13.1 mi. long. Colorado also claimed the speed record for driving a tunnel through hard rock. The 6-mi. Carlton tunnel, draining the deep gold mines of the Cripple creek district, was blasted out at the average rate of 50 ft. per day, with a top speed of 74 ft. per day, all from one portal, which made the achievement all the more remarkable.

Chicago got a good start on its subway system, the longest in the U.S. to be completely in tunnel (in contrast to the conventional "cut-and-cover" system of construction in New York and Philadelphia) with the completion of 7.7 route mi. of line involving 15.4 mi. of tunnel, of which the 3.7-mi. State St. link of twin tunnels was put into service. Wartime lack of track and signal equipment delayed opening of the Dearborn St. link, although work on this section was resumed. In Detroit the phenomenal speed of 50 ft. per 20-hr. day was averaged in driving a big sewer tunnel through soft clay with a shield. Primary lining of this bore was concrete blocks instead of the cast-iron or steel segments usually used for shield-driven tunnels, with a monolithic lining of reinforced concrete following close behind the shield. A new high record of 67½ ft. in one day (20 hr.) for shield driving was established on this project.

An unusual tunnel project was completed in Pennsylvania on the Pennsylvania turnpike, a 160-mi. 4-lane superhighway. Here, out of the seven mile-long bores, six were enlargements of old headings partly driven 50 years before for the projected South Pennsylvania railroad, abandoned early in the construction stage.

The record for the fastest overall tunnel driving was set on the Charleston, S.C., aqueduct, where 18½ mi. of tunnel were driven in 7 months at an average of 500 ft. per day. The ground was ideal for tunnelling, a marl formation which could be mined with pneumatic spades, yet was firm enough to stand unsupported. The tunnel was attacked at 36 faces, two each from 17 shafts and one from each portal.

Largest of all tunnels in cross section driven during the decade was the connecting bore through Yerba Buena island between the east and west bay crossings of the San Francisco-Oakland bridge. Though only 540 ft. long, the tunnel had 58 x 76 ft. inside dimensions, carrying interurban and vehicle traffic at two levels.

One of the most spectacular methods of tunnel driving was developed on the Minneapolis-St. Paul intercepting sewers, lying in a white sandstone formation. The rock, standing hard and firm, had the peculiar characteristic of breaking down with a fine sand when disturbed. Instead of customary drilling and blasting the contractor on this project excavated the heading faces with high-pressure air jets and pneumatic chisels, then sluiced the resulting sand into sumps with water jets. From the sumps, the mixture of sand and water was pumped along the heading and up shafts to the surface by special rubber-lined centrifugal pumps, which eliminated hauling and hoisting of the spoil. At the surface, the mixture was pumped into high bins, the water drained off, and the sand dumped into trucks for disposal.

Water supplies for the U.S. fleet based on Guam were provided by a series of tunnels constructed by Seabees on the island in 1945

Notable subaqueous vehicle tunnels were built under the Maas river at Rotterdam, Neth., at Mobile, Ala., and at New York city. At New York city, twin tubes were completed under both the Hudson and East rivers, and another pair was started under New York bay between Brooklyn and Manhattan. A vehicle tunnel started across the Thames Estuary below London became a war casualty, as did also Blackwell No. 2, at London.

Tunnelling in Europe was seriously interrupted by World War II. Because most tunnels were of military significance, censorship drew a veil over many projects that were under way or planned when hostilities broke out. In addition to the Thames and Rotterdam projects, a 7-mi. railroad tunnel in the department of Vosges, France, was completed. The short Bommerstein railroad bore was finished in Switzerland. The second and third sections of the Moscow subway were completed, and another, to encircle the six radial lanes of the first three, was started.

Elsewhere in the world tunnelling was relatively inactive during the decade. In Mexico, the 7-mi. Tequixuiac water tunnel was completed and the 7-mi. El Mirador irrigation bore was practically finished. The Cañon del Pato hydroelectric tunnel in Peru, 6 mi. long, was started. In Japan, a 2-mi. railroad bore under Kwammon straits, between Kyushu and Honshu, was placed in service.

Numerous tunnels became important military factors. Several extensions of London subways were started, to be used temporarily as air-raid shelters, later to be incorporated into the transportation system. Germany built extensive underground factories, laboratories and offices. Numerous tunnels in Japan, crude but effective, were built for underground aeroplane assembly plants and for ammunition, bomb and plane storage. Many tunnels in the U.S., especially those connected with water supply, were speeded up to serve rapidly-built war plants. In Hawaii, both the U.S. army and navy excavated large underground oil storage vaults.

Railroad construction, long a prolific source of tunnel projects, was practically dormant during the decade. The Northern Pacific replaced its half-mile tunnel at Bozeman, Mont., with a new bore, and the Denver and Rio Grande Western did likewise with its Tennessee pass tunnel under Colorado's continental divide. Relocation of the Southern Pacific around Shasta dam reservoir in California required 12 short tunnels, and the Chesapeake & Ohio built a new mile-long tunnel at Afton, Va. This completed the roster of new U.S. railroad tunnels.

Progress in Tunnelling.—The art of tunnel driving advanced steadily during the decade, despite the fact that new machinery development ceased with the outbreak of war. Perhaps most significant was the complete mechanization of small tunnel operations. Formerly all muck (broken rock) was usually loaded by hand into small cars. Drilling was done by hand-held drills or by larger drills mounted on columns or bars wedged against the tunnel walls and roof. With the introduction of small, but efficient overhead-loading type power shovels (known as mucking machines), hand loading no longer paid. Drill carriages, rail-mounted, carrying heavy drills strategically spaced to cover the round of holes in the face, were produced in small size, and column-and-bar drill mounting became a rarity.

Drill carriages or "jumbos" became a universal rig on all tunnels, both large and small. Their development, along with better shoring and bracing systems, resulted in full-face mining operations on all sizes of tunnels. Formerly, in large headings, the customary procedure was to cut out the top half of the face ahead of the lower half, the so-called heading-and-bench method of driving. Drill carriages changed this slower method to full-face driving. The drills were mounted on salvaging arms at the front end of the carriage which, when the "jumbo" was pushed close to the face, enabled each drill to bore several holes without being dismounted. On some large tunnels, trucks were used to carry the "jumbos" instead of railroad cars.

The use of detachable bits for rock drilling also speeded up tunnel driving. Formerly the drill rods had to be heated in oil furnaces and then sharpened, which required the entire rod and its bit to be taken out of the tunnel, into the shop for sharpening and back to the heading. Detachable bits, which screw onto the end of the drill rods, could remain and be attached at the "jumbo," and only the small bit end needed to be taken out of the heading for sharpening. These bits could be resharpened by grinding or hot milling, and could be used over again five or six times. Pneumatic rock drills of the large or drifter type became automatic feed, thus eliminating the necessity of the drill runner's turning a hand crank to feed the drill rod into the hole. Dynamite and blasting accessories became efficient and safer.

Ventilation equipment greatly improved to make driving long headings safe and practical. Modern ventilating plants were so arranged that foul air could be exhausted from the heading, close to the face, following the blast. Then, by reversing the fans or by changing dampers in the pipe layout, the air stream could be increased to blow fresh air through the vent pipe while the men were drilling or mucking out.

Great advances were made in hauling and hoisting equipment, especially on the Delaware aqueduct. Occasionally, the contractor preferred to hoist loaded cars to the surface for muck disposal, but the customary practice was to install skips into which the muck was dumped at the bottom of the shaft. This method eliminated hoisting the cars. Mucking machines, both air and electric operated, became increasingly efficient.

Temporary support of ground during driving operations was greatly improved with the adoption of pressed-steel liner plates and steel ribs and posts for the timbering system, and liner plates curved to fit the tunnel contour were almost universally used to hold soft ground, especially in the U.S. They were essentially ribbed shallow pans, whose edges and ends bolted together in a solid sheet, though steel beams were often installed between adjacent rings of plates for additional strength and stiffness.

Concrete lining operations became largely mechanized. Collapsible steel forms, strong and rigid, easily moved and set up, speeded up this phase of tunnel work. Forms were available which permitted passage of muck trains through them, thus permitting concrete lining to proceed in one part of the tunnel while running operations continued at the face. Pneumatic placers, forcing concrete through a pipe into the forms with compressed air, became more efficient, and the concrete pump, accomplishing the same result by reciprocal action, became a common piece of equipment. Placing the concrete mixer at the forms, so dry-batched materials were hauled into the tunnel instead of wet-mixed concrete, was found advantageous. Where wet concrete was hauled to the forms, many ingenious arrangements were worked out for handling, including ramps and automatic car dumpers for charging the placing machines.

Safety in tunnel driving increased through the years. Good ventilation and lighting became requisites. Blasting accessories were made almost foolproof, and premature explosions became a rarity. Personal protection, such as hard-shell hats, rubber clothing and boots, reduced accidents. Acceptance of compressed air codes virtually eliminated the bends or compressed air illness.

Tests were made on addition of helium to the atmosphere of compressed air tunnels, to reduce the proportion of nitrogen, whose excess presence in the human body after locking out into free air results in the bends. Pure oxygen administered to the lungs after locking out proved beneficial. Improvements in haulage, hoisting and drilling equipment all promoted safety in the tunnel.

Projects of Outstanding Interest.—Tunnel driving is not a fixed and rigid procedure, such, for example, as building construction; it is uncertain and often difficult because the crust of the earth is highly variable and sometimes treacherous. A few examples of the more interesting projects of the decade 1937–46 will be cited.

A disastrous fire at the face of the north Manhattan heading of Queens-Midtown tunnel in New York, being driven with a shield under compressed air, burned through the timber face breasting during a Sunday shutdown. When the timbers burned out, the face collapsed with resultant flooding of the heading. Only after several barge loads of clay had been dumped into the river bed to partly seal the break could the heading be again placed under air and entered. The first crews to investigate the face entered through the top emergency lock in a small rowboat, and cautiously rowed their way through the dark along the top of the tunnel while the compressor plant raced at full capacity to maintain the delicate balance between inside tunnel pressure and outside river pressure. By working under water the men finally got the face sealed so the entire heading could be pumped out and tunnelling resumed, though three months' valuable time was lost in the disaster.

In the nearby south heading, the shield ran into large rock fragments dumped into the river bed from an old subway project, which made a porous face with resulting difficulty in holding the compressed air in the heading. The face was sealed with wet clay, then as workmen gingerly removed the rock fragments one at a time, others stood by with gobs of wet clay to seal the hole from which the rock came. Any slip-up in this procedure would have meant a blowout of the face and flooding of the heading.

In the San Jacinto tunnel in California a most elaborate installation of pumping equipment had to be made to take care of inrushes of water ranging as high as 10,000 gal. per min. After the tunnel headings at the foot of Potrero shaft repeatedly had been flooded out, a waterproof chamber was finally built to house seven pumps having a total capacity of 15,000 gal. per min., which could be controlled and operated from the surface when the tunnel was flooded.

In driving through New York's Hudson river silt, the contractor on the Lincoln tunnel adjusted the shield openings to admit only 20% of the displaced silt, shoving the remainder aside. The admitted muck was allowed to remain on the tunnel floor until shield driving was completed and the compressed air taken off. A flying gangway high on the tunnel side carried railroad trains of liner segments and other supplies. After driving was completed, the muck was removed and concrete roadway building operations were carried on in a normal manner.

In the Maas tunnel at Rotterdam, concrete sills were placed under water in a dredged trench. Huge prefabricated tunnel sections, 81 ft. wide, 31 ft. high and 202 ft. long, were then floated to place and sunk. Hydraulic jacks in the walls, resting on the sills, levelled each section to correct position. The sections were joined inside a huge diving bell lowered from the surface.

Special ventilation equipment was developed for the 13-mi. Alva B. Adams tunnel in Colorado. Booster fans were installed at 5,000-ft. intervals in the ventilating pipe, so hooked up that they would start and stop in sequence rather than simultaneously. Thus, the column of moving air was treated as a hydraulic fluid rather than air. Also on this project was a signal block system, operated by electric eyes, which controlled movement of muck trains.

At Fort Peck, Mont., instant application of a bituminous sealing compound was necessary on all freshly-exposed faces of shale through which the big diversion tunnels were driven. If exposed to air for only a few minutes, the shale would slake and crumble, making it impossible to hold in place.

Extremely cold water flowing into the Leadville, Colo., drainage tunnel defied sealing off by usual cement grout methods; for the cement would not hydrate and set under the temperature conditions before the grout was forced out by water. The problem of sealing off water flows was solved by putting oats into the mix, which swelled upon becoming wet and

Major Tunnels Completed or Under Construction 1937–1946

Name	Location	Purpose	Fin. size (Ft.)	No. of bores	Unit Lgth. (Mi.)	Total Lgth. (Mi.)	Completed
Delaware aqueduct	New York	Water	13 to 26	1	85.0	85.0	1944*
Colo. river aqueduct:							
Colo. river	California	"	16.0	"	1.1	1.1	1939†
Copper basin #1	"	"	"	"	0.1	0.1	"
" " #2	"	"	"	"	2.2	2.2	"
Whipple Mt.	"	"	"	"	6.1	6.1	"
Iron Mt.	"	"	"	"	10.6	10.6	"
Coxcomb	"	"	"	"	3.4	3.4	"
East Eagle Mt.	"	"	"	"	1.8	1.8	"
West Eagle Mt.	"	"	"	"	7.1	7.1	"
Hayfield #1	"	"	"	"	1.8	1.8	"
" #2	"	"	"	"	1.1	1.1	"
Cottonwood	"	"	"	"	3.8	3.8	"
Mecca pass #1	"	"	"	"	0.1	0.1	"
" " #2	"	"	"	"	0.2	0.2	"
" " #3	"	"	"	"	0.9	0.9	"
Coachella	"	"	"	"	18.3	18.3	"
1,000 Palms #1	"	"	"	"	2.8	2.8	"
" " #2	"	"	"	"	0.7	0.7	"
Wide canyon #1	"	"	"	"	2.7	2.7	"
" " #2	"	"	"	"	0.2	0.2	"
Seven Palms	"	"	"	"	3.2	3.2	"
Long canyon	"	"	"	"	2.9	2.9	"
Blind canyon	"	"	"	"	1.3	1.3	"
Morongo #1	"	"	"	"	1.0	1.0	"
" #2	"	"	"	"	0.3	0.3	"
Whitewater #1	"	"	"	"	0.4	0.4	"
" #2	"	"	"	"	1.6	1.6	"
San Jacinto	"	"	"	"	13.5	13.5	"
Bernasconi	"	"	"	"	1.2	1.2	"
Valverde	"	"	"	"	7.0	7.0	"
Monrovia #1	"	"	10.0	"	0.8	0.8	"
" #2	"	"	10.0	"	0.9	0.9	"
" #3	"	"	10.0	"	6.1	6.1	"
Pasadena	"	"	10.0	"	2.3	2.3	"
Sierra Madre	"	"	13.0	"	1.3	1.3	"
San Rafael	"	"	10.0	"	1.7	1.7	"
Mono Craters	"	"	9.0	"	11.3	11.3	"
Chicago	Illinois	"	10 to 16	"	12.0	12.0	1946
Alva B. Adams	Colorado	"	9.8	"	13.1	13.1	" ‡
Rams Horn	"	"	10.0	"	1.3	1.3	§
Prospect Mt.	"	"	12.5	"	1.1	1.1	"
San Diego Aqueduct:							
Rainbow	California	"	6.0	"	0.9	0.9	"
Lilac	"	"	"	"	0.1	0.1	"
Red Mt.	"	"	"	"	0.6	0.6	"
Oat hills	"	"	"	"	0.7	0.7	"
Poway	"	"	"	"	0.6	0.6	"
Fire hill	"	"	"	"	1.1	1.1	"
San Vicente	"	"	"	"	0.5	0.5	"
James pass	Colorado	"	8x9	"	3.0	3.0	1938
Montebello	Baltimore, Md.	"	12.0	"	12.6	12.6	1940
Charleston	South Carolina	"	7.0	"	18.5	18.5	1937‖
Stanislaus	California	"	9.5x10.7	"	11.0	11.0	1940
Pit river #5	"	"	19.0	"	5.4	5.4	1943
Duchesne	Utah	"	11.0	"	3.0	3.0	1941
Alpine Draper	"	"	6.5	"	3.0	3.0	"
Olmstead	"	"	6.5	"	0.6	0.6	"
Bacon	Washington	"	23.0	2	1.9	3.8	§
Ft. Peck	Montana	"	24.7	4	1.2	4.8	1937
El Mirador	Mexico	"	16.0	1	7.0	7.0	"
Canon del Pato	Peru	"	18.5	"	5.7	5.7	"
Elton	Utah	Drain	10x11	"	1.5	1.5	1941
Carlton	Colorado	"	10x11	"	6.1	6.1	"
Leadville	"	"	9x10.5	"	2.6	2.6	1945
Tequixquiac	Mexico	"	18.0	"	6.8	6.8	"
S.W. Interceptor	Chicago, Ill.	Sewer	17.3x19.2	"	12.4	12.4	1937
Bronx	N.Y. city	"	8.5	"	5.0	5.0	"
Wards Island	" "	"	8.5	"	0.7	0.7	"
Memphis Sew.	Memphis, Tenn.	"	6.7x7.8	"	2.7	2.7	1940
Interceptor	St. Paul, Minn.	"	5.5 to 14	"	15.0	15.0	1937
Interceptor	Minneapolis, Minn.	"	5.5 to 14	"	15.2	15.2	"
Jefferson	Detroit, Mich.	"	16.0	"	1.9	1.9	"
Oakland	Michigan	"	5.5	"	6.0	6.0	1944
State St.	Chicago, Ill.	Subway	15x15.5	2	3.7	7.4	1943
Dearborn St.	"	"	15x15.5	"	2.8	2.8	§
Moscow #2	Moscow, U.S.S.R.	"	18.0	"	5.0	10.0	1939¶
" #3	" "	"	18.0	"	4.0	8.0	1943¶
" #4	" "	"	18.0	"	10.0	20.0	§¶
Tennessee pass	Colorado	Railroad	16x23	1	0.5	0.5	1945
Bozeman	Montana	"	18x24	"	0.6	0.6	"
Afton	Virginia	"	18x22	"	0.8	0.8	1943
Shasta dam	California	"	18x22	12	...	3.6	1940♀
Vosges	France	"	25x20	1	7.0	7.0	1940
Kwammon Straits	Japan	"	16x22	"	2.0	2.0	1942
Whittier #1	Alaska	"	16x22	"	0.5	0.5	1943
" #2	"	"	16x22	"	1.5	1.5	"
Bommerstein	Switzerland	"	16x22	"	0.3	0.3	1940
Lincoln	N.Y. city	Vehicle	21.5x13.5	2	1.7	3.4	1945δ
Queens Midtown	" "	"	21x13.5	"	1.3	2.6	1940□
Battery Brooklyn	" "	"	21x13.5	"	1.2	2.4	§□
Yerba Buena	San Francisco, Calif.	"	58x76	1	0.1	0.1	1937◊
Broadway	Oakland, "	"	25.0	2	0.6	1.2	1937
Bingham	Utah	"	16x10	1	1.2	1.2	1939
Bankhead	Alabama	"	27.0	"	0.4	0.4	1941▲
Lake Washington	Seattle, Wash.	"	30.0	2	0.5	1.0	1940

(Table concluded on next page)

Major Tunnels Completed or Under Construction 1937-46—Continued

Name	Location	Purpose	Fin. size (Ft.)	No. of bores	Unit Lgth. (Mi.)	Total Lgth. (Mi.)	Completed
Pennsylvania Turnpike:							
Blue Mt.	Pennsylvania	Vehicle	28.5x14.5	1	0.8	0.8	1941+
Kittatinny	"	"	"	"	0.9	0.9	"
Tuscarora	"	"	"	"	1.0	1.0	"
Sideling hill	"	"	"	"	1.3	1.3	"
Rays hill	"	"	"	"	0.7	0.7	"
Allegheny	"	"	"	"	1.1	1.1	1941
Laurel hill	"	"	"	"	0.9	0.9	1941+
Maas	Rotterdam	"	81x27.5	"	0.4	0.4	1941▲
Thames estuary	England	"	—	"	1.1	1.1	§
Blackwell #2	London, Eng.	"	24.0	"	0.5	0.5	"

The above list does not include numerous short tunnels driven for U.S. irrigation projects, river diversion around dams or for subways built by cut-and-cover method.

*World's longest tunnel. †Completion dates on Colorado river aqueduct are date project was put into service. Some tunnels were actually completed earlier. ‡Longest ever driven from two portals only, without intervening shafts or adits. §Tunnels not completed at the close of 1946. ‖18.5-mi. tunnel driven in remarkable time of 7 mo. from 17 shafts and two portals. ¶Record not clear as to exact lengths or proportions of twin-tube single-track line and single-tube double-track line. First unit 6.2 route mi. built in tunnel completed 1935. ♀12 tunnels, from 0.2 to 0.5 mi. long for relocation Southern Pacific railroad around Shasta dam reservoir. ♁Size given is roadway opening; tunnel is 31 ft. outside diameter; south tube completed 1937; north tube opened 1945. □Size given is roadway opening; tunnel is 31 ft. outside diameter. ◇Believed largest cross-section in world. ▲Built by sinking prepared sections into dredged trench. +Part of tunnel was enlarged from old railroad bore.

thus checked the water pressure until the cement could slowly set. (H. W. Rn.)

Bibliography.—S. H. Ash, *Safety Factors in Construction and Ventilation* (1940); B. Chase, *Sandhog* (1938); O. Kommerell, *Statische Berechnung von Tunnelmauerwerk* (Berlin, 1940); G. E. McElroy, *Dilution of Stack Effluents*, Bureau of Mines Tech. Paper 657 (1944); H. W. Richardson, *Practical Tunnel Driving* (1941). For specific periodical references consult *Engineering Index; Industrial Arts Index* (1937, *et seq.*)

Turkestan, Chinese

See Sinkiang.

Turkey

The Turkish republic lies between the meridians 26° and 44° 48 min. E. of Greenwich and between the parallels of latitude 36°–42° N. Its area is 296,185 sq.mi. Ankara with a population of 226,000 (1940 census, 157,242) is the capital of the republic. Other principal cities are Istanbul, Izmir, Adana, Bursa, Eskişehir, Gaziantep, Konya, Sivas, Erzurum, Kars, Diyarbakir, Trabzon and Samsun.

The population of the country, according to the census of 1945, was 18,861,609 (1940 census, 17,820,950). Classification of the 1945 census had not been completed at the end of 1946, but according to the census of 1935 the proportion of the Turkish-speaking population was 90% and the proportion of Mohammedans was 98%.

Legal and administrative authority in the Turkish republic was vested in the grand national assembly, to be exercised by the council of ministers nominated by the president of the republic (himself elected by the assembly). The term of the presidency was set at four years, with the president elected from among the members of the assembly. Persons of either sex, on completion of their 22nd year, were given the right to vote. The elections for the assembly were required to be held every four years.

Between 1937 and 1946 the following were presidents of the republic: Kemal Atatürk (Oct. 29, 1923–Nov. 10, 1938), Ismet Inönü (after Nov. 11, 1938). The following were prime ministers: Celâl Bayar (Oct. 25, 1937–Jan. 25, 1939), Dr. Refik Saydam (Jan. 25, 1939–July 8, 1942), Sükrü Saraçoğlu (July 9, 1942–Aug. 6, 1946), Recep Peker (after Aug. 6, 1946).

Death of Atatürk.—The most important historical event in Turkey's domestic politics during the early part of the decade 1937–46 was the death of President Kemal Atatürk on Nov. 10, 1938.

Due honour was accorded by the nation to this unrivalled hero of the War of Independence for the idealism and courageous guidance he had shown in the introduction of great reforms. All civilized nations, regardless of past friendship or enmity, made Turkish hearts swell with pride by showing their admiration and respect for Atatürk. The whole world wondered how, after Atatürk's death, Turkey would develop in the social and political fields, but events proved once more the stability of the republic. On Nov. 11, 1938, the national assembly unanimously elected Ismet Inönü, premier during most of Atatürk's administration and the latter's chief aide, as president of the republic.

Policy of Peace.—The foreign policy of the Turkish republic during the decade was based upon a sincere peace policy, genuinely devoted to the maintenance of good relations with its neighbours. The five-centuries-old struggle with Greece was brought to an end, and as desired by both parties, was superseded by a search for friendship and common security.

An atmosphere of good neighbourliness was created with Arab countries and Iran; Turkey's relations with Bulgaria were normal and very satisfactory compared with the latter's relations with other Balkan states.

Turkey's situation in 1937, as regards its relations with the great powers, could be summed up as follows: relations of good friendship continued with the soviet union. With Great Britain, no trace had remained of the enmity felt toward it all through the War of Independence, and a friendship that manifested itself conspicuously was established between the two countries. The Hatay question was the only cause of dispute between Turkey and France, and the relations between the two countries began to improve following the equitable solution of this problem. On June 23, 1939, a pact was signed at Paris together with an agreement by which France ceded Hatay (the sanjak of Alexandretta) to Turkey. Formal cession took place a month

British Gen. Sir James H. Marshall-Cornwall reviewing Turkish troops at Ankara in Jan. 1941, as the shadow of nazi aggression in the Balkans lengthened

later at Antioch. The relations between the Turkish republic and Italy varied from time to time. State visits were mutually paid, but the expansionist policy and the clamorous speeches of the fascist regime kept the Turks in a state of considerable uneasiness. Mutual confidence was lost altogether when, during the Ethiopian campaign, Turkey adhered to the decision of the League of Nations regarding the application of sanctions against Italy, and openly supported the British view as well as the coercive measures suggested by Great Britain.

Until 1937, the relations of Turkey with Germany were mostly of an economic nature. As a result of the great economic crisis that began in 1929, Turkey like other countries had to resort to a planned economy in its trade with foreign countries, and the difficulties it encountered in procuring foreign currencies finally compelled it to establish commercial relations with Germany. Trade with that country was, therefore, of great importance to Turkey.

Relations with the U.S. remained cordial throughout the decade. Every ambassador who had represented the U.S. in Turkey since the first days of the republic expressed admiration and encouragement for the Turkish people's new way of life.

As a member of the League of Nations, Turkey worked fervently for the realization of collective peace, while supporting all such organizations as were designed to secure collective peace along its frontiers. Turkey, with Rumania, Greece and Yugoslavia, founded the Balkan Entente in 1934. The main object of the Entente was to safeguard the security of common frontiers and to try to win over Bulgaria, in time, as a friend, failing which the members of the Entente would take steps to neutralize that country.

But so far as the relations with the great powers flanking the outer borders were concerned, members of the Entente were under no obligation whatsoever, unless complications with Bulgaria arose. Reservations were even made by Greece and Turkey in respect of Italy and the soviet union respectively.

Moreover, should one of the members of the Entente get involved in single-handed war against Germany or Italy, the others remained free from any obligations.

Turkey: *Statistical Data*

Item	1938 Value (000's omitted)	1938 Amount or Number	1940 Value (000's omitted)	1940 Amount or Number	1945 Value (000's omitted)	1945 Amount or Number
Exchange Rate						
U.S.		1 Turkish pound = 80.1 cents		1 Turkish pound = 72.59 cents		1 Turkish pound = 80 cents
Gt. Britain		6.10–6.22 Turkish lb. = £1		5.20–5.24 Turkish lb. = £1		
Finance						
Government revenues	$262,691 (£53,731)		$320,661 (£83,723)		$721,209 (£178,960)	
Government expenditures	$238,236 (£48,729)		$303,993 (£79,372)		$761,948 (£189,069)	
Gold reserves	$27,958 (£5,719)		$81,928 (£21,391)			
National debt	$427,473 (£87,436)		...		$1,114,010 (£276,429)*	
Transportation						
Railroads		4,366 mi.		4,522 mi. †		4,551 mi.‡
Highways		10,191 "		25,393 " †		...
Communication						
Telephones		...		23,396§		28,857
Telegraph lines		19,233 mi.		19,704 mi.§		18,795 mi.‡
Radio sets		29,000		91,216§		176,262
Minerals						
Coal		2,853,855 tons		2,766,348 tons†		4,099,454 tons
Cement		294,940 "		232,423 " †		299,689 "
Chrome		229,339 "		159,511 " †		86,313 "
Mineral water		258,940 gal.		264,587 gal.†		173,708 gal.
Crops						
Wheat		4,739,890 tons		4,634,069 tons		3,525,592 tons‡
Sugar beets		3,026,916 "				676,101 " ‡
Barley		2,843,934 "		2,529,779 "		1,546,581 " ‡
Potatoes		1,858,478 "		241,404 "		211,352 " ‡
Livestock						
Sheep		23,138,450		18,857,000		22,450,000‡
Goats (ordinary)		11,329,241		8,999,000		12,250,000‡
Cattle		9,310,966		7,724,000		9,549,000‡
Goats (mohair)		4,945,351		3,773,000		4,975,000‡
Forest Products						
Licorice		213 tons‖				...
Hazelnuts		25,353 "				...
Firewood		36,971,315 cu. ft.				26,128,740 cu. ft.‡¶
Timber		24,682,588 "				112,320,073 " ‡
Charcoal		2,317,496 "				26,128,740 " ‡¶
Manufactures						
Total	$219,365 (£44,869)	...	$383,275 (£95,058)§	...		
Food	$127,194 (£26,016)	...	$218,258 (£54,131)§	...		
Textile	$42,356 (£8,664)	...	$85,933 (£21,313)§	...		
Wood and paper	$10,517 (£2,151)	...	$12,851 (£3,187)§	...		
Exports—total	$116,158 (£23,759)	1,237,000 tons	$80,899 (£21,122)	...		
Tobacco (leaf)	$31,467 (£6,436)	47,000 "	$17,583 (£4,591)	30,000 tons		
Sultunas (seedless)	$10,837 (£2,217)	85,000 "	$3,299 (£861)	34,000 "		
Hazelnuts (shelled)	$9,762 (£1,997)	25,000 "	$4,790 (£1,251)	19,000 "		
Cotton	$8,193 (£1,676)	29,000 "	$5,092 (£1,330)	13,000 "		
Imports—total	$120,003 (£24,546)	...	$50,031 (£13,063)	...		
Iron and steel manufactures	$17,142 (£3,506)	214,471 tons	$4,373 (£1,142)	...		
Cotton textiles	$11,005 (£2,251)	11,588 "	$3,930 (£1,026)	3,967 tons		
Machinery and parts	$10,125 (£2,071)	19,940 "	$6,472 (£1,690)	13,099 "		
Mineral oils	$4,419 (£904)	184,313 "	$2,102 (£549)	47,695 "		
Defense						
Standing army personnel		132,375		750,000		
Reserves		529,425		...		
Standing navy		9,200		...		
Standing air force		8,383		8,500		
Military expenditures	$66,010 (£13,502)		$95,569 (£24,953)			
Education						
Elementary schools		6,700		9,418		10,948†
Students		764,691		905,139		939,829†
Secondary schools		282		314		334†
Students		94,868		118,563		122,859†
Normal, technical and professional schools		92		103		131†
Students		15,591		19,986		30,806†
University of Istanbul Students		4,927		6,471		8,713†

*1943. †1942. ‡1944. §1941. ‖Exports only. ¶Combined measure of firewood and charcoal.

Among the political combinations of the middle east, the Saad-Abad pact to which Turkey, Iran, Iraq and Afghanistan were parties, merited special attention. This pact was meant to bring about mutual aid and *rapprochement* in the political and social spheres by establishing friendship and good relations. It, however, did not contain any military clause to operate automatically.

Montreux Convention.—Of great importance for Turkey was the signature of the Montreux convention in 1936, which revised the straits regime imposed on Turkey by the treaty of Lausanne. The straits were demilitarized under that treaty and were opened to the warships of the Mediterranean states, provided that the tonnage did not exceed that of the strongest Black sea power. The soviet union did not ratify that treaty. But the convention of Montreux, duly signed and ratified by the soviet union, had recognized Turkey's right to fortify and defend the straits. Full freedom was recognized for merchant ships. As regards the passage of warships in peacetime, the ships of the Black sea powers could pass through without any restriction on tonnage; other powers could not, as a rule, have the right of passage for ships with an aggregate tonnage of over 30,000. In war, in the event of Turkey being neutral, the ships of belligerents would not be allowed to pass. If Turkey were a belligerent, or considered itself threatened by imminent danger of war, the passage of warships was left to the discretion of the Turkish government.

An annex was added to the Montreux convention (No. 2), wherein the essential points of the London Naval treaty of 1936 were incorporated almost identically; *i.e.*, the tonnage and characteristics of warships and auxiliary craft were specified. During World War II these descriptions were found to be insufficient. The fact that the period of 1937–38 was teeming with the portents of an imminent second world war was realized by Turkey.

Turkey attached importance to maintaining good relations with both the soviet union and Great Britain. The nation was anxious to avoid taking up a position between two opposing parties; the political situation after the Munich agreement of 1938 began to cause anxiety. But Turkey thought that this would give rise to no substantial difference in the stand taken by the soviets, Great Britain and France vis à vis the axis powers.

Early Phases of World War II.—The spring of 1939 occasioned great uneasiness in Turkey and in the Balkan countries. Germany and Italy had invaded Czechoslovakia and Albania respectively. Britain, having given up all hope of finding Germany trustworthy, was giving unilateral guarantees to the small powers exposed to aggression in eastern Europe. No such power excepting Poland, however, responded to the proposed guarantees. Certain small powers even went further and refused to accept them.

The republic of Turkey on the one hand and Great Britain and France on the other began to open negotiations with regard to mutual declarations of guarantee. These declarations made clear before the whole world the attitude of the signatories towards each other and were to be complemented by treaties of alliance. As soon as the negotiations on these declarations opened up, Turkey stressed at the very outset the necessity of co-operation with the soviet union and was convinced that Great Britain and France intended to co-operate with Russia as well.

Declarations were signed between Turkey and Great Britain and between Turkey and France on May 12, 1939, and June 23, 1939, respectively, but preparations for the treaty of alliance did not advance with the speed anticipated. Meanwhile the British and French delegations had gone to Moscow and had started negotiations with the soviet union.

Turkey was not aware of the real nature of the negotiations of 1939 between the soviet union and the western powers, but it firmly believed that the negotiations would be crowned with success.

The declarations aligning Turkey with Great Britain and France were received with great resentment by Germany and Italy. Through broadcasts and publications, grave accusations and threats were levelled against Turkey, and it was in such an atmosphere that the outcome of the negotiations among Great Britain, France and Russia was awaited. Then the cessation of the negotiations was announced, and the Russo-German pact of nonaggression was announced to a surprised world on Aug. 24, 1939.

When the Polish war broke out on Sept. 1, Turkey was disappointed at seeing the frustration of its wishes for co-operation and unity of policy between Great Britain and Russia. In Sept. 1939, while the war in Poland was still in progress, negotiations for a treaty of alliance between Turkey, Britain and France were resumed and proceeded quickly. According to this plan, Great Britain and France accepted the condition that Turkey should be supplied with military equipment to a certain agreed extent, and

Lend-lease shipment of U.S.-made bombs for Turkey being unloaded by Turkish troops in 1943

that it should not be dragged into armed conflict with Russia. Meanwhile the soviet union invited Turkish Foreign Minister Sükrü Saraçoğlu to Moscow with a view to concluding a treaty of alliance. The Turkish foreign minister informed the soviet union of the arrangements made with Great Britain and France, and stated that he would require the inclusion of a reservation concerning Great Britain and France in the prospective soviet treaty. Then, before signing the treaty with Britain and France, Saraçoğlu informed the latter nations that he was going to Moscow for a talk with the Russians, and that in the interest of his country's relations with both parties he wished to avoid the danger of hasty decisions.

Saraçoğlu arrived at Moscow on Sept. 25 and left on Oct. 17. The initial negotiations continued without a hitch, but before concluding a treaty of alliance the Russians asked for certain amendments in the plan drawn up with Great Britain. Turkey asked Great Britain and France to agree with the said amendments, which they did after lengthy negotiations.

Turkey therefore felt that the conditions for a treaty with the soviet union were all fulfilled. At that point the soviet union suggested an arrangement in its favour concerning the provisions of the Montreux convention, and it furthermore desired that a reservation regarding Germany be included in the treaty. After these points had been accepted, the U.S.S.R. stated that there would be one or two more points to be discussed.

In the face of this entirely new and unexpected situation, negotiations for the treaty were interrupted, and Foreign Minister Saraçoğlu left Moscow.

The Turkish, British and French treaty was signed in Ankara on Oct. 19, 1939. It became known through official speeches that the conclusion of this agreement displeased the soviet union.

The Year 1940.—After the fall of France, the Vichy government maintained its hold in Syria, taking up a position against Turkey, the ally of Great Britain. At the same time Rashid Ali launched a rebellion in Iraq.

Thus, Turkey had been isolated on its Syrian and Iraqi frontiers. The most important development for Turkey, however, was the very menacing political aggression of Germany. During the occupation of France, certain documents purporting to show the support of Turkey for French and British intentions directed against Russia were made public. France and Great Britain were dissatisfied at the delivery of materials to Germany in accordance with the Russo-German pact. The soviet union did not conceal its displeasure at Turkey's alliance with the western democracies. The Germans, when they published the French documents, were working zealously in a tense political atmosphere to create armed conflict between Turkey and Russia, and seeing Turkey isolated, they believed that, as was the case with Rumania, she would be drawn closer to them against an eventual Russian aggression. Turkey met these developments with calmness and tried to convince the Russians of the correctness of its policy toward them and the invalidity of the published documents, pending further developments. Contrary to German expectations, Turkey did not show any inclination whatever to side with the nazi government. On the contrary, after the Italian aggression against Greece in Oct. 1940, Turkey made known its position with renewed determination and courage.

President Inönü, in a speech delivered to the national assembly on Nov. 1, 1940, made the following statement about Great Britain: "It is my bounden duty to state, that at a time when Great Britain is compelled to struggle gallantly for existence under difficult conditions, the ties of alliance that bind us to her are sound and unshakeable."

Axis Ring.—The spring of 1941 witnessed the descent of the Germans into the Balkans and the occupation of Greece and Yugoslavia. Thus Turkey was surrounded on land and sea by Germany and Italy. The Germans did their utmost to come to the assistance of Syria and Iraq through Turkish territory, both by land and air, and every occasion gave rise to incessant and insistent *démarches* and negotiations. In April 1941, Turkey had mobilized its entire army and concentrated its forces in Thrace and on the shores of the Aegean. The nation was waiting with resolution for its turn to come after the fall of the Balkan countries. Blowing up the bridges on the Meric river, it withdrew its forces in Thrace to defensive lines further to the rear. Such was the military situation, and yet Turkey categorically refused to comply with the German demands.

After the occupation of Rumania, soviet-German relations, which seemed to have been quiet for a period, assumed new activity during the winter of 1940–41. Soviet-Bulgarian relations during the months of Feb. and March 1941 were also active. After some soviet politicians had gone to Bulgaria in an official capacity, various anti-Turkish rumours were circulated in Bulgaria. In short, everything pointed to preparations for an attack on Turkey. Meanwhile the British were fighting in Iraq and Syria and were meeting with success.

At this juncture, the Germans made it known that they would not attack Turkey and then proposed a pact of friendship. Turkey declared that it would consent to this agreement with its far-reaching provisions on condition that the terms of the treaty of alliance with Great Britain were not prejudiced. The Germans accepted this condition. It was understood that the Germans had put off their attack on Turkey to a later and more suitable time; Turkey also considered it necessary to gain time both for its own security and for the benefit of its allies.

After the German invasion of the U.S.S.R., and during the various axis campaigns in Africa, Turkey steadfastly refused to give passage to the Germans. As a guardian of the Montreux convention, Turkey on the one hand did not allow the Italian fleet to pass from the Mediterranean to the Black sea, and on the other guarded its frontiers with all its forces against a surprise attack by land or by sea. While resisting German attacks, Russia and Great Britain were maintaining safe communications through the Arab countries and in Iran. They were using all their forces against the axis on the war fronts.

At the end of 1941, after the U.S. had been attacked and had entered the war, the three great Allies began to be interested in Turkey's position, and they were satisfied with its attitude.

Franklin D. Roosevelt had stated in Dec. 1941 that as the defense of Turkey assisted the struggle of the U.S., he would help Turkey with lend-lease. On Jan. 19, 1942, the soviet government, through its ambassador in Ankara, transmitted a message to the Turkish government that it was satisfied with the Turkish attitude and was of the opinion that this attitude of itself merited reward. The axis states in 1941 and 1942 had not been able to agree on their intentions toward Turkey. Italy found that the cause of all its disasters was the fact that the axis had not penetrated into Arab countries by land after overrunning Turkey. Japan was very anxious that the Indian ocean should be reached following the invasion of Turkey and urged that time once lost could never be recovered. In the days

U.S. marines from the U.S.S. "Missouri" at Istanbul. The battleship arrived in Turkey during April 1946, with the body of Mehmet M. Ertegün, former Turkish ambassador to the U.S.

of El Alamein, it was understood that the handing of an ultimatum to Turkey was seriously considered. All these plans depended on one condition. It was necessary to pass through Turkey by force and in great strength, but the favourable moment had not arrived. The Turkish republic in the fourth year of the war, was still striving to protect its own territory against all eventualities and by means of its own unaided financial resources was already rendering services to the United Nations.

The Germans retreated from El Alamein and Stalingrad. The Americans landed in Africa (Nov. 1942), and so the axis tide began to recede.

Final Years of the War.—When, at the beginning of 1943, Winston Churchill visited Adana, he made it known that he appreciated Turkey's position. He had arrived from Casablanca after reaching a full understanding with Pres. Roosevelt. Churchill promised to supply Turkey with as much military equipment as it needed; Turkey had barred the road to further German expansion eastward. A vast program of armament for the Turkish army was to be elaborated and put into effect within a short time. In the coming phase of the conflict Turkey would decide for itself the time to enter the war.

The greatest service to the Allied cause during World War II was rendered by Turkey at the beginning of 1943. The Germans and Italians, now in control of the whole of Europe, had not been able to penetrate into the middle east. This was one of the principal factors influencing the outcome of the war, both from a political and military point of view. The Turks were able to keep the road to the middle east barred until the battles of Stalingrad and El Alamein were won, and North Africa was occupied by U.S. and British forces.

The year 1943 witnessed the advance operations of the Allies in the Mediterranean and in the plains of Russia. At each meeting of leaders of the great powers, Turkey was among the subjects of discussion. It was decided at Tehran, at the end of 1943, to ask Turkey to enter the war, and this decision was communicated to Turkey. The Turkish president was invited to go to Cairo, where he discussed this subject with Roosevelt and the British prime minister. At Cairo, Turkey pointed out that it had been impossible to fulfil the armament program as set forth in 1943. Nevertheless, not insisting on the previous arms program, it agreed in principle to enter the war on the side of the Allies. Turkey demanded to be equipped with a minimum supply within the first two or three months in order to be able to cope with a probable combined German-Bulgarian attack, and asked that arrangements be made for joint operations and close collaboration.

A British military mission visited Ankara and discussed this subject at length. It found that it could not supply Turkey with the needed material.

The manner in which these conversations were conducted was most unfortunate. Turkey's entry into the war had already been discussed at Tehran and the discussions had been recorded, but what had been said and put on paper was kept secret. In Feb. 1944, the Ankara conversations failed to produce any results, and newspaper criticism started. The past five years had been forgotten.

In Aug. 1944, Great Britain and the U.S. asked Turkey to sever diplomatic and economic relations with Germany. Turkey acquiesced and even manifested an inclination to enter the war immediately. Great Britain made it clear that the first step toward Turkey's entry had been taken, and that when the proper time arrived it would request further action. It was understood that Turkey's participation, at this time, constituted a thorny problem between Great Britain, the U.S. and Russia. In Feb. 1945, at the request of Great Britain and the U.S., Turkey declared war against Germany and Japan. Turkey consequently became a member of the United Nations and was invited to participate in the San Francisco conference.

After Germany's Defeat.—Turkey's most important problem during the immediate postwar period was its relations with soviet Russia which, in March 1945, denounced the friendship and nonaggression pact existing between the two countries since 1925 and informed Turkey of its refusal to renew the pact. Russia announced to Turkey that this pact, which terminated in Nov. 1945, did not comply with prevailing conditions and required drastic alterations of its terms. Turkey agreed. What these new terms were was not made known for a long time. Finally, in June 1945 information was obtained regarding the terms in question, which caused great disappointment in Turkey.

In the meantime, Russia opened a war of nerves on the radio. No mention was made in May and June 1945 of the services rendered by Turkey to the Allied cause and of the sacrifices it had made during the war. Turkey did its utmost to weather with patience the storm of unfair and unwarranted accusations. In the summer of 1945, the Big Three decided at Potsdam to enter into conversations with Turkey regarding the revision of the Montreux convention. Great Britain and the U.S. made known their opinions and manifested a desire to revise the Montreux convention.

The soviets in their note of Aug. 7, 1946, also outlined their position. Expounding an essentially different point of view, they proposed that the straits regime should be discussed, to the exclusion of others, by the Black sea powers only, and that the defense of the straits should be undertaken jointly by Turkey and the soviet union. In a second note the Russians confirmed this. Turkey did not accept these demands; it contended that revision should be made in accordance with the procedure prescribed by the convention itself. (I. I.)

Bibliography.—H. Froembgen, *Kemal Ataturk* (1937); L. Linke, *Allah Dethroned* (London, 1937); J. Parker, *Modern Turkey* (1940); J. T. Shotwell, *Turkey at the Straits* (1940); *Statesman's Yearbook;* B. Ward, *Turkey* (1942); D. E. Webster, *Turkey of Ataturk* (1939). *See* also *Asia* (Aug. 1946), *Foreign Policy Reports* (Nov. 1, 1944), *Nat. Geog. Mag.* (Sept. 1941).

Turkeys

See Poultry.

Turkmen S. S. R.

See Union of Soviet Socialist Republics.

Turks and Caicos Islands

See West Indies, British.

Turner, Richmond Kelly

Turner (1885–), U.S. navy officer, was born May 27, 1885, in Portland, Ore. A graduate of the U.S. naval academy at Annapolis (1908), he was commissioned an ensign in 1910; he served on a number of battleships during World War I and after the armistice trained at the Naval Aviation school in Pensacola, becoming a naval aviator in 1927. He was commander of the Asiatic fleet's aircraft squadron (1928–29) and chief of the navy's bureau of aeronautics planning division (1929–31).

On July 1, 1935, he was promoted to a captaincy, and was assigned to the Naval War college. In 1940 Turner became director of the navy's war plans division and the following year he was promoted to the rank of rear admiral. Returning to active sea duty after the U.S. entry in World War II, he commanded amphibious forces that landed on Guadalcanal, Aug. 7, 1942.

Turner also commanded amphibious operations in the New Georgia, Kwajalein, Saipan and Iwo campaigns. He was made a full admiral on May 15, 1945.

TVA

See Tennessee Valley Authority.

Tweedsmuir, 1st Baron

Baron Tweedsmuir of Elsfield (1875–1940), British statesman, was born John Buchan in Perth, Scotland, Aug. 26, 1875. He was educated at Glasgow university and Brasenose college, Oxford, and after graduation was admitted to the bar in 1901. From 1927 to 1935 he was member of parliament for the Scottish universities. When he was appointed governor-general of Canada and raised to the peerage in 1935 he was one of the best known men of letters in Great Britain. Among his better known novels were *The Thirty-Nine Steps* (1915) and *Greenmantle* (1916); he also wrote several histories, including one of World War I. He died in Montreal, Feb. 11, 1940.

Twentieth Century Fund

See Societies and Associations.

Twining, Nathan Farragut

Twining (1897–), U.S. army officer, was born in Monroe, Wis., Oct. 11, 1897. Graduated from the U.S. Military academy in 1919, he later studied at the Infantry school (1919–20). Leaving the infantry to join the air corps in 1924, he studied at the Air Corps Tactical school, 1935–36, and at the Command and General Staff school, 1936–37. Twining served in the South Pacific in the early days of World War II and was commander of the 13th air force in the Solomon Islands from July 25 to Nov. 20, 1943. During this period, his air force knocked out all the Japanese air fields on Bougainville, for which exploit he was awarded the Distinguished Flying cross. Sent to the Mediterranean theatre of war, he was made commander of the 15th air force in Italy, 1944–45, and on July 24, 1945, the army air forces announced that he had been made commander of the 20th air force in the Marianas. That same year, Twining was promoted to the rank of a lieutenant general.

After the close of World War II, Twining led a flight of three superfortresses in Oct. 1945 which completed a 13,167-mi. flight from Guam to Washington, D.C. (via India and Germany) in 59 hr. and 30 min.

Typhus Fever

See Military Medicine.

Tyrol

See Austria; South Tyrol.

U-Boats

See Submarine Warfare.

Uganda

See British East Africa.

Ukraine

The Ukrainian Soviet Socialist Republic is one of the constituent members of the Union of Soviet Socialist Republics. It is inhabited by the Ukrainians, a branch of the Slavonic nations, distinct in language, character and history from the Russians. Its area is 214,633 sq.mi. with a population (1939) of 30,960,221. Capital: Kiev (pop. 846,293). Other important cities: Kharkov (833,432), Odessa (604,223), Dnepropetrovsk (500,662). During World War II the Ukraine formed a decisive battleground in 1941 and in 1944.

For almost three years the land was under German occupation and suffered far-reaching devastation.

The Ukrainian Soviet Socialist Republic increased its territory in 1939 by the inclusion of parts of Poland extending to nearly 40,000 sq.mi. with a population of 7,000,000. On the other hand, the Moldavian Soviet Socialist Republic, until then an autonomous part of the Ukrainian Soviet Socialist Republic, was constituted on Aug. 2, 1940, with the addition of large parts of Rumanian Bessarabia, into one of the constituent members of the Union of Soviet Socialist Republics and separated from the Ukraine. But the Bessarabian districts of Khotin, Akerman and Ismail, together with northern Bukovina, were incorporated into the Ukraine, which also gained in 1945 by the annexation of the Czechoslovak Carpatho-Ukraine, a territory of 12,617 sq.mi. with a population of 725,357. Thus for the first time all lands inhabited by Ukrainians were united in the Ukrainian Soviet Socialist Republic. Several of these lands like eastern Galicia (formerly Austrian and Polish), northern Bukovina (formerly Austrian and Rumanian) and Carpatho-Ukraine (formerly Hungarian and Czechoslovak) never before formed part of the Russian empire.

The Ukrainian Soviet Socialist Republic was admitted as a member to the United Nations organization in 1945 and participated in the United Nations Conference on International Organization in San Francisco. Chairman of the Ukrainian delegation was Dmitry Zacharovich Manuilsky, one of the well-known old bolshevik leaders and member of the former Communist international, and, in 1945, deputy chairman of the Council of People's Commissars of the Ukrainian Soviet Socialist Republic. (H. Ko.)

Bibliography.—W. H. Chamberlin, *Ukraine, a Submerged Nation* (1944); Clarence A. Manning, *The Story of the Ukraine* (1947). Periodical: *Ukrainian Quarterly*.

Ulster

See Ireland, Northern.

Umezu, Yoshijiro

Umezu (1882–), Japanese army officer, was born in Jan. 1882 at Oita. He attended the Japanese Naval academy and the Naval Staff college, graduating from both, but instead of making a career in the navy he joined the army as commander of an infantry regiment. He was later chief of military affairs and in 1930 was made a major general attached to the Military Staff board. In 1934 he was assigned to command of a Japanese garrison in north China and there directed many of the intrigues designed to provide Japan with a legitimate excuse for invading China. In 1936, he was returned to Tokyo as vice-minister of war, but in 1939 was again shifted to the Manchurian scene where he held command of the Kwantung army and the title of Japanese ambassador. In reality, he was virtual ruler of the Nanking regime, then nominally headed by Wang Ching-wei. After Tojo's removal in July 1944 as chief of general staff, which post he held concurrently with his premiership, Umezu was appointed his successor.

To Umezu fell the task of signing, on behalf of the imperial general staff, the Japanese surrender document in the ceremonies aboard the U.S. battleship "Missouri" in Tokyo bay, Sept. 2, 1945.

Later he was taken into custody by the Allies and indicted for war crimes.

U. N.

See United Nations.

Undistributed Profits Tax

See Taxation.

Undulant Fever (Brucellosis)

See Veterinary Medicine.

Unemployment

See Employment.

Unemployment Insurance

See Relief; Social Security.

U. N. E. S. C. O. (United Nations Educational, Scientific and Cultural Organization)

See Education; United Nations.

Unfederated Malay States

See Malayan Union.

Union of South Africa

See South Africa, The Union of.

Union of Soviet Socialist Republics

The U.S.S.R., as the heir to the former Russian empire, is an Eurasian state which covers the whole of eastern Europe and northern Asia and much of central Asia. As a result of World War II it expanded its frontiers and above all its influence far into central and southeastern Europe and throughout the far east. Constitutionally it represents a federation of soviet socialist republics, the number of which varies with historical circumstance. It began with 7, and amounted in 1946 to 16. Actually the U.S.S.R. was held together by the strictly centralized Communist party which was the only party admitted in the U.S.S.R. and formed the core of the totalitarian structure of state and society.

The official head of the U.S.S.R. is the chairman of the praesidium of the supreme soviet. In that position Mikhail Ivanovich Kalinin was followed on March 19, 1946, by Nikolai Mikhailovich Shvernik. Prime minister (formerly chairman of the council of people's commissars): Generalissimo Joseph Vissarionovich Stalin, re-elected on March 19, 1946.

Vice-chairman of the council of ministers and foreign minister: Vyacheslav Mikhailovich Molotov.

In 1939, before the start of World War II, the area of the U.S.S.R. was 8,173,550 sq.mi. Its population, according to the census of Jan. 17, 1939, amounted to 170,467,186. The U.S.S.R. consisted then of the following 11 union republics: Russian S.F.S.R. (Capital Moscow; area 6,372,860 sq.mi.; pop. 109,278,914); Ukrainian S.S.R. (Kiev; 171,777 sq.mi.; pop. 30,960,221); White Russian S.S.R. (Minsk; 49,022 sq.mi.; pop. 5,567,976); Azerbaijan S.S.R. (Baku; 33,196 sq.mi.; pop. 3,209,727); Georgian S.S.R. (Tiflis; 27,020 sq.mi.; pop. 3,542,289); Armenian S.S.R. (Erivan; 11,580 sq.mi.; pop. 1,281,599); Turkmen S.S.R. (Ashkhabad; 171,384 sq.mi.; pop. 1,253,985); Uzbek S.S.R. (Tashkent; 145,908 sq.mi.; pop. 6,282,446); Tadzhik S.S.R. (Stalinabad; 55,584 sq.mi.; pop. 1,485,091); Kazakh S.S.R. (Alma-Ata; 1,059,184 sq.mi.; pop. 6,145,937); Kirghiz S.S.R. (Frunze; 76,042 sq.mi.; pop. 1,459,301). The Russian S.F.S.R. was thus by far the largest (78% of the whole territory and 64% of the population). Of the remaining 36% of the population, almost one-half lived in the Ukrainian republic in 1939 (2% of the territory) and the other half in the nine other union republics (20% of the territory).

The last previous census in the U.S.S.R. had been held on Dec. 17, 1926, when the population was 147,027,915. Thus the increase during this period of 12 years and 1 month was 15.9%. But the largest increase was, according to soviet figures, in the first half of the period when the population increased by 18,700,000. In the following six years the increase amounted to about 4,700,000. This fall in the rate of increase was due to the famine of 1933–34 and to the heavy burdens of the five-year plan and of agrarian collectivization. According to the second five-year plan the population of the union should have grown to 180,700,000 by the end of 1937, including 134,600,000 rural population. The census of 1939 showed, however, only a population of 170,500,000, including only 114,500,000 rural population.

On the other hand, the increase of the urban population was vast. In 1897 the urban population of Russia formed 11.5% of the entire population; in 1926, 17.9%; in 1939, 32.9%. Table I shows that this increase of urban population took place throughout the union, even in territories formerly entirely rural or even nomadic.

Asiatic parts, with capital and skilled labour forces coming from the European part of the union.

The population of Moscow doubled in 12 years, and amounted in 1939 to 4,137,018. Ten other cities had a population of more than 500,000 in 1939 and showed an increase of one and one-half to three times during the 12 years. The cities were: Leningrad, formerly St. Petersburg (3,191,304); Kiev (846,293); Kharkov (833,432); Baku (809,347); Gorki, formerly Nizhni Novgorod (644,116); Odessa (604,223); Tashkent (585,005); Tbilisi or Tiflis (519,175); Rostov-on-Don (510,253); Dnepropetrovsk (500,662). In 1939 there were 81 cities in the U.S.S.R. with a population of more than 100,000 inhabitants, 92 cities with a population of 50,000 to 100,000 inhabitants. Thirty-four cities showed in the period of 12 years a population increase varying from 3 to 10 times; Prokopevsk, Dzerzhinzk, Murmansk, Stalinabad, and Stalinsk increased by more than 10 times. Four cities totalling 459,000 inhabitants were newly built in the period between 1926 and 1939. They were Komsomolsk, Stalinogorsk, Magnitogorsk, and Karaganda.

The U.S.S.R. is inhabited by almost 100 different nationalities speaking different languages. The Slav element and the Slav languages prevail. The three branches of the Slav family living in the U.S.S.R. formed in Jan. 1939 78.1% of the population—the Great Russians 58.4%; the Ukrainians 16.6%; the Byelo- or White Russians 3.1%. None of the other nationalities, all of them non-Slavic and most of them non-European, reached 3% of the total population. The most important were Uzbeks 2.9%; Kazaks 2.8%; Tartars, 2.5%; Jews 1.8%; Azerbaijans 1.3%; Georgians 1.3%; Armenians 1.3%.

During World War II the U.S.S.R. had not only part of its economic productive capacity destroyed by military action and by the scorched-earth policy, but lost also an indeterminate number of its population. These losses were largely made up by new territorial conquests during World War II.

Table I.—*Population of the U.S.S.R. According to the Censuses of Dec. 17, 1926 and Jan. 17, 1939*

Soviet Socialist Republics	Rural Population 1926	Rural Population 1939	Rural % of Increase or Decrease (−)	Urban Population 1926	Urban Population 1939	Urban % of Increase	Total Population 1926	Total Population 1939	Total % of Increase	Area† 1939 (up to Sept.) Thousand sq.mi.	Density of Population per sq.mi. 1926	Density of Population per sq.mi. 1939
R.S.F.S.R.	76,672,807	72,620,606	− 5.3	16,785,189	36,658,008	118.4	93,457,996	109,278,914	16.9	6,374.7	14.6	17.1
Ukrainian	23,669,381	19,764,601	−16.5	5,373,553	11,195,620	108.3	29,042,934	30,960,221	6.6	171.9	168.9	180.0
White Russian	4,135,410	4,195,454	1.5	847,830	1,372,522	61.9	4,983,240	5,567,976	11.7	48.9	101.8	113.7
Azerbaijan	1,664,187	2,049,004	23.1	649,557	1,160,723	78.7	2,313,744	3,209,727	38.7	33.2	69.7	96.7
Georgian	2,083,012	2,475,729	18.9	594,221	1,066,560	79.5	2,677,233	3,542,289	32.3	26.9	99.6	131.8
Armenian	714,192	915,183	28.1	167,098	366,416	119.3	881,290	1,281,599	45.4	11.5	76.1	110.6
Turkmen	861,172	837,609	− 2.7	136,982	416,376	204.0	998,154	1,253,985	25.6	171.3	5.8	7.3
Uzbek	3,553,158	4,837,382	36.1	1,012,274	1,445,064	42.8	4,565,432	6,282,450	37.6	146.1	31.2	43.0
Tadzhik	926,213	1,233,209	33.1	106,003	251,882	137.6	1,032,216	1,485,091	43.9	55.5	18.6	26.7
Kazakh	5,554,905	4,439,787	−21.1	519,074	1,706,150	228.7	6,073,979	6,145,937	1.2	1,059.6	5.7	5.8
Kirghiz	879,364	1,188,714	35.2	122,333	270,587	121.2	1,001,697	1,459,301	45.7	75.9	13.2	19.2
Total for the U.S.S.R.*	120,713,801	114,557,278	− 5.1	26,314,114	55,909,908	112.5	147,027,915	170,467,186	15.9	8,175.5	17.98	20.85

*Exclusive of population incorporated in the U.S.S.R. after Sept. 1939.
†According to an official soviet computation (1939), which differs from previous figures.

The census showed a general displacement of population (1) to the Urals, Siberia and the far east, which received in these twelve years more than 3,000,000 migrants and increased in population by 33%, and (2) to the central Asiatic republics, which absorbed 1,700,000 migrants and increased in population by 38%. This migration highly increased the proportion of Russian elements in these Asiatic union republics. This trend of the spread of Russian and Ukrainian elements throughout the formerly non-Russian territories was increased during World War II. The war also accelerated the eastward movement of large-scale industry, which was continually and rapidly built up in the

Expansion.—In the years between 1939 and 1945 the U.S.S.R. expanded its territory considerably. At the beginning of the period it annexed in Europe the three Baltic republics of Estonia (18,353 sq.mi., pop. 1,126,413), Latvia (20,056 sq.mi., pop. 1,950,502) and Lithuania (22,959 sq.mi., pop. 2,879,070) and acquired from Finland 16,173 sq.mi. with a pop. of *c.* 500,000; from Poland 77,703 sq.mi. with a pop. of *c.* 12,775,000; from Rumania 19,300 sq.mi. with a pop. of *c.* 3,500,000. In 1945 the U.S.S.R. added to its territory the Carpatho-Ukraine from Czechoslovakia (12,617 sq.mi. with a pop. of 725,357) and the northern part of eastern Prussia from Germany (*c.* 7,000 sq.mi. with a pop. of *c.* 1,000,000). From Japan the U.S.S.R. acquired in 1945 Karafuto (southern Sakhalin), an area of 13,935 sq.mi. with a pop. (1935 census) of 331,943, and the Chishima or Kurile Islands (47 islands of 3,944 sq.mi.). Southern Sakhalin abounds in timber and petroleum; its most important industry is fishing. The importance of the Kuriles is strategic. In addition the formerly independent republic of Tannu-Tuva in Outer Mongolia (64,000 sq.mi.) was annexed and transformed into the Tuvinian autonomous region.

By a treaty of alliance with the national government of the Chinese republic on Aug. 14, 1945, the two main railroads in Manchuria, the Chinese Eastern railway and the South Manchuria railway, were to be joined into one railway system under the name of the Chinese Changchun railway, to be the joint property of the U.S.S.R. and China and to be jointly exploited by them. The managing director was to be a Russian. The important naval base of Port Arthur, which had been in Russian imperial control from 1898 to 1904, was to become a naval base at the exclusive disposal of the battleships and merchant ships of the soviet union and of China. It was to be administered by a commission of three Russians and two Chinese with the chairman a Russian. The Russian government alone was to be responsible for the defense of Port Arthur. The nearby port of Dairen was to become a free port in which the Russians would lease piers and warehouses and which would be administered by a soviet citizen. All these agreements were to run for 30 years.

The changes wrought by World War II in the size and composition of the U.S.S.R. and the lack of loyalty on the part of some of the peoples of the union brought about a reorganization of the federal structure. The following represents the composition of the U.S.S.R. at the end of 1946.

Reorganization.—The U.S.S.R. was reorganized during World War II into a federation of 16 republics. To the 11 republics existing in 1939 were added: the Karelo-Finnish S.S.R., consisting of the territory ceded by Finland and the former autonomous S.S.R. Karelia (cap. Petrozavodsk; area 75,656 sq.mi.); the Moldavian S.S.R. consisting of most of Rumanian Bessarabia and the former Moldavian autonomous S.S.R. (area 13,124 sq.mi.); the Estonian S.S.R.; the Latvian S.S.R.; and the Lithuanian S.S.R.; while the U.S.S.R. in 1939 comprised three European republics and eight Asiatic republics (three Trans-Caucasian and five central Asiatic), in 1945 the federation included an equal number of European and Asiatic republics.

On the other hand, several former autonomous republics and regions in the U.S.S.R. lost their autonomy during World War II. The German Volga A.S.S.R., one of the oldest autonomous administrations in bolshevik Russia, was abolished after the German invasion, and its inhabitants dispersed into Siberia. Apparently the soviet authorities thought that the soviet citizens of German descent would be more influenced by their race than by their class allegiance, and proceeded with their transfer although the invading Germans never reached the territory of the former German Volga A.S.S.R. The four other abolished autonomous administrations were those of the Crimean Tatar A.S.S.R., of the Kalmyk A.S.S.R. with the capital of Elista, of the Chechen-Ingush A.S.S.R. around the important oil wells of Grozny in the Caucasus and of the Karachaev autonomous region around Mt. Elbrus in the Caucasus. All these four regions were occupied by the Germans during World War II. The termination of their autonomy was probably due to the disloyalty of the populations. What happened to the populations was unknown; the indigenous languages seemed doomed because the soviet government renamed all the towns with Russian names.

The Crisis of 1937–38.—At the beginning of the ten eventful years soviet domestic policy had apparently found a new stability. On Dec. 5, 1936, the eighth extraordinary all-union congress of soviets in Moscow had adopted a revised constitution. The solemn day was declared a public holiday throughout the soviet union. The constitution introduced universal and equal suffrage but it kept the totalitarian dictatorship intact. Stalin, its author, praised the constitution because it "preserved both the working class dictatorship and the dominance of the Communist party." Art. 126 of the constitution declared that "the most active and politically conscious citizens in the ranks of the working class . . . unite in the Communist party, which is the vanguard of the workers in their struggle to strengthen and develop the socialist system and which represents the leading core of all organizations of the working people, both public and state."

The new elections were held one year later. In the fall of 1937, in all the cities and villages of the vast land, mass meetings were held, at which the candidates for the new supreme council were nominated unanimously by cheering

Inside Stalingrad during the six-month siege of the city which began in Aug. 1942

"Still No Fur Coat" was Orr's title for this cartoon in the *Chicago Tribune* as the German army faced its second Russian winter in 1942–43

crowds. No opposition candidates were presented, nor were any foreseen. The elections were an emotional demonstration of mass loyalty to the regime. With the help of the whole apparatus of propaganda, the Moscow government sought to insure a 100% electorate, to show the "foreign fascists and their agents that a united people stand behind the Red army." In fact, 96.8% of the approximate 97,500,000 franchised persons voted on Dec. 12, 1937, in the elections for the Supremem Countil. Naturally they all voted enthusiastically for the official candidates. The total number of deputies elected was 1,143. Among them were 184 women. Of the deputies 55% were officials of the party and of the government; 7½% members of the armed forces; 30½% workers and peasants; 7% "intelligentsia and illustrious citizens."

At the beginning of March 1937, in two speeches much commented upon, Stalin himself had subjected the increasing bureaucratization of the party to sharp criticism, and had demanded a closer contact of the party with the masses.

That the U.S.S.R., however, did not present a picture of unity and harmony was shown in 1937 and 1938 by the merciless extermination of real or supposed opposition elements. This purge hit equally all ranks, including the highest, of the party, the government, economic and industrial management, and the army and navy. All the accused were declared enemies of the people plotting against its security. In a number of trials an incredible situation was alleged to exist; most of the highly renowned followers of Lenin who for 20 years had been held up to the world as examples of socialism or communism were in reality persons of shabby character and complete unreliability.

The year 1937 began with a sensational trial against 17 leading communists, including Yuri Pyatakov, former vice-commissar for heavy industry, Karl Radek, mouthpiece of the Kremlin in foreign affairs, and Gregory Sokolnikov, former ambassador to Great Britain who, according to the indictment, had sought on the instigation of Trotsky to overthrow the government in order to re-establish capitalism in the U.S.S.R., and had promised to Germany and Japan, in exchange for their support, considerable territorial compensation (Ukraine, Amur territory) as well as great economic privileges and concessions. In order to hasten the removal of the soviet government, these communist leaders were said to have followed a policy of espionage, wrecking, and terror. All the accused fully admitted their guilt and made exhaustive confessions. On Feb. 1, thirteen of them, including Pyatakov, were shot; the remaining four, including Radek and Sokolnikov, were sentenced to periods of imprisonment ranging from eight to ten years. On March 5, Nikolai I. Bukharin, former chief editor of the official *Izvestia,* and Alexei Rykov, former chairman of the all-union council of people's commissars, were expelled from the party for counterrevolutionary activities. Great excitement was caused then by the arrest at the beginning of April 1937, of the all-powerful Henry Yagoda, general commissar of state security, on account of the "discovery of criminal activity." On May 31, Marshal I. B. Gamarnik, the "basest and most dangerous Trotskyist," the first vice-commissar for defense, took his own life, and—a great shock for public opinion abroad—Marshal Mikhail N. Tukhachevsky, together with seven other highly placed men of the Red army, after a four-day secret trial by court-martial, were condemned to death and shot on June 12, having been found guilty of betraying military secrets to Germany, undermining the power of the Red army, and preparing a military defeat with a view to the partition of the U.S.S.R.

On Dec. 19, the shooting of eight more highly placed soviet officials, including L. M. Karakhan, former ambassador to Turkey, and A. S. Yenukidze, Stalin's one-time right-hand man and secretary of the central executive committee of the union, was announced. Also the religious revival, several times mentioned in the Russian press, called forth oppressive measures by the government against the clergy. The hunt for "enemies of the people and socialism," "traitors to the fatherland," wreckers, "agents of fascism" and spies was not, however, confined to the above-mentioned cases, but was carried out systematically throughout the union and operated in all departments of public, economic, and cultural life. The number of victims was not announced, but it was believed to have amounted to several hundred thousand.

The purges continued in 1938. In its first session in Jan. 1938 the supreme council elected Andrei Vishinsky as chief prosecutor of the U.S.S.R. (In the same session Mikhail Kalinin was re-elected chairman of the praesidium of the supreme council and Vyacheslav Molotov was appointed chairman of the council of peoples' commissars of the U.S.S.R.) Under Vishinsky the purge was directed with fanatical zeal against all who were suspected of Trotskyism. The name of the former closest collaborator of Lenin in the first years of the Russian revolution and of the consolidation of the bolshevik regime became now the generally accepted designation for everything regarded hostile or hateful by Stalin's regime. In the soviet press and over the soviet radio, which generally used language of unbelievable coarseness against political opponents or persons out of favour with the regime, no name was too vile, no accusation too fantastic, not to be repeated again and again against Trotsky and against most of the older leaders of the bolshevik party.

Greatest political mass trial of 1938, that of the so-called "right Trotskyist bloc," took place in Moscow before the military tribunal of the soviet supreme court from March 2 to 13. Of the 21 accused persons most were old bolsheviks and until recently leading figures in Russia, among them being Rykov, Nikolai Krestinsky, formerly assistant commissar for foreign affairs and ambassador in Berlin; C. G. Rakovsky, former ambassador in London and Paris; A. P. Rosengolz, former commissar for foreign trade and chargé d'affaires in London; Bukharin, Yagoda and others. All the accused—including Krestinsky after some hesitation—admitted their guilt and played up very well even to the most fantastic accusations of the prosecutor Vishinsky. Eighteen of them were shot. Rakovsky and two others were sentenced to terms of imprisonment ranging from 15 to 25 years.

Among the other more prominent victims of the sweeping purge in 1938 were Nikolai Krylenko, one of Lenin's old guard, himself till recently commissar of justice, accused of deliberately discrediting soviet law; and the 35 year old A. V. Kosarov, since 1926 secretary and leading spirit of the Young Communist league, "liquidated" in November together with two of his secretaries and two other members of the central committee of the league, on political charges of violation of democratic principles, bureaucratic practices, self-glorification, incompetence and lack of vigour in combating the soviet's enemies. Considerable personnel changes took place even in the higher ranks of the secret police, where many officials had been replaced by staunch supporters of the Stalin regime. And at the beginning of Dec. 1938, Nikolai Yezhov, chief organizer of the above-mentioned trial of the "right Trotskyist bloc," was forced himself to resign from his post as commissar for internal affairs and head of the secret police. He was succeeded by Lavrenty Beria, a Georgian like Stalin and the former party secretary for Trans-Caucasia.

In such a way was the ruling class of the country and the leadership in party, government, economics and the armed forces completely overhauled. Large scale terror and mass executions had been well known throughout the bolshevik regime; but in 1937 and 1938 they were for the first time directed not against "enemies" but against party members, even the most renowned and trusted collaborators of Lenin. Thus Stalin strengthened his hold on the party and on the country's leadership. The old bolsheviks were replaced by young men who had grown up under the Stalin regime and were regarded as moulded by it and completely faithful to it. It was only an outward sign of the structural transformation of the bolshevik regime and of the U.S.S.R. when Stalin, who since 1922 had been general secretary of the central committee of the Communist party, stepped into the full limelight of governmental and military office. He assumed the titles of marshal and later of generalissimo, and on May 7, 1941, was appointed chairman of the council of the peoples' commissars, a title later changed to prime minister, and people's commissar for defense.

The Third Five-Year Plan.—The second five-year plan ended on Dec. 31, 1937. It was declared a success for food and heavy industries, which were reported to have surpassed the official goal of the plan by 8 and 10% respectively. The year 1938 was the first year of the third five-year plan, the outlines of which, however, were not published until Jan. 1939. The last data about the progress of the plan were published in 1940, together with the expectations for 1941. As they were the last figures published before World War II engulfed Russia, they gave a picture of the economic development of the soviet union as viewed in the official soviet statistics. They are therefore of general interest.

The number of workers and office employees engaged in national economy increased to 30,400,000 in 1940 as compared with 27,000,000 in 1937. According to the plan for 1941, the number of workers was to be increased to 31,600,000; 350,000 new students were to be enrolled in trade and railway schools and 537,000 in factory training schools. It was estimated that in 1941 industry would obtain 794,000 young skilled workers from factory training schools.

In the first three years of the third five-year plan, the industrial output of the U.S.S.R. increased from a value of 95,500,000,000 roubles in 1937 to 137,500,000,000 roubles in 1940, or by 44%, including an increase in the output of the machine building and metal working industry by 76%.

In 1940, despite the continuation of military hostilities with Finland at the beginning of the year, the value of the industrial output of the U.S.S.R. increased by 13,600,000 roubles, or by 11%, as compared with 1939, including an increase in the output of the machine building and metal working industry by 19%.

Foreign Relations before World War II.—During 1937 and 1938 the soviet union continued in its foreign policy to follow the line of *rapprochement* with the democracies—a policy adopted after Hitler's rise to power in Germany. Nevertheless, there were frequent signs of Russia's turning towards a policy of isolation. Relations with Germany and Japan, which in Nov. 1936 signed a pact directed against the Communist International with which the U.S.S.R. was regarded as closely linked, continued to be very tense. The long-established direct air line between Moscow and Berlin was suspended in the summer of 1937. The U.S.S.R. actively supported the Spanish republican government, while Germany and Italy lent their aid to the Spanish rebel forces under General Francisco Franco. In 1935 the U.S.S.R. had signed mutual assistance pacts with France and Czechoslovakia, the latter contingent on the first.

On July 17, 1937, the U.S.S.R. signed a bilateral naval agreement with Great Britain, and reserved only special rights with regard to her far eastern fleet. In the middle of November, it was stated in the house of commons that the whole financial credit of £10,000,000 granted to the U.S.S.R. by the British government in July 1936 had been utilized for purchasing British goods. On Aug. 4, 1937, after long negotiations, an important trade agreement was concluded with the U.S. by which the soviet union, in exchange for the granting of unconditional most-favoured nation treatment, pledged itself to purchase during the next 12 months U.S. goods to the value of at least $40,000,000. On July 29, a U.S. warship visited a Russian port, Vladivostok, for the first time since the revolution. On Aug. 21, China and the U.S.S.R. signed a five-year treaty of nonaggression, in which both pledged themselves "to refrain from any attack upon each other, whether singly or in conjunction with one or several other powers." The reported cooling in relations between Turkey and the soviets was contradicted at the time by the visits to Moscow of the Turkish ministers of the interior and foreign affairs in July. The signing of a new trade agreement with Turkey followed on Oct. 8.

The year 1938 brought several changes in soviet relations with the outside world. In his famous letter of Feb. 12 to a young communist, Ivanov, Stalin discussed the external tasks of communism. All foreign consulates within the soviet union were closed, and thus one of the last remaining avenues for some slight contact between the Russian people and the outside world was shut off. More and more even the few and tenuous ties which had been established between the two worlds (Russia on the one hand, and the non-Russians on the other) in the years between 1922 and 1937 were broken. At the beginning of 1939 Russia was a more jealously closed world in itself than ever in its history.

The Czechoslovak crisis strengthened these tendencies. The soviet union declared its determination to come to Czechoslovakia's help, if Czechoslovakia were attacked by Germany, and provided France did likewise. Soviet Russia was deeply distrustful of the efforts to conclude a four-power pact among Britain, France, Germany and Italy to stabilize conditions in Europe. Its exclusion from the pact of Munich which settled the fate of Czechoslovakia at the end of Sept. 1938 in no way lessened the growing antagonism between soviet Russia and the democracies.

Relations with Poland, on the other hand, changed notably and significantly in the course of 1938 from mutual mistrust and elementary antagonism to a display of friendship. The summer brought an exchange of diplomatic notes about the surveillance to which officials of the soviet as well as of the Polish embassies in the respective capitals were subjected. On Sept. 23 Moscow gave Warsaw definitely to understand that the soviet union would at once denounce its nonaggression pact with Poland if the latter invaded Czech territory, which actually amounted to a veiled war threat. However, the issue of the Czech crisis, the disappearance of Czechoslovakia as an independent factor to be reckoned with in the immediate future in high politics, the danger of a further German expansion in a southeasterly direction, and the apparent plan of Hitler

Men and women of Leningrad hauling peat supplies in the beleaguered city. German encirclement of Leningrad was broken on Jan. 18, 1943

to use Czechoslovakia's eastern province of Carpatho-Ukraine as a kind of Ukrainian Piedmont for the formation of an independent greater Ukraine at the expense of Poland and of the soviet union, forced these two eastern states to revise their former policy and, as it seemed, not without success, to seek a *rapprochement.* On Nov. 26, after exhaustive negotiations, the conclusion of a Soviet-Polish agreement of friendship was announced in Moscow and Warsaw. On Dec. 21, 1938, after five days' preliminary talks with a Polish trade delegation in Moscow, it was agreed to increase 20-fold the former commercial turnover between the two countries.

At the beginning of 1939 Russia and Japan went through a period of strained relations. One of the reasons was the question of the far eastern fishing grounds. On April 2 the existing fisheries agreement of 1928 was extended until Dec. 1939, but with Japan paying a higher rental for a smaller area than it had previously. Other disputes arose in connection with the Japanese oil concessions in northern Sakhalin. They were settled by an agreement on Aug. 12 with the Japanese-owned Northern Sakhalin Petroleum company. More serious were border clashes between troops of Russia and her satellite, Mongolia, on the one hand, and Japan and her satellite, "Manchoukuo," on the other. Early in 1939 there were mutual recriminations regarding the Japanese landing on an island in the Argun river, and a reported crossing of the Manchoukuo frontier by Russian troops; and there was some local fighting. There was also intermittent air fighting from May onward, accompanied by some infantry clashes, the most serious being occasioned by the reported crossing of the Outer Mongolian frontier southeast of Lake Buir by Japanese and Manchoukuo troops in July. On Sept. 16 an armistice was signed in Moscow providing for the immediate cessation of hostilities and for the setting up of a mixed commission to demarcate the frontier, and on Nov. 20 it was announced that an agreement had been reached by this commission.

When the German army, breaking the pact of Munich, occupied Prague and the remainder of Czechoslovakia in March 1939, the British government and the democratic peoples gained finally the definite impression that Hitler could not be trusted and that he was out for expansion into territory not inhabited by Germans. From that moment, Britain became the determined leader in the movement for the preservation of European peace against German aggression, and declared herself ready to guarantee any country threatened by that aggression. With the approaching struggle between Germany and the democracies, both sides began to try to win Russia as an ally in the forthcoming conflict. The future course of Russian policy seemed foreshadowed when on May 3, 1939, Maxim Litvinov was released from the office of foreign commissar which he had occupied since 1930. Litvinov had been a proponent of soviet collaboration with the democracies and with the League of Nations, as was his assistant commissar, Vladimir Potemkin. The change of policy became clear when Potemkin did not succeed his chief, and Molotov was appointed in his stead. Difficulties between the democracies and Russia arose when the latter demanded special guarantees for the Baltic republics which would bind them to the soviet union. The Baltic states themselves had refused such a guarantee, which they felt would compromise the strict neutrality they desired. Britain and France declared it manifestly impossible to impose a guarantee on small states against their will. Another question separating Russia and the democracies was the method of support for Poland in case of German aggression. Poland demanded help through supplies and weapons, while Russia insisted on sending her armies into Poland for that purpose, an offer which the Poles did not think they could accept. In Aug. 1939 British and French military missions arrived in Moscow for staff talks regarding common actions against aggression, and political discussions were to be held concurrently with military conversation. They were still going on when the German foreign minister, Joachim von Ribbentrop, arrived in Moscow as the honoured guest of the Russian government and was cordially received by Molotov and Stalin. On Aug. 24, the Russo-German pact of nonaggression and friendship was signed for a duration of 10 years.

The pact encouraged Germany to proceed with war in the west. All anticommunist and anti-Russian propaganda in Germany came to an abrupt end, as did all antifascist and anti-German talk and action in Russia and among the communists and their friends all over the world. The two totalitarian states, Germany and Russia, were regarded as united against the "imperialistic capitalism of plutocratic states," as representing "proletarian, young and revolutionary" nations fighting against the exploiters. When Germany started World War II by her invasion of Poland on Sept. 1, 1939, the soviet union and its communist followers continued for two years to attack diplomatically, morally and propagandistically all the nations which resisted and fought German fascist aggression.

Moscow on the Sidelines of the War.—Russia's agreement with Germany in 1939 led to the absorption of a great portion of Poland and of the Baltic republics into the soviet union. Thereby the two great powers, Germany and Russia, were brought face to face along an extended frontier, and thus the danger of a fateful clash between them was hastened.

In spite of the Polish-Russian treaty of nonaggression, Molotov handed the Polish ambassador in Moscow on Sept. 16 a note to the effect that soviet troops were about to enter Polish territory. In a broadcast to the nation, Molotov explained this action by the fact that the Polish state and its government "had virtually ceased to exist," and that consequently all treaties with the Polish government were void. More interesting, because of the light which it cast on the soviet policy of that time, were the two other reasons given. The soviet government, it was said, could not remain indifferent to the fate of its "blood brothers," the Ukrainians and Byelorussians inhabiting Poland. Thus a theory of racial kinship, not of class allegiance, motivated the Red army in invading Poland and taking under its protection the Ukrainian and Byelorussian populations of eastern Poland. Secondly, the Russians wished to deliver the Polish people from the war into which their unwise leaders had plunged them. Thus the Poles were blamed for having offered courageous resistance to the demands and aggression of nazi Germany. On Sept. 29 Ribbentrop visited Moscow again. Poland was officially partitioned between her totalitarian neighbours, who jointly declared that they would consider Britain and France responsible for any continuation of the war for which there no longer existed any reason, and that they would consult together regarding the measures to be taken if the war were continued. An economic program was drawn up according to which Russia would furnish raw materials to Germany and thus help overcome any shortages caused by the British blockade.

At the end of Nov. 1939 soviet Russia called attention ominously to alleged frontier incidents on the part of Finland. Though Finland denied the incidents, the U.S.S.R. denounced the 1932 treaty of nonaggression between the two countries, and on Nov. 30 invaded Finland. The Finns fought with great heroism; the Red army was checked both in the sparsely populated north and on the strongly fortified Karelian isthmus—everywhere save in the Petsamo region. The difficulties of a winter campaign, and,

Foreign Commissar Vyacheslav Molotov of the U.S.S.R. signing the Four-Power Pact of Moscow, terms of which were announced Nov. 1, 1943. Others seated at the table, left to right: Fu Ping Sheung, Chinese ambassador to the U.S.S.R.; U.S. Secretary of State Cordell Hull and British Foreign Minister Anthony Eden in particular, the valour, equipment and fortifications of the Finns, had evidently been underrated by the soviet authorities. Not till Feb. 1940 did they establish the superiority in numbers, artillery and aviation which enabled them to effect a break-through on the isthmus, leading to the peace treaty (signed March 12, 1940) which transferred to Russia approximately 16,175 sq.mi. of Finnish land and lakes with an original population estimated at 450,000. The new frontier ran from west of Viipuri along a line roughly coinciding with that laid down at the Peace of Nystad between Peter the Great and Sweden (1721). In the north the region of Kuolajarvi and the Fisherman's and Middle peninsulas were ceded to the U.S.S.R., together with transit rights to Norway and to Sweden. Moreover, the U.S.S.R. obtained a 30 years' lease of the Hangö peninsula which was of utmost strategic importance. These peace terms considerably restricted Finland's ability to resist Russia in case of future misunderstandings or further demands; but though much heavier than the original terms, they were lighter than those canvassed by the U.S.S.R. at the outset of the war.

The violation by the U.S.S.R. of the Soviet-Finnish nonaggression pact and the general sympathy for a weak and profoundly democratic neighbour evoked much opposition to Russia in the European democracies and in the U.S.A. Diplomatic relations with Britain and France became strained to the utmost, and the League of Nations excluded the U.S.S.R. from membership and called for help for the victim of aggression. The soviet union countered by invoking the necessity of security. Having settled with Poland and Finland, the soviet union turned to the Baltic republics and to Rumania.

Early in the fall of 1939 Estonia, Latvia and Lithuania had been requested to send their foreign secretaries to Moscow, where they signed pacts of mutual military assistance and ceded to Russia certain naval and air bases and the right to maintain "strictly limited soviet forces in them." On Oct. 31 Molotov declared soviet Russia's respect for the independence of the three Baltic republics. But with the collapse of France in June 1940, Russia presented ultimata to the three Baltic republics, soviet troops occupied them, and "friendly" new left wing governments were set up. The new regimes arranged for the election of national assemblies following the methods of the soviet union. These national assemblies unanimously voted to liquidate the national independence and to join the soviet union on July 21, 1940.

Meanwhile, on June 26, Molotov demanded from Rumania within 24 hours the cession of Bessarabia, which had formerly been a part of the Russian empire, and northern Bukovina, which had never been under Russian domination. The Rumanian government agreed to surrender the two provinces. Thus, in the first 10 months of World War II, the U.S.S.R. had gained a territory of about 170,000 sq.mi. (almost double the area of Britain) and more than 20,000,000 inhabitants. The economic importance of these gains was of course overshadowed by their strategic significance. On Aug. 1, 1940, Molotov made the following statement on the Russian-German pact: "This agreement . . . has done away with the possibility of friction in the application of soviet measures of security along our western frontiers, at the same time guaranteeing to Germany tranquillity in the east. The course of events in Europe has not only not weakened the pact of nonaggression between the U.S.S.R. and Germany but on the contrary it has underlined the meaning of its existence and further development."

But German-Russian relations were soon to be strained by the conflicting interests of the two nations in the Balkans. Molotov's visit to Berlin in Nov. 1940 did not clear away the causes of possible friction. When Germany began her active expansion into Bulgaria, Yugoslavia and Greece, the soviet union repeatedly expressed opposition.

When the Japanese foreign minister, Yosuke Matsuoka, visited Berlin, Rome and Moscow in the spring of 1941, his presence in Moscow on his return journey was used for the conclusion of a Russian-Japanese pact of friendship and neutrality on April 13, to last for five years if not renewed. By this pact Russia gained Japanese neutrality in case of involvement in war with Germany; on the other hand, Japanese action was diverted by the pact to expansion towards the south. Such a course might involve Japan in a war with the U.S.—which would weaken U.S. help to Britain and be fatal to Japanese power in the long run—and might weaken decisively the European position in Asia, a goal long pursued by the soviet union. Stalin showed his great satisfaction with the pact by the unusual gesture of bidding farewell to Matsuoka personally at the time of his departure from Moscow.

On May 6, 1941, the praesidium of the supreme soviet nominated Stalin president of the council of the people's commissars. A few days later the soviet government took an unprecedented step to express its sympathy for the German point of view. It withdrew recognition from the governments of Norway, Belgium and Yugoslavia, though these governments legally still existed, and closed their legations in Moscow. In June, when Britain and the U.S. warned the soviet union of an impending German attack, the official Russian news agency *Tass* stigmatized these warnings as "absurd and hostile propaganda spread by forces hostile to Russia and Germany."

On June 22, a Sunday, in the early morning hours, German troops crossed the soviet border without any warning and attacked the soviet union. Italy, Rumania and Hungary followed the German example, while Finland, in spite of statements of intended neutrality, allowed itself to become involved in the war. On that fateful day of June 22, in the evening, Prime Minister Churchill made his historic broadcast in which he put the might of Britain behind the soviet union in its life and death struggle with the German invader.

The U.S.S.R. at War.—The German attack caught Russia by surprise and partly unprepared, as did the Japanese attack on the U.S. at Pearl Harbor. In the first night of the invasion the German air force destroyed many of the first-line soviet planes on the ground. The German armies poured victoriously over the frontiers and penetrated deep into soviet-held territory. The annexation of the buffer states by the soviet union and the expansion of her frontiers did not provide much help for the soviet union. The Russian armies were defeated everywhere, immense numbers of Russian war prisoners were taken, the Ukraine was occupied by the Germans, and at the beginning of December German armies stood before Moscow. (For details of the German campaign in Russia, *see* WORLD WAR II.)

On June 30 the soviet government had announced the formation of a state defense council consisting of Stalin, Molotov, Beria, Malenkov and Marshal Voroshilov. On July 11 this council appointed Marshals Voroshilov, Timoshenko and Budenny commanders respectively of the northwestern, central and southwestern sectors of the front; for some time Timoshenko acquired a good reputation as a military leader, but eventually all three were replaced by new and more successful men. On July 20 a government decree appointed Stalin defense commissar in place of Marshal Timoshenko, and in Aug. 1942 General Zhukov, commander in chief of the central front, was appointed Marshal Stalin's chief deputy as commissar of defense. On July 17, 1941, the office of political commissar in the army (which had been abolished in Aug. 1940) was reintroduced. In view of the extreme gravity of the position on the central front, most of the government departments, together with the foreign embassies, were moved in October from Moscow to Kuibyshev (formerly Samara) on the middle Volga.

On Dec. 8 the Germans retreated from their advanced positions before Moscow. An unexpectedly early winter, reputedly more severe than for a whole century, caught the Germans unprepared for its hardships and inflicted great sufferings on the German army. It afforded Russia time for a reorganization and re-equipment of the army and gave Britain and the U.S. the opportunity to pour into Russia huge quantities of badly needed planes and tanks, armaments and supplies, which helped to make Russian survival and ultimate victory possible. Yet the year 1942 witnessed further German advances. The German high command abandoned the idea of a frontal attack on Moscow. It tried to conquer Leningrad in the north, and the German armies spread out throughout the south, conquering the Don basin and the northern Caucasus and approaching the Volga at Stalingrad and the oil fields of Grozny. The turning point came at the end of 1942 with the heroic defense of Stalingrad. At the same time Field Marshal Montgomery's British armies defeated the Germans at El Alemein and drove them back across Italian North Africa; and U.S. and British armies landed, under the command of General Eisenhower, in North Africa. Early in 1943 the sixth German army at Stalingrad surrendered to the Russians; at about the same time the long siege of Leningrad was raised; and during 1943 the Russian armies regained much territory and recaptured the cities of Smolensk and Kiev. While the western Allies invaded Italy in 1943 and France in 1944, the relentless Russian offensive pushed westward, across the Russian borders and into the axis capitals, into Bucharest and Budapest, Vienna and Berlin. Almost four years after Germany attacked the U.S.S.R. the war came to an end with the complete defeat of Germany and her satellites. (*See* WORLD WAR II.)

Internal Development during World War II.—The years of the war with their immense sufferings and privations and their heroic efforts and legendary deeds stirred the soviet people deeply. As far back as the middle of the thirties, the intellectual climate in the soviet union had begun to change. A new emphasis had been put on conservative forces in complete opposition to the radical tendencies of the first decade of the revolution. The importance of family and marriage, of strict discipline in schools, and authority and rank in the army was now stressed. In its beginning the revolution had regarded marriage and divorce as private affairs. Now abortion, formerly favoured, was made heavily punishable; marriage ties were strictly enforced and highly praised; the raising of big families was promoted by exhortation and rewards; divorce was frowned upon and made practically impossible by protracted court procedure and exorbitant fees. The emphasis on internationalism, entirely dominant in the first period of the revolution, relaxed. Instead, patriotism was preached and the soviet fatherland glorified. Marxist historiography after 1917 had rejected and vilified the Russian past as a dark age of feudal and Tsarist reaction and of religious bigotry and oppression. In the '30s this interpretation of history was officially declared wrong; its writers were persecuted. The Russian past was re-interpreted; the great Tsars, especially those who had ruthlessly waged war for the expansion of the Russian empire and had suppressed all tendencies of liberty for the sake of the unity of the nation, were highly praised, and the church was recognized as an important element in building the Russian nation. In 1939 the antireligious propaganda officially ceased.

When the actual war began in 1941, these tendencies gained the upper hand. The emotional forces of Russian history and nationalism were put fully into the service of the defense of "the sacred soil of the fatherland." The soviet fatherland now gave way to the Russian fatherland; attachment to the Russian past and to the Russian soil became the favourite theme of Russian poetry and of the Russian stage. The war fought by the soviet union was not called a war for socialist revolution or for a better world order; it was called a "war of national liberation," the "great patriotic war," a name which it shared with the war of 1812 when the Russian empire had successfully withstood the invasion of Napoleon and had, with the help of its allies, pursued the defeated enemy into its capital. The heroes of the Russian past were put up as examples for the soviet youth; they were not revolutionary fighters, liberals or socialists, but feudal lords and saints of the church, Tsarist generals and aristocratic conquerors of revolutions and mass uprisings. Prince Alexander Nevsky, who had defeated the Germans in the Middle Ages and was a saint of the Orthodox church; Count Alexander Suvorov, the great Russian general who had suppressed the uprising of the Russian masses under Pugachev in rivers of blood, who had dealt the death blow to Polish independence and almost to the French revolution and its armies; Count Mikhail Kutuzov, who had led the Russian army in the name of its Tsar against Napoleon in 1812: they were the most widely invoked names in Russia during the war. Holy Russia and the Russian common folk, the Russian peasant, again entered the centre of soviet thought and feeling. The great and ruthless Tsar Ivan the Terrible was glorified on screen and stage and was regarded as Stalin's ancestor as empire builder.

The Russian Orthodox church was recognized as one of the most important elements for strengthening the Russian state and the Russian aspirations. In Nov. 1942, on the occasion of the 25th anniversary of the bolshevik revolution, the metropolitan Sergei of Moscow wrote a letter to Stalin which was published in the whole soviet press: "In the name of our clergy and of all believers of the Russian Orthodox church, true to the spirit of our fatherland, I heartily and with blessings greet you, the God-chosen leader of our military and cultural forces who is leading us to victory over the barbarous invaders of our peaceful and blossoming country, and to a bright future for this nation." This metropolitan Sergei was officially installed as patriarch of all the Russias on Sept. 12, 1943.

In the Russian army the old titles, gold braided uniforms and class privileges of the Tsarist officers were reintroduced. There were few armies of World War II in which the officer class was as privileged as in the Red army, in which discipline was so strictly enforced, and military etiquette, especially saluting, so highly emphasized. The same tendency showed itself throughout the educational system. In all elementary and secondary schools coeducation was abandoned because it was declared that the aims of education were different for the two sexes: boys were to be educated to become soldiers, girls had to look forward above all to future motherhood. In July 1944 increased government aid for expectant mothers and parents of large families was introduced. Mothers of large families were granted honourary titles and special medals. Military drill and military games were made compulsory for the children and the youth in the country.

To these changes corresponded the dissolution of the Communist International on May 22, 1943. The famous monthly *Communist International* which had been founded by Lenin in 1919 appeared for the last time in July 1943. It was replaced by *War and the Working Class* which after World War II changed its name to *New Times.* On March 15, 1944, the revolutionary song "The Internationale," written by a French revolutionary, ceased to be the official anthem of the soviet union. The new national anthem, written in Russia, glorified the mighty homeland and the great Stalin.

On Feb. 1, 1944, the republics constituting the U.S.S.R. were authorized to enter into direct diplomatic relations with foreign states and to form and maintain their own commissariats of foreign affairs and of defense. However, the direction of their foreign affairs and of their armed forces, and the financing of them, would rest in the future exclusively with the central authorities in Moscow. Thus no practical changes were introduced. Yet the new arrangement proved to be useful in foreign relations. On the strength of it the soviet union could claim additional representation in international bodies.

Economic and Living Conditions.—The first years of the war were chiefly occupied behind the front in rapid development of industry at new centres beyond the Volga. It was a winter of grave sacrifices for the civilian population, especially in cities in or near the front line like Moscow and Leningrad and Sevastopol — sacrifices borne with heroic fortitude. It was a winter of enormous efforts on the production front by workers in the key industries, both near and distant from the battle zone. The blow which the German advance aimed at some of the most important industrial centres of the country was to a large extent parried by the evacuation of key factories from the threatened areas to sites in the new industrial districts around Kuibyshev on the Volga, in the Urals, or farther east still in Siberia. This was an evacuation of both the personnel (with their families) and the equipment of whole factories by a railway journey of sometimes 1,000 mi. or more. In its planning and organization as well as in its dimensions this evacuation was extraordinarily impressive, as was also the speed and efficiency with which new sites were prepared for the "leapfrog" factories, as they were called (often temporary structures of timber to economize in steel). The buildings to house them in some cases were already completed by the time the evacuated plant and personnel had arrived.

The economic losses suffered from the German advance, especially from the occupation of the Ukraine, were very serious, especially in the raw materials of heavy industry and in basic products. With the loss of the Ukraine went between one-half and two-thirds of the soviet union's prewar output of coal and iron ore and pig iron, and nearly half of its prewar steel output. The Dnieper region was an important centre of aluminum production, of ferroalloys and of rolled steel. With the German advance to the Don and into the north Caucasus in the summer offensive of 1942, more than half of the former wheat production and about 40% of rye production was lost to the U.S.S.R. More than half the pigs and more than a third of all cattle were in territory overrun by the invaders.

The soviet position in engineering was considerably bet-

Table II.—*U.S.S.R.: Statistical Data*

Item	1938		1940	
	Value (000's omitted)	Amount or Number	Value (000's omitted)	Amount or Number
Exchange rate				
United States		1 Rouble = 18.87 cents		1 Rouble = 18.87 cents
Great Britain		24.89 Roubles = £1		
Finance				
Government revenues	$11,452,276 (£2,342,458)		$11,409,031 (£2,978,859)	
Government expenditures	$11,322,762 (£2,315,967)		$11,227,836 (£2,931,550)	
Transportation				
Railroads		51,887 mi.		62,500 mi.
Highways		806,100 mi.*		...
Navigable waterways		256,200 mi.		...
Airways		69,845 mi.		88,125 mi.
Communication				
Telephones		1,272,500*		
Radio sets		5,950,000		
Minerals				
Pig iron and ferro-alloys		16,732,755 tons		16,424,270 tons
Petroleum		31,811,276 „		37,698,660 „
Gold		5,235,909 oz.		4,250,000 oz.
Iron ore		29,762,100 tons		...
Crops				
Wheat		45,062,024 tons		
Rye		23,071,139 „		
Oats		18,728,077 „		
Sugar beets		18,386,364 „		
Livestock				
Sheep and goats		102,500,000		
Cattle		85,900,000		
Swine		30,600,000		
Exports				
Total	$115,000 (£23,522)	...		
Grains (including rice)	$25,191 (£5,153)	...		
Lumber and timber	$19,361 (£3,960)	...		
Furs (raw and dressed)	$11,386 (£2,329)	...		
Petroleum and products	$9,128 (£1,867)	...		
Imports				
Total	$122,780 (£25,114)	...		
Machines and industrial equipment	$32,852 (£6,720)	...		
Iron and steel	$12,603 (£2,578)	...		
Wool	$6,465 (£1,322)	...		
Electrical machines and parts	$5,196 (£1,063)	...		
Defense				
Standing army personnel		2,000,000		4,600,000
Reserves		...		5,500,000
Standing navy personnel		23,600*		...
Standing air force personnel		80,000		150,000
Military expenditures	$2,334,979 (£477,598)		$3,565,541 (£930,951)	
Education				
Elementary and secondary schools students		34,260,000*		36,200,000†
University students		2,053,000*		657,000†

*1939. †1942.

Red army troops crawling through the snow during action on the eastern front in 1944

ter; probably not more than one-fifth of the prewar soviet capacity lay in areas occupied by the Germans. Moreover, engineering plants, even heavy engineering, were generally easier to evacuate than blast furnaces, so that a larger proportion of equipment was probably capable in this case of being salvaged and removed. The same was true of the nonferrous metal industry and of the most modern armament plants, most of which were located in the newer industrial centres east of the Volga. More than two-thirds of soviet lead, zinc and nickel, and nearly all the chrome, copper and cotton came from the eastern part; and even in the case of aluminum a new plant in the Urals was under development at the outbreak of war, based on newly exploited bauxite deposits on the eastern slopes of the range. Large tungsten and tin deposits had recently been discovered and opened up in eastern Siberia, and synthetic rubber plants were in the unoccupied zone. Even in the case of oil, although in 1940 the Caucasus region accounted for about 30,000,000 out of 34,000,000 metric tons, there was a rapidly developing and rich new area between the Urals and the Volga called "the second Baku" which was scheduled to produce 7,000,000 tons by 1942 and might have exceeded this figure. The Urals are especially rich in minerals, which had been rapidly developed. Kusbas, 1,000 mi. farther east, had iron ore, manganese and coal.

Light industries seem mostly to have gone to the Volga region and also factories making grenades and shells; for example, this was apparently the destination of most Moscow factories, some of which were evacuated completely, while others evacuated part of their machinery and staff to form the nucleus of new daughter factories. The Urals became a centre of tank, artillery and aircraft manufacture; and Kusnetsk of machine tools and the production of high grade steels. The latter centre at the end of 1942 was in a position to meet three-quarters or more of its ore requirements from adjacent mines, while the Urals were able to overcome their previous coal deficiency by drawing supplies from the rich anthracite region of Karaganda along the newly built railway from Karaganda to Magnitogorsk. A new wave of the Stakhanovite movement, known as the "thousand per-centers" of workers, who themselves took the initiative in multiplying their normal output standards many times by improved methods of working, did a great deal to augment the capacity of plants. Strenuous efforts were made to train new labour supplies, especially women, by training courses in the factory and by a system of patronage by Stakhanovites and skilled workers over newcomers.

About a third of the population of the U.S.S.R. lived in the occupied regions at the end of 1942. Of the urban population a large proportion, probably more than half, was evacuated eastward; but the proportion of the rural population evacuated must have been much smaller. Somewhere between 30,000,000 and 50,000,000 persons must, therefore, have been living in the occupied zones, many of them serving as guerrillas, harassing the German lines of communication. The plight of this population was even more grim than that of other German-occupied countries of eastern Europe. Not only were they subject to pillage and starvation on a scale quite unprecedented in modern warfare, but they were victims of a concerted campaign of terrorism and extermination to which it was hard to find a parallel since the middle ages. Virtual serfdom to German overlords was introduced into the villages on the ruins of collective farming; thousands of men, women and girls were transported under compulsion to Germany as slave labour. In Nov. 1941 Foreign Commissar Molotov, on behalf of the soviet government, issued his first note to the world powers, protesting against the barbaric treatment of Russian prisoners by the Germans. On April 27, 1942, the Moscow radio announced a new note by Molotov, charging the German government with a premeditated policy of atrocity, which included wholesale plunder of occupied territories, complete destruction of whole villages with their populations, introduction of slave labour and serfdom for workers and peasants, forcible transfer of civilians to Germany and their treatment as prisoners of war; extermination of prisoners by torture and starvation, and mass execution of soviet citizens regardless of position, age or sex. The note declared that the soviet government had documentary proof that these were not merely isolated cases of brutality by individuals or undisciplined units, but acts committed on instructions from the German high command.

With the German retreat from the Kuban and the Don regions, the problem arose of restoring not only communications but civilian life in the ravaged and depopulated areas. With the soviet offensive of the late summer of 1943 liberating half the Ukraine, the problem acquired high priority on the agenda of immediate tasks. Rebuilding was undertaken largely in the form of temporary wood structures, rapidly assembled from prefabricated parts, transported from regions where these could be mass-produced. A good deal of attention was paid to improvised and novel building methods. A special research institute in industrial building at Moscow introduced numerous innovations in wood, concrete and stone construction, in the use of substitutes for cement and brick, and in the extended utilization of three-ply boarding. A parallel institute concerned with house building experimented with "orgalite" building blocks made from waste paper, with building blocks made from slag and with aluminum-foil coatings for walls in postwar building. A special decree of the council of people's commissars outlined in considerable detail immediate measures to be taken for the restoration of national economy in the districts liberated from the Germans.

By May 1944 the "first-aid" phase of restoration of towns liberated in 1943 seemed to have been completed. Essential buildings and factories had been partially repaired or rebuilt, and public utilities were in operation. A high proportion of the population had returned. Towards the end of 1943, 300,000 people lived in Kharkov (Jan. 17, 1939: pop. 833,432). On the anniversary of its liberation (Feb. 2, 1944) the population of Stalingrad numbered 250,000 (Jan. 17, 1939: pop. 445,475). Plans for the layout of the cities showed some common features: Stalingrad, Kharkov, Rostov and Sevastapol would include green belts, a wide boulevard leading into a main square with a victory monument, etc. Railway stations were to be placed outside the city. Emphasis was placed on the use of local building materials. Production of prefabricated houses had begun. Reconstruction in the Ukraine proceeded apace. The greater part of the power stations was restored.

In Sept. 1945 the fourth five-year plan was announced. As in former plans, the emphasis was on heavy capital goods, steel production and armaments, especially also on a great increase in navy and naval bases. Labour productivity and industrial efficiency were to be improved as a condition "for expanding the soviet economy and developing its great new frontier" in Asia. To fulfil the requirements, the competitive methods in wages and other incentives known to capitalistic society were developed. Russia also intended to become an export centre of machines for all the countries in eastern and southeastern Europe where Russia wished to replace Germany as the chief supplier of industrial goods. At the same time new constructions were to continue to shift eastward beyond the Urals; from these Asiatic centres Russia could supply the markets of Asia.

Consumers' goods continued to be subordinate to the production of heavy capital goods. Yet the soviet government hoped to raise slowly the very low standard of living of the Russian people to the much higher standard of the masses in the democracies. Efforts were made to meet the constantly rising demand for better living conditions, and by the end of 1946 there had been a noticeable improvement in the food situation and in the supply of consumers' goods. Living conditions were eased. The eight-hour working day was restored and the payment of increased wages for overtime was reintroduced. The special war tax on workers was repealed on Jan. 1, 1946—a saving of about 15% for the worker.

Throughout the soviet union the reconstruction of the devastated provinces was progressing with great energy. Production increased in all fields. Of decisive aid was the great help given by U.N.R.R.A. to the Ukraine and Byelorussia. U.N.R.R.A.'s vast supplies prevented starvation in western Russia and made reconstruction possible.

Foreign Relations during the War.—The German attack of June 1941 and the new war in the Pacific occasioned considerable diplomatic activity in Moscow, London and Washington; the new alignments which followed Churchill's declaration of assistance to the soviet union on June 22, 1941, were in some respects quite startling. On July 13 the Anglo-Russian pact of mutual assistance was signed. A week later the soviet government resumed diplomatic relations with the *émigré* governments of countries occupied by Germany, and on July 18 a soviet-Czech treaty of mutual assistance was signed by the Russian ambassador in London, Ivan Maisky, and the Czech foreign minister, Jan Masaryk, providing for mutual aid and support in the war against Germany, and for Czech military units to be formed on soviet territory under the soviet high command.

On July 30, 1941, Harry Hopkins arrived in Moscow as the personal emissary of President Roosevelt to Stalin. On Aug. 16 there followed an Anglo-Soviet trade agreement under which Britain extended an initial credit of £10,000,-

"E Pluribusky Unumovich." The reaction of Darling of the *New York Herald-Tribune* to the soviet union's decision on Feb. 1, 1944, to permit each of its 16 constituent republics to establish its own army and maintain separate diplomatic representatives abroad

000 to the U.S.S.R. at 3% for five years. On Sept. 26 an exchange of letters took place between Maisky and General Charles de Gaulle in which the soviet government extended recognition to the Free French government and promised the latter full aid and support. On Aug. 10 the British and soviet ambassadors in Ankara presented identical declarations to the Turkish foreign office, confirming their fidelity to the Montreux convention and assuring the Turkish government that they cherished "no aggressive intentions or claims whatever with regard to the Straits," were "prepared scrupulously to observe the territorial integrity of the Turkish republic," and would render Turkey every help and assistance in the event of its being attacked by a European power. In view of German intrigues in Iran, British and Russian forces jointly entered Iranian territory on Aug. 25, 1941, and on Sept. 17 reached Teheran, the capital. Both Britain and Russia pledged scrupulous respect for Iranian independence and territorial integrity and the complete evacuation of the country after the war. On Sept. 28 Lord William Beaverbrook and W. Averell Harriman, representing the British and U.S. governments respectively, arrived in Moscow for a three-power conference on supplies, and on Oct. 3 it was announced that the U.S.A. and Great Britain had agreed to send large war supplies to the U.S.S.R.

German prisoners, captured on the Russian front, marching through Moscow in 1944 en route to a permanent soviet prison camp

In Nov. 1941 Maxim Litvinov was appointed Russian ambassador to the U.S.

The final weeks of 1941 witnessed the visit of the British foreign secretary, Anthony Eden, to Moscow, where in a series of meetings with Stalin and Molotov there took place an "exhaustive exchange of views on questions relating to the conduct of the war and postwar organization of peace and security in Europe," in the course of which "identity of views" was reached between both parties. On his return to England, Eden was accompanied by the soviet trade union leader, Nikolai Shvernik, with a soviet trade union delegation, to pay a return visit following that of Sir Walter Citrine and British trade unionists to Moscow a few months before. Six months later, Eden was able to inform the house of commons of the signature of a new treaty of alliance, collaboration and mutual assistance between Great Britain and the U.S.S.R., extending over a period of 20 years. This was signed in London on May 26, 1942, following the arrival of Foreign Commissar Molotov in England five days previously and a series of what Eden described as "long and friendly exchanges of views with Molotov," in the course of which "complete mutual confidence was established." Three days after the signature of the treaty, Molotov arrived in Washington, where he stayed at the White House as guest of President Roosevelt. The first fruit of these Washington conversations was the signature on June 11, 1942, of a "master lend-lease" agreement by Cordell Hull and Ambassador Litvinov. On the same date General Wladyslaw Sikorski, head of the Polish government, issued a statement welcoming the British-Soviet treaty.

The chief clauses of the historic Anglo-Soviet treaty provided that the two countries should undertake to afford one another military and other assistance and support of all kinds in the war against Germany and all those states associated with it in acts of aggression in Europe; affirmed that "the high contracting parties undertake not to enter into any negotiations with the Hitlerite government in Germany that does not clearly renounce all aggressive intentions, and not to negotiate or conclude except by mutual consent any armistice or peace treaty with Germany or any other state associated with her in acts of aggression in Europe," and declared the desire of both countries "to unite with other like-minded states in adopting proposals for common action to preserve peace and resist aggression in the postwar period, . . . to work together in close and friendly collaboration after the re-establishment of peace for the organization of security and economic prosperity in Europe," and "to render one another all possible economic assistance after the war." The foreign office statement which accompanied the announcement of the treaty stated that "full understanding was reached between the two parties with regard to the urgent tasks of creating a second front in Europe in 1942."

On Feb. 25, 1943, the foreign affairs committee of the Polish national council had issued a declaration that "from the moment of the conclusion of the Polish-Soviet treaty of July 30, 1941," they had "maintained the unchangeable attitude that so far as the question of frontiers between Poland and soviet Russia is concerned the *status quo* previous to Sept. 1, 1939, is in force." While the committee thus insisted on the territorial integrity of Poland, for which Poland and its allies had gone to war with Germany, it repudiated any hostile intentions toward the U.S.S.R. and denied that the Polish government harboured

Prime Minister Churchill, President Roosevelt and Premier Stalin with members of their advisory staffs at the conference near Yalta in the Crimea during Feb. 1945

any designs to extend Poland's eastern frontiers to the Dnieper and the Black sea. The soviet news agency replied that the declaration bore witness to "the fact that the Polish government refuses to recognize the historic rights of the Ukrainian and White Russian peoples to be united within their national states." On April 12, 1943, the German news agency announced the discovery near Smolensk (in the Katyn district) of mass graves of 10,000 Polish officers whom they alleged had been killed by the Russians in 1939, an announcement characterized by the soviet information bureau as a "vile fabrication." On the other hand the Polish government issued a statement calling for an investigation into the Katyn graves by the International Red Cross. The International Red Cross declined to act in the matter. The soviet press proceeded to charge General Wladyslaw Sikorski's cabinet with "swallowing a carefully baited hook thrown out by the German propaganda agencies"; and on April 25 Foreign Commissar Molotov handed a note to the Polish ambassador, Tadeusz Romer, severing diplomatic relations with the Polish government on the ground that "the recent behavior of the Polish government with regard to the U.S.S.R." was "entirely abnormal and violated all regulations and standards of relations between two allied states." This was followed by a statement by Andrei Vishinsky to representatives of the British and U.S. press, attacking the Polish government but denying that the soviet authorities had any intention of forming another Polish government on soviet soil, and accusing representatives of the Polish embassy of having conducted espionage activities in the U.S.S.R. under the guise of charitable activities. Six days later, on May 13, Moscow announced the formation of a body known as the Union of Polish Patriots in the Soviet Union, which published a declaration of aims in the paper called *Wolna Polska,* including the following: "to help the Polish people under German occupation to achieve their liberation; to wage war side by side with the Red army against the enemy; to strive for the independence and sovereign rights of the Polish state and its parliamentary and democratic structure, and for the material and cultural well-being of Poles in the U.S.S.R.; and to strengthen the bonds between the soviet and Polish peoples." On the same day the formation of a Polish division—the Kosciusko division—on soviet soil, under the command of Colonel S. Berling, was announced.

In Oct. 1943 the foreign ministers of the U.S.S.R., Britain and U.S.A. met in Moscow. Their meeting was followed in less than a month by a conference of Stalin, Churchill and Roosevelt at Tehran, Iran, Nov. 28–Dec. 1, 1943. This long-expected meeting of the "Big Three" resulted in a declaration, dated Dec. 1, in which the three powers pledged mutual assistance "in the war and in the peace that will follow . . ." and concerted action to bring about the final destruction of all German armed forces.

No mention was made of Japan; a separate statement guaranteed independence and postwar economic assistance to Iran. (For details of the Moscow, Tehran and subsequent conferences, *see* INTERNATIONAL CONFERENCES, ALLIED [WORLD WAR II].)

Other diplomatic events in the course of 1943 included the recall of Ivan Maisky as ambassador in London, following his appointment as a deputy commissar for foreign affairs, and his replacement by Fyodor Gusev, who had previously been appointed first soviet minister to Canada in Oct. 1942; also the recall of Maxim Litvinov as ambassador extraordinary to the government of the U.S.A. and his replacement by Andrei Gromyko, who had already acted as chargé d'affaires at the soviet embassy in Washington. On June 21 Constantine Oumansky, formerly soviet ambassador in Washington, presented his credentials to the president of Mexico as first soviet ambassador to the Mexican government; while Alexander Bogomolov, soviet ambassador to the Allied governments in London, presented his credentials to King Peter of Yugoslavia on June 8, 1943.

The problem of Poland and a crisis in Soviet-Iranian relations created considerable difficulties between the great powers in 1944. Chances of a reconciliation between the U.S.S.R. and the Polish government, never very bright, faded toward the end of 1944. When in January of that year the Red army was about to enter Poland, the U.S.S.R. proposed the acceptance by Poland of a frontier based on the Curzon line and compensations in the west at Germany's expense. The Polish government would not accept this proposal, and an offer of mediation by the U.S. was rejected by the soviet government. When soviet forces were approaching Lublin, the soviet government declared it had no further territorial aspirations in Poland—outside the eastern Polish provinces annexed in 1939—and did not intend to change the social order of that country. It recognized the Polish committee of national liberation, and the Byelorussian, the Ukrainian and the Lithuanian S.S.R. concluded agreements with the committee concerning an exchange of population (Sept. 9 and 22). The Polish prime minister, Stanislaw Mikolajczyk, visited Moscow twice. His second visit, undertaken when Churchill was in Moscow (Oct. 1944) raised some hopes of a settlement which, however, were dashed upon his resignation (Nov. 24). On Dec. 31, 1944, the Polish committee of national liberation was declared in Lublin the provisional government of Poland. Further inter-Allied difficulties arose in consequence of a demand for an oil concession in northern Iran made by S. I. Kavtaradze, U.S.S.R. deputy commissar for foreign affairs, in Tehran in Sept. 1944. In reply the Iranian government pointed out that its constitution forbade the granting of concessions while the country was occupied by foreign troops and therefore asked to postpone the granting of all oil concessions until after the war. This led to bitter criticism of the Iranian government in the soviet press, and to significant demands for a "friendly" government in Iran.

A soviet delegation headed by Andrei Gromyko, U.S.S.R. ambassador in Washington, took part in the Dumbarton Oaks conference (Aug.–Sept., 1944). The conference proposals were welcomed by the soviet press, which, however, considered that the whole structure of the organization would be undermined if a great power should not be allowed to vote in a dispute to which it was a party. (*See* UNITED NATIONS.) The Franco-Soviet treaty of alliance and mutual assistance was signed during General de Gaulle's visit to Moscow on Dec. 10, 1944. Drawn on the lines of the Anglo-Soviet treaty of 1942, its obligations of mutual aid in the event of German aggression were immediate and automatic. It referred to the United Nations organization, but did not state, as the Anglo-Soviet treaty did, that the parties did not seek territorial aggrandizement and would not interfere in the internal affairs of other states.

"Mr. Red Chips Goes to Town," as Plaschke of the *Chicago Herald-American* pictured soviet foreign policy in 1945

After World War II.—Victory found the Russian troops in occupation of large parts of Germany and Austria, and of the former German satellites, Rumania, Bulgaria and Hungary. In these countries, as well as in Poland, Yugoslavia, Albania and Czechoslovakia, regimes came into power which were regarded as friendly to the soviet union. In Yugoslavia, Poland, Rumania, Bulgaria and Albania, these regimes were under communist control. The soviet union maintained large armies of occupation, probably as a consequence of the domestic food situation, for the armies lived largely on the occupied lands. In Asia the soviet union concluded a favourable treaty with China which gave Russia economic and strategic positions of importance in Manchuria. Russia did not support officially the Chinese communists in their struggle with the Chinese government; it gave correct support to the legitimate government. Russia also occupied the northern, highly industrialized part of Korea and claimed a share in the occupation and control of Japan proper. Much international concern was caused by Russia's claims on Turkey and Iran, where Moscow apparently tried to realize the far-reaching aspirations of the former imperial government which revolutionary Russia in 1918 had officially and solemnly repudiated. From Turkey Russia demanded—on the strength of "historical rights" of Georgians and Armenians for which soviet scholarship and propaganda were mobilized in characteristic fashion—vast territories in eastern Anatolia and bases on the Straits of Constantinople, while in Iran the Russians were believed to favour autonomous and perhaps even separatist movements in the north which might lead either to the disintegration of Iran or to the establishment of a friendly government under soviet control over the whole of Iran. The principle of national self-determination was invoked in the case of the Iranian Azerbaijani and Kurds to foster Russian aims. Russia's demands on Turkey and Iran threatened to keep the tensions with the democracies acute.

With the defeat of the common enemies, the wartime alliance of the soviet union, Great Britain and the U.S. was subjected to much strain. This was the result not only of opposite ideologies but of conflicting national interests and security requirements. Nevertheless, co-operation among the Big Three was maintained. They met during 1945 in not less than four conferences. In the first two (Yalta in the Crimea and Berlin [Potsdam] in Germany) the heads of the three nations conferred. At Yalta Marshal Stalin met with President Roosevelt and Prime Minister Churchill; at Berlin, where again the Russians were hosts in their zone of occupation, Marshal Stalin met with President Truman, and it was during that conference that Prime Minister Attlee replaced Churchill. As a result of the decisions of the Berlin conference the foreign ministers of the Big Three met in London in Sept. 1945. When this conference ended without agreement, the foreign ministers met again, at the suggestion of the U.S. secretary of state, at Moscow in December. Their partial agreement there smoothed the way for the opening of the United Nations assembly in London in Jan. 1946. But there, as in the succeeding conferences of the foreign ministers in Paris in 1946, opposite ideologies and interests clashed again and little progress was made towards the writing of peace treaties with the defeated enemies.

At the United Nations conference in San Francisco in the spring of 1945 the soviet union was represented by a delegation under the leadership of Foreign Commissar Molotov. In addition to the U.S.S.R., two of its constituent republics, the Ukrainian S.S.R. and the Byelorussian or White Russian S.S.R., became members of the United Nations organization and were represented at the United Nations conference. The U.S.S.R. did not join, however, some of the international bodies organized in connection with the United Nations like the educational and food organizations. Nor did it ratify the Bretton Woods agreement. (*See* also INTERNATIONAL CONFERENCES, ALLIED [WORLD WAR II]; UNITED NATIONS; WORLD POLITICAL ALIGNMENTS, POSTWAR.)

Conflict with Democracy.—Much of the international tension could be explained by the lack of communication between the soviet union and the democracies. The U.S.S.R. and the territories occupied by its armies were on the whole inaccessible to outsiders. Travel in these territories was discouraged as was travel of soviet citizens abroad. U.S. and British press representatives in Moscow complained about the restrictions imposed upon their work in gathering and transmitting information. Thus the split of the world into two regions was increased by the soviet unwillingness to allow any contact similar to that existing between other nations and civilizations in the modern world. The soviet land and people were in 1946 more hermetically sealed off from contact with the outside world than at any other previous time in Russian history. Little was known abroad about conditions; no free flow of information was allowed to reach the Russian people from the outside and especially from the democratic world.

The disagreement about freedom was fundamental. The Russians maintained that true freedom, including freedom of the press, existed only in the soviet union. When the 10,000th issue of the official Bolshevik party newspaper, *Pravda,* appeared on Sept. 24, 1945, an occasion on which

the paper received from the government the Order of Lenin, its editor, David Zaslavsky, declared that freedom of press in the western countries was only an illusion, and that the soviet union, with journalists who did not sell themselves and were not bound to obedience by capitalist publishers, alone enjoyed such freedom.

When in the absence of Marshal Stalin, who was resting in the Caucasus, Molotov delivered in Nov. 1945 the great annual address in celebration of the anniversary of the bolshevik revolution of Nov. 1917, he stressed the point that only the soviet union represented true democracy. He spoke of "a flourishing of true democracy of the people (in the U.S.S.R.) that they did not know in the old days and that cannot exist in any other states, divided as they are into classes of oppressors and oppressed, a thing that soviet power has long put an end to in our country. . . . Unlike parliamentary democracy, the democracy of the soviets is a true democracy of the people."

Though Molotov in his speech mentioned the patriotic character of World War II, he stressed emphatically that it was the soviet government and the bolshevik revolution which had given Russia and the Russian people the strength for their great victories. "The soviet people called its war . . . the great patriotic war. By the example of the soviet people, patriots of other states learned how one must fight for one's motherland, for its liberty and independence." This Russian strength was, in Molotov's opinion, due to "the leadership of the party of Lenin and Stalin," above all to "the great Stalin, the farseeing and tried leader of the soviet union."

Accordingly the efforts of communist indoctrination and of teaching the pure doctrine of Marx and Lenin in the official interpretation were intensified. The strict unity and regimentation of the soviet state rested on the monolithic unity and discipline of the Communist party, of which Marshal Stalin was general secretary. With the end of the war the emphasis shifted again to party doctrine and party leadership.

At the beginning of 1946 the soviet people were prepared for the forthcoming elections to the supreme soviet, held on Feb. 10. Marshal Stalin and the other speakers in their election addresses stressed the need to devote the next 15 or 20 years to develop above all the military power of the soviet union. Lazar Kaganovich, one of Marshal Stalin's foremost collaborators, declared that "we must always remember, our country continues within a capitalist encirclement. We should not relax but strengthen bolshevist vigi-

Convoy of Russian trucks making the dangerous night trek to besieged Leningrad across the frozen surface of Lake Ladoga during the winter of 1941–42

 lance." Due praise was given to the Communist party and its great leader for having saved Russia by transforming the country into a highly industrialized arsenal and having led the people to victory. President Kalinin pointed out the superiority of soviet elections over democratic elections, which "are not calculated to arouse and develop the political mind of the masses but to deaden and blind them and crush the slightest sign of independent political thought." In the elections in the U.S.S.R. 99.7% of the people qualified to vote actually did vote according to official figures, and 99.18% of them voted for the party in power.

On Feb. 25, 1946, the people's commissariat for defense was transformed into a people's commissariat of the armed forces, under which the land army, the air forces and the navy were united. Generalissimo Stalin was named people's commissar of the armed forces and supreme commander in chief of the armed forces of the U.S.S.R. On March 15 the term minister was substituted for the term of people's commissar, which was introduced by the Russian revolution of Nov. 1917. On the same day the supreme soviet was told that Russia's new five-year plan called for increasing the nation's production to one and one-half times the prewar level by 1950 and for providing the Red army with the most modern armaments. The head of the state planning department declared that "monopolistic capitalism can produce a new aggressor," while by taking advantage of the superiority of the soviet discipline, the U.S.S.R. could outstrip the capitalist countries in all types of progress, including technology. On March 19 Generalissimo Stalin was re-elected prime minister, while the resignation of the critically ill President Kalinin was accepted, and Nikolai Mikhailovich Shvernik was elected as his successor. All elections were unanimous.

In May 1946, a new 20,000,000,000 rouble internal loan (nominally $3,774,000,000) was oversubscribed on the first day. The bonds were non-interest bearing but entitled holders to participation in the semiannual lottery prize drawings. *Izvestia* saw in the success of the loan proof of Russian determination to maintain its military power. (*See* also COMMUNISM.)

BIBLIOGRAPHY.—Philip Grierson, *Books on Soviet Russia 1917–1942* (London, 1943); *Information Bulletin of the Embassy of the U.S.S.R.* (Washington, D.C.); *The Anglo-Soviet Journal* (London); George B. Cressey, *The Basis of Soviet Strength* (1945); Joseph Stalin, *The Great Patriotic War of the Soviet Union* (1945); M. I. Kalinin, *The Soviet President Speaks* (London, 1945); N. Voronin, *Rebuilding the Liberated Areas of the Soviet Union* (London, 1945); Frederick I. Schuman, *Soviet Politics* (1946); William Henry Chamberlin, *The Russian Enigma* (1943); Maurice Hindus, *Mother Russia* (1943); Nicholas S. Timasheff, *The Great Retreat* (1946); Arthur Koestler, *Darkness at Noon* (1940), *The Yogi and the Commissar* (1945); Alexander Barmine, *One Who Survived* (1945); Victor Kravchenko, *I Chose Freedom* (1946); George Soloveytchek, *Russia in Perspective* (London, 1946); Walter Kolarz, *Stalin and the Eternal Russia* (London, 1944); Grigore Gafencu, *Prelude to the Russian Campaign* (London, 1945); David J. Dallin, *Soviet Russia's Foreign Policy 1939–1942* (1943), *The Real Soviet Russia* (1947); Robert J. Kerner, "Russian Naval Aims," *Foreign Affairs* (Jan. 1946); Michael T. Florinsky, "The Soviet Union and Europe," *Forum* (Dec. 1945); "What Does Alexii Want?" *The Christian Century* (Jan. 2, 1946); Michael T. Florinsky, "The Soviet Union and International Agreements," *Political Science Quarterly* (March 1946); Clarence Manning, "The Soviet Union and the Slavs," *The Russian Review* (New York, spring, 1946).
(H. Ko.)

Unitarian Church

In 1937, Unitarianism was still in the stage of parochial development; by 1946, it had taken its place as a numerically small but potentially significant factor in the field of religion on a world-wide scale. In many ways, Unitarianism came of age during this turbulent decade, especially as an organized force. The most striking evidence of this was in the work of the Unitarian Service committee, which was organized in Boston, Mass., in 1940, and which in 1946 was carrying on humanitarian service in 12 countries, with a budget that had increased more than tenfold. The nonsectarian, nonpolitical program which the Unitarian Service committee conducted made the word Unitarian known to a vast number of people in all parts of the world who, prior to 1940, had never even heard of it.

In 1937, when the triennial Congress of the International Association for Liberal Christianity and Religious Freedom was held in Oxford, England, it was clear to all the delegates that the storm clouds were gathering over Europe so threateningly that the plans for the next congress, scheduled to be held in Budapest in 1940, would have to be made subject to the course of events. No congress was held in 1940, nor in 1943, nor in 1946. But in the latter year a smaller planning conference was held in Cambridge, England, with 35 delegates from the U.S., Great Britain, Holland, Czechoslovakia, Denmark, Switzerland, Belgium, Sweden and India. It was decided that the earliest date at which a congress could be held was 1948, and plans were laid to hold it in that year in Prague. Dr. John Howland Lathrop, the head of the U.S. delegation, was elected president and the secretariat was continued in Holland.

The tremendous sufferings endured after the outbreak of the war by Unitarians and other religious liberals, not only in occupied countries but by all, were obvious. Certain countries, such as Hungary and the Philippine Islands, which were unable to send representatives, had perhaps suffered most of all. But from all reports it became clear that the spirit of free religion had not been crushed; indeed it was apparent to all that the effect of the war in many lands had been to deepen the determination of the liberals to strengthen and extend their influence. The line between the religions of authority and the free faith were drawn more sharply, and the opportunity facing the liberal forces was far greater and more challenging than ever.

In Britain, a flying bomb destroyed Essex hall, general headquarters of the church, on July 28, 1944. Six churches were completely destroyed and many others damaged. With varying details this general story applied throughout, and there were, of course, many losses other than in the material fabric of the churches. The ranks of the ministry were depleted—30 fewer in 1946 than in 1939. But the spirit of the British Unitarians was shown in the appointment in 1943 of a Commission on the Work of the Churches, which brought in a thorough and heartening report, and in the effort to raise a special fund of £100,000 to strengthen the churches.

The development of organized Unitarianism in the U.S. and Canada during this period was much less affected by the war and could be summarized in the phrase "Unitarian Advance," which first came into general use in 1937 and received great additional impetus as the result of the reports of three special committees in 1944. An excellent picture of the general forward movement, not only in the U.S. but throughout the world, was in a volume published in 1946 by the Beacon press, Boston, Mass., entitled *Together We Advance,* edited by Stephen H. Fritchman.

Organizationally, the ten-year period saw the carrying out of many of the recommendations of the Commission of Appraisal which reported to the American Unitarian association in 1936. Special emphasis was given to the newly organized Division of Publications, to the Unitarian Service committee, to a sound policy of establishing new churches, recruiting the additional ministers needed for the advance program and the rapid development of new curriculum material in the field of religious education.

Among the specific accomplishments of the decade 1937–46, mention should be made of the organization of the United Unitarian Appeal—a co-operative enterprise to raise the operating funds for the several Unitarian agencies, on the basis of a community chest—which had now become an accepted part of the denominational machinery. The total raised in 1945 was $235,000 and the amount for 1946 was $376,000. In 1946 the Appeal was incorporated. The denominational journal, *The Christian Register,* in its 125th year at the end of the decade, had doubled its circulation since 1937. The Unitarian Service committee, organized in 1940 as a standing committee of the American Unitarian association, showed remarkable growth. During the year ending April 30, 1946, funds were entrusted to it for humanitarian service and relief totalling nearly $1,000,000. The staff, at home and abroad, numbered over 200 in 1946.

During 1946 the Service committee expanded its work with the following functions and in the following countries; a service centre in Holland for food and clothing distribution, a children's home and a medical teaching team in Czechoslovakia, a dental clinic for displaced people in Innsbruck, Austria, established at the request of the Austrian government, and a service centre for clothing and food distribution in the city of Vienna. In Germany, the committee established a program in co-operation with U.N.R.R.A. for the displaced people in the refugee assembly centres of the occupied zones. A medical team and a child welfare group were operating under this program. In Budapest, there was a service centre for the distribution of clothing and food, and in Poland a medical teaching mission. All this was in addition to the maintenance and expansion of the work for refugees in the countries where the committee had operated for several years.

Branches of the Service committee were established in Czechoslovakia, Holland, England and Canada. Special mention should be made of the work of the Canadian Unitarians through their Service committee, carried on over and above their share in the United Appeal. The executive director of the Unitarian Service committee in Canada was successful in mobilizing a broad public support through the dominion for the program of the Unitarian Service committee.

By the summer of 1946, 213,640 lb. of canned food had been received in the warehouse in New York and shipped abroad. In addition, $46,993 had been received as unsolicited contributions for the purchase of canned food; 31 shipments, totalling 285 tons, had been made. The food was allocated as soon as it was received to relief and food distribution offices overseas. During a 15 months' period, 623,032 lb. of used clothing were received, processed, baled and shipped; 297 Unitarian churches took part in this clothing collection campaign. (F. M. E.)

United Church of Canada

The account of the life and growth of the United Church of Canada during the years 1937–46 can best be presented by considering the work of the church in several spheres of endeavour. In 1937 there were approximately 457,373 families, 698,738 members and 1,729,248 persons under pastoral oversight. During the following ten years these figures steadily increased so that in mid-1946 there were 43,179 more families than in 1937. There were 231,919 persons received into church membership on profession of faith, bringing the total to 505,686, with the year 1944 showing the largest increase. Moreover, the dominion census figures of 1941 revealed that 2,204,875 persons, comprising about one-fifth of the Canadian population (40% Roman Catholic in 1946) claimed some connection with the United Church. Furthermore, the 1941 census disclosed that in the province of Manitoba a larger number of people of non-Anglo-Saxon origin were identifying themselves with the United Church than with any other denomination.

At the outbreak of World War II in 1939, the church rallied to the support of the government and sought to provide spiritual ministrations and material aid for those serving in the three branches of the armed forces. There were 233 ministers commissioned as chaplains. Of this number, 3 paid the supreme sacrifice, 14 received military decorations and 8 were mentioned in military dispatches. More than 1,000 war service units were organized throughout the congregations which sent forth 6,000,000 articles for the material aid of the Canadian forces, as well as for the comfort of refugees and the victims of bombing raids. More than $50,000 was raised as an aid to British churches, and at the end of the decade more than $150,000 had been contributed for the restoration of Protestant churches in Europe.

During the depression years, which included the period of the drought on the prairies of Saskatchewan, the United Church accumulated a deficit of $1,700,000. In 1940 it was suggested that an effort be made to clean up this indebtedness by encouraging members and adherents to purchase government war savings certificates and to donate them to the church. The amounts paid and pledged would be invested to mature in 1950. The plan was launched in 1941 and continued until 1944. At the close of that period the whole of the deficit had been underwritten.

The pension fund of the church began to show signs of financial weakness soon after union. The annual revenue to be received from the missionary and maintenance fund fell short of expectations; interest rates on investments declined sharply as a result of the depression; legacies also decreased. Since each minister was assessed for pensions on a percentage basis of his salary, and since salaries generally were lowered during the depression years, revenue from this source declined. To meet liabilities, encroachments were made on capital reserves. These began in 1935 and continued until 1945. The total withdrawals from capital amounted to $800,000. Early in 1946 a campaign capital committee, composed exclusively of laymen, was set up to launch a drive to secure $3,500,000 new capital. The campaign was launched in April, and $4,000,000 was soon subscribed.

The first official paper of the United Church of Canada, following the union of 1925, was known as *The New Outlook.* In spite of the fact that it was a well edited paper, subscriptions declined. In addition, *The United Church Record and Missionary Review* represented the continuance of preunion missionary publications. In 1939 it was decided to merge these periodicals into *The United Church Observer* to be issued semimonthly and to feature the news of the church at home and abroad in attractive fashion with a liberal use of pictures. This modern trend in journalism proved popular. During the period 1941–46, the circulation of the new paper increased from 15,000 to more than 50,000.

The years of 1937–46 indicated that the United Church

had not been recruiting a sufficient number of ministers to undertake adequately the task which was visualized when the Congregationalists, Methodists and Presbyterians came together to form the new church. This shortage of ministers manifested itself throughout the 11 conference areas, but was particularly critical in the 3 prairie provinces, a section which, because of pioneer conditions, could least afford such decrease. This situation was partially met by the employment of laymen and deaconesses, but in spite of this effort congregations in western Canada were left without pastoral oversight. With the end of the war and the return of chaplains, the situation eased somewhat. It was clear, however, that in this matter of an adequate supply of candidates for the ministry, the church was facing a spiritual problem.

* * *

THE PERIOD of utopianism in religious outlook which characterized the churches during the years immediately following World War I, had given way to a temper more radical and discerning. This manifested itself in the field of religious education by a strong trend toward the biblical and the doctrinal. By the year 1940 there was a marked yearning throughout the United Church for a deeper faith. To meet this need four educational documents were produced: a short *Statement of Faith* and an exposition of the same by Prof. John Dow under the title *This Is Our Faith.* Early in 1944 a *Catechism* was published by a commission at work in that field. In the first year and a half after publication, 140,000 copies of the *Catechism* were sold.

The 1941 Canadian census revealed that approximately 600,000 people in Canada claiming to be attached to the United Church were lapsed from any visible connection with it. To meet this challenge a vigorous campaign of visitation evangelism was undertaken. Encouraging results were reported throughout the length and breadth of the church. The years 1944–46 showed a marked increase in the number of persons received into membership on profession of faith.

In 1944 the United Church responded to an appeal sent forth by the General synod of the Church of England in Canada to all other churches to discuss, through chosen representatives, the possibilities of closer unity. These conversations resulted in a report covering the procedure whereby the ministries of the two churches could be conferred each upon the other. (G. A. SI.)

United Kingdom

See GREAT BRITAIN AND NORTHERN IRELAND, UNITED KINGDOM OF.

United Nations

The term "United Nations" was coined by Pres. Franklin D. Roosevelt to describe the allied nations fighting the axis powers. It was first formally used in the Declaration by United Nations of Jan. 1, 1942, when the representatives of 26 countries pledged their governments to employ their full resources for the prosecution of World War II, to co-operate with one another and not to make a separate peace. Other governments subsequently adhered to the declaration.

It was not, however, until Oct. 30, 1943, that the need for establishing an international organization to maintain peace and security after the cessation of hostilities was formally recognized in an international declaration. On that date the foreign ministers of the soviet union, the United Kingdom and the United States and the Chinese ambassador to the soviet union issued, on behalf of their governments, the "Declaration of Four Nations of General Security" (commonly known as the Moscow declaration). They declared that their united action pledged for the prosecution of World War II would be continued for the organization and maintenance of peace and security

In the period which followed, various unofficial schemes for a world organization were prepared and circulated for information and study.

Dumbarton Oaks.—Concrete steps to formulate an agreed plan were taken by the four signatories of the Moscow declaration in the late summer of 1944. Conversations regarding a possible world organization were held at Dumbarton Oaks from Aug. 21 to Oct. 7. The first phase of the conversations, from Aug. 21 to Sept. 28, was between officials representing the soviet union, the United Kingdom and the United States; the second phase, from Sept. 28 to Oct. 7, between officials representing China, the United Kingdom and the United States. The reason for holding the conversations in two parts was that the soviet union was not at that time at war with Japan.

As a result of these conversations, the four powers reached agreement on a detailed plan for the proposed international organization. This plan was made public on Oct. 10, 1944, in the form of "Proposals for the Establishment of a General International Organization," commonly known as the Dumbarton Oaks proposals.

These proposals set forth the purposes and principles of the international organization, and stated that its membership should be open to all peace-loving states. They provided that the organization should have as its principal organs: a general assembly, a security council, an international court of justice and a secretariat, as well as such subsidiary organs as were found necessary.

The composition, functions, powers and procedure of the general assembly and the Security council were outlined, as was also the voting procedure for the general assembly. Agreement was not, however, reached at Dumbarton Oaks on voting procedure for the Security council.

The general assembly was to be composed of all the members of the United Nations, each of which was to have one vote. Among the functions assigned to the assembly were: to consider the general principles of co-operation in the maintenance of international peace and security; to discuss questions relating to the maintenance of peace and security brought before it by members or by the Security council and to make recommendations on them (except on a matter being dealt with by the Security council); to admit, suspend or expel members on the recommendation of the Security council; to elect the members of the Economic and Social council and the non-permanent members of the Security council, and, on recommendation of the Security council, the secretary-general; to apportion among members the expenses of the organization; and to make recommendations to promote international co-operation in political, economic and social fields.

Decisions on important questions were to be made by a two-thirds majority, on other questions by a simple majority.

The Security council was to be composed of 11 members. Five—the representatives of the United States, the United Kingdom, the U.S.S.R., China and "in due course" France—were to have permanent seats. The remaining six would be elected for two-year terms by the general assembly. On the Security council was to be conferred "primary responsibility for the maintenance of international peace and security." The council was to function continuously.

It was proposed that the international court of justice should be the principal judicial organ of the organization, and that its statute should be either that of the Permanent Court of International Justice, or a new statute, based on that of the permanent court. All members of the organization should *ipso facto* be parties to the court's statute.

The secretariat was to be composed of a secretary-general and such staff as might be required. The secretary-general, who was to be the chief administrative officer of the organization, was to be elected by the general assembly on recommendation of the Security council. It was proposed that he should have the right to bring to the attention of the Security council "any matter which in his opinion may threaten international peace and security."

One of the most important chapters of the Dumbarton Oaks proposals related to "Arrangements for the Maintenance of International Peace and Security, including Prevention and Suppression of Aggression." This chapter included three sections, the first dealing with the pacific settlement of disputes, the second with the determination of threats to the peace or acts of aggression and the action to be taken regarding them and the third with regional arrangements. The chapter provided for the steps which might be taken to maintain or restore international peace and security by the Security council in fulfilment of the primary responsibility conferred on it by the members of the organization.

They included in the last resort action by land, air or sea forces. Members were to undertake to make available to the Security council in accordance with special agreements the necessary armed forces, facilities and assistance. A military staff committee composed of the chiefs of staff of the permanent members of the Security council was to advise the council.

A further chapter, dealing with "Arrangements for International Economic and Social Co-operation," provided for an Economic and Social council to act under the authority of the general assembly. It was also provided that various specialized economic, social and other organizations should be brought into relationship with the organization.

Other chapters provided for the coming into force of amendments when adopted by two-thirds of the members of the organization and ratified by the permanent members of the Security council and a majority of other members, and for joint action to be taken to maintain peace and security by the four signatories of the Moscow declaration pending the conclusion of agreements making armed forces available to the Security council.

Crimea Conference.—Agreement on the question of voting in the Security council was reached at the Crimea conference between Prime Minister Churchill, President Roosevelt and Marshal Stalin in Feb. 1945. At the same time, the report issued at the conclusion of the conference stated that it had been agreed to call a conference of United Nations to meet at San Francisco on April 25, 1945, to prepare a charter for a world organization along the lines proposed at Dumbarton Oaks.

China and France would be consulted and invited to join the British, soviet and United States governments in sponsoring the invitations to the San Francisco conference.

The consultations took place, and the Chinese government agreed to join in sponsoring the invitations. The French government, which had not taken part in the Dumbarton Oaks conversations, agreed to attend the conference but decided not to act as a sponsoring power.

The countries qualifying for invitations to the San Francisco conference were those which had adhered to the declaration by United Nations of Jan. 1, 1942, and had declared war on Germany or Japan by March 1, 1945.

The invitations were issued on March 5, 1945, and contained the voting proposals for the Security council. It was proposed that each member of the Security council should have one vote, that decisions on procedural matters should be made by an affirmative vote of seven members, and that decisions on all other matters should be made by an affirmative vote of seven members including the concurring votes of the permanent members. In decisions concerning peaceful settlement or settlement through regional agencies or arrangements, however, a party to a dispute was to abstain from voting.

Poland's name was included among the countries listed as having qualified for invitations, but at the same time it was stated that the invitation to it was being held over until the projected Polish Provisional Government of National Unity was constituted.

Suggestions for Supplementing Dumbarton Oaks Proposals.—Throughout the world the Dumbarton Oaks proposals were discussed, criticized, commended and attacked in press and pamphlet and on the radio, and suggestions for their emendation were being worked out by governments, both severally and individually.

The Dumbarton Oaks proposals had left open the question of whether the statute of the international court of justice should be that of the permanent court or a new statute based upon it. Accordingly the United States government, acting on behalf of the governments sponsoring the San Francisco conference, invited a committee of expert jurists to meet in Washington on April 8 for preliminary discussions. Jurists from 44 countries attended, and proceeded to a revision, article by article, of the statute of the permanent court, making adaptations of form and introducing new features considered desirable. The question of whether the court should be established as a new court or as a continuance of the permanent court was left to the San Francisco conference to decide.

The question of trusteeship was placed tentatively on the agenda of the Dumbarton Oaks conversations, but the Dumbarton Oaks proposals contained no trusteeship provisions. At Yalta it was agreed that the five governments having permanent seats on the Security council should consult each other prior to the United Nations conference on providing machinery for territorial trusteeships. This would apply only to: existing mandates of the League of Nations; territory to be detached from the axis as a result of World War II and any other territory which might voluntarily be placed under trusteeship. They agreed further that there would be no discussions concerning any specific territory, but only on the machinery and principles of trusteeship. It would be a matter of subsequent agreement which territories would actually be placed under trusteeship.

In the second phase of the Dumbarton Oaks conversations, the Chinese government had put forward certain proposals which were agreed to at that time between China, the United Kingdom and the United States. The soviet union agreed to join in sponsoring the proposals, and they were submitted to the San Francisco conference on May 1 as a supplement to the Dumbarton Oaks proposals.

In addition the conference had before it amendments submitted by 40 national delegations and including an estimated total of some 1,200 items. The sponsoring powers themselves submitted 24 joint amendments.

 The San Francisco Conference.—In addition to the 4 sponsoring powers, 42 nations were invited to the United Nations Conference on International Organization at San Francisco. On April 30 the conference approved the admission of Argentina, the Byelorussian Soviet Socialist Republic and the Ukrainian Soviet Socialist Republic. Denmark, which had just been liberated, was invited to attend the conference on June 5. Fifty nations, therefore, were represented at the San Francisco conference and took part in drawing up the United Nations charter (*see* p. 403 for list of members).

The organization of the conference was in the hands of four committees. First there was a steering committee, composed of the heads of all the national delegations, which considered major questions of policy and procedure. It elected an executive committee composed of the chairmen of 14 delegations which took interim decisions and prepared recommendations for consideration by the steering committee. The members of the executive committee were: Australia, Brazil, Canada, Chile, China, Czechoslovakia, France, Iran, Mexico, the Netherlands, U.S.S.R., United Kingdom, United States and Yugoslavia. A co-ordination committee consisting of the deputies of the 14 members of the executive committee supervised the final drafting of recommendations made by the commissions of the conference and harmonized divergent drafts. In addition there was a credentials committee which verified the credentials of delegations.

The substantive work of the conference was divided among 4 commissions, and the work of these 4 commissions was in turn divided among 12 technical committees. Each nation had the right to be represented on each commission and each committee.

Commission I dealt with the general provisions of the world organization. It had two committees which dealt with (1) preamble, purposes and principles and (2) membership and general.

Commission II was concerned with the general assembly. It had four committees, which dealt with (1) structure and procedures, (2) political and security functions, (3) economic and social co-operation and (4) trusteeship system.

Commission III considered the Security council. It had four committees, which dealt with (1) structure and procedures, (2) peaceful settlement, (3) enforcement arrangements and (4) regional arrangements.

Commission IV dealt with judicial organization. It had two committees which dealt with (1) international court of justice and (2) legal problems.

To each committee were assigned as a basis for discussion the relevant sections of the Dumbarton Oaks proposals. The terms of reference of the committee on the trusteeship system, for which no provision was made in the Dumbarton Oaks proposals, were to prepare "draft provisions on principles and mechanism of a system of international trusteeship for such dependent territories as may by subsequent agreement be placed thereunder." The committee on legal problems had to consider proposals and documents presented by participating governments on various legal problems not touched upon in the Dumbarton Oaks proposals. The committee on the international court of justice had before it in addition to the relevant chapter in the Dumbarton Oaks proposals the draft statute prepared by the committee of jurists.

English and French were adopted as the working languages of the conference; the official languages were Chinese, English, French, Russian and Spanish.

The secretary-general of the conference was Alger Hiss of the United States department of state. The United States as host government met the general expenses of the conference which were estimated at somewhat less than $2,000,000, and was responsible for the recruitment of the secretariat.

The charter emerged from the San Francisco debates a broader, more liberal document than the Dumbarton Oaks proposals. Among the many changes made at San Francisco to the Dumbarton Oaks draft, the following may be noted:

A preamble was added to the charter, setting forth the declared common intentions of its drafters. The chapter on purposes was liberalized. Thus, the adjustment of international disputes by peaceful means was to be brought about "in conformity with the principles of justice and international law." Friendly relations "based on respect for the principle of equal rights and self-determination of peoples" were to be developed. The purpose of achieving international co-operation "in promoting and encouraging respect for human rights and for fundamental freedoms for all without distinction as to race, sex, language or religion" was added.

Similarly, changes were made in the chapter on principles. Members undertook to fulfil "in good faith" the obligations assumed by them under the charter. They agreed to settle their disputes by peaceful means in such a manner that not only international peace and security, but also "justice" were not endangered. The principle that members should refrain from the threat or use of force was expanded to read "refrain from the threat or use of force *against the territorial integrity or political independence of any state.*" Nonintervention in matters within the domestic jurisdiction of any state became one of the principles; in the Dumbarton Oaks proposals this question had been dealt with in the chapter on peaceful settlement.

As regards membership, the conference drew a distinction between "original" members and new members. Original members were to be those states which participated in the conference or had previously signed the United Nations declaration and signed and ratified the charter. New members were not only required to be "peace-loving" as specified in the Dumbarton Oaks proposals; they had also to accept the obligations contained in the charter and in the opinion of the organization to be able and willing to carry them out.

The powers of the general assembly were amplified. Thus, the assembly was empowered to "discuss any questions or any matters within the scope of the present charter or relating to the powers and functions of any organs provided for in the present charter." With the exception of matters under consideration by the Security council (an exception contained in the Dumbarton Oaks proposals) the assembly was also empowered to make recommendations on any such matters to the Security council or to members or to both. Subject to this same reservation it was also empowered to make recommendations "for the peaceful adjustment" of any situation it thought likely to impair the general welfare or friendly relations among nations, including situations resulting from violation of the charter.

As regards the Security council, the Dumbarton Oaks proposals were in the main adopted. It was, however, decided that France should from the outset be a permanent member of the council instead of "in due course," as proposed at Dumbarton Oaks. A clause was added providing that in the election of the non-permanent members of the council due regard should be "specially paid, in the first instance, to the contribution of members of the United

Nations to the maintenance of international peace and security and to the other purposes of the organization, and also to equitable geographical distribution."

The voting procedure in the Security council was one of the most controversial issues at San Francisco, several delegations opposing in particular the rule that the permanent members of the council must be unanimous in recommending measures for peaceful settlement. In an effort to clarify the voting formula agreed upon at the Crimea (Yalta) conference, the sponsoring powers and France issued an interpretation in reply to a list of 22 questions drawn up in the sub-committee considering the question. This interpretation, which was taken as embodying the views of these 5 governments, upheld the provision for unanimity of the permanent members except that a party to a dispute would not vote on a recommendation involving peaceful settlement, and no member of the council could prevent consideration and discussion by the council of any dispute brought to its attention by a member state.

Although several delegations were opposed to it on principle, the Yalta formula was eventually adopted, as the sponsoring powers made it clear that they could not accept any of the amendments proposed.

A new paragraph was added to the chapter on enforcement measures, providing that the Security council before deciding on such measures might call on the parties to a dispute to comply with provisional measures. The article relating to the provision of national contingents of armed forces was re-drafted to make it more specific. A paragraph was also inserted providing that the Security council before calling on a member to provide armed forces should invite that member to take part in the discussions concerning the employment of these forces. Another paragraph safeguarded "the inherent right of individual or collective self-defence" in case of armed attack until the Security council had taken the necessary measures, but any measures taken in self-defense were to be reported to the council.

The Dumbarton Oaks proposals had suggested that no enforcement action should be taken under regional arrangements or by regional agencies without the approval of the Security council. One exception was approved at San Francisco—action taken under regional arrangements directed against the renewal of aggressive policy by any enemy-state, until the Security council should be charged by the governments concerned with the responsibility for such action.

The economic and social provisions of the charter were given a greater importance at San Francisco. Thus, the Economic and Social council was made one of the principal organs, and the objectives of the United Nations in the economic and social field were enlarged.

The functions of the Economic and Social council were also extended. It was to initiate studies and make recommendations with respect to international economic, social, cultural, educational, health and related fields. It was decided, however, that the general assembly and not the Economic and Social council should examine the administrative budgets of specialized agencies. The specialized agencies to be brought into relationship with the United Nations were described more precisely as inter-governmental agencies having wide international responsibilities, as defined in their basic instruments, in economic, social, cultural, educational, health and related fields.

The charter provisions on international trusteeship and the declaration on non-self-governing territories were the product of the San Francisco conference. On the basis of a number of proposals the delegations of Australia, China, France, the U.S.S.R., the United Kingdom and the United States submitted a working paper which served as a basis for discussion in the committee on trusteeship. Changes, however, were made to the working paper. Thus, a statement of general policy, contained in the paper, was separated from the provisions for a trusteeship system and became a separate chapter of the charter under the title "Declaration regarding Non-Self-Governing Territories," binding on all powers administering non-self-governing territories. These territories were defined as those "whose peoples have not yet attained a full measure of self-government." The clauses defining the obligations of powers administering such territories toward the inhabitants were considerably expanded, and two new clauses were added, obliging the administering powers to promote constructive measures of development and to transmit regularly to the secretary-general statistical and other information relating to the economic, social and educational conditions of the territories administered by them.

After some controversy it was decided that the objectives of the trusteeship system should include the promotion of the progressive development of the peoples of trust territories toward "independence" as well as "self-government." It was decided that the Trusteeship council should be a principal organ of the United Nations.

The conference, after considering the recommendation

Interpreters providing simultaneous translations of United Nations proceedings at Lake Success, N.Y., in 1946. Delegates were provided with headphones; dials enabled them to tune in on translations in the language which they preferred

of the committee of jurists and the draft statute prepared by them, decided that the advantages of establishing a new court of justice outweighed those of retaining the permanent court. A provision was added to the charter that each member should undertake to comply with the decision of the court in any case to which it was a party, and that if any party should fail to comply with a decision the other party could have recourse to the Security council.

To the Dumbarton Oaks provisions concerning the secretariat the conference added clauses providing that the secretary-general and his staff should not seek or receive instructions from any authority external to the organization, and should refrain from any action reflecting on their position as international officials; that members should undertake to respect the exclusively international character of the secretariat; and that the paramount consideration in the employment of staff should be the necessity of securing the highest standards of efficiency, competence and integrity, due regard being paid to recruitment on as wide a geographical basis as possible.

On the question of amendments, certain delegations opposing the voting formula in the Security council felt that they could more readily accept the charter if the process of amendment were made easier. To meet their wishes, provision was made for the calling of a general conference to review the charter. The conference would be called by a two-thirds vote of the general assembly and any seven members of the Security council, and it was agreed that if such a conference had not been called before the tenth annual session of the general assembly, the question of calling it should be placed on the agenda of that session.

Other provisions of the charter drafted at San Francisco concerned the registration of treaties, obligations inconsistent with the charter, the privileges and immunities of the United Nations, its legal status and the signature and ratification of the charter.

The charter was signed on June 26, 1945, by the representatives of the 50 nations participating in the conference. A space was left among the original signatories for Poland, which signed on Oct. 15, 1945.

The terms of the charter provided that it should come into force when the five permanent members of the Security council and a majority of other signatory states had ratified it and deposited their ratifications with the U.S. department of state. This took place by Oct. 24, 1945, and the United States secretary of state on that date signed the Protocol of Deposit of Ratifications, bringing the charter into force.

At the same time as they signed the charter, delegates to the San Francisco conference affixed their signatures to an agreement on interim arrangements. This agreement established a preparatory commission, consisting of one representative of each signatory of the charter, to prepare for the first sessions of the general assembly, Security council, Economic and Social council and trusteeship council, for the establishment of the secretariat and for the convening of the international court of justice. The commission was to have an executive committee composed of the representatives of the 14 members of the executive committee of the conference.

The Preparatory Commission.—The preparatory commission ("Preco") met in San Francisco on June 27, 1945, and made arrangements for its executive committee to meet in London.

The executive committee convened in London on Aug. 16, 1945. It reported to the preparatory commission, which met in London from Nov. 24 to Dec. 23 and, on the basis of the executive committee's report, drew up recommendations for the general assembly. These recommendations were embodied in the "Report of the Preparatory Commission of the United Nations."

The commission and its executive committee were assisted by an executive secretary, appointed by the executive committee, and an international secretariat appointed by him.

The preparatory commission recommended that the general assembly should meet as early as possible, and it submitted the provisional agenda for the first session and provisional rules of procedure. It recommended that the assembly establish six main committees (political and security; economic and financial; social, humanitarian and cultural; trusteeship; administrative and budgetary; legal), two procedural committees (credentials committee and general committee), two standing committees (advisory committee on administrative and budgetary questions and committee on contributions) and such *ad hoc* committees as might be required.

The commission also recommended a provisional agenda and provisional rules of procedure for the Security council. It suggested that the representative of the first member of the Security council in the English alphabetical order of the names of members should act as temporary chairman of the council. At its first meeting the council should adopt a directive requesting the chiefs of staff of the permanent members of the Security council to meet at a given place and to constitute the military staff committee. The recommendations concerning the Security council were less detailed than those concerning the other organs of the United Nations, partly because it was felt that the council would meet continuously and would be able to develop its own organization and program of work.

The preparatory commission submitted a provisional agenda and rules of procedure for the Economic and Social council. It recommended that at its first session the council establish the following commissions: human rights, economic and employment, temporary social, statistical, and narcotic drugs, and that it consider the desirability of establishing a co-ordination commission and a fiscal commission. While not accepting a proposal that there should be a commission on refugees, the preparatory commission recommended that the problem should be studied by the Economic and Social council and also by the general assembly in view of the political questions involved.

The commission submitted provisional rules of procedure for the Trusteeship council and a draft resolution for adoption by the general assembly, calling on mandatory powers to take practical steps, together with the states directly concerned, so that trusteeship agreements could be submitted for approval preferably not later than the second part of the assembly's first session.

The preparatory commission had been authorized to issue invitations for the nomination of candidates for the international court of justice. The statute of the court required that three months should elapse from the date of the issue of invitations for nomination until the election of judges. Accordingly, the invitations were issued on the instructions of the executive committee. This action was endorsed by the preparatory commission, which recommended that the general assembly take the necessary steps for convening the court. It also adopted a resolution stating that it would welcome the taking by the League of Nations of appropriate steps to dissolve the Permanent Court of International Justice.

The commission recommended that the secretary-general

should work out the details for registration and publication of treaties, to be registered in accordance with the terms of the charter. It also recommended that the general assembly consider inviting non-members to send treaties and international agreements for registration with and publication by the secretariat, and inviting all governments to send for publication treaties and international agreements concluded before the date of entry into force of the charter and not included in the League of Nations Treaty series.

The commission transmitted to the general assembly for its consideration a study on privileges and immunities presented by the executive committee and a draft convention on privileges and immunities. It also recommended that the privileges and immunities of specialized agencies should be reconsidered and that the agencies should be granted only those privileges necessary to the fulfilment of their functions.

The commission recommended that the secretariat should be organized on a functional basis, and that its principal units should be: department of security council affairs, department of economic affairs, department of social affairs, department of trusteeship and information from non-self-governing territories, department of public information, legal department, conference and general services, administrative and financial services. The secretary-general, it was recommended, should take the necessary steps to co-ordinate the work of the departments of economic and social affairs.

The commission appointed a technical advisory committee on information to make recommendations concerning the functions, policies and activities of the department of public information. The committee's recommendations were transmitted to the general assembly for its consideration.

The preparatory commission considered that the secretary-general's freedom to organize the secretariat should not be restricted by too much detail. The question of salaries, allowances and pensions was referred for preliminary study to an advisory group of experts appointed by the preparatory commission to assist the executive secretary in the development of administrative, budgetary and personnel policies. The preparatory commission submitted provisional staff regulations, which it suggested for adoption by the assembly and provisional staff rules to implement these regulations which it suggested the assembly should transmit to the secretary-general for his information. The commission recommended that the secretary-general establish an international civil service commission, after consultation with the heads of specialized agencies, to advise him on methods of recruitment for the secretariat.

One of the functions specifically assigned to the commission was to make studies and prepare recommendations on the location of the permanent headquarters of the organization. After considerable debate both in the executive committee and in the preparatory commission it was decided to recommend that the permanent headquarters should be located in the east of the United States. Since it was felt that more time was required to determine an exact site, an interim committee of 12 members was appointed to function after the close of the preparatory commission's session. It was to determine the exact requirements for the site and to examine specific sites in the light of these requirements. On Dec. 25, 1945, the interim committee approved three possible areas (near Boston, Princeton and New York, respectively) for the site and appointed an inspection group of seven members. The inspection group, after studying the areas, recommended that the permanent headquarters should be established (1) near New York city and (2) in the North Stamford-Greenwich district.

Another task assigned to the preparatory commission was to make recommendations concerning the transfer of functions, activities and assets of the League of Nations which it was considered the new organization should take over. The commission recommended that the United Nations should assume only custodial, technical and non-political functions performed by the League under international agreements and that the general assembly reserve the right, after due examination, not to assume any particular function or power. It recommended that the Economic and Social council survey the non-political functions of the league, other than those arising from international agreements, to determine which should be assumed by the organization or by the specialized agencies. Pending the conclusion of this survey, the council should provisionally continue certain of these functions.

On Dec. 18, 1945, the commission appointed a committee of eight members to enter into discussions with the League of Nations supervisory committee for the purpose of establishing a common plan for the transfer of the assets of the League of Nations to the United Nations. The common plan was to be submitted to the general assembly at the first part of its first session.

Thus, by the time the general assembly met in London on Jan. 10, 1946, for the first part of its first session, the preliminary work had been accomplished and the way prepared for the establishment of the United Nations as a working organization.

MEMBERSHIP OF THE UNITED NATIONS

Original Members

Argentine Republic
Australia
Belgium
Bolivia
Brazil
Byelorussian Soviet Socialist Republic
Canada
Chile
China
Colombia
Costa Rica
Cuba
Czechoslovakia
Denmark
Dominican Republic
Ecuador
Egypt
El Salvador
Ethiopia
France
Greece
Guatemala
Haiti
Honduras
India
Iran
Iraq
Lebanon
Liberia
Luxembourg
Mexico
Netherlands
New Zealand
Nicaragua
Norway
Panamá
Paraguay
Peru
Philippine Republic
Poland
Saudi Arabia
Syria
Turkey
Ukrainian Soviet Socialist Republic
Union of South Africa
Union of Soviet Socialist Republics
United Kingdom
United States of America
Uruguay
Venezuela
Yugoslavia

Members subsequently admitted by the General Assembly on recommendation of the Security Council

Afghanistan	admitted Nov. 19, 1946
Iceland	admitted Nov. 19, 1946
Sweden	admitted Nov. 19, 1946
Siam	admitted Dec. 16, 1946

STRUCTURE OF THE UNITED NATIONS
(as of Jan. 1947)

Principal Organs

General Assembly
Security Council
Economic and Social Council
Trusteeship Council
International Court of Justice
Secretariat

404 STRUCTURE OF THE UNITED NATIONS—Continued

GENERAL ASSEMBLY

Membership (the General Assembly consists of all Members of the United Nations)

Main Committees (all Members have right to be represented)
- First—Political and Security
- Second—Economic and Financial
- Third—Social, Humanitarian and Cultural
- Fourth—Trusteeship
- Fifth—Administrative and Budgetary
- Sixth—Legal

Procedural Committees
- General Committee (President, seven vice-presidents and chairmen of six main committees)
- Credentials Committee (nine members)

Standing Committees
- Advisory Committee on Administrative and Budgetary Questions (nine members)
- Committee on Contributions (ten members)

Ad hoc Commissions and Committees established during the First Part of the First Session
- Permanent Headquarters Committee (all Members have right to be represented)
- League of Nations Committee (all Members have right to be represented)
- Committee on UNRRA (eleven members)
- Committee on Negotiations with the U.S.A. (ten members)
- Committee on Negotiations for the transfer of League of Nations assets, and the premises in the Peace Palace at The Hague (eight members)
- Headquarters Commission (nine members)

Ad hoc Committees established during the Second Part of the First Session
- United Nations Staff Benefit Committee (nine members and six alternates)
- Committee on Transmission of Information from Non-Self-Governing Territories (sixteen members)
- Advisory Committee on Permanent Headquarters (sixteen members)
- Committee on Development and Codification of International Law (seventeen members)
- Committee on Procedures and Organization (fifteen members)
- Committee to meet with ad hoc Sub-Committee of Security Council on Rules Governing Admission of New Members (five members)
- Special Technical Committee on Relief Needs after the Termination of UNRRA (ten members)

SECURITY COUNCIL

Membership

Permanent Members
- China
- France
- Union of Soviet Socialist Republics
- United Kingdom
- United States

Non-Permanent Members elected on Jan. 12, 1946, to serve until Dec. 31, 1946
- Egypt
- Mexico
- Netherlands

Non-Permanent Members elected on Jan. 12, 1946, to serve until Dec. 31, 1947
- Australia
- Brazil
- Poland

Non-Permanent Members elected on Nov. 19, 1946, to serve from Jan. 1, 1947, to Dec. 31, 1948
- Belgium
- Colombia
- Syria

Military Staff Committee (consists of Chiefs of Staff of the permanent members of the Security Council or their representatives)

Atomic Energy Commission (established by the General Assembly, but reports to the Security Council and takes its directions from the Security Council in matters affecting security) (consists of all members of the Security Council and Canada when that state is not a member of the Council)

Committees of the Atomic Energy Commission (consist of representatives of the twelve members of the Commission; the Scientific and Technical Committee consists of one scientific adviser appointed by each of the members)
- Working Committee
  - Sub-Committee 1
  - Committee 2
  - Scientific and Technical Committee
  - Legal Advisory Committee
- Committee on Rules of Procedure

Standing Committees of the Security Council (consist of eleven members of the Council)
- Committee of Experts on Rules of Procedure
- Committee on the Admission of New Members

Ad hoc Committees and Commissions, such as Sub-Committee on the Spanish Question (five members) and Commission of Investigation concerning Greek Frontier Incidents, are established to deal with temporary questions.

ECONOMIC AND SOCIAL COUNCIL

Membership

Elected on Jan. 14, 1946, to serve until Dec. 31, 1946
- Colombia
- United States
- Greece
- Lebanon
- Ukrainian Soviet Socialist Republic
- Yugoslavia

Elected on Jan. 14, 1946, to serve until Dec. 31, 1947
- Cuba
- Czechoslovakia
- India
- Norway
- Union of Soviet Socialist Republics
- United Kingdom

Elected on Jan. 14, 1946, to serve until Dec. 31, 1948
- Belgium
- Canada
- Chile
- China
- France
- Peru

Elected on Dec. 12, 1946, to serve from Jan. 1, 1947 to Dec. 31, 1949
- Byelorussian Soviet Socialist Republic
- Lebanon
- New Zealand
- Turkey
- United States
- Venezuela

Elected on Dec. 12, 1946, to fill vacancy caused by the resignation of Belgium
- Netherlands

Commissions
- Economic and Employment Commission (fifteen members)
  - Sub-Commissions
    - Economic Reconstruction of Devastated Areas
    - Employment and Economic Stability (not yet functioning)
    - Economic Development (not yet functioning)
- Transport and Communications (fifteen members)
- Statistical Commission (twelve members)
  - Sub-Commission
    - Statistical Sampling (not yet functioning)
- Human Rights (eighteen members)
  - Sub-Commissions
    - Freedom of Information and of the Press (not yet functioning)
    - Prevention of Discrimination and Protection of Minorities (not yet functioning)
- Social (eighteen members)
  - Sub-Commission
    - Child Welfare (not yet functioning)
- Status of Women (fifteen members)
- Narcotic Drugs (fifteen members)
- Fiscal (fifteen members)
- Population (twelve members)

Standing Committees
- Committee on Organization of the Council
- Committee on Negotiations with Specialized Agencies
- Committee on Arrangements for Consultation with Non-Governmental Organizations

Ad hoc Committees, such as Committee on the Finances of the International Refugee Organization (ten members) and the Committee of the Whole on Devastated Areas (all members of the Council), are established to deal with temporary questions.

International Children's Emergency Fund (established by the General Assembly, but reports to the Economic and Social Council) (twenty-five members)

Specialized Agencies in relationship with the United Nations

International Labour Organisation

United Nations Educational, Scientific and Cultural Organization

Food and Agriculture Organization of the United Nations

International Civil Aviation Organization (agreement approved by the General Assembly, subject to the compliance of ICAO with any decision of the General Assembly concerning Franco Spain; has still to be approved by the Assembly of ICAO)

International Monetary Fund (negotiations for agreement authorized by Economic and Social Council)

International Bank for Reconstruction and Development (negotiations for agreement authorized by Economic and Social Council)

Universal Postal Union (draft agreement approved by Committee of Governmental Postal Experts; subject to approval of UPU Conference, Economic and Social Council, and the General Assembly)

International Telecommunications Union (plans for ITU Conference in July 1947 include consideration of agreement)

World Health Organization (to be established; Interim Commission functioning) (Constitution of WHO provides for establishment of relationship)

International Trade Organization (to be established)

Non-Governmental Organizations in consultative status with the Economic and Social Council (Category "A")

International

World Federation of Trade Unions
International Co-operative Alliance
International Chamber of Commerce

National

American Federation of Labor.

TRUSTEESHIP COUNCIL

Membership

Members of the Trusteeship Council by virtue of their position as *Administering Authorities*

Australia
New Zealand
Belgium
United Kingdom
France

Members of the Trusteeship Council by virtue of their position as permanent members of the Security Council.

China
U.S.S.R.
United States

Elected on Dec. 14, 1946, to serve until Dec. 31, 1949

Iraq
Mexico

(As the first meeting of the Trusteeship Council will not be held until March 1947, it has not yet established any subsidiary organs)

INTERNATIONAL COURT OF JUSTICE Chamber of Summary Procedure

Membership

Elected on Feb. 6, 1946, to serve for three years

Abdel Hamid Badawi Pasha (Egypt)
Mr. Hsu Mo (China)
Mr. John E. Read (Canada)
Mr. Bohdan Winiarski (Poland)
Mr. Milovan Zoricic (Yugoslavia)

Elected on Feb. 6, 1946, to serve for six years

Mr. Isidro Fabela Alfaro (Mexico)
Mr. Green H. Hackworth (United States)
Mr. Helge Klaestad (Norway)
Mr. Sergei Borisovich Krylov (U.S.S.R.)
Mr. Charles de Visscher (Belgium)

Elected on Feb. 6, 1946, to serve for nine years

Mr. Alejandro Alvarez (Chile)
Mr. Jose Philadelpho de Barros Azevedo (Brazil)
Mr. Jules Basdevant (France)
Mr. Jose Gustavo Guerrero (El Salvador)
Sir Arnold Duncan McNair (United Kingdom)

SECRETARIAT

Department of Security Council Affairs

General Political Division
Administrative and General Division
Enforcement Measures Division
Atomic Energy Commission Group

Department of Economic Affairs

Statistical Office
Division for Co-ordination and Liaison (jointly with Department of Social Affairs)
Division of Economic Stability and Employment
Division of Economic Reconstruction and Special Studies
Division of Economic Development
Division of Transport and Communications
Fiscal Division
Secretariat for International Trade and Employment Commission

Department of Social Affairs

Division for Co-ordination and Liaison (jointly with Department of Economic Affairs)
Division of Human Rights
Division of Refugees and Displaced Persons
Division of Demography
Division of Social Affairs
Division of Narcotic Drugs

Department of Trusteeship and Information from Non-Self-Governing Territories

Division of Trusteeship
Division of Non-self Governing Territories

Legal Department

Division of General Legal Problems
Division for the Development and Codification of International Law
Division of Immunities and Registration

Department of Conference and General Services

Employee Housing Staff
Headquarters Planning Staff
Bureau of Technical Services
- Library Service
- Presentation Service
- Editorial Division
- Languages Division
- Documents and Sales Division

Overseas Offices Division
Bureau of General Services
- Communications and Registry Service
- Transportation Service
- Maintenance and Engineering Service
- Conference Co-ordination Division
- Purchase and Supply Division

Department of Administrative and Financial Services

Bureau of Administrative Management and Budget
- Procedures Division
- Estimates and Organization Division
- Budget Division

Bureau of Personnel
- Recruitment Examining and Placement Division
- Salary Administration Division
- Staff Relations and Services Division
- Training Division

Bureau of the Comptroller
- Regulations and Inspections Division
- Audit Division
- Treasury Division
- General Accounts Division
- Tax and Staff Pensions Division
- Budget Control and Accounts Division

Department of Public Information

Press Division
Radio Division
Liaison Division
Films and Visual Media Division
Reference and Publications Division

The First Year

The first year of the United Nations was of necessity largely concerned with the establishment of its principal and subsidiary organs, and with organizational questions; nevertheless many substantive questions in the political, economic and social fields were actively considered.

The charter came into force on Oct. 24, 1945, and the preparatory commission completed its work on Dec. 23, 1945, so arrangements were made for convening the first session of the general assembly. This session was divided into two parts; the first part was held in London from Jan. 10 to Feb. 14, 1946, and the second part from Oct. 23 to Dec. 15, 1946. It was planned that the first part of the session should deal largely with organizational problems, and the second with substantive questions, but decisions on certain substantive questions were in fact taken at the first part of the session.

The necessary steps were also taken to bring the other organs of the United Nations into being. Thus the non-permanent members of the Security council were elected by the assembly on Jan. 12. The council held its first meeting on Jan. 17, and was in continuous session for the rest of the year. After its 23rd meeting on Feb. 16, the council adjourned and reconvened in New York on March 20, 1946.

The members of the Economic and Social council were elected by the general assembly on Jan. 12 and 14. This council held three sessions: the first from Jan. 23 to Feb. 18 in London; the second from May 25 to June 21 at Hunter college, the Bronx, New York; and the third from Sept. 11 to Oct. 3 at the United Nations temporary headquarters at Lake Success.

Before the Trusteeship council could come into existence, it was necessary in accordance with the terms of the charter that trusteeship agreements should be drawn up and approved by the general assembly (or, in the case of agreements for "strategic areas," the Security council). The charter specified that the Trusteeship council should be composed of those members of the United Nations administering trust territories with, in addition, those permanent members of the Security council not administering trust territories and enough other non-administering states elected by the general assembly to make the membership on the council of administering and nonadministering states equal. It was not until the second part of the general assembly's first session that this condition was fulfilled, and the Trusteeship council established.

The judges of the international court of justice were elected by the general assembly and the Security council, voting independently, on Feb. 6, and the court held its inaugural sitting on April 18. On Feb. 1, the general assembly, on recommendation of the Security council, appointed Trygve Lie as the first secretary-general of the United Nations.

General Assembly—First Part of First Session.—At the first part of its first session, the general assembly held 33 plenary meetings and 102 committee meetings. Paul-Henri Spaak of Belgium was elected president of the first session of the general assembly, and the chief delegates of China, France, the Union of South Africa, the U.S.S.R., the United Kingdom, the United States and Venezuela were elected vice-presidents.

The general assembly established six main committees: political and security; economic and financial; social, humanitarian and cultural; administrative and budgetary; trusteeship; legal. It set up two *ad hoc* committees: a League of Nations committee and a permanent headquarters committee. The general assembly established two procedural committees: a general committee and a credentials committee.

As non-permanent members of the Security council, the general assembly elected Australia, Brazil and Poland for a term of two years, and Egypt, Mexico and the Netherlands for a term of one year.

It elected as members of the Economic and Social council the following 18 members: Belgium, Canada, Chile, China, France and Peru for a term of three years; Cuba, Czechoslovakia, India, Norway, the U.S.S.R. and the United Kingdom for a term of two years; Colombia, Greece, Lebanon, the Ukrainian S.S.R., the United States and Yugoslavia for a term of one year.

The general assembly and the Security council, voting independently, elected the following 15 persons as judges of the international court of justice: Alejandro Alvarez (Chile), Jose Philadelpho de Barros Azevedo (Brazil), Jules Basdevant (France), Jose Gustavo Guerrero (El Salvador), Sir Arnold Duncan McNair (United Kingdom), for a term of 9 years; Isidro Fabela Alfaro (Mexico), Green H. Hackworth (United States), Helge Klaestad (Norway), Sergei Borisovich Krylov (U.S.S.R.), Charles de Visscher (Belgium), for a term of 6 years; and Abdel Hamid Badawi Pasha (Egypt), Hsu Mo (China), John E. Read (Canada), Bohdan Winiarski (Poland), Milovan Zoricic (Yugoslavia), for a term of 3 years.

The general assembly decided that members of the councils elected in Jan. 1946 should hold office for 12 months and that elections of their successors should be held at the second part of the general assembly's first session.

Procedural Questions. — Two procedural questions aroused considerable discussion in the general assembly: the composition of the general committee and the question of nominations.

The preparatory commission had recommended that the general committee should consist of the president of the general assembly, the seven vice-presidents and the chairmen of the six main committees. Delegates supporting this recommendation stressed that a small general committee would be more efficient, and that the work of this committee was organizational and not political. On the other hand, certain delegates felt that all delegations should be represented on the general committee, as this would make for more democratic handling of the general assembly's business, and maintained that it would in practice be difficult to define what constituted an important political question. The general assembly decided that the general committee should consist of 14 members, but added a proviso that it should not decide any political question. It also decided that a member which had no representative on the general committee and which had requested the inclusion of an additional item on the agenda should participate without vote at meetings of the general committee when its request was being discussed.

Two opposing views were held on the question of nominations—the one that nominations would prevent the formation of blocs and would make for democratic voting; the other that complete secrecy was the best method of ensuring freedom and independence of vote. After considerable discussion, the general assembly decided that "there shall be no nominations."

A third procedural question decided by the general assembly was the adoption of rules of procedure concerning languages. The rules adopted provided that in all organs of the United Nations other than the international court of justice, Chinese, French, English, Russian and Spanish

Organization of the United Nations, 1945. Unbroken channels represent direct relationship as defined in the Charter. Broken channels represent relationship to be determined

should be the official languages, and English and French the working languages. Speeches made in either of the working languages should be interpreted into the other working language, and speeches made in any of the other three official languages should be interpreted into both working languages. A representative making a speech in a language other than the official languages should himself provide an interpreter into one of the working languages; interpretation into the second working language would be based on the first interpretation.

Political and Security Questions.—The general assembly on Jan. 24, 1946, unanimously adopted a resolution establishing a commission on atomic energy. This resolution had been agreed upon by the Moscow conference of the ministers of foreign affairs of the U.S.S.R., United Kingdom and United States, and the governments of China, France and Canada had agreed to join in sponsoring it. The resolution was adopted without change by the general assembly. The commission was to submit its reports and recommendations to the Security council. They were to be made public unless the Security council in the interest of peace and security directed otherwise. Where appropriate the Security council was to transmit the reports to the general assembly and other organs of the United Nations. On matters affecting security the commission would receive directions from and be responsible to the Security council. The commission was to be composed of the states represented on the Security council and Canada, when Canada was not a member of the council. Its rules of procedure were to be approved by the Security council.

The commission was to proceed with the utmost dispatch and enquire into all phases of the problems of atomic energy. In particular, it was to make proposals for extending the exchange of basic scientific information for peaceful ends, for controlling atomic energy to the extent necessary to ensure its use only for peaceful purposes, for the elimination of atomic weapons from national armaments and for effective safeguards; *e.g.,* by inspection, against violations and evasions.

The general assembly also recommended that members of the United Nations should "take all the necessary measures" to ensure that war criminals should be arrested and sent back for trial to those countries where their crimes had been committed, and called upon governments not members of the United Nations to take similar steps.

A further resolution endorsed the resolution adopted at the San Francisco conference and the statement made at the Potsdam conference to the effect that countries whose governments (*i.e.*, the Franco government in Spain) had been installed with the help of the axis powers were not eligible for membership in the United Nations. It recommended that members should, in the conduct of their future relations with Spain, act in accordance with these statements.

Economic and Social Questions.—Acting on the recommendations of the preparatory commission, the general assembly recommended that the Economic and Social council establish the following commissions: a commission on human rights, an economic and employment commission, a temporary social commission, a statistical commission, a commission on narcotic drugs; and that the council should consider the desirability of establishing the following commissions: demographic commission, temporary transport and communications commission, fiscal commission, co-ordination commission. Delegates expressed the view that the Economic and Social council should be allowed the widest possible freedom to carry out its work, and that the recommendation to consider setting up a co-ordination commission should not be regarded as a directive. Similarly the preparatory commission's recommendation that the commissions contain a majority of highly qualified governmental representatives was approved on the understanding that it would not be regarded as binding and that no limitation should be put on the council in choosing the members of commissions.

The general assembly recommended that the Economic and Social council should make arrangements for the negotiation of agreements bringing specialized agencies into relationship with the United Nations. It transmitted to the Economic and Social council for guidance in its negotiations a number of observations and a list of items submitted by the preparatory commission and deemed appropriate for inclusion in the agreements.

Requests for participation in the work of the Economic and Social council were received from the World Federation of Trade Unions, the International Co-operative alliance, the International Federation of Women and the American Federation of Labor. In a prolonged debate on the question, it was contended that the World Federation of Trade Unions, representing 65,000,000 workers all over the world, was in a unique position and should be accorded a special status. The general assembly recommended that the Economic and Social council should, as soon as possible, adopt suitable arrangements enabling the World Federation of Trade Unions, the International Co-operative alliance and other international non-governmental organizations, as well as the American Federation of Labor and other national and regional organizations whose experience the council found necessary to use, to collaborate with it for purposes of consultation.

In order to facilitate the final stages of the United Nations Relief and Rehabilitation administration's (U.N.R.R.A) work, the general assembly established a committee to consult with the states signatory to the U.N.R.R.A. agreement and urge them to make the further contribution of 1% of their national income to U.N.R.R.A.'s funds, which had been recommended by the council of U.N.R.R.A. in Aug. 1945. At the same time the committee was to urge members which had not signed the U.N.R.R.A. agreement to join that organization.

After prolonged debate on the subject of refugees and displaced persons in which, on the one hand, the inadequacy of the existing machinery was stressed and, on the other, it was contended that all displaced persons could now return to their homes, the general assembly decided to refer the question to the Economic and Social council for study and report. The assembly drew a distinction between genuine refugees and displaced persons, and traitors and war criminals. It recommended that the council establish a special committee to report on the problem, and outlined certain general principles to be taken into consideration.

The general assembly approved unanimously a draft resolution on the world shortage of cereals presented by the delegations of China, France, the U.S.S.R., the United Kingdom and the United States. It urged all governments and peoples to take immediate and drastic action both directly and through the international organizations concerned to conserve supplies and to ensure maximum production of grain.

A resolution was also adopted recognizing that the problem of full reconstruction of member countries of the United Nations which had suffered substantial war damage was a grave and urgent matter which should be given high priority among postwar problems.

Trusteeship and Non-Self-Governing Territories.—As trusteeship agreements had not yet been submitted, it was not possible for the general assembly to take steps to bring the Trusteeship council into being, but the representatives of the United Kingdom, Belgium, Australia and New Zealand made declarations stating that their governments intended to take steps to place mandated territories under the trusteeship system. The French representative stated that France was studying arrangements for placing the French Camerouns and French Togoland under trusteeship, on the understanding that this would not entail any diminution of the rights of the inhabitants and that the agreements would be submitted to the representative organs of the populations of the territories. The South African representative explained the particular circumstances of the territory of South-West Africa, and stated his government's intention of consulting the people of the territory on the form their future government should take.

The general assembly declared that the obligations undertaken by members under chapter XI of the charter were not contingent on the conclusion of trusteeship agreements.

Administrative and Budgetary Matters.—The general assembly decided that the secretary-general should receive a net salary of $20,000 with a representation allowance of $20,000 per annum. In addition he should be provided with a furnished residence. The first secretary-general was to be appointed for five years, renewable for a further five-year term. It was agreed that the general assembly and the Security council were free to modify the term of office of future secretaries-general.

The general assembly resolved that there should be eight principal units of the secretariat, as proposed by the preparatory commission, each under an assistant secretary-general. It authorized the secretary-general to appoint assistant secretaries-general and such other officials and employees as were required and to prescribe their responsibilities and duties.

Salaries of assistant secretaries-general were fixed at $13,500 (U.S.) net, with a representation allowance varying at the secretary-general's discretion from $7,000 (U.S.) to $11,500 (U.S.). Top-ranking directors were to receive a net salary of $11,000 (U.S.) with an allowance varying from $3,000 (U.S.) to $6,000 (U.S.) at the secretary-general's discretion.

The general assembly adopted a provisional budget of $21,500,000 for the financial year 1946, and established a working capital fund of $25,000,000 to cover the expenses of the organization during the first year as provided in the budget. It established a provisional scale of advances to the working capital fund, and approved the provisional financial regulations submitted by the preparatory commission. The secretary-general was instructed to prepare the first and second annual budgets, and a committee on contributions was appointed to prepare a scale for the apportionment of expenses among the members of the United Nations.

Legal Matters.—The general assembly adopted and proposed for accession by members a convention on the privileges and immunities of the United Nations. The convention provided that the United Nations should possess juridical personality; that its property and assets should enjoy immunity from legal process except when that immunity was waived; that the premises and archives of the United Nations should be inviolable, and that its property and assets should be free from all direct taxes and customs duties. The United Nations was to enjoy in the territory of each member treatment not less favourable for its official communications than that accorded by the government of that member to any other government. No censorship was to apply to United Nations official correspondence, and the United Nations was to have the right to use codes and dispatch and receive its correspondence by courier or in bags. The representatives of members, officers of the United Nations and experts on missions for the United Nations were to enjoy such immunities and privileges as were necessary for the independent exercise of their functions. The United Nations was to be entitled to issue a *laissez-passer* to its officials. Provision was made in the convention for the settlement of disputes which might arise out of contracts of a private law character to which the United Nations was a party.

The secretary-general was authorized to negotiate, subject to approval by the general assembly, the arrangements required as a result of the establishment of the seat of the United Nations in the United States of America. A committee was appointed to assist him in the negotiations, and a draft convention was approved by the assembly as a basis for discussion.

The general assembly instructed the secretary-general to open negotiations for the reconsideration of the privileges and immunities of specialized agencies, with a view to coordinating them with those of the United Nations. It invited the members of the international court of justice to make recommendations concerning the privileges, immunities and facilities necessary for the exercise of the court's functions.

The general assembly fixed the salaries of the president, vice-president and members of the court at 54,000 Netherlands florins. The president was in addition to have a special allowance of 15,000 Netherlands florins and the vice-president an allowance of 100 florins for every day on which he acted as president, up to a maximum of 10,000.

The secretary-general was instructed to take the necessary steps to summon a first meeting of the court at The Hague as soon as possible after the election of the members; to appoint a secretary and other necessary temporary officers pending the appointment of the court's registrar and officers; and to conduct preliminary negotiations with the board of directors of the Carnegie foundation to fix conditions, subject to the general assembly's approval, on which the premises in the Peace palace required by the court could be placed at its disposal.

League of Nations.—The general assembly dealt with the transfer of functions, activities and assets of the League

of Nations under these headings: functions and powers belonging to the league under international agreements; other non-political functions and activities and assets.

The assembly declared that the United Nations was willing to undertake certain functions and powers entrusted to the League of Nations under international agreements. Such functions would include the custody of documents and the performance of functions pertaining to a secretariat. It declared itself willing to take the necessary measures to ensure the continued exercise of certain non-political functions and powers of the league, subject to a careful examination of which organ of the United Nations or which specialized agency should be entrusted with these functions and powers, and referred the matter to the Economic and Social council. The assembly decided to examine any request that the United Nations should take over functions or powers of the league under international agreements of a political character.

The Economic and Social council was requested to survey those functions and activities of a non-political character, other than those exercised under international agreements, to determine which of them should be assumed by organs of the United Nations and which should be entrusted to specialized agencies. The council was provisionally to assume the work done by the following league departments: the economic, financial and transit department, particularly the research and statistical work; the health section, particularly the epidemiological service; the opium section and the secretariats of the Permanent Central Opium board and supervisory body.

The assembly requested the secretary-general to make provision for taking over and maintaining in operation the library and archives of the League of Nations and for completing the league treaty series.

The general assembly approved the common plan for the transfer of the league assets agreed upon between the committee established by the preparatory commission and

Recording the verbal proceedings of the United Nations at Hunter college, New York city. Sound filming and phonograph recording were supervised by U.S. army technicians

the supervisory commission of the League of Nations. This provided for the transfer on or about Aug. 1, 1946, of all material assets of the league in accordance with an agreed valuation. The shares in the total credit established were to be distributed between states entitled to participate in accordance with percentages to be laid down by the league at its next assembly. The shares of states which were members of the United Nations were to be credited to them in the books of the United Nations, and the purpose to which they were to be applied was to be decided by the general assembly.

It was agreed that the International Labour organization could use the Assembly hall, with the necessary committee rooms and office accommodation, on financial terms to be agreed between that organization and the United Nations. The International Labour organization was to use the library under the same conditions as other official users.

The League of Nations undertook to discharge its obligations as soon as practicable, to settle the question of contributions of member states in arrears, and to separate the interests of the International Labour organization in the assets of the league, before transfer to the United Nations.

Work of *Ad Hoc* Committees.—*League of Nations Assets.*—A preliminary agreement was reached on March 5 by the negotiating committee on League of Nations' assets with the directors of the Carnegie foundation for the use of the premises in the Peace palace at The Hague. On April 19 an agreement on the Ariana site and an interim arrangement on the privileges and immunities of the United Nations in Switzerland were signed by the United Nations and the Swiss authorities. These agreements were subject to the approval of the general assembly.

The common plan for the transfer of the League of Nations assets to the United Nations was approved by the league assembly on April 18, 1946, and the following arrangements were made:

It was agreed that the buildings would be transferred on July 31, 1946. Until that date maintenance costs would be borne by the League of Nations and afterward by the United Nations. The total value of the contents at the date of transfer would be agreed between the two secretaries-general. The library of the League of Nations would continue to function in Geneva until the question of its transfer was considered in connection with the permanent headquarters of the United Nations. Extended use would be made of photostatic and microfilm processes for copying books and documents required in New York and elsewhere, and the staff would be increased for this purpose.

Headquarters.—The representatives of the secretary-general sent to New York to find an interim headquarters were of the opinion that Hunter college was the best available site to provide a meeting place for the Security council, the Economic and Social council and its commissions and to house the secretariat. A lease was signed on March 6 taking over the premises at Hunter college until May 15, 1946. The Hunter college gymnasium was converted into a council chamber for the Security council and the Economic and Social council.

On April 11 the mayor of New York offered to make available the City building at Flushing meadow for the general assembly if the secretariat would move to the Sperry plant at Lake Success. The mayor announced that the city was ready to expend $1,200,000 on the Flushing meadow site. This offer was accepted on the same day, and at the same time a request was made to extend the lease of Hunter college from May 15 to Aug. 15, 1946.

A lease was taken of certain parts amounting to approximately 572,000 sq.ft. of the Sperry plant for a period of 3 years from July 1, 1946, with an option to renew for 2 further years, and the secretariat and councils were moved there on Aug. 15. The City building at Flushing meadow was altered for the general assembly to meet there on Oct. 23. New York city contributed $1,010,000 for the alterations to the City building and $900,000 for the roads and grounds.

Meantime the headquarters commission studied possible sites for a permanent headquarters on the basis of the desiderata laid down by the general assembly. The commission considered 25 potential sites and selected 15 for closer study—3 of each size (2, 5, 10, 20 and 40 sq.mi.) specified by the general assembly. Finally one site in each group was judged to be the best for its size. The final recommended sites were all in Westchester county.

The Security Council.—From its first meeting on Jan. 17, 1946, until the end of Dec. 1946 the Security council held 88 meetings, during which political, organizational and procedural matters were discussed.

The permanent members of the Security council were China, France, the U.S.S.R., the United Kingdom and the United States. The following non-permanent members were elected by the general assembly at the first part of its first session: Egypt, Mexico and the Netherlands for one year; and Australia, Brazil and Poland for two years. At the second part of its first session the general assembly elected Belgium, Colombia and Syria to replace Egypt, Mexico and the Netherlands, retiring members.

At its first meeting the Security council set up a committee of experts. At its second meeting the council adopted a directive to the military staff committee. The proceedings of the committee of experts and of the military staff committee are dealt with later.

On Jan. 31, 1946, the council unanimously recommended to the general assembly the appointment of Trygve Lie as secretary-general of the United Nations. On Feb. 6 the Security council and the general assembly, voting independently, elected the judges of the international court of justice.

The political questions dealt with by the Security council were concerned with Iran, Greece and the Balkans, Syria and Lebanon, and Spain.

The Iranian Question.—In a letter of Jan. 19, 1946, the representative of Iran to the United Nations brought to the attention of the Security council a situation which might lead to international friction owing to the interference of the soviet union in Iranian internal affairs. The complaint was considered at the council's third and fifth meetings, the Iranian representative participating in the discussion. The soviet representative denied interference and stated that the soviet union was willing to resume direct negotiations with the Iranian government. The council unanimously resolved on Jan. 30, 1946, that since both parties had expressed their readiness to solve the matter by negotiation, the council should be kept informed of such negotiations, while retaining the right to request information on their progress.

In a letter dated March 18, 1946, the Iranian ambassador to the United States brought to the attention of the Security council a dispute between Iran and the soviet union. He stated that the soviet union was maintaining troops in Iran after March 2, contrary to the provisions of the Tripartite Treaty of Alliance between the soviet union, the United Kingdom and Iran of Jan. 29, 1942, and alleged the continued intervention of the soviet union in the internal affairs of Iran.

The application was discussed at the 25th to the 30th meetings. Soviet objections to the inclusion of the matter on the agenda on the ground that negotiations were still proceeding were rejected by the council, as was also a request for postponing examination of the matter until April 10. The soviet representative stated that he was unable to participate in the discussion and left the council chamber. The Iranian ambassador was invited to take part in the discussion. On April 4 the council resolved, the representative of the soviet union being absent and the representative of Australia abstaining, to defer further proceedings until May 6, at which time the soviet and Iranian governments were requested to report to the council whether the withdrawal of all soviet troops from the whole of Iran had been completed.

By a letter dated April 6, 1946, the soviet representative proposed that the Iranian question be removed from the Security council's agenda on the ground that an understanding had been reached between the soviet and Iranian governments on the evacuation of soviet troops from Iran. On April 15, 1946, the Iranian ambassador also stated that his government withdrew its complaint. At the 32nd and 33rd meetings, the Security council examined the question of the removal of the Iranian appeal from the agenda, and the secretary-general submitted a memorandum on the matter in which the opinion was expressed that the council under the circumstances could not remain seized of the question. The council referred this memorandum to the committee of experts which submitted a report in which it was stated that it had been unable to reach a common opinion on the arguments advanced by the secretary-general. The report was considered by the council at its 36th meeting. A French resolution requesting the secretary-general to collect the necessary information to complete the Security council's report on the case to the general assembly was defeated and the council remained seized of the question. The soviet representative stated this was contrary to the charter and that his delegation could not take any further part in the discussion.

By a letter dated May 6, the Iranian ambassador reported the withdrawal of soviet troops from certain Iranian provinces. Regarding Azerbaijan, the Iranian government had been unable to verify by direct observation reports of its evacuation. At the 40th meeting on May 8, the council decided (the soviet representative being absent) to defer proceedings in order to allow the Iranian government to ascertain whether all soviet troops had been withdrawn from the whole of Iran. The Iranian government was requested to submit a complete report on the subject immediately it obtained the necessary information and in any case to report by May 20.

On May 20 and 21 the Iranian ambassador submitted the information asked for by the council. In his letter of May 21, he stated that, according to investigations, soviet

Andrei Gromyko resuming his seat at the United Nations security council on April 9, 1946, after boycotting several sessions in protest over the presence of the Iranian question on the agenda

troops had evacuated Azerbaijan on May 6, 1946. At the council's 43rd meeting on May 22, it was resolved to adjourn "until a date in the near future" discussion of the Iranian question.

First Greek Question.—By a letter of Jan. 21, 1946, the soviet representative brought to the attention of the Security council the situation in Greece, on the grounds that the presence of British troops in Greece after the termination of World War II constituted an interference in the internal affairs of Greece and caused tension fraught with grave consequences both for the Greek people and for the maintenance of peace and security.

The matter was brought up at the sixth meeting of the council on Feb. 1, 1946, and a final decision was taken on Feb. 6 at its tenth meeting. A representative of Greece participated without vote in the discussion.

The representative of the United Kingdom stated that British troops were in Greece after previous agreement with an all-party Greek government and with Marshal Stalin. If the Greek government decided that British troops were not wanted, they would not impose themselves upon them. He demanded that the council say whether the British government, by lending some of its forces, at the request of the Greek government, to secure order and economic reconstruction in Greece, had endangered peace. The representative of Greece denied that there had been any intervention in the internal affairs of Greece, adding that the Greek people regarded the continued presence of British forces in Greece as a factor in the consolidation of public order and security and full restoration of normal political conditions.

On Feb. 6 the president made a statement taking note of the views of members, and considering the matter as closed. This was found satisfactory.

Second Greek Question.—By a telegram of Aug. 24, 1946, the foreign minister of the Ukrainian S.S.R. called the attention of the Security council to the situation in the Balkans resulting from the policy of the Greek government which, he considered, constituted a grave danger to peace and security in this part of Europe. Border incidents allegedly provoked by Greek troops, mainly on the Greek-Albanian border, and the persecution of minorities in northern Greece were mentioned. It was stated that the principal factor conducive to this situation was the presence of British troops in Greece.

The matter came up for discussion at the 58th meeting of the council on Aug. 30, 1946. The representatives of Greece and the Ukrainian S.S.R. were invited to take part in the discussion without vote. Debate on this question continued until the 70th meeting of the council.

The Ukrainian representative developed the charges contained in the telegram. The representative of Greece rejected them, stating that if a threat to peace existed in the Balkans, it should be sought outside the confines of Greece. The representative of Albania was invited to state his views at the 64th meeting on Sept. 9.

On Sept. 20, at the 70th meeting, four draft resolutions were put to vote. A soviet resolution condemning the Greek government and requesting it to cease its provocative activities was not accepted by the council, which also rejected a Netherlands proposal calling on Greece and Albania to do their utmost to stop frontier incidents, and a Polish proposal to keep the matter under observation, and to retain it in the list of matters of which the council remains seized. A United States resolution proposing to send a commission of three individuals to investigate border incidents along the frontier between Greece on the one hand and Albania, Bulgaria and Yugoslavia on the other was not adopted by the council because of the negative vote of the soviet representative. The Greek question was considered closed.

The Balkan Question.—By a letter of Dec. 3, 1946, the acting chairman of the Greek delegation to the general assembly called to the attention of the Security council the situation in northern Greece resulting from the aid provided by Greece's northern neighbours to armed bands operating there.

The Greek complaint was brought up at the 82nd meeting of the council on Dec. 10, 1946, and a final decision was taken on Dec. 19 at the 87th meeting.

The representatives of Greece and Yugoslavia were invited to participate in the discussion without vote. The representatives of Albania and Bulgaria were invited to make statements on the matter, and on the council's decision that the question under examination was a dispute, were also asked to participate in the discussion without vote.

The Greek representative developed the charges made, and Yugoslav, Albanian and Bulgarian representatives denied them, declaring that the responsibility for the situation in northern Greece lay with the policy of the Greek government.

At the 85th meeting of the council on Dec. 18, the representative of the United States formally proposed the establishment of a commission of investigation to proceed to the area and submit a report of its findings to the council. At the 87th meeting on Dec. 19, 1946, the United States proposal was adopted by the council with two amendments proposed by the representatives of Mexico and Poland, respectively. By this resolution a Balkan commission was established, consisting of one representative of each member of the Security council. The commission was to proceed to the area not later than Jan. 15, 1947, and conduct investigations in northern Greece and in other parts of Greece which it believed should be included, and also in Albania, Bulgaria and Yugoslavia. It was to submit a report at the earliest possible date and to make any proposals it deemed wise for averting a repetition of border violations and disturbances in these areas.

The Indonesian Question.—By a letter of Jan. 21, 1946, the representative of the Ukrainian S.S.R. brought to the attention of the Security council a situation in Indonesia, which, it was alleged, created a threat to the maintenance of international peace and security.

The letter was placed on the agenda of the 12th meeting of the Security council on Feb. 7, 1946. The Ukrainian representative was invited to participate in the discussion without right of vote. He stated the case against the intervention of British and Indian troops to repress the popular movement in Indonesia. The representative of the United Kingdom denied that British troops were in Indonesia for the suppression of the Indonesian national movement. The Netherlands representative stated that there was no "dispute" or "situation" threatening peace and security with which the Security council was competent to deal.

A Ukrainian resolution, presented at the 18th meeting on Feb. 13, 1946, proposed the establishment of a commission of inquiry. This was lost, as was also an Egyptian proposal stating that British troops in Indonesia should only be used for the united purposes which brought about their presence there and that the council should be informed of the results of negotiation between the Netherlands government and the chiefs of the Indonesian movement. A soviet amendment to this resolution providing for a commission of inquiry also lost. The question was then considered as closed.

The Syrian and Lebanese Question.—By a letter of Feb. 4, 1946, the heads of the Lebanese and Syrian delegations to the United Nations brought to the attention of the Security council the presence of French and British troops in Syria and the Lebanon. The letter stated that the governments of Syria and the Lebanon had expected that these troops would be withdrawn immediately on the cessation of hostilities with Germany and Japan, but that a Franco-British agreement of Dec. 13, 1945, made the withdrawal of troops subject to conditions which were inconsistent with the spirit and the letter of the charter.

The question was discussed at the 19th to 23rd meetings of the council, Feb. 14, 15, 16, 1946, and the representatives of Syria and the Lebanon participated in the discussion without vote. Several resolutions were presented and defeated, one submitted by the United States representative receiving seven votes. This resolution expressed the confidence of the council that foreign troops in Syria and the Lebanon would be withdrawn as soon as practicable and that negotiations to that end would be undertaken by the parties without delay. It also requested the parties to inform the council of the results of the negotiations. Since the soviet representative had not voted in favour of this resolution, it was not adopted, but the representatives of France and the United Kingdom stated that their governments would give effect to this decision of the council.

The French and British governments entered into negotiation with the governments of Syria and the Lebanon, reporting on the matter to the council by letters of April 30 and May 1, respectively. By a telegram dated May 19, 1946, the Syrian prime minister and minister for foreign affairs stated that the evacuation of foreign troops from Syrian territory had been completed during the first two weeks of April 1946. By a letter of May 9, 1946, the Lebanese minister for foreign affairs stated that the negotiations with the French foreign minister had resulted in an agreement established by an exchange of letters of March 23, 1946. In conclusion, he stated his government's satisfaction with the outcome of the negotiations.

The Spanish Question.—By letters of April 8 and 9, 1946, the representative of Poland brought to the attention of the Security council the situation arising from the existence of the Franco regime in Spain. When the matter was brought up at the 34th meeting on April 17, 1946, the Polish representative formally proposed that the Security council should declare that the existence and the activities of the Franco regime in Spain had led to international friction and endangered international peace and security, and should call upon all members of the United Nations which maintained diplomatic relations with the Franco government to sever such relations immediately.

At the 39th meeting an Australian resolution was adopted by the council providing for the appointment of a sub-committee of five to examine the Spanish question. It was agreed that the sub-committee should be composed of the representatives of Australia (chairman), Brazil, China, France and Poland.

By May 31, 1946, the sub-committee completed its report, which was submitted to the council at its 44th meeting on June 6, 1946. Its conclusions were that the activities of the Franco regime constituted a potential menace to international peace and security and that the Security council was therefore entitled to recommend appropriate procedures or methods of adjustment to improve the situation.

The sub-committee also recommended that the Security council endorse the principles contained in the declaration by the governments of the United Kingdom, the United States and France of March 4, 1946; that the council transmit to the general assembly the evidence and reports of the sub-committee with the recommendation that unless the Franco regime was withdrawn and other conditions of political freedom set out in the declaration were, in the opinion of the general assembly, fully satisfied, a resolution be passed by the assembly recommending the severance of diplomatic relations with the Franco regime by each member of the United Nations.

At the 45th meeting, on June 13, the recommendations of the sub-committee were put to vote at the proposal of the sub-committee's chairman. They were not adopted because of the negative vote of the representative of the soviet union. At the 48th meeting, on June 24, 1946, the original resolution proposed by the Polish representative was put to the vote and was lost.

A new Polish resolution was introduced, proposing that the situation in Spain should be kept under continuous observation, and that it should remain on the list of matters of which the council was seized. Moreover, the Security council should take up the matter not later than Sept. 1, 1946. After the proposal of certain amendments by the representative of the United Kingdom, a drafting committee of Australia, Poland and the United Kingdom was appointed to prepare an agreed text. The drafting committee reported at the 49th meeting of the Security council on June 26 that its 3 members had been unable to agree on a text.

The Security council decided to keep the situation in Spain under continuous observation, in order to be ready at all times to take such measures as might become necessary to maintain international peace and security. Any member of the council could bring the matter up for consideration by the council at any time.

A resolution proposed by the representative of Australia that the resolution adopted did not prejudice the rights of the general assembly under the charter was then put to vote. As the soviet representative voted against it, the resolution was not carried.

At its 79th meeting on Nov. 4, 1946, the Security council unanimously decided to delete the Spanish question and to place at the disposal of the general assembly all records and documents of the case in order to enable the assembly to make recommendations on the matter.

Polish Emigré Army in Italy.—By a letter of Feb. 15, 1946, the soviet representative brought to the attention of the Security council the movements and activities of the Polish emigré army in Italy which the Yugoslav government regarded as detrimental to peaceful Yugoslav-Italian relations.

Border Incidents between Siam and Indo-China.—On May 31, 1946, the chargé d'affaires of Siam in Washington brought to the attention of the council a number of border incidents between Siam and the French authorities in Indo-China.

Armed Forces of the United Nations on Territories of Other States.—At the 57th meeting of the Security council on Aug. 29, 1946, the soviet representative proposed that the council request the members of the United Nations to submit within two weeks information on the number and location of their armed forces on the territory of other United Nations members or other states, not including former axis territories. After discussion at the 71st and 72nd meetings on Sept. 23 and 24, 1946, the Security council decided not to place the matter on the agenda.

Other Matters Considered by the Security Council.—*Admission of New Members.*—Up to Dec. 30, 1946, the Security council had received the applications of the following countries for membership in the United Nations: (1) Albania, Jan. 25, 1946; (2) Siam, May 20, Aug. 5 and Nov. 29; (3) Mongolian People's Republic, June 24; (4) Afghanistan, July 2; (5) Trans-Jordan, July 8; (6) Eire, Aug. 2; (7) Portugal, Aug. 2; (8) Republic of Iceland, Aug. 2; (9) Sweden, Aug. 9.

At its 42nd meeting, on May 17, 1946, the Security council decided to refer all applications for membership to a committee composed of representatives of each of the members of the council for examination.

The committee on the admission of new members met on July 31 and held its 14th and last meeting on Aug. 20. The Security council considered the committee's report at its 54th, 55th, 56th, 57th and 58th meetings on Aug. 28–29, 1946. The question of recommending the admission of all applicants *en bloc* was discussed and it was decided to study each application separately and in the chronological order in which they were submitted. The council then proceeded to discuss the merits of each applicant and unanimously recommended Afghanistan, Iceland and Sweden for membership in the United Nations. The other applicants were not recommended, Albania and Mongolia not securing the necessary majority, and the U.S.S.R. voting against Portugal, Trans-Jordan and Eire.

On Aug. 28, Siam requested that consideration of its application be adjourned pending settlement of a territorial dispute with France. It applied anew on Nov. 29 for membership in the United Nations. At its 83rd meeting on Dec. 12, the Security council unanimously recommended its admission to the United Nations.

Following a request from the general assembly, the Security council at its 81st meeting instructed the committee of experts to name a small committee from its own members to confer with a committee on procedures of the general assembly to prepare rules on the admission of new members acceptable to both council and assembly. The committee was to report back to the Security council. China, Brazil and Poland were appointed to the committee.

At the same meeting the Security council decided to adopt the general assembly's recommendation that it should re-examine the application for membership in the United Nations of Albania, Trans-Jordan, the Mongolian People's Republic, Eire and Portugal, on their respective merits. On Dec. 10, however, the president of the council announced that informal consultation among the members of the council indicated general agreement that consideration of these applications should be deferred.

Non-members and the International Court of Justice.—By a letter of May 1, 1946, the president of the court of international justice requested the Security council to define the conditions under which the court would be open to other states in accordance with article 35, paragraph 2 of the statute.

At its 50th meeting on July 10 the council referred the matter to the committee of experts. At its 76th meeting on Oct. 15, the council unanimously adopted a resolution on the matter submitted by the committee of experts.

The resolution stated that the court would be open to a state which was not a party to the statute on condition that it had previously deposited with the registrar of the court a declaration accepting the court's jurisdiction in accordance with the charter and under the terms and conditions of the statute and rules of the court, undertaking to comply with the court's decisions and to accept the obligations of a member of the United Nations under article 94 of the charter. This declaration might be made in respect of a particular dispute or disputes or might be general.

By a letter of Oct. 26, 1946, the Swiss consul general in New York brought to the attention of the Security council and of the general assembly the desire of the Swiss Federal council to know the conditions under which Switzerland could become a party to the statute of the international court of justice. This matter was referred by the Security council to the committee of experts, whose report the council adopted at its 80th meeting on Nov. 15, 1946. The council's recommendations were adopted by the general assembly.

The Military Staff Committee.—By article 47 of the charter, the United Nations agreed to the establishment of a military staff committee to advise and assist the Security council. It was to consist of the chiefs of staff of the permanent members of the Security council or their representatives. At its second meeting on Jan. 25, 1946, the Security council adopted a directive for the establishment of the committee.

The committee met in London on Feb. 4, 1946. It adjourned on Feb. 14 and reconvened in New York on March 25. The committee, as instructed by the council, drew up proposals on its organization and procedure and submitted them to the council for approval. At the council's 23rd meeting on Feb. 16, 1946, it instructed the committee of experts to examine the report. Pending approval of the report by the council, the military staff committee was authorized to carry on its business along the lines suggested.

At the same meeting the Security council directed the military staff committee, as its first task, to examine from the military point of view the provisions of article 43 of the charter concerning the conclusion of an agreement or agreements between the United Nations for making available to the Security council armed forces, assistance and facilities for the maintenance of international peace and security.

The military staff committee by Dec. 1946 had concluded consideration of the principles governing the composition of the armed forces to be made available to the Security council by members of the United Nations, and began consideration of the principles which should govern the strength of these forces.

Atomic Energy Commission.—On Jan. 24, 1946, the general assembly of the United Nations unanimously resolved to establish a commission to deal with the problems of atomic energy and related matters. This commission was to be composed of one representative of each of the states represented on the Security council and Canada when the latter was not a member of the Security council. The commission was requested to submit its report and recommendations to the Security council.

The Atomic Energy commission first met on June 14, 1946, and held ten meetings up to Dec. 31, 1946. A committee on rules of procedure was appointed at the first meeting and the draft rules submitted by it were approved by the commission on July 3 and by the Security council on July 10, and were officially adopted by the commission at its fifth meeting on July 18.

At the first meeting of the Atomic Energy commission, the representative of the United States presented a plan for the creation of an International Atomic Development authority entrusted with all phases of the development and use of atomic energy. The authority would conduct continuous surveys of world supplies of uranium and thorium, and would bring the raw materials under its dominion. It would control and operate all primary plants producing fissionable products in dangerous quantities. It would possess exclusive right to conduct research in the field of atomic explosives, and all other research would be open only to nations under licence of the authority which would furnish them with denatured materials. Dangerous activities of the authority and its stockpiles would be decentralized and strategically distributed. All nations would grant the freedom of inspection deemed necessary by the authority. The representative of the United States stressed the importance of immediate punishment for infringements of the rights of the authority.

At the second meeting of the commission on June 19, 1946, the representative of the U.S.S.R. suggested that the first measure to be adopted should be the conclusion of an international agreement to forbid the production and use of atomic energy weapons. Within three months from the entry into force of the agreement, all atomic weapons should be destroyed. Violation of the agreement would be considered a serious threat against humanity and would be severely punished under the domestic legislation of the contracting parties. The agreement should be of indefinite duration, coming into force after approval by the Security council and ratification by its permanent members. All states would be obliged, whether or not members of the United Nations, to fulfil all provisions of the agreement.

After various delegations had expressed their views on the two proposals, it was decided to establish a working committee to consider the proposals made and to establish, if necessary, sub-committees.

The working committee set up: (1) sub-committee 1 to study all proposals put forward by the delegations to the commission and to prepare the framework of a working plan by presenting to the working committee a list of headings or topics to be considered; (2) committee 2 to examine questions associated with the control of atomic energy activities and to make specific recommendations for such control; (3) a legal advisory committee to examine the legal aspects of atomic energy control; (4) a scientific and technical committee to advise on the scientific aspects of the problem.

Sub-committee 1 held three informal meetings during July 1–11, and presented a report to the working committee on the results of its discussions. Committee 2 continued the work begun in the working committee and sub-committee 1 and examined at length the proposals made. At its fourth meeting on July 31, it decided that before proceeding with further discussions, it was advisable to clarify the scientific and technical facts underlying control of atomic energy. It requested, therefore, the scientific and technical committee to prepare a report on the question of whether effective control of atomic energy was possible, together with an indication of the method by which it considered that effective control could be achieved. On Aug. 2, committee 2 deferred further meetings until it had received the report of the scientific and technical committee.

After eight weeks of intensive study, the scientific and technical committee, on Sept. 26, 1946, unanimously adopted a report for submission to committee 2. The scientific and technical committee concluded that it did not find a basis in the available scientific facts for supposing that effective control of atomic energy was not technologically possible. Whether or not it was politically feasible was for the Atomic Energy commission to decide.

At its sixth meeting on Oct. 2, committee 2 considered the report of the scientific and technical committee and decided to continue its discussions on the basis of the report. At its seventh meeting on Oct. 8, committee 2 unanimously decided to examine and report on the safeguards required at each stage in the production and use of atomic energy for peaceful purposes to prevent the possibilities of misuse. In accordance with this decision, a program of work was outlined by the secretariat and adopted by committee 2 at an informal meeting on Oct. 14. Under this outline, committee discussions on safeguards to prevent diversions of materials would follow a seven-step plan: uranium and thorium mines, concentration plants, refineries, chemical and metallurgical plants, primary reactors and associated chemical separation plants, isotope separation plants and secondary reactors.

On Oct. 15 at an informal meeting of committee 2, the representative of the U.S.S.R. proposed that atomic energy control should begin at the most basic stage—unmined mineral resources—and called for a world-wide report on uranium deposits. From that date, informal conversations were held about twice weekly to discuss in detail the types of necessary safeguards and to hear statements by experts. The discussions resulted in a draft report completed Dec. 13 dealing with safeguards against diversions and clandestine activities.

In the meanwhile the legal advisory committee held three meetings (June 18 and 30 and Aug. 2). With the assistance of the secretariat, it drew up a provisional list of topics under these headings: (1) drafting, including ultimately the preparation of a draft treaty or treaties; (2) the study of specific legal questions arising in the course of the work of the commission and its committees; (3) the study of the relationship between the system of measures of control recommended by committee 2 and the United Nations. This was submitted to the working committee, with a request for guidance on the next stage of the committee's work so that it might be co-ordinated with the work of other committees. The working committee considered the matter on Aug. 9 and decided that it was not necessary for the legal advisory committee to make recommendations on topics on the provisional list until further advised by the working committee.

At its sixth meeting on Nov. 13, 1946, the Atomic Energy commission decided by ten affirmative votes with two abstentions to submit to the Security council before Dec. 31, 1946, a report on its work, its findings and recommendations. Committee 2 was requested to draft the report.

While this report was being prepared, the second part of the first session of the general assembly was considering various proposals concerning the regulation and reduction of armaments, including atomic weapons. At the Atomic Energy commission's seventh meeting on Dec. 5, the chairman of the commission invited comments on the implications for the commission of the assembly discussion. The sense of the meeting was that the chairman should convey to the appropriate committees of the general assembly the view of the commission that its work should not be judged and that no action should be taken which would preclude or delay the commission from the early completion of its work.

At the same meeting, the United States representative put forward a resolution on the principles to be included in the findings and recommendations of the report of the commission to the security council. These proposals, based, as were the first United States proposals, on the prospective establishment of an International Atomic Development authority, were discussed at the eighth and ninth meetings of the commission on Dec. 17 and 20.

At the latter meeting, the United States draft resolution

was modified by a Canadian amendment, slightly revised at the suggestion of the Mexican representative. According to the Canadian amendment, the commission resolved that, for drafting purposes, the principles on which the United States resolution was based and not necessarily its exact text should be incorporated by the working committee in the report in order that the wording be in conformity with that used in the relevant parts of the text of the general assembly resolution of Dec. 14 on the principles governing the general regulation and reduction of armaments. According to the amendment proposed by the Mexican representative, it was stated in the resolution that these proposals had been made by the United States representative. The United States resolution, as amended, was adopted by the commission. Poland abstained from voting. The representative of the U.S.S.R., who had declared that he would not take part in the discussion, did not participate in the voting. The working committee was instructed to include these proposals in the draft of the commission report to be submitted to the Security council.

The report described the work of the commission, approved the report of the scientific and technical committee on scientific and technical aspects of control and the report of committee 2 on safeguards to ensure the use of atomic energy only for peaceful purposes, and made recommendations. In its general findings, it stated that scientifically, technically and practically it was feasible to extend among all nations the exchange of basic scientific information on atomic energy for peaceful ends; to control atomic energy to the extent necessary to ensure its use only for peaceful purposes; to accomplish the elimination from national armaments of atomic weapons; and to provide effective safeguards by way of inspection and other means to protect complying states against the hazards of violations and evasions. It was also stated that an effective system for control of atomic energy must be international and must be established by an enforceable multilateral treaty or convention which in turn must be administered and operated by an international organ or agency within the United Nations. An international agreement to outlaw national production, possession or use of atomic weapons was considered as essential for an international system of control or inspection but would not be sufficient to ensure the use of atomic energy for peaceful purposes or to provide effective safeguards to protect complying states against the dangers of violations and evasions.

Based upon its findings, the commission recommended the creation of a strong and comprehensive international system of control and inspection by a treaty or convention in which all members of the United Nations would participate on fair and equitable terms. This treaty should include provisions establishing an international authority possessing powers and the responsibility necessary and appropriate for the prompt and effective discharge of its duties imposed upon it by the terms of the treaty or convention. The treaty should provide that the rule of unanimity of the permanent members of the Security council should have no relation with the work of the authority.

The authority would promote among all nations the exchange of basic scientific information on atomic energy and should have positive responsibilities of research and development in order to promote the beneficial uses of atomic energy and eliminate the destructive ones. It would establish safeguards against the dangerous use of atomic energy but would not interfere with the prosecution of pure scientific research or the publication of its results.

Decisions of the authority, however, should govern the operations of national agencies for atomic energy with the minimum interference.

The treaty or convention would also provide the representatives of the authority with unimpeded rights of ingress, egress and access for the performance of their inspections. It would prohibit the manufacture, possession and use of atomic weapons by all nations which were

Correspondents at work in the United Nations pressroom at Hunter college, New York, N.Y., during meetings of the Security council in April 1946

parties to the treaty and would provide for the disposal of any existing stocks of atomic weapons and for the proper use of fissionable materials.

The treaty would also specify the methods of determining violations of its terms and would establish the measures of enforcement or swift and certain punishment for violators. Enforcement and punishment of violators would not be subject to veto.

Finally, the treaty should provide a schedule for the completion of the transitional process leading step by step to the full and effective establishment of international control of atomic energy.

Economic and Social Council.—The Economic and Social council held its first session from Jan. 23 to Feb. 18, 1946, in London; its second session from May 25 to June 21 at Hunter college in New York city; and its third session from Sept. 11 to Oct. 3 at Lake Success.

The initial members of the council, elected by the general assembly on Jan. 12 and 14, 1946, were: Belgium, Canada, Chile, China, France and Peru for a three-year term; Cuba, Czechoslovakia, India, Norway, U.S.S.R. and United Kingdom for a two-year term; and Colombia, Greece, Lebanon, Ukrainian S.S.R., United States and Yugoslavia for one year.

To replace the members who were to serve for a one-year term the general assembly on Nov. 19 and Dec. 7 and 12 elected the following six states: Byelorussian S.S.R., Lebanon, New Zealand, Turkey, United States and Venezuela. As there had been a tie vote between Turkey and the Netherlands, Belgium offered to resign so that both countries could be elected. On Dec. 12 the general assembly elected the Netherlands to fill the vacancy caused by the resignation of Belgium.

The council at its first session elected Sir Ramaswami Mudaliar (India) president; and Dr. Andrija Stampar (Yugoslavia) and Dr. Lleras Restrepo (Colombia) first and second vice-presidents, respectively, for the first period of office. Sir Ramaswami Mudaliar was unable to be present at the third session of the council and Dr. Stampar acted as president.

The council at its first session established five "nuclear" commissions and one temporary sub-commission, each consisting of nine experts appointed in their personal capacity to explore the fields to be covered by the proposed permanent commissions and to recommend to the council the composition and competence of these commissions.

The "nuclear" commissions were as follows: human rights, with a sub-commission on the status of women; economic and employment; temporary social; temporary transport and communications; statistical. During its first session, the council established one permanent commission, the commission on narcotic drugs, consisting of representatives of 15 governments.

The "nuclear" commissions met at Hunter college in the latter part of April and the first three weeks in May 1946 and submitted their reports to the second session of the council.

During its second session, the council, on the basis of the reports from the "nuclear" commissions determined the terms of reference and composition of the following commissions: economic and employment, transport and communications, statistical, human rights, social. It established a full commission on the status of women, and determined its terms of reference and composition. The council established a temporary sub-commission of the economic and employment commission on the economic reconstruction of devastated areas. It empowered the commission on human rights to set up sub-commissions on freedom of information and the press, on the protection of minorities and on prevention of discrimination and the statistical commission to establish a sub-commission on statistical sampling. It requested the social commission to take steps to create a sub-commission on child welfare.

During its third session, the council established population and fiscal commissions and determined their terms of reference and composition. It selected the member states to constitute the other permanent commissions, with the exception of the commission on narcotic drugs, which had been constituted at the first session. The council directed the economic and employment commission to set up sub-commissions on employment and economic stability and on economic development, and to consider further the question of establishing a sub-commission on the balance of payments.

With the exception of the commission on narcotic drugs, which held its first meeting in Nov. 1946, the commissions were scheduled to hold their first meetings in Jan. and Feb. 1947.

The council decided that members of the commissions should consist of members of the United Nations selected by the council with a view to securing a balanced representation in the fields covered by the various commissions. The secretary-general was directed by the council to consult with the governments selected for membership on the commissions before their representatives were finally nominated by those governments. The council held an *ad hoc* meeting on Dec. 10, 1946, to confirm the nominations after the secretary-general had carried out his consultations.

Members of the commissions, it was decided, were to serve for three years and to be eligible for re-election. In the initial period, one-third of the members were to serve for two years, one-third for three years and one-third for four years, the term being determined by lot. Members of the commission on narcotic drugs were, however, all elected for three years.

During its third session, the council decided to recommend to the general assembly that travelling expenses and subsistence allowances should be paid by the United Nations for the members of the commissions and sub-commissions of the council.

The council established standing committees on organization, on negotiations with specialized agencies, and on relations with non-governmental organizations at the first session. It made use of a number of *ad hoc* committees, in particular the committee on refugees and displaced persons and the committee on the finances of the International Refugee organization.

Economic and Employment Commission.—The following members were elected to this commission by the council at its third session: Belgium, Brazil, France, Poland, United Kingdom for two years; Canada, China, Czechoslovakia, India, Norway for three years; and Australia, Byelorussian S.S.R., Cuba, U.S.S.R., United States for four years.

At its second session the council decided that the commission's terms of reference should be: to advise the council on economic questions in order to promote higher standards of living; to make recommendations on economic questions involving concerted study or action by more than one specialized agency or commission of the council. In particular it was to advise on the prevention of wide fluctuations in economic activity and the promotion of full employment.

At the third session, the Economic and Social council

directed the economic and employment commission to establish a sub-commission on employment and economic stability to study national and international full employment policies and fluctuations in economic activity, analyze the causes of these fluctuations and advise the commission on appropriate methods of promoting full employment and economic stability.

Reconstruction of Devastated Areas.—At its second session the council itself established a temporary sub-commission of the economic and employment commission on the economic reconstruction of devastated areas, consisting of Australia, Belgium, Canada, China, Czechoslovakia, Ethiopia, France, Greece, India, Netherlands, New Zealand, Norway, Peru, Philippines, Poland, Ukrainian S.S.R., U.S.S.R., United Kingdom, United States and Yugoslavia. The sub-commission was to advise on the nature and scope of the economic reconstruction problems in those countries where they were acute because of occupation or physical devastation, and on the progress of reconstruction and how it might be helped by international co-operation.

The sub-commission was authorized to make inquiries with the consent of the governments concerned, in the countries which had been occupied or devastated, except Germany and Japan, and to make a preliminary report on their reconstruction problems, bearing in mind the special claims of countries who were members of the United Nations. The sub-commission was to consider the economic relations of those countries with Germany and Japan and with neutral countries.

The sub-commission met in London on July 29. It consisted of two working groups, one for Europe and Africa, and one for Asia and the far east. It was decided to confine the work of the second group to preliminary discussion on how later inquiries might be conducted, and to concentrate on writing the preliminary report on Europe. Accordingly, a detailed analysis was made of the material submitted by governments, inter-governmental agencies and the United Nations secretariat, and on-the-spot inquiries to supplement this information were made in Belgium, Czechoslovakia, France, Greece, Luxembourg, the Netherlands, Poland and Yugoslavia. The sub-commission presented its report to the council at its third session, the U.S.S.R. and Ukrainian delegates reserving their position. It also referred to the council a proposal for the establishment of an economic commission for Europe.

The council at its third session also endorsed a recommendation made by the U.N.R.R.A. council that the general assembly should designate some agency or agencies to review the needs in 1947 for financing urgent imports of the basic essentials of life, particularly food and supplies for agricultural production, after the termination of the U.N.R.R.A. program, and to recommend what additional financial assistance was necessary.

Assistance to the Food and Agriculture Organization.—At its second session the Economic and Social council requested the secretary-general to offer all possible assistance to the Food and Agriculture organization in making a survey of the world food position and in preparing proposals concerning longer-term international machinery with reference to food.

The secretary-general reported to the council's third session on the discussions which had taken place, and referred to the establishment by the Food and Agriculture organization of a preparatory commission to consider the proposals made for the establishment of a world food board. Representatives of the council were invited to participate in the work of this commission, and the council appointed the chairman of the economic and employment commission to take part in its discussions. The secretary-general was requested to report on these discussions to each session of the council until the preparatory commission completed its work.

Transport and Communications Commission.—The council at its third session elected as members of this commission: Brazil, India, Netherlands, Poland, United Kingdom to serve for two years; Chile, China, France, Norway, Union of South Africa to serve for three years; and Czechoslovakia, Egypt, U.S.S.R., Yugoslavia to serve for four years.

At its second session the council decided that the commission's terms of reference should be to assist the council in its tasks concerned with transport and communications problems; to advise on the co-ordination of the work of specialized agencies in these spheres; to advise the council in fields where no permanent international organization yet existed and on problems concerning more than one sphere of transport; to suggest to the council the creation of new agencies, or the conclusion of new conventions or the revision of existing conventions; to perform the task of conciliation when so authorized, in cases of dispute between states or specialized agencies on international transport and communications questions; and to assist the Security council and the trusteeship council, if desired by the Economic and Social council.

The council considered what inter-governmental organizations should operate in five fields of transport and communications: aviation, telecommunications, postal, inland transport and shipping; and which of the agencies operating in these fields should be brought into relationship with the United Nations.

In the case of aviation, it directed that negotiations should be entered into with the Provisional International Civil Aviation organization. It recommended that a world conference be held to review the organization of the existing International Telecommunications union and its radio regulations, and directed the secretary-general to convene meetings of experts to draft proposals for bringing the International Telecommunications union and the Universal Postal union into relationship with the United Nations.

Postal experts of 39 member states met at Lake Success from Dec. 10–18, 1946, and drew up a draft agreement for submission to the congress of the Universal Postal union to be held in Paris in May 1947.

It was decided that the transport and communications commission should give further study to the question of international organizations in the inland transport and shipping fields.

The council at its second session agreed that a commission of experts should prepare the ground for a world conference on passport and frontier formalities, and at its third session requested the secretary-general to convene such a meeting and to take into account in preparing its agenda the discussions and recommendations of various international organizations.

At the same session the council asked the transport and communications commission to examine the situation and the machinery needed to co-ordinate activities in aviation, shipping and telecommunications with respect to safety at sea and in the air.

The council drew to the attention of interested governments the problems of the re-establishment and reorganization of inter-governmental and other international machinery for the co-ordination of rail problems in Europe, and need for improvement of European inland waterways.

At its third session the council adopted a resolution recommending that a conference of representatives of interested states meet not later than Nov. 1, 1946, to resolve the problems of the resumption of international traffic on the Danube and establish provisional operating and navigation regulations. (The rules of procedure of the general assembly required that before such a conference could be held members of the United Nations should be consulted.)

The continuation of the activities of the League of Nations organization for communications and transit were entrusted in some instances to the relevant specialized inter-governmental organizations and in others to organs of the United Nations.

Fiscal Commission.—This commission was established at the third session of the council, with the following membership: Belgium, Czechoslovakia, India, New Zealand, United States for two years; Colombia, Cuba, Lebanon, Poland, U.S.S.R. for three years; and China, France, Union of South Africa, Ukrainian S.S.R., and United Kingdom for four years.

The council decided that the commission's functions should be to advise the council in the field of public finance; to advise the council and other commissions on the fiscal implications of recommendations made by the commissions in their own fields, and in general to co-operate with other commissions of the council, organs of the United Nations and specialized agencies.

Statistical Commission.—The council at its third session elected as members of this commission: China, Netherlands, U.S.S.R., United States for two years; Canada, India, Mexico, Ukrainian S.S.R. for three years; and France, Norway, Turkey and the United Kingdom for four years.

It decided that the commission's purposes should be to assist the council in promoting the development of national statistics and the improvement of their comparability, in the co-ordination of the statistical work of specialized agencies and the development of the central statistical services of the secretariat; to assist the council in advising the organs of the United Nations on general questions relating to the collection, interpretation and dissemination of statistical information in promoting the improvement of statistics and statistical methods. It was also to make recommendations on methods of relating the activities of quasi-governmental and non-governmental statistical organizations to those of the United Nations.

The council also decided that a central statistical unit should be organized within the secretariat of the United Nations, and that the secretariat should maintain the statistical work of the League of Nations.

Population Commission.—This commission was established at the third session of the council, with the following membership: China, U.S.S.R., United Kingdom, United States for two years; Australia, Canada, France, Ukrainian S.S.R. for three years; and Brazil, Netherlands, Peru and Yugoslavia for four years.

The council decided that the commission was to advise it on population changes, the factors associated with such changes and the policies designed to influence these factors, inter-relationships of economic and social conditions and population trends; migratory movements of populations and factors associated with such movements; and any other population problems on which organs of the United Nations or specialized agencies might seek advice.

Social Commission.—The following were elected as members of this commission at the council's third session: Czechoslovakia, France, Greece, Union of South Africa, U.S.S.R., United States for two years; Colombia. Netherlands, New Zealand, Peru, United Kingdom, Yugoslavia for three years, and Canada, China, Denmark, Ecuador, Iraq and Poland for four years.

The council decided that the terms of reference of the commission should be to advise the council on social questions of a general character, and in particular on all matters in the social field not covered by specialized agencies; and also on practical measures needed in the social field, and on measures needed for co-ordinating activities in this field. It was also to advise the council on such international agreements and conventions on any of these matters as might be required and on their execution, and to report on how far recommendations of the United Nations on social policy were being carried out.

The commission was instructed by the council at its second session to consider the best way of carrying on the functions of the League of Nations relating to traffic in women and children and measures designed to prevent such traffic. It was also instructed to consider how work in the field of child welfare could effectively be carried out, in co-operation with the international organizations concerned with particular aspects of these problems, and to create a sub-commission for work in the child welfare field. It was also to consider and make recommendations on how effective machinery could be developed for studying on a wide international basis the means for the prevention of crime and the treatment of offenders. The commission was requested to give special attention to problems in countries directly affected by World War II and in countries which were underdeveloped, and in particular to give special attention to the urgent need for finding some way of dealing with the important aspects of the work of the United Nations Relief and Rehabilitation administration after it was brought to a close. It was also asked to consider the desirability of setting up international machinery in the fields of housing and town and country planning.

The Economic and Social council at its third session took note of a resolution passed by the U.N.R.R.A. council in Aug. 1946. The resolution emphasized the desirability of the social welfare functions of U.N.R.R.A. being transferred to the United Nations. These functions would include work connected with the training of social welfare personnel, the rehabilitation of the physically handicapped, the restoration of social welfare activities and institutions, the co-ordination of the activities of voluntary agencies and child welfare.

The Economic and Social council requested the secretary-general to consult immediately with the director-general of U.N.R.R.A., to undertake the necessary studies and investigations, and to submit recommendations to the general assembly on matters requiring its authorization or special financial provisions. In the light of these studies and investigations and of the general assembly's decisions he was to take such further action as seemed desirable and to report to the next session of the council.

A further resolution passed by the U.N.R.R.A. council recommended the creation of an International Children's fund for the rehabilitation of the children and adolescents of countries which were victims of aggression, and set up a standing committee to prepare the necessary recommendations in agreement with the United Nations. The Economic and Social council recommended that the general assembly should arrange for the creation of such a fund, subject to the council's control. The secretary-general was to prepare in consultation with the director-general of

Mrs. Vijayalakshmi Pandit, chairman of the Indian delegation to the United Nations general assembly, addressing the opening session at Flushing, N.Y., on Oct. 23, 1946

U.N.R.R.A., the president of the Economic and Social council and the U.N.R.R.A. standing committee a draft resolution for submission to the general assembly providing for the establishment of the necessary machinery.

Commission on Human Rights.—The following were elected members of this commission at the council's third session: Byelorussian S.S.R., China, Lebanon, Panamá, United Kingdom, Uruguay for two years; Egypt, France, India, Iran, Ukrainian S.S.R., U.S.S.R. for three years; and Australia, Belgium, Chile, Philippines, United States, Yugoslavia for four years.

At its second session the council decided that the terms of reference of the commission should be to submit proposals, recommendations and reports on: an international bill of rights; international declarations or conventions on civil liberties, the status of women, freedom of information, and similar matters; protection of minorities; prevention of discrimination on grounds of race, sex, language or religion; and any other matters concerning human rights.

The council requested the secretary-general to arrange for the compilation and publication of a yearbook on law and usage relating to human rights; and the collection and publication of information on the activities concerning human rights of all United Nations organs.

At its second session the council empowered the commission to establish a sub-commission on freedom of information and of the press; on protection of minorities; and on the prevention of discrimination on the grounds of race, sex, language or religion.

Commission on the Status of Women.—The Economic and Social council at its third session elected the following as members of this commission: Australia, Byelorussian S.S.R., China, Guatemala, India for two years; Mexico, Syria, U.S.S.R., United Kingdom and United States for three years; and Costa Rica, Denmark, France, Turkey and Venezuela for four years.

The council decided at its second session to establish a full commission on the status of women, which was to prepare recommendations and reports to the council on promoting women's rights in political, economic, social and educational fields.

It was also to make recommendations to the council on urgent problems requiring immediate attention in the field of women's rights.

The "nuclear" sub-commission on the status of women had made recommendations for a policy and program of work to be undertaken by the sub-commission when fully constituted. It considered that in practice priority had to be given to political rights since little progress could be made without them, but recommended that the problems of obtaining improvements in civil, educational, social and economic fields should be attacked simultaneously. The program of work outlined by the "nuclear" sub-commission would provide *inter alia* for a survey of laws pertaining to the status of women and the practical application of such legislation, polls to sound public opinion, the calling of a United Nations women's conference, the international exchange of all categories of manual and intellectual women workers and the creation of a world-wide opinion through the various information media.

Commission on Narcotic Drugs.—Canada, China, Egypt, France, India, Iran, Mexico, Netherlands, Peru, Poland, Turkey, U.S.S.R., United Kingdom, United States and Yugoslavia were elected as members of this commission for a three-year term by the council at its first session.

The council at its first session decided that the commission's functions should be: to assist the council in exercising such powers of supervision over the application of international conventions and agreements dealing with narcotic drugs as might be assumed by or conferred on the council; to carry out such functions entrusted to the League of Nations advisory committee on traffic in opium and other dangerous drugs by the international conventions on narcotic drugs as the council might find necessary to assume; to advise the council on all matters pertaining to the control of narcotic drugs and draft such international conventions as might be necessary; and to consider and make proposals on any changes that might be required in existing machinery for the international control of narcotic drugs.

The commission held its first session at Lake Success from Nov. 27 to Dec. 13, 1946. The following officers were elected: Col. C. H. L. Sharman (Canada), president; Dr. Stanislaw Tubiaz (Poland), vice-president, and Dr. Szeming Sze (China), *rapporteur.* As well as considering organizational questions, the commission reviewed the control of narcotic drugs since 1940. A special review was made of the limitation of the production of raw materials, opium smoking in the far east, illicit traffic and drug addiction, with the general purpose of establishing at its prewar level the international control of narcotic drugs. Resolutions were adopted proposing the insertion of provisions for the control of narcotics in the peace treaties with Japan and Germany.

The council at its first session empowered the secretary-general, acting in accordance with the resolution of the general assembly, to take the steps necessary to continue provisionally the work of the opium section of the League of Nations and the secretariats of the Permanent Central Opium board and the supervisory body. Accordingly, arrangements were made for the narcotics division of the United Nations secretariat to assume the work of the opium section of the League as from Aug. 1, 1946, and the competent services of the League secretariat were instructed by the secretary-general of the League to give the narcotics division any assistance it might need.

Arrangements were also made for the fusion of the secretariats of the Permanent Central Opium board and the supervisory body, and for the provisional administrative and financial arrangements required to continue the work of these two organizations.

The assembly had referred to the Economic and Social council the taking of the necessary measures to ensure the continued exercise of the powers and functions of the league under international agreements including those on the international control of narcotic drugs.

The council considered the question at its third session and submitted a draft resolution and draft protocol to the general assembly, recommending that the assembly approve the assumption of the league's functions in this field. The council expressed the view that the Franco government should not become a party to the protocol. It invited the present members of the Permanent Central board and the supervisory body to continue in office for the time being and requested the general assembly to make the necessary financial provisions to enable these organizations to carry on their functions. (The protocol amending the international conventions and agreements on narcotic drugs was approved by the general assembly. During the first session of the commission on narcotic drugs it was signed by the representatives of 49 member nations.)

Relations with Specialized Agencies.—The council during its first session appointed a committee on negotiations with specialized agencies, consisting of representatives of 11 members. The committee was to enter into negotiations with the Food and Agriculture organization of the United Nations, the International Labour organization, the International Monetary fund, the International Bank for Reconstruction and Development and the United Nations Educational, Scientific and Cultural organization, and to submit a report, including a draft preliminary agreement, for consideration at the council's second session.

The committee met with the negotiating delegates of the International Labour organization on May 28 and 29, 1946, the United Nations Educational, Scientific and Cultural organization on June 3 and the Food and Agriculture organization on June 6 and 7. The draft agreements were submitted to the Economic and Social council at its second session; the council recommended that the general assembly approve them.

At its third session the council approved a draft agreement negotiated with the delegation of the Provisional International Civil Aviation organization, and recommended its approval by the assembly.

The main provisions of the agreements, which were based on principles contained in the Report of the Preparatory Commission, covered such items as reciprocal representation, admission of states not members of the United Nations; proposal of agenda items; recommendations of the United Nations made with a view to co-ordinating the work of specialized agencies, exchange of information and documents; assistance to the Security council, the Trusteeship council and co-operation with regard to non-self-governing territories; authorization to the agency to request advisory opinions from the international court of justice; headquarters and regional offices, personnel arrangements; statistical services; budgetary and financial arrangements and liaison.

At the request of the International Bank for Reconstruction and Development and the International Monetary fund, the council at its second session decided to postpone negotiations with these organizations but instructed the secretary-general to continue exploratory discussions.

Refugees and Displaced Persons.—Following the general assembly's recommendation referring the question of refugees to the Economic and Social council for examination, and setting forth certain principles for consideration, the council established a special committee on refugees and displaced persons. This committee met in London from April 8 to June 1. It decided that it was necessary to establish an international body of a nonpermanent character to deal with the problem of refugees and displaced persons. The report of the committee was presented to the council's second session. It dealt with the definition of the categories of persons entitled to international protection and assistance; the numbers and location of refugees and displaced persons, conditions governing speedy repatriation, the possibilities of resettling non-repatriables, and the general problems in the far east; the form and constitution of the new international body and its relationship to the United Nations; examination of various statements and memoranda submitted by private organizations.

In discussing the committee's report at its second session, the council concentrated on the suggestions for a draft constitution for a new international body, to be called the International Refugee organization, and on the definition of persons coming within the mandate of the new organization. It recommended to the general assembly that such an organization should be created on a non-permanent basis, as a specialized agency in relationship with the United Nations.

The secretary-general's report as well as the report of the committee on finances of the International Refugee organization, which met in London from July 6–20, and the comments from governments on the draft constitution, were considered at the council's third session. The secretary-general was requested to plan in consultation with U.N.R.R.A. and the intergovernmental committee on refugees the initiation of the work of the International Refugee organization (I.R.O.).

The draft constitution, with some further revisions, and the arrangements for a preparatory commission were transmitted by the council to the general assembly for its approval. The council also transmitted to the general assembly for final decision the report of the committee on finances of the I.R.O., which had prepared administrative and operational budgets for the first financial year and suggested scales of contributions to each, and the report of the *ad hoc* committee on finance, which revised the estimates by reducing the operational budget for large-scale resettlement from $60,000,000 to $5,000,000 and for other operational expenses from $193,954,000 to $151,-051,000.

Certain differences of opinion characterized the council's discussions on refugees and displaced persons. These chiefly revolved around the question of how far the problem could be solved by repatriation, and, on the other hand, whether there would remain a large number of genuine non-repatriables which should become the concern of the International Refugee organization, leaving out of account quislings and war criminals.

International Health Conference.—At its first session, the council established a preparatory technical committee, consisting of experts appointed in their personal capacity to prepare documentation for an International Health conference which was to consider proposals for establishing an international health organization. The committee met in Paris in March and drew up a draft constitution which was submitted to the International Health conference, convened by the Economic and Social council. The conference met in New York from June 19 to July 22 and was attended by representatives of all the members of the United Nations and of certain other states, and by observers from international organizations. It adopted the final act of the conference, which incorporated a resolution regarding the activities of the League of Nations health organization; the constitution of the World Health organization, which was signed by 61 states, 2 without reservation as to acceptance; an agreement establishing an interim commission of the organization, which was signed by 61 states; and a protocol concerning the *Office International d'Hygiène publique,* which was signed by 60 states.

The council requested the general assembly to recommend to all members the earliest possible acceptance of the constitution of the World Health organization; to transfer to this organization those functions and activities of the League of Nations health organization which the United Nations had assumed; to recommend that members accept the protocol concerning the *Office International d'Hygiène publique;* to approve the necessary funds for the interim commission and for the health organization during 1947; and to authorize the secretary-general to transmit to the general assembly recommendations to those who sent representatives or observers to the conference.

Preparatory Committee of the International Trade Conference.—The Economic and Social council at its first session decided to call an International Conference on Trade and Employment and established a preparatory committee consisting of the representatives of 19 members to prepare an agenda including a draft convention for the consideration of the conference. The council suggested that the agenda should include international agreements relating to the achievement and maintenance of high and stable levels of employment and economic activity; regulations, restrictions and discriminations affecting international trade; restrictive business practices, and inter-governmental commodity arrangements; and also the establishment of an international trade organization as a specialized agency of the United Nations.

The preparatory committee met in London from Oct. 15 to Nov. 26, 1946, and set up a committee to meet in New York on Jan. 20, 1947, to prepare a draft convention on the basis of the report and other documents of the first session of the preparatory committee.

Non-Governmental Organizations.—To implement the general assembly's resolution recommending that the Economic and Social council should adopt arrangements for consultation with non-governmental organizations, the council appointed a committee consisting of the president and 11 members to draw up proposals for consultation in particular with those organizations mentioned in the general assembly's resolution.

The council, at its second session, adopted the report of this committee. The report outlined certain principles governing arrangements for consultation. The organization should be concerned with matters falling within the competence of the Economic and Social council, its aims should be in conformity with the United Nations charter, and it should represent a substantial proportion of the organized persons within its particular field and have authority to speak for its members through its authorized representative. National organizations were eligible for consultation if they covered a field not covered by any international organization or had special experience.

Non-governmental organizations would not be given the same rights of participation accorded to states not members of the council or to specialized agencies. The objects of consultation would be to secure expert information or advice and to enable organizations representing important elements of public opinion to express their views.

At its second session the council set up a new committee with a smaller membership, being composed of the president and representatives of China, France, the U.S.S.R., the United Kingdom and the United States, and instructed the committee to review and make recommendations on applications for consultative status. At the third session the council decided that the committee, in addition to reviewing and making recommendations on applications, should be a standing committee to carry on consultations with organizations given consultative status. The committee on Oct. 2 held consultations with the

World Federation of Trade Unions.

Transfer of Non-Political Functions of the League.—The Economic and Social council at its first session requested the secretary-general to undertake a survey of the non-political functions of the League of Nations other than those exercised under international agreements, and to take the necessary steps to assume and continue the work of the league departments, as recommended in the resolution of the general assembly.

In a memorandum dated Sept. 26, 1946, the secretary-general appraised the council of the action taken in compliance with these resolutions. The memorandum surveyed the league committees, commissions, departments and publications relating to economic and social questions, and referred to the action taken to assume and continue provisionally the work of the league in these fields. It also referred to the action taken as regards league activities by various commissions of the United Nations. The report of the secretary-general was placed on the agenda of the general assembly.

The council, at its third session, recommended that the preparatory commission of the United Nations Educational, Scientific and Cultural organization (U.N.E.S.C.O.) and the International Institute of Intellectual Co-operation be requested to undertake negotiations for the future transfer to U.N.E.S.C.O. of the functions and activities of the institute.

Trusteeship Council.—Trusteeship agreements submitted by Australia, Belgium, France, New Zealand and the United Kingdom were approved by the general assembly at the second part of its first session, and these states automatically became members of the Trusteeship council.

China, the U.S.S.R. and the United States were members of the Trusteeship council, by virtue of their position as permanent members of the Security council. To make the number of states on the council not administering trust territories equal that of the administering powers, the general assembly elected Iraq and Mexico for a three-year term.

The Trusteeship council was scheduled to hold its first meeting on March 26, 1947. The agenda for the first session of the council included the adoption of rules of procedure; the election of president and vice-president; the formulation of questionnaires on the political, economic, social and educational advancement of the inhabitants of each trust territory, in accordance with article 88 of the charter; the consideration of such petitions concerning trust territories as might have been presented; and the consideration of the relations between the Trusteeship council on the one hand and the Economic and Social council and the specialized agencies on the other.

The General Assembly—Second Part of the First Session.—The second part of the first session of the general assembly was convened on Oct. 23 and adjourned on Dec. 16, 1946. During that period, the assembly held 35 plenary meetings and 357 committee and sub-committee meetings. It admitted four new members to the United Nations: Afghanistan, Iceland, Sweden and Siam.

As non-permanent members of the Security council, the general assembly elected Belgium, Colombia and Syria to replace Egypt, Mexico and the Netherlands, retiring members. It elected new members to replace the retiring members of the Economic and Social council—Colombia, Greece, Lebanon, the Ukrainian S.S.R., the United States and Yugoslavia. The Byelorussian S.S.R., Lebanon, New Zealand, the United States and Venezuela were elected in the first instance, and Turkey and the Netherlands tied for the sixth place. Thereupon Belgium offered to resign if both Turkey and the Netherlands were elected. Turkey was elected to the sixth vacant position, and the Netherlands was elected to fill the vacancy caused by the resignation of Belgium.

The assembly had approved trusteeship agreements submitted by Australia, Belgium, France, New Zealand and the United Kingdom.

The general assembly received reports from the Security council, the Economic and Social council and the secretary-general. It decided that the terms of office of members of councils should begin on Jan. 1 following their election and end on Dec. 31 following the election of their successors.

The third Tuesday in September was fixed as the date for convening the regular annual session of the general assembly.

Political and Security Matters.—The general assembly adopted unanimously a resolution recognizing the necessity of an early general regulation and reduction of armaments and armed forces. The assembly's unanimity was the result of a compromise between the U.S.S.R., which considered as the primary objective in the general reduction of armaments the prohibition of the production and use of atomic energy for military purposes, and the United States, which insisted that emphasis must be placed on the creation of effective safeguards by way of inspection and other means to protect complying states against violations and evasions, before any general system for the regulation of armaments could be planned effectively.

The resolution recommended that the Security council should give prompt consideration to formulating the practical measures, according to their priority, essential for two specific purposes: first, to provide for the general regulation and reduction of armaments and armed forces, and, second, to assure that such regulation and reduction would be generally observed by all participants, and not unilaterally by only some of the participants.

The resolution urged the fulfilment by the Atomic Energy commission of its objectives, and recommended that the Security council expedite consideration of the commission's reports, and also that it should expedite consideration of a draft convention or conventions for the creation of an international system of control and inspection. This convention should include the prohibition of atomic and all other major weapons adaptable to mass destruction, and provisions for the control of atomic energy to the extent necessary to ensure its use only for peaceful purposes.

An international system of control and inspection was to be established within the framework of the Security council.

It was to operate through special organs which were to derive their powers and status from the international conventions under which they were established.

The general assembly recommended that the Security council accelerate as much as possible the placing at its disposal of the armed forces mentioned in article 43 of the charter. It recommended that members undertake the progressive and balanced withdrawal, taking account of the needs of occupation, of their armed forces stationed in former axis territories and the withdrawal without delay of armed forces stationed in the territories of members. It further recommended a corresponding reduction of national armed forces and a general progressive and balanced reduction of national armed forces.

Finally the assembly stated that nothing in the resolution was to alter or limit the general assembly's resolution establishing the Atomic Energy commission.

A further resolution adopted by the assembly on information on the armed forces of the United Nations called on the Security council to determine, as soon as possible, the information which the states members of the United Nations should be called upon to furnish, in order to give effect to the resolution on the general regulation and reduction of armaments.

The general assembly, while admitting Afghanistan, Iceland, Sweden and Siam to membership in the United Nations, recommended that the Security council re-examine the applications for membership of Albania, Ireland, Mongolia, Portugal and Trans-Jordan on their respective merits in accordance with the provisions of article 4 of the charter. It also requested the Security council to appoint a committee to confer with a committee on procedures of the general assembly with a view to preparing rules acceptable both to the assembly and the council governing the admission of new members. The assembly committee appointed on Dec. 15 was composed of representatives of Australia, Cuba, India, Norway and the U.S.S.R.

The general assembly recommended that the Franco government of Spain be debarred from membership in international agencies established by or brought into relationship with the United Nations and that all members of the United Nations immediately recall from Madrid their ambassadors and ministers plenipotentiary accredited there.

After considering the application of India regarding the treatment of Indians in South Africa, the general assembly expressed the opinion that such treatment should be in conformity with the international obligations under the agreements between the two countries and requested the two governments to report at the next session of the assembly the measures adopted to this effect.

Economic and Social Matters.—Recognizing that the food situation was still unsatisfactory, the general assembly urged governments and international agencies to adopt or continue measures to alleviate world food shortages in 1947 and to facilitate the equitable allocation and prompt distribution of available food supplies.

The assembly approved the resolution of the Economic and Social council on economic reconstruction of devastated areas, and directed the secretary-general to inform the International Bank for Reconstruction and Development (*q.v.*) that the assembly considered that the bank should come into effective operation as soon as possible. It recommended that the Economic and Social council consider undertaking a general survey of raw material resources needed for the economic reconstruction of devastated areas, and that it give prompt and favourable consideration to the establishment of an economic commission for Europe and an economic commission for Asia and the far east.

The general assembly, recognizing the need for relief after the termination of U.N.R.R.A., established a special technical committee of ten experts to study the minimum import requirements of the basic essentials of life in countries requiring assistance and to report on the financial assistance required.

The general assembly created an International Children's Emergency fund, to be utilized for the benefit of children and adolescents of countries which were the victims of aggression, or which were receiving assistance from U.N.R.R.A., and for child health purposes generally. The fund was to consist of any assets made available by U.N.R.R.A. or any voluntary contributions from governments, voluntary agencies, individuals or other sources. The fund was to report to the Economic and Social council.

By a majority vote the general assembly approved the constitution of the International Refugee organization and an interim arrangement for a preparatory commission, and urged members to sign both instruments. The assembly authorized the secretary-general to make the necessary staff available to the preparatory commission. It urged members to consider favourably receiving on their territory for permanent settlement their fair share of non-repatriable persons. The assembly approved for the first financial year of the organization an administrative budget of $4,800,000, and an operational budget of $151,060,500 for other than large-scale resettlement and $5,000,000 for large-scale resettlement expenses.

The assembly also recommended that members accept the constitution of the World Health organization at the earliest possible date, and instructed the secretary-general to take the necessary steps to effect the transfer to the interim commission of the organization those functions of the League of Nations health organization assumed by the United Nations. The assembly approved a loan by the United Nations of a maximum sum of $300,000 to finance the activities of the interim commission from its inception to the end of the financial year 1946, and approved a further loan of $1,000,000 for 1947 either to the commission, or, if established, to the World Health organization itself.

The agreements entered into by the Economic and Social council with the International Labour organization, the United Nations Educational, Scientific and Cultural organization, the Food and Agriculture organization of the United Nations and the International Civil Aviation organization were approved by the general assembly, provided that in the case of the International Civil Aviation

"Replanting World Trade." Bishop in the *St. Louis Star-Times* signified his approval of the Bretton Woods arrangements, which congress accepted in a bill approved on July 20, 1945

organization it complied with the assembly's resolution barring the Franco regime from membership in agencies affiliated with the United Nations.

The general assembly recommended that the Economic and Social council give to the World Federation of Trade Unions the right to submit to the council questions for inclusion on its agenda.

In order to continue and develop the international control of narcotic drugs, the general assembly approved a protocol amending the agreements, conventions and protocols on narcotic drugs concluded at The Hague on Jan. 23, 1912, at Geneva on Feb. 11, 1925, and Feb. 19, 1925, and July 13, 1931, at Bangkok on Nov. 27, 1931, and at Geneva on June 26, 1936.

Trusteeship and Information from Non-Self-Governing Territories.—The general assembly approved individually the following eight trusteeship agreements: (1) for New Guinea submitted by Australia, (2) for Ruanda-Urundi submitted by Belgium, (3) for the Camerouns under French mandate submitted by France, (4) for Togoland under French mandate submitted by France, (5) for Western Samoa submitted by New Zealand, (6) for Tanganyika submitted by the United Kingdom, (7) for the Cameroons under British mandate submitted by the United Kingdom and (8) for Togoland under British mandate submitted by the United Kingdom.

Australia, Belgium, France, New Zealand and the United Kingdom, by virtue of their position as administering authorities, and China, the U.S.S.R. and the United States, as permanent members of the Security council, became *ipso facto* members of the Trusteeship council. To make the representatives on the council of states not administering trust territories equal to the number of administering powers, in accordance with the terms of the charter, the assembly elected Iraq and Mexico for the three-year term of office. It directed the secretary-general to convoke the first session of the Trusteeship council not later than March 15, 1947.

The Union of South Africa, in accordance with its undertaking to the assembly in January, reported to the general assembly the outcome of its negotiations with the people of South-West Africa. The outcome of these negotiations, it was stated, was that a majority of the inhabitants desired the incorporation of the territory in the Union of South Africa. The general assembly, however, decided that it was unable to accede to this incorporation and recommended that the mandated territory of South-West Africa be placed under the International Trusteeship system, inviting South Africa to submit a trusteeship agreement of the territory.

The general assembly noted that information had been transmitted by certain governments under chapter XI of the charter concerning conditions in non-self-governing territories and other governments had declared their intention of submitting such information. It invited members transmitting information to send to the secretary-general by June 30 of each year the latest information at their disposal, recommended that this should be summarized, analyzed and classified by the secretary-general and included in his report to the assembly's next session, and that the information should be transmitted to the specialized agencies. The assembly also established an *ad hoc* committee composed in equal numbers of members submitting information and members elected to the assembly, to examine the secretary-general's summary and analysis and recommend procedures to be followed in the future. Representatives of the specialized agencies were to sit on the committee in an advisory capacity.

The general assembly recommended that members responsible for the administration of non-self-governing territories should convene conferences of representatives of non-self-governing peoples so that expression might be given to the views and aspirations of the peoples.

Administrative and Budgetary Matters.—The general assembly approved the granting of privileges and immunities to all members of the staff of the United Nations, excepting those recruited locally and assigned to hourly rates of pay; recommended that all members grant full immunity from national taxation to their nationals employed in the secretariat; established a provisional staff retirement and insurance scheme for the secretariat; and adopted provisions relating to children's allowances and education.

The assembly appropriated an amount of $19,390,000 (U.S.) for 1946 and an amount of $27,740,000 for 1947 to finance the activities of the United Nations. It adopted a working capital fund of $20,000,000 for 1947, and approved a scale of assessments for the 1946 and 1947 budgets and the working capital fund.

The secretary-general was requested to append to the United Nations budget for 1948 the budgets of the specialized agencies and to explore arrangements by which the budgets of the agencies might be presented to the assembly for approval.

Legal Matters.—The general assembly approved the agreement between the United Nations and the Carnegie foundation concerning the use by the international court of justice of premises in the Peace palace at The Hague. It approved the agreements between the court and the Netherlands government concerning privileges and immunities and recommended that members of the court, the registrar and officials, agents and counsel of parties, assessors, witnesses and experts should be accorded such privileges and immunities as were necessary for the exercise of their duties.

The general assembly, on recommendation of the Security council, resolved that Switzerland might become a party to the statute of the international court of justice by depositing with the secretary-general of the United Nations an instrument containing (a) acceptance of the statute, (b) acceptance of the obligations of the charter under article 94, and (c) an undertaking to contribute to the expenses of the court.

After considering the application of articles 11 and 12 of the statute of the court, the assembly resolved, subject to the concurrence of the Security council, that "any meeting of the General Assembly held in pursuance of the Statute of the International Court of Justice for the purpose of the election of the members of the Court shall continue until as many candidates as are required for all the seats to be filled have obtained in one or more ballots an absolute majority of votes."

The assembly authorized the Economic and Social council to request advisory opinions of the court on legal questions arising within the scope of the council's activities. The assembly affirmed the principles of international law recognized by the charter of the Nuernberg tribunal and the judgment of the tribunal, and directed the committee on the codification of international law to treat these principles as of primary importance in the formulation of a general codification of offenses against the peace and security of mankind. The assembly affirmed that genocide is a crime under international law for which those guilty are punishable. It invited members to enact the necessary legislation, and recommended international co-operation to facilitate its prevention and punishment. It requested the Economic and Social council to draw up a draft convention on the crime of genocide for submission to the assembly.

The general assembly adopted detailed regulations for the registration and publication of treaties and international agreements. It also adopted an official seal and emblem of the United Nations and recommended that members should prohibit the use of the emblem, name and initials of the United Nations without the authorization of the secretary-general.

Assets and Functions of the League of Nations.—The general assembly approved the agreement and protocol transferring League of Nations assets to the United Nations. It requested the secretary-general to assume the non-political functions and activities of the League secretariat, and the Economic and Social council to assume those of the League committees and commissions, excepting in both cases those functions exercised in pursuance of international agreements and those entrusted to specialized agencies. The assembly authorized the United Nations Educational, Scientific and Cultural organization to utilize the assets of the Institute of Intellectual Co-operation transferred by the League of Nations to the United Nations.

Headquarters of the United Nations.—The general assembly accepted the offer of John D. Rockefeller, Jr. to give the United Nations $8,500,000 to acquire land in New York city in the area bounded by First Avenue, East 48th street, the East river and East 42nd street. It was a condition of this offer that certain adjacent parcels of land which were not available to Mr. Rockefeller were to be given to the United Nations by the city of New York.

The assembly authorized the secretary-general to negotiate with the appropriate authorities of the United States an agreement concerning the arrangements required as a result of the establishment of the permanent headquarters in New York.

Specialized Agencies

During World War II, steps were being taken, not only to found a general international organization to maintain peace and security, but also to establish specialized organizations to deal with specific postwar problems.

A United Nations Conference on Food and Agriculture held at Hot Springs, Va., from May 18 to June 3, 1943, set up an Interim Commission on Food and Agriculture to draw up a constitution for the Food and Agriculture organization of the United Nations.

The conference of allied ministers of education, which first met in London in the fall of 1942, considered plans for a permanent education organization.

The first United Nations agency to be fully created, however, was the United Nations Relief and Rehabilitation administration (*q.v.*). The agreement establishing it was signed Nov. 9, 1943, and the following day the first meeting of the U.N.R.R.A. council took place.

Articles of agreement for an International Monetary fund and an International Bank for Reconstruction and Development (*qq.v.*) were drawn up by the United Nations Monetary and Financial conference held at Bretton Woods, N.H., during July 1–22, 1944.

From Nov. 1 to Dec. 7 of the same year, the International Civil Aviation conference met in Chicago and drafted a convention on international civil aviation and an interim agreement providing for the coming into force of a Provisional International Civil Aviation organization.

Account was taken at Dumbarton Oaks and again at San Francisco of the possible contributions of these international agencies to the general over-all world organization. Article 39 of the charter provided that various intergovernmental agencies having wide international responsibilities in their specific fields should be brought into relationship with the United Nations. Accordingly, the Economic and Social council instructed a committee to negotiate agreements with certain of these agencies.

Agreements with three agencies were signed and approved by the general assembly and the organizations themselves. These were the Food and Agriculture organization of the United Nations, the International Labour organization (*q.v.*) and the United Nations Educational, Scientific and Cultural organization. An agreement with a fourth agency, the International Civil Aviation organization, was negotiated on its behalf by the Provisional International Civil Aviation organization, which was to function until the permanent organization came into being. The general assembly approved this agreement subject to the compliance of the International Civil Aviation organization with any decision of the general assembly regarding Franco Spain.

Negotiations were authorized with the International Monetary fund, the International Bank for Reconstruction and Development, the Universal Postal union and the International Telecommunications union. In addition, those organizations which were being formed through the machinery of the United Nations—the World Health organization, the International Refugee organization and the International Trade organization—were also to be brought into relationship with the United Nations.

Food and Agriculture Organization.—The Food and Agriculture organization (F.A.O.) of the United Nations officially came into being on Oct. 16, 1945, with the signing of its constitution at the first session of the conference. The United Nations Interim Commission on Food and Agriculture, set up in July 1943, had prepared the constitution for the permanent organization and had sent it for approval to the various countries which had been present at the Hot Springs conference.

The Food and Agriculture organization at the beginning of 1947 had a membership of 47 nations. Additional members might be admitted by a concurring vote of a two-thirds majority of the members of the conference and upon their acceptance of the constitution.

The constitution provided that the organization was to collect, analyze, interpret and disseminate information relating to food and agriculture. It was to promote and make recommendations on scientific, technological and economic research and to improve education and administration in these fields. It also was to promote the conservation of natural resources and the adoption of improved methods of agricultural production, as well as the improvement of processing, marketing and distribution, the provision of adequate agricultural credit and international policies concerning agricultural commodity arrangements.

The organs of the Food and Agriculture organization were specified as a conference, an executive committee and a staff headed by a director-general. The conference, composed of one representative from each member nation, was made the policy-making body of F.A.O.; it was to meet at least once each year. Each nation was given one vote in the conference. The executive committee of 9 to 15 members was to act for the conference between sessions.

The first session of the conference took place from Oct.

16 to Nov. 1, 1945. At this conference, rules of procedure and financial regulations were established; the budget for the first and second financial years and the bases for the first year's activities were worked out. The conference appointed the executive committee and the first director-general, Sir John Boyd Orr.

The conference divided into six committees covering nutrition and food management, agriculture, forestry and forest products, fisheries, marketing and statistics. Numerous recommendations were made in each of these fields, out of which emerged two dominant lines of thought: (1) expansion of production and consumption, the one to be adjusted to the other in various specific ways—through international commodity arrangements and expanded trade, raising the nutrition level of vulnerable and low-consumption groups, reorientation of production and new uses of commodities, and (2) recognition of the principle that agriculture and industry are interdependent and that, therefore, agricultural and industrial development must go hand in hand in the less developed countries.

The second session of the conference met in Copenhagen during Sept. 2–13, 1946. It approved the *Appraisal of the World Food Situation, 1946–47;* endorsed the recommendations of the special meeting on urgent food problems for the maximum use of the year's food supplies and noted the need for continued allocation measures; endorsed the report of the special F.A.O. mission for Greece on the development of agriculture and fisheries in that country; and adopted the reports of the technical committee on the various programs of work for the coming year.

The conference established a preparatory commission on world food proposals to develop and organize production, distribution and utilization of the basic foods and to stabilize agricultural prices at levels fair to producers and consumers alike. The commission, which met Oct. 28, 1946, to Jan. 24, 1947, made a number of recommendations regarding industrialization and economic development in relation to purchasing power for food; stabilization of prices and expansion of trade by specified types of international commodity arrangements; and development of programs to increase production and provide better distribution of the world's food.

The budget of the Food and Agriculture organization, as approved by the first session of the conference for the period from Oct. 16, 1945, to June 30, 1946, was $1,954,696. The second session approved a budget of $6,782,000 for the period from July 1, 1946, to Dec. 31, 1947.

United Nations Educational, Scientific and Cultural Organization.—A conference to consider the establishment of an educational and cultural organization was called by the United Kingdom government, in association with the French government, for Nov. 1, 1945. Previously, the conference of allied ministers of education in London, in association with a United States educational delegation, had drawn up and circulated to governments a draft constitution for a permanent educational organization. The French government at San Francisco had proposed a United Nations Educational and Cultural organization and also submitted a draft constitution to the conference.

The conference met in London during Nov. 1–16, 1945, and on the basis of these proposals drew up the constitution of U.N.E.S.C.O. At the same time, the conference established a preparatory commission of the United Nations Educational, Scientific and Cultural organization and decided that the seat of the new organization would be in Paris.

The purpose of the organization, as set out in its constitution, was to contribute to peace and security by promoting collaboration among the nations through education, science and culture in order to further universal respect for justice, for the rule of law and for the human rights and fundamental freedoms.

U.N.E.S.C.O. established a general conference and an executive board. The general conference, meeting annually, was to determine the policies and main plans of work of the organization and summon international conferences. The executive board, consisting of 18 members elected for 3-year terms by the general conference, was made responsible for the execution of U.N.E.S.C.O.'s program. It was to meet in regular session at least twice a year. The director-general was to be appointed by the general conference, on nomination of the executive board, for a period of six years.

The preparatory commission was charged with making arrangements for the first session of the general conference, preparing recommendations on the program and budget of the organization, and providing for immediate action on urgent needs of educational, scientific and cultural reconstruction in devastated countries. The seat of the organization was transferred from London to Paris in Sept. 1946.

The constitution of the United Nations Educational, Scientific and Cultural organization came into force on Nov. 4, 1946, when 20 governments had accepted its terms. The constitution provided that member states of the United Nations might become members of U.N.E.S.C.O.; other states might become members of the organization, subject to its agreement with the United Nations, by a two-thirds majority vote of the general conference. Thirty countries were members of U.N.E.S.C.O. at the beginning of 1947.

In accordance with the plans made by the preparatory commission, the first session of the general conference met in Paris from Nov. 19 to Dec. 10, 1946. It elected the director-general of the organization, Julian Huxley, and developed a comprehensive program of work for 1947. The conference adopted reports of the commissions on educational reconstruction and rehabilitation, on program, legal and external relations, and administration and finance. A budget of $6,000,000 was approved for 1947 and a revolving fund of $3,000,000 was authorized.

Provisional International Civil Aviation Organization.—The International Civil Aviation conference, held at Chicago from Nov. 7 to Dec. 1, 1944, drew up a convention on international civil aviation providing for the establishment of a permanent International Civil Aviation organization and an interim agreement on international civil aviation providing for the establishment of a Provisional Civil Aviation organization to operate until the permanent organization came into being, but in any case not longer than two years. Two additional agreements were adopted by the conference: the International Air Services Transit agreement providing for the mutual exchange of the first two freedoms of the air, the right to fly across foreign territory and the right to land for non-commercial purposes; the International Air Transport agreement providing for the mutual exchange of the five freedoms of the air—the two mentioned above, and in addition the rights to disembark and to take up in a foreign country traffic from the state of origin of the aircraft, and the right to carry traffic between two foreign countries. Various technical annexes were also adopted at the conference.

The provisional organization came into being on June

16, 1945, in accordance with the terms of the interim agreement, when it had been ratified by 26 countries.

The governing bodies of the Provisional International Civil Aviation organization (P.I.C.A.O.) were the interim assembly, composed of delegates from each member state and the interim council, composed of not more than 21 member states elected by the assembly for 2-year terms. The assembly, meeting annually, was to approve the financial arrangements of the organization and deal with all matters not specifically assigned to the council.

The interim council was made the executive body of the organization; it supervised the work of its committees and made recommendations concerning technical matters to member states. The interim council was deemed to function continuously. Its first session convened on Aug. 15, 1945. The interim council established three permanent committees: air navigation committee, air transport committee and committee on international convention.

In addition to these permanent committees, the interim council established administrative and standing council committees.

Considering that some of the problems of international civil aviation are regional in character, the interim council decided to hold a number of regional air navigation meetings. During 1946 meetings were held in the North Atlantic (Ireland), European-Mediterranean (France) and middle eastern (Egypt) regions.

The first session of the interim assembly was held from May 21 to June 7, 1946. It adopted 53 resolutions. In addition to administrative and budgetary matters, the resolutions dealt with such substantive questions as a multilateral agreement on commercial rights in international civil air transport, facilitation of international air transport, problems of international air mail and P.I.C.A.O. recommendations for standards, practices and procedures.

The interim assembly approved a budget of $1,960,000 to cover the financial year 1946–47.

World Health Organization.—The constitution of the World Health organization was adopted by the International Health conference, convened by the Economic and Social council, which met in New York during June 19–22, 1946. It was to come into force after 26 members of the United Nations had become parties to it "by signature without reservation as to approval; signature subject to approval followed by acceptance; or acceptance." Acceptance was to be effected by the deposit of a formal instrument with the secretary-general of the United Nations.

The organization was to act as the directing and co-ordinating authority on international health work; to collaborate with other organizations and assist governments in strengthening health services; to provide technical assistance, on request, to governments and provide health services for special groups, such as the people from trust territories. It was to maintain epidemiological, statistical and other services; help eradicate epidemics and diseases; assist in preventing accidental injuries; and promote the improvement of nutrition, housing, sanitation, recreation and other aspects of environmental hygiene.

The constitution provided that the World Health organization was to consist of a world health assembly, an executive board and a secretariat, as well as technical committees. The assembly, to be composed of delegates of all members, was to meet annually and be the policy-making body of the organization. The executive committee was to consist of 18 members elected by the assembly for a term of 3 years.

The interim commission established by the International Health conference consisted of 18 states. It was to convoke the first session of the World Health assembly and to take the necessary steps for the transfer to the World Health organization of the necessary functions and activities of the League of Nations and the *Office International d'Hygiène publique*.

In response to the application of the interim commission the general assembly approved a loan by the United Nations of $300,000 to finance the activities of the interim commission from the beginning of its work to the end of the financial year 1946; a further loan of $1,000,000 was approved to finance the activities of the interim commission of the World Health organization during the year 1947.

The general assembly at the second part of its first session approved the constitution of the International Refugee organization and recommended it to governments for signature. The committee was to come into force when 15 states had become parties to it.

The constitution recognized that genuine refugees and displaced persons should be assisted by international action, but that the main task as regards displaced persons was to encourage and assist them to return to their country of origin.

The functions of the International Refugee organization were to be the repatriation, identification, registration and classification, care and assistance, legal and political protection, transport and resettlement and re-establishment in countries able and willing to receive them, of refugees and displaced persons.

The principal organs of the organization were to be the general council, the policy-making body in which each member was to be represented, and the executive committee, consisting of representatives of nine members. A director-general, nominated by the executive committee and appointed by the general council, was to be responsible for appointing the staff and carrying out the administrative and executive functions of the International Refugee organization.

The general assembly approved a budget for the first financial year in the amount of $4,800,000 for administrative expenses, $151,060,500 for operational expenses and $500,000 for large-scale resettlement expenses.

The establishment of a preparatory commission for the International Refugee organization, to consist of one representative from each government signatory to the constitution, was approved by the general assembly. This agreement was to come into force when signed by eight governments signatory to the constitution.

The director of the intergovernmental committee on refugees, the director-general of U.N.R.R.A. and the director-general of the International Labour organization were to be invited to sit with the preparatory commission in a consultative capacity. The commission was to take the necessary measures for bringing the organization into effective operation and was empowered to take over the functions, activities, assets and personnel of existing organizations dealing with refugees and displaced persons where it considered this essential. The commission was to be convened as soon as possible and would cease to exist upon the election of the director-general of the organization. (*See* also EDUCATION; INTERNATIONAL COURT OF JUSTICE; INTERNATIONAL BANK FOR RECONSTRUCTION AND DEVELOPMENT; INTERNATIONAL LABOUR ORGANIZATION; INTERNATIONAL LAW; INTERNATIONAL MONETARY FUND; LEAGUE OF NATIONS.)

BIBLIOGRAPHY.—*The United Nations:* Dumbarton Oaks Proposals for a General International Organization, to be the subject of the United Nations Conference at San Francisco, April 25, 1945, Department of State Publication 2297, Conference Series 66 (Washington, D.C., 1945); *Documents* of the United Nations Conference on International Organization, San Francisco, 1945, published in co-operation with the Library of Congress, 16 vols. United Nations Information Organizations (London, New York, 1945–46.); *Facsimile* of the Charter of the United Nations, Statute of the International Court of Justice and Interim Arrangements, in five languages . . . San Francisco, 1945, Department of State Publication 2368, Conference Series 76 (Washington, D.C., 1945); *Report* by the Executive Committee to the Preparatory Commission of the United Nations, Preparatory Commission of the United Nations (H.M. Stationery Office, London, 1945) (PC/EX/113/Rev.1, Nov. 12, 1945); *Report* of the Preparatory Commission of the United Nations (London, H.M. Stationery Office, 1945) (PC/20, Dec. 23, 1945); *United Nations*, Report of the Secretary-General on the work of the Organization (1946) (Document No. A/65, June 30, 1946); *Journal of the General Assembly*, first session (1st part) no. 1–34, Jan. 10–March 7, 1946, (H.M. Stationery Office, London, 1946) English and French in parallel columns; *Resolutions* adopted by the General Assembly during the first part of its first session from Jan. 10 to Feb. 14, 1946 (*Résolutions adoptées par l'Assemblée Générale pendant la première partie de sa première session du 10 janvier au 14 février 1946*) (London, Church House, Westminster, 1946) (A/64, July 1, 1946) English text followed by French text; **Resolutions* adopted by the General Assembly during the second part of its first session from Oct. 23 to Dec. 15, 1946 (*Résolutions adoptées par l'Assemblée Générale pendant la seconde partie de sa première session du 23 octobre au 15 décembre 1946*) (Lake Success, New York, 1947) (A/64/Add.1, Jan. 31, 1947) English and French in parallel columns; *Journal of the United Nations (Journal des Nations Unies)* No. 1 *et seq.* Oct. 8, 1946 *et seq. 8 octobre 1946 et seq.* (Lake Success, New York, 1946 *et seq.*) English and French in parallel columns; *Journal of the Security Council*, first year, No. 1–42, Jan. 18–July 11, 1946 (*Journal du Conseil de Sécurité, première année, 18 janvier–11 juillet 1946*) (London, New York 1946) English and French in parallel columns; *Security Council*, official records, first year: second series, (*Conseil de Sécurité, procès-verbaux officiels, première année: seconde série*) *No.* 1 *et seq.* July 10, 1946 *et seq. 10 juillet 1946 et seq.* (New York, Hunter college, the Bronx, 1946 *et seq.*) English and French in parallel columns; *Journal of the Economic and Social Council*, first year, No. 1–30, Jan. 31, 1946–July 23, 1946 (*Journal du Conseil Économique et Social, première année, no. 1–30, 31 janvier 1946–23 juillet 1946*) (London, New York 1946) English and French in parallel columns. (T. L.)

United Nations Educational, Scientific and Cultural Organization

See EDUCATION; UNITED NATIONS.

United Nations Food and Agriculture Organization

See AGRICULTURE; FAMINES; UNITED NATIONS.

United Nations Monetary and Financial Program

See INTERNATIONAL BANK FOR RECONSTRUCTION AND DEVELOPMENT; INTERNATIONAL MONETARY FUND; UNITED NATIONS.

United Nations Relief and Rehabilitation Administration

The United Nations Relief and Rehabilitation administration (U.N.R.R.A.) was established on Nov. 9, 1943, as the first service agency of the United Nations. In 1946 it was composed of 48 member governments, each of which participated in U.N.R.R.A.'s policy-making council. Nine governments—the U.S., the United Kingdom, the soviet union, China, France, Canada, Australia, Brazil and Yugoslavia—were also represented on the Central committee, which was empowered to make emergency policy decisions between sessions of the council. Executive responsibility was vested in the director general, assisted by his staff, composed of more than 12,000 persons and about 30 different nationalities. Herbert H. Lehman served as director general from the inception of the administration until his resignation in March 1946. He was succeeded by Fiorello H. La Guardia.

U.N.R.R.A. was organized to provide relief and rehabilitation to the people of liberated territories in Europe and the far east, concentrating primarily on assisting those nations without adequate foreign exchange resources to finance their own relief imports. This assistance consisted of relief supplies—food, clothing, fuel, medicines; relief services—health and welfare services, repatriation of displaced persons; and rehabilitation supplies and services—seeds, fertilizers, insecticides, farm tools, repair parts, etc.

To finance these supplies and services, each member country not occupied by the enemy was asked to contribute 1% of its national income for the year ending June 30, 1943. Later, each was asked to make a second contribution in the same amount. Meanwhile all countries, invaded and uninvaded alike, contributed proportionately to U.N.R.R.A.'s administrative budget. As of July 31, 1946, the total operating and administrative contributions authorized by U.N.R.R.A.'s member governments amounted to $3,691,866,918. The total amounts subscribed by the three largest contributors were: U.S. $2,700,000,000; United Kingdom, $624,650,000; and Canada, $138,738,739.

After a period of planning and training, U.N.R.R.A. took over relief operations from the military in Greece on April 1, 1945, and in Yugoslavia on April 15, 1945. V-E day paved the way for increasing supplies and shipping to meet the needs of liberated countries in Europe. V-J day made possible relief and rehabilitation operations on a global basis.

In 1946, U.N.R.R.A. was providing general relief aid to the following countries: Albania, Austria, the Byelorussian Soviet Socialist Republic, China, Czechoslovakia, the Dodecanese Islands, Greece, Italy, Poland, the Ukrainian Soviet Socialist Republic and Yugoslavia. Programs of limited emergency aid were in effect on behalf of Finland, Hungary and the Philippines, and a special program was being operated to help Ethiopia in the fields of medicine, welfare and transport.

In 1946, U.N.R.R.A. personnel assisted the military in the care of more than 1,000,000 displaced persons, and administered hundreds of displaced persons assembly centres, however over-all responsibility for the displaced persons operations in Germany and Austria was lodged in the military authorities, who provided the basic supplies and transportation.

The acceleration of U.N.R.R.A.'s operation was borne out by the following cumulative statistics of supplies shipped overseas:

End of first quarter, 1945	37,000 long tons
End of second quarter, 1945	964,269 long tons
End of third quarter, 1945	2,067,786 long tons
End of fourth quarter, 1945	3,920,902 long tons
End of first quarter, 1946	7,787,198 long tons
End of second quarter, 1946	12,430,773 long tons
End of third quarter, 1946	17,107,648 long tons
End of fourth quarter, 1946	19,885,870 long tons

Operations in 1946 were seriously affected by the critical world food shortage. U.N.R.R.A. was unable to obtain sufficient allocations of bread grains to meet its minimum overseas commitments during the first half of the year. The fourth session of the U.N.R.R.A. council, held in March 1946, underscored the necessity for the supplying and receiving countries to take all possible measures to conserve and make available more food to avert widespread famine in Europe and the far east. La Guardia, elected director general at this session, devoted most of his time in the succeeding months to overcoming the food shortage.

Loaves of bread supplied by U.N.R.R.A. being distributed at Weimar to displaced persons temporarily quartered at Buchenwald during July 1945

He also called attention to the necessity of finding a permanent solution to the displaced persons problem in Europe.

Extraordinary efforts on the part of the major wheat growing countries and the arrival of harvests in liberated areas materially eased the food crisis in the last half of 1946, although U.N.R.R.A. officials warned that the danger of hunger would remain at least through 1947.

The U.N.R.R.A. council held its fifth session at Geneva in Aug. 1946, principally to adopt policies regarding the termination of the organization and the transfer of its remaining functions to permanent international bodies. Among the resolutions adopted were: (1) transfer of U.N.R.R.A.'s major health activities to the World Health organization or its interim commission; (2) authorization of the transfer to the United Nations of such social welfare functions as the United Nations desire to undertake; (3) continuation of displaced persons operations until undertaken by the International Refugee organization or by any other appropriate body, provided that none of these operations was to be continued by U.N.R.R.A. after June 30, 1947; (4) rehabilitation of children and adolescents of liberated countries by the creation of an International Children's fund to which such assets would be transferred as the central committee might determine, to be available after completion of the work of U.N.R.R.A.; and (5) recommendation that the general assembly of the United Nations establish the appropriate agency, or agencies, to review the needs in 1947 for financing urgent imports of the basic essentials of life, after the termination of U.N.R.R.A. programs, and to recommend the financial assistance required to meet such future relief needs. (*See* also DISPLACED PERSONS; FOOD SUPPLY, WORLD [POSTWAR].)

(H. H. L.)

BIBLIOGRAPHY.—K. E. Beer, *UNRRA in Action* (1945); H. W. Briggs, "UNRRA Agreement and Congress," *Amer. Jl. of Intl. Law*, 38:650–58 (1944); Natl. Planning Assoc., *UNRRA: Gateway to Recovery* (1944); T. A. Sunberg, "Financial Experience of UNRRA," *Am. Jl. of Intl. Law*, 39:698–712 (1945); UNRRA, *Emergency Welfare Services* (1944), *Report* (Nov. 1943), *UNRRA at Work* (London). *See* also *Journal* of the UNRRA council.

United Service Organizations

U.S.O. was chartered Feb. 4, 1941. Months before, when the plan to mobilize U.S. manpower was taking form, representatives of leading social service agencies met to discuss ways of providing for the recreational and religious welfare of the new armed forces. The idea of joint operation emerged, and the group drew up plans for an agency in which the three major religious faiths would have equal participation and responsibility. That the required agency should be a civilian organization financed by voluntary gifts of the U.S. people also seemed requisite to the founders, in spite of opposition from some quarters.

The six great humanitarian service agencies, representing the major faiths, which combined their resources and experience in the constitution of U.S.O. were the Young Men's Christian associations, the National Catholic Community service, the National Jewish Welfare board, the Young Womens Christian associations, the Salvation army and the National Travelers Aid association. Every step was taken with the support and concurrence of the war department. Later the welfare and recreational activities of U.S.O. and the Red Cross were defined to prevent overlapping of effort. Roughly, U.S.O. services were limited to the U.S. and to noncombat zones in the Atlantic and Pacific areas, such as Hawaii, Panama, Newfoundland, the Caribbean, Alaska, and, in general, South America. The Philippines were added after their liberation in 1945. An exception to the above was U.S.O.-camp shows, the sole agency to take professional talent from the U.S. for entertainment of troops overseas, performing only on military posts, in military hospitals and in the several war theatres.

In June 1941, U.S.O. launched the first of the financial campaigns which resulted in the receipt of more than $200,000,000 through the war years and in the period following the end of hostilities. For its first two years, 1941 and 1942, U.S.O. conducted its own campaigns. In the succeeding three years, its fund raising efforts were combined with those of a number of other war related agencies in the National War fund. In 1946, U.S.O. engaged in a campaign of its own to finish its wartime tasks and carry through until it received its "honourable discharge" at the end of 1947.

Original plans for U.S.O. called for the establishment of less than 500 clubs to provide a "home away from home" atmosphere for service men. As the war progressed, however, and the largest fighting force in the history of the nation was trained and deployed to the far corners of the earth, it became imperative to revise these plans. Eventually, practically every feature of recreational welfare had its place in the organization's plans and program. At its peak, in March 1944, U.S.O. reached a total of 3,035 operations, and expenditures climbed to $5,800,000 a month. The organization was serving 1,000,000 a day, and at one time 730,000 volunteers were on its rolls.

In addition to more than 1,500 clubs in the continental U.S., there was a series of U.S.O. lounges for troops in transit, working with U.S.O.-Travelers Aid bureaus in transportation terminals; mobile service—U.S.O. clubs-on-wheels—which carried recreation, supplies and good will to men and detachments on outpost duty; and overseas service, which had its clubs, smaller centres and mobile units outside the continental U.S. During wartime, in some 200 industrial communities, U.S.O. activities helped maintain the morale of men and women working in great war plants and living in overcrowded boom towns. Not only were there distinct religious programs, but U.S.O. and its member agencies distributed religious literature in almost uncountable quantities and religious articles—more than 20,000,000 annually in the U.S. and overseas—to those who desired them.

U.S.O.-Camp Shows, Inc., had a similar record. More than 5,000 entertainers in more than 700 units toured army camps, navy installations and service hospitals from just prior to Pearl Harbor until long after hostilities ended. In addition, early in 1946, U.S.O.-Camp Shows entertainment was extended at the request of the Veterans' administration to all V.A. hospitals. At the peak of its service in 1945, entertainers were giving 700 shows a day to service personnel; these performances ranged from individual specialty acts to full Broadway shows whose casts were rehearsed and perfected before they set foot on shipboard. Troupers entertained total audiences of more than 200,000,000 service men and women. Some 200 widely known artists, enrolled in the U.S.O.-Camp Shows Hospital Sketching program, made nearly 250,000 portraits of hospitalized service men. (L. F. K.)

U.S. troops forgot the rain and mud of Luzon for a short while as they laughed at the antics of U.S.O. entertainers during a camp show

Bibliography.—J. M. Carson, *Home Away from Home* (1946); R. Kendall, "Music for the Armed Services," *Musical Quarterly* 31:150–154 (April 1945); B. Klaw, "Camp Follower—USO," *Atlantic* 172:100–104, 90–95, (Nov., Dec. 1943); *USO: Five Years of Service, Rept. of the Pres.* (1946).

United States

The decade 1937–46 was fraught with events of tremendous import for the United States, both in its domestic affairs and in its foreign relations. For a third of the period —from Dec. 1941 to Aug. 1945—the nation was engaged in the most terrible war of human history, with armed forces fighting on world fronts from the Aleutians to the South Pacific islands and from the coasts of France and western Africa to the heart of the German reich. The postwar casualty roll released on June 27, 1946, by the war department listed as killed or missing 308,978 of the 10,000,000 men and women mobilized: a toll far exceeding the combined losses in all of the nation's previous foreign wars.

But aside from the years of actual combat, the whole decade was dominated by war psychology. In fact, the year 1937 may be taken to mark the shift of emphasis in government policy from the domestic to the foreign scene. It was on Oct. 5 of that year that President Franklin D. Roosevelt made his "quarantine" speech in Chicago, calling on the peace-loving nations to check the epidemic of military aggression which was spreading in Europe and Asia. Hitler had moved his troops into the Rhineland the summer before in violation of the treaty of Versailles and the pact of Locarno. In the late spring of 1937, Prince Fumimaro Konoye, a tool of the extreme militarists, became premier of Japan, and the expected attack on China south of the Great Wall followed on July 7 with the clash at the Marco Polo bridge, near Peiping. The Rome-Berlin-Tokyo axis had been formed with the determination to subject all Europe and Asia to the rule of the totalitarian despots. President Roosevelt receded momentarily from his defiant attitude at Chicago; but from 1937 on, his main efforts were directed toward rousing his fellow-countrymen to the danger which would threaten the U.S. in the event of the success of the axis powers, and in furthering a policy of military preparedness, conscription, revision of the hampering neutrality legislation and all-out aid to the Allies short of actual participation in the war.

Pres. Roosevelt's third-term election conceded, neighbours gathered outside his home at Hyde Park, N.Y., to offer congratulations on the night of Nov. 5, 1940

Little by little, in spite of the determined opposition of noninterventionist groups, public opinion as recorded by public opinion polls came to the support of the President's policies. His smashing victory over Alfred M. Landon in the election of 1936 had been followed in 1940 by his triumph over Wendell Willkie to shatter the tradition observed since George Washington's day of the limitation of the presidential tenure of office to two terms. Four years later, when the nation was in the very thick of the world struggle, he was elected for a fourth term over Gov. Thomas E. Dewey of New York; but less than three months after the inauguration he succumbed to a cerebral haemorrhage at Warm Springs, Ga. (April 12, 1945), and was succeeded by Vice-President Harry S. Truman of Missouri.

Trends in Population.—According to the decennial federal census of 1940 the continental population of the United States was 131,669,275, an increase of 8,894,229 or 7.3% over the 1930 census. In Aug. 1946 the official figures given out by the census bureau showed that the population had passed the 141,000,000 mark. If possessions and dependencies were included—and the Philippine Islands, although granted formal independence on July 4, 1946, were still in effect a dependency of the United States—the total population would reach approximately 160,000,000.

Two trends were noticeable in the population. First, the rate of increase was declining. For several decades it had averaged only about 7%, whereas in the early years of the republic, decennial gains of 20% to 25% were registered. It was this rapid growth that led Thomas Jefferson to predict that by the end of the 19th century the nation would have a population of over 200,000,000. Furthermore, U.S. demographic experts were now of the opinion that the nation was approaching a "saturation point," and that by 1980 the population might be stabilized at something like 170,000,000. The reasons for this lag in increase could not be determined with accuracy; but the closing of the inviting frontier toward the end of the 19th century, the restrictions imposed on immigration in the 20th century and the shift of population to urban centres, in which various social and economic conditions made for smaller families than those raised in the rural districts, might all be contributing causes to the slowup.

The second trend was toward a higher proportion of elderly people in the population. A falling birth rate combined with a longer expectancy of life (made possible by medical advance and government benefits to the aged and infirm) resulted in some rather startling statistics. For example, while the population as a whole increased 7.3% in the decade 1930–40, the number of persons 65 years old

Appraisal of the dispute between U.S. interventionists and non-interventionists prior to Pearl Harbor. The cartoon, by Hungerford of the *Pittsburgh Post-Gazette*, was captioned "A Strange Race Horse"

and over increased 35%; and while at the beginning of the 20th century only 4% of the people were in this old age group, by 1940 the proportion had grown to over 7%; sociologists predicted that by 1980 the proportion would rise to over 9%. In other words, instead of the 10,000,000 aged people of 1946, there would be about 18,000,000 a generation later. The significance of this trend for public and private institutions of social security, hospitals and charities could not be ignored. Moreover, while most of the citizens who were too young to work were also too young to vote, the oldsters had the ballot and might exercise an influence on legislation comparable to a major lobby. (*See* also BIRTH STATISTICS; CENSUS DATA, U.S.; CHURCH MEMBERSHIP; DEATH STATISTICS; INDIANS, AMERICAN; NEGROES, AMERICAN.)

Congress, 1937–46

During the entire decade, the control of both houses of congress was in the hands of the Democrats. Their majorities varied from session to session. In the 75th congress (elected in the year of Roosevelt's amazing victory over Landon) the Democrats held 334 of the 435 seats in the house and 76 of the 96 in the senate; and in none of the four succeeding congresses of the decade did they fall behind a majority of 100 in the house, except in the 78th congress (1943–45) when the parties were fairly balanced at 222 Democrats and 209 Republicans. The 79th congress, however, elected in the presidential year of 1944, saw the Democrats recover their wide margin with 243 seats to 190 for the Republicans. In the senate the Democratic strength varied from 70 in the 75th congress (when several of the Democratic senators had to find seats on the Republican side) to 58 in the 79th congress. These large majorities were not an unmixed blessing for the Democrats, since they gave occasion for frequent dissensions within their own ranks.

"Breathing Spell."—By 1937, the major measures of the New Deal for the relief of the small business men, the farmers, the unemployed, the underpaid, and the aged and infirm had been passed. Though some of these measures, like the Agricultural Adjustment act and the National Industrial Recovery act of 1933, had been held unconstitutional by the supreme court, the New Dealers had found valid substitutes for them in the Soil Conservation act of 1936 and the Wagner National Labor Relations act of 1935. The Social Security act of 1935, which President Roosevelt declared to be the "supreme achievement" of his administration, was designed to remedy the glaring inequalities between great wealth and dire poverty. The Securities act protected the investor in the stock market. The Home Loans act provided government aid for home owners overburdened with mortgages. The Works Progress administration was furnishing jobs for thousands of idle men in the construction of roads, bridges, schoolhouses, hospitals, playgrounds and public buildings. The Tennessee Valley authority and the Civilian Conservation corps (recruited from young men without a job) were making lasting contributions to the preservation of U.S. natural resources.

Although the president had declared in his final address of the 1936 campaign that he had "just begun to fight" for adequate wages, the abolition of farm tenancy, crop insurance, slum clearance, collective bargaining and the proper distribution of the ample products of U.S. industry, he was soon speaking as if the work of the New Deal was virtually accomplished except for a "machining down" of the measures; he was assuring the opposing business interests that they might look forward to a "breathing spell." The tapering off of the president's and of congress's occupation with the program of domestic reform from the year 1937 on was because of a rising concern over the aggressions of the fascist and nazi dictators. Nevertheless, the final session of the 75th congress (Jan. 3–June 16, 1938) saw the passage of two important measures in furtherance of the New Deal program: the elaborate Agricultural Adjustment act of Feb. 14, which Secretary of Agriculture Henry A. Wallace called "the best farm program that the nation has ever had," and the Wagner Fair Labor Standards (or Wages and Hours) act, which President Roosevelt hailed as, "with the exception of the Social Security act, the most far-sighted program for the benefit of workers ever adopted." Large sums were appropriated by congress for work relief, slum clearance, low cost housing, farm loans, and various benefit payments. In a "fireside chat" of June 24, 1938, the president lauded the 75th congress as having "achieved more for the future good of the country than any congress between the end of the [first World] war and 1933." (*See* NEW DEAL.)

Futile Neutrality.—The next year (1939), the storm broke in Europe with Hitler's invasion of Poland and the prompt declaration of war on Germany by Great Britain and France. Recalling the futile efforts of President Woodrow Wilson to keep the United States out of World War I, and remembering that in former European wars (1812, 1914) when England's defense of the Atlantic lines of trade had been threatened, the United States had been eventually involved, the government and people became immediately concerned with the problem of U.S. neutrality. As early as

The White House blazed with lights on the night of Dec. 8, 1941, as the chief executive conferred with national leaders following the U.S. declaration of war on Japan

Aug. 1935 congress had passed a temporary act forbidding the export of arms and ammunition to European belligerents and closing U.S. ports to belligerent warships. And in Jan. 1937 the embargo provisions were extended to cover the Civil War in Spain—a serious handicap for the ill-armed loyalist forces when Hitler and Mussolini were pouring in weapons and battalions to reinforce Franco's fascist armies.

Since the temporary neutrality law was to expire on May 1, 1937, it was necessary for congress to provide a new act by that date. The will to preserve U.S. neutrality was unanimous: the only question was as to the means best calculated to achieve that end. Some members of congress favoured a strict mandatory law, tying the president's hands; others would adhere to the traditional policy of leaving the president and the state department free to conduct foreign relations through the channels of diplomacy; still others advised a compromise which would give the president a certain amount of discretion in carrying out a program within the general provisions prescribed by congress. This third counsel prevailed in the new act passed on May 1, 1937, and reluctantly signed by President Roosevelt, who felt that it would unduly hamper his negotiations with foreign powers and prove more likely to get the nation into war than to keep it out. The act provided: (1) that *when* the president should proclaim that a state of war existed between any nations of the old world, no arms should be exported or loans made to the belligerents; (2) that the president *might* forbid U.S. citizens to travel on ships of nations at war; (3) that he *might* forbid U.S. ships to carry goods purchased in the United States by belligerents and compel the latter to pay cash for such goods before shipment (the "cash and carry" plan); (4) that armed merchantmen and war vessels of the belligerents be denied entrance to U.S. ports; and (5) that the president *might* extend the embargo provisions to certain other materials than arms. Note the extent of the discretionary power left to the president by the italicized words of the above clauses.

Convinced that this power was inadequate, President Roosevelt persisted in his efforts to persuade congress to repeal the embargo provisions of the act, his appeal of July 1939 being rejected by a vote of 12 to 11 in the senate committee on foreign relations. When the European war broke out in September, however, he called congress in extra session on the 21st of the month, for the express purpose of securing the repeal. His personal pleas to Hitler and Mussolini to refrain from aggressions which would plunge Europe into war had been met with cynical silence or insulting advice to mind his own business; and he had become convinced that the combined action of the peace-loving states was the only hope for the defeat of the dictators. The United States had to "play a part" in this concerted effort. Its hands had to be free to furnish all aid short of war to the democracies in their struggle for existence. Roosevelt would still maintain such safeguards of neutrality as the closing of danger zones to U.S. vessels and the cash and carry provision of the act of 1937; but the embargo on arms and ammunition would no longer be allowed to prevent Great Britain and its allies from buying the materials of war in the United States. The change which had taken place in public opinion in the two years following the act of 1937 was reflected by the unexpectedly large majorities by which the repeal of the embargo was voted by the senate (Oct. 27) and the house (Nov. 2).

When the fury of Hitler's blitz was launched on Norway, the Netherlands, Belgium and France in the spring of

1940, and his bombers began to rain destruction on the English cities, there came an increasing sense of the danger to U.S. security. It was an infamous pact with Stalin in Aug. 1939 that had given Hitler, the professed saviour of Europe from bolshevism, a free hand to crush Poland and launch his attack on western Europe. The fall of France on June 22, 1940, extended his empire to the Pyrenees and left Great Britain to battle alone, under the inspiration of the indomitable Winston Churchill, for the survival of liberty and democracy. If England should share the fate of France, the whole burden of resistance to world tyranny would fall on the shoulders of the U.S., which was woefully unprepared for such an emergency.

The regular army and national guard comprised less than 750,000 men. Secretary of the Navy Charles Edison was calling for the construction of 100 warships at an estimated cost of $1,300,000,000. The nation was building fewer than 1,000 planes a month, and of the 5,000 on hand in May 1940 Chief of Staff George Marshall declared that only 1,500 were fit for use. Congress responded readily to the president's recommendations for increased war matériel, authorizing appropriations of more than $13,000,000,000 for national defense. But the proposal to resort to conscription to augment the armed forces met with bitter opposition in congress and in the country.

On June 20, 1940, Sen. Edward Burke of Nebraska introduced a conscription bill, based on the Selective Service act of 1917, and declaring that adequate forces could not be raised by voluntary enlistments. After a spirited debate of three months the Selective Training and Service bill of 1940 was passed by votes of 47 to 25 in the senate and 232 to 124 in the house and was signed by the president on Sept. 16. It was the first time in U.S. history that peacetime conscription had been adopted. The act provided that "every male citizen and alien between the ages of 21 and 36 residing in the United States," with certain specified exceptions, should be obliged to register for military service. Those to be inducted into the service were to be drawn by lot, in the same way that the lottery had been conducted in 1917. In fact, the same "goldfish bowl" that held the capsules containing the fateful inducting numbers in 1917 was used in the drawing of Oct. 29, 1940. On that day, 19,670 men were called into the service as the first contingent of the 900,000 which might be raised in any one year in time of peace.

Nonshooting War.—The next year (1941) saw the adoption by congress of another piece of legislation of prime importance: the Lend-Lease act of March 11, 1941. Less than two weeks after the meeting of the first session of the 77th congress, which was to last through the entire year, a bill was introduced into the house "to promote the defense of the United States." It marked a drastic departure from the policy of neutrality. Hitherto the Allies had been permitted to purchase supplies for cash and to carry them in their own vessels, but U.S. ports were closed to their warships, and U.S. vessels were forbidden to enter the danger zones. The new bill proposed to put the enormous industrial resources of the United States at the disposal of the Allies, thus making the nation a virtual partner of the nations fighting the axis powers.

The terms "lend" and "lease" in the title of the bill were somewhat misleading as to the nature of the aid rendered, for the ordinary conditions of a loan were absent from it. There was no limit placed upon the amount of money or material to be furnished; no specification of the terms of payment; no time set for the expiration of the act; no restriction made on the geographical destination of the supplies. The United States, in President Roosevelt's words, was to become "the arsenal of democracy." For two months a bitter battle was waged in congress over the bill, and amendments without number were proposed. Hours were consumed by opponents who declared that the nation was heading straight for war and was preparing to part with the materials needed for its own defense. The entire country was aroused. Organizations like "America First" and "No Foreign Wars" were combated by groups with the names of "Fight for Freedom" and "Defense of America by Aid to the Allies." The Gallup poll showed a majority of 70% in favour of lend-lease. The bill passed by a vote of 60 to 31 in the senate and 317 to 17 in the house and was immediately signed by the president. On March 27, congress appropriated $7,000,000,000 for lend-lease, and on Oct. 28 supplemented it by a further appropriation of $5,985,000,000. The British were jubilant over the act, and Winston Churchill called it "Hitler's death warrant."

That the country was "heading for war," however, seemed evident from the orders of the president and the measures of congress which marked the months of 1941. On April 10, U.S. troops occupied the Danish island of Greenland to protect Atlantic shipping. On May 7, congress ordered the seizure of 92 German and Italian ships in U.S. ports. On June 14, assets of the axis countries in the United States were frozen, and two days later their consulates in the U.S. were closed. On July 7, U.S. troops occupied Iceland. During August and September, German submarines sank several U.S. merchant ships, and the president gave orders (Sept. 11) to "shoot on sight" at these marauders. Then, in October, the submarines began to attack U.S. war vessels, missing the destroyer "Greer" off Iceland, but hitting the "Kearny" on Oct. 17 and killing 11 men, and two weeks later sinking the destroyer "Reuben James" with the loss of more than half her crew.

In Nov. 1941, congress, by the close vote of 212 to 194 in the house, repealed the last remnants of the neutrality law and extended the service time of the drafted men to two and a half years. The following figures told the story of the spurt in preparedness. On June 30, 1940, the army numbered less than 300,000 men; a year later, 1,462,347. On June 30, 1940, the tonnage of combat ships was 823,335; in Oct. 1941 it was 2,138,590. During World War I, the United States spent $22,000,000,000; by May 1941 congress had appropriated $52,000,000,000—and the United States was still at peace!

"Date of Infamy."—It was not the depredations of the German submarines, however, that brought the nation into the war, but the treacherous raid of the Japanese planes on the base at Pearl Harbor on Dec. 7, at the very moment when the Japanese envoys at Washington, D.C., were deceiving Secretary Cordell Hull with conciliatory words. The next day congress, with but a single dissenting vote, declared war against Japan, and three days later both houses by unanimous votes declared war on Germany and Italy. The following June, war was declared on the axis Balkan satellites, Hungary, Rumania and Bulgaria.

During the war years congress was occupied almost entirely with legislation to implement the president's recommendations for the successful prosecution of the war. It promptly created the federal agencies which he called for to control prices and mediate between management and labour. It extended lend-lease until no fewer than 33 countries were benefiting by the act. It raised the number of registrants under the Selective Service act to a total of 42,000,000 men, by including those between the ages of 36 and 65, and created the women's auxiliary corps for the army (WACS), the navy (WAVES) and the coast guard (SPARS). Congress had made but little progress on the program recommended by President Roosevelt in his message of Jan. 6, 1945, when the surrender of Japan in August brought the war to a close. President Truman called the legislators back to Washington, D.C., on Sept. 5 and presented them with a long message containing 21 proposed measures, to which he added 5 more in his annual message of Jan. 21, 1946. Congress had readily endorsed foreign commitments, ratifying the San Francisco charter and the Bretton Woods agreement, extending the reciprocal trade pacts, and providing liberally for U.N.R.R.A. But it did "distressing little," in the president's words, to implement his overloaded program for domestic reform and recovery. Southern Democrats, resisting the trend toward New Deal policies in the program, joined with the Republicans in sabotaging four-fifths of the proposals. Week after week was spent in hearings before investigating committees, the Pearl Harbor case alone running to 16,000,000 words of testimony. And the approaching midterm congressional elections combined with the distressing labour situation made the legislators chary of risking any measures which might injure their chances of returning to Washington. So the vast and slow business of reconversion, redeployment, readjustment of wages, revision of taxes, restraint of inflationary prices and a hundred other remedial measures to help the country on the way to the realization of an era of prosperity awaited the assembling of the 80th congress in Jan. 1947, a congress in which the Republicans had a majority in both branches. (*See* also ELECTIONS; LAW.)

The Executive

For 12 years and 39 days before his death on April 12, 1945, Franklin D. Roosevelt occupied the presidential chair. During these years he made 15 replacements in his cabinet, the most sensational being the appointment of two prominent Republicans in the midsummer of 1940: Henry L. Stimson, Herbert Hoover's former secretary of state, to be secretary of war, and Col. Frank Knox, Republican vice-presidential candidate in 1936, to be secretary of the navy. Soon after assuming office, President Truman began to recast the cabinet, and by the autumn of 1946 no Roosevelt appointee was left in it, the last to go being Wallace, secretary of commerce, who was dismissed by President Truman on Sept. 20, 1946, for making a speech in New York in which he criticized the administration's policy toward soviet Russia. He was replaced by W. Averell Harriman, then ambassador to London and former ambassador to soviet Russia.

President Roosevelt belonged to what his distant cousin Theodore had called the Lincoln-Jackson type of executive, in contrast to the Taft-Buchanan type: that is, a president not content merely to "execute" the mandates of congress, but taking the initiative himself, as spokesman for the U.S. people, in proposing and urging legislation for the general welfare of the country. In pursuance of his domestic policies, President Roosevelt, especially in the earliest years of his administration, often met with determined opposition by conservatives in congress and on the supreme court. For the framers of the constitution, remembering the arbitrary conduct of many of the royal governors in colonial days, had taken pains to limit the power of the executive at home by the famous system of "checks and balances."

At the same time, the crying need for a central authority to speak for the United States as a truly united nation had led the founding fathers to give the president very large powers in the field of foreign relations. He was to appoint all ministers, consuls and special envoys to foreign states, subject in most cases to the consent of the senate (which was rarely refused). He likewise was to name all the high officials in the army and navy, and as commander-in-chief of the armed forces of the country he could order them to any region that he chose. He had the sole initiative in diplomatic negotiations, and though a vote of congress was necessary for the declaration of war, he could, and often did, so shape his diplomatic policy that the actual declaration by congress was hardly more than an inevitable ratification of his acts. It was only logical, then, that when the aggressions of Germany, Italy and Japan in central Europe, Spain and China brought a shift in the primary interests of the administration from the domestic problems of the New Deal to the need for protection against the designs of the axis powers, the attention of congress and the public should be turned chiefly to the international situation. Not that the president abandoned his program of the New Deal. At the opening of the year 1937 he declared, in the language of John Paul Jones, "I have just begun to fight!" And a year later he told congress that his domestic reform measures were not to be "put away in a filing cabinet." Nevertheless, his own prime concern during the ensuing years was to supply the maximum of material aid to democracies at war until the nation was compelled by Japan's sneak attack at Pearl Harbor to abandon its futile efforts to remain neutral in the midst of an embattled world.

President Roosevelt was a breaker of precedents. In the summer of 1932 he flew to Chicago to accept his first nomination in a speech before the Democratic convention; and

"The Crash," an interpretation of one of the factors in the swing toward Republicanism in the congressional elections of 1946. Cartoon by Summers of the *Buffalo Evening News*

shortly after his inauguration he began a series of "fireside chats" or intimate talks to the U.S. people broadcast from his desk in the White House. In his capacity as chief of his party as well as head of the nation, he intervened by speeches and letters in the mid-term campaign of 1938 to compass the defeat of certain southern senators, like Millard E. Tydings of Maryland, Walter F. George of Georgia and Ellison Smith of South Carolina, who had been hostile to his policies, since the summer before he had proposed a drastic change in the composition of the supreme court. He was the first of United States presidents to run for a third consecutive term (1940), though twice in former years congress had passed resolutions condemning such a course as fraught with danger to the republican form of government. Before the United States entered the war he took the responsibility, without consulting congress, of transferring to Great Britain 50 overage destroyers in exchange for the lease of eight naval bases along the Atlantic coast from Newfoundland to British Guiana. And during the war he made distant trips to Morocco, Cairo, Tehran (Iran) and Yalta to confer in person with Churchill, Chiang Kai-shek and Stalin on the conduct of the war and the territorial and political arrangements which should follow. Shortly after his fourth inauguration in Jan. 1945 President Roosevelt died. There had been no thought of supplanting him in the Democratic convention of 1944, when the war was at its peak—the first time since 1864 that a presidential election was held with the country actually at war. The president's own preference was to have Vice-President Wallace again as his running mate, but Wallace was not acceptable to the conservative wing of the party, and Sen. Truman of Missouri was substituted for him.

Truman's elevation to the presidency, leaving the country for the seventh time in its history without a vice-president, revived the question (still unsettled) of the presidential succession. Congress had passed a law in 1792 providing that in case of vacancy in the offices of both president and vice-president, the presiding officer of the senate and after him the speaker of the house should succeed to the presidency. But since either of these men might be in opposition to the policy of the administration (as would have been the case had President Andrew Johnson's impeachment in 1868 been sustained by the senate), the law was changed in 1886, providing for the succession of the cabinet officers in the order of the creation of their departments. But, since the president appointed the cabinet members, this law enabled him to name his successor in case of his own death or resignation. Various suggestions were made for remedying the situation: that the senate should choose the new president; that he should be elected by a joint ballot of the two houses of congress; that the office should go to the man who had received the next highest vote to that of the successful candidate in the nominating convention; or that the convention be reconvened to name a president. Fortunately, the nation had never been confronted with a vacancy in both the presidency and the vice-presidency.

National Finance

The Budget and Accounting act of 1921 had set up a bureau of the budget and required the president to submit to congress at the time of his regular annual message in January a special budget message with estimates of the government's expenditures and receipts for the fiscal year beginning the following July 1. During the prosperous decade of the 1920s, the increase in the national income from some $50,000,000,000 in 1922 to $81,128,000,000 in

Harry S. Truman being sworn in as thirty-second president of the U.S. at 7:09 p.m., April 12, 1945. The oath was administered by Chief Justice Harlan F. Stone in the presence of members of the cabinet, a few hours after the death of Pres. Roosevelt

1929, and the rise in treasury receipts from $356,000,000 to over $600,000,000, resulted in surpluses which made possible not only a substantial reduction of the national debt of $22,000,000,000 incurred in World War I, but also a considerable abatement of income taxes.

But the great depression of the early 1930s brought distress to the treasury. The national income fell in 1932 to less than half its peak figure of three years before, and there began a series of deficits totalling $27,000,000,000 in the years from 1933 to 1939, an amount larger than the national debt at the end of World War I. President Roosevelt in these years deliberately resorted to the policy of "deficit financing"; that is, of pouring out large sums of government money for the relief of unemployment, the stimulation of the people's buying power, subsidies to the farmers, benefits to the aged and infirm, pensions for retired railroad men, public works on roads, dams, buildings and parks, aid to mortgaged-oppressed home owners, and many other projects designed to start the stalled wheels of production, raise wages and bring the national income back to the $80,000,000,000 level. State and local governments and private charities were unable to cope with the depression. The national government was the only agency competent to do so. Thus the balancing of the budget was deemed a minor consideration as compared with the rescue of the American people from their distress and their fear of the future.

The annual budget deficits of $3,000,000,000 or $4,000,000,000, however, incurred by the financing of the various measures of the New Deal (some of which were self-liquidating), were as a drop in the bucket when compared with the mounting deficits of the decade 1937–46. The expenses of preparedness for war, then of actual participation in war during the decade, were colossal. While the nation was still at peace, the national debt increased from $36,427,000,000 in 1937 to $57,938,000,000 at the end of 1941, and the deficit for the latter year was nearly $11,000,000,000. After Pearl Harbor the daily rate of the war expenses rose to $150,000,000 (or $1.15 for every man, woman and child in the country), while taxes were bringing in only $49,000,000 a day to the treasury. In 1944 the war was taking 45% of the national income of $116,000,000,000, whereas in the peak year of World War I the expenses were but 9.5% of the income of $56,700,000,000. And by 1945 the national debt had risen to $2,116 per capita. The total cost of the government (including its five major wars) from 1789 to 1940 was $154,000,000,000; the cost of World War II from Dec. 8, 1941, to Aug. 14, 1945, according to the research staff of the American university at Washington, D.C., was $317,600,000,000.[1] The 13 budgets of President Roosevelt totalled $461,000,000,000, or nearly four times the amount of the combined budgets of his 30 predecessors!

During this hectic decade, the statutory debt limit was steadily raised in the attempt to keep pace with the mounting national debt. In 1937 the limit was $45,000,000,000, and the debt $36,427,000,000. In Feb. 1941 the limit was raised to $65,000,000,000, and by the end of the year the debt of $57,938,000,000 was again close to the limit. Then, after the limit had been raised to $240,000,000,000 in 1944 and the debt had passed the $250,000,000,000 figure in 1945, congress gave up the Canute's attempt to stem the rising tide. On June 30, 1946, the debt, according to the figures of the treasury, was $275,000,000,000, an increase of more than 600% in a decade.

It had been President Wilson's policy in World War I to provide for one-third of the expenditures by taxation and two-thirds by loans. That ratio was almost exactly maintained; the treasury collected $11,280,000,000 in taxes, while the four Liberty Loans from May 1917 to Oct. 1918, together with the postwar Victory Loan of April 1919, brought in approximately $23,000,000,000. But, even with the great increase in the national wealth since President Wilson's day, the Roosevelt administration could not hope to make taxation pay anything like one-third of the staggering cost of World War II. It was not until the outbreak of war in Europe in 1939 and the consequent beginning of serious activity for the defense of the country that a policy of taxation was entered, one which grew more drastic each succeeding year.

In the revenue acts of 1940 congress, with the usual reluctance to increase taxes in a presidential election year, proceeded rather gingerly. It lowered the exemptions on individual incomes to add about 2,000,000 taxpayers to the list, imposed a 10% special defense tax to expire at the end of 1944, and moderately increased the surtaxes on the brackets from $600 to $100,000. In Sept. 1941, though Secretary Henry Morgenthau, Jr., had asked for a 33⅓% increase, the Revenue act made little change in the rates. But three months later the United States entered the war, and taxes began to soar. The act of Oct. 1942, designed to add $9,000,000,000 to the revenue, raised the normal income tax from 4% to 6%, imposed a special victory tax on all incomes above $624, and lifted the surtax from 6% to 13% on incomes of $2,000, and from 77% on incomes of $500,000 to 82% on incomes of $200,000. Whereas in 1940 there were only 7,437,307 taxable returns, it was estimated that 27,000,000 persons would pay on 1942 incomes and that 43,000,000 would pay the victory tax. A single man with an income of $2,000, who paid a tax of $20 in 1917, would now have to pay $287.50.

President Roosevelt urged that no one be allowed to have an income of more than $25,000 after taxes were paid. In his budget message of Jan. 1943 he asked for $16,000,000,000 in new taxes; but after this amount was cut to $10,500,000,000 by Secretary Morgenthau, congress in the autumn of 1943 granted hardly a fifth of the treasury's demand. Again an election year was approaching. President Roosevelt, breaking a precedent of 50 years, vetoed the revenue bill, calling it a bill for the relief of the "greedy." But congress immediately passed the bill over the veto. The revenue collected in the fiscal year ending June 30, 1945, was $46,500,000,000 as against $5,400,000,000 in 1940, and 37% of the people were paying income taxes in 1945 as compared with 11% in 1940.

With the end of the war in sight, the President's budget message of 1945 was the first since 1938 to call for a reduced revenue. And when the war ended in August the U.S. taxpayer hoped for a substantial relief. The Revenue act of Nov. 8, 1945, did, to be sure, remove some 12,000,000 persons in the lowest brackets from the list of taxpayers, and slightly reduced surtaxes, at the expense of some $5,000,000,000 to the treasury. But for two good reasons congress was unwilling to scale taxes down precipitously. First, because of continuing obligations and fixed charges, such as the interest on the enormous national debt, and second, because it regarded high taxes as the most efficient way of closing the "inflationary gap" created by the savings of $125,000,000,000 in the hands of the American people bidding for the scarce supplies of consumers' goods.

Besides taxation, the government resorted to loans for its revenue—for in neither of the World Wars did it adopt the expedient, so embarrassing in the American Revolution and the Civil War, of issuing unsupported paper currency; nor did it have to seek loans from foreign countries. Between Dec. 1942 and Dec. 1945 it floated eight enormous war loans, calling for a total of $106,000,000,000. The American people responded by subscriptions of $156,900,000,000, or nearly 150% of the quotas. Two out of every three persons in the United States subscribed to the popular Series E bonds, first issued in the Third War Loan of Sept. 1943. Whereas in World War I the average rate of interest on the war bonds had been 4.25%, the treasury financed World War II at the astonishingly low interest rate of 1.8%—a testimony both to the abounding wealth of the country and to the confidence of its citizens in their government. (*See* also BANKING; BUDGETS, NATIONAL; BUSINESS REVIEW; DEBTS, NATIONAL; INCOME AND PRODUCT; PRICES; STOCKS AND BONDS; TAXATION; WEALTH AND INCOME, DISTRIBUTION OF.)

Labour Relations

The decade 1937–46 was the most fertile in U.S. history in the development of labour relations. Realizing that the word "labour" in its general sense is synonymous with human effort exerted in any manner and that the men who toil on farms or experiment in scientific laboratories or teach in colleges or create forms of art or volumes of lit-

[1] Figures on the cost of the war varied. The secretary of the treasury reported the cost as of V-E day (May 8, 1945) as $275,900,000,000, while the *United States News* of Washington, D.C., set the cost from June 30, 1941, to Dec. 1946 at $341,491,000,000. The lower figure of the treasury report was due to the fact that it included only the actual monetary transactions of the treasury. The amount given in the text above is probably as near an estimate as could be made at the end of 1946.

erature are just as much "workers" as those who labour for wages in industrial plants, nevertheless we follow here the customary use of the terms "labourers" and "workers" to denote the great mass of wage earners who are dependent for their daily living upon the pay envelopes which they receive. Labour relations will be treated under three heads: the relations between labour and the government, between labour and management and between the organized groups of labour themselves.

The Intervention of Government.—Although in the 19th century several of the states had passed laws regulating labour conditions, such as the establishment of a minimum wage, the prohibition of child labour, the liability of the employer for injury to workers through defective machinery or the neglect of safety devices, it was not until the 20th century that the federal government began to intervene in labour relations by legislation. A separate department of labour was added to the cabinet in 1913, but for a score of years its chief function was the collection of statistics and the proffer of advice. The constitution gave the president no power to interfere in labour controversies, except when it was necessary (as in the case of the great railroad strike of 1877 or the Pullman strike of 1894) to call upon troops to preserve law and order; and the only authority that congress had to exercise control (indirect) over labour relations was its constitutional grant of power to regulate interstate commerce.

With the advent of the New Deal, however, the government began to interest itself seriously in the problems of labour. For it was a major policy of President Roosevelt to further industrial democracy by the relief of unemployment, the securing of a living wage and the promulgation of fair codes of dealing in business. Although the National Industrial Recovery act of June 1933 had been declared unconstitutional by unanimous decision of the supreme court on May 27, 1935, the latter year saw the passage of the National Labor Relations act, which compelled employers to bargain collectively with the labour unions. It was hailed by labour leaders as their Magna Carta, and was upheld by a 5 to 4 decision of the supreme court in April 1937. By that date the National Labor Relations board, set up to implement the act, had handled some 2,000 labour disputes and settled three-fourths of them amicably; and by July 1940 the board had a record of having settled by agreement more than 90% of the 28,000 cases handled.

A further step in the government's policy of advancing the interests of labour was the Fair Labor Standards act (popularly called the Wages and Hours act) of June 14, 1938.

The object of this act was "to put a floor under wages and a ceiling over hours." After the first year of its operation, wages were to be increased on a sliding scale from 25 cents to a minimum of 40 cents an hour, and hours were to be reduced from 44 to a maximum of 40 a week. Numerous classes were exempt from the act: farmers, seamen, transportation workers, domestic servants. Children under 16 were not to be employed in industries whose products entered into interstate commerce. Overtime work was to be paid 50% higher per hour. Though critics of the act complained that the government was overstepping its constitutional power in prescribing wages and hours, the act was not (like its predecessor, the NIRA) invalidated by the supreme court, now "liberalized" by Roosevelt appointments.

The Fair Labor Standards act was notable as the first act of congress in U.S. history for the federal regulation of wages and hours.

"Pep talks" by army and navy officials were frequently scheduled to help speed U.S. war production. These aircraft workers were on their lunch hour as they listened to an address by an army officer in 1942

With the year 1940 and its serious attention to the problems of national defense came a decided change in the relations of government and labour. The government itself became the largest employer of labour, allotting billions of dollars worth of contracts for war materials, erecting thousands of manufacturing plants and creating new agencies for the maintenance of uninterrupted production and industrial peace. It sought the co-operation of organized labour. Sidney Hillman, vice-president of the C.I.O., was appointed a member of the advisory defense committee and in Jan. 1941 was made assistant director of the Office of Production Management. On March 19, 1941, a National Defense Mediation board was set up, consisting of 11 members representing management, labour and the public.

The extraordinary number of strikes (five times as many in the first 7 months of 1941 as in the corresponding months of 1940) moved congress to consider measures of coercion. Rep. Leland Ford of California proposed a bill to make strikes in war industries punishable with 25 years of imprisonment and even with death in case the strike produced fatalities. In June, federal troops occupied the plant of the North American Aviation company at Inglewood, Calif., and in August the navy took over the federal shipyards plant at Kearny, N.J., both of which held large government contracts. During October and November John L. Lewis, president of the powerful miners' union, held over the head of the government the threat of a strike of 400,000 bituminous coal miners, and on Dec. 5, two days before the Japanese attack at Pearl Harbor, a strike of 100,000 railway workers was averted only by the direct appeal of President Roosevelt.

When war was declared, however, the tension between the government and labour was relieved. In a December conference representing 12 industrial leaders and 6 members each from the two great federations of labour, both labour and management agreed to refrain from strikes and lock-outs for the duration of the war, and recommended the establishment of a more efficient agency to replace the NDMB.

The latter was abolished by the president in Jan. 1942, and its functions were transferred to a National War Labor board headed by William H. Davis.

The no-strike pledge, however, was honoured more in the breach than in the observance. The "little steel" formula of July 1942 limited wage increases to 15% above the levels of Jan. 1, 1941; but labour contended that prices had risen by nearly 40%. Moreover, labour feared that the loss of overtime wages and the return of millions of veterans after the war would endanger its gains, and it resented the Smith-Connally act of 1943 which forbade strikes in essential war industries. As a result, there were three times as many strikes in 1943 as in the preceding year, and in the first five months of 1944 they increased by 42%. John L. Lewis, the stormy petrel of labour, led his 400,000 bituminous miners out of the pits three times in 1943, cutting the production of coal by over 30,000,000 tons. Encouraged by Lewis' success in securing wage increases, the five railroad brotherhoods voted by a majority of 97.5% to begin a strike on Dec. 30 which would have tied up all the roads of the country. It was not until President Roosevelt had put the railroads under army control that the brotherhoods called off the strike on the eve of the deadline.

These labour revolts roused great indignation (directed chiefly against Lewis) among the public and among U.S. soldiers abroad. The Germans and Japanese took advantage of them to broadcast to the world that the economic system of the United States had broken down in chaos. The last year of the war brought no pause in labour's demands for higher wages, which it declared industry could well afford to pay out of its enormous war profits. And when hostilities ceased, an epidemic of strikes broke out in the automobile, steel, oil, coal, lumber, traction, radio,

Pres. Truman reading a message announcing the end of the railroad strike on May 25, 1946. The news came as he addressed congress, asking for legislation to forbid strikes against the government

telegraph, electric and building industries. From Oct. to Dec. 1945 the NLRB conducted as many strike votes as it had during the first two years of the operation of the Wagner act of 1935.

President Truman tried to stem the tide by the appointment of fact-finding committees to investigate the merits of the workers' demands. Immediately after V-J day he had defended in a radio address his "deliberate refusal" to step in and "lay down the law to business and labour," declaring that we must "get away as quickly as possible from government controls and get back to the free operation of our competitive system" through collective bargaining. But now he extended "government controls" to the point of insisting that labour and management should abide by the decisions of the fact-finding commissions without question—a challenge which neither labour nor management was disposed to accept.

The dawn of the year 1946 saw major strikes in progress or threatened involving nearly 2,000,000 workers. No longer deterred by the plea of war emergency and determined to have what they believed to be their just share of the war profits, the men in a score of the leading industries of the country were making demands for wage increases which management declared would bankrupt their companies. The spring months of 1946 marked the peak of the government's embarrassment. President Truman's advisers were at sixes and sevens over the proper policy to pursue, and the Democratic congress, with the autumn elections approaching, was wary of alienating the labour vote, 72% of which had been cast for Democratic candidates in 1944. When the soft coal contract expired on March 31, Lewis again led his 400,000 miners out of the pits, demanding, besides wage increases, the levy of 10 cents a ton on all coal mined, to constitute a "health and welfare fund" of $60,000,000, to be administered by the union. As soft coal furnished 95% of the locomotive power and more than half the electrical and mechanical power of the country, the new strike threatened a general industrial paralysis. Steel production fell to 54% of capacity, 350,000 automobile workers were thrown out of employment, and train schedules were drastically cut.

At the same time the engineers and trainmen of the railroad brotherhoods refused arbitration, and a walkout of 200,000 maritime workers was set for June 15. On May 17 the president again took over the railroads, and a week later seized the mines; he declared that he would use the army, navy and coast guard to keep the ships running if the maritime strike materialized. Lewis was undisturbed by the government's action, repeating his defiant slogan of 1943: "You can't mine coal with bayonets." The critical labour situation roused President Truman to unwonted assertiveness. On May 24 he addressed the nation by radio: "This is a contest," he said, "between a small group of men and their government. The strike is a strike against the government. It must meet the challenge or confess its impotence."

When on May 29 Lewis signed a contract with the solid fuels administrator, Secretary of the Interior Julius A. Krug, granting substantial benefits to the union, the men went back to work.

But on Nov. 15, 1946, Lewis, for the eighth time since 1940, again precipitated a crisis. He declared that the government had not lived up to the agreement of May 29 and arbitrarily annulled the Krug-Lewis contract. He did not order the miners to leave the pits, for that would have made him liable to the penalties of the Smith-Connally act of 1943, which forbade the incitement to strikes in government-managed industries. Nevertheless, his action was a direct encouragement to the men to leave the mines on the ground of "no contract, no work." With the cold weather approaching and supplies of coal dangerously low, the 400,000 miners quit work. Factories were closed down, train schedules were cut, brownouts were ordered in 28 states, and appeals were made by governors and mayors for the utmost conservation of fuel. This time the government was determined to have a final showdown to test the power of one man to cripple the industries of the country and cause suffering for 140,000,000 people. A federal court order enjoined Lewis to cancel his annulment of the Krug-Lewis contract, and when he refused to obey, he was summoned to stand trial for contempt of court. On Nov. 25 he appeared in court, silent while his attorneys argued that the government's action violated the Clayton act of 1914 and the Norris-La Guardia act of 1932 forbidding injunctions in labour disputes. The government, on the other hand, maintained that the acts did not apply, since the case was not a labour dispute but a move of the government to protect the public welfare. Judge T. Alan Goldsborough on Dec. 4 imposed a fine of $10,000 on Lewis and $3,500,000 on the United Mine Workers union. With appeal to the supreme court pending, and the announcement that President Truman would address the nation on the radio on the evening of Dec. 8, Lewis surrendered on Dec. 7, and ordered the miners to return to work under the terms of the Lewis-Krug agreement of May 29. The country breathed a sigh of relief; the President cancelled his address. The crisis had been passed; but a government policy for the curbing of industrial strife was still to be found.

Management on the Defensive.—Labour-management relations could be summed up in one phrase: mutual defiance. It was not simply a question of wages. Beneath the conflict over dollars and cents there was a bitter battle of charges and countercharges as to the ultimate aims of the two parties. Labour leaders repeatedly accused the managers of plotting to "smash the unions," while the managers charged labour with the presumption to dictate to them how to run their own businesses. A new type of strike (imported from France) was introduced in 1937 by the newly created Committee for Industrial Organization headed by Lewis. This was the "sit-down" strike, in which the men quit work but intrenched themselves in the factories to prevent strikebreakers from taking their places. Although it was a case of trespassing on the property of the owners, Secretary of Labour Frances Perkins hesitated to condemn the sit-down strike as illegal, and Governor Frank Murphy of Michigan refused to call out troops to evict the strikers. The sit-down strikes soon died down; but they left a wariness in the minds of the owners which increased their opposition to organized labour. Conferences called to compose the strife ended in failure.

With U.S. entrance into World War II, the unions pressed their demands for the closed shop, which was anathema to the employers, and for the participation of labour in the management of industry. For example, Walter Reuther of the United Automobile Workers, largest C.I.O. union, urged that his union be authorized to make a survey of the industry and submit a plan for its conversion into war production. Better relations between labour and industry were promised when, at the invitation of Eric Johnston, president of the United States Chamber of Commerce, the president of the American Federation of Labor (William Green) and the president of the C.I.O. (Philip Murray) met Johnston at Washington late in July 1942

"Back to Normal." Shoemaker of the *Chicago Daily News* painted with dry humour the postwar continuation of friction between labour and management at Montgomery Ward & Co.

and agreed to work together for increased production and sustained employment. But fair words were not enough. The year 1943 saw an epidemic of strikes in essential war industries like steel, coal and rubber, which moved congress to pass (over the president's veto) the Smith-Connally bill outlawing strikes in war industry plants.

The strife between labour and management continued unabated during the war years, and grew still more intense after V-J day. President Truman called a conference in Washington on Nov. 5, 1945, but it ended in the usual deadlock. Charles Edward Wilson and Alfred P. Sloan, Jr., of the General Motors corporation published a large-type advertisement in the metropolitan papers on Dec. 31, declaring that if business were to surrender responsibility for its management to any government agency or labour union it would mean the death of the U.S. system of competitive enterprise. "General Motors," they said, "will not assume the role of initiating such a policy." Both management and labour protested that they had no intention of trespassing on the other's rights and privileges.

Management, realizing that the time had passed when it alone could dictate rates of pay and hours of labour, accepted the principle of collective bargaining as prescribed by the Wagner act of 1935; and labour leaders from Lewis down asserted that they were not aiming to deprive management of its proper functions. Nevertheless, the record showed an increasing encroachment of the unions on the domain of management. They had made demands for the unionization of foremen, for union participation in company policies, for union-controlled benefit funds at industry's expense, and for access to company balance-sheets. Organized labour, with some 15,000,000 of the 58,000,000 workers enrolled in its ranks, and with large sums of money in its treasuries, showed no disposition to relax its drive for an equal, if not a decisive, voice in the conduct of U.S. business.

Labour *vs.* Labour.—In the house of labour itself, dissension was rife all through the decade. For 50 years the A.F. of L. had been the dominating labour organization, comprising all the major unions except the railroad brotherhoods and the Western Federation of Miners. Green, president since 1924, had followed the conservative policy of his predecessor Samuel Gompers, eschewing political action and depending wholly on economic bargaining to secure benefits for the workers. But a serious split in the A.F. of L. came in 1937, when ten unions, expelled from the federation for noncompliance with the rules, proceeded to form the Committee on Industrial Organization (later renamed Congress of Industrial Organizations) under the leadership of Lewis. As against the "horizontal" type of craft unions of the A.F. of L., the C.I.O. adopted the "vertical" or mass type, organizing the workers, both skilled and unskilled, in any one industry into one big union.

The more democratic and aggressive C.I.O. grew by leaps and bounds, drawing many unions from the A.F. of L., until by the end of the decade the organized workers of the country were almost equally divided between the two great federations. Naturally, the rivalry between them was intense and the disputes over membership recruiting and spheres of jurisdiction were constant. The A.F. of L. accused the C.I.O. of harbouring communists in its ranks and frowned on the manoeuvres of its Political Action committee under the vigorous leadership of Sidney Hillman. Those in favour of unity argued that if the labour organizations had stopped quarrelling and presented a united front, as President Roosevelt urged them to do, they might have figured prominently in governmental agencies or even had representation in the cabinet, like the labourites Ernest Bevin, Clement Attlee and Herbert Morrison in Churchill's British cabinet.

Shortly after Pearl Harbor Lewis did, indeed, write to Philip Murray (who had succeeded him as president of the C.I.O.) and Green proposing a union of the two federations, but on the impossible condition that the two presidents step out and leave him to compose a new slate of officers. The brash proposal only widened the rift between the organizations, and Murray retorted in a talk to the Press club in Washington a few days later: "Mr. Lewis is hell-bent on creating national confusion and national disunity." Management, too, tried to heal the breach. In March 1945, when the Allies were closing in on the retreating nazi armies, Eric Johnston and Henry Kaiser met with Murray and Green and signed a labour-management charter for industrial peace. President Roosevelt sent his congratulations, but Lewis sneered at the charter as a fake, and Ira Mosher, president of the National Manufacturers association, called it a collection of "generalities" and rebuked Johnston for publishing it at just the moment when management was planning new moves for the curbing of the unions. (*See* also EMPLOYMENT; LABOUR UNIONS; RELIEF; SOCIAL SECURITY; STRIKES AND LOCK-OUTS; WAGES AND HOURS.)

The Farmers' Fortunes

Agriculture had been the Cinderella of the U.S. economic household. In the era of industrial expansion which followed the Civil War, the manufacturer enjoyed the protection of high tariffs, the banker profited by both the interest on government bonds and the loans of currency based on them, the railroad builders were granted immense blocks of public land and advances of millions of dollars for construction; coastwise and internal shipping was restricted to vessels of U.S. registry, and labour was safeguarded against the competition of the low wages which prevailed in the European countries. But the farmer, aside from his free homestead, enjoyed no government favours. As a pioneer he was in debt for his equipment. His mortgaged land bore heavy interest charges. He suffered under what he believed to be excessive railroad and elevator rates. He was obliged to sell his crops at prices determined by world markets, while paying for his tools and fencing and building materials in a sellers' market, protected by the tariff. U.S.-made plows and reapers were actually sold in Canada and Europe at prices lower than those charged to the U.S. farmer. The "agrarian crusades" of the Grangers in the 1870s and the Populists in the 1890s against these grievances were met with a scornful hostility by the moneyed interests of the east and with uninformed indifference on the part of the government at Washington.

True, World War I had brought a moment of prosperity to the farmer, with wheat at $2.20 a bushel; but when the war was over and the farms of Europe were again in full production, his plight was worse than before. In the flush period he had extended his acreage to land purchased at a price too high for its crop values and bought on credit farm equipment which left him deeper in debt. He had no part in the "boom" of the 1920s. And if the "farm bloc" did arouse congress to the seriousness of the agricultural situation and secure the appointment of a Federal Farm board and the passage of a few acts ostensibly for farm relief, the latter were less in the nature of any direct aid by the government than of expedients to "help the farmer borrow himself out of debt." Every attempt of the farm bloc to get effective federal aid for agriculture, like the McNary-Haugen bills, met with failure. When the great depression came, the farmer's plight was so desperate that he was burning his corn for fuel, pouring his milk into the streets and meeting with shotguns the sheriff who arrived to sell his foreclosed property.

In striking contrast to the apathy of the Coolidge and Hoover administrations toward the farm problem, President Roosevelt, a city-born aristocrat (both Coolidge and Hoover were born on a farm), made effective federal farm relief a major aim of his administration. To bring farm prices up to the level of the years 1909–14 was the purpose of the Agricultural Adjustment act of 1933, which provided government subsidies for farmers who agreed to eliminate surplus production of certain enumerated commodities like grain, cotton and hogs. The act was annulled by the supreme court in Jan. 1936, a majority of six justices (against Stone, Brandeis and Cardozo) holding that congress had no power to regulate agricultural production or to levy a tax on the processing of raw agricultural products to provide funds for subsidies to the farmers.

Undeterred by this setback, the advocates of farm relief got through congress a second Agricultural Adjustment act in Feb. 1938, which eliminated the objectionable tax provision and which Secretary of Agriculture Wallace declared to be the most beneficent piece of legislation ever passed for the benefit of the farmer. It was an elaborate act of more than 130 pages, inviting the raisers of surplus producing crops like cotton, wheat, corn, tobacco and rice, to agree by plebiscites to limit their production to quotas prescribed by the administrative agency, in return for subsidies from the government. It contained also provisions for soil conservation and for the maintenance of what Secretary Wallace called "an ever normal granary": the application of Joseph's plan in Egypt to balance the poor yields of bad seasons with the stored surpluses of the good seasons. The government, through the Commodity Credit corporation, was authorized to extend loans on stored surpluses and even, through the Surplus Commodities corporation, to purchase surpluses to distribute to persons on relief. In the fiscal year 1938 the latter agency purchased $47,000,000 of such products to help feed an average of 2,000,000 needy families a month.

Under the new act the situation of the farmers was greatly improved. Whereas in 1860, agriculture had represented one-half the national wealth and had enjoyed nearly a third of the national income, its share of the country's wealth had dropped to 7% in 1933, and its income had declined to a paltry $4,300,000,000. In 1938, however, in spite of the floods and droughts of 1934 and 1936, the farm income rose to $8,880,000,000. Prices for farm products had increased from an index of 65 (based on the figures for 1910–14) in 1932 to 121, and there were over 10,000 farmers' co-operatives with a membership of 3,270,000 doing a yearly business of over $2,500,000,000.

There were, to be sure, two large drawbacks. The first was the burden of farm mortgages, which had risen to more than $7,000,000,000 and on which high charges were made for interest and renewals. Secondly, there was the growing evil of farm tenancy. About 40% of U.S. farmers were landless tenants or sharecroppers, without the incentive to continuous effort for improved operation which comes from actual possession of the land. The Bankhead-Jones act of 1937 provided a measure of relief by loans through the Federal Farm Security administration of some $10,000,000 to 1,840 landless farmers; but it was only a drop in the bucket. Tenancy increased steadily, until by 1940, out of the 32,000,000 people living on farms, 13,000,000 were landless. Though all parts of the country were plagued by farm tenancy, it was in the southern states that the evil was prevalent; President Roosevelt spoke of the agricultural situation of the south as the U.S. number one problem. In 1940, the government held first mortgages representing $40,000,000 loaned to over 13,000 tenants for purchases of land, and had in storage 18,000,000 bales of cotton.

War and Prosperity.—The effects of World War II on agriculture, as on every phase of life, were revolutionary. By 1940, grain fields in Europe and Asia were devastated by bomb craters and rolling tanks; animals were slaughtered by the millions; and countless peasants were driven into an exile of starvation. The United States, as yet uncommitted to the struggle, had an overabundance of food of all kinds; the years from 1937 to 1940 had seen an increase of 27% in crop production (because of favourable weather and improved farm machinery), in spite of a reduction in farm acreage and farm labourers. President Roosevelt recommended an appropriation of $50,000,000 to feed destitute people in Europe, as after World War I; but objection to this humanitarian proposal was voiced on the ground that whatever food was sent to the countries under Hitler's control would probably be seized by the nazis.

Soon after the meeting of congress in Jan. 1941, however, a bill was introduced into the house authorizing the shipment of unlimited supplies of food, as well as of munitions, tanks, lorries and other military equipment. After a heated debate in congress, the lend-lease bill was passed and signed by President Roosevelt. The United States undertook to furnish Great Britain during the ensuing year 5,000,000,000 lb. of processed milk, 1,500,000,000 lb. of pork and lard, 500,000 dozen eggs, and millions of pounds of poultry. Up to 1946, the value of agricultural products allocated to a score of countries by lend-lease reached the huge sum of $5,426,000,000. At that, only about 7% of the nation's food was so used, while 80%

was consumed by the civilian population at home and 13% by the U.S. armed forces.

Farm prices reached a peak in the midsummer of 1945, when wheat sold at $1.51 a bushel as against 65 cents in Oct. 1940, corn at $1.13 as against 59 cents, and cotton at 22.3 cents a pound as against 9.3 cents. The problem was not low prices but the lack of manpower and machinery for the farmer. Though local draft boards were asked to exempt agricultural labourers as far as possible, the farms lost some 2,000,000 workers who either joined the armed forces or went into war industries, and whose place was only partially filled by women and children, and labour imported from Mexico. A second embarrassment for agriculture was the shortage of farm machinery, caused by the demands of the factories for steel and other metals, which resulted in a reduction of about 20% in the allotment for tractors, reapers and combines. For all that, in the year 1943, a farm population 10% less than that of 1918 produced 50% more food on 2% fewer acres. "Food will win the war and write the peace" was the slogan of Secretary of Agriculture Claude Wickard.

From a figure of about $10,000,000,000 a year in the period 1936–41, the farm income rose to $24,000,000,000 by 1946. But this gross income was cut down to a net of $13,000,000,000 by the increased cost of fertilizer, labour and machinery. However, it meant a per capita income of more than $1,500 a year for the farmer, as against an average of $550 in the period 1936–41. The burden of farm mortgage debt was steadily reduced, until at the close of 1945 it was only half the peak figure of $10,780,000,000 of 20 years earlier, while the department of agriculture estimated that the total assets of the farms had increased from $53,700,000,000 in 1940 to $82,800,000,000 in 1945.

In an address at New York city, Dec. 6, 1945, the new Secretary of Agriculture, Clinton P. Anderson, predicted a bright future for the farmer. The production of meat, he said, in the first quarter of 1946 would be sufficient to leave a balance of 150 lb. per capita for domestic consumption, after feeding U.S. occupation troops abroad and contributing the U.S. quota to U.N.R.R.A. But neither Secretary Anderson nor anyone else could foresee the shortages in food supplies which would be created during the year by a combination of circumstances. Trucking strikes prevented the delivery of many common articles of daily consumption to the groceries; maritime strikes stopped the unloading of ships containing millions of pounds of sugar. The end of ceiling prices with the expiration of the OPA controls on June 30, 1946, led to an expansion of black market operations, until modified controls were imposed a few weeks later, only to be taken off again in October, first from meat and then from all other commodities except sugar and rents. There were more cattle, sheep and hogs in the country than ever before, but they were withheld from the market in speculative anticipation of higher prices. Thousands of butcher shops were closed, or had no meat for customers who were unwilling to pay the exorbitant black market prices. The public pressure for relief became so strong that President Truman himself made the supply of meat at reasonable prices a major item of the government agenda in the autumn of 1946 and the subject of a nation-wide address on the radio. As the year drew to a close there was promise that the abnormalities in supply and demand would be remedied and that the abundant crops and the abounding herds of livestock would ensure the country a stabilized and sufficient diet for all its people. (*See* AGRICULTURE; also articles on separate crops and agricultural products.)

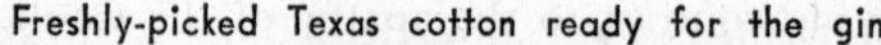
Freshly-picked Texas cotton ready for the gin

Progress in Transportation

At the beginning of the decade 1937–46, U.S. railroads were in a precarious situation. Only 13% of them showed a profit, and 30% of the mileage was in the hands of receivers. The average price of railroad bonds had fallen from $95.50 in 1930 to $55.90, and stocks from $91.56 to $26.06. Billions of dollars were needed for new equipment. The competition of buses, trucks, pipe lines and planes was causing heavy inroads on freight and passenger service. Taxes and wages were rising faster than revenues. To meet the crisis, the railroads made heroic efforts. Mammoth locomotives were built to haul long trains of freight at express speed. Road after road put into service luxury trains and comfortable overnight coach trains like the New York Central's "Pacemaker" and the Pennsylvania's "Pathfinder," which carried thousands of people for whom lower fares were more important than lower berths. In spite of all their efforts, however, the railroads were hardly better off at the beginning of the 1940s than they had been three years before. They were realizing only 2.25% on their investment.

It was the U.S. preparation for and participation in World War II that offered the roads the opportunity for unexampled prosperity and put on them a load which it hardly seemed possible for their depleted resources to bear. Thousands of tons of food and war material had to be brought daily to camps and ports of shipment. Millions of troops had to be moved. The danger of submarines on the Atlantic coast threw upon the railroads the transportation of vast quantities of material which had gone by water, and the war in the Pacific required 30% of U.S. rail facilities to service the ports of the west coast, as against 7% in World War I. On Dec. 18, 1941, President Roosevelt created the Office of Defense Transportation under Joseph B. Eastman to act with the chief railroad heads in co-ordinating transportation policies. The government did not take over the roads, as it had done (with rather unsatisfactory results) in World War I. Instead, the managers worked in close co-operation with Eastman's aides in Washington, D.C., and other cities of the country. With the flow of goods for lend-lease and U.N.R.R.A., with one-half the Pullman and one-third the coach accommodations needed for the movement of troops, the people were urged to refrain from unnecessary travel and, except for commuters' short distances, civilian train schedules were drastically cut.

Naturally, the rising cost of living brought demands from the railroad workers for increased wages. Three times after U.S. entrance into the war, the nation's vital transportation system was threatened by railroad strikes. A nation-wide strike was set for Dec. 7, 1941, on a demand for a 30% rise in wages; but a settlement was made just prior to the attack on Pearl Harbor, by an increase of 76 cents an hour, at an estimated cost of $300,000,000 to the roads. A second and more serious crisis came in the second week of Dec. 1943, when the workers voted by a majority of 97.7% to strike for a 30% rise. On Dec. 19 President Roosevelt called in conference the representatives of the five railroad brotherhoods and the carriers, after having two days before ordered the secretary of war to take over the roads. It was not until Christmas Eve that the brotherhoods called off what President Roosevelt warned was a strike against the government. The roads were returned to the owners the next month.

The third and most serious problem arose in the spring of 1946. With the war over, the appeal to patriotism lost much of its force. In the welter of strikes that characterized the early months of the year, that of the railroad trainmen and the locomotive engineers, with a combined membership of 293,000, threatened to be even more crippling to the nation's industries than those in steel, motors or coal. After all the steps provided in the Railway act of 1926 had failed to bring agreement, the strike, tying up the 230,000 miles of rail in the country, began on May 23. President Truman immediately turned the railroads over to Col. J. Monroe Johnson (who had succeeded Eastman as ODT director), and the next evening spoke to the nation on the air. "This is a contest," he said, "between a small group of men and their Government. . . . The Government is challenged as seldom before in our history. It must meet the challenge or confess its impotence. If sufficient workers to operate the trains have not returned by 4 P.M. tomorrow . . . I shall ask our armed forces to furnish protection to every man who heeds the call of his country in this hour of need." The president then went before a joint session of congress to reiterate his strong stand. As he was speaking a message was handed to him which he read to the cheering members. The brotherhoods had accepted the 18½ cents an hour raise which had been agreed on in the steel and motor industries.

Merchant Marine.—The development of the U.S. merchant marine during the decade was well nigh incredible. In 1937, only 22% of U.S. imports and 36% of U.S. exports were carried in U.S. ships. A maritime commission set up the previous year planned a 10-year program for the construction of 50 ships a year, purchased the Dollar Line, and opened schools for the training of marines. The "Good Neighbour" fleet of fine vessels (the "Argentine," the "Brazil" and the "Chile") was built, and the "America," largest merchant ship ever constructed in U.S. yards, was christened by Mrs. Roosevelt in Dec. 1939.

The outbreak of World War II, however, brought embarrassment to the merchant marine. The Neutrality act of Nov. 1939 barred U.S. ships from belligerent ports and combat areas, shutting them out of English, French, Dutch, German and Belgian harbours. Submarine attacks raised insurance rates sharply and took a toll of nearly 4,000,000 tons of U.S. shipping during the war. At the peak of the danger in 1942, some 500 German submarines were destroying merchant vessels faster than they were being built.

With the repeal of the Neutrality act on Nov. 17, 1941, and the threat of war with Japan impending, there was a remarkable spurt of energy in U.S. shipyards. President Roosevelt called for the construction of 8,000,000 tons in 1942 and 16,000,000 tons in 1943; and both these figures were exceeded. Shipyards had launched 28 cargo ships in the year 1939; in the single month of Dec. 1943 they launched 208. About 30% of U.S. cargo space in 1943 was devoted to lend-lease shipments, which reached a total of $14,000,000,000 in July of that year. When the war ended, the United States had a merchant tonnage of some 50,000,000, by far the largest in the world. It had grown from 17% of the Allied tonnage in 1940 to over 60% in 1945; at the peak of building, 700,000 workers (14% women) were employed in shipyards. Great Britain, starting in 1939 with double the tonnage of the United States, was able during the war to construct only 9,300,000 tons against submarine losses of 11,700,000 tons; while new U.S. construction of 38,250,000 tons offset U.S. losses of 3,800,000, ten-fold. As a result, on Jan. 1, 1946, the nation had a net gain of 34,400,000 tons against Great Britain's loss of 2,400,000 tons.

A report on wartime trade released by the U.S. Chamber

of Commerce on Aug. 19, 1946, showed that U.S. exports during the war (not including supplies for armed forces abroad) reached a total of $45,000,000,000—more than the combined value of exports during the 14 previous years. Nearly three-fourths of the sum represented lend-lease exports to the Allies. However, there was a serious imbalance between exports and imports. The latter amounted to only $4,300,000,000, compared with an export figure of some $10,000,000,000.

Airlines.—The progress of civil aviation during the decade was also phenomenal. From a network of 2,000 miles in 1936, the routes grew steadily until they covered not only the United States and South America, but extended to the far parts of the world. Pan American Airways took the lead. In the spring of 1939, P.A.A. clippers inaugurated a regular transatlantic service for passengers and mail, which was soon extended to Alaska, South America and the far east. The next year P.A.A. flew 69,500 miles of routes.

When the war came, the company was busy ferrying bombers across the Atlantic to Africa, and then on to Cairo and over the Indian ocean to Burma and China. Naturally, military aviation had priority during the war, but, limited as it was in plane construction, civil aviation by no means withdrew from the field. On the contrary, the depredations of submarines on merchant shipping made air service the more necessary. By the end of 1944, P.A.A. was linked to 61 countries and during that year it carried more than 3,500,000 passengers.

La Guardia field on Flushing bay, Long Island, was opened on Dec. 2, 1939, and before the end of the year was handling 150 flights a day. Congress recommended an appropriation of $435,000,000 for the construction of 3,500 airports and the training of 20,000 young pilots. Before the war was over, work was begun on the Idlewild field on Jamaica bay, designed to be the "air hub of the world," with an area eight times that of La Guardia field and a capacity of 1,000 flights a day on its 13 mi. of runways.

On June 23, 1938, the government created a Civil Aeronautics authority to function in somewhat the same way as the ICC did in the case of the railroads. Some of the railroad magnates, regarding the airways as a serious competitor, advocated putting the CAA under the authority of the ICC; but the airways managers resisted this, maintaining that their lines were supplementary to rather than competitive with the railroads, since they carried only lighter and perishable freight which called for speedy delivery.

For six weeks in Nov. and Dec. 1944 an International Civil Aviation congress, representing 52 nations, sat at Chicago to devise rules to govern the "freedom of the air." A majority of the nations accepted the articles which resulted from the conference: namely, the abolition of closed air zones, the right of free passage across national boundaries, the privilege of taking on or discharging freight at intermediate points on a flight, and many other provisions designed to make the air as free as the seas.

On V-J day, the U.S. aircraft industry was the biggest industry in the world, chiefly, of course, because of the enormous production of military planes, the 150,000th of which was completed on the second anniversary of Pearl Harbor. But with the close of the war and the rapid cancellation of aircraft contracts by the army and navy, civil aviation was in a position to make giant strides and to profit by the remarkable inventions made during the war for the increase of speed and safety. In Oct. 1945 priorities for air travel were abolished. (*See* also AVIATION, CIVIL; RAILROADS; SHIPPING, MERCHANT MARINE.)

The Armed Forces

Partly as a result of the U.S. heritage of distrust of standing armies and partly because of a sense of security in isolation from the turmoil of the old world, the weight of U.S. public opinion and governmental policy had been traditionally opposed to military preparedness. In every war in which the nation had been involved, the same pattern had been followed: a belated and feverish effort to meet the danger after it had become acute, and a rapid demobilization of the armed forces after the war was over. The situation in respect to World War II conformed to type.

The active army forces in 1938 comprised 183,500 men, or 0.3% of the population, as compared with 17.6% in Italy and 14.2% in France. President Roosevelt was in advance of public sentiment in realizing the danger of the aggression of the Berlin-Rome-Tokyo axis. Not only did he make personal appeals to the dictators to stay their course of conquest, but he sought to alert congress and the U.S. people to the necessity for military and industrial preparedness.

When Hitler launched his blitzkrieg in the spring of 1940, rapidly subduing Denmark, Norway, the Netherlands and Belgium, a Council of National Defense was set up on May 28, consisting of six cabinet members and seven advisers, patterned after the council of 1916. But instead of following the example of President Wilson in making Bernard Baruch an industrial "czar," the administration entrusted the task of industrial preparedness to a board called the Office of Production Management, consisting of William S. Knudsen, Sidney Hillman and Secretaries Henry Stimson (war) and Franklin Knox (navy).

Ever since World War I the question of compulsory military training had been under discussion; but it took the tragic events of the summer of 1940 to bring it into existence. In Sept. 1938 (the month of Munich) a Gallup poll revealed that only 37% of the respondents favoured universal military training; but when France fell in June 1940, leaving Great Britain alone to withstand Hitler in the west, the figure rose to 64%. On Sept. 16, 1940, President Roosevelt signed the Burke-Cochran Selective Training and Service act.

The procedure of registration and induction followed closely the precedent of 1917. On Oct. 16 some 16,000,000 men between the ages of 21 and 36 were registered at 125,000 centres. Twelve days later Secretary Stimson, blindfolded, drew the first number (158) from the same glass bowl that had been used in 1917. The law divided the inductees into a number of classes ranging from those wholly fit for military service (I-A) to those exempt, as ministers or theological students (IV-D) and those disqualified by physical or moral defects (IV-F). By June 1941 there were 1,500,000 men in the camps, and congress authorized (by a vote of 203 to 202 in the house) extension of the law for two and a half years. It had already, in March, voted an appropriation of $4,000,000,000 for an army of 4,000,000.

After the United States entered the war in Dec. 1941, the armed forces increased by leaps and bounds, until on V-J day the army numbered more than 8,000,000 men, and the 3,866,000 in the navy and the marines and the 2,250,000 in the air force brought the total military strength up to more than 14,000,000. Three years of fighting from the frozen Aleutians to the hot sands of Africa and the steaming jungles of the Pacific islands, and from the coast of

Normandy to the heart of Germany had made the soldiers eager to get back to their wives and families. Demobilization brought the army down to less than 2,500,000 men by April 1, 1946, distributed in the Pacific area, Germany, Austria, and the countries of the middle and far east.

Presidents Roosevelt and Truman had committed the United States at Yalta and Potsdam to the policy of keeping sufficient troops in the conquered countries to prevent any resurgence of aggression and guarantee the establishments of governments chosen by the people in fair elections. But U.S. soldiers abroad had no relish for this job of policing after the war was over. In spite of the repeated pleas of Secretary of War Robert Patterson and Chief of Staff General Dwight Eisenhower, voluntary enlistments fell short of the numbers needed for the replacement of the men who had earned their discharge. It was estimated that a monthly quota of 35,000 to 40,000 recruits would be necessary to bring the army to an anticipated strength of 1,070,000 in July 1947. But the enlistments for the first two weeks of Nov. 1946 were only 9,295. Moreover, the 272,000 volunteers who enlisted for a year or 18 months would be lost to the army by July 1947.

The Navy.—The expansion of the navy, the branch of the service closest to the heart of President Roosevelt, kept pace with that of the army during the decade. From his boyhood, Roosevelt had been passionately fond of everything connected with the sea, and his seven years as assistant secretary of the navy in Wilson's cabinet had made him familiar with naval resources and problems. Large appropriations had been made in the Wilson administration for the building of "a navy second to none in the world"; but with the end of World War I, interest shifted to plans for disarmament. The United States had led the way in the Washington conference of 1921 by scrapping a large tonnage of war vessels already building or authorized. The Harding-Coolidge-Hoover administrations had given no encouragement to naval expansion; and when Roosevelt acceded to the presidency the economic condition of the country was so distressing that his first term was necessarily devoted to the relief and rehabilitation measures of the New Deal. The return of fairly stable conditions at home coincided with the threatening aspects of nazi and Japanese aggression in Europe and the far east. From then on, U.S. military and economic preparedness to thwart Hitler and his satellites became the president's major concern. "No combination of the dictator countries of Europe and Asia," he declared in his Columbus day address of 1940, "will stop the help we are giving to almost the last free people (the British) now fighting to hold them at bay."

There was little expectation that U.S. soldiers would be called upon to fight overseas, but it was the task of the navy to be alert in the protection of U.S. interests all over the globe. In his budget message of Jan. 1938 the president asked for a naval appropriation of $1,000,000,000, or double that of the previous year; in May he signed a bill providing for an expenditure of $1,126,546,000 for the increase of naval construction and personnel over a period of ten years. By the end of 1939, the nation had already passed its nearest competitor, Great Britain, in battleships, destroyers and submarines. The 674 fighting ships of 1937 had grown to 2,674 by 1943, and at the end of 1945 the nation had over 15,000 war craft of all types—a navy larger than the combined navies of the rest of the world. Some 2,200,000 tons of war vessels had been built in the three years from 1942 to 1945; and the navy personnel, including the marine corps and the coast guard, totalled nearly 4,000,000 men.

On signing the naval bill of 1938, President Roosevelt

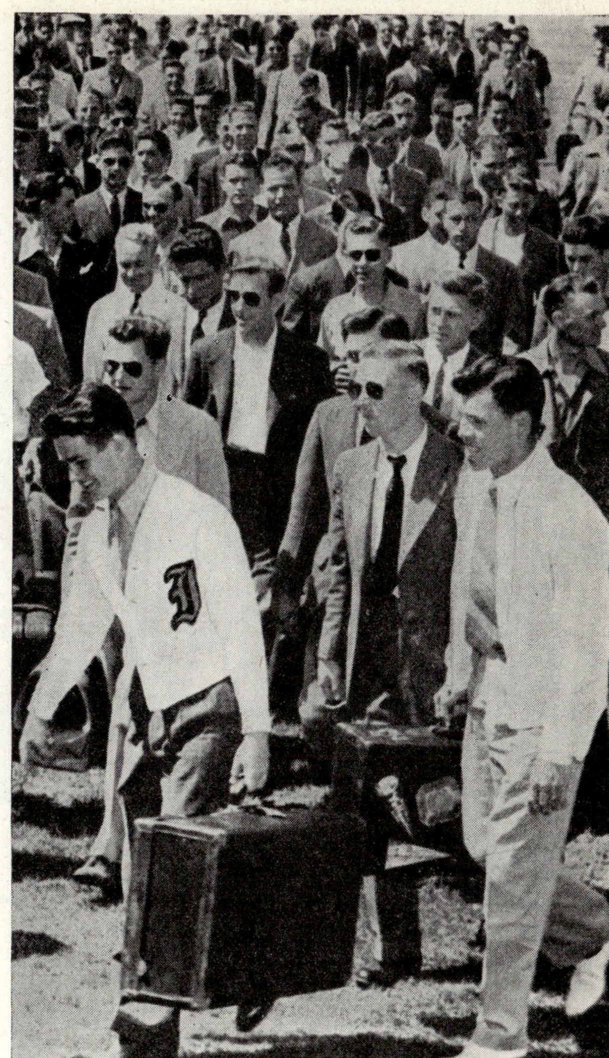

Air cadets volunteering for pilot service with the U.S.A.A.F. are shown arriving at Randolph field, Tex., three months before the signing of the Selective Training and Service act in 1940

had said that any potential enemy should be kept many hundreds of miles from U.S. shores. Hence the drive to secure naval bases within what were held to be U.S. defense areas. In Sept. 1940 the president secured from Great Britain a 99-year lease of eight such bases along the Atlantic coast from Newfoundland to British Guiana in exchange for 50 over-age destroyers. In April and July 1941, U.S. forces occupied Greenland and Iceland, thus extending the "defense area" far out to sea. After sinking eight U.S. freighters, German submarines began in Sept. 1941 to attack U.S. war vessels, though the nation was still at peace. The destroyer "Kearny" was hit on Oct. 11 and 11 of her crew were killed. A few days later the "Reuben Jones" was sunk off the coast of Ireland with the loss of 76 men. President Roosevelt thereupon announced in his Navy day address of Oct. 27 that he had given the navy orders to "shoot at sight" at any submarine appearing in U.S. defense waters.

In the surprise attack of the Japanese at Pearl Harbor (Dec. 7, 1941), the U.S. navy suffered the greatest losses in its history: two battleships, three destroyers, a training ship and a mine-layer sunk, with nearly 3,000 casualties. This was followed by the rapid seizure of Wake, Guam and the Philippines by the Japanese; and the stage was set for the long hard struggle of the U.S. navy and marines to drive

Enthusiastic reception for Wendell L. Willkie in downtown Chicago, Ill., during his campaign as Republican presidential candidate in 1940

the Japanese step by step from their fortified atolls in the Pacific, until the atomic bombs dropped on Hiroshima and Nagasaki compelled surrender on board the battleship "Missouri" in Tokyo harbour on Sept. 2, 1945.

Air Force.—The third major arm in the war was the air force. Here again, as in the case of tanks, ships and guns, almost incredible expansion was characteristic of the decade. In 1940 less than 1,000 military planes a month were being built; but during the war years, with appropriations from congress rising from a few hundred million to several billions of dollars, construction was accelerated, new bases were established, tens of thousands of pilots and mechanics were trained, and enormous improvements were made in the speed, range, carrying capacity and safety devices of all types—bombing, fighting, pursuit, patrol and transport planes. By V-J day, the army air force was at a peak of more than 80,000 planes, with a total personnel of 2,400,000 (more than the entire armed forces in World War I). Naval planes had increased from less than 2,000 to over 20,000.

In the 1920s, General William Mitchell had resigned from the air corps because his views on the supremacy of air power over naval power were not approved by the government. When such tragedies as Pearl Harbor and the sinking of the British ships "Renown" and "Repulse" off Malaya showed the vulnerability of the battleship to aerial attack, the contention of General Mitchell was revived, notably by Alexander P. Seversky in his *Victory Through Air Power*.

Still the naval authorities held to the view that the battleship was not an obsolete fighting unit.

Merger?—Another controversy concerned the organization of the armed forces. Should there be a single cabinet department of national defense, combining army, navy and air services? The army and the administration generally favoured the plan; but the navy opposed it, insisting on keeping its air force separate from that of the army. Naval officers pointed to the difference in function between the two services, and expressed fear that the merger would result in subordination of the lesser naval air force to the stronger army one. A poll of over 8,000 citizens, conducted by the *Saturday Evening Post* in the autumn of 1946, showed 95.4% answering in the affirmative the question: "Do you believe that we should maintain a military force during peacetime as an aid to insuring peace?" (*See* also Aviation, Military; Coast Guard, U.S.; Marine Corps, U.S.; National Guard, U.S.; Navies of the World; Submarine Warfare; World War II.)

Social Security

Though the preamble to the constitution declared one of the government's purposes to be "to promote the general welfare," it was not until the 20th century that the federal government took any steps to implement this recommendation by giving aid to the great number of its citizens who were unable to find employment or were handicapped by poverty, illness or old age. Such help as these unfortunates needed was left to local relief agencies or private charity. Inured to the doctrine of laissez-faire, the government felt no responsibility for their economic condition. This attitude was summed up in one of President Grover Cleveland's aphorisms: "It is the duty of the people to support their government, but not of the government to support the people." When the worst depression in the country's history came, however, in the early 1930s, the government was shaken out of its complacent policy. The wheels of industry were stopped; 15,000,000 men were out of employment; the funds of local relief agencies and charitable organizations were exhausted. When the Roosevelt administration came into power in 1933, the president and his secretary of labour, Frances Perkins, set to work on a federal program for rehabilitation of the "forgotten man."

The Social Security act was signed by President Roosevelt on Aug. 14, 1935, and declared by him to be the "supreme achievement of his administration." It provided direct government aid for such needy and disabled persons as invalid mothers, crippled or homeless children, the blind and halt, as well as contributing from the national treasury to match state appropriations, and for a system of old-age and unemployment insurance financed by taxes on pay rolls. In 1939, the act was enlarged to include wives, widows and children in the benefits of old-age insurance, and the date of the initial payments was advanced from Jan. 1942 to Jan. 1940. Early in 1945 the Wagner-Murray-Dingell bill advocated a ten-year program of federal grants and loans to hospitals, sanitariums and health centres, the government paying up to 50% of the cost of construction, and the extension of the social security benefits to agricultural workers, seamen, and domestic servants. President Truman favoured also the coverage of 3,000,000 federal employees. In Dec. 1946 the Federal Security agency reported some 35,500,000 salary and wage earners insured under the act, and the reserve funds in the treasury from the tax assessments amounted to $14,000,000,000. In 1944, the Servicemen's Readjustment act (popularly known as the G.I. Bill of Rights) was passed, to continue for five years after the war, guaranteeing to the veterans aid in obtaining employment, educational and training opportunities, hospitalization and loans for business, farms and homes.

Adequate housing, a prime necessity for social health, had been a major problem of the federal, state and local governments ever since the great depression. A United States Housing authority was set up in the department of the interior in 1937, and an appropriation of $800,000,000 was made to provide for the clearance of slums, the construction of low cost houses and loans to local housing authorities. Under normal conditions, steady and rapid progress might have been made toward providing decent living quarters for rent or purchase at prices within the means of the "one-third" of the people of the country whom President Roosevelt described as "ill housed." But the sudden demands made by the program of national defense well nigh paralyzed the business of civilian construction. Camps had to be built for the men called up by the draft. The government spent billions on the construction of war plants. Some kind of housing had to be improvised for the vast number of workers flocking to the shipyards and the aircraft factories.

After the attack on Pearl Harbor the building of houses for the general public virtually ceased. All available material and manpower was requisitioned by the National Housing agency, set up by the president's executive order of Feb. 1942.

As the war was drawing to a close, it was estimated that no fewer than 12,600,000 houses and apartment units would be needed in the first postwar decade to take care of the waiting list and the increase in population and to replace substandard buildings. From 1940 to 1945, such construction averaged only 427,000 a year; and when veterans returned by the hundreds of thousands from the war, many of them married, they were faced with a desperate housing situation. (*See* also HOUSING; RELIEF; SOCIAL SECURITY.)

Threats to U.S. Democracy

The troubled generation which passed through two devastating wars and an interval of precarious truce saw the emergence of two "ideologies," or theories of political and economic organization which sharply challenged the traditional U.S. democratic-capitalistic system. Both these ideologies exalted the totalitarian state and spurned the liberal principles of free speech, representative government, parliamentary debate, an uncensored press, and tolerance of diverse party organizations, religious and racial minorities, labour unions, and in general those civil liberties guaranteed in the bills of rights of U.S. federal and state constitutions. The nazi-fascist type of totalitarianism, sponsored by Hitler and Mussolini, was primarily a political phenomenon, aimed at the abolition of the "rotten" corpse of democracy; while the communism of Stalin claimed to be the only genuine form of democracy and concentrated on the economic program of the triumph of the working class over their capitalist masters.

Though in the days of World War I, a number of plots of pro-German emissaries and associations were uncovered in the United States, the virus then did not spread, as it did during the decade 1937–46, to thousands of U.S. citizens. The term "fifth column" originated in the Spanish Civil War of 1936–39 to denote a regiment in Madrid which was to come to the support of the rebel general's attack on the city. Thence the term was applied to any group of agents of a foreign country working under cover to undermine the civilian morale and patriotism of their fellow citizens. It was through his fifth column of nazi propagandists that Hitler "softened up" the countries which he was about to overrun with his armies. Investigators exposed with sizable documentation the alarming extent of the activities of the fascist and communist fifth column in the U.S., especially the efforts of these subversive groups to capture the allegiance of the often disillusioned returning veterans of the war. The leaders of these groups masqueraded as 100% patriots. They wrapped themselves in the U.S. flag. Their pamphlets and manifestoes carried the words "American," "Christian" and "Patriot" conspicuously on their pages. Yet they were filled with hatred and abuse of Jews, Catholics, Negroes, public officials and labour leaders. They hailed the revival of the Ku Klux Klans and appealed to the worst traits in human nature: undisciplined emotion, intolerance, class hatred, denunciation and deceit.

It was a critical hour for the fate of democracy all over the world. The United States, which had emerged from World War II as the most powerful champion of democracy, had a special responsibility for the preservation of government "of the people, by the people and for the people." Abraham Lincoln in his message to congress of July 4, 1861, declared that the struggle which the nation was then facing was "essentially a people's contest . . . to elevate the condition of men . . . to lift artificial weight from *all* shoulders." More than 80 years later, Winston Churchill acknowledged that the salvation of democracy depended chiefly upon the leadership of the United States. And Pope Pius XII in his allocution of Christmas Eve 1945 said: "God has entrusted to the hands of the American people the relief of suffering humanity." But the nation could not fulfil such solemn obligations to the world at

"The Opposition Views the Opposition." Crawford of the *Newark Evening News* caricatured the Republican party's claim that Roosevelt was too old to be president and the Democratic party's charge that Dewey was too young in 1944

large unless it preserved its birthright of freedom at home. (*See* also COMMUNISM; DEMOCRACY; FASCISM; LIBERALISM.)

Latin-American Relations

The huge continental land mass from the Rio Grande to Cape Horn, with an area nearly three times that of the United States and a population nearly as large, had been too little known to the U.S. people. From the publication in 1823 of the Monroe Doctrine, which guaranteed the republics newly liberated from Spanish rule against interference by European powers, down to the announcement of the "good neighbour" policy by President Roosevelt 110 years later, Latin America (except for Mexico and Cuba) had occupied the attention of the U.S. government only on rare occasions. Its commercial, and especially its cultural ties were with the nations of western Europe. Few U.S. citizens read the history, spoke the language or visited the countries of the sister republics to the south. These republics generally regarded the government at Washington with a not unjustified suspicion of "Yankee imperialism," disguised as benevolent protection, while the U.S. people allowed their contempt for the political instability of the Latin-American states to obscure the appreciation of their remarkable cultural achievements.

Beginning with a meeting of 19 of the American republics at Washington, D.C., in Oct. 1889, called by President Benjamin Harrison's secretary of state, James G. Blaine, Pan-American conferences were held from time to time: at Mexico City (1901, when the Bureau of American Republics was established), Rio de Janeiro (1906), Buenos Aires (1910). These conferences were occupied with economic questions such as trade, currency, copyrights and reciprocity pacts. It was not until World War I had raised the problem of hemispheric defense that emphasis in the conferences was laid on the political and military relations of the republics to the United States and to one another. President Calvin Coolidge went to Havana to open the sixth conference in Jan. 1928, and the chairman, former Secretary of State Charles E. Hughes, declared: "We have no policy of aggression. Nothing could be happier for the United States than that all the countries in the region of the Caribbean should be strong and self-sufficient, settling their problems with peace at home and the fulfilment of their obligations abroad." President-elect Herbert Hoover, in November of the same year, made a good-will tour of a dozen of the South American countries.

Good Neighbour Policy.—The cultivation of a genuine Pan-Americanism, in which the "Colossus of the North" should abandon any attempt to dominate the policies of the southern republics, was the aim of the "good neighbour" policy announced by President Roosevelt in his inaugural address of March 4, 1933. During the Taft administration, some coercive measures had been taken to protect U.S. investments in Latin America ("dollar diplomacy"), and in Wilson's day U.S. marines were stationed in Puerto Rico, Haiti and Nicaragua, dictating policies and supervising elections. Now, in implementation of the good neighbour policy, the last of the marines were withdrawn, the Platt amendment (giving the U.S. the right to intervene in Cuban affairs) was abrogated in 1934, and at the seventh Pan-American conference in Montevideo, Uruguay, under the chairmanship of Secretary of State Cordell Hull, the ties between the American republics were strengthened.

It was the eighth conference at Lima, Peru, in the closing days of 1938 that marked the greatest advance in hemispheric solidarity. The Latin-American countries had been inclined to look to the League of Nations for the orientation of their policy, and several of their statesmen had held high positions in the League. But with the evident failure of the League to halt the aggressions of Mussolini, Hitler and the Japanese war lords, the Latin-American states one after another withdrew from the League and sought closer co-operation with the United States. At Lima, a declaration was signed by all of the 21 republics which was virtually an American League of Nations. They agreed not only to reduce trade barriers and to improve the machinery for preserving peace among themselves, but, most important of all, they pledged themselves in case of threatened aggression by a foreign power to meet and consult for common protection. The Declaration of Lima paid good dividends when the European war broke out the next year. Conferences at Panamá (1939), Havana (1940) and Rio (1942) emphasized Pan-American solidarity and promised united action to oppose aggression against any of the republics. Brazil, Argentina and Uruguay forbade belligerent operations in waters within 300 mi. of their shores and pooled their navies to patrol the 6,000 mi. of coast from the mouth of the Amazon river to Cape Horn.

The Caribbean republics declared war on Hitler at once after the Japanese attack on Pearl Harbor. Mexico and Brazil followed in Aug. 1942, and Colombia and Bolivia the next year. Eleven of the republics received military and naval missions from the United States, and several of them put their naval and aviation bases at the disposal of that country. Some 500 Latin-Americans travelled to the U.S. for aviator training. A landmark in the development of Pan-American solidarity was the Inter-American Conference on Problems of War and Peace which met at Mexico City on Feb. 21, 1945. The Act of Chapultepec which resulted from this conference provided for quadrennial meetings of the American states, for a permanent economic and social council, and for the integration of the inter-American organization into the framework of the United Nations charter, which was to be drafted at San Francisco the following April. It further provided that a board draft a scheme for the closer political, economic and social co-operation of the states, to be submitted to the ninth Pan-American conference at its meeting at Bogotá (Colombia) in 1947.

U.S. relations with Mexico were far from satisfactory at

the beginning of the decade 1937–46. In March 1938, President Lázaro Cárdenas announced that the state would seize the oil properties of the British and U.S. companies, which were valued by the companies at $450,000,000. Though compensation was promised, not a penny was paid for the $25,000,000 worth of land confiscated from the U.S. owners. Great Britain broke off relations with Mexico; but Secretary Hull, hopeful of avoiding discord at the coming Lima conference, pursued a waiting policy. On Dec. 2 the Mexican supreme court upheld the expropriations by a unanimous vote and denied the companies the right to compensation for concessions granted in former years. But this intransigent policy resulted only in injury to Mexico itself. U.S. importers, as well as some Europeans, boycotted Mexican oil while a Hull trade agreement with Venezuela, reducing by 50% the duty on certain quotas of foreign oil imported into the United States, cut still further into the Mexican business. In the year following the expropriations, Mexican foreign trade fell off 40% and imports, 60% of which were normally from the United States, declined by $60,000,000. It was evident that Mexico lacked the managerial talent to run the oil properties successfully. When General Manuel Ávila Camacho succeeded Cárdenas as president in 1940, a settlement was reached in which Mexico agreed to pay $37,000,000 for the expropriated lands and the United States agreed to purchase $25,000,000 of Mexican silver a year. The hearty co-operation of Mexico in the war against the axis served to dispel the ill feeling which had existed for more than a score of years between the two nations.

Sore Spot.—It was with Argentina that U.S. relations were especially strained. That republic was the richest and most powerful of the Latin-American states; it had a larger proportion of whites than did the United States. Its great capital of Buenos Aires, with nearly 2,500,000 persons, was second in size only to New York and Chicago in the Western hemisphere. Its railroad mileage was 43% of the total in South America.

There were two main causes of friction between the United States and Argentina: one economic and the other political. First, Argentina's livestock, meat and cereals, which comprised about nine-tenths of its exports, competed with the products of the United States, as the coffee and rubber of Brazil and the tin of Bolivia did not. This meant that its exports to the U.S. fell below those to Great Britain, which needed Argentina's grain and meat; and that its demand for U.S. oil, machines, electrical equipment and factory products generally created for this nation an unfavourable balance of trade which was an embarrassment for its finances. Furthermore, the situation was made worse when in 1927 the U.S. banned the entrance of Argentine meat into the United States on the ground of the prevalence of the hoof and mouth disease among its cattle.

The economic friction was relieved to some extent when World War II threatened to dislocate Argentina's trade with Europe and emphasized the necessity for the solidarity of the western hemisphere. A reciprocal trade agreement with Argentina in Oct. 1941 cut by roughly 50% the tariff duties on 84 articles which comprised over 90% of Argentine exports to the United States, while Argentina reduced by 25% to 50% its duties on a variety of imports from the U.S. In 1942 the discrimination against Argentine meat was removed.

Then occurred the second and more serious check to the desired good relations with Argentina. Though the mass of its people and the majority of its national assembly were well disposed to the democratic ideals of the United Nations, its high officials, with a few conspicuous exceptions, sympathized with the axis. The Argentine army, which exercised an enormous political influence, was shot through and through with fascist propaganda. Fifth columnists were ceaselessly at work among the 250,000 Argentines of German nationality. The German embassy spent more than 30 times as much money in 1941 as in 1938 in subsidizing Argentine newspapers and paying nazi agents. Already at the Lima conference of 1938 the Argentine delegates showed their reluctance to adopt any resolutions offensive to the totalitarian powers. Argentina declared its neutrality in 1940 and refused to seize the ships of the axis.

At the same time, Argentina pursued a vacillating policy, not wishing to break with the United Nations. In fact, President Ramon Castillo on Dec. 31, 1941, formally declared the "solidarity" of his country with the United States. But actions spoke louder than words. On June 3, 1943, a military coup d'état overthrew the government of President Castillo, and out of the revolutionary turmoil which followed, Juan D. Perón emerged as a fascist dictator: the Franco of Argentina. The United States did not recognize the regime of "the colonels" and denied lend-lease assistance to it. Secretary Hull scored the country as the "focus of fascism" in the western hemisphere, and President Roosevelt denounced the rule of the colonels. U.S. Ambassador Norman Armour was recalled in June 1944.

Though the Argentine government had, for the sake of conciliating the democracies, broken with the axis in Jan. 1944, the coup of the army the next month frustrated any possibility that the country would co-operate faithfully in the United Nations' program. German agents were still allowed to work under cover. Liberal newspapers were suppressed. Democratic rallies were dispersed. Argentina was not invited to the Inter-American conference at Mexico City in Feb. 1945, but it was decided that if it would sign the Act of Chapultepec, would declare war on the axis, and would adhere to the United Nations pact, it might be readmitted to the community of American states. Eager to participate in the conference of the United Nations scheduled to meet at San Francisco in April, Argentina declared war on the axis on March 27, 1945, and on April 19 President Truman, after Argentina had signed the Act of Chapultepec, sent Spruille Braden as ambassador to Buenos Aires. Argentina thus won a seat at San Francisco; but Braden, during the five months that he remained in Buenos Aires, was highly critical of the good faith of the Perón regime.

Meanwhile, many forces were at work to strengthen the political, economic and cultural ties between the United States and Latin America. Reciprocal trade agreements were negotiated with half the republics. Loans were extended to Argentina, Brazil, Chile, Peru, Bolivia, Cuba and Nicaragua. In May 1942, the Columbia Broadcasting system opened a net-work of 76 Latin-American stations. Nelson A. Rockefeller's Office of Inter-American Affairs (*q.v.*) encouraged a better mutual understanding of the history and civilization of the various countries. Some 8,200 mi. of the 11,500 mile highway from New York to Buenos Aires were completed in 1940. In the summer of the same year U.S. students were registered at the universities of Bogotá, Santiago and San Marco, Peru (the oldest university on the western continent), and more than 1,000 South American students were enrolled at 158 universities and colleges in the United States. Delegations of business men, professors, lawyers, doctors and scientists travelled from Latin America to study U.S. institutions. A genuine Pan-Americanism was rapidly supplanting the spirit of dominating patronage which had too often in the past characterized the attitude of the "Colossus of the North" toward the Latin-American countries (*see* also PAN-AMERICAN CONFERENCES, 1937–46).

Foreign Policy

Disturbing events in Europe and Asia in the years immediately preceding the eventful decade—Mussolini's unprovoked attack on Ethiopia (1935), Hitler's armed occupation of the Rhineland (1936) and the outbreak of the Spanish civil war (1936)—turned the attention of the administration at Washington to the possible danger of these aggressive moves to the nation's own security. President Roosevelt's speech at Chicago on Oct. 5, 1937, sounded the note of the responsibility for checking the epidemic of aggression which was spreading in the totalitarian countries.

While a large part of the U.S. people, nurtured on the traditional policy of nonintervention and not yet grasping the fact that Hitler's aim was world conquest, believed that the Neutrality act of 1937 guaranteed immunity from the contagion of war, the president and other high officials responsible for U.S. foreign policy were convinced that the nation had to exert all possible influence to halt the march of the aggressors, and take positive measures of preparedness for national defense.

As the nazis proceeded, in spite of the Munich pact, to extinguish the republic of Czechoslovakia (1939) and overrun Poland, President Roosevelt interceded no less than three times with personal messages to Hitler, Mussolini, the president of Poland and the king of Italy, pleading with them to settle their differences peaceably, and offering Hitler the pledge of 31 listed nations to refrain from attacks against him. But all that the president got for his pains was either contemptuous silence or rude rebuke from the two totalitarian despots.

Toward War.—After Hitler's crushing defeat of Poland, Roosevelt called congress in extra session on Sept. 21, 1939, and secured the repeal of the embargo provisions of the Neutrality act by substantial majorities in both houses. And when the nazi hordes were launched against western Europe in the spring of 1940, rapidly subduing Denmark, Norway, the Netherlands, Belgium and France, and leaving Great Britain alone to withstand the savage assaults of Goering's luftwaffe, the president abandoned persuasion for prompt action. The U.S. must come to the support of the democracies. Its factories must be converted as rapidly as possible to war production.

Its army and navy must be expanded to meet all possible contingencies.

The 76th congress responded with enormous appropriations. On May 28, 1940, a Council of National Defense was set up and the next month, a Selective Training and Service bill was introduced in the house, and signed by the president on Sept. 16. (*See* above.)

The nation was only technically at peace in the autumn of 1940. Actually, it was already a partner of Great Britain, as was shown by Roosevelt's transfer to that power of 50 U.S. destroyers in exchange for leases of naval bases along the Atlantic coast. The Lend-Lease bill of the following March swept away the last pretense of neutrality, although it was not until Nov. 1941 that the provisions forbidding the arming of merchant vessels and their entrance into combat zones were repealed.

The legal fiction of neutrality was contradicted by event after event in 1941: by the closing of the nazi consulates in June, the deportation of 450 axis agents in July, the president's order to "shoot at sight" on German submarines in September. After Pearl Harbor, Prime Minister Winston Churchill spent the Christmas holidays in Washington and received an ovation when he addressed congress on Dec. 26, celebrating the solidarity between his country and the United States. He and President Roosevelt had met on a war vessel off the Newfoundland coast the previous August and drawn up the Atlantic charter (*q.v.*), parent document of the international association for the maintenance of world peace.

On New Year's day, 1942, the representatives of 26 nations (increased to 55 by the end of 1946) adhered to the principles of the Atlantic charter, and the United Nations was born.

U.S. relations with Japan had been growing more critical from year to year as it became evident that the military clique in Tokyo was determined to subjugate China, whatever the western powers might say or do. The doctrine of the "open door" was repudiated, and the Nine Power treaty of 1922 and the Kellogg pact of 1928 (both of which Japan had signed) were denounced. In retaliation, the United States terminated in Jan. 1940 the commercial treaty with Japan in effect since 1911.

Still, the United States was Japan's largest customer, buying 70% of its chief export commodity of raw silk. U.S. foreign trade with Japan was more than three times that with China, and the nation continued to send Japan oil, scrap iron and other materials needed in building its war industries.

When the treacherous attack on Pearl Harbor on Dec. 7, 1941, put an end to the insincere protests of friendship for the United States, congress on the next day declared war on Japan, and five days later on its axis partners, Germany and Italy. For the campaigns of the global war, in which U.S. officers, soldiers, sailors, marines and airmen distinguished themselves on a score of fighting fronts, *see* WORLD WAR II.

U.S. foreign policy during the war could be summed up in a single phrase: all-out endeavour, without regard to party or economic interest, to send the axis down to utter defeat.

In World War I only a few men, with President Wilson in the lead, had concerned themselves with the kind of peace that should follow. The "Big Four" (Wilson, Georges Clemenceau, Lloyd George and Vittorio Orlando) who were the architects of the Treaty of Versailles had never met until they came together at the peace table. But in the later war, frequent conferences were held, not only for the discussion of the conduct of military operations but to formulate plans for the building of a better world when the conflict should be over. The U.S. and British staffs were combined. Roosevelt and Churchill met for conferences no less than six times, in the U.S. or Canada or Africa, between Aug. 1941 and Aug. 1943.

At the end of October of the latter year Secretary Hull flew to Moscow to meet the foreign ministers of Great Britain (Anthony Eden) and Russia (Vyacheslav Molotov). The declaration which they drew up advocated the establishment "at the earliest practicable date" of "a general international organization . . . for the maintenance of international peace and security." The United States senate endorsed the proposition on Nov. 5 by a vote of 85 to 5.

Late in the same month, Roosevelt, Churchill and Chiang Kai-shek met at Cairo and agreed that Japan should be stripped of all the islands in the Pacific which it had seized and should restore all the land that it had stolen from China. From Cairo, Roosevelt and Churchill flew on to Tehran (Iran) to meet Marshal Stalin and pledge their three countries to co-operate fully in the destruction of the German army, fleet and air power, and the conclusion of a peace which should "command good will from the overwhelming masses of the world and banish the scourge and terror of war for many generations." In Feb. 1945, when the doom of Germany was practically assured, the same men held a conference at Yalta in the Crimea, where they adopted resolutions for the occupation and control of Germany, the restoration of free governments in Poland and the liberated Balkan countries, the periodic meetings of foreign ministers, and the calling of a conference at San Francisco on April 25 to draft a charter for the United Nations.

On his return from Yalta, President Roosevelt addressed the nation (March 1), reporting on the close accord of the conference and declaring that "this time we are not making the mistake of waiting until the end of the war to set up the machinery of peace." The president, worn out by his incessant labours, died 13 days before the delegates from 50 nations assembled at San Francisco. (*See* also INTERNATIONAL CONFERENCES, ALLIED [WORLD WAR II].)

World Responsibility.—In two months at San Francisco, the delegates completed an elaborate charter, based on the outline proposed at Dumbarton Oaks six months before, and President Truman went to San Francisco to close the final session on June 26. A month later the U.S. senate ratified the charter by a vote of 89 to 2. And on Oct. 24, a majority of the nations having adhered to the charter, Secretary James F. Byrnes announced that it had the force of law. For the first meeting of the general assembly of the United Nations, convened at London on Jan. 10, 1946, the U.S. delegation appointed by President Truman consisted of Secretary of State Byrnes, former Secretary Edward Stettinius, Senator Tom Connally of Texas (chairman of the senate foreign relations committee), Senator Arthur Vandenberg of Michigan, and Mrs. Franklin D. Roosevelt. The second eight-weeks meeting at Flushing Meadows, Long Island, ended on Dec. 16, 1946, and left to the 11-member Security council at Lake Success the task of completing a program for the reduction of the armed forces of the world and controlling the production and use of atomic energy. The main results of the prodigious labour of the assembly were: agreement on the principles of disarmament and the outlawing of the atomic bomb, establishment of a ten-nation Trusteeship council for the administration of the former League of Nations mandates, recommendation that the U.N. members recall their ambassadors and ministers from Spain until Franco was driven from power, adoption of a site on the east side of Manhattan, presented by John D. Rockefeller, for the capital of the United Nations, recommendation of the sparing use of the veto power by the Big Five, plans for the continuation of famine relief on the expiration of U.N.R.R.A., adoption of a budget of $47,130,000 for expenses in the succeeding year, enlargement of the Security council and the Economic and Social council, and the admission of five new states to the U.N., bringing the total membership up to 56.

(*See* also UNITED NATIONS.)

The president and the state department incurred a vast

Marshal Stalin, President Roosevelt and Prime Minister Churchill at the Tehran conference, Nov. 28-Dec. 1, 1943

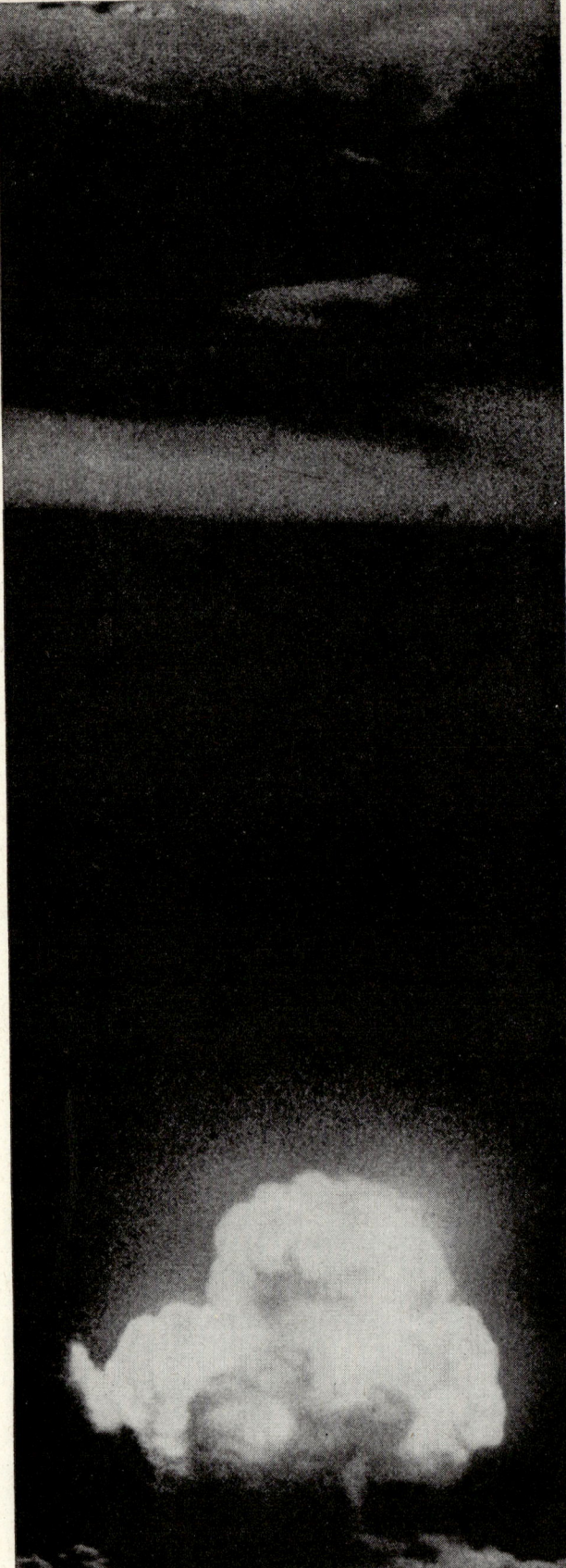

Test explosion of the first atomic bomb in history. Detonation took place at Alamogordo, N.M., on July 16, 1945

amount of criticism during the decade for their handling of several delicate and difficult problems of diplomacy as well as for the use of the atomic bomb to end World War II. The failure to insist on sanctions against Mussolini in his aggression on Ethiopia was disapproved by many as a dereliction of duty to promote the restraint of international brigandage above the profits from the sale of oil and munitions. The administration was criticized for sending Admiral William Leahy as ambassador to Vichy, thereby virtually recognizing the puppet regime of Henri Pétain and Pierre Laval. The acceptance by Roosevelt of Admiral Jean Darlan, a determined fascist foe of the democracies and a partisan of Pétain, as French chief of state in North Africa was justified by the administration at Washington as a necessary "temporary expedient" (in view of Darlan's apparent conversion to the side of the Allies) for preventing military resistance by the French to the U.S. campaign through Morocco, Algeria and Tunisia. But U.S. indignation against the employment of such a questionable "ally" was outspoken, and the assassination of Darlan by a young Frenchman on Christmas Eve of 1942 removed a leader who might well have proved a hindrance rather than a help to Allied occupation of North Africa.

Sumner Welles, former under secretary of state, in his book *Where Are We Heading?* (1946), excoriated the administration at Washington for its ignorant and bungling policy in Latin America, especially Argentina, which, he said, bid to frustrate all the gains of the "good neighbour" program of President Roosevelt.

In China, according to many critics, the United States had lamentably failed to formulate a policy to bring order out of chaos. The fundamental mistake, critics declared, had been U.S. assumption of the role of partisan instead of mediator, supporting Chiang Kai-shek (albeit ineffectually) in his intransigent attitude toward the communists of the north, with the result that neither the boisterous Patrick Hurley nor the judicious General Marshall made any headway in bringing to an end the civil war which increased in violence after the defeat of Japan. It had long been a reproach voiced against the U.S. government that it had no consistent foreign policy.

The charge may have been true. But in mitigation of the charge it had to be borne in mind that it was only during World War II that the nation had renounced its traditional refuge from world responsibility, and now found the burden of such responsibility all the greater because of the leading part which U.S. wealth and power were destined to play in the building of a new world of peace and security.

The time had come for fulfilment of the prophetic words of Theodore Roosevelt nearly half a century before:

"The question is not whether America shall play a great part in the affairs of the world, but whether she shall play it well or ill."

BIBLIOGRAPHY.—*United States Foreign Policy, 1931–1941,* Government Printing Office (1942); Samuel I. Rosenman, *Public Papers and Addresses of Franklin D. Roosevelt* (1938); William Crane Johnstone, *United States and Japan's New Order* (1941); Alexander P. de Seversky, *Victory Through Air Power* (1943); Forest Davis and E. K. Lindley, *How War Came* (1942); Thomas Arthur Bisson, *American Policy in the Far East, 1931–41* (1941); Hans Kohn, *Revolutions and Dictatorships* (1938), *Not by Arms Alone* (1940), *World Order in Historical Perspective* (1942); Theodore Clarke Smith, *United States as a Factor in World History* (1941); William Dilworth Puleston, *Armed Forces of the Pacific* (1941); William Edward and Martha Dodd, *Ambassador Dodd's Diary, 1933–38* (1941); Francis Trevelyan Miller, *Eisenhower: Man and Soldier; General Douglas MacArthur* (1944); George Edward Taylor, *America in the New Pacific* (1942); Carl Dreher, *The Coming Showdown* (1942); Henry William Spiegel, *Economics of Total War* (1942); Edward S. Cornell, *America's Future Pattern* (1942); Douglas Lurton, *Roosevelt's Foreign Pol-*

icy (1942); Frederick Lewis Schuman, *Design for Power* (1942); John B. Condliffe, *Agenda for a Postwar World* (1942); Louis P. Lochner, *What About Germany?* (1942); Josef Hanč, *Eastern Europe and the United States* (1942); Carl Crow, *Japan's Dream of World Empire* (1942); Stanley Kuhl Hornbeck, *United States and the Far East* (1942); Joseph Clark Grew, *Report From Tokyo* (1942), *Ten Years in Japan* (1944); Denys Smith, *America and the Axis War* (1942); James Barrett Reston, *Prelude to Victory* (1942); Hanson Weightman Baldwin, *Strategy for Victory* (1942); Henry A. Wallace, *The Price of Free World Victory* (1942), *Democracy Reborn* (1944), *Sixty Million Jobs* (1945); William Bernard Ziff, *Coming Battle of Germany* (1942); John Richard Hersey, *Men on Bataan* (1942), *Bell for Adano* (1944), *Hiroshima* (1946); William Lindsey White, *Queens Die Proudly* (1943), *They Were Expendable* (1942); Herbert Hoover and Hugh Gibson, *Problems of Lasting Peace* (1942); John Rotherford Bellerby, *Economic Reconstruction* (1943); David Hinshaw, *The Home Front* (1943); Eve Curie, *Journey Among Warriors* (1943); Ralph McAllister Ingersoll, *Battle is the Payoff* (1943); Herbert Matthews, *The Fruits of Fascism* (1943); Otto David Tolischus, *Tokyo Record* (1943); Ernest T. Pyle, *Here is Your War* (1943), *Brave Men* (1944); Aimee Crane, *Marines at War* (1943); K. Banning, *Our Army Today* (1943); H. A. Saunders, *Combined Operations* (1943); Alexander Clifford, *Conquest of North Africa* (1943); Richard Tregaskis, *Guadalcanal Diary* (1943), *Invasion Diary* (1944); Darryl Francis Zanuck, *Tunis Expedition* (1943); Joseph Driscoll, *War Discovers Alaska* (1943); John M. Redding and H. I. Leyshon, *Skyways to Berlin* (1943); Joao F. Normano and Antonello Gerbi, *Japanese in South America* (1943); Walter Lippmann, *United States Foreign Policy* (1943); Henry Clarence Cassidy, *Moscow Dateline* (1943); Harry Paxton Howard, *America's Role in Asia* (1943); John Maurice Clark, *Demobilization of Wartime Economic Controls* (1944); Eric Allen Johnston, *America Unlimited* (1944); Edward Reilly Stettinius, *Lend-Lease, Weapon for Victory* (1944); Gilbert Cant, *The American Navy in World War II* (1943); John Mason Brown, *Many a Watchful Night* (1944); Frederick Mears, *Carrier Combat* (1944); John Gunther, *D-Day* (1944); Quentin Reynolds, *The Curtain Rises* (1944); George Fielding Eliot, *Hour of Triumph* (1944), *The Ramparts We Watch* (1938), *The Strength We Need* (1946); Sumner Welles, *The Time for Decision* (1944), *Where Are We Heading?* (1946); Henry Merritt Wriston, *Strategy of Peace* (1944); Jan Smuts, *Toward a Better World* (1944); Pitirim A. Sorokin, *Russia and the United States* (1941); Foster Rhea Dulles, *Road to Teheran* (1944); Carl Becker, *How New Will the Better World Be?* (1944); Harold Glen Moulton and Louis Marlio, *The Control of Germany and Japan* (1944); Owen Lattimore, *Solution in Asia* (1945); Henry Morgenthau, *Germany Is Our Problem* (1945); Kenneth Davis, *Soldier of Democracy (Eisenhower)* (1945); Paul Scott Mowrer, *House of Europe* (1945); Emery Reves, *Anatomy of Peace* (1945); George Marshall, *Report to the Secretary of War* (1945); William Henry Mauldin, *Up Front* (1945); C. J. H. Hayes, *Wartime Mission in Spain, 1942–1945* (1945); Joseph F. St. John, *Leyte Calling* (1945); David Breger, *G I Joe* (1945); Carleton Beals, *What the South Americans Think of Us* (1945); Frances Perkins, *The Roosevelt I Knew* (1946); William Bernard Ziff, *Two Worlds* (1946), *Rape of Palestine* (1938); William Christian Bullitt, *Great Globe Itself* (1946); Julian Sebastian Bach, *America's Germany* (1946); Jerome Davis, *Behind Soviet Power* (1946); Robert Ducharme Potter, *The Atomic Revolution* (1946); Louis Dolivet, *United Nations* (1946); L. Balogh Bain, *Chaos or Peace* (1943); Bernard Newman, *The New Europe* (1943); Foster Bowman Hailey, *Pacific Battle Line* (1944); Waverly Root, *The Secret History of the War* (1946); Sir Bernard Pares, *Russia and the Peace* (1944); James Thomson Shotwell, *The Great Decision* (1944); T. H. Chamberlain, *The Generals and the Admirals* (1945); Carlos Pena Romulo, *I Saw the Fall of the Philippines* (1942); Nathaniel Peffer, *Must We Fight in Asia?* (1935), *The Basis for Peace in the Far East* (1942). (D. S. Mu.)

United States Antarctic Service

See EXPLORATION, POLAR.

United States-British War Boards

See BRITISH-U.S. WAR BOARDS.

United States-Canadian War Committees

See CANADIAN-U.S. WAR COMMITTEES.

United States Government Departments and Bureaus

See GOVERNMENT DEPARTMENTS AND BUREAUS. Also *see* under specific name, *i.e.*, COAST GUARD, U.S., etc.

United States Housing Authority

See FEDERAL WORKS AGENCY; HOUSING; MUNICIPAL GOVERNMENT.

United States Office of Education

See EDUCATION; FEDERAL SECURITY AGENCY.

Universal Postal Union

See INTERNATIONAL ORGANIZATIONS.

Universities and Colleges

Below and on the following pages is a selected list of universities, colleges, junior colleges and technical schools of college grade in the U.S. and Canada, with salient data for 1937 and for 1946. The symbol * designates 1945 data (listed in the 1946 column); || 1944 (in 1946 column); + 1938, ‡ 1939, §1940 (in the 1937 column).

Institution and Location	Year Founded	Chief Executive 1946	1946				1937			
			Full Time Students	Faculty	Endowment	Library Volumes	Full Time Students	Faculty	Endowment	Library Volumes
A										
Acadia University, Wolfville, N.S., Can	1838	F. W. Patterson	896	60	$ 1,083,021	87,000	460	48	968,168	70,000
Adams State Tch. Col., Alamosa, Colo.*†	1921	Ira Richardson	295	23	—	21,485	199	24	—	12,601
Adelphi College, Garden City, N. Y.	1896	Paul D. Eddy	1,909	108	—	40,003	433	42	—	31,537
Agnes Scott College, Decatur, Ga.	1889	James R. McCain	540	68	2,225,000	42,400	491	61	1,566,455	33,250
Akron, University of, Akron, Ohio	1870	H. E. Simmons	3,202	167	134,450	74,900	1,400	93	153,000	50,716
Alabama, University of, University, Ala.	1831	Raymond R. Paty	8,624	482	6,000,000	329,851	4,873	292	5,346,075	235,000
Alabama College, Montevallo, Ala.	1896	A. F. Harman	803	73	636,930	50,950	842	71	582,722	36,000
Alabama Polytechnic Inst., Auburn, Ala.	1872	L. N. Duncan	6,273	285	580,022	108,000	2,583	189	267,058	69,300
Alabama State Tch. Col., Florence, Ala.	1872	J. A. Keller	1,574	60	—	45,000	490	32	—	28,000
Alabama State Tch. Col., Jacksonville, Ala.†	1892	Houston Cole	861	29	—	30,000	560	26	—	25,000
Alabama State Tch. Col., Livingston, Ala.	1835	W. W. Hill	431	26	—	25,000	300	30	—	24,000
Alaska, University of, College, Alaska	1917	Charles E. Bunnell	300	37	—	20,000	200	25	—	15,000
Albany State College, Albany, Ga.	1903	Aaron Brown	425	40	—	12,000	255	14	—	4,000
Alberta, Univ. of, Edmonton, Alta., Can.	1906	Robert Newton	4,210	399	500,000	106,000	1,670	231	500,000	63,789
Albertus Magnus Col., New Haven, Conn.	1925	Sister M. Samuel	260	39	6,140	20,000	148	31	2,866	17,000
Albion College, Albion, Mich.	1835	W. W. Whitehouse	1,070	54	2,678,000	66,000	738	44	1,546,000	46,023
Albright College, Reading, Pa.	1856	Harry V. Masters	627	46	913,648	25,000	376	30	332,291	22,026
Alcorn A. and M. College, Alcorn, Miss.	1871	William H. Pipes	750	44	—	14,000	599	42	113,575	10,000
Alfred University, Alfred, N.Y.	1836	J. E. Walters	1,314	127	842,000	65,902	619	66	1,084,625	56,700
Allegheny College, Meadville, Pa.	1815	John R. Schultz	1,007	66	2,000,000	110,819	654	50	1,500,000	114,000
Allen University, Columbia, S.C.†	1870	Samuel R. Higgins	720	35	—	13,000	290	22	—	6,000
Alma College, Alma, Mich.	1886	Roy W. Hamilton	536	35	700,000	52,000	292	22	—	45,000
Alverno College, Milwaukee, Wis.	1936	Mother M. Corona	86	19	—	23,045	46	11	—	11,203
Amarillo College (Jr.), Amarillo, Tex.	1929	A. M. Meyer	626	37	—	10,900	312	20	—	9,000
American International Col., Springfield, Mass.	1885	William Gellermann	1,086	47	—	14,000	494	30	—	10,386
American University, Washington, D.C.	1893	Paul F. Douglass	988	172	866,237	112,558	522	91	938,078	52,002

Institution and Location	Year Founded	Chief Executive 1946	1946				1937			
			Full Time Students	Faculty	Endowment	Library Volumes	Full Time Students	Faculty	Endowment	Library Volumes
Amherst College, Amherst, Mass.	1821	Charles W. Cole	1,170	120	$12,837,000	245,000	839	74	$ 9,713,000	207,700
Andrew College (Jr.), Cuthbert, Ga.	1854	S. C. Olliff	102	13	155,000	5,000	124	13	34,000	4,500
Antioch College, Yellow Springs, Ohio	1853	A. D. Henderson	1,033	68	2,235,000	71,000	680	59	200,354	50,688
Appalachian State Tch. Col., Boone, N.C.	1903	B. B. Dougherty	947	77	—	37,000	901	44	50,000	22,000
Arizona, University of, Tucson, Ariz.	1885	Alfred Atkinson	4,487	266	73,516	180,000	2,827	198	—	125,339
Arizona State Tch. Col., Flagstaff, Ariz.*	1899	Tom O. Bellwood	146	33	—	28,000	486	40	—	26,217
Arizona State Tch. Col., Tempe, Ariz.	1885	Grady Gammage	2,172	108	—	50,000	1,116	54	—	20,045
Arkansas, University of, Fayetteville, Ark.	1872	Arthur M. Harding	4,700	275	—	250,000	2,637	210	—	138,000
Arkansas A. and M. College, Monticello, Arkansas	1909	W. E. Morgan	590	30	—	14,000	500	32	—	12,000
Arkansas Polytechnic Col. (Jr.), Russellville, Ark.	1909	J. W. Hull	1,186	62	—	15,674	571	31	—	10,657
Arkansas State Agri. and Mech. Col. (Jr.), Magnolia, Ark.	1910	Charlie S. Wilkins	573	25	—	13,700	398	21	—	7,925
Arkansas State College, Jonesboro, Ark.	1910	W. J. Edens	1,061	51	—	20,900	548	44	—	10,275
Arkansas State Tch. Col., Conway, Ark.	1907	Nolen M. Irby	1,020	53	—	33,330	623	42	—	16,000
Armstrong Junior College, Savannah, Ga.	1935	Foreman M. Hawes	428	22	41,000	6,000	217	9	—	4,500
Asbury College, Wilmore, Ky.	1890	Z. T. Johnson	800	33	748,000	30,000	520	23	383,474	17,761
Ashland College, Ashland, Ohio	1878	Raymond W. Bixler	520	51	416,500	22,402	300	29	416,084	14,026
Atlanta University, Atlanta, Ga.	1867	Rufus E. Clement	171	39	4,307,727	85,301	96	32	3,364,641	58,106
Augusta, Junior College of, Augusta, Ga.	1925	Eric W. Hardy	343	21	—	11,000	255	20	—	9,000
Augustana College, Sioux Falls, S.D.	1860	L. M. Stavig	916	52	450,715	25,183	403	36	437,438	29,165
Augustana College and Theological Seminary, Rock Island, Ill.	1860	Conrad Bergendoff	1,147	68	1,626,000	90,000	609	51	1,500,000	98,000
Aurora College, Aurora, Ill.	1893	T. P. Stephens	460	31	75,000	31,000	141	16	83,000	22,000
Averett College (Jr.), Danville, Va.	1859	Curtis V. Bishop	270	27	80,000	8,375	181	22	80,000	5,305
B										
Baker University, Baldwin City, Kan.	1858	Nelson P. Horn	615	34	1,306,000	68,000	308	31	2,000,000	60,000
Baldwin Wallace College, Berea, Ohio	1845	Louis C. Wright	1,500	62	2,140,000	60,000	625	46	1,667,126	25,000
Ball State Teachers College, Muncie, Ind.	1918	John R. Emens	1,838	136	—	100,728	1,239	101	—	64,051
Barat College of the Sacred Heart, Lake Forest, Ill.	1904	Mother Reilly	301	27	—	21,565	60	8	—	8,000
Barber-Scotia College (Jr.), Concord, N.C.	1867	L. S. Cozart	154	17	800,000	12,000	165	21	800,000	7,000
Bard College, Annandale-on-Hudson, N.Y.	1860	Edward C. Fuller	268	44	196,675	60,000	140	32	208,430	57,000
Barnard College, New York, N.Y	1889	F. D. Fackenthal	1,229	132	5,309,389	65,000	986	134	4,802,994	58,500
Bates College, Lewiston, Maine	1864	Charles F. Phillips	773	52	2,133,164	80,000	665	46	1,875,152	70,000
Bay City Junior College, Bay City, Mich.	1922	Geo. E. Butterfield	746	26	—	12,000	358	31	—	10,240
Baylor Univ., Waco, Dallas, and Houston, Tex.	1845	Pat M. Neff	4,124	295	3,087,952	157,589	1,978	85	1,680,288	90,000
Belmont Abbey Col. (Jr.), Belmont, N.C.	1878	Vincent G. Taylor	275	20	—	30,000	180	17	—	25,000
Beloit College, Beloit, Wis.	1846	Carey Croneis	912	68	2,410,207	140,000	598	50	2,350,000	92,000
Benedict College, Columbia, S.C.†	1870	J. A. Bacoats	650	28	337,018	18,093	335	25	140,000	25,000
Bennett College, Greensboro, N.C.	1873	David D. Jones	470	34	893,495	20,510	305	23	253,412	8,591
Bennington College, Bennington, Vt.	1932	Lewis W. Jones	318	47	100,100	27,000	270	43	100,094	14,929
Berea College, Berea, Ky.	1855	Francis S. Hutchins	1,012	80	7,850,000	100,992	742	58	9,863,123	71,000
Bethany College, Bethany, W.Va.	1840	Wilbur H. Cramblet	708	42	3,072,000	41,802	374	31	2,182,328	26,315
Bethany College, Lindsborg, Kan.	1881	Emory Lindquist	366	34	446,651	23,504	291	35	355,751	19,188
Bethel College, North Newton, Kan.	1887	Edmund G. Kaufman	385	30	613,165	25,000	322	28	317,918	17,500
Bethune-Cookman Col., Daytona Beach, Fla.*	1904	James A. Colston	268	30	136,211	13,595	223	14	88,028	6,213
Birmingham-Southern Col., Birmingham, Ala.	1856	George R. Stuart	1,481	62	580,548	60,000	930	40	624,530	42,000
Bishop College, Marshall, Tex.	1881	Joseph J. Rhoads	1,275	45	14,000	21,000	600	35	—	21,000
Bishop's College, University of, Lennoxville, Que., Can.	1843	A. H. McGreer	210	19	1,250,000	20,000	157	16	1,020,000	20,000
Blackburn College (Jr.), Carlinville, Ill.	1857	Robert W. McEwen	320	21	1,312,997	14,600	271	20	906,000	10,700
Black Hills Teachers College, Spearfish, S.D.	1883	Russell E. Jonas	300	30	—	21,000	250	25	—	12,000
Blue Mountain Col., Blue Mountain, Miss.	1873	Lawrence T. Lowrey	304	28	503,000	17,820	297	26	290,000	14,100
Boise Junior College, Boise, Idaho	1932	Eugene B. Chaffee	724	52	—	11,500	149	17	—	4,000
Boston, Teachers College of the City of, Boston, Mass.	1852	W. H. J. Kennedy	280	28	—	26,495	533	39	—	25,500
Boston College, Newton and Boston, Mass.	1863	Wm. L. Keleher	4,326	450	1,000,000	202,500	4,000	298	750,000	144,388
Boston University, Boston, Mass.	1839	Daniel L. Marsh	21,211	850	6,148,288	255,500	6,217	594	4,055,248	170,400
Bowdoin College, Brunswick, Maine	1794	Kenneth C. M. Sills	965	74	8,928,384	203,258	588	61	8,041,602	170,000
Bowling Green St. Univ., Bowling Green, O.	1910	Frank J. Prout	3,964	172	—	80,000	1,123	65	—	48,476
Bradford Junior College, Bradford, Mass.	1803	Dorothy M. Bell	280	32	116,000	17,000	230	24	116,000	11,358
Bradley University, Peoria, Ill.	1897	David B. Owen	2,948	149	2,429,439	65,000	768	49	2,578,205	42,060
Brewton-Parker Junior Col., Mt. Vernon, Ga.*	1904	R. L. Robinson	187	10	29,000	4,000	256	12	—	4,000
Briar Cliff College, Sioux City, Iowa	1930	Sister Jean Marie	350	26	—	17,000	98	17	4,768	—
Briarcliff Junior College, Briarcliff Manor, N.Y.	1933	Clara Tead	200	27	—	8,000	150	25	—	5,000
Bridgewater College, Bridgewater, Va.	1880	Jacob I. Baugher	434	28	509,771	15,000	235	24	511,517	15,000
Brigham Young University, Provo, Utah	1875	Howard S. McDonald	4,350	212	285,229	142,000	2,461	127	274,982	101,526
British Columbia, Univ. of, Vancouver, B.C., Can.	1915	N. A. M. MacKenzie	8,986	292	225,894	170,000	2,223	213	96,560	115,000
Brooklyn, Polytechnic Inst. of, Brooklyn, N.Y.	1854	H. S. Rogers	1,510	250	1,513,480	40,000	3,037	56	1,520,000	25,000
Brooklyn College, Brooklyn, N.Y.	1930	Harry D. Gideonse	7,714	450	19,135	165,388	5,003	299	5,584	48,727
Brown University, Providence, R.I.	1764	Henry M. Wriston	4,070	243	12,034,051	658,348	2,129	136	11,693,000	542,359
Bryn Mawr College, Bryn Mawr, Pa.	1885	Katharine E. McBride	688	86	7,476,470	196,623	475	85	6,738,826	160,000
Bucknell University, Lewisburg, Pa.	1846	Herbert L. Spencer	2,013	141	1,482,150	110,000	1,235	73	1,394,313	80,000
Bucknell Univ. Jr. Col., Wilkes-Barre, Pa.	1933	Eugene S. Farley	797	45	275,000	9,500	197	14	—	550
Buffalo, University of, Buffalo, N.Y.	1846	Samuel P. Capen	5,538	600	7,000,000	212,009	1,650	513	5,740,354	140,177
Butler University, Indianapolis, Ind.	1855	Maurice O. Ross	3,600	195	3,000,000	90,000	1,496	88	2,000,000	63,000
C										
California, University of, Berkeley, Los Angeles, Santa Barbara, San Francisco, Davis, Mount Hamilton, La Jolla, and Riverside, Cal.	1868	Robert G. Sproul	40,800	2,567	36,147,157	2,158,820	24,358	2,385	23,796,809	1,380,455
California Inst. of Tech., Pasadena, Calif.	1891	Lee A. DuBridge	1,383	200	17,000,000	70,000	909	168	7,512,620	43,747
Calvin College, Grand Rapids, Mich.	1876	Henry Schultze	1,247	50	—	35,000	400	25	250,000	25,000
Campbell College (Jr.), Buie's Creek, N.C.	1926	Leslie H. Campbell	372	29	167,371	10,032	452	27	11,511	6,000
Canal Zone Junior Col., Balboa Heights, C.Z.	1933	Roger C. Hackett	215	32	—	9,000	98	7	—	5,000
Canisius College, Buffalo, N.Y.*	1870	Timothy J. Coughlin	427	47	—	39,000	734	55	—	15,232
Capital University, Columbus, Ohio	1850	Harold L. Yochum	997	85	637,912	44,800	696	72	554,174	24,000
Carleton College, Northfield, Minn.	1866	Laurence M. Gould	1,143	91	3,606,303	143,236	801	70	3,168,240	115,500
Carnegie Institute of Tech., Pittsburgh, Pa.	1900	Robert E. Doherty	3,428	273	27,316,244	50,000	2,254	221	16,934,108	24,099
Carroll College, Helena, Mont.	1910	Emmet J. Riley	325	18	500,000	18,000	152	14	500,000	15,000
Carroll College, Waukesha, Wis.	1846	N. V. Russell	772	48	953,720	32,000	560	27	834,000	15,000
Carson-Newman Col., Jefferson City, Tenn.	1851	James T. Warren	645	30	664,968	23,000	435	26	533,666	18,581
Carthage College, Carthage, Ill.	1870	Erland Nelson	617	35	750,000	35,000	270	25	864,576	25,825
Case School of Applied Science, Cleveland, O.	1880	Wm. E. Wickenden	1,279	165	5,971,618	35,000	849	88	3,893,000	32,865
Catawba College, Salisbury, N.C.	1851	A. R. Keppel	668	38	444,071	25,249	409	32	407,562	14,818
Catholic Univ. of America, Wash., D.C.	1887	Patrick J. McCormick	2,070	400	3,938,818	398,000	1,500	164	3,297,270	338,365
Cedar Crest College, Allentown, Pa.	1867	Dale Hendry Moore	374	37	126,260	25,000	242	22	76,359	20,425
Centenary College of La., Shreveport, La.	1825	Joe J. Mickle	1,287	61	473,484	27,800	545	42	463,826	20,000

Institution and Location	Year Founded	Chief Executive 1946	1946 Full Time Students	1946 Faculty	1946 Endowment	1946 Library Volumes	1937 Full Time Students	1937 Faculty	1937 Endowment	1937 Library Volumes
Centenary Junior Col., Hackettstown, N.J.	1867	Hurst R. Anderson	297	25	$ 25,000	9,324	157	21	$ 26,310	7,000
Central College (Jr.), Conway, Ark.	1892	Robert L. Whipple	100	13	—	6,000	110	21	—	—
Central College, Fayette, Mo.	1854	Harry S. DeVore	754	64	1,020,422	50,000	605	41	1,321,000	31,386
Central College, Pella, Iowa	1853	G. T. Vander Lugt	486	32	390,000	22,500	295	23	253,000	13,000
Central Michigan College of Education, Mt. Pleasant, Michigan	1892	Charles L. Anspach	1,847	126	—	53,259	985	80	—	36,119
Central Missouri St. Col., Warrensburg, Mo.	1871	G. W. Diemer	928	73	—	103,902	779	58	—	81,540
Central State College, Edmond, Okla.	1890	R. R. Robinson	817	70	—	26,600	1,121	60	—	31,916
Central Washington Col. of Educ., Ellensburg, Wash.	1891	Robert E. McConnell	906	66	—	43,952	548	48	—	21,570
Centre College of Kentucky, Danville, Ky.	1819	James H. Hewlett	560	37	1,844,343	60,000	386	29	1,375,530	32,000
Chaffey College, Ontario, Calif.	1883	Gardiner W. Spring	948	52	—	39,000	795	55	—	35,000
Charleston, College of, Charleston, S.C.	1770	George D. Grice	368	26	532,500	31,597	328	23	361,000	28,000
Chattanooga, Univ. of, Chattanooga, Tenn.	1884	David A. Lockmiller	1,490	90	850,000	120,000	605	40	750,000	35,000
Chestnut Hill College, Philadelphia, Pa.	1871	Sister Maria Kostka	450	50	—	30,800	280	33	—	21,950
Chicago, School of the Art Inst. of, Chicago, Ill.	1879	C. Hubert Ropp	872	76	—	51,000	757	58	—	33,850
Chicago, University of, Chicago, Ill.	1892	Robert M. Hutchins	12,366	898	72,521,247	1,500,000	7,754	690	65,389,498	1,100,000
Chicago Teachers College, Chicago, Ill.	1867	James I. Swearingen	1,013	57	—	68,000	710	38	—	63,500
Christian College (Jr.), Columbia, Mo.	1851	J. C. Miller	343	36	100,000	13,000	225	27	80,000	9,000
Cincinnati, University of, Cincinnati, Ohio	1819	Raymond Walters	7,480	825	10,817,500	592,425	4,169	647	9,455,170	425,329
Citadel, The, Charleston, S.C.	1842	C. P. Summerall	1,841	92	—	38,787	987	61	—	19,000
Clark College, Atlanta, Ga.	1869	James P. Brawley	777	40	676,457	16,000	389	27	450,000	14,000
Clarke College, Dubuque, Iowa	1843	Sister Mary Ambrose	483	39	—	26,000	286	36	—	—
Clarkson Col. of Technology, Potsdam, N.Y.*	1895	John A. Ross, Jr.	385	31	1,400,000	10,000	383	32	1,520,507	11,990
Clark University, Worcester, Mass.	1887	Howard B. Jefferson	825	65	6,048,135	200,000	352	42	5,237,806	160,000
Clemson Agricultural Col., Clemson, S.C.	1889	Robert F. Poole	2,961	224	281,000	75,206	1,869	136	58,539	39,713
Coe College, Cedar Rapids, Iowa	1851	Byron S. Hollinshead	803	55	2,000,000	54,000	646	59	1,750,000	50,000
Coker College, Hartsville, S.C.	1908	Donald C. Agnew	360	33	700,000	22,000	234	27	473,000	16,000
Colby College, Waterville, Maine	1813	Julius S. Bixler	893	59	3,459,974	122,334	618	44	2,456,261	92,087
Colby Junior College, New London, N.H.	1837	H. Leslie Sawyer	390	43	375,000	20,000	315	33	275,000	15,000
Colgate University, Hamilton, N.Y.	1819	Everett N. Case	1,401	107	5,784,332	150,888	1,064	97	6,635,326	11,564
Colorado, University, Boulder, Colo.	1876	Robert L. Stearns	8,162	475	927,600	425,000	3,890	381	487,324	282,983
Colorado College, Colorado Springs, Colo.	1874	Thurston J. Davies	1,016	79	2,929,512	136,000	614	61	2,790,000	109,134
Colorado School of Mines, Golden, Colo.*	1874	M. F. Coolbaugh	235	43	—	50,000	659	61	—	30,000
Colorado State College of Agriculture and Mechanic Arts, Fort Collins, Colo.	1870	Roy M. Green	3,518	237	—	125,000	2,816	120	295,714	86,589
Colorado State Col. of Educ., Greeley, Colo.	1890	George W. Frazier	1,609	98	—	111,917	1,358	94	—	82,250
Colorado Woman's College (Jr.), Denver, Colo.	1888	James E. Huchingson	406	45	107,000	10,400	298	27	101,000	5,004
Columbia University, New York, N.Y.	1754	Frank D. Fackenthal	28,201	2,407	88,793,711	1,747,932	17,244	2,386	86,688,932	1,563,167
Compton Junior College, Compton, Calif.	1927	Scott Thompson	5,051	128	—	32,000	2,799	81	—	20,000
Concord College, Athens, W.Va.†	1872	Virgil H. Stewart	820	36	—	20,000	76	35	—	17,942
Concordia College, Moorhead, Minn.	1891	J. N. Brown	935	54	567,087	31,081	480	38	591,984	23,416
Concordia Collegiate Inst., Bronxville, New York	1881	Arthur J. Doege	160	21	—	14,000	234	16	—	14,000
Connecticut, Junior Col. of, Bridgeport, Conn.	1927	James H. Halsey	1,200	60	—	8,958	87	10	—	4,000
Connecticut, Tch. Col. of, New Britain, Conn.	1850	Herbert D. Welte	1,040	65	—	35,000	575	31	—	15,701
Connecticut, University of, Storrs, Conn.	1881	A. N. Jorgensen	6,622	449	307,394	105,000	885	123	300,707	45,000
Connecticut College, New London, Conn.	1911	Rosemary Park	843	96	2,142,609	113,535	716	67	1,315,881	75,000
Converse College, Spartanburg, S.C.	1889	Edw. M. Gwathmey	447	45	643,000	32,578	333	30	634,923	30,500
Copiah-Lincoln Junior College, Wesson, Miss.	1928	J. M. Ewing	410	28	—	8,000	343	24	—	6,000
Cornell College, Mount Vernon, Iowa	1853	Russell D. Cole	813	62	2,751,174	60,000	612	45	2,212,503	60,000
Cornell University, Ithaca, N.Y.	1865	Edmund Ezra Day	9,719	1,214	35,369,309	1,221,361	5,506	981	30,975,376	966,349
Cottey Junior College, Nevada, Mo.	1884	Marjorie Mitchell	156	21	59,091	8,635	101	17	—	6,719
Creighton University, Omaha, Neb.	1878	William H. McCabe	2,826	338	2,322,500	145,182	2,305	223	4,000,000	101,877
Culver-Stockton College, Canton, Mo.	1853	W. H. McDonald	455	30	1,000,000	30,000	254	20	1,012,000	23,000
Cumberland College, Williamsburg, Ky.	1889	J. M. Boswell	243	16	645,000	7,500	203	17	483,803	7,000
D										
Dakota Wesleyan University, Mitchell, S.D.	1885	Samuel H. Hilburn	398	30	567,532	30,981	334	28	590,000	28,600
Dalhousie Univ., Halifax, N.S., Can.‖	1818	Carleton Stanley	668	140	3,591,968	67,923	853	165	2,510,917	53,000
Danbury State Tch. Col., Danbury, Conn.	1906	Ruth A. Haas	253	17	—	25,000	146	40	—	13,000
Dartmouth College, Hanover, N.H.	1769	John Sloan Dickey	2,822	300	23,292,248	616,570	2,442	261	15,175,914	434,947
Davidson College, Davidson, N.C.	1836	John R. Cunningham	910	55	2,750,000	45,000	665	43	2,750,000	40,000
Dayton, University of, Dayton, Ohio	1850	George J. Renneker	2,104	135	—	40,000	614	45	—	32,450
Delaware, University of, Newark, Del.	1833	William S. Carlson	1,677	177	5,120,795	107,129	823	101	605,637	76,000
Delta State Tch. Col., Cleveland, Miss.	1924	William M. Kethley	482	46	—	25,000	375	32	—	20,000
Denison University, Granville, Ohio	1831	Kenneth I. Brown	1,190	76	3,490,861	111,000	891	58	2,942,229	86,000
Denver, University of, Denver, Colo.	1864	Caleb F. Gates	6,877	694	2,631,645	186,194	2,215	301	2,529,274	117,652
De Paul University, Chicago, Illinois	1898	Comerford J. O'Malley	6,230	340	—	80,513	2,782	172	—	66,440
DePauw University, Greencastle, Ind.	1837	Clyde E. Wildman	1,999	118	6,000,000	100,165	1,231	82	5,996,005	85,151
Detroit, University of, Detroit, Mich.	1877	William J. Millor	5,584	334	1,610,000	126,800	1,972	196	1,640,000	93,921
Dickinson College, Carlisle, Pa.	1773	William W. Edel	821	54	2,033,891	75,639	577	34	1,115,911	61,169
Dillard University, New Orleans, La.	1930	Albert W. Dent	446	47	3,000,000	30,000	290	21	—	19,159
Dixie Junior College, St. George, Utah	1911	Glenn E. Snow	493	26	—	10,000	143	12	—	9,500
Doane College, Crete, Nebr.	1872	Bryant Drake	428	37	1,305,982	30,859	227	24	867,532	27,610
Drake University, Des Moines, Iowa	1881	H. G. Harmon	3,500	190	1,955,000	111,000	1,008	114	1,852,070	72,302
Drew University, Madison, N.J.	1867	Arlo Ayres Brown	603	52	7,299,425	196,000	405	43	5,299,321	174,312
Drexel Institute of Tech., Philadelphia, Pa.	1891	James Creese	3,049	206	3,004,796	88,388	1,662	132	3,331,940	57,354
Drury College, Springfield, Mo.	1873	J. F. Findlay	712	46	1,200,000	70,000	409	36	1,200,000	37,000
Dubuque, University of, Dubuque, Iowa	1852	Dale D. Welch	644	41	868,581	30,000	325	29	745,142	20,000
Duchesne College, Omaha, Neb.	1881	Mother Helen Casey	239	20	—	18,100	122	18	—	11,750
Duke University, Durham, N.C.	1838	Robert Lee Flowers	4,797	637	47,685,097	722,000	3,493	449	30,880,031	529,060
Duluth Junior College, Duluth, Minn.	1927	R. D. Chadwick	797	40	—	8,800	384	23	—	5,375
Dunbarton College of Holy Cross, Wash., D.C.	1935	Sr. Mary Frederick	198	24	—	19,017	55	19	—	—
Duquesne University, Pittsburgh, Pa.	1878	Francis P. Smith	2,908	237	—	49,162	1,357	185	—	43,800
D'Youville College, Buffalo, N.Y.	1908	Sister Grace	423	34	—	25,000	260	26	—	20,190
E										
Earlham College, Richmond, Ind.	1847	Thomas E. Jones	642	44	1,438,445	70,000	388	40	1,255,572	58,000
East Carolina Tch. Col., Greenville, N.C.	1907	Dennis H. Cooke	1,187	67	—	50,692	1,767	50	—	17,500
East Central Junior Col., Decatur, Miss.	1928	L. O. Todd	506	25	—	5,500	449	19	—	4,500
East Central State College, Ada, Oklahoma	1909	A. Linscheid	1,196	64	—	47,000	1,100	61	—	19,000
Eastern Illinois State Tch. Col., Charleston, Ill.	1895	Robert G. Buzzard	1,218	105	—	65,318	741	86	—	46,341
Eastern Kentucky State Tch. Col., Richmond, Ky.	1906	W. F. O'Donnell	1,095	89	—	73,678	1,294	79	—	49,352
Eastern Montana St. Normal Sch., Billings, Mont.†	1927	A. G. Peterson	320	21	—	13,000	277	16	—	10,000
Eastern Nazarene College, Wollaston, Mass.	1919	Samuel Young	472	29	—	17,500	170	14	—	9,500
Eastern Oregon Col. of Educ., LaGrande, Ore.	1929	Roben J. Maaske	613	38	1,000	24,763	356	20	—	483,509
Eastern State Normal School, Madison, S.D.	1881	V. A. Lowry	178	25	1,050	27,340	241	30	9,351	20,863
Eastern Washington Col. of Educ., Cheney, Wash.	1890	Walter W. Isle	782	69	—	69,000	724	57	—	41,000

Institution and Location	Year Founded	Chief Executive 1946	1946				1937			
			Full Time Students	Faculty	Endow-ment	Library Volumes	Full Time Students	Faculty	Endow-ment	Library Volumes
East Tennessee St. Col., Johnson City, Tenn.	1911	C. C. Sherrod	1,084	54	—	34,000	785	45	—	33,000
East Texas State Tch. Col., Commerce, Tex.	1889	A. C. Ferguson	1,585	101	—	90,392	1,242	89	—	45,765
Edinburg Junior College, Edinburg, Tex.	1927	H. A. Hodges	507	26	—	10,110	225	14	—	7,000
Elmhurst College, Elmhurst, Ill.	1871	Timothy Lehmann	534	40	$ 266,000	40,000	248	28	$ 185,000	29,135
Elmira College, Elmira, N.Y.	1855	W. S. A. Pott	393	48	579,656	58,497	375	53	1,039,298	46,500
Emmanuel College, Boston, Mass.	1919	Sr. Margaret Patricia	754	69	—	27,045	387	44	—	19,029
Emmanuel Missionary Col., Berrien Spgs., Mich.	1874	Alvin W. Johnson	728	43	425,975	33,800	417	26	300,000	21,834
Emory and Henry College, Emory, Va.	1836	Foye G. Gibson	531	23	553,485	24,000	274	21	312,222	18,500
Emory at Oxford (Jr.), Oxford, Ga.	1836	Virgil Y. C. Eady	302	18	—	5,650	188	13	—	3,142
Emory University, Emory University, Ga.	1836	Goodrich C. White	3,404	463	9,626,233	261,830	1,428	302	5,000,000	150,000
Erskine College, Due West, S.C.	1839	R. C. Grier	460	34	380,000	32,000	300	25	353,000	25,000
Evansville College, Evansville, Ind.	1854	Lincoln B. Hale	1,446	90	409,341	23,549	349	29	430,000	17,919
Eveleth Junior College, Eveleth, Minn.	1919	O. H. Gibson	232	14	—	12,000	275	16	—	10,000
F										
Fairmont State College, Fairmont, W.Va.‖†	1867	Joseph Rosier	430	41	—	26,500	575	43	—	32,056
Fayetteville State Tch. Col., Fayetteville, N.C.	1867	J. W. Seabrook	601	25	—	21,921	455	20	—	12,681
Fenn College, Cleveland, Ohio	1881	Cecil V. Thomas	1,211	225	809,060	27,000	551	52	807,260	10,617
Finch Junior College, New York, N.Y.	1900	Jessica G. Cosgrave	265	44	—	8,500	143	24	—	4,000
Findlay College, Findlay, Ohio	1882	Carroll A. Morey	350	20	440,990	20,000	212	21	400,766	19,000
Fisk University, Nashville, Tenn.‖	1866	Thomas E. Jones	652	72	3,326,784	80,553	423	48	1,847,586	63,200
Flat River, Junior Col. of, Flat River, Mo.	1922	Irvin F. Coyle	195	18	—	9,000	140	11	—	8,000
Flint Junior College, Flint, Mich.	1923	L. A. Pratt	848	36	—	13,058	375	15	—	30,000
Florida, University of, Gainesville, Fla.	1853	John J. Tigert	6,334	463	298,000	250,000	2,992	320	288,348	140,884
Florida Agri. and Mech. College for Negroes,* Tallahassee, Fla.	1887	Wm. H. Gray, Jr.	1,092	138	—	16,350	819	104	—	11,683
Florida Normal and Industrial College,* St. Augustine, Fla.	1892	John Lee Tilley	337	27	—	6,000	193	16	—	2,742
Florida Southern College, Lakeland, Florida	1885	Ludd M. Spivey	1,590	76	1,200,000	65,000	904	45	500,000	25,000
Florida State Col. for Wom., Tallahassee, Fla.	1905	Doak S. Campbell	3,090	222	206,000	107,429	1,778	140	205,702	65,500
Fontbonne College, Saint Louis, Mo.	1923	Mother Mary Berenice	363	48	—	24,850	198	41	—	13,201
Fordham University, New York, N.Y.	1841	Robert I. Gannon	8,612	376	780,000	225,450	4,489	416	490,500	177,000
Fort Hays Kansas State Col., Hays, Kansas	1901	L. D. Wooster	941	80	—	60,000	878	70	—	25,000
Fort Valley State College, Fort Valley, Ga.	1895	Cornelius V. Troup	515	50	38,529	10,000	250	20	34,500	5,000
Frances Shimer Col. (Jr.), Mount Carroll, Ill.	1853	Albin C. Bro	306	24	189,473	12,396	172	18	25,822	9,477
Franklin and Marshall Col., Lancaster, Pa.	1787	Theodore A. Distler	1,256	63	1,587,664	105,000	806	37	1,092,791	73,100
Franklin College, Franklin, Ind.	1834	William G. Spencer	516	34	1,149,784	39,894	245	35	815,386	31,000
Fresno State College, Fresno, Calif.	1911	Frank W. Thomas	2,679	140	—	59,845	1,884	88	—	35,935
Fullerton Junior College, Fullerton, Calif.	1913	W. T. Boyce	1,550	51	—	13,500	1,046	58	—	7,174
Furman University, Greenville, S.C.	1826	John Laney Plyler	1,323	68	3,236,038	60,000	911	80	2,650,000	37,000
G										
Geneva College, Beaver Falls, Pa.	1848	M. M. Pearce	864	44	663,488	36,000	480	36	657,879	26,600
George Peabody Col. for Tch., Nashville, Tenn.	1875	Henry H. Hill	1,752	114	5,014,088	618,762	833	128	4,629,148	102,805
Georgetown College, Georgetown, Ky.	1829	Samuel S. Hill	600	40	617,000	18,000	362	26	535,000	18,000
Georgetown University, Washington, D.C.	1789	Lawrence C. Gorman	4,276	500	3,387,650	200,000	2,429	450	—	200,000
George Washington Univ., Washington, D.C.	1821	Cloyd H. Marvin	5,883	580	2,500,000	160,000	7,542	398	2,511,456	100,000
George Williams College, Chicago, Ill.	1890	Harold Coe Coffman	299	30	231,101	24,000	230	17	199,547	13,000
Georgia, University of, Athens, Ga.	1785	Harmon W. Caldwell	6,780	441	2,520,000	210,000	3,497	185	728,598	134,640
Georgia Military Col. (Jr.), Milledgeville, Ga.	1879	J. H. Jenkins	580	30	—	5,000	500	31	—	3,500
Georgian Court College, Lakewood, N.J.	1908	Mother Mary John	250	38	—	35,000	—	26	—	—
Georgia School of Tech., Atlanta, Ga.	1885	Blake R. VanLeer	4,555	315	640,000	76,638	2,459	121	524,303	36,673
Georgia Southwestern Col. (Jr.), Americus, Ga.	1924	Peyton Jacob	475	22	—	16,367	344	15	—	6,657
Georgia State Col., Industrial College, Ga.†	1891	Benjamin F. Hubert	885	58	—	13,483	530	41	—	7,288
Georgia St. Col. for Wom., Milledgeville, Ga.	1889	Guy H. Wells	1,068	117	—	38,500	1,343	103	—	30,000
Georgia State Womans Col., Valdosta, Ga.	1906	Frank R. Reade	354	28	—	22,690	308	20	—	20,000
Georgia Teachers College, Collegeboro, Ga.	1908	Marvin S. Pittman	604	38	—	35,000	644	40	—	17,000
Gettysburg College, Gettysburg, Pa.	1832	Henry W. A. Hanson	1,090	58	500,000	60,000	638	44	760,000	55,000
Glendale College (Jr.), Glendale, Calif.	1927	Basil H. Peterson	2,362	70	—	12,500	1,297	44	—	10,000
Glenville State College, Glenville, W.Va.	1872	D. L. Haught	405	25	—	22,500	312	23	—	16,044
Gonzaga University, Spokane, Wash.	1887	Francis E. Corkery	1,506	85	—	50,000	1,010	86	1,300,000	38,156
Good Counsel College, White Plains, N.Y.	1923	Mother M. Aloysia	343	37	48,000	15,085	151	34	—	10,618
Gordon Military College (Jr.), Barnesville, Ga.	1852	J. E. Guillebeau	420	22	—	6,000	100	18	—	2,000
Goshen College, Goshen, Ind.	1894	Ernest E. Miller	501	32	216,187	31,000	267	25	124,807	15,700
Goucher College, Baltimore, Md.	1885	David A. Robertson	616	67	2,096,919	83,738	668	72	2,483,362	66,133
Graceland Junior College, Lamoni, Iowa	1895	E. J. Gleazer	591	32	253,662	19,255	258	210	233,399	18,000
Grand Rapids Jr. Col., Grand Rapids, Mich.	1914	Arthur Andrews	1,422	65	—	16,000	650	35	—	12,000
Great Falls Col. of Educ., Great Falls, Montana	1932	James J. Donovan	429	32	—	50,000	350	32	—	20,000
Green Mountain Junior Col., Poultney, Vt.	1834	Howard C. Ackley	294	24	97,294	11,400	243	24	51,560	6,000
Greensboro College, Greensboro, N.C.	1838	Luther L. Gobbel	366	33	579,059	28,000	306	26	399,799	16,733
Greenville College, Greenville, Ill.	1892	H. J. Long	430	33	130,000	18,200	246	24	100,677	10,000
Grinnell College, Grinnell, Ia.	1846	Samuel N. Stevens	918	90	5,093,537	120,000	783	66	2,134,352	97,852
Grove City College, Grove City, Pa.	1876	Weir C. Ketler	1,228	55	842,000	45,000	898	56	763,524	36,158
Guilford College, Guilford College, N.C.	1837	Clyde A. Milner	551	32	682,125	28,000	345	25	610,000	16,600
Gulf Park College, Gulfport, Miss.	1921	Richard G. Cox	265	30	—	6,259	258	26	—	4,523
Gustavus Adolphus Col., St. Peter, Minn.	1862	Edgar M. Carlson	970	58	560,436	25,112	502	31	545,341	15,326
H										
Hamilton College, Clinton, N.Y.	1812	David Worcester	583	49	4,255,733	209,265	425	48	4,327,574	179,282
Hamline University, St. Paul, Minn.	1854	Charles N. Pace	1,089	75	2,158,701	49,535	590	47	1,860,732	37,086
Hampden-Sydney Col., Hamp.-Sydney, Va.	1776	Edgar G. Gammon	410	24	621,148	35,000	350	20	388,000	32,000
Hampton Institute, Hampton, Va.	1868	Ralph P. Bridgman	1,516	135	9,835,177	73,413	1,024	133	8,414,478	59,040
Hanover College, Hanover, Ind.	1827	Albert G. Parker, Jr.	608	31	3,200,000	46,000	350	26	1,200,000	40,000
Hardin Junior College, Wichita Falls, Tex.*	1922	James B. Boren	346	36	360,000	11,000	300	19	—	49,878
Hardin-Simmons University, Abilene, Tex.	1891	Rupert N. Richardson	1,655	74	1,250,000	37,500	1,168	42	1,000,000	28,000
Harris Teachers College, St. Louis, Mo.	1857	Charles H. Philpott	867	37	—	25,800	263	26	—	18,030
Harvard University, Cambridge, Mass.	1636	James B. Conant	12,076	2,190	178,297,925	4,702,229	8,289	1,878	141,941,867	3,861,438
Hastings College, Hastings, Neb.	1882	Wm. M. French	654	55	661,165	33,000	480	46	813,000	25,950
Haverford College, Haverford, Pa.	1833	Gilbert F. White	495	50	5,000,000	167,000	334	48	4,429,559	138,236
Hawaii, University of, Honolulu, Hawaii	1907	Gregg M. Sinclair	2,381	207	66,791	169,253	2,256	179	13,759	103,897
Heidelberg College, Tiffin, Ohio	1850	Nevin C. Harner	660	45	1,000,000	35,000	426	37	1,000,000	33,000
Henderson St. Tch. Col., Arkadelphia, Ark.‖	1929	Matt L. Ellis	483	44	—	24,891	501	35	—	16,685
Hendrix College, Conway, Ark.	1884	Matt L. Ellis	555	41	753,694	48,841	371	32	980,000	38,000
Hershey Junior College, Hershey, Pa.	1938	A. G. Breidenstine	132	15	30,000	15,234	85	10	30,000	7,000
Hibbing Junior College, Hibbing, Minn.	1916	S. A. Patchin	498	28	—	6,283	467	33	—	3,500
Highland Park Junior Col., Highland Pk., Mich.	1918	G. O. Withey	1,550	97	—	8,500	237	16	—	8,000
Hillsdale College, Hillsdale, Mich.	1844	Harvey L. Turner	520	40	750,000	30,000	373	44	816,480	28,000
Hinds Junior College, Raymond, Miss.	1917	G. M. McLendon	645	32	—	6,417	527	23	—	5,000
Hiram College, Hiram, Ohio	1850	Paul H. Fall	587	43	1,044,000	50,000	353	29	1,060,410	28,750
Hofstra College, Hempstead, N.Y.	1935	John C. Adams	1,667	120	775,000	21,760	567	28	—	7,946

Institution and Location	Year Founded	Chief Executive 1946	1946				1937			
			Full Time Students	Faculty	Endowment	Library Volumes	Full Time Students	Faculty	Endowment	Library Volumes
Hollins College, Hollins College, Va.	1842	Bessie C. Randolph	367	42	$ 505,915	41,300	322	39	$ 412,067	28,000
Holy Cross, Col. of the, Worcester, Mass.	1843	William J. Healy	1,510	117	—	170,000	1,250	90	97,946	118,591
Holy Names, Col. of the, Oakland, Calif.	1868	Sr. Rose Emmanuella	326	37	—	29,326	248	36	—	13,350
Holy Names College, Spokane, Wash.†	1907	Sister Clare	154	24	—	—	110	16	30,000	14,000
Hood College, Frederick, Md.	1893	Henry I. Stahr	496	52	864,959	27,000	432	49	313,184	17,883
Hope College, Holland, Mich.	1866	Irwin J. Lubbers	1,148	59	945,580	37,465	493	26	820,000	31,000
Houghton College, Houghton, N.Y.	1883	Stephen W. Paine	695	36	300,000	22,008	396	32	250,000	11,100
Howard College, Birmingham, Ala.	1842	Harwell G. Davis	1,275	56	753,329	32,000	712	50	733,767	21,800
Howard University, Washington, D.C.	1867	Mordecai W. Johnson	5,230	365	1,039,372	226,053	1,625	290	959,594	106,360
Hunter College of the City of New York, New York, N.Y.	1870	George N. Shuster	5,743	359	179,401	156,643	7,000	378	—	99,256
Huntingdon College, Montgomery, Ala.	1854	Hubert Searcy	685	65	400,000	26,000	300	25	300,000	14,000
Huron College, Huron, S.D.	1883	George F. McDougall	350	26	792,656	25,000	266	20	835,688	20,463
I										
Idaho, College of, Caldwell, Ida.	1891	William W. Hall, Jr.	479	30	532,450	22,000	390	30	545,673	14,000
Idaho, Univ. of; So. Br. (Jr.), Pocatello, Ida.	1927	Carl W. McIntosh	1,535	84	—	24,000	934	56	—	17,134
Idaho, University of, Moscow, Ida.	1892	J. E. Buchanan	3,458	214	4,743,870	96,000	2,994	162	—	100,000
Illinois, University of, Urbana, Ill.	1867	George D. Stoddard	24,189	1,887	2,071,884	2,003,622	13,823	808	1,115,746	1,086,212
Illinois College, Jacksonville, Ill.	1829	Harris G. Hudson	524	31	1,228,016	34,964	388	32	1,066,544	33,000
Illinois Institute of Technology, Chicago, Ill.§	1892	Henry Townley Heald	3,072	215	1,806,200	125,000	1,750	217	1,500,000	92,200
Illinois State Normal Univ., Normal, Ill.	1857	R. W. Fairchild	1,687	208	—	83,822	1,853	193	—	77,000
Illinois Wesleyan Univ., Bloomington, Ill.	1850	William E. Shaw	1,092	80	1,606,765	45,000	855	52	1,388,000	37,000
Immaculata College, Immaculata, Pa.	1920	V. L. Burns	343	44	—	21,200	241	36	—	13,525
Immaculata Junior Col., Wash., D.C.	1920	Sister St. Philomene	96	14	—	8,000	53	15	—	5,000
Incarnate Word College, San Antonio, Tex.	1900	Sister M. Columkille	649	66	99,524	35,338	512	38	118,800	27,000
Indiana State Tch. Col., Terre Haute, Ind.	1865	Ralph N. Tirey	2,266	158	—	150,000	1,275	104	—	128,822
Indiana University, Bloomington, Ind.	1820	Herman B. Wells	13,110	675	2,500,000	500,000	7,005	396	2,422,591	301,854
Iowa, State University of, Iowa City, Ia.	1847	Virgil M. Hancher	9,783	818	1,283,964	654,410	8,734	716	818,981	500,421
Iowa State College, Ames, Ia.	1858	Charles E. Friley	9,300	700	1,250,000	390,000	6,907	600	1,100,000	260,000
Iowa State Tch. Col., Cedar Falls, Ia.	1876	Malcolm Price	2,477	178	—	122,268	1,863	141	—	121,039
Iowa Wesleyan College, Mount Pleasant, Ia.	1842	Stanley B. Niles	497	50	800,000	40,000	291	20	400,000	22,000
J										
Jackson Junior College, Jackson, Mich.	1928	G. L. Greenawalt	519	30	—	5,207	300	14	—	4,000
James Millikin University, Decatur, Ill.	1901	J. Walter Malone	1,288	78	2,000,000	30,361	473	43	2,000,000	30,115
James Ormond Wilson Tch. Col., Wash., D.C.	1873	Walter E. Hager	372	51	—	26,651	419	45	—	19,000
Jamestown College, Jamestown, N.D.	1883	Howard J. Bell, Jr.	494	32	1,200,359	20,500	420	28	1,000,000	29,000
John B. Stetson University, DeLand, Fla.	1883	W. S. Allen	1,623	103	1,000,000	47,000	900	63	850,000	33,000
John Carroll University, Cleveland, Ohio*	1886	Thomas J. Donnelly	187	35	2,500,000	38,738	479	45	1,500,000	27,281
Johns Hopkins University, Baltimore, Md.	1876	Isaiah Bowman	2,535	784	33,447,498	737,760	1,684	604	29,874,438	535,243
Johnson C. Smith University, Charlotte, N.C.	1867	Henry L. McCrorey	813	35	2,000,000	26,108	345	29	450,000	22,370
John Tarleton Agri. Col. (Jr.), Stephenville, Tex.	1899	E. J. Howell	1,540	62	137,626	29,000	1,162	71	100,000	20,000
Joliet Junior College, Joliet, Ill.	1901	Donald M. Sharpe	627	44	—	11,900	287	34	—	—
Jones County Junior Col., Ellisville, Miss.	1927	J. B. Young	1,410	50	—	15,000	499	45	—	8,000
Judson College, Marion, Ala.	1838	J. I. Riddle	310	30	544,000	20,000	195	30	524,000	14,387
Juniata College, Huntingdon, Pa.	1876	Calvert N. Ellis	570	43	789,097	51,460	415	46	696,562	50,000
K										
Kalamazoo College, Kalamazoo, Mich.	1833	Paul L. Thompson	629	40	1,133,272	38,500	354	53	1,434,163	27,515
Kansas, University of, Lawrence, Kan.	1865	Deane W. Malott	8,985	758	256,000	370,000	4,654	306	250,000	291,900
Kansas City, Junior College of, Kansas City, Mo.	1915	A. M. Swanson	1,875	55	—	31,012	1,075	51	—	29,000
Kansas City, University of, Kansas City, Mo.	1929	Clarence R. Decker	2,055	186	—	140,000	553	40	1,088	45,000
Kansas State College, Manhattan, Kan.	1863	Milton S. Eisenhower	6,512	335	547,842	152,000	3,869	325	505,509	110,000
Kansas State Tch. Col., Emporia, Kan.	1863	D. L. MacFarlane	1,147	98	250,000	92,000	1,450	120	250,000	100,000
Kansas State Tch. Col., Pittsburgh, Kan.	1903	Rees H. Hughes	1,872	125	—	88,000	2,546	108	—	47,338
Keene Teachers College, Keene, N.H.	1909	Lloyd P. Young	400	40	—	20,000	348	52	—	15,456
Kemper Military School (Jr.), Boonville, Mo.	1844	A. M. Hitch	525	52	—	7,000	429	30	—	6,000
Kent State University, Kent, Ohio	1910	George A. Bowman	5,437	259	—	80,000	1,949	100	—	58,000
Kentucky, University of, Frankfort, Ky.	1865	H. L. Donovan	6,616	360	190,864	383,103	3,550	293	194,200	212,738
Kentucky St. Col. for Negroes, Frankfort, Ky.	1886	R. B. Atwood	671	33	—	16,575	590	27	—	9,807
Kenyon College, Gambier, Ohio.	1824	Gordon K. Chalmers	552	49	1,964,595	92,972	300	34	1,894,756	47,000
Keuka College, Keuka Park, N.Y.	1890	Katherine G. Blyley	428	32	363,804	34,353	212	25	304,790	23,899
Keystone College (Jr.), La Plume, Pa.	1868	Blake Tewksbury	568	33	—	15,000	180	17	—	8,013
Kilgore College (Jr.), Kilgore, Tex.*	1935	B. E. Masters	353	30	—	11,000	484	27	—	2,298
King's College, Univ. of, Halifax, N.S., Can.	1789	A. Stanley Walker	166	12	1,000,000	32,000	96	10	1,000,000	30,000
Knox College, Galesburg, Illinois	1837	Lyndon O. Brown	832	68	2,651,135	70,000	623	56	2,156,543	50,000
Knoxville College, Knoxville, Tenn.	1875	William L. Imes	337	18	500,000	13,849	316	20	500,000	12,000
L										
Lafayette College, Easton, Pa.	1826	Ralph C. Hutchison	1,442	107	4,506,678	114,906	825	97	3,734,804	94,628
Lake Erie College, Painesville, Ohio	1856	Helen D. Bragdon	224	20	815,086	36,361	136	26	807,000	27,000
Lake Forest College, Lake Forest, Ill.	1857	Ernest A. Johnson	636	40	1,356,000	56,686	365	28	1,462,267	48,605
Lamar College (Jr.), Beaumont, Tex.	1923	John E. Gray	1,572	66	—	6,100	500	17	—	4,231
Lane College, Jackson, Tenn.	1882	Dean S. Yarbrough	437	20	28,000	11,040	461	17	—	3,000
La Salle College, Philadelphia, Pa.	1863	Brother G. Paul	1,216	40	—	27,400	371	31	650,000	10,000
Lasell Junior College, Auburndale, Mass.	1851	Guy M. Winslow	531	53	—	10,682	390	44	100,000	6,000
La Sierra College, Arlington, Calif.	1922	G. T. Anderson	621	42	—	15,200	182	21	—	6,950
Laval University, Quebec, Can.	1852	Ferdinand Vandry	4,975	810	2,500,000	824,706	2,295	212	2,250,000	221,322
Lawrence College, Appleton, Wis.	1847	Nathan M. Pusey	1,031	77	1,550,000	74,361	679	72	1,500,000	59,836
Lebanon Valley College, Annville, Pa.	1866	Clyde A. Lynch	693	39	1,141,837	32,398	407	35	916,756	19,655
Lehigh University, Bethlehem, Pa.*	1865	E. K. Smiley	675	117	7,287,000	258,000	1,750	170	5,000,000	216,000
LeMoyne College, Memphis, Tenn.	1871	Hollis F. Price	379	20	—	18,000	50	17	—	9,000
Lenoir Rhyne College, Hickory, N.C.	1891	P. E. Monroe	761	41	709,457	27,000	592	33	700,000	25,000
Lewis and Clark College, Portland, Ore.	1867	Morgan S. Odell	749	65	300,000	20,000	314	24	200,000	—
Lewiston St. Normal Sch., Lewiston, Ida.	1892	Glenn W. Todd	390	33	—	23,000	380	28	—	10,250
Limestone College, Gaffney, S.C.	1845	Robert C. Granberry	414	30	698,000	22,000	314	27	426,810	18,209
Lincoln College (Jr.), Lincoln, Ill.	1865	M. D. McLean	149	14	326,000	12,000	73	14	200,000	9,850
Lincoln Memorial Univ., Harrogate, Tenn.	1897	S. W. McClelland	507	27	790,046	21,873	382	20	859,691	18,000
Lincoln University, Jefferson City, Mo.	1866	Sherman D. Scruggs	1,023	85	—	62,880	415	31	—	15,600
Lincoln University, Lincoln University, Pa.	1854	Horace M. Bond	507	35	1,000,000	40,000	324	29	1,045,825	40,000
Lindenwood College, St. Charles, Mo.	1827	Guy C. Motley	481	52	4,000,000	27,800	438	45	1,913,195	20,600
Linfield College, McMinnville, Ore.	1857	Harry L. Dillin	705	40	1,125,000	35,000	592	40	675,000	30,000
Little Rock Junior College, Little Rock, Ark.	1927	John A. Larson	1,012	40	1,800,000	18,000	300	18	1,225,000	14,000
Livingstone College, Salisbury, N.C.	1879	William J. Trent	375	26	46,500	21,384	281	20	46,000	16,415
Long Beach City Col. (Jr.), Long Beach, Calif.	1927	George E. Dotson	2,750	226	—	35.000	1,264	74	—	18,664
Lon Morris Col. (Jr.), Jacksonville, Tex.*	1873	C. E. Peeples	159	12	150,000	6,783	238	14	106,821	5,967
Loras College, Dubuque, Ia.*	1839	M. J. Martin	344	70	1,400,000	97 000	400	22	1,200,000	70,000
Loretto Heights College, Loretto, Colorado	1918	Sister Frances Marie	354	43	—	18,752	108	24	—	13,590
Los Angeles City Col. (Jr.), Los Angeles, Calif.	1929	Einar W. Jacobsen	8,242	240	—	60,000	4,628	187	—	50,000
Louisiana College, Pineville, La.	1906	Edgar Godbold	689	36	403,000	14,941	425	22	286,943	10,000

Institution and Location	Year Founded	Chief Executive 1946	1946				1937			
			Full Time Students	Faculty	Endowment	Library Volumes	Full Time Students	Faculty	Endowment	Library Volumes
Louisiana Polytechnic Institute, Ruston, La.	1894	Claybrook Cottingham	2,327	141	—	36,605	1,340	73	—	17,188
Louisiana State University and A. and M. College, Baton Rouge, La.	1860	Wm. B. Hatcher	10,599	703	$ 14,644	307,799	8,168	313	—	189,033
Louisville, University of, Louisville, Ky.	1837	Frederick W. Stamm	3,999	439	1,200,000	130,692	1,557	327	$ 930,338	77,023
Loyola College, Baltimore, Md.	1852	Edward B. Bunn	668	35	2,603,000	36,500	203	19	1,375,000	28,000
Loyola University, Chicago, Ill.	1870	James T. Hussey	5,187	582	—	79,000	4,694	695	—	—
Loyola University, New Orleans, La.	1912	Thomas J. Shields	1,818	180	5,331,675	102,875	984	163	2,154,387	80,794
Loyola Univ. of Los Angeles, Los Angeles, Calif.	1911	Edward J. Whelan	1,455	72	—	43,000	566	38	—	23,280
Luther College, Decorah, Ia.	1861	O. J. H. Preus	656	47	550,000	82,000	433	38	635,667	65,000
Lynchburg College, Lynchburg, Va.	1903	Riley B. Montgomery	489	33	321,949	23,358	218	19	292,398	15,000
Lyons Township Junior Col., La Grange, Ill.	1929	Harold L. Bitting	433	26	—	8,000	178	15	—	—
M										
Macalester College, St. Paul, Minn.	1885	Charles J. Turck	1,227	94	2,324,000	41,000	679	51	1,574,344	22,700
McGill University, Montreal, Que., Can.	1821	F. Cyril James	7,110	853	41,028,514	447,199	2,914	520	20,183,857	377,000
McMaster University, Hamilton, Ont., Can.	1887	G. P. Gilmour	1,121	71	1,934,679	61,500	624	40	1,800,000	42,800
MacMurray Col. for Wom., Jacksonville, Ill.	1846	C. P. McClelland	761	63	4,049,096	44,399	544	51	665,887	24,038
McPherson College, McPherson, Kan.	1887	W. W. Peters	384	28	508,929	15,225	289	28	260,000	12,000
Madison College, Harrisonburg, Va.	1908	Samuel P. Duke	1,169	80	68,083	39,563	863	62	—	20,307
Maine, University of, Orono, Me.	1865	Arthur A. Hauck	3,993	291	1,243,768	209,540	1,620	150	973,839	127,332
Manchester College, N. Manchester, Ind.	1889	V. F. Schwalm	825	40	600,604	30,000	659	41	500,000	30,000
Manhattan College, New York, N.Y.	1853	Brother B. Thomas	2,142	130	—	93,000	1,258	79	—	50,000
Manhattanville Col. of Sac. Hrt., N.Y., N.Y.	1841	Mother E. M. O'Byrne	552	77	400,900	70,195	310	37	219,726	29,980
Manitoba, University of, Winnipeg, Man., Can.	1877	Albert W. Trueman	6,495	350	1,338,584	116,000	2,706	200	820,481	60,000
Marietta College, Marietta, Ohio	1835	William A. Shimer	1,000	61	1,740,121	127,753	375	32	1,871,460	110,938
Marin Junior College, Kentfield, Calif.	1926	Ward H. Austin	945	40	—	20,000	412	25	—	8,602
Marion Institute (Jr.), Marion, Ala.	1919	James T. Murfee, II	401	24	—	4,439	266	21	—	4,000
Marquette University, Milwaukee, Wis.	1864	Peter A. Brooks	6,382	520	2,934,179	155,000	3,397	320	—	115,000
Marshall College, Huntington, W.Va.*	1837	John Davis Williams	1,088	84	—	55,000	1,609	94	—	34,000
Mars Hill College, (Jr.), Mars Hill, N.C.	1921	Hoyt Blackwell	902	36	150,000	20,000	652	24	104,999	10,000
Mary Baldwin College, Staunton, Va.	1842	Mrs. M. S. Grafton	346	35	515,000	33,000	325	28	520,496	19,000
Marygrove College, Detroit, Mich.	1910	Sister M. Honora	819	86	—	47,350	494	50	—	28,000
Mary Hardin-Baylor College, Belton, Tex.	1845	Gordon G. Singleton	438	42	1,230,981	32,034	652	50	507,000	29,000
Maryland, University of, College Park and Baltimore, Md.	1807	H. C. Byrd	8,245	2,100	4,114,000	125,000	4,834	552	2,080,000	65,065
Maryland State Tch. Col., Salisbury, Md.	1925	J. D. Blackwell	234	13	—	21,000	239	17	—	11,823
Marylhurst College, Marylhurst, Ore.	1930	Sister M. Rose Augusta	261	33	54,450	22,000	144	22	50,000	16,000
Mary Manse College, Toledo, Ohio	1922	Sister Kaley	186	46	—	21,000	110	26	—	12,644
Marymount College, Salina, Kan.	1922	Mother Chrysostom	221	30	—	21,000	121	26	—	18,000
Marymount College, Tarrytown, N.Y.‖†	1907	Mother M. Thérèse	488	57	1,000,000	19,500	121	26	—	14,688
Maryville College, Maryville, Tenn.	1819	Ralph W. Lloyd	829	46	1,937,312	50,000	800	42	1,724,182	42,000
Maryville Col. of the Sac. Hrt., St. Louis, Mo.	1872	Mother Odeide Mouton	300	38	—	27,046	111	27	—	12,875
Mary Washington College of the University of Virginia, Fredericksburg, Va.	1908	Morgan L. Combs	1,477	90	75,000	62,002	1,024	54	—	24,261
Marywood College, Scranton, Pa.	1915	Sister M. Sylvia	558	54	75,000	37,000	463	47	50,000	20,000
Mason City Junior Col., Mason City, Ia.*	1918	Harold J. Snyder	78	14	—	6,557	167	15	—	3,877
Mass. Institute of Tech., Cambridge, Mass.	1861	Karl T. Compton	5,100	925	46,000,000	385,000	2,966	598	35,567	332,007
Mass. State College, Amherst, Mass.	1863	Hugh P. Baker	3,319	159	160,000	141,684	1,120	133	20,298	109,626
Mass. State Tch. Col., Fitchburg, Mass.	1895	William J. Sanders	385	43	—	30,000	294	46	—	20,000
Mass. State Tch. Col., Framingham, Mass.	1839	Martin F. O'Connor	452	35	—	20,000	450	35	—	18,000
Mass. State Tch. Col., N. Adams, Mass.	1894	Grover C. Bowman	150	10	—	13,000	150	20	—	20,000
Mass. State Tch. Col., Worcester, Mass.	1871	Albert Farnsworth	164	19	—	16,000	234	22	—	12,350
Medical Evangelists, College of, Loma Linda and Los Angeles, Calif.	1909	W. E. MacPherson	612	430	—	35,000	519	375	—	19,227
Memphis State College, Memphis, Tenn.	1912	J. M. Smith	1,506	66	—	22,000	890	45	—	19,000
Mercer University, Macon, Ga.	1833	Spright Dowell	1,184	63	2,000,000	76,000	481	23	1,000,000	70,000
Mercyhurst College, Erie, Pa.	1926	Mother M. F. Borgia	300	32	1,650,000	18,500	175	30	1,500,000	15,000
Meredith College, Raleigh, N.C.	1899	Carlyle Campbell	504	47	568,123	30,000	498	43	530,000	20,000
Meridian Municipal Jr. Col., Meridian, Miss.	1937	J. B. Pearson	1,037	41	—	10,000	666	30	—	8,000
Miami, University of, Coral Gables, Fla.	1925	Bowman F. Ashe	5,205	234	—	52,060	934	72	—	15,767
Miami University, Oxford, Ohio	1809	Ernest H. Hahne	4,834	327	—	194,000	2,935	203	—	145,131
Michigan, University of, Ann Arbor, Mich.	1817	Alexander G. Ruthven	18,757	977	17,258,716	1,267,518	11,339	755	13,058,078	987,921
Michigan Col. of Min. and Tech., Houghton, Mich.	1885	Grover C. Dillman	1,881	138	—	52,400	577	65	—	36,000
Michigan State College, E. Lansing, Mich.	1855	John A. Hannah	13,280	864	3,225,792	201,801	5,216	386	1,055,274	116,050
Michigan St. Normal Col., Ypsilanti, Mich.	1849	John M. Munson	2,115	192	70,000	157,013	1,693	161	70,000	90,000
Middlebury College, Middlebury, Vt.	1800	Samuel S. Stratton	1,188	69	4,204,000	180,549	788	60	4,300,000	101,311
Middle Georgia College (Jr.), Cochran, Ga.	1928	Leo H. Browning	470	18	—	9,191	413	18	—	6,000
Middle Tennessee St. Col., Murfreesboro, Tenn.	1911	Q. M. Smith	1,200	49	—	3,500	626	44	—	25,000
Millsaps College, Jackson, Miss.	1892	Marion L. Smith	777	35	962,000	35,000	452	26	750,000	30,000
Mills College, Oakland, Calif.	1852	Lynn White, Jr.	688	107	2,423,057	98,500	636	100	1,989,218	68,325
Milwaukee-Downer Col., Milwaukee, Wis.	1851	Lucia R. Briggs	431	48	2,370,055	48,931	310	44	2,052,772	36,000
Miner Teachers College, Washington, D.C.	1851	Eugene A. Clark	506	49	—	37,025	45	48	—	22,182
Minnesota, Univ. of, Minneapolis, Minn.	1851	James L. Morrill	27,103	2,678	27,641,897	1,364,930	14,714	644	15,819,747	924,174
Minnesota State Tch. Col., Bemiji, Minn.	1919	C. R. Sattgast	574	50	—	23,000	472	26	—	15,595
Minnesota State Tch. Col., Duluth, Minn.	1895	Raymond C. Gibson	917	62	—	30,000	511	45	—	21,500
Minnesota State Tch. Col., Mankato, Minn.*	1868	Frank D. McElroy	351	51	—	28,565	566	57	—	19,737
Minnesota State Tch. Col., Moorhead, Minn.	1887	O. W. Snarr	601	50	—	30,000	931	52	—	25,467
Minnesota State Tch. Col., St. Cloud, Minn.	1869	Dudley S. Brainard	1,120	75	—	50,000	1,521	73	—	36,219
Minnesota State Tch. Col., Winona, Minn.	1858	Nels Minné	560	46	—	28,972	699	46	—	16,000
Misericordia College, Dallas, Pa.	1923	Sister Mary Gonzaga	376	47	1,100,000	22,090	252	37	1,100,000	14,601
Mississippi, University of, University, Miss.	1848	J. D. Williams	2,750	154	755,710	110,000	1,361	85	4,750	56,492
Mississippi College, Clinton, Miss.	1826	D. M. Nelson	845	51	750,000	31,000	397	24	630,000	15,000
Mississippi Southern Col., Hattiesburg, Miss.	1912	R. C. Cook	1,188	66	—	38,000	700	60	—	28,000
Mississippi State Col., State College, Miss.	1878	Fred T. Mitchell	3,002	171	239,798	78,215	2,174	143	239,790	68,585
Mississippi St. Col. for Wom., Columbus, Miss.	1884	B. L. Parkinson	1,100	87	—	65,000	952	64	—	37,992
Missouri, University of, Columbia, Mo.	1839	F. A. Middlebush	10,081	600	2,373,980	525,557	4,918	336	1,885,789	380,649
Missouri Valley College, Marshall, Mo.	1889	J. Ray Cable	484	29	600,000	27,000	291	22	650,000	20,000
Modesto Junior College, Modesto, Calif.	1921	Dwight C. Baker	1,160	61	—	25,000	940	51	—	13,733
Monmouth College, Monmouth, Ill.	1853	James Harper Grier	775	53	2,013,000	50,000	485	42	1,900,000	45,000
Montana School of Mines, Butte, Mont.	1895	Francis A. Thomson	397	25	850,000	19,000	360	20	800,000	15,457
Montana State College, Bozeman, Mont.	1893	Roland R. Renne	3,119	216	—	70,554	1,243	107	—	55,094
Montana State Normal Col., Dillon, Montana	1893	Rush Jordan	135	14	—	24,100	314	26	—	25,000
Montana State University, Missoula, Mont.	1893	James A. McCain	3,276	149	881,422	257,497	2,116	88	114,046	230,000
Monticello College (Jr.), Godfrey, Ill.	1838	John R. Young	360	38	100,000	25 000	83	23	60,000	8,105
Montreal, University of, Montreal, Que., Can.	1876	Olivier Maurault	5,460	580	—	250,000	4,019	562	—	225,000
Moravian College and Theological Seminary, Bethlehem, Pa.	1807	Raymond S. Haupert	312	24	571,986	25.000	135	11	496,442	22,000
Morehead State Tch. Col., Morehead, Ky.*	1923	W. H. Vaughan	222	50	—	32,000	428	53	—	21,044
Morehouse College, Atlanta, Ga.	1867	Benjamin E. Mays	860	37	1,656,002	85,301	375	23	1,138,056	175,000
Morgan Park Junior College, Chicago, Ill.	1933	Albert G. Dodd	341	19	—	6,000	158	12	—	—

Institution and Location	Year Founded	Chief Executive 1946	1945				1937			
			Full Time Students	Faculty	Endowment	Library Volumes	Full Time Students	Faculty	Endowment	Library Volumes
Morgan State College, Baltimore, Md. . .	1867	D. O. W. Holmes	1,111	60	—	36,000	460	27	$ 70,000	13,276
Morningside College, Sioux City, Ia. . . .	1889	E. A. Roadman	1,083	65	$ 482,996	51,000	789	43	325,707	37,000
Morris Brown College, Atlanta, Ga. . . .	1881	W. A. Fountain, Jr.	653	31	243,886	7,468	458	21	—	6,659
Morton Junior College, Cicero, Ill.	1924	Wm. P. MacLean	911	60	—	14,792	417	42	—	11,223
Mt. Allison Univ., Sackville, N.B., Can. . . .	1840	W. T. R. Flemington	881	82	1,084,471	53,741	420	38	775,288	35,825
Mt. Holyoke College, S. Hadley, Mass. . .	1837	Roswell G. Ham	1,124	132	6,036,000	199,533	1,014	119	5,168,396	145,973
Mt. Mary College, Milwaukee, Wis. . . .	1915	Edward A. Fitzpatrick	630	53	—	34,756	369	52	—	18,592
Mt. Mercy College, Pittsburgh, Pa.	1929	Mother M. Irenaeus	406	38	—	25,000	215	31	—	12,864
Mt. St. Agnes Col. (Jr.), Mt. Wash., Md. . .	1867	Sister M. Placide	175	20	—	11,000	150	14	—	12,000
Mt. St. Joseph-on-the-Ohio, Col. of, Mt. St. Joseph, Ohio*†	1920	Sister M. Corona	332	43	690,000	31,000	263	37	578,675	16,750
Mt. St. Mary's College, Emmitsburg, Md. . .	1808	John L. Sheridan	570	35	600,000	45,000	300	36	600,000	45,000
Mt. St. Mary's College, Los Angeles, Calif. .	1925	Sister Marie de Lourdes	418	38	—	15,500	373	28	—	10,000
Mt. St. Scholastica College, Atchison, Kan. .	1863	Mother Lucy Dooley	403	38	—	26,000	225	31	—	18,000
Mt. St. Vincent, College of, New York, N.Y. .	1847	Francis Cardinal Spellman	683	60	240,986	29,457	498	51	1,581,500	23,512
Mt. Union College, Alliance, Ohio	1846	Charles B. Ketcham	850	50	1,500,000	71,814	637	41	1,350,000	65,000
Muhlenberg College, Allentown, Pa. . . .	1848	Levering Tyson	1,207	86	1,100,000	72,000	429	34	998,000	50,000
Multnomah College (Jr.), Portland, Ore.. .	1897	Edward L. Clark	871	81	25,565	6,100	496	25	25,000	3,600
Mundelein College, Chicago, Ill.	1930	Sister M. Josephine	1,118	76	—	26,734	535	64	—	14,697
Murray State Tch. College, Murray, Ky.. .	1923	Ralph H. Woods	1,545	88	—	37,000	816	70	—	24,477
Muskegon Junior Col., Muskegon, Mich. . .	1926	A. G. Umbreit	560	25	—	250,000	270	14	—	143,294
Muskingum College, New Concord, Ohio .	1837	R. N. Montgomery	900	70	930,000	35,000	700	65	910,000	35,000
N										
National College of Educ., Evanston, Ill. . .	1886	Edna Dean Baker	342	48	138,782	32,163	316	52	43,628	15,732
Nazareth College, Louisville, Ky.	1920	Sister Mary Anastasia	290	52	15,000	22,426	248	26	—	18,452
Nazareth College, Nazareth, Mich. . . .	1924	Sister M. Kevin	298	30	—	25,000	193	29	—	18,000
Nazareth Col. of Rochester, Rochester, N.Y.	1924	Mother Rose Miriam	400	40	—	20,439	237	34	—	13,425
Nebraska, University of, Lincoln, Neb. . .	1869	Reuben G. Gustavson	9,576	480	1,870,000	422,000	7,018	350	961,067	318,577
Nebraska State Tch. Col., Chadron, Neb. .	1911	Wiley G. Brooks	325	45	—	30,000	849	55	—	22,285
Nebraska State Tch. Col., Kearney, Neb.. .	1905	Herbert L. Cushing	667	42	70,000	33,000	867	60	80,000	31,750
Nebraska State Tch. Col., Peru, Neb.. . .	1867	W. L. Nicholas	292	41	—	52,000	449	45	—	48,000
Nebraska State Tch. Col., Wayne, Neb. .	1910	Victor P. Morey	588	35	—	33,173	952	51	—	18,092
Nebraska Wesleyan University, Lincoln, Neb.	1887	John L. Knight	721	38	945,312	35,890	474	48	1,000,000	29,301
Nevada, University of, Reno, Nev.	1874	John O. Moseley	1,668	102	752,711	75,867	1,221	100	334,468	60,700
Newark Col. of Engineering, Newark, N.J..	1881	Allan R. Cullimore	1,403	100	96,316	19,642	866	81	1,137,000	23,000
Newark Colleges of Rutgers Univ., Newark, N.J.	1934	George H. Black	2,601	98	250,000	36,000	594	34	250,000	4,133
Newberry College, Newberry, S.C. . . .	1859	James C. Kinard	550	28	300,000	25,000	318	18	330,000	18,000
New Brunswick, University of, Fredericton, N.B., Can.†	1800	Milton F. Gregg	1,350	95	—	17,000	390	32	—	14,000
New Hampshire, University of, Durham, N.H.	1866	Harold W. Stoke	3,450	227	1,424,771	140,175	1,659	187	1,237,155	92,084
New Haven State Tch. Col., New Haven, Conn.	1893	Owen W. McDowell	546	54	—	21,000	345	67	—	12,000
New Jersey State Tch. Col., Glassboro, N.J..	1923	Edgar F. Bunce	375	26	—	25,000	289	27	—	15,000
New Jersey State Tch. Col., Jersey City, N.J.*	1929	Chris. C. Rossey	528	36	—	40,000	342	34	—	15,092
New Jersey State Tch. Col., Montclair, N.J. .	1908	Harry A. Sprague	1,123	80	45,000	50,000	797	46	—	34,496
New Jersey State Tch. Col., Newark, N.J.. .	1912	John B. Dougall	534	32	—	40,000	471	46	—	30,925
New Jersey State Tch. Col., Paterson, N.J. .	1855	Clair S. Wightman	542	31	—	21,000	272	21	—	16,000
New Jersey State Tch. Col., Trenton, N.J. . .	1855	Roscoe L. West	821	67	—	50,660	755	60	—	27,594
New Mexico, University of, Albuquerque, N.M.	1889	J. Philip Wernette	3,437	233	949,100	115,000	1,582	96	16,647	60,364
New Mexico College of Agriculture and Mechanic Arts, State College, N.M. . .	1889	Hugh M. Milton	1,421	98	519,619	55,000	802	70	181,142	36,557
New Mexico Highlands Univ., Las Vegas, N.M.	1893	Edward Eyring	762	49	57,864	30,662	313	36	—	22,128
New Mexico Military Inst. (Jr.), Roswell, N.M.	1893	D. C. Pearson	196	41	—	23,492	261	50	—	15,075
New Mexico School of Mines, Socorro, N.M.	1889	E. J. Workman	201	16	—	8,500	170	14	—	5,000
New Mexico State Tch. Col., Silver City, N.M.	1893	H. W. James	344	52	—	23,743	203	35	—	20,000
New Rochelle, Col. of, New Rochelle, N.Y. .	1904	Francis W. Walsh	894	70	105,000	56,541	735	52	37,000	33,976
New York, Col. of the City of, N.Y., N.Y. . .	1847	Harry N. Wright	10,500	670	—	401,616	9,566	1,044	—	194,718
New York State Col. for Tch., Albany, N.Y. .	1844	John M. Sayles	1,321	113	—	39,888	1,373	98	—	—
New York State Tch. Col., Brockport, N.Y. .	1866	Donald M. Tower	588	52	—	25,000	340	28	—	2,200
New York State Tch. Col., Buffalo, N.Y. . .	1872	Harry W. Rockwell	1,388	97	—	31,135	1,000	75	—	32,000
New York State Tch. Col., Cortland, N.Y. . .	1863	Donnal V. Smith	850	62	—	25,235	400	38	—	15,000
New York State Tch. Col., Fredonia, N.Y. .	1866	Leslie R. Gregory	550	52	—	18,771	500	44	—	20,000
New York State Tch. Col., Geneseo, N.Y. .	1867	Herbert G. Espy	443	52	—	34,296	658	33	—	30,000
New York State Tch. Col., New Paltz, N.Y. .	1885	Wm. J. Haggerty	550	49	—	19,667	650	39	—	19,240
New York State Tch. Col., Oneonta, N.Y. . .	1889	Charles W. Hunt	338	45	—	30,289	544	43	—	16,935
New York State Tch. Col., Oswego, N.Y.. .	1861	Ralph W. Swetman	826	62	—	33,733	509	36	—	18,315
New York State Tch. Col., Plattsburgh, N.Y..	1889	Charles C. Ward	581	53	—	20,338	334	28	—	10,820
New York State Tch. Col.. Potsdam, N.Y.. .	1816	Frederick W. Crumb	525	50	—	16,591	593	52	—	15,568
New York University, New York, N.Y.. . .	1831	Harry W. Chase	31,746	2,497	10,499,803	714,157	13,110	2,096	9,218,621	541,690
Niagara University, Niagara Univ., N.Y.* .	1856	Joseph M. Noonan	1,701	112	—	70,000	928	80	—	21,572
Norfolk Division, Col. of William and Mary (Jr.), Norfolk, Va..	1930	L. W. Webb, Jr.	1,038	55	—	12,059	452	27	—	2,000
North Carolina, Agri. and Tech. Col. of, Greensboro, N.C..	1891	F. D. Bluford	2,191	145	—	35,000	717	40	—	20,742
North Carolina, Univ. of, Chapel Hill, N.C. .	1793	Frank Porter Graham	6,802	423	3,325,000	473,028	3,240	276	1,619,510	257,871
North Carolina, Woman's College of the University of, Greensboro, N.C.	1892	W. C. Jackson	2,123	185	—	120,000	1,865	167	—	74,620
North Carolina Col. for Negroes, Durham, N.C.*	1910	James E. Shepard	778	72	—	29,969	418	20	—	—
North Carolina State College of Agri. and Eng., Raleigh, N.C.	1889	J. W. Harrelson	4,902	333	—	75,000	2,099	84	—	46,921
North Carolina State Tch. Col., Elizabeth City, N.C.	1892	S. D. Williams	503	26	—	14,000	516	20	6,000	—
North Central College, Naperville, Ill. . .	1863	C. H. Geiger	815	57	1,486,580	38,387	527	34	993,800	22,000
North Dakota, Univ. of, Grand Forks, N.D. .	1883	John C. West	2,670	155	1,700,000	150,000	1,953	132	1,700,000	122,000
North Dakota Agricultural Col., Fargo, N.D.	1889	John H. Longwell	2,362	118	1,571,575	67,000	1,615	116	1,566,720	58,246
North Dakota, State Normal and Industrial College, Ellendale, N.D.	1899	J. C. McMillan	250	21	—	18,000	213	22	—	16,220
North Dakota State Tch. Col., Dickinson, N.D.*	1918	Charles E. Scott	211	24	—	15,980	342	27	—	9,874
North Dakota State Tch. Col., Mayville, N.D.	1889	John W. Headley	289	24	—	22,000	517	24	—	18,000
North Dakota State Tch. Col., Minot, N.D. .	1913	C. C. Swain	610	55	—	18,328	767	52	—	19,128
North Dakota State Tch. Col., Valley City, N.D.	1889	R. L. Lokken	356	43	—	38,000	992	55	—	25,349
Northeastern State College, Tahlequah, Okla.†	1909	John Vaughan	897	55	—	39,808	954	53	—	22,979
Northeastern University, Boston, Mass. . .	1898	Carl S. Ell	3,002	335	1,119,659	41,000	5,420	262	587,062	19,957
Northeast Junior Col., L.S.U., Monroe, La. .	1931	Rodney Cline	814	41	—	10,000	450	28	—	5,000
Northeast Missouri State Tch. Col., Kirksville, Mo.	1867	Walter H. Ryle	887	58	—	75,000	1,100	59	—	37,053
Northern Illinois State Tch. Col., DeKalb, Ill. .	1895	Karl L. Adams	1,442	85	—	61,529	806	69	—	43,302
Northern Michigan Col. of Educ., Marquette, Mich..	1899	H. A. Tape	930	62	20,000	40,212	608	52	20,000	28,417

(Above) Registration at Harvard university for the fall semester, 1945, 75% of those entering were war veterans

(Below) Commencement exercises for disabled veterans at American university, Washington D.C., in Feb. 1946

Institution and Location	Year Founded	Chief Executive 1946	1946				1937			
			Full Time Students	Faculty	Endow-ment	Library Volumes	Full Time Students	Faculty	Endow-ment	Library Volumes
Northern Montana Col. (Jr.), Havre, Mont.	1929	G. H. Vande Bogart	323	20	—	20,000	432	19	—	8,723
Northern State Tch. Col., Aberdeen, S.D.	1901	N. E. Steele	706	50	—	29,000	700	48	—	24,260
North Georgia Col. (Jr.), Dahlonega, Ga.	1873	J. C. Rogers	678	35	—	17,847	416	20	—	8,200
North Idaho Junior Col., Coeur d'Alene, Idaho	1933	George Oliver Kildow	214	15	—	2,000	48	7	—	15,625
North Park College (Jr.), Chicago, Ill.	1891	Algoth Ohlson	1,351	46	$ 315,698	17,500	988	55	$ 300,000	12,000
North Texas Agri. Col. (Jr.), Arlington, Tex.*	1917	E. E. Davis	795	50	—	24,705	1,045	54	—	12,950
North Texas State Tch. Col., Denton, Tex.	1890	W. J. McConnell	3,810	210	—	170,000	2,448	125	—	64,370
Northwestern State College, Alva, Okla.	1897	Sabin C. Percefull	571	38	—	22,900	900	51	—	15,000
Northwestern State Col., Natchitoches, La.	1884	Joe Farrar	1,467	88	—	44,939	1,344	98	—	34,716
Northwestern Univ., Evanston and Chgo., Ill.	1851	Franklyn B. Snyder	10,100	1,235	65,000,000	987,465	5,983	1,210	25,900,000	331,003
Northwest Missouri St. Tch. Col., Maryville, Mo.	1905	J. W. Jones	751	52	—	30,582	778	54	—	25,000
Northwest Nazarene College, Nampa, Ida.	1913	Lewis T. Corlett	472	21	—	10,000	241	19	—	6,250
Norwich University, Northfield, Vt.	1819	Homer L. Dodge	614	48	1,029,206	40,750	293	27	800,626	30,000
Notre Dame, University of, Notre Dame, Ind.	1842	John J. Cavanaugh	4,541	379	3,654,000	224,223	3,167	277	1,010,000	197,638
Notre Dame College, South Euclid, Ohio	1922	Mother Mary Vera	271	38	—	24,000	144	34	—	17,458
Notre Dame College of Staten Island, Staten Island, N.Y.C.	1931	Mother Saint Egbert	291	26	—	9,680	140	26	—	3,548
Notre Dame of Maryland, Col. of, Baltimore, Md.	1873	Sister Mary Frances	435	53	61,000	26,980	176	26	2,649	13,539
O										
Oakwood College (Jr.), Huntsville, Ala.	1896	F. L. Peterson	254	33	37,066	7,158	248	24	—	6,250
Oberlin College, Oberlin, Ohio	1833	William E. Stevenson	2,058	166	23,419,103	457,168	1,764	177	20,116,983	381,306
Occidental College, Los Angeles, Calif.	1887	Arthur G. Coons	1,140	75	1,300,394	78,000	693	66	1,235,575	46,000
Ohio State University, Columbus, Ohio	1870	Howard L. Bevis	22,643	900	2,162,108	717,073	12,826	870	1,281,435	475,000
Ohio University, Athens, Ohio	1804	John Calhoun Baker	4,933	283	86,000	160,323	3,024	177	85,000	107,020
Ohio Wesleyan University, Delaware, Ohio	1842	H. J. Burgstahler	2,097	91	3,890,000	173,550	1,408	98	3,041,263	154,381
Oklahoma, University of, Norman, Okla.	1890	George Lynn Cross	10,245	513	4,322,862	330,000	6,212	296	3,782,917	180,210
Oklahoma Agri. and Mech. College, Stillwater, Okla.	1891	Henry G. Bennett	10,421	573	4,162,891	183,500	5,056	363	—	116,761
Oklahoma Col. for Women, Chickasha, Okla.	1908	Dan Procter	701	57	—	33,565	951	54	—	23,666
Omaha, University of, Omaha, Neb.	1908	Rowland Haynes	1,882	63	140,578	78,000	683	51	19,186	51,957
Oregon, Univ. of, Eugene and Portland, Ore.	1872	Harry K. Newburn	6,500	330	1,204,441	370,000	3,120	221	461,365	275,000
Oregon College of Educ., Monmouth, Ore.	1861	Charles A. Howard	343	39	—	30,000	567	48	—	21,218
Oregon State College, Corvallis, Ore.	1868	A. L. Strand	7,128	438	—	212,447	4,150	266	223,494	152,095
Ottawa, University of, Ottawa, Ont., Can.	1866	J. C. Laframboise	2,300	198	—	130,000	803	128	—	85,000
Ottawa University, Ottawa, Kan.	1865	A. B. Martin	480	28	435,747	20,000	321	23	462,280	17,973
Otterbein College, Westerville, Ohio	1847	J. Gordon Howard	857	54	1,500,000	33,000	324	40	1,135,326	27,259
Ouachita College, Arkadelphia, Ark.	1886	James R. Grant	850	40	500,000	25,000	500	30	500,000	20,000
Our Lady of the Elms, Col. of, Chicopee, Mass.	1928	Thomas M. O'Leary	243	22	—	—	113	—	—	—
Our Lady of the Lake College, San Antonio, Tex.	1896	John L. McMahon	332	54	392,361	48,087	367	43	183,495	38,625
P										
Pacific, College of the, Stockton, Calif.	1851	Robert E. Burns	953	90	581,173	50,135	1,330	78	576,000	—
Pacific Lutheran Col., Parkland, Wash.	1894	S. C. Eastvold	589	36	70,000	33,000	285	26	50,000	14,000
Pacific Union College, Angwin, Calif.	1909	P. W. Christian	716	55	—	33,082	537	32	—	18,315
Pacific University, Forest Grove, Ore.	1849	Walter C. Giersbach	609	40	600,000	30,000	301	24	300,000	27,000
Packer Collegiate Inst. (Jr.), Brooklyn, N.Y.	1853	Paul D. Shafer	113	24	1,414,862	12,303	123	28	1,300,408	12,900
Paine College, Augusta, Ga.	1882	Edmund C. Peters	360	20	35,000	21,000	161	10	30,000	7,500
Palm Beach Jr. Col., W. Palm Beach, Fla.	1933	John I. Leonard	265	20	—	5,166	85	19	—	—
Paris Junior College, Paris, Tex.	1924	J. R. McLemore	1,200	46	—	8,124	365	15	—	3,000
Park College, Parkville, Mo.	1875	G. I. Rohrbough	530	37	1,985,000	35,660	465	44	1,720,000	28,793
Parsons College, Fairfield, Ia.	1875	Herbert C. Mayer	416	27	547,045	24,480	245	26	530,312	21,572
Pasadena Junior Col., Pasadena, Calif.	1924	John W. Harbeson	5,295	228	—	40,000	357	24	—	10,000
Pearl River Junior Col., Poplarville, Miss.	1922	R. D. McLendon	390	26	—	6,000	246	20	—	4,000
Pennsylvania, Univ. of, Philadelphia, Pa.	1740	George W. McClelland	9,279	1,985	25,000,000	1,013,653	8,199	1,530	20,452,000	881,781
Pennsylvania Col. for Wom., Pittsburgh, Pa.	1869	Paul R. Anderson	460	48	1,092,000	30,000	282	35	553,875	18,594
Pennsylvania State Col., State College, Pa.	1855	R. D. Hetzel	10,519	887	517,000	250,000	5,904	553	517,000	175,000
Pa. State Tch. Col., Bloomsburg, Pa.	1839	Harvey A. Andruss	750	50	—	25,000	641	41	—	17,014
Pa. State Tch. Col., California, Pa.	1852	Robert M. Steele	727	50	—	25,500	688	40	—	16,200
Pa. State Tch. Col., Cheyney, Pa.	1837	Leslie Pinckney Hill	301	20	—	15,930	139	13	—	14,000
Pa. State Tch. Col., Clarion, Pa.	1867	Paul G. Chandler	681	38	—	20,632	186	25	—	18,000
Pa. State Tch. Col., E. Stroudsburg, Pa.	1893	Joseph F. Noonan	803	46	—	23,667	537	39	—	17,233
Pa. State Tch. Col., Edinboro, Pa.	1862	L. H. Van Houten	739	37	—	23,000	312	26	—	18,244
Pa. State Tch. Col., Indiana, Pa.	1871	Joseph M. Uhler	1,297	93	—	30,654	596	113	—	17,760
Pa. State Tch. Col., Kutztown, Pa.	1866	Q. A. W. Rohrbach	743	43	—	27,894	450	30	—	24,000
Pa. State Tch. Col., Lock Haven, Pa.	1877	Richard T. Parsons	707	45	—	19,000	426	35	—	17,000
Pa. State Tch. Col., Mansfield, Pa.	1854	James G. Morgan	778	63	—	32,000	602	58	—	22,808
Pa. State Tch. Col., Millersville, Pa.	1855	D. L. Biemesderfer	736	35	—	29,432	527	42	—	25,182
Pa. State Tch. Col., Shippensburg, Pa.	1871	Levi Gilbert	710	43	—	30,000	436	35	—	19,339
Pa. State Tch. Col., Slippery Rock, Pa.	1889	Dale W. Houk	777	61	—	21,330	544	53	—	20,114
Pa. State Tch. Col., West Chester, Pa.*	1871	Charles S. Swope	1,613	93	—	34,000	1,303	79	—	34,000
Pfeiffer Junior College, Misenheimer, N.C.	1903	C. M. Waggoner	290	19	500,000	7,800	180	14	—	4,500
Phillips University, Enid, Okla.	1907	Eugene S. Briggs	977	54	839,000	46,000	389	37	652,705	25,698
Phoenix Junior College, Phoenix, Ariz.	1920	E. W. Montgomery	1,090	40	—	16,620	642	27	—	8,039
Pikeville College, Pikeville, Ky.	1889	A. A. Page	282	28	356,000	11,000	323	26	300,000	7,000
Pine Manor Junior Col., Wellesley, Mass.	1911	Marie Warren Potter	268	35	—	7,000	205	39	—	3,828
Pittsburgh, University of, Pittsburgh, Pa.	1787	John G. Bowman	10,426	1,609	3,552,429	460,000	4,727	858	2,618,998	227,797
Plymouth Teachers College, Plymouth, N.H.	1870	Howard R. Jones	250	30	—	15,000	211	30	—	8,000
Pomona College, Claremont, Calif.	1887	E. Wilson Lyon	1,122	80	4,463,084	114,000	834	78	2,830,015	84,550
Port Huron Junior Col., Port Huron, Mich.	1923	John H. McKenzie	429	18	—	6,178	195	14	—	4,076
Portland, University of, Portland, Ore.	1901	Theodore J. Mehling	1,642	77	—	25,000	355	49	—	12,000
Potomac State School of West Virginia University (Jr.), Keyser, W.Va.	1901	E. E. Church	559	29	—	9,500	203	20	—	7,000
Prairie View University, Prairie View, Tex.	1876	E. B. Evans	1,480	107	41,000	25,380	937	92	—	19,432
Princeton University, Princeton, N.J.	1746	Harold W. Dodds	4,003	437	40,000,000	1,000,000	2,665	352	30,000,000	1,000,000
Principia College, Elsah, Ill.	1898	Frederic E. Morgan	446	33	866,651	36,000	278	28	561,265	17,000
Providence College, Providence, R.I.	1917	Frederick C. Foley	1,280	70	—	32,660	818	65	75,000	30,000
Puget Sound, College of, Tacoma, Wash.	1888	R. Franklin Thompson	1,489	89	1,496,147	48,000	732	42	1,200,000	25,000
Purdue University, Lafayette, Ind.	1869	Frederick L. Hovde	11,472	804	340,000	228,000	6,524	554	340,000	140,158
Q										
Queens College, Charlotte, N.C.	1857	Hunter B. Blakely	426	46	500,000	22,300	348	32	325,000	13,797
Queens College, Flushing, N.Y.	1937	Paul Klapper	2,853	221	—	65,000	400	26	—	3,652
Queen's University, Kingston, Ontario, Can.	1841	R. C. Wallace	3,019	185	5,100,000	214,473	1,694	170	3,297,830	174,807
R										
Radcliffe College, Cambridge, Mass.	1879	Wilbur K. Jordan	1,276	400	7,071,243	97,000	1,001	400	4,984,576	81,191
Radford College, Woman's Division of Virginia Polytechnic Institute, Radford, Va.†	1911	David W. Peters	703	49	—	30,113	417	53	—	26,818
Randolph-Macon College, Ashland, Va.	1830	J. Earl Moreland	467	25	1,022,300	39,989	312	17	1,064,576	30,159

Institution and Location	Year Founded	Chief Executive 1946	1946 Full Time Students	1946 Faculty	1946 Endowment	1946 Library Volumes	1937 Full Time Students	1937 Faculty	1937 Endowment	1937 Library Volumes
Randolph-Macon Woman's Col., Lynchburg, Va.	1893	Theodore H. Jack	694	75	$ 1,264,000	65,000	670	74	$ 1,205,630	46,000
Redlands, University of, Redlands, Calif.	1907	George H. Armacost	1,065	66	2,493,078	71,173	561	51	3,170,416	49,373
Reed College, Portland, Ore.*	1904	Peter H. Odegard	389	43	1,636,185	77,000	507	33	1,873,826	56,649
Regis College, Weston, Mass.*†	1927	Sister Mary Honora	583	51	—	25,000	417	42	—	19,800
Rensselaer Polytechnic Inst., Troy, N.Y.	1824	Livingston W. Houston	3,434	289	10,500,000	39,000	1,236	145	5,886,000	29,615
Rhode Island Col. of Educ., Providence, R.I.	1854	Lucius A. Whipple	357	58	—	23,782	526	35	—	45,490
Rhode Island State College, Kingston, R.I.	1892	Carl R. Woodward	2,145	215	—	83,701	1,114	95	—	51,846
Rice Institute, Houston, Tex.	1912	William V. Houston	1,487	103	30,000,000	179,400	1,343	82	15,400,000	142,250
Richmond, University of, Richmond, Va.*	1832	F. W. Boatwright	820	76	2,936,316	100,000	1,056	60	2,815,833	70,000
Ricker Junior College, Houlton, Me.	1926	Roy A. Bither	207	14	40,000	2,000	47	6	32,000	12,500
Ricks College (Jr.), Rexburg, Ida.	1888	John L. Clarke	385	20	376,310	6,798	269	15	239,389	7,540
Ripon College, Ripon, Wis.	1851	Clark G. Kuebler	639	50	854,614	43,170	366	34	756,442	33,127
Riverside College (Jr.), Riverside, Calif.	1916	A. G. Paul	938	43	—	18,130	617	39	—	11,900
Roanoke College, Salem, Va.	1842	Charles J. Smith	601	38	700,000	25,000	390	23	650,000	18,000
Rochester, University of, Rochester, N.Y.	1850	Alan Valentine	3,703	739	55,944,524	449,995	2,234	495	55,079,900	313,233
Rockford College, Rockford, Ill.	1847	Mary Ashby Cheek	453	47	1,000,000	34,300	302	36	1,007,000	25,776
Rockhurst College, Kansas City, Mo.	1910	Thomas M. Knapp	745	31	—	17,680	170	24	—	20,000
Rollins College, Winter Park, Fla.	1885	Hamilton Holt	593	75	932,960	73,569	377	72	991,800	50,000
Rosary College, River Forest, Ill.	1901	Sister Mary Peter	748	76	100,000	55,000	441	52	92,112	37,000
Rosemont College, Rosemont, Pa.	1921	Mother Mary Boniface	305	41	—	36,500	230	36	—	22,475
Rose Polytechnic Institute, Terre Haute, Ind.	1874	Donald B. Prentice	559	36	2,150,000	23,600	228	27	2,000,000	23,000
Russell Sage College, Troy, N.Y.	1916	Helen McKinstry	880	90	1,054,071	45,321	540	54	911,176	16,445
Rutgers University, New Brunswick, N.J.	1766	Robert C. Clothier	15,865	457	6,060,361	475,582	2,711	309	4,560,000	261,467
S										
Sacramento Col. (Jr.), Sacramento, Calif.	1916	Nicholas Ricciardi	2,506	106	—	26,000	2,030	83	—	18,000
St. Ambrose College, Davenport, Ia.	1882	Ambrose J. Burke	1,116	60	600,000	25,000	425	42	600,000	17,000
St. Anselm's College, Manchester, N.H.*	1893	Bertrand C. Dolan	90	20	—	12,000	280	30	—	10,000
St. Augustine's College, Raleigh, N.C.	1867	Edgar H. Goold	334	20	200,000	17,200	223	13	165,000	14,000
St. Benedict, College of, St. Joseph, Minn.*	1913	Mother R. Pratschner	241	36	10,800	30,000	200	34	—	19,850
St. Benedict's College, Atchison, Kan.	1856	Cuthbert McDonald	410	40	—	100,000	272	35	125,000	90,000
St. Bernard College (Jr.), St. Bernard, Ala.	1892	Boniface Seng	152	14	—	24,300	85	14	—	15,500
St. Bernardine of Sienna Col., Loudonville, N.Y.	1937	Mark Kennedy	2,043	84	761,833	15,000	95	8	500,000	1,046
St. Bonaventure Col., St. Bonaventure, N.Y.	1859	Thomas Plassmann	1,268	82	—	78,933	378	55	—	40,000
St. Catherine, College of, St. Paul, Minn.	1911	Sister Antonius	875	81	644,552	67,440	609	54	580,584	50,305
St. Charles College (Jr.), Catonsville, Md.	1831	George A. Gleason	395	26	—	40,000	235	20	—	40,000
St. Edward's Seminary, Seattle, Wash.	1931	John P. McCormick	52	10	—	15,000	102	15	—	5,000
St. Elizabeth, Col. of, Covent Station, N.J.	1899	Sister Marie J. Byrne	614	48	—	31,000	387	38	—	20,040
St. Francis, College of, Joliet, Ill.	1874	Sister M. Aniceta	403	45	16,000	35,000	171	33	—	18,965
St. Francis College, Loretto, Pa.‖	1847	John P. J. Sullivan	72	18	—	10,000	225	28	—	—
St. Francis Xavier Col. for Wom., Chicago, Ill.	1912	Sister Mary Huberta	356	45	—	52,000	255	25	—	30,000
St Francis Xavier Univ., Antigonish, N.S., Can.	1853	P. J. Nicholson	874	35	510,000	35,000	307	26	453,000	30,000
St. Helen's Hall Junior Col., Portland, Ore.	1932	Gertrude Houk Fariss	89	15	—	5,500	115	18	—	5,000
St. John College, Cleveland, Ohio	1928	Edward F. Hoban	163	27	—	26,000	126	24	—	22,000
St. John's University, Brooklyn, N.Y.	1870	William J. Mahoney	3,759	189	500,000	72,720	5,920	317	500,000	36,352
St. Joseph College, W. Hartford, Conn.	1932	Sister M. Rosa	416	37	—	18,415	220	29	—	6,860
St. Joseph Junior Col., St. Joseph, Mo.	1915	Nelle Blum	630	21	—	8,000	343	21	—	4,627
St. Joseph's College, Collegeville, Ind.	1889	Henry A. Lucks	514	52	1,425,815	23,307	154	18	1,075,435	18,000
St. Joseph's College, Emmitsburg, Md.	1809	Francis J. Dodd	193	32	—	15,210	177	35	—	12,202
St. Joseph's College, Philadelphia, Pa.	1851	John J. Long	1,209	63	—	18,250	492	33	—	9,000
St. Joseph's Col. for Women, Brooklyn. N.Y.	1916	William T. Dillon	520	52	29,713	22,861	449	45	—	16,015
St. Lawrence University, Canton, N.Y.	1856	Eugene G. Bewkes	1,088	72	1,793,070	82,839	653	55	2,279,312	70,612
St. Louis University, St. Louis, Mo.	1818	Patrick J. Holloran	9,497	857	10,725,035	423,694	3,876	777	1,743,328	157,252
St. Martin's College, Lacey, Wash.	1895	Raphael Heider	305	27	—	20,000	78	25	—	8,000
St. Mary College, Xavier, Kan.	1923	Arthur M. Murphy	405	41	—	33,000	165	36	—	14,481
St. Mary of the Springs, Col. of, Columbus, Ohio	1925	Sister M. Anacletus	284	44	—	31,000	124	27	—	18,000
St. Mary-of-the-Wasatch, Col. of, Salt Lake City, Utah	1926	Sister Mary Benedictus	90	17	—	12,200	95	18	750,000	11,212
St. Mary-of-the-Woods Col., St. Mary-of-the-Woods, Ind.	1840	Mother Mary Bernard	374	44	500,000	64,600	289	40	563,000	49,600
St. Mary's Col., Notre Dame, Holy Cross, Ind.	1844	Sister M. Madeleva	511	71	115,000	36,400	351	51	37,500	17,365
St. Mary's College, Winona, Minn.‖	1912	Brother Joel	220	30	—	25,000	289	26	—	18,000
St. Mary's Junior College, O'Fallon, Mo.	1929	Mother M. Borgia	19	7	—	10,570	21	7	—	—
St. Mary's Junior College, Raleigh, N.C.	1842	Richard G. Stone	170	24	18,407	10,791	300	30	160,000	6,557
St. Michael's College, Winooski, Vt.	1904	Daniel P. Lyons	518	40	150,026	40,000	100	20	50,000	10,000
St. Norbert College, West De Pere, Wis.	1898	B. H. Pennings	725	41	—	30,000	251	27	—	—
St. Olaf College, Northfield, Minn.	1874	Clemens M. Granskou	1,587	99	1,030,527	65,500	1,033	68	950,359	42,955
St. Patrick's Seminary, Menlo Park, Calif.	1898	Thomas C. Mulligan	85	13	—	32,640	139	13	—	24,000
St. Petersburg Jr. Col., St. Petersburg, Fla.	1927	Roland A. Wakefield	425	23	—	10,000	307	24	—	8,000
St. Peter's College, Jersey City, N.J.	1872	Vincent Hart	944	57	120,000	21,500	399	39	—	18,000
St. Rose, College of, Albany, N.Y.	1920	Edmund F. Gibbons	502	52	—	16,450	319	32	—	7,578
St. Scholastica, College of, Duluth, Minn.	1912	Mother M. Athanasius	498	41	—	25,000	434	42	—	—
St. Teresa, College of, Winona, Minn.	1910	Sr. M. Rachael Dady	530	58	—	35,000	380	49	—	—
St. Thomas, College of, St. Paul, Minn.	1885	Vincent J. Flynn	1,694	94	302,000	35,000	650	55	296,798	21,967
St. Vincent College, Latrobe, Pa.	1846	Alfred Koch	1,065	71	—	65,782	390	38	1,942,256	63,010
Salem College, Winston-Salem, N.C.	1772	Howard E. Rondthaler	400	43	706,250	31,500	340	37	443,523	15,264
Sam Houston State Tch. Col., Huntsville, Tex.	1879	Harmon Lowman	1,839	96	—	70,736	920	60	—	53,218
Samuel Huston College, Austin, Tex.*	1900	Karl E. Downs	267	32	6,861	10,820	271	20	—	8,375
San Angelo College (Jr.), San Angelo, Tex.	1928	W. H. Elkins	509	33	—	7,000	173	12	—	4,500
San Bernardino Valley Junior College, San Bernardino, Calif.	1927	John L. Lounsbury	1,195	55	—	25,000	800	37	—	20,000
San Diego State College, San Diego, Calif.	1897	Walter R. Hepner	3,428	154	—	95,318	1,683	72	—	44,740
San Francisco, Univ. of, San Fran., Calif.	1855	William J. Dunne	1,619	77	—	44,950	762	55	—	36,518
San Francisco Col. for Wom., San Fran., Cal.‖	1930	Mother Leonor Mejia	254	38	—	100,000	132	30	—	24,050
San Francisco State Col., San Francisco, Calif.	1899	J. Paul Leonard	2,393	136	—	45,294	1,544	89	—	36,887
San Jose State and Jr. Col., San Jose, Calif.	1862	T. W. MacQuarrie	5,741	261	—	87,459	3,206	150	—	60,000
San Mateo Junior Col., San Mateo, Calif.	1922	Charles S. Morris	1,810	74	—	13,000	790	54	—	10,000
Santa Ana Junior Col., Santa Ana, Calif.	1915	John H. McCoy	896	35	—	15,000	1,062	35	—	10,000
Santa Clara, Univ. of, Santa Clara, Calif.	1855	William C. Gianera	947	75	—	34,973	511	48	600,000	35,000
Santa Rosa Junior Col., Santa Rosa, Calif.	1918	Floyd P. Bailey	961	39	—	12,170	466	25	—	7,000
Sarah Lawrence College, Bronxville, N.Y.	1926	Harold Taylor	343	62	330,603	47,550	277	61	315,566	27,728
Saskatchewan, University of, Saskatoon, Sask., Can.	1907	James S. Thomson	4,204	165	253,345	93,000	1,776	115	76,098	61,655
Scarritt College, Nashville, Tenn.	1892	Hugh C. Stuntz	164	20	500,000	470,365	162	11	250,683	10,607
Schreiner Institute (Jr.), Kerrville, Tex.	1923	J. J. Delaney	438	26	175,000	10,000	351	22	175,000	6,500
Scranton, University of, Scranton, Pa.	1888	W. Coleman Nevils	2,673	75	—	20,616	560	33	1,500,000	11,000
Scripps College, Claremont, Calif.	1926	Frederick Hard	238	28	984,400	32,297	218	25	732,707	19,005
Seattle College, Seattle, Wash.	1892	Harold O. Small	2,447	65	—	28,361	900	25	—	4,000
Seattle Pacific College, Seattle, Wash.	1891	C. Hoyt Watson	510	35	200,000	20,100	306	28	—	9,000
Seneca, Colleges of the, Geneva, N.Y.	1822	John Milton Potter	1,111	65	704,737	87,034	527	51	1,350,731	100,000

Institution and Location	Year Founded	Chief Executive 1946	1946				1937			
			Full Time Students	Faculty	Endowment	Library Volumes	Full Time Students	Faculty	Endowment	Library Volumes
Seton Hall College, South Orange, N.J. . .	1856	James F. Kelley	5,273	144	—	34,000	402	48	—	15,000
Seton Hill College, Greensburg, Pa. . . .	1918	James A. Reeves	511	59	$ 500,000	31,268	471	41	$ 500,000	27,752
Shaw University, Raleigh, N.C.	1865	Robert P. Daniel	776	77	325,000	15,000	493	35	325,000	14,000
Shepherd College, Shepherdstown, W.Va..	1872	W. H. S. White	325	23	—	18,000	265	18	—	15,300
Shorter College, Rome, Ga.	1873	Paul M. Cousins	239	30	540,000	22,500	231	30	377,500	14,000
Siena Heights College, Adrian, Mich.. . .	1898	Mother Mary Gerald	375	24	—	25,000	107	23	—	14,000
Simmons College, Boston, Mass.	1899	Bancroft Beatley	1,494	160	3,392,883	95,975	1,585	124	3,536,625	58,000
Simpson College, Indianola, Ia.	1860	Edwin E. Voigt	580	39	1,413,849	32,119	579	43	1,200,000	36,147
Sioux Falls College, Sioux Falls, S.D. . . .	1883	Ernest E. Smith	307	30	122,000	18,000	241	25	283,260	12,140
Skidmore College, Saratoga Springs, N.Y..	1911	Henry T. Moore	1,015	92	872,368	58,401	739	69	805,728	51,119
Smith College, Northampton, Mass. . . .	1871	Herbert Davis	2,249	272	6,822,230	326,392	2,061	258	6,068,781	245,317
Snead Junior College, Boaz, Ala.	1935	Festus M. Cook	318	23	210,000	8,152	139	12	—	1,986
Snow College (Jr.), Ephraim, Utah	1888	James A. Nuttall	360	23	—	10,298	226	20	—	8,000
Sophie Newcomb College for Women, New Orleans, La..	1886	Logan Wilson	862	83	2,311,387	325,000	639	65	3,016,022	40,000
South, University of the, Sewanee, Tenn. .	1857	Alexander Guerry	492	37	2,250,000	57,000	225	33	1,570,091	44,000
South Carolina, Univ. of, Columbia, S.C. . .	1801	Norman M. Smith	4,167	226	—	180,663	1,700	98	—	150,000
South Carolina State Agri. and Mech. Col., Orangeburg, S.C.	1896	M. F. Whittaker	1,338	100	—	24,000	741	53	—	—
South Dakota, Univ. of, Vermillion, S.D. . .	1882	I. D. Weeks	1,658	118	—	120,000	799	98	—	95,000
South Dakota School of Mines and Technology Rapid City, S.D.	1885	Joseph P. Connolly	537	34	250,000	20,000	382	28	250,000	16,000
South Dakota State College of Agri. and Mech. Arts, Brookings, S.D.	1881	H. M. Crothers	1,858	102	634,452	83,256	1,176	143	597,998	50,000
Southeastern State College, Durant, Okla.*	1909	T. T. Montgomery	524	46	—	34,272	999	52	—	28,491
Southeast Missouri St. Col., Cape Girardeau, Mo.	1873	W. W. Parker	1,230	71	—	85,000	1,460	65	—	70,000
Southern California, University of, Los Angeles, Calif.	1879	R. B. von KleinSmid	14,000	1,050	1,600,000	346,093	4,707	568	1,600,000	153,265
Southern Christian Inst. (Jr.,) Edwards, Miss.	1875	John Long	517	18	—	4,928	222	21	—	4,263
Southern Illinois Normal University, Carbondale, Ill.	1874	Chester F. Lay	2,649	140	—	63,380	1,523	126	—	36,980
Southern Methodist Univ., Dallas, Tex. . .	1911	Umphrey Lee	6,686	334	4,455,341	186,450	1,462	125	2,219,215	90,000
Southern Oregon Col. of Educ., Ashland, Ore.	1926	Elmo N. Stevenson	523	31	—	20,000	506	30	—	10,859
Southern St. Normal Sch., Springfield, S.D..	1881	J. Howard Kramer	125	23	134,212	13,000	325	22	120,000	12,000
Southern University and Agri. and Mech. College, Scotlandville, La.	1880	Felton G. Clark	1,318	94	668,000	31,000	663	42	—	19,109
South Georgia College (Jr.), College, Ga..	1907	J. M. Thrash	514	18	—	8,573	350	18	—	4,787
Southwestern at Memphis, Memphis, Tenn. .	1848	Charles E. Diehl	723	44	2,303,000	57,016	549	31	437,849	40,450
Southwestern College, Winfield, Kan.. . .	1885	Mearl P. Culver	484	36	583,198	23,650	578	49	600,000	23,000
Southwestern Inst.of Tech., Weatherford, Okla.	1901	R. H. Burton	871	59	—	29,171	900	50	—	22,012
Southwestern Louisiana Inst., Lafayette, La.	1898	Joel L. Fletcher	3,167	190	—	63,772	1,409	72	—	27,000
Southwestern University, Georgetown, Tex.	1840	J. N. R. Score	1,557	111	1,011,561	89,000	410	33	250,000	45,920
Southwest Missouri St. Col., Springfield, Mo.	1906	Roy Ellis	1,609	96	—	60,598	1,194	78	—	43,420
Southwest Texas State Tch. Col., San Marcos, Tex.*	1899	John G. Flowers	536	60	—	57,800	1,121	60	—	40,200
Spelman College, Atlanta, Ga.	1881	Florence M. Read	438	35	3,238,653	78,266	333	37	3,163,057	60,500
Springfield College, Springfield, Mass. . .	1885	Paul M. Limbert	808	44	1,067,256	30,387	506	42	1,169,096	23,018
Springfield Junior Col., Springfield, Ill. . .	1929	Mother M. De Pazzi	531	35	—	11,500	161	18	—	7,032
Spring Hill College, Spring Hill, Ala. . . .	1830	Wm. Patrick Donnelly	643	34	250,000	48,000	282	33	280,000	40,000
Stanford University, Stanford Univ., Calif. .	1885	Donald B. Tresidder	7,156	900	34,229,000	925,000	4,194	450	35,384,809	686,000
Stephens College (Jr.), Columbia, Mo. . .	1833	J. M. Wood	2,225	219	217,750	49,045	935	95	113,219	21,875
Stevens Institute of Tech., Hoboken, N.J.. .	1870	Harvey N. Davis	1,159	116	—	32,000	526	65	—	30,000
Stillman Institute (Jr.), Tuscaloosa, Ala. . .	1876	A. L. Jackson	193	21	100,000	10,734	225	24	100,000	11,000
Stout Institute, Menomonie, Wis.	1893	Verne C. Fryklund	805	51	—	28,536	533	42	—	18,943
Stowe Teachers and Jr. Col., St. Louis, Mo. .	1890	Ruth M. Harris	600	25	—	16,000	400	20	400	14,000
Sue Bennett College (Jr.), London, Ky. . .	1897	Oscie Sanders	113	14	—	10,142	102	14	—	6,050
Sullins College (Jr.), Bristol, Va.	1870	W. E. Martin	409	38	450,000	10,000	350	40	—	8,000
Sul Ross State Tch. Col., Alpine, Tex. . . .	1923	R. M. Hawkins	672	37	—	26,800	427	30	—	25,000
Sunflower Junior College, Moorhead, Miss.*	1927	W. B. Horton	230	20	—	5,500	279	24	—	—
Susquehanna University, Selinsgrove, Pa. .	1858	G. Morris Smith	464	30	475,000	24,000	297	30	400,211	14,700
Swarthmore College, Swarthmore, Pa. . .	1864	John W. Nason	1,022	90	8,125,000	142,500	695	74	7,744,800	112,567
Sweet Briar College, Sweet Briar, Va. . .	1901	Martha B. Lucas	449	53	915,978	64,491	447	54	423,737	40,588
Syracuse University, Syracuse, N.Y. . . .	1870	William P. Tolley	15,228	1,092	—	380,000	6,607	735	4,641,227	299,724
T										
Talladega College, Talladega, Ala. . . .	1867	A. D. Beittel	350	35	1,157,716	30,000	286	30	1,146,109	18,000
Tarkio College, Tarkio, Mo..	1883	M. Earle Collins	320	24	670,000	18,591	219	23	657,000	15,556
Temple University, Philadelphia, Pa. . . .	1884	Robert L. Johnson	8,650	850	1,268,542	272,000	5,179	—	—	99,870
Tennessee, University of, Knoxville, Tenn. .	1794	Cloide E. Brehm	7,344	350	612,945	207,288	2,737	230	468,128	174,091
Tennessee Agricultural and Industrial State Col., Nashville, Tenn.	1912	W. S. Davis	2,126	103	—	30,000	1,262	48	—	25,822
Tennessee Jr. Col., Univ. of, Martin, Tenn. .	1927	Paul Meek	649	41	—	15,000	304	21	—	8,446
Tennessee Polytechnic Inst., Cookeville, Tenn.	1915	Everett Derryberry	1,460	78	—	30,000	452	29	—	20,000
Tennessee Wesleyan Col. (Jr.), Athens, Tenn.	1866	James L. Robb	470	28	150,000	16,000	236	19	101,000	8,935
Texarkana College (Jr.), Texarkana, Tex. .	1927	H. W. Stilwell	396	23	—	7,000	178	12	—	4,690
Texas, Agri. and Mech. College of, College Station, Tex..	1876	Gibb Gilchrist	8,653	455	208,000	128,561	5,192	330	209,000	67,850
Texas, University of, Austin, Tex..	1881	Theophilus S. Painter	16,858	670	70,080,000	804,009	9,720	491	35,265,300	531,454
Texas Christian University, Fort Worth, Tex.	1873	M. E. Sadler	4,000	174	4,000,000	105,000	900	67	3,587,999	45,056
Texas College, Tyler, Tex.*.	1894	D. R. Glass	656	23	—	10,000	476	25	—	8,000
Texas College of Arts and Industries, Kingsville, Tex..	1925	E. N. Jones	1,720	76	—	31,265	1,041	61	—	18,685
Texas Col. of Mines and Met., El Paso, Tex. .	1914	D. M. Wiggins	1,764	80	620,000	48,000	952	47	599,200	19,151
Texas Lutheran College (Jr.), Seguin, Tex. .	1892	William F. Kraushaar	251	17	20,000	18,000	155	13	20,000	13,460
Texas State Col. for Wom., Denton, Tex. .	1901	L. H. Hubbard	2,629	186	—	120,000	2,621	92	—	70,000
Texas Technological Col., Lubbock, Tex.. .	1923	William Marvin Whyburn	5,365	200	—	98,233	3,154	186	—	85,000
Thiel College, Greenville, Pa..	1866	Wm. F. Zimmerman	495	32	170,000	20,000	274	24	170,000	15,000
Tillotson College, Austin, Tex..	1877	William H. Jones	589	38	—	23,000	348	21	—	9,000
Toledo, University of, Toledo, Ohio . . .	1872	Philip C. Nash	5,900	256	—	126,117	1,979	123	—	64,403
Toronto, University of, Toronto, Ont., Can. .	1872	Sidney E. Smith	17,111	1,329	—	448,786	8,136	876	—	339,261
Tougaloo College, Tougaloo, Miss.	1869	Judson L. Cross	319	24	47,009	14,149	120	15	43,325	10,255
Transylvania College, Lexington, Ky. . . .	1780	Raymond F. McLain	515	33	750,000	53,774	522	36	750,000	40,000
Trinity College, Hartford, Conn.	1823	G. Keith Funston	827	70	3,849,219	160,000	509	54	3,278,000	120,000
Trinity College, Toronto, Ontario, Can. . .	1851	R. S. K. Seeley	675	36	2,774,481	42,500	380	28	2,313,024	38,195
Trinity College, Washington, D.C.*. . . .	1897	Sr. Catherine Dorothea	480	58	530,531	44,000	350	58	406,203	42,679
Tufts College, Medford 55, Mass.	1852	Leonard Carmichael	3,555	760	9,558,400	200,000	2,135	598	7,605,275	183,229
Tulane Univ. of Louisiana, New Orleans, La.	1834	Rufus C. Harris	4,954	751	10,884,533	450,000	3,008	462	10,541,873	178,000
Tulsa, University of, Tulsa, Okla..	1894	C. I. Pontius	2,856	125	1,300,790	52,259	884	62	1,049,146	35,075
Tusculum College, Greeneville, Tenn. . . .	1794	Geo. K. Davies	412	24	1,407,968	22,500	263	23	1,259,702	15,000
Tuskegee Institute, Tuskegee Institute, Ala. .	1881	Frederick D. Patterson	2,591	450	7,476,267	70,000	1,440	151	7,005,353	43,525

Institution and Location	Year Founded	Chief Executive 1946	1946				1937			
			Full Time Students	Faculty	Endowment	Library Volumes	Full Time Students	Faculty	Endowment	Library Volumes
Tyler Junior College, Tyler, Tex.	1926	H. E. Jenkins	513	27	—	6,782	206	17	—	4,520
U										
Union College, Barbourville, Ky.	1879	C. Boatman	400	30	$ 500,000	18,000	276	20	$ 372,972	12,873
Union College, Lincoln, Neb.	1891	Robert W. Woods	838	48	—	35,500	432	28	—	25,000
Union College, Schenectady, N.Y.	1795	Carter Davidson	1,306	116	6,000,000	110,000	812	65	2,000,000	97,828
U.S. Coast Guard Acad., New London, Conn.	1876	James Pine	300	35	—	27,000	126	25	—	7,700
U.S. Military Academy, West Point, N.Y.	1802	Maxwell D. Taylor	2,093	259	—	126,000	1,786	275	—	105,400
U.S. Naval Academy, Annapolis, Md.	1845	Aubrey W. Fitch	2,712	419	—	110,000	2,231	247	—	85,700
Upsala College, East Orange, N.J.	1893	Evald B. Lawson	1,330	78	200,000	25,000	360	28	—	11,862
Ursinus College, Collegeville, Pa.	1869	Norman E. McClure	880	49	750,000	35,000	520	43	605,000	30,000
Ursuline Col. for Women, Cleveland 6, Ohio	1871	Mother Marie Sands	278	31	—	20,000	197	—	—	14,100
Utah, University of, Salt Lake City, Utah	1850	A. Ray Olpin	8,576	480	791,283	180,000	3,935	281	880,000	132,000
Utah State Agricultural Col., Logan, Utah	1888	Franklin S. Harris	3,725	173	—	96,525	3,458	126	—	67,721
V										
Valparaiso University, Valparaiso, Ind.	1859	O. P. Kretzmann	1,406	86	499,118	40,000	524	46	555,491	26,275
Vanderbilt University, Nashville, Tenn.	1872	Harvie Branscomb	3,010	468	30,469,405	470,365	1,617	416	22,567,564	192,042
Vassar College, Poughkeepsie, N.Y.	1861	Sarah G. Blanding	1,424	192	12,400,000	255,000	1,216	181	9,048,047	203,416
Vermont, University of, and State Agricultural Col., Burlington, Vt.	1791	John S. Millis	2,065	245	2,500,000	200,000	1,395	189	3,365,544	145,000
Victoria University, Toronto, Ont., Can.	1836	Walter T. Brown	2,690	58	3,681,976	100,000	986	47	2,774,588	90,000
Villanova College, Villanova, Pa.	1842	F. X. N. McGuire	1,963	97	—	86,000	904	72	—	50,000
Virginia, University of, Charlottesville, Va.	1819	John L. Newcomb	4,308	336	13,000,000	461,691	2,574	247	10,890,413	284,462
Virginia Intermont College (Jr.), Bristol, Va.	1884	Rabun L. Brantley	427	34	499,674	12,000	397	35	172,000	7,000
Virginia Junior College, Virginia, Minn.	1921	Floyd B. Moe	435	27	—	20,000	379	28	—	10,862
Virginia Military Institute, Lexington, Va.	1839	R. J. Marshall	791	63	357,858	75,512	709	54	209,732	48,407
Virginia Polytechnic Inst., Blacksburg, Va.	1872	John R. Hutcheson	4,121	212	349,312	696,947	2,526	148	344,312	75,094
Virginia State College, Petersburg, Virginia	1882	Luther H. Foster	1,676	119	173,000	33,531	921	71	—	18,949
Virginia State Tch. Col., Farmville, Va.	1884	D. S. Lancaster	866	81	—	38,198	805	49	—	30,489
Virginia Union University, Richmond, Va.*	1865	John M. Ellison	697	38	786,476	19,700	548	34	700,000	24,562
Voorhees Normal and Industrial School (Jr.), Denmark, S.C.	1897	J. J. Gravatt	96	36	47,706	3,400	114	21	41,467	2,988
W										
Wabash College, Crawfordsville, Ind.	1832	Frank H. Sparks	501	42	2,785,700	93,000	373	29	1,992,000	83,188
Wagner College, Staten Island, N.Y.	1883	Walter C. Langsam	800	56	400,000	40,000	203	20	394,717	13,597
Wake Forest College, Wake Forest, N.C.	1834	Thurman D. Kitchin	1,712	139	3,000,000	91,050	933	40	2,285,582	60,000
Walla Walla College, College Place, Wash.	1892	G. W. Bowers	996	43	—	23,590	514	31	—	14,000
Ward Belmont School (Jr.), Nashville, Tenn.	1913	Robert C. Provine	526	77	—	16,958	533	62	—	13,841
Washburn Municipal University, Topeka, Kan.	1865	Bryan S. Stoffer	1,416	101	1,377,372	61,106	686	76	1,200,000	49,245
Washington, State Col. of, Pullman, Wash.	1891	Wilson Compton	5,891	260	7,000,000	450,000	3,896	227	3,271,000	330,000
Washington, University of, Seattle, Wash.	1861	Raymond B. Allen	15,594	950	972,778	490,000	10,703	50	—	410,613
Washington and Jefferson Col., Wash., Pa.	1780	James H. Case, Jr.	1,040	75	1,800,000	66,843	494	36	1,742,861	55,417
Washington and Lee Univ., Lexington, Va.	1749	Francis P. Gaines	1,160	75	3,528,749	150,000	958	63	2,938,171	77,887
Washington College, Chestertown, Md.	1782	Gilbert Wilcox Mead	465	28	—	30,000	297	25	—	14,000
Washington Missionary Col., Tacoma Pk., D.C.†	1904	W. H. Shephard	642	39	—	32,000	491	32	—	12,694
Washington University, St. Louis, Mo.	1853	Arthur H. Compton	7,077	800	23,442,583	725,398	3,187	603	21,073,515	364,842
Wayne University, Detroit, Mich.	1868	David D. Henry	8,431	950	4,824	274,001	4,552	659	—	76,014
Weber College (Jr.), Ogden, Utah.	1889	H. A. Dixon	1,470	63	—	16,000	705	36	—	15,000
Webster College, Webster Groves, Mo.	1915	George F. Donovan	428	58	—	26,787	215	36	—	20,484
Wellesley College, Wellesley, Mass.	1870	Mildred M. Horton	1,685	204	10,566,735	236,254	1,503	178	10,191,157	182,801
Wells College, Aurora, N.Y.	1868	Richard L. Greene	318	52	1,553,268	100,893	313	49	1,466,238	85,200
Wentworth Mil. Acad., Lexington, Mo.	1880	J. M. Sellers	106	16	—	7,500	184	22	—	5,100
Wesleyan College, Macon, Ga.	1836	Silas Johnson	595	64	1,074,788	33,081	496	43	450,000	23,006
Wesleyan University, Middletown, Conn.	1831	Victor L. Butterfield	895	95	9,400,000	330,000	704	70	7,894,948	216,099
Westbrook Junior College, Portland, Me.	1831	Milton D. Proctor	384	35	61,466	7,600	133	24	28,000	4,000
Western Carolina Tch. Col., Cullowhee, N.C.	1889	Hiram T. Hunter	500	30	—	18,000	740	44	—	13,276
Western College, Oxford, Ohio	1853	Philip E. Henderson	527	51	917,524	46,662	315	42	910,622	40,937
Western Illinois State Tch. Col., Macomb, Ill.	1899	Frank A. Beu	1,227	95	—	49,698	732	80	—	41,932
Western Kentucky State Tch. Col., Bowling Green, Ky.	1906	Paul L. Garrett	1,684	102	—	63,000	1,800	107	—	54,786
Western Maryland Col., Westminster, Md.	1867	Fred G. Holloway	779	59	880,000	45,144	523	47	898,253	29,274
Western Michigan College, Kalamazoo, Mich.	1903	Paul V. Sangren	4,000	250	—	75,000	1,952	194	—	44,130
Western Ontario, University of, London, Ont., Can.	1878	W. Sherwood Fox	2,935	285	1,194,000	167,500	1,321	109	447,711	130,000
Western Reserve Univ., Cleveland, Ohio	1826	Winfred G. Leutner	6,596	817	16,885,000	590,800	4,124	714	9,349,161	510,000
Western State College of Colorado, Gunnison, Colo.	1901	H. L. Dotson	540	30	—	33,330	386	35	—	24,500
Western Washington College of Education, Bellingham, Wash.†	1893	Wm. W. Haggard	319	57	—	67,551	865	59	—	53,476
West Georgia College (Jr.), Genola, Ga.	1933	I. S. Ingram	520	22	—	9,584	392	18	—	3,885
West Liberty State Col., W. Liberty, W.Va.	1837	Paul N. Elbin	520	25	—	20,000	202	20	—	10,000
Westminster College, Fulton, Mo.	1851	Franc L. McCluer	550	29	615,800	40,000	309	18	703,000	27,000
Westminster College, New Wilmington, Pa.	1852	H. Lloyd Cleland	1,255	78	900,000	34,000	541	48	590,000	17,800
Westminster College, Salt Lake City, Utah.	1875	Robert D. Steele	207	23	150,000	15,500	194	20	150,000	11,000
Westminster College (Jr.), Tehuacana, Tex.	1895	W. D. Blunk	100	12	—	7,114	143	8	—	5,300
West Texas State Tch. Col., Canyon, Tex.	1912	J. A. Hill	1,435	75	—	56,001	950	60	—	38,000
West Virginia State Col., Institute, W.Va.	1891	John W. Davis	1,398	52	—	35,377	706	42	—	18,500
West Virginia Univ., Morgantown, W.Va.	1867	Irvin Stewart	5,862	533	—	191,000	2,683	251	99,900	180,294
West Virginia Wesleyan Col., Buckhannon, W.Va.	1890	W. J. Scarborough	725	35	220,000	30,000	420	26	—	20,000
Wheaton College, Norton, Mass.	1834	A. Howard Meneely	478	67	1,236,414	59,528	445	57	1,127,825	37,717
Wheaton College Wheaton, Ill.	1860	V. Raymond Edman	1,472	133	670,776	90,000	1,047	77	713,436	45,000
Wheelock College, Boston, Mass.	1889	Winifred E. Bain	328	19	—	10,000	290	27	—	2,000
Whitman College, Walla Walla, Wash.	1859	Winslow S. Anderson	816	55	1,400,000	80,000	584	51	1,048,000	64,400
Whittier College, Whittier, Calif.	1901	William C. Jones	799	46	600,000	52,000	485	48	500,000	35,000
Whitworth College, Spokane, Wash.	1890	Frank F. Warren	639	44	50,000	30,000	242	28	—	—
Wichita, Municipal Univ. of, Wichita, Kan.	1895	W. M. Jardine	2,810	144	94,274	74,000	1,181	75	104,626	42,809
Wiley College, Marshall, Tex.	1873	E. C. McLeod	792	60	650,000	19,071	540	25	300,000	17,000
Willamette University, Salem, Ore.	1842	G. Herbert Smith	987	67	2,100,000	47,000	834	58	1,600,000	35,000
William and Mary, Col. of, Williamsburg, Va.	1693	John Edwin Pomfret	1,770	120	1,700,000	315,116	1,290	96	755,183	110,000
William Jewell Col., Liberty, Mo.	1849	Walter Pope Binns	767	39	1,985,518	57,476	397	24	1,109,429	40,799
Williams College, Williamstown, Mass.	1793	James P. Baxter	1,059	113	12,453,000	200,000	826	90	11,196,000	161,991
Williamsport-Dickinson Seminary and Junior Col., Williamsport, Pa.	1929	John W. Long	744	49	396,456	10,701	157	20	317,088	6,954
William Woods College (Jr.), Fulton, Mo.	1890	H. L. Smith	361	34	550,000	13,000	216	23	485,000	10,000
Willimantic St. Tch. Col., Willimantic, Conn.*	1889	George H. Shafer	135	40	—	9,000	161	15	—	17,655
Wilmington College, Wilmington, Ohio	1870	S. A. Watson	530	30	336,000	22,000	245	21	325,000	16,000
Wilson College, Chambersburg, Pa.	1868	Paul Swain Havens	474	53	878,632	56,000	408	45	804,165	40,000

Institution and Location	Year Founded	Chief Executive 1946	1946				1937			
			Full Time Students	Faculty	Endow-ment	Library Volumes	Full Time Students	Faculty	Endow-ment	Library Volumes
Winston-Salem Tch. Col., Winston-Salem, N.C.*	1892	Francis L. Atkins	587	26	—	22,244	518	23	—	8,367
Winthrop College, Rock Hill, S.C.	1886	Henry R. Sims	1,535	117	—	66,000	1,345	73	—	46,000
Wisconsin, University of, Madison, Wis.	1848	Edwin Broun Fred	18,672	1,209	$ 4,991,032	597,000	10,679	899	—	493,000
Wisconsin State Tch. Col., Eau Claire, Wis.	1916	W. R. Davies	790	57	—	31,000	519	43	—	20,078
Wisconsin State Tch. Col. LaCrosse, Wis.	1909	Rexford S. Mitchell	975	66	—	37,261	672	55	—	22,298
Wisconsin State Tch. Col., Milwaukee, Wis.	1880	J. Martin Klotsche	1,704	104	—	70,880	1,250	83	—	65,350
Wisconsin StateTch. Col. Oshkosh, Wis.	1871	Forrest R. Polk	894	60	—	37,884	693	54	—	25,129
Wisconsin State Tch. Col., Platteville, Wis.	1866	C. O. Newlun	518	48	—	30,000	526	40	—	25,000
Wisconsin State Tch. Col., River Falls, Wis.	1874	E. H. Kleinpell	683	46	—	25,000	562	39	—	23,200
Wisconsin State Tch. Col., Stevens Point, Wis.	1894	W. C. Hansen	878	53	—	40,000	614	47	—	35,000
Wisconsin State Tch. Col., Superior, Wis.	1893	Jim Dan Hill	878	58	—	28,503	725	54	—	31,750
Wisconsin State Tch. Col., Whitewater, Wis.	1868	R. C Williams	689	52	—	36,917	785	53	—	33,514
Wittenberg College, Springfield, Ohio	1845	Rees Edgar Tulloss	1,248	85	2,401,767	73,640	830	92	$ 1,555,989	55,659
Wofford College, Spartanburg, S.C.	1854	W. K. Greene	600	32	865,708	40,000	510	29	781,950	38,000
Wooster, College of, Wooster, Ohio	1866	Howard F. Lowry	1,237	80	3,673,281	102,995	950	82	3,722,930	80,301
Worcester Polytechnic Inst., Worcester, Mass.*	1865	Wat T. Cluverius	861	89	4,000,000	35,000	615	67	3,582,840	24,000
Wyoming, University of, Laramie, Wyo.	1887	G. D. Humphrey	3,019	247	4,250,000	127,922	1,852	156	4,883,848	89,586
X										
Xavier University, Cincinnati, Ohio	1831	Celestin J. Steiner	1,498	49	—	83,400	485	57	—	47,000
Xavier University, New Orleans, La.*	1925	Mother M. Agatha	499	65	470,655	44,069	642	49	60,036	20,874
Y										
Yale University, New Haven, Conn.	1701	Charles Seymour	8,651	1,244	123,112,371	3,539,600	5,230	900	105,000,000	2,650,000
Yankton College, Yankton, S.D.	1881	James C. Graham	360	32	700,000	42,000	483	45	798,281	29,000
Young L. G. Harris Col. (Jr.), Young Harris, Ga.	1886	J. W. Sharp	349	15	130,000	12,000	410	19	60,000	8,000
Youngstown College, Youngstown, Ohio.	1908	Howard W. Jones	2,241	172	12,500	34,550	272	53	—	7,100
Yuba Junior College, Marysville, Calif.	1927	J. J. Collins	592	34	—	6,159	191	18	—	4,124

U.N.R.R.A.

See UNITED NATIONS RELIEF AND REHABILITATION ADMINISTRATION.

Uranium

After the announcement of the explosion of the first atomic bomb over Hiroshima on Aug. 6, 1945, uranium filled more newspaper headlines than had ever been the lot of any other metal.

Even at the end of 1946, however, security reasons still prevented the publication of anything more than basic fundamentals relating to the metal.

For many years uranium had been recognized as a standard colouring agent in ceramics, as a useful ingredient in certain photographic processes, as a catalyst in a few chemical reactions, and in a few other minor uses. Plentiful supplies of the material were available as a by-product from vanadium and radium ores, and there was no incentive to search for ores of uranium.

In the 1930s, the unstable isotope U-235 was discovered to accompany the normal variety in the proportion of 1 to 140, but though the problem of isolating U-235 and making use of its peculiar properties received much attention as a scientific problem, it was not seriously attempted as a practical problem on a practical scale until 1942.

Starting out primarily as a problem of the separation of the scarce isotope U-235 from the plentiful variety U-238 in quantities of sufficient size to be of practical rather than of scientific value, there were a number of more or less startling developments.

Early in the research it was found that under neutron bombardment U-238 could be converted into the unstable isotope U-239, which in turn was transformed into a hitherto unknown element, No. 93, which was given the name neptunium.

Another step in the transformation converted the unstable neptunium into another new but more stable element, No. 94, called plutonium.

While plutonium is more stable than neptunium, it is still enough on the unstable side to be fissionable, like U-235, and since it is obtainable from the plentiful U-238, rather than from the scarce U-235, the discovery of this procedure simplified the problem greatly. Later it was reported that the bombardment cycle also produced smaller amounts of two more new elements, Nos. 95 and 96. Still later it was announced that some 150 different isotopes of about 35 different elements had been identified in the by-products of the chain reaction piles used for the production of plutonium.

Little information was made public concerning these isotopes, but sufficient amounts of some of them were collected to make it possible to use them in medical and biological experimentation.

Uranium played its part in World War II, and regardless of whether one agreed with the group that held this part to have been a major and decisive one, or with those who maintained it was unnecessary and unjustifiable, the fact remained that the two outstanding problems facing the postwar world were the legacy of uranium's role in the war.

The first of these problems was the necessity of adjusting international relations on such a basis as to preclude the possibility of the metal playing a major role in a third world war; the second problem, possibly even greater than the original one of creating the atomic bomb, was the adaptation of its destructive properties to peaceful pursuits, where they might be used for the benefit of mankind, rather than for its destruction.

(*See* also ATOMIC BOMB; CHEMISTRY; METALLURGY; PHYSICS.) (G. A. Ro.)

BIBLIOGRAPHY.—J. A. DeMent, *Uranium and Atomic Power* (1945); R. W. Dodson, *Studies in Nuclear Chemistry: Products of Uranium and Thorium Fissions* (1940); M. L. Eidinoff, "Uranium Fission: Discoveries Leading to a Chain Reaction," *Journal of Chemical Education*, 23:60–65 (Feb. 1946); M. H. Kanner, *Some Experiments on the Fission of Uranium and Thorium* (1940); N. B. Keevil, "Thorium-Uranium Ratios in Rocks and Minerals," *American Journal of Science*, 242:309–321 (June 1944); S. C. Lind, "Uranium and Radium in the Postwar Period," *Electrochemical Society Transactions*, 89: (preprint 14) 167–169 (1946); L. Meitner, *On the Products of the Fission of Uranium and Thorium under Neutron Bombardment* (Copenhagen, 1940); E. Orban, *Standard Electrode Potential of the Uranous-Uranyl Sulfate Redox Electrode* (1944); C. W. Sill, *Fluorescence Test for Uranium* (Bureau of Mines Incorm. Circ. 7337, 1945); U.S. Bureau of Mines, *Minerals Yearbook;* "Uranium," Chap. 63, p. 1–138, in J. W. Mellor, *Comprehensive Treatise on Inorganic and Theoretical Chemistry*, vol. 12 (1932).

468 Urology

Probably the most important advance in the field of urology during the decade 1937–46 was in chemotherapy. In no field of medicine were chemotherapeutic agents used to greater advantage than in the treatment of infections involving the genito-urinary tract.

Urinary Antisepsis.—Urinary antisepsis began with the use of the ketogenic diet as a bactericidal agent; then the discovery of mandelic acid presented the medical profession with the first specific therapeutic compound for the treatment of urinary infections. This was soon followed by the discovery of the sulfonamides and, later, the powerful antibiotics, penicillin and streptomycin.

When a patient who had infection in the urinary tract was placed on the ketogenic diet, the urine often became sterile. M. L. Rosenheim found subsequently that mandelic acid was the predominant factor in causing urinary antisepsis with ketosis. Mandelic acid, in conjunction with drugs given to acidify the urine to a pH of 5.5 or less, was found to be bactericidal to many gram-negative organisms, particularly of the colon bacillus group. Although uncomplicated bacillary infection of the urinary tract and infections caused by streptococcus faecalis, were frequently eliminated by this drug, it had no effect on other types of coccal or streptococcal infection. Unfortunately, however, mandelic acid often was not well tolerated and caused systemic reactions. Although it was largely replaced by the sulfonamides and antibiotic agents, nevertheless it was still employed in some cases. It was also used in combination with hexamethylenamine under the name of mandelamine, with good results in some cases.

Not long after the employment of mandelic acid in treatment of urinary infections, Gerhard Domagk discovered that the sulfonamides possess powerful bactericidal qualities. These drugs soon were applied to infection in the urinary tract with excellent results. A great variety of sulfonamide drugs was synthetized and replaced such early forms as sulfanilamide and sulfapyridine. Such drugs as sulfadiazine, sulfamerazine, sulfathiazole and sulfacetimide became generally employed. These newer sulfonamides caused fewer systemic reactions and permitted higher levels of the drug in the blood than the compounds first discovered. The sulfonamide drugs are easily administered and are advantageous in that they are bactericidal to both coccal and bacillary organisms. One of the disadvantages of the sulfonamide drugs is the systemic reaction which they sometimes cause. Some individuals are definitely allergic to sulfonamide drugs, and cases were reported in which one or another of the following complications appeared: profound toxaemia, extensive eruptions of the skin, fever, agranulocytosis, or haemolytic anaemia. Sulfonamides also may cause crystalluria with microscopic haematuria, and this complication should be searched for by routine urinalysis. Crystalluria is observed infrequently in the treatment of urinary infections because of the comparatively low dosage of sulfanilamide employed. It was found that alkalinization of the urine by administering sodium bicarbonate prevents crystallization in the kidneys. Sulfamerazine was advocated because a smaller dose is required to maintain effective levels in the blood than for other sulfonamide compounds, and it is excreted more slowly. It is imperative that careful medical supervision should be given in all cases in which sulfonamide compounds are administered.

Antibiotic agents, best represented by penicillin and streptomycin, were proved particularly valuable in combating infections in the genito-urinary tract. Although the antibacterial action of penicillin was discovered by Alexander Fleming in 1929, it was not applied clinically until its therapeutic value was determined by H. W. Florey and his co-workers in 1940. Penicillin, which at first was produced in limited amounts, became available in large quantities and was widely applied. The generally accepted method of administration of penicillin for urinary infections was by means of intermittent intramuscular injections. A simpler method was adopted later—a single intramuscular injection of a preparation which combines penicillin with a solution of beeswax and peanut oil sustained a high level of penicillin in the blood for more than 24 hr. Oral administration of penicillin was tried with a variable degree of success. Although penicillin failed to eliminate urinary infection in many cases, it was often found valuable in controlling acute infections when other measures had failed. It also was proved of value in combating acute infection in the prostate gland, renal cortex and perinephric tissues and in controlling periurethral inflammation, such as sometimes occurs after transurethral manipulation.

In 1944, S. A. Waksman and his co-workers, in a search for a substance which would be bactericidal to organisms of all types, isolated a new antibacterial substance, streptomycin, which was obtained from the culture filtrate of actinomyces griseus. They found that this antibiotic had relatively low toxicity and exerted a definite antibacterial action on many gram-negative and some gram-positive organisms.

Although streptomycin was not as widely applicable as penicillin, nevertheless, it was found to be particularly valuable in the treatment of infections caused by certain gram-negative bacilli. It had almost a specific effect in combating proteus ammoniae, which formerly had been difficult to control. It was shown to have a distinctly deterrent action on the activity of myco-bacterium tuberculosis. In the few reported cases of renal tuberculosis in which it was administered, definite improvement was noted in symptoms and in the patient's general condition, and in some cases tubercle bacilli were eliminated temporarily from the urine. Streptomycin usually is administered parenterally because when given by mouth practically none of it is absorbed from the gastro-intestinal tract. After one parenteral injection a high percentage of the drug is excreted in the urine within 12 hours. In some cases it produced a moderate degree of toxicity, and a few patients complained of histamine-like reactions. It is best given in a dosage of 1 or 2 gm. daily by intramuscular injection, at intervals of three hours. It is necessary that the drug be given in large doses at the beginning if the desired effect is to be obtained. It should be emphasized that self-administration of these antibiotics is inadvisable. Careful supervision by a physician is essential to their successful employment.

Since these agents had specific action for various types of bacteria, a careful study of the bacteria involved was found to be fundamental to successful treatment. By dividing the bacteria into two groups—namely, gram-negative bacilli and gram-positive cocci—it was found that mandelic acid was effective against gram-negative bacilli only; the sulfonamide drugs against both gram-positive cocci and gram-negative bacilli; penicillin largely against gram-positive cocci, and streptomycin against selected gram-negative organisms and occasionally gram-positive cocci.

It was found that all these drugs eliminate bacteria from the urinary tract only in acute and subacute infections.

In chronic infections, with extensive cicatricial changes in the renal parenchyma, the improvement usually is only temporary. Moreover, it should be repeated that no antibacterial medication can be efficacious without adequate surgical drainage, in the presence of retained urine, or in the presence of foreign bodies. In the treatment of infection in the urinary tract, the large dosage of these agents, indicated in the treatment of systemic infections, was not found necessary. This may be explained by the excretion of the agent in the urine, which permits it to come in direct contact with the infected tissue.

Treatment of Gonorrhoea.—Elimination of gonorrhoeal infection, which defied all previous efforts for centuries, was achieved during the decade. With the discovery of the sulfonamide drugs, it was soon found that they had a bactericidal effect on the gonococcus, and their administration was followed by rapid elimination of this infection in from 50% to 70% of cases. By this treatment the various complications resulting from gonorrhoeal infection so often observed in former years were prevented or speedily controlled. The sulfonamide compounds, however, frequently were administered inadequately, both in dosage and in the length of time during which the drug was employed. Although the infection often was apparently eliminated, evidence of the disease reappeared later and one or two subsequent courses of sulfonamide therapy were necessary to eradicate the infection. It soon became apparent that some strains of gonococci were resistant to the sulfonamide drugs and they were ineffective against these strains.

With the advent of penicillin, it was found that this antibiotic agent was even more efficient in eliminating gonorrhoeal infection than the sulfonamides were. In fact, it was found that penicillin would overcome gonorrhoeal infection in almost 98% of cases if given in adequate dosage. It is usually administered by subcutaneous injection at intervals of three hours. The total dosage for 24 hours is from 100,000 to 150,000 units. In 1945–46 it was demonstrated that when penicillin was injected in a solution of peanut oil and beeswax, it was absorbed continuously for from 8 to 10 hours. In most cases a single injection of from 100,000 to 200,000 units sufficed to eliminate the infection. Penicillin, therefore, largely replaced the sulfonamides in the treatment of gonorrhoea. It was particularly efficient in overcoming infections resistant to the sulfonamides. A combination of the sulfonamides with penicillin was reported to be of value in some infections which had been resistant to either drug when used alone. In the treatment of this disease adequate dosage and subsequent re-examination after the urethral discharge ceases are of primary importance. It is essential that the treatment is carried out under the guidance of a physician.

Urinary Calculi.—Although the factors fundamental to formation of calculi in the urinary tract were not determined, important pathologic and bacteriologic studies offering possible clues were reported during the decade. Attention was called to the frequent occurrence of milk patches in the renal papillae which in some cases seem to form a nucleus for the development of calculi. The importance of infection in the formation of some calculi was definitely established in cases in which urea-splitting organisms, such as staphylococcus and proteus, are present. Increased emphasis was placed on the role of calcium metabolism in the pathogenesis of stones in the urinary tract. Quantitative estimation of calcium excreted in the urine was shown to be of diagnostic and therapeutic value. Calcium metabolism was found to be greatly affected by pathologic changes in the parathyroid gland. The presence of such lesions usually cannot be determined by physical examination but can be detected by increase in the levels of calcium and phosphatase, together with decrease in phosphate in the blood. Increase in the amount of calcium in the urine, as indicated by the Sulkowitch test, proved to be a valuable diagnostic aid in recognizing parathyroid disease. Parathyroid tumour was discovered to be the aetiologic factor in cases in which renal stones had formed repeatedly, and surgical removal of the tumour was followed by cessation of formation of stones.

The dissolution of calculi in the urinary tract by the continuous application of chemical solutions was attempted, without signal success. Later, a buffered solution of citric acid was used for this purpose. When applied to renal calculi through ureteral catheters or nephrostomy tubes, it proved successful in only occasional cases of soft, recently formed stones. The solution can be used only intermittently, since it is capable of causing renal irritation. In incrusted cystitis, however, it was found useful in dissolving calcified deposits. Dietary regimens proved to be efficacious in preventing recurrence of stones only in selected cases. Reduction in intake of calcium and acidification of the urine by means of a high acid, ash diet were of value in preventing the formation of phosphatic stones in some cases.

Hormonal Therapy.—Hormonal therapy was widely employed during the decade in the treatment of various lesions of the genito-urinary tract. Although an anterior pituitary-like substance with gonad-stimulating action was successful in occasional cases in the treatment of undescended testes when employed prior to the age of puberty, in most cases mechanical impediment by surrounding tissues prevented complete descent. Use of gonadotropic or androgenic hormones was accompanied by disagreeable complications in immature patients. The female sex hormone, estrone, proved to be of value as an adjunct in the treatment of vulvovaginitis in children.

The use of female hormones in the treatment of benign prostatic hypertrophy was the subject of widespread clinical investigation. Although some observers reported reduction in size of the enlarged prostate gland, together with reduction in symptoms of urinary obstruction in some cases after administration of estrogenic substances, such treatment was not followed by permanent improvement. The deformity at the vesical neck caused by prostatic hyperplasia usually remained in spite of some reduction in the volume of the gland.

The discovery of the relation of the sex glands to the development of carcinoma in the prostate gland and its biochemical relations proved to be an advance of tremendous importance. It was found that when androgens were administered, hyperplasia of the carcinomatous tissue occurred. Elimination of the testicular source of androgen by orchectomy, or control by estrogenic drugs, caused definite regression in the size and consistency of the prostate gland, cessation of pain caused by metastasis and improvement in the patient's general condition. It was found that in the presence of carcinoma of the prostate gland, the level of acid phosphatase in the serum was elevated to a variable degree. In the presence of osseous metastasis, the value for alkaline serum phosphatase also was elevated to a degree corresponding to the extent of metastasis. With the control of androgenic sources, the concentration of serum phosphatase was reduced in most cases and often returned to normal. Although the carcinomatous prostate gland decreased in size, the mechanical obstruction at the neck of the bladder usually persisted, and operative removal of the obstructing tissue, preferably by transurethral procedures, was required.

Transurethral Resection.—During the decade, transurethral resection of tissues causing obstruction at the neck of the bladder was widely employed and became firmly established as the operation of choice in most cases. With improvement in technique of transurethral resection and with better methods of controlling haemorrhage and other complications, the operative mortality was reduced to a remarkably low figure, and the postoperative functional complications were largely overcome by experienced urologic surgeons.

In a group of patients who had retention of urine caused by lesions in the spinal cord, the function of the bladder was restored in dramatic fashion by transurethral resection. Many of these unfortunate victims of spinal disease or injury, in addition to paralysis of the extremities, were unable to urinate and were burdened with drainage tubes and usually had secondary infection in the urinary tract. Cystoscopic examination revealed obstruction at the neck of the bladder. This obstruction apparently was caused by a spastic condition of the edges of the detrusor muscles, resulting in contracture with rigidity of the tissues at the neck of the bladder. Although the commissural tissues were most involved, it was found necessary to remove tissue from all segments at the outlet of the bladder. As a result of this operation, the bladder would empty in most cases with the aid of pressure by the abdominal muscles and the diaphragm. The relief was striking in most cases. The value of the operation was demonstrated in many cases of injuries to the spinal cord among sailors and soldiers during World War II. Many, with the aid of orthopaedic and rehabilitation measures, were transformed from hopeless cripples to self-supporting citizens.

Radical Prostatectomy.—Carcinoma in any part of the body has offered the best opportunity for cure when discovered early. In spite of the technical difficulties involved, an attempt to remove localized early carcinoma of the prostate gland received greater recognition during the decade. The operation is a radical prostatectomy through a perineal approach, with excision of the seminal vesicles. A large factor in the success of this operation is the selection of early cases in which there is no periprostatic extension. Such clinical selection, however, was difficult and was largely limited to those cases in which a small nodule in the prostate gland had been discovered accidentally in the course of routine rectal palpation. It was found applicable in less than 5% of the cases of prostatic carcinoma encountered at clinical examination. As the result of refinements in operative technique, complications such as urinary incontinence and urethro-rectal fistula were largely overcome by the surgeon experienced in this operation.

Carcinoma of the Bladder.—Treatment of carcinoma of the bladder, a most difficult problem, tended to become more radical during the decade. From the therapeutic standpoint, tumours of the bladder were divided into discrete papillary tumours of low grade of malignancy and the infiltrating type of carcinoma. In the treatment of the former type, the best procedure was found to be electrocoagulation by transurethral methods. A systematic follow-up plan by means of which the patient was urged to return for cystoscopic inspection was of great value in eliminating early recurrence. Implantation of radium and roentgen therapy were not used so widely as in former years. For the infiltrating type of carcinoma, the treatment tended to become more radical and the operation was improved. In the first place, it was found that preparation of the bowel prior to transplantation of the ureters was followed by definite improvement in operative results. This preliminary treatment included hospitalization, restricted diet and employment of intestinal antiseptics, such as succinylsulfathiazole, for four or five days; and it apparently reduced the virulence of the bacterial flora in the field of operation.

Advances in operative technique included the simultaneous intraperitoneal transplantation of the ureters into the sigmoid, together with cystectomy, prostatectomy and vesiculectomy, all at the same operation. This new operation shortened the convalescence and, in the hands of an experienced surgeon, was followed by comparatively low mortality rate. The complications which caused the most trouble were postoperative. In spite of precautions, constriction of the lower part of the ureter, with retention of urine and development of pyelo-ureterectasis, occurred in a considerable number of cases. The low operative mortality rate and the frequent excellent results, however, made this procedure worthy of consideration in every case of infiltrating carcinoma of the bladder. (*See* also Bacteriology; Cancer; Endocrinology: Venereal Diseases.)

Bibliography.—M. L. Rosenheim, "Mandelic Acid in the Treatment of Urinary Infections," *Lancet*, 1:1032–1037 (May 4, 1935); Gerhard Domagk, "Eine neue Klasse von Desinfektionsmitteln," *Deutsche med. Wchnschr.*, 1:829–832 (1935); Alexander Fleming, "On the Antibacterial Action of Cultures of a Penicillium, with Special Reference to Their Use in the Isolation of B. Influenzae," *Brit. J. Exper. Path.*, 10:226–236 (June 1929); E. Chain, H. W. Florey, A. D. Gardner, N. G. Heatley, M. A. Jennings, J. Orr-Ewing and A. G. Sanders, "Penicillin as a Chemotherapeutic Agent," *Lancet*, 2:226–228 (Aug. 24, 1940); S. A. Waksman, Elizabeth Bugie and Albert Schatz, "Isolation of Antibiotic Substances from Soil Micro-Organisms, with Special Reference to Streptothricin and Streptomycin," *Proc. Staff Meet., Mayo Clin.*, 19:537–548 (Nov. 15, 1944); M. J. Romansky and G. E. Rittman, "Penicillin Blood Levels for Twenty-Four Hours Following a Single Intramuscular Injection of Calcium Penicillin in Beeswax and Peanut Oil," *New England J. Med.*, 233:577–582 (Nov. 15, 1945); Alexander Randall, "The Origin and Growth of Renal Calculi," *Ann. Surg.* 105: 1009–1027 (June 1937); C. Huggins and C. V. Hodges, "Studies on Prostatic Cancer: I. The Effect of Castration, and of Estrogen and of Androgen Injection on Serum Phosphatases in Metastatic Carcinoma of the Prostate," *Cancer Research*, 1:293–297 (Apr. 1941); J. L. Emmett, E. N. Cook, T. L. Pool and L. F. Greene, "Transurethral Surgery in 1945," *Proc. Staff Meet., Mayo Clin.*, 21:353–355 (Sept. 4, 1946); J. L. Emmett, "Urinary Retention from Imbalance of Detrusor and Vesical Neck: Treatment by Transurethral Resection," *J. Urol.*, 43:692–704 (May 1940); G. J. Thompson, "Cord Bladder: Restoration of Function by Transurethral Resection," *U.S. Nav. M. Bull.*, 45:207–214 (Aug. 1945). (W. F. Br.)

Uruguay

A republic in the southeastern part of South America, Uruguay is bounded by the Atlantic on the east, the Río de la Plata on the south, Argentina on the west and Brazil on the north. Area 72,172 sq.mi. (the smallest of any South American republic); pop. (1944 est.) 2,235,000. No census had been taken since 1908; official population estimates included the following: 1938, 2,122,628; 1939, 2,147,000; 1940, 2,164,000; 1942, 2,185,626; 1943, 2,202,936. Nine-tenths of the population was of European ancestry; mestizos constituted most of the remainder. There was a large number of foreign-born inhabitants, most of them Italians and Spaniards, with smaller numbers of Brazilian, Argentine and French birth. The population density for the entire country was officially estimated in 1941 to be 30.28 per sq.mi., varying from 12.69 in the department of Artigas to 2,095.83 in the department of Montevideo, although the only other department with a density of more than 100 per sq.mi. was Canelones, with 108.57. The capital and chief port is Montevideo (pop., 1945 est., 747,665); other important cities (with 1945 pop. estimates unless otherwise stated) are Paysandú (50,000), Salto (48,000), Mercedes (33,000), Minas (1942 est., 32,000), Tucuarembó (30,000), San José (1942 est., 30,000), Rocha (28,500), Melo (28,000), Durazno (1942 est., 27,000); Santa Lucía (1942 est., 27,000).

The constitution of 1934 provided for a centralized republic composed of 19 departments, a bicameral congress with a senate of 30 and a chamber of deputies of 99 members. Presidents during the decade 1937–46 were Gabriel Terra, to June 19, 1938; Alfredo Baldomir, June 19, 1938–March 1, 1943; Juan José Amézaga, after the latter date.

Democracy for Dictatorship.—Pres. Gabriel Terra, who had been elected in 1931 on a platform of support for the constitutional system of 1919, found himself at odds in March 1933 with the national administrative council and the congress, and forcibly dissolved both bodies after a *coup d'état.* He thereafter ruled as a virtual dictator, although both the country and the government in the closing years of the administration manifested a desire to return to more democratic practices. Pres. Terra declared his intention of permitting free elections in 1938. The principal candidates in the campaign culminating in the election of March 27, 1938, were Gen. Alfredo Baldomir, a brother-in-law of Pres. Terra, and Dr. Blanco Acevedo, the president's son-in-law. Despite the relationships, the election was vigorously contested and was generally conceded to be fairly conducted. Gen. Baldomir had campaigned on a platform of anti-fascism, which proved popular in Uruguay's traditionally democratic atmosphere, and in the three-way contest he received 37% of the popular vote; he was inaugurated June 19. Pres. Baldomir in October joined in inter-American efforts to mediate the Ecuador-Peru boundary controversy.

Uruguayan national prosperity remained largely dependent on competitive world markets, inasmuch as meat products normally provided about 95% of the exports, and in 1938 the country was adversely affected by the world economic recession and price decline of 1937, accentuated by bad weather conditions which reduced production. The government consequently directed its policy toward stabilization of markets through restriction of imports to products of countries buying from Uruguay. An arrangement was made with Mexico for the purchase of all Uruguayan oil needs for 1939, with 30% of the price to be covered by Uruguayan goods. The government late in December announced conclusion of a barter agreement with Italy, exchanging wheat for armaments, following the return of former Pres. Terra from a visit to Italy. Violent foreign criticism resulted from the announcement, coming as it did immediately after the Lima conference declaration, subscribed to by Uruguay, against such agreements.

The outbreak of war in Europe in Sept. 1939 had a generally, although not entirely, favourable effect, especially in the increased sale of livestock products. The government imposed a 25% tax on wartime profits of the pastoral industry in order to provide subsidies for adversely affected industries. Wool sales increased in the meantime, and in November the British government purchased £862,938 of Uruguayan beef.

Uruguay participated in the first inter-American foreign ministers' conference at Panamá in September–October, and was a leader in the expulsion of the soviet union from the League of Nations in December. One of the most dramatic developments of World War II occurred when on Dec. 13, 1939, the German pocket battleship "Admiral Graf Spee" engaged in a running battle with three British cruisers off the Uruguayan coast and, after being crippled

Student demonstration in Montevideo on June 6, 1941, against a pro-axis newspaper

by gunfire, fled to Montevideo for refuge. The government rejected German demands for time for repairs and ordered the "Spee's" internment unless the ship departed by Dec. 17. As the British warships were still lying in wait off the port, the crew of the "Spee" scuttled the battleship soon after leaving the harbour and within sight of the city. The government on Dec. 30 gave the German merchant vessel "Tacoma," an auxiliary ship to the "Spee," 48 hours to leave port or be interned, and did intern the vessel on Jan. 1, 1940.

War Complications.—Uruguay was torn throughout 1940 by issues arising from the European war. Serious difficulties were experienced at the beginning of the year in handling the interned German sailors from the "Tacoma." Pres. Baldomir as early as February made strenuous efforts to advance Uruguayan defenses, but a proposal for compulsory military service was rejected by an apathetic congress. The revelation in June 1940 of widespread fifth-column activities and a pro-nazi plot to overthrow the government and convert Uruguay into an agricultural colony of Germany aroused great excitement, which was calmed only by Brazilian loan of arms and munitions, the calculated arrival of two United States cruisers, and formal pledges by U.S. Minister Edwin C. Wilson on June 23 of United States aid in suppressing any attempt to overthrow the government. Following these developments, conscription was enacted into law without serious opposition. The revelations of June lent colour to the charges earlier made by Prof. Hugo Fernández Artucio in a sensational book, *Nazis en el Uruguay,* that widespread German activity existed in the republic.

The chief issue late in the year was the proposed granting to the United States of naval base rights at Punta del Este, on the Atlantic coast, as part of the hemisphere defense program. Pres. Baldomir pushed the project in the face of strong Argentine protests, based on the fear that the Plata river could thus effectively be closed, and of bitter opposition within his own cabinet, some of whose members resigned. The congressional opposition, led by Dr. Luis Alberto Herrera, also vigorously opposed the proposal. Foreign Minister Alberto Guani, an ardent democrat, announced on Dec. 14, after several days of conference at Colonia with the Argentine foreign minister, the conclusion of an Argentine-Uruguayan agreement for the joint defense of the Plata river against possible non-American aggression.

Various cabinet and congressional crises occurred during 1941, usually originating in the peculiar constitutional provisions giving the minority party (the Blancos, led by Herrera) one-third of the cabinet posts and one-half of the senate seats. Pres. Baldomir actively supported constitutional amendment to correct this situation. Herrera, well known for his opposition to the United States, steadily opposed the administration's foreign policy, the central feature of which was hemispheric co-operation. Baldomir as early as June 9 formally reiterated Uruguay's traditional policy of granting bases and other facilities for defense of the American continent against external aggression, in line with the principles of continental solidarity. Nationalist opposition and Argentine protests prevented the direct granting of bases to the United States, but in September the latter government made a $17,500,000 lend-lease grant for construction of a large naval-air base at Laguna Negra, close to the Brazilian border. Title to the base was to remain in Uruguayan hands, but it was reported that the United States would be allowed full use of its facilities.

German and Italian propaganda and other activity, meanwhile, became pronounced. Though Italians were far more numerous than Germans (the minorities were estimated at 100,000 Italians plus 500,000 citizens of Italian descent, and 6,000 Germans plus 10,000 citizens of German descent), the better organization and greater aggressiveness of the latter made them the more serious problem. The establishment of a pro-axis propaganda journal caused riots in June; its editor, a member of the chamber of deputies, was later suspended by that body. Various incidents occurred in the meantime, notably serious fascist rioting at Durazno on June 28, 1941, in which two persons were killed. After the revelations in the Hugo Fernández Artucio book and disclosure of widespread nazi intrigue in Argentina, the chamber of deputies appointed a special committee on Oct. 8, 1941, to investigate anti-Uruguayan activities in the republic. Uruguayan declarations of American solidarity were issued promptly after the Japanese attack on Pearl Harbor. The government continued diplomatic relations with the axis powers for the time being, but Pres. Baldomir and Foreign Minister Guani formally expressed the country's intention to follow its own precedent of 1917 and regard any American states at war as still possessing full nonbelligerent rights.

A regional development of great importance occurred in late January and early February 1941 when Uruguay was host to the Río de la Plata regional conference at Montevideo, a meeting of the four Platine republics of Argentina, Bolivia, Paraguay and Uruguay, attended also by Brazil, and with observers present from Chile and Peru. The conference resulted in an Argentine and Uruguayan grant of special trade treatment for ten years to landlocked Bolivia and Paraguay, with provisions for reciprocal preferential treatment of each nation's products and freedom of transit, and laid a general groundwork for a possible eventual customs union of the whole area.

The almost continuous political conflicts of the two main groups in Uruguay came, on the whole, as the result of a difference of opinion over foreign policy. The obstructionist tactics of the opposition, which had led during the preceding year to several cabinet and congressional crises, threatened to do the same in 1942. In February, Pres. Baldomir consequently dissolved the congress and postponed to November the presidential election which had been scheduled for March. The constitutional provisions giving the leading minority party a minimum of three cabinet seats and half the positions in the senate permitted the Herreristas to block governmental action simply by refusing to attend congressional sessions and thus breaking a quorum. During the eight months between the dissolution of the congress and the November elections, Pres. Baldomir ruled with the aid of a state commission, composed of a large number of prominent citizens, which he had selected to share with him the responsibilities of government.

The campaign got under way in September with the naming of Juan José Amézaga and Luis Alberto Herrera as the presidential candidates of the two main parties, respectively the traditionally liberal Colorado and the strongly nationalistic and conservative Blanco Nacionalista. The Colorado party, with its ticket supported by Pres. Baldomir, nominated an even more distinguished Uruguayan as its vice-presidential candidate; this was Foreign Minister Alberto Guani who, in addition to his outstanding record in the foreign office, had made a notable international record as chairman of the inter-American Advisory Committee for the Political Defense of the Hemisphere, with its headquarters at Montevideo. The election was held

Nov. 29, with only about 65% of the total electorate voting, partly because of the concurrent record-breaking nation-wide rainstorms. The election indicated strong approval of the administration's policies, with the government party not only electing Amézaga and Guani but also capturing control of both houses of the congress and most departmental and municipal offices; the voters, in addition, approved by decisive majorities the constitutional changes proposed by the president to remedy the legislative impasses which had frequently occurred.

At the conclusion of the third Foreign Ministers' conference at Río de Janeiro in late Jan. 1942, Uruguay severed its diplomatic relations with Germany, Italy and Japan, and announced a policy of close co-operation with the other American states against axis aggression. The army, which in 1941 had included only about 8,000 troops, was considerably strengthened and modernized with new weapons obtained largely by means of a lend-lease grant from the United States. Uruguay on July 21, 1942, signed a reciprocal trade agreement with the United States which, it was hoped, would help to offset its lost European markets and also partially to prepare for eventual postwar conditions.

Amézaga's Administration.—Pres. Amézaga took over the executive office on March 1, 1943, and continued the active collaboration in inter-American defense laid down by his party in 1941 and 1942. The vice-president elect, Dr. Alberto Guani, had visited the United States in January and signed agreements with the Export-Import bank providing for a loan of $20,000,000 to be used for a public-improvements program in Uruguay. The government announced early in 1943 that diplomatic relations would be resumed with the soviet union, with which such contacts had been broken in 1936 following sensational charges that Uruguay was being used as a base for communist propaganda in South America. The government severed its relations with the Vichy regime in France on May 12.

The new administration began its internal program with serious obstacles to overcome. The country was faced, in addition to the usual problems of wartime, with the most severe drought in a number of years. The government, in an effort to decrease unemployment, began a public-works construction program, and the president on May 3 proposed legislation which would control monopolies and would serve as a basis for price and wage controls. The labour situation remained unsatisfactory during the first half of 1943, in view of low wages, a steady increase in living costs, and only slight improvement in regard to employment. Conditions improved, however, toward the latter part of the year. The drought was broken and agricultural prospects grew brighter; wool production proved to be excellent in both quality and quantity. The United States Board of Economic Warfare in July released the former ban on South American wools which had been in effect, and Uruguay was allowed to ship to the United States 60% of the amount of the 1941–42 export. The United States also began once more to import Uruguayan sheepskins. Great Britain in October signed a contract on behalf of the United Nations to take meats available for export in Uruguay for the year. The steadily increasing favourable foreign trade balance caused some concern over inflation in 1943, with some leaders favouring nationalization of foreign-owned utilities as a desirable measure to prevent it, and others wishing the surplus to be applied to repatriation of the sterling debt of £18,000,000. Rationing continued in force, especially on gasoline and kerosene, and price controls were applied on many items. The shortage of motor fuels seriously curtailed bus and truck transportation. The government also decreed reduction of railway speeds in order to conserve irreplaceable steel rails.

Uruguay was primarily concerned in 1944 with the maintenance of its democratic position and social gains and at the same time the pursuing of a careful international policy. Domestic and foreign affairs were further complicated by the location at Montevideo of the Committee for Political Defense, presided over by Vice-President Guani. The government late in Jan. 1944, following the recommendation of the Committee for Political Defense, refused recognition to the revolutionary regime set up in Bolivia in Dec. 1943, allegedly with pro-axis support from Argentina. On June 26, however, Uruguay, in conjunction with the other American republics, recognized both the Bolivian government and a new revolutionary regime in Ecuador.

Pres. Amézaga on Jan. 13, 1944, ordered the establishment of a national committee on Uruguayan economic, financial and social postwar problems; the committee members were named June 12. The government on Jan. 29 appointed a three-man committee to fix wage ceilings in Montevideo. Some other labour difficulties occurred during the year, most serious of which was a strike of 10,000 meat-packing house workers in April; they returned to work, after a five-day stoppage, on April 17, having gained some concessions including seasonal unemployment insurance. The government on Feb. 11 began negotiations with members of the United Nations to reduce meat exports in order to relieve the domestic shortage. The senate on May 11 passed a bill aimed at restoring the eight-hour day and raising wages.

Occasional echoes of earlier Uruguayan involvements with Germany and Italy were heard in 1944. Seven Germans, including the notorious Arnulf Fuhrman, were sentenced on Feb. 5 for having engineered the sensational plot revealed in May and June 1940; Fuhrman, the alleged South American director of anti-Semitic operations, had confessed to complicity in the plot but contended that it was a joke. Two Italians were arrested on Feb. 26 for espionage. The government on April 15 seized radio sending and receiving sets, arms and nazi literature in a raid on the home of an Argentine national in Montevideo. Relations with Spain were strained at times. The Batllista, or liberal, wing of the Colorado party on Feb. 15 urged a diplomatic break with the Franco regime, and a congressional group on Oct. 17 issued a statement opposing the incumbent Spanish government. The opposition Blanco Nacionalista party, under Herrera's leadership, resolved on March 7, 1944, to continue attacking the government on domestic policies, and on March 15 its members absented themselves from the congress, thus forcing an adjournment for lack of a quorum. The senate on March 9 resolved to interpellate the foreign minister on the government's attitude toward the Farrell-Perón regime in Argentina and its relations with the Committee for Political Defense; the minister later received a vote of confidence. The government on Sept. 28 released a comprehensive proposal for postwar international organization.

Political developments in 1945 continued to be influenced largely by Uruguay's delicate geographical balance between Brazil and Argentina. The militaristic regime in the latter country aroused considerable popular opposition in Uruguay, but the government felt impelled to move cautiously. The General Workers' Union (U.G.T.) held a 15-minute general strike Jan. 9 in protest against the Argentine regime. Foreign Minister Eduardo Rodríguez Larreta aroused great interest throughout the hemisphere by his proposal on Nov. 22, supposedly with Argentina in mind, that the principle of collective intervention be adopted for the Americas in case of "the notorious and repeated violation by any republic of the elementary rights of man and of the citizen." Several other foreign ministries gave qualified endorsement of the suggestion, most notably U.S. Secretary of State James F. Byrnes on Nov. 27; but the sentiment among Latin American chancelleries, traditionally opposed to all forms of domestic intervention, gradually crystallized in opposition to the proposal, and nothing ultimately came of it.

The Uruguayan congress on Feb. 21, 1945, approved a declaration of war against Germany and Japan; Juan Carlos Blanco, ambassador to the United States, signed the United Nations pact for his government on Feb. 24. The Uruguayan delegation at the inter-American conference in Mexico City in February–March took a leading part in urging a plan for a hemispheric pact of peace and mutual guarantees. A newly formed Latin Republican union urged at Montevideo on March 22 that democratic governments should be established in Italy, Spain, France and Portugal. A serious diplomatic crisis developed between Uruguay and Spain late in September. Widespread labour unrest, accompanied by strikes, prevailed in September, caused primarily by the high cost of living. As a means of long-range attack on unemployment and labour problems in general, the government announced a comprehensive five-year public-works program, contemplating large expenditures especially for highway construction and improvement. Deficit financing continued in 1945 for the sixth successive year and caused serious concern in business and financial circles. The government's anti-inflation program, led by the Bank of the Republic, involved the issuance of monetary defense bonds against deposits; the government also imposed an excess-profits tax but rejected an income tax.

Social unrest continued in Uruguay, especially in Montevideo, in the early months of 1946 because of the increasingly high cost of living. A one-day general strike in the capital on Feb. 28, protesting living costs, involved from 50,000 to 70,000 people. The government took steps in April to expropriate and nationalize the British-owned Montevideo waterworks. The most serious threat to order in the first half of the year was revealed by the government's announcement on July 1 that it had suppressed an antigovernment coup headed by a former head of the air force and apparently supported by the Asociación Pro-Renovación del Espíritu, a supposedly totalitarian lodge embracing army officers; about 30 arrests resulted. The officers gained some concessions, however; Pres. Amézaga managed to obtain a 30% pay increase for commissioned officers and also instituted an obligatory retirement system to make room for younger officers.

The second consecutive poor wheat harvest left an estimated deficit of that important cereal of 130,000 metric tons and by early in the year threatened the necessity of wheat rationing if additional stocks could not be obtained from Argentina. The Bank of the Republic subsequently contracted for purchase of 90,000 metric tons of wheat from Argentina, but that country refused to honour its commitment, allegedly because of prior obligations.

Uruguay: *Statistical Data*

Item	1938 Value (000's omitted)	1938 Amount or Number	1940 Value (000's omitted)	1940 Amount or Number	1943 Value (000's omitted)	1943 Amount or Number
Exchange Rate						
United States		1 peso = 64.37 cents U.S.*		1 peso = 65.83 cents U.S.*		1 peso = 65.83 cents U.S.*
Great Britain		7.6 gold pesos = £1		7.63 pesos = £1 (1941)		7.66 pesos = £1 (official special account rate)
Finance						
Government revenues	$50,703 (£10,371)		$60,959 (£15,916)		$49,240 (£12,203)	
Government expenditures	$50,589 (£10,348)		$60,037 (£15,675)		$63,732 (£15,795)	
Gold reserves	$58,679 (£12,002)		$68,000 (£17,755)		...	
National debt	$199,492 (£40,804)		$270,528 (£70,634)		$278,535 (£69,030)	
Transportation						
Railroads		1,800 mi.				
Highways		8,710 mi.				
Waterways (rivers)		700 mi.				
Airways		719 mi.				
Communication						
Telephones		44,068		46,656†		...
Telegraph lines		7,320 mi.		5,966 miles†		...
Radio sets		90,000		...		125,000
Minerals						
Gold		657 oz.				
Crops						
Wheat		497,137 tons		287,039 tons		330,690 tons‡
Corn		146,385 "		...		261,245 " ‡
Flaxseed		123,899 "		148,295 tons		79,366 " ‡
Oats		57,430 "		49,163 "		85,979 " ‡
Livestock						
Sheep		17,931,327§				
Cattle		8,296,890§				
Poultry		6,091,842§				
Exports—Total	$54,886 (£11,226)	...	$72,725 (£18,988)	...	$100,022 (£24,789)	...
Wool	$23,935 (£4,896)	59,000 tons	$35,739 (£9,331)	61,000 tons	$39,270 (£9,732)	62,000 tons
Meat and meat extracts	$12,482 (£2,553)	113,000 "	$16,034 (£4,186)	107,000 "	$24,407 (£6,049)	83,000 "
Hides	$6,386 (£1,306)	30,000 "	$6,605 (£1,725)	27,000 "	$10,407 (£2,579)	30,000 "
Grains and cereals	$4,349 (£890)	129,000 "	$333 (£87)	14,000 "	$1,968 (£488)	42,000 "
Imports—Total	$42,688 (£8,731)	...	$48,865 (£12,758)	...	$63,807 (£15,813)	...
Sugar (refined)	$2,943 (£602)	57,000 tons	$3,508 (£916)	...	$4,178 (£1,035)	51,000 tons
Textiles	$2,426 (£496)	3,000 "	$4,134 (£1,079)	...	$4,575 (£1,134)	2,000 "
Crude petroleum	$1,968 (£403)	152,000 "	$4,113 (£1,074)	275,469 tons	...	...
Coal	$1,902 (£389)	368,000 "	$2,988 (£780)	500,363 "	$5,392 (£1,336)	315,000 tons
Defense						
Standing army		8,832		8,093		
Personnel reserves		24,047		26,300		
Standing navy personnel		938		938		
Standing air force personnel		318		463		
Military expenditures	$5,415(£1,108)		...			
Education						
Primary schools		1,648		1,768‖		
Students		209,651		220,833‖		
Intermediate schools		...		98‖		
Students		...		27,000‖		
Universities		1		1‖		
Students		10,000		2,670‖		

*Value of controlled currency. †1941. ‡1944. §1937. ‖1942.

BIBLIOGRAPHY.—*The Inter-American* (monthly); Pan American Union, *Bulletin* (monthly); *Foreign Commerce Weekly; The South American Handbook* (annual); S. G. Hanson, *Utopia in Uruguay* (1938). (R. H. FN.)

USHA (United States Housing Authority)

See FEDERAL WORKS AGENCY; HOUSING; MUNICIPAL GOVERNMENT.

U.S.O.

See UNITED SERVICE ORGANIZATIONS.

U.S.S.R.

See UNION OF SOVIET SOCIALIST REPUBLICS.

Utah

A Rocky mountain state, Utah was admitted to the union in 1896, popularly known as the "Beehive state." Area 84,916 sq.mi., including 2,570 sq.mi. of water. Population (1940) 550,310; the rural (nonfarm) population was 150,465, (farm) 94,352; urban 305,493, with the following origins: white (native) 510,662, (foreign-born) 32,298; Negro (native) 1,225, (foreign-born) 10. Estimated population of the state on Dec. 1, 1945, 620,000. Capital, Salt Lake City (149,934). Other principal cities: Ogden (43,688), Provo (18,071), Logan (11,868).

The 21st legislature which met in 1937 was characterized by its progressive character. The progressives, led by Dr. Herbert Maw, president of the senate, enacted their program, but the conservative minority, led by Governor Henry H. Blood, controlled patronage. Notable measures enacted were a direct primary law, which provided for run-off primaries and an increase in the number of districts in counties having more than one representative in the legislature; a social security act passed in conformity with federal legislation; a "little Wagner act," which provided for recognition by employers of employee-established bargaining agencies and set up agencies with power to subpoena witnesses and hear disputes; and a fair trade practices act to curb monopoly and prevent discrimination against buyers. Governor Blood vetoed a measure exempting from taxation homesteads up to $2,000 and personal property up to $300. The legislature was criticized for enacting a budget of $7,651,328, the largest in the state's history and more than $1,300,000 above the governor's figure, which was based on a revenue expectancy of about $6,000,000. In 1937, E. E. Monson was secretary of state; John W. Guy, auditor; Reese M. Reese, treasurer; Joseph Chez, attorney-general; and Charles H. Skidmore, superintendent of public instruction.

The elections of Nov. 8, 1938, the first under the new direct primary law, left Democrats still entrenched, controlling approximately two-thirds of the elective county positions, and considerably more patronage than this figure would indicate. New Deal Senator Elbert D. Thomas, chief target of the campaign, was returned for a second term, and Representatives Abe Murdock and J. W. Robinson were re-elected from the first and second congressional districts respectively. William H. Folland, incumbent Republican supreme court justice, was defeated by Judge Roger I. McDonough, Democrat. With 21 Democrats and 2 Republicans in the senate, and 45 Democrats and 15 Republicans in the house, the 23rd legislature followed a more conservative course than its predecessor. Gov. Henry H. Blood counselled economies, warning that the surplus in the general fund could no longer be expected to absorb excessive appropriations.

Efforts in 1939 to prohibit married women from receiving public employment resulted only in the adoption

Utah: *Statistical Data*

Table I.—*Education (Public)*

	1938	1940	1942	1943	1944
Elementary school pupils	96,850	78,394	148,632	143,448	122,414
High school pupils	42,057	59,040			
Elementary teachers	2,519	4,608	4,110	4,102	4,168
High school teachers	1,910				

Table II.—*Public Welfare*
(Money figures in thousands of dollars)

	1937	1938	1939	1940	1941
Cases on general relief	4,496	3,535	5,020	5,418	4,855
Cost of general relief	$100	$70	$102	$110	$131
Recipients of old-age pensions		13,368		13,639	14,284
Dependent children receiving aid		7,307		8,389	10,483
Blind receiving aid		200		202	183
Workers under unemployment compensation		75,381	69,342	79,800	

Table III.—*Communications*
(Money figures in thousands of dollars)

	1938	1939	1941	1942	1943	1944
Highway mileage	5,109	5,164	5,106	5,106	5,450	5,438
Expenditure on highways	$6,967	$11,332	$4,230	$6,051	$7,739	$6,617
Railroad mileage	2,157	2,086		2,157	2,005	2,214

Table IV.—*Banking and Finance*
(Money figures in thousands of dollars)

	1937	1938	1939	1942	1944	1945
State revenue	$24,385	$27,300	$28,237	$40,401		$50,265
State expenditure	$21,216	$20,911	$22,097	$37,383		$47,415
Number of banks	59	59	59	60	57	57
Total bank deposits	$144,600	$139,700	$149,100	$212,112	$384,379	$465,376
Number of national banks	13	13	13	13	12	12

Table V.—*Agriculture*
(All figures in thousands)

	1937	1939	1940	1942	1943	1944
Income from crops and livestock	$46,200	$43,996	$45,379	$83,134	$104,904	$110,370
Leading crops (bu.):						
Barley	2,379	2,516	2,812			
Celery (crates)	115	90	90	132	183	204
Hay (tons)	1,171	968	1,062	1,174	1,158	1,234
Onions (cwt.)	342	276	220	264	300	1,056
Peas (tons)	18	12	14	20	26	24
Potatoes	2,128	2,016	2,040	2,312	3,430	2,765
Sugar beets (short tons)	570	683	504	570	478	396
Tomatoes	80	55	32	35	130	66
Wheat	5,459	3,989	4,861			

Table VI.—*Manufacturing*
(Money figures in thousands of dollars)

	1937	1939	1941	1942	1943	1944
Wage earners	13,094	11,555	20,300	30,700	28,739	24,376
Wages paid	$14,479	$11,968	$27,543	$50,939	$66,960	$51,346
Value of manufactures	$204,857	$167,172				

Table VII.—*Mineral Production*
(All figures in thousands of dollars)

	1937	1938	1939	1940	1941	1944
Value of mineral production	$105,652	$59,236	$80,222			$111,036
Leading products (value):						
Copper	$49,851	$21,193	$35,753	$52,401	$61,443	
Gold	11,297	7,022	9,721	12,442	12,172	
Silver	9,954	6,260	7,303	8,656	7,967	
Lead	10,556	6,040	6,358	7,569	7,777	
Zinc	6,240	3,231	3,591	5,517	6,024	
Coal	8,648	6,875	7,114			

of a resolution urging state agencies to spread work as much as possible. Other laws provided for a fair trade practices act for agriculture by which farmers hoped to stabilize farm products prices, the relief of business from the average monthly inventory tax by substituting a year-end inventory tax, the control of small-loan agencies by the state banking department, and extension of the eight-hour day for women to all occupations.

In the 1940 presidential election, Roosevelt received 154,277 votes; Willkie 93,151; Thomas 198 and Browder 191. The veteran U.S. Senator William H. King, conservative Democrat, failed to receive renomination and his seat went to Representative Abe Murdock. Walter K. Granger was sent to congress from the 1st district, and Representative J. W. Robinson was returned by the 2nd district. Herbert B. Maw, liberal Democrat, attorney, educator and former president of the state senate, was elected governor by a plurality of 10,806 votes over Don B. Colton (Rep.). The new governor was prepared to offer the overwhelmingly Democratic legislature a progressive program including sweeping reforms in state government with a view toward efficiency and economy, and development of the state's natural resources. Composition of the legislature in 1940: senate, Democrats, 19; Republicans, 4; house, Democrats, 44; Republicans, 16.

In 1940 E. E. Monson was secretary of state; Reese M. Reese, auditor; Oliver G. Ellis, treasurer; Grover A. Giles, attorney-general; and Charles H. Skidmore, superintendent of public instruction.

In 1941, the 24th legislature adopted the sweeping governmental reorganization scheme recommended by Governor Maw, in the regular and two special sessions, It created departments of finance and publicity and industrial development and effected greater executive control over finance.

Greater co-ordination of boards and commissions was also effected.

After U.S. entry into World War II, the administration of Governor Maw co-operated with federal authorities in essential war measures and continued to perfect the governmental reorganization plan adopted by the 24th legislature in 1941.

Japanese resettlement centres were established at Topaz and Abraham.

In the 1944 presidential election, 150,088 votes were cast for President Roosevelt and 97,891 for Governor Dewey. Governor Maw was especially active in the rehabilitation of returning war veterans and the retention of permanent phases of war industrial expansion. In 1945, Ferrell H. Adams succeeded Reese M. Reese as state auditor and Dr. E. Allen Bateman succeeded Charles H. Skidmore as superintendent of public instruction; Reese M. Reese became state treasurer. E. E. Monson continued as secretary of state and Grover A. Giles as attorney-general in 1945 and 1946.

In 1946, the administration of Governor Maw co-operated with federal authorities in essential postwar measures and in all vital reconversion programs, particularly the return of Utah's gigantic Geneva Steel plant to private industry, and preliminary work on the great reclamation project of central Utah, known as the Central Utah project.

The state continued to aid business and industrial interests in the expansion of manufacturing, mining, metallurgical and transportation industries and in encouraging eastern and Pacific coast industrialists and manufacturers to establish branch factories in Utah.

(F. W. GA.; J. C. AR.; X.)

BIBLIOGRAPHY.—Council of State Govts., *Book of the States* (bienn.); Federal Writers' Program, *Utah: Guide to the State* (1941); Dept. of Public Instruction, *Utah: Resources and Activities* (1933); Secy. of State, *Utah Official Roster* (bienn.); W. E. Stegner, *Mormon Country* (1942). Periodical: *Monthly Checklist of State Publications.*

←

Copper mining installations in the Carr Fort canyon, Utah, the state which ranked first in U.S. copper production during 1937–46

Utilities, Public

See PUBLIC UTILITIES.

Uzbek S.S.R.

See UNION OF SOVIET SOCIALIST REPUBLICS.

Vaccination

See MEDICINE; MILITARY MEDICINE.

Van Acker, Achille H.

Van Acker (1898–), Belgian statesman, became a Socialist member of the chamber of deputies in 1927. Minister of labour in the Pierlot government, he formed a coalition government on Feb. 11, 1945, after Pierlot's resignation, and assumed personal charge of the production and distribution of coal. He presented the resignation of his cabinet (June 16, 1945) in protest against King Leopold's proposed return to the throne. After the chamber of deputies voted to continue the regency, Van Acker formed a new government.

After the elections of Feb. 17, 1946, Van Acker resigned; failure of other candidates to form a government acceptable to parliament led to his recall and on March 31 he formed a new cabinet without Catholic representation. His cabinet fell again on July 9 after losing a vote of confidence in the senate by one vote; he refused to form another cabinet and was succeeded by Camille Huysmann as premier.

Vanadium

Aside from small irregular amounts from Mexico and Argentina, the world output of vanadium continued to come from the four countries listed in the following table:

World Production of Vanadium
(Short tons of metal content)

	1937	1939	1941	1943	1945
Northern Rhodesia	259	423	377	533	232
Peru	643	1,097	1,121	943	684
South-West Africa	652	567	297	636	463
United States	544	992	1,257	2,793	1,482
Total	2,150	3,190	3,100	4,950	2,870

In general the United States consumed its domestic output and that of Peru (more than two-thirds of the total), while Rhodesia and South-West Africa supplied the rest of the world.

The trend of the industry in the United States is indicated by the following data, in short tons of vanadium content:

	1937	1939	1941	1943	1945
Mine shipments	543	992	1,257	2,793	1,482
Imports	629	1,066	1,069	1,058	789
Peru	629	1,066	1,068	1,026	776
Consumption	?	?	?	3,631	2,547

Vanadium supply was worked on a narrow margin throughout World War II. Consumption accounted for during 1942–45 actually added to somewhat more than production plus imports. The Metals Reserve company was able to accumulate a small emergency stock pile, which reached a peak of about 670 tons of contained metal; but this was sold out in 1945.

Consumption of vanadium continued to be practically entirely in the compounding of alloy steels. With the cessation of war uses, demand naturally declined sharply but could be expected to approximate the prewar level of demand, with some additions to cover civilian uses that were cut short by war demands, and for the extension of war applications to new peacetime uses. (G. A. Ro.)

Vandegrift, Alexander Archer

Vandegrift (1887–), U.S. marine corps officer, was born March 13, 1887, in Charlottesville, Va. He studied at the University of Virginia for two years and later was graduated from the basic school and the field officers' school of the marine corps. He entered the marine corps as a second lieutenant in 1909, participated in the landing in Nicaragua in 1912 and at Veracruz, Mexico, in 1914. In World War I he was stationed in Haiti and in the 1920s he held assignments in China. Advancing through the grades, he was promoted to brigadier general in 1940 and the following year he became assistant commandant of the marine corps.

In 1942 Vandegrift, a major general, commanded U.S. marine forces that landed in the Solomon Islands. For his achievements on Guadalcanal, he earned the congressional medal of honour and a promotion to lieutenant general. On Nov. 1, 1943, he led the marines again in their first landing on Bougainville. Shortly thereafter, he was recalled to Washington, D.C., to succeed (Jan. 1, 1944) Lt. Gen. Thomas Holcomb, retired, as commandant of the marine corps. He was raised to the rank of a full general March 29, 1945. On March 28, 1946, Vandegrift was appointed to President Truman's newly established ten-man military committee to plan national defense. His status as a four-star general was made permanent on April 2, 1946.

Vandenberg, Arthur Hendrick

Vandenberg (1884–), U.S. statesman, was born March 22, 1884, in Grand Rapids, Mich. He studied at the University of Michigan law school, but lack of funds forced him to leave school after the end of his first year. He joined the *Grand Rapids Herald* as a reporter, becoming editor and general manager of the paper by the time he was 22. Later he became active in Michigan state politics. In 1928 he was appointed to fill the senate vacancy caused by the death of Sen. Woodbridge Ferris and in November of that year he was elected to serve the remainder of the term as well as the following term. He was re-elected in 1934, 1940 and 1946.

Prior to U.S. entry into World War II, Vandenberg was one of the noninterventionist leaders in congress and had attacked the lend-lease bill and aid to Britain. After the attack on Pearl Harbor, however, he upheld the Rooseveltian line on foreign policy, and in 1944 he was instrumental in getting the Republican party to favour employment of force to maintain peace. The following year Roosevelt appointed Vandenberg as a delegate to the United Nations conference in San Francisco.

Secy. of State James Byrnes relied heavily on Vandenberg for advice during the sessions of the Council of Foreign Ministers in London in the late fall of 1945 and at the U.N. sessions in London (Jan.–Feb. 1946). On his return from the London sessions of the U.N., Vandenberg told the senate that the U.S. and the soviet union could live together in "reasonable harmony if the United States speaks as plainly on all occasions as Russia does."

After the Republican triumph in the elections of Nov. 1946, Vandenberg was regarded as one of the outstanding G.O.P. candidates for the presidential nomination in 1948.

Van Devanter, Willis

Van Devanter (1859–1941), U.S. jurist, was born April 17, 1859, at Marion, Ind. He graduated from the Cincinnati law school in 1881, and later practised law with his father in Marion. In 1884 he left for Wyoming, where he supervised revision of the state's statutes, became city attorney of Cheyenne, a member of the territorial legislature, and later chairman of its judiciary committee. In 1889 he became chief justice of the Wyoming supreme court, but resigned the next year to resume private practice. Active campaigning for McKinley brought him appointment as U.S. assistant attorney-general in 1897. In 1903 Theodore Roosevelt appointed him judge of the eighth circuit court of appeals. He was named to the supreme court by President Taft in 1910. Van Devanter was not a prolific writer of opinions. A conservative, he dissented frequently in decisions regarding New Deal legislation, and he resigned in 1937. Van Devanter was dean of the supreme court after the resignation of Justice Oliver Wendell Holmes in 1932. After his retirement he occasionally sat in the New York federal court. He died in Washington, D.C., Feb. 8, 1941.

Van Mook, Hubertus Johannes

Van Mook (1894–), Netherlands statesman and colonial official, was born in Semarang, Java, and was educated at Surabaya college in the East Indies and at Amsterdam, Leyden and Delft universities in the Netherlands. He joined the Netherlands Indies civil service in 1918 and held a number of colonial posts in Indonesia. A member of the People's council from 1931 to 1934, he was chief of the bureau of economic affairs, 1934–37, and director of economic affairs, 1937–42.

Van Mook headed the Netherlands delegation that handled negotiations with the Japanese in 1940 and 1941. The Japanese delegates, strengthened by Vichy's cession of bases in French Indo-China, attempted to frighten the Netherlands mission into yielding to their demands for economic concessions. But Van Mook refused to agree to any moves that would imperil the economic and territorial sovereignty of the Indies and the negotiations ended in a stalemate.

After the Japanese attack in Dec. 1941 against U.S., British and Dutch possessions in the Pacific, the Netherlands government-in-exile in London appointed Van Mook lieutenant governor of the Indies in Jan. 1942 and later as minister of colonies. He resigned from the latter post in Feb. 1945.

On his return to the East Indies following the close of World War II, Van Mook was the principal Netherlands delegate in negotiations with members of the Indonesian "republic."

Van Zeeland, Paul

Van Zeeland (1893–), Belgian statesman and economist, was born at Soignies in 1893. Educated at the University of Louvain and at Princeton university, N.J., he entered the Belgian national bank in 1922, becoming a director in the institution in 1926. He also joined the faculty of law at Louvain as a professor in 1928 and founded the Louvain Institute of Economic Sciences.

Van Zeeland represented Belgium at various international conferences between 1922 and 1933. On March 25, 1935, he became prime minister of a coalition cabinet in which he also held the portfolios of foreign affairs and foreign commerce. This government resigned in May 1936, and Van Zeeland formed a new one on June 14 of that year. At the request of Britain and France, he undertook an exploratory economic mission to investigate ways and means of overcoming obstacles hindering world trade and visited the U.S. in June 1937 to confer with President Roosevelt. After his return, he faced political opposition in the parliament; unable to get a vote of confidence, he resigned Oct. 25, 1937.

After the German occupation of Belgium in 1940, Van Zeeland associated himself with the Belgian government-in-exile in London and was named chairman of the Belgian commission on war problems. Following the close of World War II, Van Zeeland made several trips to the U.S., presumably for discussion of economic and political problems. On April 20, 1946, the Egyptian government announced that he had accepted its offer to become a consultant and adviser on financial problems.

Vargas, Getulio Dornelles

Vargas (1882–), Brazilian politician, was born at São Borja, Brazil, on Apr. 19, 1882. He entered the army at the age of 16 and studied for a year at the Rio Parde military college. In 1903, he left the army to study law at the University of Porto Alegre, obtaining his degree in 1907. In 1923, he was elected federal deputy for the state of Rio Grande do Sul.

Rising rapidly in the Brazilian political arena, he was minister of finance in 1925 and governor of Rio Grande do Sul in 1927. He became president of Brazil in 1930 by virtue of a *coup d'état* that he himself inspired and led. Proceeding to strengthen his power, Vargas put down a revolt in 1932 and introduced a strongly nationalistic constitution in 1934. He repudiated the terms of that charter (which prohibited a president from succeeding himself) by establishing himself as dictator in 1937 and calling off scheduled elections. He dissolved the houses of parliament, and drafted a new constitution which perpetuated his dictatorship, although it provided for a plebiscite at some "future date."

Vargas' rule was modelled on near-absolutist lines. In foreign policy, however, he supported the United Nations and declared Brazil at war with the axis nations in 1942.

Toward the end of World War II, he set the date for the long-delayed presidential elections for Dec. 2, 1945. He resigned on Oct. 29, 1945, leaving José Linhares, chief justice of the supreme court, as interim president until after the voting.

Vargas was elected senator of the state of Rio Grande do Sul and was sworn into office June 4, 1946.

Vargas Diamond

See Mineralogy.

Varnishes

See Paints and Varnishes.

Vasconcellos Mottas, Carlo Carmelo de

Cardinal Vasconcellos (1890–), Brazilian prelate, was born July 16, 1890, in the state of Minas Gerais. He was ordained priest in 1918 and was appointed auxiliary bishop of Diamantina in 1932. Four years later he was elevated to archbishop in the metropolitan see of São Luiz de Maranhão. After the death of Archbishop Affonseca e Silva, he was transferred by the Holy see to the metropolitan see of São Paulo, second largest in South America, and was installed in his new post in Oct. 1944. Named to the Sacred College of Cardinals Dec. 23, 1945, he was created cardinal on Feb. 18, 1946.

Vasilevsky, Alexander Mikhailovich

Vasilevsky (1905–), soviet army officer, was a tsarist soldier during World War I and joined the Communists during the revolution of 1917. After the war he studied at soviet general staff schools and assisted in the reorganization of soviet armies following the Russo-Finnish war of 1939–40. Attached to the soviet high command in 1941, Vasilevsky served under Marshal Georgi Zhukov. He held the rank of major general in 1941, rising to the highest grade, marshal of the soviet union, in 18 months. In Nov. 1942 he was named deputy chief of staff, and became chief of staff upon the retirement of Marshal Boris Shaposhnikov. Vasilevsky's appointment to this high post was regarded as part of Stalin's plan to revitalize his general staff with younger men.

Vasilevsky retired from his post as chief of staff in 1944 to assume command of one of the soviet armies that reconquered the Crimea and Sevastopol. In early 1945 he assumed command of the 3rd White Russian army and led the drive that culminated in the capture of Königsberg, April 9, 1945.

Following the defeat of Germany in Europe, Vasilevsky was shifted to the far eastern front, where he was commander in chief of soviet forces that invaded Manchuria in Aug. 1945. In the merger of the soviet armed forces, decreed by the soviet council of ministers, March 22, 1946, Vasilevsky was elevated to the post of chief of staff of the newly-unified services.

Vatican City State

A tiny area of 108.7 ac. situated in the heart of Rome and completely surrounded by Italian territory, the Vatican City state is the official seat of the Roman Catholic Church and the official residence of the pope and the College of Cardinals. The city state, whose extraterritorial rights were restored by the Lateran treaty of 1929, enjoys the full rights of a sovereign state. Recognized in international law, the Lateran accord legalized the status of the reigning pope as temporal ruler over this area.

Physically, Vatican City consists of the papal palace, the Vatican library, museums and gardens, St. Peter's basilica and the immediately adjacent area (including the spacious Piazza di San Pietro). Castel Gandolfo, the papal summer estate, and certain basilicas in Rome enjoy extraterritorial privileges, although they are beyond the physical confines of the city state.

Vatican City is administered by a civil governor appointed by the pope. The governor, who rules with executive powers, deals with purely secular matters. The law of the Vatican area derives basically from canon law and ecclesiastical procedures rather than from Italy's civil code.

Vatican City's independence is reflected in a variety of ways; it has its own railroad depot, radio station and postal service. It mints its own coins (although Italian currency is accepted as legal tender within its confines), issues its own stamps and publishes its own newspaper, *Osservatore Romano.*

Its "defense forces" consist of Swiss guards and papal gandarmes. During World War II, this force, normally comprising about 100 guards and 70 gendarmes, was substantially increased. The small Vatican "army," however, does not police the Piazza di San Pietro. While the large square is recognized as part of the Vatican City under the Lateran treaty, it is subject to the authority of the Italian police.

The population of Vatican City in 1932 was 1,025. Ten years later (1942), the population was estimated at about 800. The latter figure did not include the Vatican diplomatic colony consisting of representatives whose countries broke off relations or were at war with Italy. All of the regular inhabitants of the city state are Italian-speaking Roman Catholics, mostly of Italian or Swiss descent. (X.)

Momentous Decade.—The decennium 1937–46 in the history of the Vatican City spanned a momentous period of world history. At its opening totalitarian dictatorships were in power in Italy, Germany, the U.S.S.R. and Spain. In other countries of Europe these dictatorships were not without many sympathizers and supporters. After the signing of the Treaty of Versailles, grave problems remained in the international society. Conferences and agreements among the nations failed to establish confidence and real peace. The period evidenced a wide loss of faith in democracy to meet the problems of the times in many parts of Europe. Underneath all the confusion was a departure in political philosophy from the traditions of western civilization. Conventions were substituted for moral principles. The dignity and rights of the individual were made at most mere concessions of the absolutistic state in some countries. Nationalisms were exaggerated and it came about that, when sacrifices for the common good were needed, stress was placed on real or fictitious national grievances. Communism, fascism and naziism were new aggressive systems based on state absolutism.

The papacy stood an uncompromising foe of these political absolutisms. Efforts were made to bring about freedom of religion even in these difficult conditions, and they failed. It may be said that the major struggle of the papacy in this decennium was with totalitarianisms. It was not the papacy entering into the political field; through modern history the popes had abstained from sanctioning any particular political form. The plain fact which faced the church was that these systems were a mighty aggression against Christian truth. It was the religious errors in them which had brought forth the condemnations of Pope Pius XI (*q.v.*). If he made every possible effort to secure religious freedom in the countries in which they had seized power, it must be kept in mind that at the very appearance of fascism in Italy, the absolutism in it was condemned by the pope.

There were some who without studying the facts accused the papacy of friendliness to fascism and naziism. Nothing could be more untrue when the facts are examined. There is a difference between trying to mitigate an evil and approving and embracing it. All efforts of the pope to secure fundamental freedoms proved unavailing. In fascist Italy there went on constantly a fascist attack on the rights of religious organizations and religious activities. Pope Pius XI never lost an opportunity to assert these rights and to point out the errors in fascist policy. After Mussolini's full acceptance of nazi racism, the pope clearly spoke out for the rights of minorities and in the plainest language condemned anti-Semitism. In Germany it became plain that naziism was an attack on Christianity. There was persecution of the church and a brutal attempt to censor even the preaching of Christian truth. The concordat with the nazi government was scarcely signed when Hitler violated it. There could be no ideological truce between the papacy and these political totalitarianisms.

On Passion Sunday, March 14, 1937, Pope Pius XI issued his encyclical letter, "Mit Brenender Sorge," written in German, condemning naziism and protesting its violation of religious freedoms. This letter made clear the mind of the papacy. The pope told its purpose: "As you kindly visited Us as we lay on our bed of sickness, so today we turn to you and through you (that is, the Bishops of Germany) to the Catholic faithful of Germany, who, like all suffering and oppressed children, are particularly close to the heart of the Common Father. In this hour when their faith is being tried like pure gold in the fire of tribulation and concealed and open persecution, when they are surrounded by a thousand forms of organized bondage in matters of religion, when the lack of true information and absence of the customary means of defense weighs heavily on them, they have a double right to the words of truth and spiritual comfort from him, to whose first predecessor the significant words of the Saviour were spoken: 'But I have prayed for thee that thy faith fail not; and thou, being once converted, confirm thy brethren.'" In this letter the pope pointed out what was well known to the Catholics of Germany, that their political leaders were trying to destroy the church in Germany. It must be kept in mind that this letter was written at a time when the leaders in many nations still thought that there could be effective compromises with Hitler.

Five days after issuing the encyclical letter, "Mit Brenender Sorge," Pope Pius XI, on March 19, 1937, issued his encyclical letter, "Divini Redemptoris," on atheistic communism. In it he called "bolshevistic and atheistic communism" an imminent danger "which aims at upsetting the social order and at undermining the very foundations of Christian civilization." After condemning the religious errors of atheistic communism, the pope, in an appeal for a great Christian social renaissance, for which he had worked so ardently, said: "It was Christianity that first affirmed the real and universal brotherhood of man of whatever race and condition. This doctrine she proclaimed by a method and with an amplitude unknown to preceding centuries; and with it she potently contributed to the abolition of slavery. Not bloody revolution, but the inner force of her teaching made the proud Roman matron see in her slave a sister in Christ. It is Christianity that adores the Son of God, made man for love of man, and become not only the 'Son of a Carpenter' but Himself a 'Carpenter.' It was Christianity that raised manual labour to its true dignity, whereas it had been hitherto so despised that even the moderate Cicero did not hesitate to sum up the general opinion of his time in words of which any modern sociologist would be ashamed: 'All artisans are engaged in sordid trades, for there can be nothing ennobling in a workshop.'"

On March 28, 1937, the pope issued his encyclical on the persecution of the church in Mexico. It was a plea to the Catholics of Mexico to strengthen in themselves deep Christian life. In it he stressed the principles underlying the Christian social program and concluded with "an appeal to unity, charity and peace, in the apostolic labour of Catholic Action, which must give Christ back to Mexico and restore there peace and also temporal prosperity."

The story of the last years of the pontificate of Pope Pius XI is a continuation of his efforts to defend and vindicate the dignity and rights of man and to stress the Christian ideal of brotherhood in social and political life. With a sad heart he saw the darkening of the clouds on

Pope Pius XII during an informal interview with Allied press correspondents and servicemen at the Vatican, two days after the liberation of Rome in June 1944

the horizon of the world, and he knew that danger was at hand. A few days before he died he sent out orders for the bishops of Italy to come to Rome and hear from him an important message The message was never delivered. Death came to him. The message remained in the archives of the Vatican, and some day historians would know the last of the works of a great, courageous pope to protect and defend the freedoms of man and proclaim the Gospel of Christ as the only safe charter for world reconstruction.

In the midst of his gigantic struggle against the new materialistic ideologies, Pope Pius XI merited the title of "The Pope of the Missions." The Mission exhibitions in the Vatican focused the attention of Catholics everywhere on the missions. His reorganization of the Pontifical Mission Aid societies brought larger resources for their support and extension. He knew intimately every mission field. In his mission program he stressed the need of native clergies, promoted natives to the episcopacy and did much to penetrate with Christian truth native cultures. His mission work brought admirable results and, while he saw cruel persecution of the church in many parts of the western world, he had the consolation of seeing the church grow and prosper in many mission fields.

Accession of Pope Pius XII.—The conclave which elected the successor of Pope Pius XI was short. There came from it Pope Pius XII (*q.v.*), who had been the secretary of state. His talents, experience, traits and virtues made him admirably fitted for the papal office in one of the most critical periods of its long history. The popes of modern times have given the program of their pontificates in their first encyclical letters. Pope Pius XII significantly began his first encyclical with the words: "Darkness over the earth." The clouds of war were gathering fast; the aggressive spirit of naziism was no secret. It respected no rights and proclaimed as its end nothing less than world domination. In his program the pope pointed out the basic errors which gave rise to totalitarianism and refuted them with masterly argument. He left no doubt as to his program. It would be to try to make men see that Christian truth alone could be the safe foundation for individual and social prosperity. In this letter he wrote: "Even as we write these lines the terrible news comes to us that, in spite of all the prayers we have offered to avert them, the fires of war have been lit. The pen might well drop from Our hand, when we reflect on the countless calamities which are overtaking those who till now, in their private lives, enjoyed some measure of prosperity. Our heart sickens, as a father's heart must, at the prospect of the harvest which will grow from the dark seeds of violence and animosity, for which war is now tracing furrows in blood. And yet, as We think of the bitter troubles that are now brewing, and shudder at the worse troubles to come, We feel it Our duty all the more to direct men's hearts and minds, where good will is still to be found among them, towards Him who alone can bring salvation to mankind."

The peace efforts of the pope failed. The invasion of Poland was a blow to him, and in it he saw all the cruel fury of the nazis' total war. Then there came the overrunning of the Netherlands and the fall of France. Mussolini joined with Hitler. Two great things the pope could do; he could do his utmost in charity for the innocent victims of aggression; and he could point out the way to a lasting peace. His relief work is so well known that it needs no mention. It is enough to say that he sought in every possible way to defend and succour the suffering victims. Cut off from communication with the bishops in many countries, with fascists and nazis in the eternal city, he worked and laboured for a just and lasting peace.

On Christmas Eve, 1939, the pope gave to the world his Five Point Peace plan, a comprehensive statement of the essentials of a good lasting peace in the international family. Year after year through World War II he enlarged and detailed this plan. Briefly the plan called for the assurance to all nations, great or small, powerful or weak, of their right to life and independence; mutually agreed, organic and progressive disarmament; the erection of a juridical institution to guarantee the loyal and faithful fulfilment of conditions agreed upon and, in case of necessity, to revise and correct them; satisfaction of the real needs and just demands of nations and populations and of racial minorities; recognition of moral values in international life. If we assemble all the peace statements of the pope, we find in them a true pattern for lasting international peace and a sound world reconstruction. As the war progressed, it became clear that the pope would admit no fatal compromises and that he recognized clearly the grave difficulties which would confront the peacemakers. It may be said that his efforts for peace were indeed a wonderful contribution to clear thinking during years when the minds of many leaders were confused.

It is remarkable that Pope Pius XII during these busy

years of his pontificate found the time to do monumental things in the life of the church. He approved a new latin translation of the Psalms and introduced it in the use of the church. His encyclical letter on the mystical body is a document which will be read and quoted through centuries. He continued the work of his predecessor for the missions. He did much in perfecting the government of the Vatican City, which quite naturally during these troubled times became a refuge for many innocent victims of unjust persecution.

A notable encyclical issued by him Nov. 1, 1939, was a letter to the hierarchy of the United States on the occasion of the 150th anniversary of its establishment. As cardinal secretary of state, he had visited the United States and travelled by aeroplane from coast to coast. His impressions on that visit gave him the highest esteem for the country and an intelligent grasp of the problems which confronted U.S. church authorities. In referring to the social question, he expressed the hope that the U.S. people "with its genius for splendid and unselfish action" would settle this question "with due regard for the public welfare and the dignity of man." It is interesting to quote his demand that "the good things of life which the Creator has created for the benefit of all men should find their way to all alike in a just proportion." In the same letter he stressed what in one of his peace statements he again repeated, that the sanctity and freedom of the family is at the base of all right social life.

Summing up the history of the Vatican City in this decennium, we may point out the unceasing, brave defense by the popes of the dignity and rights of man, the warning to the world that justice and charity must inspire social life and its activities, the uncompromising condemnation of the excesses and unreasonable demands of the totalitarians, the call for a true Christian social renaissance, the courageous stand for justice and truth in the midst of dangers and threats, the constant pastoral solicitude for all souls, and the proclamation to the whole world that in Christian civilization alone is there the hope of lasting peace and a right ordering of the lives of nations. (*See* also ROMAN CATHOLIC CHURCH.)

BIBLIOGRAPHY.—*Acta Apostolica Sedis* 1936–46; *Sixteen Encyclicals of His Holiness Pope Pius XI*, 1926–37 (N.C.W.C.); Rankin, *The Pope Speaks; Principles for Peace;* Gonella, *A World to Reconstruct.* (SA. S.)

Vatutin, Nikolai Fedorovich

Vatutin (1901–44), soviet army officer, was born Dec. 16, 1901, in the Valuiki district of the Kursk region. In April 1920 he was drafted into the Red army as a private. Virtually unknown outside of the U.S.S.R. during the early phase of World War II, Vatutin achieved fame after Stalin reshuffled his general staff and moved him and others of the "younger generals" up to command posts.

As commander of the North Don army, he engineered the break-through of German defenses northwest of Stalingrad, Nov. 19, 1942, and the offensive launched in Feb. 1943 that carried his army to the approaches of the Dnieper river.

During the summer of 1943, Gen. Vatutin's forces beat back the last major German offensive in the Orel-Belgorod sector. His 1st Ukrainian army then counterattacked and crossed into Poland by Jan. 1944. Vatutin, in failing health, relinquished his command in March 1944 to Marshal Georgi Zhukov. He died in Kiev following an operation, on April 14, 1944.

Veal

See MEAT.

V-E Day

See WAR PRODUCTION; WORLD WAR II.

Vegetable Oils and Animal Fats

The vital importance of oils and fats, and the wide disruption of world production and trade in these materials was one of the most striking changes of the decade 1937–46. The plentiful supplies of the prewar period were inadequate to meet the increased demand of the war period for food and industrial uses. World War II disrupted the normal flow of trade and cut off the United Nations from 40% of the world's export supplies of vegetable oils and a considerable part of animal fats.

The war needs were met by widespread changes and expansion of vegetable oil crops in the United States and some other areas accessible to the Allies. Before the war, most of the international trade in oils and fats consisted of vegetable oils and marine oils. Animal fats were mainly consumed in the countries which produced them.

United States fats and oils production in 1937 was about 7,000,000,000 lb. and increased slowly to 8,780,000,000 lb. in 1940. Imports in 1937 were 2,695,000,000 lb., which declined to 1,897,000,000 lb. in 1941, then dropped to about half this amount annually through the war period. Imports from the far east were cut off by the Japanese invasions, by the shortage of shipping and by submarine warfare. Whale-oil production practically ceased. The United States imports had consisted primarily of copra from the Philippines, palm oil from the Netherlands Indies, flaxseed from Argentina and tung oil from China. The United States became a net exporter in 1943 and 1944.

Total consumption of primary fats and oils for all uses was estimated at 9,203,000,000 lb. in 1937, then declined slightly to 9,035,000,000 lb. in 1938 and increased again in 1941 to 10,924,000,000 lb., which level was well maintained through 1944. The part of this supply used for food products was at its peak in 1941 at 6,883,000,000 lb., then declined to the end of the war. Industrial uses took an increasing part of the total, nearly 4,000,000,000 lb. in 1941 and 3,682,000,000 lb. in 1945. Measured by per capita consumption, the supply was 44.7 lb. in 1937 and only 41 lb. in 1945, while the industrial uses took 22.8 lb. per capita in 1937 and 26.2 lb. in 1945.

The production of oil-bearing crops was increased to 10% more than the previous record by 1942, but this amount was inadequate to meet the need. By 1943, the output of oil-bearing crops was 300% more than in 1937. Price incentives were offered by the War Food administration in 1942 in the form of support prices for cottonseed, soybeans and peanuts. In 1943, the Commodity Credit corporation became the sole purchaser of peanuts from growers and handled the subsidies through the handlers, crushers and shellers. Imports of oils and oilseeds were placed under control. The Combined Food board controlled all purchases from other countries and allocated the exports among the United Nations. The use of fats by industries was restricted to amounts less than the average for 1940–41. Certain amounts were set aside for government purchase for lend-lease and military purposes. Consumer rationing was begun in 1943, and a system of collecting used fats from householders was started, these amounts to be used for industrial purposes.

The United States supply of oils and fats continued short through 1945 and well into 1946. The smaller supplies of lard, butter and flaxseed and the heavy demands for export made it necessary to continue strict rationing into 1945 and to limit the supplies to manufacturers. The government continued to stimulate production of both vegetable and animal fats.

The vegetable oil crops of the United States of chief importance during the decade 1937–46 included cottonseed, soybeans, flaxseed, peanuts and tung. With the shrinking cotton crop, the production of seed declined steadily during the decade from 7,844,000 tons in 1937 to 3,664,000 tons in 1945 and 3,452,000 tons in 1946. The proportion crushed was larger after 1940, amounting to 3,465,000 tons in 1945. The higher price of the oil stimulated more crushing. The price of cottonseed was supported to stimulate crushing. After 1940, the season price was above parity—$52.50 per ton compared with parity at $39 per ton in 1945.

Soybean production increased steadily and rapidly after 1927, and the quantity crushed for oil was at a high point in 1937. The total production of beans was 46,164,000 bu., of which 30,310,000 bu. was crushed. The crop doubled by 1939, then receded a little before making the great increase from 77,468,000 bu. in 1940 to 191,722,000 bu. in 1945. The 1946 crop was smaller. During 1944 and 1945, more than 150,000,000 bu. were crushed for oil each year. In terms of oil, soybean oil production rose from an average of 419,000,000 lb. in 1937–41 to 1,392,000,000 lb. in 1945. The price of soybeans rose from 67 cents per bushel in 1937 to $2.06 in 1945. A subsidy was paid to processors equal to 30–35 cents per bushel. Exports were up to 11,833,000 bu. in 1939 but dropped to only 85,000 bu. in 1940 with the outbreak of the war and then began to recover in 1944, when 3,000,000 bu. were exported. Imports of oil were about 3,000,000 lb. in 1937, exceeded by exports of 6,650,000 lb. The big exporters of soybeans in the prewar years were Manchuria and China.

Peanut oil was an important food oil through the decade 1937–46; it was usually too expensive for industrial uses. United States production in 1936 was 77,912,000 lb., of which 55,747,000 lb. were imported. The production of oil increased to 85,467,000 lb. in 1938 while imports dropped off sharply. Total peanut production averaged 1,392,000,000 lb. in the period 1937–41 and increased to 2,091,075,000 lb. in 1946. The peanut crop for crushing increased from 195,000,000 lb. in 1937 to 558,000,000 lb. in 1940 and then averaged around 400,000,000 lb. through 1946. The demand for peanuts for peanut butter and salted nuts increased during the early war years. Prices of peanuts were supported at 90% of parity, the average season price rising from 3.3 cents in 1937 to 8 cents in 1945. World production of peanuts increased steadily and frequently was the largest single oil crop. Most of the crop was produced in India, West Africa, China and the United States; and about one-third was crushed for oil.

By 1945 flaxseed and linseed oil production had increased rapidly to five times the production of the seed in 1937 and nearly twice the amount crushed for oil. The flaxseed crop of 1937 was 7,070,000 bu., which expanded to the record of 51,946,000 bu. in 1943 and then declined to 22,842,000 bu. as estimated in Sept. 1946. United States flaxseed production had been at a low level during the dry years 1934–38 in the flax belt of the northwest. Imports were large since Argentina, the principal producer, had large crops. The price of flaxseed rose from $1.87 per bushel in 1937 to a high of $2.90 in 1944. While prices to growers had reached parity, the government offered a special payment of $5 per acre for the 1945 crop which would bring prices up to about $3.40 per bushel for 1946. Linseed oil was in demand as a food principally in the soviet union and India. In the United States it continued to be used in paints, varnishes, etc.; hence the demand was expected to increase during the reconstruction period and the government stimulated production.

The tung oil supply of the United States consisted chiefly of imports from China in 1937, amounting to 129,213,000 lb. Imports declined rapidly after the outbreak of war to 8,345,000 lb. in 1943. The production of tung nuts in Georgia and other gulf coast states amounted to 11,000 tons in 1940 and increased to 33,100 tons in 1945. Large numbers of young trees were coming into bearing, and production was expected to increase rapidly. The United States output of oil was about 5,000,000 lb. in 1937, 8,600,000 lb. in 1945 and more than 10,000,000 lb. in 1946. The price of the oil averaged 16.7 cents per pound during 1935–39 and then increased in 1942 to 39.6 cents, where it remained through the war. China continued to dominate world production of tung oil and the United States took most of the exports after 1924. Small amounts of the nuts were produced in Argentina and Brazil. The exports from China became a government monopoly in 1938, when this product was balanced against a loan of $25,000,000. Imports to the United States had an average annual value of nearly $20,000,000 during the period 1935–39.

Olive oil production increased from an average of about 4,000,000 lb. during 1935–39 to 10,900,000 lb. in the peak year 1940, then declined again to 4,500,000 lb. in 1944 and about the same in 1945 and 1946. Imports averaged more than 61,000,000 lb., 1935–39, then dropped to 600,000 lb. in 1943. By 1944 imports were recovering and 8,800,000 lb. were imported. The crop of the Mediterranean area was low in 1945 because of the drought and imports continued below the prewar level. Olive production can be increased only slowly and the crop varies greatly from year to year. Olive oil was also meeting increased competition from other oils because of technical improvements and was not likely to become an important United States crop.

Animal Fats and Oils.—Lard and butter are the principal animal fats of United States production. Since the output of butter was restricted during the war period, lard became of vital importance. The enormous expansion of the hog industry supplied a large output of lard at the time of vital need. From 1935 to 1938, lard production was lower than it had been in the previous 15 years. In 1937 the output was 1,417,000,000 lb. and exports were at a low level. As hog production increased, the lard output rose but not at the same rate, since the high price of pork led to less careful trimming, and the ratio of lard production declined. At one time in 1944 the lard output was about 30 lb. per hog slaughtered, while in later months the output was up to more than 35 lb. per hog. Production rose to a record of 3,200,000,000 lb. in 1944, then declined to about 2,100,000,000 lb. in 1945 and 1946. Military and lend-lease needs took a large part of the lard output, reaching a maximum of 894,400,000 lb. in 1944. Of this total, 293,900,000 lb. were sent to the soviet union, 393,900,000 lb. to Britain and 170,000,000 lb. to other countries. Exports began to decline in 1945 and were only 530,000,000 lb. About half of this lard came from stocks accumulated in 1944. The reduced production in 1945 was the result of the decline of about 29% in the pig crop.

The use of lard in manufactured products changed markedly during the war years. During 1935–39 the total amount used averaged 5,800,000 lb. and increased to 240,600,000 lb. in 1944, then dropped to 112,100,000 lb. in 1945. Most of that used in 1944 was for soapmaking, which was restricted in 1945 to only low-grade lard. The supply of lard for civilians was 10.5 lb. in 1937 and increased to more than 14 lb. from 1940 to 1944, then declined to 12 lb. in 1945. During the war years the military and relief consumption increased up to 159,000,000 lb. in 1945.

U.S. Oils and Fats Production, 1937–46
(In millions of pounds)

	Average 1937–41	1942	1943	1944	1945	1946
Butter	2,211	2,130	2,015	1,815	1,699	1,502
Lard	1,964	2,469	3,056	3,215	2,132	2,167
Edible tallow	213	277	259	198	202	124
Inedible tallow	1,167	1,742	1,650	1,943	1,751	1,654
Marine oils	243	158	175	214	172	127
Corn oil	155	248	237	211	205	198
Cottonseed oil	1,472	1,386	1,313	1,132	1,273	964
Peanut oil	87	77	153	108	95	101
Soybean oil	419	762	1,234	1,246	1,392	1,449
Linseed oil	277	699	715	729	454	516
Other	21	35	40	34	40	34
U.S. total	8,230	9,983	10,848	10,845	9,427	8,846

Butter production increased from 1937 to 1941 and then declined to the lowest output in 15 years because of restrictions on creamery operations and the strong demand for whole milk and cheese. The decline was from 2,096,000,000 lb. in 1937 to about 1,502,000,000 lb. in 1946. Military supplies absorbed 145,000,000 lb. in 1942, 263,000,000 lb. in 1943, 312,000,000 lb. in 1944 and 249,000,000 lb. in 1945. In late 1945 some of the military stocks were released for civilian use. The civilian supply was 16.3 lb. per capita in 1937 and declined to 10.9 lb. in 1945, the smallest in more than 30 years. Margarine production doubled from 1939 to 1943, but the per capita consumption increased only from about 3 lb. to 4 lb. during the decade. The amount of shortening fats remained constant through the decade, but civilians received about a pound less. Other fats increased slightly during the period. Household fat collections amounted to 7%–8% of the total output of inedible tallow and grease. (*See* BUTTER; COCONUTS; COTTON; MARGARINE; PEANUTS; SOYBEANS.) (J. C. Ms.)

BIBLIOGRAPHY.—U.S. Dept. of Agriculture, *Agricultural Statistics;* A. E. Bailey, *Industrial Oil and Fat Products* (1945); K. Brandt, *Fats and Oils in the War* (1943).

Vegetables

Total production of all vegetable crops in the United States for sale fresh and for processing increased through the decade 1937–46 somewhat irregularly to a new high record in 1946. Total commercial truck crops were estimated by the U.S. department of agriculture at 10,130,400 tons in 1937 compared with 15,532,000 tons in 1946. The total acreage planted to truck crops increased from 3,272,000 ac. in 1937, a record to that time, to 3,810,650 ac. in 1944. Production increased faster than did acreage because of increasing yield per ac. During the last five years of the decade, truck crop production amounted to 26% of all food crop production compared with an 18% average for the previous five years. The increase was greatest in the Pacific states and next in the west south central region, during the five-year period 1939–44. Measured by carlot shipments, fresh vegetables of all kinds increased during the decade 1937–46. In total volume, the potato crop was most important, lettuce second and onions third, closely followed by cabbage, tomatoes, carrots and celery.

Stocks of frozen vegetables in storage rose from 32,503,000 lb. on Dec. 1, 1937, to 195,509,000 lb. on the same date in 1943, reflecting the large reserves. The quick-freezing process increased to a high point in 1944, when a total of 257,767,000 lb. was frozen.

Vegetable production, particularly potatoes, was the first form of food production to be restored in the countries devastated by World War II. Gardens were planted to beans and potatoes as fast as the land and seeds were available, since these crops required the minimum of machinery and fertilizers. Beans and potatoes became the staff of life in many areas in Italy and Germany after hostilities ceased, particularly in rural areas not reached by relief supplies. Vegetables furnished a palatable supplement to the types of foods provided by the United Nations Relief and Rehabilitation administration and other agencies. The supplies in the cities were generally low because of the lack of transport, on farms, and on railroads and boats.

Truck Crops for the Fresh Market.—The acreage of U.S. vegetables grown for sale fresh expanded from 1,710,340 ac. in 1937 to 1,872,720 ac. in 1944. Production was 6,294,000 tons in 1937 and rose to a record of 7,859,000 tons in 1944, to be exceeded by 8,446,000 tons in 1945 and an even greater crop in 1946. The output in 1945 was 30% more than the ten-year average 1934–43. The aggregate value of 25 commercial truck crops for sale fresh exceeded $625,000,000 in 1945 and compared with a total value of $212,881,000 in 1937. The strong consumer buying demand supported by high wages kept the markets firm in the face of the increasing volume of shipments. The per capita consumption of fresh vegetables increased for almost all kinds during World War II. The greatest increases were in tomatoes and green vegetables. The estimated per capita civilian consumption of all vegetables (excluding potatoes and dry beans) was 235 lb. in 1937, 254 lb. in 1944 and about 260 lb. in 1946.

Truck Crops for Processing.—Acreage of crops grown for processing expanded faster than did the area grown for sale fresh. This was due to the war demand for food in portable form as well as to the expansion of year-around consumption. From 1,562,470 ac. in 1937 the acreage expanded to 1,937,930 in 1944, followed by a decline in 1945 and 1946. The production was 3,835,500 tons in 1937 and increased to a high of 5,817,900 tons in 1942. Average prices of crops for processing advanced steadily and reached a top in 1945. The total pack of canned vegetables more than doubled, from 96,122,000 cases in 1939 to about 227,000,000 cases in 1946. The most notable increases were in tomato juice, spinach, green beans, carrots and peas. The pack of frozen vegetables expanded greatly during the decade, from about 85,000,000 lb. in 1937 to 272,000,000 lb. in 1945. Cold storage stocks of frozen vegetables were only 32,503,000 lb. in 1937 and about 200,000,000 lb. in 1946. The output of dehydrated vegetables rose to a record of 196,000,000 lb. in 1945 and then dropped quickly when the military demand declined. Civilians did not use these products to any great extent except in the form of soup mixtures and seasonings. It was doubtful that they could compete with the fresh product, except for export. In 1944 the amounts produced of the several vegetables were as follows: potatoes 132,012,000 lb.; onions 18,830,000 lb.; sweet potatoes 13,699,000 lb.; carrots 13,655,000 lb.; cabbage 7,333,000 lb.; beets 6,832,000 lb.; and rutabagas 1,801,000 lb. The quick-freeze processes were being rapidly adapted to retail marketing through stores and promised to take a larger proportion of the product prepared at the point of production.

Production of Individual Vegetables.—*Artichokes.*—Acreage planted to artichokes was expanded to more than 10,600 ac. in 1940, but the yield was lower than in the previous decade. Production of artichokes was 808,000 boxes in 1937 and about 700,000 boxes in 1946. The acreage declined steadily after 1940 to about 6,000 ac. in 1946. Prices fluctuated widely from $1.60 per box in 1937 up to $3.25 per box in 1944 and $4.16 in 1946. Artichokes did not gain much in popularity during the decade 1937–46.

Asparagus.—Production of asparagus for sale fresh (only about one-eighth of the total crop) amounted to 6,553,000 crates in 1937. The acreage increased from 67,170 ac. in 1937 to 92,260 ac. in 1941, then declined to 77,000 ac. in 1946. The yield steadily increased, however, bringing the total crop for 1943 to the record of 9,880,000 crates, followed by a slight drop to 9,414,000 crates in 1946. This crop showed a remarkable stability in price, which advanced steadily after 1937, when growers received an average of $1.42 per crate, to 1945, when the price averaged $2.36 per crate.

The crop for processing, chiefly canning, changed less during the decade. The high record had been made in 1929, when production was 66,790 tons. The acreage increased after that year, but the yield was not so good, and the crop of 1937 was only 51,190 tons. By 1941 it had declined to 37,970 tons but then recovered to 63,960 tons in 1946. The shortage of labour for harvesting was a factor in holding the crop in check during the war years. Considerable quantities of asparagus were frozen. The commercial crop continued to be grown chiefly in California, which produced about one-third of the total, New Jersey, producing one-sixth, and the rest widely scattered from the early areas in South Carolina to the late in Michigan. The pack of canned asparagus rose steadily from about 3,000,000 cases in 1937 to 4,300,000 cases in 1944 and then declined slightly. More than 13,256,000 lb. were frozen in 1944.

Beans, Lima.—For sale fresh, lima beans amounted to only about a third of the total crop of this vegetable after 1937. In that year the crop was 998,000 bu., or about the average of the previous ten years. The acreage increased until 1941, when the crop was 1,531,000 bu., followed by a slight decline. Prices rose from the low of $1.30 per bu. in 1939 to $2.92 per bushel in 1944, then declined. The larger crop of these beans grown for processing was sometimes drawn upon for fresh marketing when prices were high. Home garden production competed with the commercial crop because of deterioration in shipping. The winter crop from Florida continued to bring a price to growers about twice the season's average. In 1944 this price averaged $5.10 per bu. The midseason crop from Georgia and South Carolina averaged $3.34, and the late crop brought $2.29 on the average. The bulk of the crop for processing continued to be grown in the north Atlantic and central states and on the Pacific coast. The acreage grown for processing in 1937 was 42,400 ac., compared with 17,950 ac. harvested for sale fresh. This was the largest acreage on record up to that time. The total acreage increased to a peak of 87,130 in 1941 then declined as labour became scarce. By 1946, the acreage was again at a new high of 90,650 ac. The latter gain was chiefly in the crop for processing; the fresh crop had declined to a total less than that of 1937. This crop was widely grown, with New Jersey leading, California second and Delaware next in order. The output of canned lima beans was 1,512,000 cases in 1937; it rose to 2,600,000 cases in 1942 before declining to about the same level as in 1937. The frozen lima output in 1944 reached a high total of 37,051,000 lb.

Beans, Snap.—Snap beans continued to be widely distributed, produced in many states from the earliest areas of Florida to New York and Michigan. The total acreage of green snap beans grown for both fresh sale and processing increased at a remarkable rate, from 221,620 ac. in 1937 to more than 340,000 ac. in 1943; thereafter it declined to about 300,000 ac. in 1946. The acreage for sale fresh was more than twice that grown for canning in 1937 but the processing demand increased much faster and was almost half the total in 1943, a record year. Prices for the fresh sales were at the low point of 82 cents per bu. in 1938 and at $2.28 for the two high years, 1943 and 1944. For processing the price per ton advanced from the low point of $42.27 per ton to $95.37 in 1944, followed by a decline in 1945 and 1946. The leaders of the 30 odd states growing the crop were Oregon, New York, Arkansas, Florida, Maryland, Texas and Wisconsin. The two parts of the crop are interchangeable so that a surplus for one purpose can be shifted to the other use. Support prices were set to reflect about $91 per ton, and the averages for 1943 and 1944 were $93.69 and $95.37 per ton respectively. The larger crops of beans went into cans in increasing totals from 1937 on. Up to 1936, the snap bean pack had averaged about 6,000,000 cases of 24 No. 2 cans each. In 1937, the total jumped to 10,052,000 cases, then was smaller in 1939 and 1940 and made a new high record of 24,000,000 cases in 1942. Subsequently, the total dropped back to 18,000,000 cases. This was the biggest increase of any green vegetable. The total of all green beans frozen amounted to 23,260,000 lb. in 1944.

Beets.—The total production of beets doubled from an average of 122,500 tons in 1933–42 to 249,300 tons in 1944, then declined to 1946. In 1937, the acreage grown for the fresh market was almost as large as that planted to the crop for processing, 10,630 ac. compared with 12,450 ac.; but processing expanded much more rapidly during the war years. Production of beets for fresh sale was but

Tomatoes being unloaded at a New Jersey cannery with the help of soldiers on furlough from nearby Fort Dix in Aug. 1943

little larger in 1945 than in 1937, but the crop for processing increased from 70,800 tons to 184,000 tons in 1944 and 186,700 tons in 1945. Prices of fresh beets advanced from an average of 52 cents per bushel in 1937 to 62 cents in 1942. In 1943, a smaller crop brought $1.21 per bu., and in 1946 the price was down to 80 cents per bu. More than half the fresh crop was grown in Texas, with Pennsylvania and New Jersey following. The crop for processing was grown chiefly in New York, Wisconsin, Oregon, New Jersey and Michigan. More than 3,210,000 cases of beets were canned in 1937; the yearly output continued to increase until a record of 8,700,000 cases was packed in 1944. About 6,832,000 lb. were dehydrated at the peak of drying in 1944.

Cabbage.—The total production of cabbage increased during the decade 1937–46 principally during the last year of World War II. The total acreage rose from an average of 179,710 ac. in 1943 to 235,950 ac. in 1944. Production at the same time increased from 1,220,300 tons to 1,508,500 tons. Most of the crop continued to be grown for the fresh market, the part used for sauerkraut being only 107,400 tons in 1943 compared with a total of 117,900 tons in 1944. Only once before 1937 had the crop been so large. In 1945 the total crop was 1,582,000 tons, due to a large acreage and a fairly good yield, stimulated by a high price in the previous year. The price of cabbage rose from the lowest in ten years in 1938, $9.26 per ton, to a top of $47.54 in 1943. Cabbage prices fluctuated from year to year as the production varied. Prices also fluctuated from month to month in the shipping season. The government supported the market at various times by purchases. Stocks in storage ranged from a top of 78,020 tons in 1939 down to 25,700 tons in 1944. Average prices paid in the fresh market were regularly about twice those paid for stock for sauerkraut. The cabbage crop continued to be widely grown, from Texas to Wisconsin and New York. Most of the sauerkraut was made in New York, Wisconsin and Ohio, which three states accounted for about 80% of the production. New York also produced most of the early fall Danish type. Texas and Florida grew the winter crop, and Tennessee the late spring supply.

Cantaloupes and Other Small Melons.—The crops of the various melons were not regarded as a vital war food, and production declined sharply in 1942 and 1943 to the smallest total for 15 years. In 1931 the crop had been 14,412,000 crates; by 1937 it was down to the average of several years, about 11,931,000 crates. By 1943, the total had dropped to 9,311,000 crates, but it recovered to 12,009,000 crates in 1945. Prices were stable from 1937 to 1941 at around $1.06 per crate, then increased to $2.60 in 1944. California continued to be the leading state of small melon production, growing about half the total crop. Arizona came into second place, with Colorado third. The rest of the crop was grown in widely scattered states. The production of honeyball melons, mostly in California and Arizona, declined steadily from 1,165,000 crates in 1931 to only 172,000 crates in 1944, followed by a slight recovery in 1945–46. Honeydew melons also declined after 1932, from 4,957,000 crates to 2,126,000 crates in 1942, but recovered to more than 4,000,000 crates again in 1945–46. This crop was also grown chiefly in California and Arizona. Production of Persian melons increased at a slow rate because of the problems of shipping this perishable form.

Carrots.—The acreage of carrots harvested grew steadily from 1937 to 1943, then declined slightly. The production reached a record total of 29,944,000 bu. in 1943, as compared with 14,822,000 bu. produced in 1937. Fewer carrots were used for processing than other vegetables, but the amount canned increased from 949,000 cases in 1937 to 3,000,000 cases in 1944. About 20,418,000 lb. were dehydrated in 1943, the year of most extensive drying. Only small quantities were frozen. Prices of carrots were remarkably stable. The average annual price received by farmers advanced from 59 cents per bushel in 1938 to $1.37 in 1944 and $1.50 in 1946. The early crop continued to be grown in Texas and California, which also produced nearly half of the fall crop.

Cauliflower.—This crop held its place through the decade 1937–46 with an expansion much smaller than that of other vegetables. Acreage in 1937 was 29,470; it rose to 32,230 ac. in 1942 and then to 36,900 ac. in 1945. Total production increased from 8,677,000 bu. in 1937 to 11,640,000 bu. in 1945. The average price was 81 cents per bu. during 1934–43 and $1.54 per bu. in 1945. Nearly half the crop was grown in California, particularly in winter and early spring. The summer crop continued to come from Colorado and New York. Very little cauliflower was processed. In 1944, 7,205,000 lb. were frozen.

Celery.—The U.S. production of celery increased less than that of other vegetables during the decade 1937–46. The areas harvested amounted to 40,180 ac. in 1937 and 40,690 ac. in 1944. Then followed a jump to 44,190 ac. From these areas the production was 15,185,000 crates in 1937, 18,040,000 crates in 1944 and 19,316,000 crates in 1945. The price was $1.28 per crate in 1937, a top of $3.24 in 1943 and $3.20 in 1945. The early and spring crops, about one-third of the total, were grown in Florida and California, while Michigan and New York produced most of the fall crop. A good method of preserving celery was developed, and it was not processed. The culture of celery continued to be largely a commercial enterprise.

Corn, Sweet.—Sweet corn made a substantial gain during the decade 1937–46, particularly for processing. Production for the fresh market was reported for only three states. The average crops (1933–42) for these states were: New Jersey, 113,210,000 ears, New York 103,910,000 ears and Pennsylvania 51,012,000 ears, a total of 268,132,000. By 1945, these three states had increased their output to 314,810,000 ears. Small quantities of extra early corn were shipped from the south, but no carlot shipments were reported. The crop for processing increased from 978,100 tons in 1937 to 1,131,600 tons in 1945. The price rose from $9.98 per ton in 1938 to $19.30 per ton in 1945. The amount canned increased from 23,541,000 cases in 1937 to 32,000,000 cases in 1942, and then declined slightly. Corn was not dehydrated to any extent and only cut-corn was frozen. In 1944, 22,586,000 lb. of the latter was reported. An average of 11,714,000 lb. was reported held in cold storage on Dec. 1, 1940–44. More corn was canned than any other vegetable except peas and tomatoes. Large quantities were used by the military forces. Prices of crops for canning were supported by the government by contracts with canners, who passed on the support price to growers under contract. The yellow or bantam varieties became standard for canning, and more than seventy-five percent of the crop for processing in 1945 was of these varieties. (*See* also CORN.)

Cucumbers.—This crop is grown for the fresh market and for pickles; the fresh market crop usually amounts to about one-third of the total. In 1937 the fresh crop was 4,216,000 bu. and by 1945 had increased to 5,384,000 bu. For pickles, the crop was 7,761,000 bu. in 1937 and about 7,700,000 bu. in 1945. The acreage of cucumbers declined during the decade from 153,100 ac. to 144,300 ac. in 1946. Prices for the fresh market increased from 80 cents per bu. in 1938 to $2.48 in 1945, and for pickles from 59 cents per bu. to about $2.00. The war demand was not sufficient to encourage production. The crop was widely grown, with the Florida and Texas crops coming to market early in the year, while New York, New Jersey and Maryland led in the summer production.

Eggplant.—Although the total production was not large (806,000 bu. in 1937 and 1,538,000 bu. in 1945) eggplant became established as a popular vegetable. Its production was largely limited to four states: Florida and Texas for the winter crop and Louisiana and New Jersey for the summer crop. Florida produced about half the total. The acreage devoted to this crop increased from 3,650 ac. in 1937 to 6,350 in 1945. At the same time, prices rose from an average of 83 cents per bu. 1934–43 to $1.93 in 1945. No good method of preserving eggplant was developed.

Escarole.—Grown chiefly in Florida, escarole was introduced into Illinois and Indiana truck areas during the decade. In 1937, only 900 ac. were reported as the crop in Florida, with a production of 408,000 hampers. By 1945 the area was 2,800 ac. and the crop 865,000 hampers. Prices to producers increased from 45 cents per hamper in 1938 to $2.15 in 1945.

Garlic.—The commercial crop of garlic from three states, California, Texas and Louisiana, declined from 4,250 ac. in 1937 to 3,400 ac. in 1944–46. The crop harvested was 187,000 sacks in 1937 and 177,000 sacks in 1945. The price in this period advanced from $2.65 per hamper to $18.25 the greatest increase of any vegetable. California produced about five-sixths of the crop and Texas and Louisiana the rest.

Kale.—For the fresh market, not including that grown for livestock pasture, kale increased from 1,300 ac. in 1937 to 2,350 ac. (mostly in Virginia) in 1944, a record year. The crop amounted to 533,000 bu. in 1937 and 822,000 bu. in 1944. The average price advanced relatively little, from an average of 39 cents per bu. during 1934–43 to 65 cents per bu. in 1945.

Vegetables were grown in downtown areas of Tokyo levelled by Allied bombings, in an effort to increase food supplies after the close of World War II

Lettuce.—This crop reflected the growing demand for salads by expanding from 20,740,000 crates production in 1937 to 29,767,000 crates in 1945. The acreage increased from 151,750 ac. in 1937 to 172,650 ac. in 1945. In 1945, the record year, lettuce was exceeded only by cabbage in volume of total production. (*See* LETTUCE.)

Onions.—The commercial crop of onions declined after reaching a peak in 1936 of 34,688,000 sacks; only 29,974,000 sacks were produced in 1943. Acreage declined more than 40,000 ac. during this period. In 1944, the acreage was increased to a new high of 176,760 ac., and the crop harvested was also a record of 46,753,000 sacks. This big crop was followed by a reduction of nearly 38,000 ac. in the planting, and a crop of 36,137,000 sacks—less than the crop of 1942. Exports were large during the period 1939–41, then dropped to the average. The price of onions rose steadily from 66 cents per bu. in 1937 to $1.67 per bu. in 1943, and then declined under the pressure of increasing supply. The big producing states were New York, Colorado, California and Texas, which together produced half the crop.

Peas, Green.—The production of green peas for sale fresh declined during the decade, particularly during the war years, but the crops for processing practically doubled. The fresh crop was grown on 111,470 ac. in 1937 with a yield of 8,687,000 bu., but the acreage dropped off to about 69,000 ac. in 1945 with a crop of 6,176,000 bu. The prices paid growers advanced during this period from $1.14 per bu. in 1937 to $2.52 in 1945. The crop of peas for processing reflected the demand for food for the war period and increased from 268,110 tons in 1937 to 490,150 tons in 1945. The cannery price rose from an average of $54.69 per ton during 1934–43 to $83.18 in 1945. Wisconsin, the leading state, produced 113,440 tons alone in 1944, which was far more than the other leading states (Washington 46,920 tons, Oregon 46,750 tons, New York 37,800 tons and Utah 24,070 tons.) These five states produced about two-thirds of the total crop. Canned peas were the most important canned vegetable. The canning of peas was increasing up to 1937, when 23,467,000 cases were packed. By 1944 the total had reached 31,700,000 cases and continued to increase in 1945 and 1946. Peas were early found suitable for freezing, and by 1944 a total of 83,598,000 lb. was frozen. Peas were also held in cold storage in large quantities; average holdings on Dec. 1, 1940–44 were 40,000,000 lb., and in 1945 the total was 64,514,000 lb.

Peppers, Green.—Green peppers were grown on 20,600 ac. in 1937, and the area gradually expanded to 28,650 ac. in 1945. The production increased from 4,805,000 bu. in 1937 to 6,635,000 bu. in 1945. From 1941 to 1943 the crop was little larger than in 1937. Most of the crop was grown in Florida and New Jersey, with California and Texas next in order. Most was consumed fresh, as no good method of processing peppers had been developed.

Pimientos.—This crop increased very rapidly up to 1938 when the high record crop of 38,840 tons was harvested. Production then declined to 1944, when only 8,580 tons was produced. The 1945 crop was 12,470 tons. The culture of this crop was centred in a limited area in Georgia where seven-eighths of the crop is grown. California produces a small crop. The canning of pimientos reached a high peak in 1938 of 1,380,000 cases, then dropped year by year to only 200,000 cases in 1943, after which there was some recovery. The prices to growers averaged $33.83 per ton in 1934–43 and $60 in 1945.

Potatoes.—*See* separate article.

Shallots.—This crop was nearly all grown in Louisiana, and increased in popularity until 1937, when a decline in both acreage and production began which lasted until 1944. The acreage was 6,000 ac. in 1937 and 4,000 ac. in 1944 but increased to 4,900 ac. in 1945. Production for the same years was 720,000 bu. in 1937, 339,000 bu. in 1944 and 609,000 bu. in 1945. The price per bu. to growers averaged 88 cents in 1934–43 and was up to $2.37 in 1944 and $1.66 in 1945.

Spinach.—Before 1937, the production of spinach for the fresh market was stabilized at about 14,000,000 bu. per year. The acreage and yield varied more than the harvested crop. In that period the amount processed, principally canned, varied from a peak of 96,900 tons in 1929 down to 20,500 tons in 1932 and averaged about 40,000 tons. In 1937, the acreage for sale fresh was up to 75,740 ac.—which was not equalled until 1943, when 73,350 ac. were harvested for the fresh market. The crop from this area was close to 14,400,000 bu. for the entire decade. The crop for processing was grown on 29,720 ac. in 1937; the area declined for a year or two, then recovered in 1942 to a record of 46,240 ac. returning a crop of 114,400 tons. Later crops averaged about 100,000 tons. Nearly half the fresh crop came from Texas, with California the next largest producer. Nearly half the processed crop came from California and the rest principally from Arkansas and Oklahoma, with smaller amounts from Texas, Virginia and Missouri. The pack of canned spinach increased from 2,892,000 cases in 1938 to 9,500,000 cases in 1942, and then declined slightly. In 1944, more than 34,000,000 lb. were frozen. An average of 9,422,000 lb. was kept in cold storage in 1940–44.

Tomatoes.—The growing production of tomatoes reflected the increasing demand for salads during the decade 1937–46. The total acreage planted to tomatoes increased from 654,060 ac. in 1937 to 824,070 ac. in 1945. At the same time the crop for sale fresh increased about 20% and that for processing more than 50%. The crop for fresh market declined after 1937 to 200,230 ac. in 1941 and then increased to 270,970 ac. in 1945. The crop harvested rose from 22,000,000 bu. to 32,975,000 bu. in 1945. Yields per ac. were very good during the war years. The price to growers trebled from $1.07 per bu. in 1938 to $3.38 per bu. in 1945. The imports of fresh tomatoes increased from 54,861,000 lb. in 1938 to 210,874,000 lb. in 1944. Most of this quantity was from Mexico and Cuba. Texas became the leading tomato state, with California a close second in 1944. The lower valley of Texas produced most of the early spring crop. Florida grew the winter crop that competed with the imported crop from Gulf countries. The main summer crop came from Maryland, New York and New Jersey. Tomatoes for processing were grown on 451,000 ac. in 1937 and 553,100 ac. in 1945. The crop was 1,742,600 tons in 1938; a record crop of 3,169,900 tons was harvested in 1944. The crop declined in 1945 and this led the government to ask for an increase of 4% for 1946—the only increase among processing vegetables. The leading states in the output of tomatoes for processing were California, Indiana, Maryland, New Jersey, Pennsylvania and Ohio. The price of tomatoes for the factories averaged $14.68 per ton during 1934–43 and $27.22 in 1944, the good year.

Tomatoes are put up in three forms: whole tomatoes, pulp and juice. The output of whole canned tomatoes

Table I.—*Vegetable Truck Crops Production, 1937–46*
(In thousands of tons)

Year	For Fresh market	For Processing	Total
1937	6,294	3,835	10,130
1938	6,718	3,623	10,341
1939	6,723	3,390	10,113
1940	6,801	3,969	10,770
1941	6,551	5,101	11,653
1942	7,018	5,817	12,836
1943	6,697	5,064	11,761
1944	7,859	5,419	13,279
1945	8,446	5,339	13,785
1946	9,217	6,315	15,532

Table II.—*U.S. Production of Truck Crops for Processing, 1944–46, with 1934–43 Average* (In tons)

Crop	1934–43 Average	1944	1945	1946
Asparagus	49,710	53,740	53,300	63,960
Beans, lima	26,440	30,200	33,330	39,550
Beans, snap	130,800	225,200	221,500	200,500
Beets	78,800	161,500	186,700	131,400
Cabbage (sauerkraut)	162,100	117,900	233,300	264,800
Corn, sweet	880,800	1,004,500	1,131,600	1,222,900
Cucumbers	148,130	183,860	191,830	241,540
Peas, green	287,760	387,200	496,620	515,650
Pimientos	17,780	8,580	12,650	22,000
Spinach	60,400	106,900	89,300	85,000
Tomatoes	2,168,800	3,169,900	2,689,200	3,528,600

Table III.—*U.S. Vegetable Truck Crop Production, 1944–46, with 1934–43 Average*
(000s omitted)

Crop	Unit	1934–43 Average	1944	1945	1946
Artichokes	boxes	897	759	682	700
Asparagus	crates	7,593	9,546	8,627	9,414
Beans, lima	bu.	1,147	1,137	1,391	1,549
Beans, Snap	bu.	15,014	15,392	17,445	18,349
Beets	bu.	2,151	2,482	2,136	2,249
Cabbage	tons	1,084	1,508	1,582	1,475
Cantaloupes	crates	11,050	11,298	12,009	15,379
Carrots	bu.	17,280	26,833	31,043	27,759
Cauliflower	crates	8,251	9,505	11,640	12,629
Celery	crates	15,817	18,040	19,316	22,722
Corn, sweet	ears	243,955	242,400	314,810	319,860
Cucumbers	bu.	4,617	4,134	5,527	6,869
Eggplant	bu.	914	1,386	1,538	1,919
Garlic	sacks	159	150	177	204
Kale	bu.	572	822	665	556
Lettuce	crates	21,572	28,690	29,767	34,504
Onions	sacks	31,847	46,753	36,594	51,182
Peas, green	bu.	8,030	6,257	6,045	5,327
Peppermint	lbs. oil	1,024	1,195	1,410	1,334
Peppers	bu.	4,770	5,414	6,563	7,288
Shallots	bu.	587	339	609	710
Spearmint	lb. oil	165	217	295	286
Spinach	bu.	14,428	15,371	14,593	14,023
Tomatoes	bu.	24,093	27,768	32,975	33,750
Watermelons	melons	64,047	70,775	72,949	81,237

averaged about 28,000,000 cases from 1937 to 1945, rising to 41,000,000 cases in one year, 1942. The pack of canned tomatoes dropped off to only 18,000,000 cases in 1945, the smallest since 1931. The output of tomato pulp was much smaller, but increased from 3,746,000 cases in 1937 to 9,500,000 cases in 1944. The production of tomato juice, which was very small before 1930, increased from 16,979,000 cases in 1937 to 30,800,000 cases in 1944. The pack was almost 27,000,000 cases in 1945, second to the record of 1944. The shortage of labour encouraged the packing of juice rather than whole tomatoes.

Watermelons.—The production of watermelons appeared to be stabilized at around 65,000,000 melons from 1930 until the war period, when the crop dropped to 48,522,000 melons chiefly because of shipping difficulties. The acreage planted was about the same from 1937 to 1943, when it was cut from an average of 260,000 ac. to 142,600 ac. Large quantities of the crop were not harvested in some years when prices were low or shipping difficult. In 1938, more than 4,000,000 melons were lost and in 1940, 4,518,000 were not harvested. Georgia continued to be the "watermelon state," with an output almost twice that of California or Florida. These three states produced more than 30,000,000 of the U.S. crop of 70,775,000 melons in 1944. The price per 1,000 melons ranged from $106 in 1937 to $411 in 1945. The volume of shipments was 32,470 cars of 1,000 melons each in 1937, and 34,590 cars in 1944. (*See* also AGRICULTURE; BEANS, DRY; CORN; HORTICULTURE; LETTUCE; POTATOES.) (J. C. Ms.)

Venereal Diseases

Both great gains and great setbacks in the control of the venereal diseases occurred during the ten-year period 1937–46. The gains resulted from increased public education as to the threat of venereal diseases to public and individual health, heightened motivation to combat their spread and extraordinary advances in treatment methods and casefinding techniques. The setbacks were caused by the disruptive influence of World War II which in many areas, particularly the eastern hemisphere, obliterated the progress of decades.

World Incidence Trends.—Among the Scandinavian countries in which syphilis had been reduced to small dimensions by the time of the outbreak of World War II, the number of cases reported had increased eightfold in Denmark and sixfold in Norway by 1944; and even in Sweden, which was not invaded, the attack rate rose sharply after 1942.

In England and Wales, the number of new syphilitic infections under treatment by 1943 was more than double the number under treatment in 1939, but after 1941 the rate of increase fell off sharply.

On the continent, the incidence of syphilis increased markedly in many areas; although inadequate morbidity reporting made it impossible to measure changes in venereal disease rates, increases of twofold or more were not uncommon.

Reports from the orient a year after the end of the war indicated high venereal disease rates among many civilian populations.

In the western hemisphere established programs of control were not disrupted so greatly as elsewhere, and actual decreases in the incidence of syphilis were effected in some areas during the ten-year period 1937–46.

In the United States, the incidence of syphilis was cut in half during the 10-year period—from an estimated 500,-000 new cases per year in 1936 to an estimated 250,000 new cases in 1946. The number of deaths caused by all forms of syphilis declined steadily from 15 deaths per 100,000 population in 1939 to a new low estimated at 10.7 deaths per 100,000 population for 1945. The percentage of infant deaths caused by syphilis was reduced by more than one-half—from 57 deaths per 100,000 live births in 1939 to 25 per 100,000 in 1943. As reflected both in admissions to institutions and in recorded deaths, there was a steady decline in the incidence of late forms of neurosyphilis. In 1920 the national paresis death rate was 6.3 per 100,000 population; by 1943 this had been reduced by nearly half to 3.5 per 100,000. The tabes dorsalis death rate per 100,000, which was 2.1 in 1920, had dropped dramatically to 0.6 per 100,000 in 1943.

Credit for the fact that increases in the incidence of syphilis in the United States during the war were prevented, and that actual decreases in the attack rate were achieved in some areas, was shared by the armed forces, the selective service system, state and local health departments, the civilian medical profession, the U.S. public health service, the Social Protection division of the Federal Security agency, the Federal Works agency, the American Social Hygiene association, medical and laboratory research workers and many other public and private co-operating groups throughout the country.

During the war, the armed forces of the United States reduced venereal disease attack rates to record lows and by application of new treatment methods made notable reductions in the amount of time lost from duty because of venereal disease. After combat had ceased and occupation begun, rises in venereal disease rates of the armed services were reported.

Much of the progress in the control of venereal disease was made possible by development and widespread application of new rapid methods for treating syphilis and gonorrhoea and by increased casefinding activities.

New Methods of Treatment.—Most significant single development in the entire field of venereal disease control was the application of penicillin therapy to both syphilis and gonorrhoea. The announcement in 1943 by J. F. Mahoney and his associates that penicillin had demonstrated spirocheticidal activity when administered to human patients precipitated a revolution in syphilis control and profoundly influenced both casefinding and treatment procedures. The fact was subsequently developed that administration of penicillin every few hours, day and night, along with small quantities of arsenic and bismuth, rendered a large majority of early cases of syphilis so treated noninfectious within a period of less than two weeks. Furthermore, in so far as could be determined within the period of follow-up up to 1946, the therapy apparently "cured" or arrested the progress of the disease. This development largely eliminated the problem of caseholding. Before the introduction of intensive inpatient treatment of syphilis, a substantial part of the effort and funds of health departments was devoted necessarily to the difficult problem of holding the patients to the schedule of 30 injections of arsenic and 40 injections of bismuth administered in a course of 70 weekly injections. Despite caseholding efforts, less than 25% of all patients brought to treatment under the 70-week schedule were held long enough to assure the minimum protective therapy. In contrast, very nearly 100% of all patients hospitalized for intensive therapy completed the treatment.

The sudden liquidation of the caseholding problem freed an important part of the facilities of health departments for redirection toward an intensification of casefinding activities. Rapid treatment gave new impetus to finding patients infected with syphilis and bringing them to treatment.

Rapid Treatment of Syphilis.—Research in the rapid treatment of syphilis had begun as early as 1933 when H. T. Hyman, L. Chargin and W. Leifer introduced the method of administering large doses of arsenic over a short period of time by the intravenous drip procedure. Later, other rapid methods, including the administration of large doses of arsenic and bismuth over a short space of time by intravenous drip and multiple injections, and the inducing of fever, were used. In 1942 the first units of a nationwide system of rapid treatment centres for the administration of various intensive schedules of arsenotherapy requiring from one day to several weeks were established as a wartime emergency measure. The purpose was rapidly to render noninfectious persons to whom or from whom syphilis infections had been spread in areas with heavy concentrations of military and war industry personnel. By 1944, 63 rapid treatment centres had been established and had treated more than 25,000 cases of early syphilis by these methods. The advent of penicillin in the treatment of syphilis, however, and the availability of the drug in 1944 not only supplanted other methods of intensive treatment of syphilis but also afforded a sufficiently rapid turnover to permit hospitalization of all infectious cases of syphilis. During the fiscal year 1946, 120,000 cases of syphilis were treated—almost all of them with penicillin—in rapid treatment facilities which had expanded to include beds in general hospitals. This represented one-third of all syphilis cases reported to state health departments for the fiscal year and, more important, represented a major portion of all early cases of syphilis treated.

In the latter part of 1945, it was realized that some changes had occurred in the proportions of the various chemical species of penicillin present in most commercial lots produced since 1944 which explained the observation that for a time the results of therapy were less satisfactory than previously. However, the difficulty was corrected promptly when manufacturing procedures were modified so that the therapeutically more effective fractions were present in larger proportions.

The ultimate efficacy of penicillin in the prevention of the late manifestations of syphilis remained to be determined, for the character of syphilis is such that a treatment cannot be regarded as fully established until many years of post treatment observation have passed. Nevertheless, the first three years of experience with penicillin indicated strongly that it was the most effective and safest antisyphilitic drug yet developed up to 1946 for the prevention of infectious relapse, and research was directed toward determining optimum time dosage schedules. The most practical and economical method of administering penicillin in the treatment of syphilis would be an outpatient procedure which could be conducted in the offices of physicians in private practice, or in clinics without the necessity for hospitalizing patients. The possibilities of such a procedure were being explored in 1946.

Treatment of Gonorrhoea.—Success in the treatment of gonorrhoea with penicillin was spectacular. In 1943 gonorrhoea was treated successfully with penicillin by W. E. Herrell, E. N. Cook and L. Thompson. The treatment required only a few days and, most important, was effective with patients who had not responded to treatment with the sulfonamides. Within a short time, penicillin had been demonstrated effective in the cure of more than 90% of all sulfa-resistant gonorrhoea cases in which it was used, and even those cases which did not respond to first courses of penicillin therapy were cured with second or third courses. The materialization of penicillin as effective in the treatment of gonorrhoea was timely and fortunate; for the sulfa drugs, after a brief period of widespread usage, had declined disappointingly in effectiveness in gonorrhoea therapy as a result either of development of sulfonamide resistance by the gonococcus or the predominance of sulfonamide-resistant strains. In 1944 M. J. Romansky and G. E. Rittman showed that a single intramuscular injection of penicillin in an oil-beeswax mixture was effective in the treatment of gonorrhoea. At about the same time C. J. Van Slyke and S. Steinberg had succeeded in reducing to three hours the time required for the treatment of gonorrhoea with aqueous penicillin solution given in four injections an hour apart. Later, treatment that could be completed within two hours was developed. These procedures largely eliminated the necessity for hospitalization of gonorrhoea patients and were readily applicable to office practice and outpatient clinic treatment.

As the use of these speedy methods of treating gonorrhoea with penicillin became widespread, a significant proportion of patients presumed to be infected with gonorrhoea failed to respond to penicillin therapy; but subsequent studies indicated strongly that the infections, if any, present in these apparent failures were not gonorrhoea infections, and thus apprehension that penicillin-resistant gonorrhoea was developing was largely dispelled.

The importance of penicillin in the control of gonorrhoea was parallel to its importance in the control of syphilis, for it made possible more emphasis on casefinding. It also made possible more active participation by physicians in private practice in the control of the disease.

New Era in Control.—The decade 1937–46 marked the end of a dark age of evasion during which the basic problems of venereal disease control in some parts of the world were obscured by euphemistic attitudes embodied in such phrases as "social diseases." In Sept. 1936 the first national conference on venereal disease control in the United States was conducted in Washington, D.C., and attended by leading health officers and physicians from all parts of the country. The president's greeting to the conference used the words "venereal diseases" for the first time in any presidential paper. Newspapers and magazines throughout the country began to abandon the "social disease" subterfuge and call syphilis and gonorrhoea by name.

Table I.—*Activities Reported for Venereal Disease Control in States and Territories for Fiscal Years 1936–46*

	1936	1937	1938	1939	1940	1941	1942	1943	1944	1945	1946
Venereal disease											
Clinics treating venereal disease	713	965	1,125	2,080	2,633	3,245	3,569	3,770	3,707	3,477	3,324
Treatment visits in clinics . . .	3,344,257	3,757,770	5,177,827	7,923,958	9,165,490	11,373,423	11,483,404	13,925,632	12,184,770	9,170,374	6,088,432
Syphilis											
Cases reported to state health depts.*	266,626§	336,147§	480,140§	485,967§	487,464§	494,813	489,172	579,147	473,993	369,924	372,264
Primary and secondary . .						89,029	92,637	108,562	91,354	83,423	102,591
Early latent (asymptomatic under four-year duration) .						136,739	126,717	164,153	138,781	111,468	117,998
Congenital						22,171	22,226	28,864	17,170	16,371	15,046
Other						246,874	247,592	277,568	226,688	158,662	136,629
Admissions to clinic service and to rapid treatment centres and other in-patient care facilities†	79,905	101,347	149,434	249,464	288,778	340,615	343,312	431,750	357,351	278,369	253,738
Arsenical drugs (doses) distributed by state health depts. .	1,313,501	1,567,030	2,799,110	4,677,757	6,895,837	8,151,202	8,733,941	11,432,498	10,083,032	9,171,323	5,914,290
Arsenical drugs (doses) administered in clinics	934,063	1,143,354	1,854,735	3,166,342	3,719,880	4,885,736	4,928,484	6,310,639	5,562,959	3,846,479	2,321,874
Serologic tests made for syphilis	2,063,837	2,618,159	3,598,198	5,588,285	10,216,978	16,520,591	20,173,769	28,427,271	22,802,074	18,796,380	17,164,534
Darkfield examinations made for syphilis	6,673	10,682	14,228	15,789	16,327	23,674	26,755	32,153	27,227	35,666	49,676
Gonorrhoea											
Cases reported to state health depts*	162,487	182,435	198,439	184,679	180,383	198,432	220,432	281,980	311,795	295,896	375,421
Admissions to clinic service and to rapid treatment centres and other in-patient care facilities†	44,358	46,039	44,752	62,835	66,811	84,418	104,421	136,766	147,267	203,291	237,586
Tests (for detection of gonococcus) in laboratories‡	383,929	410,970	490,258	605,631	1,038,086	1,224,227	1,371,844	1,653,055	2,005,716	2,089,823	2,246,394

*Known military cases excluded.

†Admissions to rapid treatment centres and other inpatient care facilities included starting in 1944. These inpatient admissions are mainly responsible for the decreases in treatment visits in clinics, arsenical drugs distributed and arsenical (doses) administered beginning in 1944.

‡From 1942 through 1946, figures include number of cultures and number of complement fixation tests.

§Data on stage of syphilis not available.

Source: *Journal of the American Medical Association.*

Public response to the new campaign against venereal diseases led by Dr. Thomas Parran, surgeon general of the U.S. public health service, was immediate and widespread. Sampling polls conducted throughout the United States by the American Institute of Public Opinion showed that majorities ranging from 79% to 92% favoured vigorous public education, free public clinics, free blood tests, blood tests as prerequisites for marriage licences and adequate congressional appropriations for venereal disease control. Major voluntary organizations pressed for definite action to establish venereal disease control programs throughout the country. Among these were the General Federation of Women's Clubs, the Young Men's Christian association, the American Legion, the United States Junior Chamber of Commerce, the Lions International and many others. Voluntary campaigns were co-ordinated through the American Social Hygiene association.

LaFollette-Bulwinkle Bill.—The public will to combat the venereal diseases was implemented by congress in 1938, when the LaFollette-Bulwinkle bill was passed unanimously by both houses and was approved by the president on May 24. This act of congress authorized as a national policy grants-in-aid to the states sufficient for the establishment and maintenance of "adequate measures for the prevention, treatment, and control of the venereal diseases."

Table I shows the enlargement of venereal disease activity and progress which was possible after passage of the LaFollette-Bulwinkle bill.

Wartime Control Measures.—The second National Venereal Disease Control conference was conducted in Oct. 1942 at Hot Springs, Ark. by the U.S. public health service in co-operation with the American Neisserian Medical society. The conference was attended by federal, state and local health officers, by physicians in private practice and by the venereal disease control officers of the armed services. The conference considered means of meeting the wartime venereal disease control problem.

The mobilization of the military forces, together with the marked increase in industrial and defense activities, introduced numerous problems which required an intensification of the venereal disease control program.

In 1940 the army, the navy, the U.S. public health service and private health and welfare agencies formulated an effective co-operative wartime venereal disease control program which subsequently was adopted by a conference of state and territorial health officers. The program, stated in a document known as the "Eight Point Agreement" provided:

(1.) Early diagnosis and medical treatment by the army and the navy of enlisted personnel infected with venereal diseases.

(2.) Early diagnosis and treatment of infected civilians by local health departments.

(3.) Reporting by medical officers of the army and navy to state or local health authorities of information regarding possible source or spread of infections.

(4.) Reporting to medical officers of the army and the navy by civilian health authorities of contacts of enlisted men with infected civilians.

(5.) Isolation of recalcitrant infected persons with communicable syphilis or gonorrhoea during the period of communicability.

(6.) Repression of commercialized and clandestine prostitution.

(7.) Aggressive education among enlisted personnel and civilians regarding dangers of, prevention of and treatment of venereal diseases.

(8.) Co-operation of social hygiene and other voluntary organizations with official agencies in stimulating public support for the program.

In order to facilitate carrying out the provisions of the sixth point in the agreement, the federal security administrator in 1941 established the Social Protection section of the Office of Defense Health and Welfare Services. In 1943 the unit was designated as the Division of Social Protection of the Office of Community War Services, and it functioned until the beginning of the fiscal year 1947.

During the war, prostitution was repressed effectively in more than 700 communities throughout the United States. The Social Protection division assisted in developing techniques in law enforcement and in encouraging self-policing policies by business interests, such as owners and operators of hotels and rooming houses, bars and taverns, which decreased opportunities for soliciting for prostitution.

In 1941 congress passed the May act. The purpose of this act was "to prohibit prostitution within such reasonable distance of military and/or naval establishments as the Secretary of War and/or Navy shall determine to be needful to the efficiency and health and welfare of the Army and/or Navy." In May 1946 the May act was amended and retained as a law. The essential provisions of the eight-point wartime agreement were reaffirmed in 1946 by all groups adhering to the original version and by the treasury department, to whose jurisdiction the coast guard had been returned.

International Control.—During World War II, international co-operation in venereal disease control continued among many nations, particularly in the western hemisphere, despite disruptive circumstances.

International co-operation consisted largely of exchange of information regarding source and spread of infections. In North America, Canada and the United States systematically exchanged epidemiologic data. Mexico and the United States co-operated in venereal disease control through the United States-Mexico Border Public Health association. Similarly, the United States exchanged epidemiologic data with other nations in the western hemisphere; and most of the other American republics participated in co-operation in venereal disease control through the work of the Pan American Sanitary bureau, the co-operative health services of the individual republics and the American Social Hygiene association.

During the war, the United States public health service developed a system for forwarding to appropriate health agencies throughout the world the names and addresses of persons reported as contacts of infected patients under health jurisdictions of the United States.

Medical information as well as epidemiologic data was exchanged among health authorities of different countries. The venereal disease division of the U.S. public health service made freely available to physicians and health agencies of other nations information regarding new treatment methods used in the United States.

Delegates from many countries attended the National Conference on Postwar Venereal Disease Control conducted in St. Louis, Mo., in Nov. 1944, under the auspices of the venereal disease division of the U.S. public health service. The increasing need for greater international co-operation in venereal disease control was stressed by delegates from many countries attending the conference.

Selective Service's Casefinding Program.—The greatest mass syphilis casefinding mechanism in the history of venereal disease control in the United States was a co-operative program conducted by the selective service system, state and local health departments and the U.S. public health service. This program comprised blood tests as part of the general physical examinations given selective service registrants; registrants with positive test results were followed up by state and local health departments for fur-

Table II.—*Syphilis Rates per Thousand White and Negro Men Aged 21-35 in the United States, Based on 1,895,778 Selectee Serologic Reports and Arranged in Descending Order by States, U. S. Census Division and Region*†

White: Area	Syphilis Rate	Negro: Area	Syphilis Rate	Total: Area	Syphilis Rate
State:		State:		State:	
1. New Mexico	54.2	1. Florida	405.9	1. Mississippi	171.5
2. Texas	53.4	2. Texas	343.2	2. Florida	158.6
3. Florida	53.3	3. Georgia	327.6	3. South Carolina	145.5
4. Arizona	48.9	4. Maryland	324.6	4. Georgia	133.2
5. South Carolina	48.8	5. Mississippi	321.6	5. Louisiana	116.5
6. West Virginia	46.9	6. Arkansas	314.3	6. Arkansas	98.6
7. Oklahoma	39.5	7. New Mexico	304.8	7. Texas	93.4
8. Tennessee	39.4	8. South Carolina	296.3	8. District of Columbia	92.7
9. Georgia	39.0	9. Arizona	295.8	9. Alabama	92.3
10. Louisiana	37.9	10. Tennessee	277.8	10. North Carolina	84.6
11. Mississippi	35.2	11. District of Columbia	272.9	11. Tennessee	81.1
12. Nevada	32.1	12. Louisiana	272.0	12. Virginia	80.8
13. Virginia	31.0	13. Indiana	267.2	13. Maryland	77.3
14. Arkansas	30.0	14. Oklahoma	254.5	14. Arizona	60.4
15. Indiana	29.9	15. Virginia	245.9	15. West Virginia	57.2
16. Missouri	28.5	16. Delaware	239.6	16. New Mexico	56.5
17. North Carolina	28.5	17. North Carolina	237.4	17. Oklahoma	54.7
18. Maryland	28.4	18. Missouri	231.6	18. Delaware	51.5
19. Alabama	28.2	19. Alabama	227.1	19. Missouri	41.6
20. California	27.0	20. California	212.3	20. Indiana	38.3
21. Maine	26.9	21. West Virginia	211.7	21. Nevada	32.1
22. Wyoming	25.8	22. Illinois	211.4	22. California	30.7
23. District of Columbia	23.8	23. Kansas	210.5	23. Ohio	30.1
24. Ohio	21.9	24. Connecticut	207.1	24. Illinois	30.0
25. Delaware	21.8	25. Nebraska	204.4	25. Kansas	26.9
26. Illinois	21.1	26. Colorado	201.3	26. Maine	26.9
27. Kansas	20.5	27. New York	197.3	27. Wyoming	25.8
28. Colorado	20.2	28. New Jersey	193.0	28. Pennsylvania	24.7
29. Pennsylvania	17.0	29. Ohio	191.2	29. Michigan	23.5
30. Michigan	16.4	30. Pennsylvania	190.5	30. New York	22.8
31. Iowa	15.9	31. Michigan	182.6	31. New Jersey	22.0
32. Washington	15.6	32. Iowa	182.1	32. Colorado	21.9
33. New York	14.7	33. Washington	174.6	33. Iowa	16.8
34. Montana	14.1	34. Wisconsin	157.0	34. Washington	16.2
35. New Jersey	12.6	35. Minnesota	141.9	35. Montana	14.1
36. Nebraska	11.2	36. Massachusetts	115.8	36. Nebraska	13.1
37. Rhode Island	9.6	37. Rhode Island	91.8	37. Connecticut	12.5
38. South Dakota	9.6	38. Maine	*	38. Rhode Island	10.6
39. Connecticut	9.0	39. Montana	*	39. Massachusetts	10.3
40. Massachusetts	9.0	40. Nevada	*	40. South Dakota	9.6
41. Minnesota	8.6	41. New Hampshire	*	41. Minnesota	9.1
42. Utah	7.3	42. North Dakota	*	42. Utah	7.3
43. North Dakota	6.9	43. South Dakota	*	43. Wisconsin	7.0
44. New Hampshire	6.6	44. Utah	*	44. North Dakota	6.9
45. Wisconsin	6.4	45. Wyoming	*	45. New Hampshire	6.6
U. S. Census Division:		U. S. Census Division:		U. S. Census Division:	
1. West South Central	45.4	1. West South Central	307.1	1. East South Central	109.5
2. South Atlantic	36.8	2. South Atlantic	296.1	2. South Atlantic	102.9
3. East South Central	34.6	3. East South Central	277.2	3. West South Central	91.9
4. Mountain	26.4	4. Mountain	270.8	4. Mountain	28.9
5. Pacific	24.7	5. West North Central	222.3	5. Pacific	27.8
6. East North Central	19.7	6. Pacific	210.6	6. East North Central	27.1
7. West North Central	17.1	7. East North Central	204.6	7. Middle Atlantic	23.4
8. Middle Atlantic	15.2	8. Middle Atlantic	194.2	8. West North Central	22.2
9. New England	10.7	9. New England	146.2	9. New England	12.2
Region:		Region:		Region:	
1. 15 Southern states and District of Columbia	39.5	1. 15 Southern states and District of Columbia	294.0	1. 15 Southern states and District of Columbia	100.5
2. 29 Northern states	17.9	2. 29 Northern states	201.4	2. 29 Northern states	24.0
Total:		Total:		Total:	
44 states and the District of Columbia	23.5	44 states and the District of Columbia	272.0	44 states and the District of Columbia	47.7

*Number tested insufficient for computation of rate.
†Reprinted from the *Journal of the American Medical Association*, Dec. 26, 1942, vol. 120, pp. 1369-72.

Table III.—*Syphilis Among 1,895,778 Selectees and Volunteers by Age Group, Race and Residence: Number Tested, Number in Whom Evidence of Syphilis was Detected and Prevalence Rate per Thousand Tested**

	Urban			Rural			Total		
Age Group	Number Tested	Syphilis Detected	Rate per 1,000	Number Tested	Syphilis Detected	Rate per 1,000	Number Tested	Syphilis Detected	Rate per 1,000
White									
21-25	594,054	5,887	9.9	350,306	3,678	10.5	944,360	9,565	10.1
26-30	309,934	6,530	21.1	162,625	3,328	20.5	472,559	9,858	20.9
31-35	172,128	6,758	39.3	81,472	2,814	34.5	253,600	9,572	37.7
Total	1,076,116	19,175	17.8	594,403	9,820	16.5	1,670,519	28,995	17.4
Negro									
21-25	63,990	13,062	204.1	53,011	9,313	175.7	117,001	22,375	191.2
26-30	42,699	12,944	303.1	23,459	6,488	276.6	66,158	19,432	293.7
31-35	29,862	10,766	360.5	12,238	4,271	349.0	42,100	15,037	357.2
Total	136,551	36,772	269.3	88,708	20,072	226.3	225,259	56,844	252.3
Total									
21-25	658,044	18,949	28.8	403,317	12,991	32.2	1,061,361	31,940	30.1
26-30	352,633	19,474	55.2	186,084	9,816	52.8	538,717	29,290	54.4
31-35	201,990	17,524	86.8	93,710	7,085	75.6	295,700	24,609	83.2
Total	1,212,667	55,947	46.1	683,111	29,892	43.8	1,895,778	85,839	45.3

*Reprinted from *The Journal of the American Medical Association*, Dec. 26, 1942, vol. 120, pp. 1369-72.

ther diagnosis and treatment if necessary. Among the first 15,000,000 registrants examined, 720,000 men with serologic evidence of syphilis were discovered. Of these, approximately 273,000 after follow-up and treatment were made available for induction into the armed services unless otherwise disqualified.

The selective service routine blood-testing procedure in conjunction with data from surveys conducted throughout the country made it possible to estimate the total prevalence of syphilis among the entire population of the United States—approximately 3,200,000 cases.

The rate of prevalence based on positive and doubtful blood tests among the selectees examined was 45.3 per 1,000. The rate of prevalence for the entire male population of the United States between the ages of 21 and 35 was estimated to be 47.7 per 1,000.

The rate of prevalence among Negro selectees was 252.3 per 1,000, among white selectees 17.4 per 1,000. The estimated rate of prevalence for the entire male Negro population aged 21–35 was 272 per 1,000, for the entire male white population 23.5 per 1,000.

The rate of prevalence among selectees from rural areas was 43.8 per 1,000, from urban areas 46.1 per 1,000. The estimated rate of prevalence among the entire male population aged 21–35 in rural areas was 49.4 per 1,000, in urban areas 46.5 per 1,000.

Highest prevalence rates (white and Negro) were found in the southeastern states, the lowest in the New England, west north central and middle Atlantic states. The prevalence rates among males 21–35 years old for states in which data were available, and for U.S. census divisions and for regions are shown in Table II. Rates by age groups are shown in Table III.

Armed Forces Blood-Testing Separation Program.—Of importance comparable to that of the selective service blood-testing and follow-up program was the co-operative program in which the army, navy and coast guard blood-tested for syphilis all members being separated from the services. Arrangements were made whereby all separatees with positive results to the serologic test for syphilis were referred to appropriate rapid treatment centres or state or local health departments for follow-up observation. During the period of most rapid demobilization, the public health service provided interviewers at all army separation centres and the larger separation points who interviewed separated soldiers with positive or doubtful results to the serologic test for syphilis and who referred them or provided transportation to the nearest rapid treatment centre.

Community-Wide Casefinding.—In 1945 a new mass method of venereal disease casefinding was introduced in the United States, in which virtually entire populations of whole cities and counties were persuaded by intensive programs of public information and education to appear voluntarily at designated stations for physical examinations for venereal disease or for blood serologic tests for syphilis.

This method was applied in a series of 45-day demonstrations conducted by state and local health departments, with medical societies, and the U.S. public health service co-operating. Paid newspaper, radio, billboard, car-card, motion picture theatre, sound truck and other forms of advertising were used to inform the people of the prevalence, dangers, symptoms and cure of the venereal diseases and to urge persons in susceptible age groups to report for diagnosis and treatment if necessary.

The first of the series of demonstrations was conducted in New Orleans, La., from March 13 to April 30 and resulted in 3,953 new cases of gonorrhoea being discovered and brought to treatment. Approximately 40% were treated by 152 physicians in private practice and the remaining 60% were treated in clinics. Penicillin was provided to both private physicians and clinics. The New Orleans campaign brought to treatment in 45 days more cases of gonorrhoea than the total number of cases reported in that city during the 2 preceding years.

The second demonstration was conducted in Birmingham, Ala., from May 15 to June 30, 1945. A state law in Alabama passed in July 1943 required blood tests for all persons in the state between the ages of 15 and 50. During the Birmingham program, 87% of the population of Jefferson county in that age group were given blood tests, among whom 35,616 persons infected with venereal disease were found, including 32,655 infected with syphilis and 2,961 infected with gonorrhoea. More than 140 physicians in private practice co-operated in the Birmingham program.

Control in Industry.—In 1937 the venereal disease division of the U.S. public health service assigned a commissioned officer with special training in industrial hygiene to the work of furthering a program for the control of venereal disease in industry. By this time it was recognized that, since more than 40% of the population of the entire country was included in the nation's potential labour force, efforts to reduce venereal diseases among such a large portion of the population should favourably influence the trend of venereal disease rates throughout the entire population.

In 1942, the surgeon general of the U.S. public health service appointed an advisory committee on the control of venereal diseases in industry. The committee was composed of physicians representing the medical profession, the public health service, industrial physicians, the American Social Hygiene association, and others concerned with the problem. The committee, on Aug. 10, 1942, made a report which embodied its "Recommendations to State and Local Health Departments for a Venereal Disease Control Program in Industry." The specific objectives of the program recommended by the committee were: to find and treat venereal disease and to prevent its spread among industrial workers and their contacts; to develop employment policies fair to both employer and employee which would assure maximum utilization of available manpower; to co-ordinate community and industrial venereal disease control programs and to bring to employees and employers such additional benefits as improved physical condition of personnel, reduction of labour turnover, working days lost and compensation costs and increase of efficiency, production and earning power.

In 1945 the American Social Hygiene association intensified its efforts to assist state and local health officers, industries and labour and management groups in establishing programs for venereal disease control in industry. This work was conducted in co-operation with the industrial hygiene division and the venereal disease division of the U.S. public health service. By 1946 the principles of control recommended by the advisory committee had been endorsed by state and territorial health officers, leading labour unions, large industrial organizations and other groups, such as national chambers of commerce, industrial and trade associations; and active programs were being conducted in almost every state in the United States.

Premarital and Prenatal Examinations.—During the decade 1937–46, great progress was made under the leadership of the American Social Hygiene association, the medical profession, health officers and legislators in securing the enactment of state laws requiring premarital and prenatal examinations to aid in the control of the venereal diseases.

The first law requiring a premarital examination and blood test for syphilis of both partners had been passed in Connecticut in 1935. In 1937 five more states passed laws requiring a premarital examination. By 1946, 36 states had premarital examination laws; of these, 32 states and Hawaii required blood tests for syphilis of both prospective bride and groom before issuing a marriage licence. The states were: California, Colorado, Connecticut, Florida, Idaho, Illinois, Indiana, Iowa, Kentucky, Maine, Massachusetts, Michigan, Missouri, Nebraska, New Hampshire, New Jersey, New York, North Carolina, North Dakota, Ohio, Oklahoma, Oregon, Pennsylvania, Rhode Island, South Dakota, Tennessee, Utah, Vermont, Virginia, West Virginia, Wisconsin and Wyoming. Alabama, Louisiana and Texas required an examination by a physician for venereal diseases or a medical certificate showing freedom from such diseases of grooms only. The state of Delaware prohibited marriage of persons infected with venereal diseases or required personal affidavit of freedom from such diseases but specified no examination. The 12 remaining states and the District of Columbia granted marriage licences without regard to possible venereal disease infection.

The first legislation requiring prenatal blood tests was passed in 1938 by New York, New Jersey and Rhode Island. By 1946 prenatal blood tests for syphilis were required in the territory of Hawaii and 35 states: Arizona, California, Colorado, Connecticut, Delaware, Florida, Georgia, Idaho, Illinois, Indiana, Iowa, Kansas, Kentucky, Louisiana, Maine, Massachusetts, Michigan, Missouri, Montana, Nebraska, Nevada, New Jersey, New York, North Carolina, Ohio, Oklahoma, Oregon, Pennsylvania, Rhode Island, South Dakota, Utah, Vermont, Washington, West Virginia and Wyoming.

The value of state premarital and prenatal laws as health measures was indicated by estimates for 1946 which showed that under these laws more than 2,500,000 persons during the fiscal year were tested, among whom were 96,000 persons with positive blood serologic test results.

In 34 states with premarital laws, 1,689,000 blood tests were made of which 83,000 were positive. In the 35 states with prenatal laws, 957,000 tests were made of which 13,000 were positive.

Public Education.—By 1946 the principles of public education and of community action in venereal disease control had been well formulated on the basis of experience gained during the preceding decade.

The Section on Education and Community Action, National Conference on Postwar Venereal Disease Control, in 1944 made public a comprehensive report and recommendations. The section made recommendations regarding family protection, welfare and social services, moral factors, social hygiene education, patient education, education in schools, training in professional schools, community organization and action, Negro participation, prevention of prostitution and promiscuity, functions of law enforcement agencies, legislation, courts, detention facilities and social protection.

In 1945 the U.S. public health service advisory committee on public education mailed to state health officers and large city health departments questionnaires relating to venereal disease education and conducted hearings to receive testimony of individuals competent in different phases of venereal disease control, education and social protection.

In Dec. 1945 a report to the surgeon general of the U.S. public health service embodying the advisory committee's recommendations was made public. The report was based largely on the national conference report, response to the questionnaires, testimony presented at the hearings and a 1944 report of the advisory committee pertaining to the use of radio and films for venereal disease informational purposes for the general public.

The advisory committee stated that it regarded the St. Louis report as the basis for a comprehensive and thorough study for the formation of a program for community action for venereal disease control and public education which are so closely interwoven as to be inseparable. Answers received to the questionnaires mailed to state and local health officers, summarized by the advisory committee, revealed the demand for:

(1.) Greater emphasis on venereal disease and social hygiene education in the control program.

(2.) Education directed largely to the population groups having the highest incidence classification (education of patients taken for granted).

(3.) Sustained, intensive, long-range education programs.

(4.) Aid for other agencies in conducting programs of education and community action.

(5.) A long-range, intensified venereal disease education program as part of a general health program.

(6.) Employment of full-time, qualified, health education personnel for community health education.

(7.) Providing this personnel by or through health departments.

(8.) Special assistance from the U.S. public health service in training locally employed health education personnel and providing increased advisory services in health education, information and community organization.

The advisory committee made recommendations for meeting the obvious great need for a large increase in trained personnel for health education, information and community work.

The committee also recommended that the U.S. public health service stimulate the production of films of high artistic, educational and moral merit suitable for showing to special groups as well as to the general public. It strongly urged that education of transients or "floating" populations concerning the various aspects of venereal disease was essential to prevent infection and for casefinding; also, that special study should be given to more effective methods of conveying venereal disease education to urban and rural Negroes. Finally, the committee recommended that every effort be made to bring venereal disease education to industrial groups. (*See* also MILITARY MEDICINE; UROLOGY.)

BIBLIOGRAPHY.—J. F. Mahoney, R. C. Arnold and Ad Harris, "Penicillin Treatment of Early Syphilis: A Preliminary Report," *Ven. Dis. Inform.*, 24:355–357 (Dec. 1943); H. T. Hyman, L. Chargin and W. Leifer, "Massive Dose Arsenotherapy of Syphilis by the Intravenous Drip Method: Five Year Observations," *Am. J. M. Sc.*, 197:480–485 (April 1939); W. E. Herrell, E. N. Cook and L. Thompson, "The Use of Penicillin in Sulfonamide Resistant Gonorrheal Infections," *J.A.M.A.*, 122:289–292 (May 29, 1943); M. J. Romansky and G. E. Rittman, "Penicillin: I. Prolonged Action in Beeswax-Peanut Oil Mixture; II. Single Injection Treatment of Gonorrhea," *Bull. U.S. Army M. Dept.*, No. 81, pp. 43–49 (Oct. 1944); C. J. Van Slyke and S. Steinberg, "Outpatient Penicillin Treatment of Gonococcic Infections in Males," *Ven. Dis. Inform.*, 25:229–232 (Aug. 1944); Lida J. Usilton, "Mortality Trends for Syphilis," *J. Ven. Dis. Inform.*, 27:47–52 (Feb. 1946); *Annual Report of the Surgeon General of the United States Public Health Service* (1946); National Conference on Postwar Venereal Disease Control, St. Louis, Mo., Nov. 1944, "Proceedings," *J. Ven. Dis. Inform.*, supp. 20, pp. 1–213 (1945); Lida J. Usilton, "Syphilis among Civilians during World War II, January 1, 1942, through June 30, 1943," *J. Ven. Dis. Inform.*, 26:263–266 (Dec. 1945); R. A. Vonderlehr and J. R. Heller, Jr., *The Control of Venereal Diseases* (1946). (J. R. HR.)

Venezia Tridentina

See SOUTH TYROL.

Venezuela

A South American republic, Venezuela is bounded on the west, south, east, and north, respectively, by Colombia, Brazil, British Guiana and the Caribbean sea. Area: 346,481 sq.mi.; pop. (1941 census): 3,951,371, including an estimated 100,600 "indigenous forest population," *i.e.*, Indians; pop. was estimated in 1942 to be 3,996,095, including 100,670 Indians and 23,320 Venezuelans living abroad. The bulk of the population is mestizo, with a considerable admixture of Negroes and mulattoes along the Caribbean coast. The capital is Caracas (1942 pop. est., 269,930, 1941 census pop. 269,030); other important cities (with 1941 census pop.) include Maracaibo (112,519), Valencia (53,938), Barquisimeto (54,176), San Cristóbal (31,344), Maracay (32,992), Cumaná (25,893), Ciudad Bolivar (19,789), Coro (18,962), Puerto Cabello (22,087), Carúpano (16,548).

The constitution of 1936 provided for the establishment of a federal republic with 20 states, with legislative power vested in a bicameral congress with a senate and a chamber of deputies, the senate including two members from each state, elected by the state legislatures for four-year terms, and the chamber 98 members, elected on a population basis. The presidential term was five years and the president (elected by congress) was ineligible immediately to succeed himself. Presidents during the decade 1937–46 included Gen. Eleázar López Contreras, 1935–May 9, 1941; Gen. Isaías Medina Angarita, May 9, 1941–Oct. 19, 1945; Rómulo Betancourt, Oct. 21, 1945 to date.

Retreat from Dictatorship.—Venezuelan development in 1937 continued to centre, as it had in 1936, around the efforts of Pres. Eleázar López Contreras to place the country on a relatively democratic basis (following the death of the dictator, Juan Vicente Gómez, on Dec. 17, 1935), and at the same time maintain internal stability. The government exiled a number of alleged communists during the year, and refused entrance to other persons previously exiled. Several strikes were peaceably adjusted, in sharp contrast to the procedure under the Gómez dictatorship. The congress, in furtherance of the reform policy launched in 1936, enacted several laws for improvement of labour and agriculture and for the better control of foreign residents.

During 1938 Venezuela continued to be economically prosperous and politically stable. Governmental revenues increased and Pres. López Contreras was enabled to present to the congress on May 7 a far-reaching "three-year plan" for Venezuelan national development. The program provided for increased national production; a reduction in the cost of living; development of sanitation, education and population. Venezuela's foreign relations in 1938 were featured by a nonaggression treaty with Brazil signed Dec. 8, and active participation in the eighth Pan American conference at Lima, Peru, in December.

The United States and Venezuela reciprocally elevated their legations to embassies early in 1939. Long-protracted negotiations between the two governments for a reciprocal trade agreement were concluded Nov. 6, and the pact took effect Dec. 16; by its terms, Venezuela reduced import duties on important products bought from the United States, while the latter government cut in half its tariff on Venezuelan petroleum, although limiting importation through a quota system. Venezuela promptly declared its neutrality after the outbreak of World War II and took a prominent part and a keen interest (partly because of the country's closeness to the Panama canal) in the work of the first inter-American foreign ministers' conference at Panamá in September–October.

War Dislocations.—Venezuela was under some economic strain in 1940 because of the effect of World War II on its foreign markets, especially in the Scandinavian countries and the Netherlands. Exports, especially of petroleum, suffered a sharp decline, and the early wartime interruption of the petroleum refining industry in the Dutch islands of Aruba and Curaçao, off the Venezuelan coast, also affected the Venezuelan industry adversely inasmuch as most Venezuelan oil was exported directly to those islands for refining. The government established an Import Control commission in Oct. 1940 to regulate and license imports. Municipal and state elections in Nov. 1940 returned heavy majorities to the Bolivarian party, headed by Pres. López Contreras.

Half of the membership of the national chamber of deputies was renewed in a nation-wide election Jan. 30, 1941. The election was of more than ordinary importance because the new congress was scheduled to elect a successor to Pres. López Contreras. Although his original election had been for a seven-year term, expiring in 1943, López Contreras voluntarily decided to end his term in 1941; he had already rejected earlier suggestions that, owing to world uncertainties, he should avail himself of legal loopholes to accept a new term. The new congress was overwhelmingly in support of the president, but on April 5 López Contreras formally reiterated his determination not to accept re-election. The congress, therefore, on April 28, chose Gen. Isaías Medina Angarita, the incumbent minister of war, as the new president by a vote of 120 out of 137.

Medina Angarita President.—Pres. Medina Angarita took office on May 9, 1941, in the first free and open transfer of presidential power from one constitutional president to another in Venezuelan history. Medina Angarita declared in his inaugural address that it was his intention to continue the liberal program of his predecessor and to cooperate with the United States. Evidence of his democratic sincerity was revealed in September when his opponent for the presidency, the novelist Rómulo Gallegos, was allowed to form, without opposition from the government, a new party, the Acción Democrática, a group with slightly leftist leanings. This group for some time thereafter constituted the only formal party opposition to the administration party, to which both López Contreras and Medina Angarita belonged.

A hundred-year-old boundary dispute with Colombia was ended by direct negotiation in April 1941; this agreement called for improved commercial relations between the two republics and proved a forerunner for added *rapprochement* in later years strengthening the sentimental ties which more than a century before had united Venezuela, Colombia and Ecuador in the single state of Great Colombia.

Upon the outbreak of war between the United States and the axis powers in December. Venezuela hastened to support the program of hemispheric solidarity. The government promptly took increased military precautions, opened Venezuelan ports to all American powers at war

Lowering the British flag during ceremonies making the formal cession of the tiny island of Patos, in the gulf of Paria near Trinidad, to Venezuela in Sept. 1942

Gymnastic drill for cadets on the parade grounds of the Escuela Militar, Venezuela

with the axis, and restricted radio communication to the Americas only. Venezuela on the last day of the year formally severed diplomatic relations with Germany, Italy and Japan. The record Venezuela had established with her lucrative petroleum royalties—of paying off her entire foreign debt—was broken in 1941 when wartime exigencies caused the government early in the year to borrow $3,600,000 in the United States. The rising cost of living (previously the highest in Latin America) led the government to create a National Price Control board in 1941.

Venezuelan developments in 1942 were concerned chiefly with adjustment, both domestic and foreign, to a world at war. Foreign policy was directed toward the strengthening, both economically and politically, of relations with other South American states. At the third conference of American foreign ministers at Rio de Janeiro in the latter half of January, Venezuela was one of the strongest advocates of hemispheric solidarity against Germany, Japan and Italy; the Venezuelan delegation at Rio formed a part of the so-called severance bloc which worked for a unanimous break in axis diplomatic relations by all American republics.

Venezuela signed a commercial treaty with Argentina during the year and also negotiated seven *modus vivendi* agreements. A treaty with Great Britain gave Venezuela undisputed title to the small island of Patos in the Gulf of Paria and also defined the boundary line in that gulf between Venezuela and the British island of Trinidad. Venezuela and the United States concluded an agreement in 1942, to remain in force through Dec. 31, 1946, providing for U.S. purchase of Venezuelan rubber. The two governments also signed a lend-lease agreement March 18.

Internal developments in 1942 were characterized by determined efforts to decrease the country's dependence upon imported foodstuffs and manufactured goods. This had been a chronic problem because of the diversion of a large part of the country's employment and economic energies to the service of the direct and indirect demands of the petroleum industry. A notable development of the year, consequently, was the increase and improvement of the government's emergency controls of prices, transportation and imports, initiated at the outbreak of World War II. The temporarily declining revenues from petroleum royalties led the congress to pass Venezuela's first income-tax law. A new civil code was also adopted during the year.

No change in general political policy took place during 1943, and the year proved to be relatively quiet. Elections held Jan. 19, 1943, resulted in the retention by Pres. Medina Angarita's administration of control of most of the seats in the congress. The most significant development of the year was the enactment on March 13 of a new petroleum law which provided that all companies and concessions be placed in an equal position under the law. Taxes were increased on surface lands, and some immunities from customs charges previously enjoyed by the companies were eliminated.

On April 15, 1943, Medina Angarita authorized the formation of a new political party, to be named the Partidários de la Política del Gobierno and designed to support the administration program. The move was partly in anticipation of the presidential election campaign of 1945, in which Medina Angarita stated that he would not be a candidate. The fact that only one opposition party had existed (the Acción Democrática, formed in 1941), led to the belief that conservatives might form another party for the forthcoming campaign. By inclusion of three men from liberal groups in cabinet appointments made in May, the administration was interpreted as moving toward the left.

In spite of shortages in many items of consumer goods, economic conditions continued relatively satisfactory in 1943, although the cost of living showed no tendency to decline; the latter index stood at 126.3 in Dec. 1943, as against 100 in 1938. The decrease in ship sinkings in the Caribbean in 1943 allowed a greater flow of goods to Venezuela, thus aiding retail trade. The government in Nov. 1943 blacklisted the so-called German railway; it became unable to operate, because of lack of fuel, and was taken over by the government Nov. 16.

Medina Angarita, at the invitation of the United States, made a visit to that country in Jan. 1944, during which he was received by Pres. Franklin D. Roosevelt at the White House on Jan. 19, and addressed the United States congress on Jan. 20. He conferred in New York with Henry J. Kaiser, and as a result three officials of the Kaiser interests went to Venezuela in March to survey postwar developmental possibilities. On March 28, Kaiser announced a three-point plan for Venezuela, including expansion and integration of the transportation system, development of hydroelectric power and gas resources and systematic mineral exploitation; certain aspects of these recommendations, especially the first part, were subsequently criticized in Venezuela. Andrew J. Higgins, New Orleans industrialist, made a trip to Venezuela in August and September for a study of similar problems.

As a consequence of a labour congress which was somewhat critical of the administration, the government on March 25, 1944, dissolved 109 workers' and farmers' groups on the charge of having included communists in their membership; some of these were later permitted to reopen after reorganization. The government began on April 19 to apply by decree a comprehensive and compulsory new social security law, designed to take effect gradually; it provided for insurance against undue financial loss as a consequence of sickness, maternity, industrial accidents and occupational diseases.

The government on Sept. 26, 1944, ordered the liquidation of six German and all Japanese firms operating in the country; this was accompanied by some slight manifestation of concern over axis economic strength in the republic, though axis minorities were not large (they were estimated at 3,000 Germans, in addition to 4,000 citizens of German descent, and 1,500 Italians, plus 1,500 citizens of Italian descent).

Diógenes Escalante, Venezuelan ambassador to the United States, proposed on July 18 that his country's frontier with British Guiana should be revised; this found some echo in Venezuela, but nothing tangible developed to revive the famous boundary controversy of 1895 and the years following. Domestic politics gained some attention in 1944, especially in view of partial congressional elections scheduled for Jan. 1945 and the anticipated beginning of the next presidential campaign later in that same year. Medina Angarita showed some tendency to align himself with labour elements instead of the military, from whose ranks he had come, a fact which undoubtedly led to his overthrow the following year. He proposed certain constitutional changes, including the direct election of deputies (they were currently elected by the councils of the municipal districts), the abolition of the ban on communist activities, woman suffrage in municipal elections and the federalization of the judiciary. Ex-Pres. López Contreras denied on Oct. 4 that he was associated with a proposed new party, that he was ambitious to be re-elected president at the end of the current term or that he opposed the Medina Angarita administration. Less discussion of the possibility of López Contreras as the "government candidate" was heard at the end of the year, however. The government on Nov. 17 announced the suppression of a small attempt at rebellion in a Caracas garrison.

Army Revolt.—The main event of 1945 was the October revolution which overthrew the administration of Pres. Medina Angarita. Revolt broke out in Caracas and the nearby military city of Maracay on Oct. 18, staged by the rank and file of the army, led by younger officers of or below the rank of major, and joined soon afterward by the liberal Acción Democrática party. After fierce fighting for three days, Medina Angarita was forced out and Dr. Rómulo Betancourt, 40-year-old lawyer and a leader of Acción Democrática, became provisional president. Casualties in the revolution were estimated at 300 killed and more than 1,000 wounded. The new regime was almost immediately granted diplomatic recognition by Cuba, Ecuador, Paraguay, and, on Oct. 30, by the United States; other governments extended recognition at about the same time. The provisional government announced that it would hold elections, as previously scheduled, in April 1946. It soon succeeded in restoring order, and apparently enjoyed popular support. Oil companies were reassured with regard to retention of their property. The revolt was allegedly caused by the belief of younger army officers that the election of Angel Biaggini, supposedly Pres. Medina Angarita's candidate as his own successor, would be engineered under any circumstances and the regime thus continued. Medina Angarita, ex-Pres. López Contreras and others were exiled to Miami, Fla. The new regime promised a new constitution within six months.

Congressional elections on Jan. 19, 1945, resulted in an overwhelming victory for the pro-administration Venezuelan Democratic party. The government on Feb. 15 declared belligerency against Germany and Japan; Ambassador Diógenes Escalante on Feb. 20 signed the United Nations pact at Washington. The government on April 6 announced plans for liberal monthly quotas for admission of Spanish Republicans and other immigrants. Some of the constitutional amendments which Medina Angarita had previously proposed—legalizing Communist party activity, granting women a municipal vote, etc.—became effective May 5.

Venezuela established diplomatic relations with the soviet union on March 13, 1945. At the United Nations conference at San Francisco, opening in April, Venezuela received the presidency of the judicial agency set up as one of the working committees to draft the United Nations charter. The government on May 25 announced the arrest of ten Germans charged with plotting to sabotage the oil fields and to blow up Allied tankers transporting fuel to Europe.

The revolutionary junta which had been in control of Venezuela since Oct. 1945, enacted a law on March 2, 1946, setting elections for 160 members of a new constituent assembly for Aug. 27; the elections were later postponed to Nov. 11. The long-standing state of siege was lifted March 15, 1946, and the government on the following day freed all political prisoners. Serious disturbances occurred within the next few days, however, between communists and police. Political lines appeared to be tightening between the conservatives and the liberal Acción Democrática (civilian spearhead of the 1945 revolution) on the one hand, and Acción Democrática and the communists on the other.

Participants in the military coup at Caracas, Venezuela, on Oct. 18–20, 1945, which overthrew the regime of Pres. Isaias Medina Angarita. A revolutionary junta, headed provisionally by Socialist leader Dr. Rómulo Betancourt, was recognized by the U.S. on Oct. 30

Venezuela: *Statistical Data*

Item	1938 Value (000's omitted)	1938 Amount or number	1940 Value (000's omitted)	1940 Amount or number	1945 Value (000's omitted)	1945 Amount or number
Exchange rate						
United States		1 bolivar = 31.35 cents		1 bolivar = 31.35 cents		1 bolivar = 29.85 cents
Great Britain		15.71 bolivars = £1		12.27 bolivars = £1		13.56 bolivars = £1
Finance						
Government revenues	$106,698 (£21,824)		$113,275 (£29,576)		$101,558* (£25,169)	
Government expenditures	$106,840 (£21,853)		$113,275 (£29,576)		$100,254* (£24,846)	
Gold reserves	$49,627 (£10,151)		...		$48,323* (£11,976)	
National debt	$878 (£180)		...		$7,448* (£1,846)	
Transportation						
Railroads		606 mi.				
Highways		5,883 "				
Waterways (rivers)		6,500 "				
Airways		2,563 "				
Communication						
Telephones		21,880		31,856†		...
Telegraph lines		7,886 mi.		8,299 mi.†		8,393 mi.*
Radio sets		85,000		138,000†		100,000*
Minerals						
Petroleum		30,943,071 tons				
Gold		114,985 oz.				
Diamonds		13,600 carats				
Crops						
Coffee		66,138 tons				
Sugar cane		24,802 "				
Cacao		22,707 "				
Livestock						
Cattle		3,090,661‡				
Goats		614,749‡				
Swine		355,551‡				
Exports—total	$278,161 (£56,895)	30,421,000 tons	$269,895 (£70,469)	29,548,000 tons	$330,694 (£82,058)	50,134,491 tons
Petroleum and derivatives	$259,661 (£53,111)	29,369,000 "	$253,628 (£66,221)	29,474,000 "	$305,941 (£75,916)	50,043,168 "
Coffee	$8,050 (£1,647)	40,000 "	$5,848 (£1,527)	32,000 "	$10,190 (£2,529)	31,116 "
Gold	$4,670 (£955)	...	$5,262 (£1,374)	...	$2,164 (£537)	87,482 oz.
Cacao	$3,128 (£640)	23,000 tons	$2,674 (£698)	17,000 tons	$4,820 (£1,196)	16,506 tons
Imports—total	$97,483 (£19,939)	660,000 "	$97,556 (£25,472)	636,000 "	$239,976 (£59,547)	960,172 "
Machines, apparatus and accessories	$27,170 (£5,557)	...	$23,428 (£6,117)	45,000 "	$46,349 (£11,501)	87,840 "
Metals and manufacture	$19,398 (£3,968)	...	$17,787 (£4,644)	172,000 "	$28,251 (£7,010)	188,211 "
Foodstuffs and beverages	$10,787 (£2,206)	...	$13,460 (£3,514)	112,000 "	$18,884 (£4,686)	108,317 "
Defense						
Standing army		13,700		11,000		
Personnel reserves		3,000		7,500		
Standing air force personnel		200		373		
Military expenditures	$12,383 (£2,516)		...			
Education						
Primary schools		6,000		5,600§		
Students		250,000		295,400§		
Secondary and technical schools		75		90§		
Students		...		7,000§		
Universities		2		2§		
Students		...		3,000§		

*1943 †1941 ‡1937 §1942

The Copei, a conservative party enjoying the support of the Catholic Church provided the strongest opposition in the October elections for members of a constituent assembly. The Accion Democrática emerged with a victory.

BIBLIOGRAPHY.—*The Inter-American*, monthly; Pan American Union *Bulletin*, monthly; *South American Handbook*, annual; Erna Fergusson, *Venezuela* (1939); H. J. Allen, *Venezuela: A Democracy* (1940); Olga Briceño, *Cocks and Bulls in Caracas* (1945); Alfred Kidder, *Archaeology of Northwestern Venezuela* (1944).

(R. H. FN.)

Vermiculite

Most of the development of fairly extensive use of vermiculite in the United States occurred in the period 1937–45, as is indicated by the following production data:

	Short tons		Short tons		Short tons
1937	25,556	1940	22,299	1943	46,645
1938	20,700	1941	23,438	1944	54,116
1939	21,174	1942	57,848	1945	64,808

Established uses prior to World War II included heat and sound insulation, both loose and as an admixture in concrete and plaster, the latter forms also serving as a fire retardant and a weight reducer. Its colour and flaky formation made vermiculite useful as an extender for aluminum and bronze paints. In petroleum-cracking units, it served as a combined refractory and insulator. A special war adaptation was in lightweight insulating concrete for deck covering and fireproof walls in oil tankers exposed to bombing attacks. Other adaptations were as a soil conditioner and as an absorbent for oil on shop floors.

(G. A. RO.)

Vermont

A north Atlantic state of the United States, Vermont was admitted to the union in 1791, the first to be added to the original 13; popularly known as the "Green Mountain state." Area, 9,609 sq.mi., including 331 sq.mi. of water. The population in 1940 was 359,231, including 235,992 rural, 123,239 urban. There were 327,079 native whites, 31,727 foreign-born, 384 Negro, 41 of other races. On July 1, 1944, the U.S. census bureau estimated the population of the state at 310,941. Capital, Montpelier (8,006). The chief cities are Burlington (27,686), and Rutland (17,082).

During 1937, Vermont passed an unemployment compensation law and increased its old-age assistance from $250,000 to $475,000 annually. It also passed a number of bills bringing its crime legislation into harmony with that of other states, and entered into an interstate compact for flood control with neighbouring states. The state park system was expanded. An $800,000 bridge was built across the northern end of Lake Champlain. The governor was George D. Aiken; William H. Wills, lieutenant governor; Rawson C. Myrick, secretary; Thomas H. Cave, treasurer.

During 1938, the important Rutland railroad, mid-state artery, went into the hands of a receivership. The New England hurricane of Sept. 1938 did much flood and wind damage to public and private property, particularly sugar orchards. The milk situation continued to occupy the attention of the extensive dairy interests, and the governor's committee made a revolutionary recommendation advocat-

→ **Quarrying near Rutland, Vt., a source of much of the finest marble used in statuary and public buildings. Marble and granite continued to be leading mineral products in the state throughout the decade 1937–46**

ing home uses of surplus milk that would yield an estimated $1,000,000 more annually to Vermont farmers. The Winooski valley flood control project, begun in 1933, was virtually completed at a cost of $15,000,000.

A total presidential vote of 143,044 was cast in the state in 1940; Willkie received 78,371; Roosevelt 64,269. William H. Wills was elected governor; Warren R. Austin and George D. Aiken, U.S. senators; Charles A. Plumley, representative to congress; Mortimer R. Proctor, lieutenant governor; Thomas H. Cave, treasurer; Rawson C. Myrick, secretary of state.

A special legislative session in 1941 granted a bonus of $10 a month to its men in service, a sum which had been voted by a previous session in case the United States went to war. During 1941 former Gov. George D. Aiken took his seat as U.S. senator from Vermont. Provision was made for a referendum on women jury service to be decided at the general elections in 1942.

The year 1942 was an off-year for the biennial sessions of the state legislature. The principal activities of the state centred around various phases of war work. A council of safety was set up, modelled on the original council of colonial days, to head up all the civilian defense work of the state. Gov. William H. Wills became the honorary chairman and Albert A. Cree, executive chairman. Vermont led the nation in the scrap metal drive and was among the leading states in the scrap rubber drive.

(L. W. D.; X.)

The state legislature in 1943 granted emergency powers to the governor, who in turn created the office of civilian defense and the council of safety. There were no changes in the constitution. Levi R. Kelley succeeded Thomas H. Cave as treasurer of the state.

A special session of the state legislature met in 1944. Bills were passed permitting members of the armed forces to vote. Other laws enacted or amended included those pertaining to flood control on the Connecticut river and benefits for veterans of World War II. The state vote for president of the United States was distributed as follows: Thomas E. Dewey, 71,527; Franklin D. Roosevelt, 53,820; others, 14. George D. Aiken was elected U.S. senator; Charles A. Plumley, representative to congress. State officers elected in the 1944 election were: Mortimer R. Proctor, governor; Lee E. Emerson, lieutenant governor; Levi R. Kelley, state treasurer; Rawson C. Myrick, secretary of state. Requests for 7,855 ballots were received from members of the armed services, and 5,309 of these applicants voted in the November election.

In 1945, the state legislature met from Jan. 3 to April 18. Legislation enacted or amended included bills relating to the establishment of a minimum salary for teachers, provision for the regulation of air commerce, provision for standard nonforfeiture and valuation laws respecting life insurance and establishment of a state veterans' board.

Legislation enacted or amended in 1946 included bills relating to student housing at the Vermont Agricultural college, at Burlington, Vt., and public welfare. Elected in Nov. 1946, were Ralph E. Flanders, U.S. senator, and Charles A. Plumley, representative to congress. U.S. Senator-elect Ralph E. Flanders was appointed by Pres. Harry S. Truman to complete the unexpired term of Senator Warren R. Austin, who had been appointed U.S. delegate to the United Nations Security council. Chief state officers elected were: Ernest W. Gibson, Jr., governor; Lee E. Emerson, lieutenant governor; R. C. Myrick, secretary of state; and L. R. Kelley, state treasurer. (C. E. Fe.; X.)

Vermont: *Statistical Data*

Table I.—*Education (Public)*

	1938	1941	1942	1943	1944	1945
Elementary school pupils	54,773	44,524	44,095	39,104	43,460	38,800
High school pupils	13,158	16,637	16,065	14,964	15,273	14,196
Elementary teachers	2,018	1,954	1,900	1,814	1,759	1,750
High school teachers	556	698	705	708	679	678

Table II.—*Public Welfare*
(Money figures in thousands of dollars)

	1938	1940	1941	1943	1944	1945
Cases on general relief	3,140	2,488	1,599	2,439		
Cost of general relief	$71	$56	$27			
Recipients of old-age pensions	5,105	5,442	5,775		5,083	5,149
Dependent children receiving aid	1,105	1,652	1,693	1,669	1,486	1,481
Blind receiving aid	135	153	158	150	160	144

Table III.—*Communications*
(Money figures in thousands of dollars)

	1938	1939	1941	1943	1944	1945
Highway mileage	1,848	1,857	1,780	1,780	1,781	1,802
Expenditures on highways	$6,889	$7,092	$5,856	$4,300	$3,222	$1,957
Railroad mileage	928	919	917	968	968	958

Table IV.—*Banking and Finance*
(Money figures in thousands of dollars)

	1937	1938	1939	1942	1944	1945
State revenue	$12,524	$15,109	$14,890	$17,454	$17,177	$19,260
State expenditure	$11,127	$13,296	$10,482	$17,008	$15,258	$18,116
Number of banks	91	91	84	81	79	80
Total bank deposits	$170,400	$165,400	$165,900			
Number of national banks	42	42	42	40	38	39

Table V.—*Agriculture*
(All figures in thousands)

	1937	1939	1940	1941	1943	1945 (est.)
Acreage, principal crops	1,115	1,102	1,093	1,048	1,003	1,014
Income from crops and livestock	$38,500	$40,401	$75,690	$49,022		
Leading crops (bu.):						
Apples	737	780	413	664	722	106
Corn	2,960	3,040	2,627	2,622	2,432	2,442
Hay (tons)	1,147	1,143	1,123	968	1,197	1,207
Oats	1,540	1,881	1,760	1,504	1,188	1,302
Potatoes	2,194	1,950	2,142	1,740	1,825	1,375
Syrup, maple (gal.)	940	916	1,080	759	1,072	351

Table VI.—*Manufacturing*
(Money figures in thousands of dollars)

	1937	1939	1942 (est)	1943 (est)	1944	1945 (est)
Wage earners	23,682	21,759	50,000	50,000	41,856	44,000
Wages paid	$24,615	$21,232	$49,500	$55,000	$77,921	$80,000
Value of manufactures	$111,876	$103,154	$175,000	$175,000	$378,018	

Table VII.—*Mineral Production*
(In thousands of dollars)

	1937	1938	1939	1940
Value of mineral products	$7,043	$6,440	$6,972	$12,284
Leading products:				
Stone	$4,216	$3,149	$3,412	
Slate	1,432	1,730	1,948	$1,948
Lime	389	416	452	
Talc	384	329	378	
Granite				7,304
Marble				1,534

Bibliography.—Council of State Govts., *Book of the States* (bienn.); Federal Writers' Program, *Vermont: Guide to the Green Mountain State* (1937); Secy. of State, *Legislative Directory* (bienn.); *Vermont Yearbook.* Periodical: *Monthly Checklist of State Publications.*

Versailles Treaty

See Germany; World War II.

Veterans' Administration

The Veterans' administration, an independent U.S. federal agency headed by an administrator of veterans' affairs, was established by an act of July 3, 1930, to unify the work of various federal bureaus administering direct benefits to veterans and their beneficiaries.

The beginning of the ten-year period 1937–46 found veterans, as a result of the business depression, increasingly concerned with having security of benefits assured. On that account, and in the interest of simplicity of administration, constant endeavour was made to evaluate disability on a permanent basis for pension purposes. Except for former soldiers of the regular establishment, veterans of all wars other than World War I were in decreasing numbers receiving monetary benefits, while the World War I group continued to increase in number of beneficiaries with growing costs. The pressure of adverse economic conditions was also reflected in increasing hospitalization and domiciliary care.

The advancing age of about 4,000,000 World War I veterans, many with natural physical handicaps, and the resultant unemployment, also constituted a serious and progressive problem, especially because of the reluctance of commercial and industrial employers to hire older men. While the Veterans' administration did not itself maintain an employment service, it co-operated with the U.S. Employment service of the department of labor and other federal agencies in an effort to find work for veterans. Many men turned to the Civilian Conservation corps, established in 1933. Veterans' eligibility was determined by the Veterans' administration, and selectees were certified to the war department for enrolment in the corps. When CCC terminated at the close of the fiscal year ending June 30, 1942, there were still about 11,000 veterans on the rolls. Altogether, there were approximately 225,000 enrolments in the veterans' contingent after the start of the corps, and almost 600,000 veterans and their dependents had received direct monetary benefits through payments and allotments.

Period of Defense Build-up.—The national defense program brought new problems. The army was not fully prepared to meet the medical and hospital requirements of an enlarged force, so the Federal Board of Hospitalization adopted a plan approved by Pres. Franklin D. Roosevelt in Sept. 1940 that would utilize the highly trained medical staff and facilities of the Veterans' administration. This program provided that the additional requirements of the armed forces would be met by the Veterans' administration's relinquishing beds it had been using in army and navy hospitals and by addition, through new construction, of beds to existing hospital services; that temporary general hospital needs of the army and navy in manoeuvre areas would be met by the nearest general hospitals of the agency; and that in the event of a major national emergency the general facilities of the agency would be utilized for members of the armed forces who were injured or incurred disabilities in service and whose physical rehabilitation by the army was not feasible. The agency's legal obligation to provide hospitalization for members of the regular establishment discharged for service-incurred disabilities or in receipt of a pension, indicated the need for more beds through building construction.

The Selective Training and Service act of Sept. 16, 1940, was followed by public laws of Oct. 8 and 17, 1940, necessitating reorganization to handle the huge volume of insurance business brought about by these laws. During the first year, through Oct. 1941, more than 662,000 applications for national service life insurance, representing approximately $2,285,000,000 of insurance, were received from persons in the armed forces, requiring immediate expansion of the insurance and finance services of the agency.

Even as the volume of work grew, considerable inroads were being made upon the personnel of the Veterans' administration to meet the needs of the armed forces.

War Duties.—The transition of the United States from a national defense to a war basis brought additional duties. Adequate authorities obtained or were promptly enacted to permit adjudication of war service claims for pension and insurance benefits and to afford hospitalization to discharged veterans disabled in line of duty. World War II veterans were granted hospitalization, domiciliary care and burial benefits on a parity with World War I veterans, and provision was made for rehabilitation of World War II veterans.

As the Allied forces began to advance on the various battlefronts, greater consideration was given plans for the civil re-establishment of returning veterans. The result was the Servicemen's Readjustment act of June 22, 1944. The act in general applied to any World War II veteran discharged under conditions other than dishonourable after 90 or more days of service, or discharged by reason of an injury or disability incurred in line of duty. Broadly, within certain limitations, it provided: educational and vocational training aid; guarantee by the Veterans' administration of loans for purchase of homes or farms or for business purposes; payment of readjustment allowances to unemployed or self-employed veterans, and other benefits.

Demobilization.—The number of persons discharged from the U.S. armed forces rapidly increased with the surrender of the axis powers in 1945 and the ensuing demobilization. By Sept. 1, 1946, the number of veterans totalled 17,492,000, of whom 13,531,000 were those of World War II. To meet the tremendous increase in claims for direct benefits by World War II veterans more effectively and more promptly, the Veterans' administration decentralized in 1945. In addition to the central office in Washington, D.C., 13 branch offices, each under a deputy administrator, were established in various parts of the United States. Under the jurisdiction of the branch offices as of Aug. 31, 1946, there were 327 field stations (regional and subregional offices, hospitals, homes and centres) and 736 contact units. Offices were also established in Puerto Rico, Alaska, the Hawaiian Islands and the Philippine Islands. During this same period the number of full-time employees increased from 68,174 in Aug. 1945 to 177,930 in Aug. 1946. Of this latter number, 152,783 were employed in field offices. As of June 30, 1937, there had been 35,190 full-time employees on the rolls.

Medicine and Surgery.—The urgent need for rapid expansion of all medical services for veterans, as a result of World War II, prompted reorganization and creation of a department of medicine and surgery under a chief medical director in Jan. 1946. This bill authorized the administrator of veterans' affairs to employ without regard to the civil service Classification act of 1923, as amended, physicians, dentists, nurses and other professional and nonprofessional personnel at such pay rates as he prescribed. It likewise authorized the administrator to establish residencies for physicians in Veterans' administration hospitals and clinics. By June 30, 1946, 650 residents had been appointed. In conjunction with the physician-training program, 890 consultants of outstanding professional ability in their individual fields of medicine and dentistry had been appointed by June 30, 1946.

As of June 30, 1936, there were 80 Veterans' administration hospitals with a total of 45,873 beds and an additional 1,876 beds in other hospitals operated by federal agencies available through reciprocal agreements. Ten years later, June 30, 1946, there were 109 hospitals with 86,439 authorized beds and 12,669 beds allotted by other agencies, and about 8,000 beds for service-connected cases available through contracts with state and civil hospitals. Disbursements for construction of new hospitals and additions during the fiscal years 1937 through 1946 totalled $95,852,-310.68.

Of the total of 346,036 hospital admissions of veterans during the fiscal year 1946, 67.6% were World War II veterans, 28.9% World War I and 3.5% were veterans of other wars and men discharged or retired from all branches of the regular military services. General medical and surgical cases constituted 80.3% of total admissions, pulmonary tuberculosis cases 4.4% and neuropsychiatric, including neurological diseases and injuries 15.3%. Sixteen percent of all admissions were for disabilities that were service-connected, that is, directly or presumptively incurred in or aggravated by military service. Hospitals operated by the Veterans' administration accounted for 87% of the veterans admitted to hospitals in the fiscal year 1937, and only 75% of those admitted in 1946. Because of the greater need for additional hospital facilities during the year ending June 30, 1946, in which period the total veteran population was augmented by about 10,000,000 World War II veterans, there was an appreciable increase in the number of beds allocated by other federal agencies and beds contracted for in state and civil hospitals.

Discharges of veterans from hospitals during the fiscal year 1946 were 132.7% more than the 1937 total. General medical and surgical patients discharged in 1946 exceeded 1937 by 144.8%; neuropsychiatric discharges were 120.2% higher in 1946, and pulmonary tuberculosis discharges were 32.5% more than the 1937 total.

Of the 85,837 veterans under treatment in hospitals at the end of the fiscal year 1946, 32.4% had service-connected disabilities. There were 28,335 general medical and surgical patients, 13.2% of which were service-connected cases; 8,103 pulmonary tuberculosis patients, 46.2% service-connected; and 49,399 neuropsychiatric cases, 41.1% of which number were service-connected. Ten years earlier, at the beginning of the fiscal year 1937, there was a total of 41,542 U.S. veterans in hospitals, 28.1% service-connected cases; 12,556 general medical and surgical cases, 7.2% service-connected; 4,539 pulmonary tuberculosis cases, 23.7% service-connected; and 24,447 neuropsychiatric cases, 39.6% service-connected.

Table I.—*U.S. Veterans: Hospital Admissions, Discharges and Patients Under Treatment in Hospitals*

Fiscal years	Admissions	Discharges	In hospitals, June 30
1946	346,036	332,366	85,837
1945	241,013	235,022	71,229
1944	193,789	188,156	63,800
1943	160,234	159,644	56,641
1942	179,274	182,928	56,073
1941	187,374	188,617	58,160
1940	179,497	178,668	56,596
1939	165,576	164,760	53,861
1938	152,966	149,956	50,670
1937	141,537	142,814	46,142
1936	...	...	41,542

For admission to a Veterans' administration home, a patient was required to have a condition essentially chronic in character, not susceptible of cure or decided improvement by hospital treatment, and to be incapacitated from earning a living for a prospective period. As of June 30, 1946, there were 11 homes with a total capacity of 15,292 beds; at the beginning of the fiscal year 1937 there were 12 homes with 18,756 beds. The greater need for hospital beds resulted in the conversion of some space into hospital wards, which accounted in part for the reduction of beds in homes. Veterans receiving home care on June 30, 1946, numbered 11,052. Admissions during the year totalled 14,056; World War II, 2,445; World War I 10,395; and all other veterans, 1,216. Ten years earlier there were 9,586 veterans in homes, of which 84% were World War I veterans.

Out-patient clinics in Veterans' administration hospitals and regional offices continued to offer medical and dental services to veterans needing treatment for service-connected illness and injury not requiring hospitalization. In addition, medical and dental examinations continued to be made to determine the need for hospital care and for disability rating for pensions and for insurance purposes.

Out-patient medical and dental treatment for the year ending June 30, 1937, totalled 816,702 and 78,506 respectively. During the year ending June 30, 1946, there were 1,502,309 medical treatments and 160,400 dental treatments. The increase, of course, was due to the greater number of veterans to be served.

Insurance.—National service life insurance was authorized by the National Service Life Insurance act of 1940 for all members of the armed forces ordered to active duty for more than 30 days, in amounts of not less than $1,000 or not more than $10,000, in multiples of $500. The passage of this law terminated the right of persons entering the armed forces after Oct. 8, 1940, to purchase U.S. government life insurance unless they otherwise were eligible as veterans of World War I.

All national service life insurance was written initially on the five-year level premium term plan with the right to convert to a permanent plan any time within the term period after the term policy has been in force for one year. On July 2, 1945, the term period was extended on all policies written before Jan. 1, 1946, for an additional period of three years at the same premium rate. All policy holders acquired the right to continue their insurance in force after discharge from active service.

The Insurance act of 1946 liberalized the provisions of the National Service Life Insurance act of 1940, as amended, to meet the needs and desires of veterans under peacetime conditions. Restrictions were removed from the choice of beneficiaries, three endowment plans were added to the ordinary life, 20-payment life and 30-payment life already authorized, provision was made for additional optional settlements and protection against total disability for six months or more was made available in a separate policy provision for an extra premium and compliance with health requirements.

The total number of applications for national service life insurance approved through Aug 31, 1946, was 18,915,869 for an aggregate amount of $147,709,774,000 of insurance. As of the same date, there were in force under premium-paying conditions an estimated 6,195,000 policies for $38,615,520,000 of insurance, an average of $6,233 per policy. As a direct result of war casualties and other deaths of more than 369,000 insured lives up to and including Aug. 31, 1946, monthly instalments were being paid to beneficiaries on more than $3,300,000,000 of insurance awarded on death claims to that date.

United States government life insurance, initially known as war risk insurance (World War I), was authorized by amendment to the War Risk Insurance act (1917) to enable those who served in the armed forces during World War I to purchase insurance from the government in amounts of not less than $1,000 or more than $10,000, in multiples of $500. Approximately 4,500,000 persons applied for almost $40,000,000,000 of war risk term insurance between Oct. 6, 1917, and Nov. 11, 1918. Under the provisions of the original act, conversion from term to permanent United States government life insurance could not be made until after the close of the war; consequently the first policy of this kind was granted in May 1919. As of Aug. 31, 1946, there were in force 547,470 United States government life insurance policies representing $2,373,366,156 of insurance.

Article IV of the Soldiers' and Sailors' Civil Relief act of 1940, as amended, provided a method whereby the government under certain conditions, upon application by the insured, guaranteed commercial life insurance policies against lapse for the nonpayment of premiums while the insured was in active service and for two years after discharge under certain conditions. Through Aug 31, 1946, approved applications under article IV of the Civil Relief act totalled 89,048 for an amount of $221,923,103 of life insurance—an average amount of $2,492 per policy.

Pensions and Compensation.—Laws enacted during the period 1937–46 considerably increased the rates of pension and compensation and liberalized the conditions of entitlement to permit the allowance of these benefits to additional classes of dependents. At the close of the ten-year period, death pensions and compensation were being paid to the widows, children and dependent parents of veterans who served in the Mexican, Civil and Indian Wars, as well as the Spanish-American War, Boxer Rebellion, Philippine Insurrection and World Wars I and II, and in addition to the dependents of those who served during peacetime.

As of June 30, 1946, 36% of the death pension and compensation benefits being paid were based on World War II service, while 42% were for World War I service, 3% for peacetime service and the balance, 19%, for service rendered during the Spanish-American War and prior wars.

Disbursements for compensation and pension from July 1, 1945, to June 30, 1946, totalled $1,260,000,000, of which $733,000,000 was for World War II service, $346,000,000 for World War I service, $24,000,000 for service in the regular establishment and $157,000,000 for service in the Spanish-American War and previous wars. Of the $733,000,000 for World War II, $698,000,000 was for service-connected cases. On June 30, 1946, pensions at the average monthly rate of $54.90 were being paid to the dependents of 180,938 deceased veterans of World War II.

Education and Training.—Two public laws provided for education and training of World War II veterans. Public Law No. 16, 78th congress, as amended by Public Laws Nos. 346, 78th congress, and 268, 79th congress, provided for eligible disabled veterans with handicaps removable by training with the purpose of restoring employability. Title II of the Servicemen's Readjustment act of 1944 (the "G.I. Bill of Rights") provided for eligible nondisabled veterans. The latter law directed the Veterans' administration to furnish guidance to veterans in educational and vocational matters, but recognized supervision of training of students studying under the law as the function of the state institutions. Under the Readjustment act, the period of education or training to which a nondisabled veteran was eligible was determined in part by his length of wartime military service, with the maximum four years. The disabled veteran eligible for vocational rehabilitation could receive a suitable course possibly extending for four years, or for a longer period, if necessary and approved by the Veterans' administration.

As of June 30, 1946, 413,613 veterans had applied for vocational rehabilitation training; 92,213 were in training; 28,253 had interrupted training; and 2,659 had been rehabilitated.

Gen. Omar Bradley visiting convalescents at a veterans' hospital in New York city. Gen. Bradley took office as administrator of veterans affairs on Aug. 15, 1945

Of the number in training, 52,150 were in training in educational institutions and 40,063 were in training on the job.

Of the number in training in educational institutions, 34,226 were in professional, technical and managerial courses; 5,521 were in clerical and sales courses; 970 were in training for service occupations; 1,386 were in agricultural and kindred courses; and 10,047 were in trade and industrial courses.

As of June 30, 1946, 2,924,115 veterans had applied for education or training; 930,512 were in training; 234,181 had interrupted training, and 985 had exhausted their entitlement.

Of the number in training, 612,690 were in training in educational institutions and 317,822 were in training on the job.

Of those in training in educational institutions, 338,158 were in university, college, professional and technological schools; 21,327 were in teacher's colleges and normal schools; 19,590 were in junior colleges; 161,602 were in business colleges, vocational and trade schools and 72,013 were in other schools below college level.

Readjustment Allowances.—Operations under Title V of the Readjustment act of 1944, were begun on a nationwide basis on Sept. 4, 1944. Subsequently the Readjustment Allowances program, which provided, within certain limitations, financial assistance to both unemployed and self-employed veterans, was extended by Public Law No. 268, 79th congress, to include U.S. citizens who were in active service with Allied governments during World War II.

In the period Sept. 4, 1944, to June 30, 1946, a total of

Table II.—*Insurance Cases on Which Death Claims Were Being Paid at the Close of Each Fiscal Year*

Kind of insurance	June 30, 1946	Amount of insurance	June 30, 1945	Amount of insurance	June 30, 1937	Amount of insurance
Yearly renewable term, automatic and gratuitous	954	$5,374,117	2,053	$12,858,422	125,436	$1,035,484,603
United States government life	14,682	103,288,353	13,035	92,856,258	4,993	35,852,814
National Service Life	357,606	3,334,419,900	223,154	2,035,991,700	...	...

Table III.—*U.S. Veterans on Roll*

(Number of living veterans and deceased veterans whose dependents were receiving compensation and pension benefits, including retirement pay for living veterans)

Wars and regular establishment	On roll June 30, 1946	On roll June 30, 1945	On roll June 30, 1937
Total	2,631,981	1,513,586	841,937
Living veterans	2,130,353	1,144,088	598,510
Deceased veterans	501,628	369,498	243,427
War of 1812:			
Deceased veterans		1	2
Mexican War:			
Deceased veterans	51	55	221
Indian Wars	3,467	3,788	7,709
Living veterans	971	1,115	3,119
Deceased veterans	2,496	2,673	4,590
Civil War	21,658	24,750	83,162
Living veterans	154	229	7,031
Deceased veterans	21,504	24,521	76,131
Spanish-American War	194,609	200,059	225,653
Living veterans	121,572	128,104	175,361
Deceased veterans	73,037	71,955	50,292
World War I	632,218	587,589	484,045
Living veterans	422,429	425,589	379,963
Deceased veterans	209,789	162,000	104,082
World War II	1,722,448	640,753	...
Living veterans	1,541,510	546,126	...
Deceased veterans	180,938	94,627	...
Regular establishment	57,530	56,591	41,145
Living veterans	43,717	42,925	33,036
Deceased veterans	13,813	13,666	8,109

5,533,136 veterans filed applications for determination of entitlement for allowances, of whom 180,798 filed during the fiscal year 1945 and 5,352,338 during the fiscal year 1946. A total of 5,231,391 veterans submitted new claims for unemployment allowances, of whom 159,739 submitted their claims during the fiscal year 1945, and 5,071,652 during the fiscal year 1946.

A total of 368,754 veterans filed new claims for self-employment allowances, of whom 12,951 filed claims during the fiscal year 1945 and 355,803 during the fiscal year 1946.

Weekly claims for unemployment totalled 46,667,570, including 1,062,481 for the fiscal year 1945 and 45,605,060 for the fiscal year 1946; monthly claims covering self-employment filed totalled 1,449,494, including 38,709 for the fiscal year 1945 and 1,410,785 for the fiscal year 1946. Veterans paid allowances for unemployment received an average of approximately ten weekly payments during the fiscal year ending June 30, 1946.

Disbursements for the fiscal year 1945 totalled $24,155,-313, of which $20,719,059 represented payments to unemployed veterans and $3,436,254 payments to self-employed veterans.

During the month of June 1945 a weekly average of 31,-832 veterans received unemployment allowances aggregating $3,572,009, while $1,059,178 was paid to 10,624 self-employed veterans. During the same period in 1946, a weekly average of 1,780,604 continued claims for unemployment allowances were filed, payments for unemployment allowances aggregated $176,774,520, while $27,663,-306 was paid to 261,811 self-employed veterans.

Loan Guarantee Activities.—Title III of the Readjustment act of 1944, amended by Public Law 268, 79th congress, made provision within certain limitations for the guarantee of loans or insurance of credit through private lending institutions to veterans of World War II for the purchase or construction of homes, farms and business property.

From Nov. 1944, when loan guarantee activities began, to the close of the fiscal year, June 30, 1945, applications for loans totalled 15,455. Of this number, 12,228 guaranteed commitments were issued for a total of $19,644,824.90, distributed by types as follows: home loans 11,220; farm loans 270; and business loans 738. From July 1, 1945 to June 28, 1946, applications received for guarantee of loans totalled 278,571. Of this number, 223,911 were guaranteed for a total of $374,332,688.20, distributed by types as follows: home loans 197,787, average guarantee $1,749; farm loans 7,500, average guarantee $1,183; and business loans 18,624, average guarantee $1,045. The over-all average guarantee was $1,672.

Through June 28, 1946, a total of 1,266 loans had been repaid in full, against which the combined guaranty commitments totalled $1,743,767.23; defaults, comprising, 26% of loans to that date, totalled 507.

Guardianship.—Reflecting the effects of World War II, the guardianship load of the Veterans' administration rose from a total of 87,346 wards June 30, 1945, to 121,006 wards June 30, 1946.

Of the 87,346 wards in the fiscal year 1945, 73,966 were entitled to benefits because of service by veterans of World War I and other wars, and included 40,771 incompetents (veterans or their dependents) and 33,195 minors; 13,380 wards were entitled to benefits on account of service by veterans of World War II and included 4,326 incompetents and 9,054 minors.

Of the 121,006 wards in the fiscal year 1946, 83,976 wards were entitled to benefits on account of service by veterans of World War I and other wars, and included 39,991 incompetents and 43,985 minors; 37,030 wards were entitled to benefits on account of service by veterans of World War II and included 6,432 incompetents and 30,598 minors.

Thus, from 1945 to 1946 there was a decrease of 780 incompetents but an increase of 10,790 minors, or a total increase of 10,010 wards from World War I service and other wars.

Within the same year, from World War II service, there was an increase of 2,106 incompetents and an increase of 21,544 minors, or a total increase of 23,650 wards.

Table IV.—*Guardianship Load 1937–46*

Fiscal year	Total wards	Incompetents	Minors	Value of estates
1946	121,006	46,423	74,583	$177,532,742.05
1945	87,346	45,097	42,249	163,158,557.78
1944	78,456	44,242	34,214	157,434,444.79
1943	77,970	43,214	34,756	155,709,290.63
1942	81,114	43,336	37,778	159,935,514.67
1941	83,439	43,476	39,963	159,370,982.23
1940	83,776	43,492	40,284	158,514,599.52
1939	84,749	43,376	41,373	157,238,769.58
1938	85,865	43,214	42,651	156,870,857.23
1937	85,977	42,937	43,040	144,072,912.69

Finance.—The grand totals of net disbursements for the fiscal years 1937–1946 were as in Table V.

Table V.—*Total Net Disbursements*

Fiscal year		Fiscal year	
1946	$4,772,072,218.89	1941	$614,357,411.24
1945	2,271,318,333.42	1940	639,126,696.89
1944	828,391,436.33	1939	600,221,534.14
1943	643,406,394.64	1938	629,829,721.73
1942	647,333,991.90	1937	893,994,175.08

The 1937 grand total included $282,656,226.02 for World War I veterans' Adjusted-Service certificates and represented payments made on the certificates and amounts reimbursed to the U.S. government life insurance fund on account of loans made from that fund on certificates under the provisions of the World War Adjusted Compensation act as amended, and the Adjusted Compensation Payment act, 1936.

(*See also* PENSIONS, WAR [BRITISH AND EUROPEAN]; REHABILITATION OF THE DISABLED.)

BIBLIOGRAPHY.—*Annual Report of the Administrator of Veterans' Affairs*, for the years 1937–46. (O. N. B.)

Veterans of Foreign Wars

See Societies and Associations.

Veterinary Medicine

The decade 1937–46 saw a rapid growth in the adoption of veterinary medicine as a profession. Several new colleges of veterinary medicine were founded, and there was a steady improvement in educational standards to meet the demands of the livestock and food industries.

An important milestone in veterinary research was the establishment of laboratories by the U.S. department of agriculture in the east, west, middle west and south to implement the work of the agricultural experiment stations on animal pathology and to encourage the use of scientific practices in animal production. Significant advances were made in the prevention and treatment of a number of animal diseases.

Bovine Tuberculosis and Brucellosis.—The U.S. campaign against bovine tuberculosis, started on a nation-wide basis in 1917, was officially declared complete in 1940. The incidence of tuberculosis among cattle had been reduced to 0.5% of the total bovine population, at a cost of approximately $60,000,000. The objective was attained by the slaughter and post-mortem inspection of all cattle that reacted to the tuberculin (Mantoux) test.

Brucellosis of cattle, known also as Bang's disease, contagious abortion, and abortion disease, continued to menace the cattle-breeding industry throughout the world despite genuinely vigorous efforts to suppress it by sanitary methods and vaccination. The attenuated culture (vaccine) of *Brucella abortus,* known as "Strain 19," developed by the Animal Disease Research laboratory of the U.S. bureau of animal industry, was approved for general use in 1940 after five years of critical field trials in widely separated parts of the country. Though its preventive value was unquestioned, lack of uniform regulations among the states was a deterrent. Medical literature testified to the growing prevalence of brucellosis (undulant fever) in human beings exposed to infected animals. A significant discovery in this connection was the high virulence of swine brucellosis (*Brucella suis* infection) in man. The swine-to-cow-to-man passage of the specific organism was definitely confirmed in endemics during the decade.

Phenothiazine.—The high vermicide properties of phenothiazine in farm animals and its low toxicity ranked among the far-reaching gains in veterinary chemotherapeutics. No worm remedy for livestock removed as many kinds of intestinal parasites from as many species of hosts as did this drug. Its worm-removing power and concurrent safety was the long-sought combination required to keep the health-sapping entozoons of domestic animals under control. The anthelmintic properties of phenothiazine, therefore, ranked among the sensational discoveries of the period in animal medicine. Worm-infected farm animals, pastoral ruminants in particular, suffered from blood-sucking nematodes of the genus *Strongylus* which took a heavy toll in death losses, emaciating gastritis, suppressed growth, and loss of weight, especially when pastured on the same ground year after year. In terms of food poundage, deaths and net income, the losses were extremely large in swine, cattle, horses, sheep, poultry and dogs, during the period of youth and adolescence.

Phenothiazine was found to be somewhat toxic in anaemic horses and mules and young pigs. Otherwise, its safety was remarkable in view of its deadly action on intestinal worms which formerly had responded only to highly poisonous drugs. An inexpensive anthelmintic for mass treatment of gregarious livestock by simply mixing it in the feed of confined animals or the salt lick of pastoral herds, belonged in the records as a useful discovery. In turkeys, important results were obtained against the caecal worm, *Histomonas meleagridis,* the causative agent of enterohepatitis. Phenothiazine was not found useful in canine and feline medicine.

Equine Encephalomyelitis.—Equine encephalomyelitis, a filtrable virus infection affecting horse, man, laboratory animals and various genera of wildlife, was a serious threat to horses during the decade 1937–46. Although this neurotrophic disease was found to be due to a filtrable virus in 1930, and in 1932 was already suspected of being transmissible to human beings, the virus was first isolated in the human corpse in 1938. In 1939, two distinctly separate viruses, eastern and western, were isolated from the brains of horses. Later, a third virus was isolated from horses in Venezuela. Each of these viruses was found to be interchangeable between animals and man. In the early 1930s, R. A. Kelser demonstrated 11 species of *Aedes* in the role of vector between horses. The disease in horses can be controlled by annual vaccination consisting of two injections of a chick-embryo vaccine, developed in 1939 by the Rockefeller Institute of Medical Research. A condensed description of the disease was published in the 1942 *Year Book* of the U.S. department of agriculture.

Poultry Meat Inspection.—Revolutionary changes took place in the sanitary inspection of poultry at the time of slaughter. Customarily, the bulk of killed fowl enter the channels of trade as "dressed poultry," which in the language of the trade signifies poultry with head, neck and internal organs intact, the latter incasing their fermentable contents untouched until "drawn" at some future time in the meat market or kitchen. The time-honoured custom of removing the visceral organs of the fresh carcass and inspecting them for clues as to the fitness of the edible parts had not been deemed economically feasible in the marketing of killed poultry until the production-line principle of the industrial arts was introduced and quick-freezing methods invented.

The invention of equipment which the small poultry-dressing plant could afford to install, rapidly changed the scheme of poultry marketing from insanitary to hygienic. In continuous flow, fowl could be bled, plucked, decapitated, eviscerated and inspected, rinsed, dried, graded, packed and frozen, and sent into the market in prime sanitary condition at reasonable cost.

The reform grew out of the fact that standard meat inspection begins with a critical inspection of the internal organs by a trained technician who, under the regulations of the U.S. bureau of animal industry, veterinary corps of the army, the U.S. public health service, and public health agencies generally, is defined as a graduate of an accredited college of veterinary medicine—a technician familiar with animal diseases and their potentiality in food hygiene. Avoiding unnecessary rejections which diminish food poundage is as much an object of meat inspection as rejecting the unfit. The evisceration and sanitary inspection of poultry at the time of slaughter made phenomenal gains. In the early 1930s there were three poultry-eviscerating plants in two large cities employing three veterinary inspectors compared with many such plants scattered throughout the U.S. from coast to coast in 1946 and supervised by a force of 135 veterinarians directed by a chief veterinarian from the headquarters of the U.S. department of agriculture.

Artificial Insemination.—Whereas the artificial insemination of farm animals had been practised on a large scale for years in the U.S.S.R., interest in the procedure among livestock farmers in the United States began in the 1930s and only among breeders of dairy cattle. Artificial insemination in other animals was resorted to only in isolated instances. In the dairy cattle field, it was promoted by forming breeding societies with centrally-located establishments equipped for the management of the bulls and for skilful collection of semen. Trained veterinarians or other technicians were employed by the society to care for the bulls, collect and transport semen, and perform the insemination on call of its members.

Methods of diluting and preserving viable semen permitted the impregnation of a number of animals from one ejaculation and the shipping of semen for long distances.

The small dairy farmer was thus saved the trouble and expense of keeping a bull the year around and of breeding cows to sires of proved prepotency. Venereal infections were prevented, and a larger number of offspring was obtainable from the given sire.

Rabies.—The prevalence of rabies in dogs, farm animals and wildlife steadily increased in the United States during the decade. Because the federal laws pertaining to animal diseases still did not classify dogs as livestock, rabies fell to the sketchy action of the states or communities where outbreaks occurred. Quoting scientists of the U.S. bureau of animal industry: "Outstanding livestock sanitarians visiting this country from abroad expressed amazement at the prevalence of rabies in the United States, a country in which such great strides have been made in the control and eradication of foot and mouth disease, tuberculosis, brucellosis and other contagious diseases of animals."

The campaign against rabies vaccination by certain dog-owning groups, and the objection to the passage of a federal law that would enable livestock sanitary officials to cope with dogs as with other animals, were blamed for the tragic situation. Little progress was made in the handling of this disease of man and animals, despite the feasibility of its complete eradication. Canada, Great Britain, South Africa and other countries prohibited the import of U.S. dogs.

DDT.—The chemical, Dichloro-diphenyl-trichloroethane, abridged to DDT, came into use in veterinary medicine in 1943. In three years, its worthiness in livestock production was proved in extensive trials. Aside from the vectors of specific infections, insects reduce the tonnage of meat and milk by molesting animals in the pasture and stable. The horn fly (*Haematobia serrata*) and the common stable fly (*Stomoxys calcitrans*) are examples of harmful insects. Swarms of the former actually make pastoral animals run themselves thin. Entomologists charged the horn fly with reducing the production of meat and milk by one-half in vast areas. The common stable fly, unless kept under rigid control, was also pronounced a major menace of the dairy farm. DDT was shown capable of destroying both. The value of this agent in veterinary medicine could be summed up from these two examples, since there were few ectoparasites of farm animals that did not yield to its diligent use.

Newcastle Disease of Poultry.—The grave virus infection of domestic fowl named Newcastle disease for the British community on the Tyne where it was first recognized in 1928, was found to exist in 20 or more states, in a somewhat milder than usual form. Identification of the respiratory-nervous disease, pneumoencephalitis, of California poultry with Newcastle disease of foreign countries caused widespread alarm among U.S. poultrymen. A conference of poultry pathologists was hurriedly convened at St. Louis, Mo., in 1946, under the sponsorship of the U.S. bureau of animal industry, to plan a definite program for its control. Although the disease was described as a special entity in the Dutch East Indies in 1926, in England in 1928, and thereafter in various parts of the world, it was previously known only as an exotic fowl plague in the United States. As the virulence varied from mild to serious in different outbreaks and its extent remained undetermined, the course of the disease in the United States was unforeseeable at the end of the decade. A review of the animal-disease situation marked the early 1940s as the period in which Newcastle disease was recognized in the western hemisphere.

Sulfonamides.—This group of chemotherapeutic agents was extensively employed after 1937, when sulfanilamide established its superior bacteriostatic action against the ambient flora surrounding domestic animals. This chemical and its numerous companions revolutioned the treatment of a long list of local and general infections of the acute type among which were surgical peritonitis, metroperitonitis, metritis, mastitis, enteritidis, dysentery, coccidiosis, pneumonia, haemorrhagic septicaemia, streptococcal meningitis and the gamut of wound infections. The drugs which achieved popularity through merit were sulfanilamide, sulfamerazine, sulfadiazine, sulfaguanidine, sulfapyridine, sulfasuxidine, and sulfathalidine. Sulfanilamide held its popularity for topical use, sulfaguanidine for intestinal infections, and sulfapyridine for acute bronchopulmonary diseases. Preferences for the others were published, but on the whole, sharp discrimination remained in the field of investigation. Competent critics pointed out that the sulfa drugs were, unfortunately, turning veterinary surgeons away from the refined technique of aseptic surgery.

Antibiotics.—While considerable experimental work was done on the therapeutic value of gramicidin (tyrothricin and tyrocidine), penicillin and streptomycin in veterinary medicine, and important responses were obtained, more extensive clinical use under natural conditions was required to establish the exact places they were destined to occupy in the practice of veterinary medicine. Up to 1947, the cost had been prohibitive. Notwithstanding the fact that bovine mastitis caused by *Streptococcus agalactiae,* for example, responded to intramammary infusions of these antibiotic agents, and significant results in other infections were demonstrated, the price remained too high for general use. With rare exceptions in individual animals of great value, the economics of therapeutic measures continued to rule in animal medicine.

Leptospirosis.—Leptospirosis, or Weil's disease of dogs, caused by the protozoon, *Leptospira canicola,* and Stuttgart disease or canine typhus were found to be identical with Leptospira infection or Weil's disease of the human being. The two practically identical microbes—*L. canicola* and *L. icterohaemorrhagiae*—both originating in rats, as a rule, were found to be interchangeable between man and dogs in natural infections. That is to say, Stuttgart disease, which is a pellagra-like malady of dogs formerly believed to be a nutritional deficiency, leptospirosis of dogs known to be caused by *L. canicola,* and leptospirosis or Weil's disease of man, which had been definitely attributed to *L. icterohaemorrhagiae,* were shown to be one and the same disease according to research carried out within the decade 1937–46. In veterinary medicine, the significance of this finding lay in proofs that man might contract leptospirosis from dogs and vice versa.

Listerellosis.—Listerellosis, or "circling disease" of sheep, cattle, chickens and swine, is an infectious meningo-encephalitis described in New Zealand in 1931, in Indiana in 1932, in Illinois in 1937, and in Iowa in 1939. *Listerella monocytogenes*, previously thought to be pathogenic in laboratory animals only, was isolated in the enzootics reported. Six outbreaks in sheep, seven in cattle, and one in chickens, were reported by animal pathologists of the University of Illinois in 1937–40. Attempts at immunization were negative. The use of sulfonamides gave promising results. The point of interest was that another infectious disease of farm animals became known in North America.

Infectious Keratitis of Cattle.—A notable advance in animal pathology was the discovery in 1944 of the specific agent of the grave ocular disease of range and other pastoral cattle known as pinkeye, infectious conjunctivitis, or infectious keratitis. The malady was ubiquitous in the United States and Canada, and was reported in South Africa, Germany, France and other countries. In range cattle it caused heavy losses by destroying the eyesight, partially or totally, temporarily or permanently. From their inability to find water and graze food, affected animals emaciated and starved, suffered severe injury on rugged terrain by falling, or died by drowning. The cause was obscure.

Bright sunlight and a mixed secondary infection summed up its aetiology, despite years of diligent search among the mixed flora of the affected eyes for a specific microorganism.

In 1944–45, E. M. Baldwin, Jr., of the College of Veterinary Medicine, Ohio State university, working with western cattle, isolated a plump, gram-negative, nonsporulating, nonmotile bacillus of the genus *Hemophilus* which proved to be the specific agent in a series of well-controlled experiments.

The discovery was heralded as a step toward the control of the disease.

Bovine Mastitis.—The prevalence of mastitis in cows supplying market milk remained high in the milk sheds supplying milk for the large cities. In the face of exacting demands for higher grade milk and the complexity of its production and distribution, mastitis continued to be a baffling problem for the dairy farmer and his veterinarian under the existing method of handling milk cows. Because cleanliness in the surgical sense was not regarded as feasible amid the swarming flora of the byre, and the prevention of teat injuries (said to be the chief cause) was not possible under the customary method of housing milking herds, the trend was toward a complete revamping of old methods, milk production having increased faster than production methods had improved. Already, dairy farmers were beginning to herd their cows in an adjacent enclosure between milkings and bring them two at a time to a clean room to be milked. Under the prevailing setup (stable, stanchion, hard floor, excrement gutter, cow, milker, udder, milk, and utensils), the assemblage became a gigantic reservoir for germs and an excellent incubator which tended to nullify local antiseptic infusions. Among the drugs employed for intramammary infusion were iodine, acridine dyes, silver oxide, sulfonamides and antibiotics (gramicidin and penicillin). Whereas these germicides had certain therapeutic values, the consensus was that reforming the customary herd management would be necessary to control mastitis.

Trichinosis.—Although trichinosis of swine was presumed to antedate the Mosaic injunction against the eating of pork, thorough cooking as a preventive measure was of later origin. *Trichinella spiralis*, the specific metazoon, was discovered in human cadavers in 1835 by James Paget in England, and Joseph Leidy in the U.S. found the adult worm in carcasses of swine in 1846, not to ignore scientists whose investigations led to these climactic findings. In 1916 B. H. Ransom of the U.S. bureau of animal industry demonstrated that refrigeration of pork at 5° F. for 20 min. destroyed the viability of trichinae and that shorter exposures at lower temperatures were likewise protective. A third preventive measure recommended by hygienists of the food industries was the quick freezing of all pork at low temperatures before releasing it to the markets. Protagonists of the frozen-food idea contended that quick freezing of pork and a short period of storage in the frozen state would solve the trichinosis problem of human medicine. *T. spiralis* is commensal in animals so far as could be detected in the living subject but, as generally known, continued to be deadly to man. According to extensive investigations of the U.S. public health service and other agencies, the incidence was higher in man than in any animal thus far critically studied.

Veterinary Service in World War II.—In order to provide the U.S. army with the stated quota of veterinary officers without depriving important livestock areas of an adequate force of veterinarians, the veterinary service of the United States in 1941 was organized and operated under national authority—the Procurement and Assignment Service for Physicians, Dentists and Veterinarians—to the end that the military forces were able to acquire the largest force of veterinarians ever mobilized for wartime duty, and animal diseases were kept under rigid control.

Whereas each infantry division of World War I had 6,719 horses and mules, the transportation of the same unit of World War II was practically all mechanical. It might be deemed strange, therefore, that a larger force of veterinarians was needed in World War II. The paradox was explained by the fact that horses, mules, donkeys, camels, pigeons, caribou, war dogs and laboratory animals, each one a precious element of the command at times and places where replacements could not be obtained at any price—called for the best medical attention possible. Among these animals there were glanders, anthrax, tetanus, African horse sickness, surra, encephalomyelitis, variola, canine distemper, and many other maladies to prevent by vaccination or other means.

The regulation that "soldiers shall not touch any food not inspected by the Veterinary Corps," explained why a highly-trained veterinary service was needed in modern warfare. Training schools were maintained at large meatpacking and food-processing centres to accomplish that end. The military rations were inspected from the source of the food to its delivery to troops at distant outposts and hospital ships, to cars, trucks and storage under unfavourable climatic conditions.

The veterinary corps was also called upon for sanitary policing of native animals surrounding faraway military stations, and for the study and possible control of exotic infections and parasitisms.

Bibliography.—H. J. Milks, *Practical Veterinary Pharmacology, Materia Medica and Therapeutics*, 5th ed. (1946); D. M. Campbell, *Veterinary Service in Wartime* (1942).

(L. A. M.)

V.F.W. (Veterans of Foreign Wars)

See Societies and Associations.

Vichy

One of the best known French spas, the alkaline waters of which helped generations of gourmets suffering from stomach catarrh or liver complaints, Vichy became famous as the temporary capital of the unoccupied zone of France after the capitulation of June 22, 1940. This chief town of the Allier *département*, with a population of 25,074, had in 1937 more than 138,000 *baigneurs*, including 13,000 foreigners. In the summer of 1940, however, quite a different kind of temporary visitor filled its palatial hotels and modest *pensions:* French politicians, generals, admirals, civil servants, journalists, and also foreign diplomats. Hôtel du Parc became the headquarters of Marshal Philippe Pétain, chief of the ephemeral "Etat Français," and of Pierre Laval, his vice-premier and minister of foreign affairs until Dec. 15, 1940, and again from April 18, 1942, when under German pressure Pétain had to restore to power the man whom he had previously dismissed "in the interest of the nation."

Admiral Jean Darlan, the other vice-premier and heir apparent to marshal's mantle as chief of state, resided as navy minister at the Hôtel du Helder. Ironically enough, the Hôtel Britannique was the seat of the ministry of colonies and the Hotel de Russie accommodated the ministry of the interior. All the foreign embassies and legations were crowded in the Hôtel des Ambassadeurs. Many Paris daily newspapers, such as the Conservative *Figaro* and *Journal des Débats,* the big business *Temps,* the royalist *Action Française,* the Catholic *Croix* and the socialist but pro-Pétain *Effort* transferred their editorial offices from the occupied capital to Vichy. Many right-wing weeklies and monthlies did the same. At the end of 1940 the wartime population of Vichy exceeded 62,000. After the occupation by the Germans of the "free zone" (Nov. 11, 1942) the population slightly declined and in the summer of 1944 was estimated at 56,000.

The Allied landings in southern France (Aug. 15, 1944) forced Pétain and his administration to leave for Belfort and later for Sigmaringen. Liberated by the French forces of the interior, Vichy recovered its municipal freedom. The city council, appointed by the Pétainist *préfet* in 1940, was dissolved, and a new council was elected on April 29, 1945; very similar to the pre-1939 political composition, it

Marshal Pétain's guard, detailed to the office of the secretary of war at Vichy in 1942

consisted of moderate republicans, Catholics and radicals. The first postwar year which could be described as normal was 1946: in this year the permanent population of Vichy was 29,391. The season was good, but far from the prewar mark; there were only 71,409 *baigneurs,* including 6,214 foreigners. No apparent changes were found by the visitors, as neither in 1940 nor in 1944 was there any fighting in Vichy, and the city was never bombed.

Victoria

A state of the Australian commonwealth, Victoria has an area of 87,884 sq.mi.; pop.: (1937 est.) 1,859,487;

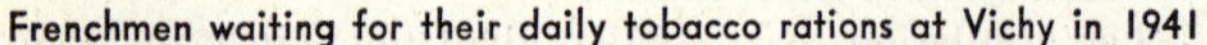
Frenchmen waiting for their daily tobacco rations at Vichy in 1941

(1946 census) 2,029,800. Chief cities (pop. 1945 est.): Melbourne (cap., 1,184,000); Geelong (41,300); Ballarat (39,500); Bendigo (30,900). Governors: Lord William Huntingfield (Dec. 1933–Nov. 1938); Maj. Gen. Sir Winston Dugan (after Nov. 9, 1938). Prime ministers: Albert A. Dunstan (1935–43); John Cain (four days only); Albert A. Dunstan (1943–Oct. 1945); Ian Macfarlan (four weeks only); John Cain (after Nov. 21, 1945).

During the life of the first Dunstan government, a new formula was introduced for settling disputes between the legislative council and the legislative assembly (upper house); it replaced plural voting for the legislative council with adult suffrage. Reform was also instituted in the Melbourne city council by the abolition of aldermen. Co-operative home building, under which the government guaranteed up to 90% of the cost of homes, was passed by the Victorian parliament in Dunstan's second ministry.

Main features of the Cain government's legislation included a comprehensive Soldier Settlement bill, liberalized benefits under workers' compensation, abolition of late Friday night trading, and independent tribunals for the public service, teachers and police. Two outstanding legislative moves in 1946 were the introduction of a bill to empower the government to take over the Victorian gas industry (electricity was already controlled by the government through the state electricity commission), and the establishment of a branch of the Melbourne university at Mildura, an important fruit-producing centre about 360 mi. from Melbourne.

A postwar program, estimated to cost £A50,000,000, was implemented by the Cain government. The greater portion of this amount was marked for water conservation, chief project being the construction at Eildon of a new dam to cost £A8,400,000. This was the biggest single engineering project ever contemplated in Australia. Other water conservation projects included in the program were enlargement of the Hume weir and construction of Cairn Curran, Eppalock, and Nambrok-Denison reservoirs. Other postwar works listed were the development of brown coal fields (to make Victoria less dependent on coal from the state of New South Wales), extension of electricity mains, forestry works, main roads, land settlement and the building of new schools and hospitals.

In 1939 and 1944 particularly, Victoria suffered devastatingly from bush and grass fires which in the latter year cost 51 lives and caused £A2,581,527 worth of loss in houses, outbuildings, livestock, fencing, grass, etc. In 1946 an elaborate fire-fighting scheme was established, which included two-way radio spotting aeroplanes, spotters in towers, 51,000 voluntary fire fighters, thousands of feet of hose and scores of motor vehicles. Experiments were made with royal Australian air force planes carrying "bombs" laden with fire extinguisher, which burst on impact. (A. R. Mn.)

BIBLIOGRAPHY.—M. L. Handsaker, "Theory of Marginal Productivity Tested by Data for Manufacturing," *Quart. Journ. of Econ.* 52:1–36, 215–254 (Cambridge, Nov. 1937–Feb. 1938); A. W. Marshall, *These Are My People* (Melbourne, 1944); *Victorian Yearbook* (Melbourne).

Victoria: *Statistical Data*

Item	1938 Value (000's omitted)	1938 Amount or Number	1941 Value (000's omitted)	1941 Amount or Number	1945 Value (000's omitted)	1945 Amount or Number
Exchange Rate						
Great Britain		£A 1.25=£1		£A 1.25=£1		£A 1.25=£1
United States		£A 1=$3.895		£A 1=$3.198		£A 1=$3.198
Finance						
State revenues	£22,000* ($107,560)		£23,147* ($93,327)		£27,991* ($112,803)	
State expenditures	£21,976* ($107,440)		£23,033* ($92,870)		£27,714* $111,687)	
State debt	£141,195* ($690,303)		£143,735* ($579,538)		£142,367* ($573,737)	
Transportation						
Railroads		4,721 mi.		4,759 mi.		4,748 mi.
Highways		104,087 „ †‡		105,043 „ ‡§		...
Communication						
Telephones		198,761		288,936		264,013
Telegraph lines		19,146 mi.*		19,185 mi.*§		19,243 mi.*
Radio sets		327,579*‖		362,790*		394,315*
Minerals						
Gold		144,243 oz.		149,769 oz.		56,511 oz.¶
Lignite		3,675,450 tons		4,565,638 tons		5,091,729 tons¶
Coal		307,258 „		326,441 „		287,100 „ ¶
Crops						
Hay		1,245,935 tons		580,237 tons		963,103 tons♀
Wheat		1,444,190 „		405,660 „		592,000 „ ♀
Potatoes		134,712 „		216,568 „		217,380 „ ♀
Apples		58,907 „		38,473 „ §		55,829 „ ♀
Raisins		48,504 „		41,342 „		48,851 „ ♀
Livestock						
Sheep		18,863,467♂		20,412,362♂		16,457,101♂
Cattle		1,880,429♂		1,922,336♂		1,903,110♂
Horses		359,106♂		318,441♂		253,782♂
Swine		285,259♂		397,945♂		296,232♂
Sea Products						
Fish		6,502 tons		5,958 tons§		4,862 tons♀
Crayfish		9,053 doz.		5,901 doz§		1,824 doz.♀
Manufactures						
Total	£50,731‖ ($224,990)	...	£85,406□ ($344,613)	...	£95,182♀ ($384,061)	...
Industrial metals, machines, implements, etc	£13,115‖ ($58,163)	...	£28,495□ ($114,978)	...	£37,728♀ ($152,231)	...
Food, drink and tobacco	£10,048‖ ($44,561)	...	£13,405□ ($54,088)	...	£15,099♀ ($60,925)	...
Clothing	£6,267‖ ($27,793)	...	£8,897□ ($35,898)	...	£8,782♀ ($35,434)	...
Textiles and textile goods	£5,039‖ ($22,348)	...	£9,070□ ($36,598)	...	£9,276♀ ($37,429)	...
Education						
State schools		2,688		2,640		2,584¶
Enrolment		234,802		225,023		198,567¶
Teachers		8,343		8,868		9,314¶
Private schools		516		518		504¶
Enrolment		80,161		81,308		84,511¶
Teachers		2,654		2,744		2,853¶
Universities		1		1□		1♀
Enrolment		3,670		3,180□		4,728♀
Teachers		295		355□		373♀
Technical schools		28		31		...
Enrolment		35,994		40,876		...
Teachers		1,214		1,383		...

*Year ending June 30. †1937. ‡Includes streets. §1940. ‖1939. ¶1943. ♀1944.
♂Year ending March 31. □1942.

Vie Femina Heureuse Prize

See LITERARY PRIZES.

Vinson, Frederick Moore

Vinson (1890–), U.S. jurist, was born Jan. 22, 1890, at Louisa, Ky. A graduate of Kentucky Normal college, 1908, he later attended Centre college, receiving his B.A., 1909, and his law degree, 1911. He was commonwealth attorney of the 32nd judicial district of Kentucky, 1921–24, and served seven terms in the federal house of representatives.

Vinson assisted in formulating revenue legislation as a member of the house ways and means committee. Strongly prolabour at that time, he voted for the National Labor Relations board, and helped push the undistributed profits tax bill through congress. In 1937 he was named by President F. D. Roosevelt to the post of associate justice in the U.S. court of appeals (Washington, D.C.), assuming his new duties in May 1938. He returned to active government service in May 1943 as director of the Office of Economic Stabilization.

President Roosevelt appointed Vinson federal loan administrator in charge of the Reconstruction Finance corporation (March 5, 1945) and director of the Office of War Mobilization and Reconversion (April 2). President Truman appointed him secretary of the treasury after Henry Morgenthau's resignation; he was sworn into this office on July 23.

On March 11, 1946, Vinson was elected chairman of the board of governors of both the International Bank for Reconstruction and Development and the International Monetary fund, whose delegates were then meeting in Savannah, Ga. He was named chief justice of the U.S. supreme court by President Truman on June 6, and was sworn into office on June 24, 1946.

Vinyl Products

See Chemistry; Industrial Research; Plastics Industry; Rayon and Other Synthetic Fibres; Textile Industry.

Virginia

Southernmost of the middle Atlantic states, Virginia was one of the 13 original United States; popularly known as the "Old Dominion" and as the "Mother of Presidents." Area, 40,815 sq.mi., including 916 sq.mi. of water. Population (1940) 2,677,773, of which 35.3% were urban and 64.7% rural; an estimate placed the white population at 2,013,723 and nonwhite at 664,050. On July 1, 1944, the bureau of census estimated the population of the state at 3,199,115. Capital, Richmond (193,042). Other cities include Norfolk (144,332), Roanoke (69,287) and Portsmouth (50,745).

At the beginning of the decade 1937–46, the leading state officials were: governor, George C. Peery; lieutenant governor, James H. Price; attorney general, A. P. Staples. In the Democratic primary election of Aug. 1937, Lt. Gov. James H. Price was nominated over Vivian Page for governor; Saxon W. Holt over Robert W. Daniel for lieutenant governor, and attorney general A. P. Staples, renominated. These nominees were elected in the usual Democratic victory which won 94 of 100 seats in the house of delegates.

On Jan. 19, 1938, Price was inaugurated governor. Legislation in 1938 included: public assistance, housing and unemployment, all acts toward carrying out programs fixed by the national government; a comprehensive county zoning act; authorization for erecting a new state library building; perfection of control granted state hospital board; regulation of outdoor advertising on public highways; and revisions in the system of dispensing justice. Judicial salaries were increased, and a voluntary retirement plan was introduced for certain judicial officers; procedure before the supreme court of appeals was amended to expedite its work; and the Bar Integration act allowed that court to organize and govern the state bar association as an administrative agency to investigate and report violations of rules and regulations adopted by that court for controlling the professional conduct of lawyers. An innovation in state law was the enabling legislation relating to the creation of the Hampton Roads sanitation district, comprising several counties, cities and towns, to eliminate pollution in adjacent waters.

Following the trend of studying subjects thoroughly before taking legislative action, the general assembly assigned topics to advisory legislative council or to special commissions as follows: apportionment of house and senatorial districts; coal industry; codification of general insurance and school laws; game and inland fisheries; jail system; labour relations; and a state civil service plan. While the federal government retained title to the property, the federal Farm Security administration allocated to Virginia 45,000 ac. in Appomattox, Buckingham, Cumberland and Prince Edward counties for state park purposes. Appomattox surrender ground, 1,000 ac., was to be turned over to the national park service.

Principal state officials serving with Gov. Price in 1939 were: Saxon W. Holt, lieutenant governor; Raymond L. Jackson, secretary of state; and A. P. Staples, attorney general.

The 1940 general assembly passed a constructive group of measures increasing appropriations for public education and welfare, bringing the unemployment compensation act in conformity with federal legislation, establishing premarital examinations, providing a comprehensive mining code and taking steps toward eliminating pollution in rivers. Bills introduced at this assembly to integrate Virginia's penal system, to place county sheriffs and city sergeants on salaries, to encourage mediation and conciliation of labour disputes, to establish a state personnel system and to create an actuarially sound retirement plan for teachers were not passed. In the 1940 national election, Virginia gave F. D. Roosevelt 235,961 votes, Wendell L. Willkie 109,363. Harry F. Byrd was returned to the senate; all nine Democratic candidates were elected to the house of representatives.

The general assembly did not meet in 1941. As usual, Democratic nominees for Virginia's three elective offices won in the general election of 1941, with Colgate W. Darden, Jr., as candidate for governor; William M. Tuck for lieutenant governor and A. P. Staples for attorney general for the third successive term. Democrats won 17 contests out of 25 in the house of delegates and 3 out of the 4 special elections for vacancies in the state senate.

The biennial session of the general assembly began Jan. 14 and ended March 14, 1942. The war program outlined by Gov. Darden in his inaugural address was substantially and quickly made law. The assembly established a state department of corrections; established a retirement system for state employees and school teachers; established a personnel and merit rating system for state employees; made the governor director of civilian defense; added $5,000,000 to the sinking fund and simplified the administration of several state departments. A special session of the assembly met from Sept. 29 to Oct. 1. Approving unanimously the governor's suggestion, the legislature provided for eventual liquidation of the state debt by transferring an additional $10,000,000 of an unobligated surplus of $18,639,879 from the treasury to the sinking fund for the purchase of federal government bonds.

The state's shipyard industry soared in 1943, and the population of Newport News increased from 35,000 to more than 55,000. Shipyard workers numbered close to 30,000, of whom 1,600 were women. War brought a marked redistribution of the state's population, as the rapid expansion of industrial localities sucked labour from farm areas. There was no session in 1943 of the general assembly, although interim commissions were active in such fields as small-loan legislation, co-operatives, medical licensing requirements and public health. The state department of corrections, which was established in 1942, ended its first year of operation with 501 prisoners on parole and 600 on probation. A general election in Nov. 1943 resulted in 15 new members in the state senate and 35 new members in the house of delegates.

(J. S. Br.; X.)

The general assembly convened for its regular biennial session early in 1944. Legislation was enacted providing a substantial increase in salary for public school teachers, and earmarking nearly $20,000,000 in the general fund for postwar expenditure on needed construction at state institutions. A program of forest protection and conservation was adopted, and industrial compensation benefits were extended to cover a score of occupational diseases. The assembly ordered interim studies of the school system, the sales tax, water pollution and general taxation. Two laws were enacted to permit Virginia servicemen to vote in 1945 elections without payment of poll taxes or compliance with registration requirements. On Nov. 20 the Virginia supreme court of appeals held these "soldier vote" laws unconstitutional, and on Dec. 14 the assembly was summoned into special session; a law was passed calling for an election to determine whether a constitutional convention should be called to amend the constitution so as to provide means for servicemen to vote. A general election in Nov. 1944 gave 242,276 votes for President Franklin D. Roosevelt, 145,243 for Gov. Thomas E. Dewey, 966 for minor party candidates. Dr. Dabney S. Lancaster was state superintendent of public instruction in 1944.

The general assembly convened in extraordinary session in March 1945, following a referendum on March 6 in which the people voted, 54,515 to 30,341 in favour of a constitutional convention to provide a means for Virginia servicemen to vote in state and local elections. In addition to arranging for the election of delegates to this convention, the legislature at this session provided a substantial increase in the state contribution to salaries of public school teachers, appropriated more than $1,200,000 for visual education equipment and paved the way for study of election laws by an interim commission. The constitutional convention in April added a new section to the constitution to validate a plan for war voting. A general election in Nov. 1945 saw William Munford Tuck elected governor by a two-to-one margin over S. Floyd Landreth, Republican, and Howard Carwile, Independent.

The general assembly convened in regular session in Jan. 1946 and wrote 400 new laws before its adjournment in March. A State Water Control board was created to reduce pollution in public waters, and a State Board of Elections to maintain general supervision over all public elections. The assembly also approved an increase in the state gasoline tax, with funds earmarked for improvement of secondary roads. The first step was taken toward abolition of the state poll tax by constitutional amendment. As 1946 ended, Gov. Tuck called the assembly back in extraordi-

Virginia: *Statistical Data*

Table I.—*Education (Public)*

	1938	1941	1942	1943	1944	1945
Elementary school pupils	469,197	438,738	449,657	428,466	423,815	425,574
High school pupils	114,359	135,701	136,525	128,244	121,049	124,081
Elementary teachers	12,405	11,894	12,416	12,165	10,942	11,064
High school teachers	4,509	5,660	5,660	5,924	4,121	4,240

Table II.—*Public Welfare*

	1938	1940	1941	1942	1943	1945
Cases on general relief	9,444	7,124	5,352	6,314	12,480	11,338
Recipients of old-age pensions	7,271	2,975	20,080	19,783	21,892	18,026
Dependent children receiving aid	2,891	9,376	12,813	14,313	17,693	13,881
Blind receiving aid	598	1,023	1,025	1,081	1,208	1,107
Prisoners	4,248		4,790	4,557	4,000	4,298

Table III.—*Communications*
(Money figures in thousands of dollars)

	1938	1941	1942	1943	1944	1945
Highway mileage			9,460	9,607	9,509	9,176
Expenditure on highways	$29,306	$24,796	$31,305	$23,528	$21,409	$23,839
Railroad mileage	4,362	4,261	4,203	4,203	4,087	4,093

Table IV.—*Banking and Finance*
(Money figures in thousands of dollars)

	1937	1939	1940	1942	1944	1945
State revenue	$65,107	$76,641	$96,234	$134,534	$138,107	$170,408
State expenditure	55,990	43,699	92,940	122,730		
State net debt	23,892		14,760	12,581		
State gross debt	29,987		19,516	18,889	18,239	$16,908
Number of banks	323	315	314	314	313	313
Total bank deposits	$552,500	$596,100	$639,800	$844,575	$1,374,807	$1,663,581
Number of national banks	132	130	130	130	130	130
Deposits of national banks	$337,039	$386,091	$423,503	$506,799	$843,986	$1,015,857

Table V.—*Agriculture*
(All figures in thousands)

	1937	1939	1940	1942	1943	1944
Acreage, principal crops	3,988	3,789	3,791	3,851	3,905	3,948
Income from crops and livestock	$126,800	$115,371	$122,565	$151,736	$274,558	$314,905
Leading crops (bu.):						
Apples	14,898	10,800	10,325	14,094	5,590	14,580
Barley	1,363	2,320	2,376	2,120	1,575	2,124
Corn	37,740	36,530	36,490	35,586	33,275	34,272
Cotton (bales)	43	13	25	34	24	29
Hay (tons)	1,206	983	1,252	1,498	1,418	1,357
Lespedeza seed (lb.)	7					
Oats	1,680	1,600	1,932	3,510	2,860	3,672
Peaches	1,599	1,025	1,392	1,936	172	2,150
Peanuts (lb.)	183,465	189,175	196,800	175,950	174,720	191,180
Potatoes, sweet	5,070	4,128	3,875	3,875	2,976	3,960
Potatoes, white	10,920	6,786	10,412	7,242	9,594	5,976
Tobacco (lb.)	111,969	143,847	100,509	104,150	109,416	148,827
Wheat	9,720	7,685	8,463	7,520	5,863	11,275

Table VI.—*Manufacturing*
(Money figures in thousands of dollars)

	1937	1939	1940	1942	1944
Wage earners	132,643	133,894			
Wages paid	$112,774	$115,539	$184,507	$397,130	$339,627
Value of manufactures	$908,222	$988,813	$1,255,355	$2,230,668	$2,273,282

Table VII.—*Mineral Production*
(All figures in thousands of dollars)

	1937	1938	1939	1942	1943	1944
Value of mineral production	$46,019	$42,370	$43,583		$82,068	$88,528
Leading products (value):						
Coal	27,177	24,054	24,608	38,494	$56,000	64,476
Stone	5,399	5,606	5,879	6,392		
Clay	2,545	1,886	2,819			
Sand and gravel	1,754	2,186	1,426	1,551		
Lime	1,248	1,015	991			

nary session to grant teachers an additional increase in pay (one had been voted at the regular session) and to consider bills guaranteeing a right to work despite "closed shop" labour union agreements and prohibiting strikes in public utilities. (J. J. KT.; X.)

BIBLIOGRAPHY.—Council of State Govts., *Book of the States* (bienn.); L. I. Capen, *Virginia, a Study of the Old Dominion* (1945); Federal Writers' Project, *Virginia; Guide to the Old Dominion* (1940); Secy. of State, *Report* (ann.); Univ. of Va., *Economic and Social Surveys of Va. Counties* (irreg.). Periodical: *The Commonwealth; Monthly Checklist of State Publications.*

Virgin Islands

A United States possession in the West Indies, east of Puerto Rico, the Virgin Islands comprise the island of St. Croix (pop. 12,902); the island of St. Thomas (11,265) and the island of St. John (722). Area, 133 sq.mi.; population in 1940, 24,889, 13.1% more than in 1930, with whites 9%, Negroes 69% (1930, 78.3%), mixed and other races, 22% (1930, 12½%). The main cities are Charlotte Amalie, the capital on St. Thomas, pop. 9,801 (1930, 7,036); Christiansted 4,495 (1930, 3,767) and Frederiksted, 2,498 (1930, 2,698) on the island of St. Croix.

On May 17, 1946, William H. Hastie was inaugurated as the fourth civilian governor of the Virgin Islands, succeeding Charles Harwood, who took office on Feb. 2, 1941. Lawrence W. Cramer was governor from 1935 to 1941.

During the decade 1937–46, there were many important changes in political organization, all of which were smoothly effected. On Jan. 1, 1937, by reason of the operation of the Organic act of the Virgin Islands enacted on June 22, 1936, the new municipal councils took office. These councils, consisting of nine members of the municipal council of St. Croix and seven members of the municipal council of St. Thomas and St. John, all elected by the qualified electors of the island, replaced the old colonial councils which were partly appointed and partly elected by a limited electorate whose qualification for voting was a property one. Universal suffrage was established in 1938, and the hitherto disfranchised majority of the population immediately showed and maintained considerable interest in government and political organization. The promise of President Truman in his first 1946 message to congress that "The people of the Virgin Islands should be given an increasing measure of self-government" was received with enthusiasm. At the end of ten years, the people of the islands were preparing their own proposals for revision of the Organic act of 1936, consistent with the president's policy.

The most significant recommendations, made by a committee appointed for that purpose, included a single legislature for the islands to meet annually in 60-day sessions, the removal of the power of the governor to send bills passed over his veto to the president for final decision, the creation of a single treasury and the establishment of the office of resident commissioner in Washington.

These suggested revisions were to be included in a comprehensive plan for modernization of the Organic act to be placed before the congress during 1947.

In 1946 there was an accelerated withdrawal of personnel from all military establishments in the Virgin Islands, until at the year's end army and navy installations, which accommodated 1,000 or more men during World War II, were reduced to essential maintenance personnel. Of approximately 800 Virgin Islanders who were conscripted for military service and sent abroad, 650 had been demobilized and returned to the islands. These figures did not include Virgin Islanders who were conscripted in the United States or those who voluntarily enlisted.

The U.S. Selective Service act was not made applicable to the Virgin Islands until Oct. 26, 1943 by a proclamation signed by Pres. Franklin D. Roosevelt on that date. Registration began on Nov. 16, 1943. The first call for men from the Virgin Islands was in 1944.

The legislative authorities of the Virgin Islands, consisting of two municipal councils and a legislative assembly, comprising the two councils in joint session, sponsored social legislation, especially in the municipality of St. Thomas and St. John, of a most important character. Outstanding pieces of legislation during the decade 1937–46 were a Workmen's Compensation act in 1941 in St. Thomas and a similar act in St. Croix in 1946; a minimum wage and maximum hour law in St. Thomas in 1942. There was no such law, however, in the municipality of St. Croix. A municipal insurance fund, for workmen's compensation, was established in St. Thomas and was successful. (E. G. A.)

BIBLIOGRAPHY.—L. H. Evans, *Virgin Islands from Naval Base to New Deal* (1945); J. A. Jarvis, *Virgin Islands and Their People* (1944); *Statesman's Yearbook.*

Virgin Islands (U.S.): *Statistical Data*

Item	1938		1941		1944	
	Value (000's omitted)	Amount or Number	Value (000's omitted)	Amount or Number	Value (000's omitted)	Amount or No.
Finance						
Government revenues	$348				$1,880	
Government expenditures	$458				$1,973	
Crops						
Limes and lemons		56 tons*†				
Sweet potatoes		53 " *				
Tanya		51 " *				
Yams		38 " *				
Manufactures						
Bay rum	...	250,000 gal.			$6,628‡	...
Sugar	$277	4,663 tons			...	...
Exports total	$1,541	...	$2,385	...		
Cane sugar	$230§	4,000 tons§	$320	5,000 tons		
Bitters	$229§	21,000 gal.§	$467	27,000 "		
Rum	$225§	127,000 gal.§	$625	643,000 gal.		
Imports total	$3,347	...	$6,308	...		
Coal	$326	83,000 tons	$638	142,000 tons		
Iron, steel manufactures	$296‖	...	$567	...		
Gasoline and kerosene	$104‖	1,042,000 gal.‖	$138	1,680,000 gal.		
Education						
Public and private		26		29		
Primary and secondary schools						
Enrolment		3,901		4,031		5,585‡

*1939 †Sold and traded ‡1945 §to U.S. only ‖From U.S. only

Virgin Islands, British

See WEST INDIES, BRITISH.

Viruses

See BACTERIOLOGY; COLD, COMMON; EPIDEMICS AND PUBLIC HEALTH CONTROL; INFANTILE PARALYSIS; MEDICINE; PNEUMONIA; VETERINARY MEDICINE.

Vishinsky, Andrei Yanuarevitch

Vishinsky (1883–), Russian statesman, was born in Kiev. He studied law at the University of Kiev and joined the Menshevik faction of the Social Democratic revolutionary movement in 1902. He participated in the abortive revolt of 1905 in the Baku area and served a year in prison. After his release, he practised as a criminal lawyer in Moscow.

When the Bolsheviks took power, Vishinsky quit the Mensheviks and served in the Red army for a year, joining the Communist party in 1920. In 1923 he was appointed attorney-general for the Russian Soviet Federated Socialist republic and he was professor of jurisprudence in Moscow university, 1925–27. He was named the All-Union deputy public prosecutor in 1933 and was public prosecutor from 1935 to 1939. He rose to fame for his prosecutions in the famed treason and purge trials, 1936–38.

In 1940 he became vice-chairman of the council of people's commissars and deputy commissar for foreign affairs in 1940. During World War II, he attended most of the important inter-Allied conferences; in 1946 he was a second to Molotov at the United Nations sessions in London, New York and Lake Success, N.Y. at the meetings of the Council of Foreign Ministers and at the 21-nations peace conference in Paris.

Throughout the meetings of the Council of Foreign Ministers and the 21-nations peace conference in Paris, Vishinsky aggressively opposed the western Allies in debate on many important questions, but at the U.N. meetings in Lake Success, he showed a more conciliatory mood, leading diplomatic observers to believe that the soviet delegation had received orders to become "more reasonable."

Vital Statistics

See Birth Statistics; Census Data, U.S.; Death Statistics; Infant Mortality; Marriage and Divorce; Suicide Statistics.

Vitamins

A rapid expansion in knowledge of vitamins occurred during the decade 1937–46, both in fundamental scientific studies of the biochemistry and physiology of these nutrients and in the application of this information to improved health. Especially outstanding in this progress was the determination of the chemical structure and the synthesis in the laboratory of practically all of the known vitamins; development of microbiologic methods for estimating many of the vitamins; development of the concept of antivitamins or vitamin inhibitors and their role as antibiotics; an understanding of the normal human needs for vitamins and the use of many of the vitamins in the nutritive improvement of some staple foods (enrichment of flour, etc.) and in the treatment of specific diseases—for example, vitamin K in certain haemorrhagic disorders, nicotinic acid or amide for pellagra and folic acid for macrocytic anaemias.

Fat Soluble Vitamins.—*Vitamin A.*—The synthesis of vitamin A was reported twice but no practicable method was available at the end of the decade. In addition to vitamin A, long known to occur in sea fish oils and to be structurally similar to the yellow pigment, carotene, another form named vitamin A_2 was found in the oils of some fresh water fish. Vitamin A_2 was crystallized in 1946; its physical properties differ from vitamin A, and it is about a 100 times less active in promoting the growth of rats than is vitamin A. The National Research council's recommended daily allowance of this vitamin was 5,000 international units for adults, probably allowing ample margin for safety. Vitamin A is used extensively in fortifying margarines. Although relatively little is known of the physiological function of vitamin A, George Wald demonstrated that the photosensitive pigment in the retina of the eye, the destruction of which originates the nerve impulse, is a protein-vitamin A complex. Some doubt was expressed as to the correctness of Wald's scheme in all of its details. It was demonstrated that vitamin A is directly concerned with bone growth. Paralysis in the deficiency is due to pressure on nerves which continue growth after bone growth has stopped.

Vitamin D.—This term is applied to substances of the sterol group which have anti-rickets properties. In 1946 at least ten such substances were known; about half were well defined as chemical entities, but only two were of outstanding nutritional importance. The two important vitamins D are activated ergosterol (vitamin D_2, calcified viosterol) and activated 7-dehydrocholesterol (vitamin D_3). Much work was done on the mode of action of vitamin D, but all that could be said is that it somehow influences the adsorption and metabolism of calcium and phosphorus. E. A. Park and associates, on the basis of histologic studies on routine postmortem examinations, reported an unusually high incidence of rickets (slightly more than 50%) in consecutive examinations of 230 children between the ages of 2 and 14 years. Little was known of the vitamin D requirement of man; however, the recommended allowance for children was 400 to 800 international units per day. Adults require perhaps half that amount or less.

Vitamin K.—This vitamin, known as the antihaemorrhagic vitamin, exists in several chemically related forms. Vitamin K_1 was originally isolated from alfalfa leaf meal and vitamin K_2 from sardine meal. Many synthetic compounds have activity. The most potent, 2 methyl, 1-4, naphthoquinone, is more active than the natural compounds, and was widely used clinically during the decade. It was shown that the low clotting ability of the blood in vitamin K deficiency was due to a low content of prothrombin. Hypoprothrombinemia in various clinical conditions, such as haemorrhagic disease of the newborn, and postoperative haemorrhage associated with liver disease, was found to respond dramatically to vitamin K. The human requirement for this vitamin was unknown but in most cases it is probably synthesized by the intestinal flora.

Vitamin E.—This vitamin, also known as tocopherol (alpha, beta, or gamma), is widely distributed in nature. In certain mammals vitamin E deficiency causes a degeneration of striated musculature, as well as sterility. Deficient chicks show a brain degeneration, encephalomalacia, or an impairment of the capillary walls which produces an edema. Since muscular dystrophy (imperfect nutrition) is one of the major signs of vitamin E deficiency in experimental animals, considerable interest was shown in possible relationships between this vitamin and muscular dystrophies in man. While numerous claims were made for the therapeutic value of vitamin E in various types of muscle dystrophies, in sterility and in heart disease, none was as yet accepted. The human requirement for vitamin E was unknown and, in fact, no proved deficiency of vitamin E in man had been reported.

Water Soluble Vitamins.—*Ascorbic Acid* (*Vitamin C*).—The absence of vitamin C eventually leads to scurvy. A search for natural sources of this vitamin and for improvement of the commercial synthesis assumed considerable importance during World War I, for in every previous war there had been large outbreaks of scurvy in armies and among civilians. It was found to exist in large quantities in a great variety of non-citrus materials, such as green walnuts, pine needles, rosehips and various berries. Citrus fruits, tomatoes, cabbage and potatoes had long been recognized as important sources. Numerous advances were made in the chemical determination of this vitamin. Additional evidence on the importance of ascorbic acid to the health of the gums was found, and while it was discovered that there are many infective types of gingivitis not related to lack of this vitamin, there was no doubt that this vitamin is important in healthy gingival tissue. The chemical function of this vitamin still remained an enigma at the end of the decade. The recommended daily allowance for man was in the range of 75 mg. per day. Ascorbic acid is easily destroyed (oxidized) and is frequently lost in the preparation of food.

B-Complex Vitamins.—*Thiamin* (*Vitamin B_1*).—The absence of this vitamin from the diet leads to beriberi, one of the classical deficiency diseases. At the beginning of the decade, events of considerable importance took place concerning this vitamin. In 1936 R. R. Williams had announced its structural formula and synthesis, and a year later K. Lohmann isolated a crystalline coenzyme from yeast which was necessary in pyruvic acid metabolism and showed that it was composed of thiamin and phosphoric acid. Numerous investigators later found that this thiamin containing coenzyme, known as co-carboxylase, is necessary for the oxidation of carbohydrate, and plays a specific role in all biological reactions involving pyruvic acid. The exact amount required is directly related to the amount of carbohydrate and protein metabolized, but fat metabolism does not require thiamin. Numerous studies were made concerning man's requirement foı this vitamin, and it was found to be in the range of one to two mg. per day. Early symptoms of thiamin deficiency in man include fatigue, muscle soreness, irritability, insomnia, paresthesias and loss of appetite. Thiamin is one of the principal B-vitamins removed in the refining of white flour, and hence it was considered in policies concerned with the nutritive improvement of flour through enrichment.

Riboflavin.—This vitamin of the B-complex is also important in oxidative reactions as it is the functioning part (prosthetic group) of a series of enzymes known as the yellow enzymes. In 1938 it was found to be of importance in man when W. H. Sebrell and R. E. Butler described riboflavin deficiency in man as being characterized by an inflamed tongue (glossitis), a fissuring at the angles of the mouth and denudation of the lips (cheilosis) and a characteristic dermatitis (seborrheic). Two years later, it was reported that in this deficiency there was an increase in the capillary blood vessels of the cornea of the eye. Few data were presented on which to base the riboflavin requirement of man, but it was generally stated to be about 2 mg. per day. Riboflavin was also used in the enrichment of white flour. Certain bacteria produce large amounts of riboflavin and this became one of the principal commercial sources.

Niacin (Nicotinic Acid or Nicotinic Amide).—A deficiency of this vitamin leads to the deficiency disease, pellagra. Niacin is also concerned with oxidative reactions in that it is the prosthetic group of two coenzymes known as the pyridine nucleotide coenzymes. In 1937 C. A. Elvehjem and co-workers made the important discovery that niacin prevented and cured the condition known in dogs as "black tongue," and which was known to be similar to pellagra in man. A few weeks after this discovery, numerous investigators reported its effectiveness in human pellagra.

However, the enigma of pellagra was not completely solved by this discovery. An interesting problem was why people consuming large amounts of corn developed pellagra. It was found again by Elvehjem and his students that there is an interrelationship between tryptophane and niacin. Apparently some niacin can be made from the amino acid, tryptophane, which is low in corn. It was also demonstrated that corn contains some material which actually increases the niacin requirement. Niacin was used in the enrichment of white flour and corn meal. The recommended daily allowance of this vitamin for man was found to be in the range of 10 to 15 mg. per day.

Pyridoxine (Vitamin B_6).—This member of the B-complex was isolated and identified chemically in 1938 and shortly thereafter was synthesized. It was first associated with growth and a characteristic dermatitis in the rat, but was later shown to be essential for the chick, dog, pig and duck. Anaemia is a symptom in all of these species. A deficiency syndrome of this factor in man was reported but not confirmed. It was found that pyridoxine existed in at least two other chemically related forms known as pyridoxal and pyridoxamine, both of which have biological activity comparable to pyridoxine.

Pyridoxine-deficient rats, dogs and pigs were found to exhibit *in vivo* a defect in the metabolism of the amino acid, tryptophane. Still another relationship of pyridoxine to amino acid metabolism was demonstrated by the discovery that the decarboxylation of tyrosine by certain bacteria is dependent on the presence of a phosphorylated pyridoxine substance. Thus, pyridoxine may function as a coenzyme in the decarboxylation of amino acids.

Rats, dogs and pigs made deficient in pyridoxine, a portion of the vitamin B complex, were found to have also a defect in the manner in which the body used tryptophane, one of the essential amino acids. It was also found that the breaking down by certain bacteria of tyrosine, another amino acid, through removal of carbon and oxygen, is dependent on a substance consisting of pyridoxine and phosphorus. A role of pyridoxine and its derivatives in enzymic reactions involving a transfer of amino groups (transamination) was also discovered.

No specific information on the pyridoxine requirement of man was available at the end of the decade.

Pantothenic Acid.—This vitamin was first associated with chick nutrition as a factor necessary to prevent a specific dermatitis. It was isolated and synthesized in 1940. In the rat, a deficiency of pantothenic acid was found to produce a greying of the hair though there is no evidence that a similar relationship exists in man. In the rat, a relationship between histologic changes in the adrenal glands and pantothenic acid deficiency was found. No data were available at the end of the decade on the requirement of man for this vitamin, and no proved case of pantothenic acid deficiency in man had been reported.

Biotin.—The feeding of large amounts of raw egg white to animals produces eczematous dermatitis which can be prevented by feeding yeast, liver and certain other foods. It was shown that the factor was the same as the growth factor for yeast, biotin, previously isolated from egg yolk by F. Kögl. Its structure and synthesis were worked out in 1942 largely by the work of V. du Vigneaud. In most animals biotin is synthesized in the intestinal tract. Egg white contains a protein, avidin, which combines with biotin and prevents its utilization, thus producing the deficiency. Certain species—the chick, duck, monkey—require biotin in the diet since an insufficient amount is synthesized in the gut. Biotin deficiency in man was reported by feeding exceedingly large amounts of raw egg white, but no information on the biotin requirements of man was available in 1946.

Choline.—This substance became of increasing interest in nutrition during the decade through the discovery that it furnishes methyl groups needed for certain necessary biological reactions and is also required for the metabolism of fat in the animal body. It was found that in the absence of choline in the diet, fat accumulates in the liver and seriously interferes with the function of this vital organ. It was also shown that other organs may also be affected under certain conditions, particularly the kidneys. Choline was also found to be of varying therapeutic value in the treatment of cirrhosis of the liver in man. Proved choline deficiency in man had not been reported at the end of the decade, and no information was available on the requirements of man.

Folic Acid.—The term "folic acid" was first used in 1941 to designate a factor necessary for the growth of certain bacteria. Subsequent studies by many investigators showed that similar preparations contained biologic activity for the chick, rat, monkey and other micro-organisms. A concentrate previously known as vitamin M, necessary for the prevention of leukopenia in monkeys, was found to have many properties similar to folic acid concentrate. A concentrate of liver known as vitamin Bc, necessary for the prevention of a macrocytic anaemia in chicks, also had properties similar to folic acid. In 1945 the chemical synthesis of *L. casei* factor, the name given to the folic acid like compound necessary for the growth of *Lactobacillus casei,* was announced, though the details of structure and synthesis were withheld until the following year. At that time, it was shown that this substance consists of one molecule each of pterin, para-aminobenzoic acid and glutamic acid. It was found in 1945 that this synthetic *L. casei* factor had pronounced haematopoietic activity in macrocytic anaemias such as occur in pernicious anaemia, sprue, pregnancy and in certain nutritional deficiencies. No data were available in 1946 on which to base any figure as to the daily requirement of man. In the treatment of macrocytic anaemias in man, as little as 2 mg. per day was effective, though generally 20 to 50 mg. daily were used.

Antivitamins or Vitamin Inhibitors.—The concept of antivitamins, antimetabolites, or vitamin inhibitors was developed during the decade. These are substances whose chemical structures are similar to a specific vitamin or metabolite and which are effective in blocking the biologic activity of the vitamin. They thus interfere with the vitamin's function. One of the vitamins which received early attention in this regard was pantothenic acid, for which several antivitamins were synthesized. Other antivitamins were found for riboflavin, thiamin, niacin, ascorbic acid and biotin. These substances became of particular practical interest in the field of chemotherapeutics, for some of them were found to penetrate the bacterial cell and block enzyme reactions vital to the life of the cell.

The chemotherapeutic effect of the sulfonamides was explained in this way, in that they interfere with the action of para-amino-benzoic acid, an essential metabolite for many bacteria.

Microbiologic Assays.—Of interest and value during the decade 1937–46 was the development of a new analytical tool for determining amounts of some of the vitamins and other essential nutrients, such as certain amino acids—namely, the microbiologic assay technique. In this procedure a micro-organism is grown in a medium deficient in the one nutrient to be assayed; then if an unknown amount of this nutrient is added to the medium, the growth of the organism will be, under appropriate conditions, proportionate to the amount of this nutrient added. Rather than measure the growth of the organism, one may measure a metabolic by-product such as the production of lactic acid by an organism such as *Lactobacillus casei.* The advantages of microbiologic techniques for the assay of vitamins are obvious. Any procedure which makes possible increased speed and accuracy of vitamin estimations is of value. This procedure was developed particularly with regard to pantothenic acid, riboflavin, niacin and pyridoxine.

Synthesis of Vitamins by Intestinal Flora.—About the beginning of the decade, the concept was developing that the bacterial flora which normally inhabit the intestinal tract synthesize a number of nutrients which are available to the host. This concept was greatly expanded, and a considerable amount of data was obtained to support it. It was shown that all the vitamins of the B-complex are, in certain animals and in varying amounts, synthesized by the intestinal flora. It was also shown that in man at least thiamin and riboflavin may be so synthesized. The synthesis of vitamins by intestinal micro-organisms may be influenced in many ways, particularly by diseases and drugs which alter the intestinal flora. The relatively insoluble sulfonamides were found to inhibit markedly intestinal synthesis of vitamins and were used as an experimental tool to produce certain vitamin deficiency diseases in animals. Differences in intestinal synthesis might explain many previously puzzling results, *i.e.* the development of deficiency signs by some individuals on diets which are apparently adequate for others.

Vitamins in Foods.—With the discovery of many new vitamins of the B-complex, a vast amount of research was done on the occurrence of these nutrients in food and on losses incurred in processing and storing food. Much of this research was carried out by the quartermaster corps of the army and the department of agriculture. The Bureau of Human Nutrition and Home Economics of the department of agriculture issued a bulletin (U.S. Department of Agriculture, Miscellaneous Publication no. 572) giving information on food composition. Losses in vitamin content during processing of foods were shown to be extremely variable depending on the nature of the processing. Nutrients were shown to be more stable if contact with heat and air are kept at a minimum. Ascorbic acid, vitamin A and thiamin are the nutrients most likely to be decreased in processing.

Enrichment of stable foods was accentuated during World War II principally as a result of the first order of the War Food administration which required the enrichment of all white flour. Thiamin, niacin, iron and later riboflavin were added in amounts approximately comparable to levels existing in whole wheat flour. Other foods improved nutritionally by the addition of vitamins were milk with vitamin D, salt with iodine, margarines with vitamin A and corn meal with thiamin, riboflavin, niacin and iron. The general policy of enriching certain stable foods was of far-reaching importance to improved public health.

Geneticists were also interested in improving the strains of various food products primarily to increase production and resistance to disease. During the decade, attention was directed to increasing nutrient content. Strains of corn were developed much richer in niacin than usual. Tomatoes and apples with greater ascorbic acid content were other examples of progress in this interesting and important development.

BIBLIOGRAPHY.—*Annual Reviews of Biochemistry,* yearly publication by Annual Reviews, Inc.; *Nutrition Reviews,* monthly publication of the Nutrition Foundation, Inc. (*See* also BIOCHEMISTRY; CHEMISTRY; CHEMOTHERAPY; DIETETICS; FISHERIES; FLOUR; GENETICS; MEDICINE; PHYSIOLOGY.)

(F. J. SE.; D. M. HD.)

V-J Day

See War Production; World War II.

V-Mail

See Photography.

V-1 and V-2

See Munitions of War; Rockets.

Vocational Education

See Education; Psychology.

Vocational Psychology

See Psychology.

Volcanoes

See Geology.

Von (in personal names)

See under proper names, *e.g.*, Ribbentrop.

Voronov, Nikolai Nikolayevich

Voronov (1899–), soviet army officer, was born in Leningrad. He joined the Red army as a private in 1918, fought in the civil war and later studied at the Leningrad Red Banner Artillery school, the Artillery High school and the Frunze Military academy. Promoted to chief of soviet artillery in 1937, he reorganized the system of artillery training and established special gunnery schools. Under his supervision, soviet artillery became the chief offensive instrument of the Red army. Voronov employed big guns to pierce the Mannerheim line during the Soviet-Finnish war, 1939–40.

The important role played by soviet batteries in turning back the Germans from Moscow in Dec. 1941 led the soviet high command to lend more weight to cannon as an offensive weapon of land armies, and in succeeding days Voronov established a reserve pool of big guns. He drew upon this reserve during the battle of Stalingrad, in which he employed 300 to 400 guns per mile of front. He employed an even greater number of guns on the Kursk sector in July 1943, pulverizing the heavy German defenses. The soviet operations that resulted in the Orel-Bryansk breakthrough in 1943 and the investment of the Yelnya-Smolensk area were under Voronov's direct command.

Voronov was raised to the rank of a marshal of the soviet union after the Stalingrad battle and was awarded two Orders of Lenin and the Order of Suvorov, first class, for his achievements.

Voroshilov, Klementiy Efremovich

Voroshilov (1881–), soviet army officer, was born Feb. 4, 1881, in Verkhnyi, Ukraine. Joining the Social-Democratic party in 1903, he was exiled to Archangel four years later for revolutionary activities but escaped to Baku. After the Russian revolution in 1917, he was made defense chairman of Petrograd, assisted Felix Dzerzhinsky in organizing the Cheka (secret police), and led guerrilla units against German armies in the Ukraine.

Voroshilov became a member of the Communist party central committee and in 1925 was named people's commissar of the army and navy. After his elevation on May 8, 1940, to the vice premiership, he was succeeded by Marshal Semyon Timoshenko as defense commissar. Two months after the German invasion in June 1941, Marshal Voroshilov was in command of the northwestern front, which included the Leningrad area; in October of that year he was charged with formation of new Russian armies.

He was later returned to the Leningrad area and was one of the soviet commanders there when the siege was broken in Jan. 1943. Voroshilov attended the Churchill-Stalin conference in Moscow in Aug. 1942, the Hull-Eden-Molotov conferences in Moscow and the Tehran parley in 1943. It was announced on Nov. 22, 1944, that Voroshilov had been relieved of his duties as a member of the eight-man defense committee of the soviet union and had been replaced by Gen. Nikolai Bulganin. He was awarded the Order of Lenin in 1945.

WAAC (Women's Army Auxiliary Corps)

See Women's Army Corps.

WAC

See Women's Army Corps.

Waesche, Russell Randolph

Waesche (1886–1946), U.S. coast guard officer, was born Jan. 6, 1886, at Thurmont, Md. He studied electrical engineering at Purdue university, Lafayette, Ind., and later entered the coast guard academy, from which he was graduated in 1906. He served as a line officer in the Atlantic, Pacific and Arctic waters and in 1916 became the first chief of the communications division. In 1928, he became chief ordnance officer in Washington and in 1931 reorganized the field forces of the service. He was appointed commandant of the coast guard in 1936, with the rank of rear admiral, and after the Neutrality act was passed in 1939, supervised the prevention of shipments of war materials from the United States to the European belligerents. Under his guidance, the coast guard grew to ten times its original size during World War II. On April 4, 1945, Waesche became the first full admiral of the coast guard and on Dec. 31, 1945, retired from the service. He was awarded the distinguished service medal. Waesche died at Bethesda, Md., Oct. 17, 1946.

WAFS (Women's Auxiliary Ferrying Squadron)

See Love, Nancy Harkness; Women's Airforce Service Pilots.

Wages and Hours

Wage developments during the decade 1937–46 were the most significant of any period in U.S. history. Both in the United States and Canada, labour fought for higher wages, vacations with pay, night shift premiums, holiday pay and various other forms of financial benefits. The movement for shorter hours was emphasized less than during many previous decades.

Underlying these developments was the fact that fundamental changes had been in process in the U.S. and Canadian industrial systems which had raised the productivity of large numbers of wage earners and increased their value to their employers. The effects of these changes came to a head in the wage conflicts of 1937–46. Brief consideration of the basic changes mentioned is essential to understanding the wage developments of that decade.

Down to the early 20th century, the differentials between the wages paid to workmen in various occupations were based principally upon two factors, skill and scarcity. In a market plentifully supplied with labour, wages varied principally with skill—including knowledges, techniques and proficiencies, acquired only through a prolonged learning period, either as an apprentice or as a learner.

But with the development of modern methods of manufacturing, a new factor came into industry. More dramatically in the mass production industries, but occurring also in thousands of factories not thought of as mass production plants, technological improvements (such as better plant layout and flow of work, highly productive machinery, line assembly and repetitive work on highly specialized tasks) multiplied the productivity of semiskilled and unskilled workers. The value of a worker was no longer determined almost exclusively by skill (which resulted in quality and also moderately increased quantity of work accomplished) but largely by quantity of output. Machines and other equipment, accurately adjusted and able to produce interchangeable units of product, could turn out quality work when manned by labour with only limited skill, and at the same time turn out many times as much work as could the skilled craftsman. Quantity of work produced had now made a multitude of semiskilled workers as valuable to their employers as skill had made the craftsman. It was the importance of quantity of output which underlay much of the successful efforts of workmen in such mass production industries as automobiles, rubber, electrical products and machinery industries, to make the rapid increase in earnings shown by the accompanying statistical tables.

Moreover, the same basic pattern which had been altering the wage situation in manufacturing was developing in transportation, mining, merchandising, large offices and other areas. Increases in the output of semiskilled and unskilled workers brought about by modernized management, equipment and work processes prepared the way for an upward shift in the wages of those groups, based primarily upon quantity of output rather than individual skill and knowledge.

Table I gives the average weekly earnings for July of each year, 1937–46, by industries. Reference to Table II on Average Hours per Week and Table III on Average Hourly Earnings, will enable the reader to determine the extent to which increases or decreases in weekly earnings resulted from variations in hours and the extent to which they were the result of changes in average hourly earnings.

Examination of Table I reveals a considerable variation in the extent to which the earnings in different industry group advanced during the decade. The increase in manufactures in general, 1937–45, was approximately 80%, while hours worked increased during the same years by 16.1%. Hourly earnings increased 66.5%. The reader is cautioned that it is earnings, *i.e.*, what the worker takes home, rather than wage rates, which are under discussion.

In iron and steel the weekly earnings increased, 1937–45, by 66%; in transportation equipment (in which aircraft manufacturers expanded enormously after 1940) 93%; in lumber 61%; in textile products, 83.5%; in anthracite coal, 108.5%; in bituminous coal, 128.5%; in building, 78%. Similar diversity appeared in the case of other industries, and in each case it is necessary to check the facts given in all three tables in order to determine the relative importance of increased hours and increased hourly earnings in the causation of the increase in weekly earnings.

Another caution is necessary. Much of the increase in weekly earnings resulted from the payment of shift premiums of five cents to ten cents per hour on night shifts and from payment of overtime rates for a substantial proportion of the work done during the war years. Overtime was paid, ordinarily, at the rate of one and one-half times the regular earning rate of the employee for hours in excess of the normal shift up to a period twice the length of the normal shift; *e.g.*, from the 8th to the 16th hour of work; and also for work on the 6th day worked in succession. It was paid at double time for hours in excess of the number covered by time and a half, for the seventh consecutive day worked, and for wartime work on holidays. During the years 1937–41, time-and-a-half was paid for Saturday work and double time for Sunday work in a large number of industries, but the amount of such overtime was far less than during the war. The government ordered during the war that overtime apply to the sixth and seventh days rather than Saturday and Sunday, because those days had to be incorporated into so many regular shifts during the war emergency.

The increase in average weekly hours worked during the war years (Table II) may be less than many citizens thought. The reasons were as follows: (1) three-shift operation was the principal means used to increase the production in factories; it made possible continuous, or nearly continuous operation of the plant, though it was not possible in most factories to get an adequate supply of labour, either in numbers or in skills and abilities to operate the entire plant three shifts; (2) part of the labour force worked only normal hours and the average minimized the length of the working week of the workers who did work overtime; (3) absenteeism, on account of fatigue and need for some relaxation from continuous long weeks, cut down the actual hours worked below the scheduled averaged hours

Table I.—*United States: Average Weekly Earnings, by Industry, *1937-46 July of each yr.*

Industry	1937	1938	1939	1940	1941	1942	1943	1944	1945	1946
All mfg	$25.31	$22.17	$23.70	$25.25	$31.24	$38.56	$42.76	$45.43	$45.42	$43.35
Durable goods	28.32	23.74	26.40	28.52	35.83	44.62	48.76	51.07	50.60	46.15
Nondurable goods	21.81	20.83	21.27	21.87	25.12	28.66	33.89	37.04	38.58	40.49
Iron and steel	30.03	21.64	25.80	28.89	35.49	40.46	47.14	49.98	50.22	46.57
Electrical mach	28.51	24.34	27.55	30.29	37.51	46.04	44.80	47.22	47.95	45.38
Machinery, not electrical	†	†	†	†	†	†	51.08	53.34	53.54	49.92
Transportation equip.†	30.89	29.54	30.95	31.88	40.51	50.93	55.93	59.26	59.64	53.46
Automobiles	†	†	†	†	†	†	57.18	56.43	53.05	51.29
Nonferrous metals	25.43	22.51	25.41	27.12	33.81	42.03	48.84	48.35	48.81	46.75
Lumber, basic	20.92	18.64	19.61	19.37	23.21	27.26	31.59	33.75	33.64	35.09
Furniture	20.09	17.80	19.30	—	—	—	32.48	35.54	36.89	38.48
Stone, clay and glass	23.41	21.90	22.61	23.55	26.97	29.90	35.49	38.14	40.32	41.77
Textile prod.	17.18	15.67	16.47	16.85	20.54	23.73	27.09	29.63	31.50	34.81
Apparel prod.	†	†	†	†	†	†	26.05	29.28	30.38	33.97
Leather	20.57	18.56	19.70	19.80	23.68	26.46	29.13	32.97	35.47	36.50
Food	24.88	24.53	24.61	24.33	26.63	30.21	35.52	38.53	39.98	43.21
Tobacco	17.33	17.18	17.48	18.36	19.45	22.10	27.41	30.04	30.73	33.24
Paper and allied prod.	25.03	23.37	23.40	29.00	31.70	33.75	35.55	38.72	40.78	43.10
Printing and publ.	29.76	28.96	30.16	—	—	—	40.08	44.14	46.62	51.77
Chemical prod.	28.34	28.48	28.99	30.12	33.81	38.80	42.04	44.01	44.99	44.65
Petroleum prod.	†	†	†	†	†	†	51.14	56.28	58.01	54.19
Rubber products	26.84	24.84	28.22	27.90	33.18	38.88	44.94	49.17	51.81	50.00
Anthracite	22.78	14.76	18.65	23.52	23.25	32.09	39.69	43.22	47.47	49.22
Bituminous	22.18	19.27	22.11	23.65	31.22	32.18	42.76	47.20	50.70	50.69
Metalliferous mining	30.17	23.84	25.11	27.34	31.62	38.90	43.43	43.46	45.64	48.17
Quarrying	22.84	21.38	21.66	22.63	31.76	26.67	36.72	40.33	42.91	45.58
Crude petroleum	33.74	33.42	33.29	33.92	39.90	36.05	49.41	54.85	54.40	52.45
Telephone	31.02	30.19	31.06	31.75	32.04	32.96	35.94	—	39.49†	44.82†
Telegraph	†	†	†	†	†	†	—	—	37.98	41.15
Electric light	33.84	33.50	33.64	34.75	36.50	39.59	44.86	48.12	50.34	51.96
Street ry	31.65	32.20	33.15	30.41	—	—	44.30	48.12	51.21	54.60
Wholesale trade	30.41	29.76	29.97	30.41	32.45	35.35	39.44	42.36	44.92	48.06
Retail trade	22.41	21.72	21.58	21.68	22.59	23.57	25.48	27.83	29.40	32.94
Hotels	14.83	14.61	15.05	15.54	16.05	20.66	28.18	22.51	24.40	26.70
Private bldg. constr.	31.31	29.52	30.85	31.78	35.38	43.42	47.97	15.81	55.57	—

*New series started April 1946, figures not strictly comparable because of changes in sample of firms reporting. Changes produce but small alterations in data, however.

†In 1943 the composition of the industry group was changed by separating automobiles from transportation equipment; apparel from textile products; telegraph from telephone and telegraph in 1945; and petroleum products from chemical products.

Table II.—*United States: Average Hours Per Week, July of Each Year, 1937–46, by Industry*

Industry	1937	1938	1939	1940	1941	1942	1943	1944	1945	1946
All mfg	37.9	34.9	36.6	37.3	40.3	42.4	44.4	44.6	44.0	39.6
Durable goods	38.6	33.6	36.1	37.9	41.5	44.7	46.0	45.7	44.9	39.2
Nondurable goods	37.1	35.9	37.0	36.7	39.0	39.6	42.1	43.0	42.8	40.1
Iron and steel	38.2	29.1	34.2	37.2	39.9	42.0	45.5	46.0	45.2	38.4
Electrical mach.	40.0	33.5	38.0	40.5	44.6	47.5	46.2	45.7	45.4	39.3
Machinery, not electrical	—	—	—	—	—	—	48.1	47.5	46.6	40.4
Transportation equip. exc. auto.	35.0	33.6	35.1	36.2	41.2	46.4	46.8	46.8	45.8	39.2
Automobiles	34.1	32.0	34.0	34.0	38.3	43.2	46.0	43.7	42.4	37.8
Nonferrous metals	38.2	34.0	37.8	38.6	42.0	44.5	46.1	46.0	45.7	40.1
Lumber, basic	39.8	36.5	36.8	37.0	39.9	41.2	42.8	42.4	41.5	38.6
Furniture	39.4	34.2	37.2	—	—	—	43.6	43.6	43.3	31.0
Stone, clay and glass	37.9	34.7	35.3	35.5	37.4	37.7	41.8	42.4	43.3	39.5
Textile prod.	33.9	32.7	35.2	33.8	27.4	38.2	40.8	41.7	41.3	39.6
Apparel prod.	30.6	30.1	33.7	31.9	35.4	34.7	36.9	37.3	36.7	36.1
Leather	38.3	36.1	37.5	35.9	38.7	38.1	39.2	41.2	41.7	38.3
Food	42.3	41.1	40.1	39.9	41.1	41.9	44.4	45.6	45.8	43.8
Tobacco	37.6	37.2	37.0	36.8	37.3	38.5	42.1	42.4	41.0	39.1
Paper and allied prod.	40.3	37.8	38.0	38.0	39.6	38.8	44.6	45.7	46.3	42.8
Printing and publ.	38.7	36.9	38.3	—	—	—	40.2	41.2	41.5	40.2
Chemical prod.	38.5	36.9	37.9	38.5	40.0	41.0	45.3	45.6	45.1	40.6
Petroleum prod.	—	—	—	—	—	—	44.9	46.9	47.7	40.0
Rubber products	34.7	32.4	36.4	35.7	39.2	41.4	44.1	45.0	45.5	39.2
Anthracite	26.0	14.9	20.1	26.3	23.2	32.3	37.7	35.8	39.4	31.3
Bituminous	25.0	21.5	24.3	26.6	28.7	30.5	37.1	39.5	40.8	34.1
Metalliferous mining	42.4	35.9	36.4	38.0	39.6	43.3	43.7	42.9	43.9	40.0
Quarrying	42.3	39.2	39.2	39.8	42.0	44.7	46.5	46.3	48.0	44.9
Crude petroleum	39.4	39.8	38.0	38.0	38.1	39.4	43.3	45.3	45.0	40.3
Telephone	39.5	38.4	39.4	40.0	40.5	40.5	42.2	—	42.2	39.7
Telegraph	—	—	—	—	—	—	—	—	46.0	45.2
Electric light	32.8	39.3	38.6	39.1	39.9	40.4	42.0	42.8	43.4	41.5
Street ry.	45.9	44.6	45.9	—	—	—	49.4	50.7	51.6	48.4
Wholesale trade	43.0	42.1	41.4	40.6	40.9	41.3	42.4	42.8	43.1	41.4
Retail trade	43.4	42.6	42.6	43.0	42.6	42.0	41.7	43.2	41.9	41.2
Hotels	43.9	46.8	46.8	46.2	46.1	45.6	44.8	44.8	44.0	44.0
Private bldg. constr.	33.8	33.0	33.6	30.8	35.4	37.5	39.0	40.6	40.1	—

Table III—*United States: Average Hourly Earnings, July of Each Year, 1937–46, by Industry*

Industry	1937	1938	1939	1940	1941	1942	1943	1944	1945	1946
	cents	cents	cents	cents	cents	cents	cents	cents	cents	cents
All mfg	65.7	63.9	64.3	66.7	74.4	85.0	96.3	101.8	103.2	109.3
Durable goods	72.2	71.1	71.8	72.7	82.6	94.6	106.0	111.7	112.6	117.7
Nondurable goods	58.8	58.2	58.1	61.5	65.7	73.2	80.5	86.2	90.2	101.0
Iron and steel	77.3	76.1	76.0	77.7	86.2	94.3	103.6	108.7	111.0	121.2
Electrical mach	71.8	72.3	72.4	74.4	83.6	96.1	97.1	103.3	105.7	115.4
Machinery, not electrical	—		—	—	—	—	106.2	112.3	114.8	123.5
Transportation equip exc. auto.	88.7	88.4	88.4	89.1	98.8	109.1	119.5	126.5	130.2	136.5
Automobiles	92.1	93.0	92.8	94.8	106.6	114.4	124.3	129.1	125.2	135.6
Nonferrous metals	65.8	65.6	67.1	70.1	80.3	93.5	101.6	105.2	106.8	116.6
Lumber, basic	53.4	51.5	53.7	51.9	57.7	66.0	73.8	79.6	81.0	90.9
Furniture	51.6	52.2	52.4	—	—	—	74.5	81.6	85.2	93.9
Stone, clay and glass	62.4	63.8	64.6	66.5	72.0	78.7	84.9	89.9	93.1	105.7
Textile prod	50.3	48.0	47.1	50.2	55.0	61.1	66.4	71.0	76.3	87.9
Apparel prod	54.1	51.4	49.5	53.4	58.2	62.8	70.6	78.5	82.9	94.1
Leather	54.2	51.6	52.1	55.3	60.9	68.7	74.3	80.1	85.1	95.4
Food	59.0	59.5	61.5	62.4	66.1	73.5	80.0	84.5	87.4	98.8
Tobacco	46.2	46.0	47.6	50.2	52.3	52.5	65.1	70.9	74.9	85.1
Paper and allied prod	62.2	61.9	61.6	79.1	82.5	89.3	79.7	84.7	88.1	100.6
Printing and publ	78.1	80.0	80.2	—	—	—	99.7	107.2	112.4	128.7
Chemical prod	74.6	77.0	77.0	78.3	83.8	94.1	92.8	96.5	99.9	100.9
Petroleum prod	96.6	—	—	—	—	—	113.9	120.0	121.7	135.5
Rubber products	79.6	77.6	77.3	78.5	84.5	93.3	101.9	109.4	113.8	129.2
Anthracite	91.5	88.5	93.1	91.8	99.8	98.4	106.3	119.4	121.9	155.8
Bituminous	88.1	88.1	90.3	89.1	102.8	105.3	115.0	119.9	125.5	147.5
Metalliferous mining	71.2	67.9	69.4	72.2	79.5	85.1	98.6	101.0	103.9	120.5
Quarrying	54.3	54.2	55.2	56.8	63.5	68.3	79.1	87.1	89.5	100.7
Crude petroleum	84.5	84.2	88.5	87.6	93.0	98.1	111.7	118.7	120.9	131.3
Telephone	81.6	85.5	81.5	79.8	79.6	81.8	85.5	—	98.4	113.5
Telegraph	—	—	—	—	—	—	—	—	82.6	91.0
Electric light	84.7	85.3	86.9	89.1	91.9	95.2	106.0	111.9	114.6	125.8
Street ry.	68.2	71.1	71.4	—	—	—	88.1	93.5	97.9	109.7
Wholesale trade	71.4	70.7	72.5	74.0	79.7	82.8	93.3	98.9	103.7	115.5
Retail trade	56.9	55.9	55.1	55.3	57.4	59.4	67.5	70.6	77.5	88.9
Hotels	39.0	31.5	31.9	33.1	34.6	36.2	44.9	50.2	54.4	60.2
Private bldg. constr.	92.5	90.4	92.0	94.7	100.0	109.7	123.1	130.2	136.7	—

of operation of the employees' departments.

The movement of hourly earnings up to a dollar an hour and higher in many industries during the late war years and 1946, probably represented a permanent shift in hourly earnings in the United States (Table III). It reflects the success of labour in the mass production and other modernized industries in forcing or inducing management to compensate their employees in some proportion to their productivity in such industries, even when the increase in productivity resulted from management's efforts more than from increases in either the effort or the skill of the wage earners.

Table III shows a sharp upward shift of hourly earnings in all industries. The intensity of labour's drive for still higher hourly earnings, characteristic of the industrial relations scene in 1946 in the United States, Canada and Great Britain alike, augured a possibly permanent substantial gain in wage earners' incomes from which they would benefit most if postwar progress in technology and the more intense competition of subsequent years brought down commodity price levels.

Great Britain.—Table IV shows the number of individuals in a substantial number of British industries who received increases in pay each year from 1939 through 1945. It was not possible to compute with accuracy the typical amounts of increase received, but the table shows a steady and substantial upward trend of wages during the war period—and the fact that increases were widely distributed.

Table V gives a closer approximation of the amount of the increases received during the period. The starting date for figures given on this table is Oct. 1938, but this is of little significance when comparison is made of the evidence given in the two tables. Examination of the monthly reports on wage increases in the *Ministry of Labour Gazette* (London) reveals that the difference between wage figures on Oct. 1938 and the average for 1939 was small. It is more than counterbalanced by the fact that Table V ends with 1945. There was fully as much increase during 1945 as there was between Oct. 1938 and the 1939 average. It is sound, therefore, to use Table V as an index of what happened between 1939 and 1945.

One significant fact stands out in the table—the much greater percentage increase in women's wages than in men's, which produced the result that women's wages had gained on men's wages by the end of World War II. The more rapid rise in women's wages was forced by the necessity of offering wages which would attract into industry some millions of new female employees to replace men called into the armed services and to make possible the necessary expansion of industries producing war materials.

Table IV.—*Great Britain: Number of Individuals Affected by Net Increases and Net Decreases in Wages by Years, 1939–46.*

Year	Number of Individuals* Reported as Affected by:		Estimated Net Weekly Amount of Change in Wages	
	Net Increases	Net Decreases	Increase	Decrease
1939	6,150,000	65,800	£980,900	18,500
1940	8,780,000	—	2,633,000	—
1941	8,855,000	—	2,485,000	—
1942	6,692,000	400	1,706,000	50
1943	7,187,000	152,100	1,619,000	2,900
1944	8,512,000	300	1,956,000	500
1945	7,164,000	400	1,756,000	50

*This is "an approximate" number. Certain large groups are not covered by the statistics. Figures afford only a general indication of movements of wages.

Table V.—*Great Britain: Average Weekly Earnings, Male and Female, by Industries, Jan. 1945; and Percentage Increase since Oct. 1938.*

Industry	Earnings, Males, 21 Yrs. and Over: Jan. 1945		% Incr. Since Oct. 1938	Earnings, Females 18 Yrs. and over: Jan. 1945		% Inc. Since Oct. 1938
	s	d		s	d	
Iron, steel, mining, quarrying products	93	8	56	—		—
Treatment of nonmetal mine and quarry prod.	108	11	64	60	9	105
Brick, pottery, glass, chemical,	106	2	68	49	9	79
paint, oil, etc.	118	0	70	62	1	90
Metal, engineering, and shipbldg.	131	2	75	70	4	111
Textiles	100	4	75	53	9	69
Leather, fur	105	2	64	52	7	51
Clothing	106	5	66	53	0	52
Food, drink, tobacco	106	7	63	54	8	66
Woodworking	103	11	57	57	6	71
Paper, printing, stationery	120	5	43	53	4	56
Building, contracting, etc	104	5	58	59	6	?
Misc. manufacturing	124	11	81	63	5	100
Transport, storage, except railways	110	10	58	78	7	125
Public utility	98	3	56	50	6	83
Governmental industrial establishments	131	6	75	84	10	90
Average	119	3	73	63	2	94

Source: Ministry of Labour Gazette: London, Aug. 1945.

The industries of particular importance for war production showed the largest percentage increases in women's rates.

An average increase of 73% in men's weekly earnings and of 94% in women's weekly earnings during a period of a little more than 6 years was a wage rise of exceptional rapidity.

It resulted, of course, from three principal factors: increases in hourly rates and piece work prices; the shifting of many thousands of workers into more highly paid classifications; and the increased hours, which frequently carried overtime premium rates.

Canada.—Two interesting series on wages were published by the Canadian department of labour, neither of which covered all of the decade of 1937–46. Table VII furnishes, by index numbers, the trend of wage rates, by industry groups.

"Now Get Them All Out!", a reference by Shoemaker in the *Chicago Daily News* to the steel strike settlement of Feb. 18, 1946. A general wave of labour unrest swept the nation in 1946 as unions fought for higher wages

Federal fact-finding board appointed by Pres. Truman to investigate claims of the International Longshoremen's and Warehousemen's union (C.I.O.) for higher wages. They are shown at a San Francisco, Calif., dock in April 1946

Table VI.—*Distribution of the National Income of the United Kingdom by Categories at Factor Cost, 1938–45*

(Million £)

	1938	1939	1940	1941	1942	1943	1944	1945
Rent of land and buildings	380	388	386	385	384	384	384	385
Interest, profits and professional earnings	1,317	1,472	1,829	2,128	2,342	2,460	2,487	2,445
Salaries	1,100	1,141	1,206	1,332	1,381	1,430	1,473	1,585
Wages	1,735	1,835	2,115	2,419	2,688	2,845	2,890	2,840
Forces, pay and allowances	78	124	386	622	805	999	1,167	1,228
Total	4,610	4,960	5,922	6,886	7,600	8,118	8,401	8,483

Table VII.—*Canada: Index Numbers of Wage Rates for Certain Main Groups of Industries: 1937–44.*

Year	Construction	Water Transportation	Elec. Ry.	Steam Ry.	Coal Mining	Metal Mining	Mfg.	Logging	Telephone	Gen. Av.
1937	96.9	92.0	97.8	96.0	95.6	99.1	96.1	93.9	98.3	96.7
1938	99.2	99.1	99.4	100.0	100.0	99.6	99.2	101.8	99.7	99.6
1939	100.0	100.0	100.0	100.0	100.0	100.0	100.0	100.0	100.0	100.0
1940	104.5	105.2	104.9	100.3	102.1	102.8	104.3	104.9	105.4	103.9
1941	111.6	113.3	110.1	104.9	109.4	112.2	115.2	114.0	110.5	113.1
1942	118.6	125.8	114.9	113.0	113.1	118.7	125.5	125.9	116.5	122.5
1943	127.7	137.3	122.4	124.4	124.8	123.1	135.6	143.1	127.3	132.8
1944	129.6	140.7	127.6	124.4	146.0	125.2	141.1	144.7	128.9	137.5

The figures are for the years 1937 through 1944. Tabulations subsequent to 1944 had not been made prior to Jan. 1947.

Table VII shows that in 1937–38, wage rates were lower than in 1939, except in the coal mining and steam railway industries. From 1939 through 1944 wage rates rose, on the average, 37.5 points. The largest increase was in coal mining (46 points), and the smallest was in the steam railways (24.4).

Table VIII.—*Canada: Average Per Capita Earnings in Eight Leading Industries and All Manufacturing, as of Aug. 1, Each Year, 1946–41.*

	1946	1945	1944	1943	1942	1941
Eight industries	32.25	32.00	31.72	30.97	28.58	25.34
All mfg.	32.37	32.73	32.38	31.72	29.01	26.05
Durable goods	34.39	35.67	35.53	34.78	31.85	28.48
Nondurable goods	30.20	29.32	28.53	27.50	25.35	23.38
Logging	29.51	27.07	26.78	26.81	22.98	19.89
Elec. light and power	38.75	36.80	37.04	35.82	33.99	—
Mining	39.41	38.93	38.04	35.94	34.55	31.49
Communications	32.40	31.16	30.73	28.90	27.56	26.50
Transportation	39.55	38.38	36.69	35.63	34.38	32.63
Construction	31.22	29.91	28.86	29.58	26.32	22.71
Services	20.87	20.95	19.08	18.54	17.26	15.64
Trade	28.72	27.35	26.54	25.77	24.25	23.00
Finance	34.66	33.54	32.65	31.58	30.34	—

Compiled from *Canadian Labour Gazette*, Sept. 1946.

Table VIII gives the average weekly earnings in major industry groups from 1941 to 1946. The table shows that from 1944 to July 1946 there was not much change in weekly earnings. Since hours worked and the amount of overtime premiums decreased between 1944 and 1946, only increases in rates could have kept 1946 earnings up to approximately the 1944–45 level.

Both 1945 and 1946 were characterized by vigorous efforts of labour unions, especially in the basic industries, to get increases in rates to counterbalance the reductions in earnings that would result from reduced overtime. (*See* also AGRICULTURE; BUSINESS REVIEW; CANADA, DOMINION OF; CENSUS DATA, U.S.; LABOUR UNIONS; LAW; STRIKES AND LOCK-OUTS.) (D. D. L.)

BIBLIOGRAPHY.—M. S. Brody, *Wage Rates and Living Costs in War Economy* (1943); Bureau of National Affairs, *Wage and Hour Manual* (1945); Canada National Labour Board, *Report* (Ottawa, 1944); M. H. Dobb, *Wages* (Cambridge, 1938); J. T. Dunlop, *Wage Determination under Trade Unions* (1944); A. Feller, *How to Operate under the Wage-Hour Law* (1938); J. O. Hopwood, *Salaries, Wages and Labor Relations* (1945); International Labour Office, *Studies and Reports, Series D: Wages and Hours* (irreg.); B. M. Stewart, *Wage and Manpower Controls in Canada* (1942); A. A. Tepper, *Wages and Hours in Wartime* (1944); U.S. Dept. of Labor, *War Time Regulation of Hours and Labor Supply in Gt. Brit.* (1941), *Wartime Regulation of Wages and Hours in Canada* (1941); J. M. Viau, *Hours and Wages in American Organized Labor* (1939). *See* also publications of National Industrial Conference board; U.S. Bur. of Labor Stat., *Wages and Hours of Labor* series. Periodical: *Monthly Labor Review*.

Wage Stabilization Board, National

See WAR AND DEFENSE AGENCIES.

Wainwright, Jonathan Mayhew

Wainwright (1883–), U.S. army officer, was born Aug. 23, 1883, in Walla Walla, Wash. A graduate of the U.S. Military academy, West Point, N.Y. (1906), he served in the Philippines during the Moro uprisings, 1909, and in France during World War I. He was stationed in the Philippines during World War II, and was second in command to General Douglas MacArthur when the Japanese invaded the islands in Dec. 1941. After MacArthur was sent to Australia, Wainwright took over command (March 17, 1942) of the U.S.-Filipino armies in Bataan peninsula. Two days later Pres. F. D. Roosevelt raised him to the rank of a lieutenant general.

Wainwright retired in April with his outnumbered U.S.-Filipino army from Bataan to Corregidor (*q.v.*). He held out under a concentrated air and artillery bombardment until May 6, when he was compelled to surrender because he had run out of food and ammunition and his exhausted forces were no longer able to fight.

After signing the surrender terms dictated by Gen. Maraharu Homma, Wainwright was moved to a prison camp in the Philippines, thence to three camps in Formosa and lastly to two in Manchuria. Shortly after Hirohito's surrender broadcast (Aug. 15, 1945), a U.S. detachment in Manchuria released him from captivity and the general took part in the Japanese surrender ceremonies aboard the battleship "Missouri" in Tokyo bay, Sept. 2. His nomination to the rank of a full general was approved Sept. 6. Wainwright returned to the United States, Sept. 8, 1945, and was given ovations on his arrival in San Francisco, Washington, D.C., and New York city.

Reception for General Jonathan Wainwright in New York city on Sept. 13, 1945. Seated in the first car beside Mayor La Guardia, the general is shown at the head of a parade passing along lower Broadway in the city's financial district

On Sept. 28, 1945, Wainwright was named commanding general of the eastern defense command; in Jan. 1946 he was given command of the 4th U.S. army.

Wake Island

Tiny, isolated Wake island was first occupied in 1935 when Pan American Airways established a seaplane base and overnight passenger facilities serving its trans-Pacific air route. Somewhat later the U.S. navy decided to develop it into an air and submarine base when it was evident that Japan was inexorably committed to a policy of aggression and conquest in the Pacific. On the eve of the attack on Pearl Harbor, the base had been half completed by the 1,146 civilian employees of contractors, Pacific naval air bases, and the navy, in late Nov. 1941, had sent in Commander W. S. Cunningham, as island commander and Major J. P. S. Devereux, with his 1st marine defense battalion of 379 men and six 5-inch coast defense and twelve 3-inch anti-aircraft guns. A task force organized about the carrier "Enterprise" and commanded by Vice Admiral William Frederick Halsey made a secret high speed run from Hawaii to Wake for the purpose of delivering marine fighting squadron (V.M.F.) 211 consisting of 12 Wildcats and 59 men (pilots and ground crews), under Major P. A. Putnam; the planes were flown ashore on Dec. 4, 1941.

The marines were woefully unprepared in numbers, training, equipment and supplies for the catastrophe which befell them at 11:58 A.M. on Dec. 8 (2:28 P.M., Dec. 7, Hawaiian time) in the form of an 18-plane Japanese air attack. A four-plane patrol had been maintained after receiving news of the attack on Pearl Harbor that same morning at 6:50 A.M., yet the lack of detection devices and the low clouds made the attack a complete surprise. Thirty-three men were killed and seven of the eight precious planes on the ground were severely damaged or destroyed during a few horrible minutes.

On Dec. 11 a Japanese task force of three cruisers, four destroyers, two patrol craft and two transports attempted to capture the island. The marines held fire until the ranges were near 5,000 yards, when they opened up with tremendous effect. Aided by planes which, by a lucky chance, started an uncontrollable fire on a cruiser, and a submarine which torpedoed a transport, the garrison sank 5 ships and inflicted casualties of 5,350 men while they suffered not a single casualty.

On all but two days the Japs sent over flights of bombers numbering between 18 and 51, each of which was opposed by all remaining flyable Wildcats, sometimes only one. The last was expended on Dec. 22, but not until the gallant airmen had destroyed 12 Jap planes, 1 light cruiser and 1 submarine. The numerous bombings were useful to the Japanese principally in the elimination of the defending planes and the exhaustion of the ground forces.

On Dec. 23 the same task force which had been repulsed on the 11th returned to the assault after having been repaired at Kwajalein and re-enforced by four heavy cruisers and two destroyers. An aircraft carrier operated in support but separately. At 3 A.M. the two patrol craft (small destroyers) and five landing craft were sacrificed by being run on the south reef to get ashore the 1,100 troops they bore. They were opposed at the landing by only 85 marines, since the remainder were obliged to man the guns variously located about the island. At this time Cunningham sent his much-quoted dispatch, "Enemy has landed, issue in doubt." After 6 hours of furious fighting, during which the marines lost only about 20 men but killed 130 Japanese, the island commander saw further resistance was useless and yielded in the interest of humanity.

The fighting at Wake had no considerable military consequence; its proximity to numerous and stronger Japanese bases determined that it probably would have fallen later even if the marines had been succoured, as the entire nation fervently prayed would happen. The battle was of supreme moment in a spiritual sense, however, for there United

Jap-held Wake Island, target of one of the most concentrated air raids of World War II on Oct. 5-6, 1943, when U.S. naval planes and ships bombed and shelled it with more than 700 tons of explosives

States forces stood before an overpowering enemy who had had an unparalleled succession of easy triumphs in all its other theatres, and proclaimed that, regardless of odds, they would have to be crushed into submission. Thus the American people, powerless to help and heartbroken that the garrison had to be abandoned to its fate, had begun to doubt their ability to cope with the Japanese, but derived new hope and inspiration from the dauntless defenders of the island, and those people went on to fight a series of campaigns over the entire Pacific and to reap victories never before recorded in history.

The Japanese captured an estimated 1,603 Americans on Wake. All but 98 were evacuated to China and Japan by Sept. 1942, when it became too dangerous to risk ships for this purpose. The Japanese fortified Otorishima, as they renamed Wake, to the utmost, moving in planes, guns, tanks, PT boats and 4,100 men under Rear Admiral Sakaibara.

Admiral Halsey attacked the island Feb. 24, 1942, with the same task force which delivered marine fighting squadron 211 the previous Dec. 4. As the Navy increased in strength and bases to the south in the Marshalls were captured, air and sea activity against the by-passed island was intensified to the establishment of an ideal blockade. It was bombarded five times by carrier task forces, and by early 1944 hardly a day passed that the island did not receive a bombing or reconnaissance mission. No Japanese ship except submarines visited it after Dec. 1943. The results were the complete devastation of the island, its uselessness for Japanese military purposes and the death of some 600 Japanese from wounds and of 1,288 from starvation.

Brigadier General Lawson H. M. Sanderson, accepted the Japanese surrender Sept. 4, 1945. The garrison was found greatly debilitated from malnutrition. Liberal U.S. treatment, food and medicines soon restored all but the few who were too far gone. Immediately the navy moved in the 85th naval construction battalion and acorn 57 to build an air base, which was commissioned Nov. 1, 1945, Captain E. A. Junghans, commanding. At once the naval air transport service and the air transport command began to use the base as a stop on the route to Tokyo in support of the occupation of Japan, and the first Pan American plane returned Nov. 25, 1945, to make preparations for re-establishment of the prewar route.

After the surrender an attempt was made to find the missing 98 civilians. At first the Japanese all told the same self-absolving story which was not given credence. At length a confession revealed that the Americans had been executed Oct. 7, 1943, when the island was under bombardment by a U.S. task force. The admiral feared the attack would develop into an assault and desired to remove a possible menace to his interior security. For this crime the admiral and two other officers were sentenced to hanging by a military commission. (E. A. Js.)

BIBLIOGRAPHY.—H. W. Baldwin, "Saga of Wake," *Virginia Quarterly Review* 3:321–35 (July 1942); J. P. Devereux, "This is How it Was," *Saturday Evening Post* (Feb. 23, March 2, 9, 16, 1946); W. S. Grooch, *Skyway to Asia* (1936); H. Major, "Isle of Paradoxes," *Country Life* 74:36–39 (Sept. 1938).

Walker, Frank Comerford

Walker (1886–), U.S. lawyer, politician and government official, was born May 30, 1886, at Plymouth, Pa. A student at Gonzaga university in Spokane, Wash. (1903–06), he later attended Notre Dame university, South Bend, Ind., where he received his law degree in 1909. He was admitted to the Montana bar in 1909 and four years later was elected to the state legislature. He became actively identified with national politics in 1932, when he became treasurer of the Democratic National committee. The following year, he was made secretary of President F. D. Roosevelt's executive council and was later executive director of the National Emergency council. On Aug. 31, 1940, Walker was named by Roosevelt to succeed James A. Farley as postmaster general, and in Jan. 1943 he was appointed chairman of the Democratic National committee, a post he held until Jan. 1944. He resigned as postmaster general June 30, 1945. On Dec. 19 of that year, President Harry Truman named Walker as one of the U.S. representatives to the United Nations general assembly meeting in London; the nomination was confirmed by the senate the following day (Dec. 20, 1945). On Jan. 7, 1946, he was assigned to the general assembly's legal committee.

Wallace, Henry Agard

Wallace (1888–), U.S. government official, was born Oct. 7, 1888, in Adair county, Ia., the son of H. C. Wallace, secretary of agriculture in the Harding and Coolidge administrations. Upon graduating from Iowa State College of Agriculture and Mechanical Arts, Ames, Ia., in 1910, he joined his grandfather's paper, *Wallace's Farmer,* as associate editor, becoming full editor in 1924. Wallace was secretary of agriculture in the Roosevelt administration from March 4, 1933 to Sept. 5, 1940, when he resigned to run for the vice-presidency. He was inaugurated with F. D. Roosevelt, Jan. 20, 1941. On July 31, 1941, he was appointed head of the Economic Defense board (later the Board of Economic Warfare) and (Aug. 28) chairman of the Supply Priorities and Allocations board.

Toward the end of 1942, a dispute developed between Wallace and Jesse Jones, secretary of commerce and chairman of the Reconstruction Finance corporation. The feud broke out into the open on June 29, 1943, when Wallace accused Jones of obstructing the war effort by hampering the BEW in its efforts to secure vital materials from foreign sources. Jones denied Wallace's accusations and came forth with charges of his own. The sensational intra-agency quarrel was quickly silenced on July 15, 1943, by Pres. Roosevelt, who abolished the BEW and withdrew from the control of the RFC all corporations which had been engaged in financing foreign purchases and imports.

Early in 1944, Wallace went on missions to China and the Asiatic parts of the soviet union. He returned in time for the Democratic National convention in Chicago, Ill., where he was defeated for renomination for the vice-presidency; although the president forsook Wallace by declaring that either Harry S. Truman or William O. Douglas would be acceptable candidates to him if Wallace were not renominated, the retiring vice-president actively stumped for Roosevelt's re-election in the 1944 campaign.

On Jan. 22, 1945, Roosevelt nominated Wallace to succeed Jesse Jones as secretary of commerce and directing head of the RFC. While the senate confirmed his nomination as secretary of commerce on March 1, 1945, his nomination as RFC head was rejected.

On Sept. 12, 1946, Wallace became involved in an intra-cabinet controversy when in a New York address he denounced the administration's foreign policy with regard to the soviet union, warned that a "get tough with Russia policy" would backfire and scored British "imperialism" in the middle east. The speech caused an international furore because of Pres. Truman's subsequent statement that he had read and endorsed it. Two days later, Truman backed down on his statement, explaining that while he

Henry A. Wallace greeting delegates at the Democratic party's national convention which opened on July 19, 1944, in Chicago to nominate candidates for the presidential election. Wallace failed to secure re-nomination for the vice-presidency

supported Wallace's right to make the speech, he did not intend to indicate that he approved the speech as "constituting a statement of the foreign policy of this country."

At the request of the president, Wallace handed in his resignation as secretary of commerce, Sept. 20, 1946. After his resignation, Wallace became editor in chief of *The New Republic.*

Walnuts

See NUTS.

Wang Ching-wei

Wang (1885?–1944), Chinese statesman, was born at Canton. He studied law in Japan and while there became interested in the revolutionary program of Sun Yat-sen, with whom he later became acquainted. By 1924 he was Sun Yat-sen's chief adviser and in 1925, after Sun's death, chairman of the Kuomintang's political council. Two years later he resigned after a quarrel with Chiang Kai-shek. Expelled from the Kuomintang in 1929 for plotting against the Nanking government, he was reinstated two years later. He was president of the executive yuan, 1932–35, and minister of foreign affairs, 1933–35. In 1939 he was again ousted by Chiang for making peace overtures to Japan. Wang then set up a puppet government, March 30, 1940, in Nanking under sponsorship of the Japanese army of occupation. Wang's regime, "the National government of China," was officially recognized by Japan in a treaty signed Nov. 30, 1940. Chiang's answer was the offer of a reward of 100,000 Chinese dollars for the capture of Wang. Dutifully following the dictates of his Japanese overlords, Wang declared war on the United States and Great Britain on Jan. 9, 1943. Wang died of diabetes in a Japanese hospital, Nov. 10, 1944, according to an announcement by Japanese Premier Kuniaki Koiso.

Wang Shih-chieh

Wang (1891–), Chinese statesman, was born in 1891 in Hupeh province. He joined the Chinese revolutionaries who forced the Manchu abdication in 1912. After the establishment of Sun Yat-sen's republican regime, Wang went to England, where he graduated from the University of London in 1917. He later attended the University of Paris, receiving his doctor of law degree in 1920. On returning to China, he joined the faculty of the Peking National university as a lecturer of comparative constitutional law, becoming dean of the law faculty.

In 1928, Wang was appointed a member of the Permanent Court of Arbitration at The Hague. In 1929, he was made a member of the legislative yuan and also president of the National Wuhan university at Wuchang. His steady rise in the Chinese educational movement was climaxed in 1933 with his appointment as minister of education. In 1939, he was given the additional portfolio of minister of information, serving until 1942. Two years later he was reappointed to this post.

Wang was named by Chiang Kai-shek as the national government's chief negotiator in dealing with the problem of the Chinese Communists in 1944. Appointed foreign minister on July 30, 1945, Wang attended the meetings of the Allied Council of Foreign Ministers in London the following September.

War

See AVIATION, MILITARY; CHEMICAL WARFARE; MUNITIONS OF WAR; NAVIES OF THE WORLD; SUBMARINE WARFARE; WAR PRODUCTION; WORLD WAR II; etc.

War, Munitions of

See MUNITIONS OF WAR.

War and Defense Agencies

The general pattern of federal administration in the United States for defense and war was one of establishing new agencies or units to carry on the principal wartime functions rather than assigning major emergency tasks to existing agencies. While the activities of the permanent agencies were greatly enlarged and accelerated, major responsibilities in such fields as production, transportation, manpower and public information were given to organizations created to meet the emergency.

The organizational basis for the development of wartime administrative machinery was in the Reorganization Act of 1939. Under the provision of this act the president, with the approval of congress, reassigned certain functions so that the number of agencies would be reduced and more efficient operation would result. Under Reorganization Plans No. I and No. II, effective July 1, 1939, and an executive order of Sept. 8, 1939, a number of activities were grouped in the executive office of the president: the

"Reduce a Little, and Then Look Around," was a suggested remedy for the U.S. labour shortage in 1942. The cartoon was by Knox of the *Memphis Commercial Appeal*

Budget Bureau (with enlarged responsibilities in the field of administrative management); the National Resources Planning board; the Office of Government Reports; the Liaison Office for Personnel Management; and the immediate White House office. The executive order of Sept. 8 also provided that there should be in the executive office, "in the event of a national emergency or threat of a national emergency, such office for emergency management as the President shall determine." This provision served as the legal basis for the erection of the major part of the government's structure for the prosecution of the war.

The *Office for Emergency Management* was formally established in the executive office of the president by administrative order on May 25, 1940. This office served two purposes: it provided the president with assistance in co-ordinating and directing the emergency agencies (through the Liaison Officer for Emergency Management); and it provided authority and an organizational location for many of the new agencies which had to be created.

The *Advisory Commission to the Council of National Defense* was re-established by the president on May 29, 1940, under statutory authority remaining from World War I for a Council of National Defense and an advisory commission "of not more than seven persons, each of whom shall have some special knowledge of some industry, public utility, or the development of some natural resource, or be otherwise specially qualified." The council (the secretaries of war, navy, interior, agriculture, commerce and labour) remained dormant; the commission consisted of advisers for industrial materials, industrial production, employment, farm products, transportation, price stabilization and consumer protection, with the Liaison Officer for Emergency Management serving as commission secretary. Several subordinate offices established by the commission served as the forerunners of later agencies or units; these included the Co-ordinator of National Defense Purchases, the Small Business Activities office, the Bureau of Research and Statistics, the Division of State and Local Co-operation, a Defense Housing co-ordinator, the Office of Co-ordination of Commercial and Cultural Relations between the American Republics and a Director of Information.

As preparations for war intensified, the advisory status of the commission became increasingly unrealistic, and the need increased for agencies with greater powers and more effective organization. Beginning early in 1941, functions of the commission were shifted in rapid succession.

Central Co-ordination; Central Services.—The *Division of Central Administrative Services* was established in the Office for Emergency Management pursuant to a letter of Feb. 28, 1941, from the president to the Liaison Officer for Emergency Management, to provide central budgetary, fiscal and administrative services for the Office for Emergency Management and its constituent agencies. As these agencies grew in size, they gradually assumed control of their own services, and an executive order of Aug. 25, 1944, terminated the division as of Nov. 30, 1944.

The *Office of Economic Stabilization* was established within the Office for Emergency Management on Oct. 3, 1942. Its responsibility was "to control so far as possible the inflationary tendencies and the dislocations attendant thereon which threatened the military effort and the domestic economic structure." An Economic Stabilization board was established by the same order with the director designated as chairman. This agency did not supersede other agencies but was expected to formulate general programs and reconcile conflicting policies and disagreements among them. An executive order of Sept. 20, 1945, abolished the office and transferred its activities to the Office of War Mobilization and Reconversion, where its functions were carried on under a stabilization administrator. The office was re-established on Feb. 21, 1946.[1]

The *Office of War Mobilization* was established by an executive order of May 27, 1943, to provide government-wide co-ordination and execution of war policies on a broader basis than the economic field covered by the Office of Economic Stabilization. Powers assigned to it included: development of unified programs and policies for maximum use of the nation's resources; co-ordination of the activities of federal agencies concerned with production, procurement, distribution and transportation; and the issuance of directives necessary to achieve these ends. The office operated with a relatively small staff as a policy-forming and co-ordinating agency; operations remained with the emergency agencies already handling them.

The *Office of War Mobilization and Reconversion* was created by the War Mobilization and Reconversion act approved Oct. 3, 1944. This legislation transferred to the new agency the functions of the Office of War Mobilization (which was terminated) and two existing agencies: the Office of Contract Settlement and the Re-employment and Retraining administration. This office exercised a general policy-forming and co-ordinative function similar to that of the Office of War Mobilization, but this function was strengthened by certain legislative grants of power extended to problems of the reconversion to peace, and enlarged by the addition of certain subordinate activities.[2]

[1]The Office of Economic Stabilization was consolidated into the Office of Temporary Controls by the executive order creating that office.

[2]The Office of War Mobilization and Reconversion was consolidated into the Office of Temporary Controls by the executive order creating that office. Certain functions of the director of war mobilization and reconversion were transferred to the president, the secretary of commerce and the reconstituted Office of Government Reports by the same executive order.

The *Committee for Congested Production Areas* was established by an executive order of April 7, 1943, to provide for the co-ordination of federal, state and local government activities in congested areas. Working through a series of area offices, the committee served to bring to the attention of Washington officials problems of these areas that needed special attention. It was terminated on Dec. 31, 1944, by act of congress.[3]

Production, Supply, Distribution, Price Control.—The *Office of Production Management* was established in the Office for Emergency Management by executive order on Jan. 7, 1941. The functions of the Advisory Commission to the Council of National Defense relating to production were transferred to it, including the activities of the Co-ordinator of National Defense Purchases, the Small Business Activities office, the Bureau of Research and Statistics and the activities of the Advisors on Industrial Materials and Industrial Production. The agency was given broad powers over the production and supply of materials required for national defense and over the co-ordination of activities throughout the government relating to production. Its functions were transferred to the War Production board by executive order on Jan. 24, 1942.

The *Office of Price Administration* was originally established as the Office of Price Administration and Civilian Supply in the Office for Emergency Management by executive order on April 11, 1941. This office inherited the functions and staff of the Advisor on Price Stabilization of the Advisory Commission to the Council of National Defense. An executive order of Aug. 28, 1941, changed its name to the Office of Price Administration and transferred its civilian supply function to the War Production board. The Emergency Price Control Act of 1942, Jan. 30, 1942, established OPA as an independent agency. Its principal functions were price control, rent control and rationing.[4] (*See* also PRICE ADMINISTRATION, OFFICE OF; PRICES; RATIONING.)

The *Supply Priorities and Allocations board* was established in the Office for Emergency Management by executive order of Aug. 28, 1941, as a policy group superimposed over the Office of Production Management. It consisted of the chairman of the Economic Defense board, the director general and associate director general of the Office of Production Management, the price administrator, the secretary of war, the secretary of the navy and the special assistant to the president supervising the lend-lease program. Its purpose was to assure unity of policy and to co-ordinate the consideration of all relevant factors involved in the supply and allocation of materials and commodities to meet military and civilian needs. It was abolished by an executive order of Jan. 16, 1942, which transferred its functions to the War Production board.

The *War Production board* was established in the Office for Emergency Management by executive order of Jan. 16, 1942. This order transferred to WPB the functions of the Supply Priorities and Allocations board, and a subsequent order of Jan. 24, 1942, transferred to the new agency the functions of the Office of Production Management. The board was largely advisory; all administrative powers of the agency were placed in the hands of the chairman. The WPB was the principal agency in the field of production and supply until Oct. 4, 1945, when it was terminated and its functions transferred to the *Civilian Production Administration*.[5] (*See* also WAR PRODUCTION.)

The *Petroleum Administration for War* was established by executive order of Dec. 2, 1942, which designated the secretary of the interior as administrator ex officio. This agency had been preceded by an Office of Petroleum Co-ordinator for War, established by presidential letter of May 28, 1941, with the secretary of the interior as co-ordinator. This earlier office was authorized to co-ordinate all federal defense activities concerned with the production, refining, transporting and marketing of petroleum; increased administrative powers were added by the executive order creating the successor agency. The Petroleum Administration for War dealt with a wide range of problems related to the production, distribution and use of petroleum products, particularly in the field of relations with the industry and co-ordination of government agencies.

The *Solid Fuels Administration for War* was established in the department of the interior by executive order of April 19, 1943, which designated the secretary of the interior as administrator. This agency absorbed the Office of the Solid Fuels Co-ordinator for War (established as Office of Solid Fuels Co-ordinator for National Defense by presidential letter on Nov. 5, 1941; title changed on May 25, 1942), a largely advisory office also under the direction of the secretary of the interior. The Solid Fuels Administration for War had powers over coal and certain other solid fuels similar to those of PAW over petroleum products. One of its activities was the supervision of operations when mines were placed under government control pursuant to the War Labor Disputes act of June 25, 1943. This control was handled from July 1, 1943, to Aug. 19, 1944, by a Coal Mines administration in the department of the interior; on the latter date that unit was abolished, and its functions were transferred to Solid Fuels Administration for War. (*See* also COAL; PETROLEUM.)

The *Office of Rubber Director* was established within the War Production board by executive order of Sept. 17, 1942. The director was given broad authority over all phases of the nation's rubber program, including direction of the existing units in the War Production board and its Division of Civilian Supply dealing with rubber and rubber products. In Sept. 1944, the office was replaced by a Rubber bureau under the WPB operations vice-chairman, and the operations of the new office were brought more closely into the WPB mechanism. (*See* also RUBBER.)

The *Reconstruction Finance corporation* (*q.v.*) provided convenient machinery for handling a number of situations in which the war agencies needed financial facilities for procurement, stock-piling, insurance and the like. One device used in a number of cases was the creation of government corporations under the auspices of RFC. These corporations included the following, the dates in parentheses being dates of their establishment: Metals Reserve Co. (June 28, 1940); Rubber Reserve Co. (June 28, 1940); Defense Plant Corp. (Aug. 22, 1940); Defense Supplies Corp. (Aug. 29, 1940); Rubber Development Corp. (Nov. 1944, later transferred to Office of Economic Warfare); War Emergency Pipe Lines, Inc. (Sept. 8, 1941); War Damage Corp. (incorporated Dec. 13, 1941, as War Insurance Corp.); United States Commercial Co. (March 26, 1942); Colonial Mica Corp. (April 17, 1942); Copper Recovery

[3]The Office of Temporary Controls was established in the Office for Emergency Management by an executive order of Dec. 12, 1946. The Office of Economic Stabilization, the Office of Price Administration and the Civilian Production Administration were transferred to it. The Office of War Mobilization and Reconversion was transferred to it, with the exception of certain powers of the director of war mobilization and reconversion, which were transferred to the president, the secretary of commerce, and the reconstituted Office of Government Reports.

[4]The OPA was consolidated into the Office of Temporary Controls by an executive order of Dec. 12, 1946.

[5]The Civilian Production Administration was in turn transferred to the Office of Temporary Controls by executive order of Dec. 12, 1946.

Corp. (April 21, 1942); Steel Recovery Corp. (July 18, 1942); War Materials, Inc. (Aug. 24, 1942); and Petroleum Reserves Corp. (June 30, 1943, later transferred to Office of Economic Warfare).

The *Smaller War Plants corporation* was created by act of congress approved June 11, 1942. Attention to the problems of small business had begun on Oct. 23, 1940, when a Small Business Activities office was established under the Advisory Commission to the Council of National Defense. A defense contract service was established in the Office of Production Management, and an executive order of Sept. 4, 1941, raised its status to that of a division of contract distribution. This division engaged in various measures, including a spectacular publicity campaign, to assist small manufacturers in war production. The Smaller War Plants corporation, which succeeded to the field of action of the Contract Distribution division, engaged in assistance to small business through publicity, loans, provision of information, liaison with other government agencies and other methods. The corporation was terminated by executive order of Dec. 27, 1945, and its functions were transferred to the Reconstruction Finance corporation and the department of commerce.

International Economic Activities.—International economic matters, including co-ordination of foreign purchases in the United States, provision of supplies for the allies, administration of alien property, and matters of economic warfare, were handled at first by a number of relatively small and informal devices. In the field of purchasing by allies of the United States, the president established, on Dec. 6, 1939, an Interdepartmental Committee for Co-ordination of Foreign and Domestic Military Purchases. This committee, generally known as the president's liaison committee, consisted of representatives of the war, navy and treasury departments. It operated under the direction of the secretary of the treasury to locate sources of supply, and to iron out competition between foreign purchasing programs and U.S. procurement activities. On May 2, 1941, the Division of Defense Aid Reports was established in the Office for Emergency Management. This division co-ordinated requests for aid from other countries, checked records and accounts, and maintained liaison among the departments concerned with the execution of the program. As policies became established, the division increased its activity in implementing them. The division was abolished by executive order of Oct. 28, 1941, which created the Office of Lend-Lease Administration.

The *Office of Lend-Lease Administration* was established by executive order of Oct. 28, 1941, to replace the Division of Defense Aid Reports within the Office for Emergency Management. This agency administered the Lend-Lease act, providing for the manufacture, procurement, lending, leasing, or selling of defense articles to such nations as were vital to the defense of the United States. This office was consolidated into the Foreign Economic administration by executive order of Sept. 25, 1943.

Export controls had other aspects besides the problem of co-ordinating foreign purchases with the U.S. domestic production program. Initially, the government possessed only a limited power to control exports, and it was necessary to broaden this authority so that materials could be controlled which were required for U.S. production, and so that critical materials would not be shipped to aggressor countries. On July 2, 1940, the president approved an act which permitted him to prohibit or curtail the export of any military equipment, machinery, tools, materials or

"End of the Line." A reference by Hal Coffman of the *Ft. Worth Star-Telegram* to the end of U.S. lend-lease shipments on Aug. 21, 1945, which left many Allied nations seeking new sources of foodstuffs and other materials

supplies necessary for the manufacture of military goods. On the same day, by military order, he designated an administrator of export control. The duties of the administrator included the control of export materials and commodities that were designated as essential to defense and could not be exported except under licence. These powers were transferred to the Economic Defense board under an executive order of Sept. 15, 1941, where they were continued in an Office of Export Control. (*See* also LEND-LEASE.)

The *Economic Defense board* was established by executive order of July 30, 1941. The board consisted of the vice-president, who acted as chairman, and the secretaries of state, treasury, war, navy, agriculture, commerce and the attorney-general. Originally a policy co-ordinating body, it moved into the area of operations on Sept. 15, 1941, when an executive order transferred to it the functions and staff of the Office of Export Control and of the Division of Controls of the department of state. The board was reconstituted in Dec. 1941, as the Board of Economic Warfare.

The *Board of Economic Warfare* was established by an executive order of Dec. 17, 1941, as the successor to the Economic Defense board. It was responsible for developing and co-ordinating policies, plans and programs to protect and strengthen the international economic relations of the United States in the interests of national defense. The board was terminated when the Office of Economic Warfare was created.

The *Office of Economic Warfare* was established in the Office for Emergency Management by executive order on July 15, 1943; it assumed the functions of the Board of

Economic Warfare. At the time of its creation, there were transferred to it the U.S. Commercial Co., the Rubber Development Corp., the Petroleum Reserve Corp., the Export-Import Bank of Washington and other subsidiaries of the Reconstruction Finance Corp. and the department of commerce engaged in financing foreign purchases and imports. OEW was succeeded by the Foreign Economic administration in Sept. 1943.

The *Foreign Economic administration* was established within the Office for Emergency Management by executive order on Sept. 25, 1943, to unify and consolidate activities relating to foreign economic affairs. The order transferred to FEA the Office of Lend-Lease Administration, the Office of Foreign Relief and Rehabilitation Operations, the Office of Economic Warfare (together with the agencies earlier transferred to that office) and the foreign economic operations of the Office of Foreign Economic Coordination in the state department. A later executive order (Oct. 6, 1943) transferred to FEA the foreign procurement activities of the War Food administration and the Commodity Credit corporation. The agency was terminated by an executive order of Sept. 27, 1945, and its functions were transferred to the departments of state, commerce and agriculture, and to the Reconstruction Finance corporation.

The *Office of Foreign Relief and Rehabilitation Operations* was established by order of the state department on Dec. 4, 1942, as announced by the White House in a press release on Nov. 21, 1942. The office was organized to plan and administer measures for the relief and rehabilitation abroad of victims of war, including the provision of food, housing, clothing and medical supplies in territories occupied by the armed forces of the United Nations. While the office was established within the department of state, it exercised a large degree of freedom of action. It was transferred to the Foreign Economic administration by executive order of Sept. 25, 1943, which established that agency.

The *Office of Alien Property Custodian* was established in the Office for Emergency Management by executive order of March 11, 1942, under the authority of the Trading with the Enemy Act of 1917. The agency had authority over businesses, patents, securities and other properties of enemy governments or nationals, with power to hold, use, administer, or sell such property under certain conditions. The office was transferred to the department of justice by executive order of Oct. 14, 1946.

Foreign Funds Control, an office within the treasury department, was established by that department Sept. 22, 1942. Among its activities were: the freezing of $8,500,000,000 held in the United States by persons in enemy-occupied, liberated and European neutral countries; the investigation and regulation of international financial transactions; co-operation, through the department of state, with other American republics in the control of enemy property and transactions; and participation in the restrictions on trading-with-the-enemy under the Trading with the Enemy act.

Transportation.—The *Office of Defense Transportation* was established in the Office for Emergency Management by executive order of Dec. 18, 1941. It succeeded the Transportation division established by the Advisory Commission to the Council of National Defense; its responsibility was "to assure maximum utilization of the domestic transportation facilities of the nation for the successful prosecution of the war." Its jurisdiction included railroad, motor, inland waterway, pipe line, air transport and coastwise and intercoastal shipping. The office continued its activities on a reduced scale into 1946, its best-known activities being the issuance of emergency orders in the case of major dislocations caused by rail and coal strikes.

The *War Shipping administration* was established in the Office for Emergency Management by executive order of Feb. 7, 1942. A shipbuilding section of the Production division of the Advisory Commission to the Council of National Defense had been established in July, 1940, with the chairman of the maritime commission as its head. During 1941, activities in the field of shipping were handled by the maritime commission, the Office of Production Management, a Shipping Priorities Advisory committee, a Cargo Clearance committee, a Strategic Shipping board, the Economic Defense board and other units. The War Shipping administration was given powers, many of them formerly exercised by the maritime commission, over the operation, purchase, charter, insurance, repair, maintenance and requisition of vessels. All vessels owned by the commission were transferred to War Shipping administration. A later executive order transferred from the coast guard to War Shipping administration certain functions pertaining to the operation of the United States Maritime service, the merchant marine cadet training program, and other nautical training schools. (*See* also MOTOR TRANSPORTATION; RAILROADS; SHIPPING, MERCHANT MARINE.)

Manpower, Labour, Selective Service.—The *Selective Service system* was established under the Selective Training and Service Act of 1940 to administer the selection of men for the armed services under that act, and to perform related duties. It was originally a separate government agency responsible directly to the president, but an executive order of Dec. 5, 1942, placed the organization under the jurisdiction of the War Manpower commission, where it was known as the Bureau of Selective Service. An executive order of Dec. 23, 1943, restored the Selective Service system to its separate status under the president. (*See* SELECTIVE SERVICE, U.S.)

The *National Defense Mediation board* was established by executive order of March 19, 1941. The board, which was charged with the responsibility of settling controversies between employers and employees, consisted of three public members, four representatives of employees, and four representatives of employers. It was instructed to act when the secretary of labour certified that a dispute threatening the production or transportation of equipment or materials essential to national defense could not be adjusted by the conciliation activities of the department of labour. During its ten months of life, the board received 118 cases, of which 96 had been adjusted when it ceased operation; the remainder were transferred to its successor, the National War Labor board. The board ceased to exist upon the creation of the National War Labor board.

The *National War Labor board* was established within the Office for Emergency Management on Jan. 12, 1942. The board consisted of four industry, four labour and four public members, assisted by a number of panels that handled much of the work except in the most difficult cases. It was authorized to take jurisdiction of a dispute after a certification by the secretary of labour that the Conciliation service had been unable to settle it. The board might also take jurisdiction of a dispute on its own motion after consultation with the secretary. It was empowered to act as final arbiter of wartime labour disputes and to control adjustments of wages and salaries under $5,000 a year, with certain exceptions. An executive order of Sept. 19, 1945, transferred the board to the department of labour to be administered as an organizational entity under the supervision of the secretary of labour. The board was terminated when the National Wage Stabilization board was established as a successor agency.

The *National Wage Stabilization board* was established within the department of labour by executive order of Dec. 31, 1945. The board contained representatives of employers, employees and the public; it succeeded to certain limited functions of the National War Labor board relating to the settlement of labour disputes. It also succeeded to the powers of that labour board relating to the stabilization of wages and salaries. These functions included acting on applications for approval of increases or decreases in wages and salaries, and carrying out the program for the enforcement of stabilization regulations.[6]

The *War Manpower commission* was created in the Office for Emergency Management by an executive order of April 18, 1942. The commission, under the chairmanship of the federal security administrator, served at first to provide general co-ordination of manpower matters as a prelude to more extensive operations at a later date. A series of executive orders, the last on Dec. 5, 1942, transformed the commission from a policy-co-ordinating body into an operating agency. These orders gave the War Manpower commission authority over a number of activities, including the National Youth administration, the Apprenticeship Training program, the Training Within Industry service and the Selective Service system. The commission was also given authority to regulate all hiring and recruitment of workers in any area designated as critical by the chairman. The commission was terminated by an executive order of Sept. 19, 1945, and most of its functions were transferred to the department of labour.

The *National Roster of Scientific and Specialized Personnel* was established on June 28, 1940, by a letter of authorization from the president to the National Resources Planning board. It was administered by the Civil Service commission, under agreement with NRPB, until its transfer to the War Manpower commission by an executive order of April 18, 1942. Later it was transferred to the department of labour, by an executive order of Sept. 19, 1945.

Public Information, Censorship, and Intelligence.—The *Office of Censorship* was established by an executive order of Dec. 19, 1941, which gave the director of censorship authority "in his absolute discretion" to censor incoming and outgoing communications by mail, cable, radio or other means of communication between the United States and other countries. Internal censorship of domestic press and radio was not subject to the same formal control but was established on a voluntary basis by a letter from the president to the director of censorship on Jan. 27, 1942. The work of the Office of Censorship thus fell into three principal areas: actual censorship of communications between the United States and other countries; the collection, investigation and circulation of information from censored communications that might further the prosecution of the war; and the development and implementation of codes to be followed by the domestic press and radio in their program of voluntary censorship. The office was terminated effective Nov. 15, 1945. (*See* also CENSORSHIP.)

Other agencies handled intelligence, espionage and the affirmative job of providing information for the public. The principal agency in the information field was the Office of War Information (*see* below), which carried on after 1942 the work of a number of predecessor agencies, particularly the Office of Government Reports, the Division of Information of the Office for Emergency Management, the Office of Facts and Figures and certain foreign information activities of the Office of the Coordinator of Information. Intelligence and propaganda behind axis lines were initiated by the Office of the Coordinator of Information and later handled by the Office of Strategic Services (*see* below). Cultural and informational relations with Latin America were handled by the Office of Coordinator of Inter-American Affairs (also *see* below).

The *Office of Government Reports* was the oldest of the agencies that were ultimately to form the nucleus of OWI activities. It was created on July 1, 1939, to perform functions formerly carried on by the National Emergency council, which had existed since 1933 and which was abolished by the president's Reorganization Plan II on that date. The office performed a number of functions in the field of public information, including the maintenance of a central press clipping service, public inquiry offices, the co-ordination of the government's film production program, and the maintenance of facilities (including field offices) for analyzing public opinion, handling federal-state relationships in the public information field and disseminating government information. This agency was transferred to the Office of War Information by the executive order creating that office.

The *Division of Information* was created in the Office for Emergency Management on March 5, 1941, by instructions given by the president in a letter to the liaison officer for emergency management dated Feb. 28, 1941. It was designed to provide a centralized information service for the emergency agencies as an alternative to separate information offices in each of the agencies. It served most of the existing emergency agencies, assisting materially in such matters as the national drive for production in the first half of 1942 and the preparation of the first general production report issued to the public in July 1942. As information activities grew in size, there was increasing pressure from the war agencies to set up their own information offices, a pattern which was substantially fixed with the establishment of the Office of War Information, to which the Division of Information was transferred.

The *Office of the Coordinator of Information* was established by presidential order of July 11, 1941, for two purposes: to co-ordinate intelligence materials from all sources, and to transmit information to other countries except to Latin America (covered by the Office of the Coordinator of Inter-American Affairs). The first function was transferred to the Office of Strategic Services by presidential order of June 13, 1942, and the second function was transferred to the Office of War Information by executive order of the same date.

The *Office of Facts and Figures* was established in the Office for Emergency Management by an executive order of Oct. 24, 1941, to co-ordinate defense information activities on the home front. It was designed to serve as a point of co-ordination for the Division of Information of the Office for Emergency Management and for other government agencies on speeches, press releases, pamphlets, posters and other information media. It served also as a clearinghouse for the activities of the press, radio and motion picture industries in support of the government's war activities. It participated in the work of the Committee on War Information, which was created to act as a war in-

[6]The National Wage Stabilization board was terminated by executive order of Dec. 12, 1946, after most of its powers had been eliminated by executive order on Nov. 9, 1946. Remaining powers were transferred to the departments of labour and treasury.

formation planning agency, composed of representatives of the state, war, navy, treasury and justice departments, the Coordinator of Information, the Coordinator of Inter-American Affairs, the Office of Government Reports, the Office of Lend-Lease Administration, the Office of Civilian Defense, and the Office for Emergency Management. The Office of Facts and Figures was transferred to the Office of War Information by the executive order creating that office.

The *Office of Coordinator of Inter-American Affairs* was established in the Office for Emergency Management by an executive order of July 30, 1941. This office was a successor to the Office for Coordination of Commercial and Cultural Relations Between the American Republics, which had been established on Aug. 16, 1940, by an order of the Council of National Defense. The functions of this agency went far beyond informational activities; it was established to serve as a centre of co-ordination for cultural and commercial relations with the other American republics. In co-operation with other agencies, particularly with the department of state, it formulated programs dealing with such fields as the arts and sciences, health and sanitation, food supply, education, transportation, press, radio and motion pictures. It assisted in the development of a number of associations and government corporations for activities in special fields, including the Institute of Inter-American Affairs, the Inter-American Educational Foundation, Inc., the Institute of Inter-American Transportation, the Inter-American Navigation corporation and Prencinradio, Inc. The name of the office was changed to the Office of Inter-American Affairs by executive order on March 23, 1945. The informational activities of the office were transferred to the department of state by executive order of Aug. 31, 1945, and the office was terminated, its remaining functions going to the state department.

The *Office of War Information* was established in the Office for Emergency Management by an executive order of June 13, 1942, to consolidate into one agency the war information activities, both domestic and foreign, of the government. Previously existing agencies that were consolidated into OWI included the Office of Facts and Figures; the Office of Government Reports; the Division of Information of the Office for Emergency Management; and the Foreign Information service, and the outpost, publications, and pictorial branches of the Office of the Coordinator of Information. The office was authorized to carry out, through the use of press, radio, motion pictures and other facilities, informational programs designed to provide an intelligent understanding, at home and abroad, of the status and progress of the government's war activities. It served as a point of co-ordination and clearance for informational activities of other agencies, developed and disseminated information in this country and abroad, and served as a point of contact with many private agencies and associations in their informational activities in furtherance of the war effort. The office was terminated by an executive order of Aug. 31, 1945. The Bureau of Special Services (originally United States Information Service in the Office of Government Reports) handling centralized public inquiry and press clipping services was transferred to the Bureau of the Budget. Foreign informational activities were transferred to the department of state.[7]

The *Office of Strategic Services* was created by presidential order of June 13, 1942, to supersede the Office of Coordinator of Information, except for the foreign informational activities of the latter office which were transferred to

News room of the OWI at Washington, D.C., where official reports were received and prepared for release through radio, newspapers, motion pictures and other channels of public information. Both the overseas and domestic branches of the OWI went out of existence in 1945

the Office of War Information on the same date. The Office of Strategic Services was placed under the jurisdiction of the Joint Chiefs of Staff to engage in intelligence operations abroad and in the analysis of strategic information. The office was terminated by an executive order of Sept. 20, 1945, and its remaining functions were transferred to the war and state departments.

Food and Agriculture.—The field of food and agriculture was the principal instance in World War II of an existing agency attempting to administer a major segment of the war economy. Nominally, at least, the department of agriculture had responsibility for the measures developed to prosecute the war in that area: production; allocations to the several major users; distribution; and the administration of loans, "set-asides" and other mechanisms. As in every major segment of the war effort, of course, various other agencies dealt with parts of the food problem; examples were the Office of Price Administration (food price control and rationing), the War Production board (machinery for food production and processing, among other activities), the Office of Defense Transportation and the War Shipping administration (transportation), and the various agencies concerned with foreign economic problems.

During the existence of the Advisory Commission to the Council of National Defense (May 1940 to May 1941), one of the advisers was responsible for agricultural matters. In May 1941, the president abolished the Agricultural division of the Advisory Commission to the Council of National Defense and transferred its functions to an Office of Agricultural Defense Relations in the immediate office of the secretary of agriculture. Originally designed to have broad functions in connection with food for war, its prin-

[7]The Office of Government Reports was re-established by executive order on Dec. 12, 1946, to carry on the functions of the Division of Special Services of the Bureau of the Budget and the Media Programming division and the Motion Picture division of the Office of War Mobilization and Reconversion.

cipal activities consisted of liaison with the War Production board and the Office of Price Administration on priorities and price problems. On June 4, 1942, a Food Requirements committee was constituted, with the secretary of agriculture as chairman, and membership comprising representatives of the war, navy and state departments, the Office of Price Administration, the Board of Economic Warfare, the Office of Lend-Lease Administration, and the War Production board. The committee was authorized to determine total food needs, the amount required to balance supply and need, and amounts of food to go to the principal claimants, including the army, the navy, other government agencies, foreign nations and civilians. The chairman of the War Production board was authorized to decide issues on which the chairman of the Food Requirements committee and the chairman of the WPB Requirements committee might be in disagreement. The staff of the Office of Agricultural War Relations (thus renamed in May 1942) served as staff for the committee and actual operations were carried on by the committee's constituent agencies rather than by the committee itself.

An executive order of Dec. 5, 1942, made a number of rearrangements in the handling of food problems, largely within the department of agriculture itself. This reorganization was built around four major responsibilities placed on the secretary of agriculture: determination of total food requirements, execution of a food production program to meet these requirements, establishment of allocation and priority controls to bring about proper food distribution, and the procurement of food for the military services and other government agencies. Many existing activities were regrouped under a Food Production administration and a Food Distribution administration.

The creation of the Food Production and Distribution administration in 1943 marked a partial step toward setting up an emergency agency to handle food problems. The administration was established within the department of agriculture; the administrator was, however, appointed by the president and was responsible directly to him. All of the powers delegated to the secretary of agriculture in Dec. 1942 were transferred to the administrator. The name of this unit was later changed to War Food administration, and it continued to handle the department's emergency functions until the end of hostilities. It was terminated by an executive order of June 29, 1945.

Civilian Defense, Housing, Health, Welfare and Internal Security.—The *Office of Civilian Defense* was established in the Office for Emergency Management by an executive order of May 20, 1941. It had been preceded by the Division of State and Local Cooperation in the Advisory Commission to the Council of National Defense, which had concerned itself primarily with federal-state-local relations in matters of production-contracts, the location of defense plants, and the like. The OCD was directed to assure effective co-ordination of federal relations with state and local governments engaged in the furtherance of war programs, to provide for federal-state-local co-operation in civilian protection, and to facilitate participation of all persons in war programs. Under this authorization, the OCD engaged in a variety of activities related to protection, morale and civilian participation in war activities. The office was terminated on June 30, 1945. (*See* also Air Raid Defense.)

In the field of housing, the Advisory Commission to the Council of National Defense announced the appointment of a housing co-ordinator on July 21, 1940, to function, as did other members of the commission's staff, in a capacity that included co-ordination, investigation and planning rather than direct administration. This office was replaced by the Division of Defense Housing Coordination established in the Office for Emergency Management by an executive order of Jan. 11, 1941. The functions of the division, like those of its predecessor, were co-ordinative and advisory. Its functions were transferred to the National Housing agency by the executive order creating that agency. (*See* Housing.)

The *Office of Defense Health and Welfare Services* was established in the Office for Emergency Management by an executive order on Sept. 3, 1941. It superseded the Office of the Coordinator of Health, Welfare, and Related Defense Activities set up by order of the Council of National Defense on Nov. 28, 1940. Its responsibility, which paralleled at many places the activities of the Office of Civilian Defense and other agencies, was to co-ordinate health, medicine, welfare, nutrition, recreation and other related activity affecting the national defense. This office was abolished by an executive order of April 29, 1943, and its functions were transferred to the Office of Community War Services, which was established within the Federal Security agency by the same order.

The *Committee on Fair Employment Practice* was originally established within the Office of Production Management by an executive order of June 25, 1941. This committee was transferred to the War Manpower commission on July 30, 1942. It ceased to exist, and a new committee of the same name was established within the Office for Emergency Management in 1943. Its purpose was to formulate and carry out policies for the prevention of racial discrimination in employment, both in government agencies and in work done under government contract.

The *War Relocation authority* was established in the Office for Emergency Management by an executive order of 1942, to provide for the supervision and, in a large number of cases, for the maintenance in relocation centres of Japanese from the Pacific coast area. This agency was transferred to the department of the interior by an executive order of Feb. 16, 1944.

Scientific Development.—The *Office of Scientific Research and Development* was established in the Office for Emergency Management by an executive order of June 28, 1941. It continued and greatly extended the work done by the National Defense Research committee created earlier by order of the Council of National Defense. The office was given a broad charter to co-ordinate and supplement the activities of other government agencies in scientific research, to develop and review plans for scientific research, and to initiate and support scientific research. Armed with the power to make contracts with commercial and university laboratories, the office stimulated and guided important research in a great variety of scientific fields.

Combined Boards.—While not strictly agencies of the United States government, a number of combined boards had an impact on the nation's war effort. The principal boards were the Combined Food board, the Combined Production and Resources board, the Combined Raw Materials board and the Combined Shipping Adjustment board. The first two were established by the president and the prime minister of Great Britain on June 9, 1942, and the last two by the same officials on Jan. 26, 1942. The termination of the first three was announced on Dec. 10, 1945, by the president and the prime minister to take effect June 30, 1946, for the first and Dec. 31, 1945, for the second and third. The Combined Shipping Adjustment board became the United Maritime authority in Aug. 1944, and extended membership to other maritime countries. (*See* also BRITISH-U.S. WAR BOARDS; CANADIAN-U.S. WAR COMMITTEES.)

There were a number of other international boards and commissions for military or economic purposes on which the United States had membership. Examples were the Joint Economic Committees—United States and Canada, the Combined Chiefs of Staff, and various inter-American defense groups.

Contract Termination and Surplus Property Disposal.— Although World War II left many large and urgent responsibilities, such as housing, veterans' affairs and international problems in its wake, only two postwar problems will be mentioned here. These two, contract termination and the disposal of surplus property, are included because they were handled by agencies of an emergency character and because work on them was begun before the cessation of hostilities.

The *Office of Contract Settlement* was established by the Contract Settlement Act of 1944, approved July 1, 1944. It was preceded by the Joint Contract Termination board, established on Nov. 12, 1943, by the Director of War Mobilization to develop unified policies governing contract terminations. The office was advised by a Contract Settlement Advisory board consisting of the heads of the departments and agencies most closely concerned with contract termination. By act of congress approved Oct. 3, 1944, the office was placed within the Office of War Mobilization and Reconversion. The function of the office was to prescribe the policies and procedures to govern the termination of war contracts by the various contracting agencies.[8] (*See* also WAR PRODUCTION.)

The *Surplus War Property administration* was established within the Office of War Mobilization by an executive order of Feb. 1944. The administrator, aided by a policy board, was directed by the order to supervise the handling and disposition of surplus war property. General policies and procedures were established by the board; actual disposition was handled by other agencies. This agency was terminated on the establishment of the Surplus Property board.

The *Surplus Property board* was established by the Surplus Property Act of 1944, approved Oct. 3, 1944. A three-man board replaced the previous administrator, and the act established a number of policies as to preferential treatment of certain groups in the disposal of surplus property. Actual disposal was handled by a number of agencies: department of commerce, Reconstruction Finance corporation, maritime commission, War Food administration, National Housing agency, and others. The board was abolished with the creation of the Surplus Property administration.

The *Surplus Property administration* was established within the Office of War Mobilization and Reconversion by act of congress approved Sept. 18, 1945. This agency continued to handle policy-making functions; disposal activities were progressively concentrated in the War Assets corporation under the supervision of the Reconstruction Finance corporation. An executive order of Jan. 31, 1946, placed the functions of the Surplus Property administration, along with those of the War Assets corporation under the jurisdiction of the War Assets administration, which was created by the same order. (*See* also SURPLUS PROPERTY DISPOSAL.)

The *War Assets administration* was established within the Office for Emergency Management by an executive order on Jan. 31, 1946, to administer the domestic surplus property disposal functions of the former Surplus Property administration and the War Assets corporation. (The latter had been established in the Reconstruction Finance Corp. in 1943 as the Petroleum Reserves Corp. Its name and functions were changed by amendment of its charter on Nov. 9, 1945, and on Jan. 15, 1946, it was designated by the surplus property administrator as the disposal agency for all kinds of surplus property for which RFC had been the disposal agency.) Thus the War Assets administration became the principal agency, both as to policy formulation and as to actual disposal, for domestic surplus property. (*See* also LAW.)

[8]The Office of Contract Settlement was transferred to the treasury department by executive order on Dec. 12, 1946.

BIBLIOGRAPHY.—Bureau of Labor Statistics, *Wartime Technological Developments,* a study made for the subcommittee on war mobilization of the committee on military affairs of the U.S. senate, U.S. Government Printing Office (May 1945); Civilian Production Administration, *Historical Reports* on war administration (series; multilithed); Committee on Records of War Administration, Bureau of the Budget, *The United States at War,* development and administration of the war program by the federal government, U.S. Government Printing Office (Jan. 1947); Leonard D. White, *Civil Service in Wartime* (1945).

(P. H. F.)

Great Britain

During World War II there was an unprecedented extension of governmental activity, and every aspect of British national life was touched at one point or another by the state fiat. Assuming responsibility for the whole organization of the war effort, the government directly and indirectly controlled all supplies, productive resources and manpower. To direct labour and productive resources, and to create the machinery required for these purposes, an immense amount of emergency and summary legislation was enacted, mainly in the form of defense regulations. These regulations gave "sub-legislative" powers to ministers of the crown, and they, in turn, delegated their authority to officials of their departments and other appointed representatives or controllers. War agencies in the U.S. sense had no exact parallel in wartime Britain, where executive and regulating powers remained in the hands of government departments acting either directly or through regional or local controllers. Advisory committees and councils were appointed early in World War

"Is There a Screwdriver in the House?" Crawford of the *Newark Evening News* illustrated the problem of gearing the world's industrial machine to a peacetime economy after the surrender of Japan in Aug. 1945

II to help the government in this work.

In assuming the full direction and regulation of the war effort, both military and industrial, the state took upon itself a large number of new functions, which necessitated the creation of new departments and an extension of the field of action of existing ones.

The most important of the departments whose powers were widened in World War II were the board of trade (control of imports and exports, control and limitation of consumer goods apart from food, and price regulation, the latter being enforced by a central price regulation committee); ministry of labour and national service (formerly the ministry of labour; it had additional responsibilities during the war of administering the National Service acts, of apportioning manpower as between the armed forces, civil defense and industry, and of organizing and controlling the supply of labour for war industries; to give effect to the powers invested in the minister by the Emergency Powers [Defense] act, 1940, a labour supply board with the minister as chairman, was formed in May, 1940); ministry of health (responsible for certain aspects of civil defense, the wartime organization of hospitals, medical treatment of air-raid casualties and the evacuation of the civilian population); and the ministry of agriculture (responsible for home food production and given wide powers of control over agricultural land; it delegated many of its powers to county war agricultural committees).

The new departments or ministries created for war purposes are given below.

Ministry of Aircraft Production.—A minister for aircraft production was first appointed in May 1940 when, on the resignation of Neville Chamberlain, a new cabinet was formed by Winston Churchill. The whole planning of the aircraft production program was placed in the minister's hands, and he was given very wide powers of control over the aircraft industry. Purchases of aircraft from the United States were also this ministry's responsibility.

Ministry of Civil Aviation.—In April 1940, the undertakings of Imperial Airways and of British Airways were transferred to the British Overseas Airways corporation. This body operated its services as required by the secretary of state for air. In 1944 a ministry of civil aviation was created to take over the air transport undertakings belonging to the B.O.A.C.; it continued to conduct the services for the air ministry.

Ministry of Economic Warfare.—Formed on the outbreak of World War II, its function was the disorganization of the economic life of Germany. It superintended the blockade of Germany, instituted the "navicert" system, made competitive purchases of war materials in neutral countries and negotiated trade agreements. It was abolished in May 1945.

Ministry of Food.—This department, created in 1939, was responsible for the control and distribution of food supplies throughout the war, and it was still carrying out these functions in 1946. It arranged the import and production of food, accumulated reserves, fixed food prices and rationed food to consumers. In Oct. 1939, the ministry set up a system of licensing for the sale of all food, and this control, as well as rationing, first introduced in June 1940, was effected by a network of local food control offices.

The ministry also made provision for the supply of food to bombed areas.

Ministry of Fuel, Light and Power.—This ministry was formed in June 1942 to take over the functions of the ministry of mines and those of the petroleum department of the board of trade. It was given full control of the coal industry. The minister was assisted by a controller-general and by regional controllers in each district. A national coal board was also appointed by the minister to advise him on all matters affecting the running of the industry. The rationing of fuel was later introduced by this ministry, and it was implemented by its regional and local fuel offices.

Ministry of Home Security.—This ministry was established in 1939 to co-ordinate all civil defense arrangements, which included air-raid precautions and similar emergency services. The post of minister was combined with that of secretary of state for home affairs. During the war the combined ministries, besides being responsible for civil defense (organization of which was placed in the hands of 12 regional commissioners), directed the operation of all security regulations, including the institution of a national registration system, the regulation of aliens, etc.

Ministry of Information.—This was one of the two ministries formed immediately on the outbreak of World War II. Its main functions were the provision of means for the communication of news to the press, censorship, the dissemination of propaganda in axis countries, and publicity in Allied and neutral countries. The department of postal and telegraph censorship of the war office was transferred to this ministry, which was abolished in 1946.

Ministry of Shipping.—The ministry was instituted in Oct. 1939 to assume functions which were previously the responsibility of the board of trade and to co-ordinate the activities of the merchant fleet. It requisitioned all U.K. shipping in Feb. 1940. It was amalgamated with the ministry of transport in May 1941 to form the ministry of war transport. The ministry of transport itself took over the control of the national railway systems and the London Passenger Transport board at the outbreak of war, the minister appointing a railway executive committee which operated the railways on his behalf.

Ministry of Supply.—Formed in July 1939 to acquire and maintain reserves of essential metals and other raw materials in connection with the defense program, the ministry was given wide powers of control over industry during World War II. It regulated the distribution of commodities, fixed commodity prices, placed war contracts and established boards of control over a number of industries. It was assisted by a supply council from Sept. 1939, and it established area committees throughout the country in Dec. 1939.

In May 1940, regulations gave this ministry power to declare all war production undertakings "controlled undertakings," and in June of that year 1,500 firms were subjected to this control.

Such controlled undertakings worked under the directions of a government department, usually the admiralty, the ministry of aircraft production or the ministry of supply.

Ministry of War Production.—All duties previously exercised by the production executive, which was a cabinet committee formed in 1941, except those of manpower, were transferred to this department when it was formed in Feb. 1942. Broadly, its tasks were the supervision and guidance of the various departments concerned with production, the allocation of available services of productive capacity and the settlement of priorities. The ministry was given even wider powers in March 1942. Thereafter it concerted the activities of the production departments, adjusted existing programs and initiated policy. It was also given control of raw materials and machine tools, and, in co-operation with the ministry of national service, of labour itself. In June 1942, devolution of the ministry's authority was effected by the creation of 11 regional boards of production. A national production advisory council to advise the minister of production on general production questions, excluding those normally handled by the joint organizations of the Trades Union congress and employers, was also formed. In March 1943 the minister conferred on himself powers to appoint three directors to the board of any firm working for the government with government capital. This ministry also made appointments to the combined production and resources board set up in Washington. The ministry was merged in the board of trade in May 1945.

Ministry of Works and Planning.—Founded in Oct. 1940 to erect all works and buildings required by government departments, and to license private building, the ministry also decided as to the priority of air-raid damage proposals. Prior to Feb. 1942 it was known as the ministry of works and buildings; in that month its functions were widened to include those of post-war planning. (C. Ns.)

War Boards, British-U.S.

See British-U.S. War Boards.

War Bonds

On May 1, 1941, the United States government began to raise the huge sums necessary to finance World War II. Between that date and Dec. 31, 1945, the government spent $350,000,000,000, of which $318,000,000,000 was for war purposes. It took in $147,000,000,000 (net) in taxes and other revenues. A net increase in the public debt of $225,000,000,000 was required to meet the deficit and to build up the cash balance to the level required by the large expenditure volume.

Three principles guided the treasury in borrowing the tremendous sums required to finance the war program. The first was that the funds should be raised in such a way as to minimize the risk of inflation. In order to accomplish this objective it was necessary to sell a large proportion of the total to investors other than banks. In order to do this the treasury initiated a campaign to sell savings bonds to the people as early as May 1941. It initiated a pay roll savings plan for the sale of war bonds to wage and salary earners, and it conducted seven war loans and a Victory Loan sales campaign.

The second principle was that the securities offered should be best suited to the needs of the investors to whom they were sold. In order to do this the treasury sold a wide variety of securities—some short term, some medium and some long. To small investors it sold savings bonds—a security which was made absolutely free from risk of price fluctuation and was redeemable on demand after a short holding period.

The third principle was that the cost of financing should be kept at a reasonable level. By the war's end the average rate of interest was 1.96%. After World War I—when the public debt had risen to $24,000,000,000—the average rate was 4.22% on June 30, 1920.

Of the $225,000,000,000 borrowed to finance the war, the funds raised in the eight drives amounted to $156,900,000,000. Of this total, $43,300,000,000, or 28%, was sold to individuals, partnerships and personal trust accounts. Sales in the First War Loan, which was the smallest, totalled $12,900,000,000. Sales in the Seventh War Loan, the largest, amounted to $26,300,000,000.

Sales of restricted issues, that is, marketable securities not eligible for bank ownership, together with the sales of non-marketable securities (savings bonds and notes) amounted to $88,700,000,000 or 57% of the total sales. In the Seventh War Loan and in the Victory Loan, the sales of restricted issues and non-marketable securities amounted to 75% and 82% of the respective total sales.

The kinds of securities purchased by the various investor groups in the eight loans combined are shown in the table below.

The Series E savings bond was the security principally relied upon for sale to small investors during the war

"They Put Him Across." Jerry Costello in the *Knickerbocker News* (Albany, N.Y.), credited the U.S. press for its effective support in government war bond drives during World War II

Purchases by Each Investor Group in the Aggregate in Seven War Loans and the Victory Loan
(millions of dollars)

Investor Groups	All Issues	Savings Bonds (issue price) E	F and G	Savings Notes	Bills	Certificates	Notes	Medium-term Bonds	Long-term Bonds (2½'s)
Nonbank investors:									
1. Individuals, partnerships and personal trust accounts	43,259	19,942	4,061	1,286	—	2,642	563	8,203	6,559
2. Savings banks	12,435	—	45	5	—	592	254	7,604	3,932
3. Insurance companies	22,121	—	72	9	—	980	407	6,115	14,538
4. Dealers and brokers	4,203	—	‡	1	—	1,605	187	1,796	612
5. State and local governments	8,164	—	162	564	—	3,455	317	1,405	2,258
6. Building and loan and savings and loan associations*	1,868	—	40	8	—	59	46	1,160	556
7. Corporations and associations†	53,462	—	1,614	15,221	—	22,303	1,724	7,951	4,650
8. Treasury investment accounts	1,219	—	—	—	—	1	—	151	1,067
9. All nonbank investors	146,727	19,942	5,995	17,095	—	31,637	3,498	34,386	34,173
Commercial banks	10,166	—	—	—	1,716	4,268	—	4,183	—
All investors	156,893	19,942	5,995	17,095	1,716	35,905	3,498	38,569	34,173

*Separate figures for this group were tabulated only for the Sixth, Seventh and Victory Loans.
†Includes federal agencies and trust funds.
‡Less than $500,000.

New Yorkers lining Fifth avenue to watch a military parade marking the start of the Third U.S. War Loan drive Sept. 9, 1943

financing period. Nearly $40,000,000,000 of E bonds were sold. Of this total, more than $19,900,000,000 were sold in the eight loans. This amount constituted 46% of all securities sold to individuals.

E bond sales were promoted through the pay roll savings plan and other sales devices so that by the end of the war, these bonds had been placed in the hands of some 85,000,000 individuals. Highest sales occurred in the Fourth, Fifth, Sixth and Seventh Loans which took place during the 18 months beginning with Jan. 1944. This was the period when wartime earnings were at their highest levels. In companies and other organizations operating pay roll savings plans, separate pay roll deduction programs were arranged for the periods of the drives, and at the same time campaigns for extra cash sales were promoted. In five loans, pay roll purchases represented the largest proportion of E bond sales; and in the last four loans pay roll sales constituted well above 50% of the total E bond sales.

In the eight loans, 61% of total E bond sales came from 11 states, in each of which sales were more than $500,000,000. Six of these states—New York, California, Pennsylvania, Illinois, Ohio and Michigan—topped the $1,000,000,000 mark. Texas, New Jersey, Massachusetts, Iowa and Indiana were included in the $500,000,000 sales category.

Sales in the eight drives entailed the issuance of more than 450,000,000 separate E bonds. The largest volume sold in a drive, $4,000,000,000 in the Seventh War Loan, was represented by 92,000,000 units. In the first four war loans, Series E bonds were issued in the following denominations: $25, $50, $100, $500 and $1,000. Beginning in the Fifth War Loan there was offered also a $10 denomination which was available only to members of the armed forces. In the Victory Loan, the $200 denomination Roosevelt Memorial bond was introduced.

A total of $54,700,000,000 of E, F and G savings bonds was sold between May 1, 1941, and Dec. 31, 1945. These sales represented 997,000,000 separate Series E bonds, 4,000,000 Series F bonds and nearly 10,000,000 Series G bonds.

By the end of World War II the net result of the U.S. war financing program was that investors generally owned securities adapted to their needs. Savings banks and insurance companies owned principally long-term marketable bonds. Individuals owned mostly nonnegotiable savings bonds, redeemable on demand. Commercial banks owned medium- and short-term securities. Nonfinancial corporations owned mostly short-term securities. The maturity structure of the debt thus obtained was in a position to play its part as an aid to smooth reconversion immediately after the close of the war. (V. L. Ck.)

Great Britain.—The policy pursued by Great Britain in financing World War II differed materially from that pursued during World War I. Instead of covering the deficit through the issue of irredeemable or long-term stocks, the British treasury raised the necessary money through the issue of medium-term bonds. The new method had been inaugurated before the war, through the issue in 1937 of £100,000,000 2½% national defense bonds for the purpose of financing the cost of rearmament. The same method of medium-term financing was pursued throughout the war, and even after the war, and the total of medium-term bonds issued exceeded £7,000,000,000. They carried interest at 2½% or 3% with the exception of the exchequer bond issue of £326,000,000, issued at 1¾%.

Throughout the war the policy was successfully followed to offer each new issue on terms slightly less favourable to the investor than the preceding one, due allowance being made for their maturity. While during World War I, government borrowing became increasingly dearer to the taxpayer, during World War II it became gradually cheaper. The explanation lay in the application of Lord Keynes's principles of public finance to the financing of war expenditure. Instead of trying to force long-term loans on a reluctant investing public, the deficit was largely financed by an increase in the floating debt bearing interest at ½%. As the capital available for reinvestment increased, the public was given an opportunity to acquire medium-term bonds at 2½% or 3%. This opportunity was eagerly taken, partly because, as a result of the control of private issues, there was no possibility of large-scale reinvestment in any other form, and partly because investors came to realize that the treasury was in a position virtually to determine the rate of interest at which to place its war bonds. This belief in the treasury's omnipotence derived from a growing realization of the possibilities of scientific monetary management.

Even before 1939 the British authorities had been able to keep interest rates steady for many years by means of controlling new capital issues and regulating the volume of bank credit. The prestige they had thus gained during the years 1932–39 was an important factor in helping them to issue war bonds at a low interest rate, notwithstanding the large amount of their financial requirements. Thanks to this policy it was possible to keep down the burden of the increased public debt. Thus the total of the national debt at the end of the financial year 1945–46 had at £24,539,400,000, almost trebled in comparison with the corresponding 1939–40 figure (£8,931,600,000), while the interest charges and management expenses had only doubled at £455,400,000 against £222,800,000; the average percentage of interest on the national debt had dropped from 2.5% (1939–40) to 1.87% (1945–46). But there were dark spots in the picture. The floating debt now represented a large proportion of the total public debt (approximately 27% against 10% before the war) and large amounts of war bonds were maturing during the early reconstruction period. So long as the investors believed in the treasury's ability of keeping down, and even reducing further, interest rates, the renewal of maturing war bonds was not likely to encounter any major difficulties. (*See* also BANKING; DEBTS, NATIONAL.) (P. EG.)

BIBLIOGRAPHY.—R. K. Merton, *Mass Persuasion: The Social Psychology of a War Bond Drive* (1946); H. Morgenthau, *War Finance Policies* (1944); *Moody's Bond Survey* (1936–*et seq.*); S. F. Porter, *How to Make Money in Government Bonds* (1939). Periodical: *The Minute Man* (U.S. Treas.). *See* also publications of the U.S. Treasury.

War Chest

See COMMUNITY CHEST.

War Committees, Joint (U.S. and Canada)

See CANADIAN-U.S. WAR COMMITTEES.

War Communications, Board of

See FEDERAL COMMUNICATIONS COMMISSION.

War Contracts

See WAR PRODUCTION.

War Crimes

On Jan. 13, 1942, an inter-Allied conference met in London, England, with delegates present from the governments of Belgium, Czechoslovakia, Free France, Greece, Luxembourg, the Netherlands, Norway, Poland and Yugoslavia. Representatives of Great Britain, Australia, Canada, India, New Zealand, the Union of South Africa, the United States of America, the Union of Soviet Socialist Republics and China were present as guests. In a joint declaration on the punishment of war crimes the conferees resolved to "place among their principal war aims the punishment, through the channel of organized justice, of those guilty of or responsible for these crimes, whether they have ordered them, perpetrated them, or participated in them."

On Aug. 21, 1942, Pres. F. D. Roosevelt made a declaration on war criminality which concluded with these words: "It seems only fair that they (the war criminals) should have this warning that the time will come when they shall have to stand in the courts of law in the very countries which they are now oppressing and answer for their acts."

Then on Oct. 7, 1942, Pres. Roosevelt for the United States and Lord Simon, lord chancellor, for the British government in separate declarations announced "the intention to apprehend and punish war criminals, as well as to create an agency to investigate war crimes."

The following year, on Oct. 20, 1943, at a meeting of government representatives at the foreign office in London, the commission was brought into being under the title, United Nations War Crimes commission.

The commission consisted of 16 members—the representatives of the governments of Australia, Belgium, Canada, China, Czechoslovakia, France, Greece, India, Luxembourg, the Netherlands, New Zealand, Norway, Poland, the United Kingdom, the United States of America and Yugoslavia. These representatives were all distinguished diplomatists and lawyers.

Sir Cecil Hurst, United Kingdom representative and vice-president of the Permanent Court of International Justice, was the first chairman of the commission. He resigned on account of ill health and was succeeded on Jan. 31, 1945, by Lord Wright, lord of appeal in ordinary, representing Australia on the commission.

Duties of the Commission.—The commission was created

General view of the International Military tribunal in Tokyo, where 28 Japanese charged with war crimes went to trial on June 13, 1946. The prisoners' dock, under military guard, is at the left

as a fact-finding body, but was later also given advisory functions. It soon became apparent that the commission could not itself investigate the mass of charges and reports of war crimes. Shortly after its formation the commission, therefore, urgently recommended to each of the member nations that it establish a national war crimes office to investigate war crimes against the citizens of its own country. Each established a war crimes office to detect, investigate and record evidence of war crimes. When a national office determined that a case was reasonably complete, it forwarded a summary to the United Nations War Crimes commission or its subcommission in the far east, which examined the information and materials.

These bodies, if they believed that a war crime had been committed and that the information showed that there was, or would be at the time of trial, sufficient evidence to justify a prosecution, placed the name or description of the individual upon their lists. The actual investigation, including the detection of crime, interviewing of witnesses, and preparation of cases, was done by the official agencies best suited to conduct investigations within the national boundaries and according to the laws of each country.

After official lists of war criminals had been prepared by the commission, they were furnished to the apprehending authorities in order that the persons named might be arrested and turned over to the proper nation for trial.

The commission had three principal standing committees: the Committee on Facts and Evidence, the Committee on Enforcement and the Committee on Legal Questions.

The Subcommission for the Far East was created in May 1944 with its location originally at Chungking. This subcommission was composed of representatives of Australia, Belgium, China, Czechoslovakia, France, India, Luxembourg, the Netherlands, Poland, the United Kingdom and the United States. Its function was to examine information against Japanese war criminals, and to prepare lists for forwarding to all participating nations. However, the main commission in London was not precluded from receiving evidence of war crimes in the far east, and considered a number of charges against Japanese.

The soviet union was not a member of the United Nations War Crimes commission but had a commission of its own—the Russian Extraordinary State commission.

After the formation of the United Nations War Crimes commission the United States had a full-time commissioner and, for most of the time, a deputy commissioner, and maintained offices and staff in London. The U.S. commissioner not only performed his duties upon instruction of the state department, but also maintained close liaison with both the war crimes organizations in the field and with the war crimes office in the civil affairs division of the war department, which furnished trained officers to represent the United States on the commission.

Herbert C. Pell, formerly U.S. minister to Portugal and Hungary and former member of congress, was the first commissioner to represent the United States. He was succeeded on May 10, 1945, by Colonel Joseph V. Hodgson, who had served both as deputy and acting commissioner since Jan. 1, 1945. Lieutenant Earl W. Kintner, then deputy commissioner, served as acting commissioner after the resignation of Colonel Hodgson on May 17, 1946. Colonel Robert M. Springer was appointed commissioner by President Harry S. Truman on July 18, 1946. (R. P. P.)

←

Nazi commander of the concentration camp at Altendorn, Germany, being taken into custody by U.S. military police in 1945, as former inmates cheered in the background. On April 1, 1946, there were 13,582 Germans on the U.N. list of war criminals

The Nuernberg Trial.—When the Nuernberg trial was opened on Nov. 20, 1945, Lord Justice Lawrence, the president, described it as "unique in the history of the jurisprudence of the world and of supreme importance to millions of people all over the globe."

Originally 24 defendants were indicted. Martin Bormann was tried and sentenced to death in his absence. It was not known whether he was a fugitive or dead. On Oct. 25, 1945, Robert Ley committed suicide in Nuernberg jail, in a cell adjacent to that in which, a year later, Hermann Goering anticipated the gallows. On Nov. 15, 1945, the tribunal decided that the aged Gustav Krupp von Bohlen und Halbach could not then be tried because of his physical and mental condition. Without Krupp, the list of defendants lost its representative character as a cross-section of nazi power. By Nov. 15, however, public impatience at the delay was so great that further postponement was considered inadvisable, though the decision to continue without an industrialist in the dock was by no means unanimous. The proceedings in the closed sessions, both of the judges and of the prosecutors, were necessarily secret. Differences between representatives of four differing legal systems and procedures, with conflicting political attitudes and speaking different languages, were inevitable. One of the outstanding achievements of the trial was the extent to which those differences were bridged, both on the bench and at the prosecution tables. Until the very last day, when the dissenting opinion of the Russian judge was published, the United Nations at Nuernberg remained united. It should be noted, however, that this dissenting soviet opinion embodied many of the submissions made by each of the Allied prosecutors. They had called unanimously for the conviction not only of the three defendants—Hjalmar Schacht, Franz von Papen and Hans Fritzsche—who were acquitted by a majority vote of the tribunal, but also for the condemnation of the *Sturm-Abteilungen* (the S.A.), the high command and general staff and the reich cabinet, which again the majority of the tribunal declined to declare criminal groups or organizations. Although there were differences between the judges as to the form of punishment of some of the convicted defendants, there was no recorded conflict as to the fact of their guilt or as to a finding of criminality against the leadership corps of the nazi party, the *Schutz-Staffeln* (the S.S.) (including the *Sicherheits-Dienst* (the S.D.) and the *Geheime Staats-Polizei* (the gestapo).

When the hearing of evidence and the speeches of counsel ended on Aug. 31, 1946, more than 400 open sessions of the tribunal had been held. Thirty-three witnesses gave evidence orally for the prosecution, among them German generals (even a field marshal), S.S. chiefs, survivors of concentration camps and those who had commanded them. Sixty-one internees, in addition to 19 of the defendants themselves, spoke for the defense; a further 143 gave evidence for the defense by means of written answers to interrogation.

There was the mountain of evidence relating to the indicted organizations, given by more than 100 witnesses and about 200,000 affidavits. Thousands of documents were submitted by each side. The prosecution case was largely founded on the researches of Allied investigators who, in the wake of the Allied armies, unearthed in salt mines, in holes in the ground, in secret places behind false walls, in hastily abandoned headquarters, most of the secrets of the third reich. It was their own documents, not the eloquence of Allied counsel or the accusations of their victims, that

Hermann Goering, chief defendant in the United Nations trial of war criminals at Nuernberg, Germany, took the stand in his own defense in March 1946, pleading not guilty

condemned the nazi chiefs; the whole atmosphere of the trial was one of fact-finding.

Such was the nature of the court's proceedings that there was unqualified acceptance of the court's authority by the accused and their counsel. "I am firm in the conviction that truth and justice will prevail before this tribunal," said Baron Konstantin von Neurath in his final plea. On Oct. 1, 1946, when the tribunal sentenced 12 of the accused to death (Hermann Wilhelm Goering, Joachim von Ribbentrop, Wilhelm Keitel, Ernst Kaltenbrunner, Alfred Rosenberg, Hans Frank, Wilhelm Frick, Julius Streicher, Fritz Sauckel, Alfred Jodl, Arthur Seyss-Inquart and Martin Bormann), not one of them protested or challenged the tribunal's authority. Before them, for ten months, history had been patiently unfolded. Their contribution to it was shown to be, first, aggressive, premeditated war against 12 nations—in Europe more than 10,000,000 soldiers, sailors, airmen and civilians killed in battle; townships wrecked from London to Stalingrad, the countryside devastated and the aftermath of war in disease and hunger felt through most of the world. Second, genocide, the deliberate nazi attempt to destroy whole nations and races. Third, mass murder: not less than 12,000,000 men, women and children exterminated scientifically; two-thirds of the Jewish race in Europe dead; most of these 12,000,000 gassed and burned in the ovens of Oswiecim (Auschwitz) and Treblinka, Dachau, Buchenwald, Matthausen, Majdanek and Marienburg, and the rest butchered in mass graves all over Europe. Fourth, 7,000,000 men, women and children taken into slavery. Finally, the moral perversion of the German people by the nazis; of their corruption into naziism, the defendant Baldur von Schirach, leader of the Hitler Youth, confessed, "It is my fault that I educated German youth for a man who committed murders millionfold."

The legal bases of the trial were the cause of much controversy. The conflicting contentions were argued by the prosecutors and by the most eminent of German counsel at the trial itself. Most of the commentators singled out as the major legal achievement of the trial the vindication of what the British chief prosecutor, Sir Hartley Shawcross, described as "the salutory legal rule that persons who, in violation of the law, plunge their own and other countries into aggressive war, do so with a halter round their necks." In the final result, however, each of the 12 defendants who was sentenced to death was found guilty of committing war crimes and (or) crimes against humanity. No one was hanged for waging aggressive war alone. Rudolf Hess, although convicted under counts one and two of the indictment of planning and waging aggressive wars, was not sentenced to death.

Many, alarmed by the persistence of persecution on political, racial and religious grounds in the postwar world, were disappointed with the tribunal's limitation of the legal conception of "crimes against humanity" under the charter, to crimes against humanity which were committed in execution of or in connection with aggressive war or war crimes. Nuernberg, however, was the beginning, not the end, of the effort described by Justice Jackson, the U.S. chief prosecutor, in his opening speech: "to put the forces of international law, its prospects, its prohibitions and, most of all, its sanctions, on the side of peace, so that men and women of good will, in all countries, may have 'leave to live by no man's leave,' underneath the law." (*See* also ALLIED MILITARY GOVERNMENT; INTERNATIONAL LAW; LAW.)

(F. E. J.)

BIBLIOGRAPHY.—L. C. Bial, *Vergeltung und Wiedergutmachung in Deutschland* (Havana, 1945); G. Creel, *War Criminals and Punishment* (London, 1945); S. Glueck, *Nuremberg Trial and Aggressive War* (1946), *War Criminals* (1944); International Military Tribunal, *Case Against the Nazi War Criminals* (1946), *Indictment* (London, 1945); R. H. Jackson, *Case Against the Nazi War Criminals* (1946); H. Kelsen, *Peace Through Law* (1944); M. Lachs, *War Crimes, an Attempt to Define the Issues* (London, 1945); M. H. Myerson, *Germany's War Crimes and Punishment* (1945); E. Rubin, *Nuremberg Trial* (1945); A. N. Trainin, *Hitlerite Responsibility under Criminal Law* (1945); Q. Wright, "War Criminals," *Am. Jl. of Intl. Law* 39:257–285 (1945); U.S. Dept. of State, *Trial of War Criminals: Documents* (1945).

War Damage Corporation

See INSURANCE.

War Damage Insurance

See INSURANCE.

War Debts (World War I)

The World War I indebtedness of foreign governments to the United States as of July, 1946, is indicated in the following table:

Country	Principal	Accrued Interest	Total Indebtedness
Funded debts:			
Belgium . . .	$ 400,680,000.00	$ 111,215,077.60	$ 511,895,077.60
Czechoslovakia	165,241,108.90	14,418,713.03	179,659,821.93
Estonia . . .	16,466,012.87	8,598,217.94	25,064,230.81
Finland . . .	7,734,932.45	683,583.56	8,418,516.01
France . . .	3,863,650,000.00	820,031,394.40	4,683,681,394.40
Germany (Austrian indebtedness) . .*	25,980,480.66	44,058.93	26,024,539.59
Great Britain	4,368,000,000.00	2,199,564,782.58	6,567,564,782.58
Greece . . .	31,516,000.00	5,793,375.10	37,309,375.10
Hungary. . .	1,908,560.00	898,748.21	2,807,308.21
Italy	2,004,900,000.00	52,295,159.34	2,057,195,159.34
Latvia. . . .	6,879,464.20	3,474,733.84	10,354,198.04
Lithuania. . .	6,197,682.00	3,082,026.11	9,279,708.11
Poland . . .	206,057,000.00	107,606,444.20	313,663,444.20
Rumania. . .	63,860,560.43	12,880,838.94	76,741,399.37
Yugoslavia. .	61,625,000.00	2,079,843.78	63,704,843.78
Total . . .	$11,230,696,801.51	$3,342,666,997.56	$14,573,363,799.07
Unfunded debts:			
Armenia . .	$ 11,959,917.49	$ 16,029,157.71	$ 27,989,075.20
Russia. . . .	192,601,297.37	265,108,005.45	457,709,302.82
Total . . .	$ 204,561,214.86	$ 281,137,163.16	$ 485,698,378.02
Total of above. .	$11,435,258,016.37	$3,623,804,160.72	$15,059,062,177.09
Germany†			
Army costs (reichsmarks)	997,500,000.00	75,606,895.25	1,073,106,895.25
Awards of Mixed Claims commission (reichsmarks)	2,040,000,000.00	216,240,000.00	2,256,240,000.00
Total (reichsmarks). .	3,037,500,000.00	291,846,895.25	3,329,346,895.25
Total (in dollars at 40.33 cents to the reichsmark)	$ 1,225,023,750.00	$ 117,701,852.85	$ 1,342,725,602.85

*The German government had been notified that the government of the United States would look to the German government for the discharge of this indebtedness of the government of Austria to the government of the United States.

†Indebtedness to the United States under agreements of June 23, 1930, and May 26, 1932.

During the ten-year period since July 1, 1937, the principal of all these debts had remained unchanged, except in the case of Finland, which had reduced its principal from $8,270,138.77. No other country with World War I indebtedness to the United States made any payments toward principal during the decade. The total of accrued interest as of July 1, 1937, was as follows: funded debts, $1,155,927,945.22; unfunded debts, $189,084,616.50; Germany, $15,637,753.31. (E. F. B.; X.)

War Department, U.S.

See GOVERNMENT DEPARTMENTS AND BUREAUS.

War Food Administration

See WAR AND DEFENSE AGENCIES.

War Information, Office of

See PSYCHOLOGICAL WARFARE; PSYCHOLOGY; WAR AND DEFENSE AGENCIES.

War Labor Board, National

See WAR AND DEFENSE AGENCIES.

War Manpower Commission

See WAR AND DEFENSE AGENCIES.

War Medicine

See MEDICINE; MILITARY MEDICINE; NURSING, WAR; PSYCHIATRY; REHABILITATION OF THE DISABLED; SURGERY.

War Mobilization and Reconversion, Office of

See WAR AND DEFENSE AGENCIES.

War Prisoners

See PRISONERS OF WAR.

War Production

The tremendous volume of war equipment produced by the United States was a major factor in the victory of the United Nations in World War II. The world's battlefronts were not only amply supplied with munitions, but the basic economy was maintained in a healthy condition, capable of sustained support of the war effort, and the total national production of goods and services rose to the highest level in the nation's history.

The U.S. Production Record.—Although the U.S. was not a belligerent until the Japanese attack on Pearl Harbor on Dec. 7, 1941, the initiation of the rearmament program dated from mid-1940, and followed closely on the German invasion of the Low Countries and France. From July 1, 1940, to July 31, 1945, just two weeks before the formal capitulation of Japan, the U.S. produced $181,000,000,000 worth of munitions. Of this total, aircraft constituted 24%; ships, 22%; clothing equipage, medical supplies and other miscellaneous equipment and supplies, 20%; combat and motor vehicles, including tanks and trucks, 12%; ammunition, 10%; guns and fire control equipment, 6%; and communications and electronic equipment including radio and radar, 6%. The year-by-year rise in munitions production (measured in dollar terms on the basis of 1945 unit costs) was as follows:

July 1, 1940—Dec. 31, 1941	$10,489,000,000
1942	30,168,000,000
1943	51,745,000,000
1944	57,594,000,000
Jan. 1—July 31, 1945	30,767,000,000

Measured by units or by weight, rather than by dollar value, the five year production achievement was even more remarkable. More than 296,000 military aeroplanes and special purpose aircraft were produced. About 97,000 were bombers, 99,000 fighters and 24,000 transports, the rest being trainer, communication and reconnaissance planes and special purpose aircraft. Naval construction amounted to 71,000 ships weighing 8,200,000 displacement tons. The great number of these were landing vessels, which also accounted for 35% of the total tonnage. Combatant vessels, though only 1,200 in number, accounted for 43% of the total tonnage. The maritime commission built 4,800 merchant ships weighing 50,400,000 deadweight tons. The bulk of the merchant vessels, more than 65%, were emergency cargo vessels specially designed for wartime mass production even at the expense of speed of movement in the water.

Other achievements included the production of 86,000 tanks, 2,500,000 trucks, 41,600,000,000 rounds of small arms ammunition, 4,200,000 short tons of ground artillery ammunition and 5,800,000 short tons of aircraft bombs.

The significance of U.S. production of munitions could best be appraised against the munitions production of other nations. In 1944, the peak year, the U.S. produced 43% of the world's $100,000,000,000 output of combat munitions. This was more than the rest of the United Nations combined; it was also more than the axis nations combined. It was estimated that the other United Nations produced almost a third, and the axis a little more than a quarter, of the world's munitions in 1944.

While exact international comparisons were not feasible, a rough comparison could be made of munitions production in the U.S. and the United Kingdom. Table I shows U.S. production of particular types of munitions in the period of July 1, 1940, to July 31, 1945, covering 61 months, and United Kingdom production of the same types of munitions in the period of Sept. 1939 to June 1944, covering 57 months. British production and that of other principal belligerents are discussed separately later.

Table I.—*Production of Selected Munitions in the United States and the United Kingdom*

(U.S. figures: 61 months, July 1, 1940, to July 31, 1945. U.K. figures: 57 months, Sept. 1939 to June 1944)

Munitions Item	United States	United Kingdom
Aircraft		
Total: Number	296,000	102,600
Airframe weight	2,474,276,000	587,700,000
Heavy bombers (number)	34,400	10,000
Medium and light bombers (number)	55,500	17,700
Fighters (number)	98,700	38,000
Naval Ships		
Total: Number	71,062	5,744
Displacement tons	8,243,000	1,807,077
Major naval vessels (number)	1,201	722
(displacement tons)	3,560,000	1,333,961
Landing vessels (number)	64,546	3,636*
(displacement tons)	2,905,000	440,320*
Tanks (number)	86,333	2,474
Small arms ammunition (million rounds)	41,585	1,411

*U.K. figures include some miscellaneous craft in addition to landing craft.

Source: U.S.: *Wartime Production Achievements and the Reconversion Outlook*: Report of the Chairman, War Production Board, Oct. 9, 1945 (U.S. Govt. Printing Office, 1945), pp. 106–109.
U.K.: *Statistics Relating to the War Effort of the United Kingdom*, Nov. 1944 (London: H.M. Stationery Office, Cmd. 6564), pp. 10–14.

The war production of the U.S. was accomplished primarily through pressing total national production to hitherto undreamed of heights, rather than by rigorous reduction of civilian living standards. Between 1939 and 1944, the total value of national output of goods and services rose from $88,600,000,000 to $198,700,000,000, a 125% increase. Inflationary influences were reflected in these figures, however. If the figures were adjusted to reflect 1939 dollar values throughout the period and thus more accurately to reflect actual production, the rise was from $88,600,000,000 to $135,000,000,000, a 52% increase. Of the total output in 1944, 40% was for war purposes, and 60% for nonwar purposes. Despite the absorption of so large a segment of national resources for war purposes, consumer purchases of goods and services were actually greater in 1944 than in 1939, but slightly less than in 1941. Though there were shortages of particular kinds of consumer items, and deterioration of the quality of goods and services, the civilian in the U.S. fared remarkably well. In contrast, the quantity of consumer goods and services purchased in the United Kingdom fell by 21% between 1938 and 1944.

The wartime emphasis on manufacturing, mining and construction meant that there were unusually great increases in these types of output. In fact, taking these activities as a single group, there was a doubling of output between 1939 and 1944. The average annual increase of this combined industrial production was more than 15%, compared with a 4% average for the 70 years from 1869–1939, and a 7% average for the 1914–18 period of World War I. The most nearly comparable increase was the 12% annual average achieved in the 1932–37 recovery from the depression of the early 1930s. Manufacturing itself (as distinct from mining and construction) trebled in output between 1939 and 1944. Production of raw materials rose in the same period by 60%. New construction doubled between 1939 and 1942, after which it fell back until in 1944 it was a third less than in 1939, reflecting the completion of war plants and the diversion of resources to use in manufacturing.

The U.S. munitions production program required conversion of many factories producing peacetime goods, construction of new plants and expansion of old ones, manufacture and installation of large numbers of machine tools, more intensive use of available plants and tools, accelerated production and importation of materials, enlargement of the total labour force of the country and raising of the productivity of the individual worker.

Conversion of plants was particularly important in the metal-working industries. In late 1944, almost three-fourths of the output of prewar metal-working plants consisted of military supplies. Almost a third of their output consisted of combat matériel, as distinct from products similar to those manufactured in peacetime. Certain industries upon which consumers in peacetime had made heavy demands shifted over to military supply to the almost complete exclusion of civilian requirements. In the last quarter of 1944, the motor vehicle and parts industry shipped 86% of its output as military supplies. The radio, radio tube and phonograph industry shipped 94% for the same purpose, while the comparable percentage for the communication equipment industry was 88%, and that for the refrigerator and refrigeration machinery industry was 79%.

The construction and equipment of new plants and the expansion of old plants were a major phase of the war program, especially from 1940–43. The manufacturing capacity of the country increased by about 50% between 1939 and 1945, at a cost of $25,000,000,000, most of it borne by the government. In terms of cost, the most substantial additions were those for aircraft, explosives and ammunition loading, ship construction and repair, guns and ammunition and iron and steel. Though smaller in amount, the expansions for other materials and products, notably synthetic rubber, aviation gasoline, aluminum and magnesium, were crucial to the success of the war program.

World War II resulted in no general shift in the geographical distribution of U.S. industry as a whole. Up to mid-1944, the major wartime facilities expansions were in Pennsylvania, Ohio, Michigan, Illinois, Wisconsin, New

Women aircraft workers finishing transparent bomber noses for fighter and reconnaissance planes at the Douglas Aircraft Co. plant in Long Beach, Calif., in 1942

York, California, Texas and Indiana. Each of these states added more than $1,000,000,000 worth of wartime facilities between July 1940 and May 1944, representing in each case more than 5% of the nation's total facilities expansion in this period. Most of such slightly industrialized states and local areas as did experience marked expansion of industrial capacity during the war owed the expansion primarily to such industries as aircraft and shipbuilding, which were not likely to have a postwar market comparable to that of wartime. In each of several states, such as Utah and Nevada, the great proportionate expansion of industrial capacity largely resulted from the construction of a single large plant, whose postwar utility was doubtful.

An important aspect of plant construction and of conversion of old plants was the provision of new machine tools adapted to the specialized needs of military production. The number of machine tools in the hands of U.S. manufacturers increased about 50% between the end of 1939 and the end of 1944. In the peak year, 1942, four times as many machine tools were shipped to U.S. factories as in 1940. These were notable achievements in the face of the fact that machine tools had been a major bottleneck in the defense period's rearmament program.

Maximum utilization of plants was another objective of the war supply program. While in 1939 factories probably were used not more than 40 hr. a week, by Dec. 1942 the plants in the war industries were averaging almost 90 hr. a week, and a number of the plants in the aviation program were averaging well above 100 hr. a week. The peak of plant utilization was reached in the spring of 1943, when 39% of the workers in metals-using industries were employed on the second and third shifts. It was estimated that this increased utilization of existing facilities added almost as much to industrial output as did the construction of new facilities.

The production of industrial raw materials, as noted above, rose by 60% between 1939 and 1944. Production of steel, basic to all major munitions as well as to many industrial equipment and civilian items, doubled in this period. Industrial chemicals production trebled. The year 1943 marked peak production for a number of key materials, among them aluminum, which was 5 times its 1939 production; magnesium, which was 55 times 1939 output; copper, whose smelting in 1943 was 40% above the rate of 1939.

The U.S. was almost wholly dependent on foreign countries for 48 of the 136 raw materials listed as strategic and critical at the beginning of the war. Examples were tin ore, natural rubber, chrome, manganese, nickel, tantalite, and burlap and rope fibres. In addition, foreign sources were called on to supplement the domestic production of such materials as copper, lead and bauxite.

The total labour force of the country was markedly expanded during the war. It rose from 54,000,000 to 64,000,000 persons between 1939 and 1944. The number of actually employed persons rose even more, for the unemployed in the total labour force fell from 9,500,000 in 1939 to 840,000 in 1944. Of the 18,700,000 persons thus actually at work in 1944 who in 1939 had been either unemployed workers or persons not connected with the labour force, the armed forces took 11,000,000, leaving 7,700,000 as net additions to the civilian working force. More than 6,500,000 workers moved into the manufacturing, mining and construction industries between 1939 and 1943, the peak year for this type of employment.

The vast expansion of the U.S. industrial output depended in part on the increased productivity of the individual worker. One way of achieving this was through lengthening the work week. In 1944, the average work week in manufacturing was more than 45 hr., a 20% increase over the 38 hr. worked in 1939. In durable goods production, especially vital to the munitions program, there was a 25% increase in the work week, from 38 hr. in 1939 to 47 hr. in 1944. Other factors in increased productivity were increased worker efficiency, provision of up-to-date plant equipment, labour-management committees sponsored by the war production drive, intercompany pooling of information on efficient production techniques, application of mass production methods to products not previously manufactured by such methods, greater use of large plants and, of course, the patriotic incentives of wartime. Whatever the factors, it was estimated that the productivity of labour increased by about 25% between 1939 and 1944.

"Defense" Period, 1940–41.—Between May 1940 and Dec. 1941, the U.S., though not a belligerent, was actively aiding the enemies of the axis and laying the foundations for the mammoth war production achievements of 1942–45. Conditioning the defense period mobilization activities were a number of factors, among them the following: The strongly noninterventionist and pacifistic sentiment of a large portion of the people, reflected in divisions of opinion within congress; the reluctance of some business men and defense officials to see "business as usual" disturbed by drastic orders of a regimenting character, particularly in view of prophecies of an early collapse of Great Britain and expectations in many quarters that the U.S. itself would not be attacked or become a belligerent; the consistently low military requirements stated as adequate by the military agencies, a result in part of the difficulty of defining when, where, for how long, and against what enemies the U.S. might have to fight; the mutual distrust between the Roosevelt administration and the business community that was part of the legacy of the New Deal, and the resulting jockeying between the president and the more conservative businessmen for control of the industrial mobilization program; and the presidential election of 1940, which precluded the establishment in mid-1940 of a strong industrial mobilization agency that might be misconstrued as a certain portent of the nation's entry into the war. Perhaps most important among these factors was the simple question of whether the U.S. would ever be a belligerent. Nobody could answer the question with certainty. Yet the doubt on the question beclouded the solution of many problems that under conditions of actual war were found to be very simple.

During the defense period, the federal government was poorly organized for the task of economic mobilization. The Army and Navy Munitions board had developed an "Industrial Mobilization Plan," which contemplated establishment of a War Resources administration to serve as the key superagency for wartime industrial co-ordination. This administration was to be set up in skeleton form as early as practicable when an emergency was envisioned. Shortly before the German invasion of Poland on Sept. 1, 1939, the assistant secretaries of war and navy, with Pres. Roosevelt's approval, called into being a War Resources board, headed by E. R. Stettinius, Jr., and principally composed of business leaders. It was expected that this board would oversee such industrial mobilization steps as might be appropriate, serving in effect as a skeletal War Resources administration. However, in November, when the formal state of war between Germany and France and England had settled down to a winter "Sitzkrieg," the president dismissed the War Resources board, which had been widely attacked for its lack of representation of labour and small business.

Welder at the Federal Shipbuilding and Dry Dock Co. at Kearny, N.J., in 1943. U.S. shipyards contributed more to Allied tonnage than any other nation during World War II

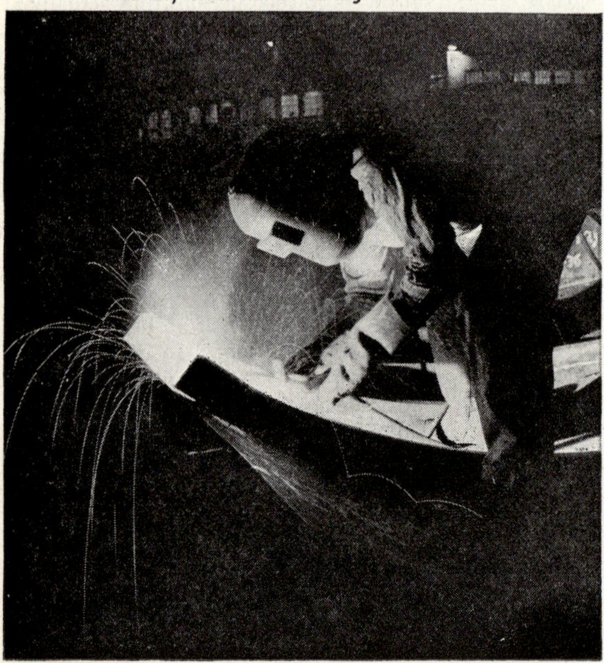

Meanwhile, on Sept. 8, 1939, Pres. Roosevelt had made provision, with congressional acquiescence, for an Office for Emergency Management as an integral part of the executive office of the president. On May 25, 1940, after German invasion of Denmark, Norway, Belgium, the Netherlands and France, the president activated the Office for Emergency Management, which provided the legal peg on which he could hang most of the agencies created in the defense period. On May 28, 1940, relying on a long dormant statute of Aug. 29, 1916, the president announced revival of the Advisory Commission to the Council of National Defense. The council itself, composed of six cabinet officers, played no more than a nominal role, but the Advisory Commission initiated the economic mobilization of the country and continued in operation until Oct. 1941. Its significant work, however, was confined to the last seven months of 1940.

The Advisory Commission was composed of seven advisers, each responsible directly to the president. The commission had no chairman. The advisers were: E. R. Stettinius, Jr., on industrial materials; William S. Knudsen, on industrial production; Sidney Hillman, on employment; Chester C. Davis, on farm products; Ralph Budd, on transportation; Leon Henderson, on price stabilization; and Harriet Elliott, on consumer protection. Donald M. Nelson, appointed coordinator of national defense purchases in June, served in effect, though unofficially, as an eighth member of the commission.

The commission as a group reviewed proposals of the war and navy departments for construction of defense plants, prescribed general policies to govern the award of defense contracts, initiated legislation to encourage construction of defense plants with private capital, stimulated the participation of small business in defense work, recommended purchases of strategic materials for stockpiling and was responsible for the establishment of a priorities board, which instituted a voluntary preference rating system. Individual members of the commission were active as advisers and co-ordinators in their respective fields.

On Jan. 7, 1941, the president established the Office of Production Management (OPM), which promptly took over the Advisory Commission's work on industrial materials, industrial production, purchases, employment and priorities. The immediate management of OPM was assigned jointly to a director general and an associate director general, posts held respectively by William S. Knudsen of the General Motors corporation and Sidney Hillman of the Amalgamated Clothing Workers of America. This so-called partnership reflected the president's belief in balancing management and labour interests in the direction of industrial mobilization. It also testified to the vital contribution of immigrants to U.S. leadership, for Knudsen had been born in Denmark, and Hillman in Lithuania. Over-all control of OPM policy was the task of a council composed of the director general and associate director general of OPM, the secretary of war and the secretary of the navy.

The OPM was reorganized in June and Aug. 1941. The June reorganization set up commodity sections, each designed to focus responsibility within OPM for control of an individual commodity or group of commodities and for contacts with the corresponding industries; it also established industry advisory committees, enabling formal consultation by OPM with industries affected by existing and proposed orders, but at the same time rejecting proposals that industrial self-regulation, rather than government directive, be the basic technique of gearing individual industries to defense production.

The August reorganization was designed to (1) provide a new policy-level board above OPM, which would take a broader view than OPM of the programming of defense requirements and press more vigorously for curtailment of less essential civilian production; (2) settle the long-disputed question of whether OPM or the Office of Price Administration and Civilian Supply should control civilian allocation and curtailment; (3) provide an escape from the morass into which priorities administration had fallen; and (4) give added impetus to the policy of bringing small business into the defense mobilization program. The president created a Supply Priorities and Allocations board, with broad policy control over programming of requirements, over priorities and allocations problems and over materials supply problems. Vice-president Henry A. Wallace, who was chairman of the Economic Defense board, was made chairman of the new board, which included the four members of the OPM council, and Leon Henderson, price administrator, and Harry Hopkins, special assistant to the president in charge of the lend-lease program. Donald M. Nelson was appointed executive director of the board. Nelson also succeeded Stettinius as OPM director of priorities, and in that role set about to effect much-needed improvements in priorities administration. To settle the summer-long controversy over civilian allocations authority, the president established in OPM a Division of Civilian Supply, headed by Leon Henderson, and transferred to it the civilian supply function previously assumed by the Office of Price Administration and Civilian Supply. The president also established in OPM a Division of Contract Distribution, designed to stimulate the award of contracts and subcontracts to small plants. Several additional changes were made in the organization and directorship of OPM divisions.

The major achievements of the defense production agencies were less in the field of munitions production than in the completion of much of the foundation for the munitions production of later years. The munitions produced in the 18 months of July 1940 to Dec. 1941, were but 12% of the production attained in the last 18 months of the war. Illustrative of the scale of defense period production of particular munitions items were the 23,000 aeroplanes produced, compared to 140,000 in a like period in 1944–45; the 136 merchant ships built, compared to almost 2,000 in the later period; and the 4,200 tanks produced, compared to 18,700 in the later period.

However, the value of manufacturing facilities put in place in the 18 month defense period amounted to $5,800,000,000, well ahead of the $4,700,000,000 worth of manufacturing facilities put in place in the war's final 18 months. Similarly, much progress was shown in machine tools alone.

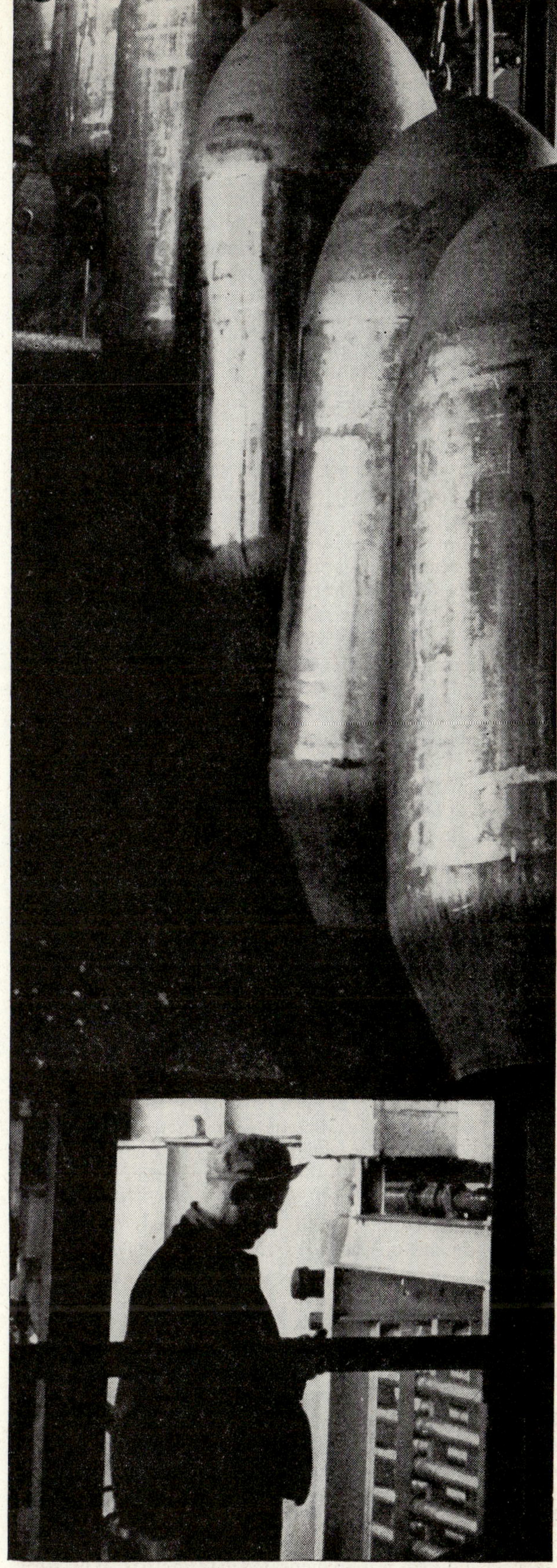

Mass production of 500-lb. bombs at the A. O. Smith Corp. plant, Milwaukee, Wis. This type of bomb was used in the air war over Europe prior to the Allied invasion of the continent in 1944

The 1941 domestic shipments of 132,000 machine tools, though less than 1942 and 1943 shipments, compared favourably with the 100,000 shipped in 1944. Raw materials production was substantially accelerated in 1940 and 1941. In 1941 the U.S. produced about 170% as much steel as in 1939, 120% as much copper, 160% as much zinc, 190% as much aluminum and 490% as much magnesium.

Industrial mobilization in the defense period encountered several major problems. One was that of relations between the civilian production agencies and the armed services. The failure of the president to put the Industrial Mobilization Plan into effect, the weak and largely advisory character of the succession of civilian mobilization agencies, the direct administration of contract awards and priorities for military items by the war and navy departments, and the services' natural reluctance to yield authority until they had more confidence in the civilian agencies—all played their part in making the problem acute.

A second problem was that of fixing upon the goals of the production program. The Industrial Mobilization plan had contemplated that 1,000,000 men would be needed for a protective mobilization force, and 4,000,000 men, if necessary, for full mobilization. On the basis of these goals, the Army and Navy Munitions board had concluded that no expansion of metal-producing capacity would be necessary to meet war needs for copper and aluminum, although well before Pearl Harbor the civilian agencies found it necessary to initiate important expansion programs for both metals. Even the Industrial Mobilization Plan goals, low as they were later found to be, were reduced in 1940, and a 1,200,000 man army was taken as the group to be fully equipped, and a 2,000,000 man army as the group for which combat items of equipment should be planned.

The strictly logical civilian agency officials argued that the armed services should be relied on for statements of military requirements, and the civilian agencies should then see that production met these requirements. Another group, however, persistently contended that military estimates of needs were far too low, and pressed for production policies geared to an independently determined set of high munitions production goals. Had the goals fixed by the military been followed, the expansion of industrial facilities, production of raw materials, stockpiling of strategic materials, curtailment of civilian consumption and related measures, would have been woefully inadequate for the emergency confronting the nation after Pearl Harbor. The need for civilian officials' improvising of production goals, coupled with the reappraisals of requirements by the military agencies, the dependence of procurement operations upon the fitful succession of appropriation acts and the appeals by Great Britain and other countries for additional war equipment, meant that there was a highly unstable basis for the planning of facilities and materials supply programs.

A third problem involved expansion of materials-producing capacity. There was a dramatic dispute over the steel industry's assurance that it had adequate capacity to meet any foreseeable demands of the defense program. The industry's position was supported by Gano Dunn, a presidential consultant, in Feb. 1941, but he reversed himself in May, with the result that an expansion program for the steel industry was inaugurated late in 1941. The steel dispute was repeated, though in more muted tones, for other commodities. In almost every case, the factors included the industry's fear of over-expansion of capacity in relation to peacetime markets, an ill-defined and low set of estimates of military requirements and a confidence that increased military needs could be met out of the "cushion" of civilian consumption.

Finally, there was contention over the curtailment of production of civilian goods. The curtailment dispute centred about industries normally producing such items as automobiles, refrigerators, radios and farm machinery. The curtailment proposal had several objectives: to free factory space and machine tools for use in munitions production; to divert steel, copper, aluminum, nickel and other critical metals from civilian use to use in munitions; and to bring able managers and skilled workmen into the munitions program. There were doubts among industrialists and OPM executives about the adaptability of the machine tools in civilian plants to specialized munitions production, and doubts about the wisdom of reducing civilian production until there could be a heavier load of military contracts to take up the production slack promptly. Labour was also concerned about the weeks-long unemployment that workers in converting industries would suffer. Until after Pearl Harbor, these objections to curtailment for facilities-conversion reasons seemed persuasive to OPM officials. However, curtailment was initiated for another reason, the growing shortage of critical metals. An agreement in May 1941 between OPM and the automobile industry to effect a 20% voluntary curtailment of automobile production was followed by mandatory OPM orders in Sept., effecting a 43% curtailment. Similarly, mechanical refrigerator production was cut 43%.

During 1941 a number of other OPM orders were issued, designed not to reduce the output of civilian end-products, but to prohibit or reduce the use of critical materials and equipment in nondefense work. Even before July 1941, such items as machine tools, aluminum, magnesium, tungsten, nickel, copper, natural and synthetic rubber and zinc were under priorities and allocations controls, and other items were added during the rest of the year.

Wartime Organization.—Pearl Harbor ended all doubts about the involvement of the U.S. in war and forced adoption of challengingly high production goals and establishment of a new agency to gear American industry to the new task.

On Jan. 16, 1942, when the U.S. had been an active belligerent for a little more than a month, the president established the War Production board. Despite its title, WPB was a single-headed agency. Its chairman had full power of decision, and the members of the board served in a merely advisory capacity. The president appointed Donald M. Nelson, former vice-president of Sears Roebuck and company, as chairman of the board. Nelson's broad social philosophy, his understanding of the political and economic factors of the modern industrial economy and his inclination toward negotiation as a technique of reaching solutions of controversial problems qualified him for the difficult role of presiding over the many agencies, industries and labour and management interests that had a share in industrial mobilization. His strengths were also his weaknesses, and some critics felt that he tolerated differences of viewpoint and delayed decisive action to an extent that interfered with vigorous and firm direction of the war production program.

Creation of the War Production board involved abolition of the Supply Priorities and Allocations board; on Jan. 24, 1942, the OPM was also abolished. Knudsen, appointed lieutenant general, was put in charge of war department production; Hillman remained in WPB until

April as director of the labour division, but then left the government.

The original War Production board consisted, in addition to the chairman, of the secretary of war, secretary of the navy, federal loan administrator, lieutenant general in charge of war department production, director of the WPB labour division (until April 1942), administrator of the OPA, chairman of the Economic Defense board (later the director of the Office of Economic Warfare and then the administrator of the Foreign Economic administration), and the special assistant to the president supervising the defense aid program. In effect, the original board had the same membership as the superseded Supply Priorities and Allocations board. In 1943 the membership was expanded to include the chairman of the War Manpower commission, director of the Office of Defense Transportation, petroleum administrator for war, war food administrator and secretary of agriculture. In late 1944, the director of the Office of Contract Settlement also became a member.

The powers of the chairman were broadly stated in two presidential executive orders, issued on Jan. 16 and 24, 1942. The chairman was to "exercise general direction over the war procurement and production program," to "determine the policies, plans, procedures, and methods of the several Federal departments, establishments, and agencies in respect to war procurement and production, including purchasing, contracting, specifications, and construction; and including conversion, requisitioning, plant expansion, and the financing thereof," and to "issue such directives in respect thereto as he may deem necessary or appropriate."

The chairman was specifically made heir to the powers earlier vested in the Supply Priorities and Allocations board and Office of Production Management. These included authority to determine total requirements of materials and commodities for all purposes, and take steps for the fulfilment of such requirements; to assign priorities to deliveries under contracts and subcontracts deemed necessary to defense of the U.S. or of other countries whose defense was vital to the U.S.; to allocate any material threatened with shortage in supply as a result of defense requirements; to requisition materials and equipment needed for defense of the U.S.; and to place compulsory manufacturing orders enforceable by plant seizure and criminal penalties.

In practice, the WPB chairman's authority was substantially limited by the breadth of production and procurement responsibility of the war and navy departments, the powers vested in coequal civilian agencies and the creation of superagencies with overriding co-ordinative authority. The actual awarding of war contracts and the scheduling and expediting of military production were responsibilities of the armed services largely because Nelson did not want WPB to become too large for effective administration and because he felt that shifting of these responsibilities to WPB in early 1942 would have caused such temporary confusion as to set back munitions production at a most critical period in the war. As a result of this decision, WPB confined itself principally to policy and program determination, production and distribution of materials, production and distribution of industrial equipment and of the components of military and civilian end-products and direct control of civilian production. WPB lacked adequate sanctions with which to assure effective control of the procurement and production work of the armed services, and found it difficult to administer its important materials-allocation powers since they needed to be integrated with the contract-awarding and production scheduling decisions of the services.

Other civilian agencies reduced the theoretical scope of WPB power. Agencies directly or in effect responsible to the president were established for petroleum and petroleum products, solid fuels, rubber and food, although their functions were not far different from those performed within WPB for other commodities equally important to the war program. In addition to these independent commodity agencies, there were agencies with responsibility for functions that directly affected war production, such as manpower, price, economic warfare, transportation and housing. Of these, the manpower function was the most vital, for in the latter years of the war it was manpower, rather than the materials and commodities under WPB control, that was the critical resource on which the fate of the production program depended.

Finally, from late 1942 to the end of the war, WPB was subordinated to superagencies established by the president to exercise portions of his responsibilities for co-ordination of war agencies. On Oct. 3, 1942, the president established the Office of Economic Stabilization with overriding authority over certain functions of such agencies as the War Production board, War Labor board and Office of Price Administration. On May 27, 1943, the president created the Office of War Mobilization with very broad powers over the war agencies. This office was further strengthened on Oct. 3, 1944, when it received statutory support and its name was changed to Office of War Mobilization and Reconversion.

For most of the war period, WPB's internal organization was focused on the following functions: (1) top management and policy control; (2) allocation of resources among the agencies serving as spokesmen for military, foreign and civilian requirements; (3) issuance of industry-regulating orders; (4) administration of board policies governing production and distribution; and (5) advisory and technical service to the units responsible for the above four functions.

Top management and policy control were vested in Nelson as chairman until Sept. 1944, when he was succeeded by J. A. Krug. From Feb. 1943 to Aug. 1944, Nelson shared his responsibility with Charles E. Wilson, president of the General Electric company, who held the WPB post of executive vice-chairman. Associated with Wilson was a production executive committee, which brought together the procurement heads of the war and navy departments and the Maritime commission, and which came to play a major role in WPB policy formation. Krug, who had been the Tennessee Valley authority's power engineer and an OPM and WPB executive through most of the war, succeeded to the chairmanship when both Nelson and Wilson resigned as a result of controversies over reconversion policy.

The functions of resources allocation and issuance of industry-wide orders were assigned to a program vice-chairman. For resources allocation purposes he was advised by a requirements committee, composed at its peak of representatives of more than a dozen agencies serving as sponsors of particular types of requirements. The committee reviewed the whole range of requirements each quarter, and, balancing these against the limited supplies of basic materials, made allocations based largely upon relative urgency of need. Much of the detailed work of reviewing requirements and allocating resources was performed by "divisional requirements committees," headed by WPB industry division directors, and composed of representatives of the claimant agencies.

Virtually all limitation and conservation orders and priorities and allocations regulations were issued under the authority of the program vice-chairman; this gave him a firm control of WPB's policies in regulating industrial activities. He was aided in this responsibility by an order clearance committee whose membership was intended to assure that each WPB order was considered from all significant points of view before issuance.

Administration of WPB policies was the responsibility of an operations vice-chairman, who supervised and worked primarily through the industry divisions of WPB. The industry divisions were the focal points for WPB's supply-stimulation activities, for the detailed work of distribution of resources to individual plants and for the initiation of industry-regulating orders and of quarterly allocations of resources among claimant agencies. More than 1,000 industry advisory committees provided a major source of advice to the divisions, but labour advisory committees were never effectively attached to the divisions and, in fact, were inactive until reconversion policy questions arose in 1944 and 1945.

Advisory and technical units aiding in the carrying out of WPB's functions were numerous. Among the more important were the planning committee, which advised Nelson in 1942 and early 1943 on major program and policy problems; the Office of Progress Reports, which appraised critically the record of performance in meeting the month-by-month production goals; the research and statistics staff, which provided the factual foundation for the difficult work of policy determination; the succession of top offices designed both to give labour a voice in WPB policy councils and to represent WPB interests in the manpower work of other agencies; and the conservation division, which sponsored standardization, simplification and substitution measures to save critical materials. During much of the war the Office of Civilian Supply served not only as a claimant agency on behalf of civilian consumers' requirements, but also as an adviser on general economic policy.

The staff of the WPB rose from 7,600 at the beginning of 1942 to a peak of 23,000 a year later, and then declined to 18,000 at the beginning of 1944, 13,000 at the beginning of 1945 and 5,400 on Oct. 31, 1945. Almost all the employees were paid regular government salaries, but several hundred business executives given key posts in WPB were allowed to continue receiving salaries from their companies and received token government salaries of $1 a year. This practice was severely criticized, but Nelson insisted that experienced business executives could not be obtained at standard government salaries and that adequate safeguards could prevent the misuse of government positions on behalf of the companies paying WPB executives. This problem, plus the fear in some quarters that men drawn from industry for wartime government work even at regular salaries might occasionally confuse the public interest with the special interests of individual industries, prevented the delegation to WPB industry divisions of the extensive powers that they themselves felt desirable for the most effective administration.

The war and navy departments reorganized early in the war in an effort, among other things, to achieve internal co-ordination among their many units participating in the production and procurement program. The war department established the army service forces (at first named the services of supply) under Lieut. Gen. Brehon Somervell, who had direct charge of the many supply services of the war department. The supply interests of army aviation, however, were handled by the army air forces. The navy department established an Office of Procurement and Material under Vice-Adm. Samuel Robinson, who had the general task of securing co-ordination of the navy department's traditionally autonomous supply bureaus. The Army and Navy Munitions board was by presidential order directed to report to the president through the chairman of WPB. In practice, however, the ANMB remained through most of 1942 a vigorous proponent of the services' point of view and endeavoured to assure a united front by the army and navy on key phases of production policy. After 1942 the ANMB had a less active role.

At the international level, the U.S. war production program was most directly affected by the work of the Combined Raw Materials board, established on Jan. 26, 1942, and the Combined Production and Resources board, established on June 9, 1942. The Combined Raw Materials board, of which W. L. Batt, a top WPB official, was the U.S. member, enabled joint British-U.S. international allocation of critical materials controlled by the two countries, and agreement upon means for increasing the supply of materials. The Combined Production and Resources board, of which the WPB chairman was the U.S. member, was intended to integrate the war production programs of the U.S., United Kingdom and Canada. Although some progress was made on this difficult assignment, the board was more successful with civilian types of production than with munitions production proper, a reflection very largely of WPB's own difficulties in exerting effective control over military production and procurement activities in the U.S.

Programs and Actual Production.—The basic planning of production goals for an all-out war effort had been completed under the Supply Priorities and Allocations board before establishment of the War Production board. The approach taken was based on measurement of the nation's war production potential, and not primarily on the stated requirements of military, foreign and civilian claimants, or on the assumption of limited appropriations for defense. As a result of this approach, it was estimated that in 1942

"Tank Traps" of 1942, as viewed by Bishop of the *St. Louis Star-Times*

the U.S. was capable of producing $40,000,000,000 worth of munitions and war construction. This was about $13,000,000,000 greater than existing programs, but the president shortly closed this gap almost twice over by fixing 1942 production goals at something more than $50,000,000,000. With an actual war at hand, the armed services quickly skyrocketed their programs, until they were far beyond even the high goals fixed by the president. Actual munitions production and war construction in 1942 was valued at $46,600,000,000,—more than three and a half times the 1941 figure, but short of the president's goal.

The president not only fixed an over-all 1942 goal for the economy but also set specific goals for production of key munitions items. Table II compares actual production of selected items with the January and May objectives fixed by the president.

Table II.—*Presidential Objectives in 1942 and Actual U.S. Production*

Munitions Items	Presidential Objectives Jan. 1942*	May 1942†	Actual Production‡
Aeroplanes	60,000	60,000	48,000
All tank-type weapons	—	46,500	33,100
Tanks	45,000	24,700	24,800
Anti-aircraft guns	20,000	17,400	14,400
Merchant ships (deadweight tons)	8,000,000	9,000,000	8,000,000

Sources: *President's message to Congress, Jan. 6, 1942.
†Letter, the President to Donald M. Nelson, May 1, 1942.
‡*Wartime Production Achievements and the Reconversion Outlook* (1945), pp. 106–109.

The laying out of a 1943 munitions program proved a difficult and hotly contested matter. In Dec. 1941 the president and Nelson had agreed that the 1943 munitions and war construction potential of the country was about $60,000,000,000. By the end of Feb. 1942, however, the armed services had already formally submitted 1943 programs totalling $110,000,000,000. Under pressure from the president, who now set a $75,000,000,000 limit to the 1943 war program, the services reduced their programs in April to $80,000,000,000, but by mid-July they had raised them again to $92,000,000,000. These developments were simultaneous with a running dispute over the size of the services' 1942 programs. In fact, the expectation of a deficit in 1942 production as against the services' objectives led to the fear that the services would simply shift this deficit to 1943, with the result that the only way of meeting the tremendous military programs would be so drastically to divert resources to war production as to have 75% of the nation's productive effort assigned to these programs by Dec. 1943. Such a diversion would wreck the economy, for, WPB economists held, neither the U.S. nor any other country could devote more than about half of its output to war production. Consequently, in Nov. 1942, the joint chiefs of staff responded to WPB's representations by reducing the 1943 program to $80,000,000,000. Subsequent changes altered the program further both to fit revised strategic requirements and to recognize that the estimated production of $75,000,000,000 to $80,000,000,000 was not going to be realized.

The importance of getting production objectives into line with production possibilities lay in the facts that unreasonable objectives provided a thoroughly false basis for strategic planning, that excessive demands on industry placed an impossible strain on the existing systems for allocating materials and scheduling production, that unrealistic goals might actually lessen total output by getting far more weapons started in production than could be completed in view of shortages of resources and that such goals would tend to encourage excessive production of easy-to-manufacture items and thus cut production of the hard-to-manufacture items, which were also the most-needed weapons. Actual munitions production and war construction in 1943 came to about $65,000,000,000, which was about $20,000,000,000 above the 1942 figure and more than $50,000,000,000 above the 1941 figure. This significant achievement, however, fell $10,000,000,000 to $15,000,000,000 short of the estimated 1943 production potential of the country.

Goals for 1943 production of major munitions items had been publicly announced by the president in his Jan. 1942 address to congress. These goals, together with actual 1943 production, are shown in Table III. However, the Jan. 1942 goals were substantially altered during 1942 and 1943 and, therefore, are not fully accurate yardsticks against which to judge 1943 actual production.

Table III.—*Initial Presidential Objectives and Actual U.S. Production in 1943*

Munitions Items	President's Objectives Jan. 1942	Actual 1943 Production
Aeroplanes	125,000	85,900
Tanks	75,000	29,500
Anti-aircraft guns	35,000	not available
Machine guns	500,000	830,000
Merchant ships (deadweight tons)	10,000,000	19,000,000

Despite the fact that 1942 and 1943 production goals were not fully met, by the end of 1943 the major pressure on the resources for which WPB was responsible eased. The year 1943 marked the peak year for munitions production and war construction, and Nov. 1943 was the peak month with more than $5,500,000,000.

In other words, from Nov. 1943 to Feb. 1945 munitions production and war construction fell off slightly each quarter. For all practical purposes this period represented a plateau between the steep ascent of 1942 and 1943 and the precipitous decline in mid-1945.

The substantial completion of the wartime construction program released materials and manpower for production of actual munitions, with the result that munitions production in 1944 was about $5,000,000,000 greater than in 1943. Nonetheless, the general trend was not significantly upward, and there was no question of the production feasibility of programs presented by the armed services. The only questions were in terms of genuineness of military needs as against the desirability of starting reconversion of portions of industry to civilian production. Actual munitions production and war construction in 1944 were valued at about $64,000,000,000.

For particular munitions items, 1944 marked the war's peak. This was true for the 95,000 aeroplanes, a doubling of 1942 production that was the more remarkable because the 1944 emphasis on heavier planes meant that by airframe weight the 1942 production had been more than trebled. The navy built 3,200,000 displacement tons of ships—more than three times the 1942 performance and well above that of 1943. Construction of merchant ships, however, was reduced to 16,200,000 deadweight tons, and of tanks to 17,600 from the 1943 peaks.

In 1945 there was a brief halting of the gradual decline of programmed and actual munitions production and war construction, and March actually witnessed a 7% rise in munitions output as compared with February. This brief spurt in response to the unexpected reverses of the United Nations forces in Germany, was succeeded by slight declines which became precipitous with victory in Europe in May 1945 and the Japanese surrender in August. April munitions production was 4% below March's; May's was 7% below that of March; and June's was 12% below that of March. By early September, however, the drop was so great that the production rate was down 65% from the spring peak.

The WPB was in a difficult position with regard to requirements programs. First, each agency responsible for stating its requirements tended to exaggerate its own needs. This stemmed partly from a mistaken concept of the importance of its own segment of the total war effort, partly from a conviction that the agency would expose itself to greater criticism if it fell short of meeting war needs than if it exceeded them and partly from a padding of estimates to assure that cutting of its stated requirements would still leave its real requirements uncurtailed.

Second, a number of agencies were slow to develop integrated and carefully considered programs, and there was inadequate machinery for integrating programs of agencies with related functions. Where an agency did not integrate its own program, the requirements were often inflated many times over, as each unit, section, division and bureau would tend to pad estimates as they moved up the administrative hierarchy, for fear that an adequate "safety cushion" had not been included at the lower levels. Where groups of related agencies did not work out mutually complementary programs, there were also difficulties. For instance, WPB received separate requirements programs from the army, navy and maritime commission, and early in the war these appeared to be principally developed by supply officers and to have a very tenuous relation to strategic considerations. Similarly, in 1942, WPB received foreign requirements both from the lend-lease administration and the Board of Economic Warfare, and it was not clear which countries filed their requirements with which agency. In addition, Russian requirements came directly through the soviet protocols negotiated by the White House. Over-all programs covering domestic consumers and industrial requirements were also slow to develop. Many of these problems eased as the war progressed. Establishment of official relations between WPB and the joint chiefs of staff in late 1942 enabled reference of important conflicts among military requirements programs to the strategists for decision; this was perhaps the most important advance in production programming for it paved the way for better understanding of the reciprocal relations of strategy and production—an understanding that had been impossible while WPB was isolated from contact with the joint chiefs. Establishment of the Foreign Economic administration in Sept. 1943 merged economic warfare and lend-lease operations. And successive efforts were made to get a more accurate formulation of requirements of civilian consumers, while industrial requirements for such purposes as maintenance and repair of industrial plants and equipment became reasonably stabilized.

Third, WPB had difficulty in probing into the justifications for stated requirements. This was a particular difficulty in connection with military requirements. Precluded from questioning essentiality of need from the strategic standpoint, from obtaining data deemed too secret for divulgence to civilian officials, or in some cases from seeking information from officials at lower military levels, WPB was often reduced to correcting strictly statistical inaccuracies in the official estimates, to encouraging voluntary yielding of claims by one military agency so that an essential requirement of another agency might be met, and, after 1942, to referring major conflicts among military requirements to the joint chiefs of staff. Short shrift was made of WPB economists who ventured to question such matters as the proposed size of the armed forces or the size of inventories of supplies held by the armed forces. Yet these and other phases of the over-all needs of the services were necessarily determinative of the disposition of resources under WPB control. In the foreign requirements field, it was often difficult because of distance and the paucity of data in the U.S. to appraise legitimacy of foreign nations' requests for materials and requirements. For civilian requirements there was also an inadequacy of information on actual needs. Much of the early calculations of consumers' needs were statistical computations from peacetime production and consumption figures. After sampling surveys indicated strong consumer demand for such items as electric irons, bobby pins, alarm clocks and telephones, it was difficult to convince other claimants that the urgency of need for these products was at all comparable to that for munitions of war. And even if urgency of need for a civilian item were established, there were few touchstones for judging the quantity of the item that should be authorized for production. Even some industrial requirements remained throughout the war a subject of sharp debate. The Office of Defense Transportation consistently condemned WPB's allocations to the railroads as utterly inadequate and as risking a breakdown of the transportation system. Allocations of materials for production of farm machinery and allocations of newsprint to newspapers were subjected to severe censure in congress on grounds of inadequacy.

Much of the progress made in the appraisal of requirements programs resulted from the able work of the WPB requirements committee and its staff. Much was also the result of the introduction in 1943 of the Controlled Materials Plan, a quarterly allocation system that forced the reduction of total requirements programs to the total supply of critical resources, while leaving to the claimant agencies the selection of the segments of their programs to be cut. However, the effectiveness of these pressures for program curtailment weakened in 1944 and 1945, when resources under WPB control became relatively plentiful in relation to crucial needs, and the problem became that of determining the degree to which consumers' less essential needs should be satisfied by direction of resources into civilian production. This in turn raised anew the question of the validity of stated requirements of the armed services in view of the accumulated supplies from previous years' production, the favourable prospects of military operations and the length of time required for munitions in production to reach the battlefronts.

Time served to ease somewhat the problem of analysis of legitimacy of requirements estimates. Significant increases in requirements by any agency above its requirements as stated in previous quarters were held to warrant explanations to WPB and the other agencies concerned in the allocation of resources. And WPB bookkeeping helped to bring into question the requirements of agencies that in a succession of quarters had proved unable to use their full allocations.

Conversion and Concentration.—Conversion to war production of a number of plants normally producing civilian goods was a major objective in the first half of 1942. To the degree that this objective was achieved, the nation could avoid building of new plants, thus saving steel, lumber and other materials critically needed in actual munitions production. It would also save the time required for building new plants, and so get quantity output of munitions at an early date. Furthermore, conversion was necessary to the continued operation of the metal-using plants, for even if a vast quantity of new war facilities had been built, there would not have been a sufficient supply of

Final assembly operations on combat plane fuselages at a Curtiss-Wright plant in Buffalo, N.Y., during 1941. These planes were earmarked for both U.S. and British air forces

metals and other resources for both the new and the old facilities to operate at capacity production.

The doubts of 1941 that the defense program warranted wholesale curtailment of civilian production and conversion of plants to defense production were succeeded in 1942 by a full awareness that the war munitions program was so large as to require drastic measures to bring existing plants, especially those in the durable goods industries, into war production. While in 1941 Knudsen and others had had to urge the armed services to increase their programs and place a heavier load of defense contracts on industry, in the first three months of 1942 the services flooded industry with a tremendous quantity of war contracts, and conversion became an obvious necessity.

Curtailment of less essential civilian production was achieved through WPB's issuance of limitation orders and conservation orders. The former prohibited or reduced the output of specific products; the latter prohibited the use of scarce materials in less essential civilian products. In some cases the materials conservation orders simply saved critical materials for war production by forcing manufacturers to shift to more plentiful materials if they wished to stay in production. But where substitution of a plentiful material for a scarce one was impracticable, the conservation order had the effect of stopping production, thus freeing plants for conversion to war production.

The early 1942 cutoffs applied to gaming machines, metal office furniture, passenger automobiles, radios, phonographs and mechanical refrigerators. The great flood of cutoffs, however, came in May and June, and by mid-1942 the production of nonessential civilian durable goods had been mostly halted. The effects of curtailment and conversion, therefore, were felt in the last five months of 1942, which were the months in which the bulk of 1942 munitions production was concentrated.

The U.S. did not follow Great Britain's and Germany's lead in obtaining still more effective use of its industrial facilities by executing a large-scale program for concentration of civilian industry. Limitation orders that substantially reduced, but did not prohibit, production of particular civilian products restricted all plants in the curtailed industries to part time civilian production. This often prevented effective conversion of the plants to war work and threatened sharp increases in prices of civilian goods because of the uneconomic rate of production imposed on the plants. Furthermore, it appeared unsound to permit continuation of civilian production in labour shortage areas when such production could be transferred to manpower surplus areas, freeing manpower for war work through shutting of civilian plants in the shortage areas.

In July 1942, the WPB adopted proposals of Leon Henderson and the planning committee for adoption of a concentration program. The program was not effectively implemented, however, and was abandoned early in 1943. By that time it was clear that the nation was not hard-pressed for plant capacity. Meantime, an awkward administrative arrangement for carrying out the program, difficulties in obtaining statistical data basic to the program, opposition by the WPB industry divisions and a ruling that WPB could not legally require plants benefiting from the program to compensate plants closed by the program, had impeded execution of the plans. The only industries covered by concentration orders were those producing stoves, bicycles, typewriters, farm machinery and pulp and paper.

Small Business in the War.—A further attempt to utilize the productive capacity of the U.S. to the full was the emphasis on the use of small business in war production. There were a number of reasons for an apparent preference of the armed services for awarding contracts primarily to large enterprises. The large manufacturing corporations were thought to have the greatest stability, the best management talents, a sense of responsibility for effective performance, the fullest understanding of mass production techniques and in many cases the only experience with production of specialized munitions. In addition, it was easier from the administrative standpoint to deal with a few score large corporations than to work with thousands of small enterprises. Nonetheless, any full scale war production effort would require mobilization of the small plants, for in the aggregate they had substantial productive capacity. Furthermore, with curtailment of civilian production and diversion of critical materials and manpower to war production, the confining of war contracts to large plants might risk a wholesale bankruptcy of small businesses, with profound repercussions on the soundness of the U.S. economic structure.

Concern over this problem led to creation of a succession of special agencies, culminating in congress' establishment of the Smaller War Plants corporation in June 1942. The corporation's board of directors was to be appointed by the chairman of WPB, who also was assigned specific statutory responsibilities in connection with mobilization of small plants. Congress also authorized higher per unit payments under contracts with small plants than under contracts with large plants.

Through much of the defense and war period, the armed services, WPB and the special agencies created for the benefit of small business were criticized for inadequate consideration for small business. Some confusion arose from the demonstrated fact that small business received a relatively small share of the prime contracts, that is, contracts awarded directly by the government's procurement agencies. A storm of criticism arose in July 1941 when statistics were released indicating that three-fourths of the dollar value of army and navy contracts had gone to 56 companies, and that almost a third of the total value had gone to 6 corporations. While efforts continued to be directed toward spreading prime contracts among more companies, the major channel for bringing small plants into the war program was subcontracting. Once the U.S. was actually at war, the services placed so heavy a load of prime contracts on large companies that the latter were forced to pass the orders along by subcontracts to other plants, many of them small.

As it turned out, smaller enterprises fared very well in the war. Business failures in the country fell steadily from 15,000 in 1939 to 1,200 in 1944. While the number of operating concerns was reduced from 3,300,000 to 2,900,000, this trend was not paralleled in the mining and manufacturing industries, which accounted for war production. In these industries, the number of operating concerns rose from 236,000 in 1939 to 251,000 in 1944. Furthermore, in the same period, the profits of smaller industrial concerns increased nearly 700% before taxes and more than 250% after taxes, a far more favourable record than that of the larger enterprises.

Facilities and Construction.—Construction of new facilities provided still another method of expanding the nation's capacity for production of munitions and of materials and components needed for munitions. The bulk of war facilities were built directly at government expense. Those built directly with private capital were substantially financed by the government. This was done by authorizing the owners to amortize the cost of the facilities over a five-year period (assuming the war did not end sooner) and thereby to charge off most of the cost against the corporations' tax payments to the government.

A major problem in construction of new facilities was the extent to which it drained resources from current production in order to permit greater production peaks a year or two later. Metals were so heavily used in construction that grave questions arose over the wisdom of thus curtailing munitions output in 1942 and 1943, when the need for munitions was acute. In 1942, about 29% of the munitions and war construction program was devoted to construction, and in 1943 the corresponding figure was 13%.

Because there had been no effective central appraisal of needs for such projects, the facilities program as a whole was not closely related to the over-all war progam, nor were individual segments of the facilities program correlated with each other. In 1942 and 1943, WPB inaugurated controls designed to keep facilities expansions to those really needed for meeting approved war production goals. WPB itself set the example by sharply cutting plans for expanding facilities designed to produce basic materials, but the agencies sponsoring expansions for military end products were slow to see the necessity of curtailment. As a result, materials-using facilities were over-expanded in relation to materials-producing facilities.

The WPB was never successful in getting all facilities construction projects incorporated in a comprehensive program. It did, however, succeed in providing central review of every major project proposed, and through this review WPB both appraised the necessity for each project and made a detailed review of construction specifications to assure minimum use of critical materials. WPB also controlled the allocations of materials for construction and actually scheduled the delivery of scarce materials and equipment to the major facilities expansion projects for production of steel, aluminum, aviation gasoline and rubber.

These controls over facilities proper were supplemented by rigorous restriction of civilian construction under limitation order L-41. WPB, however, had no substantial control over the military construction program, which was excluded on the ground that decisions as to essentiality of military construction were strategic in character.

Materials and Manpower.—As the adequacy of the nation's plant capacity was demonstrated fairly early in the war, the major wartime bottlenecks proved to be materials, components and manpower. Broadly speaking, the overall shortages developed in that order, with materials shortages dominating 1942 and early 1943, components shortages reaching major prominence in the first half of 1943 and manpower shortages gaining and retaining the spotlight from late 1943 to the end of the war in 1945.

For each of the resources, the character of the shortage problem altered from year to year, and even at shorter intervals. In materials, *e.g.,* two trends were especially notable. One was the shift from shortage of raw materials to shortage of fabricated forms and shapes of the materials (*e.g.,* tubing, sheets, plates, wire). The other trend was the shift from shortage of metals to shortage of nonmetals such as lumber, pulp and paper, textiles and plastics, which early in the war had been thought so plentiful as to warrant use as substitutes for the critical metals. To some extent the trend from plenty to scarcity was evident even within the metals field. Lead, which early in the war had been plentiful, turned out to be critically short in 1944 and 1945.

The supply of materials was augmented through importation and stockpiling, expansion of domestic capacity and fuller utilization of existing capacity. These methods of providing an over-all increase in supply of materials were supplemented by the curtailment of use of critical materials for civilian products and by conservation practices adopted by the armed services. Both of these means of reducing consumption of critical materials had the effect of increasing the availability of materials for the most important military and essential civilian uses.

Importation was facilitated by payment of subsidies to stimulate foreign production, payment of incentive prices for sales to the U.S., abolition of tariff duties on war materials and an elaborate system of priorities and scheduling to control the precious space on ships and planes carrying imports to the U.S. Importation was subject to two major limitations as a reliable means of meeting materials shortages. One was the fact that many major sources of imports came under axis control. The other was that during the height of the submarine attacks on United Nations shipping in 1942, the flow of imports was very seriously interrupted. Both of these limitations lost their weight as territory was regained and as merchant ships were increasingly freed of the hazard of submarine attack.

Stockpiling of materials proved only a modest help in World War II, partly because foreign supplies had not been sought aggressively enough during the defense period, the loss of Malaya and the Philippines had not been anticipated, civilian consumption of imported materials had not been curtailed soon enough and drastically enough and industry's rate of use of materials in war production prevented husbanding of materials in stockpiles. Although at the beginning of 1942 the official stockpile goals were

Blast furnace at the Bethlehem steel works in Pennsylvania which poured out much of the raw material needed in enormous quantities for the conduct of mechanized combat during World War II

generally intended to assure a three years' supply of the principal imported materials, actual stockpiles in most cases never exceeded a year's supply. Consequently, WPB realistically reduced the objectives on the basis of accumulating one year's supply. And, in 1944, after the threats to availability of foreign materials had been substantially reduced, the stock piles of materials wholly imported from abroad were as a general rule cut to a six months' supply.

Expansion of domestic capacity was not only complementary to the importation program, but was in part competitive with it. This was because for certain materials produced both at home and abroad, such as copper, there was serious debate over whether the U.S. should stimulate foreign production at highly profitable price levels or should stimulate the development of submarginal mining properties and the discovery and exploitation of new domestic sources.

The extent to which the materials supply was substantially increased by facilities expansion varied greatly among the individual materials. For such relatively unanticipated demands as synthetic rubber and aviation gasoline, facilities construction accounted for the major share of the increased supply. A great expansion was also achieved for aluminum, whose primary ingot capacity rose from 400,000,000 lb. in 1940 to 2,300,000,000 lb. in 1944. However, in such an industry as steel, the 17% war-time increase in steel ingot capacity was not as great a contribution to war production as was the ability to take advantage of the 50% under-utilization of capacity that had characterized the steel industry in the 1930s.

Fuller utilization of existing materials production capacity was attained principally through price incentives, measures to meet manpower shortages and shifting of facilities from production of less needed types of materials to those most needed for the manufacture of munitions. Price incentives were provided not only through general price increases, but through special subsidy schemes. The most notable of these grew out of the Office of Price Administration's concern that the effort to stimulate nonferrous metal mining from relatively unprofitable mines and veins might result in a general inflation of metals prices. This danger was largely overcome through a premium price plan that enabled subsidizing of marginal production of copper, lead and zinc, while at the same time requiring that the normal output of these metals be sold under the regular ceiling prices.

Manpower shortages dogged nonferrous metals production and, later in the war, such metals industries operations as those of foundries, forges and brass mills. Unfavourable wages and working conditions in metals in-

Wearing face shields to protect them from burns, these Negro war workers at Edgewood arsenal, Md., are shown filling shells with white phosphorus for use in chemical warfare. The chemical was handled under water because it ignited when in contact with air

dustries, especially mines, accounted for the loss of workers to aircraft, shipbuilding and other industries. A number of skilled miners were also drafted. Adjustment of wages with the approval of the War Labor board, revision of Selective Service regulations to recognize the essential character of mining work and even furloughing of miner-soldiers back to the mines were among the remedial measures adopted.

The most notable example of shifting of existing facilities to increase the production of critically needed types of materials occurred in the steel industry early in the war, when steel plates were critically short for shipbuilding, tank production and plant construction. To meet the problem, steel plate capacity was increased from 460,000 tons in Aug. 1941 to 1,167,000 tons in March 1943. Eighty per cent of this increase was obtained by converting steel strip mills to the production of steel plates, rather than by the building of new plate facilities.

The major resource limiting war production achievements in the last years of the war was manpower. The major manpower problem was not one of inadequacy of total labour supply, but the maldistribution of workers among industries, among geographical areas and between industrial and military service. Generally workers gravitated to those industries that had favourable wages and working conditions and were clearly recognized in Selective Service deferment regulations as contributory to the war effort. While these factors aided the factories producing finished munitions, they created acute problems in factories and mines whose work was basic to war supply.

To adjust to the problem of labour surplus areas and labour shortage areas, WPB in late 1943 established Area Production Urgency committees and the War Manpower commission established complementary Area Manpower Priorities committees. The urgency committees tried to prevent prime contracts from being placed in labour shortage areas, to control the volume of facilities construction in shortage areas and to advise the manpower priorities committees on the relative war urgency of production of individual plants in the area. The manpower priorities committees endeavoured to guide available workers to the most critical plants and to set employment ceilings on individual plants. The War Manpower commission lacked statutory authority to enforce its employment ceilings and hiring regulations. Late in 1944, though, the director of war mobilization and reconversion authorized a policy of withdrawal of WPB priority ratings and allocation rights from plants that, by violating the War Manpower commission rulings, were making ineffective use of materials and facilities in support of war production.

Under the stabilization program the adjustment of wages was under the control of the War Labor board, but the War Production board was active in sponsoring wage increases for industries lagging in war production because of manpower difficulties.

Priorities and Allocations.—The major controls over industry were exercised under the priorities and allocations authority vested by statute in the president and delegated by him to the chairman of the War Production board. This authority was provided by statutes of June 28, 1940, and May 31, 1941, and took final form in section 2 (a) of the Second War Powers Act of March 27, 1942. Priorities could be assigned to deliveries under contracts or orders of the army and navy, or "contracts or orders for the government of any country whose defense the President deems vital to the defense of the United States" under the Lend-Lease act, or "contracts or orders which the President shall deem necessary or appropriate to promote the defense of the United States," or "subcontracts or suborders which the President shall deem necessary or appropriate to the fulfillment of any contract or order" covered by other provisions of the section. Acceptance of and performance under such contracts and orders in preference to other contracts and orders could be required of individual manufacturers.

Allocation of materials and facilities was provided for by the following provision: "Whenever the President is satisfied that the fulfillment of requirements for the defense of the United States will result in a shortage in the supply of any material or of any facilities for defense or for private account or for export, the President may allocate such material or facilities in such manner, upon such conditions and to such extent as he shall deem necessary or appropriate in the public interest and to promote the national defense."

Priorities were largely relied on until mid-1942; thereafter allocations became the principal instruments of production control. However, allocations were used for some materials as early as 1941, and priority ratings continued throughout the war as a buttress to the allocation system. The priorities system proved adequate only so long as the materials under priority control were not really scarce in relation to essential needs. Under such conditions, the priority ratings merely diverted materials from nonessential uses to essential uses. However, the ratings proved unsatisfactory as instruments for controlling the division of the available supply of materials among essential needs when nonessential uses had already been squeezed out of the picture. Priority ratings were qualitative, rather than quantitative, controls. That is, they could establish that tanks were more important than, say, merchant ships or locomotives, but they were not suitable for limiting the amount of materials to go to tanks in a given month, quarter, or year. What was much the same thing, priorities did not recognize that while the first hundred tanks might be more important than the first hundred ships or locomotives, an additional hundred tanks after 20,000 tanks were on hand would be less important than the first hundred ships or locomotives.

Finally, as materials became scarcer and manufacturers and procurement officers found that their existing ratings could not get them needed materials, there was a steady cheapening of priorities "currency," because all producers and their governmental sponsors pressed for award of higher ratings.

Allocations were developed to cure these defects of the priorities system. Ideally, allocation of a material involved a periodic consideration of the total supply of the material for a given time period, and the firm allocation of that supply among all essential users of the material, such allocation to be guided by the relative importance of products and the marginal war value of additional output of each product.

Although a number of allocation devices for individual materials were used in the course of the war, the two principal allocation schemes for controlling the major output of U.S. industry were the Production Requirements Plan and the Controlled Materials Plan. The Production Requirements Plan was in use on a voluntary basis in the first half of 1942 and on a mandatory basis from July 1942 to March 1943; it was in partial effect from April to June 1943, when the Controlled Materials Plan was also getting started. From June 1943 to the end of the war the Controlled Materials Plan was in full effect.

Under the Production Requirements Plan, WPB required all industrial users of more than $5,000 worth of basic metals per quarter to apply to WPB for allocation of basic materials and for preference ratings. Each plant's application indicated such facts as recent rate of use of each material, size of inventories, volume of orders on hand and quantitative distribution of the plant's output. These applications, tabulated on an industry basis, enabled the requirements committee to make policy-level allocations of total supplies of material among the 200 principal industries of the country for a given quarter. These over-all allocations were then used as guides by WPB industry divisions, which made specific allocations to individual plants and authorized the use of priority ratings to obtain the approved quantities of materials in the following quarter.

The Production Requirements Plan was distinguishable from most other allocation proposals by its use of the "horizontal allocation" principle, under which WPB directly dealt with every important metal-using plant in the country, regardless of whether it produced end-products or produced components of end products. This method was thought helpful to manufacturers since each plant was treated as a unit, even if it produced more than one product or component. It provided effective control of inventories, since materials allocations to plants were reduced if inventories were excessive. And it assured civilian control of the economy through WPB's detailed control of the flow of materials.

Although it remained in effect for almost a year, pending completion of plans for a substitute method of control, the Production Requirements Plan was officially abandoned in Nov. 1942, when WPB adopted the Controlled Materials Plan. Under this new plan, WPB allocated total quarterly supplies of steel, copper and aluminum among about a dozen claimant agencies, such as the war department, navy department, Office of Civilian Supply and Board of Economic Warfare. Each claimant agency determined how its allocation should be distributed among its principal programs, and also determined and made allotments to the manufacturers of end-products under the claimant agency's jurisdiction. In turn, each end-product manufacturer divided his allotment under a particular contract among his subcontractors and suppliers, and so on down the production chain. This was a "vertical allocation" system. However, it was supplemented by horizontal allocation of materials to some manufacturers whose production methods would not fit readily in the vertical allocation system, principally because they manufactured such items as nuts and bolts well in advance of receipt of orders.

The Controlled Materials Plan had important virtues. It enabled WPB policy-level allocations to be made in terms of end-product programs such as aircraft, naval ships, merchant ships, ordnance, lend-lease needs and civilian consumer requirements. This meant that these quarterly allocations could reflect the annual production objectives for the whole war production program and could be readily adjusted to changes in strategic objectives by the joint chiefs of staff. In this regard it was superior to the Production Requirements Plan, which had required that quarterly allocations be directed to industries, rather than to claimant agencies responsible for end-product programs. The second principal advantage of the Controlled Materials Plan was that it co-ordinated the flow of materials allocations with the methods already developed for awarding contracts and assigning production schedules. For munitions, the latter two methods had been largely adminis-

Canadians assembled at Malton, Ont., on Aug. 6, 1943, to witness the dedication of the first Lancaster built in Canada for overseas use

tered by the procurement organizations of the war and navy departments. And under the Controlled Materials Plan, the services gained the additional function of allocating materials to munitions producers and indirectly to all producers tied to munitions plants as subcontractors and suppliers. From one point of view, the supplanting of the Production Requirements committee by the Controlled Materials Plan meant a lessened role for WPB in direction of industry. But it also gave WPB a firmer control over end-product programs and, by forcing reduction of production schedules to fit materials allocations, assured real control over the production of U.S. industry.

Abandonment of the Production Requirements Plan was caused by temporary difficulties as much as by inherent defects in the plan. It had the misfortune to be in operation in a period when the total munitions production demands by the armed services were far beyond the capacity of U.S. industry, and when the preference ratings already outstanding throughout industry were being supplanted by new ratings sponsored by the Army and Navy Munitions board. As the first over-all allocation system it also encountered numerous administrative problems that were spared the Controlled Materials Plan. In any event, it was the Production Requirements Plan that guided the flow of materials during the great production build-up of 1942 and part of 1943. And the Controlled Materials Plan carried the nation through the balance of the war with apparent satisfaction to industry, military agencies and civilian agencies.

Production Scheduling and Components.—In late 1942 and early 1943, WPB attempted to recapture firm control of production scheduling, which up to that time had been handled in a relatively independent manner by the armed services. This was in effect a continuation of the battle over reduction of the services' programs to a reasonable approximation of the nation's productive capacity. As the war progressed, materials and components became so heavily demanded for essential programs that WPB felt it must not only bring total requirements into balance with supplies on a yearly basis, but see to it that the month-by-month schedules for production of individual items were in line with resources availability and were in balance with the production prospects for complementary items. Despite strong resistance from the services, Donald M. Nelson and Charles E. Wilson, then the production vice-chairman of WPB, won broad authority in the production scheduling field. In practice, however, WPB concentrated on expediting particular programs, particularly aircraft, destroyer escort vessels and radar equipment, and scheduling deliveries of critical common components.

In Feb. 1943, WPB issued general scheduling order M-293, which enabled WPB to control the order boards of manufacturers of critical common components. Such components were selected manufactured items that were in acute competitive demand for incorporation into such end-products as naval vessels, merchant ships, aircraft and rubber and aviation gasoline plants. WPB analyzed the outstanding orders for such components, directed which orders were to be filled first, and "froze" plants' order boards so that the plants could schedule their production operations without fear that new orders would unsettle the schedule. It also rationalized the distribution of orders by shifting orders from heavily loaded plants to underutilized plants, and by shifting orders for easy-to-make items from highly skilled plants to less skilled plants, thereby freeing the former's machines for work on the most difficult items. By mid-1943 this procedure had resulted in almost completely breaking the components bottleneck.

Despite these successes, WPB had not used its hard-won powers to fix production schedules from end-products down through components to materials. For this it relied on the Controlled Materials Plan's requirement that production schedules be adjusted to fit the amounts of materials allocated. This, however, fell far short of WPB's earlier desire to exercise such detailed surveillance of monthly production scheduling by the services as to assure balance in the flow of complementary items.

Industrial Demobilization.—In 1943 and 1944, most resources other than manpower began to come into easy supply, and the shortages, while requiring vigorous attention, were not of an economy-wide character. Furthermore, as United Nations military advances brought the end of the European war in sight, there was growing concern lest the nation be unprepared either for scattered cutbacks in munitions production or for the wholesale cutbacks expected to follow immediately the final victory in Europe. There was, therefore, a problem with many facets: how to use surplus materials, such as aluminum; how to guide cutbacks of military production, as between government-owned and privately owned plants, as between large and small plants, and as among local areas; how to use plants no longer needed in military production; what plans to lay for adapting the economy to the one-front war against Japan, which was expected to last for a considerable period after the victory in Europe; and what role to anticipate for the WPB and its staff as the greater part of the economy returned to civilian production.

Nelson held to the view that materials, facilities and manpower no longer needed in military production should be diverted to the production of civilian goods. The armed services held a contrary view, believing that munitions production would suffer because relaxation of restrictions on civilian products would lead to the impression that the war was over for all practical purposes and war workers would shift to jobs in civilian industries. Nelson acceded to the services' position pending successful invasion of western Europe. Immediately after the success of the beachhead in France was assured, Nelson announced his intention to issue four reconversion orders. The most controversial of the orders provided for "spot authorization" of civilian production; that is, for granting of permission by WPB field offices to local manufacturers to resume or expand civilian production, despite WPB limitation orders, where local investigation established that such action would not interfere with war production.

The services opposed all four orders, but took particular exception to the "spot authorization" proposal. Their main contention was that, as manpower was still inadequate in some areas for war production, surplus workers should be encouraged to migrate to such areas, and that to expand civilian production in labour surplus areas would discourage such migration. Nelson, on the other hand, contended that most workers, when thrown out of employment by plants whose military contracts had been cut back, would not migrate but would drift out of the industrial labour force into other less essential types of work in their own communities or would completely leave the labour market. He also felt that if a setback in Europe should occur and demands for munitions programs be again stepped up, the nation would profit most by having maintained its industrial labour force intact, rather than by having dissipated a substantial part of it in order to get a few workers to migrate to labour shortage areas.

The "spot authorization" order was on its face a departure from proposals that WPB postpone resumption of civilian production in an industry until all plants in the industry could start simultaneously in the race for the postwar market. The order, therefore, was adverse to the interests of established firms in civilian industries, since it would facilitate the entry of newcomers into the industries, and to the interests of large corporations still heavily engaged in war work.

Although all four orders were in effect by Aug. 15, 1944, the "spot authorization" order had slight effect, for restrictions on its use were imposed by the director of war mobilization, the services steeply increased their munitions requirements, and WPB itself agreed to suspension of the order in the more critical labour areas.

Issuance of the reconversion orders in the summer of 1944 was opposed not only by the services, but by most of the WPB vice-chairmen. The publicizing of the dispute was popularly assumed to lie behind the president's Aug. 19 announcement that he was sending Nelson on a mission to China, and it was the direct cause of Wilson's resignation as executive vice-chairman. J. A. Krug was appointed acting chairman of WPB, and on Sept. 30, 1944, replaced Nelson as chairman.

In the spring of 1944, WPB established machinery to guide the distribution of cutbacks of military production contracts, so as to protect munitions programs, ease manpower problems and facilitate reconversion. This activity was relatively ineffectual, however, as there were in many cases no alternatives to the cutbacks proposed, there was inadequate information on subcontracting under specific prime contracts, and WPB lacked effective control over contract run-outs (as distinguished from cancellation of contracts only partly fulfilled).

Planning for the partial reconversion to follow victory in Europe turned largely on the question of the degree to which WPB would continue controls over industry. One group argued that controls would be necessary not only to protect munitions production for the one-front war against Japan, but also to prevent a chaotic scramble for scarce materials, to prevent hoarding of materials, to assure that essential civilian needs were met before nonessential needs and to bolster price control. The other group argued that, while a minimum of controls would be needed to protect munitions production, the bulk of the other controls should be scrapped so that U.S. enterprise might return as rapidly as possible to a relatively free competitive system with reliance placed on individual initiative and ingenuity rather than on governmental directives.

A major factor determining the choice of policy was the production requirements of the armed services for continuing the war against Japan. If these requirements were to be so low as to release large amounts of materials for civilian production, there would be little need for continuance of controls, save for a priority system to assure first preference to the meeting of military orders. But if military requirements were to be so high as to leave only modest amounts of materials for civilian production, there would be much more weight to the argument that WPB controls would be needed to assure that civilians' essential needs were met before their nonessential needs, and to provide fair and noninflationary distribution of the limited supplies of materials.

Estimates of military requirements, however, proved to be unstable. The munitions needs for the year following victory in Europe, and assuming continuance of the war with Japan, were variously estimated as 14%, 30%, 40% and even 50% below 1944 munitions production.

In practice, WPB looked in both directions at once, planning for a sweeping away of most controls, but reserving the right to reinstate controls if the scramble for materials threatened to get out of hand. Much the same policy characterized WPB's development of plans for the period following victory over Japan. Here, however, the critical question was not the size of military requirements, but the desirability of using a number of WPB controls to guide the U.S. economy through the difficult problems of the transition period to maximum peacetime production and full employment.

Victory in Europe initiated a general relaxation of controls, and this was accelerated following the victory over Japan. Between May and Aug. 1945, more than 200 orders and regulations were revoked, and all steel, copper and aluminum not needed for Controlled Materials Plan allocations were thrown on the free market; the plan itself was completely abandoned at the end of Sept. 1945. By Nov. 3, when WPB was succeeded by the Civilian Production administration, there remained only 52 orders and priorities regulations out of the 650 WPB controls that had been in effect at the war's peak. A third of the retained orders concerned textiles, clothing and leather; another group controlled such scarce materials and products as rubber, tin, lead, newsprint and certain chemicals and containers; a third group provided inventory and scheduling controls, and authorized priority ratings for breaking reconversion bottlenecks.

Paralleling the policy of removal of most WPB controls was a policy of liquidating most of the WPB staff. Some 2,000 employees were separated in the fall of 1944, and then the staff was stabilized at about 12,000 employees for the first half of 1945—approximately half the size of WPB at its peak. By the end of Oct. 1945, the staff had been cut to about 5,000 employees, and a large part of WPB's experienced executives had returned to their posts in industry.

By an executive order dated Oct. 4, 1945, the president terminated the WPB, effective as of the close of business on Nov. 3, 1945. The board's remaining functions were assigned to a new Civilian Production administration, which was directed "to further a swift and orderly transition from wartime production to a maximum peacetime production in industry free from wartime Government controls, with due regard for the stability of prices and costs." The task of war production, and of unwinding most of the wartime controls, was finished. (J. W. Fr.)

Contract Terminations.—Early in World War II, shifts in the tide of warfare, changes in terrain and tactics, and, above all, the growth of new weapons and supplies led to the need for terminating war contracts at the convenience of the government before they had been completed. This was a necessary adjunct to the war production program and saved a great deal of time, effort and money. Further, the cessation of hostilities resulted in termination of the vast majority of contracts then outstanding. By Sept. 30, 1946, in the U.S., 318,000 contracts involving cancelled commitments of $65,300,000,000, which the government had entered into for war production purposes, had been terminated. At the same date, 312,000 (98%) of these contracts, with cancelled commitments of $59,000,000,000 (90%), had been settled for gross allowances of $5,900,000,000.

During the early days of the war, the major contracting agencies of the government—the war and navy departments, the maritime commission, the treasury department and the Reconstruction Finance corporation—began to develop their own termination policies. However, the need for uniform planning soon made itself felt, and the Joint Contract Termination board, under the Office of War Mobilization, was established by the principal contracting agencies. The board's work was largely summarized in the "Report on War and Post-War Adjustment Policies" by Bernard M. Baruch and John M. Hancock. The so-called Baruch-Hancock report stressed the need for speed in the settlement of war contracts and for fairness to the contractor and to the government. These general conclusions served as a basis for subsequent legislation and regulation.

The Contract Settlement Act of 1944, which became effective on July 21, 1944, established the Office of Contract Settlement to supervise policy-making for the entire government. However, the actual operation of terminations was left to the various contracting agencies. Robert H. Hinckley, a vice-president of the Sperry corporation and former assistant secretary of commerce for air, was appointed director of Contract Settlement and assumed his duties on July 28, 1944. Hinckley retired as director in the early part of 1946. Col. H. Chapman Rose, general staff corps, deputy director, became his successor. On Oct. 1, 1946, Roger L. Putnam, former mayor of Springfield, Mass., and wartime deputy director of the OCS, assumed the duties of director.

Although the termination of war contracts first received widespread attention in World War II, the procedure had been recognized as far back as the Civil War, and to a further extent in World War I. In 1918 when the end of World War I seemed close at hand, hasty efforts were made to devise a system of settling the sudden termination of contracts which would be effected at the Armistice. Only by the most frantic measures was the government able to avoid total injustice to manufacturers, and to prevent the production of vast quantities of unneeded supplies. As it was, the government found itself compelled, after the Armistice, to continue manufacture and receipt of millions of dollars' worth of new but useless munitions. While the agencies responsible for termination and settlement proceeded as expeditiously as the meagre early preparations would allow, the bulk of settlements took many months to make. Many claims and disputes resulted in litigation which wound its costly way through the courts for 20 years after the Armistice. The whole experience was an object lesson pointing to the vital necessity for formulating the basis of a contractual program which could be used in any future emergency.

During the 1920s and 1930s, termination of government contracts for reasons other than the default of the contractor played a small part in the peacetime procurement. However, the confused settlement experience of 1918 had indicated clearly that cancellation arrangements should be considered. As a result, the draftsmen for war contract forms during the interwar period included some termination provisions in their agreements.

Immediately following the declaration of war on Dec. 7, 1941, the First War Powers act was passed authorizing the president "to enter into contracts and into amendments or modifications of contracts . . . and to make advance, progress and other payments thereon." Executive orders, issued shortly after the act was passed, implemented the provisions of this legislation. These orders reaffirmed the government's power to terminate and settle.

As the purchasing program of World War II increased in early 1942, terminations began to occur. Before long, the contracting agencies sensed the eventual need for an orderly procedure which would facilitate settlements. Moreover, contractors anticipated the danger of possible time lags between actual termination dates, settlement payments and the clearance of plants for the resumption of other production.

The early efforts expended by individual contracting agencies in formulating termination policies were eventually consolidated in the work of the Joint Contract Termination board and elaborated into the Contract Settlement Act of 1944. The act stated broadly that: "It is the policy of the Government, and it shall be the responsibility of the contracting agencies and the Director, to provide war contractors with speedy and fair compensation for the termination of any war contract. . . ."

Generally, the Contract Settlement act provided that termination claims should be settled by negotiation between contracting agency and contractor to the maximum extent feasible. Such settlements would be final in the absence of fraud. In case an agreement could not be reached, the amount due could, subject to right of appeal, be fixed by determination upon the part of the contracting agency. Wherever it would facilitate settlements, the contracting agencies had power to deal directly with subcontractors. The act provided for prompt plant clearance and liberal financing for the contractor in the interval between termination and settlement. Still another important feature of the legislation was a broad provision for the settlement of defective, informal and quasi contracts.

In accordance with further provisions of the act, the Office of Contract Settlement was established in Aug. 1944, along with a contract settlement advisory board and an appeal board. Broad discretionary powers were given the director to organize the settlement program so that it would not hamper war production.

At the same time that wide authority was put into the hands of the director, it was maintained strongly that the OCS should remain on a policy-making level. The firm belief was that actual settlement operations could best be carried through by the agencies which had made the contracts originally. Termination policies were similar to those of the former Joint Contract Termination board. Interagency committees under the Contract Settlement advisory board met with the specialized divisions (accounting, legal, financial, etc.) of the OCS. Members of the individual divisions of the OCS, in turn, consulted with representatives of industry and trade associations in considering the formulation of contract settlement policy. In this way, 20 regulations covering fair compensation, interim financing, plant clearance and other subjects were worked out during the first two years of operation of the OCS.

Termination Articles and Settlements.—The basis for the formulation of uniform termination clauses and articles was established by the Joint Contract Termination board. Under the board's aegis, the basic Uniform Termination Article for Fixed-Price Supply Contracts was devised. Shortly after the establishment of the OCS, similar termination articles were drawn up for insertion into cost-plus-a fixed-fee contracts, construction contracts, preliminary contractual instruments and subcontracts. These termination articles assured uniform handling of claims by all government agencies, eliminated possible conflict and confusion over varying contract provisions and led to swifter and more equitable settlements. Moreover such articles promised to save time, effort and money for prime contractors and their subcontractors.

In 1942, shortly after Pearl Harbor, the first large government terminations took place. It became evident that some simplifying technique had to be substituted for the overwhelming work required in conjunction with full-audit settlements. As a result, negotiated settlements were proposed as a means of simplification and speed. Negotiation allowed the government to make settlements on the basis of certain relevant facts and data; the exact accounting methods of settlement by formula were reserved only for cases of negotiation breakdown. The finality of these negotiated settlements, in the absence of fraud, was confirmed by the attorney general in 1942. It was pointed out that negotiated contract settlements could be effected with an optimum of speed and fairness to both contractors and the government if a reviewing agency were limited to checking for fraud.

After several termination accounting guides had been put into use by various agencies during the war, the Joint Contract Termination board early in 1944 devised a uniform "Statement of Principles for Determination of Cost upon Termination of Government Fixed-Price Supply Contracts." This statement was part of the Uniform Article for Fixed-Price Supply Contracts. It recognized costs "sanctioned by commercial accounting practices" including "the direct and indirect manufacturing, selling and distribution, administrative and other costs incurred which are reasonably necessary for the performance of the contract, and are properly allocable or apportionable, under such practices to the contract."

Generally, the provisions of the statement of cost principles endured the test of thousands of terminated fixed-price war contracts.

Both government and industry agreed as to the fairness of the allowances and disallowances. Reasonable profits were paid for work actually done on the terminated portion of contracts.

Under no-cost settlements, the contractor retained all termination inventory and waived his termination claim. The minimization of effort in this method of settlement was of advantage to all concerned. More than 217,000 terminated contracts, or about two-thirds of the total, were settled at no-cost. These accounted for a cancelled commitment value of $10,000,000,000 out of the over-all figure of $59,000,000,000 in cancelled commitments settled by Sept. 30, 1946.

In the termination of a large prime contract, subcontractors of various tiers would sometimes number in the hundreds or even thousands. For example, upon termination of tank production by the International Harvester company in March 1943, representing contracts aggregating $217,000,000, there were 428 immediate subcontractors located in 100 cities in 20 states, and an estimated 2,000 second and third tier subcontractors.

Inasmuch as the government had no direct contractual relationship with subcontractors, fair and fast settlements of their claims had to be effected primarily through the cooperation of procurement agencies and prime contractors. Just as prime contractors aided subcontractors in securing priorities, financing and engineering, so in contract settlement "primes" had to assist their "subs" with interim financing, filing claims, plant clearance and other termination problems.

The principal machinery utilized for the settlement of subcontractors' claims was the method known as the "vertical settlement system." This procedure utilized the normal connections and relationships of business in the settlement of contracts up the subcontractor chain.

During the war, several termination settlement variations were fostered by the government and industry. In Oct. 1943 the war department took the first steps in establishing a closer relationship between the government and contractors with what later came to be known as the "Consolidated Termination Program." Under this program, field accounting representatives were installed in the plants of war contractors with authority to make accounting examinations of all war department contracts. This was broadened to include the handling of plant clearances. Later, the navy department joined in administering the program. Almost 100 of the country's largest war contractors operated in varying degrees under this termination system.

Another variation to vertical settlements was "Company-wide Settlements," offered as a solution for the contractor who found himself in the position of having a large volume of terminated prime and subcontracts with various customers and contracting agencies.

The Company-wide Settlement program provided for the assignment of selected contractors to one service or bureau of the war or navy departments for direct settlement of all claims resulting from termination of both its prime and subcontracts. This method differed from the Consolidated Termination program primarily in that under the latter, the assigned contractor's claim, after accounting review and plant clearance, passed through normal vertical settlement channels. Under the Company-wide procedure, final settlement was made by the designated service or bureau. By Sept. 30, 1946, more than 69,000 claims had been settled under a total of 31 Company-wide Settlement assignments.

The contracting agencies also made direct settlements with subcontractors on individual contracts when necessary, in the interest of expeditious and equitable settlement. Moreover, contractors were given blanket authority to settle claims of less than $1,000, without governmental approval, where the subcontractor retained or disposed of all inventory. In addition, contracting agencies allowed selected contractors to make final settlement of their subcontractors' claims of $10,000 or less.

Termination Financing.—One of the primary needs of war contractors was financial assistance during the period when their working capital was tied up in cancelled contracts or subcontracts. In addition to private banking sources, the government provided its own means of interim financing including guaranteed loans; utilization of advance payments; and partial payments.

During the spring of 1945, surveys showed that interim financing was readily accessible to all war contractors. Shortly after V-E day, and again after V-J day, the demand for financ-

Table IV.—*Status of U. S. Contract Settlement, Sept. 30, 1946*
(All Terminations and Settlements; All Reporting Agencies)

	TERMINATED		SETTLED		PENDING	
	Number of Contracts (approximated to nearest thousand)	Cancelled Commitment Value (approximated to nearest billion)	Number of Contracts (approximated to nearest thousand)	Cancelled Commitment Value (approximated to nearest billion)	Number of Contracts (approximated to nearest thousand)	Cancelled Commitment Value (approximated to nearest billion)
Dec. 31, 1944	128,000	$25.5	117,000	$13.9	11,000	$11.6
April 30, 1945	145,000	29.7	137,000	19.4	8,000	10.3
(V-E day May 7)						
June 30, 1945	165,000	37.0	150,000	22.3	15,000	14.7
July 31, 1945	174,000	38.5	157,000	23.6	17,000	14.9
(V-J day Aug. 14)						
Aug. 30, 1945	271,000	60.9	165,000	24.7	106,000	36.2
Dec. 31, 1945	303,000	63.9	250,000	30.4	53,000	33.5
June 30, 1946	317,000	65.2	305,000	54.2	12,000	11.0
Sept. 30, 1946	318,000	65.3	312,000	59.0	6,000	6.3

ing increased sharply. Partial payments, utilized in termination financing to a far greater extent than advance payments or government-guaranteed loans, were made promptly to the satisfaction of contractors. By Oct. 1946 more than $3,000,000,000 in partial payments had been made on terminated war contracts.

Inventory Disposal.—A termination notice brought prompt cessation of all work allocable to a contract in both the prime contractors' factory and in the plants of subcontractors. The disposition of the raw materials, work in process, machinery and equipment presented one of the war's major tasks. Seven billion dollars of inventory, or 95% of the expected total, had been cleared by Oct. 1946. Of this, about 56% was sold to third parties or retained by the contractors in possession; 16% was retained by the contracting agencies; and 28% was declared to War Assets administration or its predecessor agencies as surplus property.

A 60-day plant clearance policy was one of the basic tenets of the government in disposing of inventories. Under this policy, the contractor could ask the contracting agency to move the inventory out of his plant and, if the government failed to do this within the 60-day period, he could then move or store the inventory at federal expense. When the bulk of plant clearance requests started to appear toward the end of the war, the OCS sponsored interagency meetings to assure co-ordinated disposal efforts both in Washington, D.C., and in the field. Problems ironed out were broad in scope; allocation of storage space, priority of handling inventories of the various agencies and shipping policies were a few of the questions considered at the inter-agency plant clearance meetings.

Information and Training.—During World War II, several methods were used by individual contractors to speed the administration of their termination settlements. Generally, these were: pretermination planning; creation of a termination unit; preparation of a termination manual; and training of personnel.

An extensive training program for contracting agency personnel was carried on by the government. In addition, more than 75,000 contractor personnel—representing about 40,000 industrial firms—attended termination training sessions given by co-ordinating committees throughout the country. Contractors, business and professional organizations and the newspaper and trade press, as well as private information publications co-operated in the program. These groups voluntarily sponsored settlement publicity and training in the form of articles, special pamphlets and promotion of conferences and instructional sessions.

By Sept. 30, 1946, 112 appeals had been made by contractors to the appeal board of the OCS in the settlement of more than 311,000 terminated war contracts. The reason for this negligible amount of litigation was attributed, in a large part, to the vast planning which went into the Contract Settlement Act of 1944 and policies and procedures thereunder. By Sept. 30, 1946, 103 cases of suspected termination fraud had been reported to the department of justice from all sources. Only 4 of the 52 cases disposed of to that date had warranted criminal or civil proceedings. Table IV gives the status of contract settlement as of Sept. 30, 1946. (R. L. Pm.)

Great Britain

During World War II, Britain mobilized its resources perhaps more fully than any other nation, and its achievement was remarkable. British armed forces and auxiliary services increased from 477,000 in June 1939 to 5,092,000 in June 1945. Of the equipment used by the armed forces of the British commonwealth and empire (8,750,000 men in all), no less than 70% was produced in the United Kingdom itself, another 10% in the empire and one-fifth from the U.S. Simultaneously, Britain succeeded in ensuring its civilian population a standard of living which was only 15% lower than before the war and much higher than in any continental country.

Table V.—*Proportions of British Gross National Income Spent in War Production*

Year	Gross National Income (at current prices)	National Cost of the War	Cost of the War. in % of National Income
	in million £		
1938	5,129	348(*)	7
1939	5,490	771(*)	14
1940	6,452	2,662	41
1941	7,434	3,668	49
1942	8,113	3,961	49
1943	8,635	4,512	52
1944	8,887	4,493	51

*For 1938 and the first 9 months of 1939 the figures in this column represent rearmament expenditure.

The different phases of Britain's war effort are best illustrated by the increasing proportions of its total gross national income spent as shown in Table V.

The increase in the United Kingdom's war effort is similarly reflected in the expansion of the armed forces and of those producing munitions (*see* Table VI).

Table VI.—*Distribution of Manpower*

Year	Labour force	Armed forces	Insured workers employed on orders of the supply departments
1939	21,000,000	600,000	1,202,400 (June)
1941	22,700,000	3,800,000	...
1942	23,500,000	4,500,000	...
1943	23,800,000	5,100,000	5,075,500 (June)
June 1944	23,500,000	5,200,000	...

The vast expansion of both the armed forces and of munition workers emerges clearly from these figures. Millions of workers in other callings of life also went into full-time war employment, such as transport workers, civil servants, etc. The comparison of the total labour force, of those in the armed forces and of those in civilian war employment, can be made for June 1944 between Britain, U.S. and Canada (*see* Table VII).

Table VII.—*Distribution of Manpower (U.K., U.S.A. and Canada)*

	Total labour force	Armed forces	Estimated civilian war employment
		in millions	
U.K.	23.5	5.2	7.8
U.S.	62.2	11.5	13.4*
Canada	5.1	0.8	1.3†

*Not including agriculture.
†Including 25% of farm employment.

Although these figures are not strictly comparable between the three countries, they indicate that in June 1944 about one-third of the U.K. labour force was employed in producing munitions and in civilian war work compared with only about one quarter in the U.S. and Canada. The total armed forces amounted to 22% of the working population in the U.K., 18.5% in the U.S. and 16% in Canada. Altogether, 55% of the working population was in the forces or on war work in the U.K., 40% in the U.S. (exclusive of agriculture) and 41% in Canada (including 25% of farm employment).

This same point, namely that there was a division of labour between the United Nations, each contributing what it could best do under the circumstances, must be

Table VIII.—*Munitions Production Indices*
1943=100

	U.K.	U.S.	Canada
1940	37.2	4.7	14.3
1941	54.3	15.1	35.0
1942	84.4	56.5	79.6
1943	100.0	100.0	100.0
1944	97.4	108.3	102.9

considered when comparing total production of munitions.

The production of munitions increased rapidly in Britain between 1939 and 1942, and there was further expansion in 1943–44. In 1944 munition production ran at more than six times the rate of production in Sept. 1939 and at about twice the 1941 rate of production. Until early in 1942, British munition production was bigger than the corresponding U.S. production, but when the U.S. entered the war the rate of its munition production increased very rapidly. The 1944 production of munitions index underestimates somewhat production in the U.K., as it did not make allowance for such construction works as the "mulberry harbour," etc., but taking the 1943 figures as typical, the volumes of munitions production in the three countries were related as follows: U.S. nearly 4 to U.K. 1; U.K. more than 5 to Canada 1.

Organization.—Britain had not prepared for total war. At the outbreak of World War II, therefore, there was not in existence a well thought-out central organization for war production; the machinery developed as needs arose and problems required solution. Broadly speaking, the supreme co-ordinating agency was the minister of defense (Winston Churchill, from May 10, 1940 to his resignation, July 26, 1945) and the defense committee of the cabinet whose business it was to define the tasks of the production ministries in relation to the broad lines of war strategy. Day-to-day co-ordination was ensured at first by different high level committees until by 1941–42 the ministry of production was established which took over a number of co-ordinating functions.

For munitions, there was no single supply organization. Broadly speaking, the ministry of supply took charge of weapons and supplies for the army. From May 1940 onward, the ministry of aircraft production did the same for the royal air force, while the provision of ships and naval stores remained the responsibility of the two comptrollers of the admiralty, the one for the navy, and the other for merchant ship building. Actual distribution of functions was, however, not quite so rigid. The resources in short supply for which all three supply departments were clamouring were usually dealt with by one agency only. Machine tools were the bottle-neck in the early stages of the war, and their production and supply was controlled for all users by the ministry of supply and later by the ministry of production. Raw materials were controlled for all users throughout by the ministry of supply. The procurement of labour, a most important factor, was for all purposes the responsibility of the ministry of labour.

Although war production proper was controlled by the above-mentioned supply departments, other government departments were for obvious reasons also deeply concerned with many of its aspects. It was the duty of the board of trade, *e.g.*, to look after the minimum civilian requirements. In this capacity it exercised control over production and distribution in order to release and divert resources such as factory space, machinery and labour from nonessential civilian production to war production. The ministries of food and agriculture played a vital role in other important spheres of the war effort, apart from the central directing department, the treasury. Without a proper financial policy that skilfully combined taxation and borrowing it would have been impossible either to mobilize all the resources of Britain for the war or to set aside such a high proportion of the national income for war purposes. Apart from the big central departments concerned with the war effort, there were the regional organizations of the different government departments whose work was later co-ordinated to a certain extent by the interdepartmental regional board. Many vital production problems, such as finding new capacity, saving transport, subcontracts, etc., could only be settled locally.

The co-ordination of Britain's war effort with that of its Allies, notably the U.S., also passed through several stages. Before Pearl Harbor, this co-ordination was informal, but in the summer and autumn of 1941 a system began to emerge. After Pearl Harbor, together with the combined chiefs of staff, a combined materials assignment board was set up, based on Washington, D.C., to allocate according to strategic needs, munitions produced in the U.S. and similarly, a board in London to allocate munitions produced in the British empire. These boards were later supplemented by a combined raw materials board and a combined production and resources board, both in Washington, mainly concerned to fit British needs from the U.S. into the total U.S. supply program. Eventually, a vast network of Anglo-U.S. supply contracts developed. Difficulties notwithstanding, a common outlook and a large measure of understanding enabled both sides to deal rationally with interallied supply problems.

Execution.—In 1939, Britain was still predominantly a free-enterprise country in the sense that the means of production were owned by private entrepreneurs. The execution of war production programs required a considerable measure of central direction and control with which the business community readily complied. But it was not then intended that the state as such should take over ownership of industry to secure the execution of the war program. Only a very small part of the munitions industry, such as the royal ordnance factories or the admiralty ship yards, were state-owned.

Although there was a central co-ordination of war production, the placing of actual production orders remained the task of the three main supply departments, whose policies followed eclectic lines. In regard to army equipment the ministry of supply and previously the director general of munition production in the war office relied for certain jobs on the state-owned royal ordnance factories. Thus the filling of ammunition and to a large extent the manufacture of small arms, ammunition and explosives were carried out by the royal ordnance factories. At the same time the ministry of supply tried to bring into the field of armament production the widest possible range of private firms, mostly engaged in the engineering and chemical trades.

In regard to aircraft and its equipment, the ministry of aircraft production and the air ministry before it, followed the policy of nursing a group of specialized private firms whose relations with the air ministry were sufficiently intimate to enable it to guide and control design and production of aeroplanes. These "family firms" were in private hands, although the state provided a substantial proportion of their capital. Eventually, a wide range of other firms were brought into this field, in particular some big motor car and electrical firms. The admiralty also relied on dividing contracts between government yards and private shipbuilders. Their big craft were mainly built by some specialized firms, the smaller craft, especially in the later stages of the war, by a wider range of other firms.

Apart from work directly contracted for the supply departments, many firms and industries were brought into war production by other methods. The raw material producing industries, such as iron and steel, nonferrous metals, while remaining in private hands, were, of course, subjected to controls and their output allocated according to war needs. Moreover, war contractors relied on subcontracting to a large extent. Originally, the main contractors themselves found their subcontractors, but at later stages, the government departments undertook the ordering and distribution of many parts, accessories and components. Relations between contractors and government, and even more, relations between contractor and contractor, were also influenced by the so-called group system. Several firms engaged in the production of the same weapon worked together as a team with departmental direction and assistance, in producing the required equipment.

The central direction of war production was, of course, not confined to the placing of orders and contracts by the supply departments. It went much beyond that stage. There was machinery for securing factory space, raw materials and labour as well as finance for war production. Thus the government provided capital for the conversion and expansion of existing plant or for building and equipping new factories. In such cases the government retained ownership of the assets. The government also provided working capital either by progress payments or advances; lastly, tax concessions were given to write off

British munitions plant which manufactured 14-inch naval guns for the armed forces during World War II

quickly building and equipment which would cease to be of value by the end of the war. In some industries, the conversion from peacetime to wartime production could be achieved overnight.

One of the main factors in the successful wartime conversion of British economy was the ability of firms and whole industries to turn to entirely new fields of production, *e.g.*, some made gun parts instead of stockings; a public transport undertaking, the London Passenger Transport board, produced bombers in its workshops. With the conversion of factories and workshops, many workers automatically turned to war production; others switched, or were switched, into war industries.

Mobilization of Manpower.—Mobilization of manpower and its allocation as between production and the armed services was one of the fundamental problems of wartime organization. In its legal aspects, mobilization was governed by the national service (armed forces) act, 1939, and its subsequent amendments which provided for compulsory enlistment into the fighting services of men of military age. As the war proceeded, the scope of this legislation had to be extended. Enlistment of women into the auxiliary women's services became compulsory in Dec. 1941. Industrial recruitment, originally on a voluntary basis, also became subject to compulsory registration (March 1941). To prevent depletion of manpower reserves and too quick a turnover of labour in defense and other essential industries, the ministry of labour, in March 1941, issued the Essential Works order under which, in such industries, employers lost the right of hiring and firing, and workers the right of quitting their jobs, except with the ministry's consent. Finally, under schedules of reserved occupations set up at the outbreak of the war, certain essential workers were maintained in civilian occupations instead of being drafted into the armed services.

Between June 1939 and June 1944, when the peak was reached, the total number of men aged 14 to 64 and of women aged 14 to 59 in the services or in industrial employment in Great Britain rose from 18,500,000 to 22,000,000, the combined result of a reduction of the number of unemployed by 1,250,000 and an expansion of the total labour force of the country by 2,250,000 persons not previously in industrial employment. In these figures two part-time workers were reckoned equal to one full-time worker. Unqualified by this distinction the addition to the labour force amounted to 4,500,000 (versus 3,500,000) units.

In addition to the increase in units, the average hours worked by the working population also increased from 46.5 in Oct. 1938 to 50 hr. in July 1943 and 48.6 in July 1944. In the munitions industries the hours worked were even longer. In extent, the mobilization of manpower achieved altogether greatly exceeded that of World War I. In this, the contribution made by women was decisive. Out of the 3,500,000 added to the labour force, 2,250,000 were women.

At the middle of 1944, of the 22,000,000 of working age, 47% or 10,300,000 were in the services or in full-time civil defense or employed in engineering, shipbuilding, metals and chemicals, *i.e.*, industries mainly concerned with the output of munitions; 26% or 5,700,000 were in agriculture, mining, national and local government service, public utilities, transport, shipping, including the merchant navy, in the manufacture of food, drink and tobacco, *i.e.*, industries which it was necessary to maintain or expand during the war; 27% or 6,000,000 were in building and civil engineering, the textile and clothing and other manufacturing industries, the distributive trades and civilian services. These figures when compared with those for 1939 represent a very important shift in the occupational distribution of the working population, as can be seen in Table IX. In mid-1944, as compared with mid-1939, the number of persons employed in the munitions industries had increased by about two-thirds; those in the basic industries and services had remained largely unchanged, and those in other industries and services had decreased by more than one-third. In 1939, of the total population subject to unemployment insurance, 1,200,000 were employed on orders for the supply departments; in 1943, 5,100,000; in the same period those employed on orders for the home market decreased from 4,400,000 to 2,300,000 and those employed on export orders decreased from 900,000 to 240,000.

Table IX.—*War-time shifts in the Working Population in Great Britain*

		Number employed ('000)	
		mid-1939	mid-1944
1. Munition industries	males	2,600	3,210
	females	506	1,851
2. Principal basic industries and services .	males	4,688	4,059
	females	852	1,644
Agriculture, horticulture etc.	males	1,046	948
	females	67	184
Mining	males	868	802
	females	5	13
National government service	males	416	520
	females	123	495
Local government service	males	225	160
	females	17	32
Transport, shipping and fishing	males	1,222	1,038
	females	51	212
Food, drink and tobacco	males	391	269
	females	263	240
3. Other industries and services (building, textiles, clothing, etc. industries, distribution, services)	males	5,798	2,900
	females	3,479	3,102

Raw Material Resources.—With Britain fully mobilized, the shortage of manpower became the chief factor limiting expansion of output. Hardly less important a factor was the supply of industrial raw materials. Except for coal and iron ore, Britain's industries had to rely almost entirely on imports. In the earlier stages of the war, in particular after the loss of the European continent and the far east as sources of supply, the Allies experienced not only relative, but also absolute, shortages of strategic raw materials, further aggravated by the shipping problem that arose on account of the intensive warfare at sea. Demands on tonnage were reduced by three methods: first, by expanding the home production of some raw materials, *e.g.*, iron ore, flax, timber, light metals, etc.; secondly, by the recovery of waste material through intensive salvage drives; thirdly, by economizing as far as possible imported, *i.e.* scarce, raw materials in the production processes (by changes in specifications, use of substitute materials, etc.) Similar considerations also applied to the importation of foodstuffs. The reduction in imports of all kinds is shown in Table X.

Table X.

1. *Reduction in Imports of dry Cargo to the United Kingdom (including imports from Eire)*

('000,000 tons)

	1934–38 average	1943	Jan.-June 1944 average
Food	22.0	11.5	5.4
Raw materials . . .	26.0	12.8	6.1
Finished goods, munitions, etc. . . .	7.0	2.0	1.3
Total	55.0	26.3	12.8

2. *Changes in the Volume of Imports during the War*

(1938 = 100)

	Retained Imports			Retained Imports	
Year	Including munitions	Excluding munitions	Year	Including munitions	Excluding munitions
1935 . .	92.0	. . .	1941 . . .	82.4	. . .
1936 . .	98.5	. . .	1942 . . .	83.2	70.5
1937 . .	104.7	. . .	1943 . . .	116.4	77.5
1938 . .	100.0	. . .	1944 . . .	143.7	80.2
1939 . .	96.8	. . .	1945 . . .	87.7	62.7
1940 . .	94.0	. . .			

Capital Equipment.—Britain fought the war largely with the industrial equipment which it had possessed before the war. There was neither time nor resources to create wholly new industries, a few cases excepted; but substantial capital investment for war purposes occurred in existing industries. This, however, was not on a scale comparable with similar investment in the U.S. In the absence of accurate statistical data the increase in the production of machine tools provides a significant pointer. The turnover of the machine tool industry rose from £19,000,000 in 1939 to £47,000,000 in 1942, the peak year of production. Over the same period the number of people employed in making machine tools increased from 25,000 to approximately 85,000. The tooling up of British war factories was not completed until 1943.

Production of Armaments.—In 1944 total armaments production, as mentioned above, ran at more than six times the rate of Sept. 1939. Table XI shows the main items produced between Sept. 1939 and June 1944 as well as the rate of production at these two dates, and the rate of production in the peak year.

Table XI.—*Armaments Production*

(Sept. 1939 to June 1944)

	Total Numbers	Monthly average (numbers)		
	Sept. 1939 to June 1944	Sept.–Dec. 1939	Jan.–June 1944	Peak
Naval vessels				
Major naval vessels . . .	722	4.2	14.6	14.6 (1944)
Mosquito naval craft . . .	1,386	0.5	21.0	33.7 (1942)
Other	3,636	2.2	151.0	151.0 (1944)
Ground munitions				
Field, medium and heavy artillery equipments . .	13,512	—	309.0	329.0 (1942)
Heavy anti-aircraft equipments	6,294	37.3	30.8	178.0 (1942)
Light anti-aircraft equipments	15,324	7.5	116.6	464.1 (1943)
Machine guns and submachine guns . . .	3,729,921	1,750.0	5,633.3	6,750.0 (1943)
Rifles	2,001,949	5,600.0	54,750.0	84,833.0 (1943)
Tanks	25,116	78.0	412.0	717.0 (1942)
Wheeled vehicles for the services	919,111	6,100.0	15,600.0	16,600.0 (1942)
Aircraft				
Total aircraft	102,609	731.0	2,435.0	2,435.0 (1944)
Heavy bombers	10,018	—	481.0	481.0 (1944)
Medium and light bombers	17,702	268.0	232.0	356.0 (1942)
Fighters	38,025	112.0	942.0	942.0 (1944)

Table XI shows a vast expansion in virtually all the categories of basic munitions. At different phases of the war it became necessary to push more energetically the requirements of one service or other, *e.g.*, the expansion of aircraft production began earlier (in 1940) than that of tank production or the building of small naval craft, but eventually, it was immense in all three categories.

War production was largely a race against time. That race was won in the end, but not without difficulties, disappointments and occasional sharp controversies, in particular over tank and aircraft production. Final success notwithstanding, the planning of production was not perfect, and the fighting services did not always secure the right equipment in right quantity and quality, at the right time. More than once, Churchill's speeches in the early stages of the war indicated the lamentable lack of aircraft and tanks. Yet, in the end, there was not only an immense increase in the quantities produced, but also a vast improvement in quality coupled with an increasingly quick response of the armament industries to changes in the design and the types of equipment produced.

In the aircraft industry, *e.g.*, there was a constant increase in the structural weight of aircraft owing to the changeover to more powerful types, particularly heavy bombers. In the case of tanks and antitank equipment, there was a similar increase in the firing power of the tanks, and similar improvements occurred among virtually the whole range of armament production. In regard to naval armament, substantial quantities of additional or wholly new equipment, such as radar, control gear and devices for protection against mines, were required in the later stages of the war. The numerous new types of armament required an equal diversification and quantitative increase of ammunition, engineers' stores, signal equipment, food stores and stores of army clothing similarly expanded.

The building of merchant ships was not perhaps armaments production in the strict sense of the term, but in Britain's position as a heavy importer of foodstuffs and raw materials from overseas, merchant tonnage constituted an important economic weapon. Table XII shows merchant tonnage lost through sea warfare and new tonnage built in Britain during World War II. New construction, in 1941–43, was greater in volume than in similar circumstances during World War I, although it required this time more specialized equipment as well as defensive armament.

Table XII.—*Shipping Losses and Merchant Shipbuilding*

	Losses of Merchant Ships Total	British	*New merchant vessels completed in the U.K.* (Tankers and nontankers of 100 gross tons and more)
	'000 gross tons		'000 gross tons
1939 Sept.-Dec.	935	498	243
1940	4,549	2,725	810
1941	4,693	3,047	1,158
1942	8,338	3,695	1,302
1943	3,646	1,678	1,204
1944			1,020
1945			744

The picture of armaments production would not be complete without mentioning the part played by repair and reconditioning services. The ships of the royal navy which were frequently in action and continuously at sea required refitting and repair. In the case of merchant vessels repairs absorbed more than half of the manpower available for the construction of such ships. The proportion of repair work was also very high in the aircraft industry, where for every six aircraft newly produced in 1943, four aircraft underwent major repairs.

Human Side of War Production.—Statistics alone cannot convey the whole story of British war production. No less impressive than its quantitative side was its human side. The endurance and the will to work of the average workman, severely handicapped by the blackout, bombing and shortages of all kinds, was matched by the inventiveness and ingenuity of scientists and engineers. Britain took the lead in developing radar, the jet propulsion engine, the drug penicillin, the Bailey temporary bridge, the "mulberry" floating harbour, and the "Pluto" pipe-line under the ocean, a record of invention and discovery that would have been highly creditable even if it had been achieved under conditions less adverse. No less creditable was the response of the whole nation to the call of its government. This wholehearted response was reflected in the excellent labour relations which prevailed in industry throughout World War II and the absence of any but minor strikes.

Two characteristics were outstanding in British war production: ingenuity in improvisation and ability in organization. The first provided the solution of some urgent problems, as when garages were converted into war factories and a big aircraft industry was created from modest beginnings, by subcontracting and other unorthodox methods. The second characteristic showed in the extensive mobilization of labour, much of it unskilled, in the satisfactory rationing arrangements of essential supplies, including food, and in a skilful financial policy. But neither ingenious improvisation nor organizing and planning ability could have succeeded without the full and conscious co-operation of the whole nation. This co-operation was largely voluntary—not the least reason for its success in quantity and quality.

Bibliography.—*Statistics relating to the War Effort of the United Kingdom* (London, 1944); *The Impact of the War on Civilian Consumption in the United Kingdom, the United States and Canada* (London, 1945); *Monthly Digest of Statistics*, of the Central Statistical office No. 1, Jan. 1946 (London); *British War Production 1939–45. A Record* (*The Times*, London, 1945); *Reports of Select Committee on National Expenditure* (1940–45); *The Economist* (weekly, London 1940–45); *Bulletins of Oxford University Institute of Statistics.*

British Empire.—Britain and the U.S. were the great arsenals of the western Allies. The British empire also produced munitions, but its main contribution lay necessarily in the supply of essential foodstuffs and raw materials, except in the case of Canada, which in a way had become the third great arsenal. In 1943–44, at its peak, Canadian war production amounted to one-fifth (or including raw materials, one-fourth) of the war production of the United Kingdom. Yet what is more amazing, virtually its whole war industry had been created after 1939.

Canada's labour force expanded from 4,300,000 to 5,100,000 between 1939 and 1944. The strength of the armed forces increased from 20,000 in 1939 to 800,000 in 1944, *i.e.*, from practically nil to 16% of the working population. In addition, 1,300,000 persons were in civilian war employment in 1944, of whom about 700,000 were in war industries proper. The biggest number were in aircraft production (118,000), shipbuilding (109,000) and mechanical transport (57,000).

Of all the munitions produced, only 30% were used by Canada, the rest by the other Allies.

Canada's war production was also an interesting example of organization. Canada was virtually the only country within the United Nations which handled all war supply problems through a single agency, the centralized department of munitions and supply. At the same time the control of all primary and secondary materials—whether for civilian or for munition use—came under the joint control of the department of munitions and supply and the wartime prices and trade board.

As distinct from the British, but similar to the U.S. case, most of the Canadian war industry was newly created and built. By the end of Dec. 1944 the department of munitions had made commitments for investment in war production facilities totalling nearly $850,000,000. Another interesting feature of Canadian war production was the setting up of crown companies to operate new war plants or to deal with the building up and distribution of stocks of key materials. Table XIII indicates both the

Table XIII.—*Canada's National Income 1939-44 and War Production 1940-44*

	1938	1939	1940	1941	1942	1943	1944
			'000,000 Canadian $				
Gross national income at current prices . .	4,150	4,550	5,520	6,830	8,710	9,470	10,270
Total Canadian war product*	—	—	1,182	2,265	3,872	5,180	5,585
Munitions	—	—	333	816	1,857	2,334	2,402
War plant expansion	—	—	106	287	246	132	30
Net war export .	—	—	370	920	530	835	1,225
Military pay and allowances . .	—	—	170	330	520	800	920
Miscellaneous war costs	—	—	92	211	380	557	602
Defense construction	—	—	88	137	226	274	126

*Some series are at current prices, some at constant prices. The value of total war product includes indirect federal taxes. Source: *The impact of the war effort on civilian consumption in the U.K., the U.S. and Canada*, p. 153 (1945).

order of magnitude and the rate of increase in the Canadian war effort.

The war production of Australia and New Zealand took a different form, owing both to their different industrial structure and to their different geographical position. In the latter respect, their war production was connected with the different phases of the war, first in the Mediterranean and then in the Pacific. Both dominions supplied Britain throughout the war with foodstuffs and raw materials. In addition, Australia bore the burden of forming the base and supply centre for the armies fighting against the Japanese. A great deal of Australia's resources went also to supply other parts of the empire through the Eastern Group Supply council. Exports to Eastern Supply (India and Ceylon) increased fivefold. Even New Zealand succeeded in providing at least in part the means of its defense and in equipping an expeditionary force. At the same time it supplied vital foodstuffs to Britain as well as to the South Pacific forces.

Table XIV shows the changes in the distribution of working population during the war for the two Pacific dominions.

Table XIV.—*Working Population (000's omitted)*

	Australia		New Zealand	
	1939 June	1944 June	1939 Dec.	1944 Dec.
Total gainfully occupied population	2,627	3,170	700	781
Forces	13	725	3	126
Industry, etc.	1,889	2,010	517	493
Agriculture	425	410	155	162
Unemployed	300	25	(25)	—

Source: C.T. Saunders, *Manpower Distribution 1939-1945. Some International Comparisons.* (Manchester Statistical Society, Feb. 1946).

In Australia, in June 1944, 736,000 persons were employed in manufacturing proper and, of these, 150,000 were directly engaged in manufacturing equipment and supplies for the forces.

Lastly, Table XV relates the war effort of the three dominions to their total mobilized resources and compares it with that of the three great Allies.

Table XV.—*Percentage of National Income devoted to War Expenditure*

Country	1939 %	1940 %	1941 %	1942 %	1943 %	1944 %
United Kingdom	15	39	49	53	54	54
United States	2	3	11	35	46	46
U.S.S.R.	22	27	35	45	48	44
Canada	2	10	19	40	54	52
Australia	2	12	25	43	48	44
New Zealand	2	9	23	50	54	49

Source: 15th *Annual Report* of the Bank for International Settlements, Basle. Table originally prepared by the U.S. Foreign Economic administration: the figures are no more than "general approximations of trends and magnitudes rather than exact statistical measurements").

In 1946 less factual information was available on the war effort of other parts of the British empire. This did not mean, however, that their contribution was in any way less important or less impressive in relation to their resources. South Africa, *e.g.,* not only contributed heavily to the arming of its own troops who fought in North Africa and the western desert, but also became the main repair shop for the middle east front. India experienced a vast industrial expansion, and its few ordnance factories and railway workshops developed into a real war industry, while the different British colonies, being mainly agricultural communities, served the war effort both by reducing their imports and by supplying more of their vital native produce.

U. S. S. R.

Although the colossal war effort of the U.S.S.R. was beyond question, more data were available on the brilliant

Assembling tanks at a soviet plant in the Urals, where workers maintained day and night schedules during World War II

feats of the soviet armies in the field than on the number of tanks or aircraft or guns produced. The western Allies helped the Russians generously through lend-lease, but obviously Russia's own war production must have been immense.

The results of soviet war production were the more impressive as the U.S.S.R., of the three main Allies, suffered by far the greatest loss of industrial potential through the invasion of its territory and the destruction of its productive economy by the Germans. The removal of industries from the invaded areas in 1941 and 1942 was successful; and, in addition to the transfer of the factories, the resources of the eastern provinces, notably the Urals, were greatly expanded, especially the production of iron and steel, coal, aluminum and water power. But these developments could not entirely make up for the loss of the industrial capacity of the Ukraine. The Donbas (Donets Basin) region had, before 1941, accounted for nearly half the coal and iron of the U.S.S.R. After the recapture of this area in 1943, the destruction found there was enormous, their rehabilitation and the renewal of their contribution to the total war production were necessarily slow. Thus, on account of the flooding of the mines by the Germans, the coal production of the Donets basin in March 1944 was no more than 13% of the prewar total although the Donets had been recaptured in Sept. 1943.

As shown in table XV the total military expenditure of the U.S.S.R. in relation to its national income was higher in 1939 than that of the western democracies, though in the decisive years all of them contributed very nearly half of their resources to the war (the U.K. a little more, the U.S. and the U.S.S.R. a little less). Table XVI shows U.S.S.R. war expenditure as a proportion of total government expenditure.

Table XVI.—*U.S.S.R. Government Expenditure in roubles* *(000,000,000 omitted)*

	1940†	1941‡	1942	1943‖	1944†	1945†
Total expenditure* . . .	173.3	216.0	no data	210.0	264.0	298.6
Defense	56.1	70.9§	108.4	124.7	137.8	128.2
National economy . .	57.1	73.2	no data	31.1	53.7	74.4
Social and cultural development	41.7	47.9	no data	37.2	51.3	62.7

* Amalgamated budget of the union and its constituent republics.

† Closed budgetary accounts. ‡ Budget estimates. § Actual 1941 expenditure on defense is stated to have exceeded budget estimates by 20,000,000,000 roubles. ‖ Provisional results.

Sources: *United Nations Monthly Bulletin of Statistics*, Nov. 1946, for 1940, 1944 and 1945 and *World Economic Survey* 1942-44 (*League of Nations 1945*) for 1941–43 inclusive.

Table XVI shows that in order to allocate such a high proportion of its resources to the war effort, the U.S.S.R. was compelled not only to reduce the consumption levels of the population, but had also to reduce the amounts spent on economic, social and cultural development.

Germany

The history of war production in continental Europe (excluding the U.S.S.R.) during 1937–45 was in the main the history of the German war effort. Having overrun the Low Countries and France in 1940, Germany launched its "new order" program which included all countries under its direct or indirect control. The long-term objective of this plan, *viz.*, the integration of the European economy, was never achieved, but the short-term objective of harnessing ruthlessly all the resources of Europe to the service of the German war effort was successful. The extent of Europe's contribution to the German war effort and the latter's increase in general, can be seen in Table XVII.

These estimates, put forward by U.S. experts using German statistical sources, indicate that the volume of the German national income (*i.e.*, its value after eliminating changes in prices) expanded less during the war than did that of the Allied countries. Without foreign contributions as shown in the table (which, incidentally, do not include the contributions of slave labour and prisoners of war employed in Germany proper), Germany would have been unable to expand its war effort.

Europe's contribution was not necessarily made in the form of producing munitions, although in the later stages of the war several new factories were set up or moved to the east (Austria, Czechoslovakia). Europe contributed men, raw materials and a variety of products which made it possible for the German industry to concentrate on producing munitions. As can be seen from table XVII, an increasing proportion of the total available product was claimed by the German government, and used largely for purposes of the war.

Views held abroad on Germany's war effort and war production underwent a material change when, after the German collapse, British and U.S. experts made a study of its war economy. The picture emerging from these studies suggested a German war effort far less "total" or "thorough" than that of either Britain or the U.S.S.R. Nor was the German war organization particularly efficient. Labour (especially female labour) was never fully mobilized, and the drastic reduction in civilian consumption standards was forced on the Germans only in the last stages of the war.

Beyond any doubt Germany had started preparations for an aggressive war at the very beginning of the nazi regime. But it appeared in retrospect, that while the army leaders believed in "rearmament in depth," Hitler was in favour of "rearmament in width," *i.e.*, of the maximum increase in immediate striking power in order to support his blitz warfare tactics. The four-year plan of 1936 provided for this type of rearmament (*i.e.*, a maximum concentration on production of finished munitions, etc.), and the Polish and western campaigns appeared to have justified Hitler's conception. In consequence, during the critical period between the French eclipse and the soviet campaign, no particular effort was made in Germany to expand war production, and the rate of armament production remained more or less stationary. It was asserted that, at the end of Sept. 1941, Hitler, believing that the war was nearly won, ordered a reduction in armament production.

Only their defeat before Moscow and the entry of the U.S. into the war in Dec. 1941 made the Germans face the prospect of a prolonged war. In Feb. 1942 Albert Speer was appointed minister of armaments, a position which he held virtually to the end, and this marked a new era and a vast expansion in Germany's armament production.

Prior to Speer's appointment, there was no central authority in charge of war production. The *Heereswaffenamt*, the traditional military procurement authority, retained the direction of armament production. The air ministry controlled

Table XVII.—*Volume of Gross National Income and of the total available Income of Germany* *(In rm. at 1939 prices, 000,000,000 omitted)*

	1936	1937	1938	1939	1940	1941	1942	1943	1944
Gross national income	107	116	128	140	141	150	152	155	159
Foreign contributions	—	—	—	—	9	19	26	29	21
Total available income	107	116	128	140	150	169	178	184	180
Total government expenditure . . .	28	33	40	45	65	89	106	114	118
Percentage of total available income used by the government	26	28	31	32	43	53	60	62	65

the aircraft industry, and the ministry of national economy controlled the industries producing basic materials for the forces or for vital civilian consumption. The general administration of industry was in the hands of 32 different "groups of industries" (*Wirtschaftsgruppen*) representing branches of production. The new minister of armaments, to start with, was given coordinating functions only, for the purpose of obtaining the most urgently needed types of munitions. But his powers were rapidly extended and came to cover all industries producing munitions for the army. In Nov. 1943 he took control of naval armaments, in March 1944 of fighter aircraft production and in July 1944 of the armament industry as a whole.

The mobilization of labour, the recruitment of foreign labour and the allocation of labour in general remained separately organized.

Speer, as minister of armaments, created a new organization of committees and "rings," subdivided according to end-products (tanks, guns, etc.) and staffed by production experts (engineers, etc.) These committees were given the task of increasing production by combining maximum economy of labour and materials (*i.e.*, thorough rationalization) with maximum utilization of capacity. A central planning bureau was also set up, the first serious attempt at a thorough planning of German war economy; but it is believed that its influence was small. This belated German all-out production effort appears to have been very successful. Despite its coincidence with the intensified Allied air offensive against Germany, there was a big increase in the total armaments produced, as can be seen from the production indices in Table XVIII.

Table XVIII.—*German Production Indices of Finished Armaments*

1940 = 100

Year	Index
1940	100
1941	101
1942	146
1943	229
1944	285
1945 March	149

(Table prepared by Dr. R. Wagenfuehr of the German armament ministry. It covers 90% of finished armaments production)

At its peak in July 1944 German armament production (mainly of tanks and aircraft) was three times as high as in early 1942. From then onward a steady decline set in as a result of the Allied air and other offensives, and German armament production never recovered.

The different stages of German war production become clear from a study of the mobilization of labour, the supply of raw materials, the availability of capital equipment for producing armaments and, finally, from a review of its results, by types of munitions.

Manpower.—At the outbreak of World War II, Germany was already mobilized. Its army of unemployed had already been mopped up during the years of war preparations, and a large proportion of its labour force had already been shifted into the war industries. Both in Britain and in the U.S., these stages were only reached during the first few years of the war. The number of workers employed in German industry rose from 9,100,000 to 11,200,000 in the ten years 1929–39; virtually the whole increase went into the capital goods industries. In July 1939 nearly a quarter of all industrial workers, *viz.*, 2,500,000 persons, were working on direct orders of the armed forces (and many others indirectly).

Germany apparently possessed substantial manpower reserves in Germany proper when war broke out, and in fact made little use of such labour reserves (*e.g.*, women) as it did possess.

The first few years of the war brought nevertheless, substantial changes in the manpower position. The first factor was the drafting of 7,500,000 men from the civilian labour force into the army. The gap thus created was made good partly by shifting more people from nonessential industries (handicraft, distribution, etc.) into the war industries. Simultaneously the German victories opened up a new large source of manpower for the reich in the form of prisoners of war and civilian labour recruited abroad. Table XIX illustrates the mobilization of manpower.

Table XIX.—*Manpower Mobilization in Germany between 1939 and 1944*

	Civilian labour force		Armed forces			
	Germans	Foreigners and prisoners of war	Total mobilized	Cumulative losses	Active strength	Total active labour force
	(1)	(2)	(3)	(4)	(5)	(6)
			(000,000 omitted)			Columns (1)+(2)+(5)
May 31, 1939	39.1	0.3	1.4	—	1.4	40.8
May 31, 1944	29.0	7.1	12.4	3.3	9.4	45.2
Sep. 30, 1944	28.4	7.5	13.0	3.9	9.1	45.0

As Table XIX shows, there was at the most an addition of 1,000,000 Germans to the total labour force after 1939 (800,000 men and 200,000 women); in fact, the number of German women employed decreased in the first two war years. The number of men in the armed forces expanded throughout the war, in spite of the severe losses, and virtually the whole gap was made good by foreign and prisoner labour. The latter went first into agriculture, but soon they were also needed in industry, and the ratio of foreign and prisoner labour (25%) in war production proper, was higher than either in agriculture (18%) or in industry in general (14%). As there was no significant strain on the labour force, the average working week increased only slightly, from 47.8 hr. in Sept. 1939 to 49.5 in Sept. 1941, 48.7 in Sept. 1942 and 47.9 in Sept. 1943 though longer hours were worked in particular industries. Later, when the wehrmacht suffered severe losses, and the recruitment of foreign workers did not fill the gaps, more determined efforts were made at mobilization. A far-reaching conscription measure was taken first in Jan. 1943 and then in July 1944, when a 60-hr. week was introduced by decree, but these measures were never fully carried out. Under the 1943 decree, 3,500,000 additional persons registered (mostly women), but the number of women in the total labour force hardly increased. In the nazi party there was strong objection to such an increase, and totalitarian Germany could not face popular resistance from inside.

Even though new recruitment yielded little result in Germany proper, the mobilization policy was successful in shifting more people into the war industries. In Jan. 1943 all enterprises not directly connected with the war effort were either shut down or concentrated, and the workers shifted into the war industries. Table XX illustrates the distribution of the nonagricultural civilian labour force as between the war, and the civilian, sectors.

Table XX.—*Distribution of German Civilian Labour Force (nonagricultural)*

	1939	1940	1941	1942	1943	1944
			Percentages			
War sector	42	45	49	53	56	59
Civilian sector	58	55	51	47	44	41

Table XXI shows the continuous expansion of manpower in the war sector, and the corresponding contraction

Table XXI.—*Distribution of Manpower in Germany and Great Britain*
1939 and 1943
(000,000 omitted)

	Great Britain			Germany		
	1939	1943		1939	1943	
	numbers	numbers	%	numbers	numbers	%
Munition industries . . .	3.1	5.2	31.7	5.8	6.9	26.9
Principal basic industries and services	5.5	5.6	27.3	7.2	7.9	31.0
Other industries and services	10.5	6.8	41.0	15.0	10.8	42.1
Total, excluding armed forces and agriculture .	19.1	17.6	100.0	28.0	25.6	100.0

Source: N. Kaldor, *German War Economy* (see bibliography).
These figures would suggest that in 1943 Germany was less thoroughly mobilized than Great Britain; Germany's last big effort came in 1944.

in the civilian sector.

It is interesting to compare the distribution of German and British manpower as between different industries in 1939 and in 1943, and this is done in table XXI.

Raw Materials.—Germany's war leaders always regarded its reliance on imported raw materials as its great strategic weakness, and great preparations were made before World War II to remedy it. First of all, stocks were accumulated. Simultaneously, under the four-year plan of 1936, Germany tried to expand the production of indigenous raw materials and to develop the output of synthetic raw materials. By contrast, Britain never thought of wasting manpower on production of synthetic materials and relied on keeping its sea lanes open for getting supplies from overseas. The German policy was successful in regard to synthetic oil and rubber, but it did not make Germany self-sufficient. Synthetic oil production increased from 1,300,000 tons in 1938 to 6,000,000 in 1944. Synthetic rubber production increased from 5,000 tons in 1939 to 134,000 tons in 1944. The German conquest of Europe made a vast contribution to nazi Germany's raw material supplies. In this way it secured big stocks all over Europe as well as important current supplies, *e.g.*, oil from Rumania, copper from Yugoslavia, Norway and Finland, bauxite from Hungary, France and Yugoslavia, ore from Lorraine and Luxembourg, etc. As the supply of materials which it was wont to produce at home (such as coal and steel) had satisfied the requirements of the armament program, the raw materials position until early in 1944 was, generally speaking, comfortable. From then onward shortages appeared. The heavy bombing of the synthetic oil plants in 1944 was regarded as one of the reasons for German collapse.

Mobilization of Capital Equipment.—Although the industrial structure of Germany was not very different from that of Britain and the U.S., its capital goods industries had always been somewhat over-dimensioned in relation to its consumption goods industries. Germany's capacity to produce capital goods was always far in excess of its normal home requirements. Germany was, of course, one of the big world exporters of heavy machinery, but this excess capacity served it well when the switch-over to wartime production took place. The supply of machine tools, of which Germany was one of the great world suppliers, provided a good example. The German machine tool industry hardly expanded during World War II, but Germany possessed an ample stock as well as a large flow of supplies throughout the war and did not experience the same difficulties in this field as Britain and the U.S. That plant facilities and general machinery were not in short supply was clearly shown by the fact that throughout the war most of the German industries worked on a single shift system. There were exceptions to this rule (*e.g.*, a small proportion of those producing tanks, aircraft engines, etc., worked on a double shift system); shortages and bottlenecks occurred in particular industries, such as oil and chemicals, and at particular times; but generally speaking there was no shortage of capital equipment.

Production of Particular Types of Munitions.—The end-products which all countries at war aim at producing in vast quantities are munitions, and the output figures, by all types of weapons, indicate their success in applying their mobilized resources to the war job.

Table XXII gives an illuminating comparison between the output of munitions in Germany and Great Britain in 1940, 1943 and 1944.

Table XXII.—*Munitions Output in Germany and the U.K.*
(in numbers of units)

	1940		1943		1944	
	Germany	U.K.	Germany	U.K.	Germany	U.K.
Aircraft	10,826	15,049	25,527	26,263	39,807	14,609
Tanks	1,467	1,397	12,061	7,467	17,459	2,474
Other armoured vehicles	no data	6,044	14,906	24,375	19,280	13,957
Guns	5,499	3,410	26,904	17,314	40,684	3,886

These figures show that already in 1940 Britain outproduced Germany in aircraft and maintained its superiority, except in 1944, when Germany made a final spurt. In tanks Germany was also behind in 1940–42, until, in 1943 and 1944 it made a tremendous effort. Virtually the same applied to guns; German output leaped up only in 1943 and 1944.

After Germany had stolen a march on the peaceful democracies and equipped itself for blitzkrieg, it was too late to prepare its people for such an all-out war effort as the democracies produced. Germany went "all out" only in the years 1942–44, but never achieved the same complete mobilization of resources as did Britain or the U.S., because from Sept. 1944 onward heavy air attacks disorganized its transport system, and destroyed part of its oil supplies. This, together with its heavy losses in the field in the east and the west led to a complete industrial collapse.

BIBLIOGRAPHY.—U.S. Strategic Bombing Survey, *The Effects of Strategic Bombing on the German War Economy* (1945); N. Kaldor, *The German War Economy* (Manchester Statistical Society, May, 1946). (L. Rs.)

Japan

Few nations had gambled more recklessly with their future than did Japan in 1941 when it launched the Pacific war. The stakes were high—the control of all east Asia. The opportunity appeared to present itself as a result of Hitler's successes in Europe and the preoccupation of the U.S., as yet unmobilized, with that threat. Only by seizing the rich producing areas of southeast Asia could Japan relieve the continued dependence of its growing military machine on overseas supplies of oil and other strategic materials.

Accordingly, in the fall of 1941 Japan's army and navy leaders decided, without effective civilian opposition, to risk all in one daring military effort.

That it was a gamble is clear from the plan determined upon.[1] This called for swift conquest of the southern zone, and the establishment of a defense perimeter on the outlying islands. With the new resources thus secured, it was hoped that Japan could successfully withstand any Allied counteroffensive until the time when U.S. indifference and

[1] Data were taken largely from the findings of the U.S. Strategic Bombing survey, as presented in its *Summary Report* (*Pacific War*) (1946) and in "The Japanese War Economy: 1940-45," by Jerome B. Cohen, *Far Eastern Survey*, Dec. 4, 1946. *See* also Supreme Commander for the Allied Powers, *Summation of Non-Military Activities in Japan* (monthly, Sept., 1945 *et seq.*).

war weariness would make possible an advantageous, negotiated peace.

To achieve this end presupposed avoiding an all-out war in which Japan's limited resources would be no match for the preponderant power of the U.S.

The history of the war was the history of the miscarriage of these plans. Japanese assumptions, of course, were in error.

Once the resources and the will of the U. S. people were fully mobilized, and the nazi empire began to crumble under Allied blows, it was only a question of time until Japan too would be overwhelmed.

Japan entered the war with an economy greatly strengthened by a decade of unprecedented industrial expansion. From 1930–41 its real gross national product nearly doubled, with military outlays and investments in munitions industry already accounting for 23% of the total in the latter year. Production of ingot steel in Japan proper rose from 2,200,000 to 6,800,000 tons. Coal output increased from 31,400,000 to 55,600,000 tons, electric generating capacity from 4,300,000 to 9,400,000 kilowatts, and aircraft production from 400 to 5,000 planes. The growing demands of war industry for raw materials led in turn to strenuous efforts to develop the potentialities of "Manchoukuo," Korea and North China. Japan remained basically dependent, however, on nonempire sources of oil (90%), bauxite, rubber and a number of ferroalloys and nonferrous metals.

This was partially compensated for by the accumulation of strategic stock piles, including at the time of Pearl Harbor an estimated two-year reserve of oil—43,000,000 barrels.

Early successes in the Pacific heightened the spirit of confidence in Japan. They apparently accounted for its failure in 1942 to step up war production to its full potentiality and to fashion effective centralized controls for this purpose. Not until the beginning of Allied advances in the South and central Pacific did Japanese leaders reluctantly abandon the hope of a war of limited liability and embark on full scale mobilization. Gross national product, discounting price changes, increased from 39,800,000,000 yen in the fiscal year beginning April 1940 to only 41,000,000,000 yen in 1942. By 1944 it had reached 50,000,000,000, with 52% devoted to war expenditures and capital outlays for munition production. Under a new munitions ministry priority controls were strengthened in favour of key industries. Monthly aircraft production rose from 700 planes of all types in the summer of 1942 to a peak of 2,572 in Sept. 1944. Construction of steel merchant ships jumped from 238,000 tons in 1941 to 1,600,000 tons in 1944. Basic industrial capacity was also enlarged; steel ingot capacity, *e.g.*, reached 14,000,000 tons in the latter year.

By 1944, however, the Japanese war economy was already beginning to sag at its foundations. The production of basic materials, in fact, had passed its peak in 1943. In part this represented failures at the top in centralized planning and allocation of resources, owing to unresolved conflicts among the army, navy and business interests. In part it reflected the growing scarcity of technical skills, and the effects of fatigue and deprivation among a people reduced by 1944 to an average per capita diet of 1,900 calories.

But the decisive factor was the progressive decline in imports of essential war materials as Allied air and submarine attacks first cut shipping lanes from the southern zone and finally isolated the home islands almost entirely from the mainland.

Japan began the war with 6,000,000 tons of merchant shipping. It built or acquired an additional 4,100,000 tons. Some 8,900,000 tons were destroyed or put out of action, 55% by Allied submarines alone. Oil shipments from the Indies began to dwindle as early as Aug. 1943. By April 1945 they had ceased entirely, and oil stocks were nearing exhaustion. Bauxite imports were virtually cut off by the end of 1944. The shrinkage in shipments of iron ore and coking coal from China cut steel ingot production from 7,800,000 tons in the fiscal year 1943 to 5,900,000 in 1944. By the first quarter of 1945 (April–June) it had slumped to an annual rate of 1,500,000 tons. Strenuous efforts to develop the production of synthetic oil, domestic iron and North China aluminous shale yielded only meagre results. The consequence was a disastrous fall in the output of fuel, aircraft, ships and munitions for the fighting forces.

Even before long-range bombing of the Japanese home islands began in earnest, late in 1944, it was clear that Japan had lost the war. By July 1945, just before the surrender, over-all industrial output had dwindled to 40% of the 1944 peak, and was dropping precipitously. In the opinion of the U.S. Strategic Bombing survey, the blockade alone would have led virtually to this result. To its strangling effects, however, was now added the systematic destruction of Japanese industries and cities by air bombardment. Some 40% of the built-up area of 66 cities was laid in ruins, largely by fire bombing. This campaign spread demoralization among the people and progressively advanced the day when Japan's military leaders would be compelled publicly to acknowledge defeat. When the atom bomb was finally released early in August and the soviet union entered the war, Japan surrendered within the week.

(*See* also AGRICULTURE; AUTOMOBILE INDUSTRY; AVIATION, CIVIL; AVIATION, MILITARY; BUDGETS, NATIONAL; BUILDING AND CONSTRUCTION INDUSTRY; BUSINESS REVIEW; IRON AND STEEL; LABOUR UNIONS; LAW; LEND-LEASE; LOGISTICS OF WORLD WAR II; MACHINERY AND MACHINE TOOLS; MUNITIONS OF WAR; PRICE ADMINISTRATION, OFFICE OF; RAILROADS; RATIONING; SHIPBUILDING; STRATEGIC MINERAL SUPPLIES; WAR AND DEFENSE AGENCIES; WORLD WAR II; *See* also separate articles on other individual industries.)

(W. W. L.)

BIBLIOGRAPHY.—*Wartime Production Achievements and the Reconversion Outlook*, Report of the Chairman, War Production Board (1945); *War Production in 1944*, Report of the Chairman of the War Production Board, June 1945; Donald M. Nelson, *Arsenal of Democracy, The Story of American War Production* (1946); Bureau of Demobilization, Civilian Production Administration, *Minutes* of the Advisory Commission to the Council of National Defense; Council of the Office of Production Management; Supply Priorities and Allocations Board; War Production Board; and Planning Committee of the War Production Board. Historical Reports on War Administration: War Production Board, Documentary Publications 1 to 5 (1946); Bureau of Demobilization, Civilian Production Administration, *Special Studies* series of Historical Reports on War Administration: War Production Board (1946); James A. McAleer, *Chronology of the War Production Board and Predecessor Agencies* (1946); Army Service Forces, *Annual Reports* for the fiscal years 1943, 1944, 1945; James Forrestal, *et al.*, *The Navy: A Study in Administration* (1946); General Economics and Planning Staff, Program and Statistics Bureau, War Production Board, *American Industry in War and Transition, 1940–1950: Part II, The Effect of War on the Industrial Economy* (July 20, 1945); John Lord O'Brian and Manley Fleischman, "The War Production Board Administrative Policies and Procedures," *George Washington Law Review* 13, pp. 1–60. (Dec. 1944). (J. W. FR.)

War Production Board

See WAR AND DEFENSE AGENCIES; WAR PRODUCTION.

War Relief, U.S.

Relief of human misery had always invoked the compassion and generosity of the American people in peace as well as in wartime. This tradition accounted in large measure for the fact that the voluntary war relief efforts of the people of the U.S. during World War II actually began in the early 1930s when political, religious and ideological persecution forced a continuously growing stream of refugees to flee from Germany. Many groups in the U.S. raised funds to help them reach places of relative security. Civil strife in Spain and Japanese aggression in China gave rise to additional efforts to help those whose lives, homes and families were broken. The invasion of Poland with the gradual spread of hostilities throughout Europe and Asia and the eventual involvement of the U.S. caused the initiation and expansion of many additional voluntary efforts. These activities were for both foreign civilian war sufferers and the servicemen and servicewomen of the U.S. and its Allies who needed a variety of hospitality, recreational welfare and protective services over and above those provided by their governments.

Volume of Relief.—During the active war years, 1939–45, Americans contributed more than $1,000,000,000 to nationwide voluntary war-relief agencies which provided a variety of services and supplies to people affected by the war. Doubtless many additional millions of dollars were solicited and received from the American people by local relief organizations which were not supervised by the wartime federal government agency, the President's War Relief Control board. These funds, in addition to the millions of dollars voluntarily donated to the American Red Cross and the millions of tax funds turned over to the American Red Cross, swelled the total amount of money spent for war relief by voluntary U.S. organizations.

Early Governmental Action.—In 1939, congress passed the Neutrality act which prohibited various forms of U.S. economic activity with countries declared belligerent by the president. One section of the act (section 8[b]) provided, however, that U.S. foreign relief work could be continued in and for belligerent countries if conducted in accordance with U.S. governmental regulations. These included registration and reporting of activities by all U.S. relief agencies (except the American Red Cross) to the department of state. Between Sept. 1939 and June 30, 1942, 545 agencies reported activities including receipt and expenditure of about $75,000,000. During the same period, agencies helping people in countries not declared belligerent collected and spent about $25,000,000.

Because of the increasing number of public charitable appeals, President F. D. Roosevelt on March 13, 1941, appointed the President's Committee on War Relief agencies to make a study of this problem in the public interest. The committee, composed of Joseph E. Davies as chairman, Charles P. Taft and Frederick P. Keppel, recommended to the president the creation of a small wartime governmental board to license and supervise all national voluntary war-relief agencies. On July 25, 1942, the president issued an executive order establishing the President's War Relief Control board. Administration of section 8(b) of the Neutrality act was transferred from the department of state to the board which was authorized to control not only relief for belligerent countries but also other war related relief activities, both domestic and foreign, except: (1) those of the American Red Cross; (2) those through established religious bodies as a part of their regular activities; and (3) those of a domestic character confined to local and intrastate areas.

The Board's Work.—The board was instructed by the president to use its authority to effect co-ordination of war relief with other established charities and to promote efficiency and economy of relief administration. As groups of organizations with similar objectives applied for registration, the board, under the president's mandate to eliminate or merge agencies when necessary in the interests of efficiency and economy, withheld licensing of competitive and overlapping organizations until their activities were adequately co-ordinated.

The board's review of the proposed programs of new applicants for war relief licences and its continuous examination of the certified reports and public audits of receipts and expenditures required from organizations operating under its jurisdiction were conducted with special attention to efficiency of administration. In some instances, examination of the record showed unjustifiable waste of relief contributions because of high overhead costs. Well-intentioned but inexperienced administration, huge expenditures for unproductive "benefits" and other promotional schemes, or other overhead expenditures out of proportion to the public support obtained were found in a number of cases to consume 50%, 60% or 70% of the contributions received. Cases of this sort were far and few between, but when the record revealed such a situation, representatives of the relief agency were called to a hearing to show reasons why registration should not be revoked for failure to comply with the board's regulations concerning reasonable efficiency and economy of operation. The effect of this action, combined with the increased efficiency of the relief organizations during the period of the board's supervision, was to reduce sharply the overhead costs of private foreign relief administration. The reduction from the high ratios of 1941 and 1942 meant that about $23,000,000 to $25,000,000 of the funds contributed in 1943, 1944 and 1945 were used for relief and welfare services rather than for overhead costs.

The second phase of the effort to reduce the number of independent appeals for war-relief funds was the formation of the National War fund in Jan. 1943 (at the instance of the chairman of the War Relief Control board). The National War fund was established as a private organization (under the leadership of Winthrop Aldrich of New York city, N.Y. and a national board of directors from each state in the union) to collaborate with established community chests in a united appeal for local charities and national war philanthropies, to organize a concurrent appeal in non-chest areas, and to distribute the resulting contributions to war-relief and welfare agencies approved by the President's War Relief Control board.

Initially as a part of the action on co-ordination of fund raising and later as a service to the officials of the many relief agencies, the War Relief Control board called upon the advice and information of other governmental agencies on problems affecting the planning and operation of foreign relief projects overseas and the development of services in the U.S. and abroad for members of the armed services. For instance, priorities and export allocations of materials in short supply were secured by the board from the departments of agriculture and commerce and reallotted to each agency; permission for the agencies to transfer funds abroad was secured from the treasury department; shipping space was obtained for the agencies on the basis of appeals by the board to the War Shipping administration and the military authorities; the board supported the agencies reasonable requests for passports, visas, priority army transportation and billeting overseas for the agencies' personnel.

Safeguarding Public Interest.—As one of the agencies of the federal government, which as a whole was directing the U.S. war effort, the board was responsible to the general public through the president, for seeing that money voluntarily donated for relief was spent efficiently and for the purpose collected—namely, relief. The board was responsible also for seeing that private relief made its maximum contribution to the furtherance of the war purpose, which included assuring that the operation of specific private relief activities of U.S. citizens was not directly inconsistent with the wartime foreign policies of the U.S. as expressed by the state department. This was a delicate task. Almost without exception, either humanitarian or religious convictions or political attitudes with respect to events in other countries, singly or in combination, motivated the U.S. leadership and support of large segments of the U.S. public for specific U.S. voluntary relief efforts. The board and its staff made every effort in the administration of its duties to be impartial in its dealings with all agencies irrespective of the religious convictions or political leanings of the individuals directing the affairs of the relief agency.

Council of Voluntary Agencies.—The board's work and that of the National War fund were greatly strengthened by the formation in 1943 of an American Council of Voluntary Agencies for Foreign Service as a nonofficial body to promote joint planning and action on matters of mutual interest to its members. The council's work was carried out through a series of country committees (on France, Poland, Hungary, etc.) and functional committees (on purchasing, displaced persons, child welfare). Through these committees, the relief agencies themselves met many problems of interagency co-ordination.

Among the major accomplishments of the council and agencies in voluntary co-ordination were the formation of two agencies through which the component agency members carried out common objectives. They were CARE (Co-operative for American Remittances to Europe, Inc.) and CRALOG (Council of Relief Agencies Licensed to Operate in Germany).

CARE was a nonprofit individual food-package service from which individuals and organizations could order standard food parcels for delivery by CARE to designated individuals and groups in several European countries. The CARE plan of relief was accepted by the governments of Norway, Finland, the Netherlands, Belgium, France, Italy, Greece, Yugoslavia, Czechoslovakia and Poland, and by the military authorities in Austria and Germany. The agreements with these authorities provided for protection of the stock piles of packages warehoused in the foreign countries, freedom from customs duties or other taxes, and freedom from ration control.

CRALOG was a joint operation primarily of church relief agencies interested in aiding German civilians. In the fall of 1946, 15 agencies jointly planned, shipped and distributed relief for Germany through approved church channels in Germany under the supervision of the various Allied military authorities. The wisdom and success of such joint operations suggested to the agencies that they voluntarily combine their operations in certain other countries, and work progressed to this end.

End of Wartime Control.—At the board's request, the president agreed to the termination of the board's wartime controls effective May 15, 1946. This request was made because of the board's conviction that the furtherance of the war purpose no longer required federal control over solicitation of contributions for private charities which had been invoked as a war measure and accepted only as such by the U.S. people.

The Advisory Committee on Voluntary Foreign Aid, composed of Charles P. Taft as chairman, Chester C. Davis and William L. Batt, appointed by the secretary of state and the secretary of agriculture, was established under authority of similar letters of May 14, 1946, from the president to the secretaries of these departments, "to tie together the governmental and private programs in the field of foreign relief and to work with the Famine Emergency Committee and other interested agencies and groups"; and for the purpose of continuing the liaison, advisory and consultative functions formerly performed by the president's War Relief Control board.

(*See* also PRISONERS OF WAR; DISPLACED PERSONS; RED CROSS; RELIEF.) (C. P. T.)

War Relocation Authority

See WAR AND DEFENSE AGENCIES.

Warren, Earl

Warren (1891–   ), U.S. politician, was born March 19, 1891, in Los Angeles, Calif. He worked his way through the University of California, Berkeley, Calif., graduating in 1912. He received his law degree in 1914 and was admitted to the bar the same year. He was a lieutenant in the U.S. army during World War I.

His first political position of importance was that of deputy city attorney of Oakland, 1919–20. In 1925 he was elected district attorney, holding this position until 1939, when he was elected state attorney general on the Republican ticket. In 1942 he was nominated as Republican candidate for governor. He also ran in the Democratic primaries but lost to the Democratic incumbent, Gov. Cuthbert Olson, by the narrow margin of 100,000 votes. However, he defeated Olson in the elections by a majority of 342,000, carrying all of California's 58 counties.

In the 1946 elections he was nominated for governor of California by both the Republican and Democratic parties. This unprecedented action projected him into the limelight as a presidential possibility for 1948 because of the near certainty that he could carry California.

War Risk Insurance

See INSURANCE.

War Savings Stamps

See POST OFFICE.

Warsaw

As capital of restored Poland, Warsaw, from 1918 onward, had made rapid progress in every respect; by absorbing neighbouring districts its area was increased from 46 sq.mi. (1920) to 54 sq.mi. (1939). Its population grew from 937,000 (1921) to 1,289,000 (est. Jan. 1, 1939). According to the 1931 census, 66.8% of Warsaw inhabitants were Roman Catholics, and 30.2% of the Jewish faith; 70.5% used Polish as their mother tongue, and 28.4% were Yiddish or Hebrew-speaking.

From the very first day of World War II Warsaw was subject to air bombing by the Germans. The damage of the first weeks increased to an appalling extent during the siege which began on Sept. 14, 1939. Two days later Gen. Julian Rómmel, the military commander of Warsaw, rejected the demand for capitulation. Stefan Starzyński, the popular mayor of Warsaw, who had done much for restor-

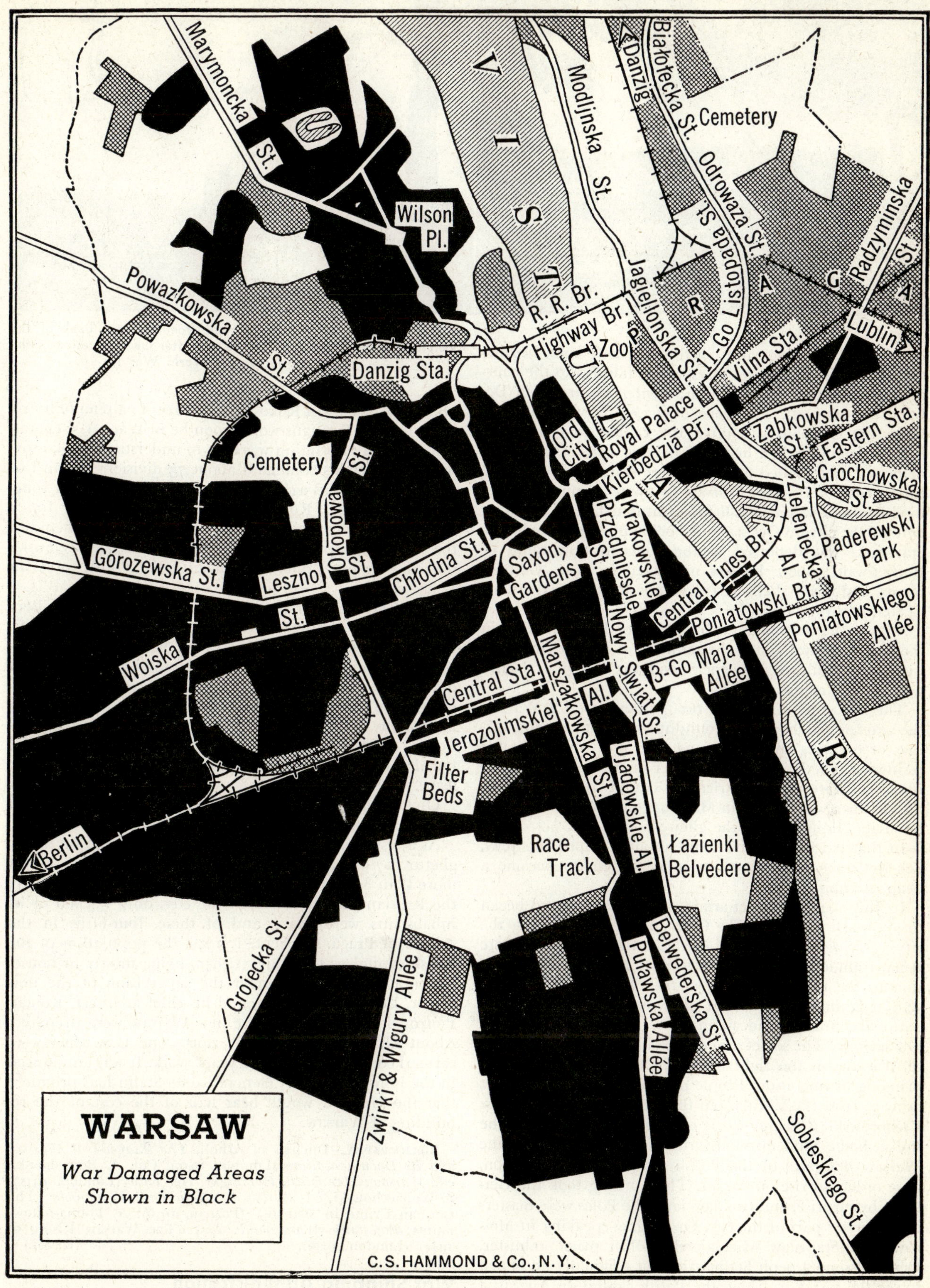
WARSAW
War Damaged Areas
Shown in Black
C.S. HAMMOND & Co., N.Y.
VISTULA R.
PRAGA
Marymoncka St.
Wilson Pl.
Powazkowska St.
Danzig Sta.
R. R. Br.
Highway Br.
Zoo
Modljnska St.
Danzig
Białołecka St.
Cemetery
Odrowąża St.
Jagiellońska St.
11-Go Listopada St.
Radzyminska St.
Lublin
Vilna Sta.
Old City
Royal Palace
Kierbedzia Br.
Zabkowska St.
Eastern Sta.
Grochowska St.
Cemetery
Okopowa St.
Górozewska St.
Leszno St.
Chłodna St.
Saxon Gardens
Krakowskie Przedmiescie
Central Lines Br.
Zieleniecka Al.
Paderewski Park
Poniatowski Br.
Poniatowskiego Allée
Woiska
Central Sta.
Nowy Swiat St.
3-Go Maja Allée
Marszałkowska St.
Jerozolimskie Al.
Filter Beds
Ujadowskie Al.
Berlin
Race Track
Łazienki Belvedere
Grojecka St.
Zwirki & Wigury Allée
Puławska Allée
Belwederska St.
Sobieskiego St.

The royal castle at Warsaw, viewed from the east bank of the Vistula river, as it appeared before and after the destruction of the Polish capital during World War II

ing the old buildings and erecting the new ones, became the soul of the resistance. Warsaw was faithful to the courageous motto of its coat of arms: *Contemnit procellas* (Defying the tempest). The worst days were Sept. 25 and 26, when the Germans submitted the capital to continuous bombardment by their heaviest artillery. Tens of thousands of people were killed and fires were started which lasted for a week. On Sept. 27 Warsaw—without ammunition and food, without water and light—capitulated. The Germans entered the city on Oct. 1, Hitler being present. The heroic Starzyński was deported to the concentration camp of Buchenwald, where he was murdered in 1942. German bombs and heavy shells destroyed about 25% of Warsaw's 24,800 dwelling houses.

Among the monumental buildings of historic value in the city, the royal castle, the ministry of finance, the ministry of agriculture, the opera and the national theatre were laid in ruins.

The five years of German occupation were for Warsaw the years of searches, street roundups, evictions, arrests, takings of hostages and executions, but also of indomitable resistance. The large Jewish quarter in Warsaw was turned into a separate police district and cut off from the rest of the city by a wall. When in May 1943 the Germans decided upon its "liquidation," the ghetto rose.

In that battle the Polish underground helped the Jews, but the struggle was unequal and the ghetto became a heap of rubble.

In July 1944 the soviet armies sweeping westward began to approach Warsaw. The Germans were evacuating the city, carrying off everything of value; the inhabitants were being rounded up to build fortifications and for deportation to the reich. On July 30 the "Kościuszko" wireless station (under the control of the Russian-sponsored Polish national council) broadcast an appeal to the people of Warsaw saying: "The soviet armies are close to Praga (a suburb of Warsaw on the right bank of the Vistula). They are bringing us liberation. People of Warsaw, assist the soviet army to cross the Vistula." In these circumstances Tadeusz Komorowski (General Bor), commander in chief of the Polish home (underground) army, in agreement with the Warsaw delegates of the Polish government in London, gave orders to rise on Aug. 1. The uprising took the Germans by surprise, and two days later the Poles were masters of the major part of the city. On Aug. 9, speaking in Moscow with Stanislaw Mikolajczyk, Polish prime minister, Generalissimo Joseph Stalin said that originally he hoped to see the soviet armies in the Polish capital on Aug. 6; a successful German counterattack from Modlin had forced Marshal Konstantin Rokossovski's forces to a temporary retreat, but the Russians would soon be in Warsaw. Generalissimo Stalin's optimism was easy to understand: Rokossovski had under his command about 75 divisions, a third of them armoured, as against 22 German divisions. For some reason, however, Rokossovski remained inactive for a month, during which the Germans, under the command of the S.S. Obergruppenfuehrer Erich von dem Bach-Zelewski, started a series of operations against the Polish forces in Warsaw.

The German commander had at his disposal artillery of the largest calibre, mortars, heavy tanks and aircraft. The defenders of Warsaw had only light weapons in insufficient numbers. On Sept. 14 Rokossovski took Praga but did not even try to cross the Vistula. Meanwhile the Germans were reducing the areas in possession of the Polish home army and destroying Warsaw with an incredible passion of hatred, dynamiting brick and stone houses and burning the wooden ones. The population was ordered to leave.

On Oct. 2, after an epic battle of 63 days, Gen. Komorowski was forced to lay down his arms.

As a result of the siege of 1939, of the liquidation of the ghetto in 1943 and of the uprising of 1944, Warsaw lost more than 80% of its dwelling houses. When in Jan. 1945 the Russians finally liberated the city, only 153,000 of its inhabitants were there, and of these, four-fifths in the suburb of Praga. On Sept. 1, 1946, the population of the Polish capital was already 522,945, living mostly in houses temporarily repaired. Under the supervision of the new mayor, Ludwik Tolwinski, and his chief architect, Roman Piotrowski, the plans for the new Warsaw were prepared. About Zl.15,000,000,000 (one zloty=one U.S. cent) were earmarked for the first three years' work. It was announced in the Polish press that Generalissimo Stalin had promised that the U.S.S.R. would bear half of the cost of the rebuilding of Warsaw.

Bibliography.—Duchess of Atholl, *The Tragedy of Warsaw and its Documentation* (London, 1945); Col. A. Boguslawski, ed., *Warsaw: Her Faith, Her Fight, Her Fate* (London, 1945); Z. Wojciechowski, ed., *Zbrodnia Niemiecka w Warszawie* (The German Crime in Warsaw) (Poznań, 1946); A. Pomian-Dowmuntt, *Powstanie Warszawskie 1944* (The Warsaw Rising of 1944) (London, 1946).

(K. Sm.)

War Shipping Administration

See War and Defense Agencies.

Washington

A state in the extreme northwest United States, popularly known as the "Evergreen state," Washington was admitted to the union Nov. 11, 1889. Total area, 68,192 sq.mi., including 66,977 sq.mi. of land. Population (1940) 1,736,191, including 1,525,812 native born and 210,379 foreign born. On Nov. 1, 1943, the bureau of census estimated the population of the state at 1,905,239. Capital, Olympia (13,254). The three largest cities are Seattle (368,302); Spokane (122,001); and Tacoma (109,408). The urban population in 1940 was 921,969 or 53.1%.

The legislature met in its 25th session from Jan. 11 to March 11, 1937. The social security system was placed under a department, administered under the merit system, and was made conformable to federal law. A maximum of 60 hours per week was prescribed for domestic labour, significant in view of the decision of the U.S. supreme court sustaining the Washington minimum wage law. A teachers' retirement system was substituted for the old arrangement of local funds. The Congress of Industrial Organizations-American Federation of Labor rivalry appeared in the strike on the *Seattle Star,* while Spokane saw the emergence of the closed shop issue in a laundry strike which failed after it had tied up the industry for two months and also witnessed a sit-down demonstration of Work Projects administration workers.

The chief state officers in 1937 were: Clarence D. Martin, governor; Victor A. Meyers, lieutenant governor; Ernest N. Hutchinson, secretary of state; Cliff Yelle, auditor; Phil H. Gallagher, treasurer; G. W. Hamilton, attorney general; A. C. Martin, commissioner of public lands; William A. Sullivan, insurance commissioner; Stanley F. Atwood, superintendent of public instruction; Edward J. Reilly, speaker of the assembly; and William J. Steinert, chief justice.

Citizens of the state acknowledged the importance of the 1938 election by registering to the number of 898,159, an all-time high, and casting 632,813 votes, a record for a non-presidential year. Homer T. Bone, Democratic incumbent and senior U.S. senator, defeated Ewing D. Colvin (Rep.) and the state returned an entire Democratic delegation of six congressmen. C. G. Jeffers defeated Ernest M. Card for position number three on the supreme court; William J. Steinert and George B. Simpson were selected for positions one and two without contest. The 1938 legislature was preponderantly Democratic, but the conservative elements of the party had a decided majority. Probably more significant than candidates were certain initiative measures submitted for popular verdict. A constitutional amendment authorizing the levy of a graduated tax on net incomes was defeated. Most controversial was measure no. 130, which would have required "a majority vote of employees concerned—before a strike may be called." Supported by a group known as "Associated Farmers and Women of Washington" and fought by organized labour, it was defeated by a narrow count of 268,848 for to 295,431 against. Reenacted was the so-called 40-mill limit bill which had a clause authorizing the legislature to drop the state levy of 2 mills and permit cities and towns to make a commensurate increase. Successful also was an act providing nonpartisian elections for state and county superintendents of schools.

Washington celebrated its 50th anniversary of statehood in 1939. The legislature met in its 26th session from Jan. 9 to March 9. To meet the serious problem of finance, former exemptions from the sales tax of such items as fruit, fresh vegetables, dairy products and unsweetened bread were removed. At the same time the 40-mill limit bill regarding property taxes was placed upon the 1940 ballot as a legislative referendum measure. A general law as regards fair trade practices, as well as acts dealing with such problems in particular industries as apple growing and livestock, were passed. Ratification was extended to the federal law of May 27, 1937, to prevent speculation in lands in the Columbia basin. Since the supreme court sustained its position as to eligibility of persons for old-age assistance regardless of need, the legislature modified the state law and also barred such claims against the state based upon the old law. A commission to prepare for the Pacific Northwest Centennial exposition, scheduled for Seattle in 1942, was created.

A record number of citizens registered and voted in the 1940 elections. In the Democratic primaries a spirited contest between Gov. Martin, presenting himself for a third term, and former Sen. Clarence C. Dill resulted in the nomination of the latter. He was, however, defeated in the final election by Arthur B. Langlie (Rep.), mayor of Seattle, by a vote so close that the outcome was not determined until the count of the unusually numerous absentee ballots was made. There were five incumbents among the seven Democratic state officers elected on party tickets. Six Democrats, five re-elected, were sent to congress. President Roosevelt's popular vote for the state's 14 electoral votes exceeded that of any candidate on the state ballot, 462,145 to 322,123 for Wendell L. Willkie. The legislature in its 27th session consisted of 38 Democrats and 8 Republicans in the senate and 70 Democrats as against 29 Republicans in the assembly.

The chief officers elected for 1941 were: Arthur B. Langlie, governor; Victor A. Meyers, lieutenant governor; Mrs. Belle Reeves, secretary of state; Cliff Yelle, auditor; Otto A. Case, treasurer; Smith Troy, attorney general; Jack Taylor, commissioner of public lands; William A. Sullivan, insurance commissioner; Pearl A. Wanamaker, superintendent of public instruction.

To meet the substantially increased old-age pensions voted in Nov. 1940 the sales and use taxes were increased in 1941 from 2% to 3%, and a gift tax was enacted. Defense legislation gave the governor authority to designate defense areas, authorized the transfer of state property to the United States, protected the interests of residents who entered the armed forces and made provision for housing those engaged in defense activity. Other reactions to the crisis were an amendment to the criminal anarchy law of 1909 and the requirement that U.S. and Washington history and government be taught in the schools.

In line with the general U.S. trend toward Republicanism, three of the six congressional districts of Washington, formerly all Democratic, elected G.O.P. candidates in Nov. 1942. The perennial 40-mill limit on the taxation of real property and a measure to increase the benefits of industrial insurance were adopted by popular referendum. The supreme court sustained the state law designed to curb chain-dentistry.

The legislature in its 28th session responded in 1943 to a popular initiative petition and passed a measure authorizing public utility districts to combine and acquire electric power projects through eminent domain procedures. Opponents of the bill filed a referendum petition. The state supreme court sustained the contention that the emergency clause in the act was not valid and therefore did not militate against a referendum on the bill. The court also declared that children suspended from a school because they did not give the flag salute were not delinquent, providing they were not disrespectful to the national emblem.

At a special session in March 1944 the legislature passed a soldiers' vote bill. In the November election, President Roosevelt carried the state by a vote of 486,774 as against 361,689 for Thomas E. Dewey. Warren G. Magnuson (Dem.) defeated Harry P. Cain (Rep.) for U.S. senator. Democrats won four of the state's six seats in the house of representatives. All state offices, likewise, fell to the party in power. The Democratic majority in both houses of the legislature reached two-thirds. State officers for 1945 were: governor, Mon C. Wallgren; lieutenant governor, Victor A. Meyers; secretary of state, Belle Reeves; treasurer, Russell M. Fluent; attorney general, Fred E. Lewis (Smith Troy on leave); superintendent of public instruction, Pearl A. Wanamaker.

In 1944 the voters adopted a constitutional amendment "limiting exclusively to highway purposes the use of motor vehicle license fees, excise taxes on motor fuels and other revenue intended for highway purposes only." Three statutory measures were rejected by the voters. Two were initiative bills which would have increased social security payments substantially. The other was a referendum bill which was designed to facilitate the formation of public utility districts. It had been submitted to the 1943 legislature by initiative petition, and although enacted into law, its operation was suspended by referendum petition.

Breaking paths for new state policies, the legislature in 1945 passed measures regulating aeronautics, authorizing the establishment of public hospital districts, declaring the ground waters of the state to be public ground waters and appropriating state funds for public libraries. Other enactments included a uniform food and drug act, a measure creating a contingent receipts fund and an appropriation of $100,000 for the conduct of a survey of the entire public educational system. The state supreme court refused to recognize the emergency clauses in three acts of the legislature and ordered the referendum petitions submitted against them to be filed. The court also declared an act liberalizing the admission to the bar for veterans unconstitutional on the score that admission to the practice of law was a judicial function. It sustained a law which permitted county officers who served on employment statistics commissions to receive compensation in addition to their regular salaries.

During Aug. 1945 it was revealed that atomic bombs had been manufactured at the mysterious war project at Hanford on the Columbia river. Recognition that the state's school system ranked first in educational efficiency came from the National Educational association. Landowners in the Columbia basin voted overwhelmingly to share with the federal government the cost of placing the Columbia Basin Irrigation project into operation. On Sept. 23 the northwest loggers and timber workers went on strike and stayed out until Dec. 3–4. A walkout of the typographical workers of the three largest Seattle newspapers on Nov. 17 closed their plants for the rest of the year.

Despite the largest registration of voters in the state's history, the numbers of votes cast at the primary and general elections of 1946 were far below those of 1944. Harry P. Cain, Republican, defeated Hugh B. Mitchell, Democrat, for the senate by a vote of 358,847 to 298,683. The Republicans elected five of the state's six congressmen. The voters rejected one initiative measure and two referendum measures. The initiative measure, upon which the two largest utility companies in the state took opposite views, would have required the approval of voters in utility districts "as a prerequisite to acquisition of any operating electrical utility properties." One referendum was intended to make the state game commission responsible to the governor; the other was to create a state timber resources board. An amendment to the state constitution "to permit the state to tax the United States and its instrumentalities to the extent that the laws of the United States will allow" was ratified by the electorate. (H. J. De.; X.)

Washington: *Statistical Data*

Table I.—*Education (Public)*

	1938	1941	1942	1943	1944	1945
Elementary school pupils	234,684	208,852				
High school pupils	105,293	127,104	266,929	265,880	279,276	288,112
Elementary teachers	6,065					
High school teachers	4,154	11,495	11,658	11,661	12,273	12,666

Table II.—*Public Welfare*
(Money figures in thousands of dollars)

	1938	1940	1941	1943	1944	1945
Cases on general relief	25,762	11,051	9,605		7,348	
Cost of general relief	$394	$154	$151			
Recipients of old-age pensions	37,610	39,192	57,488	62,422	60,391	60,657
Dependent children receiving aid	13,040	11,813	12,653	14,551	7,986	14,564
Blind receiving aid	1,032	1,037	1,041	921	684	597
Prisoners	2,166	2,442		2,080	2,001	2,400

Table III.—*Communications*
(Money figures in thousands of dollars)

	1937	1938	1939	1940	1941	1944
Highway mileage		6,341	6,297	6,297	6,304	
Expenditure on highways	$22,128	$24,468	$24,289	$39,925		
Railroad mileage	5,280	5,281	5,268	5,268	5,215	5,215

Table IV.—*Banking and Finance*
(Money figures in thousands of dollars)

	1937	1938	1939	1942	1943	1944
State revenue	$74,740	$90,021	$88,413	$147,802	$147,583	$214,050
State expenditure	$71,033	$74,780	$67,230	$130,012	$127,697	$186,426
Number of banks	179	153	146	135	132	127
Total bank deposits	$512,900	$491,500	$540,600	$855,093	$1,578,638	$1,732,368

Table V.—*Agriculture*
(All figures in thousands)

	1937	1939	1940	1942	1944	1945 (est.)
Income from crops and livestock	$162,700	$146,616	$145,342	$325,804	$449,901	
Leading crops (bu.):						
Apples	29,346	26,000	28,804	27,552	31,100	25,840
Barley	2,074	3,120	3,915	12,560	8,550	7,175
Cherries (tons)	14	27	29		29	35
Hay (tons)	1,735	1,891	1,864	1,966	1,916	2,073
Hops (lb.)	8,785	9,212	12,480	11,788	16,975	21,060
Oats	8,060	11,221	8,658	10,080	7,728	7,200
Pears	5,600	5,779	6,100	6,723	8,665	7,922
Potatoes	9,400	7,350	8,325	7,800	10,340	12,255
Wheat	50,824	43,822	41,808	55,148	64,030	68,427

Table VI.—*Manufacturing*
(Money figures in thousands of dollars)

	1937	1939
Wage earners	101,260	90,324
Wages paid	$128,472	$118,326
Value of manufactures	$675,640	$636,650
Saw mills, etc.		$123,605
Pulp mills	$48,412	37,288
Paper and paperboard mills	37,048	33,961
Meat packing	28,175	26,125
Grain mill products	31,775	25,018

Table VII.—*Mineral Production*
(All figures in thousands of dollars)

	1937	1938	1939	1943
Value of mineral production	$26,658	$21,167	$31,590	$37,547
Leading products (value):				
Sand and gravel	$6,818	$2,861	$6,049	
Coal	6,325	4,939	5,256	
Gold	1,271	2,596	3,165	
Stone	1,910	1,849	2,020	
Copper	15	1,179	1,872	
Clay	1,120	1,018	1,084	
Zinc	535	1,095	1,054	

Bibliography.—Council of State Govts., *Book of the States* (bienn.); Bur. of Statistics and Immigration, *Washington: Its People, Products and Resources* (1940); Federal Writers' Project, *Washington: Guide to the Evergreen State* (1941); J. W. Goddard, *Washington, the Evergreen State* (1942); *The State of Washington, a Review of the State's Natural Resources* (1939); *Washington State Government* (state manual) (1940). Periodical: *Monthly Checklist of State Publications.*

Washington, D.C.

By 1945 the total land area of the District of Columbia was 61 sq.mi. and the population was 926,260 (1940 census 663,091). In 1922 the federal government had contributed 40% of the budget for the government of the District of Columbia; by 1945 this had decreased to 9.45%. During the decade 1937–46 congress contributed $6,000,000 each year; but, as the budget inevitably increased, this amount became a progressively smaller proportion of the total expenses. In 1946, for the 1947 budget, the senate voted to contribute $10,000,000 and in conference the amount agreed upon was $8,000,000.

The District of Columbia continued to be governed by a commission of three, two residents of the district appointed by the president and a third officer from the U.S. army engineering corps nominated by the chief of engineers.

A revised master plan had been prepared by the national capital park and planning commission, based largely on the plan of 1901, which in turn revived the essential features of the original L'Enfant plan by which the city was laid out for its first occupation in 1800.

The war years 1941–45 brought dislocation of the population and violence to the master plan of Washington. Government activities expanded so rapidly that many private buildings were rented and apartment houses were taken over for offices, only to leave shortages in housing units even more acute. The public mall was studded with temporary buildings for offices and dormitories. New public and private buildings were often located without regard to the plan.

Before World War II, the Alley Dwelling authority had cleared out certain inhabited alleys and built nearly 2,500 housing units. During the war 57,537 dwelling units were erected by private enterprise and 8,493 by public agencies in addition to 9,048 dormitories.

The nation's capital, besides being served by the national capital park and planning commission, was also fortunate in having the Commission of Fine Arts, established by congress in 1910, which continued to function as the guardian of the art, architectural and landscape development of the capital. In 1944 the chairman, Gilmore D. Clarke, explained that the commission had not approved the abandonment of the city's classical background and had continued to stress attributes of architecture of the past. The Fine Arts commission, in addition to authorization of the original act of congress and a series of executive orders, was also aided by the Shipstead-Luce act of 1930, under which the commission was to exercise an effective control over the design of all buildings erected on private property opposite designated public buildings and grounds.

After 1922–23, the American Planning and Civic association had an active Committee of One Hundred on the Federal City, under the chairmanship (until 1940) of Frederic A. Delano, who was succeeded by Associate Justice Owen J. Roberts of the supreme court and in 1945 by Clifton Woodrum, a member of congress from Virginia. In 1940 the committee sponsored a dinner at which the first report of the committee in 1924 was examined and compared with accomplishments in the succeeding 16 years. The first task of the committee had been to secure legislation for the national capital park and planning commission. The result was the legislation of 1924 authorizing park purchase, supplemented by the Capper-Cramton act of 1930, and the legislation of 1926 setting up the commission. This legislation was sponsored jointly by the Civic association working with leaders in the American Institute of Architecture, the American Society of Landscape Architecture, the American Institute of Planners, the American Society of Civil Engineers, the Garden Club of America and others.

In 1940 it was reported that the acquisition of 70% of the park system, as planned by the commission, had been completed, with an expenditure of 52% of the funds authorized. During this period, also, the Civil War forts surrounding the city had been acquired, and work was begun on the connecting parkway. The Mount Vernon Memorial highway was completed, and the Chesapeake and Ohio canal was acquired for recreational purposes. Schools and schoolgrounds were located in accordance with the plan, and a number of joint school and recreational centres were established.

The Washington Zoning act, originally adopted in 1920 and modernized by congress in 1938, continued to maintain a comparatively low skyline and to prohibit skyscrapers which might dominate the dome of the capitol and the Washington Monument.

In 1940 the Committee of One Hundred on the Federal City announced a new program, which, however, was soon to be interrupted by World War II.

Realizing the importance of the problems facing the federal city and the interest of the U.S. people in their capital, a joint committee on the national capital was set up in 1943, consisting of representatives of ten national organizations: American Federation of Arts, American Institute of Architects, American Institute of Planners, American Planning and Civic association, American Society of Civil Engineers, American Society of Landscape Architects, the Garden Club of America, National Association of Real Estate Boards, National Sculpture society, and National Society of Mural Painters. This committee was not to act as a unit on pending matters but was to secure data and make recommendations to the constituent organizations so that they might be in a position to act intelligently.

In the early 1940s a citizens' council for community planning brought together most of the local organizations interested in planning and housing in Washington.

During the decade 1937–46 several controversies developed concerning the character of the federal city. In 1936 congress had directed the corps of engineers of the U.S. army to make studies of the river basins of the country in order to develop plans for flood control. The reports of the division and district engineers not only recommended flood-control measures but proposed extensive power development along many miles of the Potomac river, involving the destruction of large aesthetic and economic values. In the 1920s, proposals to develop power on the Potomac by private companies had been defeated in congress. The proposal of the 1940s was to develop public power, but the physical works were similar. At the hearings before the board of engineers for rivers and harbours in April 1945, there was unanimous expression of opinion against the proposal, and consequently the board made an adverse report on the proposals for power on the Potomac.

This was a recognition of the residential and monumental character of the federal city, which, apparently, the U.S. people wished to protect from unrelated industrial development, at the same time preserving the features of natural beauty which had made the city famous.

In 1946 another controversy developed over plans to erect large extensions to the White House to be used for office buildings. This brought to public attention the proposals growing out of the Senate Park report of 1901 that the office wings erected in the White House grounds be considered temporary until such time as a proper site could be secured for permanent executive offices, even then rapidly outgrowing space in the White House. The Committee of One Hundred on the Federal City and the D.C. chapter of the American Institute of Architects circulated accurate information, with the result that most of the important newspapers in the country presented articles and editorials against further encroachments on the White House grounds. Congress withdrew its appropriation for new building, and the national capital park and planning commission was committed to a restudy of the entire White House area in order to develop a detailed plan for permanent development.

In 1946 the Urban Redevelopment and Housing bill was passed by congress, after several years of bitter controversy, to set in motion plans for redevelopment of blighted areas in the federal city.

Still another controversy concerned the building of new bridges across the Potomac. The proposed location and plans of the District of Columbia highway engineer's office failed to receive the approval of the national capital park and planning commission as conforming to the master plan, and, according to the commission, focused too large a volume of traffic on the already overcrowded business district.

In Jan. 1944 the bureau of the budget made a report to the president, at his request, recommending certain measures to strengthen the powers of the national capital park and planning commission, but the confusion of World War II and its aftermath prevented the action of congress on these important recommendations.

BIBLIOGRAPHY.—Commission of Fine Arts, *Reports;* National Capital Park and Planning Commission, *Reports;* Bureau of the Budget, *Report to the President on the National Capital Park and Planning Commission* (1944); Gilmore D. Clarke, *Aesthetic Standards for the National Capital, Planning and Civic Comment* (April 1944); Maj. Gen. Philip B. Fleming, *Federal Works for the Federal City, Planning and Civic Comment* (April 1944); J. E. Greiner Co. and DeLeuw, Cather & Co., *Report on Transportation to the District Commissioners* (1944); Maj. Gen. U. S. Grant, 3rd, "Washington a Planned City in Evolution," *American Planning and Civic Annual* (1943); Chas. D. Maginnis, *The Nation's City, Planning and Civic Comment* (April 1944); and numerous articles on the federal city in the *American Planning and Civic Annual* and *Planning and Civic Comment; Washington, City and Capital* (1937); M. F. Parton, *Your Washington* (1938). (H. Js.)

WASP

See WOMEN'S AIRFORCE SERVICE PILOTS.

Water-Borne Commerce of the United States

See CANALS AND INLAND WATERWAYS; RIVERS AND HARBOURS.

Water Power

Water-power development in the decade 1937–46 proceeded on the largest scale in history. U.S. Federal Power commission reports showed that ten years' increase in hydroelectric generating capacity was approximately 4,800,000 kilowatts—from 10,037,165 in 1936 to 14,839,744 in 1946—a growth of 47.3%. Boulder, Grand Coulee, Bonneville, the Tennessee Valley authority dams and other large federally-constructed projects accounted for most of this increase. Privately-owned hydroelectric utility plants increased only 4.4%—from 8,494,068 to 8,867,290 kw.—while publicly-owned water-power installations mounted from 1,543,097 to 6,044,327 kw., or 292%.

Steam and other fuel plants still produced nearly 70% of the U.S. electric energy, although in 1945, owing to favourable water conditions, water power produced 37% of the total. But the amount produced by water power rapidly increased. Hydro production for public use in 1936 was only 39,057,647,000 kw.hr. In 1945 it reached 79,970,312,000 kw.hr., an increase of 105%. Publicly-owned hydro plants in the same period increased their output from 3,894,756,000 to 32,710,897,000 kw.hr., or 740%. Privately-owned plants still generated more than 80% of the country's total energy requirements and an even larger percentage when the output of industrial plants was included.

The Boulder dam project on the Colorado river was the largest U.S. power plant at the end of the decade. With more than 1,000,000 kw. of generating capacity, its vast output was transmitted 270 mi. to Los Angeles, Calif., supplying the electric needs of southern California. Columbia river developments made the Pacific northwest the greatest of power-producing areas. Bonneville (522,400 kw.) began operations in 1933, followed in 1941 by Grand Coulee (743,000 kw. installed) which, with its ultimate installation of 1,964,000 kw., was to be the largest in the United States. Beginning with Norris (100,800 kw.) and Wheeler (129,600 kw.) completed in 1936, the Tennessee Valley authority constructed some 14 major dams, including Pickwick (144,000 kw), Watts Bar (150,000 kw), Fontana (135,000 kw.), Kentucky (96,000 kw.), Chickamauga (81,000 kw.), Apalachia (75,000 kw.), Guntersville (72,900 kw.), Fort Loudoun (64,000 kw.), Cherokee (60,000 kw.), Douglas (60,000 kw.) and Hiwassee (57,000 kw.). With Wilson dam (335,200 kw.) at Muscle Shoals, 6 steam plants, and hydro projects acquired or TVA-operated, the Tennessee Valley authority system by 1946 had a total installed capacity of 2,500,000 kw. producing more than 12,000,000,000 kw.hr. a year—the largest output of any integrated system in the world.

Other large hydroelectric projects constructed were Grand river dam in Oklahoma (72,400 kw.), and Denison dam on the Red river in Texas (71,000 kw.) which were to be connected by Southwestern Power administration transmission lines with Norfolk dam (ultimate capacity 70,000 kw.), under construction at the end of 1946 on the White river in Arkansas. In Texas, the Lower Colorado River authority built a series of dams developing more than 117,000 kw. constituting an integrated system, and the Brazos river project (22,500 kw.) was completed. Santee Cooper (132,615 kw.), constructed with federal funds by the South Carolina Power authority, was the largest new plant completed in the southeast. In Montana, on the upper Missouri river, army engineers built Fort Peck dam, with incidental power capacity of 50,000 kw. Nebraska, developing its water resources through the Loup river, Platte valley and Central Nebraska Public power districts, became, with the purchase of the Nebraska Power company by the city of Omaha, the first public-power state.

Largest of all projects under construction at the end of 1946 was the Central Valley project in California, where Shasta dam (154,000 kw. installed) was to have an ultimate installation of 379,000 kw., to be followed by Keswick (75,-

←

Gen. Dwight D. Eisenhower placing a wreath at the Lincoln Memorial in Washington, D.C., on Feb. 12, 1946, to commemorate the 137th anniversary of the president's birth

000 kw.) and other dams utilizing the Sacramento river and other waters for irrigation and power. Parker dam, on the Colorado river in California, was completed (120,000 kw. installed) and Davis dam on the Arizona-Nevada border was under construction, designed for an ultimate capacity of 225,000 kw.

Hydroelectric projects authorized by congress, but awaiting appropriations for construction in 1946, included Clark Hill on the Savannah river in Georgia and South Carolina, designed for 200,000 kw.; Bugg's Island on the Roanoke river (Virginia and North Carolina), 204,000 kw.; Wolf Creek on the Cumberland river in Kentucky, 270,000 kw.; Bull Shoals on the White river in Arkansas, 336,000 kw. and Blakely on the Ouachita river, 63,000 kw. Georgia's capacity was to be increased 108,000 kw. by construction of the Allatoona dam on the Etowah river.

Missouri river projects authorized included Garrison dam in North Dakota, 320,000 kw., and Fort Randall dam in South Dakota, 400,000 kw. In the Columbia river basin, Montana was to get 150,000 kw. by construction of Hungry Horse dam, while development of the Umatilla (McNary) dam was to give Oregon its largest hydro plant, 690,000 kw.

River basin development by multipurpose projects providing for flood control, irrigation, navigation, power, water supply, soil conservation, reforestation and recreation was rapidly superseding the wasteful, piecemeal single-purpose undertakings. Regional programs covering entire drainage areas could stimulate local enterprise and promote every element of the region's economy.

Power remained the principal money earner in such programs.

The Tennessee Valley authority furnished the best example of unified multipurpose development. With an electric system of 2,500,000 kw., selling power to 92 municipalities and 46 co-operatives and serving 650,000 homes, farms, stores and factories in 7 states, its 26 dams assured effective flood control. Nine-foot navigation was provided for a distance of 650 mi., through a series of pools connected by locks, extending from Knoxville, Tenn., to Paducah, Ky. Farming and forestry were fostered, many new local industries were established and the large lakes made by its reservoirs created a new recreation area, with 115,000 ac. of game or wildlife areas and 55,000 ac. of public parks.

Considered from an over-all regional standpoint, the undeveloped water-power resources of the United States were still immense. The Federal Power commission's roster of river basin projects studied and found favourable for multipurpose development offered the possibility of ultimately increasing the nation's hydroelectric generating capacity to 100,000,000 kw., with an annual output of more than 500,000,000,000 kw.hr.—nearly twice as much electric energy as the entire country used for all purposes in 1946.

By far the largest proportion of undeveloped U.S. water power was in the Pacific and Rocky mountain states. As compared with their total of about 9,000,000 kw. of hydro and steam electric power in 1946, their rivers, principally the Columbia river and its tributaries, offered the possibility of an additional 50,000,000 kw., producing annually 300,000,000,000 kw.hr. From the streams which drain the Missouri-Mississippi basin and their tributaries, rivers in New Mexico, Texas, Colorado, Oklahoma, Kansas, Missouri, Arkansas and Louisiana, the nation could expect projects producing 120,000,000,000 kw.hr. and from the east and south coasts, on rivers which drain into the Atlantic ocean and the east coast of the Gulf of Mexico, additional production of approximately 80,000,000,000 kw.hr.

These estimates looked to the distant future when the United States would require many times the electric energy that its people and industries used at the end of the decade 1937–46. But there were many important sites calling for early development. Most outstanding, perhaps, was the St. Lawrence seaway and power project. An agreement between the governments of the United States and Canada for joint development of the water in the Great Lakes-St. Lawrence river basin for navigation and power was signed March 19, 1941. The agreement provided for a power development in the International Rapids section of 1,650,000 kw., or 875,000 kw. apiece for the two countries, and contemplated an almost equal amount of additional power through the redevelopment of the Niagara river. St. Lawrence power, to the extent of 6,500,000,000 kw.hr. a year, could be generated and delivered throughout New York state and New England at an average cost of about 2.2 mills.

Power transmission over longer distances would greatly increase hydroelectric service areas. Maximum transmission in the United States in 1946 was approximately 300 mi. at 287,000 volts, the longest line in operation running from Boulder dam to Los Angeles.

Engineers were studying plans developed in Germany to transmit electric energy up to 500 mi. over lines carrying 400,000 volts.

Power grids, connecting the generating and distribution facilities of entire systems and areas, were coming into use. Through the Tennessee Valley authority, publicly and privately-owned systems from Ohio to the Gulf were linked by connections which relieved the wartime power shortage in the south. A power pool which connected public and private systems aided substantially in meeting Pacific northwest war power demands. Grids proved successful in various regions.

Forward-looking engineers expected some day to see all the hydro developments and steam generating plants in the Pacific and mountain states, from Canada to California, Utah and Colorado, linked together in the largest power pool the world had ever seen. (*See* also DAMS; ELECTRIC INDUSTRIES.) (L. O.)

BIBLIOGRAPHY.—H. K. Barrows, *Water Power Engineering* (1943); Federal Power Commission, *Laws and Hydroelectric Power Development Laws* (1941), *National Power Survey*, 4 vol. (1935–36), *Opinions and Decisions* (1940 *et seq.*); C. H. Pritchett, *Tennessee Valley Authority* (1943); Sou. Appalachian River Conf., *Proceedings* (irreg.); U.S. Engineer Dept., *Potential Water Power Sites* (1935). Periodical: *Water Resources.*

Water Supply

See PUBLIC HEALTH ENGINEERING.

Wavell of Cyrenaica and Winchester

Viscount Wavell (Archibald Percival Wavell) (1883–), British army officer, was born May 5, 1883. He was educated at Winchester college and the Royal Military college, Sandhurst, and joined the Black Watch regiment in 1901. His career thereafter was both variegated and adventuresome. He fought in the South African War (1901–02), in India's northwest frontier (1908) and in France during the first part of World War I (1914–16), in which he suffered the loss of his left eye. In 1916, he served as military attaché with Russian armies in the Caucasus and was transferred to Palestine in 1917. Following the end of World War I, Wavell was made commander of a brigade and later a division at Aldershot. In 1936, he went to the soviet union as a military attaché; the following year, he was dispatched to Palestine and Trans-Jordan,

Viscount Wavell (second from left) chatting with Mohammed Ali Jinnah (third from right) and other leaders of the All-India Moslem league who attended the conference at Simla in June 1945

but returned to England in 1938 to head the southern command.

With war impending, Wavell was made commander of British armies in the middle east in the summer of 1939. Wavell's small force of British imperial troops fell back before Marshal Graziani's attack, launched Sept. 12, 1940, and retreated beyond Sidi Barrani in Egypt. On the night of Dec. 8–9, 1940, Wavell opened a lightning counter-attack, sweeping the Italians out of Cyrenaica and driving them all the way back to El Agheila west of the Libyan hump by Feb. 10, 1941.

Marshal Rommel, who replaced Graziani at the head of the axis forces, counterattacked on March 25, 1941, forcing Wavell to relinquish the gains he had won at Graziani's expense.

Wavell also directed the successful Allied operations in East Africa, in Iraq and (in part) in Syria, but suffered serious defeats at the hands of the Germans in Greece and Crete.

On July 1, 1941, Wavell was transferred to the post of commander of British forces in India and the following month, he headed British forces in the joint British-soviet campaign in Iran. After the Japanese attack on Britain and the U.S. in Dec. 1941, he was named supreme commander of Allied forces in the far east on Jan. 3, 1942; the following March he returned to his former position as commander of British forces in India and, additionally, Burma. Promoted to the rank of field marshal on Jan. 1, 1943, he was appointed viceroy of India on June 19 of that year and the following July he was elevated to the peerage as Viscount Wavell of Cyrenaica and Winchester.

WAVES

See Women's Reserve of the Navy.

W.C.T.U. (Women's Christian Temperance Union)

See Societies and Associations.

W.D.'s (Women's Division, Royal Canadian Air Force)

See Canadian Women's Services, World War II.

Wealth and Income, Distribution of

Although there had been very great interest in this subject and wide recognition of its importance, no entirely satisfactory study of the size distribution of the income in the U.S. had been made up to the end of the decade 1937–46. All the available studies suffered to some extent from a lack of basic information, and in addition the numerous technical difficulties in the field contained many unsolved problems. Nonetheless, considerable progress was made during the decade, and various studies became available which provided much useful information, even though their results had to be considered more or less tentative.

Stimulus to research in the distribution of income was given by the publication in 1934 of a study made by the Brookings institute, entitled *America's Capacity to Consume*. This study examined the distribution of income for the year 1929 and found that there was a high degree of inequality even in that year of national prosperity. Out of the 36,462,000 spending units in the U.S. in 1929, it was estimated that 27% were in the income group of less than $1,000 and received only 5.2% of total income. Furthermore, 55% of the income units were in a group with earnings less than $2,000 and received only 27.1% of total income. The proportion of families earning under $3,000 was 72% and this large group accounted for but 42.9% of total income. On the other hand, the remaining 28% of families received 57.1% of total income.

The most comprehensive study of the distribution of income was that issued by the National Resources committee. It provided a wide variety of data on both the distribution of income and the distribution of expenditures for the year 1935–36. Three reports were published: *Consumer Incomes in the United States, Consumer Expenditures in the United States* and *Family Expenditures in the United States*. These studies were based upon income data for about 300,000 consuming units, augmented by income tax information for the high income groups, and expenditures data for about 60,000 consuming units. Summary data from this study are given in Tables I and II.

The relatively high degree of concentration of income is evident from the data in Table I. It may be calculated that the average income per consumer unit for the year 1935–36, that obtained by dividing the aggregate income by the total number of consumer units, was $1,502. Yet half of the consumer units had incomes of less than $1,070 because of the large incomes received by a relatively small number of consumer units at the upper end of the income scale. The largest number of consumer units was in the group receiving incomes from $500 to $1,000. This group contained almost 30% of all consumer units and received a little less than 15% of aggregate income. Slightly more than 17% of the consumer units received income of less than $500 and, as a group, received less than 3½% of aggregate income. At the upper end of the income scale it may be noted that the number of individuals included in the various groups fell off sharply after the $3,000 level was reached. Altogether, less than 7% of the consumer units had incomes of more than $3,000. This group received more than 30% of total income.

The disparity of incomes was strikingly revealed by grouping the total number of consumer units by tenths. The poorest tenth of the consumer units received incomes up to $340 and in the aggregate accounted for less than 2% of total income. The second tenth had incomes ranging from $340 to $545 and received 3% of the total. On the other hand, the tenth of consumer units with the highest incomes included those receiving $2,600 and more and in the aggregate accounted for 36% of the total income. This highest tenth received about the same total income as the 70% at the bottom of the income scale.

As much public discussion had been concerned with the lower third of the population, it was interesting to compare the size distribution of income on the basis of the three thirds of consumer units. Each of these thirds contained 13,000,000 families and single individuals.

During 1935–36 the lower third of the nation received incomes of less than $780, with an average income for the group of $471. The share of the aggregate income received by this lower third of the nation was just more than 10% of the total of $59,000,000,000. It should not be thought that these 13,000,000 families and single individuals constituted a distinct and unusual group. All types of consumer units, from single individuals to large families, were included in the group; they lived in all types of communities; and they worked in all the major types of occupations. Apart from receiving less income, they differed from the other two thirds of the nation principally in that a larger proportion received relief for some part of the year; a larger number lived on farms and a smaller number had occupations in the professional, business and clerical fields. Although the proportion receiving relief in this group for some part of the year was relatively large, it was not essentially a group dependent upon relief, since 70% of the total number were completely nonrelief families and individuals.

In the middle third of the nation were the 13,000,000 consumer units receiving from $780 to $1,450 during the year. They had an average income of $1,076. As contrasted with the lower third, only 13% were at all dependent upon relief; twice as many lived in large cities and twice as many worked at professional, business and clerical occupations.

The upper third of the consumer units contained all those with incomes of more than $1,450. In total, this group received about two-thirds of the aggregate income

Table I.—*Average Disbursements of Consumer Units* in Each Third of Nation, 1935–36*

Category of Disbursement	Average disbursements of families and single individuals in: Lower third, incomes under $780	Middle third, incomes of $780 to $1,450	Upper third, incomes of $1,450 and over	Percentage of income: Lower third	Middle third	Upper third
Current consumption:						
Food	$236	$404	$642	50.2	37.5	21.7
Housing	115	199	408	24.4	18.5	13.8
Household operation	54	108	240	11.4	10.0	8.1
Clothing	47	102	251	10.0	9.5	8.5
Automobile	16	57	215	3.3	5.3	7.2
Medical care	20	41	106	4.3	3.9	3.6
Recreation	9	28	89	1.8	2.6	3.0
Furnishings	9	28	72	1.8	2.6	2.4
Personal care	12	22	44	2.5	2.1	1.5
Tobacco	10	23	40	2.2	2.1	1.4
Transportation other than auto	11	19	37	2.4	1.7	1.3
Reading	6	12	23	1.3	1.2	.8
Education	2	7	30	.5	.6	1.0
Other items	3	6	15	.6	.5	.5
All consumption items	550	1,056	2,212	116.7	98.1	74.8
Gifts and personal taxes†	13	39	181	2.8	3.7	6.1
Savings	−92	−19	566	−19.5	−1.8	19.1
All items	471	1,076	2,959	100.0	100.0	100.0

Source: Consumer Expenditures in the United States, National Resources committee, 1939.

*Includes all families and single individuals, but excludes residents in institutional groups.

†Taxes shown here include only personal income taxes, poll taxes and certain personal property taxes.

Table II.—*Size-Distribution and Utilization of Consumer Incomes in the U.S., 1935–36*
(In millions)

Income Level (Dollars per Year)	Consumer Units: Number (Millions)	% of Total	Aggregate Income: (Million Dollars)	% of Total	Income Utilization: Current Consumption	Gifts and Personal Taxes*	Savings
Total	39.46	100.00	$59,259	100.00	$50,214	$3,067	$5,978
Under $ 500	6.71	17.01	2,061	3.48	2,817	44	−800
500— 1,000	11.65	29.52	8,745	14.76	9,097	284	−636
1,000— 1,500	8.73	22.12	10,698	18.05	10,294	406	−2
1,500— 2,000	5.19	13.15	8,875	14.98	8,072	362	441
2,000— 3,000	4.44	11.25	10,577	17.85	9,043	465	1,069
3,000— 4,000	1.35	3.42	4,599	7.76	3,631	226	742
4,000— 5,000	.46	1.17	2,045	3.45	1,494	117	434
5,000—10,000	.60	1.52	4,092	6.90	2,604	270	1,218
10,000—20,000	.22	0.56	2,922	4.93	1,532	238	1,152
20,000 and up	.11	0.28	4,645	7.84	1,630	655	2,360

Source: Consumer Incomes in the U.S. and Consumer Expenditures in the U.S., National Resources committee.

*Personal income taxes, poll taxes and certain personal property taxes.

of all consumer units.

In interpreting the above data on the distribution of income, it should be kept in mind that the figures refer to dollar income. As the cost of living and the mode of living differed widely from community to community, the dollar incomes did not accurately measure the differences in real income or economic well-being.

It may be seen in Table I that more than two-thirds of the nation's consumer units spent considerably more than their aggregate income in 1935–36 for all purposes. In other words, as a group they had negative savings. The proportion of savings to aggregate income became relatively large with those receiving more than $5,000 during the year and in the income group of more than $20,000 approximately half of the aggregate income was saved.

The average expenditures of each third of the nation for various categories of consumption are shown in Table II. These data reveal the very high proportion of income expended on the necessities of life by the lower third of the nation, as well as the low dollar expenditure totals of this group. Almost 75% of its income went for food and housing, and the addition of household operation and clothing brought this to more than 95%. On the other hand, the upper third of the nation spent only a little more than 50% of its income for these purposes.

During the years of World War II two surveys of the distribution of U.S. income were made on the basis of a small sample of spending units, which were illuminating in showing the tremendous shift in the distribution of income that occurred under conditions of economic prosperity. The first of these studies covered the year 1941 and was made by the bureau of labour statistics, and the bureau of home economics. At the end of World War II, a survey covering the year 1945 was made by the bureau of agricultural economics, for the board of governors of the federal reserve system. This survey was entitled *National Survey of Liquid Asset Holdings, Spending and Saving.*

A comparison of the distribution of income during World War II with that of 1935–36 is shown in Table III. The most striking result of the expansion of total income which occurred during the period of wartime prosperity was to move family units out of the small income classes. By 1945 the family units were much more evenly distributed among the income classes than was the case in either 1941 or 1935–36. At the beginning of the decade 1937–46, more than 50% of the units had annual incomes of under $1,000, while by 1941 only 35% of the units were in this income class. By 1945 only 20% of the units were in the group earning under $1,000. This change was a reflection of not only the increase in average incomes during this period but also of the virtual elimination of unemployment in 1945 as compared with 1935–36.

The income groups receiving $2,000 or more showed the largest increases in the proportion of spending units over this ten-year period. Only 16% of the spending units were in this income group in 1935–36. However, by 1941 35% of the spending units had incomes of more than $2,000, and this percentage had risen to 53 in 1945. It may be noted that the greatest gain occurred in the $3,000 to $5,000 income group which had more than 20% of the spending units in 1945 as compared with 4% ten years earlier.

Inasmuch as the rise in incomes had the effect of shifting family units out of the smaller income groups, the families remaining in those groups received a much smaller proportion of the total income in 1945 than they did in 1935–36. For example, the spending units with incomes of less than $2,000 received 20% of total income in 1945, while the much larger number of units in this income class received 30% of total income in 1941 and 53% in 1935–36. This did not mean that the low income families failed to participate in the increase in income but rather that, by participating in the increase in income, they had been shifted out of the low income category.

In a period like the decade 1937–46, the vast changes in the cost of living and tax liabilities must be kept in mind in analyzing data on the distribution of income. In cautioning about these difficulties, the bureau of agricultural economics stated the following in its report: "In interpreting these shifts between income classes, it should be realized that income refers to money income received and does not take into account price and tax changes that have occurred during the war years. The Consumers' Price Index of the Bureau of Labor Statistics shows prices in 1941 to be about 7 percent higher than prices prevailing in 1935–36, and prices in 1945 to be roughly 30 percent higher. Because of these substantial price rises, a spending unit which was shifted from the under $1,000 income group to the $1,000 to $2,000 income group may not have materially improved its buying power or financial position. Furthermore, taxes increased substantially during the war. This increased tax burden undoubtedly affected the spending habits of some lower income groups and to an even greater extent affected total saving, particularly of the highest income brackets."

U.S. State Distribution of Income.—Statistics on the geographic distribution of income in the U.S. continued to be published annually by the U.S. department of commerce. A summary of these statistics for the years 1937–45

Table III.—*Distribution of Spending Units, Income and Saving by Income Classes in 1935–36, 1941 and 1945**

Annual income (money income before taxes)	1935–36 Spending units	1935–36 Total income	1935–36 Total saving	1941 Spending units	1941 Total income	1941 Total saving	1945 Spending-units	1945 Total income	1945 Total saving
	Percentage of total								
Under $1000	53%	20%	−30%	35%	9%	− 6%	20%	4%	− 1%
$1,000–$1,999	31%	33%	15%	30%	21%	9%	27%	16%	11%
$2,000–$2,999	10%	17%	21%	20%	24%	11%	23%	23%	14%
$3,000–$4,999	4%	11%	22%	10%	18%	18%	22%	32%	36%
$5,000 and over	2%	19%	72%	5%	28%	68%	8%	25%	40%
All classes	100%	100%	100%	100%	100%	100%	100%	100%	100%

*Figures for 1935–36 and 1941 are taken from *Spending and Saving of the Nation's Families in Wartime*. Bureau of labour statistics bulletin #723, Oct. 1942. Table I of this BLS Bulletin gives the distribution of income by income classes, and Tables I and IV were used to estimate total net saving by income classes.

The 1935–36 data were originally developed in the *Study of Consumer Purchases*, 1935–36, made by the National Resources committee. The material for 1941 represents a combination of the results of two surveys—the one a survey of spending units in urban areas made by the bureau of labour statistics, and the other a survey of spending units in rural areas made by the bureau of home economics, U.S. department of agriculture. For 1945 the data are taken from the national liquid assets survey.

Readers are cautioned that the findings of these three surveys are not strictly comparable. The various surveys differ somewhat in the definition of spending units, in the coverage of spending units and in the methods used in collecting the data. The figures in this table, therefore, cannot be used to measure precise changes in income and saving by income classes. However, it is believed that the table accurately shows the nature of certain broad changes which occurred in the pattern of income and saving during the years of World War II. In the table, income refers in all cases to money income before taxes and excludes income in kind.

Table IV.—*Total Income Payments to Individuals, by States and Regions, 1937–45, Selected Years*

(Millions of dollars)

State and region	1937	1939	1940	1941	1942	1943	1944	1945
United States	72,211	70,601	75,852	92,269	115,301	139,285	149,660	152,704
New England	5,900	5,729	6,124	7,367	8,908	10,159	10,624	10,744
Connecticut	1,356	1,301	1,417	1,837	2,329	2,632	2,688	2,608
Maine	408	400	431	505	667	847	853	830
Massachusetts	3,193	3,106	3,309	3,846	4,499	5,107	5,416	5,592
New Hampshire	272	268	269	309	348	373	411	446
Rhode Island	494	480	511	651	814	915	950	948
Vermont	177	174	187	219	251	285	306	320
Middle east	23,481	22,783	24,319	28,203	33,079	38,446	41,671	43,036
Delaware	205	203	239	278	316	372	400	398
District of Columbia	792	813	905	1,040	1,251	1,447	1,509	1,617
Maryland	1,067	1,074	1,222	1,516	1,997	2,388	2,509	2,467
New Jersey	2,835	2,859	3,138	3,676	4,519	5,333	5,739	5,655
New York	11,635	11,301	11,830	13,384	15,132	17,542	19,280	20,308
Pennsylvania	6,174	5,819	6,225	7,404	8,783	10,137	10,878	11,134
West Virginia	773	714	760	905	1,081	1,227	1,356	1,457
Southeast	8,457	8,414	9,043	11,580	15,421	19,201	21,051	21,703
Alabama	711	681	763	1,037	1,419	1,743	1,902	1,980
Arkansas	479	478	493	658	888	971	1,098	1,171
Florida	773	819	900	1,062	1,464	2,082	2,283	2,387
Georgia	920	901	986	1,241	1,632	2,110	2,336	2,369
Kentucky	902	839	880	1,042	1,322	1,675	1,826	1,916
Louisiana	792	828	847	1,066	1,400	1,846	1,967	1,931
Mississippi	442	436	444	630	881	1,079	1,147	1,159
North Carolina	1,077	1,090	1,131	1,436	1,859	2,218	2,484	2,575
South Carolina	485	493	545	703	954	1,122	1,245	1,265
Tennessee	880	853	927	1,221	1,508	1,951	2,202	2,353
Virginia	996	996	1,127	1,484	2,094	2,404	2,561	2,597
Southwest	3,804	3,756	3,908	4,734	6,421	8,391	9,078	9,095
Arizona	232	227	237	287	433	588	566	581
New Mexico	177	179	190	222	295	371	404	431
Oklahoma	841	796	829	956	1,305	1,579	1,781	1,820
Texas	2,554	2,554	2,652	3,269	4,388	5,853	6,327	6,263
Central	20,620	20,090	21,664	26,800	32,886	39,327	41,763	42,610
Illinois	5,395	5,285	5,740	6,889	8,035	9,342	10,223	10,589
Indiana	1,713	1,688	1,858	2,437	3,067	3,731	3,946	3,985
Iowa	1,092	1,185	1,233	1,527	1,956	2,349	2,287	2,516
Michigan	3,257	3,054	3,425	4,271	5,432	6,829	7,080	6,672
Minnesota	1,362	1,378	1,424	1,626	2,022	2,360	2,426	2,666
Missouri	1,824	1,832	1,914	2,363	2,898	3,394	3,602	3,806
Ohio	4,406	4,154	4,448	5,646	6,933	8,314	8,901	8,925
Wisconsin	1,571	1,514	1,622	2,041	2,543	3,008	3,298	3,451
Northwest	3,238	3,099	3,363	4,109	5,832	7,104	7,365	7,676
Colorado	584	563	589	695	973	1,134	1,131	1,238
Idaho	223	213	232	278	408	478	521	512
Kansas	781	692	757	974	1,427	1,830	1,931	1,938
Montana	299	288	321	372	459	508	549	539
Nebraska	549	523	569	655	975	1,214	1,272	1,347
North Dakota	217	209	237	331	432	526	559	588
South Dakota	202	227	242	301	430	510	518	599
Utah	247	243	265	329	512	661	622	641
Wyoming	136	141	151	174	216	243	262	274
Far west	6,711	6,730	7,431	9,476	12,754	16,657	18,108	17,840
California	5,047	5,047	5,606	7,044	9,205	12,075	13,175	13,124
Nevada	77	84	92	107	196	203	198	196
Oregon	580	587	633	824	1,178	1,537	1,602	1,549
Washington	1,007	1,012	1,100	1,501	2,175	2,842	3,133	2,971

Source: U.S. department of commerce.

Table V.—*Per Capita Income Payments by States and Regions, 1937-45,* Selected Years*
(Dollars)

State and region	1937	1939	1940	1941	1942	1943	1944	1945
United States	561	539	575	693	862	1,040	1,133	1,150
New England	704	680	725	866	1,044	1,210	1,285	1,288
Connecticut	808	764	827	1,059	1,305	1,479	1,513	1,449
Maine	490	474	509	602	806	1,036	1,079	1,051
Massachusetts	737	719	766	883	1,034	1,200	1,291	1,321
New Hampshire	562	548	546	629	720	808	893	971
Rhode Island	714	678	715	900	1,097	1,218	1,288	1,268
Vermont	493	483	521	613	734	868	982	1,023
Middle east	740	709	752	873	1,031	1,212	1,336	1,370
Delaware	795	771	896	1,023	1,133	1,323	1,408	1,381
District of Columbia	1,107	1,031	1,080	1,101	1,141	1,274	1,303	1,361
Maryland	635	634	713	851	1,064	1,214	1,241	1,212
New Jersey	750	746	803	912	1,093	1,291	1,416	1,373
New York	861	825	863	994	1,155	1,353	1,519	1,595
Pennsylvania	629	589	628	751	903	1,071	1,176	1,199
West Virginia	417	378	398	477	587	699	791	839
Southeast	310	303	322	404	529	656	737	761
Alabama	256	242	268	359	482	602	677	700
Arkansas	249	246	252	332	448	519	617	654
Florida	445	442	471	531	684	879	950	996
Georgia	301	290	315	389	507	654	730	745
Kentucky	325	297	308	369	474	613	701	735
Louisiana	346	354	357	433	549	722	788	785
Mississippi	207	201	202	283	396	483	541	556
North Carolina	312	308	316	397	521	610	702	732
South Carolina	262	261	286	354	473	575	652	663
Tennessee	311	295	317	413	513	659	768	813
Virginia	405	402	450	565	738	833	888	903
Southwest	397	386	399	477	642	810	901	906
Arizona	482	461	473	562	787	865	890	918
New Mexico	353	341	356	415	558	694	759	812
Oklahoma	358	340	356	417	590	728	860	889
Texas	409	401	413	497	655	840	925	917
Central	589	565	605	745	914	1,122	1,204	1,217
Illinois	691	671	726	865	1,002	1,214	1,324	1,360
Indiana	508	495	541	705	879	1,098	1,157	1,152
Iowa	434	468	485	609	806	1,013	1,011	1,109
Michigan	659	591	649	790	982	1,259	1,308	1,212
Minnesota	500	497	509	589	759	915	968	1,061
Missouri	488	486	505	621	763	905	1,006	1,063
Ohio	646	603	643	815	998	1,207	1,301	1,289
Wisconsin	510	485	516	649	815	999	1,113	1,161
Northwest	438	418	454	564	822	992	1,048	1,101
Colorado	532	505	524	620	877	975	1,000	1,100
Idaho	444	411	440	543	854	961	1,008	1,054
Kansas	430	383	422	549	814	1,027	1,101	1,113
Montana	541	515	574	682	891	1,049	1,179	1,172
Nebraska	412	397	433	510	784	988	1,049	1,117
North Dakota	333	325	368	534	738	968	1,061	1,123
South Dakota	306	351	376	484	734	883	932	1,083
Utah	459	443	480	592	887	1,042	1,019	1,023
Wyoming	560	567	605	696	857	957	1,027	1,096
Far west	714	692	750	925	1,181	1,402	1,491	1,443
California	769	741	805	974	1,198	1,426	1,513	1,480
Nevada	733	767	836	912	1,441	1,418	1,244	1,243
Oregon	552	544	579	752	1,075	1,244	1,318	1,266
Washington	597	588	632	833	1,152	1,398	1,519	1,407

*Per capita income payments are derived by division of total income payments by total population, excluding federal civilian and military personnel stationed outside the continental United States.
Source: U.S. department of commerce.

is shown in Table IV. The tremendous variations in the income of the various states may be seen from these data, the range in the prewar year of 1937 being from $77,000,000 in Nevada to $11,635,000,000 for the state of New York. The major factor behind these variations was, of course, the large differences in the population of the various states. The heavily populated states like New York, Pennsylvania, Illinois, Massachusetts, California, Michigan and Ohio were the states with the larger total income. Hence, from the standpoint of revealing differences in the standard of living from area to area, the per capita income data shown in Table V is more meaningful.

Even on a per capita basis, the differences in income among the various states were very substantial. In the prewar year of 1937 these differences ranged from $207 per capita in Mississippi to $1,107 in the District of Columbia. The southeastern region of the nation had the lowest per capita income average in the country with $310, and the southwest region with $397 was well below the national average of $561. On the other hand, New England, the middle eastern states and the far west region with per capita incomes of $704, $740, and $714 were significantly above the national average.

The major factor explaining these differentials in income was the variation in the industrial structure of the states. This is brought out by the information in Table VI, which shows the industrial distribution of the employed labour force for the states with per capita incomes less and more than the national average. It can be seen that the high-income states generally had a larger proportion of the labour force in manufacturing, mining, construction and the distributive and service industries and a smaller proportion in agriculture and domestic services. In the low-income states, on the other hand, these proportions were generally reversed. For example, the low average income in the southeastern region was explained primarily by the large dependence upon agriculture and domestic services as a source of income in that area. Approximately two-fifths of the persons employed by private industry in the region were in agriculture, while in the rest of the country this industry accounted for only one-seventh of total employment. Furthermore, the states in this region had relatively fewer workers in the manufacturing, distributive and service industries, where earnings were much higher than in agriculture and domestic services.

There were, of course, other factors accounting for the low income level in the south. For example, average farm income in the region was substantially lower than in other areas of the country, and the south was still a low wage area. It was significant, too, that the south had a greater proportion of manufacturing industries which had been traditionally low wage industries.

A tremendous expansion of income which occurred after 1940 lifted the per capita income of the country to a record high level. From 1940 to 1945, the per capita income of the nation as a whole doubled, rising from $575 to $1,150. All areas of the country participated in this expansion, though they did so in unequal proportions. There was a general tendency for the differences in per capita income to be narrowed during the years of World War II, with the lower income states gaining relatively to the higher income areas. This tendency had been in evidence during the '30s, but the changes in this direction were accelerated as income expanded under the stimulus of government war spending. The characteristics of the expansion in the various regions and the extent to which the pattern of change differed from prewar trends can be brought out by analyzing the income changes in the various regions.

Over the period 1933–45, there was a continuous decline in New England's proportionate share of total income payments. The relative decline was small up to 1940 but was sharply accelerated in the subsequent period. For all of the New England states, the gains in total income

Table VI.—*Industrial Distribution of Employed Labour Force (Excluding Government) in 1940, by States*

State	Percent of employed labour force (excluding government)			
	Agriculture, forestry and fisheries	Manufacturing, mining and construction	Distribution and service, excl. domestic service*	Domestic service
Continental United States.	19.8	31.7	43.0	5.5
High income states† . . .	8.6	38.6	48.1	4.7
California	11.6	26.2	57.5	4.7
New York	4.6	34.5	55.3	5.6
Washington	15.7	30.9	49.9	3.5
Connecticut	4.2	51.0	39.5	5.3
Delaware	14.8	38.2	39.2	7.8
New Jersey	3.4	44.3	47.5	4.8
Nevada	16.6	29.2	51.8	2.4
Illinois	10.4	36.1	49.7	3.8
Michigan	12.4	45.2	38.7	3.7
Oregon.	19.9	28.5	48.0	3.6
Massachusetts	2.9	44.0	48.3	4.8
Rhode Island.	2.3	53.9	39.7	4.1
Ohio	11.5	41.0	43.1	4.4
District of Columbia . .	.3	19.5	67.5	12.7
Maryland	11.5	35.5	45.7	7.3
Pennsylvania.	6.3	46.8	42.2	4.7
Indiana	18.7	37.2	40.4	3.7
Low income states† . .	33.7	23.2	36.8	6.3
Montana	34.3	20.7	42.5	2.5
Wisconsin	27.1	30.7	38.4	3.8
Kansas	33.3	16.9	45.9	3.9
Maine	15.1	39.8	38.9	6.2
Wyoming	32.8	19.3	45.2	2.7
Nebraska	39.4	11.5	45.3	3.8
Utah	20.7	24.7	52.4	2.2
Missouri.	24.7	25.3	45.4	4.6
Iowa	37.5	17.2	41.4	3.9
Colorado	22.7	21.3	52.0	4.0
Idaho	39.1	17.6	40.8	2.5
Vermont	26.3	29.4	37.1	7.2
Minnesota	31.9	18.2	45.7	4.2
North Dakota	56.1	5.3	34.9	3.7
Florida	20.1	19.6	48.9	11.4
Texas	31.4	18.8	42.6	7.2
New Hampshire . . .	9.6	47.3	37.4	5.7
Virginia.	26.8	30.5	35.1	7.6
Arizona.	23.2	24.3	47.7	4.8
South Dakota	50.7	9.4	36.7	3.2
Oklahoma.	35.1	18.1	42.0	4.8
West Virginia	16.0	45.2	34.2	4.6
Louisiana	34.6	20.1	36.1	9.2
Tennessee	34.5	25.3	32.9	7.3
New Mexico	34.3	19.9	41.4	4.4
Georgia	36.8	23.7	29.2	10.3
North Carolina	35.1	32.2	25.7	7.0
Kentucky	38.2	24.3	32.5	5.0
Alabama	41.3	24.9	25.4	8.4
South Carolina	41.0	27.4	22.9	8.7
Arkansas	53.5	14.3	26.8	5.4
Mississippi.	59.6	13.1	20.1	7.2

*Include trade, transportation, public utilities, finance and service (except domestic).

†A state is classified as high income or low income according to whether its per capita income of civilians in 1944 was more or less than the national average. States are ranked by size of 1944 per capita civilian income.

Source: U.S. department of commerce.

from 1940 to 1945 were less than the national average. The rate of income expansion in Connecticut, however, was greater than the national average in 1940–42 because of the fact that the rearmament program greatly stimulated income in this highly industrialized state.

The middle east region likewise received a smaller share of the nation's income payments in both the prewar and war periods. The small prewar decline was attributable to the fact that New York, Pennsylvania and the other states in the region had higher proportions of the total in 1940 than in 1929. As in the case of New England, the proportionate decline was accelerated during World War II when every state in the region had an increase in income that was lower than the national average. In the early war period, the large expansion of the aircraft and shipbuilding industries in Maryland produced a larger than average increase in income of that state, but this trend was reversed in 1944–45 as the growth of these industries levelled off and declined. On the other hand, the proportionate increase of income in New York turned upward in 1944–45 for the first time since 1938. This was because of the fact that the great diversification of industry in New York made that state less vulnerable to the decline in war production.

The states of the southeast region experienced gains during World War II that were substantially higher than the national average. In fact, the rise in total income was larger in the southeast than in any other region of the country. This trend was a continuation of prewar developments. In 1940 income payments in the southeast region were 4% higher than in 1929 as against a decline of 10% for all other areas of the nation. It reflected largely the expansion of manufacturing activity in the south, where factory pay rolls were 12% higher than in 1929 as compared with a drop of 7% for the other regions. During World War II, factory pay rolls in the southeastern states continued to expand more rapidly than for the nation as a whole, and, in addition, the large volume of military payments in this area contributed to its greater rise of income payments.

The states of the southwestern region also increased their share of total income payments in both the prewar and wartime periods, though their relative wartime gain did not begin until 1942. As in the southeast, military payments were an important source of income expansion during World War II. But this factor did not determine the trend as there was a substantial expansion of war production in the area. Factory pay rolls by the end of 1945 were one and a half times the 1940 total, the largest increase of manufacturing pay rolls in the country.

Income payments in the central states region moved approximately in proportion to the national totals. For example, the region showed a decline of 11% during 1929–40 as compared with an 8% decline for the nation as a whole, while from 1940–45 income payments expanded 97% in the region and 101% in the nation. The relative change in income of the various states in the region did not move similarly throughout this period. Up until 1943 Illinois gained less rapidly while Michigan and Indiana experienced rising income shares. In 1944 and 1945, however, Illinois gained relative to the other two states. As the central states region included highly industrialized as well as agricultural areas, the expansion of war industries and agriculture were the primary sources of its increased income during World War II. Military payments were less important than in any other area in their contribution to the expansion of income.

The northwest region was a conspicuous exception to other regions in that the relative movement of income during World War II was not in accordance with prewar trends. The region experienced a larger than average rise in income during the war in contrast to its relative loss in income in 1929–40. The experience of agriculture largely accounted for this difference. In the prewar period, the severe loss of farm income in Kansas, Nebraska, North Dakota and South Dakota affected the income of the region adversely. During 1939–43, however, farm income in the northwest tripled, with the result that the region made record gains in income payments.

The large expansion of war industry in the far west contributed to an increase in income of 144% from 1940–44, in contrast to a rise of 97% for the nation. This rapid advance during World War II continued at an accelerated rate the relative gains made by the region during 1929–40. In the earlier period, too, the growth of the industrialization was the primary factor explaining the trend. By 1940 the factory pay rolls of the far west region were 7% higher than the 1929, while for the entire nation there was a 6% decline over this period.

An important result of these diverse trends during World War II was to narrow the differentials among the states and regions in per capita income. The reduction in geographic inequality can be seen by the changes during the period 1940–45 in the relationship of regional per capita incomes to national per capita income. Per capita income in New England and the middle eastern states declined as a percentage of the national average over this period. On the other hand, in regions with low income such as the southeast, southwest and northwest, the per capita incomes rose by much more than the national average. The experience on a state basis was similar. In 1940 there were 17 states with per capita incomes higher than the national average. The gains of 14 of these states were less than the national average during 1940–45. On the other hand, out of the 32 states with per capita incomes below the national average, 28 experienced wartime increases that were greater than the national average. (M. Gt.)

Bibliography.—American Economic association, *Readings in the Theory of Income Distribution* (1946); M. D. Anderson, *Dynamic Theory of Wealth Distribution* (1938); Brookings institution, *Distribution of Wealth and Income in Relation to Economic Progress* (1935); Conference on Research in Income and Wealth, *Studies in Income and Wealth* (1937 *et seq*); W. L. Crum, *Distribution of Wealth* (1935); J. A. Ryan, *Distributive Justice* (1942).

Great Britain.—On distribution of income and wealth in the period immediately preceding World War II, facts were more complete for the United Kingdom than for any other country. British income tax continued to be a tax on personal income where the size of the income must be ascertained for administrative purposes. Also the definition of income for income tax purposes agreed on the whole with the economist's definition, and an efficient administration left little scope for evasion of assessment. Hence income tax returns provided the statistical raw material for calculating the distribution of income in the United Kingdom. By 1937 some 10,000,000 incomes out of an estimated total of 25,000,000 (including the incomes of recipients of unemployment benefit, sickness benefit, pensions for old age and widows and orphans) were above the income tax exemption limit, and this figure rose temporarily to 15,000,000 during World War II. It was the larger incomes which were assessed, which meant that about 70% of the total private income distributed to persons was brought into assessment.

Until a study of tax returns for 1938 was made, no official figures on income distribution extracted from in-

Table VII.—*Distribution of Income in Australia, 1933*

Income £ (Australian)	Number of persons (000's omitted)	Income £ (Australian)	Number of persons (000's omitted)
Under 52 . . .	1,070	156–208	321
52–104	633	208–260	250
104–156	403	260 and over . . .	346
		Total	3,023

come tax data had been published since those for 1919. These figures were completed for the lower ranges of income by using national income estimates published in 1942. Later annual estimates of the distribution of private income were published by the Central Statistical office in the White Papers, called *National Income and Expenditure of the United Kingdom,* and issued annually in April. There was a necessary time lag between the year to which the figures referred and the date of publication. The distribution for 1944 is given in Table VIII in comparison with the distribution for 1938. Figures for 1944 were subject to revision.

In interpreting Table VIII it should be borne in mind that the bulk of the income not assessed as the income of individuals consisted of the income of companies not paid out to shareholders but paid in company taxation or

Table VIII.—*Distribution of Private Income by Ranges of Incomes, United Kingdom, 1938 and 1944*

Range of Income £	1938		1944	
	Number of incomes 000's	Amount of incomes £ million	Number of incomes 000's	Amount of incomes £ million
Under 250	(22,500)	2,681	(18,250)	3,569
250–500	1,745	595	5,200	1,830
500–1,000	500	350	1,400	995
1,000–2,000	195	270	520	729
2,000–10,000	97	360	117	415
10,000 and over	8	170	8	155
Unallocated income	—	605	—	1,301
Total	(25,000)	5,031	(26,500)	8,994

Source: National Income and Expenditure of the United Kingdom, 1938–45 (Cmd. 6,784, 1946), except for figures in brackets which are approximate estimates.

Notes.—Incomes from national insurance and assistance benefits are included in the range below £250. Unallocated income includes the undistributed profits of companies, liabilities for national defense contribution and excess profits tax, the income from investment of nonprofit-making bodies and assurance funds and other income that cannot be allocated to different ranges.

put into general reserves.

These incomes were properly attributable to the higher income brackets where shareholders could usually be found.

The main drawback of the estimates in Table VIII lies in the absence of reliable information on the distribution of income less than £250, which was regarded as the upper limit of working class income in 1938. At that date over four-fifths of British families fell into that class—less than the proportion indicated by Table VIII, as the average number of earners per family was greater in the lower than in the higher ranges of income. Income tax statistics did not cover most of the lower ranges and statistics of wages referred to averages for groups without disclosing individual variation. As there was, in spite of standardized wage rates, great variation in annual earnings because of unemployment, sickness and similar factors, it was very difficult to dovetail statistics of wages into income tax data.

It should be mentioned that the incomes of man and wife were assessed as a single income. For the ranges above £250 the concept "number of incomes" should be interpreted in this sense. For most families in the higher ranges this represented the family income; the distribution of incomes under £250 could to some extent be obtained from sample studies of family income, as was done in the U.S.A. No such study existed for the United Kingdom as a whole but some information was obtainable for selected towns, for instance York, from social surveys carried out in the years preceding 1939. Valuable information might also be forthcoming from the official family budget inquiry carried out in 1937–38 the results of which were not analyzed during World War II. On the other hand, detailed annual information existed for incomes of more than £2,000. These incomes were subject to surtax. The figures obtained from the administration of this tax appeared in the annual inland revenue reports.

The information disclosed by Table VIII, it should be remembered, referred to incomes before tax. The distribution for 1938 compared with that for 1919 as far as the two distributions were comparable showed little change. The wartime distribution for 1944 showed, on the face of it, certain changes, notably a tendency toward a more equal distribution of income. However, if allowance was made for changes in the price level and for the fact that the income not allocated to the different ranges was properly attributed to the higher ranges of income, the change from 1938 to 1944 was very small. It could be said that no statistically significant change was exhibited during World War II in the distribution of income; but the distribution of incomes available for disposal by individuals became distinctly more equal during World War II, primarily because of the operation of the excess profits tax and higher income tax. Some of the effects of wartime taxation were likely to be retained.

As the administration of the United Kingdom income tax supplied the data for a distribution of incomes, so the administration of estate duties yielded information on the distribution of capital owned by persons. Since 1894 estate duties had been payable on estates valued over £100 at the death of the owner. In 1946 the exemption limit was raised to £2,000. At death a valuation of the estate was made for tax purposes; this valuation was on the whole satisfactory from the economist's point of view, and little scope was left for evasion. For certain years the annual inland revenue reports published tables showing the number of estates and the amount of estates "falling in" at death, classified both according to size and according to sex and age of the owner. Assuming that the persons dying in a particular year (or during, say, three years) represented a fair sample of their respective sex and age groups, a distribution of capital owned by persons could be obtained by dividing the mortality rate of sex and age groups into the number of estates or into the amount of estates left at death by persons in that group. To obtain more accurate results, mortality rates for the higher occupational classes and not general mortality rates were used.

Publication of the basic tables required for these estimations was suspended during the early '30s but was resumed for England and Wales for 1936 and 1938. No such tables were published for the years of World War II. The only figures relating to Scotland were published for 1938, and these were not sufficiently complete. H. Campion, following his previous work carried out in conjunction with Professor G. W. Daniels, published in 1939 distributions for 1936, together with comparable figures for earlier years. Although in 1936 all except 5% of the total capital in personal ownership was above the estate duty exemption limit, it was very difficult to relate the number of estates in that class to the total in the country. The reason was that the ownership of estates by women and minors was common among the rich and hence it was not possible to estimate the number of families which were in the ownership of 95% of all personal property. As a device to overcome part of this difficulty, Campion took estates owned by persons over 25 and related them to all persons over 25

Table IX.—*Distribution of Property of Persons over 25 by Ranges of Capital England and Wales, 1911–13 and 1936*

Range of capital £	1911–13 Number of estates %	1911–13 Amount of capital %	1936 Number of estates %	1936 Amount of capital %
More than 100	11.6–13.4	89.7–93.4	23.5–25.9	94.6–97.2
More than 1,000	2.9–3.3	79.7–83.0	6.8–7.4	83.3–85.8
More than 5,000	0.8–0.9	64.0–67.0	1.8–2.0	65.3–67.5
More than 10,000	0.4	54.3–57.0	1.0	54.8–56.7
More than 25,000	0.1	40.3–42.4	0.4	39.1–40.5
More than 100,000	0.03	21.6–22.9	0.05	18.0–18.8

Source: H. Campion, *Public and Private Property in Great Britain* (1939). Where two figures are given these represent minimum and maximum estimates.

in the country. In Table IX cumulative percentage figures are given showing the distribution of property of persons over 25 for 1911–13 and 1936. Prices were about 50% higher in 1936 than in 1911–13 and incomes about doubled during the period.

It can be seen that the distribution of capital was much more unequal than the distribution of income. Whereas 0.4% of the number of persons had 12% of all personal income, they owned 40% of all personal capital; and the working classes (that is, those in the range of incomes less than about £250 in 1938) which had some 60% of the total income had only 5% of the total capital in personal ownership. Comparing 1936 with 1911–13, a tendency toward more equal distribution was noticeable. In 1911–13, about 1% of the number of persons owned almost 70% of the total capital; by 1936 this was reduced to 55%. But during the same period the ownership of estates by women became more common; allowing for this effect, the distribution of capital between families changed very little. There could have been some changes at the top of the pyramid, but the fundamental division between the top and the base did not change.

When all factors were taken into account it could be estimated that one-third of the number of families in Great Britain had estates over £100 in 1936 or thereabout; very little was known about the other two-thirds. Of 12,000,000 families in the country, 4,000,000 had more than £100 and sufficient details existed about the distribution of this number. Another 4,000,000, according to the estimate of J. Hilton (1944), owned just less than £100 in the period considered, while the remaining 4,000,000 had practically nothing.

British Commonwealth.—Turning to other British countries, no late information was available in 1946 for Australia. In connection with the census of 1933, data relating to the distribution of incomes were obtained, but C. Clark and J. G. Crawford (1944) showed conclusively that these data were defective; in particular there was a serious understatement of income by small independent producers. For the sake of completeness the figures are given in Table VII.

As the estimated number of occupied persons was only 2,175,000, it was clear that a large number of persons with small pensions or allowances must have been included, possibly in the lowest group.

In Canada, a pioneer study was carried out for 1942 and published alongside the national income estimates in 1946. The drawback of the publication was that agricultural incomes were not covered, as it was found impossible to obtain reliable information. The estimates, a summary of

Table X.—*Distribution of All Income Recipients in Non-Agricultural Occupations (including the Armed Services) by Ranges of Incomes, Canada, 1942.*

Range of Income $	Number of Incomes 000's	Number of Incomes %	Amount of Incomes $ million	Amount of Incomes %
Under 500	756	18.4	203	3.6
500– 1,000	1,091	26.5	828	14.8
1,000– 2,000	1,603	39.0	2,318	41.5
2,000– 5,000	598	14.6	1,595	28.5
5,000–10,000	47	1.1	311	5.6
10,000–25,000	14	0.3	205	3.7
25,000 and over	3	0.1	132	2.3
Total	4,112	100.0	5,592	100.0

Source: National Accounts: Income and Expenditure, 1938–1945 (Dominion bureau of statistics, Ottawa, 1946.)

which is given in Table X, were prepared by L. M. Read and were the result of co-operation between academic and government statisticians. Figures for higher ranges of income were based on income tax statistics. These were supplemented by data from the census of 1941 showing wage earners by income classes. The information coming from two distinct sources was then suitably adjusted. As agricultural incomes were excluded, together with income not allocated to the different ranges, the total of Canadian $5,600,000,000 in Table X covered only about one-half of the national income. In the original publication detailed distributions were given distinguishing married men on the one hand, and single men and women on the other. Also, separate distributions were given for each of the provinces. Starting from the study for 1942 it was expected that annual estimates would be published by the dominion bureau of statistics.

No estimates of the distribution of capital existed for Canada and Australia, except the 1915 Australian figures which were subject to gross understatement. Information on the distribution of income and wealth in other British countries, as far as it existed, was not sufficiently reliable to warrant inclusion.

Europe.—Statistics of European countries, other than the United Kingdom, were either discontinued during World War II or made irrelevant by postwar conditions. Such information as was available for prewar years was summarized and published in comparative form by C. Clark (1940). Owing to unsettled economic and financial conditions in most European countries, it was impossible, in 1946, to obtain useful figures. The Netherlands national income estimates, which follow the example of the British White Paper, did not contain the required information.

The outstanding exception was Sweden, where conditions remained stable during World War II and where excellent statistics existed already before the war. The Swedish *Statistical Yearbook* (in Swedish and French) published annual estimates and those for 1943 are summarized in Table XI.

Table XI.—*Distribution of Income by Ranges of Incomes, Sweden, 1943*

Range of income	Number of incomes		Amount of incomes	
Kr.	000's	%	Kr. million	%
Under 1,000	289	9.8	233	2.2
1,000– 2,000	750	25.4	1,108	10.2
2,000– 4,000	1,056	35.7	3,086	28.5
4,000– 8,000	683	23.1	3,647	33.7
8,000–15,000	131	4.4	1,359	12.6
15,000–30,000	37	1.2	720	6.6
30,000 and over	11	0.4	667	6.2
Total	2,957	100.0	10,820	100.0

Source: *Swedish Statistical Yearbook of 1945.*

The estimates are given in more detail in the original, distinguishing important occupational and social classes. The latest figures for distribution of capital referred to 1930 and were given in great detail in the same publication.

An attempt has been made in Tables X and XI to arrange the Canadian and Swedish income distribution in categories comparable with the relatively few categories of the British distribution in Table VIII. Approximately $5 or kr.15 could be taken as the equivalent of £1. Both the Canadian and the Swedish statistics disclosed a more equal distribution than the British, though it must be remembered that the Canadian distribution did not cover agricultural incomes. The richest 0.4% of the population had 6.0% of the total income in Canada, 6.2% in Sweden, but 12.0% in the United Kingdom. About one-quarter of the total income accrued to the richest 6% in Sweden and the richest 3% in the United Kingdom.

Table XII.—*Distribution of Taxation and Public Expenditure, United Kingdom, 1937*

Range of income	Amount of incomes	Amount of taxation	Amount of allocated expenditure			Excess of taxation over expenditure
			Social	Roads, etc.	Total	
£	£ million	£ million	£ million	£ million	£ million	£ million
Under 250	2,465	479	509	31	540	−61
250– 500	645	130	26	17	43	+87
500– 1,000	350	96	2	13	15	+81
1,000– 2,000	275	94	2	8	10	+84
2,000–10,000	450	199	1	9	10	+189
10,000 and over	225	160	0	2	2	+158
Total	4,410	1,158	540	80	620	+538

Source: T. Barna, *Redistribution of Incomes through Public Finance in 1937*(1945).

But the tables show distributions of income before taxation, and it was known that the taxation of the rich is highest in the United Kingdom. Apart from the distribution of incomes given in Table VIII, important statistics were available for the immediate prewar years in the form of family budget studies and social surveys which made it possible to prepare estimates as to the distribution of total taxation in the United Kingdom, as well as to the distribution of benefits derived from public expenditure, on the basis of which it was possible to estimate the amount redistributed from the rich to the poor. No similar estimates, except those showing the amount of taxation at selected levels of income, were available for other countries.

The estimates are given in summary form in Table XII. The number of incomes in the different ranges was about the same in 1937 as in 1938 and these are not shown. The amount of incomes differs from the figures shown in Table VIII in so far as here undistributed profits and other nonpersonal incomes are allocated to the different ranges but income from national insurance is excluded (and included in social expenditure). Of the total taxation of £1,160,000,000, some £480,000,000 was paid by those below £250 and £680,000,000 by the rest, about 15% of the population. Most social expenditure obviously benefited the poor. In addition to the bulk of social expenditure it was possible to allocate £80,000,000 in other expenditure, chiefly on the maintenance of roads. But certain other expenditure (for instance, expenditure on defense or general administration) could not be allocated to ranges of income without making certain assumptions. Even without these, the classes less than £250 received £60,000,000 more in benefits than they paid in taxation. Expenditure on defense and similar items together with the excess of interest on government debt over government interest on government property and the savings of public authorities came to £540,000,000. After making reasonable assumptions as to the allocation of this sum, it was estimated that, in 1937, £200,000,000–£250,000,000 was transferred from those above the £250 limit to those below it. This was equivalent to 5% of the national income. All taxation and public expenditures were included, that by central as well as local government. (*See* also BUDGETS, NATIONAL; CENSUS DATA, U.S.; INCOME AND PRODUCT.)

BIBLIOGRAPHY.—T. Barna, *Redistribution of Incomes through Public Finance in 1937* (1945); H. Campion, *Public and Private Property in Great Britain* (1939); C. Clark, *Conditions of Economic Progress* (1940); J. R. Hicks, *The Social Framework* (1942); J. Hilton, *Rich Man, Poor Man* (1944). (T. BAR.)

Weather

See METEOROLOGY.

Wedemeyer, Albert Coady

Wedemeyer (1897–), U.S. army officer, was born July 9, 1897, at Omaha, Neb. He was graduated from the U.S. Military academy in 1918, and from the Command and General Staff school in 1936. During World War II, he participated in the Sicilian landings (July 1943) as a combat commander under Gen. George S. Patton, Jr., and was appointed deputy chief of staff to Admiral Lord Louis Mountbatten, Allied commander in the Southeast Asia theatre in Oct. 1943. The following year, Wedemeyer succeeded Gen. Joseph W. Stilwell as commander of U.S. forces in China and as chief of staff to Generalissimo Chiang Kai-shek in the China theatre of operations. In Jan. 1945 he was promoted to the temporary rank of lieutenant general.

Weed Killers

See CHEMISTRY.

Welding

See ELECTRICAL INDUSTRIES; ELECTRONICS; METALLURGY.

Welles, Sumner

Welles (1892–), U.S. diplomat, was born Oct. 14, 1892, at New York city. Educated at Groton school in Massachusetts and at Harvard university, he started his career in the U.S. foreign service as a secretary in the U.S.

embassy at Tokyo (1915–17). He was chief of the Latin-American affairs division of the state department (1921–22), U.S. commissioner to the Dominican Republic in 1922, and President Coolidge's personal representative in Honduras in 1924. Welles was appointed assistant secretary of state April 6, 1933, holding this post, save for a short interim appointment as ambassador to Cuba in 1933, until May 1937, when he was appointed undersecretary of state.

In the spring of 1940, he undertook a "fact-finding" mission to Germany, Italy, France and Great Britain, conferring with both Allied and axis leaders. During 1941, he held many interviews with sundry European and Asiatic diplomats, and also initiated moves to settle the Ecuador-Peru clash in the summer of 1941. He headed the U.S. delegation to the Pan-American parley that opened at Rio de Janeiro on Jan. 15, 1942.

Increasing friction with Secretary Hull over questions of policy was said to have resulted in Welles' resignation, announced Sept. 25, 1943. Shortly afterward Welles began a syndicated column on foreign affairs. He also wrote two books, *The Time for Decision* (1944) and *Where Are We Heading?* (1946), both dealing with U.S. foreign policy.

West Africa, British

See BRITISH WEST AFRICA.

Western Australia

Politically, Western Australia ranks among the smaller states of the commonwealth. Physically it is the largest state of all; *c.* 975,920 sq.mi. in area and roughly one third of Australia. Pop.: (1937 est.) 462,500; (1946 census) 493,700 of whom 235,000 lived in the metropolitan area of Perth, the capital. During the decade 1937–46 the governorship was vacant. The position of lieutenant-governor was held by Sir James Mitchell (appointed July 1933). Prime ministers; John Collings Willcock (1936–45); Frank Joseph Scott (after Aug. 3, 1945).

Like all other Australian states, Western Australia's production during World War II reflected the heavy drain of manpower for military services and the intense concentration of available labour on the claims of other war activities. Western Australian enlistments were the highest in the commonwealth in proportion to population. Gold mining suffered heavily owing to voluntary enlistments and diversion of labour and machinery for military purposes. Before the outbreak of war the gold yield, mainly from the Golden Mile line of lode of Kalgoorlie, had reached its peak. Mining processes had been greatly improved, enabling the profitable working of ore of less than 8 dwt. The Big Bell, near Cue, owned by a U.S. company, was treating ore of as low a grade as 4 dwt. average and at a handsome profit.

In relation to the area of Western Australia, the population is small, but a great proportion of the state is suitable only for pastoral pursuits in which the percentage of labour to the square mile is low. Disastrous drought in the far northwest and the Murchison district, hit this primary industry heavily. Great areas of the pastoral districts in the northwest were without useful rain for seven years, and in parts of Murchison, drought lasted for ten years. The recuperative power of the pastoral country was amazing. In the Murchison district the country had been virtually denuded of vegetation, but within a few months heavy rains early in 1945 made the country ablaze with wild flowers of every colour and carpeted with herbage, all splendid sheep feed. The sheep "runs" in Western Australia, ranged from 500,000 to 1,000,000 ac. and in good seasons the larger properties carried 70,000 sheep. The long drought reduced sheep numbers by two-thirds, and all the skill and patience of pastoralists were required to preserve a nucleus of breeding ewes.

Western Australia had become a comparatively big wheat producer after World War I, but this industry too

Western Australia: *Statistical Data*

Item	1938		1941		1945	
	Value (000's omitted)	Amount or Number	Value (000's omitted)	Amount or Number	Value (000's omitted)	Amount or Number
Exchange rate						
Great Britain		£A 1.25 = £1		£A 1.25 = £1		£A 1.25 = £1
U.S.		£A 1 = $3.895		£A 1 = $3.198		£A 1 = $3.198
Finance						
State revenues	£8,619* ($42,140)		£9,067* ($36,560)		£11,073* ($44,625)	
State expenditures	£8,628 ($42,183)*		£9,059* ($36,524)		£11,069* ($44,609)	
State debt	£74,659* ($365,008)		£77,564* ($312,739)		£76,097* ($306,672)	
Transportation						
Railroads		4,374 mi.		4,381 mi.		4,381 mi.
Highways		2,973 mi.†		3,062 mi.†		...
Communication						
Telephones		34,210		38,116		42,934
Telegraph lines		12,057 mi.*		12,040 mi.*§		12,435 mi.*
Radio sets		79,262*‡		91,368*		98,210*
Minerals						
Gold		1,167,791 oz.		1,109,318 oz.		546,475 oz.‖
Coal		604,792 tons		556,574 tons		531,546 tons‖
Arsenic		3,999 tons		...		2,283 tons‖
Crops						
Wheat		1,086,750 tons		631,800 tons		496,500 tons¶
Hay		450,419 tons		375,143 tons		314,359 tons¶
Oats		69,830 tons		52,000 tons		63,425 tons¶
Apples		22,336 tons		26,842 tons§		37,451 tons¶
Livestock						
Sheep		9,177,531		9,722,780		10,020,299♀
Cattle		767,680		839,731		850,863♀
Horses		143,674		124,402		96,453♀
Swine		64,598		217,910§		163,604♀
Sea products						
Fish		2,921 tons		...		1,248 tons‖
Pearl-shell		1,015 tons		700 tons§		616 tons‖
Crayfish		56,202 doz.		...		39,223doz.‖
Manufactures—total	£6,479‡ ($28,733)	...	£7,514 ($30,320)♂	...	£9,400 ($37,928)¶	...
Industrial metals, machines, Implements, etc.	£1,858‡ ($8,241)	...	£2,554♂ ($10,304)	...	£4,037¶ ($16,291)	...
Food, drink and tobacco	£1,742‡ ($7,725)	...	£1,874 ($7,560)♂	...	£2,169¶ ($8,750)	...
Woodworking and basketware	£658‡ ($2,919)	...	£713 ($2,875)♂	...	£751¶ ($3,032)	...
Paper, printing and binding	£536‡ ($2,375)	...	£480 ($1,938)♂	...	£478¶ ($1,928)	...
Education						
State schools		836		762		680‖
Enrolment		61,580		57,490		55,827‖
Teachers		2,379		2,378		2,050‖
Private schools		146		159		146‖
Enrolment		14,320		15,688		16,861‖
Teachers		644		688		675‖
Universities		1		1♂		1‖
Enrolment		924		604♂		833‖
Teachers		67		71♂		77‖
Technical schools		5		8		...
Enrolment		5,382		6,299		...
Teachers		155		229		...

*Year ending June 30. †Declared main roads only. ‡1939. §1940. ‖1943. ¶1944. ♀Year ending March 31. ♂1942.

had suffered from seasonal variations, and the reduction of the area cropped when the price of wheat fell to an unprofitable figure. Production in the southwest, where the rainfall exceeds 50 in., had made considerable progress, and there are great forests of hardwoods, notably the tough and heavy jarrah and the magnificent karri, towering straight as gun barrels, to 140 ft. to the first branch. A sound forest policy assured the permanence of the valuable timber industry. Dairying had also made strides in this fertile part of western Australia.

BIBLIOGRAPHY.—*Statistical Register of Western Australia* and *Pocket Year Book of Western Australia,* both published annually by the Government Statistician; *Quarterly Statistical Abstract,* published by the Government Statistician; J. Gintilli, *Atlas of Western Australian Agriculture* (1941). (GE. B.)

West Indies

An archipelago between Florida and the South American coast opposite the mouth of the Orinoco River, the West Indies group is less commonly known as the Antilles. The West Indies include the Greater Antilles (in order of size, Cuba, Haiti or Hispaniola, Jamaica and Puerto Rico), the Lesser Antilles including a large number of islands between Puerto Rico and the Venezuelan coast, the Bahama group northeast of Cuba, and certain more distant islands, including Curaçao, Aruba and Bonaire near the mouth of Lake Maracaibo in Venezuela. The land area is approximately 92,000 sq.mi. The population, estimated in 1945 at more than 15,000,000, is approximately 75% white and 25% Negro and mulatto in Cuba and Puerto Rico and from 80% to 100% Negro and mulatto elsewhere, except that in Trinidad about 40% is of East Indian origin. The religion is predominantly Roman Catholic; the languages used include Spanish, English, French and Dutch, in addition to various African dialects. Politically, the West Indies include the three independent republics of Cuba, Haiti and the Dominican Republic, two United States territories (Puerto Rico and the Virgin Islands), six British colonies (the Bahamas, Barbados, Jamaica, the Leeward Islands, Trinidad and Tobago and the Windward Islands), two French colonies (Guadeloupe and Martinique) and one Netherlands colony (Curaçao). In addition to prewar bases, five of the eight U.S. naval bases, sites for which were obtained from Great Britain in 1940, were built in the West Indies.

Economic Disruption.—The West Indies, an area of colonial economy, suffered grave economic dislocation in 1937 and later. The considerable oversupply of sugar in the world's markets especially seriously affected Cuba and other West Indian islands, where sugar is the principal agricultural product. The British islands in particular were adversely affected. One consequence of the disturbed economy was the greater fluidity of the agricultural population, resulting in considerable peasant migration from one island to another and from the islands to mainland areas. The most serious result was the massacre of several thousand Haitian peasant farm workers in the fall of 1937 after they had filtered across the border of the Dominican Republic for longer or shorter periods. Several of the units in the West Indies, notably Cuba, however, expelled migratory agricultural labourers in 1937–38 in order to reduce competition with their own labouring classes.

The economic impact of the European war brought serious repercussions in the West Indies, depending, as most portions of the area did, either on export of staple agricultural products or on the tourist trade. Certain islands, notably Cuba and the Bahamas, anticipated that the arbitrary cessation of a tourist flow to Europe would divert much of it to them. It was also expected that the blocking of normal extra-American sources of supply of products in which the West Indies competed would ultimately result in an improvement of that area's commercial position.

Effects of World War II upon the West Indies during 1940 were primarily of three sorts: the acquisition by the United States of several sites for development of naval and air bases, the plight of the French colonies following the collapse of France in June and the general problem of the future of European possessions in the Caribbean, as climaxed in the second Inter-American conference of foreign ministers at Havana, Cuba, in July. The development involving naval bases concerned primarily the British colonies (where all of the leased sites were located), but in a general way it affected the entire archipelago as constituting a potential defense arc off the Atlantic terminus of the Panama canal. The executive agreement between Prime Minister Winston Churchill and President Roosevelt for the 99-year lease of naval base sites in exchange for 50 overage destroyers was formally consummated by an exchange of notes on Sept. 2, 1940, following which inspections, surveys and construction proceeded rapidly in the locations immediately involved. The institution of the Vichy regime in France posed a problem for the American republics because of the presence of a pro-Vichy administrator, Adm. Georges A. Robert, as governor of Martinique. The strategic location of Martinique and Guadeloupe, the internment there of various planes and units of the French fleet and the storage of large amounts of French gold made those colonies of concern to the hemisphere until 1943, when agents of Gen. Charles de Gaulle succeeded to the administration of the colonies.

Political-Strategic Question Marks.—The rapid conquest of the Netherlands and France in the spring of 1940 and the fear that Great Britain might soon suffer the same fate caused the convening at Havana on July 21, 1940, of the second foreign ministers' conference, with the question of the disposition of European possessions in Middle America, in the case of a German attempt to control them, as the chief topic on the agenda. Other and more remote European possessions, such as the Falkland Islands, the mainland colonies of British Guiana and British Honduras, and the northern French colony of St. Pierre and Miquelon, were theoretically involved, but the main attention of the conference centred on the European colonies in the West Indies. The formula for "provisional administration" of those possessions by one or more American republics, in the case of later contingencies, represented a considerable advance in international co-operation in the hemisphere.

The political and military contingencies anticipated by the American foreign offices in 1940 did not materialize, but the West Indies felt a more extreme economic impact from World War II in 1941. The normal trade of the European colonies had been largely with their respective mother countries. Although inevitable wartime reorientation threw it chiefly to the United States, it was seriously interrupted by the lack of adequate shipping because of submarine losses and diversion to more important wartime purposes; normal imports were also severely curtailed by the unavailability of consumer goods to be imported from the U.S. Large surpluses of many products began to accumulate, but by the latter part of 1941, and especially after the spread of the war to the Pacific, sugar (the most important product), long under restriction because of world overproduction, came into heavy demand. Piled-up stocks were generally cleared, and 1942 crops were contracted for in advance. Cuba, Trinidad and some other islands where mineral resources were known to exist undertook more careful surveys of such resources in order to learn more definitely what might be exploited for the war effort. The Netherland islands of Curaçao and Aruba, long famous as one of the world's largest centres of the oil refining industry, were especially subject to economic dislocation, but ultimately began a huge program of enlargement of their industrial facilities and capacity. Communications facilities by sea were seriously interrupted as early as 1941 but those by air began to be expanded.

The course of developments in the West Indies during 1942 continued to be dominated by the war. With the exception of the French colonies, the position of which remained anomalous, the entire archipelago was not only at war with the axis powers, but was a combat area as well. Submarine attacks and ship losses became commonplace. These, coupled with the extensive diversion of shipping needed for more immediate belligerent purposes, served to disrupt trade seriously. Sugar continued to be in abnormally heavy demand, but shipping shortages prevented the export of a large portion of the crop from many of the islands, even from Cuba, one of the world's largest producers and located only about 100 mi. from the United States mainland. The greatly increased need for mineral resources focused some attention during the year on Jamaica, where existence of bauxite deposits was reported. Perhaps the most important political development of the year affecting the West Indies was the creation by Great Britain and the United States, on March 9, 1942, of the Anglo-American Caribbean commission, designed to study and make recommendations with regard to the economic and social problems and needs of the possessions of those two countries in the Caribbean area. By 1944 the scope of the commission's activity and support became enlarged to include the possessions of France and the Netherlands in the West Indies and the Guianas on the South American mainland.

The main political development in 1943 was the shift in the political status of the French colonies from allegiance to the Vichy regime to control by the French Committee of Liberation under Gen. Charles de Gaulle. Popular reaction in the French islands had long been sympathetic to the Allied cause, and the change in administration brought the entire archipelago, for the first time in its history, into war with a common enemy. The effectiveness of the Allied naval and air patrol in Caribbean and Atlantic waters considerably reduced the submarine menace to West Indian shipping, although the sector continued to be a combat area. Construction work on naval and air base facilities, in the British leased sites and elsewhere, tapered off before the end of 1943, and United States and other Allied use of such bases greatly increased the effectiveness of defense of the islands and the Middle American mainland. Employment and other economic conditions during 1943 showed great variation in different parts of the West Indies. Trinidad and Curaçao, for example, were centres of war production and hence flourishing, but Jamaica, more nearly completely agricultural, suffered greatly from inability to ship her products.

The year 1944 was marked by a continued decline of the submarine activity which had harassed the West Indies for three years, with a consequent recovery in exporting and other economic activity. Restoration of more nearly normal peacetime trade was hampered in part, however, by a serious hurricane which swept through parts of the West Indies in the latter half of Aug. 1944, ravishing large agricultural areas and adversely affecting production and exporting for months thereafter; Jamaica was especially hard hit by the hurricane. The various West Indian colonies and independent states were all concerned in 1944 with efforts to effect readjustments in anticipation of peace. An important step toward that end was the holding of the first West Indian conference, at Bridgetown, the capital of Barbados, in March, under the auspices of the Anglo-American Caribbean commission, but participated in by representatives of French and Netherland possessions as well. The conference was concerned mainly with economic and social problems and proposals for long-range planning and public-works construction.

Readjustment to Peace.—Economic dislocation was general in many parts of the West Indies in 1945, with the ending of World War II, and the principal general problem was readjustment to peacetime conditions. The return to their previous island homes of many persons employed during the war in the Canal Zone or in the United States aggravated an unemployment condition which already was serious in certain areas. Another factor intensifying the impact was the cessation or tapering off of various wartime agricultural ventures by the United States, especially its programs of encouragement of rubber and abacá production in various West Indian islands. The British government took steps in certain of its colonies to grant a liberalized franchise and increased autonomy. Tentative suggestions were advanced in various quarters during 1945 for mutual tariff reductions among the several West Indian units, with the eventual objective of creation of a free trade area. It was difficult to approach that problem, however, since it involved not only the British colonies, but the other three powers as well; the independent states did not figure in such discussions to any important extent. The end of the war brought the prospect of considerable improvement in communications and transportation facilities, especially with regard to air services. Both the British West Indian airways and KLM (Royal Dutch air lines) announced plans for expansion of their services, while Pan American airways in certain instances enlarged and in others contracted its services.

A joint conference, with participation by representatives of British, United States, French and Netherland possessions in the West Indies, met at St. Thomas, U.S. Virgin Islands, beginning Feb. 21, 1946, to consider problems of the area. Parts of the West Indies, but very largely the Dominican Republic, were severely affected by a series of earthquakes (with resulting tidal waves) beginning Aug. 4, 1946; the quakes were among the heaviest ever recorded in the West Indies, although loss of life was far less than in the volcanic eruption in Martinique in 1902.

(*See* also BAHAMAS; CUBA; CURAÇAO; DOMINICAN REPUBLIC; FRENCH COLONIAL EMPIRE; HAITI; PUERTO RICO; VIRGIN ISLANDS; WEST INDIES, BRITISH.)

BIBLIOGRAPHY.—*The West Indies Year Book* (annual); *The South American Handbook* (annual); (*Foreign Commerce Weekly; The Inter-American* (New York, monthly); *Canada-West Indies Magazine* (Montreal, monthly); *Colonial Review* (London, quarterly); W. M. Macmillan, *Warning from the West Indies* (1938); A. Macmillan, *The West Indies, Past and Present* (1938); J. W. Vandercook, *Caribbean Cruise* (1938); J. F. Rippy, *The Caribbean Danger Zone* (1940); R. R. Platt (ed.), *The European Possessions in the Caribbean Area* (1941); H. Follett, *Islands on Guard* (1943). (R. H. FN.)

West Indies, British

Single islands and groups in the Caribbean sea, the British West Indies are organized politically as six British crown colonies. They are: Bahama Islands (*q.v.*), Barbados,

 Jamaica and dependencies, the Leeward Islands, Trinidad and Tobago and the Windward Islands. Jamaica is the third in size of the four islands comprising the Major Antilles. The Leeward Islands and the Windward Islands (and Barbados) form a large part of the Lesser Antilles. Trinidad is a single island just north of the Orinoco river delta. The total area (excluding the Bahamas) is approximately 8,065 sq.mi. and the total estimated pop. (1946), 2,397,567; earlier estimates of pop. were: 1940, 2,233,000; 1944, 2,347,113; 1945, 2,366,949. No census had been taken, except in 1943 in Jamaica and dependencies, after 1931 (in some cases earlier); the British government made plans in 1945 to take early census in the remaining units. Density of the different islands varies greatly, that of Barbados (almost 1,300 per sq.mi.) is one of the highest of any political unit in the world. The racial composition of the population is from 75% to almost 100% Negro, although the population of Trinidad was estimated to include 180,509 East Indians and a small number of Chinese. Aboriginal Indians have almost entirely disappeared, though on St. Vincent and Dominica a few Indian-white and Indian-Negro descendants remain.

The political organization of the different islands reflects no uniformity and various anomalies. Each of the colonies has a royally appointed governor. Barbados has an executive council, a legislative council of 10 nominated members and a house of assembly with 24 elected members. Jamaica has an executive council of 10 members (5 elected by the house of representatives from their own members), a legislative council (with a majority of non-officials) and a house of representatives with 32 members elected by universal suffrage. The Cayman Islands and the Turks and Caicos Islands are political dependencies of Jamaica; the latter, 450 mi. northeast of Jamaica, are geographically a part of the Bahamas. The Leeward Islands have a general federal type of government. A general legislative council with an ex officio membership of eight plus nine elected non-officials represents all of the islands in the colony; a separate legislature for local affairs serves each of three of the constituent presidencies (all except the Virgin Islands, for which the governor is directly responsible). The Leeward and Windward Islands have joint police and judicial officials. Trinidad has an executive council of 8 members and a legislative council of 18, each council including some officials ex officio and some non-official members, both nominated and elected. The Windward Islands are not federalized, lacking a common legislature, laws, revenues, or tariffs; they do unite for certain purposes, however. The governor of the colony is ex officio administrator of Grenada. Each of the constituent islands or island groups has its own legislative council. British Guiana (on the South American mainland) and British Honduras (adjoining Guatemala) are for some purposes regarded as within the British West Indies; after 1940, for example, they, together with the island colonies, had a common comptroller for development and welfare, with whom were associated advisers in special fields.

Post-Depression Turmoil.—The effects of the world depression of the 1930s were felt especially heavily in the West Indies, with their primary reliance on export of agricultural staples, particularly sugar, which were largely at the mercy of world markets. The result was that low price levels for exports accentuated an already severe unemployment problem. This in turn led to general unrest and to serious labour riots in Jamaica, Trinidad, Barbados and elsewhere. The British government in consequence established on Aug. 5, 1938 a West-Indies royal commission (informally known as the Moyne commission from its chairman, Lord Walter G. Moyne) to investigate social and economic conditions in the British Caribbean colonies and British Honduras and British Guiana. The commission made a prolonged study and published a portion of its formal report in Feb. 1940. Its main recommendations were for the establishment of a West Indies welfare fund, to be financed by an annual grant of £1,400,000. In the field of social services, it urged improvement of educational facilities, the establishment of a unified health policy and betterment of housing conditions. Great stress was put on the acute problem of labour relations, with recommendations for a labour adviser, a system of wage boards and industrial courts, and consideration of unemployment insurance, improved factory regulations and workmen's compensation. In the economic field, the commission took cognizance of world overproduction of the principal West Indies agricultural products and the problem of increasing overpopulation, and, after approving an increased sugar quota, gave qualified endorsement to government support of industrial enterprises. For agriculture itself, the commission recommended a centralization of agricultural policies and direction and increase of agricultural education, along with special soil surveys and inquiries into various means of developing forms of agriculture best suited to the region, with stress on the production of foodstuffs for local consumption, and development of a comprehensive land settlement program. Consideration was also given to an improved communications policy.

The long-continued agitation for complete self-government based on universal suffrage was met by a commission recommendation of political federation as an ultimate, but not immediate, end, with a greater actual participation of elected representatives and a substantial reduction in the qualifications required of elected members of legislative councils. Political federation, the commission felt, should first be given a practical test through merger of the Leeward and Windward Islands administration, using the existing Leeward Islands government as a model. Need for betterment of appointive administrative personnel was also stressed. The Moyne report was generally well received in both Great Britain and the West Indies, and its recommendations were the bases of the subsequent Colonial Development and Welfare act, passed by parliament in July 1940. This act authorized sums for colonial research, development and welfare, with an immediate expenditure in the tropical American colonies of £350,000 through grants-in-aid, including £27,810 in the Windward colonies.

In Jan. 1939 following the end of a general strike which had paralyzed Jamaica economically, the insular government promised economic and social reforms, but when it failed to put them into effect immediately a strike of water front workers in mid-February brought new disturbances and obliged the governor to proclaim a state of emergency for several days. Underlying unrest continued until after the Moyne report. Following the Moyne report and the parliamentary legislation of 1940, Sir Frank Stockdale, a comptroller and a veteran in colonial service, proceeded to the West Indies and, with his advisers, visited practically every island in that area. In a report published as a white paper in 1943, he outlined approved schemes for bettering public health, agriculture and communications. The report was prefaced by a brief description of the natural advantages and disadvantages of each colony and an account of the problems to be solved. In the meantime, instead of setting up the proposed welfare fund, it had been decided that the West Indies were to share in the general financial provisions made by the development and welfare act of 1940, fixed at £5,000,000 annually for ten years.

Immediate Impact of War.—The outbreak of World War II in Sept. 1939 had prompt repercussions throughout the British West Indies, and the colonies at once put themselves on a war footing. Jamaica and Trinidad granted their respective governors emergency powers and imposed press censorship. Price regulation was resorted to in an effort to hold down the mounting cost of living, and a licence system for imports was established. This system was made necessary by the decline of the pound sterling in terms of the dollar, and the consequent shortage of dollar exchange. In spite of the various restraints imposed, the first month of war saw heavy price increases, especially in Jamaica, and a retrenchment in that colony's public works program and other governmental activity as a result of rising costs. Nevertheless, the agricultural situation was regarded as satisfactory, especially in Trinidad, where the outlook was for higher agricultural prices. A sharp wave of indignation swept the entire British West Indies in Oct. 1939 when it was proposed in the United States senate that the United States should seize the British islands as the only means of obtaining repayment of the British debt to that country.

A much more significant development involving the British West Indies was the Roosevelt-Churchill agreement of mid-summer in 1940 for the trade of overage destroyers for naval base sites. The executive agreement was crystallized and definitely formulated in an exchange of notes between the two governments on Sept. 2, 1940, under which Great Britain made available to the United States "for immediate establishment and use of naval and air bases and facilities for entrance thereto and protection thereof" sites in Newfoundland, Bermuda, the Bahamas, Jamaica, the Leeward and Windward Islands, Trinidad and British Guiana. These were to be leased to the United States for 99 years, free of all charges other than those necessary to compensate owners of private property. Several high United States naval and other officials, including Secretary of the Navy Frank Knox, visited the West Indies during the remaining months of 1940, and in December President Roosevelt himself made a tour of inspection. Some difficulties were encountered in selection of a specific site on Trinidad, regarded by many as the most important location of all. United States officials objected to allocation of a swampy area for an air and naval base, though colonial officials preferred that because of its isolation from heavily populated districts.

These difficulties were adjusted in Jan. 1941 and a definitive agreement was signed at London on March 27 replacing the tentative agreements of the previous year. Sites in Jamaica included a fleet anchorage of two sq.mi. in Portland bight, the Portland ridge peninsula shoreline, Manatee bay shoreline and adjacent areas and the 50-ac. Pigeon Island; the total area was about 55 sq.mi. Two tracts on Antigua in the Leeward Islands were obtained at Parham harbour and on Judge's bay, totalling about 700 ac. Trinidad facilities, totalling about 25,000 ac., included 4 air and naval base areas on the west coast, special anchorage rights in the Gulf of Paria and wharfage facilities at Port of Spain. Six areas on St. Lucia in the Windwards aggregated about 1,300 ac. and included Gros Islet bay and an airfield at Vieux port.

Prior to 1940 the only fortified places in the British West Indies had been Barbados, St. Lucia and Jamaica, all used primarily as coaling stations. The United States in 1940 rushed construction at the sites it had gained, and affected formal occupation during that year. Economic effects of the construction work were felt in some instances, notably in Trinidad, with labour shortages, rising wage scales and stimulated buying power. The labour shortage in Trinidad—the greatest single centre of development with an expenditure of more than $17,000,000 involved—necessitated relaxing of the immigration restrictions to permit the entry of Barbadian and other agricultural labour. The local expenditure alone in Jamaica was estimated at in excess of £1,000,000. Construction work was largely completed in 1941, and the tapering off of employment in 1942 brought repercussions, accentuated by the fact that construction wages had been greatly in excess of local standards. Heavy pay rolls for United States defense personnel and some continuing construction were an economic factor almost throughout World War II, however, and continued to swell savings bank deposits in several islands.

Caribbean Commission.—An Anglo-United States agreement of March 9, 1942, established the Anglo-American Caribbean commission (A.A.C.C.). This body, consisting of six members (three from each country), was designed to deal primarily "with matters pertaining to labour, agriculture, housing, health, education, social welfare, finance and related subjects in territories under British and United States flags," and to advise the respective governments. Sir Frank Stockdale and Charles W. Taussig of the United States served as the original co-chairmen of the commission. Stockdale's headquarters were in Barbados, but a permanent secretariat was established in Washington, with secretaries of the British and United States sections respectively. Confronted with urgent problems arising from the submarine menace in the Caribbean, the commission concerned itself with the regulation of food imports and increasing local production, with the importation of goods from Canada and the United States and the ships to carry them, and with formation of a schooner pool for the better utilization of local vessels in interisland trade. A fishing survey was also organized, the position of the sugar industry was examined, and the problem of venereal disease was attacked. Organization of the commission was modified somewhat in June 1945. Membership for each country was increased to four, with two of the British representatives nonofficial West Indians. Sir John Stuart Macpherson succeeded Sir Frank Stockdale in 1945 as British co-chairman, with headquarters in Kingston, Jamaica. The territorial scope of the commission's interests had been broadened to include, first, Netherlands, and then French representatives; it then functioned as a Caribbean commission and on July 15, 1946, Lawrence W. Cramer, former governor of the (U.S.) Virgin Islands, was appointed secretary general.

The Caribbean Research council was established provisionally in 1943 as an advisory body to the A.A.C.C. It was made permanent on March 1, 1945, with headquarters and a central secretariat in the West Indies and with five subcommittees dealing with agriculture, nutrition, fisheries, and forestry; building and engineering research; industries; public health and medicine and social sciences. A further development was the formation of the West Indian conference in 1944 to discuss and formulate plans for inter-colonial co-operation. Membership included two delegates from each British colony and each United States territory in the West Indies. The first meeting of the

Members of the Trinidad royal volunteer reserve servicing guns aboard a minesweeper after patrol duty in 1944. The service was organized in 1939 and operated by the British admiralty with recruits drawn from all areas in the West Indies

conference was at Bridgetown, Barbados, March 21–30, 1944, with delegates and representatives from Great Britain and the United States, the various British Caribbean colonies, and observers from Canada and the Netherlands West Indies (including Surinam). Included in the agenda were plans for raising nutritional levels and increasing local food production, fisheries development, postwar absorption of war workers and veterans, industrial development, quarantine and health protection, and long-term public works construction through regional planning boards and an international Caribbean planning commission as part of the A.A.C.C. To these various ends, the conference recommended enactment of uniform legislation in the various political units affected and a continued interchange of the results of different research projects already sponsored by the commission. It urged the development of secondary industries, where feasible, as a means of diversification and of satisfying local needs, and recommended economic surveys and development of transportation and resources in British Guiana and British Honduras which, though mainland colonies, came within the scope of the commission.

The War Moves Closer.—The British West Indies were much more acutely affected by World War II in 1942 than at any time previously. For the first time, actual hostilities were carried on within their territorial waters. Submarine sinkings and the diversion of ships for the transportation of supplies to overseas war fronts seriously impeded the exportation of agricultural products and sharply reduced the volume of imports. Submarines were active especially in the middle months of 1942. Shipping anchored in Carlisle bay, Barbados, was attacked in September. Later in the year the submarine menace abated but did not disappear. Interisland and external trade was badly disrupted. The islands undertook programs of agricultural self-sufficiency. Barbados made it compulsory to devote fixed percentages of land area to food crops and livestock. Other colonies subsidized acreage put in foodstuffs and guaranteed minimum price returns. Licensing of imports curtailed or prevented use of shipping space for non-essentials, and, to achieve maximum efficiency in the importation of necessities, official buying pools were set up. Exportation of commodities needed for local consumption was forbidden. As an antidote to the acute economic ailments, the British government undertook to purchase the entire crops of certain agricultural products in 1942, notably Jamaica's bananas, citrus and sugar, even when shipping space and available markets were entirely lacking. Financial advances were made for specific projects, especially those furthering agricultural diversification and self-sufficiency.

The decreased menace of axis submarines in West Indian waters in 1943 resulted in a less acutely felt shipping shortage than in 1942. Living costs soared in many of the islands, and rationing and price controls were necessary on many commodities. Employment and other economic conditions were varied in 1943; Trinidad, for example, suffered from a manpower shortage that seriously affected harvesting of crops, while Jamaica was faced with an unemployment problem. Jamaican banana exports by 1943 had fallen to about 6% of the 1938 figure. Some 9,435 Jamaican agricultural labourers went to the United States under contract in mid-1943, and by the end of the year their money order remittances to the island exceeded £100,000. The West Indian colonies continued to be the principal recipients of colonial development and welfare loans and grants during 1943, being allotted more than £2,500,000 of a total of £4,500,000. These included projects for road construction in the Leewards, rural health, a food storage plant in Grenada and numerous others. The total cost of West Indian schemes approved by 1943 was about two-thirds of all expenditures sanctioned under the parliamentary act for the whole empire down to that date. The trend toward nationalization was further evidenced by the action of the government of Trinidad in acquiring 50% of the shares of the British West Indian airways, principal aviation company operating in the British West Indies, and offering them for sale by popular subscription or to such West Indian colonial governments as might be interested. Several imperial grants were made in 1944 under the development and welfare act in furtherance of the general recommendations of the Bridgetown conference. Especially noteworthy was a £525,000 free grant for a five-year agricultural program in Jamaica recommended by the agricultural adviser for the West Indies.

Reform Measures.—Improvement of West Indian educational facilities began to receive official consideration in 1944. The West India committee of the royal commission on higher education in the colonies, headed by Sir James C. Irvine, visited the various colonies in that year and in its report, published in July 1945, recommended that a University of the West Indies be established in Jamaica, with faculties of agriculture and agricultural sciences, arts and sciences, and medicine, and departments of education and extramural studies. The capital cost of the project was estimated at £1,130,000; the committee proposed that it should be provided by the British government, although maintenance would be met by contributions from the colonial governments involved and by endowments and fees. A further educational proposal advanced in 1945 was that the government and denominational teacher-training institutions in Trinidad should be replaced by a central training institute which would serve the Leeward and Windward Islands as well.

Discussion of domestic and inter-colonial constitutional

West Indies (British), Windward Islands: *Statistical Data*

Item	1938 Value (000's omitted)	1938 Amount or Number	1940 Value (000's omitted)	1940 Amount or Number	1944 Value (000's omitted)	1944 Amount or Number
Exchange rate		£1 = $4.889		£1 = $3.83		£1 = $4.035
Finance						
Government revenues						
Grenada	£169 ($825)				£287 ($1,160)*	
St. Lucia	£94 ($462)				£194 ($781)*	
St. Vincent	£102 ($499)				£117 ($473)*	
Government expenditures						
Grenada	£172 ($841)				£236 ($952)*	
St. Lucia	£105 ($514)				£166 ($668)*	
St. Vincent	£97 ($473)				£138 ($555)*	
Crops						
Grenada						
Cacao		4,781 tons				3,234 tons
Nutmegs		2,315 "				3,054 "
Bananas		2,927 "				220 "
St. Lucia						
Sugar cane		88,511 tons				61,765 tons
Bananas		4,125 "				...
St. Vincent						
Sugar cane		26,880 tons				24,640 tons
Arrowroot (starch)		4,425 "				3,600 "
Dominica†						
Bananas						1,134 tons
Exports						
Grenada—total	£315 ($1,539)	...	£292 ($1,120)	...	£592 ($2,389)*	...
Cocoa (raw)	£127 ($621)	4,781 tons	£113 ($434)	3,139 tons	£192 ($775)*	3,937 tons*
Nutmegs	£75 ($365)	2,031 "	£80 ($305)	2,347 "	£269 ($1,085)*	2,543 tons*
Mace and other spices	£39 ($192)	559 "	£40 ($152)	307 "	£70 ($282)*	375 tons*
St. Lucia—total	£127 ($619)	...	£140 ($538)	...	£142 ($573)*	...
Sugar (vacuum pan)	£65 ($316)	8,743 tons	£69 ($266)	7,768 tons	£67 ($270)*	6,849 tons*
Lime oil	£8 ($41)	1,327 gal.	£3 ($13)	6,301 gal.	£9 ($36)*	875 gal.*
St. Vincent—total	£211 ($1,030)	...	£238 ($913)	...	£166 ($670)*	...
Arrowroot	£92 ($448)	4,090 tons	£110 ($423)	4,606 tons	£97 ($391)*	3,807 tons*
Cotton (sea island)	£60 ($295)	344 "	£68 ($261)	332 tons	£42 ($169)*	193 tons*
Dominica†—total	£78 ($381)	...	£92 ($354)‡	...	£144 ($581)*	...
Lime oil (distilled)	...	13 tons	£20 ($77)	12 tons	£47 ($190)*	17 tons*
Lime juice (raw)	...	150,424 gal.	£10 ($38)	179,830 gal.	£8 ($32)*	183,067 gal.*
Limes	...	3,789 bbl.	£7 ($27)	5,370 bbl.	£1 ($4)*	605 bbl.*
Imports						
Grenada—total	£304 ($1,485)	...	£355 ($1,359)	...	£429 ($1,731)*	...
Flour	£39 ($192)	3,696 tons	£44 ($169)	4,050 tons	£62 ($250)*	3,544 tons*
Cotton cloth	£20 ($97)	1,103,123 yd.	£22 ($84)	946,920 yd.	£53 ($214)*	898,569 yd.*
St. Lucia—total	£189 ($926)	...	£242 ($925)	...	£387 ($1,562)*	...
Wheat flour	£21 ($102)	1,669 tons	£26 ($99)	2,222 tons	£48 ($194)*	2,626 tons*
Cotton cloth	£16 ($77)	767,007 yd.	£19 ($74)	732,056 yd.	£50 ($202)*	845,395 yd.*
St. Vincent—total	£199 ($972)	...	£249 ($952)	...	£327 ($1,319)*	...
Wheat flour and meal	£21 ($105)	1,822 tons	£23 ($88)	1,117 tons	£37 ($149)*	2,051 tons*
Cotton cloth	£16 ($79)	828,665 yd.	£20 ($78)	679,417 yd.	£49 ($198)*	1,216,012 yd.*
Dominica†—total	£103 ($504)	...	£114 ($438)	...	£244 ($985)*	...
Grain, flour, etc.	...	968 tons	£14 ($55)	1,164 tons	£35 ($141)*	1,865 tons*
Cotton piece goods	...	...	£11 ($42)	416,705 yd.	£46 ($186)*	792,660 yd.*
Education						
Grenada						
Primary schools				53		53*
Students				16,785		17,135*
Secondary schools				4		4*
Students				493		561*
St. Lucia						
Primary schools				45§		45*
Students				10,808§		11,477*
Secondary schools				2		2*
Students				188		223*
St. Vincent						
Primary schools				36§		37*
Students				10,791§		10,603*
Secondary schools				2§		2*
Students				176§		263*
Dominica						
Primary schools				33§		33*
Students				7,420§		7,545*
Secondary schools				3§		3*
Students				73§‖		86*‖

*1943. †Part of Leeward Islands before Jan. 1, 1940.
‡Including re-exports of £112 ($43).

§1941.
‖Figures for 2 schools only.

changes in the British West Indies had crystallized as early as 1940; Jamaica and Trinidad were the colonies first concerned. Changes proposed in that year (and in 1941 for Jamaica) did not entirely meet the demands of the island's semi-socialistic People's National party, although they generally met with qualified approval. Discussion of political modernization in Jamaica proceeded through 1942 and 1943 but it was not until Nov. 20, 1944, that the new constitution could be promulgated. It was understood that it would be tried out for a full electoral period of five years. Elections for the Jamaican house of representatives in Dec. 1944 resulted in an overwhelming victory for the Labour party, which obtained 23 seats; the People's National party won 4, the Independents 5 and the Democratic party none.

Proposals for inter-colonial political federation, either functional or organic, extended back to the time of the Moyne report and earlier. A short initial step had been taken through the establishment of limited joint administrative and judicial services for the Leeward and Windward Islands. Later in World War II, however, and especially in 1945, more far-reaching proposals were repeatedly and thoroughly discussed. Oliver Stanley, secretary of state for the colonies, addressed a letter in March 1945 to the governors of the eight British Middle American colonies (six in the West Indies plus British Honduras and British Guiana) proposing that their peoples give consideration to the advantages of political federation. He argued that greater economic stability would result, administrative costs could be cut and efficiency increased, and that such a federation might anticipate an ultimate status of self-government comparable to that of a dominion. The proposal was not too well received in the Bahamas but met a generally favourable reaction elsewhere. The British proposals were motivated in part by the desire to make the colonies more nearly self-supporting financially. The British government indicated in 1945 that it would gradually cease extending subsidies to Jamaica over a five to ten-year period. On the other hand, the mother government's financial assistance in certain directions continued on a generous scale. Under the terms of the Development and Welfare act of 1940, the West Indian colonies had received, to March 31, 1945, a total of £8,690,113 (including £1,263,-492 in loans, £60,030 for grants for research, and the re-

West Indies (British), Trinidad and Tobago: *Statistical Data*

Item	1938 Value (000's omitted)	1938 Amount or Number	1941 Value (000's omitted)	1941 Amount or Number	1943 Value (000's omitted)	1943 Amount or Number
Exchange rate		1 trinidad $* =$1.7165		1 trinidad $* =84.06 cents		1 trinidad $* =84.06 cents
Finance						
Government revenues	£4,721 ($23,079)		£3,405 ($13,043)†		£6,076 ($24,517)	
Government expenditures	£4,294 ($20,993)		£4,503 ($17,248)†		£6,019 ($24,288)	
National debt	£6,927 ($33,867)		£4,207 ($16,112)†		£5,652 ($22,806)	
Transportation						
Railroads		123 mi.		123 mi.		123 mi.
Highways		1,846 mi.		1,845 mi.		1,841 mi.
Communication						
Telephones		5,869				9,678‡
Telegraph lines		119 mi.				119 mi.‡
Radio sets		3,305				8,269‡
Minerals						
Petroleum		17,737,000 bbl.				21,385,000 bbl.
Asphalt		117,000 tons				56,000 tons
Crops						
Sugar cane		149,662 tons				83,173 tons‡
Cacao		21,218 „				5,311 tons‡
Rice		6,720 „				15,798 tons‡
Copra (export)		4,694 „				14,656 tons‡
Exports—total	£12,417 ($60,709)	...	£9,860 ($39,757)	...	£7,641 ($30,832)	...
Fuel oil	£4,440 ($21,707)	494,678,000 gal.	...	...	...	...
Gasoline	£3,506 ($17,143)	162,012,000 gal.	...	...	...	...
Sugar	£1,741 ($8,510)	135,000 tons	£1,410 ($5,687)	121,000 tons	742 ($2,993)	61,000 tons
Imports—total	£12,463 ($60,931)	...	£1,985 ($48,322)	...	£12,456 ($50,258)	...
Machinery	£2,589 ($12,656)	...	£1,103 ($4,449)	...	£455 ($1,837)	2,000 tons
Metals	£763 ($3,730)	...	£378 ($1,523)	13,000 tons	£857 ($3,460)	...
Grain, flour, and preparations	£742 ($3,628)	...	£818 ($3,300)	...	£1,176 ($4,747)	60,000 tons
Education						
Primary and secondary schools				292		291
Students				80,736		82,137

*Sterling is legal tender. †1940. ‡1944.

West Indies (British), Leeward Islands: *Statistical Data*

Item	1938 Value (000's omitted)	1938 Amount or Number	1942 Value (000's omitted)	1942 Amount or Number	1944 Value (000's omitted)	1944 Amount or Number
Exchange rate		£1 =$4.889		£1 =$4.035		£1 =$4.035
Finance						
Government revenues	£337 ($1,650)				£500 ($2,017)*	
Government expenditures	£332 ($1,623)				£448 ($1,809)*	
National debt	£354 ($1,733)				£103 ($417)*	
Crops						
Sugar cane		102,450 tons		61,476 tons†		
Tomatoes		720 tons‡		69 tons‡		
Cotton		639 tons		656 tons		
Manufactures						
Sugar	£416 ($2,032)	...				
Rum	£2 ($9)	...				
Tobacco	£1 ($6)	...				
Exports—total	£577 ($2,821)	...	£608 ($2,452)	...	£772 ($3,114)	...
Sugar	£376 ($1,840)	53,000 tons	£412 ($1,663)	42,000 tons	£632 ($2,551)	...
Cotton	£92 ($448)	649 tons	£129 ($521)	632 tons	£60 ($241)	...
Molasses	£17 ($83)	1,872,000 gal.	£18 ($72)	1,108,000 gal.	£5 ($19)	...
Imports—total	£734 ($3,587)	...	£774 ($3,125)	...	£777 ($3,134)	...
Grain, flour, etc.	£67 ($326)	...	£131 ($530)	2,000 tons	£163 ($656)	...
Cotton manufactures	£40 ($196)	...	£70 ($284)	...	£62 ($249)	...
Butter, lard, edible oils, and substitutes	£22 ($109)	...	£35 ($141)	181 tons	£11 ($46)	...
Education						
Primary schools				97§		85
Students				19,803§		18,857

*1943. †Sugar crystals. ‡Exports only. §1942.

mainder as grants). A new Colonial Development and Welfare act, effective April 25, 1945, more than doubled the sums available from the British treasury and extended the terminal date for development projects to March 31, 1956. In the meantime, discussions proceeded with regard to a unified West Indian currency, uniform quarantine regulations, a unified radio service, and a customs union. A department of civil aviation was established during 1945 to serve all of the British West Indies; government subsidies enabled the British West Indian airways to expand its services, and the obvious governmental policy was to favour an aviation monopoly. The incorporated Chambers of Commerce of the British Caribbean met at Basseterre on St. Kitts-Nevis in May 1945 to discuss development of travel, the proposed customs union, commerce with Canada, etc. The Trinidad legislature in 1945 unanimously approved the Stanley proposal for federation. A somewhat less favourable reaction resulted from a conference of two delegates from each of the four constituent colonies of the Windward Islands which met at St. George's on Grenada in Jan. 1945 to discuss federation with the Leeward Islands; the conference recommended that the matter be further discussed at a meeting of the non-official members of the several legislatures concerned. Under Secretary Arthur Creech Jones reported on March 1, 1946, that a closer union of the Leeward and Windward Islands would later be formally proposed. A joint conference, including British, French, Netherlands and United States representatives, met in the U.S. Virgin Islands beginning Feb. 21, 1946.

The other major concern of the British West Indies in 1945, in addition to federation, was the restoration of a peacetime economy. The important economic policy committee rendered its report (the "Benham report") for Jamaica early in 1945, proposing a comprehensive plan for the economic rehabilitation of the island. The incorporated Chambers of Commerce gave important consideration to economic problems in view of the imminent end of the war in Europe. The Caribbean commission held an important series of meetings in Washington at the end of July 1945 to consider political and economic problems as

West Indies (British), Jamaica: *Statistical Data*

Item	1938 Value (000's omitted)	1938 Amount or Number	1940 Value (000's omitted)	1940 Amount or Number	1943 Value (000's omitted)	1943 Amount or Number
Exchange rate		£1 = $4.889		£1 = $3.83		£1 = $4.035
Finance						
Government revenues	£2,476 ($12,107)		£3,081 ($11,802)		£5,655 ($22,818)*	
Government expenditures	£2,271 ($11,105)		£3,164 ($12,119)		£5,949 ($24,005)*	
National debt	£4,605 ($22,513)		£6,495 ($24,876)		£7,441 ($29,024)*	
Crops						
Sugar cane (sugar content)		132,371 tons				
Oranges		14,719 "				
Coffee		4,731 "				
Forest products						
Logwood extract†		879 tons				
Logwood (dyewood)†		6,449 "				
Sea products						
Sponges†		10 tons				
Lobsters†		808 cases				
Manufactures						
Leather		61 tons				
Textile		244 "				
Exports—total	£5,033 ($24,607)‡	...	£3,038 ($11,635)	...	£4,040 ($16,303)	...
Bananas	£2,917 ($14,262)	23,811,000 bunches	£1,045 ($4,004)	6,849,000 bunches	£47 ($191)	289,000 bunches
Sugar (unrefined)	£859 ($4,202)	118,000 tons	£848 ($3,249)	91,000 tons	£1,832 ($7,391)	157,000 tons
Rum	£248 ($1,212)	1,081,000 gal.	£338 ($1,296)	1,280,000 gal.	£462 ($1,866)	496,000 gal.
Imports—total	£6,486 ($31,709)	...	£6,154 ($23,570)	...	£7,311 ($29,501)	...
Grain and flour (except rice)	£452 ($2,210)	40,536 tons	£494 ($1,893)	50,602 tons	£689 ($2,779)	50,189 tons
Cotton cloth	£388 ($1,896)	25,846,680 yd.	£345 ($1,321)	16,585,938 yd.	£987 ($3,983)	19,189,290 yd.
Motor cars and trucks	£237 ($1,161)	1,436	£101 ($388)	535	£4 ($15)	18
Education						
Public elementary schools				667§		668*
Students				164,000§‖		164,000*‖

*1944.
†Exports only.
‡Includes re-exports with a value of £107 ($522).
§1942.
‖Approximate.

West Indies (British), Barbados: *Statistical Data*

Item	1938 Value (000's omitted)	1938 Amount or Number	1941 Value (000's omitted)	1941 Amount or Number	1944 Value (000's omitted)	1944 Amount or Number
Exchange rate		1 barbados $ = $1.7165*		1 barbados $ = 84.06 cents*		1 barbados $ = 84.06 cents*
Finance						
Government revenues	£528 ($2,583)		£591 ($2,382)		£942 ($3,802)	
Government expenditures	£546 ($2,671)		£819 ($3,304)		£874 ($3,526)	
National debt	£442 ($2,162)		£585 ($2,359)		£86 ($346)	
Minerals						
Petroleum		1,568 bbl.		...		...
Manjak (asphalt)		59 tons		71 tons		20 tons†
Crops						
Sugar cane		124,784 tons‡		83,544 tons§		149,266 tons†‡
Sea products—total	£17 ($81)	...				
Flying fish	£15 ($73)	...				
Manufactures						
Rum		126,155 gal.‖		405,815 gal.¶		
Biscuits		1,997 tons		1,814 tons♀		
Sugar and molasses		...		127,281 tons♀		
Exports—total	£1,218 ($5,957)	...	£1,881 ($7,585)	...	£2,097 ($8,463)†	...
Sugar	£674 ($3,294)	102,000 tons	£841 ($3,392)	75,000 tons	£1,498 ($6,045)†	130,000 tons†
Molasses	£462 ($2,260)	6,980,000 gal.	£723 ($2,914)	8,638,000 gal.	£416 ($1,678)†	4,363,000 gal.†
Rum	£10 ($48)	105,000 gal.	£59 ($237)	587,000 gal.	£168 ($679)†	985,000 gal.†
Imports—total	£2,087 ($10,204)	...	£2,317 ($9,344)	...	£2,937 ($11,851)†	...
Flour	£95 ($464)	11,948 tons	£144 ($582)	17,615 tons	£148 ($597)†	9,658 tons†
Cotton cloth	£80 ($393)	3,302,286 sq.yd.	£92 ($371)	2,439,940 sq.yd.	£185 ($745)†	3,015,246 sq.yd.†
Implements, tools, and machinery	£66 ($324)	...	£51 ($204)	...	£57 ($231)†	...
Education						
Primary schools				126♁		126
Students				28,494♁		29,695
Secondary schools				11♁		11
Students				1,659♁		2,089

*British currency also legal tender. †1943. ‡Sugar content. §Sugar produced. ‖Exports only. ¶1939. ♀1940. ♁1942.

conditioned by the end of World War II. Consideration was subsequently given to the holding of a second West Indian conference comparable to the one at Bridgetown in March 1944. Considerable numbers of Barbadians and some from other islands were recruited for work in the United States, especially in the second quarter of 1945, although other islands' residents were at the same time returning after periods of employment in the United States. Jamaica was in certain ways harder hit economically in 1945 and 1946 than were the other colonies, especially because of the disastrous hurricane of Aug. 20, 1944, which destroyed some 90% of the island's banana trees and 40% of the coconut palms. The injury to the banana industry came just at the time when the more favourable shipping picture might have permitted a considerable recovery from the wartime slump in exports. As it was, no shipments of Jamaican bananas to Great Britain could be resumed until Dec. 15, 1945. The Mona reservoir on the Hope river at Kingston, Jamaica, construction of which was begun during the war period, was the largest engineering project ever undertaken in that island; when completed at an estimated cost of £460,000 it would impound 700,000,000 gal. of water. Economic unrest in Kingston, Jamaica, in Feb. 1946 culminated in a week-end "reign of terror" shortly after the middle of the month. A subsequent general strike ended only on March 10, but further violence broke out early in July.

BIBLIOGRAPHY.— *The West Indies Year Book* (annual); W. M. Macmillan, *Warning from the West Indies* (1938); A. Macmillan, *The West Indies, Past and Present* (1938); J. W. Vandercook, *Caribbean Cruise* (1938); J. F. Rippy, *The Caribbean Danger Zone* (1940); *West India Royal Commission, 1938–39;* Sir F. A. Stockdale. *Development and Welfare in the West Indies* (H.M.S.O., 1943). (R. H. FN.)

Westmark

See GERMANY.

West Point

See MILITARY ACADEMY, U.S.

West Virginia

A state in the Appalachian mountain region in the eastern part of the United States, West Virginia is popularly known as the "Panhandle state" or the "Mountain state." West Virginia was formed from Virginia during the American Civil War and was admitted to the union, June 20, 1863. Area, 24,282 sq.mi.; population (1940) 1,901,974, of which 1,742,320 were white (41,782 foreign born). The total urban population was 534,292. On July 1, 1944, the bureau of census estimated the population of the state at 1,715,984. Its capital is Charleston (population 67,914 in 1940). Other chief cities are Huntington (78,836) and Wheeling (61,099).

Principal state officers in 1937–40 were: governor, Homer A. Holt; secretary of state, William S. O'Brien; treasurer, R. E. Talbott; auditor, Edgar B. Sims; attorney-general, Clarence W. Meadows; commissioner of agriculture, J. B. McLaughlin; state superintendent of schools, W. W. Trent.

All these officials except the governor were re-elected in Nov. 1940. M. M. Neely was elected governor. In the presidential election of 1940, Franklin Delano Roosevelt received 496,146 votes and Wendell Willkie received 372,662 votes. For governor of the state the vote stood 496,028 for Neely and 383,698 for D. Boone Dawson. Other state officials (Democrats) were elected by majorities ranging

West Virginia: *Statistical Data*

Table I.—*Education (Public)*

	1938	1941	1942	1943	1944	1945
High schools	360	413	387	383	391	385
Elementary school pupils	359,864	306,942	302,230	292,608	281,859	279,205
High school pupils	83,925	144,111	141,107	134,509	127,221	126,366
Elementary teachers	10,248	10,842	10,717	10,519	10,191	10,059
High school teachers	4,635	5,359	5,402	5,312	5,133	4,994

Table II.—*Public Welfare*
(Money figures in thousands of dollars)

	1937	1938	1939	1940	1941
Cases on general relief	18,100	22,185	14,137	15,650	12,572
Cost of general relief	$180	$204	$112	$143	$119
Recipients of old-age pensions		17,977		17,816	19,278
Cost of pensions		$248		$247	$287
Dependent children receiving aid		17,246		21,526	24,992
Blind receiving aid		754		807	862
Workers under unemployment compensation		278,587	268,695	299,600	

Table III.—*Communications*
(Money figures in thousands of dollars)

	1937	1938	1939	1942	1944	1945
Highway mileage				13,872	16,986	17,090
Expenditure on highways	$22,618	$25,313	$24,720			
Railroad mileage	3,832	3,849	3,847	4,171	4,230	3,229

Table IV.—*Banking and Finance*
(Money figures in thousands of dollars)

	1937	1938	1940	1942	1944	1945
State revenue	$60,456	$68,288				
State expenditure	$49,661	$64,952				
State net debt	$76,019	$81,136		$68,748	$62,807	$59,579
State gross debt	$84,056		$80,893	$73,963	$67,981	$64,754
Number of banks	186	184	182	180	180	178
Number of national banks	79	79	77	77	77	76

Table V.—*Agriculture*
(All figures in thousands)

	1937	1939	1940	1942	1943	1944
Income from crops and livestock	$42,300	$40,831	$41,052	$64,698	$78,461	$84,621
Income from government payments	$800	$1,800	$1,920	$2,595	$2,774	$4,417
Leading crops (bu.):						
Apples	6,384	5,670	4,868	4,686	2,046	4,356
Barley	135	270	306	312	209	225
Buckwheat	298	248	245	209	209	185
Corn	14,245	13,994	12,852	14,042	13,294	10,426
Hay (tons)	1,206	722	833	946	964	805
Oats	1,700	1,460	1,462	1,848	1,599	1,430
Potatoes	3,264	3,040	3,630	3,808	2,775	2,040
Wheat	2,736	2,102	2,016	1,457	1,053	1,680

West Virginia: *Statistical Data* (continued)
Table VI.—*Manufacturing*
(Money figures in thousands of dollars)

	1937	1939	1940
Wage earners	83,464	74,989	
Wages paid	$102,511	$88,487	$396,885
Value of manufactures	$480,526	$441,840	$898,722

Table VII.—*Mineral Production*
(All figures in thousands of dollars)

	1937	1938	1939	1944 (est.)
Value of mineral production	$306,591	$254,995	$275,563	$600,000
Leading products (value):				
Coal	$223,055	$179,356	$189,971	
Natural gas	$58,639	$55,910	$63,194	
Petroleum	$8,800	$5,600	$6,000	
Coke	$7,054	$4,820	$4,700	
Stone	$3,697	$4,392	$4,478	
Clay	$2,770	$2,183	$3,094	
Sand and gravel	$2,349	$1,803	$2,036	
Natural gasoline	$2,528	$2,063	$2,017	

from 141,745 for secretary of state to 112,000 for commissioner of agriculture. For U.S. senator, Judge Harley M. Kilgore received a vote of 492,413 and Thomas B. Sweeney received a total of 381,806.

In June 1942 Clarence W. Meadows, attorney-general was succeeded by William S. Wysong, who had been serving as president of the board of control.

In the elections of 1944, Clarence W. Meadows was elected governor. Ira J. Parthlow was elected attorney-general. Re-elected were: secretary of state, William S. O'Brien; treasurer, R. E. Talbott; auditor, Edgar B. Sims; state superintendent of schools, W. W. Trent. In the 1944 presidential election Roosevelt received 392,777 votes and Thomas Dewey received 322,819. (J. M. CA.; X.)

BIBLIOGRAPHY.—C. H. Ambler, *West Virginia, The Mountain State* (1940); Council of State Govts., *Book of the States* (bienn.); Federal Writers' Project, *West Virginia: Guide to the Mountain State* (1941); State Legislature, *West Virginia Blue Book* (annual). Per.: *Monthly Checklist of State Publications* (Washington, D.C.).

Weygand, Maxime

Weygand (1867–), French soldier, was born at Brussels, Belgium, Jan. 21, 1867. He studied at the St. Cyr Military academy and at the Cavalry school at Saumur. He was commander of a hussar regiment in 1912. A month after the outbreak of World War I, he was appointed a temporary colonel (Sept. 1914) and was chief of staff of a French army. In 1916, he was promoted to general of a brigade. He succeeded Marshal Ferdinand Foch in 1917 as French representative on the Inter-Allied General staff. In April 1918, he was appointed Foch's chief of staff.

In 1920, Weygand reorganized the Polish army and directed the Polish counter-offensive that turned back the soviet forces from Warsaw. Later, he held a number of high posts in the French army; he was high commissioner to Syria (1923–24), inspector-general of the army (1931–35) and commander of French forces in the Levant (1939–40).

On May 19, 1940, nine days after the start of the German invasion of the Low Countries and France, Weygand succeeded Gen. Maurice Gamelin as commander in chief of the Allied armies. He promptly dismissed 15 generals and planned a "defense in depth" but was no more successful in stopping the German blitzkrieg than was his predecessor. When Marshal Henri Pétain replaced Paul Reynaud as premier, Weygand was named minister of defense in the cabinet. He was "relieved" of this post, Sept. 6, 1940, and dispatched to Africa to deal with the revolt of various French colonies whose governors joined Gen. Charles de Gaulle's Free French movement. Pétain appointed Weygand French pro-consul in Africa in 1941 and then governor-general of Algeria in July of that year. However, Weygand retired as pro-consul on Nov. 20, 1941.

After the Allied landings in French North Africa, Weygand was arrested by the Germans. He was freed by Allied troops in May 1945, but was arrested on his return to Paris on charges of "attempts against the internal security of the state."

The following July, the French high court ordered seizure of his property and assets.

Wheat

The world wheat situation changed completely during the decade 1937–46. A large and growing supply piled up during the years 1937 to 1942 and then suddenly was used up in three years. The world's supply became short. In 1937, the world crop was about the average of the previous decade, although the United States had small crops in 1933 and 1934. A big crop in Europe in 1938 raised the world's total in excess of 4,559,000,000 bu., a high point that had not been equalled for ten years. This estimate did not include China and the soviet union, both large producers of wheat consumed domestically for the most part. Total world exports were estimated at 519,000,000 bu. in 1937, principally from Australia, the United States, Canada and Argentina. An estimate for 1938 which included 1,500,000,000 bu. for the soviet union and 640,000,000 bu. for China gave 6,587,000,000 bu. as the world's total wheat crop. After 1938, estimates for the soviet union were omitted and those for China were mere approximations. The world crop of 45 countries, which represented about 95% of world production, excluding China and the soviet union, was put at an average of 3,774,000,000 bu. in 1935–39.

An increase was reported in 1941 and 1942, a decline to less than the prewar average in 1943 and an increase to 3,797,000,000 bu. in 1944. Drought cut the production in Europe and Africa in 1945, bringing the total down to 3,570,000,000 bu.

Better crops were reported in nearly all countries in 1946, but mid-year reports indicated that exports might not be as large as in 1945. The world stocks of wheat reached the high total of 1,740,000,000 bu. in 1943, about three times the average before 1937. By 1945, these stocks had been exhausted, and exports declined accordingly. The crops of many countries were larger for domestic use, which was expected to reduce the demand for relief wheat by another year. By July 1945 wheat stocks in the big four exporting countries were 25% less than the prewar average.

Canada contributed a large share of the supplies of wheat for Britain. The crop of Canadian wheat was very small in 1937, only 180,210,000 bu. compared with an average of 312,399,000 during 1935–39. Production recovered in 1938, and a crop of 520,623,000 bu. was harvested in 1939. Prices were low and a support program was started; a trade agreement was signed with Britain. The 1940 crop increased further, but that of 1941 was off to 314,825,000 bu. Again in 1942 the Canadian crop was large, 556,684,000 bu., followed in 1943 by a reduction of more than half, to 284,460,000 bu. Again in 1944, production recovered to 435,535,000 bu., but slumped again in 1945. The acreage was increased in 1946 and the crop once more was in the higher levels. Throughout the decade, the Canadian crop was a succession of large and small yields.

Australia played a less important role in the wheat trade because of two factors; the shipping shortage in the early days of World War II, and the droughts of 1944 and 1945. The prewar average production of Australia was 169,744,000 bu., which was increased to 210,000,000 bu. in 1939. The crop of 1940 was poor—only 83,192,000 bu. Then followed three almost normal crops, but production was cut again by the drought of 1944 to only 53,000,000 bu., the smallest in two decades. Seeding was increased for the 1946 crop, and an output of 135,000,000 bu. was expected, of which about 55,000,000 bu. was likely to be available for export.

In 1946, the Food and Agriculture organization made a world food survey to determine the actual food consumption of different countries, also the needs, shortages, and probable needs in 1960. A sufficient supply of wheat to meet world demands was expected after the 1948 crop was harvested. There was believed to be considerable possibility of increasing production. The report stated that in areas containing more than half the world's population, the supply of food in good years before World War II was sufficient only to supply 2,250 calories per day per capita. Another third of the world's people had an average of 2,750 or more calories daily while the remaining sixth were somewhere between these levels. The conclusion was that the world needed a larger food supply, of which wheat would form a very important part.

United States.—The U.S. wheat crop, second only to corn as the most important crop, supplied almost a third of the world's crop in 1946. A record yield on a near-record acreage returned high-record crops at a time of vital need. Both stocks and production reached unprecedented heights. Wheat was grown on about one-sixth of the nation's cropland, in every state. The use of machinery proceeded further with wheat than with any other major U.S. crop. It was the sole cash crop in many areas and was grown in rotation with other crops almost everywhere.

A large world wheat crop in 1938 caused prices to drop from 96 cents per bu. for the 1937 crop to 56.2 cents for the 1938 crop. Reduction of acreage was advised by the Agricultural Adjustment administration, and the harvested area dropped to about 52,668,000 ac., where it remained for two years, and did not rise much until 1944. In the early years of World War II, wheat-adjustment programs were continued in effect as stocks on hand were very large. The war needs were for other crops, and farmers were advised to limit wheat acreage and plant feed crops and oil-seeds wherever possible. Prices of other crops were supported, and the whole educational program was directed toward limiting wheat. Favourable weather, however, in these early war years brought excellent yields which offset the acreage reduction to a large extent. By 1944, acreage restrictions were removed, the price increased and the crops began to increase rapidly. By 1946, the harvested area was up to 65,680,000 ac., and the department of agriculture set a goal for 1947 at 71,000,000 ac. to be seeded; this was about the same area as was seeded for the 1946 harvest. The regional changes in wheat acreage after 1937 included a steady decline in the northwest, Pacific northwest and in the soft red winter or central wheat states. The south increased its wheat area steadily. In Kansas, the centre of wheat production in the United States, the decline was less in the western third of the state than in the eastern or central thirds. This was due primarily to the lack of competing crops.

The acre yield of U.S. wheat averaged higher in 1937–46 than for a long period previously: 16.2 bu. per ac. with two high years, 19.8 bu. in 1942 and 18.2 bu. in 1944. For the 30 years before 1937 the average yield had been 14.3 bu. per acre. Wide fluctuations, however, had ranged from a low of 11.3 bu. in 1933 to a top of 16.3 bu. in 1931. The high average during World War II was due to unusually favourable weather. This was also shown by the percentage of the seeded area abandoned, which was high in 1936 but declined steadily to 1946. Drought continued to be the greatest hazard for grain, but there were no serious droughts during the decade 1937–46. Losses from rust were not heavy after 1938. Floods caused some abandonment in 1941–43 in the central states. Winter-killing was also serious in 1933 but was not an important cause of loss after 1937. In general, favourable precipitation in the plains, particularly in Kansas, from 1940 on, maintained the high yields in these states. Some increases in yield recorded in certain areas were because of the use of better seed. Rust-resistant varieties with stiff straw gave good returns. Improved cultural methods also showed results. Summer fallow was beneficial in the hard winter and spring wheat regions. The use of commercial fertilizers increased in the central states, where wheat continued to be grown in rotation. The average size of wheat farms increased in the specialized areas. In the spring wheat belt they averaged 437 ac. in 1920 and 500 ac. in 1940. In the Pacific northwest, the average size increased from 727 ac. in 1920 to 1,134 ac. in 1940.

The chief changes in wheat farming came in the use of machinery. In the spring wheat belt, about 97% of farms used tractors and 71% had grain combines. In the hard-winter belt of Kansas and Nebraska, 75% had tractors and 80% used combines. The hours of labour per ac. declined accordingly. In the Kansas area, 8 hrs. per ac. were expended in 1909 and only 3.6 hrs. in 1936. On the wheat farms of the plains country, the amount of work stock in the form of horses and mules almost disappeared during World War II with the decline of animal-drawn machinery.

The total production of wheat averaged about 800,000,000 bu. from 1910 to 1944, ranging from a low of about 551,600,000 bu. in 1933 to a high of 1,008,000,000 bu. in 1915. During 1915–19 the crops had averaged 824,000,000 bu. from an average of 59,000,000 ac. During 1942–46, the crops averaged 1,035,000,000 bu. from 57,000,000 ac. Three 1,000,000,000-bushel crops were added to stocks which were at high-record levels in 1942 and 1943. No effort was made to increase wheat production until 1943.

The fear of great surpluses led to the drafting of a world wheat agreement between Britain, the chief buyer, and the United States, Canada, Australia and Argentina in 1942. Quotas of the amounts to be sold to Britain by the four exporters were set up and observed to a general extent. The Combined Food board directed allocations as the shipping problem changed.

The regional changes in U.S. wheat production were of importance in explaining the fluctuation of the crop. While the total U.S. crop increased after 1937, the output of the soft, red winter states of Iowa, Missouri east to Ohio and Michigan, were declining in production. The greatest increases were in the hard-winter and spring belts, including the Dakotas, Nebraska, Kansas and Oklahoma in the plains. During the drought years 1933–36, production in the plains was extremely low—only 43% of the national total—while in 1941–44 the production in this area rose to 65% of U.S. production. The output of this area, and particularly Kansas, largely determined whether the national output would be high or low. The variations in the plains were due more to changes in yield than in acreage, and the yield in turn depended on the degree of precipitation. The nation was fortunate that the drought period which had struck this area regularly did not occur during the war period.

Hard winter wheat made up about 44% of the total acreage seeded in 1935–39; spring wheat 28%; soft red winter wheat 15%; Pacific 7% and all other east and south 6%. Of the spring wheat, only a small part was durum, nearly all of which was grown in the three states of Minnesota and the Dakotas. For the period 1935–44 the average amounts of each class of wheat were: hard red 359,476,000 bu.; soft red 200,727,000 bu.; hard red spring 158,979,000 bu.; durum 32,832,000 bu.; and white 91,678,000 bu., a total of 843,692,000 bu. Most of the increase during the war years was in the hard winter wheat. Durum amounted to 39,715,000 bu. in 1938 and increased to 44,600,000 bu. in 1942 but yielded only 35,600,000 bu. in 1946. Spring wheat was grown to a very limited extent outside of the northwest.

U.S. domestic wheat consumption was relatively stable, in contrast with production, and the surplus was used for export, feed or industrial purposes in varying degrees. The amount needed for the increasing population was less than the rate of rise in population since the per capita consumption declined with the expansion in the variety of foods produced. In 1937 the per capita consumption as food was down to 3.65 bu. from 3.94 bu. in 1930. The consumption declined further to 3.58 bu. in 1940, then turned upward to 4 bu. per capita in 1944. In 1937, 474,644,000 bu. was consumed as food; 132,398,000 bu. as feed for livestock; 94,146,000 bu. for seed and only 39,000 bu. for industrial uses. This made a total of 701,227,000 bu. for domestic use. The rest of the crop of 1937 went into stocks for carry-over, which increased before 1938; about 103,000,000 bu. was exported as wheat and flour. The changes in wheat distribution brought about by World War II is shown by the uses made of the big 1944 crop. In the year 1944 food requirements took 558,869,000 bu.; feed 281,923,000 bu.; seed 80,830,000 bu.; and industrial uses, principally for industrial alcohol, 95,772,000 bu.; making a total of 1,017,394,000 bu. Exports were 138,900,000 bu., but stocks were low. The great increase in the use of wheat for livestock feed came in 1943, when the amount reached a high total of 480,000,000 bu., almost equal to the total wheat crops of some earlier years.

Wheat exports disappeared in 1935 and 1936, when the imports of flour more than offset the exports of grain. This was the period of real shortage of supply. In 1943, the balance was again in favour of imports, but this was due to the heavy food and feed utilization and the restrictions on shipping abroad. The July 1 stocks of wheat (carry-over) were dammed up in 1941–42 and 1943, and created larger reserves than had been seen for 30 years. In 1942, the carry-over was 632,103,000 bu. and in 1943, 621,659,000 bu. The big stock of 1943 was fed to livestock to balance the situation. The demand for wheat for relief in early 1946 became so strong that special efforts were made by the government to get more wheat delivered by growers and to move stocks being held in grain elevators. Three orders were issued by the government, the first directing millers to use 80% of the grain in flour, the second limiting the use of wheat in mixed feeds and the third prohibiting the use of wheat to make alcohol or spirits.

It was estimated that 15,000,000 to 20,000,000 bu. of wheat were saved by the milling order, and about an equal amount by the restrictions on alcohol. The U.S. department of agriculture offered a bonus of 30 cents per bu. for wheat delivered between April 19 and May 25. On May 13, the ceiling price of wheat was raised 15 cents per bu. and other grain prices were adjusted accordingly. These actions resulted in a total of exports for the year ending June 30, 1946, at an all-time high of more than 400,000,000 bu. Exports in 1945 were 385,800,000 bu., the record to that year. At the same time, the stocks of wheat were down to 101,500,000 bu., the smallest in 20 years except for 1937, when stocks were down to 83,000,000 bu. because of the droughts. Prospects for another record crop of wheat in early May 1946 justified the government's shipping out the reserved stocks to a low point. World stocks of wheat were at a record peak of more than 1,700,000,000 bu. in 1943, of which more than 1,200,000,000 bu.

Table 1.—*World Wheat Production, 1941–46, with 1935–39 Average*
(In millions of bushels)

	Average 1935–39	1941	1942	1943	1944	1945	1946
United States	759	943	974	841	1,079	1,108	1,155
Canada	312	315	557	284	435	305	440
Mexico	14	16	17	13	14	13	13
Europe†	1,570	1,340	1,212	1,370	1,348	949	1,288
United Kingdom	62	75	96	130	117	81	72
North Africa	120	133	110	108	86	77	115
Asia†	1,442	1,404	1,433	1,495	1,530	1,430	1,500
Argentina	222	238	235	250	150	143	200
Union of South Africa	16	14	20	18	14	10	20
Australia	170	167	156	110	53	144	160
World Total†	5,940	5,700	5,700	5,400	5,650	3,570*	4,200*
Total	4,687	4,645	4,810	4,619	4,826	4,260	4,963

*Excludes U.S.S.R. and China.
†Estimate.

Table II.—*U.S. Wheat Production by States, 1937–46*
(In millions of bushels)

	1937	1939	1941	1942	1943	1944	1945	1946
U.S. Total	875.6	751.4	943.1	974.1	841.0	1,078.6	1,108.	1,155.
Kansas	158.0	111.6	173.3	206.7	144.2	191.6	207.9	216.7
North Dakota	57.0	79.0	144.7	149.8	156.7	161.6	154.5	139.8
Nebraska	47.1	36.3	36.2	69.9	61.2	35.9	82.3	90.6
Oklahoma	65.4	60.4	48.6	57.3	31.7	85.9	73.8	88.2
Washington	50.8	43.8	61.1	55.1	51.6	64.0	77.9	61.5
Ohio	46.1	37.1	48.9	36.2	26.4	46.8	57.4	48.5
Montana	21.9	51.4	68.2	73.7	77.0	73.8	57.1	62.3
South Dakota	15.3	18.9	35.3	45.2	31.5	38.8	49.6	53.1
Texas	41.6	29.0	27.1	47.4	36.3	74.7	48.1	62.9
Indiana	34.7	27.6	34.6	13.8	15.2	26.4	34.9	29.6
Colorado	15.1	12.9	25.0	27.8	31.6	19.1	35.4	37.0
Idaho	28.3	21.3	27.8	20.7	22.1	30.3	32.7	34.8
Michigan	18.6	15.7	16.2	15.3	11.1	23.0	27.0	22.8
Illinois	45.6	41.4	34.3	12.8	17.0	24.6	24.8	19.5
Missouri	42.5	30.4	18.0	9.0	12.6	23.8	18.2	18.7
Minnesota	35.7	22.1	20.1	23.1	18.0	20.6	21.2	27.0
Oregon	20.4	16.1	23.5	19.9	19.7	23.1	21.8	25.1
Pennsylvania	23.5	19.4	16.8	15.3	13.4	20.2	20.0	19.9
California	17.8	12.1	11.6	9.9	8.4	10.3	10.6	12.5
New York	8.2	6.3	6.6	7.5	4.5	8.9	9.1	5.6
Virginia	9.7	7.6	7.6	7.5	5.8	11.2	7.5	8.3
Maryland	9.0	7.3	7.2	5.9	4.9	8.9	6.7	7.3
Utah	5.4	3.9	7.0	5.0	5.4	7.3	6.7	6.9
North Carolina	5.8	5.1	7.3	8.0	5.8	8.9	5.7	6.3
Tennessee	6.7	4.1	5.4	5.2	4.1	6.7	4.5	3.8
Kentucky	10.2	4.0	7.1	5.1	3.9	7.9	5.0	4.1
Wyoming	3.0	2.8	4.8	4.2	4.0	3.1	4.2	5.4
South Carolina	1.4	2.4	3.1	3.3	2.8	3.6	2.9	2.7
Iowa	14.6	6.9	2.3	4.7	2.4	2.2	2.6	3.3
Georgia	1.4	1.7	2.1	2.5	2.1	2.9	2.4	2.0
New Mexico	3.1	3.7	2.7	4.8	2.4	3.1	2.7	2.8
West Virginia	2.7	2.1	1.6	1.4	1.0	1.6	1.6	1.5
Wisconsin	2.0	2.0	1.3	1.7	1.3	1.4	1.4	2.2
New Jersey	1.4	1.1	1.2	1.7	.9	1.3	1.3	1.5
Delaware	1.3	1.2	1.3	1.2	1.0	1.2	1.3	1.2
Arizona	.9	.8	.3	.5	.4	.5	.5	.5
Arkansas	1.0	.3	.3	.2	.01	.05	.4	.4
Nevada	.4	.4	.4	.4	.5	.4	.4	.5
Alabama	.07	.06	.09	.1	.01	.02	.3	.1
Maine	.07	.08	.03	.04	.04	.04	.01	.02
Mississippi	—	—	.09	.1	.2	.4	.3	.1

were in the United States and Canada. The heavy war utilizations reduced this reserve rapidly until, in 1946, the world stocks were estimated at only about 400,000,000 bu., approximately the level of 1937 and the prewar period 1922–27.

The total use of wheat in the 1945–46 fiscal year was the largest in U.S. history, although it was only slightly more than 1943–44, when the large quantity was used for feed. The amount used for feed dropped to prewar levels in 1946, and the industrial use was down to 21,000,000 bu. The food consumption was down to 495,000,000 bu. compared with the 550,000,000 bu. used in 1944–45.

The distribution of exported wheat in the year ending June 30, 1946, included the following principal destinations: Europe 277,700,000 bu.; far east 33,400,000 bu.; Latin America 34,900,000 bu., and various other countries 39,800,000 bu. Of the amount shipped to Europe, 98,000,000 bu. went to the United Nations Relief and Rehabilitation administration; 56,700,000 bu. to the United States military civilian feeding; 52,600,000 bu. to France and French North Africa; 20,200,000 bu. to Belgium; 11,300,000 bu. to the Netherlands, and 11,400,000 bu. to Britain. In the far east, U.N.R.R.A. received 4,700,000 bu. and the U.S. military forces 16,600,000 bu. for civilian feeding. The total U.S. contribution to relief was estimated at about 200,000,000 bu. About 1,300,000 bu. went to the soviet union.

The price of U.S. wheat to growers advanced each year during the decade from a low of 56.2 cents per bu. in 1938. Prices had advanced from 39.1 cents per bu. in 1931 to $1.025 per bu. in 1937, then declined with the increasing crops of 1937 and 1938. By 1942, the average price had recovered to $1.098 per bu., slightly more than the 1937 level. It then moved up to $1.42 per bu. in 1944. The average for 1945 was $1.45 per bu. By April 1946, the farm price was $1.58 per bu., or 99% of parity. As the ceiling was raised 15 cents in May 1946, prices continued to advance and by mid-1946 were reported at $1.74 per bu., the highest since 1920. When price ceilings were removed, wheat prices advanced 5% to 10%, but the improved crop outlook held them in check. The movement of wheat became as large as shipping and storage facilities would allow, and in some areas open-air storage was resorted to. The world need for wheat was expected to extend through 1947, and the price advance was encouraged to direct grains into human food rather than livestock feed, since more people could be fed with the grain than from the livestock produced from the same amount of grain. When the Office of Price Administration was restored in Aug. 1946, price ceilings were put on meats, but grains were left free. It was recognized that this would produce less meat, but the policy was adopted for the purpose of conserving grain for human consumption. To assure more wheat for 1947, the national goal was set for 717,000,000 ac., the largest acreage since 1938.

The world wheat agreement planned for an export quota for the United States at 16% of the total amount to be exported by the big four wheat exporting countries. This was estimated to amount to from 64,000,000 to 80,000,000 bu. in the postwar years after 1947. During the period 1935–39, net exports averaged 42,000,000 bu. per year. With the increasing domestic use this was expected to take care of the U.S. surplus should the wheat area be reduced to the prewar level. The U.S. department of agriculture estimated that 64,000,000 ac. would yield 925,000,000 bu., which would care for maximum needs; there would be no serious threat of surpluses. With a U.S. population of 146,000,000 in 1955, the need for wheat was estimated at 785,000,000 to 925,000,000 bu. including 60,000,000 to 80,000,000 bu. of exports. The use of wheat as a livestock feed was demonstrated to many farmers during World War II, and larger quantities could be used in years of surplus and low prices. (*See* also AGRICULTURAL RESEARCH ADMINISTRATION; FLOUR.) (J. C. Ms.)

BIBLIOGRAPHY.—U.S. Dept. of Agric., *Agricultural Statistics; Handbook Official Grain Standards* (1941); *Intl. Wheat Agreement,* Wheat Meeting (1941–42); *Wheat Studies,* eight Nos. per yr.

Wheat Advisory Committee

See INTERNATIONAL ORGANIZATIONS.

Wheeler, Burton Kendall

Wheeler (1882–), U.S. politician, was born in Hudson, Mass., on Feb. 27, 1882. A graduate of the University of Michigan Law school (1905), he was admitted to the bar in Montana in 1906 and was a member of the Montana house of representatives (1911–13). After serving as district attorney for the state (1913–18), he ran unsuccessfully for governor in 1920 on the Non-Partisan league ticket. Two years later (1922), he was more successful in his campaigning for the U.S. senate, to which he was elected and was subsequently re-elected four times. Although generally a member of the Democratic party, he ran for vice-president of the U.S. on the Progressive ticket in 1924.

Wheeler was a strong supporter of President F. D. Roosevelt and New Deal measures until 1937, when he broke sharply with the president over the latter's plan to reorganize the supreme court, and was instrumental in defeating the measure. Subsequently, he voted with the farm bloc, although he gave active support also to pro-labour measures. Wheeler strongly disapproved the administration's foreign policy in the critical years preceding the U.S. entry into World War II and became an active leader of the U.S. noninterventionist group in 1941.

Senator Wheeler was favoured to win his bid for renomination for a fifth term in the senate in the Montana primaries and on July 11, 1946, Pres. Harry S. Truman threw his support to the Montana senator. However, the C.I.O.-P.A.C. withdrew its endorsement from the senator, charging that he was no longer a "liberal" and stumped for his opponent, Leif Erickson, who won the nomination on July 17, 1946.

Wheeler, Raymond Albert

Wheeler (1885–), U.S. army officer, was born in Peoria, Ill., on July 31, 1885, and was graduated from the U.S. Military Academy in 1911. He was graduated from the Command and General Staff school in 1927 and the Army War college in 1937. He served overseas in World War I, 1917–19, and later held a number of military engineering posts in the United States and Panamá. He became chief regional engineer for the Work Projects administration in Chicago, Ill., in 1935 and attended the Permanent International Association of Navigation congress in Brussels, Belgium, in 1936 as the U.S. delegate.

Following the outbreak of World War II, he was chief of the U.S. military mission to Iraq, Iran and India, 1941–42, with the task of speeding supplies to the soviet union and China. He was appointed to the staff of Lord Louis Mountbatten in the southeast Asia command in 1942, as director of supply forces. Promoted to the rank of a lieutenant general in 1944, he was named deputy commander of the southeast Asia theatre in Feb. 1944.

In June, 1945, he succeeded Gen. Daniel Sultan as commander of the India-Burma theatre. The following October he was sworn in as chief of the U.S. army engineers.

Wheeler-Lea Amendment

See ADVERTISING.

Whisky

See LIQUORS, ALCOHOLIC.

White Russian S.S.R.

See BYELORUSSIA.

Wholesale Prices

See INCOME AND PRODUCT; PRICES.

Wholesale Trade

See BUSINESS REVIEW.

Whooping Cough

See MEDICINE.

Wickard, Claude Raymond

Wickard (1893–), U.S. government official, was born Feb. 28, 1893, near Delphi, Indiana and was graduated from Purdue university in 1915. He was appointed to the Agricultural Adjustment administration in 1933 and later became director of the AAA's conservation program for the north central states.

Appointed undersecretary of agriculture on Feb. 1, 1940, Wickard was named by Pres. Roosevelt to succeed Henry A. Wallace as secretary of agriculture on Aug. 19, 1940. In March 1941, the new secretary took charge of the production and distribution of lend-lease food to Britain and her allies. On Dec. 6, 1942, he was appointed war food administrator with full control over the nation's food program.

Wickard was named "neutral chairman" of the United Nations war food board on Oct. 29, 1943. A little more than a month after he assumed office, Pres. Truman named Clinton P. Anderson as secretary of agriculture (May 23, 1945), and on July 2 of that year, Wickard assumed his new post as head of the Rural Electrification administration.

Wildlife Conservation

During the decade ending in 1946, wildlife conservation in the United States became more firmly established as a public policy than ever before. Disastrous results of a negligence that had led some conservationists to call wildlife "the forgotten resource" had, just before this decade, prodded not only conservationists but the general public into formulating and implementing a program to restore these resources. When preparations for war began to interfere with continuance of the program as planned, the evaluation demanded of all such enterprises resulted in general recognition that an abundant wildlife was an invaluable part of the American heritage, a resource upon which the "American way of living" was dependent.

Although World War II brought drastic curtailments in projects requiring materials and many man-hours, it was the occasion of a conscious treasuring of these resources. As a result, wartime exploitation was not as serious as had been feared (partly also because of the vigilance resulting from the fears); when postwar opportunities were being visualized, wildlife conservation was taken for granted as one of the national objectives. Furthermore, distracting as the prewar and war years had been for such long-time undertakings, there were many constructive developments upon which future progress could be based.

In 1937, at the beginning of the decade, the wildlife agency of the federal government reported a settling down to the more prosaic but essential task of carrying out the details of a national wildlife program. The condition of waterfowl seemed most precarious, and so drastic had been

Ducks over a refuge near Sacramento, Calif., during the migration season in 1946

the decline of these birds that public opinion was aroused. Out of the disaster of the waterfowl arose the national wildlife program.

The national program was in its simplest broad terms a co-ordination of measures to reduce and control the number of animals taken by hunters and to restore and preserve large areas of land and water for the increase of wildlife. These measures were based on the results of scientific investigation and intensified research, and they were fortified by widespread educational programs, both in schools and among the general public.

The program was best exemplified by its major component—the waterfowl restoration program. Most conspicuous in conservation discussions throughout these years were the ducks and geese. The outstanding species threatened by extermination was the trumpeter swan (*see* below). Being migratory birds, the waterfowl were protected by the federal government under international treaties with Canada and with Mexico. Their conservation was thus in a peculiar sense a national undertaking, and the resulting program developed was larger than any comparable program ever organized in any part of the world.

The restoration and preservation of wildlife lands resulted in a remarkable enlargement of the federal refuge system. Areas added either primarily or partly for the increase of waterfowl made up the most notable group of acquisitions, although other species of birds, and mammals also, were benefited. Including refuges of all kinds, the government reported in 1937 that at the beginning of the fiscal year (*i.e.*, on July 1, 1936) there were 164 refuges, whereas at the close of the year (on June 30, 1937) there were 231. On July 1, 1935, there had been only 106. The refuge acquisition program thus begun continued throughout the following ten years (seriously impeded but not entirely interrupted by World War II) until by 1946 the refuges totalled 291 with an area of 17,819,495 ac. Acquisition was followed by developments that included both measures to restore or create national conditions favouring the wildlife and also the installation of buildings and other facilities for protecting and managing the areas, refuge managers and other personnel being established on most of them. This program from the start and throughout the ten years was under the direction of J. Clark Salyer, II, and was credited with a considerable part of the increase in wildlife, particularly waterfowl, noted until the great increase of hunting began in 1945.

Yet the critical factor in affecting waterfowl populations during the ten years was the restrictions on hunting determined annually by the federal government in accordance with hunting demands and investigations of the numbers of birds. At the end of the shooting season of 1937 the continental waterfowl numbers were estimated at 40,000,000 and the waterfowl hunters numbered 603,623. (In accordance with the Migratory Bird Hunting Stamp act of 1934 all hunters over 16 years of age were required to purchase a $1 stamp—the "duck stamp," sales of which helped finance the refuge program and incidentally provided an index to hunting pressure). In 1938 the ducks increased to 50,000,000, the hunters to 783,039. In the three succeeding years duck numbers went to 57,000,000, to 65,000,000 and to 70,000,000, while the number of hunters was climbing to 1,002,715, to 1,111,561 and 1,257,161. The upward surge of hunters reached 1,437,362 in 1942 and was then halted by the war, falling to 1,380,222 in 1943 and 1,169,362 in 1944. In 1942 the duck numbers increased to 100,000,000, and when war brought not only a decrease in hunters but also restrictions on gasoline, tires and ammunition, the duck increases continued to 120,000,000 in 1943 and reached a peak of 125,350,000 in 1944. By 1945, however, the number of hunters grew to 1,487,029 and the bird numbers started a decline to 105,500,000 that year and to only 80,000,000 in 1946, while later figures revealed a total of 1,686,368 waterfowl hunters—the largest number on record.

In 1937 the shooting season was limited to 30 days (in each of three transcontinental zones in the United States) and other restrictions were severe. During the succeeding years continued restrictions made possible the steady increase of birds. As bird populations grew, however, these restrictions were relaxed, until by 1945 the three seasons provided were for 80 days each. The 1946 waterfowl hunting seasons were reduced to 40 days in each of three zones; daily bag limits were reduced from 10 to 7; and the shooting days were ended a half-hour earlier. Albert M. Day, who became director of the fish and wildlife service on April 1, 1946, pointed out in June that "the only quick means of adjusting hunting pressure is provided through the annual hunting regulations." He made the following prediction: "In the years immediately ahead, the wild ducks and geese of this country are going to face the greatest army of hunters in all history. A declining period in waterfowl is all too plain. Increased hunting pressure is fact and not fiction. It is going to take the best kind of management possible to prevent further cuts into the breeding stocks of waterfowl."

Ostensibly there had thus occurred during these ten years a cycle from scarcity of waterfowl through relative abundance to a drastically declining population (reflected in a 36% decrease from 1944 to 1946), yet actually there was not apparent a return of the crisis of a previous decade, since the refuge system was in existence as a much enlarged area of special protection. Forecasts of increasingly severe hunting restrictions were received with less opposition than similar predictions in the 1930s, and waterfowl conservation, like all wildlife conservation, was more firmly established as a national policy.

* * *

CONSERVATIONISTS during these years followed closely the reports on the trumpeter swan—largest American wildfowl, which in 1935 was apparently doomed to extermination in the United States, only 73 individuals being then known. Protected by every legal restriction possible on shooting, this species was also provided with a refuge—the Red Rock Lakes National Wildlife refuge in Montana—sometimes described as the trumpeter swan's refuge. This refuge was established on an area used by the few remaining trumpeter swans, an area not far from Yellowstone national park, where these birds also were completely protected and given special attention. Thus aided, the trumpeter swan began to win the battle against extinction. A report early in 1946 showed "at least 301 birds" in the United States in 1945—including 60 in Yellowstone national park and 163 on the Red Rock Lakes refuge. The remainder were scattered in the vicinity of these sanctuaries and on two other refuges to which a few swans were transplanted in 1939—the National Elk refuge in Wyoming and the Malheur National Wildlife refuge in Oregon. So tense was the interest in this bird that special annual counts

→

Trumpeter swan on the Red Rock lakes national wildlife refuge in Montana. In 1945, 301 of the species, formerly believed to be extinct, were counted at the Red Rock lakes refuge, in Yellowstone national park and other refuges

 were made leading to reports that there were 114 in the United States in 1936, 168 in 1937, and in succeeding years 148, 199, 185, 211, 199, 221, 283 and finally 301 in 1945.

Game species in general during these years were not subject to the nation-wide co-ordinated protection afforded the migratory birds by the federal government, the protection of other species being the concern of the individual states. There was thus not available year-by-year data for all wildlife in the U.S. comparable with the estimates and statistics relating to waterfowl.

An understanding of conditions and trends among big-game animals was, however, made possible to a great extent by an annual inventory begun by the fish and wildlife service in 1937 on the basis of data from state and federal agencies. Counts were made while animals were on their winter range, as near to the last day of each calendar year as possible, although it was found better to wait till early spring for estimating the numbers of some species.

A variety of methods was adopted. Aeroplanes were used in many regions without heavy forest cover and proved successful with regard to deer, elk, caribou, antelope, bighorns, mountain goats and buffalo. Men on skis or snowshoes elsewhere made ground counts of deer, elk and antelope, and on horseback made buffalo estimates. High slopes frequented by bighorn sheep and mountain goats were reached on foot. Bears were sometimes counted on feeding grounds in parks, but elsewhere it was usually necessary to locate their dens or trace the bears by tracks and claw marks on trees.

The first of the inventories, compilation of data for the year 1937, resulted in an estimate of 5,044,000 big-game animals of 15 groups and races. The latest one completed at the end of the decade—that for 1943—suggested an increase to 7,148,422, although it was surmised that some of the apparent increase might have been because of improvements in making the estimates. Dr. Hartley H. T. Jackson, who conducted the inventories, analyzed the trends during the first five years in *Big-Game Resources of the United States: 1937–1942*, published in 1944 as Research Report 8 of the fish and wildlife service. "At the close of the 5-year period," he wrote, "three species seemed to be in a precarious status. The number of moose had decreased throughout the United States 11.3 percent since 1937, and that of bighorn sheep 14.6 percent. The grizzly bear population had increased 12.1 percent; nevertheless, it is in constant danger of extirpation in the United States outside of national parks. The prong-horned antelope showed an increase of 51.6 percent in numbers over those of 1937; black bear, 45.1 percent; elk, 42.8 percent; deer, 30 percent; peccary, 23.8 percent; mountain goat, 23.6 percent; and American bison, 21.4 percent. Big game as a whole increased 30.8 percent."

A basis for detailed estimates of other game species throughout the country was not available, yet there were good grounds for concluding that the ten years had been a period of improvement in general game conditions as a result of the Federal Aid to Wildlife Restoration act of 1937. This act, designed primarily to increase and improve conservation work by the states, authorized a federal grant to any state which had enacted certain legislative measures to promote conservation. By 1946, 47 states were thus participating and receiving grants for purchasing and developing lands and for conducting research in wildlife management, the federal government paying 75% and the state 25% of the costs of the authorized projects—conducted in accordance with federal standards.

Two international agreements consummated during these years not only involved the United States further in conservation as a hemisphere concern but also established its own national policies more firmly. On March 15, 1937, the United States and Mexico exchanged ratifications and proclaimed a convention for protecting migratory birds and regulating shipments of game mammals between the two countries. On May 1, 1942, the Convention on Nature Protection and Wild Life Preservation in the Western Hemisphere became effective. One of the proposals of this convention was "to protect and preserve in their natural habitat representatives of all species and genera of the native fauna and flora" of the contracting states, "including migratory birds, in sufficient numbers and over areas extensive enough to assure them from becoming extinct through any agency within man's control."

There continued throughout these years a widening interest in song birds, in the birds noted for their plumage, and in wildlife in general for its own sake—an interest stimulated and served by such organizations as the National Audubon society and such magazines as *Nature*. Such general conservation organizations and publications prospered during the decade and continued in the war years to serve the U.S. through their influence for conservation, the circulation demand of the periodicals actually increasing beyond the wartime limitations on the use of paper.

Two significant general developments were the increased emphasis on the technology of wildlife management and the keener recognition that land-use management was of critical importance in wildlife management.

The intensified and enlarged public programs for wildlife restoration—both federal and state—were accompanied by a greatly increased demand for wildlife-management technologists. At the same time it was more generally recognized that sound conservation programs could be realized only by basing them on research. The annual publications of the proceedings of the North American wildlife conferences were, for example, to a great extent compilations of technical or semitechnical papers. A new organization of professional personnel, the Wildlife society, successfully established the *Journal of Wildlife Management*, and such earlier scientific publications as the *Journal of Mammalogy* and *The Auk* (ornithology) published much that was pertinent to wildlife management and conservation. Research units for the development of trained personnel (as well as for the prosecution of needed studies) were maintained at ten land-grant colleges, and training at other colleges and universities was further developed. So important, in fact, had science and special training become in wildlife conservation that Ira N. Gabrielson, director of the fish and wildlife service in 1945, called the loss of trained personnel the "most serious effect of the war on the conservation of United States animal resources."

Assuming of course a proper regulation of hunting, wildlife conservationists came more and more to see their central problem as largely one of land management. National parks, national forests and similar state areas were ranked with wildlife refuges. Establishment of a new conservation organization, the Wilderness society, for the preservation of wilderness and wild areas, was supported by many wildlife conservationists. The Committee on Bird Protection of the American Ornithologists' union in its report for 1944 pointed out that the ornithologist's "objective is a kind of conservation which assumes that land comes first and that its proper use must be the basis of all conservation."

Public law 732 enacted by the 79th congress made it

mandatory to have biological surveys made and reports thereon prepared, before multiple purpose or other high dams could be constructed or major diversions of water effected.

Pollution control was vigorously demanded, and an anti-pollution measure prepared by the house committee on rivers and harbours on the basis of three earlier bills was reported to congress, but failed to be enacted. At the close of 1946 the Izaak Walton league was mobilizing support for a similar measure to be introduced in the 80th congress. Thus in many ways the wildlife problem was recognized as one of providing suitable environment; this aspect of conservation seemed destined to be of increasing importance.

Bibliography.—The best source of brief but critical information regarding publications on wildlife conservation during this ten-year period is in the files of the fish and wildlife service's *Wildlife Review* authoritatively prepared by W. L. McAtee as a listing and critical annotation of books, articles in journals, and other publications. *See* also A. F. Gustafson, C. H. Guise, W. J. Hamilton, Jr., and H. Ries, *Conservation in the United States* (1939, revised 1944); Margaret Morse Nice, *The Watcher at the Nest* (1939); Ira N. Gabrielson, *Wildlife Conservation,* (1941) and *Wildlife Refuges,* (1942); *Fading Trails: The Story of Endangered American Wildlife,* by a committee from the National Park Service and the Fish and Wildlife Service, edited by Charles Elliott (1942). (H. Z.)

Other Countries.—In 1938 a conference met in London, England, to take stock of progress in the implementation of the convention for the conservation of the fauna and flora of Africa, signed in 1933, and to consider further measures of protection. The progress reported was not, except in the case of the Belgian Congo, remarkable, but the existence of the conference proved that the question of conservation was occupying the minds of the signatory governments. Various provisional agreements were reached for the purpose of making the convention more effective and it was agreed that the conference should reassemble in 1939 concurrently with a projected wider conference, which was to consider the extension of the protection afforded by the existing convention to the flora and fauna of tropical Asia and the western Pacific. Owing to the outbreak of World War II, neither conference materialized.

The incidence of war was inevitably prejudicial to the conservation of wildlife in many parts of Africa and in Europe. One important species, the magnificent European bison, almost certainly suffered through the war. This animal had been present in considerable numbers before World War I in the Russian forests, protected as hunting grounds of the tsars; during that war its numbers were already very seriously reduced by marauding soldiers and poachers, so that in 1939, in spite of the activities of an international society for their protection, there were no more than approximately 100 in existence, of which about 30 were in the forest of Bialowieza, Lithuania, and about 30 in Germany. On the whole the species survived World War II better than was to be expected. A group of 13 in Germany was protected by the British control commission; another 23 were reported to be in the Bialowieza forest under Russian protection. Other small groups and individuals survived in various zoos in Sweden and elsewhere and in England a herd of 21 was kept in the duke of Bedford's park at Woburn. Because of the tendency of the species to breed a preponderant number of males, however, the existing remnant was still in some danger of eventual extinction.

In British Africa the conservation of wildlife suffered a very serious setback in World War II. Not only did the conditions of war deplete the staffs of the various colonial game departments, so that the enforcement of the laws and ordinances for the protection of wildlife were weakened, but also in various territories—notably in Southern Rhodesia and in part of South Africa—a policy of game slaughter was enforced in the belief that, by this means, the disease-bearing tsetse fly could be eradicated or controlled. The officially published figures of the numbers of animals slaughtered in Southern Rhodesia were alarming: in 1945 more than 28,000 head were lost. It was by no means certain that such measures would have the effect desired, or that competent organized scientific research would not reveal other means for controlling the tsetse fly menace; yet the ideas underlying the slaughter policy were gaining ground in other territories.

It was widely feared that, as a result of the Japanese invasion and occupation, the wildlife of Malaya and of the Netherlands East Indies would be seriously threatened. According to reports received by 1946, however, it appeared that, in Malaya at least, the position had not deteriorated and might rather have improved because of the strictly-enforced Japanese embargo on the carrying of firearms of any description.

Bibliography.—On fisheries, *see International Convention for the Regulation of Fishing Nets and the Size Limits of Fish* (Cmd. 5494, H.M.S.O., London, 1937); *Final Act and Convention of the International Overfishing Conference* (Cmd. 6791, H.M.S.O., London, 1946). On Whaling, *see International Agreement for the Regulation of Whaling* (Cmd. 5857) and *Protocol* amending this agreement (Cmd. 5993, H.M.S.O., London, 1937 and 1938 respectively); *Protocol on the International Regulation of Whaling, with the Final Act of the Conference* (Cmd. 6510, H.M.S.O., London, 1944); *Protocol amending the Agreement of 1937 and Protocol of 1938* (Cmd. 7009, H.M.S.O., London, 1945). On wildlife in general, *see Journal* of the Society for the Preservation of the Fauna of the Empire, new series, parts XXXI to LIV (London, 1937–46). (H. G. M.)

Wilhelmina

Queen Wilhelmina (Wilhelmina Helena Pauline Maria of Orange-Nassau) (1880–), of the Netherlands, was born Aug. 31, 1880, the daughter of King William III of the Netherlands and Queen Emma. Succeeding to the throne in 1890, she ruled under the regency of her mother until 1898 when, at the age of 18, she was formally enthroned. She married Henry, duke of Mecklenburg-Schwerin in 1901 and in 1909 Crown Princess Juliana was born. Prince Consort Henry died in 1934.

The queen successfully steered her country along a path of absolute neutrality during World War I (1914–18), but the Netherlands' efforts to remain neutral during World War II were frustrated by the German invasion of May 10, 1940; the royal family fled to London for refuge. The queen proclaimed on May 13, 1940, that the seat of the Netherlands government had been transferred to London; Netherlands forces carried on the war from there until the liberation of the country.

As the war in Europe was drawing to a close, the queen took up residence near Breda, in April 1945, and moved to the royal palace at The Hague, July 7, 1945. On Dec. 25, 1946, she proclaimed the existence of the provisional state of East Indonesia, comprised of all of the Netherlands Indies east of Java and Borneo, excepting New Guinea.

Wilkinson, Ellen C.

Miss Wilkinson (1891–1947), British member of parliament, was born in Manchester, England. The daughter of a millworker, she won a scholarship at the University of Manchester, where she obtained her master of arts degree. Upon completion of her studies she became a trade union organizer. An early advocate of women's suffrage, she organized the National Union of Women's Suffrage in 1913 and she was elected in 1924 as Labour member for Middlesbrough, one of the few women ever elected to the British parliament. Miss Wilkinson was returned to commons in 1935 as Labour member for Jarrow and later agitated in parliament for more effective relief for the unemployed in that shipbuilding community. She was made parliamentary secretary to the ministry of pensions in the Churchill coalition government in May 1940, but left this post a few months later to join the ministry of home security in order to assist in providing food and shelter for bombed out Londoners. Early in 1945, she was made a member of the privy council, and in April she attended the San Francisco conference of the United Nations as a member of the British delegation. After Prime Minister Attlee formed the Labour government (July 26, 1945), he appointed Miss Wilkinson to the post of minister of education. At the opening session in London of the United Nations education conference, Nov. 1, 1945, she was elected president of the parley. She was also one of the British delegates to the United Nations general assembly sessions that opened in London Jan. 10, 1946. Miss Wilkinson died Feb. 6, 1947, at London.

Willkie, Wendell Lewis

Willkie (1892–1944), U.S. politician and business executive, was born Feb. 18, 1892, in Elwood, Ind. After graduating from the University of Indiana with an A.B. degree in 1913, he taught history in the high school at Coffeyville, Kan., and attended Oberlin college for a short time in 1915; he then became a laboratory assistant in a Puerto Rican sugar plant. In 1916 he received his law degree from the University of Indiana and joined his father's law firm in Elwood. On the day in 1917 that the U.S. entered World War I, Willkie enlisted; in France he became a captain in the 325th field artillery and after the armistice he continued in service to act as counsel for enlisted men who had been court-martialled. Meanwhile, on Jan. 14, 1918, he had married Edith Wilk of Rushville, Ind.

Back in civilian life, Willkie worked for a short time in the legal department of the Firestone Tire and Rubber company in Akron, O., then joined the law firm of Mather and Nesbitt in that city. Among Willkie's legal clients was an Ohio utilities company, and through this relationship he was persuaded in 1929 to go to New York city as a member of the legal staff of Commonwealth and Southern, a large utilities holding company with operating units in 11 states. Four years later he was president of the company. In this $75,000-a-yr. office he more than doubled the amount of electricity sold by the company. He also entered into a controversy with the Tennessee Valley authority (which had set up extensive power developments in competition with Commonwealth and Southern) and attracted national notice and considerable sympathy for the cause of public utilities. Always ready to concede the need for proper control of utilities, he presented his arguments against excessive governmental regulation in such a logical manner that he became known, in the words of one publication, as the "most articulate" of the New Deal's critics, and, by 1939, as a potential candidate for president.

He was nominated for the presidency by the Republican convention June 28, 1940, in the face of much opposition by regular politicians. (*See* Republican Party and Elections.) His campaign was an unusually active one. Although he was defeated by a substantial margin in the election of Nov. 5, 1940, the 22,333,801 votes cast for him exceeded the largest number ever cast for a presidential candidate except Franklin D. Roosevelt. After the election, Willkie retired to private life (he had resigned as president of Commonwealth and Southern) and issued a call to his followers to co-operate in national unity.

At the request of Pres. Roosevelt he became the latter's special emissary and toured England, the middle east, the U.S.S.R. and China in 1941–42. His book, *One World,* the story of this trip, pleaded for postwar co-operation among all nations. While Willkie criticized Roosevelt's domestic policies, he urged the Republican party to support the president in the war effort. This appeal and his views on international co-operation alienated the G.O.P. leaders, and they opposed his efforts to obtain the Republican nomination for president in the 1944 campaign. Willkie struggled against the tide, but after his overwhelming defeat in the Wisconsin primaries in April, he withdrew from the race. He died of coronary thrombosis in New York city, Oct. 8, 1944.

Wilson, Charles Edward

Wilson (1886–), U.S. industrialist, was born Nov. 18, 1886, in New York city. At the age of 12, he went to work as a shipping clerk with the General Electric company, later becoming a factory manager and assistant superintendent. He became executive vice-president of General Electric in 1937 and president Jan. 1, 1940.

Wilson was selected by Chairman Donald Nelson for the post of War Production board vice-chairman in full charge of production, Sept. 17, 1942, and the following December was made chairman of WPB's Production Executive committee. On Dec. 1, 1942, he was also made chairman of the U.S.-Canada Joint War Production committee, succeeding James S. Knowlson.

Soon a policy dispute over control of production and materials developed between Wilson and Ferdinand Eberstadt, vice-chairman in charge of materials. Chairman Nelson resolved the dispute in Feb. 1943 by removing Eberstadt and transferring his functions to Wilson, who shortly thereafter became executive vice-chairman.

Wilson resigned in Aug. 1943 in protest against "a campaign of vilification" picturing him as an exponent of big business in plans for postwar reconversion. President F. D. Roosevelt, in accepting the resignation, lauded Wilson for "outstanding service" to the nation.

Wilson, 1st Baron

Baron Wilson of Libya and of Stowlangtoft (Henry Maitland Wilson) (1881–), British army officer, was born Sept. 5, 1881, at Stowlangtoft hall in the county of Suffolk. Educated at Eton and the Royal Military college at Sandhurst, he joined a rifle brigade in 1899 and served in the Boer War (1899–1902). During World War I, he served in France (1914–17), was cited three times and received the distinguished service order.

Promoted to lieutenant general in 1939, Wilson was made commander of the British army of the Nile. He organized the western desert defenses and, under Gen. Archibald Wavell's direction, led the drive that swept Rodolfo Graziani's Italian armies out of Cyrenaica. Gen. Wilson was then made commander in chief and military governor of Cyrenaica. In 1940 he commanded British troops in the ill-fated Greek campaign and he also directed Allied armies that won Syria (June–July 1941). He was appointed commander of the Iran-Iraq theatre in Aug. 1942.

Returning to Egypt in Feb. 1943 as commander in chief

of the middle east, he was appointed supreme allied commander in the Mediterranean theatre in December of that year. On Nov. 26, 1944, he was appointed head of the British joint staff mission in Washington and was elevated to the rank of field marshal on Dec. 29, 1944. He was elevated to the peerage March 12, 1946, as 1st Baron Wilson of Libya and of Stowlangtoft. On Oct. 9, 1946, Lord Wilson was succeeded in his post as British army member of the joint staff mission by Lt. Gen. Sir William D. Morgan.

Winant, John Gilbert

Winant (1889–   ), U.S. diplomat, was born on Feb. 23, 1889, in New York city. He studied at Princeton university, Princeton, N.J., and in 1912 joined the faculty of St. Paul's school as a teacher of English and assistant rector. He entered the U.S. army during World War I, becoming captain of the 8th air observation squadron in France. After the war he was elected to the New Hampshire legislature, serving in both the lower and upper houses between 1917 and 1923.

He was governor of New Hampshire in 1925–26 and from 1931 to 1934.

Winant joined the International Labour organization in 1935, serving as assistant director and then director. In 1941 he was appointed ambassador to Great Britain by President Roosevelt. In Dec. 1944 he submitted to the British, French and soviet governments a detailed U.S. proposal for shaping the postwar economy of the reich.

On Jan. 12, 1946, Winant was appointed as U.S. representative on the United Nations Economic and Social council.

He held this post concurrently with his position as ambassador until March 23, 1946, when he was succeeded as ambassador by W. Averell Harriman.

Windsor, Duchess of

The duchess of Windsor (1896–   ), was born June 19, 1896, in Monterey, Pa., as Bessie Wallace Warfield, daughter of Mr. and Mrs. Wallis Warfield. In 1916, when she was 20, Miss Warfield was married to Lieut. E. Winfield Spencer, whom she divorced in 1931. A year later, she married Ernest Simpson, a well-to-do London broker. Some time later she met the prince of Wales and on Oct. 27, 1936, she was granted an uncontested divorce from Simpson. While waiting for her divorce decree, the prince, who had become King Edward VIII, had announced to the cabinet his intention of marrying Mrs. Simpson. The marriage was opposed by Prime Minister Stanley Baldwin and other high British dignitaries. At the height of the crisis, marked by the king's insistence and the government's unalterable opposition to the marriage, Mrs. Simpson offered on Dec. 8, 1936, "to withdraw from a situation that had been rendered both unhappy and untenable." However, the king decided to reject the throne and on Dec. 11, 1936, abdicated and assumed the title duke of Windsor.

Baldwin subsequently prohibited any official recognition of the duke's forthcoming marriage, and the archbishop of Canterbury declined to authorize a Church of England ceremony on the grounds that the bride was a divorcee. The Baldwin government also issued a decree forbidding the American woman and "her descendants if any" from any right to the title of "Royal Highness." They were married June 3, 1937, in the Chateau de Candé in Monts, France. After a trip to Austria, they took up residence in France.

After the start of World War II, she went in Aug. 1940 to Nassau with her husband who had become governor of the Bahamas. After the war they returned to France.

Windsor, Edward, H.R.H., The Duke of

The duke of Windsor (1894–   ), who reigned for 46 weeks and 4 days in 1936 as King Edward VIII of England, was born June 23, 1894, at White Lodge, Richmond Park, England, the first child of King George V and Queen Mary, who at the time were the duke and duchess of York. He was baptized Edward Albert Christian George Andrew Patrick David. He was sent to Osborne, a naval preparatory college, in 1907 and two years later entered the Royal Naval college at Dartmouth. On completing his training at Dartmouth in July 1911, he was invested prince of Wales and earl of Chester. He entered Magdalen college, Oxford, 1912, but left the university upon the outbreak of World War I in 1914 and was gazetted to the Grenadier Guards in Aug. 1914. He served as aide-de-camp to Sir John French for 18 months on the western front; later he was on the staff of the general officer commanding the Mediterranean expeditionary force. After the war the prince visited Canada and the United States in 1919, Australia and New Zealand in 1920, India and Japan in 1921–22 and British possessions and dominions in Africa and South America in 1925.

On Jan. 20, 1936, George V died and the prince of Wales ascended the throne as King Edward VIII. In the summer of that year gossip connected the king's name with that of Mrs. Wallis Warfield Simpson. In October and November Prime Minister Stanley Baldwin conferred with the king on the issue and was informed by Edward that he intended to marry Mrs. Simpson. Baldwin objected to the marriage, not because of Mrs. Simpson's status as a commoner or an American, but because she already had been twice divorced. (Mrs. Simpson had obtained a decree *nisi*, Oct. 27, 1936.) Given a choice between his proposed marriage and the crown, Edward chose the former, abdicating, Dec. 11, 1936, in favour of his brother, the duke of York, who became King George VI.

Taking the title of duke of Windsor, he married Mrs. Simpson in a ceremony at the Chateau de Candé, Monts, France, on June 3, 1937.

On Sept. 12, 1939, nine days after the outbreak of World War II, the duke returned to England for a brief family reunion. He returned to France Sept. 22 as liaison officer between the British and French armies. After the Germans began to overrun France in June 1940, the Windsors fled to Spain and thence to Portugal. He was later appointed governor and commander in chief of the Bahamas, assuming this post in Aug. 1940. The duke resigned in March 1945.

Windward Islands

See West Indies, British.

Wines

In spite of wars and other catastrophes, the hardy vine continued to survive during the decade 1937–46 and to produce its grapes which the indefatigable vignerons of the world pressed into wine. Viticulture continued to give a direct livelihood to 30,000,000 people in Europe alone. The violence and scope of World War II, however, naturally dislocated every phase of normal trade and production. The true extent of the damage was not known, as it was impossible to obtain exact statistics from all the wine-producing regions of the world.

Algeria.—France had always counted on Algeria to supplement its own wine harvest and to make up the difference between its production and the consumption of the French people. Conditions in Algeria deteriorated rapidly after 1940, and the yield dropped from an average of well over 400,000,000 gal. per year to about 250,000,000 gal. in 1945. Efforts were made after the end of the war to increase production, but several years would be required before normal harvests were again possible.

Argentina.—Unaffected by the rigours of war, Argentine production was maintained at approximately the normal 200,000,000 gal. annually. The 1945 vintage was somewhat less, because of early frost and mildew, but this was offset by substantial carry-overs from the previous vintages. Consumption of wine in Argentina increased steadily until by 1946 it exceeded 12 gal. per capita as compared to less than 1 gal. in the U.S. Quality-wise, Argentina steadily improved its wines. An important contributing factor was the increasing amount of bottled wine shipped from the wineries in Mendoza, San Juan and Rio Negro to the distributing centres of the country. By 1946, this amounted to nearly 50% of the wine as opposed to the former system of shipping almost everything in wood for bottling by the retail establishments. As usual, the wines of Argentina did not vary greatly in quality from one vintage to another.

Australia.—Although Australia was deeply involved in World War II from Sept. 1939 onward, production and consumption of wine was maintained at a fairly normal rate until 1945, when there was a disastrous vintage in quantity although excellent in quality. Normal and even increased consumption was aided by the fact that the government placed restrictions on the consumption of beer and spirits so that the loss of Australia's foreign markets was more than made up for by its increased home consumption. By 1946, Australia found itself with an actual shortage of wine, but with the lifting of restrictions on beer and spirits it hoped to find itself in a position to resume its flourishing prewar export trade. During the decade 1937–46, fair to good wines were produced every year, with wines of exceptional quality being produced in South Australia in 1945 and wines of vintage quality being produced in the Hunter river district in 1940.

Chile.—Viticulturally, Chile was still perhaps the most favoured nation in the world insofar as climatic conditions were concerned. It also remained unique in possessing the only vineyards in the world that had never known the ravages of the phylloxera. Production of wine increased to such a point that the government restricted the amount of wine which could be marketed, to prevent excessive consumption on the part of the poor people. All excess production had to be distilled for industrial purposes or exported. The principal European grape varieties were cultivated, and wines of excellent quality were obtained. A large export market was developed; after the war, Chile's exports to its neighbouring South American countries, to the U.S. and to Europe increased substantially. Among its outstanding wines were Riesling and Sauterne among the white wines, and a full-bodied red wine of the Burgundy type.

France.—Traditionally the largest producer and consumer of wines in the world, France probably suffered most during the war period. In no way could this be demonstrated better than by the fact that wine was rationed in France, each person receiving only one litre (just over a quart) per month, a quantity normally consumed in two or three days. From 1935 to 1939, the average production of wine in France was 1,468,160,000 gal., with the 1939 vintage 1,796,371,000 gal. In 1945, the first peacetime vintage after liberation was only 661,494,000 gal., almost 1,000,000,000 gal. less than the 1939 vintage and about 45% of the normal production. The reasons for this decline were several: (1) Lack of manpower to care for the vineyards; France's men were prisoners of war or in forced labour battalions in Germany; (2) vines too old or diseased could not be replaced when they died, partly for the previous reason; (3) copper sulphate and other disease-combating sprays and chemicals were not available, and vines that could have been saved were lost. It was estimated that more than 10,000,000 vines had to be planted, in addition to the normal annual replantings, before France's vineyards could be brought back to prewar production. It was economically impossible to do this at once, and at least 10 years would pass before the total number of vines in production approached the prewar figure. The resulting short production, in addition to inflation, naturally caused huge increases in price. France's large prewar export trade in wines was adversely affected.

Even though the Germans requisitioned substantial quantities of fine wines, they were unable to carry off much of what they wanted because of lack of transport facilities. Therefore, excellent stocks of very fine wines still remained in France. From a quality standpoint, the vintages of 1937, 1943 and 1945 were outstanding for all wines. In addition to these years, very good wines were produced in the Bordeaux region in 1940, 1942 and 1944, while in the Champagne region, excellent wines were produced in 1938, 1941 and 1942. It should be noted that the 1945 vintage promised to be the finest of the 20th century up to that year.

Germany.—For obvious reasons, it was not possible to obtain satisfactory information regarding production of wines in Germany. The situation was further confused because of the fact that part of the Rhine-Moselle wine-growing regions lay in the French zone of occupation, while the rest lay in the U.S. zone. With regard to quality, the outstanding vintages of the decade were 1937, 1943 and 1945, with 1942 and 1944 producing very good wines as well.

Greece.—Exact production figures from 1939 onward were unobtainable. However, it was estimated that production averaged between 50,000,000 and 80,000,000 gal. per yr. The German and Italian occupational forces seized large quantities of wines which were shipped to Germany and Italy; because of lack of other vitamin-containing foods, a large quantity of the grapes produced in Greece was consumed by the Greek people to replace bread and other vital foods which they did not have. Further, because of lack of disease-combating chemicals and sprays, many of the vineyards suffered. In Greece, as in France, it was economically impossible for the vineyard owners to bring their plantings up to prewar par for a number of years.

Hungary.—No definite information was obtainable regarding Hungary's wine production after 1939, other than the fact that wine continued to be an important part of Hungary's agriculture. The 1945 vintage, as in the rest of Europe, was very favourable from a quality point of view. The quantity produced was estimated to be about 4,000,000 hectolitres (105,671,000 gal.). In the Tokajhegyalja, the weather was favourable for the drying of the grapes on the vine, so that it was possible to produce better than average quantities of the rich, sweet Aszu Tokaji wines.

Italy.—Wine production in Italy during the war years suffered a slowdown resulting from lack of manpower and from destruction by phylloxera, which, far from diminishing, reached a greater intensity because of prolonged dry spells and the scarcity of irrigation which could not be properly carried on. In many zones where actual battles raged, hardly a trace of the vines remained. The arduous campaigns fought on the Italian peninsula ravaged many of the vineyards, and no actual census was made. It appeared that the most heavily-damaged parts of Italy were in Tuscany and Emilia, where some of the best wines of Italy were produced, particularly Chianti from Tuscany. However, the vineyards of Apulia seemed to have suffered little or no damage. This region of Italy produces the largest quantity of wine, although very few of the wines reach the export market; they are either consumed in Italy or reach foreign markets in the form of vermouth. There are less violent variations in climatic conditions in Italy from year to year than in other European wine-producing regions, and for that reason vintages are more uniform.

Palestine.—The art of viticulture had been practiced in Palestine since prebiblical times, and all references to wine in the Bible are to the wines produced in Palestine. For many centuries, however, viticulture was neglected, and it was only re-established on a commercial basis in 1882 by Baron Edmond de Rothschild of Paris, who installed a modern plant and large cellars.

Cultivation of the vine in Palestine made its most outstanding progress during the ten years preceding 1946; production more than doubled from the 61,574,000 gal. produced in 1936 to an average of 140,000,000 gal. produced in 1944 and in 1945, largely because of the increase in labour made possible by the influx of refugees from western Europe. Whereas prior to 1936 the wines produced were labelled port, malaga, sherry, tokay, etc., the tendency developed after that year to label wine with Palestinian names such as Kallia, Adom Atik, etc., the object being to cease the selling of Palestinian wines under foreign names and to endeavour to develop the world markets on the basis of the original Hebrew names. Because of the even-tempered climate there is very little variation in quality among vintages.

Champagne stored in wicker baskets in a French wine cellar where U.S. troops of liberation found it in 1944. The proprietor is shown talking shop as two U.S. army nurses look on

Portugal.—Physically untouched by the ravages of war, Portugal had the good fortune to be favoured with several of its most abundant vintages at the very moment when there was the greatest demand for its wine in export markets. The country of the Lusitanians has perhaps some of the most uneven climate of Europe; there were such wide variations in production figures as 126,809,000 gal. in 1940 and 344,995,000 gal. in 1944. The U.S. alone, normally importing about 125,000 gal. of wine from Portugal, imported 1,763,326 gal. in 1943 and 3,861,718 gal. in 1944. These abnormal importations of Portuguese wines by the U.S. were due to the fact that its normal sources of supply were cut off because of occupation by the axis nations, and the production of spirits in the U.S. was greatly curtailed because of the entire use of distilling facilities for the war effort.

The 1938, 1940, 1942, 1944 and 1945 Portuguese wines were good. Of these, the 1938 and 1940 wines were bottled as vintage wines; the 1942 was good enough to be declared a vintage, and the 1944 or 1945 probably would be shipped as a vintage wine.

Spain.—Official production figures after the 1941 vintage were unobtainable, but presumably they were about 400,000,000 gal. on the average. Spain, too, was untouched by the physical aspects of World War II. During the Civil War of 1936–39, little fighting took place in the principal export wine-producing region, in and about Jerez, where sherry is produced. Like Portugal, Spain's exports to the U.S. enjoyed an unprecedented increase during 1943 and 1944, when they totalled 1,264,215 gal. and 2,392,715 gal. respectively, as compared to a normal shipment of approximately 500,000 gal. The importation of table wines from Spain also increased by 600% to 700% during 1943–44.

The relative merits of one sherry vintage as compared to another have only minor importance because of the fact that all commercial sherry is produced by the Solera system of continual blending.

Union of South Africa.—No great change was noted in the production figures of the vineyards of the Union of South Africa, probably because of the fact that the export market remained small. The principal market was still England, where wines labelled Empire Claret, Empire Burgundy, etc., continued to be shipped. South African wines generally have a spicy quality and are quite full-bodied.

United States.—The vine is cultivated in all 48 states of the union; commercial wine making in 1946 was practised in 27. California's soil and climate were found to be so suitable to wine-producing grape culture that it accounted for more than 90% of the wine made in the U.S. New York and Ohio remained the most important producers among the other states.

Wine production on a commercial basis was resumed in 1933 after 14 years of prohibition. In the first few years it was inevitable that large quantities of wines had to be made from grape varieties better suited for eating or drying. Great strides were made in the replanting of vineyards to wine-producing varieties, but with the advent of World War II, this program suffered a setback, because of the government requirements of vast tonnages of raisins, which were found to be one of the best concentrated vitaminous rations for troops.

Wine Production of the Principal Wine-Growing Countries of the World
In thousands of American Wine Gallons
1,000 American Gallons equals 833⅓ British (Imperial) Gal.

Country	1936	1937	1938	1939	1940	1941	1942	1943	1944	1945
*Algeria	304,512	407,447	565,577	470,446	370,744	280,120	325,281	174,251	244,657	250,974
†Argentina		208,320	243,120			200,000	201,036	285,635	285,000	191,000
†Australia	20,947	16,196	23,803	17,949	16,730	19,188	19,034	23,841	23,837	15,616
†Chile		93,082	94,342			61,000		72,633	127,000	100,000δ
*France	1,043,474	1,357,228	1,531,677	1,796,371	1,185,556	1,136,863	890,442	999,500	1,075,310	661,494
‡Germany	110,643	89,775	87,045δ	Exact figures unobtainable						
‡Greece	45,543	88,410	106,181	Exact figures unobtainable—production estimated between 50,000 and 80,000 gal.						
‡Hungary	119,122	117,416	85,548	Exact figures unobtainable						
§Italy	887,753	961,843	1,103,812	1,128,488	804,011	967,078	1,003,213	996,124	879,116	773,038
†Palestine	61,574	90,613	81,631	90,613	99,859	97,217	98,274	115,446	145,298	135,808
†Portugal	149,712	255,220	203,848	146,402	126,809	175,659	198,543	333,217	344,995	240,363
‖Spain		427,285	420,000		532,349	374,290				
¶Union of South Africa	34,122	32,585	27,954	31,179	37,811	35,339	29,456	40,429	45,982	40,522
♀U.S.A.	52,031	95,308	60,396	80,778	113,998	118,182	66,926	88,279	97,425	129,334δ

δEstimated.

Sources: *Syndicat International, Paris, Comite Interprofessionnel de Vin de Champagne, Epernay, & La Journee Vinicole, Montpellier.
†Private trade sources. Data unofficial, but reliable.
‡Exact figures unobtainable.
§Associazione Italiana Industriale ed Esportatori di Vini, Liquori e Derivati, Rome.
‖Estadistica de Produccion del Ministerio del Trabajo, Madrid.
¶Ko-opertieve Wijnbouwers Vereniging van Zuid-Afrika, Beperkt, Zuider Paarl.
♀Wine Institute Bulletin of The Wine Advisory Board, San Francisco.

Wine production in the U.S. had a difficult time keeping ahead of consumption. Whereas in 1936 about 52,000,000 gal. were produced, consumption was more than 60,000,000 gal. The peak of consumption was reached in 1941 and 1942, with taxpaid figures of 101,674,303 gal. and 113,270,677 gal. respectively. Consumption figures fell off somewhat during the war years. This was due to a series of causes, such as shortage of supply, the order to produce raisins for the war effort, shortages of labour, bottles and cartons and transportation difficulties. The lifting of the restrictions of the grape order was immediately reflected in an increase of more than 30% in production in the 1945 vintage. The marketing of wine was aggressively pursued by the California producers. A national advertising program was conducted under the supervision of the California Wine Advisory board.

American wine producers continued their efforts to offer wines so crystal bright that they would never have any sediment. This sedimentation can be prevented by pasteurizing, and a vast majority of the wines produced in the U.S. are so treated, but when a wine is pasteurized, almost all its character is lost. Nevertheless, distinguished wines were produced in the U.S. (*See* also LIQUORS, ALCOHOLIC.)

BIBLIOGRAPHY.—(Australia): J. L. Williams, *The Establishment of Vineyards under Australian Conditions* (1946); (Italy): F. Carpentieri, *Theoretical-Practical Oenology* (1941); (Palestine): J. Shapira and David Judelevitz, *Wine and Almonds in Palestine;* (Portugal): G. M. Tait, *Port from the Vine to Glass* (London, 1936); (Spain): Gordon Manuel Gonzalez, *Sherry* (Spain, 1936); (United States): M. A. Amerine and M. A. Joslyn, *Commercial Production of Table Wines* (1940); Mary Frost Mabon, *A.B.C. of America's Wines* (1942); Frank Schoonmaker and Marvel Tom, *American Wines* (1941). (O. J. W.)

Wisconsin

One of the north central states, Wisconsin, popularly known as the "Badger state," was admitted to the union in 1848. Area, 56,154 sq.mi., including 1,439 sq.mi. of water. Population (1940) 3,137,587, of which 1,679,144 were urban and 1,458,443 rural. Only 24,835 were nonwhite. Foreign-born whites numbered 288,774. On July 1, 1944, the bureau of census estimated the population of the state at 2,975,910. Capital, Madison (pop. 1940, 67,447). The largest city is Milwaukee with a population of 587,472. Other cities: Racine (67,195); Kenosha (48,765); Green Bay (46,235); La Crosse (42,707); and Sheboygan (40,638).

State officers in 1937 (elected in 1936) were Philip Fox La Follette, governor; Henry A. Gunderson, lieutenant governor; Theodore Dammann, secretary of state; Solomon Levitan, treasurer; and Orland S. Loomis, attorney general. The election of 1936 had represented a triumph for the newly organized Progressive party, which also gained a controlling voice in the legislature. But Roosevelt, Democratic candidate for president, received 802,984 votes to Landon's 380,826, and 74,748 for all others.

The general election of Nov. 8, 1938, however, brought serious reverses to the state administration. Three parties had nominees for the state offices: the Progressive, Republican and Democratic. The actual race proved to be between the Progressive and Republican parties, the latter winning an overwhelming victory. Julius P. Heil, Republican candidate for governor, emerged with a plurality of approximately 187,000 over La Follette, incumbent candidate for a fourth term. Republican candidates for the offices of secretary of state, attorney general and state treasurer received heavy pluralities also, and the Republicans elected 8 out of 10 congressmen, defeating all Progressive candidates save one. The state senate and assembly both secured Republican majorities. The Democratic party ran a poor third; even its candidate for the U.S. senate, F. Ryan Duffy, who was endorsed by Pres. Roosevelt, had a smaller vote than the Progressive candidate, Herman L. Ekern, and the combined votes of these two proved decidedly less than the votes polled by Alexander Wiley (Rep.).

In the presidential election of 1940, Roosevelt received 704,821 votes, Wendell Willkie (Rep.) 679,206, Norman Thomas (Soc.) 15,071, Earl Browder (Comm.) 2,394, Roger Babson (Proh.) 2,148, John W. Aiken (Soc. Lab.) 1,882. The 11 electoral votes of Wisconsin were given to Roosevelt by a smaller majority than in 1936 and 1932. Robert M. La Follette, Jr. (Prog.) was returned to the U.S. senate by a plurality vote, his Republican opponent, Fred M. Clauson, trailing by some 45,000 and the Democratic contender being left far behind. In the three-cornered race for the governorship the Republican incumbent, Julius P. Heil, had the plurality, Orland S. Loomis, the Progressive candidate, running second and Francis E. McGovern, Democrat, third. Again, as in the session of 1939, the Republicans gained control of both houses of the legislature, but by more impressive majorities. (J. Sc.; X.)

The legislature in 1941 passed a number of important measures. The Model Sabotage Prevention act prohibited and penalized intentional interference with the defense program. The State Guard act created a militia in the absence of the national guard. Communists were barred from the ballot. Military training was made compulsory

Blackhawk winter wheat, a disease-resistant hybrid developed by Dr. R. G. Shands at the University of Wisconsin college of agriculture to increase Wisconsin farm feed supplies. Seed raised in 1945 by certified growers was being cultivated in sufficient quantity for general farm distribution

Wisconsin veterans of World War II arriving at the capitol building in Madison to discuss grievances which included the question of bonuses and the rate of unemployment compensation

at the state university. Various civil service laws were passed to protect the rights of those in the military services. Safety and traffic regulations included a law under which all drivers had to renew their licences every four years. An amendment to the constitution permitting instalment payment of real estate taxes was submitted to the electors and ratified. The Unfair Sales act was clarified and strengthened. The teachers' tenure law of 1937 was repealed. Upon the death of Stephen Bolles, congressional representative from the 1st district, a special election was held in 1941. Lawrence H. Smith (Rep.) was opposed by a Progressive, Thomas R. Amlie, who ran on the Democratic ticket. Amlie, who stressed support of Roosevelt's foreign policy, was defeated by a 2-to-1 vote. (L. KN.; X.)

The election of Nov. 3, 1942, was marked by bitter discussion of the prewar nonintervention attitude of Wisconsin members of the lower house of congress, but all were re-elected except three. The state elections showed a Republican gain in the legislature, so that Republicans held 74 of the 100 assembly seats and 23 of 33 senate seats. The state officers were all re-elected save Governor Heil (Rep.), who lost to Orland P. Loomis (Prog.), by a plurality of 100,000. Heil was criticized politically for allowing the conservation commission to remove Commissioner H. W. MacKenzie, for his frequent absence from the capital at Madison, for his expenditures in the contingent fund and for his administration of civilian defense. The death of Governor-elect Loomis on Dec. 7 raised a constitutional question as to his successor, and the supreme court decided that under the constitution Lieutenant Governor W. S. Goodland should serve as acting governor for the full two-yr. term.

The legislature, urged by the acting governor to put the state on a war footing and to set aside the money pouring in from the income tax for postwar construction and rehabilitation of war veterans, passed 566 acts in 1943. Of the governor's 36 vetoes, 21 were overridden by the legislature, one more than the total overridden in the entire history of the state, and the legislature insisted upon reconvening on Jan. 12, 1944. Yet much of the governor's program was obtained. The 60% emergency surtax on incomes was not re-enacted, but its yield for 1942 was set up as a postwar rehabilitation trust fund for returning veterans. A state trunk highway fund, estimated to contain $17,450,000 by the end of the 1943–45 biennium, was created for postwar construction. The state Civil War debt of $1,183,700 was retired. Unemployment insurance contribution rates and payments were increased, as were workmen's compensation payments. Aid to high schools was raised from $1,385,000 to $3,500,000 yearly. Civil service employees were voted a cost-of-living bonus, a pension-retirement plan, and a regulated system of annual increases. A controversial bill requiring all attorneys to be members of the state bar was passed over a veto and upheld by the supreme court.

The legislature convened for six days in Jan. 1944, enacting laws providing absentee ballots for soldiers in the 1944 elections and establishing a $7,000,000 trust fund for building and modernizing state mental institutions. In March, Wendell L. Willkie focused national interest on Wisconsin by conducting a 1,500-mi., 13-day campaign to secure the state's 24 delegates to the national Republican convention on a frankly anti-isolationist platform. In April voters repudiated Willkie, electing 17 delegates pledged or friendly to Thomas E. Dewey, 4 pledged to Harold E. Stassen and 3 pledged to Douglas MacArthur. On the next day Willkie withdrew from the presidential race. In the August primary the vote was about 70% Republican, 23% Democratic, and less than 7% Progressive. In November Dewey received a 24,000-vote lead over Pres. Roosevelt and 50.91% of the popular vote. U.S. Senator Wiley (Rep.) was re-elected by 97,000 votes despite bitter attacks on his isolationist record by H. J. McMurray (Dem.).

The Republican state ticket swept to an easy victory in 1944, led by Acting Governor Goodland, 82 years old, who became governor in his own right with a plurality of 161,000 over D. W. Hoan, Democrat and former Socialist. Oscar Rennebohm was elected lieutenant governor, and the secretary of state, treasurer and attorney general were retained. The new assembly

Wisconsin: *Statistical Data*

Table I.—*Education (Public)*

	1936	1938	1941	1942	1943	1944
Elementary school pupils	408,707	387,526	374,854	361,599	354,692	348,774
High school pupils	168,636	172,942	160,311	158,248	151,398	142,022
Elementary teachers	14,313	14,999	15,415	15,312	14,466	14,245
High school teachers	6,586	6,498	6,162	5,924	6,322	6,162

Table II.—*Public Welfare*

(Money figures in thousands of dollars)

	1938	1940	1941	1943	1944	1945
Cases on general relief	48,948	45,352	24,106	8,669	6,428	5,235
Recipients of old-age pensions	43,659	51,545	54,018	50,495	47,324	44,923
Dependent children receiving aid	25,108	28,128	28,383			
Blind receiving aid	1,965	2,008	1,983	1,728	1,525	1,400

Table III.—*Communications*

(Money figures in thousands of dollars)

	1937	1938	1939	1942	1944	1945
Highway mileage		10,326	10,289			
Expenditure on highways	$39,208	$35,991	$32,706	$34,394	$25,195	$31,347
Railroad mileage	6,828	6,754	6,667	6,639	6,502	6,479

"Prodigal's Return," a Shoemaker cartoon which appeared in the *Chicago Daily News* in March 1946 following the return of the Wisconsin Progressives to the Republican party, ending 12 years of independent existence

included 75 Republicans (gain of 3), 19 Democrats (gain of 4) and 6 Progressives (loss of 7). The senate consisted of 22 Republicans (loss of 1), 6 Democrats (gain of 2) and 5 Progressives (loss of 1). The election showed clearly the decline of the Progressive party, which polled less than 6% of the vote for governor. The state as a whole appeared anti-Roosevelt and anti-New Deal rather than non-interventionist. The Progressives in most cases had stronger non-interventionist records than did the Republicans.

The legislature met on Jan. 10, 1945, recessed on June 20 until Sept. 5, and adjourned on Sept. 6, having passed 590 acts. Though overwhelmingly Republican, it engaged in considerable controversy with the Republican governor. He presented the largest budget in state history and it was adopted in substantially the same form. He advocated a building program for state education and welfare institutions calling for $23,193,050 to be financed from the balance on hand and the high yield of existing taxes. But the advocates of highway construction passed a bill over his veto segregating motor vehicle tax yields in a separate fund for highway purposes. The legislature then trimmed the building program to $16,473,500, which included $8,000,000 for the university, $4,600,000 for the department of public welfare and $3,150,000 for the teachers colleges.

The legislature also approved a rather strict anti-gambling bill, strengthened laws against lobbying, but failed to pass over the governor's veto a bill to prevent candidates changing parties readily. The state elections in April 1945 witnessed an exciting race for justice of the supreme court between Elmer Barlow, the incumbent, and F. R. Zimmerman, secretary of state, who was not an attorney. Barlow won by more than 70,000 votes. John Callahan, 79, superintendent of public instruction from 1921, defeated Arthur Jorgensen by about 60,000. (E. P. A.; X.)

The Progressive party, established in 1934 under the leadership of the La Follette brothers, dissolved itself at a convention at Portage, March 17, 1946, and voted to rejoin the Republican party. In the ensuing primary on Aug. 13, the ex-Progressive forces were turned back in an effort to capture the key nominations. Governor Goodland, denied renomination by the Republican convention, defeated the former Progressive, Ralph Immell, in a three-way race in which the organization candidate ran a poor third, while Judge Joseph V. McCarthy upset Senator La Follette in a very close contest for the senatorial nomination. The state's representation in congress consisted at the end of 1946 of 2 Republican senators and 10 Republican representatives.

(C. L. L.)

Bibliography.—Council of State Govts., *Book of the States* (bienn.); Federal Writers' Project, *Wisconsin: Guide to the Badger State* (1941); Legislative Reference

Table VII.—*Mineral Production*

(All figures in thousands of dollars)

	1937	1938	1939	1942	1943	1944
Value of mineral production	$15,240	$10,637	$12,705	$17,998	$18,925	
Leading products (value):						
Stone	4,284	3,881	3,564	6,309	6,677	$7,741
Iron ore	4,474	1,886	3,527	3,937	3,822	4,190
Sand and gravel	3,292	2,800	2,616	3,497	2,596	4,128
Zinc	902	199	614		3,108	3,545
Lime	509	483	542			
Clay	557	407	494			

Table IV.—*Banking and Finance*

(Money figures in thousands of dollars)

	1937	1938	1939	1942	1943	1944
State revenue	$94,524	$106,537	$103,137	$140,867	$141,028	$146,070
State expenditure	79,484	92,604	74,856	126,867	129,123	141,865
Number of banks	605	595	582	564	562	559
Total bank deposits	$865,300	$855,400	$916,200	$1,450,933	$1,897,974	$2,369,721
Number of national banks	105	105	105	98	97	96
Deposits of national banks	$462,126	$490,153	$536,460	$779,289	$1,034,078	$1,262,942

Table V.—*Agriculture*

(All figures in thousands)

	1937	1939	1940	1942	1943	1944
Acreage, principal crops	10,472	10,175	10,166	9,009	10,165	10,367
Income from crops and livestock	$322,700	$269,721	$308,260	$615,171	$766,064	$774,153
Leading crops (bu.):						
Alfalfa (tons)	1,720	1,972	2,866	2,859	2,132	1,730
Barley	22,022	22,591	24,525			
Corn	76,356	85,970	93,582	103,544	108,924	116,536
Hay (tons)	4,989	5,829	7,416	7,513	7,033	6,549
Oats	79,360	71,012	96,793	100,577	100,347	118,938
Peas (lb.)	148,000	100,000	182,000	260,480	261,240	243,200
Potatoes	18,031	17,336	15,054			
Tobacco (lb.)	25,102	32,391	36,260	29,200	27,145	
Wheat	2,043	1,350	1,743			

Table VI.—*Manufacturing*

(Money figures in thousands of dollars)

	1935	1937	1939	1942 (est.)	1943 (est.)	1944 (est.)
Wage earners	196,972	234,076	200,897	322,700	345,000	364,700
Wages paid	$204,201	$296,365	$251,947			
Value of manufactures	$1,313,815	$1,772,310	$1,604,507			
Leading products (value):						
Motor vehicles		$90,701	$162,081			
Paper and paperboard mills		97,934	101,302			
Meat packing		72,387	80,235			
Condensed and evaporated milk		57,355	68,493			
Malt liquors		42,710	53,446			
Creamery butter		63,932	48,218			

Library, *Wisconsin Blue Book* (bienn.); Wisconsin Regional Planning Committee, *Report* (1934). Periodical: *Monthly Checklist of State Publications* (Washington).

WLB (War Labor Board)

See WAR AND DEFENSE AGENCIES.

Woman's Christian Temperance Union, National

See SOCIETIES AND ASSOCIATIONS.

Women, Freedom of

The women of the world made great advances during the decade 1937–46, particularly during and after World War II. Wars sometimes have this curious effect, partly because the mould of habit breaks up in wartime and it becomes comparatively easy to form new moulds; and partly because women's enormous contribution to victory in this particular war earned them recognition in quarters where it had heretofore been lacking. Much the same phenomenon occurred in the U.S. following the Civil War, when educational institutions for women had a sudden flowering and when the foundations were laid for the development of the profession of nursing and the Red Cross, one of the first great humanitarian efforts ever organized by women. World War I in its turn hastened the entry of women into many new fields of work, in which many of them remained and made good. It also precipitated the granting of suffrage to the women of Great Britain and the U.S. World War II merely accelerated these same trends.

Hitler's Ideas about Women.—But our story begins before the war. In 1936, the U.S. was still in the depths of the greatest depression in history and the menace of Hitlerism was increasingly blackening the world sky. The trend of work for women outside the home had been on the increase ever since the industrial revolution in the middle of the 19th century. The tens and twenties of the 20th century had seen advances by women in every field. But in depressions women are the first to be fired, and this depression was no exception to the rule. No matter how much they needed their jobs, no matter how many dependents they had to support, women were fired in great numbers, in order, so the theory went, to give more jobs to men. The fact that most women worked because they had to, because they had to support themselves and their dependents, was all too frequently overlooked.

The situation was aggravated during the '30s by the rise of fascism with its philosophy of the degradation of women. In Hitler's Germany, women were legally classified not as citizens but as subjects. A woman's world, said Hitler, "is her husband, her family, her children and her home. . . . We do not find it right when the woman presses into the world of the man. Rather we find it natural when these two worlds remain separate. . . . Reason is dominant in man." All that mattered to a woman, in Hitler's opinion, was "the child that must come into being and that must thrive." And Mussolini, not to be outdone, added his echo: "Women must play a passive part. . . . Of course I do not want women to be slaves but . . ." and so on.

Dictatorship, however, had never bothered about consistency. At first a passionate advocate of woman's place in the home, Hitler gradually lost interest in keeping women in it as his need for guns increased. It suited his purposes better to put them to work in factories, mostly as heavy, unskilled, cheap labour. As a Berlin newspaper of the period said, "Women are generally cheap, and manufacturers appreciate cheap labour." Whether in the kitchen or in the factory mattered very little; women under Hitler were definitely second-rate citizens. But the era of Hitler passed, and with its passing came great victories for women.

Political Advances.—Women's most striking victories of the decade occurred in the political field. Before World War II, in addition to the U.S. and Great Britain, votes for women had come only to Australia, Austria, Brazil, Canada (with the exception of Quebec), China, Cuba, Czechoslovakia, Denmark, Estonia, Finland, Germany (where it was meaningless under Hitler), Iceland, Latvia, Lithuania, Luxembourg, the Netherlands, New Zealand, Norway (the first European country to enfranchise women), Poland, Russia, Spain, Sweden and Turkey. Other countries granted them a limited franchise, restricted either to local elections or to limited age groups or to those with special educational or property qualifications. Among these countries were included South Africa, Chile, Greece, Hungary and Portugal. India granted a limited franchise of this sort to both men and women. But in many countries women had no right of franchise whatever. This was true of Afghanistan, Albania, Argentina, Belgium, Bolivia, Colombia, Costa Rica, the Dominican Republic, Egypt, El Salvador, France, Guatemala, Haiti, Honduras, Iran, Iraq, Lebanon, Mexico, Saudi Arabia, Syria, and Switzerland. In other countries, such as Italy, where women theoretically had the vote, they seldom used it. And while the constitution of the Spanish republic of 1931 gave women the vote, the practice after 1939 under Franco was not to encourage it. Thus the battle for suffrage was barely half won.

But World War II changed this picture with startling rapidity. What happened in France was perhaps typical of the revolution that took place all over the world. During the German occupation of 1940–45, women had played a prominent role in France. Swept almost bare of its men of fighting age, the country found itself a country of women and children—and older men. Women were therefore the heart of the resistance. When the tide turned and victory was on its way, De Gaulle decreed that women should vote in the first elections to be held in free France. And vote they did—in overwhelming numbers—electing many of their sex to the assembly. The new constitution of France, drafted by the delegates for whom the women voted, provided for universal suffrage.

Voting for the first time in French history, women outnumbered men at the polls during the municipal election of April 29, 1945, the first French election after liberation

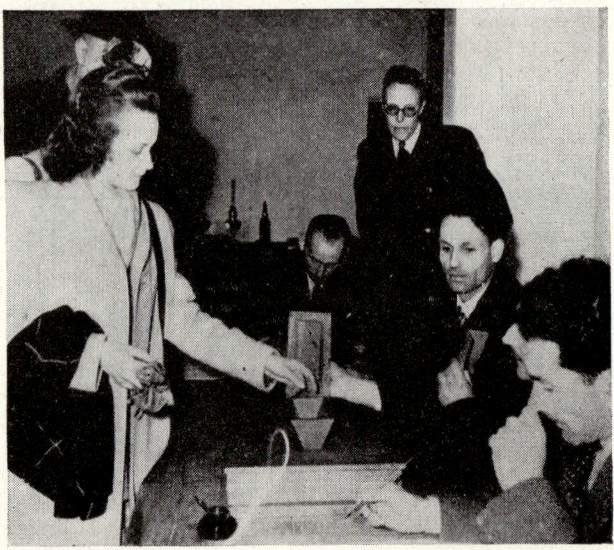

Japanese women were enfranchised for the first time on Dec. 11, 1945. Women who gained seats in the diet during the elections of April 1946 are shown during a conference devoted to the problems of their countrywomen

Other countries also rushed to give women the vote or to expand their previous limited voting powers. Argentina gave them the vote in 1946, Belgium was in process of so doing; in Canada the province of Quebec joined the procession; the Dominican Republic granted the vote in 1942, El Salvador in 1939, Guatemala in 1945 and most surprising of all, following its occupation by the U.S. in 1945, Japan followed suit. At the end of 1946 Mexico was also about to give women the right to vote in local elections. It was estimated that of the members of the United Nations at the end of 1946, 37 countries had granted women the vote in one form or another by the end of 1946 and 16 had not. Of those not members of the United Nations, four (Finland, Eire, Italy and Japan) had given women the vote, four (including Switzerland) had not and the rest had granted a limited voting power.

In most countries, eligibility to hold public office had run parallel with the right to vote. This had always been true in all the states of the U.S. with the single exception of Oklahoma. That state had long had a law on its statute books forbidding women to hold certain public offices, including those of governor, lieutenant-governor, secretary of state, attorney-general, state treasurer, and one or two others. This anachronism was removed from the statute books and, except for minor positions in a few states, women were eligible at the end of the decade for practically all elective and most appointive public offices.

A curious situation existed in Belgium, where women were eligible for public office and were elected and appointed to them, but could not themselves vote for such offices. This anomaly was in process of change, however.

In Great Britain, one of the long prohibited fields for women had been the diplomatic service. This taboo was successfully broken down during World War II, and women became eligible for diplomatic and consular appointments overseas. Their appointments by the end of the decade had been to posts of modest rank, and no woman minister or ambassador had as yet appeared on the scene. In the U.S., where no legal bar existed, there had been two women ministers to foreign countries, one to Denmark and the other to Norway, where she was caught by the German invasion in 1940 and forced to flee with the king of Norway and his court to England. Both of these appointments were made before the war.

In Canada, where women had previously been barred from the senate on the ground that an old statute governing eligibility used the word "person" in the sense of a male person only, a woman nominated to the senate contested this interpretation of the statute to the highest court in the land and won her case. Women were now persons in Canada, for this purpose at least, and a woman accordingly sat in the dominion senate.

Military Service.—Perhaps the most interesting aspect of the war years (and proof, if proof were needed, of the war's quality of totality) was the service of women not only with but actually within the armed forces. This was more striking in those countries which were in the actual war theatres than it seemed in the more remote U.S. But the phenomenon was universal. In the U.S.S.R., for instance, women fought in the armies side by side with men; women doctors performed feats of heroism in the front lines under fire, and women everywhere were organized for defense of the fatherland. This was also true to a varying extent in every invaded country. In France, the women of the resistance worked side by side with the men. In England, invaded by bombs if not by armies, the women in the various branches of the armed forces, while in theory noncombatants, actually frequented the danger zones quite as much as the men. It would have been impossible to keep them in a safe place. When raids were on, they manned and often fired the anti-aircraft guns. Had there been an invasion, they would have fought as surely and to as deadly effect as their Russian sisters. The WRENs in the navy, the A.T.S. in the army, the WAFs in the air service and the special corps of women ferrying bomber planes, the Women's Land army, the fire and air raid wardens, all contributed to the heroic defense.

The same thing happened in only lesser degree in the U.S. In World War I there had been a few female yeomen (mostly clerical workers) in the navy. In World War II, women's services were recognized from the start as indispensable and were eagerly sought after. First to be formed were the WAACs, an auxiliary service outside the army. Then came the WAVES, a woman's division *within* the navy, although, somewhat like Gilbert and Sullivan's admiral, not allowed to serve at sea. This was followed by the SPARS, a subdivision of the coast guard, and finally by the full-fledged women members of the marines. These woman marines spurred the WAACs to abandon their auxiliary status, and they secured legislation making them full-fledged members of the U.S. army, known as the WACs, their chief officer a colonel and themselves regular officers and enlisted personnel of the armed forces. There was also a small auxiliary force of women flyers who instructed army flyers, ferried bomber planes and otherwise did everything short of fighting in this most hazardous of wartime jobs.

Women doctors had perhaps a harder struggle for recognition than did any other group of American women. Although many volunteered for service with the armed forces, they were at first refused commissions on the ground that the statute covering the situation used the word "person" in a purely masculine sense. It was necessary to pass special legislation in order to qualify them for commissions in the medical corps of the army and navy. While the legislation was passed too late in the war to secure the services of many women doctors, those who served did so with distinction.

But it was not only the women in actual military service who acquitted themselves with credit. The civilian and voluntary services of women reached an all-time peak. The Red Cross, the British and American Women's Voluntary services, in the U.S. the C.D.V.O. (Civilian Defense Volunteer's organization), the women's land armies, the air raid wardens' organizations and many others supplemented the war effort and were indispensable to it. The air raid wardens' service in England, in particular, which fought fires night after night and dug in the ruins by day for victims of the bombings, was a service of women quite as much as men. (*See* also British Women's Services, World War II; Canadian Women's Services, World War II; Coast Guard, U.S.; Marine Corps, U.S.; Women's Airforce Service Pilots; Women's Army Corps; Women's Reserve of the U.S. Navy.)

Other Civil Rights.—The decade also saw an advance in the field of nationality. The Cable act of 1922 had given women in the U.S. the right to choose their own nationality independent of their husbands. Another act was passed in 1934 which gave to children born out of the U.S., whose nationality had previously followed that of their father or of the country in which they had been born, the power to choose their father's or their mother's nationality. An advance was also made along similar lines in Great Britain, where women, whose nationality had always followed that of their husbands, were first given power during World War II to recover their nationality if married to an enemy alien and, second, were later given full power to retain their nationality under any and all circumstances.

The service of women on juries was considerably expanded in the U.S. during the decade 1937–46 by the addition of six states to the group of those admitting women to such service. While four of these six did not require such service to be compulsory and made it purely optional, nevertheless their inclusion in the ranks of women jury states left only 17 states which limited jury service to men.

A variety of other small changes in the laws of the different states were all in the direction of removing obsolete and outmoded discriminations against married women. Georgia passed a law safeguarding a married woman's right as an individual to her personal earnings; New Jersey passed a law forbidding discrimination against married women in the holding of public office, and North Carolina and West Virginia passed similar laws relating to married women teachers. The trend of judicial decisions was in the same direction—that of recognizing women's rights and responsibilities as independent human beings. Thus an increasing number of judges were tending to award alimony to the husband in cases where the wife had means and the husband was ill or for some other good reason was without earning power.

The fight for a blanket equal rights amendment to the U.S. constitution continued, with the forces opposed to special labour laws for women lined up in favour of the amendment and those favouring retention of the power to enact such laws lined up on the other side. The amendment for the first time in its history came up for vote on the senate floor in the summer of 1946 and failed to receive the required two-thirds majority.

Economic Advances.—Equally striking, although more difficult to assess and perhaps in part impermanent, were the gains made by women on the economic front.

The trend of women's work outside the home continued steadily on the increase. In 1870 women formed 14.8% of the entire working population of the U.S. By 1930 their numbers had grown to 22%. The depression which was then commencing constituted a serious setback. But by 1940 the percentage had gone up again and beyond, to 24.3%; by 1945, at the peak of the war effort, it was 34.7%. More than 6,000,000 women (one-half the former total) had been added to the labour force. A higher percent probably prevailed in Great Britain, where the manpower shortage was even more acute and the conversion of the country to munitions making even more complete.

The occupations of women also underwent a change. In 1940 the entire labour force of women amounted to about 12,750,000 as compared to a masculine labour force of about 40,000,000. Of these women, over one-half worked in domestic service and at clerical or selling jobs of one sort or another. The rest of them furnished almost all nurses, the bulk of social workers, a majority of teachers, a large proportion of factory workers in the needle trades and practically all telephone operators. Comparatively few of them were employed as labourers, craftsmen or farmers. In the fields of transportation and heavy industry and in the higher executive posts, women were practically unknown. But World War II changed the picture with surprising speed. War needs took women out of domestic service and into munitions factories. Great numbers of women worked in aircraft and gun and electrical equipment factories. They riveted ships in shipyards, helped run the railroads and harvest the crops. They were increasingly called upon for engineering and scientific skills of all sorts. As the manpower shortage increased, they moved into one new occupation after another until eventually there were very few which they had not touched.

This invasion into new fields necessitated a number of changes, including the opening of the doors of trade unions to them. Some old-line unions, the boilermaker's among them, not only had never had women members, but actually had bylaws excluding women. These bylaws had to be changed or else honoured in the breach.

Another problem was that of pay. The notion that women were cheap unfortunately was not confined to Hitler. Ever since their first advent into industry women had to struggle for equal pay for equal work. The tradition of paying them less than men, even for identical work, was hoary and well entrenched. It was even written into some union contracts. During the war, the principle was laid down by the U.S. government that there should be equal pay for equal work, and the National War Labor board acted upon this theory when it ruled that wage increases granted to women workers for the purpose of bringing them up to the general level prevailing in particular plants were not to be considered wage increases as such but merely the removal of unjust inequalities. This principle of equal pay for equal work mounted in public favour, and four states enacted equal pay laws. A bill was introduced into the federal congress in 1946 to accomplish the same result nationally.

The close of World War II brought an abrupt loss of jobs to a substantial number of women. It was estimated that from the high of nearly 19,000,000 in the U.S., 4,000,000 women were displaced. The demand for labour in other fields was so great, however, that many of these women did not remain unemployed long. By the end of 1946, about 2,000,000 had been re-employed in civilian occupations, and the woman labour force was only slightly under 17,000,000, or about 30% of the total U.S. labour force. Of the remaining 2,000,000, only about 250,000 were listed as unemployed and seeking work, which suggested that the others were never a part of the permanent labour force but took jobs in wartime as a patriotic duty.

The United Nations.—The United Nations charter, as first drafted, contained no reference to human rights. But when it came up for final approval at San Francisco in 1945, the statesmen were faced with a great ground swell of popular demand for the addition of what in effect amounted to a bill of rights. The preamble therefore listed among its objectives the achievement of international co-operation "in promoting and encouraging respect for human rights and for fundamental freedoms for all without distinction as to race, sex, language, or religion."

This principle was repeated several times in the body of the charter. In its implementation, a Commission on Human Rights was set up as a permanent part of the machinery of the United Nations. In further implementation of that portion of it relating to sex, the following clause, taken in modified form from the covenant of the old League of Nations, was also incorporated in the charter:

"Article 8:

The United Nations shall place no restrictions on the eligibility of men and women to participate in any capacity and under conditions of equality in its principal and subsidiary organs."

At the first meeting of the general assembly in London early in 1946, the Human Rights commission was set up. The assembly also set up, under it, a subcommission on the status of women, which was later changed to a full commission on a par with all the other commissions of the United Nations. But the assembly did not stop there. At its second meeting held in New York late in 1946, it adopted the following resolution: "That all Member States which have not already done so, adopt measures necessary to fulfill the purposes and aims of the Charter in this respect by granting to women the same political rights as to men."

Bibliography.—Sophonisba Breckenridge, *Marriage and Civic Rights of Women* (1931); Sophonisba Breckenridge, *Women in the Twentieth Century* (1933); Hilary Newitt, *Women Must Choose* (1937); *Dictatorships in the Modern World*—Edited by Guy Stanton Ford (Includes *Women Under the Dictatorships* by Mildred Adams) (1939); Eve Curie, *Madame Curie* (1939); Ethel Mannin, *Women and the Revolution* (1939); Isabel de Palencia, *I Must Have Liberty* (1940); Dr. Maude Glasgow, *The Subjection of Women and Traditions of Men* (1940); *Victory: How Women Won It—A Centennial Symposium* (1940); Pearl Buck, *Of Men and Women* (1941); *Yale Review*—Ada Comstock, "Women in This War" (1942); Konrad Bercovici, *Women and the Fall of France* (1943); Mary Grey Peck, *Carrie Chapman Catt* (1944); Mary R. Beard, *Women as Force in History* (1946).

(D. Kn.)

Women's Airforce Service Pilots

For more than two years women pilots served with the U.S. army air forces (AAF) and, by their contribution to the war effort, proved that women could be trained in large numbers and utilized for most noncombat military pilot operations. In training, safety and in operations, their performance was comparable to the over-all record of the AAF flying within the continental limits of the United States. At the time of deactivation, 938 WASP were on duty, 637 in operations for the training command, 164 with the air transport command, 118 in domestic air forces, 3 in proving ground command, 3 in air technical service command, 11 in weather wing and 2 in headquarters AAF.

The women's pilot program was first considered by the army air forces in connection with possible demands of global warfare in the summer of 1941, but because there was at the time a lack of aircraft and an ample supply of male pilots, the program was not activated until the fall of 1942, when two experimental groups, one in operations and one in training, were formed. In the interim between conception and activation of the program, 25 qualified U.S. women pilots entered the service of Great Britain's ferrying operations and demonstrated that a select group of qualified women pilots could serve a military purpose.

The experimental operational group of the AAF women pilot program was organized by the ferrying command at New Castle, Del. It was made up of about 30 qualified commercial licensed pilots. The group was known as WAFS, Women's Auxiliary Ferrying squadron, and was under the leadership of Nancy Harkness Love. After four to six weeks' orientation training they were assigned to ferrying light liaison and training planes within the continental limits of the United States. All subsequent operational groups were processed through the women pilot training program.

The first training group enlisted pilots of less experience and was directed by Jacqueline Cochran (Mrs. Floyd B. Odlum). When both experimental groups had proved the feasibility of employing women for noncombat military operations, the program was enlarged, and unified; the official name WASP was adopted, and the whole was placed under the direction of Miss Cochran.

More than 2,500 young women between 18 and 35 years of age applied for WASP training; 1,830 were accepted. During training about 30% were eliminated for flying deficiency and about 2% for other reasons—a lower rate than among male cadets. Of the women accepted, 80 resigned and 1,074 were graduated. Of the graduates, over 83% were with the program at time of deactivation in addition to 16 pilots from the original ferrying group. During training, 11 WASP trainees lost their lives; during operations 27 WASP were killed.

After graduation from training, the WASP flew 60,000,000 mi. in such operations as ferrying, target-towing, tracking and searchlight missions, simulated strafing, smoke laying and other chemical missions, radio control flying, basic and instrument instruction, engineering test flying, administrative and utility flying. They flew all types of military aircraft from light training and liaison planes to the rocket propelled and the superfort B-29, including B-17, B-26, C-54, the Mustang and Thunderbolt.

The program was deactivated Dec. 1944 at a time when the WASP were prepared to give maximum service, because a fortunate change in the demands of war had made surplus many more trained AAF male pilots than had been anticipated. The WASP had proved the worth of their service, but were no longer needed. A congressional bill to militarize the WASP was defeated. (H. TA.)

Women's Army Corps

The Women's Army corps (WAC), originally created as the Women's Army Auxiliary corps by public law 554, 77th congress, approved on May 14, 1942, became a part of the army of the United States when public law 110, 78th congress, was signed by President Roosevelt on July 1, 1943.

The purpose of the corps was to make available to U.S. national defense, for the duration of World War II and six months thereafter, the knowledge, skill and special training of U.S. women.

Mrs. Oveta Culp Hobby, former Texas newspaper woman, legislator, civic leader and organizer, who, at the time of the writing of the bill, was directing the activities of the women's interest section in the bureau of public relations of the war department, was named director of the Women's Army Auxiliary corps on May 14, 1942. She took the oath of office with rank equivalent to that of colonel in the army of the United States, the first U.S. woman to hold such rank.

After three full years of service, Colonel Hobby resigned from active duty on July 12, 1945. She was succeeded by the deputy director of the WAC, Lt. Col. Westray Battle Boyce, who was simultaneously elevated to the rank of colonel.

To be eligible for enlistment, applicants had to be between the ages of 20 and 50, U.S. citizens, with at least 2 years of high school; no women with children under 14 years of age were accepted, unless the full care and custody of the children had been in other hands for 18 months prior to making application for enlistment.

In addition, because women were assigned to jobs requiring specific skills, they were also required to meet certain high standards of intelligence, stability and personal integrity. These standards were determined by means of written test and interview, to bring into the army only women who could readily adjust themselves and do the job happily and well.

At its top strength, the Women's Army corps numbered 100,000, of whom approximately 18,000 served overseas in 21 different countries. The Wacs in the United States served at more than 400 army installations, and were engaged in 239 noncombatant army jobs.

WACS were trained first at Fort Des Moines, Ia. Then, as the corps expanded, other training centres were opened at Fort Oglethorpe, Ga.; Daytona Beach, Fla.; Fort Devens, Mass., and Camp Polk, La. Enlistments in the WAC were closed on Aug. 29, 1945, following the cessation of hostilities.

Basic training for women in the army was six weeks, during which the transition from civilian to military life was made.

The basic military program was, with some adaption, the same as the first six weeks of military training given to men in the army. The courses were largely the same, the drill the same (except for shorter steps and without weapons) and the daily routine likewise the same.

In the course of training the women were taught military customs and courtesies, organization of the army, defense against chemical and air attack, first aid, barracks sanitation and wear and care of the uniform. They learned to dress in 15 minutes, to march in formation and to master simple physical conditioning exercises designed especially for women to keep them fit for army duties.

Following basic military training, the woman soldier was assigned directly to a post, camp or station somewhere within the United States, or given additional training in

Group exercises for members of the Women's Army corps in training at Fort Des Moines, Ia.

Parade of overseas WACs on the Champs Élysées in Paris, celebrating the third anniversary of the Women's Army corps, May 1945

one of the basic technical courses conducted at the training centre, or sent to a specialist school.

If her civilian skills were such that she needed no more than on-the-job training at an army post, she was assigned directly to an army job. The majority of women fell into this category. If she qualified in one of the fields for which additional training was required, she was sent to a specialist school. As women acquired proficiency on an army job, they became eligible for advanced military specialists' training at any of the army schools open to enlisted men. Officers were eligible to attend the Command and General Staff school or any officers' school, except the wholly tactical schools available to men of the army.

The type and extent of advanced military training given members of the Women's Army corps depended on the need for such advanced skills in the command to which the individual was assigned. She was sent to a small arms repair school, for example, if the post to which she was assigned saw that there was or would be need for personnel with such training. The extent of training was gauged always by army needs.

Whether a member of the Women's Army corps acquired new skills by attending a school or by learning on the job, each new military specialty she acquired was entered on her classification card. It was by these military specialist numbers that she might later be selected for reassignment to a more important job in the United States or overseas. Overseas theatre commanders placed requisitions for WAC personnel by these military occupation specialties (MOS).

There were 239 of these specialties in which women in the army were found equally adept, sometimes more so, than men. Many of them had civilian counterparts (stenography and typing, for example) which had long been a field for women rather than men. Many others were army jobs which had no civilian counterpart, but for which women were readily trained.

The first class of officer candidates began on July 20, 1942, at Fort Des Moines, Ia. This class and eight succeeding classes were made up of eligible women selected directly from civilian life. The tenth, which started early in Nov. 1942 and all subsequent classes were composed of women selected from the ranks of the corps. Beginning in Sept. 1943 all officer candidate classes were held at the 3rd WAC Training centre, Fort Oglethorpe, Ga. They continued there until they were shifted back to Fort Des Moines, where the 57th class began on March 5, 1945. The last and final class of officer candidates, the 60th, was commissioned on Nov. 17, 1945.

At peak strength of approximately 100,000 (6,800 officers and 93,000 enlisted women), members of the Women's Army corps were serving at more than 400 installations in the United States and in all theatres of operation. They performed practically every type of task except actual combat. Enlisted women were assigned, for headquarters work, to combat elements in overseas theatres. The women of the corps served with army ground force installations, with the army air forces, corps of engineers, the ordnance department, chemical warfare service, the signal corps, military intelligence, the provost marshal general's office, the transportation and quartermaster corps, the judge advocate general's and the inspector general's departments, the surgeon general's office, office chief of finance, in the adjutant general's office, in civil affairs and with the general staff corps.

WACS were present at many of the historic moments of

World War II. Twenty-seven of them operated the switchboard at the Potsdam conference; 432 worked on the atomic bomb project; others were present at the meetings of the Big Three at Yalta, in Canada, at Potsdam, at the German surrender at Reims and at the Japanese surrender at Baguio, P.I. Still others were on duty as legal stenographers and aides at the war crimes trials in Germany and in Manila.

One of the unusual jobs held by WACS was in the prisoner of war camp at Chartres (France), where they handled administration in connection with 500 German women prisoners. In the 8th air force, WACS worked as watch officers, staying with a mission from the planning stage to the return of the bombers. A former University of Illinois coed directed a fleet of taxis in Paris. In the United States, women served as radio operators in transport planes, on bombers at training fields and on hospital ships.

Before any WAC was sent overseas, she must have spent at least three months on an army job in this country, to enable her to acquire a general knowledge of army procedure, improve her occupational skill and so adapt herself to army work methods that she was equipped to adjust herself to new surroundings.

It never proved necessary to send any woman to a foreign theatre who, for personal or family reasons, might undergo great hardship in leaving the United States. So many women were eager for overseas service that for the most part selection was made from those who had volunteered.

Not all of the willing and capable volunteers were sent overseas. However, nearly 18% of the army's 100,000 WACS did go, and some had more than 3 years of overseas service. WAC officers and enlisted women served in Bermuda, Puerto Rico, Italy, North Africa, Alaska, the Netherlands Indies, Belgium, Scotland, Germany, England, France, Egypt, India, China, Ceylon, New Guinea, Australia, Hawaii, Labrador, British Columbia and Yukon territory, Leyte and Luzon in the Philippines, Japan and Korea, New Caledonia, African Gold coast, New Zealand, Austria and Panama.

More than 9,000, the largest number in any 1 overseas theatre, were serving in the European theatre of operations just after V-E day. At the same time there were approximately 5,600 in the Pacific theatre.

Pay for members of the Women's Army corps was exactly the same as that of men in the army for the corresponding grade or rank. Where their duties warranted it, WACS drew flying pay and all of those serving overseas received the same additional overseas pay as the men.

Although originally the head of Pallas Athene, official WAC insignia, was worn by all members of the corps, after Sept. 1943 it was replaced by many for the insignia of other branches of the army to which they had been assigned. For example, women serving with the army air forces, wore the air force wings; those with the signal corps, the crossed semaphores; women with ordnance, the bursting bomb and those with the general staff corps, the insignia of the general staff.

Women in the army were subject to all army regulations, had the privileges of free medical care, free postage, leave and furlough. They were entitled to benefits under the Soldier's and Sailor's Relief act as well as all benefits provided under the GI Bill of Rights. They were eligible also for National Service Life insurance.

Service in the predecessor Women's Army Auxiliary corps did not entitle former members to veterans' rights and benefits. However, they were entitled to mustering out pay and hospitalization, if they were honourably discharged for physical disability.

As of March 1, 1946, one member of the corps had been awarded the Distinguished Service Medal; 33 the Legion of Merit; 479 the Bronze Star; 7 the Soldier's Medal; 2 the Air Medal; 2 the French Legion of Honour; 5 the French Croix de Guerre; 16 the Purple Heart; 2 had received letters of commendation from the United States navy; 7 wore the Most Excellent Order of the British Empire and 31 Meritorious Service Unit Plaques had been awarded.

On June 1, 1946, the strength of the Women's Army corps was approximately 20,000. While recruiting was discontinued after V-J day, on April 1, 1946 the war department announced a re-entry program, permitting honourably discharged WACS to re-enter the corps at the grade held upon discharge.

On July 24, 1946, the WAC Integration Act of 1946, establishing the Women's Army corps in the regular army, was introduced in the senate by Chairman Elbert Thomas of the senate military affairs committee. The same bill was introduced in the house of representatives on July 26, 1946. The bill called for an initial corps strength of 5,000 enlisted women and 500 officers, and established the maximum strength at 2% of the regular army male strength authorized from time to time. (W. B. Be.)

Bibliography.—*Establishing a Women's Army Corps* (U.S. 78 cong., 1 sess., H. Rept. 267) (1943); F. Hess, *WACS at Work* (1945); Infantry Journal, *You Must be Fit* (1943); E. R. Pollock, *Yes, Ma'am: Personal Papers of a WAAC* (1943); N. B. Shea, *WAACS* (1943).

Women's Auxiliary Ferrying Squadron (WAFS)

See Love, Nancy Harkness; Women's Airforce Service Pilots.

Women's Clubs, General Federation of

See Societies and Associations.

Women's Reserve of the United States Coast Guard Reserve (Spars)

See Coast Guard, U.S.

Women's Reserve of the U.S. Marine Corps Reserve

See Marine Corps.

Women's Reserve of the U.S. Navy

The women's reserve of the United States naval reserve (WAVES) was established as an amendment to the Naval Reserve act of 1938 on July 30, 1942. Although enlisted women served with the navy in World War I this was the first time they were enlisted and appointed as officers on an equal basis with men. The legislation originally limited ranks to 1 lieutenant commander, not more than 35 lieutenants, and lieutenants (junior grade) not in excess of 35% of the total number of commissioned officers. However, this limitation proved too restrictive as numbers increased, and on Nov. 8, 1943, the original legislation was amended removing restrictions on ranks up to captain and limiting that rank to one officer. This amendment likewise provided more liberal allowances and benefits comparable to those for male officers and enlisted men rather than to those for civil service employees. The restriction of assignments to continental United States which was in the original legislation was not removed until Sept. 1944, when another amendment authorized assigning women outside the continental limits of the United States to the American area and the territories of Hawaii and Alaska.

Three WAVES, trained as machinist's mates in the repair and overhauling of aeroplane engines, working on a navy plane at the naval air station in Jacksonville, Fla., during 1944

Under the authority of this act, women could serve in the navy "during the present war and for six months thereafter or until such earlier time as the Congress by concurrent resolution or the President by proclamation may designate." It was planned to continue on active duty a limited number of officers and enlisted women volunteering until July 1, 1947.

The first woman to be sworn into the navy on Aug. 3, 1942, was the director, the former Mildred H. McAfee (later Mrs. Douglas Horton), president of Wellesley college, Wellesley, Mass. She served in this capacity first as a lieutenant commander and later as a captain until Feb. 1946, when she resigned from the service to resume her full time duties at Wellesley college. Her place was taken by Jean T. Palmer, who had served as an assistant to Mrs. Horton since the beginning of the program.

The standards for the appointment of women officers were the same as for male officers in the naval reserve, while the educational qualifications of enlisted women were higher than those for enlisted men. Some of the physical requirements were slightly lowered for women since their service was to be confined to shore based naval activities.

Training.—The training of WAVES began less than a month after the passage of the necessary legislation, when an advance class of approximately 100 women reported to the Naval Reserve Midshipmen's school (WR) on the campus of Smith college, Northampton, Mass., prior to their assignment to recruiting and procurement offices and to the staffs of schools for WAVES which were to open soon. A two-month course for officer candidates was developed there which gave women a practical introduction to navy life and to their responsibilities as naval officers.

WAVES were also classified for their future duties through interviews with trained personnel officers. This officer school continued until Dec. 1944 and at one time also utilized facilities at Mount Holyoke college in South Hadley, Mass. It was later replaced on a much smaller scale by an officer candidate school in Washington, D.C., from April to Oct. 1945. The classes at the school in Washington varied in number from 20 to 30 WAVES and were composed of former enlisted women and of occupational and physical therapists drawn from civilian sources. Altogether over 9,000 women officers were trained, 12% of whom came from enlisted status. Many women officers were assigned directly to their duty stations at the completion of their indoctrinal period but others needed further training in their specialized fields before assuming their new duties. A communications school operated at Northampton, Mass., under the same command as the midshipmen's school.

The first class of women entered the Radcliffe branch of the supply corps school at Harvard university, Cambridge, Mass. during Jan. 1943. In Sept. 1943 training of aerological engineers was established at Massachusetts Institute of Technology in Cambridge, and other aerology classes later entered the University of Chicago and the University of California at Los Angeles. Other programs included the preparation of officers for duties in technical and administrative radar, Japanese language, air combat information, educational services and as instructors in air navigation, link celestial navigation, ships and aircraft recognition, aviation radio, photographic interpretation and gunnery.

The first schools for enlisted women opened Oct. 9, 1942, and combined both recruit and specialized training. WAVES learned to be radiomen on the campus of the University of Wisconsin at Madison; they became yeomen at Oklahoma A. & M. College at Stillwater and they prepared for duties as storekeepers at the University of Indiana at Bloomington. The first recruit school for WAVES opened on the campus of Iowa State Teachers college in Cedar Falls, Ia., in Dec. 1942; this school later trained yeomen when recruit training was transferred to New York city, where larger facilities were available. Other yeoman and radioman schools were established later.

The Naval Training school (WR), the Bronx, N.Y., on the uptown campus of Hunter college, was commissioned on Feb. 9, 1943. There a recruit training program was organized which provided WAVES with instruction in naval customs, regulations and history. In addition, the WAVES were classified for their future assignments to specialized training or to duty in the field as the result of interviews and standard navy tests. The length of this recruit training was originally four weeks, but was lengthened first to six weeks and later to eight weeks. This school remained the largest of those for WAVES, and at the peak of procurement for the women's reserve as many as 5,000 WAVES were in training there at one time.

During later months other training units for enlisted WAVES were located on the station at the Bronx. Specialists (S) V-10 (personnel supervisors) mailmen, cooks and bakers received instruction at schools there, and hospital corps WAVES were prepared for general duties in medical activities, or received advanced training for rehabilitation work.

The first specialized training for the aviation ratings began in Feb. 1943. Future aviation machinist's mates and aviation metalsmiths learned to repair planes and engines at the school at the Naval Training station, Norman, Okla., and in Memphis, Tenn. The first of many classes of link trainer instructors began learning the fundamentals of teaching flight by instruments at the Naval Air station, Atlanta, Ga. Training for assignments in aviation continued to expand and later included preparation for duties as parachute riggers, aerographer's mates, control tower operators, fixed and free aircraft gunnery instructors, aircraft instrument repairmen, link celestial navigation operator-maintenance personnel, aerial camera repairmen and carrier pigeon trainers.

The training of women for the hospital corps was originally done at naval hospitals. This program, however, was gradually superseded by the concentration of initial hospital corps training at the school which opened in Bethesda, Md., Jan. 12, 1944. In the summer of 1945 when hundreds of new recruits were sent to this type of training, the activity at Bethesda was supplemented by schools at Camp Moffett, Great Lakes, Ill., and the Bronx, N.Y.

The graduation of the last class of WAVES from the Hospital Corps school at Bethesda, Md., Jan. 10, 1946, brought to a close the training program for members of the women's reserve, which at its peak in 1944 was carried on at approximately 40 naval activities. In the three-and-a-half years this program was in effect, 86,000 WAVES received either recruit or midshipmen's training, and many were also assigned to specialized training for duties in aviation, supply, medical and administrative activities. The schools for WAVES followed the pattern of those for navy men and were either established on the campus of a college or university or at a naval activity. The curricula at the specialized schools duplicated those set up for men in order that WAVES would be prepared to assume the same duties as men. In a number of cases, particularly in the aviation ratings and in advanced training for officers, WAVES studied at schools for navy men.

Duty of WAVES.—Shortly after V-J day the women's reserve reached its peak strength when there were a total of 8,000 officers and 78,000 enlisted women on active duty in 900 shore establishments throughout the continental United States and in the territory of Hawaii. At this time WAVES composed 18% of the total naval personnel assigned to shore establishments in the continental United States. They released 50,500 men for duty afloat or overseas and took over about 27,000 other jobs in the greatly expanded naval shore establishment service. Although WAVES were assigned to regular overseas duty only in the 14th naval district, they were also on temporary duty in such places as Alaska, the Aleutians, Puerto Rico and Bermuda.

WAVES and marines receiving instruction in control tower operation at Gordon field, Ga., in 1943

The largest group of enlisted women were seamen, who filled a variety of billets which ranged from serving as general office workers to acting as film projectionists and chauffeurs. Thirty-eight ratings were open to enlisted women, with approximately 14,500 WAVES serving as yeomen. Others included storekeepers, radiomen, specialists, telegraphers, electrician's mates, cooks, bakers and printers. Approximately 30% of the WAVES were assigned to naval aviation. They repaired planes, packed parachutes and collected weather information. WAVE link trainer instructors gave lessons in instrument flying to approximately 4,000 men a day. Under the guidance of WAVE gunnery instructors additional navy men learned the essentials of aerial gunnery. WAVES directed air traffic from control towers and served as flight orderlies on almost all Naval Air Transport service routes in continental United States as well as on the Bermuda and Hawaii runs.

Getting supplies to the fleet and to the advanced bases, paying navy personnel and accounting for the expenditures of the navy were the primary duties of 1,000 WAVE officers assigned to the supply corps. Also assisting in the work of supplying the fleet were several thousand enlisted women, storekeepers, yeomen and seamen, whose work was identical with that of enlisted men on similar duty. The officers were assigned to general supply duties or to disbursing duty in which their responsibilities sometimes entailed expenditures aggregating millions of dollars each month. Supply corps WAVES became familiar with all types of navy materials, which ranged in variety from spare parts for plane engines to dry provisions. The majority of the WAVE officers served as line officers in billets which used their knowledge and training as administrators, language specialists, radio and radar technicians, lawyers, communicators and educational services officers. However, many officers were medical specialists serving as laboratory technicians, dental hygienists, occupational and physical therapists. There were 41 women doctors in the medical corps; two dentists in the dental corps and two women in the civil engineer corps.

WAVE officers in air activities included those who served as aerologists, assistant air transport officers and air navigation and link celestial navigation instructors. WAVE officers were designated as naval air navigators and were the first women officers in any United States military organization entitled to perform duties as part of a military air crew. They wore the wings of the naval air navigator on their uniforms. Of unusual interest was the increasingly important part played by women in the secret fields of technological research and development, particularly in the application of radar to the perfection of night fighter tactics and in controlled approaches and landings of aeroplanes.

WAVES in the hospital corps served in the wards, laboratories and offices of naval hospitals and dispensaries throughout the United States and in Hawaii. At the peak of the women's reserve program in July 1945 there were approximately 13,000 WAVES in the hospital corps.

When the navy's demobilization plan was announced shortly after V-J day, women were scheduled to be separated from the service in the same percentage to total numbers as for the men. Separate centres were established for the women, and the point scores were lowered in order to complete the navy's plan for demobilization in an orderly flow by Sept. 1, 1946. (J. Pal.)

Bibliography.—*Amending the Naval Reserve Act* (U.S. 78 cong., 1 sess., H. Rept. 527) (1943); J. Angel, *Angel of the Navy: Story of a WAVE* (1943); M. V. Harris, *Guide Right, a Handbook of Etiquette* (1944); N. W. Ross, *WAVES* (1944); U.S. Navy Dept., *Story of You in Navy Blue* (1944).

Women's Royal Naval Service

See British Women's Services, World War II; Canadian Women's Services, World War II.

Wood, Sir Kingsley

Sir Kingsley Wood (1881–1943), British statesman, was admitted as a solicitor in 1903, entered public life as a London county councillor for Woolwich in 1911 and was elected to Parliament as Conservative member for Woolwich West in 1918, the year in which he was knighted. Between 1919 and 1929 he was parliamentary private secretary to various ministers of health; from Sept. to Nov. 1931 he was parliamentary secretary to the Board of Education in the national government. In Nov. 1931, he became postmaster-general and during his tenure effected many reforms which put the post office on a profit-making basis for the first time in many years. When Stanley Baldwin became prime minister in June 1935, Sir Kingsley was transferred to the ministry of health. He retained that office until 1938, when he succeeded Lord Swinton as minister for air. His policies and leadership in the air ministry were harshly attacked by both government and opposition leaders, and he was shifted to the post of chancellor of the exchequer in May 1940, where he was given the difficult task of financing Britain's war expenditures. Sir Kingsley died in London, Sept. 21, 1943.

Wood, Robert E.

Wood (1879–), U.S. army officer and business executive, was born June 13, 1879, at Kansas City, Mo. A graduate of the U.S. Military academy in 1900, he was on active duty in the Philippines the following two years. During the construction of the Panama canal, he was assistant chief quartermaster and chief quartermaster and director of the Panama Railroad Co.

He left the army in 1915 to engage in private business, but rejoined the service upon the entry of the U.S. into World War I and was promoted to the rank of brigadier general. Gen. Wood was acting U.S. quartermaster general in 1918–19. He re-entered business in 1919 as vice-president of Montgomery Ward and Co., in Chicago, and later joined Sears, Roebuck and Co., also in Chicago, as vice-president (1924–28) and president (1928–39). He became chairman of the board in 1939.

Gen. Wood supported the Roosevelt administration in 1932 and 1936, but split with the New Deal in 1940 because he disapproved its foreign policy. Fearing that all-out aid to Britain would weaken U.S. defenses and involve the nation in war, he organized the America First committee to oppose intervention in the European conflict. He maintained his opposition to Franklin D. Roosevelt's conduct of foreign policy throughout 1940 and 1941, but after the Japanese attack on Pearl Harbor, Dec. 7, 1941, he gave unqualified support to the government in its prosecution of the war.

Wool

Overproduction and the warlike situation in Europe caused U.S. wool prices in 1937 to decline 35% from the peak. Early in the year, expected government contracts for the army, navy and Civilian Conservation corps caused wool industrialists to make heavy purchases of cloth, with a backlog of 50,000,000 linear yd. of men's wear at the middle of the year—a continuance of the immense business placed during 1936.

Germany, at the same time, was acquiring wool and other import commodities by the barter system, principally from South America. In the U.S., strikes, tying up intercoastal boats, caused at one time 30,000 to 40,000 bales of Australian wool to be held at west coast ports. Heavy floods in the midwest and sit-down strikes in the automobile industry, together with strikes in wool warehouses in June, added to the general instability of wool prices.

Six months of depreciation in wool prices in 1938 were followed by six months of appreciation. The contemplated British Trade treaty, lowering the tariff on wool fabrics, noils and wastes, caused uneasiness among growers and manufacturers. The growers were especially alarmed by the adverse trend of wool prices and urged legislation to secure a commodity loan on wool through the Commodity Credit corporation. In Feb. 1938 the secretary of agriculture assured growers that such a loan would have favourable consideration. The wool market continued to slump. Loan terms were announced about June 1, halting the decline in values, and an upward trend took place on the theory that the loan had placed a floor on prices. The removal of $10,000,000 worth of surplus clothing for relief distribution caused the market to become more liquid for the regular operators in wool textiles.

Hearings in May 1938 by the Adams committee, investigating practices in the wool trade, for the purpose of separation of consignment accounts from direct purchases, were held in Washington. Little evidence was brought forth to substantiate the claims of growers that they had been subjected to unfair practices in part. The Australian-Japanese agreement for the year commencing July 1, 1938, allotted 350,000 to 400,000 bales of wool for shipment to Japan. Germany continued to purchase large weights of wool in the South American market. In the U.S., the wool labelling, or "truth in fabrics," issue was again renewed.

The wool industry during 1939 was saved to a great extent by the outbreak of World War II. In the U.S. the wool textile business was retarded because of the threat of lowering textile tariffs in the British treaty. This threat did not mature, as the declaration of war by Great Britain and France turned practically all of their production of textile machinery into war work.

Upon the declaration of war in Europe, U.S. wool textile manufacturers realized that there would be a continuation of their home market for fabrics, and the probability of immense orders from the belligerents. Orders for wools at that time caused prices to advance 50% above the market prices of June 1. Every effort was made by England to continue its export trade, with fabrics on hand or in process, and to take over the German business previously obtained in South America and in South Africa. In the U.S., former importers of British fabrics placed orders with domestic manufacturers, causing a demand for domestic-grown wools. From Sept. 1 to 30, 1939, fine territory wools jumped from 68 to 70 cents to $1.05 to $1.08, clean basis. Australia, in Dec. 1939, released 75,000 bales of wool, approximating 30,000,000 lb., for immediate shipment to the U.S. More than 100,000 bales of South African wools were purchased for U.S. use. Argentina shipped 46,500 bales and Uruguay 11,000, a total of over 55,000,000 lb.

In Australia, the British government agreed to purchase every bale of wool for the duration of the war and one year after. The customary auction sales were indefinitely postponed. In the U.S., the government announced the extension of the Commodity Credit corporation loans on domestic grown wools to Feb. 15, 1940. Prices advanced considerably in the west. In September, the British government set up the English Wool Control plan with full control of all wool stocks in England, these stocks to be allocated directly to individual manufacturers. The Australian Wool commission established 848 different types of Australian wools.

The discouraging daily reports received from the battle fronts in Europe similarly affected the wool market during the first six months of 1940. Machinery output in U.S. mills was woefully below normal, and the lack of business had forced a number of small mills to shut down. The New York buyers of wool fabrics made but few commitments and only enough yardage to cover immediate needs. The rapid thrusts by the nazis through the Low Countries and France caused deep apprehension throughout England. This fear spread to the U.S., and Washington decided to conscript manpower as a protective measure against possible invasion, should England be attacked by invading forces. Congress went into action immediately, appropriating huge sums for the proper equipment of its army and navy. It was figured that it would take 10 sheep, growing approximately 75 lb. of wool, to clothe one soldier.

Start of U.S. Army Purchases.—As soon as the appropriations were signed by Pres. Roosevelt, the army requested bids for clothing and blankets. On June 13, 1940, the Quartermaster depot in Philadelphia announced that bids were to be opened for 10,500,000 yd. of overcoating, serge and shirting. The wool market immediately reversed itself from its previous position earlier in the year. At the same time, the British government negotiated for U.S. storage space for 250,000,000 lb. of Australian wool, to be held as a strategic reserve.

In August the Quartermaster depot advertised for bids on 1,000,000 blankets, later increased by 200,000. During the same month, invitations were published to furnish 8,000,000 yd. of material requiring 16,000,000 lb. of grease wool. Shut-down mills immediately reopened to secure a portion of this immense government business. These orders instilled confidence in the New York goods market, and civilian business in volume was resumed. Awarding of these government contracts showed that 70% of the men's wear business in the mills was scheduled for the army and navy. On Oct. 1, less than 10% of the season's domestic wool clip was unsold.

On Oct. 9, 1940, the army opened bids for an additional 2,000,000 blankets, requiring over 8,000,000 lb. of scoured wool. The following day the Quartermaster depot issued invitations to bid on 18,000,000 yd. of flannel, olive drab serge and elastique. On Oct. 11 the top futures exchange reacted to these purchases by an advance of 19 to 55 points. On Dec. 5 orders for 13,000,000 yd. of materials, specifying the use of foreign wool, were announced. These wools included those grown in Australia, South Africa and South America. Wools were cheaper in these markets, especially in South America, compared with the prices of U.S.-grown wools. This was due to the impossibility of shipping wools from these markets to England and approved nonbelligerents on account of the submarine menace and blockades. Thus, only the market in the U.S. remained open for reasonable shipment. Because of the demand for South American wools, more than 50% of the season's clip was sold between Nov. 15 and Dec. 31. The bulk of the government orders for uniforms called for 18 oz. of serge, 32 oz. of overcoating and 18 oz. of elastique.

During the first six months of 1941, U.S. wool textile manufacturers were busy on orders placed during the last quarter of 1940. This heavy backlog of orders placed by the government, together with civilian requirements, placed the manufacturers in a very strong position. Buyers for civilian fabrics found but little idle machinery available for their needs. Approximately one-half of the 55,000,000 yd. of fabrics included in the backlog of orders was for men's wear which was held up by the precedence of government orders. The manufacture of women's wear suffered to a similar extent. Unfilled orders exceeded by 50% those of a year previous. The prospect of additional orders for the defense supplies caused the mills to withhold any offerings of fabrics for civilian purposes. During the month of May, U.S. mills were producing 4,000,000 yd. of fabric weekly.

The trade agreement with Argentina in Oct. 1941 reduced the tariff on lower grades of wool shipped from that country. Japan, a few months prior to Pearl Harbor, had freighters in seaports of Peru and Chile, loading all types of commodities, including wool and alpaca. The Defense Supplies corporation, a subsidiary of the Reconstruction Finance corporation, completed negotiations with the British government to transfer ownership of 176,000,000 lb. of British-owned wool stored in the United States or afloat.

Huge Military Demands.—The outbreak of war with Japan in Dec. 1941 resulted in a withdrawal of offerings of wool piece goods in New York, with the belief that the bulk of the textile machinery would necessarily be confined to government fabrics to equip at least 5,000,000 men. There was talk at this time of the government's taking over all wool supplies. The Office of Price Administration announced the temporary establishment of ceiling prices of wool and wool fabrics based on the approximate level of prices in effect during the period of Oct. 1 to Dec. 6. Immediately after the declaration of war with Japan, added names were appended to the British list of blocked nationals, the so-called blacklist of names considered by both governments to be within the Trading with the Enemy act. Prices remained fixed on wools in Australia, New Zealand and South Africa. The rise in war risk insurance did not stop U.S. purchasing of wools in these markets.

Orders for army cloth for the year amounted to 88,748,257 yd. and 5,848,784 blankets, with the navy and marine corps taking 3,355,000 yd. and 384,000 blankets. Wool consumption in the U.S. was 1,018,553,000 lb., as compared with a normal peacetime consumption of approximately 600,000,000 lb.

During 1942, wool was considered as a strategic material by all nations engaged in the global war. As such, free trading was stopped and was controlled for home use and export by the nations involved. The wool producing countries in South America were free to trade with the world on this commodity, but because of the circumstances of the times could ship only to the U.S. Some wool was shipped to Sweden from South America in ships flying the Swedish flag and having the required British navicert. A few ships carrying large weights of wool destined for Germany were seized by British and U.S. patrols, and the cargoes were confiscated.

At the beginning of 1942, the transition from defense to actual war economy took place. The OPA issued maximum prices on shorn wool, effective Feb. 28. Mills, under adjustment to the conservation program, experimented with substitutes for virgin wool. The use of 100% virgin wool for civilian fabrics was restricted during the year because of greater military requirements. During the period from Aug. 3, 1942, through Jan. 31, 1943, worsted manufacturers were permitted to use not in excess of 25% of such basic poundage for the manufacture of fabrics and yarns of any wool content, and an additional amount of wool owned, not in excess of 30% of such basic quarterly poundage, for fabrics containing not more than 65% wool. For woollen manufacture an amount of wool not in excess of 5% of such basic quarterly poundage could be used for the manufacture of fabrics and yarns, with an additional amount of wool, not in excess of 25% of such basic poundage, for the manufacture of fabrics and yarns containing not more than 65%.

War risk insurance rates on wool reached a peak of 25%, principally because of the submarine menace, but were reduced later in the year to 12½% as sinkings by submarines lessened. Insurance was established by the U.S. government at 1½% up to 4%, thus re-establishing heavy purchases of wool in Australia, South Africa and South America. Orders placed in March by the government called for 74,182,000 yd. of woollen and worsted fabrics, 10,000,000 blankets and 10,000,000 pairs of wool socks. A reciprocal trade agreement between Peru and the U.S. included the reduction in duty of alpaca, used extensively in the manufacture of aviators' uniforms. An agreement between the U.S. and Uruguay was ratified in Washington, wherein the U.S. agreed to purchase from Uruguay a part of the 1941–42 and 1942–43 wool clips, covering 30,000 bales of the older clip and 37,500 bales of the newer clip, providing the latter was unsold by June 1, 1943.

In Dec. 1942, the secretary of agriculture assumed full control over the U.S. food program (wool being included). The government's stock pile of wool was announced to be 450,000,000 lb., principally Australian, New Zealand and South African. Of this, 33,000 bales, or 11,000,000 lb., of Australian wool were sold by public auction in Boston during December. In addition to this holding, there were 225,000,000 lb. in storage intended for transshipment to the United Kingdom. The War Production board's general imports order M-63, covering government control of shipping space for the importation of strategic materials, including wool, required importers to obtain the necessary authorizations or licences to import wool. These licences were granted only on grades of wool, including certain types of alpaca and wool-wastes, suitable only and deemed necessary and appropriate in the public interest and to promote national defense.

U.S. wool consumption during 1942 amounted to 1,021,200,000 lb. of greasy, 22% of which was for civilian fabrics and 78% for military. An army blanket required 10½ lb. of shorn wool; 1 yd. of 18 oz. serge, 4½ lb.; 1 yd. 32 oz. melton, 3⅕ lb.

The year 1943 again showed a consumption of over 1,000,000,000 lb. of wool in the U.S. In bids for government fabrics, preference was given to those containing domestic-grown wool. Nevertheless, of the 445,000,000 lb. of scoured wool consumed during the first three-quarters of the year, the National Association of Wool Manufacturers reported that 37% was domestic and 63% imported.

CCC Control.—To assure the effective distribution of wool for the fulfilment of war and civilian requirements in the U.S., the War Food administration, in 1943, issued an order requiring that U.S.-grown wool not sold prior to April 25 should, with certain exceptions, be sold to and purchased only by the Commodity Credit corporation. The order applied to both shorn and pulled domestic wool, the wool being purchased through handlers on the basis of ceiling prices, less handling costs. It then would be sold directly to manufacturers at ceiling prices. In addition to the purchase of approximately 250,000,000 lb. of U.S.-grown wool, an additional amount of foreign-grown wool was purchased by the government. This stock pile consisted of 290,000,000 lb. of Australian, 6,000,000 of Argentinian and 32,000,000 of Uruguayan, 20,000,000 still remaining in Uruguay at the end of 1943. The total of 328,000,000 lb. of foreign wool did not include an estimated amount of 525,000,000 lb. of Australian, New Zealand and South African wool owned by Great Britain and stored in the United States. This large accumulation of wool was held in storage in the United States for British use should the mills in Yorkshire become incapacitated through German action. Low priced wools from South America, in comparison with domestic wool prices, were attractive to importers, and sizable orders were placed. Deliveries were slow on account of the scarcity of ship bottoms and other circumstances. The War Production board stopped shipments in March from South America of 44s quality and below, and finer than 58s, because shipping space was badly needed for other strategic materials, and the lower and finer qualities of wools from South America were not deemed necessary for the war effort.

The surrender of Italy in Sept. 1943 accentuated a conservative feeling throughout the trade. Manufacturers faced demands for civilian goods over and above those which could be filled, pending calls for military and lend-lease fabrics.

Overoptimism concerning the possible end of the war in Jan. 1944 caused many manufacturers to accept sizable civilian orders. The estimated early defeat of Germany did not take place, however, and by the end of the year these same mills were more concentrated on military goods than at any time during the previous war period. Shortage of manpower affected the mills. New machinery and parts for repairs were practically unobtainable. Necessary soaps and oils were scarce, causing bottlenecks in scouring and in topmaking. This was the fourth successive year in which over 1,000,000,000 lb. of wool was consumed in the United States.

On Jan. 18, 1945, the Defense Supplies corporation offered 1,900,287 lb. of greasy and 3,620,859 lb. of scoured Uruguayan wool by auction. This lot of wool was understood to be originally destined for axis accounts. Statistics showed that the use of imported wool amounted to 64% and domestic 36%. Large military supplies were lost during the "battle of the bulge." New government orders were immediately placed for early delivery, disrupting mill plans for civilian output. With large supplies of the merino type of wools in Australia and South Africa, these orders caused continued activity in these primary markets. The larger amount of business was placed by the U.S. in Australia because of speedier deliveries. Orders for wool placed in both the Cape and South America were taking from five to six months for delivery.

Australian and other foreign apparel wools could be imported into the U.S. at 10 to 20 cents lb. clean basis, including the duty, which was under the ceiling prices in force of domestic-grown wools. The growers in the U.S. urged a centralized control of foreign and domestic wool under one control. The so-called "Hill plan" was offered as another expedient in the manipulation of foreign wools brought into the U.S.

The world wool surplus was estimated to be 2,500,000,000 lb. at the close of 1945. The stock pile of domestic-grown wool was estimated to be slightly under 300,000,000 lb.

Reconversion.—In 1945 the consumption of wool in the U.S. again showed the use of over 1,000,000,000 lb. The mills used approximately 90% of imported wools, because of lower conversion cost and higher yield. After the defeat of Germany in May, the government demands for wool fabrics subsided. By the end of November, 400,000,000 lb. of domestic wool were on hand from the three clips commencing in 1943. In Aug. 1945, after the capitulation of Japan, the manufacturers looked ahead to reconversion of their plants for postwar needs. Wartime orders not in process were immediately cancelled, but there still remained a bottleneck in scouring and combing, as well as time spent in making suitable samples to offer for the civilian trade.

During April and May the British empire group laid the foundation for the orderly marketing and disposal of the war-controlled surplus of wool and the forthcoming clips. A long-term basis was agreed upon for the disposal of these surplus wools, estimated to take at least 12 years to market. It was shown that as of June 30, 1945, there were approximately 3,315,000,000 lb. of United Kingdom owned wool on hand, of which 3,245,000,000 lb. were of dominion origin. Auction sales were recommended as the best medium of marketing this accumulation, and it was expected that the dominions would begin theirs soon after July 1, 1946, and in London prior to that date.

The surplus stock of wool owned by the U.S. government at the end of 1945 amounted to 425,000,000 lb. This consisted of the balance of the 1943–45 clips purchased by the Commodity Credit corporation at established ceiling prices and resold on the same basis. During the week beginning Nov. 26, a new price schedule took effect, lowering the established ceiling prices from 15 to 20 cents clean basis.

A general strike in the woollen and worsted mills was threatened at the beginning of 1946. The New York Western Union strike delayed cable service to Great Britain and the wool centres in South America and South Africa. Manufacturers were hesitant to make wool purchases because of the uncertainty in the labour situation.

As of Jan. 7, 1946, the Commodity Credit corporation reported its unsold stock of domestic-grown wool as 419,115,000 lb., although nearly 22,000,000 lb. had been sold since Nov. 27 of the preceding year, when prices were reduced. Total purchases by this bureau from the beginning of the 1943 program to Dec. 15, 1945, aggregated 895,000,000 lb.

World competition brought about great changes in the wool supply. Australia sold 300,000 to 400,000 bales to France during two weeks in Jan. 1946. The U.S.S.R., Holland and Spain purchased large weights in South America, causing the market in Montevideo to advance 10% almost immediately. U.S. orders placed in Australia during the 7 months ending March 31 totalled 1,408,350 bales or approximately 460,000,000 lb.

Considerable interest was shown in a proposed U.S. government policy on domestic wools, as prepared by the departments of agriculture and commerce. Under this proposal, wool parity prices would be advanced to a level equivalent to other farm products. Many favoured a direct subsidy on sheep to continue to encourage production of wool.

Large weights of foreign wools were re-exported to Italy and to other European countries from the United States. Considerable barter business was being done, exchanging the raw material for yarns or finished fabrics. Mills on the continent were running at 60% of capacity, with labour supply best in Italy. The wool manufacturing industry was practically undamaged in France, Belgium and Italy. The British mills, at the middle of the year, had 158,000 wage earners, with an additional 66,000 needed to restore the prewar complement of 224,000.

The return of auction sales commenced in Sept. 1946 at the various centres in Australia, South Africa and London. Continental competition for these wools caused them to advance from 10% to 20% above the former issue prices of June 30. Ceiling prices in the U.S. were decontrolled on domestic-grown wool by the OPA, but controls were maintained over foreign wools under a regulation which held that, while products might be judged to be agricultural if produced domestically, they did not necessarily come under that category when produced abroad. (*See* also SHEEP; TEXTILE INDUSTRY.) (C. M. AN.)

BIBLIOGRAPHY.—U.S. Dept. of Agric., *Agricultural Statistics;* H. S. Davis, *Wool and the War* (1942); *Wool Yearbook; National Wool Grower* (mo.).

Woolton, 1st Baron

Baron Woolton (Frederick James Marquis Woolton) (1883–), British economist, businessman and government official, was born Aug. 24, 1883. Educated at Manchester university, he was awarded a research fellowship in economics by that institution and became warden of the university settlement in Liverpool. Later, he started the first children's dental clinic in Liverpool and with his wife inaugurated the city's first prenatal clinic.

During World War I, Woolton, who was rejected as medically unfit for military service, joined the war office and became secretary of the Leather Control board. After the war, he went to the U.S. for a study of industrial conditions and on his return he joined the board of Lewis, Ltd., a department store. He became managing director in 1927 and chairman of the board in 1934. He was raised to the peerage as 1st Baron Woolton in 1939.

In early 1939, he joined the war office as director-general of equipment and stores and in April 1940, he was appointed minister of food. Winston Churchill named Woolton to the post of minister of reconstruction in Nov. 1943. Woolton was lord president of the council from May 1945 to the accession of the Attlee government in the following July.

Words and Meanings, New

The words listed in this article were chosen as most typical of the years 1937–46 from some thousands which came into the English language during that period, either by coinage, by extension of meaning, by new combinations or by borrowing from other languages.

The words became prominent or were seemingly used for the first time during the decade 1937–46. Dates within the parentheses following a word or definition indicate the first recorded use of the new word known. A preceding hyphen means that the word or meaning is at least as old as the date given.

In general, the new words of 1937 reflected unrest—dissatisfaction with working and living conditions following a long period of economic depression and widespread unemployment. Some of the new expressions revealed a desire for security, as in government pensions for the old. There was a new feeling of hemispheric solidarity as turmoil increased in Europe. On the other hand, much advance in science was indicated by the many coinages in the fields of aviation, radio, motion pictures, chemurgy and the new synthetics.

In many cases, the individual word or term was first used prior to the year of the listing in which it appears. It is included in that listing, however, because it became prominent or generally definable in that particular year.

1937

Airacuda. An experimental bimotored fighter-bomber built by Bell Aircraft corporation for the U.S. army air corps. Named for the ferocious barracuda.

ad lib, *v. i.* & *t.* To speak lines not in the script during a radio broadcast (–1937; older in theatre); to insert a "lick" in playing a jazz music score. (–1935) *Colloq.*

air poll. Survey of radio program popularity, with listeners checked by a device called a *radiovoter.*

Ambassador-at-Large. A representative of the United States on a special mission abroad.

artificial heart. The Lindbergh-Carrel mechanism for medical experiments in blood circulation. Also **glass heart** and **robot heart.** (1936)

audition, *v. i.* & *t.* To compete in any sort of trial, as ice-skating. Originally a trial of a candidate for employment as a vocalist or instrumentalist.

avoidance of taxes. To be distinguished from "evasion of taxes." The U.S. treasury published the names of 67 wealthy taxpayers who "avoided" full payment of taxes by transferring personal assets to corporations.

bacteriological warfare. The spreading of pestilential germs endangering the enemy's life, both directly and through his food and water supply. First employed in 1340's against Turks by the Tartars, who catapulted corpses of Black Death victims over city walls. Also **germ warfare.**

bank night. A copyrighted form of lottery in motion picture theatres with prizes awarded to members of the audience previously registered. **Banknighter.** The winner in such a lottery. (–1935)

barrelhouse. Playing without regard for what others are playing in a jazz orchestra. *Slang.*

Battey Ball. A form of paddle ball which was a national fad of 1937. Also **Bo-Lo, Fli-Back, Hi-Li, Rapatap, Rick-Rack, Sockit.**

Bauhaus, New. A school of design opened in Chicago in 1937, based on the ideas of the German school. Also **American Bauhaus.**

Bemberg. Trade name of a rayon fabric made by the cuprammonium process.

B film. A film produced quickly and cheaply, without star performers, with routine plot and treatment.

bingles. Token money paid by the U.S. government to settlers in Matanuska valley, Alaska.

blind landing. An aeroplane landing with the pilot guided wholly by the radio homing-type compass. See **DF.**

boogie-woogie. A type of jazz music characterized by free improvisation in the treble range against a pronounced rhythm bass.

bracket, high- and low-, *n.* Those bracketed together as of the same age, size, price, amount of income, etc.

break, *n.* & *v.* Those improvisations distinguishing "hot" jazz music from "sweet." They broke from the basic melody, and each solo was a "lick" for some player. *Slang.*

broken homes. Those homes disrupted by divorce.

Brown Shirt. (Ger. *Braunhemd.*) A member of the *Sturmabteilung,* in nazi Germany.

Bund, The German-American. A pro-nazi organization in the U.S., formed in 1936 as the *Amerikadeutscher Volksbund* with a "culture centre" at Camp Siegfried, L.I.; headed by Fritz Kuhn.

camelback. An uncured compound of rubber for mending pneumatic tires. (–1937)

candid-camera. A small camera for taking unposed photographs. Legislation was urged to curb its use. Also, **candid-cameraman, -craze, -fan.**

captive mine. A coal mine owned and operated by a large industry consuming the entire output. Opposed to **domestic mine.**

cash-and-carry-provision. A clause in the Pittman Neutrality act requiring nations at war to pay in cash for and to transport goods bought from the U.S.

ceiling. A maximum limit on prices, wages or hours, fixed by the government as legal. Opposed to **floor.**

chemurgy. Chemical utilization of farm products in industry. Term coined in 1935 from **chemistry** plus **ergon** (Greek for **work**). Also **chemurgic** and **chemurgical.**

coaxial cable. An insulated cable used to transmit telegraph, telephone and television signals.

commercial, *n.* Radio entertainment paid for by advertisers. Opposed to **sustaining program.**

commercial band. A large well-known jazz band playing "compromise swing"; opposed to serious jazz players.

composite. A seaplane for ultra-long-range flights, consisting of two aeroplanes, one mounted on the other's back and released therefrom in flight.

compressibility burble. A disturbance of the airflow as a plane approaches the speed of sound.

contact lens. Thin plastic lens fitting invisibly over the eyeball and moving with it; designed to correct errors of vision.

court-packing. President F. D. Roosevelt's proposal to add a new justice to the U.S. supreme court for every existing member who persisted in sitting beyond the permissible retirement age of 70 yr. *See* **Nine Old Men.**

crop control. Secretary of Agriculture Wallace's system of limiting planting and fixing prices of farm crops. Farmers who accepted the plan were called **co-operators.**

cyclotron. Atom-smashing machine invented by Dr. E. O. Lawrence, of the University of California in 1932.

Dead End. A grimly realistic play and film on juvenile delinquency, in New York's slums; by extension, used to describe underprivileged, delinquent children.

death sentence. Section 11b of the Securities and Exchange Commission's Public Utilities act, limiting the operation of utility holding companies, effective Jan. 1, 1938.

de-icer. An air-driven device to melt the ice forming on the wings and tail surfaces of an aeroplane in flight. Also **de-icing overshoes.** (1934)

DF. (Direction-finder.) A radio device located on the ground to guide a plane from any point within transmitting range. (–1928 in England)

Du Prene. Trade name for a synthetic rubber manufactured by du Pont. (1935)

dust bowl. a region suffering from prolonged drought and dust storms; *specifically,* the western border of the great plains from 1934 to 1937.

economic rent. Cost of interest, amortization and maintenance of property. Opposed to **social rent,** the sum which low-income families can afford.

economic royalist. One believing himself superior by virtue of wealth. (–1936) Also **ducal economic overlord,** and **tory.**

Eire. Ireland, an independent and sovereign republic, superseding the Irish Free State. Pronounced *Airy.*

electroencephalograph. An apparatus for detecting brain activity and recording it on a visible screen.

emcee, *n.* & *v.* To act as master of ceremonies at a night club, on a radio program, etc. Also **M.C.**

epiallopregnanolone. Male hormone No. 3. Also **EAP.**

Epok. Outdoor advertising sign operated by photoelectric cells, showing a series of animated cartoons. *See* **spectacular.**

estrone. One of the most important female sex hormones. Also **oestrone.**

ever-normal granary. The plan of Secretary of Agriculture Wallace to maintain a federal reserve or reservoir of such crops as cotton, corn, wheat, rice and tobacco to equalize shortages and surpluses.

facsimile broadcasting. A method of transmitting the printed page, with maps and diagrams, by radio and of reproducing them in the home or office. *See* **wirephoto.**

Fair Trade Act. Miller-Tydings act prescribing a minimum price for the resale of a commodity bearing the trade-mark of the manufacturer.

fever therapy. The treatment of disease by artificially induced fever called **machine fever.** Also, **fever cure.**

fifth column. General Franco's sympathizers within Madrid (General Emilio Mola); thus, those who seek to undermine a nation in the interests of a foreign power.

fighter. A military pursuit plane.

fireside chats. President Roosevelt's informal radio addresses in which he appealed to the people for support of certain measures. (1936)

flight recorder. An aeroplane device to keep automatic records of altitude, use of the plane's radio transmitter and reception of beacon signals. Also **flight analyzer.**

floor. A minimum level, as of prices, wages, hours of work. *Colloq.*

Flying Fortress. Boeing trade-mark for Model 299 four-engine bomber. Also **destroyer of the skies, flying dreadnought,** etc. (1935)

flying laboratory. Experimental aeroplane to test new safety devices, **flying fatigue** of aviators, etc.

freeze. To fix by order, as prices, wage scales, capital.

frequency modulation. A system of radio transmission depending upon controlled variation of wave frequency, as opposed to the conventional system of varying wave amplitude. Frequency modulation virtually eliminated static and offered listeners very high fidelity. Also, **FM.**

Gestapo. (Ger. *Geheime Staatspolizei.*) The nazi secret police.

Good-neighbour policy. President Roosevelt's policy of friendship and business co-operation with the Latin American countries and Canada. (–1933)

goon. A labour union representative using violence and illegal coercion. *Slang.*

grass-roots Republicans. The "People's party," embracing all kinds of Republicans from old guardsmen to labourers, with Glenn Frank as chief in 1937 (name itself possibly dated from the 1920s).

groove, in the. Descriptive of swing music played in an inspired fashion; later applied to persons. Also **groovey, going to town** and **out of this world.** (–1936) *Slang.*

guinea pig. The subject of any sort of experimentation.

gutbucket. "Low-down" jazz music. (–1936) *Slang.*

halter. The upper half of a woman's abbreviated swimming suit; or any woman's sport blouse designed for maximum legal skin exposure.

heavy electron. An atomic particle believed to constitute a large part of cosmic rays. Also X particle.

hep cat. A swing music addict. (–1936) *Slang.*

horse opera. A "western" film, or any melodramatic thriller. Also **hoss opera.**

Horst Wessel song. Official nazi rallying song, composed by Horst Wessel, most famous nazi martyr. (–1933)

hot jazz. A series of variations on a basic theme, often improvised, played or sung with gusto. (–1935)

hot money. Foreign capital invested in the U.S.

hydroponics. Growing of plants in nutrient solutions for commercial purposes. Also **tray agriculture.**

ickie. One pretending to like jazz but having no knowledge of true jazz. Opposed to jitterbug. *Slang.*

incident. Undeclared or unauthorized war, border clashes; especially, Japanese and German aggression, as the *Mukden incident* and the *Panay incident.*

Isograph. A machine for solving complex equations, invented by Dr. T. C. Fry.

ivory hunter. Personnel officer of a business firm interviewing likely candidates on college campuses.

jam, *n.* & *v. i.* Free improvisation in swing manner against a rhythm background; to make music in this fashion. **jam session**—An unrehearsed, unplanned, experimental ensemble performance by ruggedly individual swing musicians. (–1936) *Cant.*

jitterbug. A person genuinely receptive to swing and interested in its technique. Also one gesticulating wildly while dancing. *Colloq.*

Keedoozle Stores. A chain grocery system composed of self-service stores employing key-operated electric vending machines.

Kinescope. Trade name attached to a form of cathode ray tube capable of converting streams of electrical particles into visible images. Used in one form of television system.

Koroseal. Goodrich's translucent flexible synthetic material. Also **rubber glass.**

lanital. An artificial wool made by Italian chemists from skimmed milk.

Liberty League, American. A conservative political group, organized in 1934, which fought the New Deal in the 1936 presidential campaign. Also, **Liberty Leaguer** and **Liberty Leaguish.**

liquidate. To kill secretly and ruthlessly, as in the soviet "blood purge."

Little TVA's. Seven proposed federal power projects similar to the Tennessee Valley authority, including the Columbia valley, the Cumberland and the Nebraska. *See* **Regional Planning.**

loss leader. Any article advertised for sale below its cost as a means of drawing customers who might buy other goods offered at profitable prices.

Lucite. Trade name of du Pont's transparent synthetic resin (polymerized methyl methacrylate). Known also as **firefly glass.**

minicam, *n.* & *v.* Short for miniature camera. As a verb, to photograph with such a camera.

neutrino. A light, chargeless particle of smaller mass than the neutron.

newscaster; sportcaster. A reporter broadcasting news or sporting events.

Nine Old Men, The. U.S. supreme court justices over 70 years of age, whom President Roosevelt wished to replace on grounds of their being overaged.

nonobjective, *n.* An abstract art form characterized by bright colours and avoidance of all physical symbols and associations. Also **nonobjectivist,** *n.* The artist. (1930)

off-the-record, *adj.* Not for publication; as of information given out in confidence by government officials during informal press conferences, etc.

Oscar. The annual award for excellence in directing or acting in motion pictures. (–1936)

parachute infantryman. A soldier trained and equipped to descend from the air behind enemy lines; first demonstrated by the soviets at their army manoeuvres near Kiev in 1935.

photomontage. A composite picture, made up of several individual photographs.

pilot error. A mistake in judgment responsible for an aeroplane accident. Flying fatigue caused by oxygen deficiency at high altitudes was held responsible for many such errors.

platter. A phonograph record. Also **wax.** *Slang.*

plexiglas. A transparent plastic material (methyl methacrylate) used in military aircraft in place of window glass.

Pliofilm. A trade name for a thin transparent rubber hydrochloride, used for raincoats and packaging material, manufactured by Goodyear. (–1936)

Polaroid. A trade name for a light-polarizing plastic material, used in eyeglasses, windshields and lamps as a glare-preventive. Also **anti-glare,** *adj.*

pressure-cabin. A sealed aircraft-cabin in which the atmospheric pressure is kept at normal ground pressure by a cabin-supercharger or pressurizer.

pulps. Magazines printed on rough-surfaced paper, and commonly devoted to crime, mystery, gangster and "spicy" detective fiction. Also **pulpwood magazines,** and **pulpdom.** Opposed to **slicks.** *Slang.*

quarantine, *v.t.* To segregate, boycott, or otherwise engage in specific punitive action against a nation. President Roosevelt made the term famous in his speech of Oct. 5, 1937, at Chicago, when he recommended quarantining "aggressor nations."

quick-freeze, *v.t.* To freeze food in a special high-speed refrigerator for storage or transportation. Clarence Birdseye, inventor of the frozen foods process, sold his rights to General Foods corp. in 1929.

quickie. A sit-down strike of labour. (–1936) *Slang.*

reefer. A cigarette containing the dried leaves and flowers of marijuana. Also **bennys, Mary Warners, muggles,** etc. *Slang.*

Regional Planning Bill. Original plan was to include seven power-producing **Little TVA's.** (Tennessee Valley Authorities.)

reliefer. An unemployed person on federal government relief rolls. Also **relief client.**

roadable aeroplane. The Waterman Arrowplane corporation produced a combination automobile and aeroplane called an *Arrowbile.* (The wings of the aeroplane were detached for road use.) A **roadable autogiro** was produced in 1936.

Rome-Berlin axis. An alliance entered into in 1936 between Italy and Germany.

Sanforizing. A mechanical patented process of preshrinking woven materials. Named after the inventor, Sanford Cluett. (1929)

schmaltz, *n.* & *v.* (Ger. *Schmalz,* grease, fat.) A derogatory term to describe playing jazz in a "sweet" or sentimental style. (–1935)

schuss, *n.* (Ger. *shoot.*) A straight, high-speed run in skiing. (1936)

send, *v.* To communicate the personal excitement of the swing musician to his listeners through inspired improvisation or "licks." *Cant.*

shadow, *n.* A skeleton or outline ready to be completed when needed, as a shadow factory or government. (–1936) *Colloq.*

short. A short subject in a moving picture program, as a **Disney short.** Also **film short.**

sit-down, *n.* & *v.* A labour strike in which the workers cease work and refuse to be ousted from the place of employment. Also **sit-in, show-down, lie-down.** Sit-down strikers were called **sitters, sit-downers,** or **trespassers.** (–1936) A possible origin of the term was traced to a strike in the General Electric plant in 1906.

smear campaign. Personal political attack. Also **whispering campaign** and **whispering campaigner.** *Slang.*

spectacular. A large outdoor advertising sign. Also **Wondersign,** trade name.

sponge rubber. Foamed latex for use in the cushions of upholstered furniture and mattresses; opposed to cast rubber.

sterilization of gold. The buying of imported gold by the U.S. federal government for the purpose of holding it in reserve to prevent glutting of U.S. bank reserves. Also **insulation.**

streamliner. Streamlined railroad train.

strip tease, *n.* & *v.* A burlesque dance act wherein a supposedly beautiful girl slowly struts across the stage, disrobing as she goes. Also, **strip-tease** and **strip-and-tease,** *adj. Slang.*

strong man. A leader in politics, sports, etc. Also, **strong-man,** *adj.*

sulfanilamide. A white crystalline compound, discovered in 1935, used successfully in the treatment of bacteria-caused diseases.

superfortress. A four-motored bombing plane built by Boeing.

sustainer. A **sustaining program** paid for by a radio network rather than an advertiser.

swing. *n.* A style of playing dance music which subordinates melody entirely to improvised variations. Opposed to sweet. **Swingster,** an advocate of swing music. Also, **swing band** and **swing fever.**

Technicolor. A patented process of making movies in natural colour; first developed in 1915 but not made commercially practical until 1937.

Thiokol. A synthetic plastic rubber manufactured by the Dow company. (–1936)

Third Reich. (Ger. *Das dritte Reich,* the third empire.) The German totalitarian state, established in 1933.

tin ear. Term applied to a jazz player with poor intonation and with a mechanical method of playing. (–1935) *Slang.*

total war. War waged with all a country's available resources and against the total population and resources of the enemy. Opposed to **limited** or **defensive** war.

Townsendite. Member of the Old Age Revolving Pension, Ltd., advocating a monthly $200 pension for person over 60 years of age not in active employment. Also **Townsendeer, Townsender, Townsendist.** (–1936) The **Townsend Clubs** were founded in 1935.

trailerite. One traveling in a trailer cottage, an automobile-drawn home. **Traileritis,** a name for this mode of living.

trucking. Dancing (usually to swing or jazz music) with a shuffling step.

ultraviolet ray screen. A barrier or screen of germ-killing ultraviolet rays created by a special lamp; used to protect the rest of a hospital from its contagious wards.

unemployment census. A registration conducted by the federal government to determine the number of unemployed in the United States.

workshop in education. An informal study group organized to help teachers apply the principles of "progressive" education to the solution of their own educational problems by the laboratory method. Also, **workshopper.** (–1936)

1938

Prominent among the new words of 1938 were many relating to war—air-raids, blackouts, gas masks, the scorched earth policy, conscription. Science had been stimulated by approaching war and its needs; thus many of the new terms dealt with the results of experiments with the atom and with medicine. A new preoccupation with race was shown, because of the conflicts of nations.

* * *

air-mass theory of weather. The Bjerknes theory; used successfully by the Germans in military aviation and by most U.S. air lines as the basis for forecasts and dispatching.

air raid shelters. Steel and cement structures used as protection against enemy bombing and gassing, in London, Paris, Leningrad and many German cities. Also **bomb shelters, bombproof shelters, shelters.**

amphibian. Amphibious tank built for use in marshlands.

area tactics. A military strategy, used by Chiang Kai-shek's army, of filtering into unprotected enemy territory.

badman. Gangster or desperado.

balloon barrage. British system of balloons and steel cables used to guard key cities from attacks by low-flying enemy aircraft.

barytron. A sub-atomic particle whose electrical shifts give off energy to cement atoms together. Or, a **heavy electron.**

bathinette. A combined dressing table and tub for babies.

battle wagon. A battleship. *Slang.*

Benzedrine. Trade name applied to amphetamine, a synthetic drug closely related to certain gland secretions, used as a nasal inhalant and as a stimulant producing alertness and wakefulness.

Big Apple, *n.* & *v.* A dance, adapted by college students from the highly imaginative dancing of Negroes, which took the United States by storm and also became popular in England.

blackout, *n.* & *v.* An air raid precaution in which all lights are extinguished or covered.

blanketing of a radio station. Silencing of a station by a more powerful station. *Fig.* Censorship, as of war news.

blind bombing. Haphazard dropping of small projectiles from above cloudbanks.

blitzkrieg. (Ger. lightning war.) A German method of war first suggested by Von Moltke and later evolved in detail by General Hans von Seeckt. Blitzkrieg involved the concentration of mobile troops, devastating air raids, together with shattering attacks of all manner of armoured vehicles.

blue-ribbon grand jury. A panel of jurors selected for special qualifications, such as alertness, intelligence and common sense. Also **Blue Ribboners.** *Colloq.*

brain wave. Electric current generated by a human brain cell. An instrument for measuring brain waves was invented by Hans Berger in 1929. *See* **electroencephalograph,** in 1937 list.

breakdown, *n.* An analysis or classification. **Break down,** *v.* To analyze or classify.

Chicago piano. An eight-barreled "pom-pom," or rapid-fire, anti-aircraft gun. *Slang.*

Chicago Plan. A system of higher education advocated by certain faculty members of the University of Chicago, providing for four years of broad cultural training, to be followed by two years of specialization in the student's chosen field.

class. A group of conscripts becoming eligible for military service in a given year.

closed-end trust. An investment trust whose securities have no right of redemption. Opposed to **open-end.**

cold Anschluss. Term applied by some newspaper correspondents to Hitler's bloodless conquest of Austria.

commentator. In radio, one who broadcasts news summaries, with or without comments.

Corrigan, Wrong Way. A nickname for Douglas Corrigan, who flew to Ireland in a decrepit plane without the authority of the U.S. department of commerce. Also **Non-stop Corrigan** and **On again, off again, up again Corrigan.** **To do a Corrigan**—to do a daring feat. **Corriganism** became synonymous with recklessness. **Manhattan Corriganitis** described the hysterical acclaim with which he was met on his return to the United States.

crab, *v.* To head an aeroplane into a cross wind to counteract drift.

Dagenan. Trade name applied in the United States to a pneumonia-combating chemical (hydroxyethylapocupreine). The British name *T693* was coded shortening of the full chemical word-formula.

Dapp. The Mexican government's system of press censorship.

deadpan. Expressionless countenance. *Slang.* (–1936)

desterilization. The release by the U.S. treasury of inactive gold reserves. *See* **sterilization of gold,** in 1937 list.

dime store. A ten cent store. Also **5-and-10,** both singly and in combination, as "Barbara Hutton, the **5-and-10** heiress."

Divinism. A nation-wide religious cult led by "Father Divine," Harlem Negro (legal name, George Baker). His followers called themselves **angels,** and the cult headquarters in a luxurious Hudson river estate became known as **paradise.** Cult slogan: "Peace, it's wonderful!"

documentary, *adj.* Applied to an artistic presentation of factual material; as the U.S. government's **documentary** film "The River."

double-talk, *n.* Talk or writing that ostensibly is meaningful but is a mixture of sense and gibberish.

drive-in, *n.* & *adj.* Roadside restaurant serving customers in their automobiles; suburban moving picture shows viewed by patrons in their cars; banking service given to customers in their cars.

Dunningcolor. Three-hue colourfilm, used in advertising.

educational orders. Government orders for war material awarded to selected firms to enable them to perfect methods of large-scale production in advance of actual need by the armed forces.

egg in your beer. An unreasonable demand. *Slang.*

enterprise capital. Proprietor's capital, risk-bearing capital, venture capital.

escapism. Turning of the mind from routine and reality to more pleasing imaginative activity. **Escapist,** *adj.,* as in escapist literature; **escape,** *adj.* as in **escape** mechanism—

any means employed in "escaping" from reality.

fact-finding, *n.* & *adj.* The process of ascertaining the facts in a case by careful investigation, as by a congressional committee. Also **fact seeker.**

Fair Labor Standards Act. U.S. federal legislation, dealing with wages, hours and child labour.

feathering, *n.* & *adj.* Pertaining to a device which enables the pilot of an aeroplane in flight to turn the propeller blades so that they present their edges rather than their flat surfaces to the resistance of the air mass.

Fiberglas. Trade name applied to fine tough strands drawn from molten glass and spun into textiles or made into sound and heat insulation.

five-suit bridge. Originated by Dr. Walter Marseilles of Vienna; a game employing a 65 card deck.

Flat Foot Floogee with the Floy-Floy. A popular swing dance and song, the latter written in **jive talk.**

Floxalan. A synthetic wool fabric made from cellulose.

fluorescent lamp. A tubular electric lamp which uses mercury vapour instead of a filament and produces much illumination.

flying squadron. A committee organized for quick and effective action; as in politics, labour union strikes and police patrols. Or **flying squad.** (–1934)

front. A figurehead.

gagaism. Modernistic art.

gangster nations. The axis. Also **international gangsters.**

Garand rifle. A semi-automatic, gas-operated rifle, used by the U.S. army.

gastrin. A hormone located in the inner lining of the lower end of the stomach, discovered by Dr. S. A. Kamarov, of McGill university.

giropilot. A mechanism for steering an aeroplane after it has gained its desired cruising altitude. Also **gyroscopic pilot** and **gyropilot.** Also **mechanical mike.** *Slang.*

glamour boys. Actors, athletes, aviators and other men appealing to the popular U.S. fancy. *Slang.*

glamour girls. Actresses and society girls noted for beauty and "oomph." *Slang.*

googol. An arbitrarily coined word intended to denote the number formed by the numeral "1" followed by 100 zeros.

green light, to give the. To grant permission to proceed with a project. *Colloq.*

hair-do. Woman's coiffure.

Ham and Eggs for Californians. An old-age pension scheme, planned by Lawrence Allen, a Hollywood lawyer, based on the stamped-scrip idea, promising "$30 every Thursday" to each jobless Californian more than 50 years old. Also **Ham-and-Eggers,** adherents of the plan.

heel. A contemptible person. *Slang.*

Henleinite. Follower of Konrad Henlein, Sudeten nazi leader. Also **Henleinist.** The **Free Corps** of nazis in Czechoslovakia were **Sudeten exiles** who demanded autonomy.

high-light, *v.* To give prominence to.

hit-and-run driver. A motorist leaving the scene of an accident illegally after striking someone.

ideology. A system of theories and aims constituting a program, as New Deal ideology. **Ideologist,** *n.,* and **ideological,** *adj.*

institutional. Descriptive of advertising aimed to create good will and prestige for a company. *Cant.*

integration. The combination of companies or industries through stock purchase. A **wagon-wheel** is such a combination in which the components are clustered around a large city or consumption area. The **clothesline type** of combination is made up of geographically separated units loosely strung together.

jitterbug. A small industrial truck for handling internal [within a factory] materials. *Slang.*

jive, *v.* To play swing music. **Jive talk,** the lingo of swing musicians.

jobholder. An employe of the U.S. federal government.

juicer. A machine to extract fruit and vegetable juices.

La Follette party. The National Progressive party, organized by Robert and Philip La Follette in 1938.

Lambeth Walk. A novelty dance imported into the United States from England; a restrained sort of Big Apple.

live, *adj.* Applied to radio network programs in which the performers actually appeared in the studio; opposed to **recorded** or **transcribed** programs.

Lovelace mask. The substratosphere oxygen mask for aviators, tested by Howard Hughes. Also **B.L.B. inhalator,** named for the three designers, Drs. Boothby, Lovelace and Bulbulian.

Ludlite. A fireproof building-sheathing material consisting of a thin sheet of stainless steel bonded to a layer of sound-deadening composition board. Full trade name, **Ludlite Bord.**

lug, *n.* Political pressure for campaign funds (–1936). Also **kickback.** *Slang.*

mercy killing. Euthanasia or painless death for the incurably ailing.

methylcholanthrene. Powerful carcinogen (cancer-producing chemical).

Metrazol. Trade name for a camphor derivative used in treating mental disorders.

Navicert. (Naval Certificate.) A maritime bill of lading devised in 1916, when the American consul-general in London persuaded the British admiralty to establish a method of determining in advance the senders, receivers and contents of cargoes carried by neutral ships, to prevent enemy receipt of such cargoes. A war word revived in 1938.

neutretto. An electrically neutral atomic particle.

Number 1. The most important member or exponent; **Number 1 educator.**

Number 2. Second in importance; **Number 2 nazi** (Goering).

Nylon. Yarn 66 of the Du Pont company. The name was coined by company chemists to designate a whole group of synthetic polyamides.

oomph. A term made by onomatopoeia to express male appraisal of female beauty and charm. Ann Sheridan was the first U.S. "Oomph Girl." (–1936) *Time* magazine used **gazoomph** and **gazoomphing.** Also **umph.**

open city or town. Undefended; hence immune under international law from attack by an enemy power.

Oslo Group. Seven powers (Denmark, Sweden, Norway, Finland, the Netherlands, Belgium and Luxembourg) banded together in 1936 to foster economic and political co-operation. Also **Oslo Powers, Oslo States** and **Non-interveners.**

outside route. An airline from the U.S. to Alaska over the open sea; opposed to **inside route.**

pickaback plane. "Composite" plane (see 1937 list). Also **piggyback.** *Slang.*

pipe, *v.* To transmit radio programs by telephone wires to restaurants, etc.

pipe line. A means of transmission of ideas; as information from abroad to the U.S. press.

predicator. Electric sighting mechanism on British anti-aircraft guns.

pressure, *v.* To force passage or defeat of legislation or alter public policy through unofficial channels. Also, **pressure campaign** and **pressure group.**

Progressivism. The theory of education holding that children learn best by their own experience. Introduced into the United States about 1918 by John Dewey, who adapted the principles of Froebel and Rousseau. Also, **progressive,** *adj.*

protective arrest. Detention, often in concentration camps of those disagreeing with the views of rulers, as Pastor Martin Niemoeller in nazi Germany. Or **protective custody.**

racism. A doctrine based on the assumption that certain races are inherently superior. Also, **racist,** *adj.,* and **racial,** *adj.*

racial fitness. The anti-Jewish policy of the Third Reich of sterilizing those persons who did not pass "racial fitness" tests.

radio knife. An electric needle used for cutting through tissue, sterilizing the edges of the wound at the same time.

rank-and-filers. Members of labour unions, as opposed to the leaders.

Revisionist, Jewish. An extremist political party in Palestine which wished to drive out the Arabs.

scorched earth. A policy adopted by retreating armies of destroying property which might have possible use to the enemy. Usually **scorched earth tactics.**

screwball. Anything acting crazily. (1) In baseball, a variety of pitched ball made famous by Carl Hubbell and "Lefty" Gomez; also **screwballist.** (2) A fanatic, eccentric or zany. *Slang.*

Siegfried Line. The nazi line of concrete fortifications along the Rhine, begun in 1936.

Silk Road. The caravan route linking Russia and China, once used by Marco Polo. Also **Silk Route** and **Marco Polo Route.**

situation. Irregularity or fraud. Also, **special situation** and **Wall Street situation.**

sound conditioning. The use of filters in air-conditioning ducts to keep sound from travelling to other parts of the building.

spiral, *n.* In economics, a rapid increase or decrease; as the **downward spiral** of the 1938 recession in the United States.

spot, *adj.* Originating in a local radio station, as **spot advertising.**

Sterilamp. The Westinghouse germ-killing, air-conditioning lamp used in hospitals and other public places.

stork derby. The contest among mothers of large families in Canada to secure a share of the $500,000 **stork derby prize** provided by the bequest of C. V. Millar. Also, **baby derby.**

subsistence homestead. A co-operative community financed by loans from the Farm Security administration. Among the projects were the Cumberland, Penderlea, Red House and Skyline homesteads. Members were known as **homesteaders.**

super-cyclotron. An atom-smashing machine of great power.

tape transmission. A narrow continuous film used in recorded radio programs (–1936).

TASS (Rus. *Telegraphnoye Agenstvo Sovyetskovo Soyuza*). The soviet news agency.

televisigraph. A patented device for writing by television.

Tergitol. Trade name for a chemical wetting agent.

thought control. Japanese censorship system in which police arrested persons suspected of having "dangerous thoughts."

Time Capsule. A seven-foot long, torpedo-shaped shell of Cupaloy (an alloy of copper, chromium and silver) buried on the grounds of the New York World's Fair, containing 10,000,000 printed words on microfilm, 1,000 photographs, a dictionary of slang, the *World Almanac,* periodicals and excerpts from the *Encyclopædia Britannica.*

Trubenizing. A patented process for producing semi-stiff collars. (1934) A patent for a method of wilt-proofing collars was taken out by the Celanese corporation in 1933.

Upsweep hair-do. A favoured coiffure of women in 1938.

Vitamins L-1 and L-2. Two new vitamins reported by Japanese scientists, extracted from liver and yeast.

Vitamin K. The diet factor influencing coagulation of blood; discovered by Dr. E. A. Doisy.

warphan. A child whose father and mother had been killed in war.

war weariness. Low morale among the general public in wartime. Also, **war-weary,** *adj.*

wire photo. A service, begun in 1935 by the Associated Press, to transmit a facsimile of a photograph by electrical signals over telephone wires.

yardstick. A unit of measure for determining the cost of production of electric power, milk, farm machinery, etc. Federal projects were set up to attempt to establish costs and prices.

1939

The new words for 1939 had a background of war. Hundreds of strange terms appeared, naming munitions, mines and anti-mine devices, mechanized war equipment and lines of fortifications in Europe.

In the U.S., however, many persons were attending the two great World's Fairs—in New York city and in San Francisco—where the exhibits showed many new wonders of science.

* * *

absolute. Measured from the ground, in aeronautics; as, the **absolute altimeter.**

abstraction. An abstract composition in art representing an idea or an emotion by means of nonrepresentational designs. **Abstractionist** and **semi-abstractionist** designated the artists. **Near abstraction** was a nonrepresentational design with recognizable elements.

aerial mine. A large bomb dropped from an aeroplane in flight and delayed in descent by a parachute. Also **chute** and **parachute mine.**

air raid bulbs. Dimmed blue street lights giving no more than two yards vision. Also **A.R.P. lights.**

air raid warden. A local officer directing air raid precautions.

Alnico. General Electric's permanent magnet alloy capable of hoisting weights nearly 1,500 times heavier than itself. It was used also in loudspeakers and phonograph pickups.

Anderson shelter. A sheet-steel hovel, sunk several feet into the ground and covered with earth. One million were distributed free in Britain by Sir John Anderson, A.R.P. head. Also **doghouse air raid shelter.** *Slang.*

antenna mine. A large naval mine with projecting wire

filaments, exploding on contact with a metal object, such as a passing ship.

anti-aircraft sound detector. A mechanism with large horns pointing skyward, mounted on a truck. Also **sound locator.** Also **mechanical ears.** *Slang.*

area bombing. The royal air force method of high-altitude bombing of large areas; opposed to **precision bombing.**

A.R.P. codes. The code word "yellow" signified the bombers were 20 minutes away; "red," 5 minutes; "green," all clear.

bail out, *v.i.* To make a parachute jump from an aeroplane in flight.

baby bonus. The offering of prizes for large families. Mussolini spent $3,000,000 for prizes to Italian mothers during a single year.

banana-town. A town in the Latin-American tropics. *Slang.*

bank. A storage place for a reserve supply; as a **blood bank,** with blood for transfusions kept in refrigerated containers.

barbiturate. A drug used as a sedative or hypnotic; sold under a variety of trade names. Also **lullaby pills.** *Slang.*

beam at, *v.* To aim a radio broadcast at certain receiving stations; as German propaganda programs beamed at North America. (–1933)

black. Illicit; as the **black bourse** in New York city, where smuggled German marks were bought from German refugees.

blackout fashions. Women's costumes in London and Paris included many white accessories as a safety measure during blackouts. White patches were also sewn on the sleeves of both women and men.

blitzkrieg, sea. Submarine mine warfare.

blueprint, *n.* and *v.* A plan for anything; as, blueprints for "Mobilization Day."

B_x vitamin. A growth vitamin of the B groups; antagonistic to the action of the sulfanilamides. Also **anti-gray-hair vitamin.**

C.A.B. (Co-operative Analysis of Broadcasting.) A confidential poll for radio advertisers and their agencies. See **Crossley rating** and **Hooper-Holmes survey.**

Chamberlain fashions. Hats, combs, and fur-handled umbrellas, named for Prime Minister Chamberlain, featured in U.S. fashions. In Belgium, citizens called an umbrella **un Chamberlain.** In Normandy, a new dance was named **La Chamberlaine.**

consumer subsidy. A plan to move surplus farm products by a two-price system; proposed by the department of agriculture. **Reliefers** (persons on government relief) were to be issued **bonus checks** or **relief stamps (blue and orange stamps),** for which they could buy surplus foods at reduced prices.

critical materials. Those materials essential to national defense which were not so difficult to secure as strategic materials. The U.S. government listed 17 in 1939, including asbestos and vanadium. Or **critical commodities.** *See* **essential materials.**

Crossley rating. A weekly index on a radio program's audience.

cyclical budgeting. The plan of Marriner S. Eccles to abandon annual budgeting for the federal treasury. Its opponents called it the **Spend and Wait** theory.

decontaminate. To free of poison gas.

Domei (*Domei Tsushin-sha*). Official Japanese Federated News agency.

dust-bowler. An inhabitant of the **Dust Bowl.**

dry shaver. An electric shaver.

Egalitarian Women's Party. Advocates of equal rights for women. Opposed to **protectionists.**

Ekarhenium. Discovered by Prof. Jean Baptiste Perrin in pitchblende ore, in a natural state; the same element as No. 93, synthesized in 1934 by Prof. Enrico Fermi.

electric apron. A powerful magnetic force that could be thrown some hundreds of feet ahead of mine sweepers to render magnetic mines inactive.

electric organ. A musical instrument using electric devices instead of wind; especially the *Hammond organ.*

electronic microscope. A supermicroscope using the invisible rays given off by electrons.

essential materials. Those materials essential to national defense which were not classified as **critical** or **strategic** but which later might be so classified.

evacuation camps. British camps in the country for women and children evacuated from bomb-threatened London.

exposition feet. A slight case of gout aggravated by excessive walking, as at the New York World's fair and the Golden Gate International exposition in San Francisco.

F.A.F. (fly-away field). Descriptive of a completed plane, ready to be flown away; as, listing at $2,995 F.A.F. Wayne, Mich.

farm, *n.* & *v.* A system, in professional sports, wherein a recruit is assigned to a minor league for training until he is needed by an associated major league.

Flying Pencil. Dornier-17 plane.

flying wing. A type of aeroplane with a specially designed wing, without fuselage and with pusher-type engine.

fog disperser. Calcium chloride to dispel fog endangering docking ships; under experimentation in 1938 at the Massachusetts Institute of Technology.

fog dispersion beam. System of sending out a beam of infra-red rays, which cuts a clear-vision channel through smoke or fog; for airmen, mariners, etc.

fortify. To improve a food in nutritive value by adding vitamins and minerals when processing destroys the factors; as pasteurized milk fortified by the addition of vitamins A and D.

Futurama. A diorama designed by Norman Bel Geddes for the General Motors exhibit at the N.Y. World's Fair, portraying superhighways and other methods of modelling traffic in the future.

ground crew. A crew of mechanics and technicians maintaining and servicing a plane. Opposed to **flight crew.**

gun, *v.* To open up the throttle of a motor to increase its speed; as to gun a plane.

Harbour Service. A German saboteur spy working in the great world ports during peacetime. More common types of secret agents were **termites** (spreading rumours to lower a country's morale) and **torpedoes** (active wreckers and assassins).

harmonic synthesizer-analyzer. A machine for solving complex mathematical equations.

Hatch Act. Act barring U.S. federal employees from engaging in national political campaigns.

Hooper-Holmes survey. An investigation of the listening habits of radio audiences. Later, **Hooper rating.**

Hydra-matic Drive. A combination of "a liquid flywheel and fully automatic transmission" to eliminate gear shifting; developed by General Motors.

infiltration, troop. Enveloping tactics combined with the encircling manoeuvre; used by the Germans in their operations in Poland in 1939. Described by the German general staff as putting the enemy in *Beutels* (bags).

Information Please. A radio quiz show born on May 17, 1938.

interceptor plane. Speedy light plane with quick-firing cannon. Also, **interceptor-pursuit, pursuit-interceptor** and **interceptor fighter.**

iron horse. The U.S. army **combat car**; a tank-type vehicle assigned to the mechanized cavalry. Also, **iron cavalry.**

Ivy Leaguer. Member of a big-time Eastern university football team. John Lardner divided them into two groups: *hedera helix* (true ivy) and *rhus toxicodendron* (poison ivy). The latter were paid players.

Janizariat. President F. D. Roosevelt's close advisers, including Tommy Corcoran, their head; borrowed from old Turkish term by Gen. Hugh S. Johnson. Also called the **Corcoran Crowd.**

Jones's corner. The spot at which the clippers changed their course in flying between California and Hawaii. *Aviators' slang.*

klystron. A super-short-wave radio transmitter.

lending-spending program. By law President Roosevelt was granted $5,000,000,000 for relief projects. Also **spend-lend.**

Limes Line. A name given by Hitler in 1939 to the Siegfried line, from the ancient term applied to the Germanic outposts of the Roman empire. Pronounced: *lee-mez.*

Lincoln Brigade. The **Abraham Lincoln Battalion of the International Brigade** (Loyalists) in the Spanish Civil War, made up of volunteers. **Spanish volunteers** fought in such numbers as to warrant the Spanish conflict's being called **Little World War** after Aug. 1936.

linear resonant accelerator. An 8-foot-high glass tube atom-smasher which impels the particles in a straight line.

macon. Mutton smoked to approximate bacon; an experiment of the British ministry of food.

magnetic mine. A naval mine designed to explode when its magnetic needle is deflected by the proximity of the metal hull of a vessel.

Mannerheim Line. The Finnish line of fortifications, named after Baron Mannerheim.

marathoner. A participant in one of the many competitions calling for endurance; as Bible-reading, bike-racing, dancing, etc.

maturism. The theory of **economic maturity** advanced by President Roosevelt at the opening of congress, Jan. 1939; the belief that the U.S. economic system was no longer capable of being self-supporting on a free-enterprise basis.

Melba toast. Very thin toasted bread, originated by Mme. Marie Ritz, and named for Mme. Melba, who was stopping at the same hotel.

microscalpel. A glass instrument with a 1/1,000,000-inch point.

microvivarium. Micro-organisms projected on a five-foot screen; a New York World's fair exhibit.

monitor, *v. t.* To check short-wave receivers; as by interpreters listening to European broadcasters for possible news flashes.

moto-rustlers. Modernized cattle thieves who packed steers into trucks. (–1936)

Munich, A. Any appeasement pact; as "a new Munich."

Neohexane. A process to increase gasoline's octane rating.

nickelodeon. A machine which plays a music record when a coin (nickel) is put in a slot.

night owl broadcast. Illegal early morning radio program. Also **bootleg broadcast.**

night raid. To bomb at night.

Nisei. A second-generation Japanese in the U.S.; a citizen of Japanese ancestry. Also **Nissei.**

Novachord. Trade name for a stringless piano with piano and harpsichord tones, invented by Laurens Hammond.

nursery school. A pre-kindergarten school which extends scientific upbringing to children aged two to five.

octane rating. Establishment in 1927 of the **octane number scale** rated the anti-knock quality of a motor fuel. **100-octane gas** was first used in 1936.

package, *n.* and *adj.* A unit containing miscellaneous elements. A package offered by brokers might contain some securities with excellent earning records, some that were speculations. General Motors produced a **packaged power** unit of engine and generator; the radio networks had **packaged programs** of transcribed numbers. Also **package-sale.**

Panelbilt House. The U.S. Steel corporation's prefabricated house.

paper bullet. A form of psychological warfare in which propaganda leaflets were dropped by plane in enemy territory. Also **bomphlet** and **throwaway.**

parentorium. A parent guidance centre where parents were taught to help cure their offspring of speech disorders.

penetration, nazi. German propaganda activities.

phony war. The "sitzkrieg," or non-active war on the western front, dating from Sept. 1939.

photogenic. Very suitable for being photographed.

pianothon. A piano-playing marathon.

pops. Concerts of popular music.

polymethylacrylate. A tough, rubberlike, transparent material made from milk; used in the manufacture of sails, balloon cloth and anti-war-gas uniforms.

polystyrene. A colourless, transparent thermoplastic made from mineral oil.

polythene. A solid hydrocarbon polymer, discovered in the laboratories of the Imperial Chemicals Industry, Ltd. of Great Britain and further developed by Du Pont; valuable for wire and cable insulation.

Polyvinyl Acetate. A Monsanto plastic, used in the manufacture of safety glass.

psychological warfare. Propaganda designed to break down the morale of the enemy, both those in the armed services and civilians. Also called **radio armament, leaflet raids, war of nerves.**

put the finger on. To point out as the intended victim. Originally racketeer slang.

radiocast, *n.* A radio broadcast.

radio photo. A facsimile of a photograph transmitted long distances by electrical impulse instead of by wire. International Radio photos offered this service.

R man. An air-wave detective of one of the Federal Communications commission monitoring stations, who watched for unlicensed operations, checked on the efficiency of ship transmitters and recorded questionable programs.

red, walking on the. A street traffic signal violation.

Republicrat. One who withdrew temporarily from the Republican party in April 1938 to vote with the Democrats. (1935)

robot plane. Crewless, radio-controlled plane, directed both from land stations and from bombers. Also **robot bomber.**

rugcutter. A swing dancer. (–1938)

safety-belt. A **safety zone** proclaimed by 21 American republics at the Panama Neutrality convention in Dec. 1938; to run from the Canadian line around both the eastern and western coasts of the Americas, at an average of 300 mi. from shore. Known also as the **hemispheric defense zone.**

safety glass, high-test. Two layers of glass with an inner layer of polyvinal acetate resin, used in automobiles.

sealed beam. Headlamps for automobiles, with the reflector, the light source and the lens in a single, hermetically sealed unit.

secret weapon, Hitler's. The magnetic mine, the parachute mine and the use of the loudspeaker for propaganda purposes were among the various **new weapons** which the allies thought might be the **secret weapon** hinted at by Hitler.

Singapore, American. Guam, which the U.S. navy hoped to fortify strongly. A **French Singapore** in Indo-China was also planned.

sitathon. A marathon motion picture show with seven full-length films.

sitzkrieg. (Sitting war.) An inactive war, as opposed to the **blitzkrieg** of the nazis.

Six-man football. Introduced by Stephen Epler, on the Columbia university campus, following the success of the six-man football game which he introduced in 1934; the latter was played by 2,100 schools in 1938.

slap-happy. Witless. Originally pugilistic slang. (–1938)

soup. Horsepower. Corruption of **supe** from **supercharge.** *Aviation slang.* (–1937)

soup up. To step up the power of an engine.

S.S. (*Schutzstaffel.*) Hitler's bodyguard; known also as the **Black Shirt Guard** (*Schwarzhemd*) because of their black uniforms. Superseded the **S.A.** (*Sturmabteilung,* **Brown Shirts, Storm Troopers**) in 1934, as Hitler's favoured group.

Stader splint. A method of clamping broken bones together by running a steel pin into both ends of the break and connecting the pins with an adjustable metal bar.

Stakhanoff movement. The speed-up system in soviet industry. **Stakhanoffite,** the Russian **superworker.**

Station wagon. An automobile with a wooden body, several cross seats and a baggage compartment.

Stock pile. A reserve supply of an essential material usually built up by a nation in anticipation that war or blockade might cut off the supply.

strategic materials. Those materials, essential to national defense, which must be largely imported and which must be strictly controlled.

Stratoliner. Trade name of the Boeing 307, a four-motored substratoplane, commercial counterpart of the army's Flying Fortress. (1938)

straw-hat theatre. Summer theatre presented in many small communities throughout the United States, often by amateurs.

suicide fleet. Mine sweepers.

supernova. A nova hundreds of times brighter than common novae (black, lightless stars).

super tank. A tank weighing 80 tons or more.

talkathon. A talking marathon; that is, a protracted legislative debate.

tank trap. Artificial obstacles of many sorts—thick vertical walls of concrete, deep shell craters, cement or steel posts, bunkers, abatis (tree branches interwoven with barbed wire), etc.

teardrop design. Streamlined, as automobile bodies.

telecast, *v.* To broadcast by television.

telegenic. Suitable for photographing for television.

third-termers; anti-third-termers. Persons in favour of President Roosevelt's being elected to a third term or opposed to it, respectively.

tin fish. A submarine. *Slang.*

T-man. (Treasury-man.) Special agent of the U.S. treasury department.

Tommie gun. A Thompson submachine gun.

video. Pertaining to the transmission of televised images. Television waves, after radio-frequency amplification, are split into **video** and **audio impulses.**

Voder, (voice operation demonstrator.) A mechanism to provide speech for persons who have lost their larynxes. Nicknamed **Pedro.** An earlier form of the machine was called *Vosyn.*

war chest. Funds deposited in U.S. by foreign governments for war materials to be bought in the U.S.

war names. Suggested by correspondents to magazines during 1939 were the following: Hitler's War, European Power War, Nervy Nazi War, Nutsy War, Ritzkrieg, Weird War, the Word War, The Little War that Wasn't There, World War II.

war of nerves. Psychological warfare, resulting **in war fever, war hysteria** and **war jitters.**

West Point of the Air. Randolph Field, Texas.

West Wall. Hitler's definition: "West wall is for all times the Reich frontier in the west." Nazi newspapers first called the German fortifications the Siegfried line, then adopted *Limes,* and rechristened them the West Wall.

wild mine. An unanchored or free sea mine.

Youth Hostel, American. An affiliate of International Youth Hostels association, which was organized in the U.S. by Monroe Smith. In 1939 300 leaders held their second annual meeting in Northfield, Mass.

(M. J. M.)

1940

AA. *See* **ack-ack.**

ack-ack. (From ack, the word used by British signallers for "a.") Short for anti-aircraft gun; also the fire of one or more anti-aircraft batteries. Also **AA.**

action station. (*Brit.*) Place on shipboard to which a man is assigned during an action against the enemy.

aeroembolism. A painful embolism consisting of bubbles of nitrogen in the blood and the tissues, resulting from a too rapid ascent to rarefied altitudes of 30,000 ft. or more; relieved by oxygen. (–1940)

airblitz. Aerial blitzkrieg.

airplot room. Room for planning air operations.

anchor. A vital military position, a base of operations for an important area.

anoxia. State of being without adequate oxygen, esp. common among fliers at altitudes over 15,000 ft. unless adequately protected.

asdic. Initials of Anti-Submarine Detection Investigating Committee, a device for detecting and locating submarines by the use of reflected inaudible sound waves. (1939)

bar-fly, *Slang.* A frequenter of bars or drinking-places.

barroon. (*Brit.*) A barrage of balloons.

basin-hat. (*Brit.*) A steel helmet. *See* **bassinet.**

bassinet. (*Brit.*) A steel helmet; also called **tin hat.** From the pronunciation of **basin-hat.**

beach-head. A foothold gained and held on an enemy beach to make possible the landing of troops and supplies in sufficient number and quantity for further advances.

billetee. (*Brit.*) One evacuated from a section in danger of being bombed.

blister turret. A small compartment, usually for a gunner, protruding above the top of the fuselage of an aeroplane and equipped with a transparent covering shaped like a blister.

blitz, *v.* (Ger. lightning.) To attack with lightning-like rapidity and force, esp. from the air. **blitz,** *n.* Short for **blitzkrieg** (*see* 1938 list).

Blitz, or The Blitz. The bombing of Great Britain by the German airforce extending from Aug. 1940, to May 1941.

blitzer. *See* **blitzkrieger.**

blitzflu. A type of influenza with quick onset and rapid recovery.

blitzkrieger. One engaging in a blitzkrieg. Also called **blitzer.**

blitzlull. (*Brit.*) A letup in a blitz.

bombardier. That crewman of a bomber who, through the use of a bombsight, drops the bombs at the proper time.

bomb bay. A bay in the bottom of the fuselage of a bomber where the bombs are stored and from which they are dropped after the bomb bay doors are opened.

bombee. One who has gone through an air raid.

brown off. *R.A.F. Slang.* To have had one's fill; to suffer from ennui; to be in low spirits. (Old Brit. slang term revived in World War II.)

buttoned up. *R.A.F. Slang.* Prepared in every detail; orders distinctly comprehended, or executed; consummated attack.

cabineteer. A member of a cabinet.

camporee. A word blended from **camp** and **jamboree** to describe a meeting of Boy Scouts drawn from a district or section of the country.

car-hop. One, usually young, who waits on patrons in parked automobiles.

cat. *Slang.* A shortening of **caterpillar tractor.**

cat skinner. *Slang.* One who drives a caterpillar tractor.

chatter-bug. (*Brit.*) Term coined by Harold Nicolson, parliamentary secretary to the minister of information, to describe a civilian whose loose talk (chatter) revealed military facts.

chutist. Short for **parachutist.**

Clara. (*Brit.*) Employed by Londoners for the all-clear signal.

combined operations. An operation in which at least two fighting services combined to assault an enemy.

conscriptee. One conscripted.

coventrate, *v. t. See* **coventrize.**

coventrize, coventryize, *v. t.* To make rubble of a city as was done by the Germans at Coventry during the night of Nov. 14–15, 1940, when an estimated 500 German bombers dropped some 1,100,000 lb. of bombs. Also **coventrate.**

crashproof. Of an aeroplane and its equipment, proof against damage as a result of crashing. (–1940)

Cunningham's comet. A comet discovered by Leland E. Cunningham.

curb, *v. t.* To take (a dog) to the curb; as, curb your dog.

curvaceous, *adj.* Well-shaped, exhibiting curves; in reference to the female body.

defrost. To remove the frost deposited around the ice compartment of mechanical refrigerator. (–1940)

de-gaussing girdle. (*de* + *gauss,* unit of magnetic flux density, named for Carl Friedrich Gauss, German scientist and mathematician, + *ing.*) A special girdle of electric cables, placed around the hull of a ship, carrying a certain kind of electricity which neutralizes the magnetic field set up by the metal of the ship and thus renders magnetic mines ineffective. **degaussisation,** *n.*

Dendroica Potomac. A new species of warbler discovered by Karl W. Haller. Also called **Sutton's Warbler.**

dive bombing. Bombing at the end of a long, steep dive during which the plane is pointed at the target.

droop, *n. Slang.* An undesirable, unattractive person.

Dunkirk throat. A sore throat, accompanied by hoarseness.

E-boat. (*Brit.*) *Slang.* Short for **enemy boat,** a German motor torpedo boat.

egg, to lay an. *Slang.* To attempt a joke, usually in commercial entertainment, that does not come off.

ferry, *v.* To fly an aeroplane to the purchaser. American planes were ferried across the Atlantic ocean for the British. **ferryman,** *n.*

fireblitzed, *adj.* (*Brit.*) Pertaining to a severely bombed area.

first termer. A public officeholder serving his first term.

flare-blitz. (*Brit.*) A blitz of flares rather than bombs dropped from nazi aircraft.

flat-footed, to catch. To catch one unprepared, or without proper defenses, or preparations.

flight deliver, *v.* To deliver a plane to a purchaser by flying it to him.

ghost town. A town economically dead as a result of the removal of all important sources of livelihood. (–1940)

Hollywood, to go. *Slang.* To praise oneself openly.

horse (or **horsed**) **cavalry.** That part of the cavalry employing horses as contrasted with that using motorized equipment.

incendiary, *n.* Short for **incendiary bomb.**

iffy, *adj.* Uncertain, dubious, contingent.

intercom. Short for **intercommunication,** the telephone system in an aeroplane.

Jaycee. A member of the U.S. Junior Chamber of Commerce. (–1940)

Joad. The name of the family of migratory labourers in John Steinbeck's *The Grapes of Wrath*; hence, any migratory labourer. Usually plural.

Killick. *Naval Slang.* Petty officer, so called from the killick (anchor) on his sleeve. (–1940)

know-how, *n.* The technical knowledge and skill to carry out a given project.

L.D.V. British Local Defense volunteers.

Lebensraum, *n.* (Ger. living space.) Land necessary to the self-sufficiency of the nazi state.

Luftwaffe (pl. *Luftwaffen*). (Ger. *Luft,* air + *Waffe,* weapon.) The air force of Germany. (–1940)

Mae West. A life preserver.

man-tailored, *adj.* Pertaining to women's clothes, tailored like those of a man.

Me. Short for **Messerschmitt,** German fighter plane.

Molotov breadbasket. A large bomb, taller than a man, so designed as to release 20 to 30 small incendiary bombs. In one type, the fire bombs were ejected by the explosion when the bomb struck the ground; in the other, the incendiaries were released by a mechanism after the breadbasket had fallen for some distance; named for Russian Foreign Minister Molotov during the "winter war" in Finland, 1939–40.

Molotov cocktail. A hand-grenade improvised from an

empty bottle, which is filled with gasoline, fuel oil, or the like, corked, and supplied with a wick which acts as a fuse.

Mona. (*Brit.*) Name given the air raid signal by Londoners.

muck. (*Slang.*) Gunfire.

Munichism. Mental state similar to that of Munich, when Hitler was appeased.

name calling. A technique, esp. used in propaganda, of setting up an attitude toward a person (or thing) by applying to him (or it) a word with the desired (usually derogatory) connotations. (–1940)

near miss. A miss by a bomb, which yet strikes so near the target that damage is inflicted.

newsworthy. Pertaining to what has news value. (–1940)

Nylons. Short for Nylon hose.

Okie. A migratory farmer, so called because from Oklahoma. (1939)

Panzer column, division. (Ger. armour.) An armoured, highly mechanized and mobile division of troops used in conjunction with the air arm in the German blitzkrieg.

parachuter. A parachutist.

paratrooper, *n.* & *adj.* A fully armed infantryman parachuted behind enemy lines.

parashooter. (*Brit.*) Civilian volunteer trained to shoot enemy paratroops. Also **parashootist, parashot, paraspotter.**

party-liner. One who follows his political party very closely in his views and voting.

Paul Pry. (*Brit.*) *Slang.* A tremendous searchlight.

peashooter. (*Brit.*) *Slang.* A pursuit plane.

peel off, *v.* To leave a formation of aircraft in a steep bank preparatory to taking up an individual position for a mission.

pep pill. A benzedrine tablet. (–1940)

P. E. T. N. Short for **pentaerythritol tetranitrate,** an extremely powerful explosive.

phantom limb. An amputated limb which the amputee imagines he can still feel.

plastic. Anything fashioned from plastic material.

pollee. One questioned in a poll, such as a Gallup poll.

possible, *n.* A plane possibly shot down.

powder, take a. *Slang.* To make off, go away, disappear, vanish.

pratfall, *v.* To fall backward, esp. on the buttocks.

prefabricator. A producer of prefabricated units, esp. houses.

priority. A prior claim, esp. on strategic materials, given by a government board to manufacturers of products necessary in war.

PT boat. A motor torpedo boat.

quisle, *v.* To betray, be a traitor, or a Quisling.

Quisling. A traitor; so called from the treachery of Maj. Vidkum Quisling, founder and head of the nazi party in Norway, who assumed headship of the puppet administration set up by the Germans after their successful occupation of Norway. Also **quisler.**

radiogenic. Highly suitable for radio; as, a radiogenic script.

radiosondage. Term adopted by international agreement for the method of obtaining meteorological data in the higher altitudes by sending into the stratosphere a small balloon equipped with instruments and a short wave set for transmitting the data to the ground.

Ration D. An emergency ration in the form of a candy bar containing 600 calories of chocolate, vanilla, sugar, milk and oat flour; developed by the U.S. army.

recap, *v.* To replace the worn surface of a tire after the top of the tread and as much of the shoulder as necessary have been filed off. *See* **top cap.** Also **recap, recapping,** *n.*

ringdom. The realm of prizefighting. (–1940)

Roger. Technically, "Your message has been received." Loosely, O.K.

Sansei. A third generation Japanese in the United States. A child of Nisei parents. (–1940)

script, *v.* To write a script; to adapt a story for radio production. **scripteur** or **scripter,** *n.*

scuttle, *v.* To wreck, destroy; impair seriously; reject.

selectee. One who had been inducted but not sworn into the U.S. army (from Selective Service).

shrapnel. Fragments falling from the explosion of antiaircraft shells.

smoke jumper. A forest fire fighter dropped by parachute.

Spit. (*Brit.*) *Slang.* Short for Spitfire fighter plane.

starlet. A young, usually quite promising, motion picture actress.

station-master. (*Brit.*) One in command of an airfield.

stick of bombs. Bombs placed in a bomber so that they can be dropped at predetermined and regular intervals.

stumble-bum, stumblebum. Awkward, clumsy, inept.

Sutton's Warbler. *See* **Dendroica Potomac.**

T4. Short for **cyclotrimethyltrinitramine,** an Italian explosive employed as a primer.

tanker. *Mil.* Member of a tank crew.

telecaster. One who telecasts, that is, broadcasts by television.

Third Termite. *Jocose.* One wishing a third term for President Roosevelt.

top cap, top capping. A resurfacing in which only the top of the wornout tread of a tire is smoothed off before the new rubber is applied. *See* **recap.**

vackie. (*Brit.*) Short for evacuee; *specif.* anyone sent from London early in the war as a precautionary measure.

wedgies, wedges. Shoes with a solid, wedge-shaped platform sole.

whistle-bomb. A bomb to which is attached a mechanism that screams or whistles as the bomb falls.

winterization. Putting in condition for the winter; as, the **winterization** of an automobile. (–1940)

wonder drug. Generic term for drugs like the sulfa drugs, with remarkable curative powers.

1941

As the United States sped its mobilization of manpower and industry and then finally entered World War II in the last month of 1941, the new words of that year indicated primary interest in things military. Some words were humorous, some deadly serious, and most had the virtue of accurate description.

* * *

Airathon. A series of five tests with point scoring for competing college fliers.

airgraph. (*Brit.*) A system developed by the British for microfilming letters to conserve space.

airtel. A place similar to a motel (*q.v.*) for travellers by plane.

alertion. The state of being on the watch for or on guard against danger, as an air attack.

all-outer. One who, impatient of half-measures, favoured a rapid move towards a complete war economy.

area. *Specif.* (*Brit.*) A part of a city or town serving as a unit in the defense program against air raid fires.

AT. Initials of anti-tank.

Atlantic Charter. The eight-point charter worked out by Pres. Franklin D. Roosevelt and Prime Minister Winston Churchill at a conference on the Atlantic ocean in 1941.

balding. Becoming bald.

battle station. One's assigned post on shipboard during battle.

beam; fly the iron beam. *Aviation slang.* Use a railroad as a guide in a plane. **fly the wet beam.** *Aviation slang.* Use a river as a guide in a plane. **off the beam.** *Slang.* Going in the wrong direction, incorrect; crazy; doing badly. **on the beam.** *Slang.* Going in the right direction, correct; sensible; doing well.

black, put up a. *R.A.F. Slang.* To commit an error; confess to a poor job in executing an assignment.

blackout. A loss of consciousness, usually of short duration, as from making a high-speed turn in an aeroplane.

blitz buggy, wagon. A car for staff purposes.

blitzfighter. (*Brit.*) A member of the fighting forces defending England against the German blitz.

bolona. (*Brit.*) A night free of bombing; coined by the Germans from *"bombenlose nacht,"* literally bombless night. Also **bombenlos.**

bomb run. That part of the course of a bomber extending from the time the bombardier assumes control until he releases the bombs over the target.

butcher wagon. *Slang.* An ambulance. Also **meat wagon.**

chatterbox. (*Brit.*) *Slang.* A machine gun used against aeroplanes.

cliff-hanging. The habit of ending an episode of a radio serial at an exciting and uncertain point (in an earlier day the hero or heroine in motion pictures would frequently be left actually hanging from a cliff). (–1941)

conventioneer. A person who goes to a convention. (1940)

contour-plow, *v.* To plow according to the contour of the land, to check or prevent erosion. (–1941)

cooling-off period. A period, usually 30 days, to allow violent emotions to subside, as following the declaration of a strike.

covered wagon. *Slang.* An aircraft carrier.

crash-land, *v.* To bring a plane down with enough of the landing gear inoperative to run the risk of at least a partial crash.

creative pause. A term used by the nazis to describe a quiet period in the fighting, sometimes after a conquest, when gains were consolidated and preparations for future engagements made.

de Gaullist. A follower of Gen. Charles de Gaulle.

deglamourize, *v.* To strip one of glamour; to make plain.

dematerialization. A direct hit that so severely damages a vessel as to make it sink.

de-Quisle, *v.* To disable an automobile for use by Quislings and the like by stripping it of spark-plugs, carburettor, or other parts necessary to its operation.

desynchronized, *adj.* Not synchronized, said of twin engines in a German aircraft.

dit da man. *U.S. army slang.* One working with dots (dits) and dashes (das), namely, a radio operator.

dogface. *U.S. army slang.* An ordinary soldier.

dream up, *v.* Make up; imagine, as in a dream; work out in one's own mind.

Dunkirk, *n.* A loss, repulse, set-back; from the Battle of Dunkirk in June 1940, when the English were forced to withdraw all their troops from the continent.

fellow-travelling, *n.* The state of being sympathetic to and co-operative with the Communists. (–1941)

ferrying command. A unit organized May 29, 1941, for the purpose of transporting planes from the United States to Canada for delivery to the British.

fireblitz. A bombing with incendiary (fire) bombs.

fire bomb. An incendiary bomb.

flak. (Ger. *Fliegerabwehrkanone,* fr. *Flieger,* aircraft+*Abwehr,* defense+*Kanone,* gun.) The fire from anti-aircraft artillery.

flash-. A combining form meaning that which happens quickly, often unexpectedly, of short duration, frequently with a suggestion of violence; as, **flash** fire, **flash** flood. (–1941)

flying boxcar. A large aeroplane hauling cargo; sometimes applied to a bomber.

four freedoms. The four essential human freedoms described by Pres. Franklin D. Roosevelt in a speech made on Jan. 6, 1941, as freedom of speech and of religion; freedom from want and from fear.

fragmentation bomb. A bomb scattering shell fragments over a wide area.

Free French. The French opposed to collaboration with Germany; the non-Vichyites.

gen.—pukka gen, real gen. *R.A.F. slang.* That highly restricted information available only to insiders, the low-down; later, supposed "low-down" that is unreliable. (pucka, pukka, of Hindu origin, had long been in use in the sense of real, genuine.)

George. *Slang.* Name given to a gyro pilot. Also called an **iron mike.**

gramicidin. One of the so-called germ chemicals obtained from soil germs, especially effective against Gram-positive micrococci.

grease monkey. Helper to an aeroplane mechanic. (–1941)

Hitleristic, *adj.* Of, relating to, or having the qualities of Adolf Hitler.

hypo-happy. Very enthusiastic about the subject of photography.

iron mike. *Slang. See* **George.**

island. The superstructure of an aircraft carrier, located on the starboard side.

jeep. A small, versatile, highly manoeuvrable combat car and truck. The word may have come from the fact that the pronunciation of the letters G. P. (general purpose) on the early jeeps recalled the habitual utterance ("jeep") of the character in E. C. Segar's comic strip, "Popeye."

jook joint. Name of uncertain origin to describe a place of entertainment, such as a roadhouse, serving drinks and equipped with a juke box for dancing. (–1941)

juke box. An automatic record player, so called from its association with a jook joint (*q.v.*), playing a record when a coin is put in a slot. In some, there was a mechanism for obtaining the record desired; in others, the records played in rotation. (–1941)

lease-lend. *See* **lend-lease.**

lend-lease, *adj.* Of or pertaining to the U.S. Lend-Lease act (March 1941), whereby supplies and services could be lent or leased to Allied powers. Also **lend-lease,** *n.* & *v. t.*; **lease-lend,** *adj.* & *v. t.*

liase, liayshe, *v.* (*Brit.*) To form a liaison with.

lid. *U.S. army slang.* A radio operator.

line, shoot a. *R.A.F. slang.* To give a blown-up account of one's part in an engagement; to brag.

lovely, *n. Slang.* An extremely attractive young girl,

esp. a model or a screen actress. (Extension of older Brit. usage.)

Loyal Opposition. Opposition to a political party in power which does not go so far as to oppose "fundamental national principles." Used to describe the followers of Wendell Willkie.

mastermind, *v.* To exercise or display superior mental qualities.

meat wagon. *Slang. See* **butcher wagon.**

motel. A motorists' hotel, a group of individual cottages, equipped with modern conveniences, for the accommodation of motorists. *See* **airtel.**

Naziphile, *n.* An enthusiastic adherent of nazi beliefs and policies.

Nip, *n.* & *adj.* Short for Nippon, Nipponese; a Japanese.

occupation money. Unsecured money printed by the Germans in occupied territories in such quantities as were necessary.

oil bomb. An oil-filled sphere in whose centre are high explosives which ignite the oil and scatter it in all directions.

old-school-tie. Pertaining to British public school graduates, esp., often derisively, to their group loyalty and their proneness to follow what is well established.

organise. (*Brit.*) An adaptation of the German *organisieren,* "to get hold of, obtain, illegally."

peep. *U.S. army slang.* Term used for a bantam car, esp. in contradistinction with the larger jeep.

penicillin. A powerful, nontoxic substance (a so-called germ chemical), obtained from a mold, which acts on various kinds of infection, including that resulting from streptococci, gonococci, meningococci and pneumococci.

Pentolite. A very high-powered explosive.

playsuit. A summer sports outfit, usually consisting of shirt, shorts and detachable skirt.

plushy, *Fig.* Smugly opulent; wealthy, luxurious.

prang. *R.A.F. slang.* To crash in a plane; to damage or smash up an aeroplane.

pump-primer. Temporary remedial action by the government designed to get the economic machine started. (–1941)

radiolocator. An instrument developed by the British to detect and locate objects, especially military, by means of radio waves.

RDX. An explosive developed by the British said to be 40% more powerful than TNT.

rheotron. A device which gives high speed (energy) to beta particles (electrons) by whirling them around in circular orbits.

Rh factor. An agglutinable factor designated as Rh because it is elicited by the sera of guinea pigs immunized with the corpuscles of rhesus monkeys; the factor was discovered by Karl Landsteiner and Alexander S. Wiener, in 1940, to be present in the erythrocytes of about 85% of human beings.

riser, *n.* & *adj.* One of the supports extending from a parachute to the parachutist.

scatter gun. *U.S. army.* A machine gun employed against aircraft (in older usage, a shotgun).

sea marker. An aluminum powder which dyes the sea and makes it possible to reckon the drift of a plane; used also as a distress signal.

shooting war. A war of battles rather than a war of nerves, or propaganda, or sanctions.

silk, hit the. *U.S. army slang.* To descend in a parachute.

ski troops. Troops operating on skis. **ski trooper.**

smooching. *Slang.* Caressing, petting, necking. (–1941)

soften, *v.* To undermine a country by flooding it with defeatist propaganda so that it might become an easy victim to actual military invasion.

strategic bombing. Long range bombing designed to bring about the collapse of an enemy country by bombing out industrial plants, means of communication and other parts of its vital economic organization.

strep throat. A throat with a streptococcus infection.

Stuka (Ger. *"Sturz,"* crash+*"Kampf,"* fight.) A German dive bomber.

sugar report. *Slang.* A letter from one's girl or sweetheart.

swing shift. The 4 P.M. to midnight shift in industrial plants, corresponding to the second trick of railroad telegraph operators.

tactical bombing. Bombing designed to aid the ground forces in a military manoeuvre.

tin can. *Slang.* A destroyer.

umbrella. A number of aircraft, usually fighters, which protect land or sea forces by operating over and around them, forming a kind of umbrella.

V-for-Victory. Slogan adopted by several Allied nations in the propaganda war against the nazis.

water wasp. The PT-10 torpedo boat, equipped with three motors, each capable of developing 1350 h.p.

withholding tax. An income tax collected at the source, that is, withheld from a payment of salary, wages and the like.

wolf pack. A small fleet (usually three or more) of submarines organized to attack enemy shipping, especially convoys.

yard bird. *U.S. army slang.* A new recruit.

zippered. Supplied with a zipper, or slide fastener.

1942

As during the three preceding years and the three succeeding years, the new words and meanings of 1942 dealt mostly with the conflict which had now spread to the most remote corners of the world.

* * *

ABDA. The Southwest Pacific area; from American, British, Dutch, Australian, the countries waging war in that area against Japan.

adtevac. A word composed from adsorption, temperature and vacuum to describe a process whereby blood can be dried on a large scale to make blood plasma.

Alcan Highway. The Alaska-Canada highway, an interior direct road from Fairbanks, Alaska, to Edmonton, Alberta, running between parallels 62° and 63° north and paralleling Canada's chain of airports, officially opened Nov. 20, 1942.

antipersonnel mine. A mine employing a hair-trigger trip-type of mechanism, which rises several feet above the ground before it explodes, scattering shrapnel over a large area.

AP. A drug, derived from coumarin, with anti-blood-clotting properties that make it useful in the treatment of thrombosis of the legs.

assault boat. A 200 lb., powered, plywood boat carrying up to 11 men, which lends itself especially to scouting and actual assault work.

Atabrine. A drug (quinacrine hydrochloride), produced in tablet form, very effective in the treatment of malaria. Trade mark.

AVG. The American Volunteer group, a group of American aviators fighting in China under Brig. Gen. Claire Lee Chenault.

backstage, *adj.* Behind the scene, hidden, not readily apparent.

betatron. A machine which gives high speed to beta particles by whirling them around in circular orbits. (The 1941 term **rheotron** was largely supplanted by **betatron.**)

blacketeer. One who buys or sells on the black market.

Burma road. The road over which supplies were transported from Burma to China; hence, *fig.,* a similar road or route for the transportation of supplies and materials; as, "An Alaska-Siberia 'Burma Road.'"

call. Available for prostitution, especially for engagement by telephone. (–1942)

car pool. A voluntary pooling of private vehicles, esp. for commuting.

Chemigum. A strong, tough, resistant synthetic rubber developed by the Goodyear Tire and Rubber company, used in the manufacture of such products as tires, hose and gasoline tanks. Trade mark.

CINCPAC. The **Commander-in-Chief** of the **Pacific** fleet.

clipper, *v. t.* & *i.* To travel, or be sent by, clipper plane.

commandoman. A member of a commando unit.

COMINCH. **Commander-in-Chief** of the U.S. fleet. (This term supplanted *Cincus* because the pronunciation of the latter suggested sink us.)

cook with gas. *Slang.* Make headway, go in the right direction. (–1942)

crash-landing, *n.* The landing of a plane when its landing gear is ineffective.

C ration. A ration for soldiers consisting of a day's supply of precooked food, including meat, vegetables, crackers, sugar, hard candy and coffee, for use in the field.

cuff, off the. *Slang.* In an informal or unstudied manner; unrehearsed.

Demerol. A synthetic analgesic, almost as potent as morphia but lacking its strong tendency to addiction, which takes effect within 15 to 20 min. and lasts several hours.

dicoumarin. A synthetic chemical (found naturally in spoiled sweet clover) which, taken through the mouth or hypodermically, reduces the tendency of the blood to form clots.

dim-out, *n.* & *v.* A decrease in the amount and extent of illumination.

door-key children. "Defense work orphans" who, lacking supervision because both parents were at work, went about carrying their house keys.

E. A joint award, symbolized by a pennant bearing an "E," made by the U.S. army and navy to those industries doing an excellent job of production in the war effort.

eagle day. *U.S. army slang.* Pay day. (From "eagle," a ten dollar goldpiece.)

expendable, *adj.* Of or pertaining to that which can be used up (expended) without regard to cost; said of materials or men to be sacrificed, or already sacrificed, in the attainment of a military objective. (–1941)

Festung Europa. *See* **Fortress Europe.**

Fighting French. Term supplanting **Free French,** the anti-Vichy group.

finger park. A residential area consisting of a landscaped central park from which extend like fingers dead-end driveways for the surrounding dwellings.

flame cultivation. A method of burning off weeds without harming the crop.

flash freezing. A method of quick-freezing of foods developed at the University of Texas. The quick-freezing of the surface juices prevents the juices and the flavour from escaping.

flat-top. An aircraft carrier, so called from its large, flat landing surface for planes.

Foamglass. A black glass, with low specific gravity, which has the properties of buoyancy and insulation. It was developed by the Pittsburgh Corning corp.

Fortress Europe. (Ger. *Festung Europa.*) An idea begun by the Italian press of considering Europe as an impregnable fortress so that the Allies, discouraged, might sue for peace.

frozen food. A food frozen so rapidly that its chemical composition, and hence its taste and food value, is unaffected.

gas hog. *Slang.* One using more than his share of rationed gasoline.

Geronimo. The name of an old Indian warrior shouted by paratroopers jumping out of a plane.

grasshopper. *Slang.* A small, low-speed, highly manoeuvrable cabin monoplane (such as the Piper Cub), supplied with a two-way radio, used for military observation.

greenhouse. *Air slang.* (1) The Plexiglas-like cover enclosing the cockpit, cabin, and other parts of a plane where visibility is desired. (2) The place so covered.

gremlin. A spiteful little creature thought by airmen to be responsible for all sorts of trouble involving aircraft.

Gyrene. *Slang.* The co-pilot of a glider transporting soldiers or freight.

heavy. Short for heavy tank, such as the 60-ton supertank of U.S. build. (1941)

Herrenvolk. (*Ger.*) Term used by the nazis in the sense of "master race" to describe what they regarded as their own position in world society.

horizontal bombing. Bombing at low altitudes (1,500 to 2,000 feet) from fighter planes which, once the two bombs with which they were equipped were away, could be manoeuvred quickly to a safe altitude to escape the effects of the exploding bombs.

igloo. A place for storing ammunition.

immersion foot. A potentially gangrenous condition similar to frostbite which comes about when the foot is immersed in sea water too long without adequate exercise.

inductee. One inducted into the U.S. armed forces. (–1942)

Japanazi, *adj.* Of or relating to the *Jap*anese and the *nazis* as copartners in World War II.

jerk, *n.* Term of disparagement for anyone, especially if stupid, regarded unfavourably.

Kenny method. A technique of treating polio developed by the Australian nurse Elizabeth Kenny, in which the paralyzed part is kept free and gently exercised.

K. P. pusher. *U.S. army slang.* One who supervises, especially the kitchen police.

K ration. (Army ration K.) An emergency ration for soldiers consisting of two pounds (in three packages, the equivalent of three balanced meals) of concentrated bread, meat, drink and dessert. Earlier, "parachute ration."

Niacin. Name recommended by the National Research council and approved by Federal Security Administrator Paul McNutt for "nicotinic acid," the anti-pellagra enriching element used in flour, to allay the fears of those who might believe nicotinic acid to be the poisonous acid derived from tobacco. For the same reason, nicotinic acid amide was to be called **Niacin Amide.**

Niacin Amide. *See* **Niacin.**

one-stop, *adj.* Pertaining to those filling stations, stores and the like where a shopper, especially a motorist, can supply all his wants in a particular line.

PAB. Short for para-aminobenzoic acid. (–1942)

paleogrostology. The study of fossilized grasses.

para-ski, *adj.* Pertaining to paratroops manoeuvring on skis.

pattern blackout. A partial blackout by means of destroying light patterns that aid aeroplane pilots in getting their bearings.

PC boat. Literally, a patrol craft boat, varying in length from 110 to 170 ft., supplied with a diesel engine, and equipped to locate and fight submarines. (–1942)

P.F.C. Private first class.

point rationing. A system of rationing of scarce articles, which could be purchased only in exchange for coupons, limited in quantity and good only for a certain period, each with a specific point value.

prefab, *n.* Shortening of *prefabricated unit,* as a house, consisting of standardized parts which can be put together at the final location.

preference rating. A rating given commodities according to the importance of the use to which they are to be put; as, steel to be used in the construction of warships would have a higher **preference rating** than that to be used in civilian building.

Promin. A drug, related to the sulfas, of some promise in the treatment of tuberculosis.

Quonset hut. A 56 by 20 foot insulated prefab produced in Quonset, R.I. (whence its name), with a semicircular metal roof, and equipped with a plywood floor and electric lighting, widely used by the U.S. army and navy for housing and hospitalization.

radar. Word derived from **Radio Detection and Ranging,** to describe the technique of finding and locating objects by sending out radio waves which are reflected from the objects in the manner of an echo.

reception centre. The centre where the U.S. inductee was given his second physical examination and numerous other tests, and where he received his civilian and military occupational classification. (–1942)

rejectee. A U.S. inductee rejected because of some disability. (–1942)

rev it up. *Slang.* To go more rapidly; speed up.

roll-back, rollback. A government-ordered reduction to former (and usually lower) levels of those commodity prices not subject to OPA regulations.

ropey, *adj. R.A.F. slang.* Disagreeable, unpleasant, unpopular (person).

sack, *adj. U.S. army slang.* Pertaining to sleeping, as in "hit the sack" (go to bed).

Saran. Trade mark of a synthetic material, which, made into cloth, has many useful properties, including resistance to water.

scrambled eggs. *U.S. naval slang.* Nickname for the intricate gold braid on the caps of high-ranking naval officers.

screen. An interview, test, or the like for the purpose of eliminating the psychologically unfit from military service.

Sixth Column. A coinage of Col. Richard C. Patterson, Jr., to describe those who gossiped and spread rumours inimical to the U.S. war effort.

skyglow. Reflection of city lights against a night sky.

slit trench. A V-shaped trench somewhat like a foxhole.

spending tax. A tax on expenditures for the purpose of promoting war savings.

staging area, base. A military depot; also a place where men are trained for an operation.

stinger turret. *U.S. army slang.* The gun-turret in the tail of a bomber.

Strato-chamber. A chamber made by the York Manufacturing company in which stratospheric conditions could be maintained.

tank destroyer. A motorized vehicle running on rubber tires, equipped with heavy guns to combat enemy tanks but without heavy armour for greater manoeuvrability.

task force. A group of military, naval and air units brought together under a single commander in any combination necessary to accomplish a specific assignment.

totaquin. A drug obtained from cinchona bark, which can be used instead of quinine in the treatment of malaria. It is not as effective as quinine.

V-day. The designation of the day when the Allies would be victorious over the axis.

victory garden. A small individual wartime garden.

victory girl. A girl who, supposedly fired by patriotism, solicited men in uniform.

V-mail. The American system, modelled on the British airgraph, for microfilming letters, sending them overseas in reduced size in a roll and enlarging them for the addressees at some distribution centre.

war time. Official name give by President Roosevelt to year-round daylight saving, adopted Feb. 9, 1942, for the war period. Abbrev. EWT, CWT, etc. for eastern war time, central war time, etc.

zack. *Australian slang.* A sixpence piece.

zip. To close or fasten by means of or in the manner of a zipper, or slide fastener. (I. W. R.)

1943

The words of 1943 showed, among other things, the great importance that aeronautics was assuming. Not only was war being waged largely in the air with block-busters, glide-bombs and pathfinders, but the new word *aeropolitics* indicated that politics and economics were strongly affected by the increased mobility afforded by aviation. The new importance of foods and the danger in their scarcity were reflected in *enrich, restore, extend* and *stretch.*

* * *

activate. To bring into active existence, as "to activate an air corps squadron"; to put into practice, get busy on, as "to activate a reconversion program." (Orig. military, –1941.)

aeropolitics. Political and economic development as influencing, and as influenced by, the development and application of aviation. (*Burnet Hershey,* Feb. 28, 1943.)

bazooka. A firearm, consisting of a metal tube slightly over 50 in. long and under 3 in. in diameter, with a shoulder stock, front and rear grips, sights, electric battery to set off the charge, and trigger, designed to launch rocket projectiles. It is operated by two men, one holding and firing the gun, the other loading. (*Major Zeb Hastings,* 1942, after the musical instrument invented by Bob Burns, 1905.)

block-buster. The 4,000-lb. bomb dropped by British Lancaster planes beginning in March 1942; a similar heavy bomb. (1942)

brief. To give formal instructions, regarding a scheduled military operation, to those about to engage in it. (–1940)

brownout. A voluntary, partial dimout. (Australia, 1942; U.S., 1943.)

cargoliner. A transport plane carrying freight exclusively. (1943)

chin turret. A gun turret mounted beneath the nose of bombers. (1943)

co-belligerent, *adj.* Fighting together (with another power) without a formal alliance, as "co-belligerent Italy." *n.* A country so fighting. (–1813)

commando. A unit of British soldiers trained in close-range fighting for raids on axis territory; loosely, a member of such a unit, or of a similar unit of another nationality. (*Winston Churchill,* Oct. 10, 1941, from Portuguese or Spanish **comando** adopted as name for defense units of Boer Republic.) Compare **ranger.**

enrich. To supply with added food value, esp. with vitamins and minerals. Government standards were promulgated in May 1941 and on July 3, 1943 for enriched flour. (*Frank L. Gunderson,* summer 1940, from *Quaker Oats Co.,* 1932.) **enrichment.**

expediter, expeditor. An official charged with keeping uninterrupted the flow of materials or of routine work in industry and government. Some expediters were agents of the U.S. army and navy; others were in direct employ within industries and government bureaus such as the War Production board. (*General Electric Co., c.* 1925.)

extend. To make a scarce or expensive food go farther by preparing in combination with a cheaper or more plentiful food, as "to extend meat with cereal." (–1934 as "to adulterate.") **extender.**

featherbedding. The limiting of work or output in order to spread jobs and thus prevent unemployment. **featherbed rules.** Union regulations to accomplish featherbedding.

feather merchant. A slacker. (After comic-strip characters of *Billy De Beck,* 1937, from earlier senses.)

G.I., G.I. Joe, *n.* An American soldier. *G.I.* was to the army as a whole what *doughboy* was to the infantry. (Short for **G.I. soldier,** –1941) *adj.* Pertaining to the army services, or ministering to its needs, as "G.I. food," "a G.I. dance." (Government issue.)

glide-bomb. To bomb, from an aeroplane, by descending at an angle of less than 65° from the horizontal when releasing bombs. Steeper dives are called *dive-bombing.* (–1940)

globaloney. Nonsense about matters affecting the world as a whole. (**Global baloney.** *Rep. Clare Luce,* Feb. 9, 1943.)

handie-talkie, *military.* A portable two-way radio telephone weighing about five lb. (–1942) Compare **walkie-talkie.**

homeostasis. The tendency of living organisms to maintain a relatively stable condition by means of mechanisms which compensate for disturbing factors. (*Walter B. Cannon,* 1926.) A similar function elsewhere, as in the social organism. (–1941)

incentive pay. Wages paid in accordance with various "incentive plans" or "systems" which reward increased production; in particular, a piece-work or modified piece-work system. (–1907)

longram, *telegraphy.* A deferred day message with a minimum charge for 100 words. (**Long telegram.** Dec. 1942; service effective Feb. 1, 1943.)

mission. The objective of an operational flight, esp. where bombing is involved; the flight itself. (–1942)

mock-up. A model of an aircraft, constructed of inexpensive material and usually full-size, for the purpose of prearranging or studying details of construction and use. (–1938) A similar model of other items of military equipment. (–1942) A model in general. (1943)

newsmap. A map issued periodically with current events depicted on it, and with accompanying text and illustrations. (**News Map** *of the Week,* a copyrighted periodical, 1938.)

pathfinder. A flare capable of illuminating the ground for bombing purposes, even through fog, when dropped by attacking planes. Called also *TI* (target-indicator). (Nov. 1943.)

pattern-bomb. To bomb, from a number of aircraft, in such a way that the relative position of the craft determines the "pattern" of the bombs when they strike, so as to cover the target in a desired manner.

pesticide. An agent for controlling farm or garden pests of whatever sort. The Canadian Fertilizers and Pesticides administrator was commissioned Jan. 20, 1942. (*Grant S. Peart,* Sept. 18, 1940.)

pin-up girl. A girl with whose picture men, esp. soldiers, liked to decorate their quarters. (–1941)

probable. A supposed casualty, esp. referring to military craft, as "there were ten destroyed and five probables."

ranger. A member of a battalion of U.S. soldiers, formed Dec. 1941, trained in close-range fighting for raids on enemy territory. (1942) Compare **commando.**

restore. To bring back a food to the original nutritive value of its ingredients. (1939)

scuttlebutt, *naval slang.* Gossip; a rumour. (–1938. **Scuttle-butt** story, –1901; scuttle butt, drinking fountain on board ship, –1843.)

Seabees (*gen. plural*). The U.S. navy construction battalions, comprising welders, carpenters, mechanics and other personnel skilled in building and supplementary trades, trained to fight as well as work in the field. (1942)

shuttle, *combining form.* Involving vehicles, esp. aircraft, making repeated trips between fixed points, as "shuttle bombing," "shuttle raid," "shuttle plane." *v.* To move a vehicle or by a vehicle in such trips. (–1941, from **shuttle** train, –1891.)

snafu, *military slang.* In a mess, haywire. (Situation normal; all fouled up.)

sortie. An operational flight by one military aircraft. Each return to base for replenishment was counted as the end of one sortie.

stretch, stretcher. *See* **extend.**

suntans. Summer uniform worn by U.S. soldiers.

TI. *See* **pathfinder.**

trainasium. A conglomerate structure of metal bars, resembling a large bird-cage, used to develop muscular co-ordination in military training. (**Training** gymn**asium.** –1942.)

triphibian. Adapted to or using the three elements, land, water and air, as "a triphibian assault." (**Tri**+**amphibian.** *Winston Churchill,* Aug. 31, 1943.)

triphibious. *See* **triphibian.** (**Tri**+**amphibious.** *Leslie Hore-Belisha,* 1941.)

underground, *n.* An outlawed political or military movement or organization operating in secret; such organizations collectively, as "the European underground struck against naziism"; underground fortifications, materials or equipment protected under ground against attack. *adv.* Into hiding, into the underground, as "the patriots had to go underground." **undergrounder.** A member of the underground.

upgrade. To raise (the name or number of a quality) without improving the quality itself, as "cheaper meats were illegally upgraded." (–1941)

walkie-talkie, walkee-talkee, walky-talky, *military.* A two-way radio telephone small enough to be transported on horseback; a smaller set carried on the back of one man. (–1940) Compare **handie-talkie.**

wolf. A determined would-be seducer, a man "on the

make." (–1937, esp. 1942, from an older underworld sense.) (D. L. Br.; X.)

1944

The terror aroused by the buzz-bomb accounted for the many names coined for the jet-propelled weapons which entered into European warfare in 1944, among them *fly-bomb, robomb* and *Vengeance* weapons *1, 2* and *3*.

In the U.S., delinquency among teen-agers and the bobby sox brigade assumed alarming proportions because of homes disrupted by the absence of parents in the armed services or war production. There was, however, a new note of confidence in *V-E day, V-J day* and *X-day*.

* * *

aerosol bomb. Bomb used in spraying insects. It contains pyrethrum extract, oil of sesame and freon. (1943)

airpark. A small airfield, in or close to a community and financed by it, for private fliers. (1944)

airstrip (also **strip**). A strip of land, frequently in a newly conquered area, hurriedly levelled off for use by aeroplanes. (–1942)

amtrac. An amphibious tractor. (1944)

bobby socks (sox) brigade. Teen-age girls, chiefly the high-school group, who engaged in such activities as listening for hours on end to recordings, and making long phone calls with boys with whom they were friends. (1944)

buzz, *v. t.* & *i.* To fly dangerously low, esp. in congested areas, frequently to show off. (–1941)

buzz-bomb. A jet-propelled bomb, designed like an aeroplane and launched like a rocket from specially built ramps. Its speed was around 300 m.p.h. and its maximum range about 150 mi. The main body contained a ton or more of explosive, which was set off by the fall of the plane when its fuel burned out. First used by the Germans in June 1944. (1944)

cannibalize. To salvage the sound parts of damaged equipment for re-use. (–1943; older in the services.)

collaborationist, *specific.* One who collaborated with an axis country, esp. Germany. (–1941)

combat fatigue (also **battle, operational, war fatigue**). Euphemism for a neurosis resulting from combat conditions. (1944)

cut back, *v.* To decrease the volume of an order in accordance with procedure provided for in the contract. Also **cutback,** *n.* (1943)

D-day. The day set for a military operation; used so that the actual day could be kept secret. (–1942) *Specific.* The day of a certain operation, as June 6, 1944, the invasion of western Europe. (*Mil.* 1918.)

DDT. Initials of a powerful insecticide, dichloro-diphenyl-trichloroethane. (–1943)

deepfreeze. Trade name of a food locker made by Motor Products corporation for maintaining temperatures around 0°. (–1942)

dim view. Unfavourable opinion of. (–1941)

ditch. Land a disabled plane on water. (–1943)

doodle (bug). The buzz-bomb, so named possibly to make light of it. (1944)

double summer time. (*British.*) Two hours ahead of Greenwich mean time. (1944)

dropping zone (also **drop zone, dropping ground**). Area where paratroops land. (1943)

duck. A two-and-a-half-ton amphibian truck made by General Motors. (–1943)

E.A.M. (*Ethnikon Apeletherotikon Metopon.*) In Greece, the National Liberation front.

earthquake bomb. A six-ton bomb which penetrates the ground, where its delayed-action fuse causes an earthquaking explosion. (1944)

E.D.E.S. (*Ellinikos Dimokratikos Ethnikos Stratos.*) In Greece, the Hellenic National Democratic army, a conservative group. (1944)

E.L.A.S. (pron. ā′las; *Ellinikos Laikos Apeletherotikos Stratos.*) Hellenic Peoples' Army of Liberation, the military arm of E.A.M. (1944)

exploded sketch, view. A picture that shows the parts of a piece of machinery slightly spread apart (exploded) so that their relation to each other is clear. (1944)

factory buster. A six-ton bomb. (1944)

F.F.I. French Forces of the Interior, organized to combat the Germans in France. (1944)

flying bomb, also **flybomb.** A buzz-bomb. (1944)

flying jeep. Army nickname of the Vultee Sentinel, a small aeroplane also known as a **grasshopper.** (1943)

geeheebee (also **Jahemy, Jeramy**). Movable dry-dock. (1943)

gobbledygook. Word coined by Maury Maverick to describe the involved and abstract language of Washington official documents. (1944)

hump. A 525-mi. skyway from Assam, India, to the Yunnanese plateau, over which the American transport command flew supplies to China. The "big hump," where the Himalayas reach nearly 20,000 ft., is the watershed between the Salween and the Mékong rivers. Fliers who cracked under the strain of flying the hump were said to be "hump happy." (1943)

jeep, *v. t.* & *i.* To ride some one in a jeep; to ride in a jeep. (–1942)

jet plane. Plane operated by jet-propulsion. Sometimes shortened to **jet.** (1944)

jet propulsion. Principle of locomotion in which air is sucked into an engine, partially heated, and compressed. Mixed with a combustion fuel, the expanded air becomes the jet whose backward push gives a forward motion. (–1932)

L.C. (Elsie). Landing craft. Other craft, all designated by their initial letters, were landing craft control, landing craft infantry, landing craft mechanized, landing craft personnel, landing craft rubber, landing craft support, landing craft tank, landing craft vehicle, landing craft vehicle personnel. (L) or (S) following the initials denoted large or small, for example: L.C.I.(L). (1943, 1944)

locust tank. Glider-borne seven-ton tank. (1944)

L.S.D. Landing ship dock. A floating dock 450 ft. long, used following an attack. (1944)

L.S.M. Landing ship medium. (1944)

L.S.T. Landing ship tank. For transporting tanks. Large doors in the bow and a ramp permitted rapid unloading. (1943)

maquis, mackey, maquisard (Fr. *maquis.* In Corsica, land covered with brush and small trees whose branches spread out from their bases. [*Larousse.*]) Guerrilla-fighter members of the French underground who, because wanted by the German police, operated in the hills and the woods. (1944)

milk run. Regular bombing of a target. (–1943)

N.P. Neuropsychosis, neuropsychiatric. (–1944)

obliteration bombing. Concentrated bombing tending to wipe out. (1943)

P.A.C. Political Action committee of the C.I.O., organized to support the interest of labour within the existing two-party system. (–1944)

p.o.w., p.w. Prisoner of war. (–1944)

reconversion. *Specific.* The change from wartime economy to the peacetime economy following the end of World War II; as, the changing of a factory converted to the production of war materials back to its peacetime manufacturing. (1943)

renegotiation. *Specific.* The renegotiation by the government of original contracts to bring them more in line with actual costs as revealed by experience. (1943)

reslooming. Trade name of a process developed by the Monsanto Chemical company, whereby textile fibres and fabrics may be treated with a water-soluble melamine type of compound so as to impregnate the resin into the fibres. This process imparted greater resilience to cotton and rayon fabrics and reduced the shrinking and felting of woollens and worsteds. (1944)

robomb (robot bomb). A buzz-bomb. (1944)

robot, robot bomb, robot plane. A buzz-bomb. (1944)

sad sack. A well-intentioned but downtrodden U.S. soldier who never seemed to do anything right; character in comic strip by George Baker. (–1943)

saturation bombing. Concentrated bombing. (1943)

S.H.A.E.F. (pron. shāf). Supreme Headquarters Allied Expeditionary force. (1944)

sky train. A train of gliders towed by a plane. (1944)

sky-troops. Airborne troops. (1944)

spot authorization. A procedure whereby local WPB agencies would give manufacturers permission to make civilian goods if they could show they had labour and machinery which was not needed for the production of war goods. (1944)

sweat it out. To await, usually with sickening apprehension and worry. (–1941: may go back to Mark Twain.)

Sytons. Trade name of a group of silica compounds developed by the Monsanto Chemical company. Fibres and fabrics given a treatment of a dilute Syton solution show less tendency to slip or fray because of the deposit of submicroscopic particles. Stockings so treated are less likely to run. (1944)

take-home pay, take-away pay. Amount left after various deductions, such as for bonds and withholding tax, have been made from wages. (1944)

tank-dozer. A medium tank equipped with a scraping blade similar to that of the bulldozer. (1944)

teen-ager. One in his teens. (1943)

teen can, teen canteen, teen town. Recreation centre for teen-agers. (1944)

triptane. A fuel (paraffinic-trimethylbutane) with nearly four times the horsepower of 100-octane gasoline. (1943)

V-1 (*Ger. Vergeltungswaffe, eins:* vengeance weapon, one). A buzz-bomb. (1944)

V-2. Vengeance weapon, two. A long rocket projectile, weighing 12 tons at the time of launching, with a bomb load of from one ton up, which, shot some 68 mi. into the super stratosphere, fell and hit the ground at 800 to 1,000 m.p.h., so fast that people were struck before they heard it. Sometimes called a **telephone pole bomb.** (1944)

V-3. Vengeance weapon, three. Said to be a projectile about 60 ft. long, 5½ ft. in diameter, and 14 tons in weight at the time of shooting. Launched straight up, it is then directed by radio. (1944)

V-bomb. Generic term for V-1, V-2, V-3, etc. (1944)

V-E day, V-J day. Victory day in Europe, Japan, respectively. (1944)

X-day. The day of peace following World War II. (1944)

1945

The Atomic age was separated from the pre-atomic era by the event of Aug. 6, 1945, the horror of its destructiveness lightened, however, by the peacetime promises of atomic energy. The United Nations showed that new world organizations were ready to cope with world problems. *Separatee, liberee, returnee* and *de-vacuee* were new terms, happier in tone than their wartime antonyms.

* * *

A-bomb. *See* **atomic bomb.**

abort. To fail to complete a mission or flight; said of an aeroplane. (1944)

ABSD. (Advance Base Sectional Dock.) A prefabricated dock where battleships could be repaired.

ABSIE. From the initials of the American Broadcasting Station in Europe, which operated from April 30, 1944, to July 4, 1945. (1944)

Admiral of the Fleet. (*U.S.*) A five-star admiral. (1944; older in British usage.)

airbrasive method. Drilling of teeth by an abrasive subjected to high pressure and pinpointed on the area to be drilled.

airedale. One who handles a plane on an aircraft carrier; a "plane-pusher."

air-sea rescue. Recovery of air crew after they had bailed out over water. Rescue was effected by a patrol plane which radioed the position of the survivors to a station. The station, in turn, sent out a rescue boat. (1944)

Alsib. Air route from Montana to Moscow so named because it passed over **Alaska** and **Siberia.**

Amvets. The **American Veterans** of World War II. (1944)

Anti-G suit. *See* **G-suit.**

ANTU. A poison, harmless to human beings, so powerful that ⅓ lb. will destroy 100,000 rats.

Ascender. An experimental fighter aeroplane (XP-55) with the propeller in the rear. Made by Curtiss-Wright Corp.

atobomb, atom bomb. *See* Atomic bomb.

atom bombing. *See* **atomic bomb.**

Atomic age. The new age dominated by atomic energy, ushered in with the dropping of the first atomic bomb, Aug. 6, 1945.

atomic bomb. A bomb releasing atomic energy with explosive force estimated to exceed that produced by 20,000 tons of T.N.T. The first such bomb to be publicly used was dropped on Hiroshima, Japan, Aug. 6, 1945. Variants include **a-bomb, atobomb, atom bomb,** the last the verb form. The bomb was at least once described as a **world-buster. Atom-bombing,** *n.*

atomize. To pulverize; destroy completely.

atomobile. Future automobile driven by atomic energy.

Azon bomb. Bomb regulated by radio waves which can be guided by the bombardier of plane. Developed by U.S. air forces.

baka bomb. (Jap. foolish.) Rocket plane driven by a Japanese suicide pilot.

bamboo telegraph, bamboo wireless. Native grapevine.

banzai. Desperate, fanatical, suicidal; usually applied to a frenzied attack of Japanese soldiers accompanied by shouts (*banzai*) and indifference to cost in life. (–1943)

B.A.R. Browning automatic rifle. (–1943) **barman.** One who operates such a rifle.

belly tank. Auxiliary gasoline tank under the belly or wing of a plane. It can be released if necessary to lighten the load. (–1945)

blow job. *Aviation slang.* A jet-propelled plane.

BMB. (Broadcast Measurement Bureau.) An organization composed of advertisers, advertising agencies and radio stations to discover a reliable index of broadcasting effectiveness.

bobby soxer. A teen-aged girl addicted to adolescent fads and crazes. (*See* 1944 list.)

bogey, bogie. Aeroplane whose identity is unknown. (1944)

bomber's moon. Moon favourable for bombing. (–1943)

bug bomb. A spray employing aerosol. (1944)

butcherette. Female butcher.

butterfly bomb. A small anti-personnel bomb dropped from a plane. (1944)

carpet bombing, carpet raid. A bombing attack which attempts to clear the way for advancing ground troops. Such attacks lay **bomb carpets.**

chosen instrument. A government-authorized air line to represent a country in the international skyways. (–1945)

cloak and dagger. Office of Strategic Services; pertaining to OSS.

Conestoga. A large cargo plane made by Edward G. Budd Mfg. Co. (1944)

De Gink Hotel. Name given to the hotels built along the the air transport command routes. (–1944)

dehumidification. Method developed by the United States navy bureau of ships for keeping materials from rusting. (1944)

de-nazification. Eradication of nazi influence. **de-nazify,** *v.* (1944)

de-requisition. Release from government occupation.

de-vacuee. (*British.*) A returned evacuee.

disintegrator. Secret weapon to oppose Kamikaze attacks.

displaced person (DP). Person brought into Germany from conquered countries, usually for purposes of slave labour. (1944)

doggy. *Slang.* Infantryman.

downgrading. Classifying of a job to a lower grade with less pay. (1944)

DP. Displaced person.

dumbo. Plane used in air-sea rescue (*q.v.*). (1944)

Electric Blanket. Blanket made by General Electric Co. electrically heated and automatically controlled.

Electronic Rat Trap. A trap made by Electronic Traps, Inc. After being entrapped, the rat electrocutes itself, following which a mechanism ejects the rat and resets itself for the next victim.

EMIC. Emergency Maternity and Infant Care Program. (1944)

Ercoupe. Trade name of a small passenger plane manufactured by Engineering and Research Corp. for civilian use. (1944)

fibrin film. A material made from blood plasma, promising to be effective in averting the convulsions following head wounds. (1944)

FIDO. From the initial letters of Fog Investigating Dispersal Operation, used by the British to disperse fog long enough for planes to land safely.

fighter bomber. A fighter plane equipped to carry a bomb, after the dropping of which the plane can operate as a fighter. (1942)

flash gear. Outfit to protect the wearer from the flames thrown by the explosion of shells and bombs. (–1945)

Fleet Admiral. Admiral of the fleet.

flight test. To test a plane in flight.

flying boxcar bomb. U.S. name for the 700-lb., 5-ft. long spigot mortar of the Japanese.

foo-fighter. Strange fire ball of undetermined origin (possibly controlled by radio) which followed Allied planes early in 1945.

formation stick. An electronically operated control stick which makes manipulation of a plane much easier and thus decreases fatigue to pilots. A joint development of the air technical service command and the Minneapolis-Honeywell Regulator Co.

Fortisan. A very strong yarn made by Celanese Corporation of America, especially for use in flare parachutes. Trade mark. (–1944)

foxhole circuit. A circuit comprising theatres at the various fighting fronts at which U.S. troupes entertained U.S. fighting forces. (1944)

Foxhole university. The United States Armed Forces institute.

fraternize. To deal socially with members of an enemy nation, especially with women; and, specifically, sexually. **fraternization,** *n.*

fringe wage. Term used by the War Labor board to describe wages the raising of which did not appreciably increase the cost of production and would not, therefore, challenge the Little Steel formula.

Gammexane. An insecticide (named from its being the gamma isomer of hexachlorene benzene) more powerful than DDT. Its discovery was made by scientists of the Imperial Chemical Industries.

General of the Army. (*U.S.*) A five-star general, one rank above a full general. (1944)

genocide (Gr. *genos,* race+*cide,* killing). A coinage of Professor Raphael Lemkin, of Duke university, Durham, N.C., to describe "the extermination of racial and national groups."

G.I. Jill. A WAC. (–1944)

Globester. Name of plane used by army air transport command in test flights looking toward passenger service extending around the world.

Goop Bomb. The M-76 incendiary bomb. (1944)

G-Suit (*G* for gravity). A suit designed by the armed services to prevent an airman from blacking out when making quick turns or precipitous dives.

homing pigeon. Button to identify discharged servicemen.

hubba, hubba. Exclamation of enthusiastic approval. (From earlier **haba, haba,** –1940)

Image Orthicon. A camera tube made by Radio Corporation of America for use in television. It is so sensitive that it can take pictures by moonlight, by the light of a match.

inspectoscope. An X-ray device used by the armed forces to discover illegal objects in packages sent home by servicemen.

island-hopping. Going from one island to another; especially military advance by seizing one island after another as a base, often by-passing one or more Japanese-occupied islands. Used in the Pacific area. (1944)

Jato. From the initial letters of "jet-assisted take-off." (1944)

jet-. Combining form for **jet-propelled** or relating to **jet-propulsion,** as **jet-booster, jet car, jet crew, jet engine.** (1944)

jungle rot. *Slang.* Any of several tropical skin diseases; also, general demoralization.

Kamikaze (Jap. divine wind). (Pron. *Kámakazē*). A suicide attack by a Japanese plane. Sometimes applied to the plane and also to the pilot.

Kriegie (Ger. *Kriegsgefangene*). Prisoner of war. (1944)

Lanaset. Trade-mark of a resin put out by the American Cyanamid Co. to make material shrink-resistant.

liberee. One liberated from a prisoner of war camp.

Lily. The pontoon-floated airstrip developed by the British.

loafer. A shoe for informal occasions. (–1944)

Loran. A device employing radar which acts as a **Long Range Aid** to **Navigation**.

Manhattan Project. Code name for the atomic bomb project.

May Day (Fr. *M'aidez,* "help"). Call for help.

meateasy. Place where black market meat could be bought.

Mickey Mouse money. Valueless Japanese money in the Philippines.

Micky. U.S. nickname for a radar bombsight which makes accurate bombing through the clouds possible. (1944)

Mixmaster. Army bomber propelled by two rear counter-revolving propellers. Made by Douglas Aircraft Co., Inc.

Mulberry Harbour or **Port.** Artificial harbour used on D-day. (1944)

MVA. Proposed Missouri Valley authority. (1944)

narco-synthesis. A method of treating a neurosis by working with a patient while he is under the influence of an injection of sodium pentathol. (1943)

Neptunium (after the planet Neptune. Cf. *Century Dictionary and Cyclopedia,* 1911, *s.v. neptunium:* "A supposed new element announced by Hermann in 1877 as present in columbite and ferro-ilemite. Its existence has not been confirmed."). Element Number 93, produced when uranium 238 takes on a bombarding neutron. This absorption causes the uranium to emit an electron, the emission changing a neutron into a proton. The element is not found naturally.

PCAU. Philippine Civil Affairs Unit.

pedal pusher. Knee-length trousers for girls. (1944)

Periston. Ersatz blood plasma, developed by the Germans.

pinpoint. To determine precisely; to give highly specialized training to, as, "to pinpoint the training of students." (Probably an extension of *pinpoint,* as in "to pinpoint bombs.")

PLUTO. From the initial letters of **Pipe Line Under The Ocean**, a gasoline line under the English channel.

Plutonium (after the planet Pluto). Element Number 94, which results when the radioactive neptunium breaks down with the emission of an electron which changes one of its neutrons into a proton. The element is not found naturally.

pre-atomic. Before Aug. 6, 1945, the date of the atomic bombing of Hiroshima.

Precipitron. Trade name of a machine made by Westinghouse Electric and Manufacturing company for purifying air by the electronics principle. (1942)

PRECO. United Nations Preparatory commission.

PREWI. Press Wireless, Inc. (1944)

Projected Books, Inc. A nonprofit group formed to furnish books on films to veterans and patients unable to use their hands. (–1944)

proximity fuse. A radio-operated fuse built in the tip of a projectile which explodes the projectile at that distance from the target where its flying fragments will do most damage. Developed by the army and the navy.

Red Ball Highway. A system of highways set up in France to expedite the movement of war materials to the fighting fronts. (1944: *red-ball* is an old railroad term for a fast freight.)

redeploy. To move fighting men from one front to another, used to describe the shifting of U.S. troops from Europe to the Pacific. **Redeployment,** *n.*

returnee. One who has returned, as from a fighting front. (1944)

ruptured duck. Identification button for discharged U.S. servicemen.

Schnorkel (also **Snort**). Device of the Germans which enabled them to keep their submarines under water for many weeks. An air pipe, when extended above the surface of the water, enabled the submarine to recharge its batteries and exhaust its fumes while remaining submerged. (1944)

selevision. The selling of citrus fruits by telegraph.

separate. To discharge or release from active duty in the armed services. Construed with *from.* (–1944)

separatee. One who has been separated from the armed services. (1944)

separation centre. A centre where U.S. servicemen were sent for discharge or release from active duty. Sometimes separation was accomplished by sending only the individual's records to the centre. (1944)

set-aside, *n.* Materials, such as meat, canned goods and vegetables, set-aside by order of the government for its use.

Shooting Star. Trade-mark of the Lockheed P-80 jet plane. (1944)

Silicones. A group of synthetic resins developed by Dow-Corning Corp., which resist water and high temperatures. (1944)

sitting duck. Something extremely easy; as easy to hit as a sitting duck. (–1944)

Skycoupe. A pusher-type monoplane for two occupants planned by Piper Aircraft Corp.

Skycycle. A monoplane for a single occupant designed by Piper Aircraft Corp.

sky-hook. Apparatus for dropping packages from planes by spinning them and thus controlling where they fall. (1944)

skymarker bomb. Bombs dropped to locate targets hard to find. It leaves a trail of coloured smoke which lasts five minutes and which can be seen by a plane five miles away. (1944)

Skysedan. Plane for four occupants designed by Piper Aircraft Corp.

squawk box. Loud speaker on board a ship. (1944)

stateside. Pertaining to the United States; in or toward the U.S. (1944)

Stratocruiser. Trade-mark of a four-motored plane built by Boeing Airplane Co., designed either for passengers or freight, cruising at 340 m.p.h. at a ceiling of 30,000 ft. and carrying 80 or more passengers or 35,000 lb. of freight. (1944)

Strato-suit. A suit, pressurized and heated by electricity, which makes it possible for flyers to be comfortable at altitudes as high as 80,000 ft. Oxygen is supplied through a special headpiece. Maj. John B. Kearby and the B. F. Goodrich Co. developed the suit.

Stratovision. Method worked out by Westinghouse Electric and Manufacturing company and Glenn Martin of using planes in the stratosphere to broadcast television.

streptomycin. A drug related to penicillin. (1944)

sub-sonic. Speeds ranging up to that of sound.

suicider. A suicide. (1943)

super-dumbo. A B-29 Superfortress used in air-sea rescue work.

superseniority. Job seniority for veterans which superseded all other seniority except that of another veteran in the same class. (1944)

supersonic. Speeds above that of sound.

talking book. A recording of a reading of a book; for use by the blind.

TCP. Trichlorophenoxyacetic acid; a weed killer.

1080. Sodium fluoroacetate, the 1,080th substance examined in a search for a new rat poison.

terminal leave. Accumulated leave given an officer in the U.S. services immediately prior to his release from active duty. In 1946, terminal leave pay was voted by congress to nonofficers for unused leave.

terror bombing. Deliberate bombing for terror effects with hope of shortening a war.

test-fly. Make a test-flight of a plane. (–1944)

top secret. A security classification used by the armed forces and the diplomatic corps to denote information or matériel of the utmost secrecy.

trans-sonic. Speeds in the range of that of sound (roughly 600–900 m.p.h.).

trusteeship plan. A plan for handling the mandated territories of the League of Nations and those newly acquired territories which might need to be controlled internationally after World War II. A council composed of nations which formerly held mandates and a like number of those which did not, would exercise control over territories voluntarily submitted to trusteeship. (1939)

TWI. (Training within Industry.) A War Production board program. (1944)

2,4-D. Laboratory designation of a synthetic hormone which destroys weeds without hurting the grass. Developed by the U.S. department of agriculture and others.

UNCIO. United Nations Conference for International Organization.

under wraps. Censored, secret.

USAFI. (United States Armed Forces Institute.) This institute supplied war department correspondence courses for service personnel, sending the courses even to remote areas. It also assisted service men and women in getting extension courses from the college or university of their choice. (–1943)

USFET. United States Forces in the European Theatre, with headquarters at Frankfurt, Germany.

USIBA. United States International Book Association, set up to aid in the distribution of U.S. books abroad.

VIP (also **Viper**). Very Important People (usually, in the army). (1943)

Viper. A rocket-propelled plane designed by the Germans to break up formations of United States bombers. The pilot, after having directed the plane, would parachute to safety.

Vista Dome. A glass-enclosed section, slightly raised above the top of a railway coach to enable its occupants to see in any direction; designed by General Motors.

volcano bomb. An 11-ton bomb made and used by the British. Also called **town-buster.**

Volkssturm (Ger. *Volks,* of the people+*Sturm,* troop). Army made up from the people; home guard. (–1943)

VT fuse. *See* **proximity fuse.**

war-weary plane. A plane beyond repair; also, one whose great damage required it to be sent home for repairs.

werewolf. Member of a German underground organization opposing the Allies.

wingman. The second of two planes, to one side and behind the leader, to protect the latter's tail. (–1945)

Zaibatzu (Jap. *zai,* wealth+*batzu,* clique). The group which controlled most of Japan's industry.

zeroed in, to be. In artillery fire, to have the exact range. (1944; to *zero,* –1925.) (I. W. R.; X.)

1946

The continuing importance of physics (especially electronics) in the creation of new words was noticeable in 1946. In aviation and medicine, also, the influence of science on word coinage was evident. In the nonscientific field an indication of postwar problems could be seen in such terms as *buyers' strike, 52-20 club* and *iron curtain.*

* * *

Able day. *See* **A-day.**

A-day. Short for Atomic day, June 30, 1946 (July 1 Bikini time), when the fourth atomic bomb was dropped in a test at Bikini to determine its effect on a fleet of war vessels. Also **Able day,** from "able," the signaller's word for "a."

aeropulse. A type of jet-propulsion motor in which the air sucked in from the atmosphere is let into the combustion chamber through shutters equipped with springs which open and close with a pulse-like movement.

americium. Element number 95, named by Glenn T. Seaborg for the two Americas.

A.S.V. air-to-surface-vessel, a radar device able to detect vessels on the surface of the water. (1945)

athodyd. *See* **ramjet.**

atomic cloud. The mushroom-shaped, radioactive cloud formed by the explosion of an atomic bomb.

bacitracin. An antibiotic substance for use against many bacteria, including those that cause pus and blood poisoning. It was first isolated in a wound of Margaret Tracey, after whom it was named. (1945)

Baker day. The day on which the second atomic bomb of Operation Crossroads was to be set off beneath the surface of the water in the midst of a fleet. So called after the signaller's word for "b," *See* **Able day.**

banana money. Japanese currency, so named because it bore the design of a banana. (1945)

Bat (bomb). A glider bomb, containing radar in its tip, which, launched from the wing of its mother ship, is electronically guided until it hits its target. It was developed by the U.S. navy and the Bell Telephone laboratories. (1945)

be-bop. *Slang.* Name of uncertain origin—possibly from a similar sound made on the trumpet—to describe a development of swing music which was unrestrained, unrehearsed, high-note and dissonant; possibly imitative of Igor Stravinsky. (1945)

benzene hexachloride. *See* **666.**

Bloc(k). Code name for a television transmitter attached to a plane which enables one to see what is going on 200 mi. away. It was developed by the U.S. navy in co-operation with the Radio Corporation of America and was used in life saving and in actual battle.

boom-and-bust, *n.* A cycle of economic inflation and deflation. (–1946)

brideship. A ship carrying a large number of brides of servicemen.

Bungalow Biddy. *See* **Tournalayer.**

buyers' strike. A movement by consumers to force prices down by not buying. (–1946)

Calutron. A word composed from **California** university **cyclotron** to describe an electrical machine that classifies atoms on the basis of their weight differences. It is manufactured by the Westinghouse Electric corp. (–1945)

carbon 14. A radioactive substance of great promise as a synthesizer of food and fuel and as a tracer in biological research.

caretaker, *adj.* Pertaining to something temporary; stopgap; as, a "caretaker government." (1945)

chalk. 1. Information, often posted in chalk on slates or blackboards, concerning the odds in horse-race betting. **chalk favourite.** A horse favoured to win. (–1936) **chalk player.** One who waits for the last writing or posting of prices or odds so that he can play the favourite. (–1934); also **chalk eater** (–1942) 2. Hence, by extension, a favourite in horse racing as indicated by such information or "chalk." (–1946)

Chromovox. An electric machine devised by Herman R. Goldberg to help teach the deaf to talk by associating voice sounds with certain colours.

cuddle seat. A contrivance for carrying small children consisting of a seat hung from a strap slung over the shoulder. It was introduced into the U.S. by Australian war brides.

curium. Element number 96, named by Glenn T. Seaborg for Pierre and Marie Curie.

cyclophon. A tube used in pulse time modulations (*q.v.*).

DANA. Initials of the ***Deutsche Allgemeine Nachrichten Agentur*** (German General News agency), sponsored by U.S. newspapermen as a successor to the DNB.

Doron. A glass-cloth armour, named for its inventor Brig. Gen. G. F. Dorion, impervious to bullets as large as .45 calibre. (1945)

drone. A plane handled by remote control from a control or mother ship (*q.v.*). (–1946)

echo. A radar wave which has been reflected from an object. It makes a pip (*q.v.*) on a radar screen. (1941)

electropult. A small car, something like a trolley, provided with a 1,400-ft.-long track and capable of developing sufficient speed (120 m.p.h.) within 500 ft. to launch a plane.

elevon. A combination **elevator** and **aileron** located in the trailing edge of the wing of a flying wing.

ENIAC. Electronic Numerical Integrator and Computer, a machine invented by John W. Mauchly and J. Presper Eckert which can solve difficult mathematical problems with great rapidity. (–1946)

Exercise Musk-Ox. A U.S. expedition into the subarctic and arctic regions to obtain scientific data. *See* **operation.**

existentialism. A pessimistic literary-philosophic doctrine in France which denied the value and significance of human existence. Jean-Paul Sartre was its chief proponent. (1945)

fact finder. One engaged, as in a labour dispute, to ascertain the facts of a case. (–1945)

52–20 club. The veterans of World War II who, rather than take low-salaried jobs, accepted the $20 a week unemployment compensation the government would pay for a year (*i.e.,* 52 weeks).

fissionable, *adj.* Pertaining to that which is subject to fission. (–1946)

Flying Ram. The U.S. army XP-79, a small jet-propelled flying wing made by Northrop Aircraft Co. Fourteen feet long, with a wing span of 38 ft., it was flown at speeds of more than 500 m.p.h. by a pilot in a prone position. The plane was welded into a simple magnesium sheet strong enough to withstand the ramming of enemy planes.

flying stove pipe. *See* **ramjet.**

Gapa. Short for "ground-to-air pilotless aircraft," a guided missile of the U.S. army air forces. It is a thin, rocket projectile, ten feet long, to be used against enemy missiles before they strike. Manufactured by the Boeing Aircraft Co.

G.C.A. Ground control approach, a radar-operated system in which a ground operator "talks in" (*q.v.*) a plane that must make a blind landing. (1945)

gray market. A modified black market.

guided missile. A missile directed by some means of remote control such as radio, radar or television. (–1945)

hoppicopter. A flying machine invented by Horace T. Pentecost which operated on the principle of the helicopter. Its source of energy was a 20-h.p., 2-cylinder engine, attached to the back of the pilot. (1945)

hot, *adj.* Pertaining to objects which have been made radioactive.

huckster. *Slang.* A radio advertising man. (–1946)

Huff-Duff, *n.* Pronunciation given by servicemen to the initials (HF DF) of "high frequency direction finder," a device which could determine the location of such objects as ships and aeroplanes as far away as 3,000 mi. Through Huff-Duff, lost planes and ships could be told where they were. It was developed by the U.S. navy and the International Telephone and Telegraph Corp.

Huks. Shortening of Hukbalahaps, a Tagalog word meaning armed peasants, people's army. (1945)

hydrobomb. A 3,000-lb. aerial torpedo with an explosive charge of 600–1,250 lb., built to withstand launching speeds as high as 350 m.p.h. In the water it is rocket-powered accurately at 40 knots.

IFF. Identification, friend or foe, equipment carried in an aeroplane which is sensitive only to corresponding sets, in another plane or on the ground, using a prearranged code. (1945)

iron curtain. (1) The supposed impenetrable censorship and secrecy dividing soviet-dominated Europe from the remainder of the world. Attributed variously to Winston Churchill and to William Joyce (Lord Haw-Haw). (–1946) (2) Any such curtain.

Mad Operator. *Slang.* Navy nickname for the magnetic air-borne detector which enabled aeroplanes to locate submerged submarines.

missile. *Specif. Mil.* Term that includes the whole class of pilotless, jet-propelled projectiles.

mop. *Slang.* A word connoting surprise; a mild sort of "hubba, hubba, hubba." (1944)

mothered, *pp.* Controlled by a mother plane.

mother ship. An aeroplane whose pilot controls a drone or push-button plane. Also **mother plane** (1945), **worker plane.**

mycocidin. A substance obtained from mould in the *aspergillaceae* family, of promise in the treatment of tuberculosis. Developed by Drs. Isadore F. Gerber and Milton Gross.

Navar. A system developed in the International Telephone and Telegraph Federal Telecommunications laboratories of controlling air navigation and airport traffic from centres containing screens on which electronic images enable a control officer to determine the position of all aircraft within a radius of 80 mi. (–1946)

operation. During the years 1939–46, new specific combinations of this word, too numerous for inclusion, occurred. (1) Such specific military uses as **Operation Neptune** (the naval aspect of the invasion of Normandy) to describe a campaign involved a sense of the word dating from 1749. (2) As a rehearsal, the term apparently went back to World War I; a new specific combination involving this sense was seen in **Operation Crossroads,** the atomic bomb test at Bikini. (3) Under the influence of the many combinations in senses 1 and 2, operation was employed to cover any specific plan or project, especially nonmilitary. Thus, **Operation Dixie** described the plan of the C.I.O. to organize the south; **Operation Friendship** was a plan of the British Travel assn. to cement friendships made in England between Americans and Englishmen.

orbit rocket. A theoretical rocket which could be sent out into space, where it would be made to act as a satellite until such time as it might be directed at an enemy.

paludrine. An antimalarial drug developed by English investigators from coal tar. (1945)

performance-observer method. A method to keep horse racing honest. For each entry in a race an observer is appointed who watches the race through binoculars to which is attached a microphone connected with a recorder to make a record of his remarks during the race. (1945)

pip. The indication of an echo (*q.v.*) on a radar screen. (–1945)

Plesianthropus. An "almost man," some of whose skeletal remains were found by Dr. Robert Broom not far from Johannesburg, South Africa. (1945)

pregnenolone. A synthetic chemical, daily doses of which improve human performance by counteracting fatigue. (1945)

psychodrama. A kind of play invented by Dr. J. L. Morens for neurotics. The patients resolve their neuroses by extemporaneously creating and acting out before their fellow patients the type of situation they fear to face in actual life. (1945)

pulse time modulation. A method of using microwaves whereby a number of phone conversations can be transmitted over a single wave band. Abbrev. **PTM.**

push-button, *adj.* Pertaining to the remote-control made increasingly possible by developments in the field of electronics; as, a **push-button** plane, **push-button** war. (1945)

radar scope. (1) Short for radar oscilloscope, a machine for viewing the images produced by radar. (2) A radar screen. (–1946)

radar screen. A fluorescent screen at the end of the radar scope on which the pips are indicated. (–1946)

radioisotope. Short for radioactive isotope.

ramjet. A jet-propulsion unit without moving parts which operates on a continuous stream of air which is compressed by the speed with which the unit "rams into the air." The higher the speed, the greater the compression and hence the efficiency. Also called **athodyd** and **flying stove pipe.**

raticide. *See* **rodenticide.**

Red Feather. The symbol of the Community Chest.

ribbon city. A city about a mile wide built along a highway. Also **strip city.**

Ring. Code name for a large, free-moving, air-borne television transmitter capable of relaying pictures as far as 200 mi. It was developed by the U.S. navy in co-operation with Radio Corporation of America and was used in lifesaving and in actual battle.

rodenticide. A rodent killer. (1945) Also **raticide.**

Sferics. Short for static direction finders, the U.S. army's electronic system for obtaining information on weather conditions; reliable for distances up to 3,000 mi. (1944)

Shock wave. A wave resulting from the fact that as a plane approaches the speed of sound, the air flows over the rear of the wing more slowly than the front, causing shocks that affect the lifting efficiency of the plane and eventually batter it to pieces. (1945)

Shoran. Short for "short-range radar," a radar device which uses high-frequency radio waves sent from a plane to ground stations to locate and measure by miles or feet any spot on the earth. Used during World War II to bomb targets through an overcast, it may be used in peacetime for mapping unknown areas. Developed by the Radio Corporation of America. (1945)

sitter. Short for **baby sitter** (1937), one, usually a teen-age girl, who sits with a baby while the grown-ups are out. (1944)

666. An insecticide (hexachlorobenzene) for intestinal parasites. (1945)

Skimobile. A mechanical chain of cars used to pull skiers up a mountain.

SN 7618. A synthetic drug (7-chloro-4-[4-diethylamino-1-methylbutylamino] quinoline) said to excel atabrine or quinine in the treatment of malaria. So called because it was the 7,618th substance tested.

snake. Nickname of a device used during an army's advance to destroy wires and detonate mines.

sniperscope. A U.S. army detection device, attached to a .30-calibre carbine, for sighting objects in the dark. Infrared rays, shot out by electronic equipment powered from a source on sniper's back, hit an object, an image of which is reflected on a screen. Soldiers thus sighted were unaware of the fact. It was manufactured by Electronics laboratories of Indianapolis, Ind.

snooperscope. A U.S. army detection device, operating on the same principle as the sniperscope, which can be attached to a soldier's helmet to enable him to see, or be used by leaders for signalling. It was manufactured by Electronics laboratories of Indianapolis, Ind.

snowmobile. Term applied also to a light tank, equipped with a glass cabin and rubber tracks in which particles of steel are imbedded for traction. (1943)

Sofar. An underwater sound system, called "Sofar" from sound fixing and ranging, developed by the U.S. navy and the Oceanographic institution, Woods Hole, Mass., which made possible the location of air and ship survivors as far as 2,000 mi. from shore and thus facilitated sea rescue.

sono-radio buoy. A buoy equipped with hydrophones which pick up sound waves from a submerged submarine and convert them into radio waves for transmitting to aircraft or surface vessels. Also **sonobuoy.** (1945)

stacking, *n.* The assigning of planes to certain altitudes, say, 1,000 ft. apart, especially over an airport when landings are delayed by bad weather conditions. As the bottom plane lands, each member of the stack drops 1,000 ft. and a new plane can then be brought in on top. Also **stack up,** *n.* (1943)

synchrotron. A new 300,000,000 electron-volt atom smasher devised independently by Prof. V. Veksler (U.S.S.R.) and Prof. Edwin M. McMillan (U.S.). (1945)

talk down, *v.t.* To aid a pilot to land a plane in overcast weather by studying the position of his plane on a radar screen and giving him directions. Also **talk in.** (1943)

target-seeking missile. A missile, equipped with a target-seeking mechanism, which is attracted toward its target when it approaches its vicinity.

Tournalayer. A huge machine, made by R. G. LeTourneau, Inc., which can "lay" a 24 ft. x 30 ft. 4-room concrete house in 24 hr. Also called **Bungalow Biddy.** The poured concrete houses are called **Tournalaids.**

transuranic, *adj.* Pertaining to elements beyond, that is, heavier than, uranium. (1945)

Truman bread (flour). The bread made from 80% wheat flour, adopted in April 1946 to make it possible to send more wheat abroad. The measure was temporary.

truth serum. Popular name for sodium pentathol, under the influence of which an individual will disclose the truth he has been suppressing. (–1946)

velvet curtain. Term used by the U.S.S.R. to describe British secrecy in British-occupied Europe and the middle east.

Wac corporal. A rocket, 16 ft. in length, 12 in. in diameter, weighing 600 lb.–1,000 lb., the nose of which contains weather instruments to determine various facts about the ionosphere at an altitude of about 43 mi. So called from its slim and graceful appearance.

wave guide. Hollow pipes through which radio waves flow.

weaponeer. The person who prepares an atomic bomb for dropping by the bombardier. (1945)

window, *n.* An antiradar device consisting of strips of aluminum foil one-half the length of a radar wave which, when scattered from a plane, confuse the enemy radar operator by producing a number of echoes on his screen. Also called **chaff, shaff.**

wire recorder. An electrically operated machine for recording sound on a thin aluminum wire strung between two spools, one of which winds and the other unwinds. The recording can be heard as often as desired, or it can be rubbed off and a new one made on the same wire. (–1943)

worker plane. *See* **mother ship.**

X-M bank. The Export-Import bank. (–1946)

(*See* also ABBREVIATIONS.) (I. W. R.)

Workmen's Compensation

See INDUSTRIAL HEALTH.

Work Projects Administration

See FEDERAL WORKS AGENCY; SOCIAL SECURITY.

Works Agency, Federal

See FEDERAL WORKS AGENCY.

World Bank

See INTERNATIONAL BANK FOR RECONSTRUCTION AND DEVELOPMENT.

World Commerce

See INTERNATIONAL TRADE.

World Council of Churches

See CHRISTIAN UNITY; RELIGION.

World Court

See INTERNATIONAL COURT OF JUSTICE; PERMANENT COURT OF INTERNATIONAL JUSTICE.

World Federation of Trade Unions

The World Federation of Trade Unions was founded at a conference held in London in Feb. 1945 and met in Paris to adopt its constitution and hold its first formal congress in Oct. 1945. It was a much more inclusive body than existed before World War II, when the world trade union movement was split between two rival bodies, the (Amsterdam) International Federation of Trade Unions, representing chiefly western Europe, and the (communist) Red International of Labour Unions, consisting mainly of the soviet trade unions, with smaller groups from other countries. There was also a separate International Federation of Christian Trade Unions, representing movements in a number of countries, mostly with a fairly small membership. A good many national trade union bodies were not affiliated to any of these internationals. Attached loosely to the I.F.T.U. were a number of trade secretariats, or international federations of particular bodies of workers; *e.g.,* transport workers, miners, textile workers, commercial employees.

The W.F.T.U. was initiated chiefly by the British and soviet trade unions, which had established a wartime joint committee, in consultation with the U.S. Congress of Industrial Organizations. The conservative American Federation of Labor, with which the British T.U.C. had a joint committee, had lately joined the I.F.T.U., but refused to take any part in forming the W.F.T.U. The Confederation of Latin American Workers, representing most parts of South and Central America, took part in forming the W.F.T.U., as did the American Railroad brotherhoods and the main body of Canadian trade unionists. In all, the Paris conference had representatives from the trade union movements of 56 countries, as compared with 37 at the earlier London conference. The number of members represented was roughly 67,000,000, of whom nearly 30,000,000 were in the soviet union, as against 7,000,000 for Great Britain, 6,000,000 for the C.I.O., and so on, down to very small numbers in some countries. The constitution laid down a system of voting and of representation on councils and committees which prevented the larger movements from exercising a preponderant control. At the congress, each national affiliated group was entitled to at least one delegate, and thereafter, up to 5,000,000 members, to one delegate for each 250,000; but beyond this figure the number of delegates was tapered off. A similar system was applicable to the general council, which was to meet at least once a year and to include at least one delegate from each country. For the smaller executive committee countries were grouped for purposes of representation, as follows: three members each for the soviet union, U.S.A. and Canada; two members each for Great Britain, France and Latin America; one member each for the near and middle east, China, India and Ceylon, Australasia, Africa, Scandinavia, western Europe, southern Europe, central Europe and southeast Europe. In addition, three members were to be chosen by the trade secretariats, and the secretary-general was to be a member. The affiliation dues were graded, to reduce the per capita sums payable by the very large bodies.

The W.F.T.U. put forward a claim for direct representation on the assembly and on the economic and social council of the United Nations. This led to considerable difference of opinion, the U.S. strongly opposing the claim. It was finally decided that the W.F.T.U., the International Co-operative alliance, and other suitable organizations, including by name the American Federation of Labor, should be associated in a consultative capacity with the economic and social council.

The W.F.T.U. at its 1945 congress adopted a comprehensive plan of world economic reconstruction providing for the universal adoption of policies of full employment and social security, for full trade union freedom and participation in the planning and control of industry, for the elimination of all "economic or social discrimination based on race, creed, colour, or sex," and for international arrangements to promote trade and orderly migration.

BIBLIOGRAPHY.—B. Wallace, *World Labour Comes of Age* (1945); Trades Union congress, *Annual Report* (1946).

(G. D. H. C.)

Delegates of 56 nations, representing an estimated 66,759,348 workers, attended the first congress of the World Federation of Trade Unions in Paris during the fall of 1945

World Government

See International Law; World Political Alignments, Postwar.

World Health Organization

See United Nations.

World League Against Alcoholism

See Societies and Associations.

World Political Alignments, Postwar

When the greatest of all wars and the second world war in a generation came to an end Sept. 2, 1945, two fundamental concepts underlay the emerging pattern of postwar political alignments. The first, adopted in the United Nations' declaration of Jan. 1942 as the policy of the alliance that was to defeat the axis, was based on the concept of One World and was to find its realization in the United Nations organization as the international authority to preserve peace. The second, referred to as the realistic concept and born of national self-interest, was based on a world divided into already-existing spheres of security, such as the U.S., the British and the Russian, and was to find recognition in bilateral treaties and in articles 52, 53 and 54 (regional arrangements) of the United Nations charter.

One World *v.* Regional Spheres.—These two concepts were reconciled by their amalgamation in the United Nations charter signed by 50 nations June 26, 1945, in San Francisco. The United Nations charter admitted to the organization all members of the coalition on a basis of sovereign equality irrespective of their military alliances, regional ties, or status of sovereignty. Adherents to the One World idea hoped that as the United Nations grew in strength, it would gradually eliminate the rival concept by making security blocs unnecessary as a prop for peace, at the same time recognizing their temporary necessity.

Supporting this point of view, U.S. Secretary of State James Byrnes, in an address in New York city on March 1, 1946, stated: "We (the United States) will gang up against no state. We will do nothing to break the world into exclusive blocs or spheres of influence. In this atomic age we will not seek to divide a world which is one and indivisible." Emphasizing that the foreign policy of the British commonwealth and empire was based on the United Nations and not on rival security spheres, Foreign Secretary Ernest Bevin said in a speech to the Labour party conference June 12, 1946: "I have deliberately not pressed for an alliance with France or the Western Powers because I have been actuated all the time in this approach not to divide Europe."

On the other hand, adherents to the concept of security spheres looked to the balance of power between blocs of states to keep peace in the final analysis and, while supporting the United Nations as a forum in which the power of these blocs could be tested, concluded bilateral security pacts. For example, the soviet union negotiated treaties with Czechoslovakia, China, France, Poland, Yugoslavia and Britain.

Victors and Vanquished.—Emanating from World War II, in addition to these two concepts which underlay the emerging pattern of postwar political alignments, was the fact of the alignment of the victors on one side, the vanquished on another and the neutrals grouped in a third cluster by virtue of their neutrality. The victorious coalition was comprised of 50 nations who had declared war on either Germany or Japan or both.[1] The vanquished were Germany, Japan, Italy and the axis satellites—Rumania, Bulgaria, Hungary and Finland. The neutrals were Sweden, Switzerland, Eire, Spain and Portugal. Finally, there was Denmark, which alone among the axis-occupied countries had neither collaborated with Germany nor established a government abroad. Of these, in considering alignments, the obvious fact was that the vanquished were not permitted to align themselves, and the neutrals were of such a scattered nature as to have no basis for postwar coalition. However, the neutrals, with the exception of Spain, would early become members of the United Nations (substantially synonymous with the victorious alliance). It remained to be seen whether such an alignment of nations bound together by a common enemy could continue in time of peace with the only binding force the will to peace. The victors comprised such a vast percentage of the area and population of the world that the effect of a continuation of this alignment would be to remove the bond of an external threat and thereby increase the divisive influences within the coalition. The United Nations charter attempted to remedy this by substituting the very real but impersonal enemies of want, ignorance, injustice and intolerance. Complicating the peacetime existence of this war-born alliance was another factor. Except in war, the victorious nations had not been united. In fact, in 1938, England and France had signed a nonaggression pact with Germany at Munich in which they gave their consent to a partial occupation by Germany of the territory of Czechoslovakia, their ally. As late as 1941 the U.S.S.R. was member to a nonaggression pact with Germany which had been already at war with England and France for two years. The real hope for peace, therefore, was whether an alignment formed during World War II, and without any prewar basis, could exist postwar.

The most significant postwar alignment was that of the soviet union with the countries following it on the one hand, and the alignment of the United States and the countries following it on the other. The first date on which this division in alignment became openly evident was April 30, 1945, just prior to the end of the war with Germany. The occasion was the vote in the United Nations conference at San Francisco on the question of the admission of Argentina to the conference. By a vote of 31–4, Argentina was invited by the United Nations to attend the conference despite repeated requests by the U.S.S.R. that Argentina be omitted until the Polish government in Warsaw was invited. The 14-nation executive committee voted 9–3 to invite Argentina; the U.S.S.R., Czechoslovakia and Yugoslavia voted against, with China abstaining. The steering committee voted 29–6 to invite, with Czechoslovakia, Yugoslavia, Belgium, Greece, New Zealand and the U.S.S.R. in the minority. In the plenary session the final vote showed the U.S.S.R., Yugoslavia, Czechoslovakia and Greece voting in the minority.

Colonial *v.* Noncolonial Powers.—Another significant issue which had come to the front as a basis of postwar political alignment was the question of the attitude of colonial and noncolonial powers to dependent peoples. Since no trusteeship policy had been formulated by the United Nations prior to the San Francisco conference, the first evidences of alignment on this issue took place at this time. Contrary to what might have been expected, the colonial powers—Great Britain, France, the Netherlands, Portugal, Belgium and the United States—did not always line up against the noncolonial states.

In general, however, China, whose future interest was related to the independence of dependent peoples in Southeast Asia; Australia, New Zealand, Egypt, Iraq, Syria, the Philippines and India, all of which had been dependencies; and U.S.S.R., whose vast empire was without overseas possessions, were sympathetic to the aspiration for independence of colonial peoples. Nevertheless, despite this cleavage in alignment between the colonial and noncolonial powers, the former accepted for the most part the provisions of the United Nations charter regarding trusteeship. They provided no change in the status of colonies except by consent of the colonial powers themselves. Some proof of the good faith with which the colonial powers ascribed to the spirit of the charter's trusteeship provisions was evidenced by the fact that within the year the world's leading colonial power, Great Britain, had agreed to place under United Nations trusteeship its mandated territories Tanganyika, Togoland and Cameroons and to give Trans-Jordan and India their independence. Following this lead, Belgium agreed to place its African mandate, Ruanda Urundi, under United Nations trusteeship; Australia, its mandates of Nauru and New Guinea; New Zealand, its mandate Western Samoa; and the Netherlands indicated that Indonesia would have the opportunity for self-determination "in our time," in the meantime offering to establish a commonwealth of Indonesia under which all Indonesians would enjoy citizenship and civil rights in all parts of the Netherlands kingdom. On the other hand, France showed reluctance to place its African mandates—French Togoland and French Cameroun—under United Nations trusteeship, and the Union of South Africa expressed an interest in establishing sovereignty over its mandate of South-West Africa. The French cabinet approved a plan to give French Indo-China autonomous self-government within a French federal union. This was in keeping with the pledge given by the French Committee of National Liberation on Dec. 8, 1943, which promised Indo-China "a new political status within the French community."

Russia and the Veto.—Other political alignments issued from the debates in the San Francisco conference, but none was as fundamental as the cleavage on the question of the veto power. The soviet union took the position that the five great powers—China, France, Great Britain, Russia, the United States—should have the right to veto not only the investigation of any dispute and decision to take enforcement action with respect to it, but also the discussion of any dispute at any stage. The formula for voting established at the Crimea conference in Feb. 1945 distinguished between procedural decisions and decisions on other matters. On procedural matters, decisions were to be reached by an affirmative vote of any seven members, permanent or nonpermanent. On all other matters, decisions were to be reached by an affirmative vote of seven members, including the five permanent members. In other words, the five permanent members had what was referred to as

---

[1] Argentina, Australia, Belgium, Bolivia, Brazil, Byelorussia, Canada, Chile, Colombia, Costa Rica, Cuba, Czechoslovakia, Dominican Republic, Ecuador, Egypt, El Salvador, Ethiopia, France, Greece, Guatemala, Haiti, Honduras, India, Iran, Iraq, Lebanon, Liberia, Luxembourg, Mexico, Netherlands, New Zealand, Nicaragua, Norway, Panama, Peru, Paraguay, Philippines, Poland, Arabia, Syria, Ukraine, South Africa, U.S.S.R., United Kingdom, United States, Uruguay, Venezuela, Yugoslavia.

"a veto power." While the lesser powers—the so-called "little 45"—reluctantly conceded the right of the permanent members of the Security council to veto enforcement action, they fought to remove all other matters from the scope of the great powers. Especially, were they determined that the great powers should have no veto over discussion of any dispute. Great Britain and the United States sided, in general, with the "little 45," taking the view that all members of the Security council should be free to discuss any dispute threatening international peace. On June 7, 1945, it was reported that Stalin had instructed the soviet delegation to abandon its request for a veto over discussion of international disputes. Once this was done and the 22 questions concerning the veto power asked by the "little 45" had been answered, the Yalta formula was incorporated in Article 27 of the charter. Despite the conciliatory attitude shown by the U.S.S.R. at this critical juncture in regard to the veto power, the division between the U.S.S.R., Czechoslovakia, Byelorussia, Ukraine, Yugoslavia and Poland on the one hand, and the other United Nations on the application of the veto was the central thread of the major alignment of countries following the U.S.S.R. and the countries following the United States. An example was the rejection by the soviet union and the countries following it of the United States' plan for control of atomic energy involving the outlawing of the veto as it pertained "to protect those who violate their solemn agreements not to develop or use atomic energy for destructive purposes."

The period following the prefatory alignments of the San Francisco conference had been marked by the ascendancy of the so-called realistic concept emphasizing regional political alignments within the great powers' spheres of security. Some of these dated back to periods long before World War II but received fresh impetus during the postwar period. The reason for the revival of the balance of power policy between regional spheres was the fact that there was no power in the United Nations charter to enforce decisions against a major power and no immediate prospect of general disarmament.

Four Regional Blocs.—What blocs or regional spheres came into existence in political alignment in this postwar period?

Inter-American System.—The Inter-American system had no formal recognition in a written charter. Though the Pan American union had been in existence since 1890, only since the Act of Chapultepec (1945) had the Inter-American system begun to assume the appearance of a regional security sphere. Part I of the act laid down the procedure American states were to adopt in the face of aggression, including the application of economic sanctions and the use of armed force during the period of war. Part II provided that for the postwar period a treaty be negotiated which would establish similar procedures for the time of peace. A proposed Inter-American conference for such a purpose scheduled to be held in Oct. 1945 was postponed when the United States state department announced on Oct. 2, 1945: "In view of recent developments in Argentina, the United States government does not feel it can properly negotiate or sign with the present Argentine government a treaty of mutual assistance." Part III contained the proviso that defined the relationship of the Inter-American system to the United Nations. It stated that regional arrangements should be "consistent with the purpose and principles of the general international organization when established." Twenty American states adhered to the Act of Chapultepec at the close of the Mexico City conference March 8, 1945. Argentina had not been invited. However, the Pan American union governing board unanimously approved a motion to open the final act of the Mexico City conference to Argentine admission on April 4, 1945. Besides the Act of Chapultepec, a resolution was passed on "reorganizing, consolidating and strengthening the Inter-American system." In the future, International Conferences of American States were to meet every four years, and the ministers of foreign affairs were to meet in every non-conference year with powers to take decisions on situations and disputes of every kind "which may disturb the peace of the American republics." Though the Act of Chapultepec still required implementation in the postwar period by an Inter-American mutual assistance treaty, the conference at Mexico City, 1945, marked the high point in the formulation of a western hemisphere security alignment. One further step was taken later. On May 6, 1946, the United States announced a proposed program for co-ordinating the military forces of the western hemisphere. It was known as the Inter-American Military Co-operation bill and provided for the integrated training of armed forces personnel, the maintenance of military or naval installations in new world countries, and the transfer to these countries of a wide variety of military equipment.

Russian Security Sphere.—During World War II, the U.S.S.R. annexed Lithuania, Latvia, Estonia, eastern Poland, Bessarabia and Bukovina, Moldavia, Carpatho-Ukraine, East Prussia, Karelo-Finland, Petsamo-Finland, Tannu Tuva, southern Sakhalin Island and the Kurile Islands. To secure its frontiers, the soviet union likewise obtained naval bases on Porkala peninsula, Finland, and at Port Arthur in China, together with joint ownership and operation of the Manchurian trunk railway lines. Russia further bulwarked its security by concluding a mutual assistance treaty with Czechoslovakia in Dec. 1943, with France in Dec. 1944, a 30-year pact of friendship with China in Aug. 1945, an assistance pact with Poland in May 1946 and an assistance pact with Yugoslavia in June 1946. In addition, the U.S.S.R. concluded in May 1942 a friendship and assistance pact with Great Britain which Great Britain twice offered to extend from 20 to 50 years. Beyond annexing bordering territory and concluding security pacts, Russia occupied Hungary, Rumania and Bulgaria—all former axis satellites.

In the east, the U.S.S.R. exerted influence in Korea, in which it held military occupation of the northern part. In Manchuria, it secured joint ownership and operation with China of the Manchurian trunk railway lines. To the south, the U.S.S.R. sought to expand its security sphere by pursuing its historical objective of warm water ports. At various times after the close of the war, the soviet union asked for partial control of Tripoli, sought trusteeships under the United Nations for Tripolitania and Eritrea, and indicated a desire for military bases in the Dodecanese Islands and the Greek Islands. In March 1945 the U.S.S.R. renounced the Turko-Soviet Pact of Friendship and Neutrality (1925). In June 1945 Russia asked Turkey to return Kars and Ardahan in eastern Anatolia and to support the soviet claim for a revision of the Montreux convention of 1936 which would give the U.S.S.R. a share in the defense of the straits as conditions for renewal of the Turko-Soviet pact. In July 1945 Turkey rejected these conditions. Finally, the U.S.S.R. exerted pressure on Iran, which stood between the soviet union and its desire for ports on the Persian Gulf and Indian ocean. In the northern province of Iran, Azerbaijan, soviet pressure succeeded in establishing an autonomous government friendly to Russia.

Alignment in Russia's security sphere was not based on any real relationship to the have and have-not division talked about between the two world wars. Raw materials studies published by the Brookings institution (*World Minerals and World Peace*), by the Royal Institute of International Affairs (*World Production of Raw Materials*), and by the United States Military academy (*Strategic and Critical Raw Materials*) indicated that no other single political area, except possibly the United States, could in case of necessity become so nearly self-sufficient in the material elements of national power as the soviet union. With the exception of tin, antimony, nickel and tungsten, there were very substantial quantities of practically every other raw material within the soviet sphere of influence. Though oil production might fall below Russia's needs, its petroleum deposits had been vastly increased and other promising areas were yet uncharted. According to the Brookings study, "No longer does Russia depend entirely on the production of the Baku district for its requirements. It is claimed by the Geological survey (U.S.S.R.) that in the Urals and area west to the Volga river, reserves have been indicated of a greater magnitude than those of the Baku district."

Any sort of an expansionist attitude on the part of the U.S.S.R. could not, therefore, be laid down to a lack of raw materials or lack of living space.

British Commonwealth and Empire.—The British Commonwealth of Nations, an association of nations tied by language, custom, race and common interests, represented an alignment of nations which far antedated the post-World War II period but continued to have great influence in that period. It included the United Kingdom, Canada, Australia, New Zealand, South Africa, Newfoundland, British Honduras, British Guiana, India, Nigeria, Kenya, Gibraltar, Malta, Jamaica, Rhodesia and other islands and dependencies. It comprised about a quarter of the habitable surface of the world, and, including India, its population was one-quarter of the world's population. As the king's prime ministers of the self-governing dominions said May 18, 1944: "The British Commonwealth of Nations finds its strength not in any formal bond but in the hidden spring from which human action flows."

The strength of the commonwealth's bonds was severely tested during World War II and the postwar period in the Mediterranean, the middle east and the far east. Centre of anti-British agitation in the middle east was Palestine, Britain's mandate since 1922. In the London conference on the Palestine problem Sept. 1946, Britain was trying to reconcile its strategic interests with its promise to the Jews made in the Balfour declaration of 1917 and its promise of independence made to the Arabs in the McMahon-Hussein agreement of 1915. In the Mediterranean, Egypt was insistent that British troops be withdrawn immediately from Egyptian territory and that the condominium over Sudan by Britain and Egypt be abolished in favour of annexation by Egypt. Britain, for its part, desired to ensure the military security of the Suez Canal Zone, a vital point in the life line to its possessions in the far east. In the far east, the focal point of British concern was India. The long struggle for the independence of India culminated in the British White Paper's proposal of May 16, 1946, for full and unrestricted independence. On August 12, 1946, Viceroy Archibald P. Wavell asked Jawaharlal Nehru, president of the dominant Congress party, to form an interim government. Riots immediately broke out in Calcutta between Moslem and Hindu factions.

The Moslem league's demands for Pakistan were difficult to reconcile with the Hindu all-India Congress party's demand for a united India free of British rule.

Within and without the framework of the British Commonwealth of Nations, there were political alignments. On Jan. 21, 1944, Australia and New Zealand completed an agreement which provided for subregional consolidation in the south seas. On Nov. 15, 1945, Britain and Canada joined with the United States in a common declaration on atomic energy, marking the first step in the development of international atomic policy. By the Ogdensburg agreement of Aug. 17, 1940, Canada and the United States had already established a permanent joint U.S.-Canada Board of Defense "to consider in the broad sense the defense of the northern half of the western hemisphere." In a speech

Paris conference of foreign ministers of Great Britain, France, the U.S.S.R. and the United States, which opened on April 25, 1946, and closed in July without having reached agreement on the German problem

in London Nov. 25, 1943, Jan Smuts, South Africa's prime minister, suggested the possible erection of a western bloc as the only means by which the British commonwealth might continue to rank as a world power. Winston Churchill, former prime minister of Great Britain, carried forward a similar sentiment in a speech at Zurich, Sept. 21, 1946:

"We must build a kind of United States of Europe. . . . There is no reason why a regional organization of Europe should in any way conflict with the world organization of the United Nations. . . . The first step in the recreation of the European family must be a partnership between France and Germany."

On March 5, 1946, in Fulton, Mo., Churchill had called for yet another political association:

"Neither the sure prevention of war nor the continuous rise of world organization will be gained without what I have called the fraternal association of the English-speaking peoples. This means a special relationship between the British Commonwealth and Empire and the United States of America. . . . The United States has already a permanent defense agreement with Canada. . . . This principle should be extended to all British Commonwealths with full reciprocity . . . eventually, there will come the principle of common citizenship."

The Arab League.—The Arab league (*q.v.*) came into existence as the first regional organization born of the postwar period. On March 22, 1945, in Cairo, a covenant was signed by Egypt, Trans-Jordan, Lebanon, Syria, Iraq, Saudi Arabia and Yemen binding themselves to co-ordinate their political action, to take common measures of defense and to resort to arbitration and conciliation in cases of conflict.

Intervention in the internal politics of member states was forbidden. Stimulating the drive to Arab unity was the necessity of presenting a common front against extensions of outside control. Anti-western feelings increased during World War II and were brought to a head in the French Lebanese crisis Nov. 1943. Two annexes to the covenant asserted the juridical right of Palestine to independence, and secondly, urged the league to strive for the national realizations of all Arab countries not yet qualified for membership.

The Arabs did not wish to be satellites of great powers. They were entitled to have their own place and proper function within a United Nations system.

Postwar world political alignments posed the fundamental question as to whether the alignment of the United Nations would become stronger than the regional alignments that had developed on the basis of ideologies and geography within the United Nations. It posed the equally fundamental questions raised at the time of the breakup of the Foreign Ministers' conference at London in Sept. 1945: whether the peace of the world would be imposed by dictate of the three great powers, or whether the world would govern itself in the spirit of the United Nations with all the peoples which were members participating in the decisions, or whether the postwar peace would be lost. (*See* also INTERNATIONAL LAW.)

BIBLIOGRAPHY.—Crane Brinton, *U.S. and Britain* (1945); Harold Sprout, *Foundations of National Power* (1945); Vera Dean, *The Four Cornerstones of Peace* (1946); H. A. R. Gibb, "Toward Arab Unity," *Foreign Affairs*, Oct. 1945; Walter Sharp, "Inter-American Systems and the United Nations," *Foreign Affairs*, April 1945; Nicholas Spykman, *American Strategy in World Politics* (1942); Robert Strausz-Hupe, *The Balance of Tomorrow* (1945); Leith, Lewis and Furness, *World Minerals and World Peace* (1943); Sumner Welles, *Time for Decision* (1944); L. S. Stavrianos, *Balkan Federation* (1944); Walter Lippmann, *U.S. Foreign Policy* (1943). (H. E. ST.)

World War II

The article which follows is divided into seven broad sections which describe the principal political and military events of World War II. The military and air operations have been treated according to three main geographical divisions—Europe, Africa and the near east; China; and the war in the Pacific. Naval operations are described in a separate section, although it is often impossible to draw a sharp line of demarcation between purely military and purely naval action in World War II, particularly in the Pacific.

Following are the main sections and divisions of the article, with page references:

I. THE ORIGINS

The years between the two great world wars covered another period in history wherein the struggle for world peace resulted in failure. It was a period during which those who had the power to enforce peace failed to act and during which the aggressors, encouraged by such failure, and heedless of the destruction and human suffering entailed, again took up war and oppression as a means of accomplishing their objectives.

The panorama of the ten eventful years from 1937 to 1946 was so vast, so packed with diverse forces, interests and personalities, so marked by significant political and social developments, that in itself it challenged measurement and description. Yet, no single decade of history can be divorced from the years which led up to it. The decade of 1937–46 represented only the brink and the falls of disaster through which there plunged the weight of all the forces which had been gathered from the many tributaries of the world's ambitions, energies and manifold mistakes.

World War I had been sufficiently vast and destructive to induce mankind to search deeply for the means of avoiding another such convulsion. Many objective and high-principled leaders, who devoted all the energies they could summon to the establishment of a form of society which would bring security and peace, arose after that conflict. If there were also men of partisan approach and background, they did not dominate the scene; and it is safe to say that all were so gripped by the full sense of the destructive power of war as to seek honestly and energetically for security. Then, as at later times, there was divergence of opinion as to method.

Then, as after World War II, acute postwar problems arose which had to be dealt with even while the discussion of the form of a world organization was taking place—problems in some instances uncannily like those which confronted the world after 1945. These problems frequently plagued the general will to set up a form of international organization which would become either a substitute for, or a moderation of, the old methods of achieving security; namely, by alliance, individual action and war.

It was the conflict, probably inevitable, between the concept of individual security and Pres. Woodrow Wilson's doctrine of collective security which compromised the settlement after World War I. They stalked across the entire period between the wars, and finally led to the outright defiance of the League by the axis powers and to virtual abandonment of it by the western democracies. The establishment of the many new small nations had been tied in with the creation of the League as the fundamental basis of fostering European peace. With these new nations and the alterations of boundaries which were necessary to produce them, and without firm adherence to the League on the part of the victors, Germany was left a wide choice of European issues to exploit.

All of the great Allied Powers, including soviet Russia, appeared to have been guilty of the most painful blunders in their vacillation between collective and individual security as the aggressors began their exploitation of Allied disunity, weaknesses and indecision. That vacillation frequently nullified effective action toward peace. It was only in the face of black disaster and the heat of actual armed conflict that unified action was forged.

The Significance of Versailles.—It is to this persistent conflict between collective and individual security and the jockeying it produced among the powers, rather than to the harshness or the softness of the treaty of Versailles in respect to Germany, that one must look for the elements most useful to the aggressors during the 1930–40 decade.

The Versailles treaty attempted to put together French and Anglo-U.S. concepts of a stable world order. France, which sought drastic modifications of Germany's political boundaries, finally settled for military guarantees of the type with which for centuries it had become familiar. These it accepted from Britain and the United States of America in return for the abandonment of its claim to strategic frontiers and of its plan for the dismemberment of Germany.

The resultant treaty, at least in French eyes, presupposed the continuance of English and U.S. military support, which in the end was not forthcoming. France, as a result, never was induced by a basic sense of security to rest its full faith in the League of Nations.

Practically from the instant of the refusal of the United States to support France by a military alliance and the consequent loss of the British guarantee, the essential elements of the whole theory on which the treaty was drafted were taken from under it. The United States refusal to ratify the treaty was a body blow of almost fatal character in itself, considering the part which the assumed adherence of the United States had played in the treaty negotiations. Even France's proposal for an international police force was rejected. The representatives of Great Britain and the United States had been rather well satisfied with the geographical and military positions of their respective countries after World War I. They were disposed to be content with the formal creation of an organization to keep the peace without placing any great emphasis on the methods by which such an organization would be made potent and dynamic. The League without U.S. participation was thus doubly undermined. To make matters worse, after U.S. withdrawal, England quickly shifted to its old concepts of the balance-of-power and of restricted intervention in European affairs which effectively deterred it from supporting France's proposals to curb the first military gestures of the renascent reich. Instead of Anglo-French integration of policy, there ensued a sort of duel between the two countries resulting in the practically unilateral and highly unsuccessful occupation of the Ruhr by France and the consequent encouragement of Germany to flout the treaty.

The Germans, especially Adolf Hitler, made much of the harshness of Versailles; but in retrospect no serious contention could be held that the political burdens of Versailles were too great for it to bear. The boundaries in some cases were awkward, as for example the Polish corridor; but they left Germany a strong national state, with a chance for complete economic recovery. Considering the conglomeration of races in Europe and the acute sense of security need which German aggression had induced, the territorial solutions attempted at Versailles could not be said to have been unreasonable or vindictive. It is true that the reparations clauses of the treaty were unrealistic, and they played a part together with other factors—most of them of German origin—in inducing the distressful inflation which Germany underwent. The reparations clauses were moderated, however, by successive plans of adjustment; and in the end Germany failed to pay by way of reparations as much as was received by it in foreign loans on which it later defaulted. It is true that the inflation under which Germany suffered and the economic collapse of Germany did serve to destroy the chief prop the German republic had in the way of political support, for it embittered the middle class against the government, and it enabled Hitler to gain ground with his joint denunciation of the republic's leaders and Germany's former enemies.

While the economic features of the treaty had serious consequences, the true defect of Versailles lay in the failure of the Allied Powers to move together in the enforcement of the settlement, even after their own moderation of its terms. The truth of the matter became apparent too late, but eventually even to Anglo-U.S. apologists for the alleged harshness of the treaty it became evident that Hitler was grossly overplaying Versailles as a justification for his depredations.

Primary German Responsibility.—Hitler, however, successfully utilized the treaty as a means of gaining power at home and disseminating publicity abroad as to the sincerity of his purposes. It was only on the verge of war that the realization arose that something deeper than modifications of the treaty of Versailles stood between peace and war in Europe. Hitler's reiteration at each crisis he precipitated that he sought no further concessions in Europe finally lost its force.

Prior to World War II, the German standard of living had substantially improved—it was measurably higher than that of the first victims of Hitler's attacks. If there was discrimination displayed by contiguous states against German residents, none of it approached Hitler's charges nor faintly suggested the brutalities Hitler was himself exerting on German minorities within his own borders. Yet these were the elements which his propagandists stressed and which readied the nation for another war.

With all this, Hitler could not have made Germany march without another factor which underlay the whole German structure. This was a still deeply seated tradition and sense of superiority fostered by Germany's military philosophers and supported generally by the people. It arose from pride in Germany's many and important military successes in the past and a conviction of superiority which was never entirely dissipated by its really thorough defeat in 1918. The unconvincing character of that defeat in German minds, and the humiliations which defeat brought Germany, supplied the chief nourishment on which Hitler's propaganda could and did thrive.

Germany had no justifiable military, political or economic cause for war and it was always within its power to avert it; but the Allied Powers made the way easy for Hitler's ambitions, first, by their failure to enforce collectively the provisions of the treaty and the agreements made subsequent to the treaty, and, second, by their refusal to take united and timely action in the way of economic concessions which would have strengthened the republic. These concessions, which were never forthcoming in unified form, were belatedly urged on Hitler when they were of no further avail as a war preventive.

In condemning the shortsightedness and indecision of the Allied Powers, it must always be borne in mind that these factors did not cause the war. They only failed to prevent it.

The utter wantonness of Hitler and the willingness of the German people to support him and condone his depredations caused the European war, and in the disappointment caused by the weakness and indecision of the Allied leaders and peoples one could not lose sight of the primary and fundamental responsibility of Germany, Japan and Italy for the years of misery they inflicted on the world.

Futility of Disarmament.—Throughout the period between the two world wars, the western democracies clung persistently to the concept that disarmament in itself would bring peace. Indeed, this became almost the only continuing element of their policy. Even in the face of the most significant acts of aggression on the part of Germany, Japan and Italy, the disarmament conferences went on. No disarmament agreements of any substance were concluded by the axis powers, a fact significant enough in itself; but all the while they went on arming. The democratic governments were informed of this rearmament, but they chose to ignore it. They fastened only the more firmly to the hope that the more convenient policy of disarmament would induce peace. Though no agreements were consummated, the two greatest of the democracies were actually disarming through their failure to maintain their military establishments at any stage which either Germany or the smaller nations, eventually to become Germany's victims, could recognize as a factor measurable in terms of time and effect in enforcing peace.

This tendency arose in large part from the expressions of great bodies of well-meaning people, in both Great Britain and the United States, who firmly believed that no arms meant no violence. It was combined with the ever-present reluctance of political parties in power to take the responsibility of imposing on the electorate the added tax and personal burdens which armament involves.

Whatever the motive, the result was clear. None of the axis powers felt that there was either a will or a capacity to enforce the peace on the part of the great democracies. This belief was transmitted to those countries which might have resisted the aggressions. It thus entered into the calculations of both aggressor and victim—the aggressor being convinced that he could make away with his gains before any retribution could overtake him and the victim being convinced that resistance was useless, since no help could or would arrive before he was overrun.

Locarno and London.—Two occurrences, rather characteristic of the trend of world politics in the period before 1937, should be referred to before reciting the sequence of the direct and immediate events which led up to the actual outbreak of war. The first was the repudiation of the Locarno pact of 1925, and the second was the failure of the World Economic conference in 1933. During the period between the wars, as indeed in most periods of history, political and economic issues went hand in hand as parallel irritants to friendly relations. In the period referred to, the economic crazy quilt of high tariffs, reparations, foreign loans and strangulation of international trade constantly created international complications and demanded rectification.

A serious effort was made, and for a time seemed successful, to deal with the political issues at Locarno. The conclusion of the pacts ushered in a period of much good feeling. It followed the evacuation of the Ruhr and the acceptance of the Dawes plan as a settlement of the reparations problem and the stability of German economy. At Locarno, Franco-German and Belgian-German boundaries were guaranteed; the permanent demilitarization of the Rhineland was provided for; war was renounced and the principle of arbitration of disputes between the countries was established, except for cases in which self-defense, League action or German violation of the demilitarization provisions was involved. Great Britain and Italy joined in to promise assistance to the country which became the victim of another's aggression. Germany was elected to the League. Thus, all but Germany's eastern boundaries were dealt with. The Soviet Union naturally was disturbed, but in spite of Russian suspicions the Locarno pact established a basis upon which much might be built and even more hoped for. Here was an agreement entered into freely by Germany as a co-equal. It had none of the aspects of the *Diktat* which Germany signed in the Hall of Mirrors at Versailles.

Hitler came to power in Jan. 1933; in 1936, not long after he had proclaimed his firm intention to observe the agreements which were made at Locarno, hardly more than ten years after the pacts had been signed, the new German leader marched his troops into the Rhineland in direct violation of the pacts. The great powers did no more than make formal protestations to this action.

The other significant event was the attempt made to solve the major economic problems then plaguing the world. To accomplish this, a great economic conference was called together to meet in London in June 1933. The conference was called by the League in a supreme effort to recognize the integral character of the world's economy. The economic dislocations brought on by World War I, and the continued nationalistic measures and counter-measures which were everywhere in force, were patently interfering with the political stability of the world. The conference was to deal primarily with the removal of trade barriers, the stabilization of currencies and disposal of other restrictions impeding world trade.

Though having high hopes and possibilities, the conference at the very outset was spiked by the action of the United States in opposing any measure leading to the stabilization of currencies. Other restrictions on the power of the U.S. delegates, together with the force and manner in which their authority respecting currencies was taken from them by their own chief, turned the conference into something of a fiasco.

The political value of Locarno was destroyed by the

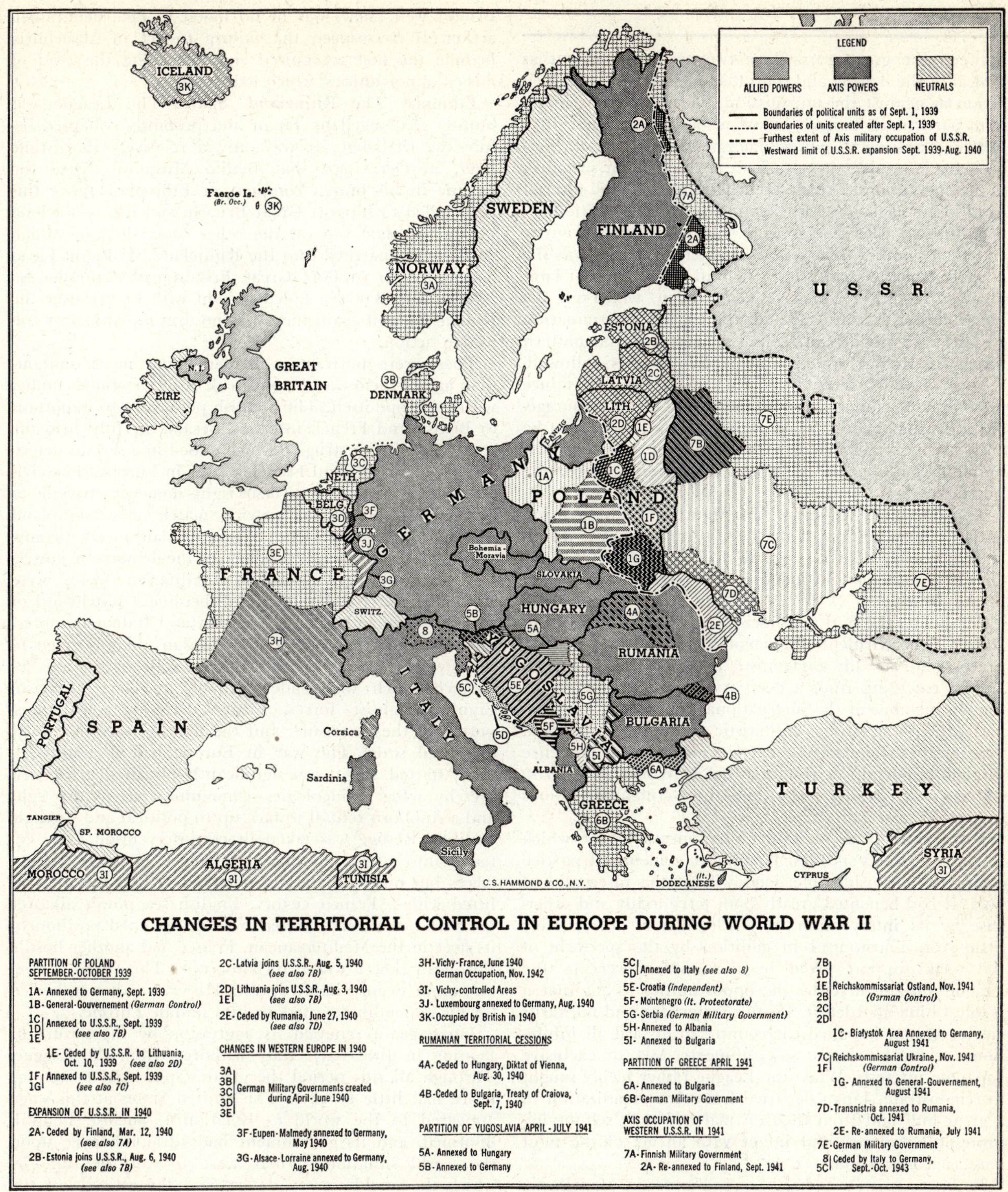

CHANGES IN TERRITORIAL CONTROL IN EUROPE DURING WORLD WAR II

determination of Hitler to prepare his way for outright aggression, whereas the attempt to deal with world economic problems was nullified at a critical time largely by a leader who had just come on the scene and who was to play such a vital part in the final overthrow of Hitler—Pres. Franklin D. Roosevelt. The president felt a compelling domestic need for higher prices and was prepared to place that consideration above the international need for stabilized world economic conditions. This event is stressed as a significant incident of the general trend of nationalistic action which tended to interfere with constructive plans for world peace. The event is the more significant in that President Roosevelt, who was later to become almost the personification of collective action and internationalism, was impelled to pursue this course. Whatever his motives, the failure of the London conference served to encourage the policies of economic nationalism. This encouragement unfortunately played into the hands of the nazi leaders of Germany. Other factors may have obstructed the possibilities of success at London, but the action of the United States made a spectacular contribution to its failure.

In the rather long array of incidents and issues marking the opportunities and patterns of the Armistice years between the great wars, these two events stood out as typical of the halting and contradictory character of Allied action as against the unequivocal evidence of axis intention, particularly as such intention became manifest after Hitler's accession to power. They were only typical, however, for it would not be difficult to find similar instances of the operation of British, French and Russian self-interest or to locate as flagrant an example of axis provocation.

Failure to Check Aggression.—Thus, first one country and then another, the western democracies as well as the U.S.S.R. (for the record shows that all were sooner or later involved) took, or failed to take, action, which set the stage for the ever-present and unrelenting determination of Hitler to divide and conquer. This was the pattern which led to war, and one step after another followed, no one of which seemed sufficient at the time to induce the powers to undertake collective action or even courageous individual action. Some of the major incidents can be only briefly summarized, with consequent risk of oversimplification, but it is impossible to misinterpret the trend.

The Japanese aggression in Manchuria in 1931 apparently was the first of the definite steps toward doom. It is necessary at this stage to look at the state of affairs in the far east to judge the part Japan was to play in the drama.

Paralleling the nazi and fascist motives of Germany and Italy, another virulent and demoralizing force was steadily at work and steadily antagonistic to peace. Comparatively late in emerging from a deep tribal isolationism to become a member of the international community and permeated with a strong militaristic tradition, Japan had persistently expanded its territories and areas of influence through opportunistic conquests before World War I; viz., China (1894), Russia (1904) and the German possessions in the far east (1914).

For a time, after obtaining the concessions for which it contended at Versailles, Japan gave evidence of participating with considerable good will in the international field. It had benefited greatly both territorially and otherwise by its intervention in World War I, at relatively little cost. Encouraged in addition by the spectacle of the weak support given by the great powers to the League and inspired by the opportunities it felt that a feeble China afforded it, Japan's materialist and militarist elements soon impelled the country to discard all inhibitions, seize Manchuria and subjugate Asia to exclusive Japanese interests. When the League rather feebly sought to remonstrate, Japan departed from that organization in a great huff and from then on matched each self-serving protestation of peaceful intent with an act of the most barefaced aggression.

Its first step was, as has been indicated, in Manchuria. In Sept. 1931 a portion of the track of the South Manchurian railway was blown up with all the marks of a manufactured incident. The Japanese army immediately took possession of important strategic positions in Manchuria. Four months later Japanese forces landed in Shanghai, bombarding the town and engaging the Chinese forces located there. All of Manchuria was occupied. The foresighted warning of Henry L. Stimson, then United States secretary of state, who called for collective action, appealed neither to Great Britain, whose stake in the Pacific areas was, if anything, greater than that of the United States, nor to the United States. In spite of Secretary Stimson's prescience, the United States, as Great Britain well knew, was in no mood to take determined action. In retrospect, the failure to act in Manchuria became the first recognized signpost along the road of missed opportunities, which led to war.

Ethiopia, The Rhineland, Spain.—The League was bluntly challenged by Japan and promptly collapsed before the challenge. It was only a relatively short time later, in Oct. 1935, that Benito Mussolini defied the League in his brazen conquest of Ethiopia. France this time failed to support Great Britain, and it was not long before the shoe was on the other foot when in March 1936 Hitler marched into the Rhineland. As Pierre Laval had failed to support Great Britain over Ethiopia, so now Stanley Baldwin failed to join with France over the Rhineland, and again there was no firm individual or collective action.

These were portentous incidents, but more ominous than any of them was the outbreak of bitter armed conflict within Europe itself. The Spanish peninsula, so important to British and French interests, became in July 1936 the scene of a violent struggle which ended in a serious deterioration of British and French power in Europe. The civil war moved from a left-versus-right domestic struggle to a sort of international proving match of strength and weapons, in which German and Italian forces became deeply involved; and the position of the democratic powers became increasingly weak as totalitarian forces were strengthened. "Nonintervention" became a watchword of Allied policy, and still the German and Italian reinforcements of men and arms grew. Russian aid was given to the loyalists (left) but never on the scale of the axis assistance which was made available to Gen. Francisco Franco's rightist forces. Entire divisions were transported to the peninsula, and the fighting was on a fully organized scale. The war in Europe had in reality already started, but it was significantly obscured in western eyes by a fog of ideologies—communism versus the right and a stubborn refusal to face up to political and strategic realities. Refuge was taken in nonintervention pacts entered into after laborious exchanges between foreign offices but only unilaterally observed. When the fog had lifted with a Franco victory, English sea power all over the world was compromised by the weakened position of its fleet in the Mediterranean. France had another hostile European power with which to cope. The Soviet Union was more deeply isolated, and Hitler was better heeled for his impending excursions into middle Europe.

Japan again renewed its aggression by the seizure of Peiping in July 1937. Italy withdrew from the League. Through all this period the greatest potential power for peace had little to offer. The United States at this stage appeared to the world as isolationist, pacifist, neutral, disarmed, and its government had little influence upon the world situation. Others were to call the tune by which the world was to dance, and the attitude of the United States was ignored by the aggressor nations who were in a few years to be destroyed by a combination of powers of which the United States was to be the chief centre of strength.

Austria and Czechoslovakia.—While Hitler was already fighting in Spain, he was preparing at home his more ambitious plans of conquest and forging the means by which they were to be carried out.

By 1936 the paramilitary organizations of Germany were in full strength. The *Sturm Abteilungen* (SA), the *Schutzstaffel* (SS) and the *Reichsarbeitsdienst* (RAD) consisted of more than 1,500,000 men disciplined as military organizations, yet intimately involved in the social and political life of the country. They were the select exponents of the nazi doctrine. Force was the keystone of their existence. Their intermittent spectacles of massed manpower with Teuton, if not barbaric, display of colour and music gave indication of the dangerous momentum of the country. At their head was the coterie of individuals which had followed Hitler to power. Strange mixtures of zealots and opportunists placed in positions of great and self-perpetuating authority, they came to feel no limit to their ambitions or the destiny of the state they ruled. Though Hitler seems to have had a design for all his conquests, the tremendous concentration of power in the hands of this relatively small group created a psychological impulse as well as a means to act promptly and drastically. With this fearful imperative it was not long before final action was forthcoming.

Austria was marked as the first victim. Chancellor Engelbert Dollfuss had made an attempt at strengthening the government in Austria in 1933 but it was not the type of strength which Hitler sought, since it involved exclusion of nazis. After Dollfuss' assassination in 1934 by nazi storm troopers, Kurt von Schuschnigg became chancellor and under heavy external pressure in July 1936, agreed to a friendship agreement with Germany.

Not content with this arrangement and in accordance with plans laid far in advance, Hitler, with a modern modification of Canossa, first humiliated Schuschnigg at his Berchtesgaden hilltop and then forced Schuschnigg's resignation. This time full collaboration with the nazis was exacted, and on the night of March 11, 1938, German troops in their new war paint marched into Austria on the pretense that Chancellor Arthur Seyss-Inquart, the new nazi chancellor, needed them to restore order.

Next in order was Czechoslovakia; nazi propaganda began its heaviest drumfire on this front in the summer of 1938. The world heard much during this period about Hitler's rages and his "patience." So great was the instinct for appeasement, so firm the determination not to be embroiled over issues in "remote" countries, that the appeal of President Eduard Beneš for assistance brought only a blunt proposal by the French minister at Prague that unless Czechoslovakia agreed to the Anglo-French plan for the surrender of the Sudetenland to Germany with the abandonment of the highly prized border fortifications and its existing military alliance, Czechoslovakia could look elsewhere for help. It was quite clear that if Czechoslovakia refused, it had to face the rearmed might of Germany alone.

Munich.—Somewhere between Sept. 21 and Oct. 1, 1938, another opportunity for France, Britain and the U.S.S.R. to join and oppose was lost. The famous Munich agreement, from which the soviet union was excluded, was entered into on Sept. 30 and incorporated a drastic concession to Germany in the Sudeten issue. It was such an abandonment of Czechoslovakia that it represented a showdown on the one hand too humiliating for the great powers long to endure and on the other, too successful for nazi politics not to exploit. Again great pressure was placed on the Czech government to conform to the Munich agreements, and just at this stage even Poland, soon itself to be engulfed, sped an ultimatum to demand the immediate cession to it of the Teschen area. Again came capitulation, and this time President Beneš resigned and fled to London. Neville Chamberlain, Edouard Daladier and the Munich capitulation were much criticized. But individuals were condemned for a policy which was largely dictated by the people of the Allied nations themselves. Munich was generally applauded in France and Britain, and the representatives of those countries were met with welcoming crowds on their return. Prime Minister Chamberlain was following the overwhelming desire of the people of Great Britain to avoid a war which they sensed would be desperate if not worse in its consequences to them. Subconsciously, they sensed the significance of air power as not only a challenge to their long dominance of the seas but as a weapon which could be employed perhaps disastrously against the homeland itself. The people of France were in a like mood. Czechoslovakia was not in the sphere of their vital interests. It was probably time, they reasoned, that such a maladjustment as the Sudetenland should be moderated. "If we have to fight it must be on larger issues than that," said Chamberlain, echoing the sentiments of the majority when he said it. A "quarrel in a far away country between people of whom we know nothing" was not a sufficient base on which to make a stand. But if Chamberlain was doing all he could to avoid a stand which might mean war, he was merely coping with a dilemma which Stanley Baldwin had had more timely opportunity to avoid. Daladier was but following a course toward which Camille Chautemps and the rationalizing spirit of France had directed him.

The illusion of "peace in our time" which it was hoped that truce had brought was soon to be dispelled. On the night of March 14, 1939, Pres. Emil Hácha of Czechoslovakia was called to Berlin, subjected to another of Hitler's set tirades and threatened with the destruction of Prague by air. In the face of these threats, and in something like six months after Munich, all Czechoslovakia was overnight made a vassal state of Germany.

Poland and the Russo-German Pact.—Great Britain and France were belatedly aroused, if not to collective European action, at least to strong joint and individual action. Poland was so obviously the next victim that this time Great Britain made its position entirely clear in advance. An attack on Polish independence resisted by the Poles, would mean active support to Poland from Great Britain, and in this action it was stated that France would join. At this point Mussolini attacked and on April 8, 1939, seized the weakest opponent at hand—Albania.

Events moved quickly. A firm military alliance was concluded between Germany and Italy on May 9, 1939. Maxim Litvinov, soviet commissar for foreign affairs, who had been an outspoken and consistent advocate of collective security, resigned on May 3, 1939, an ominous note if one had the foresight to interpret it, for shortly thereafter and almost in the midst of protracted Allied-Soviet negotiations for collective action in the event of further German aggression, Moscow announced on Aug. 21, 1939, a ten-year treaty of nonaggression and neutrality with nazi Germany. Left out of the Austrian settlement and the Munich negotiations, suspicious of the western powers and desirous of a free hand in the Baltic states, soviet Russia joined hands with Germany on the verge of battle. Its motives were destined to be debated and its conduct alternately supported and condemned at least until the time, if ever, when history might disclose definitive proof of their true character.

The great hope of Russia from the time of the treaty of Brest-Litovsk had lain in the spread of great revolutionary movements. It was Nicolai Lenin's thought that his action in withdrawing as a participant from World War I would be followed by revolutionary developments in Germany and the German army. Subsequently, it became a tenet of the soviet faith that such movements must occur throughout the world if the full concept of soviet philosophy were to develop. In the interval between the two world wars such upheavals were not forthcoming to the degree soviet concepts required. The soviet leaders set about implanting agents and propagating soviet doctrine in the countries and dependencies of the western democracies. This doctrine of revolution, mixed with some rather involved interpretations of its own self-interest, constantly ran counter to the soviet need for collective action to meet the recrudescence of German strength. There was inculcated in its people the fear of the "imperialism" of the western democracies which rather outdid in rivalry, as the chief enemy concept, the strength of fascism or the growth of German industrial and military power. If the western European powers had been very slow to recognize the need for a soviet rapproachement, their reluctance could be understood when all the while soviet agents fomented destruction of their governments.

If Litvinov, a liberal diplomat of wide experience, did see the need and worked toward collective action, there were others in the soviet union who inspired actions which gave the democracies as much cause for suspicion as the exclusion of soviet representatives from important councils gave the soviet union.

Another strong element in Allied suspicions was the constantly recurring suggestion of soviet desire for continuing "imperialistic" wars. Indeed, until Hitler made it so unmistakably clear that the object of his chief animosity was the soviet union, Joseph Stalin seemed not to fear the nazi development in Germany. With this background it was not surprising that both British and Russian leaders should harbour the unexpressed hope that matters would so fall out that their respective countries could stand aloof while Germany became embroiled in war with the other.

After many unfortunate failures to co-operate in the solution of European problems, this conflict was put to the final test. The soviet union held out for guarantees which Britain did not feel it could give. Not receiving the price of its support, it spectacularly stood aside to permit Germany to have its way with Poland. Germany was not long in acting, and the failure of any combined Anglo-French-Russian policy to check the aggressor was to cost the soviet union unbelievable destruction and death, France utter defeat and bring England and the whole civilized world to the brink of ruin.

Hitler, with his border problems now in order, struck at Poland on Sept. 1, 1939. Great Britain and France, no longer hesitant, declared war on Germany two days after the attack; but no steps could be taken to save Poland from its fate. (*See* under section VI below, p. 763, for a discussion of the general trends of World War II.)

(J. J. McC.)

II. THE WAR IN EUROPE, AFRICA AND THE NEAR EAST

A. The German Campaign in Poland

The German conquest of Poland in Sept. 1939 was the first demonstration in war of the theory of high-speed armoured warfare which had been conceived by the British tank exponents after World War I and adopted by the Germans when their rearmament began. Although the senior German generals took a cautious view of the new technique and had developed the means for it in a measure much more limited than the tank exponents visualized, it sufficed to produce a startlingly quick victory. Poland was all too well suited for such a demonstration. Its frontiers were immensely wide—about 3,500 mi. in all. The stretch of 1,250 mi. adjoining German territory had recently been extended to 1,750 mi. by the occupation of Czechoslovakia. This had also resulted in Poland's southern flank's becoming exposed to invasion as the north flank, facing East Prussia, already was. Western Poland had become a huge salient that projected between Germany's jaws.

1. Polish Dispositions.—It would have been wiser for the Polish army to assemble farther back, behind the broad river lines of the Vistula and the San, but that would have entailed the definite abandonment of some of the most valuable parts of the country. The Silesian coal fields were close to the frontier, while most of the main industrial zone, though farther back, lay west of the river barrier. It was difficult to conceive that the Poles could have maintained their hold on the forward areas even in the most favourable circumstances, but the economic argument for making the attempt, and delaying the German approach to the main industrial zone, was heavily reinforced by national pride and military overconfidence, as well as by an exaggerated idea of what Poland's western allies could do to relieve the pressure.

The Polish army at peace strength was as large as the French and not much smaller than the German. It comprised 30 infantry divisions and 12 cavalry brigades. But Poland's industry was insufficient to make full use of its manpower or even furnish an adequate scale of equipment for its active forces. On mobilization it could increase its number of divisions by only a third, whereas Germany could more than double its divisions, except for the armoured and motorized ones; but this limitation on Germany's side was offset by Poland's almost complete lack of such modern type forces. Poland had no armoured or

German mechanized unit rolling through a Polish town battered by luftwaffe raids during the opening weeks of World War II

motorized divisions—merely a sprinkling of light tanks, while only one of its cavalry brigades was motorized; and its old-style formations were very short of both anti-tank and anti-aircraft guns. Yet many of its leaders gallantly but absurdly clung to the double belief that their preponderance of horsed cavalry was an important asset and that they could take the offensive against the German mechanized forces. They also tended to discount the effect of Germany's vastly superior air force, which was nearly ten times as powerful as their own.

The unrealism of such an attitude was repeated in the Polish dispositions. Approximately a third of the forces were concentrated in or near the Corridor (Polish Pomorze), where they were perilously exposed to a double envelopment—from East Prussia and the west combined. This indulgence of national pride was inevitably at the expense of the forces available to cover the areas more vital to Poland's defense. For in the south, facing the main avenues of approach, the forces were thinly spread. At the same time nearly another third of Poland's forces were massed in reserve north of the central axis, between Lodz and Warsaw, under the commander in chief, Marshal Edward Smigly-Rydz. This grouping embodied the offensive spirit; but its aim of intervening with a counterattack did not correspond to the Polish army's limited capacity for manoeuvre, even if this had not been cramped by German air attack on the rail and road routes of movement. The Poles' forward concentration in general forfeited their chance of fighting a series of delaying actions, since their foot-marching army was unable to get back to the positions in the rear, and man them, before being overrun by the invader's mechanized columns. In the wide spaces of Poland the unmechanized state of its forces was a heavier handicap than the fact that it was caught by surprise before all its reserves had been called up. By the same token, the 40-odd infantry divisions of normal pattern which the Germans employed in the invasion counted for much less than their 14 mechanized or partially mechanized divisions. These included six armoured divisions, four light divisions (motorized infantry with two armoured units) and four motorized divisions. It was their deep and rapid thrusts that decided the issue, in conjunction with the overhead pressure of the luftwaffe which wrecked the Polish railway system, besides destroying most of the Polish air force before it could come into action.

2. The German Offensive.—The German forces crossed the frontier shortly before 6 A.M. on Sept 1, 1939; air attacks had begun an hour earlier. In the north, the invasion was carried out by Gen. (later Field Marshal) Fedor von Bock's army group, which comprised the 3rd army under Gen. (later Field Marshal) Georg von Keuchler, and the 4th army under Gen. (later Field Marshal) Guenther von Kluge. The former thrust southward from its flanking position in East Prussia, while the latter pushed eastward across the Polish Pomorze to join it in enveloping the Poles' right flank. The greater role was given to Gen. (later Field Marshal) Karl Rudolf Gerd von Rundstedt's army group in the south. This was nearly twice as strong in infantry, and more in armour. It comprised the 8th army under Gen. (later Field Marshal) Johannes von Blaskowitz, the 10th under Gen. (later Field Marshal) Walter von Reichenau and the 14th under Gen. (later Field Marshal) Siegmund List. Blaskowitz, on the left wing, was to push toward the great manufacturing centre of Lodz and help to isolate the Polish forces in the Poznan salient, while covering Reichenau's flank. On the right wing, List was to push for Cracow and simultaneously turn the Poles' Carpathian flank, using an armoured corps to drive through the mountain passes. The decisive stroke, however, was to be delivered by Reichenau, in the centre; and for that purpose he was given the bulk of the armoured forces.

The success of the invasion was helped by the way that the Polish leaders, despising the defensive, had devoted little effort to the construction of defenses, preferring to rely on counterattacks—which they believed their army, despite its lack of machines, could effectively execute. Thus, the mechanized invaders had little difficulty in finding and penetrating open avenues of advance, while most of the Polish counterattacks broke down under the combined effect of a repulse to their forward movement and a deepening German threat to their own rear. By Sept. 3, when Britain and France entered the war, Kluge's advance had cut the Corridor and reached the lower Vistula, while Keuchler's pressure from East Prussia toward the Narew was developing. What was more important, Reichenau's armoured forces had penetrated to the Warta and forced the crossings there. Meanwhile, List's army was converging from both flanks on Cracow, forcing Gen. Antoni Szylling's army in that sector to abandon the city and fall back to the line of the Nida and the Dunajec.

By Sept. 4 Reichenau's spearheads had reached and crossed the Pilica, 50 mi. beyond the frontier. Two days later his left wing was well in the rear of Lodz, after capturing Tomaszow, and his right wing had driven into Kielce. Thus, the Polish Gen. Juliusz Rommel's army, covering the Lodz sector, was outflanked, while Gen. Stanislaw Kutrzeba's army was still far forward near Poznań, and in danger of being isolated. The other German armies had all made progress in fulfilling their part in the great enveloping manoeuvre planned by Gen. Franz Halder, the chief of the general staff, and directed by Gen. (later Field Marshal) Walther von Brauchitsch, the commander in chief. The Polish armies were splitting up into unco-ordinated fractions, some of which were retreating while others were delivering disjointed attacks on the nearest German columns.

The German advance might have travelled still faster but for a lingering conventional tendency to check the mobile forces from driving far ahead of the infantry masses that were backing them up. But as newly gained experience showed that such a risk was offset by the opponents' confusion, a bolder course was pursued. Exploiting an open gap between Lodz and the Pilica, one of Reichenau's armoured corps raced through to the outskirts of Warsaw on Sept. 8; it had covered 140 mi. in the first week. By the following day the light divisions on his right wing reached the Vistula farther south, between Warsaw and Sandomierz. They then turned northward. Meanwhile, near the Carpathians, List's mobile forces had swept across the Dunajec, Biala, Wisloka and Wislok in turn, to the San on either flank of the famous fortress of Przemysl. In the north, Keuchler's army had pushed across the Narew and was attacking the line of the Bug, in the rear of Warsaw. Thus, a wider pincer movement was strongly developing outside the inner pincers that were closing on the Polish forces in the bend of the Vistula west of Warsaw.

On Sept. 10 Marshal Smigly-Rydz issued orders for a general retreat into southeastern Poland, where Gen. Kazimierz Sosnkowski was placed in charge, with the idea of organizing a defensive position on a relatively narrow front for prolonged resistance. But this was now a vain hope. While the big encirclement west of the Vistula was being tightened, the Germans were now penetrating deeply into the area east of the Vistula. Moreover, they had

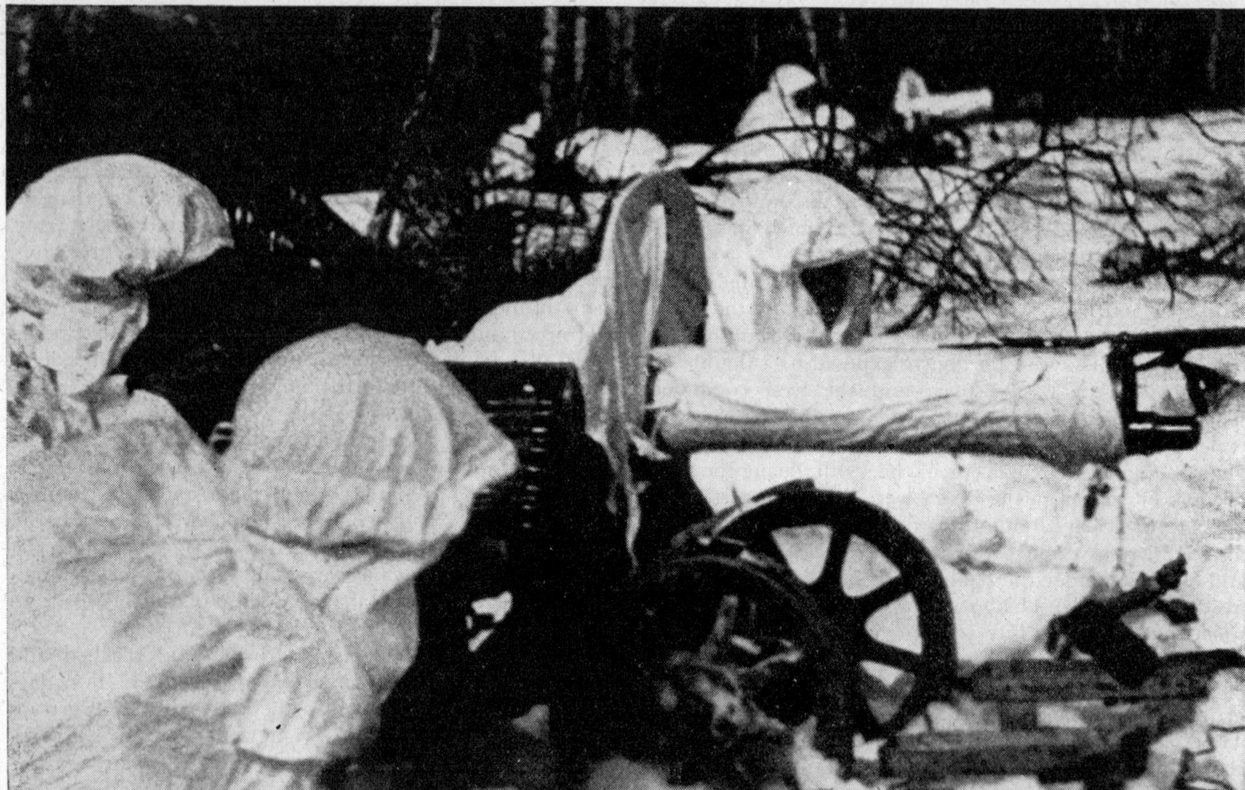

Camouflaged Red army troops manning machine guns along the Mannerheim line during the Russo-Finnish winter war of 1939–40

turned both the line of the Bug in the north and the line of the San in the south. On Keuchler's front, an armoured corps drove southward in a wide outflanking thrust to Brzesc-nad-Bugiem (Brest-Litovsk). On List's front, Gen. (later Field Marshal) Paul von Kleist's armoured corps reached the city of Lwow on Sept. 12. There the Germans were checked by Sosnkowski, but they spread northward to meet Keuchler's forces. Although the invading columns were feeling the strain of their deep advances and were running short of fuel, the Polish command system was so badly dislocated that it could not profit either by the Germans' temporary slackening or by the stubbornness that many isolated bodies of Polish troops still showed. These dissipated their energy in random efforts while the Germans were completing the encirclement.

3. The Russian Invasion.—On Sept. 17 the soviet armies crossed Poland's eastern frontier. That blow in the back sealed its fate, for there were scarcely any troops there to oppose this second invasion. Next day the Polish government and high command crossed the Rumanian frontier, the commander in chief sending back a message to tell his troops to fight on. Perhaps it was as well that it did not reach most of them, but many gallantly fulfilled its intention in the days that followed, although their resistance collapsed bit by bit. The garrison of Warsaw held out until Sept. 28, despite heavy bombardment from the air and the ground; and the last considerable Polish fragment did not surrender until Oct. 5, while guerrilla resistance continued into the winter. About 80,000 escaped over neutral frontiers. The German and Russian forces had met and greeted each other, as partners, on a line running south from East Prussia past the Narew-Bug line and Przemysl to the Carpathians. That partnership was sealed, but not cemented, by the mutual partition of Poland.

B. The Russo-Finnish Winter War

Following the partition of Poland, the soviet government made haste to underwrite its forward security policy by re-establishing strategic control of Russia's former buffer territories in the Baltic. By Oct. 10, 1939, Estonia, Latvia and Lithuania were induced to allow soviet forces to garrison key points on their soil. On Oct. 14 similar demands were presented to Finland. Considered from the viewpoint of strategic safeguards—against Hitler's possible use of Finnish territory as a springboard for attack on the U.S.S.R.—they were moderate, and the small cessions of territory required of Finland were to be compensated by the U.S.S.R.'s giving up strips elsewhere. But national sentiment made it hard for the Finns to agree to a settlement on these lines. When they continued to argue the points, the soviet forces invaded their country on Nov. 30.

1. Early Finnish Successes.—The original advance ended in a check that astonished the world. A direct push from Leningrad up the Karelian isthmus came to a halt in the forward layers of the deep and well-fortified Mannerheim line. A flanking advance north of Lake Ladoga made no better progress. At the other end of the front the Russians cut off the small port of Petsamo on the Arctic ocean, as a means of blocking the entry of help to Finland by that route. Two more immediately menacing thrusts were delivered across the waist of Finland. The more northerly thrust penetrated past Salla to Kemijärvi, halfway to the Gulf of Bothnia, before it was driven back by the counterattack of a Finnish division which had been switched up by rail from the south. The southerly thrust, past Suomussalmi, was interrupted in turn by a counterstroke, early in Jan. 1940. Circling round the invaders' flanks, the Finns blocked their line of supply and retreat, waited until their troops were exhausted by cold and hunger, then attacked and broke them up.

Sympathy with Finland as a fresh victim of aggression had rapidly developed into enthusiasm at the apparent success of the weak in repulsing the strong. This impression had far-reaching repercussions. It prompted the French and British governments to consider the dispatch of an expeditionary force to this new theatre of war with the object, not only of aiding Finland, but of securing the Swedish iron mines at Gällivare from which Germany drew supplies, while establishing themselves in a position that threatened Germany's Baltic flank. Partly because of the objections raised by Norway and Sweden, this project did not materialize before Finland collapsed. France and Britain were thus spared entanglement in war with the U.S.S.R. as well as with Germany—at a time when their own powers of defense were perilously weak. But the obvious threat of an Allied move into Scandinavia precipitated Hitler's decision to forestall it by occupying Norway. Another effect of Finland's early successes was that it reinforced the tendency in western quarters to underrate the soviet military strength. The general view was epitomized in Winston Churchill's broadcast assertion of Jan. 20, 1940, that Finland "had exposed, for the world to see, the military incapacity of the red army." His misjudgment was to some extent shared by Hitler—with momentous consequences the following year.

More dispassionate examination of the campaign, however, provided better reasons for the ineffectiveness of the original advance. There was no sign of proper preparation to mount a powerful offensive, furnished with large stocks of munitions and equipment. There were clear signs that the soviet authorities had been misled by their sources of information about the situation in Finland, and that, instead of reckoning on serious resistance, they imagined that they might have to do no more than back up a popular rising of the Finnish people against an unpopular government. The country cramped an invader at every turn, being full of natural obstacles that narrowed the avenues of approach and helped the defense. Between Lake Ladoga and the Arctic ocean the frontier appeared very wide on the map but in reality was a tangle of lakes and forests, ideal for laying traps as well as for stubborn resistance. Moreover, on the soviet side of the frontier the rail communications consisted of the solitary line from Leningrad to Murmansk, which in its 800-mi. stretch had only one branch leading to the Finnish frontier. This limitation was reflected in the fact that the "waist-line" thrusts which sounded so formidable in the highly coloured reports from Finland were made with only one division apiece, while only two were employed in the outflanking manoeuvre north of Ladoga.

2. Mannerheim Line Crushed.—Much the best approach to Finland was through the Karelian isthmus, but this was blocked by the Mannerheim line, while the Finns' six active divisions were concentrated there at the outset. The Russian thrusts farther north, though they fared badly, served the purpose of drawing part of the Finnish reserves thither while thorough preparations were being made, and 14 divisions brought up, for a serious attack on the Mannerheim line. This was launched on Feb. 1, under the direction of Gen. Kizil A. Meretskov. Its weight was concentrated on a ten-mile sector near Summa, which was pounded by a tremendous artillery bombardment. As the fortifications were pulverized, tanks and sledge-carried infantry advanced to occupy the ground, while the Russian air force broke up attempted countermoves. After little more than a fortnight of this methodical process a breach was made through the whole depth of the Mannerheim line. The attackers then wheeled outward to corner the Finnish forces on either flank, before pushing on to Viipuri (Viborg). A wider flanking operation was carried out across the frozen Gulf of Finland by troops who advanced from the ice-bound island of Hogland and landed well in the rear of Viipuri. Although an obstinate defense was still maintained for several weeks in front of Viipuri, Finland's limited forces had been worn down in the effort to hold the Karelian isthmus. Once a passage was forced, and their communications menaced, eventual collapse was certain. Capitulation was the only way in which it could be averted, since the proffered Anglo-French expeditionary force had not arrived, though almost ready to sail. Field Marshal Carl Gustav Emil von Mannerheim, the Finnish commander in chief, had been too optimistic in estimating that Finland could hold out with its own resources until after the spring thaw. On March 6, 1940, the Finnish government sent a delegation to negotiate peace, and on March 13 it was announced that the soviet terms had been accepted. They were not much more severe than those proposed in the first place.

C. German Campaigns in Denmark, Norway

As the Nuernberg trials later brought out, the German conquest of Norway and Denmark was the first of Hitler's aggressions which was not long premeditated. He was led into it unwillingly by the combined effect of persuasion from some of his followers and provocation from his opponents' moves. The persuasion started from the arguments of Vidkun Quisling, the Norwegian pronazi, about the possibility of the British occupying the Norwegian coast, with or without the consent of the Norwegian government. It was reinforced by Adm. Erich Raeder who, in Oct. 1939, pointed out both the danger of such a development and the advantage to Germany of occupying that coast to loosen the grip of the British blockade. Further incitement came from British and French talk of various moves to rally the neutrals to their side and threaten Germany's flanks. This possibility was increased by Allied offers of aid to Finland.

As late as Dec. 18, 1939, Hitler—in private discussions with the advocates of the Norwegian project—emphasized that he would prefer that Norway, as well as the rest of Scandinavia, remain completely neutral; he did not intend to enlarge the theatres of war and draw other nations into the conflict—unless "the enemy took such steps with the aim of further throttling and threatening Germany." But in Jan. 1940 Winston Churchill, in a broadcast, addressed the neutrals on their duty to join in the fight against Hitler, while other signs of an Allied move multiplied. Toward the end of the month Hitler approved a preparatory study of the problem of seizing the Norwegian ports. Then on Feb. 18, 1940, the British destroyer "Cossack," on orders from the admiralty, pushed up Josing fjord and forcibly rescued naval prisoners from the "Altmark," a German vessel which had taken refuge there. This action infuriated Hitler and was the spark that ignited the powder trail. On Feb. 21 he appointed Gen. Nikolaus von Falkenhorst to prepare the forces for an invasion of Norway, and of Denmark too, as a necessary strategic steppingstone. On April 2 he gave the order for the invasion to be launched a week later.

When the Germans later captured the French archives they found reason for self-justification and self-congratulation in the evidence of how narrowly they had forestalled the Allies. These documents showed that from Jan. 1940 onward the latter had been discussing plans for extending the expedition to help Finland, which they were preparing, into "the seizure of ports and aerodromes on the west coast of Norway," and the further step of "occupying the iron ore mines at Gällivare," in the north of Sweden. On Feb. 21 the French prime minister, Edouard Daladier, urged that the "Altmark" incident should be used as a ground for the immediate seizure of the Norwegian ports. This initiative was regarded with some doubt in London, as the forces were not ready and Neville Chamberlain still hoped that the Scandinavian governments would agree to the entry of Allied troops. At a meeting on March 11, however, Churchill unfolded a scheme of arriving in force off Narvik and throwing a detachment ashore immediately, on the principle of "displaying a strength in order to avoid having to use it." These projects were temporarily upset by Finland's capitulation on March 13, but a fortnight later it was agreed that fresh pressure should be applied to the governments of Norway and Sweden. A mine-laying operation in Norwegian waters was to be carried out on April 5, and the first convoy of troops was to sail for Narvik three days later.

1. German Invasion.—These dreams were abruptly dispelled. The mine laying did not take place until April 8. In the dark hours of the following morning small detachments of German troops, carried mostly in warships, arrived in or near the chief ports of Norway, from Oslo right up to Narvik, and captured them with little difficulty. Their commanders announced to the local authorities that they had come to take Norway under German protection against an Allied invasion that was imminent. A similar announcement had been made by the German minister in Oslo when, just after 4 A.M., he paid a sudden call on the Norwegian foreign minister; and the same was done in Denmark at the same hour. The total force that executed this string of coups was very limited. It comprised 7 cruisers, 14 destroyers, a number of auxiliary craft and the leading elements of 6 divisions—amounting altogether to about 10,000 troops. One parachute battalion was also employed, the first time that parachute troops had been used in war. While they made an important contribution to the German success, the most decisive factor, as in Poland, was the luftwaffe. It overawed the Norwegian people in the first phase and later paralyzed the Allies' countermeasures.

The most astonishing of the opening series of coups was that at Narvik, for this far northern port was about 1,200 mi. distant from the German naval bases. On the evening of April 8 the Norwegian naval authorities were notified by the British admiralty that a number of German warships appeared to be making for Narvik. One of the two Norwegian coast-defense ships went out to the mouth of the fjord as a precaution but was quickly sunk by the attacking force, which comprised six of Germany's latest destroyers. The other Norwegian warship met them on their arrival in the harbour and scored some damaging hits before it was sunk. But the shore defenses made no attempt at resistance; the local commander was a close friend of Quisling. Next day a British destroyer flotilla steamed up the fjord and fought a mutually damaging action with the Germans, and then on April 13 these were finished off by the inroad of a stronger flotilla supported by the battleship "Warspite." But the opportunity for a landing was not exploited and the German troops were allowed time to establish themselves firmly in and around Narvik.

Farther south, Trondhjem was captured with ease after the German ships had run the gauntlet of the batteries dominating the fjord—a hazard that had dismayed Allied experts who had considered the problem. By securing Trondhjem, the Germans had possessed themselves of the strategic key to central Norway, though the question remained whether their handful of troops there could be reinforced from the south. At Bergen, Stavanger and Kristiansand the Germans suffered some damage from the Norwegian warships and batteries but had little trouble once they were ashore. They also landed small detachments at Arendal and Egersund on the south coast. In the approach to Oslo, however, the main invading force suffered a jolt. For the large cruiser "Bluecher," carrying many of the military staff, was sunk by torpedoes from the Oscarsborg fortress, and the attempt to force the passage was then given up until this fortress surrendered in the afternoon, after heavy air attack. Thus, the capture of Norway's capital devolved on the troops who had landed on the Fornebu airfield; in the afternoon this token force staged a parade march into the city, and their bluff succeeded. But the delay at least enabled the king and the government to escape northward with a view to rallying resistance.

The capture of Copenhagen was timed to coincide with the intended arrival at Oslo. The Danish capital was easy of access from the sea, and shortly before 5 A.M. three small transports steamed into the harbour, covered by aircraft overhead. The Germans met no resistance on landing and a battalion marched off to take the barracks by surprise. At the same time Denmark's land frontier in Jutland was invaded, but after a brief exchange of fire resistance was abandoned. The occupation of Denmark went far to ensure the Germans' control of a sheltered sea corridor from their own ports to southern Norway and also gave them advanced airfields from which they could support the troops there. While the Danes might have fought longer, their country was so vulnerable as to be hardly defensible against a powerful attack with modern weapons.

Norway should have been a much tougher problem. But at all points the invaders' path was eased because, despite the warnings from the Norwegian minister in Berlin and urgings from the chief of the general staff, no order for mobilization was given until the fateful night of April 8–9. The Allies were also caught napping. Although for three months they were busy with schemes for establishing themselves in Scandinavia, and thus threatening Germany's flank, they failed to make adequate preparations and have suitable forces ready for a prompt counter to a German invasion. Speaking in the house of commons on April 11, Winston Churchill, then first lord of the admiralty, dwelt on Hitler's "grave strategic error" and declared: "I feel we are greatly advantaged by what has occurred, provided we act with increasing and increasing vigour to turn to the utmost profit the strategic blunder into which our mortal foe has been provoked." The final word was of historical significance. But it was soon made clear that such "vigour" did not mean a willingness to venture into the Skaggerak and Kattegat with surface warships in an effort to interrupt the flow of German reinforcements to Norway. Fear of German air attack forbade it. Caution also prevailed to cancel an attempt to force an entry into the Trondhjem fjord and eject the Germans from that key point before it was too late.

2. Allied Landings in Norway.—The land effort was even more feeble. It was not until April 12 that the first convoy of the force under Gen. P. J. Mackesy which had been allotted for Narvik originally, before the German invasion, sailed from the Clyde. It comprised only two infantry brigades, and on the way to Narvik one of these, the 146th, was diverted to Namsos. This was the result of a new plan for a further expedition, under Gen. Sir Adrian

Carton de Wiart, to regain Trondhjem. Before the direct attack, the 146th was to be landed north of it, at Namsos, together with a further brigade. But then the plan was changed, and the latter was sent to land at Andalsnes, south of Trondhjem, the idea being that the two thrusts would act as diversions to cloak and assist the attack on Trondhjem. These landings began on April 16 and 18, respectively, after naval detachments had earlier occupied the harbours. Both were made without loss. Then the plan was changed again. It was decided to exploit these footholds for a pincer move against Trondhjem and thus avoid the risks of forcing a passage into the Trondhjem fjord. The landing at Namsos was reinforced by a demi-brigade of French *chasseurs alpins*, also diverted from Narvik; and a second British brigade was sent to Andalsnes. Gen. Sir Bernard Paget was sent to handle the latter pincer while Gen. Carton de Wiart was left in charge of the former, and Lieut. Gen. H. R. S. Massy was to command the whole.

On paper the chances looked good, for there were less than 2,000 German troops in the Trondhjem area, whereas the Allies had 13,000. The advance south from Namsos, however, was clogged by the deep snow and then upset by the threat to its rear produced by the landing of several small German detachments near the top of the Trondhjem fjord, supported by the one destroyer which the Germans had in the area. Carton de Wiart's forces fell back north of Steinkjer and were so harried by air attacks that on April 23 he suggested their evacuation. The advance from Andalsnes reached Dombas in the Gudbrand valley on April 19 but instead of being able to wheel north on Trondhjem, it quickly turned into a defense of its own communications against the German troops who were pushing up the valley from Oslo and brushing back the Norwegians. From Dombas the 148th brigade was sent down the valley to support the Norwegians at Lillehammer but was soon driven back on the 15th brigade, which had taken up a position at Kvam, south of Dombas. On April 25 General Massy reported that the British lodgment in central Norway could be maintained only if sufficient air support was provided to check the luftwaffe, which was severely harassing the valley and the base. As this was not possible, two days later he advised evacuation, and the authorities at home agreed. The decision naturally met with strong protest from the indomitable Norwegian commander in chief, Gen. Otto Ruge, but was justified by a realistic view of the prospect, now that the invaders' strength was growing. After covering the northward retreat of the scattered Norwegians, Paget's force began its withdrawal down the Rom valley to the sea. The re-embarkation at Andalsnes was completed on the night of May 1, and the force at Namsos was evacuated on the following night. The Germans were thus left in complete control of southern and central Norway.

3. Narvik Episode.—The Allies now concentrated on gaining Narvik, more for "face-saving" purposes than from any continued hope of reaching the Swedish iron mines. The original Allied landing in that area had been made on April 14, and the Allied forces were eventually built up to a strength of about 15,000 men (including a French and a Polish brigade), while the Norwegian forces there were on similar scale. But progress was slow. The 2,000 Austrian alpine troops who had been used to seize Narvik had been reinforced by as many sailors from the disabled German destroyers; skilfully handled by Gen. Eduard Dietl, they made the most of the defensive advantages of the difficult country. Heavy snowstorms also delayed both preparations and operations so that Narvik was not wrested from the Germans until May 28. By this time the German offensive in the west had driven deep into France, and the Allies were now more concerned with saving themselves from decisive defeat there than in saving their faces in Scandinavia. So on June 7 the Allied forces were evacuated from Narvik. The king and the government had left Norway for England, and the Norwegian forces laid down their arms.

Nazi troops (background) in Oslo shortly after the occupation of Norway in April 1940. The two unarmed Norwegian policemen in the foreground were helpless onlookers

D. The Western Front, First Phase

1. The "Phony War."—When the Germans invaded Poland on Sept. 1, 1939, they left only 23 divisions in the west. The French mobilized nearly five times as many divisions. The German generals themselves felt that their western front was dangerously underinsured, but they could see no way of increasing the insurance without forfeiting their chance of a quick victory over Poland. Their anxiety proved excessive. The French had hardly dented the foremost layers of the defense before the Germans had overrun Poland and returned in force to the west. The French advance was confined to the 100-mi. stretch of the common Franco-German frontier between the Rhine and the Luxembourg border, and any pressure was limited to narrow sectors of this stretch. At the end of the month, following the collapse of Poland, the French command decided to withdraw its divisions to the shelter of its own Maginot line. Then stagnation settled on the western front for the next seven months.

The German command felt that the French had never seriously tried to attack and had thereby let slip a great opportunity. The first assumption was true; the second more doubtful. The French army was a ponderous machine, with a tactical doctrine to match, and thus had little capacity for rapid action. Even if the French army had been fitted for manoeuvre, room for manoeuvre was lacking as long as Belgium remained neutral. On Sept. 1 Gen. Maurice Gustave Gamelin, the French commander in chief, addressed a memorandum to his government which

German frontier sentries on duty along the western front during the winter of 1939–40, the period of the "phony war" which was described in communiques of the day as "the usual inactivity"

argued that the only way of success would lie in "extending our front of attack" from the Moselle to Maastricht, for an advance through Belgium and Dutch territory to the lower Rhine. If Belgium and the Netherlands would not agree to this, and the French government was unwilling to override their neutrality, the prospect was dim. As this wider alternative was ruled out, Gamelin did not see any point in courting heavy loss and wearing down the French army's morale by pressing the attack on the Rhine-Moselle sector.

While Germany clearly benefited from the neutrality of Belgium and the Netherlands at this stage of the war, it was doubtful whether the alternative that Gamelin desired would have made any important difference to the fate of Poland. For the mobilization of the French army was not completed until Sept. 20, and the leading British army corps arrived at the front only in the first week of October, whereas most of Poland was overrun by the third week of September. But the prospects of subsequent resistance to a German offensive in the west might have been greater if the French armies had been permitted to advance into Belgium in September. The situation was radically changed with the collapse of Poland. The scales of forces in the west now tilted heavily to the German side, and the primary problem of the French was to assure their own defense. In these different circumstances, however, they still favoured the idea of an advance into Belgium, even if it could be carried out only *after* a German invasion of Belgium. That was a more questionable decision. Their own army was not well fitted to execute such a racing manoeuvre and establish itself firmly on a fresh line at short notice.

The widespread view that the French leaders were too defensive minded is a fallacy. During the months that followed the fall of Poland, Gamelin showed a hankering for the offensive and mooted various provocative moves to threaten Germany's flanks, even though he had to admit that the means were lacking. That urge to do something, however unpromising the chances, was stimulated by political criticism of Gamelin's "caution," particularly from Paul Reynaud, whose cry for bold and early action brought him growing political influence, as usually happens in a democracy at war. The pressure of such tendencies could be traced in the development of the French plan to meet a German invasion of Belgium. The first idea was that the two armies on the extreme left, the French 7th army and the British, should advance a short distance across the frontier and occupy a position along the Escaut river as far as Ghent, there linking up with the Belgian army, which was expected to fall back on the line Antwerp-Ghent. This was extended by November into plan D, which embraced a 60-mi. advance to the line of the Dyle, east of Brussels, and a general wheel forward of the French left centre to correspond. In March a third development in the plan gave it a still more venturesome turn. The French 7th army was to dash up the Belgian coast past Antwerp into the Netherlands, so that it could not only buttress the joint between the Belgian and Dutch armies, but strike at the flank of the Germans advancing into Belgium.

The plan and the distribution of forces expressed the twin convictions of the French high command. One was that the Germans would make their main effort in the plain of Belgium, north of Namur, as in 1914. The other was that no serious stroke could be delivered south of Namur, through the Ardennes, because of the difficulties presented by that hilly and wooded belt of country. This proved a fatal delusion. Yet if the German offensive had been launched when Hitler intended, in November, Gamelin's plan might well have succeeded in checking it on the Dyle, while at the worst a decisive defeat of the French would have been unlikely. But Hitler's desire was repeatedly postponed by the weather, coupled with the hesitation of his generals. And when at last the German offensive was delivered, six months late, its plan had been so changed as to profit decisively from the nature of the French plan.

The centre of gravity was shifted from Gen. (later Field Marshal) Fedor von Bock's army group B on the right, facing the main plain of Belgium, to Gen. (later Field Marshal) Gerd von Rundstedt's army group A facing the wooded hill-belt of Belgian Luxembourg. The change was suggested by Gen. (later Field Marshal) Fritz Erich von Manstein, Rundstedt's chief of staff, who argued that the tank forces could be effectively used in the Ardennes, contrary to orthodox ideas, and that the risk of a check would be less than if they met the main mass of the Allied forces head-on in the centre of Belgium. Manstein's proposal was regarded as too hazardous by the heads of the German army; but its boldness appealed to Hitler, who, in March, secured its adoption. The French advance into Belgium now played into the hands of the Germans in the same way that the French advance of 1914 into Lorraine and the Ardennes had done. It was, however, the employment of fast-moving armoured vehicles, instead of foot-marching infantry masses, that made the vital difference to the result in 1940 compared with 1914.

The period that popular opinion christened the "phony war" was far from being such in reality. It was a period when the Allies were projecting offensive schemes which they lacked the power to execute, and when Hitler was repeatedly mounting an offensive, only to be compelled to defer it, contrary to his desire, but to his advantage.

2. German Conquest of the Low Countries and France. —Following the dramatic success of his April coup in Norway, Hitler became more eager to attempt the deferred stroke in the west. But it was not until May 7, 1940, that the first warning order since January was actually issued. On May 8 Hitler was "very agitated" by reports that the Dutch were accelerating their precautions and might allow the British to reinforce them. The invasion was launched in the early hours of May 10. Under the remodelled plan, Bock's army group B comprised two armies instead of the former three. The 18th army, under Gen. (later Field Marshal) Georg von Keuchler, invaded the Netherlands with the aid of an armoured division and air-borne forces, while the 6th army (Gen. Walter von Reichenau) advanced along the main avenue into Belgium, with the aid of an armoured corps. These two German armies had to deal with the Dutch and Belgian armies, the British expeditionary force (now grown to 13 divisions, of which 9 were available there) and 2 of the best-equipped French armies. Lacking superiority of numbers there, the Germans depended on surprise and superior skill. Rundstedt's army group A covered the stretch between the middle Meuse and the Moselle. Its strength had been raised to more than 80 divisions, of which 7 were armoured. Once it had brushed aside the screen of Belgian troops in the Ardennes it had only to deal with two French armies consisting of 12 infantry divisions—half of them low-grade—and 4 horsed cavalry divisions. Against this weak hinge of the Allied wheel forward into Belgium were massed nearly two-thirds of Germany's forces in the west, and nearly three-quarters of its armoured punch. Along the Franco-German frontier, between the Moselle and Switzerland, stood Gen. (later Field Marshal) Wilhelm von Leeb's army group C, comprising two armies. Its task was merely to threaten an attack on the Maginot line and thus pin down the excessively large proportion of the French forces that were arrayed there. For 41 divisions were posted in and behind that well-fortified sector, compared with 39 on the longer sector between the Maginot line and the Channel coast, while the larger part of the French general reserve was also on this flank. The responsibility for those fatal dispositions lay more directly with Gen. Alphonse Joseph Georges, the commander in chief of the armies on the northeast front, than with Gamelin. For the moment that danger was obscured by the dramatic opening of the campaign in the Low Countries.

(*a*) *Conquest of the Netherlands.*—The Dutch army comprised ten divisions and the equivalent of a further ten in smaller formations. It should thus on paper have had a very good chance of withstanding the German invasion, since its front was covered by successive rivers, while the attacking army comprised only seven divisions, apart from the air-borne forces. But the Dutch had a wide front, very sensitive and densely crowded rear, poor equipment in modern weapons and no experience of modern war. Apart from air superiority, the German offensive depended for its success primarily on the air-borne forces. Contrary to popular imagination after the event, these forces were on a small scale. Four parachute battalions were used, together with a regiment of air-transported infantry, to seize the bridges at Moerdyk, Dordrecht and Rotterdam, on the main road artery from the south into the heart of the Netherlands, with the aim of opening the way for the mobile ground forces. One parachute battalion, followed by two air-transported regiments, descended on the airfields around The Hague with the aim of capturing the main government buildings. The attack on the capital did not succeed, though it caused a lot of confusion and thus aided the invader's purpose. But the bridges were captured with very slight loss, and the defense was too disorganized to dislodge the troops who had dropped out of the sky before they were reinforced by forces arriving overland.

While the invasion could hardly have triumphed without this capture of the backdoor, the air-borne coup would have mattered little if the Dutch front had not broken down at a specially vulnerable spot.

Gen. Hendrik Gerard Winkelman, the Dutch commander in chief, was mainly concerned to cover the direct approach into the heart of the Netherlands. Out of his four army corps, two were massed on the Geld valley position, between the Maas (Meuse) and the Zuider Zee, while another was in reserve behind them. The remaining corps had held the Peel line south of the Maas; but, just before the invasion came, the Dutch command came to the conclusion that it would be safer to concentrate on holding the central part of the Netherlands, covered by the great rivers. So the army corps in the south was withdrawn, leaving the Peel line to be held by a screen composed of lower-grade troops who lacked antitank and anti-aircraft guns. Nothing could have been better designed to suit the German aim of bringing quick reinforcement to the air-borne troops near Rotterdam.

On May 10 the Germans penetrated the Peel line. The next day the defenders retreated due west past Tilburg toward Breda, thus leaving a clear road by which the solitary German armoured division could drive northwestward to the Moerdyk bridge. That same afternoon the leading mobile troops of Gen. Henri Giraud's French 7th army reached Tilburg, after a remarkable 140-mi. dash from the French frontier. Disconcerted by the Dutch retreat and German air attack, they fell back on Breda. By May 12 they had been reinforced but made no serious attempt to advance over the farther ten-mile strip to the Maas and bar the German armoured division's passage to Moerdyk. This reached the outskirts of Rotterdam soon after midday. Meanwhile, the main German forces had spent two days in closing up to the Geld valley line. On May 12 they made a narrow breach in it. Lacking reserves on the spot for effective counterattack, the Dutch command decided to abandon this line and fall back on the "fortress of Holland" line, just in front of Amsterdam and Utrecht. Its defense was never tested; for by the time the Germans closed up to it, late on May 14, the campaign had been brought to an end.

The Germans had made no progress at Rotterdam on May 13, and their situation there might have again become precarious since it formed a narrow wedge thrust far forward between the Dutch and French forces. But it was difficult for the Dutch to see the situation in such a light. They were more conscious that most of their country had been swiftly overrun and that the roar of German aircraft filled their ears. The queen and the government sailed for England on May 13, leaving the country in charge of General Winkelman. By the next afternoon he had decided to surrender. That decision was produced not only by the blackness of the outlook but by the threat of bombing the cities of Rotterdam and Utrecht if resistance continued. Such action was in accord with the old laws of warfare governing the bombardment of besieged places, since both cities were now in the fighting zone. But its technical legality did not diminish its inhumanity as a means of moral pressure. Rotterdam was actually bombed, through a fault in signal communications, after the Dutch had yielded to the threat. The horror it produced was shown in the way the statement that this bombing, by a mere 30 planes, had killed 30,000 people was credited, and continued to be believed long after bombings of 10 times such a scale had been found to kill only a fraction of the figure.

(*b*) *Conquest of Belgium, First Phase.*—The direct invasion of Belgium was made with stronger forces than were used against the Netherlands, but with only a handful of air-borne troops. Reichenau's 6th army deployed 4 army corps abreast on the 30-mi. Roermond-Aachen front and also included Gen. Erich Hoeppner's armoured corps. The air-borne troops consisted of a mere 500. To compensate for the shortage, dummy parachutists were dropped over a wide area, thus accounting for the reports that "thousands of parachutists" were descending on the country. At the start of the invasion of the west, the main weight of the German air force, of the dive bombers in particular, was concentrated on the gateway into Belgium, before being switched south to help in the passage of the upper Meuse around Sedan. That concentration of air bombardment was the invaders' biggest asset in gaining an ascendancy over the Belgian defense. The tiny element of air-borne troops, however, counted for almost as much. For it was they who secured the keys to the gate.

The most delicate point of the Belgian forward position lay north of Liége, where the Maastricht "appendix" of Dutch territory protruded between the Belgian and German frontiers, forming an indefensible strip that could mask an approach to the Albert canal, which there formed the Belgian frontier line. The invaders' chances turned on gaining the bridges at that point before they could be blown up, and preventing the guns of Eben Emael, Belgium's most modern fort, from dominating them subsequently. Early on May 10, before it was light, a platoon in gliders landed at the back of each bridge and captured each intact. Other gliders landed on the top of Eben Emael and dropped explosives into the guns and the exits unobserved by the garrison inside—which was thus helplessly imprisoned in its now useless fort. By the morning of May 11 sufficient German troops had accumulated beyond the canal to burst through the Belgian line. The leading armoured division now drove through to the west, while part of the infantry wheeled south and entered Liége from the rear. That evening the Belgian command (King Leopold III, commander in chief; Gen. F. F. O. Michiels, chief of staff) ordered a general withdrawal to the Antwerp-Namur (or Dyle) line, where the leading Allied divisions had just arrived—the French 1st army (under Gen. Georges Blanchard) occupying the sector from Namur to Wavre, the British (under Viscount Gort) occupying the sector from Wavre to Louvain, while the Belgians wheeled back to hold the sector from Louvain to Antwerp.

In view of the imminent collapse of the Belgians' forward position, the French advance to the Dyle line had been accelerated on May 11, and from there Gen. René Prioux's cavalry corps (of two light mechanized divisions) pushed on eastward to meet the Germans. It was too late to check the break-through on the Albert canal, but it helped to cover the Belgians' retreat from Liége. Falling back by stages, Prioux checked a series of German tank thrusts on May 12–13. During the second night his corps withdrew to an antitank obstacle a few miles in front of the main position. On May 14 the Germans made a powerful effort to break through in the direction of Gembloux, and a big tank battle developed. Although Prioux prevented a complete break-through, his corps was so badly mauled by the afternoon that it had to be withdrawn to reorganize behind the main position, which was now solidly occupied by the rest of the 1st army. When the Germans attacked the next morning, they were checked. Immediately afterward, Hoeppner's armoured corps was sent south to join Rundstedt's army group. Its disappearance appeared to increase the French prospects of holding this end of the Dyle line, while no pressure at all had yet developed on the British sector. But on the evening of May 15 Gamelin ordered its abandonment. For by then Rundstedt's armoured forces, which had crossed the Meuse at Sedan on May 13, were driving deep into France. It had now become a question for the Allies, not whether they could hold out in Belgium, but whether they could escape being cut off there.

(*c*) *Thrust into France.*—The break-through from the Ardennes across the Meuse turned more on the approach march than on the battle. The passage of such great forces through such a difficult belt of country as the Ardennes was an amazing feat of staff work. Rundstedt's army group comprised, from right to left, the 4th army (Gen., later Field Marshal, Guenther von Kluge), the 12th army (Gen., later Field Marshal, Siegmund List) and the 16th army (Gen., later Field Marshal, Ernst Busch), while the 2nd army (Gen., later Field Marshal, Maximilian von Weichs) was in reserve. But its thrust was provided by two armoured groups: a large one under Gen. Paul von Kleist and a smaller one under Gen. Hermann Hoth. The solution of the approach march problem was both bold and ingenious. While the armoured divisions used such roads as were available through that hilly and wooded belt, infantry divisions started alongside them by using field paths and marched so fast across country that the leading ones reached the Meuse only a day after the armoured divisions.

Early on May 10 Kleist's leading troops crossed the frontier of Luxembourg, where they met only road obstructions. In three hours they reached the frontier of Belgian Luxembourg, 30 mi. beyond. There they found bridges blown up and met opposition, first from the Belgian *Chasseurs Ardennais* and then from French horsed cavalry. The French paid forfeit for pushing old-fashioned cavalry divisions deep into the Ardennes in face of armoured divisions. By the next evening they were driven back across the Semois in disorder and had suffered such losses as to ease the Germans' task in forcing the difficult passage of that river. Georges now ordered reinforcements to that sector, but their arrival was too slow to match the German rate of movement.

By the evening of May 12 the Germans were across the French frontier, and overlooking the Meuse. The blow was about to fall not only on the hinge of the French advance into Belgium but on the joint between two armies: Gen. Charles Huntziger's 2nd army and Gen. André Corap's 9th. Huntziger's left wing, from Sedan eastward, was composed of two reserve divisions of oldish men. Corap's right wing, west of Sedan, was of similar composition. The defenses were rudimentary; it was the least fortified stretch of the whole French front. Worse still, they had hardly any antitank guns and no anti-aircraft artillery. Such was the measure of the trust placed in the unlikelihood of an armoured thrust through the Ardennes.

On May 13 Kleist's forces achieved a three-fold crossing —by Gen. Heinz Guderian's corps at two points near Sedan, and by Gen. Georg Hans Reinhardt's corps at Monthermé. At Sedan, wave after wave of dive bombers swooped on the defenders of the south bank. These could not stand the nerveracking strain, and the German troops were able to push across the river in rubber boats and on rafts. The tremendous air bombardment was the decisive factor in the crossings. A thousand aircraft supported Kleist's forces while only a few French aircraft intervened in a gallant but hopeless effort to aid their troops on the ground. On May 14 the breakout began, after the tanks had crossed the bridges. Guderian's corps swung westward, its nose pointed to the Channel coast. The French collapse spread next day as Reinhardt's corps joined in the pressure.

There was no "battle of the bulge," such as was vividly described in the Allied reports at the time. It was a procession in quick time along an almost empty corridor behind the backs of the Allied armies in Belgium. Meanwhile, further crossings had been made to the west, between Givet and Namur. Thus, in two days the breach had widened to 60 mi., and any French positions remaining had become mere islets lapped and left behind by the waves of the armoured torrent that was now sweeping through the corridor between the Sambre and the Aisne. Giraud was now sent to replace Corap and reinforcements followed. But there again the measures were inadequate and taken too late. When he arrived, on May 15, he drew up a plan for a counteroffensive to block the corridor on a line 25 mi. west of the Meuse. But a day later he found that the forces were not available, while the Germans had advanced in strength far beyond their line. So he now decided to withdraw to the line of the Oise, 30 mi. farther back, and block the Germans there. Once again he was too late, for the German armoured divisions outran his retreating troops and were across that barrier on May 17. Even if the French had been able to mount a counteroffensive, they would not have found it easy to crush the invaders' flank. For Kleist's southern flank was progressively lined by his motorized divisions, which in turn were relieved by the infantry corps that were marching on as fast as possible.

This lining of the Aisne had an important indirect effect—by playing on the most instinctive fear of the French. For on May 15 Gamelin received an alarming report that the Germans were crossing the Aisne between Rethel and Laon. He told the government that he had no reserves between that sector and Paris and that he could not guarantee the security of the capital for more than a day. After Gamelin's startling message the French premier, Reynaud, hastily decided to evacuate the government from Paris to Tours. By evening more reassuring reports came from the Aisne, and Reynaud went to the radio to broadcast a denial of "the most absurd rumours that the government is preparing to leave Paris." At the same time he seized the opportunity to replace Gamelin, and for that purpose summoned Gen. Maxime Weygand from Syria. Weygand did not arrive until May 19; and thus for three critical days the supreme command was in a state of mental, though not actual, suspense.

While the Allied statesmen, like their peoples, were still dreaming of an attack that should cut off the "bulge," the German armoured forces raced on to the sea and cut off the Allied forces in Belgium. The remaining obstacles that could have blocked the tanks were not manned in time on an adequate plan. After crossing the Oise on May 17, Guderian's advanced troops reached Amiens the next day. On May 20 they swept on and reached Abbeville, thus blocking all communications between north and south. By the next day the motorized divisions had taken over the line of the Somme from Péronne to Abbeville, forming a defensive flank barricade; and Guderian's corps turned north up the coast in a drive for Calais, while Reinhardt's, swinging south of the British rear position at Arras, headed for Dunkirk.

(*d*) *Conquest of Belgium, Final Phase.*—After abandoning the Dyle line on May 16 the Allied armies in Belgium had wheeled back to the line of the Escaut (or Schelde). By the time they arrived there, the position had been undermined by the cutting of their communications. On May 19 Gort began to consider the necessity of evacuating the British expeditionary force by sea, and the preparatory steps entailed. Next day, however, orders came from the cabinet that the B.E.F. was to march south on Amiens. Gort argued that such a long-range drive in reverse was not practicable, either tactically or administratively. All he could manage was an attack by two divisions, which had just been rushed south to Arras for the purpose, led by a brigade of infantry tanks, the only armoured troops he had. When this riposte was launched on May 21, it comprised no more than two tank battalions backed by two infantry battalions, while elements of one French light mechanized division covered its flanks. Nevertheless, this small drive into the corridor momentarily shook the nerve of the German higher command. The effect showed that if two or three armoured divisions had been available for a concentrated counterstroke, the German advance might have been dislocated.

After this flash-in-the-pan the Allied armies in the north made no further effort to break out of the trap, while the belated relieving push from the south was so feeble as to be almost farcical. The prevailing confusion was increased by Weygand's arrival to take over supreme command. This veteran of 1914–18 was better in expounding theory than in grasping reality, and even his theory was out of date. His grandiloquent orders had no more chance of being translated into practical terms than those of Reynaud and Churchill. While the governments and commanders got into a tangle of divergent views and orders, the cut-off armies in the north fell back on a slant closer to the coast under increasing pressure from Reichenau's advance through Belgium. More dangerous still was the backdoor approach of Kleist, whose armoured forces were sweeping north past Boulogne and Calais. So three of Gort's divisions were pulled out of the front and sent south to strengthen the line of canals that covered Dunkirk and the Allies' rear. Two more were allotted for Weygand's renewed project of a Franco-British drive down into the German corridor. But then the Belgians' extended right flank, adjoining the British, gave way under Reichenau's pressure; so these two divisions were rushed north again. By the time they arrived on May 27, the Belgian centre had cracked; and there were no reserves to fill this fresh gap. With their country overrun and their backs to the sea, in a small strip crowded with refugees, the Belgians were driven to sue for an armistice that evening; and the "cease fire" was sounded early next morning.

Even before the Belgian capitulation, the British government had decided to evacuate the B.E.F. by sea from Dunkirk, and the admiralty had been collecting every kind of small craft to help in bringing away the troops. The retreat to the coast now became a race to re-embark before the German pincers closed. As the troops had to be taken off from the beaches, it was a slow and difficult process, extending from May 26 to June 3. In the end 233,039 British troops were brought away, as well as 112,546 Allied troops, mainly French, though most of the equipment had to be left behind. The evacuation could not have been achieved but for the air cover provided by fighter aircraft from the English coast, the indomitable efforts of the seacraft and the good discipline of the troops. It was Hitler, however, who did most to make their escape possible. For the German armoured forces had reached and crossed the canal defense line close to Dunkirk as early as May 23, when the bulk of the B.E.F. was still far distant from the port. Just as they were expecting to drive into Dunkirk, they were suddenly halted by Hitler's order and actually pulled back to the canal line. Hitler subsequently explained his intervention as the result of his desire to preserve the armoured forces for the next stage of the offensive in France; but some of his generals believed that he had a deeper reason, the idea that Britain would be more likely to make peace if its pride was not wounded by seeing its army surrender. After three days Hitler withdrew his veto and Kleist started to advance again, but the opposition was now reinforced, and almost immediately he received fresh orders—to turn south for the attack on the Somme line. Reichenau's army followed, leaving Keuchler's to clear up things in the north, where more than 1,000,000 prisoners had been taken in the 3 weeks' campaign, at a cost of 60,000 German casualties.

(*e*) *Collapse of France.*—The new French front along the Somme and the Aisne was longer than the original one, while the forces available to hold it were much diminished. The French had lost 30 of their own divisions in the first stage of the campaign, beside the help of their Allies. (Only two British divisions remained in France, though two more that were not fully trained were now sent over.) In all, Weygand had collected 49 divisions to cover the new front, leaving 17 to hold the Maginot line. The Germans, by contrast, had brought their 10 armoured divisions up to strength again with relays of fresh tanks, while their 130 infantry divisions were almost untouched. For the new offensive the forces were redistributed, two fresh armies (2nd and 9th) being inserted to increase the weight along the Aisne sector (between the Oise and the Meuse); Guderian was given command of a group of two armoured corps that were moved to lie up in readiness there. Kleist was left with two corps, to strike from the bridgeheads over the Somme at Amiens and Péronne respectively, in a pincer move aimed to converge on the lower reach of the Oise near Creil. The remaining armoured corps was to advance between Amiens and the sea.

The offensive was launched on June 5, initially on the western stretch between Laon and the sea. Resistance was stiff for the first two days, but on June 7 the most westerly armoured corps broke through on the roads to Rouen. The defense then collapsed in confusion, and the Germans met no serious resistance in crossing the Seine on June 9. Kleist's pincer stroke did not, however, go according to plan. The left pincer, from Péronne, was hung up by tough opposition north of Compiègne. The German supreme command then decided to pull back Kleist's group and switch it east to back up the break-through that had been made in Champagne. The offensive there did not open until June 9, but then the collapse came quickly. As soon as the infantry masses had forced the crossings, Guderian's tanks swept through the breach toward Châlons-sur-Marne and then eastward. The drive continued at racing pace, over the Langres plateau to Besançon and the Swiss frontier, cutting off all the French forces in the Maginot line.

On June 10 Italy declared war. An Italian offensive, however, was not launched until ten days later and was then easily held in check by the weak French forces. On June 11 Churchill flew to Tours in a vain effort to encourage the French leaders. Next day Weygand addressed the cabinet, told them the battle was lost, blamed the British for both defeats and then declared: "I am obliged to say clearly that a cessation of hostilities is compulsory." There was little doubt that he was correct in this estimate of the military situation, for the French armies were now splitting up into fragments. The cabinet was now divided between capitulation and a continuance of the war from North Africa but decided only to move itself to Bordeaux.

The Germans entered Paris on June 14 and were driving deeper on the flanks. Two days later they reached the Rhône valley. Meanwhile Weygand had continued his pressure for an armistice, backed by all the principal commanders. Reynaud resigned, whereupon a new cabinet was formed by Marshal Henri Philippe Pétain, and the request for the armistice was transmitted to Hitler on the night of June 16. Hitler's terms were delivered to the French envoys on June 20. The German advance proceeded beyond the Loire while discussion continued, but on June 22 the German terms were accepted. The armistice became effective at 1.35 A.M. on June 25, after an accompanying armistice with Italy had been signed the day before.

3. The Siege of Britain.—No plans had been made for the invasion of Britain when the Germans launched their offensive. Nor were any made even when the collapse of France was assured. It is clear that Hitler counted on the British government's agreeing to a compromise peace on the favourable terms he was disposed to offer and had no desire to press the conflict to a decisive conclusion. The German army was given to understand that the war was over, leave was granted and part of the luftwaffe was shifted to other quarters. Even when Churchill's determination to continue the war was manifest, Hitler still clung

Ominous vapour trails in a London sky during a raid by the German luftwaffe. Until the 1944 campaign of flying bombs, the nazi "air-blitz" over England was most concentrated during 1940–41, with heaviest damage occasioned by night raids

to the belief that it was merely a bluff, feeling that Britain must recognize "her militarily hopeless situation." That hope of his was slow to fade. It was not until July 2, 1940, that Hitler even ordered a consideration of the problem of invading England, and he still sounded a note of doubt about its necessity when at last, on July 16, he ordered preparations to begin for such an invasion, christened Operation "Sealion." But he said that the expedition must be ready by mid-August 1940.

The German army was in no way prepared for such an undertaking. The staff had not contemplated it, the troops had been given no training for landing operations and nothing had been done to build landing craft for the purpose. So all that could be attempted was a hurried effort to collect shipping, bring barges from Germany and the Netherlands and give the troops some practice in embarkation and disembarkation. It was only the temporary "nakedness" of the British forces, after losing most of their equipment in France, that offered such an improvisation the possibility of success. The main operation was entrusted to Field Marshal von Rundstedt's army group A, which was to use the 9th and 16th armies, comprising 25 divisions. Starting from the various harbours between the Schelde and the Seine estuaries, they were to converge on the south coast of England between Folkestone and Worthing, while air-borne troops were to capture the cliff-covered Dover area. According to the plan, ten divisions were to be landed in the first four days, to establish a wide bridgehead. After about a week the main advance inland would begin, its first objective being to gain the high ground along an arc from the Thames estuary to Portsmouth. In the next stage, London was to be isolated from the west. If opposition were stiff, the 6th army (from army group B) might be landed west of Weymouth for a push northward to the Severn.

The German generals were very apprehensive of the risks that their forces would run in crossing the sea. They had little confidence in the capacity of either their own navy or the luftwaffe to keep the passage clear. The German admirals were even more frightened about what would happen when the British navy appeared on the scene. They had no confidence in their own power to stop it and insisted that the responsibility must be placed on the luftwaffe. Hermann Goering, however, expressed assurance that the luftwaffe could check British naval interference as well as drive the British air force out of the sky. So it was agreed that he could try his preliminary air offensive, which did not commit the other services to anything definite, while the time for the invasion attempt was postponed to mid-September.

During July and early August a rising stream of air attacks was delivered against Britain's convoys and ports. Then on Aug. 13 the main offensive was unleashed, initially against air bases. Although targets and tactics were changed in different phases, the underlying object was always to wear down Britain's air defense, and the effort was maintained far into September. Although it severely strained the limited resources of fighter command, under Air Chief Marshal Sir Hugh Dowding, the German losses in both bombers and fighters were disproportionately heavy. Aug. 15 and 18, Sept. 15 and 27 were the luftwaffe's days of greatest loss in the long series of air battles over Britain. As the expensiveness of the daylight attacks came to be impressed on the luftwaffe, the offensive effort was increasingly diverted into the channel of night raids on Britain's industrial centres. Although the nightly "blitz" imposed a great strain on the civilian population, beside impairing war production and food supply, it contributed little to the main purpose that had prompted the air offensive. (*See Battle of Britain,* below.)

The evident inability of the luftwaffe to dominate the sky increased Hitler's hesitation to take a decision on Operation "Sealion." Orders he issued on Aug. 16 hinted at further delay. On Sept. 3 the date of invasion was deferred to Sept. 21, and then on Sept. 19 he ordered the shipping to be dispersed. On Oct. 12 he announced that the operation was off for the winter, though a pretence of preparations was to be kept up. Long before the spring came he had decided to turn eastward against Russia, and plans for the invasion of Britain were definitely discarded. Rundstedt and other generals had doubted all through whether his intentions were serious, in view of the apparent lack of interest and impetus on his part compared with the way he had spurred on the preparations for other offensives. The campaign against Britain henceforth became purely a blockade of its sea approaches, conducted mainly by the German submarines, supplemented by the luftwaffe.

4. British Amphibious Raids.—The number of operations carried out by the commandos (*q.v.*) during World War II was small, but they had a tonic effect on British national morale during the depressing period of isolation and siege that followed the enforced evacuation of the continent by the British forces in 1940. They helped to show that the German hold on the continental coast line was not completely secure, and they secured valuable experience for future amphibious operations on a larger scale. While the German command had reason to welcome these occasional raids as a help in keeping its own troops alert, it became uncomfortably impressed by such evidence of the excessive stretch of coast it had to cover as a result of its conquests. The commando operations were also valuable as a school in the application of irregular tactics to regular warfare, correcting the normal tendency of armies to develop formal habits and stereotyped methods.

The earlier raids had as their main target the fish-oil plants in Norway that were used in the making of glycerine for explosives; destruction of shipping was one of the subsidiary aims. The first raid was carried out—by the British commandos, light naval forces and Norwegian marines—at the head of the Vestfjord off Narvik, on March 7, 1941. The next was a purely Norwegian raid, at Oksfjord, between Tromsö and Hammerfest on the night of April 11. On Dec. 27, a larger raid, mainly by British forces, was delivered against the island of Vaagsoey. In 1942 commando operations were switched to the Atlantic shores of occupied France. The first was on the night of Feb. 27 at Bruneval, near Le Havre, where the secrets of the radar station formed the main objective. Some parachute troops co-operated in this very successful small operation. A more ambitious one was attempted at St. Nazaire on March 28 and did considerable damage to the harbour works, though at a rather high cost. On April 22 there was a small raid near Boulogne.

A much bigger operation was attempted at Dieppe on Aug. 19, 1942. Officially described as a "reconnaissance in force," it furnished useful lessons for the future in the problem of invading a well-defended coast. Although the cost was very high, it showed the possibility of achieving a large-scale landing under modern conditions, while bringing out mistakes that were to be avoided. In this operation, the commandos played only the preparatory

Troops debarking from an invasion barge on a British beach after the Allied raid on Dieppe Aug. 19, 1942

role, in the form of a dual flanking move. The right-hand thrust was successful in disabling the coastal guns on its sector, but the left-hand thrust miscarried; it unluckily ran into a German flotilla before the landing. The main assault was carried out on the beaches of Dieppe, by a mainly Canadian force of about 7,000 men, and tanks were employed to help it, though their efforts were seriously obstructed by the sea wall. Nearly half the assaulting force was lost, largely as prisoners. Losses in landing craft and aircraft were also heavy, though in the air a compensating toll was taken by the great Allied "umbrella" of about 1,000 fighters. (B. H. L. H.)

5. Air Warfare over Western Europe, Germany, Mediterranean and Italy.—Germany used its air force from 1939 to 1944 mainly as an adjunct to offensive military and naval operations; but by the beginning of 1944 it was forced to switch to the defensive because of the Allied air campaign against its industrial area. Thereafter, German offensive action was largely limited to mechanical weapons, first the flying bomb or V-1 and later the big rocket or V-2. Allied air strength in the earlier period had been built up from a condition of numerical inferiority to an overwhelming preponderance. Victory in the long run depended largely on the Allies' success in expanding and deploying their air forces and on the failure by Germany to prevent this. If the German air force could have smashed the British aircraft industry between 1940 and 1942 or the Russian aircraft industry after 1941, or stopped the flow of U.S. aircraft to Britain after 1941 or prevented the movement of air forces to North Africa, the eastern Mediterranean and Russia, it could have changed the course of the war. It achieved none of these tasks; as a strategical weapon, German air power failed.

Allied air effort, whether its strength warranted it or not, always took account of strategical as well as tactical needs until the two merged into one with the invasion of Germany. By that time it had disorganized German production and transport, safeguarded Allied bases and had given vital support to the ground forces in a series of campaigns.

This continuous and mounting attack on the sources of axis power formed the background to the campaigns. It went on in retreat and in advance. It rose at last to an intensity never before imagined. While the armies of Germany and Italy were being forced back, the whole economy of their homelands was being destroyed. High on the program of destruction were the aircraft industry and the oil needed by the axis air forces. When finally the Allied armies crossed the Rhine in the last stages of the war, there was practically no interference from the German air force.

(*a*) *The Success of the Blitzkrieg.*—Most of the nations Germany attacked between 1939 and 1941 were in a position similar to that of Germany at the end of the war. The one exception was Russia. When Germany invaded Poland in Sept. 1939 it had about 5,000 first-line aircraft. Nearly 2,000 of these were used in the campaign. Poland could muster at most 600 aircraft; the German aim was to put these out of action first. In two weeks this purpose had been achieved, and German air units could concentrate on turning retreat into confusion and on spreading terror among civilians. The entire campaign cost Germany only about 200 aircraft. When the Germans invaded Norway in April 1940 the air defense was equally inadequate, and it was impossible for the British to reinforce the Norwegian army.

Ship-based aircraft, few in numbers, backed up by only two land-based fighter squadrons, could not compete with the German land-based aircraft of superior performance. Thus, a second campaign was decided in the air.

When the main thrusts were delivered into the Netherlands, France and Belgium, the German air operations resembled those of the Polish campaign, with some innovations. Again the resistance was weak. About 3,500 aircraft were used by the Germans. Against these France had a total of 2,500, but never many more than 1,000 aircraft in its first-line strength. The British air strength in France did not exceed 500 aircraft. Heavy air fighting took place, and the Germans suffered serious losses especially among their dive bombers; but they were too well supplied with aircraft to be checked.

In the Netherlands, parachute troops were used in force for the first time. About 20,000 were dropped chiefly in the neighbourhood of Rotterdam; this action was preceded by an intense bombing of the dock area of the city which caused great loss of life. On other parts of the 250-mi. front, German aircraft attacked airfields and communications, broke down resistance in front of their troops, put up a defensive umbrella over their advancing columns, bombed and fired at refugees on the roads and took every opportunity to create chaos in the rear of the opposing armies. By way of breaking the spirit of the French, there were raids on certain towns, including one by 120 bombers on military objectives around Paris. Meanwhile the relatively small force of the royal air force continued to cover the British retreat to Dunkirk and to oppose to the limit of its powers the advance of the Germans. The bombing of towns by the luftwaffe had released the British from their inhibitions concerning targets where civilians might be involved. During the German advance there were frequent attacks on railway yards, oil supplies and road junctions in western Germany. In the air fighting near Dunkirk, the Germans had a taste of the opposition they were henceforth to meet. British victories in the air made the evacuation possible but could not impede the collapse of France. The German air force lost 2,000 aircraft in 6 weeks of fighting, yet after 6 weeks' refitting it was ready for the next venture, to prepare the way for the invasion of England.

(*b*) *The Battle of Britain.*—The Germans had available for this task about 3,000 aircraft. The British could put against them a fighter force about 800 strong; but this force was extremely well armed with 8-gun fighters, its aircraft carried armour over vital parts, its pilots were well trained and, perhaps most important of all, it was equipped with radar which had been brought secretly to a remarkably high state of efficiency. This apparatus detected formations at a distance of 50–60 mi. and revealed their strength, height and direction.

The Germans opened the battle of Britain on Aug. 8, 1940, with attacks on shipping and on south coast ports. For ten days they kept up this onslaught. From Aug. 12 they combined their campaign against shipping with raids on airfields, aircraft factories and radar stations in southeast England. On the whole they used about 500 aircraft a day; on some days, the figure reached 1,000. Throughout, losses were heavy. Failing to obtain the success they had expected, the Germans tried out various plans—night attacks on industrial towns in the Midlands, raids on the airfields of the home counties.

Early in September came attacks on London itself. The first was made by more than 400 aircraft; of these nearly a quarter were brought down. So heavy were the losses of the Germans in their daylight assaults that they turned to night bombing. Daylight raids continued, but they were more a nuisance than a threat; the night raids were to trouble Britain for two years. Meanwhile an invasion fleet of barges had been assembling on the French and Belgian coasts and British bombers had been attacking it. Many barges were destroyed, but the danger of invasion remained an influence in British policy for many months and, together with the German campaign against shipping, curtailed British activity in other theatres of war. (*See* also *Siege of Britain*, p. 672.)

(*c*) *The Defensive Phase.*—When Italy entered the war in June 1940 there were fewer than 400 British aircraft in the whole middle east command; these had to look after the defense of Malta, the Suez canal and the Sudan and to undertake offensive operations in Libya, Eritrea, Italian East Africa and Ethiopia. The Italians, on the other hand, had a front-line strength of about 1,500 aircraft. Reinforcements from the air forces of Australia, New Zealand, South Africa and Rhodesia soon arrived in North and East Africa. Under the "cash-and-carry" arrangement a certain number of U.S. aircraft, chiefly fighters and long-range reconnaissance types, were taken in British ships to Britain and thence to Africa. Later, under the lend-lease scheme, the flow was greatly increased.

The Italian air force was roughly handled wherever the British forces came into conflict with it. Axis ports on both sides of the Mediterranean were bombed. The British air units made up in dash what they lacked in numbers and equipment. Ship-borne aircraft had one outstanding success in Nov. 1940, when British planes caught some ships of the Italian navy at anchor in Taranto harbour and torpedoed seven, including two battleships. In the following April they took a major part in the battle of Cape Matapan. But for the most part, the British forces were at a disadvantage, especially in protecting convoys and in preventing the movement of traffic from Italian ports.

These difficulties came to a climax with the advance of the Germans through Yugoslavia to the Greek coast in April 1941 and with the capture of Crete by an air-borne force in May. This was the first example of an entirely air-borne campaign; it was preceded by intense bombing of the three airfields from which the small British fighter force operated. The latter became so reduced in size as to be ineffective against a raiding force about 500 aircraft strong and had to be withdrawn. Then the Germans dropped paratroops and glider troops, so that by the end of a week they had nearly 23,000 men on the island.

This evidence of German skill in air-borne invasion increased the anxiety felt in Britain. Night bombing had meanwhile grown in strength. Sometimes as many as 450 bombers attacked London in a night. A large part of the City had been destroyed by fire at the end of 1940. There had been heavy raids on other towns such as Coventry, Bristol, Birmingham, Liverpool and Birkenhead. Defense against night attacks was having little success mainly because single-seat fighters were being used and there was no room in them for an air-borne radar set and its operator. The possibility of an air-borne invasion by night was acknowledged. Home defense then remained a priority and alongside it stood the need to give more attention to the Atlantic battle.

German submarines were now working in packs, guided by scouting aircraft from advanced bases. Some of these aircraft made bombing attacks on merchant ships approaching Europe. With coastal bases all the way from Norway to the Spanish border in its hands, the German air force came near to making good the claim that air power could neutralize sea power. In the end, air power from British bases held down the German aircraft and checked the operations of the German submarines as well. Small escort carriers—converted merchant ships—came to be used in addition to naval escorts, and the R.A.F. steadily increased its long-range patrols until they were not only locating but fighting the submarines. By the end of the war, 415 out of the total of 781 submarines accounted for had been destroyed by air action. In this defense of Britain as a base, operations began near the shores of Britain and were gradually extended into the oceans until air cover was provided along all the convoy routes.

In the Mediterranean in 1941 there was a parallel situation in which the Germans held the majority of bases for controlling traffic in that sea, and the British were even less well equipped than they were at home. The Germans failed to knock out Malta and they paid heavily in every attempt they made to do so. Although the British were unable to prevent the transport of German troops from Italy to Africa, they did destroy the ships supplying these forces.

(*d*) *The Offensive Phase.*—The process of building up a British striking force in the middle east was slow and laborious. For two years the bulk of the fighting strength was in Britain and had to be used from Britain. Bombers and fighters went out whenever the weather was fit, by day and by night, to hamper German production and communications and to challenge the German air force in France. The daylight raids were intended to tie down units in France which might otherwise have been moved to the Mediterranean and Russia. Most British scruples were removed by the German incendiary attacks and so with the night raids began the campaign of systematic, wide-spread destruction which was afterward to make Germany the most devastated area in Europe.

Strategic bombing, aimed at Germany's power to feed the war machine, was gathering weight by the end of 1941. The first of the four-engined bombers had gone into action. Mounting production in Britain was adding to the numerical strength of the attack building up; new ideas in technique were also being introduced. The raid by 1,000 British bombers on Cologne on the night of May 30–31, 1942, introduced the "saturation" attack; the 1,000 aircraft delivered more than 2,000 tons of bombs within a period of 90 min. There was a repetition at Essen the following night and again at Bremen on June 25. This time the attack was completed in 75 min. It was the last 1,000-bomber raid, but all this was the prelude to the series of heavy night raids which the R.A.F. continued right up to the end of the war. These were based on the "pathfinder" technique, by which radar was used to enable a specially trained advance party to locate the target and mark it with distinctive ground or sky markers, flares so powerful that their light could often be seen through clouds. On those marker flares the main body dropped its bombs.

During this period bigger and bigger bombs were used. At the end of June 1942 the 4,000-lb. bomb was introduced. By September the 8,000-lb. bomb was in use and a year later there was first a 12,000-lb. bomb and then a 22,000-lb. bomb for the uprooting of particularly difficult structures such as viaducts. Another important development in the early part of 1942 was the arrival of heavy bomber units of the United States army air forces and of fighter units to escort them on daylight attacks. The B-17 four-engined bombers specialized in precision bombing, and this was a consideration in deciding that the U.S.

heavy bombers should undertake the day bombing while the British Lancasters and Halifaxes should continue their night campaign. From Sept. 1942 the daylight campaign of the Americans, continually growing in volume, was carefully co-ordinated with the mounting night offensive of the R.A.F. It was also supplemented by high-speed, unprotected attacks in daylight and in darkness by R.A.F. Mosquito bombers, each capable of carrying one 4,000-lb. bomb or a selection of smaller bombs.

While these developments were taking place in the west, Germans and Russians were both using their air forces to help their armies, much in the way that Germany had applied air power in its earlier campaigns. Air losses on both sides were heavy. The Russians, for instance, admitted the loss of 4,500 aircraft in the first 2 months of the fighting in 1941. German losses in the same period were nearly 2,000. That winter and in subsequent winters, Germany withdrew some of its best air units from Russia to the western and Mediterranean fronts to be used against Britain.

On both these fronts, however, by the beginning of 1942 the British were beginning to assert superiority in the air. On the French front, this was shown in a series of provocative sweeps by day bombers and fighters, which were later amplified by the addition of U.S. army air forces and which cleared the way for the Normandy landings of June 1944. In the Mediterranean, the Allied air superiority expressed itself first in a close co-operation with the army and later also in the complete isolation of the axis forces in Tunisia from their sources of supply in Sicily and on the Italian mainland. It also amounted to air supremacy during the Allied crossing from Tunisia to Sicily, a crossing in which paratroops and glider troops were used in large numbers.

The technique of close co-operation with the army had been carefully worked out during the see-saw battles of the desert campaign. Both strategical and tactical operations had been planned by the air force to serve the general military scheme. Soon after the opening of the British offensive at El Alamein, the Anglo-U.S. landings in Morocco and Algeria took place Nov. 1942 and the limited axis air forces in Africa had to serve two fronts. They were already outnumbered in Egypt, and such was the spirit of the Allied air forces that they were outfought as well. As the Allied air forces moved up always within a few miles of the forward troops, their effectiveness against the axis line of supply from Italy was improved until neither reinforcement nor escape was possible for the troops in Tunisia. The process of making the front too hot for the axis air forces was repeated in Sicily so that within a fortnight of the Allied landings not a single axis aeroplane was based on the island.

In the African campaign, the air operations of the Allies differed from those which the Germans had applied to their offensives in the sense that they stretched out farther beyond the battlefields and that they dealt with air opposition which, on occasions, was strong. In supporting the armies the Allied air forces employed fighter bombers which gave better help than the axis dive bombers and made successful use of rocket projectiles against armour and against shipping. As the Allies advanced northward through Italy, the Germans experimented with radio-controlled bombs in attacks on ships; but the strength of Allied air cover soon made these of little consequence.

British and U.S. air forces were now working together. The performance of the British air forces in the advance from El Alamein and of the united air forces in Sicily and Italy set the standard for subsequent operations in western Europe, where the numbers of aircraft were greater and where powerful forces of heavy bombers could be fitted into the strategic plan. Before the Allied landings were made in Normandy, the German air force had been bombed out of its forward bases, its radar had been disorganized and its sources of supply and reinforcement had been attacked. Railways in the whole of northwest France had been reduced by attacks on junctions and on rolling stock. Coastal fortresses were smothered. A regular patrol of aircraft in the English channel kept submarines out of the course the invasion fleet was to follow. The whole scheme of air protection and preparation was co-ordinated and directed toward the threefold end of pushing back the axis' air defense, of preventing air or sea interference and of isolating the battlefield chosen by the supreme commander.

It succeeded beyond expectations, although Germany had had two years in which to convert its air force from an offensive into a defensive weapon. Its success undoubtedly owed much to its comprehensiveness. It brought Germany's production to a standstill, it crippled German communications; at the same time, it provided effective cover for allied strategy and close tactical support for the ground forces. In the Mediterranean, the method had been evolved and tested. In France and on through Belgium to the Rhine and beyond, it was applied with the full weight of the Allied resources and with the skill derived from experience.

The one factor which tended to divert and dissipate part of the Allied air effort was the introduction by the Germans of mechanical air weapons. Launching sites of the flying bombs and the rockets had to be attacked and fast fighters had to be used to intercept the flying bombs. When the armies advanced far enough to put these weapons out of action, the war was nearly over, and Germany's air power had been largely destroyed by air action.

(E. C. Sd.)

6. The German Occupation of Western Europe.—Under the terms of the Franco-German armistice, the northern half of France together with the whole of its Atlantic seaboard remained in German occupation. "Unoccupied France" was economically the poorer part, and at the time of the armistice its problems were complicated by the fact that its population had been swollen by several million refugees from the north and from Belgium. The French government under Marshal Pétain, which was established at Vichy (*q.v.*), retained a nominal independence but was naturally subject to German control and interference. It was permitted to retain an army similiar in size (100,000) to that which Germany had been allowed under the Versailles treaty, and also its navy, as well as its colonial empire. This concession, which proved of great importance for the future, was prompted not only by a desire to secure French co-operation but by the Germans' naval weakness and consequent difficulty, when faced by the British navy, in extending their tide of conquest to the French territories overseas.

The other conquered countries of western Europe were completely occupied, but the Germans sought, for their own convenience, to get the administration carried on by officials of these countries, subject to German control. A policy of conciliation was at first pursued. It corresponded to the ideas of the German military chiefs, who had learned the drawbacks of repression from the experience of World War I, while it also represented Hitler's desire to get these countries to accept their intended place in his "new European order." At first, that policy made considerable progress—largely because of the way the German troops fulfilled the high command's instructions to behave with restraint and courtesy in the conquered countries. This polite behaviour, combined with the German efforts to restore normal conditions, began to win over a much larger proportion of the peoples than merely the instinctive collaborators. Its prospects, however, were frustrated by the combination of Britain's continued defiance with nazi impatience and intolerance. Overbearing demands provoked resistance in occupied Europe, leading to more drastic measures and thus to more widespread resistance, in a rising spiral. This resistance became increasingly organized, with British support, and caused the occupying forces more and more trouble as the war went on. Beside the more active forms, sabotage and guerrilla warfare (*q.v.*), there was a much more general passive resistance which had on the whole greater effect, without the legacy of licensed violence that in the former case often complicated the restoration of order after liberation.

In France, where the resistance eventually became strongest, it started with the handicap imposed by the Vichy government's tendency to avoid any such direct opposition to the conquerors as might worsen the plight of the French people. At the same time, prior to June 1941, the leaders of the large Communist party advocated collaboration with the Germans against Britain—as the last European stronghold of "western plutocracy." After the German invasion of Russia its attitude changed, and it started its own resistance movement. Others were also doing so on separate lines—Radical, Socialist or Catholic. The disunity of these movements hampered their effectiveness, and in their discords they often played into the hands of the occupying forces, until a later stage.

Outside France, Gen. Charles de Gaulle had started his "Free French" (later "Fighting French") movement as early as June 18, 1940. But he was able to collect only a few hundred in England, at Morval camp near Aldershot, and support for him elsewhere was at first small. The censure of the Vichy government was a deterrent to many, while confidence was shaken by the fiasco of De Gaulle's July attempt, under the protection of a British fleet, to seize Dakar, on the West African coast. But his prospects gradually improved as German impositions and the Vichy government's subservience brought an increasing flow of converts to his cause. The British entry into Syria in 1941 and Madagascar in 1942 paved the way for extension of his authority. Still more decisive was the U.S.-British occupation of French North Africa, in reply to which the Germans rushed to occupy the whole of France (Nov. 11, 1942) and turned the French people more definitely against them. Although the French fleet at Toulon did not escape to join the Allies, it was scuttled rather than allow it to fall into German hands (Nov. 27). Henceforth, there was a great development of the resistance in France, which was now better coordinated, while being more plentifully equipped with arms dropped by air. All the different bodies were now unified under the C.N.R. (*Conseil National de la Résistance*), while the guerrilla sections were combined in a single organization entitled the F.F.I. (*Forces Françaises de l'Intérieur*)—though the Communist partisans retained a measure of autonomy.

At the same time the regular forces under De Gaulle were growing fast. A brigade under Gen. Joseph-Pierre Koenig played a gallant part in the British campaign of 1942 in Libya. Larger forces were employed in the Tunisian campaign. The following year an army corps under Gen. Alphonse Juin went to Italy and achieved the decisive manoeuvre through the mountains in the Allied offensive of May 1944 that led to the capture of Rome. Meanwhile Koenig had taken over command of the F.F.I., which severely harassed the German communications in France before and during the Allied invasion of Normandy. On Aug. 18, as the Allied armies approached, the people of Paris rose in arms to liberate their city, and a French armoured division was hurried thither to support their efforts. In the same week a French army under Gen. Jean de Lattre de Tassigny formed part of the Allied landing in the south of France. It later achieved striking successes in the Rhine campaign. (B. H. L. H.)

E. British African Campaigns

1. East African Campaigns. East Africa developed into an important battle arena in Aug. 1940, about six weeks after the collapse of France. At that time the British, in desperate straits and girding for an expected nazi invasion of their homeland, were too hard pressed to spare troops for the African theatre. To Mussolini, the time therefore seemed propitious to attempt an attack on British possessions in Africa, and in August he launched an offensive against British Somaliland.

The Italian strategy was simple and direct. While their East African armies were to seize the British protectorate and close the southern outlet to the Red sea, Marshal Rodolfo Graziani's armies in the north were to advance across Egypt and seize the Suez canal. Lacking adequate arms and troops in that area, the British had no choice but to depend upon a delaying action in order to maintain intact a strong concentration of troops in north Egypt for the protection of Suez.

How unevenly matched were the Italian and British forces in that critical period is graphically illustrated by the following figures. Italy had an army of approximately 110,000 men in its East African empire. About 35,000 of these were stationed in Eritrea. An estimated 50,000 more were encamped in Ethiopia and the garrison in Italian Somaliland was said to amount to 10,000 troops. Additionally, the Italians had numerous outposts near Kenya and Lake Tana, the chief reservoir of the Blue Nile in western Ethiopia. The British, on the other hand, had only the merest handful of men in East Africa. The peacetime strength of their forces in British Somaliland amounted to only 1,200 African soldiers led by 47 British officers. Although this force was later implemented by some volunteers, it was no more than a token-size army in Aug. 1940.

The actual invasion of British Somaliland began on Aug. 4 along three routes. The Italians, using the greater part of two divisions, including some mechanized forces, converged on Berbera, capital of the British protectorate. The British retreated hastily and by Aug. 19 they were evacuated by sea from the threatened port.

Substantial Italian forces also crossed into Kenya near Moyale, forcing the withdrawal of the weakly manned British outposts from the arid belt along Kenya's northern frontier. At the same time, Italian troops in Eritrea penetrated the southern part of the Anglo-Egyptian Sudan, capturing Kassala and Gallabat. Fighting in East Africa for the next five months was confined mostly to patrol skirmishes along the wild Sudanese and Kenya frontier regions.

By Dec. 1940, the British had gathered together a considerable army of British, Free French and Belgian regulars as well as Bengalis, Sikhs, Ethiopians and South Africans. The Allied armies in the Sudan consisted of about 40,000 men. Another 30,000 had been massed in the Kenya regions. In addition, a royal navy squadron weighed anchor for the task of blockading the sea outlets of Italian East Africa on the Red sea and the Gulf of Aden.

The Allied offensive began in early Jan. 1941 after Gen. Sir Archibald Wavell's drive against Italian armies in North Africa was well underway. Wavell commanded operations in both the North and East African theatres. Striking southward from Sudan, an Allied force recaptured Kassala by Jan. 17, invaded Eritrea and started a rapid thrust toward the heavily defended Cheren-Asmara-Massawa triangle. Other Allied contingents operating from Kenya bases attacked Italian positions in Italian Somaliland and Ethiopia.

While Allied forces on the north met sharp resistance before Cheren in Eritrea, those invading Italian Somaliland broke through with relative ease. By Feb. the Allies crossed the Juba river and on Feb. 26 captured Mogadiscio, capital of the colony, climaxing a 220-mi. dash in 48 hours. By March 7 all Italian Somaliland fell to the British and most of the Italian troops in the colony were either killed or captured in the fighting. The Allied forces then swung inland, following the Webi Shebeli river into Ethiopia. Marching rapidly through the jungle wastes at a rate of 50 mi. daily, they sped toward the Addis Ababa-Djibouti railway. Meanwhile, British naval units in the Gulf of Aden succeeded in attacking and recapturing Berbera. This action, coupled with the other Allied offensives, served to immobilize and prevent counterattacks from the Italian occupation forces holding the rest of the British protectorate.

Meanwhile, the Italian garrison at Cheren, the key defense point of Eritrea, fought stubbornly, but on March 27 it evacuated the town after a seven-week siege. The capture of Cheren enabled the British to sweep up rapidly the remaining important points of Eritrea. Asmara, declared an open city, surrendered April 1 without a fight; a British-Free French detachment took Massawa May 9.

In Ethiopia the Italians were falling back toward Addis Ababa. The city of Harar fell the same day that Cheren was captured, and Allied troops moving on Diredawa captured that town and cut the Addis Ababa-Djibouti railway on March 30. Meeting little serious resistance, the British took Addis Ababa April 6, while the duke of Aosta, the Italian commander, retreated with the bulk of his army, most of whom were Ethiopians, toward Amba-Alagi. Although he rejected the initial British surrender terms, Aosta was hopelessly trapped and on May 19 he surrendered.

The capitulation of Aosta virtually sealed the East African campaign, although sporadic fighting by isolated Italian units continued until the end of September. By mid-July, the Allies not only reconquered British Somaliland but all of Italy's East African empire as well. Militarily, the British had secured the Suez canal from attack by the south and had gained an additional number of ports on the Red sea that could relieve Aden's overworked docks of the burden of naval repairs. (X.)

2. Egypt and Libya.—The campaigns under this head were dominated by three gifted commanders whose careers overlapped but whose ascendancy fell into three marked periods: Gen. Sir Archibald Wavell (until Feb. 1941), Field Marshal Erwin Rommel (March 1941–Aug. 1942) and Lt. Gen. Bernard L. Montgomery (from Aug. 1942).

Between El Agheila, near the Tripolitanian frontier, and El Alamein, about 60 mi. west of Alexandria, there was no naturally defensive position which could not be readily turned. There was only one road, along the coast. There were several small, but, with the exception of Benghazi, only two large ports, Tripoli and Alexandria (each at the end of the respective lines of communication) by which to maintain major forces. Water supplies were, in parts, sparse. Apart from the Jebel Akhbar, the "bulge" of Cyrenaica which the Italians had attempted to colonize and which was outflanked regularly throughout the campaigns, the terrain was, in the main, flat and arid desert. Between Agheila and Alamein there was ample room for manoeuvre, particularly for mechanized forces; airfields were readily confected; moreover, save a small number of Arabs and, at first, a few Italian settlers, there were no civilians. The nature of the country with its solitary coastal road and the dispersion of its small ports gave the campaigns their pattern: a series of mechanized turning movements, outflanking "hooks" from inland while infantry hugged the coast, to secure a port which would nourish a further advance. "North Africa," said von Ravenstein, the commander of the 21st panzer division, "is a tactician's paradise and a quartermaster's hell."

(*a*) *First Italian Offensive* (*Sept.–Dec. 1940*).—When Italy declared war on June 10, 1940, there were more than 200,000 Italian troops in Libya and a considerable numerical superiority in aircraft. Thenceforward, British reinforcements had to reach Egypt via the Cape of Good Hope. With a detachment of the 7th armoured division on the Cyrenaican frontier, the main British positions were at Mersa Matruh 120 mi. farther east. From June 11, small British columns established an early dominance by harassing raids over the frontier, but on Sept. 13 after a heavy artillery program against the deserted escarpment above Es Sollum, the Italians invaded Egypt on a narrow front along the coast with two divisions up, two in rear and a further division and the Maletti group in reserve. Sidi Barrani was reached by Sept. 16. These forces, subsequently increased by 2 further divisions to a strength of 80,000 men, then distributed themselves, to remain for more than 2 months with ill-assured supply, in a series of fortified camps from Maktila, on the coast east of Sidi Barrani, to the escarpment about Sofafi, about 50 mi. away, in echelon from the left flank. Defenses lacked depth and mutual support. A gap of more than 20 mi. lay between Sofafi on the right and the next camp at Nibeiwa.

(*b*) *British Counteroffensive* (*Dec. 1940–Feb. 1941*).—After an approach march by night over open desert two highly mobile British divisions (7th armoured and 4th Indian) advanced on the gap. Complete surprise resulted in the rapid capture of Nibeiwa early on Dec. 9; and by nightfall the Tummar camps, immediately north, had almost completely fallen. Next day Sidi Barrani was retaken, and the ragged road to the west had been cut. In quick pursuit, the 7th armoured division intercepted a long Italian column between Buq Buq and Sollum, making its way back to the frontier. "Something is wrong with our Army," wrote Count Galeazzo Ciano on Dec. 11, "if five divisions allow themselves to be pulverized in two days." By Dec. 15 all Italian troops had been driven from Egypt, leaving more than 38,000 prisoners in British hands, and the majority of the Italian army remaining in Cyrenaica had withdrawn within the invested 17-mi. perimeter of Bardia. There was a pause for maintenance, reliefs and to utilize the port of Sollum, before Bardia fell, after a naval bombardment and a heavy attack from the west, to the 6th Australian division (which had relieved the 4th Indian division) on Jan. 5. About 45,000 prisoners and 462 guns were captured.

By the next day, the 7th armoured division had cut the road Tobruk-Derna and the track Tobruk-Mechili while the Italians abandoned their airfields at Gazala, Tmimi and Bomba. The southern face of the 28-mi. perimeter of Tobruk was attacked by the Australians on Jan. 21, with effective air and naval support, to capture the road junction Sidi Mahmoud 8,000 yd. inside the perimeter. The town capitulated next day with 38,000 more prisoners.

The remaining Italian forces in Cyrenaica fell into two main elements: the majority of the infantry east of Derna and a mechanized group about Mechili, the nodal point of the tracks south from the Jebel Akhdar and the direct westward route to Benghazi. While the Australians pushed into the Jebel, the 7th armoured division moved on Mechili. By Feb. 3 it was evident that the Italians were abandoning the "bulge," and great risks offered complete victory. The 7th armoured division was therefore swiftly directed on Msus with a tight maintenance margin to cut off the Italians south of Benghazi by moving northwest on Soluch or southwest on Agedabia as required. By Feb. 5, after a gruelling march in unreconnoitred desert, detachments were astride the main routes southwest of Beda Fomm, blocking escape into Tripolitania. Eighty-four Italian tanks were put out of action next day by the British pincers closing from Soluch and Beda Fomm. After an abortive attempt by 30 Italian tanks to break through at dawn on Feb. 7, Gen. Annibale Bergonzoli surrendered unconditionally. The Italian 10th army had thus been wiped out, and Cyrenaica was in British hands. During the two months following Dec. 7 the Army of the Nile advanced about 500 mi. It had destroyed an Italian army comprising 9 divisions and part of a tenth and had taken 130,000 prisoners, 400 tanks and 1,290 guns. In these operations Gen. Sir Richard O'Connor, Wavell's tactical commander, had never employed more than 2 divisions at a time, the 7th armoured division, "the Desert Rats," being engaged throughout. British casualties totalled 1,928 men. The bombardment and supply work of the royal navy had been remarkable while the royal air force, though most inferior in numbers, had gained complete superiority over the Italian air force.

(*c*) *Second Axis Offensive* (*March–April 1941*).—Wavell was compelled to gamble on a strategic shoestring. Uncertain on the one hand when German ground forces would reach Africa (where their aircraft were already operating) and pledged on the other, although Keren and Kismayu had still to be taken, to send to Greece what he could scramble together, he risked leaving the newly gained Cyrenaica with an understrength armoured brigade covering its western approaches and a new Australian division forming in the Jebel. British and German armoured cars first met on Feb. 20 and, before the month was out, German aircraft had made the port of Benghazi unusable. The maintenance of the slender British forces had therefore been thrown back on the long line to Tobruk when Rommel recaptured Agheila on March 24 and advanced in force through Marsa Brega on March 31 with the 5th light division (an experimental German formation subsequently converted into the 21st panzer division) and two mobile Italian divisions.

The British attempts to delay, first around Agedabia, to cover Benghazi, then on the line Derna-Mechili to cover Tobruk, were foiled by the faster and more powerful German tanks on the open flank. The Germans thrust in two main groups, one forcing its way through the Jebel on Derna, the other dashing via Msus across the open desert on Tobruk. Having captured a British divisional headquarters at Mechili on April 8 and driven a small delaying force back from El Adem to the Egyptian frontier, Rommel launched an ill-prepared attack on Tobruk on April 10–11, which was worsted after three tense days by the British gunners and Australian infantry who had withdrawn within the perimeter.

Their tanks requiring overhaul, the Germans, with Italians in attendance, settled down to prepare a less impetuous assault while the 15th panzer division moved up from Tripoli. The renewed attack went in on the night of April 30–May 1, but the Germans narrowly failed in their purpose, and Tobruk settled down to the rhythm of its long siege.

The escarpment running southeast from Sollum was generally impassable to vehicles for about 50 mi. inland save at Sollum itself and at Halfaya. While Tobruk remained besieged, operations on the Egyptian frontier developed into battles for possession of the two passes. Sollum and Capuzzo were captured by the British on May 15, only to be regained by the Germans next day. On May 27 the Germans took Halfaya in an operation ("Scorpion") beginning as a diversion for the battle of Crete. As a result of political pressure to relieve Tobruk, Wavell ordered an attack ("Battleaxe") over the frontier on June 15 designed to defeat the German armour in detail before advancing on El Adem. Capuzzo fell, but Halfaya and Sollum remained in German hands, and by the evening of June 16 additional German armour had arrived from outside Tobruk. Following an armoured battle south of Sidi Omar that night, the British began to withdraw after heavy tank losses, particularly from the German 88-mm. gun.

Rommel had already revealed the qualities which were to stamp his desert career: a forceful and inspiring personal leadership, disdaining either risk or advice, the requirements of maintenance and of his allies alike; a roughshod capacity to take advantage of his opponents' mistakes as rapidly as he recovered from his own; a tendency to improvise and to repeat his tactics; a liability to obsession.

Preoccupation with Tobruk conditioned the reorganization and accumulation of strength to which both sides devoted the long hot summer: one to capture, the other to relieve, the fortress. While eight Allied battalions in the front line dominated the four Italian divisions and three German battalions besieging the perimeter, the Allied naval and air forces tackled with redoubtable success the double task of keeping Tobruk alive and hamstringing the build-up and maintenance of the axis forces preparing to assault its mettlesome garrison. The Italian navy was not risking another Matapan; and between May and November no single axis convoy reached Tripoli or Benghazi unscathed; no single axis formation arrived in Africa complete. Meanwhile, Sir Claude Auchinleck succeeded the sagacious Wavell, who had been involved in six campaigns between February and July, and steadily built up his striking force (which became the 8th army), undisturbed in the desert itself save by an abortive raid to investigate his preparedness by the 21st panzer division over the frontier as far as Rabia on Sept. 14, and by the urgent and political need to change the personnel holding Tobruk.

The Italian forces under Gen. Ettore Bastico's supreme command (for the North African littoral as an Italian domain was perforce also in name an Italian theatre) totalled eight divisions, of which three (Ariete, Trieste and Trento) were formed into a mobile corps. The axis frontier defenses were strengthened by the fortification of Halfaya and Sidi Omar to increase the difficulty of frontal assault and to extend any turning attempt. To release the 15th and 21st panzer divisions for their proper role, the 90th light division was created from positional battalions about Tobruk. Rommel proposed to hold off the British at the frontier while he attacked Tobruk on Nov. 23.

(*d*) *Second British Counteroffensive* (*Nov. 1941–Jan. 1942*).—The British attack ("Crusader") at dawn on Nov. 18, 1941, achieved complete surprise. Swinging an armoured corps wide across the frontier from Maddalena, the British sought to bring the German armour to battle, while on the inner flank another corps, having masked the frontier defenses, attacked northward to isolate Sollum and Bardia. The Tobruk garrison was to break out approximately southeast to join the relieving armoured corps. By Nov. 19 the British had seized the vital area of Sidi Rezegh southeast of Tobruk. Rommel replied by ordering the junction of the 21st panzer and Ariete divisions west of Bir el Gobi for attack eastward, while the 15th panzer division moved west from Sidi Omar.

By Nov. 23 the British plan had gone agley. Sidi Rezegh had been retaken, the sortie from Tobruk was stuck and the spearhead of the corps which had attacked north over the frontier was held at Gambut. While uncertainty existed in the British command, a mood relieved by Auchinleck's decision to take over personally, Rommel threw away his opportunity in a characteristic gamble to finish the battle quickly. Collecting all the armour he could muster on Nov. 24, he led a "dash to the wire," a raid over the frontier through the British lines, then swept north on a wide, incoherent front. His disruptive columns, having failed to unseat the British from their essential purpose, swung back on Nov. 26 against the rear of the New Zealanders, who had by then pushed beyond Gambut to retake Sidi Rezegh. Next day the Tobruk garrison captured El Duda, making junction with the relieving forces on Nov. 27. The 21st panzer and Ariete divisions were therefore east and the 15th panzer division west of the corridor: the reverse of their dispositions when Sidi Rezegh had first been captured and some measure at once of the disruption which Rommel had created for himself and of the whirligig of desert warfare.

By Dec. 1, however, the 15th panzer and the 90th light divisions managed to break through the corridor to join the 21st panzer division at Zaafran. Rommel then again overreached himself and had to pull in his horns by abandoning the area east of the general line Bir El Gobi-El Adem. He began to withdraw from Tobruk on Dec. 7–8 and by Dec. 12, after expensive rearguard actions, the Germans had reached a line running southwest from Gazala with an open right flank. A heavy battle for disengagement ensued, but by Dec. 15 it was evident that Rommel's lines were both pierced and turned. He retreated to Agedabia, picking up a delivery of tanks from Benghazi en route. The British failed to cut him off and, after another enveloping attempt about Agedabia on Dec. 28–30, tried to contain the main axis forces in western Cyrenaica while they proceeded methodically to eliminate the isolated axis positions masked in the rear: Bardia, Sollum and Halfaya. Refreshed by the arrival of a convoy at Tripoli and by two Italian divisions, Rommel then withdrew into the strong Agheila position to refit: back where he had started.

(*e*) *Third Axis Offensive* (*Jan.–Aug. 1942*).—Nearer to his base, Rommel was ready first. Having probed British strength astride the coastal road on Jan. 21, he seized his advantage next day and rapidly captured Saunnu and Antelat. By Feb. 4 he had retaken Benghazi and driven the Allied forces back to their chosen line of resistance south from Gazala. He did not press home his attack on Feb. 14–15, and both sides settled down to prepare again for further advances while the race for supply was run, a phase demonstrating the immense significance of Malta, the "unsinkable aircraft carrier."

The Allied defenses were a straggle of irregularly spaced strongpoints, "boxes" linked by minefields. Most important was that at "Knightsbridge," a track junction where the Trigh Capuzzo running west from El Adem crossed the north-south track between two further "boxes," Acroma and Bir Hacheim. South and east of Bir Hacheim the left flank lay open. Rommel planned a swift drive round this flank to capture Bir Hacheim and roll up the Allied posi-

Firing from ground position, these British troops manned a British six-pounder antitank gun in the El Alamein sector, Egypt, before the 8th army's great drive against Rommel's Afrika Korps began Oct. 23, 1942

tions from south and rear. Tobruk was to fall on May 30.

The attack began on May 25, the German armour swinging round Bir Hacheim, one division making for Acroma, another for El Adem. By May 28 it was obvious that rapid success had escaped him, and the slim margin of supply which Rommel had allowed himself might be turned to Allied advantage. To ensure his continued maintenance, or if necessary his retreat, he had to cut a corridor back westward through the British mine fields. A fierce four-day armoured battle about Knightsbridge resulted. Within an ace of victory, the 8th army failed to prevent Rommel from keeping open, indeed widening, his feedpipe to the "cauldron." Instead of his enforced withdrawal, Rommel regained the initiative with a modification of his original plan by regrouping his main strength in a salient east of his corridor while he proceeded to eliminate Bir Hacheim, which extended and hobbled his southern supply line. While the Free French hung on tenaciously against repeated attacks on Bir Hacheim from June 2 to 10, farther north the British were trying unsuccessfully to pinch out the axis salient. The evacuation of Bir Hacheim on the night of June 10–11 offered Rommel the opportunity to destroy the remaining positions piecemeal. A series of heavy armoured battles, in which once again the inferiority of British tanks was revealed, covered the fighting withdrawal of the exposed Allied infantry. The British then attempted to repeat 1941 by holding Tobruk and delaying on the Egyptian frontier. But Tobruk, so long the symbol of British resistance to Rommel, fell with suddenness on June 21. With the forces thus released and the booty thus secured, Rommel could be stopped at the frontier neither by Allied arms nor by Italian advice. Once again Auchinleck rose to the crisis and assumed personal command. He decided to pause at Mersa Matruh while the last ditch was manned, the El Alamein line which Wavell had reconnoitred and Auchinleck himself had made ready.

By June 26 Rommel had reached Matruh, where he attempted to repeat the enveloping manoeuvre which had just gained him Tobruk. He was foiled by the remarkable rearguard action of the New Zealanders at Minqar Qu'aim and because the British, who had retreated hundreds of miles under the magnificently offensive protection of the desert air force, despite the loss of 80,000 men, were still full of fight. Although Matruh and Daba fell before the end of June, by the time the Germans reached El Alamein their drive was almost spent. The first few days of July saw desperate fighting, but by July 5 the Germans had begun to establish a defensive screen. Both sides set about developing their defensive layout, and the heavy fighting which continued throughout July centred upon possession of the key ridges of Tel El Aisa in the north and Ruweisat, the backbone of the British defenses in the central sector.

The El Alamein line was the organization of a naturally defensive position about 60 mi. west of Alexandria between the sea coast and the Qattara depression 35 mi. south. Like the Gazala position, it had been originally laid out as a series of mutually supporting "boxes," but with the significant difference that the southern flank was closed by a sand sea generally impassable to large forces. Astride the coastal road lay Rommel's obsession, the El Alamein "box" itself, upon which the remaining defenses pivoted.

Once again the battle of supply bulked foremost. Rommel was now at the end of a long and frequently punctured pipe line (although an Allied combined operation to take Tobruk failed in September), whereas the Allies were defending their very base. While the toll of axis shipping mounted rapidly, the Allied build-up was for the first time swifter. Nevertheless, Rommel attacked first.

The 8th army, now under Montgomery's command, knew how the battle was to proceed. When Rommel advanced in strength on Aug. 31 to complete the "final annihilation," he was met on the strongly held Alam Halfa ridge which dominated the southern sector, by massed artillery and tanks which refused to react to his design but fought a model defensive battle on ground of Montgomery's choosing. Close air support was employed as never before. As in May, Rommel had impulsively disregarded his maintenance in the rapid hope of a glittering prize: this time Egypt itself. Far in the rear, the *coup de grâce* was delivered by Air Marshal Arthur Tedder's Wellingtons, which sank the petrol convoy in Tobruk which was Rommel's last hope of effective resupply. On Sept. 3 he began to withdraw. Montgomery had become a power in the sand, and the 8th army had acquired the morale and the master it needed for the battle of El Alamein.

(*f*) *Final British Offensive (Oct. 1942–April 1943)*.—To ensure the safe passage of the last convoy which could renew Malta's almost exhausted aviation spirit, the Allies needed possession of the Martuba group of airfields in the Jebel Akhdar by mid-November. Moreover, the North African landings ("Torch") were to take place early in the month. These requirements and the state of the moon and of Allied readiness set the date for Oct. 23.

By then the axis defenses were deeper and stronger. In the northern sector any Allied attack was intended to lose both force and direction within the system itself; in the south, where the defenses were less intricate, they were sited to canalize Allied penetration. Five Italian divisions were held in position by thick mine fields and a corset of German infantry. In the rear were four armoured divisions and the 90th light division. A further Italian infantry division stood on the frontier. Montgomery's design ("Lightfoot") was to feint in the south while he cut two corridors through the northern axis positions in a moonlit break-in operation with massed artillery support; to hold off the German armour during the "crumbling" operations which would ensue and, in this dogfight, lasting perhaps ten days, to destroy the axis infantry and thus leave Rommel's armour without firm bases from which to manoeuvre or within which to refurbish. Then only did Montgomery purpose to release his own armour.

Before Oct. 23 the desert air force had conclusively won the air battle and thereafter devoted its full and successful attention to the close support of the land forces shown so effective at Alam Halfa. By Oct. 25 Montgomery had established a bridgehead in the northern axis positions and the dogfight was going well. He then developed his northern thrust by a series of fierce attacks, mainly by the 9th Australian division, the veterans of Tobruk, into a salient which menaced the coastal road and railway. Misled about his ultimate line of advance, the German Africa corps steadily congregated, not without severe losses, in the northern sector about Sidi Abd el Rahman. Switching his thrustline swiftly, Montgomery, who by shrewd regrouping since Oct. 26 had been accumulating reserves as steadily as Rommel had been committing his, early on Nov. 2 (Operation "Supercharge") cut south of the German strength into the Italian positions. A quickly improvised axis antitank screen prevented the immediate breakthrough, but by Nov. 4 the 51st highland and the 4th Indian division had forced back the screen, and the Sherman tanks of the British armoured divisions swept with the motorized New Zealanders out into open country. Heavy rain on Nov. 6 and 7 saved the axis forces from annihilation; but 4 German and 8 Italian divisions had been drastically defeated, and 30,000 prisoners were taken.

The pursuit was rapid. The Martuba group of airfields were in Allied hands by Nov. 15, in time to support the convoy which left Alexandria next day. Benghazi fell on Nov. 20 and by Nov. 23 Rommel was back once more at Agheila. The capture of Agheila was psychologically important to the 8th army, with its memories of the annual retreat of the past, as the gateway to Tripoli, its perennial target. In the event, Rommel partially false-fronted the British attack, and the remarkable December outflanking march of the New Zealanders over inland desert never before traversed by large forces failed to entrap many of the Germans who retreated to the Buerat position covering Tripoli. The main Allied difficulty was now administration, and the size of the force which could be maintained as far as Tripoli was small. By the morning of Jan. 16, however, the "left hook" was beyond the Wadi Zem Zem, the main natural obstacle, and on Jan. 23, exactly three months after the Alamein battle had begun, the 8th army entered Tripoli.

The next objective was the Mareth line, but first Tripoli had to be "uncorked." Only light forces advanced into southern Tunisia. Between Feb. 28 and March 4, the 8th army was therefore not well disposed for axis counterattack, yet it was increasingly evident that Rommel, having broken off his Tebessa attack against the 1st army, was turning south to deal the 8th army a blow before the united weight of Gen. Dwight D. Eisenhower's command could be brought against him. He was too late, for when he attacked on March 6 at Medenine with the 10th, 15th and 21st panzer divisions, Montgomery had made ready. In Rommel's last attack in Africa, he was decisively defeated in a single day in an engagement which again demonstrated Montgomery's mastery of the defensive battle.

The Long Range Desert group, a remarkable body of military explorers, had already found a way through the uncharted desert west of the Matmata hills which closed the western end of the Mareth line, which the French had originally prepared. With Gen. Jacques Leclerc's Free French, who had joined Montgomery after their astounding march from Lake Chad, screening at Kasr Rhilane, a large outflanking force was built up with Maj. Gen. Bernard Freyberg's New Zealanders as a nucleus. A heavy frontal attack on the Mareth line proper was launched across the water-filled Wadi Zigzaou on March 20, but the German reaction was heavy. Montgomery straightway reinforced his left hook and by March 26, with the most effective close support by aircraft till then ever employed, he was able to force the axis switchline west of the hills before El Hamma and release an armoured division by moonlight through the disorganized axis forces. German reinforcements were too late; the 52 tanks they had lost at Medenine on March 6 were badly missed at El Hamma. The Mareth line had been turned, and only the axis forces holding the Wadi Akarit position (the "Gabes gap" between the Shott el Fejaj and the sea) stood between the 8th army and their U.S. comrades. The position was stormed in the dark early morning of April 6. The Germans held on throughout the day, but on April 7 British armoured cars made contact with tanks of the 2nd U.S. corps on the Gabes-Gafsa road. (For the rest of the Tunisian campaign, *see* p. 696 fol.) (E. T. W.)

3. Occupation of Madagascar.—The British had reason to believe that the Japanese, after the capture of the Andaman Islands, would seize the island of Madagascar either by force or through Vichy collaboration and thus cut off the last supply route to the middle east. In order to forestall a Japanese invasion, a British naval and military force under the command of Adm. Sir James F. Somerville attacked Diégo Suarez on May 6, 1942. The next day Diégo Suarez surrendered. After the occupation of this important naval base in the Indian ocean it was hoped that some degree of collaboration with the French administration would supervene which would enable the British to secure certain military objectives while still maintaining the machinery of French government in the island. By July it became obvious that the governor general, Armand Annet, although toying with the idea of collaboration, was really playing for time until the rains began in October, and that no sincere *rapprochement* could be expected from him.

Lieut. Gen. Sir William Platt, who since July 1, 1942, had been in command of all British troops in Madagascar, therefore advised the chiefs of staff that further operations were essential. The plan proposed by General Platt, Admiral Somerville and Air Commodore M. L. Taylor was accepted. The offensive began on Sept. 10, and the same day the port of Majunga was conquered after slight resistance. Eight days later Tamatave surrendered; on Sept. 23 the British entered Antananarivo, the capital, where they were enthusiastically received by the population. Annet, however, and the pro-Vichy French forces withdrew southward, blocking all roads heavily as they went. At the end of September the British advance from Antananarivo was resumed. Antsirabe was occupied on Oct. 2 and Fianarantsoa on Oct. 29. On Nov. 4 Annet sent a plenipotentiary to obtain terms for an armistice. The British terms were accepted and hostilities ceased on Nov. 5. Annet was interned at Durban, and on Jan. 8, 1943, General Platt handed over the responsibility for the administration of Madagascar to Gen. Paul Legentilhomme, a representative of Fighting France under Gen. Charles de Gaulle. (K. Sm.)

F. The Near East Campaigns

1. Iraq.—Influenced by axis successes during 1940, the Iraqi government continued to maintain diplomatic relations with Italy, whose legation became the centre of axis intrigue and propaganda. Early in 1941, Rashid Ali el-Gailani became prime minister; backed by four Iraqi generals, known as the Golden Square, he began to collaborate openly with the axis.

On March 31, 1940, the regent of Iraq took refuge on a British warship at Basra to evade arrest by his government. The British government, in accordance with its treaty rights, ordered an Indian brigade to Basra which arrived on April 18. Rashid Ali, on hearing that further troops were coming from India, ordered the Iraqi army to attack the British air base at Habbaniya 40 mi. west of Baghdad. The Iraqi forces consisted of more than 9,000 troops with 50 guns while the garrison of Habbaniya numbered 300 British infantry (flown up from Basra), 1,000 royal air force personnel, 1,000 levees (mainly Assyrians) and no artillery.

On April 30 the Iraqi forces occupied a ridge overlooking Habbaniya and commenced bombardment by air and artillery. Until May 7 the position was critical; then the garrison, supported by British air forces from Egypt, drove the Iraqi forces, which had been reinforced by the German air force, back to Al Falluja on the Euphrates. Meanwhile, the Indian brigade advancing from

Basra was delayed by floods and demolitions.

On May 18 a mechanized column consisting of British cavalry and the Arab legion of the emir of Trans-Jordan, reached Habbaniya after marching about 560 mi. from Haifa, mostly across desert. This force secured Falluja bridge on May 19 and continued its advance, reaching the outskirts of Baghdad on May 30. The government of Rashid Ali, disheartened by the lack of adequate support from the Germans, thereupon fled the country. Resistance ceased and the regent was able to return and form a new government.

2. Syria.—During May 1941 the French (Vichy) had assisted the passage of German air forces to support Rashid Ali in Iraq. After the evacuation of Crete, the strategical importance of Syria increased; if occupied by the axis, it would constitute a threat against Turkey or Egypt. The Allies decided therefore that the country could not be left open to German infiltration and should be occupied. The degree of resistance to be expected from the French (Vichy) could not be assessed, but the presence of Free French forces with the Allies was expected to have a stiffening effect. The garrison of Syria consisted of about 30 battalions with 90 tanks. The Allies had available for this operation about 15 battalions made up of British cavalry, the 7th Australian division, 5th Indian infantry brigade and Free French forces, but no tanks. On June 8 the Allies crossed the frontier in three columns. The right column (Indian and Free French Brigade), moving via Deraa on Damascus, was checked on June 10 ten miles short of that city. The centre (Australian) column captured Merjayoun on June 9, while the left column (Australian), moving up the coast, captured Tyre and forced the passage of the Litani river. Resistance to the advance stiffened thereafter, and Merjayoun was recaptured by a French counterattack. Only along the coast was slow progress maintained.

On June 21 a bold night attack by the 5th Indian brigade reached the outskirts of Damascus and captured the airfield, causing the French (Vichy) to evacuate the city. By the end of June the coastal column, supported by fire from a cruiser squadron of the royal navy, had taken Sidon and faced a strong position covering Beirut. The Allied force in the meantime had been augmented by a British infantry brigade from Egypt and farther east by forces released from the Iraq operations. The British mechanized column turned back across the desert and took Palmyra after hard fighting, while an Indian column moved unopposed up the Euphrates valley to capture Deir ez Zor.

British Bren tank parked amid the ancient ruins of Palmyra during the Syrian campaign of June-July 1941

On June 7, the 7th Australian division on the coast launched an attack to secure Beirut and was closely supported by effective fire from the cruisers, in the face of which resistance began to crumble, causing the French (Vichy) to ask for an armistice on July 11. This armistice was signed at Acre on July 14, and Syria passed into Allied occupation.

3. Iran.—During June and July 1941, reports began to reach the Allies of axis activity in Iran and of the infiltration of Germans described as "tourists." By the end of July, German activities had increased to an extent that compromised the neutrality of the Iranian government. After previous warning, on Aug. 16 the British and soviet governments asked the government to expel all Germans. This request was answered on August 16 by an assertion on the part of the Iranian government of strict neutrality together with a denial of German subversive activities.

As a result of this unsatisfactory reply, British and soviet troops moved into Iran on Aug. 25. British columns starting from Iraq were directed in the south on Abadan and Ahwaz and farther north on Kermanshah and Hamadan, while soviet columns advanced south on Tabriz and Pahlevi. After slight initial resistance, the Iranian army ceased fighting. A fresh government was formed in Tehran, and by Sept. 2 the basis of a settlement with the Allies had been reached.

On Sept. 16 the shah abdicated in favour of his son and on the same day British and soviet troops arrived at Tehran. All axis nationals, with the exception of 80 Germans who had disappeared into the mountains, were evacuated.

G. The Balkan Campaigns (1940-41)

1. The Greek-Italian War.—The occupation of Albania by Italian forces on April 7, 1939, caused a reorientation of the defense plans of the Greek government, which hitherto in accordance with previous Balkan agreements had been considered in face of Bulgaria as a possible adversary. The distribution of troops was altered to deploy, for defensive purposes on the Albanian front, eight infantry divisions and two infantry brigades. The timing for concentration on this front was 22 days. The Greek air force comprised about 156 planes for all purposes, many of them of an obsolescent type.

In early Aug. 1940 Mussolini discussed in Rome the possibilities of an attack on Greece. The Greek light cruiser "Helly" was torpedoed by an unknown "alleged Italian" submarine on Aug. 15, the day of the Feast of the Assumption. The Greek government, on advice from Berlin, acted with caution over this incident, but the event had an important psychological effect on the whole of the Greek populace and added a religious zeal to the prosecution of the coming war against Italy.

On Oct. 12, 1940, and subsequent days Mussolini held conferences in Rome planning the attack on Greece. The date was fixed for October 28. The Italian forces taking part were on a war footing, while the Greek army had not mobilized. The main Italian thrust, consisting of two divisions and an armoured division, was directed through Epirus and was successful in forcing back Greek forces of one infantry division and one infantry brigade to the river Acheron. In the centre on the Pindus mountains, an Italian mountain division drove in initially through two Greek battalions and penetrated to the Metsovo pass but was unable to hold the ground gained in face of counterattacks. In the northeast, in the vicinity of the Prespa lakes, two Italian divisions attacked a Greek force consisting of one infantry division and one infantry brigade with similar results.

After two weeks of fighting, the Italian invasion had been checked and held by the Greek forces, whose divisions had concentrated on their respective battlefronts and gone straight into action. The mountainous nature of the terrain, with its lack of communications, made their supply difficulties acute. Greek peasants, men, women and children from the villages adjacent to the lines, carried up ammunition and rations to the forward troops. The Greek air force, which by this time was reduced to low numbers, was reinforced by five British squadrons from the middle east.

After Nov. 14, 1940, the initiative passed to the Greek forces. On the northeast front, in a hard battle in which five divisions were engaged on each side, the Greek forces captured the town of Koritza (Corcia); on the Epirus and central fronts, the Greeks forced back the Italians toward the frontier and by Nov. 16 had retaken Konitsa. At this juncture the Greek command was faced with having to decide whether to continue the defensive in the northeast, where the greater successes had been achieved but where they were faced with very mountainous terrain and no definite objective, or to concentrate on the Epirus front for a thrust against the port of Valona. The maintenance of communications for such an operation could be assisted by using sea transport. The latter course was decided upon and resulted in the capture of Port St. Quantara and the town of Argyrocastro by Dec. 8, while on the rest of the front parallel advances were made in the course of heavy fighting through mountains. In the centre progress had been made in the Aoos valley and Premeti was captured. Further attempts to reach Valona secured the port of Chimara on Dec. 28, but further offensive was brought to a standstill by heavy snow conditions. The strength of the forces engaged at the end of the year was as follows: Italians, 16 divisions; Greeks, 11 divisions, 2 infantry brigades and one cavalry division.

In Jan. 1941, the Greek command transferred the axis of attack to the centre sector. The offensive, initially successful, came to a halt by the end of the month after the capture of Boubessi but short of Tepelini, where it encountered many divisions freshly arrived from Italy. During February the Italians were still further reinforced and between March 9 and 25 launched a counteroffensive on a narrow front between Trebesina mountain, east of Tepelini and Boubessi, employing 12 divisions. This attack was stopped with heavy losses and no appreciable gain by six Greek divisions, while spasmodic fighting flared up all along the front. The forces engaged at the end of March were: Italian, 26 divisions; Greek, 14 divisions, 2 infantry brigades and a cavalry division.

The hard fighting, combined with bitter conditions prevailing in the Pindus mountains during the winter, had taken its toll of Greek manpower in casualties from battle and frostbite. Throughout the campaign, because of the lack of communications in the mountainous country, the maintenance of front-line troops imposed a great strain on all transport resources as well as on the troops themselves, who frequently had to resort to manhandling supplies.

The Italians were better situated in this respect, as the port of Valona and the communications radiating from it were not seriously disrupted. It was this background of conditions that the Greek command had to face when, at the end of March, the Germans were ready to strike from Bulgaria and the action of Yugoslavia was uncertain.

2. German Occupation of Rumania and Bulgaria.—During 1940 the occupation by the U.S.S.R. of the two Rumanian provinces of Bessarabia and Bukovina in June and the Italian attack on Greece on Oct. 28 disposed of any German intention of avoiding a commitment in the Balkans.

The joining of the axis by Rumania on Nov. 23, 1940, followed shortly by the infiltration into that country of German troops, secured the oil supply from the Ploesti fields and was a preliminary to the occupation of Bulgaria and eastern Thrace.

On March 1, 1941, Bulgaria joined the axis and the following day German troops commenced to cross the river Danube. In the occupation of Bulgaria the German forces found themselves in contact with two states, Yugoslavia on the west and Turkey to the southeast, whose attitude was so far undetermined. Forces therefore had to be detailed to cover these frontiers and had to be in sufficient strength to overawe the respective governments and prevent their taking action.

The German forces which entered Bulgaria consisted of 17 divisions (including five panzer) of which 8 were intended for the operations in Grecian Thrace. Their deployment was completed within approximately a week of crossing the Danube, but the build-up of air forces and supplies necessitated a pause; the stage was thus set for carrying out the occupation of the northern Aegean coast line at the end of March.

3. German Conquest of Yugoslavia and Greece.—The attitude of the Bulgarian government to the German infiltration into Rumania, which was nearly completed by the end of Jan. 1941, left no doubt that the German armies would be granted a free passage through that country for an attack on either Turkey or Greece. The Greek armies at that time were heavily engaged in Albania, where 300,000 troops were deployed on the front between Lake Ochrid and the Adriatic.

To replace heavy casualties in the Albanian fighting, the Greek garrisons of the fortified line in eastern Macedonia covering Salonika against an attack from Bulgaria, had been heavily drawn upon. Faced with the possibility of a German attack from this direction, the Greek government on Feb. 8, 1941, asked the British government what help could be afforded to it in case of such a development. As a result it was agreed that a British force would be sent to Greece to hold a position west of Salonika, which included the Aliakmon river and the Vermion range. This force was to be augmented by the Greek garrison from Thrace and eastern Macedonia, considered strategically indefensible in view of the forces available. This plan envisaged Yugoslavia, whose attitude was in doubt, either acting as an ally or a strict neutral, to cover the northern flank. In face of the menace of a German attack from Bulgaria, the soundest strategical course would have been to withdraw the Greek armies on the Albanian front to a shorter line and thereby produce reserves which could be used as required for operations in northeast Greece. The Greek commander in chief, Gen. Alexander Papagos, however, had to discard this plan in view of the disastrous effect it might have on the morale of the Greek soldiers.

The force for holding the Aliakmon-Vermion line was altered subsequently to three Greek divisions and seven independent battalions. The eastern Macedonia defense was held by three divisions. On March 7 the first British contingent (1st armoured brigade group) began to arrive in Athens and moved to an area west of the river Vardar, where it completed its concentration by March 21.

Meanwhile, heavy pressure was being brought to bear by the Germans on the Yugoslav government to join the Tripartite pact which, after much vacillation, was signed in Berlin on March 25. The Yugoslavs considered this agreement an infringement of their sovereignty. On March 27, a coup d'état organized by Gen. Dushan Simovitch expelled the regent and overthrew the government. A new government was formed in Belgrade but a paralysis of indecision descended on it, and several days were lost while a state of uncertainty existed as to what courses should be adopted politically or strategically. Meanwhile, the German high command had ordered an attack on Yugoslavia to be ready in eight days. The Yugoslav armies were in a semistate of mobilization, ill equipped and lacking in modern weapons, tanks, antitank and anti-aircraft guns.

On April 6 the axis attack started with heavy bombing attacks on Belgrade, while land operations took the form of thrusts inward from all round the perimeter. These thrusts were successful in dividing the Yugoslav army and eliminating it in detail. The German columns which moved through Stip were directed on Skoplje and Bitolj with the object of getting in touch with the left flank of the Italian armies in Albania and isolating the Yugoslav forces from Greece. The head of these columns reached Bitolj on April 8 and by April 9 had completed its task of cutting off the Yugoslav forces, who, by this time, were no longer capable of organized resistance. The inevitable result was that Yugoslavia passed under German domination on April 17, within 11 days of being attacked.

The German column moving via Strumica bypassed the Greek defenses in eastern Macedonia and erupted down the Vardar valley into the Salonika plain, where it came into contact with British troops on April 9.

The collapse of Yugoslav resistance and the occupation of Bitolj by German forces threatened the Anglo-Greek army in process of getting into the Aliakmon-Vermion position, as any advance down the valley running from Bitolj to Kozani would take that position in flank and reverse, the terrain offering easy movement for armoured fighting vehicles except for a gap with poor facilities for defense near Florina.

The imperial forces had meanwhile been augmented by the arrival of the New Zealand division and two-thirds of the 6th Australian division, which enabled a hastily improvised flank guard to be collected and established to watch the Florina gap. This detachment was in position by April 9 and in touch with the 20th Greek division on the Vermion range on the right, and a Greek cavalry division with one Greek infantry brigade under command detached from the Albanian front on the left, about Nymphaion.

A heavy bombing attack by the German air force on Piraeus harbour on April 7 caused considerable dislocation to the working of the port, which never regained its former capacity. From April 8 to 11, air operations were on a low scale because of bad weather.

The collapse of resistance in Yugoslavia placed the Anglo-Greek army in a difficult situation. Its flank was threatened by a force of one armoured and one infantry division from the direction of Bitolj, while on its front a German corps was west of the river Vardar and in contact. The Aliakmon-Vermion position was held too lightly for its length of front to offer protracted defense, and it was doubtful how long the detachment guarding the Florina gap could hold on in face of the superior forces opposed to it. It was decided therefore to fall back to a line running from Mount Olympus through Servia and then northward along the mountain ridge east of and parallel to the upper section of the Aliakmon river.

The German advance from Bitolj crossed the frontier on April 10 and became heavily engaged with the flank guard. A two-day battle was fought in a snowstorm in which the Germans were able to make some slight progress. While this fighting was taking place, the withdrawal from the Aliakmon-Vermion position started on the night of April 11–12 and was completed by the morning of April 13; the flank guard covered by the 1st British armoured brigade thereupon fell back on Kozani.

German panzer units moving southward through Greece in April 1941, despite heavy spring rains and muddy roads

During these three days' operations, the forecast of General Papagos as to the effect a withdrawal would have on the morale of the Greek army became manifest. His divisions had not been trained to carry out such a complicated manoeuvre as a retreat, and signs of disintegration were beginning to appear. In consequence it was decided to withdraw all forces east of the Upper Aliakmon river to its western bank.

Up to April 14, except for the heavy bombing of Kozani, the activity of the German air force was limited while the small British air force engaged German columns. With the improvement of weather conditions, the German air force came into operation again; and its attacks became continuous, widespread and intense, directed mainly on road and rail communications.

Though the Anglo-Greek army in central Macedonia still presented an intact front, the general situation was far from satisfactory. The weakness of the left of the Greek forces in the Upper Aliakmon valley and the gap between the left of the Greek cavalry division and the armies in Albania were being exploited by the Germans and would shortly become a menace. To meet this situation it became necessary to withdraw all Allied armies to a shorter line in order to retain an intact front.

On April 14, General Papagos approved the further withdrawal of the Anglo-Greek army to a line through Thermopylae to which the armies in Albania would conform. He suggested at the same time that the British forces should withdraw from Greece to save the country from devastation.

On April 15, fighting developed in the Mount Olympus area, in which Australian and New Zealand troops were engaged. The withdrawal commenced on April 17 and was largely carried out by night to avoid German air attacks. By April 20 the occupation of the new position was complete with the New Zealanders holding the famous Thermopylae pass and the 6th Australian division the Brailos pass farther inland.

On April 18 Alexander Korizis, who had succeeded Gen. John Metaxas as prime minister, committed suicide; and King George II became acting head of the government. As a result of conferences following this crisis it was decided with the full approval of the Greek king and government that the evacuation of the imperial forces was essential, and the first night for embarkation was fixed for April 28. Events in Epirus, however, caused the evacuation to be advanced four days; on April 21 the German Adolf Hitler division had reached Yannina and the local commander, without reference to the high command in Athens, had ordered the capitulation of the whole of the Greek army in Epirus. The embarkation was set therefore to commence on the night of April 24–25 and to be completed in three nights. The port of Piraeus was unusable but still remained a target for German bombing. Nine embarkation points, consisting of small ports and open beaches, were selected on the coast line between Marathon to the north, east of Athens, and Kalamati in the south of the Peloponnesus.

The rearward movement to the beaches began on the night of April 22–23 and was carried out without interference until April 24, when a German attack in force with tanks along the coast on Thermopylae was repulsed by the 6th New Zealand infantry brigade.

The royal navy with the light forces of the Mediterranean fleet carried out the embarkation and transport of troops by sea. By using fast warships for the journey to and from Crete, rigidity in the plan could be avoided and embarkation points altered to suit the tactical situation on land. The movement by sea was subjected to continuous attacks by the German air force by day and cost the loss of some warships and transports. The destruction of the remaining British fighters on an airfield at Argos gave the Germans complete superiority at this time.

The evacuation was completed by April 28–29, but at Nauplion and Kalamati the Germans were successful in cutting off certain detachments which could not be embarked.

The number of British commonwealth troops sent to Greece was approximately 57,660. Of these, 43,000 were taken off, but all equipment had to be jettisoned. Of those embarked, 27,000 were landed in Crete and the remainder transported to Egypt.

The inability of the Italian forces in Albania to achieve success over the Greeks, the Yugoslav coup d'état and the presence of British forces in central Macedonia forced the German high command to a commitment considerably in excess of its original concept. In all, 27 German field divisions (including 7 panzer divisions) became involved in the campaign against Greece and Yugoslavia, in terrain which precluded rapidity of movement, thereby causing difficulties when it came to extrication.

By April 21, information had reached Athens through Balkan railway sources that a comprehensive and carefully worked out railway movement of troops from southeast Bulgaria to Galicia had been dislocated by the diversion of these troops to the Greek and Yugoslav fronts. That such a concentration was contemplated could portend only that a German attack on the U.S.S.R. was imminent. It could be assessed that in the extrication of their divisions from the Balkans, the German high command lost from four to five weeks before completing their preparations for the attack on Russia, which took place on June 22. This delay, if studied in conjunction with the German attempt to take Moscow before the end of 1941 and the advent of an early winter, played no inconsiderable part in the final outcome of World War II.

4. The Conquest of Crete.—The capture of Crete became necessary to the German high command after the occupation of Greece in order to secure sea communications in the Aegean and to provide fields for air action against the middle east and Mediterranean shipping routes. Crete, a mountainous island 160 mi. long by 40 mi. broad, offered poor facilities for defense against an attack from Greece since its one lateral road, harbours and airfields were all located along its northern shore. All Allied shipping therefore had to pass through the narrow waters between either Greece or Rhodes, held by axis forces.

The imperial garrison consisted of 28,000 troops, most of whom, having been evacuated from Greece, were short of equipment and supporting weapons. The defense was disposed along the northern coast to cover the airfields of Malemi and Retimo, the port and harbour of Heraklion and the naval base at Suda bay. The German air force was in such superiority in attacking shipping and airfields that all British aircraft were withdrawn before the main operation. The main attack started with the heavy bombing of Malemi aerodrome in the northwest corner of the island at dawn on May 20 and was followed by parachutists and gliders. In the afternoon similar tactics were employed against Retimo and Heraklion. In all about 7,000 troops were landed during the day. Casualties were extremely heavy, and only at Malemi had the attack established itself. At night counterattacks by New Zealand troops were at first successful, but at dawn they were compelled to abandon ground because of heavy bombing.

During May 21–22, heavy fighting took place around Malemi aerodrome while German forces were continually landing from troop carriers. This enabled a sufficient force to be built up at Malemi to advance toward the town of Canea.

During the nights May 21–22 and 22–23, German attempts to reinforce by sea, using a large number of small craft, were frustrated by the royal navy, which caused considerable casualties but at the same time suffered losses itself from bombing after daylight.

Heavy fighting continued through May 24–25, the German attacks on Canea continuing to make progress; at Heraklion two British battalions landed on the south coast, marched overland and eased the pressure. German detachments, however, isolated the Retimo garrison by cutting the road east and west of the airfield.

On May 27, the Germans succeeded in breaking through the Allied defenses covering Canea and thereby rendered Suda bay untenable. The continuous fighting and uninterrupted air bombing were beginning to exhaust the power of the defense with the result that on that day the decision was made to evacuate. The losses suffered by the royal navy from axis bombing made it imperative that the evacuation should take place in the shortest possible time and it was decided that all should be completed by the night of May 31–June 1. The imperial forces in the Canea area, consisting of Australian and New Zealand brigades, British marines and commandos with tank and artillery units, withdrew over the mountains to the small port of Sphakia on the south coast, where embarkation started on the night of May 28–29 and was carried out without undue interference. At Heraklion the evacuation was completed on the night of May 28–29 from that port in warships, thereby avoiding a German attack which was in preparation. The isolated Australian and Greek garrison at Retimo, having received no orders to withdraw, continued fighting until May 31, when it was overwhelmed.

There were 27,550 imperial troops in action at the commencement of the attack; of these, 14,580 were evacuated. The German losses were estimated at between 12,000 and 15,000, which included a very high percentage of killed.

The German success was attributable to the manner in which a completely superior air force was handled in conjunction with air-borne troops. Success against troops ill supplied with supporting arms took longer to achieve and cost more than the German high command anticipated. The troops employed could not be reconstituted before late in the autumn, and an operation on such a scale was never again attempted. (H. M. Wn.)

H. The German-Russian War

The course of history was changed when Hitler invaded the U.S.S.R. on June 22, 1941, a day ahead of the anniversary of Napoleon's invasion. That move ultimately proved as fatal for him as it had for Napoleon. The effect was most immediate on Britain's situation. Until then its prospects had appeared hopeless in the eyes of most people except its own, for its situation was far worse under modern conditions of war than it had been in Napoleon's time. Its government's decision to continue the struggle after the fall of France, and reject Hitler's peace offers, could spell only slow suicide unless relief came from one or other of the two remaining great powers. Otherwise, even if a German sea-borne invasion failed, the concentrated development of submarine and air pressure on Britain's sea communications was bound to produce eventual collapse.

Hitler brought Britain relief by turning east, just as the strain was becoming severe. That eastward turn was influenced by Britain's stubborn resistance but had deeper promptings. He had always contemplated the overthrow of soviet Russia. Though he had brought himself to make the 1939 pact as a matter of expediency, anti-Bolshevism was his most profound emotional conviction, arising from fear even more than from ambition. It had been stirred up afresh before he even considered the question of invading Britain. For early in June 1940, while he was still engaged in the French campaign, Stalin had seized the opportunity to occupy the three Baltic states. Then on June 26, again without notice to Hitler, Russia addressed a 24-hour ultimatum to Rumania demanding the restoration of Bessarabia, together with the surrender of northern Bukovina. The Russian forces poured in immediately, as Rumania yielded. That placed them ominously close to the oilfields on which Germany depended. Hitler became acutely suspicious of Stalin's intentions and began to feel that he could not afford to wait to complete the subjugation of the west before dealing with Russia.

A provisional plan for a stroke against Russia was worked out in the late summer of 1940, and elaborated in the autumn. The doubts of his generals merely served to give the new turn of his mind a more definite bent. Their doubts suggested that they still distrusted his military judgment; he must prove them wrong once again, and more strikingly. When they argued that it meant war on two fronts, he retorted that to overcome Britain would require an expansion of the air force and navy at the expense of the army, and that this could not be risked while Russia remained a menace. In that mood he did not share his diplomatists' moderate satisfaction over the result of the November discussions with Vyacheslav Molotov in Berlin, but only noted the Russians' hesitation to join the axis. On Dec. 18 he issued "Directive No. 21, Case Barbarossa," which opened with the statement: "The German armed forces must be prepared to crush soviet Russia in a quick campaign before the end of the war against England."

On Feb. 3, 1941, Hitler approved the final draft of the plan, and had it expounded by Field Marshal Wilhelm Keitel to a conference of his chief soldiers. Their anxieties were not diminished by Keitel's balance sheet, which showed that the invasion would have to be made with an inferiority of numbers, in tanks as well as men, and must trust to an offsetting superiority of quality. That deficiency of strength became a handicap even before the offensive was launched. For Hitler was anxious to safeguard his Balkan flanks before striking at Russia and had hoped to secure this by power-diplomacy alone, without fighting. That hope was impaired, to his annoyance, by Mussolini's independent aggression against Greece which opened up the prospect of a British army's being landed there. This threat led Hitler to decide that he must overcome Greece and clear out the British before he could proceed with his eastern plan. But the effort entailed was much increased when Yugoslavia's adhesion to the axis was upset by a military coup d'état in that country on March 27. Larger forces had now to be sent south to crush Yugoslavia simultaneously with Greece. Both nations were quickly overrun while the British were hustled back into their ships. But Hitler's decision, on April 1, to mount this double offensive had entailed the postponement of the Barbarossa plan from the middle of May to late June. By the swiftness of his Balkan victories he was able to keep to this revised timetable, but the five weeks' delay went far toward for-

feiting his subsequent chance of victory over Russia.

1. To the Outskirts of Moscow.—The German offensive was delivered on June 22, 1941, by three army groups under the same commanders as in the 1940 invasion of the west. Field Marshal Gerd Rundstedt was on the right, in southern Poland. Field Marshal Fedor von Bock was in the centre, north of the Pripet marshes. Field Marshal Wilhelm von Leeb was on the left and drove through the Baltic states. But this time the main weight, and the decisive role, was committed to Bock's army group. Two armoured groups (later rechristened "armies"), under Gen. Heinz Guderian and Gen. Hermann Hoth, were allotted to Bock's front compared with only one, under Kleist, to Rundstedt's front. Once again the issue turned, not on the infantry masses, but on the armoured forces. These had now been increased from 10 divisions to 20, but only by halving the scale of tanks in each division.

On Bock's front, the invasion profited at the start from the way that the Russian position in Poland formed a projection. Cutting quickly into the flanks of this Bialystok salient, Bock's armies attempted their first pincer stroke around Slonim, 100 mi. beyond the initial front line. But they were not quick enough to complete the encirclement before the bulk of the enveloped Russian armies forced their way out of the trap. Although these were clumsily handled and frittered their tank strength away in piecemeal action like that of the French in 1940, the isolated troops fought with a stubbornness that the French had not shown, and their resistance imposed a brake by the way it continued to block road centres long after the German tide had swept on.

The armoured groups of Guderian and Hoth, on the wings, now drove 100 mi. farther to produce an envelopment round Minak, which fell on June 30. But the effort to close the ring failed, though many prisoners were taken, and with the miscarriage of this intended decisive manoeuvre, Hitler's dream of a quick victory faded. A series of rainstorms came to the aid of the Russians, turning the sandy soil into mud. Even when the tanks could push on, they were often held back because their transport, composed of heavy-wheeled vehicles, was bogged. The Germans had owed their success to the measure in which they were mechanized but now paid forfeit for not being sufficiently mechanized; that is, on tracks. The frustration of Hitler's "grand design" now drew him into that advance beyond the Dnieper which he had hoped to avoid. In mid-July a third encirclement was executed around Smolensk. This time a much larger bag of Russians was secured but more escaped to help in forming a fresh block across the road to Moscow. The Germans were now 400 mi. deep into Russia, and Moscow lay 200 mi. ahead. Bock wanted to push on, but Hitler hesitated in a state of indecision.

Meanwhile, Rundstedt's army group had been driving forward through southern Poland with little difficulty despite the greater strength of the Russian armies there. These were thrown off their balance by the invasion and fell back eastward in confusion. In the next phase, Rundstedt's advance was delayed by flank counterattacks from the Pripet marshes. But at the end of July, Kleist's tanks broke through Gen. (later Marshal) Simeon M. Budenny's front south of Kiev and made a scythe-like sweep down through the Ukraine toward the Black sea. The mouths of the Bug and the Dnieper were reached by mid-August, trapping a large part of the southern Russian armies which were opposing the advance from Rumania. This striking success suggested to Hitler the idea of shifting his centre of gravity and carrying out another great encircling manoeuvre near the junction of Bock's and Rundstedt's army groups. Kleist was ordered to wheel northward again, and Guderian southward, to close the pincers behind the Russian armies assembled around Kiev. This trap succeeded, and 600,000 prisoners were taken. But it was late in September before the victory was completed, and winter was approaching.

Elated by this great success, Hitler decided to resume the advance on Moscow, while Kleist was again sent south, to form the spearhead of a continued advance southeastward by Rundstedt, from the Dnieper to the Don, on the road to the Caucasus. Leeb's advance through the Baltic states had reached the outskirts of Leningrad, but Hitler cancelled the intended assault, fearing to become entangled in city fighting. Rightly, he deemed it wiser to rely on the German superiority of manoeuvre in the open, but he had lost the best two months of the summer, when the open country was good going. He also handicapped his chances by splitting his effort in divergent directions.

The renewed advance on Moscow began on Oct. 2. Its prospects looked bright when Bock's armies brought off a great encirclement round Vyazma, where a further 600,000 Russians were captured. That left the Germans momentarily with an almost clear path to Moscow. But the Vyazma battle had not been completed until the end of October; the German troops were tired, the country became a morass as the weather got worse, and fresh Russian forces appeared in the path as they plodded slowly forward. Most of the German generals wanted to break off the offensive and take up a suitable winter line. But Hitler could not resist the temptation of Moscow, now so close in front of his eyes, and was convinced that the Russians were on the verge of collapse. Bock, as the commander who was given the role of honour, had a natural tendency to agree with Hitler. On Dec. 2 a further effort was launched, and some detachments penetrated into the suburbs of Moscow; but the advance as a whole was held up in the forests covering the capital.

2. Russian Winter Counteroffensive.—This was the signal for a Russian counteroffensive of large scale, prepared and directed by Gen. (later Marshal) Georgi K. Zhukov. It tumbled back the exhausted Germans, lapped round their flanks and produced a critical situation. From generals downward, the invaders were filled with ghastly thoughts of Napoleon's retreat from Moscow. In that emergency Hitler forbade any retreat beyond the shortest possible local withdrawals. His decision exposed his troops to awful sufferings in their advanced positions facing Moscow, for they had neither the clothing nor equipment for a Russian winter campaign; but if they had once started a general retreat it might easily have degenerated into a panic-stricken rout.

In the south, Kleist's drive had reached Rostov, near the mouth of the Don, on Nov. 23; but it had exhausted its fuel in plowing through the mud. The glamour of attaining this "gateway to the Caucasus" impelled Hitler to insist on staying there, although Rundstedt tendered his resignation rather than commit such a folly. Within a week the Germans were thrown back by a Russian counterstroke there. For a moment their situation looked grave, but they managed to hold on to the defensive line of the Mius river, which Rundstedt had chosen before his removal.

The soviet army's winter counteroffensive continued for more than three months after its December launching, though with diminishing progress. By March 1942 it had advanced more than 150 mi. in some sectors. But the Germans maintained their hold on the main bastions of their winter front—such towns as Schlüsselburg, Novgorod, Rzhev, Vyazma, Briansk, Orel, Kursk, Kharkov and Taganrog—despite the fact that the Russians were often many miles in the rear. In retrospect, it became clear that Hitler's veto on any extensive withdrawal worked out in such a way as to restore the confidence of the German troops and probably saved them from a widespread collapse. Nevertheless, they paid a heavy price indirectly for that rigid defense. Its success encouraged the belief that it could be as successfully repeated in the more adverse conditions of the following winters. A more immediate handicap was that the strength of the luftwaffe was drained in the prolonged effort to maintain supplies by air, under winter conditions, to the garrisons of these more or less isolated bastion towns. The tremendous strain of that winter campaign, on an army that had not been prepared for it, had also a serious delayed effect in other ways. Before the winter ended, many divisions were reduced to barely a third of their original strength. They were never fully built up again. The unfavourable aspects of the situation were realized by the German general staff, but its heads now had less power to influence Hitler's decision. Hitler's pressure was too strong for them to resist, and the pressure of events was too strong for Hitler. He was compelled to go on and on. The weight of military opposition was weakened by the changes in the higher commands which followed the miscarriage of the 1941 campaign. When the failure of the whole campaign was plain to the world, the removal of Field Marshal Walther von Brauchitsch was announced. That act served the dual purpose of furnishing Hitler with a scapegoat and opening the way for him to take over direct command of the army.

3. German Advance to the Caucasus.—The plan to launch another great offensive crystallized in the early months of 1942. Hitler's decision was influenced by pressure from his economists. They told him that Germany could not continue the war unless it obtained oil supplies from the Caucasus, a view that was proved mistaken by the fact that Germany failed to secure the Caucasus oil yet managed to continue the war for three more years. But Hitler was the more responsive to such economic arguments because they coincided with his instinctive urge to do something positive and offensive. He was led, however, to recognize the limitation of Germany's resources to the extent of admitting the necessity of limiting the scope of his new offensive. The main effort was to be made on the southern flank near the Black sea.

The most effective factor in clearing the path for the German advance was a Russian offensive toward Kharkov, which began on May 12. This was a premature effort, beyond the powers of the soviet army at this stage in face of the Germans' defensive skill. The prolongation of this Kharkov offensive played into the Germans' hands, absorbing too large a part of the Russians' reserves. Moreover, although the Russians succeeded in parrying the immediate counterstroke which the Germans launched against the southern flank, this gained a valuable leverage for the future by reaching the Donetz river near Izyum. On June 3, preliminary to the main offensive, a siege assault was launched against the fortress of Sevastopol though it was not until July 3 that the fortress, and with it the whole Crimea, was completely in German hands. On June 10 the Germans exploited their Izyum wedge by forcing the passage of the Donetz and gaining a bridgehead on the north bank. This created an invaluable flanking leverage to assist the easterly thrust of their main offensive, which was launched on June 28.

The 4th panzer army broke through in the sector between Kursk and Byelgorod, and swept rapidly across the 100-mi. stretch of plain to the Don near Voronezh. It then wheeled southeastward into the corridor between the Don and the Donetz, followed by the 6th army, which had the mission of taking Stalingrad. These operations tended to cloak the menace that was developing on the right wing. For a more dangerous thrust was being delivered by Kleist's 1st panzer army from the Kharkov sector. After achieving a quick break through, it drove toward the lower Don at and above Rostov. There it gained a crossing, with little opposition, on July 22, after an advance of about 250 mi. from the starting line. The German armies now forked on divergent courses: part for the Caucasus oil fields, and part for the Volga at Stalingrad. After crossing the lower Don, Kleist's right column drove southward through Armavir to the great oil centre of Maikop, 200 mi. beyond Rostov, which it reached on Aug. 9. On the same day the van of his centre column swept into Pyatigorsk, 150 mi. to the east of Maikop, on the outskirts of the Caucasus mountains.

The pace of this early August onrush beyond the Don was terrific. But it slowed down almost as suddenly as it had developed. The prime causes were a shortage of fuel and an abundance of mountains. That dual brake was subsequently reinforced by the distant effect of the struggle for Stalingrad, which drained off a large part of the forces that might have been used to give a decisive impetus to the Caucasus advance. The first serious check occurred on reaching the Terek river, which covered the approaches to the mountain road over to Tiflis. Kleist then tried a manoeuvre to the east, downstream, and succeeded in forcing a passage near Mozdok, in the first week of September. But his forces were held up again in the densely wooded hills beyond the Terek. Throughout September and October, Kleist went on trying to push south from Mozdok, by surprise attacks at different points. At each attempt he was blocked. The front was then stabilized, with the Germans still facing the mountain barrier which they had vainly tried to pierce. This final repulse in the central Caucasus coincided with the opening of the great Russian counteroffensive at Stalingrad.

4. Turning Point at Stalingrad.—The German command might have captured Stalingrad with little difficulty at the end of July if it had not overestimated the capacity of the Russians to hold Rostov and the lower Don. For the 4th panzer army was temporarily diverted southward to help the 1st, which, in fact, needed no such help. When the postponed thrust to Stalingrad developed a fortnight later, the Russians had gathered just sufficient forces to check the advance. Another fortnight passed before their resistance was loosened by the advance of the German 6th army, under Gen. (later Field Marshal) Friedrich Paulus, eastward across the Don bend. The last week of August had thus arrived before the Germans were ready to begin the final stage. The tenseness of the situation was manifested in the tone of the call of the Russian troops to hold on at all costs to the last man. They responded to the call with wonderful endurance. Attack followed attack in seemingly endless succession, with frequent changes of site and method, but with only slight progress to compensate for the attackers' cost. The more closely the Germans converged on the city, the more their own power of manoeuvre became cramped, whereas the narrowing of the frontage helped the defender in moving his reserves more quickly to a threatened point on the diminished arc. At the same time, the Germans' concentration at Stalingrad increasingly drained reserves from their flank cover, which

The German caption on this photograph showing nazi soldiers in Stalingrad during the siege of 1942 noted that "one step at a time, every foot of ground in Stalingrad had to be fought for"

itself was already strained by having to stretch so far, nearly 400 mi. from Voronezh along the Don to the Stalingrad "isthmus," and as far again from there to the Terek.

On the surface, the defenders' position came to appear increasingly perilous, or even desperate, as the circle contracted and the Germans came closer to the heart of the city. The most critical moment was on Oct. 14. The defenders now had their backs so close to the Volga that they had little room left in which to practice shock-absorbing tactics. But beneath the surface fundamental factors were working in their favour. The attackers' morale was being sapped by heavy losses, a growing sense of frustration, and the coming of winter, while their reserves were so fully absorbed as to leave the overstretched flanks without resiliency. They were thus becoming ripe for the counterstroke which the Russian command was preparing. It was launched on Nov. 19 and was well timed. It started in the interval between the first strong frosts, which hardened the ground for rapid movement, and the heavy snows, which clogged manoeuvre. A pair of pincers, each composed of several prongs, was inserted in the flanks of the Stalingrad attack, so as to isolate the 6th army and 4th panzer army. The pincers were driven in at places where the flank cover was largely provided by Rumanian troops. The plan was devised by a brilliant triumvirate of the Russian general staff, Zhukov, Gen. (later Marshal) Alexander M. Vasilevsky and Gen. (later Marshal) Nikolai N. Voronov. By Nov. 23 the encirclement was completed. It was welded more firmly in the days that followed, enclosing more than 200,000 Germans.

Meanwhile, another powerful Russian force had burst out of the Serafimovichi bridgehead and spread over the country west of the Don bend. This outer-circle movement was of vital importance, for it dropped an iron curtain across the more direct routes by which the relieving forces might have come to the aid of Paulus. Thus, the German reply, in mid-December, was delivered from the southwest, beyond the Don, up the line from Kotelnikovo to Stalingrad. But this hastily improvised advance was checked a long way short of the beleagured army and then gradually forced back by Russian pressure on its own flank. With the frustration of this attempt any hope of relieving Paulus passed, for the German command had no reserves for another attempt.

Hitler was at last brought to realize the inevitability of a disaster greater even than the Stalingrad encirclement if he persisted in his dream of conquering the Caucasus and compelled the armies there to cling on while their flank was exposed for 600 mi. back. So, early in Jan. 1943, the order was sent that they were to retreat. The decision was taken just in time for them to escape being cut off. Their successful extrication prolonged the war, but it preceded the actual surrender of the Stalingrad armies in making clear to the world that the German tide was on the ebb. Paulus' army at Stalingrad surrendered on Jan. 31, 1943, at the same time as Kleist's army from the Caucasus recrossed the Don at Rostov. The latter could hardly have escaped if Paulus' army had yielded any time during the first seven weeks after its encirclement. Its sacrifice detained Russian forces that could otherwise have poured down upon Kleist's line of retreat and swamped Field Marshal Fritz Erich von Manstein's army which was covering Kleist's rear. Even as it was, those two armies held off the Russians' outflanking pressure by the narrowest of margins. In terms of time, space, force and weather conditions that Xenophon-like retreat was an amazing performance.

5. Russian Reconquest of the Ukraine.—After Kleist's army had passed safely through the Rostov bottleneck, it had still to ward off dangers that were developing farther back on its line of retreat. In the last half of Jan. 1943 Gen. Nikolai F. Vatutin's armies had struck southward

Red army troops in Kharkov after its first capture by Russian troops Feb. 16, 1943. The city was retaken by the Germans a month later, but occupied again by the Russians the following Aug. 23

from the middle Don to the Donetz. At the same time Gen. Filip I. Golikov's armies, farther west, broke through the front of the 2nd Hungarian army, and within a week drove forward 100 mi., halfway from the Don to Kharkov. Before the end of the month the Russians struck westward from Voronezh, across the upper Don, and advanced on Kursk, the starting point of the last German summer offensive, which they captured on Feb. 7. Two days earlier Vatutin had crossed the Donetz southward at Izyum and then spread westward to capture Lozovaya junction on Feb. 11. Besides undercutting the German position at Kharkov, which fell into the Russians' hands on Feb. 16, these advances came near to intercepting the armies of Manstein and Kleist. Their retreat became a race, with the odds against them.

But a dramatic change came over the scene in the last half of February. An early thaw intervened to hamper the Russians in bringing up supplies and reinforcements to maintain their momentum. Thus, the retreating armies gained time to get back to the Dnieper, with the help of the better communications in the coastal strip, and mount a counteroffensive just as the Russian advance had lost its impetus. This counteroffensive snapped off the Russian wedges southwest of Kharkov and recovered the line of the Donetz. If the Germans could have crossed the river quickly and cut astride the rear of the soviet armies that were pushing westward, they might have produced a Russian disaster comparable to their own at Stalingrad. But they were baulked in the attempt, lacking the strength to storm such a barrier. Although they squeezed the Russians out of Kharkov, their own drive petered out in the slush of the spring thaw.

Further evidence of their shrinking strength was seen in the withdrawal they were now compelled to carry out in the north. Gen. Kurt Zeitzler, who had succeeded Gen. Franz Halder as chief of the general staff, persuaded Hitler that it was no longer possible to maintain their advanced position facing Moscow. So in March the Germans abandoned their salients there and fell back to a straighter line close to Smolensk. What the Germans gained by this shortening of their front was, however, more than offset by the fresh extension caused by the success of their counteroffensive in the south. Although its results had been limited, it had secured a promising set of offensive springboards that looked all too tempting to a leader who instinctively clung to the hope that an offensive success in summer might still turn the war in his favour. By recapturing Byelgorod and retaining Orel the Germans had suitable flank positions for a pincer stroke against the big salient in which the Russians were left around Kursk.

Following this line of thought, Hitler concentrated all efforts on that offensive without regard to the risk that the cost of an unsuccessful attack would leave him without reserves to maintain any subsequent defense of his long front. His generals had become more doubtful than ever of his policy, though the two who were chosen to play the leading roles, Kluge and Manstein, naturally tended to swallow their doubts—professional opportunity always nourishes hope. But the increasing difficulty in building up the forces, with fresh drafts of men and equipment, was reflected in the increased delay that year in opening the summer offensive. Three months' pause followed the close of the winter campaign.

By contrast, the soviet army had improved a lot since 1942, both in quality and quantity. The flow of new equipment had greatly increased as well as the number of new divisions, and its numerical superiority was now about four to one. Better still, its leadership had improved with experience. Generals and junior commanders alike had become more skilled tacticians. That was foreshadowed in the way the Russians, in the summer of 1943, waited to let the Germans lead off and commit themselves deeply, while they themselves kept well poised to exploit the Germans' loss of balance in lunging.

The German offensive was at last launched on July 5, and into it Hitler threw 17 armoured divisions, almost all he had. Both the pincers got entangled in the deep mine fields which the Russians had laid, forewarned by the long preparation of the offensive, and failed to secure any large bag of prisoners since the Russians had withdrawn their main forces out of reach. After a week of effort the German armoured divisions were seriously reduced.

On July 12, as the Germans began to pull out, the Russians launched their own offensive, which thus had the recoil-spring effect of a counterstroke. The Germans just managed to check the northern thrust from cutting their communications behind Orel, and they were not squeezed out of that city until Aug. 5. The southern thrust began more gradually but then quickened into a deep drive past Byelgorod. The danger of a general collapse was narrowly averted by the arrival from the south of the Germans' one remaining armoured corps, though Kharkov had to be abandoned. In the second half of August the Russian offensive was more widely extended; and though it did not make headway very fast, its alternating strokes kept the scanty German reserves scurrying from sector to sector.

In September the shrinkage of German reserves was reflected in an acceleration of the Russians' advance. Skilful commanders like Vatutin, Gen. (later Marshal) Ivan S. Koniev and Gen. (later Marshal) Konstantin Rokossovski were quick to exploit thin stretches of the broad front. Before the end of the month they had reached the Dnieper and established a wide range of bridgeheads beyond it. While attention was focussed by Vatutin's threat to the famous city of Kiev, Koniev burst out of his bridgehead at Kremenchug and went halfway to severing the great bulge formed by the Dnieper bend. Although Manstein rushed reserves there in time to stem the advance and extricate the imperilled garrisons, it was at the price of a breakdown between the Dnieper bend and the sea. The Russians' fresh stroke there reached the mouth of the Dnieper early in November, closing the exits from the Crimea and isolating the German forces there.

At the same moment Vatutin advanced from his bridgeheads near Kiev, broke into the city from the rear and drove 100 mi. westward in a week to capture the junctions of Zhitomir and Korosten, not far from the Polish frontier. Manstein was left without reserves to meet this crisis, but ordered one of his best young generals, H. von Manteuffel, to scrape together such armoured fragments as he could find for a flank counterattack. This light stroke profited by the Russians' overstretch and tumbled them out of both junctions. Manstein tried to develop the opportunity by organizing a larger counteroffensive when reinforcements arrived from the west; but although it pushed the Russians back toward Kiev it was never so dangerous as it appeared on the surface, and early in December it petered out in the mud.

Hitler's chief consolation that autumn was that his northern armies, after falling back from Smolensk in September to a line covering the upper Dnieper, succeeded in repelling five successive Russian offensives between October and December. The assaults there were mainly delivered astride the Moscow-Minsk highway. As they came along an obvious line and on a narrow front, the well-knit defense proved superior despite a numerical inferiority of about one to six. It showed how Hitler might have spun out the war if his strategy had been wiser, and less self-exhausting.

6. Russians Enter Poland and Rumania.—The dominant factor in the campaign of 1944 was that the German front remained as wide as ever, while the German forces were shrinking. As a natural result the Russian advance continued with little check except from its own supply problem; and, because of the Russians' simpler requirements, that problem was less of a handicap than in any other great national army. On Dec. 24, 1943, Vatutin's armies, now reinforced, burst out of the Kiev salient and within a week had regained Zhitomir and Korosten. On Jan. 4 they crossed the prewar Polish frontier. Scraping up reserves, Manstein produced another inner flank counterstroke that checked Vatutin's progress, but only at the price of thinning the line both north and south. The Russians soon profited by the opportunity. On the north, they drove forward and captured Luck, 100 mi. beyond the frontier, by Feb. 5. On the south, Vatutin's left wing converged with Koniev's right wing to pinch off a force of ten weak German divisions that was still clinging, by Hitler's order, to the Dnieper line near Korsun. This produced a miniature "Stalingrad." The effort to bring help to this trapped force entailed, in turn, the abandonment of Nikopol, in the Dnieper bend, and its valuable manganese ore.

Early in March 1944 the Russians started a new combined manoeuvre, of still wider scope. It began with a thrust toward Tarnopol that outflanked the defensive line of the upper Bug. This was delivered by Zhukov, who had taken charge of Vatutin's armies when the latter was stricken with a fatal illness. Meanwhile, at the southern end of the front, Gen. (later Marshal) Rodion Y. Malinovski's armies pushed forward across the mouths of the Dnieper and the Bug. Between these two horns, Koniev drove suddenly forward to the central stretch of the Bug, crossed it, drove on to the Dniester 70 mi. beyond and crossed this difficult river by seizing pontoon bridges intact in the confusion caused by his swift onrush.

Before the end of March, Koniev's spearheads had penetrated to the line of the Pruth near Jassy, in Rumania, while Zhukov had crossed the upper reaches of that river. This advance brought them close to the foothills of the Carpathians, the ramparts of Hungary. Hitler promptly reacted to the danger by occupying Hungary. The preservation of this mountain barrier was essential, not only to check a Russian surge into the plains of central Europe, but to ensure any continued hold on the Balkans.

On April 1 Zhukov's advance reached the entrance to the Tartar pass, and it looked as if he might repeat Sabutai's exploit of 1241, when the Mongols swept through the Hungarian plain to the Danube in a few days. But his spearhead failed to penetrate the pass, and there was not sufficient weight behind it to renew the impetus. His forces were feeling the effects of their prolonged advance, while the Germans benefited by falling back on their supply lines. The following week they succeeded in mounting a flank counterstroke from the Lwów area that broke off the tip of Zhukov's spearhead and enabled them to extricate a part of their forces which had been trapped by the Russians' rapid advance. After this the front in southern Poland was stabilized from April to July. Koniev, also, was halted in his effort to penetrate the northern stretch of the Rumanian frontier. But his left wing wheeled south down the Dniester, toward the Black sea, thus threatening the rear of the German forces that were facing Malinovski's advance toward Odessa. This leverage squeezed the Germans out of that great port, which was regained by the Russians on April 10.

April also saw the liberation of the Crimea, to which Hitler had insisted on clinging. Gen. (later Marshal) Fedor Tolbukhin attacked southward, from the mainland, and unhinged the defenses of the Perekop isthmus by a crossing of the Siwash lagoon. Then Gen. Andrey Yeremenko struck westward from his foothold on the Kerch peninsula. The Germans were thrown into confusion, and most of the Crimea forces were quickly overrun, up to the outskirts of Sevastopol. Hitler still believed that the fortress itself could be maintained, though he let the Rumanians be evacuated by sea and relied on the stubbornness of the German garrison. But when the Russians breached the southeast approaches, between Inkerman and Balaklava, the garrison abandoned Sevastopol on April 10 and fell back into the Khersonese peninsula. The Germans' resistance there, with their backs to the sea, was as brief as on the Cape Bon peninsula in Tunisia the year before.

On the other flank of the eastern front, a January offensive broke the Germans' encircling grip on Leningrad. There, however, they achieved an orderly withdrawal, at the end of which they stood fast on the line of lakes from the Gulf of Finland to Pskov. This straightening and shortening of their front much improved their situation for the moment. But it left the Finns in isolation and prompted them to approach the Russians for an armistice in February. Although the Finns baulked at accepting the Russian conditions and did so again after the renewed negotiations that followed a Russian advance to Viipuri in June, it was only a postponed capitulation. Moreover, Finland's attempted breakaway set an example that Germany's other satellites soon followed. The general stabilization of the eastern front that the Germans apparently achieved in May 1944 was unstable, both politically and militarily, under the surface.

7. The Russians on the Vistula.—The Russians' main summer offensive was launched two and a half weeks after the Anglo-U.S. invasion of Normandy. Contrary to general expectation the offensive began, not from the Russians' great wedge in southern Poland, but from their relatively backward line north of the Pripet marshes, in White Russia. This was the best-fortified sector of the German front and had withstood repeated assaults in 1943; but for that very reason it was less likely to be reinforced, now that the German reserves were so scanty. Moreover, the German communications there were long stretched and suffered much interference from the Russian partisans, whereas the Russian communications were shorter there than in the south, so that their offensive could have greater momentum. Four groups of armies were massed there for the Russian offensive. Realizing the danger, the German commanders wanted to carry out a withdrawal before the blow fell, to the line of the Berezina, which would have thrown the Russian advance out of gear; but Hitler forbade it.

The offensive opened on June 23, 1944. Exploiting wedges driven in the previous autumn, the right wing began by pinching out the famous bastion town of Vitebsk and then swung south across the highway from Moscow to Minsk. On the other flank Rokossovski's armies broke through just north of the Pripet marshes and then drove 150 mi. deep, in a week, to cut the highway farther back on the stretch from Minsk to Warsaw. Minsk itself fell on July 3. Although a large part of the enveloped armies managed to find a way back by secondary routes, the Russian mechanized spearheads raced ahead, bypassing any attempted blocks. By mid-July they had overrun half of northeast Poland and pressed deep into Lithuania.

On July 14 the Russian armies south of the Pripet marshes joined in the offensive; and within a fortnight were across the San, besides capturing Lwów. This multiple pressure at so many points gave Rokossovski's mobile columns an opening to slip through the centre, past the end of the marshes, and reach the Vistula. On July 31 one of them penetrated to the suburbs of Warsaw, and the Polish underground leaders there were encouraged to give the signal for a rising.

It was a moment of general crisis for the Germans. In the west their front in Normandy was collapsing, while their rear was shaken by the repercussions of the plot to kill Hitler and the purge that followed. But an astonishing rally came in August, beginning at Warsaw. Three *Schustztaffel* armoured divisions arrived at the crucial moment and delivered a counterstroke which threw back the Russian advanced forces. This gave the Germans a breathing space in which to suppress the Polish rising. But the change was not confined to that sector, for by the end of the first week of August the Russians were held up almost everywhere. They had advanced up to 450 mi. in 5 weeks—the longest and fastest advance they had yet achieved. They were now suffering the natural effect of overstretching their communications and had to bow to that strategic law. Six months were to pass on the Vistula before they were ready to mount a fresh drive.

8. The Hungarian Plain Reached.—The reprieve which Hitler obtained on the main front, however, was offset by the advent of a fresh menace on his Balkan flank. On Aug. 20, 1944, Malinovski and Tolbukhin launched a converging attack on the German salient that still projected into Bessarabia. Aug. 23 saw a change of government in Rumania, which thereupon made peace and simultaneously changed sides as a sequel to negotiations that had been proceeding for some time. With their passage thus cleared, the Russians pushed through the mountain barrier into Transylvania and, more quickly, up the Danube valley to the Yugoslav frontier. At the same time they occupied Bulgaria, where they met no resistance.

The autumn of 1944 saw the gradual development of a great wheel, by the Russian left wing, through the vast spaces of southeastern and central Europe. All that the Germans could do was to put a brake on it, by holding the successive communication centres as long as possible, and gain time to extricate their forces from Greece and Yugoslavia. Belgrade was liberated on Oct. 20. Meanwhile, the inner flank of the wheel had reached the edge of the Hungarian plain. From there the Russians made a strong spurt, which reached the suburbs of Budapest on Nov. 4. But, like other cities that had been stubbornly defended, Budapest proved a hard nut to crack. It was still unconquered at the end of the year, though by then deeply enveloped, and did not fall until Feb. 13, 1945.

The autumn of 1944 also saw a similar flank-sweeping process at the northern end of the eastern front. Finland capitulated early in September, and the Russians then concentrated on clearing the Baltic states and, if possible, cutting off the German army group which still clung there. Although it managed to evade several dangerous scythe strokes, the remains of it were cornered, by mid-October, in the Courland peninsula. The Russians then tried to break into East Prussia, but their attacks there were repelled and deadlock ensued.

The year 1944 had seen a tremendous shrinkage in Germany's *lebensraum.* Yet it had avoided the total collapse that seemed almost certain at the end of the summer. Its subsequent rally—in the east, and the west and the centre of Europe—was proof of the combined effect of its contracted defensive front and the attackers' extended communications. It also showed how the Allies' demand for "unconditional surrender" had helped Hitler to stiffen the Germans' resistance. That might have continued longer, gaining time for the development of his new weapons, if he had planned a strategy of elastic defense, instead of insisting on the rigid defense of untenable positions.

9. From the Vistula to the Oder.—The year 1945 opened with a German counteroffensive to relieve Budapest. This did not succeed in its local aim, and it was made with armoured divisions that had formed the main reserve available to meet a renewed Russian offensive in Poland. Yet Hitler, while dictating this abortive effort in Hungary, would not permit any withdrawal from the Vistula line, to forestall the expected Russian offensive there. He thus, in a double way, played into the hands of Stalin.

After nearly six months' interval for preparation, the Russians had built up their communications in Poland and assembled abundant resources for a long drive. Besides a numerical superiority of nearly five to one, they had greatly increased the output of their new "Stalin" tanks, which the Germans considered the best in the world, while the inflowing stream of U.S. trucks enabled them to motorize many more of their infantry brigades, to back up the armoured thrust.

The offensive was initiated on Jan. 12, 1945, by Koniev's three armies, from the Baranow bridgehead. A breach was soon made, and armoured corps poured through it, some driving westward, while others threatened the rear of the Germans who were facing Zhukov. On Jan. 14 both Zhukov and Rokossovski joined in the offensive, and the breach became 200 mi. wide. Warsaw was isolated and fell on Jan. 17, by which time Zhukov's spearheads were close to Lodz. Two days later Koniev's spearheads crossed Germany's Silesian frontier besides driving into Cracow, while Rokossovski reached the southern frontier of east Prussia. Too late, Hitler allowed German divisions to be rushed north from Slovakia; they were too few to fill such an immense gap.

Rokossovski entered east Prussia by the same route, toward Tannenberg, that Gen. Alexander Samsonov had taken with fatal results in 1914, but Tannenberg was to be reversed this time, for Rokossovski swept on past that battlefield and reached the Baltic on Jan. 26, thus isolating all the German forces east of Danzig. Meanwhile, Koniev had already reached the Oder, isolating the industrial area of Upper Silesia.

Between these two far-stretched wings, Zhukov's armoured columns drove through the corridor between the Vistula and the Warta, bypassed the great fortified communication centres of Torun and Poznan, which were thus surrounded by the motorized forces following on, and on Jan. 30 crossed the Brandenburg frontier, 220 mi. from Warsaw and barely 100 from Berlin. Next day one of his spearheads reached the lower Oder near Kuestrin, only 40 mi. from Berlin.

10. Fall of Berlin.—But the advance had gone so far and so fast that it no longer had the momentum needed to overcome the defense of this great river, which was aided by a sudden thaw. Although Zhukov gained footholds near Kuestrin and Frankfurt in the following week, his advanced forces lacked sufficient weight to burst out. Koniev then sought to develop a flanking leverage by a push down the west bank of the Oder from Breslau, but his forces in turn were held up on the Neisse, which there provided the Germans with a convenient switch line. The Germans were much helped at this stage by the fact that their front had been forcibly contracted to only a fraction of its former extent. That contraction went far to balance their losses for the moment, giving their defense a better proportion of force to space than it had ever enjoyed since the tide of the war had turned and thrown them on the defensive. Although the Russians were baulked, it was the menace of their imminent approach to Berlin that led Hitler to decide that most of his fresh drafts must be sent to reinforce the Oder whatever the risk to the defense of the Rhine. The way was thus eased for the passage of the Rhine by the U.S. and British armies.

Early in March 1945 Zhukov enlarged his bridgehead over the Oder but did not succeed in breaking out. Russian progress on the far flanks continued, and Vienna was entered early in April. Meanwhile, the German front in the west had collapsed; and the Allied armies there were driving eastward from the Rhine with little opposition. They reached the Elbe, 60 mi. from Berlin, on April 11. There they halted. On April 16 Zhukov resumed the offensive, in conjunction with Koniev, who forced the crossings of the Neisse. This time the Russians burst out of their bridgeheads and within a week were driving into the suburbs of Berlin, where Hitler chose to remain for the final battle. By April 25 the city had been completely isolated by the encircling armies of Zhukov and Koniev, and two days later Koniev's forces joined hands with the Americans on the Elbe. But in Berlin itself desperate street-by-street resistance was put up by the Germans and was not completely overcome until the war itself ended, after Hitler's suicide, with Germany's unconditional surrender. (B. H. L. H.)

I. The North African Campaign (1942-43)

1. Securing of Morocco, Algeria, French West Africa.—When the British chiefs of staff visited Washington, D.C., in Jan. 1942 the invasion of northwest Africa was debated. In July the desperate situation of the Russians and the unfavourable turn of events in Libya prompted the combined chiefs of staff to suspend preparations for the invasion of Europe and to launch an expedition into northwest Africa.

Lieut. Gen. Dwight D. Eisenhower, who was commanding U.S. forces in the United Kingdom, was designated to command the Allied forces in this "Torch" operation with orders to gain, in conjunction with the Allied forces in the middle east, early and complete control of North Africa from the Atlantic to the Red sea.

Intensive measures were instituted for the preparation, under strictest secrecy, of three task forces—western, centre and eastern. The western task force was American, including the 3rd infantry, 2nd armoured and most of the 9th infantry divisions, with supporting troops and, commanded by Maj. Gen. George S. Patton, Jr., was organized in the United States. Under Rear Adm. H. K. Hewitt this force totalling 34,000 assembled at sea on Oct. 24, 1942, and departed on its missions of capturing Casablanca and establishing communications with the centre task force, which was to land at Oran. This latter force, also U.S., included the 1st infantry, and part of the

1st armoured divisions, with supporting troops, was commanded by Maj. Gen. Lloyd R. Fredendall and numbered 31,000. The eastern task force, under British Lieut. Gen. K. A. N. Anderson, consisted of British commando and infantry units and U.S. infantry and rangers, totalling 32,000 and was to capture Algiers. In view of lingering French hostility to the British the first landings of this force were to be commanded by an American. The centre and eastern task forces sailed from England on Oct. 25 under British naval escort.

Since the ultimate objective was the capture of Tunisia, some thought was given to making other landings farther east, but lack of shipping and landing craft and the axis capability of attacking communications via proaxis Spain discouraged this project.

Adm. Sir Andrew B. Cunningham was naval commander in chief for the operation; his responsibilities included protection against attack by the Italian and Vichy French fleets. The assigned air forces were commanded by Air Marshal Sir William L. Welsh and Brig. Gen. James H. Doolittle, respectively. The western task force was supported by 171 aircraft from 4 U.S. navy carriers and the centre task force by 57 British planes from 3 carriers and by 2 U.S. fighter groups from Gibraltar. At Algiers the British furnished air support from 4 carriers and from Gibraltar.

To clinch clandestine negotiations which had been opened with a few French officials Maj. Gen. Mark W. Clark landed near Algiers on the night of Oct. 22–23

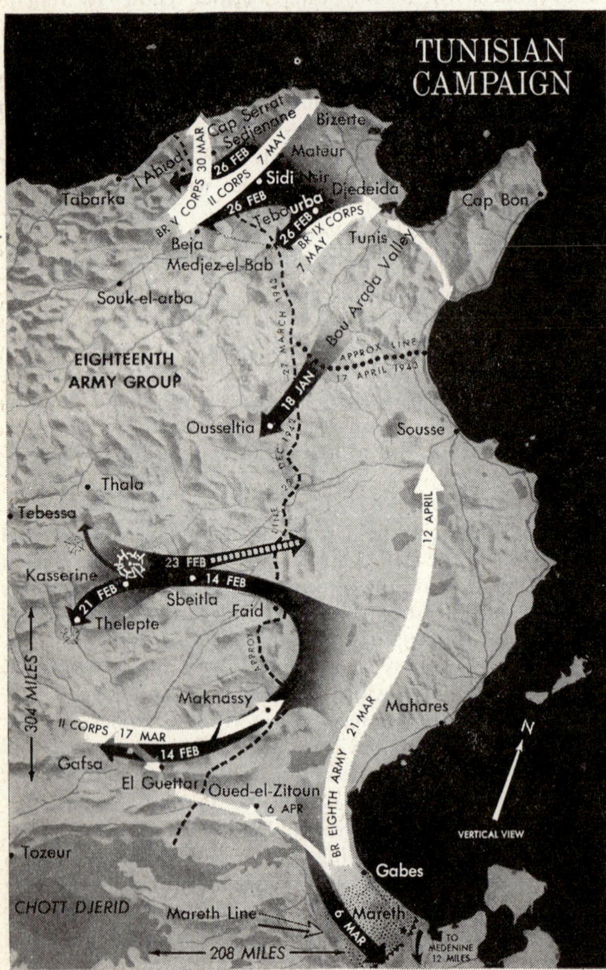

after a voyage by air and submarine. The peculiar relationship between Vichy and Berlin, the schism between the pro-Vichy and Free French elements, the veneration with which Marshal Henri Pétain was regarded by many Frenchmen and the deep-rooted antagonisms of the mixed populations of Morocco and Algeria presented political problems which were to prove insoluble.

On Nov. 5 Eisenhower established his command post at Gibraltar. Undetected, the central and eastern task forces reached the Straits, and, passing eastward, at 1 A.M. on Nov. 8 landed their assault forces. Simultaneously, President Roosevelt broadcast an assurance to the French people that the Allies sought no territory. At the same time the Spanish government was notified that no operations were contemplated against its territory. At 4:35 A.M. the western task force began its landings.

(*a*) *Eastern Task Force.*—Landings were made at two beaches west, and one east, of Algiers, against spotty opposition. One of two British destroyers carrying commando and antisabotage parties into the port was sunk by shellfire.

Adm. Jean Darlan, Pétain's designated successor, was discovered in Algiers and agreed to cease resistance at 7 P.M.

(*b*) *Centre Task Force.*—Landings against slight opposition were made at Arzeu, 30 mi. east of Oran and at 2 beaches west of the city. A U.S. paratroop mission flying 1,500 mi. from England to help capture the airfields was scattered by a storm, but such troops as landed locally aided in seizing the Tafaraoui airfield.

Two British cutters, carrying rangers and antisabotage parties into Oran to seize the port facilities, were disabled by fire from shore batteries and French naval craft; most of the personnel either became casualties or were captured. Three French destroyers which took to sea were destroyed. At noon on Nov. 10 the city surrendered.

(*c*) *Western Task Force.*—Landings were made on Nov. 8 at Fedala and Mehdia northeast of Casablanca and at Safi to the southwest. By 10:15 A.M. Safi had been captured. At Fedala, which fell at 3 P.M., and at Mehdia (near Port Lyautey airfield) there was considerable opposition from aircraft and shore batteries, the latter being silenced by naval gunfire.

Off Casablanca three cruisers and five destroyers were engaged by the U.S.S. "Brooklyn," "Augusta" and two destroyers. One French cruiser was damaged. Later three cruisers and two destroyers were taken under fire by the U.S.S. "Massachusetts" and by naval aircraft, one French destroyer being sunk; a heavy cruiser, "Primaguet," was set afire.

Port Lyautey was finally captured on Nov. 10. A planned attack on Casablanca became unnecessary when, on Nov. 10, Darlan broadcast that hostilities should cease by 7:00 A.M. Nov. 11.

Under the armistice, Darlan agreed that Gen. Henri Giraud's forces should render active assistance in the conquest of Tunisia, the next Allied objective. He responded to the German invasion of unoccupied France by rejecting the Vichy government. Subsequently Gov.-Gen. Pierre Boisson announced the adherence of French West Africa to the Darlan regime. When Darlan was murdered on Dec. 24, 1942, control passed to Giraud, although many extremists of Gen. Charles de Gaulle's Free French party refused to compromise with him.

2. The Tunisian Campaign.—Hope of anticipating the axis in Tunisia lay in acting with utmost speed, not only against a build-up of axis forces but also against the weather. Unfortunately, the French made no resistance to the German air landings which began on Nov. 9, 1942. On that day Lt. Gen. Anderson took over command of the British 1st army. Troops were rushed to capture Bougie on Nov. 11 and Bone the next day. Already axis air reaction was making itself felt on Allied shipping at sea and in port.

On Nov. 15 the U.S. 503rd parachute battalion dropped at Youksles-Bains and seized the airfield there; two days later it occupied the airfield at Gafsa. On Nov. 16 the 1st army encountered German patrols 60 mi. west of Tunis. Operations developed along the axes Beja-Medjez-Tebourba, Beja-Sidi Nsir, Tabarka-Djebel Abiod-Mateur. On Nov. 25, after several clashes with axis troops, Anderson's leading elements seized Medjez-El-Bab, 30 mi. southwest of Tunis and 3 days later captured the airfield at Djedeida, 16 mi. from that capital. On Nov. 25 Eisenhower moved his headquarters from Gibraltar to Algiers. The advance had now developed the axis defensive position created by the reinforcements which had been steadily pouring into Tunisia from Italy by sea and air. Further progress was checked. Winter rains set in. Eisenhower now directed Anderson to withdraw his forces to more defensible ground but to hold Medjez-El-Bab. This movement was accomplished under axis harassment and in heavy mud which resulted in a serious loss of armoured vehicles. After an unsuccessful renewal of pressure eastward from Medjez on Dec. 22, the advance on Tunis was definitely abandoned for the winter.

The ensuing months were devoted to the intensive build-up of supply installations and to bringing up reinforcements. Up until this time the advancing elements had been relatively weak, their line of communications installations necessarily sketchy. Meanwhile, the axis continued to augment its strength and to harass the Allied forces. In the latter mission it profited by its excellent modern airfields.

By contrast, Allied air forces operated under the handicap of improvised runways which frequently were mere mud strips.

On Jan. 1, 1943, Clark was appointed to command the newly created U.S. 5th army, in which the remainder of the centre task force was consolidated with the western task force, with the missions of guarding the lines of communication and of training for future offensive operations. The same day Fredendall was appointed to command the U.S. 2nd corps, which included a French division and a British paratroop brigade, with the mission of protecting the U.S. right flank and attacking axis lines of communication.

Meanwhile, Allied naval and air forces had embarked upon their task of protecting supply routes and disrupting those of the axis. With ever-increasing intensity they hammered at axis air bases in Tunisia, Sicily and Sardinia and on the Italian mainland and harassed axis sea and air communications.

At the turn of the year the French 19th corps was holding a sector on the eastern dorsal between Anderson's 1st army and Fredendall's 2nd corps. The Allied battle position ran generally along the line Medjez-Ousseltia-Faid-Gafsa. Gen. Erwin Rommel, the German commander, had sensed the lack of equipment of the French, and although retreating before Gen. Bernard L. Montgomery through Tripolitania, on Jan. 18, 1943, he struck down the Bon Arada valley at the junction between the British and French, causing both to fall back several miles and relinquish Ousseltia. In this attack the German Mark VI Tiger tank made its debut. In order to improve the organization of command and communications, Eisenhower thereupon vested in Anderson operational control over all U.S., French and British forces in Tunisia east of the line Bone-Chott (Salt Lake) Djerid. These were grouped from north to south into the British 5th corps, French 19th corps (French and U.S. troops), U.S. 2nd corps (U.S. and French troops).

The growing strength of the U.S. forces began to make itself felt. After a successful axis attack on Jan. 30 against the French who were holding Faid pass, U.S. troops, among them the U.S. 1st armoured division, reacted to divert axis pressure by attacking eastward from Gafsa. At this moment Rommel's retreating forces arrived in southern Tunisia from Libya.

On Feb. 4 the combined chiefs of staff separated the North African theatre of operations from the European theatre.

At dawn on Feb. 14 the axis launched a determined armoured attack from the Faid area toward Sbeitla-Kasserine and a subsidiary attack from Maknassy southward. U.S. forces suffered heavily and retired through Kasserine pass; Gafsa also was relinquished. The axis, following up its advantage, captured Sbeitla and Kasserine as well as Thelepte with its airfield. After debouching from the west end of Kasserine pass on Feb. 21, axis troops encountered stiffening resistance to which some hastily gathered British reinforcements contributed, and on the morning of Feb. 23 began to withdraw under the heavy pressure of Allied armour strongly supported from the air. Renewed attacks by Allied ground troops and the combined efforts of all air forces maintained the German retreat, which was skilfully covered by lavish use of mines, and by March 3 contact was regained at Faid. Rommel's intention apparently had been merely to disrupt the Allied dispositions by attacking the invitingly thin line of the U.S. 2nd corps and thus gain time and space for the reorganization of the merging axis forces in Tunisia. Fired by his initial success he evidently tried to exploit it by an attack on the Allied communications in the Tibessa-Thala-Le Kef region.

With the approach of the British 8th army to the German-Italian Mareth defense line, a command reorganization became necessary. Under Air Chief Marshal Sir Arthur W. Tedder, the Mediterranean air command was created on Feb. 19 to control all Allied air forces based in the middle east, northwest Africa and Malta. Under Lieut. Gen. Carl Spaatz the Northwest African air force was formed to unify the activities of the various air elements including the British eastern air command, and the U.S. 12th air force. This command comprised a strategic air force, a tactical air force and a coastal air force. Doolittle commanded the heavy and medium bombers whose particular mission was the destruction of strategic targets such as axis naval and air bases, communications and convoys. Air Marshal Sir Arthur Coningham commanded the tactical air force with the particular mission of closely supporting the ground troops. Air Vice-Marshal Sir Hugh P. Lloyd commanded the coastal air force with the task of defending ports and convoys, conducting continual reconnaissance and carrying out shipping sweeps and antisubmarine patrols.

On Feb. 20, Admiral of the Fleet Sir Andrew B. Cunningham became commander in chief, Mediterranean, his area of command being extended to longitude 16° E. and including Malta.

On the same day, Gen. Sir Harold R. L. G. Alexander, commander in chief, middle east, became deputy commander in chief, allied forces, and commander in chief, 18th army group, which was composed of the British 1st (Anderson) and 8th (Montgomery) armies, the U.S. 2nd corps (Fredendall) and the French 19th corps (Alphonse Juin). Thus, the command of the forces which had pursued Rommel from Egypt through Tripolitania and of the 500,000 troops which had been built up from the landings in North Africa was unified under Eisenhower. A large proportion of the Allied strength was operating on the lines of communication.

On Feb. 26 the Germans began an attack on a wide front west of Tunis, making new gains in the Medjez-El-Bab and Beja areas and capturing Sedjenane near the north coast. The fighting was bitter and cost the axis heavily in tanks which it could ill spare. The Allied positions at Djebel Abiod and Medjez were critically exposed. On March 28, the 46th division and other units of the British 5th corps attacked to re-establish their positions and, fighting through heavy rains, recaptured Sedjenane two days later and pushed on to Cap Serrat. Following powerful artillery preparation, the 5th corps on April 7 launched the British 78th division on a ten-day advance of about ten miles which removed the axis threat to Medjez. In a despairing effort to ensure its hold on its Tunisian beachhead the Afrika Korps on March 6 made an armoured attack on Medinine, south of Mareth; the attempt failed. Four days later an axis armoured column struck patrols of Gen. Jacques Leclerc's Fighting French column which had trekked across the Sahara from Lake Chad. Again the axis forces were defeated after being mauled by Allied aircraft. This setback marked the end of axis freedom of action. On March 17 the U.S. 2nd corps, under Patton, who had taken command on March 6, attacked the German lines of communication and recaptured Gafsa; Maknassy fell five days later.

Capture of Long Stop Hill (Djebel el Ahmera), a key to the approaches of Tunis, was accomplished by the Allies after a bitter three-day battle, April 23–26, 1943

On the night of March 20–21, Montgomery's 8th army attacked the Mareth line following a heavy air bombardment by the western desert air forces. After ten days of powerful frontal assaults and a brilliant outflanking manoeuvre by the New Zealand corps on the west, covered by overwhelming air support, the Mareth positions were breached and turned. On April 6 patrols of the 8th army and the U.S. 2nd corps joined in the region of Oued-el-Zitoun. The 8th army continued to pursue Rommel's forces up the coast while the 18th army group maintained its pressure from the west. Sousse was occupied April 12. Allied air forces meanwhile were striking hard at the German attempts to reinforce their garrisons in Tunisia by air and by sea, climaxing their achievements on April 18 when nearly 100 Junkers-52 transports were shot down.

The advance of the 8th army freed the U.S. 2nd corps for transfer to the north. With its four divisions (9th, 1st, 34th infantry, 1st armoured) this corps moved across the rear of the 1st army to reappear on the extreme left flank.

When the general offensive was resumed on April 22, such resistance was met by the 8th army that Alexander transferred to the 1st army the major offensive role, reinforcing it with divisions from the 8th. The assaults were everywhere successful and by the afternoon of May 7, units of the U.S. 2nd corps (under Maj. Gen. Omar N. Bradley, who had assumed command on April 15) had captured Mateur and were entering Bizerte while the British 9th corps was entering Tunis. Axis troops retreated into Cap Bon peninsula and on May 12 Col. Gen. Juergen von Arnim was captured. The next day organized resistance ended.

In this campaign the axis suffered more than 320,000 casualties; 252,415 German and Italian troops and their equipment were included in the final surrender. The conquest of the African continent was complete, and the Allies were in a favourable position to invade the continent of Europe. The Mediterranean was again open to Allied shipping. The French army had been reborn. U.S. troops had demonstrated their battle efficiency and had gained invaluable experience. The allied air forces had demonstrated their effective co-ordination with ground forces and the strategic application of air power. And this campaign had fully demonstrated the practicability of unifying both in command and in staff work the efforts of three Allied forces.

Allied casualties were approximately as follows:

	Killed	Wounded	Missing	Total
British	5,920	19,000	7,680	32,600
U.S. Nov. 8–11	526	837	41	1,404
Nov. 12–May 13	2,715	8,978	6,528	18,221
French	6,307	8,077	4,482	18,866
Total	15,468	36,892	18,731	71,091

The following major ground units served in these campaigns:

	Armies	Corps	Divisions
British	1st	5th, 9th	1st, 4th, 46th, 78th infantry; 4th Indonesian; 1st, 6th, 7th armoured
	8th	10th, 30th N.Z.	51st, 56th infantry; 2nd N.Z.; 1st French
U.S.		2nd	1st, 3rd, 9th, 34th infantry; 1st armoured
French		19th Corps d'Afrique	Moroccan; Algerian, Oran

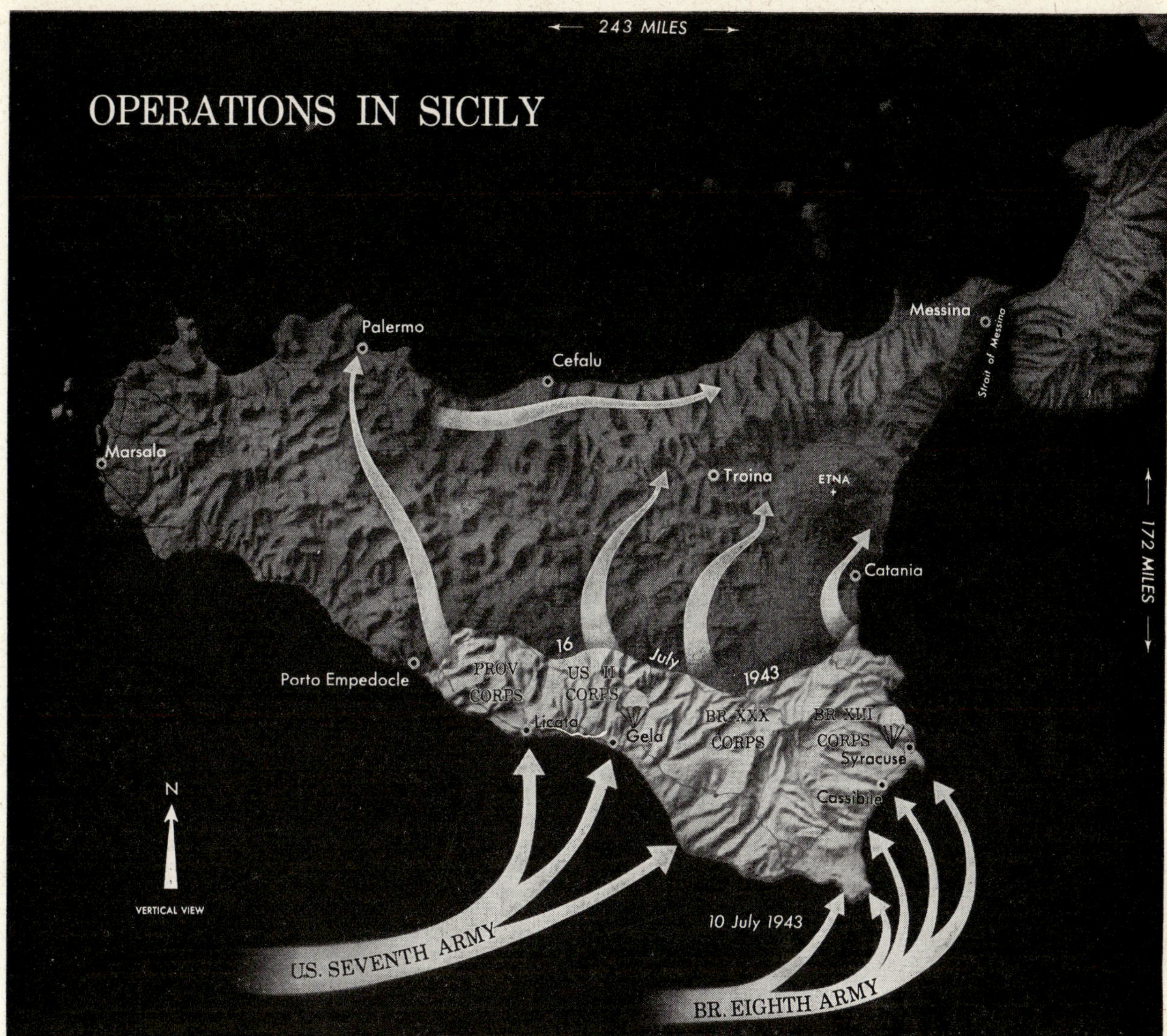

3. Pantelleria, Lampedusa, Lingosa, Lampion.—The nuisance constituted by the radar stations and airfields on Pantelleria, reputed to be a second Gibraltar, and its neighbouring small islands was next to be removed. A crescendo of air attacks begun on May 20 was climaxed by continuous air and naval bombardment from June 7 to 11. At 11:55 A.M. on June 11 elements of the British 1st division landed to receive the surrender of the 11,000 defenders of Pantelleria, whose losses of less than 200 killed revealed the moral effect of the bombardment.

The air and naval attack then turned upon Lampedusa, which surrendered with 4,600 prisoners next evening. Lingosa yielded as U.S. naval craft approached; Lampion was found deserted on June 13.

On July 10, fighters based at Pantelleria supported Allied landings in Sicily.

J. The Sicilian Campaign

At the Casablanca conference in Jan. 1943 the imperative need to relieve pressure upon the U.S.S.R. had been recognized. With reasonable prospects for early success in Tunisia, consideration was given to Sardinia or Sicily as the logical next stepping stone. The fairly obvious decision was made to attack Sicily, with target date the July moon period.

For "Husky" operation Gen. Sir Harold Alexander was to be Eisenhower's deputy in command of ground forces (15th army group).

Adm. Sir Andrew B. Cunningham and Air Chief Marshal Sir Arthur W. Tedder were to be naval and air commanders, respectively.

Although assaults upon both Palermo and Catania were considered initially, it became evident that the airfields in the southeastern corner of the island must be captured promptly lest the entire operation be imperilled. This, together with the shortage of landing craft and available troops, led Eisenhower to favour a single expedition against the 100 mi. of coast line extending from just south of Syracuse westward around to Licata. Thus, he assumed the risk of putting a substantial force ashore without the prospect of early seizure of a major port to ensure its logistical support. Success in this venture was to provide a precedent for the later landings at Salerno and in Normandy.

Allied air forces now enjoyed more than a two-to-one local superiority over those of the axis. In the air preparation, which began while operations in Tunisia were still in progress, Brig. Gen. James A. Doolittle's strategic air force hammered axis air bases and communications, while Air Marshal Sir Arthur Coningham's tactical air force performed close-range missions more directly preparatory to the assault.

On June 12 Doolittle began the intensive destruction of airfields in Sicily, rendering most of them unserviceable on D-day, July 10.

Adm. Sir Bertram Ramsay's eastern naval task force transported Gen. Bernard L. Montgomery's 8th army, which was assigned the eastern sector and which consisted of the British 13th and 30th corps. In the assault of the 13th corps were the 5th and 50th divisions and commandos; the 30th corps attacked with its 231st brigade, 51st and Canadian 1st divisions and commandos. Adm. H. K. Hewitt's western naval task force convoyed Gen. George S. Patton, Jr.,'s 7th army, consisting of the 2nd corps (U.S. 1st and 45th infantry divisions) plus a provisional corps (U.S. 3rd infantry division and part of 2nd armoured division).

The armada of Allied ships and landing craft reached the unprecedented total of 2,500. British naval forces guarded against a possible gesture by Mussolini's six battleships.

At 11 P.M. on July 9 a brigade of the British 1st Airborne division was scheduled to drop by parachute and glider south of Syracuse and seize a vital bridge and dominating points. Although many of the gliders were released off shore the bridge was captured. In the U.S. sector four battalions of the U.S. 82nd air-borne division were to parachute beyond Gela to clear obstacles for the advance on the airfields; despite scattering caused by bad weather, the paratroops prevented axis reinforcements from reaching the landing beaches. During a renewed attack two nights later U.S. planes were fired upon by U.S. naval craft through faulty identification, 23 failing to return. A similar mishap befell a second attack by the British air-borne forces.

Wind of near-gale proportions sprang up during the night preceding D day on July 10, but fortunately subsided somewhat toward H hour. In compensation the weather put the beach defenders off their guard.

The landings which began at 2:45 A.M. on July 10 met little opposition. Licata was seized and opened to shipping that day; Syracuse was opened two days later. The occupation of axis airdromes on D day gave Allied fighters bases from which to cover further operations. Allied aircraft maintained close support, flying up to 1,200 sorties daily.

The Allies found themselves confronted by two German and nine Italian divisions. After several counterattacks against the 7th army, only one of which, northeast of Gela, became critical, the Germans disengaged and moved into positions opposite the 8th army, where, recognizing the threat against Messina, they brought in heavy reinforcements.

Problems of supply were acute during the first few days, when adverse weather and occasional axis air attacks made unloading of ships difficult and hazardous. In these operations the 2½-ton amphibious "DUKW" ("duck") trucks made their debut with phenomenal success. During the first 2 days more than 80,000 men, 7,000 vehicles and 300 tanks were landed.

Racing into the hills of western Sicily, the 7th army occupied Palermo on July 22. Patton then turned east and in hard mountain fighting, particularly in the Troina area, between Aug. 1 and 6 aided the 8th army in crumbling German resistance before Catania. Along the north coast the 7th army leapfrogged the axis defenses by amphibious operations on Aug. 8, 11 and 16; on the last date the 8th army also made an "end-run" south of Messina. On Aug. 17 the U.S. 3rd division entered Messina from the west simultaneously with British patrols from the south. In 39 days the Sicilian campaign had ended.

Under heavy anti-aircraft protection the Germans withdrew thousands of first-line panzer and air-borne troops across the strait of Messina. Nevertheless, the loss of Sicily was a major military disaster for the axis, whose casualties totalled 167,000, of which 37,000 were Germans. Losses of German heavy equipment included 78 tanks and armoured cars, 287 artillery pieces and 3,500 motor vehicles.

U.S. infantry conducting mopping up operations in the streets of Messina during the conquest of Sicily in 1943

Allied casualties in Sicily were as follows:

	Killed	Wounded	Missing	Total
U.S.	2,059	5,373	2,332	9,764
British	2,721	7,939	2,183	12,843
French	21	54	12	87
Total	4,801	13,366	4,527	22,694

During these operations the U.S. 9th and the British 78th divisions reinforced the original assault forces.

The shock of the invasion accompanied by the heavy bombing of the Italian mainland exposed the bankruptcy of the fascist regime and on July 25, 1943, Mussolini resigned and was succeeded by Marshal Pietro Badoglio.

K. The Italian Campaign

The Trident conference held in Washington, D.C., during the latter part of May 1943 resulted in a directive to Gen. Dwight D. Eisenhower to plan such operations in exploitation of the conquest of Sicily as would be best calculated to eliminate Italy from the war and to contain the maximum number of German divisions. Available to him would be 19 British and Allied, 4 U.S. and 4 French divisions in the Mediterranean and middle east. Much of this force, however, would be involved in garrison and internal security duties. In addition, four U.S. (1st and 9th infantry, 2nd armoured, 82nd air-borne) and three British (7th armoured, 50th and 51st infantry) divisions were to be returned to the United Kingdom by Nov. 1 in preparation for the cross-channel operation.

An attack on Italy offered tempting fruits. The collapse of a major axis partner would have staggering moral effect upon the satellites. The Italian air bases, particularly those in the Foggia region, could be put to excellent use. The Allies could render more substantial support to the Yugoslav guerrillas and could seriously threaten axis positions within the Balkans.

1. Strategic Drawbacks.—The risks were evident. The Allies still had to maintain North Africa behind them. Not since the fighting in Greece had the Allies challenged the axis when its lines of communication did not cross the sea. In the first attack upon the European mainland the axis could be expected to exert every effort to maintain its prestige. The inevitable drain upon Allied shipping and manpower had to be reckoned with, plus the lengthening lines of communication entailing a heavy proportion of administrative troops—and the corresponding advantages to the axis as its own lines shortened. The political problems which had beset Italy could easily impede the conduct of military operations.

The terrain was not at all favourable for offensive warfare. The towering masses and narrow defiles of the Appennines, the countless streams, flooded in winter, flowing from them, and the marshlands along the coast offered a series of natural defensive positions against which it would be difficult to exploit to the full the anticipated Allied superiority in artillery and armour. During the winter, communications would be still further hampered by heavy snowfall. Nevertheless, the exposure of the axis flanks to amphibious attack was a weakness of which it was always sensitive.

On June 5, 1943, the 15th army group was directed to prepare plans for an assault across the Strait of Messina to capture the ports of Reggio di Calabria and San Giovanni and then to move northeastward, seizing the airfield at Crotone.

The landing-craft situation presented an acute problem. No replacements from the United Kingdom or the United States could be expected; in fact, Eisenhower had been directed to send to the United Kingdom and to India a large proportion of the craft already allotted to him. Throughout the next year operations in the Mediterranean were to be conditioned by the chronic shortage of landing craft. Not only the Salerno operation but also the Anzio and southern France expeditions were to give rise to repeated demands upon the combined chiefs of staff for additional L.S.T.'s, and were to be shaped to fit the numbers of landing craft which could be available at the respective target dates.

With the collapse of the Mussolini regime, new prospects opened. An early assault upon the Naples area now offered reasonable chances of success. However, a direct attack upon the city would certainly meet stiff opposition since the Germans could be counted upon to hold this focal point to cover the withdrawal of their forces from the south. The plain to the north of Naples was beyond the range of Allied fighter aircraft and its beaches were unsuitable for landings. To the south lay the Gulf of Salerno which, although landlocked about 2–10 mi. from shore by high mountains across which the routes to Naples passed through narrow defiles, possessed a 20-mi. stretch of ideal beach. It was calculated that if all available fighter aircraft with detachable tanks were used, a continuous patrol of 36 aircraft could be maintained over the area during daylight for the few days before an air strip could be captured. Gen. Mark Clark was therefore ordered to prepare plans for a landing in the Gulf of Salerno with target date of Sept. 7. The Messina crossings would be made several days before the Salerno landings in order to release landing craft for the latter operation.

2. Invasion and Italian Surrender.—Following heavy air preparation against axis airfields, batteries and communications in the "toe" of Italy, the British 13th corps (Canadian first infantry division and British 5th infantry division) swarmed ashore at 4:30 A.M. on Sept. 3, 1943. Negligible resistance was encountered, and the strait was opened to shipping on Sept. 6. On Sept. 12 Crotone was in Allied hands.

Marshal Pietro Badoglio had established contact with Eisenhower on Aug. 19 in an effort to negotiate a surrender without the knowledge of the Germans. The combined chiefs instructed Eisenhower to accept the unconditional surrender of Italy (which was signed at Cassibile in Sicily on Sept. 3) and to obtain the maximum military advantage from this development. Responding to Badoglio's plea that the capital be seized to prevent the capture of the king and government, Eisenhower offered to fly an air-borne division into the Rome area provided that the Italians would seize the necessary airfields and silence the anti-aircraft batteries. The 82nd air-borne division was alerted to make this drop.

Meanwhile, Allied air forces had intensified their blows against axis marshalling yards, airfields, gun positions, military installations and communications. Pisa, Benevento, Salerno, Foggia, and Brenner pass, were among the many places heavily attacked. Field Marshal Albert Kesselring's headquarters at Frascati, south of Rome, were bombed out. Axis fighter opposition progressively decreased.

On Sept. 8 the unconditional surrender of Italy was announced. That day Badoglio reported that he was unable to guarantee the Rome airdromes for the air-borne landings. It was now too late to put the 82nd division on its original objective, the Volturno river, where it was to have guarded the north flank of the Salerno landings. Thus, it was rendered inactive at this critical moment.

3. The Salerno Beachhead.—At 3:30 A.M. on Sept. 9 Clark's U.S. 5th army landed on the beaches at Salerno.

A street in Naples where debris was so heavy after the city's capture in 1943 that labour corps had to clear a path before U.S. troop movements could proceed

The northern assault force which had sailed from Sicily and Bizerte under command of Commodore G. N. Olliver consisted of the British 10th corps with the 46th and 56th infantry divisions in the assault. The southern assault force which had been convoyed by Rear Adm. John L. Hall, Jr., from Oran consisted of the 6th U.S. corps with the 36th division in the assault followed by the 45th division. U.S. rangers and British commandos landed on Sorrento peninsula, the former to seize the passages leading through to the Naples plain, and the latter to capture Salerno. Having suspected that the Allies might undertake an amphibious operation against the Naples area, the Germans' reaction was swift and vigorous. Withstanding several counterattacks, both corps by nightfall had established a bridgehead four miles deep although a dangerous five-mile gap at the Sele river separated them.

Eisenhower and his ground force commander, Gen. Sir Harold Alexander, estimated that eight German divisions were available to oppose the landing. Two were in the Rome area, two were in the Naples area and four were in the south. The axis forces were heavy in armour. Shortage of shipping prevented the Allies from putting their own heavy armour into the fight until the British 7th armoured division began to unload on D-plus-5. On Sept. 10 the two Allied corps made contact at the Sele river, but the vigour of the German defensive measures increased. Every available aircraft of both the strategical and tactical air forces was thrown into the battle to halt the arrival of axis reinforcements, and heavy naval gunfire lent its support. By Sept. 12 an airstrip had been placed in operation in the beachhead; in the preceding 3 days 3,000 fighter sorties had been flown from Sicily and from carriers. On the nights of Sept. 13 and 14 air-borne troops were flown to critical parts of the defense and by Sept. 15 the crisis had passed.

4. Progress up the Peninsula.—As the Italian battle fleet vacated Taranto on Sept. 9, the port was occupied by the British fleet carrying the British 1st air-borne division, which two days later occupied Brindisi. On Sept. 9, 3 Italian battleships, 6 cruisers and 13 destroyers from Spezia and Genoa, steaming southward to surrender, were bombed by German aircraft, which sank the battleship "Roma." The remainder of the fleet escaped to the Balearic Islands and to Bone. From Bone the Italian fleet moved on to Malta, where it was joined by other surrendering elements. Only a small proportion, 320 planes, of the Italian air force complied with the surrender terms by flying over to the Allies. The Italian army made apathetic resistance to the Germans; because of its lack of leadership Rome was denied to the Allies for many months to come.

On Sept. 12 Capri and other islands in the Bay of Naples surrendered. Four days later patrols of 5th and 8th armies met 40 mi. southeast of Salerno, uniting Alexander's 15th army group into a single front. On Sept. 18 the axis evacuated Sardinia to the French, and on Oct. 6 Corsica followed suit.

The 5th and 8th armies now moved forward abreast. Bari fell on Sept. 13. On Sept. 28 the 8th army occupied the Foggia airfields and on Oct. 1 the 5th occupied Naples and its harbour. Repairs to the demolished port structures were immediately begun, and on Oct. 14 unloading ceased over the Salerno beaches, where, during the period Sept. 9–Sept. 26, a total of 108,000 tons of supplies, 30,000 motor vehicles and 189,000 troops had been landed.

Capture of the Foggia airfields confirmed the Allied hold on the mainland. Large numbers of fighters could now be based relatively close to the battle area, and heavy bombers could easily strike at the passes across the Alps, add their attacks to those of the 8th and 9th air forces against Germany and disrupt industry and transportation in the Balkans to the benefit of the Red army.

German resistance, however, began to stiffen. To avoid a costly frontal attack on the port of Termoli, the British made an amphibious landing north of the city, but the axis delayed its capture until Oct. 6.

At 4 P.M. on Oct. 13, Italy declared war on Germany. One outstanding advantage brought by this cobelligerency was to obviate the need for the Allies to establish military government.

On Nov. 1 the U.S. 15th air force was established. Primarily, this force was to be employed strategically against targets of the combined bomber offensive as directed by the combined chiefs of staff. However, its use by Eisenhower in strategical or tactical emergencies was authorized.

New divisions arrived to join the Allied forces, while the Germans hastily reinforced their own defenses. On the night of Oct. 12–13, the U.S. 2nd and 6th corps forced a crossing of the Volturno river in hard fighting. Destroying every bridge and culvert en route, the Germans withdrew to their winter line athwart the peninsula which they had been preparing since the Allied landings on the mainland. This deep position followed generally the lines of the Garigliano and Sangro rivers. The 5th army's efforts to gain control of the lower Garigliano began on Nov. 6; the 8th army crossed the Sangro two weeks later. Communications were almost nonexistent, winter was coming on and heavy rains and snows added to the handicaps. To deal with axis defenses, Allied artillery was heavily reinforced by batteries of the heaviest field pieces produced in the United States; 240-mm. howitzers and 8-in. guns were rushed to Italy. The 5th army continued to shove the axis from the succession of mountains which still barred the Cassino corridor to Rome and finally, in December, arrived before its entrance. In the same month the first of eight French infantry and armoured divisions which the United States had agreed to equip arrived in Italy.

The build-up of Allied ground forces was delayed by the necessity for using shipping to import not only the huge quantities of equipment, supplies and personnel to establish and man the air bases, but also the foodstuffs to keep the Italian civil population from starvation. A setback was suffered on Dec. 2 when a German air attack confused Allied radar detectors at Bari and sank or damaged 22 freighters. By this time Adriatic ports were unloading 70,000 tons and Naples 80,000 tons weekly.

U.S. troops marching northward on an Italian highway in Jan. 1944

On Dec. 5, 1943, the combined chiefs of staff vested in Eisenhower responsibility for all operations in the Mediterranean other than strategic bombing. On Dec. 10 he was appointed supreme allied commander for the cross-channel invasion, and on Jan. 8, 1944, Gen. Sir Henry Maitland Wilson succeeded him as supreme commander in the Mediterranean. Lieut. Gen. Jacob L. Devers became Wilson's deputy. Gen. Bernard L. Montgomery and Air Chief Marshal Sir Arthur W. Tedder followed Eisenhower to England, Lieut. Gen. Sir Oliver W. H. Leese succeeding Montgomery in command of the 8th army. Gen. Carl Spaatz was designated to command the U.S. strategic air force with headquarters in London. Gen. James Doolittle replaced Gen. Ira C. Eaker in command of the 8th air force and Eaker assumed command of the Mediterranean air forces.

Early in January Gen. Alphonse Juin's French corps took over the right sector of the 5th army from the U.S. 6th corps, which was withdrawn to prepare for the Anzio landing.

5. Anzio and Cassino.—In order to disrupt communications in the rear of the German forces in the Cassino area, the 6th corps landed on the beaches near Anzio on Jan. 22; its troops included the U.S. 3rd division, British 1st division and U.S. rangers. To divert the attention of the local axis forces from this operation the 5th army had mounted a series of local operations. The British 10th corps on Jan. 17 gained a bridgehead over the Garigliano but made no further progress. The U.S. 2nd corps (36th division) on Jan. 20–21 unsuccessfully attempted to force the Rapido. East of Cassino the French corps made considerable gains.

The Germans reacted swiftly to the landings and by the end of January the 6th corps had been sealed in by strong forces which were able to deliver persistent and accurate artillery fire throughout the flat beachhead—18 mi. long by 9 mi. deep—and against ships off shore. Axis counterattacks reached the peak of their intensity on Feb. 17, but the beachhead was held. During the four months of its existence the beachhead was reinforced by the U.S. 1st armoured, 34th, 36th and 45th divisions and by the British 5th and 56th—the last being later withdrawn.

Farther south the 5th army offensive had been halted before the strong defenses of Cassino, where raged some of the bitterest fighting of the war. The U.S. 34th division in early February and the New Zealand corps for four weeks thereafter tried unsuccessfully to capture the site. Despite pulverizing attacks by air and artillery the German defenders held on.

6. Pursuit North from Rome.—As spring approached the Allied air forces systematically destroyed all the important axis railroad yards south of Florence. Then, after thoroughly regrouping their forces, the 5th and 8th armies launched a co-ordinated offensive on May 11. As the attack gained momentum the U.S. 6th corps on May 23 struck out from the Anzio beachhead. In a swift advance over the mountains west of the Liri river, the U.S. corps on the left of the French corps joined hands with the beachhead forces. On June 4 Rome fell to the 5th army.

Both the 5th and 8th armies took up the pursuit of the

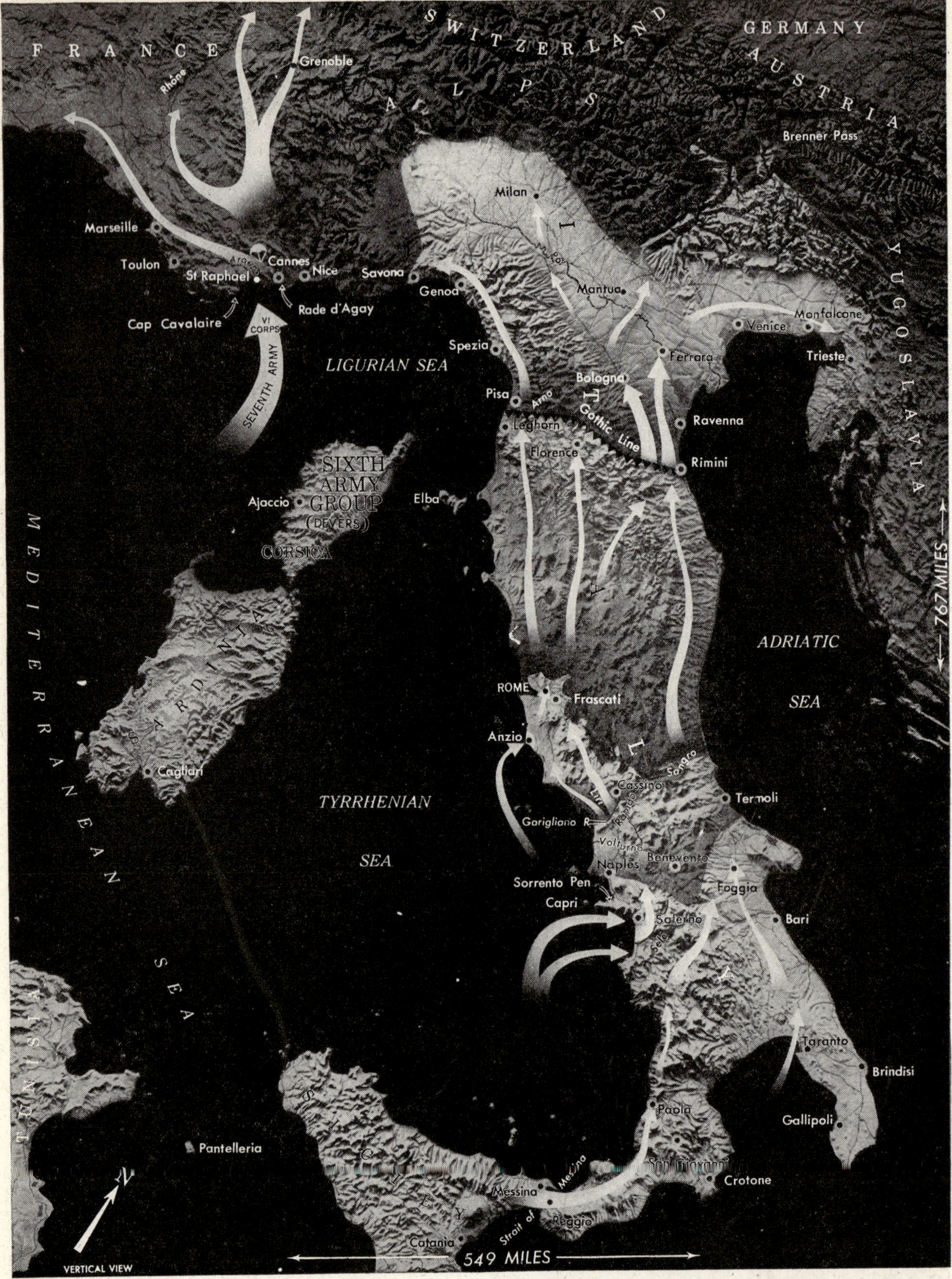

Operations in Italy and southern France, 1943–45

retreating Germans and in July the Allied forces reached the Arno. In mid-June a French amphibious force recaptured Elba. Leghorn fell on July 19, Florence on Aug. 13 and Pisa on Sept. 3. The 8th army passed through the Apennine divide and on Sept. 21 captured Rimini. On Sept. 15 the Brazilian division had begun to move into the 5th army line.

While the pursuit was in progress it had been necessary to withdraw troops in preparation for the "Anvil" attack on southern France. The U.S. 4th corps replaced the 6th corps, and the 45th, 3rd and 36th divisions were withdrawn from the line during the last half of June. The French corps and its four divisions were withdrawn during July. Some of these troops were replaced by new units from the U.S. and by British and other forces.

On July 20, 1944, allied force headquarters moved from Algiers to Caserta.

7. The "Gothic Line."—The 15th army group now stood before the "Gothic Line," which the Germans had been preparing since early in 1944. On Sept. 10, 1944, the 5th army attacked this powerful line frontally, and the 8th army, now commanded by Lieut. Gen. Sir R. L. McCreery, pushed northwest from Rimini. Although after three months of costly fighting the line was breached, the axis had been able to establish a new defensive position.

On Dec. 12, 1944, Alexander replaced Wilson as supreme commander, Wilson moving to Washington, D.C., as field marshal to represent the British chiefs of staff. Clark was promoted to 15th army group commander, and command of the 5th army passed to Lieut. Gen. Lucian K. Truscott.

During the fall and winter months the air forces continued to pound axis communications across the Alps and in northern Italy, as well as oil and rail targets in Austria and southern Germany. In Jan. 1945 the Canadian 1st corps with the Canadian 1st infantry, Canadian 5th armoured and British 5th infantry divisions were ordered to France to reinforce the attacks on Germany.

On April 9, 1945, the 8th army launched a general attack west of Ravenna. Five days later the 5th army joined the offensive and after a week of heavy fighting drove into the Po valley and entered Bologna. Bridgeheads were established across the Po southwest of Mantua on April 23. Both armies raced across the Po valley and into the foothills of the Alps. On April 28 Italian antifascists captured Mussolini and executed him. On April 29 the Allies entered Milan; 5th army forces along the Ligurian sea captured La Spezia on April 25, swept through Genoa and Savona and advanced to make contact with the French. On every side effective support was received from Italian patriots. By May 1, 8th army troops advancing on Trieste had made contact with Yugoslav partisans at Monfalcone and the next day at noon the commander of the German armies in northern Italy capitulated. On May 4, patrols of the U.S. 88th division met those of the 7th army south of the Brenner pass.

By the dogged pressure which they had maintained for 20 months the Allied forces in Italy had made a major contribution to the common effort. Pinning down substantial strength which Hitler had needed to reinforce both his eastern and western fronts, they had accomplished the mission given them at the Trident conference.

During these operations the axis lost more than 47,000 known dead, 170,000 wounded and probably some part of the 209,000 reported missing prior to the German surrender.

Allied casualties were as follows:

	Killed	Wounded	Missing	Total
U.S.	21,389	92,589	40,079	154,057
British	30,782	99,773	15,071	145,626
French	6,255	23,500	998	30,753
Polish	2,108	8,270	274	10,652
Brazilian	432	1,353	20	1,805
Others	1,032	3,376	773	5,181
Total	61,998	228,861	57,215	348,074

The following major units participated in the ground fighting in Italy under the 15th army group:

	Armies	Corps	Divisions
U.S.	5th	2nd, 4th, 6th	3rd, 10th, 34th, 36th, 45th, 85th, 88th, 91st, 92nd infantry; 1st armoured; 82nd air-borne.
British	8th	5th, 10th, 13th; 1st Canadian, New Zealand	1st, 4th, 5th, 46th, 56th, 78th infantry; 1st, 6th, 7th armoured; 1st air-borne; 1st Canadian infantry; 5th Canadian armoured; 2nd N.Z. infantry; 6th S. African armoured; 4th, 8th, 10th Indian infantry;
French	—	expeditionary corps	1st motor; 3rd Alger. infantry; 2nd Moroccan; 4th Moroccan Mountain;
Polish	—	2nd	3rd Carpathian; 5th Kresowa
Brazilian	—	—	1st infantry.
			Other units
U.S.			442nd infantry (Jap.-Amer.)
U.S.—Can.			1st Sp. Service Force
Italian			Legnano Gp., 1st Motor Gp.
Jewish			Palestine Brig.

(T. N.)

L. Balkan Operations (1942-44)

1. Resistance in Yugoslavia and Greece.—With their mountains and lack of modern means of communication, with their populations having age-long traditions to conspire and to resist the invader, Yugoslavia and Greece were ideally fitted for guerrilla warfare. Unfortunately, the political situation did not favour a unified underground movement in either. In Yugoslavia, particularly, the resistance was divided first by the Serbo-Croat feud and secondly by the tendency of the Communist party to pursue its aims without any compromise. The German advance in April 1941, in its very swiftness, left in its rear tens of thousands of Yugoslav soldiers who hid with their arms. A month later Col. (later Gen.) Draja Mikhailovitch started to organize his *chetas* (companies) to fight the enemies of Yugoslavia. For the Chetniks, however, the enemies were not only the Germans but also the *ustashe* (insurgents) of the Croat quisling Ante Pavelitch. From the beginning, then, Mikhailovitch, who had a unique chance to be a national Yugoslav leader, appeared in the narrower role of a Serbian patriot.

This situation was skilfully exploited by the leader of the rival underground movement, Josip Brozovich, called Tito. This Moscow-trained Communist and veteran of the Spanish Civil War, where he served with the international brigades, organized his partisans and started guerrilla operations only after the German attack on the U.S.S.R. A meeting between Tito and Mikhailovitch held in Oct. 1941 was fruitless. Although at first Chetniks and partisans sometimes fought the Germans together, their relations now became strained and they even fought each other. Mikhailovitch was anxious to avoid reprisals against the civil population; he also considered that the menace of communism was at least as great as the menace of naziism or fascism. For this, after Aug. 1942, he was denounced as pro-German by the "Free Yugoslavia" radio (speaking from Tiflis). In Nov. 1942 in the small Bosnian town of Bihach, Tito convened an Antifascist Assembly of National Liberation of Yugoslavia (AVNOJ or *Antifashistichko Veche Narodnog Oslobodyenya Jugoslavye*), which proclaimed that the Yugoslav National Army of Liberation was fighting for a "truly democratic and federal Yugoslavia in which equal national rights not only of Serbs, Croats and Slovenes, but also of Macedonians and Montenegrins would be recognized."

The first British officer to be parachuted into occupied Yugoslavia, in Sept. 1941, was Col. S. Hudson; he was instructed by the general headquarters, middle east, to coordinate the sabotage operations of Chetniks and partisans, but soon discovered how difficult was his assignment. Until March 1943, however, the British helped with money and munitions only Mikhailovitch's forces. At this time a first British emissary to Tito, Lt. Col. F. W. D. Deakin, was parachuted into Yugoslavia. He reported that the partisans had both a political and a military organization on a large scale; he also recognized that Tito's soldiers were really fighting the Germans, despite setbacks and the sufferings of the civilian population. In Sept. 1943 a larger mission headed by Brig. Fitzroy Maclean was parachuted into Bosnia and soon after came important material help to the partisans. By this time the Allies had established for the purpose a special base near Bari in southern Italy; it was no longer necessary to fly the supplies from Egypt. The British mission to Mikhailovitch was withdrawn in May 1944 and entire support was transferred to Tito. Speaking in the house of commons on Feb. 22, 1944, Winston Churchill stated that the partisans were the only people who were doing any effective fighting against the Germans and that they were checking no fewer than 14 German divisions out of the 20 in the Balkan peninsula.

In Oct. 1944 all southern and eastern Yugoslavia was liberated by the joint effort of Russians (Marshal Fedor Tolbukhin's army), Bulgarians (now fighting with the Russians) and partisans of Tito. In April 1945 all Yugoslavia was free, and although many Chetniks took refuge in Allied-occupied Italy, Mikhailovitch remained in his Serbian mountains. (He was arrested on March 13, 1946, condemned to death by a partisan court on July 16 and executed the next day at dawn.)

Compared with that of Yugoslavia, the situation in Greece was simpler in one respect; there was no feud similar to the Serbo-Croat. The political divisions were, however, serious enough not only to endanger the national unity but also to paralyze any large-scale operations against the axis. It must be remembered that Greece before the war had a dictatorship opposed by all Greek political parties. But while the royalists were ready to forgive the king for supporting Gen. John Metaxas if they were given power, the liberals and socialists were against both the dictatorship and the monarchy. After the occupation of Greece by the Germans and Italians the Communist party exploited this situation by sponsoring an underground national liberation movement (E.A.M. or *Ethnikon Apeleutherotikon Metopon*) which proclaimed the necessity, after the war, of a Greek republic allied with the U.S.S.R. and other Balkan republics. The E.A.M. organized its own national popular liberation army (E.L.A.S. or *Ethnikos Laikos Apeleutherotikos Stratos*), the commander in chief of which was Gen. Stefanos Serafis.

When the first British military mission was parachuted into Greece during the night of Sept. 30, 1942, they found that both E.A.M. and E.L.A.S. were firmly established, capably organized, not badly armed and entirely controlled by the Communist party. The G.H.Q., middle east, decided to support them with gold, arms and ammunition in the hope that they would start a large guerrilla campaign against the axis powers. In actual fact they were mainly fighting the royalist guerrilla bands such as that of Col. Dimetrius Psaras, who was murdered by the E.L.A.S., or the more important E.D.E.S. (*Ellinikos Dimokratikos Ethnikos Stratos* or Hellenic Democratic National army) led by Col. Napoleon Zervas. In the house of commons Jan. 18, 1945, Churchill said that the E.L.A.S. leaders "were simply taking our arms, lying low and awaiting the moment when they could seize power in the capital."

2. British Reconquest of Greece.—There was no large-scale fighting for the liberation of Greece; it was not necessary. With two Allied armies north of Florence in Italy, with the Russians holding Rumania and Bulgaria, Hitler gave Field Marshal Maximilian von Weichs, commander in chief, Balkans, the order to abandon Greece. At the beginning of Oct. 1944 small British forces under Maj. Gen. Sir Ronald MacKenzie Scobie started the liberation of the country. On Oct. 18, coming from Cairo, the legal Greek government returned to Athens. (K. SM.)

M. Allied Reconquest of Western Europe

During the British-U.S. staff conversations held at Washington, D.C., in March 1941 to outline the application of the united efforts of the British commonwealth and the United States in the event that the latter was forced into the war, the cardinal principle postulated was that the defeat of Germany must be the paramount objective. With this achieved the destruction of any remaining enemies would be a less formidable task.

Meeting in London in April 1942, the combined chiefs of staff agreed that plans should be prepared for a major invasion of the continent in 1943 (Operation "Roundup"). They reaffirmed that, subject to necessary measures being taken to hold the front against Japan, all resources had to be concentrated upon the defeat of Germany. Since the Red army was at that moment sustaining the full force of the German offensive, it was decided that an operation against the continent on as large a scale as possible should be planned, for execution by the late summer or early fall of 1942 in the event that conditions so deteriorated as to render it necessary. To this contingent operation was given the name "Sledgehammer."

In June 1942 Prime Minister Churchill and Gen. Sir Alan F. Brooke, chief of the imperial general staff, went to Washington and reopened previous discussions of an operation in the Mediterranean, where the British were now falling back before Field Marshal Erwin Rommel's attack. The situation of the soviet forces was becoming rapidly worse. In this emergency Gen. George C. Marshall and Adm. Ernest King went to London to examine what could be done. Gen. Dwight D. Eisenhower had arrived in England on June 24, assuming command of U.S. forces in the European theatre. It had become obvious by this time that sufficient resources could hardly be massed in the United Kingdom during 1942 for even the "Sledgehammer" operation. The combined chiefs, therefore, reluctantly agreed to delay the cross-channel operation and to launch an expedition against North Africa in the fall of 1942. Eisenhower left England on Nov. 5, 1942, to lead this force.

In Jan. 1943, the situation in North Africa having turned definitely in favour of the Allies, it was decided at the Casablanca conference that the build-up for the invasion of northwestern Europe should be resumed and that to the same end the bombing of Germany should be continued and intensified; submarine construction yards and critical war industries which sustained German efforts were selected as initial objectives.

At the Trident conference in Washington in May 1943 a target-date of May 1, 1944, was set for "Overlord," as the revived cross-channel operation was called. At Quebec, Canada, in September (Quadrant conference) it was directed that the bombing of Germany from the United Kingdom should be supplemented by strategic bombing from bases in the Mediterranean theatre. In 1943 Lieut.

→

U.S. troops wading ashore to the Normandy beachhead on D-day, 1944

Gen. Sir F. E. Morgan had been appointed chief of staff for the supreme allied commander (Cossac); his outlined plans were now approved. The Sextant conference at Cairo, Egypt, in Nov. 1943 decided that an operation against southern France should be carried out in conjunction with the cross-channel effort. To these operations, priority over all others in the world was to be given. At Tehran in Dec. 1943 Stalin concurred in this program.

Meanwhile, the combined air attacks of the British and U.S. air forces were reaching their climax. Submarine yards and bases were heavily damaged during 1943 and the effort of the U.S. precision bombers was then concentrated against German aircraft and ball-bearing plants, aerodromes and communications. Royal air force bombers concentrated upon the destruction of industries in the Ruhr and the Rhineland and upon the undermining of the morale of the German industrial workers. The German fighter command was progressively weakened by the Allies' attacks upon its basic industries and by air combat.

1. Plans for "Overlord."—On Dec. 10, 1943, Eisenhower was appointed supreme commander of the allied expeditionary forces. Returning to England by way of Washington, he received on Feb. 14, 1944, his directive to "enter the Continent of Europe and, in conjunction with the other United Nations, undertake operations aimed at the heart of Germany and the destruction of her armed forces. The date for entering the Continent is the month of May 1944. After adequate channel ports have been secured, exploitation will be directed towards securing an area that will facilitate both ground and air operations against the enemy." Eisenhower's headquarters in England, known as S.H.A.E.F., absorbed Cossac's planning staff.

His experience in the Mediterranean theatre led Eisenhower to believe that the assault force of three divisions proposed by the Cossac planners should be increased to five and that the assault beaches should be extended from the Caen area, which they had proposed, so as to include part of the east coast of the Cotentin peninsula. These landing beaches, selected after study of the European coast from Denmark to Brittany, had the advantages of being less obvious than the strongly defended Pas de Calais area, yet were within supporting range of fighter aircraft based in England. They included no major port, but the plan contemplated early capture of Cherbourg. To seize the constricted exits from the Cotentin peninsula beaches which were isolated by floods and to assist in subsequent operations, two air-borne divisions were to land by parachute and glider. Another air-borne division would seize the bridges over the Orne river and Caen canal and protect the left flank.

Selection of the date for the assault was based upon tidal and light conditions. The tide had to be sufficiently low to enable the initial assault elements to land and prepare gaps through the beach obstacles at low-tide level. This condition had to coincide with a date having sufficient light to permit visual bombing by aircraft and bombardment by naval vessels, and sufficient moonlight on the preceding night for the air-borne landings. Chiefly because of the shortage of landing craft, some of them to come from the Mediterranean, the date of the attack was postponed from early May to early June. June 5, 6 and 7 corresponded with the requisite tide and light conditions. When rough weather developed in the channel on June 5, the date provisionally set, Eisenhower postponed D-day until June 6.

As organized for the attack, the ground forces, both British and U.S., were placed under Gen. Bernard L. Montgomery's command. Within his 21st army group were the Canadian 1st army (2nd corps) under Lieut. Gen. H. D. G. Crerar, the British 2nd army (1st, 8th, 12th and 30th corps) under Lieut. Gen. Sir Miles C. Dempsey, British air-borne troops (1st and 6th divisions) under Lieut. Gen. F. A. M. Browning and United States 1st army (5th, 7th, 8th and 19th corps) together with the 82nd and 101st air-borne divisions, commanded by Lieut. Gen. Omar N. Bradley. Adm. Sir Bertram Ramsay was commander of the allied naval expeditionary force. Air Chief Marshal Sir Trafford Leigh-Mallory commanded the allied expeditionary air force. The strategic air forces (R.A.F. bomber command, under Air Chief Marshal Sir Arthur Harris, and U.S. 8th and 15th air forces, under Lieut. Gen. Carl A. Spaatz) remained directly responsible to the combined chiefs of staff; after April 13, 1944, the supreme commander was authorized to call upon them when needed.

From right to left, Maj. Gen. J. L. Collins' 7th corps was to land with the 4th infantry division in the assault on "Utah" beach just north of the Vire estuary, and Maj. Gen. Leonard T. Gerow's 5th corps was to attack "Omaha" beach west of the Vire river with one combat team of the 29th infantry division on the right and one combat team of the 1st division on the left in the assault. Dempsey's British 2nd army was to land on Ouistreham ("Sword"), Courseulles ("Juno") and Asnelles ("Gold") beaches with the Canadian 3rd and British 3rd infantry divisions of the 1st corps and 50th infantry division of the 30th corps in the assault. The beaches measured about 50 mi. in length.

The objective of the 7th corps, supported by the air-borne divisions, was to cut the Cotentin peninsula and seize Cherbourg. The 5th corps was to push south toward St. Lô and, with the forces from the Cotentin peninsula, drive to a line extending from Avranches eastward. Gen. George S. Patton, Jr.,'s 3rd army during this period was to build up in the beachhead with the prospective mission of capturing the Brittany ports. The British and Canadian forces were to gain ground in the Caen area and protect the left flank against an expected main German counter-attack. These forces faced terrain favourable for the operation of armoured units, and it was in this region that the first strong German reaction was expected.

The navies divided the assault area between the western (U.S.) task force under Rear Adm. A. G. Kirk and the eastern (British) task force under Rear Adm. Sir P. L. Vian. Each task force was subdivided to provide for an assault force to land the troops on each of the five beaches. More than 5,000 ships and 4,000 "ship-to-shore" craft were employed in the assault and build-up, including 6 battleships, 2 monitors, 22 cruisers and 93 destroyers.

At the moment of the invasion there were 47 divisions (26 British, Canadian, Polish; 21 U.S.) in the United Kingdom. U.S. forces, including air and lines of communication troops, numbered about 1,600,000. The table on p. 709 shows the progressive build-up of the combat forces in the theatre until the German surrender in May 1945. With attached anti-aircraft, tank destroyer and tank units the divisions approximated 17,000 men each.

On May 8, 1945, the strength of Allied forces under Gen. Eisenhower's command was approximately as follows:

U.S.	2,585,000
British	890,000
French	413,000
Canadian	183,000
Italian	37,000
Polish	15,000
Belgian	7,000
Czech	6,000
Dutch	2,000
Total	4,138,000

Allied Forces in Northwest Europe

	U.S. On continent	U.S. In U.K.	BRITISH On continent	BRITISH In U.K.	FRENCH On continent
June 6, 1944					
Armies . .	1st	3rd	2nd	1st Canadian	0
Corps. . .	5th, 7th	8th, 12th, 15th, 19th, 20th, 23rd	1st, 30th	2nd, 8th, 12th, 2nd Canadian, 1st Polish	
Divisions. .	1st, 4th, 29th Infantry 82nd, 101st Air-borne	2nd, 5th, 8th, 9th, 28th, 30th, 35th, 79th, 83rd, 90th Infantry; 2nd, 3rd, 4th, 5th, 6th, 7th Armoured	3rd, 50th Infantry; 6th Air-borne; 3rd Canadian	15th, 38th, 43rd, 45th, 47th, 51st, 52nd, 53rd, 55th, 49th, 59th, 61st, infantry; 7th, 9th, 11th, 79th, Guards Armoured; 1st Air-borne; 2nd Canadian Infantry; 4th Canadian Armoured; 1st Polish Armoured; 2nd Polish Grenadier Armoured.	
Sept. 30, 1944					
Armies . .	1st, 3rd, 7th, 9th	0	2nd, 1st Canadian	0	1st
Corps. . .	3rd, 5th, 6th, 7th, 8th, 12th, 15th, 18th, 19th, 20th	13th, 16th	1st, 8th, 12th, 30th; 1st Air-borne; 2nd Canadian	2nd	1st, 2nd
Divisions. .	1st, 2nd, 3rd, 4th, 5th, 8th, 9th, 26th, 28th, 29th, 30th, 35th, 36th, 44th, 79th, 80th, 83rd, 90th, 94th, 95th, 102nd, 104th Infantry; 82nd, 101st Air-borne; 2nd, 3rd, 4th, 5th, 6th, 7th, 10th Armoured	95th Infantry; 17th Air-borne; 9th Armoured	3rd, 15th, 43rd, 49th, 50th, 51st, 52nd, 53rd, 59th Infantry; 1st, 6th Air-borne; 7th, 11th, 79th, Guards Armoured; 2nd, 3rd Canadian Infantry; 4th Canadian Armoured; 1st Polish Armoured	38th, 45th, 47th, 52nd, 55th, 61st Infantry; 2nd Polish Grenadier Armoured	1st, 2nd Armoured; 1st Motorized; 2nd Moroccan; 3rd Alg.; 9th Col.
Dec. 31, 1944					
Armies . .	1st, 3rd, 7th, 9th, 15th,	0	2nd, 1st Canadian	1st, Allied Air-borne	1st
Corps. . .	3rd, 5th, 6th, 7th, 8th, 12th, 13th, 15th, 16th, 18th, 19th, 20th, 21st	22nd, 23rd	1st, 8th, 12th, 30th, 2nd Canadian	2nd, 1st Air-borne	1st, 2nd
Divisions. .	1st, 2nd, 3rd, 4th, 5th, 8th, 9th, 26th, 28th, 29th, 30th, 35th, 36th, 44th, 45th, 75th, 78th, 79th, 80th, 83rd, 84th, 87th, 90th, 94th, 95th, 99th, 100th, 102nd, 103rd, 104th, 106th Infantry; 17th, 82nd, 101st Air-borne; 2nd, 3rd, 4th, 5th, 6th, 7th, 9th, 10th, 11th, 12th, 14th Armoured	66th, 69th, 76th Infantry; 8th Armoured	3rd, 15th, 43rd, 49th, 50th, 51st, 52nd, 53rd Infantry; 6th Air-borne; 7th, 11th, 79th, Guards Armoured; 4th Canadian Armoured; 1st Polish Armoured	38th, 45th, 47th, 48th, 55th, 61st Infantry; 1st Air-borne; 2nd Polish Grenadier Armoured	1st, 2nd, 5th Armoured; 1st Motorized; 2nd Moroccan; 4th Moroccan Mtn; 3rd Alg.; 9th Col.; 27th Alp.
March 26, 1945					
Armies . .	1st, 3rd, 7th, 9th, 15th, 1st Allied Air-borne	0	2nd, 1st Canadian	0	1st
Corps. . .	3rd, 5th, 6th, 7th, 8th, 12th, 13th, 15th, 16th, 19th, 20th, 21st, 22nd, 23rd; 18th Air-borne.	0	1st, 8th, 12th, 30th, 1st, 2nd Canadian	2nd, 1st Air-borne	1st, 2nd
Divisions.	1st, 2nd, 3rd, 4th, 5th, 8th, 9th, 26th, 28th, 29th, 30th, 35th, 36th, 42nd, 44th, 45th, 63rd, 65th, 66th, 69th, 70th, 71st, 75th, 76th, 78th, 79th, 80th, 83rd, 84th, 86th, 87th, 89th, 90th, 94th, 95th, 97th, 99th, 100th, 102nd, 103rd, 104th, 106th Infantry; 13th, 17th, 82nd, 101st Air-borne; 2nd, 3rd, 4th, 5th, 6th, 7th, 8th, 9th, 10th, 11th, 12th, 13th, 14th, 16th, 20th Armoured	0	3rd, 15th, 43rd, 49th, 51st, 52nd, 53rd Infantry; 6th Air-borne; 7th, 11th, 79th, Guards Armoured; 2nd, 3rd Canadian Infantry; 4th, 5th Canadian Armoured; 1st Polish Armoured	38th, 45th, 47th, 48th, 50th, 55th, 61st Infantry; 1st Air-borne; 2nd Polish Grenadier Armoured	1st, 2nd, 5th Armoured; 1st Motorized; 2nd Moroccan; 4th Moroccan Mtn; 3 Alg.; 9th Col.; 27th Alp; Gironde
May 8, 1945					
Armies . .	Same as March 26, 1945	0	2nd, 1st Canadian	0	1st
Corps. . .			1st, 8th, 12th, 30th; 1st, 2nd Canadian	1st Air-borne	1st, 2nd
Divisions. .			3rd, 5th, 15th, 43rd, 49th, 51st, 52nd, 53rd Infantry; 6th Air-borne; 7th, 11th, 79th, Guards Armoured; 1st, 2nd, 3rd, Canadian Infantry; 4th, 5th Canadian Armoured; 1st Polish Armoured	38th, 45th, 47th, 48th, 50th, 55th, 61st Infantry; 1st Air-borne; 4th Polish	1st, 2nd, 5th Armoured; 1st Motorized; 2nd Moroccan; 4th Moroccan Mtn; 3rd Alg.; 9th Col.; 27th Alp; Gironde; 1st, 10th, 14th Infantry—(for occupation duty)

Available to the air forces were 4,900 fighter aircraft and 5,800 bombers.

Supplies for this operation of unprecedented size had been accumulating in the United Kingdom since 1942. In June 1944 the monthly import reached a total of 1,900,000 tons. For the invasion 2,500,000 tons were required in addition to the normal loads carried by the troop units.

In France and the Low Countries there were on D-day about 60 German divisions, of which 36 infantry and 6 panzer divisions were located in the coastal area opposite England. In the immediate area of Allied assaults Germany had nine infantry divisions and one panzer. Its 15th army was held in the Pas de Calais area to cope with what it anticipated would be the main Allied assault. This error of judgment was to prove a major factor in German defeat in Normandy. Against an invasion the Germans had built their Atlantic wall which, according to Hitler, consisted of "a belt of strong points and gigantic fortifications from Norway to the Pyrenees." Along the beaches were successive rows of various types of obstacles, many of them with mines attached.

In the late spring of 1944 the Allied air forces directed their efforts against synthetic fuel plants and crude oil refineries, reducing production during the summer of 1944 by 95%. In the spring of 1944 they also began directly to pave the way for the invasion. Attacking bridges and rail centres, they isolated the invasion coasts and thus crippled the efforts of the Germans to reinforce this critical area.

For some months prior to the invasion the Germans had created a diversion by constructing launching sites for flying bombs and rockets near the channel coast, particularly in the Pas de Calais area. Heavy bombing by Allied air forces delayed until June 12 the initial launching of these missiles which, unimpeded, could have crippled the invading fleets, or reduced London to ruins in a brief period.

The Germans fired about 18,335 V-1 (flying bombs) between June 13, 1944, and March 29, 1945; 7,840 were fired at England, about 4,260 being destroyed in the air, and 10,595 at targets on the continent. Between Sept. 8, 1944,

Devastation at St. Lo, France, after U.S. forces broke through heavy German defenses in July 1944. After its capture, the city became an important Allied communications centre

and March 29, 1945, about 3,000 V-2 rockets were fired, of which about 1,250 were fired against England and 1,750 at the Antwerp, Belgium, area. The V-1 and V-2 missiles caused about 31,612 casualties, civilian and military, in England and probably at least as many on the continent.

2. The Assault Begins.—At 1:30 A.M. on June 6, 1944, parachutists of the U.S. 101st and 82nd air-borne divisions began to drop beyond Utah beach and those of the British 6th air-borne division east of the Orne river. Shortly after midnight 1,136 R.A.F. bombers started to unload 5,853 tons of bombs on coastal batteries between Cherbourg and Le Havre, and as day broke 1,365 U.S. heavy bombers dropped 2,796 tons on the shore defenses during the half-hour preceding the landings. Then medium, light and fighter bombers swarmed in to attack individual targets among the defenses. So thoroughly had the air forces done their work during the preceding months that the Germans reacted little in the air.

The troops made their first touchdowns at 6:30 A.M. under heavy supporting fire of naval guns as well as of tanks and artillery pieces firing from tank landing craft. Although still heavy, the sea had moderated. Some of the craft mislanded, partly because of the force of the current, but in the main the landings were made as planned. First came tanks (some with jettisonable flotation attachments—most of this type were lost), next came infantry to cover the engineers and naval crews who were to blast gaps through the beach defenses and then came successive waves of the assault infantry with their supporting weapons. Heavy resistance at some points caused serious losses to the assault waves. With great gallantry the attacking forces stormed or worked their way through the defenses and by nightfall the five sea-borne assaulting divisions were firmly ashore. Integrating their efforts with those of the ground forces and of the navies, aircraft of all types contributed in large measure to the success of this critical day.

Pinning their faith to the defensive strength of the coast fortifications, the Germans, under Rommel, had prepared relatively few inland defenses with the result that once Allied troops had breached the Atlantic wall, operations became fluid. Aggressively attacking the Germans through the difficult hedgerow country, the British and Canadians pressed toward Caen, taking Bayeux on June 8 while U.S. forces moved toward a junction of the beaches near Carentan. Outmanoeuvred, their efforts to bring in reinforcements disrupted by Allied air attacks, the Germans threw in piecemeal such troops as were available; thus, they were never able to amass a mobile reserve sufficiently large to endanger the Allied beachheads. On June 11 all beachheads were linked up in a solid front.

There followed six weeks of gruelling fighting in which the Allies expanded the lodgement area and built up forces for their future breakout. The U.S. 7th corps cut the Cotentin peninsula on June 17 and, pushing northward, captured Cherbourg nine days later. The port's installations had been thoroughly demolished by the Germans, and unloading could not begin until July 19.

Delay in the acquisition of a major port had been anticipated, and to meet this deficiency the novel expedient had been devised of preconstructing two artificial ports (Mulberries), each of the size of Dover, one for the U.S. and one for the British forces. The components had been built in the United Kingdom and were towed to the Normandy coast and there assembled. A heavy storm on June 19 completely wrecked the Mulberry serving the U.S. beaches, but that serving the British was repaired and kept in service until Antwerp became available in the fall. Throughout the summer months major reliance was placed upon the arrival of reinforcements and supplies over the beaches or via this Mulberry. During the first 6 days of the invasion 326,000 troops, 54,000 vehicles and 100,000 long tons of supplies passed over the beaches. By July 4 the totals had reached 1,000,000 men, 200,000 vehicles and 700,000 tons of supplies; and by November, 2,628,240 men, 549,664 vehicles and 4,522,192 tons.

During the latter days of June the British maintained their pressure toward Caen despite desperate but piecemeal efforts of German armoured units which revealed the German resolve to prevent, at all costs, a breakthrough up the Seine valley toward Paris. Caen fell on July 9. After the capture of Cherbourg the U.S. 7th corps turned toward the south and with the U.S. 8th and 19th corps cleared the Cotentin peninsula. On July 18 St. Lô was taken.

3. Breakout from St. Lô.—The moment had now arrived for a breakout from the lodgement area. Eisenhower decided to put to good account the German tenacity on the east flank by continuing to punch hard in that region and

following with a smashing right-hand blow. Preceded by a powerful air assault by bombers and lighter aircraft, on July 18 British and Canadian forces renewed their drive in the Caen area. Dogged resistance was aggravated by bad weather but on July 25, again preceded by a powerful air bombardment, the attack of Bradley's forces against the Germans beyond St. Lô was launched. Complete success was achieved. Coutances was captured on July 28, parts of several German divisions being cut off to the north. Only now did the Germans recognize the Allied main effort and decide to bring reinforcements to this region from the army which had been retained in the Pas de Calais. Their decision came too late.

Patton's 3rd army officially came into existence on Aug. 1 when he took command of the U.S. 8th, 12th, 15th and 20th corps; the 5th, 7th and 19th corps remained with Lieut. Gen. Courtney H. Hodges' 1st army, both under Bradley's 12th army group. Crerar's Canadian 1st army had become operational on July 23, and he now commanded the British 1st and Canadian 2nd corps on the east flank. With Dempsey's British 2nd army these formed Montgomery's 21st army group. On Sept. 1 Eisenhower was to assume personal direction in France of all operations, at which date S.H.A.E.F. was established officially on the continent.

Pouring through the breach in the St. Lô-Coutances line, the 3rd army seized Avranches on July 31 and, in a swift amputation of the Brittany peninsula, reached Nantes on Aug. 10.

With the collapse of the Germans on the west flank, Eisenhower decided once more to adapt his plan to his opportunities and, despite his need for the Brittany ports, to turn his back upon them and make a wide encirclement of the German 7th army and panzer group west, which were still showing fanatical obstinacy, resisting in place. Leaving to his 7th corps the task of reducing the Brittany ports, Patton in a rapid advance overran Mayenne, Laval and Le Mans and on Aug. 13 reached Argentan.

As part of the manoeuvre, the U.S. 1st army and the British forces had maintained their pressure from the north and west. In a desperate effort to checkmate this offensive, Field Marshal Gerd von Rundstedt, who had succeeded Rommel, launched a panzer attack, supported by infantry, from the Mortain area toward Avranches with the hope of cutting off Patton's army from the rear. Prepared for the blow, Bradley attacked the flanks of the moving German columns and at the same time the Allied air forces blasted them from above.

4. Falaise-Argentan Pocket.—After this failure the Germans strove desperately to hold open the gap between Falaise and Argentan in order to extricate the forces caught

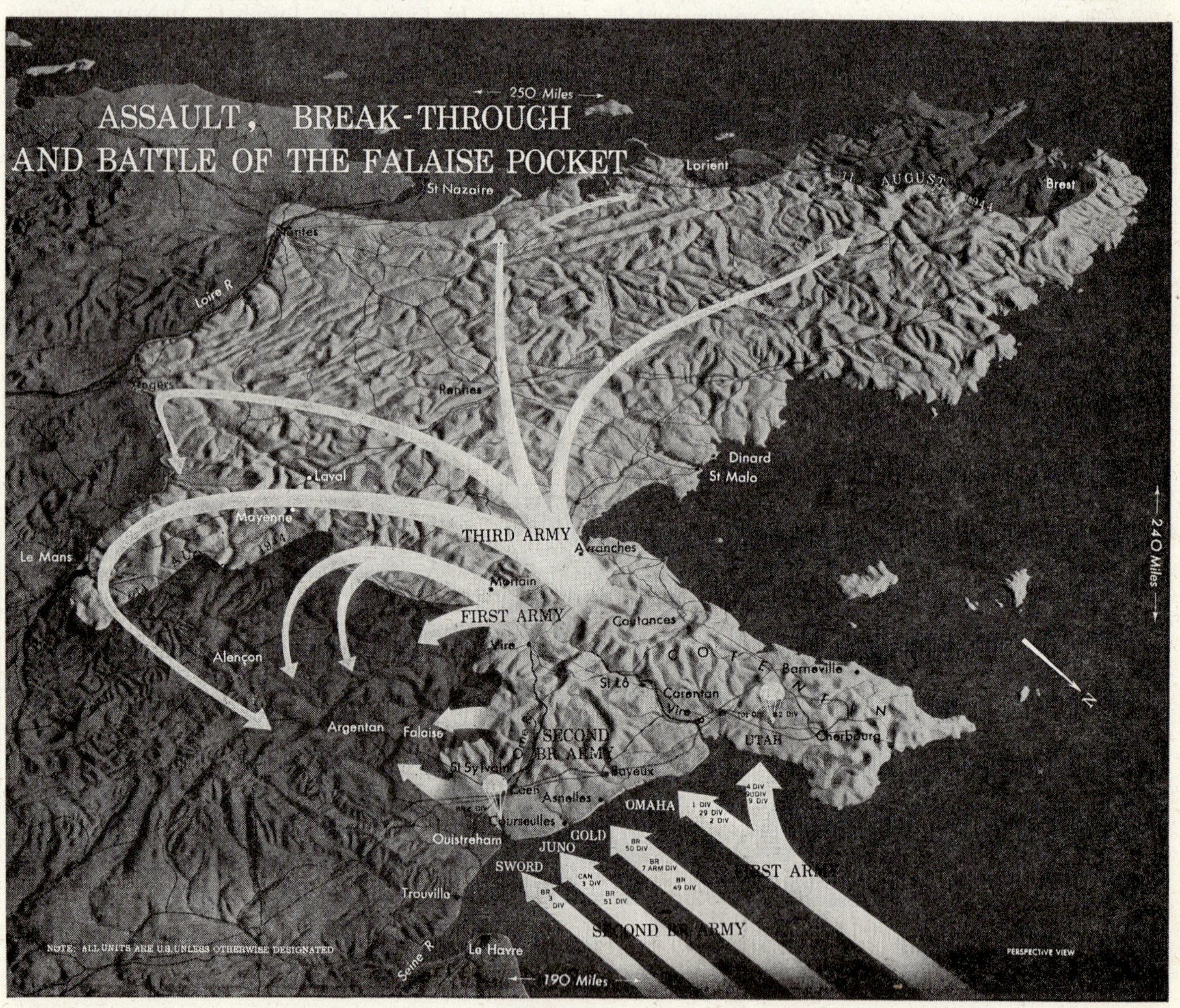

The opening of the second front, showing the invasion of Normandy on June 6, 1944, the breakthrough at St. Lô, and the offensive aimed at the Falaise pocket

in the pocket which the Allies were steadily squeezing. Although many were able to escape, the Germans lost a great proportion of their equipment, and their 7th army was virtually annihilated as an organization. By Aug. 22 the pocket was eliminated. An interesting feature of the rapid advance of the 3rd army was the protection of its open right flank by the 19th tactical air command. Air power also played its part in the catastrophe of the German 7th army by persistent attacks against German communications and by raking German columns as they retreated across the Seine.

5. Attack on Southern France.—Meanwhile, on Aug. 16, the Allies had launched a heavy supporting attack in southern France.

As early as the Quadrant conference at Quebec in 1943 the combined chiefs of staff had contemplated an attack on southern France in conjunction with the proposed cross-channel invasion. At the Cairo (Sextant) conference in Nov. 1943 the plan began to take shape, and the scheme for the two operations received Stalin's approval. The demands of the operations in Italy together with the necessity for transferring forces and landing craft for the cross-channel expedition repeatedly overshadowed the plans for the southern France invasion and finally occasioned its postponement from the originally planned date of early June. However, Eisenhower's needs for additional port capacity soon pointed to the desirability of the early capture of Marseilles. Such an operation would also contain and destroy German forces which might otherwise oppose him and would threaten the flank and rear of the main forces which already faced him.

Measures were taken to organize and arm a large force of French patriots who were to lend valuable support to Allied operations. On July 30, 1944, Lieut. Gen. Jacob L. Devers organized the 6th army group headquarters in Corsica. To command the landing forces Lieut. Gen. Alexander M. Patch was placed in command of the U.S. 7th army.

After prolonged aerial attacks against the communications serving this region, on Aug. 15 at 8 A.M., the 7th army, escorted by a powerful fleet of British and U.S. warships and under their gunfire, landed on the beaches between Cap Cavalaire and Agay, the area which offered the most favourable approach to the Rhône valley. The assault forces consisted of the U.S. 6th corps with the 36th division on the right, 45th division in the centre and 3rd division on the left. Most of the U.S. forces had been loaded at ports in the Naples area, the French forces at Oran, Taranto and Brindisi. A British-U.S. air-borne task force jumped astride the Ardens river west of St. Raphael the night preceding the assault and seized the pass through which the Allied forces would debouch.

Gen. Sir Henry Maitland Wilson estimated that there were 11 German divisions in southern France, two of them armoured, but that only three would be ready to oppose the landing immediately. Weak resistance was actually encountered, the beachheads were promptly established and the main forces moved west toward the Rhône valley.

On the heels of the 6th corps the four divisions of Gen. Jean de Lattre de Tassigny's French 1st army went ashore. By Aug. 28 Toulon and Marseilles were in Allied hands and by Sept. 1 Nice had fallen. Meanwhile, part of the 36th division headed directly north, seized Grenoble and turned northwest to cut off the Germans who were retreating up the Rhône valley. This drive into the rear of the German 19th army, already under pressure from the south, together with the havoc caused by the air forces, caused it to fall back in confusion. On Sept. 3 Lyons fell.

On Sept. 15, after effecting a junction with Patton's forces, the U.S. 7th and French 1st armies, forming Devers' 6th army group, passed to Eisenhower's command. Devers was succeeded as deputy theatre commander in the Mediterranean by Lieut. Gen. Joseph C. McNarney, former deputy chief of staff in Washington.

Allied casualties to Sept. 15 in the southern France campaign were:

	Killed	Wounded	Missing	Total
U.S.	1,395	4,798	1,081	7,274
French	1,300†	5,000*	†	6,300*
British	156	141	—	297
Total	2,851	9,939	1,081	13,871

*Estimated.
†Killed and missing figures combined.

6. Advance to the German Border.—In northern France, meanwhile, the Allied armies were hard on the heels of the retreating Germans. Eisenhower's strategy called for his main effort on his north flank. In a rapid sweep the

Casualties of U.S. army ground forces during the drive on the Rhine, from D-day to Jan. 29, 1945

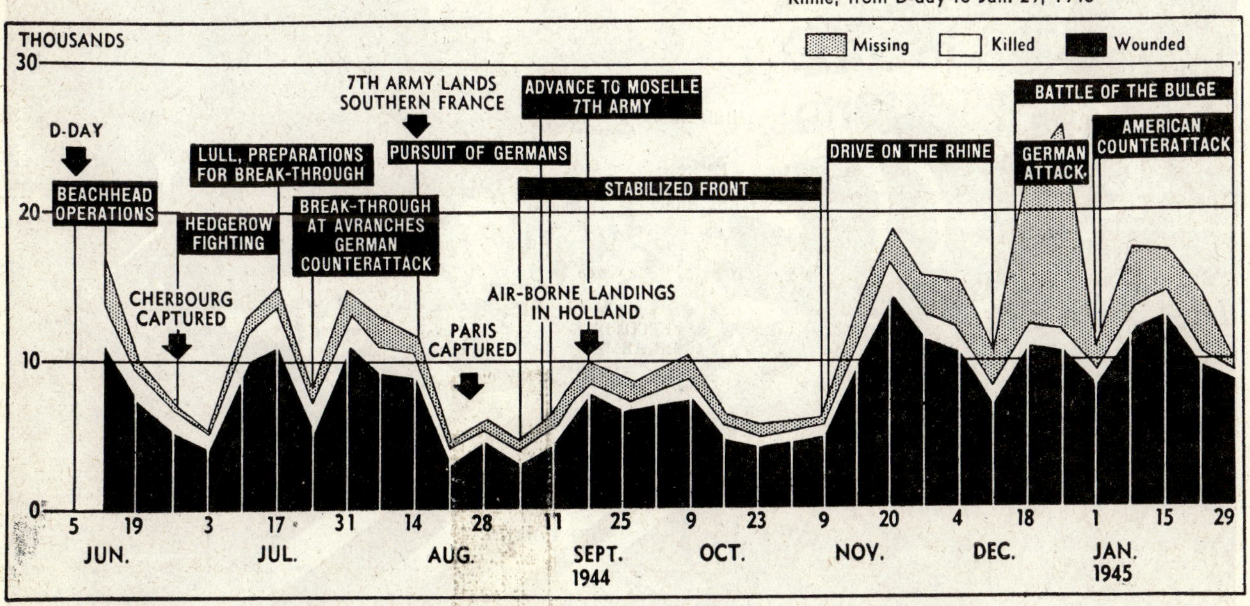

Canadian army cut off Le Havre (captured Sept. 12), Dieppe (captured Sept. 1), Boulogne (captured Sept. 23) and Calais (captured Sept. 30), reaching Bruges on Sept. 9 and overrunning a large portion of the Pas de Calais flying-bomb sites. The British 2nd army advanced simultaneously, took Amiens on Aug. 31 and on Sept. 4 occupied Antwerp virtually intact. The U.S. 1st army crossed the Seine east and west of Paris, captured Soissons and, turning east, freed Namur on Sept. 5, Liége on Sept. 8 and Luxembourg two days later. Eisenhower had left to a French division, the 2nd armoured, the honour of receiving the surrender of the city of Paris on Aug. 25. In pursuit the 1st army cut off and surrounded a large pocket of the retreating Germans between Compiègne and Mons, taking 25,000 prisoners. The 3rd army swept eastward, captured Reims and Châlons, overran Verdun on Sept. 1 and gained a foothold beyond the Moselle on Sept. 7. Patch's 7th army and De Tassigny's French 1st army (constituting Devers' 6th army group), which had made a phenomenal advance up the Rhône valley, from the Riviera to establish contact with Patton's forces at the little village of Sombernon near Dijon on Sept. 11, came under Eisenhower's command on Sept. 15 (*see* above). A continuous front now ran from the Netherlands along the French frontier to Switzerland and from Switzerland to the Mediterranean. Large German forces were isolated, of which one block of 20,000 surrendered along the Loire. Most of the ports along the channel and Atlantic coasts were still held by the Germans, Eisenhower making no attempt to reduce them after the experience at Cherbourg and Brest, where the Germans reduced their installations to ruin.

On Sept. 5 the U.S. 9th army was created under the command of Lieut. Gen. W. H. Simpson. His 8th corps (2nd, 8th and 29th divisions) finally reduced Brest on Sept. 19. Thereupon, the 9th army on Oct. 3 took over a sector of the line in the 12th army group between the 1st and 3rd armies.

Not only was resistance stiffening as Allied troops approached the threshold of Germany, but the unprecedented speed of their advance had caused them to outrun their supplies. Slowly the armies came to a halt. Herculean measures were taken to carry supplies from the beaches to the troops, including the use of aircraft and the establishment of the famous Red Ball route, a virtually continuous line of trucks operating day and night over the highways. Gasoline pipe lines were laid under the channel and carried forward behind the troops as fast as the engineers could establish them.

The direction of Eisenhower's main effort now lay across the series of Dutch rivers which included the Meuse, the Waal and the lower Rhine. On Aug. 8 he had created the 1st air-borne army under command of Maj. Gen. Lewis H. Brereton, consisting of the U.S. 18th corps (17th, 82nd, 101st air-borne divisions) and the British air-borne troops command (1st and 6th air-borne divisions). Successively, it had been intended to use this army in the seizure of the Paris-Orléans gap after Patton's break-through, then at the Seine crossings after the Falaise pocket operation and then to cut off the German 15th army in the Pas de Calais; but the swift advance of the Allied ground forces made these operations unnecessary. Eisenhower now decided upon a rapid crossing of the Dutch rivers. The name "Market-Garden" was given to this operation. In "Market," the air-borne operation, the British 1st air-borne division was dropped in the Arnheim area, the U.S. 82nd air-borne division in the Nijmegen area and the U.S. 101st air-borne division north of Eindhoven, on Sept. 17. In "Garden," the land operation, British ground forces advanced through Eindhoven and Nijmegen and made contact with the air-borne units, the combined forces seizing the Waal river bridge at the latter town; but after desperate efforts to hold the lower Rhine crossings the forces at Arnheim were withdrawn. More than 20,000 troops were dropped by parachute and nearly 14,000 by gliders, together with their equipment and vehicles.

Montgomery (promoted to Field Marshal Sept. 1) now turned to opening the port of Antwerp. With naval and air support, Canadian and British forces attacked South Beveland and Walcheren Islands at the mouth of the Scheldt and completed their capture on Nov. 9. The estuary was swept and the first ship unloaded at Antwerp on Nov. 26. This important step materially eased the supply situation. Appreciating its importance to the Allies, the Germans for many months maintained a harassing bombardment of Antwerp with flying bombs and rockets but were unable to prevent, or even appreciably delay, unloading operations.

By Sept. 30 the Germans had sustained a million casualties. The U.S. 1st army entered Germany near Trier on Sept. 11, breached the Siegfried line north of Aachen on Oct. 2 and captured that German city on Oct. 21. With the approach of winter unusually heavy rains now set in.

South of Metz, the 3rd army fought its way across the Moselle, taking Nancy on Sept. 15. In the Vosges the 7th army came up abreast of the 3rd.

With Antwerp operating, Eisenhower could now complete his drive to the line of the Rhine. Rather than maintain a flexible defense, the Germans once more elected to contest every foot of the ground, with the result that they were decisively defeated west of what would have been for them a formidable natural defense and conversely yielded to the Allies that barrier behind which the latter could, with relative impunity, concentrate their forces at any point they desired for the final assault.

On Oct. 23 the 9th army was moved to the north flank of the 1st army and on Nov. 16 the 1st and 9th armies resumed their drive toward the Rhine in the Aachen sector. Aided by powerful air support, U.S. troops in bloody fighting moved forward into Hurtgen forest, and on Dec. 3 the 9th army reached the Roer river. The Germans still held the series of dams higher up this river near Schmidt; and after air attacks had failed to destroy them, the 1st army on Dec. 13 undertook their capture lest the Germans, by releasing the waters, should flood the Roer at the moment of the 9th army's crossing.

East of Thionville the 3rd army had crossed the German frontier on Nov. 18 and reached the Siegfried line near Saarlautern. The last forts of isolated Metz finally fell on Dec. 13.

Belfort was captured on Nov. 22 by the French 1st army which reached Mulhouse the same day while the U.S. 7th army, which had reached the Rhine, took Strasbourg on Nov. 27. Between the prongs of the Allied advances at Strasbourg and Mulhouse the Germans were able to maintain a bridgehead west of the Rhine, known as the Colmar pocket, which was not liquidated until Feb. 9, 1945.

7. [illegible] ffensive in the Ardennes.—In order to make the [illegible] attacks in the Aachen sector and in the Saar, the [illegible] ont had necessarily been left thin in some regi[illegible] was the case in that sector of the hilly Eifel betw[illegible] nschau and the Moselle. It was there that Hitl[illegible] d to launch a desperate counteroffensive, presum[illegible] the hope of capturing Liége and Antwerp and [illegible] upting the Allies' supply system and severing

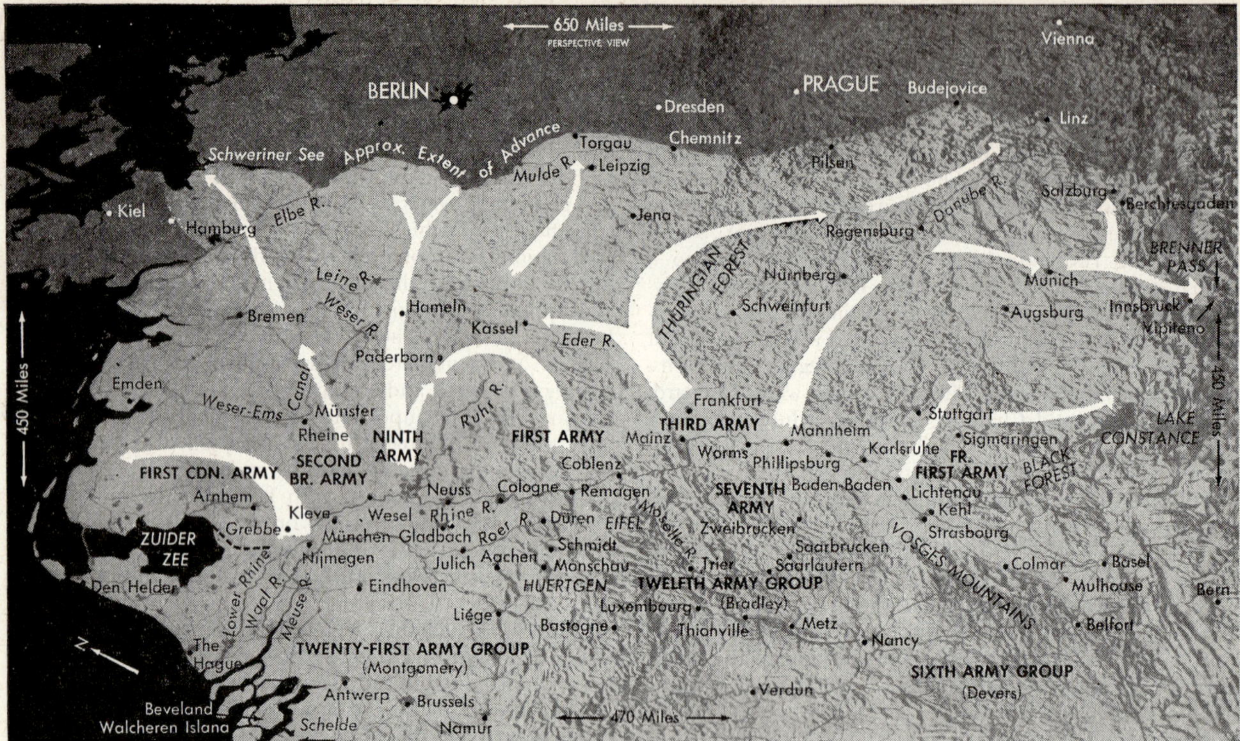

Encirclement of the Ruhr and the meeting of the Allied armies of the west with the Russians, in the spring of 1945

their forces. Important, too, was the prospect of dampening the offensive determination of the Allied command. S.H.A.E.F. was alive to the possibilities of such an attack but felt that the German military leaders would hesitate to undertake a counteroffensive in this unfavourable terrain and with such faint hope of success. The Germans had taken fantastic precautions to ensure the secrecy of their preparations. Volksgrenadier divisions had gradually replaced panzer divisions in this sector and the knowledge that the attack was to be made had been limited to a very few senior commanders.

On Dec. 16, aided by phenomenally heavy fog, the Germans attacked. The first brunt of the assault was borne by the U.S. 4th, 28th, 106th infantry and 9th armoured divisions. Eisenhower at once alerted the army commanders to hold their free divisions ready for support if needed, and the 101st air-borne division was rushed into Bastogne, where it held out for five days. Eisenhower directed that the shoulders of the penetration be held, and all attacks elsewhere halted. Patton was to make a major counterattack in the direction Bastogne-Cologne. An attack by Montgomery from the north was to follow. A monumental piece of staff work was performed by the 3rd army, which, during a period of six days, broke off its general attack in the Saar region, faced to the left and mounted this new attack with six divisions. Devers was instructed to extend his left flank to cover the front vacated by the 3rd army. By Dec. 19 the German penetration had become so deep as to impair Bradley's communications with his armies. Eisenhower therefore placed under Montgomery's command all U.S. troops north of the salient, leaving to Bradley's control troops on the south face, thus placing under Montgomery the U.S. 9th and most of the 1st [illegible]

The Germans in their attack used three ar[illegible] 5th and 6th panzer and the 7th armies, includ[illegible] 4th infantry and 10th panzer divisions. They al[illegible]yed a panzer brigade using U.S. equipment with[illegible]sion of spearheading German combat units and spr[illegible]anic and confusion behind U.S. front lines. Paratroops, dropped throughout the battle area as far to the rear as Paris, were to sabotage important bridges and headquarters. Although the penetration at its maximum reached a depth of about 50 mi. it never reached the Meuse; and since Bradley had not established any major installations east of the river in that region, this advance was not alarming. After the war it was learned from Von Rundstedt that the German high command privately conceded its failure when within 48 hours it had failed to reach the Meuse. Eisenhower's prompt measures proved successful and by Jan. 25, 1945, the original front had been re-established. Simultaneously with this attack, Devers' front had also received a German assault but had reacted promptly and successfully.

The net effect of the German effort was a delay in Allied operations of perhaps 6 weeks but a loss to the Germans of nearly 250,000 men, 600 tanks and assault guns and about 1,600 aeroplanes which they could ill afford. The attack cost the Allies about 60,000 casualties. Of greater significance was the disillusionment of the Germans at the failure of their last offensive venture.

After this battle, the German 6th panzer army departed for the eastern front taking seven panzer and three infantry divisions and virtually removing the last threat to the continuous advance of the Allied forces on the western front.

8. Drive for the Rhine.—Eisenhower now resumed his manoeuvres to destroy the Germans west of the Rhine and to reach the banks of that river. These operations were performed in three successive steps. First came Operations "Veritable" and "Grenade." On Feb. 8 "Veritable" was launched in difficult thaw and flood conditions resulting from the heavy January snows. Attacking from the Nijmegen area southeastward between the Rhine and the Meuse, the Canadian 1st army, in bitter fighting, forced its way through the Reichswald to the outskirts of Kleve and on Feb. 14 reached the Rhine at the site of the Allies' future major crossing. On Feb. 23, "Grenade" was launched. As a prerequisite, the U.S. 1st army had captured the Roer dams by Feb. 10 after the Germans had opened the sluices of the Schwammenauel dam, causing the level of the Roer to rise about 4 ft. and thus delaying "Grenade" by 13 days. The 7th corps of the U.S. 1st army and the 19th and 13th corps of the 9th army crossed the flooded river, cleared Juelich and Dueren on Feb. 24 and 25 and rapidly gained momentum. By March 1 the 9th army had cleared Muenchen-Gladbach and had reached the Rhine at Neuss. This threat to the Germans' rear, coupled with frontal pressure, resulted in their withdrawal across the Rhine of all units below Neuss.

The next operation was "Lumberjack," in which the 1st army advanced on the right flank of the 9th army and by March 7 had captured Cologne. Farther south, on the same day, troops of the U.S. 9th armoured division seized an opportunity by crossing at Remagen the one bridge spanning the Rhine that the Germans had not yet demolished. Bradley was ordered to put not less than five divisions promptly on the far bank. Despite the Germans' frantic efforts to retrieve their error, by March 23, when the main crossings of the Rhine were begun, the 1st army had 3 corps beyond Remagen in a bridgehead 25 mi. long and 10 mi. deep. On the right the 3rd army was pushing through the rugged Eifel, crushing the German front north of the Moselle, and on March 9, reached the Rhine just below Koblenz.

The third step was Operation "Undertone," a combined offensive by the U.S. 3rd and 7th armies. Instead of further exploiting the Remagen bridgehead, as the Germans might have expected, the 3rd army attacked southward across the Moselle behind them in the Saar region; on March 15 the Germans were attacked frontally by the 7th army. Zweibruecken and Saarbruecken were occupied by March 20. The Siegfried line defense collapsed and by March 22 Mainz had been occupied by the 3rd army. That night Patton sent his 5th division across the Rhine. By March 25 all organized resistance ceased west of the river.

In all of these activities the air forces had played a conspicuous part. Particularly in the Saar offensive the tactical air units effected noteworthy destruction upon German rail and road traffic. On Feb. 22 Operation "Clarion" had involved nearly 9,000 aircraft from bases in England, France, the Netherlands, Belgium and Germany which attacked targets over an area of 250,000 sq.mi. extending from Emden to Berlin, Dresden, Vienna and Mulhouse. Their widespread blows struck minor communications facilities such as railroad signal points and grade crossings, canal locks and junctions. Against such attack the Germans could make no defense.

9. Across the Rhine; the Ruhr Pocket.—Maintaining his main effort on the north flank, Eisenhower now forced the Rhine. Under Montgomery the U.S. 9th army and British 2nd army began their crossing at 9 P.M. on March 23 near Wesel. Shortly after the ground assault the allied 1st air-borne army dropped the 18th air-borne corps (U.S. 17th and British 6th air-borne divisions) north and northwest of Wesel. On the left flank the Canadian army guarded the Scheldt estuary and then followed the other two armies across the river. The whole operation was preceded by air attacks which severed all communications with the Ruhr. Since the Germans still had a number of jet aircraft which effectively assisted their defense, the airfields possessing the long runways necessary for jet operation and upon which Allied intelligence had detected that these aircraft were being concentrated, were heavily bombed from the air, thus effectively prohibiting their operation. The crescendo of air attacks reached a climax at the moment of the assault of the Rhine; from March 21 to 24 British and U.S. air forces based in the United Kingdom and the continent flew more than 42,000 sorties against Germany.

The major crossing met relatively light resistance. Contact was made promptly with the air-borne troops. Meanwhile, the U.S. 1st army attacked in the Remagen area and, breaking out to the southeast on March 26, raced toward Frankfurt. Farther up the Rhine the 3rd army crossed at several points and, clearing Frankfurt, joined hands with the 1st army in a plunge toward Kassel. On March 26 the 7th army crossed the Rhine near Worms and three days later captured Mannheim. On April 1 the French 1st army crossed the Rhine at Phillipsburg.

Now occurred another brilliant operation which constituted one of the outstanding military successes in history. Racing toward Muenster, the armoured elements of the 9th army charged around the north flank of the Ruhr and near Paderborn made contact with 1st army elements which had swept around the south flank of that area. Within the industrial heart of Germany were trapped the whole of German army group C and two corps of army group H. On March 30 the 15th army under Gerow had moved into the line along the Rhine opposite the Ruhr. Leaving strong forces to contain and reduce the defenders in the Ruhr, the 9th and 1st armies swept eastward and, with this huge operation still continuing at their backs, maintained their momentum toward the Mulde and Elbe valleys. On April 18 the Ruhr pocket was finally liquidated, German prisoners totalled 325,000, including 30 generals.

10. The Death Blow.—Berlin was no longer a military objective. The Russians were hammering at its gates. Eisenhower therefore decided to throw the weight of his advance toward Leipzig and thus cut the remainder of Germany in half. Jena, Chemnitz and Leipzig fell; and on April 18 the Allied armies set foot in Czechoslovakia. On April 25 patrols of the 273rd regiment, 69th division, 5th corps, of the U.S. 1st army met Russian patrols in the vicinity of Torgau on the Elbe, thus effecting the junction of the eastern and western allies.

Meanwhile, Montgomery's forces were sweeping the northern German plains. The British 2nd army crossed the Weser and reached the Elbe on April 19, Bremen was captured on April 26 and Hamburg one week later. Pushing northward through the Netherlands, the Canadian army cleared the area east of the Zuider Zee by April 21. Arnheim fell on April 15 and the Germans withdrew into Fortress Holland beyond the Grebbe and New Water defense lines which had been built by the Dutch prior to the war. There an attempt to follow the Germans would have caused them to open the dykes. Eisenhower therefore reached an agreement with Arthur Seyss-Inquart, the nazi commissioner for the Netherlands, on April 30, whereby the Allied forces were to stand on the Grebbe line and the Germans were to cease flooding the country and thus causing unnecessary distress to the inhabitants. The Germans also agreed to the introduction of food to the Dutch by land, sea and air. No further progress was made in the western Netherlands until the German troops surrendered simultaneously with those in northern Germany.

Covering the right flank of the 12th army group, the 7th army in early April pushed through Schweinfurt to Nuernberg, where stiff fighting delayed its fall until April 20. Karlsruhe fell to the French 1st army on April 4, Kehl on the 15th; and the Germans along the upper Rhine retired to the Black Forest.

The German surrender at Reims, France, on May 7, 1945. Seated at the extreme left, and proceeding clockwise around the table: German representatives Maj. Gen. W. Oxenius, Col. Gen. A. Jodl, Gen. Adm. H. G. von Friedeburg; Allied officers Lieut. Gen. Sir F. E. Morgan, Maj. F. Sevez, Adm. Sir H. M. Burrough, Lieut. Gen. W. B. Smith, Lieut. Gen. I. Chermiaeff (at a distance from table), Maj. Gen. I. Susloparoff, Gen. C. A. Spaatz, Air Vice-Marshal J. M. Robb, Maj. H. R. Bull and Senior Lieut. Col. Ivan Zenkovitch

Evidence had reached S.H.A.E.F. of a German government intention to leave Berlin and seek refuge in the "national redoubt" in the Berchtesgaden area. Into this mountainous region of western Austria and southern Germany Eisenhower directed the 6th army group. On April 30 the 7th army captured Munich. On May 4 Berchtesgaden and Salzburg fell, and by this swift advance the possibility of resistance within the redoubt was dissipated. On the same day, elements of the 103rd division, 6th corps, which had pushed through Innsbruck and the Bruenner pass to Vipiteno in Italy, met the 88th division of the U.S. 5th army.

Simultaneously, the French 1st army broke through resistance in the Black Forest and pushed along the southern boundary of Germany to Lake Constance, making contact with the 7th army at the western end of the redoubt. Farther east the western Allies had extended their contacts with the soviet forces.

On April 14 the French forces with powerful air assistance had launched an attack against the Germans resisting at the mouth of the Gironde, which was cleared with the reduction of the island of Oleron on May 1. St. Nazaire and Lorient held out until the final surrender of the German army.

Hitler having disappeared, the German forces surrendered piecemeal. On May 5 Adm. Hans von Friedeburg arrived at Reims representing Adm. Karl Doenitz, who had taken over the direction of the German state. Gen. Alfred Jodl arrived the following day. These emissaries attempted to play for time in negotiating the surrender, presumably to allow the remaining German forces to surrender to the western Allies rather than to the Russians. Upon the threat that General Eisenhower would seal his front within 48 hours Doenitz authorized the acceptance of Eisenhower's demands for unconditional surrender, and at 2:41 A.M. on May 7 the Act of Surrender was signed by Jodl, to become effective at midnight May 8–9. This act was ratified at Berlin on the night of May 9.

Among the purely military reasons which may be given for the defeat of the Germans are: (1) Imperfect German intelligence concerning Allied intentions; this resulted largely from Allied air superiority; (2) destruction of German industries and communications by Allied air forces; (3) German failure to provide defenses in depth to meet the Allied attack once the Atlantic wall had been breached; as a result German reserves, when available, were used piecemeal; (4) German stubbornness in fighting to retain ground; (5) superior generalship on the part of the Allies, inexhaustible supplies, care in planning and the two-front war which Hitler himself had invoked.

During these operations the Germans lost more than 80,000 known dead, 265,000 wounded and probably some part of the 491,000 reported missing prior to the German surrender.

The Allied land and air forces suffered these casualties:

	Dead	Wounded	Missing	Total
U.S.*	133,482	369,773	88,366‡	591,621§
British†	41,754	128,972	16,670	187,396
French†	10,138	42,021	4,225	56,384
Poles†	1,251	4,158	313	5,722
Belgians†	75	259	32	366
Dutch†	33	147	—	180
Czechs†	169	447	9	625
	186,902	545,777	109,615	842,294

*1941–May 8, 1945.
†June 6, 1944–May 8, 1945.
‡Practically all have returned. Those who died in captivity are included under dead.
§Includes about 60,000 of army air forces.

(T. N.)

III. THE CHINESE-JAPANESE WAR (1937-45)[1]

A. Prior to Pearl Harbor

The overt act which made the Chinese-Japanese war inevitable was the "Mukden Incident" of Sept. 18, 1931, when Japanese garrisons in the vicinity of that important northeast city forcibly took over control from the Chinese authorities. But this incident was only a manifestation of a long-planned Japanese policy for continental Asia which became evident after the Chinese-Japanese war of 1894–95. This war resulted in Japan's occupation of Korea and gave the island empire a foothold on the mainland.

1. Background of War.—After the Russo-Japanese War of 1904–05, Japan officially proclaimed the annexation of Korea. At the same time it began to exploit China's three northeastern provinces, obviously with a view to converting them into a base for the establishment of its continental empire. In the wake of World War I, Japan extended its tentacles from the northeast to north China. At this time it acquired a mandate over the German islands in the Pacific which it began to fortify. Thus, with the simultaneous execution of Japan's twin programs of northward and southward expansion, what were later publicized as the "New Order in East Asia" and "Sphere of Co-Prosperity in Greater East Asia" gradually assumed physical shape. Because of abundant coal and iron deposits and the agricultural products in the northeast which Japan needed, together with its available manpower, in order to fight for world hegemony, the northeast became the first victim of Japan's ambition for territorial conquest. But no sooner had it considered its exploitation of the northeast complete, than it began to proclaim that north China was its "lifeline."

The Japanese adopted a policy of *divide et impera* in interfering with political and military affairs in China. Throughout the years of internal strife after the inauguration of the republic, Japanese intrigue or instigation in one form or another was always present. The Northern Punitive expedition, led by the Chinese Kuomintang, came to a successful end in 1928, and two years later national unification, though in crude outlines, became a reality in China. A unified China, however, was anything but agreeable and tolerable to Japan. The foreign policies of European and American nations were none too harmonious following the world economic depression of 1929. Capitalizing on this situation, Japan took a bold step forward and invaded the northeast on Sept. 18, 1931.

After taking Mukden, Japan adopted an attitude of caution and "pulse feeling." Not being prepared for the invasion, China, on the one hand, offered what resistance it could muster to the onslaughts in Heilungkiang (northernmost province) and other places. On the other hand, it tenaciously maintained its adherence to the League covenant, the Nine Power treaty and the Anti-War pact and appealed to the League of Nations and the world at large.

In a proclamation to the world on Nov. 14, 1931, China pledged full support of the "sanctity of treaties" and urged the friendly nations signatory to the various pacts to "fulfill their obligations undertaken thereunder in order that peace in the Far East and the world may not be endangered by Japan and that international justice and humanity may not be bludgeoned into submission by brute force." For China was thoroughly aware of Japan's designs. Consistently it warned the world that the northeast issue and the Sino-Japanese conflict constituted a vital, integral part of the over-all problem of world peace.

China demanded the application of Articles XV and XVI of the covenant of the League of Nations, which would mean imposing economic sanctions against Japan, but without success. As the second choice, Article X of the covenant was invoked. The result was the organization of the Lytton Inquiry commission of the League of Nations.

On the eve of the arrival in China of the commission, Japan moved again. It occupied still more cities and towns in the northeast. It started hostilities in and around Shanghai (Jan. 1932) in an attempt to menace the Chinese national capital. Determined resistance by the Chinese brought Japan to the bitter realization of the futility of intimidation. So it signed an agreement with China for cessation of hostilities in and around Shanghai.

Frustrated in the south, Japan turned its attention to the north. In March of the same year, it established puppet "Manchukuo" at Changchun, northeast railroad centre, with Henry Pu Yi, last emperor of the deposed Ching (Manchu) dynasty, on the throne. In addition, under Japanese instigation and coercion, a puppet Mongolian autonomous government appeared in Inner Mongolia.

Meanwhile, the general attitude of the League of Nations was one of appeasement and timidity. It was slow to act. Worse still, the proposal of Henry L. Stimson, then U.S. secretary of state, which called for an appeal to the Nine Power treaty and the adoption of joint action by the member states, brought no response from the powers in Europe. The impotency of international treaties and the League structure made Japan all the more audacious.

Thus, the existing peace structure, the League of Nations, was flouted by Japan. Then the inevitable took place. Other aggressive, ambitious nations were encouraged to follow suit. Benito Mussolini invaded Ethiopia. Adolf Hitler marched into the Rhineland, annexed Austria and dismembered Czechoslovakia.

China, although not adequately equipped to wage a major war, was nevertheless impelled to hasten its preparation for such an eventuality. In so doing it had to trade space for time. For instance, in the hostilities of 1933, despite the desperate resistance of its soldiers, China had to yield the provincial seat of Jehol, Chengteh and the Great Wall region to the invading Japanese.

In this interval, Japan feverishly pushed forward its program of "specialization of North China," while China applied itself assiduously to consolidating its national unification. With national defense as their objective, the Chinese renovated the army, developed an air force, improved ordnance by maximum possible standardization of

[1] This section, prepared by the secretary general of Chiang Kai-shek, was read and approved in manuscript by the latter.

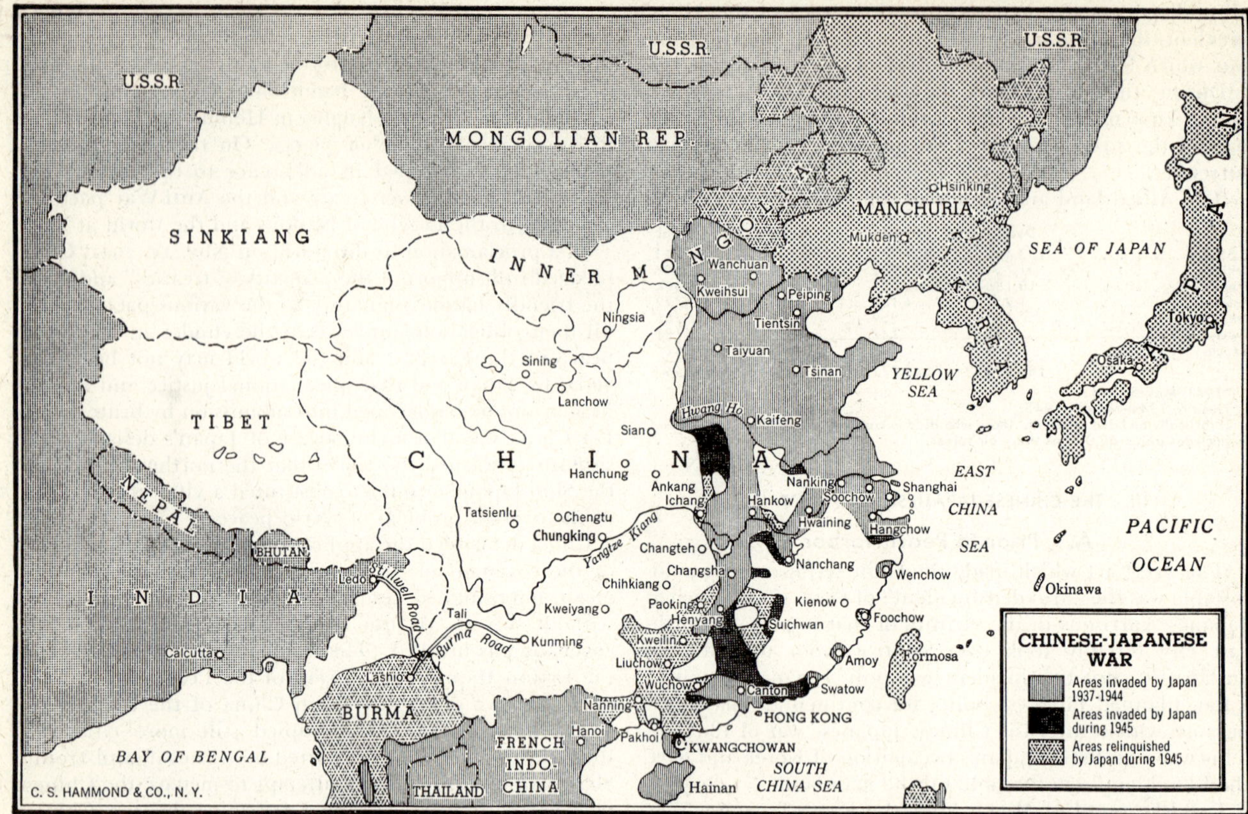

arms, unified the national currency through the adoption of a *fapi* (legal tender) policy and within two-and-a-half years rushed to completion the Canton-Hankow railway, beating a schedule which called for four years.

2. The "Loukouchiao Incident."—At this moment, Koki Hirota, Japan's foreign minister, adopted toward China a "Three Point Program" for "readjustment" of Sino-Japanese relations. Under Point One, "abandon the policy of playing one foreign country against another," Japan demanded that China recognize the existence of "Manchukuo" and its relation to Japan as protégé.

Point Two, "jointly devise effective measures for preventing the spread of Communism," was a demand for the privilege of stationing troops in certain northern provinces, apparently aimed at soviet Russia. It was tantamount to a Sino-Japanese military alliance in the cloak of "joint defense against Communism," which would have pressed China into the aggressor camp as a satellite. Hirota's third point, calling for "economic co-operation," aimed at expelling from China the economic interests of Great Britain, the United States and other countries and giving Japan a monopolistic position in their stead.

In order to maintain a national independent existence while upholding international justice and the interests of all friendly nations in China, the Chinese government flatly refused to consider these three points This taxed further the "endurance" of the Japanese Samurai. Encouraged by the ever-deteriorating situation in Europe and the mounting influence of noninterventionism in the United States, Japan took another determined step forward and precipitated the Loukouchiao (Marco Polo Bridge) incident.

On July 7, 1937, a party of Japanese troops held a large-scale manoeuvre at Loukouchiao, on the outskirts of Peiping, and, declaring that a soldier was missing, attacked the county seat of Wanping (at the southern end of Loukouchiao). The Chinese garrison resisted. The full-scale war which resulted was inevitable in view of the fact that Peiping, besides having been the Chinese capital for 700-odd years, was the centre of Chinese culture and civilization and a vital strategic base in north China.

In a statement made at Lushan, Kiangsi province, on July 17, to the nation's leaders in all walks of life, who had been invited to the famed summer resort for consultation on important problems confronting the nation, Generalissimo Chiang Kai-shek proclaimed the "arrival of the stage where it is impossible to avoid the inevitable." The generalissimo specifically defined the war as "a war between right and wrong, between good and evil, between right and might, between justice and brute force, between the treaty abider and the treaty violator." He further asserted: "Once war has begun there will be absolutely no premature cessation or compromise. For we should realize that terms for such an alternative will be nothing but terms for a total surrender and destruction of the nation." Again, in his message of Oct. 10, 1937, to the people of China, Generalissimo Chiang called their attention to the fact that the war was one of "seeking life from the jaws of death" and that it "can by no means be concluded within a short time."

Thus, with a determination steeled by indignation and the fight for survival, China went into the war. This determination sustained it through the more than eight years of hard and bitter fighting.

3. Strategy.—That China had to fight a long-term war was decided on the outset. This determined its strategy of attrition. In view of the lack of time necessary for building up coastal and river defenses, the shortage of both heavy industries and heavy armament, the deficiency of the air force, a loosely knit transportation system founded on inadequate means of communication, and the slowness and difficulties in obtaining foreign aid, the Chinese supreme command took the vital decision that the Chinese should not fight decisive battles in the coastal and river regions but should fight city by city and town by town, thereby luring the Japanese into deep inland penetrations. This strategy, not only wearing down but also spreading thin Japanese strength, was then known as "magnetic warfare."

Quite the reverse was the Japanese strategy. Encouraged by the easy success of their earlier adventures and whetted by sheer arrogance, the Japanese militarists were confident that the China campaign would not last more than three months. Following the conquest of China, they calculated that they could make use not only of their victorious forces but also of the newly subjugated manpower and material resources in their coming struggle for world hegemony. The Japanese, therefore, adopted a strategy of "a quick, decisive war" during the initial stage of the conflict. This strategy gave way to that of "a quick peace, a quick end" when Japan found China as undaunted and stubborn as ever despite the loss of Nanking, its national capital, and Wuhan, its heart. Japan, therefore, tried to employ all means and devices to entice China into a negotiated peace. This attempt, however, failed. And in view of the rapidly changing world situation, the Japanese strategy for the third stage of hostilities changed again into that of "a war to sustain war." This strategy was accompanied by the much-vaunted "mopping-up warfare." Comparable to task force operations, this latter strategy called for grouping of a sizable force to launch surprise attacks on vital strategic points, its main tasks being the dislodging of field forces, the nullifying of counteroffensive preparations and the plundering of materials. Such strategy was resorted to only when there was a shortage of military strength for distribution and when the best defense was offense.

To meet the strategic changes of Japan, Chinese strategy also varied in formula from stage to stage, but its fundamental principle remained unchanged. Without grasping this fact, there can be no true understanding of the evolution of the various battles during the Chinese-Japanese War.

During the first days of the war, when the Japanese employed the strategy of a quick, decisive war, China avoided, wherever possible, large-scale, decisive battles. This was because Chinese military preparations in north China were yet incomplete, and Japanese heavy armament could easily be brought into full play on the vast plateaus there. Furthermore, the Japanese Kwantung army with its base in the already occupied northeast would have no difficulty in furnishing reinforcements. When the Japanese drove westward into Shansi province, however, the Chinese were not hesitant to hit back and, in an east-west flanking assault in September in the vicinity of Pinghsingkwan (one of the Great Wall passes in northeastern Shansi) pounded the invaders severely. In Oct. 1937 three Japanese divisions, including two crack Kwantung army divisions, were dislodged from their stronghold, Sinkow, on the north-south Tatung-Puchow railway, after suffering numerous casualties. When the Japanese fought back with large reinforcements, the Chinese withdrew to their bases in the Taihangshan and Chungtiaoshan ranges and clung like barnacles to the south Shansi triangle, which placed them in control of the four rail lines, the Peiping-Hankow, the Lunghai, the Chengting-Taiyuan and the Tatung-Puchow. These lines were used as bases for harassing and counterattacking the Japanese from behind. Another portion of the Chinese forces, following the loss of the northern section of the Tientsin-Pukow railway, retreated into the mountains south of Shantung and controlled the basins of the Yangtze and Huai rivers in anticipation of future fighting.

China also offered stout resistance to the ruthless Japanese invasion of Shanghai on Aug. 13, 1937, begrudging no sacrifice. In this unfortified region, the Chinese defenders stood their ground for three months in defiance of the combined onslaught of the Japanese land, navy and air forces. Time and again reinforcements arrived from Japan, totalling approximately 200,000 men. The Chinese retreated only after having exacted a large toll from the Japanese. China, too, paid very heavily in men. The battle, nevertheless, had a tremendous bolstering effect on the morale of both the fighting services and the civilians throughout the country.

4. Fall of Nanking.—With Shanghai and adjoining Woosung in their pocket, the Japanese rumbled westward by land and by river and, with their mechanized units, swooped down on Nanking, allowing the Chinese frontline troops little breathing spell to regroup themselves. They took Nanking on Dec. 13, 1937, and plunged into the biggest slaughter ever known in human history. Even civilians were roped together and mowed down by Japanese machine-gun fire for sport. Shocking crimes were committed against women. Hardly any female, with the exception of some of those concealed within mission compounds, escaped violation. Even the very aged and the very young received no mercy from the invaders. What was worse, a great many were ruthlessly butchered after they had been raped. This wrote, in every sense of the term, the blackest page in the modern annals of mankind.

China appealed to the League of Nations on Aug. 30, while hostilities were going on in and around Shanghai. On Oct. 30 the member nations signatory to the Nine Power treaty met in Brussels, Belgium, but came to no agreement. The British ambassador, Sir Hughe Knatchbull-Hugessen, while travelling on the Nanking-Shanghai highway on Sept. 7, was machine-gunned by Japanese planes near Wusih (industrial town on the Nanking-Shanghai railway). A similar incident occurred on Dec. 12, when the U.S.S. "Panay," Yangtze river gunboat, was bombed and sunk by Japanese planes near Wuhu (rice town in southern Anhwei). These incidents well reflected Japan's flagrant, open defiance of the United States and Great Britain.

On the eve of the fall of Nanking, the Japanese sent peace overtures through the German ambassador, Dr. Oscar P. Trautmann, but these were rejected flatly by the Chinese government.

To show its determination to fight the war to the end, even over a long period, China at this juncture announced the removal of the government to Chungking, 1,200 mi. up the Yangtze from Nanking. On the night before he evacuated Nanking, Generalissimo Chiang Kai-shek in a press statement asserted that in entering Nanking the Japanese were inviting ultimate defeat. By that he ruled out completely the possibility of peace negotiations.

China, naturally, suffered a grievous blow in the loss of its national capital. Most of its troops, notwithstanding, succeeded in redeploying themselves in western Chekiang and southern Anhwei. These areas were held, till the end of the war, as bases of guerrilla warfare and counteroffensives against the Japanese rear. By virtue of its strategic location, Wuhan (the triple cities of Hankow, Wuchang and Hanyang) became the new headquarters of the Chinese supreme command.

5. Victory at Taierhchwang; Defeat at Wuhan.—In April 1938 Chinese forces in Shantung and Hopei, taking advantage of the opportunity of moving into the hilly region of southern Shantung, scored a major victory near

Taierhchwang, on the Tientsin-Pukow line. Two Japanese ace divisions crumbled in the battle. The significance of this victory was that it restored the morale of the entire Chinese rank and file, which had been impaired by the fall of Nanking.

A Japanese drive was launched against Hsuchow (important rail junction in northern Kiangsu) in May in an attempt to destroy the bulk of the Chinese strength in that sector but the invaders fell short of their objective. The fact was that the Chinese main force, after having given the Japanese considerable mauling, had long since retired to predesignated hill bases in southern Honan and northern Hupeh.

Hsuchow won, the Japanese made for the Wuhan cities, still bent on the realization of their fond hope of a quick, decisive war.

According to the original plans of the Chinese supreme command, the Chinese were to build up their counter-offensive strength west of the Peiping-Hankow and Canton-Hankow railways and to bide their time for fighting a decisive battle against the Japanese. Chinese resistance, however, was to continue east of the two railroads by capitalizing on the topographical advantages of the region, thus making the invasion as expensive as it could be for the Japanese and also trading space for time. Since Wuhan was the heart of China and a vital point on the Canton-Hankow railway and, moreover, since hills and marshlands were abundant on both sides of the Yangtze around Wuhan, it was decided to direct telling blows against the invading columns at the outer perimeter of the triple cities.

The Japanese offensive started in June 1938, with the navy blasting its way up the Yangtze to penetrate the Chinese river defenses. In a pincers movement, the invaders pushed one column from south of the Yangtze to attack the northern section of the Kiukiang-Nanchang railway with the object of covering the left flank as well as poising for a westward thrust. North of the Yangtze, the Japanese made a two-pronged advance. One prong wheeled westward along the river and another column fringed the northern foot of the Tapiehshan range on the Honan-Hupeh border in an attempt to seize Sinyang, on the Peiping-Hankow railway, and thus make a detour to the north of Hankow. The battle for the Wuhan cities began.

The Japanese lunge at Teian, on the northern Kiukiang-Nanchang line, was a costly failure, while on the north side of the Yangtze the invaders also received setbacks in a number of sectors. All in all, as many as 12 Japanese divisions were called in, with repeated regroupings and replenishments. On Oct. 25, 1938, after a campaign lasting four-and-a-half months, the Japanese won control of the Wuhan cities.

Meanwhile, in south China, Canton, seat of Kwangtung province, also fell on Oct. 21 when the Japanese attacked the southern section of the Canton-Hankow line. This marked Japan's seizure of China's last seaport.

With the conclusion of the battle of Wuhan, the Chinese-Japanese War entered a new stage, in which terrain gradually became strategically favourable to China. The Chinese main strength retired to previously-built positions west of the Peiping-Hankow and Canton-Hankow lines. The supreme command moved to Chungking. Further westward penetration by the Japanese was prevented by hazards and dangers in the Yangtze gorges. The fertile plain of Chengtu, provincial seat of Szechwan, afforded a granary in the interior; and the Yunnan-Indo-China railway and the Burma road brought to China, though in dribbles, supplies from other countries, thereby sustaining the Chinese resistance.

Large Chinese forces, however, remained deployed in areas east of the Peiping-Hankow and Canton-Hankow railways, retaining strategic regions. To protect the left and the right flanks of Szechwan, the Chinese also massed considerable strength in the Siang river valley, north of the Yangtze, in Shensi west of the Yellow river (Hwang-Ho) as well as in the basin of Tungting lake (China's "rice bowl") and mountainous western Hunan. In fact, vast territory behind the Japanese lines remained under Chinese control. South of the Yangtze, the Chinese held southern Anhwei, eastern Chekiang and areas in Fukien, Kiangsi and Kwangtung; on the lower reaches of the Yellow river, they retained hilly southern Shantung, most of the Huai river valley and certain areas north of the Yellow river; in north China, they preserved the southern Shantung triangle despite several unsuccessful Japanese penetrations. On top of all this, the Chinese held off the Japanese for six years in the Taihangshan range (eastern Shansi) and more than four years in the Chungtiaoshan range (southwestern Shansi).

All of the guerrilla operations to harass the Japanese rear were initiated by Chinese national troops which operated behind the Japanese lines or in adjacent areas. This Chinese strategy of advance through infiltration into the Japanese rear yielded excellent results. Its execution narrowed the Japanese occupation of any locality down to the extent of a point or line rather than a large piece of territory. Thus, even after the loss of a *hsien* or county, the original magistrate could continue his official duties in the surrounding villages inasmuch as the Japanese occupied only the county seat. Likewise, the governor of a province would still be able to carry on his administration within his province even though his capital had been lost.

In the costly capture of Wuhan, Japan began to realize the difficulties of military subjugation. Therefore, the war cabinet under Prince Fumimaro Konoye changed to the program of a quick peace, a quick end. To that end, every artful strategem was exploited; and, in order to slacken the Chinese army's will to fight, propaganda was dosed out that Japan was willing to cease fighting first. All these overtures of peace were spurned by the Chinese generalissimo.

Realizing that it could no longer hope for a negotiated peace, Japan, in the winter of 1938, entered into liaison with the Chinese arch defeatist, Wang Ching-wei. Wang deserted from Chungking to the Japanese side, and March 1940 saw the inauguration of his puppet regime in Nanking and the conclusion of a Japan-Wang secret treaty. In these events the Japanese designs for establishment of a "New Order in Greater East Asia" were fully exposed.

Japan, on the one hand, tried to work for the disintegration of the central government in Chungking. On the other, beginning in May 1939, the Japanese carried out unremitting and indiscriminate bombing of Chungking and other cities in the interior.

China at this time was under most trying circumstances, both internally and externally. Its official invocation of Articles XVI and XVII of the League covenant in Sept. 1938 had failed to bring any tangible result from the League except denunciation of the Japanese use of poison gas and adoption of a report urging the member states to abstain from any action that would weaken China. The League council meetings the following year, in January, May and September, again failed to achieve the collective application of Article XVI of the covenant, aside from the passing of a resolution requesting the member states to "hold consultations to consider individually measures to aid China." As it was, China's only consolation was the branding of Japan as an aggressor.

What tormented China most at this juncture was the growing paucity of war supplies. Although it was capable of producing acceptable light arms and ammunition, there was an acute shortage of raw materials. Conversely, Japan, through its open sea lanes, shipped in all the U.S. scrap iron and metals and all the U.S. and Netherlands Indies gasoline it could possibly get.

Having attained its objective of blockading the south China coast through the occupation of Canton, Japan plunged headlong into the planned realization of its "Greater East Asia Co-Prosperity Sphere" design. It occupied Hainan Island and the Spratley Islands, respectively, in Feb. and March 1939. Upon the invasion of Hainan Island, Generalissimo Chiang Kai-shek sounded a warning to the world that it was "the 'Mukden Incident' of the Pacific," but it drew no attention from the nations concerned.

6. Situation After Outbreak of European War.—The outbreak of war in Europe in Sept. 1939 removed the big nations still farther from the far eastern arena. They strengthened their so-called appeasement policy and continued to give up pawns to Japan.

China, on the other hand, wavered not a whit in its determination to carry on resistance. In an address of the Chinese generalissimo before the People's Political council on Sept. 10 of the same year, he asserted: ". . . The Sino-Japanese conflict is not merely a world issue but one of the utmost importance. The present turmoil in the world is due mainly to Japan's wanton invasion of Chinese territory and violation of international pacts, thereby jeopardizing world peace. We of China are fighting to perpetuate our national independence and existence, and also to check the rise of international gangsterism, of which Japan is the ringleader, as well as to uphold justice and peace under the sun. In short, the Sino-Japanese war was the starting point of a general conflict, and is the real center of the present world-wide struggle." In that same year, on Oct. 29, the generalissimo declared at a military conference at Hengshan (southwest of Changsha, seat of Hunan province) that "we must fight on till the world war is ended and righteousness and justice fully vindicated, and only then shall we have attained our final victory."

In the continued execution of the appeasement policy of the big powers, Great Britain, on June 19, 1940, signed a Tientsin agreement with Japan and on July 18 declared closure of China's only remaining international outlet, the Burma road, for a period of three months. On the day following the signing of the Anglo-Japanese Tientsin agreement, France, too, concluded a Franco-Japanese agreement, which closed the Yunnan-Indo-China route of transit. On Sept. 22, an agreement was concluded between Japan and Indo-China, permitting Japanese troops to enter Indo-China in three columns and to use the airfields in southern Indo-China as bases for bombing southwest China. On Sept. 29, in full appreciation of nazi Germany's military supremacy, Japan officially signed a Tripartite pact with Germany and Italy.

Following a directive to stop the licensing of aviation gasoline shipments to Japan in August, the United States on Oct. 16, 1940, placed an embargo on the export of scrap iron and steel to the island empire. Two days later, on Oct. 18, the Burma road was reopened, after three months of closure. Not until July 1941, however, did the Netherlands Indies begin to stop shipping oil to Japan.

In this period, Japan was becoming increasingly aware of the futility of its plan for a quick peace, a quick end, and of the tremendous development of a global struggle. With the view, therefore, of conserving its military strength and, simultaneously, of exploiting the material and manpower resources in occupied China through the various puppet regimes, Japan reoriented its China program and decided upon a war-to-sustain-war plan. This new program, as announced, was also one for long-term warfare. long-term reconstruction. In the northeast, fresh impetus was given to the development of the coal and iron industries. In the other occupied areas the Japanese established so-called national policy companies to issue paper currency and readjust taxation in order to absorb resources and materials.

Meanwhile, Japan's military blockade and pressure against Chungking continued. In the month following the outbreak of the European war (Oct. 1939), the Japanese staged a big drive on the Hunan capital, Changsha. But they were thrown back with heavy losses as the result of fierce Chinese resistance and encircling operations at the perimeter of the city. In November, a fresh Japanese push started in south China, resulting in the occupation of Nanning, Kwangsi capital, and other localities in southern Kwangsi. However, in the ensuing encounters at Kunlunkwan, strategic mountain pass (northeast of Nanning), which culminated in the Chinese recapture of the pass and the Japanese retreat to the city of Nanning, the Japanese lost very heavily. (The Chinese regained Nanning in the following October and, three years later, in Oct. 1944, lost it to the Japanese again.) In May 1940, in order to remove the Chinese threat to the Wuhan cities, the Japanese started separate drives in southern Honan and northern Hupeh. Taking advantage of their mountainous positions in Tungpehshan and Tahungshan on the Honan-Hupeh border, the Chinese, in a flanking movement, sent the Japanese back.

But at that time the war situation took a very critical turn. In June China lost Ichang, trading town in western Hupeh and gateway to the Yangtze gorges, thus giving the Japanese a greater threat against Chungking. Thereupon, in August, the Japanese subjected Chungking to successive, terrific air bombardments but again failed to break China as anticipated. Rather, the Chinese went on building industries in the interior in preparation for a protracted struggle.

7. Japan's Pre-Pearl Harbor Offensives.—In 1941, desirous of playing its part in the global theatre, Japan made repeated attempts to crush the Chinese field forces and eliminate the Chinese menace to their rear. In January they staged a fresh drive in southern Honan, throwing in huge forces. Chinese operations taking advantage of the mountainous terrain of Tungpehshan and Tahungshan again compelled the Japanese to retreat from Nanyang to the Sinyang sector on the Peiping-Hankow railway. A violent battle was fought in northern Kiangsi in March when the Japanese attempted to seize Shangkao, southwest of Nanchang (provincial seat), with the aim of clearing up the hilly northwestern part of the province, a mounting threat to the flank of the Japanese in case of a swoop on Changsha. The Japanese not only failed in this attempt but suffered greatly as the result of a Chinese task force attack. In May, the Japanese carried out another operation on the worst appendix behind their lines, the Chungtiaoshan range, against which they had during the preceding 5 years launched more than 15 unsuccessful attacks. This last appendectomy proved a success, but part of the Chinese defensive force broke through and infiltrated into the Japanese rear.

However, the Chinese remained hostilely entrenched in the Taihangshan range, an additional thorn in the flesh of the Japanese. Consequently, in Oct. 1941, when the Japanese in the Yellow river valley crossed over the flooded areas to attack Chengchow, key city in central Honan and rail junction of the Peiping-Hankow and Lunghai lines, they were intercepted and forced to retreat. This was partly because of frontal Chinese resistance and partly because of the harassing of the Chinese in the Taihangshan range, another testimony to the success of the Chinese strategy of advance through infiltration into the Japanese rear.

In the same year, in September, the Japanese made another drive on Changsha but took another defeat at the beginning of October.

On April 13, 1941, Japan and the soviet union signed a neutrality pact. They mutually recognized "Manchoukuo" and Outer Mongolia. Two days later, Pres. Franklin D. Roosevelt declared that the United States had begun listing materials for China under the Lend-Lease act such as had been extended to Great Britain and Greece. He said: "China likewise expresses the magnificent will of millions of people to resist the dismemberment of their nation. China, through Generalissimo Chiang Kai-shek, asks our help. America has said that China shall have our help."

B. After Pearl Harbor

1. One World War.—The bold Japanese attack on Pearl Harbor in Dec. 1941 marked the realization of Generalissimo Chiang Kai-shek's premonition of the Mukden Incident of the Pacific. To other nations, it was a sheer surprise; to China, a logical certainty. For the stupid and arrogant Japanese militarists were seasoned at adventurism and opportunism. Nevertheless, the incident changed not merely the war situation of the world but also, in a much greater degree, the war situation in the far east. It marked the integration of the far eastern front and all other fronts into the global theatre.

In conformity with its consistent stand for international pledges and commitments, China on the day following the sneak Japanese attack declared war against the three major axis nations, Japan, Germany and Italy. Until this date China had not formally declared war on Japan lest the latter's belligerent status permit interception and seizure of China-bound military supplies on the high seas. There was no ground for such apprehensions now. Although the outbreak of war in the Pacific had a most stimulating effect on China, it entertained no overoptimism as to the conduct of the war during the initial stage. Rather, it was anticipating another interval of great tribulation.

Inadequate preparation in the beginning of the Pacific war caused a series of Allied reverses and setbacks—the successive fall of Guam, the Philippines, Hong Kong, Singapore and Rangoon. Not only was the Burma road closed, but the hostilities spread to China's back door, Yunnan province.

Its own difficulties and hazards notwithstanding, China assembled three of its crack armies, the 5th, the 6th and the 66th, which it had reserved for a general counteroffensive, and force-marched them to the Burma border to assist the Allied forces. Repeated negotiations with the Allied authorities gained the Chinese expeditionary force entrance into Burma and had it placed under the U.S. general, Joseph W. Stilwell. By that time the Japanese had already penetrated into Burma from Indo-China and Siam.

The Chinese on March 25, 1942, launched a vigorous offensive against the Japanese converging on Toungoo, important rail city in lower Burma. But because of the lack of time for developing an Allied air force capable of supporting ground troops and the disunity of Allied command coupled with army supply difficulties, the general battle order deteriorated into fighting by isolated units. The disparity between the Allied and the Japanese forces widened even more because of the latter's superior air might and easy sea supply. After a bitter defense of more than ten days the Chinese expeditionary force retreated because of lack of reinforcements.

Undaunted, the Chinese carried on the campaign on the Burma border. In the middle of April, at great risk, they rushed to the rescue of a besieged Allied force at Yenangyaung on the Irrawaddy river. After two days and nights of terrific fighting the Chinese breached Japanese defenses and reached the Allied troops, including several high-ranking commanding officers.

Western Yunnan was invaded when Lashio, Burmese terminal of the Yunnan-Burma highway (April 29), and Wanting, highway town on the Yunnan border, fell to the Japanese. Enormous losses were suffered by the Chinese expeditionary force, including the loss of Divisional Commander Tai An-lai of the 200th division. When the Burmese campaign was pronounced definitely lost, a part of the Chinese troops withdrew to Chinese soil, and another, led by Lieutenant General Stilwell, retreated to Ledo on the eastern Indian border. This latter Chinese force, upon regrouping and training in India, later played a vital role in the Allied counteroffensive in Burma.

Generalissimo Chiang Kai-shek accepted supreme command of the China theatre of war on Jan. 3, 1942, and the Pacific war command was established in Washington, D.C., on March 30. Thenceforth, a more co-ordinated strategy was made possible between China and its allies.

Nevertheless, China's chief problem remained. It was the complete paralysis of its overland communication with the outer world and the inadequacy of its air transport. The most effective aid it received then was from the American Volunteer group (later known as the "Flying Tigers") formed in Kunming (Yunnan capital) by the U.S. Maj. Gen. Claire L. Chennault in Aug. 1941. Scores of air victories were won by these airmen over the Kunming region, thereby reducing Japanese air raids on other interior cities. On July 4, 1942, the duties of the American Volunteer group were taken over by the 23rd fighter squadron of the United States army air force. In March 1943 the 14th air force of the United States army was officially inaugurated, and, by the latter half of that year, China had gradually gained control of its air domain.

2. New Japanese Objectives.—After the Pearl Harbor outrage the Japanese continued and intensified their war to sustain war program on the China front whereby Chinese resources and manpower were exploited to sustain Japanese military operations on other fronts. At this stage the Japanese war blueprint had a threefold objective: (1) to intensify its military blockade and blows against China; (2) to destroy the Chinese air bases in order to curb U.S. air activity in China and (3) to make maximum exertions to put a corridor through the continent in view of the growing shortage of seaworthy vessels and the mounting U.S. air menace. The Chinese formulated a new operational plan aiming at smashing these Japanese objectives and thus achieving their twin objectives of protracted warfare and attrition. In the meantime, they tried to build up their combat strength, paving the way for a coordinated action with the anticipated Allied general counteroffensive.

Toward the close of 1941, Japan, intent upon accomplishing its first military objective as outlined above, pitted a large army against Changsha for a third time. Against this fresh drive the Chinese prepared a much better timetable than on the previous two occasions. The Chinese garrison in the city of Changsha stubbornly resisted the invasion, thus neutralizing large Japanese forces, while its own position remained firm and unshaken. Other Chinese units, deployed on the exterior lines, closed in on the Japanese in a counterencircling movement and gave heavy blows to group after group of Japanese reinforcements. On Jan. 15, 1942, came the wholesale debacle of the invading army after having suffered heavy casualties.

With a view to consolidating their hold on north China, the Japanese launched so-called mopping-up operations against the Chinese-held Taihangshan range in the summer of 1943. This was the third drive the Japanese had made against that region. Outnumbered, and with their supply line severed, the Chinese gave up their mountain base in early August.

Simultaneously in western Hupeh, the Japanese, in heavy strength, lunged forward from the south side of the Yangtze, along the northwestern corner of the province, reducing the important pass of Yuyangkwan (southwest of Ichang). The Japanese push was aimed at a westward thrust against Enshih, war capital of Hupeh, thereby threatening Chungking, and also at a southward thrust against Changteh on the west bank of Tungting lake. The Chinese struck back, taking advantage of their mountainous positions, delivered a serious blow to the invaders and compelled them to retreat on May 31.

On Nov. 2, 1943, the Japanese massed a strength of more than 100,000 men and hurled them against Changteh in a full-scale attempt to seize the rice bowl of Tungting lake and to threaten the left wing of Changsha. Changteh changed hands several times but was finally retaken by the Chinese after five days. The battle ended late in December in favour of the Chinese. Japanese losses were high and, testifying to the severity of the fighting, the Chinese lost three division commanders. Effective Chinese air support was the most important factor for this victory: it was the first time throughout the China war, which had entered its 6th year, that as many as 280 interior-based bombers had been thrown into a single battle.

The Japanese northern Burma and western Yunnan campaigns were also integral parts of their general operations during this period.

In order to attain its second post—Pearl Harbor military objective on the China front, the Japanese carried out wide-spread sorties and sweeps against the Chinese air bases, particularly those built for the U.S. air force. At a time when there was a critical shortage of machinery and instruments in China because of the Japanese blockade, construction of these air bases in many cases involved use of hundreds of thousands of labourers, and oftentimes several months were spent for the completion of a single base.

These bases presented a positive menace to the Japanese, all the more so since the Doolittle raid on Tokyo, Yokahama and Osaka on April 18, 1942. The battle of the Chekiang-Kiangsi border in the summer of 1942, though in itself a mopping-up operation, was primarily designed to neutralize the largest seaboard airfield at Chuhsien in eastern Chekiang. Likewise, the Japanese objective in the drives on Suichuen and Kanchow in southern Kiangsi in Jan. 1944 was the destruction of the airfields in those localities. In addition, they sought to achieve full possession of the Canton-Hankow railway. The 35 days of fighting that ensued took a heavy Japanese toll.

In October of the same year, the Japanese attacked and took the twin Kwangsi cities of Kweilin and Liuchow, also because they were important strongholds of the Chinese and U.S. air forces. In May 1945 the Japanese threw their last stakes into an all-out assault on the Chihkiang airfield in western Hunan but underwent a disastrous defeat at the hands of newly trained Chinese ground forces supported by air operations.

As a necessary move toward the attaining of its third military objective in post-Pearl Harbor China operations, Japan tried to gain full control of first the Peiping-Hankow line and then the Canton-Hankow line, thereby forming

The recapture of Changteh from the Japanese in Dec. 1943 was an important Chinese victory in the Sino-Japanese War. Chinese refugees are shown re-entering the ruined city

a corridor from the south to the north of China to be linked with the main military transportation artery of Indo-China and Burma. This need became all the more pressing to the Japanese in view of the extensive U.S. bombing operations in the Pacific theatre. Thereupon, the Japanese, at the end of April 1944, took Chengchow, Honan, strategic city on the northern section of the Peiping-Hankow railway, and, in May, fought into Loyang with the object of consolidating their defenses west of the railway. By June 17, 1944, they had won complete control of the entire line.

Moving toward its next objective, full possession of the Canton-Hankow railway, Japan brought up ten divisions early in May and threw them into what was its fourth drive on Changsha. The Hunan capital fell on June 19 as the result of a flanking movement by large Japanese forces from the east and west wings. Pushing south along the Canton-Hankow line, the invaders converged on Hengyang, important rail centre in southern Hunan, with good airfields. The Chinese garrison of the city, the 10th army, was ordered to make a determined stand at all costs in order to upset the Japanese military timetable for occupation of the entire length of a transcontinental line of communication. This lone Chinese force checkmated the Japanese advance for 48 days and fought virtually to the last man. The battle for Hengyang, though finally lost on Aug. 8, went down in history as one of the most heroic defense actions in the Chinese-Japanese War.

Though the Japanese succeeded in occupying the whole Canton-Hankow line, the lack of time for repairs prevented through traffic even by the conclusion of the war. The four Changsha battles, the Hengyang defense and several major encounters on the Peiping-Hankow line, therefore were closely related to the global war.

3. Shansi Front.—A summary of the Shansi front is essential before we describe the general war situation in China on the eve of the all-out counteroffensive.

Ever since the Japanese invasion of Shansi and seizure of the Tatung-Puchow railway in 1938, practically the whole of western and northern Shansi, with the exception of a handful of hsien (counties), had been under Japanese control. In reality, the contending forces kept a vigilant watch on each other across the Yellow river.

That the Japanese never pushed across the Yellow river for westward thrusts was the result of two causes. In the first place, such attempts would have made heavy claims on men and caused an overextension of their supply line. The other cause was purely political in character. The Chinese Communist party possessed armed troops, which at the outbreak of war hardly exceeded 10,000 men. When the hostilities began, the Communist party had announced its acceptance of the Three People's principles of Dr. Sun Yat-sen, its support of the national government and its obedience to the command of Generalissimo Chiang Kai-shek in the nation's united resistance to Japanese aggression.

The Chinese Communists participated in the battle of Pinghsingkwan in northeastern Shansi; but, after the Wuhan battle, they went counter to their promises. Instead of obeying the supreme command, they tried to develop their own strength to be used in a future struggle for political power and to carry out their Communist revolution. For that purpose they made frequent attacks on national troops in order to seize weapons from them. Being fully preoccupied with the resistance campaign against a powerful foe, the Chinese government was unable to prevent such attacks. The Communist activities, therefore, sorely grieved the government. It was precisely with the purpose of exploiting and intensifying this internal strife in China that the Japanese had abstained from crossing the Yellow river and attacking Shansi Province.

4. Increased Air Transport.—Beside devising effective measures to thwart the three major Japanese military moves in the post-Pearl Harbor period, China held to the strategy of protracted warfare pending aid from the Allies and, at the same time, reorganized and renovated its army in order to co-ordinate it with the future Allied counteroffensive. But everything hinged upon the reopening of international communication lines and the inflow of Allied arms and war materials.

From July 1942 on, U.S. supplies began trickling by air into Kunming, Chinese terminal of the China-India shuttle, via the Himalayan Hump. Not until the formation of the United States 14th air force in the following year, however, was there air cover or protection and a subsequent increase in air cargo tonnage. Hardships and hazards undergone by these Hump fliers wrote a brilliant record of bravery and self-denial. Most of the cargo flown in was aviation gasoline and equipment, which were sorely needed by the Chinese. There was no way of bringing in heavy arms, and only limited quantities of other arms were flown over the Himalayas. For these reasons, China pooled its resources with its allies to hack out the Stilwell road from Ledo on the eastern frontier of India to Yunnan and laid an oil pipe line through the entire length of the highway. It also fought a bitter battle to reopen the old Burma road and even had to fight for control of certain sections of the Stilwell road.

By then the United States had a fairly large and powerful air fleet based in China, and the huge airfields under construction in various places in Szechwan came into use one after the other. And by 1944 China-based U.S. Superfortresses were shuttling back and forth between China's interior and the Japanese empire on bombing missions. Contributory to the success of these raids was the intimate collaboration between the Sino-American Co-operation organization and the United States navy, which supplied military intelligence and reports on weather conditions along the China coast.

5. Japan's Last Adventure.—The Chinese army that was regrouped and trained by U.S. instructors for the general counteroffensive was composed of two portions. One portion comprised, in addition to the India-based Chinese troops as its nucleus, air-borne men and officers selected for their good qualities from among various units within China. The second portion consisted of a selected number of interior-based units transferred to Kunming and vicinity to be re-equipped and given intensive training by U.S. army personnel. Both were intended for performing China's role in a co-ordinated Allied counteroffensive against Japanese-held Burma.

Just as these picked troops were in training in Yunnan and the Chinese were still nursing their wounds sustained in the battle of Changteh, the Japanese, in the winter of 1944, drove with a powerful force into Kweichow from northwestern Kwangsi, heading toward Tushan, railroad and highway junction. The sudden and swift Japanese advance threatened the rear of Kweiyang (provincial seat of Kweichow) and China's war capital, Chungking. The Chinese fought back, making use of the favourable topography, and, by the beginning of December, forced the Japanese to retreat. Thus, the last Japanese adventurous move in China failed.

At that time Generalissimo Chiang Kai-Shek sent out a

"Join the Army!" call to the students of universities and secondary schools throughout China. It instantaneously brought to the colours nine divisions of students. This marked another forward step which China took to pit its strength against the Japanese in co-ordination with future Allied landings and counteroffensive operations against Japan.

China's six India-based divisions and about 10 Yunnan-based divisions (there were 36 divisions at the time of the Japanese surrender), in co-ordination with Allied forces, opened up well-timed assaults and counteroffensives separately in north Burma and western Yunnan.

On the north Burma front, they captured Maingkwan on March 5, 1944, and Kamaing shortly afterward. On June 26 they took Mogaung, important Japanese base in northern Burma, virtually putting out of existence the Japanese 18th division. Meanwhile, a Chinese task force, in collaboration with U.S. units, made a daring penetration against Myitkyina, important rail town in northern Burma, and in one swoop captured the city's airfield. The city itself fell on Aug. 3, thereby removing for the Allied air transport command the danger of Japanese air interception and the hazards of Hump flying.

On the western Yunnan front, on May 10, 1944, the Chinese effected a forced crossing of the swift Salween river and battled their way, inch by inch, through the most difficult mountainous terrain and under adverse weather conditions. By Sept. 7, Sungshan, Japanese stronghold in western Yunnan, was recaptured, thus re-opening the important Huitung bridge spanning the Salween. On Sept. 14, another Japanese stronghold, Lungling, fell. With these achievements, the Chinese were now able to start the construction of the northern section of the Stilwell road.

In Jan. 1945 Wanting, the last Japanese base on the old Burma road, was recovered. By the end of that month the historic juncture of Chinese forces striking from the north Burma and Salween fronts took place at Maymyo in eastern Burma, which marked another significant Allied success and rendered possible the repairing of the old Burma road. These troops from the two fronts, fighting in well-nigh unnegotiable territory and inclement weather, demonstrated a tenacious combat spirit and achieved an excellent battle tally that formed an important chapter in the war history of the Allies.

Attesting further to the combat strength of these newly trained Chinese troops on their own soil, which had already been well demonstrated in the Salween offensive and the battle for Chihkiang (allied air base in western Hunan), were the Chinese counterattacks against Kweilin and Liuchow (Kwangsi cities) at the end of April 1945. The Chinese advanced in two separate columns. One prong restored Nanning, border town near Indo-China, toward the close of May and by the middle of June was converging on the Liu river. Another prong made for Ishan, rail town northwest of Liuchow on the Kweichow-Kwangsi railway, which changed hands time and again. Well-co-ordinated assaults by both columns caused the Japanese to evacuate Liuchow at the end of June and Kweilin at the end of the following month. By then the weakening of the Japanese fighting strength became even more obvious.

6. Surrender.—Following the capitulation of nazi Germany in May 1945, sea battles moved ever closer to the Japanese homeland while intensified air assaults were made upon important Japanese cities. In China, increasingly high-degree co-ordination of Sino-U.S. combat strength for the continental counteroffensive was being attained. Japan itself realized that it had lost the contest.

China, the United States and Great Britain, on July 26, jointly announced the Potsdam declaration. On Aug. 6 the first atomic bomb was dropped on Hiroshima, and, three days later, the second atomic bomb fell on Nagasaki. On Aug. 9, the soviet government declared war on Japan. On the afternoon of Aug. 10, Japan's surrender offer, accepting the Potsdam terms, was forwarded to the Allies through the governments of Switzerland and Sweden. After four days, the Japanese government officially proclaimed Japan's unconditional surrender on Aug. 14.

On Sept. 2, the representatives of China's supreme command participated in the formal signing of the instrument of Japanese surrender aboard the U.S.S. "Missouri" in Tokyo bay. In Nanking, on Sept. 9, Gen. Yasutsugu Okamura, commander in chief of the Japanese expeditionary army in China, officially signed the surrender instrument for the China theatre in the presence of Gen. Ho Ying-chin, commander in chief of the Chinese army and personal representative of Generalissimo Chiang Kai-shek, supreme commander of the China theatre. Thus, the Chinese-Japanese War of 8 years and 2 months or, rather, the continuous Chinese-Japanese hostilities of 14 years after the Mukden incident, were brought to a victorious conclusion.

The area in which China was to accept the Japanese surrender comprised China and Indo-China north of latitude 16° N., but excluded the Japanese Kwantung army in the northeast, which was to surrender to the soviet union. The surrendering Japanese troops, which represented the entire remaining Japanese strength during the closing stage of the war, totalled about 1,300,000 (including about 30,000 in northern Indo-China but excluding those in the northeast). These were the troops which had been pinned down in China during the final phase of the war and which otherwise could have been used in other war theatres. This was the net result achieved through China's magnetic warfare strategy.

Throughout the war of more than 8 years, 22 large-scale battles, 1,117 major encounters and 38,931 minor engagements took place. China's total casualties amounted to 3,211,419 officers and men, including 1,319,958 killed, 1,761,335 wounded and 130,116 missing. Altogether, 14,-050,521 able-bodied men were conscripted. Civilian casualties were far heavier; they included victims of shellfire, air raids and slaughter; those who were killed while constructing roads and airfields or transporting military and food supplies to the front and war refugees who fell exhausted by the wayside. Losses of public and private property, including that either destroyed or wasted, were incalculable.

Aside from its strategical blunders, Japan's failure may be traced to four fundamental causes: (1) the militarists' excessive underrating of the opponent's strength, and their opportunistic and speculative mentality, led to their reckless moves and ultimate self-ruin; (2) the absence of far-sighted, firm-willed statesmen at the helm of the state and the frequent conflicts inside of the militarist groups which controlled the government, as evidenced by the repeated cabinet changes in wartime Japan; (3) Japan's blind faith in the supremacy and dominance of military force over everything else; (4) a nationalistic education and narrow-gauged patriotism which centred on loyalty to the emperor and developed a feudalistic national character. Added to these was the blending of technological research with the worship of military force, which rendered it difficult for the Japanese to live peacefully with other racial groups in the modern society of nations.

The Japanese claimed that they knew China and were well grounded in China, having an understanding of the individual habits and traits of Chinese political and social figures. As a matter of fact, they saw only the individual trees, not the whole forest. China's military might at that time was far weaker in comparison with Japan's, but Japan did not know: (1) that China's vast territory was a force; (2) that China's teeming population was a force and (3) that China's national characteristic of tenacious resistance against any foreign rule, a legacy of China's long, continuous history and culture, when blended with national consciousness developed by the Three People's principles of Dr. Sun Yat-sen, was also a vital force. That any aggressive act in China would constitute a threat to world peace and therefore a grave world problem baffled Japan's understanding and appreciation even more.

It seemed a miracle to many that China, despite its inferior military might, was able to resist the Japanese aggression for more than eight years. Of course, the final victory was won by China in co-ordination with its allies. Nevertheless, during the first four-and-a-half years of war China fought singlehanded against powerful Japan. Especially during the two years and more following the war in Europe, it struggled with a prospect darkened almost completely with gloom and dismay. But it never weakened or cringed from the Japanese. The integration of the China front with the other sectors of the world after the outbreak of war in the Pacific, the initial reverses of the Allies and the subsequent "Europe first" strategy—these forged China ahead, with greater hope but in more intense tribulation, until the winning of the ultimate triumph.

Machine gun nest operated by U.S. soldiers during the Japanese attack on Oahu, Hawaii, Dec. 7, 1941

It was the firm will of the entire Chinese nation that made this indomitable and bitter resistance possible. In this gigantic struggle China staked what it had and what it was against the aggressors. The whole Chinese people endured stoically all privations and sacrifices because they wished not only to preserve their national sovereignty and existence but also to perpetuate that sense of righteousness which was the blended product of Chinese history and culture. (C. P. Li.)

IV. THE WAR IN THE PACIFIC

A. The Period of Japanese Victories

The Japanese attack in the Pacific was initiated by a dawn surprise raid of two hours' duration against the United States Pacific fleet at anchor in Pearl Harbor, Hawaii, on Dec. 7, 1941. The raid was carried out by 105 planes, launched from 6 carriers which, together with the necessary protecting warships, formed a task force under the command of Vice-Adm. Chuichi Nagumo. This task force was covered by an advance expeditionary force commanded by Vice-Adm. Mitsumi Shimiza, which consisted of 3 light cruisers, 20 submarines and 5 midget submarines.

Present in Pearl Harbor at the time of the attack were 94 ships of the United States Pacific fleet. Eight battleships, three light cruisers, three destroyers and four other vessels were either sunk or damaged. The army and navy also lost 155 planes with 81 additional out of commission after the attack because of extensive damage. Personnel casualties amounted to 2,335 killed, 1,236 wounded and 982 missing.

Coincident with the attack on Pearl Harbor, the Japanese struck at Manila, Hong Kong and Malaya.

1. Hong Kong.—The attack on Hong Kong, which was garrisoned by 12,000 British and Canadian troops, started with a dive-bombing raid that destroyed the air power of the garrison, leaving the city at the mercy of the Japanese bombers. Pushing down Kwangtung peninsula, Japanese ground troops penetrated the Kowloon defense lines and forced the British defending forces to withdraw to the island of Hong Kong. By Dec. 24 the Japanese had established themselves firmly on the island, and by bombing and artillery fire had destroyed water supply facilities. Faced with overwhelming force and a total lack of water, the remnants of the British garrison surrendered on Dec. 25, 1941.

2. Malaya.—On Sept. 22, 1940, the Vichy French government signed an agreement with the Japanese by which the latter were allowed to place a garrison of 60,000 troops in French Indo-China. They soon gained control of the port of Saigon, which they immediately converted into a naval base. A long-standing border dispute between Thailand (Siam) and French Indo-China was seized upon by the Japanese in early 1941 as an opportunity to gain control of the former country. Thus, Japan stood poised to strike at the rich southeast Asia empire (Burma, Malaya and the Netherlands Indies), whose natural resources it had long coveted. On Dec. 8–9, 1941 (Malayan time), Japanese troops landed on the east coast of the long, narrow Malay peninsula, in order to secure the airfields of Kota Bharu, Singora and Patani. They immediately pushed troops across the narrow Kra isthmus, cutting land communications between Burma and Malaya.

During the ensuing six weeks, the Japanese forces in a two-pronged advance down the east and west coasts of

Pearl Harbor naval air station after it had become a target for Japanese high explosive and incendiary bombs on Dec. 7, 1941

the peninsula pushed back the British defenders, whose successive defense lines were made untenable by leapfrog amphibious landings along the coast and swift flanking movements through the Malayan jungles. The Japanese gained an early advantage in the campaign when the two strongest units of the British fleet in the Pacific, the battleship "Prince of Wales" and the battle cruiser "Repulse" were sunk off Kwantung by Japanese torpedo planes, on Dec. 10, 1941. The two ships had been sent north from Singapore to strike the invasion fleet. An inexplicable failure to provide air protection permitted them to fall an easy prey to Japanese air power. The destruction of these two ships assured the safety of the Japanese sea communications with their invading forces.

On Jan. 3, following U.S.-British-Dutch discussions in Washington, D.C., the command structure of Allied forces in southeast Asia was unified, with the title A.B.D.A.C.O.M. (Australian, British, Dutch, American command). Supreme command was entrusted to Gen. Sir Archibald Wavell, British army. Lieut. Gen. George H. Brett, U.S. army, was designated as deputy commander in chief. Air Marshal Sir Richard Pierse, R.A.F., commanded the allied air force, while Adm. Thomas C. Hart, U.S. navy, was in command of the woefully weak combined naval forces. Generalissimo Chiang Kai-shek commanded the ground and air forces located in China.

On Jan. 31, 1942, the hard-pressed British troops in Malaya withdrew to Singapore Island, destroying the causeway connecting with the mainland and leaving the Japanese in complete possession of the Malayan peninsula.

The attackers lost no time in making preparations for the attack on the island stronghold. Under an unceasing aerial siege, ground forces were concentrated for an all-out assault across the Straits of Johore. Protected by an intense artillery bombardment, successful landings on a ten-mile front were made during the night of Feb. 8–9, 1942. The Japanese quickly repaired the causeway and rushed reinforcements, including armour, to their extensive bridgehead. They pushed rapidly south toward the city of Singapore and forced its unconditional surrender on Feb. 15. Japanese military forces employed in the conquest of Malaya totalled approximately 80,000. The British casualties numbered 127,000, of which 64,000 were natives and Indians. Japanese losses totalled 31,200.

3. The Philippines.—On Dec. 8, 1941 (Philippines time), eight hours after the Pearl Harbor attack, Japanese planes struck heavily at the United States airfields in the Philippines, destroying the majority of the bomber and fighter planes. Two days later, the naval base at Cavite was destroyed in another raid. However, the weak United States Asiatic fleet, commanded by Admiral Hart, had evacuated the base, moving southward to cover the convoys bringing British reinforcements to Singapore.

On Dec. 10, Japanese troops landed on the north coast of Luzon, and the next day strong Japanese forces were put ashore at Legaspi, on the island's east coast. However, Gen. Douglas MacArthur, who commanded all forces in the Philippines, correctly interpreted these efforts as diversionary attacks and kept the major portion of his forces concentrated in the central Luzon plain. A minimum of strength was detached to cover the eastern and southeastern approaches to Manila.

The assault on Luzon began in earnest on Dec. 21, 1941, when Japanese troops from 70–80 transports began landing on the eastern shore of Lingayen gulf. Faced by overwhelming superiority of strength, the defending Filipino-U.S. forces fought a delaying action which permitted an orderly regrouping of troops. On Dec. 25, 1941, Manila was declared an open city in a futile attempt to save it from further bombing. Manila was abandoned on Dec. 31, 1941, and a skilful withdrawal was executed into the mountainous Bataan peninsula, which, together with Corregidor, controlled the entrance to Manila bay. Manila was occupied by the Japanese Jan. 2, 1942.

The siege of Bataan, which began on Jan. 1, 1942, and continued until April 9, was characterized by the courageous and skilful defensive action of the defending forces. Lacking ammunition, medicine, food, transport and many other military essentials, they withstood the continuous assaults of the Japanese attackers.

On Feb. 22, 1942, orders were issued from Washington for Gen. MacArthur to proceed to Australia to become supreme allied commander of the newly created Southwest Pacific area. However, it was not until March 11 that MacArthur left Bataan and Gen. Jonathan M. Wainwright assumed command of the hard-pressed garrison as well as the forces still resisting on the other Philippine Islands.

The complete exhaustion of the physical and material resources of the defenders, coupled with an all-out Japanese attack which crushed the entire right flank of the U.S. final defensive position, compelled surrender on April 9, 1942. Approximately 1,367 individuals escaped to Corregidor *(q.v.)* from a total strength on Bataan of 30,853 combat troops and 40,795 ineffectives.

The Japanese immediately brought heavy artillery to bear on the fortified island of Corregidor. On May 5, 1942, after nearly a month of heavy artillery and air bombardment, Japanese landing forces gained a secure foothold on the island. The next day the defenders capitulated, followed on May 10 by the surrender of the Filipino-U.S. forces on the southern islands commanded by Brig. Gen. William F. Sharp.

The defending U.S.-Filipino forces incurred approximately 53,250 military casualties, including killed, wounded, missing and captured, while the attackers lost 31,500 killed and wounded. (W. A. WR.)

4. Burma.—The early phases of the war in Burma were shaped before it began by the brief campaign in Malaya. In those few disastrous weeks Britain had lost command of the Indian ocean. Its hastily gathered land and air forces had also been depleted, either to reinforce Singapore or to hold the chain of airfields which still connected it with Burma and India.

When in Jan. 1942 the Japanese struck from Siam across the jungle ranges toward Rangoon, they were opposed by forces which were little more than a light defensive screen. The outlying airfield garrisons were evacuated barely in time to escape annihilation or capture. The Japanese were close upon Moulmein, at the mouth of the Salween river, before the British could oppose the invasion with more than a single brigade. Though this was reinforced up to the strength of a division, it was forced into retreat almost at once to avoid encirclement. Fighting a desperate rear-guard battle, the 17th Indian division was almost destroyed in February at the Sittang river, the last moat lying between the invaders and Rangoon. The interlude, however, had been sufficient for the deployment of a second weak division which lay farther northward in the Shan states. The reinforcement of an armoured brigade still left the British outnumbered and unable to contain the Japanese drive on Rangoon, the only seaport remaining to the British in southern Burma. Its fall became certain when fresh Japanese forces began to pass across the only two roads which ran north from it toward India.

Rangoon had already been bombed by the superior Japanese air force and was burning. Gen. Sir Harold Alexander (later Field Marshal Viscount Alexander of Tunis), who assumed command of the British troops at this critical moment, ordered its evacuation. He drew back his army upon a line covering both roads. By this decision, he averted a second Singapore trap and permitted a rather disorderly retreat northward. Alexander was thus able: (1) to bar what might otherwise have developed into a Japanese rush upon India; (2) to scorch the oil fields along his line of march and (3) to gain time for Chinese reinforcements to enter Burma at a point farther north, from the neighbouring province of Yunnan. The fall of Rangoon of course deprived his army of all means of communication with India except by land, and beyond Mandalay no roads of any kind led across the Chindwin and over the wild mountains of Manipur into Assam. The problems of retreat were further complicated by the 100,000 Indian, Burmese and British refugees who fled before the Japanese sword and the knives of the Burmese guerrillas whom the invaders had organized. By this time the air forces which supported the British army as it trudged toward the frontier were reduced to a few fighter planes manned by the royal air force and the American Volunteer group, under Col. Claire L. Chennault, which had been in Rangoon en route for China at the time of the invasion and had distinguished itself in the air battles over the city.

By swift outflanking marches and infiltrating tactics, the Japanese had driven the Allies completely out of Burma by the end of May. The British made their way into India along a road hastily constructed by planter labour to meet them. Their rear-guards still fought, but it was the onset of the monsoon which finally halted the Japanese advance. A curtain of rain divided the two armies for the next six months. Most of the Chinese withdrew up the gorges of the Salween river into their own country, though a number marched with their U.S. commander, Gen. Joseph W. Stilwell, over the Naga hills into India. During the lull which followed, both sides built up their strength for the next encounter. This came when Field Marshal Lord Wavell, then commander in chief in India, launched a limited offensive down the Arakan coast, with the object of recapturing the island of Akyab with its port and airfields. Lacking equipment, combined operations on a serious scale were not possible. The land forces made a rapid initial advance but were soon held up by the strong Japanese defenses. Malaria took a still heavier toll among the British and Indian troops. The Japanese vigorously exploited the change of fortune. Driving up the British land flank, they cut their communications and disrupted their rear. The British were compelled to fall back and take up new positions along the Indian frontier to guard against a Japanese advance up the coast to Calcutta.

This second reverse in Burma was barely offset by the success of two other enterprises, one British, the other U.S. The first of these was Brig. Orde Wingate's intruder march deep into the Japanese-held country east of the Chindwin river. Moving in several columns, Wingate's raiding force blew up bridges, railways and dumps behind the Japanese lines for three months. About one-third of his force made its way back to India. The chief value of this daring mission, however, was not the disruption which Wingate caused to the Japanese rear. It was to prove, first, that with effective leadership and training, British and Indian troops could master the Japanese in jungle warfare; second, that it was not necessary to rely upon a supply train moving laboriously (and because of Japanese raids, dangerously) along the floor of the jungle. Once across the Chindwin, Wingate's expedition was supplied entirely by air. Thus the pattern was set for that complete air-army strategy which two years later was to revolutionize the fighting in Burma and the art of war itself.

The U.S. innovation was also in the air. In the last days of the retreat from Burma, a U.S. pilot had flown a military aircraft from Assam across the Himalayas to China. He thus blazed the pioneer trail across the vast mountain barrier known in the armies as "the Hump." During that summer, Dakota aircraft brought more than 13,000 Chinese troops back over the Hump to India. This regular air service was carried on without loss throughout the fierce monsoon storms and with no fighter protection in an area where the Japanese held air mastery. It was the beginning of a two-way traffic that developed into one of the greatest war supply achievements of all time. A fleet of 300 planes plied the sky to China; they took across the 18,000-ft. mountains field guns and every other kind of weapons, ammunitions, motor transports, tank parts, staff officers, expert instructors. An aerial shuttle run was established from Patterson field, O., to Assam, delivering aeroplane parts to the end of the longest supply line in the world within five days. From beyond the Hump, on the return passage, came thousands of Chinese soldiers to be trained in India under General Stilwell. Another U.S. project, though one which was not to bear decisively on the campaign for many months, was the building of the Ledo road. This magnificent military highway started in Assam and was designed to climb the mountain wall of Burma, descend into the northern valleys and link with the old Burma road. (F. O.)

5. Netherlands Indies.—The Japanese strategy for the conquest of the Netherlands Indies consisted of an encirclement, coupled with a thrust through the centre. Their initial move was a landing, on Dec. 22, on the northwestern coast of Borneo in British Sarawak. This landing, preceded by a heavy bombing, followed by two days the Japanese capture of Davao, on Philippine Mindanao, where they immediately organized a strong air and sea base. From this base they began heavy bombing raids on Jan. 10, 1942, striking at Dutch Borneo and the Celebes in order to gain control of the Macassar strait passage to the Java sea. From their base at Truk in the Caroline Islands, Japanese amphibious forces landed at Rabaul, New Britain and Kavieng, New Ireland, on Jan. 23, 1942, and on Bougainville in the Solomons on Jan. 29, 1942. These latter operations made the sea lanes from Australia to the Indies most hazardous.

In the Java sea, the Allied navy, consisting of what U.S., British, Dutch and Australian ships could be scraped together, attempted to stop the Japanese advance. In the battle of Macassar strait on Jan. 23–25, Allied sea forces struck, under cover of darkness, at a Japanese invasion fleet lying off Balikpapan, Borneo, inflicting severe damage and forcing the Japanese to withdraw northward. However, this attack was too late to prevent the Japanese capture of Balikpapan on Jan. 22 by troops which had been landed before the sea battle. (For more extended discussions of the battle of the Java sea and other naval engagements mentioned in this section, *see* under section V, "The War at Sea," p. 751 *fol.*)

Aboina and Ceram Islands in the Banda sea were occupied by the Japanese on Feb. 1, 1942.

On Feb. 4, a Dutch-U.S. fleet, consisting of four cruisers and seven destroyers, commanded by Rear Adm. Carel W. F. M. Doorman of the royal Netherlands navy, attempted an attack on another invasion fleet which air reconnaissance had discovered at Balikpapan. The Allied fleet was intercepted by Japanese bombers and forced to turn back. The U.S. cruiser "Houston" and the U.S. light cruiser "Marblehead" were damaged.

Previous agreements had provided that, when the focal point of Japanese attack became the Netherlands Indies, the Allied defensive forces would be commanded by Dutch officers. On Feb. 11, 1942, in compliance with this agreement, Admiral Hart turned over operational command of Allied naval forces to Vice-Adm. C. E. I. Helfrich, royal Netherlands navy. A few days later, General Wavell turned over his command to Lieut. Gen. Hein ter Poorten, royal Netherlands army, and departed for India.

Japanese paratroopers were dropped on southern Sumatra on Feb. 14, one day before Singapore surrendered, and were quickly followed by sea-borne troops. They rapidly overran the Palambang oil fields and forced the Dutch defenders to withdraw to Java.

On Feb. 18, the Japanese seized a Dutch airfield on the island of Bali and on the 20th landed on Timor. Occupation of this latter island completed the southern encirclement of Java, cutting its communications with Australia. Also, the seizure of these two islands gave the Japanese air power a base within easy striking distance of Java. Thereafter, the bombing of key points on that island was intensified.

Admiral Doorman led his composite naval force in an attack on a Japanese convoy, bringing reinforcements to Bali, striking the Japanese in Bandung straits on the night of Feb. 19–20. This attack inflicted extensive damage on the Japanese, but the Allied fleet suffered the loss of one Netherlands destroyer, the "Pict Hein," and damage to two Netherlands cruisers, the "Java" and "Tromp" and the U.S. destroyer "Stewart." The U.S. seaplane tender "Langley" was sunk on Feb. 26 while attempting to reach Java with reinforcements of fighter planes.

Admiral Doorman's Allied fleet, now consisting of two heavy cruisers, three light cruisers and nine destroyers, sortied against a superior Japanese force lying off Surabaya on Feb. 27, in an attempt to intercept Japanese convoys closing in on Java. This engagement resulted disastrously for the Allies and marked the end of organized naval resistance in the Netherlands Indies. Two cruisers and two destroyers were sunk and one cruiser damaged. While the Japanese covering fleet suffered some damage, its invasion convoys were untouched.

On Feb. 28 one Allied cruiser and two destroyers were sunk in Sunda straits while attempting to flee the Java sea. Again, on March 1, two cruisers and one destroyer were lost in the same locality. Of the entire Allied fleet, only four U.S. destroyers managed to make their way to Australia by way of Bali strait.

Japanese invasion forces landed at three points on the north Java coast on Feb. 28 and quickly made their way across the island. Reinforcements were landed rapidly until the Japanese strength exceeded 100,000 troops. The defensive efforts of the Allied forces, isolated by the rapid thrusts of the invaders, were quickly dealt with, and on March 9, 1942, Java surrendered. Allied military casualties approximated 18,000 killed, wounded and captured: Dutch 11,300; British 5,600; Australian 300; U.S. 800. No Japanese casualty figures became available.

6. The Tokyo Raid.—On April 18, 1942, the Japanese home islands were raided by 16 U.S. B-25 medium bombers. These planes were transported to within 850 mi. of the Japanese shore on the United States carrier "Hornet," with planes from the carrier "Enterprise" furnishing scouting and fighter cover. Under command of Col. James H. Doolittle, the planes completely surprised the Japanese and dropped their bombs on Tokyo and other industrial cities with little effective opposition. After the raid the planes flew to China, except one which landed in Russian territory, where it crash landed as its gasoline supply was exhausted. Of the 80 crew members, 64 returned to United States control, being aided by friendly Chinese. While the raid had little strategic value, its morale effect in the dark days of 1942 was inestimable. (*See* Tokyo.)

Meanwhile, Gen. MacArthur had reached Australia March 17, 1942, to find that that continent was being systematically isolated by the Japanese sweep through the Southwest Pacific islands. The Australian port of Darwin on the north coast was heavily raided by Japanese planes on Feb. 19, 1942, and was virtually neutralized. The airport, warehouses, docks and practically every ship in the harbour was destroyed. Advancing from their New Britain and New Ireland bases, the Japanese struck at the northern New Guinea coast, landing at Lae and Salamaua on

Survivors of the battle of Midway paying their last respects to those who were killed in the action of June 1942

March 8, 1942, and pushing the Australian defenders inland on the road to Port Moresby.

B. Allies on the Offensive-Defensive

On May 3, 1942, the Japanese began to occupy Florida Island in the southern Solomon Islands. This advance constituted a threat to the bases which had been established by the United States in the New Hebrides and Fiji Islands as well as New Caledonia, to protect the shipping lanes connecting the United States with Australia. Further, Japanese appearance in the southern Solomons area constituted a direct threat to the northeast coast of Australia, with a probable initial thrust to eliminate Port Moresby, the Allied base on the southeast coast of New Guinea. A United States naval force under Rear Adm. Frank J. Fletcher, consisting of 1 carrier, 3 cruisers and 6 destroyers, initiated on May 4 a plane attack which sank or damaged 12 of the 15 Japanese ships in Tulagi harbour, with a loss of 3 aircraft. On May 5, Admiral Fletcher's fleet joined with a task force commanded by Rear Adm. Thomas C. Kinkaid and an additional naval group under the command of Rear Adm. J. G. Grace. The combined fleet of 2 carriers, 11 cruisers (including 2 Australian cruisers) and 15 destroyers struck a Japanese force of 1 carrier, 3 cruisers and 6 destroyers, sinking the carrier and 1 cruiser on May 7. The next day the Allied fleet struck another Japanese force consisting of two carriers, four cruisers and several destroyers, damaging one carrier. The Japanese carrier plane attack on the Allied fleet resulted in the sinking of the United States carrier "Lexington," the U.S. destroyer "Sims" and one other vessel. The United States carrier "Yorktown" was damaged. The Japanese forces withdrew to the north after suffering extensive losses. The battle of the Coral sea, which definitely stopped the Japanese advance, was, in the words of Adm. Ernest J. King, commander in chief, United States fleet, "the first major engagement in naval history in which surface ships did not exchange a single shot."

The battle of the Coral sea marked the beginning of the end of the period of Japanese victories. The setback they suffered there delayed further aggressive action and allowed the Allies to mass strength and assume the offensive.

1. Midway.—Following the battle of the Coral sea, the Japanese decided on an offensive attempt in the central Pacific. However, the United States Pacific command had foreseen the possibility of such a Japanese attempt and had recalled the carriers with their supporting vessels from the South Pacific. The total United States force consisted of 3 carriers, 1 heavy cruiser, 7 light cruisers, 14 destroyers and 20 submarines. The Japanese forces were picked up several hundred miles southwest of Midway Island (*q.v.*) on the morning of June 3. The next day another attacking force was developed northwest of that island. On June 5–6, United States land-based and carrier planes hammered the Japanese vessels until they withdrew to the westward in thick weather. The battle of Midway, like that of the Coral sea, was entirely fought by aircraft. Surface vessels did not exchange a shot. It also marked the first decisive defeat of the imperial Japanese navy in 350 years.

2. Guadalcanal.—In July 1942, the Japanese moved a force consisting of troops and labourers to Guadalcanal Island in the Solomon Islands (*q.v.*) and commenced the construction of an airfield. The Allies immediately recognized that land-based aeroplanes operating from this field would seriously menace the bases in the New Hebrides and New Caledonia as well as Port Moresby in New Guinea.

Immediate steps were taken to eject the Japanese, utilizing forces available in the South Pacific area. On Aug. 7, 1942, the U.S. 1st marine division reinforced, commanded by Maj. Gen. A. A. Vandergrift, made surprise landings on Guadalcanal and Florida Islands. The landings were made with strong naval and air support and met little initial opposition. The airfield on Guadalcanal and Tulagi harbour at Florida Island were seized in the first 36 hours.

The Japanese reacted quickly and on the night of Aug. 9 struck hard at the Allied naval force supporting the operation. A Japanese force of cruisers and destroyers engaged the Allied fleet and, in 30 minutes of intensive activity (battle of Savo sea), sank one Australian and three U.S. cruisers.

The concentration of Japanese forces in the Rabaul area to the north foreshadowed further attempts to force the Allies to relinquish the seized islands. On Aug. 24, Allied carrier-based aircraft intercepted a transport convoy about 250 mi. north of Guadalcanal. An intensive bombing attack, in which land-based army and marine planes also participated, inflicted extensive damage, and forced the convoy to turn back to Rabaul. This engagement was named the battle of the eastern Solomons. The Japanese, however, continued to reinforce their Guadalcanal forces, transporting troops in by night from the near-by islands with light surface craft, and by the end of September had succeeded in moving what amounted to a complete new division into the area. They also continued their attempts to provide naval support to their ground forces, which led to a series of engagements with the Allied naval forces engaged in the same mission. In the battles of Cape Esperance on Oct. 11–12; Santa Cruz Island, Oct. 26; Guadalcanal, Nov. 13–14–15, and Tassafaronga on Nov. 30, the Allied sea forces established undisputed naval superiority in the southern Solomons area. Japanese losses were 46 ships of all types sunk or damaged, while Allied losses totalled 1 battleship damaged, 1 carrier sunk and 1 damaged, 3 cruisers sunk and 4 damaged, 11 destroyers sunk and 3 damaged—a total of 24 vessels.

Meanwhile, the land action on Guadalcanal had steadily increased in intensity as the United States marine forces stubbornly resisted the increasing pressure of the numerically superior Japanese. The defense was aided by improved air support and by United States army reinforcements (Americal division) which began arriving Oct. 13. Japanese effort to eliminate the U.S. foothold reached its peak on Oct. 26, when an all-out attack pierced the Allied defense lines and the possession of Henderson field hung in the balance. Allied counterattacks, however, restored the position and defeated the last serious ground offensive effort on the part of the Japanese. During the remainder of 1942, the Japanese forces were steadily pushed back toward the northwestern part of the island. During the period Dec. 18, 1942–Jan. 4, 1943, the U.S. 25th infantry division moved to Guadalcanal. These reinforcements increased the Allied combat strength to two army divisions and one U.S. marine regiment, the 1st marine division being withdrawn in December after more than four successive months of intensive combat. Offensive operations continued through Jan. 1943, narrowing and compressing the Japanese defensive positions. During the first week of February, Japanese light surface craft began evacuating the small forces remaining, and on Feb. 8, 1943, the last Japanese pocket of resistance was eliminated and Guadalcanal was firmly in Allied hands.

3. Papua.—Even though the Japanese were heavily engaged in their attempt to hold Guadalcanal, they were determined to continue the push toward Australia. The battle of the Coral sea had frustrated the initial Japanese attempt at a sea-borne invasion of the southern coast of New Guinea. Their next effort was an overland advance from New Guinea's northeast coast across the Owen Stanley mountains. Port Moresby, with its excellent harbour on the south coast, was the immediate Japanese objective. Its possession would provide the Japanese with a potential invasion base within 350 mi. of the Cape York peninsula in Australia.

On July 21–22, 1942, Japanese invasion forces, with a strength of 4,400, landed at Buna, Gona and Sanananda on the northeast coast. Additional troops poured in until by Aug. 13 the Japanese strength totalled more than 11,000, and the drive toward Port Moresby began. Australian soldiers in greatly inferior numbers put up a desperate resistance but were slowly pushed back across the summit of the precipitous Owen Stanley range and down the southern slope to within 30 mi. of Port Moresby by Sept. 14. At this point, logistical difficulties coupled with stiffened resistance by the Australians, who had received timely reinforcements, halted the Japanese advance.

Additional Japanese forces were landed at Milne bay

Supplies pouring onto the beachhead at Guadalcanal after advance landings by U.S. marines in 1942. The army and marine corps were preparing for joint action in wiping out remaining Japanese resistance on the island

on the eastern tip of New Guinea, on Aug. 25, with the intention of enveloping Port Moresby from that direction. The landing forces suffered heavy losses from strafing by Allied planes and after three days of stiff fighting were forced to re-embark. This was the first time that a Japanese force, which failed to accomplish its mission, had ever been evacuated.

During the two weeks' stalemate, Sept. 14–28, while the Australians held the main Japanese forces east of Port Moresby, the Allied air forces had continuously attacked the tortuous Japanese supply line stretching over the mountains to Buna and Gona. Under this heavy pounding, the Japanese supply system had broken down completely. The half-starved Japanese were in no condition to resist the Australian attack, which started on Sept. 28, and they began a hasty withdrawal, closely pursued by the Allies.

Reinforcements of U.S. troops (elements of the U.S. 32nd infantry division) reached Port Moresby on Sept. 28, and plans were made for an offensive designed to eliminate the Japanese in the Papuan peninsula. While the Australians drove them back along the mountain trail, U.S. troops undertook a wide envelopment on the east flank, attacking in the vicinity of Buna.

The Australian 7th division, reinforced, steadily followed up the retreating Japanese, who made only a brief stand in front of Kokoda, which was captured on Nov. 3, and then retreated to the coast without offering battle. By Nov. 18, the Japanese had been penned up in isolated pockets at Gona, Sanananda and Buna. Because of Japanese preoccupation with the struggle on Guadalcanal, no reinforcements were reaching their forces in Papua. However, the perimeter defenses of Japanese pockets along the coast were skilfully adapted to the jungle terrain and were garrisoned by determined troops who would fight to the death before surrender. The U.S. attack to reduce the Buna beachhead began Nov. 19. It required 45 days of constant, determined attack by 9,000 U.S. soldiers before the Buna pocket with its defending garrison of 2,200 Japanese was finally eliminated on Jan. 2, 1943.

Meanwhile, the Australians had pushed on toward the much more weakly held Gona pocket (estimated garrison was 650 Japanese). A co-ordinated attack launched on Nov. 28 smashed the Gona defenses and eliminated the pocket by Dec. 3, 1942.

The two forces (Australian 7th division and elements of the U.S. 32nd and 41st infantry divisions) then joined up to wipe out the Sanananda perimeter, the strongest of the three being garrisoned by an estimated 5,000 Japanese. The attack, which commenced Jan. 4, 1943, was resolutely pushed by the Allied forces; and all resistance was overcome on Jan. 23.

The Papua campaign cleared the coast of New Guinea of Japanese as far north as Gona and, together with the capture of Guadalcanal, removed the threat of a Japanese invasion of Australia. The Allied air force, though limited in strength, had been skilfully employed to assist the campaign. The destructive raids on Japanese lines of communication had forced the Japanese to resort to submarines and air-drops to supply the fanatical defenders of their isolated beachhead pockets. In addition, the air transport, supply and evacuation of Allied troops had added materially to the handicaps imposed by limited communication facilities in the undeveloped jungles of New Guinea.

4. **Aleutians.**—Simultaneously with their thrust across the mid-Pacific which culminated in the battle of Midway, the Japanese also threatened the Aleutians. Their immediate objective appeared to be Dutch Harbor, which was attacked by bombers June 3, 1942. Repeated attacks by U.S. aircraft commencing June 4, 1942, despite most unfavourable weather conditions, inflicted heavy losses and forced the withdrawal of this force. Subsequent to this attack, it was discovered that Japanese forces had occupied the Aleutian Islands of Kiska, Attu and Agattu. The occupation of these barren islands was of little strategical importance, provided defensive measures were taken to prevent a build-up in the Japanese strength which would permit further infiltration along the island chain. Therefore, immediate provision was made to bring the Japanese-held islands within effective range of combat aircraft. U.S. troops were landed on Adak Island on Aug. 30, 1942, and immediately commenced the development of advanced airfields, from which the first mass air raid against Kiska was launched on Sept. 14, 1942.

U.S. forces establishing their beachhead on Attu Island in the Aleutians May 11, 1943

In order to facilitate the air attacks further, a U.S. task force occupied Amchitka Island, 70 mi. west of Kiska, on Jan. 11, 1943. This action effectively cut the Japanese supply lines and ensured that there could be no further development of Japanese strength in that area. The air blockade proved so effective that the Japanese ceased all attempts to supply their garrisons by surface ships, in March 1943.

The extreme shortage of ships, aeroplanes and trained troops, coupled with the more pressing requirements needed to maintain the Allied position in other areas, precluded any attempt to recapture the occupied islands at this time. After the successful completion of the operations on Guadalcanal and in Papua, a limited amount of personnel, matériel and shipping were made available to contest the Japanese occupation of the Aleutians. The main Japanese garrisons were located on Kiska, with an estimated strength of 7,800, and Attu, occupied by 2,200. Military operations on either island presented tremendous problems because of climate, distance from suitable staging facilities and extremely rough and difficult terrain. The decision was to bypass Kiska, where intelligence reports indicated the Japanese expected an attack, and assault Attu. On May 11, the U.S. 7th infantry division, with strong naval and air support, landed on Attu and fought its way across the island, in three weeks of desperate fighting, to encircle the Japanese at Chichagof harbour. On May 31, 1943, the campaign ended with the annihilation of 2,350 Japanese defenders. U.S. casualties totalled 2,900, including 513 dead. Nonbattle casualties accounted for 40% of the above total.

The capture of Attu sealed off Kiska and rendered the Japanese position on the latter untenable. When a U.S. task force made a combat landing on the west coast of Kiska on Aug. 15, it discovered that the Japanese had evacuated by submarine under the protection of bad weather and fog. The threat to Alaska and the Pacific northwest coast had been first checked and then eliminated.

These new bases in the western Aleutians placed the Japanese northern Kuriles within effective range of heavy bombers. Throughout the remainder of the war, air attacks were made on these islands, especially on the main base at Paramushiro, whenever weather conditions permitted. The attacks possessed a high degree of deceptive value and contributed to the general attrition of Japanese military strength.

C. Road Back to Tokyo

The successful termination of the fight for Guadalcanal, coupled with Allied success in the naval battles of the South Pacific and Midway, marked the first step on the long road back to Tokyo. In itself, the battle of Guadalcanal was strategically defensive in character, being fought to protect the United States-Australia lines of communication. The same was true of the Papua campaign. Success in these struggles had gained for the Allies footholds from which to launch their next attack on the Japanese defense perimeter in the Pacific.

From Dec. 7, 1941, until early 1943 the Japanese had held the initiative. The Allies had little opportunity to plan operations, being forced to use their limited means wherever and whenever Japanese activities dictated.

At the Casablanca conference in Jan. 1943, the United States and British chiefs agreed that there must be increased supplies for China. Strategic plans for operations in the South and Southwest Pacific were also drawn up. Even though preoccupied with the task of eliminating Germany from the war, the needs of the Pacific as to troops, matériel, ship tonnage, naval dispositions, etc., were given consideration.

In March 1943, commanders and staff officers of the Central, South and Southwest Pacific areas were called to Washington, D.C., to co-ordinate their theatre plans with the over-all strategical plan which guided the Allied prosecution of the war.[1] This conference resulted in developing a plan which included allotment of available resources, definition of command structures and a statement of operational objectives. It was subsequently approved by the joint chiefs of staff and furnished guidance to the field forces for the immediate future.

In April 1943, Gen. Joseph Stilwell and Gen. Claire L. Chennault were called to Washington to give first-hand information regarding conditions in China to a conference of United States and Great Britain heads of state and the combined chiefs of staff. Field Marshal Sir Archibald Wavell presented the situation in India and Burma while Dr. T. V. Soong pleaded for more aid to China. At this conference, an integrated plan for logistical support and military operations was evolved to guide future Asiatic activities.

At the Trident conference in Washington, May 12–25, 1943, there was further development of the logistic and operational plans designed to aid China.

The Quadrant conference at Quebec, Aug. 1943, resulted in the formation of the southeast Asia command under Adm. Louis Mountbatten, with General Stilwell as deputy commander. The latter retained command of the United States-China-Burma-India theatre as well as his position as deputy to Generalissimo Chiang Kai-shek, who continued in command of operations in China. The royal air force and United States army air force combat units operating against Japanese-held Burma from bases in India were combined into the eastern air command under Maj. Gen. George E. Stratemeyer, U.S. army.

Also at the Quadrant conference, the strategic plans for the Pacific offensive against the Japanese were developed. General MacArthur's operations along the north New Guinea coast were to continue on a schedule which contemplated that he would reach the Philippines by the late fall of 1944.

The South Pacific forces, both army and navy, were commanded by Adm. William F. Halsey, United States navy. While retaining operational autonomy, these forces were under the strategical control of General MacArthur. Their axis of advance through the Solomons would protect the eastern flank of the New Guinea forces and aid in the ultimate isolation of the Japanese stronghold in the Rabaul-Kavieng area.

Adm. Chester W. Nimitz, United States navy, commanding Pacific ocean area, was to strike across the central Pacific through the Gilbert, Marshall and Marianas Islands with the objective of securing a foothold in the Ryukyus in the spring of 1945. Adm. Ernest R. King, chief of naval operations, United States navy, accurately forecast at that time that a major collision with the Japanese navy, resulting in a decisive defeat for the latter, would occur during either the Marianas or Philippine phase of this advance.

Another major development of the Quadrant conference was the proposed air plan of Gen. H. H. Arnold, chief of the United States army air forces, to soften Japan by extensive B-29 Superfortress bombing raids from bases in China and the Marianas. This proposal was later approved and led to the formation of the 20th air force, which operated as a strategic air force under the direction of the U.S. joint chiefs of staff.[2]

---

[1] Gen. Douglas MacArthur did not attend, being represented by a senior staff officer.

[2] While the combined U.S.-British chiefs of staff controlled the broad strategic distribution of resources to the various theatres, the U.S. joint chiefs of staff directed actual operations in the Pacific.

1. After Guadalcanal.—Subsequent to the elimination of the Japanese at Guadalcanal and Buna, there ensued a lull in sea and ground activities, while supplies, ships and troops were being augmented and regrouped for future operation. However, large-scale and effective operations were carried on by the Allied air forces, which stifled Japanese attempts to reinforce and supply their garrisons in the outer ring of their Pacific defenses.

By July 1, 1943, the Allied forces in the Southwest Pacific consisted of four U.S. and six Australian divisions under General MacArthur's control. In the central Pacific, Admiral Nimitz had nine U.S. army and marine divisions, the U.S. 7th air force and the U.S. Pacific fleet. With this force, the Allies advanced to the threshold of the Philippines within a year.

On June 22–23, 1943, a U.S. amphibious thrust from the newly won New Guinea base easily secured the small Kiriwina and Woodlark Islands to the east of New Guinea. Airfields were quickly constructed, which permitted the rapid interchange of fighter aircraft between the Solomons and New Guinea, as the situation demanded.

The South Pacific forces, operating from Guadalcanal, initiated operations to secure New Georgia Island on June 30, 1943, by landing on near-by Rendova Island to secure artillery positions which would support the main attack. The initial landings on New Georgia by the elements of two U.S. divisions (37th and 43rd) met slight resistance. However, opposition stiffened and it was only after the attacking forces had been reinforced by the U.S. 25th division that the main objective, Munda airfield, was captured on Aug. 5, 1943. This series of operations in the Solomons was concluded when the U.S. 14th corps, commanded by Maj. Gen. Oscar W. Griswald, captured Vella Lavella Island on Oct. 9, after bypassing Kolombangara Island, which was strongly garrisoned by the Japanese. The capture of Vella Lavella forced the Japanese to evacuate Kolombangara, which was occupied without resistance.

Allied forces in New Guinea had not been idle. Supported by a U.S. regimental combat team, Australian troops advancing overland had captured Salamaua on Sept. 11, 1943. While the Japanese garrison at Salamaua still offered strong resistance, additional Australian troops made an amphibious landing just east of Lae, 30 mi. north of Salamaua, on Sept. 4. This landing was followed by the drop of a U.S. parachute regiment, the next day, to seize the Nadzab airport, about 20 mi. northwest of Lae. An Australian division was immediately moved by air to Nadzab and after some arduous and difficult combat occupied Lae on Sept. 16.

Without pausing to reorganize, MacArthur quickly moved his hard-fighting Australians on Finschhafen. Landing near the town on Sept. 22, the Australians secured it on Oct. 2. The remarkable achievements of the limited Allied air force in neutralizing Japanese supply lines and airfields, as well as transporting and supplying the Allied ground troops, had contributed materially to the success of the campaign. The considerable Japanese forces which had fled inland to escape the Allied attacks along the coast continued to offer strong resistance until Feb. 1944.

Keeping step with General MacArthur's advance, the Allied troops in the Solomons pushed forward. New Zealand forces seized two islands in the Treasury group, northwest of Vella Lavella, on Oct. 23, 1943. After successful diversionary landings on Choiseul Island, the United States 3rd marine division struck the western coast of Bougainville Island at Empress Augusta bay on Nov. 1, 1943. No attempt was made to occupy the entire island. The planned objective was to secure a lodgment of sufficient size to permit the building of airfields which were within fighter range of Japanese concentrations in the Rabaul-Kavieng area. Two United States army divisions, the 37th and the Americal, reinforced the initial landing force during the ensuing six weeks. Supported by a naval task force under Admiral Halsey, which completely blanketed the Japanese sea and air strength at Rabaul, the beachhead was successfully defended against a series of desperate Japanese counterattacks. These attacks culminated in an all-out assault on the Allied defense lines in March 1944 which was beaten back with heavy and irreplaceable losses to the Japanese.

2. Central Pacific.—In the fall of 1943, the United States sea and land forces under Admiral Nimitz, commander in chief, Pacific ocean area, initiated operations designed to

U.S. marines on Tarawa preparing to attack Japanese positions from their bitterly-won beachhead. The 76-hour battle for this coral atoll in the Gilberts in Nov. 1943, was one of the bloodiest in the history of the marine corps to that date

carry out the directive which had been evolved in the Quadrant conference at Quebec the preceding August.

The first objective was to gain control of the Gilbert Islands (*q.v.*) group. The strategic directive originally issued by the joint chiefs of staff called for simultaneous assaults on Tarawa and Nauru Islands. Upon representations by Admiral Nimitz that the distance between the two islands was so great that the covering naval forces would be exposed to the danger of defeat in detail by Japanese forces based in the Marshall Islands, Makin Island was substituted for Nauru. On Nov. 21, 1943, U.S. forces made simultaneous landings on the two islands. Elements of the 27th division landing on Makin Island met stubborn but ineffective opposition from the relatively weak Japanese garrison. The U.S. 2nd marine division landed on Tarawa Island, where the much stronger garrison fought with grim determination. The defense was aided by the restricted area of the island which precluded the employment of large numbers of attacking troops. Skilfully constructed defensive works protected by mines and underwater obstacles commanded the practicable landing areas. From these defensive positions an intense cross fire of automatic weapons could be brought to bear on the landing forces. The positions were taken by direct infantry assault under the cover of a shattering air and naval bombardment. The losses of the attacking forces were so heavy that Tarawa may be considered one of the bloodiest battles in U.S. history. Its successful outcome constituted a memorial to the unflinching courage of the U.S. fighting man. When the island was finally secured on Nov. 24, the casualties of the United States 2nd marine division totalled 913 killed and missing and 2,037 wounded.

The next blow in this central Pacific advance fell on Kwajalein atoll in the Marshall Islands (*q.v.*). Preceded by an intensive two-day air and naval bombardment which threw 14,500 tons of high explosives, a composite U.S. army and marine landing force struck the islands on Jan. 31, 1944. The U.S. 7th infantry division landed on Kwajalein Island in the southern part of the atoll while the U.S. 4th marine division attacked the islands of Namur and Roi at the northern tip. By Feb. 9, all resistance had been overcome. Operations to secure the Marshall Islands were completed on Feb. 22, when Eniwetok atoll was secured by amphibious U.S. marine and army forces, dispatched from Kwajalein, which had landed on Feb. 19, 1944. U.S. casualties in these operations totalled 2,016 killed, wounded and missing. Estimated Japanese casualties were approximately 9,000.

Control of the Marshall Islands brought the great Japanese naval and air base at Truk within effective bombing range. It was thus effectively neutralized until further U.S. advances into the Caroline Islands could definitely isolate it and render it totally useless.

3. Southwest Pacific.—After the capture of Finschafen, further advance westward along the New Guinea coast could not be attempted until control of the Vitiaz and Dampier straits, separating New Britain from New Guinea, had been obtained. This necessitated mounting operations to secure the western end of New Britain Island, including the extensive air base at Cape Gloucester. A reinforced cavalry regiment was landed on the southern shore of New Britain, near Arawe village, on Dec. 15, 1943, followed 11 days later by the landing of the U.S. 1st marine division in the Cape Gloucester area. This force occupied the aerodrome on Dec. 30 and immediately struck south to link up with the Arawe force. Mainly because of terrain difficulties rather than Japanese resistance, it was not until mid-March that these joint operations secured western New Britain and made the straits safe for the passage of Allied vessels.

Prior to the completion of the western New Britain operations, an amphibious expedition, consisting of a regimental combat team from the U.S. 32nd division, pushed westward 100 mi. from Finschafen to land near Saidor on the north New Guinea coast on Jan. 2, 1944. By Jan. 7, an air strip was in operation, and Allied air power intensified its interdiction of the Japanese supply lines to the remaining New Guinea garrisons.

Allied possession of the Saidor-Cape Gloucester area isolated the Japanese-Kavieng-Rabaul concentrations from the west. The airfields captured or constructed permitted the basing of Allied planes within 300 mi. of Rabaul. Meanwhile, the Allied South Pacific forces under Admiral Halsey had arrived within 125 mi. of Rabaul to the eastward when on Feb. 15, 1944, a U.S. force landed in the Green Islands, meeting only minor opposition. This operation, coupled with the activities of U.S. naval forces in the central Pacific, made any Japanese attempts to supply their beleaguered forces from the east or northeast extremely hazardous.

On Feb. 29, 1944, elements of the U.S. 1st cavalry division landed on Los Negros in the Admiralty Islands to conduct a reconnaissance in force. The initial success of this landing was followed up by the commitment of the remainder of the division. The major Japanese aerodrome was secured and held against fanatical counterattacks. By April 17, 1944, organized Japanese resistance on the main island of Manus had ceased. U.S. casualties were 321 killed, 1,189 wounded and 4 missing. The Japanese lost 3,280 killed and 75 captured.

The capture of the Admiralties, an operation which General MacArthur referred to as "putting the cork in the bottle," placed Allied forces squarely across Japanese supply lines to the Bismarcks from the north and northwest, leaving 100,000 of their seasoned troops in isolated impotence. As an offensive base for Allied sea and naval power, the islands controlled the Bismarck sea and protected Allied advances toward the Philippines. Manus Island, with its protected Seeadler harbour anchorage, became the major Allied naval supply base in the Southwest Pacific.

The next move westward along the New Guinea coast involved a leapfrog advance of more than 400 mi. On April 22, 1944, U.S. forces (24th, 32nd and 41st divisions), landing on a front of 175 mi., secured beachheads at Aitape, Hollandia and Tanahmera bay. The operation came as a complete surprise to the Japanese, and the landings were practically unopposed. These landings were beyond the effective range of army fighters. Therefore, their air support was provided from naval carriers, many of which had been borrowed from Admiral Nimitz' Pacific fleet and attached to Adm. Thomas C. Kinkaid's Southwest Pacific forces. By April 30, Allied forces had captured the three excellent airfields which were put into immediate use as Allied air bases. Simultaneously, an Australian division was landed near Madang and advanced overland toward Wewak and Aitape. This force reached Hansa bay on June 15, 1944.

The advance westward continued without pause with the landing on May 17, 1944, of elements of the U.S. 41st division at Arara, 125 mi. west of Hollandia. A few days later, on May 21, a regiment of this same division landed on Wakde Island, just off shore from Arara, and captured its airstrip. Meanwhile, the force left on the main island of New Guinea pushed the perimeter of the initial Arara beachhead westward to include Maffin bay.

Without delaying to regroup, Allied forces (U.S. 41st division) pushed on westward 200 mi. under naval and air cover to land on Biak Island, which controlled the entrance to Geelvink bay, on May 27, 1944. The island was taken, despite the fierce resistance of the garrison of 8,000 Japanese, on June 20. The three airstrips captured in this operation were quickly placed in operational condition, furnishing Allied bases for air strikes against Japanese concentrations in the Moluccas and Celebes. After Allied air power had hammered for three weeks at Noemfoor Island, a U.S. combat team supported by paratroops landed on July 2 and seized an airstrip in three hours, completing the capture of the island three days later. Possession of that island, 100 mi. west of Biak, gave necessary depth to Allied air deployment in the area and provided advanced bases which permitted deeper penetration of the Japanese-held Pacific island empire.

On July 30, 1944, elements of the U.S. 6th division effected another surprise landing at Sansapor, on Vogelkop peninsula, at the extreme western end of New Guinea. Resistance was slight, despite the presence of 18,000 Japanese troops in the area. This operation marked the strategic end of the New Guinea campaign which had brought the Allied forces 1,200 mi. closer to the ultimate objective, Tokyo. The technique employed resulted in the isolation of more than 60,000 Japanese along the north New Guinea coast. This force was so disorganized and separated by the successive leapfrog landings at key points that it was incapable of offering any co-ordinated and unified resistance. Allied air and sea power completely controlled the Japanese supply lines to these bypassed units, leaving them to starve and die in the jungles.

A prime factor in the Allied successes in the Southwest Pacific was the brilliant and efficient employment of the limited Allied naval and air resources allocated to the area. The co-ordinated teamwork of the land, sea and air power available did much to overcome the matériel and personnel shortages, as also did the practice of combining naval and air resources of the various Pacific areas for certain operations. Each operation attempted was preceded by air attacks. Initially, the U.S. 5th air force under Lieut. Gen. George C. Kenney in the Southwest Pacific and the U.S. 13th air force, commanded by Brig. Gen. Nathan F. Twining in the South Pacific, operating in close unity with their respective Australian and New Zealand air forces, functioned as separate but co-operative commands. On June 25, 1944, these two air forces, while maintaining their separate identities, were merged together with the royal Australian air force and royal New Zealand air force into the Far East air forces, commanded by General Kenney. Maj. Gen. Ennis C. Whitehead succeeded to the command of the U.S. 5th air force, while the U.S. 13th air force was commanded by Maj. Gen. St. Claire Streett, who had succeeded General Twining. The combined air forces swept the Japanese from the skies and struck far to the westward against Japanese supply bases and airfields in the Celebes, Timor, Java, Sumatra and Borneo. By these attacks, the Japanese were seriously hampered in their attempts to supply and control their widely separated island garrisons and were prevented from concentrating their forces to meet the Allied thrusts.

4. The Marianas.—The lull in ground operations in the central Pacific area, which followed the capture of the Marshall Islands, was broken on June 15, 1944, when an amphibious force which consisted of the United States 2nd and 4th marine divisions and the U.S. 27th infantry division landed on Saipan Island in the Marianas Islands (*q.v.*). The attacking forces forged ahead despite stubborn opposition from the garrison consisting of two Japanese divisions. The island was secured on July 9, after 25 days of extremely difficult combat. The prize of this operation was possession of the well-developed Aslito airstrip in the southern portion of the island.

The Japanese fully recognized the significance of this thrust into the western Pacific and took immediate steps to counter it. On June 19 their carrier planes hit the United States naval forces supporting the landing operations and, in the terrific aerial battle which ensued, lost 402 aircraft as against 27 planes lost by the U.S. forces. In addition, one United States battleship and two carriers suffered slight damage. The Japanese fleet fled toward the Philippines, pursued by the United States carrier fleet commanded by Vice-Adm. Marc A. Mitscher. On June 20, United States planes located the fleeing Japanese vessels and sank one carrier and two tankers. In addition, three Jap carriers, one battleship, three cruisers, three destroyers and a tanker suffered damage. This was the third decisive naval victory for the Allied sea power that was fought entirely by carrier planes. Like the battles of Coral sea and Midway, the surface vessels involved did not exchange a shot. The U.S. armada, assured of complete control of the Marianas waters, returned to support the attack of the land forces.

On July 24, 1944, the U.S. 2nd and 4th marine divisions landed on the small island of Tinian, lying approximately three miles south of Saipan. The landing was supported by heavy artillery fire from Saipan and met little initial resistance. The island was captured after 9 days of fighting in which U.S. casualties were relatively light—195 killed, 1,526 wounded and 24 missing—as compared with 5,745 counted Japanese dead.

On June 21, 1944, a landing force, which consisted of the United States 2nd marine division reinforced the U.S. 77th infantry division, landed on Guam (*q.v.*), to reconquer that former United States possession which had been in Japanese hands since Dec. 11, 1941. Because of the intensive 17-day air and sea bombardment which preceded the landing, there was little initial resistance. However, when the landing forces had advanced beyond effective range of the naval support, the Japanese resisted stubbornly. The island was fully secured on Aug. 10, after 20 days of combat during which Japanese casualties were 10,693 killed and 98 captured. United States forces lost: 1,288 killed, 5,648 wounded and 145 missing.

Before these operations to capture the Marianas were complete, United States forces had begun the construction of heavy duty airfields, which would be bases for the strategic bombing of the Japanese home islands by the newly developed Superfortresses. In the meantime, the U.S. 7th air force, under Maj. Gen. Robert W. Douglass, was already conducting bombing operations against the Japanese outposts of Iwo Jima and Chichi Jima in the Bonin Islands.

Changed conditions which resulted from the Allied successes in the Pacific made it necessary at this time to change the command set-up in the area. On Aug. 1, 1944, the army forces in the Pacific and South Pacific areas were consolidated into one command as the United States army forces, Pacific ocean area, under Lieut. Gen. Robert C. Richardson. The over-all command remained under Admiral Nimitz as commander in chief, Pacific ocean area. At the same time, all United States army air forces in

The Pacific theatre of operations, 1941–45

the area, except the strategic U.S. 20th air force, were combined to form the United States army air forces, Pacific ocean area, under the command of Lieut. Gen. Millard F. Harmon.

The U.S. 20th air force remained under the direct command of General Arnold, commanding general, United States army air forces, with General Harmon as deputy commander to supervise field operations.

The next step westward in the central Pacific area was aimed directly at the Philippines. On Sept. 15, 1944, a joint landing force struck the western Carolines with the United States 1st marine division landing on Peleliu Island, while the 81st infantry division went ashore on near-by Angaur Island two days later. The operation was supported by the greatest naval armada ever assembled in United States history to that date; more than 800 vessels were actively engaged in direct support, neutralizing far-flung Japanese bases which might contribute to the defense.

Angaur Island was rapidly overrun, being practically secured by Sept. 20. Initial progress on Peleliu Island was satisfactory also but slowed down when the attacking forces reached the main defensive positions near the centre of the island.

This was largely because of the Japanese reinforcements transported in barges from the heavily garrisoned island of Babelthuap to the north. The island was fully secured by Sept. 30, 1944, in spite of the difficulties of heavy resistance and rough terrain.

5. Morotai.—Simultaneously with the operations in the western Carolines, MacArthur's Southwest Pacific forces made their next jump. On Sept. 15, 1944, the United States 31st infantry division landed on Morotai Island in the Moluccas.

The island was seized against only slight ground opposition while the far eastern air force effectively neutralized the main Japanese airfield on Halmaheira Island to the south. Morotai, located 350 mi. south of the Philippine island of Mindanao, was a logical steppingstone on the move northward. Also, as an air base it protected MacArthur's western flank from attacks by Japanese concentrations in the Celebes and Netherlands Indies.

6. Return to the Philippines.—On Sept. 12, 1944, planes from Admiral Halsey's 3rd fleet struck heavy blows in the central Philippines. This operation, which was carried out to cover the Allied landings in the western Carolines and on Morotai, developed weaknesses in the Japanese dispositions. Admiral Halsey immediately recommended the cancellation of projected attacks against Yap, Mindanao and other islands to the south in favour of an early attack against Leyte Island in the central Philippines. Admiral Nimitz approved the recommendation and offered General MacArthur the forces which were at the time loading in Hawaii to strike Yap. In two days, General MacArthur revamped his plans and notified the joint chiefs of staff that he was ready to strike Leyte on Oct. 20 instead of Dec. 20 as originally planned. The message from General MacArthur reached the joint chiefs of staff at Quebec, Canada, where they were assembled for the Octagon conference with the British. In 90 min. the change in schedule was approved.

(*a*) *Leyte.*—On Oct. 20 as scheduled, the United States 10th and 24th corps of the 6th army (Gen. Walter Krueger commanding) landed on the east coast of Leyte, following a heavy drumfire, naval bombardment that battered down Japanese resistance. The naval armada which transported the landing forces consisted of more than 800 vessels, including 6 battleships and 18 escort carriers. In addition, the United States 3rd fleet was ready to counter any attempt by Japanese naval forces to oppose the landings.

The ground troops pushed rapidly inland and met little opposition from the Japanese defending forces, who were demoralized by the preparatory air and sea bombardment. After three days' advance, General MacArthur directed the forces ashore to hold their ground until the outcome of the impending naval battle was determined.

The Japanese committed the major portion of their naval force in an effort to drive U.S. troops out of the Philippines. The Japanese Singapore fleet, under Adm. Kurita, struck eastward in two forces, one south of Leyte through Surigao strait, the other to the north through San Bernardino strait, against the 7th fleet. At the same time, a third Japanese fleet sailed south from the Japanese main islands to engage the 3rd fleet. On Oct. 24–26, in three almost simultaneous engagements (grouped as the battle for Leyte gulf), the Japanese navy suffered another decisive defeat. The safety of the land forces on Leyte was assured.

The forces on Leyte resumed their advance along two main axes. While the 24th corps under Maj. Gen. J. R. Hodge struck straight westward and drove the defending forces into the mountains, the 10th corps, commanded by Maj. Gen. F. C. Sibert, pushed on Limon on the north coast, aided by short amphibious operations. Seven U.S. divisions (7th, 24th, 32nd, 77th and 46th infantry, 1st cavalry and 11th air-borne divisions) were assembled on Leyte by Dec. 1, 1944. Five airfields were in operation and everything was set for the final push on Ormoc, the Japanese stronghold and supply base on the west coast. Meanwhile, the determined efforts of the Japanese to reinforce their Leyte garrison with troops from other Philippine islands had resulted in a substantial increase in effective strength. This was accomplished in the face of staggering losses in shipping, personnel and supplies, inflicted by Allied land and carrier planes. The Japanese fiercely resisted the advance down the Ormoc valley from the north. On Dec. 7, the United States 77th infantry division, which was transported by water from Tarragona on the east coast of Leyte to the west side of the island, landed south of Ormoc and in four days captured the town and large quantities of supplies. Although the capture of Ormoc sealed the fate of the Japanese defenders, they continued to resist until the end of December.

(*b*) *Luzon.*—On Jan. 9, 1945, the United States 6th army assaulted Luzon, landing at the head of Lingayen gulf. On the first day, 68,000 troops had landed and gained possession of a beachhead 15 mi. long and 1½ mi. deep. The amphibious assault forces had assembled off the east coast of Leyte and sailed westward through the Surigao strait, which separated the islands of Leyte and Mindanao. Throughout their movement northward, traversing the Mindanao, Sulu and North China seas, all precautions possible to deceive the Japanese as to disposition and ultimate destination were undertaken. Land-based and carrier-based aircraft blanketed the skies over Luzon to prevent any Japanese attempts at air reconnaissance. All activities, air, naval and guerrilla, were directed toward creating the impression that the impending operations were directed at southern Luzon.

Little opposition to the landing was met, because of the inability of the Japanese to concentrate their forces with sufficient rapidity. While the assault forces were en route, U.S. air attacks had been directed against Japanese lines of communications. Coupled with these air attacks were the increased guerrilla sabotage operations against railroads, bridges and tunnels. These activities aided materially in immobilizing the dispersed and misplaced Japanese troops.

During the three weeks following the landing, U.S. forces pushed steadily southward across the central plain of Luzon. Strong forces were deployed to contain the large Japanese troop concentrations in the mountainous terrain to the east and north of the zone of advance. The only serious Japanese resistance was encountered on the front of these forces and in the vicinity of Clark field and Fort Stotsenburg, where broken terrain favoured the defenders. On the main front, Japanese troops were committed to action piecemeal as they arrived from the south and were defeated in detail.

On Jan. 29, 1945, elements of two United States infantry divisions (the 38th and 24th) landed on the west coast of Luzon, near Subic bay, and drove eastward against light opposition to cut off Bataan peninsula and thus prevent the Japanese from making the same use of it as General MacArthur had three years previously. This advance pushed through the mountains of western Luzon with unprecedented speed and by Feb. 2 had linked up with elements of the 6th army on the north shore of Manila bay.

On Jan. 31–Feb. 3, U.S. forces (elements of the U.S. 11th air-borne division) made a combined amphibious-air-borne landing in Batangas, south of Manila, and immediately pushed on Cavite. On the latter date, advanced elements of the 6th army reached the northern outskirts of Manila. On Feb. 6, the U.S. forces from Batangas had reached Nichols field in the southern part of the city. Although attacked from all landward sides of the city, the Japanese garrison fought bitterly in a house-to-house defense, until their final elimination on Feb. 23.

The campaign in the Philippines, 1944-45 →

0 50 100 200
MILES
N
LUZON
Aparri
10 DEC 1941
GUERRILLAS
26 JUNE 1945
22 DEC 1941
9 JAN 1945
Baguio
Lingayen Gulf
Belete Pass
Clark Field
Ft. Stotsenburg
29 JAN 1945
Bataan
Nichols Field
Manila
(23 FEB 1945)
SUBIC BAY
Corregidor
Cavite
15 FEB 1945
31 JAN 1945
Batangas
SOUTH
CHINA
SEA
MINDORO
11 DEC 1941
Legaspi
San Bernardino Straits
SAMAR
PANAY
Limon
Ormoc
Tarragona
LEYTE
20 OCT 1944
CEBU
MARCH 1945
NEGROS
Surigao Straits
PALAWAN
28 FEB 1945
Puerto Princesa
MINDANAO SEA
Cagayan
SULU SEA
MINDANAO
Cotabato
Zamboanga
BORNEO
Macassar Straits
CELEBES SEA

Fording a tank trap laid for U.S. forces by the Japanese 14th army in its retreat across Leyte. Invasion of the island in Oct. 1944 constituted a critical threat to Japanese supply lines and dogged resistance was offered in its defense

Meanwhile, operations designed to open Manila bay were initiated when a landing force, consisting of troops of the U.S. 38th division, seized the tip of Bataan peninsula on Feb. 15. On the following day, a parachute regiment dropped on Corregidor and at the same time an amphibious force assaulted the shore. After two weeks of vicious fighting the island was secured, and Manila bay was opened.

An important minor operation was the seizure in late February of Puerto Princesa peninsula on Palawan Island, with its two airfields. Aeroplanes based on these fields were able to control a major portion of the South China sea, disrupting Japanese communications with Malaysia and Burma.

During March 1945, landings were made on other major islands in the Philippines, including Mindanao, Panay, Cebu and Negros. Meanwhile, on Luzon, the 6th army drove north and east from the central Luzon plain against the mountain strongholds of the one remaining Japanese force of consequence in the vicinity of Baguio and Balete pass. At the same time, other troops cleared the area southeast of Manila, reaching the eastern shore of Luzon on May 13, 1945. These operations split the Japanese forces and rendered them incapable of cohesive action.

The Japanese forces isolated in the mountains of northern Luzon still controlled the Cagayan valley, and operations were continued to eliminate them. United States infantry and Philippine guerrillas engaged in fierce fighting to force the southern entrances to the valley while other guerrilla forces reconquered northwest Luzon. These latter, with the assistance of rangers from the United States 6th army, captured the port of Aparri on June 21, 1945. Two days later, elements of the United States 11th airborne division dropped just south of Aparri and in the ensuing 3 days pushed 25 mi. up the valley to link up with the forces which had forced their way northward through the mountain passes. The juncture of these two forces completed the conquest of the Cagayan valley and to all intents terminated the Luzon campaign, although many large pockets of Japanese remained to be mopped up.

The reconquest of the Philippines was accomplished in eight months of bitter fighting. In that time, 317,000 Japanese had been killed and 7,200 captured. United States casualties totalled 60,600 killed, wounded and missing.

7. Iwo Jima.—While the occupation of Saipan, Tinian and Guam in Aug. 1944 had provided bases from which long-range bombers could operate against the home islands of Japan, it was recognized that bombing sorties could operate with greater effectiveness and minimum losses if they were provided with fighter support. On Feb. 19, 1945, the United States 5th marine corps (3rd, 4th and 5th marine divisions) landed on the east coast of Iwo Jima (*q.v.*), one of the Volcano Islands, 750 mi. south of Tokyo. Japanese resistance on this small island, only 2 mi. wide by 5 mi. long, was exceptionally severe. The advantages of superior forces could not be exploited with so little room to manoeuvre. The landings were preceded by heavy air and sea bombardments, which battered down the initial resistance, but once the marines were ashore the Japanese counterattacks were made with unprecedented ferocity, and the sanguinary campaign lasted until mid-March before organized resistance was overcome. On April 7, 1945, the B-29 raids on Tokyo were being covered by fighter planes based on Iwo Jima. In addition, many battle-damaged B-29s were saved by being able to land on Iwo Jima airfields when they were incapable of flying back to their home bases in the Marianas about 800 mi. farther south.

8. The Ryukyus.—All planning for an assault on the home islands of Japan had developed the necessity for a base from which land-based aeroplanes could provide continuous support for the assaulting troops. The island of Okinawa (*q.v.*) in the Ryukyu group was ideally situated for this purpose. On March 26, 1945, the attack to secure the Ryukyus was launched by the United States 10th army (3rd marine corps, consisting of the 1st and 3rd marine division; 24th corps, consisting of the 7th, 27th, 77th and 96th infantry divisions), commanded by Lieut. Gen. Simon B. Buckner, when infantry elements landed on the small islands of Kerama Retto, off the west coast of Okinawa. Possession of these small islands provided positions from which land artillery could support the landings on the key island of Okinawa. Under cover of an intense land and naval bombardment, the United States 3rd marine corps and 24th army corps went ashore on Okinawa on April 1, 1945. After pushing across the island, the marine corps moved rapidly northward, quickly overrunning that portion of the island. The army corps which was directed to the south was held up by the main Japanese position. Progress against the elaborate defensive positions was slow, and it took until mid-June to break through the successive Japanese defensive lines. On June 18, General Buckner was killed by Japanese shellfire while he was in a forward observation post. Three days later, organized resistance on Okinawa ceased. U.S. casualties totalled 10,585 killed, 36,715 wounded and 1,302 missing, as compared to 109,600 Japanese killed and 7,870 taken prisoner.

The intense ground fighting on Okinawa was paralleled by the heavy and frequent Japanese air attacks on the Allied shipping supporting the assault. The Japanese operated from the relatively close bases on Kyushu and employed large numbers of suicide or Kamikaze planes. These planes carried only enough gasoline for a one-way trip to the attack area and were loaded to their remaining carrying capacity with explosives. The sole object of the pilot was to dive his plane into an Allied ship. In addition, the Japanese employed a small short-ranged aircraft called the "Baka," which was hung under a medium bomber until within range of its target and then guided into a rocket-assisted diving attack by its suicide pilot. It carried more than a ton of explosives in its nose. In 2 months of intensive air warfare, the Japanese lost 20% of their combat aircraft strength. More than 3,400 Japanese planes were shot down over Kyushu and the Ryukyus, and 800 others were destroyed on the ground. Allied losses totalled more than 1,000 planes. More than 250 Allied vessels had suffered damage from Japanese air attacks, including 34 destroyers and smaller craft which were sunk.

9. Borneo.—Preliminary operations for the recapture of Borneo began on May 1, 1945, when elements of the Australian 9th division landed on the island of Tarakan to establish a fleet and air base to support future operations. The operation was strongly supported by Australian and U.S. fleet units and met only slight opposition.

On June 10, preceded by a heavy naval bombardment, the 9th Australian division, reinforced, made an unopposed landing at Brunei bay on the northwest Borneo coast on June 10, 1945. They immediately secured the naval anchorage and airfields against slight resistance and drove toward Seri and Miri, where important oil fields were located. On July 1, additional Australian forces attacked Balikpapan in southeastern Borneo. By mid-July, Allied forces were in complete control of Balikpapan harbour. From their new Borneo bases, Allied air and naval forces were able to interdict the main Japanese land and sea routes of communication to Indo-China and Malaya. No attempt was made to mop up the remnants of the Japanese forces, which had fled to the interior of the island. Isolated from their supplies and without chance of reinforcement, they were no threat to the Allied beachhead. As in Bougainville, New Guinea and New Britain, they were left to "rot on the vine."

10. Reconquest of Burma.—The Japanese conquest of Burma in 1942 had isolated China except for the 500 mi. of hazardous air route over the towering Himalayas. This made it impossible to supply the critical heavy equipment that China desperately needed. While the Allied strategy makers realized that first priority should be given to the defeat of Germany, they also recognized that it was highly important that material assistance be given China in order to keep it in the war. At the Casablanca conference in Jan. 1943, the Washington Trident conference in May 1943 and the Quadrant conference of Aug. 1943, held in Quebec,

First aid station on Iwo Jima, Feb. 1945

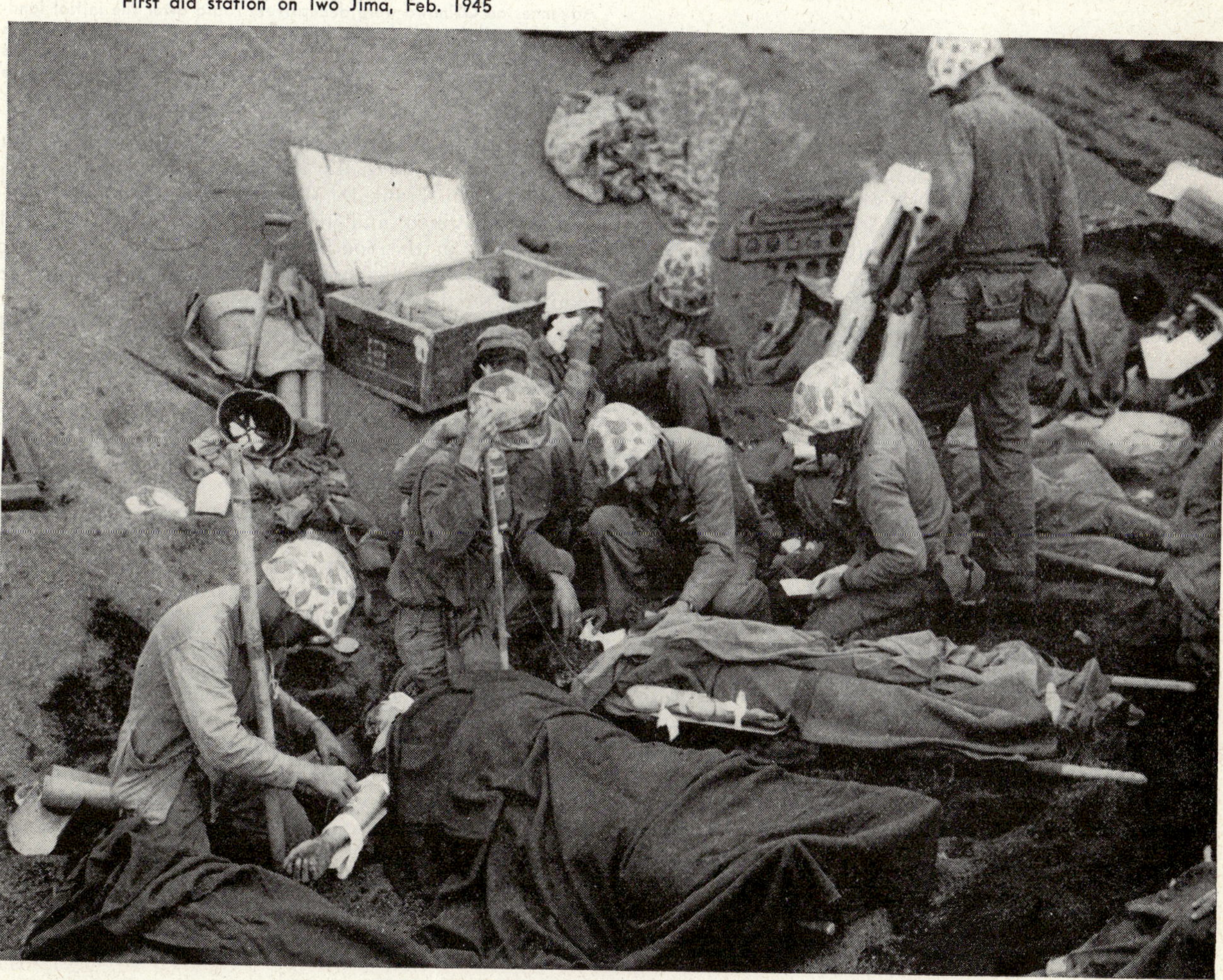

Advances on Okinawa were deceptively rapid after the initial landings of April 1, 1945, as is shown in this picture of U.S. marines covering rough terrain almost on the double. Fierce resistance was not encountered until Naha and Shuri were reached in the drive southward

plans were initiated and developed not only to reinforce the air transport route to China but also to open the land route.

At the Quadrant conference, the command set-up to accomplish the herculean tasks which confronted the Allies in Burma was created. Admiral Mountbatten was named commander of the newly organized Southeast Asia command (S.E.A.C.), and General Stilwell was made deputy commander, while still retaining his position as chief of staff to Generalissimo Chiang Kai-shek, who retained command of operations in the China theatre. All British and U.S. combat air elements in India were combined into the eastern air command, with Maj. Gen. George E. Stratmeyer as commander.

The initial Allied ground operations against the Japanese in Burma were a series of long-range raids against the Japanese supply lines feeding their forces in northern Burma. A specially trained force, known as the "Chindits," consisting of Gurkhas, Burmese and an English regiment and commanded by Brigadier Orde C. Wingate, secretly penetrated the Japanese lines and invaded Burma in March 1943. Supplied entirely by air, this force played havoc with Japanese communications and operated for several weeks without being caught by the Japanese in force. This original raiding expedition penetrated to within 120 mi. of the Burma road before being ordered to return (*see* above, p. 728).

The success of General Wingate's air-supported operations inspired the formation in Aug. 1943 of the first air commando force of the U.S. Army air forces, commanded by Col. Philip G. Cochran. This force of transport, glider, fighter, medium bomber and liaison aircraft was especially designed to support operations such as General Wingate's. Also, in Aug. 1943, the decision was made to form a U.S. long-range penetration unit similar to Wingate's 77th Indian infantry brigade. This unit, officially entitled the 5307th composite unit (provisional) but popularly called "Merrill's Marauders," after its commander, Brig. Gen. Frank D. Merrill, was formed by recruiting jungle-trained and tested volunteers from United States forces in the Southwest Pacific, the South Pacific and the Caribbean defense command. By Feb. 1, 1944, five months after the initial decision to organize this force, it had been formed, transported to India, trained and turned over to General Stilwell to assist the advance of his Chinese divisions already pushing down the Hukawng valley.

General Stilwell's plans for the 1944 campaign were keyed entirely to the construction of the "Ledo Road." This effort to construct a new land route to China by connecting Ledo in the upper Brahmaputra valley of India with the old Burma road near Bhamo, in northern Burma, involved the building of nearly 300 mi. of heavy duty highway through virgin jungle and precipitous mountains. The route selected crossed the Patkai Mountains, forming the boundary between India and Burma, through Pangsan pass, then south and east through the Hukawng and Mogaung valleys to Myitkyina in the upper Irrawaddy valley and continuing south to Bhamo, then southeast to the junction with the old Burma road.

Operations begain in Oct. 1943, when two U.S.-trained Chinese divisions moved into the Hukawng valley. By Feb. 1, 1944, these troops had advanced 60 mi. against increasing opposition from approximately 7,000 Japanese troops concentrated in the area. Aided by the wide flanking and deep enveloping movements of the "Marauders," the advance continued at the rate of about one mile per day until Myitkyina was reached on May 19, 1944. Both Myitkyina and Mogaung fell to Allied forces in July 1944, after a two-months siege, and the besieging forces immediately moved on Bhamo, farther south. Meanwhile, troops along the Burma-Chinese border initiated an offensive in May 1944 and drove westward astride the old Burma road.[3] The link-up of these forces on Jan. 27, 1945, assured the success of the Ledo road venture.

General Stilwell's position in the command set-up in the China-Burma-India area placed him squarely in the middle of the political crosscurrents of two great governments, neither of which was his own. His inescapable involvement in complex political and military problems which he was in no position to solve or control inevitably led to conflicts of personalities that rendered a change advisable. On Oct. 28, 1944, General Stilwell was recalled to Washington. At the same time, the U.S. Asiatic administrative area was divided into two theatres, the India-Burma, commanded by Lieut. Gen. Daniel I. Sultan, and the China theatre. The latter was commanded by Maj. Gen. Albert C. Wedemeyer, who succeeded General Stilwell as chief of staff to the generalissimo. (W. A. Wr.)

(a) *Arakan*.—The most important field command, that of the 14th army, was assigned to Lt. Gen. (later Gen. Sir) William Slim.

In Jan. 1944, aggressive British operations opened with the lifting of the monsoon clouds when the British forces began to press down the Arakan coast. They ran headlong into a Japanese advance intended to seize southern Bengal. Two British divisions were encircled. This time, however, they did not yield their ground. They stood fast as ordered, and were supplied entirely by air throughout a three-week siege. At the end of this time the Japanese themselves were trapped. Fresh British troops, descending from the north, pressed them against the anvil of the still intact British positions and hammered them to pieces. Thus ended, disastrously, the first Japanese "March on Delhi."

(b) *Imphal to Rangoon*.—The second march was not long in coming; indeed, it hinged upon the first. A further purpose of the Japanese in invading south Bengal had been to draw off the British reserves while they delivered their main blow against the central front. This was based upon the Plain of Imphal, a plateau in the Manipur mountains.

In mid-March 1944 the Japanese crossed the Chindwin at several points with 100,000 troops and converged upon Imphal. They also struck farther north at Kohima, a hill station on the mountain road from Assam to Imphal. Within a few days the Japanese had isolated the British army corps centred around Imphal plain; from Kohima they threatened to descend into the Brahmaputra valley and cut off the U.S.-Chinese force which had begun its march over the mountains into the northern valleys, building the Ledo road as it went. The Japanese invasion would also have overrun the chain of airfields in Assam which were the Indian terminal of the Hump air-route. Thus all communication with China would have been severed at a blow, and the republic possibly forced out of the war.

General Slim had anticipated the Japanese plan and had ordered his outlying divisions to withdraw into the plain, which he had prepared as a jungle Stalingrad. He had not foreseen the speed or strength of the Japanese drive upon Kohima, where a garrison of 3,000 assorted troops, many of them already wounded, received the impact of a crack Japanese division of 18,000. The little garrison at Kohima held the gate to India for three weeks, when they were relieved by the advance of Lt. Gen. Sir Montagu Stopford's 33rd Indian corps. Storming the Kohima heights by frontal assault, Stopford passed on to break the siege of Imphal after three months of the fiercest fighting seen upon the Burma battlefields.

The severe struggle upon Imphal plain smashed the spine of the Japanese army in Burma. The victorious British, Indian and African regiments of the 4th Indian corps (Lt. Gen. Sir Geoffrey Scoones's command) pressed hard in pursuit of the beaten Japanese, and by the end of August the last organized units had been expelled from India. While this long slogging battle was raging, an airborne invasion of 10,000 men under Wingate had landed in the rear of the Japanese army and caused continuous havoc there. Wingate himself was killed in a flying accident, but his Chindits remained beyond the Chindwin for four months.

The condition of the Japanese was now everywhere desperate. The 14th army had broken their front and the integrated British-U.S. air force had disrupted their rear. As the Chinese-U.S. forces under Stilwell forced their way into Myitkyina, the last remaining Japanese stronghold on the upper Irrawaddy and the key to the Burma road, the 14th army fought its way down to the Chindwin river.

By the beginning of 1945 the 14th army was deployed in strength in the plains north of Mandalay and had forced a bridgehead across the Irrawaddy 40 mi. above the city. Farther northward, Stilwell's U.S.-Chinese forces had cut their way through to the Burma road and reopened the land link to China. At this point an urgent new problem arose for the quartermasters; the armies were now 1,000 mi. from their main sea base at Calcutta. The sappers and pioneers had performed miracles of road building, but to supply by overland route a host which now numbered close to 1,000,000 men had become an insuperable difficulty. The air force was called upon to bridge the gap. Men, weapons, ammunition, rations, mules and oxen were borne through the skies above the jungle to keep the armies marching. This air lift rose in the end to a peak of 80,000 tons a month. But since there was an economic limit for air supply, it now became imperative to wrest airfields from the Japanese where the transport aeroplanes could be serviced and refuelled. Admiral Mountbatten therefore ordered a series of amphibious operations, supported by Lt. Gen. Sir Philip Christison's 15th corps, down the Arakan coast to secure these objectives.

By March General Slim had massed the greater part of his 14th army along the western bank of the Irrawaddy, threatening Mandalay. Beyond the river, the Japanese concentrated to meet the expected thrust against the city. But Slim by a secret march of 200 mi. passed a whole corps across their front, and, forcing the passage of the river south of Mandalay, fell upon the key point of the Japanese rear at Meiktila. This was the decisive battle of the campaign; afterward, the Japanese army disintegrated.

The 14th army stormed southward in two columns upon Rangoon. As it went, the Karen tribesmen of the hills along the China frontier, organized and led by British officers who had parachuted among them, rose and barred the hurried retreat of the remaining intact Japanese forces. Meantime, Rangoon itself had been seized on May 3 by an air and sea assault. The remnants of the Japanese army, now shattered beyond repair, sought to escape across the Sittang river. The last battle of the campaign was fought by the 17th Indian division upon the banks of the river which three years before they had passed in retreat.

Admiral Mountbatten had prepared two further opera-

[3]In Jan. 1945, Generalissimo Chiang Kai-shek renamed the Burma-Ledo road the Stilwell road in honour of its greatest protagonist.

tions, one across the jungle toward Siam, the second by sea and air against Singapore, when the atom bomb fell upon the first Japanese cities. This ended the war. Within a few days the remaining organized Japanese forces in southeast Asia, which still numbered close to 700,000 men, had laid down their arms in unconditional surrender.

No notable naval engagements marked the course of the Burma campaign, but from 1943 onward the royal navy re-asserted its mastery of the Indian ocean and its approaches. This command of the sea was the prerequisite of military success. (F. O.)

11. Operations in China.—With the exception of a small number of U.S. ground troops who acted as instructors and advisers in training the Chinese army in modern military techniques, British and U.S. support to their Chinese ally consisted exclusively of air activities, including the air transport of supplies and equipment. Allied strategy, as determined soon after the United States became an active participant, called for concentration of resources on the defeat of Germany. Only after the demands of this task had been met could men and supplies be spared for offensive operations against the Japanese. An important feature of this strategy was the necessity of supplying sufficient military support to keep China in the war and thus contain as many Japanese divisions and aeroplanes on the Asiatic mainland as was possible with China's meagrely equipped and poorly trained forces. Air support was not only the most essential but also the most economical assistance that could be furnished China in accomplishing this strategical objective.

In 1941 and early in 1942, the only effective land air force opposing the Japanese on the Asiatic mainland was the American Volunteer group organized by Col. Claire L. Chennault, whose services had been engaged by the Chinese government. The group consisted of volunteers, mainly former United States army air corps personnel employed under contract by the Chinese. Under the tutelage of Col. Chennault, a master air tactician, this group compiled an enviable combat record, using hit-and-run aerial guerrilla tactics against a vastly numerically superior enemy.

In April 1942 Chennault was recalled to active duty with the U.S. Army air forces and promoted to brigadier general, and on July 4, 1942, the A.V.G. was disbanded and a small number of its personnel absorbed in the 10th air force. The latter had been established in India the preceding March under the command of Maj. Gen. Lewis H. Brereton. The major mission of Chennault's portion of the 10th air force was the protection of the air transport operations, the only remaining means of moving military supplies to China.

Throughout the remainder of 1942 and all of 1943, the tenuous supply situation precluded any major Allied air offensive in China. However, effective air support aided the ground troops materially in stopping the annual Japanese "rice offensives."

In late 1943, work was begun on the airfields needed for the operations of the newly developed B-29 Superforts. Employing more than 700,000 native labourers, 5 fields in India and 4 in China were completed in April 1944. The long-range bombing operations against Japan by the 20th bomber command, U.S. Army air forces, were initiated on June 15, 1944, with a damaging raid on Yawata.

12. Japanese Offensive Operations, 1944.—The Japanese reacted immediately to the threat of China-based bomber operations and launched powerful offensives against the air bases in China. A secondary objective was to secure an inland supply route to their forces in southeast Asia. A southward advance from Hengyang occupied the major base at Kweilin on Sept. 17, 1944. By Nov. 26 the airfields at Tanchuk, Luichow, Kweiping and Nanning had been evacuated. On Dec. 10, 1944, Japanese forces, moving north from Indo-China, met columns advancing south from Nanning and opened a through corridor from Korea to Malaya.

This operation marked the successful termination of the last Japanese offensive effort in the war. In the spring of 1945, the armies of China assumed the offensive with a strong attack on the southern front. The Chinese advance recaptured Nanning on May 27, 1945, and during the months of June and July wiped out practically all the gains made by the Japanese in 1944. The sudden cessation of hostilities in Aug. 1945 ended this Chinese offensive, which had steadily gathered momentum. Before it ended, Chinese forces had reached the China sea at Fort Bayard, near the base of the Luichow peninsula.

13. Victory in the Pacific.—Early in 1945 the Allied high command began to put in final form their detailed plans for the operations that would bring victory. The collapse of Germany in the spring or early summer was forecast, and the tremendous task of rapidly transferring the huge Allied military potential to the Pacific area was planned and developed in all its complexity.

Changes in the Pacific command structure to meet the new conditions were directed by the joint chiefs of staff. General MacArthur was placed in command of all United States army forces and Admiral Nimitz of all naval forces in the Pacific on April 6, 1945. At the same time they were directed to prepare for the invasion of the Japanese home islands under guidance of the over-all strategic directive furnished them.

On July 10 the joint chiefs of staff revised the air force command structure. The 20th air force headquarters, which had been in Washington furnishing strategic direction to the 20th and 21st bomber commands in the Pacific, moved to Guam and, under the command of Lieut. Gen. Nathan F. Twining, absorbed the 21st bomber command. The personnel of the deactivated 20th bomber command was transferred to the 8th air force, redeployed to Okinawa from Europe under the command of Lieut. Gen. James H. Doolittle. The two air forces were combined into the United States strategic air force, commanded by Gen. Carl Spaatz. Strategic control of this huge bombing fleet was retained by the joint chiefs of staff.

Throughout July 1945, preparatory operations to soften the main Japanese islands for the contemplated landings continued to build up. Air attacks by very heavy bombers from the Marianas; heavy, medium, light bombers and fighters from the newly developed Okinawa airfields and fighters from Iwo Jima filled the Japanese skies. The United States 3rd fleet, which had been joined by a powerful British contingent, pounded at Japan from Hokkaido to Shikoku. Many Japanese coastal towns were bombarded by the Allied warships.

The plans for the invasion of Japan called for initial landings on the southeast and southwest shores of Kyushu of a force of five United States infantry, one cavalry and three marine divisions, while three additional infantry divisions were held in reserve. The operation, known as "Olympic," was scheduled for early Nov. 1945. This operation was to be followed in early March 1946 by the landing of two armies on plains of Honshu Island east of Tokyo. The contemplated strength of the initial landing force was nine infantry, two armoured and three marine divisions. The follow-up force was to consist of the United States 1st army, transferred from Europe, and composed of ten infantry and one air-borne division. This landing force had the major mission of destroying Japanese military strength on the main home island and occupying the highly important Tokyo-Yokohama area.

Meanwhile, a project formally initiated in 1941 came to fruition. Research and development of the possibility of releasing, instantaneously, huge amounts of energy through the principle of atomic fission had been conducted in great secrecy in isolated and closely guarded installations in the United States. By an agreement reached in 1940, the project was a joint Anglo-U.S. undertaking—the knowledge and resources of the United States, Great Britain and Canada being pooled under the control of a combined policy committee.

The first successful explosion of an experimental atomic bomb (*q.v.*) was on July 16, 1945, just three weeks prior to its first operational employment. A report of the results of this experiment was rushed to Potsdam, where the chiefs of state of Great Britain, the United States and Russia were meeting in conference to decide future policies. A quick decision was reached to use this new weapon with the aim of shortening the war and saving lives. On July 26 a joint ultimatum to Japan to end the war unconditionally was issued by the United States and Great Britain and was promptly rejected. Meanwhile, instructions were issued to the commanding general of the U.S. army strategic air force to drop the new bomb on an important Japanese industrial installation of his own choosing, on any date subsequent to Aug. 3.

On Aug. 6, a lone B-29 Superfortress flew high over Hiroshima (*q.v.*), and dropped a single bomb. It was exploded at a predetermined height above the ground, with devastating results. Of the city 4 sq.mi. were utterly destroyed, and more than 80,000 inhabitants were killed.

Soviet Russia, in compliance with commitments made at Potsdam the preceding month, declared war on Japan on Aug. 8. Russian forces in the far east immediately began the invasion of Manchuria from both the east and the west. Additional forces crossed the Korean-Siberian border on Aug. 10.

Meanwhile, on Aug. 9, a second atomic bomb struck the city of Nagasaki, an important seaport and industrial centre of Japan. Destruction comparable to that wreaked on Hiroshima resulted, with 3.3 sq.mi. of urban area completely pulverized.

The following day, Aug. 10, the Japanese government sued for peace, accepting, in general, the Allied terms set forth in the Potsdam declaration, with the proviso that the prerogatives of the Japanese emperor as a sovereign ruler would be maintained. After conferring with the other Allied governments, the United States answered the Japanese appeal on Aug. 11, reaffirming the position taken in previous declarations, and stating that the emperor's authority would be subject to the commands of the supreme commander of the Allied Powers (S.C.A.P.).

On Aug. 14, 1945, Japan declared its acceptance of the Allied terms.

Combat activities continued unabated during the interchange of notes. Land-based bombers continued their destructive raids while the Allied fleet inflicted heavy damage with its planes and guns. By agreement, General MacArthur was named supreme commander for the Allies.

Following receipt of the Japanese acceptance, General MacArthur instructed the Japanese surrender envoys to proceed to Manila, where detailed procedure to accomplish the cessation of hostilities was presented to them. These included the formal signing of the general surrender in Tokyo bay, on Aug. 31. However, a typhoon caused a postponement of the ceremony for 48 hours. The ceremony took place at 9:08 A.M., Sept. 2, 1945, on the deck of the U.S. battleship "Missouri," flagship of the United States 3rd fleet. The instrument of surrender was signed on the part of Japan by representatives of the civil and military authorities, while General MacArthur signed for the Allied Powers. Representatives of all nations which

Scheduled invasion of Japan which became unnecessary after the use of the atomic bomb in Aug. 1945. Planned in two phases, operation Olympic called for landings on southern Kyushu in the fall of 1945 and Operation Coronet for the invasion of eastern Honshu early in 1946

had engaged in the war against Japan affixed their signatures to the document as witnesses.

One hundred and eighteen days after the collapse of Germany, the war in the Pacific was terminated. Japan surrendered while still possessing a capable army of 2,000,000 men and an air force of more than 3,000 planes of all types. Its navy was, however, for practical purposes nonexistent. The nation's military and industrial potential had been completely demoralized by the air and sea power of the Allies. In addition to the destruction Japan suffered in the home islands, the tight and effective blockade imposed during the last six months of the war denied it the raw materials and resources essential to modern war.

(W. A. Wr.)

V. THE WAR AT SEA

A. Prior to U.S. Entry into War

For many decades it had been a keystone of Britain's policy to maintain a fleet equal to any combination of two opponents likely to be brought against it. This policy rested on the belief that Britain could exist only by the importation of a large proportion of its food and could maintain the unity of its world-wide commonwealth of nations only by the mobile power of a dominant navy. The Washington Naval treaty (1922) accepted equality with the United States while limiting the navies of France, Italy and Japan in proportion to their needs. The German navy already, by the Versailles treaty, had been reduced to impotence. The treaty of London (1936) imposed further limitations on cruisers and destroyers; but Italy, under fascist influence and expansionist ideas, declined to be bound, being already engaged in developing a fleet which might in favourable conditions give it mastery of the Mediterranean. The growing nationalism of Germany and the feeling that that country could be made peaceful only by allowing it a navy sufficient to satisfy national self-respect, resulted in the Anglo-German agreement of 1935 and declaration of 1937. These gave Germany the right to build up to 35% of Britain's strength in all categories and to 100% in submarines. Germany had already started to rebuild its fleet and had produced the pocket battleships "Deutschland," "Admiral Graf Spee" and "Admiral Scheer," nominally 10,000-ton cruisers but in fact powerful commerce raiders of considerably larger tonnage. It now settled down in earnest to construct a modern fleet. The "Scharnhorst" and "Gneisenau," 26,000-ton battle cruisers, were completed in 1938, the "Tirpitz" and "Bismarck," capital ships more powerful than any afloat or contemplated elsewhere, were laid down. Submarines were built in great numbers.

Britain became conscious of the inevitability of war as early as 1936 when a rearmament program was begun, but the recovery of the navy was slow. As forecast in 1938 the naval strength of the countries likely to be involved in the coming struggle would in 1940 be as follows:

	Battleships	Aircraft carriers	8-in. cruisers	Light cruisers	Destroyers	Submarines
British empire . . .	17	7–11	15	63	188	69
Germany	7	2	5	10	22	119–129
France	10	1	7	12	66	94
Italy	6	—	7	28	99	120–130

The British battleships were old, and the new program of battleship construction, introduced by Lord Chatfield when first sea lord, could not reach completion till 1941–42.

1. Two Great Strategic Aims.—British strategy had a threefold object: to ensure the safe arrival of supplies of all kinds to the home country, to prevent the landing of any enemy military expedition on its coasts and to provide force whereby a British expedition could be landed and maintained on enemy territory. Long experience had taught Britain that these essentials were best met by seeking out and destroying any enemy force which showed itself at sea.

German strategy aimed at cutting off Britain's supplies, primarily by submarines, secondly by surface raiders and thirdly by aircraft. Britain could thus be reduced to impotence, after which an actual invasion, well supported by air, could destroy its power forever. This plan involved disregard of the limitations on the use of submarines agreed on at Washington and demanded not only a large fleet of U-boats but an invincible army and overwhelming air power, all of which Germany had attained by 1939 when it invited war with Britain and France by its invasion of Poland.

The events which followed all took their place in the struggle between these two great strategic aims. Either one might be successful; both could not.

Britain declared war on Germany on Sept. 3, 1939; but before that date Germany had already stationed its fleet for the attack on British merchantmen. The "Admiral Graf Spee" was at sea in the South Atlantic with a number of improvised commerce raiders. U-boats were on the trade routes, and supply ships were in position. Britain had a battle fleet based on Scapa Flow to contain the German fleet, another at Malta to contain the Italian fleet, which, in view of the axis treaties, could not be ignored. A number of cruiser squadrons were formed for trade protection and the hunting of raiders. Britain's greatest weakness lay in the absence of escort craft for merchant-ship convoys. Nevertheless, it was British policy to establish convoys as soon as possible for all except fast merchant ships.

On the opening day of the war the "Athenia," a British passenger liner outward bound carrying 1,480 passengers and crew, was torpedoed off Ireland; and in the first fortnight Britain lost 27 merchant ships totalling 131,000 tons. By Sept. 7, however, the first outward-bound convoy had been assembled and sailed, and by the end of the first fortnight the convoy system was in regular operation and being extended daily. Convoys were escorted by destroyers and trawlers from British waters to longtitude 20°–30° W., and thereafter by cruisers, battleships or armed merchant cruisers as defense against raiders. Many U-boats were attacked, a few were sunk, but as the war developed it became evident that the U-boats could and would operate right across the North Atlantic and that antisubmarine escort must accompany convoys for the whole journey. To meet this threat, the range of action of a number of destroyers was increased by the sacrifice of a boiler to permit added oil stowage, and a simple type of escort vessel known as the corvette was designed and laid down in large numbers in British building yards. A separate organization, coastal convoy, was created for the protection of coastal traffic resulting from the assemblage and dispersal of the great ocean convoys which took place off the west coast of Scotland.

On Sept. 6 Britain suspended its obligations under the London Naval treaty. On Sept. 17 the great aircraft carrier "Courageous" was torpedoed by a U-boat and sunk in the North Atlantic. On Oct. 14 a German U-boat under the command of Kapitan-Leutnant Guenther Prien made a daring entry into Scapa Flow through a narrow channel between two islands and there found and torpedoed the battleship "Royal Oak." This proof that Scapa Flow was not impregnable came as a shock to the British. Urgent measures were then taken to strengthen the base.

The "Admiral Graf Spee," German pocket battleship which was blown up by her own commander near the Montevideo harbour on Dec. 17, 1939, four days after the ship was disabled in a running fight with three British cruisers

Germany meanwhile had developed new types of mines, and on Nov. 19 came the first announcement of sinkings by magnetic mines. Fifteen ships, largely neutrals, were lost in four days by the indiscriminate use of this secret weapon, laid sometimes by aircraft and sometimes by ships. The British secured a mine, discovered its secret and in a very short time developed an antidote and equipped their rapidly swelling fleet of mine sweepers with the means to explode it and so clear a safe channel.

The surface raiders too were active; a German battle cruiser sank the A.M.C. (armed merchant cruiser) "Rawalpindi" off Ireland on Nov. 26, and about the same time the "Admiral Graf Spee" sank the Polish liner "Pilsudski," the British "Doric Star" and a number of other ships. But despite these setbacks Winston Churchill was able to report on Dec. 6 that the convoy system was in full operation and only 1 ship per 750 sailings had been sunk. In addition, the British expeditionary force had been safely conveyed to France.

2. Battle of the River Plate; the Altmark.—On Dec. 13, 1939, a British cruiser squadron under Comm. Henry H. Harwood, consisting of "Ajax," "Exeter" and "Achilles," fought the pocket battleship "Admiral Graf Spee" in the South Atlantic. The "Ajax" and "Achilles" had 6-in. armament, the "Exeter" 8-in., while the "Graf Spee's" armament of six 11-in. and eight 5.9-in. exceeded in broadside weight that of all 3 British cruisers. The action opened soon after dawn; the British divided their force, the "Exeter" taking one side and the two six-in. cruisers the other so as to force the "Graf" to split its fire. The "Exeter" received the brunt of the fire and was heavily hit and eventually forced out of action while the three British, together, so pummelled the German that it turned away and made for the neutral port of Montevideo with the British in pursuit. On Dec. 17 the "Admiral Graf Spee" left harbour and to the surprise of the British, waiting outside, scuttled itself in mid-channel. Its crew was interned and its commander, Capt. Hans Langsdorff, committed suicide. The action was remarkable for the tactical handling of the cruisers which enabled them to defeat the much more heavily armed "Graf Spee."

The problem of transporting large contingents of troops from overseas was now urgent and was met throughout the war by the use of large fast liners specially fitted up for troop transport. The first Canadian consignment arrived in Britain on Dec. 17, 1939, and the method proved extremely successful, the liners' speed rendering U-boat attacks very difficult.

In Jan. 1940 the British requisitioned all British shipping capable of overseas trade, and in February the Germans announced that all British ships would be sunk without warning.

On Feb. 16 an incident occurred which, though relatively unimportant, created considerable stir. The armed merchantman "Altmark," returning to Germany after its campaign in the South Atlantic with 300 British prisoners of war, was known to be working its way down the Norwegian coast to Germany, inside territorial waters. It put into Josing fjord, and thereupon the British destroyer "Cossack," Commander Philip Vian, entered the fjord, ranged alongside and rescued the prisoners.

3. Operations off Norway and Denmark.—On April 9 Germany invaded Norway and Denmark. It claimed that it was forced to this action because the British had laid mines in Norwegian waters. In fact, however, the mines were laid only on the morning of April 8, when some of the German invading force had already left for Norway. The Germans occupied Oslo, Trondhjem and Narvik as well as a number of other ports. On April 9 the battle cruiser "Scharnhorst" was engaged and severely damaged in an action with H.M.S. "Renown" but escaped under the cover of smoke screens laid by the cruiser "Hipper." On April 10 a British destroyer force led by Capt. H. Warburton-Lee in the "Hardy" entered Narvik fjord to attack German naval forces. In the ensuing battle, one German destroyer was sunk, three were set on fire and a number of supply ships sunk or burnt. The British lost the "Hardy" and "Hunter" and Captain Warburton-Lee was killed. On the same day German troopships were sunk by submarines in the Skagerrak and the cruiser "Koenigsberg" was sunk by the fleet air arm at Bergen.

On April 13 the battleship "Warspite" and a strong force of destroyers made a second attack on Narvik under Vice-Adm. William Whitworth and succeeded in sinking seven German destroyers and capturing the fjord. On the same day the cruiser "Bluecher" was sunk in Oslo fjord. The "Karlsruhe" was sunk by the British submarine "Truant" while the British lost the aircraft carrier "Glorious," by U-boat, and the cruisers "Curlew" and "Effingham." Two days later a British, French and Polish force was landed in Norway, and the British occupied the Faroe

Islands. The German invasion had been successful, though at a heavy cost, including 26 transports. It remained to establish their position, and in the ensuing struggle on land, assisted by greatly superior air support, they forced the Allies to evacuate between June 1 and 4.

The Norwegian adventure gave Germany a long Atlantic coast line and many harbours. It greatly facilitated the submarine campaign and improved the flow to Germany of the important Swedish iron ore. These advantages were bought at the cost of a serious dispersion of force in all three arms, as well as the moral stigma of having invaded two peaceful countries without the slightest justification, an action which shocked the neutral world.

4. Germany on the Atlantic.—By May 13, 1940, the Netherlands, overrun by German troops, capitulated; four days later Brussels was taken and German forces had broken through in France. The royal navy was doing all in its power to evacuate Dutch and Belgian merchantmen to British ports and succeeded in saving very considerable tonnage. On May 28 Belgium surrendered. The British army, split off by the German advance from its French allies, was compelled to retreat to the coast. Dunkirk was chosen as the place of evacuation. The British mobilized every available small vessel to assist their destroyers in this evacuation. The operation started on June 1 and lasted 4 days, during which 345,585 men were brought back, mostly from open beaches; but their equipment was lost.

On June 10 Italy declared war on Britain and France; four days later Paris surrendered and on June 15 the British completed their army's evacuation from Brest and St. Nazaire. On June 24 an armistice was concluded between Germany and France. Britain then stood alone, its army without equipment, and only its navy and its air force (greatly reduced by losses in France) between it and invasion. The occupation of the Netherlands, Belgium and France, as well as Denmark and Norway, now gave Germany a vast Atlantic coast line. Its U-boats need no longer run the gauntlet of the Dover straits or the Fair Island channel, and it promptly developed U-boat bases at Brest, St. Nazaire, Lorient and Bordeaux. Its aircraft based near the coast in the Netherlands, Belgium and France could operate over the North sea, English channel and Bay of Biscay, while its fast coastal craft, based on Dutch and Belgian ports, were well placed to attack British coastal convoys moving in and out of the port of London. The British prepared to meet invasion. They kept a close watch on channel ports where invasion barges were collecting and harried them by bombing.

5. Immobilization of French Navy.—Now that Italy was in the war the French navy presented a serious problem; for if Germany obtained possession of it, the combined Italian and German-French navies would be superior in every arm to the royal navy. The French armistice provided that the French fleet was to be assembled in French and Italian ports and demilitarized except for units which the Italian or German governments desired for the protection of French colonial interests. This obvious loophole and the distrust in German promises prompted the British to take decisive action. On July 3 all French warships in British ports were boarded and placed under British control. Ships in North African ports were offered alternative conditions designed solely to keep them out of German hands. An important contingent, including the battle cruiser "Dunkerque," lay at Oran; Adm. Marcel-Bruno Gensoul, in command, refused to accept any conditions and prepared his ships for sea and for action. A British force under Adm. Sir James Somerville, after eight-and-a-half hours' delay, opened fire; a battle ensued in which the majority of the French force was destroyed. The battleship "Richelieu" lay at Dakar, and there again the French admiral refused the alternatives offered. On July 8 a launch manned by British personnel entered Dakar, placed depth charges against the "Richelieu's" hull and seriously damaged it. Naval aircraft completed the damage which kept the ship immobilized for two-and-a-half years.

On July 9 a British fleet was at sea to the east of Malta covering an important convoy, when a mixed Italian force of two battleships, cruisers and destroyers was encountered. The British force gave chase, but the Italians turned away, covering their retreat with smoke screens. One Italian battleship was hit and a cruiser torpedoed by aircraft. The British pursued to within sight of land and although heavily attacked by aircraft suffered no loss. Ten days later the cruiser "Sydney," Capt. J. A. Collins, accompanied by destroyers, encountered two Italian cruisers and sank the "Bartolomeo Colleoni."

6. Operations during Battle of Britain.—In Aug. 1940, the threatened invasion of Britain appeared imminent. The Germans had reorganized their armies for the task, and embarkation was being practised. On Aug. 8 the campaign opened with mass air raids, and the battle of Britain began. In this, British fighter aircraft created havoc in the German bombing forces, which were eventually so weakened that the German high command was forced to abandon its plans for invasion, a fact which became apparent to the British as the autumn wore on. In November Germany concentrated its air attacks on British ports. Southampton was the first to suffer. Portsmouth, Plymouth, Portland and Bristol all experienced severe raids and were gravely damaged. The London docks were frequently attacked and immense fires caused. None of these ports, however, was entirely immobilized; and work continued.

The battle of the Atlantic also continued. In June 1940 the liner "Lancastria," carrying troops, was bombed and sunk, as was the A.M.C. "Andania." In July the "Arandora Star" was sunk, in August the A.M.C. "Transylvania," and in September the "City of Benares" carrying evacuee children, all by U-boat. In October the "Empress of Britain" was sunk by bombing. Against these successes the British could claim the capture of the German liner "Weser" in the Pacific.

The British were desperately short of escort vessels, and on Sept. 3 an agreement with the U.S.A. was announced leasing a number of bases to the latter in exchange for 50 overage U.S. destroyers, transferred to the royal navy. These vessels, after a good deal of modernization, helped greatly to fill the void.

7. Mediterranean Operations.—In the Mediterranean the British continued to command the sea, operating by extensive sweeps in search of the Italian fleet. On Oct. 12 the cruiser "Ajax," Capt. E. D. B. McCarthy, encountered three large Italian destroyers south of Sicily and sank two of them. In a subsequent action against a cruiser and four destroyers it crippled one, the remainder escaping in darkness. Next day the cruiser "York" found the crippled destroyer and sank it after allowing time for its crew to abandon ship. British submarines maintained continuous pressure against Italian supply ships plying to the African coast and sank three in October.

These results did not satisfy the British naval commander in chief, Sir Andrew Cunningham. The Italian battle fleet of two new and four reconstructed battleships constituted an ever-present threat to his supremacy. A carefully prepared attack by carrier-borne torpedo aircraft was delivered against the great Italian base at Taranto on the night of Nov. 11. At least three battleships lay in the outer harbour; all were hit and left in a sinking condition. Only the shallowness of the water prevented their final loss. In the inner harbour two cruisers were badly damaged and two fleet auxiliaries sunk. The British lost only two aircraft. This shattering blow established British naval supremacy in the Mediterranean, but shore-based aircraft operating from Sicily, Sardinia, the African coast and the Dodecanese still interfered with free movement of British transports. The majority of these, including troop transports and ammunition ships, now made the long journey round the cape in order to maintain and reinforce the British armies operating against Ethiopia, Eritrea and Libya.

In the North Atlantic the struggle continued to be severe. On Nov. 5 the A.M.C. "Jervis Bay," Capt. E. S. F. Fegen, was escorting a convoy of 38 ships when the pocket battleship "Admiral Scheer" was sighted closing to attack. Captain Fegen at once ordered his convoy to scatter and make smoke, while he steamed rapidly toward the raider and opened fire. It was evident from the first that the odds were hopeless; nevertheless, he engaged the "Scheer" for nearly an hour and held the Germans' fire. When at last the "Jervis Bay," crippled and in flames, sank beneath the waves, the merchantmen had had time to scatter so that of the whole 38 only 4 were sunk.

In the Mediterranean the British now scored a series of successes. The offensive launched from Egypt on Dec. 9, 1940, led to a rapid advance culminating in the capture of Benghazi. This advance was strongly supported by the royal navy whose main base was now, by agreement with the Egyptians, at Alexandria. But at this point, because of the pressure on Greece from German and Italian forces, the British decided to send reinforcements there. There followed a number of contacts between naval forces in which the Italians invariably retired behind smoke screens. Powerful forces of Italian and German aircraft, however, attacked with determination; and on Jan. 14, 1941, while protecting a convoy en route for Greece, the aircraft carrier "Illustrious" was damaged and the cruiser "Southampton" set on fire so heavily that the British sank it. On Feb. 9 Vice-Admiral Somerville led a heavy bombardment on the naval base at Genoa which caused great destruction. In the Red sea Kismayu was captured on March 6, and ten axis ships were sunk or captured.

8. Battle of Cape Matapan.—On March 19, 1941, aircraft reported Italian cruisers southeast of Sicily steaming to the southeastward. The British commander in chief despatched a force of four cruisers, a carrier and some destroyers under Vice-Adm. H. P. Pridham Whipple to make contact and followed with three battleships screened by destroyers. The light forces sighted an Italian battleship and two cruisers, and while attacking the battleship by torpedo aircraft, led the cruisers toward the British battle fleet. The Italian battleship received several hits in the course of the day's fighting but escaped, badly damaged, to its base.

A second Italian force of two battleships and several cruisers was now sighted some distance to the northward, and a chase ensued until the 8-in. cruiser "Pola," which had been attacked by torpedo aircraft, was sighted, stopped and heavily damaged, and the British battle fleet closed on it. Night had already fallen when three more large cruisers crossed the British battle fleet's bows, possibly in support of the "Pola." The battleships opened fire and the cruisers were quickly destroyed. The result of this action was that the three 8-in. cruisers "Pola," "Zara" and "Fiume," one or two smaller cruisers and two destroyers were sunk. The remaining Italian forces escaped northwestward. The British lost 2 aircraft but had no other casualties; they picked up more than 900 Italian officers and men next morning. The action was notable in having been brought on by the delay imposed on the Italians by torpedo aircraft. The Italians had 3 battleships, 11 cruisers and 14 destroyers at sea against the British 3 battleships, 1 aircraft carrier, 4 cruisers and a number of destroyers. Greek destroyers co-operated effectively with the British.

On April 1, 1941, Asmara, the capital of Eritrea, surrendered; and an Italian flotilla in the Red sea was engaged and sunk.

The necessity for reinforcing Greece seriously weakened the British forces in Africa. The Germans were coming to the rescue of their Italian allies and pouring panzer troops and ammunition into Tripoli. This supply line had Malta on its flank, and although the island had suffered severe bombing and was no longer used by the battle fleet, it remained the base of destroyers and submarines. These harried the Italian convoys. On the night of April 15–16 a force of four British destroyers led by the "Jervis" sighted a convoy of five large ships escorted by four destroyers. In the first few minutes of the British attack the leading Italian destroyer was overwhelmed and sunk, then every ship of the convoy was set on fire and a battle ensued between the remaining destroyers. The British lost the "Nubian" by torpedo. All the Italian destroyers were sunk or set on fire, while the entire convoy which consisted of ammunition ships, motor transport and German troops was destroyed.

But despite naval victories the British position in the Mediterranean now suffered a decline. On April 3, 1941, the British evacuated Benghazi; and a retreat to the Egyptian frontier followed. Tobruk held out and was supplied from the sea.

9. Operations off Greece and Yugoslavia.—On April 6, 1941, the Germans invaded Greece and Yugoslavia, the Yugoslav army withdrawing. Salonika fell to the Germans on April 9, and Monastir was reached the next day. The British forces in Greece now fell back fighting, and on April 23 the Greek government was evacuated to Crete. Two days later the Germans occupied Lemnos Island and shortly afterward the whole of the Dodecanese group. The British were forced to evacuate their army in Greece, and about 43,000 escaped to Egypt and to Crete, 3,000 being left. The Germans then brought overwhelming air superiority to bear on Crete and made parachute and glider landings. Their sea-borne troops suffered heavy losses, but they gained a foothold and the British found it necessary to evacuate Crete also. This proved a most costly operation. In the course of May and June the British lost by aerial attack three cruisers and eight destroyers, proving beyond all doubt that naval operations within the reach of shore-based aircraft could not be carried out without air support. By June 1, however, the evacuation of Crete was complete.

In the summer months of 1941 the air attacks on Malta were intense, but the fortress held out and the British fought their convoys through and took a heavy toll of Italian supply ships to Africa. In the course of these operations the battleship "Nelson" was torpedoed on Sept. 27, but not fatally. The aircraft carrier "Ark Royal" was torpedoed and sunk on Nov. 14. The "Barham" was torpedoed and sunk on Nov. 25.

On the reverse side, Capt. W. C. Agnew in the cruiser

"Aurora," patrolling on the night of Nov. 9 in the central Mediterranean with a force of two cruisers and two destroyers, encountered two convoys of ten supply ships escorted by destroyers and covered by two 8-in. cruisers. In the resulting action all the supply ships were destroyed and three destroyers sunk, a fourth being subsequently sunk by a British submarine. The British suffered no casualties. An armed merchant cruiser and several supply ships were sunk two days later. British submarines had many successes.

Supported by the fleet, the British attacked in Libya on Nov. 18 and gained much ground. Severe fighting followed but by Dec. 1 the German and Italian tank forces had pressed the British back once more to the Egyptian frontiers and beyond, and Tobruk was again invested.

Turning to the Atlantic, the British had planned a raid on the Lofoten Islands where, under German occupation, quantities of fish oil and other products were made and sent to Germany. On March 4 the raiding squadron fell upon the islands, captured the garrison, sank ten merchant ships and some armed trawlers, revictualled the Norwegian inhabitants, destroyed the fish-oil plant and withdrew with their prisoners. The operation was sudden, swift and precise. There were a few German but no British casualties.

10. The "Hood" and "Bismarck."—In the middle of May 1941 the battleship "Bismarck," which for some time had been sheltering at Bergen, set out on a commerce-raiding expedition, and the task of finding and bringing it to action fell to the commander in chief of the home fleet, Adm. Sir John Tovey. He sent the cruisers "Norfolk" and "Suffolk" to the Denmark straits, while three groups containing capital ships took up intercepting positions. On the evening of May 24 Adm. W. F. Wake-Walker in the "Norfolk" sighted the "Bismarck" and a cruiser and started to shadow, and as a result the battlecruiser "Hood" and the new battleship "Prince of Wales" made contact and engaged next morning. The engagement was fortunate for the Germans, for while both the "Bismarck" and "Prince of Wales" received only slight damage the "Hood" was hit in a magazine and blew up. The "Bismarck" turned southwestward and broke off action; but it was shadowed, and the "Prince of Wales" again engaged toward evening. The Germans turned to the west and then to the south in an endeavour to shake off pursuit. But during the night the "Victorious" launched a torpedo aircraft attack which scored a hit. At 3 A.M. on May 25 in misty weather, contact was lost, the "Bismarck" being then about 350 mi. S.S.E. of the southern point of Greenland. Admiral Tovey's squadron, led by the "King George V," was closing in from the north, while another group under Admiral Somerville was converging from the south. It was not until 10:30 A.M. on May 26 that the quarry was again located by aircraft. The "Bismarck" was now alone and steering east, about 550 mi. W. of Land's End. In the course of the day the "Ark Royal" sent off two striking forces, the second of

The "Ark Royal," British aircraft carrier torpedoed by an axis submarine off Gibraltar, shown listing before it sank in the Mediterranean on Nov. 14, 1941

which succeeded in making two torpedo hits. Cruisers were then in touch, and during the night successful torpedo attacks were led by Captain Vian in the "Cossack," after which the "Bismarck" was reduced to eight knots though its gun armament was still intact. At 9 A.M. on May 27, the "King George V" and "Rodney" engaged and silenced it; finally the "Dorsetshire" sank it with torpedoes. About 100 officers and men were rescued. This lesson made the German grand commander in chief, Adm. Erich Raeder, very chary of sending out commerce-raiders.

11. Naval Help for Russia.—On June 22, 1941, the war entered a new phase when Germany invaded Russia. Russia was desperately short of munitions and means had to be found to help it. Stretched to the limits though it already was, Britain organized a system of convoys to Archangel, the first convoy sailing in August. These convoys continued throughout the war. The Germans based on Norway were well placed to interfere by aircraft, surface ships and submarines. Each successive convoy was attacked, but the great majority of ships got through.

On Aug. 15 President Roosevelt met Prime Minister Churchill in Argentia bay, Newfoundland, and drew up the Atlantic charter. That these two leaders, so vital to their countries' welfare, could risk an Atlantic voyage was a measure of the mastery of the submarine menace which had been attained. But while fast and well-escorted ships could travel with relative safety, the slower convoys, still inadequately protected, were far from safe. In the first 11 months of the war, Britain lost 1,500,000 tons of shipping, out of a total of 21,000,000. Losses averaging 500,000 tons a month were sustained in the early part of 1941, when Germany had developed its Atlantic bases and its production of U-boats had become gigantic. Adm. Karl Doenitz, directing the U-boat war, constantly introduced new tactics, while, step by step, the British countered them. April 1940 had seen the first corvette at sea; by 1941 they were afloat in large numbers, and many U-boats had been sunk. In the latter months of that year losses diminished markedly to 180,000 tons per month and it seemed that, for the time being at least, the British had the upper hand in the unending struggle.

Mine sweeping had developed to vast dimensions, the sweepers now being equipped to destroy magnetic and acoustic mines as well as the older contact mines.

In British waters hundreds of motor gunboats had been built and were at sea guarding the coastal convoys and fighting the E-boats which operated from Dutch and Belgian harbours. The struggle to protect shipping was at a peak. The percentage of losses on a voyage was never great, but cumulatively they were serious.

British eyes were turning to the east, where Japan was becoming increasingly menacing. On Aug. 24, 1941, Churchill warned Japan that opposition to the passage of supplies to Russia must stop. Such reinforcements as could be spared were sent to Hong Kong and Singapore.

(C. V. U.)

B. War at Sea after Pearl Harbor

In Dec. 1941 the United States was confronted with war at sea in both the Atlantic and Pacific oceans. The geographical position of the nation necessarily required control of the seas before U.S. troops could fight offensively upon land.

In the Atlantic, United States strategy involved maintaining lines of communication to Great Britain and to future bases of operations against the continent of Europe, in opposition to the vigorous efforts of the German submarine and air forces to secure and maintain control of that ocean. In the Pacific, not only the initial success of the Japanese attack upon Hawaii but the lack of any well-developed bases in Australia and in the South Pacific islands, combined with the immense distances, placed Allied naval forces immediately upon the defensive. However, before the end of 1942 the offensive had been seized in both oceans.

1. Defensive Phase in the Pacific.—After the Pearl Harbor attack, which resulted in the permanent loss of two battleships of the United States Pacific fleet and the incapacitation of six others for varying periods of time, the Japanese withdrew from the central Pacific and, except for the capture of Guam and Wake Island, devoted their attentions to the Philippine Islands, the Malay region and the Netherlands Indies. The Allied naval forces in that part of the world were hopelessly outnumbered, but though incapable of permanently checking the Japanese advance, they undertook with great gallantry to delay it as long as possible. The British battleship "Prince of Wales" and battle cruiser "Repulse"—sent to Singapore as a token force, without adequate escorts or air support—were sunk on Dec. 10, 1941, by Japanese torpedo-carrying planes before they had an opportunity to give any account of themselves. With no hope of predictable reinforcement from the United States Pacific fleet, the small U.S. Asiatic fleet (commanded by Adm. Thomas C. Hart, consisting of 3 cruisers, 13 overage destroyers, 29 submarines, 2 squadrons of patrol planes and a few gunboats and auxiliaries, operating in conjunction with equally slender British and Dutch forces) was all that was available to stem the Japanese tide. At the outbreak of war Admiral Hart's forces in the Philippines were already skilfully deployed in anticipation of a possible attack, which soon came. On Dec. 10 the navy yard at Cavite was practically wiped out by Japanese bombing, and the Asiatic fleet (save for units which remained to assist in support of the army's positions on Bataan and Corregidor) moved south to the Netherlands Indies. On Jan. 3, 1942, Gen. Sir Archibald P. Wavell of the British army assumed supreme command of the Australian, British, Dutch and U.S. forces in the theatre, and Admiral Hart became commander of the Allied naval forces.

During the next few months, the Japanese advanced rapidly in many directions by overcoming the inferior Allied air opposition at a given point of attack and then sending heavily screened amphibious forces to make landings. As soon as they were in control of a new area, they would repair the airfields and move on to still another. With totally inadequate air support, the Allied naval forces could only attempt to delay the Japanese advance by breaking up landing operations wherever possible. In the battle of Macassar strait, early in the morning of Jan. 24, 1942, and in Madura strait on Feb. 4, naval attempts were made to disrupt Japanese invasion forces. Though one drive might be impeded by one of these gallant delaying actions, others would go forward almost simultaneously, and by mid-February the Japanese were in a position to advance on Java. At this point, in accordance with previously made international agreements, the command of the Allied defensive was assumed by Netherlands officers, and Admiral Hart relinquished operational command of the Allied naval forces to Vice-Adm. C. E. L. Helfrich of the royal Netherlands navy. Attempts to halt the Japanese invasion of Java were made in Bandung strait on the night of Feb. 19–20 and in the battle of the Java sea on Feb. 27. Allied losses were heavy, and on Feb. 28 the

Japanese landed on the north coast of Java. As no suitable base for naval surface forces remained, the Allied naval command was dissolved, and the surviving U.S. naval vessels proceeded to Australia.

In the course of March 1942 Java was occupied, and the Japanese continued their plan of conquest in directions as widely separated as Burma and New Guinea. A British fleet including old battleships and aircraft carriers under command of Adm. Sir James Somerville had been assembled in the Indian ocean to prevent the westward spread of the Japanese offensive. This force suffered the loss of the cruisers "Dorsetshire" and "Cornwall" in the Japanese attack on Colombo, Ceylon, on March 28, and of the aircraft carrier "Hermes" and other smaller vessels in a Japanese raid on Trincomalee, Ceylon, on April 9. The possibility that the Japanese would follow up this successful offensive in the Indian ocean by threats farther west emphasized the strategic importance of Madagascar, which was in Vichy-French possession. Consequently, to forestall any Japanese aspirations in that direction, a British force, under command of Rear Adm. E. Syfret, successfully occupied the main base at Diego Suarez at the northern end of Madagascar on May 5–7. However, the April raid on Trincomalee proved to be the last blow struck by the Japanese in the Indian ocean; and it was to the eastward in the Pacific, where the United States navy was gathering its strength, that the war at sea was to be decided.

No United States aircraft carriers had been at Pearl Harbor during the Dec. 7 attack, and so Adm. Chester W. Nimitz, who had become commander in chief, United States Pacific fleet, late in Dec. 1941, was able to use these ships in the first offensive strikes of the Pacific war, while the situation was still going from bad to worse in the far east. A force consisting of the carriers "Enterprise" and "Yorktown," cruisers and destroyers, under the command of Vice-Adm. William F. Halsey, Jr., struck various points in the Marshall and Gilbert Islands beginning Feb. 1, 1942, with such success that several similar raids were conducted during the following weeks on Wake Island, Marcus Island and the New Guinea ports of Salamaua and Lae, where Japanese troops were landing in early March. On April 18 United States army bombers, which took off from the carrier "Hornet," struck Tokyo.

By the middle of April 1942 the Japanese had extended their conquests into New Guinea, New Britain and the Solomon Islands and had attained a position from which they could threaten the whole of Melanesia as well as the continent of Australia; they were moving their forces in anticipation of an offensive to the southeast that would threaten the lines of sea communication between the west coast of the United States and Australia and New Zealand. To protect these lines of communication, advance bases were being developed in the Fijis and New Caledonia to serve as fuel and troop staging stations, and consequently any Japanese movements in that direction were anxiously watched.

2. Battle of the Coral Sea.—Thus, when the Japanese began to occupy Florida Island in the Solomons on May 3, 1942, Rear Adm. Frank Jack Fletcher, who was cruising in the Coral sea with a force consisting of the carrier "Yorktown," cruisers and destroyers, undertook to hinder them. Planes from "Yorktown" on May 4 sank and damaged various Japanese vessels at Tulagi, and on the following day Fletcher's force joined other United States and Australian units, including the carrier "Lexington." The concentration of Japanese forces in the Bismarck archipelago—New Guinea area indicated that an amphibious operation, possibly against Port Moresby, New Guinea, was in prospect. Consequently, Rear Admiral Fletcher placed part of his force within striking distance of the probable course of the invasion fleet and moved his remaining ships northward in search of the Japanese covering forces. On the morning of May 7 aircraft from the "Lexington" and "Yorktown" located and sank the Japanese carrier "Shoho." The carrier "Shokaku" was attacked and damaged to such an extent that it could not be used, as planned, in the forthcoming operation against Midway. In a counterattack by Japanese carrier planes, both the "Lexington" and "Yorktown" were damaged, and it later became necessary to abandon the "Lexington" and have it sunk by one of the United States destroyers.

The battle of the Coral sea, from which the Japanese forces withdrew with heavy losses, was the first major check that Japan had received in an otherwise successful campaign of aggression. It was, moreover, the first major naval engagement in history between aircraft of opposing fleets, with no contact between the surface vessels of the fleets. Thus ended the period in which the United States navy was entirely upon the defensive in the Pacific, save for the operations of its submarines, which from the very beginning brought the war to regions that the Japanese thought they controlled. Although entirely unpublicized, for reasons of operational security, the activities of these submarines reduced the Japanese supply of fuel from the East Indies and decimated their shipping. Postwar interrogations of Admirals Osami Nagano and Soemu Toyoda, successively chiefs of the Japanese naval general staff, indicated that during the first half of the war U.S. submarines caused the greatest difficulty, just as naval aviation did in later years. (*See* SUBMARINE WARFARE.)

3. Battle of Midway.—During the lull which followed the battle of the Coral sea, it was correctly assumed that the Japanese were preparing for a large-scale operation somewhere, and the best evidence seemed to indicate that they would strike in the central or northern Pacific or both. In consequence the carriers and supporting vessels that had been operating in the South Pacific were recalled, and the ships available—carriers "Enterprise," "Hornet" and "Yorktown," 8 cruisers, 14 destroyers and about 20 submarines—were organized into task forces commanded by Rear Adm. Raymond A. Spruance and Rear Admiral Fletcher. A marine corps air group based on Midway Island and army bombers from Hawaii were made ready for active operations.

Scouting and patrol lines, which had been established to the westward of Midway, sighted a large Japanese attack force on the morning of June 3 which was bombed later in the day by a squadron of army B-17's. On the following day Japanese aircraft bombed Midway, while army, navy and marine corps planes from Midway attacked the Japanese fleet. Planes from the "Hornet," "Enterprise" and "Yorktown" attacked a force of four Japanese carriers with telling results, though planes from a Japanese carrier inflicted damage on the "Yorktown." Throughout June 5 and 6, army and navy aircraft, which had now won control of the air, pursued and attacked the fleeing Japanese. Although the damaged "Yorktown" and the destroyer "Hammann," which was aiding it, were fatally torpedoed by a submarine on June 6, the score was heavily against the Japanese, for United States carrier planes sank the carriers "Akagi," "Hiryu" and "Kaga" and the heavy cruiser "Mikuma," while the carrier "Soryu," which was damaged by carrier planes, was later sunk by the submarine "Nautilus." These losses, plus damage to other ships, were the first serious setback to the Japanese fleet since the outbreak of the war.

4. Solomon Islands Campaign.—The landing of the U.S. 1st marine division, reinforced, on Guadalcanal and Tulagi Islands in the Solomons on Aug. 7, 1942, marked the first Allied offensive move in force in the Pacific war. In this so-called offensive-defensive phase of the war, United States forces had seized the initiative, though progress was slow since they were still obliged to use a large part of their efforts to defend recent gains. Just before the battle of the Coral sea in early May the Japanese were occupying Tulagi Island in the Solomons, and in July they began the construction of an airfield on Guadalcanal, from which land-based planes could have endangered Allied control of the New Hebrides and New Caledonia. This penetration toward Allied lines of communication to Australia and New Zealand represented a peril that had to be stopped at all costs, and prompt steps were taken to eject the Japanese from that area.

This operation, under the command of Vice-Adm. R. L. Ghormley, involved moving the marines, under Maj. Gen. A. A. Vandergrift, from New Zealand, with naval surface and air support. The landings on Aug. 7 took the Japanese by surprise, and good progress was made in the early stages. Later the Japanese reacted strongly, and for many months there followed intense ground fighting, with frequent actions at sea between the fleets that were endeavouring to reinforce and support the opposing land forces. An initial reverse occurred in the battle of Savo Island in the early hours of Aug. 9, when Japanese cruisers and destroyers attacked Allied naval forces protecting the landings, and sank the cruisers "Quincy," "Vincennes," "Astoria" and "Canberra." After this action the U.S. positions were under frequent attack from air and sea, but the marines held their ground, and in a battle beginning on Aug. 20 were successful in repelling counterattacking Japanese troops. In anticipation of a further Japanese reinforcement, Vice-Admiral Ghormley concentrated southeast of Guadalcanal two task forces, which included the carriers "Saratoga" and "Enterprise," the battleship "North Carolina," cruisers and destroyers. On Aug. 24 contact was made with a powerful Japanese force, and the battle of the eastern Solomons ensued, during which planes from the "Saratoga" sank the Japanese carrier "Ryujo." Marine and army land-based planes joined in, and the Japanese, after the loss of carrier support, broke off the action, although not before inflicting damage on the "Enterprise."

Pacific fleet carrier U.S.S. "Yorktown" after a direct hit from Japanese planes which braved a barrage of anti-aircraft fire during the battle of Midway, June 3–6, 1942. Despite the U.S. loss of two carriers, the Japanese suffered their first naval setback of World War II

During the next six weeks, no major action took place in the Solomons, although Japanese planes and submarines, which were harassing U.S. supply lines, were responsible for the loss of the carrier "Wasp" and several destroyers. The Japanese also succeeded in reinforcing their positions on Guadalcanal by almost nightly runs of the so-called "Tokyo express." On the night of Oct. 11–12 United States cruisers and destroyers, in a surprise attack, engaged a sizable force in the battle of Cape Esperance, near Guadalcanal, but the Japanese showed no signs of discontinuing their efforts to launch a full-scale attack. A fortnight later, on Oct. 26, while Japanese troops were actively attacking the marine positions on Guadalcanal, the carriers "Hornet" and "Enterprise" exchanged blows with carriers operating with a powerful naval force moving to support land operations on Guadalcanal. In this action, known as the battle of Santa Cruz Island, although damage was done to Japanese carriers, the United States carrier "Hornet" was lost.

The climax of sea fighting in the Solomons came in the battle of Guadalcanal, Nov. 13–15, 1942, when the Japanese, having concentrated an invasion force at Rabaul, were met by United States naval forces (covering reinforcements for troops on Guadalcanal) and defeated in a series of violent engagements which caused heavy losses on both sides. On Nov. 11 and 12, two contingents of reinforcements and supplies were landed at Guadalcanal. When strong Japanese forces were located approaching Guadalcanal from the northwest, a force of cruisers and destroyers under the command of Rear Adm. D. J. Callaghan (who was, with Rear Adm. Norman Scott, killed in the ensuing action) was assigned to fight a delaying action to cover the withdrawal of the transports and cargo vessels. Shortly after midnight on the morning of Nov. 13 the opposing forces met in a surface engagement of great violence. During the 24 min. that it lasted, gunfire was exchanged at close range, and though the Japanese battleship "Hiyei" was lost in consequence of this action, so were the United States cruisers "Atlanta" and "Juneau," as well as several destroyers.

On the morning of Nov. 14 Japanese cruisers and destroyers shelled Henderson field on Guadalcanal, and an invasion force, preceded by an escort of battleships, cruisers and destroyers, was discovered to the north of the island. This was subjected to air attack throughout the day, and on the evening of Nov. 14 the battleships "Washington" and "South Dakota" and the carrier "Enterprise" reached the scene of the action. Shortly after midnight, contact was made north of Savo Island, and in another fierce night action, which resulted in the loss of the Japanese battleship "Kirishima" and three United States destroyers, the Japanese were turned back. Although United States losses were heavy, the battle of Guadalcanal was decisive in that U.S. positions in the southern Solomons were never again seriously threatened. After this action, United States forces on Guadalcanal retained the offensive, gradually driving the Japanese westward.

On Nov. 30 a Japanese effort at reinforcement was broken up by the battle of Tassafaronga (Lunga point), although at the cost of the loss of the cruiser "Northampton." Through December and January the Japanese ground forces found themselves in an increasingly unfavourable position, as U.S. troops were reinforced, and the 1st marine division was gradually replaced by fresh army forces. However, in anticipation of another Japanese effort to retake the island, Admiral Halsey (who had replaced Vice Admiral Ghormley as commander, South Pacific force, on Oct. 18) maintained considerably augmented naval forces in adjacent waters. On Jan. 29, 1943, the heavy cruiser "Chicago," escorting a convoy from New Caledonia to Guadalcanal, was torpedoed and sunk; but no further major action developed in the southern Solomons since on the night of Feb. 7–8, 1943, exactly six months after the initial U.S. landings, the Japanese withdrew their remaining forces from Guadalcanal. So ended the first Allied offensive campaign of the Pacific war.

5. Defensive War in the Atlantic.—When the year 1942 opened, the Allied navies were fighting a defensive war in the Atlantic, as they were in the Pacific. The Germans, who had been unable in their years of rearmament to build up a powerful and balanced fleet, had concentrated upon submarine construction and counted upon this underseas force to cut the sea routes to Great Britain. The German U-boat campaign followed the submarine strategy of World War I, which had been so nearly successful in isolating the British Isles. As the basic Allied strategy of the war called for the defeat first of Germany and then of Japan, it was essential that the control of Atlantic sea lanes be maintained to ensure the safe passage to Great Britain of U.S. troops and supplies. The shipment of supplies to Russia could be accomplished only through the northern ports of Murmansk or Archangel and required naval protection against German forces based in Norway, while the royal navy had heavy commitments to maintain the vital supply line to the Mediterranean.

Germany was able to operate a large number of submarines in the Atlantic, and sustained attacks on German shipyards by the British bomber command did not appear materially to have reduced production. In the winter and spring of 1942 submarine attacks were extended westward to the Atlantic coast of the United States and continually reduced the available total of Allied tonnage throughout the rest of the year. At that point increased Allied forces, improved antisubmarine measures and the growing production of U.S. and British shipyards turned the tables, and from 1943 onward new construction of merchant ships far outweighed the tonnage sunk by German submarines.

The battle of the Atlantic was a war of wits and of scientific devices, in which new measures and countermeasures were constantly evolved by the opposing navies, but upon its success depended the outcome of the military operations that eventually led to the defeat of Germany. Its pattern throughout the entire war may most clearly be seen in the following statistical table included in Adm. Ernest J. King's third report to the secretary of the navy:

Year	German submarines Sunk	Allied shipping sunk	New construction U.S.	British	Total	Net gains or losses
	(Number)		(In thousands of tons)			
1939 (4 months)	9	810	101	231	332	−478
1940	22	4,407	439	780	1,219	−3,188
1941	35	4,398	1,169	815	1,984	−2,414
1942	85	8,245	5,339	1,843	7,182	−1,063
1943	237	3,611	12,384	2,201	14,585	+10,974
1944	241	1,422	11,639	1,710	13,349	+11,927
1945 (4 months)	153	458	3,551	283	3,834	+3,376
Totals	782	23,351	34,622	7,863	42,485	+19,134

Although the major German naval effort was devoted to submarine warfare, German shore-based aircraft were a menace to shipping, and a small number of powerful surface ships had to be taken into account. On Feb. 12, 1942, the German battleships "Scharnhorst" and Gneisenau" and the cruiser "Prinz Eugen" made a successful dash from Brest, France, through the English channel to German waters, despite gallant attacks by British destroyers and Swordfish aircraft. The new battleship "Tirpitz," based in Norway, with cruisers, destroyers, submarines and aircraft, constituted a continuing menace to Allied north Russian convoys, which ran a gauntlet on every voyage requiring a strong covering force. The protection of these convoys was the main task of the British home fleet, which was from time to time augmented by U.S. heavy ships. Particularly vicious attacks were made upon these north Russian convoys in July and Sept. 1942, and during the last quarter of 1942 they were discontinued because of the requirements of shipping and escorts elsewhere. When they were resumed in December the Germans were on the alert, and on Dec. 31, 1942, a convoy was attacked by the German pocket battleship "Lutzow," the cruiser "Hipper" and six destroyers. In a series of short, sharp engagements, these forces were held off for four hours by six British destroyers commanded by Capt. Robert Sherbrooke, and eventually were driven out of the area by two 6-in.-gun cruisers of Rear Adm. Sir R. Burnett's covering force.

In Sept. 1943, royal navy volunteers manning midget submarines entered Aalten fjord, Norway, and torpedoed the "Tirpitz," putting it out of action for six months; on April 3, 1944, when repairs were advancing, fighters and bombers of the naval air arm operating from carriers attacked the battleship again and mauled it severely, thus neutralizing one of the potential threats to the north Russian convoys. The "Tirpitz" was attacked three times in July and Aug. 1944 by carrier planes and finally sunk on Nov. 12, 1944, by royal air force bombers.

The most dramatic action of the royal navy in arctic waters occurred on Dec. 26, 1943, when the German battleship "Scharnhorst" attempted to molest a convoy. Adm. Sir Bruce Fraser was at sea with the battleship "Duke of York" and other ships, providing distant cover for a convoy escorted by four cruisers under Rear Admiral Burnett. The "Scharnhorst" was sighted when the convoy was to the southeast of Bear Island, and was shadowed by the British cruisers, while the "Duke of York" moved up from the southwest at high speed to intercept. The British battleship obtained a hit at long range, and the "Scharnhorst" was prevented from escaping by destroyers which delivered a torpedo attack that reduced its speed enough to allow the "Duke of York" to close the range and renew the battle. In a short time the German battleship had been set on fire and almost stopped, and it was then sunk, 60 mi. northeast of North Cape, by a torpedo fired by the cruiser "Jamaica."

Throughout 1942, while the German navy was impeding the progress of north Russian convoys in Norwegian waters, the Italian navy constituted a potential threat to supplies and reinforcements in the Mediterranean. The fluctuations of the land fighting in the North African campaign emphasized the vital importance of a naval base in the central Mediterranean and the necessity of maintaining Malta at all costs. A Malta convoy got through in Jan. 1942, but the February convoy was driven back. On March 22, 1942, Vice-Adm. Sir Philip Vian, with inferior forces, outwitted and repelled a larger Italian naval force. The convoy that he was covering, though subsequently attacked by German aircraft, got through to Malta. In the spring Spitfires were flown in to the island from carriers that penetrated the Mediterranean, the United States carrier "Wasp" taking part in these operations with the royal navy. In June an attempt was made to relieve Malta simultaneously from the west and from Gibraltar, and in August a heavily escorted convoy was sent from England. Although these attempts involved heavy fighting and losses and were only partially successful, some ships got through, and by September the situation at Malta had improved. The Italian navy at no time made adequate use of its extensive resources, and until its surrender in the autumn of 1943 remained in the character of a potential threat rather than a true adversary of the numerically inferior British Mediterranean naval forces.

During the defensive period of 1942, two operations of very limited scope against the continent of Europe were attempted. On March 27–28 an attack was made upon the French port of St. Nazaire to put the graving docks there out of action; the British destroyer "Campbeltown," loaded with high explosives, rammed the lock gates and scuttled itself. On Aug. 19 a commando raid upon Dieppe was carried out, with very heavy casualties. Though continuous fighter cover was maintained by the royal air force, this raid indicated the necessity of being able to support landings of troops by naval gunfire.

6. Amphibious Assaults upon North Africa and Europe. —World War II was characterized by a series of successful amphibious operations of unparalleled magnitude, which were made necessary by the geographical extension of axis aggression on both sides of the world. In the Pacific, the Japanese could be reached only by crossing thousands of miles of ocean. In Europe, the rapid successes of German arms in 1940 had driven the Allies from the continent and had penetrated Africa. There also, Allied ground troops could come to grips with the axis only after transportation over water and landings on hostile shores. Amphibious landings required the most complicated planning and co-ordination between the various branches of the armed forces of the United States and Great Britain.

(*a*) *North Africa.* The combined chiefs of staff decided in July 1942 to effect landings in force in French North Africa in the autumn of that year, and to postpone the assault upon the continent of Europe until a later date. Lieut. Gen. Dwight D. Eisenhower was appointed commander in chief of the Allied force, with Adm. Sir Andrew Browne Cunningham as his principal naval subordinate. Three points were to be attacked: Oran and Algiers by U.S. army troops supported by British naval forces, and Casablanca by U.S. troops under Maj. Gen. George S. Patton, Jr., supported by naval forces commanded by Rear Adm. H. Kent Hewitt, who commanded United States naval units in all subsequent amphibious operations in the Mediterranean. The Oran and Algiers forces proceeded from the British Isles, but the Casablanca force came entirely from United States ports and crossed the Atlantic without untoward incident. Landings were made early in the morning of Nov. 8, and though there was resistance ashore and a naval action off Casablanca with French ships, good progress had been made before an armistice was negotiated with the French forces on Nov. 11. By this operation, the largest overseas expedition ever dispatched to that time, the axis was denied the use of northwest Africa, and ports and bases had been secured which were essential for the control of the Mediterranean and subsequent entry into Europe.

(*b*) *Sicily and Italy.*—Within six months after the North African landings, German forces had been driven from Tunisia, and Allied strength was augmented to a point that made it possible to plan for a movement across the Mediterranean into axis territory. During May and June naval forces were assembled at Algerian and Tunisian ports for the invasion of Sicily. The specially designed landing craft, which allowed the landing of troops and tanks directly upon assault beaches, had just begun to emerge from U.S. and British shipyards and were used for the first time in large numbers in the Sicilian operation. The larger types of these craft were capable alike of crossing the ocean under their own power and beaching themselves in shallow water for the discharge of their loads by means of ramps. The development of these highly specialized vessels contributed immeasurably to the amphibious successes of the war.

Landings took place on July 10, the United States forces having objectives at Scoglitti, Gela and Licata, on the south coast of Sicily, while British forces attacked beaches

Cargo ship laden with supplies for U.S. troops ashore at Anzio after the invasion of Jan. 1944. The vessel lay at anchor, guarded from sea or air attack by amphibious craft (foreground) and a barrage balloon overhead

on the southeastern coast. Naval gunfire was extensively used before the landings; and for several weeks afterward, as troops were pushing across the island toward Messina, cruisers and destroyers assisted them by bombarding axis positions.

Messina was occupied on Aug. 17; with Sicily under control, immediate invasion of the Italian mainland was planned. British forces began crossing the Straits of Messina, and to assist them in their advance up the Italian peninsula, amphibious landings were made in the Bay of Salerno on Sept. 9. In spite of counterattacks, some of which naval fire succeeded in breaking up, the port of Salerno was captured on Sept. 10, and on Oct. 1 Allied troops entered Naples.

After the Italian surrender, the greater part of Italy's fleet sailed to Malta to surrender, arriving on Sept. 11. Thus ended the astonishing and ignominious career of a powerful navy, which gave no useful account of itself in the day of battle. The Mediterranean was free once more of axis surface vessels, though German aircraft were still to be reckoned with.

There were no further amphibious operations against the Italian peninsula on the scale of the Sicilian and Salerno landings, although on Jan. 22, 1944, a joint force landed at Anzio, south of Rome, and established a beachhead behind the German lines. Resistance and counterattacks were so severe that it required great effort to support the troops at this point.

(*c*) *The Normandy Landings.*—In Jan. 1944 General Eisenhower arrived in Britain from the Mediterranean and assumed the duties of supreme commander, Allied expeditionary force. His principal naval subordinate in the planning for the cross-channel invasion of France was Adm. Sir Bertram H. Ramsay, designated as Allied naval commander in chief. The site chosen for the attack was the Baie de la Seine in Normandy, near the ports of England and within easy range of fighter-plane bases; but, since there was no adequate harbour for a quick build-up after the initial assault, it was necessary to devise artificial harbours which could be quickly constructed once the beachhead was secured. This involved a naval problem of great magnitude. Added to the large numbers of ships and craft needed to move the troops and their supplies were those necessary to tow the hollow concrete caissons that had been secretly built in England for sinking at designated points to establish breakwaters. The scale of the operation was indicated by the fact that 5,000 ships and about 200,000 officers and men of the Allied navies and merchant fleets were involved. After the first landing about 2,000 merchant ships (totalling 4,000,000 tons) were continually employed in supplying the armies.

The beaches on the western half of the Baie de la Seine were assigned to United States troops, landed from U.S. vessels, while the eastern half of the area was taken by British and Canadian troops, transported chiefly in British vessels. Loading of troops began on June 1, 1944, and by June 3 all had been loaded and briefed. D day had been initially set for June 5, but because of unfavourable weather was postponed 24 hr. This great armada, setting sail from various ports in the British Isles upon an intricately timed and involved schedule, was preceded by great numbers of mine sweepers, clearing the channels, and by about 80 fire support vessels—battleships, cruisers and destroyers—which brought 800 guns, ranging in calibre from 4-in. to 16-in., to batter shore defenses and cover the landing of the troops. On June 6 the initial landings took place, substantially according to schedule, closely followed by the build-up convoys of transports and cargo ships. On June 7 all the elements of the artificial harbours, or "Mulberries" as they were called in code, had been towed from England, and the work of installation began.

For many days after the landings, while the Allied troops were still within range of ships' guns, the battleships, cruisers and destroyers furnished highly useful fire support, and on June 25 Cherbourg was bombarded to assist the army forces that were advancing on the port from the land side. Cherbourg fell on June 27, and naval salvage forces began clearing the port, as they subsequently did at Le Havre when that city surrendered on Sept. 12. The build-up following the invasion proceeded so rapidly that 100 days after the initial landings more than 2,000,000 men, nearly 500,000 vehicles and 4,000,000 tons of stores had been landed in France; and the Allied armies were far advanced in their drive across France to Germany.

(*d*) *Southern France.*—Landings on the south coast of France were also involved in the plan for the penetration of the continent, and consequently the fire support ships and landing craft of the Normandy invasion were deployed to the Mediterranean as soon as they could be spared from the English channel operations. On Aug. 15 United States and French troops were put ashore on beaches near St. Tropez, Fréjus and St. Raphael, on the southern coast of France in the area between Toulon and Nice. These operations, of which the naval commander was Vice-Admiral Hewitt, were successful in establishing a firm beachhead. With strong air support, the army pressed rapidly inland up the Rhône valley and eventually effected a junction with troops from the Normandy beachhead. By the end of August Toulon and Marseille had surrendered, and by the end of September the last beaches were closed and the amphibious phase of the campaign had ended.

With no further large-scale amphibious operations in prospect in the area, ships left the Mediterranean as rapidly as possible for further service in the Pacific. Though naval forces assisted in the crossing of the Rhine river in March 1945, and in various coastal operations in France and Germany, the war in Europe passed into the hands of the Allied air and ground forces. The United States navy was free to concentrate its attentions upon the Japanese, while the royal navy prepared to send a force to the Pacific to assist in operations there.

7. Offensive-Defensive in the Pacific.—Although the landings in the Solomon Islands in Aug. 1942 had wrested the initiative from Japan, progress in the Pacific was necessarily slow for more than a year thereafter. When the Japanese evacuated Guadalcanal on Feb. 8, 1943, it remained to eject them from the northern Solomons, and then (as it seemed at that time) from an almost endless chain of island positions. The Japanese had held some of the latter since World War I and had fortified them in defiance of mandate agreements.

Throughout the spring of 1943 naval forces bombarded Japanese positions in the central Solomons, while the Japanese still continued air attacks upon Guadalcanal. On June 30 amphibious landings were made on Woodlark and Trobriand Islands (between the Solomons and New Guinea), at Nassau bay on New Guinea and at Rendova harbour and Viru harbour in the central Solomons. On July 2 and 3 landings were made on New Georgia and at Vangunu Island near by. This movement to the northward soon brought contact between United States naval forces and the "Tokyo expresses" that were making nightly runs to supply and reinforce Japanese positions in the central Solomons. The battle of Kula gulf on July 6 and the battle of Kolombangara (also called second battle of Kula gulf) on July 12–13 discouraged interference with U.S. operations on New Georgia and prevented the Japanese from using Kula gulf as a route for supply runs. The former action, however, resulted in the loss of the cruiser "Helena," and the latter in the loss of the destroyer "Gwin" and damage to other ships.

The capture of Munda airfield on Aug. 5, six weeks after the invasion of New Georgia, marked the climax of the central Solomons campaign, which ended with the Japanese evacuation of Kolombangara and Vella Lavella Islands on Oct. 6.

8. The Pacific Offensive.—In the autumn of 1943, United States strength in the Pacific had reached a point where it was possible for the army and navy to attack at points of their own choosing. Allied strategy called for an advance upon the core of the Japanese positions from two different directions, which, reduced to the simplest terms, consisted of a movement northward from Australia by forces under the command of Gen. Douglas MacArthur, and a thrust westward across the central Pacific from the Hawaiian Islands by forces under the command of Admiral Nimitz. During the next year these two great advances from different points in the Pacific rapidly converged, finally closing in a gigantic pincer movement upon the Philippine Islands in Oct. 1944. From that point onward, there was but a single route to Tokyo.

Both routes involved a constant succession of amphibious landings, though in the move northward from Australia the large land masses of New Guinea entailed a greater amount of ground fighting than in the central Pacific, where the distances were greater and the island groups of diminutive size. The central Pacific campaign consequently offered more points of naval interest, for it was there that the technique of the fast carrier striking forces was evolved.

In Oct. 1942 United States carrier strength was at its lowest point; four of the seven U.S. aircraft carriers in commission at the outbreak of war had been lost in the Pacific. New and more powerful types were, however, under construction in large quantities, and by the late summer of 1943 a sufficient number had joined the fleet to make large-scale offensive operations possible. Since the battle of Midway in June 1942 there had been no naval operations of importance in the central Pacific. At the time of Midway, the Japanese, in a thrust into the north Pacific, had occupied Kiska and Attu in the Aleutians; but Attu had been recaptured by United States forces in May 1943 and Kiska was reoccupied in Aug. 1943 after its evacuation by the Japanese. The North Pacific was therefore no longer a threat, but in the central Pacific the Japanese were thoroughly established in the Marshall, Gilbert, Caroline, Palau and Marianas Islands. The great distances between groups of islands required the development of a special technique for attack. The new carriers, accompanied by fast battleships and cruisers, were formed into mobile striking forces that were able to travel far afield, deliver a powerful attack from the air, or by naval gunfire, and give a good account of themselves with any Japanese ships that might be encountered.

(*a*) *Gilbert and Marshall Islands.*—In Aug., Sept. and

Advance units of the U.S. marine corps wading across a reef on the shore of Tarawa during the invasion of Nov. 1943

Oct. 1943 the first large-scale carrier-based air strikes were made against Marcus Island, Tarawa in the Gilbert group, Apamama and Wake Island. Following in rapid succession, they were designed to soften Japanese installations and to confuse the Japanese as to U.S. intentions. During October and November major units of the Pacific fleet were placed under the command of Vice-Adm. Raymond A. Spruance, who was designated commander, central Pacific force (later commander, 5th fleet); and plans were made for an amphibious assault upon the Gilbert Islands. This group of coral islands, lying athwart the equator, which had been seized by the Japanese from the British in Dec. 1941, was of great strategic importance since it lay to the north and west of Allied bases in the South Pacific and to the south and east of Japanese bases in the Caroline and Marshall Islands. During the second week in November, the central Pacific force headed west from the Hawaiian Islands and on Nov. 20, 1943, attack groups were off Tarawa and Makin Islands in the Gilberts. After heavy shore bombardment, army units were put ashore on Makin and marines on Tarawa. The fighting on Tarawa was particularly severe and casualties were heavy, but after four days the island was captured. The capture of Makin was announced on Nov. 22. Upon completion of the assault phase of the operation, the naval covering forces withdrew to their bases, en route to which carrier task groups attacked Kwajalein and Wotje atolls in the Marshall Islands, where future landings were projected. During the remainder of the year army and navy land-based planes continued to attack positions in the Marshalls.

On Jan. 29, 1944, Admiral Spruance's forces began the most intensive offensive operations yet conducted against the Marshall Islands. Carrier planes simultaneously struck Kwajalein, Roi, Taroa and Wotje, while cruisers bombarded Taroa and Wotje, and shore-based aircraft bombed all four islands as well as Mille and Jaluit. The attacks were resumed the next day, with battleship bombardment of Kawajalein and Roi in addition. On Jan. 31 an unopposed landing was made on Majuro, and on Feb. 2 landings were made on Roi, Namur and Kawajalein. Resistance on Roi and Namur was quickly overcome; although it was stiffer on Kawajalein, that entire atoll was secured by Feb. 8.

It was now possible for Admiral Spruance's forces to venture further with impunity. His fast carriers, battleships, cruisers and destroyers on Feb. 17–18 carried out an attack upon the Japanese base at Truk, far to the westward in the heart of the Caroline Islands. Similar strikes against the western Carolines were made at the end of March, when carrier-based planes attacked shipping in the Palau group on March 30 and 31, while others attacked Yap and Ulithi. In April these forces were in New Guinea waters, in support of General MacArthur's assault upon Hollandia. For an understanding of the significance of this operation, it is necessary to leave the central Pacific temporarily, and turn back to the beginning of accelerated operations in the South and Southwest Pacific.

(*b*) *New Guinea.*—While forces of the South Pacific area were attacking the central Solomons in the summer of 1943, General MacArthur's troops in the Southwest Pacific were launching powerful attacks in New Guinea to the westward. Landings had taken place at Nassau bay on June 30. Early in September amphibious forces moved against the Huon gulf area. On Sept. 11 Salamaua was captured, and Lae fell five days afterward. Finschhafen was captured on Oct. 2.

With the conclusion of the central Solomons campaign, South Pacific forces continued the northward advance through the Solomons in order to protect the eastern flank of the Allied troops in New Guinea and to aid in the ultimate isolation of the Japanese stronghold in the Rabaul-Kavieng area. At the end of October, United States marines landed at Empress Augusta bay, on the west coast of Bougainville, and so established a position in the northern Solomons. The intention there was not so much to eject the Japanese from Bougainville as to gain a perimeter in which air facilities could be established for attacking the port of Rabaul, which had until that time been in a key position to control the area to the south. On Nov. 5, and again in the following week, carrier forces of the Pacific fleet attacked Rabaul, and during the last ten days of December it was struck by land-based planes operating from bases in the Solomons. Carrier strikes were made against Kavieng, another important base on the northern tip of New Ireland, on Dec. 25 and 28, 1943, and Jan. 1, 1944.

Amphibious landings were made on the western end of New Britain Island at Arawe on Dec. 15 and at Cape Gloucester on Dec. 26, while on Jan. 2 an unopposed landing was made at Saidor on the New Guinea coast. On Feb. 13, 1944, the final occupation of the Huon peninsula in northeast New Guinea was completed by United States and Australian troops. Thus, from the Solomons (to the eastward) and from New Guinea (to the westward) Allied pincers were closing upon Rabaul. Although not directly assaulted and captured, its usefulness was neutralized, and it no longer represented a major threat to Allied progress along the northern coast of New Guinea. Landings were made on Green Island, 120 mi. from Rabaul, on Feb. 15, on the Admiralty Islands on Feb. 29 and on Emirau (in the St. Matthias group north of New Britain) on March 20. The capture of the Admiralty Islands, which established Allied forces in a position to interfere with Japanese supply lines to the Bismarck archipelago from the north, isolated large numbers of troops in the region.

This same leapfrog strategy was pursued with telling effect by General MacArthur in a series of amphibious landings which carried his troops westward along the northern coast of New Guinea. In accordance with it, the next major bypassing move was directed at the coastal area in the vicinity of Aitape and Hollandia, about 200 mi. beyond Wewak, where the Japanese had concentrated a considerable force. The assault on Hollandia involved three separate attacks; one at Tanahmerah bay and a second at Humboldt bay (30 mi. to the eastward) secured the Hollandia airstrips, while a third at Aitape (90 mi. to the eastward) won another airfield. On April 21 the Pacific fleet carriers that were supporting the operation attacked the area, which had previously been bombed for some days by land-based aircraft. The actual landings, which took place on April 22, were virtually unopposed. By this operation approximately 50,000 Japanese troops were cut off, and airfields indispensable for future progress were obtained.

Returning north from the support of the Hollandia landings, the fast carrier task force attacked Truk again on April 29 and 30, carrier planes dropping 740 tons of bombs on land installations. Similarly, cruisers and destroyers of the force bombarded Satawan Island on April 30, while battleships and destroyers bombarded Ponape on May 1. The task force then returned to the central Pacific, in anticipation of impending operations against the Marianas Islands, for which preparations had begun as soon as bases in the Marshall Islands were secured.

Rescue workers aboard a cruiser directing streams of water at the light carrier U.S.S. "Princeton," hit by Japanese bombs during the battle of Leyte gulf in Oct. 1944, and later sunk

(*c*) *The Marianas; Battle of the Philippine Sea.*—The Marianas Islands provided the Japanese with a series of highly useful airfields and bases that afforded protected lines of air and sea communication to distant possessions. Allied occupation of the group would not only hamper Japanese communications, but provide United States forces with bases from which aircraft could bomb Tokyo; also, the sea areas farther to the west could be controlled. The operation for the capture of the Marianas, which involved more than 600 ships, 2,000 aircraft and 300,000 navy, marine and army personnel, was under the command of Admiral Spruance, who had already conducted the Gilberts and Marshalls operations. Japanese air bases on Marcus Island and Wake Island to the northward, which might have threatened the operation, were attacked by carrier planes, cruisers and destroyers during the third week in May 1944. Marcus was struck on May 19 and 20 and Wake on May 23. From the beginning of June, land-based aircraft from the Admiralty Islands and Hollandia kept neighbouring bases at Truk, Palau and Yap under attack, while the fast carrier task force began attacks on the Marianas on June 11. As the island of Saipan had been in Japanese hands since World War I, it was formidably fortified; and an intensive attack was necessary before landings could take place. Surface ships began bombardment on June 13, and early on the morning of June 15 marine and army troops were put ashore. The Japanese resisted vigorously; and, though initial beachheads were established, progress inland was slow.

At this point it became apparent that the Japanese fleet was en route to the Marianas, apparently bent upon provoking a full-scale action. This presented a problem in objectives, for although Admiral Spruance's ships and planes were entirely ready and able to meet the Japanese at sea, his basic mission was to capture the Marianas, and therefore the forces attacking Saipan had to be protected from interference at all costs. In consequence, he operated aggressively to the westward of the Marianas, but did not move so far away from the islands that he could not protect the amphibious forces from any possible attack. While some of the fast battleships and carriers were operating to the westward in anticipation of the arrival of the Japanese fleet, other carriers went north and struck Iwo Jima and Chichi Jima, thus eliminating temporarily the threat of air attack from the Bonin and Volcano Islands. Upon completion of this attack, the carriers rejoined Admiral Spruance's other ships west of Saipan.

On June 19, 1944, the battle of the Philippine sea began in the form of a large-scale attack by Japanese carrier aircraft on Admiral Spruance's fleet. Four hundred Japanese planes were shot down, with only very moderate United States air losses and minor damage to surface vessels, while the Japanese carriers, "Taiho" and "Shokaku" were sunk by United States submarines. Because of these substantial carrier plane losses, further Japanese attacks upon Saipan seemed unlikely; and Admiral Spruance's forces therefore headed to the westward in the hope of intercepting and destroying the Japanese fleet in a decisive engagement. Search planes did not locate the Japanese surface ships until afternoon, and it was nearly sunset by the time carrier strikes were launched. These attacks had to be made at extreme range; nevertheless, they sank the carrier "Hiyo," damaged the carrier "Junyo," sank two fleet tankers and damaged one. Nightfall cut short the attack. Although only a small number of United States planes were lost to Japanese anti-aircraft fire, 73 were lost while returning to their carriers when they ran out of fuel and crash landed in the darkness, although a high percentage of the personnel of planes that landed in the water near their carriers was rescued. The Japanese fleet continued its retirement during the night of June 20, and on June 21 was out of range. Though it had not been destroyed, its effort to reinforce the Marianas had been very thoroughly broken up, and its corps of carrier-plane pilots had been practically eliminated. Japanese naval aviation never entirely recovered from this severe blow. The occupation of the Marianas, in consequence of the battle of the Philippine sea, then proceeded without further threat of naval interference, although the land fighting on Saipan was bitter and protracted. All organized resistance finally ceased on the island on July 9.

Landings on the neighbouring island of Guam (which

had been captured by the Japanese in Dec. 1941) had been scheduled for June but had been postponed because of the unexpectedly intense resistance on Saipan and the threat of the battle of the Philippine sea. Because of the postponement, a long period of preliminary bombardment and air attacks was possible, beginning on June 16. From July 8 until July 21, when U.S. troops landed, battleships, cruisers and destroyers shelled the island daily, while planes from fast and escort carriers, as well as from the newly won fields on Saipan, bombed defense installations. Japanese resistance, although stubborn, was less intense than on Saipan, and on Aug. 10 all organized resistance ended. Guam was rapidly developed as a naval and air base for further offensive operations.

Amphibious operations in the Marianas Islands were completed by the capture of Tinian, an island located across the narrow channel to the south of Saipan. There also there were heavy advance air and surface attacks before the actual landings, which began on July 24. Resistance was less severe there than in the other islands, and in a fortnight the assault and occupation phase was completed.

(*d*) *The Carolines.*—The next major objective in the central Pacific was the western Caroline Islands, the capture of which would complete the isolation of Truk and other Japanese positions in the central and eastern Carolines. This operation was commanded by Admiral Halsey (commander, 3rd fleet) who, having completed the mission in the South Pacific that had begun in Oct. 1942, thereafter alternated with Admiral Spruance in command of the great striking forces of the Pacific fleet. As new ships were constantly joining the fleet, the forces available for the western Carolines operation were even greater than those used in the Marianas; nearly 800 vessels were employed.

Prior to the landings, which were scheduled for Sept. 15, air and surface strikes were made in many directions to divert and eliminate Japanese forces that might have interfered. Attacks were made by the fast carrier task force on the Bonin and Volcano Islands, to the northward, between Aug. 31 and Sept. 2, and on Yap on Sept. 7 and 8. As the plan for a landing on Peleliu Island in the Palau group of the western Carolines by Admiral Halsey's forces was co-ordinated with a simultaneous landing on Morotai Island (between New Guinea and the Philippine Islands) by General MacArthur's forces, who had advanced the length of New Guinea, the fast carrier task force made strikes on Mindanao Island in the southern Philippines on Sept. 9 and 10 to prevent opposition from that direction. Because of the slight resistance encountered at Mindanao, further carrier strikes were made against the Visayas, in the central Philippines, from Sept. 12 to 14, which achieved tactical surprise and inflicted considerable damage on Japanese installations, ships and planes.

Preceded by three days of surface bombardment, air bombing, mine sweeping and clearing of beach obstacles, landings took place on Peleliu Island on Sept. 15, and on Angaur Island, six miles south of Peleliu, on Sept. 17. No landings were made on Babelthuap, the largest of the Palau group, since the bases obtained on Peleliu and Angaur made possible the domination of the group and neutralized Japanese ground forces on the other islands. Progress ashore on Peleliu was slow, and it was the middle of October before the assault phase of the operation was completed, but the island of Angaur was overrun by Sept. 20. An unopposed landing was made on Ulithi atoll on Sept. 23, and steps were immediately taken to develop it as an anchorage for large surface forces.

Simultaneously with the landings on Peleliu, General MacArthur's forces landed on Morotai Island, in a move calculated to isolate Japanese forces on Halmahera Island, which were in a position to impede any movement into the southern Philippines. This operation was the result of a succession of amphibious landings that had been made along the north coast of New Guinea after the capture of Hollandia five months before. The landings, designed to prevent Japanese air and troop movements in New Guinea and to secure the southern flank of the offensive operations to the northward in the central Pacific, were in general not heavily opposed. Consequently, they involved the support of no ships larger than heavy cruisers, unlike the Hollandia operation in April, which had been supported by battleships and carriers of the Pacific fleet. The Wakde Island area, 70 mi. west of Hollandia, was occupied on May 17–19, and on May 27 an amphibious assault was made on Biak Island to secure a forward base for the operation of heavy bombers. On July 2 a landing was made on Noemfoor Island, southwest of Biak, and on July 30 an amphibious force landed in the Cape Sansapor area on the Vogelkop peninsula in western New Guinea. Thus, during the spring and summer, General MacArthur's forces had reached the western extremity of New Guinea, neutralizing that great island as a base for Japanese operations and obtaining airfields that facilitated the attack on the southern approaches to the Philippines.

(*e*) *Leyte.*—After supporting the western Carolines landings, the fast carrier task force resumed the attack upon the Philippine Islands, making the first carrier strike of the war on Manila and Luzon Island on Sept. 21 and 22. On Sept. 24, carrier planes hit the central Philippines and photographed the area around Leyte and Samar, where landings were to take place in October. It had originally been planned to attack the Philippines at a somewhat later date, but Admiral Halsey's air strikes had revealed an unexpected weakness of Japanese defense in the islands; and, accordingly, the joint chiefs of staff, acting with the greatest rapidity, undertook to capitalize upon this situation. Plans were quickly revised, and preparations were made for the invasion of Leyte Island in the central Philippines on Oct. 20. The east coast of Leyte had a free undefended approach from the east, and adequate anchorages, as well as good access to the other islands in the central Philippines. Moreover, the seizure of Leyte would bypass and isolate Japanese forces in Mindanao.

The Leyte operation marked the joining of the two advances upon Japan from different directions. It was under the command of General MacArthur, to whom Admiral Nimitz made available strong forces of the Pacific fleet. Admiral Halsey's 3rd fleet covered and supported the landings by air strikes over the northern and central Philippines and Formosa and provided protection against an attack upon the landings by the Japanese fleet. Preparatory carrier strikes occupied the period from Oct. 9 to 20. The Ryukyu Islands (including Okinawa) were attacked on Oct. 9 and 10, northern Luzon on Oct. 11, Formosa and the Pescadores on Oct. 12 and 13. On Oct. 13 and 14 a part of the fast carrier task force was attacked by Japanese planes and two cruisers were damaged. To prevent further attacks while these damaged ships retired, U.S. carrier aircraft attacked airfields in Formosa and the northern Philippines repeatedly during Oct. 14 and 15. On Oct. 18 and 19 further strikes were made against objectives in the central and northern Philippines, and during and after the actual landings on Leyte some of the fast

Refuelling a destroyer during 1945 operations in the China sea. The U.S. carrier slacked its oil lines to reduce tension caused by the rough waters

carriers furnished direct support while others conducted searches for Japanese fleet units.

On Oct. 20, after heavy bombardment and air bombing, forces of the central Philippine attack force, commanded by Vice-Adm. Thomas C. Kinkaid (commander, 7th fleet, and General MacArthur's principal naval subordinate), went ashore on the east coast of Leyte Island. The initial landings were entirely successful, but they were soon challenged by the Japanese navy in a full-scale operation, designed to drive U.S. forces from the Philippines.

(*f*) *Battle of Leyte Gulf*.—There followed the battle of Leyte gulf, the greatest naval engagement of the war, which resulted in the complete and thorough defeat of the Japanese. This battle, which consisted of a series of surface and air engagements taking place between Oct. 23 and 26, culminated in three actions, designated as the battle of Surigao strait, the battle off Samar and the battle off Cape Engaño.

The Japanese attack came from three directions. One force (the southern) approached Leyte from the south through Surigao strait; another force (the central) came through San Bernardino strait, while a third (the northern) approached from the direction of Japan. As the battle of the Philippine sea had resulted not only in the sinking of three Japanese carriers, but in the virtual destruction of the air groups of three carrier divisions, the fleet had been reorganized for surface action. The Japanese plan for driving U.S. forces from the Philippines was consequently dependent upon surface ships' provoking a decisive naval engagement. The only Japanese carriers involved were in the northern force, which was intended chiefly for a decoy since the only air support counted upon by the Japanese was from land-based planes.

Early in the morning of Oct. 23 the Japanese central force was discovered off Palawan by two United States submarines, "Darter" and "Dace." The "Darter" sank the heavy cruiser "Atago" and damaged the heavy cruiser "Takao," but in manoeuvring went aground and was itself lost. The "Dace" sank the heavy cruiser "Maya." On the following day 3rd fleet carrier planes located and attacked the central force in the Sibuyan sea and the southern force in the Sulu sea. In the course of the Sibuyan sea action heavy damage was inflicted, and the Japanese battleship "Musashi," equipped with 18-in. guns and one of the two largest battleships in the world, was sunk. Nevertheless, the central force pushed doggedly onward toward San Bernardino strait and Leyte. The Japanese southern force entered Surigao strait in the early hours of Oct. 25 and was annihilated there in a surface engagement with destroyers and battleships of the 7th fleet. The battleships "Yamashiro" and "Fuso" and three destroyers were sunk almost immediately in this battle of Surigao strait, which was one of the few actions of the war in which aircraft did not participate.

The central force, having passed through San Bernardino strait, moved southward off the coast of Samar and shortly after daybreak attacked a group of lightly armed escort carriers of the U.S. 7th fleet. This battle off Samar was finally broken off by the retirement of the greatly superior Japanese force.

During the night of Oct. 24–25, Admiral Halsey's carrier task force had been moving northward to meet the Japanese northern force. In the resulting battle off Cape Engaño the Japanese carriers "Zuikaku," "Zuiho," "Chitose" and "Chiyoda" were sunk; but upon receiving word of the battle off Samar, Admiral Halsey sent a detachment of carriers and battleships to assist the 7th fleet escort carriers. These ships were unable to intercept the retiring Japanese central force before it had re-entered San Bernardino strait, but on the afternoon of Oct. 25 and during Oct. 26 carrier planes attacked the fleeing Japanese and inflicted further damage. At the end of the battle of Leyte gulf, three Japanese forces had either been destroyed or had retired out of range. While 6 U.S. vessels (the light carrier "Princeton," 2 escort carriers, 2 destroyers and 1 destroyer escort) had been sunk, the Japanese had lost in the course of the battle 3 battleships, 4 carriers, 10 cruisers and 9 destroyers—a total of 26 combatant ships. The battle of Leyte gulf represented the end of the Japanese navy as a powerful element in the Pacific war.

During the remainder of 1944 no major naval actions developed, but the fast carriers were constantly employed in support of the Leyte campaign; and, because of delays in establishing airfields on shore, because of unfavourable weather, naval aircraft gave direct support to the troops on Leyte for a considerably longer period than had been anticipated. Manila and other targets on Luzon were attacked repeatedly. In furtherance of the Leyte operation, an amphibious landing was made at Ormoc bay, on the west coast of the island, on Dec. 7, while on Dec. 15 a further landing was made on Mindoro Island, nearly 300 mi. to the northwest.

(*g*) *The Philippines*.—The attacks upon Manila in December had caused the Japanese to expect landings in that area, but the next large amphibious operation entirely bypassed Manila and was directed against Lingayen gulf, in the northern part of Luzon Island. In preparation, the 3rd fleet attacked Formosa and the southern Ryukyu Islands on Jan. 3 and 4, 1945; and on Jan. 9, while troops were going ashore on beaches in the Lingayen gulf area, Formosa was again attacked by carrier planes. A thrust by the fast carrier task force into the South China sea then followed, during which the coast of Indo-China between Saigon and Camranh bay was attacked on Jan. 12, Formosa on Jan. 15 and Hong Kong and Canton on Jan. 16. The complete inability of the Japanese to resist the movements of the United States navy on the very shores of the continent of Asia was indicated by the fact that Admiral Halsey's forces traversed 3,800 mi. in the South China sea during this series of attacks without receiving damage to any ship.

Although U.S. forces were securely established in the Philippines, large land areas and innumerable islands remained to be cleared; and until the end of the war land fighting, accompanied by amphibious landings, was going on in various parts of the group. Landings to accelerate the capture of Manila were made in the vicinity of Subic bay on Jan. 29 and 30 and at Nasugbu, south of Manila bay, on Jan. 31. On Feb. 13 cruisers and destroyers bombarded the entrances to Manila bay; on Feb. 15 troops landed on the Bataan peninsula and on Feb. 16 on Corregidor Island—the scenes of bitter United States reverses three years earlier. Subsequent operations were undertaken to gain control of the straits leading into the waters of the central Philippines and to seize coastal cities and strongly held Japanese positions in various central and southern islands. Landings were made at Zamboanga on Mindanao Island on March 10, at Iloilo on Panay Island on March 18 and at Cebu Island on March 26. On April 17 a landing at Malabang in southern Mindanao resulted in the seizure of the important Davao gulf area. In May similar operations were extended to the westward into Borneo to recover Japanese conquests in the Netherlands Indies and cut off Japanese oil supplies. The first Borneo landings were against the island of Tarakan on May 1; the second large operation was against the Brunei bay area on the northern coast on June 10, and on July 1 a large amphibious force attacked Balikpapan on Makassar strait.

(*h*) *Attacks on the Home Islands.*—While the Philippine Islands were still being fought over, the war was simultaneously being carried not only to the inner defenses of the Japanese empire but to the home islands themselves. The occupation of the Marianas Islands in the summer of 1944 had furnished bases from which U.S. long-range bombers could attack Japan, but to increase the effectiveness with which these planes could operate, fighter support was desirable. The island of Iwo Jima in the Volcano Islands, only 750 mi. from Tokyo, offered an ideal site for a fighter base to support the Marianas-based B-29's, as well as for the operation of medium bombers. An amphibious assault upon Iwo Jima was therefore undertaken in Feb. 1945, although it was known that the island was heavily fortified and would be vigorously defended. The operations for the capture of Iwo Jima were under the command of Admiral Spruance, who had relieved Admiral Halsey in command of the fast carrier task force of the Pacific fleet after the latter's successful sweep through the South China sea. Although the island was only 2 mi. wide and 5 mi. long, such severe fighting was anticipated that a landing force of 60,000 United States marines, put ashore by a naval force of more than 800 ships, was provided for its capture. Iwo Jima had been intermittently attacked since June 1944 by surface ships and carrier planes, and from December onward the attacks had been intensified. Landings were scheduled for Feb. 19; as a preliminary move the carrier aircraft of Admiral Spruance's 5th fleet struck Tokyo on Feb. 16, one year to the day after the first attack on Truk. This attack was renewed on Feb. 25. Meanwhile, surface ships and planes were attacking the defenses of Iwo Jima. As soon as the marines were ashore, severe fighting developed which continued for several weeks; but on March 16 all organized resistance ceased. The airfields which were immediately developed on the island greatly facilitated the air attack upon the Japanese home islands.

To bring Japan even more closely under attack, a very large amphibious operation was directed against Okinawa, in the Ryukyu Islands, in the spring of 1945. The capture of the Marianas and Philippine Islands had brought U.S. forces within 1,300 mi. of the Japanese homeland. The capture of Iwo Jima placed them 640 mi. from Tokyo, while Okinawa offered sites for airfields within 350 mi. of Kyushu, the southernmost of the main islands of Japan. The difficulty of this assault was considerable, for Okinawa was heavily defended, and its proximity to Japan meant that any attack upon it could readily be resisted by the main strength of the Japanese air force.

After preliminary strikes by the fast carriers, and intensive naval bombardment, landings were effected on the southwest coast of Okinawa on April 1. Though there was relatively light resistance on the beaches, and the northern two-thirds of the island was occupied in a matter of three weeks, Japanese resistance in the southern portion of Okinawa, where strong defensive positions had been established, was extremely bitter and protracted. It was not until June 23 that the entire island was captured. During this long period, many naval vessels were required for the support of the troops ashore. More than 1,200 had been employed in the initial landings, and a considerable number were required for many weeks thereafter. These ships were subjected to heavy air attack by Japanese suicide planes and received considerable damage. There was relatively little danger from Japanese naval vessels in consequence of the defeat inflicted the previous October in the battle of Leyte gulf, and through April, May and June the fast carrier task force constantly operated in support of the Okinawa assault, frequently launching attacks upon Kyushu. On April 7, in a last attempt to make some use of surviving surface vessels, the great Japanese battleship "Yamato" (sister ship of "Musashi," which had been sunk in the battle of Leyte gulf) sortied, but was promptly sunk in the East China sea off Kyushu, together with the accompanying cruiser "Yahagi" and four destroyers.

With the approaching conclusion of the war in Europe, major units of the royal navy had been dispatched to the Pacific and organized as a British Pacific fleet, under the command of Adm. Sir Bruce Fraser. These ships were placed under the operational control of the commander in chief, United States fleet, and in the spring of 1945 a British carrier task force was assigned to Admiral Spruance's 5th fleet to assist in the air support of the Okinawa operation. This British force attacked Sakishima Gunto, southwest of Okinawa, from March 26 to April 20 and again from May 4 to 25 in order to neutralize Japanese air installations there.

After the conclusion of the Okinawa operation, Admiral Halsey's 3rd Fleet, the greatest assembly of sea power in

Dawn breaking over a U.S. armada moving toward Luzon in 1945, as a coast guard lookout stood at his watch

the history of naval warfare, moved northward toward Japan to conduct a preinvasion campaign aimed at the destruction of the remaining units of the Japanese navy and of industrial sites. Strikes were made against airfields and factories in the vicinity of Tokyo on July 10, and against northern Honshu and southern Hokkaido on July 14–15. On July 17, in company with units of the British Pacific fleet, 3rd fleet ships conducted the first U.S.-British bombardment of the Japanese home islands. Carrier planes attacked the Yokosuka naval base in Tokyo bay on July 18; the Inland sea area on July 24, 25 and 28; northern Honshu on Aug. 9 and 10 and Tokyo on July 30 and Aug. 13 and 15. These 3rd fleet operations were in preparation for Operation "Olympic," a vast amphibious landing projected against southern Kyushu, which was to be followed later in 1945 by Operation "Coronet," an amphibious assault into the Tokyo plain area. These last great efforts were not required, for on Aug. 14 Japan accepted the terms of the Potsdam proclamation, which involved the absolute surrender of all military forces. The cease-fire order was given on Aug. 15.

Amphibious forces were organized for the occupation, which began on Aug. 28. On Sept. 2, on board the battleship "Missouri" in Tokyo bay, the formal surrender was signed. (W. M. W.)

VI. GENERAL CHARACTER OF THE WAR

The conclusions as to the general character of World War II and its major trends reached from as close a perspective as the end of 1946 could not be final, but even if they might be somewhat distorted because of the closeness of view, they could furnish a record of contemporary thought and serve a definite purpose. The more measured accounts of the future would have the benefit of wider knowledge and thus almost certainly a better balance of judgment. But without opportunity for comparison with the contemporary appraisals such accounts might lack some reality.

Axis Initiative.—At the outset of the war, the initiative and the power of the offensive lay completely with the axis powers. The intensity of Germany's great preparations, the confidence of success and the sense of destiny with which Hitler had imbued the reich were fully disclosed to the world as Hitler's armies plunged across the Polish frontiers.

The Germans are a persistent people, and despite the great failure of 1914–18, the short-war concept of Frederick the Great, Karl von Clausewitz and Alfred von Schlieffen again enticed them into a new effort to conquer Europe. The mistakes of the past were studied and avoided. This time there was to be no accident of the Marne to block success. So well were the preparations laid that they operated to destroy without a pause a sturdy opponent, who by World War I standards was well equipped and well trained, and, finally to wipe out all organized opposition between the Rhine and the Atlantic. The German army had been freed from the stifling hold by which old weapons and old techniques frequently had hampered armies in the past. The new reichswehr had the immense advantage of building from scratch, with no attachment to old forms and old matériel. In consequence, the German armies at the outbreak of the war possessed more fire power, greater mobility and a far heavier weight of armoured columns than any of their opponents had been able to amass in their tentative progress toward modernization.

The Polish invasion took the immediate form of a devastating air blow, followed by fast, hard-hitting armoured and infantry columns, against which the Polish army, substantial as it was, could only reel and become confused.

On paper the advantages of manpower, industry and wealth lay with the Allies; but their lack of integration spelled only destruction for Poland. Britain's strength was diffused and had to be accumulated over long water routes, and France was to prove itself utterly incapable of generating anything comparable to the German power. The Allied world was still stunned by the political-military strokes of Hitler, particularly by the nazi-soviet nonaggression pact; the small nations of western Europe, who were not without considerable political and military power, were enfeebled by the wishful thinking that their only salvation lay in taking as little action as possible to defend themselves. Hardly had Poland begun to feel the full force of the German blow, when it found its rear overrun by the Russian armies. The collapse was complete.

Even after the Polish campaign had come to an end, the western powers could offer no dynamic defense to the German threat. French and British forces began to take up positions in and outside the permanent fortifications of the continent. Behind the lines efforts were hastily made to prepare, but no mobilization or striking capacity comparable to the German power resulted. In the meantime, the German armies were regrouping, obviously for blows in the west. But while this period of the war carried over some of the aspects of the earlier peace in the way of uncoordinated defense to German aggression, there appeared certain factors which gave faint signs of Allied potentialities. The British blockade tactics began to take form. Although the central powers had greater continental resources on which to draw than in World War I, still the generally restrictive effects of the blockade were again impressed and again began to play their part. Unified British public opinion and determined leadership emerged. Signs of U.S. concern increased, and the importance of superior industrial capacity became more and more apparent.

Denmark had signed a ten-year non-aggression pact with Germany providing that "under no circumstances" would either country resort to war or any other form of violence against the other. It took just one hour's ultimatum on April 9, 1940, for Germany to destroy that pact and for King Christian to order a cease-fire. Norway, however, was a different story, and in the Norwegian campaign the pattern of things to come was further unfolded. In defiance of Britain's sea power and the proximity of English naval bases, German troops had seized all but northern Norway within less than a month, and in another month all Allied forces were compelled to withdraw from the country. The unchallengeable air supremacy of the Germans in the area told the tale; and, if the lesson was a dismal one for Britain and its navy, properly interpreted it pointed also to Germany's doom, for as the emphasis on naval supremacy diminished, the significance of air power took form. In spite of an immediate and pronounced inferiority in planes, it was in Allied not German hands that the great potentialities of air power lay.

While the fighting was still progressing in Norway, Hitler launched his great attacks to the west, attacks proclaimed by him to fix Germany's destiny for a thousand years. His plans were made and his objectives were still clear. The Netherlands, Belgium and France were promptly overrun. In three short weeks the armies of four important countries were completely defeated.

Again, however, in the defeat of one of those armies lay Allied hope of the future; that army, huddled together on the beaches at Dunkirk, was significantly evacuated to England with almost no loss of life. In a few days 233,039 British and 112,546 French and Belgian soldiers were taken safely across the channel. It was Britain's surface command of the channel which accomplished it, but it was Britain's air superiority at the spot which made it possible.

The Critical Point.—It was at Dunkirk that Britain was directly threatened, and it was there that it first utilized its small but decisive air fighter superiority in its full strength. The fast and heavily armed British fighters swept clean the air above the evacuation beaches. The German bombers which had wreaked such destruction on Rotterdam and the communication lines of the Allied armies on the continent could not measurably interfere with the evacuation. And in attempting to do so, the luftwaffe, in a few days in the end of May and the beginning of June 1940, lost something in the neighbourhood of ten times as much in air personnel and planes as did its opponent.

After a respite, the air attack on the British mainland began, and again the overworked fighter command took its toll—a toll so great that though the fight was long and painful and pressed with all the determination and courage of the best German military tradition, by October of the same year the luftwaffe substantially abandoned the field. The bravery, endurance and skill of the British pilots were the main contributing factors to the result; but great credit must also go to those whose plans made available at the critical time the excellent planes which the pilots used, and particularly to those who had seen the need and designed the means by which the German planes could be detected day or night, through the use of radar. The luftwaffe had an impressive record to register; 35,000 British civilian casualties, severe damage to docks, to airdromes, to factories and to London generally, but with it all no decisive result.

As the perspective lengthens, this phase of the war stands out perhaps as deeply significant of the ultimate course of the conflict as any development which came later. Until then, Hitler had called the tune and his conquests which had matched some of the very greatest of all military history lost much of their momentum at just this point. Thereafter his complications accumulated, and he was compelled to improvise new avenues of conquest. Relying on what he assumed would be the inability and unwillingness of Britain to continue to oppose him after the collapse on the continent, Hitler apparently had made no adequate plans for a timely or full-scale invasion of England. The luftwaffe, well conceived for bombing over the battlefield and rear areas in the field, was not adequately designed for the defeat of a nation like Great Britain. Britain stood, resolute, if shaky, and with it stood hope and the vast strategic consequences of its continuous lines of communication and bases around the world. Its stand signified the preservation of a great bastion in the Atlantic by which re-entry to the continent was possible, a great and firm base in, through and from which its own continued strength and the great powers of the North American continent could be delivered.

Including Dunkirk, the battle of Britain had cost Britain the lives of approximately 500 pilots, while the Germans had lost at the minimum 3,000 planes and most of their occupants. (The German planes were mostly bombers containing on the average from four to six occupants.)

The forces of Britain were later to be deployed in Africa and the middle east, on the continent and in the Pacific and Asia. The British victory at El Alamein, Egypt, was to give new hope to the Allied cause, but no other contribution was ever to be so critically important as was this repulse of the luftwaffe over England in the summer and fall of 1940.

Russian Fiasco.—Out of the enigma of the east evolved the next great development of the war. In 1936 Hitler had consummated the Anti-Comintern Pact uniting Germany, Japan and Italy against the U.S.S.R. In Aug. 1939 Hitler and Stalin produced a mutual nonaggression pact which had made it possible for Hitler to attack Poland and the west unhindered by any eastern involvements. And in the early morning of June 22, 1941, without prior warning or demands, the German army attacked Russia along the entire border with full strength. Precisely what motivated Hitler to attack Russia at this stage of the war remained obscure, although there were many explanations. Whatever the motive, by so doing he uncovered new forces of opposition, the extent of which he had greatly underestimated. Not only were those forces underestimated, they became a wearing burden on the German energy, which, with the growth of the military power of the United States was to crush Germany as no other great nation save Japan was crushed in modern times. The German attacks in Russia were supported by their full forces, and they accomplished the destruction of several armies in the course of their deep advance into the country. They crippled the area west of the Don without which, till then, it had been thought the soviet union could not carry on organized resistance. Yet, the Red army still fought on with matériel and personnel always at hand to continue the struggle. The failure to capture Leningrad, the repulse at Rostov and Moscow, showed Germany that there were great centres of Russian resistance still to be taken and, more clearly, that the soviet armies were yet to be annihilated. The early severe winter, the lateness of the German attack, German tactical mistakes and the means of trading space for time accumulated to account in large part for the effectiveness of the Russian resistance in the face of terrible losses. Without, however, the persisting will of the people of the soviet union to endure and conquer their enemy, all of the foregoing would have been unproductive; in the final analysis it was that will which inspired all the vast effort which led to victory.

An offensive through 1942 which took German forces 1,000 mi. into the heart of Russia over a front of even greater length, severely taxed the strength of both Russia and Germany. In terms of both extent and numbers of troops engaged, the energies expended in this tremendous campaign were far greater than the land campaigns in the west. There were no wide general withdrawals to entice the wehrmacht over a "scorched earth" to eventual destruction. It was hard continuous fighting all the way.

That the Red army was capable of conducting this fighting retreat and then of extricating itself to undertake first a winter and then a summer offensive of the magnitude of those of 1942 and 1943, bespoke a nation of first rank, strength and unity. It is true that the African and Italian invasions effected a most helpful diversion of German strength. It is also true that large shipments of motor vehicles from British and U.S. sources played an important part in enabling the Red army to forestall the enemy, but its own vast sacrifices and real military skill were the fundamental factors of the soviet union's strength. With the German failure to take Stalingrad, the Verdun of the east, Hitler's dream of the Ukraine and the Caucasus was shattered; but more than this was involved. With this great block thrown in the German path, the impossibility of a complete subjugation of the country came in sight, for thereafter Germany was never again to possess the capacity for great strategic offensives, or, indeed, decisive defensives, in either the east or the west. With the final Anglo-U.S. and Russian offensives in the spring of 1945, it was Germany's turn to reel and become confused.

Hitler had plunged Germany into the Russian venture confident of results comparable to the French collapse. These failed to materialize, and the growing power of the west left him with a two-front war—the eternal phobia of German military thinking since Bismarck—a two-front war of a magnitude and scope which even Hitler's own general staff had never envisaged.

United States Underrated.—The importance of the United States as a military power had not been taken fully into account even after the decisive role played by it in World War I. Its full emergence as a recognized military power of vast potentiality did not occur until World War II.

In the period between the two world wars, its nonaggressionism, unpreparedness and uncertain foreign policy had diluted its effectiveness as a factor in the prevention of war. Its new role under the leadership of President Roosevelt did not come about readily. In the fall of 1940, for the first time in history, the United States adopted compulsory military service as a peacetime measure. This was the first expression of its power. The second came in the form of the so-called Lend-Lease legislation, whereby countries whose defense was deemed important or vital to the defense of the United States were supplied with arms, munitions of war and other supplies on a basis which meant almost unlimited aid to those fighting the axis. The legislation was enacted in March 1941, and it is difficult to overstate the enormous influence it had on the course of the war.

The United States had been concerned over the plight of Poland but thought of war on such an issue was largely excluded from the public mind. With Britain beleaguered, however, a deep uneasiness pervaded the country, which gradually became sensitive to its own danger. This sense of danger was paralleled by a general abhorrence of nazi methods. Though late in the day, the tremendous energies of the country began to be applied to the objective of Hitler's defeat. President Roosevelt was a strong leader, and in his now fully aroused internationalism and antagonism to Germany he led the nation in its new role. The United States was to become the "arsenal of democracy."

 Not only were the goods to be made available to the anti-axis belligerents; they were to be delivered. The Atlantic charter was compounded in the summer of 1941 by Roosevelt and Churchill as the pattern for "a better future for the world."

The final spur to the full expression of U.S. energies came, however, only with the surprise Japanese attack at Pearl Harbor on the morning of Dec. 7, 1941. Though matters had been clearly heading for a crisis of some sort, the country was stunned by the news that Japan had deliberately and without warning attacked the United States. Thenceforward without stint the country formed its armies, navies and air forces, forged its weapons and greatly multiplied its already vast general production facilities.

The full effect of this effort on the outcome of the war was difficult to measure. That it was the greatest single factor in the winning of the war for the Allies there can be no doubt. Britain continued to perform its full and potent share, but it did not possess the population and the resources to conclude the battle decisively. The soviet union, for all its rugged power, did not possess the capacity to effect a complete defeat of Germany. The victory was obviously the result of the combined effort of all the powers including resistance forces, but it is a fact that where both Britain and Russia produced matériel and manpower in vast quantities, the United States produced far more than both combined in the way of most munitions of war, including planes, motor vehicles and ships. At the same time the country had 14,000,000 men under arms in its own military services. With its first-line navy wiped out at Pearl Harbor, it ended the war with a balanced fleet incomparably the largest in the world. Its men fought in every corner of the world, and while it furnished the weight of men and materials to bring about the final victory in western Europe, it almost singlehanded defeated the forces of the Japanese empire utterly in the Pacific. Its airplanes soon were flying in greater quantities over Germany than those of Great Britain, and many of those flown by Britain were either U.S.-built or U.S.-equipped. Much of the equipment of the British armies was U.S.-made, and almost all of the new equipment of the French army was of U.S. manufacture. The Chinese armies were largely maintained by U.S. supplies, and besides thousands of aircraft and great shipments of raw materials the Red army was made mobile in a modern sense by the constant stream of locomotives, rails, rolling stock and approximately 300,000 U.S. motor vehicles to the soviet union. Deprived of normal imports and trade, the very economy of Britain during the war was substantially supported by U.S. materials and foodstuffs.

In all, more than $40,000,000,000 of U.S. equipment and supplies were sent abroad to the Allies during the course of the war. Of the military items alone, which together constituted less than half the entire shipments, some concept of the extent of United States contribution can be obtained from the fact that the equivalent in United States cost of 588 armoured divisions or 2,000 infantry divisions were dispatched and delivered to U.S. allies in addition to the munitions shipped abroad for the use of the United States forces.

Lest it be thought that this contribution was rendered more in terms of weight of manpower and matériel than military skill, it is necessary to record that the armies and navies of the United States were led by men whose genius for military and naval accomplishments were certainly not excelled by the leaders of any of the Allied or axis powers. Gen. George Marshall's strength of character, vision and administrative ability, Gen. Dwight D. Eisenhower's genius for combined command and Gen. Douglas MacArthur's brilliance in the Pacific campaigns left no doubt as to the strength and skill with which the armies were led. Adm. Ernest J. King's strategic and tactical direction of the U.S. fleets and Adm. Chester W. Nimitz's operation of them—their application of carrier air power and their mastery of amphibious attacks under many complicated situations—testified to the effective employment of U.S. sea power. New concepts and tactics on the use of air power, largely the result of Gen. H. H. Arnold's driving inspiration, became a most important element in the U.S. contribution.

Much as Germany had overrun vast areas in western Europe and Russia, so Japan had conquered by brilliant tactics a vast area on the mainland of Asia, the Malay peninsula and the Pacific Islands. Japan's incursions in China had dated from 1931 and continued intermittently until 1940, when Japan turned south to prepare its jumping-off bases for its coming attacks on the Dutch and British possessions in the Pacific. Like Germany, Japan felt that its hope lay in a quick and decisive victory, preferably to be achieved when its chief opponents were concerned elsewhere. With timing suited to the occasion, when Britain and the U.S.S.R. were fully engaged in Europe, and with the United States sleeping late of a Sunday morning, Japan struck out in many directions at once in the hope of achieving a decisive result. By Aug. 1942 Japan controlled a new area which in geographical extent and numbers of people subjugated rivalled the conquests of Germany. Japan accomplished this largely through its control of the sea and air throughout the area, and it was able to achieve it at very little cost in lives. In doing so, however, it strained its own capacities and stirred to vigorous action the United States, whose industrial capacity exceeded Japan's at least tenfold. By a combination of sea and air power, and a development of amphibious tactics on a scale which dwarfed the same type of Japanese operations, the Japanese were driven completely on the defensive in less than two years' time. As an example of what great flexibility was attained through U.S. superiority on the sea and in the air it is significant to note that at the time of the surrender, the Japanese still had an army of about 5,000,000 men under arms. They had been able to deploy only between 600,000 and 700,000 of these against their principal enemy in the Pacific, and the United States forces at no time were called upon to fight more than 300,000 of them. Mainly through control of the air and sea, the United States forces in the Pacific were able to defeat those they met in the field (most of whom were killed), and they could largely choose where and when their battles were to be fought. It required many men, long lines of communication, vast wealth and skilful leadership to accomplish this, but in the long and interesting study of the importance of logistics in warfare, this is one of the most interesting case studies to be found in military history.

Combined War Policy.—Another outstanding feature of the war which determined the course of most of its campaigns was the prompt and effective manner in which the energies of the Allied Powers were combined to achieve their objectives, once the United States had become engaged.

Whereas the period between the wars was marked by the dearth of effective collective action, the importance of close integration of Allied war policy, particularly Anglo-U.S., was quickly recognized and acted upon once all were engaged. The early meetings of Churchill and Roosevelt, followed later by meetings at which these two were joined by Stalin and Chiang Kai-shek, resulted in strong co-ordinated action. This co-ordination greatly expedited victory and reduced misunderstandings. It served to convert the necessarily defensive attitudes which German and Japanese aggression had initially forced on the Allied Powers into a mighty 'round-the-world offensive which finally overwhelmed all of the axis powers completely.

During and immediately after the war, a number of differences of view between the United States and Great Britain were disclosed and commented upon. More disclosures of this nature would no doubt be made and exploited as time went on. But the fact remained that during the war these divergences of view were ironed out, controlled and finally merged into a close association of the leaders of the states and their military staffs in the conduct of the war. In the meetings of the chiefs of state, their individually firm adherence to the principle of combined action, particularly in the case of President Roosevelt and Prime Minister Churchill, and in their frequent interchanges, lay the key to this integration. The integration was carried out by means of the almost continuous sessions of the combined chiefs of staff. (*See* Chiefs of Staff, Combined and Joint.)

Of the number of important decisions taken in this combined form, perhaps the greatest, apart from the underlying determination to pool and administer Anglo-U.S. resources on a combined basis, was the determination to treat the European theatre as the primary theatre, and the defeat of Germany and its armies as the primary objective.

This plan was first proposed at the Anglo-U.S. staff talks in Feb. and March 1941 and was approved in the talks at the Atlantic conference that summer. When Churchill and the British staff arrived in Washington after Pearl Harbor, there was considerable doubt as to whether the U.S. point of view had changed as a result of the Japanese attack. They were surprised and relieved by the immediate assurance that Pearl Harbor had not altered matters, and that no alteration in the grand strategy was proposed.

So vast were U.S. resources that a wise use of the forces available made it possible to establish a sound temporary defense in the Pacific and at the same time commence the development of immense offensive power in that area. The decision to throw the greatest strength against Germany ensured the decisive character of the victory in the European theatre and never seriously prejudiced the operations in the Pacific. Continuous Russian pressure combined with the effects of this decision to keep Germany's strategy invariably out of balance. Germany was capable of serious threats such as the submarine and the V-1 and V-2 attacks, but it never could give sufficient time and resources to develop any threat into an effective means of averting defeat.

The second most important decision taken by the combined chiefs of staff was to invade the European continent from the west. Once made, it was carried out effectively by all the elements on whose co-operation it was to depend.

Lack of Axis Integration.—In contrast to the unity of purpose and action thus carried out by the Allied Powers was the almost totally unrelated activities of the axis powers. There is no evidence that any close integration of strategy and policy existed between Germany and Japan, and surprisingly little between Germany and Italy. Japan's attack on Pearl Harbor was known to Germany but seems not to have been integrated with German plans. Italy quickly became a burden rather than an aid to Germany, and Italy's unilateral actions in Greece and Africa substantially complicated Germany's strategic problems.

Even within Germany itself there appears to have been only a limited strategic concept. Hitler had in mind Germanic domination of Europe and pursued a policy of successful opportunism in respect of the Rhineland, Austria and Czechoslovakia. By his successes in these areas he beguiled the nation into deeper waters. His initial conquests were highly co-ordinated affairs, with the wehrmacht operating in accordance with familiar German tradition, but once these were accomplished Hitler's much vaunted will outran Germany's military capacities and even its plans. By the end of 1946, no German strategic plan encompassing the war as a whole had been disclosed. It is doubtful if one existed, for the evidence indicated that Hitler's personal desires rather than seasoned judgment determined the course of the war for Germany. Not since Napoleon had there been combined in one person such a dictatorship of the state and its military force, and rarely had any individual leader exacted such ultimate defeat of his country as Hitler demanded of Germany. Indeed, the final battles surged up to the very porticos of his office in Berlin.

Whereas there was an orderly development of Allied strategy, Hitler's grand intuitions and concepts culminated as the tide ran against him into a bankruptcy of military and political policy, and at the end it was merely his perversity which governed.

Development of Air Power.—The enormous development of air power in World War II and the new strategical concepts it provoked deeply affected the entire course of the war.

World War II mobilized greater forces in all categories than had ever been amassed before, but the increase in strength in air and naval forces was particularly marked. This was the first war in which aircraft on decisive missions ranged far at sea and operated over many hundreds of miles. The new strategic and political consequences of air power fell far short of eliminating the profound influence of sea power upon the outcome, but the predominant position which sea power had formerly played in warfare was greatly affected by the developments in the air arm.

In the spring of 1940, the Germans, largely through air power, accomplished the successful invasion and occupation of Norway. This was followed in the spring of 1941 by the seizure and occupation of the island of Crete, again, largely through the concentration of air-borne troops. Norway and Crete were each situated in sea zones whose control since Lord Nelson's day were considered indisputably British. Yet each, largely by reason of German plane superiority in the area, was quickly wrested from Britain's domination. The sinking of the "Prince of Wales" and the "Repulse" off the Malay coast in Dec. 1941 (not to mention Pearl Harbor) and the British attacks on the Italian navy at Sardinia, Taranto and Naples by Adm. Sir Andrew B. Cunningham's somewhat antiquated torpedo planes furnished further impressive evidence of the vulnerability of ships to air attack.

The early German attacks on Poland and Britain were the first manifestation of strategic bombing forces in operation. But the supreme manifestation of modern air power came with the British and U.S. long-range bombing over Germany. From the spring of 1942 to the summer of 1944 the operation of these bombers made it possible to carry on a powerful offensive against what otherwise would have been an unreachable enemy. This bombing caused terrible destruction and inflicted during the war a little more than 1,000,000 civilian casualties, 5,000,000 evacuations and severe privations to many millions of others. Industries, railroads, oil refineries and storages and industrial cities generally felt the weight of these attacks. In times of emergency the great bombing squadrons were diverted to deal with targets which directly supported Germany's offensive operations, such as the submarine warfare and subsequently its missile warfare. Indeed, on occasions the strategic forces were even thrown against German tactical forces in the field. In the course of destroying German ground targets through their own fire power and their accompanying fighters, these great bombers played a large part in wearing out the German air forces.

By 1943 Great Britain had become an enormous air base from which many thousands of U.S. and British bombing planes were operated. Until the end of the war these concentrations constituted the greatest demonstration of modern air power the world had ever seen. It took months of effort and heavy casualties to achieve it, and the demonstration could never have been made without the control of the seas. The result, however, was to carry home to Germany an offensive which sea power alone could not accomplish. It was primarily through air power that the full impact of modern war with all its horror and suffering was brought home to the German people.

In the Mediterranean, the employment of long-range as well as tactical planes permitted landings to be made and held which but for the use of such air power might have had disastrous results. The landings in Africa, Sicily and at Salerno and Anzio were all hazardous affairs, and in each case Allied air superiority greatly helped to maintain the foothold. And, finally, the great Normandy invasion of 1944 was, as General Eisenhower testified, made possible through the use of Allied air power. There were other elements which contributed to the success of that invasion, without some of which it could not have been successful, but air power furnished the determining factor that made the conquest of the continent by the ground forces feasible.

In combination with naval power the use of air weapons also contributed much to end what was perhaps Germany's greatest threat, namely, its U-boat warfare, and in combination with the ground forces air power greatly assisted the progress of troops over the ground.

In eastern Europe the Russian armies were heavily supported by medium-range bombers and tactical planes. Soviet air power, however, had been created primarily to assist the infantry over the ground, and though most effective for the role it was designed to play, it never reached the power or flexibility which the air forces of the western powers were able to bring to bear.

On the other side of the globe as air bases became available, particularly in the Marianas, the bombing of Japan rivalled the attacks on Germany. A new type of very long-range bomber of large bomb capacity was placed in operation, and toward the end of the war, with these bombers supplemented by air strikes from carrier-based planes, the air offensive on the Japanese mainland became intense. It laid waste large sections of 66 of the more important cities of Japan. Finally, it was from two of these long-range bombers that the atom bombs were dropped on Hiroshima and Nagasaki.

In stressing the development of air power, it is necessary in order to measure the development to draw comparisons with the sea and ground forces. But while the growth of air power in World War II was great and deeply significant, it is important to record that the victory was not achieved and could not have been achieved without the co-ordination of all arms. Though control of the air was vital to almost every operation of the war, it was still necessary to transport the energies of Britain and the United States by means of ships to the point where those energies could be made effective. Ships had to be maintained and seaways kept open throughout the world for the greatest transportation of men, food and munitions ever undertaken in the history of warfare. While this transport was being accomplished, the Allied navies met and effectively dealt with all axis sea-borne objectives, including the serious threat of the U-boat. They greatly assisted in the establishment of landing forces ashore through highly skilful amphibious tactics and shore bombardment. Moreover, with complete control of the air and complete control of the seas, the final objectives in World War II had to be taken as in all previous wars by men moving over the ground. (J. J. McC.)

VII. CONCLUSIONS

The full cost of World War II will never be known, either in intrinsic values or in intangibles. Even the best estimates will continue to be guesses. At the end of 1946, a discussion of the political, economic and psychological impact of the war on different nations and on the world as a whole had to be recognized as a matter primarily of surmise based on the trends which had thus far developed.

The costs of war could not be measured alone in such mathematical terms as battle casualties, dollar expenditures and similar data. Such figures were but partial and inadequate yardsticks. The data regarding casualties among civilians were only partially available. They were known to be very great, often exceeding the military losses. The loss of life because of the privations, cruel treatment and mass murders which were a feature of the axis concentration camps had to be included in any comprehensive record of costs in terms of human lives. A more difficult problem was to appraise the losses occasioned by the displacement and dislocation of populations. Recognition had to be given to the long-term effects of devoting the major portion of the world's over-all capabilities for a period of years to the objective of destruction.

Costs, computed in terms of dollars, of raising and supporting armed forces, lost their significance as the conflicts of war extended from high in the air to the depths of the oceans and over most of the earth's surface. The destruction of homes, industries and means of livelihood of millions of people probably represented a greater monetary cost factor than the support of armed forces. The destruction common to World War II could not be measured in terms of the replacement cost alone.

The figures in the succeeding paragraphs must be considered in light of the foregoing factors.

Fifty-seven nations, Allied and axis, were belligerents in World War II. In the final compilation of figures as to casualties and expenditures of resources, the data for each nation should be viewed in the light of that nation's total manpower and national wealth. The major portion of the cost was borne by the United States, the British commonwealth, the Union of Soviet Socialist Republics, China and France and by the three major axis powers, Germany, Italy and Japan. The battle dead gave a partial picture of that cost.

The cost of victory for the United States in battle deaths and missing personnel was 295,904 lives, or 1 in every 500 of the 1940 population.

The cost to the British commonwealth in military personnel killed and missing during the period Sept. 3, 1939, to V-J day was 452,570. This represented 0.08% of the population of the British commonwealth. These casualties came from all parts of the empire, but the majority were suffered by the people of the home islands. The figures for those killed and missing were approximately 305,770 from the United Kingdom itself, or 1 in every 150 of the population; 39,300 from Canada, 29,400 from Australia, 12,200 from New Zealand, 8,700 from South Africa, 36,100 from India and 21,100 from the remainder of the empire.

The Union of Soviet Socialist Republics reported its losses as approximately 7,500,000 military personnel killed and missing, or 1 in every 22 of its 1940 population.

France had 200,000 military personnel killed and missing, or 1 in every 200 of its 1940 population.

Germany lost 2,850,000 military personnel killed and missing, or 1 in every 25 of its 1940 population.

Italy had 300,000 military personnel killed and missing, or 1 in every 150 of its 1940 population.

During the course of the war, China suffered the second largest number of casualties of any of the Allied nations. Its battle losses numbered 2,200,000 or 1 in every 200 of its 1940 population, excluding Manchuria. These figures covered the period during which time China was formally at war with Japan and did not include the six years of undeclared hostilities beginning in 1931.

As a result of its aggression, Japan had lost 1,506,000 military personnel killed and missing since 1937, or 1 in every 46 of the 1940 population of its home islands.

The total number of military personnel of the major Allied powers killed and missing during World War II was about 10,650,000. The total number of military personnel of the major axis powers killed and missing during the war was approximately 4,650,000. The total cost to the principal belligerents, both Allied and axis, in military personnel killed and missing in battle exceeded 15,000,000.

The very considerable costs to the smaller countries, particularly Poland and the nations in southeastern Europe, added hundreds of thousands more to the total.

As a result of the nazi method of obtaining slave labour during World War II and the battles which were fought over so much of the European continent, on V-E day approximately 10,000,000 civilians were displaced beyond the national boundaries of their own country by reason of war. Approximately 6,000,000 of these displaced persons had been returned to their homes at the end of 1946 by the occupying powers, plus the numbers handled within the soviet zone, on which no figures were available. As of the end of 1946, approximately 1,200,000 persons were still being cared for by the three western Allies in Germany.

In the far east, approximately 5,000,000 Japanese, about half civilians, had been returned to Japan from Asia and

Signing of the Japanese surrender document aboard the U.S.S. "Missouri" in Tokyo bay, Sept. 2, 1945. Gen. Douglas MacArthur is shown broadcasting the ceremonies as Japanese Foreign Minister Mamoru Shigemitsu signed for the emperor

the Pacific Islands. Approximately 1,000,000 Koreans had been returned to Korea. At the end of 1946, about 1,500,000 Japanese remained on the continent, and about 500,000 Koreans were still in Japan.

One military lesson to be drawn from the war indicated that, if war came again, crippling and perhaps decisive blows might be struck in the opening moves. The English channel was now not much more of an obstacle to destructive fire power than the Rhine would have been in World War I. The seas and polar wastes guarding North America would, in a few years, be not much more of an obstacle to the destructive weapons of the future than was the English channel in bygone years.

Of great importance to a nation's security in the future was the shrinkage in the time conceivably available to mobilize for defense. Mass destruction weapons, when considered together with available and potential means of delivery, made it evident that if war came, there would not be time for a nation on the defensive initially to mobilize on the basis of World War II schedules, as did the United States in 1940, 1941 and 1942. The great nations of the world had the choice between the constant maintenance of a high state of readiness in industry and military forces, or, alternately, the evolution of some international arrangement which would give mutual assurance against aggression.

World War II, both in the operations and in the weapons developed, demonstrated that, with the exception of the wealthy powers, a nation could no longer depend on its armed forces alone for security against external aggression. The Netherlands, Norway, even Poland, fell in a matter of a few days. Modern methods of war required large populations, large national areas and great industrial capacity not only to support these methods, but to sustain the impact when attacked. Hence, the majority of the nations in the world had to depend primarily on international action for their security. Even if all other elements were available to them, they would not possess the wealth to support the costly modern weapons and forces. A growing recognition of this situation might result in a decreasing emphasis on armed forces and installations except for those necessary to internal security and for the support of agreements for collective security.

Turning to the political results of World War II—for political objectives are the basic objectives of every war—the outcome was still far from clear at the end of 1946. The world was left with two great political forces: soviet communism and western democracy in its various forms. Although the stated purposes of these two political systems might be approximately the same, their concepts were difficult to reconcile in practice. Some system of international collaboration was essential if another war were to be avoided. Perhaps a solution lay in some sort of world commonwealth. It appeared, however, that the alternative could only be continuation of the struggles for ascendancy or survival.

Pending the proven development of some sort of world order, the world had to deal with a drastic shift in the world power situation. Germany, which at the beginning of the decade was a great power, had been eliminated from that category. France, which was recognized as a great power in the 1930s, one of the victorious allies of 1918, was now weaker than before the war. Italy, a cobelligerent at the end of the war, was definitely a minor power. Thus, the four great powers on the European continent in 1937 had in ten years been reduced to one—soviet Russia.

The destruction of Germany and the impact of the war on other European countries left a weak western Europe overshadowed by the military power of the U.S.S.R. The soviet union emerged as one of the two greatest world powers, although with temporary weaknesses to overcome resulting from its enormous expenditures and losses during the war. All Europe suffered from the economic ills of dislocation and scarcity and from the artificial barrier separating eastern and western Europe as established by the occupation forces. Stability could not be achieved until Europe's economic problems were solved and until military power ceased to be the dominant factor in political considerations.

Great Britain had been weakened, not only directly by the cost of the war but also relatively by the shifts in the power potential of other nations and the impact of the war on the controls through which it had long made its influence felt throughout the world. The British empire was in a process of evolution. Witness the grant of self-government to India and the formula being worked out mutually with the Egyptian government. It remained to be seen whether in the long run the evolution of the British empire might develop into a loosely knit federation of states which in turn might point the way to a practicable solution for the remainder of the world. Pending the development of such a world solution, Great Britain would continue to be gravely preoccupied with Europe, since its vulnerability to modern weapons was all too apparent. Equally the portions of the British commonwealth, such as Canada and Australia, without loosening their commonwealth ties, appeared to be faced with the necessity of undertaking independent action in order to look after their own interests.

World War II gave a great impetus to the awakening of backward and colonial peoples, and the generation of a feeling of nationalism and some cohesion in such peoples. This was true in the far east and in the middle east and even in Africa. In the long run the development of this situation should make for a more stable world, providing an over-all solution to the problem of security as between the great powers could be found. For the immediate future, this lively force further complicated the already chaotic world political scene.

The war left the middle eastern area as one of the most troubled areas of the world. It was shadowed by the military power of the U.S.S.R. The new influences had lessened British power in the area.

At the beginning of the decade in the far east, Russia and Japan were recognized as the great powers. The war eliminated Japan, at least for the time being, and brought China forward as a power to be reckoned with. China was weak and split by internal strife. Also it had made important treaty concessions to the U.S.S.R. The future structure in the far east would depend in great part on whether China could fill the void created by the elimination of Japan as a military power.

It was U.S. industrial and military power which provided the additional strength necessary to stem the high tide of initial axis successes and finally to bring the war to a victorious conclusion. The direct military cost to the U.S. for the mobilization of more than 12,000,000 men and the supply of war matériel to its allies was approximately $350,000,000,000 between 1939 and 1946. It required three to five years for the United States to bring the various components of its power actually to bear against the axis. It was U.S. industry which was called to the colours to equip and support not only U.S. forces, but considerable portions of allied forces, and earned the title of "the arsenal of democracy." But all this required time, since the total mobilization of a nation's force is dependent on mobilization of its industry.

An important economic result of World War II was the tremendous expenditure of resources, either through destruction or through absorption in the manufacture of implements of war. Some resources such as timber might be replenished in time, but other resources such as minerals and oil were gone for good.

The majority of the nations which were damaged as a result of military action were in the throes of rehabilitation and of meeting the necessity of establishing adequate living standards for their peoples. This was particularly difficult for the defeated axis powers, now heavily dependent on the Allies for many of the essentials of life. Until such time as these nations could provide for their share of the economic load, the stability of the world would continue uncertain.

During the struggle there was developed to a high degree of efficiency a form of psychological warfare, or the war of nerves. Extensive use was made of propaganda in all its forms, both during the war and after cessation of hostilities. This war of words had an unhappy after-effect seriously complicating and retarding the negotiations concerning the terms for peace settlements. This comparatively new phase of diplomacy would continue to influence the political relations of the world powers through the moulding of public opinion along predetermined lines. This procedure could develop into an evil force of serious moment in international affairs. A free press remained the best defense against this danger.

Emerging from the most widespread and most disruptive war in history, the world faced many major political, economic and social problems of great importance to the peace and well-being of humanity. The growth of nationalism and the desire of backward peoples to improve their political position and their standard of living was a factor which presented varied problems throughout the world. The tremendous advancement in communication facilities during the decade, greatly accelerated by the demands of military necessity, had brought all peoples close together in their human relationships. Technological progress had leaped forward under the pressure of war. It was a sobering thought that world political and moral developments had lagged behind technological developments.

A definite concept for the establishment of international peace had been outlined in the charter of the United Nations. This concept recognized the power of the great nations and the sovereign rights of the small. If it could survive the clash of ideologies, it gave promise of leading the world to a peaceful solution for many of its problems and, finally, to a world without war. (G. C. ML.)

(*See* also AIR RAID DEFENSE; AIR TRANSPORT COMMAND; ALLIED MILITARY GOVERNMENT; ATOMIC BOMB; AVIATION, MILITARY; BIOLOGICAL WARFARE; BLOCKADE; BRITISH-U.S. WAR BOARDS; BRITISH WOMEN'S SERVICES, WORLD WAR II; CAMOUFLAGE; CANADIAN-U.S. WAR COMMITTEES; CANADIAN WOMEN'S SERVICES, WORLD WAR II; CENSORSHIP; CHEMICAL WARFARE; COAST GUARD, U.S.; COMMANDOS, BRITISH; DISPLACED PERSONS; GUERRILLA WARFARE; INCENDIARY WARFARE; INTERNATIONAL CONFERENCES, ALLIED [WORLD WAR II]; JET PROPULSION; LOGISTICS OF WORLD WAR II; MARINE CORPS, U.S.; MILITARY MEDICINE; MUNITIONS OF WAR; NATIONAL GUARD, U.S.; NAVIES OF THE WORLD; PEACE NEGOTIATIONS, WORLD WAR II; PRISONERS OF WAR; PSYCHOLOGICAL WARFARE; REPARATIONS [WORLD WAR II]; ROCKETS; STRATEGIC BOMBING; STRATEGY OF WORLD WAR II; SUBMARINE WARFARE; TACTICS OF WORLD WAR II; WAR AND DEFENSE AGENCIES; WAR CRIMES; WAR PRODUCTION; WAR RELIEF, U.S.: WOMEN'S AIRFORCE SERVICE PILOTS; WOMEN'S ARMY CORPS; WOMEN'S RESERVE OF THE U.S. NAVY.)

BIBLIOGRAPHY.—*I. The Origins.*—*Foreign Affairs* (1937–41) contains pertinent articles. *See* also issues of *International Conciliation;* H. Abend, *Japan Unmasked* (1941), *Ramparts of the Pacific* (1942); H. Agar, *A Time for Greatness* (1942); T. A. Bisson, *American Policy in the Far East, 1931–1941* (1941); E. L. Bogart, *Economic History of Europe, 1760–1939* (1942); R. D. Butler, *The Roots of National Socialism* (1942); W. S. Churchill, *Step by Step, 1936–1939* (1939), *While England Slept* (1938); G. Tanaka (C. Crow, ed.), *Japan's Dream of World Empire: The Tanaka Memorial* (1942); F. Davis, *How War Came: An American White Paper; from the Fall of France to Pearl Harbor* (1942); G. E. R. Gedye, *Betrayal in Central Europe* (1939); J. C. Grew, *Ten Years in Japan* (1944); A. W. Griswold, *Far Eastern Policy of the United States* (1938); J. Gunther, *Inside Asia* (1942), *Inside Europe* (1940); C. G. Haines, *Origins and Background of the Second World War* (1943); J. C. Harsch, *Pattern of Conquest* (1941); R. Heberle, *From Democracy to Nazism* (1945); W. C. Johnstone, *The United States and Japan's New Order* (1941); K. London, *Backgrounds of Conflict* (1945); H. J. MacKinder, *Democratic Ideals and Reality* (1942); W. Millis, *Why Europe Fights* (1940); F. Munk, *Economics of Force* (1940); A. Nevins, *America in World Affairs* (1942); H. A. L. Fisher, *et al., The Background and Issues of the War* (1940); C. Randau, *Setting Sun of Japan* (1942); F. D. Roosevelt, *Roosevelt's Foreign Policy, 1933–1941* (1942); F. L. Schuman, *Design for Power: The Struggle for the World* (1941); W. L. Shirer, *Berlin Diary* (1941); U.S. War Dept., Bur. of Public Rel., *The Background of Our War* (1942); A. Wolfers, *Britain and France between Two Wars* (1940).

II. The War in Europe, Africa and the Near East.—*A. The German Campaign in Poland.*—R. L. Buell, *Poland: Key to Europe* (1939); J. Ciechanowski, *Defeat in Victory* (1947); *German Occupation of Poland* (Polish Whitebook) (1942); J. Karski, *Story of a Secret State* (1944); *Soviet Occupation of Poland* (London, 1940); A. L. Strong, *I Saw the New Poland* (1946). Periodical: *Polish Review* (1941 *et seq.).*

B. The Russ.-Finnish Winter War.—W. P. Coates, *Soviet-Finnish Campaign, Military and Political, 1939–1940* (London, 1942); H. B. Elliston, *Finland Fights* (1940); J. Langdon-Davies, *Invasion in the Snow* (1941); V. A. Firsoff, *Ski Track on the Battlefield* (1943).

C. German Campaigns in Denmark, Norway.—A. Fen, *Nazis in Norway* (1943); J. Goodell, *They Sent Me to Iceland* (1943); C. J. Hambro, *I Saw It Happen in Norway* (1940); F. J. Harriman, *Mission to the North* (1941); H. Koht, *Norway, Neutral and Invaded* (1941); H. K. Lehmkuhl, *Hitler Attacks Norway* (1943); T. Myklebost, *They Came as Friends* (1943); P. Palmer, *Denmark in Nazi Chains* (London, 1942). *See* also *American Mercury* (Jan. 1945); *Foreign Affairs* (Jan. 1943).

D. The Western Front, First Phase.—R. Aghion, *Fighting French* (1943); Gt. Brit. Ministry of Information, *Air Battle of Malta, Official Account* (1944); Allied Forces, *Report of the Supreme Commander to the Combined Chiefs of Staff on the Operations in Europe* (London, 1946); A. B. Austin, *We Landed at Dawn* (Dieppe raid) (1943); K. Ayling, *Bombardment Aviation* (1944); *Battle of Britain* (British Air Ministry, London, 1941); V. Brittain, *England's Hour* (1941); L. E. O. Charlton, *Royal Air Force*, 3 vol. (London, 1941-44); E. K. Chatterton, *Epic of Dunkirk* (London, 1940); W. S. Churchill, *Blood, Sweat, and Tears* (1941); G. N. Clark, *Belgium and the War* (1942); P. Cot, *Triumph of Treason* (1944); A. P. de Seversky, *Victory through Air Power* (1943); C. Gardner, *First Blood for the R.A.F.* (1941); D. Garnett, *War in the Air, Sept. 1939–May 1941* (1941); J. A. Goris, *Belgium in Bondage* (1944); Gt. Brit. Combined Operations Command, *Combined Operations: The Official Story of the Commandos* (London, 1943); G. Holman, *Commando Attack* (1942); T. D. Kernan, *France on Berlin Time* (1941); J. Lorraine, *Behind the Battle of France* (1943); L. Marchal, *Vichy: Two Years of Deception* (1943); A. Maurois, *Tragedy in France* (1940); F. O. Miksche, *Paratroops* (1943); A. A. Michie, *The Air Offensive against Germany* (1943); J. M. Redding and H. I. Leyshon, *Skyways to Berlin* (1943); Q. Reynolds, *Dress Rehearsal* (1943); J. Scott, *Duel for Europe* (1942); J. M. Spaight, *Battle of Britain, 1940* (1941); J. M. K. Strabolgi, *The Campaign in the Low Countries* (London, 1940); *Target: Germany* (U.S. Army Air Forces) (1943); R. Thruelsen and E. Arnold, *Mediterranean Sweep* (1944); E. N. van Kleffens, *Juggernaut over Holland* (1941).

E. British African Campaigns.—*Battle of Egypt* (British Information Services, 1943); A. G. Clifford, *Conquest of North Africa, 1940–1943* (1943), *Crusader* (London, 1942); S. Fielding, *They Sought out Rommel* (London, 1942); Gt. Brit. Ministry of Information, *The First to Be Freed: The Record of British Military Administration in Eritrea and Somalia 1941–3* (London, 1944); Gt. Brit. Air Ministry, *RAF Middle East* (London, 1945); Gt. Brit. War Office, *Destruction of an Army: The First Campaign in Libya* (London, 1941), *The Abyssinian Campaigns* (London, 1942); R. Hill, *Desert War* (1942); C. Hollis, *Italy in Africa* (London, 1941); A. Q. Maisel, *Africa, Facts and Forecasts* (1943); E. G. Ogilvie, *Libyan Log* (London, 1943); E. S. Pankhurst, *British Policy in Eritrea and Northern Ethiopia* (Woodford Green, England, 1946); E. Rosenthal, *The Fall of Italian East Africa* (London, 1942); W. B. K. Shaw, *Long Range Desert Group: The Story of Its Work in Libya* (1945); J. Y. Case, *Written in Sand* (1945).

F. The Near East Campaigns.—E. J. Byng, *The World of the Arabs* (1944); P. W. Ireland (ed.), *The Near East: Problems and Prospects* (1943); C. M. Tobin, *Turkey: Key to the East* (1944).

G. The Balkan Campaigns (1940–1941).—S. Casson, *Greece against the Axis* (London, 1942); G. Christopoulos, *Battle of Greece* (1941); Gt. Brit. War Office, *Campaign in Greece and Crete* (London, 1942); J. A. Hetherington, *Airborne Invasion: The Story of the Battle of Crete* (1943); F. W. L. Kovacs, *The Untamed Balkans* (1941); C. Mackenzie, *Wind of Freedom: The History of the Invasion of Greece by the Axis Powers, 1940–1941* (London, 1943); H. Rowan-Robinson, *Wavell in the Middle East* (1942); R. St. John, *From the Land of Silent People* (1942).

H. The German-Russian War.—W. E. Allen, *Russian Campaigns of 1941–1943* (1944); E. Caldwell, *All-out on the Road to Smolensk* (1942); W. B. Kerr, *The Russian Army: Its Men, Its Leaders, and Its Battles* (1944); G. Meiksins, *Baltic Riddle* (1943); B. Skomorovsky, *Siege of Leningrad* (1944); L. Stowe, *No Other Road to Freedom* (1941); Officers of the Red army and soviet war correspondents, *Strategy and Tactics of the Soviet-German War* (1942); A. Yugow, *Russia's Economic Front for War and Peace* (1942).

I. The North African Campaign.—R. Aghion, *War in the Desert* (1941); H. C. Butcher, *My Three Years with Eisenhower* (1946); A. Clifford, *Conquest of North Africa, 1940–1943* (1943); K. Crawford, *Report on North Africa* (1943); R. Gosset, *Conspiracy in Algiers, 1942–1943* (1945); J. MacVane, *Journey into War* (1943); H. P. Marshall, *Over to Tunis: The Complete Story of the North African Campaign* (London, 1943); A. Moorehead, *The End in Africa* (1943), *Mediterranean Front* (1942); G. W. Price, *Giraud and the African Scene* (1944); E. Pyle, *Brave Men* (1944); G. H. Ramsey, *One Continent Redeemed* (1943); H. Rowan-Robinson, *From Tunisia to Normandy* (1945); M. T. Wordell, *Wildcats over Casablanca* (1943).

J. The Sicilian Campaign.—T. Blore, *Turning Point—1943* (1945); I. Hay, *Malta Epic* (1943); R. L. Oliver, *Malta Besieged* (London, 1945); L. S. B. Shapiro, *They Left the Back Door Open* (1945); R. W. Tregaskis, *Invasion Diary* (1944).

K. The Italian Campaign.—Allied Forces, *Report of the Supreme Allied Commander, Mediterranean, to the Combined Chiefs of Staff on the Italian Campaign* (1946); C. Buckley, *Road to Rome* (London, 1945); J. M. K. Strabolgi, *Conquest of Italy* (London, 1944); U.S. War Dept. General Staff, *From the Volturno to the Winter Line* (1945), *Salerno, American Operations* (1944).

L. Balkan Operations (1942–44).—F. Daley, *Greece—Gallant, Glorious* (1941); M. Padeo, *Marshal Tito* (1945); S. S. Petrovitch, *Free Yugoslavia Calling* (1941); M. Pezas, *Price of Liberty* (1945); David Martin, *Ally Betrayed* (1946).

M. Allied Reconquest of Western Europe.—H. W. Baldwin, "America at War: Victory in Europe," *Foreign Affairs* 23:527–539 (July 1945); *From D-Day through Victory in Europe* (CBS War Correspondents) (1945); E. Holles, *Unconditional Surrender* (1945); W. Millis, *The Last Phase: The Allied Victory in Western Europe* (1946); A. Moorehead, *Eclipse* (1946); U.S. Strategic Bombing Survey, *Summary Report* (European War) (1945); B. G. Wallace, *Patton and His Third Army* (1946).

III. The Chinese-Japanese War (1937–45).—C. A. Buss, *War and Diplomacy in Eastern Asia* (1941); Chiang Kai-shek, *Resistance and Reconstruction* (1943); Chinese Ministry of Information, *China Handbook* (1944); C. Crow, *China Takes Her Place* (1944); H. Forman, *Report from Red China* (1945); A. R. Hager, *Wings for the Dragon* (1945); Lin Yutang, *Vigil of a Nation* (1945); H. S. Quigley, *Far Eastern War, 1937–1941* (1942); E. Snow, *Battle for Asia* (1941); H. K. Tong (ed.), *China after Seven Years of War* (1945).

IV. The War in the Pacific.—J. Belden, *Retreat with Stilwell* (1943); D. Crisp, *Why We Lost Singapore* (1944); H. Daniel, *Islands of the Pacific* (1943); N. Deck, *South from Guadalcanal* (1946); J. Driscoll, *Pacific Victory, 1945* (1945); F. Eldrige, *Wrath in Burma* (1946); F. B. Hailey, *Pacific Battle Line* (1944); H. Handleman, *Bridge to Victory: The Story of the Reconquest of the Aleutians* (1943); J. R. Hersey, *Hiroshima* (1946), *Men on Bataan* (1942); G. E. Hubbard, *British Far Eastern Policy* (1943); F. Hunt, *MacArthur and the War against Japan* (1944); W. Karig and W. Kelley, *Battle Report, Pearl Harbor to Coral Sea* (1944); S. L. A. Marshall, *Island Victory* (1944); C. P. Romulo, *I Saw the Fall of the Philippines* (1942), *I See the Philippines Rise* (1946); G. S. Seagrave, *Burma Surgeon* (1943), *Burma Surgeon Returns* (1946); R. L. Sherrod, *On to Westward: War in the Central Pacific* (1945); N. Smith and T. B. Clark, *Into Siam, Underground Kingdom* (1946); H. Templeman, *Return to Corregidor* (1945); R. Tregaskis, *Guadalcanal Diary* (1943); G. McMillan, *et al*, *Uncommon Valor: Marine Divisions in Action* (1946); U.S. War Dept., *Merrill's Marauders* (1945); W. L. White, *They Were Expendable* (1942); I. Wolfert, *Battle for the Solomon Islands* (1943); D. O. Woodbury, *Builders for Battle* (1946).

V. The War at Sea.—G. Cant, *America's Navy in World War II* (1945), *Great Pacific Victory* (1946); E. Huxley, *Atlantic Ordeal: The Story of Mary Cornish* (1942); W. Karig, *et al.* *Battle Report: The Atlantic War* (1946); *Navy Yearbook* (1944 *et seq.*); F. Pratt, *Fleet against Japan* (1946); Q. Reynolds, *Convoy* (1942); P. Schubert, *Sea Power in Conflict* (1942); U.S. Office of Naval Operations, *Reports* (1941 *et seq.*); U.S. Strategic Bombing Survey, *Campaigns of the Pacific War* (1946).

VII. Conclusions.—J. M. Clark, *Demobilization of Wartime Economic Controls* (1944); Gt. Brit. Prime Minister, *Strength and Casualties of the Armed Forces and Auxiliary Services of the U.K. 1939 to 1945* (Papers by Command, Cmd. 6832) (London, 1946); S. E. Harris (ed.), *Postwar Economic Problems* (1943); E. J. Howenstine, *Economics of Demobilization* (1944); A. Lauterback, "The Aftermath of War Finance," *South Atlantic Quarterly* 44:250–259 (July 1945); L. L. Lorwin, *Economic Consequences of the Second World War* (1941); John F. Bell, *et al.* (G. A. Steiner, ed.), *Economic Problems of War* (1942); U.S. Navy Dept., *State Summary of War Casualties* (1946 *et seq.*); U.S. Office of War Information, *Army-Navy War Casualties: State Group* (1945); U.S. Treasury Dept., *Summary Report* (World War Finance) (1945); University of Chicago Round Table, *Psychiatric Cost of War* (Nov. 19, 1944); A. Vagts, "Battle and Other Combatant Casualties in the Second World War," *Journal of Politics* 7:256–294, 411–438 (Aug.–Nov. 1945); "War Casualties," *League of Nations Mo. Bul. of Statistics* 27:189–191, 233 (May, June 1946); A. P. Youngman, *The Federal Reserve System in Wartime* (1945).

WPA (Work Projects Administration)

See FEDERAL WORKS AGENCY.

WPB (War Production Board)

See WAR AND DEFENSE AGENCIES; WAR PRODUCTION.

WRA (War Relocation Authority)

See WAR AND DEFENSE AGENCIES.

Wrens (Women's Royal Naval Service)

See BRITISH WOMEN'S SERVICES, WORLD WAR II; CANADIAN WOMEN'S SERVICES, WORLD WAR II.

Wrestling

The state of Oklahoma in general, and Oklahoma Agricultural & Mechanical college, Stillwater, Okla., in particular dominated amateur wrestling from 1937 to 1946. Of the 17 national championships staged over the 10-year period, Oklahoma representatives won 11 of them. Oklahoma A. & M. captured each of the seven national intercollegiate championships held during the span.

Only eastern wrestlers broke into the team dominance of Oklahoma in the Amateur Athletic Union championships. The West Side Young Men's Christian Association annexed three titles; the New York Athletic club two, and the Baltimore Y.M.C.A. the other in A.A.U. competition.

Dean of amateur wrestling was Coach Ed Gallagher, who guided his Oklahoma Aggies to eight national intercollegiate championships before he died in 1943. One of Gallagher's pupils, Art Griffith, carried on with a team victory in 1946, the year the intercollegiate meet was resumed after a three-year recess because of the war.

Weight divisions in wrestling changed frequently, the most noteworthy changes being increases from 112 to 115 lb., 118 to 123 lb. and 158 to 160 lb.

Southwestern State Teachers college of Weatherford, Okla., narrowly overcame the Buffalo Y.M.C.A., 11½ to 11, in the 1937 A.A.U. tournament. The meet marked the first national championship for the state of Utah when Merrill Croft won the 118 lb. division. Willard Duffy of the University of Indiana, Bloomington, Ind., was judged the tourney's outstanding wrestler.

Led by Joe McDaniels, a 123-lb. winner in both tournaments, Oklahoma A. & M. scored the only double of the 10-year period by winning both the national A.A.U. and intercollegiate titles in 1938. The Aggies repeated in 1938 in the intercollegiates, but the New York A. C. made good a 5,000 mi. journey to San Francisco, Calif., to win the A.A.U. championships.

Henry Wittenberg led the West Side Y.M.C.A. of New York city to successive A.A.U. team titles in 1940 and 1941, and started a string of five individual championships in doing it. Wittenberg won the 175-lb. divisions in 1941 and 1942, and repeated as 191-lb. champion in 1943, 1944 and 1946.

Oklahoma A. & M. collegians made a landslide of 1942 wrestling, easily winning the college phase of national championships and competing for the Crescent club of Tulsa, Okla., to win the A.A.U. crown. Dave Arndt, 145 lb., and Vernon Logan, 155 lb., won titles in both meets. Collegiate competition also marked repeat titles for the University of Michigan's (Ann Arbor, Mich.) brother team of Merle and Burl Jennings in the 121- and 128-lb. divisions, respectively.

The east dominated A.A.U. championships in 1943 and 1944, the West Side Y.M.C.A. of New York city taking the 1943 title and Baltimore "Y" wrestlers winning in 1944. Midshipman Malcolm McDonald, in the 121-lb. class, became the first wrestler from the U.S. Naval academy to win a National A.A.U. mat title, and also was judged the outstanding wrestler of the 1944 tournament.

A.A.U. championships in 1945 and 1946 featured a series of repeat championships, topped by Wittenberg's fifth national crown as titlist of the 191-lb. division in 1946. Three triple champions were crowned in the 1945 national A.A.U.—Dr. A. M. Northrup of San Francisco, Calif., 175 lb.; Richard Vaughan of Lancaster, Pa., heavyweight, and Douglas Lee of Baltimore, 155 lb. Lee, who won his first A.A.U. title as a 135-pounder in 1941, highlighted the 1946 tournament by defeating Dr. Northrup in the 175-lb. final. The Oklahoma City Y.M.C.A. captured the 1945 team title, while the New York A. C. won in 1946.

Professional Wrestling.—The paid-to-wrestle fraternity fared poorly during the ten-year period. Claimants of world titles in 1938 included Jim Londos, Strangler Lewis, "Doc" Len Hall, Bronko Nagurski, Jack Sherry and Hans Stenke. Most of them had retired by 1946, at which time the former heavyweight boxing champion of the world, Primo Carnera, had become the chief pro mat attraction. (M.P.W.)

Team Wrestling Champions, 1937–46

Year	National A.A.U.	National Intercollegiate
1937	Southwestern State Teachers college	Oklahoma A. & M.
1938	Oklahoma A. & M.	Oklahoma A. & M.
1939	New York A. C.	Oklahoma A. & M.
1940	West Side Y.M.C.A., New York city, N. Y.	Oklahoma A. & M.
1941	West Side Y.M.C.A.	Oklahoma A. & M.
1942	Crescent club, Tulsa, Okla.	Oklahoma A. & M.
1943	West Side Y.M.C.A.	No contests
1944	Baltimore, Md., Y.M.C.A.	No contests
1945	Oklahoma City Y.M.C.A.	No contests
1946	New York A. C.	Oklahoma A. & M.

WSA (War Shipping Administration)

See WAR AND DEFENSE AGENCIES.

Wyoming

A Rocky mountain state, Wyoming was admitted to the union on July 10, 1890, as the 44th state. Leadership in the extension of rights to women gave it the name "Equality state." Land area, 97,506 sq.mi.; water area, 408 sq.mi. Population (1940) 250,742, including 157,165 rural and 93,577 urban; 229,818 native white; 950 Negro; 17,107 foreign born; and 2,345 Indians. On July 1, 1944, the bureau of census estimated the population of the state at 257,108. Capital, Cheyenne (1940: 22,474). Other cities of 10,000 or more: Caspar (17,964); Laramie (10,627); Sheridan (10,529).

Elective state officials in 1937–38 were: governor, Leslie A. Miller; secretary of state, Lester C. Hunt; auditor, William Jack; treasurer, J. Kirk Baldwin; and superintendent of public instruction, Jack R. Gage. In the election of Nov. 1938, the following state officers were chosen: governor, Nels H. Smith (Rep.); secretary of state, Lester C. Hunt (Dem.); auditor, William Jack (Dem.); treasurer, Mart T. Christensen (Rep.); and superintendent of public instruction, Esther Anderson (Rep.). The Republican party was given the balance of power on administrative boards and a majority in both houses of the 1939 legislature.

The 1939 session of the state legislature combined the state planning board with the state conservation board, and gave the new board power to make surveys of water, transportation needs, recreational facilities, soil, adaptability of various parts of the state for crops, range and recreation, mineral resources, possible improvement of the public service, and fish and game. Attempts to remove the sales tax on foods and to require the use of coal instead of gas in public buildings failed in the legislature.

In the general election of Nov. 1940, the Republicans retained control of the state senate, but were forced to take a position of equality in the state house of representatives, since 28 Democrats and 28 Republicans were returned. The state voted Democratic in the national election, giving President F. D. Roosevelt 59,287 votes; Wendell L. Willkie 52,633; Roger Babson 172; Norman Thomas 148. Sen. J. C. O'Mahoney was re-elected to the U.S. senate with the largest majority ever given a Wyoming candidate—more than 19,000—despite the fact that his Republican opponent, Milward Simpson, carried on one of the most active campaigns in the state's history. In the congressional election John J. McIntyre (Dem.) defeated Representative Frank Horton (Rep.). Many celebrations were held in July 1940, in honour of Wyoming's 50th year of statehood.

The state legislature enacted few laws in 1941. A teachers' retirement act was passed, but was vetoed. Communists were barred from primary and general election ballots. Defeated were attempts to replace the 2% sales tax with a gross receipts tax, to establish a drivers' licence law, to legalize gambling, to move the college of agriculture and to remove regulations on trucking. Ninety per cent of the more than 300 bills introduced in both houses were designed to correct defects in existing laws.

Principal state officers elected in Nov. 1942 were: governor, Lester C. Hunt (Dem.); secretary of state, Mart T. Chistensen (Rep.); auditor, William Jack (Dem.); treasurer, Earl Wright (Rep.); superintendent of public instruction, Esther Anderson (Rep.). There was no meeting of the state legislature in 1942.

In the general election of 1942, 30,771 Republican and 23,684 Democratic votes were cast.

Mart T. Christensen (Rep.), secretary of state, died on Oct. 12, 1944, and William Jack (Dem.), state auditor, was appointed secretary of state by the governor on Oct. 16, to finish Christensen's term, a little more than two years. On Oct. 17 the governor appointed Carl Robinson (Dem.) as state auditor to finish William Jack's term. In the general elections of 1944, 51,921 Republican (Thomas E. Dewey) and 49,419 Democratic (Roosevelt) votes were cast. Ralph Kimball (Rep.), supreme court justice, and Frank Barrett (Rep.), congressman, were re-elected.

State officials elected in Nov. 1946 were: governor, Lester C. Hunt, second term (D.); secretary of state, Dr. A. G. Crane (R.); auditor, Everett T. Copenhaver (R.); treasurer, C. J. Rogers (R.); superintendent of public instruction, Edna B. Stolt (R.). Fred H. Blume was re-elected associate justice of the supreme court. A Republican legislature was elected. (A. T. L.; M. H. E.; X.)

BIBLIOGRAPHY.—Council of State Govts., *Book of the States* (bienn.); S. Burt, *Powder River* (1938); Federal Writers' Project, *Wyoming: Guide to Its History, Highways and People* (1941); Secy. of State, *Official Directory* (bienn.). Periodical: *Monthly Checklist of State Publications.*

Wyoming: *Statistical Data*

Table I.—*Education (Public)*

	1938	1941	1942	1943	1944	1945
Elementary school pupils	41,448	39,617	40,125	37,780	39,275	40,420
High school pupils	15,522	15,910	15,123	12,670	13,154	14,103
Elementary teachers	2,023	2,697	1,887	1,725	1,009	1,016
High school teachers	745		820	813	743	750

Table II.—*Public Welfare*

(Money figures in thousands of dollars)

	1938	1940	1941	1943	1944	1945
Cases on general relief	2,379	1,322	870	568	560	540
Cost of general relief	$42	$19	$14			
Recipients of old-age pensions	3,006	3,403	3,523		3,366	
Cost of pensions	$65	$81	$85			
Dependent children receiving aid	1,479	1,846	1,968			
Blind receiving aid	162	148	150	122	125	128

Table III.—*Communications*

(Money figures in thousands of dollars)

	1938	1939	1940	1942	1943	1945
State highway mileage	3,791	3,930			4,082	4,082
Expenditure on highways	$5,415	$4,639	$6,272	$3,000		
Railroad mileage	2,010	2,010	1,993	1,992	1,996	1,996

Table IV.—*Banking and Finance*

(Money figures in thousands of dollars)

	1937	1939	1940	1942	1944	1945
State revenue	$14,010	$14,056	$15,468	$30,543	$15,258	$16,312
State expenditure	$13,161	$9,359	$14,260	$28,260	$14,156	$15,102
State gross debt	$ 3,886		$ 3,878	$ 3,529	$ 2,520	$ 2,520
Number of banks	58	58	58	57	56	56
Number of national banks	26	26	26	26	26	26

Table V.—*Agriculture*

(All figures in thousands)

	1937	1939	1940	1942	1944	1945
Income from crops and livestock	$48,500	$47,944	$54,455			
Leading crops (bu.):						
Beans (cwt.)	649	460	605	1,024	1,251	1,400
Corn	2,480	1,771	1,930	2,013	1,260	1,300
Potatoes	2,400	1,620	2,400	2,240	2,170	2,200
Sugar beets (short tons)	684	539	667	451	305	310
Wheat	3,060	2,812	3,410	4,259	3,198	3,290

Table VI.—*Manufacturing*

(Money figures in thousands of dollars)

	1937	1939	1941 (est.)	1942 (est.)	1943 (est.)	1944 (est.)
Wage earners	3,795	3,484				
Wages paid	$5,219	$4,757				
Value of products	$49,129	$45,423	$26,000	$10,000	$26,000	$27,000

Table VII—*Mineral Production*

(All figures in thousands of dollars)

	1937	1938	1939	1943	1944	1945
Total value mineral production	$41,088	$37,364	$39,425	$46,247	$51,743	$55,140
Leading Products (value):						
Petroleum	18,860	18,000	18,150	26,962	28,850	30,892
Coal	11,600	9,851	10,766	16,363	18,671	18,900
Natural gas	4,997	4,853	4,901	1,215	1,359	1,900

X-Ray

The 50th anniversary of the discovery of the X-ray was celebrated throughout the world in 1945. On Nov. 8, 1895, Wilhelm Konrad Roentgen at the University of Würzburg discovered the new form of energy which he called "X-rays."

The atomic bomb had served to recall in a dramatic way the effect which the discovery of X-rays had upon knowledge of the structure of the physical universe. Arthur H. Compton recalled how Professor Albert Michelson, when dedicating the Ryerson Physical Research laboratory at the University of Chicago, Chicago, Ill., in 1893, had stated that the fundamental principles of physics were then well established and that it remained only to make more precise measurements of the known physical constants. As Dr. Compton observed in his article, "Modern Physics and the Discovery of the X-Rays" in the Nov. 1945 issue of *Radiology,* we were living up to that time in a "determined world, precisely predictable according to laws that were clearly known." It was a world neatly arranged in known patterns, made up of a certain number of elements, each of which in turn was composed of a certain number of atoms. Roentgen's discovery fell into that neatly arranged world with an effect upon the physical theories of the day comparable to the effect of the explosion of the atomic bomb upon the social and political life of a half century later. Soon we were living, not in a world of inert elements, but of electrons, protons and neutrons. The world which had been fixed and determined became a world in flux, seething with constant change in its ultimate structure. The continuing effects of this revolutionary discovery were disclosed as the results of the explosion of atomic bombs were published and as scientists explored the far-reaching nonmilitary possibilities of atomic fission.

The effects of the use of X-rays in medicine had been almost, if not quite, as dramatic and important as their effects on physical science. The decade which ended in 1946 witnessed inventions and discoveries which constituted important advances in the field of medical radiology.

New Apparatus.—From the earliest days of the use of the X-rays in medicine attempts were made to construct an X-ray tube with a rotating anode but it was not until about 1937 that a practical rotating anode tube was devised. Important improvements were made in the tube during the next ten years so that it became standard equipment. It made possible a rapidity of exposure and a fineness of detail in roentgenograms representing a radical improvement over the performance of tubes with stationary anodes.

An automatic timing device to control X-ray exposures was invented and placed in practical use on photoroentgenographic apparatus in 1944 by Dr. Russell Morgan and Dr. Paul C. Hodges. The device consisted of a photoelectric timing mechanism controlling electronically the length of photoroentgenographic exposures. It assured films of uniform density regardless of the thickness of the patient's chest. Its use greatly facilitated the application of photoroentgenography to mass surveys of the chest. At the close of the decade Drs. Morgan and Hodges had completed the necessary research and had constructed several phototimers for use in general roentgenographic work. These were still in a somewhat experimental stage but there seemed no doubt that eventually the automatic electronic timer would be a part of standard X-ray equipment.

Photoroentgenography was one of the most important advances in medical roentgenology during the decade. It consisted in photographing the X-ray image produced on the fluorescent screen and was found especially applicable to examination of the chest and in mass surveys. About 20,000,000 chest examinations were made by this method of members of the U.S. army and navy during World War II. Its value for the detection of pulmonary tuberculosis was so thoroughly demonstrated that it became the chief weapon in the battle against this disease. It was found practical with a single apparatus to make photoroentgenograms of the chests of approximately 500 persons per day. The method came into use in various parts of the world, notably in the United States and in Sweden, in mass surveys of high school children and of industrial employees. It demonstrated its value as a public health measure by disclosing about 100 persons with pulmonary tuberculosis, not before suspected, in each 10,000 examined.

Photoroentgenography brought about renewed interest in cinemaroentgenography. At the beginning of the decade Maurice L. Van de Maele, of Brussels, and Russell J. Reynolds, of London, had succeeded in constructing different types of apparatus which were used successfully in diagnostic studies. The methods used were (1) photoroentgenography, in which the X-ray images were projected on a fluorescent screen and photographed and (2) the direct or roentgenographic method, which registered a considerable number of roentgenograms on a reel or series of films. The great improvement in the photoroentgenographic method which occurred from 1940 to 1946 made it readily adaptable to roentgenocinematography of the heart and intrathoracic blood vessels and of the oesophagus and stomach.

Angiocardiography.—A new method, called angiocardiography, for study of the anatomy and physiology of the heart and great blood vessels and for use in diagnosis of the circulatory system, was devised by George P. Robb and Israel Steinberg in 1938. It was the result of research carried out by them at the New York university college of medicine and the Third Medical Division of Bellevue hospital. The method depended upon the injection of a 70% solution of diodrast into one of the large veins of the arm and the making of roentgenograms when the chambers of the heart and the blood vessels were opaque to the X-rays. Diodrast is an organic compound containing iodine which renders it opaque to the X-rays; its chemical formula is 3.5-diiodo-4-pyridone-N-acetic acid and diethanolamine. It was demonstrated that the following structures become visible upon roentgenograms taken at proper intervals following the injection: the superior vena cava and its tributaries, the four chambers of the heart, the ventricular walls and the interventricular septum, the tricuspid, pulmonic and aortic valves, the pulmonic and aortic sinuses, the pulmonary artery and the entire thoracic aorta and the branches from the arch.

X-raying a wounded veteran of Iwo Jima at the naval hospital, Bethesda, Md. The X-ray technician was a WAVE pharmacist's mate

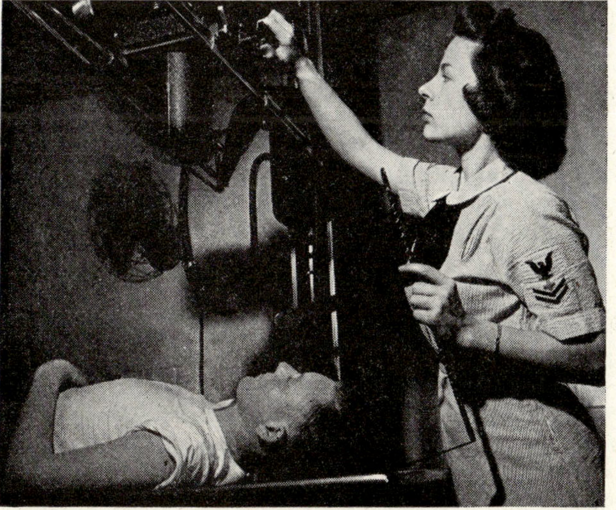

The method was found to be safe and practical, and later reports by the originators and other investigators corroborated its value in diagnosis of a considerable number of intrathoracic diseases and abnormalities. They include congenital heart disease, coarctation of the aorta, aneurysm and various other conditions with associated changes in the size, position and contour of the heart and great vessels. Others reported on the use of the method in various heart diseases and still others on its use in diagnosing pulmonary embolism. At the end of the decade it was clear that angiocardiography had become of real value as a diagnostic aid in diseases within the chest, but it had not yet come into common use because of mechanical and technical difficulties. Improvements which were on the way in photoroentgenography gave promise of overcoming these difficulties and making the method generally available.

Myelography.—In Dec. 1936 Aubrey O. Hampton and J. Maurice Robinson had published a report on the diagnosis of protruding intervertebral disc by injection of lipiodol into the spinal canal. Lipiodol had been used for diagnosis of tumours and other intraspinal lesions ever since its first introduction by J. A. Sicard and J. Forestier. Its use to demonstrate rupture and protrusion of an intervertebral disc, which often causes great pain and disability, was a definite advance. There were objections to the introduction of lipiodol into the spinal canal because of the fact that it is never absorbed and remains as a "foreign body" in the canal. To overcome this objection, Hampton and his co-workers later advocated the removal of the lipiodol through the lumbar puncture needle immediately after the diagnostic procedure was completed. This was not constantly successful because of the viscidity of the lipiodol. The objections to lipiodol for myelography were completely overcome in 1942 when a new contrast medium called "pantopaque" (ethyl iodoundecylate) was devised—an iodized oil much lighter and less viscid than lipiodol. Because of its fluidity it could be manipulated to any locality within the arachnoid sac by tilting the patient on the movable table. It especially facilitated examination of the dorsal and cervical regions of the spine.

The greatest advantage of "pantopaque" was the ease with which it could be withdrawn through the same needle with which it was injected when the diagnostic procedure was finished. There was also evidence that even if a small amount remained in the spinal canal it disappeared after a few weeks, either disseminated in the spinal fluid or absorbed.

Cholecystography.—Advance was made during the decade in diagnosis of diseases of the gall bladder by the use of a new opaque medium named priodax (beta-[4-hydroxy-3.5-diiodophenyl]-alpha-phenyl propionic acid). At the end of the decade priodax had largely replaced tetraiodophenolphthalein for cholecystography. It was found to have the following advantages:

1. Since it does not contain phenolphthalein it does not act as a cathartic. This assures better absorption since it remains in the small intestine for a longer time than tetraiodophenolphthalein.

2. It is less toxic than tetraiodophenolphthalein although in some patients it does produce nausea and diarrhoea.

3. It is almost completely absorbed from the intestinal tract and therefore does not produce opacities which conflict with the gall bladder shadow.

4. It is easily and simply administered in tablet form.

5. The gall bladder filling is better than with the older dye because of the complete absorption of the drug from the intestinal tract.

"Virus" Pneumonia.—During the latter half of the decade 1937–46 there were numerous reports, especially in the United States, from widely separated localities, of an acute disease of the respiratory tract. It was most commonly named "virus pneumonia" but received other names, among them "acute diffuse bronchiolitis," "influenzal pneumonitis," and "atypical pneumonia." Good descriptions of the disease were given by Worth B. Daniels and by Ben E. Goodrich and Henry A. Bradford. It differs from the common types of pneumonia in the absence of identifying organisms in the sputum, in giving few physical signs other than râles, in leukopenia instead of leucocytosis and in its relatively low mortality. It also differs from other pneumonias in its complete failure to respond to the sulfonamide drugs and to penicillin.

The X-ray changes in the lungs include small, diffuse, patchy areas of increased density; a fine, hazy or cloudy appearance which may involve an entire lobe; dense areas which closely simulate the consolidation seen in lobar pneumonia; and widespread miliary dissemination. Another characteristic is its tendency to persist in the lung and to show X-ray evidence of its presence long after clinical signs have disappeared.

X-ray Therapy.—Progress was made during the decade in the treatment of cancer by X-rays produced at very high voltage. A summary of 3½ years' experience with 1,000,000 volt X-ray therapy at Memorial hospital in New York city, published in 1944, may be accepted as a consensus of the status of this type of therapy at the end of the decade. It was demonstrated by physical measurements that deep-seated tumours could be given a much larger dose of X-rays with safety to the normal structures than was possible with lower voltages. The report indicated that the 1,000,000 volt machine was not a substitute for the 200,000 volt unit. At not to exceed 7 or 8 cm. depth, the 200,000 volt unit gave nearly as great a dose as the 1,000,000 volt unit and because of its ease of manipulation was to be preferred. For deep-seated tumours, especially those near vital organs, the 1,000,000 volt machine was better than one giving lower voltages. It could not be stated that treatment at 1,000,000 volts constituted a spectacular advance, but the opinion was generally held by radiotherapists that the improvement was nevertheless real for treatment of deep-seated tumours. (*See* also CANCER; PHOTOGRAPHY; RADIOLOGY; STANDARDS, NATIONAL BUREAU OF; TUBERCULOSIS.)

BIBLIOGRAPHY.—Arthur H. Compton, "Modern Physics and the Discovery of the X-Rays," *Radiology*, 45:534–538 (Nov. 1945); M. J. Gross, and Z. J. Atlee, "Progress in the Design of Rotating Anode Tubes," *Am. J. Roentgenol.*, 41:276–282 (Feb. 1939); Herman E. Hilleboe and Russell H. Morgan, *Mass Radiography of the Chest* (1945); George P. Robb and Israel Steinberg, "Visualization of the Chambers of the Heart, the Pulmonary Circulation, and the Great Blood Vessels in Man: A Practical Method," *Am. J. Roentgenol.*, 41:1–17 (Jan. 1939); Aubrey O. Hampton and J. Maurice Robinson, "The Roentgenographic Demonstration of Rupture of the Intervertebral Disc into the Spinal Canal After Injection of Lipiodol," *Am. J. Roentgenol.*, 36:782–803 (Dec. 1936); Worth B. Daniels, "Bronchopneumonia of Unknown Etiology in a Girls' School," *Am. J. M. Sc.*, 203: 263–276 (Feb. 1942); Ben E. Goodrich and Henry A. Bradford, "The Recognition of Virus Type Pneumonia," *Am. J. M. Sc.*, 204.163–179 (Aug. 1942); Alfred F. Hocker and Ruth J. Guttman, "Three and One-Half Years' Experience with the 1000 Kilovolt Roentgen Therapy Unit at Memorial Hospital," *Am. J. Roentgenol.*, 51:83–94 (Jan. 1944). (A. C. CH.)

Yachting

While many important events in yachting took place during the decade 1937–46, the most important single fact in connection with the period was the growth of the sport itself in spite of wartime conditions during more than half the decade. At the beginning of the period the sport was in full swing, but gathering war clouds soon put a damper on the international aspects. With the actual outbreak of the conflict, all except the most local and restricted kind of sailing became impossible.

Yet the sport was never wholly suspended. Large yachts were laid up or turned over to the naval services and did valuable work as patrol boats, etc. Even in American waters, large coastal areas were closed to pleasure craft, and others were available only under strict regulations. Most of the younger adult yachtsmen were in the services, and many others were in war industries far from their usual sailing grounds. Gasoline, sailcloth, rope, good paint and many other essentials of yacht equipment were either unobtainable or rationed.

For all that, sailing went on. The Englishman, barred from his coastal waters, occasionally managed a sail in a dinghy or other small craft in the lakes and rivers. (Incidentally, the evacuation of Dunkirk was in considerable part a "yachting event" which demonstrated what small craft, handled by amateurs, could do in a deadly emergency. The Blue Water medal of the Cruising Club of America was awarded to "British Yachtsmen at Dunkerque" for their part in the rescue of an army.) Some sailing managed to exist even in occupied countries, like the Netherlands, and the Star class international organization learned, after the war, that new boats had been built and sailed in the unoccupied part of France during the war. The United States, farther from the actual conflict, continued with a considerable amount of local racing throughout the war, although long distance events were impossible except on the Great Lakes; and some cruising was done in small boats, whose activities were restricted to daylight hours. The fleets were manned largely by under-service-age juniors, but many older men bowed down with wartime work and many servicemen home on furloughs, found relaxation in occasional sailing and racing.

In the years between 1940 and 1946 the trend, already evident in the earlier 1930s, was to smaller boats, but there were many more of them and they were sailed by many more people. Although the average tonnage of sailing craft in 1946 was only a fraction of what it had been in 1937, the numbers had multiplied many times. Already a popular sport at the beginning of the decade, the sailing of small yachts was established by the end of 1946 on a far broader and stronger basis than ever before, with many thousands of people of very modest incomes forming the backbone of what had once been considered a rich man's game. The spread of the sport during the ten years demonstrated beyond doubt its vitality and its appeal to the ordinary man.

A minor but significant example of this was "G.I. yachting." From the dismal islands of the Pacific, where soldiers and sailors patched together all manner of strange craft out of odds and ends of salvaged equipment, to the lakes of Germany, where the occupation forces went out in "liberated" yachts, army and navy men from many lands found a way to go sailing.

The America's Cup.—In the opening year of the decade, the outstanding event was the 16th match for the historic America's cup, blue ribbon of international yachting since 1851. In that year T. O. M. Sopwith, a British yachtsman who had been defeated in his first "Endeavour" in 1934, tried again with "Endeavour II," designed and built, like her predecessor, by Charles E. Nicholson. To meet the challenge, Harold S. Vanderbilt, skipper of the last two syndicate-owned defenders of the cup, "Enterprise" and "Rainbow," built "Ranger," designed jointly by W. Starling Burgess and Sparkman and Stephens, and built by the Bath Iron Works.

With the experience of his previous challenge, and with the first "Endeavour" for a trial horse in tuning up the new boat in U.S. waters, Sopwith was a more formidable challenger than he had been in 1934. But he was up against even tougher competition. In her early trials against "Rainbow" and "Yankee," "Ranger" never lost a race, and gave every indication of being a phenomenally fast yacht. She proved it against "Endeavour II." In four races held between July 31 and August 5, 1937, the issue was never in doubt. "Ranger" won by the margins of 17 min. .5 sec.; 18 min. 32 sec., 4 min. 27 sec., and 3 min. 27 sec. respectively in the four races. In contrast to the 1934 series, both the America's cup match and the less formal racing which followed, with the two British and three U.S. class J sloops taking part, was marked throughout by cordial good will and excellent sportsmanship.

"Ranger" was universally acclaimed the fastest Class J sloop ever built. Yet so abnormal were these huge and costly Class J sloops in the modern yachting scene that she was never commissioned again after her one triumphant America's cup season, and was broken up for junk early in World War II. The war forestalled another possible challenge, and there was no immediate postwar indication of early resumption of racing in yachts of this size.

Ocean Racing.—Ocean and long distance racing was one of the most prominent phases of the sport throughout the nonwar years of the decade, from the standpoint of increased participation, public interest and the development of new yachts and gear. The classic fixtures of the sport, such as the Bermuda and Honolulu races from the U.S. coasts, and the British Fastnet race, drew big fleets and fine competition up until the actual start of hostilities, and the Bermuda race was revived with 34 starters in 1946, after the war's end.

In the 1938 Bermuda race, which drew 43 starters, the winner was Henry C. Taylor's 72-foot yawl "Baruna," which continued to be an outstanding boat in cruising class competition throughout the period. The Class B prize winner, Richard J. Reynolds' "Blitzen," also started a career which subsequently included victories in the Honolulu and Mackinac races. The postwar revival of this event in 1946 saw Howard Fuller's sloop "Gesture," built in 1941, take top honours and Robert F. de Coppet's little yawl "Suluan," one of the few ocean racing craft built after the war and completed in time for the race, win in Class B. The fleet included a number of yachts built in the 1920s and early '30s, but they were generally outclassed by the more modern ocean racing type sloops and yawls built after 1936.

The "Vim," Harold S. Vanderbilt's yacht (foreground) which won the annual regatta of the New Rochelle Yacht club in Long Island sound June 29, 1940, despite a broken spinnaker pole

The Fastnet, British equivalent of the Bermuda race, attracted fast fleets both in 1937 and 1939, with a Dutch entry, G. Bruynzeel's "Zeearend," winning in 1937. In 1939, Isaac Bell's yawl "Bloodhound," one of the most modern British ocean racers, was the winner with "Zeearend" second and a German entry, "Roland von Bremen," third. In the Honolulu races, from west coast ports, "Blitzen" was the winner in 1939 and D. W. Elliott's sloop "Escapade" defeated a small fleet that sailed the course in 1941. Both the Fastnet and Honolulu races were scheduled for revival in 1947.

Great Lakes yachtsmen were fortunate in having their waters open for sailing during the war, and the Mackinac Island races from Chicago, Ill., and Port Huron, Mich.—fresh water counterparts of the ocean events—went on uninterrupted. Among the notable winners were Henry Rubinkam's "Rubaiyat," John B. Ford Jr.'s "Royono II," James R. Lowe's "Manitou," Herman Kronstedt's "Hope," Fred S. Ford's "Evening Star," E. B. Lumbard's "Bangalore," A. Herrmann's "Gloriant," O. Dreher's "Lively Lady," "Blitzen" (then owned by Murray Knapp and Ernest Grates), Sumner Scott's "Breeze," the Timken brothers' "Kitty Hawk," C. E. Sorenson's "White Cloud," James Rider's "Carina" and others.

In addition to these few major events, scores of shorter races, from overnight to several days' duration, took an increasingly prominent place in the yachting calendars in U.S. and British waters and, after the conclusion of the war, to some extent in Scandinavian waters.

Six-Metre Internationals.—The International Rule six-metre class, for many years a leading factor in international yachting, was as active as ever up to the outbreak of war in Europe. In 1937 the Scandinavian Gold cup and the Seawanhaka International Challenge cup were both held by the Seawanhaka Corinthian Yacht club at Oyster Bay, N.Y., and were successfully defended. Briggs S. Cunningham's "Lucie" defeated a fleet of boats from several countries for the former trophy, and Paul Shields's "Rebel" won a match for the latter.

In 1938, again off Oyster Bay, George Nichols' "Goose" successfully defended the Gold cup; a British-U.S. team

race was won by the Seawanhaka trio of "Goose," H. S. Morgan's "Djinn" and "Rebel"; and J. H. Thom, a Scottish challenger, sailing "Circe," took the Seawanhaka cup in a match series with "Goose."

By mutual agreement, the Gold cup races were held in Scandinavian waters in 1939, and again "Goose" was the winner.

Late in 1946 Seawanhaka challenged the Royal Northern Yacht club of Scotland for the Seawanhaka cup, the race to be sailed in six-metres the following year, and a challenge was expected for the Gold cup as well. However, postwar conditions had made six-metre racing an even more expensive sport than before the war, and there was a movement among yachtsmen on both sides of the Atlantic to attempt to establish another class of somewhat smaller and considerably lighter and less expensive yachts which should in time supplant the Sixes.

Other International Events.—The visit of Harold Vanderbilt's 12-metre sloop "Vim" to British waters in 1939 was so successful, from a racing standpoint, that it brought from Charles E. Nicholson, dean of British designers, the comment that there was little use in trying to beat U.S. yachts until the British had a model testing tank similar to those in which U.S. designs were tested and developed before the boats were built.

A Beverly Y.C. team of 30-square-metre yachts defeated a team of Swedish sloops of that class in a series on Buzzards Bay, Mass., in 1938.

The Star class functioned throughout the decade as a popular small boat world racing organization. The 1937 world's championship was marked by the appearance of Walter von Hutschler's German Star "Pimm," with a revolutionary rig having flexible mast and boom. "Pimm" broke down in that series, which was won by Milton Wegeforth's "Lecky," of San Diego, Calif., but she won the next two years in a row, with the result that the bending rig was adopted by most of the keener skippers of the world-wide class, which now included more than 2,000 boats. The visiting Star sailors in the 1939 world series at Kiel got out of Germany just as the German army marched into Poland. Starting with 1940 world champion Star skippers were James Cowie and George Fleitz, both of Los Angeles, Calif., Harry G. Nye of Chicago, A. M. Deacon of the Long Island Sound fleet, and Gerald Driscoll and Malin Burnham, both of San Diego.

The 14-ft. international sailing dinghies long popular in the British Isles and to a lesser extent in other European countries, Canada, the United States and elsewhere, were in the midst of an expansion in 1946 which indicated that these boats might figure more prominently in the international sailing picture.

Material, Designs, Rules.—World War II and its aftermath greatly increased costs of building and maintaining boats—approximately double prewar figures in some cases—and caused scarcities of materials and equipment. As a result, many experiments in new materials and methods were undertaken in 1945 and 1946. Hulls were built of moulded and sheet plywood, plastics of various sorts and aluminum, and steel was used in much smaller boats than had been common prewar practice. Nylon made its appearance in sails and rope, and aluminum spars became common in small craft.

Whether any or all of these materials would permanently replace the old standards of lumber, cotton and hemp, when the latter materials were again available, was a source of considerable speculation. At least some of the substitutes seemed satisfactory and likely to become standard material.

A notable trend of the decade was the increase in the numbers and popularity of stock boats. Small stock one-design sailing craft, such as the Comets, Snipes, Lightnings, dinghies and other types, multiplied manifold, and a number of such classes each included several thousand boats by the end of the decade. They were organized on a national basis in many countries and, in some cases, on an international basis which promised further competition among yachting nations.

This swing to stock boats, partly for more equitable racing and partly for economy, spread during the decade from the small racing and day sailing classes to cruising auxiliaries up to 40 feet or more in over-all length. Many designers and builders offered such boats, and several hundred were built, some of which raced successfully among themselves and in coastwise and port-to-port races. Though a detriment to the progress of yacht design, the spread of these stock classes helped to popularize the sport.

The rules of the sport remained practically static during the decade, but 1946 saw a movement on both sides of the Atlantic to consider changes. These proposed changes embraced both the right-of-way rules of racing, which were practically standardized among all the active yachting countries, and the measurement rules, some of which were also international in scope. The changes appeared likely to be slow in taking final form and general acceptance, but national and international yachting organizations were working toward the desired ends at the close of the decade.

BIBLIOGRAPHY.—Harold S. Vanderbilt, *On the Wind's Highway* (1938); Alfred F. Loomis, *Ocean Racing*, new ed. (1946); Maurice Griffiths, *Little Ships and Shoal Waters* (British); T. Harrison Butler, *Cruising Yacht, Design and Performance* (British, 1946); Harvey Flint, *Winning Yacht Races* (1946); Dennis Puleston, *Blue Water Vagabond* (1939); Capt. and Mrs. Irving Johnson, *Westward Bound in the Schooner Yankee* (1936); Capt. and Mrs. Irving Johnson, *Sailing to See* (1939); Alan Villiers, *Cruise of the Conrad* (1937); Maurice Griffiths, *Post War Yachting* (British, 1946). (H. L. ST.)

The "Gesture" and the "Niña" just after the start of the 1946 races from Newport, R.I., to Bermuda. The "Gesture" took class A honours

Yalta Conference

See INTERNATIONAL CONFERENCES, ALLIED (WORLD WAR II).

Yamamoto, Isoroku

Yamamoto (1884–1943), Japanese naval officer, was born April 4, 1884, at Nagoaka, Japan. He was graduated from the naval academy in 1904 and fought as an ensign in the Russo-Japanese war. He was naval attaché in the Japanese embassy in Washington, 1925. As Japanese delegate at the London naval conference in 1934–35, he successfully fought the Anglo-U.S. proposal to extend the naval "holiday." Yamamoto thereafter won rapid promotion. Foremost Japanese advocate of combining air and sea power in naval attacks, he was promoted to commander in chief of the fleet in 1939. Referring to the Japanese surprise attack on Pearl Harbor, Domei (Japanese) news agency revealed in a dispatch on Dec. 17, 1941, that the strategy of surprise carried out by Adm. Yamamoto was planned by him earlier (in Jan. 1941, according to Japanese documents seized after V-J day).

A Tokyo radio report of 1943 announced that he had been mortally injured in action while directing naval operations from a plane on a "far southern front," in

April 1943, and that he had died shortly afterward. The real facts of his death became known after V-J day in 1945. Through an intercepted Japanese message, Yamamoto's exact air itinerary was learned in advance by U.S. intelligence officers, who forwarded the information to the army air forces in the Solomons. A precise rendezvous with death was thus arranged for Yamamoto, whose plane was shot down by Lt. Col. T. G. Lanphier, Jr., over the Solomons on April 18, 1943.

Yamashita, Tomoyuki

Yamashita (? -1946), Japanese army officer, was a close student of German military tactics. An able strategist, he conceived the military plan for the Japanese invasion of Malaya, 1941–42. After a 10-wk. campaign, Singapore surrendered to Gen. Yamashita on Feb. 15, 1942. On March 9, Gen. Yamashita assumed command of the Philippine campaign. With a numerically superior army and air force, he won the battle of Bataan, April 9, and conquered the Corregidor island fortress, May 6, 1942.

After Gen. MacArthur's surprise landing of U.S. troops on Leyte in the Philippines Oct. 20, 1944, Gen. Yamashita assumed personal command of the resisting Japanese forces. His army was badly defeated in both the Leyte and Luzon campaigns and he surrendered at Baguio, Luzon, to Lt. Gen. Jonathan M. Wainwright on Sept. 3, 1945. Arraigned Oct. 8 in Manila before a military court on charges of being a war criminal, Yamashita pleaded not guilty and subsequently denied that he knew of atrocities committed in his command. Found guilty (Dec. 7) and sentenced to be hanged, he immediately filed an appeal through his counsels with the U.S. supreme court to contest the decision.

The U.S. supreme court on Dec. 17 granted Yamashita a stay of his execution until a decision could be made on its intervention in the case. But on Feb. 4, 1946, the supreme court finally turned down his plea, and he was hanged Feb. 23.

Yap

See Pacific Islands, Mandated; World War II.

Yarnell, Harry Ervin

Yarnell (1875–), U.S. naval officer, was born Oct. 18, 1875, at Independence, Ia. He was graduated from the U.S. Naval academy in 1897 and from the Naval War college in 1915. Commissioned an ensign in 1899, Yarnell served in the Spanish-American war, the Philippine insurrection, the Boxer rebellion and in the occupation of Vera Cruz (1914).

During World War I, he commanded the U.S.S. "Nashville" on patrol duty at Gibraltar and in 1918 he was appointed to Adm. Sims' staff in London. Yarnell was named chief of the Naval Bureau of Engineering and raised to the rank of rear admiral in 1928. Three years later, he became commander of the aircraft squadrons of the battle fleet and in 1933, he was appointed commandant of the Pearl Harbor naval station. Advanced to commander-in-chief of the U.S. Asiatic fleet in 1936, he achieved renown for his consistent refusals in 1938–39 to submit to early Japanese efforts to restrict U.S. commercial and naval privileges in China.

Upon his retirement in 1939, congress voted him a distinguished service medal. After the close of World War II, Adm. Yarnell urged that the U.S. retain its Pacific island bases until such time as the United Nations trustee council had reached a stage of maturity and responsibility.

Yeast

Fundamental studies of yeast metabolism during the decade 1937–46 helped explain not only the mechanisms of fermentation and respiration, but also the basic relationships existing between vitamins and enzymes. The enzyme hydrogenase was isolated from yeast in pure form. The chemical nature of yeast ribonucleic acid was explored. Establishment of the stimulating effect of certain B complex vitamins upon either growth or alcoholic fermentation by yeast led to use of yeast in microbiological assay methods for these vitamins.

Numerous secondary sterols of yeast were studied, and improved methods were perfected for manufacturing ergosterol from yeast. Other industrial advances were development of active dry yeast for baking, and cultivation of torulopsis yeasts for feed and food uses. Progress in utilization of by-products for yeast cultivation included the use of wastes from fruit processing industries and the invention of a speedy method for hydrolyzing wood wastes to make carbohydrates for growing yeast. New types of yeast extracts and yeast derivatives were perfected. A process was invented for manufacturing bakers' yeast high in thiamin (vitamin B_1) by growing in a substrate containing thiamin intermediates.

The *Pharmacopoeia* of the U.S. set up specifications for dry yeast for pharmaceutical use. Nutritive and therapeutic values of yeast were clarified by establishment of its content of the vitamins folic acid, biotin, choline, inositol, pyridoxine and pantothenic acid, and of the essential amino acids. Use of irradiated dry yeast to produce metabolized vitamin D milk was discontinued, but irradiated dry yeast gained increased use as a source of vitamin D for four-footed animals.

Bibliography.—F. G. Walter, *The Manufacture of Compressed Yeast* (1940); S. C. Prescott and C. G. Dunn, *Industrial Microbiology* (1940). (F. W. N.)

Yellow Fever

See Entomology; Epidemics and Public Health Control.

Yemen

See Arabia.

Yeremenko, Andrei Ivanovitch

Yeremenko (1892–), Russian army officer, was born Oct. 14, 1892, at Markova, in the Ukraine. He was conscripted into the Imperial Russian army in 1913 and saw service in World War I on the eastern front. After the peace of Brest-Litovsk, Yeremenko became a guerrilla and joined the Red army during the revolution, serving later as an officer in a cavalry unit. Yeremenko subsequently studied at the High Cavalry school, the Military-political academy and the Frunze Military academy. He was given command of a field army on the northwest front in 1941 and was assigned to the Stalingrad front in late 1942. Yeremenko was wounded seven times in the historic struggle for the Volga city. Decorated with the Order of the Red Banner, he was promoted first to the rank of colonel general and then full general in Aug. 1943.

In 1944, Yeremenko directed the special maritime army in the Crimean drive that culminated in the recapture of Sevastopol. In July of that year, he was given command of the 2nd Baltic army and participated in the reconquest of Latvia. Toward the close of the war early in 1945,

Yeremenko took over command of the 4th Ukrainian army from Gen. Petrov.

Y.M.C.A.

See YOUNG MEN'S CHRISTIAN ASSOCIATION.

Yonai, Mitsumasa

Yonai (1880–), Japanese naval officer and politician, was born in March 1880 in Morioka, Iwate prefecture. Graduated from the Naval academy (1901), he served in the Russo-Japanese war, 1904–05, subsequently rising rapidly through the grades. He was navy minister in the Hayashi cabinet, 1937–39, and was named supreme war councillor in Aug. 1939. Emperor Hirohito called on Yonai on Jan. 14, 1940, to form a cabinet. His selection as premier was regarded as a surprise victory for the so-called moderates as opposed to the army extremists. Yonai assertedly objected to extremist demands that Japan join the Rome-Berlin axis, and he was forced from the premiership on July 16, 1940, by Gen. Hideki Tojo, who was then the acknowledged leader of the ambitious military clique. Subsequently, when Tojo was ousted from the premiership (July 1944), both Gen. Kuniaki Koiso and Adm. Yonai were asked (July 20) to form a cabinet and rule as co-premiers. However, Gen. Koiso assumed the premiership and Yonai was allocated the post of navy minister. Yonai was also navy minister in the Suzuki government and in the surrender cabinet formed by Prince Naruhiko Higashi-Kuni, Aug. 16, 1945. He was retained in the Shidehara cabinet formed in Oct. 1945, but not in the succeeding Yoshida government (May 1946) in which the navy portfolio was dropped.

York, Archbishop of

See GARBETT, CYRIL FORSTER.

Yoshida, Shigeru

Yoshida (1878–), Japanese politician, was born Sept. 22, 1878, in Tokyo. He was educated at Tokyo Imperial university, graduating from the Law college in 1906. The same year, he entered the diplomatic service, and from 1916 to 1917 he was a second secretary at the Japanese embassy in Washington. He was Japan's minister to the Scandinavian countries in 1928, vice-foreign minister, 1928–30, and ambassador to Italy, 1930–32. Yoshida made a special tour of Europe in 1934, trying to justify Japan's seizure of Manchuria and to soothe diplomatic feelings ruffled by his country's subsequent departure from the League of Nations. From 1936 to 1939 he was ambassador to London.

Toward the close of World War II, Yoshida was arrested as a peacemonger. After Japan's surrender, he was freed and became foreign minister in the Shidehara cabinet, Oct. 6, 1945. There was some tepid criticism of Yoshida's appointment because of his previous associations with the Zaibatsu (Japanese "big business").

On May 15, 1946, Yoshida accepted the presidency of the Japanese Liberal party; the following day he was named successor to Shidehara as premier; his cabinet was sworn in May 22.

Young Men's Christian Association

In 1937, there were 10,380 local Young Men's Christian associations in 66 countries, with more than 2,000,000 members, chiefly youth. In that year, the 21st world conference was held at Mysore, India, evidencing an interracial, intercultural, international and interreligious bond that had continued and grown stronger for almost a century.

Such an organization was among the first to feel the impact of World War II. Except in a few neutral lands, the young men of the membership were first under arms and in combat. The various Y.M.C.A. national alliances promptly made their experience and facilities available to their governments, and the record of their contribution to the youth of their respective countries, whether under arms or in civilian life, became notable.

Among the Allied nations, the national Y.M.C.A. organizations of England, Canada, China, Australia, New Zealand, India, Poland and other countries accompanied the armed forces everywhere. Veterans of Dunkirk, El Alamein, the North African campaign and the defense of England found the services of tea vans in the field, clubs in the staging points and cities and at leave centres. When Japanese occupation of China caused whole cities to trek westward into the interior, Y.M.C.A. members and leaders among them were immediately active in organizing new centres and services. The direct service among the Chinese armies was extensive and included distant contingents in Thailand, Burma and India. When Poland was overrun, Y.M.C.A. activity was at once begun among the army remnants and refugees who made their way into Hungary and Rumania until finally this Polish Y.M.C.A. service was continued in 151 centres in Palestine, Syria, Egypt and in five countries in East Africa, as well as in western Europe.

In America, where government policy did not permit direct service by religious organizations and groups as such or allow them to go with military expeditions abroad, much was done within continental U.S. and in offshore bases, by the United Service Organizations (*q.v.*), a newly-formed body of which the Y.M.C.A. was one of the six founding member bodies. With official recognition by the government, this service provided extensive social, recreational, educational and religious programs adjacent to military establishments, in leave centres, in transit and in certain army bases from Iceland and Brazil to Alaska, Hawaii and the Philippines.

In Germany and other central and occupied countries in Europe, ruling regimes began, even before the outbreak of the war, to place certain restrictions upon Y.M.C.A. activities. Programs for boys were prohibited in Germany. A limited program among young men was allowed for a time, protected in a measure by church sponsorship. However, even after occupation, as in Czechoslovakia, Poland, France and other countries in western Europe, some activity continued, though usually with considerable risk. In Japan, where the Y.M.C.A. had earlier been included by government order in the general framework of the National Church of Christ, it was possible to continue some service among Japanese in Manchuria, China and Korea. Local Y.M.C.A. work continued in China and the Philippines under Japanese occupation, sometimes under great deprivations and in the midst of destruction. More than 80 Y.M.C.A. buildings in various countries were wholly or partially destroyed, 13 of them in the Philippines alone. Many secretaries were long imprisoned. Most of them suffered infamous cruelties, and some of them lost their lives.

War Prisoners' Aid.—In World War II, as in World War I, the Y.M.C.A.'s work among prisoners of war became an outstanding feature. Under the World's Alliance of Y.M.C.A.s, in accordance with provisions of the Geneva convention of 1929, the Y.M.C.A. accepted responsibility for conducting recreational, educational and religious programs among war prisoners wherever reciprocal agreements negotiated with belligerent nations opened the way. Using more than 150 neutral staff representatives as visitors, with service and supplies costing almost $17,000,000, this grateful activity reached its crest in the spring and summer of 1945. Official permission was granted to visit prisoner of war camps and supply material was granted for 33 countries, while prisoner contingents in 20 more received shipments of supplies. These visits and services were not allowed in the case of soviet Russia, nor were visits allowed in Italy. Earlier restrictions by Japan were gradually liberalized to permit visits and supplies in certain areas.

Wartime Centennial.—The Y.M.C.A.'s world centennial in 1944 found the association's own members in nearly all countries engulfed in unprecedented wartime demands. Nevertheless the observance was world-wide. A solemn service of thanksgiving and dedication, in which the king of England and other international notables took part, was broadcast from St. Paul's cathedral in London, almost on the spot where young George Williams and 11 fellow-workers in Hitchcock's store organized the first Young Men's Christian association in 1844. On every continent and unto the uttermost parts of the earth, friends in community and public life joined with members and leaders of every race and faith in a tribute that represented gratitude and expectancy.

Reconstruction.—Long before the war's end, association leaders of many nations had begun to plan for reconstruction and the future. An enlarged executive meeting of the World's committee at Geneva, Switzerland. Feb. 28 to March 8, 1946, laid plans for reconstruction and extension around the world. The steadily diminishing work among prisoners of war was voted continuance through 1947 with a budget of $800,000. Fresh opportunities among prisoners returning home were widely reported. A petition for reinstatement in the World's Alliance of Y.M.C.A.s, by representatives of the German Y.M.C.A., which had abruptly withdrawn from the World's Alliance of Y.M.C.A.s in June, 1939, was granted after searching consideration. Plans for visitation and survey among seven major regional divisions of the world were activated. From North America was reported the launching of a World Youth Fund for Restoration and Advance with a goal of $8,650,000 for restoring personnel and buildings in war-occupied countries and for emergency assistance in meeting war-created needs now faced by Y.M.C.A.s in their service among youth around the world.

BIBLIOGRAPHY.—*The Hundred-Year Book, a Synoptic Review of the History of the Young Men's Christian Association*, Reprint from *YMCA Year Book* (1944); *Gazetteer of YMCA Work Around the World*, and *Report on 1944 Centennial Observance*, Reprint from *YMCA Year Book* (1945); *Actions of Enlarged Executive Meeting of the World's Committee of Young Men's Christian Associations* (Switzerland, 1946); Andre Vulliet, *The Y.M.C.A. and Prisoners of War* (1946). (O. E. P.)

Young Womens Christian Association

During nearly the whole of the ten years from 1937 to 1946 the Young Womens Christian association was involved in the problems of war. In 1937, when China was invaded by Japan, the Y.W.C.A. of the United States began to raise special funds to help the Y.W.C.A. leadership of China to meet their problems, one of which was moving westward into free China in 1941.

In the fateful days of Sept. 1938 the World's council met in Canada, working at that meeting on the problems of the Y.W.C.A. throughout the world, such as the needs of youth and the desirability of co-operating with youth organizations, the Y.W.C.A. as a Christian women's movement, its contribution in the oecumenical and social fields, and its responsibility in the field of international relations. But surrounding these discussions was the impending horror of war.

Through the months and years that followed, the Y.W.C.A. throughout the world endeavoured to relieve suffering, provide cheerful and homelike atmosphere in clubs and hostels for women in the services of the Allied nations, and in all possible ways to mobilize the services of women as leaders and to meet the needs of war victims everywhere.

The Y.W.C.A. in Great Britain was early requested by the government to work as a private agency with girls and women in munitions factories and in the war services, both in Britain and overseas. The house built on the Nile for nurses worn out by their arduous duties, the hostel in Eritrea, vacation lodges in India and Italy, wherever they could be set up, and club centres for service women and Red Cross nurses just back of the front lines in Africa, Italy, Europe and southeast Asia—all were examples of the type of work carried on. In this work of the British War services the Y.W.C.A. of the U.S. co-operated by assigning American staffs to them and grants of money for their programs.

In the U.S. the Y.W.C.A. was one of the six organizations in United Service Organizations (*q.v.*), working with men and women in the vicinities of the camps and in war production areas. Through its participation in the National War fund it was possible for the Y.W.C.A. to work overseas in connection with the British War services and independently, and also to serve war victims in the U.S.—refugees, interned enemy alien women and Japanese evacuees. In the U.S. the Y.W.C.A. worked also through American War-Community Services, Inc., in industrial communities. Meanwhile, in the U.S., in Great Britain and in other countries, the Y.W.C.A. endeavoured to maintain its so-called regular work with women and girls—recreation, housing, club centres, discussion groups, personal counselling. Much of the work carried on in these years was in co-operation with other organizations. Never before had the Y.W.C.A. drawn so close to the other organizations with a similar purpose, the churches, the Y.M.C.A., the youth movements and many government agencies.

Three national conventions were held in the United States during the decade 1937–46: in 1938 at Columbus, O., where special emphases recommended for the following biennium were religion, democracy and building a world community; in 1940 at Atlantic City, N.J., the world already at war and the question being asked "Should the United States participate?", the Y.W.C.A. considered the tremendous needs it was endeavouring to meet overseas; and in 1946, when the actual hostilities were over, another large meeting in Atlantic City with more than 2,300 delegates from the U.S. and representatives from 26 foreign countries coming together to look at the situation facing this international Christian women's organization, and to determine its task for the following three years. Of particular significance was the report on interracial practices in the U.S. and the determination to move forward in the light of this report. At the end of the decade, the Y.W.C.A. was working in 69 countries and in the U.S. alone had a constituency of nearly 3,000,000. (M. S. Ss.)

Youth Administration, National

See NATIONAL YOUTH ADMINISTRATION.

Yugoslavia

Yugoslavia was established after World War I as the kingdom of the Serbs, Croats and Slovenes, and received the name Yugoslavia officially in 1929. Under King Peter II in 1941 it rejected German demands for collaboration; as a result of German aggression it was defeated and partitioned in 1941. It was liberated in 1945 by Russian and British armies and by the partisans under leadership of Marshal Tito (Josip Brozovich or Broz). Area 95,558 sq.mi.; pop. (est. Jan. 1, 1940) 15,703,000. Capital (1931 census): Belgrade, 238,775. Other chief cities: Zagreb, 185,-581; Subotica, 100,058; Ljubljana, 59,767; Sarajevo, 78,173. Religion: 6,785,501 Greek Orthodox; 5,217,910 Roman Catholic; 1,561,166 Mohammedans; 231,169 Protestants; 68,405 Jews.

At the beginning of the fateful decade in 1937, Yugoslavia was a constitutional monarchy; the king, Peter II, had succeeded to the throne on Oct. 9, 1934, at the age of 11. During his minority a Regency council governed under the king's uncle Prince Paul; the premier and minister of foreign affairs was Dr. Milan Stoyadinovitch. The year 1937 seemed to strengthen the country's interests and position. A treaty of friendship with Bulgaria, signed on Jan. 24, secured her eastern flank, and inaugurated an era of genuine good feeling. On March 26, a political and a commercial treaty was signed with Italy. The two countries undertook to respect their common frontiers on land and in the Adriatic. If either were attacked without provocation by one or more powers, the other would abstain from action calculated to help the aggressor. Each would inform the other of measures taken to safeguard itself in international crises. Both agreed not to resort to war as an instrument of their national policies, and to settle their differences by peaceful means. They would not tolerate on their territories activities directed against each other's territorial integrity or political independence, or calculated to disturb their existing relations. It was understood that they exchanged assurances to respect the integrity of Albania, and not to seek exclusive advantages in that country. Under the trade agreement, Yugoslavia got increased exports to Italy, participation in the benefits of the Rome protocols and an active trade balance with Italy.

While remaining formally faithful to the Little Entente and Balkan Entente, Yugoslavia leaned more and more toward the fascist powers and also improved her relations with Hungary. But many Yugoslavs felt that Stoyadinovitch was going too far in cultivating the friendship of Italy and Germany, which he visited on Jan. 15, 1938, being warmly received. Hitler stressed Germany's interest in "a strong and independent Yugoslavia," while after the occupation of Austria he declared Germany's new frontier with Yugoslavia inviolable. The premier therefore expressed no misgivings about the occupation, although the opposition was less complacent, particularly in view of nazi agitation among the Germans of Yugoslavia, and alleged oppression of the Slovenes in Carinthia. Yugoslavia in 1938, at the time of the Czechoslovak crisis, abandoned the Little Entente and thought that she could watch the Czechoslovak crisis (in which she declared herself neutral) with comparative detachment.

Serb-Croat Problem.—Internally Yugoslavia enjoyed considerable prosperity, largely owing to her increased trade with Germany, and her industrialization proceeded. But Yugoslavia's most vexing problem remained unsolved: the relations between the two leading Slav peoples forming Yugoslavia, the Serbs and the Croats. There the political deadlock continued. Vlatko Machek, the Croat leader, who had been in touch with the Serb opposition during 1938, visited Belgrade on Aug. 14, and the arrangements for collaboration concluded in 1937 were confirmed. In the December elections the Popular Entente representing Machek's Croat Peasant party and the Serb democratic opposition, increased its vote considerably, polling 40.21% of the total votes cast, and gaining very large majorities in Croatia and Dalmatia. The government list, which polled 59.8% of the votes, was successful chiefly in Serbia and Slovenia. The government bloc secured 304 seats in the new chamber, the opposition 68 seats.

Though the electoral law gave the government a disproportionate majority of seats, the necessity of an understanding with the Croats was generally recognized. On Feb. 4, 1939, the government was reconstructed with Dragisha Cvetkovitch as premier in place of Stoyadinovitch. It was at once announced that the government meant to solve the Croat question; it was understood also that it hoped to return to more constitutional methods. Serbo-Croat negotiations began at once, but many difficulties arose, including that of delimiting the Serb and Croat areas. On April 27, 1939, it was announced that agreement had been reached, but a later announcement stated that the prince regent had refused his consent to the agreement, which included provision for a representative government of concentration. Only on Aug. 25, after feeling had risen very high, were fresh proposals sanctioned. A new government was now formed, including five members of the government party, five representatives of the Croat party, and three of the Serb opposition. Cvetkovitch remained premier and Alexander Cincar-Markovitch foreign minister. The two Croat banovinas (provinces), with seven adjacent districts, amounting to 20% of the area of Yugoslavia, with a population of 4,423,000 (3,052,000 were Croats and 360,000 Serbs) were formed into a new banovina under a Croat ban (appointed and dismissible by the crown), and with its own diet at Zagreb. The banovina enjoyed very wide autonomy, but foreign affairs, defense, foreign trade, public security, religion, commerce, transport, mining, weights and measures and general educational policy were reserved to the central authorities. The first ban was Ivan Shubashitch. Parliament was dissolved and the government was empowered to hold new elections. The agreement was hailed with wide-spread enthusiasm, although it left many questions to the future: the organization of a Slovene banovina, the position of the Voivodina, Montenegro, Macedonia, and above all of Bosnia and Hercegovina, a bone of contention among Serbs, Croats and Moslems.

Efforts to Remain at Peace.—In Feb. 1939 the government had stated that its foreign policy would be unchanged, but the departure of Stoyadinovitch was generally interpreted as meaning less enthusiasm for Germany and more for the democracies. Visits were, however, exchanged between the Yugoslav and Italian foreign ministers, and Italy's occupation of Albania was taken quietly. Yugoslavia continued efforts to reconcile Bulgaria and to mediate between Rumania and Bulgaria, and also between Rumania and Hungary, with whom her relations improved remarkably. On the outbreak of World War II, Yugoslavia declared her intention to remain neutral.

In the following year Yugoslavia's main concern was, in view of the war, her foreign policy. Yugoslavia pursued a policy of strict neutrality, although it leaned toward the axis, partly out of weakness and geographic conditions, partly out of the inclinations of a certain group of political leaders like the former Prime Minister Stoyadinovitch and the Slovene leader Father Anton Koroshetz, the minister of public education and president of the senate, who died on Dec. 14, 1940. At the conference of the Balkan Entente in Belgrade at the beginning of February, Yugoslavia opposed all moves toward stronger Balkan solidarity against any outside aggression, and generally took a line in harmony with Italy. But the Belgrade government took energetic measures when, in the middle of April 1940, the Yugoslav police unearthed a fascist plot under the leadership of Stoyadinovitch, who was exiled from the capital to a distant provincial town. The great successes of Germany in the late spring of 1940, Italy's entrance into the war and France's surrender, induced Yugoslavia to follow a more cautious policy and to release Dr. Stoyadinovitch.

The grave reverses suffered by the Italian army in its war against Greece awakened in the Yugoslav army and the war minister, General Milan Neditch, the desire for an active policy on the part of Yugoslavia to prevent a fate similar to that which had befallen Rumania, but the tendency of Father Koroshetz prevailed and General Neditch resigned. A commercial pact with Germany on Oct. 19, 1940, subordinated Yugoslav economic life to the exigencies of German economy. At the beginning of December the Hungarian foreign minister, Count Csáky, visited Belgrade and concluded on Dec. 11 a treaty of "everlasting friendship" between the two countries.

On Feb. 13, 1941, Premier Cvetkovitch and Foreign Minister Cincar-Markovitch went to visit Hitler. Long negotiations followed, and meanwhile Bulgaria's adherence to the axis pact put Yugoslavia into a very unfavourable strategic position. At the same time, the agitation of Croat extremists and the fascist-terrorist group of the Croat Ustashi under the leadership of Dr. Ante Pavelitch, who directed the movement from Italy, caused concern to the Yugoslavs.

The Yugoslav government tried to arrive at a compromise with Germany, which demanded not only signature of the axis pact but permission to send troops down the Morava and Vardar valleys into Greece, and additional military, political and economic concessions binding Yugoslavia firmly to the "new order." While the government deliberated, the democratic Serb parties, who represented the vast majority of the Serb population, organized an opposition to Yugoslavia's submission to Germany. The German minister to Yugoslavia, Viktor von Heeren, negotiated secretly with minority groups in Yugoslavia, promising freedom to the separatist groups in Croatia and Bosnia in exchange for their promise of neutrality in case of a Yugoslav-German conflict. The Yugoslav government tried to substitute a friendship and nonaggression pact with Germany for the demanded full membership in the axis. For several days the nation seemed to fluctuate between acceptance and resistance. Popular temper among the Serb civilians and the Serb army definitely changed in the latter direction. When, on March 20, 1941, the Yugoslav cabinet accepted the German final terms for a settlement which would take into account the nonactive character of Yugoslav co-operation with the "new order," the unrest of the Serb people grew hourly.

In the early morning hours of March 27, 17-year-old King Peter II took over the government of the country, Prince Paul fled, and a new government under Gen. Dushan Simovitch, chief of the Yugoslav air force, was formed. In the new cabinet the Croat leader, Dr. Vlatko Machek, was first vice-president. Thus the Serbs under King Peter and the Serb army officers dared to challenge Germany, then at the peak of power, opposed only by Britain, with Russia still friendly to Germany.

The German Blow Falls.—The time left to the new government to prepare for the struggle with Germany was much too short. On April 6, 1941, the German invasion began simultaneously through Hungary and Bulgaria, and by April 16 the Yugoslav army had disintegrated. King Peter and his cabinet were forced to flee and to continue their struggle against Germany from abroad. (For an account of the Yugoslav campaign, see WORLD WAR II.)

Large parts of the country were annexed outright by Bulgaria, Hungary, Germany and Italy. Southern Serbia (Macedonia) was annexed by Bulgaria; northeastern Yugoslavia and the fertile plains of the Bachka, were annexed by Hungary, while Slovenia was divided between Germany, which annexed the northern part, and Italy, which annexed the southern part as an autonomous province of Ljubljana. Out of the remaining part of Yugoslavia, an "independent" new kingdom of Croatia was created, while in rump Serbia, under a German-instituted government of General Milan Neditch, the Serb population under Chetnik leadership continued the struggle against the German invaders with an indomitable courage and an unparalleled heroism. Meanwhile the legal Yugoslav government functioned in London, where it had found temporary refuge as one of the allied governments.

Life in Yugoslavia throughout the following years presented a very unhappy picture. The country was divided into several parts, occupied by the troops of four foreign nations and in addition torn by bitter internal strife. Croatia was organized as an outright fascist state with Ante Pavelitch as fuehrer or poglavnik. The fascist militia, the ustasha, terrorized the population, especially the Serbs and the Jews. Many Serbs and Jews were ruthlessly massacred. Officially Croatia was under Italian influence. On May 15, 1941, the restoration of a monarchy in Croatia, which had become extinct in A.D. 1089, was officially announced in Rome. The crown of Zvonimir, the last Croatian king, was offered to the Italian Prince Aimone, Duke of Spoleto, who became King Aimone I on May 17

Partition of Yugoslavia among Germany, Italy, Hungary, Rumania and Bulgaria after the axis conquest of April 1941

without, however, ever setting foot in his kingdom. Croatia had, at the beginning, an area of 44,454 sq.mi. with 7,000,000 inhabitants, but large parts of Dalmatia though inhabited by Croats were either annexed to Italy or controlled by the Italian army. Croatia aligned itself completely with the axis; a small part of the new Croatian army fought in Russia with the Germans, but its main part was used for the suppression of internal opposition. After the surrender of Italy in Sept. 1943, King Aimone was deprived of his throne and Croatia became a republic under German protectorate. Throughout the war a number of German, Italian, Hungarian and Bulgarian divisions were kept busy in Yugoslavia suppressing and counteracting the military activities of the Serbs. The unrest was increased by the internal struggle between Croats and Serbs which led to much bloodshed and bitterness.

Split Among the Patriots.—It was most difficult to get an exact picture of the operations conducted by the Yugoslav patriots against the axis forces and the satellite governments. The Serb patriots (Chetniks) were under the command of General Draja Mikhailovitch, who had been recognized by the Yugoslav government as commander in chief of the Yugoslav armies. Under his leadership the troops of the patriot army succeeded in breaking up axis communications, controlling at various times large parts of the country and supplying themselves from provisions captured from the axis. They also maintained a broadcasting station which was in communication with the Yugoslav government in London. Yet the problem of getting supplies became more and more difficult, as it was almost impossible to send any supplies from outside. During 1942 a serious split occurred within the patriot army. Groups of Partisans, some inspired by communism, others by nationalism and others again probably only by the general misery and unrest, undertook operations on their own account and found themselves soon in opposition to General Mikhailovitch.

Toward the end of the year accusations were levelled against Mikhailovitch of abandoning the struggle and seeking terms with the axis powers. The Yugoslav government in London, however, expressed its unchanged confidence in Gen. Mikhailovitch's loyalty. By the end of 1942 the internal situation of Yugoslavia presented a rather confused picture, yet in different parts of the country, especially in those occupied by Italians, the struggle went on relentlessly, and the patriot forces could always point toward some local successes.

Meanwhile the Yugoslav government in London was reorganized at the beginning of 1942. General Dushan Simovitch was succeeded as premier by Slobodan Yovanovitch, a former professor of the university of Belgrade. At the same time General Mikhailovitch was appointed minister of war, and Milan Gavrilovitch, former Yugoslav minister in Moscow, was made minister of justice. The new premier was well known as a promoter of Balkan unity. In July General Mikhailovitch was named chief of staff and was given full military and administrative power in the Yugoslav territory. In recognition of Yugoslavia's importance the U.S. raised its diplomatic mission to the Yugoslav government from a ministry to an embassy, and the Yugoslav minister in Washington, Constantin Fotitch, became Yugoslav ambassador.

The situation in Yugoslavia continued throughout 1943 in a troubled state, further complicated by the collapse of Italy. The unrest and bitterness produced by the occupation of Yugoslavia was also much increased by the continued internal struggle among the Yugoslavs themselves. Mikhailovitch continued as commander of the Chetniks, but a new figure had arisen to challenge his leadership of the Yugoslav resistance. This was Tito, who, by 1943, had secured firm control of the oppositionist Partisans.

The forces of Mikhailovitch represented mainly the Serb army and guerrillas, while those of Tito included Serbs, Croats and Slovenes and were of a more leftist political conviction, often representing communism, yet accepting in their ranks men of all parties and classes, peasants, workers, intellectuals, officers and priests.

The exile government in London, recognized as one of the United Nations, reflected the internal strife of the homeland and was frequently reorganized. The cabinet of Slobodan Yovanovitch resigned on June 17, 1943, because it was unable to define a satisfactory postwar policy. On June 26 a new cabinet was formed with Milosh Trifunovitch, deputy leader of the Serb radical party, as premier and Milan Grol, leader of the Serbian democratic party, as minister of foreign affairs. In a broadcast on June 28, a national holiday of the Serbs, King Peter promised his people that after their liberation they would be free "to decide on their own fate in conformity with the principles of democracy."

As a result of Serb-Croat tension the new cabinet resigned on Aug. 10, 1943, and was followed by a cabinet with Dr. Bozhidar Puritch, a Serb diplomat, as premier. The Yugoslav government transferred its seat at the beginning of October from London to Cairo. From there on Oct. 7 King Peter called on his people to "obey Mikhailovitch and other national leaders of your resistance to the enemy and refrain from internal struggles." Thereby the king recognized officially the existence of other liberation movements, especially that of Tito. On Oct. 16 the Yugoslav government was broadened by the inclusion of three new members, two Croats and one Slovene.

Meanwhile the struggle in Yugoslavia went on. The partisan armies were able to wrest important territory from the Germans, and at times many important cities in Dalmatia and Bosnia were entirely under patriot control. But the attempts of creating a united front of the patriots failed. On Dec. 4, 1943, the Partisan movement announced that it had set up a provisional regime in opposition to the existing Yugoslav government in exile. It was reported that 240 delegates had created in Jajce, Bosnia, a parliament and government for the territory already won back from the Germans. Dr. Ivan Ribar, first president of the constitutional assembly of Yugoslavia since World War I, was elected head of the government of the Antifascist Council for the National Liberation of Yugoslavia (Antifašističko Vječe Narodnog Oslobodjenja Jugoslavje or A.V.N.O.J.), and Tito was named field marshal and chairman of the committee for national defense. A regular cabinet was formed, the three vice-presidents being respectively a Serb, a Croat and a Slovene. In the British parliament it was disclosed officially on Dec. 8, 1943, that the larger part of British supplies and arms sent to Yugoslavia had been going for some time to Tito's forces, with whom the British had established military liaison earlier in the year. On Dec. 14 Foreign Secretary Anthony Eden announced that the British military mission was headed by Fitzroy Maclean, a former member of the British foreign office. The soviet government followed the British example and announced on Dec. 14 that it would also send a military mission to Yugoslavia. By the end of Dec. 1943, the hostility between Tito's Partisans and the government in exile took on more and more violent form. Tito's council issued a manifesto depriving the government in exile of all rights and accusing Mikhailovitch openly of a hostile attitude and of organizing civil strife. The government in exile denied these charges and maintained the legitimacy of its position.

Tito Eclipses Mikhailovitch.—In the following months, British and Russian backing of Marshal Tito became more and more pronounced. British pressure was increased on the royal Yugoslav government under King Peter to drop General Draja Mikhailovitch as minister of war and to seek an agreement with Marshal Tito.

At the end of Jan. 1944 a national congress was held secretly in Serbia by the followers of Mikhailovitch. The delegates expressed their loyalty to King Peter and to the exile government. Dr. Zhivko Topalovitch, a Serb labour leader, was elected president and Rusomir Yankovitch, a member of the Serb peasant party, vice-president of the congress. A constitution was drafted for Yugoslavia as a federation based upon the equality of Serbs, Croats and Slovenes. On the other hand several Serb leaders, including General Dushan Simovitch, who led the coup d'état in 1941 against collaboration with Germany, came out in favour of Yugoslav unity under Tito's leadership. The Yugoslav ambassador to the soviet union, Stanoye Simitch, took a similar stand against Mikhailovitch and against King Peter's government, still headed by Puritch. Marshal Tito demanded the recognition of the National Liberation committee headed by Dr. Ivan Ribar. He wished this committee to be recognized as the provisional government of Yugoslavia with representatives in the different inter-Allied commissions.

A decisive turn of events occurred in May 1944, when King Peter dismissed the government of Puritch and asked the Croat leader, Dr. Ivan Shubashitch, to form a government and to try to arrive at a reconciliation with Marshal Tito. General Vladimir Velebit, who was in London as Marshal Tito's ambassador, had a number of conversations with Churchill, who decided to back Tito openly. The United States, following the British and Russians, established a military mission at Tito's headquarters in 1944, headed by Col. Ellery C. Huntington, Jr.

On July 7, 1944, Dr. Shubashitch succeeded in forming a government in which he himself took the portfolios of foreign affairs and war. The new cabinet consisted of six members, two from each of the three national groups, Croat, Slovene and Serb. In his statement the new premier recognized the principle of a federated Yugoslavia but expressed also his attachment to the king and the monarchy. Thus the groundwork was laid for apparent collaboration between the royal government in exile and Tito's Committee of National Liberation. But part of Serb public opinion was apparently not satisfied. Constantin Fotitch, Yugoslav ambassador to the U.S., resigned his position in protest against the formation of the new government, which in his opinion did not represent the Serbs.

The temporary agreement between the royal government and Marshal Tito followed a meeting between Dr. Shubashitch and Tito in Yugoslavia on June 16, 1944. As its result the decisive influence in Yugoslavia shifted more and more to Tito and his forces. They fought during the whole time against the German invaders with varying success, mostly supported by small British forces on land and by the British navy in the Adriatic, as well as by Allied air forces from Italy. The advance of the Russian army through Rumania marked a turning point, as did Bulgaria's desertion of the German alliance; Russian and

Yugoslav representatives at their desks before the new republic's first regular parliamentary session opened at Belgrade in May 1946

Yugoslav forces combined in the liberation of Belgrade and of the eastern parts of Yugoslavia, while the Bulgarian army began to collaborate with the Yugoslavs. By the end of 1944 much of Yugoslavia had been liberated. Tito was able to establish his administration on firm foundations. On Jan. 2, 1945, King Peter agreed to the formation of a regency, an act which definitely confirmed the abdication of the monarchy in favour of the movement led by Tito.

A coalition cabinet was established in Belgrade in March, 1945. Of its 28 members, 6 represented the London government. The two most prominent of these were Shubashitch, who became minister of foreign affairs, and Milan Grol, a Serb democrat. But all the power remained in the hands of Marshal Tito and other members of the Communist party. The secret police, the O.Z.N.A. (Odelenje Zastite Narod—Department of Defense of the People), was responsible for the maintenance of order and of the "right spirit." By the end of the summer Dr. Shubashitch and Dr. Grol had resigned from the cabinet.

Russian Ascendancy.—On April 11, 1945, Yugoslavia concluded a 20-yr. treaty with the U.S.S.R. Yugoslav policy was conducted throughout 1945 and 1946 in complete agreement with Russian policy. The huge Yugoslav army was not demobilized. Very much in the country had been destroyed and the economic and transportation situation suffered heavily from losses inflicted by the German-Italian occupation. The government evolved far-reaching plans for the improvement of economic conditions of the country and with great energy went after their realization.

Meanwhile, the nationality problem which had afflicted Yugoslavia for 20 years led to the formation of a federation in which the various nationalities and regions were put on an equal basis. Yugoslavia was divided into six federal states, Bosnia-Hercegovina, Croatia, Macedonia, Montenegro, Serbia and Slovenia, each with its own administration, but united through the direction by Communist party members. The Croatian Peasant party which represented the overwhelming majority of the Croats was in opposition; its famous leader, Dr. Machek, went into exile. In Macedonia, Macedonian was recognized as a separate Slav language and was made the official language of south Serbia. A special alphabet was evolved for the new language. The creation of this new national Macedonia was to serve as a centre of attraction for Greek and Bulgarian Macedonia, which was coveted by Yugoslavia. The ministry of national education in Skoplje, the capital of the new Macedonia, published on July 1, 1945, the first issue of *Prosvetno Delo* in the new alphabet, the central Macedonian dialect being used as the new literary language.

On Nov. 11, 1945, elections were held for the constituent assembly. Only candidates of Marshal Tito's Liberation front which formed the government, presented themselves. The electorate voted overwhelmingly for the single list of candidates. On Nov. 29 the constituent assembly proclaimed the federal People's Republic of Yugoslavia and abolished the monarchy. King Peter protested this act as a violation of the agreement concluded between Shubashitch and Tito in June 1944 under guarantees of the Allies, and charged that a totalitarian tyranny reigned in Yugoslavia.

International complications were caused by Yugoslavia's demands for territory from Austria and Italy. When Germany collapsed, Marshal Tito's forces occupied the Italian province of Venezia Giulia and the Austrian province of Carinthia, claiming these lands as inhabited by Yugoslavs (Slovenes and Croats). After protracted controversies the Yugoslav armies abandoned the Austrian territory, and the decision regarding its sovereignty was left to the peace conference. As regards the Italian territory, the justice of Yugoslav claims to a large part of it was generally recognized on ethnographic grounds, and all the districts with an undisputed Yugoslav majority were put under Marshal Tito's administration. The remaining much smaller part which, however, included the important port of Trieste, was left under Allied administration until a final decision by the peace conference.

Yugoslavia: *Statistical Data*, 1938

Item	Value (000's omitted)	Amount or Number
Exchange rate		
U.S.		1 Dinar = 2.31 cents
Great Britain		204 to 214 Dinars = £1
Finance		
Government revenue	$277,080 (£56,674)	
Government expenditures	$256,184 (£52,400)	
Gold reserves	$44,150 (£9,030)	
National debt	$543,203 (£111,107)	
Transportation		
Railroads		6,436 mi.
Highways		26,047 "
Waterways (rivers)		1,220 "
Communication		
Telephones		67,588
Telegraph lines		11,873 mi.
Radio sets		147,572
Minerals		
Copper ore (copper content)		54,564 tons
Copper		46,297 "
Gold		78,318 oz.
Crops		
Corn		5,242,429 tons
Wheat		3,339,859 "
Potatoes		1,875,784 "
Livestock		
Poultry		22,763,164
Sheep		10,137,357
Cattle		4,267,339
Exports—Total	$116,671 (£23,864)	4,081,000 tons
Wood and wood products	$19,001 (£3,886)	...
Live animals	$12,644 (£2,586)	556,000
Corn	$11,116 (£2,274)	516,000 tons
Imports		
Total	$115,005 (£23,523)	1,400 tons
Cotton and manufactures	$18,212 (£3,725)	43,000 "
Iron and manufactures	$13,201 (£2,700)	151,000 "
Machines, instruments and apparatus	$11,481 (£2,348)	27,000 "
Defense		
Standing army personnel		166,237*
Reserves		1,649,000*
Standing navy personnel		5,987*
Reserves		734*
Standing air force personnel		812*
Reserves		16,795*
Military expenditures	$55,890* (£11,432)	
Education		
Elementary schools		8,727
Students		1,393,422
Secondary schools		320
Students		156,287
Universities		3
Students		16,207

*In 1940: Army personnel: 600,000; Reserves: 1,240,000; no data for navy personnel; Air force personnel: 6,500; Reserves: 500; Expenditures: $65,767 (£17,172).

On Dec. 22, 1945, the British and the U.S. governments recognized the new "Federative People's Republic of Yugoslavia." According to the new constitution the praesidium of the constituent assembly, elected by both houses, was empowered, among other executive functions, to represent the new state inside and outside the country. President of the praesidium was Ivan Ribar, a Croat lawyer; the six vice-presidents were Mosha Pijade, a Jewish Serb journalist and secretary of the Communist party; Philip Lakus, a former deputy of the Croat Peasant party; Dr. Josip Rus, a Slovene liberal and a judge by profession; Djure Pucar, a Bosnian Serb; Dimiter Vlahov, a Macedonian communist; and Marko Vujachitch, an agrarian from Montenegro.

At the time of the recognition of Marshal Tito's government, U.S. Acting Secretary of State Dean Acheson made public the instructions sent to U.S. Ambassador R. C. Patterson, Jr., in Belgrade, declaring that in view of conditions existing in Yugoslavia, it could not be said that the guarantees of personal freedom and of liberties of speech, press and assembly, promised in the Tito-Shubashitch agreement and underlying the Yalta declaration, had been honoured. Nor did the elections of Nov. 11, 1945, provide, in the opinion of the U.S. government, an opportunity for a free choice of the people's representatives. Under those circumstances the U.S. government warned that the establishment of diplomatic relations with the regime in Yugoslavia "should not be interpreted as implying approval of the policies of the regime, its methods of assuming control or its failure to implement the guarantees of personal freedom promised its people."

On March 24, 1946, the Yugoslav government announced that General Mikhailovitch had been taken a prisoner on March 13 and would face trial for treason. The U.S. government requested permission for American army personnel connected with General Mikhailovitch during the war to testify at his trial. The Yugoslav government rejected this request. Mikhailovitch was found guilty on July 15 and was executed two days later. On May 9, the first anniversary of the victory over Germany, a huge military parade was held. Many types of heavy Russian tanks and much motorized artillery were on display. On the same day a mutual assistance pact between Yugoslavia and Czechoslovakia was signed and the brotherhood of the two Slav peoples was emphasized.

BIBLIOGRAPHY.—Rebecca West, *Black Lamb and Grey Falcon* (1941); Nicholas Mirkovich, "Jugoslavia's Choice," *Foreign Affairs* (Oct. 1941); Robert St. John, *From the Land of the Silent People* (1942); Dinko Tomasitch, "Croatia in European Politics," *Journal of Central European Affairs* (April 1942); Josip Broz Tito, "The Yugoslav People's Fight to Live," *Free World* (June 1944); Correspondence between C. L. Sulzberger and General Draja Mikhailovitch, *The New York Times* (Aug. 6, 1944); Winifred N. Hadsel, "The Struggle for Yugoslavia," *Foreign Policy Reports* (March 1, 1944); Bernard Newman, *Balkan Background* (1945); Hal Lehrman, "Yugoslav Democracy, Limited," *The Nation* (Sept. 8, 1945); Sam Pope Brewer, "The Ordeal of Yugoslavia," *The American Mercury* (Nov. 1945); Temple H. Fielding, "Tito, A Portrait from Life," *Harper's* (Oct. 1945); A Pomerantsev, "Yugoslav Democracy Combats Reactionary Intrigues," *New Times* (Oct. 15, 1945); Stoyan Pribichevich, "Rise and Fall of Mikhailovitch," the *N. Y. Herald Tribune* (April 8, 1946); Allen Raymond in the *N. Y. Herald Tribune* (Jan. 2 and 3, 1946); David Martin, *Ally Betrayed* (1946). (H. Ko.)

Yugoslav Literature

See CENTRAL EUROPEAN AND BALKAN LITERATURE.

Yukon Territory

Popularly called "the Yukon" by Canadians, Yukon Territory is the most westerly political division of the Dominion of Canada. Slightly more than one-half the size of the province of Ontario, the territory's 207,076 sq.mi. (of which 1,730 sq.mi. are fresh water) are bounded on the north by the Arctic ocean, the east by the Northwest Territories, the south by British Columbia and Alaska, the west by Alaska. Capital is Dawson, other centres of population being White Horse, Mayo and Carcross. English is the chief language, and the population is predominantly Anglican.

World War II speeded the rate of population increase; at one time during the building of the Alaska highway and the Canol project, the population of the Yukon went over the 10,000 mark. But this was only temporary, and in 1945 the majority of the military personnel was withdrawn. Nevertheless, the permanent population in the 1941 census reported growth to 4,914, and in 1944 the dominion bureau of statistics officially estimated the population to be not less than 5,000.

The Yukon, formerly part of the Northwest Territories, was made a separate territory in 1898, with a local government of an appointed controller and three legislative council members elected for three years. Elections during the 1937–46 decade were held in 1938, 1941 and 1944. Controller for the same period was George Allen Jeckell.

* * *

DURING the first part of the 1937–46 decade, the Yukon followed pretty much its well-established economic trends. Placer gold-mining, using electrically-powered hydraulic equipment, was the largest single activity, with lumbering, fishing and fur trading far behind. There were also important consolidations within the placer mining activity. By 1937 only a few individual miners operating pick and shovel and cradle remained: mechanization had replaced the romantic methods of the big gold rush. By 1946 this mechanization, with its demands for electric power, had resulted in a modest expansion of the hydroelectric potentials of the territory.

When World War II cut the usual lines of supply for scarce raw materials, there was widespread search for new sources, and deposits of Yukon scheelite, from which vital tungsten was extracted, were exploited, bringing a flurry of activity to various regions. But the territory was not greatly affected by the war until Japan attacked the U.S. and brought Alaska into the orbit of military strategy. The initiation of joint Canadian-U.S. defense projects in 1942 was followed by a period of great activity.

Work on the Alaska highway commenced in March 1942, and construction of 1,523 mi. of road from Dawson Creek, B.C., to Fairbanks, Alaska, was rushed forward. Of this distance, 1,220 mi. were constructed in Canada, including 560 in the Yukon. The highway was completed as a pioneer road in Nov. 1942, with many of the bridges only temporary wooden structures. During 1943 the highway was developed until it met the standard requirements of a gravelled military route. Steel bridges were prefabricated in sections in Edmonton, Calgary and Winnipeg, shipped to railhead, and transported to river sites on special trucks. In addition, a cut-off road was constructed from Haines, Alaska, on Lynn canal, to meet the highway about 95 mi. west of White Horse. This route, 154 mi. in length, was completed late in 1943. Access roads, totalling more than 200 mi., were constructed to link airports and intermediate aerodromes along the Northwest Staging route with the Alaska highway.

Travel on the Alaska highway and connecting roads was restricted and controlled by the Joint Traffic Control board, set up in 1943 with headquarters at Edmonton. On April 3, 1946, however, Canada took over the jurisdiction of the Alaska highway, and immediately began to build numerous refuelling depots, comfort stations and accommodation camps, anticipating removal of tourist travel restrictions over the great scenic route.

In 1946, also, Canada took over jurisdiction of the Edmonton to Alaska section of the telephone system which the U.S. military authorities had set up along the Alaska highway. This provided an important communications link between the Yukon and the rest of Canada, supplementing the department of national defense radio stations operated at Dawson, White Horse and Mayo.

Major world aviation developments during the decade brought the Yukon to the fore. An early defense project of World War II was the so-called Northwest Staging route, which was a series of military airports connecting Edmonton and U.S. defense installations along the Alaska coast. North America-Asia commercial routes began circling the top of the globe in 1946, and the military flight strips constructed during the war along the Alaska highway and the staging route aerodromes became part of the emergency landing system established between principal commercial airports.

Probably the most spectacular war development affecting the Yukon was the effort to make the northwest corner of North America self-sufficient in gasoline in case the coast should be attacked and occupied by Japanese forces. On March 31, 1944, the Canol project, being a 600-mi. pipe line pumping oil from Norman wells, Northwest Territories, across the Mackenzie mountains to White Horse, was completed; and the following May a White Horse oil refinery began operating. But this hope of industrial expansion faded when in March, 1945, the pumping of oil from Norman wells was discontinued, and the operation of the refinery suspended. (C. CY.)

BIBLIOGRAPHY.—W. R. Curtin, *Yukon Voyage* (1938); F. Fieldhouse, *Yukon Holiday* (1940); H. C. Lanks, *Highway to Alaska* (1944); *Statesman's Yearbook.*

Yukon: *Statistical Data*

Item	1938 Amount or Number	1941 Amount or Number	1944 Amount or Number
Exchange Rate			
Great Britain	4.867 Canadian $ = £1	4.45 Canadian $ = £1	4.45 Canadian $ = £1
U.S.	1 Canadian $ = 99.4 cents	1 Canadian $ = 90.9 cents	1 Canadian $ = 90.9 cents
Transportation			
Railroads	58 mi.	58 mi.	58 mi
Communication			
Telephones	171	180	114
Telegraph lines	...	...	582 mi.†
Radio sets*	386	585	459†
Minerals‡			
Gold	72,368 oz.	68,022 oz.	23,818 oz.
Silver	2,844,659 oz.	856,772 oz.	32,066 oz.
Tungsten concentrates	...	...	3 tons
Lead	...	...	53 tons
Education			
Schools (public)		5	
Roman Catholic schools		1	
Students		185	

*Includes Northwest Territories.
†1945.
‡Mineral production in Northwest Territories:
1938, gold, 6,800 oz.; silver 581,902 oz.
1941, gold, 77,354 oz.; silver, 15,327 oz.; petroleum, 23,664 bbl.
1944, gold, 20,775 oz.; silver, 13,677 oz.; petroleum, 1,223,675 bbl.

Y.W.C.A.

See YOUNG WOMENS CHRISTIAN ASSOCIATION.

Zanzibar and Pemba

See BRITISH EAST AFRICA.

Zeitzler, Kurt

Zeitzler (1895–), German army officer, was born in Luckau, Brandenburg, Germany. He joined the army in World War I, serving as infantry lieutenant, and gave up his commission after the Armistice in 1918. Rejoining the Reichswehr in 1926 as a captain, he rose through the grades, becoming a major general in early 1942 and then a full general. Zeitzler commanded an infantry unit during the Polish campaign (Sept. 1939), and was chief of staff to Gen. Paul L. von Kleist in the French campaign (May-June, 1940). Later he was assigned as chief of staff to Marshal Karl R. von Runstedt, when the latter was commander of German armies in the west in 1942. In the winter of 1942, Zeitzler, who was virtually unknown outside Germany, was made chief of the German general staff, replacing Gen. Franz Halder. On Jan. 31, 1944, Hitler promoted Zeitzler to the rank of colonel general; the following March, he was replaced by Gen. Alfred Jodl as chief of the army general staff.

Zeolites

See Chemistry.

Zeppelins

See Aviation, Civil.

Zhdanov, Andrei Alexandrovich

Zhdanov (1896–), soviet politician, was the son of a Russian Orthodox clergyman. He fought in the Russian imperial army as a noncommissioned officer and at the outbreak of the revolution in 1917 urged soldiers to join the bolshevists. He enrolled in the Communist party and was party secretary in the industrial city of Gorki. After the assassination of Sergei Kirov in 1934, Zhdanov became party leader for Leningrad. That same year, he was also elected to the politburo of the Communist party and was named by Stalin as an alternate party secretary. In 1937, he was elected to the supreme soviet, and the following year he became head of the foreign affairs committee in the soviet of the union (lower house of the soviet parliament). Later, he was elected president of the R.S.F.S.R. (Russian republic).

During the German attack on Leningrad, Zhdanov was appointed head of the Leningrad Military council with the rank of major general. He was credited by many sources as having organized the successful defense of the city, and he signed the soviet-Finnish armistice in 1944. He was made chairman of the Allied control commission for Finland, and resigned as Leningrad party secretary to devote more of his time to his new post. In 1945 and 1946, rumour was current in Moscow that Zhdanov was Stalin's first choice as his successor. Zhdanov was elected (March 12, 1946) as chairman of the soviet of the union.

Zhukov, Georgi Konstantinovich

Zhukov (1895–), soviet army officer, was born in 1895 in the village of Strelkova, central Russia. He left school at an early age, and was inducted into the Russian imperial army in 1915. After the revolution in 1917, he enlisted in a Red Guards cavalry division, joined the Communist party in 1919 and fought in the civil war. He continued in the army after the bolshevist victory, studied at the Frunze Military academy, attended German general staff lectures in Berlin and was soviet military observer in the Spanish Civil War.

In 1939, Zhukov led Red army tank units that surrounded and destroyed the 6th Japanese army in the fighting along the Mongolian-Manchurian border. During the Russo-Finnish war of 1939–40, he served on Semyon K. Timoshenko's staff and in Feb. 1941, he was appointed chief of the army general staff, vice-commissar for defense, and alternate member of the Central committee of the Communist party.

After the German invasion of the U.S.S.R., Zhukov was made commander of the western front army, with the special task of defending Moscow in Oct. 1941. Zhukov's counteroffensive, launched Dec. 6, turned back the Germans from the capital. In Aug. 1942, Zhukov was made first vice-commissar for defense and directed the defense of Stalingrad as well as the counteroffensive that drove the Germans from the Don-Volga area.

Zhukov was then sent to the Leningrad front, where he co-ordinated the soviet operations which resulted in lifting the siege of the city on Jan. 18, 1943. Two days later he was promoted to the rank of marshal of the soviet union.

He participated in the soviet summer offensive of 1943 and in March 1944, took command of the 1st Ukrainian army, launching a drive that went through Poland to the borders of Czechoslovakia. On April 10, 1944, Zhukov received the Order of Victory, the highest award of the soviet union, and in July he returned to Moscow to act as Stalin's deputy commander in chief. In this capacity he co-ordinated the strategy of the numerous soviet armies in the field.

In early Jan. 1945, when his plans for invasion of Germany were completed, he left his desk job to lead the 1st White Russian army in the drive on Berlin. The offensive, launched Jan. 12, 1945, by five large armies, was successful. Berlin fell to soviet forces May 2, and Zhukov headed the Allied delegation that accepted the German surrender in the ruined city, May 8, 1945.

Zhukov was then appointed head of the soviet occupation forces in the reich, and after the merger of the soviet armed forces (announced on March 22, 1946), he was made commander of soviet ground forces. Thereafter, his star apparently declined. On April 10, 1946, he relinquished his post as soviet occupation chief in Germany, and on Nov. 18, 1946, it was disclosed that he had been succeeded as commander of ground forces by Marshal Ivan Stepanovich Konev.

Zinc

World production of zinc continued to be concentrated in a relatively few countries during the decade 1937–46, so far as major producers were concerned. While there were a few other small producers, 99% of the world output was accounted for by the countries listed in Table I. However, attention should be called to the fact that this is a table of smelter output, and not mine output; the latter would be dispersed a little more widely. There were a number of gaps in the table during the war years, and it was impossible to arrive at a reliable figure for the world total after 1940. The totals shown in parentheses in the table are rough approximations, based on the year-to-year changes in the figures reported, and so include the assumption that over-all changes in other countries were in the same proportion. While there were certainly some variations from this assumption, the reporting countries represented about 85% of the total, and variations of the estimates from the true totals should not be great.

Zinc differed from other metals in that a larger proportion of its smelting capacity was in the active war zones than was the case with any other major metal. However,

Table I.—*World Smelter Production of Zinc*
(Short tons)

	1937	1938	1939	1940	1941	1942	1943	1944	1945
Australia	78,120	78,199	79,766	85,072	87,022	83,196	84,847	88,162	93,826
Belgium	248,659	231,926	205,052	84,305	52,051	40,587	48,248	9,766	11,398
Canada	158,542	171,933	175,641	185,722	213,608	215,795	206,510	168,517	182,265
France	66,661	60,311	67,262	41,715	28,570	25,165	19,588	9,223	8,889
Germany	180,574	214,256	254,600	350,100	350,100	346,200	343,900	321,900	?
Great Britain	69,598	61,939	58,296	66,166	75,703	79,848	77,542	80,678	69,483
Italy	41,868	36,781	39,020	43,363	42,770	34,779	?	?	?
Japan	50,200	59,749	56,500	65,811	67,342	64,152	68,652	66,746	?
Mexico	40,330	39,552	38,988	36,804	42,635	57,037	60,020	54,287	53,901
Netherlands	27,166	27,900	22,600	5,566	4,098	5,680	5,032	2,320	?
No. Rhodesia	15,715	11,441	14,219	14,773	15,170	14,381	15,013	16,217	17,067
Norway	45,499	51,283	50,615	18,992	7,125	8,480	16,949	12,982	?
Poland	118,139	119,128	120,002	132,300	?	?	?	?	40,108
Spain	2,032	8,457	14,767	13,583	21,102	21,109	21,164	19,901	19,028
U.S.S.R.	77,600	88,000	93,700	93,700	?	?	?	?	?
United States	556,904	446,341	507,236	675,275	822,020	891,872	942,309	869,302	764,561
Total	1,789,000	1,726,000	1,819,000	1,925,000	(2,100)	(2,200)	(2,200)	(2,000)	(2,000)

Table II.—*Data on the Zinc Industry in the United States*
(Short tons)

	1937	1938	1939	1940	1941	1942	1943	1944	1945
Mine production	626,362	516,703	583,807	655,068	749,125	768,025	744,196	718,642	614,358
Smelter production	556,904	446,341	507,236	675,275	822,020	891,872	942,309	869,302	764,561
Domestic ores	551,165	436,007	491,058	589,988	652,599	629,957	594,250	574,453	467,084
Foreign ores	5,739	10,334	16,178	85,287	169,421	261,915	348,059	294,849	297,477
Imports	46,251	26,039	66,998	196,788	323,767	404,749	595,204	486,325	478,835
In ore	8,812	18,583	36,100	180,320	289,213	368,355	539,049	422,699	381,719
Argentina	...	...	1,544	6,723	20,579	23,395	53,452	22,253	...
Australia	...	...	...	1,749	8,933	32,212	122,305	42,216	15,377
Canada	84	...	1,613	33,993	49,764	78,744	110,310	112,299	90,200
Mexico	338	7,253	23,221	93,789	148,201	160,713	166,168	177,628	177,003
Newfoundland	...	...	...	23,640	7,267	30,103	32,949	19,013	23,515
Peru	8,373	11,330	9,722	17,285	28,883	27,506	21,901	43,889	35,415
Metal	37,439	7,456	30,898	16,468	34,554	36,394	56,155	63,626	97,116
Canada	?	?	6,402	6,938	7,236	2,392	8,570	18,099	46,594
Mexico	?	?	16,556	8,948	25,621	34,002	45,344	39,703	36,105
Exports	8,521	8,124	13,910	90,073	97,456	140,477	106,466	25,891	14,347
Available supply	570,219	375,004	607,464	677,168	762,265	730,938	806,265	845,008	826,627
Secondary recovery	171,532	206,933	206,933	222,013	283,967	330,526	368,488	345,469	360,444
Metal	79,782	53,263	69,556	68,942	89,656	81,445	78,892	79,513	83,936
In alloys	61,750	98,879	98,879	112,306	145,807	215,726	257,986	229,218	234,642
In compounds	30,000	54,791	38,498	40,765	48,504	33,355	31,610	36,738	41,866
Consumption	610,000	421,000	626,000	719,000	827,435	728,169	816,777	888,626	852,311
Stocks									
Producers	81,113	159,426	86,283	19,973	25,102	84,440	170,606	233,696	256,216
Consumers	?	?	?	76,615	66,854	75,489	90,356	64,772	73,543
In bond	12,452	25,529	10,148	92,221	?	?	?	?	?

since much of this capacity normally used a large proportion of imported ores (most of which originated from without the war zones), smelter output in the war zones was cut sharply through lack of ore supplies, when war conditions stopped importation of ores. Conversely, ores that normally would have gone to these areas were diverted to other smelting centres, especially the U.S. While there was much shifting of ore supplies from one country to another, the production trend seemed to have been continuously upward from 1937 to 1943, except for 1938, followed by moderate declines in 1944 and 1945, after the peak of war demand had been passed.

United States.—Mine production of zinc in the U.S. suffered a 17% decline in the recession year 1938, from which it had not recovered in 1939. Production continued to respond to the increasing war demand that followed, up to 1942, with declines in the following years, the total for 1945 being less than for 1937. Demand far exceeded the domestic supply, which was supplemented by imports, both of ore and metal. Smelter output from domestic and foreign ores reached a peak in 1943, but the subsequent decline was relatively much less than with mine output, because of greater imports of ore.

Prewar imports were negligibly small, but expanded rapidly from 1940, reaching a maximum in 1943, when the zinc content of ore imported was 73% of the domestic mine output.

The chief sources of ore imports were Australia, Canada and Mexico. Metal imports increased moderately, mostly from Canada and Mexico.

Consumption of zinc continued to increase up to 1944, and showed only a 4% decrease in 1945.

The decline in domestic mine production, under way since 1942, continued into 1946, though with some improvement after midyear, bringing the Oct. 1946 output back to the average rate for 1945. The total for the 10 mo. was 470,218 short tons, equivalent to an annual rate of 564,300 tons, or 8% less than in 1945. Smelter output in the first three quarters of 1946 was 568,802 tons, and consumption was 563,394 tons. Imports continued the 1945 trend, with ore decreasing and metal increasing.

Canada.—In addition to the metal output shown in Table I, Canada exported a large percentage of the mine output as concentrates. Total mine production increased from 185,169 short tons in 1937 to 305,377 tons in 1943, and decreased to 254,815 tons in 1945 and 235,917 tons in 1946, 9% less than in 1945.

(G. A. Ro.)

BIBLIOGRAPHY.—E. V. Gent, *Zinc Industry* (1940); J. D. Sumner, "Wartime Price Control of Copper, Lead and Zinc," *Mining and Metallurgy*, 24:9–11 (Jan. 1943); U.S. Bureau of Mines, *Minerals Yearbook*.

Zionism

At the beginning of 1937, the Jewish population of Palestine numbered 404,000, or 30.6% of the total settled population. Of this number, no fewer than 144,000 had entered during the previous four years, for the most part from nazi Germany and from Poland. In the period which followed, as one country after another succumbed to the nazis, the situation of the Jews in Europe continued rapidly to deteriorate, with a corresponding increase in the pressure to emigrate. Nevertheless, political developments within Palestine itself resulted in a relative contraction in the rate of Jewish immigration into that country, though a steady stream of immigrants continued to arrive even during World War II. In all, during the decade ending in Dec. 1946, 104,000 additional registered immigrants entered Palestine. At the latter date the estimated Jewish population of Palestine totalled approximately 620,000, or 32% of the whole.

At the end of the decade, land in Jewish ownership in Palestine amounted to approximately 687.5 sq.mi. out of Palestine's total area of 10,100 sq.mi., an increase during the ten years of approximately 156 sq.mi. More than 100 new Jewish settlements were established in this period, bringing the total number of such settlements to 320 scattered throughout Palestine. Despite increasing legislative and other difficulties, land purchases by Jews and Jewish organizations continued to be made on the open market though, generally, at highly inflated prices.

About 45% of all Jewish-owned land at the end of 1946 belonged to the Jewish National fund (a public body leasing land to settlers for 49 yrs., with a renewal option for a similar period). During the period 1936–46 the population settled on Jewish National fund land more than doubled, from a figure of 44,200 to more than 100,000. With other

Jewish bodies, the fund invested large sums in drainage, afforestation and in otherwise ameliorating the land.

Jewish urban development also showed marked advances. As compared with the 1936 figure, the Jewish population of Jerusalem had increased in 1944 by 30% to a total of 97,000, while Haifa, with a Jewish population of 66,000, had recorded a 20% increase in the same period. The growth of the all-Jewish city of Tel-Aviv was even more striking; founded in 1909 and proclaimed a municipal corporation in 1932, its estimated population in 1946 was 208,000, an increase of about 40% more than in 1936.

Particularly impressive were the developments in the character and scope of Palestinian industry. The economy of Palestine had within a few years been transformed from a predominantly agricultural into that of a semi-industrialized country. This development was associated with the immigration into Palestine from central and eastern Europe of large numbers of manufacturers, skilled workers and experts of various kinds. It was greatly accelerated by World War II when, as the only territory in the middle east with a considerable reservoir of technically trained personnel, Palestine became an important centre of production for the war effort. The effect of war conditions, further, was for the time being to create in Palestine itself a highly protected market at a time of severe shortage of consumer goods. While this resulted in a considerable measure of inflation, it also stimulated the development of a remarkable variety of new industries, many of which would appear to have good prospects to establish themselves firmly and to survive the change-over to peace conditions. The number of workers employed in Jewish industry and handicrafts increased from 33,000 in 1935 to 66,000 in 1945, while the value of manufactured goods produced in the same period rose from £9,000,000 ($36,000,000) to a total of £50,000,000 ($200,000,000).

Decade of Disorder.—The decade 1937–46 was one of almost uninterrupted tension and difficulty for the Zionist movement. Reflecting faithfully the deterioration in the general international situation, events in Palestine had taken an ominous turn for the worse early in 1936 following Mussolini's successful invasion of Abyssinia. Violent disturbances broke out in Palestine which lasted for the better part of three years. During this period 134 British, 462 Jews and 1,082 Arabs were killed; in addition, considerable numbers from among Arab terrorist gangs were killed by military and police action.

The reaction of the Zionist leadership was to organize resistance to the terrorists by all means at their disposal but, at the same time, firmly to reject a policy of indiscriminate retaliation by killing innocent Arabs in revenge for the murder of innocent Jews. Despite great provocation, this self-imposed policy of self-restraint was, with few exceptions, rigorously observed.

In the winter of 1936–37, a British royal commission, under the chairmanship of Lord Peel, was sent to Palestine to inquire into the situation and to make recommendations. In its report, issued in July 1937, the commission stated that "unquestionably . . . the primary purpose of the Mandate as expressed in its Preamble and Articles is to promote the establishment of the Jewish National Home." Nevertheless, adopting a broad view of its terms of reference, it expressed the opinion that the irreconcilable aims of Arabs and Jews in Palestine had made the mandate unworkable and that it should be abrogated. The commission therefore recommended the partition of Palestine and the setting up of independent Jewish and Arab states.

The partition proposal created deep differences of opinion among Zionists throughout the world. It was realized that a turning point had been reached in the relations of the Jews and the mandatory power. But there were many who, on historical, religious and economic grounds, were strongly opposed to what was regarded as a further partition of the area of the Jewish national home, the first having taken place in 1922, with the political separation of Trans-Jordan from western Palestine. On the other hand, there were those, led by Dr. Chaim Weizmann, president of the Jewish Agency for Palestine and of the World Zionist organization, who saw in the early prospect of Jewish statehood, even though in a relatively small area, the best hope for rescuing large numbers of their fellow Jews from the impending calamity and at the same time achieving that national status for the Jewish people in Palestine which was fundamental to the Zionist idea.

By a majority of nearly two to one the Zionist congress, which met in Zurich, Switzerland, in the summer of 1937, adopted a resolution which, while rejecting the plan of partition proposed by the Peel commission, nevertheless authorized the Zionist executive to negotiate with the British government. However, despite its own announced acceptance of the royal commission's proposal, the British government postponed action and finally, with the sending out a year later of a new commission, the proposal was abandoned. Instead, there followed early in 1939 the London conferences, held at St. James's palace, between representatives of the British government on the one hand and of Jews and Arabs, respectively, on the other, which culminated finally in the White Paper of 1939.

White Paper of 1939.—The crux of the problem was obviously immigration. Ever since the confirmation of the mandate in 1922 the criterion by which the biannual immigration quotas had been determined by the Palestine government was Palestine's economic capacity to absorb additional immigrants. As had been stated in the letter from the prime minister to Dr. Weizmann, in 1931, that was the sole limitation admissible in terms of the mandate, and this position had been confirmed by the Permanent Mandates commission and the council of the League.

The 1939 White Paper proposed to abandon this criterion and, after providing for the admission within a five-year period of an additional 75,000 immigrants, to put a stop to all further Jewish immigration into Palestine except with the acquiescence of the Arabs. Moreover, Jewish settlement and land development in Palestine was to be severely curtailed as a result of provisions designed to restrict Jewish purchase of land to an area of 500 sq.mi., approximately 5% of the total area of Palestine west of the Jordan. For this policy the government obtained approval in parliament by the relatively small majority of 268 votes (as against its usual voting strength of 413) to 181.

Jewish reaction to the White Paper was one of bitter disillusionment. The proposals were condemned as a betrayal and as calculated to lead to the liquidation of the Jewish national home. In Palestine itself there were sporadic disorders, and the leadership of the Jewish agency made it clear that it would seek, whatever the obstacles, to bring Jewish immigrants into Palestine and to extend Jewish agricultural colonization. Among those who criticized the White Paper were Winston Churchill, Herbert Morrison and other leading members of parliament.

In Aug. 1939 the Permanent Mandates commission of the League of Nations, having exhaustively considered the issues involved, expressed the unanimous opinion that the policy of the White Paper was not in accordance with the interpretation of the mandate agreed upon by the council of the League, the Permanent Mandates commission and the mandatory power.

Before the matter could be considered by the council of the League of Nations, World War II broke out. Dr. Weizmann, in a letter to Prime Minister Neville Chamberlain, dated Sept. 1, 1939, immediately offered the assurance that the Jewish agency wished its differences with the mandatory to give way before "the greater and more pressing necessities of the time"; and he pledged Jewish manpower, technical ability and economic resources to the cause of the world democracies. In Palestine a Jewish national register of volunteers was opened, and more than 134,000 Jews between the ages of 18 and 50 expressed their readiness to volunteer for immediate service, for the most part in a combatant capacity. It was not until some time later, however, that under stress of war needs Jewish volunteers from Palestine began to be accepted in small scattered Jewish units of the British army. And finally, late in 1944, the British government announced the formation of the Jewish brigade group which, as part of the 8th army, participated in the fighting in Italy. In all, about 30,000 Jewish volunteers from Palestine served in the British forces during the war, a creditable record in the light of a total population of 600,000.

Biltmore Program.—A major development in Zionist policy during World War II was the adoption of the so-called Biltmore program in favour of the establishment of Palestine as a Jewish commonwealth. The program was first formulated at a conference of American Zionists held in New York in May 1942. It was formally endorsed a few months later on behalf of the whole movement, by the Inner Zionist General council in Jerusalem and by the World Zionist conference held in London in Aug. 1945. The first postwar congress of the World Zionist organization, held in Basle, Switzerland, in Dec. 1946, also confirmed this formulation.

The significance of this development lay in the fact that formerly the Zionist organization had studiously refrained from defining the aims of the movement in final terms. As long as Jewish immigration and land settlement could proceed uninterruptedly within the framework of the mandate, it was felt that such a definition would be premature and might be harmful. The White Paper of 1939, however, with its far-reaching restrictions on further Jewish immigration and land settlement made it imperative, in the view of the Zionist leaders, that Zionist aims be defined in clear and authoritative terms. It was urged that the gates of Palestine be opened to Jewish immigration; that the Jewish agency be vested with the control of immigration into Palestine and with the necessary authority for the upbuilding of the country and that Palestine be established as a Jewish commonwealth integrated in the structure of the democratic world and based upon full equality of rights for all its inhabitants without distinction of religion or race.

Deterioration in Palestine.—The end of World War II in Europe revealed the terrible fate which had befallen European Jewry at the hands of the nazis. Of the 7,500,000 Jews of Europe (outside the soviet union) 6,000,000 had perished in the most barbarous mass slaughter in history. The condition of the survivors, many of whom remained herded in "displaced persons" camps, was in general of the most miserable description. The reports of successive investigators made it clear that for many of them the prospects were slender of an early integration into the economic and social life of the countries where they had lived. Hundreds of thousands wished, above all, to emigrate, the great majority of them to Palestine.

As the full horror of what had happened in Europe became known, the demand that the White Paper be abrogated and the surviving Jews of Europe allowed freely to enter Palestine gathered momentum. Palestine Jewry made it clear that it was united in its determination to do whatever lay in its power to give succour to the tragic remnant of its brethren. As successive transports of would-be immigrants arrived off the shores of Palestine and sought to break through the British air and naval blockade of the Palestinian coast, tension mounted to a dangerous pitch. In the case of the extremist Jewish groups, resistance began to assume the form of terrorist outrages directed against the British authorities who, in turn, sought by repressive measures to stem the growing agitation.

Hopes that the new Labour administration of Prime Minister Clement Attlee would, in fulfilment of the policy set out in its party platform, repudiate the White Paper and take positive action in behalf of the immediate entry of large numbers of Jews into Palestine, were disappointed. The Palestinian administration continued severely to restrict the grant of immigration certificates and the discriminatory land regulations remained unchanged.

In the meantime, the growing interest of the United States in the related issues of Palestine and the Jewish survivors in Europe had become an important factor in the situation. On Sept. 2, 1945, Pres. Harry Truman sent a personal letter to Prime Minister Attlee, urging the admission of 100,000 Jewish refugees into Palestine. This request was not granted, but in November it was announced that a joint Anglo-U.S. committee of inquiry would be set up "to examine the question of European Jewry and to make a further review of the Palestine problem in the light of that examination." The report of the joint committee, issued at the end of April 1946, recommended *inter alia* the immediate entry of 100,000 Jewish displaced persons from the camps in Europe and the virtual abrogation of the White Paper of 1939. On the question of larger policy, the committee declared that Palestine should be neither a Jewish state nor an Arab state and recommended that for the time being the existing mandate be continued "pending the execution of a Trusteeship Agreement under the United Nations."

President Truman immediately indicated his approval of the recommendation of the committee for the transfer of the 100,000 Jews to Palestine, but the British government again delayed action. Instead, a new joint committee was set up, which, though ostensibly appointed to give effect to the recommendations of the earlier body, in fact put forward entirely new proposals for the division of Palestine, apart from the Negev, into semiautonomous Jewish and Arab provinces under the ultimate control of a central British administration in Jerusalem. In outlining this plan to parliament on July 31, 1946, Herbert Morrison announced that the British government proposed to submit it as a basis for negotiation to a conference of representative Jews and Arabs which would be convened in the near future in London.

The Morrison plan was acceptable neither to Jews nor to Arabs. It was condemned by the Zionist leaders both because of the very small area, 15% of western Palestine, which it was proposed to allocate to the Jewish province and also as having all the disadvantages without any of the advantages of partition.

The situation in Palestine in the meantime continued to deteriorate. The government's failure to implement the

Above: Tiny fortress-like settlement of Gouloth erected in primitive fashion in 1946 on land purchased from Arabs in the Negev desert area when such purchases by Jews were still legal

Right: Agricultural workers on a Jewish farm settlement in Palestine. There were 320 such communities in the Holy Land in 1946

Lower Right: Calisthenics class for children of Jewish settlers in Palestine. Child care was a prime consideration in the autonomous social order followed in these settlements

Below: Young Zionists assigned to work in the hatchery on their communally worked farm. Most Jewish settlements aimed at self-sufficiency in supplying their own food requirements

recommendations of the Anglo-U.S. committee in regard to immigration and the abrogation of the land restrictions had further embittered Palestine Jewry and strengthened the hands of the terrorists. Nor were matters improved by the arrest and detention for months without trial of several of the leading members of the Jewish agency.

In Aug. 1946 the Jewish agency executive, apart from those members still under detention, met in Paris. It rejected the Morrison plan as a basis for discussion, but in an effort to break the impasse expressed its readiness to negotiate a proposal for the establishment "of a viable Jewish State in an adequate area of Palestine." In a statement dated Oct. 4, 1946, President Truman indicated that a solution along these lines would have the support of the U.S. government. Informal conversations which followed between the British foreign and colonial secretaries on the one hand, and representatives of the Jewish agency on the other, were inconclusive, and the question of Jewish participation in the London conference was finally deferred until after the 22nd Zionist congress scheduled to be held in Basle in Dec. 1946.

The Basle congress was the first congress of the World Zionist organization held in seven years. Its composition reflected the change in the structure of the Jewish people brought about by the destruction of many of the great Jewish communities of central and eastern Europe and the consequent increase in the influence and authority of the U.S. segment of world Jewry. Disillusionment with a policy which looked to an arrangement with Great Britain was shown in the failure of congress to re-elect the veteran and distinguished leader of the Zionist movement, Dr. Chaim Weizmann, to the position of president of the organization which he had occupied practically since the time of the Balfour declaration. No other president, however, was elected in his stead. After prolonged, and, at times, stormy discussions, it was resolved by a small majority not to participate in the London conference "in the existing circumstances." At the same time, authority was given to the general council of the Zionist organization to determine the conditions under which the Zionists would be ready to participate. Twenty-nine years had passed since the Balfour declaration. The character of the partnership which for most of that period had existed between the Jewish people and Britain in regard to the Jewish national home and Palestine was apparently about to enter a new phase. (*See* also ARAB LEAGUE; JEWISH RELIGIOUS LIFE; JEWS, DISTRIBUTION OF; PALESTINE.)

BIBLIOGRAPHY.—Paul L. Hanna, *British Policy in Palestine,* American Council on Public Affairs (1942); *Palestine Royal Commission Report,* Cmd. 5479 (London, 1937); Alfred Bonne, *The Economic Development of the Middle East,* Jewish Agency for Palestine, Economic Research Institute (Jerusalem, 1943), revised edition (London, 1945); Dr. Walter Clay Lowdermilk, *Palestine, Land of Promise* (1944); Robert R. Nathan, Oscar Gass, Daniel Creamer, *Palestine, Problem and Promise,* American Council on Public Affairs (1946); *A Survey of Palestine,* prepared in Dec. 1945 and Jan. 1946 by the Palestine Government for the information of the Anglo-American Committee of Inquiry (Jerusalem, 1946); London Office of the Executive of the Jewish Agency for Palestine, to the 22nd World Zionist Congress, *Political Report* (London, 1946); Executives of the Zionist Organization and the Jewish Agency for Palestine, submitted to the 22nd Zionist Congress, *Reports* (Jerusalem, 1946); Jewish Agency for Palestine, to the Permanent Mandates Commission of the League of Nations, *Report* (London, 1930–39); *Hearings* before the Committee on Foreign Affairs, House of Representatives, 78th Congress (1944); Prof. Carl J. Friedrich, *American Policy Toward Palestine,* American Council on Public Affairs (1944); *The New Judaea* (periodical), Zionist Organization, monthly (1936–46). (A. LOU.)

Zirconium

For the first time the production of zircon in the United States attained significant proportions during the decade 1937–46. A war-born project for recovery of the zircon content of Florida beach sands delivered several thousand tons of concentrates to consumers in 1945, and in the first half of 1946 domestic production was about on a par with imports in supplying the demand.

U.S. Imports of Zircon and Baddleyite, 1940-45
(In short tons)

	Zircon from			Total	Baddleyite	Total
	Australia	India	Brazil	Zircon	from Brazil	Imports
1939	1,526	241	*	1,767	706	2,473
1940	7,387	3,609	*	10,996	1,591	12,587
1941	14,689	963	*	15,652	5,002	20,654
1942	11,145	196	...	11,341	15,283	26,624
1943	11,472	...	110	11,582	8,821	20,403
1944	11,317	...	101	11,418	2,231	13,469
1945	17,138	...	...	17,144	792	17,936

*Included with baddleyite.

Previously, U.S. supplies had been furnished by imports, as indicated in the accompanying table.

Shipments of domestic and imported concentrates to consumers reached a record high of 16,000 tons in 1945, one-fifth of which was used in the production of zirconium ferrosilicon and other alloys, and the remainder in ceramics, mainly porcelains and refractories. In the first half of 1946 shipments to consumers increased to 8,600 tons, but imports declined to 5,208 tons. (G. A. Ro.)

Zog I

King Zog of Albania (1895–) was born Oct. 8. Educated at a Monastir military school and at the Turkish Lycée in Constantinople, he fought with the Austrians in World War I. After the armistice, he became minister of the interior, retaining this office from Jan. to Nov. 1920 and organized Albanian resistance to Yugoslav raids. The following year, he was made commander in chief of the Albanian forces. Returning to the interior ministry, he suppressed a revolt in early 1922.

Zog became prime minister in Dec. 1922 but resigned after an attempt against his life in Feb. 1924 and fled to Yugoslavia. Returning to his homeland, he regained power, was elected president of the Albanian republic, Feb. 1, 1925, and was proclaimed king of Albania, Sept. 1, 1928.

He married Countess Geraldine Apponyi of Hungary on April 27, 1938. A son, Prince Skander, was born to them April 5, 1939. Three days later the Italians invaded Albania and the royal family fled to Greece. Later, they went to France where they were forced into flight to England by the German invasion in 1940. Zog then moved to Alexandria, Egypt. While he frequently expressed the conviction that the Albanian people would re-establish the throne, his hopes were dashed by the establishment of a republic, Jan. 11, 1946, by the Albanian constituent assembly.

Zonta International

See SOCIETIES AND ASSOCIATIONS.

Zoological Gardens

See ZOOLOGY.

Zoology

At the beginning of the decade 1937–46, zoological research was exhibiting its most rapid advances in the fields of genetics and experimental embryology. From these main currents of research, however, several important new streams of investigation were taking form. A few of these may be thought of as branches separating from their parent streams to assume a relative independence, but others took their origin from the confluence of the main currents and these latter, providing an important integration between previously widely separated fields, were strengthening rapidly at the beginning of the decade and showed promise of results of broad significance.

With the exigencies of World War II the course of zoology, like that of every science, was necessarily altered. Fortunately most of the chief lines of investigation did continue some advance, but much of the work in fundamental zoology was, perforce, suspended. The attention of many workers in the field was turned to subjects of more immediate practical importance. As a result, certain of the problems which seemed destined for rapid solution remained unanswered, and the rate of advance in some lines was considerably decreased. On the other hand, certain fields of zoological research which had previously been somewhat neglected took great strides forward during World War II. For obvious reasons such subjects as parasitology, entomology (both in relation to agriculture and to insect-borne diseases) and animal husbandry were intensively studied and greatly advanced. Moreover, certain techniques and materials developed as a result of war research influenced the course of zoological investigation by providing tools previously unknown or unavailable. The most noteworthy example of this was the use of radioactive tracers in physiological studies, a technique which came into wide use with the increased production of radioactive isotopes by the numerous cyclotrons employed in researches in nuclear physics. Finally it may be mentioned that knowledge of the geographical distribution of many plants and animals was increased by the spread of troops into isolated and little-known regions. This was particularly true with reference to the smaller islands of the Pacific. Interested naturalists, both professional and amateur, took advantage of whatever opportunities for collecting they were afforded in these out-of-the-way parts of the world, and a number of important additions to the fauna and flora of the Pacific thus found their way into museums, to be of value in future studies.

Embryology.—The initiation of embryonic development, the process of fertilization, was rather intensively studied from a chemical point of view during the decade. The work of R. Kuhn, F. Moewus and D. Jerchel (1938), demonstrating that the fusion of the male and female gametes of the alga Chlamydomonas is brought about through the mutual attraction exerted by specific chemical substances secreted by the two gametes, aroused interest in similar substances in animal eggs. Earlier work on the sea-urchin egg led F. R. Lillie to advance the theory that it contains a substance which, upon passing into the surrounding water, causes agglutination of the spermatozoa of the same species. This substance he named fertilizin. M. Hartmann and O. Schartau (1939) showed that there are in fact two substances produced by the egg; one which activates and attracts the spermatozoa and another which causes agglutination. Kuhn and K. Wallenfels, working with a species found at Naples, identified the sperm-activating principle as echinochrome. The agglutinating principle was investigated by Albert Tyler and his collaborators, who found it to be of protein nature. Tyler also studied substances produced by the sperm of marine invertebrates and found that the sperm elaborates a chemical which reacts with the agglutinating principle of the egg somewhat in the manner of antigen and antibody.

The traditional view that gastrulation in the bird is accomplished by a process of inturning at the posterior end of the blastodisc was controverted by several investigations. K. Peter, J. Pastells and W. Jacobson all found that the entoderm is formed by certain cells of the blastodisc giving rise to a new layer beneath the surface by a process which was variously termed "delamination," "polyproliferation" or "diffuse polyinvagination."

One of the most active fields in embryology during this period was that concerned with the study of morphogenetic stimuli. The pioneering work of Hans Spemann revealed that the primary organizer of the amphibian embryo lies in the roof of the archenteron. A chemical stimulus exerted by this tissue is responsible for the initiation of neural tube formation in the overlying ectoderm. J. Holtfreter showed that the presence of this organizer chemical can be demonstrated not only in the archenteron-roof but also in all other parts of the egg. The idea was advanced that the substance ordinarily exists in the form of some inactive precursor and is only liberated in tissue which passes over the dorsal lip of the blastopore. To test this hypothesis, several workers turned to studies of the metabolic characteristics of different parts of the egg. J. Brachet and H. Shapiro and F. G. Fischer and H. Hartwig reported a slight difference in oxygen consumption at the dorsal lip as compared with other parts of the egg but other workers failed to confirm this. Joseph Needham, E. J. Boell and V. Rogers, using the Linderstrom-Lang Cartesian diver technique, demonstrated that anaerobic glysolysis and anaerobic ammonia production are at much higher levels in the dorsal lip region than they are in ventral ectoderm. Transplantation of various chemical substances to regions beneath the ectoderm showed that many purified chemicals can cause neural tube formation if used in sufficiently high dosage but only a few are effective in minute doses. Needham interpreted this as meaning that the former substances act indirectly, by liberating the "masked" organizer-substance within the tissue itself, while only the latter may be considered as acting directly in a way similar to the natural organizer. On this basis, the primary organizer itself was considered to be a steroid, the most active substances found in these experiments being some of the polycyclic hydrocarbons such as methylcholanthrene, one of the powerful carcinogens.

Work on the development of the sea-urchin egg, somewhat paralleling that which led to the discovery of the organizer phenomenon in amphibians, was carried out by S. Horstadius and other workers in Sweden. It was found that in this egg, material from the animal pole causes production of ectodermal structures while material from the vegetal pole causes production of entodermal and mesenchymal structures. In normal development these two balance each other so as to give a normally proportioned larva, but by transplantation of one or the other of these materials into another egg the balance may be shifted so as to give, in the one case an "animalized" larva with abnormally large and abundant ectodermal parts and in the other case a "vegetalized" larva with overdeveloped gut and skeleton. Various chemical treatments can also shift the balance. Horstadius' interpretation of the situation was on the basis of a double gradient system, one gradient having its high point in the animal pole the other in the vegetal pole.

Studies on morphogenetic factors at stages after gastrulation were numerous and only a few can be mentioned. One of the noteworthy series of studies in this field was that of

F. R. Lillie and his co-workers, in which the regenerating feather germ of the bird was employed to elucidate problems of morphogenesis. As an example of experiments dealing with morphogenetic factors in invertebrates, the work of L. von Ubisch on the skeleton of the echinoderm may be noted. He found that the viscosity of the protoplasm is of importance in determining the nature of the skeletal spicules of the larva and that this is the basis for the variations in skeletal structures found in hybrids and chimeras. The inductive ability of the eye-cup in amphibia was studied by O. E. Schotté and F. C. Hummel, who found that when the eye lenses of adult salamanders are removed and replaced by regenerating tissue from the stumps of amputated limbs or tails, new lenses are formed by the regenerate under the organizing action of the eye cup. The regenerating tissue thus behaves like undifferentiated embryonic tissue.

The process of regeneration itself, which offers another experimental approach to the problem of differentiation, was investigated from several aspects. The source of the blastema cells in regenerating amphibian limbs and the inhibiting effects of X-rays on limb regeneration were studied by a number of workers. A. Striganova and several other Russian investigators added much to knowledge of the enzyme systems and the metabolic processes involved in the formation of the regeneration blastema. The role of the nerve supply in limb regeneration was studied by Schotté and E. G. Butler, who found that the nerve functions in stopping the regressive changes initiated at the time of amputation and thus makes possible the formation of the regeneration blastema. Study of regeneration in invertebrates centred about the problem of the function of gradient systems in determining the regenerative capacity at different levels along the axis. The Japanese investigator J. Watanabe found that eye-spot formation in the planarian occurs at different rates depending upon the level, the rate decreasing from anterior to posterior but rising somewhat near the tail. A. Goldin and L. G. Barth studied regeneration in a coelenterate, *Tubularia,* and obtained significant results showing that the polarity of the regenerate can be controlled by oxygen tension.

An extraordinarily rapid advance was made during the decade in knowledge of the origin and development of the pigment cells and the pigment patterns of vertebrates. F. Dorris showed, by means of explantation and transplantation experiments, that the pigment cells which give rise to the melanophores in the feathers of the bird, take their origin in the early embryo from the cells of the neural crest. M. E. Rawles successfully traced them to still earlier stages when they are localized in the surface of the blastoderm in the region of Hensen's node. The precise way in which the melanoblast cells migrate to reach their final position in the epidermis and the time required for this migration was studied by B. H. Willier and Rawles and by R. L. Watterson. Willier and his co-workers also investigated the origin of melanophores in regenerating feathers and found evidence that these are derived from a reserve supply of melanoblasts lying in the dermis. Since there are, in the domestic fowl, a great many colour varieties in which the colour pattern depends upon known genetic factors, work of this type offered an opportunity for analysis of the methods by which the genes control development to produce the characteristic adult structure. Willier and Rawles found that, in transplantation of ectoderm from one embryo to another of a different breed, the behaviour of the melanophore accords with its own genic type regardless of the genic constitution of the feather germ which it supplies. Neural crest origin of skin melanophores in amphibians is also well substantiated and experiments by F. Baltzer at Berne showed that, when neural crest material is transplanted from frog to salamander larvae, the pigment cells retain the cellular characteristics of the donor but their arrangement is determined by the host pigment pattern.

Genetics.—The experimental study of gene mutations and chromosome aberrations continued to be a fruitful field of investigation, and the fundamental problem of the nature of gene mutation was attacked with a number of diverse techniques. An increasing number of cases of the "position effect," that is, effects upon the genetic system attributable not to genic differences but to differences in the spatial relations of the genes, was reported. This led R. Goldschmidt to suggest the possibility that all mutations are position effects and that indeed, such effects might account for all hereditary modifications in the chromosome. Most geneticists, however, preferred the view that mutations arise as definite rearrangements within the molecule while recognizing, however, that many so-called mutations are actually minute deficiencies or rearrangements in the chromosome. The intensive study of viruses led to many comparisons between the virus and the gene based originally on the similarity in self-reproducing ability in the two. The X-ray dosage inactivation curves were also shown to be similar, and chemical investigations revealed that the reproduction of both is associated with nucleoproteins.

There was much interest during the decade in studies of haploid and polyploid animals produced as a result of parthenogenetic development. G. Pincus and his co-workers carried out experiments in which rabbit eggs were artificially activated and after implantation in the uterus went on to develop to give normal living female rabbits. Breeding experiments with the females so produced indicated that these individuals were diploid, despite their parthenogenetic origin, the diploid condition probably arising by fusion of the chromosomes produced at the second maturation division. T. Kawamura investigated the chromosomal condition in parthenogenetic frogs and found that though most of these were haploids many were diploids or triploids. The formation of the diploids was apparently the result of suppression of the first cleavage but the triploids seem to have been produced by fusion of three of the sets of chromosomes formed during meiosis. G. Fankhauser produced haploidy and polyploidy in amphibians by subjecting the eggs to various treatments such as exposure to cold or heat shortly before fertilization. The nucleoplasmic ratio in such animals was found to be constant, and the body size was affected in the haploids only. The developmental rate and viability of haploids was lower than normal, but the viability of triploids appeared normal. This material shed light upon the problem of sex determination in amphibia for the sex conditions in the triploids indicated that, in the newt, the female sex is heterogametic.

A new field of genetic investigation was opened with the discovery by T. M. Sonneborn, in 1937, of mating types in the ciliate protozoan, *Paramecium aurelia.* It was found that the individuals of this species fall into three groups, the members of which, when mixed, do not conjugate with each other. However, within each group there are two

Flamingos (left foreground), snowy egrets and other tropical American birds at the Lincoln Park zoo in Chicago, Ill., where tropical plants and spanish moss were used in outdoor cages for the first time in 1946

mating types, and when clones consisting of these two types are mixed they clump together in large masses from which conjugating pairs later emerge. H. S. Jennings found a similar but more complex situation in *Paramecium bursaria* in which there are as many as eight different mating types within a single group. Conjugation will occur between any two of the eight types but not within a single type. Sonneborn showed that it is the macronucleus which determines the mating type and there is considerable evidence for attributing the mating type to a mutable gene.

A new approach to the study of the mode of action of genes was found in the work of D. F. Poulson, who followed the developmental history of *Drosophila* eggs in which there were known deficiencies in the X chromosome. All these deficiencies were lethal, but the exact stage at which development became abnormal differed, depending on the extent and location of the deficiency. Thus in the complete absence of the X chromosome, abnormality was observed during early cleavage. Lack of half the X chromosome affected blastoderm formation or separation of the germ layers depending upon which half was missing. Smaller defects in specific regions of the chromosome affected specific processes; for example, the deficiency "Notch-8" resulted in failure in mesoderm differentiation and abnormalities in the nervous system. This work indicated that individual genes directly control particular events in development, although this point was not definitely proved at the end of the decade.

Another lethal effect, that found in the homozygous "Creeper" fowl, was investigated in a series of studies by V. Hamburger and was found to be due to abnormalities in development of the splanchnic mesoderm which result in inhibition of the yolk-sac circulation.

An outstanding example of a research which contributed to knowledge in several of the main fields of zoology and provided an important integration of genetics, development and biochemistry was the study of the differentiation of eye colour in the fruit-fly. This investigation, which had its beginning in 1935, produced extremely significant results due to the carefully planned and executed experiments of B. Ephrussi and his co-workers in Paris and of G. W. Beadle and his collaborators in California. The normal wild fruit-fly has brownish-red eyes, but it has long been known that various other eye colours are produced in flies having certain recessive genes. The eyes develop embryonically from the optic imaginal discs of the larva and first become pigmented during the pupal stage. Ephrussi and Beadle devised a method by which these eye discs could be transplanted from one larva to another. They found that, when the eye-discs of different eye-colour mutants are transplanted into wild-type hosts, certain of these mutants, namely "vermilion" and "cinnabar," differentiate into wild-type eyes instead of giving their characteristic colour. Further transplants indicated that this results from the presence, in the lymph of the host, of two different substances (designated v^+ and cn^+) which cause the change from vermilion to wild-type and from cinnabar to wild-type respectively. Transfusions of lymph from one larva to another and the preparation of active extracts from the lymph confirmed this idea. Feeding experiments indicated that tryptophane is in some way related to the v^+ substance and finally, through the work of A. Butenandt and his collaborators in Berlin the v^+ substance was identified as kynurenine, a tryptophane derivative. The cn^+ was known to be itself a derivative of the v^+ substance but its exact chemical nature was still unknown at the end of the decade. It is probable that this method of eye-colour determination occurs generally in insects, for A. Kuhn, E. Caspari and E. Plagge found a similar situation in the moth *Ephestia.*

Animal Behaviour.—Several studies of the migratory behaviour of different animals are noteworthy. The migration of butterflies was investigated by C. B. Williams, G. F. Cockbill, M. E. Gibbs and J. A. Downes by means of tagging experiments carried out in England. The migration and spawning of the salmon was studied and reviewed by E. B. Powers, who found evidence that the carbon dioxide concentration in the water is a controlling factor. A comprehensive book by C. Elton presented an account of the population cycles and mass movements in certain small rodents. C. S. Chadwick found that the migration of newts from land to water in the autumn could be influenced by injections of prolactin or pituitary extracts.

Studies of the "social hierarchy" in the fowl were extended by the finding of W. C. Allee, N. Collias and C. Z. Lutherman, that the "pecking order" in a group of hens may be modified by injecting the birds which stand low in the hierarchy with the male hormone, testosterone. Such individuals then become increasingly pugnacious and rise to dominant positions. Similar results were obtained in experiments on certain fishes.

The long-discussed problem of the mechanism by which flying bats are able to avoid obstacles in the dark was solved by the ingenious experiments of D. R. Griffin and R. Galambos who showed that the bat, during flight, is continuously emitting supersonic cries and that its obstacle-avoidance results from its ability to accurately localize objects by perception of the reflected supersonic waves.

Morphology and Evolution.—A number of important studies of the phylogeny of specific animal groups appeared during this period. Among these may be mentioned the monograph of W. Garstang and R. Gurney on the relationships of the trilobites and crustacea, R. E. Snodgrass' review of the phylogeny of the annelids and arthropods and the extensive study of T. Dobzhansky and C. Epling on the taxonomy and interrelationships of the races of *Drosophila pseudobscura.* Several fossil groups of particular interest in relation to vertebrate evolution became better known through monographic treatment. The most primitive of the vertebrates with movable jaws, the Acanthodian fishes, were studied by D. M. S. Watson. E. C. Olson discussed the structure of the mammal-like reptiles, and found indications that the early mammals may have originated from several reptilian stocks rather than a single one. R. Broom continued his extensive studies of the manlike apes of the Pleistocene of South Africa. In relation to studies of fossil groups, the discovery in 1939 in the deep waters off South Africa, of a living coelacanth fish was noteworthy. The animal is a member of a group previously known only from fossil forms. The phylogeny of the musculature of the tetrapod limb was elucidated by morphological studies on various vertebrate types by A. B. Howell and by A. S. Romer.

A study of cave fishes of Mexico by C. M. Breder, Jr. and Z. B. Gresser was of interest since the authors found a complete gradation from blind, eyeless fishes to normal individuals. The blind individuals showed a definite avoidance of light, despite the absence of eyes, and this was considered an important factor in the segregation of the cave forms. Beadle investigated the problem of osmotic regulation in the body fluid of aquatic animals in relation to the adjustments necessary in passing from marine to fresh-water habitats.

The use of serological techniques in the study of relationships became of increasing value. H. P. Levine and P. A. Moody, using this method with rodents, found that the serological relationships follow closely the accepted classification on the basis of morphology. R. W. Wilhelmi utilized precipitin tests in studying the relationships of echinoderms, arthropods, annelids and prochordates, and found corroboration for the generally accepted theory of echinoderm ancestry for the prochordates. R. W. Cumley applied the complement fixation method to investigate the taxonomy of *Drosophila.* M. M. Mahr found the serological technique sufficiently delicate to detect species differences in tapeworms.

BIBLIOGRAPHY.—C. M. Child, *Patterns and Problems of Development* (1944); E. J. Cole, *A History of Comparative Anatomy* (1944); A. M. Dalcq, *Form and Causality in Early Development* (1938); T. Dobzhansky, *Genetics and the Origin of Species* (1937); C. Elton, *Voles, Mice and Lemmings: Problems in Population Dynamics* (1942); B. Hanstrom, *Hormones in Invertebrates* (1937); R. Hesse, W. C. Allee and K. P. Schmidt, *Ecological Animal Geography* (1937); J. Huxley, *The New Systematics* (1940); R. S. Lillie, *General Biology and Philosophy of Organism* (1945); L. Loeb, *The Biological Basis of Individuality* (1945); J. Needham, *Biochemistry and Morphogenesis* (1942); G. G. Simpson, *Tempo and Mode in Evolution* (1944); C. H. Waddington, *Organisers and Genes* (1940); G. L. Walls, *The Vertebrate Eye and its Adaptive Radiation* (1942); P. Weiss, *Principles of Development* (1939). (W. G. L.)

Scene at the Washington Park zoo in Milwaukee, Wis., where polar bear Sultana II and her half-year-old cub attracted crowds in 1945

Zoological Gardens.—The decade saw far-reaching changes in concepts of zoological gardens in the United States. The hampering effects of building restrictions prevented extensive physical changes but provided a much-needed opportunity for reconsideration of underlying philosophies and means for giving them effective expression. Previously the aim of every such institution had been to exhibit a series of living creatures as extensive as its facilities would allow. Ranking was accorded almost solely on the basis of the number of species included in collections. The enforced pause in building operations, coupled with nearly complete cessation of the importation of fresh specimens, gave time for thought. The result was a sweeping revision of understanding of the functions of the zoological garden in its relation to the public. Fewer animals to exhibit brought realization that there was no merit in mere numbers. The necessity for preserving existing specimens brought marked improvements in the techniques of animal care, breeding and exhibition.

Realization that the primary purpose of the zoological garden is to arouse interest in natural history and to meet the resulting desire for information with factually correct material, resulted in several definite advances. Further development of the printed label, probably first used at the Zoological Garden of Philadelphia, resulted in improved readability and better utilization of space. Carefully done illustrations in colour added greatly to readiness of identification. Larger labels, giving the story behind especially notable exhibits, were used to great advantage. This effort resulted in a flood of requests for further information. In the New York Zoological park, the reaction was met by the installation of a Question house, where trained attendants answered thousands of inquiries annually.

To satisfy the need for a means to encourage the natural interest of children in animals, a "Baby Pet zoo" was opened in the Philadelphia Zoological garden in 1938 and a "Children's zoo" in the New York Zoological park in 1941. Here children were allowed to come into contact with tame, living animals. Since this was often a first experience, carefully selected personnel maintained close and constant supervision.

In the exhibitional field, important advances were made. Many plans remained in the drawing stage, yet there was enough actual construction to establish the general soundness of ideas. The moated, barless area, originally devised by Carl Hagenbeck in 1907 and later used by several U.S. gardens, was seen in improved form in the African plains opened in the New York Zoological park in 1941. Further development of this idea, on an extensive scale, was indicated in the plans of many institutions.

The most revolutionary idea in exhibitional technique had to do with those creatures which must be shown indoors. The use of glass-fronted enclosures, naturally or artificially lighted and viewed from a darkened space to avoid disturbing reflections, had had limited use for public aquariums and for the exhibition of reptiles. However, it was not fully applied to warm-blooded creatures until the opening of the Jewel room in the New York Zoological park in 1945. Here, brilliantly coloured birds were shown with excellent effect against a carefully arranged background of tropical planting. A similar plan was developed for the anthropoid apes and small mammals in the same institution. Animals and public were fully insulated from each other, to mutual advantage. The use of fluorescent lighting made this development possible, since a negligible degree of heat was generated.

Isolation from world sources of supply during most of the decade resulted in intensified efforts on the part of U.S. zoological gardens to increase the animals in hand and brought about the foundation of breeding stocks of many kinds. The zoological gardens of Chicago (Brookfield) and St. Louis were especially successful with various species of antelopes. The San Diego Zoological garden had notable results with monkeys and numerous birds. Deer, wild cattle and antelopes were well established in the New York Zoological park, where the rare wattled crane of Africa was bred in captivity for the first time in 1945.

In a decade marked by a paucity of animal importations into the United States it was remarkable that the few arrivals should number several great rarities. Giant pandas came from China to the zoological gardens of Chicago, St. Louis and New York. The first and only okapi to be seen in the U.S. was received at the New York Zoological park in 1937. The first specimens of the very rare Pere David's deer arrived in New York in Dec. 1946. Among birds, rarities included the quetzal, the umbrella bird, the scarlet cock of the rock and the emperor penguin, the latter at the National Zoological park in Washington.

(L. S. C.)

During World War II, zoos—not only in Europe but all over the world—suffered from general depletion of their collections owing to the impossibility of obtaining new specimens from other countries to replenish the normal losses incurred by old age and sickness. In addition, many of the zoos in the immediate theatre of war suffered severely from the many and varied forms of destruction which the war produced.

Of the European zoos in the immediate war zone, that of Antwerp suffered severely in the final stages from flying bombs. The Rotterdam gardens, which had been moved from the centre of the city to the suburb of Blijdoorp, escaped the fate of the city in 1940. The gardens at Amsterdam also escaped. The intensive bombing of German cities by the British and U.S. air forces resulted in the destruction of several of the most famous of the German zoos. The Berlin zoo was reduced to ruins and the Hamburg, Hanover and Munich zoos were considerably damaged. In Paris both the Jardin des Plantes and the new zoo at Vincennes, with its amazing structures, escaped damage, but the Jardin d'Acclimatation was used as a barracks by the nazi troops, who did much wanton damage there.

In spite of the many wartime difficulties, the London zoo remained open throughout World War II, providing entertainment, relaxation and education for many thousands of war workers and members of British and Allied forces, who were admitted at specially reduced rates. From Sept. 1939 to the cessation of hostilities in Europe in May 1945, visitors to the London zoo numbered 6,500,000. During the bombing of London in 1940–41, the zoo at Regent's park received 26 direct hits from high-explosive bombs and upward of 400 incendiary bombs. In 1944 even greater damage was caused by flying bombs, one of which fell in the centre of the gardens and was responsible for an enormous amount of material damage, though fortunately little loss of life. In Aug. 1940 the council of the Zoological society of London revised the rule whereby Sundays were reserved for fellows of the society. The gardens were opened to the public in the afternoon and it was decided to continue this practice indefinitely.

Whipsnade park, the society's new venture which was completed in 1931, also remained open throughout World War II, with the exception of the winter months of 1939–40. The elephants from London were sent there for safety and also the famous giant panda "Ming," one of the first specimens of this rare animal to be shown alive in Europe. Another rare animal in the London zoo at the outbreak of war was the okapi, which had been presented in 1937 by the Belgian king to King George VI. It was decided in this case that the risk of moving the animal from London to Whipsnade was greater than the risk of bombing, and fortunately it survived. Visitors to Whipsnade park during the war numbered approximately 1,250,000. Before the war the average annual attendance was 500,000. The considerable falling off in numbers was due to the rationing of gasoline which made it difficult for visitors to make the 30-mi. journey from London.

At the outbreak of World War II, the aquarium and reptile house in the London zoo were closed, and all the poisonous snakes were destroyed. This was a fortunate precaution, as a high-explosive bomb later fell in the aquarium's freshwater hall and the glass of the reptile house dens was shattered by a flying bomb. The children's zoo, introduced during the secretaryship of Dr. Julian Huxley, was closed in 1939 but re-opened in 1944 and continued to prove a great attraction to young visitors.

Dr. Huxley's predecessor, Sir Peter Chalmers Mitchell, who was the society's secretary from 1903 to 1935 and was responsible for many innovations in the keeping of animals in captivity and for the formation of Whipsnade park, died as the result of an accident in July 1945.

In spite of paper restrictions and printing difficulties, the Zoological society of London continued its scientific meetings and publications throughout World War II, although both meetings and scientific papers submitted were reduced in number. The replanning of the Regent's park gardens, which was started in 1939 with the proposed construction of a new elephant house, had to be postponed. The rebuilding of the elephant house on the old site was abandoned.

The zoos at Bristol, Edinburgh and Chester came through the war unscathed but with their collections much depleted. The outstanding exhibit at the Bristol zoo during this period was the male gorilla "Alfred" which was 18 years old in 1946 and considered to be the finest gorilla in captivity anywhere. In addition to the above-mentioned zoos which were run by private societies and were non-profit-making, the zoos at Manchester, Dudley, Chessington and Maidstone remained open through World War II. (*See* also ENDOCRINOLOGY; ENTOMOLOGY; GENETICS; MARINE BIOLOGY; PALAEONTOLOGY; PHYSIOLOGY.)

BIBLIOGRAPHY.—Bridges and Hollister, *Big Zoo* (1941); *Who's Who in the Zoo* (WPA Federal Writers' Project, 1942); *Proceedings of the Zoological Society of London* (quarterly) and *Zoo Life* (quarterly); *Fauna*, published by the Philadelphia Zoological Society (quarterly); *Animal Kingdom*, bulletin of the New York Zoological Society (every two months).

(G. M. V.)

INDEX

INDEX

THIS INDEX gives the exact location of information to be found in *Ten Eventful Years* by volume, page and section of the page. The section of the page is indicated by the letters "a," "b," "c" and "d," signifying respectively the upper and lower halves of the first column and the upper and lower halves of the second column. Thus, 4:365c indicates that the information will be found in volume 4, page 365, top half of the second column.

Information dealing with the subject as a whole is given first after the main entry. Secondary entries are indented and follow the main entry alphabetically, each giving page reference to specific information. Cross references are to the index only.

A page number in italic type indicates an entire article on the subject. A page number with "fol." after it indicates that other references to the subject follow within the same article. References to pictures are indicated by "*illus.*"

All index entries whether consisting of a single word or more are treated for the purpose of alphabetization as single complete headings. Names beginning with "Mc" and "Mac" are alphabetized as "Mac"; "St." is treated as "Saint"; "Mt." as "Mount."

A

B

C

D

E

G

H

I

J

L

N

P

Q

R

S

T

U

V

Printed in the U.S.A.